n Publication

duced under the direction of

Timeform Organisation

B.A., G. F. Walton, Dip.A.D.
. Newton, B.A. (Editor-in-Chief),
B.A. (Editor), D. P. Adams, S. N.
wther, G. J. Cunningham, LL.B.,
3.Sc., W. Hughes, G. M. Johnstone,
O. C. Pennant Jones, B.A. and C. S.

Limited 1993

2

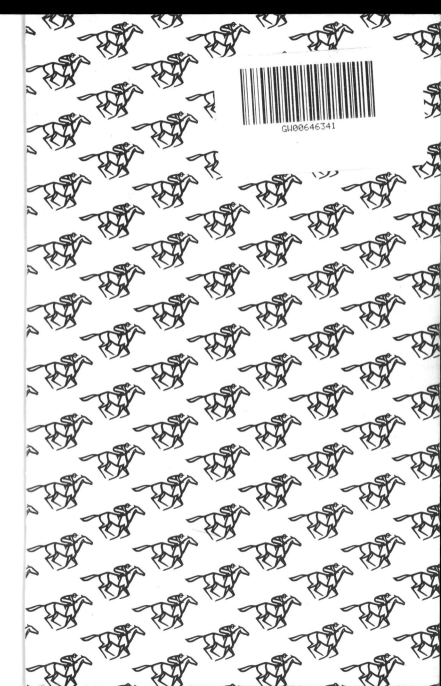

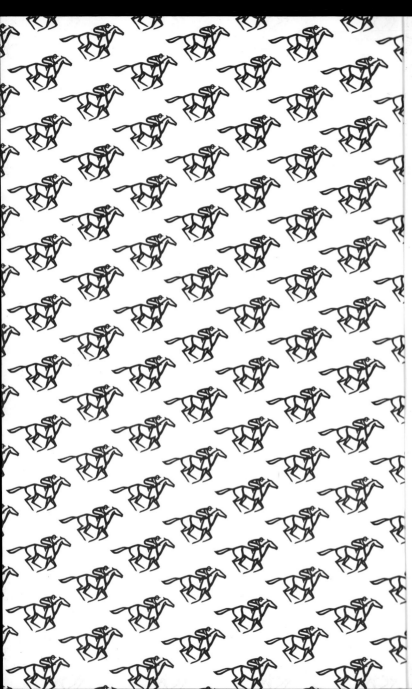

A Timefor

Compiled and pr
Reg Griffin

by members of the

G. Greetham,
(Directors), J. I
R. J. C. Austen,
Copeland, G. Cr
P. R. Entwistle, I
G. J. North, B.Sc.,
Williams

The annual volume
Hall, is published by I
Yorkshire HX 1 1XE; prin
Beccles. Every care is take
no responsibility is accept
or their consequences.

© Portway Press

ISBN 0 900599 63 4

CONTENTS

4	Age, Weight and Distance Tables
7	Foreword
8	Index to Photographs
17	Explanatory Notes
21	The Form Summaries and Rating Symbols
23	Racehorses of 1992
957	Timeform Champions of 1992
958	The Timeform 'Top Hundred'
960	Timeform Computer Timefigures
962	1992 Statistics
964	The Free Handicap, British and International Classifications
971	Selected Big Races 1992
996	Trainers
1003	Jockeys
1006	Apprentices
1010	Flat Fixtures 1993
1014	Characteristics of Racecourses
1023	Stallion Section
1038	Timeform Champions

AGE, WEIGHT & DISTANCE TABLE

Timeform's scale of weight-for-age for the flat

Dist	Age	Jan 1-16	Jan 17-31	Feb 1-16	Feb 17-28	Mar 1-16	Mar 17-31	Apr 1-16	Apr 17-30	May 1-16	May 17-31	June 1-16	June 17-30
5f	4	10-0	10-0	10-0	10-0	10-0	10-0	10-0	10-0	10-0	10-0	10-0	10-0
	3	9-5	9-5	9-6	9-7	9-7	9-8	9-8	9-9	9-9	9-10	9-10	9-11
	2						8-0	8-1	8-3	8-4	8-5	8-6	8-7
6f	4	10-0	10-0	10-0	10-0	10-0	10-0	10-0	10-0	10-0	10-0	10-0	10-0
	3	9-2	9-3	9-4	9-5	9-5	9-6	9-7	9-7	9-8	9-8	9-9	9-9
	2									8-0	8-2	8-3	8-4
7f	4	9-13	9-13	10-0	10-0	10-0	10-0	10-0	10-0	10-0	10-0	10-0	10-0
	3	9-0	9-1	9-2	9-3	9-4	9-4	9-5	9-6	9-6	9-7	9-8	9-8
	2											7-13	8-1
1m	4	9-13	9-13	9-13	9-13	10-0	10-0	10-0	10-0	10-0	10-0	10-0	10-0
	3	8-12	8-13	9-0	9-1	9-2	9-2	9-3	9-4	9-5	9-5	9-6	9-7
	2												
9f	4	9-12	9-12	9-12	9-13	9-13	9-13	9-13	10-0	10-0	10-0	10-0	10-0
	3	8-10	8-11	8-12	8-13	9-0	9-1	9-2	9-2	9-3	9-4	9-5	9-5
	2												
1¼m	4	9-11	9-12	9-12	9-12	9-13	9-13	9-13	9-13	9-13	10-0	10-0	10-0
	3	8-8	8-9	8-10	8-11	8-12	8-13	9-0	9-1	9-2	9-2	9-3	9-4
	2												
11f	4	9-10	9-11	9-11	9-12	9-12	9-12	9-13	9-13	9-13	9-13	9-13	10-0
	3	8-6	8-7	8-8	8-9	8-10	8-11	8-12	8-13	9-0	9-1	9-2	9-2
1½m	4	9-10	9-10	9-10	9-11	9-11	9-12	9-12	9-12	9-13	9-13	9-13	9-13
	3	8-4	8-5	8-6	8-7	8-8	8-9	8-10	8-11	8-12	8-13	9-0	9-1
13f	4	9-9	9-9	9-10	9-10	9-11	9-11	9-11	9-12	9-12	9-12	9-13	9-13
	3	8-2	8-3	8-4	8-5	8-7	8-8	8-9	8-10	8-11	8-12	8-13	9-0
1¾m	4	9-8	9-8	9-9	9-9	9-10	9-10	9-11	9-11	9-12	9-12	9-12	9-13
	3	8-0	8-2	8-3	8-4	8-5	8-6	8-7	8-8	8-9	8-10	8-11	8-12
15f	4	9-7	9-8	9-8	9-9	9-9	9-10	9-10	9-11	9-11	9-11	9-12	9-12
	3	7-13	8-0	8-1	8-2	8-4	8-5	8-6	8-7	8-8	8-9	8-10	8-11
2m	4	9-6	9-7	9-7	9-8	9-9	9-9	9-10	9-10	9-11	9-11	9-11	9-12
	3	7-11	7-12	7-13	8-1	8-2	8-3	8-4	8-5	8-6	8-7	8-8	8-9
2¼m	4	9-5	9-5	9-6	9-7	9-7	9-8	9-9	9-9	9-10	9-10	9-10	9-11
	3	7-8	7-9	7-11	7-12	7-13	8-0	8-2	8-3	8-4	8-5	8-6	8-7
2½m	4	9-3	9-4	9-5	9-6	9-6	9-7	9-7	9-8	9-9	9-9	9-10	9-10
	3	7-5	7-7	7-8	7-9	7-11	7-12	7-13	8-1	8-2	8-3	8-4	8-5

For 5-y-o's and older, use 10-0 in all cases
Race distances in the above tables are shown only at 1 furlong intervals.
For races over odd distances, the nearest distance shown in the table should be used:
thus for races of 1m to 1m 109 yards, use the table weights for 1m;
for 1m 110 yards to 1m 219 yards use the 9f table

AGE, WEIGHT & DISTANCE TABLE

Timeform's scale of weight-for-age for the flat

Dist	Age	July 1-16	July 17-31	Aug 1-16	Aug 17-31	Sept 1-16	Sept 17-30	Oct 1-16	Oct 17-31	Nov 1-16	Nov 17-30	Dec 1-16	Dec 17-31
5f	4	10-0	10-0	10-0	10-0	10-0	10-0	10-0	10-0	10-0	10-0	10-0	10-0
	3	9-11	9-12	9-12	9-12	9-13	9-13	9-13	9-13	10-0	10-0	10-0	10-0
	2	8-8	8-9	8-10	8-11	8-12	8-13	9-0	9-1	9-2	9-2	9-3	9-4
6f	4	10-0	10-0	10-0	10-0	10-0	10-0	10-0	10-0	10-0	10-0	10-0	10-0
	3	9-10	9-10	9-11	9-11	9-12	9-12	9-12	9-13	9-13	9-13	9-13	10-0
	2	8-5	8-6	8-7	8-8	8-9	8-10	8-11	8-12	8-13	9-0	9-1	9-2
7f	4	10-0	10-0	10-0	10-0	10-0	10-0	10-0	10-0	10-0	10-0	10-0	10-0
	3	9-9	9-9	9-10	9-10	9-11	9-11	9-11	9-12	9-12	9-12	9-13	9-13
	2	8-2	8-3	8-4	8-5	8-6	8-7	8-9	8-10	8-11	8-12	8-13	9-0
1m	4	10-0	10-0	10-0	10-0	10-0	10-0	10-0	10-0	10-0	10-0	10-0	10-0
	3	9-7	9-8	9-8	9-9	9-9	9-10	9-10	9-11	9-11	9-12	9-12	9-12
	2			8-2	8-3	8-4	8-5	8-6	8-7	8-8	8-9	8-10	8-11
9f	4	10-0	10-0	10-0	10-0	10-0	10-0	10-0	10-0	10-0	10-0	10-0	10-0
	3	9-6	9-7	9-7	9-8	9-8	9-9	9-9	9-10	9-10	9-11	9-11	9-12
	2					8-1	8-3	8-4	8-5	8-6	8-7	8-8	8-9
1¼m	4	10-0	10-0	10-0	10-0	10-0	10-0	10-0	10-0	10-0	10-0	10-0	10-0
	3	9-5	9-5	9-6	9-7	9-7	9-8	9-8	9-9	9-9	9-10	9-10	9-11
	2							8-1	8-2	8-4	8-5	8-6	8-7
11f	4	10-0	10-0	10-0	10-0	10-0	10-0	10-0	10-0	10-0	10-0	10-0	10-0
	3	9-3	9-4	9-5	9-5	9-6	9-7	9-7	9-8	9-8	9-9	9-9	9-10
1½m	4	10-0	10-0	10-0	10-0	10-0	10-0	10-0	10-0	10-0	10-0	10-0	10-0
	3	9-2	9-2	9-3	9-4	9-5	9-5	9-6	9-7	9-7	9-8	9-9	9-9
13f	4	9-13	9-13	10-0	10-0	10-0	10-0	10-0	10-0	10-0	10-0	10-0	10-0
	3	9-0	9-1	9-2	9-3	9-4	9-4	9-5	9-6	9-6	9-7	9-8	9-8
1¾m	4	9-13	9-13	9-13	10-0	10-0	10-0	10-0	10-0	10-0	10-0	10-0	10-0
	3	8-13	9-0	9-1	9-2	9-3	9-3	9-4	9-5	9-5	9-6	9-7	9-7
15f	4	9-12	9-12	9-13	9-13	9-13	10-0	10-0	10-0	10-0	10-0	10-0	10-0
	3	8-12	8-13	9-0	9-1	9-1	9-2	9-3	9-4	9-4	9-5	9-6	9-6
2m	4	9-12	9-12	9-13	9-13	9-13	9-13	10-0	10-0	10-0	10-0	10-0	10-0
	3	8-10	8-11	8-12	8-13	9-0	9-1	9-2	9-3	9-3	9-4	9-5	9-5
2¼m	4	9-11	9-12	9-12	9-12	9-13	9-13	9-13	9-13	10-0	10-0	10-0	10-0
	3	8-8	8-9	8-10	8-11	8-12	8-13	9-0	9-1	9-2	9-2	9-3	9-4
2½m	4	9-10	9-11	9-11	9-12	9-12	9-12	9-13	9-13	9-13	9-13	10-0	10-0
	3	8-6	8-7	8-8	8-9	8-10	8-11	8-12	8-13	9-0	9-1	9-2	9-3

For 5-y-o's and older, use 10-0 in all cases

Race distances in the above tables are shown only at 1 furlong intervals.

For races over odd distances, the nearest distance shown in the table should be used:

thus for races of 1m to 1m 109 yards, use the table weights for 1m;

for 1m 110 yards to 1m 219 yards use the 9f table

The

Sporting Life

BEST RUNNER OF ALL EVERY YEAR

YOU'RE LIFELESS WITHOUT IT

FOREWORD

"Racehorses of 1992" deals individually, in alphabetical sequence, with every horse that ran under Jockey Club Rules (including on the all-weather tracks) in 1992, plus a number of foreign-trained horses that did not race here. For each of these horses is given (1) its age, colour and sex, (2) its breeding, (3) a form summary giving details of all its performances during the past two seasons, (4) a rating of its merit, (5) a commentary upon its racing or general characteristics as a racehorse, with some suggestions, perhaps, regarding its prospects for 1993 and (6) the name of the trainer in whose charge it was on the last occasion it ran. For each two-year-old the foaling date is also given.

The book is published with a twofold purpose. Firstly, the book is intended to have permanent value as a review of the exploits and achievements of the more notable of our thoroughbreds in 1992. Thus, while the commentaries upon the vast majority of the horses are, of necessity, in note form, the best horses are more critically examined, and the short essays upon them are illustrated by half-tone portraits and photographs of the finishes of some of the races in which they were successful; and secondly, the book is designed to provide data for practical use in analysing the racing programmes from day to day, and instructions as to its use in that capacity will be found in the Explanatory Notes.

The attention of foreign buyers of British bloodstock, and others who are concerned with Timeform Ratings as a measure of absolute racing class in terms of a standard scale, is drawn to the section headed "The Level of the Ratings" in the Explanatory Notes.

February, 1993

INDEX TO PHOTOGRAPHS

PORTRAITS & SNAPSHOTS

Horse		Breeding	Copyright	Page
Alflora	3 b.c.	Niniski–Adrana (Bold Lad)	John Crofts	36
All At Sea	3 ch.f.	Riverman–Lost Virtue (Cloudy Dawn)	John Crofts	43
Andros Bay	3 b.c.	Alleged–Montage (Alydar)	Jacqueline O'Brien	57
Approach The Bench	4 b.c.	Law Society–Arguing (Pharly)	Jacqueline O'Brien	60
Arazi	3 ch.c.	Blushing Groom–Danseur Fabuleux (Northern Dancer)	P. Bertrand	66
Armarama	3 ch.f.	Persian Bold–Rossitor (Pall Mall)	John Crofts	71
Arrikala	3 br.f.	Darshaan–Alruccaba (Crystal Palace)	Jacqueline O'Brien	75
Barathea	2 b.c.	Sadler's Wells–Brocade (Habitat)	John Crofts	91
Basim	2 b.c.	Capote–Mer Belle (Far North)	Jacqueline O'Brien	96
Bezelle	3 b.f.	Dominion–Ideal Home (Home Guard)	Jacqueline O'Brien	111
Bonny Scot	3 b.c.	Commanche Run–Scots Lass (Shirley Heights)	John Crofts	129
Brief Truce	3 b.c.	Irish River–Falafel (Northern Dancer)	Jacqueline O'Brien	136
Calling Collect	3 ch.c.	Phone Trick–My Little Guest (Be My Guest)	John Crofts	146
Captain Horatius	3 b.c.	Taufan–One Last Glimpse (Relko)	Rex Coleman	150
Cardoun	3 b.c.	Kaldoun–Cable Car (Fabulous Dancer)	John Crofts	153
Corrupt	4 b.c.	Lear Fan–Nirvanita (Right Royal V)	Rex Coleman	184
Cunning	3 ch.f.	Bustino–Vice Vixen (Vice Regent)	John Crofts	197
Desert Secret	2 b.c.	Sadler's Wells–Clandestina (Secretariat)	John Crofts	219
Dr Devious	3 ch.c.	Ahonoora–Rose of Jericho (Alleged)	John Crofts	237
Drum Taps	6 b.h.	Dixieland Band–Lavendula Rose (Le Levanstell)	Rex Coleman	242
Duke of Eurolink	3 b.c.	Jupiter Island–Lady Eurolink (Kala Shikari)	John Crofts	244
El Prado	3 gr.c.	Sadler's Wells–Lady Capulet (Sir Ivor)	Jacqueline O'Brien	256
Environment Friend	4 gr.c.	Cozzene–Water Woo (Tom Rolfe)	John Crofts	260
Exit To Nowhere	4 b.c.	Irish River–Coup de Folie (Halo)	John Crofts	267
Fatherland	2 b.c.	Sadler's Wells–Lisadell (Forli)	Jacqueline O'Brien	278
Flashfoot	4 ch.c.	Rousillon–Miellita (King Emperor)	Rex Coleman	289

Name	Age/Desc	Pedigree	Photographer	No.
Forest Wind	2 ch.c.	Green Forest–Pompoes (Belmont)	*John Crofts*	296
Frenchpark	2 b.c.	Fools Holme–Piffle (Shirley Heights)	*Jacqueline O'Brien*	302
Guilty Secret	3 ch.f.	Kris–Miss Toshiba (Sir Ivor)	*Rex Coleman*	337
Guislaine	3 br.f.	Tropular–Clodette (Ben Trovato)	*P. Bertrand*	338
Hatoof	3 ch.f.	Irish River–Cadeaux d'Amie (Lyphard)	*P. Bertrand*	348
Hazaam	3 b.c.	Blushing Groom–Sonic Lady (Nureyev)	*John Crofts*	352
Humam	2 ch.c.	Nijinsky–Passamaquoddy (Drone)	*John Crofts*	369
Hydro Calido	3 b.f.	Nureyev–Coup de Folie (Halo)	*John Crofts*	370
Inchinor	2 ch.c.	Ahonoora–Inchmurrin (Lomond)	*W. W. Rouch & Co*	378
Ivanka	2 b.f.	Dancing Brave–Diamond Land (Sparkler)	*John Crofts*	389
Ivory Frontier	2 ch.c.	Imperial Frontier–Ivory Home (Home Guard)	*Jacqueline O'Brien*	390
Ivyanna	3 b.f.	Reference Point–Ivy (Sir Ivor)	*Jacqueline O'Brien*	391
Jeune	3 ch.c.	Kalaglow–Youthful (Green Dancer)	*John Crofts*	399
Jolypha	3 b.f.	Lyphard–Navajo Princess (Drone)	*P. Bertrand*	405
Kenbu	3 gr.f.	Kenmare–Tarlace (Targowice)	*John Crofts*	419
Knifebox	4 b.c.	Diesis–Matoki (Hail To Reason)	*John Crofts*	429
Kooyonga	4 ch.f.	Persian Bold–Anjuli (Northfields)	*Jacqueline O'Brien*	433
Lahib	4 b.c.	Riverman–Lady Cutlass (Cutlass)	*Rex Coleman*	441
Landowner	3 b.c.	Kris–Laluche (Alleged)	*John Crofts*	445
Lochsong	4 b.f.	Song–Peckitts Well (Lochnager)	*Rex Coleman*	463
Lost Soldier	2 b.c.	Danzig–Lady Winborne (Secretariat)	*John Crofts*	469
Love of Silver	2 ch.f.	Arctic Tern–Silver Clover (Secretariat)	*John Crofts*	472
Market Booster	3 b.f.	Green Dancer–Final Figure (Super Concorde)	*Jacqueline O'Brien*	503
Marling	3 b.f.	Lomond–Marwell (Habitat)	*John Crofts*	506
Masad	3 b.c.	Sadler's Wells–Marmolada (Sassafras)	*John Crofts*	510
Needle Gun	2 b.c.	Sure Blade–Lucayan Princess (High Line)	*John Crofts*	566
Norwich	5 b.h.	Top Ville–Dame Julian (Blakeney)	*Rex Coleman*	582
Oumaldaaya	3 b.f.	Nureyev–Histoire (Riverman)	*Rex Coleman*	595
Pistolet Bleu	4 b.c.	Top Ville–Pampa Bella (Armos)	*P. Bertrand*	623
Polytain	3 ch.c.	Bikala–Paulistana (Pretense)	*John Crofts*	631
Pursuit of Love	3 b.c.	Groom Dancer–Dance Quest (Green Dancer)	*Laurie Morton*	648

Name	Age/Colour	Breeding	Photographer	Page
Rain Rider	3 b.c.	Fools Holme–Moon Parade (Welsh Pageant)	*Rex Coleman*	661
Rami	5 br.h.	Riverman–Ancient Regime (Olden Times)	*Jacqueline O'Brien*	665
Rodrigo de Triano	3 ch.c.	El Gran Senor–Hot Princess (Hot Spark)	*John Crofts*	692
Rudimentary	4 b.c.	Nureyev–Doubly Sure (Reliance II)	*Laurie Morton*	702
Sapience	6 ch.h.	Niniski–Claretta (Roberto)	*W. W. Rouch & Co*	717
Sayyedati	2 b.f.	Shadeed–Dubian (High Line)	*John Crofts*	724
Seattle Rhyme	3 ch.c.	Seattle Dancer–Golden Rhyme (Dom Racine)	*W. W. Rouch & Co*	731
Second Set	4 b.c.	Alzao–Merriment (Go Marching)	*John Crofts*	733
Selkirk	4 ch.c.	Sharpen Up–Annie Edge (Nebbiolo)	*Fiona Vigors*	739
Shambo	5 b.h.	Lafontaine–Lucky Appeal (Star Appeal)	*John Crofts*	747
Shanghai	3 b.c.	Procida–Korveya (Riverman)	*John Crofts*	749
Sheba Dancer	3 b.f.	Fabulous Dancer–Elisheba (Nonoalco)	*John Crofts*	754
Shuailaan	3 ch.c.	Roberto–Lassie's Lady (Alydar)	*John Crofts*	763
Sikeston	6 b.h.	Lear Fan–Small Timer (Lyphard)	*John Crofts*	767
Sillery	4 b.c.	Blushing Groom–Silvermine (Bellypha)	*P. Bertrand*	769
Silver Wizard	2 b.c.	Silver Hawk–Cherie's Hope (Flying Paster)	*Rex Coleman*	774
Sonus	3 b.c.	Sadler's Wells–Sound of Success (Successor)	*John Crofts*	789
Sought Out	4 b.f.	Rainbow Quest–Edinburgh (Charlottown)	*John Crofts*	792
St Jovite	3 b.c.	Pleasant Colony–Northern Sunset (Northfields)	*Peter Mooney*	813
Subotica	4 b.c.	Pampabird–Terre de Feu (Busted)	*John Crofts*	821
Supreme Choice	4 b.c.	Sovereign Dancer–Editor's Choice (Sir Ivor)	*Rex Coleman*	830
Surrealist	4 b.c.	Tate Gallery–Natuschka (Authi)	*Rex Coleman*	832
Tel Quel	4 br.c.	Akarad–Best Girl (Birdbrook)	*John Crofts*	849
Terimon	6 gr.h.	Bustino–Nicholas Grey (Track Spare)	*John Crofts*	854
Thourios	3 b.c.	Green Desert–Graecia Magna (Private Account)	*Rex Coleman*	861
Up And At 'Em	2 b.c.	Forzando–Ergo (Song)	*Jacqueline O'Brien*	887
User Friendly	3 b.f.	Slip Anchor–Rostova (Blakeney)	*John Crofts*	894
Witness Box	5 b.h.	Lyphard–Excellent Alibi (Exceller)	*John Crofts*	926
Wolfhound	3 ch.c.	Nureyev–Lassie Dear (Buckpasser)	*John Crofts*	930
Young Buster	4 b.c.	Teenoso–Bustara (Busted)	*John Crofts*	938

Zaahi	3 b.c.	Slew O' Gold–Alghuzaylah (Habitat)	John Crofts	942
Zafonic	2 b.c.	Gone West–Zaizafon (The Minstrel)	P. Bertrand	946
Zieten	2 b.c.	Danzig–Blue Note (Habitat)	John Crofts	950

RACE PHOTOGRAPHS

Race and Meeting	Copyright	Page
A. F. Budge Park Hill Stakes (Doncaster)	John Crofts	575
Airlie/Coolmore Irish Two Thousand Guineas (the Curragh)	Caroline Norris	689
Arlington Million (Arlington)	Four Footed Fotos, Inc	213
Ascot Stakes (Ascot)	John Crofts	325
Aston Upthorpe Yorkshire Oaks (York)	John Crofts	891
Autumn Stakes (Ascot)	George Selwyn	844
Baring International Darley Stakes (Newmarket)	John Crofts	521
Beefeater Gin Celebration Mile (Goodwood)	John Crofts	737
Ben Marshall Stakes (Newmarket)	John Crofts	382
Bentinck Stakes (Newmarket)	Alec Russell	343
Berkeley Stakes (Handicap) (Ascot)	George Selwyn	795
Bessborough Stakes (Handicap) (Ascot)	John Crofts	799
Blandford Stakes (the Curragh)	Caroline Norris	56
Blue Seal Stakes (Ascot)	George Selwyn	652
BonusPrint Easter Stakes (Kempton)	John Crofts	474
BonusPrint September Stakes (Kempton)	George Selwyn	398
BonusPrint Sirenia Stakes (Kempton)	George Selwyn	773
Bovis Handicap (Ascot)	George Selwyn	78
Bradford & Bingley Handicap (York)	Alec Russell	232
Britannia Handicap (Ascot)	John Crofts	250
Budweiser International (Laurel)	Laurel Racecourse	953
Budweiser Irish Derby (the Curragh)	George Selwyn	809
Butlins Southcoast World Prestige Stakes (Goodwood)	John Crofts	471
Carmelites Kildare 7th Centenary Desmond Stakes (the Curragh)	Caroline Norris	901
Castrol St Simon Stakes (Newbury)	John Crofts	886
Challenge Stakes (Newmarket)	John Crofts	738
Cheveley Park Stud Sun Chariot Stakes (Newmarket)	Alec Russell	671
Child & Co Superlative Stakes (Newmarket)	George Selwyn	69
Ciga Grand Criterium (Longchamp)	P. Bertrand	851
Ciga Prix de l'Abbaye de Longchamp (Longchamp)	P. Bertrand	548
Ciga Prix de l'Arc de Triomphe (Longchamp)	P. Bertrand	819
Ciga Prix de l'Opera (Longchamp)	John Crofts	347
Ciga Prix de Royallieu (Longchamp)	John Crofts	270
Ciga Prix Dollar (Longchamp)	John Crofts	768
Ciga Prix du Cadran (Longchamp)	P. Bertrand	791
Ciga Prix du Rond-Point (Longchamp)	P. Bertrand	65
C. L. Weld EBF Park Stakes (the Curragh)	Caroline Norris	77
Coalite Handicap (Doncaster)	George Selwyn	520
Coalite St Leger Stakes (Doncaster)	Alec Russell	892
Colmans of Norwich Nursery (Newmarket)	Alec Russell	840
Coral Autumn Cup (Newbury)	W. Everitt	157
Coral-Eclipse Stakes (Sandown)	John Crofts	431
Coral 1st Sunday Race (Doncaster)	Alec Russell	720
Coral Sprint Trophy (York)	Alec Russell	216
Cork And Orrery Stakes (Ascot)	Alec Russell	745
Cornwallis Stakes (Ascot)	George Selwyn	886
Coronation Stakes (Ascot)	John Crofts	505
Coventry Stakes (Ascot)	George Selwyn	612

Craven Stakes (Newmarket)	*John Crofts*	46
Criterium de Maisons-Laffitte (Maisons-Laffitte)	*P. Bertrand*	411
Criterium de Saint-Cloud (Saint-Cloud)	*P. Bertrand*	496
Dalham Chester Vase (Chester)	*John Crofts*	881
Daniel Prenn Royal Yorkshire Stakes (York)	*Alec Russell*	122
Derby Italiano (Rome)	*John Crofts*	376
Dewhurst Stakes (Newmarket)	*Alec Russell*	945
Diadem Stakes (Ascot)	*George Selwyn*	928
Diomed Stakes (Epsom)	*John Crofts*	941
Doncaster Bloodstock Sales Scarbrough Stakes (Doncaster)	*John Crofts*	553
Doncaster Cup (Doncaster)	*John Crofts*	306
Doonside Cup (Ayr)	*Alec Russell*	458
Dubai Champion Stakes (Newmarket)	*Alec Russell*	691
Dubai Poule d'Essai des Poulains (Longchamp)	*John Crofts*	748
Dubai Poule d'Essai des Pouliches (Longchamp)	*P. Bertrand*	194
Duke of York Stakes (York)	*Alec Russell*	745
Earl of Sefton EBF Stakes (Newmarket)	*John Crofts*	831
EBF Chesterton Maiden Stakes (Newmarket)	*John Crofts*	95
EBF Halifax Maiden Fillies Stakes (Ascot)	*Ed Byrne*	825
EBF Timeform Charity Day Stakes (York)	*Alec Russell*	456
Emirates Prix du Moulin de Longchamp (Longchamp)	*John Crofts*	42
European Free Handicap (Newmarket)	*John Crofts*	647
Ever Ready Derby (Epsom)	*Ed Byrne*	234
Ever Ready Derby (Epsom)	*John Crofts*	235
Falmouth Stakes (Handicap) (York)	*John Crofts*	914
Falmouth Stakes (Newmarket)	*John Crofts*	339
Federation Brewery L.C.L. Pils Lager Beeswing Stakes (Newcastle)	*Alec Russell*	156
Festival Handicap (Ascot)	*John Crofts*	751
Fillies' Mile (Ascot)	*Alec Russell*	368
Flanders Maiden Stakes (Div. 1) (Doncaster)	*Alec Russell*	865
Flying Childers Stakes (Doncaster)	*George Selwyn*	626
Forte Mile (Sandown)	*John Crofts*	701
Foster's Silver Cup Stakes (York)	*Alec Russell*	883
Fred Archer Stakes (Newmarket)	*John Crofts*	393
Galtres Stakes (York)	*John Crofts*	196
Gardner Merchant Hungerford Stakes (Newbury)	*John Crofts*	538
General Accident Jockey Club Stakes (Newmarket)	*John Crofts*	716
General Accident One Thousand Guineas Stakes (Newmarket)	*John Crofts*	347
General Accident Two Thousand Guineas Stakes (Newmarket)	*John Crofts*	688
Gladness Stakes (the Curragh)	*Caroline Norris*	110
Goffs Irish One Thousand Guineas (the Curragh)	*Caroline Norris*	504
Gold Cup (Ascot)	*John Crofts*	241
Gold Seal Oaks (Epsom)	*John Crofts*	889
Goodwood Cup (Goodwood)	*John Crofts*	306
Grand Prix de Deauville Lancel (Deauville)	*P. Bertrand*	537
Grand Prix de Paris Louis Vuitton (Longchamp)	*John Crofts*	365
Grand Prix de Saint-Cloud (Saint-Cloud)	*P. Bertrand*	622
Gran Premio di Milano (Milan)	*Perrucci*	511
Great Voltigeur Stakes (York)	*Alec Russell*	128
Grosser Mercedes Benz Preis Bayerisches Zuchtrennen (Munich)	*Zeno-Turffoto*	432
Grosser Preis von Baden (Baden-Baden)	*Zeno-Turffoto*	512
Hackwood Stakes (Newbury)	*John Crofts*	541
Hanson Coronation Cup (Epsom)	*John Crofts*	708
Hardwicke Stakes (Ascot)	*John Crofts*	686
Haydock Park Sprint Cup (Haydock)	*Alec Russell*	757
Heinz 57 Phoenix Stakes (Leopardstown)	*Caroline Norris*	619
Homeowners Dante Stakes (York)	*George Selwyn*	47
Hoover Cumberland Lodge Stakes (Ascot)	*George Selwyn*	592
Hoover Handicap (Ascot)	*George Selwyn*	663
Ibn Bey Geoffrey Freer Stakes (Newbury)	*John Crofts*	746
Insulpak Victoria Cup (Ascot)	*John Crofts*	89
Irish Independent Newspapers Pretty Polly Stakes (the Curragh)	*Maymes Ansell*	502

12

Jacobs Goldene Peitsche (Baden-Baden)	*John Crofts*	252
Jefferson Smurfit Memorial Irish St Leger	*John Crofts*	513
(the Curragh)		
Jersey Stakes (Ascot)	*John Crofts*	640
Jockey Club Cup (Newmarket)	*John Crofts*	307
John Mallinson Stakes (Limited Handicap) (Haydock)	*Alec Russell*	814
John of Gaunt Stakes (Haydock)	*Alec Russell*	581
John Smith's Magnet Cup (Handicap) (York)	*Alec Russell*	549
Juddmonte International Stakes (York)	*Alec Russell*	690
Juddmonte Lockinge Stakes (Newbury)	*John Crofts*	737
July Cup (Newmarket)	*John Crofts*	547
July Stakes (Newmarket)	*John Crofts*	915
Keeneland Nunthorpe Stakes (York)	*Alec Russell*	481
Kensington Palace Graduation Stakes (Ascot)	*George Selwyn*	656
Kerry Group Irish Champion Stakes (Leopardstown)	*Caroline Norris*	236
Kildangan Stud Irish Oaks (the Curragh)	*Caroline Norris*	890
King Edward VII Stakes (Ascot)	*John Crofts*	109
King George Stakes (Goodwood)	*John Crofts*	301
King George V Stakes (Handicap) (Ascot)	*John Crofts*	793
King George VI and Queen Elizabeth Diamond Stakes	*Ed Byrne*	810
(Ascot)		
King George VI and Queen Elizabeth Diamond Stakes	*John Crofts*	811
(Ascot)		
King's Stand Stakes (Ascot)	*John Crofts*	756
Krug Trophy (Handicap) (Ascot)	*George Selwyn*	655
La Coupe (Longchamp)	*John Crofts*	924
Ladbroke Autumn Handicap (Newmarket)	*John Crofts*	147
Ladbroke Bunbury Cup (Newmarket)	*Ed Byrne*	181
Ladbroke Chester Cup (Handicap) (Chester)	*John Crofts*	912
Ladbrokes (Ayr) Gold Cup (Handicap) (Ayr)	*Alec Russell*	463
Ladbrokes (Ayr) Silver Cup (Handicap) (Ayr)	*Alec Russell*	368
Lanson Champagne Vintage Stakes (Goodwood)	*George Selwyn*	508
Laurent-Perrier Champagne Stakes (Doncaster)	*Alec Russell*	612
Leslie And Godwin Spitfire Stakes (Handicap)	*John Crofts*	602
(Goodwood)		
Lowther Stakes (York)	*John Crofts*	571
Mail On Sunday Trophy Stakes (Doncaster)	*Alec Russell*	937
March Stakes (Goodwood)	*W. Everitt*	660
Maxims Club Derby Trial Stakes (Lingfield)	*George Selwyn*	79
May Hill Stakes (Doncaster)	*John Crofts*	499
Meadow Meats EBF Flying Five (Leopardstown)	*Maymes Ansell*	291
Moet & Chandon-Rennen (Baden-Baden)	*John Crofts*	753
Monks Cross Stakes (York)	*Alec Russell*	835
Moorestyle Convivial Maiden Stakes (York)	*Alec Russell*	676
Moyglare Stud Stakes (the Curragh)	*Maymes Ansell*	721
Newbury Sales Super Sprint (Newbury)	*Ed Byrne*	479
Newcastle Brown Ale Northumberland Plate	*Alec Russell*	925
(Handicap) (Newcastle)		
Newgate Stud Middle Park Stakes (Newmarket)	*John Crofts*	949
Norwest Holst Trophy (Handicap) (York)	*Alec Russell*	536
Old Newton Cup (Handicap) (Haydock)	*Alec Russell*	516
Ormonde EBF Stakes (Chester)	*Alec Russell*	707
Palace House Stakes (Newmarket)	*Alec Russell*	540
Personnel Selection Stakes (Ascot)	*George Selwyn*	377
Phil Bull Trophy (Pontefract)	*Alec Russell*	275
Polo Mints Yorkshire Cup (York)	*Alec Russell*	685
Premio Ellington (Rome)	*John Crofts*	734
Premio Parioli (Rome)	*International Racing Bureau*	37
Premio Presidente Della Repubblica (Rome)	*International Racing Bureau*	765
Prince of Wales's Stakes (Ascot)	*W. Everitt*	609
Princess of Wales's Stakes (Newmarket)	*John Crofts*	708
Princess Margaret Stakes (Ascot)	*John Crofts*	500
Prix Daphnis (Evry)	*P. Bertrand*	807
Prix d'Aumale (Longchamp)	*P. Bertrand*	423
Prix de Diane Hermes (Chantilly)	*P. Bertrand*	403
Prix de Fontainebleau (Longchamp)	*P. Bertrand*	659

13

Prix de la Foret (Longchamp)	*John Crofts*	929
Prix de la Grotte (Longchamp)	*P. Bertrand*	26
Prix de la Porte Maillot (Longchamp)	*P. Bertrand*	223
Prix de la Salamandre (Longchamp)	*P. Bertrand*	945
Prix de Malleret (Longchamp)	*John Crofts*	875
Prix de Meautry (Deauville)	*P. Bertrand*	880
Prix de Pomone (Deauville)	*P. Bertrand*	485
Prix de Saint-Georges (Longchamp)	*P. Bertrand*	252
Prix de Seine-et-Oise (Maisons-Laffitte)	*John Crofts*	760
Prix des Tourelles (Longchamp)	*George Selwyn*	903
Prix d'Ispahan (Longchamp)	*John Crofts*	952
Prix du Conseil de Paris (Longchamp)	*P. Bertrand*	311
Prix du Haras de Fresnay-le-Buffard Jacques le Marois (Deauville)	*P. Bertrand*	266
Prix du Jockey-Club Lancia (Chantilly)	*P. Bertrand*	630
Prix du Petit-Couvert (Longchamp)	*John Crofts*	927
Prix du Prince d'Orange (Longchamp)	*John Crofts*	68
Prix Eclipse (Saint-Cloud)	*P. Bertrand*	255
Prix Eugene Adam (Saint-Cloud)	*P. Bertrand*	629
Prix Foy Escada (Longchamp)	*George Selwyn*	486
Prix Ganay (Longchamp)	*P. Bertrand*	818
Prix Guillaume d'Ornano (Deauville)	*P. Bertrand*	330
Prix Jean de Chaudenay (Saint-Cloud)	*P. Bertrand*	212
Prix Jean Prat (Longchamp)	*John Crofts*	428
Prix Le Fabuleux (Saint-Cloud)	*John Crofts*	677
Prix Lupin (Longchamp)	*John Crofts*	401
Prix Marcel Boussac (Longchamp)	*P. Bertrand*	323
Prix Maurice de Gheest (Deauville)	*P. Bertrand*	647
Prix Maurice de Nieuil (Maisons-Laffitte)	*John Crofts*	899
Prix Morny Agence Francaise (Deauville)	*P. Bertrand*	944
Prix Omnium II (Saint-Cloud)	*P. Bertrand*	65
Prix Royal-Oak (Longchamp)	*P. Bertrand*	79
Prix Saint-Alary (Longchamp)	*P. Bertrand*	695
Prix Saint-Roman (Evry)	*P. Bertrand*	678
Prix Vermeille Escada (Longchamp)	*P. Bertrand*	404
Queen Anne Stakes (Ascot)	*Alec Russell*	440
Queen Elizabeth Handicap (Kempton)	*W. Everitt*	230
Queen Elizabeth II Stakes (Ascot)	*John Crofts*	440
Queen Mary Stakes (Ascot)	*John Crofts*	478
Queen Mother's Cup (York)	*Alec Russell*	729
Racecall Gold Trophy (Redcar)	*Alec Russell*	620
Racecall Melrose Handicap (York)	*George Selwyn*	208
Racing Post Trophy (Doncaster)	*John Crofts*	73
Reference Point Sceptre Stakes (Doncaster)	*Alec Russell*	607
Reference Point Strensall Stakes (York)	*Alec Russell*	797
Ribblesdale Stakes (Ascot)	*Alec Russell*	70
Richmond Brissac Trophy (Handicap) (Goodwood)	*W. Everitt*	833
Ripon Horn Blower Stakes (Ripon)	*Alec Russell*	475
Rockfel Stakes (Newmarket)	*Alec Russell*	934
Rokeby Farms Mill Reef Stakes (Newbury)	*W. Everitt*	295
Rothmans International (Woodbine)	*Michael Burns*	784
Rous Stakes (Newmarket)	*John Crofts*	120
Royal Hunt Cup (Ascot)	*John Crofts*	176
Royal Lodge Stakes (Ascot)	*John Crofts*	218
Schweppes Golden Mile (Handicap) (Goodwood)	*George Selwyn*	459
Scottish Equitable Gimcrack Stakes (York)	*John Crofts*	800
Scottish Equitable Richmond Stakes (Goodwood)	*John Crofts*	788
Sea World International Stakes (the Curragh)	*Caroline Norris*	766
Shadwell Stud Firth of Clyde Stakes (Ayr)	*Alec Russell*	919
Shadwell Stud Nell Gwyn Stakes (Newmarket)	*John Crofts*	81
Singer & Friedlander Greenham Stakes (Newbury)	*John Crofts*	458
Smurfit National Stakes (the Curragh)	*Caroline Norris*	277
St James's Palace Stakes (Ascot)	*John Crofts*	135
Sunset Boulevard Solario Stakes (Sandown)	*John Crofts*	918
Sussex Stakes (Goodwood)	*John Crofts*	505
Tattersalls Cheveley Park Stakes (Newmarket)	*John Crofts*	722
Tattersalls Musidora Stakes (York)	*John Crofts*	41
Tattersalls Rogers Gold Cup (the Curragh)	*Caroline Norris*	591

Tattersalls Sales Stakes Nursery (Final) (Newmarket)	*John Crofts*	24
Tennents Scottish Classic (Ayr)	*Alec Russell*	752
Tetley Bitter Doncaster Mile (Doncaster)	*Alec Russell*	207
T.G.I. Friday's Gordon Richards EBF Stakes (Sandown)	*George Selwyn*	211
Thresher Classic Trial (Sandown)	*John Crofts*	628
Timeform Futurity (Pontefract)	*Alec Russell*	577
Timeform Harry Rosebery Trophy (Ayr)	*Alec Russell*	308
Tote Cesarewitch (Newmarket)	*Alec Russell*	904
Tote Ebor (Handicap) (York)	*Alec Russell*	654
Tote Gold Trophy Stakes (Handicap) (Goodwood)	*John Crofts*	798
Tote Great St Wilfrid Handicap (Ripon)	*Alec Russell*	332
Tote-Portland Handicap (Doncaster)	*Alec Russell*	462
Troy Stakes (Doncaster)	*Alec Russell*	415
UB Group Temple Stakes (Sandown)	*John Crofts*	782
United Breweries Fillies Stakes (Sandown)	*John Crofts*	834
Van Geest Criterion Stakes (Newmarket)	*John Crofts*	871
Vodac Chesterfield Cup (Handicap) (Goodwood)	*W. Everitt*	430
Vodafone Nassau Stakes (Goodwood)	*John Crofts*	700
Washington Singer Stakes (Newbury)	*John Crofts*	851
William Hill Cambridgeshire Handicap (Newmarket)	*John Crofts*	663
William Hill Golden Spurs Trophy (Handicap) (York)	*Alec Russell*	188
William Hill Lincoln Handicap (Doncaster)	*Alec Russell*	360
William Hill November Handicap (Doncaster)	*Alec Russell*	879
William Hill Stewards' Cup (Goodwood)	*John Crofts*	462
Windsor Castle Stakes (Ascot)	*John Crofts*	719
Wokingham Handicap (Ascot)	*Alec Russell*	670

THE LEADER
IN
TELEPHONE RACING

COMMENTARIES

MAINLINE
0891·500·300
All the action from all the courses on just one number

INDIVIDUAL COURSE COMMENTARIES
0891·500·PLUS
Course Number available in Daily and Racing Press

COMMENTARY CALL-UP
0891·500·368
Missed a live race commentary? Dial into the Racecall Daily
Commentary Library and follow the computer instructions for
a re-run of the race of your choice.

RESULTS

COURSE LINES
Results from just the one course, starting with
the most recent race.

RESULT FLASH
0891·500·350
A rapid round-up from all meetings starting with the latest race and
working backwards through the day.

CLASSIFIED
0891·500·345
Complete course by course results service.

THE MOST COMPREHENSIVE SERVICE AVAILABLE

TIS plc., 24 West Smithfield, London EC1A 9DL. Calls cost 36p per minute cheap rate and 48p per minute at all other times

EXPLANATORY NOTES

To assess the prospects of any horse in a race it is necessary to know two things about him: first, how good he is; and second, what sort of horse he is. In this book the merit of each horse is expressed in the form of a *rating* (printed on the right) and the *racing character* of the horse is given in the commentary.

TIMEFORM RATINGS

The Timeform Rating of a horse is simply the merit of the horse expressed in pounds and is arrived at by careful examination of its running against other horses using a scale of weight for distance beaten which ranges from 3 lb a length at five furlongs and 2 lb a length at a mile and a quarter to 1 lb at two miles. We maintain a "running" handicap of all horses in training throughout the season, or, to be strictly accurate, two handicaps, one for horses aged three years and over, and one for two-year-olds.

THE LEVEL OF THE RATINGS

At the close of each season all the horses that have raced are re-handicapped from scratch, and each horse's rating is revised. It is also necessary to adjust the general level of the handicap, so that all the ratings are kept at the same standard level from year to year. Left to itself, the general level of the ratings, in each succeeding issue of Timeform, tends to rise steadily. For technical reasons it is desirable to allow it to do so during the season: but, in winter, when the complete re-handicap is done, the ratings must, of course, be put back on their proper level again.

This explains why, in this book, the ratings are in general, different from those in the final issue of the 1992 Timeform series.

RATINGS AND WEIGHT-FOR-AGE

The reader has, in the ratings in this book, a universal handicap embracing all the horses in training it is possible to weigh up, ranging from tip-top classic performers, with ratings from 130 to 145, down to the meanest selling platers, rated around the 20 mark. What we now have to explain is the practical use of these ratings in the business of weighing up a race.

Before doing so, it is important to mention that all ratings are at weight-for-age, so that equal ratings mean horses of equal merit: perhaps it would be clearer if we said that the universal rating handicap is really not a single handicap, but four handicaps side by side: one for 2-y-o's, one for 3-y-o's, one for 4-y-o's and one for older horses. Thus, a 3-y-o rated, for argument's sake, at 117 is deemed to be identical in point of "merit" with a 4-y-o also rated at 117: but for them to have equal chances in, say, a mile race in May, the 3-y-o would need to be receiving 9 lb from the 4-y-o, which is the weight difference specified by the Age, Weight and Distance Tables on pages 4 and 5.

USING THE RATINGS

In using Timeform Ratings with a view to discovering which horses in any race have the best chances at the weights, we have two distinct cases, according to whether the horses taking part are of the same age or of different ages. Here is the procedure in each case:-

A. Horses of the Same Age

If the horses all carry the same weight there are no adjustments to be made, and the horses with the highest ratings have the best chances. If the horses carry different weights, jot down their ratings, and to the rating of each horse add one point for every pound the horse is set to carry less than 10 st, or subtract one point for every pound it has to carry more than 10 st. When the ratings have been adjusted in this way the highest resultant figure indicates the horse with the best chance at the weights.

Example (any distance: any week of the season)

2 Good Girl (9-6)	....	Rating 119	....	add	8	....	127
2 Paulinus (9-4)	....	Rating 113	....	add	10	....	123
2 Abilene (8-11)	....	Rating 107	....	add	17	....	124
2 Bob's Joy (8-7)	....	Rating 108	....	add	21	....	129
2 Time Warp (8-2)	....	Rating 100	....	add	26	....	126
2 Eagle Eye (7-7)	....	Rating 92	....	add	35	....	127

Bob's Joy (129) has the best chance; Good Girl (127) and Eagle Eye (127) are the next best.

B. Horses of Different Ages

Take no notice of the weight any horse receives from any other. Instead, consult the Age, Weight and Distance Tables on pages 4 and 5. Treat each horse separately, and compare the weight it has to carry with the weight prescribed for it in the tables, according to the age of the horse, the distance of the race and the month of the year. Then, add one point to the rating for each pound the horse has to carry less than the weight given in the tables: or, subtract one point from the rating for every pound it has to carry more than the weight prescribed by the tables. The highest resultant figure indicates the horse most favoured by the weights.

Example (1½ miles on June 30th)

(Table Weights: 5-y-o 10-0; 4-y-o 9-13; 3-y-o 9-1)

6 Nimitz (10-2)	....	Rating 115	....	subtract 2	.	113
4 Red Devil (9-9)	....	Rating 114	....	add 4	....	118
6 Sweet Cindy (9-5).	...	Rating 115	....	add 9	....	124
3 Jailhouse (9-2)	....	Rating 120	....	subtract 1	.	119
4 Haakon (8-11)	....	Rating 101	....	add 16	....	117
3 Fine Strike (8-7)	....	Rating 108	....	add 8	....	116

Sweet Cindy (124) has the best chance at the weights, with 5 lb in hand of Jailhouse.

TURF AND ALL-WEATHER RATINGS

When a horse has raced on turf and on all-weather and its form on one is significantly different from the other, the two ratings are given, the all-weather set out below the turf preceded by 'a'.

Thus with FREE FOR ALL 47

a55

the top figure, 47, is the rating to be used in turf races, and the one below, a55, is for use in all-weather races.

JOCKEYSHIP AND APPRENTICE ALLOWANCES

There is just one further point that arises in evaluating the chances of the horses on the basis of their ratings: the question of jockeyship in general, and apprentice allowances in particular. The allowance which may be claimed by an apprentice is given to enable apprentices to obtain race-riding experience against experienced jockeys. For the purposes of rating calculations it should, in general, be assumed that the allowance the apprentice is able to claim (3 lb, 5 lb, or 7 lb) is nullified by his or her inexperience. Therefore, the *weight adjustments to the ratings should be calculated on the weight allotted by the handicapper, or determined by the conditions of the race,* and no extra addition should be made to a rating because the horse's rider claims an apprentice allowance.

The above is the general routine procedure. But, of course, there is no reason why the quality of jockeyship should not be taken into account in assessing the chances of horses in a race. Quite the contrary. Nobody would question that the jockeyship of a first-class rider is worth a pound or two, and occasionally an apprentice comes along who is riding quite as well as the average jockey long before losing the right to claim. Once the age and weight adjustments have been made to the ratings, small additional allowances may, at the discretion of the reader, be made for these matters of jockeyship. Please note, though, that if a horse is regularly ridden by a claiming apprentice, the fact will have been taken account of when its previous performances have been assessed by our handicappers.

WEIGHING UP A RACE

The ratings tell you which horses in a particular race are most favoured by the weights; but complete analysis demands that the racing character of each horse, as set out in the commentary upon it, is also studied carefully to see if there is any reason why the horse might be expected not to run up to its rating. It counts for little that a horse is thrown in at the weights if it has no pretensions whatever to staying the distance, or is unable to act on the prevailing going.

These two matters, suitability of distance and going, are no doubt the most important points to be considered. But there are others. For example, the ability of a horse to accommodate itself to the conformation of the track. Then there is the matter of pace versus stamina: as between two stayers of equal merit, racing over a distance suitable to both, firm going, or a small field with the prospect of a slowly-run race, would favour the one with the better pace and acceleration; whereas dead or soft going, or a big field with the prospect of a strong gallop throughout the race, would favour the sounder stayer. There is also the matter of temperament and behaviour at the start: nobody would be in a hurry to take a short price about a horse with whom it is always an even chance whether it will give its running.

A few minutes spent checking up on these matters in the commentaries upon the horses concerned will sometimes put a very different complexion on a race from that which is put upon it by the ratings alone. We repeat, therefore, that the correct way to use Timeform, or this annual volume, in the analysis of individual races is, first to use the ratings to discover which horses are most favoured by the weights, and second, to check through the comments on the horse to discover what factors other than weight might also affect the outcome of the race.

Incidentally, in setting out the various characteristics, requirements and peculiarities of each horse in the commentary upon it, we have always expressed ourselves in as critical a manner as possible, endeavouring to say just as much, and no whit more than the facts seem to warrant. Where there are clear indications, and definite conclusions can be drawn with fair certainty, we have drawn them: if it is a matter of probability or possibility we have put it that way, being careful not to say the one when we mean the other; and where real conclusions are not to be drawn, we have been content to state the facts. Furthermore, when we say that a horse *may not* be suited by hard going, we do not expect the reader to treat it as though we had said that the horse *is not* suited by hard going. In short, both in our thinking and in the setting out of our views we have aimed at precision.

THE FORM SUMMARIES

The form summary enclosed in the brackets shows for each individual horse the distance, the state of the going and where the horse finished in each of its races on the flat during the last two seasons. Performances are in chronological sequence, the earliest being given first.

The distance of each race is given in furlongs, fractional distances being expressed in the decimal notation to the nearest tenth of a furlong. Races on an all-weather surface are prefixed by letter 'a'.

The going is symbolised as follows: h = hard or very firm; f = firm (turf) or fast (all-weather); m = on the firm side of good; g = good (turf) or standard (all-weather); d = dead, or on the soft side of good; s = soft, sticky or holding (turf) or slow (all-weather); v = heavy, very heavy or very holding.

Placings are indicated, up to sixth place, by the use of superior figures, an asterisk being used to denote a win.

Thus [1991 NR 1992 10s* 12f³ 11.7g a11g²] signifies that the horse was unraced in 1991. He ran four times in 1992, winning over 10 furlongs on soft going first time out, finishing third over twelve furlongs on firm going next time out, unplaced, not in the first six, over 11.7 furlongs on good going, and then second over eleven furlongs on standard going on an all-weather track.

Included in the pedigree details are the highest Timeform Annual ratings during their racing careers of the sires, dams and sires of dams of all horses, where the information is available.

Where sale prices are given F denotes the price in guineas sold as a foal, Y the price in guineas sold as a yearling. The prefix IR denotes Irish guineas.

THE RATING SYMBOLS

The following symbols, attached to the ratings, are to be interpreted as stated:-

p   the horse is likely to make more than normal progress and to improve on its rating.

P   there is convincing evidence, or, to say the least, a very strong presumption that the horse is capable of form much better than it has so far displayed.

+   the horse's form may be rather better than we have rated it.

d   the horse appears to have deteriorated, and might no longer be capable of running to the rating given.

§   a horse of somewhat unsatisfactory temperament; one who may give its running on occasions, but cannot be relied upon to do so.

§§   an arrant rogue or thorough jade; so temperamentally unsatisfactory as to be not worth a rating.

?   the use of a query without a rating implies that although the horse has form, its merit is impossible to assess with confidence. If used in conjunction with a rating this symbol implies that the rating is based upon inadequate or unsatisfactory data, or that the rating is suspect.

THE AGENCY WITH A TRADITION OF BUYING GOOD HORSES

CURRAGH

BLOODSTOCK AGENCY

RACEHORSES OF 1992

Horse	*Commentary*	*Rating*

A A BAMBA 3 b.f. Slip Anchor 136 – Enchanting Dancer (FR) (Nijinsky (CAN) **57**
138) [1991 7g⁶ 8.1g 8g⁴ 10m* 1992 12v 12g² 13m⁴ 15.8d 14d³ 16f 12g⁴ 14.1d a12g⁶
a14g] tall, angular, unfurnished filly: modest performer: in frame in claimer and 3
handicaps: stays 1¾m (set too strong a pace over 15.8f): below form on extremes of
going: blinkered (tailed off) final start: has run well for apprentice: looks one paced.
N. A. Callaghan

AAHSAYLAD 6 b.h. Ardross 134 – Madam Slaney 92 (Prince Tenderfoot (USA) **81**
126) [1991 17.1m² 18f² 14g⁶ 16.5m* 16m⁴ 16.1m² 15g² 13g* 13.9g 13.9g 17.5m² 18m
1992 11.9g 18f* 20m 16.1f 15m² 17.5d³ 15s² 18m 14.6g⁴] big, good-topped horse:
impresses good deal in appearance: moderate mover: fairly useful handicapper: won
at Doncaster in May: best runs when placed at Ayr: sold to join J. White 20,000 gns
Newmarket Autumn Sales: effective at 13f, and stays really well: acts on any going:
effective visored or not: tough and genuine. *F. H. Lee*

AAL EL AAL 5 br.h. High Top 131 – Last Card (USA) 56 (Full Out (USA)) [1991 **–**
NR 1992 14.1d] second foal: half-brother to a winner abroad by Ela-Mana-Mou: dam
maiden: ran as if something amiss when tailed off in Redcar maiden: won NH Flat
race later in autumn: sold 2,000 gns Ascot November Sales. *P. J. Hobbs*

AALU (IRE) 2 b.f. (Apr 12) Sure Blade (USA) 130 – Hopeful Search (USA) 71 **36**
(Vaguely Noble 140) [1992 6g 5g⁴ 7d 6v] smallish, leggy, unfurnished filly: first foal:
dam, disappointing maiden possibly best at 1¼m, is daughter of temperamental
Quest, a sister to high-class 1983 French 2-y-o Treizieme and half-sister to Gold
Cup second Eastern Mystic: form only in 5f Folkestone maiden: outclassed next
start, eased significantly final one: will stay 1m: may be capable of better. *C. E.
Brittain*

AARDVARK 6 ch.g. On Your Mark 125 – Vaguely Jade (Corvaro (USA) 122) **66**
[1991 NR 1992 9.9g³ 8m² 8m] lengthy gelding: winning handicapper as 4-y-o: placed
at Beverley and Newbury (apprentices) within a week in June: ran poorly in July:
effective from 1m to 1¼m: seems unsuited by soft going, acts on any other: effective
visored or not, didn't wear them in 1992: suitable mount for inexperienced rider. *R.
M. Whitaker*

AASFF (USA) 3 b.c. Sovereign Dancer (USA) – Ecstatica (USA) 81 (Damascus **68**
(USA)) [1991 7m 7m⁶ 7f² 7f³ 8m* 7.6d 1992 7f⁵ 8.1d 8g 10g⁶ 9.9m³ 9d 10m]
well-made, lengthy colt: moderate walker: fair handicapper: well below form in
Cambridgeshire at Newmarket and apprentice event (no chance after slow start) at
Pontefract last 2 starts: stays 1¼m: acts on firm going, seemingly not on dead: ran
poorly in blinkers final start: takes strong hold. *D. Morley*

ABBEY GREEN 4 ch.g. Gabitat 119 – Getaway Girl 63 (Capistrano 120) [1991 **–**
NR 1992 8.3m 6g⁴ 7.1s 8.1d] workmanlike gelding: poor maiden: has twice reared in
stalls. *C. J. Hill*

ABBEY'S GAL 2 b.f. (May 2) Efisio 120 – Outward's Gal (Ashmore (FR) 125) **77**
[1992 6m³ 6g² 6m² 5d* 7.3g⁴] lengthy filly: has a round action: fourth foal:
half-sister to 3-y-o Princess of Orange (by Master Willie) and 1¾m NH Flat race
winner Hell of A Guy (by Absalom): dam poor maiden: fair form: odds on, niggled
along throughout to win at Wolverhampton in August: set plenty to do and got poor
run when never-nearer fourth in slowly-run nursery at Newbury following month:
will stay 1m: acts on good to firm and good to soft ground. *I. A. Balding*

ABBEY STRAND (USA)   3 b.f. Shadeed (USA) 135 – Christchurch (FR) 88 (So   **73**
Blessed 130) [1991 6s 7m³ 1992 11.5d5 10m 7g⁵ 7s² 7d 7m a8g² a8g³ a8g³ a8g*]
leggy, quite good-topped filly: fair handicapper: odds on, easily won weak maiden at
Lingfield in December, making all: stays 1m well (remote last in listed company
over further): acts on soft ground and all-weather surfaces: well below form in visor
once. *Lord Huntingdon*

ABBOTSHAM   7 b.g. Ardross 134 – Lucy Platter (FR) (Record Token 128) [1991   –
22.2m 16.2g 1992 16.2m] big, lengthy gelding: lightly raced and no form on flat:
winning (1990/1) hunter chaser. *W. R. Williams*

ABELONI   3 ch.g. Absalom 128 – Agreloui 59 (Tower Walk 130) [1991 5m⁶ 5m⁵ 5g   **58**
1992 7g 8.2g a8g² a7g 10.5d⁶ 8f 8m⁴ 10g 7d* 8.2s a8g⁶] leggy, workmanlike gelding:
modest handicapper on his day: trained until after sixth 3-y-o start by A. Scott:
visored first time, won at Catterick in October: stays 1m: acts on good to firm and
dead ground and on fibresand: fair effort in blinkers final start: sold to join W.
Williams 2,600 gns Doncaster November Sales. *J. A. Glover*

ABERDEEN HEATHER   2 b.g. (Mar 22) Absalom 128 – Scotch Thistle 73   **78**
(Sassafras (FR) 135) [1992 5d 5g 6g 7d⁵ 7m⁴ 7.3g⁶ 8.1d 7d³ 7s³ 8m⁵ a8g* a7g*]   a91
9,800F, 10,500Y: sturdy gelding: half-brother to 3-y-o Green's Exhibit (by Song) and
several winners, including (from 1m to 10.4f) Flying Scotsman (by Tower Walk):
dam placed at up to 1½m: progressive performer: won maiden and (easily beat
effort) nursery at Lingfield in November: will stay 1¼m: acts on good to firm and
soft ground, and particularly well on equitrack: has run well for 7-lb claimer. *D. R. C.
Elsworth*

ABERFOYLE (IRE)   4 b.g. Vision (USA) – Princess John (Run The Gantlet   –
(USA) [1991 12d⁵ 11g² 15g* 14.1m² 14.1f⁵ 12g 16.1g 1992 a14g⁴ 18g 21.6g] leggy
gelding: poor mover: moderate fourth in amateurs handicap at Southwell (wore
eyeshield) for I. Campbell: should stay beyond 2m: acts on good to firm and dead
ground, and on fibresand: well beaten in blinkers: trained second start by P.
Kelleway. *Miss Gay Kelleway*

ABERGELE   2 gr.g. (Mar 11) Absalom 128 – Clare Celeste 73 (Coquelin (USA)   **86** p
121) [1992 a6g² a7g* 6s⁵ 7s³ 6m*] 18,000Y: workmanlike gelding: has a round
action: first foal: dam poor maiden best effort at 7f at 2 yrs, is half-sister to very
useful 6f and 7f winner Braddells: progressive form: won maiden at Southwell in
July and nursery (staying on strongly having been one of first off bridle) at
Newmarket in October: will stay 1m: acts on good to firm and soft ground, and on
fibresand: probably capable of further improvement. *J. G. FitzGerald*

ABERLADY   2 b.f. (Mar 24) Sizzling Melody 117 – Peep of Day (USA) (Lypheor   **65**
118) [1992 5g³ 5m⁶ 5g* 5g² 5m* 5m 5.1d⁵] angular, workmanlike filly: moderate
walker: first foal: dam French 9f winner: modest form: successful in maiden (for
apprentice) and claimer at Wolverhampton in summer: will stay 6f: ran respectably
when sweating final start: sold 2,300 gns Newmarket Autumn Sales. *M. A. Jarvis*

ABERLEMNO   2 ch.c. (May 3) Absalom 128 – Campagna (Romulus 129) [1992 8g   **37**
8.5m] 8,200Y: sturdy colt: brother to a modest maiden and half-brother to several

*Tattersalls Sales Nursery (Final), Newmarket —
the grey Abergele stays on strongly from Benzoe*

winners, including quite useful middle-distance filly Carlingford Rose (by Dance In Time): dam French 1¼m winner: well beaten in maiden events in the North in late-summer: sold 520 gns Doncaster November Sales. *J. Berry*

ABET (USA)   2 b.f. (Feb 1) Alleged (USA) 138 – Reactress (USA) (Sharpen Up **64 p** 127) [1992 8g³ 8.1d³] quite attractive filly: second reported foal: dam minor sprint stakes winner: 9 lengths third of 10 to River Delta in maiden at Haydock in September: will stay 1¼m: likely to improve again. *Major W. R. Hern*

ABIGAILS BOY (HOL)   3 gr.c. Superlative 118 – Heartbreaker 71 (Steel Heart **50** 128) [1991 6m 6m⁴ 6m 5.7g 5d⁵ 1992 6v 6d* 6g 6d⁶] strong, close-coupled colt: modest handicapper: won at Hamilton in April: will probably prove best at around 6f: acts on good to firm and dead ground: not seen out after May. *Dr J. D. Scargill*

ABIGAIL'S DREAM   5 gr.m. Kalaglow 132 – Moss Pink (USA) (Levmoss 133)   **–** [1991 a12g⁵ 11.8g⁶ a12g⁵ 1992 a12g] lightly-made mare: quite modest performer at best: well beaten in Lingfield claimer in January: stays 1¼m well: acts on firm going: sold 2,000 gns Doncaster May Sales. *J. R. Jenkins*

ABILENE   2 ch.f. (Apr 23) Primo Dominie 121 – Burnt Amber (Balidar 133) [1992   **46** 5g⁶ 6m⁴ 7g⁴ 7d] leggy filly: third foal: sister to 3-y-o Ming Blue: dam unraced half-sister to Lockton: modest plater: stays 7f: sold 1,100 gns Newmarket Autumn Sales. *J. A. R. Toller*

ABINGDON FLYER (IRE)   4 b.g. Pennine Walk 120 – Busca (USA) 49 (Mr   **73** Prospector (USA)) [1991 10f⁶ 10g 10d⁴ 8m 10g 10s 11.7f² 10m² 10f* 10.3m 10g 1992 10.3g 11.9g⁴ 11.9m* 10m* 11.5f* 8f³ 11.9f² 10m³ 11.6m³ 10d] lengthy gelding: consistent performer, successful in spring in handicap at Brighton and claimers at Windsor and Lingfield: stays 1½m: needs top-of-the-ground: takes a lot of driving: probably best in blinkers: not seen out after July. *R. Hannon*

ABJAR   2 br.c. (Mar 22) Dominion 123 – Rye Tops 97 (Ile de Bourbon (USA) 133)   **65 p** [1992 6g⁴ a6g³] 2,200 2-y-o: angular, quite good-bodied colt: fourth foal: half-brother to 3-y-o Speedy Beauty (by Rousillon) and 11f winner Wassifa (by Sure Blade): dam 10.5f winner stayed 1½m, is sister to Most Welcome and daughter of Topsy, smart winner at up to 1¼m: bandaged, better effort when third in claimer at Lingfield, slowly away and behind, then finishing very strongly: will be well suited by middle distances: will do better. *P. A. Kelleway*

ABLE CHOICE (IRE)   2 b.c. (Feb 15) Taufan (USA) 119 – Great Land (USA)   **68 p** (Friend's Choice (USA)) [1992 6m⁴ 6m³] 31,000Y: good-topped colt: fifth foal: half-brother to unreliable sprint plater Land Sun (by Red Sunset): dam won 9 races at up to 9f in North America: odds on, better effort when keeping-on third in maiden at Newmarket in July: looked sure to improve again, particularly at 7f. *R. W. Armstrong*

ABLE LASSIE   4 gr.f. Grey Desire 115 – Clairwood (Final Straw 127) [1991 8m²   **70** 9.2d* 8.3d* 10.9g² 8g* 10.1m 1992 8.3m³ 10g⁵ 11f³ 12f⁶ 11.1m* 11.5g² 10.5d³ 12.1g³ 10.5s⁴] smallish, angular filly: moderate mover: fair handicapper: won Hamilton claimer in July: ran well afterwards, claimed £8,010 out of Haydock claimer final start: effective from 1¼m to 1½m: acts on any going: has won for apprentice: effective forcing pace or held up: tough. *Mrs M. Reveley*

ABLE PLAYER (USA)   5 b. or br.g. Solford (USA) 127 – Grecian Snow (CAN)   **–** (Snow Knight 125) [1991 7h 7m 10f³ 11.9g* 12.3m 12m 12.1g 1992 11.9d] leggy, quite good-topped gelding: none too consistent handicapper (rated 51) at 4 yrs: well beaten in September: will probably be suited by 1¾m: acts on hard ground: below form when blinkered once: progressive winning hurdler, including after being sold to join Mrs S. Bramall 32,000 gns Doncaster November Sales. *C. W. Thornton*

ABLE PRINCESS   4 ch.f. Music Boy 124 – Glamorous Girl (Caliban 123) [1991   **–** 5m⁴ 6s⁴ 5f 6m² 6m⁵ 5m² 5m 5m⁶ 6.1m a6g a5g a5g 1992 a7g] workmanlike filly: moderate mover: modest maiden (rated 53) at 3 yrs: stays 6f: below form on very firm going: effective blinkered or not: usually bandaged: retained 1,000 gns Doncaster January Sales and not seen after. *Mrs N. Macauley*

A BRIDGE TOO FAR (IRE)   2 b.f. (Mar 20) The Noble Player (USA) 126 –   **47** Miss Galwegian (Sandford Lad 133) [1992 5g⁶ 5f³ 6.1g* a6g⁴ 7.5s⁵ a7g⁴] 2,000Y: workmanlike filly: fifth foal: sister to 3-y-o Jubal Early, 7f winner at 2 yrs: dam placed over 6f at 2 yrs in Ireland: modest plater: narrowly won at Nottingham (no bid) in May for W. Pearce: seems suited by 6f: below best on fibresand (twice) and on soft ground: twice looked a hard ride, including final start (July): sold 520 gns Doncaster September Sales. *B. Beasley*

Prix de la Grotte, Longchamp—
Absurde (black cap), by a narrow margin from Guislaine, Verveine and Euphonic

ABSALOUI 4 gr.f. Absalom 128 – Agreloui 59 (Tower Walk 130) [1991 5m 7d 8m 7.1g⁴ 7.1m 9.7m⁶ 1992 a8g] leggy, workmanlike filly: probably of little account these days. *W. G. M. Turner* —

ABSENT RELATIVE 4 ch.f. Absalom 128 – Relatively Smart 76 (Great Nephew 126) [1991 10d 10g 10.1m 11.4m⁵ a12g⁴ 12d 1992 11.5m 10.1d³ 9d 9d] workmanlike filly: shows knee action: fair maiden: best effort at 4 yrs when third in Epsom handicap: effective from 1¼m to 1½m: acts on good to firm and dead ground and on equitrack: below form for amateur: won handicap hurdle in October. *Miss B. Sanders* **64**

ABSO 4 b.g. Absalom 128 – Classical Vintage 80 (Stradavinsky 121) [1991 8g⁶ 8m 8f 7f⁶ 7.1g 6g* 7m² 7m² 6m² 7f⁴ 7g 6m 7g* 7d² 1992 8g³ 7g³ 8s⁶ 8m³ 8.1f⁴ 8f² 8m⁶ 8.1g² 7.6m 7.1s⁵] strong, lengthy gelding: fair handicapper: has won 2 of 29 starts: effective from 7f to 1m: acts on firm and dead ground: effective blinkered/visored or not: often hangs and is irresolute. *R. Hannon* **69** §

ABSOLUTELY FACT (USA) 2 ch.c. (Apr 3) Known Fact (USA) 135 – Chilly Welcome (General Assembly (USA)) [1992 6f⁵ 7d a6g³ 7m a8g² a8g* a8g² a7g²] $7,500Y: smallish, stocky colt: fourth reported foal: half-brother to winners in North America by Proud Truth and Irish River: dam, Irish 12.8f winner, is sister to Irish stayer Security Clearance and daughter of Freeze The Secret: fair performer: sold out of W. Haggas' stable 3,200 gns Newmarket Autumn Sales after fourth outing: improved afterwards, easily winning a claimer at Lingfield and runner-up in 2 nurseries: will stay 1¼m: best efforts on all-weather surfaces. *C. C. Elsey* **61** a76

ABSOLUTELY NUTS 3 ro.f. Absalom 128 – Double Stitch 74 (Wolver Hollow 126) [1991 5d⁵ 5m⁵ 5m⁵ 5.1g³ 5m² 5d⁶ 1992 5g² 5g* 5f⁴ 6m* 5g⁴ 5m 5s⁴ 6f² 6d 5d³ 6.1s] lengthy filly: carries condition: fair performer: made all in good style in maiden at Thirsk and minor event at Leicester in May: good second in handicap at Ripon, having moved poorly to post on firm ground: well below form afterwards: suited by 6f: probably unsuited by a soft surface: tough and genuine. *B. A. McMahon* **73**

26

ABSOLUTELY RIGHT 4 ch.c. Absalom 128 – Sun Worshipper (Sun Prince **56 d**
128) [1991 10g 6f⁵ 7g 8f 7m 7g 8.3m 9.7f² 10.8m 9s 10.8g³ 11d² 10m 9.7s³ a12g² a10g³
1992 a10g⁶ a12g³ 11.9g* 11.9d² 11.9m³ 9.7g² 8.3g 18g 10.2f⁴] small, sturdy colt: has a
quick decisive turn of foot: moderate performer: successful in claimer at Brighton in March, only
win of career: trained until after sixth start by R. Akehurst: well below form after:
stays 1½m: seems to act on any going. *J. White*

ABSOLUTE MAGIC 2 b.c. (Feb 17) Doulab (USA) 115 – Trickster 92 (Major **60 p**
Portion 129) [1992 6m²] 17,500Y: sturdy colt: half-brother to numerous winners,
mostly at sprint distances, including smart Jester (by Song): dam sprinter: springer
in market though very green, 10 lengths second of 10 to Forest Wind in maiden at
Goodwood in August, keeping on well: seemed sure to improve. *W. J. Haggas*

ABSOLUTION 8 gr.h. Absalom 128 – Great Grey Niece 74 (Great Nephew 126) **83**
[1991 a5g⁶ 5g⁵ 5g 5f 5d 5f 5d 5m³ 5g* 5m 5m* 5g 5f 5f 5m 5.2g² 5d 1992 5f⁵ 5m³ 5g
5f³ 5g 5g* 5m⁵ 5d 5.1g 5g 5m 5s⁵ 5s 5g² a5g⁴ a6g a5g⁵ a5g⁵] workmanlike, good-
quartered horse: moderate walker and mover: fair but inconsistent handicapper:
won at Ayr in July: best at 5f: acts on any going: has won for apprentice: used to be as
effective in blinkers, didn't wear them in 1992: visored (well beaten) once at 8 yrs:
tries to dominate. *M. P. Naughton*

ABSONAL 5 gr.g. Absalom 128 – Aldbury Girl 79 (Galivanter 131) [1991 8d 8g⁵ **81**
8d⁶ 8g 1992 8.1m 7f⁶ 8f 8g⁶ 8s⁴ 8d 8g* 9d 9s 7d a10g³ a10g³ a10g³ a7g* a8g²]
strong, good-topped gelding: fairly useful performer: won claimers at Wolverhampton and Lingfield in the autumn: stays 1¼m: acts on firm ground and all-weather
surfaces, seems unsuited by a soft surface: held up. *R. Hannon*

ABSURDE (FR) 3 b.f. Green Desert (USA) 127 – Absolute (FR) 105 (Luthier **114**
126) [1991 8g* 6.5g* 6m² 7v³ 1992 8g* 8m⁴ 8f⁵ 6d] strong, close-coupled, rather
plain filly: smart performer: won Group 3 Prix de la Grotte at Longchamp in April:
good fourth to Culture Vulture in Poule d'Essai des Pouliches there and fair fifth to
Marling in Coronation Stakes at Royal Ascot: subsequently off course 3 months and
behind in Group 3 event at Maisons-Laffitte: will probably stay 1¼m: acts on good
to firm and heavy ground. *F. Boutin, France*

ABTAAL 2 b.c. (Mar 20) Green Desert (USA) 127 – Stufida (Bustino 136) [1992 **81**
6g² 7g* 8s³ 7g] 165,000Y: medium-sized, good-bodied, attractive colt: has scope:
fluent mover: fourth foal: half-brother to 1989 2-y-o 6f and 7f winner Fearless Rival
(by Cozzene): dam very good Italian filly, winner of 1¼m Premio Lydia Tesio at 3
yrs: fairly useful performer: narrowly won minor event at Kempton in August:
creditable third of 4 in moderately-run minor event at Ayr month later: travelled
strongly 4f then found little when last in £8,900 event at Ascot final start: stays 1m:
yet to race on top-of-the-ground. *H. Thomson Jones*

ABURY (IRE) 2 b.f. (Feb 19) Law Society (USA) 130 – Bay Shade (USA) 90 **91**
(Sharpen Up 127) [1992 7m³ 7m* 8m 8s⁵] leggy, useful-looking filly: has a fluent
action: first foal: dam 2-y-o 7f winner: fairly useful performer: seemed ill at ease on
track despite winning maiden at Chester in August: very good 6 lengths fifth of 8 to
Ivanka in Fillies' Mile at Ascot in September: will stay 1¼m: acts on good to firm
and soft ground. *P. W. Chapple-Hyam*

ACANTHUS (IRE) 2 b.c. (May 28) Slip Anchor 136 – Green Lucia 116 (Green **– p**
Dancer (USA) 132) [1992 8d⁵ 8m] 41,000Y: medium-sized, good-quartered colt:
brother to 4-y-o 1½m/1¾m performer Luchiroverte, closely related to Irish 1¾m
winner Euromill (by Shirley Heights) and half-brother to 2 winners: dam placed in
Irish Oaks and Yorkshire Oaks: poor form in autumn maidens at Goodwood and
Newmarket: will be well suited by middle distances: looks sort to need time. *J. L.
Dunlop*

ACARA (IRE) 3 b.f. Alzao (USA) 117 – Glencara 104 (Sallust 134) [1991 NR 1992 **56**
7g 7.1g⁴ 6m⁶ 7d³ 7s⁶ 8s] IR 12,000F, 43,000Y: rangy filly: half-sister to several
winners, including 5f winner Mrs Sauga (by Derrylin) and bumpers winner Admiral
James (by Julio Mariner): dam, useful at up to 1m in Ireland, is half-sister to useful
NH performer Rathconrath: modest maiden: should stay 1m: acts on good to firm
and dead ground, below form in handicaps on soft. *C. James*

ACCESS CRUISE (USA) 5 ch.g. Wajima (USA) – Lady of Meadowlane (USA) **43**
(Pancho Jay (USA)) [1991 10m⁵ 13d⁵ 10.2m⁶ 14.6m* 14.6m 14.1m³ 16.1m 1992 14.1g
14.1m 12.3m* 14.6d 14.1d 12f 14.1d] tall, sparely-made gelding: moderate mover:
poor form: soundly beaten in handicaps after winning weakly-contested claimer at
Wolverhampton in June: stays 1¾m: best efforts on good to firm ground: keen sort:
tried in a tongue strap: sold to join P. Clarke 2,500 gns Ascot September Sales. *B. A.
McMahon*

ACCESS FESTIVALS   2 b.g. (Apr 23) Tina's Pet 121 – Merency 75 (Meldrum   –
112) [1992 6m] 4,500Y: tall gelding: brother to 5-y-o Petmer, 10.2f winner at 4 yrs,
and half-brother to several winners, including 2-y-o 5f winners Tachywaun (by
Tachypous) and Carribean Tyme (by Tyrnavos): dam 2-y-o 5f winner: 25/1, always
behind in 16-runner maiden auction at Yarmouth in September: has been gelded. *R.
Boss*

ACCESS SKI   5 b.h. Bustino 136 – Crimson Lake (FR) 71 (Mill Reef (USA) 141)   –
[1991 16g⁶ 18.4d 18f* 1992 14d 11.5m 16.5g 20m⁶ 16.1m³ 15.9m 18m⁴ 14.1d]
close-coupled, robust horse: fluent mover: fairly useful handicapper at 4 yrs: not
worth a rating in 1992: stud. *R. Boss*

ACCESS SUPREME   4 b.g. Law Society 130 – Honeypot Lane 91 (Silly   –
Season 127) [1991 14m⁴ 14g³ 14.1f⁶ 1992 14.6g] tall, leggy, sparely-made gelding:
broke down in handicap on reappearance: dead. *R. Boss*

ACCESS VOYAGER   3 b.c. Ballad Rock 122 – Marseillaise (Artaius (USA) 129)   –
[1991 8.2m³ 1992 6.1g a7g⁵ a10g 9g] lengthy colt: moderate mover: reappeared in
September and ran well below debut form: finished last in visor final start: sold 1,900
gns Doncaster November Sales. *R. Boss*

ACE GIRL   3 ch.f. Stanford 121§ – Lucky Candy 61 (Lucky Wednesday 124) [1991   55
5m² 5d² 7.5f² 6.1m⁵ 5.1f a7g a5g⁵ 1992 8.5g 8m* 10m⁶ 8g⁴ 7.5d² 6m⁶ 7g² 7g² 8m⁴]
sparely-made filly: fair performer in claiming/plating company, and also ran well on
only outing in handicap (penultimate start): won maiden claimer at Ripon in May:
stays 1m: acts on firm and dead going: below form in blinkers final 2-y-o start:
usually makes the running. *S. R. Bowring*

ACE REPORTER   3 b.f. Double Schwartz 128 – Strapless 84 (Bustino 136) [1991   56
NR 1992 6.9d² 6m 8s⁶ 9.7s² 10d⁵ 8v] leggy filly: fourth foal: half-sister to ungenuine
Elenos (by Trojan Fen), a winner in Austria: dam 6f winner out of Cheveley Park
second Dame Foolish: easily beat efforts when second in maiden at Carlisle and
seller (for 7-lb claimer) at Folkestone: stays 9.7f: visored once, running moderately:
sometimes mulish at stalls: sold 1,600 gns Doncaster November Sales. *M. H.
Tompkins*

ACHELOUS   5 b.g. Dominion 123 – Siren Sound (Manado 130) [1991 a11g³ a12g³   –
a12g⁵ 13.8d³ 11s* 10d 12.3d 1992 10.5s 10.3g a12g] workmanlike gelding: poor
mover: rated 65 at 4 yrs: off course 18 months: best at 11f: acts on soft ground and on
fibresand: suited by forcing tactics: has won when blinkered, tailed off in visor last
time. *J. A. Glover*

ACHY BREAKY   2 b.f. (May 28) Northern Tempest (USA) 120 – Be My Sweet 78   40 p
(Galivanter 131) [1992 10d⁶] unfurnished filly: eighth foal: half-sister to several
winners, including 1988 2-y-o 6f winner Sola Mia (by Tolomeo) and plating-class 6f
and 7f winner Sugar Token (by Record Token): dam, 1m and 1¼m winner, is
half-sister to Gunner B: 33/1, never-nearer sixth of 19 in seller at Leicester in
October: unseated rider prior to start and pulled hard early on: should improve. *S. R.
Bowring*

ACKERS WOOD   4 b.g. Castle Keep 121 – Gloria Maremmana (King Emperor   –
(USA)) [1991 10.2g⁶ 8.1s⁴ 7m⁴ 7.1g 7m 1992 10d 7g 9g a8g] rangy gelding: seems of
little account nowadays. *K. R. Burke*

ACQUA NOIR   5 ch.g. Kings Lake (USA) 133 – Late Sally 101 (Sallust 134) [1991   –
7m⁴ 8.3m 10g 10.8g 1992 9d] sparely-made gelding: moderate mover: poor
handicapper at best: dead. *A. W. Jones*

ACQUISITION   5 b.g. Petorius 117 – Steady The Buffs 62 (Balidar 133) [1991 9s   –
8f² 8m 8h⁴ 8s⁴ 8g⁴ 10.8m⁴ 9m² 11.1f³ 10.3m 1992 9.2v³ 8d⁵ 14.1g⁶] quite
good-topped gelding: poor form: stays 10.8f: probably acts on any going: effective
blinkered or not. *S. G. Payne*

ACROBATE (USA)   3 ch.g. Arctic Tern (USA) 126 – Musical Medicine (USA)   73
(Margouillat (FR) 133) [1991 10g 1992 12m⁵ 12g⁴ 12g6 12.8g* 14d 12d⁵ 11d] big,
rather leggy, workmanlike gelding: fair form: trained first 2 starts in 1992 by P.
Kelleway: won maiden at Wexford in August: should stay 1¾m: acts on good to firm
and dead ground: has run creditably for apprentice. *Mrs A. M. O'Brien, Ireland*

ACROSS THE BAY   5 ch.g. Krayyan 117 – Siofra Beag (Steel Heart 128) [1991   73
5g⁴ 5.3f 6g 6v⁶ 1992 a6g a8g⁴ a8g a8g 6v* 6d² 5.3m² 5d⁴ 6s⁴ 6g* 6d⁶ 7m* 7d 7d⁴
7.1d² 7m 7m⁶ 8g 7g²] close-coupled gelding: carries condition: moderate mover:
fair handicapper: successful in first half of year at Folkestone, Lingfield and
Goodwood (claimer): effective from 5f to 7f: acts on any going: nearly always
visored. *S. Dow*

ACROSS THE BOW (USA)   2 b.c. (Mar 19) Fit To Fight (USA) – Crooning   **51**
Water (USA) (Riva Ridge (USA)) [1992 7m 7g] third foal: dam, successful at up to 9f,
is half-sister to Clare Bridge and Song of Sixpence: modest form, well beaten, in
maidens at Wolverhampton and Lingfield (slowly away): sold 5,200 gns Newmarket
Autumn Sales. *I. A. Balding*

ACTEUR FRANCAIS (USA)   4 b.c. Al Nasr (FR) 126 – Kilmona (USA) 121 **116**
(Bold Bidder) [1991 8g² 8d² 8g⁴ 8g* 8g 1992 8g⁵ 8g⁵ 8g* 8s* 8s⁵] rather
lightly-made colt: smart French miler: successful in 1992 in minor race at
Saint-Cloud and Group 3 event at Baden-Baden: set plenty to do when below-form
fifth to Arazi in Prix du Rond-Point at Longchamp final start: acts on good to firm and
soft ground. *A. Fabre, France*

ACTINELLA (USA)   2 b.f. (May 28) Seattle Slew (USA) – Aerturas (FR)   **57**
(Manado 130) [1992 6m⁵ 7.1d³ 7m⁶] $125,000Y: leggy, lengthy, unfurnished filly:
good mover: second reported foal: dam graded-placed winner at up to 1m, is
daughter of sister to Noalcoholic: modest maiden, last seen out in July: will stay at
least 1m. *R. Hannon*

ACTION NIGHT   2 b.f. (Apr 6) Night Shift (USA) – Rosie Black 80 (Roan Rocket   **56**
128) [1992 6m⁴ 5g⁵ 5g² 6g] 34,000Y: neat filly: moderate walker: good mover:
half-sister to fairly useful 1987 2-y-o 6f and 7f winner Rose of Ebony (by Tap On
Wood) and a winner abroad: dam best at 2 yrs, successful over 1m: modest form in
maidens: didn't handle bend at all when well beaten in nursery at Catterick final
start (August): will stay 7f. *M. Moubarak*

ACT OF UNION (IRE)   3 b.c. Green Desert (USA) 127 – Carnival Dance 69   **71**
(Welsh Pageant 132) [1991 6f³ 6f⁴ 8.3g⁴ 7g² 1992 7g² 7m³ 5.9f* 8.1d 7.1g⁵ 7m* 7m
7g 6s 7s] rather leggy colt: fair handicapper: won at Carlisle (maiden) in May for W.
Pearce and Newcastle in July: ran poorly last 4 outings, visored last 2 occasions:
suited by 7f: acts on firm ground, possibly not on a soft surface: tends to hang under
pressure: has joined D. Bell. *B. Beasley*

ADAMPARIS   2 b.f. (Feb 20) Robellino (USA) 127 – Mrs Darling 70 (Mummy's   **57** p
Pet 125) [1992 7m 7g⁵] 6,200Y: good-bodied filly: second foal: half-sister to 3-y-o
6.1f winner Sharling (by Sharrood): dam, maiden winner at 6f, is out of Portland
Handicap winner Matinee: springer in market, though still bit backward, when fifth
in maiden auction at Leicester in September, prominent throughout: will improve
again. *A. N. Lee*

ADAM SMITH   4 b.c. Sadler's Wells (USA) 132 – Krakow 85 (Malinowski (USA) **107**
123) [1991 10g² 10g⁵ 1992 9g² 10g⁵ 10d* 10g² 11f⁶ 12f⁶ 8.5g* 8.5d*] strong,
compact, good sort: very useful performer: dead-heated in £9,150 event at Newbury
in July: won allowance races at Belmont Park in October and Aqueduct 3 weeks
later: sixth in Grade 1 events at Belmont previous 2 starts, final effort in 11f Man o'
War Stakes: should stay 1½m: acts on good to soft going, fair effort on firm: remains
in USA. *L. M. Cumani*

ADDICTED TO LOVE   3 b.f. Touching Wood (USA) 127 – Fleur Rouge 71   **66**
(Pharly (FR) 130) [1991 NR 1992 10.2m⁶ 10g* 10s 12g² 10g⁴ 11.8d³ 11.5d²] angular
filly: second living foal: half-sister to temperamental maiden Masroug (by
Dunbeath): dam 2-y-o 6f winner well beaten at 3 yrs: consistent handicapper: won
claimer at Leicester in July: worth a try at 1¾m: below form on very soft going: ran
well in blinkers final start. *P. J. Makin*

ADELINA PATTI   3 b.f. Top Ville 129 – Gertrude Lawrence (Ballymore 123)   **–**
[1991 NR 1992 11.9m⁵ 16.9d] leggy, sparely-made filly: moderate mover: half-sister
to 10.2f winner Komombo (by Sadler's Wells), quite useful Irish 6f and 1m winner
Lady Ambassador (by General Assembly) and Irish 1¾m winner Gertrudes
Daughter (by Niniski): dam unraced daughter of Sarah Siddons, dam also of
Seymour Hicks and Princess Pati: well beaten in maidens in August: sold 5,800 gns
Newmarket December Sales. *A. C. Stewart*

ADIEU AU ROI (IRE)   3 ro.c. Kenmare (FR) 125 – Pomme Royale (Shergar **116** §
140) [1991 7.5g 8g⁵ 8s⁴ 1992 10.5s⁴ 10s* 10.5s 10.5g⁶ 12g* 12g 10m⁴ 10s] 950,000
francs Y: second foal: dam unplaced at 3 yrs in France is a half-sister to Noir Et Or:
smart at his best: won minor event at Maisons-Laffitte in March and Group 2 Prix
Hocquart at Longchamp in May: best effort when fourth to Homme de Loi in Grand
Prix de Paris Louis Vuitton there following month: refused to race final start: stays
1½m: best efforts on a sound surface, though probably acts on any going: evidently
unreliable. *J. Lesbordes, France*

ADJACENT (IRE)   4 ch.f. Doulab (USA) 115 – Near The Door (USA) (Stage   **45**
Door Johnny) [1991 10g⁵ 8m⁶ 10.2g* 9.9f² 10.5g⁴ 12f⁶ 10m³ 10.5g⁶ 9g a10g⁴ a12g*

a12g 1992 a12g² a13g⁵ a13g⁴ a12g⁵ 11.9g] sturdy, lengthy filly: one-time fair handicapper, very much on the downgrade: not seen out after being withdrawn lame at start in April: stays 1½m: acts on firm going and equitrack, ran moderately on fibresand. *M. Dixon*

ADJARISTAN   5 b.g. Akarad (FR) 130 – Adjarida (Red God 128§) [1991 11.8g a14g² 12g 16.2d 1992 a12g a16g 16f⁶ 18.2m⁶] small gelding: lightly-raced maiden and no worthwhile form: not seen out after June. *R. Simpson*   –

ADMINISTER   4 b.f. Damister (USA) 123 – Apply 87 (Kings Lake (USA) 133) [1991 10g 11m⁴ 12.1g* 1992 10.3v 12g 12g] lengthy, angular filly: moderate mover: modest form at 3 yrs for R. Charlton: off course 16 months, well beaten in 1992: blinkered and reluctant to race final start. *L. J. Codd*   –

ADMIRAL ALBERT (IRE)   3 gr.g. Slip Anchor 136 – Magic Spell (FR) (Dancer's Image (USA)) [1991 5m 7d⁴ 8m⁴ 6.9f⁵ 7d 1992 6m 10m] sturdy, quite attractive gelding: quite modest maiden at 2 yrs: of no account. *R. Akehurst*   –

ADMIRAL FROBISHER (USA)   2 b.c. (Feb 20) Eskimo (USA) – Roadability (USA) (Gnome's Gold (USA)) [1992 5g 5.3m 5s² 6g⁵ 6s] $4,000F, $19,000Y: leggy, unfurnished colt: first foal: dam unraced: sire (by Northern Dancer) minor stakes winner at up to 1m: modest plater here: ran moderately last 2 starts, blinkered first occasion: sent to Italy and ran well in 1m listed race on heavy at Turin in November. *C. F. Wall*   ?

ADMIRAL'S MISTRESS (IRE)   4 ch.f. Sexton Blake 126 – Little Cygnet (My Swanee 122) [1991 a12g* 1992 a12g6] quite modest form when winning claimer at Southwell in November, 1991: well beaten in apprentice handicap there 3 months later: stays 1½m. *P. J. Makin*   –

ADMIRALS REALM   3 gr.g. Another Realm 118 – Bedeni 100 (Parthia 132) [1991 NR 1992 5m a7g 5s³ 5g⁴ 6.1g² 6s³ 6m* a7g] 2,400F, 8,200Y: lengthy, unfurnished gelding: half-brother to several winners, notably very useful 1976 2-y-o 5f to 7f winner Sky Ship (by Roan Rocket) and smart 1¼m filly Upper Deck (by Sun Prince): dam disappointing half-sister to smart Admirals Launch, Torpid and the dam of Cut Above: consistent form: won poor contest at Pontefract in October: should stay 7f: acts on good to firm and soft ground, ran poorly on fibresand. *B. A. McMahon*   59

ADMIRALS SEAT   4 ch.g. Ardross 134 – Sombreuil 95 (Bold Lad (IRE) 133) [1991 8d⁴ 7.5g⁶ 8.5f 8m 8.2g⁴ 12d⁵ 1992 10s 10.5s* 11.9d³ 11.9s⁵ 10.9s⁶ 10.5s] big, strong, workmanlike gelding: usually looks very well: won apprentice handicap at Haydock in April: off course 4 months, best of last 3 starts when fair sixth: stays 1½m: acts on good to firm and soft ground. *Mrs J. R. Ramsden*   68

ADMIRALS SECRET (USA)   3 ch.c. Secreto (USA) 128 – Noble Mistress (USA) (Vaguely Noble 140) [1991 7m 7.1s 7m 1992 a8g* 10f 10m² 12g² 12g³] good-quartered colt: has a round action: fair handicapper: won maiden at Southwell in February: tongue tied down, hung left when second at Leicester in May (demoted from first for interference) and Pontefract: well-beaten third in Austrian Derby at Vienna in June: stays 1½m: below form on firm ground. *C. F. Wall*   69

ADMIRALTY WAY   6 b.g. Petorius 117 – Captive Flower 99 (Manacle 123) [1991 10.4d* 10.8m⁵ 10.1f 10g⁴ 1992 10.8v 10s 10.3g 10g 8g 10m⁶ 11.7f² 9.7m a12g] leggy gelding: thoroughly unreliable handicapper: stays 11f: acts on firm and dead going: has been tried in blinkers/visor, not in 1992: sold out of M. O'Neill's stable 5,000 gns Doncaster May Sales after third start. *R. Brotherton*   40 §

ADMIRED   2 ch.f. (Feb 20) Good Times (ITY) – Sandy Looks 69 (Music Boy 124) [1992 7s 5.1s³ 6d] compact filly: third reported foal: dam, winning jumper lightly raced on flat, is daughter of Irish 1000 Guineas second Hannah Darling: keeping-on third in minor event at Bath in September, only form: should be well suited by further than 5f. *M. R. Channon*   48

ADMISSION (IRE)   2 br.g. (Feb 9) Glow (USA) – Admit (Welsh Pageant 132) [1992 7g⁵ 6g 7g] IR 4,600Y, 15,000 2-y-o: strong, lengthy gelding: closely related to 9f to 1¾m winner Light Romance (by Be My Guest) and Italian listed winner Mon Coeur (by Try My Best): dam, once raced at 3 yrs in Ireland, is granddaughter of Valoris: bit backward at least, well beaten in minor event and maiden auctions in the North: gives impression needs time: has been gelded. *N. Chamberlain*   40

ADWICK PARK   4 b.c. Blazing Saddles (AUS) – Ana Gabriella (USA) (Master Derby (USA)) [1991 7m⁴ 6g² 6g 6g 1992 6s 6g 6g 5g6 6g⁴ 6m 6.1m³ 6m³ 6g] robust, good-quartered colt: impresses in appearance: fairly useful handicapper: best efforts when third, unlucky at Newmarket in August: ideally suited by 6f/7f: acts on   87 firm ground, seems unsuited by a soft surface: used to go well with forcing tactics, but held up of late: has joined M. Bell. *T. D. Barron*

AEDEAN   3 ch.g. Risk Me (FR) 127 – Finlandaise (FR) (Arctic Tern (USA) 126)   **53**
[1991 6d 5g5 6d4 6.1s3 6m* 6.1g3 7m 6g3 6g 1992 6s 7.6s 7f3 7d 10g 8f 12.3m] tall, leggy gelding: moderate mover: form in 1992 only when third in claimer at Warwick: trained until after following start by C. C. Elsey: visored third and fourth 3-y-o starts: won juvenile hurdle in November. *C. A. Horgan*

AEGAEN LADY   3 b.f. Lochnager 132 – Gamma (GER) (Zank) [1991 5m2 6f 5h5   **59**
6.1m 5g a8g2 a7g4 a7g5 a8g4 1992 6.9d 7.1m 6g4 a7g a6g 10d4 8.9d6 10m2 10s 10.5s2 10d6 9.2v* 9.7v2] sturdy filly: modest handicapper: won at Hamilton in November by 6 lengths: best efforts at 9f/1¼m: goes well on heavy ground, acts on fibresand: has run poorly in blinkers (at 2 yrs) and visored. *J. Etherington*

AFFA   3 b.f. Local Suitor (USA) 128 – Pine (Supreme Sovereign 119) [1991 6f 7.1d6   **56**
6s a7g 1992 10d2 11.6g a12g6 a12g5 12.1s 8.9d2 9.7m] leggy, unfurnished filly: modest maiden: claimer ridden, good second of 20 in handicap at Wolverhampton: not seen out after kicked at start (withdrawn) in September: suited by 9f/1¼m: best efforts on good to soft ground: usually bandaged. *T. Thomson Jones*

AFFAIR OF HONOUR (IRE)   4 ch.c. Ahonoora 122 – Good Relations (Be My   **–**
Guest (USA) 126) [1991 8g6 10m6 12d 10.1g2 10d3 10g5 1992 13f5 13.8d] strong colt: has a round action: rated 68 at 3 yrs for P. Cole: tailed-off last in handicaps as 4-y-o: stays 1¼m: acts on hard and dead ground: winning (1991/2) hurdler for present trainer. *J. J. O'Neill*

AFFAIR OF STATE (IRE)   3 b.f. Tate Gallery (USA) 117 – All Hat (Double   **–**
Form 130) [1991 5m3 5d* 5m2 5g 6m* 6m 1992 5.2g a7g] neat filly: fairly useful performer at 2 yrs, when winner of very valuable 6f Tattersalls Breeders Stakes at the Curragh: never dangerous in minor event at Newbury in September, tailed off in Southwell handicap almost 3 months later: needs further than 5f: best form on good to firm ground, has won on dead. *M. R. Channon*

AFFIDARE (IRE)   3 b.g. The Noble Player (USA) 126 – Cala-Vadella (Mummy's   **62**
Pet 125) [1991 6g4 5f3 1992 7g2 7d] smallish, useful-looking gelding: 13/2 from 10/1 on first run for 14 months, second in maiden at Catterick: well beaten in handicap at Newmarket later in autumn: stays 7f. *S. M. Hillen*

AFFIRMED'S DESTINY (USA)   3 b.g. Affirmed (USA) – Grand Destiny   **47**
(USA) (Grand Central) [1991 7d5 7g2 8.1g 7.3m 7.6d6 1992 10f5 11.6m3 12.3m6 10m 9.7m5 12s a10g] leggy gelding: inconsistent maiden: should stay 1½m: acts on good to firm and dead ground, never comfortable on equitrack: blinkered (fair effort but found little) once at 2 yrs: a tricky ride and often finds little: sold 3,700 gns Ascot November Sales. *J. L. Dunlop*

AFFORDABLE   4 b.g. Formidable (USA) 125 – Ophrys 90 (Nonoalco (USA) 131)   **65**
[1991 5m3 5m 5s5 7g4 7d3 7g* 8s 7g4 7g6 7.1m6 7m* 7m 7g4 1992 8s 7m 7g 7f*
7g 7g 7m] strong, good-quartered gelding: has a quick action: inconsistent handicapper: won at Redcar in June: well below form after: stays 7f: acts on firm and dead ground, possibly unsuited by soft: ran badly when blinkered at 2 yrs: has joined S. Norton. *W. Carter*

AFIF   3 b.c. Midyan (USA) 124 – Alpine Sunset (Auction Ring (USA) 123) [1991 5g3   **85**
6g5 5d* 5m* 5m3 5g6 6g6 6f* 6m* 6m 6.1s* 1992 6s3 7g4] neat, attractive colt: usually looks very well: has a round action: fairly useful performer: ran creditably in spring: will prove ideally suited by 6f: probably acts on any going: effective with or without blinkers: goes well for claimer. *Mrs J. Cecil*

AFORE JANE   3 b.f. Lomond (USA) 128 – Dabbiana (Fappiano (USA))   **54**
[1991 NR 1992 8s 9.7m4 12m3 12m3 11.5m5 a16g3 16.2d] strong, lengthy filly: second foal: half-sister to 1990 2-y-o 7f winner Alton Bay (by Al Nasr), also successful over hurdles: dam winner at around 7f in USA: modest maiden: appears to stay 2m: best efforts on top-of-the-ground. *G. Harwood*

AFRICAN CHIMES   5 b.h. Kampala 120 – Rynville (Ballymore 123) [1991 a8g2   **80**
a7g5 a7g* a7g a8g5 8m 6g 7g6 7m* 7m3 7m3 a7g2 a7g* a6g2 a6g* 1992 a7g* a6g*   **a94**
a7g* a7g2 a8g a7g* a6g* 7g 5.7f* 5g 5m5 5m2 5m4 5m a7g* a6g2 a6g*] leggy, angular horse: has round action: useful and consistent performer on all-weather tracks: had a tremendous season: successful in 4 claimers at Southwell (claimed £13,002 to join M. Chapman final start) and 3 at Lingfield: not so good on turf, but won Bath handicap in June: very best form at up to 7f, though has won at 1¼m: acts on firm ground and all-weather surfaces: effective blinkered or not: ran poorly when visored once: usually held up, and has turn of foot: usually ridden by E. O'Gorman. *W. A. O'Gorman*

AFTER THE FIRE   3 ch.g. Dunbeath (USA) 127 – Cinderwench 95 (Crooner   –
119) [1991 NR 1992 10d 9.7m 8g] quite good-topped gelding: has been tubed: fourth
foal: half-brother to 8.5f to 1½m winner Planet Ash and 4-y-o 5f (at 2 yrs) and 1m
winner Broad Appeal (both by Star Appeal): dam won from 1m to 1½m: tailed off in
maidens and claimer: not seen out after June. *A. N. Lee*

AFTER THE LAST   2 b. or br.c. (Feb 21) Infantry 122 – Era 70 (Dalsaan 125)   **82** p
[1992 5f 7g4 6f* 7.3g* 7g* 8f4 7.3g3 6m4] 3,500F, 4,000Y, 10,000 2-y-o: good-
bodied colt: second foal: dam placed over 5f at 2 yrs: fairly useful handicapper: won
auction event at Brighton and nurseries at Newbury (in good style) and Chester
(plenty to do entering straight, quickened impressively) within 16 days in August:
remained bang in form through the autumn: will stay 1¼m: acts on firm ground:
genuine, and type to go on at 3 yrs. *R. Hannon*

AGAINST YOU   5 b.m. Auction Ring (USA) 123 – Saranita 70 (Thatch (USA) 136)   –
[1991 10d6 8f6 14g4 10m 13.3d5 12v 11.7m 1992 a13g] lengthy, workmanlike mare:
poor mover: no form for long time and not seen out after March. *R. Akehurst*

AGENDA ONE   2 b.f. (May 21) Precocious 126 – Glint of Victory 96 (Glint of   **50**
Gold 128) [1992 6m 7g5 8.2s] workmanlike filly: second foal: half-sister to 3-y-o
Ipsilante (by Mansooj): dam 1¼m winner stayed 1½m: modest maiden: stays 8.2f.
Miss A. J. Whitfield

AGHAADIR (USA)   4 b.c. Private Account (USA) – Kris Kris (USA) (Hoist The   –
Flag (USA)) [1991 8d4 7d 7m* 1992 7m 7d 8s5 8g] leggy, useful-looking colt:
moderate mover: rated 99p when gamely dead-heating for York handicap in
October, 1991: off course nearly a year, nowhere near so good in October: should
prove as effective over 1m as 7f: acts on good to firm and dead ground: raced freely
in visor final start. *J. H. M. Gosden*

AGHAR (IRE)   2 ch.c. (Feb 25) Ahonoora 122 – Foliage (Thatching 131) [1992   **69** p
6g3 6s] 30,000F, 26,000Y: useful-looking colt: has scope: third foal: half-brother to
French 3-y-o 9f winner Tra Fiori (by Law Society) and a middle-distance winner in
Germany by Commanche Run: dam unraced sister to Grade 1 winner (at 9f)
Fitzwilliam Place: much better effort when keeping-on third to stable-companion
Rustic Craft in newcomers race at Ascot: moved fluently to post at Newbury later in
October and not knocked about once fading final 2f: will stay 1m: may well do better.
D. R. C. Elsworth

AGIL'S PET   2 b.f. (Jan 21) Tina's Pet 121 – High Voltage 82 (Electrify) [1992 5m6   –
6m4 5g] 5,000Y: leggy filly: moderate mover: half-sister to 3 winning sprinters,
including one-time useful Dorking Lad (by Cawston's Clown): dam won 3 times at
5f: no worthwhile form: not seen out after July. *J. Sutcliffe*

AGINCOURT SONG (USA)   3 b.c. Al Nasr (FR) 126 – La Francaise (USA)   **76**
(Jim French (USA)) [1991 7.1m2 7.1s4 1992 8m 7g2 8.5f2 7.9f2 8.1d2 9.7d* 8d 8m3
10s] useful-looking colt: fair form: 9/4 on, won maiden at Folkestone in July: most
inconsistent in handicaps afterwards: unlikely to stay much beyond 1¼m: acts on
firm and dead ground: usually makes the running: sold 12,000 gns Newmarket
Autumn Sales, to Italy. *J. L. Dunlop*

AGNES FLEMMING (USA)   3 b.f. Al Nasr (FR) 126 – Placer Queen (Habitat   **74**
134) [1991 NR 1992 8g 8m 7g6 8g* 8m3 8.1d 8.1g] useful-looking filly: third known
foal: half-sister to 1989 2-y-o 6f winner Invisible Halo (by Halo): dam ran 3 times
here before winning at up to 1¼m in Canada: fair form: won maiden at Kempton in
July, gamely making most: ran very well in handicap next start, soundly beaten
after: stays 1m well: acts on good to firm ground: sold 8,000 gns Newmarket Autumn
Sales. *P. W. Harris*

AGWA   3 b.c. Local Suitor (USA) 128 – Meissarah (USA) (Silver Hawk (USA) 123)   –
[1991 NR 1992 7f5 8d 6f5] sturdy colt: second foal: brother to 8.2f to 13f winner
Magic Secret: dam never ran: no worthwhile form: sold to join J. Gillen 500 gns
Newmarket July Sales after final start. *B. Hanbury*

AHBAB (IRE)   3 b.f. Ajdal (USA) 130 – Magic Slipper 97 (Habitat 134) [1991 7g5   **81**
1992 6m3 6.9g* 6g3 8g5 7.1g 7g2 7.1s3 7.3g 6m6 6g5] big, heavy-topped filly: fairly
useful handicapper: won apprentice maiden at Folkestone in April: should have
stayed 1m: acted on good to firm and soft ground: effective visored or not: visits
Lycius. *P. T. Walwyn*

AHJAY   2 br.c. (Mar 31) Tina's Pet 121 – City Link Rose (Lochnager 132) [1992 6s   **49** p
6d 6v6] workmanlike colt: fourth foal: brother to 5f sprinter City Link Pet and
half-brother to 3-y-o 5f winner Bodari (by Prince Sabo): dam showed signs of ability
on last of 3 starts: modest form in maidens: yet to race on top-of-the-ground: can
improve further. *D. A. Wilson*

AHKAM (IRE) 3 ch.f. Persian Bold 123 – Ghanayim (USA) 107 (Sharpen Up 127) –
[1991 7g⁵ 7g 5m 6s⁶ 1992 5v 5m 5g] good-bodied filly: moderate mover: no
worthwhile form here in 1992, blinkered final start: sold out of T. Thomson Jones's
stable 1,700 gns Newmarket July Sales, resold 6,800 gns Newmarket December
Sales having won races over 7f and 9f in Belgium. *H. Thomson Jones*

AIDE MEMOIRE (IRE) 3 b.f. Don't Forget Me 127 – Pharjoy (FR) 85 (Pharly 58
(FR) 130) [1991 6g 7m 6d a8g 1992 12m⁴ 16f⁴ 12.1s² 17.5s³ 16.1s 15.8d³ a16g⁶] leggy
filly: modest handicapper: thorough stayer: goes well on soft ground: acts on
fibresand, well beaten on equitrack final start: sold to join Mrs B. Broad 4,500 gns
Doncaster November Sales. *C. B. B. Booth*

AIN'TLIFELIKETHAT 5 gr.h. Godswalk (USA) 130 – Blue Alicia (Wolver 56
Hollow 126) [1991 7m³ 7g⁵ 7.6m⁶ 7d³ 6g⁵ 7g⁵ 7f² 7m* 7g⁶ 7m⁵ 6.9f⁵ 7f a7g³ 8g⁶ 7g
a8g⁴ a7g⁶ 1992 a7g* 5.9d⁶ a7g³ 7m³ 7.1m⁵ a7g³ 8f⁴ 7f 7f² 6m* 7g² 6d⁵ a7g 6g⁶
a6g⁵] workmanlike, good-quartered horse: untrustworthy handicapper at 4 yrs,
proved consistent in 1992: successful at Lingfield in April and Folkestone in August:
effective from 6f to 1m: acts on hard ground and all-weather surfaces, not ideally
suited by dead: visored (below form) once, usually blinkered nowadays: often slowly
away: best with extreme waiting tactics, and suited by strongly-run race. *T. J.
Naughton*

AIR COMMAND (BAR) 2 br.c. (Feb 1) Concorde Hero (USA) 101 – Hubbar- 57
dair 60 (Town And Country 124) [1992 5d³ 7.1g 6g³ 6d⁶ a6g⁶ a6g] close-coupled
colt: first known foal: dam 2-y-o 1m winner: modest form in varied events: bred to be
suited by 1m +: blinkered (ran poorly) final start. *R. Hannon*

AISLABIE AIRBORNE 3 br.g. Kalaglow 132 – Expensive Gift (Record Token –
128) [1991 NR 1992 10d a7g 10m 14.1g 11.5g⁶ 10m 16.9d] 1,000F: leggy gelding:
second reported living foal: half-brother to a winner in Austria by Longleat: dam no
sign of ability in 2 races: of little account: blinkered last 2 starts. *Mrs N. Macauley*

AITCH N'BEE 9 ch.g. Northfields (USA) – Hot Case 92 (Upper Case (USA)) 79
[1991 a7g⁶ 8g* 7s⁶ 8g² 7m 8g³ 1992 8.1d² 8m⁶ 8f³ 8d⁴ 7f² 8f² 8g* 8m 7g⁴] small,
strong gelding: consistent old handicapper: successful at Kempton in September:
effective at 7f/1m: acts on any going: also goes very well on fibresand, ran
moderately once on equitrack: tried visored/blinkered early in career: goes well
fresh. *Lady Herries*

AJAAD (USA) 4 ch.c. Nureyev (USA) 131 – Execution (USA) (The Axe II 115) 102
[1991 7g² 7f* 8m* 8m* 7f 1992 7.1d³ 8m] leggy, angular colt: moderate walker:
progressed really well as 3-y-o until never travelling fluently final start: off course 9
months and looking really well, creditable third in listed event at Haydock: last in
Lockinge Stakes later in May: stays 1m: acts on firm and dead ground: sold 24,000
gns Newmarket December Sales. *M. R. Stoute*

AJALAN (IRE) 2 ch.c. (Feb 6) Be My Guest (USA) 126 – Intensive (USA) (Sir 76 p
Wiggle (USA)) [1992 8s⁵] IR 135,000Y: leggy colt: half-brother to 3-y-o 9f winner
Prince of Darkness (by Shadeed) and 3 winners abroad, including Grade 3 winner
Intensive Commander (by Dust Commander): dam never ran: 16/1, 7 lengths fifth of
8 to Arusha in minor event at Newbury in October, running green off bridle 2f out
and not knocked about: will improve. *M. R. Stoute*

AJANTA 2 ch.f. (Mar 5) Rousillon (USA) 133 – Ajuga (USA) 102 (The Minstrel 74
(CAN) 135) [1992 6.1m⁴ 8.2g* 7s³ 7.3s] small, lightly-made filly: good walker: fluent
mover: first foal: dam, 6f and 7f winner, is daughter of Cairn Rouge: fair performer:
won minor event at Nottingham in September: well beaten in face of stiff task in
Newbury listed event final start: sold 5,200 gns Newmarket Autumn Sales: will
prove better suited by 1¼m: acts on soft going: one of first off bridle last 3 starts. *B.
W. Hills*

AJFAN (USA) 2 ch.f. (Apr 9) Woodman (USA) 126 – Misinskie (USA) 84 101
(Nijinsky (CAN) 138) [1992 7f* 7d³ 8s²] 88,000Y: well-made filly: has scope: fifth
living foal: closely related to a winner in USA by Conquistador Cielo and half-sister
to 2 winners, including useful 1987 2-y-o 5f and 6f winner Space Cruiser (by Foolish
Pleasure): dam, best at 2 yrs, is half-sister to high-class sprinter/miler Clever Trick:
useful performer: won maiden at Yarmouth in August in good style: progressed well
afterwards in Group 3 event at Goodwood and particularly so when battling-on 1½
lengths second of 8 to Ivanka in Fillies' Mile at Ascot: will stay beyond 1m: may
improve further. *H. Thomson Jones*

AJIB (USA) 3 ch.c. Woodman (USA) 126 – Shelbiana (USA) (Chieftain II) [1991 –
6m 7.9m* 1992 7.6g⁵] close-coupled, quite attractive colt: won maiden at York in

autumn, 1991: sweating profusely, took good hold when well beaten in minor event at Lingfield in May: bred to stay 1¼m: sent to N. Drysdale in USA. *J. H. M. Gosden*

AJMAAN (USA) 2 br.c. (Mar 12) Arctic Tern (USA) 126 – Melodina 118 (Tudor **70 p** Melody 129) [1992 8.2s3] $225,000Y: brother to useful 1988 2-y-o 7f winner Polar Run, later stayed 2m, and half-brother to several winners, notably triple champion hurdler See You Then (by Royal Palace) and Oaks third Dubian (by High Line): dam won over 5f at 2 yrs and stayed 1½m well: 9/2, 7½ lengths third of 13 to Revere in maiden at Nottingham, staying on from mid-division under considerate ride: will be well suited by middle distances: certain to improve. *A. C. Stewart*

AJO (IRE) 3 b.c. Ajdal (USA) 130 – Betty's Secret (USA) (Secretariat (USA)) **81** [1991 6d6 7d 1992 10g3 10.2m4 10.5g2 7.9f4 8.5d3 10m] leggy, workmanlike colt: fairly useful maiden: stays 10.5f: acts on firm ground, seemingly not on dead: wears tongue strap: last seen out in July. *M. R. Stoute*

AJZEM (USA) 3 gr.c. Blushing Groom (FR) 131 – Nobiliare (USA) (Vaguely **97 ?** Noble 140) [1991 NR 1992 10d3 8.5s* 10d] rather leggy, unfurnished colt: sixth reported living foal: half-brother to 2 winners, notably top-class 1¼m winner Indian Skimmer (by Storm Bird): dam unraced daughter of half-sister to Dark Image, 1968 champion 3-y-o filly in USA: useful form in maiden at Kempton on debut: 6/4-on winner of 4-runner maiden at Beverley in July: virtually pulled up, something badly amiss, in minor event following month: stays 1¼m: has raced only on a soft surface: bandaged last 2 outings. *M. R. Stoute*

AKENSIDE 2 b.g. (Apr 18) Kings Lake (USA) 133 – One Last Glimpse 73 (Relko **50** 136) [1992 6m 7g 7d6 6.1m6] 14,500Y: well-made gelding: fourth foal: half-brother to 3-y-o middle-distance colt Captain Horatius (by Taufan) and 4-y-o sprint winner Running Glimpse (by Runnett): dam second from 8.2f to 10.6f: modest maiden: will be suited by 1m +: best effort on dead ground: sold 4,200 gns Newmarket Autumn Sales. *D. R. C. Elsworth*

AKKAZAO (IRE) 4 b. or br.f. Alzao (USA) 117 – Akka (Malacate (USA) 131) **77** [1991 8s 7m2 7m2 9f2 7g 10.1g4 10g 8m2 8.1g3 8.3m2 8g 1992 8g 9g* 8.1f* 8f4 8g3 8g 8.3g 9d4 8.1g3 a10g] workmanlike filly: largely consistent handicapper: won at Goodwood and Sandown (gamely) in June: stays 9f: best efforts on a sound surface, below form (after 3-month break) on equitrack: tried blinkered earlier in career: usually forces pace. *W. Carter*

AKURA (IRE) 3 b.f. Vision (USA) – Bebe Altesse (GER) (Alpenkonig (GER)) **62** [1991 5m 7.5f 8.1m 1992 10g6 a8g* a8g6 9s3 8s2 8d a7g4 8g 8f* 8f 9.2m*] quite good-topped filly: modest performer: won maiden at Southwell in February, then selling event (no bid) at Ripon and claimer at Hamilton in June: stays 9f: acts on any going, including fibresand: makes running/races prominently: sold to join A. Forbes 6,200 gns Doncaster June Sales. *M. Johnston*

ALAMEL (USA) 2 b.f. (Mar 16) Shadeed (USA) 135 – Albadeeah (USA) 85 **–** (Nashua) [1992 6d] big, lengthy filly: has scope: fifth foal: dam 2-y-o 6f winner: 7/1 from 4/1 and green, thirteenth of 19, outpaced from 2f out, in maiden at Haydock in October: sold 2,700 gns Newmarket Autumn Sales. *H. Thomson Jones*

ALAMSHAH (IRE) 4 b.c. Lashkari 128 – Alannya (FR) (Relko 136) [1991 **–** 15.3m5 1992 12s 14.1m5] compact colt: no worthwhile form since 2 yrs. *J. A. Glover*

ALASAD 2 ch.c. (Mar 28) Kris 135 – Midway Lady (USA) 126 (Alleged (USA) 138) **65 p** [1992 8m] big, good-topped colt: has plenty of scope: half-brother to 3-y-o Sharayif and useful 7f and 1m winner Umniyatee (both by Green Desert): dam won 1000 Guineas and Oaks: 10/1, around 12 lengths eleventh of 19 to Bashayer in maiden at Newmarket, taking strong hold under restraint then handled considerately when beaten: looks sort to leave this form well behind in due course. *B. Hanbury*

ALASIB 2 gr.f. (Feb 2) Siberian Express (USA) 125 – Fahrenheit 69 (Mount **66 p** Hagen (FR) 127) [1992 5f* 5.1g4 5g3] good-topped filly: third foal: half-sister to 1989 2-y-o 6f winner Full Blast (by Sayyaf) and 6f (at 2 yrs) and 1m winner Start-Rite (by Comedy Star): dam ran twice at 3 yrs, placed around 7f and 1m: fair form: well-backed favourite, easily won maiden at Pontefract in June: off course 2 months and easily better effort afterwards when third in nursery at Wolverhampton: will stay 6f: may do better. *M. Moubarak*

ALASKA BAY 2 b.g. (Apr 21) Northern State (USA) 91 – Bay Blues 62 (Cure The **–** Blues (USA)) [1992 5.1m 7d 8s] workmanlike gelding: moderate mover: first foal: dam, maiden, stayed 7f: no form in maidens. *R. J. Holder*

AL BADETO   5 b.m. Hays 120 – Atedaun (Ahonoora 122) [1991 a7g a11g 7d 7m   **33**
10d 12.3f 12m⁵ 1992 8.5d⁵ 12m 12.2g 12m⁴ 12s] lengthy, sparely-made mare: poor
handicapper, and still a maiden: stays 1½m. *J. Norton*

ALBANY SPARK   3 br.g. Sparkling Boy 110 – Lauriston Cottage (Welsh Saint   **–**
126) [1991 a7g 1992 a7g a8g⁵ 11g 8d 8g] big gelding: of little account: tried
visored/blinkered. *G. H. Eden*

ALBEMINE (USA)   3 b.g. Al Nasr (FR) 126 – Lady Be Mine (USA) 76 (Sir Ivor   **72**
135) [1991 6m 1992 9s⁵ 8s* 9s] good-topped gelding: good walker: half-brother to 2
winners, including leading 1989 2-y-o (unbeaten in 6 starts from 6f to 1m) Be My
Chief (by Chief's Crown): dam 1m winner out of half-sister to dam of Lord Seymour
and Marwell: easily won maiden at Pontefract: well beaten facing stiffish task in
£11,700 handicap at Newbury later in October: should prove as effective at 9f as 1m.
Mrs J. Cecil

ALBERSTAN   2 b.g. (Apr 29) Stanford 121§ – Afrabela 76 (African Sky 124) [1992   **–**
5m] leggy gelding: first foal: dam 6f winner: green, beaten around 15 lengths in
maiden at Ripon in May. *M. H. Easterby*

ALBERT   5 b.g. Kings Lake (USA) 133 – Darine 114 (Nonoalco (USA) 131)   **53 §**
good-bodied gelding: has a round action: thoroughly unreliable handicapper: won
(for second successive year) amateurs event at Goodwood in June: effective from
8.5f to 1½m: acts on any going, except perhaps heavy. *D. A. Wilson*

ALBERTITO (FR)   5 b.g. Esprit du Nord (USA) 126 – Aranita (Arctic Tern   **–**
(USA) 126) [1991 NR 1992 14.6g⁵] leggy, workmanlike gelding: fourth foal: dam won
over 9f at 2 yrs in Ireland: ex-French maiden: progressive winning hurdler in 1991/2:
well-backed outsider but no form in maiden at Doncaster in March: worth a try at
1½m. *R. Hollinshead*

ALBERT THE BOLD   3 b.g. Never So Bold 135 – Alcassa (FR) (Satingo 129)   **67**
[1991 5d⁵ 5m⁵ 1992 a7g* a7g* a7g⁵] fair performer: off course 14 months and
wearing eyeshield, won maiden and handicap (gamely) at Lingfield in late-summer:
never dangerous in handicap there 3 months later: will stay 1m: acts on equitrack.
Mrs L. Piggott

AL BILLAL   4 b.c. Enchantment 115 – Liana Louise (Silly Season 127) [1991 a14g   **–**
1992 5g⁶ 7s 12v a10g a12g] good-topped colt: shows knee action: no worthwhile form
since 2 yrs: blinkered last 3 starts. *J. J. Bridger*

ALBURY GREY   5 gr.m. Petong 126 – Infelice (Nishapour (FR) 125) [1991 9s   **–**
10.1m⁵ 11.9g⁶ 1992 11.9d 12v] workmanlike mare: no worthwhile form on flat, little
over hurdles. *R. Curtis*

ALCOY (IRE)   3 b.g. Glow (USA) – Organdy 84 (Blakeney 126) [1991 7m⁶ 7f⁶   **60 d**
8m² 1992 11d 10g⁴ 10f³ 14.1m³ 10g 10f⁶ 14.1d] big, good-topped gelding: moderate
maiden at best: no form since being tubed after fourth start: probably stays 1¾m:
acts on firm ground: has had tongue tied down: last seen out in July. *P. A. Kelleway*

ALDAHE   7 ch.g. Dalsaan 125 – Alanood 85 (Northfields (USA)) [1991 7f⁴ 7.5g⁵   **46**
10.8m 8f⁵ 7.1m 7m* 7v⁴ 7.6g* 7f³ 7g 7g 7.6m³ 7.1g* 8m 7g 8m 7g 1992 8g 8.1m 7f⁴
7.1f⁴ 8f³ 7f⁶ 8f⁵ 7g 7g 8d⁴ a7g] sparely-made gelding: has a round action: poor
handicapper these days: effective from 7f to 1m: acts on any going: best form
without blinkers: often hangs, but has gone very well for claimer: trained until after
ninth start by B. Millman: tough. *B. Forsey*

AL-DAHLAWIA (IRE)   3 b.f. Cyrano de Bergerac 120 – Dancing Sun (Will   **–**
Somers 114§) [1991 6s 6d 1992 6d 7m⁶ 5g⁵] neat filly: of little account. *G. A.
Pritchard-Gordon*

ALDAVERA   3 ch.g. Executive Man 119 – Springle 83 (Le Johnstan 123) [1991 NR   **–**
1992 10d 11.6g⁶ 10d⁵ 16d 12s] workmanlike gelding: second foal: dam 2-y-o 1m
winner: of little account. *M. Dixon*

ALDERBROOK   3 b.c. Ardross 134 – Twine (Thatching 131) [1991 NR 1992   **74**
a12g³ a12g² 14.1d⁵ 11.5m⁴ 10d* 10.2d² 9.7v*] rather unfurnished colt: moderate
walker: brother to lightly-raced 7f winner Duckey Fuzz and half-brother to very
useful 6f (at 2 yrs) and 1¼m winner Native Twine (by Be My Native) and a winner in
Spain: dam unraced granddaughter of Mesopotamia: fair performer: won handicaps
at Goodwood (claimer) and Folkestone in October: sold to join Miss S. Hall 38,000
gns Newmarket Autumn Sales: stays 1½m: goes well on a soft surface. *Mrs J. Cecil*

ALDERNEY PRINCE (USA)   2 ch.c. (Feb 1) Trempolino (USA) 135 –   **85 p**
Princess of Man 104 (Green God 128) [1992 6.1m* 7d³ 7m⁴ 8.1d² 9g²] close-
coupled, workmanlike colt: fluent mover: closely related to 6f (at 2 yrs) to 11.5f
winner Ausherra (by Diesis) and a winner in USA by Sharpen Up and half-brother to

4 winners including 3-y-o Ardisia (by Affirmed), successful at around 1¼m: dam won Musidora Stakes: odds on, won modest 4-runner maiden at Chepstow in June: best efforts when second in Sandown nurseries in late-summer: strong-galloping sort and will be well suited by 1½m: acts on good to firm and dead ground: will continue to progress. *P. F. I. Cole*

ALDINGTON NOBLE 5 b.g. Creetown 123 – Mae Mae 69 (Communication 119) [1991 NR 1992 a12g⁶ a12g] second foal: brother to a poor animal: dam won over 5f at 2 yrs: seems of little account. *C. C. Trietline* –

ALDINGTON PEACH 3 ch.f. Creetown 123 – Aldington Cherry (Legal Eagle 126) [1991 NR 1992 a6g 6d 5m a5g] plain filly: fourth foal: sister to plating-class 1991 3-y-o maiden Ashgrove Cherry: dam unraced: no worthwhile form (trained by B. McMahon on debut, off course 7 months afterwards), including in claimers. *P. D. Evans* –

ALESSANDRINA (USA) 3 b.f. Alydar (USA) – Best Decision (USA) (Best Turn (USA)) [1991 7m 1992 10d⁵ 9g4 10.1d⁵ 9m* 12m 11.9f] leggy, lengthy, angular filly: much improved form to win 4-runner handicap at Goodwood in June: well beaten in handicaps afterwards, visored last time (August): should stay 1¼m: acts on good to firm ground. *M. R. Stoute* 78

ALFAARI (USA) 3 b. or br.c. Danzig (USA) – Life's Magic (USA) (Cox's Ridge (USA)) [1991 NR 1992 6.1g³ 8s4 10.3g] big, lengthy colt: third foal: half-brother to 4-y-o Alrayed (by Alydar) and North American winner Magic Prospect (by Mr Prospector): dam champion 1984 3-y-o filly in USA, won from 6f to 1¼m: modest form in maidens first 2 starts: snatched up early on and never got into Doncaster minor event last time: sold to join D. Murray-Smith 9,800 gns Newmarket December Sales: may well be capable of better. *Major W. R. Hern* 54 +

ALFLORA (IRE) 3 b.c. Niniski (USA) 125 – Adrana 86 (Bold Lad (IRE) 133) [1991 7g³ 7f4 7m³ 6.1m* 7m 7m³ 1992 7d⁵ 10g 10.4m⁵ 12g⁶ 12m³ 10m² 12m² 11.9g4 10d³] big, rangy colt: impresses in appearance: strong-galloping type, shows knee action: a smart and most consistent performer: contested only pattern events in 1992, putting up best effort in Irish Champion Stakes at Leopardstown in September, finishing around 9 lengths third of 8 behind Dr Devious and St Jovite: also placed in King Edward VII Stakes, Scottish Classic and Gordon Stakes: stays 112

Circlechart Ltd's "Alflora"

1½m: acts on good to firm and dead ground: very tough and genuine: likely to pick up a pattern event at 4 yrs. *C. E. Brittain*

ALGAIHABANE (USA)   6 b.g. Roberto (USA) 131 – Sassabunda 108 (Sassafras   –
(FR) 135) [1991 6m² 7g² 8g* 8g* 8d⁴ 1992 10g⁴ 8.5g 10g² 10s³ 12d 10d*] lengthy,
fair maiden, only poor nowadays: probably stays 2¼m: acts on firm going: below
form when blinkered once. *P. J. Hobbs*

AL GUSWA   3 ch.f. Shernazar 131 – Nuit d'Ete (USA) 90 (Super Concorde (USA)   **98**
128) [1991 6m² 7g² 8g* 8g* 8d⁴ 1992 10g⁴ 8.5g 10g² 10s³ 12d 10d*] lengthy,
workmanlike filly: second living foal: dam 2-y-o 5f and 6f winner: useful Irish
performer: off course 3 months after finishing fourth of 6 to All At Sea in listed race
at Newmarket in April: won handicap at the Curragh in October: better at 1¼m than
shorter: acts on soft going. *J. S. Bolger, Ireland*

ALHAAJIB (USA)   3 ch.c. Blushing Groom (FR) 131 – Lady Cutlass (USA)   **95** ?
(Cutlass (USA)) [1991 NR 1992 7.9g³ 8g⁴ 10.4d⁵ 10s⁵] rangy, attractive colt: good
mover: brother to fairly useful 7f and 1m winner Sajjaya and half-brother to several
winners, including very smart 4-y-o 1m/1¼m performer Lahib (by Riverman): dam,
5f to 7f winner in North America, is half-sister to high-class middle-distance
performer General Holme: disappointing maiden: easily best effort in 1m minor
event at Newbury: never travelling fluently either start afterwards: should prove
better at 1¼m than shorter: sold to join G. Pistoletti 12,500 gns Newmarket
December Sales. *J. L. Dunlop*

AL HAAL (USA)   3 b.c. Northern Baby (CAN) 127 – Kit's Double (USA) (Spring   **68**
Double) [1991 7.1d 8d 1992 10d³ 12g⁴ 9.9m³ 10g] lengthy, angular colt: fair maiden:
edgy, always behind final start: probably stays 1½m: acts on good to firm ground:
sold to join J. Joseph 5,800 gns Newmarket July Sales. *P. T. Walwyn*

ALHAMAD   3 b.c. Slip Anchor 136 – Dafinah (USA) 89 (Graustark) [1991 8m 8m²   **101**
1992 12m² 10g³ 10m* 10.1f* 12m² 12m⁴] rangy colt: really good mover: useful
performer: successful in small fields in handicap (sweating) at Windsor and minor
event at Newcastle in June: best efforts in minor event at Newmarket and listed
race at Goodwood following month: stays 1½m: acts on firm ground: hung first 3
starts this year, and wore a special bit on final one: sold only 2,200 gns Newmarket
December Sales. *H. R. A. Cecil*

ALHIJAZ   3 ch.c. Midyan (USA) 124 – Nawara 75 (Welsh Pageant 132) [1991   **122**
6g* 7m² 7m* 8m³ 8v* 8s* 1992 7d 8d* 8g⁴ 10m 8d⁴ 8s³ 8s* 10v²]

As in 1991, one had to travel to the Continent to see the best of Alhijaz.
This was no great surprise seeing as in the latest season he was sent overseas
for six of his eight starts. One of the exceptions was the Greenham Stakes on
his reappearance, a race he needed to put him right for his classic challenge
just over three weeks later, not at Newmarket, but at Rome for the Premio
Parioli. Already the winner of one Group 1 event in Italy, the Gran Criterium,
Alhijaz found the second well within his capabilities as well, comfortably
accounting for Spendaccione by two lengths in a ten-runner field with the
favourite Irish Memory only ninth. On the same weekend that Rodrigo de

Premio Parioli, Rome—Alhijaz wins by two lengths from Spendaccione

Triano won at the Curragh, Alhijaz lined up for his own, rather less acclaimed Guineas double, in the Mehl-Mulhens Rennen at Cologne. This was only the second year that the German Guineas had been open to foreign competition (Alhijaz's stable-companion Flying Brave won the first) but some sardonically questioned whether this was still practically the case after the latest running when, having beaten the odds-on German colt Platini by a short head, Alhijaz was controversially demoted and Carson given a one-day ban having apparently hampered the fourth home, Distinct Thatcher. An appeal against the decision failed.

These performances still left Alhijaz with plenty to find on form against the principals from the more important Guineas, a position that was not altered by his last of ten in the Grand Prix de Paris. As in 1991, however, autumn and soft ground revealed Alhijaz in a new light. The first two of three very smart efforts came in the Celebration Mile at Goodwood and Prix du Rond-Point at Longchamp. These races were basically exhibitions by Selkirk and Arazi, but Alhijaz was beaten only about two and three quarter lengths, receiving just 3 lb, at Goodwood, and four lengths, *giving* 7 lb, at Longchamp. One week after the Rond-Point, Alhijaz was back in Italy to win a third Group 1 prize in the Premio Vittorio di Capua at Milan. In this he faced far stronger opposition than on his previous Group 1 victories, notably from Shanghai and Rudimentary, winners respectively of the Poule d'Essai des Poulains and Forte Mile, and the top older horse in Italy, Misil. Alhijaz's ability to stay a mile thoroughly was proven already and he certainly needed it to win here, some five lengths behind Rudimentary entering the straight before wearing him down and staying on strongly for a three-and-a-half-length victory, Misil another two and a half lengths back in third and the remainder tailed off. With top-of-the-ground conditions now looking just as likely an explanation as the trip for his poor showing in the Grand Prix de Paris, Alhijaz was tried again at a mile and a quarter for his final appearance of 1992, in the Premio Roma in mid-November. On this occasion, however, it was Misil, on his first attempt at the distance, who proved much better suited by conditions, striding five and a half lengths clear of a below-form Alhijaz who had every chance.

Alhijaz (ch.c. 1989)	Midyan (USA) (b 1984)	Miswaki (ch 1978)	Mr Prospector Hopespringseternal
		Country Dream (b 1970)	Ribot Equal Venture
	Nawara (ch 1980)	Welsh Pageant (b 1966)	Tudor Melody Picture Light
		Bright Decision (ch 1973)	Busted Miss Klaire II

The close-coupled, quite good-topped Alhijaz is by the same owner Prince Faisal's Jersey Stakes winner Midyan, from a first crop which also includes the Prix de Seine-et-Oise winner Central City. Alhijaz has extended Nawara's one hundred per cent record of winners to foals, the best of the previous four being Usran (by Valiyar) and Usaylah (by Siberian Express) who showed useful form for Dunlop as three-year-olds; Usran won three handicaps and should have stayed a mile and three quarters while Usaylah, although not so good, won four at up to an extended mile and a quarter. The responsibility for carrying on this record rests with the Legend of France filly Flashella, an Irish 1,550-guinea foal and 1,800-guinea yearling who has had one run so far for Fairhurst. She is followed by a filly then a colt by Waajib. Nawara won a maiden at Bath over a mile and a quarter, a distance at which her dam Bright Decision won six times, showing useful form, as a four-year-old. Bright Decision also won over a mile at both three and four years, and is half-sister to the very useful miler Miracle and sister to the useful middle-distance handicapper Buss whose 1990 foal Beauchamp Hero is also by Midyan and in training with Dunlop. Alhijaz remains in training. *J. L. Dunlop*

ALICANTE 5 b.h. Alzao (USA) 117 – Safe And Happy (Tudor Melody 129) [1991 **42** 10.1m[3] 10.8m[2] 1992 12.3g 9.2g[5] 10.3g 10.8g 10g] small horse: poor maiden: trained first 4 starts by F. Yardley: worthwhile form in 1992 only when close seventh in Leicester handicap final start: stays 10.8f: acts on firm going: ran moderately in blinkers earlier in career: has looked none too keen. *M. C. Chapman*

ALICE BAY   2 ch.f. (Feb 3) Ballacashtal (CAN) – Halka (Daring March 116) [1992   **45**
5s⁴ 6g a7g a7g⁴ a7g 7d³ 8d] 3,000Y: medium-sized, workmanlike filly: fourth foal:
half-sister to winning sprinters Rose of High Legh and 5-y-o Nuclear Express (both
by Martinmas): dam unraced: poor form in varied company, including selling: stays
7f: best effort on good to soft ground. *D. Haydn Jones*

ALICE'S MIRROR   3 gr.f. Magic Mirror 105 – Pousdale-Tachytees 60   –
(Tachypous 128) [1991 6s 1992 7g⁵ 7f 9.7m] rather leggy filly: poor form: should stay
at least 1m: winner over hurdles in September. *T. P. McGovern*

ALIF (IRE)   3 b.c. Ajdal (USA) 130 – Pilot Bird 86 (Blakeney 126) [1991 NR 1992   –
10g⁴ 10m 14s 12s] leggy, attractive colt: moderate mover: second foal: dam 1¼m
winner, is daughter of Oaks third The Dancer: no worthwhile form: sold 5,600 gns
Newmarket Autumn Sales. *J. L. Dunlop*

ALIGHT (IRE)   3 b.f. Alzao (USA) 117 – Pitaka (Pitskelly 122) [1991 6m⁶ 7m⁵   –
8s* 1992 8f 11.6g 10.3m] leggy, rather angular filly: easy winner of Yarmouth maiden
at 2 yrs: not seen out until August and no form facing stiff tasks in handicaps, not
taking the eye in appearance last 2 starts: sold 4,400 gns Newmarket December
Sales. *A. C. Stewart*

ALILISA (USA)   4 b.f. Alydar (USA) – Balletomane (USA) (Nijinsky (CAN) 138)   –
[1991 10g² 10m³ 12m³ 11m³ 12g² 12d² 11g 12g² 12.8m* 1992 11.9g 14m⁶] lengthy,
sparely-made filly: fourth foal: half-sister to 2 minor winners in USA: dam
successful at up to 9f in graded-stakes company: ex-Irish filly, blinkered last 6 starts
at 3 yrs and successful in Wexford maiden for J. Bolger: bandaged and behind in
handicaps at York and Sandown in May: stays 12.8f: acts on good to firm and dead
ground. *W. J. Haggas*

A LITTLE PRECIOUS   6 b.g. Precocious 126 – The Silver Darling 75 (John   **56**
Splendid 116) [1991 6g 6g⁶ 8.3d 7m 7g³ 6g² 6g* 6d⁵ 7g⁴ 7s⁴ 7d 1992 6v 8d 6g⁴
a7g 6g³ 6g 8m 7.1s] strong, close-coupled gelding: poor mover: inconsistent
handicapper: has won one of last 33 starts: stays 7f: yet to race on firm going, acts on
any other. *J. R. Bostock*

ALIZARIN   3 ch.f. Noalto 120 – The Crying Game 55 (Manor Farm Boy 114) [1991   –
NR 1992 8v 10.3g 10g 11d] smallish, close-coupled filly: third reported foal: dam,
plater, stayed 1m: seems of little account. *B. C. Morgan*

ALIZARI (USA)   3 b.c. Topsider (USA) – Alia 112 (Sun Prince 128) [1991 NR 1992   **76** d
12g⁵ 14.9m³ 14.1f² 17.9d⁶ 16.2m⁵ 18m] sturdy colt: half-brother to 11.9f winner
Scimitarlia (by Diesis) and 1¼m/1½m winner Apply (by Kings Lake): dam won 5
races from 1¼m to 1½m: disappointing maiden: sold out of G. Harwood's stable
2,400 gns Newmarket September Sales after fourth start: probably stays 2m: may
prove best on a sound surface: blinkered second, third and final starts. *G. Fleming*

ALJADEER (USA)   3 b. or br.c. Alleged (USA) 138 – Return The Roses **115**
(USA) (Carry Back) [1991 8m* 8g* 1992 10g² 10.4m³]

Reports from the sales ring tend to be dominated by those horses which
sell best, such as Lyric Fantasy who made 340,000 guineas at Tattersalls in
December, but the returns at the opposite end of the market often take the
eye too. In 1992 there was the 8,000 guineas that was enough to buy Royal
Ascot winner Romany Rye, and the 2,000-odd guineas for one-time talking
horses Alhamad and El Cortes. Most striking of all though must have been the
8,400-guinea sale of lot 752 at the Newmarket Autumn Horses In Training
Sales, Aljadeer. Aljadeer's was not one of those nosedives from grace that
often lies in wait for an expensive yearling—he made 50,000 dollars, half the
average price for a yearling by Alleged in 1990—but, although a precise figure
cannot be placed on it, his was just as dramatic a reappraisal because only
three weeks before the race Aljadeer had been 9/2 favourite for the Derby. By
that stage (the morning of the Dante Stakes) Aljadeer had been talked about
as a Derby colt for some time, having spreadeagled large fields in a maiden at
Leicester and minor event at Newbury as a two-year-old. His reappearance
effort in the Thresher Classic Trial at Sandown brought him to the top of the
ante-post lists, even though he was beaten: the margin between him and the
winner Pollen Count was a head, and Aljadeer was widely reckoned to be
unlucky as his jockey had had to rein back when short of room over two
furlongs out then, having quickened well to take a slight advantage, Aljadeer
jumped a path inside the final furlong and was caught close home. Five lengths
and more adrift of this pair were Assessor, Beyton and Bonny Scot who all

went on to win important races in the next few months, as indeed did Pollen Count. Aljadeer was reckoned to have an excellent opportunity in the Dante Stakes at York eighteen days later, starting 5/4 in a field of seven, but, contrastingly, he could not reproduce the Sandown form, let alone improve on it as anticipated, being unable to match the pace of Alnasr Alwasheek over the final three furlongs and beaten five and a half lengths into third. Misgivings about the reliability of Alnasr Alwasheek's all-the-way success as a Derby guide were soon expressed, however, and Aljadeer, who seemed far more likely to be suited by the distance, remained prominent in the Derby betting. On May 18th it was announced that Michael Roberts had been booked to ride, then three days later Roberts was temporarily without a Derby mount. Aljadeer had jarred a suspensory ligament at York, and tendon trouble with his near-fore ensured that that was the last time his name appeared on the front pages.

Aljadeer is the sixth foal and fourth winner out of the minor American three-year-old winner Return The Roses, clearly the best of the remainder being No More Flowers (by My Gallant) who was placed in three graded contests, including the Grade 1 nine-furlong Florida Derby, in the spring as a three-year-old yet ended his racing career without a stakes win. Return The Roses is a daughter of Garland of Roses, who won the Grade 2 nine-furlong Black Helen Handicap as a six-year-old, and that celebrated racehorse of the early-'sixties Carry Back. One of the best at two years and winner of both the Kentucky Derby and Preakness Stakes at three years, Carry Back caused a stir in Europe as well as a four-year-old when he ran in the Arc. Rated second only to Kelso among the older horses in North America that season, Carry Back started third favourite in the Arc but finished tenth of twenty-four. A strong body of evidence suggests that he did not stay, but connections apparently blamed the ride given him by Scobie Breasley and their response was to challenge the first five home to a rematch with each of the owners contributing 25,000 dollars to the purse. This spectacular failed to materialise when only one of the five accepted. Carry Back went to stud the following year but was back on the track when the breeding season ended and won two out of six starts, a second bid for the Arc being ruled out only when he sustained an injury in another race eight days earlier.

Aljadeer (USA) (b. or br.c. 1989)	Alleged (USA) (b 1974)	Hoist The Flag (b 1968)	Tom Rolfe
			Wavy Navy
		Princess Pout (b 1966)	Prince John
			Determined Lady
	Return The Roses (USA) (ch 1977)	Carry Back (br 1958)	Saggy
			Joppy
		Garland of Roses (b 1969)	Beau Gar
			Bully For Rosy

Aljadeer is an attractive colt, though rather leggy and lacking in substance compared to some of his rivals in the Dante. He is a fluent mover, and should stay a mile and a half. It is doubtful, however, whether Aljadeer will run on the flat in 1993: he is now in training with Mick Easterby, his future over hurdles. *H. R. A. Cecil*

ALJAZZAF 2 b.c. (May 14) Mtoto 134 – Ibtisamm (USA) 71 (Caucasus (USA) 127) **82**
[1992 6f4 6g6 8m3] quite attractive colt: fifth foal: half-brother to 6f winner Dosha (by Touching Wood) and 3-y-o 7f winner Al Sadi (by Sharpo): dam 1m winner: fairly useful maiden: contested 6-runner Chesham Stakes at Royal Ascot and July Stakes at Newmarket (where got upset in stalls) first 2 starts: keeping-on third in moderately-run maiden at Doncaster in September, making most: will be well suited by middle distances: sure to win a maiden. *C. E. Brittain*

ALJERNAAS 3 ch.c. Rousillon (USA) 133 – Little White Star (Mill Reef (USA) **80**
141) [1991 7m 8m* 1992 10.3m 8.1g3 10g] lengthy colt: has a long stride: not seen out until late-July and failed to live up to 2-y-o promise, form only when third in handicap at Haydock: stays 1m well: sent to Dubai. *L. M. Cumani*

ALKARIF (USA) 3 ch.c. Diesis 133 – Mystery Mood (USA) (Night Invader **78**
(USA)) [1991 7m6 8m6 7.1s2 1992 8d5 8s4 7g4dis 5.9f2 6g3 8f* 8f* 8d* 8f3 7.9m 8m6 10.3m4 9d] lengthy, workmanlike colt: fair performer: won Redcar maiden and 2 handicaps at Warwick in the summer: subsequently sold out of A. Scott's stable 19,000 gns Newmarket July Sales: ran well on occasions afterwards: effective from

1m to 1¼m: acts on any going: takes keen hold: resold 22,000 gns Newmarket Autumn Sales after final start. *Mrs J. R. Ramsden*

AL KARNAK (IRE)   3 b.g. Darshaan 133 – Texly (FR) (Lyphard (USA) 132)   **95**
[1991 NR 1992 10g⁵ 10m³ 11g* 12m 13.9g² 14.6f³ 13.3g³] IR 54,000Y: big, strong gelding: moderate walker: fluent mover: half-brother to several winners here and abroad, including useful 1984 2-y-o sprinter Cameroun (by African Sky): dam, granddaughter of brilliantly speedy Texana, showed no form in France: useful performer: 11/2-on winner of maiden at Redcar in July: subsequently contested good-quality handicaps, running well when placed: should stay 2m: acts on firm ground: has run well for apprentice. *M. Moubarak*

ALKHAFJI   3 b.c. Ardross 134 – Eljazzi 92 (Artaius (USA) 129) [1991 NR 1992   **75 p**
a12g²] fourth foal: half-brother to Prix de Diane winner Rafha (by Kris) and 4-y-o 1½m to 14.6f winner Sarawat (by Slip Anchor): dam 2-y-o 7f winner disappointing at 3 yrs, is half-sister to high-class miler Pitcairn and very smart middle-distance stayer Valley Forge: 10/1 from 6/1, length second of 5 to Quadrant in maiden at Lingfield in September, slowly away, shaken up to have every chance approaching straight and running on: likely to improve. *H. R. A. Cecil*

ALL AT SEA (USA)   3 ch.f. Riverman (USA) 131 – Lost Virtue (USA)   **124**
(Cloudy Dawn (USA)) [1991 8g* 1992 10d* 10g* 10.4g* 12d² 10m² 10.4g² 8s* 8s⁴]

All At Sea was sent to the United States in the autumn, to go into training with Bobby Frankel in California. She took with her a record of model consistency and substantial achievement capped by a win in the Emirates Prix du Moulin de Longchamp on her penultimate start. That win put her among the season's best fillies at a mile. But another of All At Sea's qualities is her versatility. Her second to Rodrigo de Triano in the Juddmonte International over a mile and a quarter at York was equally good form, while her second to User Friendly in the Oaks was no mean performance even if it did raise the possibility of stamina limitations. Provided she acclimatizes, she should be a moneyspinner for her new stable.

All At Sea started 11/10 favourite in an unusually small Oaks field after setting up an unbeaten sequence in mile-and-a-quarter races commemorating Oaks winners—the Oh So Sharp Stakes at Nottingham, the Pretty Polly Stakes at Newmarket and the Musidora Stakes at York. A rangy filly with

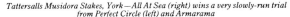

Tattersalls Musidora Stakes, York—All At Sea (right) wins a very slowly-run trial from Perfect Circle (left) and Armarama

Emirates Prix du Moulin de Longchamp—a well-deserved Group 1 win for All At Sea; Brief Truce makes a strong challenge in second, ahead of Hatoof

scope, she became ante-post favourite for the classic in late-April when a very impressive display in the Pretty Polly confirmed the promise of a five-length win at Nottingham, which itself had been preceded by an equally easy one in a back-end maiden at Wolverhampton on her debut. All At Sea looked in a different league from the opposition in an apparently under-strength race at Newmarket, sprinting clear up the hill. Further clues to her Oaks prospects were limited by the very slow pace in the following month's Musidora, when she clashed with another Oaks fancy Perfect Circle in a five-runner affair. All At Sea settled well as usual and again showed a good turn of foot to beat her main rival by a length in what developed into a two-furlong sprint. Of the two, All At Sea seemed the more likely to get a mile and a half; in fact, on breeding, racing style and temperament (she is always notably relaxed in the preliminaries) there seemed few grounds to doubt that she would get it. However, on the day she was beaten by not just a better filly but by a stouter stayer. The race was a true test, run at a good gallop on softish going. As User Friendly was sent on approaching three furlongs out, All At Sea, who'd cruised along in mid-division, responded and began to look a serious threat a furlong later; but the challenge only brought out more from the leader and All At Sea herself came under pressure with still a furlong and a half to go, running on willingly. Through the final furlong it became increasingly clear that User Friendly was the stronger and in the end she won going away by three and a half lengths, All At Sea tending to edge left. Although the first two drew twenty lengths clear, All At Sea's jockey and trainer both expressed the view that she'd failed to stay. She was duly returned to shorter distances, first of all in the Nassau Stakes at Goodwood in which she and the equally genuine Ruby Tiger stood out on form. The spoils went narrowly to the older mare, who snatched a clear advantage three furlongs out and held on as All At Sea, having travelled strongly, tucked away, couldn't get into contention quite so comfortably as at Epsom and only gradually managed to reduce Ruby Tiger's advantage under pressure. Cecil reportedly felt the ground too firm for the runner-up. All At Sea's performance was not far out of line with her previous best. However, she improved on easier ground in the Juddmonte International three weeks later in finishing only a length behind Rodrigo de Triano, turning the tables on a below-par Ruby Tiger. There was plenty in her display to encourage connections to run her back at a mile. She cruised through to track Alnasr Alwasheek as he tried to crack the high-class field half a mile out, and she was virtually on the bridle on narrowly taking over in front two furlongs from home. In the end Rodrigo de Triano proved to have an even better turn of foot, but All At Sea battled on until eased slightly near the line.

So to the Moulin in September. The withdrawal of Arazi because of a training knock left All At Sea facing nine opponents, six of whom were Group 1 winners, something that All At Sea was not. But those six—Brief Truce, El Prado, Shanghai, Hatoof, Kitwood and Misil—were a very mixed bag, and four of them had recently been beaten by Exit To Nowhere in the Prix Jacques le

Mr K. Abdulla's "All At Sea"

		Never Bend	Nasrullah
	Riverman (USA)	(b 1960)	Lalun
	(b 1969)	River Lady	Prince John
All At Sea (USA)		(b 1963)	Nile Lily
(ch.f. 1989)		Cloudy Dawn	Grey Dawn II
	Lost Virtue (USA)	(gr 1969)	Creme Brulee
	(gr 1977)	Aunt Tilt	Tulyar
		(b 1963)	Kerala

Marois at Deauville, along with two more of the field, Cardoun and Take
Risks. The betting gave the visitors the edge, with All At Sea second favourite
close behind Brief Truce who was running for the first time since his win in
the St James's Palace Stakes. In testing conditions All At Sea soon proved
well able to lie up, and Eddery had her second on the heels of Brief Truce's
pacemaker Sharp Review on the home turn. Shortly afterwards, Eddery made
the decisive move by attacking for the lead. All At Sea quickened very well,
and as she slipped into the lead below the distance she had the favourite in
trouble on the outside of the bunch. He still turned out to be the main threat,
finishing best, but All At Sea ran on under the whip and held on by a neck.
Back-to-form Hatoof took third place without being able to land a blow. To a
certain extent All At Sea had had the run of the race and it came as little
surprise to see Brief Truce turn the tables in the Queen Elizabeth II Stakes at
Ascot later in the month, when they finished second and fourth respectively
behind Lahib in a stronger field than the Moulin's. All At Sea finished six
lengths behind the winner. Her coat had just begun to go by then and she was
less outstanding in appearance than during the summer.

All At Sea's sire Riverman has been responsible for some good race-mares over the years, some as good at a mile and a half as Triptych, Gold River and Detroit. The dam, the unraced Lost Virtue, was seldom covered by such a high grade of stallion previously, and in the circumstances she has a superb record as a producer—eight winners from eight runners, including the stakes winner Full Virtue (by Full Out) and the 1985 Free Handicap winner Over The Ocean (by Super Concorde). Barren in 1990, she foaled a colt by Blushing Groom in 1991. The second dam Aunt Tilt was useful on the track and in the paddocks in the States, and was one of eight winners out of Kerala, foremost among them Aunt Tilt's half-brother, the 1967 Horse of the Year Damascus. *H. R. A. Cecil*

ALL BAILEYS 2 b.f. (Mar 12) Jalmood (USA) 126 – Council Rock 74 (General   –
Assembly (USA)) [1992 5d⁶ 5s⁵ 6s] 4,200F, 2,100Y: very small filly: first foal: dam, maiden suited by 1¼m, is daughter of Nassau Stakes winner Dancing Rocks: no worthwhile form, including in claimers, in the spring. *M. Johnston*

ALL EARZ (IRE) 3 b.g. Auction Ring (USA) 123 – Classic Choice (Patch 129)   –
[1991 5m 6.1m⁵ 6m⁶ 6g 1992 7g 8.1g 8g 7g⁴ 5m 6d 7s] lengthy gelding: moderate mover: poor maiden: stays 7f: well beaten in blinkers once: sold 900 gns Doncaster November Sales. *R. Earnshaw*

ALLEGAN (USA) 3 b. or br.c. Alleged (USA) 138 – Artiste 95 (Artaius (USA) **107**
129) [1991 NR 1992 10d* 12g* 14d² 13.9s* 15.5s⁶] good-topped colt: second live foal: half-brother to minor French 12.2f winner Sedova (by Nijinsky): dam 1m winner stayed 1¼m, is daughter of Oaks winner Val's Girl: well-backed favourite, won maiden at Kempton in April and minor events at Newmarket in May and York (12/1 on in match) in October: best effort when beaten head by Rain Rider in 4-runner listed race at Goodwood: well beaten in Prix Royal-Oak at Longchamp final start: stays 1¾m well: yet to race on top-of-the-ground. *H. R. A. Cecil*

ALLEGATION 2 b.c. (Apr 20) Dominion 123 – Pageantry 83 (Welsh Pageant   **75**
132) [1992 8s⁵ 8s⁴ 8d³ 8m⁵] 32,000Y: medium-sized, good-bodied colt: carries condition: fourth foal: brother to useful 7f and 1m winner Just Class, later graded winner in USA, and half-brother to smart 3-y-o Up Anchor (by Slip Anchor), successful from 8.2f (at 2 yrs) to 1½m: dam ran only at 2 yrs when placed over 5f and 6f: fair maiden: best effort third start: will be suited by 1¼m+: one paced. *P. F. I. Cole*

ALLEGRAMENTE 3 b.c. Music Maestro 119 – Eastern Romance 73 (Sahib 114)   **57**
[1991 5g⁶ 6g 6m 7f⁶ 7m 7f 6g 1992 7.5m 8m² 7g⁴ 8.5d² 8m 10s 7g] rather lightly-made colt: modest performer: in frame in seller and handicaps: stays 8.5f: acts on firm and dead going. *R. O'Leary*

ALLEGRISSIMA 2 b. or br.f. (Mar 18) Sharpo 132 – Hasty Key (USA) (Key To **71** d
The Mint (USA)) [1992 a7g* 7.1g* 7f a7g² 7d* 7m 7d] leggy, unfurnished filly: moderate mover: fifth foal: half-sister to 3-y-o Believe It (by Bellypha), 2-y-o 7f winners Cutting Note (by Diesis) and Hasty Vessel (by Raise A Cup) and a winning hurdler: dam minor winner at up to 9f in USA: made all or close up throughout when winning seller (retained 3,600 gns) at Southwell, claimer at Edinburgh and selling nursery (very gamely and easily best effort, subsequently retained 3,400 gns) at Wolverhampton in summer: well below even previous form afterwards: will stay 1m: acts on fibresand but easily best effort on dead ground, ran moderately both starts on top-of-the-ground: sold 5,400 gns Newmarket Autumn Sales. *J. Berry*

ALLENSEA (IRE) 2 b.g. (May 25) Simply Great (FR) 122 – Quai Des Brumes   **48**
(USA) (Little Current (USA)) [1992 7g 7g 10g] 1,600F: leggy, close-coupled gelding: half-brother to several winners abroad by Be My Guest: dam placed once at 3 yrs in France: soundly beaten in minor event and maidens in autumn: will stay 1½m: has been gelded. *C. A. Horgan*

ALLE-ROY 4 b.g. Alleging (USA) 120 – Loyal And Regal 51 (Royal And Regal   **65**
(USA)) [1991 8m⁵ 10.1g⁴ 10.1m² 12m³ 11.9m 15.9d 12.1s 1992 a12g* a11g³ a14g⁴] leggy, workmanlike gelding: fair handicapper on his day: won twice at Southwell in January: below form after, last seen out in February: should stay 1¾m: acts on good to firm ground and fibresand: visored (below form) once. *J. C. Gillen*

ALLESCA 2 b.f. (Jan 28) Alleging (USA) 120 – Hitesca 110 (Tesco Boy 121) [1992 **52** p
7m 6g] 1,400F: workmanlike filly: half-sister to out-and-out stayer Hydrangea and winning stayer/hurdler Broctune Grey (both by Warpath) and fair miler Referendum (by Reform): dam, very game filly, stayed 1½m: carrying condition, better effort, though bumped and eased inside last, when in mid-division in 6f maiden at Newbury

in September: bred to be very well suited by longer distances, and is likely to improve. *M. D. I. Usher*

ALLEZ BIANCO 2 ch.f. (Mar 19) Precocious 126 – Tripolitaine (FR) (Nonoalco 50 (USA) 131) [1992 5m3 6d2 5.7g4 6m 6.1g] 4,600Y: sturdy filly: half-sister to several winners, including 3-y-o sprinter Walk In The Park (by Valiyar) and 1989 2-y-o 5f winner Western Music (by Music Boy): dam won twice at around 11f in France: consistent, albeit plating-class form, first 3 starts: off course nearly 8 weeks and finished last in nursery (very stiff task) and maiden (visored) in September: may do better over further. *R. J. Holder*

ALL GREEK TO ME (IRE) 4 b.g. Trojan Fen 118 – Do We Know (Derrylin – 115) [1991 7v4 8s 9d* 12.3d 12g5 9.2d2 10g 10.5g 1992 8s5] leggy, rather good-topped gelding: modest handicapper (rated 59 in 1991): never-nearer fifth of 22 in Pontefract handicap in October: stays 9f: acts on dead ground: winning (1991/2) hurdler. *C. W. Thornton*

ALLIMAC NOMIS 3 b.g. Daring March 116 – Game For A Laugh 72 (Martinmas 39 128) [1991 7f 8m 1992 8.3d 6.1d 10g6 a10g6 10g3 8f* 8m 10m 10g 8g] leggy, angular gelding: modest plater: won at Brighton (no bid) in May: sold out of N. Callaghan's stable 1,800 gns Newmarket July Sales after seventh 3-y-o start: effective from 1m to 1¼m: acts on firm ground: winner over hurdles in September: resold 900 gns Ascot December Sales. *I. Campbell*

ALLINSON'S MATE (IRE) 4 b.c. Fayruz 116 – Piney Pass (Persian Bold 123) 78 [1991 6d2 6m 7m2 7m3 8m 6d 6m 6.1m 6f 7m6 6m 1992 5m4 6g 6g 7m 5m2 6d 6d 6m a85 a6g* a7g*] small, robust colt: carries condition: moderate mover: fairly useful performer, but none too consistent on turf: won claimer and handicap in late-season at Southwell: effective from 5f to 7f: acts on firm and dead ground and on fibresand. *T. D. Barron*

ALLMOSA 3 b.f. Alleging (USA) 120 – Wimosa 92 (Mossborough 126) [1991 NR 52 1992 7s4 8d3 10d a8g a12g4 a12g4 12.3s* 12v3 14.1s3] leggy, close-coupled filly: has a round action: half-sister to several winners, including fairly useful 7f and 1m winner Master Golfer (by Swing Easy) and Irish 9f and 1½m winner Samantha's Flutter (by Beldale Flutter): dam suited by 1½m +: fair and largely consistent plater: won (no bid) at Wolverhampton in September: stays 1½m well: acts on heavy ground and equitrack. *T. J. Naughton*

ALL PROMISES 2 br.f. (Feb 24) King Among Kings 60 – Market Blues (Porto 33 Bello 118) [1992 5g 6g6 6m5 5h 6d a6g] 400Y: smallish, lengthy filly: poor mover: second reported foal: sister to 3-y-o 6f and 7f winner Palacegate King: dam poor: sire 11.7f winner: poor plater: stays 6f: acts on good to firm ground. *P. Butler*

ALLTHRUTHENIGHT (IRE) 3 ch.c. Precocious 126 – Time For Pleasure 85 (Tower Walk 130) [1991 5g 5g3 5m 5g* 5m4 5d 1992 5v2 6d4 5g 5g* 5m 5f5 5m5 5m 5d6 5d3 5g] good-quartered colt: fairly useful and consistent handicapper: won at Epsom in June: probably best at 5f: acts on heavy going and good to firm: gets on toes and has sweated up. *L. J. Holt*

ALL WELCOME 5 b.g. Be My Guest (USA) 126 – Pepi Image (USA) (National) – [1991 NR 1992 12.3m] angular gelding: poor mover: modest maiden (best efforts at 1m on top-of-the-ground) as 3-y-o for J. Fanshawe: fair winning hurdler in 1991/2: backed at long odds but never able to challenge in Ripon handicap in August: effective blinkered or not. *G. M. Moore*

ALMAMZAR (USA) 2 b.c. (Jan 16) Theatrical 128 – Promising Risk (USA) 71 p (Exclusive Native (USA)) [1992 7m4 8m*] $75,000Y: quite attractive colt, shade unfurnished: third reported foal: half-brother to 4-y-o River Island (by Spend A Buck), winner at 1¼m at 3 yrs: dam unraced half-sister to Belle's Gold, stakes winner from 6f to 9f, including of Grade 3 events: odds on after promising debut at Newmarket, narrowly won maiden at Yarmouth in September, setting modest pace, then running on well when shaken up: will be well suited by middle distances: sure to continue improving. *M. R. Stoute*

ALMANOT 5 ch.m. Remainder Man 126§ – Coumenole (Beau Chapeau) [1991 NR – 1992 14f4] lengthy, rather sparely-made mare: second foal: dam behind in NH Flat races: third in NH Flat race in January: 50/1, tailed off in 4-runner minor event at Salisbury in June. *R. Curtis*

ALMANSOUR (USA) 2 b.c. (May 4) Al Nasr (FR) 126 – Grausdee (USA) 73 (Graustark) [1992 7g4 7f2 7g2 7.5m3 7m4 7m 8s3 8.1g] $11,000Y: close-coupled colt: sixth reported foal: half-brother to 3 minor winners in North America: dam unraced: fair maiden: very good third to Sudbury in nursery at Warwick on penultimate start:

will require good test of stamina: acts on firm and soft going: sold 6,000 gns Newmarket Autumn Sales. *H. R. A. Cecil*

ALMASA 4 b.f. Faustus (USA) 118 – Superfrost 49 (Tickled Pink 114) [1991 7g⁴ **64** 6d⁴ 6g⁴ 6d⁴ 6d 5.2f 5m 8m 6m 7m 6m⁶ 1992 6m 6g 6m² 6g⁴ 6m² 6m² 6d³ 7m 6.1g² 6s⁶ 6d 5v] sparely-made filly: poor mover: fair handicapper: ran well when in frame, moderately otherwise: stays 6f: acts on good to firm and dead going: tends to drift right: has run creditably for apprentice: visored (well beaten) once. *D. Morris*

ALMONTY (IRE) 2 b.c. (May 13) Mazaad 106 – Nordic Maid 84 (Vent du Nord) **–** [1992 a7g a8g] 4,100 2-y-o: half-brother to Irish 1½m winner Ballinascreena (by Kampala): dam 1m winner: soundly beaten in maidens at Lingfield. *W. R. Muir*

ALMOOJID 6 b.h. Sadler's Wells (USA) 132 – Irish Bird (USA) (Sea Bird II 145) **–** [1991 NR 1992 12.3v] big, leggy ex-Irish horse: soon tailed off in Wolverhampton handicap on first run on flat since 3 yrs: has run well in blinkers. *R. J. Baker*

ALMOST A PRINCESS 4 b.f. Alleging (USA) 120 – Rabab (Thatching 131) **–** [1991 8g 10g⁶ 8g³ 8d² 10g⁴ 8.1g 8.3m 8g 8.1s 1992 8.3g⁶] leggy filly: retained 1,550 gns Ascot February Sales but probably of little account nowadays. *J. Akehurst*

AL MOULOUKI 2 b.c. (May 29) Efisio 120 – Prejudice 83 (Young Generation **40** 129) [1992 6g 7d 6s⁵ 7d] 14,000Y: good-topped colt: has scope: has a round action: second foal: half-brother to 3-y-o 6.1f and 7f winner Hob Green (by Move Off): dam maiden suited by 1m: poor maiden. *J. W. Payne*

ALMUHTARAMA (IRE) 3 ch.f. Rainbow Quest (USA) 134 – Bold Lady (FR) **84** (Bold Lad (USA)) [1991 NR 1992 10f* 11.9d⁵ 10g² 12g] rangy filly: half-sister to several winners, including very useful 1984 French staying 2-y-o Hello Bill (by Bellypha): dam won 3 times at up to 9f in France: fairly useful performer: won 4-runner maiden at Pontefract in August: best effort when short-head second in handicap at Sandown: ran moderately final start: should have stayed 1½m: visits Lycius. *A. C. Stewart*

AL MUTAHM (USA) 4 b.g. Green Dancer (USA) 132 – Musical Medicine (FR) **104** (Margouillat (FR) 133) [1991 10m³ 12m* 16.2g 13.3g⁵ 11.9g³ 12g 1992 14.9v 12.3v* 14g² 16.2d*] tall, rangy gelding: much improved for new stable: successful in April in handicap at Warwick (most impressively) and Group 3 Sagaro Stakes at Ascot: stayed on determinedly to lead close home at Ascot, beating Supreme Choice a neck: much better at 2m than shorter: dead. *J. A. B. Old*

ALNASR ALWASHEEK 3 b.c. Sadler's Wells (USA) 132 – Someone **117** Special 105 (Habitat 134) [1991 7d² 7g* 7m³ 1992 8g* 8g 10.4m* 12g 10.4g 9.7s]

   Alnasr Alwasheek's career in Europe was ultimately a disappointment, all the more so for its having, on occasions, given so much. An occupational hazard with winning a race that carries that unofficial but persuasive title 'classic trial' is the expectation it engenders. And Alnasr Alwasheek's wins

Craven Stakes, Newmarket—Alnasr Alwasheek takes the measure of Dr Devious, Irish Memory (check cap) and Muhtarram

Homeowners Dante Stakes, York—Alnasr Alwasheek makes all this time; Great Palm is a clear second

in the Craven and Dante Stakes, the two most prestigious classic trials in the Calendar, engendered considerable expectations. The Craven Stakes attracted an eight-runner field with one of the top two-year-olds of 1991, the Dewhurst winner Dr Devious, taking on some far less experienced but highly promising individuals including Muhtarram, Bold Pursuit, Badie and Forest Tiger, the last of whom had won a newcomers race at the Doncaster Lincoln meeting and was so well touted that he started favourite on this, only his second start. Alnasr Alwasheek was a 5/1 joint-third choice following a two-year-old season that had brought victory in a Kempton maiden and a third in the Tattersalls Tiffany Highflyer Stakes. Bubbles were burst (Forest Tiger finished last) as Alnasr Alwasheek became the Two Thousand Guineas favourite with a length-and-a-half beating of Dr Devious. The best at the weights, giving 5 lb, was Dr Devious but he was bound for Churchill Downs and Alnasr Alwasheek had won in style, travelling strongly in rear before being eased towards the outside and bursting through into the lead a furlong out. The timefigures for the first two, equivalent to ratings of 126 and 127, were the fastest recorded by three-year-olds over the distance all year. None of which stopped Alnasr Alwasheek from being beaten nearly ten lengths in the Guineas just over two weeks later. We considered Alnasr Alwasheek a worthy favourite (he started 5/2) but he never got in a blow, becoming involved in some bumping before halfway and stumbling slightly in the Dip, but basically wanting for an obvious excuse.

Whatever the explanation was, it could not have been anything too serious physically because Alnasr Alwasheek was on the racecourse again inside two weeks. Muhtarram was a late absentee because of injury but the Homeowners Dante Stakes at York, like the Craven, promised much as a classic trial. With tactics quite unlike those employed in the Craven, Alnasr Alwasheek made all. The Thresher Classic Trial runner-up and Derby favourite Aljadeer and the Dewhurst second Great Palm (having his first run of 1992) kept close tabs, but they didn't take on Cauthen and Alnasr Alwasheek for the lead and, when the pace quickened from over three furlongs out, it soon became clear that nothing would. Running on strongly, Alnasr Alwasheek passed the post three lengths up on Great Palm with another two and a half back to Aljadeer. It was the Maktoum family's first success in the race. 'Dante building into ultimate Derby test' had been the headline in *The Sporting Life* four days earlier but the conclusions to be drawn from the result of this test were far from clear. His pedigree, worries about his adapting to the Epsom track, and the way in which he had been able to dictate the pace in the Dante all made Alnasr Alwasheek a less attractive proposition for the Derby than he had been for the Guineas. Cauthen preferred him to Twist And Turn, a sensible decision on grounds of proven ability, but the doubts proved well founded as Alnasr Alwasheek hung markedly in the last two furlongs and tired into seventh of eighteen. Alnasr Alwasheek had failed his two classic tests and he could not regain the winning thread in two races after Epsom. Considering that he set a fast pace, was harried from an early stage and capitulated only approaching the furlong marker, his seventh of twelve in the International Stakes at York wasn't at all a bad effort, but Alnasr Alwasheek's season ended in a whimper on soft ground at Longchamp in the Prix Dollar.

Alnasr Alwasheek was purchased for 175,000 guineas at the Highflyer Sales, a sum which does not seem exceptional, for, although the dam's only previous foal Someone Brave (by Commanche Run) broke his duck as late as September 1992 in a three-runner novice hurdle, Alnasr Alwasheek is by Sadler's Wells out of a famously-related dam. Someone Special was a useful miler, third to Sonic Lady in the Coronation Stakes, but one whose achievements pale beside those of both her half-sister and dam. The half-sister is Milligram who won the Coronation Stakes, by seven lengths, and was one of only two fillies in 1987 to beat Miesque, by two and a half lengths when Miesque was 4/1 on in the Queen Elizabeth II Stakes. Milligram was also second in the Marcel Boussac, One Thousand Guineas and Irish One Thousand. Her dam One In A Million went one better at Newmarket but one worse (until Buz Kashi's controversial disqualification) in the Coronation Stakes. Milligram's first foal was a colt by Alleged, still unnamed with Weatherbys when he was exported to Japan in March 1991, and her second is the Alysheba filly Alligram in training with Stoute, One In A Million's latest of racing age being the Reference Point colt Number One Spot who is with Roger Charlton. Someone Special had an early abortion after her 1989 covering; bidding for her 1991 filly by Alzao reached 130,000 guineas, but not her reserve, at the Houghton Sales. She threw a Night Shift filly in 1992.

Alnasr Alwasheek (b.c. 1989)			
	Sadler's Wells (USA) (b 1981)	Northern Dancer (b 1961)	Nearctic / Natalma
		Fairy Bridge (b 1975)	Bold Reason / Special
	Someone Special (b 1983)	Habitat (b 1966)	Sir Gaylord / Little Hut
		One In A Million (b 1976)	Rarity / Singe

It has been said that Alnasr Alwasheek, a lengthy, lightly-made colt, takes more after his dam's family than his sire in looks and, although he has had only the one race at a mile and a half, the same is almost certainly true of his optimum racing distance. He is a fluent mover, possibly unsuited by soft ground. What is known for certain is that Alnasr Alwasheek is a very talented performer on his day—he should win a good race in the United States, where he is to be trained by Neil Drysdale. *M. R. Stoute*

ALNASRIC PETE (USA) 6 b.g. Al Nasr (FR) 126 – Stylish Pleasure (USA) **55** (What A Pleasure (USA)) [1991 6g 7d 7m 7m5 7f 9d 8m4 8.3m 7m* 8g 7f 8m 8m* 8m 8m3 6.9s 1992 8g 7g 8m5 7f4 7d 7.1s 7d3 8g5 7s2 7d 8d2] rather leggy, good-topped gelding: carries condition: has a round action: none too consistent handicapper overall, though ran creditably 4 of last 5 starts: sold to join G. Humphrey 4,400 gns Newmarket Autumn Sales: best form at 7f/1m: acts on firm and soft going: found nothing when blinkered once: sometimes bandaged: has run well for lady rider: takes keen hold, and best held up in strongly-run race. *D. A. Wilson*

ALOUETTE 2 gr.f. (Apr 29) Darshaan 133 – Alruccaba 83 (Crystal Palace (FR) **89** 132) [1992 7s3 8d2 7d2 8d*] 21,000Y: fourth foal: sister to Irish 3-y-o Arrikala, successful at up to 1¾m, and half-sister to fair 1½m winner Allegra (by Niniski): dam 2-y-o 6f winner: fairly useful performer: ran an excellent race when 3 lengths third of 8 to Sayyedati in Moyglare Stud Stakes at the Curragh in September: narrowly won maiden at Leopardstown following month: will be well suited to middle distances and may be capable of better. *J. S. Bolger, Ireland*

ALPHA HELIX 9 b.g. Double Form 130 – Daidis 66 (Welsh Pageant 132) [1991 **30 §** 13.8d 12g 12m5 13f 15g5 13m 1992 13d 13m 15.1m5 13.1m 12.1m 15.1m4 15.1m2 15.1g* 15.1f2 15g 17.5d4 12.1d4 17.9d 15.8d 15.1d] deep-girthed gelding: moderate mover: poor handicapper: successful at Edinburgh in July: stays 15f: acts on firm and dead ground: has worn blinkers, visored nowadays: has put head in air and found very little: not one to trust. *Miss L. A. Perratt*

ALPHARD 3 gr.c. Kalaglow 132 – Julia Flyte 91 (Drone) [1991 8.2m* 1992 11.9f* **105** 12m5 11.9f* 12m6] good-topped colt: moderate mover: useful performer: successful in small fields in minor event at Brighton in May and listed race (made all to beat Bobzao 2½ lengths) at Haydock: reportedly very lame after running poorly in Gordon Stakes at Goodwood later in July: well worth a try at 1¾m. *H. R. A. Cecil*

ALQAIRAWAAN 3 b.g. Ajdal (USA) 130 – Clare Island 108 (Connaught 130) **84** [1991 7m 8.1g⁴ 7.9m³ 8m³ 1992 13.3d 14m² 16.2s 14.1d³ 14.6g³] lengthy, well-made gelding: fair maiden: easily best 3-y-o effort in handicap second start: should stay 2m: seems not to act on a soft surface: sold to join J. Sutcliffe 28,000 gns Newmarket Autumn Sales and gelded: will win a handicap at 4 yrs. *J. L. Dunlop*

AL RAMIS (IRE) 3 b.g. Crystal Glitters (USA) 127 – Diamond Spring (USA) **73** (Vaguely Noble 140) [1991 7g 8s² 7m 7.6d* 1992 8.9g 11.4m⁵ 9.9m 8g² 7f* 8.1s] close-coupled, quite good-topped gelding: usually impresses in appearance: fair performer: won claimer at Yarmouth in June: stiff task, last in £10,500 handicap at Sandown following month: headstrong on occasions, and seems best at up to 1m: acts on any going: wore tongue strap last 3 starts: has been gelded. *C. E. Brittain*

ALRAYED (USA) 4 b.c. Alydar (USA) – Life's Magic (USA) (Cox's Ridge – (USA)) [1991 12m³ 11.7g 1992 8.1g 12f] big, strong, rangy colt: good mover, with a light action: well bred, and rated 86 when third in Newmarket maiden: split a pastern on way to post next start and tailed off in 1992. *Major W. R. Hern*

ALREEF 6 b.g. Wassl 125 – Joey (FR) 110 (Salvo 129) [1991 10.8g⁵ 10g⁶ 9.7f 1992 – a12g] sparely-made, rather dipped-backed gelding: plating-class handicapper (rated 48) at 5 yrs: well beaten in Lingfield handicap in November: should stay 1½m: acts on good to firm and dead ground, probably unsuited by very soft: effective blinkered/visored or not: has run well for amateur: fair winning (1991/2) hurdler. *T. Thomson Jones*

ALSAARM (USA) 3 b.c. Danzig (USA) – Lucky Lucky Lucky (USA) (Chieftain **87** II) [1991 7g* 8m³ 7m⁶ 6m³ 1992 8d 7.3g⁶ 6.1m³ 6m³] lengthy, good-quartered colt: usually looks well: fairly useful performer: easily best 3-y-o effort in 6.1f minor event at Nottingham: bred to stay 1¼m: sent to USA. *J. L. Dunlop*

AL SADI (USA) 3 ch.c. Sharpo 132 – Ibtisamm (USA) 71 (Caucasus (USA) 127) [1991 6m⁶ **79** 1992 8d⁵ 7g³ 7g* 6d 8m 7g⁶] leggy colt: fair form: off course 5 months after winning maiden at Kempton in May: faced stiff tasks afterwards, never placed to challenge nor knocked about in minor event final start: should stay 1m. *C. E. Brittain*

AL SENAFI (IRE) 2 b.c. (Feb 23) Persian Bold 123 – Sheer Innocence (Shirley **76 p** Heights 130) [1992 7m 8.2s²] IR 105,000Y: unfurnished colt: first foal: dam, Irish maiden placed mostly at 1½m, is out of Princess Elizabeth winner Varishkina: followed promising debut at Newmarket with running-on second to Azzilfi in maiden at Nottingham later in October: will stay 1½m: will improve again. *L. M. Cumani*

AL SHAATI (FR) 2 b.f. (Feb 10) Lead On Time (USA) 123 – With You All (Free **61 p** Round (USA)) [1992 6s³ 6d⁵] 750,000 francs (approx £75,300) Y: leggy, unfurnished filly: good mover: third foal: dam French 8.2f winner: better effort when fifth of 21, ridden soon after halfway, eased close home, to Specified in maiden at Redcar in October: will stay 1m: will improve again. *M. R. Stoute*

AL SHAREEF 7 b.g. Shareef Dancer (USA) 135 – Tarpoon (USA) (Vaguely – Noble 140) [1991 10s 9s² 10d² a7g⁴ a8g⁶ 10.3d⁶ a10g a13g 1992 a11g] quite attractive gelding: has a round action: no form since spring 1991: retained 1,350 gns Ascot July Sales. *D. Burchell*

AL SKEET (USA) 6 b.g. L'Emigrant (USA) 129 – Processional (USA) **33 §** (Reviewer (USA)) [1991 10g 12g a12g 1992 10d 10m 10.3m² 12.1s² 11.7d 10g] lengthy, quite attractive gelding: poor handicapper: sold out of A. Moore's stable 3,000 gns Ascot June Sales: form since 3-y-o only when second in apprentice races in August: stays 1½m: acts on any going: ran poorly in blinkers earlier in career: won selling handicap hurdle in October. *R. J. Price*

ALTA VICTORIA (IRE) 2 b.f. (May 18) Fairy King (USA) – Sunland Park **51 p** (Baragoi 115) [1992 6g] IR 3,000F, 19,000Y: smallish, angular filly: half-sister to several winners, including one-time fairly useful middle-distance performer Gulfland (by Gulf Pearl): dam unraced: 50/1, backward and green, beaten around 9 lengths in mid-division of 20-runner Newmarket maiden in October, fading closing stages: bred to stay middle distances: should improve. *R. Charlton*

ALTERMEERA 4 br.g. Noalto 120 – Mac's Melody (Wollow 132) [1991 8.2d² **60** 10g⁶ 8g 9.7m⁴ 7m² 7f 7.1m² 1992 9m 8.1f 10.2g⁶ 10g⁴ 10m⁵ 14.1d 12s³ 11.8d 11.8s] tall, rangy gelding: shows knee action: none too consistent handicapper, and still a maiden: stays 1½m: acts on good to firm and soft ground: visored final start, finishing tailed off. *Mrs Barbara Waring*

ALTERNATION (FR)　3 ch.f. Electric 126 – Alanood 85 (Northfields (USA))　**54** d
[1991 a8g³ a8g 1992 a10g² a10g* a10g⁵ 12v⁶ a12g² 12g² 14.1g⁴ 16.1d² 14.1g a12g⁵]
lengthy filly: plating-class performer: consistent early in year and won claimer at
Lingfield in January: should stay beyond 1½m: acts on all-weather surfaces, below
form on a soft surface: blinkered (2 fair efforts) last 3 starts: sold to join J. Webber
5,200 gns Newmarket September Sales. *P. F. I. Cole*

ALTNAHARRA　2 gr.f. (May 3) Sharrood (USA) 124 – Embroideress 80　**47**
(Stanford 121§) [1992 8.2s a7g] fourth foal: half-sister to ungenuine 3-y-o 1m and
9.9f winner Milanese and fair sprinter Sacque (both by Elegant Air) and 1m and 1¼m
seller winner Tom Clapton (by Daring March): dam 5f to 7f winner: beaten around
15 lengths in maiden at Nottingham in October: pulled up at Southwell following
month. *D. Morley*

ALTO　3 ch.g. Superlative 118 – Rose Music 86 (Luthier 126) [1991 6g 1992 7f⁵ 8g　**37**
a11g⁶ a12g⁴] well-made gelding: worthwhile form only when fourth in handicap at
Southwell in July: better at 1½m than shorter: wore blinkers last 3 starts, also
eyeshield last two. *J. G. FitzGerald*

ALTO JANE　3 ch.f. The Minstrel (CAN) 135 – An Empress (USA) (Affirmed　**76**
(USA)) [1991 7f* 7m⁴ 1992 8m 10m 10s 10m² 10m] quite good-topped, rather angular
filly: fair form at her best: stays 1¼m: acts on good to firm ground, well beaten on
soft: sweating (well beaten) final start: lacks turn of foot, best racing close to pace.
G. Harwood

ALTONA GOLD　2 b.f. (Mar 14) Domynsky 110 – Wayleave (Blakeney 126) [1992　–
8.1d 7d a8g] smallish, sturdy filly: seventh reported living foal: half-sister to a
winning middle-distance plater: dam race once: no worthwhile form in maidens. *R.
Earnshaw*

ALTON BELLE　3 b.f. Blakeney 126 – Oscilight 112 (Swing Easy (USA) 126)　–
[1991 7f 8.9m 8g 1992 10g⁶ 16m 10d 8m 6g 9.7s] close-coupled, sparely-made filly: of
little account: blinkered last 4 starts. *P. Howling*

ALTO PRINCESS　3 b.f. Noalto 120 – Queen of The Hills 72 (Connaught 130)　–
[1991 NR 1992 10.2f⁶ 12.5g⁵ 10.2f 7d 5g 6.9g⁶ 6g] workmanlike filly: half-sister to
winners abroad by Swing Easy and King of Spain: dam won 1m seller: no worthwhile
form on flat: visored and wore tongue strap (edgy) final start. *A. P. Jones*

ALTRUISTIC (IRE)　2 b.f. (Feb 6) Alzao (USA) 117 – Overseas Wealth (USA)　**40**
(Forli (ARG)) [1992 6g 5d 6s 6m] 10,000Y: smallish, sturdy filly: poor mover: first
foal: dam unraced daughter of Irish 1000 Guineas winner Miralla: poor form,
including in large-field seller at Newmarket final start: will stay 7f: has had tongue
tied down: sold 800 gns Newmarket Autumn Sales. *C. F. Wall*

ALUM BAY　3 b.c. Reference Point 139 – Bella Colora 119 (Bellypha 130) [1991　**89**
NR 1992 10f² 10m⁵ 12f³ 10.1g² 10.4g³] 46,000Y: good-topped colt: third foal:
half-brother to high-class 1¼m performer Stagecraft (by Sadler's Wells) and closely
related to very useful 1991 3-y-o miler Hyabella (by Shirley Heights): dam 6f to
1¼m winner is half-sister to Irish Oaks winner Colorspin: fairly useful but
inconsistent form: mulish in paddock and at stalls, well below-form third at York last
time, tending to hang fire: should prove better at 1½m than 1¼m: acts on firm
ground: sold to join N. Tinkler 20,000 gns Newmarket Autumn Sales. *H. R. A. Cecil*

ALWAL　2 b.f. (Apr 13) Pharly (FR) 130 – Debate (High Line 125) [1992 7s 8d] tall,　–
leggy filly: first reported foal: dam 3-y-o 10.5f and 11f winner in French Provinces:
well beaten in maidens in September, racing too freely second occasion. *C. James*

ALWATAR (USA)　3 b.f. Caerleon (USA) 132 – Klarifi 91 (Habitat 134) [1991 NR　**64**
1992 10s³ 12v⁴] 104,000Y: workmanlike filly: fourth foal: half-sister to 1990 2-y-o 7f
winner Kashteh (by Green Desert) and Irish middle-distance winner Ezy Koter (by
Lomond): dam Irish 7f winner, is out of disqualified Irish Oaks winner Sorbus:
better effort in autumn maidens when third at Newbury (moved moderately to post):
visits Slip Anchor. *A. C. Stewart*

ALWAYS ALEX　5 b.m. Final Straw 127 – Two High 89 (High Top 131) [1991　–
10.1g 11.5g⁵ 11.8g⁶ 10.8m⁴ 12m³ 10.5g 12.5g 13.8m 11.5s² 1992 a10g 10.5s 12g 10g
11.5g 12.3g] smallish, workmanlike mare: poor mover: hasn't won on flat since debut
at 2 yrs and no form in 1992, including in blinkers once: stays 1½m: acts on good to
firm and soft ground: won over hurdles in August. *P. D. Evans*

ALWAYS FRIENDLY　4 ch.f. High Line 125 – Wise Speculation (USA) (Mr　**111**
Prospector (USA)) [1991 10s* 10f³ 11.9g² 14.6m⁴ 12d* 12g³ 1992 12g⁴ 12g⁵ 12d⁴
12g⁴ 13.5s³ 14.6m⁶ 12.5s⁴ 15.5s²] workmanlike filly: has a markedly round action:
very useful and consistent performer: competed only in pattern company in 1992:
flattered in Coronation Cup at Epsom second start: placed in Prix de Pomone at

Deauville (around a length behind Magic Night) in August and Prix Royal-Oak at Longchamp (beaten 2½ lengths by Assessor) in October: effective from 1½m to 15.5f: has form on any going, but goes well on an easy surface: held up. *H. Candy*

ALWAYS LYNSEY (IRE) 3 b.f. Mansooj 118 – Kilcurley Lass (Huntercombe 133) [1991 NR 1992 8d5 7f4 7.5d 7g5 10m 8m] IR 8,500F, 10,000Y: workmanlike filly: tubed since debut: moderate walker: half-sister to several winners, including useful 7f and 1m winner Lance (by Main Reef) and middle-distance performer Kalzao (by Alzao): dam unraced half-sister to high-class 1969 2-y-o Divine Gift: of little account. *Miss L. C. Siddall*   –

ALWAYS READY 6 b.g. Tyrnavos 129 – Merchantmens Girl 58 (Klairon 131) [1991 5g 5d5 5f2 5g5 5m3 5d* 5m5 5g4 5m3 5f 5g6 1992 9d2 10.5s4 8m 9d 10.5d5] strong, good-bodied gelding: poor handicapper: best form at up to 9f: acts on any going: usually visored/blinkered as 5-y-o: won over hurdles in October. *R. Lee*   **40**

ALWAYS RISKY 2 ch.f. (Mar 19) Risk Me (FR) 127 – Minabella (Dance In Time (CAN)) [1992 5v2 5g 5g a6g4 5g 8.2d* 8.3s2 7.6v6] 1,200Y: smallish, sparely-made filly: has a quick action: second foal: dam once-raced half-sister to Ribblesdale winner Miss Boniface: useful plater: won at Nottingham (retained 4,000 gns) in September: good second (possibly unlucky, had to be switched) at Hamilton 6 days later, and claimed out of P. Kelleway's stable £6,200: ran poorly in Chester nursery following month: will probably stay beyond 8.3f: has raced only on an easy surface. *A. Bailey*   **63**

ALYAFILL (USA) 3 br.f. Stately Don (USA) 122 – Creature Comfort (USA) (Ack Ack (USA)) [1991 NR 1992 7g 6.9h2 10.2g2 11.9m3 12.3g2 14.1d* 12.2d2 13.3s4] $47,000Y: leggy filly: ninth foal: half-sister to 5 winners, notably 1988 3-y-o 6f stakes winner Ofelia Girl (by Peterhof) and multiple Canadian stakes winner Winmor Miss (by Royal Ski): dam placed once from 12 starts: fair performer: won maiden at Redcar in October: ran well afterwards: will be well suited by 2m: acts on good to firm and soft ground: has run well for apprentice. *B. Hanbury*   **79**

ALYAKKH (IRE) 2 b.f. (May 25) Sadler's Wells (USA) 132 – Al Bahathri (USA) 123 (Blushing Groom (FR) 131) [1992 6g2] leggy filly: fourth foal: half-sister to very useful 7f/1m performer Hasbah (by Kris): dam, thoroughly genuine front runner, won Lowther Stakes and Irish 1000 Guineas: 7/2 from 7/4, short-headed by Easy Access in 11-runner maiden at Doncaster in November, soon recovering from slow start and staying on strongly final 2f: will improve, particularly at 7f/1m and win a maiden at least. *H. Thomson Jones*   **78 p**

ALYCIDA (USA) 3 b.g. Topsider (USA) – Alycette (USA) (Alydar (USA)) [1991 NR 1992 8g 7m* 8.1m2 8.3g 8m 10s 8m] rangy, good-topped gelding: has rather round action: second foal: dam, half-sister to a Grade 2 winner, successful twice in minor company at up to 1m in North America: won maiden at Redcar in April: no worthwhile form last 4 starts: should stay beyond 1m: has been gelded: sent to Dubai. *L. M. Cumani*   **84**

AMAAM AMAAM 2 b.c. (May 13) Last Tycoon 131 – What A Pity 97 (Blakeney 126) [1992 7g3 7.9s2 8.1g4] 42,000Y: leggy, angular colt: moderate mover: fifth foal: brother to useful 1990 2-y-o 6f and 7f winner Junk Bond, subsequently winner in Italy, and half-brother to 3-y-o Millyrous (by Rousillon) and a winner in Italy: dam lightly-raced 7f winner from sprinting family: fair maiden: will stay beyond 1m: yet to race on top-of-the-ground: bandaged last 2 starts: looks pace paced. *J. H. M. Gosden*   **75**

AMADEUS AES 3 b.c. Dublin Lad 116 – Kind Lady 56 (Kind of Hush 118) [1991 5m6 6g3 6g2 6g 6f4 7m2 7m6 7m3 7m2 7g2 7d a7g2 1992 a7g 7g* 7m 6.9m2] smallish, sturdy colt: has a roundish action: fair handicapper: won Yarmouth maiden in July: stays 7f: acts on good to firm ground: effective visored or not: below form when blinkered once: tends to carry head bit high. *D. Morris*   **81**

AMALFI 3 ch.f. Sayf El Arab (USA) 127 – Good Natured § (Troy 137) [1991 7m 7m5 1992 9.9g 11.6m 12m 11.8m 11d] leggy, lightly-made filly: poor plater: stays 11f. *J. Pearce*   –

AMATORIAL 3 b.f. Local Suitor (USA) 128 – Wolverene 114 (Relko 136) [1991 7m2 7.5f5 7m* 8m 1992 10f5 14.1f3] big, leggy filly: had a markedly round action: quite modest handicapper: broke knee in May: stayed 1¾m: dead. *Sir Mark Prescott*   **58**

AMAZE 3 b.g. Natroun (FR) 128 – Entrancing 95 (Posse (USA) 130) [1991 7g2 8.1g2 7m3 1992 8d* 9g6 8.1d3 8m 10m 10d3 10g6 10d2 8s] light-bodied, leggy gelding: has a round action: won handicap at Newbury in April by 8 lengths: stays 1¼m: needs a soft surface: bandaged: edgy sort: possibly best fresh: none too consistent. *Lady Herries*   **97**

AMAZING AIR (USA) 2 ch.c. (Apr 12) Air Forbes Won (USA) – Amoriah —
(USA) (Norcliffe (CAN)) [1992 7s] $27,000Y: lengthy colt: has scope: brother to
useful stakes winner at around 1m Buck Forbes: dam won at up to 9f: sire 6f to 9f
(Grade 1 event) winner: 20/1, ridden by 7-lb claimer and very green, slowly away and
always well behind in 16-runner maiden at Salisbury in September. *D. R. C. Elsworth*

AMAZING BABY (USA) 2 b.f. (Feb 26) Northern Baby (CAN) 127 – Amazing **79**
Love (USA) (Advocator) [1992 5.7f* 6g4 7d6] $30,000Y: rather leggy, good-topped
filly: has a round action: half-sister to 3 minor winners in North America, 2 by
Alydar: dam, sister to fairly useful 1984 2-y-o sprinter Balqis, won at up to 9f: fair
performer: narrowly won maiden at Bath in August: best effort when tenderly
handled 6 lengths fourth to Silver Wizard in listed race at Kempton: should be suited
by 7f+: possibly unsuited by dead ground. *D. R. C. Elsworth*

AMAZING FEAT (IRE) 3 b.g. Petorius 117 – Mountain Chase (Mount Hagen **95** p
(FR) 127) [1991 6m5 6f4 5m5 1992 5g* 7g 8m 7g* 7d4 7m3 8g* 7v*] tall,
workmanlike gelding: fluent mover: not seen out until August but progressed
extremely well: successful in Catterick maiden (hampered and awarded race) and
handicaps at Redcar, Doncaster (idled) and Redcar (£9,200 event, very impressively
by 8 lengths easing down): will prove better at 1m than 7f: has form on good to firm
going, but goes really well on heavy ground: hasn't stopped improving yet. *Mrs M.
Reveley*

AMAZON EXPRESS 3 b.c. Siberian Express (USA) 125 – Thalestria (FR) 91 **72** p
(Mill Reef (USA) 141) [1991 a8g5 a7g5 1992 a7g4 12v4 12.3s 10g6 9.7g3 10g5 10m*
11.5m6 10d a10g4 8d6 9.7g* 11.5d* a13g*] leggy colt: moderate mover: progressive
performer: successful in claimer at Kempton, seller (sold out of C. Brittain's stable
3,400 gns) at Folkestone and handicaps at Yarmouth and at Lingfield in second half
of season, as well as over hurdles: stays 13f: acts on good to firm and dead ground,
and on equitrack: below form when blinkered once: capable of better still. *R.
Akehurst*

AMBASSADOR ROYALE (IRE) 4 gr.g. Pennine Walk 120 – Hayati 94 **80**
(Hotfoot 126) [1991 9g4 10.2f* 10d4 11.9m2 12d 1992 11.1m3 11.5m2 12f 10.2f] big,
lengthy gelding: fair handicapper: well below best final 2 starts: stays 1½m: acts on
firm going: below form when blinkered: sold to join D. R. Tucker's stable 3,800 gns
Newmarket September Sales. *P. F. I. Cole*

AMBER GLOW (IRE) 3 ch.g. Glow (USA) – Sea Queen (FR) (Le Fabuleux —
133) [1991 NR 1992 a8g6 8g 10g a7g 7d 12h6] 18,000F, IR 24,000Y: tall,
shallow-girthed gelding: closely related to a winner abroad by Glenstal and
half-brother to several winners, notably smart French 1980 2-y-o 9f winner
Mariacho (by Mariacci): dam French maiden: no worthwhile form, including in
sellers. *L. J. Codd*

AMBER MILL 4 b.f. Doulab (USA) 115 – Millaine 69 (Formidable (USA) 125) **81**
[1991 5m* 6g5 6m 5.1g2 5g 5m4 5d 5d 1992 5g 5m 5.1m4 5f5 5.6m 5m] lengthy, quite
good-topped filly: rated 96 at 3 yrs: below best in 1992: speedy: best form on a sound
surface. *J. Berry*

AMBIGUOUSLY REGAL (USA) 3 b.c. Vaguely Noble 140 – Kazatska (USA) **83**
(Nijinsky (CAN) 138) [1991 NR 1992 11d3 12m2 13.9g* 16.2f6 13.3g 14m] leggy,
unfurnished colt: third reported foal: half-brother to a minor winner in North
America by Tom Rolfe: dam, daughter of top-class French middle-distance filly
Comtesse de Loir, won over 12.5f in France: consistent in first half of 1992, winning
York minor event and sixth in Queen's Vase at Royal Ascot: well below form in
handicaps final 2 starts after 3-month absence: stays 2m: acts on firm and dead
ground: front runner. *Mrs J. Cecil*

AMBIVALENTATTITUDE 2 b.c. (Apr 20) North Briton 67 – Bestena 70 **40**
(Bustino 136) [1992 5.1d 7g 5.7g 5m5 7d a8g] 2,100Y, 5,200 2-y-o: small, stocky colt:
first foal: dam 10.2f winner, is sister to good-class middle-distance performer
Bustomi: took a while to show even poor form: sold out of M. Usher's stable 775 gns
Ascot September Sales after penultimate start: will stay 1m: acts on dead ground,
stiff task and well beaten on equitrack. *D. C. Jermy*

AMBUSCADE 6 ch.g. Roberto (USA) 131 – Gurkhas Band (USA) **68**
(Lurullah) [1991 16.2g 16m4 16.2f4 17.6m 18f 1992 17.5s 16.1s2 17.1s* 18m2 15.1d3]
lengthy gelding: consistent handicapper: won (first time on flat) at Pontefract in
October: needs thorough test of stamina: probably acts on any going: has run well
when blinkered: improved into a smart hurdler, winning handicap at Ayr and placed
in 2 Grade 2 events. *Mrs M. Reveley*

AMENABLE 7 b.g. Kampala 120 – Kirin (Tyrant (USA)) [1991 a8g a8g* a8g* –
a8g* a8g* 8d* 1992 a8g5] sturdy, compact gelding: most progressive handicapper
in spring, 1991, culminating in an impressive win in Lincoln at Doncaster: well
beaten in claimer at Southwell in December: suited by 1m: acts on any going and
all-weather surfaces: usually held up: well ridden by A. Greaves. *T. D. Barron*

AMERICAN BOOGIE (FR) 3 b.c. Baby Turk 120 – Santa Musica (Luthier 61
126) [1991 NR 1992 9.7v5 10m 10.3g6 12m6 10m 10.2f3 8f4 8g*] tall, workmanlike
colt: sixth foal: half-brother to 1986 2-y-o 6f winner Rumboogie (by Sharpo) and
1¼m winner Air Music (by Fabulous Dancer), both useful, and a winner in France:
dam French 9f and 11f winner: largely consistent performer: won Leicester claimer
in July: best form at 1m/1¼m: acts on firm ground. *C. E. Brittain*

AMERICAN HERO 4 ch.g. Persian Bold 123 – American Winter (USA) 78 73
(Lyphard (USA) 132) [1991 6g 10m2 8f* 10.2f5 8.5m2 9.2d4 8m 8.9m4 8f* 8m2 8m
1992 11m 7.5m 8f* 7.5g2 8f 9m5 8.1d] tall, quite good-topped gelding: has a round
action: won handicap at Doncaster in May: ran poorly last 3 starts: stays 8.5f: acts on
firm and dead going: usually a front runner: trained first 6 starts by C. Tinkler. *R.
Allan*

AMERICAN SWINGER (USA) 2 b.c. (May 6) Dixieland Band (USA) – 56 p
Cassoway (USA) (Cormorant (USA)) [1992 7g 7d 6d5] $32,000Y: strong colt:
half-brother to 3 minor winners in North America: dam won at up to 9f: sire (by
Northern Dancer) won from 5.5f to 9f: modest form, apparently not fully wound up,
in maidens: will prove capable of better at 1m + . *P. W. Harris*

AMERIGUE 2 gr.f. (Mar 12) Absalom 128 – Caroline Lamb 74 (Hotfoot 126) 59
[1992 5g 5m3 6d* 7.5d2 7m6 7.5d2 7g5 7s] 600Y: small, close-coupled filly: small
reported foal: sister to winning chaser/hurdler Master Lamb and half-sister to 4-y-o
11f winner Radio Caroline (by All Systems Go): dam won over 1m and over hurdles:
modest performer: won maiden claimer at Hamilton in May: below form last 2
starts: will stay beyond 1m: acts well on good to soft ground: has run well for
claimer. *Miss S. E. Hall*

AMETHYSTINE (USA) 6 ch.m. Barachois (CAN) – Amathus (Song 132) [1991 63
6g 7m 8f3 7.1m* 8.5m 6.1d2 7v 7.1g* 8g 7.6m* 7g 5f 8g 6g 6.1d 1992 6.1m 7.6m4 6d
6m4 7f* 6f3 7g 6d2 6.1m 7g 7d 7s6 a7g3 a10g] sparely-made, angular mare: in good
form in handicaps in the summer, successful at Brighton: below best afterwards:
effective from 6f to 1m: acts on firm and dead ground, well below form on heavy:
goes well at Chepstow: suitable mount for claimer. *R. J. Hodges*

AMIARGE 2 b.c. (Jan 29) Reference Point 139 – Scotia Rose (Tap On Wood 130) 61
[1992 8f 7.9s5] 21,000Y: small colt: fourth foal: half-brother to Irish 3-y-o Rose
Society (by Caerleon) and 1989 2-y-o 6f winner Fanellan (by Try My Best): dam
Irish middle-distance winner, is half-sister to dam of Greenland Park (dam of
Fitnah) and Red Sunset: modest form in autumn maidens in Yorkshire: will be well
suited by middle distances. *M. Brittain*

AMIGO MENOR 6 ch.h. Whistling Deer 117 – Chive (St Chad 120) [1991 6s 5g 110
6g* 6m* 6g 6m* 6f6 6d4 7g 1992 6d2 6m3 6f2 6d 6s 6s3 6d5 6d] leggy, lengthy
horse: useful and largely consistent performer: placed in minor race at Kempton,
Duke of York Stakes at York, Cork And Orrery Stakes at Royal Ascot and Prix de
Meautry at Deauville: best racing up with pace over 6f: acts on any going: best in
blinkers: tough and genuine: sold 36,000 gns Newmarket Autumn Sales, reportedly
to race in USA. *D. J. G. Murray-Smith*

AMIGOS 4 ch.g. Nordance (USA) – Hi Gorgeous (Hello Gorgeous (USA) 128) –
[1991 a7g3 8g4 7.6g 11.5s3 a10g* 9.7f2 9m6 11.5g2 1992 11.5s6] leggy gelding:
modest handicapper: stays 11.5f: acts on any going, including equitrack. *P. Mitchell*

AMILLIONMEMORIES 2 br.g. (Apr 14) Macmillion 110 – March Memories 64
(Mandamus 120) [1992 6.1d 6m 8.1d3 8.1d5 10g] smallish gelding: first reported foal:
dam seemed of little account over jumps: modest maiden: easily best efforts over
8.1f on dead ground. *Mrs Barbara Waring*

AMIRATI (USA) 2 b.f. (May 1) Danzig (USA) – Weekend Surprise (USA) 69
(Secretariat (USA)) [1992 5.2g* 5f 6g6] $425,000Y: useful-looking filly: sister to a
graded stakes-placed winner at up to 1m, closely related to Preakness winner
Summer Squall (by Storm Bird) and half-sister to Belmont Stakes and Breeders'
Cup Classic winner A P Indy (by Seattle Slew): dam won 7 races, including graded
events at 6f and 8.5f as 2-y-o: favourite, won maiden at Newbury in June in good
style: well beaten in Queen Mary Stakes (lost a shoe) at Royal Ascot and Cherry
Hinton Stakes (looked very well, raced freely over 3f) at Newmarket later in
summer: should stay 1m. *A. A. Scott*

AMISTINA 2 b.f. (Feb 5) Damister (USA) 123 – Poplina (USA) (Roberto (USA) **38**
131) [1992 7s⁶ 7d] leggy, close-coupled filly: first foal: dam French 11f winner, is
half-sister to 1985 champion older male in USA (stayed 1½m) Vanlandingham: sixth
of 14 in maiden at Salisbury: soon driven along and hung throughout in seller at
Redcar later in autumn: sold 2,200 gns Newmarket Autumn Sales. *R. Charlton*

AMLAK (USA) 3 b.c. Riverman (USA) 131 – Ruwiyda (USA) 73 (In Reality) [1991 –
NR 1992 8g⁵] lengthy colt: first foal: dam thrice-raced maiden: in need of race and
prominent 6f in 8-runner maiden at Kempton in August, only run: sold to join J.
Banks 3,200 gns Newmarket Autumn Sales. *A. C. Stewart*

AMORUCCIO (USA) 3 ch.c. Affirmed (USA) – A Little Affection (USA) (King **77**
Emperor (USA)) [1991 NR 1992 10d⁵ 11.8g⁶] lengthy colt with plenty of scope:
moderate mover: brother to high-class 5-y-o Zoman and half-brother to 1988 2-y-o
Grade 1-placed Love And Affection (by Exclusive Era): dam smart American
sprinter: very green when 3¾ lengths fifth of 16 in Kempton maiden: weakened 2f
out in Leicester maiden later in summer: seems not to stay 11.8f. *G. Harwood*

AMOUR DU SOIR (USA) 5 b.g. L'Emigrant (USA) 129 – Evening Kiss (USA) –
(Saggy) [1991 NR 1992 5.7d 5s 5s 5.1d 5.1g] rather leggy gelding: on the downgrade:
should stay 6f + : acts on hard ground. *R. Lee*

AMOUREUSE (IRE) 3 b.f. Petorius 117 – Amorak 85 (Wolver Hollow 126) **59**
[1991 5m 5d² 5m⁶ 5g* 6.1g² 6m⁵ 7g 1992 5v⁴ 6.1g⁴ 6m 6d 5s 7s] tall, leggy, plain
filly: moderate mover: inconsistent handicapper: should stay 7f: best form with
some give in the ground: tends to sweat: has gone well at Chester: refused to enter
stalls twice as a 2-y-o: trained until after third start by E. Owen jun. *T. H. Caldwell*

AMPHIGORY 4 b.g. Gorytus (USA) 132 – Peculiar One (USA) (Quack (USA)) **50**
[1991 11.6m² 10.2f² 12m⁵ 1992 a8g³ a10g³ 11.9g⁴ 14.6g] lengthy gelding: fluent
mover: rated 78 as 3-y-o: well below form in spring of 1992: stays 11.6f: acts on firm
ground: below form when visored: sold to join P. Rodford's stable 6,200 gns Ascot
May Sales: won over hurdles in September. *Lord Huntingdon*

AMPLE (IRE) 2 b.f. (Mar 26) Alzao (USA) 117 – Apple Peel 109 (Pall Mall 132) **51**
[1992 8.1s 7.1s³ 8.2d] IR 16,000Y: lengthy filly: moderate mover: half-sister to
several winners, including very useful 6f to 8.5f winner Eve's Error (by Be My
Guest) and 6-y-o 11f to 13f winner Discord (by Niniski): dam 1m and 1¼m winner:
plating-class form in soft-ground maidens at Chepstow: favourite but hampered
early on and always behind in Nottingham seller later in September: shapes like a
thorough stayer: sold 4,100 gns Newmarket December Sales. *P. F. I. Cole*

AMRAH 2 b.f. (Mar 24) Midyan (USA) 124 – Ranyah (USA) 84 (Our Native (USA)) **49** p
[1992 6d] leggy filly: first foal: dam 2-y-o 7f winner, became unreliable: backward,
signs of ability after missing break in maiden at Newbury in August: should
improve. *J. L. Dunlop*

AMRON 5 b.g. Bold Owl 101 – Sweet Minuet (Setay 105) [1991 5d* 5g 6d* 6m* 6g **91**
6m 6m 6m³ 6m⁶ 6g⁴ 6d 1992 5g* 5d* 6s⁶ 6g 6g 6f 6g⁶ 6d 6d² 6d 6d 6m]
sparely-made gelding: fairly useful handicapper: won at Doncaster and Newcastle in
March: mostly disappointing after: effective at 5f and 6f: has won on good to firm
ground, but suited by some give: suitable mount for claimer. *J. Berry*

AMTHAAL (USA) 3 b.c. Mr Prospector (USA) – Maysoon 121 (Shergar 140) –
[1991 7d⁵ 7m⁴ 7m² 1992 7g 7m 7g 8g] leggy colt: has a smooth action: maiden
handicapper: below form in 1992, visored once: should stay 1m: acts on good to firm
ground. *M. R. Stoute*

AMWAG (USA) 3 ch.f. El Gran Senor (USA) 136 – Mazzei Mood (USA) (Roberto **106**
(USA) 131) [1991 NR 1992 7m* 8.1d* 8s⁵] rather leggy filly: second foal: dam minor
winning sister to smart 1981 American 2-y-o filly Mystical Mood and half-sister to
very smart miler Maximilian: not seen out until August: showed good turn of foot to
win Newmarket maiden (by 8 lengths) and Sandown listed race (by 2 lengths from
Melpomene): ran creditably in Prix Perth at Saint-Cloud, first run for 3½ months:
stayed 8.1f: acted on good to firm and soft ground: visits Nashwan. *A. C. Stewart*

AMYS DELIGHT 4 b.f. Idiot's Delight 115 – Amy Gwen (Master Buck) [1991 NR –
1992 8f] second foal: dam of little account: soundly beaten in Warwick amateurs
event, only run. *A. J. Chamberlain*

ANAHEIM (IRE) 2 b.c. (Mar 16) Auction Ring (USA) 123 – Hajjar 58 (Valiyar **80**
129) [1992 5d³ 7m* 7g 7d⁴] 29,000Y: quite attractive colt: first foal: dam,
maiden, stayed 7f, is half-sister to Kooyonga: fairly useful performer: comfortably
made all in 19-runner Kempton maiden in August: may stay 1m: acts on good to firm
and dead ground: sold 26,000 gns Newmarket Autumn Sales. *R. Hannon*

ANAR (IRE) 3 ch.c. Sharpo 132 – Only A Dream (FR) (Green Dancer (USA) 132) **52**
[1991 5m 5m⁵ 6g⁵ 7s⁵ 7m³ 7m 8g 7m 1992 9.7v⁶ 12.3s 11.6g 14.1f* 14.1g 13.8f⁴ 13.8g
14.1d³ 16.1s⁶] leggy colt: poor mover: modest handicapper: won for claimer at
Yarmouth in June: stays 1¾m: acts on any going: has joined S. Norton. *W. Carter*

ANATROCCOLO 5 b.m. Ile de Bourbon (USA) 133 – Art Deco (Artaius (USA) **47**
129) [1991 7s 6.9f 7s 1992 a7g 8.3d 8f⁴ 9.7m² 8g* 7g] unfurnished mare: modest
handicapper: gamely made all in Brighton selling event (no bid) in August: stays
9.7f: acts on firm going: trained reappearance by C. Horgan. *R. A. Bennett*

ANAXAGORAS 2 b.c. (Apr 14) Mtoto 134 – I'll Try 71 (Try My Best (USA) 130) **84**
[1992 6g⁶ 6g 7s* 7.6v²] 30,000Y: close-coupled, attractive colt: third foal:
half-brother to 3-y-o Steel Mirror (by Slip Anchor): dam 2-y-o 5f winner later
successful in USA, is out of half-sister to Irish 1000 Guineas winner Katies: much
improved in October: 1½-length winner of Warwick maiden and headed post in
Chester nursery: will stay 1¼m: acts well on soft ground. *A. A. Scott*

ANCESTRAL DANCER 2 gr.f. (Feb 10) Siberian Express (USA) 125 – **86**
Exuberine (FR) 82 (Be My Guest (USA) 126) [1992 5g* 5m² 5m³ 6g* 7.5g* 7.5g*
7m⁴ 7s⁴ 7m⁶] 10,000Y: workmanlike filly: moderate walker: half-sister to 2m seller
winner Pharoah's Guest (by Pharly) and Irish 1½m and 1¾m winner Classy Trick
(by Head For Heights): dam 1m winner: fairly useful performer: successful in
Newmarket maiden in April and listed races at Milan and Turin in July: ran very well
after in Lanson Champagne Vintage Stakes at Goodwood, Moyglare Stud Stakes at
the Curragh and Rockfel Stakes at Newmarket: will stay 1¼m: probably acts on any
going: consistent. *M. Bell*

ANCHORAGE (IRE) 3 b.f. Slip Anchor 136 – Cartridge (FR) 108 (Jim French **86**
(USA) [1991 7g 1992 12.3f* 12.3m* 14.1g² 10s⁶ 12.1d³ 12.3v²] angular filly: good
walker: consistent performer: won Redcar apprentice maiden and Wolverhampton
minor event in June: effective at 1½m to 1¾m: acted on any going: visits Rock
Hopper. *H. R. A. Cecil*

ANCHORITE 3 b.c. Slip Anchor 136 – Elysian 94 (Northfields (USA)) [1991 6m³ **98**
7f² 8.1f* 8g⁴ 1992 10m² 10g 11.5s⁵ 10.3f² 11.6g² 12m⁴ 10d] leggy colt: poor mover:
useful performer: fourth to Kasmayo in Doncaster listed event: stays 1½m: suited
by a sound surface. *P. T. Walwyn*

ANCHOR STONE 2 b.c. (May 1) Slip Anchor 136 – Doumayna 79 (Kouban (FR)) **– p**
[1992 8m⁵] smallish, sturdy colt: has a quick action: fourth foal: half-brother to
useful middle-distance stayer Bondstone (by Miller's Mate): dam, 2m winner, is
half-sister to Darshaan and Darara: easy to back when around 10 lengths fifth of 8 in
Yarmouth maiden in September, slowly away and outpaced from 2f out, not knocked
about: will stay well and improve. *H. R. A. Cecil*

ANDARE 3 ch.c. Precocious 126 – Betty Jane 92 (Morston (FR) 125) [1991 NR **–**
1992 10.2f] first foal: dam 1m (at 2 yrs) and 1½m winner: always behind in Bath
maiden claimer in June, only run. *R. J. Hodges*

ANDERSON ROSE 4 b.f. Kind of Hush 118 – Fille de Bourbon 71 (Ile de **–**
Bourbon (USA) 133) [1991 a8g a8g⁶ 10d 12.3s 10m 15g* 15s 12g 13.8f³ a12g 11.9f⁵
16m 12.3g 12m⁵ a14g 1992 a12g] sturdy filly: has a round action: poor plater: stays
15f: acts on firm going: below form when blinkered once. *D. J. Wintle*

ANDES 3 b.c. Heights of Gold – Edna 92 (Shiny Tenth 120) [1991 6g⁶ 1992 8d 10f] **–**
big, strong colt: behind in spring maidens. *W. G. R. Wightman*

ANDITISITIS (USA) 3 gr.c. Verbatim (USA) – Enamor (USA) (Drone) [1991 **71 d**
NR 1992 10s³ 10s 10.2g⁵ 12.5g³ 16d] $35,000Y: sturdy colt: eighth reported foal:
half-brother to several winners, including useful 7f to 8.2f winner Pentaquod (by
London Company), later successful in USA: dam unraced: regressive maiden:
should prove suited by 1½m+: acts on soft ground: sold to D. Browning 7,600 gns
Newmarket September Sales. *D. W. P. Arbuthnot*

AND ME 3 ch.f. Don't Forget Me 127 – Nicola Wynn 83 (Nicholas Bill 125) [1991 **–**
a6g 6g a6g⁵ 7g 7g a7g a8g 1992 a10g 10d 6m 12s 14.1s⁶] leggy, rather sparely-made
filly: bad maiden: ran creditably when visored once: won poor selling hurdle (bought
in 2,300 gns) in November. *D. T. Thom*

ANDRATH (IRE) 4 b.c. Commanche Run 133 – Rathvindon 93 (Realm 129) **83 d**
[1991 8g⁵ 11.9g* 10m⁵ 14m 1992 10.3g 10.4m* 10.1g⁶ 10f⁴ 10.4d 10.5s] big, strong
colt: fluent mover: well beaten after dead-heating in £8,200 York handicap in May:
stays 11.9f: acts on firm going: sold only 4,400 gns Newmarket Autumn Sales. *C. E.
Brittain*

ANDREA'S GIRL 2 b.f. (Mar 21) Faustus (USA) 118 – Don't Tell Daddy (Song **32** 132) [1992 5g 6s⁶ a6g 8d 8.1d⁶ a8g] 3,000Y: workmanlike filly: moderate mover: first foal: dam unraced: poor form, including in sellers: probably stays 1m: sold to join M. Tate 1,100 gns Doncaster November Sales. *J. Berry*

ANDRELOT 5 b.h. Caerleon (USA) 132 – Seminar 113 (Don (ITY) 123) [1991 – 12.3g 14.6g 1992 16.9g] leggy horse: poor handicapper: stays 1¾m: best form with give in the ground: tried visored/blinkered. *K. White*

ANDREW'S EXPRESS (IRE) 2 b.c. (Apr 30) Hatim (USA) 121 – Fast Bay – (Bay Express 132) [1992 6g 6g 7s 8.3s 8d] IR 5,000Y, 4,400 2-y-o: workmanlike colt: fifth foal: half-brother to 3-y-o Believe In Me (by Don't Forget Me) and a winner in Macau: dam lightly raced: no form, including in selling nursery: tried blinkered. *S. E. Kettlewell*

ANDROMAQUE (USA) 2 ch.f. (Apr 3) Woodman (USA) 126 – Heaven's Mine **83** p (USA) (Graustark) [1992 8s²] leggy, unfurnished filly: second foal: dam unraced: shaped promisingly when 33/1-shot in 8-runner Newbury minor event in October, smooth headway and looking likely winner 1f out but green and caught near line by Arusha: sure to improve, and win a maiden. *R. Charlton*

ANDROS BAY (USA) 3 b.c. Alleged (USA) 138 – Montage (USA) (Alydar **116** p (USA)) [1991 7d² 1992 10v² 12d* 10g² 12s* 12d*] $110,000Y: third reported foal: half-brother to fair 1m winner Mahrah (by Vaguely Noble): dam, winner at around 1m in USA, is closely related to a multiple graded-race winner and half-sister to another: won maiden at Leopardstown (by 6 lengths), minor event at Listowel (nowhere near best) and put up an improved performance to land Group 2 Blandford Stakes at the Curragh by ½ length from Arrikala, leading halfway: stays 1½m: yet to race on top-of-the-ground: progressive. *M. V. O'Brien, Ireland*

*Blandford Stakes, the Curragh—further progress from Andros Bay (left),
who beats Arrikala (right) and Ebaziya*

Mr A. J. O'Reilly's "Andros Bay"

ANDRULA MOU   2 gr.f. (May 6) Fairy King (USA) – Madame Sinclair (Homing   **48**
130) [1992 6g 5d3 6f] 6,000Y: plain, angular filly: moderate mover: first foal: dam ran
once: poor maiden: found nothing off bridle final start: should be better suited by 6f
than 5f: gives impression probably capable of better: tail swisher. *R. Boss*

ANDY JACK   3 ch.g. Risk Me (FR) 127 – Gemma Kaye 91 (Cure The Blues   **–**
(USA)) [1991 8.1g4 7.1d4 7d 1992 11.6m 8g 10g 7g] lengthy, workmanlike gelding: on
the downgrade: stays 7f: sold 1,050 gns Ascot July Sales, resold 1,600 gns Ascot
December Sales. *M. J. Heaton-Ellis*

ANEESATI   2 b.f. (Apr 13) Kris 135 – Dabaweyaa 118 (Shareef Dancer (USA) 135)   **62** p
[1992 6d4] strong filly: first foal: dam, 7f/1m winner and second in 1000 Guineas, is
half-sister to Oaks second Acclimatise: bandaged and better for race when over 5
lengths fourth of 9, one pace, to Nicer in maiden at Newmarket in October: moved
moderately down: sure to improve, particularly over further. *C. E. Brittain*

ANGELICA PARK   6 b.m. Simply Great (FR) 122 – Rosana Park 83 (Music Boy   **37**
124) [1991 a14g 14d 17m 14.6m3 12g* 13.6m3 12f3 1992 13.8d 14.1g 12m5 14.1m3
14.6d 17.9d5] stocky mare: poor stayer: acts on firm and dead ground. *J. Wharton*

ANGELO'S DOUBLE (IRE)   4 b.c. M Double M (USA) – Bebe Altesse (GER)   **–**
(Alpenkonig (GER)) [1991 8m3 7.1g* a8g6 1992 10.2s] strong, workmanlike colt: has
a round action: rated 81 at 3 yrs: well beaten in Bath apprentice handicap in
September, only run in 1992: should stay 1m: sometimes bandaged. *G. A. Ham*

ANGELS ANSWER (IRE)   3 b.f. Stalker 121 – Greek Music (Tachypous 128)   **–**
[1991 5m 5m 6d3 6m 5g2 5d2 5d* 5d2 5m3 1992 5g5 6g 6d 5s 6d] sparely-made filly:
little form in 1992: should stay 6f: acts on dead ground: trained first 3 starts by Mrs J.
Jordan. *Mrs M. Reveley*

ANGEL'S WING   3 ch.f. Precocious 126 – Razor Blade 65 (Sharp Edge 123)   **36**
[1991 6f 7g 8m 1992 8d 7d 8m2 8d] smallish, lengthy filly: moderate mover: poor

plater: stays 1m: acts on good to firm ground: sold 1,000 gns Doncaster November Sales. *R. M. Whitaker*

ANGEL TRAIN (IRE)   4 ch.f. Burslem 123 – Senama (FR) (Sanctus II 132)   **36**
[1991 a8g⁶ 7d 8.2s 7.5g 8.2m⁴ 10f 7g² 8d 8f⁶ 1992 7g 8v⁶ 8.5g⁴ 7m 8.1m 7.1m² 6g³ 7g 7d a8g] smallish, angular filly: very poor mover: inconsistent handicapper: stays 8.5f: best efforts on a sound surface: sometimes blinkered. *J. Parkes*

ANGHAAM (USA)   3 b.f. Diesis 133 – Taylor Park (USA) (Sir Gaylord) [1991 NR   **80**
1992 10g 10s* 10s 12g³ 10.3g] $160,000Y: unfurnished filly: fifth foal: half-sister to 1½m winner Howjal (by Conquistador Cielo): dam won 5 times at up to 7f at 2 yrs, including in minor stakes company: won Sandown maiden in August: form after only when third in Newmarket handicap: effective at 1¼m to 1½m: visits Soviet Star. *A. C. Stewart*

ANGUISH (IRE)   3 b.f. El Gran Senor (USA) 136 – Naval Light (USA) (Majestic   **56**
Light (USA)) [1991 6s⁵ 6f 8m 7g³ 7m 1992 8.1m⁶ 11.1f³ 10f4 a12g 8.5d³ 9.7d* 10m 9.7g] angular, workmanlike filly: has a round action: poor walker: none too consistent handicapper: won selling event at Folkestone (bought in 3,900 gns) in July: should prove as effective at 1½m as 1¼m: acts on firm and dead ground: ran poorly on equitrack: sold 30,000 gns Newmarket December Sales. *N. A. Callaghan*

ANGUS DUNDEE (IRE)   2 b.c. (Apr 13) Nordico (USA) – Trina's Girl (Nono-   **59**
alco (USA) 131) [1992 6m² 6m⁴ 7d 6s] robust colt: good mover: sixth foal: closely related to 6f and 7f winner Albyn Lady (by Be My Guest) and half-brother to 1¼m winner My Ratbag (by Main Reef): dam 2-y-o 5f winner: regressive form in maidens, tried blinkered final start: sold 9,000 gns Newmarket Autumn Sales: should be suited by further than 6f: may well be unsuited by soft ground. *H. R. A. Cecil*

ANIMA   3 b.f. Ajdal (USA) 130 – Cocotte 111 (Troy 137) [1991 NR 1992 7d 7.6g³]   **–**
rangy filly: second foal: half-sister to fairly useful 1m (at 2 yrs) and 7f winner Glowing Ardour (by Dancing Brave): dam 1¼m winner: 15 lengths third in Chester maiden: withdrawn lame at start 3½ months later: sold 5,800 gns Newmarket December Sales. *Major W. R. Hern*

ANLACE   3 b.f. Sure Blade (USA) 130 – Ascot Strike (USA) 85 (Mr Prospector   **81**
(USA)) [1991 7m* 1992 8.1d 8d³ 8d⁵] rather leggy filly: most promising 2-y-o: suffered a set-back in spring and form after only when third in Milan listed event: should have stayed beyond 1m: visits Shareef Dancer. *L. M. Cumani*

ANNABELLE ROYALE   6 b.h. Anfield 117 – France (Milesian 125) [1991 8s   **75**
7g⁵ 8d⁵ 7m 7f* 8g⁵ 7m² 6m² 7f⁶ 6f* 7f* 7g 6f⁶ 1992 7g 7m 7f 6f 7f² 7m* 7m 7.6m² 7.1m 8f⁵ 7g 7.6d a7g 10d 7d] small, strong, lengthy horse: carries condition: moderate mover: won Yarmouth minor event in July: mostly below best after: effective at strongly-run 6f, and stays 1¼m: goes particularly well on top-of-the-ground: goes well at Lingfield (turf) and Yarmouth: tough and genuine. *Mrs N. Macauley*

ANNA COMNENA (IRE)   3 b.f. Shareef Dancer (USA) 135 – Anna Paola   **71**
(GER) (Prince Ippi (GER)) [1991 NR 1992 10.1g⁶ 10m² 12d] angular, quite good-topped filly: fifth foal: sister to useful 1¼m to 1½m winner Atlaal, and half-sister to 10.5f winner Anna Petrovna (by Wassl): dam, leading filly at 2 and 3 yrs in Germany, wins including 11f Preis der Diana: looked a promising filly, ninth second in Newmarket maiden, until disappointing on dead ground: probably best on a sound surface: visits Ela-Mana-Mou. *L. M. Cumani*

ANNACURRAGH (IRE)   3 b.f. Shardari 134 – Forest of Arden (Tap On Wood   **74**
130) [1991 NR 1992 10.2f² 10g³ 10d² 10d³ a10g* a10g⁵] 6,200Y: angular filly: first foal: dam Irish 7f winner out of half-sister to Irish 1000 Guineas/Yorkshire Oaks winner Sarah Siddons: inconsistent performer: won a weak claimer (claimed out of A. Stewart's stable £6,500) at Lingfield in December: should stay 1½m: looks difficult ride, and not one to trust implicitly. *C. J. Hill*

ANNA OF SAXONY   3 ch.f. Ela-Mana-Mou 132 – Anna Matrushka (Mill Reef   **109**
(USA) 141) [1991 NR 1992 10g⁴ 12g* 14m² 14.6m³ 12s 12g² 12f] leggy filly: second foal: half-sister to fairly useful (at up to 9f) performer Andrassy (by Ahonoora): dam unraced daughter of champion German filly Anna Paola: progressed really well after winning Kempton maiden in July: third in Park Hill Stakes at Doncaster and beaten neck by Cunning in Princess Royal Stakes at Ascot: behind in valuable handicap at Gulfstream Park final start: stays 14.6f: acts on good to firm ground, well below form (sweating, pulled hard) on soft: carries head high and tends to hang fire under pressure. *J. H. M. Gosden*

ANNE BONNY   3 b.f. Ajdal (USA) 130 – Sally Brown 120 (Posse (USA) 130) [1991   **105**
7m⁴ 1992 8g* 10g³ 10f² 10g 9d² 10g* 12g³] big, lengthy filly: has a round action:

capable of useful form: won Newmarket maiden in May and Sandown minor event in September: excellent third to Cunning in Princess Royal Stakes at Ascot: better suited by 1½m than shorter: acts on firm and dead ground: headstrong on occasions. *J. R. Fanshawe*

ANNE'S BANK (IRE)   4 b.f. Burslem 123 – West Bank (Martinmas 128) leggy – ex-Irish filly: moderate walker: poor handicapper: should stay 1½m: acts on good to firm ground. *A. Moore*

ANNE'S BAY (IRE)   2 b.f. (Apr 19) The Noble Player (USA) 126 – Depaypur – (Touch Paper 113) [1992 6m³ 6f³ 7g] first foal: dam Irish 8.5f winner: soundly beaten in modest company. *D. Moffatt*

ANN HILL (IRE)   2 ch.f. (May 10) Bob Back (USA) 124 – Yuma (USA) (Caro 133)   **58** [1992 5v⁶ 6f³ 6g 6m⁴ 6f⁶ 7g² 7.6v 8g² 8.3v a7g⁴ a8g²] IR 1,300F, IR 2,000Y: smallish filly: first foal: dam showed ability at 2 yrs in Ireland, placed at 7.9f: modest performer: will be well suited by 1¼m + : best form on good ground (no form at all on heavy) and fibresand. *R. Hollinshead*

ANNIE ROSE   2 ch.f. (Mar 26) Clantime 101 – Penset (Red Sunset 120) [1992 5d²   **46** 5g 5f⁶ 6f² 7f⁶ 6.1m⁴ 5g a6g 6g] 5,000Y: leggy, lengthy filly: first foal: dam unraced: poor plater: stays 6f: acts on firm and dead ground: effective blinkered or not: sold 650 gns Doncaster October Sales. *T. D. Barron*

ANNIVERSAIRE   2 b.c. (Apr 15) Petong 126 – Etta's Pet 76 (Mummy's Pet 125)   **63** [1992 6.1m³ 5d⁴ 7s⁵ 6v] 5,200Y, 15,000 2-y-o: useful-looking colt: has a round action: first living foal: dam, maiden, stayed 1¼m: modest form in varied company: never dangerous but not discredited in Racecall Gold Trophy at Redcar final run: will stay 1m: probably acts on any going. *Bob Jones*

ANNYBAN   2 b.f. (May 14) Bairn (USA) 126 – Mandrian 103 (Mandamus 120)   – [1992 7g] lengthy, unfurnished filly: seventh foal: half-sister to 3-y-o 1¼m winner Handy Lass (by Nicholas Bill) and 1m to 19f winner Autonomous (by Milford): dam 8.2f and 12.2f winner: backward and green, always behind in Wolverhampton maiden in September. *E. J. Alston*

ANONYMOUS   2 b.f. (Apr 3) Night Shift (USA) – Princess Lieven (Royal Palace   **89** ? 131) [1992 5g⁵ 6m² 5d* 6g 5m⁶ 6s⁵ 6m⁴] leggy, workmanlike filly: has a quick action: fifth living foal: sister to 9.7f winner St Patrick's Day and half-sister to 11.5f winner Beau Ideal (by Brigadier Gerard) and 3-y-o La Cousine (by R B Chesne): dam unraced daughter of sister to Brigadier Gerard: inconsistent after winning 3-runner £7,300 event at Epsom in June: never-dangerous last of 4 in Cheveley Park Stakes at Newmarket: stays 6f: acts on good to firm and dead ground, apparently not on soft. *C. E. Brittain*

ANORAK (USA)   2 b.c. (Feb 12) Storm Bird (CAN) 134 – Someway Somehow   **55** p (USA) (What Luck (USA)) [1992 6g] $80,000Y: brother to 7-y-o 7f/1m performer Cape Pigeon and half-brother to 2 winners: dam winning sister to 1983 champion older mare Ambassador of Luck: 50/1, claimer ridden, burly and green, beaten around 10 lengths in mid-division of 20-runner Newmarket maiden in late-October, soon pushed along: likely to improve. *L. M. Cumani*

ANOTHER EPISODE (IRE)   3 b.g. Drumalis 125 – Pasadena Lady (Captain   **90** James 123) [1991 5s³ 5m⁵ 5m* 5m² 5m* 5d* 5g² 5g* 5g* 5m⁵ 1992 5g 5f⁵.1d⁴ 5d² 5d* 5d* 5.2g a5g a5g² a5g*] leggy, lengthy gelding: useful sprinter as 2-y-o: odds on, successful in small fields for claimers at Ayr, Epsom and Lingfield in second half of season: best efforts on an easy surface and acts on equitrack. *J. Berry*

ANOTHER JADE   2 ch.f. (May 7) Beveled (USA) – Zamindara (Crofter (USA)   **63** 124) [1992 5g 5g 5.7d⁵ 5s 5.1d* 5g 5g] smallish, sturdy filly: third foal: half-sister to sprinter Greetland Rock (by Ballacashtal): dam poor maiden stayed 1m: ran moderately after winning Chepstow nursery in October: speedy: acts on dead ground. *A. P. Jarvis*

ANOTHER KINGDOM   2 gr.g. (Feb 19) Another Realm 118 – Chiquitita 44   **52** (Reliance II 137) [1992 6g⁶ a5g³ a5g⁴ 6m* a7g* 7m a7g⁴ a6g⁶ a7g⁴] 2,100F, 1,500Y: lengthy, rather unfurnished gelding: half-brother to 1986 2-y-o 5f winner Quite So (by Mansingh), later ungenuine: dam won 1¼m seller: modest form: ran moderately after winning Warwick selling nursery (bought in 3,800 gns) and Southwell claimer in July, apart from final start: stays 7f. *J. Wharton*

ANOTHER NICK   6 ch.g. Nicholas Bill 125 – Another Move 69 (Farm Walk 111)   – [1991 13d 10.5d 1992 15.1d] tall, lengthy, sparely-made gelding: no worthwhile form on flat. *J. M. Jefferson*

ANOTHER NUT   3 b.f. Blushing Scribe (USA) 107 – Manageress 74 (Mandamus   –
120) [1991 5m 5f 5g⁴ 6m 7m a7g⁵ a6g a7g⁴ 1992 7v a6g 7m 8g⁶ 10d⁶ 8g] small filly:
poor plater: stays 1¼m: acts on dead ground and fibresand: ran well when visored
once. *P. D. Evans*

ANOTHER RYTON   3 gr.g. Another Realm 118 – Gemgem 54 (Lochnager 132)   –
[1991 5f 5m 5f 1992 6m 7.5m] small, stocky gelding: has round action: poor plater:
sold 1,000 gns Doncaster October Sales. *M. W. Ellerby*

ANOTHER VINTAGE   3 ch.g. Risk Me (FR) 127 – Meanieminymoe 66 (Star   42
Appeal 133) light-framed gelding: none too consistent handicapper: stays 6f: acts on
dead ground and fibresand: effective blinkered or not: below form when visored. *P.
D. Cundell*

ANSELLMAN   2 gr.c. (Apr 13) Absalom 128 – Grace Poole (Sallust 134) [1992   100
5.2d 5g⁵ 6f³ 5d* 6g³ 5m² 6s⁵ 5g² 5g⁴ 5d*] 8,500Y: close-coupled, sturdy colt:
carries condition: has a round action: half-brother to several winners, including (at
5f to 9f) Olore Malle (by Camden Town) and (at 5.1f at 2 yrs in 1988) Ranweli Reef
(by Superlative): dam Irish 1m and 1½m winner: progressive colt: won Salisbury
maiden in July and Doncaster listed race (gamely by ½ length) in October: good
fourth in Cornwallis Stakes at Ascot: effective at 5f and 6f: probably acts on any
going, though goes well with give in the ground: genuine. *M. J. Haynes*

ANSILLO   2 b.c. (May 15) Rousillon (USA) 133 – Vian (USA) (Far Out East (USA))   70 p
[1992 7d 8.1d*] 11,500Y: third foal: half-brother to 3-y-o Bold Steve (by Never So
Bold): dam unraced half-sister to Optimistic Lass, herself dam of Golden Opinion:
confirmed debut promise with very easy win in Edinburgh maiden in November:
probably capable of much better: sent to France. *J. H. M. Gosden*

ANSWERSNOTPROBLEMS (IRE)   4 b.f. Runnett 125 – Gossip (Sharp   –
Edge 123) [1991 7.1g 8m a6g 1992 a7g] sturdy, lengthy filly: no worthwhile form:
tried blinkered. *R. Tate*

ANTESTER (IRE)   2 b. or br.c. (Apr 27) Soviet Star (USA) 128 – Haneena 118   92 p
(Habitat 134) [1992 7g³ 7g* 6m⁶ 7g*] IR 85,000Y: good-topped colt: has scope: has
a roundish action: half-brother to several winners, including very useful French
miler North Haneena (by Far North) and splendidly tough 5-y-o 7f/1m winner
Doulab's Image (by Doulab): dam sprinter, later raced in USA: successful at Ayr in
summer in small-field maiden and minor event: never able to challenge but ran very
well when last of 6 in Richmond Stakes at Goodwood: will be suited by 1m: sort to do
better. *P. W. Chapple-Hyam*

ANTE UP (IRE)   4 b.c. Sharpen Up 127 – Petillante (USA) (Riverman (USA) 131)   §§
[1991 8d⁶ 8m³ 8m* 8m 1992 10.8v 8.1d 12.1s] tall, close-coupled colt: ungenuine and
one to avoid. *J. Akehurst*

ANTICO NATIVO (IRE)   4 b.g. Be My Native (USA) 122 – David's Pleasure   55
(Welsh Saint 126) [1991 8f 8g 7g 10g a12g³ 14.1m a12g 1992 12d4 11.7f³ 12g] leggy
gelding: moderate walker: largely consistent handicapper: stays 1½m: acts on firm
and dead ground. *S. Dow*

ANTIGUAN FLYER   3 b.c. Shirley Heights 130 – Fleet Girl (Habitat 134) [1991   85
7g 7g⁶ 1992 11.7d* 13.9g² 13.1s* 16.1s 13.3s⁶ a16g⁵] lengthy colt: good mover: won
Bath maiden in June and Ayr amateurs race in September: disappointing in
handicaps last 3 starts, sold to join J. Bostock 12,500 gns Newmarket Autumn Sales
before final one: stays 13.9f: acts on soft ground. *J. R. Bostock*

ANTIQUE SONG (USA)   3 b.f. Palace Music (USA) 129 – Lucky Ole Axe   –
(USA) (The Axe II 115) [1991 NR 1992 10g] $26,000Y: closely related to a winner by
The Minstrel and half-sister to several winners: dam, successful at up to 1m, is
half-sister to useful middle-distance stayer Kudz: last in Windsor maiden in May:
dead. *C. F. Wall*

ANUSHA   2 b.f. (Apr 24) Alzao (USA) 117 – Arita (FR) (Kronzeuge) [1992 6d⁴ 6v*   62
a6g] leggy filly: fifth foal: half-sister to 3-y-o winning sprinter Arctic Appeal (by
Ahonoora), and 1m (at 2 yrs) and 9f winner Aribie (by Henbit), and a winner in
Germany: dam won in Germany: comfortably won Hamilton maiden: never able to
land a blow in nursery at Southwell later in November: will stay 7f: clearly acts well
in the mud. *J. Berry*

ANY DREAM WOULD DO   3 b.f. Efisio 120 – Pasha's Dream (Tarboosh   48
(USA)) [1991 NR 1992 6.9d⁵ 8g⁶ 8m* 8m 10m] 1,700Y: angular filly: moderate
mover: seventh living foal: half-sister to 1m and 1¼m winner Obeliski (by
Aragon) and 5f winner Davill (by Record Token): dam half-sister to smart
middle-distance performer Jimsun: well beaten in handicaps after winning Thirsk

seller (no bid) in July: stays 1m well: refused to enter stalls once in May: trained by C. Thornton and bandaged behind first 3 starts. *P. Beaumont*

A NYMPH TOO FAR (IRE) 3 b.f. Precocious 126 – Faraway Places (Flair Path 122) [1991 5d 5.7f3 6d 7g 7.1m a8g4 1992 a10g5 a8g3 a8g* a7g5 8g4 8f 8f3 9.7g6 8.9g5 8f4 8g] angular, sparely-made filly: inconsistent handicapper: won Lingfield claimer in February: stays 1m: acts on equitrack: well below form when visored once. *Dr J. D. Scargill* **47** d

APACHEE FLOWER 2 ch.f. (Mar 9) Formidable (USA) 125 – Molucella (Connaught 130) [1992 8.1s 8g 7s] compact filly: moderate walker: third foal: half-sister to 3-y-o Hidden Flower (by Blakeney): dam poor half-sister to smart miler Fair Season: soundly beaten in maidens. *J. D. Roberts* **35**

APACHE MAID 3 b.f. Reach 122 – Hopi 68 (The Brianstan 128) [1991 NR 1992 6f 6g 8.3g] 500Y: plain, lengthy filly: moderate mover: second foal: dam barely stayed 6f: no sign of ability. *J. S. Moore* **–**

APACHE MYTH 2 b.f. (Feb 26) Salse (USA) 128 – Peak Squaw (USA) (Icecapade (USA)) [1992 6d 6d4 7d5] lengthy, good-bodied filly: second foal: half-sister to 3-y-o Forgetful (by Don't Forget Me): dam Irish 2-y-o 6f winner: modest form in maidens: still not fully wound up when fifth of 17 at Leicester in August: stays 7f. *R. Hannon* **58** p

APACHE SQUAW 2 br.f. (Apr 2) Be My Guest (USA) 126 – Siouan 78 (So Blessed 130) [1992 6g4 7d] leggy filly: has scope: sister to 12.3f winner Tomahawk and half-sister to several winners, including very smart middle-distance colt Apache (by Great Nephew): dam 1½m winner, is half-sister to high-class middle-distance stayer Dakota and very useful Warpath: shaped encouragingly in maidens at Ayr and Catterick nearly 3 months later: will do better. *C. W. Thornton* **52** p

APIFERA 2 b.f. (Feb 24) Norwick (USA) 120 – Miss Hippolyta 82 (High Line 125) [1992 5.1m 6.1m 7m 6g 5.1d 7s] leggy filly: has a round action: fifth living foal: sister to 11.5f winner Kniphofia: dam 10.8f winner: poor form, including in sellers: should stay 7f: acts on dead ground. *R. J. Hodges* **40**

APOLLO DE ORIENTE 2 b.c. (May 6) Siberian Express (USA) 125 – Marie Galante 73 (Shirley Heights 130) [1992 6s a6g6 5d a5g a6g4] 4,200Y: compact, workmanlike colt: third foal: half-brother to 3-y-o 7.5f winner Round By The River (by Superlative): dam maiden stayed 14.8f: poor maiden: stays 6f: acts on fibresand: ran well when visored penultimate start. *J. S. Wainwright* **48**

APOLLO RED 3 ch.g. Dominion 123 – Woolpack (Golden Fleece (USA) 133) [1991 NR 1992 10d 9g 8.2d5 8.3g 8m] 20,000F, 38,000Y: smallish, sturdy gelding: first foal: dam unraced daughter of Klairone, in frame in Irish 1000 Guineas/Oaks: no worthwhile form: sold 2,100 gns Ascot November Sales. *P. W. Harris* **–**

APOLLO'S SISTER 2 b.f. (Apr 16) Then Again 126 – Cruise Port 73 (Homeric 133) [1992 5g 7f a7g] leggy, unfurnished filly: fourth foal: half-sister to 1990 2-y-o 6f and 7f winner Port Vauban (by Tumble Wind) and poor 1½m winner Almetingo (by Touching Wood): dam placed here at 2 yrs, won over 1m at 4 yrs in France: no form, including in sellers. *Mrs J. Jordan* **–**

APPEALING BUBBLES (IRE) 3 b.c. Last Tycoon 131 – Bubbling (USA) (Stage Door Johnny) [1991 7g 9g* 8g3 9d6 1992 12m2 16.2f 12m 12g3 12g*] IR 40,000Y: lengthy, attractive colt: half-brother to 3 winners, including useful Irish 7f and 1¼m winner Raconteur and useful Irish 7.6f and 1m winner Midnight Tiger (both by The Minstrel): dam, half-sister to high-class 6.5f and 1½m winner Effervescing, was smart stakes winner over 1m: fairly useful performer: won minor event at Galway in July: prominent to 2f out in Queen's Vase at Royal Ascot and set pace in Irish Derby at the Curragh second and third starts: stays 1½m: acts on good to firm and dead ground: usually blinkered. *J. S. Bolger, Ireland* **89**

APPEALING TIMES (USA) 3 ch.g. Timeless Moment (USA) – Appealing One (USA) (Valid Appeal (USA)) [1991 6m3 5m2 5g4 6f2 6m5 7d a5g* a6g2 a5g2 1992 a6g3 a5g2 a6g4 a6g3 a7g* a7g* 6d4 7m a7g6 5.7g 8m] smallish gelding: in fine form in early-March, successful in 2 claimers and a handicap at Lingfield: well below form after on turf: better at 7f than shorter, and may well stay 1m: acts on firm ground and all-weather surfaces: effective blinkered or not. *W. A. O'Gorman* **–** a76

APPLE 3 b.g. Balliol 125 – Crabtree (King of Spain 121) [1991 5s 5m6 5g 7m3 6f6 8.2m 1992 8g 12.2g 11.5s] lengthy, plain gelding: shows knee action: no form in 1992: stays 7f: acts on firm ground. *W. Holden* **–**

APPLEDORN 5 ch.m. Doulab (USA) 115 – Mythical Lady 86 (Track Spare 125) [1991 7g 7g3 7.2g 7.3f 7g 7m5 7d 1992 7g 7.1g5 6f 6f2 6.1d 6m 6g 6g 6d 6g2 6g a6g6] a76 **84**

a6g* a6g²] leggy, angular ex-Irish mare: has quick action: most inconsistent handicapper but fairly useful on her day and, well backed, won claimer at Southwell late in year: effective at 6f and 7f: acts on firm ground and fibresand: below form when blinkered. *B. A. McMahon*

APPLE TREE (FR) 3 ch.c. Bikala 134 – Pomme Rose (Carvin 127) [1991 8d 8g* **120** 10v⁶ 1992 10.5g* 10.5m³ 12g 12m³ 12g*] big, good-topped colt: closely related to a French 2-y-o 7.5f winner by Kalamoun and half-brother to the dam of smart but seemingly unreliable French 3-y-o Adieu Au Roi and several winners, notably high-class French 1m (at 2 yrs) to 1½m winner Noir Et Or (by Rheingold): dam smart 5f to 1¼m winner: very smart French performer: won Prix Greffulhe at Longchamp in April: off course around 3 months, best efforts when ½-length third of 8 to Songlines in moderately-run Prix Niel at Longchamp and when winning Geno Europa Preis (by 1¾ lengths from Platini) at Cologne in September: stays 1½m: best efforts on a sound surface: has twice unseated rider in preliminaries: reportedly stays in training. *A. Fabre, France*

APPLIANCEOFSCIENCE 5 b.g. Bairn (USA) 126 – Moonlight Serenade 66 **41** (Crooner 119) [1991 13.8f⁵ 10g³ a12g 1992 a10g a16g⁶ a10g³] workmanlike gelding: moderate walker: inconsistent handicapper: stays 1¼m: acts on good to firm ground: effective blinkered or not. *A. S. Reid*

APPROACH THE BENCH (IRE) 4 b.c. Law Society (USA) 130 – Arguing 71 **113** (Pharly (FR) 130) [1991 7g⁴ 7g⁵ 10g 8g 8g⁵ 10m² 8m³ 7m² 7g 8d³ 9.7d⁵ 1992 10v² 8d⁴ 9m* 8m⁵ 8m 9g* 10g⁴ 8g⁴ 10g⁴] small, quite attractive Irish colt: smart performer: successful in 1992 in listed race and IR £16,600 handicap at Leopardstown: also ran well when fifth of 9 in Queen Anne Stakes at Royal Ascot and on final start when close fourth to Karinga Bay in Group 3 race at Baden-Baden: effective at stiff 1m, to 1¼m: acts on good to firm ground and dead. *J. E. Mulhern, Ireland*

Mr J. E. Mulhern's "Approach The Bench"

A PRAYER FOR WINGS 8 gr.g. Godswalk (USA) 130 – Late Swallow (My **94** +
Swallow 134) [1991 NR 1992 6d 6f 6g* 6m*] tall, rather leggy gelding: useful
performer nowadays: successful in claimers at Kempton and Doncaster in July:
suited by 6f: acts on any going: looked difficult ride when tried in blinkers: bandaged
in 1992. *J. Sutcliffe*

APRIL CITY 3 b.f. Lidhame 109 – Gay City 99 (Forlorn River 124) [1991 NR 1992 **56**
9.7s* 10.3g 9.7v] half-sister to several winners, notably useful sprinter Boezinge
(by Derrylin): dam sprinter: below form in sellers after winning one at Folkestone
(no bid) in October. *M. J. Heaton-Ellis*

APRIL DOUBLE (IRE) 2 ch.f. (Apr 16) Double Schwartz 128 – Laputa **34**
(Kashiwa 115) [1992 7g³ 6.1d 7g 8.2d] IR 2,000Y: leggy, short-backed filly:
half-sister to a winner in France by Commanche Run: dam Irish maiden, half-sister
to April Run: third in Yarmouth seller: sold 650 gns Newmarket Autumn Sales. *M.
H. Tompkins*

APRIL POINT (IRE) 2 b.f. (Feb 24) Fools Holme (USA) – Highland Girl (USA) **51**
(Sir Ivor 135) [1992 5d 5g⁶ 7.5d 6.1d 6s 6m] 24,000Y, 9,500Y: leggy filly: half-sister
to 3 winners in France, including listed 1989 2-y-o 6f winner Cut My Heart (by
General Assembly): dam twice-raced sister to Princess Ivor, a smart winner at up to
9f in USA: plating-class maiden: best effort at 7.5f: acts on good to soft ground. *R.
Hollinshead*

APRIL SHADOW 3 b.f. Shardari 134 – X-Data 93 (On Your Mark 125) [1991 6d **51**
6m 5f 1992 8m⁴ 8.2g 7g² 7g 8m⁵ 8m⁴ 7g³ 7g] leggy, angular filly: inconsistent
maiden: should stay beyond 1m: acts on good to firm ground: sometimes wears
tongue strap: sold to join Mrs P. Sly 2,500 gns Doncaster October Sales. *C. W.
Thornton*

AQUADO 3 b.c. Green Desert (USA) 127 – Meliora 73 (Crowned Prince (USA) **–**
128) [1991 NR 1992 8g⁶] good-topped colt: seventh live foal: half-brother to 5
winners, notably good-class stayer Weld (by Kalaglow): dam 7f winner: very coltish
and readily outpaced in 8-runner Kempton maiden in August, only run: sold 1,400
gns Newmarket Autumn Sales. *W. Jarvis*

AQUAMARINE 3 ch.f. Shardari 134 – Green Rock (FR) (Mill Reef (USA) 141) **89**
[1991 7m 1992 11.4g* 11.9m⁵ 14.6m] rangy filly: looked a stayer when ¾-length
winner from Juniper Berry of Cheshire Oaks in May: off course 3½ months and well
beaten after in York listed race and Park Hill Stakes at Doncaster: stud. *B. W. Hills*

ARAADH (USA) 2 b.f. (Apr 12) Blushing Groom (FR) 131 – Idle Gossip (USA) **70**
(Lyphard (USA) 132) [1992 8s³ 8d] small filly: has quick action: third foal: dam, won
from 6f to 9f in USA, from good family: failed by long way to repeat debut form when
favourite in Yarmouth maiden in October. *H. Thomson Jones*

ARABAT 5 b.g. Habitat 134 – Kalamac (FR) (Kalamoun 129) [1991 8d 7m 6g⁴ 8d **65**
7m 7.1m⁶ 7g 5d 1992 7.1m 7f³ 7g 7g 6g* 6m 6s 6s* 6d 6v⁵] robust, attractive
gelding: successful in handicaps at Redcar (claiming event) and Hamilton but
unreliable: headstrong, and best at 6f/7f: acts on good to firm and soft ground: has
gone well visored, below form when blinkered including final start. *M. P. Naughton*

ARABELLAJILL 3 b.f. Aragon 118 – Crackerjill 37 (Sparkler 130) [1991 5m 5m³ **93**
6.1d⁴ 6g⁴ 5m* 5m² 5.1m² 6.1m* 6m² 6g⁶ 1992 6g 6m* 6m³ 6.1m⁶ 6d³ 6g* 6g⁶ 6m
6g 6g] leggy filly: consistent handicapper: successful at Windsor and Newmarket in
summer: stays 6f well: acts on good to firm ground and dead. *R. Hannon*

ARABIAN BOLD (IRE) 4 br.g. Persian Bold 123 – Bodham 88 (Bustino 136) **69** +
[1991 10m² a12g* 11.7g* 1992 11.1m⁶ 12f 12.3g⁶ 12f⁴] leggy, quite attractive gelding:
rated 90 as 3-y-o: well below form in handicaps in 1992: should stay beyond 1½m:
acts on good to firm ground and equitrack: front runner. *W. J. Haggas*

ARABIAN CASTLE 2 b.c. (May 31) Sayf El Arab (USA) 127 – Magnifica (Sandy **–**
Creek 123) [1992 7g 7d] second reported foal: dam half-sister to very useful
performer (at up to 1m) Milk of The Barley: no form in maidens. *M. J. Heaton-Ellis*

ARABIAN KING 4 b.c. Sayf El Arab (USA) 127 – New Edition 72 (Great **–**
Nephew 126) [1991 a8g² 6g⁴ 7.5g* 7m² 8m⁶ 7m³ 7f⁴ 7m³ 1992 7.5g 7g 7.5g]
workmanlike colt: modest handicapper: probably stayed 1m: acted on firm going:
dead. *M. Brittain*

ARADANZA 2 ch.c. (Feb 13) Aragon 118 – Divine Fling (Imperial Fling (USA) **92**
116) [1992 5.2d⁵ 5g³ 5g² 5m* 5.2d² 6g 6s 6g⁶ 5s* 5d] 4,200Y: quite attractive,
good-quartered colt: has scope: has a round action: third foal: brother to 1m winner
Conquista: dam poor maiden: inconsistent performer: successful in Sandown
maiden auction in June and Pontefract minor event in October: also good sixth in

Mill Reef Stakes at Newbury: stays 6f: easily best efforts on an easy surface. *M. R. Channon*

ARAGONA 3 b.f. Aragon 118 – Polly Worth 55 (Wolver Hollow 126) [1991 5.7m⁴   **42**
5.7m 7g 7.1m 1992 7s* 7g 8d 6g⁶ 8.3m 7g 7d] leggy filly: below form after winning
Salisbury apprentice handicap in April: stays 7f: best effort on very soft ground:
below form when blinkered: retained 800 gns Ascot November Sales. *P. D. Cundell*

ARAGON AYR 4 b. or br.g. Aragon 118 – Brig of Ayr 90 (Brigadier Gerard 144)   **43**
[1991 10g⁵ 9f⁴ 1992 11.1s 8.3s 9.2d² 9.2s 8s 12.1s 9.2v] compact gelding: poor mover:
poor handicapper: stays 9f: acts on firm and dead ground. *P. Monteith*

ARAGON COURT 4 b.g. Aragon 118 – Balatina 85 (Balidar 133) [1991 10g 7m   **52**
8.2g a8g⁴ 7m⁶ 7m 7d⁶ 8m⁶ 1992 8.3m 8.3d³ 8g 8f3 9.7m* 10.8g 9.7g⁵ 9.7s 10.3g]
compact, good-topped gelding: poor mover: well backed when winning Folkestone
seller (no bid) in August: no form after: stays 9.5f well: acts on good to firm and dead
ground: has pulled hard and drifted left: sold 2,700 gns Ascot November Sales. *J. Pearce*

ARAGON KING 2 b.g. (Mar 11) Aragon 118 – Cadasi 68 (Persian Bold 123) [1992   **44** p
a8g⁵] 3,000Y: fifth foal: half-brother to 3-y-o Karamoja (by Auction Ring), modest 7f
winner, and winning Irish sprinter Bold Starlet: dam 2-y-o 6f winner later placed at
up to 1m in Ireland, is half-sister to smart Irish sprinter Back Bailey: fifth of 10 in
Lingfield maiden in December won by Convoy, outpaced straight: may improve.
Miss Gay Kelleway

ARAGROVE 2 b.c. (Apr 22) Aragon 118 – Grovehurst (Homing 130) [1992 5g   **70**
5.1g⁵ 5g 6d 5.2g⁴ 5s³ a6g*] 15,500Y: compact colt: has scope: has a round action:
first foal: dam ran once: improved late in year and ran out emphatic winner of a
modest Lingfield maiden, making all and quickening clear off home turn: withdrawn
at start after reportedly having broken a blood vessel later in November: stays 6f:
has run well for 7-lb claimer: acts on equitrack and has raced only on an easy surface
on turf. *L. J. Holt*

ARAK (USA) 4 b.c. Clever Trick (USA) – Twilight Flight (USA) (Quack (USA))   **76**
[1991 10g⁵ 7g² 8m 1992 8.1d 8g 8.1m 10.1g⁴ 10.3f* 10.1m* 9.9d5] lengthy, quite
attractive colt: has a long stride: fair handicapper: successful in small fields at
Doncaster and Yarmouth in summer: better suited by 1¼m than shorter: acts on
dead going, but goes very well on top-of-the-ground: front runner: sold to join D.
Moffatt only 4,000 gns Newmarket Autumn Sales. *R. W. Armstrong*

ARANY 5 b.g. Precocious 126 – Bellagio 68 (Busted 134) [1991 8d 8g 8g⁵ 7.6d* **101** d
8.5f 7g² 7g 7m 8g 7g 7m 7d 8m 7.6d 1992 7g⁵ 7.6g² 7g⁴ 8f 10.4d⁶ 7.9m 8s³ 7.1s
8s 7.9s] lengthy, quite attractive gelding: poor mover: inconsistent handicapper
nowadays: best form at around 1m: needs an easy surface: below form when
visored/blinkered. *M. H. Tompkins*

ARAWA 2 b.f. (Mar 21) Doulab (USA) 115 – High Heather (Shirley Heights 130)   **43**
[1992 6m 6g 6m a5g⁴ 7g 6g a7g⁵ a8g³] unfurnished filly: first foal: dam unraced: poor
maiden: probably stays 7f: acts on good to firm ground and fibresand. *D. Marks*

ARAZI (USA) 3 ch.c. Blushing Groom (FR) 131 – Danseur Fabuleux (USA) **124**
106 (Northern Dancer (CAN)) [1991 5m² 6g* 5g* 5.5g* 6g* 7m* 8d* a8.5f*
1992 8s* a10f 8m5 10g³ 8s* 8f]
  There is an old saying that if something looks too good to be true it
probably is. So what of Arazi, hailed as the wonder of the age after a spectacular victory in the Breeders' Cup Juvenile but regarded as a flop as a
three-year-old? Arazi's demonstrable superiority over the best two-year-
olds in North America—following a string of victories in the top races in
France—kindled the imagination of the racing public on both sides of the
Atlantic. To some in America Arazi was 'the new Secretariat'. The conviction
that Arazi was destined to join the gallery of the famous was echoed the racing
world over. Drawing on Benjamin Franklin's famous observation, Geoff
Lester introduced his preview in *The Sporting Life* of the Kentucky Derby
with the statement: 'If there is a third certainty after death and taxes, it is
surely that Arazi will win the 118th Kentucky Derby at Churchill Downs
today'.
  Odds-on Arazi's eighth-of-eighteen placing behind Lil E Tee in the
Kentucky Derby left the racing world stunned. The reasons for his finishing
so far down the field—he folded abruptly after surging through to dispute
second on the home turn—were debated fiercely. Some blamed Valenzuela

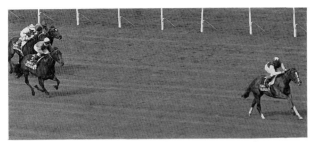

Prix Omnium II, Saint-Cloud—a good work-out for Arazi

for having had Arazi too far back early on and then moving him up too quickly. Valenzuela countered that he had ridden Arazi much the same as in the Breeders' Cup Juvenile. 'He ran by horses easily and it was only at the quarter pole that I really asked him to run . . . I thought I was just going to inhale them. I thought there was no way I could get beat,' Valenzuela said. Valenzuela's explanation for the defeat was that 'Arazi didn't get home', meaning he didn't stay a mile and a quarter. The question of Arazi's state of readiness also came up. The much-publicised operation on the horse's knees after the Breeders' Cup Juvenile kept him on the side-lines longer than his trainer would have liked. Boutin's protestations after the race that Arazi had had a 'hurried preparation' might have been received more sympathetically, however, had he not been widely quoted beforehand as saying that the colt was in tip-top form. Arazi had been warmed up in a listed event at Saint-Cloud in early-April: none of his seven rivals, whom he met at levels, had won a pattern race and Arazi completed a straightforward task in the style expected. Arazi's untaxing preparation contrasted with the much more demanding schedule of most of the American-trained Kentucky Derby runners. The winner Lil E Tee, for example, had four races before Churchill Downs, while the second and third, Casual Lies and Dance Floor, had three apiece.

Arazi's running in the Kentucky Derby didn't immediately suppress expectations that he would prove himself a great three-year-old. The Kentucky Derby was the first poor race he'd run. The next step could have been to send Arazi on to the second leg of the American triple crown, the Preakness

Ciga Prix du Rond-Point, Longchamp—
Arazi produces an impressive change of pace

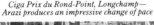

Stakes at Pimlico. One noted American commentator, Andrew Beyer of the *Washington Post*, asserted that 'Arazi would annihilate his rivals in the manner that had been expected of him at Churchill Downs'. It was Beyer's view that 'a more fit, more seasoned Arazi would have won the Kentucky Derby . . . I cannot believe that the awesome running machine we saw last fall is congenitally incapable of running a final quarter mile in 26.4 sec and out-finishing the likes of Lil E Tee'. Britain's leading owner Sheikh Mohammed had taken a half-share in Arazi with the original owner Allen Paulson before the Breeders' Cup Juvenile and there had been some talk of Arazi's attempting the Churchill Downs-Epsom 'Durby-Darby' double. As things turned out, Arazi wasn't seen on a racecourse again until Royal Ascot where he started odds on for the St James's Palace Stakes, which also attracted Rodrigo de Triano, winner of the Two Thousand Guineas at both Newmarket and the Curragh before disappointing in the Derby. The St James's Palace received enormous publicity but neither Arazi nor Rodrigo de Triano reached a place behind the 25/1-shot Brief Truce. Arazi looked fit and on good terms with himself beforehand but managed only fifth, beaten about two and a half lengths by the winner, leaving the impression that the best had probably been seen of him. There were many who thought Arazi would bow out. 'Europeans,' Beyer had told his readers, 'seem obsessed with avoiding defeat. They habitually duck and dodge competition and retire their horses prematurely; when they run and lose they respond with a litany of excuses'. The damage that can be done to a horse's value for stud by a number of defeats is something that top European racehorse owners generally seem much more concerned about than their American counterparts. The decision to carry on with Arazi after Royal Ascot was praiseworthy but, alas, it proved largely unproductive. After an eleven-week absence, Arazi was declared for the Prix

Sheikh Mohammed's "Arazi"

du Moulin at Longchamp, only to be withdrawn at the eleventh hour. He did run a fortnight later in the Prix du Prince d'Orange, a recognised Prix de l'Arc trial over a mile and a quarter at Longchamp in September, and came a disappointing third, his trainer saying the horse needed the race after recovering from the set-back that had kept him out of the Prix du Moulin. Connections fired the last shots in their locker in October. Arazi turned in his best effort of the season in the Ciga Prix du Rond-Point, the opening race on the Prix de l'Arc day programme, producing a good turn of foot to win by four lengths from Calling Collect. Victory earned him a place in the field for the Breeders' Cup Mile at Gulfstream Park but he was again disappointing, starting favourite and beating only three home.

		Red God	Nasrullah
Arazi (USA) (ch.c. 1989)	Blushing Groom (FR) (ch 1974)	(ch 1954)	Spring Run
		Runaway Bride (b 1962)	Wild Risk
			Aimee
	Danseur Fabuleux (USA) (b 1982)	Northern Dancer (b 1961)	Nearctic
			Natalma
		Fabuleux Jane (ch 1974)	Le Fabuleux
			Native Partner

Arazi is no oil-painting—he's close-coupled and lightly made—but he's an impressive mover with a powerful, extravagant action. He has a good pedigree too, being by the now-deceased Blushing Groom, an outstanding sire, out of a Northern Dancer mare from a first-rate family. Arazi's dam Danseur Fabuleux never won a race but showed useful form at up to a mile and a half. Arazi's grandam Fabuleux Jane was a good middle-distance performer who reached a place in the Prix de Diane and Prix Vermeille; she was a half-sister to the champion sprinter Ajdal, as she was to the Middle Park winner Formidable and the American filly Flying Partner who was placed in the CCA Oaks and Kentucky Oaks. Arazi was bred to stay further than a mile; he won on good to firm going but showed his best form on turf with some give in the ground (the Breeders' Cup Juvenile is run on dirt). Sheikh Mohammed purchased Arazi outright after his final start and has retired him to stud. He will stand at Dalham Hall, Newmarket, at a fee of £20,000 (October 1st terms) in 1993. Arazi's career as a three-year-old may have fallen a long way short of fulfilling the expectations held for it, but his outstanding achievements in 1991 ensure that his name will be recalled as long as racing is talked about. He was the best European-trained two-year-old for many a year. *F. Boutin, France*

ARBORETUM (IRE)   3 b.f. Green Desert (USA) 127 – Fear Naught 99 (Con-   **83** naught 130) [1991 6f5 6.1f 7m 1992 6s6 7f2 7m* 7g6 6f* 6m] small, sparely-made filly: fairly useful performer: won Lingfield maiden in August and Doncaster handicap in September: stays 7f: acts on firm ground. *R. Charlton*

ARBUSHA (USA)   3 b.f. Danzig (USA) – Lulu Mon Amour (USA) (Tom Rolfe)   **103** [1991 6m4 1992 8d* 8.1m4 8g* 10d4 8v] unfurnished filly: useful performer: won £9,700 contest at Ascot in April and listed race at Hoppegarten in August: good fourth to Oumaldaaya in Rome Group 2 event: stays 1¼m: acts on good to firm and dead ground, possibly unsuited by heavy. *Lord Huntingdon*

ARCADIAN HEIGHTS   4 b.c. Shirley Heights 130 – Miss Longchamp 94 **114** § (Northfields (USA)) [1991 12m 14.1f3 14.8g* 14g2 13.4m* 14.6m 1992 12g4 16.2d 13.4m2 16.4m2 20f2 16m4] lengthy, good-topped colt: usually impresses in appearance: has a fluent round action: smart performer: best efforts in 1992 when second to Drum Taps in Henry II Stakes at Sandown and Gold Cup at Royal Ascot: went with little zest when tried in net muzzle final start: stays 2½m: acts on firm ground: twice bit opponent in 1992, and not one to trust. *G. Wragg*

ARCADIAN PRINCESS   3 b.f. Teenoso (USA) 135 – Top Shot 84 (Grundy 137)   **–** [1991 7.1m 1992 10g] sturdy, lengthy filly: no sign of ability: sold 600 gns Newmarket Autumn Sales. *Miss A. J. Whitfield*

ARCANGUES (USA)   4 ch.c. Sagace (FR) 135 – Albertine (FR) 117 (Irish River **121** (FR) 131) [1991 9d* 10g* 10g2 12m3 12s3 1992 10s6 9.2d2 10s 10g* 12s] angular French colt: very smart performer: 6-length winner of Prix du Prince d'Orange at Longchamp in September: best other efforts in 1992 also there, second to Zoman in Prix d'Ispahan and staying-on seventh of 18 in moderately-run Prix de l'Arc de

Prix du Prince d'Orange, Longchamp—Arcangues wins by six lengths; Arazi (outside) is only third

Triomphe: effective from around 9f to 1½m: acts on good to firm and soft ground. *A. Fabre, France*

ARC BRIGHT (IRE)　2 b.c. (Mar 12) Trempolino (USA) 135 – Brillante (FR) 118　**66**
(Green Dancer (USA) 132) [1992 7m 8m⁴ 8.1d² 8s⁶ 7.6s⁴ 8.2s⁵] 24,000Y: rather leggy, workmanlike colt: half-brother to 1989 French 2-y-o 6f winner Bazilia (by Mr Prospector) and a winner in USA: dam French 1m (at 2 yrs) and 11f winner, is half-sister to Bellypha and Bellman: modest maiden: will be suited by middle distances: probably acts on any going. *R. Hollinshead*

ARCHIPELLAGO GIRL　2 ch.f. (Apr 18) Music Streak (DEN) 116 – Fields of　–
Grain (Final Straw 127) [1992 5m 6f] small filly: first foal: dam won over 11f in French Provinces at 3 yrs, placed in Scandinavia at 4 yrs: sire (by Music Boy), Scandinavian sprinter/miler pattern winner: last in northern sellers in June: trained debut by W. Pearce. *B. Beasley*

ARC LAMP　6 b.g. Caerleon (USA) 132 – Dazzling Light 116 (Silly Season 127)　**62**
[1991 a6g² a6g a5g³ 6g 5m⁴ a5g² 5m a5g a6g 6g 5g⁴ 5g* 5m² 5s⁵ 5d a6g a6g⁵ 1992 6v⁵ 5g⁵ 5d 5f⁶ 6g⁴ a5g* 7m 5f³ 5m* 5f² a5g⁶ 5.6m 5f² 6m⁵ 5s⁴ a6g³ a5g³ a5g a6g] workmanlike, angular gelding: not a good walker: largely consistent handicapper: successful at Southwell and Wolverhampton in June: below form last 2 starts: best at 5f: has form on soft ground and fibresand, but goes well on a sound surface: below form when blinkered once: genuine. *J. A. Glover*

ARCTIC AGNES (USA)　2 b.f. (Mar 21) Arctic Tern (USA) 126 – Nice Noble　**37**
(USA) (Vaguely Noble 140) [1992 6m⁶ 5g 6m⁵ 6d 6s 10d 8d] $30,000F, 4,500Y: leggy filly: fifth foal: half-sister to a winner in North America by Cresta Rider: dam, winner in Italy, is daughter of Cherry Hinton: poor plater: suited by 1¼m: acts on good to firm and dead ground: joined S. Dow. *R. Akehurst*

ARCTIC APPEAL (IRE)　3 b.f. Ahonoora 122 – Arita (FR) (Kronzeuge) [1991　**87**
5m* 5g 5f⁵ 6.1m² 6.1d³ 1992 5v* 6g² 5g² 6.1g 5f⁵ 6g³ 6m² 6g* 6d² 6d⁵ 6d⁶ 6s] rather sparely-made filly: moderate mover: fairly useful handicapper: won Folkestone minor event in March and Hamilton claimer in August: ran poorly final start and sold 7,800 gns Newmarket Autumn Sales: stays 6f: best on an easy surface. *J. Berry*

ARCTIC CIRCLE (IRE)　3 ch.g. Northern Baby (CAN) 127 – High Quail (USA)　**52**
(Blushing Groom (FR) 131) [1991 7f 7m 8m 10m⁶ 1992 10d⁴ 10.2d 13.3m³ 14.1g] leggy gelding: has a long stride: poor maiden on flat, not seen out after July: shapes like a stayer: acts on good to firm ground and dead: well beaten when blinkered once: won 3 times over hurdles in autumn. *Miss A. J. Whitfield*

ARCTIC GUEST (IRE)　2 ch.f. (Mar 20) Arctic Tern (USA) 126 – Sojourn 87　**51**
(Be My Guest (USA) 126) [1992 6f⁵ 7f⁵ 6g 7m* 7f² 8d 7s 7s] IR 2,000Y: leggy filly: has scope: moderate walker: second reported foal: dam 2-y-o 7f winner later successful in USA: easily best efforts at Redcar in summer when winning seller (no bid) and second in nursery: seemed unsuited by soft ground after: will be better suited by 1¼m: well handicapped on top-of-the-ground form. *M. Johnston*

ARCTIC OATS　7 ch.m. Oats 126 – Arctic Festival (Arctic Slave 116) [1991 16.2g⁴　**49**
22.2m 11f 1992 16.2g 16m⁴ 19m³] leggy, sparely-made mare: modest handicapper: stays very well: acts on good to firm ground. *W. W. Haigh*

ARCTIC SPLENDOUR (USA)　3 b.f. Arctic Tern (USA) 126 – Field Dancer　**66**
110 (Northfields (USA)) [1991 7g⁴ 8.1s⁴ 1992 7.5g³ 12f⁴ 12f⁵ 13.1m⁶ 14.9g* 16.4m² 16.1g* 17.5s 17.2s⁴] small, sparely-made filly: fair handicapper: won at Warwick in

July and August: stays 2¼m: possibly suited by an easy surface: usually held up: sold 7,800 gns Newmarket December Sales. *P. W. Chapple-Hyam*

ARDENT GROOM (IRE) 4 ch.g. Coquelin (USA) 121 – Arminiya (Roan – Rocket 128) [1991 7s 1992 a10g] dipped-backed gelding: seems of little account. *T. M. Jones*

ARDISIA (USA) 3 ch.f. Affirmed (USA) – Princess of Man 104 (Green God 128) **87** [1991 7.1m³ 8m 8.9d⁴ 1992 10g² 10.2h* 9.9d* a10g* 11.9m⁴ 10.1m³ 8d] lengthy filly: easy mover: fairly useful performer: won Bath maiden and minor events at Beverley and Lingfield in summer: should prove better suited by 1½m than shorter: acts on hard and dead ground. *P. F. I. Cole*

ARDKINGLASS 2 b.c. (Feb 11) Green Desert (USA) 127 – Reuval 102 (Sharpen **108** p Up 127) [1992 5g² 6m* 6m⁴ 7g* 7g*] leggy, sparely-made colt: not a good walker: fourth foal: half-brother to useful 1¼m winner Jura (by Rousillon): dam suited by 1m: progressive colt: won York maiden, Newcastle minor event and Child & Co Superlative Stakes (by 2½ lengths from White Crown) at Newmarket in first half of 1991: also fourth in Coventry Stakes at Royal Ascot: will be well suited by 1m. *H. R. A. Cecil*

AREA GIRL 2 ch.f. (Jan 25) Jareer (USA) 115 – Shannon Lady 67 (Monsanto (FR) **76** 121) [1992 5f* 5f⁶ 5m* 5m² 5.1m* 5m³ a5s⁵ 5d⁶ 5g] IR 6,700Y: leggy, lengthy filly: first live foal: dam poor maiden: successful in summer in maiden auction at Carlisle, minor event at Windsor and claimer at Bath: will stay 6f: acts on firm and dead ground, below par on fibresand. *Sir Mark Prescott*

AREMEF (USA) 3 b. or br.g. Northern Baby (CAN) 127 – Bambina Linda (ARG) **81** (Liloy (FR)) [1991 7m 1992 10d* 10.5d² 12m⁴ 14d⁵ 12f² 10g 11.5g⁴ 10g⁵ 12g⁶] workmanlike gelding: good mover: won Leicester maiden in April and largely consistent in handicaps and a graduation race after: caught eye, never placed to challenge, final start: should stay beyond 1½m: acts on firm and dead going: usually forces pace: has been gelded. *Mrs J. Cecil*

AREWENEARLYTHERE (IRE) 2 b.f. (Mar 8) Robellino (USA) 127 – **45** Shahrood (Prince Tenderfoot (USA) 126) [1992 6m 7g 7g 8.1s 6m] 2,000F, 5,200Y: smallish, workmanlike filly: has a markedly round action: half-sister to 3 winners in USA: dam sister to Icing, the dam of Al Hareb: poor form, including in sellers: should stay 1¼m: probably well suited by soft ground. *M. Blanshard*

ARFEY (IRE) 3 b.c. Burslem 123 – Last Gunboat 50 (Dominion 123) [1991 8m **61** 1992 12d* 12d² 11.1f⁴ 11.6g⁶ 16.1g⁶] angular, workmanlike colt: quite modest handicapper: won Beverley median auction in July: effective at 1½m, but should prove ideally suited by 1¾m/2m: acts on dead ground: bandaged. *T. Thomson Jones*

ARGYLE CAVALIER (IRE) 2 b.c. (Apr 7) Simply Great (FR) 122 – Fete **77** Champetre 80 (Welsh Pageant 132) [1992 5g⁵ 5m⁵ 6f⁴ 6d⁶ 7.5d* 7.5d⁶ 7.9d⁵ 8s²] IR 18,500Y: leggy, angular colt: second living foal: half-brother to 1990 2-y-o 6f winner

Child & Co Superlative Stakes, Newmarket —
Ardkinglass looks useful in beating White Crown and Humam (noseband)

Ribblesdale Stakes, Royal Ascot—Armarama makes all from Niodini

Jim's Wish (by Heraldiste): dam twice-raced half-sister to very smart sprinter Le Johnstan: progressive colt: claimer ridden when winning Beverley nursery in July: excellent second at Pontefract in October: will be suited by middle distances: probably acts on any going. *F. H. Lee*

ARIGHI BOY   3 b.c. Aragon 118 – Varushka 74 (Sharpen Up 127) [1991 NR 1992 – a7g⁶ a7g 8g] 520Y, 5,200Y: lengthy colt: third foal: half-brother to a winner in Switzerland by Formidable: dam ran once: no sign of ability. *J. E. Banks*

ARINTHOD (FR)   2 b.c. (Jun 5) Baillamont (USA) 124 – Rose River (FR) **112** (Riverman (USA) 131) [1992 6m 7.5g² 8g² 8s³ 8g³ 8s³ 9d* 10v³] fourth foal: brother to French 3-y-o Mirabello, successful at 1m (at 2 yrs) and 9f, and half-brother to 1989 French 2-y-o 7f winner Lituanien (by King of Macedon): dam unraced granddaughter of La Lagune: won minor event at Évry in October: much-improved third to Marchand de Sable in Criterium de Saint-Cloud in November: suited by a good test of stamina. *F. Boutin, France*

ARISTOCRATIC PETER (USA)   5 b.g. Sir Ivor 135 – Glimmer Glass (USA) – (The Axe II 115) [1991 a8g a14g 10m 9m 9s 1992 10.2f] good-topped gelding: has quick action: poor maiden nowadays: stays 11.7f: tried blinkered: sold 2,000 gns Ascot July Sales. *D. C. Jermy*

ARJJIL   3 b.g. Beldale Flutter (USA) 130 – Miss Deed 83 (David Jack 125) [1991 **46** NR 1992 8d⁵ 6g⁴ 8.1d² 8g 8m] leggy, unfurnished gelding: seventh reported foal: half-brother to 1¼m winner Jack's Luck (by Lucky Wednesday) and 2 sprint winners: dam, placed at 5f, half-sister to middle-distance performer Tesoro Mio: poor maiden: stays 1m: acts on dead ground: below form when visored once. *M. H. Tompkins*

ARJUZAH (IRE)   2 b.f. (Feb 8) Ahonoora 122 – Saving Mercy 101 (Lord Gayle – p (USA) 124) [1992 6g] 150,000Y: good-topped filly: has scope: fifth foal: half-sister to Irish 1m/1¼m winner Ormsby (by Ela-Mana-Mou): dam won Lincoln Handicap and stayed 1¼m: well backed but on backward side, shaped well under tender ride in Newmarket maiden in July: seemed sure to improve. *J. H. M. Gosden*

ARKAAN (USA)   2 b.c. (May 2) Nijinsky (CAN) 138 – It's In The Air (USA) (Mr **70** p Prospector (USA)) [1992 7d⁴] leggy, unfurnished filly: sixth living foal: closely related to winners abroad by Northern Dancer and Shareef Dancer and half-sister to 3 winners, notably smart French 6.5f and 7f winner Bitooh (by Seattle Slew): dam high-class filly, successful from 6f to 1¼m: 12/1, shaped really well in 15-runner Leicester maiden won by Gabr in October, finishing strongly under considerate handling and beaten 5 lengths: sure to improve and win races, particularly over further. *M. R. Stoute*

ARK CELESTE   2 b.f. (May 17) Celestial Storm (USA) 132 – Scrummage 64 **51** (Workboy 123) [1992 7g 8.5m 8d] leggy, close-coupled filly: second foal: dam, unraced until 4 yrs, later 7f and 1m winner: form in autumn maidens only at Beverley second start: will stay well. *W. W. Haigh*

ARKENDALE DIAMOND (USA)   2 b.c. (Feb 13) Derby Wish (USA) – **66** Dimpled Out (USA) (Full Out (USA)) [1992 5g 5g³ 5d⁴ 5g² 5f⁶ 5f² 5g⁴ 5m⁶ 5g⁵ 5g 5g* 5d 6g⁶ 7g] $4,500F, 6,400Y: good-bodied colt: moderate mover: first foal: dam ran 3 times: sire (by Lyphard's Wish) very smart 1m to 1¼m winner: modest performer: won Redcar nursery in September: effective at 5f, and probably stays 7f: acts on firm and dead ground: below form when blinkered once: often has tongue tied down: trained until after eleventh start by W. Pearce/B. Beasley: sold 5,400 gns Doncaster November Sales, reportedly to Czechoslovakia. *C. B. B. Booth*

ARMAITI   4 b.f. Sayf El Arab (USA) 127 – Almitra (Targowice (USA) 130) [1991 6f² 7f² 7g* 7f* 7m² 7m 7g⁵ 7m⁵ 7.5f⁶ 7d⁴ 7d 7m³ 7.1m⁵ 7g² 7d 1992 a8g a8g a7g 6d 8d 8g 8m 8.9s] leggy, dipped-backed filly: rated 78 at 3 yrs for M. Johnston: well below form in 1992: should stay 1m: acts on firm and dead going: has joined C. J. Hill. *D. R. Tucker*   –

ARMAN'S SAX (IRE)   2 b.c. (Apr 16) Waajib 121 – Miss Sandman 86 (Manacle 123) [1992 6s⁵ 7g* 8v* 8v] IR 5,000Y, 28,000 2-y-o: tall, leggy colt: fluent mover: half-brother to several winners, including Reel of Tulloch (by Salmon Leap), 7f (at 2 yrs) and 9f winner, and Spanish Mariner (by Julio Mariner), successful at up to 1½m in Ireland: dam 5f winner at 2 yrs: progressed really well in autumn, successful in Leicester maiden auction and Milan listed race, until tailed off in Gran Criterium at Milan: stays 1m. *J. L. Dunlop*   **98** ?

ARMARAMA   3 ch.f. Persian Bold 123 – Rossitor 78 (Pall Mall 132) [1991 5m⁵ 8s² 1992 8d² 10g² 10.4g³ 12g² 12f* 11.9g² 12g⁶] good-topped filly: very useful performer: won Ribblesdale Stakes at Royal Ascot by 2 lengths from Niodini: also placed in Musidora Stakes at York, Oaks d'Italia (beaten a length by Ivyanna) at Milan and Lancashire Oaks at Haydock: rare modest effort in Irish Oaks, second run in a week: will stay 1¾m: has form on soft ground, but best efforts on a sound surface: game: usually forces pace. *C. E. Brittain*   **111**

ARMASHOCKER   4 ch.c. Electric 126 – Armalou 54 (Ardoon 124) [1991 10v⁵ 9s⁵ 10g³ 7.5g³ 7v 7s⁵ 8g⁶ 10.5g⁵ 9.5g 10.5g⁶ 9v⁴ 8v 9v³ 15s 10s² 10.5v⁴ 1992 10m 11.5f a8g 9d⁴ a14g a8g⁶ a12g 8m⁶] leggy colt: fourth foal: half-brother to 1987 2-y-o 6f seller winner Annacando (by Derrylin), later suited by 1½m, and to a winner in Italy: dam won at 1¼m: raced on numerous occasions at 2 and 3 yrs in Italy for   –

Mr C. T. Olley's "Armarama"

present trainer, mostly in modest company: no form here in 1992: stays 10.5f: acts on heavy ground. *D. Sasse*

ARMENIAN COFFEE (IRE) 2 b.c. (May 1) Ela-Mana-Mou 132 – Streamer- **72** p
tail 81 (Shirley Heights 130) [1992 7m8.1s 8.2g³ 8.1d²] sparely-made colt: third foal: half-brother to fairly useful 6f (at 2 yrs) to 1¼m winner Jacamar (by Jalmood) and 3-y-o Battle Colours (by Petorius), successful at 6f (at 2 yrs) to 1m: dam 8.2f and 9f winner: best efforts when placed in moderately-run maidens at Nottingham and Haydock in autumn: will be well suited by middle distances: acts on good to soft ground: likely to do better. *J. L. Dunlop*

ARMIGER 2 ch.c. (Feb 15) Rainbow Quest (USA) 134 – Armeria (USA) 79 **131** p
(Northern Dancer (CAN)) [1992 8m* 8d*]
History demands that a six-length winner of the Racing Post Trophy should be afforded maximum respect. In its thirty-one-year life under various titles, the race has been won by many good animals, but only Vaguely Noble and Reference Point were able to stamp themselves on their rivals as Armiger did on the nine which faced him at Doncaster in October. Both Vaguely Noble and Reference Point, of course, went on to prove themselves amongst the outstanding middle-distance colts of the post-war era; Vaguely Noble, who won by a long-looking seven lengths in 1967, wasn't entered in the classics but won four of his five races as a three-year-old and meted out a brilliant three-length beating to Sir Ivor in the Arc; and Reference Point, also a seven-length winner in 1986 (when the judge surprisingly returned his winning margin as only five lengths) went on to win five of his seven races the following season including the Derby, King George and St Leger treble last achieved by Nijinsky in 1970. Armiger, too, looks a top-class middle-distance prospect. In common with his illustrious predecessors he won the Racing Post Trophy in utterly comprehensive fashion, coming clear early in the straight from a useful field, many of whom had already shown a good level of form under the prevailing softish conditions, in a manner that was reminiscent more of Reference Point's unstoppable pillar-to-post gallop than of Vaguely Noble's spectacular surge clear. In the process Armiger showed the best form from a two-year-old over any distance all year, some 5 lb or 6 lb better than that achieved by his stable-companion and deposed Derby favourite Tenby in the Grand Criterium or by Zafonic in the Dewhurst; and his timefigure was the best by a middle-distance-bred two-year-old for several seasons. All this on only his second appearance on the racecourse!
The field that was assembled against Armiger in the Racing Post Trophy may not have been so strong as some of those that have contested the race in the past, and perhaps wasn't quite so strong as that which Zafonic had beaten in the Dewhurst two weeks previously, but it was a representative one, nonetheless, and certainly good enough to ensure a rigorous examination of the classic pretensions of any of its participants. That Armiger should win so handsomely, unchallenged virtually from the point he took up the running with three furlongs to go, his rider needing to do no more than keep him running straight, on only his second run is testimony to his tremendous potential. As Armiger relentlessly galloped further and further clear of the Fillies' Mile winner Ivanka, a progressive filly with proven form over the distance and on the ground, the only question that remained to be answered was the small matter of the winning distance, which we measured as almost exactly six lengths. Behind Ivanka, the remaining eight runners passed the post outclassed. Ten lengths behind Armiger in third came Zind, a progressive colt who two weeks previously had finished just three lengths off second place in the Dewhurst, but who had been made to look thoroughly one paced here; eleven lengths back in fourth came one of the first under pressure, the Royal Lodge winner Desert Secret; and sixteen and more lengths behind were the fairly useful York nursery winner Noyan; Newton's Law, an established soft-ground performer who'd run a good second under the conditions to the Dewhurst fifth Fatherland in the Futurity Stakes at the Curragh; the wide-margin Newbury minor event winner Redenham; the fairly useful and consistent Mukhamedov; the May Hill winner Marillette and the pacemaker Wahem, none of whom played a part once the race went beyond five furlongs. Since all of the beaten runners with the exception of Marillette,

Racing Post Trophy, Doncaster —
no danger from Ivanka or Zind as Eddery looks round on Armiger

who looked past her best for the season, and Wahem, could be demonstrated to have improved upon, or run virtually up to, their best form we don't feel that Armiger was in any way flattered. And if further confirmation of the merit of his performance was required it was provided by the classic-standard timefigure of 125, overwhelmingly the best by a two-year-old all season and as encouraging an endorsement of the form as one could wish to find.

Armiger went to Doncaster with a victory in the Soltykoff Stakes over a mile at Newmarket on the final day of September behind him. The Soltykoff Stakes is usually an informative contest—it was won by Dancing Brave in 1985—and the latest running looked well up to standard with an interesting combination of lightly-raced, promising animals and well-bred newcomers from most of the largest southern stables. Armiger, a finely-made, quite attractive colt, started second favourite behind Zind, who had finished a promising fourth to Armiger's stable-companion Dakar Rally in a similar event at Doncaster earlier in the month. Zind made the expected improvement, but he was powerless to stop Armiger's winning comfortably by three and a half lengths, with the remainder well strung out four lengths and more further behind. Keen and well beforehand, showing no signs of inexperience, Armiger soon held a good position close to the leaders, quickened immediately when shaken up with three furlongs to run, leading soon afterwards, and ran on with great strength and enthusiasm despite edging slightly off a true line. Significantly, Armiger recorded a timefigure of 107 at Newmarket, an exceptional figure for a newcomer.

There's little doubt that Armiger will be extremely well suited by a mile and a half. His sire Rainbow Quest built up an extremely impressive record over the distance, winning the Coronation Cup, Great Voltigeur Stakes and Arc (somewhat fortuitously on the disqualification of Sagace) and running into a place in the Irish Derby, Prix du Jockey-Club and King George. Rainbow Quest has sired plenty of good animals suited by a mile and a half or more, including the Irish Oaks winner Knight's Baroness, the Arc winner Saumarez and the Derby winner Quest For Fame, who, out of a mare by Green Dancer, is bred on similar lines to Armiger. Armiger's dam Armeria, whose first foal he is, was tried twice over a mile and a half but was eventually brought back to a mile and a quarter, a distance which suited her better and over which she showed fair form in winning a minor event at Windsor. Armeria's family has thrown up several good middle-distance stayers over the years, one of the more recent being her half-sister I Want To Be, who won the Park Hill Stakes and was placed in the Irish St Leger as well as the Prix Royal-Oak. Their dam Frontonian, placed in a minor ten-and-a-half-furlong race in France, is a daughter of the minor stakes winner and top-class broodmare Treasure Chest. Treasure Chest has produced numerous winners, among them Diomedia, a smart performer at up to nine furlongs in the States; Gold Treasure, a very useful winner at up to a mile; Kanz, a winner of two races

73

including the Princess Elizabeth Stakes and second in the Yorkshire Oaks; and Carefully Hidden, a winner of two races in the States. Diomedia and Carefully Hidden have since foaled the Earl of Sefton winner Media Starguest and the Irish One Thousand Guineas winner Enscombe; another of Treasure Chest's daughters, Crown Treasure, has produced the top-class middle-distance stayers Diamond Shoal and Glint of Gold.

		Blushing Groom	Red God
	Rainbow Quest (USA)	(ch 1974)	Runaway Bride
	(b 1981)	I Will Follow	Herbager
Armiger		(b 1975)	Where You Lead
(ch.c. Feb 15, 1990)		Northern Dancer	Nearctic
	Armeria (USA)	(b 1961)	Natalma
	(b 1985)	Frontonian	Buckpasser
		(b 1974)	Treasure Chest

According to his trainer, Armiger will always be best with some give underfoot. While often quite enlightening, especially from someone like Cecil, trainer's opinions tend to be repeated in the Press so regularly that they become accepted as fact long before they are established as fact. We've also seen it written that Rainbow Quest's progeny seem particularly well suited by an easy surface. While many of his offspring may well show their form when the ground is good or softer, it's equally clear that most of them don't have an established preference for such conditions. Armiger's extravagant, slightly round action, is one that is usually associated with a soft-ground performer, and time may indeed show him to be suited by some give in the ground. But there weren't many who would have suggested he needed it soft after his runaway win on the good to firm at Newmarket, and all that can usefully be said on the scanty racecourse evidence available is that his form on dead ground is much better than his form on good to firm. Here's to finding out more about Armiger in 1993. He looks a ready-made classic prospect, and except for his stable-companion and same owner's Tenby, whom he is most unlikely to encounter anyway, we honestly can't see at this stage what will beat him in the Derby. *H. R. A. Cecil*

ARMY OF STARS   7 b.h. Posse (USA) 130 – Starawak 68 (Star Appeal 133) [1991   **86** d
12.3s² 12g* 12s² 16g² 16.1m 16d 16.2g⁴ 11.9g⁴ 1992 a10g⁴ a12g² a12g³ 14.9v* 16d
12.5g 12d⁵ 14.6m⁵ 14s] tall, useful-looking horse: impresses good deal in
appearance: moderate mover: disappointing in handicaps after winning at Warwick
in March by 7 lengths: effective at 1½m to 2m: acts on any going: tried blinkered:
suitable mount for apprentice: usually races up with pace. *C. E. Brittain*

AROGANT FOOL   2 b.c. (Apr 19) Aragon 118 – Footstool 61 (Artaius (USA) 129)   **–**
[1992 5.3d 5.1d 6d 9g] 1,500Y: leggy colt: first foal: dam won 3 races at 1¼m at 6 yrs:
well beaten, including in sellers: bolted for girl apprentice before final start: sold
700 gns Ascot November Sales. *D. A. Wilson*

AROOM   2 gr.c. (Feb 7) Sharrood (USA) 124 – Babycham Sparkle 80 (So Blessed   **77** p
130) [1992 6s⁵ 6g³] 28,000Y: close-coupled, unfurnished colt: fourth foal: half-
brother to 6f winner Number Eleven (by Local Suitor): dam, 2-y-o 5f and 6f winner,
half-sister to smart French middle-distance colt El Famoso: still better for race
when always-prominent third of 20 to Serious in maiden at Newmarket in October:
should improve again. *C. J. Benstead*

ARRANVANNA   4 ch.f. Primo Dominie 121 – Smoke Creek 67 (Habitat 134)   **110**
[1991 8g² 8v* 8v³ 8g 8g⁶ 8g* 8v⁵ 8s 6v* 1992 6g² 5g 6g 5s* 6s²] big, lengthy filly:
very useful Italian performer: gained most notable success at 3 yrs in Italian 1000
Guineas at Rome: off course nearly 5 months at 4 yrs after falling on second start:
won Group 3 event at Milan in October by 3 lengths from Flowing: fair second in
Group 2 contest at Rome following month, 2½ lengths behind Swing Low: effective
from a testing 5f to 1m: acts on any going. *A. Renzoni, Italy*

ARRAS ROYALE   2 ch.c. (May 23) Arrasas (USA) – Sheer Class (Victor Hugo)   **53**
[1992 6d 7d 6g 6d⁵] workmanlike colt: has a round action: first reported foal: dam,
plater, stayed 9f: well beaten, including in a seller: visored final start. *J. E. Long*

ARRASTRA   4 b.f. Bustino 136 – Island Mill 79 (Mill Reef (USA) 141) [1991 10m²   **59**
10f⁴ 11.7m⁴ 13.1m² 14m* 14g³ 14m 14.6m 1992 14d 11.5f³ 14m 9d³ 12f⁵ 12f 10s
12g⁵] smallish, rather sparely-made filly: has quick action: none too consistent
handicapper: stays 1¾m: acts on firm and dead going: sold to join R. Lee 7,000 gns
Newmarket Autumn Sales. *I. A. Balding*

ARRIKALA (IRE)   3 br.f. Darshaan 133 – Alruccaba 83 (Crystal Palace **113** (FR) 132) [1991 8m* 7d⁵ 9d² 8m* 7d⁵ 9d² 1992 9s² 10v* 12g³ 11s 12f⁶ 14m* 12g³ 12s⁵ 14s⁶ 12d² 10g³]

Arrikala was some way removed from the top filly of 1992, but one would not have known it entering the straight in the Irish Oaks where she made smooth headway from the rear; not at the two-furlong marker where she was travelling strongly on the heels of the leaders; and not at the winning post where Arrikala was still under restraint on the rails trying to nose through a gap that wasn't there. She was beaten only about three quarters of a length into third behind User Friendly. One has to conclude that Arrikala was unlucky, although the need to hold her up as long as possible, which connections stressed afterwards, was clearly a contributory factor in jockey Kevin Manning's opting for the inside. Victory in the Irish Oaks would have transformed Arrikala's record. Finishing third in the race stands out as it is. She won a Leopardstown maiden as a two-year-old and added a handicap and listed race at the Curragh, but the only form that can be compared with that Irish Oaks run is her half-length second to Andros Bay in the Blandford Stakes at the same course in October. On this occasion Arrikala raced on the outside most of the way up the straight!

		Shirley Heights (b 1975)	Mill Reef Hardiemma
	Darshaan (br 1981)		
		Delsy (b or br 1972)	Abdos Kelty
Arrikala (IRE) (br.f. 1989)		Crystal Palace (gr 1974)	Caro Hermieres
	Alruccaba (gr 1983)		
		Allara (gr 1973)	Zeddaan Nucciolina

D. H. W. Dobson's "Arrikala"

Arrikala's dam Alruccaba had far less chance to prove her merit, running four times for Michael Stoute and winning a six-furlong maiden at Brighton before being let go by the Aga Khan for 19,000 guineas at the December Sales on the close of her two-year-old season. Her dam Allara was lightly raced as well, the winner of a seven-furlong maiden in the French Provinces at three years, but she was a half-sister to the dams of Aliysa and Nishapour. Prior to Arrikala, Alruccaba produced two foals by Niniski in the one-and-a-half-mile Southwell winner Allegra and four-year-old maiden Ballymac Girl. Since Arrikala, there has been her sister Alouette, who got off the mark at the fourth attempt in a one-mile maiden at Leopardstown in October, also for Jim Bolger, and a colt by Slip Anchor who was purchased by Darley Stud Management for 65,000 guineas at Goffs in the same month. Arrikala herself fetched 29,000 at the Highflyer. A workmanlike filly, she has shown useful form in winning over one and three quarter miles but her best is at one and a half. She was well below form on firm ground in the Ribblesdale Stakes but probably acts on any other. *J. S. Bolger, Ireland*

ARROCHAR 2 b.f. (May 7) Belfort (FR) 89 – Arachova 71 (High Line 125) [1992 5f a7g] 1,000Y: leggy, unfurnished filly: third reported foal: dam won at 1½m at 4 yrs: well beaten in sellers. *J. G. FitzGerald* –

ARROGANT DAUGHTER 3 b.f. Aragon 118 – Sea Aura 89 (Roi Soleil 125) [1991 NR 1992 8g a7g3] 7,800Y: sixth foal: half-sister to 2-y-o 6f winners Caspian Grey (by Absalom) and Koracle Bay (by Kind of Hush) and to a winner in Norway by Song: dam probably best at 7f: poor form in first half of 1992: stays 7f. *J. W. Payne* –

ARROW DANCER 6 b.g. Gorytus (USA) 132 – Rose And Honey (Amber Rama (USA) 133) [1991 NR 1992 11.1v 13d 8.3g 8s5] lengthy gelding: poor maiden on flat: stays 1m: acts on good to firm and soft going: tried blinkered: won selling hurdle in September. *J. J. O'Neill* –

ARSAAD (USA) 3 ch.f. Topsider (USA) – Bar J Gal (USA) (Key To The Mint (USA)) [1991 6m 8g2 8.9d5 1992 10.2s 10f 10d6] small, quite attractive filly: moderate mover: soundly beaten in handicaps in first half of 1992, tried visored final run: stays 8.9f: acts on dead ground: sold 1,100 gns Newmarket July Sales. *P. T. Walwyn* –

ART CRITIC (IRE) 3 b.c. Tate Gallery (USA) 117 – Point of View (FR) (Sharpman 124) [1991 6m 8.1m6 1992 7g 11.8g 10.3m] smallish, good-bodied colt: poor maiden: should have stayed 1¼m: dead. *M. J. Heaton-Ellis* –

ART FORM (USA) 5 b.g. Little Current (USA) – Christi Dawn (USA) (Grey Dawn II 132) [1991 a14g* 16g a12g* 12g* 14.1f* 16.5m5 14.1g5 18.8f* a16g* 20g5 16m4 16.1m* 14m 17.2g 16m3 18m a16g3 a12g a14g* 1992 a16g 16m* 14.1g] tall, angular gelding: has a round action: grand handicapper: won at Goodwood in May: not seen out again after running poorly following month: effective at 1¾m to 2½m: seems to need a sound surface on turf and goes well on all-weather surfaces. *C. A. Cyzer* 80

ARTIC TRACKER (USA) 3 b.c. Eskimo (USA) – Andy's Find (USA) (Buckfinder (USA)) [1991 7g* 7g* 7.1m3 7m3 1992 7g4 8g 10.4f5 10m3 10m 6d] smallish, sturdy colt: good mover: useful performer: easily best efforts as 3-y-o when in frame in European Free Handicap at Newmarket and Kempton listed event: stays 1¼m: acts on good to firm ground: below form when blinkered once: sold 44,000 gns Newmarket Autumn Sales. *C. R. Nelson* 101

ARTISTIC REEF 3 ch.c. Claude Monet (USA) 121 – Kellys Reef 92 (Pitskelly 122) [1991 5m 5g** 5g3 1992 5.1g2 5m3 5.2g2 5m3 5d*] strong, workmanlike colt: moderate mover: useful performer: best efforts when third in King George Stakes (narrowly beaten by Freddie Lloyd) at Goodwood and Newmarket listed race: straightforward task in Haydock minor event in October: very speedy: hung left final 2 starts. *G. H. Eden* 106

ARUSHA (IRE) 2 b.f. (Apr 14) Dance of Life (USA) – African Doll (African Sky 124) [1992 8s*] 15,000Y: leggy, unfurnished filly: half-sister to several winners, notably 2000 Guineas winner Don't Forget Me (by Ahonoora): dam Irish 1½m winner: 25/1, ½-length winner of 8-runner Newbury minor event in October, steadied rear after slow start then finishing really strongly to collar Andromaque close home: sure to improve. *D. R. C. Elsworth* 84 p

ASAASY (USA) 3 b. or br.c. Danzig (USA) – Carduel (USA) (Buckpasser) [1991 7g6 1992 8s* 8.1d4 8.9g2 10f2 8m] strong, close-coupled colt: moderate mover: 96

useful performer: won Ripon maiden in April: not seen again after running poorly in Britannia Handicap at Royal Ascot: stays 1¼m well: acts on any going. *M. R. Stoute*

AS ALWAYS (IRE) 4 ch.f. Hatim (USA) 121 – Red Magic (Red God 128§) [1991 10g 8f 10m 13.1f⁵ 14g² 16.2f* 18.5g² 16g³ 15.4f 16m⁶ 1992 11.9m 12g 16.9g 16.1m⁵ a16g⁶] good-topped filly: easy mover: well below best in handicaps in 1992: stays 2¼m: acts on firm going: tried blinkered: trained until after penultimate start by G. Lewis. *D. T. Thom* –

ASCOM PAGER (IRE) 2 b.f. (May 7) Colmore Row 111 – Milveagh 92 (Milesian 125) [1992 5m 5d] 10,000Y: half-sister to numerous winners, including (at 6f as a 2-y-o in 1987) useful Madam de Seul (by Pas de Seul) and (at 5f) Coming About (by Right Tack): dam won at up to 1m: nearly fell at halfway in Sandown maiden: last of 19 in similar event at Lingfield over 3 months later: joined P. Howling. *G. Lewis* –

ASCOM PAGER TOO 2 b.f. (Feb 2) Kings Lake (USA) 133 – Intoxication 73 (Great Nephew 126) [1992 6m 6.1m 6.1m 6m 6m⁴ 7d 7m³ 7s⁴ 7d a8g] 5,200Y: smallish, lengthy filly: third foal: half-sister to 14.6f winner Innerglow and middle-distance maiden Inkala (both by Kalaglow): dam stayed 1½m, is daughter of Princess Royal winner Shebeen: plating-class maiden: will stay well: acts on good to firm ground, ran poorly on equitrack. *P. Howling* **55**

A SECRET WEAPON (USA) 2 b.c. (Feb 17) Pass The Line (USA) – Who Am I (USA) (Old Bag) [1992 6g⁵ 6d²] close-coupled colt: first foal in North America: dam won in USA before export to Columbia: sire very smart 1m to 1¼m performer: much improved effort in autumn when strong-finishing second of 19 to Vayavaig in maiden at Haydock: should improve again, particularly over further. *J. M. P. Eustace* **58** p

ASEMA (USA) 2 b.f. (Feb 17) Theatrical 128 – Lady of The Light (USA) (The Minstrel (CAN) 135) [1992 6m* 7g² 8d* 7s*] $37,000Y: second reported foal: dam unraced close relative of top-class filly Sabin and half-sister to Fatah Flare, an excellent family: progressive filly: successful in maiden at Gowran Park in June and Meadow Meats EBF Killavullan Stakes (by 2 lengths from Alouette) at Leopardstown and C L Weld Park Stakes (by 1½ lengths from Miami Sands) at the Curragh in September: withdrawn from Moyglare Stud Stakes at the Curragh earlier in September after bolting to start: suited by a test of stamina: acts on good to firm and soft ground. *D. K. Weld, Ireland* **93** p

AS GOOD AS GOLD 6 ch.g. Oats 126 – Goldyke 63 (Bustino 136) [1991 12.1d⁴ 1992 12.1s] robust, workmanlike gelding: poor maiden: should stay well. *T. M. Jones*

ASHDREN 5 b.h. Lochnager 132 – Stellaris (Star Appeal 133) [1991 6s² 7m 7m⁶ 6g⁶ 7g³ 5m 6g* 6d³ 6g 6m 6f⁵ 6m⁶ 7m 8.1s² 1992 8g⁴ 8s⁴ 8g 7g² 7m 7.9m 6d 6s³ 7d 7d] angular horse: good walker: moderate mover: largely consistent handicapper: effective at 6f to 1m: probably acts on any going: effective visored or not: swishes tail. *A. Harrison* **83**

ASHGORE 2 b.c. (Jan 31) Efisio 120 – Fair Atlanta 73 (Tachypous 128) [1992 6s 6s⁵ 5v³] 4,800F: good-topped colt: has scope: second foal: dam 10.2f winner: best **60**

C. L. Weld EBF Park Stakes, the Curragh—the progressive Asema (second left) stays on strongly

Bovis Handicap, Ascot—rejuvenated Ashtina is an emphatic winner

effort when third in Redcar maiden in October: should prove as effective at 6f+ as 5f. *M. Johnston*

ASHGROVE PLUM 2 b.f. (May 8) Smackover 107 – Aldington Cherry (Legal **31** Eagle 126) [1992 a6g a6g] fifth foal: dam never ran: no form in claimer and maiden at Southwell late in year. *B. A. McMahon*

ASHOVER 2 gr.c. (Mar 14) Petong 126 – Shiny Kay 65 (Star Appeal 133) [1992 **53** 6m² 6g 7g] 13,500Y: compact colt: second foal: half-brother to 1991 2-y-o 6f and 1m winner Lady Linnet (by Nomination): dam 1½m winner, is half-sister to K Battery: second of 3 in maiden at Newcastle in July, best effort. *T. D. Barron*

ASHTINA 7 b.g. Tina's Pet 121 – Mrewa (Runnymede 123) [1991 5f⁵ 5.8d 6v* 6g⁵ **96** 5d⁵ 5d 1992 5g 6g⁶ 5m⁴ 5g³ 5f 5.1m⁵ 6d⁵ 5g 5m 5m³ 5d⁴* 5.1s³ 5d² 5m* 5g* 5m 5g] leggy, good-topped gelding: had excellent season in 1992, successful in autumn handicaps at Epsom, Newmarket and Ascot (£16,700 race): ran very well in Newmarket listed race penultimate run: effective at 5f to 6f: acts on good to firm and heavy ground and equitrack: usually forces pace. *R. J. Hodges*

ASIAN PUNTER (IRE) 3 ch.g. M Double M (USA) – Centenary Year **70** (Malinowski (USA) 123) [1991 6f² 7m 1992 10f⁶ 11.4d² 12.3f* 12g⁴ 12g 14m⁶ 12g⁵] sturdy gelding: consistent handicapper: won Ripon minor event in August: will prove best at up to 1¾m: acts on firm and dead going. *A. Hide*

ASPIRANT 4 b.g. High Top 131 – Yen (AUS) (Biscay (AUS)) [1991 NR 1992 7f **–** 10.2f 9.7g] second known foal: dam maiden, raced in Australia: no worthwhile form, including in seller. *K. G. Wingrove*

ASSESSOR (IRE) 3 b.c. Niniski (USA) 125 – Dingle Bay (Petingo 135) **118** [1991 7s* 7f³ 8.1m² 7d* 8g³ 1992 10g³ 11.5s* 12g 11.9g³ 14.6m⁶ 15s³ 15.5s*]
Assessor failed to make up into so good a horse as he'd promised when winning the Lingfield Derby Trial by seven lengths, but with conditions in his favour he is a much better one than he showed in either the Derby or St Leger. His win in the Prix Royal-Oak at Longchamp in typical back-end conditions confirmed him essentially a soft-ground stayer. Up to Epsom, Assessor's record was one of steady improvement and included a creditable third place behind Seattle Rhyme in the Racing Post Trophy on his final start as a two-year-old. The improvement at Lingfield coincided with an appreciably stiffer test of stamina. Assessor ran as though he needed it, for he had to be scrubbed along virtually from the start in a seven-runner race and made no significant headway until approaching the straight. From then on, the further they went the more impressive he became; he took the lead two and a half furlongs out, soon got well on top and proceeded to win easing up from the Newbury maiden winner Tapis Rouge who wasn't entered in the Derby. In retrospect, it wasn't a strong classic trial; the third horse Bonny Scot would have been a much tougher proposition later on in the season. However, at the

78

Maxims Club Derby Trial Stakes, Lingfield—Assessor gets well on top in the end

time Assessor's Derby prospects looked as bright as most, and he started among the favourites at 9/1. His supporters must have been bitterly disappointed with his performance, as well as puzzled by it. Hampered on two separate occasions early on, he dropped out after a furlong and seemed reluctant to pick up his bit. He was last going into Tattenham Corner, second last out of it and ran by just a few stragglers in the straight.

Assessor's respectable third to Bonny Scot in the Great Voltigeur Stakes at York in August on his next start raised hopes of a better run in the St Leger, but he again never travelled with any fluency and finished well beaten. He went more sweetly (bandaged in front) on soft going in the Ciga Prix du Lutece on Arc weekend, but the form didn't look good enough to give him a major chance in the Prix Royal-Oak even though he was meeting the two that beat him, Dadarissime and Jamshid, on better terms. Sought Out, who'd beaten Drum Taps by four lengths in the Prix du Cadran on the same card as the Lutece, started at odds on while Assessor was a near-43/1 outsider. He and the other challengers from British and Irish stables—Allegan and Balnibarbi (19/4 coupled), Witness Box (9/1), Always Friendly (15/1) and Ivyanna (37/1)—made up half the field. The race proved such a severe test of stamina that the runners finished strung out like washing behind second-home Always Friendly, with a below-par Sought Out six lengths adrift in third,

Prix Royal-Oak, Longchamp—distance and ground suit Assessor;
Always Friendly comes second

eight lengths clear of the rest. The first three could be named a long way out. Unlike Sought Out, neither Assessor nor Always Friendly figured among the early leaders, but after a mile and a quarter both had begun to improve significantly and on straightening for home they occupied the first two places, Always Friendly in front. Quinn had blamed himself for going too soon on Assessor in the Lutece. On this occasion he made the challenge halfway up the straight; Assessor responded to lead over a furlong out and ran on under firm driving to stay two and a half lengths up.

Assessor (IRE) (b.c. 1989)	Niniski (USA) (b 1976)	Nijinsky (b 1967)	Northern Dancer / Flaming Page
		Virginia Hills (b 1971)	Tom Rolfe / Ridin' Easy
	Dingle Bay (b 1976)	Petingo (b 1965)	Petition / Alcazar
		Border Bounty (b 1965)	Bounteous / B Flat

Assessor's sire Niniski won the Prix Royal-Oak in very similar conditions in 1979. He failed in a repeat bid the following year having had some success over shorter distances in between, notably on firm going in the John Porter Stakes. We shouldn't imagine that Assessor will be doing much racing at a mile and a half, and certainly not on firm ground, in future. He could develop into a Cup horse, though, if he continues to race as kindly as he did in the Royal-Oak. Looking at the Calendar, an obvious early opportunity presents itself in Italy, in the Coppa d'Oro di Milano, a race won in the latest season by Drum Taps on his way to Royal Ascot. Assessor, physically a useful sort with a fluent action, cost IR 50,000 guineas as a yearling. His maternal grandam Border Bounty is a well-known mare. Bred to stay all day, she won four races at up to a mile and a half and finished second in the Yorkshire Oaks and Park Hill Stakes. Her eight winning produce include three by Petingo—the high-class miler Pitcairn, the stayer Valley Forge, who ran his best race when third in the Irish St Leger, and Assessor's dam Dingle Bay—as well as Eljazzi, the dam of the 1990 Prix de Diane winner Rafha. Dingle Bay was successful over a mile and a mile and a quarter at Navan. She made a slow start at stud before producing the quite useful Irish filly Walliser, Assessor's sister and immediate predecessor, who seemed best at up to a mile and a quarter. Dingle Bay's foal of 1990, a filly by King of Clubs called Bay of Storms, has yet to race. *R. Hannon*

ASSIGNMENT 6 b.h. Known Fact (USA) 135 – Sanctuary (Welsh Pageant 132) **80**
[1991 a7g2 a5g* a7g3 a6g* 6s 6g 7.6m 6g 6f3 6f3 6m6 8d 6m2 a7g a6g3 a6g3 1992 a6g3 a8g6 a6g5 6d2 6g3 5.7g 6f a6g2 6d4 6g* 6d3 6d 6m] strong, deep-girthed horse: fair handicapper: won £15,530 event at Goodwood in September: suited by 6f: acts on firm and dead ground and equitrack. *J. Ffitch-Heyes*

ASTERIX 4 ch.g. Prince Sabo 123 – Gentle Gael 97 (Celtic Ash) [1991 8s4 8g 7d **56**
8m 6g3 8.3m 6f5 7g* 7.6m 7.6g 1992 a6g5 6d 8.9g 9g 8.1m 7.1m3 7d6 7g 8f 7g] smallish, lengthy gelding: moderate mover: seems on the downgrade: effective at 6f to 1m: has form on any going: often visored. *J. M. Bradley*

ASTRAC TRIO (USA) 2 ro.c. (May 7) Timeless Moment (USA) – Fairway Flag **73**
(USA) (Fairway Phantom (USA)) [1992 6g a6g* 7g 7d 7g] $10,000F, $9,000Y: big, lengthy colt: second foal: half-brother to American 3-y-o Post The Colors (by Air Forbes Won): dam 2-y-o sprint winner: sire (by Damascus) very smart at up to 1m: well beaten in nurseries after winning Southwell maiden in July: should stay 1m: visored final start. *S. G. Norton*

ASTROID 2 b.f. (Feb 14) Sayf El Arab (USA) 127 – Priors Dean 61 (Monsanto **–**
(FR) 121) [1992 6m 6m] good-bodied filly: fifth foal: half-sister to a winner abroad: dam ran only at 2 yrs, when best at 6f: tailed off from halfway in Newbury maiden in May. *W. R. Muir*

ASWAMEDH 4 ro.c. Ore 116 – Asmalwi 61 (Averof 123) [1991 12m 16g4 16.2s3 **60**
16.9g2 15.9d 1992 16.2d* 20m] big, good-bodied colt: shows knee action: won amateurs handicap at Haydock in May: not seen again after running moderately in June: stays 2m: acts on soft going: sold 1,150 gns Doncaster October Sales. *P. J. Hobbs*

ATALL ATALL 9 b.h. Kampala 120 – Bint Africa 71 (African Sky 124) [1991 6m* **–**
6m2 7m5 1992 6d] rather leggy, attractive horse: not a good walker or mover: rated

74 at 8 yrs: last in handicap in September, only run in 1992: stays 6f: acts on any going: tailed off when blinkered. *G. M. Moore*

ATAN'S GEM (USA) 3 ch.f. Sharpen Up 127 – Fidelity (USA) (Sir Ivor 135) [1991 NR 1992 7f 10.3g⁶ 9.9m 13.8d] close-coupled filly: has a markedly round action: third reported foal: closely related to Irish 1¼m winner Wicked Smile (by Kris): dam winner at about 1¼m in USA: no worthwhile form. *J. Norton* –

ATHAR (IRE) 3 b.f. Master Willie 129 – Walladah (USA) 71 (Northern Dancer (CAN)) [1991 7m 1992 8d 12s⁵ 10f 10m 9.7h⁴ 8f 8f⁴ 12d 12.1s* 10.2s² 12s⁴ 10.2d] leggy, workmanlike filly: moderate mover: modest handicapper: won Chepstow apprentice event in August: ran very well next 2 outings: effective at 1¼m to 1½m: suited by soft going: sold out of P. Walwyn's stable 1,000 gns Newmarket July Sales after fifth start. *R. J. Baker* 67

ATHCLARE (IRE) 4 ch.c. Glow (USA) – Athry (Be Friendly 130) [1991 6v⁴ 9v⁴ 7d⁵ 9d² 8.5g⁵ 10g⁴ 13m³ 12m 10g⁶ a10g³ 1992 a11g⁵] poor ex-Irish colt: sold only 625 gns Ascot March Sales after only run in 1992: probably stayed 13f: acted on good to firm ground and heavy: tried blinkered: dead. *J. Akehurst* –

ATHENE NOCTUA 7 b.m. Aragon 118 – Lady Lorelei 105 (Derring-Do 131) [1991 10.2s 1992 10.5m 9.9g 12s³ 11.8g⁶] leggy, light-framed mare: poor mover: poor handicapper nowadays: stays 1½m: acts on any going: has joined R. Hollinshead. *B. A. McMahon* 32

ATHENS BELLE (IRE) 2 b.f. (Jan 29) Groom Dancer (USA) 128 – Greektown (Ela-Mana-Mou 132) [1992 7g*] leggy, attractive filly: first foal: dam French 1¼m and 1½m winner: weak 8/1-shot, impressive winner of 19-runner minor event at Kempton in September, good progress 2f out and running on really well to beat Society Lady by ¾ length, pair clear: moved well to post: sure to leave that form well behind, particularly when tried over further. *R. Charlton* 77 p

ATHERTON GREEN (IRE) 2 ch.c. (May 8) Shy Groom (USA) – Primacara 58 (Rusticaro (FR) 124) [1992 6d 6g* 6f³ 7.5d⁵ 8m³ 8f 8.2d] small, close-coupled colt: first foal: dam, half-sister to smart 7f to 1¼m performer Trucidator, stayed 1¼m: sire won from 6f to 9f: inconsistent performer: won Pontefract maiden auction in June: best form at 1m: acts on good to firm and dead ground. *J. A. Glover* 70

ATLANTIC SUNSET (IRE) 2 ch.g. (Feb 18) Red Sunset 120 – Restless Lady (Sandford Lad 133) [1992 6f 5m³ 6f²] 10,500F, 15,000Y: strong gelding: half-brother to 3 winners, including fairly useful Catherines Well (by Junius): dam showed little form: plating-class maiden: dead. *M. W. Easterby* 54

ATLANTIC WAY 4 gr.f. Bold Owl 101 – Overseas 48 (Sea Hawk II 131) [1991 10.2d 8m 12.3m⁶ 10.2g 10m 1992 a14g a12g* 12d³ a12g³ 10s² 11.9g* 12d³ 11.9d 11.8d a12g a12g² a16g³] leggy filly: has a round action: inconsistent handicapper: successful at Southwell and Brighton in summer: stays 1½m: acts on soft ground and fibresand: has been mulish to post and looked temperamental. *C. J. Hill* 47

A-TO-Z (IRE) 3 b.f. Ahonoora 122 – Zenga (Try My Best (USA) 130) [1991 6m* 5g⁴ 6m⁵ 6g⁵ 6.3s 1992 7m* 8g⁶ 8g⁴] big, good-topped filly: hobdayed late in 1991 101

Shadwell Stud Nell Gwyn Stakes, Newmarket—
A-To-Z comes from behind to beat Perfect Circle (rails)

and much improved in spring as 3-y-o: ¾-length winner of Nell Gwyn Stakes at Newmarket and not discredited in English and Irish (beaten 2¾ lengths by Marling) 1000 Guineas: reportedly cracked near-fore pastern, and not seen again: stays 1m: acts on good to firm ground: held up. *M. Bell*

AT PEACE 6 b.g. Habitat 134 – Peace 113 (Klairon 131) [1991 a7g a8g⁵ 10.8m 8d 10g 9.2d² 8g² 8.3g 1992 9.2d 10.2f⁶] robust gelding: carries plenty of condition: no show in handicaps in 1992: stays 9f: best form on an easy surface: below form when visored once. *J. White* –

ATTADALE 4 b.g. Ardross 134 – Marypark 93 (Charlottown 127) [1991 10g 12m⁵ 14.1g⁶ 16.1m* 16.1g⁵ 17.9f⁴ 16m³ 16.1g³ 1992 15.1m³ 15.1m² 16.2d⁴ 15m⁴ 17.5d² 16.1g³] rangy, good-topped gelding: has a round action: consistent staying handicapper: acts on firm and dead going. *L. Lungo* **61**

ATTIC WIT (FR) 6 b.g. Shirley Heights 130 – Laughing Matter 56 (Lochnager 132) [1991 NR 1992 12.3g 8fa14g] stocky, well-made gelding: first foal: dam sprinter: no form in 1992. *R. J. Holder* –

AUCTION KING (IRE) 3 b.g. Auction Ring (USA) 123 – Brigadina (Brigadier Gerard 144) [1991 5d³ 5g³ 5g² 5f² 5m⁶ 5f⁴ 5m⁵ 5f² 7g⁶ 5d 5m² 5g⁴ 5d 1992 5v⁶ 5g² 6m⁵ 5f³ 5g⁵ 5s² 6g 7m² 7f³ 7g⁴ 10.3m a8g*] workmanlike gelding: consistent handicapper: won Southwell maiden in September: effective at 7f to 1m: acts on fibresand and any turf going, except possibly heavy: ran moderately in blinkers. *A. Smith* **59**

AUDE LA BELLE (FR) 4 ch.f. Ela-Mana-Mou 132 – Arjona (GER) (Caracol (FR)) [1991 10f³ 10f⁶ 8g⁵ 10g³ 10g 10m 1992 a12g⁵ a12g³ a13g² a14g* a16g* a16g³ a14g⁴ 14d* 16.2m* 16m* 16.2g⁴ 15.9m² 18f⁴ 16.2s 16.2d³ 18m] small, light-framed filly: has a quick action: had really good season in handicaps, successful at Southwell, Lingfield, Sandown, Beverley and Kempton (gamely in £10,950 event): effective at 1¾m to 2¼m: acts on firm and dead ground and all-weather surfaces: below form when sweating once: held up: a credit to her trainer. *Mrs A. Knight* **81**

AUGHFAD 6 b.h. Millfontaine 114 – Saulonika 94 (Saulingo 122) [1991 6s 5g 5m⁶ 5m 6d 5g* 6m* 5f⁴ 6d* 5d* 5m⁶ 5.2g 6g 6g³ 6m 5d 5d 5.2g 5g 1992 5.2d 5g 6f 5m⁴ 6g* 6g 6f 6d⁴ 5g* 5.2d* 6m 6d 6g 5g 5.2s] strong, workmanlike horse: poor mover: won handicaps at Goodwood, Newmarket and Newbury in first half of 1992: lost his form completely after: effective at 5f and 6f: acts on hard and dead ground: effective visored or not: has won for apprentice. *T. Casey* **95** d

AUNTIE CHRIS 2 ch.f. (Apr 25) Bold Owl 101 – Basin Street (Tudor Melody 129) [1992 6m 7d] 1,600Y: close-coupled filly: sister to 8.2f (at 2 yrs) to 15.3f winner Bold Street Blues and half-sister to several winners: dam bad maiden: soundly beaten in modest company: sold to join J. Allen 1,200 gns Doncaster October Sales. *A. W. Potts* –

AUNTIE GINGER 2 ch.f. (Apr 19) Blushing Scribe (USA) 107 – Soho 63 (Camden Town 125) [1992 5d² 5m 6g⁵ 5g] 400Y: angular filly: fifth foal: dam lightly raced: well beaten after second in Kempton maiden auction in April: should stay 6f. *P. Butler* **49**

AUNTIE LORNA 3 b.f. Uncle Pokey 116 – Bronze Tango (Bronze Hill 96) [1991 NR 1992 8m] leggy filly: first reported foal: dam of little account in 4 races over jumps: well beaten in Ripon maiden claimer in May, only run. *Mrs P. A. Barker* –

AURORA LAD 5 ch.h. Free State 125 – Hawthorne Vale (Richboy 117) [1991 NR 1992 7.5m a14g] close-coupled, angular horse: first foal: dam bad plater at 2 yrs: twice raced and no sign of ability. *Mrs S. J. Smith* –

AUSSIE AISLE (IRE) 4 gr.f. Godswalk (USA) 130 – Scoby Lass (Prominer 125) [1991 7v 7v 10m 10m 9g 10g* 8g 10s 1992 10.1s 7.1g 12f] sturdy, plain filly: has round action: half-sister to 6-y-o sprint handicapper Barrys Gamble and Irish 1m winner Productivity (both by Nishapour) and 2 other winners abroad: dam never ran: ex-Irish handicapper, successful at Down Royal as 3-y-o for E. O'Grady: no show on flat here in spring at 4 yrs, visored in seller final start: stays 1¼m: best effort on good ground: sold 1,400 gns Doncaster June Sales. *D. Moffatt* –

AUSTRAL JANE 2 b.f. (Apr 14) Dominion 123 – Dabbiana (CAN) (Fappiano (USA)) [1992 7d 7.1s² 7s²] strong, good-bodied filly: has scope: third foal: half-sister to 1990 2-y-o 7f winner Alton Bay (by Al Nasr): dam winner at around 7f in USA: easily best effort in maidens on second start when runner-up at Chepstow: will stay 1m. *G. Harwood* **74**

AUVILLAR (USA) 4 br.g. Temperence Hill (USA) – Exquisita (USA) (Cougar (CHI)) [1991 8.2d 8h⁵ 12g² a11g* a12g* 1992 12.3v a12g] compact gelding: has a –

roundish action: rated 58 at 3 yrs: no form on flat in 1992, though won claiming hurdle in between: stays 1½m: acts on fibresand, best turf effort on good ground: often visored: ran well when blinkered once. *D. Burchell*

AVIATOR'S DREAM 2 b.g. (Mar 26) Valiyar 129 – Maputo Princess (Raga Navarro (ITY) 119) [1992 6.1d⁵ 6d⁴ 7.5m 7s 7m] 1,200Y: robust gelding: sixth foal: half-brother to 1989 2-y-o 6f winner Qualitair Dream (by Dreams To Reality): dam maiden: plating-class maiden: probably stays 7.5f: acts on dead ground: refused to enter stalls on intended debut. *J. F. Bottomley* **52**

AVICE CARO (USA) 3 gr.f. Caro 133 – Outstandingly (USA) (Exclusive Native (USA)) [1991 NR 1992 8g³ 8.5d³ 10f* 10f* 10g4 10m 10m] big, lengthy filly: second foal: dam won from 5.5f (at 2 yrs) to 9f, including Breeders' Cup Juvenile Fillies: successful at Brighton in July maiden and August handicap: below form in apprentice handicaps final 2 starts: better at 1¼m than shorter: acted on firm ground: visits Diesis. *J. H. M. Gosden* **85**

AVILA 3 b.f. Ajdal (USA) 130 – Sweet Habit (Habitat 134) [1991 NR 1992 7d³ 7g⁶] lengthy filly: half-sister to Chester Vase winner Nomrood and very useful 1m to 1¼m winners Alleging (both by Alleged) and Monastery (by General Assembly): dam unraced daughter of Prix de Diane winner Sweet Mimosa: promising third in Newbury newcomers race but not seen again after disappointing in Newmarket maiden later in April: visits Shirley Heights. *J. H. M. Gosden* **76**

AVISHAYES (USA) 5 b.g. Al Nasr (FR) 126 – Rose Goddess (Sassafras (FR) 135) [1991 10.2s 11s 8g⁵ 7m³ 8h* 8g* 8m⁶ 8m³ 9m* 10m4 10g³ 8.2f² 9.2f* 8m⁶ 1992 8g 9g] big, lengthy gelding: moderate mover: rated 60 at 4 yrs: no form in 1992: effective at 1m to 1¼m: acts on hard ground: blinkered early in career: best efforts with waiting tactics. *M. D. Hammond* **–**

AVRIL ETOILE 2 ch.f. (Apr 1) Sharpo 132 – Alsiba 68 (Northfields (USA)) [1992 5.1m 5f³ 5g 5g³ 6s⁵] leggy, good-topped filly: moderate mover: third foal: half-sister to fairly useful 1¼m and 1½m winner Smart Blade (by Elegant Air): dam staying daughter of half-sister to Irish 2000 Guineas winner Northern Treasure: modest maiden: stays 6f: probably acts on any going. *L. J. Holt* **60**

AVRO ANSON 4 b.g. Ardross 134 – Tremellick 87 (Mummy's Pet 125) [1991 8d 10f 10.2g 1992 14.1d* 16.2m² 16d*] big, workmanlike gelding: progressive staying handicapper: successful at Nottingham in April and Redcar in October: will stay beyond 2m: acts on good to firm and dead ground: also on the upgrade over hurdles, winner twice later in the autumn. *M. J. Camacho* **61 p**

AWESOME POWER 6 b.g. Vision (USA) – Majestic Nurse 80 (On Your Mark 125) [1991 9m 7g 6m 8m 8.5g² 9m4 7g4 9m⁵ 7.5g a6g4 a8g a7g⁶ 1992 a8g² a8g² a10g² a10g* a10g² a10g² 9d a10g³ 10s a10g* a10g² a10g* a10g²] ex-Irish handicapper: goes really well on equitrack and won at Lingfield in February (amateurs), October (when still with C. Nelson) and, by 5 lengths in a claimer, November: likely to stay 1½m: acts on firm ground and all-weather surfaces, seemingly not a soft surface: below form when blinkered. *J. W. Hills* **–** a81

AWESOME RISK 2 b.f. (Mar 27) Risk Me (FR) 127 – Gemma Kaye 91 (Cure The Blues (USA)) [1992 5.3d³ 5.1d³ 6g⁵ 6m a7g³ a6g³ 6m* 7g³ 6.1m³ 7.1s³ 8.5d 8s 6d*] 3,400Y: lengthy, sparely-made filly: third foal: sister to 3-y-o Andy Jack: dam, lightly-raced maiden, best effort at 7f at 2 yrs, is half-sister to Irish Oaks winner Olwyn: modest performer: won seller at Lingfield (no bid) in July and claimer at Leicester in October: sold 4,400 gns Newmarket Autumn Sales: seems suited by 6f: acts on good to firm and soft ground, and on all-weather surfaces. *G. Lewis* **58**

AWESOME VENTURE 2 b.c. (Mar 20) Formidable (USA) 125 – Pine Ridge 80 (High Top 131) [1992 7g] 64,000Y: sixth foal: half-brother to several winners, notably In The Groove (by Night Shift), Group 1 winner from 1m to 1½m, and fairly useful miler Spanish Pine (by King of Spain): dam 1½m winner: 10/1 and in need of race, around 11 lengths eleventh of 18, slowly away, progress into mid-division halfway, no nearer, to Azilian in maiden at Doncaster in November: will improve. *B. J. McMath* **44 p**

AWESTRUCK 2 b.c. (Feb 13) Primo Dominie 121 – Magic Kingdom 76 (Kings Lake (USA) 133) [1992 5m⁶ 6f* 7g³ 7d* 7m² 7g 7.6v] sturdy, useful-looking colt: first foal: dam, second over 1m on all 3 starts, is daughter of very useful French middle-distance performer Darine: successful in Epsom maiden and Yarmouth nursery (made all) in summer: below form last 2 starts: best form at 7f: acts on firm and dead ground, well beaten on heavy. *W. J. Haggas* **68**

AWOL 3 b.f. Slip Anchor 136 – Strigida 120 (Habitat 134) [1991 NR 1992 12s³ 12f* 12f³ 14g²] angular, rather sparely-made filly: fifth foal: sister to 1½m winner Owler **79**

and half-sister to a winner in Hungary by Nureyev: dam, grandam and great grandam all won Ribblesdale Stakes: won Thirsk maiden and ran well after, second in Sandown handicap in July: will be suited by further: probably acts on any going: sold 9,000 gns Newmarket December Sales. *H. R. A. Cecil*

AY BEAT   3 ch.g. Bairn (USA) 126 – Thorny Rose 81 (Tap On Wood 130) [1991 5g⁴   – §
7.1s 6.9f 1992 10s] compact gelding: no worthwhile form: blinkered once: probably ungenuine. *E. A. Wheeler*

AYR RAIDER   5 ch.g. Claude Monet (USA) 121 – Thimothea (FR) (Timmy My   69
Boy 125) [1991 8m 8m⁶ 8s⁵ 5g* 6d 5d³ 5m³ 6f⁵ 5f 5g⁴ 5m⁵ 5m* 5m 5m 1992 5f⁵ 5m⁴
5m³ 6.1d² 6.1g² 5.6m 6d⁵ 6m³ 6s 6.1d⁵ a7g a7g] strong, workmanlike gelding: modest handicapper: effective from 5f to 7f: acts on firm and dead ground: effective with or without blinkers: below form when visored: rather inconsistent. *W. R. Muir*

AZHAR   2 b.c. (Apr 7) Night Shift (USA) – Aunt Jemima (Busted 134) [1992 6m*   88
7d² 7m 7m] 140,000Y: compact, useful-looking colt with scope: third foal: dam unraced: easily landed odds in 3-runner maiden at Newcastle and good second of 3 at Salisbury in summer: off course almost 2 months and below form after: will stay 1m: slowly away first 3 starts. *M. R. Stoute*

AZILIAN (IRE)   2 b. or br.c. (Mar 15) Top Ville 129 – D'Azy 91 (Persian Bold   72 p
123) [1992 7g*] 30,000Y: first foal: dam, 2-y-o 7f winner, is half-sister to smart middle-distance performer Sirk: 9/2 but bit backward, length winner from Foreshore of 18-runner maiden at Doncaster in November, niggled along at halfway and staying on well to lead entering last: will be well suited by middle distances: certain to improve. *J. H. M. Gosden*

AZRAG (IRE)   2 b.c. (Mar 4) Bluebird (USA) 125 – Red Val 101 (Red God 128§)   43
[1992 6m 6.1m] 7,000F, 56,000Y: lengthy, rather unfurnished colt: half-brother to several winners, including useful 7f/1m winner Carpet General (by Sallust) and 12.2f winner Astral (by Ela-Mana-Mou): dam stayed 1½m: poor form in maidens: bandaged behind on debut. *T. Thomson Jones*

AZURE ROYAL   2 ch.g. (May 7) Prince Sabo 123 – Cloudless Sky 67 (He Loves   –
Me 120) [1992 6g] 6,800Y: second foal: half-brother to 3-y-o Smudgemupum (by Green Ruby): dam miler: slow-starting last of 7 in Folkestone minor event in September. *G. Lewis*

AZUREUS (IRE)   4 ch.g. Horage 124 – Effortless (Try My Best (USA) 130) [1991   82
8d³ 7g⁴ 8m 11m² 7m⁵ 8m² 11s 11.9m⁶ 10g² 8m⁴ 11.9g 10.9m 1992 10s 8f* 11.9f*
10m* 10.5g³ 11.1m² 10.5d 8.9m] strong, attractive gelding: joined present trainer and improved handicapper in 1992: successful at Carlisle, York and Ayr: seems ideally suited by 1¼m to 1½m: acts on hard and dead ground: usually ridden by 7-lb claimer: won over hurdles in October but has also been reluctant to race. *Mrs M. Reveley*

AZZILFI   2 ch.c. (Mar 13) Ardross 134 – Tanouma (USA) 114 (Miswaki (USA) 124)   82 p
[1992 8d² 8.2s*] leggy colt: second foal: dam, 6f (at 2 yrs) and 7f winner (at 4 yrs) stayed 1m, is daughter of very speedy French 2-y-o Diffusion: favourite, won 14-runner maiden at Nottingham in October by 2½ lengths from Al Senafi, leading inside final 1f and running on well: will be suited by middle distances: capable of better. *J. L. Dunlop*

B

BABAROOMS PARADISE (NZ)   5 b.m. Babaroom (USA) – Our Paradise   –
(NZ) (Belmura 112) [1991 NR 1992 10m] leggy mare: of little account on flat. *J. R. Jenkins*

BABA'S LADY (NZ)   5 b.m. Babaroom (USA) – Windsor Lady (NZ) (Silver   –
Dream 107) [1991 NR 1992 10m] leggy, plain New Zealand-bred mare: has a round action: no worthwhile form on flat. *J. R. Jenkins*

BABYTALKER   2 b.c. (Apr 28) Bairn (USA) 126 – Soothing Word (USA) (Sensi-   –
tive Prince (USA)) [1992 5d⁵ 5.3f] 3,300Y: close-coupled colt: second foal: half-brother to a winner in Italy: dam poor daughter of half-sister to champion Canadian colt Giboulee: always behind in claimer and seller in spring. *N. A. Callaghan*

BABY WIZZARD   3 b.f. Scottish Reel 123 – Wizzard Art 71 (Wolver Hollow 126)   49
[1991 NR 1992 10f 10.2f⁴ 12m* 11.5m⁶ 11.7f⁴ 11.8g] leggy, angular filly: first foal: dam won from 7f to 1¼m, including in Belgium: modest performer: sweating, narrowly

won claimer at Goodwood in June: below form last 2 starts: stays 1½m: acts on firm ground: has joined R. Rowe. *I. A. Balding*

BACK BILLY (IRE) 3 b.c. Bob Back (USA) 124 – Island Time (USA) (Bold **85** Hour) [1991 NR 1992 8g 12m⁵ 12m⁴ 10m⁴ 10s] IR 9,000F, IR 24,000Y: rangy, workmanlike colt: fourth reported foal: half-brother to Irish 7f to 13f winner Sapor (by Nishapour), Irish 7f to 11f winner Islet Time (by Burslem) and a winner in Italy: dam Irish 1m winner: fairly useful maiden: easily best effort third start, when fourth in minor events at Newmarket in July: better at 1½m than shorter: dead. *C. E. Brittain*

BACKSTABBER 2 ch.g. (Apr 13) Flash of Steel 120 – Guest List 85 (Be My **63** Guest (USA) 126) [1992 6d 6m 8d² 7.6s] 580Y: close-coupled, workmanlike gelding: moderate mover: first foal: dam 6f (at 2 yrs) and 7f winner, is half-sister to high-class sprinter/miler Sanedtki: modest maiden: form only in 23-runner auction event at Redcar in October, making most from halfway and caught close home: had worst of draw in Lingfield nursery: much better suited by 1m than 6f: acts on dead ground. *Dr J. D. Scargill*

BACK TO FORM 7 ch.g. Homing 130 – Alezan Dore 82 (Mountain Call 125) **26** [1991 NR 1992 12f³ 18.2g⁵ 11.9m⁶] robust, lengthy gelding: poor maiden: seems to stay 2¼m: acts on firm ground: has looked none too keen. *W. G. M. Turner*

BADAWIAH 3 gr.f. Siberian Express (USA) 125 – Jawhara 93 (Upper Case **73** (USA)) [1991 7m² 7m 1992 7g⁵ a7g* 7g a6g 6g 8g⁵ 6.9v⁵ a10g⁶ a10g²] tall, leggy filly: fair performer, though none too consistent: 11/4 on, won maiden at Lingfield in June: easily best effort when second in handicap there in November: stays 1¼m: best turf efforts on a sound surface: often wears crossed noseband: has been bandaged. *W. A. O'Gorman*

BADAWI (FR) 2 ch.c. (Apr 27) Script Ohio (USA) – Beautiful Bedouin (USA) **46 p** (His Majesty (USA)) [1992 a7g4] second foal: dam unraced half-sister to Silver Hawk: sire good-class 2-y-o: 10/1 from 16/1, around 8 lengths fourth of 11 behind Dance To Order in maiden at Southwell in December, running on under pressure to be nearest finish: should improve, particularly over further. *C. N. Allen*

BADAWI (USA) 4 ch.f. Diesis 133 – Begum (USA) (Alydar (USA)) [1991 8.5m² **103** 8g* 1992 8g* 7.9m 10g⁶ 8f³ 8g* 8.1d² 8.9m* 8.9d² 8m³ 9m⁶ 8g2] lengthy, sparely-made filly: has long stride: useful and consistent performer: progressed really well, winning Pontefract minor event in the spring and Ascot ladies race and £12,300 handicap at York in midsummer: subsequently placed in 3 listed races: stayed 9f: acted on firm and dead ground: won when sweating: held up: game and genuine: visits Green Desert. *J. H. M. Gosden*

BADENOCH BURNER 2 b.c. (Apr 19) King of Spain 121 – Nocturnal Bliss **–** (Pyjama Hunt 126) [1992 5g a5g] 4,800F, 5,200Y: workmanlike colt: fourth foal: half-brother to winning 2-y-o sprint platers Midnight Violet (by Sulaafah) and Ballet Bliss (by Balidar): dam ran twice: last in seller in March and maiden (wore bandages, hung badly left) in July: looks a hard ride. *N. Tinkler*

BADIE (USA) 3 gr.c. Blushing Groom (FR) 131 – Desirable 119 (Lord Gayle **103 ?** (USA) 124) [1991 7g* 7d 1992 8g⁵ 8g 12m 10m⁵] close-coupled, good-topped colt: good mover: useful form at Newmarket in Craven Stakes and 2000 Guineas: subsequently looked unco-operative under pressure in King Edward VII Stakes at Royal Ascot, then weakened tamely final 2f in minor event at Newmarket in July: should be suited by further than 1m: below form on dead ground: not one to trust. *J. L. Dunlop*

BAEZA 2 ch.c. (May 10) Arctic Tern (USA) 126 – Tashinsky (USA) (Nijinsky **–** (CAN) 138) [1992 7f 8.1s] 15,000Y: second foal: half-brother to 3-y-o 11.1f winner Sovereign Page (by Caro): dam, showed some ability in France, is closely related to smart Mukaddamah: well beaten in maidens in August: has joined D. Loder. *H. R. A. Cecil*

BAFFIE 3 b.f. Doc Marten 104 – Phyl's Pet (Aberdeen 109) [1991 NR 1992 8v] fifth **–** reported foal: half-sister to 8-y-o Invertiel (by Sparkling Boy), successful from 7f to 11f and over hurdles: dam well behind all starts: 33/1, tailed off in maiden at Newcastle in November. *P. Monteith*

BAGALINO (USA) 2 ch.c. (Mar 13) Lyphard (USA) 132 – Bag of Tunes (USA) **75 p** (Herbager 136) [1992 6m⁵ 7g³ 8.2g*] smallish, good-topped colt: fluent mover: brother to useful 7f (at 2 yrs) and 1½m winner Andaleeb and half-brother to 1¼m winner Reed Player (by Quack) and a winner in USA: dam won Kentucky Oaks: progressive form: well-backed favourite, won maiden at Nottingham in September, making all, quickening 4f out and battling on well: will be well suited by middle distances: may well improve further. *R. Charlton*

BAHARLILYS 3 gr.f. Green Dancer (USA) 132 – April Wind 91 (Windjammer (USA)) [1991 7.1m⁵ 8m 8d⁶ 7m 1992 8d 6m 10f 7.6g] leggy, unfurnished filly: nervy type: no worthwhile form in 1992, and not seen out after July. *N. C. Wright* –

BAHER (USA) 3 b.c. Damister (USA) 123 – Allatum (USA) 81 (Alleged (USA) 138) [1991 NR 1992 9.7v 12m 9.7m³ 11.1f² 12.3f² 14.8f⁶] leggy, quite good-topped colt: second reported foal: half-brother to winning hurdler TV Pitch (by Fast Topaze): dam 2m winner: fair maiden: weakened rapidly over 3f out in 1¾m handicap: stays 1½m: blinkered last 3 starts: joined C. Brittain, but didn't run for him and sold to join Mrs A. Swinbank 4,600 gns Newmarket Autumn Sales. *N. A. Callaghan* **74**

BAHI (IRE) 3 b.c. Tate Gallery (USA) 117 – Spear Dance (Gay Fandango (USA) 132) [1991 6g 8s² 1992 12v³ 12d² 10g* 14m³ 12m* 11m* 12.3g² 10g⁵ 11d 10g³ 12.3g² 10s³] IR 46,000Y: third foal: half-brother to plating-class 1991 3-y-o 6f winner Lambada Girl and Irish 11f to 1¾m winner Masai Warrior (both by Petorius): dam Irish 7f and 1m winner, is sister to Jersey Stakes winner Rasa Penang: progressive form to win maiden and minor event at Leopardstown then handicap at the Curragh: ran creditably, including in listed races, most starts afterwards: probably stays 1¾m: best efforts on a sound surface: has been sent to D. Hayes in Australia. *K. Prendergast, Ireland* **103**

BAIE PETITE 3 b.f. Bay Express 132 – Little Newington 51 (Most Secret 119) [1991 NR 1992 6s 6d 6.1g 7m 6d 8s] workmanlike filly: first foal: dam 6f and 1m winner: seems of little account. *A. W. Jones* –

BAILEYS COLOURS 2 b.f. (Feb 3) Damister (USA) 123 – The Yellow Girl 102 (Yellow God 129) [1992 6m 6f⁴ 7m 7.1s⁵ 7d⁴ 7g a6g 8.2s a8g] 3,000Y: workmanlike filly: has a round action: half-sister to several winners, including St Leger Italiano winner Comme L'Etoile (by Star Appeal), Derby Italiano second Teofane (by Wolver Hollow) and 8.5f winner Asbaab (by Young Generation): dam won 3 times at 7f: modest plater: stays 1m: acts on firm and soft ground, and on equitrack: has run well for 7-lb claimer: sold 1,650 gns Doncaster November Sales: consistent. *B. J. McMath* **42**

BAJAN AFFAIR 2 b.f. (Feb 12) Bold Owl 101 – Silvery Moon (Lorenzaccio 130) [1992 5d⁶ 6m 5f⁶ 5m⁶ 8.1d] 4,400Y: leggy filly: sister to 7f (at 2 yrs) and 1m winner Premiere Moon, modest sprinter Cotton On Quick and quite modest 1¼m performer The Mague and half-sister to a winner abroad: dam of little account: seems of little account. *Miss L. C. Siddall* –

BAJKA 2 b.f. (Feb 12) Elegant Air 119 – Chase Paperchase 79 (Malinowski (USA) 123) [1992 6d⁵ 5g 7d 8g a6g] good-bodied filly: has scope: third foal: sister to 1990 2-y-o 6f winner Zloty: dam maiden stayed 6f: plating-class maiden: soundly beaten in 1m selling nursery: trained until after then by W. Jarvis: stays 7f: acts on dead ground. *R. C. Spicer* **47**

BALAAT (USA) 4 b.g. Northern Baby (CAN) 127 – Bar J Gal (USA) (Key To The Mint (USA)) [1991 7m 10g² 8m 9d 7.9m 1992 a11g a8g a12g⁵ a14g⁴ 16.2d 11.9g 14.6g 10.3g a16g⁵ a14g⁴] quite good-topped gelding: moderate mover: only a poor handicapper nowadays: seems to stay 1¾m: seems ill at ease on top-of-the-ground. *M. C. Chapman* –

BALADEE PET 3 gr.g. Petong 126 – Baladee (Mummy's Pet 125) [1991 6f⁵ 5m 5f² 5f⁵ 5g³ 6f² 6f 5h 1992 5m⁶ 6d⁴ 6m 5g⁴ 5m 5s⁴ 5m] leggy, close-coupled gelding: modest maiden: off course 2½ months and blinkered, tailed off in handicap in September final start: stays 6f: acts on firm ground. *Mrs V. A. Aconley* **51**

BALIANA 2 b.f. (Apr 11) Midyan (USA) 124 – Okosan (USA) 72 (Far Out East (USA)) [1992 5g² 5m² 5s² 5d] 1,500F, 7,800Y: useful-looking filly: second foal: dam, maiden, seemed best as 2-y-o at 7f/1m: fair maiden: visored, tailed off (never travelling well having been hampered leaving stalls) in Doncaster listed event final start: well worth a try at 6f+: best effort on soft ground. *C. B. B. Booth* **75**

BALIGAY 7 b.m. Balidar 133 – Gaygo Lady 113 (Gay Fandango (USA) 132) [1991 7m 5.8f² 6.1m* 6m 6d² 6.1g 6.1m² 5f* 5m 1992 6g 5.7f³ 6f⁶ 5.7g 6.1m² 6g² 7s 5d 6d 5.2s³ 5g] lengthy, workmanlike mare: moderate mover: inconsistent handicapper: effective from 5f to 7f: probably acts on any going: effective blinkered or not: good mount for claimer. *R. J. Hodges* **80**

BALLACASCADE 2 b.g. (Mar 25) Ballacashtal (CAN) – Pasha's Dream (Tarboosh (USA)) [1992 a7g⁶ a8g⁵ a7g⁶] 4,000F: eighth living foal: half-brother to 3-y-o 1m seller winner Any Dream Would Do (by Efisio), 1m and 1¼m seller winner **46**

Obeliski (by Aragon) and 5f winner Davill (by Record Token): dam half-sister to smart middle-distance performer Jimsun: easy to back and well beaten in maidens at Southwell and Lingfield. *P. C. Haslam*

BALLAD DANCER   7 ch.g. Ballad Rock 122 – Manx Image (Dancer's Image   **56** (USA)) [1991 a6g⁶ 6s* 6d 6d⁵ 6m 5g* 5.1g 5s³ 5d² a5g² 6f 5m² 5m 1992 5s 6d 6s⁵ 5d² 7m⁵ 5m⁵ 5m⁵ 7.6g⁴ 8m⁴ 7g⁴ 5g² 5g* 7g³ 5d⁵ 5s³ 7f 6d 6s] angular, lengthy gelding: moderate mover: modest handicapper: consistent in summer and successful at Ayr in August: well beaten last 3 starts: effective at up to 1m: acts on good to firm (not on firm) and soft ground: has run well for a claimer: sometimes starts slowly. *E. J. Alston*

BALLAINDY   2 ch.f. (May 3) Ballacashtal (CAN) – Indy 77 (Indigenous 121)   **33** [1992 5s⁶ 5s 5g 5.3m 5f] leggy, sparely-made filly: fourth foal: dam 5f winner at 2 yrs: poor maiden: very edgy in blinkers final start, in May: sold 650 gns Ascot November Sales. *W. G. M. Turner*

BALLA JIDAAL (USA)   3 b.c. Shadeed (USA) 135 – Hiaam (USA) 110 (Alydar   **97** (USA)) [1991 5m⁴ 6m* 6m⁵ 1992 a10g⁴ 7g²] smallish, quite attractive colt: has a quick action: useful performer: in frame in minor event at Lingfield (held up pulling hard) and in £7,200 contest at Newmarket (made most) in spring: probably stays 1¼m. *M. R. Stoute*

BALLASECRET   4 ch.f. Ballacashtal (CAN) – Soft Secret (Most Secret 119)   **84** [1991 a6g² a5g* a7g² 5d⁴ 6d⁴ 6m* 5m⁵ 5d⁵ 5m* 5m 5.1g 5.7m 7m 5.1s³ 5.2g⁴ 5d a5g 1992 5g³ 5g 7f⁵ 5.2g 5m* 5d* 5g³ 6g 6d] lengthy filly: fairly useful handicapper: clearly best efforts when successful in apprentice events at Pontefract and Goodwood within 3 days in August: probably ideally suited by 5f: acts on good to firm and dead ground, has also won on equitrack: front runner. *R. Dickin*

BALLERINA BAY   4 ch.f. Myjinski (USA) – Lady Seville 64 (Orange Bay 131)   **72** [1991 a12g 10d 11.5g⁴ a12g³ 11.5m* 11.6m⁴ 8g⁵ 11.6m 9m⁴ 9m* 8.9m⁴ 10m 8m 9g⁵   **a60** a10g a7g a8g² 1992 a10g a8g² a8g* a8g 10.3g⁶ 9d⁴ 9d 8d⁶ 9m⁴ 7g* 8m 8g⁵ 9g⁵ 7d⁴ 7m* 8g 7d³ 7d³ 8m³ 7d* 7g 7g a8g⁴ a8g] lengthy filly: carries condition: has round action: consistent handicapper: successful in the spring at Southwell and Lingfield (in amateur events) and twice in the autumn at Yarmouth: effective from 7f to 11.5f: acts on good to firm and dead ground and on all-weather surfaces: effective visored or not: has worn bandages: good mount for a claimer/amateur. *D. T. Thom*

BALLERINA ROSE   5 b.m. Dreams To Reality (USA) 113 – Ragtime Rose   **–** (Ragstone 128) [1991 10f⁴ 1992 a14g a10g⁶] leggy mare: has a round action: little show on flat: modest winning (1991/2) hurdler. *O. O'Neill*

BALLET   3 b.f. (Apr 24) Sharrood (USA) 124 – Silk Stocking 109 (Pardao 120)   **61** p [1992 6m 6d 5g² 7s] leggy, unfurnished filly: has long stride: half-sister to several winners, including useful 1983 2-y-o 7f and 1m winner Satinette (by Shirley Heights) and useful 1982 2-y-o 7f winner Silk Pyjamas (by Queen's Hussar), later minor stakes winner in USA: dam (stayed 1½m) half-sister to good sprinter Shiny Tenth: modest maiden: easily best effort when keeping-on second at Sandown: favourite, never a factor in nursery at Wolverhampton later in September: should be suited by further than 5f: possibly unsuited by soft ground: likely to do better. *Lord Huntingdon*

BALLET SHOES (IRE)   2 b.f. (May 12) Ela-Mana-Mou 132 – River Dancer 118   **71** p (Irish River (FR) 131) [1992 6d²] lengthy, attractive filly: third foal: half-sister to 1¼m winner Snow Plough (by Niniski): dam French 5f (at 2 yrs) and 1m winner from family of Sun Princess and Saddlers' Hall: favourite, keeping-on 2 lengths second of 10 to Bright Spells in maiden at Goodwood in October, headed 1f out: will stay at least 1m: will improve. *R. Charlton*

BALLET SOCIETY (FR)   3 b.f. Sadler's Wells (USA) 132 – Gwydion (USA) 118   **–** (Raise A Cup (USA)) [1991 NR 1992 8d] IR 460,000Y: sturdy, good-topped filly: first foal: dam sprinter: weak 14/1, very green and never better than mid-division, well beaten, in maiden at Kempton in September: visits Taufan. *J. H. M. Gosden*

BALLON   2 b.f. (Feb 17) Persian Bold 123 – La Vosgienne (Ashmore (FR) 125)   **63** [1992 6m³ 7d 5.2g⁴ 6g] IR 7,800Y: quite good-topped filly: has scope: half-sister to 3 winners, including 1½mile winner Emven (by Dara Monarch) and 1988 2-y-o 7f winner Shelbourne Lady (by Coquelin): dam, showed some ability in France, is half-sister to Royal Lodge winner Bengal Fire: modest maiden: easily best effort when around 10 lengths fourth of 6 in listed race at Newbury in August: bred to be suited by 1m + : ran wide into straight first 2 outings. *C. E. Brittain*

BALLYCASTLE MARY (IRE)   3 ch.f. Music Boy 124 – Apple Rings 97   **–** (Godswalk (USA) 130) [1991 NR 1992 6m 7f 6m 9.7d] IR 13,000Y: sturdy filly: first foal: dam, 6f and 7f winner, is half-sister to very useful 6f to 8.5f winner Eve's Error: no worthwhile form: not seen out after July: sold 775 gns Ascot November Sales. *T. J. Naughton*

BALLYGRIFFIN BELLE 3 gr.f. Another Realm 118 – Illiney Girl 66 (Lochnager 132) [1991 NR 1992 6m] second foal: half-sister to 4-y-o 6f and 7f winner Quick Steel (by Alleging): dam winning sprinter: 33/1, always behind in maiden at Folkestone in August. *T. P. McGovern* —

BALLYKETT PRINCE (IRE) 4 ch.g. Thatching 131 – Flower Petals (Busted 134) [1991 8d 8g 7g 10m⁶ 7d* 9d* 9g⁶ 8s⁴ 10g* 1992 9d* 9g³ 9m² 8f 9g² 8.5g² 9g² 10g⁶ 8s² 8d*] big, workmanlike gelding: half-brother to modest 1¼m and 11.7f winner Arnaldo (by Upper Case): dam, Irish 1¼m winner, is sister to smart middle-distance performer Bog Road: very consistent and useful Irish handicapper: successful at Leopardstown in May and the Curragh in October: stays 1¼m: acts on good to firm and soft ground: wears blinkers: tough. *J. S. Bolger, Ireland* **108**

BALLYMAC GIRL 4 gr.f. Niniski (USA) 125 – Alruccaba 83 (Crystal Palace (FR) 132) [1991 9g 12g 13g⁵ 12g³ 12s 1992 8f 14.1d⁵ 14.1m² 16.2g³ 12.1s³] leggy, sparely-made ex-Irish filly: second foal: sister to modest 1½m winner Allegra: dam 6f winner, raced only at 2 yrs: trained by B. Kelly at 3 yrs: poor handicapper: stays 2m: acts on good to firm and soft ground. *C. T. Nash* **47**

BALLYMONEYBOY 3 ch.g. Ballacashtal (CAN) – Honeybuzzard (FR) (Sea Hawk II 131) [1991 6g 1992 8.3s* 8g 9.7v⁶] rangy, angular gelding: favourite, easily won claimer at Hamilton in May: below that form in autumn: will stay 1¼m. *M. H. Tompkins* **68**

BALLYMUST (IRE) 3 ch.f. Muscatite 122 – Bally 74 (Balidar 133) [1991 6m 6m 1992 5g] compact filly: poor mover: of little account: tried blinkered. *J. White* —

BALLYRANTER 3 ch.g. Bold Owl 101 – Whipalash 73 (Stephen George 102) [1991 7g 8m a7g² a8g⁵ a8g³ 1992 12.3s a8g a8g³ 8.9m 14.1d 10.5d⁶ 8s² 8.1g* 8v a7g] strong, workmanlike gelding: modest performer: won 5-runner maiden at Edinburgh in October: stays 10.5f: acts on soft ground (well beaten on heavy) and on fibresand. *H. J. Collingridge* **53** a57

BALLYSTATE 4 ch.f. Ballacashtal (CAN) – Brandenbourg 66 (Le Levanstell 122) [1991 10g³ 10m⁵ 12m³ 12g 16g 11.6m 7f 11.5g 1992 11.8d] angular filly: still a maiden on flat, and rated 69d at 3 yrs: stays 1½m: tried blinkered: fair hurdler, and won 2 handicaps in the autumn. *C. James* —

BALNIBARBI 3 b.c. Rainbow Quest (USA) 134 – Balabina (USA) 110 (Nijinsky (CAN) 138) [1991 NR 1992 9g* 10.3f⁴ 10.8s* 15.5s] leggy colt: good mover: first foal: dam 1½m winner, is sister to good middle-distance performers Quiet Fling and Peacetime: useful performer: won maiden (edgy) at Kempton in May and 3-runner minor event at Warwick after 4½-month break in October: stiff task, set pace when tailed off in Prix Royal-Oak at Longchamp: will be better suited by 1½m than 1¼m: probably acts on any going. *H. R. A. Cecil* **95** +

BALUGA 3 ch.c. Don't Forget Me 127 – Miss Zadig 102 (Thatch (USA) 136) [1991 6g 7g⁵ 1992 7d² 8d 8m* 8g⁴ 9m* 10f* 8d* 8g 8f⁶ 8.1g 8g] lengthy, good-quartered colt: carries condition: impresses in appearance: good mover: fairly useful handicapper: front-running efforts to win at Goodwood, Sandown and Salisbury (2) in first half of season: kept on most gamely under very hard ride on last of those: below form (including in visor once) afterwards: effective from 1m to 1¼m, on firm and dead ground: sold 26,000 gns Newmarket Autumn Sales. *G. Harwood* **85**

BALUSTRADE BOY (IRE) 2 b.c. (Apr 12) Bold Arrangement 111 – Norman Native (FR) (Bourbon (FR) 129) [1992 5m 6g 6m a8g³ 8d 8d] 925Y: small, lightly-made colt: half-brother to 3 winners in France by Moulin, including 1¼m winner Mill of The North: dam once raced at 2 yrs in France: plating-class maiden: bandaged, ran moderately final start: looks a thorough stayer: acts on dead ground, and on equitrack. *B. Stevens* **50**

BALZINO (USA) 3 ch.g. Trempolino (USA) 135 – Royal Procession (USA) (Lyphard (USA) 132) [1991 NR 1992 7d⁶ 8s⁶ 10d⁵ 10s a12g³] 50,000Y: sturdy, lengthy gelding: third foal: half-brother to Windsor Forest (by Spectacular Bid), placed from 6f to 1m in France at 2 to 4 yrs: dam unraced half-sister to very smart middle-distance stayer Orban: modest performer: best effort on debut: sold out of L. Cumani's stable 4,200 gns Newmarket Autumn Sales: showed he retains ability when staying on from rear in Southwell claimer: will prove suited by 1½m: has been gelded. *Mrs J. R. Ramsden* **62**

BAMAN POWERHOUSE 4 b.g. Bold Owl 101 – Bella Abzug (Karabas 132) [1991 NR 1992 a8g] angular gelding: half-brother to numerous winners, including —

Irish 1½m and 1¾m winner Jamie's Lady (by Ashmore) and 1988 2-y-o 1m winner Les Mains Douces (by Free State): dam placed over 5f at 2 yrs in Ireland: tailed off in Southwell maiden in May. *M. Scudamore*

BAMBURGH (USA) 2 ch.c. (Feb 20) Alysheba (USA) – Golden Dust (USA) **77 p** (Dusty Canyon) [1992 7d2] $400,000Y: lengthy, attractive colt: has scope: half-brother to several winners, notably Bet Twice (by Sportin' Life), top-class performer successful in Belmont Stakes: dam minor winner at 2 yrs: sire (by Alydar) top class at around 1¼m: 8/1, 2 lengths second to Gabr in 15-runner maiden at Leicester, held up travelling comfortably then galloping on strongly without being given an unduly hard race: will improve, particularly when granted 1¼m+, and looks certain to win races. *M. R. Stoute*

BANANA CUFFLINKS (USA) 6 b.g. Peterhof (USA) 116 – Heather Bee **39** (USA) (Drone) [1991 18s 9g 7.6g 12m6 10g 1992 8m6 8m6 9.9f5 14.1h2 11.9f2 11.5g4] lengthy, attractive gelding: maiden: stayed 1¾m: acted on hard ground: ran well when visored: dead. *M. H. Tompkins*

BANBURY FLYER 4 b.g. Mummy's Game 120 – Haddon Anna (Dragonara **63** Palace (USA) 115) [1991 6g 6m5 6g2 5d3 5g 6m6 5g5 6m* 6f 6f 5d 1992 5d 5.1d6 5.3m4 5m 5g 5g6 6.1m4 6d6 5g 6f4 5m3 5.7d2 5s a6g2 a6g* a6g2] smallish gelding: has a quick action: none too consistent handicapper, but took well to equitrack, winning in November and failing only narrowly to follow up: stays 6f: acts on firm and dead ground: blinkered (not entirely discredited) once: suitable mount for claimer. *Mrs A. L. M. King*

BANDAO 3 ch.c. Kind of Hush 118 – Mellow Girl 88 (Mountain Call 125) [1991 NR **–** 1992 16m3 15.1m6] deep-girthed colt: eighth foal: half-brother to 9.4f winner Riva Renald (by Try My Best) and 6-y-o 1¼m to 12.4f winner Daisy Girl (by Main Reef): dam 5f and 6f winner at 2 yrs: favourite after promising debut, tailed off before straight in maiden claimer at Edinburgh (reportedly finished in distress) in July. *J. Mackie*

BANDOLINE 3 br.f. Top Ville 129 – Chic Belle (USA) (Mr Prospector (USA)) **78** [1991 7m 8.1s5 1992 7.5m5 12.2g* 13.3d3 14.1g* 16.2s2dis 15s* 14d5 16.5g6] tall, lightly-made filly: has a markedly round action: moderate walker: progressive form to win maiden at Catterick in July and handicaps at Yarmouth (amateurs, sweating badly) in August and Ayr in September: suited by a test of stamina: went well on soft ground: twice very much on toes, but ran well: game and consistent: visits Caerleon. *B. W. Hills*

BAND ON THE RUN 5 ch.h. Song 132 – Sylvanecte (FR) 70 (Silver Shark 129) **102** [1991 8d3 7d2 8g4 8g 8.1g2 7.9g 7.1f3 1992 7d* 7.9m* 8f 7f4 8m5 7.3d5 8.9d5] rather angular, good-topped horse: poor mover: consistent performer: better than ever at 5 yrs: successful in the spring in Victoria Cup at Ascot and Hambleton Stakes (Limited Handicap) at York: ran particularly well in Group 3 events at Newmarket and Newbury in the summer: effective from 7f to 1m: acts on firm and dead ground: has hung left: game and genuine. *B. A. McMahon*

BAND SARGEANT (IRE) 3 b.g. Nashamaa 113 – Indian Honey (Indian King **–** (USA) 128) [1991 5m5 7d4 5m6 6m 1992 12.2g] big, lengthy gelding: off course 12 months and no form in amateurs handicap in August: seems suited by an easy surface: subsequently showed modest ability in juvenile hurdles. *G. Richards*

Insulpak Victoria Cup, Ascot—Band On The Run goes one better than in 1991;
High Low (right) makes a race of it

BANGLES 2 ch.f. (Feb 25) Chilibang 120 – Vague Lass 85 (Vaigly Great 127) **77**
[1992 5f³ 5.1g² 5m* 5.2g⁵ 5m* 5.2g³ 5m⁴ 5g⁶] workmanlike filly: has scope: good
mover: first foal: dam sprinter: fair handicapper: successful in maiden at Windsor
and nursery at Newcastle in summer: will stay 6f: yet to race on a soft surface:
consistent. *Lord Huntingdon*

BANG ON TIME 2 b.g. (May 21) Green Ruby (USA) 104 – Mount of Light 61 **36**
(Sparkler 130) [1992 6g 7s] close-coupled gelding: seventh living foal: half-brother
to 3-y-o Call The Bureau (by Gorytus), 6f winner at 2 yrs, and 1987 2-y-o 5f and 6f
seller winner Rustic Dawn (by Rusticaro): dam, half-sister to smart miler Richboy,
stayed 1½m: 50/1 and backward, always behind in maidens at Newbury and
Salisbury in September: has joined P. Murphy. *G. B. Balding*

BANHAM COLLEGE 6 b.g. Tower Walk 130 – Baby Flo 67 (Porto Bello 118) **61**
[1991 5d³ 5g⁵ 6g 5f² 6m 5g* 1992 5m² 5g⁶ 5m² 5s⁴ 5.1g³] robust, rather
dipped-backed gelding: moderate mover: modest handicapper: off course 14 months
and returned better than ever in autumn: best at 5f: acts on firm and dead ground,
fair effort on soft: wandered badly final start: has run well for apprentice. *B. A.
McMahon*

BANISH 3 b.c. Don't Forget Me 127 – Busca (USA) 49 (Mr Prospector (USA)) **–**
[1991 7.1d 1992 8d] good-bodied colt: no form: sold 1,250 gns Newmarket July Sales.
B. W. Hills

BANKER MASON (USA) 6 b.h. Sadler's Wells (USA) 132 – Alwah (USA) **–**
(Damascus (USA)) [1991 9s 12d 1992 a12m 12g] smallish, sparely-made horse: of
little account: tried in blinkers. *W. L. Barker*

BAN RI (IRE) 2 gr.f. (Feb 5) Gairloch 122 – God Save (USA) (Empery (USA) **42**
128) [1992 5g² 5m³ 6m 6s⁵ 6d] angular, rather sparely-made filly: third foal: half-
sister to a minor winner in France: dam, French maiden, is daughter of very smart
French miler Reine Imperiale and granddaughter of Prix de Diane winner/Arc
second Rescousse: modest plater: well beaten, racing too freely, when visored in
non-selling nursery at Haydock final start: will stay 7f +: sold 600 gns Newmarket
Autumn Sales. *M. H. Tompkins*

BANTEL BRIGADIER 3 ch.g. Mandrake Major 122 – Bantel Baby (Warpath **–**
113) [1991 5f 6d 5m⁵ 6f 1992 9s⁶ 5g 6.9d³ 5s] good-bodied gelding: no worthwhile
form, blinkered final start: dead. *R. Allan*

BARAHIN (IRE) 3 b.c. Diesis 133 – Red Comes Up (USA) (Blushing Groom **86**
(FR) 131) [1991 NR 1992 8g³ 8d³ 10d* 10.8s² 12.3v⁴] 225,000F: rangy, attractive
colt: good mover: second known foal: dam French maiden, sister to Rainbow Quest:
fairly useful performer: off course 5 months after debut: 11/10 on, took plenty of time
to get on top in maiden at Brighton in September: made most and ran well on form,
but looked reluctant when second of 3 in minor event at Warwick: stays 10.8f: yet
to race on top-of-the-ground: sold to join R. O'Sullivan 13,500 gns Doncaster
November Sales. *J. L. Dunlop*

BARASSIE 2 b.f. (Apr 8) Presidium 124 – Always A Lady 66 (Dominion 123) **35**
[1992 5.2s 7g 7d] small filly: first foal: dam soft-ground sprinter: poor maiden: green
all starts. *P. Mitchell*

BARATHEA (IRE) 2 b.c. (Mar 2) Sadler's Wells (USA) 132 – Brocade 121 **107** p
(Habitat 134) [1992 7m* 7m*]

The Sadler's Wells roadshow rolled up at Newmarket's Cambridgeshire
meeting with several new faces on the bill, and, true to form, unearthed
another promising talent in Luca Cumani's Barathea, who took the second
division of the seven-furlong Taxi News Westley Maiden Stakes by a length
and a half from another newcomer Gabr. Backward and green beforehand,
and weak at 12/1 in a market headed by the York runner-up Black Dragon,
Barathea upstaged his better-fancied rivals with an impressive success
characterised by a useful turn of foot. Barathea's second and only other
appearance as a two-year-old came in the Philip Cornes Houghton Stakes
over the same course and distance later in October. The Houghton Stakes,
traditionally contested by lightly-raced, well-regarded animals, often throws
up a horse or two who go on to make an impact in good company as a three-
year-old, and we have few misgivings that both Barathea and the runner-up
Storm Canyon fall into that category. Storm Canyon, beaten a length and a half
by Placerville in the other division of the Westley Maiden on his only previous
appearance, started favourite at 5/4 on receiving 7 lb from Barathea; but it was

Sheikh Mohammed's "Barathea"

Barathea, carrying the second colours of Sheikh Mohammed, who once again stole the show. The pair had the race to themselves in the final furlong, and though Storm Canyon had first run, half a length up with two hundred yards to run, Barathea fought back strongly on the rising ground, nosing ahead with fifty yards left and passing the post the winner by a neck with Thaleros seven lengths behind in third. Significantly, Barathea recorded a timefigure of 114 in the Houghton Stakes, one of the best by a two-year-old all season and further evidence of his potential as well as his ability.

		Northern Dancer	Nearctic
	Sadler's Wells (USA)	(b 1961)	Natalma
	(b 1981)	Fairy Bridge	Bold Reason
Barathea (IRE)		(b 1975)	Special
(b.c. Mar 2, 1990)		Habitat	Sir Gaylord
	Brocade	(b 1966)	Little Hut
	(b 1981)	Canton Silk	Runnymede
		(gr 1970)	Clouded Lamp

Barathea is Brocade's fourth foal and third winner following the French eleven-furlong winner Zabar (by Dancing Brave) and the smart filly Free At Last (by Shirley Heights), who gained all her successes here and in the States between seven furlongs and a mile and a quarter. Brocade, a daughter of the leading broodmare sire Habitat, possessed a really good record on the racecourse, where, campaigned only at seven furlongs and a mile, she won five of her eleven races including the Challenge Stakes at Newmarket and the Prix de la Foret at Longchamp. Brocade's family isn't a particularly distinguished one, though her dam Canton Silk, four times a winner over five furlongs, has produced plenty of winners, including Brocade's full brother Cause Celebre, a very useful performer at up to seven furlongs here, and the useful two-year-old sprinter Royal Pinnacle, both of whom stayed a mile when sent abroad. Canton Silk's dam Clouded Lamp, who stayed a mile but did all her winning at seven furlongs, produced plenty of minor winners, of whom the northern sprint handicapper Irma Flintstone was probably the best known. The deep-bodied Barathea seems sure to make up into a good three-year-old. He has the physical scope, he'll be better suited by a mile and a mile and a quarter, he's stabled with one of the best trainers in the land and he possesses a turn of speed. Clearly he's very much one to keep on the right side. *L. M. Cumani*

BARBARA'S CUTIE 4 ch.f. Tina's Pet 121 – Eucharis 41 (Tickled Pink 114) **43** [1991 5s2 5m5 5g 5g6 5m 5.1m 5g 5m3 5d2 a5g4 a5g4 1992 a5g a5g4 5s 5.1d 5m 5m 6.1g6 5.2g3 5.1m5 5.1m 5g 5g6 5g* 5.2m3 6.1g4 5s 5s6 5.1g4 a5g a8g a6g] sturdy, close-coupled filly: formerly an inconsistent handicapper: visored, held her form well after winning (for first time) at Folkestone in September until well beaten final 2 starts: seems best at 5f: acts on good to firm and soft ground. *M. Blanshard*

BARBARY REEF (IRE) 4 b.g. Sarab 123 – Brown's Cay 71 (Formidable (USA) **51 d** 125) [1991 9d 14.1g 10g* 10.1m* 10.1m5 8m 10m2 9ga 12g6 1992 10.4m 10m3 10.1g 11d 10m4 11f] strong gelding: moderate walker: poor handicapper nowadays: mulish stalls and looked none too enthusiastic in blinkers final start, in August: stays 1¼m: acts on good to firm ground: visored (ran poorly) once at 3 yrs. *G. H. Eden*

BARBEZIEUX 5 b.h. Petong 126 – Merchantmens Girl 58 (Klairon 131) [1991 5g – 5m 5f 5g 5m 5.1m 5g5 5g3 5d* 5d6 5m2 5m* 5m4 5m4 6g4 5f 7g 6m 5f 5.3g 1992 a5g a5g 5s3 a5g 5m 6f 5g 6.1g 5m6 5m 5g 5g] strong, workmanlike horse: moderate mover: poor sprinter: no worthwhile form in 1992: acts on good to firm and good to soft going. *T. J. Naughton*

BAR BILLIARDS 3 b.c. Bold Arrangement 111 – Green Teable (FR) (Green **71** Dancer (USA) 132) [1991 7m 1992 11.7s3 12.1m3 12d6 14.8f3 15.8m* 14.6g 19m6 16d 14.6d5 12s*] leggy, useful-looking colt: modest performer: successful in small-field maiden at Catterick in July for F. J. Houghton and apprentice handicap (made all) at Ascot in September on first start for new stable: stays 15.8f: acts on good to firm and soft ground: blinkered last 7 starts. *G. Lewis*

BARBOUKH 2 ch.f. (Mar 15) Night Shift (USA) – Turban 80 (Glint of Gold 128) **75 p** [1992 6s6 6d4 7.3s] rangy filly: has plenty of scope: moderate mover: first foal: dam, 1¼m winner stayed 1½m, is half-sister to smart Irish middle-distance filly Green Lucia and to Old Vic: fair maiden: carrying plenty of condition, easily best effort when keeping-on fourth in Blue Seal Stakes at Ascot: pulled too hard in listed race at Newbury later in autumn: bred to be well suited by 1m +: worth another chance. *D. R. C. Elsworth*

BARDIA 2 b.f. (May 14) Jalmood (USA) 126 – Bauhinia 70 (Sagaro 133) [1992 5.9f **42** 6m5 7g 8f 7s] small, sturdy filly: half-sister to several winners here and abroad, including fairly useful sprinter Sylvan Mistral (by Aragon): dam lightly raced: plating-class maiden: looks a thorough stayer: seems unsuited by soft ground. *Don Enrico Incisa*

BARDOLPH (USA) 5 b.g. Golden Act (USA) – Love To Barbara (USA) **87** (Stevward) [1991 9d6 12d* 16.2d4 14s* 16.2g5 18m2 16.5d5 1992 18g2 16d2 18.5g2 16m6 20m 16s4 20m* 15.9m4 16.2s3 18m6 a16g8*] compact gelding: moderate mover: consistent handicapper: won Goodwood Stakes (Handicap) in July and at Lingfield in October: suited by a test of stamina: acts on any going: effective blinkered or not, didn't wear them in 1992: has run well when sweating: has won for amateur: usually bandaged off-hind: game and genuine. *P. F. I. Cole*

BARFORD LAD 5 b.g. Nicholas Bill 125 – Grace Poole (Sallust 134) [1991 10.1g2 **82** 10m5 8f3 8.9g 8.1m4 9m5 8g3 1992 8g 8s 9d* 7d 8.5g2 10f* 10m5 10.1m4 9d 10.3v3] good-topped gelding: fairly useful handicapper: blinkered twice, returning to form when winning at Kempton, well beaten in valuable event at Ascot later in April: also successful at Newmarket in June: effective from 1m to 1¼m: acts on any going: has won when sweating: pulled hard when visored once at 3 yrs: has found less than seemed likely, and is none too easy a ride. *J. R. Fanshawe*

BARGA 3 b.f. Dancing Brave (USA) 140 – Sylvatica 99 (Thatching 131) [1991 NR – 1992 10g 9.9m 10.5d 10.5d 11.8s] leggy, angular filly: moderate mover: first foal: dam Irish 2-y-o 6f winner later stayed 1¼m, is from family of Ardross: no worthwhile form: sold out of D. Elsworth's stable 2,900 gns Newmarket July Sales after debut. *W. Clay*

BARIK (IRE)   2 b.c. (Feb 6) Be My Guest (USA) 126 – Smoo 84 (Kris 135) [1992   **70** p
7d⁴ 7d 6s*] 54,000F: smallish, sturdy, attractive colt: first foal: dam, twice-raced and placed at 1m, is from family of Bedtime: well-backed favourite, comfortable winner of maiden at Folkestone in October, smooth progress to lead 1f out: will stay 1m: yet to race on a sound surface: will improve again. *A. C. Stewart*

BARJONAL   3 gr.f. Absalom 128 – Hum 69 (Crooner 119) [1991 5d 6g 6g 1992 8v   –
8m 12s] plain filly: poor mover: no worthwhile form: blinkered (edgy) penultimate start: sold to join C. Weedon 725 gns Ascot July Sales. *J. J. Bridger*

BARKSTON SINGER   5 b.m. Runnett 125 – Miss Flirt (Welsh Pageant 132)   – §
[1991 7f 7m 9m⁴ 10.5d 10m⁴ 8m² 9g a8g a10g 1992 a11g⁵ 8m 11.8g 8.9g 9f⁶] tall, leggy, lightly-made mare: poor walker: rated 65 at best at 4 yrs: very much on the downgrade: trained reappearance by Mrs N. Macauley: has looked temperamental. *J. L. Harris*

BARLEY CAKE   2 b. or br.f. (Mar 30) Midyan (USA) 124 – Fancy Flight (FR) 74   **53**
(Arctic Tern (USA) 126) [1992 6m a6g a7g] 2,100Y: shallow-girthed, leggy filly: fourth foal: half-sister to a winner in Sweden by Prince Sabo: dam 1¼m winner: keeping-on ninth of 29 in seller at Newmarket: well beaten in claimers later in autumn: should stay 1m: has joined T. Fairhurst. *W. A. O'Gorman*

BARLOGAN   4 b.f. Dunbeath (USA) 127 – Corinthia (USA) (Empery (USA) 128)   **58**
[1991 6m 7g³ 8g³ 7.6m³ 7g* 8m⁴ 8g 1992 6v 7m a8g 6.9d²] workmanlike filly: modest handicapper: should stay beyond 1m: acts on good to firm and dead ground: won when sweating: not seen out after July. *C. F. Wall*

BARMBRACK   3 ch.g. Doulab (USA) 115 – Irish Cookie 80 (Try My Best (USA)   **39**
130) [1991 6.1m 6m 5g 1992 8m 8.5f 8h⁴ 8m 8f 10s 6.9g 6.1m] useful-looking gelding: poor mover: poor maiden: stays 1m: acts on hard ground: visored sixth 3-y-o start: retained 1,350 gns Doncaster September Sales. *R. M. Whitaker*

BARNEY O'NEILL   6 gr.g. Ballad Rock 122 – Lapis Lazuli 84 (Zeddaan 130)   –
[1991 NR 1992 10.1s 8f 6.9f] big, workmanlike gelding: was effective at 7f and 1m: acted on top-of-the-ground: dead. *J. J. O'Neill*

BARNIEMEBOY   2 ch.c. (Jan 15) Donor 47 – Form Up (Gold Form 108) [1992   –
5m 7d] lengthy colt: poor mover: second reported live foal: dam probably of no account over jumps: tailed-off last in minor event at Windsor and maiden at Salisbury in midsummer. *R. A. Bennett*

BARNSVIEW   3 ch.g. Doulab (USA) 115 – Ridans Girl 89 (Ridan (USA)) [1991 5d   –
5g 5m⁴ 5h⁶ 5g 1992 5g 5m a5g 6g⁶] leggy gelding: of little account in 1992: blinkered final start, in July: sold 1,000 gns Doncaster November Sales. *M. W. Ellerby*

BARON FERDINAND   2 ch.c. (Apr 29) Ferdinand (USA) – In Perpetuity 90   **73** p
(Great Nephew 126) [1992 7g³ 7s³] quite good-topped colt: has scope: third foal: half-brother to a winner in North America by Linkage: dam 1¼m and 10.8f winner, is half-sister to Shirley Heights: sire (by Nijinsky) won Kentucky Derby, later Horse of the Year as 4-y-o, best at 1¼m: fair form, rather keen early on, in minor event at Kempton and maiden (had poor run, finished strongly) at Salisbury in September: will be well suited by at least 1¼m: will improve, and has a maiden at least. *R. Charlton*

BARRAAK   2 b.c. (Apr 7) El Gran Senor (USA) 136 – Rosia Bay 102 (High Top   **52** p
131) [1992 7m 8m] smallish, sturdy colt: has a quick action: eighth foal: half-brother to several winners, including Ibn Bey (by Mill Reef), Roseate Tern (by Blakeney) and 1984 2-y-o 5f winner Cerise Bouquet (by Mummy's Pet): dam, miler, is half-sister to Teleprompter: modest form in maiden at Yarmouth: still burly, well beaten at Newmarket later in September, eased from 2f out. *Major W. R. Hern*

BARRISH   6 b.h. Wassl 125 – Rowa 83§ (Great Nephew 126) [1991 12s 12m 12m²   **78**
12g 14g² 13.9g 14m* 14.6m⁴ 13.3m 12m⁶ 12g 1992 11.1m** 12d 16.2m 12g⁶ 11.9f* 11.4g 13.3g] angular horse: formerly a consistent handicapper, not so in 1992: won at Kempton in May and Brighton in August: stays 1¾m (ran as if something amiss over 16.2f): seems best on a sound surface: often sweats. *R. Akehurst*

BARRYS GAMBLE   6 gr.h. Nishapour (FR) 125 – Scoby Lass (Prominer 125)   **79**
[1991 5g 5f 5m 5f⁴ 1992 a5g 5g 5m 5f* 5m⁶ 5f⁶ 5m⁴ 5g] robust, good-quartered horse: carries plenty of condition: poor mover: reportedly injured fetlock in 1991: fair handicapper: won at Thirsk in May: best on top-of-the-ground: sometimes blinkered: usually claimer ridden: twice spoilt chance at start: stud. *T. Fairhurst*

BARSLEY 2 ch.c. (Mar 16) Kalaglow 132 – Mycenae Cherry 69 (Troy 137) [1992 –
5g] 2,300Y: rather sparely-made colt: second foal: half-brother to 3-y-o Mypeto (by
Petong): dam, 1¼m winner, is daughter of Cherry Hinton: coltish, behind in maiden
at Warwick in April. *J. R. Jenkins*

BAR THREE (IRE) 3 b.g. Lafontaine (USA) 117 – El Prat (Royal Match 117) –
[1991 NR 1992 10m a12s 14s] IR 2,000F, IR 4,000Y, resold 2,000Y: poor mover:
second reported foal: dam poor maiden in Ireland: no form in maidens, blinkered last
time. *L. J. Codd*

BARTOLOMEO (USA) 3 b.g. Vaguely Noble 140 – Stonechurch (USA) 44
(Naskra (USA)) [1991 7f 7g 8g4 1992 8.9s 9.2d5 10.1s5 10g 12.1s 12.1m² 14.1g 11.1m³
10g] strong, workmanlike gelding: inconsistent handicapper: not seen out after July:
stays 1½m: probably acts on good to firm ground and dead: below form when
visored and blinkered (at 2 yrs) once: sold 7,000 gns Newmarket Autumn Sales. *Mrs
J. R. Ramsden*

BARTON PRIDE (IRE) 3 b.g. Phardante (FR) 120 – Ginosa 62 (Kalamoun –
129) [1991 7m 7.6d5 1992 10v5 14.6g6 14.6f3 14.1g] close-coupled gelding: no
worthwhile form in 1992, final start in June: should be suited by middle distances. *R.
Hollinshead*

BARTON ROYAL (IRE) 2 b.c. (May 8) Petorius 117 – Royal Sensation 103 46
(Prince Regent (FR) 129) [1992 8.2g 8d 7g] 5,000Y: angular, short-backed colt:
brother to 1989 2-y-o 5f and 8.2f winner Chou-Chou Royale and half-brother to
several winners on flat and over hurdles, including sprinters Royal Rouser and
Hello Cuddles (both by He Loves Me): dam stayed 1¼m: poor form, well beaten, in
maidens: best effort on dead ground. *R. Hollinshead*

BARUD (IRE) 4 b.g. Persian Bold 123 – Pale Moon 58 (Jukebox 120) [1991 7d –
8.2d 6g 6.9s 1992 7f] leggy gelding: sold out of C. Smith's stable 2,800 gns Ascot
June Sales: still a maiden, and well beaten in amateurs handicap in August: bred to
stay 1m+ but rather headstrong: refused to race in selling hurdle in October. *D.
Burchell*

BASHAMAH (IRE) 3 b. or br.f. Nashamaa 113 – Raja Moulana 75 (Raja Baba 48
(USA)) [1991 7g 7m 1992 9s 12f6 14.1f4 14.1m 16m6] leggy, sparely-made filly:
moderate mover: plating-class maiden: stays 1¾m (stiff task at 2m): acts on firm
going: blinkered (ran poorly) penultimate start: sold to join I. Jones 2,100 gns Ascot
November Sales. *C. E. Brittain*

BASHA (USA) 3 b.f. Chief's Crown (USA) – My Darling One (USA) (Exclusive –
Native (USA)) [1991 NR 1992 8f 8m] fourth foal: dam high-class winner at up to 9f:
bandaged behind, well beaten in maiden at Salisbury and minor event at Kempton
(sweating) in June: visits Robellino. *J. L. Dunlop*

BASHAYER (USA) 2 b.f. (Jan 30) Mr Prospector (USA) – Height of 90 P
Fashion (FR) 124 (Bustino 136) [1992 8m*]
    The EBF Chesterton Stakes over Newmarket's straight mile is just one
of several usually-informative late-season maiden races for two-year-olds on
which it can pay to keep a keen eye—and not necessarily just upon those
horses fighting out the finish, of course—but in the latest renewal one had to
be struck first and foremost by its beautifully-bred winner Bashayer. By Mr
Prospector out of a mare who'd already produced Nashwan and Unfuwain,
Bashayer was very much the pick of the nineteen runners on pedigree, but
with her inexperience glaringly evident in the preliminaries and her stable in
the middle of a bad run, she was weak in the market and drifted from 5/1 to
twice that price in the face of strong support for Henry Cecil's good-looking
newcomer Princess Borghese. That Bashayer, a leggy, unfurnished filly,
should win by two and a half lengths augurs well for her as a three-year-old.
Things didn't look too bright at halfway where Bashayer held a prominent
position but was just starting to be pushed along; she responded swiftly,
however, quickened smoothly to take up the running with over two furlongs
to run then stayed on strongly under firm hand riding to come home
unchallenged from another newcomer Silverdale, in the process earning
quotes of 20/1 for both the One Thousand Guineas and the Oaks. The bare
form of the Chesterton Maiden is a world away from that required to win a
classic—fifth-placed Aberdeen Heather, for example, had had plenty of
chances previously, and eighth-placed Maastricht, not beaten that far, was
well beaten twice subsequently, once at Southwell—but Bashayer has plenty

EBF Chesterton Maiden Stakes, Newmarket—
Nashwan's half-sister Bashayer makes an impressive debut

going for her, and is better placed than most late-season maiden winners we saw to make a successful transition into stronger company. Bashayer's victory certainly provided a welcome tonic for her stable which struggled to find form all year; reportedly, Bashayer herself had been held up in her work for some considerable time.

Bashayer (USA) (b.f. Jan 30, 1990)	Mr Prospector (USA) (b 1970)	Raise A Native (ch 1961)	Native Dancer / Raise You
		Gold Digger (b 1962)	Nashua / Sequence
	Height of Fashion (FR) (b 1979)	Bustino (b 1971)	Busted / Ship Yard
		Highclere (b 1971)	Queen's Hussar / Highlight

Bashayer is Height of Fashion's sixth foal. Besides Nashwan (by Blushing Groom) and Unfuwain (by Northern Dancer), the dam has been represented by the smart middle-distance performers Alwasmi (a full brother to Unfuwain) and Mukkdaam (by Danzig), and only her fifth foal Manwah (by Lyphard) failed to make it five winners out of five. Height of Fashion was purchased by the Maktoum family during her racing days, in which she was beaten only twice in seven races. Her most noteworthy victories came in the May Hill Stakes and the Hoover Fillies' Mile as a two-year-old, and in the Princess of Wales's Stakes the following season, in which race she showed herself to be a high-class filly at a mile and a half. Height of Fashion is stoutly bred—she's by the Coronation Cup and St Leger winner Bustino out of the One Thousand Guineas and Prix de Diane winner Highclere, who, like Bustino, also finished second in the King George. For the record, Highclere, a cornerstone of the breeding operation of the Royal Studs in the last twenty years, is also the dam of the smart middle-distance performer Milford and the Ribblesdale Stakes runner-up Highbrow. Bashayer seems to be regarded by her trainer as a middle-distance filly and not a miler, even though she is by Mr Prospector. Certainly, there's every reason, given the strong stamina influences in the bottom half of her pedigree, to anticipate her staying a mile and a half. We await her reappearance with interest. *Major W. R. Hern*

BASILICA 3 b.c. Bold Arrangement 111 – Sunset Reef (Mill Reef (USA) 141) **63** [1991 8m⁶ 8m⁶ 6g 1992 a8g⁶ a10g 10v³ 8m 7.3g⁴ 8f⁶ 10d a8g 11g⁶ 10g 8g] **a–** workmanlike, sturdy colt: modest maiden: ran in France last 3 starts, leaving C. Brittain after penultimate one: should stay 1½m: best effort on heavy ground, below form on all-weather surfaces: wore eyeshield on reappearance. *J. E. Hammond, France*

BASIM (USA) 2 b.c. (Apr 9) Capote (USA) – Mer Belle (USA) (Far North **119** (CAN) 120) [1992 6g* 5d² 6.3s* 8s³]
For the second year in succession the best performance by an Irish-trained two-year-old came in the Ciga Grand Criterium at Longchamp in October. Basim, the horse responsible, finished an excellent third to the two-and-a-half-length winner Tenby after holding a prominent position throughout, managing one place better than stable-companion St Jovite had in a much smaller field of six the year before. We rather doubt that Basim can scale the

Maktoum Al-Maktoum's "Basim"

		Seattle Slew	Bold Reasoning
	Capote (USA)	(b or br 1974)	My Charmer
	(b or br 1984)	Too Bald	Bald Eagle
Basim (USA)		(b or br 1964)	Hidden Talent
(b.c. Apr 9, 1990)		Far North	Northern Dancer
	Mer Belle (USA)	(b 1973)	Fleur
	(b 1984)	Caracciola	Zeddaan
		(gr 1978)	Cendres Bleues

same heights as his illustrious stable-companion who patently found the mile at Longchamp a minimum, but he's almost as good as St Jovite was at the same stage, and quite possibly open to a little more progress.

Basim was sent to Longchamp with two wins behind him from his three starts. First time up he'd won a maiden race over six furlongs at Leopardstown in July by three lengths but had then gone down by two and a half lengths to the improving Up And At 'Em, who'd finished third in the race Basim had won over two weeks before, in the five-furlong Eaton Two-Year-Old race at the same venue in August. Up And At 'Em went on to show himself a much better sprinter at five furlongs than six furlongs, while Basim clearly needed at least the latter distance, and he reversed the form when he met Up And At 'Em for the third time in just under a month in the Anglesey Stakes over an extended six furlongs at the Curragh later in August. In a disappointing turnout even before Unusual Heat was withdrawn because of the soft ground, Basim won by six lengths from an eased Up And At 'Em, with the only other runner, the once-raced Curragh maiden winner El Zorro Dorado, another six lengths back in third. The resolute manner in which Basim strode right away in the closing stages was indicative of one who'd be suited by longer distances, and in the one-mile Criterium, on the back of a strong pace on very soft ground, Basim came up with easily his best effort. He had no answer once Tenby took up the running from him with around two furlongs left, but he stuck to his task in the straight, and, despite losing second to Blush Rambler on the line, made it a clean sweep for the foreign challengers two and a half lengths ahead of the remainder.

First-foal Basim was the only yearling by the 1986 Eclipse Award winner and leading 1991 first-season stallion Capote to be sold at public auction in Britain and Ireland in 1991, falling to a bid of 165,000 guineas from Gainsborough Stud Management at Newmarket's Highflyer Sales. As a son of Triple Crown winner Seattle Slew, who's steadily making a name for himself as a sire of sires, and a half-brother to the established stallions Baldski and Exceller, Capote was tipped to make the grade as a stallion; the success of his first crop may be judged by the fact that his covering fee was one of the few actually raised in 1992. Capote's original owners, who paid Calumet Farm 4,000,000 dollars for the remaining half-interest in him when it came up for auction at the end of 1991, will be hoping his success as a stallion will endure longer than his form on the racecourse. Capote won three of his four races as a two-year-old when his season culminated in front-running Grade 1 victories in the Norfolk Stakes and the Breeders' Cup Juvenile. He failed to continue in the same vein as a three-year-old, though, when a viral infection and a lack of stamina thwarted his classic hopes. If Capote's exploits on and off the track aren't familiar to European racegoers then the achievements of some members on the female side of Basim's pedigree certainly should be: the dam Mer Belle is a close relative of the 1991 Two Thousand Guineas winner Mystiko. Furthermore, Mystiko's dam Caracciola is a half-sister to the middle-distance filly Calderina (since the dam of the smart French middle-distance colt Hello Calder) and the mile-and-a-quarter performer Pasakos, both of whom showed good form in France. The third dam Cendres Bleues was a very useful middle-distance performer back in the early-'seventies in Italy. It's quite likely that Basim will stay middle distances, too; certainly a mile and a quarter. He acts particularly well when the mud is flying, and it may be significant that as a two-year-old he raced only on an easy surface. *J. S. Bolger, Ireland*

BASMA (USA) 3 b.f. Grey Dawn II 132 – Tilting (USA) (Seattle Slew (USA)) [1991 6g* 6s⁴ 6f* 6m³ 1992 6m⁶] big, close-coupled, attractive filly: useful form at 2 yrs, including third in Cheveley Park Stakes at Newmarket: wearing net muzzle, poor last of 6 in minor event at Newbury in May, pulling hard early and weakening tamely 2f out: bred to stay beyond 6f: unsuited by soft ground: visits Dayjur. *Major W. R. Hern*   –

BASSETLAW BELLE 3 b.f. Lucky Wednesday 124 – Delayed Action 113 (Jolly Jet 111) [1991 NR 1992 5.1d 6m 7.5m 8d 5d⁶ a5g] leggy, unfurnished filly: eighth living foal: sister to 4-y-o 5f (at 2 yrs) and 7f winner MCA Below The Line and half-sister to fairly useful sprinter Force of Action (by Galivanter) and a winner in Isle of Man: dam won seven 5f races: no form. *S. R. Bowring*   –

BASSIO (BEL) 3 b.c. Efisio 120 – Batalya (BEL) (Boulou) [1991 5d⁴ 5s⁵ 5f⁴ 6m² 6g⁴ 6f* 6g* 7g⁶ 7.5f* 7f³ 8f⁶ a8g³ 1992 a10g⁴ a8g* a8g⁴ a8g³ a7g 8.1s a12g a10g] neat colt: fair performer: won claimer at Southwell in February: well beaten last 4 starts: stays 1¼m: best on firm ground and all-weather surfaces: blinkered/visored once: suitable mount for a claimer. *C. N. Allen*   **67**

BATABANOO 3 ch.g. Bairn (USA) 126 – For Instance (Busted 134) [1991 5m² 6g³ 7f* 7m* 7m* 7m³ 8m* 8m³ 8g 1992 8m 8f 11m² 10.5g 11.1f⁶ 9.2m³ 8m² 8m³ 10m* 8m³ 10.3m] leggy, sparely-made gelding: has a quick action: fair handicapper: dropped in class, won seller (bought in 9,600 gns) at Ripon in August: likely to prove best over 1¼m + : yet to race on a soft surface: won novice hurdle in November. *Mrs M. Reveley*   **70**

BATCHWORTH BOUND 3 b.f. Ballacashtal (CAN) – Treasurebound 63 (Beldale Flutter (USA) 130) [1991 NR 1992 7g 8m 8.1g³ 6m³ 6m 6d⁶ 7d⁶ 7g 6.1s³ 5.3g* 6s⁶ 6.9v] tall filly: rather nervy type: first foal: dam, placed over 6f at 4 yrs, is daughter of very useful 6f and 7f performer Miss Tweedie: poor form: won maiden at Brighton in September: never dangerous in handicaps following month: ideally suited by further than 5f: acts on soft ground: blinkered twice, running creditably first occasion. *E. A. Wheeler*   **49**

BATHSHEBA EVERDENE 4 gr.f. Monsanto (FR) 121 – Gill Breeze (Farm – Walk 111) [1991 NR 1992 6m] sparely-made, dipped-backed filly: still a maiden: well beaten in Folkestone handicap on first run since 2 yrs. *K. O. Cunningham-Brown*

BATON BOY 11 ch.g. Music Boy 124 – Lobela 77 (Lorenzaccio 130) [1991 7f³ 6g⁵ 7.6g³ 8f 6m 7m 8.3f⁵ 7m 10.5d 1992 7.1f⁶] lengthy, rather sparely-made gelding: poor mover: poor handicapper nowadays: effective from stiff 6f to 1m: probably acts on any going: has run moderately in blinkers. *S. G. Norton*

BATTLE COLOURS (IRE) 3 b.c. Petorius 117 – Streamertail 81 (Shirley 90 Heights 130) [1991 5g⁶ 6s² a5g² a6g* 1992 7d⁵ 6d³ 7f* 7.1m* 7.1m³ 8m³ 7.6m³ a7g⁴ 8m*] smallish, quite attractive colt: fairly useful handicapper: successful at Thirsk and Haydock in May and Newcastle (gamely, best effort) in July: suited by 1m: acts on firm and dead ground (fair effort on equitrack): genuine and consistent. *Sir Mark Prescott*

BATTLE ON 5 b.m. Blakeney 126 – Perfect Picture (FR) 78 (Hopeful Venture – 125) [1991 16v 12d⁵ 16m* 14m* 16m* 16g* 20g 16g² 14d* 14g³ 16g* 16g⁵ 16m⁴ 16s 1992 20m] lengthy Irish mare: prolific winner as 4-y-o: twice well beaten in Ascot Handicap, including on only start in 1992: stays 2m: acts on firm and dead ground: ran creditably when blinkered once. *J. S. Bolger, Ireland*

BATTLE STANDARD (CAN) 5 b.g. Storm Bird (CAN) 134 – Hoist Emy's 80 Flag (USA) (Hoist The Flag (USA)) [1991 8d* 8g 9g⁵ 8g³ 9m⁶ 9g⁶ 8g⁶ 10g* 10g 1992 a8g*] ex-Irish gelding: half-brother to 3 winners in USA: dam successful 9 times, including in 7f stakes race at 3 yrs: successful 3 times in Ireland, trained as 4-y-o by T. Stack: best effort to win claimer at Southwell in February: stays 1¼m: acts on good to firm, dead ground and fibresand: sold to join Mrs S. Bramall 6,800 gns Doncaster May Sales: won 2 selling hurdles in October. *C. Tinkler*

BATTLING BELLA (USA) 3 b.f. Fighting Fit (USA) – Belle Marina 82 – (Lochnager 132) [1991 6g³ 5g⁴ 6.1m 1992 5.3m 5m 5.7m 5m 5m] sturdy, workmanlike filly: has a round action: modest maiden: no worthwhile form in 1992, blinkered on final start, in June: tends to sweat and get on edge. *J. Sutcliffe*

BATTUTA 3 ch.f. Ballacashtal (CAN) – Valpolicella 63 (Lorenzaccio 130) [1991 42 5m³ 6m⁴ 6m³ 6.1m⁴ 7m 1992 5v 7g⁶ 7m³ 7g 7m⁵ 7m³ 8m³ 6.9g⁵ 9g] leggy, lightly-made filly: plating-class maiden: stays 1m: acts on good to firm ground: has run creditably for 7-lb claimer. *R. Earnshaw*

BAULKING TOWERS 2 b.g. (Mar 20) Kala Shikari 125 – Carrula (Palm Track – 122) [1992 6m⁵ 7d 8.1s 7m] 3,200Y: big gelding: has a round action: fifth foal: half-brother to winners abroad by Dublin Taxi and Marching On: dam unraced: well beaten in maidens: sold 1,500 gns Ascot November Sales and gelded. *M. McCormack*

BAWAETH (USA) 2 b.f. (Jan 19) Blushing Groom (FR) 131 – Last Feather 70 p (USA) 120 (Vaguely Noble 140) [1992 7g⁴ 7d³] small, sparely-made filly: sixth foal: sister to fairly useful 1m winner Contessa and half-sister to French 9f winner Phar Feather (by Lyphard) and Irish 1¼m winner Limbir Dancer (by Nijinsky): dam 7.3f and 10.5f winner also third in Oaks: fair form in minor event at Newbury and maiden at Leicester (stayed on having been checked 2f out) in the autumn: will prove capable of better, particularly over 1m+ . *B. W. Hills*

BAYADERE (USA) 3 b.f. Green Dancer (USA) 132 – Azallya (FR) (Habitat 134) 61 [1991 7m 1992 12s⁵ 14m⁶ 14.1g² 16.9d³ a16g] lengthy, sparely-made filly: modest maiden: stays 17f: acts on dead ground, seemingly not on fibresand: visored last 3 starts. *M. R. Stoute*

BAYAIREG (USA) 3 ch.c. Diesis 133 – Cacti (USA) (Tom Rolfe) [1991 7g⁶ 87 8.1m³ 7g⁶ 1992 8m³ 10g³ 9.9f* 10.3f* 12f⁴ 10g⁴ 10m 10g 10.3m] compact colt: has a quick action: fairly useful handicapper: held up when successful at Beverley and Doncaster in May: better form when fourth at Royal Ascot and Newmarket's July meeting: unimpressive in appearance, ran moderately last 2 outings: may prove ideally suited by 1¼m: acts on firm ground: wears crossed noseband. *A. A. Scott*

BAYDON BELLE (USA) 2 br.f. (Apr 21) Al Nasr (FR) 126 – Vague Prospect 64 (USA) (Vaguely Noble 140) [1992 6m⁶ 8g⁴ 8.2g⁴] $130,000Y: leggy, sparely-made filly: first foal: dam half-sister to Dowsing and Fire The Groom: modest maiden: will stay 1¼m. *G. Lewis*

BAYFAN (IRE) 2 b.c. (Mar 3) Taufan (USA) 119 – Laurel Express 76 (Bay – Express 132) [1992 6s] IR 1,000F, IR 6,500Y, resold 6,000Y: tall colt: fifth foal: half-brother to 3-y-o 1m and 1½m winner Take By Storm (by Bluebird): dam second over 7f from 2 starts: 33/1 and burly, soon pushed along and behind throughout in 16-runner maiden at Newbury in October. *J. S. Moore*

BAYIN (USA)   3 b.c. Caro 133 – Regatela (USA) (Dr Fager) [1991 NR 1992 8g 8g⁶   –
14.1m a8g⁵] $2 10,000Y: leggy, lengthy colt: has a round action: seventh foal: brother
to a winner in North America and half-brother to several winners, including good
1982 2-y-o Wings of Jove (by Northern Jove): dam, winner 9 times, from good South
American family: behind in maidens: sold out of R. Armstrong's stable 5,200 gns
Newmarket Autumn Sales after penultimate start. *M. D. I. Usher*

BAY MOUNTAIN   6 b.g. Tyrnavos 129 – Just You Wait (Nonoalco (USA) 131)   –
[1991 NR 1992 a7g a8g a10g⁵ a7g] tall, well-made gelding: shows knee action: still a
maiden: blinkered last 2 starts, in the spring. *M. Dixon*

BAY QUEEN   2 b.f. (Apr 30) Damister (USA) 123 – Be My Queen 84 (Be My   61
Guest (USA) 126) [1992 7s⁴ 8d] leggy, unfurnished filly: fifth foal: half-sister to 1991
2-y-o 9f winner Sarasota Bay (by Petoski): dam 1m winner out of half-sister to
Derby second Cavo Doro: swishing tail repeatedly in paddock, fourth in auction at
York, much better effort in maiden events in October: will stay at least 1¼m. *M. Bell*

BAYRAK (USA)   2 b.c. (May 12) Bering 136 – Phydilla (FR) 126 (Lyphard (USA)   –
132) [1992 8.2s] $110,000Y: closely related to French 1¼m and 10.5f winner Cupid
Sea (by Arctic Tern) and half-brother to useful maiden Mysteries (by Seattle Slew)
and 3-y-o Landed Gentry (by Vaguely Noble): dam won from 6f to 1m, and is
daughter of good broodmare Godzilla: 9/1, beaten around 20 lengths in maiden at
Nottingham in October, never dangerous and tending to run right. *A. C. Stewart*

BAY RUM   2 br.f. (Feb 14) Green Ruby (USA) 104 – Cuba Libre (Rum (USA))   41
[1992 6m a7g 7g3 6m a8g] good-topped filly: ninth living foal: half-sister to several
winners here and abroad, including (at 7f and 1m) Grey Rum (by Absalom) and (at 6f
and 1m) Hudsons Mews (by Young Generation): dam ran 3 times in Ireland: modest
plater: better suited by 7f than 6f: well beaten on equitrack: ran creditably in
blinkers: trained until after penultimate start by B. Beasley. *K. O. Cunningham-
Brown*

BAYSHAM (USA)   6 b.g. Raise A Native – Sunny Bay (USA) (Northern Bay   79
(USA)) [1991 6s 6g⁴ 6g* 6m⁴ 6d³ 6g* 6g⁴ 6g 6m 5.6m² 7d⁵ 5d 5.2g 1992 6d⁴ 5d⁶ 6s*
6f⁶ 7g 6f 5s 6m 6g⁶ 6g 5.1s⁴ 7d 5.1d] tall, close-coupled gelding: impresses good deal
in appearance: consistent handicapper at 5 yrs, not so in 1992: won at Salisbury (all 3
of wins there) in April: best short of 7f: acts on firm and soft going: wears
blinkers/visor these days: has run well when sweating. *B. R. Millman*

BAY TERN (USA)   6 b.h. Arctic Tern (USA) 126 – Unbiased (USA) 81 (Foolish   43
Pleasure (USA)) [1991 15m⁵ 14.1m⁴ 1992 16.2d³ 13.1m⁴ 15.8m 13.1s⁴] rangy horse:
only a poor handicapper nowadays: stays 2m: acts on good to firm and soft ground:
joined T. Dyer and won handicap hurdle in October. *M. H. Easterby*

B B GLEN   2 b.f. (Feb 14) Hadeer 118 – Damaska (USA) (Damascus (USA)) [1992   48
7m² 7d² 7g²] lengthy, plain filly: fourth foal: half-sister to 3-y-o 11.5f winner
Resplendent (by Sharrood) and 11f winner Taskalady (by Touching Wood): dam
unraced: consistent form in sellers in midsummer: will probably stay 1¼m+: acts
on good to firm and dead ground. *D. Morris*

BE A HONEY   4 ch.f. Be My Guest (USA) 126 – Reltop 72 (High Top 131) [1991   87
10d 12m 11.8m* 12f* 14.6m 12m 1992 13.3g⁴ 11g 15.9d⁶ 14m³ 14s³ 14.6f 12m] rangy
filly: fairly useful but inconsistent handicapper: stays 1¾m (stiff task over 15.9f):
acts on firm and soft ground: sold 30,000 gns Newmarket December Sales. *N. A.
Graham*

BEAM ME UP SCOTTY (IRE)   3 br.g. Orchestra 118 – Bright Path 64 (He   55 d
Loves Me 120) [1991 6g 5m⁵ 6f² 7m 6.1m 10m³ 8m 1992 10g³ a10g³ a10g³ a12g³ 12g 10g⁵
12m 12m⁵ 12g 12d] close-coupled, quite attractive gelding: modest maiden: below
form in handicaps last 4 starts, including when blinkered once: stays 1¼m: acts on
firm going, and equitrack: looks a difficult ride: sold 3,100 gns Newmarket Autumn
Sales and gelded. *P. Mitchell*

BEANSHOOT   2 gr.f. (Apr 18) Precocious 126 – Meanz Beanz (High Top 131)   –
[1992 5f³] quite good-topped filly: fifth live foal: half-sister to useful middle-distance
stayer Bean King (by Ardross): dam unraced half-sister to Chilibang out of Chili
Girl: green, remote third of 4 in maiden at Pontefract in August: withdrawn lame on
intended debut. *J. Berry*

BEAR WITH ME (IRE)   3 ch.f. Ahonoora 122 – Bear's Affair (Gay Fandango   64
(USA) 132) [1991 6s 7g 1992 6.1d 6.9m³ 7.1m* 6.9h⁵ 8g² 8m] workmanlike filly:
modest handicapper: won at Edinburgh in June: stays 1m: acts on good to firm
ground: tongue tied down last 3 starts, reportedly choking first occasion: usually
bandaged behind: not seen out after July: sold 10,500 gns Newmarket December
Sales. *M. Bell*

BEATLE SONG 4 b.f. Song 132 – Betyle (FR) (Hardicanute 130) [1991 6f4 a8g2 **64** 8g a8g* a7g3 5.7g* 5d6 6g 5.1m 5.2f a6g4 1992 a7g4 6d 6v 6s 7m6 5.7m 7.1m 7f4 6m 7.1m* a7g 7g 7.1s] good-quartered, workmanlike filly: inconsistent handicapper: trained reappearance by C. J. Hill: won at Chepstow in June: effective from 7f to 1m: acts on firm ground and on fibresand: sometimes pulls hard. *R. J. Hodges*

BEAT THE BAGMAN (IRE) 2 b.c. (Mar 9) Bob Back (USA) 124 – Dacani 118 **39** (Polyfoto 124) [1992 5f 6m5 a6g6 7g 6m 6s6 6v4] 6,400F, 6,000Y: close-coupled, sturdy colt: good mover: half-brother to 3 winners here and abroad, including 1986 2-y-o 6f seller winner Fantine (by Hard Fought): dam smart sprinter here won over 7f in USA, is sister to very smart sprinter Valeriga: poor maiden: will stay 7f: best form on very soft ground: has run creditably for 7-lb claimer: consistent. *L. J. Holt*

BEAUCHAMP FIZZ 4 ch.c. Jalmood (USA) 126 – Buss 102 (Busted 134) [1991 – 9m 12g 12f5 12f* 14g 14m4 12g 12m2 16d 12g4 15.8d] small, angular colt: rated 75 at best for J. Dunlop as 3-y-o: no worthwhile form in 1992: trained first 2 starts by N. Callaghan: not seen out after June. *W. Storey*

BEAUCHAMP GRACE 3 b.f. Ardross 134 – Buss 102 (Busted 134) [1991 NR **72** 1992 10g 12g3 11.6g5 14.1g* 16d3] tall filly: shows knee action: half-sister to numerous winners, including fairly useful 1m winner Imperial Ace (by Derring-Do) and 17.6f winner Beauchamp Cactus (by Niniski): dam game performer at up to 11f: fair performer: landed odds in maiden at Carlisle in September: suited by test of stamina: acts on dead ground: sold to join D. Nicholson 14,500 gns Newmarket Autumn Sales and won juvenile hurdle at Cheltenham in December. *J. L. Dunlop*

BEAUCHAMP HERO 2 b.c. (May 6) Midyan (USA) 124 – Buss 102 (Busted **65** p 134) [1992 7m 7d4] half-brother to numerous winners, including 3-y-o 14.1f winner Beauchamp Grace (by Ardross), fairly useful miler Imperial Ace (by Derring-Do) and stayer Beauchamp Cactus (by Niniski): dam game performer at up to 11f: fourth of 20 in maiden at Lingfield in September, staying on very well last 300 yds: will improve again, particularly over middle distances. *J. L. Dunlop*

BEAU DADA (IRE) 4 b.f. Pine Circle (USA) – Beauvoir (Artaius (USA) 129) **55** [1991 a6g3 7f3 8g 8.3g* 10g 8.3m6 8.3m6 8s 9s 1992 a8g3 a8g5 a8g2 a10g3 10g 10f4] neat, quite attractive filly: modest handicapper, largely consistent in 1992: effective from 1m to 1¼m: acts on firm going and equitrack: tends to get on edge: below form when visored twice at 2 yrs: not seen out after May. *J. White*

BEAUFAN 5 br.g. Taufan (USA) 119 – Beaume (FR) (Faraway Son (USA) 130) – [1991 NR 1992 12.3g] brother to Irish 5f to 1m winner Erindale, later successful in Australia, and fair 1987 2-y-o 7f winner Be My Fan: dam unraced granddaughter of Sweet Solera: in frame in sprint maidens at Phoenix Park and the Curragh for L. Browne at 2 yrs: winning hurdler in 1991/2: 100/1, soundly beaten in Wolverhampton claimer in April. *C. F. C. Jackson*

BEAUMAN 2 b.c. (Mar 10) Rainbow Quest (USA) 134 – Gliding 94 (Tudor **72** p Melody 129) [1992 7d3 8m 8.1d*] 28,000F: leggy, workmanlike colt: has a round action: half-brother to 3-y-o Pleasuring (by Good Times) and several winners, including (at 7f) useful Rose of Montreaux (by Habat) and (at 7f and 8.5f) useful Bay Street (by Grundy): dam sprinting half-sister to very smart 1973 2-y-o Splashing (dam of Bassenthwaite): fair form: ridden by 7-lb claimer, easily won maiden at Haydock in September, leading 2f out and staying on well: will stay beyond 1m: well below form on good to firm ground. *B. A. McMahon*

BEAUMONT (IRE) 2 br.c. (May 2) Be My Native (USA) 122 – Say Yes (Junius **58** p (USA) 124) [1992 7.5m] 14,000Y: leggy, unfurnished colt: good walker: second foal: dam Irish 2-y-o 1m winner, is half-sister to Molecomb winner Hatta: keeping-on seventh of 10 in maiden at Beverley in July, not knocked about: went well to post: looked sure to improve. *J. Pearce*

BEAUMONT'S KEEP 6 b.g. Castle Keep 121 – Powderhall 81 (Murrayfield **29** 119) [1991 8s 8.2s3 10m 7f6 9m 5f* 6g 6g5 6d6 6f2 6m2 6m5 6g 6g 6m 6s 1992 a5g a6g2 a6g] good-topped gelding: carries plenty of condition: moderate mover: poor handicapper: best at sprint distances: acts on firm and dead going and on equitrack: often slowly away: not one to trust implicitly: not seen out after February and sold 1,100 gns Doncaster June Sales. *T. D. Barron*

BEAUMOOD 6 b.g. Jalmood (USA) 126 – Falcon Berry (FR) (Bustino 136) [1991 – 12s 14d 12.3s 13.8m6 12g2 11.9m 15g3 12g* 12.1s5 12.3m3 12f 12.1g 1992 a14g] neat gelding: good mover: rated 52 at 5 yrs: soundly beaten at Southwell in February: stays 13f: suited by an easy surface: goes very well with forcing tactics: effective visored or not: sold 2,800 gns Doncaster May Sales. *C. Tinkler*

BEAU QUEST 5 b.h. Rainbow Quest (USA) 134 – Elegant Tern (USA) 102 (Sea **68**
Bird II 145) [1991 a12g² a14g³ a14g² a14g² a14g² 14.8g² 14m² 16.2f² 16.5m⁵ 12.2d*
12.3g* 12.3f 13.9g 15.9m⁶ 11.9g 11.9m 1992 11.9s⁴ 18.5g⁵ 12f² 14g³ 14.1m* 13.1m*
16.1f] small horse: has quick action: fair handicapper: successful in June at
Nottingham and Ayr: not seen out after finishing behind in Northumberland Plate at
Newcastle: effective from 1½m to 2m: probably acts on any going: effective with or
without blinkers or visor: tail flasher: found little on occasions earlier in career, but
did nothing wrong in 1992: suited by waiting tactics. *R. M. Whitaker*

BEAU VENTURE (USA) 4 ch.c. Exploded (USA) – Old Westbury (USA) **99**
(Francis S) [1991 5m⁵ 5m² 6m² 5g 5g 6m⁵ 5g 5g* 5d 1992 5g 5m³ 5m² 6f³ 5m* 5g*
6m 5d² 6g 5.6m 5d 6g 5g] leggy, quite good-topped colt: moderate mover: improved
handicapper in first half of season, successful at Ayr and York (£9,080 event): well
below form last 5 starts: suited by 5f: acts on firm and dead ground: held up, and has
turn of foot: good mount for claimer. *F. H. Lee*

BEAVER BROOK 2 gr.c. (Apr 19) Bairn (USA) 126 – Lucky Song 91 (Lucky **63**
Wednesday 124) [1992 5.2d 5.1m⁴ 5m4 6m 7m³ 8.2d] 20,000Y: tall, lengthy,
unfurnished colt: has a quick action: third foal: half-brother to 1991 2-y-o 6f and 7f
winner X My Heart (by Aragon) and fair 1990 2-y-o 5f and 6f winner Level Xing (by
Stanford): dam 5f and 7f winner: generally progressive maiden: stays 8.2f: acts on
good to firm and dead ground: ran well when sweating penultimate start: sold 4,200
gns Newmarket Autumn Sales. *R. Hannon*

BECKINGHAM BEN 8 gr.g. Workboy 123 – Pickwood Sue 74 (Right Boy 137) **39**
[1991 a5g⁵ 5g⁶ 5d⁶ 5m⁵ 5g⁵ a5g⁵ a6g a5g 1992 a6g a5g a5g² a5g³ 5g 5m] tall gelding: **a48**
poor handicapper: has won one of last 42 starts: suited by 5f: acts on firm and dead
going and on all-weather surfaces: effective with or without visor or blinkers: has
looked none too keen: not seen out after April. *J. P. Leigh*

BECKSWHITE ABBEY 2 ch.f. (Apr 23) Absalom 128 – Spare Wheel 67 (Track **–**
Spare 125) [1992 5d 5f 6m] 500F: plain filly: fourth reported foal: sister to 1m (at 2
yrs) and 6f winner Pacific Rim: dam 1½m seller winner also successful over
hurdles: backward, well beaten, including in seller: trained by W. J. Pearce first 2
starts: sold 550 gns Doncaster June Sales. *B. Beasley*

BECKY BOO 2 b.f. (May 4) White Mill 76 – Aber Cothi (Dominion 123) [1992 5g] **–**
leggy, unfurnished filly: first foal: dam poor maiden on flat won over hurdles: always
well behind in seller at Leicester in April. *D. Burchell*

BECKYHANNAH 2 b.f. (Feb 12) Rambling River 111 – Munequita (Marching **33**
On 101) [1992 6d 6.1g 7d] 1,100Y: plain filly: first foal: dam ran once at 2 yrs: poor
maiden, ran in seller last time. *R. Bastiman*

BEDOUIN PRINCE (USA) 5 b.h. Danzig (USA) – Regal Heiress 81 (English **–**
Prince 129) [1991 a8g a11g² a11g² a12g* a11g² a12g³ a14g³ a12g 12s 12.3s 10f³ 11f²
a11g² 16g⁶ 12g a12g 13.6g⁴ 16.1m a12g² a12g³ a12g 1992 a12g a12g⁶] heavy-topped
horse: carries condition: poor mover: rated 53 at best at 4 yrs: well beaten in
Southwell in 1992: stays 1¾m (stiff tasks over 2m): acts on firm going and fibresand:
effective with or without visor, has been tried in blinkers. *B. Richmond*

BEE BEAT 4 ch.g. Bairn (USA) 126 – Thorny Rose 81 (Tap On Wood 130) [1991 **– §**
a6g³ a8g⁴ 7s⁵ 10.2g³ 10m⁵ 11.5m 11.7g² 11.7m² 11.7m² 11.6m² 13.1f⁶ a12g⁶ 13.3m
12g⁴ 12.1d 1992 12m 11.6g 12d⁶ 12f⁴ 15g 11.6g⁵] leggy, lightly-made gelding: still a
maiden: best at around 1½m: acts on good to firm ground: blinkered nowadays:
tends to wander, has seemed reluctant to race and is one to avoid. *E. A. Wheeler*

BEEBOB 4 b.f. Norwick (USA) 120 – Anzeige (GER) (Soderini 123) [1991 8g² **–**
10g* 10g* 11.5g* 14g* 13.9g⁵ 14m² 14.6m² 16.2g 1992 16d 12.5g 18.5g 16m]
sparely-made filly: fair performer (rated 85) as 3-y-o for G. Lewis: in good form over
hurdles in 1991/2 for present trainer: no form on flat in 1992: should stay 2m: acts on
good to firm ground (injured on heavy): sometimes bandaged. *M. C. Pipe*

BEECHWOOD COTTAGE 9 ch.g. Malinowski (USA) 123 – Drora (Busted **54 d**
134) [1991 a7g a7g⁵ a8g* a7g⁵ a8g⁶ a10g⁶ a8g a7g³ 7f 8g 7f 7m 5m 6m 8f 7g 6.9m 6f
7f³ 10f³ 10.5f 10m 8g 1992 a7g⁶ a8g* a8g a8g⁵ a8g 7d³ 8g 7g a7g⁶ a8g⁶ 10.5g⁶ 7d
8.9g 10f² 8f3] small, sturdy gelding: poor mover: unreliable handicapper: won
claimer at Lingfield in January: stays 1¼m: acts on any going and on equitrack:
effective with or without blinkers: visored once at 8 yrs, running below form:
usually starts slowly and gets behind: a difficult ride, and needs tender handling. *A.
Bailey*

BEE DEE DANCER 2 ch.f. (Apr 15) Ballacashtal (CAN) – Albion Polka (Dance **–**
In Time (CAN)) [1992 6d] 2,600Y: tall, leggy filly: second foal: dam unraced: green,
last of 13 in maiden auction at Ayr in September. *Miss L. A. Perratt*

BEE DEE ELL (USA) 3 b.g. Lemhi Gold (USA) 123 – Truth Above All (USA) **42**
(Far North (CAN) 120) [1991 6d⁶ 5s³ 7d⁶ 6g 5f⁶ 8.3g⁶ 8.1m 6s a6g 1992 5m 7m³
11.1m⁵ 9.2f⁴ 8.1m³ 10m⁵ 6m³ 8.1m⁵ 7g⁴ 8.3f⁴ 5f³ 7d⁶ 8.1d⁴ 8.3s⁵ 5d] sturdy gelding:
poor maiden: headstrong, and should prove best at about 1m: acts on firm and soft
ground: no improvement in blinkers/visor: has run creditably for 7-lb claimer: sold
1,500 gns Doncaster September Sales: not one to be too interested in. *Miss L. A.
Perratt*

BEE UPSTANDING (IRE) 3 b.f. Standaan (FR) 118 – Buzzing Around (Prince   –
Bee 128) [1991 NR 1992 a8g⁶] IR 5,400F, 12,500Y: angular filly: first foal: dam Irish
7f winner from family of Time Charter and Nicholas Bill: blinkered and bit
backward, tailed-off last in maiden at Southwell in July: moved poorly to post: sold
875 gns Ascot December Sales. *Dr J. D. Scargill*

BEGGARMAN THIEF (USA) 2 b.c. (Mar 16) Arctic Tern (USA) 126 – **112** p
Rascal Rascal (USA) (Ack Ack (USA)) [1992 6g 7m* 7m⁴ 7.3s*]
  Beggarman Thief proved a real handful when he made his debut in a
minor event at Newmarket in August. After getting worked up in the preliminaries, so much so he was difficult to mount, he gave his rider a thoroughly
torrid time in the race as well, refusing to settle, and ended up beating just two
home. Less than two months later Beggarman Thief lined up as 5/1
joint-second favourite for the Vodafone Horris Hill Stakes at Newbury, gave
no trouble beforehand, settled well once the race was under way, and won
comfortably. The key to Beggarman Thief's tremendous improvement in form
in the intervening period, in which time he easily won a maiden at Yarmouth
and finished an unlucky fourth in the Somerville Tattersall Stakes at
Newmarket, was his becoming gradually more amenable to restraint.
Beggarman Thief still took a fierce hold for three furlongs at Yarmouth
(where he wasn't brought into the paddock until very late), but he settled
much more quickly in behind a strong pace at Newmarket and did so again at
Newbury where, turning into the straight, he brought up last place racing
keenly but under control. As the favourite Urgent Request, Nominator and
New Capricorn battled it out in front, Beggarman Thief made steady progress
towards the leaders, and once he was produced with his effort with over a
furlong to run he quickly went past the new leader Bin Ajwaad and went on to
beat him by two lengths; Port Lucaya finished a further three lengths behind
in third. Beggarman Thief would probably also have won the Somerville
Tattersall Stakes had he not been bumped and then denied a clear run with
less than two furlongs to go; he finished strongly, just over a length down on
the winner Nominator at the line, form he reversed in no uncertain fashion at
Newbury.

Beggarman Thief (USA) (b.c. Mar 16, 1990)	Arctic Tern (USA) (ch 1973)	Sea Bird II (ch 1962)	Dan Cupid Sicalade
		Bubbling Beauty (ch 1961)	Hasty Road Almahmoud
	Rascal Rascal (USA) (b or br 1981)	Ack Ack (b 1966)	Battle Joined Fast Turn
		Savage Bunny (b or br 1974)	Never Band Tudor Jet

  In spite of being by Arctic Tern, an influence for stamina and sire of such
as Bering, Harbour, Escaline, Glacial Storm and Khairpour, Beggarman Thief
is reportedly regarded by his trainer purely and simply as a miler. Significantly, perhaps, two of the dam's previous foals, the 1990 two-year-old one-
mile winner Alpha Rascal (by Alphabatim) and the extended seven-furlong
winner Key Suspect (by Alleged) were also trained by Gosden, neither
staying so far as could reasonably have been anticipated. Rascal Rascal, whose
two other foals include the Miswaki filly Wakia, successful at up to seven
furlongs, was a useful racemare at up to nine furlongs and stayed further than
her own dam Savage Bunny, whose four wins all came at sprint distances. In
keeping with most recent Horris Hill winners, Beggarman Thief's form is still
several pounds below the best of his contemporaries. Few recent Horris Hill
winners have possessed such thoroughly progressive form as he, though, and
if he remains tractable, then there's a fair chance there's still plenty of
improvement to come. A leggy, lengthy colt, Beggarman Thief will most likely

prove best at up to a mile and a quarter. He acts on good to firm and soft ground. *J. H. M. Gosden*

BEHAANIS (USA) 2 ch.c. (Apr 8) Java Gold (USA) – Dusty Gloves (USA) (Run Dusty Run (USA)) [1992 7f4 7g 7g 7g 8f 8s] $67,000F, $135,000Y: lengthy, rather unfurnished colt: fourth reported foal: half-brother to a winner by Clever Trick: dam, winner of 6 races at up to 11f, is half-sister to very smart middle-distance performer Spruce Needles: sire (half-brother to Spicy Story) top class at 3 yrs from 9f to 1½m: plating-class maiden: will stay 1¼m+: soundly beaten on soft ground. *A. A. Scott*   **46**

BEIJA FLOR 5 gr.g. Busted 134 – Rusticello 94 (Rusticaro (FR) 124) [1991 8.5f4 8.5f* 10.1f3 10g2 1992 12.3g 8.9g 10.2m 6.9h6 10g] lengthy, good-bodied gelding: poor mover: rated 79 at 4 yrs for H. Cecil: no form in 1992: stays 1¼m: acts on firm ground: blinkered penultimate start. *F. Jordan*   **–**

BELAFONTE 5 br.g. Derrylin 115 – Ulla Laing 107 (Mummy's Pet 125) [1991 10d3 10m2 12m* 11.9m2 12g* 16.5g4 11.9g 11.4m* 10m 1992 12.3v2 14m4 11.9f4 14.9f2 11.6g5 16m3 14s6 12.1s5] compact gelding: modest handicapper: largely consistent until below par last 2 runs: effective from 1½m to 2m: acts on any going: below best when blinkered or visored at 3 yrs: suitable mount for claimer: won over hurdles in October. *R. J. Holder*   **63**

BELARIUS 4 b.g. Bellypha 130 – Celebrity 101 (Troy 137) [1991 10g 8.1s5 10.3g6 1992 a11g 12.1g 12g] lengthy, workmanlike gelding: seems of little account these days. *R. E. Barr*   **–**

BELATED 3 gr.f. Bellypha 130 – Enchanted 116 (Song 132) [1991 NR 1992 8g2 7m6 7g5 6h3 6m* 5m2 6g3 5d* 5.2s2 5g4 a6g4 a6g] small, compact filly: half-sister to several winners, including useful 11f and 11.7f winner Woodpecker (by Touching Wood): dam sprinter, best at 2 yrs: progressed really well through the season, winning at Thirsk (maiden, hanging markedly left) in July and Goodwood in October: sold out of H. Thomson Jones's stable 14,500 gns Doncaster November Sales and well beaten on all-weather tracks afterwards: best form at around 5f with give in the ground: genuine. *P. C. Haslam*   **90**

BEL BARAKA (IRE) 3 ch.g. Bering 136 – Typhoon Polly 117 (Lord Gayle (USA) 124) [1991 7g 1992 8d 10s3 11.4m6 11.4d 8m6 11.6g3 8d2 10s5 9g a7g6 a10g3] compact gelding: modest maiden: changed hands 4,200 gns Newmarket July Sales: takes keen hold, and seems best at up to 1¼m: acts on soft going. *D. R. C. Elsworth*   **60**

BELDALE STAR 9 b.g. Beldale Flutter (USA) 130 – Little White Star (Mill Reef (USA) 141) [1991 16.2g 16.2d 16m* 1992 16d 14d 16.2g 16.4s 16.4g 16s 16.5g] deep-girthed, quite attractive gelding: good mover: rated 74 at 8 yrs: very much on the downgrade: stays 2m: acts on any going: usually bandaged nowadays. *R. Akehurst*   **–**

BELDI (USA) 3 ch.c. Diesis 133 – Margie Belle (USA) (Vaguely Noble 140) [1991 7g3 7g3 8.1f 7.9m2 8g 1992 10m* 10m3 12g 8m] strong, close-coupled colt: useful performer: won minor event at Brighton in April: ran well in listed race at Goodwood, moderately in Derby Italiano at Rome: no chance at Royal Ascot final start: stays 1¼m: acts on good to firm ground. *C. E. Brittain*   **99**

BELFORT RULER 5 b.g. Belfort (FR) 89 – Call Me Kate 72 (Firestreak 125) [1991 6m5 6m 1992 5.3m3 6g 7m4 7m4 7g6 7g5 7d4 6d 7m* 7m 7m2 7d 6g 7.3g] close-coupled, workmanlike gelding: fair handicapper: successful in Goodwood apprentice handicap in July: well below best last 2 starts: stays 7f: acts on good to firm and dead ground: has run well when sweating. *B. Gubby*   **71**

BELGRAN (USA) 3 b.c. El Gran Senor (USA) 136 – Belle of Dodge Me (USA) (Creme Dela Creme) [1991 NR 1992 10m3 10g* 12m* 16.2f2] strong, good-topped colt: moderate walker: eighth reported foal: closely related to useful 1984 2-y-o 7f winner Gallant Archer (by Nijinsky), later Grade 3 11f winner in USA, and a winner in Germany: dam smart winner at up to 1m, is sister to high-class filly Barely Even: fairly useful performer: won maiden at Nottingham and handicap at Newbury in the spring: mulish at stalls, creditable second in Queen's Vase at Royal Ascot: stays 2m: looks rather lazy: suffered tendon trouble and sold only 3,000 gns Newmarket Autumn Sales. *H. R. A. Cecil*   **90**

BELIEVE IN ME (IRE) 3 b.c. Don't Forget Me 127 – Fast Bay (Bay Express 132) [1991 7g 1992 6s 10.3g a8g a8g a12g4 a8g2] strong, useful-looking colt: good walker: modest form in 1992 only at Southwell on last 2 starts: stays 1m: acts on fibresand. *B. A. McMahon*   **56**

BELIEVE IT 3 b.c. Bellypha 130 – Hasty Key (USA) (Key To The Mint (USA)) –
[1991 8m⁴ 1992 9g 12m] leggy, quite attractive colt: no form in maidens in 1992:
should stay 1¼m: sold to join N. Waggott 4,200 gns Newmarket July Sales. *C. E.
Brittain*

BELJINSKI 4 b.f. Myjinski (USA) – Lady Bedale (Comedy Star (USA) 121) [1991 –
7g⁴ 6s⁵ 6g 1992 5.1d a5g a7g 6m 7.6m 7.5d] leggy, lengthy filly: poor plater. *B. J.
McMath*

BELLA BALLERINA 2 b.f. (Mar 21) Sadler's Wells (USA) 132 – Bella Colora 85 p
119 (Bellypha 130) [1992 7d⁵] rangy, attractive filly: has scope: sister to high-class
1¼m performer Stagecraft and half-sister to smart 1m winner Hyabella (by Shirley
Heights) and 3-y-o Alum Bay (by Reference Point): dam 6f to 1¼m winner, is
half-sister to Colorspin and very useful Rappa Tap Tap: 4/1, over 10 lengths fifth of 6
to Yawl in minor event at Newmarket in October: showed a fluent action to post:
sure to benefit greatly from the experience. *M. R. Stoute*

BELLA BAMBOLA (IRE) 2 ch.f. (Mar 31) Tate Gallery (USA) 117 – Sciam- 42
bola (Great Nephew 126) [1992 5m 5m⁴ 7f⁵ 5f⁶ 5g⁴ 6g] IR 2,200Y: useful-looking
filly: fifth foal: half-sister to a winner in Scandinavia: dam ran in Italy without
success: modest plater: put up best effort when blinkered in a maiden fifth start:
trained first 3 starts by S. Norton, next 2 by B. Beasley. *N. Tinkler*

BELLA BETTINA 3 ch.f. Doulab (USA) 115 – Barbara Zapolia (ITY) (Great –
Nephew 126) [1991 5d 6f 7g 7.6m 1992 5m 6g] leggy, rather sparely-made filly:
seems of little account: blinkered final start, in July: sold 600 gns Ascot November
Sales. *J. S. Moore*

BELLA RUN 3 ch.f. Commanche Run 133 – Bonne de Berry (Habitat 134) [1991 –
8d 7g 1992 8d⁶ 10d 7s 10.2f 8f 6g] lengthy filly: little form. *R. J. Hodges*

BELLA'S BOY 2 b.c. (Mar 9) Green Ruby (USA) 104 – Ty-With-Belle 67 –
(Pamroy 99) [1992 5v] smallish, lengthy colt: fourth foal: half-brother to 3-y-o
Bella's Match (by Royal Match) and 1989 2-y-o 5f seller winner Starchy Belle (by
Starch Reduced): dam quite modest maiden at 2 yrs, later placed over hurdles:
green, soon outpaced in maiden at Warwick in March. *B. Palling*

BELLA'S MATCH 3 b.f. Royal Match 117 – Ty-With-Belle 67 (Pamroy 99) [1991 –
5m 6m 7g 1992 8g 5.7f] sparely-made filly: has quick action: of little account:
blinkered final start, in August. *B. Palling*

BELLATRIX 4 b.f. Persian Bold 123 – Sorebelle 95 (Prince Tenderfoot (USA) 45
126) [1991 7g⁶ 1992 8m 8.5g⁵ 7m 7.5m 7f 7m³ 7.6m 10s 7m] big, rangy filly: poor
maiden: below form last 3 starts: likely to prove best at 7f/1m: acts on good to firm
ground. *C. E. Brittain*

BELLE ISIS (USA) 3 br.f. Sir Ivor 135 – Bemissing (USA) (Damascus (USA)) 77
[1991 NR 1992 12g 10.1d* 10s] $72,000Y: small, sturdy filly: first foal: dam unraced
half-sister to Jet Ski Lady: fair form: still better for race, won maiden at Haydock:
well tailed-off last in handicap at Ascot later in September, struggling before
halfway: will stay 1½m. *Lord Huntingdon*

BELLE SOIREE 2 ch.f. (Mar 21) Night Shift (USA) – Party Game 70 (Red Alert 53
127) [1992 6m⁴ 5d² 5f 6m a7g] sturdy, good-topped filly: fourth foal: half-sister to
fairly useful 4-y-o sprinter Very Dicey (by Tremblant) and to a winner in Belgium by
Daring March: dam 6f winner stayed 7f: modest form: strong-finishing second in
maiden at Epsom: well beaten afterwards, off course almost 5 months before final
start: will stay 6f: hung on firm ground. *S. Dow*

BELL LAD (IRE) 2 ch.c. (May 3) Common Grounds 118 – Quack Shot (USA) –
(Quack (USA)) [1992 5s 5g a7s⁶] IR 2,000Y, 2,500 2-y-o: close-coupled, rather leggy
colt: eighth foal: dam of little account: well beaten in sellers. *C. A. Smith*

BELLSABANGING 2 b.c. (Feb 25) Chilibang 120 – Bells of St Martin 89 61
(Martinmas 128) [1992 5.1h² 5.7f⁵ 5g⁵ 5g⁵ 5g⁶ 5s³ 5d³] lengthy colt: fifth foal:
half-brother to 3 winners, including sprinters My Ruby Ring (by Blushing Scribe)
and Bells of Longwick (by Myjinski): dam 2-y-o 5f winner: modest maiden: will stay
6f: acts on any going: has run well for apprentice: fairly consistent. *D. R. Laing*

BELLS OF LONGWICK 3 b.f. Myjinski (USA) – Bells of St Martin 89 (Martin- 92 ?
mas 128) [1991 6.1g 6g³ 7f 6g 6g⁴ 1992 6m 6f⁴ 7f⁵ 8f⁶ 7m⁵ 5m* 5.1f* 5g² 5.2f² 5d²
5s* 5.1s⁶ 5.2g³ 5d⁶ 5.1d] leggy filly: moderate mover: probably flattered when third
to Wolfhound in £7,000 conditions event at Newbury: fairly useful handicapper on
most form: successful at Wolverhampton and Bath in summer and Salisbury
(visored first time) in September: below form in visor next time: suited by 5f: acts

104

on any going: well beaten when sweating and edgy final start: has been bandaged behind. *D. R. Laing*

BELL TURRET 5 b. or br.g. Beldale Flutter (USA) 130 – Base Camp 80 (Derring-Do 131) [1991 8g 9s[6] 9m[3] 10g 9.9m 9.2d 9m 9m[4] 10.8m 10m 8m 10g 10.3g 1992 a12g a8g] good-topped gelding: one-time fair plater: no longer of much account. *A. W. Potts* –

BELMOREDEAN 7 ch.g. Be My Guest (USA) 126 – Hanna Alta (FR) (Busted 134) [1991 11.5m[6] 10d[5] a10g* 11.7m[6] 12g[5] a10g[5] 11.5m* 11.4m a10g[2] a10g a10g[3] 1992 a12g[3] a10g[2] 10.3g a10g[2] 12g a10g[3] a10g[6]] angular, sparely-made gelding: fair handicapper, best on equitrack: effective from 1¼m to 1½m: best form on turf on top-of-the-ground: races prominently: won 2 novice chases in the autumn. *R. J. O'Sullivan* – a80

BELPENEL 6 ch.g. Pharly (FR) 130 – Seldovia (Charlottown 127) [1991 NR 1992 16d] quite attractive gelding: tailed off in Nottingham handicap on first run on flat since 3 yrs: has been blinkered: winning (1989/90) selling hurdler. *C. A. Smith* –

BELTHORN 3 ro.f. Belfort (FR) 89 – Blowing Bubbles 72 (Native Admiral (USA)) [1991 5g 7.1s 5g 5m[4] 1992 5g 5.1m[6] 5.7h[3] 5g[4] 5.1g[2] 5m 5.1m[2] 5g[2] 5.2g 5s] tall, plain filly: modest maiden: best at 5f: acts on hard ground, probably not on soft: usually makes the running. *J. J. Bridger* 51

BE MY ERA (IRE) 4 b.g. Be My Guest (USA) 126 – Ribera (FR) (Wittgenstein (USA) 123 [1991 NR 1992 10m] second living foal: dam staying maiden out of sister to Ribot: won NH Flat race at Lingfield in February: showed nothing in Kempton claimer in August. *A. W. Denson* –

BE MY EVERYTHING (IRE) 3 b.f. Be My Guest (USA) 126 – Everything Nice 107 (Sovereign Path 125) [1991 7m[6] 1992 8f[3] 8.1d[4] 8d[2] 7m[3] 8g 10.5g 7g* 8g 10s[4] 7s] small filly: moderate mover: fair performer: won apprentice maiden at Thirsk in August: may prove ideally suited by shorter than 1¼m: acts on good to firm and soft ground. *R. Hollinshead* 67

BE MY HABITAT 3 ch.g. Be My Guest (USA) 126 – Fur Hat (Habitat 134) [1991 NR 1992 9g 8g[5] 10m 10g[4] 11.8g 10g 12.3s] IR 20,000F, 21,000Y: neat, sturdy gelding: second foal: half-brother to 4-y-o Wild Sable (by Kris), 1¼m winner at 3 yrs: dam unraced half-sister to Teenoso and sister to Topsy: twice showed signs of ability when with N. Graham first 5 starts: soundly beaten afterwards, blinkered in seller last time: won juvenile hurdle at Ascot in November. *Miss L. C. Siddall* –

BEN BLUFF 3 b.g. Cyrano de Bergerac 120 – Makalu 79 (Godswalk (USA) 130) [1991 6f[4] 6d 7.1d 1992 5.7s[6] a6g[3] 7g[5] 6f 5.7f 5.7d] strong gelding: poor maiden: should stay 7f: best efforts on soft surface: visored (always behind) penultimate outing: tends to hang left. *L. G. Cottrell* –

BEND SABLE (IRE) 2 b.c. (Apr 1) Mtoto 134 – Chrism (Baptism 119) [1992 6m[6] 7g[5]] 35,000Y: close-coupled colt: fourth foal: dam Irish maiden half-sister to Shining Finish: off course 2½ months, around 14 lengths fifth of 18 in maiden at Doncaster in November: will be better suited by 1¼m: will improve again. *P. C. Haslam* 52 p

BENEFACT (USA) 3 b.c. Known Fact (USA) 135 – Beneficence (USA) (Majestic Prince) [1991 6m[2] 6g 7m 8.2m 8m 1992 14.6g 10.2f a12g[6] 6g] leggy, close-coupled colt: of little account these days: tried blinkered/visored: sold 1,000 gns Newmarket July Sales. *W. P. Arbuthnot* –

BENEFICIAL 2 b.c. (Apr 6) Top Ville 129 – Youthful (FR) (Green Dancer (USA) 132) [1992 7f[2] 7g* 8.2g*] smallish, well-made colt: fourth foal: half-brother to very smart 3-y-o Jeune (by Kalaglow) and fairly useful 5-y-o miler Dorset Duke (by Beldale Flutter): dam, French 1½m winner, is out of high-class French staying 2-y-o First Bloom: progressive performer: narrowly won maiden at Wolverhampton in July, carried wide into straight then finishing strongly despite hanging left: off course nearly 3 months and better for race, followed up in minor event at Nottingham, taking time to hit top pace then staying on in fine style: looks a useful middle-distance colt in the making. *G. Wragg* 82 p

BENEVOLENT 2 b.c. (Mar 30) Robellino (USA) 127 – Ragged Moon 72 (Raga Navarro (ITY) 119) [1992 a7g 7f[6] 7d* 7g 8s[3] 7.3s[3] 7s* 7g] 11,500F, 41,000Y: well-made colt: good mover: fourth foal: closely related to 4-y-o Devil's Soul (by Faustus), unreliable in 1992, and useful 3-y-o Misterioso (by Forzando), successful at 6f at 2 yrs: dam won 1m sellers: fairly useful performer: successful in maiden at Yarmouth in August and nursery at Leicester in October: as effective at 7f as 1m: acts well on soft ground: tends to hang left: wears special bridle: tricky ride. *Sir Mark Prescott* 85

BENGAL TIGER (IRE)   4 b. or br.g. Petoski 135 – Heart 'n' Soul (Bold Lad   **52**
(IRE) 133) [1991 10.1m⁴ 10.1m 12g 13.3g 10d* 10.3d a10g⁵ a12g⁶ 1992 8g 9d* 7g 8m
9.2m² 9d⁵ 10f⁵ 8.3m⁶ 10g² 9.7d⁶ 9.7m⁴ 9g] lengthy gelding: bad mover: modest
handicapper: won girls apprentice event at Kempton in April: best at 9f/1¼m: acts
on firm and dead ground (yet to race on very soft going): wears blinkers: races
prominently: sold to join P. Evans 2,000 gns Newmarket Autumn Sales. *J. Akehurst*

BEN'S BEAUTY   4 b.g. Aragon 118 – Aunt Charlotte 85 (Charlottown 127) [1991   –
NR 1992 10.5d 13.6f a12g] leggy gelding: seems of little account. *Mrs S. Oliver*

BENTICO   3 b.g. Nordico (USA) – Bentinck Hotel 74 (Red God 128§) [1991 7d   **67**
1992 10d⁶ 10g 10m 12g³ 11.6m* 11.6m² 13.3d⁵ 10.3m* 8g 9d 10s] lengthy, well-made
gelding: poor mover: fair handicapper: won at Windsor (making all) in June and
Doncaster (led 3f out, held on gamely) in July: well below form afterwards: effective
at 1¼m and 1½m: probably needs a sound surface. *M. A. Jarvis*

BENZOE (IRE)   2 b.c. (Apr 28) Taufan (USA) 119 – Saintly Guest (What A Guest   **86** p
119) [1992 6g 5f3 a5g³ 5m³ 5d⁴ 6d* 6m²] 4,600Y: tall, unfurnished colt: has a
roundish action: second foal: half-brother to 3-y-o 8.5f winner King's Guest (by
Tender King): dam lightly raced in France from family of Sandford Lad: generally
progressive form: travelled strongly throughout when easy winner of Ayr maiden
auction in September: very good second of 17 in nursery at Newmarket following
month, keeping on strongly: much better suited by 6f than 5f, and will stay 7f: acts
on good to firm and dead ground: sure to progress further. *M. W. Easterby*

BE POLITE (IRE)   2 b.f. (Apr 13) Taufan (USA) 119 – Say Thanks (Thatching   **53**
131) [1992 5g 5g³ 6m⁶ 6m² 5m² 5m 5.3f² 5.2g² 6d² 6m 6s³ 7d] IR 6,800Y: small,
leggy filly: second foal: dam unraced half-sister to Molecomb winner Hatta: modest
maiden: runner-up in nurseries and sellers: suited by 6f: probably acts on any going:
blinkered (ran well) twice, visored (ran moderately) once: largely consistent: sold
4,000 gns Newmarket Autumn Sales. *M. Bell*

BERCEAU (USA)   3 b.f. Alleged (USA) 138 – River Lullaby (USA) (Riverman   **105**
(USA) 131) [1991 NR 1992 10s* 10.5v² 10.5g⁵ 12s* 12m⁶ 12.5s] $150,000Y: first foal:
dam Irish 2-y-o 6f winner, third in 1¼m listed race at 3 yrs: useful French
performer: won minor event at Maisons-Laffitte in March and Prix de Royaumont at
Saint-Cloud in June: not discredited in Prix de Royallieu at Longchamp in October
final start: stays 12.5f: acts on soft ground. *A. Fabre, France*

BERDANSK (USA)   2 b.c. (Feb 18) Bering 136 – Madame Premier (USA) (Raja   **106**
Baba (USA)) [1992 6g³ 8s² 8d⁴ 8v³] $310,000F: half-brother to several winners in
France and America, notably smart 6.5f (at 2 yrs) to 1m winner Northern Premier
(by Northern Baby): dam 2-y-o 5f stakes winner: useful French maiden: in frame in
Prix La Rochette at Longchamp and Prix Thomas Bryon (2½ lengths third to Mil
Foil) at Saint-Cloud in autumn on last 2 starts: will stay 1¼m. *A. Fabre, France*

BERGLIOT   2 b.f. (Mar 6) Governor General 116 – Come North 72 (Track Spare   **51**
125) [1992 5g 6m³ 5d⁵ 5m⁵ 5d] heavy-topped filly: tenth living foal: dam best at up to
1m: modest maiden: ran moderately last 2 starts, off course 10 weeks in between:
stays 6f. *J. Berry*

BERKELEY HILL BOY   5 ch.g. Castle Keep 121 – Brown Velvet 68 (Mansingh   –
(USA) 120) [1991 6g 6f⁵ 7f⁴ 7m 1992 6d] rangy gelding: no worthwhile form since 3
yrs: usually blinkered. *R. Hollinshead*

BERLIN WALL (IRE)   4 b. or br.c. Thatching 131 – Friedrichsruh (FR)   **81** d
(Dschingis Khan) [1991 a8g* 7.1g 8m* 1992 8d⁴ 7.9m 8f 8g⁶ 9d⁶ 7d 8g] sturdy,
good-bodied colt: fair handicapper: chipped a knee bone final start at 3 yrs: ran well
in Spring Handicap at Newbury on reappearance, well below that form after: should
stay 1¼m: has form on good to firm, easily best effort in 1992 on dead: edgy in a
visor second start, well beaten in blinkers final one: sold 4,200 gns Newmarket
Autumn Sales. *P. W. Chapple-Hyam*

BERNIE SILVERS   3 ch.g. Risk Me (FR) 127 – Vacation 102 (Remainder 106)   **43**
[1991 6m⁵ 7.1d 1992 9.7v⁴ 9.7g 5.1d⁴ a5g⁵ 8m 7d⁴ a11g 7f⁴ 6m] leggy gelding:
modest plater: sold out of G. Lewis's stable 1,100 gns Ascot May Sales after third
start, resold 720 gns Doncaster August Sales after final outing: may prove best at
6f/7f: acts on firm and dead ground. *M. C. Chapman*

BERNSTEIN BETTE   6 b.m. Petong 126 – Glenfield Portion 86 (Mummy's Pet   **76**
125) [1991 6d 6f 6g 6m⁴ 6f⁵ 6g* 6m* 6m⁴ 6m 6f³ 7g 7s 1992 6.1d 7.5m 7f⁶ 6d*
6m⁶ 6.1d³ 7g⁵ 7g⁵ 6m⁴ 6.1g 7d*] good-quartered mare: carries condition: fair
handicapper: won at Leicester in June and October: effective from 6f to 7f: probably
acts on any going: usually held up. *P. S. Felgate*

BET

BERSETO (USA) 3 b.c. Secreto (USA) 128 – Bergid (USA) (Cool Moon (USA)) –
[1991 8m⁵ 7d* 1992 8.1d 8m⁴ 6g 8.1g 7.9s] sturdy, good-bodied colt: moderate
mover: promising when making all in Doncaster maiden in 1991, but well beaten in
minor events this campaign in 1992: may need further than 1m: tongue tied down
final start: best left alone. *H. R. A. Cecil*

BERTIE WOOSTER 9 ch.g. Homeboy 114 – Peace of Mind 81 (Midsummer 89
Night II 117) [1991 5m³ 6g⁶ 6m 6g³ 6m 6g⁶ 6g 6g² 6g 6m 6m 6g 1992 6f 6.1m⁵ 7f 6f 7d
6g* 6m 6g 6g² 6d 6d³ 6m] strong, compact gelding: carries condition: moderate
mover: inconsistent handicapper: successful at Ascot in July: suited by 6f: not at his
best on very soft going, acts on any other: effective with or without blinkers: gets
behind and wins rarely. *R. J. Holder*

BESCABY BOY 6 b.g. Red Sunset 120 – Charo (Mariacci (FR) 133) [1991 10s⁴ 69
8d* 8m² 10g 9m³ 10g 8m³ 8m⁴ 8g³ 10m³ 8.5f³ 10.5g 9g* a8g⁵ a12g³ 1992 10g²
9.9m³ 9m⁶ 12g² 10.5g² 11.6g² 10f³ 10m³ 12.3d] strong gelding: carries condition:
very consistent handicapper: probably best at middle distances these days: acts on
any going: effective with or without blinkers: sold 7,800 gns Ascot September Sales.
J. Wharton

BESOTTED 3 b.f. Shirley Heights 130 – Bold And Beautiful 105 (Bold Lad (IRE) 96
133) [1991 NR 1992 10.2m* 10d² 10g² 10.3g³] lengthy filly: second foal: half-sister to
1991 French 3-y-o 1m (including listed event) winner Silly Bold (by Rousillon): dam
suited by 1m, is out of half-sister to very smart animals Western Jewel and Mr
Fluorocarbon: useful performer: won maiden at Bath in May: put up best effort in
minor event at Nottingham over 3 months later: ran in snatches next outing, then
hung left when fair third after another lengthy absence: will stay 1½m: has joined H.
Pantall, in France. *B. W. Hills*

BEST APPEARANCE (IRE) 2 b.c. (Apr 18) Try My Best (USA) 130 – Reli- 57 p
able Rosie (Relko 136) [1992 6f⁴ 6m⁴ 6g⁴ 7.9d] IR 10,500F, 14,000Y: sturdy, close-
coupled colt: brother to 1988 Irish 2-y-o 6f winner Try My Rosie and half-brother to
several winners, including Irish 1½m winner Camden Loch (by Camden Town):
dam won from 8.5f to 11.5f in Ireland: progressive form in maidens first 3 starts:
creditable effort in nursery at York, but gave impression would have done better
ridden more patiently: will stay further than 1m: likely do do better. *J. G. FitzGerald*

BEST EFFORT 6 ch.g. Try My Best (USA) 130 – Lunaria (USA) (Twist The Axe 66
(USA) [1991 6s⁴ 8d 5m⁴ 5d⁵ 5s* 5g³ 5s⁴ 5f⁶ 6f* 6m⁴ 5g* 7g 5m 1992 5g 5s³ 5s⁶ 5g
7m⁵ 5m² 5m* 5m* 5g⁵ 5d 5d 6d 5g 5d³ a8g] strong, workmanlike gelding: fair
handicapper: twice successful in small fields at Edinburgh in July: ideally suited by
5f nowadays: acts on firm and soft going: often soon ridden along: seems a hard ride
but won for amateur and claimer. *M. P. Naughton*

BEST GUN 3 b.g. K-Battery 108 – Ribonny (FR) 33 (Fast Hilarious (USA)) [1991 71 d
NR 1992 14.1m* 12f 16.1s 16d 14m 15.1d⁶] rather leggy gelding: half-brother to 4-y-o
Bonnys Game (by Mummy's Game): dam staying maiden, placed over hurdles: won
4-runner maiden at Redcar in June: failed to reproduce that form in handicaps, in
blinkers last 2 starts: should stay 2m. *C. W. C. Elsey*

BETALONGABILL 3 b. or br.g. Lir 82 – Cornish Susie (Fair Season 120) [1991 42
6m² 6m⁶ 7m 6g 8g 1992 8m⁴ 10m⁵ 8g³ 10m 8.1g 8f⁶] leggy gelding: poor maiden:
should stay 1¼m: blinkered last 4 starts. *M. Madgwick*

BETELGEUSE 3 br.f. Kalaglow 132 – Feather Flower 74 (Relkino 131) [1991 NR 86
1992 10f⁵ 12m³ 16m² 14.1g* 16.2d⁶] 5,800F: leggy, angular filly: shows knee action:
third foal: sister to 7f (at 2 yrs) and 10.6f winner Corcina, and half-sister to a winner
in Brazil: dam placed at 1¼m here before winning at 11.8f in France, is closely
related to very smart middle-distance stayer Relay Race: fairly useful performer:
sweating, easily won maiden at Yarmouth in July: well-beaten last in handicap 3
weeks later: carries head high. *H. R. A. Cecil*

BE THE BEST 4 b.g. Rousillon (USA) 133 – Shadywood 96 (Habitat 134) [1991 40
7g⁶ 7g³ 8m³ 1992 10.1s 8s 9m⁵ 9.9f³ 11f⁴ 13.8g³ 10g⁴ 10f 12.2g] lengthy, leggy
gelding: moderate mover: still a maiden: well below form in amateur handicaps last
2 starts, in visor final one: effective at 1¼m, and probably stays 1¾m: acts on firm
ground. *M. P. Naughton*

BETRAYED 2 b.f. (Feb 25) Beveled (USA) – Davemma 81 (Tachypous 128) [1992 39
5m⁶ 5m³ 5g] 2,000F, 1,700Y: close-coupled, sparely-made filly: third foal: half-
sister to 3-y-o Brilliant Disguise (by Ballacashtal), 8.1f seller winner at 2 yrs, and
1990 2-y-o 7f winner Melting Tears (by Noalto): dam disappointing maiden, stayed
1½m: achieved poor form only on debut: last in seller final start, in July. *P. C.
Haslam*

BETTER STILL (IRE)   3 b.f. Glenstal (USA) 118 – That's Better (Mourne 126)   –
[1991 NR 1992 a6g a10g5] 8,200Y: half-sister to 3 winners, including 1977 2-y-o 6f
and 1m winner Dolly Dewdrop (by On Your Mark): dam 2-y-o 5f winner in Ireland:
soundly beaten in claimers in November. *P. C. Haslam*

BETWEEN TWO FIRES   3 br.f. Sulaafah (USA) 119 – Bluebell Time (Good   52
Times (ITY)) [1991 5d 6m4 6g5 7m3 6.9m5 7.5f* 7m5 a7g5 8m5 8m3 7.5f2 8.3g 10.5d
1992 8s 7g3 8.1g5 10d2 8.3s4 8.1m4 10g] smallish, rather dipped-backed filly:
moderate mover: fair plater: stays 8.3f: best form on a sound surface: effective
blinkered or not: ran well for 7-lb claimer at 2 yrs: sold 2,500 gns Doncaster June
Sales. *J. Berry*

BEVANNO (IRE)   2 gr.g. (Feb 25) Salse (USA) 128 – Talina (General Assembly   –
(USA)) [1992 6s 7s] 4,200Y: first foal: dam, successful at 9f to 10.7f in France, is
half-sister to Zino: no worthwhile form in autumn maidens. *Pat Mitchell*

BEVELED EDGE   3 ch.f. Beveled (USA) – Best Offer 96 (Crepello 136) [1991   49
6.1d6 1992 7f6 5.1m4 6.1g 5.1m4] leggy, sparely-made filly: modest maiden: best
form at 5.1f though is bred to stay at least 7f: sweating last 2 starts. *B. Palling*

BEWARE OF AGENTS   3 b.c. Tremblant 112 – Saltation 111 (Sallust 134) [1991   91
6m2 6d 6d2 6d* 1992 7m* 7v2 7m5 7.6g3 6f 8f 9g2 7d] big, strong, lengthy colt:
usually looks well: fairly useful performer in the spring, winning handicap at
Newmarket: off course nearly 3 months after finishing behind in Group 3 6f event:
form afterwards only when fair second in weak minor event at Redcar: should prove
equally effective at 1m: acts on good to firm and heavy ground. *M. Johnston*

BEYOND OUR REACH   4 br.g. Reach 122 – Over Beyond 78 (Bold Lad (IRE)   –
133) [1991 6g 8m4 6.1m 8m* 7g 7f 8m3 8d3 7d 9g 1992 8d] small, sturdy gelding:
moderate mover: fair form (rated 84) at 3 yrs: in rear in Spring Handicap at
Newbury, running as if something amiss: better at 1m than shorter: acts on good to
firm going: ran moderately on fibresand at 2 yrs: sweated and hung badly once. *R. J.
Hodges*

BEYOND THE LIMIT   2 b.f. (Feb 19) Aragon 118 – Height of Folly 81 (Shirley   55
Heights 130) [1992 7.1d5 7s4 7d a8g a8g] smallish, sparely-made filly: good walker:
first foal: dam stayer: modest maiden: one paced, and will be suited by 1¼m +: sold
out of Lady Herries' stable 2,100 gns Ascot November Sales after third start. *D.
Marks*

BEYOND THE MOON (IRE)   3 b.f. Ballad Rock 122 – Vivi (Welsh Saint 126)   –
[1991 6m4 6m 1992 6g 7g 6d 7d 8.3g] strong, good-bodied filly: no worthwhile form
in 1992. *M. J. Fetherston-Godley*

BEYTON (USA)   3 b.c. Alleged (USA) 138 – Ann Stuart (USA) (Lyphard **116**
(USA) 132) [1991 7g4 7.1s4 8.1g* 7.3m* 7m 10g3 1992 11d* 10g4 12.3g4 12m*
12m3 12g2 12d6]

Beyton's win in the King Edward VII Stakes might have upset the
devotees of ten-year trends. The previous ten editions of the race had been
won by Derby runners (Cacoethes, Sheriff's Star, Love The Groom, Lanfranco, and Head For Heights who had contested the French Derby) or
lightly-raced, unexposed sorts (Saddlers' Hall, Private Tender, Bonhomie,
Shareef Dancer and Open Day), but the 1992 winner could not be placed in
either category. Beyton had had nine runs before Royal Ascot, at least two
more than any of those previous ten winners, and had had more racecourse
experience than eight of them with his six two-year-old races alone. He had
not been entered for the Derby, and if he had, defeats in classic trials at
Sandown and Chester ensured that he would have been an outsider. With only
thirteen days between races, the sixth home, Alflora, was the only Derby
runner to figure in an twelve-runner field for the King Edward VII which
comprised mainly young pretenders such as Alphard, Badie, Peto, Sonus and
Sun Seeker. A twenty-length winner on soft ground on his latest start, Peto
started a heavily-backed favourite and was soon at the head of affairs, but he
was beaten two furlongs out, at which point it was Beyton, always in the first
four, who swept to the front. It was a critical stage of the race as the Predominate Stakes winner Jeune, half a length down on Beyton and travelling
strongly on the turn, ran out of room on the inside. When Jeune emerged
between Alflora and the rails in the final furlong, Beyton had gone beyond
recall. The final distances were two lengths and three quarters. It was an
improved effort from Beyton—and his fourth win, following those in a maiden

King Edward VII Stakes, Royal Ascot—Beyton bursts clear of Jeune (noseband) and Alflora

at Chepstow and nursery at Newbury in 1991, and a minor event at Newbury on his reappearance—but one that left him still some way beneath the top rank. Tough, genuine and consistent though he is, Beyton was found wanting after Royal Ascot. He carried a 5-lb penalty when both Bonny Scot and Alflora proved too good for him in the Gordon Stakes, then was beaten four lengths by the top German three-year-old Platini in an extremely valuable contest at Hoppegarten. Beyton's final start, in the Rothmans International at Woodbine, saw a performance on a par with his best, but that was still only good enough for sixth. He's now been sold and will remain in Canada.

		⌈ Hoist The Flag	⌈ Tom Rolfe
	⌈ Alleged (USA)	{ (b 1968)	{ Wavy Navy
	{ (b 1974)	{ Princess Pout	{ Prince John
Beyton (USA)	{	⌊ (b 1966)	⌊ Determined Lady
(b.c. 1989)	{	⌈ Lyphard	⌈ Northern Dancer
	{ Ann Stuart (USA)	{ (b 1969)	{ Goofed
	⌊ (b 1980)	{ Miss Carmie	{ T V Lark
		⌊ (b 1966)	⌊ Twice Over

The strong, well-made Beyton impresses in appearance as well as attitude. He will stay beyond one and a half miles, acts on good to firm ground and good to soft. Beyton failed to find a buyer at Keeneland in September two months before his 52,000-guinea purchase at Tattersalls as a yearling. Two of his dam's previous five foals made over 300,000 dollars as yearlings but Beyton is clearly the best on the racecourse. Two of the others showed fair form in winning here, River Loch (by Riverman) over nine furlongs and Secret Obsession (by Secretariat) over a mile and a quarter. Two more by Alleged are winners, Ann Alleged also gaining a third placing in a Grade 3 turf contest over nine furlongs. The unraced Ann Stuart is the fourth mare out of Miss Carmie to produce a pattern or graded winner. Among the others to have done so are the dams of Kentucky Derby winner Winning Colors and Prince of Wales's Stakes winner Two Timing, while those who have not include the Champion North American three-year-old filly of 1974 Chris Evert who has an additional claim to fame as the grandam of Chief's Crown. *R. Hannon*

BEZELLE 3 b.f. Dominion 123 – Ideal Home 104 (Home Guard (USA) 129) [1991 **113** 6g⁵ 5d* 6m* 1992 7v* 8g 6f⁶ 6s* 5s⁴ 7s⁴] leggy filly: very useful performer: successful over the Curragh in 1992 in Gladness Stakes in April and listed race in September: below-form sixth in Cork And Orrery Stakes at Royal Ascot: best effort when strong-finishing fourth to Mr Brooks in Prix de l'Abbaye at Longchamp penultimate start: effective at 5f (at least when conditions are testing) and stays 7f,

109

Gladness Stakes, the Curragh—
close between Bezelle (centre), Norwich (right) and Street Rebel

ran poorly in Irish 1000 Guineas: has won on good to firm ground, seems best with
plenty of give. *C. Collins, Ireland*

BEZIQUE (USA)   2 gr.c. (Jan 11) Caro 133 – Card Played (USA) 82 (Lyphard   **80** ?
(USA) 132) [1992 6g⁴ 6s³ 7s*] $200,000Y: medium-sized, workmanlike colt: second
foal: half-brother to American 3-y-o Count Play (by Private Account): dam, placed
at 7f and 1m here before winning at 1m in USA, is daughter of Table Hands,
second-best 2-y-o of 1979 in USA: blinkered, raced alone on far rail when winning
10-runner maiden at Lingfield in October by 8 lengths: will be at least as effective at
1m: yet to race on top-of-the-ground: ran creditably in visor second start. *J. H. M.
Gosden*

B GRADE   7 b.m. Lucky Wednesday 124 – Hitravelscene (Mansingh (USA) 120)   **44**
[1991 6d 7m 6m² 6m 6g⁶ 6d 6s 1992 5g⁴ 6g 6s⁶ 6m⁵ 5d² 5s⁶ 5v] leggy, plain mare:
has a round action: poor handicapper: last win came 39 starts ago, at 3 yrs: stays 7f:
probably best with give in the ground, and acts on soft: often hinders chance with
slow start. *J. Balding*

BIBLICAL TIMES   3 b.c. Ahonoora 122 – Sacristy 54 (Godswalk (USA) 130)   –
[1991 NR 1992 9g⁶] 11,000Y: close-coupled colt: first foal: dam thrice-raced half-
sister to Park Appeal and Nashamaa (both by Ahonoora), Desirable and Alydaress:
running-on sixth in maiden at Kempton in May: showed round action to post: sold to
join R. Simpson 3,000 gns Newmarket Autumn Sales. *C. R. Nelson*

BICHETTE   2 b.f. (Mar 22) Lidhame 109 – Freely Given 69 (Petingo 135) [1992   **66**
6m⁴ 6g³ 5g³ 7f⁶ a6g³ a7g* a7g³ a7g³] 4,200F, 6,800Y: leggy filly: half-sister to fair
Irish 3-y-o maiden Nightman (by Night Shift) and 3 winners, including (at 1½m)
New Zealand (by Dominion) and (from 7f to 15f) fair Bloodless Coup (by Free State):
dam lightly-raced half-sister to very useful stayer Tom Cribb: fair performer: won
maiden at Lingfield in November: subsequently ran creditably in nurseries: stays 7f:
acts on good to firm ground and on equitrack. *R. Hannon*

BID FOR SIX (USA)   3 br.c. Saratoga Six (USA) – Savage Bunny (USA) (Never   **85** d
Bend) [1991 6f⁴ 6g 1992 8g⁵ 7g² 8f² 8g⁶ 8m 8.3g 10m 8g] workmanlike colt: looked a
fairly useful maiden when second at Newmarket and (in handicap) Newbury in May:
lost his form completely: suited by 1m: acts on firm going: has joined G. Thorner. *R.
Hannon*

BIDWEAYA (USA)   5 b.m. Lear Fan (USA) 130 – Sweet Snow (USA) (Lyphard   **44**
(USA) 132) [1991 NR 1992 8.5s² 8.1g* 7f³ 10f⁶ 8.3g⁴ a7g 8g 10.3g⁶ a8g] angular,
sparely-made mare: poor handicapper: successful at Edinburgh in July: stays 1¼m:
probably acts on any going: has won for claimer. *J. L. Eyre*

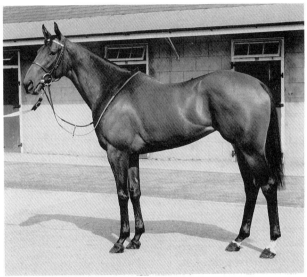

Mr James McNeil's "Bezelle"

BIG BEAT (USA) 4 br.g. Super Concorde (USA) 128 – Embroglio (USA) –
(Empery (USA) 128) [1991 8m 10g⁶ 12m⁴ 10g³ 10g³ 10g 1992 10g³ 12s] rangy, rather
angular gelding: rated 68 at 3 yrs, gelded after looking somewhat unsatisfactory
final start: stays 1½m: acts on good to firm ground, possibly not on soft: wears
dropped noseband: rather headstrong: progressed into a useful novice hurdler,
winning twice late in the year. *D. R. C. Elsworth*

BIG BLUE 3 b.g. Bluebird (USA) 125 – Cassina 91 (Habitat 134) [1991 6f⁶ 7m² **94**
1992 8g³ 8. 1g⁵ 8. 1m² 8g⁴ 10.3m² 9m* 7.9m 8. 1g⁶ 9d] lengthy, good-topped gelding:
fairly useful performer on his day: looked none too genuine fifth start: made all in
maiden at Ripon in July: below form in handicaps afterwards: should stay 1¼m: acts
on good to firm ground: blinkered third (ran very well) and final 3-y-o starts: has
been gelded. *C. E. Brittain*

BIG EASY (IRE) 3 ch.c. Ela-Mana-Mou 132 – Babilla (USA) (Raja Baba (USA)) **86**
[1991 8.1s a7g² a7g² 1992 10g³ 10. 1d² 10m² 10m* 10.4d] lengthy, workmanlike colt:
fairly useful performer: favourite, won minor event at Windsor in June, making all:
set strong pace and weakened quickly 4f out in £38,500 handicap at York 12 days
later: strong-galloping type and should be suited by 1½m: acts on good to firm and
dead ground: wore eyeshield on fibresand. *Mrs J. Cecil*

BIG GEM 2 ch.c. (Apr 23) Sayyaf 121 – Gemgem 54 (Lochnager 132) [1992 6m a6g –
a5g⁶ a7g a6g 6m 8s] 1,750Y, 3,500 2-y-o: compact colt: fourth foal: half-brother to
3-y-o Another Ryton (by Another Realm): dam 7f seller winner: seems of little
account. *M. C. Chapman*

BIG HAND (IRE) 3 b.g. Tate Gallery (USA) 117 – Clonsella Lady (High Top **91**
131) [1991 5f² 6f³ 6m² 6m³ 1992 7g⁶ 7f² 6m* 6g* 5s⁵] well-made gelding: much
improved to win £11,500 handicaps at Newcastle and Ayr (battled on well) in

summer: not entirely discredited back over 5f at Haydock: best at 6f: acted on firm ground: tended to get on edge, and carry head high: dead. *J. W. Watts*

BIGHAYIR 5 gr.g. Petong 126 – Nook (Julio Mariner 127) [1991 10.1s 10.8m³ **80** 8.5m* 10m² 8g⁴ 8g² 12g 10f³ 10.2m³ 8g 10.2s³ 12.1d² 1992 10.2f* 10.2g* 11.8g* 12f⁶ 10.3s² 11.8s a12g⁴] sturdy gelding: fairly useful handicapper: successful twice at Chepstow and in Leicester claimer in midsummer: off course nearly 3 months before very good second at Chester: below form afterwards: effective from 1m to 1½m: probably acts on any going: wears blinkers nowadays: won claiming hurdle (claimed £12,101, probably to Scandinavia) in December. *M. C. Pipe*

BIG LEAP (IRE) 3 b.g. Auction Ring (USA) 123 – Bristle 96 (Thatch (USA) 136) **96** [1991 6m* 7m 1992 7g* 8d² 8f³ 8g² 8m* 7m 8d5] rather leggy, quite attractive gelding: progressed really well to win handicaps at Doncaster in March and Newmarket (£20,100 contest, came from towards rear to win by a short head) in July: needs further than 7f and stays 1m well: acts on firm and dead ground. *M. Moubarak*

BIG PAT 3 b.c. Backchat (USA) 98 – Fallonetta 41 (Tachypous 128) [1991 7f 10m **59** 8m 1992 11g³ 12m 10f³ 9.4d* 10g³ 10.1g³ 12m³ 11m* 14.1d² 12g5 11.8m* 12s² 12.1g6] leggy colt: useful plater: won sellers at Beverley (handicap, bought in 5,400 gns) and Wolverhampton (no bid) in summer and claimer (best effort) at Leicester in September: may be ideally suited by 1½m (hung left when running fairly well at 1¾m): possibly unsuited by very soft ground: usually claimer ridden. *J. Pearce*

BIG-W 2 b.g. (May 9) Stanford 121§ – Lucky Saran 72 (Lucky Wednesday 124) **–** [1992 a8g] third foal: dam, plater suited by 1m, is half-sister to useful sprinter Cyril's Choice: 33/1, slowly away and well beaten in 10-runner claimer at Southwell in December. *Ronald Thompson*

BIGWHEEL BILL (IRE) 3 br.g. Last Tycoon 131 – Get Ahead 58 (Silly **83** Season 127) [1991 7g² 7m⁴ 7m 1992 8s² 9.9f5 10.5g³ 12f4 11.9s² 15s4 11.9s* 11.8s] leggy, lengthy gelding: fairly useful handicapper: favourite, made virtually all in apprentice contest at York in October: best form at 1½m: easily best 3-y-o efforts on an easy surface: visored (best effort at that time) final start at 2 yrs. *J. W. Watts*

BIJOU PRINCESS 4 b.f. Glint of Gold 128 – Likeness 101 (Young Generation **– §** 129) [1991 10.5g 12g 7g 1992 12f 16.2d 10m 10.8g] sparely-made filly: no worthwhile form and is ungenuine: tried in blinkers. *A. Bailey*

BILATERAL (USA) 3 ch.c. Blushing Groom (FR) 131 – Double Axle (USA) **90** (The Axe II 115) [1991 7.1s³ 7g* 8g² 7m² 1992 10m³ 10.8f² 8m³] sturdy colt: impresses in appearance: has a quick action: fairly useful performer: ran only in midsummer at 3 yrs: stays 1¼m: acts on firm ground: sold 4,000 gns Newmarket Autumn Sales. *H. R. A. Cecil*

BILBERRY 3 b.f. Nicholas Bill 125 – Snow Tribe 94 (Great Nephew 126) [1991 **46** NR 1992 a8g a10g5 7m³ 9.9g 12.2g² 12.3m5 11.8g 13.8g5 16.1s 13.8d 15.1d4] leggy filly: closely related to Yorkshire Cup winner Line Slinger (by High Line) and half-sister to several winners, including fair middle-distance winner/good hurdler Past Glories (by Hittite Glory): dam staying daughter of St Leger third Cold Storage: plating-class maiden: trained first 2 starts by J. Hetherton: stays 15f: possibly unsuited by soft ground: carried head awkwardly final start. *C. W. C. Elsey*

BILHAB (USA) 3 b. or br.c. Topsider (USA) – Pour Me Out (USA) (Raise A Cup **–** (USA) [1991 NR 1992 7.9g] $110,000Y: medium-sized, workmanlike colt: first foal: dam minor 2-y-o 1m stakes winner, also successful at 3 yrs: 20/1 and green, moved badly to post and little promise in 8-runner maiden at York in September. *A. C. Stewart*

BILJAN (USA) 2 b.c. (Feb 26) Alydar (USA) – Best Decision (USA) (Best Turn **61** p (USA) [1992 8.1s4] $125,000Y, resold $150,000Y: fourth foal: brother to 3-y-o 9f winner Alessandrina and half-brother to a winner in USA by Believe It: dam, won 4 races at up to 1¼m, is half-sister to Grade 1 winning juvenile Dream Team: favourite, fourth of 14 in maiden at Chepstow in August, racing in front rank then one pace and green under fairly considerate ride closing stages: will do better. *P. F. I. Cole*

BILL MOON 6 ch.g. Nicholas Bill 125 – Lunar Queen 96 (Queen's Hussar 124) **62** [1991 7.6g 6f4 7.1d4 a8g* 8.5f5 7m 6m4 7m*dis 8m³ 6.1d² a7g 1992 7g³ 6f3 7.1m² a8g3 8f² 8.5d 7f³ 7g² 7d 8g³ 8g² 7d 6.1d* 7s a8g] leggy, quite attractive gelding: fair handicapper: gained reward for series of good runs when landing Chepstow ladies race in October: ran moderately afterwards: effective from 6f to 1m: acts on firm ground, and on equitrack: overall record on a soft surface is most inconsistent: good mount for amateur: tough. *P. J. Feilden*

BILLYBACK 2 b.g. (Feb 9) Absalom 128 – Petit Secret 64 (Petingo 135) [1992 6s **56**
6v⁶ 6d⁶ 6v⁵] brother to sprint maiden Libran Star, closely related to useful 1982
2-y-o 5f and 6f winner Secret Miracle (by Abwah) and half-brother to several
winners here and abroad, including (from 6f to 1¼m) fair Terminator (by
Tachypous): dam placed over 1m: modest maiden: will stay at least 7f: acts on heavy
ground, yet to race on a sound surface. *M. J. Ryan*

BILLY BLAZER 3 ch.g. Nicholas Bill 125 – Flaming Peace 104 (Queen's Hussar **83**
124) [1991 6g⁴ 6f³ 6m* 8m² 1992 8m 10m⁴ 10.3m³ 11.9d² 10.9s* 10s⁶ 11.9s] leggy
gelding: moderate mover: fairly useful handicapper: won at Ayr in September:
stayed 1½m: had plenty of form on good to firm ground, but very best efforts with
some give: was held up: tended to carry head awkwardly: dead. *M. H. Tompkins*

BILLY BUNTER 3 ch.g. Nicholas Bill 125 – Cosset 56 (Comedy Star (USA) 121) **66**
[1991 NR 1992 10s³ 11.8g⁵ 10s 11.8g 12s⁶] rather leggy gelding: fifth living foal:
brother to 1¼m and 1½m winner Billet: dam ran 3 times at 2 yrs: modest maiden:
should stay 1½m: sold to join R. Akehurst 8,000 gns Newmarket Autumn Sales. *H.
Candy*

BILLY LOMOND (IRE) 4 b.g. Lomond (USA) 128 – Relko's Belle (FR) (Relko **–**
136) [1991 8m⁵ 9d 7m⁵ 8m⁶ a12g³ a12g⁵ a10g* 10.8m a10g⁶ 16m a12g 1992 a12g a13g
12.3g⁵] smallish, strong-quartered gelding: carries condition: has a quick action: no
worthwhile form in 1992: stays 1½m: acts on good to firm ground and on equitrack:
blinkered 5 times, winning on first occasion. *C. A. Cyzer*

BIN AJWAAD (IRE) 2 b.c. (Apr 16) Rainbow Quest (USA) 134 – Salidar (Sallust **108** p
134) [1992 8s² 7.9s* 7.3s²] 84,000Y: tall, good-topped colt: has plenty of scope:
sixth foal: brother to 1½m winner Hidden Quest and half-brother to 6f and 7f winner
Budapest (by Diesis): dam winner over 9.5f in Ireland, is half-sister to Park Appeal,
Desirable (dam of Shadayid) and Alydaress: favourite, though carrying condition
still, impressive winner of maiden at York in October: looking in fine shape,
excellent 2 lengths second to Beggarman Thief in Horris Hill Stakes at Newbury 2
weeks later, leading 1½f out until close home: will stay middle distances: yet to race
on a sound surface: very much on the upgrade: has good turn of foot and is an
interesting prospect for 1993. *B. Hanbury*

BINEYAH (IRE) 3 b.f. Sadler's Wells (USA) 132 – Clandestina (USA) 98 **109**
(Secretariat (USA)) [1991 NR 1992 11.5g* 10m⁴ 12g⁴ 11.9m² 14.6m⁵ 12g] lengthy
filly: good walker: moderate mover: fourth living foal: closely related to fair 1¼m
winner Night Secret (by Nijinsky) and half-sister to 1¾m and 2m winner Bestow (by
Shirley Heights): dam Irish 1¼m winner, is half-sister to Seattle Slew and Lomond:
useful performer: won maiden at Yarmouth in June: beaten 3¼ lengths then 2½
lengths behind User Friendly in Irish Oaks at the Curragh and Yorkshire Oaks
(stayed on strongly) in the summer: struggling long way from home in Park Hill
Stakes at Doncaster, well beaten in Princess Royal Stakes at Ascot: should be
suited by further than 1½m. *M. R. Stoute*

BINKHALDOUN (IRE) 3 ch.c. Roberto (USA) 131 – Aviance 112 (Northfields **111**
(USA)) [1991 6f* 7m 1992 8.1g⁴ 10.4m² 10.3f* 12g⁶] robust, good-bodied colt: useful
form in minor events, winning 4-runner race at Doncaster in May: best
effort when 5 lengths sixth of 17 to Polytain in Prix du Jockey-Club at Chantilly,
every chance 1f out: stays 1½m: acts on firm going: wears bandages. *H. Thomson
Jones*

BINT ALBADOU (IRE) 2 b.f. (Mar 9) Green Desert (USA) 127 – Cistus 123 **91**
(Sun Prince 128) [1992 6g³ 6m* 5g² 6m* 6s⁵] 650,000 francs (approx £65,500) Y:
half-sister to 2 middle-distance winners and winning jumper Celsius (by Ile de
Bourbon): dam won from 6f (at 2 yrs) to 1¼m and is half-sister to Lancastrian: won
maiden at Leopardstown and nursery at the Curragh: second to Tropical in pattern
event at the Curragh in between: ran moderately on final start (August): will stay
1m. *J. S. Bolger, Ireland*

BIRCHWOOD SUN 2 b.c. (Feb 28) Bluebird (USA) 125 – Shapely Test (USA) **71**
(Elocutionist (USA)) [1992 5m² 5.1f² 6.1m 6m 5m* 5.1m 6d 6m² 6s* 6m⁶ 7g]
9,600F, 3,200 2-y-o: compact colt: moderate mover: half-brother to 3 winners
abroad: dam Irish 1m winner: fair handicapper: won maiden auction at Haydock in
August and nursery (despite ducking sharply right when taking lead 1f out) at York
in October: should stay 7f: probably acts on any going: inconsistent. *R. Hollinshead*

BIRD HUNTER 2 gr.c. (May 11) Never So Bold 135 – Blushing Cousin (Great **61**
Nephew 126) [1992 5.3d 5.2d⁴ 5s* 5.1g⁶ 6d² 7g²] angular, well-grown colt: has
scope: third foal: dam (showed a little ability in USA) is out of half-sister to Blushing
Groom: modest performer: won claimer at Newcastle in April: creditable second in

seller at Newmarket final start, in July: stays 7f well: yet to race on top-of-the-ground: suitable mount for a claimer. *N. A. Callaghan*

BIRD WATCHER   3 b.c. Bluebird (USA) 125 – Grayfoot 87 (Grundy 137) [1991   **66** NR 1992 10s⁴ 10m 12.3s⁵] heavy-topped colt: easy mover: third foal: dam, maiden half-sister to Irish Oaks winner Swiftfoot, was possibly temperamental: easily best effort in maidens on debut, hanging left over 1f out: blinkered final start: sold 5,000 gns Newmarket Autumn Sales. *Major W. R. Hern*

BIRLING ASHES   4 gr.g. Magic Mirror 105 – Morning Miss 59 (Golden Dipper   – 119) [1991 a8g⁴ 7d 8m 8f⁵ 8g⁴ a12g⁶ 9.7m 12f 1992 10g] small, angular gelding: inconsistent plater, still a maiden after 24 starts: never placed to challenge at Windsor in July: stays 1m: acts on firm going: blinkered twice, hooded once at 2 yrs. *J. R. Jenkins*

BIRTHDAYS' CHILD   4 b.f. Caerleon (USA) 132 – Shaara (FR) (Sanctus II 132)   – [1991 8g³ 10g 10m 11.5s 1992 8.9g 8g 7d a12g] leggy filly: of little account these days. *J. R. Fanshawe*

BISHOPSTONE BILL   3 b.g. Skyliner 117 – Sybilly (Nicholas Bill 125) [1991   – 6.1g 5.7m 7g a7g 1992 7g 5s⁵ 5m⁵ 6.1m 5.1f⁵ 6.9d⁶ a10g⁵] leggy, good-topped gelding: poor maiden: stays 7f. *S. Mellor*

BITMAC BOY   3 gr.g. Another Realm 118 – Hedonist 74 (Mandamus 120) [1991   – 6d 7f 1992 a7g a6g⁶] leggy, angular gelding: seems of little account: sold 1,050 gns Doncaster March Sales. *Mrs P. A. Barker*

BIT OF A LARK   4 b.g. Nomination 125 – Straffan Girl (Sallust 134) [1991 6m⁴ **102** 6m 6g 5g 5.6m 5.2m³ 1992 6f 5.1f* 6s³ 6g 5d* 6g 5.6m] sturdy gelding: moderate walker: useful handicapper: successful at Chepstow and Haydock (£9,500 race) in summer: creditable seventh of 13 in Newmarket listed race next start: effective at 5f and 6f: acts on firm and soft ground: effective ridden from front or held up: has won for 7-lb claimer. *R. Hollinshead*

BIT ON THE SIDE (IRE)   3 b.f. Vision (USA) – Mistress (USA) (Damascus   **64** (USA)) [1991 NR 1992 10m 10f 10g 10g⁶ 11.6g² 11.8g* 11.4g 11.8d⁵ 11.8s²] leggy, lengthy filly: second foal: half-sister to a winner in Italy by Glow: dam unraced: fair handicapper: held up when winning at Leicester in September: ran well final outing: better at 1½m than shorter: acts on soft going. *W. J. Musson*

BITTER ALOE   3 b.c. Green Desert (USA) 127 – Sometime Lucky 89 (Levmoss   **72** 133) [1991 NR 1992 10g⁶ 10f⁵] 9,000Y: strong, lengthy colt: half-brother to 3 winners, including 1m to 1½m winner/smart hurdler Pike's Peak (by High Top): dam lightly raced: staying-on fifth in maiden at Newbury in May: looked likely to improve again. *J. L. Dunlop*

BITTER'S END (IRE)   2 b.c. (Mar 16) Waajib 121 – Annsfield Lady (Red Sunset   **68** p 120) [1992 7g] rangy, useful-looking colt: first foal: dam Irish 9f/1¼m performer, is closely related to very useful middle-distance colt Beeshi: 10/1, promising eighth of 18 in maiden at Newbury in August, prominent and travelling well to past halfway, green when shaken up after 2f out and eased near finish: sure to do better. *R. Hannon*

BIXBY (USA)   2 b.c. (Mar 8) Seattle Dancer (USA) 119 – Golden Secretariat   **56** p (USA) (Secretariat (USA)) [1992 7g⁵ 8d 8s] $27,000Y: rangy, attractive colt, rather unfurnished: has plenty of scope: good mover: sixth foal: half-brother to very useful 1989 French 2-y-o 1m winner Golden Era (by Hero's Honor) and quite modest 1m winner Shine On Brightly (by Majestic Light): dam ran 5 times: showed plenty of promise in 7f Kempton minor event in September: subsequently gave strong impression unsuited by soft ground: looks sort to do good deal better. *D. R. C. Elsworth*

BLACK BOY (IRE)   3 br.g. Auction Ring (USA) 123 – Relic Spirit (Relic) [1991   **52** NR 1992 5d 6m 5g² 5m 5g³ 6d⁵ 5s 7d a8g a6g⁶ a5g a5g⁶ a7g⁴ a7g] 16,500F, 15,500Y: angular, good-quartered gelding: brother to fairly useful 1983 Irish 2-y-o 5f winner Malang-Lou and half-brother to several winners, including fair 6f to 1m winner African Spirit (by African Sky): dam second 4 times over sprint distances in Ireland: inconsistent performer: first past post in Catterick maiden in August but demoted a place for interference: probably stays 7f: below form when visored once: hangs left, and not an easy ride. *J. A. Glover*

BLACK CORAL (IRE)   3 b.f. Double Schwartz 128 – Countess Olivia 80   **53** (Prince Tenderfoot (USA) 126) [1991 6m⁵ 1992 5g³ 6m⁵ 6g³ 6s] leggy, lengthy, unfurnished filly: has been hobdayed: modest maiden: should stay 7f: sold 1,700 gns Newmarket Autumn Sales. *C. F. Wall*

BLACK DRAGON (IRE)   2 ch.c. (Feb 22) Ela-Mana-Mou 132 – Indian Lily 100   **90** ?
(Indian King (USA) 128) [1992 7d² 7m] lengthy, useful-looking colt: rather unfurnished: second foal: half-brother to 3-y-o Indian Jack (by Bustino): dam 2-y-o 5f
winner: ½-length second of 7 to Kusamba in York minor event in September: disappointing favourite in Newmarket maiden following month: will stay 1¼m. *B. W.*
Hills

BLACK JEWEL   9 b.g. Welsh Captain 113 – New York Rose (Pieces of Eight 128)   –
[1991 NR 1992 5d 5.9s 7g 5g 14g 5g⁵ 8d⁶ 8s 12g⁶] big, lengthy ex-Irish gelding: poor
performer: trained until after fifth start by L. Reilly: stays 1m: often blinkered, tried
visored: won 2 selling hurdles (sold to join R. Hollinshead 5,200 gns after second) in
autumn. *M. D. I. Usher*

BLACK MISCHIEF   2 b.f. (Feb 19) Salse (USA) 128 – Cameroun 106 (African   **82** p
Sky 124) [1992 7s²] compact filly: second foal: half-sister to 7f/8.5f winner
Eternal Flame (by Primo Dominie): dam 2-y-o 5f winner: 2/1 but burly, beaten ½
length by Great Steps in 3-runner minor event at York in October, running on well
despite tending to carry head high: will improve, and can win a race. *H. R. A. Cecil*

BLACKPATCH HILL   3 br.g. Efisio 120 – Myrtlegrove (Scottish Rifle 127)   –
[1991 6g 7f⁵ 8g 1992 9.7g⁵ 9.7g⁶] lengthy gelding: has a round action: modest
maiden: not seen out again after running poorly in July: should stay 1½m. *J. L.*
Dunlop

BLACK SAPPHIRE   5 ch.g. Lomond (USA) 128 – Star of India (General   –
Assembly (USA)) [1991 NR 1992 11.5m 12s⁶ 16.2g 18m] lengthy, quite attractive
gelding: moderate mover: rated 78 as 3-y-o: no form in handicaps in autumn: should
stay beyond 1½m: acts on firm going: visored final start. *M. H. Tompkins*

BLADE OF FORTUNE   4 b.g. Beldale Flutter (USA) 130 – Foil 'em (USA)   –
(Blade (USA)) [1991 8.2f⁶ 6m 1992 7m] leggy, rather unfurnished gelding: poor
maiden: stays 7f. *F. H. Lee*

BLAKE END (USA)   3 b.c. Valid Appeal (USA) – Fine Singing (USA) (Diplomat   **80**
Way) [1991 6m² 6m³ 1992 a6g² 6g* 5m² 6m 5m⁵] sturdy colt: landed odds in
Brighton maiden in April: somewhat disappointing after next start, and not seen out
after May: may prove best over 6f/stiff 5f: below form on fibresand: sold 6,200 gns
Doncaster November Sales. *W. A. O'Gorman*

BLAKENEY BOY   2 b.c. (Apr 20) Blakeney 126 – Leylandia 69 (Wolver Hollow   –
126) [1992 7m 8s] 4,200Y: close-coupled, workmanlike colt: brother to very useful
7f (at 2 yrs) to 1¾m winner Thetford Forest and half-brother to 2 winners: dam
4-y-o 2m winner: tailed off in maidens at Redcar and Newcastle. *R. R. Lamb*

BLAKES BEAU   2 br.g. (May 8) Blakeney 126 – Beaufort Star 95 (Great Nephew   **54** p
126) [1992 6g 6d 7s⁴ 7s 7d] 6,400Y: compact gelding: closely related to a winner in
Italy by Julio Mariner and half-brother to 3 winners, including Kaths Choice (by
Dunbeath) and Kiveton Komet (by Precocious), successful at up to 7f: dam sprinting
sister to Uncle Pokey: caught the eye in maidens and nursery (stiff task) last 3
starts: will be well suited by middle distances: remains capable of better in handicap
company. *M. H. Easterby*

BLAKES REACH   2 b.c. (Jan 19) Blakeney 126 – Carib Flash (Mill Reef (USA)   –
141) [1992 7d⁶ 6g 8m] 5,000 2-y-o: smallish colt: moderate walker and mover:
second foal: dam unraced: no form in maidens. *R. R. Lamb*

BLAKE'S TREASURE   5 b.g. Mummy's Treasure – Andamooka (Rarity 129)   –
[1991 9s 10m 10g 10g 8.1g 8.3g 8.2f* 8.5f 8g 1992 a8g 8m] good-topped gelding:
moderate mover: poor handicapper nowadays: stays 1m: acts on firm ground:
usually visored, also tried blinkered. *T. Thomson Jones*

BLANCHLAND   3 gr.c. Bellypha 130 – Premier Rose 117 (Sharp Edge 123) [1991   –
NR 1992 10.4d] tall colt: fifth foal: half-brother to 9 winners, including stayer
Provence (by Rousillon) and fairly useful middle-distance 6-y-o Opera Ghost (by
Caerleon): dam stayed 1m: 50/1, well beaten in 8-runner maiden at York in October
on belated debut, always behind and not knocked about: may be capable of better. *P.*
W. Harris

BLANC SEING (FR)   5 b.g. Shirley Heights 130 – Blanche Reine (FR)   **55**
(Nureyev (USA) 131) [1991 NR 1992 8.5g 7.9g 8.3s 12.1s* 17.1s³] strong gelding:
first foal: dam French 1m winner: winning ex-French horse, formerly with Mme C.
Head: blinkered for first time and well backed, first form here when comfortably
winning handicap at Hamilton in October: again blinkered, set plenty to do when
creditable third in Pontefract handicap: clearly effective over 17f, but should prove
better returned to around 1½m: goes well on a soft surface: often bandaged. *M. W.*
Easterby

115

BLAZING FEN 4 ch.c. Myjinski (USA) – Clipsall 57 (Petitioner 83) [1991 a6g   –
a7g⁶ a8g³ a10g³ a10g² a12g³ 8.5f a10g a12g 1992 a7g] neat colt: poor mover: poor
handicapper: probably stays 1½m: best form on all-weather surfaces: carries head
high, and sometimes looks none too keen. *Mrs N. Macauley*

BLAZING PEARL 4 b.f. Blazing Saddles (AUS) – Ring of Pearl (Auction Ring   –
(USA) 123) [1991 6f 5d 8m 7d 10m³ 11.8m⁴ a14g 1992 6d 10.8d a10g 10g 7f 10g] small
filly: poor mover: poor plater: stays 11.8f: acts on good to firm ground: below form
blinkered/visored. *J. L. Harris*

BLAZING SENSATION 4 br.c. Blazing Saddles (AUS) – La Reine de France
(Queen's Hussar 124) [1991 NR 1992 5v⁵ 6.1d] smallish, strong colt: fourth foal:
half-brother to 3 modest 2-y-o sprint winners by Sayf El Arab, Absalom and Rectory
Maid: dam never ran: twice raced and no form in modest company in spring: joined
R. O'Sullivan. *D. W. P. Arbuthnot*

BLAZING SOUL (IRE) 2 ch.f. (May 2) Common Grounds 118 – Regal Way   59
(Sovereign Path 125) [1992 6m 5g² 6d³ a6g⁵] IR 2,200Y: tall, leggy filly: half-sister
to 2 middle-distance winners and a bumpers winner: dam Irish 1¾m winner, is
sister to useful 7f performer Oldstock: modest maiden: stays 6f: acts on dead
ground: trained first 2 starts by P. Kelleway: sold 2,800 gns Ascot November Sales.
R. Hannon

BLAZON OF TROY 3 b.c. Trojan Fen 118 – Mullet 75 (Star Appeal 133) [1991 6s   67
1992 9.7g* 12d⁵ 11.7d⁶] won Folkestone maiden in July: ran creditably in handicaps
after: stays 1½m. *T. Thomson Jones*

BLESSINGTON (USA) 3 b. or br.c. Alydar (USA) – Blessings (FR) 83   76
(Floribunda 136) [1991 NR 1992 10m⁶ 10g³ 10g⁶] $300,000Y: rangy colt: half-brother
to several winners in Argentina: dam 6f winner here: promising third in Newmarket
maiden: well-backed favourite and visored, ran moderately in £10,000 race at Ascot
later in July: should stay 1½m. *J. H. M. Gosden*

BLETCHLEY PARK (IRE) 3 b.c. Caerleon (USA) 132 – Enigma 87 (Aho-   100
noora 122) [1991 6g² 5m⁵ 6f³ 6m* 7m⁵ 1992 6s 5m* 7.3d⁶ 6s 6d 5.2g] close-coupled,
attractive colt: poor mover: useful performer: won minor event at Haydock in July
and very good sixth in Group 3 event at Newbury: stiff tasks after: needs further
than 5f, but not certain to stay any further than 7.3f: acts on good to firm and dead
ground: bandaged near-fore: usually wears tongue strap. *A. A. Scott*

BLIMPERS DISCO 3 gr.c. Grey Desire 115 – In A Spin 59 (Windjammer   –
(USA) [1991 5d 6m⁴ 7m 7.6d 1992 8s⁶ 7g 10.5d 7.6g 8g] tall colt: moderate mover:
no worthwhile form in 1992, blinkered once. *E. H. Owen jun*

BLOCKADE (USA) 3 b.g. Imperial Falcon (CAN) – Stolen Date (USA) (Sadair)   85
[1991 7m 7g² 7f* 8f* 8g* 7d⁴ 8g⁴ 1992 8.2d³ 10m⁵ 10m* 9m³ 8g* 8f³ 8g* 8f* 7.9m⁶
8g 8d] leggy, close-coupled gelding: tubed: had very good season in handicaps in
1992, winning at Goodwood (claimer), Newmarket (2) and Bath: in process of
running very well but saddle slipped when sixth in £25,000 handicap at York: stays
1¼m: best efforts on a sound surface: sometimes sweating: front runner. *M. Bell*

BLOOMSBURY SQUARE 2 ch.g. (Jan 21) Persian Heights 129 – Artistic   46 p
Licence (High Top 131) [1992 6m 6d 5v] 22,000F, IR 56,000Y: good-topped gelding:
good walker: first foal: dam, lightly raced, placed at 12.2f, is out of half-sister to
Circus Plume: never a factor in autumn maidens, bandaged and soon ridden along
final start: bred to stay middle distances: looks sort to do better. *J. W. Watts*

BLOW DRY (IRE) 2 b.c. (Feb 19) Glenstal (USA) 118 – Haco 104 (Tribal Chief   86 ?
125) [1992 5f² 6m⁶ 6d 5s*] IR 7,200F, 7,000Y, 27,000 2-y-o: good-topped colt:
has a fluent, round action: half-brother to 1½m winner Timsah (by Solinus), Irish
bumpers winner Paget (by Taufan) and a winner in France: dam, from excellent
family, useful maiden at up to 1m: soon ridden along when sixth of 8 to Splendent in
Gimcrack Stakes at York: no comparable form, neck winner of Redcar maiden in
September: will stay beyond 6f. *J. Hanson*

BLOWEDIFIKNOW 2 b.c. (Feb 16) Prince Rupert (FR) 121 – Ballys Princess   51
(Salvo 129) [1992 5m 6f⁶ 8s³ 10g a8g⁴ a8g] 7,000F, 8,200Y: leggy, lengthy colt:
moderate mover: half-brother to winning stayer Reform Princess (by Reform) and
1m and 9f winner Camallino Rose (by Dominion): dam ran twice: modest maiden:
probably stays 1¼m. *J. Wharton*

BLUEBELLA 2 ch.f. (May 10) Mummy's Game 120 – La Bleu 67 (Blue   42
Cashmere 129) [1992 5f 5m 5m³ 6m⁴ 5g² 6m 5g³ 6g 6s 7d] strong, lengthy filly: third
foal: dam won 9f and 1¼m sellers: poor plater: stays 6f: acts on good to firm ground:
below form when visored once. *Mrs P. A. Barker*

BLUE BLAZER 2 b.c. (Mar 31) Bluebird (USA) 125 – View 88 (Shirley Heights 89
130) [1992 6g 7g^3 7m 7g^4 8.2d^2 8.1d* 9v] close-coupled, quite attractive colt:
half-brother to 1m winner Namaste (by Petoski) and a winner in Italy by Bellypha:
dam 6f and 1m winner: easily best efforts when second in Nottingham nursery and
2-length winner of maiden at Haydock in autumn: ran poorly in listed race at Milan
final start: strong-galloping stayer: possibly suited by an easy surface. *B. Hanbury*

BLUE CROSS 3 b.f. Mansingh (USA) 120 – Rosslayne Whisper (Donibristle 96) –
[1991 6g 6m^5 6f^5 6f 1992 8v 10g] small, sturdy filly: bad maiden. *P. S. Felgate*

BLUE DISC 7 br.g. Disc Jockey 95 – Kaotesse (Djakao (FR) 124) [1991 7.1m 1992 –
a11g^6 a16g a14g] workmanlike gelding: winning hurdler but bad maiden on flat: has
joined R. Hollinshead. *C. R. Beever*

BLUE DRIFTER (IRE) 3 b.g. Bluebird (USA) 125 – Sea Swallow (FR) 90 (Dan 41
Cupid 132) [1991 NR 1992 7f^6 a7g^4 6h^4 6g 6.9m 8m a7g a10g^4 a8g] 16,500F: smallish
gelding: half-brother to several winners, including fairly useful 1983 2-y-o 6f and 7f
winner Meraval (by Ahonoora): dam won over 1¼m: poor maiden: below form of
late, in blinkers last time: should prove suited by further than 7f. *J. Sutcliffe*

BLUEFAULDS 3 bl.g. Noalto 120 – Parma Nova 58 (Dominion 123) [1991 NR –
1992 7.1m] 1,000Y: second foal: dam poor maiden: last in Edinburgh seller, only run.
T. Craig

BLUE FLAG (USA) 3 b.c. Dixieland Band (USA) – Stuttsman County (USA) 71 +
(Damascus (USA)) [1991NR 1992 10m 11.8g^2 a12s^2 14d] $42,000F, $80,000Y: sturdy
colt: first foal: dam sprint winner: sire Grade 2 stakes winner at up to 9f: modest
form when second in summer maidens at Leicester and Southwell: stiff task in
Kempton handicap: stays 1½m: may be capable of better. *Lord Huntingdon*

BLUE GRIT 6 b.g. Thatching 131 – Northern Wisdom (Northfields (USA)) [1991 63
a12g a8g 10.2s 9s 8g^2 9f* 8.5f* 8.2m^2 9f4 8m^5 8f4 9f^3 8f^2 8h^4 1992 8.3d^3 7.5g 9m^6
8f4 9f 8.1m* 8.1m 8.3m 6g* 5.9f^2 6f4 6g^5 6m* 5g 7g* 7s 7d 7.1g^3] good-topped
gelding: had a good season in handicaps in 1992, first past post at Edinburgh,
Pontefract (2), Carlisle and Catterick: best from stiff 6f to 9f: acts on dead ground
but goes well on a sound surface: effective blinkered or not: below form when
visored: good mount for inexperienced rider: has won when sweating: very tough.
M. Dods

BLUE GROTTO (IRE) 2 ch.c. (Feb 28) Bluebird (USA) 125 – Ganna (ITY) 75 p
(Molvedo 137) [1992 7g^3 8d^2] 12,000F, IR 20,000Y: useful-looking colt: fourth foal:
half-brother to Irish 7f winner Slash And Burn (by Thatching): dam unraced sister to
John Porter winner Salado and Italian St Leger winner Gallio: shaped well in
maidens at Newcastle and Redcar (finished strongly when beaten short head by
Tomos): will be suited by test of stamina. *J. W. Watts*

BLUE IS TRUE (IRE) 3 b.f. Bluebird (USA) 125 – Royal Wolff (Prince Tender- 54
foot (USA) 126) [1991 6f^3 1992 7.1g 8g^5 6m^3 6.1g^5 5s^2 6s^5] angular, long-backed
filly: poor mover: modest maiden: stayed 6f: acted on good to firm and soft ground:
dead. *L. J. Barratt*

BLUE LAWS (IRE) 2 b.c. (Apr 16) Bluebird (USA) 125 – Claretta (USA) 82 63 p
(Roberto (USA) 131) [1992 6f^3 7g 8.1d^3] 28,000F: leggy colt: brother to 3-y-o
Zaffarancho and half-brother to several winners, notably Sapience (by Niniski):
dam, a 2-y-o 7f winner, is half-sister to Italian 1000 Guineas winner Rosananti and
good English/German performer Claddagh: staying-on third to Soul Emperor in
Haydock maiden in September, final start: will be suited by good test of stamina. *J.
G. FitzGerald*

BLUE LYZANDER 3 b.f. Petrizzo 109 – Ol' Blue Eyes (Bluerullah 115) [1991 –
NR 1992 15.4d^6 14.1g] third reported foal: dam twice-raced at 2 yrs in Ireland and
winning pointer: well beaten in autumn maidens. *R. Brotherton*

BLUE MARINE 3 b.f. Bellypha 130 – Opale 117 (Busted 134) [1991 7d 1992 7f* 79
8g^2 7m^4] lengthy filly: moderate walker: fluent mover: ran creditably in small-field
minor events after winning Epsom maiden in July: bred to stay middle distances, but
may prove best over strongly-run 6f/7f: sold 25,000 gns Newmarket December
Sales. *A. C. Stewart*

BLUE NOVA (IRE) 2 b.c. (Feb 6) Bluebird (USA) 125 – Res Nova (USA) 65
(Blushing Groom (FR) 131) [1992 7.1s^2 8s] 15,500Y: compact colt: first foal: dam
unraced half-sister to Grade 3 winner in USA, is daughter of top-class racemare
Track Robbery: clear second in maiden auction at Chepstow: always struggling
when favourite in similar event at Bath later in September: sent to Italy. *P. W.
Chapple-Hyam*

BLUE RADIANCE 2 b.f. (May 22) Skyliner 117 – Stellaris (Star Appeal 133) **60**
[1992 5s⁶ 6f* 5m³ 7f³ 6s² 6d] angular, unfurnished filly: fourth living foal: sister to
3-y-o Celestine and half-sister to 5-y-o Ashdren (by Lochnager), both of them
winners at up to 7f: dam lightly raced: won Ripon seller (no bid) in June: only
below-par effort after when last final start: will stay 1m: acts on any going. *T.
Fairhurst*

BLUES BREAKER 2 b.f. (May 5) Sizzling Melody 117 – Dominion Blue 66   **–**
(Dominion 123) [1992 6s 5d] compact filly: third foal: half-sister to a winner in
Belgium: dam 1¼m winner: well beaten in October maidens. *D. Sasse*

BLUE SEA 3 b.g. Bluebird (USA) 125 – Sophonisbe (Wollow 132) [1991 NR 1992 **80**
8g³ 8.3f² 10.2f² a12g³] IR 25,000Y: sparely-made gelding: fourth foal: half-brother
to a winner in Germany: dam French 11f winner, is half-sister to Steinlen: fair
maiden: off course 6 months, easy to back and below form at Lingfield last time:
should stay 1½m. *M. A. Jarvis*

BLUE SOMBRERO (IRE) 2 b.f. (Apr 29) Reasonable (FR) 119 – Jep Chapeau **49**
(Viking (USA)) [1992 6.1m 7d⁵ 7g⁶ 8.2d 8d⁶ 10.5d] good-topped filly: first foal: dam
Irish maiden: stays 1m. *R. J. Holder*

BLUES TRAVELLER (IRE) 2 b.c. (May 10) Bluebird (USA) 125 – Natuschka **105** p
(Authi 123) [1992 6g³ 6g* 7m] 100,000Y: useful-looking colt: good walker:
half-brother to 3 middle-distance winners, including very useful 4-y-o Surrealist (by
Tate Gallery), also successful at 7f at 2 yrs: dam won from 9f to 2m in Ireland:
progressive type: heavily-backed favourite when ½-length winner of 20-runner
maiden at Newbury: outclassed in Dewhurst Stakes at Newmarket won by Zafonic
month later, but ran very well to finish over 8 lengths seventh of 11: will be much
better suited by 1m +: sure to win another race or two. *B. W. Hills*

BLUE TESS (IRE) 2 br.f. (Apr 12) Bluebird (USA) 125 – Royaltess (Royal And **70**
Regal (USA)) [1992 6.1m² 6d² 6m²] IR 32,000Y: quite attractive filly, rather
angular: easy mover: third foal: half-sister to useful 1989 2-y-o 6f winner Makbul (by
Fairy King): dam unraced sister to useful Irish sprinter winner Regaltess: fair form
in maidens: will be suited by further: bandaged behind final start. *M. Moubarak*

BLUE TOPAZE 4 ch.f. Fast Topaze (USA) 128 – Forever Mary 81 (Red Alert **69**
127) [1991 7d 1992 5m³ 6g 6d* 5.7g* 7m³ 6g⁵ 7s 6m³ 6.1d³] good-topped filly:
consistent handicapper: successful in July at Salisbury and Bath: should prove
better suited by 7f than shorter: acts on good to firm and dead ground, seems
unsuited by soft: suitable mount for lady rider. *R. J. Holder*

BLUE TRUMPET 2 b.g. (Mar 29) Respect 95 – Sans Blague (Above Suspicion **49**
127) [1992 6m 6g² 6m] 2,300Y: compact gelding: half-brother to 2 winners abroad:
dam Irish 1½m and 1¾m winner: sire sprinter: easily best effort when second in
seller at Redcar in September on debut: will be suited by 7f. *A. Hide*

BLUNHAM EXPRESS 3 b.f. Never So Bold 135 – Park Parade 94 (Monsanto **39**
(FR) 121) [1991 5g 5m⁴ 6m² 6g² a6g⁵ 6m³ 8.1g⁴ 7m 1992 7.1m 6.9h³ 8.3f² 10m 6g 7d]
robust filly: has a round action: poor maiden: stays 1m: acts on hard ground: below
form when blinkered once: sold 1,200 gns Doncaster October Sales. *T. Fairhurst*

BLUSHING BARADA (USA) 2 br.f. (May 1) Blushing Groom (FR) 131 – **53** p
Galletto (USA) 111 (Nijinsky (CAN) 138) [1992 6g 7m] $315,000Y: rather leggy filly:
half-sister to several winners, notably Irish St Leger winner Authaal (by Shergar):
dam, won Galtres Stakes, is half-sister to useful stayer Sir Daniel out of Irish Oaks
winner Gaia: bandaged behind, in midfield for big-field maidens at Newbury and
Newmarket in autumn, eased once held: will stay 1m: should prove capable of
better. *A. A. Scott*

BLUSHING BELLE 4 b.f. Local Suitor (USA) 128 – Shuteye 91 (Shirley **56** d
Heights 130) [1991 10g³ 12.2m³ 12.2m³ 12m² a14g 1992 16d 10.8d⁴dis a12g² 10f2 12f⁶ 10.2f4
14.6d 12f² 11m⁴ 11.9g 14g⁵ 17.2s] rangy, workmanlike filly: has a very round action:
inconsistent handicapper: should stay beyond 1½m: acts on any going, including
equitrack: below form when visored once, usually blinkered: sold to join J. White's
stable 3,800 gns Newmarket Autumn Sales. *P. F. I. Cole*

BLUSHING GOLD 3 ch.f. Blushing Scribe (USA) 107 – Nonpareil (FR) 92   **–**
(Pharly (FR) 130) [1991 NR 1992 12g⁶ 12.2m⁶ 14.1m⁴ 10f] 2,300Y: lengthy, rather
sparely-made filly: fourth foal: brother to 2-y-o sprint winners Access Leisure and
Mister Lawson: dam best at 2 yrs: looks of little account. *Mrs J. Jordan*

BLUSHING STORM (USA) 3 b.f. Blushing Groom (FR) 131 – Witwatersrand **102**
(USA) (Mr Prospector (USA)) [1991 NR 1992 10s⁶ 10.2m³ 11.5g² 12f³ 11.9g³ 10d³]
long-backed filly with scope: has round action: third reported foal: dam minor
winner at 1¼m from family of Sir Harry Lewis: easily best efforts fourth and fifth

starts in Ribblesdale Stakes at Royal Ascot and Lancashire Oaks (soon tailed off after jockey had been injured leaving stalls but finished with a flourish and beaten only 3 lengths) at Haydock: needs at least 1½m, and will stay further: acts on firm ground. *J. R. Fanshawe*

BLUSH RAMBLER (USA)   2 b.c. (Feb 26) Blushing Groom (FR) 131 – **119** p Romanette (USA) (Alleged (USA) 138) [1992 7d² 7g² 7g* 8d* 8s²]
It could not have been reasonably anticipated from Blush Rambler's first two performances that he would go on to show himself to be one of the best two-year-olds in training, but with time and distance his form improved tremendously, so much so that on his final outing he emerged best of the ten runners that chased home Tenby in the Grand Criterium at Longchamp in October. The first indication that Blush Rambler was on the upgrade came when he strolled home unchallenged in a nineteen-runner maiden at Newcastle in August on his third outing. The race might have been a weaker affair than those in which he'd been second at Salisbury and Ascot—when at Ascot he'd pulled too hard and was reportedly suffering from corns—but Blush Rambler ran out a very impressive winner, settling much better before quickening around ten lengths clear, eased to seven at the post. Less than two weeks later, when given the opportunity to tackle a mile for the first time, Blush Rambler confirmed that he was a rapidly-improving colt by running away with the Stardom Stakes at Goodwood, a listed event contested by a smaller but much stronger field than he'd beaten at Newcastle; the Acomb winner Woodchat, who'd beaten Blush Rambler by two and a half lengths at Salisbury, the progressive stayer Futurballa, a runaway winner under 9-7 of an Epsom nursery on his previous outing, and the tough and genuine Nominator looked to be his most dangerous opponents. As they began the descent into the straight none in the field was travelling so easily as Blush Rambler, second favourite to Woodchat in the betting, and once he was switched left at the two-furlong pole he sprinted clear, passing the post four lengths ahead of Nominator with Woodchat, suffering a turnaround of seven lengths on their Salisbury running, a neck behind in third. Blush Rambler was no match for the two-and-a-half-length winner Tenby in the Grand Criterium, but he ran a gallant race, improving significantly on anything he'd achieved previously and, after turning into the short straight in the middle of the field, stayed on well to deny the Irish-trained colt Basim second on the line. As at Goodwood, Blush Rambler tended to hang to his right in the run for home.

		Red God	Nasrullah
	Blushing Groom (FR)	(ch 1954)	Spring Run
	(ch 1974)	Runaway Bride	Wild Risk
Blush Rambler (USA)		(b 1962)	Aimee
(b.c. Feb 26, 1990)		Alleged	Hoist The Flag
	Romanette (USA)	(b 1974)	Princess Pout
	(b or br 1982)	Laughing Bridge	Hilarious
		(b or br 1972)	Brook Bridge

The close-coupled, quite attractive Blush Rambler is the best so far from the penultimate crop of Blushing Groom, who was put down in May at Gainesway Farm after a long fight against cancer. Blushing Groom was a top-class racehorse and stallion. On the track he won the Prix Robert Papin, Prix Morny, Prix de la Salamandre and Grand Criterium (the last to achieve the feat, incidentally, before his son Arazi in 1991) as a two-year-old and the Prix Fontainebleau and the Poule d'Essai des Poulains at three, when he also ran third to The Minstrel in the Derby and second to Flying Water in the Prix Jacques le Marois. Blushing Groom's achievements at stud have been no less impressive: he's sired around eighty stakes winners, of whom the best include Blushing John, Rainbow Quest, Al Bahathri, Mt Livermore, Baillamont, Jalmood, Crystal Glitters, Groom Dancer, Snow Bride and, of course, Arazi. Blushing Groom had a quiet year by his high standards in 1992, although the victories of Arazi, Gold Splash and Sillery at the Arc weekend brought him back briefly into the spotlight. Blush Rambler's dam Romanette was a useful mare who won five races at up to eleven furlongs, including the Jersey Oaks over nine furlongs, from twenty-five starts. She's one of several winners produced by Laughing Bridge, a smart two-year-old in the States in

1974 when she won two Graded races at six furlongs and ended the year rated 8 lb below the top filly Ruffian in the Experimental Free Handicap. Romanette is easily the best of Laughing Bridge's several winners; the others, most of whom were run-of-the-mill, include the five-furlong winner Bridge Master. Not many of Blush Rambler's predominantly American-based family have run over here in recent years, but among those who have are the fair mile to mile-and-a-quarter winner Ninth Saga, who's a daughter of Bridge Master, and the 1992 three-year-old Empeeka, a daughter of Romanette's five-furlong winning half-sister Laughing Ruler.

Blush Rambler was only just coming to himself in the autumn so he could well be capable of more improvement in his second season (he was sent to spend the winter in Dubai). He'll be very well suited by a mile and a quarter. He's a fluent mover but has raced only on an easy surface, showing his best form when the ground was softest. *M. R. Stoute*

BLYOSTKA (USA)   3 ch.f. Gone West (USA) – Calypsa (USA) 83 (The Minstrel   –
(CAN) 135) [1991 7m³ 7f⁴ 6f⁶ 7f 1992 6g²] leggy, close-coupled filly: poor maiden: bred to stay 1m + : acts on firm ground. *G. A. Pritchard-Gordon*

BLYTON LAD   6 b.g. Skyliner 117 – Ballinacurra (King's Troop 118) [1991 **119**
5m⁶ 5g 5g³ 5m³ 5m* 5m² 1992 5g³ 5m² 5f 5m² 5m 5m³ 5m* 5m² 6g*]
The tough and genuine northern sprinter Blyton Lad was better than ever as a six-year-old and really came into his own in the autumn. He won the Rous Stakes at Newmarket for the third year running, staying on resolutely after being driven firmly from some way out, and the Remembrance Day Stakes at Doncaster, keeping on gamely to get the better of Keen Hunter. Blyton Lad's successes in the Rous Stakes have been for three different trainers, John Balding (who had care of the horse until the end of his four-year-old days), Will Pearce and, in the latest season, Maurice Camacho. Blyton Lad ran for Pearce on his first two starts in 1992 (placed in the Palace House Stakes and the Temple Stakes) and was saddled on his third by Beasley, who picked up the reins at Hambleton House stables after Pearce's tragic death. Blyton Lad was transferred to Camacho after running poorly in the King's Stand Stakes at Royal Ascot. Kept to five-furlong conditions events, Blyton Lad was placed in the King George Stakes at Goodwood and the Scarbrough Stakes at Doncaster (running poorly in between the Nunthorpe) before his success in the Rous Stakes. He'll reportedly be aimed at a fourth Rous Stakes as a seven-year-old but his success in the Remembrance Day Stakes, his first race at six furlongs since his three-year-old days, gives connections a wider choice of races to aim at.

Rous Stakes, Newmarket—Blyton Lad wins for the third successive year;
Garah (right) pips Artistic Reef for second place

	Skyliner	African Sky	Sing Sing
	(b 1975)	(b 1970)	Sweet Caroline
Blyton Lad		Keep Going	Hard Sauce
(b.g. 1986)		(br 1966)	Whistle Stop
	Ballinacurra	King's Troop	Princely Gift
	(ch 1972)	(b 1957)	Equiria
		All Royal	Primera
		(b 1966)	Moonlit

Blyton Lad is a big, rangy gelding—among the biggest racing on the flat—and usually takes the eye in the paddock, despite often spoiling himself by sweating and being on edge. He has a tendency to be unruly in the preliminaries and sometimes gives trouble going into the stalls, though he is much more tractable nowadays than he used to be. His sire Skyliner was a sprinter-miler, probably best known as the sire of the useful two-year-olds Mamma's Too and Sky Royale, prolific winners for the Berry stable. Blyton Lad's dam Ballinacurra ran only once. Her other winners include Blyton Lad's sister She Is The Boss, successful over five furlongs in Ireland. Blyton Lad acts on firm and dead going; somewhat surprisingly, in a lengthy career he's never encountered soft or heavy ground. Blyton Lad's sheer size makes him difficult to keep balanced. The task of riding him has been unfashionable northern jockey Stuart Webster's ever since Webster became the first to win on him back in 1989. *M. J. Camacho*

BLYTON STAR (IRE) 4 b.g. Horage 124 – Saintly Angel 87 (So Blessed 130) –
[1991 5g 5m⁶ 5m a7g 1992 5s 8.2s a16g a14g] sturdy gelding: moderate mover: seems of little account. *S. R. Bowring*

BOARDING SCHOOL 5 b.g. Glenstal (USA) 118 – Amenity (FR) 76 (Luthier –
126) [1991 16.5m² 1992 16.5g⁵] good-topped ex-Irish gelding: rated 92 at 4 yrs: soundly beaten only run on flat in 1992: stays 2m: acts on good to firm and dead ground. *C. Parker*

BOBBIE BOLD 4 ch.g. Noalto 120 – Silk Imp 72 (Imperial Fling (USA) 116) 38
[1991 10f a12g 1992 8m 8g³ 6.9h³ 7d⁴ 8g 8f 10m a7g 7d 10.3g] lengthy, angular gelding: poor handicapper: stays 1m: acts on hard and dead ground: raced too freely when tried blinkered: sold out of R. O'Leary's stable 1,600 gns Doncaster August Sales after sixth run. *T. Kersey*

BOBBIE DEE 2 b.f. (Mar 1) Blakeney 126 – Aldbury Girl 79 (Galivanter 93
131) [1992 6m⁶ 7g³ 7d⁵ 8m⁴ 10g² 10s] workmanlike filly: has scope: sister to 3-y-o Royal Seaton, stays 1½m, and half-sister to fairly useful 6f to 1m winner Absonal (by Absalom): dam 2-y-o 5.9f winner: improved with every run in 1992 until running poorly in Italy final outing: fourth in Group 3 event at Doncaster and second to Bob's Return in listed race at Newmarket in autumn: will be suited by 1½m: acts on good to firm and dead ground: certain to win a race. *D. R. C. Elsworth*

BOBBY ON THE BANK 6 ch.g. Monsanto (FR) 121 – Dewberry 68 (Bay –
Express 132) [1991 10d 10m³ 8h⁶ a12g⁶ 8.9m 10.5m 1992 11.1v 8d] small, rather sparely-made gelding: moderate mover: poor handicapper: stays 1¼m well: acts on any going: sold 1,100 gns Doncaster October Sales. *S. G. Payne*

BOBBYSOXER 2 b.f. (May 12) Valiyar 129 – Beveridge (USA) 86 (Spectacular 59 p
Bid (USA)) [1992 7g 8d 7d⁶] 20,000Y: tall, close-coupled, good-topped filly: fourth foal: half-sister to 3-y-o 1¼ and 11.5f winner Rainridge (by Rainbow Quest) and 2-y-o 6f winners Safa (by Shirley Heights), useful at 1m, and Between Time (by Elegant Air): dam 2-y-o 7f winner from good family: beaten around 6 lengths when sixth of 16 in maiden at Leicester in October: backward and green previously: will do better. *J. L. Dunlop*

BOB'S RETURN (IRE) 2 br.c. (Mar 5) Bob Back (USA) 124 – Quality of Life 99 p
(Auction Ring (USA) 123) [1992 5g⁵ 6m⁴ 8m* 10g*] IR 14,500Y: good-topped colt: moderate walker: third foal: dam Irish 2-y-o 6f winner: really progressive colt: made all in big-field maiden at Pontefract and listed event (by ¾ length from Bobbie Dee) at Newmarket in October: will stay 1½m. *M. H. Tompkins*

BOBZAO (IRE) 3 b.c. Alzao (USA) 117 – Brilleaux 73 (Manado 130) [1991 6s* 106
7g⁴ 8.1m³ 7d² 7s 1992 8d⁴ 7g 6.1g⁵ 10.4f* 11.9f² 10g 10.4g 10d 10g] useful-looking colt: 3-length winner of York listed race in June: mostly faced stiff tasks after but

Daniel Prenn Royal Yorkshire Stakes, York—Bobzao stays on from Polish Blue

well below form in £18,200 Newbury handicap final start: effective at 1¼m to 1½m: acts on any going. *W. Carter*

BODANDERE 2 b.f. (Mar 24) Hallgate 127 – Tarvie 101 (Swing Easy (USA) 126) **45** [1992 5.2g6 5d5 5g4 5.3f4 6g 6d6 6d 7.3s] smallish, plain filly: moderate mover: half-sister to several winners, including very speedy 1985 2-y-o Stalker (by Kala Shikari) and 1989 Irish 2-y-o 5f winner Regal Peace (by Known Fact): dam game sprinter: poor form, including in sellers: should stay beyond 6f (stiff task over 7f): acts on firm and dead ground: below form when blinkered/visored: sold 3,600 gns Newmarket Autumn Sales. *M. J. Fetherston-Godley*

BODARI 3 b.c. Prince Sabo 123 – City Link Rose (Lochnager 132) [1991 5m6 5m4 **81** 1992 6s5 5m 5g3 5f3 5m5 5f* 5d* 5m3 5m2 6d2 5m5 5d4 5d4 5g4 5.2s5 5g] good-quartered colt: really consistent handicapper: made virtually all to win at Newmarket and Sandown in summer: effective at 5f and 6f: acts on firm and dead ground, below form on soft: suitable mount for apprentice: tough. *D. A. Wilson*

BODY LANGUAGE 2 ch.f. (Jan 30) Petoski 135 – Whipp's Cross 93 (Kris 135) **48** [1992 5.2m6 5.7g 7g 5.1d] 10,000Y: compact filly: first foal: dam, 1¼m and 11f winner, is half-sister to very useful middle-distance stayer Glowing With Pride: poor maiden: bred to be well suited by middle distances: sold to join Mrs J. Ramsden's stable 2,000 gns Newmarket Autumn Sales. *I. A. Balding*

BOETHIUS (USA) 3 ch.g. The Minstrel (CAN) 135 – Bechamel (USA) 91 **–** (Sauce Boat (USA)) [1991 NR 1992 7g] lengthy, heavy-topped gelding: dam sprinter: tailed off in Newmarket maiden in April: sold 840 gns Newmarket Autumn Sales. *J. R. Fanshawe*

BOG TROTTER (USA) 4 ch.c. Irish River (FR) 131 – Chaleur (CAN) (Rouge **107** Sang (USA)) [1991 7g* 8g 7m* 6s 7m5 1992 7m3 7.6m4 7f] angular, good-topped colt: impresses in appearance: rated 119 at 3 yrs: below form in 1992 after fair third in Longchamp Group 3 event: should prove as effective at 6f as 7f: acts on good to firm ground and dead: takes keen hold, and seems best when allowed to dominate: bandaged near-fore second start. *W. J. Haggas*

BOHEMIAN CROWN (USA) 2 b.c. (Mar 16) Danzig (USA) – Infantes (USA) **69** p (Exclusive Native (USA)) [1992 7m5 7d] $450,000Y: rangy colt: closely related to fairly useful 1989 2-y-o 5f winner Tatwij (by Topsider) and half-brother to Tejano (by Caro), second best 2-y-o of 1987 in USA and graded-stakes placed several times at 3 yrs: dam won at around 1m at 2 yrs: not fully wound up when beaten around 9 lengths in October maidens won by Placerville at Newmarket and Gabr at Leicester: gives impression will stay middle distances and do better. *M. R. Stoute*

BOHEMIAN QUEEN 2 ch.f. (Feb 8) Doulab (USA) 115 – Tittlemouse 86 **47**
(Castle Keep 121) [1992 5.1f 6m 7.5s⁴ 7d 7d⁵ 10.5d 10d⁴] 5,400Y: small, light-framed filly: first foal: dam 1¼m winner: plater: made fourth of 19 at Leicester final start (October): will stay well: acts on soft ground. *J. L. Spearing*

BOISTEROUS 2 b.c. (Mar 14) Sizzling Melody 117 – Balgreggan (Hallez (FR) –
131) [1992 6g 6s 7.1d 6m] 12,000Y, 13,000Y: good-bodied, quite attractive colt: closely related to 2 winners by Song, including useful 6f to 1m winner Sailor's Song, and half-brother to several winners, including sprinters Manton Dan (by Tower Walk) and Street Market (by Porto Bello): dam twice-raced half-sister to smart stayer Golden Love: poor maiden: blinkered final start. *W. R. Muir*

BO KNOWS BEST (IRE) 3 ch.g. Burslem 123 – Do We Know (Derrylin 115) **68**
[1991 5d 6g⁴ 7m³ 7g 7m 1992 7m 6.9m 8.3m 8.3m 10d* 10d* 12s² 11.4g* 12s* 12s] leggy gelding: tends to be unimpressive in appearance: progressed well in handicaps in 1992, successful at Nottingham (selling event, bought in 7,200 gns), Goodwood (claiming event), Sandown and Salisbury, until disappointing favourite final start: effective at 1¼m to 1½m: acts on soft ground: tends to be lazy once in front. *J. Sutcliffe*

BOLD ACRE 2 ch.g. (May 18) Never So Bold 135 – Nicola Wynn 83 (Nicholas Bill **56**
125) [1992 5.1d4 5g 6f4 6.1m4 7d² 7m² 7m5] 4,800Y, 7,000 2-y-o: leggy gelding: has a round action: second foal: half-brother to 3-y-o And Me (by Don't Forget Me): dam 1½m winner, is half-sister to dam of Brocade: modest maiden: will be suited by 1m: acts on firm and dead ground: ran creditably when blinkered once. *D. R. Laing*

BOLD A MAIDEN 2 ch.f. (Apr 18) Never So Bold 135 – Al Nuwaibi (USA) 71 (Sir **36**
Ivor 135) [1992 5.7f5 6g 6g a6g 7d 6s] 3,200F: unfurnished filly: moderate walker: third foal: dam won over 6f on debut but showed nothing after: well beaten in modest company: tried blinkered/visored. *D. R. Laing*

BOLD AMBITION 5 br.g. Ela-Mana-Mou 132 – Queen of The Dance (Dancer's **41**
Image (USA)) [1991 NR 1992 10m 10.4m 11f 8m 10.3m5 12d 12.3g4 12.3d3 12m 13.8g² 13.8d 14.6g] good-bodied gelding: poor mover: inconsistent handicapper: effective from 1¼m to 14.6f: acts on good to firm and dead ground: sold out of D. Elsworth's stable 3,200 gns Doncaster January Sales. *T. Kersey*

BOLD AMUSEMENT 2 ch.c. (Apr 6) Never So Bold 135 – Hysterical 68 (High **71** p
Top 131) [1992 6g*] 42,000Y: fifth foal: half-brother to 3 winners, including (at 7f to 9f) useful Comic Talent (by Pharly) and 3-y-o Rully (by Rousillon), 7.6f winner at 2 yrs: dam won over 1½m at 4 yrs, only season to race: 5/1-winner of maiden at Hamilton in August, always prominent and staying on well to beat Robix by 2 lengths: looks sure to improve. *Mrs M. Reveley*

BOLD ANGEL 5 b.g. Lochnager 132 – Lobela 77 (Lorenzaccio 130) [1991 6m5 **86**
6m² 7f³ 8d6 7.1g 6g* 6.1m³ 7g 7.5f4 6m² 6g5 7g 1992 7f* 7g³ 7f4 7.1m*] strong, close-coupled gelding: carries condition: has a round action: improved handicapper in 1992: successful at Thirsk and Haydock: effective at 6f and 7f, and should stay 1m: acts on firm and dead ground: ran moderately when blinkered once: game. *M. H. Easterby*

BOLD ANSWER 9 b.g. Bold Owl 101 – Subtle Answer (Stephen George 102) –
[1991 a8g 1992 a11g 8.5m] seems of little account nowadays. *M. C. Chapman*

BOLD ARABELLA 4 b.f. Never So Bold 135 – Nativity (USA) (Native Royalty –
(USA)) [1991 7v³ 8d 7g³ 7g* 7d 1992 8.5m 9g] big, workmanlike filly: little sign of retaining ability in handicaps in 1992: stays 7f: tried blinkered once: sold 850 gns Newmarket Autumn Sales. *J. L. Spearing*

BOLD BORIS 3 br.g. Never So Bold 135 – Pride of Paris (Troy 137) [1991 a7g –
1992 a8g6 a10g6] lengthy, quite attractive gelding: poor maiden: not seen out after January: sold 800 gns Newmarket September Sales. *R. W. Armstrong*

BOLD BOSS 3 b.c. Nomination 125 – Mai Pussy 91 (Realm 129) [1991 NR 1992 8g **88**
7s³ 10.5d² 8m² 8.3g* 10g 7.1m4 7m² 8d6 7d³] strong, good-bodied colt: impresses in appearance: has a roundish action: seventh foal: half-brother to several winners, including smart 7f to 1¼m performer Beau Sher (by Ile de Bourbon): dam stayed 6f: fairly useful handicapper: won at Windsor in July: best at up to 1m: acts on good to firm and dead ground: tongue tied down last 3 starts: joined G. Moore and won 2 juvenile hurdles in December. *B. Hanbury*

BOLD BOSTONIAN (FR) 4 b.c. Never So Bold 135 – Miss Boston (FR) –
(River River (FR) 117) [1991 8s 8g 12d 8d² 8g³ 8.9g6 10m² 8.9m² 11g 1992 8.1d5 11f5]

quite good-topped colt: good mover: rated 88 as 3-y-o: below best in handicaps in May: stays 1¼m: acts on good to firm ground and dead. *P. J. Hobbs*

BOLD CELT   9 b. or br.h. Brave Shot – Pearl Locket (Gulf Pearl 117) [1991 6d⁴ 1992 6s] leggy horse: poor maiden: stays 7f: acts on dead ground. *C. B. B. Booth* —

BOLD COOKIE   4 b.f. Never So Bold 135 – Irish Cookie 80 (Try My Best (USA) 130) [1991 6m³ 6m⁴ 6m⁵ 1992 5.9d⁶] lengthy filly: still a maiden, and not seen again after giving temperamental display in claimer in April: should stay 7f+: acts on good to firm ground: not one to trust. *Miss S. E. Hall* —

BOLD COUNTY   2 b.f. (May 23) Never So Bold 135 – Hants 111 (Exbury 138) [1992 5m* 5m⁴ 5m⁶ 5f* 5m* 5.7m⁶ 6g 5.1d 5g³ 5g²] IR 2,000Y: leggy, unfurnished filly: has scope: half-sister to several winners, including 6f to 1m winner Potemkin (by Sir Gaylord) and 7f and 1½m winner Tants (by Vitiges), both very useful: dam won 4 times at about 1¼m: successful in Catterick maiden, Hamilton median auction and Windsor nursery: good placed efforts in nurseries in autumn: stays 6f: takes keen hold, and has hung badly: sometimes mounted on track. *M. Johnston*   **70**

BOLD DANCER (FR)   3 ch.f. Bold Arrangement 111 – Dancela 74 (Ela-Mana-Mou 132) [1991 NR 1992 8m] sturdy, lengthy filly: third foal: half-sister to 4-y-o Loudest Whisper (by Reach): dam disappointing half-sister to useful Irish middle-distance winner Sir Simon: always beaten in Kempton maiden in May, only run: sold 1,000 gns Ascot November Sales. *P. J. Makin* —

BOLD ELECT   4 b.g. Electric 126 – Famous Band (USA) (Banderilla (USA)) [1991 9s 10f 13.9m⁵ 10f⁴ 9.9f² 12.3f* 12m 10.9m 13.9m⁴ 1992 12g 16.2m⁶ 12.3m⁴ 12.3f⁴ 12s* 14.1d⁴ 12.3m* 12m* 12d⁴ 11.9d 12d] sturdy, lengthy gelding: carries condition: in excellent form in handicaps in summer, successful at Beverley (2) and Ripon: lost his form after: best form at around 1½m/1¾m: acts on any going: held up. *P. Wigham*   **76**

BOLD FACE (IRE)   2 br.c. (Jan 31) Persian Bold 123 – Siva (FR) (Bellypha 130) [1992 5.1m⁵ 5g⁴ 6.1d³ 7f² 8.1d 7m 6.1m³ 7d] IR 16,000Y: small, sparely-made colt: first foal: dam French 1m to 11.2f winner: modest performer: will prove suited by 1m: has form on dead ground, but seems best on a sound surface: effective with or without blinkers: sold 4,600 gns Newmarket Autumn Sales. *R. F. Johnson Houghton*   **68**

BOLD FLASH   2 ch.g. (May 4) Flash of Steel 120 – Amenaide 79 (Known Fact (USA) 135) [1992 5.9g 8.5m⁵ 7s a7g] 5,000Y: sturdy, lengthy gelding: first foal: dam 2-y-o 5f winner stayed 7f, is out of half-sister to Irish Oaks winner Swiftfoot: poor maiden: should stay 1¼m: acts on good to firm ground, very stiff task on fibresand. *P. C. Haslam*   **48**

BOLD HABIT   7 ch.g. Homing 130 – Our Mother 95 (Bold Lad (IRE) 133) [1991 7m 7.6g* 8g 5g* 7g* 6m⁶ 5f* 6m 7m a7g³ a7g² 1992 a7g* a6g² a7g² 7g⁶ 6g 7g³ 6f 5g³ 7m⁶ 5g⁶ 5d 7.1s⁶ 7f 7.3g 7d⁵ 7m a6g a6g] sturdy, strong-quartered gelding: moderate mover: won Southwell claimer in January: shaped promisingly on several starts on turf after but lost his form late in the year: effective at up to 1m: acts on firm and dead going and all-weather surfaces: good mount for claimer: trained until after fourteenth start by W. Pearce/B. Beasley, next 2 by S. Kettlewell: held up. *Mrs J. R. Ramsden*   **89**

BOLD LEZ   5 b.h. Never So Bold 135 – Classy Nancy (USA) (Cutlass (USA)) [1991 6g 5g* 5m² 6g6 6m 5g4 5.6m⁵ 6m 5d 5d³ 5.2g 1992 5g 6g* 6g² 6f 5s³ 6m 6g⁵ 6g 5m 6m] leggy horse: usually looks well: poor mover: useful sprinter: successful in Lingfield handicap in May and good efforts when placed in Lingfield and Sandown listed races after: effective at 5f and 6f: acts on any going. *M. J. Haynes*   **102**

BOLD LINE   2 br.f. (Jan 31) Never So Bold 135 – Known Line 100 (Known Fact (USA) 135) [1992 6.1g 7d] 16,000Y: leggy, lengthy filly: shows knee action: second foal: dam 8.2f winner at 2 yrs later better at 1½m, is out of Park Hill winner Quay Line: in midfield in autumn maidens at Nottingham and Leicester: sold 3,000 gns Newmarket Autumn Sales: should stay 1¼m. *R. J. R. Williams*   **44**

BOLD MAC   6 b.g. Comedy Star (USA) 121 – Northern Empress 80 (Northfields (USA)) [1991 NR 1992 12v] tall gelding: on the downgrade. *M. Blanshard* —

BOLD MELODY   3 b.f. Never So Bold 135 – Broken Melody (Busted 134) [1991 a6g a8g⁵ 1992 a7g⁵ 8h⁶ 8.3f* 8.3g* 8.3g 8.3s⁴] ran moderately after winning maiden claimer and handicap at Hamilton in July: stays 8.3f: acts on firm ground: winning hurdler in August. *P. C. Haslam*   **57**

BOLD MEMORY   3 br.c. Never So Bold 135 – Try To Remember (Music Boy 124) [1991 6m 6d⁴ 1992 5g² 5m 6m 5m 6d 7d 7m 7m 8m 6v] leggy, good-topped colt: ran well in minor event at Kempton on reappearance, good eighth of 18 in handicap   **91**

124

at Newmarket seventh start: well below form otherwise: stays 7f: acts on good to firm ground and dead. *M. Johnston*

BOLD MOOD 3 br.g. Jalmood (USA) 126 – Boldie 81 (Bold Lad (IRE) 133) [1991 –
8.3g 6d³ 6.1d⁵ 6s a7g 1992 6.9v 8s 7f 10m 7.5d⁶ 9.2g] leggy, close-coupled gelding: no form in 1992: bred to stay 1¼m: sold 1,300 gns Doncaster August Sales. *J. Berry*

BOLD N'FLASHY (CAN) 3 b.c. Bold Ruckus (USA) – Flashy Chestnut (USA) **114** (Briartic (CAN)) [1991 a5.5f* a6s⁴ a6f³ a6.5s⁵ 1992 a4.5f³ a4.5f* a4.5s* a6s* a7f⁵ a6f⁶ a6f⁴ a6f⁵ 5f* 5s⁶ 6s² 5.5f⁴] robust, strong-quartered colt: first foal: dam winning sprinter from 2 to 4 yrs in claiming and allowance company: sire smart performer from 5f to 9f: very useful Canadian sprinter: won maiden at Woodbine at 2 yrs: successful in 1992 in 2 allowance races at Greenwood and minor stakes event at Woodbine: tried for the first time on turf at The Meadowlands, USA, in September, winning Mercer Raceabout Stakes by 5¾ lengths: led 3f when about 3½ lengths sixth of 9 to Mr Brooks in Prix de l'Abbaye at Longchamp: acts on any going. *Deborah England, Canada*

BOLD PHILIP 2 b.c. (May 20) King of Spain 121 – Our Mother 95 (Bold Lad **50** (IRE) 133) [1992 5s 5f⁶ 5m 5g³ 7m⁵ 6g⁶ 6g⁵ 7g] 7,200Y: strong, lengthy colt: has scope: moderate mover: half-brother to several winners here and abroad, including fairly useful 7-y-o 5f to 7.6f handicapper Bold Habit (by Homing): dam ran only at 2 yrs, winning at 5f: poor maiden: will prove best at up to 6f: acts on good to firm ground. *B. Beasley*

BOLD PROSPECT 2 b.c. (May 16) Never So Bold 135 – Petite Hester 85 **50** (Wollow 132) [1992 5d 6v⁴] angular, lightly-made colt: sixth living foal: half-brother to several winners here and abroad, including 6f winner Miss Daisy (by Final Straw) and fair stayer Siesta Key (by Glint of Gold): dam won 4 times at 7f: easily better effort in late-season maidens when fourth at Hamilton: should stay beyond 6f: sold 3,600 gns Doncaster November Sales, reportedly to Scandinavia. *P. Calver*

BOLD PURSUIT (IRE) 3 b.c. Thatching 131 – Pursue 78 (Auction Ring (USA) **95** 123) [1991 7m³ 8m* 1992 8g⁶ 8.1d⁵ 7d³ 8g² 7g⁵] tall, lengthy colt: most promising 2-y-o: generally disappointing in 1992, best efforts after 4½-month absence when placed at Ascot: best form at 1m: acts on good to firm ground and dead: sold 20,000 gns Newmarket Autumn Sales. *R. Hannon*

BOLD REALITY 2 ch.g. (Apr 27) Dreams To Reality (USA) 113 – Naturally Bold –
(Bold Lad (IRE) 133) [1992 7g] 1,900Y: second foal: dam unraced: bandaged, green and always behind in Doncaster maiden auction in July. *J. S. Wainwright*

BOLD RESOLUTION (IRE) 4 b.g. Shardari 134 – Valmarine (FR) (Val de **77** Loir 133) [1991 10g⁶ 12f⁴ 11.7s 10g² 12f⁴ 12m 11.9g⁴ 11.9m⁶ 12f a12g 1992 16.2g 11.9m⁶ 12g* 10.8g⁶ 11.8m² 12m⁴ 12d* 12f⁵ 11.8g 12g² 14g* 16.2s* 16.2g* 16g⁶] big, close-coupled gelding: moderate walker: poor mover: much improved handicapper in 1992: successful at Folkestone (2), Sandown and Ascot (2 quite valuable events): stiff task final run: suited by test of stamina: acts on any turf going (tailed off on equitrack). *C. A. Cyzer*

BOLDRULLAH 3 b. or br.g. Auction Ring (USA) 123 – La Neva (FR) (Arctic –
Tern (USA) 126) [1991 NR 1992 8g⁶ 8g 10f 10m 10g] 10,000Y: leggy gelding: first foal: dam French 12.5f winner: no worthwhile form. *D. W. P. Arbuthnot*

BOLD SETKO (IRE) 3 b.c. Bold Arrangement 111 – Ribamba 82 (Ribocco 129) **57** d [1991 5h³ a6g 5.7m 1992 7d² 7g⁴ 8d 7g 8s] rather sparely-made colt: has a round action: regressive maiden: should stay 1m: acts on dead ground: sold 3,100 gns Newmarket Autumn Sales. *J. M. P. Eustace*

BOLD SEVEN (IRE) 2 ch.f. (Apr 1) Never So Bold 135 – First Blush **73** (Ela-Mana-Mou 132) [1992 5g⁶ 5f* 6m⁵ 5g³ 5m² 6f² 6g² 6m* 6g³ 6.5m⁵ 6d 7d] IR 5,000Y: small, leggy, angular filly: moderate mover: half-sister to fairly useful 1m winner Cooley's Valve (by Pennine Walk) and a winner in Italy: dam half-sister to Chief Singer: held her form well, winning Thirsk median auction and £8,350 York seller (bought in 16,200 gns) in summer, until running poorly on dead ground last 2 starts: should prove suited by further than 6f: seems to need a sound surface: often slowly away, and usually gets behind. *F. H. Lee*

BOLD STAR 2 b.c. (Feb 26) Persian Bold 123 – Star Arrangement (Star Appeal · – 133) [1992 6g] 60,000Y: strong, good-bodied colt: first foal: dam half-sister to Bold Arrangement (by Persian Bold): behind throughout when last of 7 in Yarmouth maiden in July: sold 4,200 gns Newmarket September Sales. *A. A. Scott*

BOLD STEVE 3 ch.g. Never So Bold 135 – Vian (USA) (Far Out East (USA)) **59** [1991 NR 1992 8f⁵ 8m² 8d 10f⁴ 7g] 27,000Y: medium-sized gelding: second foal: dam unraced half-sister to Optimistic Lass, herself dam of Golden Opinion: modest maiden: gives impression should stay beyond 1m: possibly needs a sound surface: joined M. Tompkins and gelded. *L. M. Cumani*

BOLD STROKE   3 br.g. Persian Bold 123 – Fariha (Mummy's Pet 125) [1991 7g² 8.2f² 8m* 8d⁶ 1992 8d⁴ 10g* 8.9g 12f 10g²] good-bodied gelding: good walker: has a fluent action: useful handicapper: won at Sandown in April: not seen again after excellent second in £15,400 event at Newmarket in July: acts on good to firm and dead ground: races up with pace. *J. L. Dunlop*   **93**

BOLD SURPRISE   3 b.c. Ballad Rock 122 – Bombshell 76 (Le Levanstell 122) [1991 6f³ 6m⁶ 7m 1992 10d 7g] lengthy, quite attractive colt: still a maiden, and below form in handicaps in spring: should stay at least 1m: sold 1,800 gns Newmarket September Sales. *R. W. Armstrong*   –

BOLD THATCHER   2 b. or br.c. (Mar 31) Thatching 131 – Bold Apple (Bold Lad (IRE) 133) [1992 6v⁴] IR 10,000F, 15,000Y: fourth foal: half-brother to 1990 2-y-o 6f winner Bess Pool (by Sayf El Arab) and a winner abroad: dam half-sister to smart 6f and 1¼m winner Sarania and to dam of Pennine Walk: 16/1, one-paced fourth of 11 in maiden at Folkestone in October: will improve. *P. W. Harris*   **61** p

BOLD TREASURE (IRE)   2 b.f. (Mar 21) Treasure Kay 114 – Granny Stock (Imperial Fling (USA) 116) [1992 a6g 8.2d 5g] leggy filly: poor mover: third foal: dam ran once in Ireland: no sign of ability: blinkered final start: refused to enter stalls intended second. *Mrs N. Macauley*   –

BOLDVILLE BASH (IRE)   2 br.c. (Mar 18) Bold Arrangement 111 – Yashville (Top Ville 129) [1992 5v³ 5s⁶ 5m³ 6g⁴ 7g* 7.5d⁴ 7m⁵ 8m 7.9d 8.2d* 8s*] IR 11,500Y: strong colt: has scope: first foal: dam unraced: progressive colt: successful in Redcar claimer in July and large-field nurseries at Nottingham and Pontefract in autumn: will be well suited by middle distances: probably acts on any going, though best form on an easy surface. *T. D. Barron*   **78**

BOLD VISIT (IRE)   2 ch.c. (May 23) Bold Arrangement 111 – Visiting 77 (Vitiges (FR) 132) [1992 7m 8m] good-quartered colt: good mover: fourth foal (previous 3 by Miramar Reef): dam 11.7f winner: poor form in maidens: ran better than tenth-of-21 position suggests at Pontefract final outing, still in fourth place entering straight and eased considerably when beaten: sure to improve. *D. R. C. Elsworth*   **44** p

BOLLIN DUNCAN   2 b.c. (Jan 27) Petoski 135 – Bollin Emily 82 (Lochnager 132) [1992 7.5m 8.1s 6d⁶] big, good-topped, workmanlike colt: has plenty of scope: second foal: dam sprinter: best effort when keeping-on sixth of 19 in maiden at Haydock in October: will prove better suited by 1m (stiff task at trip): bandaged off-hind second start: sort to keep improving. *M. H. Easterby*   **51** p

BOLLIN MAGDALENE   4 b.f. Teenoso (USA) 135 – Klairlone 116 (Klairon 131) [1991 12m 10g 12.3g⁴ 13d 12m⁴ a14g⁴ 17.9f 17.1m⁴ 15.8g³ 15.1s 1992 13.8d² 16.1s² 15.8d] leggy, rather angular filly: moderate mover: out-and-out staying handicapper: ideally suited by give in the ground: visored or blinkered nowadays: won over hurdles in October. *M. H. Easterby*   **47**

BOLLIN PATRICK   7 b.g. Sagaro 133 – Bollin Charlotte 79 (Immortality) [1991 10.5d 10m 1992 11.9s³ 16d³] strong, workmanlike gelding: has a quick action: modest form in handicaps in April: stays 2m: possibly needs an easy surface nowadays. *M. H. Easterby*   **71**

BOLLIN WILLIAM   4 b.c. Nicholas Bill 125 – Bollin Charlotte 79 (Immortality) [1991 10.5g 10.4m 1992 11.9d 11.9s⁵] big, good-topped colt: lightly raced and no form on flat, but showed signs of ability in handicaps in autumn: worth a try beyond 1½m: useful hurdler, winner of 3 handicaps in the autumn. *M. H. Easterby*   – p

BOLOARDO   3 b.c. Persian Bold 123 – Northshiel 85 (Northfields (USA)) [1991 NR 1992 10d² 11d⁶ 10d⁵ 9m* 10.4f⁴ 12m] 54,000Y: leggy, good-topped colt: first foal: dam 2-y-o 7f winner is closely related to Waajib: useful performer in first half of 1992: won maiden at Goodwood and very good fourth of 5 in York listed race: soundly beaten in Irish Derby at the Curragh: stays 10.4f: acts on firm and dead ground. *C. E. Brittain*   **91**

BOLTON FLYER   6 b.m. Aragon 118 – Linda's Romance (USA) (Restless Restless (USA)) [1991 7.9g 10s⁴ 10g 9d 1992 a7g 10.8v a8g] second foal: half-sister to modest 1988 3-y-o 7f winner Native Romance (by Be My Native): dam well beaten: ex-Irish handicapper: no form in 1992: stays 1¼m: acts on soft ground and good to firm. *O. O'Neill*   –

BOLTROSE   2 b.c. (May 15) Electric 126 – Garnette Rose 74 (Floribunda 136) [1992 8s 7.1s] 6,000Y: compact colt: brother to 4-y-o 6f/7f performer Surrey Racing   **45**

126

and half-brother to several winners here and abroad, including fairly useful 1985 2-y-o 5f winner Camilla's Boy (by Faraway Times): dam seemed to stay 1m: soundly beaten in October maidens at Warwick and Chepstow. *K. White*

BOMOH 2 b.c. (Apr 4) Valiyar 129 – See The Tops (Cure The Blues (USA)) [1992 **39** 8.1d⁶ 8m] leggy, close-coupled colt: second foal: half-brother to 3-y-o Classic Exhibit (by Tate Gallery): dam never ran: soundly beaten in October maidens at Haydock and Pontefract: sold 640 gns Newmarket Autumn Sales. *S. P. C. Woods*

BONANZA 5 ch.g. Glenstal (USA) 118 – Forliana 75 (Forli (ARG)) [1991 12g⁵ **–** 16s⁴ 1992 17.1d] lengthy, attractive gelding: no worthwhile form on flat: dyed-in-the-wool stayer: won novice chases in October and November. *Mrs M. Reveley*

BONAR BRIDGE (USA) 2 b. or br.g. (Feb 26) Quadratic (USA) – Merririver **75** (USA) (Taylor's Falls (USA)) [1992 7.3m⁵ 7.1s³ 7.1g⁵ 8.1d] $8,000F: workmanlike gelding: good walker: first known foal: dam ran twice in North America: sire very smart stakes winner from 5.5f to 9f: modest maiden: should prove better suited by 1m than shorter: acts on soft ground: has been gelded. *R. Hannon*

BONARME (IRE) 2 b.c. (Mar 11) Vacarme (USA) 121 – Bonvin (Taufan (USA) **67** p 119) [1992 6d 7.5m⁴ 7g⁴ 8d*] IR 3,400Y: leggy, unfurnished colt: dam 5f (at 2 yrs) and 1m winner in Ireland: progressive colt: gamely won 23-runner maiden auction at Redcar in October by a neck from Backstabber: will be better suited by 1¼m: acts on good to firm and dead ground: strong-galloping sort. *M. H. Easterby*

BONASA (IRE) 2 b.f. (Mar 1) Persian Heights 129 – Sand Grouse (USA) (Arctic **–** Tern (USA) 126) [1992 7f] unfurnished filly: first foal: dam, French 1¼m winner: well beaten in maiden at Brighton in August: sold 840 gns Newmarket Autumn Sales. *B. W. Hills*

BONICA 3 b.f. Rousillon (USA) 133 – Flaming Rose (USA) (Upper Nile (USA)) **–** [1991 5m⁵ 6m⁴ 6m⁶ 1992 8m⁶] small, leggy filly: poor maiden: should be suited by 7f +.*J. R. Fanshawe*

BONITA BEE 2 b.f. (Mar 1) King of Spain 121 – Lady Annie Laurie (Pitcairn 126) **50** [1992 5m 5m⁴ 5d⁵ 6d] rangy filly: half-sister to Irish middle-distance winner Arowvale (by Aragon): dam Irish 2-y-o 6f winner: poor maiden: stays 6f. *L. J. Holt*

BONJOUR 2 br.g. (Feb 12) Primo Dominie 121 – Warm Welcome 89 (General **71** Assembly (USA)) [1992 6m⁵ 6d* 6g 6g] useful-looking gelding: excellent mover: second foal: dam, 1¼m winner, is granddaughter of 1000 Guineas winner Full Dress II: didn't progress after impressively winning Haydock maiden in August: should stay beyond 6f: cocked jaw and found little third start: visored final one. *J. H. M. Gosden*

BONNY PRINCESS 2 br.f. (Apr 3) Petoski 135 – True Queen (USA) 79 (Silver **47** Hawk (USA) 123) [1992 7d 6m⁵ 8.2d 8g 8s⁵ a8g] unfurnished filly: moderate mover: first foal: dam 1¼m winner probably stayed 11.5f: poor maiden: will be suited by 1¼m + : seems stained by a soft surface, tailed off on fibresand.*J. D. Bethell*

BONNY SCOT (IRE) 3 b.c. Commanche Run 133 – Scots Lass 79 **119** (Shirley Heights 130) [1991 8m³ 8.1d* 10g* 1992 10g⁵ 11.5s³ 12m⁶ 14.8g² 12m* 11.9g* 14.6m³ 12s⁴]

Commanche Run and his 1984 St Leger win was a piece of family history which began to loom large when a leading candidate for the latest running emerged in the shape of his son Bonny Scot. The last St Leger winner sired by a St Leger winner had been Indiana (by the 1947 winner Sayajirao) in 1964. By the time they lined up for the 1992 race, Bonny Scot's three-year-old season had taken on some marked similarities to that of his sire. Both reached the second half of the season before they really found their stride. Bonny Scot had begun the year already with classic aspirations following his victory in a mile-and-a-quarter listed race at Newmarket, and was given every chance to show himself a Derby horse, contesting trials at Sandown and Lingfield, but falling a long way short of the required standard. The King Edward VII Stakes at Royal Ascot had a similar outcome but there was much more to enthuse about with his second in a listed race at Newmarket in July, both in the way he went through the race and, despite the drop in class, his form; Bonny Scot looked an assured winner when quickening clear over two furlongs out in this near-fifteen-furlong test but, conceding 5 lb, he was found out by Rain Rider's renewed effort in the last hundred yards. 'I was pleased that he showed a turn of foot', Cumani told us in a *Timeform Interview* later that month, 'and it could

Great Voltigeur Stakes, York—
Bonny Scot shows a good turn of foot against Sonus, Assessor and Alflora (right)

be he's going to turn out like his sire in that he's a late developer. Commanche Run seemed to have no kind of speed or acceleration early on as a three-year-old.'

Commanche Run had also contested the King Edward VII Stakes (finishing third) but the similarity between the two on paper became a lot more convincing after Bonny Scot's fifth start of the season, in the Gordon Stakes at Goodwood. Commanche Run had won the race by five lengths easing down and, although Bonny Scot's winning distance was three lengths less, he too was impressive, given a confident ride after a modest early pace and sprinting clear of Alflora and Beyton in the final furlong. Bonny Scot was bang in the reckoning for the St Leger after these last two runs, a point he reiterated with a Group 2 success against two St Leger rivals in the Great Voltigeur Stakes at York, but although his record might now have been superior to Commanche Run's at the same stage in terms of 'black type', beating Sonus and Assessor by one and a half lengths and two and a half lengths at level weights certainly did not prove that Bonny Scot was yet in the same class. Bonny Scot started at 5/2 in the St Leger and would have been favourite without User Friendly whose participation was still in doubt in the morning. He would have gone close to winning the race without her, but without her this would also have been (as Sonus' second in a listed race and Bonny Scot's fourth in the Cumberland Lodge further demonstrated) the lowest-rated St Leger since *Racehorses* began. The return to the longer distance failed to coax any further improvement from Bonny Scot who, having tracked User Friendly into the straight, was simply outclassed over the last two and a half furlongs, eventually beaten three and a half lengths and a neck.

A sturdy, attractive colt who really impressed in condition before his last six starts, Bonny Scot is a fluent mover. He has comparable form at a mile and a half and an extended mile and three quarters, on soft ground and good to firm. Bonny Scot is very much the standard bearer for Commanche Run at stud although the sire's representatives in the latest season also included two graded winners in South Africa. Bonny Scot himself is now bound for Qatar. One does not have to retreat far in the stud or form books to find a noteworthy

Lord Weinstock's "Bonny Scot"

Bonny Scot (IRE) (b.c. 1989)	Commanche Run (b 1981)	Run The Gantlet (b 1968)	Tom Rolfe First Feather
		Volley (b 1965)	Ratification Mitrailleuse
	Scots Lass (b 1982)	Shirley Heights (b 1975)	Mill Reef Hardiemma
		Edinburgh (b 1974)	Charlottown Queen's Castle

winner in the dam's family; her half-sister Sought Out won three good staying races in 1992, including the Prix du Cadran. Scots Lass's first foal Border Mate (by Be My Guest) gained victories in 1992 in the United States and her third, Dragon's Teeth (by Caerleon), made the frame in a couple of two-year-old maidens. Her 1991 foal is a filly by Be My Guest. Scots Lass, like Bonny Scot, was a mile-and-a-half winner who stayed a mile and three quarters, but one with a rather unsatisfactory temperament as well as a lot less ability. *L. M. Cumani*

BONNY'S GAME 4 b.f. Mummy's Game 120 – Ribonny (FR) 33 (Fast Hilarious (USA)) [1991 9.1s⁵ 12.2g 14f 15g³ 13.8f³ 16.2f³ 14m⁶ 13.8m⁵ 1992 13.8d 12g⁵] small, workmanlike filly: poor maiden: stays 2m: acts on firm going: usually blinkered/visored: sold 700 gns Ascot May Sales. *C. W. C. Elsey*   –

BONUS POINT 2 ch.g. (Apr 30) Don't Forget Me 127 – Blue Aria (Cure The Blues (USA)) [1992 5g⁴ 5m* 6f 7.5d⁵ 7g 7s 7m] 4,500F, 13,000Y: big, rather leggy gelding: good mover: first foal: dam middle-distance maiden: off course 3 months after winning maiden at Redcar in April and didn't progress: should stay 1m: sold 4,200 gns Newmarket Autumn Sales. *Mrs M. Reveley*   58

BONZER 3 br.g. Electric 126 – Lady Doubloon (Pieces of Eight 128) [1991 8m 7m
8m 1992 11.8g] leggy, close-coupled gelding: fourth reported foal: brother to
winning hurdler Bright-One and half-brother to 1986 2-y-o 5f winner Peter's Blue
(by Riki Lash): dam unraced: little worthwhile form on flat, but showed clear signs
of ability in Leicester handicap in September: subsequently third over hurdles:
should be capable of improvement. *J. G. FitzGerald* **– p**

BOOGIE BOPPER (IRE) 3 b.g. Taufan (USA) 119 – Mey 78 (Canisbay 120)
[1991 6m 7m² 6f⁵ 1992 a8g 6d³ 7g⁴ 8g⁴ 7d 8f 10.1g² 12m⁴ 10.1d² 10s³ 10g 10s³ 10.4s²
10.3g³] leggy, sparely-made gelding: modest maiden: worth another try at 1½m:
possibly suited by give in the ground: ran poorly when blinkered once: sold to join
M. Pipe's stable 7,500 gns Newmarket Autumn Sales and won selling hurdle
(bought in 6,800 gns) in December: not one to trust implicitly. *M. Bell* **64**

BOOGIE WOOGIE BOY 5 ch.g. Mr Fluorocarbon 126 – Gosforth Lady 73
(Linacre 133) [1991 NR 1992 12f⁶] big, plain gelding: brother to modest 11.7f winner
Another Nonsense and half-brother to 4 winners, notably Norsk St Leger winner
Statecraft (by Sheshoon): dam, half-sister to Giacometti, won at up to 9f: no sign of
ability in Carlisle claimer in June, only run. *P. Beaumont* **–**

BOOGY LADY (IRE) 4 b.f. Glenstal (USA) 118 – Lady Regrets (FR) (Sir
Gaylord) [1991 10m⁴ 11.5m⁵ 10m 1992 10d 11.9m] workmanlike filly: no worthwhile
form: should stay 1½m. *I. Campbell* **–**

BOOKCASE 5 b.g. Siberian Express (USA) 125 – Colourful (FR) 108 (Gay
Mecene (USA) 128) [1991 12g* 12v 12g³ 11.7m³ 14f 12f⁴ 11.4m² 12g* 1992 a10g⁶]
big, good-topped gelding: usually looks very well: rated 76 at 4 yrs: never nearer
under 7-lb claimer in handicap in December: probably stays 13f: acts on firm ground:
tried in blinkers at 3 yrs: has shown signs of unsatisfactory temperament: suited by
extreme waiting tactics. *D. R. C. Elsworth* **–**

BOON HILL 3 b.g. Green Ruby (USA) 104 – Nyota 97 (Reform 132) [1991 5m⁴
6m⁶ 7g⁵ 7.5f 7.5f a6g⁴ 8m 1992 8.2g 9f a8g] rangy gelding: moderate walker: poor
maiden: stays 7f. *M. W. Ellerby* **–**

BOOTIKIN 4 ch.f. Relkino 131 – Galosh 86 (Pandofell 132) [1991 NR 1992 14.8f]
plain, angular filly: sister to a modest hurdler and half-sister to 3 winners, notably
very useful 5f to 1m winner Silly Prices (by Silly Season): dam needed long
distances: in frame in 2 NH Flat races before scant promise on flat debut in June. *C.
W. C. Elsey* **–**

BORDER DREAM 2 b.g. (Apr 29) Electric 126 – Be Still (Derring-Do 131) [1992
5d 5.1s⁶ 6f 7g] 1,500F, 1,500Y: leggy gelding: poor mover: sixth live foal:
half-brother to 2 winners abroad: dam unraced: poor maiden: should be suited by
6f+: acts on soft ground. *W. G. M. Turner* **32**

BORING (USA) 3 ch.c. Foolish Pleasure (USA) – Arriya (Luthier 126) [1991 NR
1992 8d 10.1s⁶ 7g 12.2m² 12.1m* 11m³ 10g⁵ 12.3m] 450,000 francs (approx £41,700)
Y: big colt: half-brother to 3 minor French winners: dam won 3 races over 10.5f at 3
yrs, and is half-sister to good-class Arokar: modest handicapper: won at Edinburgh
in May: stays 1½m: acts on good to firm ground: trained first 3 starts by N.
Callaghan. *W. Storey* **56**

BORN TO BE 3 b.f. Never So Bold 135 – Beryl's Jewel 86 (Siliconn 121) [1991
5m* 1992 6m⁴ 5g 6d 5g⁵] close-coupled filly: moderate mover: modest sprinter:
acts on good to firm ground. *S. Dow* **65**

BORN TO DANCE 3 b.f. Dancing Brave (USA) 140 – Oh So Bold (USA) (Better
Bee) [1991 NR 1992 7g⁶ 8.1d* 8m] leggy, close-coupled filly: half-sister to several
winners, including fairly useful 1¼m winner Spearman (by Diesis) and 1988 2-y-o 6f
winner Hope And Glory (by Well Decorated): dam, minor winner in USA, is
half-sister to Law Society, Legal Bid and Strike Your Colors: easily landed odds in
maiden at Haydock: not seen out again after well-beaten favourite in handicap at
Goodwood later in May: should stay 1¼m+. *M. R. Stoute* **76**

BOROCAY 4 b.g. Lochnager 132 – Maybehandy 66 (Some Hand 119) [1991 NR
1992 8d 6d 6s⁴ 7s 8s 8v] strong, good-topped gelding: second reported living foal:
dam 7f and 1m seller winner: not seen out until 1992, and no worthwhile form:
should stay beyond 6f. *M. J. Camacho* **–**

BORODISLEW (USA) 2 b.f. (Jan 19) Seattle Slew (USA) – Breath Taking (FR)
119 (Nureyev (USA) 131) [1992 6.5s* 5d⁴ 6.5g³ 8s³] fourth reported foal: half-sister
to French 7.5f and 1m winner Further Love (by Kris): dam, stayed 7f, is daughter of
versatile Australian performer Cap d'Antibes: won newcomers race at Deauville in
August: in frame in pattern and listed company after, running well on final start **110**

when very close third to Corrazona in Prix des Reservoirs at Longchamp in October: stays 1m: has raced only on easy surface. *Mme C. Head, France*

BORRAM (IRE) 3 b.g. Persian Bold 123 – Silken Topper (High Hat 131) [1991 5m⁵ 6m 6d 1992 10m 10.2m 11.8g] useful-looking gelding: poor maiden: bred to stay middle distances. *D. Nicholson* —

BOSAMBO (USA) 4 b.c. Our Native (USA) – Grey Dawn Girl (USA) (Grey Dawn II 132) [1991 8g⁶ 10f² 8m 11.9f³ 9d 1992 14.6g] tall, strong colt: easy mover: untrustworthy maiden, on the downgrade: sold 950 gns Ascot June Sales. *C. L. Popham* — §

BOTH BARRELS 2 b.c. (Apr 14) Sayf El Arab (USA) 127 – Gunner Girl 85 (Gunner B 126) [1992 5.1d 5.1m 7g] sturdy, good-bodied colt: third live foal: dam 7f to 1¼m winner: no sign of ability in maidens: sold 700 gns Doncaster November Sales. *R. J. Holder* —

BOULABAS (IRE) 3 ch.f. Nashamaa 113 – Betty Bun (St Chad 120) [1991 5m⁴ 5g* 5f² 5f² 5d 5d⁶ 1992 5g⁶ 7g 6s 5m] small, sturdy filly: on the downgrade: sold 850 gns Doncaster June Sales. *M. O'Neill* —

BOULMERKA 2 ch.f. (Feb 5) Farajullah 113 – The Victor Girls (Crofthall 110) [1992 5f 5g] workmanlike filly: first reported foal: dam lightly raced: green and always well behind in northern claimers in August: has joined B. Cambidge. *M. Johnston* —

BOUNDER ROWE 5 b.g. Henbit (USA) 130 – Arita (FR) (Kronzeuge) [1991 10m 8g 14s⁶ 8g 1992 8.3d 7f⁴ 8g 8d⁵ a10g⁶] rather leggy, quite attractive gelding: moderate mover: no worthwhile form in 1992. *J. Ffitch-Heyes* —

BOURBON JACK 2 b.c. (Feb 27) Robellino (USA) 127 – Bushti Music 63 (Bustino 136) [1992 5g⁴ 5g⁴ 6m* 6m 6d* 6m⁵ 7m⁵ 8.1d 7.5g] 9,000Y: quite good-topped colt: half-brother to 3-y-o Storm Drum (by Celestial Storm) and 1½m to 16.2f winner Kingsley (by Kings Lake): dam, who stayed 9f, is half-sister to very useful sprinters Hanu and Sanu: modest performer: successful in claimers at Goodwood in May and Warwick in July: sent to Italy afterwards, behind in listed races there: stays 1m: acts on good to firm ground, but may be ideally suited by an easy surface. *J. W. Payne* 70

BOURSIN (IRE) 3 b.g. Taufan (USA) 119 – Cloven Dancer (USA) (Hurok (USA)) [1991 NR 1992 7g 7m⁵ 7f* 7g* 7f³ 6g 7m⁵ 7g⁶ 8g] IR 10,000Y: tall, leggy gelding: good mover: third foal: half-brother to 1989 Irish 2-y-o 7f winner Bop Shop (by Prince Tenderfoot): dam Irish 1m winner: fair performer: made all in maiden at Redcar in May and minor event at Catterick in June: should stay 1m. *P. Calver* 79

BOWDEN BOY (IRE) 4 b.g. Never So Bold 135 – Glebehill 76 (Northfields (USA)) [1991 6d* 7m⁵ 8g⁵ 8g 8g 7g⁶ 8m 1992 8d 8g a8g³ 10f* 10.5g* 10m 10.1g* 10.1g⁵ 10m 10g³ 10.2s⁶ 9.7g³] lengthy, rather angular gelding: poor mover: in very good form in handicaps in summer, successful at Newmarket (claimer), Haydock and Yarmouth: below form final 2 starts and sold only 1,800 gns Doncaster October Sales: suited by around 1¼m: acts on firm and dead ground and equitrack: usually blinkered: sometimes slowly away: hangs. *N. A. Callaghan* 73

BOXBOY 2 b.c. (Mar 26) Kings Lake (USA) 133 – Majan 67 (Brigadier Gerard 144) [1992 6m 7s] IR 4,000F, 1,700Y: good-bodied colt: has a round action: half-brother to several winners, including 1½m winner Standard Breakfast (by Busted) and useful 6f/1m performer Ajanac (by Known Fact): dam placed over 1¾m from 2 starts: well beaten in maidens. *K. O. Cunningham-Brown* 31

BOYHOOD (IRE) 3 b.c. Sadler's Wells (USA) 132 – Infanta (USA) (Intrepid Hero (USA)) [1991 NR 1992 10.4g] IR 430,000Y: sturdy, lengthy colt: sixth foal: half-brother to 1986 2-y-o 5f winner Take A Hint (by Pitskelly) and 1m winner Forty Or More (by Yashgan): dam twice-raced half-sister to dam of Robellino: burly and decidedly leery, reminders after 3f when tailed-off last in York maiden in September, only run. *J. H. M. Gosden* —

BOY MARTIN 3 ch.g. Local Suitor (USA) 128 – Mary Martin (Be My Guest (USA) 126) [1991 NR 1992 5g⁵ 6m² 5m² 5.9f* 6g⁵ 5m 7g 7g 6g⁵ 7d² 7d⁴ 7d a7g³ a6g* a7g⁶] good-bodied gelding: moderate mover: reportedly fractured off-hind cannon bone at 2 yrs: third foal: brother to 2-y-o Marina Park and half-brother to 4-y-o Maria Cappuccini (by Siberian Express) and winning sprinter Pacific Gem (by Valiyar): dam unraced half-sister to Greenland Park and Red Sunset: inconsistent handicapper: won at Carlisle (maiden) in June and at Lingfield in November: should stay 1m: acts on firm and dead ground and equitrack: ran fairly well when blinkered once: sold to join S. Kettlewell 5,200 gns Doncaster November Sales. *M. Johnston* 73

131

BRACING (IRE) 3 b.f. Dancing Brave (USA) 140 – Almagest 72 (Dike (USA)) – [1991 NR 1992 8g 11.9m6] 58,000Y: rangy filly: closely related to Tolomeo (by Lypheor): dam 1½m winner: green and no form in maidens at Kempton and Haydock: sold 3,600 gns Newmarket December Sales. *G. Harwood*

BRACKEN BAY 5 ro.m. All Systems Go 119 – War Bird (Warpath 113) [1991 NR – 1992 a7g a6g 5g 7g 7f] sturdy mare: of little account nowadays. *T. Kersey*

BRACKENTHWAITE 2 ch.g. (May 16) Faustus (USA) 118 – Cosset 56 **53** (Comedy Star (USA) 121) [1992 5d 5m 6d6 8g4 8.3v a8g a7g6] strong, good-quartered gelding: sixth living foal: half-brother to 1¼m to 1½m winner Billet (by Nicholas Bill): dam very lightly raced: modest maiden: failed to confirm form of fourth in selling nursery at Doncaster: much better suited by 1m than less: may be unsuited by heavy ground. *T. D. Barron*

BRADAWN BREEVER (IRE) 3 b.c. Salmon Leap (USA) 131 – Ozone **109** ? (Auction Ring (USA) 123) [1991 5v4 5d2 6g*dis 6g* 6g2 6m3 5m4 6m* 5d3 5d 6g 1992 5m 7g5 5g3 6.5g 6g6 6g 5g] useful performer: made all in Heinz '57' Phoenix Stakes at Leopardstown eighth outing at 2 yrs: good third of 8 to Flowing in listed race at Tipperary third start in 1992: below form after in pattern events and listed race: stays 6f: acts on good to firm ground and dead: best form in blinkers. *K. Prendergast, Ireland*

BRADMORE'S VISION 6 b.g. Vision (USA) – Plum Run (USA) (Run The – Gantlet (USA)) [1991 NR 1992 10.3m] leggy, narrow gelding: seems of little account nowadays. *L. J. Barratt*

BRAMBLEBERRY 3 gr.c. Sharrood (USA) 124 – Labista 116 (Crowned Prince **66** (USA) 128) [1991 NR 1992 8g3 10.3g4 10m2 11.8g4 8.1g6 10.4g4 10s 8d] 5,000Y, 5,000 2-y-o: close-coupled, plain colt: has a round action: sixth foal: half-brother to middle-distance winner Rushluan (by Kalaglow) and 1m winner Poniard (by Kris): dam speedy 2-y-o, appeared not to train on: modest maiden: better at around 1¼m than shorter: below form on a soft surface. *Mrs S. J. Smith*

BRAMBLES WAY 3 ch.g. Clantime 101 – Streets Ahead 67 (Ovid 95) [1991 5m4 **56** d 5f6 6g 6f5 5m 1992 7g2 7m 7f 7m3 7g5 6g5 7m3 7f4 7g 7g 8s6 7d3 8.1g2 8.1d4] compact gelding: has a quick action: poor maiden: stays 1m: acts on firm and dead ground: usually visored. *W. L. Barker*

BRANDONHURST 2 b.c. (Feb 20) Elegant Air 119 – Wolverina 71 (Wolver **82** Hollow 126) [1992 7g2 6f* 7g4 7d2 8g] 5,000Y: good-topped colt: half-brother to 4 winners abroad: dam 2-y-o 5f winner: landed odds in Pontefract maiden auction in August: creditable efforts after, in listed race at Ascot final start: will stay beyond 1m: acts on firm and dead ground. *I. A. Balding*

BRANDON PRINCE (IRE) 4 b.g. Shernazar 131 – Chanson de Paris (USA) **85** (The Minstrel (CAN) 135) [1991 8g 11.7s6 13.1f4 11m* 16.2g2 16g* 16.5g* 14f5 16.1m6 16.2g* 18m 1992 16d 16m 20m 16.4s* 16.2g3 15.9m6 14g] close-coupled gelding: fair handicapper: successful at Sandown in July: ideally suited by around 2m and some give in the ground: usually blinkered: held up. *I. A. Balding*

BRANSBY ROAD (IRE) 2 ch.c. (Mar 27) Salt Dome (USA) – Ivory Smooth **48** (USA) (Sir Ivor 135) [1992 7g 6.1g 7d] 7,500F, IR 7,500Y: neat colt: half-brother to 1m and 1½m winner North Pacific (by Hawaii), 1987 2-y-o 6f winner Foujita (by Tap Shoes), and a winner in USA: dam 1m winner in USA: sire smart sprinter: behind in varied events in autumn. *R. Akehurst*

BRANSTON ABBY (IRE) 3 ch.f. Risk Me (FR) 127 – Tuxford Hideaway 102 **99** (Cawston's Clown 113) [1991 5g3 5m* 5g2 6m6 5f3 8m 6.1m6 5m6 6g 1992 5f* 6f 5g6 5.6m 5g2 5m 5s* 5.1d* 5m* 6.1s* 5g* a5g5] tall, lengthy filly: useful performer: has had a tremendous year winning minor event at Beverley in June (when with J. Wharton), 4 races in October (handicaps at Pontefract and Chepstow, claimer at Pontefract and minor event at Chepstow), then 22-runner handicap at Doncaster (best effort) 9 days later: not discredited under 7 lb penalty at Southwell: stays 6f: has won on firm going, but goes particularly well on soft: highly strung and often mounted on track of late. *M. Johnston*

BRANTFELL 4 b.c. Say Primula 107 – Jendor 82 (Condorcet (FR)) [1991 6.9f3 – 13.6m2 13.8m5 11m 12.1m6 11d6 a12g6 1992 a12g] compact colt: good walker: poor maiden: stays 13.6f: acts on firm going: sold 1,000 gns Doncaster January Sales. *T. Fairhurst*

BRAVE BIDDER 2 b.f. (Feb 16) Gabitat 119 – Queen's Bidder 84 (Auction Ring **39** (USA) 123) [1992 5g a5g3 5m6 a6g 5m 6d] workmanlike filly: poor mover: sixth live foal: dam 2-y-o 5f winner: poor sprint maiden: sold 700 gns Ascot September Sales. *B. Gubby*

132

BRAVEBOY 4 b.g. Never So Bold 135 – Relkina (FR) 85 (Relkino 131) [1991 8g² –
1992 9m 7g] quite attractive gelding: rated 74 as 3-y-o: stiff tasks in October, 1992:
should stay beyond 1m: has been gelded. *C. E. Brittain*

BRAVE THE WIND 3 b.f. Dancing Brave (USA) 140 – English Spring (USA) –
116 (Grey Dawn II 132) [1991 7.1m 7f⁵ 7g* 8.1d⁴ 1992 10.2s⁵ 10.3f 10m⁴ 10s⁶ 8f 8g]
rather leggy, quite attractive filly: good walker: has a fluent action: rated 67 at 2 yrs:
well below form in handicaps in 1992: should be suited by 1¼m+: acts on firm and
dead ground: twice below form when blinkered: sold 18,000 gns Newmarket
December Sales. *I. A. Balding*

BRAVO STAR (USA) 7 b.g. The Minstrel (CAN) 135 – Stellarette (CAN) –
(Tentam (USA)) [1991 NR 1992 14m 17.2f 12f 12g] sturdy, close-coupled gelding:
seems of little account on flat nowadays: twice winner over hurdles in autumn. *P. Leach*

BRAVURA 3 b.g. Never So Bold 135 – Avahra 108 (Sahib 114) [1991 7g 7m³ 1992   78
7g⁴ 7m⁶] lengthy gelding: lightly-raced maiden: capable of winning a race but not
seen out after being badly hampered in £19,400 York handicap in May: gave
impression worth a try at 1m. *W. J. Haggas*

BRAYOWSKI 2 gr.c. (Jan 30) Siberian Express (USA) 125 – Cataclysmic 78   71 p
(Ela-Mana-Mou 132) [1992 7g⁴] 3,600Y: smallish, sturdy colt: first foal: dam 1½m
winner: 20/1, stayed on well when fourth of 14 to Pamzig in maiden at Doncaster in
late-October: will improve. *J. R. Fanshawe*

BREAK BREAD (USA) 3 b.c. Bering 136 – Troyanna 109 (Troy 137) [1991 8g* 111
8m³ 9d³ 1992 10.5g² 10m* 12g 10g⁵ 9g⁶ 8s⁵] useful French colt: won Group 3 Prix
La Force at Longchamp in May: unplaced in Prix du Jockey Club following month:
fair efforts in 1¼m Prix Eugene Adam at Saint-Cloud and 1m Prix Quincey (though
last of 5) at Deauville afterwards: stays 1¼m: acts on good to firm ground, probably
on soft. *D. Smaga, France*

BREAKDANCER (IRE) 3 b.g. Fabulous Dancer (USA) 124 – Bennetta (FR)   60
(Top Ville 129) [1991 NR 1992 10g 11.1m⁴ 8.9s 10g² 11.1m⁴ 10m* 10f⁴ 10d 6.9m 8g⁴
a10g⁵ 8d 8d³ 10.8s³ a12g* a12g] workmanlike gelding: first foal: dam unraced
daughter of useful French 1979 2-y-o 7.5f and 1m winner Indigene: modest
handicapper: won claiming events at Ayr in June (claimed out of Mrs J. Ramsden's
stable £8,600) and Lingfield in the autumn: effective from a testing 1m to 1½m: acts
on good to firm and soft ground and on equitrack: retained 3,500 gns Newmarket
Autumn Sales. *W. R. Muir*

BREAKFAST BOOGIE 2 b.f. (Apr 16) Sizzling Melody 117 – Bonne de Berry   46
(Habitat 134) [1992 5g 5.1g² 5g⁶ 6m⁴ 5s⁵] close-coupled filly: moderate mover:
fourth foal: half-sister to 3-y-o Bella Run (by Commanche Run) and French 1989
2-y-o 5.5f winner Sabaya (by Vayrann): dam French 1¼m winner: poor maiden:
stays 6f: acts on good to firm and soft ground: tends to hang, and not easiest of rides.
J. R. Fanshawe

BREAKING HEARTS (IRE) 2 ch.f. (May 5) Broken Hearted 124 – Rags To   41
Riches (High Hat 131) [1992 5m⁴ 6f⁵ 6g] IR 700Y: small, leggy, lightly-made filly:
has a round action: half-sister to 1979 Irish 2-y-o 6f winner Horatio Alger (by
Karabas): dam 7f to 9f winner in Ireland: poor form in maiden auctions in the North:
will be much better suited by further. *A. P. Stringer*

BREAK MY HEART 2 b.c. (Apr 10) Broken Hearted 124 – Migiyas 87 (Kings   64
Lake (USA) 133) [1992 5.1m 6d⁴ 6f*] good-quartered, useful-looking colt: third foal:
half-brother to 3-y-o 1¾m winner Last Conquest (by Slip Anchor): dam 5f (at 2 yrs)
and 7f winner: won Brighton claimer in June: will stay 7f: heavily bandaged near-
fore second start: sold 2,400 gns Newmarket Autumn Sales. *P. F. I. Cole*

BRECON BEACONS (IRE) 3 b.f. Shirley Heights 130 – Welsh Daylight   59
(Welsh Pageant 132) [1991 6m² 7g² 7f 1992 10g² 9.9m³ 11.8s³] leggy filly: modest
maiden: should stay at least 1¼m: acts on good to firm ground: sold 20,000 gns
Newmarket December Sales. *R. Charlton*

BREEZE AWAY 3 b.f. Prince Sabo 123 – Ballad Island 83 (Ballad Rock 122)   56
[1991 6m⁶ 5g³ 5m³ 1992 7f⁵ 8.2g 7m⁴ 6.1g*] strong, lengthy filly: modest handicapper: won selling event at Nottingham (no bid) in July: best form at up to 7f: acts
on firm going. *R. M. Whitaker*

BREEZE BY 2 br.f. (Mar 20) Elegant Air 119 – Bracey Brook (Gay Fandango   51
(USA) 132) [1992 7g 8.5m] leggy, good-topped filly: third foal: half-sister to 13f NH
Flat race winner Brook Dance (by Mashhor Dancer) and a winner abroad: dam poor
Irish maiden: behind in September maidens at Kempton and Beverley: sold 4,000
gns Newmarket Autumn Sales. *I. A. Balding*

BREEZED WELL   6 b.g. Wolverlife 115 – Precious Baby (African Sky 124) [1991   **59**
a8g⁴ a8g⁵ a10g 8d 10g 9m 8f⁴ 8d³ 8d² 8g 8m³ 8m 1992 a7g⁵ 9.7v⁵ 8m 8m 8f 8.5d⁴
8m⁶ 10m² 8f⁶ a10g⁴ 9.7m³ 11.9g⁴ 10.8g⁵ 9g² 8d⁶ 9.7m a8g⁵] smallish, sparely-made
gelding: poor mover: modest handicapper: has won one of last 58 starts: best at stiff
1m to 1¼m nowadays: acts on firm and dead going: below form when blinkered
once: successful for claimer: trained until after penultimate start by C. Allen. *B. R.
Cambidge*

BREEZY DAY   6 ch.m. Day Is Done 115 – Bedouin Dancer 79 (Lorenzaccio 130)   **81**
[1991 5g 5d* 5m 6g² 6d³ 5.1d* 6.1g⁴ 5.2g² 5m⁵ 6f 5.6m 6m 5g 6.1d* 5d a6g a6g 1992
a5g a5g⁶ 5g 5d* 5.1m 5m 6g* 5.9h² 6f² 6g* 5.6m 6.1m⁴ 5.1g 6d⁶ 5d* 6d 6.1s⁴ 5g]
compact mare: has round action: fair sprint handicapper: successful in 1992 at
Warwick, Kempton (claimer), Catterick and Haydock: acts on any going, including
fibresand, but suited by some give: goes well at Chester: suitable mount for
apprentice. *B. A. McMahon*

BREEZY SAILOR   6 ch.g. Tumble Wind (USA) – Bouganville (Gulf Pearl 117)   **–**
[1991 NR 1992 7m 11.5m 7d 6g] robust, good-quartered gelding: has been tubed: of
little account on flat nowadays. *R. Thompson*

BRENDA FROM HUBY   4 ch.f. Tina's Pet 121 – Dominion Blue 66 (Dominion   **38**
123) [1991 7m 7m³ 8g 6m 1992 8g a7g³ 7s] good-topped filly: poor maiden: stays 7f:
acts on good to firm ground and fibresand: sometimes wears tongue strap. *B. C.
Morgan*

BRIDGE PLAYER   5 ch.m. The Noble Player (USA) 126 – Auction Bridge 76   **47**
(Auction Ring (USA) 123) [1991 a8g⁵ 9s⁵ 13d⁶ 9.9m⁵ 12.3d³ 13d² 12.1f³ 12.2g³   a52
13.6d⁵ 15.1s² a16g² a14g* 1992 a14g* a14g⁵ 13.8d⁴ 16.2m² 13d² 15g⁶ 12.1d⁶ 17.1s
15.8d² 15.1d a14g a14g] close-coupled ex-Irish mare: none too consistent
handicapper: won at Southwell in January: stays 2m: acts on good to firm and soft
ground, and on fibresand: well beaten in visor last time: usually held up: good mount
for claimer. *D. Moffatt*

BRIDGE STREET BOY   3 ch.g. Risk Me (FR) 127 – Bridge Street Lady 93   **–**
(Decoy Boy 129) [1991 NR 1992 6m 5d a8g] sturdy gelding: first foal: dam sprinter:
no worthwhile form, for D. Murray-Smith first 2 starts. *J. R. Bosley*

BRIDLE TALK (IRE)   3 b.f. Runnett 125 – Gossip (Sharp Edge 123) [1991 5m³   **44 §**
5g⁶ 5d³ a5g³ a5g² 5.3f 5m 1992 5.1m 5g⁴ 5m 5m⁴ 5.1g³ 5.3f⁵] rather lightly-made
filly: has a round action: poor sprint maiden: reluctant to race and persistently hung
left fourth start: one to be wary of. *M. McCormack*

BRIEF HABIT (IRE)   2 b.f. (Mar 14) Carmelite House (USA) 118 – Bold And   **– §**
Brief (Bold Lad (IRE) 133) [1992 5g] IR 4,200Y: leggy, close-coupled filly: has scope:
fifth live foal: half-sister to Irish 3-y-o Nordic Brief (by Nordico), 5f winner at 2 yrs
who now stays 1¾m, and a winner in Czechoslovakia: dam Irish 1¼m winner:
showed clear signs of ability in maiden at Sandown in April: got loose and twice
withdrawn after: sold 820 gns Doncaster November Sales: clearly one to have
reservations about. *M. R. Channon*

BRIEF TRUCE (USA)   3 b.c. Irish River (FR) 131 – Falafel (CAN)   **126**
(Northern Dancer (CAN)) [1991 6d* 19d 7d² 8d* 8g³ 10d* 8m* 8s² 8s² 8f³]
    The finish to the St James's Palace Stakes was the sort of head-to-head
which, in a race for which hopes had run very high, only the greatest optimist
could have anticipated. All that was missing in the drama were both the
expected leading protagonists. Dual Guineas winner Rodrigo de Triano and
11/10-on shot Arazi could finish only fourth and fifth. Up front it was Diomed
Stakes winner Zaahi versus the Gallinule winner Brief Truce. Zaahi had set
out to make all, stretching the field approaching the straight at which point
Brief Truce was pushed along in fourth before being switched to the outside,
Arazi and Rodrigo de Triano in indian file behind him. Brief Truce, however,
was the only one who looked like getting to the leader, and in the final stride,
responding gamely to Kinane's urgings, he thrust his head in front. One and a
half lengths behind, Ezzoud short-headed Rodrigo de Triano, Arazi three
quarters of a length adrift of them.
    Brief Truce was a 25/1-shot at Royal Ascot. He had won three of his five
races, a maiden at Fairyhouse as a two-year-old and a listed race at Leopardstown before the Gallinule. Ironically, though, it was his best effort which led
to Brief Truce's being so readily dismissed in the St James's Palace, his
two-and-a-half-length third to Rodrigo de Triano in the Irish Two Thousand

St James's Palace Stakes, Royal Ascot—
Brief Truce wins very gamely from Zaahi (rails) and Ezzoud;
out wide are Rodrigo de Triano and Arazi

Guineas in which Rodrigo de Triano's superiority appeared to be greatly understated and Ezzoud finished in front of him as well. Brief Truce had been one of the first under pressure that day, and had idled in front when beating Firing Line by a length at 2/1 on in the mile-and-a-quarter Gallinule. Blinkers were fitted for the first time at Royal Ascot. Whether it was the blinkers that were chiefly responsible for his improvement or a continuation of the progress he'd already shown, one cannot, of course, be certain, but Brief Truce's season after Royal Ascot left one thing crystal clear—that performance was no flash in the pan.

Brief Truce did not win again but the form he showed in defeat was an improvement again on that he'd shown in the St James's Palace. After a near three-month break, he came on the outside from a position seventh of ten entering the straight to run All At Sea, second entering the straight and three lengths clear a furlong out, to a neck in the Prix du Moulin de Longchamp. The Queen Elizabeth II Stakes produced a similar finale to the St James's Palace, with Brief Truce battling on gamely up the Ascot straight in pursuit of one of Sheikh Hamdan's colts, but a different outcome as Lahib stayed on strongly for a two-length victory. All At Sea, incidentally, this time finished four lengths behind Brief Truce. The sight of Brief Truce putting in his best work at the death was becoming a familiar one; also becoming familiar in the top mile races of 1992 was speculation about what the result *should* have been. As far as Brief Truce is concerned, the one race where the result clearly should have been different and his position improved was the Breeders' Cup Mile. To get to post in a condition to do themselves justice was a task that proved beyond most of the European runners at Gulfstream Park. That was not the case, however, with Brief Truce. Instead, things went wrong when he was in the stalls. It had reportedly been requested that Brief Truce be attended by no handler in the stalls, but one was with him when the stalls opened; distracted according to Kinane, Brief Truce was very slowly away. He lost any chance of winning there—whether he'd have beaten the three-length winner Lure anyway is obviously open to doubt—but Brief Truce produced a tremendous late challenge from the rear to capture some of the sizeable place money, only narrowly failing to get up for second.

Brief Truce's sire Irish River also had Hatoof, Exit To Nowhere, the Oak Tree Invitational winner Navarone and Paradise Creek, the colt who finished a neck up on Brief Truce in the Breeders' Cup Mile, to fly the flag for him in 1992. The dam's side of Brief Truce's pedigree has hardly been wanting for an advertisement either in recent years; the family has now been discussed in each of the last four editions of *Racehorses* as his grandam Queen's Statute is also the third dam of Snow Bride and the fourth dam of Hector Protector and Shanghai. A hatful of other good winners have emerged since Queen's Statute

135

Moyglare Stud Farms Ltd's "Brief Truce"

was sent, unraced, to be covered in Canada as a three-year-old. She herself had a perfect winners-to-runners record, Brief Truce's dam Falafel being the thirteenth and last to get in on the act. She had five starts in France and won a fillies maiden over an extended mile as a three-year-old. She had four winners from nine foals before Brief Truce, easily the most noteworthy of them being Again Tomorrow (by Honest Pleasure) who Weld sent out to win the Premio Parioli in 1985.

Brief Truce (USA) (b.c. 1989)	Irish River (FR) (ch 1976)	Riverman (b 1969)	Never Bend River Lady
		Irish Star (b 1960)	Klairon Botany Bay
	Falafel (CAN) (b 1973)	Northern Dancer (b 1961)	Nearctic Natalma
		Queen's Statute (b 1954)	Le Lavandou Statute

Brief Truce may have missed out on classic success at the Curragh, but he ended the season with form well up to standard for the average Irish Guineas winner and a record in the big races afterwards considerably in advance. He will be in training in 1993, but with D. Wayne Lukas in the United States, when his Breeders' Cup target could be either the Mile or the Classic. Although Brief Truce's form at a mile and a quarter does not compare with that at a mile, he has, of course, had only the one race over the longer trip and seemed to stay well enough that day. Whether Brief Truce will take to racing on dirt is more problematical. His record on turf is that of one who acts on any going, although his trainer has expressed the view that he will prove best on a sound surface. He decided not to fit Brief Truce with the blinkers at Gulfstream Park. *D. K. Weld, Ireland*

BRIER CREEK (USA) 3 b.c. Blushing Groom (FR) 131 – Savannah Dancer **106** (USA) (Northern Dancer (CAN)) [1991 7m⁵ 1992 10d³ 10g 10m 12g* 12g* 12f* 14.8g³ 12m³ 13.9m² 14.6f* 12m 12g] good-topped colt: easy mover: progressed really well in 1992 to win handicaps at Pontefract, Newmarket and Doncaster (2, £9,400 event on second occasion): placed in Newmarket listed event and Ebor Handicap (beaten head by Quick Ransom) at York: ideally suited by around 1¾m: acts on firm going: held up: a credit to his trainer. *J. H. M. Gosden*

BRIERY FILLE 7 b.m. Sayyaf 121 – Zeddera (FR) (Zeddaan 130) [1991 10.2s⁵ **–** 10m⁵ a12g⁶ a12g 1992 10m 12.3g 12.3d] lengthy, angular mare: soundly beaten in 1992: stays 1½m: acts on firm going: below form when blinkered/visored. *B. J. McMath*

BRIGADORE GOLD 2 br.f. (Apr 6) Petong 126 – Brigado 87 (Brigadier Gerard **51** 144) [1992 6m 5m⁴ 5g³ 5.1f⁴ 6h³ 5d 6d⁴ 5m⁶ 7g] 3,500Y: leggy filly: moderate walker and mover: sixth foal: sister to 1989 2-y-o 7f winner Garscube and half-sister to 1½m seller/hurdles winner Vado Via (by Ardross): dam 2-y-o 1m winner: regressive maiden: should stay 7f: acts on hard ground: sold 3,000 gns Newmarket Autumn Sales. *R. Hannon*

BRIGANTE DI CIELO 2 b.c. (Feb 10) Robellino (USA) 127 – Follow The Stars **81** 86 (Sparkler 130) [1992 5.7m⁵ 5g* 6g³ 7.3g² 7g* 7.3s] 6,800Y, 9,200 2-y-o: good-bodied colt: sort to carry condition: fourth foal: dam, 8.5f and 1¼m winner, is half-sister to very useful French 9f to 1¼m winner Schoeller: progressed well in second half of 1992, successful in Windsor maiden auction and 16-runner Ascot nursery, until well below form on heavy ground (also raced on possibly unfavoured part of track) at Newbury: will be better suited by at least 1m. *R. Hannon*

BRIGG FAIR 2 b.c. (Feb 9) Aragon 118 – Brig of Ayr 90 (Brigadier Gerard 144) **95** [1992 5g 6g³ 6g⁵ 6m* 5.2g* 5g] 4,800Y: leggy, workmanlike colt: progressed well physically: has a quick action: closely related to 1984 2-y-o 6f winner Ever So (by Mummy's Pet) and half-brother to 3 winners, including 1983 2-y-o 5f winner Pageantic (by Welsh Pageant): dam won from 1m to 11f at 4 yrs: progressed really well to win nurseries at Doncaster and Newbury (by 4 lengths, having quickened in excellent style 1f out) in September: well-beaten favourite in Cornwallis Stakes at Ascot final start: stays 6f. *R. Hannon*

BRIGGSCARE 6 b.g. Chief Singer 131 – Magonis 74 (Blakeney 126) [1991 NR **62 §** 1992 14.1g 16f² 14.1m² 14.1g⁴ 16m² 16.2g⁴ 18.2m⁵] leggy gelding: maiden handicapper: carries head high and twice looked unwilling when asked for effort in 1992: effective at 1¾m to 2¼m: seems to act on any going: below form when blinkered: seems beset with waiting tactics. *W. Jarvis*

BRIGGS LAD (IRE) 3 ch.g. Be My Native (USA) 122 – Zestino (Shack (USA) **69** 118) [1991 7m⁴ 8.3g⁵ 8m³ 1992 10m³ 11.1f* 12.3f² 14.1g⁴ 14.6g 12m⁴ 12v⁴] good-bodied gelding: modest handicapper: won maiden at Edinburgh in June: stays 1¾m: acts on firm going, possibly not on heavy: well below form when blinkered once: sold to K. Bailey 8,600 gns Newmarket Autumn Sales. *W. Jarvis*

BRIGGSMAID 4 b.f. Elegant Air 119 – Merry Yarn 64 (Aggressor 130) [1991 **65** 10m² 12m³ 12f* 16.2g 13.1m³ 16m 14.1f³ 14m⁶ 12f⁵ 12g 1992 11.8d 12g 14.1m⁵ 14.6d³ 15.1g² 13f* 13.1d* 14.1f* 14.1d² 16.1g² 17.5s 14.6s] lengthy, workmanlike filly: shows high knee action: had a good season in handicaps, successful in summer at Hamilton, Ayr and Yarmouth: effective from 13f to 2m: acts on firm and dead ground: sometimes edgy: usually held up. *J. M. P. Eustace*

BRIGHT GEM 2 b.f. (Jan 30) Heraldiste (USA) 121 – Spring Bride 57 (Auction **52** Ring (USA) 123) [1992 5d* 5m⁵ 6d⁵ 5f³ 5d² 5m⁴ 5f² 6m 7.1g⁶ a6g* a6g⁴ a5g⁴] leggy, lengthy filly: half-sister to useful sprinter Hafir (by Tender King) and 1986 2-y-o 7f winner Lightning Laser (by Monseigneur): dam, raced only at 2 yrs, is sister to very useful 1979 2-y-o 7f Highest Bidder: modest performer: won maiden at Catterick in the spring and nursery at Southwell in the autumn: probably stays 7f: acts on firm and dead ground and on fibresand: ran poorly when blinkered once: has put head in air and looked ungenuine. *T. Fairhurst*

BRIGHT GENERATION (IRE) 2 b.f. (Mar 23) Rainbow Quest (USA) 134 – **93** New Generation 91 (Young Generation 129) [1992 6.1m* 7.1g* 7s² 8s⁴] leggy, close-coupled filly: fourth foal: half-sister to 3-y-o Tales of Wisdom (by Rousillon),

1988 2-y-o 5f winner Noble Habitat (by Formidable) and winning stayer Moving Out (by Slip Anchor): dam won at up to 1m: wide-margin winner of Chepstow maiden and Sandown minor event in early-summer: ran well after in Moyglare Stud Stakes (beaten 1½ lengths by Sayyedati) at the Curragh and Fillies' Mile (5 lengths behind Ivanka) at Ascot: will be well suited by middle distances: probably acts on any going: tail flasher. *P. F. I. Cole*

BRIGHTNESS   3 gr.f. Elegant Air 119 – Jove's Voodoo (USA) 74 (Northern Jove   **75** d
(CAN)) [1991 NR 1992 7.5g* 8m 8.3g⁵ 8m 9.7m a8g] 24,000F: tall filly: third foal: sister to 10.4f winner Vermont Magic and half-sister to 1½m winner Spirit Away and Zamore, successful over 1m later over hurdles (both by Dominion): dam 6f winner: failed to progress after winning maiden at Beverley in March: stays 1m: wore tongue strap once: trained until after penultimate start by M. Moubarak. *Miss Gay Kelleway*

BRIGHT PARAGON (IRE)   3 b. or br.g. Treasure Kay 114 – Shining Bright   **49**
(USA) (Bold Bidder) [1991 NR 1992 6d 6s 5f⁴ 5g 7g 6g² 6m⁵ 5s* 5.1g a7g⁵ a7g⁶ a44
a7g³] 4,000Y, 1,000 2-y-o: workmanlike gelding: fourth foal: half-brother to modest 1990 2-y-o 5f winner Miss El Arab (by Sayf El Arab) and 5f and 8.2f winner Shawniga (by Lyphard's Wish), also successful in France at 2 yrs: dam never ran: modest handicapper: trained first 4 starts by B. Richmond: won at Lingfield in October: stays 7f: best efforts on an easy surface, ran creditably on equitrack. *H. J. Collingridge*

BRIGHT SEA (USA)   4 b.g. Secreto (USA) 128 – Muriels Dream (USA) (Blue   –
Prince II 123) [1991 6d 8g⁵ 11.5g 7g⁵ 7m⁴ 11.6m 7f 10g 5.1s 8.1d 1992 8.1g⁵ 6.9d 7f 6g 6g⁵ 5s] small, sturdy gelding: seems of little account. *Billy Williams*

BRIGHTSIDE (IRE)   2 b.f. (Apr 1) Last Tycoon 131 – Wedgewood Blue (USA)   **67** p
(Sir Ivor 135) [1992 6d 8g*] 62,000Y: lengthy, angular filly: sister to Irish 3-y-o Vasarelli, 7f winner at 2 yrs, and half-sister to several winners here and in USA, including middle-distance stayer Spode's Blue (by Sadler's Wells): dam, 2-y-o 7f winner, is out of top-class filly Furl Sail and half-sister to dam of Green Line Express: well backed when 4-length winner of 10-runner maiden at Leicester in September, never far away and leading under 2f out: sure to progress again. *P. F. I. Cole*

BRIGHT SPELLS   2 ch.f. (Feb 4) Salse (USA) 128 – Scattered Showers 86   **93** p
(Ardross 134) [1992 5d⁴ 7s² 6d* 7.3s²] leggy filly: has a fluent, quick action: first foal: dam, 1¼m winner here also successful in France at 4 yrs, is out of half-sister to Play It Safe and Providential: really progressive filly: comfortably won maiden at Goodwood: second of 8 to 5-length winner Criquette in listed race at Newbury later in October, caught flat-footed when pace quickened early in straight then staying on strongly: will be better suited by 1m: likely to improve again. *D. R. C. Elsworth*

BRIGHT WALES   2 b.f. (May 8) Precocious 126 – Galesa 90 (Welsh Pageant   **39**
132) [1992 6g 8.1s] compact filly: second foal: sister to 3-y-o Early Gale: dam 1½m winner: always behind in maidens at Kempton and Chepstow: sold 725 gns Ascot November Sales. *M. McCormack*

BRIGINSKI   3 b.f. Myjinski (USA) – Raunchy Rita (Brigadier Gerard 144) [1991   –
6g 6m⁴ a8g a7g 1992 8v 7g 7d] leggy filly: moderate mover: no worthwhile form: blinkered final start. *K. R. Burke*

BRIGTINA   4 b.g. Tina's Pet 121 – Bristle-Moss (Brigadier Gerard 144) [1991 14f⁵   –
10d³ 10d 1992 10.2s a12g] angular gelding: moderate mover: poor maiden on flat: bought 1,600 gns Ascot June Sales before reappearance: stays 1¼m: acts on good to firm and dead ground: won selling handicap hurdle (no bid) in October. *J. M. Bradley*

BRILLIANT   4 ch.f. Never So Bold 135 – Diamond Hill 82 (High Top 131) [1991   **75**
7m 7g 7g² 7g⁶ 7g³ 8.9g 7m 9m 10.3g 1992 8f* 9m 8.5s* 8.5d² 10f² 8.9g² 8g 9d] rangy filly: fair handicapper: successful in amateur events at Warwick and Beverley: well below best last 2 starts: effective from 1m to 1¼m: acts on any going: below form when visored once. *J. Pearce*

BRILLIANT DISGUISE   3 ch.f. Ballacashtal (CAN) – Davemma 81 (Tachy-   **49**
pous 128) [1991 5s³ 6m⁶ 6g 7f 8m 8.3g* 10.5d 7.1m⁶ 1992 9.2d 9.2m 9.2f⁵ 10m 15.1m 12.1g²] rather sparely-made filly: poor handicapper: stays 1½m: acts on good to firm ground: effective visored or not: below form when blinkered once. *P. Monteith*

BRISAS   5 ch.g. Vaigly Great 127 – Legal Sound 85 (Legal Eagle 126) [1991 a6g*   **48** §
a5g² 5f4 5m⁶ 5g 5m a5g⁶ 5m 5f⁶ 5m 5m 5h* 5g 5m a5g 5g a5g⁵ a6g* a6g³ 6d 5g a63 §
5m 6g 5m⁵ 5f 5.9h² 6m⁶ 5m⁴ 6f a6g a5g] strong-quartered, attractive gelding: has a quick action: untrustworthy handicapper: won at Southwell in February: effective at

5f and 6f: acts on hard going and fibresand, possibly unsuited by heavy: blinkered: has looked none too keen, and refused to enter stalls once. *T. Fairhurst*

BRISTOL FASHION 2 b.c. (Mar 1) Slip Anchor 136 – Fettle (Relkino 131) **70** [1992 7g⁵ 7d² 8.1s] 10,500F: workmanlike colt: half-brother to 3 winners, including (at 11f) Indian Plume (by Commanche Run) and (at 6f as 2-y-o in 1986) Khakis Love (by Dominion): dam unraced half-sister to Circus Plume: best effort when staying-on second in maiden at Chester: pulled very hard and found little final start: sold 11,000 gns Newmarket Autumn Sales. *M. Bell*

BROAD APPEAL 4 ch.f. Star Appeal 133 – Cinderwench 95 (Crooner 119) [1991 **51 §** a7g⁵ a5g 1992 10g 8.1m 8g 7g⁵ 7d 9.2m⁴ 8f 8f² 8g³ 8d* 8g 8s 8.2g⁵ 8g] angular filly: moderate mover: reluctant to race after winning Goodwood handicap in September: stays 9f: acts on firm and dead ground: effective blinkered or not: trained first 7 starts by W. Pearce/B. Beasley: best left alone. *R. C. Spicer*

BROADSTAIRS BEAUTY (IRE) 2 ch.g. (Apr 11) Dominion Royale 112 – **62** Holy Water (Monseigneur (USA) 127) [1992 a5g⁴ a6g 7s 5g a5g² a6g*] IR 2,900Y, 3,500 2-y-o: angular, workmanlike gelding: fourth foal: half-brother to 4-y-o 1m (at 2 yrs) to 12.3f winner Drinks Party (by Camden Town): dam unraced daughter of sister to Deep Diver and half-sister to Irish 2000 Guineas winner King's Company: ridden by 5-lb claimer, best effort to win nursery at Southwell in November: speedy type, likely to prove best at sprint distances for time being: may improve further. *M. C. Chapman*

BROAD STORY (NZ) 5 b.h. Diesis 133 – Broadway Hit (Hittite Glory 125) – [1991 a7g² a8g³ 6m⁴ 6m 6d⁴ 6g 6g⁴ 1992 6g] lengthy, short-legged horse: modest handicapper: sustained leg injury in £12,200 event at York in May and has been retired: stayed 1m: acted on good to firm and soft ground. *P. Calver*

BROADWAY RUCKUS (CAN) 3 br.f. Bold Ruckus (USA) – Broadway **61** Beauty (USA) (Chompion (USA)) [1991 6m⁶ 1992 12d 8d⁶ 6d* 6.1s 6.9v] rangy filly: first sign of ability when winning maiden at Redcar in October: never placed to challenge after: should prove suited by further than 6f: acts on dead ground. *D. R. Laing*

BROCKTON DANCER 2 b.f. (Mar 29) Fairy King (USA) – Susie's Baby **73 ?** (Balidar 133) [1992 5m 5.2g⁴ 5f⁴ 5.2s² 6m³ 5.7f* 6.5m⁶ 6d 7m⁵ 6d³] 10,500Y: workmanlike filly: moderate mover: fifth foal: half-sister to 4-y-o 5f performer Sir Tasker (by Lidhame) and two 2-y-o 5f winners by Kafu: dam lightly raced: modest performer on balance of form, successful in Bath median auction event in August: appeared to show vastly improved form in moderately-run York listed race won by Rain Brother final start: stays 7f well: probably acts on any going: didn't find much off bridle when visored once: occasionally bandaged behind. *R. Hannon*

BROCTUNE GREY 8 gr.m. Warpath 113 – Hitesca 110 (Tesco Boy 121) [1991 **75** 16.1m 16m 1992 16.1s³ 16f* 14.1h* 14.1m* 16m* 19m² 16.2m4] angular, sparely-made mare: successful in 1992 in claimers at Redcar, Carlisle and Yarmouth and handicap at Redcar: stayed really well: acted on hard and soft ground: below form when visored once: usually held up: dead. *Mrs M. Reveley*

BRODESSA 6 gr.g. Scallywag 127 – Jeanne du Barry 74 (Dubassoff (USA)) [1991 **69** 12.1d² 12.4m⁵ 9m⁴ 12m⁶ 12m³ 12.4m⁴ 13.6d 1992 13m² 13.6f* 14.1d³ 12m³] big, workmanlike gelding: moderate walker: consistent handicapper: won (for first time) at Redcar in June: will stay 2m: acts on firm and dead ground: suitable mount for amateur. *Mrs M. Reveley*

BRONZE MAQUETTE (IRE) 2 b.f. (Apr 27) Ahonoora 122 – Working Model – **p** 99 (Ile de Bourbon (USA) 133) [1992 7s] IR 25,000Y: quite good-topped filly: good walker: first reported foal: dam 1¼m winner probably ideally suited by 1½m: 13/2 and bit backward, shaped better than eighth-of-14 position suggests in Salisbury maiden in October, front rank to over 2f out and eased when beaten: showed a round action: will improve. *P. F. I. Cole*

BRONZE RUNNER 8 gr.g. Gunner B 126 – Petingalyn (Petingo 135) [1991 **37** 11.7g 11.5g⁴ 10.2f⁵ 11.7m⁵ 10.8m* 11m* 9.7f⁴ 10m⁶ 10.2g* 12ga 12ga 13g⁴a 12g⁴a 14g 1992 10m 10f 11.4f³ 10f⁶ 10.2f⁵ 10g⁴ 10s⁴ 11.7d⁵ 12.2g⁶ 10m] leggy gelding: poor mover: tough old handicapper: effective at 1¼m to 1½m: acts on any going: excellent mount for inexperienced rider: visored or visored. *E. A. Wheeler*

BROOKLANDS EXPRESS 2 gr.c. (May 20) Absalom 128 – Lucy's Melody 39 **51** (On Your Mark 125) [1992 5d⁵ 5v a6g] sturdy colt: has a round action: second foal: dam won 8.2f seller: modest maiden: failed to win off equitrack. *J. D. Bethell*

BROOKS EXPRESS (FR) 3 b.c. Siberian Express (USA) 125 – Brook's **44** Dilemma 80 (Known Fact (USA) 135) [1991 NR 1992 8d 8g 10m 7d⁶ 8d 7d³ 7s 7g] rather leggy colt: has a quick action: second foal: half-brother to 4-y-o 1m winner Kay's Dilemma (by Ya Zaman): dam 6f winner: poor maiden: should stay beyond 7f: acts on dead ground. *R. Akehurst*

BROOMHOUSE LADY 2 b.f. (Apr 19) General Wade 93 – Dairy Queen 76 (Queen's Hussar 124) [1992 7s 7d] leggy filly: half-sister to several winners, including useful 7f and 1m performer Parlour Game (by Birdbrook): dam placed from 6f to 1¼m: no promise in Redcar maidens in autumn. *M. Johnston* —

BROOM ISLE 4 b.f. Damister (USA) 123 – Vynz Girl 82 (Tower Walk 130) [1991 10g 12.3d 12g⁶ 12m⁴ 12.3m 10m⁴ 10.5g³ 12f⁶ 1992 a12g² a12g³ 12d³ 14.6g² 12m² 12m² 12f³ 15.9m² 14.9f* 18.5d⁵ 14g³ 12m] lengthy, quite good-topped filly: carries condition: moderate mover: consistent handicapper: successful at Warwick in June: effective at 1½m to 2m: acts on firm ground and fibresand, seems unsuited to dead. *Mrs A. Knight* **67**

BRORA ROSE (IRE) 4 b.f. Drumalis 125 – Run Swift (Run The Gantlet (USA)) [1991 8m⁴ 10f 10d⁶ 11.7d² 11.7m⁶ 12s³ 12d⁴ 12g 17.2g a14g a12g* 1992 a14g* a13g⁴ 13.8d 14.1d a12g⁶] leggy, close-coupled filly: below form after winning Southwell handicap in January: reluctant to race final start: stays 1¾m: best turf efforts on a soft surface: has run creditably in blinkers: sold to join R. Frost's stable 2,300 gns Doncaster May Sales: later joined Mrs F. Walwyn. *J. D. Bethell* **42 d**

BROTHERLYAFFECTION 3 ch.g. Brotherly (USA) 80 – Lady Peggy (Young Nelson 106) [1991 8.2f 7.1s a8g³ a8g⁴ 1992 a8g³ a7g³ a7g⁵ a7g* a7g 8s 8v⁴ 12.2g 10m 12.3d] big, rangy gelding: modest handicapper on all-weather, successful at Southwell in February: little form on turf after: stays 1m: best form on fibresand: changed hands 2,160 gns Doncaster January Sales after second start. *R. Hollinshead* a54 —

BROUGHPARK AZALEA 3 b.g. Song 132 – Slip The Ferret 109 (Klairon 131) [1991 6m⁵ 6f⁴ 7m 8m 8.3g 1992 12.3s 12g] good-topped gelding: good walker: has a round action: poor maiden: below form blinkered final start (April): stays 1m: acts on firm ground. *J. J. O'Neill* —

BROUGHTON BLUES (IRE) 4 ch.g. Tender King 123 – Princess Galicia 82 (Welsh Pageant 132) [1991 a7g* a10g a8g⁴ 8g 7.5g 9d 8d* 8m⁴ 10g 10.9g⁴ a10g² 10.3m 9m 10m⁴ 10g² 10m² 1992 a12g a12g a12g⁶ 9d⁶ 10d³ 10g 10g⁵ 9.7h³ 10d a10g a13g a12g] sparely-made gelding: poor handicapper: lost his form last 4 starts, twice wearing eyeshield: stays 1¼m well: acts on hard ground and soft: effective blinkered or not. *W. J. Musson* **36 a–**

BROUGHTONS FORMULA 2 b.c. (Mar 19) Night Shift (USA) – Forward Rally 84 (Formidable (USA) 125) [1992 6m a6g⁶ a7g a7g a7g] 42,000Y: small, close-coupled colt: second foal: dam 8.2f to 1¼m winner: modest maiden at best: will stay 1m+: has run creditably for 7-lb claimer. *W. J. Musson* **50**

BROUGHTON'S GOLD (IRE) 4 b.f. Trojan Fen 118 – Smash Hit (Roan Rocket 128) [1991 a8g 7v 8.2d 12g 12m 1992 10g] lengthy, angular filly: moderate mover: poor maiden: probably stays 1½m. *W. J. Musson* —

BROUGHTON'S TANGO (IRE) 3 b.c. Tender King 123 – Topless Dancer (Northfields (USA)) [1991 5g 6g 6m 7m⁵ 6g 6m 8m 6g⁵ 1992 7.5g a8g 7d⁶ 8.3m² 8g⁴ 10d 9.7g* 10.2s³ 10m⁴ 9g²] leggy, lengthy colt: modest handicapper: won apprentice event at Folkestone in September: sold out of W. Musson's stable 6,000 gns Newmarket Autumn Sales before good second in similar event at Newmarket final start: stays 1¼m: acts on good to firm ground, probably on soft: not discredited in blinkers: joined M. Heaton-Ellis. *C. G. Cox* **56**

BROUGHTONS TURMOIL 3 b.g. Petorius 117 – Rustic Stile (Rusticaro (FR) 124) [1991 NR 1992 7.9g4] 16,000F: workmanlike gelding: second foal: half-brother to 7.9f and 9.2f winner Henbury Hall (by Bellypha): dam unraced half-sister to King's Island and Bengal Fire: wearing crossed noseband, one-paced fourth of 8 in claimer at York in September, only run: should improve. *W. J. Musson* **59 p**

BROWN AS A BERRY (IRE) 4 b.g. Glow (USA) – Sun Bed (Habitat 134) [1991 a7g³ a7g⁵ a6g⁵ 10f 1992 8.3v 8.1m 10.3m⁵ 7d 8f 7f] robust gelding: well beaten in 1992: stays 7f: tried in eyeshield, visor and blinkers. *W. Storey* —

BROWN CARPET 5 b. or br.g. Never So Bold 135 – Geopelia 109 (Raffingora 130) [1991 7g² 10m 8g 8.1g 8.3g 1992 10.3g 9m² 11.5m³] smallish, workmanlike gelding: has a quick action: maiden handicapper: probably stays 11.5f: acts on firm ground: ran creditably when blinkered. *C. A. Horgan* **32**

BROWN FAIRY (USA) 4 b.f. Northern Baby (CAN) 127 – Chepstow Vale (USA) 97 (Key To The Mint (USA)) [1991 7.5g* 7.6g⁴ 8g² 8.5m⁴ 7.5f* 8m 7g 8g⁶ 7d* 7d a6g⁵ a7g³ 1992 a7g 8.5g 7g* 7f⁴ 8.5g⁵ 8f⁶ 7m³ 8g⁴ 10.3m 10g] leggy filly: **67**

none too consistent handicapper: won at Thirsk in May: needs strongly-run race at 7f, and effective at 1¼m: acts on firm and dead going: below form when sweating: retained 3,000 gns Newmarket Autumn Sales. *Mrs N. Macauley*

BROWN'S (FR)   2 b.c. (Mar 23) Sicyos (USA) 126 – Charlata (FR) (Chaparral (FR) 128) [1992 6m 6m⁵ 7m⁴ 8d⁶ 8m²] 300,000 francs (approx £30,100) Y: leggy, unfurnished colt: half-brother to several winners, including prolific Italian winner Charlo Mio (by Sole Mio), successful from 5f to 1¼m, including in Group 3 event: dam French 10.5f winner from good family: much improved after joining present trainer (with N. Callaghan first 2 starts), in frame in maidens won by Barathea at Newmarket and Bob's Return at Pontefract: stays 1m: best form on good to firm ground, pulled hard on dead. *P. W. Chapple-Hyam*   **80**

BRUSH WOLF (USA)   3 ch.g. Blushing Groom (FR) 131 – Swept Away 106 (Kris 135) [1991 NR 1992 7g 11g 8.1m 8g] close-coupled gelding: shows knee action: first foal: dam, daughter of smart French miler Costly Wave, won at 9f and 1¼m: bought out of N. Graham's stable 2,200 gns Newmarket Autumn (1991) Sales: no form, including in sellers. *J. M. Bradley*   **–**

BRUSQUE (USA)   8 b.g. Assert 134 – Cecelia (USA) (Royal Levee (USA)) [1991 13d² 16.5m 13d⁴ 13.6g 12.1s* 13d⁵ 12.1m² 12.1f⁴ 15.1g² 16.1m 1992 16.1s 13d 12.1s⁴ 13m 15.1m³ 15.1g⁴ 17.9d² 17.5s⁵ 17.1s] compact gelding: none too consistent handicapper: stays well: acts on any going. *Don Enrico Incisa*   **38**

BUCKINGHAM BAND (USA)   4 ch.g. Palace Music (USA) 129 – Intensive (USA) (Sir Wiggle (USA)) [1991 10m 10.5g⁵ 12.3d⁵ 12.1s⁶ 1992 16.1s 13d 14.1d 21.6g 17.1m 12f³ 10.5d³ 10m² 10.1f² 13.1g³ 10.9d⁶] big, leggy gelding: poor handicapper: effective at 1¼m, and should stay further than 13f: probably acts on any going: suitable mount for amateur: goes well blinkered, below form visored: sold 2,000 gns Doncaster September Sales. *F. H. Lee*   **46**

BUCKSKI ECHO   2 b.g. (Mar 2) Petoski 135 – Echoing 93 (Formidable (USA) 125) [1992 5g 5g 6m 6m] 1,000Y: compact gelding: second foal: dam 2-y-o 5f winner from family of Time Charter: well beaten in varied events in first half of 1992. *T. M. Jones*   **–**

BUCK THE TIGER   2 b.g. (Jan 27) Risk Me (FR) 127 – Grey Twig 68 (Godswalk (USA) 130) [1992 5s 6s 6f⁶] 3,300F, 580Y: smallish, sturdy gelding: fifth living foal: half-brother to several winners, including 2-y-o sprint winners Mr Burfield (by Faustus) and Grey Wolf Tiger (by Rolfe): dam ran only at 2 yrs: soundly beaten in maiden and sellers: blinkered final start. *R. Hannon*   **–**

BUDDY (IRE)   3 b.c. Double Schwartz 128 – Silk Trade (Auction Ring (USA) 123) [1991 5m 5m* 6g 6g 1992 a8g* a7g³ a6g* a7g² a5g a7g⁴ 7g 6d⁴ 6g 8.1d⁶ 7g 8d 6s] workmanlike colt: moderate mover: successful twice in handicaps at Southwell in January: no form on turf and sold 4,500 gns Newmarket Autumn Sales: should prove best at 7f/1m: acts on good to firm ground and all-weather surfaces: below form visored/blinkered: often claimer ridden. *M. Bell*   **– a59**

BUDDY'S FRIEND (IRE)   4 ch.c. Jester 119 – Hasta (Skymaster 126) [1991 8m 7f⁶ 10g⁶ 8m 10d a10g⁵ 1992 a7g³ a8g³ a8g⁶ a8g⁴ a8g* a10g⁵ a10g a8g² a8g² 8.1m* 7.9d⁶ 8m² 8m a8g⁵ a8g⁵] smallish, workmanlike colt: poor mover: modest handicapper: won at Southwell (maiden) in February and Chepstow in June: effective from 1m to 1¼m: acts on all-weather surfaces and good to firm ground, unsuited by a soft surface: good mount for lady rider. *R. J. R. Williams*   **61 a53**

BUDGET   4 ch.g. Bustino 136 – Australia Fair (AUS) (Without Fear (FR) 128) [1991 a12g 1992 8.1d] leggy, angular gelding: thrice raced on flat and no worthwhile form. *A. J. Chamberlain*   **–**

BUFFALO RIVER   2 b.c. (Mar 2) Robellino (USA) 127 – Strapless 84 (Bustino 136) [1992 5m⁵ 7m³ 7g] 8,000F, 7,000Y: workmanlike colt: good mover: fifth foal: half-brother to ungenuine maiden here Elenos (by Trojan Fen), later successful in Austria: dam 6f winner, is out of Cheveley Park second Dame Foolish: off bridle at halfway when staying-on third of 8 in maiden auction at Catterick: helped set too strong a pace later in July: should stay well. *M. H. Tompkins*   **45**

BUGLET   2 b.f. (Mar 2) Taufan (USA) 119 – Blue Bell Girl (Blakeney 126) [1992 8d⁵ a8g² a8g³ a8g] IR 4,000Y: first foal: dam, placed over 1m at 2 yrs in Ireland, is half-sister to one-time smart sprinter Ever Sharp: modest maiden: acts on fibresand: looks a staying type. *G. C. Bravery*   **52**

BUNDERBURG (USA)   2 b. or br.c. (May 19) Nureyev (USA) 131 – Hortensia (FR) 119 (Luthier 126) [1992 6m] tall, lengthy, angular colt: eighth foal: half-brother to 3-y-o Glacial Moon and Derby second Glacial Storm (both by Arctic Tern), latter successful at 15.5f in France, and 3 middle-distance winners: dam smart at around   **– p**

1¼m in France: 20/1, around 13 lengths eleventh of 14, outpaced soon after halfway and not knocked about, to Felucca in maiden at Newmarket in October: will improve. *P. W. Chapple-Hyam*

BUNTY BOO   3 b.f. Noalto 120 – Klairove 74 (Averof 123) [1991 6d4 6.1m2 6g2   **96** 1992 6.1d* 6.1g 6m6 5m6 5.1g* 5m2 5s2 5s* 5m3 6g] leggy filly: useful performer: won maiden at Nottingham in April and handicaps at Chester in July and York (wearing crossed noseband and ridden by 7-lb claimer) in October: also good third in listed race at Newmarket: best at 5f: acts on good to firm and soft ground: consistent. *B. A. McMahon*

BUONARROTI   5 b.g. Ela-Mana-Mou 132 – Amiel (Nonoalco (USA) 131) [1991   – 14s 1992 16d] strong, lengthy gelding: moderate walker: lightly raced on flat nowadays, well beaten in Newbury handicap in April: won over hurdles in December: should stay beyond 2m: acts on dead ground. *J. A. B. Old*

BURBAGE (IRE)   2 ch.c. (Apr 29) Caerleon (USA) 132 – Princesse Timide   **66** p (USA) (Blushing Groom (FR) 131) [1992 7m 6v*] close-coupled colt: closely related to smart French 11f and 1½m winner Louis Cyphre (by Niniski): dam French 7.5f and 1¼m winner: very easy to back when neck winner of 13-runner Folkestone maiden in October, reminder halfway then staying on well to lead near line: will improve again, especially over 1m+: sent to race in USA. *P. W. Chapple-Hyam*

BURBLE   2 b.f. (Mar 1) Kabour 80 – Mrs Buzby 71 (Abwah 118) [1992 a6g a6g a7s   **34** a5g] compact filly: third living foal: dam 6f and 7f winner: poor form, including in sellers: blinkered first 3 starts. *D. W. Chapman*

BURISHKI   2 gr.f. (Mar 2) Chilibang 120 – Hunza Water 70 (Relko 136) [1992 5s   **49** 6s 6m 6g* 6f3 6m2 a6g4 6m] 1,700Y: small, sturdy filly: has a round action: third foal: half-sister to 3-y-o Up The Punjab (by Daring March), successful at 1m, including at 2 yrs: dam 11.5f winner: plater: won at Yarmouth (no bid) in June: ran badly final start (July): stays 6f: acts on firm ground: best in blinkers: sometimes slowly away. *G. A. Pritchard-Gordon*

BURMESE PEARL   4 b.f. Good Times (ITY) – Hampton Court (Town And   – Country 124) [1991 NR 1992 12f] leggy, angular filly: second foal: sister to NH Flat race winner Burmese Ruby: dam lightly-raced maiden: bandaged, soon tailed off in Thirsk seller in May, only run on flat. *P. T. Dalton*

BURN BRIDGE (USA)   6 b.g. Linkage (USA) – Your Nuts (USA) (Creme Dela   – Creme) [1991 12m 12g3 1992 12.3m] small gelding: no worthwhile form on flat for long time: acts on soft going: usually blinkered over hurdles, winner in August. *M. D. Hammond*

BURNING COST   2 br.f. (Apr 27) Lochnager 132 – Sophie Avenue (Guillaume   **51** Tell (USA) 121) [1992 7g 8.2d 8d] 1,300Y: leggy, angular, rather plain filly: moderate mover: fifth foal: half-sister to 8.2f and 10.5f winner Parking Bay and 1½m winner Bayphia (both by Bay Express): dam French 2-y-o 7f winner: poor form, staying on from rear, in maidens: shapes as though will stay beyond 1m. *G. A. Pritchard-Gordon*

BURNING SAND   2 br.f. (Apr 19) Forzando 122 – Bernarda (GER) (Priamos   – (GER) 123) [1992 6m] lengthy filly: first foal: dam ran several times at 2 yrs in Germany: mulish and blinkered, pulled very hard in maiden at Yarmouth in September: sold 660 gns Newmarket Autumn Sales. *J. M. P. Eustace*

BURNT IMP (USA)   2 ch.c. (Feb 22) Imp Society (USA) – Flaming Reason   **76** p (USA) (Limit To Reason (USA)) [1992 8m 8g] $100,000Y: angular, good-bodied colt: fourth foal: brother to 2 winners, notably smart 1990 2-y-o Mac's Imp: dam won at up to 7f: sire very smart at up 1¼m: much better effort in October on final run when never-dangerous eighth of 9 to Shaiba in Newmarket minor event: may progress again. *G. Harwood*

BUROOJ   2 br.c. (Mar 23) Danzig (USA) – Princess Sucree (USA) (Roberto (USA)   **82** p 131) [1992 7d* 7g5] big, leggy colt: fluent mover: fifth foal: closely related to useful 1988 2-y-o 6f and 7f winner Rasheek (by Topsider) and 1986 2-y-o 7f winner Tipatina (by Northern Baby) and half-brother to 3-y-o Mashaaer (by Shadeed): dam, placed over 6f and 8.5f at 4 yrs in USA, is half-sister to Kentucky Derby winner Cannonade: comfortable 1½-length winner of 20-runner maiden at Lingfield: ran well when staying-on fifth of 16 to Brigante di Cielo in nursery at Ascot later in autumn: will be suited by 1m: has plenty of scope, and sure to do better. *D. Morley*

BURRACOPPIN   5 b.g. Niniski (USA) 125 – Favorite Prospect (USA) (Mr   – Prospector (USA)) [1991 12m 8.2f 12m5 14.6g 12g 1992 a12g 14.6g a12g a16g4] leggy, rather sparely-made gelding: seems of little account nowadays. *Mrs Barbara Waring*

BURSANA 6 b.m. Burslem 123 – Lady of Surana (Shirley Heights 130) [1991 –
a 12g^2 a 16g^2 a 13g* 10.2s a 12g 1992 a 16g a 13g] sparely-made mare: poor mover: poor
handicapper nowadays: stays 2m: acts on good to firm and soft going. *J. L. Spearing*

BUSHFIRE MOON 4 ch.g. Julio Mariner 127 – Flea Pit (Sir Lark 101) [1991 –
14.1m 10m 12s^4 1992 14.1d] tall, leggy gelding: no worthwhile form. *C. N. Williams*

BUSMAN (IRE) 3 ch.c. Be My Guest (USA) 126 – Cistus 123 (Sun Prince 128) 74
[1991 8g 7d^5 1992 10g 10m^5 10.2g 10g* 10d] workmanlike colt: modest handicapper:
easily best run in 1992 when winning maiden at Brighton in August: should be
suited by 1½m: sold 13,500 gns Newmarket Autumn Sales. *Major W. R. Hern*

BUSTED ROCK 7 b.h. Busted 134 – Mexican Two Step (Gay Fandango (USA) 89
132) [1991 a 11g^3 a 12g^4 10.8m^2 10.8m* 10m* 10d^2 10m^2 10.1g* 10g 10m^3 10.4m^3
1992 10d^4 10d 10.1g^2 10g^2 10.1m^2 11.9d^6 10.1g^4 10f^5 10.1m^3] rangy, quite attractive
horse: moderate mover: usually impresses in appearance: consistent handicapper:
effective at 1¼m: acts on firm and dead going: wore eyeshield on all-
weather: suited by waiting tactics and firm handling: tough and genuine: finished
lame over hurdles in November and has been retired to stud. *Mrs L. Piggott*

BUSTER 4 br.g. Macmillion 110 – Valsette (Anfield 117) [1991 7g* 6g^6 7m 8g^6 8g –
6d 1992 a 6g] lengthy, sparely-made gelding: looked potentially useful when winning
4-runner minor event at Doncaster in July, 1991: fair at best otherwise and always
outpaced at Lingfield in December: needs further than 6f, and should stay 1m: acts
on firm going: tends to wander. *Mrs Barbara Waring*

BUSTINETTA 3 b.f. Bustino 136 – Butsova 93 (Formidable (USA) 125) [1991 NR 89 ?
1992 10d 10m^2 10s^2 11.1f* 12.3g^3 14.6m 12s^4 14m^3 16g^3] 30,000Y: leggy, lengthy
filly: has a quick action: first foal: dam 6f winner, is out of Italian Oaks second
Nicholas Grey, dam also of Terimon (by Bustino): consistent handicapper: won
maiden at Edinburgh in July: appeared to run extremely well in moderately-run
Newmarket listed race won by Specificity final start: suited by further than 1½m:
acts on good to firm ground and soft: sold 50,000 gns Newmarket December Sales. *J.
R. Fanshawe*

BUSTINO BAY 4 b.g. Bustino 136 – Betsy Bay (FR) 107 (Bellypha 130) [1991 –
10.2s 10m 12g 1992 10d] sturdy gelding: poor mover: little worthwhile form. *D. Shaw*

BUTLERS WHARF 7 b.g. Burslem 123 – Regal Promise (Pitskelly 122) [1991 – §
12f 12f^5 1992 12m 11.8m] big, lengthy gelding: thoroughly untrustworthy
handicapper: stays 1½m well: acts on any going: below form in blinkers and visor. *K.
W. Hogg, Isle of Man*

BUY NORDAN 8 ch.m. Camden Town 125 – Mivanwy (Welsh Saint 126) [1991 –
NR 1992 11.1m] leggy, close-coupled mare: poor maiden: broke leg in May. *F.
Watson*

BUY SUNDAY SPORT 2 b.f. (May 12) Rich Charlie 117 – Tricky Tracey –
(Formidable (USA) 125) [1992 a 5g 6f a 6g] IR 550Y: smallish, unfurnished filly: poor
mover: fifth foal: half-sister to French 1m winner Trickiest (by Try My Best) and
quite modest 1990 2-y-o 5f winner Domino Trick (by Primo Dominie): dam unraced:
seems of little account. *Miss Gay Kelleway*

BUZZARDS BELLBUOY 3 b.c. Buzzards Bay 128§ – Bella Travaille 82 77
(Workboy 123) [1991 NR 1992 a 8g^4 a 8g^4 8g^4 9s^6 7.6s^5 10.1m 8m^2 8d* 8d 7d
8g^2] quite good-topped colt: moderate mover: fifth foal: half-brother to fair 1987
2-y-o 5f winner Magna Travaille (by Mr Fluorocarbon) and 5f and 6f winner On The
Record (by Record Token): dam, best at 2 yrs, won 3 times at 5f: modest
handicapper: won at Newmarket in July and Yarmouth in August: suited by 1m: acts
on good to firm and soft going: effective held up or forcing pace. *H. J. Collingridge*

BUZZARDS CREST 7 ch.g. Buzzards Bay 128§ – Diamond Talk (Counsel 118) 31
[1991 10.2s* 10.2s* 12m^3 9d 11.9m 12d 10.5g^5 a 12g 1992 a 8g^3 10.3g 12d 12.4s 9.7h
10.9d^3 12.1v a 8g] lengthy gelding: poor mover: inconsistent handicapper: stays
1½m: acts on good to firm and soft going. *Bob Jones*

BUZZ-B-BABE 2 ch.c. (Jan 21) Buzzards Bay 128§ – Bella Travaille 82 52
(Workboy 123) [1992 6g^5 6.1m^5 7d^5 7g^6 7g^5 6m^5 8f a 7g] 1,350 2-y-o: robust colt:
sixth foal: brother to 3-y-o 1m winner Buzzards Bellbuoy and half-brother to sprint
winners by Mr Fluorocarbon and Record Token: dam, best at 2 yrs, won 3 times at
5f: modest maiden: very stiff tasks last 3 starts: should stay 1m: acts on good to firm
and dead ground: looked reluctant on occasions. *B. Ellison*

BWANA KALI 10 b.g. Kala Shikari 125 – Modom 81 (Compensation 127) [1991 –
NR 1992 10m 6.1g] angular gelding: moderate mover: poor handicapper: stays 1¼m:
acts on any going: sometimes blinkered/looks none too keen. *J. A. Bennett*

BY ARRANGEMENT (IRE) 3 b.f. Bold Arrangement 111 – Eulalie 85 **52** (Queen's Hussar 124) [1991 6m3 6g3 7m4 1992 8f5 a11g6 8g3 10f4 8g3 8m* 10.1g* 12m 10d2 10d] leggy, unfurnished filly: ridden by 7-lb claimer, won claimer at Newmarket and seller (no bid) at Yarmouth in July: left R. Guest after penultimate run and rare poor effort final start: effective at 1m/1¼m: acts on firm and dead going: well beaten on fibresand. *S. Woodman*

BY FAR (USA) 6 b.m. Far North (CAN) 120 – Countess Babu (USA) (Bronze **34** Babu) [1991 a12g a16g6 1992 11.8g5 14.1d5 a12g5] smallish, close-coupled, sparely-made mare: poor handicapper: stays 1¾m: acts on dead ground. *O. O'Neill*

BY HAND 3 ch.g. Sayf El Arab (USA) 127 – Madame Laffitte 54 (Welsh Pageant **77** 132) [1991 6f a6g* 7m* 6m6 7d 1992 a7g3 8d5 8.1s 7m2 7.1m6 7.6m2 7.6d2 7m4 7g5 7.1g*] well-made gelding: moderate mover: fair handicapper: won at Sandown (apprentices) in September: should have stayed 1m: acted on good to firm and dead ground: dead. *W. J. Haggas*

BY RUBIES 2 br.f. (Mar 12) Green Ruby (USA) 104 – Bystrouska (Gorytus **54** (USA) 132) [1992 5.2m 6g2 a6g5 7.1s2 7d] leggy, workmanlike filly: has round action: first foal: dam once-raced (at 2 yrs) daughter of speedy 2-y-o Labista (didn't train on): plating-class maiden: likely to stay further than 7f: acts well on soft ground: sold 3,600 gns Newmarket Autumn Sales. *B. W. Hills*

C

CABOCHON 5 b.g. Jalmood (USA) 126 – Lightning Legacy (USA) 78 (Super **80** Concorde (USA) 128) [1991 16g6 14.8m3 18.4d 20g* 17.2g2 16.2d 18m6 16.5d3 1992 18g 17.1d20m5 16.1f2 16.2d3 16.2g6 18.2m2 18m] lengthy gelding: has a round action: largely consistent handicapper: very free to post when well-beaten second favourite for Cesarewitch final start: effective from 2m to 2½m: acts on firm and soft ground: sold to join R. Frost 17,000 gns Newmarket Autumn Sales. *D. Morley*

CACHOU (USA) 3 b.f. Roberto (USA) 131 – Scierpan (USA) 86 (Sharpen Up 127) **74** [1991 NR 1992 8g3 8m3 7m6 8m2 8.9m* 9s2 10.3s3 9g5] has a quick action: first foal: dam maiden placed at 5f and 6f at 2 yrs, only season to race, is half-sister to smart middle-distance performers Tralos and Polemic (both by Roberto): fair and consistent handicapper: won at Wolverhampton in September: should have proved best at 1¼m+: acted on good to firm and soft ground: suitable mount for an apprentice: stud. *J. H. M. Gosden*

CADENCY 4 b.g. Teenoso (USA) 135 – Mullet 75 (Star Appeal 133) [1991 10m **70** + 10.1g4 11.6m* 12m5 10d 12d 12g 1992 10s2] small, sturdy gelding: moderate mover: rated 90 at his best in 1991: neck second in slowly-run handicap at Salisbury in September, 1992: stays 11.6f: acts on good to firm ground: won handicap hurdle in October. *M. H. Tompkins*

CAERLINA (IRE) 4 b.f. Caerleon (USA) 132 – Dinalina (FR) (Top Ville 129) **113** [1991 8d2 8d3 10.5d* 10m* 12m 1992 8g2 9.2d 8g5 9.5f] small French filly: rated 120 at 3 yrs when successful in Prix de Diane Hermes at Chantilly: shaped encouragingly on reappearance when going down by 1½ lengths to Exit To Nowhere in Prix du Muguet at Saint-Cloud: never a threat in Prix d'Ispahan at Longchamp later in May, fair efforts in Prix d'Astarte at Deauville in August and Grade 1 Beverly D Stakes at Arlington following month: best form at 1¼m: acts on good to firm ground and dead. *J. de Roualle, France*

CAERULIA 4 gr.f. Absalom 128 – Liberation 63 (Native Breeder) [1991 a7g6 a7g **–** a6g 7d 1992 a5g4 a7g6] smallish, good-quartered filly: of little account: blinkered in 1992. *W. J. Pearce*

CAHEREA SCHOOL 3 ch.f. Country Classic – Morse Princess 69 **–** (Communication 119) [1991 a7g a8g 1992 6f 8.5d 8m] leggy filly: of little account. *R. O'Leary*

CAITHNESS ROCK 3 ch.g. Ballad Rock 122 – Thessaloniki 94 (Julio Mariner **–** 127) [1991 6d 6g6 7f3 8f4 7d 1992 10d 10.1d 9f 12.1m6 12.1s] close-coupled, stocky gelding: looked of little account in 1992: trained until after penultimate start by M. Jarvis. *C. Parker*

CALACHUCHI 5 b.m. Martinmas 128 – Seleter (Hotfoot 126) [1991 12f2 9s* **–** 12.3d5 10.6g* 10.3d2 12.2g* 10.5g* 10.5f 1992 10f 12.2g5] leggy mare: genuine claimer (rated 74) as 4-y-o: off course over 9 months and tubed, well below form in midsummer in 1992: stays 1½m: acts on any going: keen sort, taken down early. *M. J. Camacho*

CALCUTTA FLYER (IRE)   2 b.c. (Mar 17) Persian Heights 129 – Imperatrice   52
(USA) (Kings Lake (USA) 133) [1992 5.1g 7m 7d4] smallish, useful-looking colt: first
foal: dam, once raced in France, is half-sister to very useful 7f and 10.5f winner
Cameo Shore and very useful middle-distance winner Iseo: modest maiden: not
seen after July: will be well suited by 1¼m. *P. W. Chapple-Hyam*

CALCUTTA QUEEN   3 ch.f. Night Shift (USA) – Happy Snap (Jalmood (USA)   51
126) [1991 NR 1992 a8g3 a8g3] 8,600F, 21,000Y: first foal: dam unraced granddaughter of 1000 Guineas second Photo Flash: third in maidens at Southwell and
Lingfield in January: will stay 1¼m: sold 1,000 gns Newmarket July Sales. *Mrs J. Cecil*

CALDERVALE   2 b.g. (Mar 28) Midyan (USA) 124 – Linguistic 95 (Porto Bello   71
118) [1992 5g 5f4 5f5 6f 7d6 7g3 6g 7s] 17,500Y: leggy, close-coupled gelding:
half-brother to several winners, including stayers Castle Douglas (by Amboise) and
Relatively Easy (by Relkino): dam won twice over 5f at 2 yrs: modest maiden: easily
best effort when third of 4 at Ayr: will stay 1m: blinkered final start, first for 8 weeks
and never a factor. *A. Bailey*

CALEMAN   3 b.g. Daring March 116 – Lillemor (Connaught 130) [1991 6g 6m3   84
7m* 7.6m* 1992 8f5 8m 7m2 6m 6s5] leggy, narrow gelding: has a round action:
fairly useful handicapper: stays 7.6f: acts on good to firm ground, probably on soft:
has been gelded. *R. Boss*

CALENICK LASS   2 b.f. (Apr 17) Elegant Air 119 – Teye (Mummy's Pet 125)   33
[1992 a7g 7m 6s 10d] 2,400Y: leggy filly: sister to 3-y-o Elegant Touch, 1m winner at
2 yrs, and half-sister to modest 6f winner Hazel Bee (by Starch Reduced): dam
showed little ability: poor plater: best run at 1¼m, though raced very freely early
on. *D. Haydn Jones*

CALIBAIRN   4 ch.g. Bairn (USA) 126 – Calibina 101 (Caliban 123) [1991 5s 6g 7g   –
6.9s 6m 1992 6g 5m 5g 5s] sparely-made gelding: no form since 2 yrs: usually
blinkered at 3 yrs: sold 1,200 gns Newmarket Autumn Sales. *D. J. S. Cosgrove*

CALIBRATE   2 b.c. (Apr 19) Blakeney 126 – Vernair (USA) 73 (Super Concorde   48 p
(USA) 128) [1992 6m] 1,200F, 13,500Y: useful-looking colt: third living foal:
half-brother to 7f winner Gavin Allen (by Heraldiste) and 3-y-o Woodlands Legend
(by Sayf El Arab): dam 6f winner also won in Italy: 33/1, soon pushed along in rear
and no danger from halfway in 14-runner maiden at Newmarket in October: looks
sort to do better. *D. R. C. Elsworth*

CALICON   6 ch.g. Connaught 130 – Calgary 63 (Run The Gantlet (USA)) [1991 NR   –
1992 14s 14g 14d 16.2g] lengthy, angular gelding: rated 86 as 4-y-o: no form in 1992:
used to be suited by a test of stamina. *I. A. Balding*

CALIFORNIA DREAMIN   3 b.f. Slip Anchor 136 – Misguided 106 (Homing   –
130) [1991 NR 1992 10s] 17,500Y: unfurnished filly: fifth foal: half-sister to 1987
2-y-o 5f and 7f winner Kajar (by Persian Bold) and winning hurdler Prime Warden
(by Blakeney): dam sprinting half-sister to smart 6f and 1m winner Missed Blessing:
13/2 from 8/1, in rear in 8-runner maiden at Newbury in July, very slowly away then
leading until over 3f out: moved moderately to post: reluctant at stalls. *D. W. P. Arbuthnot*

CALISAR   2 br.g. (Feb 20) Mummy's Game 120 – Maycrest (Imperial Fling (USA)   51
116) [1992 5g* 5v2 6d5 6g4 6.1f3 6.1g4 7g2 8g] 2,600F, 2,500Y: leggy, angular
gelding: moderate mover: third foal: half-brother to 4-y-o Foursingh (by Mansingh),
juvenile 5f winner: dam ran once: modest performer: won maiden auction at
Beverley in March: largely consistent afterwards: stays 7f: acts on any going. *W. G. M. Turner*

CALL FOR ROONEY   4 b.g. Music Maestro 119 – Sally Bowles 87 (Blakeney   54
126) [1991 5f3 7f3 7f3 8f4 7f4 10.3m 1992 a7g 5m5] lengthy, good-topped
gelding: modest maiden: off course 4 months and 33/1, creditable never-nearer fifth
at Beverley in May: really needs further than 5f and stays 1m: acts on firm ground:
sold 1,050 gns Doncaster October Sales. *A. Smith*

CALLING COLLECT (USA)   3 ch.c. Phone Trick (USA) – My Little Guest   115
(Be My Guest (USA) 126) [1991 7g* 6g3 6g4 9s* 10v2 1992 9.2s4 9.2d4 10.5d4 8g*
8s2 9m3] rather sparely-made ex-French colt: has a quick action: very useful
performer: transferred from E. Lellouche's stable after second start: won listed
event at Kempton in September: good efforts later in autumn in Prix du Rond-Point
at Longchamp (beaten 4 lengths by Arazi) and listed race at Newmarket (length

Miss G. Gatto-Roissard's "Calling Collect"

third to Mellottie): effective at 1m and stays 1¼m: acts on good to firm ground and heavy: best held up for turn of foot: stays in training. *L. M. Cumani*

CALLIPOLI (USA)   5 br.m. Green Dancer (USA) 132 – Minstrelete (USA)   –
(Round Table) [1991 10m 10g 10f² 12.3g⁶ 10.1g³ 10g³ 9.9f³ 8.9g⁵ 10.1f³ 10m² 1992
10d 10.1d⁵ 10g] close-coupled, rather sparely-made mare: rated 72 at 4 yrs: no
worthwhile form in 1992. *R. Guest*

CALL ME BLUE   2 gr.c. (Feb 10) Kalaglow 132 – Woodfold 80 (Saritamer (USA)   **46**
130) [1992 6m 6g] leggy, angular colt: second reported living foal: dam sprinter: in
need of race, poor form in maidens at Goodwood and (3 months later) Newmarket:
may do better. *T. J. Naughton*

CALL ME DICKINS   3 gr.g. Rusticaro (FR) 124 – Bad Start (USA) (Bold   –
Bidder) [1991 NR 1992 10m 10d⁴ 12m] 2,100F: sparely-made gelding: third foal: dam,
unplaced on 6 starts in France, is daughter of smart French 9f and 10.5f winner
North Sea: well beaten in maidens, hint of ability only on dead ground: reluctant
stalls all starts, coltish on debut. *R. Hollinshead*

CALL ME I'M BLUE (IRE)   2 b.c. (May 19) Reasonable (FR) 119 – Bluebutton   **65** p
65 (Blue Cashmere 129) [1992 6g* 6s] IR 4,600Y: sturdy colt: half-brother to Irish 7f
and 1m winner Blue Sceptre (by Tender King) and a winner in Hong Kong: dam
placed over 5f at 2 yrs: heavily-backed favourite, easily made all in 25-runner seller
(sold out of B. Beasley's stable 9,200 gns) at Redcar: helped set possibly too strong
a pace when well beaten in nursery at York later in autumn: worth another chance.
N. Tinkler

CAM

CALL THE BUREAU 3 ch.g. Gorytus (USA) 132 – Mount of Light 61 (Sparkler **65**
130) [1991 5g 6m* 6.1s² 1992 7f³] compact gelding: good mover: off course 11
months and bandaged, third of 8 in handicap at Salisbury in June, prominent
throughout: will be better suited by 1m: acts on any going. *M. J. Heaton-Ellis*

CALL TO THE BAR (IRE) 3 b.g. Kafu 120 – Papun (USA) (Mount Hagen (FR) **55**
127) [1991 NR 1992 6g 6g³ 5.1g 6m 5g⁶ 5m⁴ 5g³ 5s* 5s] 2,200F, 1,900Y: leggy,
sparely-made gelding: first foal: dam, ex-Italian filly, stayed 1m: modest handicapper: won apprentice event at Wolverhampton in September, always prominent
and wandering under pressure: well held at Warwick week later: stays 6f: below
form when blinkered (bolted) and visored once. *C. G. Cox*

CALPELLA 3 b.f. Ajdal (USA) 130 – Calandra (USA) 114 (Sir Ivor 135) [1991 NR **81**
1992 8g⁴ 8m⁴ 8g* 8m* 10g 7m 8g] big, good-topped filly: sixth foal: half-sister to
1¾m winner Reef Lark (by Mill Reef) and useful Irish 1m winner Golden Temple
(by Golden Fleece): dam Irish 1m and 1¼m winner and fourth in Irish Oaks: fairly
useful form in first half of season: won maiden at Pontefract and £11,700 handicap
(awarded race having been checked) at Ascot in June: below form afterwards,
though shaped encouragingly penultimate start: stayed 1m: acted on good to firm
ground: visits Thatching. *J. A. R. Toller*

CAL'S BOY 3 b.g. Green Ruby (USA) 104 – Green Gypsy 83 (Creetown 123) **–**
[1991 5d⁵ 6m 5d⁴ 5g 8d 1992 5m 5m 8g a8g] tall, leggy gelding: blinkered, no form in
handicaps and claimers in 1992. *J. P. Smith*

CALVANNE MISS 6 b.m. Martinmas 128 – Blue Empress (Blue Cashmere 129) **–**
[1991 6g 5.8f 7.1m 1992 a5g] leggy, sparely-made mare: quite modest handicapper at
4 yrs: no show since: effective from 5f to 7f: acts on firm going, possibly unsuited by
a soft surface. *C. J. Hill*

CAMBRIAN 3 b.c. Ajdal (USA) 130 – Cambretta (USA) (Roberto (USA) 131) **98**
[1991 NR 1992 8g 8g* 8.1m 7.9s 8m* 8g*] leggy colt: moderate walker: seventh
living foal: closely related to smart French winner at up to 1¼m Pluralisme (by The
Minstrel) and half-brother to 4 winners, including very useful performers Classic
Tale (by Blushing Groom) and Singletta (by Nodouble): dam, Irish 9f winner, is
sister to high-class 1m and 1½m winner Critique: progressive colt: won maiden at
Kempton in May: off course 4½ months after next start, but better than ever when
landing handicaps at Newmarket in October, gamely making all to beat Jdaayel a
head in £29,500 contest last time: will probably be well suited by 1¼m: should win
more races. *Mrs J. Cecil*

CAMBRIAN HILLS (IRE) 3 b.f. Caerleon (USA) 132 – My Therape 112 **93**
(Jimmy Reppin 131) [1991 6d* 6d* 6m⁴ 1992 7m 7.1d⁴ 8m⁶ 6d 8g⁶] smallish, sturdy,
good-quartered filly: carries condition: fairly useful performer on her day: sixth in
moderately-run listed races at Doncaster and Ascot: should have stayed 1¼m:
acted on good to firm and dead ground: to stud. *P. W. Chapple-Hyam*

CAMBUS BAY 2 b.f. (Feb 11) War Hero 116 – Harbour Girl (Quayside 124) [1992 **–**
5m⁵ 5f 7g 5.9g] 480F: workmanlike, unfurnished filly: has a markedly round action:
first reported foal: dam no sign of ability over jumps: seems of little account: sold
600 gns Doncaster November Sales. *W. T. Kemp*

CAMDEN KNIGHT 7 b.g. Camden Town 125 – Motionless 109 (Midsummer **–**
Night II 117) [1991 10.2s 12.4v⁴ 11s⁴ 12d 13d³ 10.2m 11.9m 14g 10.3d 1992 a12g 12.4v]

Ladbroke Autumn Handicap, Newmarket—a good prize, hotly contested;
it goes to Cambrian (centre, star on cap) from Jdaayel (extreme right)
and Heart of Darkness (noseband)

leggy, good-topped gelding: poor mover: rated 55 at best at 6 yrs: no form in 1992. *N. Bycroft*

CAMDEN'S RANSOM (USA)   5 b.g. Hostage (USA) – Camden Court (USA)   **76**
(Inverness Drive (USA)) [1991 a8g⁴ a10g* 10g 10g⁴ 10g3 10g⁴ 10.4m 10g 1992 11.9m 10.8d 8m* 9g⁴ 8m* 8f⁶ 10d⁴ 8g⁵ 8m⁴ 8.9m 10s⁶ 8.1g² 8d⁴ 9d 8g] good-bodied gelding: has a long stride: fair but inconsistent handicapper: won at Bath in May and Newbury (apprentices) in June: effective from 1m to 1¼m: acts on good to firm and dead ground and on equitrack: has run well when sweating: a tricky ride. *D. R. C. Elsworth*

CAMEO KIRBY (FR)   2 b.c. (Mar 7) Lead On Time (USA) 123 – Nofret (FR)   **62**
(Meautry (FR) 109) [1992 7d⁶ 7d⁵ 8.1g⁶] 800,000 francs (approx £80,300) Y: leggy colt: half-brother to 2 middle-distance winners in France: dam won from 1½m to 15.5f in France: modest maiden: will be suited by 1¼m. *A. A. Scott*

CAMEO SHADES   5 b.g. King of Spain 121 – Sweet Ecstasy 79 (Rarity 129)
[1991 NR 1992 a10g a10g] second foal: dam won over 6f (at 2 yrs) and 1½m: tailed off at Lingfield late in the season, visored last time. *M. McCormack*

CAMINO A RONDA   3 ch.f. Hallgate 127 – Viva Ronda 67 (Kampala 120) [1991   –
NR 1992 a6g a5g a6g 7g 7m⁴ 5m 6g a5g] leggy filly: first foal: dam 2-y-o 5f seller winner: of little account. *Pat Mitchell*

CAMOMILE   4 b.f. Bay Express 132 – Hot Spice (Hotfoot 126) [1991 10g 1992   –
a12g] lengthy filly: has shown little in 2 starts, in claimer at Lingfield in January. *D. Morley*

CANAAN LANE   3 gr.g. Northern Tempest (USA) 120 – Milnsbridge (Dragonara   **66**
Palace (USA) 115) [1991 NR 1992 7.5g⁵ 7g⁴ 7s⁴ 9f3 8.3f3 11.1f² 8g²] leggy, close-coupled gelding: third foal: half-brother to 1988 2-y-o 5f to 7f winner Crowthers (by Mandrake Major): dam poor maiden: consistent maiden: may prove best at around 1m (ran in slowly-run match over 11.1f): acts on any going: tends to get on edge. *A. Harrison*

CANAAN VALLEY   4 ch.g. Absalom 128 – My Pink Parrot (Pirate King 129)   –
[1991 6g3 7m² 7m⁶ 7g* 7.9m3 7f 1992 7m⁴ 8.1m a8g] lengthy, well-made gelding: has high knee action: fair handicapper at best: not so good as at 3 yrs, and well beaten last 2 starts: stays 1m: acts on good to firm ground: tried in eyeshield and blinkers: twice refused to enter stalls, when fitted with net muzzle in July on final intended outing: sold 2,500 gns Doncaster November Sales: one to have reservations about. *J. G. FitzGerald*

CANADIAN BOY (IRE)   3 b.c. Commanche Run 133 – Canadian Guest 74 (Be   –
My Guest (USA) 126) [1991 NR 1992 10d 10d⁶ 10g] 3,000F: big, workmanlike colt: moderate mover: second foal: brother to 1½m winner Commanche Guest: dam maiden stayed 1m: of little account. *D. Shaw*

CANADIAN CAPERS   3 ch.f. Ballacashtal (CAN) – Carolynchristensen 58   **60**
(Sweet Revenge 129) [1991 6g⁴ 6m3 6g² 5.7f* 6m⁶ 1992 5g 6m3 7f 7d3 7.6m* 7d 7.6s 8.1d3 7.1s a10g a8g⁵ a10g⁶] big, angular filly: moderate mover: modest handicapper on her day: made all in claimer at Lingfield in June: below that form afterwards: stays 7.6f: best efforts on top-of-the-ground: has run well when sweating and on toes. *M. R. Channon*

CANADIAN EAGLE   2 ch.f. (Mar 20) Risk Me (FR) 127 – Princess Lily 65   **48**
(Blakeney 126) [1992 7g 7m 6m] 5,400Y: close-coupled, angular filly: second foal: sister to 3-y-o Personal Hazard, 7f winner at 2 yrs: dam, maiden, stayed 1½m, is sister to very useful 1½m winner Believer: always towards rear in large fields, in seller at Newmarket last time: will stay 1m+: sold 1,500 gns Newmarket Autumn Sales. *G. Lewis*

CANASKA STAR   2 b.c. (Apr 11) Doyoun 124 – North Telstar 104 (Sallust 134) **105**
[1992 6m² 6m⁶ 6g² 6m² 7m⁴ 8s] 22,000F, 56,000Y: well-made colt: second foal: half-brother to fair Irish 3-y-o maiden Magnum Star (by Damister): dam Irish 6f (at 2 yrs) and 9f winner: useful performer: in frame in July Stakes at Newmarket, Richmond Stakes at Goodwood and Prix de la Salamandre at Longchamp: not discredited in Grand Criterium final start: stays 1m: acts on good to firm and soft ground. *P. A. Kelleway*

CANAZEI   2 b.f. (Mar 15) Mazaad 106 – Captain Bonnie 60 (Captain James 123)   **33**
[1992 5d 5.1d 5m 6g 5g3 6g⁵ 7m 6s 6g 7d] 1,500Y: close-coupled filly: carries condition: sixth foal: half-sister to 3-y-o 5f winner Doesyoudoes (by Bay Express) and 1988 2-y-o 6f seller winner Check The Gate (by Blushing Scribe): dam ran only at 2 yrs, placed over 5f: poor plater: stays 6f: best efforts on good ground: tried in a visor. *Don Enrico Incisa*

CANBRACK (IRE) 3 b.g. Glenstal (USA) 118 – Cottage Style 65 (Thatch (USA) **50** d
136) [1991 6f⁶ 6m 6m³ 7m 1992 7.1m 9m 8.5d⁵ 9d 12.2d 12.4v a8g⁵ a6g] workmanlike
gelding: plating-class form in 1992 only when fifth: stays 8.5f. *W. A. Stephenson*

CAN CAN CHARLIE 2 gr.c. (Apr 12) Vaigly Great 127 – Norton Princess 76 **56** p
(Wolver Hollow 126) [1992 6m 7s 6d 7g⁵] 4,800F, 7,000Y: big, strong, good-topped
colt: has plenty of scope: fifth foal: half-brother to 1990 2-y-o 5f winner Princess
Who (by Lidhame) and 1½m winner Pan E Salam (by Ile de Bourbon): dam 2-y-o 6f
winner seemed not to train on: modest form in maidens on last 2 starts: burly
previously: stays 7f: looks sort to keep improving. *M. Johnston*

CANDARELA 2 b.f. (Apr 4) Damister (USA) 123 – Guestimate (FR) (Be My **41**
Guest (USA) 126) [1992 7g 8m⁶ 7s] 750Y: leggy, close-coupled filly: has a round
action: second foal: dam unraced half-sister to Kingscote, dam of smart 3-y-o
Rainbow Corner: poor maiden. *P. Howling*

CANDESCO 6 b.m. Blushing Scribe (USA) 107 – Madame Mim 57 (Artaius **–**
(USA) 129) [1991 a7g a7g² a8g 1992 10.1d a8g a8g⁶ a8g³ a12g] strong, close-coupled a53
mare: modest performer, easily best on fibresand: best at around 1m. *R. C. Spicer*

CANDLE KING (IRE) 4 b.g. Tender King 123 – Candelaria (FR) (Touch Paper **–**
113) [1991 6g⁶ 6g 8d 8g⁶ 7m 7g* 7d* 8m³ 8m 7m 1992 6d 8s 7m 7g 8g 8f⁵ 7g 7g 8f]
leggy, sparely-made gelding: keen walker: moderate mover: rated 71 in 1991 but no
worthwhile form in 1992: stays 1m: acts on good to firm ground and dead: often
blinkered: bought for 3,200 gns by H. Manners after winning selling hurdle in
August. *M. J. Fetherston-Godley*

CANNONALE (IRE) 3 b.c. Mummy's Treasure – Sierra Princess (Vital Season **–**
105) [1991 6f 7m 1992 8.1g 7g 8g 8.9s] lengthy colt: no worthwhile form. *J. Pearce*

CANNON CAREW 2 ch.g. (May 30) Gunner B 126 – Molly Carew (Jimmy **74**
Reppin 131) [1992 6s⁶ 8d 7v²] close-coupled gelding: first reported foal: dam was a
strong-pulling jumper: easily best effort behind very easy winner Shintillo in
maiden at Newcastle in November: should stay 1m: acts on heavy going: ridden by
7-lb claimer all starts. *D. Moffatt*

CANNY CHRONICLE 4 b. or br.g. Daring March 116 – Laisser Aller (Sagaro **85**
133) [1991 8m⁴ 8.2g³ 8m⁶ 12.4m* 12f⁴ 13.9g 10.9m³ 12d* 12m 12d³ 1992 11.5g*
13.3g 10g⁶] leggy gelding: moderate mover: fairly useful handicapper: impressive
winner at Lingfield in August: fair one-paced sixth in £8,500 race at Ascot, easily
better subsequent effort: really needs further than 1¼m, and should stay 1¾m (ran
as if something possibly amiss over 13.3f): acts on firm and dead going. *M. H.
Tompkins*

CANNY LAD 2 b.c. (Apr 8) Green Ruby (USA) 104 – Young Whip (Bold Owl 101) **56**
[1992 5f³ 6g⁵ 5d⁵] 1,700Y, 6,200Y 2-y-o: angular, workmanlike colt: first foal: dam
unraced: showed plenty of dash in maiden auction maidens in the summer, showing
better form at 5f: wasn't seen after July. *J. G. FitzGerald*

CANONISED 8 b.g. Welsh Saint 126 – Forest Glen (Tarqogan 125) [1991 NR **–**
1992 a12g a12g] half-brother to several winners, including useful 6f and 7f winner
Inside Quarter (by Tyrant), later successful in USA: dam placed over middle
distances in Ireland: of little account. *R. G. Brazington*

CANON KYLE (IRE) 3 ch.g. Music Boy 124 – Crymlyn 68 (Welsh Pageant 132) **59**
[1991 NR 1992 7g⁶ 7m 6.9d³ 6f⁶ 7g⁴ 6m² 6.9f*] leggy gelding with scope: third foal:
dam maiden stayed 7f: modest performer: won 3-runner maiden at Carlisle in July:
stays 7f: acts on firm and dead ground: blinkered (ran creditably)/visored (well
below form) once: sold 3,100 gns Newmarket September Sales: carries head rather
high. *M. H. Easterby*

CANOPUS 2 ch.c. (Apr 21) Kalaglow 132 – Jacinth 133 (Red God 128§) [1992 7m⁵] **79** p
20,000Y: workmanlike colt: brother to fair middle-distance stayer Rubelite and
half-brother to several winners, including fair 1½m winner Spinelle (by Great
Nephew) and fairly useful 6f winner Jacquinta (by Habitat): dam best 2-y-o of 1972
and high-class miler at 3 yrs: 50/1 and backward, around 8 lengths fifth of 10, green
off bridle and never dangerous, to Barathea in £8,850 event at Newmarket in
October: will improve. *W. Jarvis*

CANTANTA 3 b. or br.f. Top Ville 129 – Sarah Siddons (FR) 122 (Le Levanstell **74**
122) [1991 NR 1992 12s⁴ 14m³ 14.1m² 16m* 16s] lengthy, deep-girthed filly: sister to
Irish Oaks winner Princess Pati and half-sister to several winners, including
high-class middle-distance performer Seymour Hicks (by Ballymore) and 5-y-o
14.6f and 2m winner Star Quest (by Rainbow Quest): dam won Irish 1000 Guineas
and Yorkshire Oaks: fair form: reportedly in season when reluctant third start,
hanging persistently: subsequently blinkered, winning 3-runner maiden at

149

Mr D. R. Hunnisett's "Captain Horatius"

Nottingham in June: stiff task in handicap following month: stayed 2m: acted on good to firm ground: to stud. *R. Charlton*

CANTORIS 6 b.m. Song 132 – Singing Witch 71 (Sing Sing 134) [1991 5g⁵ 6m³ **97** 5m⁵ 5g⁴ 5m 5f* 6g 5g* 5g³ 5m² 5d⁴ 5m⁵ 5d 6m 5d 1992 5g 5.6m³ 5d²dis 5.1g³ 5.6m³ 6d 5m 5g 5.2s 5g³] leggy, close-coupled mare: has a quick action: largely consistent handicapper: worth another try at 6f: acts on any going: has run well for claimer: held up and is suited by strongly-run race. *R. J. R. Williams*

CAPABLANCA 2 br.g. (Jan 30) Chief Singer 131 – Madam Trilby (Grundy 137) **65** [1992 7m⁵ 7d⁶] lengthy, unfurnished gelding: first foal: dam out of half-sister to Circus Plume: fifth of 19 in maiden at Kempton, in August, keeping on strongly under hand riding: remote sixth in similar event at Lingfield following month, disputing lead 5f: sold 6,600 gns Newmarket Autumn Sales. *I. A. Balding*

CAP CAMARAT (CAN) 3 ch.f. Miswaki (USA) 124 – Cap d'Antibes (AUS) **59** (Better Boy 91) [1991 5m⁶ 5m⁴ 5g⁶ 5g⁴ 8f5 1992 7f5 8.1d* 8f4] leggy, quite close-coupled filly: clearly best effort in midsummer to win apprentice handicap at Sandown, staying on really strongly: will probably be suited by 1¼m: may need a soft surface: blinkered (best effort to that point) final start at 2 yrs. *P. F. I. Cole*

CAPE PIGEON (USA) 7 ch.g. Storm Bird (CAN) 134 – Someway Somehow **90** (USA) (What Luck (USA)) [1991 7g⁶ 7.6s* 7.1g² 7.6m* 7g 7g⁴ 7m² 7.6d⁶ a7g 1992 8s² 7m* 7g⁶ 8f 7.1f* 7.1d⁴ 8m⁴ 7m³ 7.6d 7.6g 8g 8.1d²] big, strong gelding: carries plenty of condition: usually looks well: fairly useful handicapper: successful in early-summer at Goodwood and Chepstow: went right off the boil final 4 starts: effective from 7f to 1m: acts on any going: tried visored earlier in career. *L. G. Cottrell*

CAPE WEAVER 2 b.f. (Feb 8) Pampabird 124 – Storm Weaver (USA) (Storm **73** p Bird (CAN) 134) [1992 6m³ 6g² 6m*] tall, leggy filly: first foal: dam, second over 9f from 3 starts in France, is closely related to smart American colt Sportin' Life: won maiden at Doncaster in July, challenging 2f out and running on well inside last: will probably be better suited by 7f: bandaged off-hind last 2 starts: looked sure to do better, but wasn't seen out again. *J. H. M. Gosden*

CAPITAL BOND (IRE)   4 b.c. Hegemony 112 – Have A Flutter (Auction Ring   –
(USA) 123) [1991 8g² 8d 8g⁶ 8g⁶ 8g⁴ 7m* 8.2f⁵ 8m⁵ 10.2g² 8g* 9.7s⁴ 1992 8g 10.8d
8s 12.3m⁴ 10.2f 10m 10d⁴ 8.9d] smallish colt: has a quick action: rated 72 at 3 yrs
(stayed 1¼m, acted on good to firm and soft ground), but appears to have
deteriorated: sold 900 gns Doncaster November Sales. *R. J. Holder*

CAPITAL IDEA (IRE)   3 b.c. Mister Majestic 122 – Star Heading 74 (Upper   48
Case (USA)) [1991 6g 6g⁵ 7m 5f* 5f³ 6m⁵ a7g 1992 5v 6m 5f 6m4 5h 5m 6m³ a5g⁵
9.2g⁶ 7.5d] strong, compact colt: moderate mover: plating-class handicapper:
appears to stay 9.2f: acts on firm going, below form on fibresand: blinkered
(successful at 2 yrs) or visored 6 of first 7 3-y-o starts: sold 950 gns Doncaster
September Sales. *Ronald Thompson*

CAPITAL LAD   3 ch.g. Dublin Lad 116 – Wellington Bear (Dragonara Palace   –
(USA) 115) [1991 5d 5g⁵ 7f⁴ 1992 12.3m 8f 12g] big, workmanlike gelding: no form
and may be ungenuine. *M. Avison*

CAPPAHOOSH (IRE)   3 ch.f. Salmon Leap (USA) 131 – Tagik (Targowice   59
(USA) 130) [1991 7g 6f 8m³ 8.2m⁵ 1992 10d⁶ 10m 10m 10d³ 8.5d* 8g³ 8m 8.9d 7.1g
8.2g 8g] good-topped filly: moderate mover: quite modest handicapper on her day:
made all at Beverley in July: well below form last 5 starts: effective from 8.5f to
1¼m: acts on good to firm and dead ground. *H. J. Collingridge*

CAPRONI   5 b.g. Lomond (USA) 128 – Helaplane (USA) 68 (Super Concorde   –
(USA) 128) [1991 NR 1992 13.1s] IR 130,000Y, 5,000 2-y-o: good-topped gelding:
second live foal: half-brother to very useful miler Strike Force (by Gorytus): dam
plating-class maiden: visored, behind in NH Flat race in January, 1991: 100/1 and
decidedly burly, tailed off in amateurs event at Ayr in September, 1992. *Miss L. A.
Perratt*

CAPS NINETY-TWO (IRE)   2 b.f. (Feb 7) Magical Wonder (USA) 125 –   57
Rahwah 73 (Northern Baby (CAN) 127) [1992 5g⁶ 6s⁴ 6m 5f* 5m³ 6f 6g⁵ 5m 6m] IR
8,000Y: sturdy filly: good mover: first live foal: dam, 1½m winner, is out of sister to
Prix Robert Papin winner Maelstrom Lake: modest performer: won maiden auction
at Salisbury in June: stays 6f: probably well suited by firm ground: has flashed tail.
Dr J. D. Scargill

CAPTAIN HORATIUS (IRE)   3 b.c. Taufan (USA) 119 – One Last Glimpse 73 **112**
(Relko 136) [1991 7.1s* 8.1f⁵ 8.1g* 10g² 1992 11d⁴ 10g* 11g* 12g 11m² 12m* 12g⁶
12g⁶ 10v⁴] tall, close-coupled colt: moderate mover: smart performer: successful in
listed Newmarket Stakes (edgy, ran on strongly despite hanging right, to beat
Shuailaan and Jeune) in May: subsequently raced only on the Continent, winning
Group 2 contests in Germany and Turkey: below form in Germany, Sweden and
Italy last 3 starts: stays 1½m: below form on heavy ground, looked ill at ease on very
firm at 2 yrs. *J. L. Dunlop*

CAPTAIN JACK   2 b.c. (May 1) Salse (USA) 128 – Sanctuary (Welsh Pageant   72
132) [1992 7.1g 7s² 8d] angular, quite good-topped colt: sixth living foal: half-brother
to 3-y-o Nest (by Sharpo) and 3 winners at up to 7f, notably 4-y-o champion sprinter
Sheikh Albadou (by Green Desert): dam unraced half-sister to Little Wolf and
Smuggler: fair maiden: stays 7f: acts on soft ground. *L. M. Cumani*

CAPTAIN LE SAUX (IRE)   2 b.c. (Mar 11) Persian Heights 129 – Casting   96
Couch (Thatching 131) [1992 6m² 6f* 6m* 6m² 7.3g³ 6g² 8s²] IR 13,000Y: leggy,
useful-looking colt: first foal: dam Irish 2-y-o 6f winner: useful performer:
well-backed favourite, won maiden at Hamilton and claimer (claimed afterwards
£40,200) at Newcastle in June: second in Tattersalls Breeders Stakes at
Leopardstown and listed race at Turin in autumn: stays 1m: acts on any going:
trained first 6 starts by M. Bell. *L. d'Auria, Italy*

CAPTAIN MARMALADE   3 ch.g. Myjinski (USA) – Lady Seville 64 (Orange   57
Bay 131) [1991 NR 1992 10m 10m a8g⁴ a7g³ a11g⁵ 8g⁵ 10s 7g a7g 8.2s 10.3g a8g⁶]
workmanlike gelding: third foal: brother to 7f to 11.5f winner Ballerina Bay: dam
maiden suited by 1½m+: modest maiden: should stay 1¼m: acts on all-weather
surfaces. *D. T. Thom*

CAPTAIN MY CAPTAIN (IRE)   4 ch.g. Flash of Steel 120 – Amanzi 94   –
(African Sky 124) [1991 8d 8.2g 12g⁵ 10g 12f⁵ 10.2g⁵ 10.8g 10m⁴ 10.3g⁶ 11.8g
14.1d 11.7d 10.2s⁵] lengthy gelding: rated 66 at 3 yrs, seems just a poor maiden
handicapper nowadays: better suited by 1½m than shorter: acts on good to firm

ground: trained until after second 4-y-o run by G. Balding: won novice hurdle in November. *R. Brotherton*

CAPTEN MORGAN (IRE)　2 b.g. (Mar 30) Governor General 116 – Grugiar 　**33**
(Red Sunset 120) [1992 6d 7g 7m 6m] sturdy gelding: carries condition: has no near eye: moderate mover: first foal: dam, ran 3 times at 2 yrs, is out of disappointing half-sister to Park Hill winner Cursorial: poor form, including in sellers. *W. J. Haggas*

CARBON STEEL (IRE)　2 b.c. (Apr 20) Sure Blade (USA) 130 – Alligatrix 　**98**
(USA) 111 (Alleged (USA) 138) [1992 6m² 5s* 6g⁵ 7m] IR 25,000Y: good-topped colt: has plenty of scope: has a free, round action: sixth foal: half-brother to 3 winners, including useful 6f winner Persianalli (by Persian Bold), later successful at 1m in USA, and useful 6f (at 2 yrs) to 1m winner Alidiva (by Chief Singer): dam well-bred 2-y-o 7f winner, stayed 1m: useful performer: heavily-backed favourite, won maiden at Haydock in September, quickening to lead over 1f out: sweating profusely, excellent keeping-on fifth in Mill Reef Stakes at Newbury: ran respectably in Dewhurst Stakes at Newmarket in October: should be better suited by 7f than less. *B. W. Hills*

CARDEA CASTLE (IRE)　4 b.f. Fayruz 116 – Yamba (FR) (Amarko (FR)) [1991 　–
10m 10.3m 12m⁶ 1992 14.6g 8.5g 7m 8d 9.2d 8f 10g] stocky filly: no worthwhile form, including in sellers: tried blinkered/visored. *B. Ellison*

CARDINAL BIRD (USA)　5 b.g. Storm Bird (CAN) 134 – Shawnee Creek 　–
(USA) (Mr Prospector (USA)) [1991 NR 1992 14.9d⁶ 16.2d⁵ 16.9g] lengthy gelding: walked over once at 3 yrs but no worthwhile form: blinkered final start, in May: won poor handicap hurdle in November, though looked reluctant and one not to be trusted. *S. Mellor*

CARDINAL DOGWOOD (USA)　2 b. or br.c. (Jan 26) Silver Ghost (USA) – 　**54**
Orinoco (USA) (Arctic Tern (USA) 126) [1992 5.1g⁶ 7m⁵ 6g 7m³ 7g 5.9g⁵ 8.1d⁴ 7d] $11,500Y: good-quartered colt: moderate mover: first foal: dam ran 3 times: sire (by Mr Prospector) won at up to 6.5f: modest maiden: stays 1m: acts on top-of-the-ground and dead: seems best in blinkers. *M. Brittain*

CARDINAL POINT (USA)　4 ch.c. Sharpen Up 127 – Lavishly Bold (USA) 　–
(Exuberant (USA)) [1991 7g* 9m* 8.1d* 8g² 1992 7v⁵] quite attractive colt: has a short, round action: progressed into useful performer as 3-y-o, second in New-market listed event on final start: well below best on heavy ground when fifth of 7, beaten around 9 lengths, to Bezelle in Gladness Stakes at the Curragh in April, only outing at 4 yrs: stays 9f: acts on dead ground (faced simple task on good to firm). *J. H. M. Gosden*

CARDMANIA (USA)　6 b.g. Cox's Ridge (USA) – L'Orangerie (USA) 115 (J O 　**110**
Tobin (USA) 130) [1991 6s² 6s³ 7g 6d 8g³ 6.5g* 6g* 6g² 5g* 5s* 1992 a7f⁴ a5.5f³ a6.5f* a6.5s* a7f⁴ a6f* 5m⁵ 6m⁴ 6.5g a6f a6f 5.5f 6f³] lengthy gelding: first foal: dam, French 5f to 1m winner, is out of half-sister to top-class Irish River: very useful performer: won handicaps at Santa Anita (2) and Hollywood Park (Grade 3) in spring: had 3 races in Europe for Mme M. Bollack-Badel in summer, including creditable fifth of 9 in Temple Stakes at Sandown: well beaten in Breeders' Cup Sprint: effective at 5f and 6f: probably acts on any going. *D. Meredith, USA*

CARDOUN (FR)　3 b.c. Kaldoun (FR) 122 – Cable Car (FR) (Fabulous Dancer **119**
(USA) 124) [1991 6g² 6g* 7g* 7g² 7m⁵ 6.5d* 7v* 1992 7g* 8g 6.5g² 8s³ 8s⁶ 6d³ 8f] strong, workmanlike colt: poor walker: smart performer: won Prix Djebel at Maisons-Laffitte but well below form in 2000 Guineas at Newmarket in the spring: very good third behind Exit To Nowhere in Prix Jacques le Marois at Deauville in August: below form after: effective at 6.5f (second in Prix Maurice de Gheest) and stays 1m: acts on heavy going: hampered and never dangerous in Breeders' Cup Mile on firm: best held up for turn of foot. *A. Fabre, France*

CAREFREE TIMES　5 b.g. Good Times (ITY) – Danaka (FR) (Val de Loir 133) 　**49** d
[1991 12d³ 10.4d³ 12g* 10.1m³ 11.9m⁵ 11s⁵ 12g⁶ 12fa 11g⁵ 10m⁵ 11.8m 11.1s 1992 12g 17.1d² 21.6g 16.2m 12.1m⁴ 15.8d⁶ 16.2d⁴ 17.9d] big, strong gelding: poor mover: one-time modest handicapper, on the downgrade: stays 17f: acts on good to firm and dead ground: visored once earlier in career. *J. Norton*

CARELAMAN　2 b.c. (Feb 16) Ela-Mana-Mou 132 – Caro's Niece (USA) 86 (Caro 　**78**
133) [1992 7.1g² 7m³ 7g* 8.2g⁵] smallish colt: first foal: dam lightly-raced 1m winner from very good family: fair performer: won maiden at Wolverhampton in September, staying on well: sweated up, went very freely to post then pulled hard when running moderately in Nottingham minor event following month: should be better suited by 1m than 7f. *J. L. Dunlop*

CARELESS SON 2 b.c. (Apr 17) Salse (USA) 128 – Careless Whisper 94 **47**
(Homing 130) [1992 6f 7g⁴ 7d 8f] small, strong, lengthy colt: first foal: dam sprinting
daughter of sister to Dominion: plating-class maiden: stays 7f: visored (well below
best) final start: sold 420 gns Doncaster September Sales. *Miss S. E. Hall*

CARIBOO GOLD (USA) 3 b.c. Slew O' Gold (USA) – Selket's Treasure (USA) **77**
(Gleaming (USA)) [1991 NR 1992 10.5d² 10.4d³ 12m³ 15.1d²] $175,000Y: lengthy,
angular colt: eighth reported foal: half-brother to several winners, including Irish
middle-distance stayer Husaam (by Run The Gantlet): dam unraced: fair maiden:
suited by test of stamina: acts on good to firm and dead ground: has joined K. Bailey.
J. H. M. Gosden

CARLINGFORD (USA) 6 ch.h. Irish Castle (USA) – Delta Sal (USA) (Delta **64**
Judge) [1991 8g 8.2m⁴ 12m 10.3m 8m⁴ 10.5d⁵ 13.8m³ 13.6d³ 15.1s⁴ a12g 1992 a14g²
a13g² a12g³ a16g* 18g 12g³ 14.1d⁴ 16.2d⁶ 12m 12h* 12.1m* 12.1m* 11.1m* 12.2g⁴
12.1g⁴ 12.3g⁶] rangy horse: has round action: modest handicapper: trained until
after third start by H. Whiting: won at Lingfield in March: in tremendous form to run
up 4-timer in handicaps at Carlisle (amateurs), Hamilton and Edinburgh (2) in
midsummer: effective from 11f to 2m: has form on dead going and fibresand, but
goes very well on top-of-the-ground and equitrack: races up with pace. *M. P.
Naughton*

CARLOWITZ (USA) 4 b.g. Danzig (USA) – Aunt Carol (USA) (Big Spruce –
(USA)) [1991 8m 8d 1992 a12g a12g² a10g² a12g⁶ a10g⁵ 11.9m 9.7s 12v 9.7v a10g² a48
a12g⁵ a10g*] big ex-French gelding: half-brother to 3 winners in North America,
notably Grade 1 1¼m winner Nostalgia's Star (by Nostalgia): behind in minor
company for A. Fabre in 1991: poor form here: won maiden claimer at Lingfield in
December, making all: stays 1¼m: acts on equitrack: ran creditably in a visor. *A.
Moore*

CARNBREA SNIP 2 b.f. (Mar 18) Robellino (USA) 127 – Morica 88 (Moorestyle **77**
137) [1992 a6g⁵ 5d* 6g⁶ a5s⁶ 5g* 5m 5d* 5d4] 2,400Y: leggy filly: moderate mover:

Daniel Wildenstein's "Cardoun"

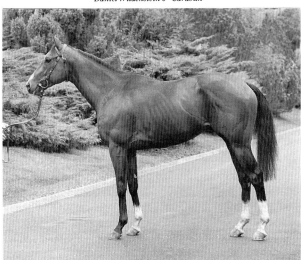

153

second foal: dam 2-y-o 6f winner, stayed 1¼m, is half-sister to Aragon out of half-sister to Song: fair performer: made all or most when successful in maiden at Warwick and nurseries at Windsor and Ayr: seems best at 5f: best form on good and dead ground. *M. Bell*

CARNEA   2 b.f. (Mar 15) Belfort (FR) 89 – Touch of Luck (FR) 69 (Tap On Wood   **32** 130) [1992 a7g³ a7s² a7g⁶ 8.2d 8.3s⁶] leggy filly: first reported foal: dam, maiden on flat stayed 1¾m, won over hurdles: poor plater: stays 1m: acts on dead ground, and on fibresand: has sweated and got on edge. *J. G. FitzGerald*

CARNFIELD   4 ch.f. Anfield 117 – Easterly Wind 94 (Windjammer (USA)) [1991   – 10.6g 5f 1992 a7g a8g⁴ a7g a7g a7g a6g³ a5g⁴ 5s 5.1d] lengthy, rather angular filly: a42 moderate mover: poor handicapper: effective at 5f to 1m: acts on fibresand: visored last 4 starts, last of them in April. *J. A. Glover*

CAROLES CLOWN   6 gr.m. Another Realm 118 – Show Business 72 (Auction   **47** § Ring (USA) 123) [1991 16.4m a16g⁶ 15.4f³ 16m² 16m² 18.1m⁴ a16g a16g⁵ 1992 a16g⁴   a– § 14.1g⁶ 16.5m³ 14.1m* 15.4h³ 18.2g⁴ 16.5g⁴ a16g⁵] leggy, lightly-made mare: has a round action: plating-class handicapper: successful at Nottingham (apprentices) in June: effective from 1¾m to 2¼m: acts on firm ground: tried visored earlier in career: often finds little off bridle and is a difficult ride. *M. J. Haynes*

CAROLES EXPRESS   4 ch.f. Scottish Reel 123 – Peregrine Falcon (Saulingo   **76** 122) [1991 7g³ 7.6d⁴ 7g² 7m* 7s* 7m 7g⁵ 7.1m² 7.6m⁴ 8d² 6m 7m³ 1992 7d 7m 7g 7m⁴ 7d⁶ 7.1g 7m 7.6d* 7.6g⁴ 7d] big, lengthy filly: moderate mover: fair handi-capper on her day: well backed and bounced back to form when winning at Lingfield in September: best at 7f/1m: acts on good to firm and soft ground: sometimes a front runner. *R. Akehurst*

CAROL'S PET (IRE)   4 b.f. Sadler's Wells (USA) 132 – Very Bissy (BRZ)   **49** d (Harken (URU)) [1991 8m³ 10.5g 1992 a10g⁴ 12.1m² 13f³ 13.1d² 11.8g⁶ 12.1g 12.1d 12.1s] leggy filly: poor walker: trained on reappearance by J. Banks: showed modest form early in season but looked an arrant rogue on her last 3 starts and is best left alone. *M. Johnston*

CAROMANDOO (IRE)   4 b.g. Simply Great (FR) 122 – Tanimara (Sassafras   – (FR) 135) [1991 a10g* a10g⁴ 10g² 12.3d 12g 10g* 10g 10m 10m 1992 10.5m 8s] big, angular, unfurnished gelding: rated 75 at 3 yrs for M. Bell: winning hurdler in 1991/2 season for B. Murray: no form on flat at 4 yrs. *A. Barrow*

CAROMISH (USA)   5 br.m. Lyphard's Wish (FR) 124 – Carom (USA) (Caro 133)   **75** d [1991 6d⁶ 6m³ 6m 6v 6g⁶ 7m 7f² 7f 7.6m 7m 7g 7d³ 6.1d 1992 6f* 6g⁵ 6m 6f³ 6m 8g⁵ 7f³ 6f 6.9m 7g] tall, rather leggy mare: first run since being tested in foal to Aragon, very easily made all in handicap at Brighton in late-May: failed by long way to reproduce that form: stays 7f: probably acts on any going. *M. D. I. Usher*

CAROUSELLA   4 b.f. Rousillon (USA) 133 – Salchow 116 (Niniski (USA) 125)   – [1991 a8g a8g⁴ 8m 8.1m* 8d 7g 6.9s 1992 a7g a12g 12g] rather leggy, close-coupled filly: has a quick action: no worthwhile form in 1992, last seen out in March. *C. E. Brittain*

CAROUSEL MUSIC   5 b.m. On Your Mark 125 – Diana's Choice (Tudor Music   **56** 131) [1991 a13g a13g³ 9g 12m⁵ 1992 11.1m⁴ 12f⁵ 11.6g* 12.3g 11.9d a12g a16g] leggy mare: modest handicapper: game winner of Windsor seller (no bid) in August: failed to confirm that form: stays 1½m: acts on firm and dead going. *J. Akehurst*

CARPENTIER (USA)   3 b.g. Fit To Fight (USA) – Mademoiselle Molly (USA) (Nashua) [1991 NR 1992 9m] $40,000Y: eleventh reported foal: half-brother to numerous winners: dam, half-sister to very useful 1974 2-y-o Highest Trump, won over 6f at 4 yrs: always behind in maiden at Lingfield in June. *M. J. Haynes*

CARPET SLIPPERS   6 br.m. Daring March 116 – Mollified 67 (Lombard (GER)   – 126) [1991 12g⁴ 11.5m³ 10d 10g⁴ 10g 10g² 10f 11.4m 10g 10m a12g⁵ a10g⁶ a12g* a13g⁴ 1992 a12g⁴] leggy, lengthy mare: rated 56 at 5 yrs: well below that form at Lingfield in January: twice below form when blinkered at 5 yrs. *J. D. Bethell*

CARRANITA (IRE)   2 b.f. (May 1) Anita's Prince 126 – Take More (GER)   **84** (Frontal 122) [1992 5g* 5g* 5f 6g* 6g⁶ 7g⁴ 7d⁶ 6s⁴ 6v] 1,300F, 850Y: leggy filly: has a markedly round action: sister to Irish 6f winner Take More Chances and half-sister to 4 winners (in Ireland and Germany): dam won 6 races in Germany: fairly useful performer: successful in maiden at Leicester and median auction event at Salisbury in spring despite having given trouble at stalls, then a minor event at Windsor in July: good fourth in listed race at Ayr penultimate start: stays 7f: may well be suited by some give in the ground, and acts on soft. *B. Palling*

CARRANTUOHILL (IRE)   3 b.f. The Noble Player (USA) 126 – Translation   –
(Fordham (USA) 117) [1991 7.1m 8m 1992 10f 10g 8g] unfurnished filly: moderate
mover: probably not of much account: blinkered last time: sold 1,100 gns Newmarket September Sales. *S. P. C. Woods*

CARROLLS MARC (IRE)   4 b.g. Horage 124 – Rare Find (Rarity 129) [1991   **61**
a8g² a8g³ 1992 a8g a8g⁵ 10.3g 12g³ 13.8m² 13.8d² 14.6g⁵ 14.1h³ 14.1g³ 12m³ 14.1g³
14.6d* 12.2g* 14.6s⁴ 13.8d² 12v 10.3g] angular gelding: poor mover: modest
handicapper: successful at Wolverhampton (seller, no bid) and Catterick (ladies) in
September: effective at 1½m and will stay 2m: acts on good to firm and dead ground
and on all-weather surfaces: suitable mount for lady rider: sometimes bandaged
behind. *P. J. Feilden*

CARTEL   5 b.g. Kris 135 – Meis El-Reem 124 (Auction Ring (USA) 123) [1991 8d   **56** d
8g 8.2f* 7m 8.2m 7m 8.2m* 8m a8g a7g 1992 8g 8g 8.2m⁴ 8m 8.2d³ 8g 8.2m a7g]
close-coupled gelding: moderate mover: inconsistent handicapper: form in 1992
only when in frame: stays 1m: acts on firm and dead ground: sold 1,450 gns
Doncaster November Sales *J. L. Harris*

CASE FOR THE CROWN (USA)   5 b.m. Bates Motel (USA) – Crown The   –
Queen (USA) (Swaps) [1991 NR 1992 12g 8m] big, angular mare: rated 70 as 3-y-o:
no form in 1992: backed down to favouritism when bandaged on first run for 4
months in handicap at Yarmouth, but never able to reach a challenging position. *B. J.
Curley*

CASE LAW   5 ch.h. Ahonoora 122 – Travesty 63 (Reliance II 137) [1991 6m* 6m   **107**
5g* 1992 6m²] strong, good-bodied horse: usually looks well: poor mover: very
useful performer: off course 9 months having reportedly had sinus operation, but
looking in magnificent shape, short-head second of 8 to Fylde Flyer in Abernant
Stakes at Newmarket in April, just losing out in last-furlong duel: stays 6f: acts on
good to firm ground: splendidly tough and genuine: fractured near-hind cannon bone
(did not require surgery) and wasn't seen out again. *Sir Mark Prescott*

CASHABLE   2 b.c. (Mar 19) Dunbeath (USA) 127 – Middleham Jewel (Swing   **60**
Easy (USA) 126) [1992 5g 6m 6m⁴ 7m⁵ 7f⁵ 7m 7g 6s a6g] 14,000Y: lengthy,
unfurnished colt: first foal: dam twice-raced half-sister to Bold Arrangement:
modest maiden: stays 7f: probably acts on any turf going, ran moderately on
fibresand: effective blinkered or not: trained until after penultimate start by J.
Jenkins. *D. T. Thom*

CASH A MILLION (FR)   4 ch.g. Crofter (USA) 124 – Zertxuna (Averof 123)   **46**
[1991 6m* 7g a7g 1992 5d 6s 6g³ 8m 7.1m 6g 6.1g³ 7g] lengthy, good-quartered
gelding: inconsistent handicapper: stayed 6f: acted on good to firm ground: tried in
near-side pricker and in blinkers: dead. *P. D. Cundell*

CASHELL   2 b.f. (Mar 5) Lomond (USA) 128 – Celtic Assembly (USA) 95   **84**
(Secretariat (USA)) [1992 7f³ 8.2d⁴ 7s³ 8d 7.6s²] sturdy filly: fifth foal: half-sister to
3-y-o Congress (by Dancing Brave), 1m winner at 2 yrs, and 2 other winners,
including (at 6f and 7f) Volksraad (by Green Desert): dam 10.6f winner, is daughter
of Welsh Garden, top 2-y-o filly in Ireland in 1975: fairly useful maiden: well drawn
and put up much improved effort when running-on second in Lingfield nursery in
October: will be well suited by 1¼m+: acts well on soft ground. *M. R. Stoute*

CASHMIRIANA (IRE)   3 b.f. Dominion 123 – Kashmiri Snow 83 (Shirley   **58**
Heights 130) [1991 6s 5g⁴ 6g⁴ 1992 6m⁶ 7g 5g² 6m 6m² 5.1d] angular, useful-looking
filly: has no near eye: modest maiden: off course 8 weeks, well beaten in handicap
final start: stays 6f: has joined J. Bosley. *Miss H. C. Knight*

CASHTAL DAZZLER   5 b.g. Ballacashtal (CAN) – Miss Meg 68 (John Splendid   –
116) [1991 8v⁵ 8m⁶ 8d⁴ 8m² 7m³ 8m⁶ 8d* 8. 1g⁵ 8m⁶ 8d 1992 8.5g 7g 7.9s 8g a8g a8g]
leggy gelding: good walker: has a quick action: rated 75 at 4 yrs, when blinkers when
successful: no form in 1992. *N. Tinkler*

CASHTAL QUEEN   3 ch.f. Ballacashtal (CAN) – Casbah Girl 79 (Native Bazaar   –
122) [1991 5g⁴ 5m³ 6f⁴ 6g² 6f* a6g² a6g⁶ 5m 6m⁵ 1992 6d 5.1d 6f⁴ 6d 6m⁶ 7f] leggy,
sparely-made filly: won sellers at 2 yrs: has deteriorated considerably, not seen out
after July in 1992. *J. Berry*

CASIENNE (IRE)   4 ch.f. Doulab (USA) 115 – Borshch (Bonne Noel 115) [1991   –
10.2g 9m 10.2d⁵ 8g⁵ 8f⁴ 8.9g³ 8f³ 8g⁶ 1992 12d 14.6g³] sparely-made filly:
moderate mover: still a maiden, but not seen out after July: stays 9f: acts on firm
ground: tried blinkered at 2 and 3 yrs. *R. J. Holder*

CASILLA   4 b.f. Liboi (USA) 76 – Sdenka (FR) (Habitat 134) [1991 10.2f⁴ 12m   –
10.2m 12g 1992 11.8m 8.2m 8m 10m⁶ 12.3d a10g⁶] small filly: moderate mover: still a
maiden: stays 1m: acts on good to firm ground. *H. Candy*

Federation Brewery L.C.L. Pils Lager Beeswing Stakes, Newcastle—
blinkers do the trick with Casteddu

CASNIKTONY 3 b.g. Ilium 121 – Scottish Belle 78 (Scottish Rifle 127) [1991 7.1s   –
7m 1992 10g 11.9f] close-coupled gelding: soundly beaten: blinkered final start. *A. Moore*

CASPIAN BELUGA 4 b. or br.g. Persian Bold 123 – Miss Thames 105 (Tower   **69**
Walk 130) [1991 8g 10.2g a12g 1992 a12g² a12g* a12g² 12g5 11.8d4 14m6 12m3 12d*
12f2 12g* 11.9m6 12m4 10.3s a12g² a13g3] strong, close-coupled gelding: has a round
action: tremendously consistent handicapper: successful at Lingfield in March and
twice at Salisbury in the summer: seems ideally suited by 1½m: acts on firm and
dead ground and equitrack: game front runner. *Mrs A. Knight*

CASPIAN TERN (USA) 3 ch.f. Arctic Tern (USA) 126 – Lady Winborne (USA)   **89** p
(Secretariat (USA)) [1991 NR 1992 10.2d* 10d*] $210,000F: rangy filly: sister to 2
winners, including 1987 French 2-y-o 1m winner Baranof, closely related to a
winner by Little Current and half-sister to 2 winners by Believe It, notably Al
Mamoon, useful sprinter here later very smart at around 1m in USA: dam, half-sister
to Allez France, won over 9f in Ireland from 2 starts: won maiden at Bath and minor
event at Leicester in the autumn: will improve again, particularly at 1½m. *H. Candy*

CASTEDDU 3 b.c. Efisio 120 – Bias 108 (Royal Prerogative 119) [1991 5g4 6g2 **111**
6g3 7m* 7d* 6g* 1992 8m3 8m6 7f3 7.6m3 7m* 7m6 7d 8g] smallish, sturdy colt:
has a round action: smart performer: blinkered first time, best effort to win
Beeswing Stakes at Newcastle in July in very good style by 5 lengths from Sure
Sharp, quickening on over 1f out: ran poorly afterwards, blinkered first 2 occasions:
stays 1m: acts on firm and dead ground: often gets on toes: not one to trust
implicitly. *J. W. Payne*

CASTEL ROSSELO 2 br.c. (Feb 22) Rousillon (USA) 133 – On The House (FR)   **73** p
125 (Be My Guest (USA) 126) [1992 6d2] sixth foal: half-brother to 3-y-o 1½m and
13.8f winner Upper House (by Shirley Heights) and quite useful 7f winner Domus
(by Kalaglow): dam, from excellent family, won 1000 Guineas and Sussex Stakes:
10/1, 5 lengths second of 12 to Half Term in maiden at Yarmouth in October, slowly
away, leading 2f out, then putting head in air and swerving right over 1f out before
keeping on to finish clear of remainder: will improve if temperament doesn't get the
better of him. *G. Wragg*

CASTILIAN QUEEN (USA) 3 ch.f. Diesis 133 – Royal Heroine 121 (Lypheor   **82** ?
118) [1991 6g* 6m6 1992 8m 7g4 6m 7m 6g 6g5] sturdy filly: fair form: easily best
effort when staying-on fourth in £11,600 handicap at Newmarket in July: got poor
run next start but disappointing afterwards: bred to stay at least 1m, but should
prove effective at 6f. *J. H. M. Gosden*

CASTILLET 3 b.c. Rousillon (USA) 133 – Strident Note 89 (The Minstrel (CAN)   **71**
135) [1991 7g 7m2 10m* 10g 1992 14g 12d 11.7d 10s 10d2 11.5d3] leggy colt: fair
handicapper: had very stiff tasks until running well placed at Redcar and (after very
slow start, travelled strongly long way) Yarmouth in the autumn: stays 11.5f: never
going well and carried head awkwardly on very soft ground: takes keen hold. *G. Harwood*

CASTING SHADOWS 3 gr.f. Chief Singer 131 – Six Ashes (Bruni 132) [1991   **44**
NR 1992 5g5 8.2m4 7m6 8m 5g4 6.1s4 5.1g 6.1s] compact filly: third foal: half-sister
to Misty Glow (by Kalaglow), plating-class middle-distance maiden later successful
over hurdles: dam unraced: plating-class maiden: ideally needs further than 5f, and
stays 1m: acts on soft ground: no improvement in blinkers. *R. Dickin*

CASTLEACRE 6 ch.g. Mr Fluorocarbon 126 – Misfired 101 (Blast 125) [1991 8m – 10.3d 1992 a10g 12.3m 12.3s] small, sparely-made gelding: of little account. *C. A. Smith*

CASTLE CARY 6 gr.m. Castle Keep 121 – Tibouchina 75 (Runnymede 123) – [1991 a5g 6v 5g 10m 5m* a5g 5m² 5f⁴ 5g 5.1s a6g 1992 6v 7.1g 7m 8.3s 5f 5m] workmanlike mare: carries condition: has a quick action: no longer of much account: sold 920 gns Doncaster September Sales. *T. Craig*

CASTLE CLOWN 7 ch.g. Castle Keep 121 – Peteona 97 (Welsh Saint 126) [1991 – 12m⁵ 10d⁵ 10m 9s 12s 11.4m² 1992 11.4g 12d] tall, lengthy gelding: rated 73 at 6 yrs: not fully wound up in handicaps in the autumn at 7 yrs: stays 11.5f: acts on good to firm and soft going: best visored: has run well for amateur. *Lady Herries*

CASTLE COURAGEOUS 5 b.g. Castle Keep 121 – Peteona 97 (Welsh Saint 93 126) [1991 12g⁶ 11d³ 13.3d* 14.8d* 14g⁴ 13.9g 14g 12d⁶ 1992 14g³ 16g³ 14g* 14g⁵ 14g³ 12m 13.9m 14.6f⁵] leggy, angular gelding: good walker: fairly useful handicapper: successful at Newmarket in May: better at 1¾m and 2m than shorter: has form on top-of-the-ground, but best efforts with some give: won novice hurdles in November. *Lady Herries*

CASTLE GALAH 5 b.m. Castle Keep 121 – My Pink Parrot (Pirate King 129) – [1991 10g 1992 10d⁶ 8m 6f] tall, leggy mare: seems of little account. *S. Woodman*

CASTLE MAID 5 b.m. Castle Keep 121 – Village Lass (No Mercy 126) [1991 5g³ 35 5g⁴ 6g 6g⁶ 5m³ 1992 7.1f⁶ 5m⁵ 5.1m⁶ 5m 5g 5.7d] rangy, workmanlike mare: poor sprint maiden: acts on good to firm ground. *R. J. Hodges*

CASTLEREA LAD 3 b.c. Efisio 120 – Halo 51 (Godswalk (USA) 130) [1991 5d² 76 5d⁴ 5m³ 6g* 6f³ 6m³ 1992 6s 5.1g⁵ 6m* 8.1d 7.6m⁵ 6g 6f⁴ 6m* 5m 6f⁴ 6d 7g] good-topped colt: fair handicapper: won at Haydock in May and (claimer) August: needs further than 5f, and ran creditably over 7.6f at Chester: easily best form at 3 yrs on top-of-the-ground. *R. Hollinshead*

CASTLE SECRET 6 b.g. Castle Keep 121 – Baffle 87 (Petingo 135) [1991 17.6m² – 22.2m⁵ 1992 18g⁵] quite attractive gelding: moderate mover: rated 83 at 5 yrs: off course 9 months, fifth of 18 at Doncaster in March: stays very well: possibly unsuited by soft going nowadays, acts on any other: has run well when blinkered, wore hood at Doncaster: useful winning hurdler in 1991/2, last seen out when very good second in valuable handicap at Haydock in May. *D. Burchell*

CASTORET 6 b.g. Jalmood (USA) 126 – Blaskette 99 (Blast 125) [1991 12g⁴ 10.4d 91 11.1g* 12g 11.5d 14g* 13.3m² 16.2d⁵ 16.5d⁶ a14g 1992 12g⁴ 14d⁵ 12d* 11.9g⁴

Coral Autumn Cup, Newbury—
Castoret and the season's leading apprentice David Harrison
make a good partnership

12d³ 12m² 13.9m 12d³ 13.3g* 12s 11s² 12g³] lengthy gelding: moderate mover: tremendously consistent handicapper who progressed steadily from April to November: successful in Northern Dancer Handicap at Epsom in June and Autumn Cup at Newbury in September, latter by 3 lengths from Welsh Mill: effective from 11f to 1¾m: acts on good to firm and soft going: usually ridden by D. Harrison: effective held up or ridden from front: tough and genuine. *J. W. Hills*

CATALANI 7 ch.m. Music Boy 124 – Two Stroke (Malicious) [1991 a7g a5g⁶ a6g⁵ **51** 1992 a6g 5f* 5.1m³ 5m² 5m³ 5m 5f³ 6f³ 5.1f⁶ 5d 5.1g a6g] workmanlike, angular mare: consistent handicapper: won at Lingfield in May: off course 2 months and well below form last 2 starts: effective at 5f and 6f: acts on firm ground, probably not at her best on heavy going: sometimes bandaged: tough. *T. J. Naughton*

CATEL RING (IRE) 3 b.c. Auction Ring (USA) 123 – Dame Kelly (Pitskelly – 122) [1991 7m 8m 8m 1992 10g a12g⁶ 8.3m] workmanlike colt: plater: well beaten all starts: 5/2 favourite from 14/1, front rank 7f at Leicester on reappearance: not at all knocked about next outing (maiden), slipped on home turn final one (June): should stay at least 1m: bandaged behind. *I. Campbell*

CATHERINEOFARAGON 2 ch.f. (Mar 6) Aragon 118 – Edna 92 (Shiny Tenth **88** ? 120) [1992 5f³ 6g³ 7m 6d² 6s* 7g⁶ 6s] rangy filly: sixth foal: half-sister to 3-y-o Andes (by Heights of Gold), 6f and 7f winner Segovian (by King of Spain) and a winner in Italy: dam soft-ground sprinter: fairly useful performer on her day: easily best effort when running away with £7,600 event at Salisbury in September by 10 lengths: should stay beyond 6f: very well suited by soft ground. *W. G. R. Wightman*

CATHERINES WELL 9 ch.m. Junius (USA) 124 – Restless Lady (Sandford **77** Lad 133) [1991 6d 6m 6m 5m⁵ 5.9m⁶ 5f⁴ 5f* 6f³ 5.1m 5f⁴ 6f* 5m⁶ 6m 6m⁵ 5g⁴ 5s 1992 5m³ 6f 5f* 6g⁵ 5f⁵ 5g³ 5g* 5f² 5.1m³ 5d⁶ 5m* 5m³] lengthy mare: went to stud in 1987 and had 3 foals, including Occhiobello (by Sadler's Wells) a winner 3 times in Italy in 1992: successful twice at Doncaster (including an apprentice event) and at Catterick: effective at 5f and 6f: probably acts on any going: has been bandaged: genuine. *M. W. Easterby*

CATHOS (FR) 7 b.g. Bellman (FR) 123 – Charming Doll (Don (ITY) 123) [1991 **58** a14g³ a13g⁴ 12m 14m 10.6g 12.3d 12d⁶ 12m 12f* 10m 16.2f² 14f 11.4m 10m 12.2m² 10.5g 12g 9.7f 10.3d 1992 12m 12.3f* 12f² 11.4s³ 10d 14d 10f⁵ 11.5m⁵ 12m² 10g 12d a12g* 12s 12v²] leggy gelding: has a rather round action: none too consistent handicapper: won at Ripon (ladies) in June and Southwell in September: best from around 1½m to 2m nowadays: acts on any turf ground and on fibresand: tried blinkered earlier in career: often starts slowly: has refused to race over hurdles. *D. A. Wilson*

CATRAIL (USA) 2 b.c. (Jan 16) Storm Cat (USA) – Tough As Nails (USA) **96** P (Majestic Light (USA)) [1992 7g*] $30,000Y, resold $250,000Y: second foal: dam unraced: sire (by Storm Bird) high-class 2-y-o: 4/1, won 9-runner mixed-aged event at Newmarket in October in good style, always travelling well and coming clear from over 1f out to win by 3½ lengths from Waterford Creek: will stay 1m: very much one to follow. *J. H. M. Gosden*

CATUNDRA (IRE) 4 ch.f. Far North (CAN) 120 – 'tis A Kitten (USA) (Tisab – (USA)) [1991 9d 8m 7m² 6.9m 7d 1992 a7g⁵ a8g⁶ a12g] leggy, angular filly: no form in handicaps in January: should stay beyond 7f. *Mrs A. Knight*

CAUSLEY 7 br.g. Swing Easy (USA) 126 – Four Lawns 77 (Forlorn River 124) **81** [1991 7.5g* 7.5f 8m² 7f⁶ 8.9m 8m⁵ 7.9m⁶ 8g³ 7.5f⁶ 8.3m³ 8f² 8.5f⁶ 8g 7.9m³ 7.6d⁴ 1992 8s² 8g 9d² 8h² 8.1g³ 8g* 7g² 8f³ 10.3g² 7.5m² 7.6v⁶ 7g³] good-topped, workmanlike gelding: has a round action: consistent handicapper: successful at Pontefract in July: best from 7f to 1m: acts on any going, except seemingly heavy: good mount for inexperienced rider: mulish behaviour at stalls does not affect performance: very tough and genuine front runner. *B. A. McMahon*

CAVALIER PRINCE (IRE) 2 b.c. (May 26) Prince Rupert (FR) 121 – Peace – Princess (On Your Mark 125) [1992 7s 7g] IR 8,000F, IR 6,000Y: second living foal: dam Irish middle-distance winner: claimer ridden, well beaten in maidens at Warwick and Doncaster in the autumn. *A. P. Jarvis*

CAVEAT VENDOR 4 b.g. Auction Ring (USA) 123 – Star Court 102 (Aureole – 132) [1991 8.3f⁶ 8m 12.1f⁶ 8m 1992 7.5m] workmanlike gelding: of little account: tried blinkered. *P. C. Haslam*

CAVO GRECO (USA) 3 b.g. Riverman (USA) 131 – Cypria Sacra (USA) 103 **52** (Sharpen Up 127) [1991 8.1d 1992 8.1m 10g³ 11.6m 12m⁶] smallish, lengthy gelding: moderate mover: form only when third of 12 in claimer at Goodwood: better at 1¼m than shorter: sold to join J. Joseph 3,100 gns Newmarket July Sales. *P. F. I. Cole*

C D SHAREPLAN (USA) 2 b.c. (Mar 27) Lucky North (USA) 101 – Lady **57** Andromeda (USA) (Nordic Prince (USA)) [1992 5m 6m 8.1s⁵ 9g 7g] $2,500F, 6,400Y: workmanlike colt: third foal: half-brother to 2 minor winners in North America: dam minor winner at around 1m in USA: form only when fifth in maiden at Chepstow in August, front rank 6f and keeping on same pace: stays 1m: possibly suited by soft ground. *M. R. Channon*

CEATHARLACH 3 b.g. Sayf El Arab (USA) 127 – Kilttaley 74 (Tower Walk 130) **51** [1991 5d 6g 6.1g³ 1992 6.1d 7d 7g 5.7d 6g⁴ 6s*] leggy gelding: trained until after penultimate start by R. Holder: easily best effort when winning 18-runner apprentice selling handicap (no bid) at Leicester in October: will stay at least 7f: yet to race on top-of-the-ground: blinkered 3 times, including final start: sold 2,000 gns Doncaster November Sales. *P. G. Murphy*

CEDAR RUN 9 b.g. Billion (USA) 120 – Sapele 73 (Decoy Boy 129) [1991 NR **–** 1992 16d] lengthy gelding: first run on flat since 6-y-o when tailed off in celebrity race at Worcester in March: ungenuine hurdler/chaser nowadays. *R. F. Johnson Houghton*

CEE BEAT 3 ch.f. Bairn (USA) 126 – Sharp Venita 84 (Sharp Edge 123) [1991 NR **– §** 1992 7d 8f⁶] fifth foal: half-sister to 7f and 7.6f winner Sharpalto (by Noalto) and quite modest 6f and 7f winner Sharp Times (by Faraway Times): dam sprinter: visored, gave roguish displays in maidens, virtually refusing to race second start (June). *E. A. Wheeler*

CEE-EN-CEE 8 b.g. Junius (USA) 124 – Lady Red Rose 87 (Pitskelly 122) [1991 **72** 7m 6g⁶ 6g 6g 7m³ 7g⁴ 7g⁵ 8.3m 6m⁵ 5.7f* 7s 5.1g⁴ a7g⁶ a7g² a7g a6g⁴ 1992 a7g a6g⁵ 5.1d* 5.7m* 6m* 6g 5.7f² 7d 5.7g 5.1f⁴ 6g 5.7d⁵ 7d 5.1d] workmanlike gelding: has a round action: overall record is none too consistent, but seldom runs a moderate race at Bath: successful twice there in the spring, and also at Kempton: effective at 5f to 6f: acts on firm and dead ground: has won for apprentice: best in blinkers or visor though has won without. *M. McCourt*

CEE-JAY-AY 5 gr.g. Free State 125 – Raffinrula 75 (Raffingora 130) [1991 a7g 7g² **61** 7.6d⁵ 8m 7g⁵ 7m² 8.1m 7d⁶ 7m 8g² 7f⁴ 7.6m⁵ 7m⁶ 7.5f* 7g⁵ 7m⁴ 7.6d⁵ 12g⁴ 1992 a65 a8g³ 7.6g⁵ 8m a7g³ 8m⁶ 8.9d 7.5m³ 8g³ 7s* 7d⁵ 7.6v² 8.1d⁶ a8g] smallish, workmanlike gelding: none too consistent handicapper: successful at Warwick (apprentices) in October: effective at 7f and 1m: acts on any going, including fibre-sand: below form when blinkered once at 4 yrs: usually slowly away: as effective for lady rider/claimer. *J. Berry*

CELESTIAL KEY (USA) 2 br.c. (Apr 27) Star de Naskra (USA) – Casa Key **87 ?** (USA) (Cormorant (USA)) [1992 5f* 5s⁵ 6d⁴ 7v⁴ 7g] $15,000F, $25,000Y: close-coupled, workmanlike colt: third foal: half-brother to a minor stakes-placed winner by Bounding Basque: dam won at up to 9f: sire champion sprinter at 4 yrs, stayed 9f: fair performer: won 4-runner maiden at Pontefract in August: visored, creditable fourth in 7f minor event at Chester: well beaten in nursery final start: will stay 1m: acts on any going. *S. G. Norton*

CELESTINE 3 b.f. Skyliner 117 – Stellaris (Star Appeal 133) [1991 5f 5f 7m⁴ 7m **62** 5g* 5m⁴ 5d 1992 7g* 7.1d⁵ 6s* 7g] leggy, close-coupled filly: modest form: won handicaps at Catterick in August and Hamilton in September: better at 6f/7f than shorter: acts on good to firm and soft ground: tried blinkered (including when successful) and visored (ran poorly) at 2 yrs. *T. Fairhurst*

CELIA BRADY 4 b.f. Last Tycoon 131 – Lucayan Princess 111 (High Line 125) **59** [1991 8m* 8.1m 1992 8g 12f 10.2g² 10m⁴ 10g⁴ 8s⁵] leggy, sparely-made filly: largely consistent handicapper: well worth another try at 1½m: acts on good to firm and soft ground. *H. Candy*

CELLIST 3 ch.g. Music Boy 124 – Chevulgan (Cheval 117) [1991 NR 1992 7g 9s] **–** sturdy gelding: half-brother to 9-y-o 1m to 1½m winner Cheerful Times (by Faraway Times): dam, plating class on flat, won over hurdles and fences: no form in the spring. *R. Thompson*

CELLITO (IRE) 3 b.c. Flash of Steel 120 – Apocalypse (Auction Ring (USA) **54** 123) [1991 a8g a7g² a8g 1992 a7g a7g⁴ a6g a6g² a6g² a6g a6g a6g a6g a7g] sturdy colt: poor mover: modest performer: visored, won Lingfield claimer in March, despite edging left: below form afterwards: stays 7f: acts on all-weather surfaces: has worn a hood and usually blinkered/visored these days: ridden by claimer of late. *W. A. O'Gorman*

CELTIC BANJO 7 br.m. Celtic Cone 116 – Allende (Grand Roi 118) [1991 NR **–** 1992 10.2s] third foal: half-sister to a winning selling hurdler: dam won over hurdles: tailed off in apprentice event at Chepstow. *J. D. Roberts*

CELTIC CHERRY 2 br.f. (Apr 7) Green Ruby (USA) 104 – Celtic Bird 77 (Celtic – Cone 116) [1992 5g⁶ 5g⁶ 5d 5d] leggy, lengthy filly: has round action: first reported foal: dam sprinter: no worthwhile form, including in a seller. *J. Balding*

CENTRAL CITY 3 b.f. Midyan (USA) 124 – Miss Silca Key 102 (Welsh Saint **111** 126) [1991 5g* 5m* 5g3 1992 7.3d3 8g 6m⁶ 6m² 6g* 6f 6d² 6s⁶ 5m 6d* 6d] tall, leggy, lengthy filly: smart performer but rather inconsistent: won £7,500 event at Newmarket and listed race at Lingfield in May and Prix de Seine-et-Oise (best effort, by ½ length from Monde Bleu) at Maisons-Laffitte in September: head-strong, and best short of 7f: acts on good to firm and dead ground: blinkered (below form, edging right) ninth start: sold to race in USA. *R. Hannon*

CERTAIN LADY 3 ch.f. Absalom 128 – Bold Duchess 78 (Persian Bold 123) **59** [1991 5g 6g 5g3 5.2g* 5s⁴ 6f 5.2f 5m 6.1m² a6g3 a6g 1992 5v⁶ 7g* 6m 8g⁶ a7g⁵ **a47** 7d* 7.6m² 7f⁶ a7g 7m* 7f² 7g* 7d5 6.9g⁶ a7g] lengthy, workmanlike filly: has a round action: useful performer in plating/claiming company, though runs the odd moderate race: apprentice ridden, won claimer at Warwick in April and sellers (bought in 4,200 gns, no bid, then 4,000 gns) at Leicester (twice) and Brighton in the summer: best at around 7f: acts on good to firm and dead ground, and on all-weather surfaces: trained until after penultimate start by G. Blum. *R. T. Juckes*

CERTAIN WAY (IRE) 2 ch.c. (Feb 12) Sure Blade (USA) 130 – Ruffling Point **59** (Gorytus (USA) 132) [1992 7g 7g 7g 8d 8.3v⁶ a7g² a8g3 a7g⁵] IR 2,500Y: good-quartered colt: first foal: dam unraced half-sister to very smart 1983 middle-distance colt John French: modest maiden: stays 1m: acts on dead ground (possbily unsuited by heavy) and fibresand: visored nowadays. *C. Tinkler*

CEZANNE 3 b.c. Ajdal (USA) 130 – Reprocolor 114 (Jimmy Reppin 131) [1991 NR **83** 1992 10g⁴ 10m* 11.8s² 8.9m] tall, useful-looking colt: half-brother to several winners, including Irish Oaks winner Colorspin (by High Top) and very smart 6f to 1¼m winner Bella Colora (by Bellypha): dam won Lingfield Oaks Trial and Lancashire Oaks: fairly useful form: won maiden at Sandown in May: off course 2½ months but looking very well, well below form in £12,300 handicap at York in August: needs further than 9f, and stays 11.8f: acts on good to firm and soft ground. *M. R. Stoute*

CHADDLEWORTH (IRE) 2 b.c. (Apr 17) Ahonoora 122 – Perlita (FR) **81** (Baldric II 131) [1992 6m*] 92,000Y: rangy, attractive colt: half-brother to several winners in France, notably high-class Persepolis (by Kalamoun): dam, placed

Prix de Seine-et-Oise, Maisons-Laffitte—
American jockey Corey Black teams up with Central City (No. 10);
they win narrowly from Monde Bleu

at up to 1m in France, is out of Poule d'Essai des Pouliches winner Pola Bella: well-backed favourite, won 7-runner maiden at Newbury in June in good style, taking closer order on bridle 2f out and quickening smartly under hands and heels to lead inside last: injured himself shortly afterwards: looked a good prospect. *P. W. Chapple-Hyam*

CHAFF 5 b.g. Final Straw 127   Silky (USA) (Nijinsky (CAN) 138) [1991 a10g a7g 7f 7f 7g⁶ 7g 8.1g 9.7m 8m³ 9.7f 8m² 8m⁶ 1992 a8g 7f⁵ 8f⁶ 8g 8f 8m 7s 8m 8d⁴ a10g] smallish, angular gelding: shows a quick action: inconsistent maiden handicapper: should stay beyond 1m: acts on good to firm and dead ground: no improvement in blinkers/visor. *D. Morris*   —

CHAIN DANCE 2 b.f. (Feb 15) Shareef Dancer (USA) 135 – Historical Fact 78 (Reform 132) [1992 6g³ 6m* 7m 7g² 7.3s⁵] workmanlike, close-coupled filly: moderate mover: fourth foal: half-sister to 3-y-o Sea Crusader (by Formidable), 5f winner at 2 yrs: dam 1¼m winner: fairly useful performer: narrowly won minor event at Windsor in June: off course 3 months afterwards, but progressed well, finishing second in nursery at Ascot and fifth in listed race at Newbury in October: will be suited by 1¼m: probably acts on any going. *M. R. Stoute*   88

CHAIN SHOT 7 b.g. Pas de Seul 133 – Burnished (Formidable (USA) 125) [1991 a7g 1992 7.5g³ 7m⁶ 7f⁴ 7g³ 6g] sturdy, workmanlike gelding: moderate mover: plating-class handicapper: ran well when in frame: stays 7.5f well: acts on any going: has run well for claimer: effective blinkered or not, tried visored: winner of 2 handicap chases in September. *M. H. Easterby*   49

CHAJOTHELYTBRIGADE (IRE) 2 b.f. (Apr 19) Electric 126 – Rampage 93 (Busted 134) [1992 7m] smallish, lengthy filly: half-sister to 3-y-o On The Rampage (by Midyan) and several winners, including 1½m winner Rambo Castle (by Castle Keep) and French 11.7f winner Catalogue (by Auction Ring): dam, winner from 11f to 1¾m, is out of half-sister to 1000 Guineas winner Full Dress II: ridden by 7-lb claimer, well-beaten last of 7 in maiden at Newmarket in August: sold to join M. Avison 625 gns Ascot December Sales. *C. N. Allen*   —

CHALLENGER ROW (IRE) 2 b.g. (Apr 1) Colmore Row 111 – Tunguska 76 (Busted 134) [1992 6m 6m 6m 8g 8.3s 10.5d³] leggy, good-topped gelding: has a round action: seventh foal: half-brother to 3-y-o 1m winner Trooping (by Auction Ring): dam 1¼m winner stayed 1½m: modest maiden: put up best effort in selling nursery at Haydock 1m start: will stay 1½m: fair efforts on good to firm ground: wears bandages behind. *C. W. Thornton*   53

CHAMPAGNE BREAK 3 ch.g. Flying Tyke 90 – Horann (Horage 124) [1991 5g 5g 1992 8v] close-coupled gelding: well behind in sellers. *M. W. Ellerby*   —

CHAMPAGNE GRANDY 2 ch.f. (May 5) Vaigly Great 127 – Monstrosa 70 (Monsanto (FR) 121) [1992 5f 5d⁶] leggy, close-coupled, sparely-made filly: has a quick action: third foal: half-sister to 4-y-o Muddy Lane (by Ilium), 5f winner at 3 yrs: dam 2-y-o 5f winner stayed 1m: poor form in maidens in early summer: will probably stay 1m. *M. R. Channon*   41

CHAMPENOISE 4 b.f. Forzando 122 – Migoletty 59 (Oats 126) [1991 8g 10g⁴ 7.6s⁶ 8f² 8s² 8.3m⁵ 8g 8.1s 8.2m⁵ 9.2s 1992 a10g 9d⁵ 8g 9g 12.3f⁶ 10.2f 8m⁴ 8g* 8.3g² 8f⁴ 7.6m 8g⁶ 8g 8d] small, sturdy filly: inconsistent maiden handicapper: gained first win in seller (no bid) at Yarmouth in July: stays 9f: acts on any going: blinkered (ran moderately) once: sold 3,300 gns Newmarket Autumn Sales. *M. Bell*   51

CHANCE REPORT 4 b.f. Beldale Flutter (USA) 130 – Report 'em (USA) (Staff Writer (USA)) [1991 8m 7g⁴ 8.2d 7m* 8f 8.2m 8m⁴ 1992 7d⁶ 10.5s 8f² 8g⁴ 8f⁶ 8m 7d 8f 8g⁴ 9g² 8g 7s a8g⁴ a7g²] leggy, sparely-made filly: poor walker: moderate mover: poor handicapper: has won one of 27 starts: stays 1m: acts on firm ground, and on equitrack: sometimes bandaged: has run well when sweating. *F. H. Lee*   38

CHANCETOBEWILD (USA) 2 b. or br.c. (Mar 23) Wild Again (USA) – Austere (USA) (Never Bend (USA)) [1992 6d³ 6v* 7s³] $26,000F, $65,000Y: half-brother to numerous minor winners: dam minor winner at 3 yrs: sire won Breeders' Cup Classic: off course 3 months before winning minor event at Maisons-Laffitte in October by 1½ lengths from Ski Paradise: 2 lengths third to Kadounor in Criterium de Maisons-Laffitte month later: will stay at least 1m. *J. E. Hammond, France*   112

CHANCE TO DREAM 3 gr.f. Petong 126 – Silken Purse (Posse (USA) 130) [1991 5m² 5g 6d 5.7f³ 5.1g 6.9f⁶ 1992 5m 7s 6g⁴ 7f* 7g 8g³] leggy, sparely-made filly: has a quick action: modest form: won maiden at Brighton in August: below form in handicap and no chance in minor event afterwards: stayed 7f: acted on firm ground: to stud. *R. Hannon*   60

CHANDIGARH   4 br.g. High Top 131 – Lady Zi (Manado 130) [1991 6.1m⁴ 7.1g³   **57**
1992 10g 7.1s² 7d 7s] good-topped, attractive gelding: modest maiden handicapper:
looked one not to place too much faith in last time: should stay beyond 7f:
headstrong, and has worn net muzzle. *R. Lee*

CHANDNI (IRE)   3 b.f. Ahonoora 122 – Jardiniere (Nijinsky (CAN) 138) [1991   –
NR 1992 7m 6.9g 8d] leggy, unfurnished filly: moderate mover: second foal: dam
once-raced sister to Kings Lake: of no account: sold 3,800 gns Newmarket Autumn
Sales. *B. Hanbury*

CHANGE THE WILL   3 ch.f. Master Willie 129 – Fresh Thoughts 77 (Young   **60**
Generation 129) [1991 NR 1992 10g 8g⁵ 7m 8m⁶ 8f⁵ 8m³ 7g³] 4,300Y: lengthy,
angular filly: has round action: first foal: dam 7.6f winner from family of High Line
and Grey Desire: consistent form in varied company, including selling: would have
stayed 1¼m: acted on firm ground: dead. *M. D. I. Usher*

CHANTRY BARTLE   6 ch.g. Say Primula 107 – Sallametti (USA) (Giacometti   –
130) [1991 12f⁴ 1992 12m⁶] sparely-made gelding: very lightly raced since 4 yrs:
stays 2m: acts on firm ground: good mount for claimer: fair handicap hurdler,
successful in October. *C. W. Thornton*

CHANTRY BELLINI   3 ch.f. Efisio 120 – Lifestyle 80 (Jimmy Reppin 131) [1991   **46**
5m 1992 6m⁴ 7m⁶ 9f 12.2g⁴ 11g³ 14.6g⁶ 13.8f⁴ 10m⁴ 10d³ 8.9d] small filly: poor
performer: stays 1½m: acts on dead and good to firm ground, seemingly not on firm:
blinkered last 3 starts, running creditably first 2 occasions: probably needs strong
handling. *C. W. Thornton*

CHAPEL MERE   2 b.f. (Apr 21) Kala Shikari 125 – Callace 51 (Royal Palace 131)   –
[1992 5g] 920Y: workmanlike filly: first foal: dam, maiden, stayed 1m: tailed off in
seller at Wolverhampton in July. *D. McCain*

CHAPKA (IRE)   2 b.f. (May 13) Green Desert (USA) 127 – Cockade 104   **68** p
(Derring-Do 131) [1992 7g⁶] compact filly: half-sister to several winners, including
Old Vic (by Sadler's Wells) and smart middle-distance performers Green Lucia (by
Green Dancer) and Splash of Colour (by Rainbow Quest): dam, 1m winner, is sister
to High Top and Camden Town: 10/1 and green, over 5 lengths sixth of 24 to Fayfa in
maiden at Newmarket in October, steadied after plunging stalls, then keeping on
well not knocked about: will improve. *Major W. R. Hern*

CHAPLINS CLUB (USA)   12 ch.g. Parade of Stars (USA) – Nautical Rose   **52**
(USA) (Henrijan) [1991 16s 6d 6g 5.9m 6d* 5g 6g 5m² 6d³ 7m³ 6g² 5m 6m 6m 6m 6m
6s 1992 a7g a7g 6v 6d² 5.9d 6s 6g⁵ 7d*] small, strong gelding: tremendously tough
handicapper, who proved a great servant to connections over the years, winning 24
times: at his best in 1988 when winning 9 handicaps and rated 99: retired after
winning Redcar selling event in July, 1992: was effective from 5f to 7f: acted on good
to firm ground, but went particularly well on an easy surface: tended to hang and
was usually blinkered off side only: usually got behind. *D. W. Chapman*

CHARETTE (USA)   2 b.f. (Mar 6) Chief's Crown (USA) – Northern Sunset   **83** p
(Northfields (USA)) [1992 8d*] half-sister to several winners, 4 at least very smart,
notably St Jovite (by Pleasant Colony) and Prix du Jockey-Club fourth Norberto (by
Roberto): dam Irish 6f and 7f winner also successful over hurdles: odds on, won
6-runner maiden at Leopardstown in September by a head: sure to do better. *J. S.
Bolger, Ireland*

CHARIOTEER   3 b.g. Formidable (USA) 125 – Aunt Charlotte 85 (Charlottown   **53**
127) [1991 NR 1992 8s⁵ 7m⁶ 8m² 10.1f⁵ 12.3m a10g a14g a12g] good-topped gelding:
brother to fairly useful 1¼m to 1¾m winner Chiclet and half-brother to 2 other
winners: dam stayed very well: modest maiden: no form last 4 starts, blinkered final
one: will probably stay 1¼m. *P. C. Haslam*

CHARITY EXPRESS (IRE)   2 gr.f. (Jan 16) Treasure Kay 114 – Arminiya   **76**
(Roan Rocket 128) [1992 5g² 5g* 6f⁶ 6m⁵ 5g⁴ 5g* 5.1m³ 6g 5.2g 5d] lengthy filly:
half-sister to several winners here and abroad, including fair 1984 2-y-o 6f winner
Armorad (by Red Alert) and 1½m winner Arifa (by Wolver Hollow): dam French
10.5f winner: fair performer: successful in maiden at Catterick and nursery at
Wolverhampton in the summer: well below form (twice slowly away) in nurseries
and a listed race last 3 starts: should prove as effective at 6f as 5f: acts on good to
firm and dead ground (ran moderately on firm): inconsistent. *J. Berry*

CHARLIE BIGTIME   2 b.g. (Apr 6) Norwick (USA) 120 – Sea Aura 89 (Roi   **86**
Soleil 125) [1992 8m 10g⁶] 1,000Y: leggy gelding: seventh foal: half-brother to 3-y-o
Arrogant Daughter (by Aragon), 2-y-o 6f winners Caspian Grey (by Absalom) and
Koracle Bay (by Kind of Hush) and a winner in Norway by Song: dam probably best
at 7f: keeping-on sixth of 9 to Bob's Return in listed Zetland Stakes at Newmarket in

October, much better effort: appears likely to prove best at middle distances. *Miss Gay Kelleway*

CHARLIE LOVE 3 ch.c. Highlands – Friendly Wonder (Be Friendly 130) [1991 NR 1992 12.2m 7.1m⁶] second foal: dam poor maiden: no worthwhile form in early-summer. *W. Storey* —

CHARLIES REWARD 2 ch.c. (Jun 4) Rich Charlie 117 – Joint Reward (Netherkelly 112) [1992 6d 6f⁶ 6g² 7m 6m 7d] 1,050Y, 1,100 2-y-o: good-topped colt: third reported foal: dam showed some ability over jumps: modest plater: trained until after third start by W. Barker: should stay 7f: acts on firm ground: sold 900 gns Doncaster October Sales. *T. Fairhurst* **46**

CHARLO 4 br.c. Chief Singer 131 – Dance Card 69 (Be My Guest (USA) 126) [1991 8d⁶ 9m² 10g* 8.9m² 1992 10m* 10d² 10g 10g 12m⁶] strong, workmanlike colt: looked a smart prospect when winning £7,370 Ascot handicap and second to Fire Top in valuable Royal Hong Kong Jockey Club Trophy at Sandown in midsummer, but well below form in handicaps afterwards: should prove at least as effective at 1½m as 1¼m: acts on good to firm and dead going. *J. H. M. Gosden* **102**

CHARLY PHARLY (FR) 5 b.g. Pharly (FR) 130 – Burnished (Formidable (USA) 125) [1991 a7g* a7g 7.6g⁵ a7g⁶ a8g* 10.5m* 8m* 8.9g 10.3m⁵ 10m 10.5d 1992 a8g⁵ 10.5g 10.8g a7g⁵ 10s 10m] good-topped, workmanlike gelding: carries condition: no worthwhile form in 1992: effective from 7f to 10.6f: acts on good to firm and dead ground: usually blinkered, once visored: sold to join B. Llewellyn 2,000 gns Newmarket Autumn Sales. *F. H. Lee* —

CHARMED KNAVE 7 b.g. Enchantment 115 – Peerless Princess (Averof 123) [1991 8m³ 7.1m² 8.1d* 8.1g² 8.3m⁴ 7.6m 7m 8f⁴ 7f* 7m⁴ 7.6m* 8g⁴ 6.9f 1992 8m 7.1m² 8.1m⁴ 8f³ 7.1m² 8f 7g⁵ 7g 7.6g² 7g⁴ 7d 7s] lengthy gelding: poor mover: largely consistent handicapper: below form last 2 starts: effective at 7f to 1m: acts on firm and dead ground: blinkered earlier in career. *D. R. Laing* **58**

CHARMED LIFE 3 b.c. Legend of France (USA) 124 – Tanagrea (Blakeney 126) [1991 NR 1992 10.1g 10g³ 12.3g* 12s 10.2d a12g] sturdy, good-quartered colt: has a quick action: third foal: half-brother to 4-y-o Tanegrus (by Dunbeath): dam unraced sister to Irish Derby winner Tyrnavos and half-sister to several other high-class performers: modest performer: set plenty to do when winning claimer (claimed out of H. Cecil's stable £8,007) at Wolverhampton in September: well beaten afterwards: will stay beyond 1½m: often bandaged near-fore. *A. Barrow* **58**

CHARMING GIFT 5 b.m. Petorius 117 – Aubretia (USA) 84 (Hatchet Man (USA)) [1991 a8g² a8g⁶ 8m² 7m⁶ 8.5m 8m* 8m⁶ 10m² 10s² 8f⁵ 10s³ 10m⁴ 10.3g⁴ 10.1s 9.7s² 1992 a11g a10g a10g⁴ a10g⁴ a12g 8m* 8f³ 8m⁵ 8m*] leggy mare: moderate mover: modest handicapper: won Newmarket celebrity event in May and at Doncaster in June: effective from 1m to 1¼m: acts on any going: below best in blinkers: has run creditably for apprentice: sold to join A. Forte 1,050 gns Doncaster November Sales. *R. J. R. Williams* **57** **a40**

CHARMONIX 3 ch.f. Scottish Reel 123 – Sand Valley (FR) (Arabian) [1991 7g 7g 8s⁶ a8g 1992 a6g⁴ a8g 7v] tall, leggy filly: no form in spring: will stay middle distances: joined J. Joseph and won selling hurdle (no bid) in October. *G. Blum* —

CHAROLLES 3 b.f. Ajdal (USA) 130 – Chalon 125 (Habitat 134) [1991 6m³ 1992 8m 12.4m² 12g⁴ 8v² 12v] sturdy, quite attractive filly: fair form when second over 1m at Newcastle, almost certainly best effort as 3-y-o: stayed 1m: acted on good to firm and heavy ground: visits Slip Anchor. *H. R. A. Cecil* **71**

CHARRUA 2 b.f. (Apr 3) Sharpo 132 – Yldizlar 77 (Star Appeal 133) [1992 6g 6m⁵ 6.1g⁵] IR 11,500Y: smallish, sturdy filly: third foal: half-sister to 3-y-o 10.3f and 12.2f winner Yildiz (by Be My Guest): dam, twice-raced 2-y-o 7f winner, is half-sister to very useful duo Petrullo and Domynsky: progressive form in maiden auctions: will be better suited by 7f: may well improve further. *J. R. Fanshawe* **55 p**

CHART CROSS 6 b.g. Millfontaine 114 – Whichcombe 79 (Huntercombe 133) [1991 8m 9.9m* 12m⁶ 10m 8.3m 8.2m² 7m 10.8m 9.9f⁴ 1992 8.5m 10.8f⁴ 9.9f] rather leggy, angular gelding: inconsistent handicapper: best at up to 11f: acts on firm and dead going: has broken blood vessel: not seen out after June. *K. S. Bridgwater* **31 +**

CHASMARELLA 7 b.m. Yukon Eric (CAN) – Miss Polly Peck (March Past 124) [1991 14g 12g 1992 20m] smallish, lengthy mare: poor and lightly-raced plater: 200/1, tailed off in Goodwood Stakes: stays 1½m: probably acts on any going. *A. R. Davison* —

CHATEAU NORD 3 ch.g. Salmon Leap (USA) 131 – Touraine (FR) (Luthier 126) [1991 5m* 6f² 6m 6d² 5d* 5f⁶ 5m³ 5g 5d 1992 5s⁵ 5s 5m 5f 6m² 5h* 5m³ 5m⁴ 5m⁵ 5m 5m 5d] lengthy, rather leggy gelding: modest handicapper: won at Carlisle **54**

in June: ran moderately last 5 starts: stays 6f: acts on any going: sold 1,500 gns Doncaster October Sales. *J. Berry*

CHATHAM ISLAND   4 ch.g. Jupiter Island 126 – Floreal 68 (Formidable (USA)   **67** 125) [1991 a7g² 8g 8d 12g 10g² 10m⁵ 8f² 8m⁶ 10m* 10g* 10.4m² 10.3d⁶ 1992 10.3g 10g 8.9g 10f⁵ 10m* 10.1f* 10.1m³ 10g⁵ 10g⁵ 10.3m*] rangy gelding: impresses in appearance: good walker: fair handicapper: had a good season, winning at Lingfield, Yarmouth and, narrowly and in game fashion, Doncaster: should stay 1½m: goes really well on top-of-the-ground: races up with pace. *C. E. Brittain*

CHATINO   3 b.f. Dancing Brave (USA) 140 – Nophe (USA) 95 (Super Concorde   **61** (USA) 128) [1991 7m² 6.1d⁵ 1992 8v⁵ 7.6g⁶ 8.2g 7f² 8f⁵] quite attractive filly: poor walker: modest maiden: easily best efforts over 7f on top-of-the-ground: sold 5,600 gns Newmarket July Sales. *C. E. Brittain*

CHATOYANT   2 b.c. (Apr 29) Rainbow Quest (USA) 134 – Ouija 104 (Silly   **– p** Season 127) [1992 7g] tall, good-topped colt, though rather light of bone: half-brother to useful miler Message Pad (by Rousillon) and high-class 1m to 1¼m performer Teleprompter (by Welsh Pageant): dam best at 1m: looking really well though heavily bandaged and burly, around 17 lengths tenth of 14 in maiden at Doncaster in October, green at halfway and not knocked about: sort to do better. *J. W. Watts*

CHATTERBERRY   2 b.f. (Feb 4) Aragon 118 – Silver Berry (Lorenzaccio 130)   **67 ?** [1992 5f⁵ 5f* 5.2g⁶ 5.1s] strong, attractive filly: sister to good sprinter Argentum and half-sister to several winners, including fair miler Eurodollar (by Sparkler): dam poor half-sister to very smart 1¼m filly Cranberry Sauce: fair performer: well-backed co-favourite, made all in maiden at Salisbury in June despite looking very green: ran as if something amiss both starts afterwards: should stay at least 6f: needs to prove her well-being. *L. J. Holt*

CHATTERER (USA)   3 ch.c. Theatrical 128 – Chateaucreek (USA) (Chateau-   **80** gay) [1991 NR 1992 12f⁴ 16m*] $100,000Y: big, rather leggy colt: fluent mover: tenth reported foal: closely related to French 10.5f winner Raneen (by Nureyev) and half-brother to several winners, notably Henbit (by Hawaii) and quite useful middle-distance stayer Henbane (by Alydar): dam minor stakes winner at up to 6f: fairly useful form: won 5-runner maiden at Nottingham in August, easing down by 7 lengths: sold to join P. Bevan only 3,100 gns Newmarket Autumn Sales. *G. Harwood*

CHATWORTH GREY   2 gr.f. (Apr 10) Taufan (USA) 119 – Reef Point 68 (Main   **–** Reef 126) [1992 5s] compact filly: first living foal: dam, best at 2 yrs, is daughter of sister to Godswalk: always behind in maiden at Lingfield in April. *P. Howling*

CHEAP METAL   7 br.g. Sonnen Gold 121 – Economy Pep 69 (Jimmy Reppin 131)   **–** [1991 NR 1992 a14g⁶ 10s⁶] big, lengthy gelding: lightly raced and no sign of ability on flat: blinkered on reappearance: won over hurdles in September. *R. Ingram*

CHECKPOINT CHARLIE   7 b.g. Artaius (USA) 129 – Clouded Issue (Manado   **62** 130) [1991 12d 12f² 12f⁶ 12f³ 11.9m³ 12f* 14.1f⁴ 11.5f⁶ 1992 11.9m² 11m² 12f* 12f⁵ 11.9f 11f 10.1f 12f⁴ 14.1g a12g] useful-looking gelding: moderate mover: inconsistent handicapper: claimer ridden, won at Thirsk in May: stays 1½m: acts on firm ground. *J. M. P. Eustace*

CHEEKA   3 ch.g. Dawn Johnny (USA) – Lallax 109 (Laxton 105) [1991 NR 1992   **47** 8g⁵ 10f⁴] leggy, angular gelding: second live foal: dam 7f (at 2 yrs) and 1¼m winner: swerved leaving stalls before running-on fifth in claimer at Leicester: reluctant at stalls, led 6f then hampered and eased in 4-runner maiden at Pontefract later in summer: has joined C. Smith. *M. R. Leach*

CHEEKY CHAPLIN   6 b.g. Anfield 117 – Saroan Meed (Midsummer Night II   **–** 117) [1991 10v 10.8d 8f⁴ 6g 7m 8f 1992 7d] leggy gelding: probably of little account these days. *D. R. Gandolfo*

CHEEKY POT   4 b.g. Petoski 135 – Pato 90 (High Top 131) [1991 10d³ 12g⁴ 12.3d   **45** 10.5g⁶ 10.5d* 10.3d 11d⁵ 12.1s² 1992 12g 12.4s 10.5m 10.5d a12g³ 12.1m⁴ a12g² a12g 12.3m 10.1m² 9.2s 13.8g] compact gelding: poor mover: inconsistent handicapper: stays 1½m: acts on good to firm and soft going and fibresand: blinkered last 3 starts, usually visored: won novice handicap hurdle in December. *Denys Smith*

CHEERFUL TIMES   9 b.g. Faraway Times (USA) 123 – Chevulgan (Cheval   **47 +** 117) [1991 10d⁴ 1992 a11g⁴ a11g⁵ 10.3g] good-topped gelding: usually looks well: poor walker: plating-class handicapper nowadays: not seen out after March: stays 1½m: acts on any going: has worn a visor, but better without: often apprentice ridden: occasionally reluctant at stalls: usually finds little off bridle: fairly useful winning hurdler in 1991/2. *B. A. McMahon*

CHELTENHAM WINDOWS   2 ch.g. (Mar 28) Risk Me (FR) 127 – Trail of   –
Blues (Cure The Blues (USA)) [1992 5g 5m 5g] 400Y: angular, close-coupled
gelding: third foal: dam unraced: looks of little account. *M. W. Easterby*

CHEQUERS (IRE)   3 b. or br.g. Red Sunset 120 – Mallabee 92 (Pall Mall 132)   71 d
[1991 5m⁶ 6m² 7.5f4 7.3m⁴ 8g 7g³ 8.3s 1992 8m² a8s⁴ 8.1g* 8m⁴ 8g 8m 8d] lengthy,
workmanlike gelding: failed by long way to reproduce form of reappearance, but
won Haydock claimer in August: sold 4,500 gns Newmarket Autumn Sales: stays
1m: acts on good to firm ground, ran respectably on soft at 2 yrs: visored (well
beaten) fifth 3-y-o start. *R. J. R. Williams*

CHEREN BOY   3 ch.g. Swing Easy (USA) 126 – Shades of Autumn (Double Form   –
130) [1991 NR 1992 8.3g 8d 8g] leggy gelding: moderate mover: second foal: dam
poor maiden: no form in claimer and sellers, last seen out in July. *B. Forsey*

CHERHILL (IRE)   2 b.f. (Feb 11) Ahonoora 122 – Battine (USA) (Topsider   –
(USA)) [1992 6g³] 5,000F, 27,000Y: rather angular filly: first foal: dam, unraced,
from family of Nureyev and Sadler's Wells: favourite, over 6 lengths third of 6 in
maiden at Ayr in July, slowly away, unable to quicken and not knocked about: moved
moderately down: looked sure to improve. *P. W. Chapple-Hyam*

CHERRY BOB   3 ch.f. Adonijah 126 – Cherry Picking 85 (Queen's Hussar 124)   38
[1991 6m 6g 1992 7g 12g 10f 12.3d⁶] leggy, rather angular filly: poor plater, last seen
out in July: stays 1½m: acts on firm and dead ground: sold 700 gns Doncaster
October Sales. *C. W. Thornton*

CHERRY GROVE LAD (IRE)   4 br.c. Caerleon (USA) 132 – Bean Siamsa 112
(Solinus 130) [1991 7d² 8g² 9g³ 9g* 10m* 10m* 12g 12.3g4 10g² 10m⁴ 8d² 10g³ 10g5
12.3g² 1992 9d⁵ 10g* 10m* 9g* 10g 11d³] IR 39,000F, IR 90,000Y: fourth foal:
closely related to 1988 2-y-o 5f winner Gorytus Star (by Gorytus) and half-brother to
7f/1m handicapper Amber King (by Indian King): dam unraced from good family:
very useful Irish handicapper: won handicaps at the Curragh in May, Naas in June
and Leopardstown (quite valuable listed event) in July: good third in Group 3 event
at Milan: better at 1¼m than shorter and stays 1½m: yet to race on extremes of
going: wears blinkers these days: genuine and consistent. *D. K. Weld, Ireland*

CHERRYWOOD LASS   4 br.f. Belfort (FR) 89 – Rainbow Vision 73 (Prince   –
Tenderfoot (USA) 126) [1991 NR 1992 9.7s a7g a6g4 a6g5] smallish filly: no
worthwhile form. *R. Curtis*

CHERUBINI   2 b.c. (Apr 20) Chilibang 120 – Edwins' Princess 75 (Owen Dudley   53
121) [1992 5f5 6g³ 7g5 8g] 8,000Y: sturdy, quite attractive colt: third foal:
half-brother to 3-y-o Pageboy (by Tina's Pet), 6f winner at 2 years: dam disappointing
2-y-o 5f winner stayed 1m: plating-class maiden: stiff task ridden by 7-lb claimer in
Warwick nursery final outing, and wasn't entirely discredited: may well prove best
at up to 7f: sold 1,800 gns Newmarket September Sales. *J. R. Fanshawe*

CHESHIRE ANNIE (IRE)   3 br.f. Double Schwartz 128 – So Valiant 80 (So   54
Blessed 130) [1991 5g 5m 5g5 6f² 6g 6g 1992 7d 5v 5m 6g 5.3f* 5g6 5m 5m5 5g² 5f²
5.7d] leggy, lightly-made filly: modest handicapper: won at Brighton in May: best at
5f: acts on firm ground, seemingly not on a soft surface. *W. Carter*

CHESTER BELLE   3 b.f. Ballacashtal (CAN) – Cascabel 82 (Matahawk 127)   –
[1991 5f 6g6 5g 6f 5m 1992 8s 6m 6m 7.1m 5h 6g 6g] sturdy filly: of little account:
tried visored. *P. C. Haslam*

CHEVELEY DANCER (USA)   4 b.g. Northern Baby (CAN) 127 – Alwah   –
(USA) (Damascus (USA)) [1991 9g* 10.5s 9g4 8g3 8g3 1992 8m5 10g5 10m6 7f a10g
10s 6.9v] big, lengthy ex-French gelding: second foal: half-brother to quite modest
1¼m winner Banker Mason (by Sadler's Wells): dam unraced half-sister to 2
winning jumpers: won a maiden in French Provinces in 1991 when trained by J.
Hammond: sold out of R. Hannon's stable 8,200 gns Ascot February Sales, then
little form: stays 9f: visored final start: pulls hard. *A. W. Denson*

CHEVEUX MITCHELL   5 ch.h. Dunbeath (USA) 127 – Hide Out (Habitat 134)   77
[1991 7m 8g5 7m* 7.6m* 7f 7d* 7.6s5 7m 8m⁴ 7f 7g 7.6m 7.6m 1992 8d 7d 8g 7m3
7g* 7g6 7m 7g 7m* 8g 7m 8.3g 7d5 7.6d 7.6g] sturdy horse: inconsistent
handicapper but is game in true finish: successful at Lingfield (fourth win there)
in May and Brighton in July: seems ideally suited by around 7f: acts on firm and dead
ground: visored nowadays: retained 7,400 gns Newmarket Autumn Sales. *M. R.
Channon*

CHEVROTAIN   2 b.c. (Apr 21) Salse (USA) 128 – Mary Mary Mouse (USA)   82
(Valdez (USA)) [1992 5g2 7g** 7.9d² 8f²] 8,400Y: strong, good-quartered, good sort:
has plenty of scope: third foal: half-brother to 1½m winner Standing Room Only (by
Stalwart): dam unraced half-sister to dam of Contract Law, family of Law Society:

progressive form: heavily-backed favourite, won 16-runner maiden auction at Doncaster in July: runner-up in nurseries at York (beaten short head) and Doncaster, on both occasions running lazily when hitting the front: didn't respond well to visor, breaking loose from stall and withdrawn from Ascot nursery later in autumn: will probably stay 1¼m: acts on firm and dead ground. *J. W. Watts*

CHEW IT OVER (IRE)   4 b.g. Taufan (USA) 119 – Stop The Cavalry (Relko   **48** d
136) [1991 8f⁴ 7m 10g a8g 10g³ 10m² 10m 8m³ 9s 8.2m⁶ 8m 1992 10d 8d⁵ 8g 8.9g
10m⁴ 10g⁶ 12m³] sturdy gelding: has a round action: plating-class maiden: stays
1½m: acts on good to firm and dead ground. *C. A. Smith*

CHEZ POLLY   6 ch.m. Homing 130 – My Pink Parrot (Pirate King 129) [1991 NR   –
1992 10m⁵ 11.8m 8g⁴] tall, workmanlike mare: probably of little account: tried
blinkered and visored. *P. R. Hedger*

CHIAPPUCCI (IRE)   2 b.g. (Apr 11) Doulab (USA) 115 – Jenny's Child (Crash   **50**
Course 128) [1992 7m 8.1d⁴ 8d 8g] IR 5,200Y: good-bodied gelding: first reported
foal: dam Irish middle-distance winner: poor maiden: will stay 1¼m: acts on dead
ground. *M. A. Jarvis*

CHICAGO (IRE)   2 gr.c. (Apr 30) Standaan (FR) 118 – Ruling Pride (Bold Lad   **41**
(IRE) 133) [1992 5f⁶ 5m] IR 5,800Y: smallish colt: second foal: dam ran once in
Ireland: poor form in maiden auctions at Redcar in midsummer. *C. Tinkler*

CHICA MIA   8 b.m. Camden Town 125 – Backwoodsgirl (Young Emperor 133)   –
[1991 NR 1992 8.3m 7.5d] lengthy, workmanlike ex-Irish mare: has been tubed: of
little account these days. *G. A. Ham*

CHICARICA (USA)   4 b.f. The Minstrel (CAN) 135 – Little Lady Luck (USA)   **103**
(Jacinto) [1991 7.3g³ 6m² 6m⁵ 1992 6m⁵ 6g³ 6g] big, strong, attractive filly: useful
performer: off course 3 months after best run of year, when third of 5 to Street Rebel
in Group 3 event at the Curragh in May: best form at 6f: acted on good to firm and
dead ground: often sweating: visits Kris. *J. H. M. Gosden*

CHIEF MINISTER (IRE)   3 br.g. Rainbow Quest (USA) 134 – Riverlily (FR)   **88**
(Green Dancer (USA) 132) [1991 8d 1992 10m 12s* 11.7s⁴ 14m*] leggy gelding:
has a round action: fairly useful performer: won maiden at Salisbury in April:
subsequently split a pastern and off course 5 months: returned in fine shape and,
wearing blinkers, won handicap at Newmarket: stays 1¾m well: acts on good to firm
and soft ground: sold to join Mrs J. Ramsden 24,000 gns Newmarket Autumn Sales
and gelded. *L. M. Cumani*

CHIEF OF STAFF   3 ch.c. Caerleon (USA) 132 – Fanny's Cove 89 (Mill Reef   **83**
(USA) 141) [1991 7m⁴ 7.1m² 1992 10s² 12g 10f 8m* 10s²] leggy, unfurnished colt:
fairly useful performer: bounced back to form when winning apprentice claimer at
Warwick in July: off course 2½ months, good second in claimer at Salisbury: sold
12,500 gns Newmarket Autumn Sales: should stay 1½m: acts on good to firm
ground and soft. *P. F. I. Cole*

CHIEFS BABU   4 ch.g. Chief Singer 131 – Nullah 71 (Riverman (USA) 131) [1991   –
8d⁶ 6m 12d* 11m* 11.5m* 12g² 10m⁴ 10m 11.9g 1992 10.4m 12.3m 10m⁵]
good-topped gelding: poor mover: rated 81 as 3-y-o for B. Hanbury: no form in 1992.
R. O'Leary

CHIEF'S SONG   2 b.c. (Mar 13) Chief Singer 131 – Tizzy 79 (Formidable (USA)   **59** p
125) [1992 6s² 6g] 5,000F, 18,500Y: tall, useful-looking colt: has scope: fourth living
foal: half-brother to 3-y-o Dizzy Penny (by Pennine Walk) and fairly useful 1989
2-y-o 5f winner La Galerie (by Glenstal): dam 9f and 1¼m winner: similar form in
maidens at Lingfield and Newmarket in October, staying on well from 2 out: will
improve when stepped up to around 1m. *B. W. Hills*

CHILD OF THE MIST   6 b.g. Lomond (USA) 128 – Lighted Lamp (USA) (Sir   –
Gaylord) [1991 NR 1992 16d⁴] strong, lengthy gelding: moderate mover: first run on
flat since being a fairly useful 3-y-o for B. Hills, fourth in celebrity race at Worcester
in March: useful but irresolute hurdler in 1991/2: sold to join J. Whyte only 1,200 gns
Ascot June Sales. *O. Sherwood*

CHILD STAR (FR)   3 gr.f. Bellypha 130 – Miss Shirley (FR) 76 (Shirley Heights   **58**
130) [1991 a7g a7g⁶ 1992 a10g² a10g a10g⁶ 14.6g² 12.3d 14.6g* 12.3m a14g⁵
14.6g 16.1s* 16s* a16g⁴] angular, light-framed filly: has a round action: modest
handicapper: won at Wolverhampton in July then Warwick and Nottingham in
October: suited by a test of stamina: acts on soft going, below best on all-weather
surfaces. *D. Marks*

CHILI HEIGHTS   2 gr.c. (Mar 4) Chilibang 120 – Highest Tender 56 (Prince   **84**
Tenderfoot (USA) 126) [1992 5g⁵ 5d⁴ 5.7g* 6g⁶ 6m³ 6d⁶ 6s* 7g⁴] 3,000F, 4,100Y,

12,000 2-y-o: compact colt: fifth foal: half-brother to a winner in Hong Kong: dam plater: fairly useful performer: won maiden auction at Bath in July and nursery at Newbury (rallied gamely) in October: very good fourth in similar event at Doncaster following month: stays 7f: has form on good to firm, but seems well suited by plenty of give in the ground. *G. B. Balding*

CHILL WIND   3 gr.c. Siberian Express (USA) 125 – Springwell 73 (Miami   –
Springs 121) [1991 5g 5m6 5m 6m3 5m 7m 1992 8.1d a12g6 10g 7.5g 6g 6s6] tall colt: no longer of much account: blinkered (edgy) last 3 starts. *N. Bycroft*

CHILLY BREEZE   2 b. or br.f. (Feb 17) Ballad Rock 122 – Chicobin (USA) (J O   50 p
Tobin (USA) 130) [1992 6g5] leggy, unfurnished filly: second foal: half-sister to 3-y-o Chicmond (by Lomond), useful 6f and 7f winner at 2 yrs: dam unraced: 11/1, around 8 lengths fifth of 9, pushed along from halfway, not knocked about when beaten, to Southern Memories in maiden at Doncaster in November: will improve. *Sir Mark Prescott*

CHILTERN HUNDREDS (USA)   2 b.c. (Mar 3) Premiership (USA) – Halo   63
Lady (USA) (Halo (USA)) [1992 5f3 6f4 6s2 6d a6g3 6v6] $26,000F, $45,000Y: smallish, sturdy colt: fifth reported foal: half-brother to 3 winners in North America: dam, minor winner at around 6f, is from family of Digression and Swing Till Dawn: sire useful sprinter: modest maiden: sold out of Mrs J. Cecil's stable 3,600 gns Newmarket Autumn Sales after running poorly fourth start: well below best afterwards: stays 6f: acts on any going. *W. J. Musson*

CHINAMAN   3 b.g. Noalto 120 – Diorina 91 (Manacle 123) [1991 5d 5d 5d 7g 6f4   –
6f3 7f2 7g 7.1s 6g 1992 7d5 10g 8f 8f 6.9m 10d 11.7d 10g5 6s 8.1d] workmanlike gelding: has a round action: no worthwhile form for long time: has been blinkered/visored. *W. G. R. Wightman*

CHINA SKY   4 b.g. Tina's Pet 121 – Buy G'S (Blakeney 126) [1991 a10g a8g a10g6   43
8.2s2 8s6 9d 12.5m 12g a8g2 a8g a8g2 a8g3 a7g4 8.3m2 8f* 8f* 8f6 8m 1992 8d 8m2 7f 8m a8g4 a8g4 8g 9.7m 8g] rather sparely-made gelding: has a round action: poor handicapper: probably stays 1¼m: acts on any going: has raced freely, including in visor once: sold 1,400 gns Newmarket Autumn Sales. *C. N. Allen*

CHINNERY (IRE)   2 gr.c. (May 1) Tate Gallery (USA) 117 – Phar Lapa 59   64
(Grundy 137) [1992 5d 5d6 5.3m2 6f3 6m 7m4 7m3 7.5d5] IR 9,200F, IR 8,000Y: neat colt: has a quick action: fourth foal: half-brother to 3-y-o Yatoo (by Ballad Rock) and 4-y-o 1¼m to 16.1f winner Mrs Barton (by Faustus): dam staying maiden: fair maiden: best effort when third in 7f nursery at Goodwood in August, quickening ahead 2f out but caught close home: will probably stay 1¼m: acts on firm ground, possibly unsuited by dead. *J. M. P. Eustace*

CHIPAROPAI (IRE)   4 b.f. Commanche Run 133 – Violino (USA) 59 (Hawaii)   –
[1991 10s3 12g 10s5 10s 1992 7d 9.2v5 8f 12.2g6 15.1m6] lengthy, sparely-made ex-Irish filly: fourth foal: dam maiden stayed 1½m: trained by J. Bolger at 3 yrs, easily best effort on debut: no worthwhile form here, visored in handicap final start: joined M. Hammond and now novice handicap hurdle in December. *W. Storey*

CHIPPENDALE LADD (CAN)   2 b.c. (Apr 26) Commemorate (USA) – Jackie   68 p
Pearl (USA) (Ruffled Feathers) [1992 7s4] IR 32,000Y: leggy, quite attractive colt: half-brother to several winners, including 1990 2-y-o 6f winner Panchos Pearl (by Pancho Villa) and Italian St Leger winner Rough Pearl (by Tom Rolfe): dam very useful winner at up to 1m: sire useful sprinter: 14/1, over 5 lengths fourth of 16 to Moorish in maiden at Salisbury in September, held up, good progress 2f out then one pace inside last: will stay 1m: will improve. *P. W. Chapple-Hyam*

CHIPPER   3 b.c. Risk Me (FR) 127 – Dunphate (Dunphy 124) [1991 8.1s6 1992   60
9.9g5 8.3d3 11.6m3 12m4 14.1g] sturdy, useful-looking colt: modest maiden: stayed 11.6f: acted on good to firm and dead ground: dead. *R. Boss*

CHIRINDA (IRE)   3 br.f. Petoski 135 – Lady Zi (Manado 130) [1991 NR 1992 8d]   –
rangy filly: fourth foal: half-sister to 4-y-o Chandigarh, Italian middle-distance winner Freeway of Love (both by High Top) and to smart 7f and 1m winner, later successful in USA, Anshan (by Persian Bold): dam, minor 1½m winner in France, is half-sister to dam of No Pass No Sale: closed leaders 5f when well beaten in apprentice maiden at Leicester in October. *R. J. Hodges*

CHLOES DIAMOND (IRE)   4 ch.f. Heraldiste (USA) 121 – Salique (Sallust   47 §
134) [1991 8m3 9m 8.1g 8m 7.9g2 9d 9m* 9m2 a10g2 a10g 12g a12g a8g4 8v 7g5 8.9g 8.1m 7f2 7g a8g 7f 8g3 8d4 8d] sparely-made filly: inconsistent plater: has won one of 26 starts: refused to race final start: effective from 1m to 1¼m: acts on firm and dead ground (below best on soft) and on equitrack: often sweats: sold 600 gns Newmarket Autumn Sales: not one to trust. *J. L. Spearing*

CHOCOLATE MINT 3 b.f. Doulab (USA) 115 – Supper Party (He Loves Me –
120) [1991 NR 1992 5g 6d⁵] 5,600F, 5,600Y: moderate mover: fourth foal: half-sister
to a winner abroad by Balidar: dam never ran: signs of a little ability in spring
maidens: sold 740 gns Doncaster November Sales. *C. W. Thornton*

CHOICE LOT 5 b.g. Auction Ring (USA) 123 – More Candy 98 (Ballad Rock 122) **42**
[1991 6g⁶ 6g 6.5s⁵ 6.5d 6s 1992 6s 5d 7.1m³ 7d a8g a6g] second foal: dam, raced only
at 2 yrs, stayed 6f: ex-Irish gelding, trained until after reappearance by F. Berry:
form in 1992 only when third in selling handicap at Edinburgh in May: stays 7f: acts
on firm ground: sold out of J. J. O'Neill's stable 1,100 gns Doncaster September Sales
after fourth start. *T. H. Caldwell*

CHOIR PRACTICE 5 ch.g. Chief Singer 131 – Good Try 92 (Good Bond 122) **72**
[1991 5g* 5g³ 5g 6g² 6m 5.2g⁶ 1992 5.2d 5g 6g 6g 7f a7g 6g 6d 7.3g⁶ 7d 7d⁶ 7.6v⁵]
big, workmanlike gelding: fair but inconsistent handicapper: effective at 6f and 7f:
acts on good to firm and dead ground. *W. J. Haggas*

CHOIR'S IMAGE 5 br.m. Lochnager 132 – Choir (High Top 131) [1991 NR 1992 –
12s] lengthy, quite good-topped mare: showed little in Pontefract seller on first run
since 2 yrs. *J. L. Eyre*

CHOKER 2 b.f. (Feb 10) Mandrake Major 122 – Beads 59 (Noalcoholic (FR) 128) –
[1992 5.9g 6g] leggy, sparely-made filly: first foal: dam, maiden stayed 6f, is
half-sister to several winners by Mandrake Major: no form in September, including
in seller at Redcar: sold 570 gns Doncaster October Sales. *C. W. Thornton*

CHOPPY CHOPPY (USA) 3 gr.f. Woodman (USA) 126 – Bien Sur (USA) **72**
(Storm Bird (CAN) 134) [1991 6g 6f² 7d⁵ 8g² 1992 10.2s² 11.9f⁴ 10.2h² 10.2f⁵ 10s]
small, stocky filly: inconsistent maiden: off course 3½ months before finishing well
beaten at Newbury final start: stays 1¼m well: acts on any going: sold 6,400 gns
Newmarket December Sales. *B. W. Hills*

CHORAL SUNDOWN 6 b.m. Night Shift (USA) – Choir (High Top 131) [1991 –
8m³ 7m⁴ 9m* 10g² 8.9m 8d 9.9f 11m³ 10.1m 8f 10.3m 11.9m³ 1992 8.5g 9.9g] stocky
mare: carries condition: moderate mover: modest handicapper (rated 64) at 5 yrs:
no form in 1992, for B. Murray on reappearance: effective from 1m to 1½m: yet to
show her form on very soft going, acts on any other: sold 1,400 gns Doncaster
November Sales. *C. W. C. Elsey*

CHOUETTE 2 b.f. (Apr 28) Try My Best (USA) 130 – Bugle Sound 96 (Bustino **54**
136) [1992 8d⁴ 8s] leggy, workmanlike filly: half-sister to several winners, including
3-y-o 1¼m winner Major Bugler (by Thatching), 1984 Irish 2-y-o 1¼m winner Over
The Waves (by Main Reef) and 2m seller winner Dari Sound (by Shardari): dam
stayed 1¾m, is out of Melodina, dam also of Dubian and See You Then: fourth in
slowly-run maiden at Goodwood in September: will stay at least 1½m. *W. J. Musson*

CHRISTIAN FLIGHT (IRE) 3 b.f. Fayruz 116 – Opening Flight (Falcon 131) –
[1991 NR 1992 8d 8g 8f⁴] IR 5,200Y: workmanlike filly: half-sister to 3 winners,
including fairly useful 1983 2-y-o 5f winner Deasy's Delight (by Tanfirion): dam
Irish 9f winner: no worthwhile form in maidens: sold 1,100 gns Doncaster August
Sales. *R. Hannon*

CHRISTIAN SPIRIT 2 gr.c. (Apr 15) Petong 126 – Hidden Asset (Hello **43**
Gorgeous (USA) 128) [1992 5.3d⁴ 6f⁶ 6d⁵ 6g 5.3f³ 6s 6g a6g⁴ a8g* a7g⁵] 4,000Y: a63
leggy colt: second foal: dam seemed of little account: looked poor over sprint
distances but showed marked improvement at 1m, making most and just holding on
to win maiden at Lingfield: ran poorly in nursery at Southwell later in December:
stays 1m: acts on equitrack: well beaten when blinkered once. *R. Hannon*

CHRISTIAN WARRIOR 3 gr.g. Primo Dominie 121 – Rashah 67 (Blakeney –
126) [1991 5g³ 6f⁵ 6d 6m² 5.1g³ 5.1m² 6g⁵ 6g³ 7.1m² 8f³ 7g² 7m 7d⁶ 1992 7d 6d⁶ 7g
7.6s 7m⁴ 7.1m 6g 10g] neat gelding: no worthwhile form in 1992: blinkered (looked
unenthusiastic) penultimate start: subsequently sold out of R. Hannon's stable
2,500 gns Doncaster August Sales. *R. E. Peacock*

CHRISTMAS CACTUS 3 b. or br.f. Dancing Brave (USA) 140 – Prickle 114 **67**
(Sharpen Up 127) [1991 NR 1992 12f⁵ 14.9m²] leggy, good-topped filly: third foal:
half-sister to fairly useful 1¼m winner Jungle Rose (by Shirley Heights): dam
Lowther winner didn't train on: shaped like a stayer when easily beaten in 3-runner
maiden at Warwick in July: sold 5,600 gns Newmarket December Sales. *J. H. M.
Gosden*

CHRISTMAS HOLS 6 b.g. Young Generation 129 – Foston Bridge 68 (Relkino –
131) [1991 NR 1992 12g] lengthy, angular gelding: rated 55 as 3-y-o: bought out of J.
Bosley's stable 1,100 gns Ascot June Sales: tailed off in amateurs handicap on first
run on flat since: tried blinkered once. *Miss L. Bower*

CHRONOLOGICAL   6 b.g. Henbit (USA) 130 – Forward Princess (USA)   –
(Forward Pass) [1991 a14g a13g* a12g⁴ a12g⁴ a14g⁶ a16g⁶ a14g* a14g² 1992 a14g⁵
a14g⁴ a14g⁶] sparely-made, angular gelding: moderate mover: none too consistent
performer: has reportedly broken blood vessel: stays 2m: acts on all-weather
surfaces: goes well visored: pulled hard when blinkered once: subsequently
reluctant and withdrawn over hurdles in March. *M. H. Tompkins*

CHUCKLESTONE   9 b.g. Chukaroo 103 – Czar's Diamond (Queen's Hussar   72
124) [1991 16g 17.1m 1992 14g⁵ 16.9g 16m³ 17.2f⁵ 17.2h* 17.2f* 16m* 13.1f* 16.1g
16d] neat gelding: has a rather round action: fair handicapper: at the top of his game
in the summer, winning at Lingfield and 3 times at Bath: well below form
afterwards: effective at 13f, and stays very well: well suited by a sound surface and
acts on hard ground: tailed off when visored earlier in career: very game and
genuine front runner. *J. S. King*

CHUMMY'S CHILD (IRE)   3 ch.g. Mazaad 106 – Corda (Current Coin 118)   47
[1991 NR 1992 7g 10m 7g 10m 8.1g 10.1g⁵ 10f* 12g⁵] IR 3,000Y, 9,800 2-y-o: sturdy
gelding: fourth reported living foal: half-brother to Irish 1m winners Rim (by Private
Walk) and Creeping Sally (by Royal Match): dam unraced half-sister to very useful
Irish 2-y-o 5f performer Wind Drift: fair plater: no form first 4 starts for B. Hills: no
bid when making all at Brighton in August: suited by 1¼m: acts on firm going. *J.
Sutcliffe*

CHUMMY'S FRIEND (IRE)   2 ch.f. (Feb 26) Be My Guest (USA) 126 – So   47
Directed 98 (Homing 130) [1992 5g⁶ 7m 5g⁴] 31,000Y: leggy, lightly-made filly: third
foal: closely related to 3-y-o Well Directed (by Sadler's Wells) and half-sister to
1¼m winner Harbour Knight (by Caerleon): dam Irish 2-y-o 5f winner: off course 4
months after debut: best effort when fourth in seller at Newcastle but will be well
suited by return to further. *B. W. Hills*

CHUMMY'S IDEA (IRE)   2 b.f. (Apr 18) Fayruz 116 – Adivara 58 (Tyrnavos   45
129) [1992 5f 6m 6s 6g⁴ 6s] IR 2,400Y, 10,000 2-y-o: small, good-quartered filly: first
foal: dam 1¼m winner: plating-class maiden: best effort, though beaten almost 9
lengths, when fourth in minor event at Folkestone in September: will stay 7f. *J.
Sutcliffe*

CHUMMY'S PAL (USA)   2 b.c. (Mar 28) Bering 136 – Miss Vestment (USA)   68 p
(Magesterial (USA) 116) [1992 7m³] 42,000Y: third foal: dam won twice at up to 9f:
10/1, under 2 lengths third of 16 to True Hero in maiden at Leicester in September,
chasing leaders travelling smoothly and finishing strongly under hand riding: would
have gone close had run begun sooner: bred to be very well suited by middle
distances: sure to improve and win races. *B. W. Hills*

CHUMMY'S SAGA   2 ch.c. (Feb 1) Caerleon (USA) 132 – Sagar 74 (Habitat 134)   44 p
[1992 7g] leggy, unfurnished colt: fifth foal: half-brother to French 1¼m winner
Suruba (by Top Ville), 1½m winner Kaleidos (by Rainbow Quest) and modest
juvenile 5f winner Gold Ducat (by Young Generation): dam 10.5f winner in France:
33/1, chased leaders over 4f then dropped right away to finish last of 11 in minor
event at Kempton in September: should do better. *B. W. Hills*

CHURCH STAR   8 b.m. Cajun 120 – Lady of Rathleek (Furry Glen 121) [1991 9g   – §
9v⁶ 9.7s 1992 10s] compact, good-bodied mare: of little account these days: tried
blinkered. *J. J. Bridger*

CICERONE   2 br.c. (Mar 30) Tina's Pet 121 – Emma Royale 69 (Royal And Regal   56 p
(USA)) [1992 5m 6s 6d] 3,700Y: leggy colt: has a round action: fifth foal: dam 1½m
winner: progressive maiden: will stay beyond 6f: hung left first 2 starts: may
improve further. *P. Calver*

CINDERS GIRL   2 b.f. (Feb 11) Presidium 124 – Salinas 65 (Bay Express 132)   56
[1992 6d³ 5d⁴ 6g 6m] small filly: first foal: dam maiden stayed 6f: plating-class
maiden: stays 6f: may well be unsuited by top-of-the-ground. *J. M. P. Eustace*

CINDORA (IRE)   3 b.f. Fairy King (USA) – West of Eden (Crofter (USA) 124)   89
[1991 6m² 5m* 5g* 6m⁴ 5m* 6f⁴ 5m³ 6g 5d 5g⁴ 1992 5g* 6g 5.1g* 5m 6d 5m 5.2s
5g] leggy, sparely-made filly: moderate mover: fairly useful handicapper: successful
at Doncaster in March and Chester (£7,000 event, gamely) in May: best effort
afterwards on final start, in November: best form at around 5f: acts on good to firm
and dead ground, never travelling well on soft: sold 9,000 gns Newmarket
December Sales and sent to Canada. *M. H. Tompkins*

CIPRIANI QUEEN (IRE)   2 b.f. (Apr 19) Seattle Dancer (USA) 119 –   –
Justsayno (USA) (Dr Blum (USA)) [1992 7m] 68,000Y: first foal: dam 5f winner at 2
yrs, later very useful at around 1m, finishing second in Grade 1 Matron Stakes: 33/1,

lost place at halfway when tailed off in 12-runner maiden at Newmarket in October: showed a quick action: sold 900 gns Ascot November Sales. *M. R. Stoute*

CIRCUS COLOURS 2 b.c. (Mar 2) Rainbow Quest (USA) 134 – Circus Plume 124 (High Top 131) [1992 8g 8m] unfurnished colt: fourth foal: half-brother to useful 1m and 9f winner Circus Feathers (by Kris) and 1990 2-y-o 8.2f winner Circus Light (by Kalaglow): dam, 7f winner at 2 yrs, won Oaks: backward, well beaten in minor event at Newbury and 19-runner Newmarket maiden in the autumn: looks sort to do better in time. *J. L. Dunlop* **58 p**

CISEAUX (USA) 3 ch.g. Nureyev (USA) 131 – Sharp Ascent (USA) 97 (Sharpen Up 127) [1991 7d⁴ 6.3m³ 6m* 6g* 1992 7m 6f 6.3g 9d] tall, leggy gelding: third foal: brother to 1989 2-y-o 5f performer Ascending Dream: dam 2-y-o 5f performer here later Grade 3 8.5f winner in USA, is daughter of Rivermande, a very useful winner at around 1m in France: looked fairly useful when successful in maiden at the Curragh and minor event at Naas in autumn at 2 yrs: towards rear in handicaps as 3-y-o, when well backed but never dangerous in Wokingham Stakes at Royal Ascot on only start here: should stay 7f: off course 4 months before final start and sold only 1,700 gns Newmarket Autumn Sales. *D. K. Weld, Ireland* **–**

CISSBURY RING 2 b.c. (Mar 9) Jalmood (USA) 126 – Celtic Ring 93 (Welsh Pageant 132) [1992 6m³ 6m² 7d* 8g] tall colt: had scope: first foal: dam 1¼m and 1½m winner from good family: won maiden at Salisbury in July by 10 lengths: had to be destroyed after breaking down in Warwick nursery following month: would have been well suited by middle distances. *Lady Herries* **81**

CITIQUEEN (IRE) 3 ch.f. Lomond (USA) 128 – Supremely Royal (Crowned Prince (USA) 128) [1991 a8g* 1992 12.5g⁶ 11.6g* 12.4m* 10.1g² 13.3s] good-topped filly: progressed into useful performer in the summer: won handicaps at Windsor and Newcastle then excellent second to Red Slippers in listed event at Newcastle: moved moderately to post, well beaten in handicap at Newbury in October: should prove suited by 1½m + . *H. R. A. Cecil* **105**

CITIZEN KING 2 b.c. (Apr 30) Local Suitor (USA) 128 – La Belle Princesse 85 (Royal Match 117) [1992 7s] 5,200F: workmanlike colt: third foal: half-brother to 3-y-o Tudor da Samba (by Sizzling Melody): dam Irish 2-y-o 7f winner, is out of half-sister to smart 7f to 1¾m performer Rocamadour: 25/1 and backward, tailed-off last of 12 in maiden auction at York in October: moved moderately to post. *G. A. Pritchard-Gordon* **–**

CITY LIGHTER 2 bl.f. (May 11) Lighter 111 – Another City 68 (Scallywag 127) [1992 5s 8.1d] workmanlike filly: first reported foal: dam 3-y-o 12.2f winner, later winning hurdler and useful and game front-running handicap chaser: 33/1, slowly away and always behind in maidens at Haydock in the autumn. *E. J. Alston* **–**

CITY LINE 3 b.g. Capricorn Line 111 – Racine City 71 (Dom Racine (FR) 121) [1991 7g 7d 1992 10.2f³ 12.1m⁶ 9.7d 11.7m* 12.3g 11.8m 17.2s³] leggy gelding: modest performer: sold out of R. Hannon's stable 1,250 gns Ascot February Sales: claimer ridden, won 4-runner maiden claimer at Bath in August: bounced back to form in Bath handicap final start: stays 2¼m: probably acts on any going: visored (ran moderately) penultimate start. *D. R. Laing* **57**

CITY ROCKET 2 b.c. (Mar 31) King of Spain 121 – Hat Hill (Roan Rocket 128) [1992 6m³ 5f⁵ 7m² 7g⁴ 7g] 19,000Y: sturdy, lengthy colt: has scope: sixth foal: half-brother to 3-y-o Red Sombrero and a winner in Macau (both by Aragon) and 1987 2-y-o 7f seller winner Nore Hill (by Town And Country): dam ran 4 times: fair maiden: creditable fifth, never able to challenge, in Windsor Castle Stakes at Royal Ascot: off course 7 weeks, ran respectably in Doncaster nursery final start, in November: stays 7f: acts on firm ground. *P. J. Makin* **70**

CITY TIMES (IRE) 2 b.f. (Jan 3) Last Tycoon 131 – Sea Harrier (Grundy 137) [1992 6g² 6d 7s] 47,000Y: useful-looking filly, rather unfurnished: half-sister to middle-distance winners Water Boatman (by Main Reef) and Glendera (by Glenstal): dam twice-raced half-sister to high-class stayer Sea Anchor: fair maiden: promising second in Ascot maiden on debut: rather disappointing next time but ran well, though no threat last 3f, in Moyglare Stud Stakes at the Curragh in September: will stay at least 1m. *B. A. McMahon* **65**

CIVIL ACTION (IRE) 2 br.c. (Apr 21) Law Society (USA) 130 – Habituee (Habitat 134) [1992 8.1d] 30,000Y: leggy, quite attractive colt: brother to a listed-placed maiden in France, and half-brother to several winners, including smart 7f and 1m winner Dabaweyaa (by Shareef Dancer) and Oaks second Acclimitise (by Shirley Heights): dam 1m winner: 13/2, 18 lengths seventh of 9 to Beauman in maiden at Haydock in September, held up after slow start, steadily outpaced under **– p**

considerate handling from 3f out: will be well suited by 1½m: will do better. *J. Hanson*

CIVIL LAW (IRE) 2 b.c. (Feb 6) Law Society (USA) 130 – Senane 86 (Vitiges (FR) 132) [1992 7m³ 7g⁴ 7d³] 18,500F, 19,000Y: quite good-topped colt: fifth foal: half-brother to 1990 2-y-o 6f winner Carole's King (by Kings Lake), later effective at 1½m, and 1989 Irish 2-y-o 9f winner Commanche Chief (by Commanche Run): dam 1m winner stayed 1½m, possibly ungenuine, is out of top 1978 2-y-o staying filly Formulate: fairly useful maiden: raced only in small fields, best effort 10 lengths third of 4 to Tenby in listed event at Newbury: withdrawn lame at York 4 days later in August and not seen out again: will be well suited by middle distances. *R. Hollinshead* **87 ?**

CIZARD (IRE) 2 b.f. (Feb 12) Jareer (USA) 115 – Abertywi 87 (Bounteous 125) [1992 5g⁶ 5f 5g 5.2g 5g⁶ 6d 6g a7g⁵] 4,000F, 1,000 2-y-o: sparely-made filly: half-sister to several winners here and abroad, including 1988 2-y-o 7f winner Down The Valley (by Kampala) and 1m and 10.2f winner Meziara (by Dominion): dam, 7f and 1m winner, is sister to Abergwaun: poor form, including in sellers. *A. W. Potts* **40**

CLAIR SOLEIL (USA) 3 b.g. Conquistador Cielo (USA) – Parissaul 75 (Saulingo 122) [1991 NR 1992 8g⁶ 12f⁴ 10d⁴] $28,000Y: workmanlike gelding: fourth foal: half-brother to Irish 7f and 1¼m winner Silken Fan (by Lear Fan): dam maiden half-sister to Musidora and Yorkshire Oaks winner Condessa, should have been suited by 1¼m +: modest maiden: should prove better at 1½m than shorter: joined A. Moore. *Denys Smith* **52**

CLANGOLD 2 ch.f. (Apr 5) Clantime 101 – Moorhill (Vaigly Great 127) [1992 5s⁴ 5f² a6g 6g⁴ 6g⁶ 5g⁵ 6s 5m 6s] 2,800Y: leggy, angular filly: first foal: dam unraced: inconsistent plater: stays 6f: probably acts on any going: below form when blinkered once. *J. Berry* **43 d**

CLANROCK 2 ch.g. (Mar 4) Clantime 101 – Petroc Concert § (Tina's Pet 121) [1992 6m⁶ 6m⁶ 5g³ 6s⁴ 5m⁴ 6g⁵ 6s² 6m] 400Y: leggy, unfurnished gelding: blind in off-eye: first foal: dam irresolute maiden probably stayed 11f: consistent plater: stays 6f: probably acts on any going. *R. M. Whitaker* **60**

CLAR DUBH (IRE) 2 ch.f. (Apr 8) Double Schwartz 128 – Tableaux (FR) (Welsh Pageant 132) [1992 7g 7m 8.9s] IR 2,000Y: tall, sparely-made filly: half-sister to French 8.7f winner Living Image (by Kenmare): dam French maiden: poor maiden: sold 1,500 gns Newmarket Autumn Sales. *M. H. Tompkins* **45**

CLARE HEIGHTS 4 b.f. Shirley Heights 130 – Clare Island 108 (Connaught 130) [1991 10.5g* 12g 12m⁴ 16g⁴ 1992 16.2d⁴ 16.2m²] workmanlike, angular filly: useful, but lightly raced: ran well in spring in Group 3 Sagaro Stakes (promoted place) at Ascot and well-contested minor event (beaten ½ length by Romany Rye) at Haydock: stayed 2m well: acted on good to firm and dead ground: visits Soviet Star. *J. R. Fanshawe* **96**

CLARE KERRY LASS 3 b.f. Alleging (USA) 120 – Gay Hostess (FR) (Direct Flight) [1991 5s³ 6g* 6f³ 6m* a6g² 6m 5m³ 6m 7g⁴ 7.6m⁵ a6g⁴ a8g² a8g³ 1992 a8g⁵ 7f 7g² 7d* 8m 7g⁶ 7d³ 8.1g⁶ 7.6v³] leggy filly: fair handicapper: won claimer (claimed out of T. Naughton's stable £12,000) at Epsom in June: stays 1m: best efforts on an easy surface. *J. R. Fanshawe* **76**

CLARE'S BOY 2 ch.g. (Apr 18) Librate 91 – Sue Clare 51 (Busted 134) [1992 6m a6g 6g] leggy, sparely-made gelding: first reported foal: dam maiden stayed 1½m: little sign of ability. *J. M. Bradley* **–**

CLASSIC ACCOUNT 4 ch.g. Pharly (FR) 130 – Money Supply (Brigadier Gerard 144) [1991 a10g² a10g* a10g⁵ a10g⁴ 10g 9d 10g 11.5s* 14.1g⁴ 11.5m⁵ 12s² 1992 a13g* 13g a12g⁴ a12g²] workmanlike handicapper: modest mover: modest handicapper: won amateurs race at Lingfield in March: sold out of J. Akehurst's stable 5,800 gns Ascot June Sales and off course 7½ months, excellent second in claimer at Southwell in December: will stay 1¾m: acts on soft ground and all-weather surfaces. *J. Pearce* **40 + a69**

CLASSICAL CHARMER 3 ch.f. Ardross 134 – Very Nice (FR) (Green Dancer (USA) 132) [1991 6f 7g 8s 1992 10d 10g 12m 10d] workmanlike filly: regressive maiden: should stay well: acts on dead ground. *B. R. Millman* **–**

CLASSIC EXHIBIT 3 b.g. Tate Gallery (USA) 117 – See The Tops (Cure The Blues (USA)) [1991 6m 7m a6g⁶ 1992 8s 8.2g 7f 6.1g 10g⁶] unfurnished, leggy gelding: poor plater: unlikely to stay beyond 1m: trained first 2 starts by A. Hide: sold 3,600 gns Newmarket September Sales: won selling hurdle in October for A. Forbes. *S. P. C. Woods* **–**

CLASSIC IMAGE (IRE) 2 b.c. (Apr 27) Vision (USA) – Braneakins (Sallust 134) [1992 6m³ 6m] IR 23,000Y: leggy colt: has fluent action: fourth living foal: half-brother to temperamental 1m (at 2 yrs) and 1½m winner Peking Opera (by Sadler's Wells) and 3-y-o Grand Honda (by Lomond): dam, Irish 1½m winner, is half-sister to Park Appeal, Desirable and Alydaress: shaped encouragingly in maidens at Ripon and Goodwood in July: sort to do better. *M. Moubarak* — 70 p

CLASSICS PEARL (IRE) 4 gr.f. Reasonable (FR) 119 – Zanskar (Godswalk (USA) 130) [1991 7m³ 8.3m 9d 8f 10m 1992 8.2g 12f] stocky filly: moderate walker: poor maiden: should be suited by further than 7f: acts on firm ground: below form when blinkered once: won selling hurdle in September. *N. A. Twiston-Davies* — –

CLASSIC STATEMENT 6 ch.h. Mill Reef (USA) 141 – Lady Graustark (USA) (Graustark) [1991 14g 1992 16.9g 13.3g 20m 18.2g³ 16.5g⁶] leggy, quite attractive horse: poor handicapper: needs extreme test of stamina: acts on good to firm and dead ground. *R. Lee* — 49

CLASSIC STORM 2 b.f. (Jan 19) Belfort (FR) 89 – Lady Tamara 114 (Kenmare (FR) 125) [1992 5g* 5d² 5m* 5g³ a5g* 5f* 6.1f* 5d* 5f³ 6g* 6d⁵] 2,500Y: angular filly: blind in near-eye: third reported foal: half-sister to 1989 2-y-o 5f winner Tamara's Twinkle (by Sharpen Up), successful at 6.2f in France in 1991: dam French middle-distance performer: had really good season, successful in sellers at Doncaster (no bid) and Beverley (retained 4,600 gns), claimers at Southwell, Edinburgh, Chepstow and Beverley and nursery at Ripon: stays 6f: acts on firm and dead ground and fibresand: tough and genuine. *J. Berry* — 73

CLASSIC STORY (USA) 2 ch.c. (Apr 25) Green Forest (USA) 134 – Million Stories (USA) (Exclusive Native (USA)) [1992 5d* 5m⁵ 5m³ 5m⁴] strong, good-quartered colt: has scope and is most likeable sort: fluent mover: second foal: dam French 7.5f winner, is daughter of Perlee, dam also of French 1000 Guineas winner Pearl Bracelet: won maiden at Beverley in July: only disappointing effort after when not finding so much as seemed likely in competitive Ripon minor event final start. *M. Moubarak* — 78

CLAUDIA MISS 5 b.m. Claude Monet (USA) 121 – Palace Travel (High Top 131) [1991 7.5g³ 7m⁴ 8m⁶ 8m² 8g⁵ 1992 8d² 7m⁴ 7m⁵ 7g⁴ 8g³ 7.5g³ 8g⁵ 7d³ a8g² a7g] workmanlike mare: poor mover: largely consistent handicapper: effective at 7f to 1m: acts on any going, with possible exception of very firm: below best when visored once and when unruly stalls and missing break final start. *W. W. Haigh* — 57 a62

CLAYBANK (USA) 3 ch.c. Vice Regent (CAN) – Captain's Mate (USA) (Turn-To) [1991 5m² 5m³ 1992 6m² 7g* 7m 6g 6g² 6d 8g] good-topped colt: won maiden at Newmarket in May: easily best effort in handicaps after when good second at Newcastle in August: should prove better at 7f than 6f: below form when blinkered once. *B. W. Hills* — 89

CLEAN GATE 3 gr.g. Hallgate 127 – Ville Air 85 (Town Crier 119) [1991 NR 1992 6m 5.1g 7g] rather leggy gelding: second foal: half-brother to quite modest middle-distance maiden Air Time (by Good Times): dam won over 6f at 2 yrs on only start: well beaten in maidens and seller. *P. D. Cundell* — –

CLEAN SINGER 3 b.f. Chief Singer 131 – Rosalka (ITY) (Relko 136) [1991 8.1g 8m 8m 1992 8m 12f 8.9d 12.1s⁵ 10.9s] close-coupled filly: poor maiden on flat: won selling hurdle in November. *N. Bycroft* — –

CLEARFOOT 2 ch.f. (Mar 30) Hotfoot 126 – Clear As Crystal 80 (Whitstead 125) [1992 7s] leggy filly: third foal: sister to fair 1990 3-y-o 1½m winner Hot Rumour and half-sister to modest 1990 2-y-o 6f winner Clyro (by Kind of Hush): dam 11.7f winner on only start: slowly away and always behind in maiden at Salisbury in September. *R. J. Holder* — –

CLEAR HONEY (USA) 2 b.f. (May 5) Palace Music (USA) 129 – Gantlette (Run The Gantlet (USA)) [1992 7g 7.1g* 7m 8f 7s] 30,000Y: rather leggy filly: has a round action: half-sister to several winners, including very useful middle-distance performer Run Don't Fly (by Lear Fan), as well as dam of Lancashire Oaks winner Pharian: dam French 2-y-o 1m winner: somewhat disappointing in handicaps after winning Edinburgh maiden in July: should stay 1m: well below form on soft ground: blinkered and sweating final start. *B. Hanbury* — 55

CLEAR IDEA (IRE) 4 ch.g. Try My Best (USA) 130 – Sloane Ranger 84 (Sharpen Up 127) [1991 a8g⁵ 10.2g⁶ 11.7g 10g 7g 1992 a10g a10g⁵ a10g⁵ 11.9d⁴ 14.1d⁶] tall, quite attractive gelding: fluent mover: poor handicapper: effective at up to 1¾m: acts on dead ground: below form when visored once. *C. R. Nelson* — 39

CLEAR LIGHT 5 ch.g. Exhibitioner 111 – Beach Light 89 (Bustino 136) [1991 a12g* 12.2d* 14.8m² 12.3d³ 17.6m⁴ 14.8d⁴ 14.6m⁶ 1992 12g 12.5g³ 12.3m 10.2m⁶ — 58

12d] angular gelding: moderate mover: modest handicapper: not seen out after being tailed off in July: effective at 1½m to 14.8f: acts on good to firm and dead ground and fibresand: effective blinkered or not: below form when visored once: good mount for claimer: often forces pace: lazy but genuine. *C. A. Smith*

CLEAR LOOK 2 b.f. (Apr 1) Green Desert (USA) 127 – Avoid (USA) **63** (Buckpasser) [1992 5d³ 6.1m³ 5g² 6g 6.5m] tall, unfurnished filly: has a roundish action: half-sister to Irish 1m winner Avoid The Step (by Go Step) and 2 winners in USA: dam unraced: regressive maiden and has shown signs of temperament: stays 6f: acts on good to firm and dead ground. *P. F. I. Cole*

CLEAR SOUND 3 b.f. Bellypha 130 – Cecilia Bianchi (FR) (Petingo 135) [1991 **61** 7m⁵ 8m⁵ 1992 8s² 9.9f³ 12.2d⁶ 12.2g⁴ 9g² 11.5m] close-coupled filly: modest maiden: seems best at around 1¼m: probably acts on any going: ran well when visored once: sold 3,800 gns Newmarket December Sales. *G. Wragg*

CLEDESCHAMPS 3 b.f. Doc Marten 104 – Cape Farewell (Record Run 127) **45** [1991 NR 1992 6m 6.9h⁴ 10m 8m⁴ 6.9f⁴ 8g* 8m⁶ 8m] smallish, lengthy filly: moderate mover: second foal: dam, daughter of a fairly useful middle-distance performer, won hurdles: poor handicapper: won selling event (no bid) at Thirsk in August: suited by 1m, possibly by give in the ground. *M. W. Ellerby*

CLEFTI'S SLIPPER 4 b.f. Skyliner 117 – Glenn's Slipper (Furry Glen 121) – [1991 a6g 1992 a6g] twice raced and no worthwhile form. *C. J. Hill*

CLEO MODENA (IRE) 4 b.f. Dalsaan 125 – Modena 66 (Sassafras (FR) 135) **50** [1991 a6g 1992 a7g⁵ a8g*] thrice raced at Southwell and easily best effort when winning claimer in January: stays 1m well: sold 1,000 gns Doncaster October Sales. *M. O'Neill*

CLEVER CLAUDE 6 b.g. Cragador 110 – La Mirabelle 92 (Princely Gift 137) – [1991 10.1s 1992 8m] leggy, shallow-girthed gelding: poor plater: seems to stay 1m. *K. S. Bridgwater*

CLIBURNEL NEWS (IRE) 2 b.f. (Mar 28) Horage 124 – Dublin Millennium **76** (Dalsaan 125) [1992 5f⁵ 5.9f* 6d⁵ 6f 6g⁵ 6s⁴ 7.1g* 7g] unfurnished filly: second reported foal: dam twice-raced Irish 12.5f winner: consistent performer: won maiden at Carlisle in June and claimer at Edinburgh in October: will be better suited by 1m: probably acts on any going. *M. H. Tompkins*

CLIFTON CHARLIE (USA) 4 b.c. Crafty Prospector (USA) – Illustrious **89** Joanne (USA) (Illustrious) [1991 6m 6g 1992 8g 6m 6f⁴ 5.1f⁵ 5s 6m 6m 6m² 6g 6g 6d* 5.6m] lengthy colt: unreliable performer: won Ripon claimer: broke down badly (reportedly shattered a pastern) later in September: stayed 6f: acted on firm ground and dead: trained first run in 1992 by C. Nelson: dead. *M. R. Channon*

CLIFTON CHASE 3 ch.c. Try My Best (USA) 130 – Mrs Cullumbine 60 (Silly **54** Season 127) [1991 6m 6d 1992 8g 10d 10.1g³ 13.8f 11.5s 15.8d a12g⁵ a10g³ a12g*] angular, workmanlike colt: inconsistent handicapper: improved form at Southwell in December, winning by 5 lengths: suited by 1½m: blinkered last 4 starts. *M. A. Jarvis*

CLIFTON CRUISER (USA) 3 ch.g. Miswaki (USA) 124 – Atomic Juice (USA) – (Sauce Boat (USA)) [1991 7g⁵ 7m 7g 1992 10g 8m 8.5d⁵] rather leggy, good-topped gelding: poor maiden: stays 7f: below form when blinkered once: joined Mrs F. Walwyn. *C. R. Nelson*

CLIFTON HAMPDEN 4 b.g. Blakeney 126 – Red Ruby 113 (Tudor Melody – § 129) [1991 10g 12m⁴ 11.5m 12m 17.2g² 18m 1992 a16g² 16.2m 22.2g 16m] compact, rather sparely-made gelding: has rather round action: untrustworthy handicapper: stays well: possibly needs give in the ground: below form blinkered/visored: none too easy ride. *Lady Herries*

CLIMBING HIGH 3 b.f. Last Tycoon 131 – Snowtop (Thatching 131) [1991 NR **64** 1992 7g² 7m² 7m² 7g² 6.9g² 7g⁵] leggy, lengthy, sparely-made filly: second foal: dam Irish sprinting half-sister to Al Hareb and smart French 9f to 1¼m winner Dr Somerville: modest maiden: rare poor effort when visored final start: will stay 1m: ran well when blinkered once: sold 13,500 gns Newmarket December Sales. *I. A. Balding*

CLIPPER ONE 4 b.f. Dreams To Reality (USA) 113 – Sleekit 78 (Blakeney 126) – [1991 7d⁴ 8f* 8m 10g a8g 1992 a7g⁶] leggy, close-coupled filly: on the downgrade: stays 1m well: retained 600 gns Newmarket Autumn Sales. *K. O. Cunningham-Brown*

CLOS DU BOIS (FR) 6 b.g. High Top 131 – Our Shirley 84 (Shirley Heights – 130) [1991 a16g⁴ a14g a16g² 12m⁶ 1992 a16g] small, sparely-made gelding: still a maiden on flat: rated 45 at 5 yrs: well beaten at Southwell in December: stays 2m: acts on good to firm and dead going: often bandaged. *Mrs N. Macauley*

CLOSE FRIEND (IRE) 4 gr.c. Law Society (USA) 130 – Bellifontaine (FR) **100** (Bellypha 130) [1991 8g² 10.5g³ 10.1m³ 12g* 14.8m⁴ 1992 12g* 13.4m⁶ 16.1g⁵ 12g 13.3g] deep-girthed colt: has a round action: well beaten after gamely winning Newmarket handicap in April: should stay beyond 1½m: likely to prove best on an easy surface: sometimes drifts right: sold 26,000 gns Newmarket Autumn Sales: to race in Saudi Arabia. *B. W. Hills*

CLOUDED ELEGANCE 2 b.c. (May 14) Elegant Air 119 – Clouded Vision 74 **72** p (So Blessed 130) [1992 8s⁶] 7,000Y: leggy, quite good-topped colt: sixth living foal: half-brother to 1½m winner Voltage (by Electric) and a winner in Italy: dam 6f winner: 16/1 and very green, never able to challenge after slow start when 9 lengths sixth of 8 to Arusha in minor event at Newbury in October: sure to improve. *I. A. Balding*

CLOUD OF DUST 3 b.f. Aragon 118 – Lady Bequick 81 (Sharpen Up 127) [1991 **108** 6d² 6m* 1992 8d* 8d 8.1m² 7f⁵ 8g² 8.1d 8s* 8g³ 8v²] leggy, quite attractive filly: useful performer: won £9,900 contest at Kempton in April and Group 3 event (beat Soiree 2 lengths) at the Curragh in September: ran creditably in German inited race and Italian Group 3 contest last 2 starts: stays 1m: acts on good to firm ground and heavy: sometimes sweating: retained by trainer 140,000 gns Newmarket December Sales. *J. L. Dunlop*

CLOUDY REEF 2 b.f. (Mar 22) Cragador 110 – Kellys Reef 92 (Pitskelly 122) **57** [1992 5m³ 5f² 5.1g³ 5g⁴ 5.1m⁴ 5g³ 5m² 5f³ 5m³ 5g³ 5m⁶] 500F: small, good-quartered filly: poor mover: fourth foal: sister to quite modest 7f winner Calypso Reef and half-sister to 3-y-o 5f winner Artistic Reef (by Claude Monet): dam sprinter: consistent performer: will be suited by 6f: acts on firm ground, yet to race on a soft surface (has given impression it would suit): ridden by claimer. *R. Hollinshead*

CLOVERMILL 4 b.f. Sayf El Arab (USA) 127 – Opinion 71 (Great Nephew 126) – [1991 7g 8.5m 8f⁵ 7m 6g 7g 10m 1992 12m] leggy, lengthy filly: had a quick action: poor maiden on flat/winning hurdler: should have been suited by further than 1m: below form blinkered/visored: dead. *W. Bentley*

CLUB VERGE (IRE) 2 ch.c. (Jan 17) Sayf El Arab (USA) 127 – Collegian 90 **53** (Stanford 121§) [1992 5.1g⁴ 5m³ 5f⁵ 5m³] IR 2,200Y: robust colt: moderate walker and mover: fourth foal (all by Sayf El Arab): brother to 5f (at 2 yrs) to 7f winner Unveiled and 6f (at 2 yrs) to 1½m winner South Sands: dam 6f and 1m winner: regressive maiden: hung throughout final start. *E. J. Alston*

CLURICAN (IRE) 3 ch.g. Dara Monarch 128 – Jane Bond 59 (Good Bond 122) **75** [1991 6d 7g⁴ 7m 7.1s 1992 10s* 10g³ 10s⁵ 14g] close-coupled gelding: fair handicapper: made all in median auction race at Leicester in June: stays 1¼m well: acts on soft going: usually sweating: fairly useful juvenile hurdler, winning twice. *D. Nicholson*

CLWYD LODGE 5 b.g. Blakeney 126 – High Caraval (High Top 131) [1991 NR – 1992 a16g] sturdy gelding: moderate mover: poor handicapper: should stay very well: acts on any going: below form when blinkered once. *R. T. Juckes*

CLYTIE (USA) 3 br.f. El Gran Senor (USA) 136 – Counting Rainbows (USA) – (Halo (USA)) [1991 7g³ 1992 8d⁵] leggy, lengthy filly: twice raced, and well-beaten last in £9,900 contest at Kempton in April: should stay 1¼m. *H. Candy*

COALISLAND 2 br.c. (Apr 2) Kind of Hush 118 – Hit The Line 71 (Saulingo 122) **51** [1992 6.1m 7g⁶ 7.1g] good-bodied colt: third reported living foal: dam winning sprinter: plating-class form in fair company. *R. Ingram*

COASTAL EXPRESS 3 ch.g. Viking (USA) – Hold Me Fast (USA) (Angle Light **60** (USA)) [1991 5m 5m a7g³ 7s³ 7.5f² 7g* 8m 7g 7m⁵ a7g 1992 9s 8d⁵ 6.9d³ a7g* a8g* **a78** 7.1f* 7.1m⁶ 7f 6d⁶ 8g a7g⁶] workmanlike gelding: shows knee action: none too consistent handicapper: won at Southwell (2) and Edinburgh in first half of 1992: stays 1m: probably acts on any turf going, but best effort on fibresand: sometimes pulls hard. *E. Weymes*

COAT OF DREAMS 3 b.g. Ballacashtal (CAN) – Montelimar 108 (Wolver **40** Hollow 126) [1991 5f⁴ 5g⁶ 6d⁵ 6m* 7m 5m 1992 6.1m 8h 7.6g 6g³ 6m] leggy gelding: inconsistent handicapper: best form at 6f: acts on good to firm ground: effective blinkered or not: looked hard ride for apprentice final start. *R. Bastiman*

COBBLERS HILL 3 gr.c. Another Realm 118 – Morning Miss 59 (Golden **54** Dipper 119) [1991 5m* 5m³ 6f³ 1992 8m* 9.2m³] plain, workmanlike colt: bandaged when winning Ayr seller (no bid): well beaten in claimer later in June: stays 1m: sold to join C. Barwell 1,000 gns Doncaster September Sales. *J. White*

CO-CHIN (IRE)   3 gr.c. Coquelin (USA) 121 – Whiffswatching (USA) (Sassafras   **75**
(FR) 135) [1991 5d² 5d² 5m³ 7m* 7g³ 7m 7.6d⁴ 8g 1992 8f 7.1d⁶ 6m 8f⁴ 6g 7d 7d⁶]
leggy, sparely-made colt: none too consistent handicapper: should prove best at up
to 1m: acts on firm and dead ground: tailed off when blinkered once: joined D.
Moffatt and won second hurdles in October. *G. Lewis*

COCKERHAM RANGER   2 b.g. (Apr 27) Roaring Riva 103 – Miss Shegas 65   **63**
(Rabdan 129) [1992 5g⁶ 5m⁶ 5d² 5d⁶ 5d⁵] leggy, rather light-framed gelding: third
foal: dam 2-y-o 5f winner: won maiden at Redcar in July: inconsistent in nurseries,
stiff tasks, after: will stay 6f. *J. Berry*

COCONUT JOHNNY   2 br.c. (Mar 19) King of Spain 121 – Gentle Gypsy 94   **55**
(Junius (USA) 124) [1992 5s 5m 5m² 5f* 5m³ 5m* 5.1d⁵ 5g] 3,600Y: good-quartered,
sprint type: moderate mover: third reported foal: dam 2-y-o 5f winner, seemed not
to train on: useful plater: no bid after winning at Thirsk and Beverley in early-
summer: well below form last 2 starts: speedy: seems to need top-of-the-ground:
best form blinkered. *G. M. Moore*

COCOS ISLAND (USA)   3 b.g. Proud Birdie (USA) – Devious Dancer (USA)   –
(Raise A Bid (USA)) [1991 7g⁵ 6g⁵ 6f⁶ 1992 5v⁴ 7g] tall, good-topped gelding:
disappointing maiden, not seen out after May: sent to USA. *P. W. Chapple-Hyam*

CODDEN LAD   2 br.c. (Apr 20) Kala Shikari 125 – Gainsborough Lady 67   –
(Camden Town 125) [1992 6m 6m 7g 5s] leggy, sparely-made colt: poor mover:
second reported foal: dam placed at up to 1½m: poor form in maidens and a nursery.
N. Tinkler

COFFEE MINT   2 gr.f. (Feb 9) Belfort (FR) 89 – Chicory (Vaigly Great 127)   –
[1992 5g³ 7g] 4,100Y: lengthy, rather sparely-made filly: fifth foal: half-sister to 17f
winner Electric Dancer and a winner in Yugoslavia (both by Norwick): dam
twice-raced half-sister to very useful animals Macmillion and Baz Bombati: well
beaten in maiden at Hamilton and Catterick seller in summer. *J. Berry*

COIN GAME (IRE)   4 b.f. Dalsaan 125 – Canhaar (Sparkler 130) [1991 NR 1992   –
a12g] no worthwhile form. *Graeme Roe*

COLD BLOW   5 b.m. Posse (USA) 130 – Warm Wind 84 (Tumble Wind (USA))   –
[1991 NR 1992 11.8m 10g] sparely-made mare: on the downgrade. *J. Wharton*

COLD MARBLE (USA)   7 b.g. Told (USA) – Coney Dell 71 (Ercolano (USA)   –
118) [1991 11.8g 12f 1992 a14g a14g 18.2g 16m³ 14.1f⁶] good-topped gelding: poor
mover: poor handicapper nowadays: seems better at 2m than shorter: acts on firm
and dead going: below form when visored: changed hands 700 gns Ascot March
Sales. *D. R. Tucker*

COLD SHOWER (IRE)   3 b.g. Kings Lake (USA) 133 – Arctic Ford (FR) 85   **77**
(Arctic Tern (USA) 126) [1991 a8g⁴ a7g³ 1992 a8g³ 8.9s⁶ a8g 10g² 9.9f* 10g* 10f²
10m² 10f 8.5m* 9g* 10m* 10.4s⁵ 10m⁶] leggy, close-coupled gelding: progressed
really well in handicaps in 1992: successful at Beverley (apprentice selling event,
bought in 4,200 gns), Pontefract (seller, bought in 4,400 gns), Beverley, Redcar and
Newmarket (apprentices): effective at 8.5f, and stays 1¼m well: acts on firm going
(not soft) and on fibresand: often apprentice ridden: sold 9,400 gns Newmarket
Autumn Sales. *J. A. Glover*

COLERIDGE   4 gr.g. Bellypha 130 – Quay Line 117 (High Line 125) [1991 11g   **75** §
11.7g⁴ 15.3m* 11.5m⁴ 16.2g³ 16.2g 14s⁴ 20g 16.1m 1992 a16g 18g* 14g 16d 16m 14g
20m 17.2s 16.2d⁶ 18m⁴ 16.5g] tall, leggy gelding: moderate mover: won handicap at
Doncaster in March and ran well when fourth in Cesarewitch at Newmarket:
thorough stayer: best form on a sound surface (yet to race on firm ground): often
visored, also effective blinkered: unreliable. *D. Shaw*

COLFAX STARLIGHT   2 gr.f. (Feb 22) Absalom 128 – Wheatley (Town Crier   **48**
119) [1992 5g⁵ 5d⁵ 5m⁵ a6g² a7g 6g² a6g³ 5m⁶ a7g a6g] 1,800Y: small, sturdy filly:
half-sister to bumpers winner/successful jumper Last Grain (by Remainder Man)
and 2 winners abroad: dam half-sister to high-class sprinter Rabdan: plating-class
maiden: runner-up in maiden auctions: well below form last 2 starts, when blinkered
last time. *B. S. Rothwell*

COLLIER BAY   2 b.c. (Jan 21) Green Desert (USA) 127 – Cockatoo Island 99   **52** p
(High Top 131) [1992 8m 8d] angular, good-topped colt: has plenty of scope: has a
round action: second foal: half-brother to 3-y-o Colonsay (by Sharpo): dam 1½m to
14.8f winner: burly and green, in rear in large-field autumn maidens won by Armiger

Royal Hunt Cup, Royal Ascot—Colour Sergeant returns after a lengthy absence; the stand-side challenge comes from Gymcrak Premiere, Dorset Duke, High Low and Cru Exceptionnel, while Marine Diver (No. 30) is first home on the far side

at Newmarket and Dyab at Leicester, racing in touch 6f on first occasion, never placed to challenge on second: sure to do better at 3 yrs. *J. H. M. Gosden*

COLMAR   2 b.f. (Mar 10) My Dad Tom (USA) 109 – Maydrum 50 (Meldrum 112)   **45**
[1992 6f a7g6 6g 6g6 7d a6g4] 700Y: leggy, lengthy filly: third foal: half-sister to
3-y-o Speed Oil (by Java Tiger): dam lightly raced: poor plater: should be suited by
7f. *R. Bastiman*

COLONEL FAIRFAX   4 gr.g. Alias Smith (USA) – Mistress Meryll 61 (Tower   **38 §**
Walk 130) [1991 6g 6s6 5m 10.2f 11g6 10m3 8m2 1992 10.3g 10.1s5 8d a8g 8m5 7m
8m3] workmanlike gelding: poor handicapper: effective at 1m to 1¼m: acts on good
to firm ground: didn't go through with effort when visored final start: sold to join N.
Henderson's stable 5,200 gns Newmarket Autumn Sales. *J. W. Watts*

COLONEL FUTURE   2 b.g. (Apr 27) Full Extent (USA) 113 – Emerin 85 (King   **34**
Emperor (USA)) [1992 5f 6g5 7m 6g] 2,400Y, resold 2,000Y: compact gelding:
half-brother to 3 winners on flat and over hurdles, including 1988 2-y-o 5f winner
Katherines Emerald (by Aragon): dam 6f winner: little worthwhile form in modest
company: visored final start. *J. W. Watts*

COLONIAL BEAUTY (FR)   3 b.f. In Fijar (USA) 121 – Exceptional Beauty 94   **–**
(Sallust 134) [1991 NR 1992 11.9m] first reported foal: dam 1½m winner: behind
when slipping up in maiden at Haydock in August, only run on flat. *G. F. H.
Charles-Jones*

COLONIAL HEIGHTS (IRE)   2 b.c. (Feb 15) Colmore Row 111 – Paradise   **–**
Regained 41 (North Stoke 130) [1992 6m 6.1m] IR 4,800F, 18,000Y: leggy colt: has a
quick action: second live foal: half-brother to quite modest middle-distance
performer Al Shany (by Burslem): dam placed at 1½m and 15.4f: well beaten in
Newbury maiden and Nottingham seller: retained 525 gns Ascot July Sales in
between, sold to join J. Glover's stable 440 gns Doncaster September Sales. *R.
Hannon*

COLONSAY 3 ch.g. Sharpo 132 – Cockatoo Island 99 (High Top 131) [1991 NR – 1992 7g] unfurnished, useful-looking gelding: first foal: dam 1½m to 14.8f winner: never going well in Newmarket maiden in April. *J. R. Fanshawe*

COLORADO INSIGHT 4 b.f. Green Ruby (USA) 104 – Holly Burton 73 (King – Emperor (USA)) [1991 12.3d 12f³ 15.8f⁵ 12.1f⁵ 12.2g 1992 a12g] small, angular filly: moderate walker and mover: no worthwhile form on flat. *Mrs V. A. Aconley*

COLORIFIC 3 b.c. Rainbow Quest (USA) 134 – Miss Petard 113 (Petingo 135) **108** [1991 7m 7f* 7m 8s² 1992 12m 12m* 11.9g] leggy, quite good-topped colt: has a round action: very useful performer: impressive 1½-length winner of slowly-run minor event at Newmarket in July: pulled up in Great Voltigeur Stakes at York following month: stays 1½m: acts on any going. *B. W. Hills*

COLOSSUS 4 ch.c. Good Times (ITY) – Adrana 86 (Bold Lad (IRE) 133) [1991 **74** 10g³ 10m 8g⁴ 8g³ 11.5m 10.1g 5s⁴ 7g 6m⁴ 7m 6f⁴ 7d 6d* 1992 7.5g* 7g 7.5g* 7.6g³ 6f⁴ 7m 7d 7f 7d 7d 6m⁵ 7.6v⁴ a7g²] robust, lengthy colt: moderate mover: fair performer: ran well in handicaps in the spring, when successful twice at Beverley: had been out of sorts before returning to form late in year: sold out of C. Brittain's stable 17,000 gns Newmarket Autumn Sales before final start: was effective from 6f to 1m: acted on firm and dead ground: tried blinkered earlier in career: usually raced up with pace: went well on a turning track: dead. *P. C. Haslam*

COLOURING BOOK (IRE) 3 ch.f. Krayyan 117 – Her Name Was Lola – (Pitskelly 122) [1991 5g 6.9f 1992 a10g⁵ a10g³ 12v a12g⁵] sturdy filly: poor maiden: stays 1¼m. *M. J. Haynes*

COLOUR OF LIFE 2 b.f. (Mar 1) Crowning Honors (CAN) – Within A Whisper – (Welsh Pageant 132) [1992 7d] unfurnished filly: third foal: dam unraced: backward and always well behind in maiden at Leicester in October. *C. C. Elsey*

COLOUR SERGEANT 4 br.g. Green Desert (USA) 127 – Tartan Pimpernel **90** 109 (Blakeney 126) [1991 6f³ 8.2m⁵ 8m⁵ a8g* 8m³ 9g 8g 1992 8f* 8g* 8m⁵ 7m] strong, close-coupled gelding: gelded late at 3 yrs and a much improved handicapper in 1992: successful in summer at Ascot in Royal Hunt Cup (by neck from Gymcrak Premiere) and £10,770 race (idled): ran well next time: better suited by 1m than shorter, and should stay further: acts on firm ground: held up: a credit to his trainer. *Lord Huntingdon*

COLOUR SOLUTIONS 3 b.f. Grey Ghost 98 – Belinda Brown 83 (Legal Eagle **42** 126) [1991 NR 1992 a6g⁵ a6g⁴ 5f⁴ 6g] tall, rather sparely-made filly: third live foal: half-sister to 1m winner Captain Brown (by Welsh Captain): dam 2-y-o 5f winner: regressive maiden: will stay 7f: acts on fibresand: joined R. Marvin. *T. D. Barron*

COLSAN BOY 5 b.g. Remainder Man 126§ – Wimbledon's Pet (Mummy's Pet – 125) [1991 NR 1992 8d] leggy, quite good-topped gelding: poor walker: poor handicapper: stays 7f: acts on firm and dead going: below form blinkered/visored. *C. G. Cox*

COLTRANE 4 b. or br.c. Dominion 123 – Rainbow's End 83 (My Swallow 134) **73** [1991 7m a8g* 9m 9g² 1992 7m 9s a10g*] leggy, quite attractive colt: lightly-raced handicapper: decisive winner at Lingfield in November: suited by 1¼m: acts well on all-weather surfaces, possibly unsuited by the mud: seems best in a visor. *Lord Huntingdon*

COLWAY BOLD 3 br.c. Never So Bold 135 – Jhansi Ki Rani (USA) 94 (Far North **99** (CAN) 120) [1991 6g* 6m* 6f* 5m³ 6.3s* 6g 1992 6m⁴ 6m⁵ 6f 7m⁶ 6g⁵ 5.2g⁵] good-topped colt: useful performer on his day: visored and ran well in quite valuable events at York (handicap) and Newbury last 2 starts: stays 6f: acts on any going: takes keen hold. *J. W. Watts*

COLWAY ROCK (USA) 2 b.c. (Mar 21) Irish River (FR) 131 – Petite Diable **83** p (USA) (Sham (USA)) [1992 7s* 7d³ 7v³] 30,000Y: strong, compact colt: has a quick action: fourth foal: half-brother to 2 winners in USA, including Grade 1 Metropolitan Mile winner Dixie Brass (by Dixieland Band): dam won at up to 1¼m in USA: bandaged behind when neck winner of Ayr maiden in September: stayed on unable to challenge in minor events at York and Chester: will be well suited by 1m+. *J. W. Watts*

COLYAN (IRE) 2 b.c. (Mar 18) Midyan (USA) 124 – Ladyfish 79 (Pampapaul 121) **87** [1992 6d* 5f³ 6g² 6g⁴] IR 60,000Y: quite attractive colt: half-brother to 3 winners here and abroad, including middle-distance stayer/winning chaser and hurdler Fishki (by Niniski) and 1¼m winner The Dara Queen (by Dara Monarch): dam, 1m winner, is half-sister to Carroll House: easily won Catterick minor event in June: better efforts when placed in Windsor Castle Stakes at Royal Ascot and listed event (hung left and carried head awkwardly last 1f) at Haydock: bit backward and found little off bridle in Doncaster minor event, first run for over 3 months: will stay 7f. *M. R. Stoute*

COMANCHE COMPANION   2 b.f. (Mar 23) Commanche Run 133 – Constant   **64**
Companion 84 (Pas de Seul 133) [1992 6g³ 5f a5g⁵ 6s⁴ 6m 6v²] 500F: plain,
close-coupled filly: moderate mover: first foal: dam 1m winner stayed 1¼m: modest
maiden: will be very well suited by 7f+: acts on heavy going: sometimes bandaged.
T. J. Naughton

COMBATIVE (IRE)   3 ch.g. Persian Bold 123 – Caranina (USA) (Caro 133)   **85**
[1991 NR 1992 8m⁵ 8.5g⁴ 8d² 8.2g* 8.1d* 8g³ 8.3g²] 33,000F: plain gelding: fourth
foal: half-brother to 6f winner Glenscar (by Glenstal) and winners in USA and Italy:
dam Irish 6f winner: progressed well in handicaps in first half of 1992, successful at
Nottingham and Haydock: suited by strongly-run race at 1m, and will prove suited
by further: acts on dead ground: wears visor: tongue tied down last 4 starts: tends to
get on edge: sold 27,000 gns Newmarket July Sales. *J. H. M. Gosden*

COMBELLINO   2 br.c. (Mar 4) Robellino (USA) 127 – Honeycomb (Valiyar 129)   **56**
[1992 6g 8.2s] 1,500F, 6,000Y: strong colt: first foal: dam unraced out of a half-sister
to high-class middle-distance stayer Attica Meli: much better effort in autumn
maidens when never-dangerous seventh of 13 in 1m event at Nottingham. *P. W. Harris*

COME ON MY GIRL (IRE)   4 gr.f. To-Agori-Mou 133 – Travelin' Joan (USA)   –
(Al Hattab (USA)) [1991 8g³ 6f* 6d 6g⁵ 7m a6g⁴ 5g 5.2f 5m³ 6.1m 6.1m⁴ 1992 5.9h
5m 7.1m⁶ 8.1m 5g⁶ 5.9f 5g] lengthy filly: little form in 1992: stays 6f: acts on firm
going: below form when blinkered: sold 950 gns Doncaster November Sales:
possibly temperamental. *T. A. K. Cuthbert*

COME TO GOOD   5 br.m. Swing Easy (USA) 126 – Demta (Astec 128) [1991 10v   –
8f 1992 12f] plain mare: seems of little account. *M. P. Muggeridge*

COMETTI STAR   8 ch.g. Giacometti 130 – Hotazur 52 (Hotfoot 126) [1991 NR   –
1992 16.2g] workmanlike gelding: sixth foal: half-brother to 1982 2-y-o 5f winner
Palace Beau (by Dragonara Palace) and Lord Ludo (by Owen Anthony), successful
at around 9f: dam plater: winning chaser as 6-y-o: tailed off in Beverley maiden. *J. Wharton*

COMET WHIRLPOOL (IRE)   2 ch.c. (Apr 30) Waajib 121 – Remember   **57**
Mulvilla (Ballad Rock 122) [1992 a5g 5d a5g⁵ 5g³ 5d⁶ 5g a5g⁴ a6g² a5g²] IR 10,000Y:
angular colt: first foal: dam Irish 2-y-o 6f winner, is granddaughter of 1000 Guineas
third Alpine Bloom, dam of Prix d'Ispahan winner Full of Hope: modest maiden:
speedy: possibly requires a sound surface: blinkered last 3 starts: trained first 4
starts by B. Beasley. *Pat Mitchell*

COMISKEY PARK (IRE)   3 ch.c. Caerleon (USA) 132 – Soba 127 (Most Secret   **35**
119) [1991 NR 1992 a6g a6g a8g⁶ 7.5g a7g⁴ 8.5f⁶ a7g] 23,000Y: plain colt: moderate
mover: fifth foal: closely related to 7f and 1½m winner Gold Dust (by Golden
Fleece) and half-brother to 2 winners, notably fairly useful 7.6f winner Water Well
(by Sadler's Wells): dam sprinter: poor handicapper: may prove better suited by
1¼m than 1m: acts on fibresand. *D. W. Chapman*

COMMANCHE CREEK   2 b.c. (Mar 29) Commanche Run 133 – Vice Vixen   **79** p
(CAN) (Vice Regent (CAN)) [1992 8m 8g⁶] sturdy, lengthy colt: second foal:
half-brother to very smart 3-y-o middle-distance filly Cunning (by Bustino): dam
unraced daughter of half-sister to smart French middle-distance winner Lichine:
carrying plenty of condition, much better effort in October when keeping-on sixth of
9 to Shaiba in minor event at Newmarket: will be well suited by middle-distances:
sure to progress. *L. M. Cumani*

COMMANCHE GOLD (IRE)   2 b.c. (May 16) Commanche Run 133 – Golden   **79** p
Braid 109 (Glint of Gold 128) [1992 8.1s³ 8d*] sturdy, useful-looking colt: second
foal: half-brother to 3-y-o Gold Belt (by Bellypha): dam 7f (at 2 yrs) and 1¼m
winner, is daughter of Silk Slipper: justified favouritism in moderately-run
16-runner maiden at Kempton in September, staying on strongly to beat Spring To
Action by 2 lengths: will improve further when tried over long distances. *Lord Huntingdon*

COMMANCHE SIOUX (IRE)   4 b.f. Commanche Run 133 – Papsie's Pet   –
(Busted 134) [1991 12.2m³ 12m* 13.8g 1992 14.1m a14g⁵ a12g a12s] small, lengthy
filly: moderate mover: on the downgrade: seems to stay 1¾m: acts on good to firm
ground: often visored. *K. A. Morgan*

COMMANCHE STAR   2 ch.g. (Mar 5) Commanche Run 133 – Lehzen (Posse   –
(USA) 130) [1992 7s] first foal: dam unraced daughter of half-sister to Gold Cup
winner Ragstone, very smart middle-distance stayer Castle Keep and dam of Moon

Madness and Sheriff's Star: soon well behind in maiden at Lingfield in October. *D. Shaw*

COMME CI COMME CA 6 ch.g. Buzzards Bay 128§ – Morstons Maid 40 – (Morston (FR) 125) [1991 NR 1992 10.3g] big, workmanlike gelding: moderate mover: twice raced and soundly beaten. *B. Ellison*

COMME D'HABITUDE (USA) 2 gr.f. (Mar 24) Caro 133 – Une Amazone **71** (USA) (Youth (USA) 135) [1992 8.1s* 8s] $67,000Y: good-topped, workmanlike filly: eighth foal: half-sister to smart middle-distance stayer Al Maheb (by Riverman) and 2 winners in France: dam unraced half-sister to Prix Royal-Oak winner Henri le Balafre: strong at finish when 1½-length winner of maiden at Chepstow: tailed off in Fillies' Mile at Ascot later in autumn: will be suited by middle distances: has joined W. Carter. *P. F. I. Cole*

COMMENDABLE (IRE) 4 b.c. Baillamont (USA) 124 – Praise (FR) 116 (Hard **111** To Beat 132) [1991 10.5g4 12m 11g6 1992 12g* 12.5s* 15.5s* 15.5g*] lengthy, good-bodied ex-English colt: rated 102 when with G. Harwood at 3 yrs: showed improved form and was unbeaten in spring, successful in amateur races at Toulouse and Saint-Cloud before pattern events at Maisons-Laffitte (Prix de Barbeville) and Longchamp (narrowly beat Last King and Mardonius in Prix Vicomtesse Vigier): better at around 2m than shorter, and should stay further: below form only run on good to firm ground, and clearly goes well with some give: blinkered nowadays. *H. Pantall, France*

COMMITTED DANCER (USA) 5 b.h. Nijinsky (CAN) 138 – Committed **109** (USA) 128 (Hagley (USA)) [1991 8d 8g6 9g* 8m 8.5g* 8m* 8m4 1992 10s 9d 9m2 8f 9g 8g* 8s5 8s5] strong Irish horse: first foal: dam top-class sprinter, also won over 7.9f: very useful but none too consistent: won listed race at Fairyhouse and good second to Approach The Bench in similar event at Leopardstown: effective at 1m/9f: needs a sound surface: successful when blinkered. *D. K. Weld, Ireland*

COMMON COUNCIL 3 br.g. Siberian Express (USA) 125 – Old Domesday **75** Book 93 (High Top 131) [1991 5g a7g3 7m3 8g6 7m* a8g* 1992 8m3 8.1d3 8m2 7.6d3 8f a8g a10g2] compact gelding: fair form in handicaps: stays 1¼m: acts on good to firm and dead ground and on equitrack: has run well for 7-lb claimer. *G. A. Pritchard-Gordon*

COMMON GAIN (IRE) 2 b.c. (May 21) Common Grounds 118 – Precious Gift – (Prince Tenderfoot (USA) 126) [1992 5g 5g] IR 2,000Y: well-made colt: moderate walker: fifth foal: half-brother to 1m and 1½m winner Must Hurry (by Kampala): dam Irish maiden: poor form in northern maiden auctions in spring. *J. Berry*

COMPANY CASH 4 ch.c. Chief Singer 131 – I'll Try 71 (Try My Best (USA) 130) – [1991 NR 1992 a7g a5g4 a7g* 8s 5g a7g 7m a7g a7g a7g5 a6g] rather leggy colt: first a48 foal: dam, 5f winner at 2 yrs, is daughter of half-sister to Irish 1000 Guineas winner Katies: mostly well beaten after making all in Southwell maiden in February: should stay 1m: below form when visored once, usually blinkered. *R. Bastiman*

COMPLETE MADNESS 2 ch.c. (Mar 1) Irish River (FR) 131 – Candle In The **79** p Wind 90 (Thatching 131) [1992 6s3] leggy, close-coupled colt: second foal: dam 2-y-o 6f winner later ran in USA: 33/1, shaped well when beaten 1½ lengths by Zarani Sidi Anna in 16-runner maiden at Newbury in October, prominent throughout and keeping on stoutly after looking green: will improve. *J. W. Hills*

COMSTOCK 5 ch.g. Coquelin (USA) 121 – Maura Paul (Bonne Noel 115) [1991 **86** d 12g3 12.3g 11.9m3 12g 13.9g 12m2 10m 12d 1992 12g2 14g 11.9g3 10.9s5 11.9d 11.9s6 12g] lengthy gelding: good mover: fair handicapper: below form after reappearance: should prove better suited by 1¾m than shorter: acts on good to firm ground: sold out of J. FitzGerald's stable 20,000 gns Doncaster May Sales after third start: won novice hurdle in December. *N. Tinkler*

COMTEC'S LEGEND 2 ch.f. (Mar 29) Legend of France (USA) 124 – Comtec **49** Princess 73 (Gulf Pearl 117) [1992 7f4 7m* 7g6 7f4 8m 7.5m3 8.3s5 7d3 a7g2] 1,200Y: small filly: half-sister to several winners, including middle-distance stayer Qualitair Aviator (by Valiyar) and 1988 2-y-o 5f seller winner Swynford Princess (by Raga Navarro): dam 1m to 1¼m winner: won seller (no bid) at Wolverhampton in June: consistent form in nurseries late in year: will stay 1¼m: acts on good to firm ground, seems unsuited by very soft: sometimes hangs left. *J. F. Bottomley*

CONBRIO STAR 2 ch.c. (Feb 21) Jester 119 – Hill of Fare (Brigadier Gerard **37** 144) [1992 5.7f3 6m 5.7f6m6 a5g 6v a8g a6g] 1,300Y, 6,000Y 2-y-o: lengthy colt: first foal: half-brother to a winner in Belgium: dam lightly raced: bad maiden: tried blinkered: sold out of C. Cox's stable 420 gns Doncaster September Sales after fifth start. *J. R. Jenkins*

CONCERT PITCH 13 ch.g. Royal Match 117 – Ballychord (DEN) (Ballymoss 136) [1991 a8g a8g³ a8g² a8g⁶ a7g⁴ 8m 8m 7.1d a8g 1992 a7g 8.5g⁶] strong, dipped-backed, lengthy gelding: has a round action: poor handicapper: stays 1m: acts on any going: has won in blinkers. *B. Palling* —

CONCINNITY (USA) 3 b.c. Hello Gorgeous (USA) 128 – Cincinnity (USA) (Shareef Dancer (USA) 135) [1991 NR 1992 7d⁴ 8d 10d⁴ 8m] rangy colt: shows knee action: first foal: dam minor 3-y-o winner in USA, closely related to useful middle-distance 4-y-o Mellaby: easily best effort when staying-on fourth in maiden at Brighton in September: stiff task in Newmarket handicap after: will be suited by return to middle distances. *L. J. Holt* —

CONCORD WENCH 4 b.f. Alleging (USA) 120 – Guest Image (Be My Guest (USA) 126) [1991 NR 1992 10d 10.3g] small filly: second foal: dam little form but seemed best at 1m: twice raced, and well beaten in maiden and seller. *P. D. Evans* —

CONE LANE 6 ch.g. On Your Mark 125 – Cee Beauty 74 (Ribero 126) [1991 a7g⁶ 7g 7m⁵ 1992 a8g⁶] workmanlike gelding: poor handicapper: stays 7f: acts on hard going: ran poorly in blinkers: winning hurdler in March. *B. Gubby* —

CONEYBURY (IRE) 2 b.c. (Apr 2) Last Tycoon 131 – Jackie Berry 97 **86 p** (Connaught 130) [1992 7g 7m³ 7g*] lengthy, well-made, good sort: fourth foal: brother to 3-y-o 7f and 1¼m winner Juniper Berry and half-brother to a winner in Italy by Lydian: dam Irish 7f and 8.5f winner is out of sister to smart 1¼m filly Cranberry Sauce: progressive colt: heavily-backed favourite when 4-length winner of 9-runner maiden at Brighton in September, quickening smartly from rear 3f out and running on strongly despite drifting left: will stay 1¼m: has plenty of scope, and will do lot better as 3-y-o. *L. M. Cumani*

CONEY DOVE 7 b.m. Celtic Cone 116 – Shadey Dove 81 (Deadly Nightshade 107) [1991 NR 1992 10.2s⁶] non-thoroughbred mare: first foal: dam useful hurdler: modest winning hurdler: well beaten in Chepstow apprentice event on flat debut. *R. J. Price* —

CONFOUND (IRE) 3 b.g. Wolverlife 115 – Arachosia (Persian Bold 123) [1991 6d 6g 5d 1992 7d 9.7g 8f 7.6m⁶ 11.9f 9.7d⁵] lengthy, plain gelding: moderate mover: no worthwhile form. *J. Akehurst* —

CONFRONTER 3 ch.c. Bluebird (USA) 125 – Grace Darling (USA) (Vaguely **87** Noble 140) [1991 7d 7.1m³ 7g² 6m⁵ 6.1d² 6s* 1992 8d 6d 7.6s³ 8m² 8.5d³ a7g* 8f² a7g* 8g² 7.1g⁴ 7d] tall, angular colt: fairly useful performer: won 2 apprentice races at Lingfield in summer: may prove ideally suited by further than 1m: acts on any turf going, and on equitrack: effective blinkered or not: ran well for lady rider. *P. F. I. Cole*

CONGRESS (IRE) 3 b.f. Dancing Brave (USA) 140 – Celtic Assembly (USA) 95 **79** (Secretariat (USA)) [1991 7g 7f³ 8m* 7m² 1992 8g³ 10d 10.3m⁴ 8.3g 8.1g] good-bodied filly: moderate mover: fair handicapper: stayed 1¼m: acted on good to firm ground: headstrong in visor final start: none too consistent: visits Robellino. *M. R. Stoute*

CONISTON LAKE (IRE) 3 ch.g. Coquelin (USA) 121 – High Lake (Quisling **63** 117) [1991 6g⁴ 6g⁴ 8m 1992 7s 8d 7f³ 7.1m⁵ 7d⁶ 7m² 7f⁴ 6g⁵ 7g* 7.1s 7.1g 7g⁵ a7g] neat gelding: inconsistent handicapper: won at Brighton in August: will prove as effective at 1m as shorter: acts on good to firm ground: best form blinkered, always outpaced (on equitrack) in visor final start. *G. Lewis*

CONISTON WATER (USA) 3 b.c. Private Account (USA) – Rivers of Mist **83 p** (USA) (Irish River (FR) 131) [1991 NR 1992 8g⁴ 8f* 9s] $180,000F: good-topped colt: first foal: dam, won over 1m in France on only start at 2 yrs (later winner in USA at 4 yrs), is granddaughter of Never Too Late: sire good-class 9f/1¼m performer, best at 4 yrs: fourth in Wood Ditton Stakes before landing odds in maiden at Yarmouth in June by ½ length: never dangerous in £11,700 handicap at Newbury 4 months later: should stay beyond 1m: should prove capable of better. *J. H. M. Gosden*

CONJURER 5 gr.g. Magic Mirror 105 – Morning Miss 59 (Golden Dipper 119) — [1991 NR 1992 a8g 9.7g⁶ 10m⁴] leggy, close-coupled gelding: poor handicapper nowadays: should stay 1¼m: acts on firm going: joined J. Joseph. *R. Simpson*

CONJURING (USA) 4 b.c. Devil's Bag (USA) – Hint (USA) (Nijinsky (CAN) — 138) [1991 8m² 10g 1992 a12g a12g⁶ 14.6g⁶ 14.1d] tall, leggy colt: has been hobdayed: has a round action: poor maiden: stays 1m: acts on good to firm ground: usually blinkered: sometimes has tongue tied down: probably one to treat with caution. *G. Thorner*

CONQUISTA 4 ch.f. Aragon 118 – Divine Fling (Imperial Fling (USA) 116) [1991 **75** 7m² 7m 8s³ 7g⁴ 7f² 7.1g³ 8m⁵ 8g* 8m⁴ 1992 8d⁶ 7.5m⁶ 8f⁵ 8.1g⁶] leggy, workmanlike filly: fair handicapper: stays 1m: best efforts on a sound surface: best blinkered: headstrong, and sometimes mounted on track: usually held up. *Lady Herries*

CONSIGLIERE 4 ch.c. Caerleon (USA) 132 – Miss Silca Key 102 (Welsh Saint **102** 126) [1991 7d² 8m* 7g 1992 6f² 6f 7g* 6m³ 7m² 6g5] lengthy, strong-quartered colt: progressed really well in 1992: successful in Bunbury Cup (Handicap) at Newmarket (beat Ashdren a head) and good efforts after in Stewards' Cup at Goodwood and listed races at York (2 lengths second to Reported) and Newmarket: best form at 6f/7f: acts on firm and dead ground: often bandaged: joined R. Frankel in USA. *R. Charlton*

CONSPICUOUS (IRE) 2 b.c. (Mar 14) Alzao (USA) 117 – Mystery Lady (USA) **69** (Vaguely Noble 140) [1992 5.2d² 5.1h³ 5.7f² 6m³ 7g³ 7.3g⁶ 8.9s5] IR 70,000Y: close-coupled colt: has a quick action: half-brother to a multiple winner in USA by Smarten: dam ran twice: fair performer: stays 9f: acts on firm and dead ground: strong-galloping sort: consistent. *P. F. I. Cole*

CONSTRUCTIVIST (IRE) 3 b.c. Fools Holme (USA) – Spire 75 (Shirley **67** Heights 130) [1991 6m 7g² a7g² 1992 8d 10.2g⁴ 11.9f² 10.2s⁴ 14g 10s] smallish, quite attractive colt: moderate mover: modest maiden: well beaten final 2 starts: should prove suited by 1½m+: probably acts on any going: sold to join M. Barraclough 7,000 gns Newmarket Autumn Sales. *B. W. Hills*

CONSULATE 6 gr.g. Absalom 128 – Maiden Pool 85 (Sharpen Up 127) [1991 6m **62** 7m 5g² 5g5 5d* 6g 5d² 5m³ 5g⁴ 5m 1992 5s² 5d 5m³ 5g5 5g⁴ 5m² 5m 5s 5d 5.1g] stocky gelding: none too consistent handicapper in 1992: effective at sprint distances, and has form over 1m: acts on good to firm and soft ground and equitrack. *J. Balding*

CONTESTED BID (USA) 3 b. or br.c. Alleged (USA) 138 – Queens Only **120** (USA) (Marshua's Dancer (USA)) [1991 8g⁴ 8d* 10v³ 8f* 1992 9.2s5 10.5m² 12g³ 12m³ 12m⁴ 10d³] quite attractive colt: good walker: very smart French performer: won maiden at Saint-Cloud and Hoist The Flag Stakes (Div.2) at Hollywood Park as 2-y-o: in frame in 1992 in Prix Lupin at Longchamp (beaten length by Johann Quatz), Prix Jockey-Club at Chantilly (2¼ lengths third to Polytain), Irish Derby at the Curragh (13 lengths third to St Jovite), Prix Niel at Longchamp and Budweiser International at Laurel (2 lengths third to Zoman): will stay further than 1½m: acts on any going: most consistent: has joined R. Frankel in USA. *M. Zilber, France*

CONTINUITY 3 b.f. Celestial Storm (USA) 132 – Tamassos 67 (Dance In Time **59** (CAN)) [1991 NR 1992 10d⁶ 10f⁴ 9.7g³ 8.9m 9.7m 12m³ 11.8d² 13.8d³ 12.4v⁶ a12g²] robust filly: moderate mover: first foal: dam, 1¼m winner, is half-sister to Ile de

Ladbroke Bunbury Cup, Newmarket—Consigliere just holds on;
behind are Ashdren (noseband) and Knight of Mercy,
with Superbrave just visible in between

Chypre: modest performer: trained first 5 starts by G. Harwood: stays 13.8f: acts on good to firm and dead ground: below form when blinkered once: sold to join E. Alston 5,200 gns Newmarket December Sales. *M. H. Tompkins*

CONTRAC COUNTESS (IRE)   2 b.f. (Apr 19) Thatching 131 – Crimson Sails   **53** (Lomond (USA) 128) [1992 6m4 5d 7f 7.5d2 7g 8.5m] IR 1,000Y: smallish, plain filly: first foal: dam Irish maiden, placed at 7f at 3 yrs: inconsistent maiden: stays 7.5f: acts on good to firm and dead ground. *B. S. Rothwell*

CONTRACT COURT (USA)   2 br.g. (May 17) Conquistador Cielo (USA) –   **64** Moth (USA) (Drone) [1992 6m4 7.1g 7m 8.2g5 8s 7m] $30,000Y: angular, good-topped gelding: half-brother to several minor winners in North America: dam minor winner as 2-y-o: modest maiden: well beaten in nurseries last 2 starts: stays 1m: acts on good to firm ground. *C. A. Cyzer*

CONTRACT ELITE (IRE)   2 b.g. (Apr 18) Dominion Royale 112 – Salote   **59** (USA) 109 (Forli (ARG)) [1992 5s3 5d* 6m6 7.5d6 6g6 7m4 7g5 8.2d6] 10,000Y: sturdy gelding: has scope: good walker: half-brother to several winners here and abroad, including (at 1½m) fairly useful Mountain Isle (by Shirley Heights): dam suited by 1½m: won maiden auction at Carlisle in May: bandaged off-fore, ran well in nurseries last 3 starts: will be well suited by middle distances: probably acts on any going. *C. W. Thornton*

CONVENIENT MOMENT   2 ch.f. (Apr 2) Clantime 101 – Panay 77 (Arch   **59** Sculptor 123) [1992 5g2 5g* 5m2 5.2g 5d 5s*] 1,500Y: small filly: sister to 3-y-o 5f winner Grand Time and half-sister to 1987 2-y-o 5f winner Hatay (by Alias Smith): dam 2-y-o 5f winner: modest performer: won seller at Wolverhampton (bought in 3,000 gns) in July and nursery at Warwick in October: speedy: acts on good to firm and soft ground: ran poorly when blinkered once. *J. Berry*

CONVOY   2 gr.g. (Mar 4) Be My Guest (USA) 126 – Be Easy 110 (Be Friendly 130)   **66** [1992 6d a7g6 a8g2 a8g*] half-brother to 6 middle-distance winners, notably very useful Glowing With Pride (by Ile de Bourbon) and Whipp's Cross (by Kris): dam best at up to 7f: improved form when blinkered and stepped up to 1m, staying on to win maiden at Lingfield in December: will be suited by 1¼m. *G. Wragg*

COOCHIE   3 b.f. King of Spain 121 – York Street (USA) (Diamond Shoal 130) [1991   **–** 5f 6g 5.7m 6m 7f5 10.5d 1992 8d 11.9d 10.8s] small, rather leggy filly: poor plater: below form when blinkered: may well be temperamental. *R. J. Baker*

COOLABA PRINCE (IRE)   3 b.g. Red Sunset 120 – Acquire 105 (Burglar 128)   **71** [1991 5g5 5g6 5m4 5f4 5g5 5d4 1992 5.9d2 5s5 6m2 6f2 7g6 6g* 6f6 6d 6d2 6.1s*] sturdy, rather angular gelding: modest handicapper: won at Ayr in July and Nottingham in October: best efforts at around 6f on a soft surface: has run creditably in blinkers/visor. *F. H. Lee*

COOL APOLLO (NZ)   5 b.g. Gay Apollo – Maple Leaf (NZ) (King's Troop 118)   **–** [1991 NR 1992 11.8s 12.3m5] workmanlike New Zealand-bred gelding: seems of little account. *J. C. McConnochie*

COOL ENOUGH   11 ch.g. Welsh Captain 113 – Sundrive (Status Seeker) [1991   **41** 7d4 8d 7.5f 6g4 7m4 7h* 7f 8d 8m 8g4 7f 7f5 1992 a7g6 a7g 7d 7.1g3 8d 8.1m 6.9f2 7.1m* 7d 7d6 7f 6m2 7g5 7s 8s] small, sturdy gelding: tough handicapper: gained twelfth career win from over 100 starts when landing selling event at Edinburgh (no bid) in May: best form at 7f/1m: acts on any going: often apprentice ridden. *Mrs J. R. Ramsden*

COOLEY'S VALVE (IRE)   4 b.c. Pennine Walk 120 – First Blush (Ela-Mana-   **92** Mou 132) [1991 8g 8d* 10.4g2 7d2 11.9g6 8m2 1992 10d 10g4] rangy, good-topped colt: impresses in appearance: good walker: moderate mover: quite useful handicapper: not seen out after creditable fourth in £11,350 event at Newmarket in May: stays 1¼m (stiff task at 11.9f): acts on good to firm and dead ground: sold to join N. Henderson 26,000 gns Newmarket Autumn Sales. *B. W. Hills*

COOL FLIGHT   3 ch.f. Absalom 128 – Fancy Flight (FR) 74 (Arctic Tern (USA)   **–** 126) [1991 NR 1992 10d a12g] 1,400Y: sparely-made filly: third foal: dam 1¼m winner: no promise in seller at Leicester and claimer at Lingfield. *R. Thompson*

COOL LUKE (IRE)   3 b.g. Red Sunset 120 – Watet Khet (FR) 82 (Wittgenstein   **82** (USA) 123) [1991 NR 1992 7s* 8d6 8.1m4 7f3 8m4 7.1s* 7s4 7d] 3,100Y: half-brother to several winners in Italy, including 1991 1m listed winner Mercorella (by Lomond): dam 12.3f winner: won maiden at Newcastle in April and £8,000 handicap at Haydock in September: rare modest effort final start: stays 8.1f: has form on firm ground, but goes particularly well on soft: sometimes hangs, and below best for claimer. *G. M. Moore*

COOL PARADE (USA) 4 ch.g. Listcapade (USA) – Yours Trudy (USA) (Star 52 Envoy (USA)) [1991 7s⁴ 10m⁵ 8.2d 8m 8.5f* 9.2d⁶ 9m⁴ 9.9f 8h 10.5d 12.2g⁴ 8m* 1992 9m² 8d⁵ 8m⁴ 9.2m⁴ 10f⁴ 10f] leggy, quite good-topped gelding: largely consistent performer: should prove best at up to 1¼m: acts on any going, except seemingly on hard: ran creditably when visored once, usually blinkered. *G. M. Moore*

COOL SOCIETY (USA) 3 ch.c. Imp Society (USA) – Icy Friend (USA) (It's 64 Freezing (USA) 122) [1991 6g⁶ 6g 6.1g⁶ 6 7g⁴ 8m* 8.1m 8.2m 1992 10f* 10d 10f4 10f4 11.4d 10m] good-quartered colt: has a quick action: inconsistent maiden: stays 1¼m: acts on firm ground: has won for apprentice: sold to join W. Musson's stable 2,800 gns Newmarket Autumn Sales. *C. R. Nelson*

COOPERS DELIGHT 2 b.c. (Mar 17) Sharpo 132 – Petrify 71 (Air Trooper 115) 43 [1992 5.2m 5g 5d⁶ 5g 8g 6d] 11,000Y: good-quartered colt: second foal: half-brother to 1¼m winner Scared Stiff (by Electric): dam lightly-raced 7f winner: poor maiden: stays 6f (raced too freely at 1m): sold 2,200 gns Newmarket Autumn Sales. *G. Lewis*

COOPERS SPOT-ON (IRE) 4 b.g. Glenstal (USA) 118 – Shikari Rose (Kala 62 Shikari 125) [1991 10v 9g 9g 1992 8d⁵ 9d 10m 16g* 16g 15.1d³] ex-Irish gelding: won Wexford maiden for J. Oxx in summer: failed to repeat that form, in Edinburgh seller final start: seems better at 2m than shorter: effective blinkered or not. *P. Monteith*

COPPERMILL LAD 9 ch.g. Ardoon 124 – Felin Geri (Silly Season 127) [1991 52 6v² 6d⁴ 6g⁶ 7g⁶ 6m 6d⁵ 6v³ 5d⁴ 6g⁵ 5g⁵ 7g 1992 5s* 6.1d 6g² 6g 6d⁴ 6m² 5m* 6d 5m⁵ 6g 5d³ 5g 6s⁵] compact gelding: carries plenty of condition: has a round action: none too consistent handicapper: successful at Lingfield (awarded race) in April and Goodwood (apprentices) in June: effective at 5f and 6f: acts on any going: usually gets behind: tough. *L. J. Holt*

COPPER TRADER 3 gr.f. Faustus (USA) 118 – Alicia Markova 64 (Habat 127) – [1991 5m⁶ 8m 6s⁵ 1992 8.5f⁶ 8.9s⁶ 10g³ a12g⁵] leggy, workmanlike filly: poor maiden: gives impression will stay 1¼m: acts on soft ground. *K. S. Bridgwater*

COPPOT TEL (IRE) 2 b.c. (Apr 7) Jareer (USA) 115 – Arctic Dark (Arctic Tern 64 (USA) 126) [1992 5.2d 7g 7d⁴ 9g⁴ 7g] IR 14,500Y: leggy colt: progressed well physically: has an easy action: fourth foal: half-brother to Irish 11f winner Smoke Screen (by Vayrann): dam unraced: modest maiden: will stay beyond 9f: acts on dead ground. *C. E. Brittain*

COP THE CASH (USA) 2 ch.c. (Apr 18) Known Fact (USA) 135 – Twilight 68 Flight (USA) (Quack (USA)) [1992 5g⁵ 5f² 5.9f4] $30,000Y: tall, useful-looking colt: half-brother to 4-y-o 1¼m winner Arak (by Clever Trick) and a winner by Tilt Up: dam unraced half-sister to Cornwallis winner Hadif and good 1985 USA 2-y-o Silent Account: second to Petardia in maiden at Doncaster in May: ran moderately in Carlisle maiden following month. *M. Bell*

COPY LANE (IRE) 3 b. or br.g. Runnett 125 – Airy Queen (USA) (Sadair) [1991 – 6m 7d 5.7f⁴ 5.7m 6m⁴ 8.2m⁵ 8g 7.6m 1992 a10g³ a10g⁵ 12v 16m 12s] leggy gelding: inconsistent maiden: stays 1¼m: acts on firm ground and equitrack: won 3 times over hurdles in autumn: subsequently sold 6,000 gns Newmarket Autumn Sales. *M. R. Channon*

CORAL FLUTTER 5 b.m. Beldale Flutter (USA) 130 – Countess Olivia 80 64 (Prince Tenderfoot (USA) 126) [1991 a7g⁶ a10g 7d4 9s 7m² 7d 8.3g⁴ 7m³ 7m 7g⁵ 6.9f⁶ 8f⁶ 7m² 8g⁵ 1992 7g⁶ 7m 7f4 8f 7m* 7g⁴ 7f* 7m* 7f3 8m² 7m a7g⁴ a7g] lengthy, good-quartered mare: has a quick action: consistent handicapper: successful in summer at Yarmouth (2) and Lingfield: effective at 7f/1m: acts on firm going: keen sort, forces pace: usually blinkered/visored. *J. W. Payne*

CORCINA 4 gr.f. Kalaglow 132 – Feather Flower 74 (Relkino 131) [1991 8s⁴ 8g⁵ 77 10f 10.6g* 12g⁴ 1992 10g 10.4d 10.1m² 9f 10g³ 10.1m⁶] leggy filly: fair handicapper: best form at 1¼m: acted on good to firm ground: took keen hold, and forced pace: inconsistent: in foal to Indian Ridge. *M. Bell*

CORDILLERO 6 b.g. Head For Heights 125 – Petipa (FR) (Habitat 134) [1991 – 9.7m 1992 9.7g 11.5f⁵ 10g] angular gelding: poor mover: no worthwhile form: stays 13.6f: acts on good to firm going: below form when blinkered. *A. Moore*

CORINTHIAN GOD (IRE) 3 b.c. Red Sunset 120 – Rathcoffey Duchy 44 (Faberge II 121) [1991 5.7f⁶ 7m 1992 10.1d⁵ 12d 13.6f* 12.3m* 12d 14.6g 10s 12s] compact colt: poor handicapper: won at Redcar and Wolverhampton in August: stays 13.6f: suited by top-of-the-ground. *D. A. Wilson*

Mr F. M. Kalla's "Corrupt"

CORLEY FLOWER   3 b.f. Sizzling Melody 117 – Dame Corley (L'Enjoleur   **31**
(CAN)) [1991 5.1m 6f 6m 8m 1992 a5g⁴ 5.1d 8d] sparely-made filly: poor plater:
probably doesn't stay 1m. *P. D. Cundell*

CORMORANT BAY   3 ch.f. Don't Forget Me 127 – Quarry Wood 89 (Super Sam   **55**
124) [1991 NR 1992 8d⁴ 9s⁴ 10d² a10g] leggy filly: fifth reported foal: half-sister to
top-class 1¼m filly Cormorant Wood (by Home Guard), dam of Rock Hopper, 10.4f
winner Cormorant Creek (by Gorytus) and good hurdler River Ceiriog (by Broxted):
dam won at up to 1¾m: modest maiden: ran poorly on equitrack debut: stays 1¼m:
acts on soft ground: often bandaged near-hind. *F. H. Lee*

CORNFLAKE   2 b.f. (Apr 29) Prince Rupert (FR) 121 – Corny Story 75 (Oats 126)   **35**
[1992 7g 7d 7g] 2,600F, 4,600Y: tall, well-made filly: half-sister to 1988 2-y-o 6f
winner Cornet (by Coquelin), later successful over jumps, and 2 other winners over
hurdles: dam, 11f winner, is half-sister to smart sprinter Pepita: always behind in
maidens. *Denys Smith*

CORN FUTURES   4 b.f. Nomination 125 – Hay Reef 72 (Mill Reef (USA) 141)   **76**
[1991 6d² 6m² 5g² 6d⁵ 7g 7f 8d⁴ 8d 7.6d² 7g 1992 a6g 7.5g 6g⁵ 7g⁴ 7.6g 6f⁶ 6f⁶ 6f²
6f⁶ 7f 7s 6v⁴dis] compact filly: has a quick action: fair handicapper: effective at 6f to
1m: acts on firm ground and dead: often visored/blinkered nowadays: often takes
keen hold. *J. P. Leigh*

CORNHILL MELODY   4 ch.f. The Minstrel (CAN) 135 – French Cutie (USA)   **31**
(Vaguely Noble 140) [1991 12h³ 14.8f⁵ 16m³ 11.5f 10g 1992 7.1g⁵ 8d 10.8g³ 10.8f 12f
10g 8.2m 10f 8.9d⁵ 9.7g 8g] angular filly: inconsistent maiden handicapper: stays
10.8f: acts on dead ground: below form when blinkered once. *J. L. Spearing*

CORN LILY   6 ch.m. Aragon 118 – Ixia 91 (I Say 125) [1991 11f² 13d² 12.3f³ 12.3f*   **73**
12m* 12f⁵ 12f* 13.8m* 1992 12.3f⁵ 12.3m⁶ 12.3g 12m* 13.8g*] tall, leggy mare: fair
handicapper: won at Thirsk and Catterick in September, both races for second
successive year: effective at 1½m to 1¾m: acts on firm and dead going: genuine and
consistent: front runner. *Mrs M. Reveley*

CORONA GOLD 2 b.g. (Mar 1) Chilibang 120 – Miss Alkie 58 (Noalcoholic (FR)   – p
128) [1992 6g] 15,000Y: sturdy gelding: first foal: dam won 6f seller: 20/1 and burly,
behind in 18-runner maiden at Thirsk in August, racing in touch 4f, eased when
beaten: will improve. *J. G. FitzGerald*

CORPORATE TYPE (IRE) 4 b.g. Last Tycoon 131 – Sherkraine 98 (Shergar   **24**
140) [1991 a10g a10g 12.2g 12m 9.9f 10m⁵ 10f 10m a11g a12g⁵ a12g 1992 a14g 9.9f
12.2g⁴ 12.1s⁶ 12.2g] sturdy gelding: maiden handicapper: stays 1½m: sold 1,500 gns
Doncaster September Sales. *G. P. Kelly*

CORPUS 3 ch.c. Ballacashtal (CAN) – Millingdale 65 (Tumble Wind (USA)) [1991   –
NR 1992 10.2g 10g] good-topped colt: fifth foal: half-brother to 1989 3-y-o 7f winner
Lady Stock (by Crofter): dam, ran only at 2 yrs, second over 5f and 6f: twice raced on
flat, and no worthwhile form. *R. J. Hodges*

CORRAZONA (USA) 2 ch.f. (Feb 7) El Gran Senor (USA) 136 – Heartbreak **111** p
(USA) (Stage Door Johnny (USA)) [1992 8d* 8s*] $550,000F: fourth foal: half-sister
to Belmont Stakes runner-up Thirty Six Red (by Slew O' Gold), winner of Grade 1
Wood Memorial: dam minor winner in USA: successful in newcomers race and Prix
des Reservoirs (by a head and a short neck) at Longchamp in autumn: a most
promising middle-distance filly. *Mme C. Head, France*

CORRESPONDENCE (CAN) 2 br.c. (Jan 27) Phone Trick (USA) – Chas'   **45**
Lady (USA) (Key To The Kingdom (USA)) [1992 6g 7.1s⁵ 6g] $82,185Y: leggy,
useful-looking colt: has a round action: half-brother to several minor winners in
North America: dam, winner at up to 7f, is half-sister to very useful middle-distance
turf performer Miss Huntingdon: sire top-class sprinter: poor form in autumn
maidens: visored final start. *J. H. M. Gosden*

CORRIN HILL 5 b.g. Petorius 117 – Pete's Money (USA) (Caucasus (USA) 127)   –
[1991 6f³ 5.8f 7g* 7m 7g* 7g 7f 7g 1992 8g 7g 7g⁵ 7.1m 7s⁵ a10g⁵] useful-looking
gelding: inconsistent handicapper: stays 7f: acts on firm going: effective with or
without blinkers: sometimes hangs, and flashes tail: sold to join P. Kelleway's
stable 1,400 gns Newmarket Autumn Sales and won novice hurdle in November. *P.
A. Kelleway*

CORRUPT (USA) 4 b.c. Lear Fan (USA) 130 – Nirvanita (FR) (Right Royal V **117**
135) [1991 8g* 11.5g* 12f6 12g5 10d² 11.9g* 14.6m6 1992 12d5 12g 10s* 11.1g4 9.7s3
10m 12f] tall, leggy colt: shows knee action: smart performer: disappointing first 2
starts (flashed tail) when with N. Callaghan but returned to form after joining
present trainer: won Group 3 race at Deauville by 1½ lengths from Sillery and ran
well in September Stakes at Kempton, Prix Dollar (third to Sillery) at Longchamp
and Champion Stakes at Newmarket: well beaten in Breeders' Cup Turf: effective at
1¼m to 1½m: best on an easy surface: sometimes bandaged. *P. W. Chapple-Hyam*

COSMIC DANCER 5 ch.g. Horage 124 – Royal Cloak (Hardicanute 130) [1991 **54**
a14g² 17m6 14.6g 1992 16.1s a16g6 a14g6 a16g2] small, good-quartered gelding:
moderate mover: modest handicapper: trained reappearance by A. Hide, blinkered,
best form for some time when second at Southwell in December: stays 2m: acts on
firm ground and fibresand. *S. P. C. Woods*

COSMIC FUTURE 3 gr.c. Siberian Express (USA) 125 – Bourgeonette 81   –
(Mummy's Pet 125) [1991 7g 7m* 1992 10d 11.8s⁵ 10g 12g 12d 10d² 10.4s6 16.5g4]
lengthy, angular colt: little form in 1992, trained first 2 starts by A. Hide: stays 1½m
(stiff task at 16.5f): acts on good to firm ground and soft: below form when blinkered.
S. P. C. Woods

COSMIC STAR 2 gr.f. (May 9) Siberian Express (USA) 125 – Miss Bunty 70 **58** p
(Song 132) [1992 6g 7f*] 4,400Y: workmanlike filly: second foal: half-sister to 3-y-o
Positive Aspect (by Jalmood): dam maiden suited by 1m, is sister to very useful
Shark Song: ¾-length winner of 10-runner maiden auction at Thirsk in July, running
on well from 2f out: should improve. *S. P. Woods*

COSSACK NOIR 4 b.g. Lidhame 109 – Almeda 54 (Martinmas 128) [1991 11g 7m **41** §
11g⁵ a6g 1992 a7g a7g⁴ a7g a7g⁶ a11g] neat gelding: ungenuine maiden: sold to join
N. Mitchell 1,400 gns Doncaster May Sales. *M. P. Naughton*

COSTA VERDE 2 b.f. (Apr 13) King of Spain 121 – Octavia (Sallust 134) [1992 5g **77**
5g² 5v⁵ 6g⁴ 6d² 5g⁴ 5g² 7.5d* 5g 8g⁵ 7.9d 7m³] workmanlike filly: sister to 1991
2-y-o 5f seller winner Peniscola Star and half-sister to several minor winners,
including modest Kinoko (by Bairn), successful at up to 12.3f: dam showed a little
ability: progressed really well in nurseries, impressively winning at Beverley:
demoted after winning claimer there sixth start: best form at 7f/1m: acts on good to
firm and dead ground: sometimes hangs in closing stages: a credit to her stable. *K.
W. Hogg, Isle of Man*

COST EFFECTIVE 5 ch.g. Burslem 123 – Perle's Fashion (Sallust 134) [1991 **38** §
14d⁵ 16s³ 13.8g 16.5m* 16.2f³ 16m 16m 14d 16.5m 16m 17.1m⁶ 12.4m³ 15.1s⁶ 1992
17.1m⁶ 16.2m⁵ 14m 16.1m 16.2g* 16.5m 16.2s⁶ 18m³ 16s 15.1d⁵] narrow,
angular gelding: poor handicapper: won at Beverley in June: probably acts on any
going: below form when visored: not easiest of rides: unreliable. *M. Brittain*

COTTAGE GALLERY (IRE) 4 b.f. Tate Gallery (USA) 117 – Cottage Style 65 **33**
(Thatch (USA) 136) [1991 7f⁶ 6m 8f² 6f⁴ 5m 6m 5m 1992 6f⁴ 5m⁶ 5g⁴ 5g³ 5g 8g 5s]
small, sturdy filly: poor sprint maiden: acts on firm ground: below form blinkered.
W. A. Stephenson

COTTON BANK (IRE) 4 ch.g. Sandhurst Prince 128 – Cotton Town –
(Takawalk II 125) [1991 7g 8m 7m⁴ 6d a6g 1992 6v 7d] workmanlike gelding: seems
of little account. *P. Butler*

COTTONWOOD 3 b.f. Teenoso (USA) 135 – Smoke Creek 67 (Habitat 134) **80**
[1991 8m 1992 10d* 12g 10m 11.4d⁴ 10.5s⁶ 9g⁶ 10g] leggy filly: won maiden at
Sandown in May: mainly disappointing after, including in handicaps last 3 starts:
should stay 1½m: acts on soft ground. *Lord Huntingdon*

COUNT BARACHOIS (USA) 4 b.g. Barachois (CAN) – Seattle Queen (USA) –
(Seattle Slew (USA)) [1991 10g 9f⁶ 10m² 12.4m³ 10.4g⁵ 10.3m 1992 a12g 10.1s] tall
gelding: on the downgrade. *D. Morris*

COUNTER BLAST 3 b.f. Valiyar 129 – Trading 74 (Forlorn River 124) [1991 a7g –
a7g 1992 a5g] no sign of ability. *W. Holden*

COUNTERCHECK (IRE) 3 b.g. Try My Best (USA) 130 – Swift Reply (He **52**
Loves Me 120) [1991 6g 6m 7.1s⁶ 6s 1992 7g⁵ 7g³ 8m⁶ 6.9m² 7f 6.9h² 6.9f² 6m⁴
7.6m³ 8.9d 7g 7.1g⁵] quite lengthy gelding: maiden handicapper: stays 7.6f: acts on
any going: ran well in blinkers once. *C. F. Wall*

COUNTESS BRUSSELS 4 ch.f. Scottish Reel 123 – Net Call 108 (Song 132) –
[1991 NR 1992 10m a7g] workmanlike filly: has a round action: no worthwhile form.
K. G. Wingrove

COUNT ME OUT 7 ch.g. Vaigly Great 127 – Balatina 85 (Balidar 133) [1991 **38** §
a6g² a7g⁵ a6g⁶ a7g⁶ a7g³ a6g 6v⁴ 7d 6d³ 6f 6.1m a6g³ a7g a6g³ a7g⁵ a7g 1992 a7g a41 §
a6g³ a8g⁴ a6g³ a6g³ a6g³ 6d³ 6.1d 6f 6f⁴ 7d 6g⁵] lengthy, sparely-made gelding:
poor mover: unreliable handicapper: probably stays 1m: acts on any going: often
blinkered: often finds little. *J. Pearce*

COUNT MY BLESSINGS 7 b.g. Touching Wood (USA) 127 – Topaz Too 78 –
(Sun Prince 128) [1991 NR 1992 14.1d⁶ 16.5g⁵ a16g] neat gelding: moderate mover:
on the downgrade. *J. L. Eyre*

COUNT ROBERT (USA) 4 ch.g. Roberto (USA) 131 – Domludge (USA) **45**
(Lyphard (USA) 132) [1991 NR 1992 8.3g 10g⁵ 8.3d⁵ 11.6g⁵ 9.7m² 10.8g] sturdy,
close-coupled gelding: poor mover: first foal: dam once-raced half-sister to Mrs
Penny as well as dam of Hatoof: poor handicapper: best form at 1m/1¼m: acts on
good to firm ground: wore a net muzzle first 2 starts: not easiest of rides. *Miss
Jacqueline S. Doyle*

COURAGEOUS KNIGHT 3 gr.c. Midyan (USA) 124 – Little Mercy 90 (No **73**
Mercy 126) [1991 7g 6f 7m⁶ 1992 6d 8.1m² 8.5d 7f* 8d⁵ 8m³ 8m⁶] lengthy colt:
modest handicapper: won maiden at Brighton in June: may well prove suited by
further than 1m: best efforts on top-of-the-ground. *R. Hannon*

COURT CIRCULAR 3 b.c. Miswaki (USA) 124 – Round Tower 93 (High Top –
131) [1991 6d 8.1g⁵ 8m² 8g 1992 7d 10f 13.3d⁶ 11.9d⁶ 12s] strong, lengthy colt:
impresses in appearance: has a round action: maiden handicapper: below form in
1992: should be suited by middle distances: acts on good to firm ground: below form
visored: sold to join W. Clay 7,000 gns Newmarket Autumn Sales. *Lord Huntingdon*

COURTENAY BEE 3 b.c. Absalom 128 – Broken Accent (Busted 134) [1991 6g –
7m⁶ 7m³ a7g⁴ a8g* 1992 10m] good-bodied colt: rated 70 at 2 yrs: tailed off in
handicap in May, not seen again: best form at 1m: acts on equitrack. *W. Jarvis*

COURTING NEWMARKET 4 b.g. Final Straw 127 – Warm Wind 84 (Tumble **45**
Wind (USA)) [1991 9d³ 8s 8m 1992 a7g a6g⁶ a6g a6g* a5g⁶ a6g⁶ a7g⁵ a6g 7g⁵ 7.1s a55
6m 9d a7g² a7g⁵ a8g⁶ a8g] leggy, good-topped gelding: moderate mover: successful
in amateurs handicap at Lingfield in February: ran as if something amiss final start:
effective from 6f to 9f: acts on equitrack, good to firm ground and dead: tried
blinkered: has worn eyeshield. *Mrs A. Knight*

COURTLINE JESTER 3 ch.g. Caerleon (USA) 132 – Bottom Line 90 (Double **82**
Jump 131) [1991 8m 8m 1992 10v² 10.5d* 12g 10d 10g 10s] angular gelding: fair
handicapper: won at Haydock in May: should be better suited by 1½m (stiff task in

Derby Italiano): goes well on a soft surface: below form when blinkered once. *M. A. Jarvis*

COURT MINSTREL 3 br.g. Hadeer 118 – Sheer Bliss 76 (St Paddy 133) [1991 **60** 5m 5m 6m 6f 6s⁴ 1992 6d 5m³ 6g⁶ 6.9m⁴ 7f* 8m* 7g⁴ 8f⁴ 7g 8d] strong gelding: good walker: modest handicapper: won at Brighton and Goodwood (sweating) in June: stays 1m: probably acts on any going. *L. J. Holt*

COURT OF KINGS 3 b.c. Green Desert (USA) 127 – Abbeydale 110 (Hunter- **–** combe 133) [1991 NR 1992 10s 7.1s 10.2d 15.4d³ 16.1s] 140,000F: compact, attractive colt: has knee action: seventh foal: half-brother to leading 1985 2-y-o Huntingdale (by Double Form), later third in 2000 Guineas, and 1m winner Totley Brook (by Habitat): dam second in 1000 Guineas: no worthwhile form: tried blinkered once: sold to join M. Bradley 3,200 gns Newmarket Autumn Sales. *P. F. I. Cole*

COURT PIANIST (IRE) 2 b.c. (Mar 2) The Noble Player (USA) 126 – Court **49** Barns (USA) (Riva Ridge (USA)) [1992 6m 7g 5.7d 6s] 4,200F, 14,000Y: half-brother to several winners, including 1½m winner Pellincourt (by King Pellinore) and 7f winner Supreme Blues (by Cure The Blues): dam, daughter of high-class Sovereign, won 3 times at 6f: well beaten in maidens: blinkered final run: sold 1,200 gns Newmarket Autumn Sales. *S. M. Hillen*

COURT RISE (USA) 3 b.g. Northern Prospect (USA) – Kal's Cornish Girl **–** (USA) (Cornish Prince) [1991 NR 1992 10.8g 11.8s 12m 14.1m] 20,000Y: lengthy, deep-girthed gelding: third foal: dam, minor winner in USA, is half-sister to U.S. graded winner Ride Sally: sire useful sprinter: no worthwhile form in first half of 1992: retained by trainer 2,400 gns Newmarket July Sales: sold to join M. James 800 gns Doncaster November Sales. *R. W. Armstrong*

COURT ROOM 3 b.g. Aragon 118 – Ladysave (Stanford 121§) [1991 5d⁴ 5m 5g **–** 7m 7g⁵ 5m 8m 1992 a10g⁶ a8g⁴ a7g a8g 10g] smallish gelding: poor maiden: stays 1m: acts on fibresand: below form blinkered/visored. *A. Moore*

COVEN MOON 2 ch.f. (Feb 9) Crofthall 110 – Mayspark 50 (Stanford 121§) [1992 **47** 7s⁶ a7g⁴ a8g⁵] lengthy filly: second foal: dam 1¼m seller winner: plating-class maiden: stays 1m: acts on soft ground and equitrack. *H. J. Collingridge*

COVENT GARDEN GIRL 2 b.f. (Apr 15) Sizzling Melody 117 – Azelly 77 **53** (Pitskelly 122) [1992 5f 7m 6g 5g² 5d³ 5g 5s³] 2,500Y: lengthy filly: third foal: dam placed over 5f at 2 yrs, failed to train on: plating-class maiden: well worth another try at 6f +: acts on soft ground. *M. W. Easterby*

COVERED WAGON (USA) 2 gr.c. (Jan 28) Gone West (USA) – Hardship **75** p (USA) (Drone) [1992 6g²] $150,000Y: compact colt: half-brother to fairly useful 1990 2-y-o 6f winner Futuh (by Diesis) and winners in USA by Plugged Nickle (very useful filly Rose Park) and Elocutionist: dam very useful 2-y-o in North America: sire (by Mr Prospector) very smart at 1m/9f: promising ¾-length second of 13 in maiden at Newmarket in June, travelling strongly long way but very green in front and soon headed: not seen again. *J. H. M. Gosden*

COV TEL LADY 3 ch.f. Celestial Storm 132 – Silette 84 (Silicon 121) **77** [1991 5d³ 6m⁵ 5m³ 8g 1992 11.6m⁶ 12d⁴ 10g² 12f* 13.1m³ 12.3d⁴ 14.1f* 14.1d³ 13.6m² 16.2m*] unfurnished filly: moderate mover: consistent and had good season as 3-y-o: won claimers at Carlisle and Yarmouth and handicap at Beverley: better at 2m shorter: very best efforts on top-of-the-ground. *M. H. Tompkins*

COXANN 6 b.g. Connaught 130 – Miss Nelski 84 (Most Secret 119) [1991 NR 1992 **–** 12f 18.2g 12g] good-bodied gelding: bad maiden: stays 1m. *J. C. McConnochie*

COX ORANGE (USA) 2 b. or br.f. Trempolino (USA) 135 – Spectacular Joke **108** (USA) 123 (Spectacular Bid (USA)) [1992 6s² 6m* 7s* 8s] close-coupled filly: third foal: half-sister to minor winner in USA by Seattle Slew: dam French 6.5f to 1m winner, later placed in USA: progressive filly: successful in minor event at Saint-Cloud in August and Prix du Calvados (by ¾ length from Rouquette) at Deauville following month: virtually pulled up and gave impression something amiss when last of 11 in Prix Marcel Boussac at Longchamp: should stay 1m: probably acts on any going. *A. Fabre, France*

COY BOY (IRE) 2 ch.g. (Mar 2) Shy Groom (USA) – North Lady (Northfields **78** (USA)) [1992 6g 5m⁶ 6m*] 7,400Y: strong, good-quartered gelding: moderate mover: half-brother to a winner in Italy by Burslem: dam poor half-sister to Lowther winner Miss Demure: favourably drawn when neck winner of maiden at Kempton in June: was progressing really well, but not seen out again. *G. Lewis*

CRABBY BILL 5 br.g. Blakeney 126 – Dancing Kathleen 53 (Green God 128) **–** [1991 12m⁴ 16.2g⁴ 14m 14m⁵ 11.4m⁵ 14m 17.2g⁵ 1992 12d⁶ 16d 11.5s⁵ a16g] leggy, lengthy gelding: none too consistent handicapper: effective at around 1½m to 2m: acts on good to firm and soft ground: usually blinkered/visored: has sometimes looked none too keen. *Miss B. Sanders*

CRAB 'N LOBSTER (IRE)   2 b.f. (Apr 24) Waajib 121 – Storm Crest 80 (Lord   **36** Gayle (USA) 124) [1992 5m 6d 7m 7.5m⁴ 6g] 4,500Y: small, leggy filly: half-sister to 4 winners by Daring March, notably very useful sprinter Ongoing Situation, as well as 3-y-o Spanish Storm (by King of Spain), fairly useful 5f to 7f winner at 2 yrs: dam won over 5f at 2 yrs and stayed 1½m: poor maiden: will probably be suited by further than 1m: acts on good to firm ground: sold 620 gns Doncaster November Sales. *Mrs J. R. Ramsden*

CRACKER JACK   2 ch.c. (May 23) Chilibang 120 – Friendly Jester 90 (Be   **42** Friendly 130) [1992 5g 5g 5.1g 5m 5.1m 5d] 8,600Y: good-topped colt: has scope: half-brother to several winners, mostly at sprint distances, including smart Fayruz (by Song): dam 5f winner, is half-sister to dam of Jester: poor maiden: often blinkered: ran well in tongue strap once. *T. Fairhurst*

CRACKLING   3 gr.f. Electric 126 – Birch Creek (Carwhite 127) [1991 5s³ 5m⁵   **57** 6.1d³ 6.1g 7g⁴ 7m³ a7g⁴ 9m⁵ 7g 8g 1992 7g 8.5d 8.9m 7d 10d² 8.9d* 11.9d³ 12s²] angular filly: has a round action: modest handicapper: in very good form in autumn, first past post at Wolverhampton and Goodwood (demoted in claimer final start): effective at 9f/1½m: acts on good to firm and soft ground, and on equitrack: sometimes wandered under pressure, but ran creditably for claimer. *D. Marks*

CRADLE DAYS   3 b.c. Dance of Life (USA) – Dream Chaser 92 (Record Token   **93** 128) [1991 5g² 6m³ 6m⁶ 5.1d² 5m⁵ 1992 5g* 5.7s 5m² 5g⁶ 5m² 5.2m* 5m² 5.2g* 5d] tall, lengthy colt: progressed really well in 1992, successful in Wolverhampton maiden and 2 handicaps at Newbury: stumbled and unseated rider early on on final outing: best form at 5f: acts on good to firm and dead ground: tends to hang. *R. Hannon*

CRADLE OF LOVE (USA)   4 b.f. Roberto (USA) 131 – Kadesh (USA) (Lucky   **76** Mel) [1991 7g 8m² 9g* 9m 10m⁴ 1992 8m⁵ 10.4d 9f⁵ 9g] leggy, light-framed filly: fair handicapper: should stay beyond 9f: acts on good to firm ground, possibly unsuited by dead: below form when blinkered once: none too consistent: has been covered by Sharrood. *J. W. Hills*

CRAFT EXPRESS   6 b.g. Bay Express 132 – Lydia Rose 68 (Mummy's Pet 125)   **68** [1991 a6g³ a7g² a7g² 6m⁵ 6g 7.6d 6d⁴ 6m³ 6d 6d⁶ 6g 6g 6f 7m 6d 1992 6f³ 8g 7.8g 6g 7g⁵ 7g⁶ a8g a8g] compact gelding: poor mover: inconsistent handicapper: last win came 40 starts ago at 3 yrs: needs stiff 5f, and stays 7f: acts on good to firm ground and heavy: effective with or without blinkers or visor: often hangs: trained by N. Meade in Ireland until after seventh start. *Miss S. J. Wilton*

CRAIGIE BOY   2 b.g. (May 7) Crofthall 110 – Lady Carol 42 (Lord Gayle (USA)   **53** 124) [1992 5g 5.1d 5g² 5m²] leggy, unfurnished gelding: fourth reported foal: dam 1m winner: modest maiden: not seen out after May. *J. P. Leigh*

CRAIL HARBOUR   6 b.g. Don 128 – Broccoli (Welsh Saint 126) [1991 6d³ 5f³   **59** d 5f⁴ 5m⁴ 6m 5f² 1992 a5g 5g³ 6v 5.9d⁵ 5s⁴ 6m 5m 8.5m 9g 7.1g 7d] angular, sparely-made gelding: mostly below best in handicaps in 1992: best at 6f or stiff 5f: probably acts on any going: has run creditably when visored/blinkered once. *P. C. Haslam*

CRANFIELD COMET   3 b.g. Beveled (USA) – Return To Tara (Homing 130)   **74** [1991 5v⁵ 5s 5m³ 6m⁵ a5g* 5m* 5g* 5m* 5m³ 1992 a5g⁵ 5.1d a5g⁶ 5s³ 6.1g² 5f* 5f⁶ 6m⁴ 5.7m⁵ 6.1d 5g* 5.7d a5g* 5s* 5d 5.1d⁶ 5m] tall, close-coupled gelding: fair handicapper: won at Redcar in June and at Wolverhampton, Lingfield and Newcastle in September: suited by 5f: acts on any going, including equitrack: effective blinkered/visored or not: sometimes wanders: sold 8,400 gns Newmarket Autumn Sales. *J. Berry*

CREAGMHOR   2 gr.c. (Mar 6) Cragador 110 – Cawstons Prejudice 53   **55** (Cawston's Clown 113) [1992 5d³ 5s⁴ 5f⁴] 2,600Y, 10,500 2-y-o: rather leggy, close-coupled colt: first foal: dam won 1m seller: failed to progress after third in Ripon maiden: not seen out again after being withdrawn lame at start (June). *J. Berry*

CREAKING BOARD   2 ch.f. (Mar 16) Night Shift (USA) – Happy Landing (FR)   **?** (Homing 130) [1992 5.5g² 5.5g* 6m² 5.5g² 6s a8.5f⁶ 8f* a8.5f*] second foal: dam showed a little ability in France: improved performances on first outings for new trainer when winning valuable Miesque Stakes in November and Grade 1 Starlet Stakes (on dirt by 8 lengths) following month, both at Hollywood Park: sixth in Breeders' Cup Juvenile Fillies previous outing: best effort in France when second in Prix Robert Papin at Maisons-Laffitte in July: earlier successful in minor event at

Evry: evidently well suited by 1m or so: seems well suited by firm ground: trained first 3 outings by D. Sepulchre, next 3 by P. Bary. *R. Frankel, USA*

CREAM AND GREEN 8 b.g. Welsh Chanter 124 – Jumana (Windjammer (USA)) [1991 6d 8m a7g 10.3d4 7.1g4 7.6g 6.1s6 1992 7s6 8.2s3] leggy, close-coupled, sparely-made gelding: untrustworthy handicapper: stays 1m: best form with plenty of give in the ground: below form when visored: headstrong: often slowly away. *K. White* **39 §**

CREAM OF THE CROP (IRE) 4 ch.g. Milk of The Barley 115 – Hua Hin (Night Star 94) [1991 NR 1992 10f] leggy gelding: first foal: dam unraced half-sister to Whitbread Gold Cup winner Andy Pandy: always behind in Newmarket claimer in June on debut. *J. Wharton* **–**

CREATIVE FLAIR (USA) 2 gr.f. (Apr 16) Seattle Dancer (USA) 119 – Rare Thing (USA) (Grey Dawn II 132) [1992 6.1m4 7m5 6g 6.1m 7.1s4 8g a6g 8s] $60,000Y: small filly: has a round action: half-sister to winners in North America by Summing and Hail The Pirates: dam won at up to 9f: poor maiden: needs further than 6f, and should stay 1m: acts on soft and good to firm ground: took keen hold when blinkered final run: sold 2,300 gns Newmarket Autumn Sales. *P. F. I. Cole* **50**

CRECHE 3 b.c. Bairn (USA) 126 – Melody Park 104 (Music Boy 124) [1991 5s4 5g 5f4 5d 6g 5m4 5.1f4 5m4 5m2 5m2 5g2 5m5 5m5 a5g* 1992 a5g* a5g* a5g2 a5g2 a5g* a5g* 5m 5m6 5g5 5m4 5m 5.1g a5g a5g* a6g a5g3 a6g2] leggy colt: moderate mover: fairly useful form on all-weather tracks: won claimer at Lingfield and claimers (2) and a handicap at Southwell: nowhere near so good on turf: will prove best at 5f: effective with or without blinkers, has worn them of late: reared stalls, injured and withdrawn once in June. *Mrs N. Macauley* **65**, **a90**

CREDIT SQUEEZE 2 ch.c. (May 12) Superlative 118 – Money Supply (Brigadier Gerard 144) [1992 5.2m 6g3 5.1f 7m* 7m 7g 7d4 6d] 5,000Y: well-grown colt: good mover: half-brother to 3-y-o Petty Cash (by Midyan) and 3 winners, including middle-distance performer Classic Account (by Pharly) and (at 6.3f at 2 yrs in Ireland) Roman Citizen (by Electric): dam unraced sister to vey useful Irish 1m winner Senior Citizen: modest performer: won maiden auction at Catterick in June: best form at 7f or stiff 6f: acts on good to firm and dead ground. *R. F. Johnson Houghton* **58**

CREEAGER 10 b.g. Creetown 123 – Teenager 71 (Never Say Die 137) [1991 16.5d 1992 18.1g* 16.9g2 18g2 20m] lengthy, good-bodied gelding: carries plenty of condition: poor mover: modest handicapper: won at Nottingham in April: stays 2¼m: unsuited by soft going, acts on any other: below form blinkered: best held up. *J. Wharton* **68**

CREEGO 3 b.c. Creetown 123 – Go Flamingo (Relkino 131) [1991 5g 6d 6m4 7m4 a6g4 7f3 1992 8.2g 7.5m4 6.1m 8f a7s 10m 7s] tall, lengthy colt: poor maiden: stays 7.5f: acts on firm ground. *J. A. Glover* **39**

CREPT OUT (IRE) 3 ch.c. On Your Mark 125 – Valbona (FR) (Abdos 134) [1991 6g 6f3 5h 6m 5s4 1992 7g5 7s5 7g3 6m* 6.9f2 a8g] sturdy colt: modest handicapper: won claimer at Catterick in July: should prove ideally suited by 7f/1m: acts on any going: sold out of Miss S. Hall's stable 3,000 gns Doncaster September Sales and well beaten in amateurs race in December. *J. L. Harris* **54**

CRESELLY 5 b.m. Superlative 118 – Gwiffina 87 (Welsh Saint 126) [1991 7f* 7m 7m2 7m 7d* 7.5f 8f 8.1g5 1992 7f 7m3 7m 7g5 a7g 10s 8s4 8.2s5 a8g* a8g4 a8g] compact, workmanlike mare: inconsistent handicapper who bounced back to form under positive ride at Southwell in November (7/1 from 12/1) when making all: effective at 7f to 1m: probably acts on any going and clearly goes well on fibresand: has been visored. *J. G. FitzGerald* **59**

CRESTED WAVE (IRE) 2 ch.f. (Feb 9) Persian Heights 129 – Sea Venture (FR) 98 (Diatome 132) [1992 5g5 5g*] IR 5,000Y: lengthy, angular, unfurnished filly: half-sister to numerous winners, including smart middle-distance performer Sailor's Mate (by Shirley Heights) and useful 1980 French 2-y-o 6f winner Grecian Sea (by Homeric): dam, from family of Reform, won over 6f at 2 yrs and stayed 1m: 2-length winner of maiden auction at Pontefract in April: seemed sure to improve again, particularly when tried at 6f: sent to Italy. *P. W. Chapple-Hyam* **56**

CRESTWOOD LAD (USA) 3 ch.g. Palace Music (USA) 129 – Sweet Ellen (USA) (Vitriolic) [1991 6m3 6g3 6g 6m6 7g 1992 7m 5d 7g 6d] strong, good-bodied gelding: moderate walker: has a round action: no form in 1992: stays 6f. *Mrs M. Reveley* **–**

CRETOES DANCER (USA) 3 br.g. Secreto (USA) 128 – Mary Read (USA) (Graustark) [1991 6f 7m 6f 6g2 5d5 6g 1992 8d 10g 10g 8d6 8d6 a8g2 a10g a10g5 a10g* **55**

a 10g3] good-bodied gelding: moderate mover: modest form: apprentice ridden, easily won claimer at Lingfield in December, making all: stays 1¼m: acts on equitrack: effective with or without blinkers. *W. R. Muir*

CRIME OF THE CENTURY   2 b.f. (Apr 23) Pharly (FR) 130 – Crime of Passion   – p
115 (Dragonara Palace (USA) 115) [1992 5d] fifth foal: sister to fair 1988 2-y-o 5f winner Cardinal Sin and half-sister to 3-y-o Master of Passion (by Primo Dominie), 5f and 6f winner at 2 yrs, and a winner in Belgium: dam sprinting 2-y-o didn't train on: co-favourite, better than tenth-of-19 position suggests in Lingfield maiden won by Go Flightline in September, slowly away and eased when starting to fade 1f out: sure to improve. *P. F. I. Cole*

CRIMSON BLADE   3 ch.c. Crever 94 – Red Velvet 114 (Red God 128§) [1991 5g   –
6g 6m 1992 7m 6m 6g] workmanlike colt: no worthwhile form. *P. W. Harris*

CRIMSON CLOUD (IRE)   4 ch.g. Red Sunset 120 – Shangara (Credo 123)   45
[1991 10.2s4 12.2d2 10d 12m* 12f2 11m 12d4 13.8g 12f6 10.9g5 12.3f 12f3 12.4m6 13.6d2 1992 12m a12g6 15.1m3] close-coupled gelding: moderate mover: poor handicapper: stays 15f: acts on good to firm ground and heavy: gets trouble at stalls: often makes the running: has joined Don Enrico Incisa. *N. Tinkler*

CRIMSON CONSORT (IRE)   3 b.g. Red Sunset 120 – Purple Princess 93   31
(Right Tack 131) [1991 5d5 5g 6m 7m 7.5f 8.9m 1992 5v6 8.3d6 10d a8g6 a7g3 7.1m3 7.1m3 a7g 7g 8s] sturdy gelding: moderate mover: bad maiden: stays 7f: acts on good to firm ground and fibresand: best runs when visored. *Don Enrico Incisa*

CRIQUETTE   2 b.f. (Apr 7) Shirley Heights 130 – Ghislaine (USA) 71 **104** P
(Icecapade (USA)) [1992 7d2 7.3s*]

     Criquette is a filly of considerable potential. That much was evident when she ran the impressive Salisbury maiden winner Thawakib to a length, the pair of them seven lengths clear, in the seven-furlong Kensington Palace Graduation Stakes at Ascot in September on her first appearance on the racecourse; but it was when she ran clean away with the listed Radley Stakes at Newbury four weeks later that she really underlined her prospects for the next season. Opposition to Criquette at Newbury consisted of: Nicer, successful in a maiden at Newmarket last time out and beaten only around five lengths when fifth to Sayyedati in the Moyglare Stud Stakes at the Curragh before that; Chain Dance, a progressive filly second in a valuable nursery at Ascot on her latest run; No Reservations, a tough and genuine filly a place behind Chain Dance at Ascot; the highly-regarded winners Ajanta and Bright Spells; and the promising maidens Barbouki and Cristal Flite. Criquette started 8/13 favourite, Nicer being the only other runner seriously backed, and won handsomely. Cristal Flite, Ajanta and Chain Dance cut out the early running at a fair gallop with Criquette settled in midfield travelling well. Little changed until the two-furlong marker where Criquete, still moving strongly, ranged upsides Cristal Flite then, in very little time at all, opened up a gap of three to four lengths. Bright Spells came through late into second, three lengths ahead of No Reservations, but never troubled Criquette who passed the post with five lengths to spare, a margin which would have been greater had she been ridden right out. Exactly what Criquette achieved isn't easy to evaluate, remembering that the very soft ground on which the race was run could well have distorted the result, but with the consistent No Reservations so far behind in third the strong probability is that it's useful form. What is certain, though, is that Criquette is a highly promising filly who'll be better suited by middle distances as a three-year-old. We've little hesitation in suggesting that she's a considerably better filly than we're able to rate her.

     As do most of Shirley Heights's progeny, Criquette's full sister Ahead improved tremendously as a three-year-old when stepped up to a mile and a half. She won a minor event at Salisbury early in the season, finished third in the Princess Royal Stakes at Ascot late on, and in between ran well in the Oaks for a long way before finishing fifth to Salsabil. Criquette is Ghislaine's fourth foal and third winner, the other being the rattling good miler Mark-ofdistinction (by Known Fact), fourth in the Two Thousand Guineas and later successful in the Queen Anne and the Queen Elizabeth II Stakes. Ghislaine won at a mile and a quarter from only two starts. Her dam, Cambretta, a full sister to the Cumberland Lodge winner Critique, won in Ireland at nine furlongs, while Cambretta's dam Cambrienne won at around seven furlongs as a two-year-old in France. This is an excellent family which has cropped up regularly in *Racehorses*, and more details can be found in the essay on Cambrienne's great-grandson Dr Devious.

		Mill Reef	Never Bend
	Shirley Heights	(b 1968)	Milan Mill
	(b 1975)	Hardiemma	Hardicanute
Criquette		(b 1969)	Grand Cross
(b.f. Apr 7, 1990)		Icecapade	Nearctic
	Ghislaine (USA)	(gr 1969)	Shenanigans
	(b 1981)	Cambretta	Roberto
		(b or br 1975)	Cambrienne

Criquette, a rangy, angular filly who looked somewhat unfurnished at two, should fill out and make an attractive three-year-old. A powerful mover, with a roundish action, she is almost certainly capable of holding her own in much stronger company. The Oaks would seem a realistic objective. *L. M. Cumani*

CRISTAL FLITE 2 b.f. (Mar 20) Niniski (USA) 125 – Julia Flyte 91 (Drone) **69** [1992 7g⁴ 6s⁴ 7.3s⁶] leggy filly: has a quick action: sixth foal: half-sister to 3-y-o 1½m winner Alphard (by Kalaglow), a winner in Italy and one over hurdles: dam 2-y-o 6f winner, is half-sister to very useful Miss Petard, dam of Rejuvenate: fair form, including in listed event final start: would have been well suited by middle distances: dead. *R. Hannon*

CRITICAL MASS 2 gr.c. (Mar 2) Petong 126 – Cut It Fine (USA) (Big Spruce **47** (USA)) [1992 5v⁵ 5m⁶ 5.2d 6g³ a6g] 10,500Y: leggy, good-topped colt: third foal: half-brother to 3-y-o Specific (by King of Spain), 7f winner at 2 yrs, and 1989 Irish 2-y-o 6f winner Close The Till (by Formidable): dam poor stayer: poor maiden: ran poorly on equitrack: stays 6f: sold 2,200 gns Doncaster September Sales. *J. Berry*

CROFTER'S CLINE 8 b. or br.g. Crofter (USA) 124 – Modena (Sassafras (FR) **–** 135) [1991 6m 9m⁴ 8h² 8h³ a8g* a7g* 8.1m⁶ 7m⁵ a8g a8g 1992 7.6g a8g 10.3g 7g a10g] strong gelding: on the downgrade: stays 1m: acts on any going: blinkered/ visored. *A. Bailey*

CROFT HOUSE 3 b.g. Sizzling Melody 117 – Isolationist (Welsh Pageant 132) **–** [1991 NR 1992 12f⁶] plain, unfurnished gelding: second foal: dam unraced daughter of a 1¾m winner: bandaged behind and soundly beaten in claimer at Pontefract, only run. *J. Dooler*

CROFT VALLEY 5 ch.g. Crofthall 110 – Sannavally (Sagaro 133) [1991 8.5f² **97** 8.5f* 8f³ 7g 8m² 8f⁴ 8m 8.5f* 8m⁵ 9m 8m* 7g⁶ 8g a8g 1992 8.3g* 8m² 8d² 8m³ 7g*] workmanlike gelding: not seen out until August in 1992 but improved with every run for new stable, showing useful form: made all in Windsor handicap and well-contested minor event at Doncaster, latter by 1½ lengths from Deprecator: effective at 7f/1m: acts on firm and dead going: ran well when visored at 3 yrs: game. *R. Akehurst*

CROIRE (IRE) 2 b.f. (Feb 4) Lomond (USA) 128 – Fighting Run (Runnett 125) **– p** [1992 6s] 35,000Y: second foal: dam from family of Braashee, Bassenthwaite and Hadeer: 20/1, well behind from halfway in maiden at Leicester in October: should do better. *G. Wragg*

CROMARTY 2 b.f. (May 7) Shareef Dancer (USA) 135 – Forres (Thatch (USA) **67 p** 136) [1992 8.5m⁴] close-coupled, quite attractive filly: eighth foal: half-sister to 12.2f winner Ailort (by Ardross) and fairly useful 1985 2-y-o 5f winner Loch Hourn (by Alias Smith): dam never ran: easy to back when one-paced fourth of 13 to Zenith in maiden at Beverley in September: will improve over further. *H. R. A. Cecil*

CROMER'S EXPRESS 3 ch.c. Mansingh (USA) 120 – Sallusteno 80 (Sallust **–** 134) [1991 5g⁴ 5m⁴ 6d 5.2g² 6m³ 6m⁶ 7m 6g⁴ 5d² 1992 5d 5g⁶ 5g 5g 6f 7g 6m 10s 8g] leggy, close-coupled colt: good mover: little form in 1992: stays 6f: acts on firm and dead ground: often blinkered or visored: sometimes mulish at stalls. *Miss L. C. Siddall*

CRONK'S COURAGE 6 ch.g. Krayyan 117 – Iresine (GER) (Frontal 122) [1991 **79** 6d² 6s² 6g* 6g⁶ 6g 6m⁶ 6d⁴ 6.1s 6g² 6f⁵ 6m 6m 6m 6.1m⁶ a6g² a6g² a6g⁴ a6g* a5g a8g* a6g 1992 6d² 6v* 7g² 6d³ 6g⁶ 5.1m² 6g⁶ 6. 1d 6m³ 5.6m² 7.1m 5g² 5.1g⁶ 6d 6g] big, strong, lengthy gelding: has a quick action: fair handicapper: won at Hamilton in April: speedy, but has won at up to 1m: visored/blinkered: tough and genuine front runner. *E. J. Alston*

CRONK'S QUALITY 9 b.g. Main Reef 126 – Ozone (Auction Ring (USA) 123) **45** d
[1991 6v⁶ 6d² 6f⁵ 7f 6g³ 6m 5.1m 6f* 6m⁵ 7.1g⁶ 7m⁵ 6.1m³ 7f* 7m 7.6m⁵ 7.1g 7.1m
6m⁴ 7g³ 7d 6.9f³ 7s 6.9s 1992 6g 5f⁶ 6f⁴ 6d 6m 7g 6.9m a6g 7.1s 5.3d⁶ 5s⁴ 5d⁶ 5.1s]
small, good-quartered gelding: moderate mover: inconsistent handicapper:
effective from 5f to 7f: acts on any going: effective blinkered or not: sold 675 gns
Ascot November Sales. *D. C. Jermy*

CROPTON 2 b.f. (Mar 29) Flash of Steel 120 – Crymlyn 68 (Welsh Pageant 132) **81** p
[1992 5.1g⁵ 7g* 7s*] leggy, close-coupled filly: fourth foal: half-sister to 3-y-o 7f
winner Canon Kyle (by Music Boy): dam maiden stayed 7f: trained on debut in May
by M. H. Easterby: vastly improved efforts in autumn, winning maiden at Lingfield
and minor event (comfortably by 3 lengths from Formal Affair) at Warwick: will stay
at least 1m: will improve again. *Mrs J. Cecil*

CROSBY 6 b.h. Music Boy 124 – Yelney 65 (Blakeney 126) [1991 a8g a7g⁴ a7g* –
a7g a7g⁵ a7g* 6d 7g² 7m⁶ 7.6g 5m 7g⁵ a6g* a7g³ a6g² a6g³ a7g⁶ a8g* a8g² a7g a52 +
1992 a8g⁵ a8g²] good-bodied horse: fair handicapper, best on all-weather surfaces:
inconsistent on turf: effective at 6f to 1m: seems to act on any going: often sweats:
sometimes wears eyeshield, including when successful: effective blinkered or not.
P. A. Kelleway

CROSBY PLACE 6 gr.m. Crooner 119 – Royal Bat 69 (Crowned Prince (USA) **43** +
128) [1991 a10g a10g² 10.2s³ 12m 12g a12g⁵ 9.7s* 10g⁵ 10m* 11.5f 10m 12g 12f*
10.3d 1992 a13g³ 10.3g] workmanlike, close-coupled mare: carries condition: none
too consistent handicapper: effective at around 1¼m to 1½m: probably acts on any
going: effective blinkered or not. *M. J. Haynes*

CROSSILLION 4 b.c. Rousillon (USA) 133 – Croda Rossa (ITY) (Grey **84**
Sovereign 128§) [1991 8d² 7m 8f* 7g³ 8m a10g* a10g* 1992 a11g⁶ 10s⁵ 9d²] lengthy,
quite attractive colt: good walker: easy mover: fairly useful handicapper: not seen
out after April: best efforts at around 1¼m: acts on firm and dead ground, and
particularly well on equitrack: effective held up or making the running: game. *G.
Wragg*

CROUPIER 5 b.h. Night Shift (USA) – Countess Walewski 85 (Brigadier Gerard –
144) [1991 9m 10m³ 10g⁶ 10m⁵ 7g 8g 10.1f 8m 1992 8g 8.1m⁶ 10f⁶ 7f] rather leggy,
attractive horse: rated 107 at best as 4-y-o: not nearly so good in 1992: stayed 1¼m:
acted on firm going: below form when blinkered once: dead. *C. E. Brittain*

CROWN BALADEE (USA) 5 b. or br.g. Chief's Crown (USA) – Naseem –
Baladee 82 (Kris 135) [1991 11.5g² 10f⁵ 1992 12g] strong, close-coupled gelding: has
round action: lightly-raced maiden: stays 11.5f: ran fairly well when blinkered once.
M. D. I. Usher

CROWN RESERVE 4 br.c. Another Realm 118 – Stardyn (Star Appeal 133) **40**
[1991 a7g⁵ 8m a10g a12g⁴ a12g 1992 a10g a10g 8s 10m⁵ 8m³ 8g* 10m] sturdy colt:
has quick action: poor handicapper: won (for first time) seller at Pontefract (no bid)
in June: stays 1¼m: acts on firm ground: below form blinkered. *M. J. Ryan*

CRUACHAN (USA) 4 b.c. Lear Fan (USA) 130 – Sugar Hollow (USA) (Val de –
L'Orne (FR) 130) [1991 10g* 10.5g* 8m² 10m² 1992 9g] strong, lengthy, good sort:
impresses in appearance: rated 124 as 3-y-o, easily best effort when second in
Champion Stakes: not seen out again in 1992 after disappointing last of 8 in Earl of
Sefton Stakes at Newmarket in April: should stay 1½m: acts on good to firm ground.
G. Harwood

CRU EXCEPTIONNEL 4 b.c. Scottish Reel 123 – Elton Abbess 86 (Tamer- **76**
lane 128) [1991 8d 7g⁵ 9s² 8m⁵ 8.5f* 1992 8s 8m³ 8f⁵ 8.1s 9d 7.6g 9d⁵ 8m⁵] strong,
good-bodied colt: moderate mover: fair handicapper: stays 9f: acts on any going:
sometimes wore tongue strap: held up: inconsistent: sold to join P. Hobbs's stable
20,000 gns Newmarket Autumn Sales. *P. J. Makin*

CRUISE PARTY (IRE) 4 b.g. Slip Anchor 136 – Cider Princess (Alcide 136) –
[1991 10g³ 11d² 13m* 12m* 16.1m⁴ 14g⁵ 11.7g 13.3g 1992 14.9d] big, lengthy gelding:
has a high knee action: fairly useful at best at 3 yrs: on the downgrade: stays 2m:
acts on good to firm ground: takes keen hold and carries head high. *W. Jarvis*

CRUSADE (IRE) 2 b.c. (Mar 14) Digamist (USA) 110 – Theda 61 (Mummy's Pet **79**
125) [1992 5.2d 5g² 6m⁶ 6g² 6f* 6g³ 6f] 10,500Y: well-grown colt: impresses in
appearance: progressed well physically, and has plenty of scope: fourth foal:
half-brother to 1990 2-y-o 5f winner Graceland Lady (by Kafu): dam stayed 7f: fair
performer: easy winner of 3-runner maiden at Brighton in June: broke blood vessel
final outing (August): stays 6f: sold to race in USA. *R. Hannon*

CRYPTIC CLUE (USA) 3 b.c. Alleged (USA) 138 – Nom de Plume (USA) 116 –
(Nodouble (USA)) [1991 NR 1992 10.8g⁶ 12.1m 10g] light-bodied colt: first foal: dam

1m to 10.5f winner, is half-sister to high-class 1982 2-y-o Total Departure: modest maiden, thrice raced: should prove suited by 1½m: bandaged last 2 starts: sold 2,800 gns Newmarket July Sales. *M. J. Heaton-Ellis*

CRYSTADO (FR) 3 ch.c. Crystal Glitters (USA) 127 – Kantado 93 (Saulingo **98** 122) [1991 7g⁶ 1992 8f³ 8.5s² 8m* 8m4] rangy, rather unfurnished colt: progressive form: 3½-length winner of maiden at Newmarket before fourth of 6 to River Falls in moderately-run minor event at Goodwood: pulls hard, and should prove as effective in strongly-run race at 7f: probably acts on any going (hung markedly on soft). *D. R. C. Elsworth*

CRYSTAL CROSS (USA) 3 b.f. Roberto (USA) 131 – Crystal Cup (USA) **84** (Nijinsky (CAN) 138) [1991 7g 7f8.2m³ 8.9d³ 1992 9g4 13.1m² 12d* 12f² 12d³ 13.3d² 12g⁵ 16d 11.7s* 13.3s] leggy, close-coupled, rather sparely-made filly: fairly useful handicapper: won at Epsom in June and Bath in September: may prove best at up to 1¾m: acts on firm and soft going: retained by trainer 52,000 gns Newmarket December Sales. *I. A. Balding*

CRYSTAL HEIGHTS (FR) 4 ch.g. Crystal Glitters (USA) 127 – Fahrenheit **85** 69 (Mount Hagen (FR) 127) [1991 a8g* a7g² a6g³ 7g* 8m4 1992 7m³ 7m⁵ 8.3g 7m³ 9d⁶ 6s² 7m 7g] big, strong, lengthy gelding: fairly useful performer: best efforts at 7f: acts on good to firm ground and fibresand: sometimes hangs right: below form blinkered: sold to join J. Joseph 5,000 gns Newmarket Autumn Sales. *W. A. O'Gorman*

CRYSTAL JACK (FR) 4 b.g. Crystal Glitters (USA) 127 – Cackle (USA) (Crow **92** (FR) 134) [1991 7m 6g 7m⁶ 6m³ 5.1g* 6.1g⁵ 6m³ 5m 5.1m⁶ 5.1m 6m4 5g 6m 6.1d⁶ 5d 1992 6d⁵ 5.1m⁶ 6f* 6d* 6f⁵ 5.1m* 6.1d⁶ 6m 5.1g* 6g⁵ 6g 6.1s²] leggy, quite good-topped gelding: has a quick action: had a good season in handicaps in 1992, successful at Doncaster, Haydock and Chester (2, course specialist there): effective at 5f to 6f: acts on any going: sometimes visored: often edgy/sweating: takes keen hold, and sometimes hangs: suited by strongly-run race. *F. H. Lee*

CRYSTAL KEY 2 b.f. (Apr 20) Bustino 136 – Minor Chord 88 (Major Portion **54** 129) [1992 6.1d³ 7g⁶] leggy, unfurnished filly: half-sister to 3 winners, including 1¼m seller winner Musical Will (by Remainder Man) and 5.8f and 1¼m winner Aldeburgh Festival (by Club House): dam 2-y-o 5f winner: tailed-off last in Yarmouth maiden having shaped encouragingly at Nottingham earlier in July: should stay middle distances. *C. E. Brittain*

CRYSTAL PATH (FR) 4 ch.f. Crystal Glitters (USA) 127 – Flower Parade (Mill **109** Reef (USA) 141) [1991 7d² 8d* 8m² 10v² 8m⁶ 8g² 8g³ 8m⁵ 1992 10d² 10m⁶ 8s³ 8g4 9.5f] workmanlike filly: useful performer: in frame in Kempton listed event, Group 3 Prix Messidor (narrowly-beaten third behind Take Risks) at Longchamp and Group 2 Prix d'Astarte (beaten 4½ lengths by Hydro Calido) at Deauville: behind in Grade 1 Beverly D Stakes at Arlington final run: effective at 1m to 1¼m: acts on good to firm ground and heavy: raced too freely when blinkered once. *M. Moubarak*

CRYSTAL SPIRIT 5 b.g. Kris 135 – Crown Treasure (USA) (Graustark) [1991 **85** NR 1992 18f⁶ 20m³] rangy, workmanlike gelding: has rather round action: fairly useful handicapper/smart hurdler: lightly raced on flat nowadays, not seen again after third in Ascot Stakes in June: suited by thorough test of stamina: acts on firm ground, possibly not good: front runner. *I. A. Balding*

CRYSTAL STONE 2 b.f. (Jan 11) Commanche Run 133 – Bonnie Banks 63 **51** (Lomond (USA) 128) [1992 6g 7.1g⁵ 8.2d 7g 7s 7m] small, sparely-made filly: first foal: dam lightly-raced half-sister to very useful sprinters Hanu and Sanu: poor maiden: should stay 1m: easily best efforts on good ground. *T. Thomson Jones*

C SHARP 5 ch.g. Song 132 – Simply Jane (Sharpen Up 127) [1991 NR 1992 6.1m 6d **–** a7g 6.1m 6.1s] sparely-made gelding: on the downgrade. *W. R. Muir*

CUBIST (IRE) 2 b.f. (Apr 18) Tate Gallery (USA) 117 – Finalist 78 (Star Appeal **71** 133) [1992 6m⁶ 7d* 7d] IR 22,000Y: leggy filly: has a quick action: first foal: dam twice-raced daughter of Galtres Stakes winner Deadly Serious, herself out of very smart Joking Apart: won maiden at Redcar in good style by 2½ lengths from La Menorquina: never dangerous in big-field Doncaster nursery later in October: will be suited by 1m +: bandaged off-hind last 2 starts. *D. Morley*

C U CORAL 3 ch.f. Hard Fought 125 – Sweet And Sour 96 (Sharpen Up 127) [1991 **55** 6g 6g⁶ 7m 1992 10d* 12.1s] sturdy filly: won handicap at Salisbury: tailed off in apprentice handicap at Chepstow later in August, and not seen out again: should stay 1½m: best effort on dead ground. *M. C. Pipe*

CUDDLY DATE 2 b.f. (Feb 16) Nomination 125 – Persane (FR) (Persepolis (FR) **51** 127) [1992 6g 5g 6g² 6f⁵ 5.2g* 5g⁵ 5g⁵ a6g⁶ 6m] 500F, 400Y: long-backed filly: first foal: dam unraced: won seller at Yarmouth (no bid) in August: in-and-out form in nurseries after: should prove as effective at 6f as 5f: has looked a tricky ride. *D. T. Thom*

CUE DIRECTORS (IRE)   3 b.f. Parliament 117 – Syllabub (Silly Season 127)   – [1991 6.9m⁶ 6m⁴ a7g 6g 8m 1992 a8g⁶] workmanlike filly: has quick action: poor maiden: should stay beyond 6f: sold 560 gns Doncaster September Sales. *B. Beasley*

CULTURED   3 b.c. Saint Cyrien (FR) 128 – Made of Pearl (USA) (Nureyev (USA)   **79** 131) [1991 8m 8m 1992 9s 9.9m² 12m³ 12.3g⁵ 9.9m⁴ a12s* 12.3g] tall, leggy colt: fair handicapper: won maiden at Southwell in August: stays 1½m: acts on good to firm ground and fibresand: sold to join J. White 15,000 gns Newmarket Autumn Sales. *M. R. Stoute*

CULTURE VULTURE (USA)   3 ch.f. Timeless Moment (USA) – Per- **118** fect Example (USA) (Far North (CAN) 120) [1991 6d* 5g² 6g* 8d* 8d* a8.5f 1992 7.3d³ 8g⁵ 8m* 8f² 8g³ a9f]

Culture Vulture failed to end her second season in Europe in anything like the same style as her first, but on two of her outings as a three-year-old she was better than ever. In May she won the Dubai Poule d'Essai des Pouliches. It was afterwards reported in several publications that Culture Vulture was the first British-trained winner of the race since Fairy Legend, owned by Sir Mortimer Davis and trained by Harry Count, in 1927. Count was, as one might guess, of British descent, but actually French-born and Chantilly-based. The 1922 British form-book records Lord Derby's winner Frisky as trained by George Lambton in its index, but with William Pratt, who trained in France, for the Pouliches, and the conclusion of our research is that Culture Vulture is almost certainly the first winner of the Pouliches trained in Britain since the Poule d'Essai split into separate races for colts and fillies in 1883. One rather more accessible piece of Longchamp history was Culture Vulture's two-year-old triumph by a short head from Hatoof in the Prix Marcel Boussac. Its relevance to their respective chance in the Pouliches, however, was widely dismissed when Culture Vulture followed a disappointing effort in the Fred Darling Stakes by being beaten over nine lengths behind Hatoof in the One Thousand Guineas, seen off shortly after the two-furlong pole having

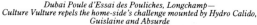

Dubai Poule d'Essai des Pouliches, Longchamp—
Culture Vulture repels the home-side's challenge mounted by Hydro Calido,
Guislaine and Absurde

taken a good hold and raced in the front rank. Not surprisingly, Hatoof started a short-priced favourite in the Pouliches with only one of the nine runners at longer odds than Culture Vulture. The race was not long underway before there were signs of an upset. Hatoof's pacemaker Plume Magique fulfilled her task admirably but Hatoof, racing in second, failed to settle and looked all at sea on the turns. Quinn on Culture Vulture, meanwhile, was biding his time in the rear. They were still there entering the straight, but not for long because, as Hatoof struggled to get past the pacemaker, Culture Vulture launched a tremendous challenge between horses to burst into the lead a furlong out, going on to beat Hydro Calido, who also came from behind, by half a length; a further three quarters of a length back Guislaine, Absurde and Euphonic finished in a bunch, just as they had done in the Prix de la Grotte three weeks earlier. It was later reported that the bit had slipped on sixth-home Hatoof. Kenbu, also well ahead of Culture Vulture at Newmarket, was seventh after meeting interference in the straight.

One month later Culture Vulture had an opportunity to turn the tables on Marling, another filly that had finished in front of her in the One Thousand Guineas. The Pouliches-Coronation Stakes double has been completed only once, by Toro in 1957, the most recent to have tried and failed being Danseuse du Soir and Ravinella. The latest Coronation Stakes was justifiably billed as a two-horse affair, between the Irish and French Guineas winners, and so it proved; it was a great battle throughout the last one and a half furlongs, the pair pulling six lengths clear, but despite running on in really genuine fashion Culture Vulture could not pull Marling back. The difference between them at the line was three quarters of a length. In these two races Culture Vulture had demonstrated a turn of foot, tenacity, and an ability to act on firm going to add to her fine record on good to soft in 1991. She has not raced on soft ground. One surface Culture Vulture has failed on twice is dirt in the Breeders' Cup; she was ninth of fourteen in the Breeders' Cup Juvenile Fillies in 1991 and tenth of fourteen in the Distaff in 1992. Marling again figured amongst the opposition in the Distaff but both went into the race under a cloud after modest efforts on their most recent outings. Culture Vulture had been off the course for nearly four months after the Coronation Stakes and when she returned it was to be beaten in an Ascot listed race. There were mitigating circumstances, not least her being some way short of peak fitness and not getting the best of runs, but nothing sufficient to give her more than an outside chance at Gulfstream Park, and like that of so many European horses, Culture Vulture's season ended with a comprehensive defeat; she never managed a challenging position.

Culture Vulture (USA) (ch.f. 1989)	Timeless Moment (USA) (ch 1970)	Damascus (b 1964)	Sword Dancer
			Kerala
		Hour of Parting (ch 1963)	Native Dancer
			Sweet Sorrow
	Perfect Example (USA) (b 1982)	Far North (b 1973)	Northern Dancer
			Fleur
		Bold Example (b 1969)	Bold Lad
			Lady Be Good

Culture Vulture progressed into a sturdy filly from two to three years. Her pedigree was discussed at length in *Racehorses of 1991* but needs some updating as Perfect Example's fifth foal, Ibraz (by Cox's Ridge), has now won a race here as well. Her 1991 foal is a colt by Slew o' Gold. The unraced Perfect Example is a half-sister to the dams of the two top milers of 1989 Zilzal and Polish Precedent. Culture Vulture's turn at stud will have to wait as she's due to be contesting more of the top races at seven furlongs and a mile in 1993, her campaign reportedly being geared to the summer months. *P. F. I. Cole*

CUMBRIAN CAVALIER 3 b.g. Mansingh (USA) 120 – Lilac Star 75 (Hard Man 102) [1991 5g 5f⁶ 5d⁶ 5g² 6.1m⁴ 6m⁶ 1992 5.1d⁵ 5m² 5g 6g 6g⁴ 6.1m 6m⁴ 6g⁶ 5.2g⁶ 5.3f a5g a7g a5g⁶ a12g] lengthy gelding: inconsistent maiden: trained fifth to tenth starts by J. Bostock: tried blinkered: ungenuine. *K. G. Wingrove*   **45 d**

CUMBRIAN CHALLENGE (IRE) 3 ch.g. Be My Native (USA) 122 – Sixpenny (English Prince 129) [1991 5g⁴ 6f³ 7m 7m² 8m* 8m³ 8g* 1992 10.1f³ 8.9d⁶ 8m² 8.9m⁴ 8m* 8m 9g* 9d] leggy gelding: has a markedly round action: useful handicapper: won £7,600 event at Newcastle in August and median auction event   **96**

(simple task) at Redcar in September: takes good hold, but will prove better at 1¼m than 1m: acts on firm and dead ground. *M. H. Easterby*

CUMBRIAN CLASSIC   3 b.g. Glint of Gold 128 – Blubella 86 (Balidar 133)   –
[1991 6g 8f 1992 8.3f⁴ 6m⁵ 7.1m] good-topped, workmanlike gelding: no worthwhile form: sold 900 gns Doncaster November Sales. *L. Lungo*

CUMBRIAN WALTZER   7 ch.g. Stanford 121§ – Mephisto Waltz 98 (Dancer's **100** Image (USA)) [1991 6d³ 5m⁵ 6m* 6m* 5m² 6g 6g 6g 6m 6m* 7g⁵ 1992 5m⁴ 6g³ 6g⁴ 6f 5g² 5g⁵ 6g⁵ 5m⁶ 5d³ 6g 6d 6d 6g⁴ 5g] leggy, good-topped gelding: often dull in coat: good mover: useful handicapper: caught eye on several occasions in 1992, but below best form after fifth outing (good second to Viceroy in Gosforth Park Cup at Newcastle): ideally suited by 6f or stiff 5f: acts on any going: very tough. *M. H. Easterby*

CUNNING   3 ch.f. Bustino 136 – Vice Vixen (CAN) (Vice Regent (CAN)) **118** p
[1991 NR 1992 8g⁵ 10.2f* 12f* 11.9m* 12m² 12g*]
There is no doubt who was the easiest winner at the latest Ebor meeting. 'Cunning basically came home in a canter through the final two furlongs' reported our race-reader after the three-year-old filly had beaten Percy's Girl six lengths and Shirley Valentine another eight in the listed Galtres Stakes. Cunning was a 5/4-on shot mainly on the strength of impressive wins in a maiden at Bath and amateurs race at Newmarket, but few could have envisaged her making this step up in class look equally undemanding. It was a performance which left one wishing that Cunning had taken on User Friendly in the Yorkshire Oaks twenty-four hours earlier, but Cunning's appearance in Group 1 company was not far away, in the Prix Vermeille, and she ran so well there that speculation that Cunning and User Friendly would clash in the Prix de l'Arc de Triomphe followed. She went down by only a head to Jolypha, who overcame trouble to get up near the finish after Cunning had taken a narrow advantage early in the straight in a very slowly-run affair. Cunning's performance fixed her in the top half dozen middle-distance fillies of her age. That conclusion certainly seemed pervasive at Ascot four weeks later where, the temptation to supplement her for the Arc having been resisted, Cunning started 13/8 on for the Princess Royal Stakes in a nine-runner field which could boast no pattern-race winner and only one other listed winner in Pearl Angel who had won the Sweet Solera Stakes as a two-year-old. Cunning duly

Galtres Stakes, York — Cunning is very impressive

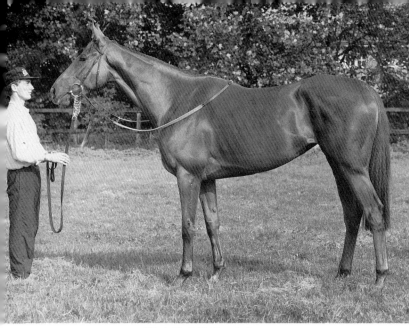

Fittocks Stud Ltd's "Cunning"

obliged, but not in the manner that had been anticipated. It looked as if her superiority would be affirmed in good style as she cruised into the lead two furlongs out, but Cunning never got clear and had only a neck to spare over Anna of Saxony at the post. Cunning looked to be running lazily in front but it is also worth bearing in mind that the going may not have been ideal for her; an excellent mover, she put up her best effort on top-of-the-ground. Either way, Cunning is better than that Ascot run suggests and looks sure to win more good races in 1993.

		Busted	Crepello
	Bustino	(b 1963)	Sans Le Sou
	(b 1971)	Ship Yard	Doutelle
Cunning		(ch 1963)	Paving Stone
(ch.f. 1989)		Vice Regent	Northern Dancer
	Vice Vixen (CAN)	(ch 1967)	Victoria Regina
	(b 1984)	Super Foxe	Blood Royal
		(b 1978)	Stylish Genie

A big, long-backed filly given plenty of time by her trainer, Cunning is the first foal out of Vice Vixen who was purchased for 175,000 dollars as a yearling and trained by Cumani at two years, but did not make the racecourse. Neither did her dam Super Foxe. Stylish Genie, the third dam, won a one-mile stakes race as a four-year-old. That is not a great deal to set the pulse racing but Stylish Genie is a half-sister to Artaius and her 1979 colt by Lyphard caught the eye of Messrs Niarchos and Sangster, passing to the former for a then world-record price for a yearling of 1,700,000 dollars. The record was bettered by three Northern Dancer colts twelve months later. The Lyphard colt, named Lichine, had still not seen the racecourse by that stage and was no

197

world-beater when he did, winning three races, the best of them a listed event, in two seasons although he did show smart form in reaching the frame in races such as the Prix Daphnis, the Ris Orangis and Foret. At stud, Lichine has had a couple of prominent winners in Belgium and, having covered just six mares in 1990, stood for the equivalent of about £750 in 1991. A Sadler's Wells colt out of Stylish Genie fetched 230,000 guineas at the latest Goffs Irish National Yearling Sale. Apart from Cunning, the family's best runner since Lichine is the useful Baltic Fox, a son of Super Foxe, second in the 1988 Gallinule Stakes and placed in graded handicaps in North America in the next two seasons as well. Cunning's 1990 half-brother Commanche Creek (by Commanche Run) has shaped promisingly on two outings and is followed by a filly by Damister. *L. M. Cumani*

CUPBOARD LOVE 2 gr.f. (Mar 24) Grey Desire 115 – Mother Hubbard (Mummy's Pet 125) [1992 5f] small filly: first foal: dam unraced: soon struggling in seller at Thirsk in May. *J. Berry*   –

CURE THE KING (IRE) 2 b.g. (Feb 26) Fairy King (USA) – Top Nurse (High Top 131) [1992 7g 7f4 7g4 8m2 8.3s* 8.9s2 9v2] IR 9,800Y: lengthy, quite good-topped gelding: has plenty of scope: fifth foal: dam unraced: progressive colt: won maiden at Hamilton in September: very good second after in claimer (claimed out of S. Norton's stable £20,150) at York and listed race at Milan: will be suited by 1¼m: has form on any going, but goes well on very soft. *C. Bjorling, Sweden*   **92**

CURRENCY BASKET (IRE) 3 b.g. Lafontaine (USA) 117 – Trouville Lady (Tap On Wood 130) [1991 9g2 8s3 1992 10v 12g2 16.2f4 14m 12g* 14d3 16s] tall gelding: first foal: dam placed over 1½m in Ireland at 3 yrs, became useful hurdler at 4 yrs winning 5 times: fairly useful performer: won amateurs maiden at Galway in July: good fourth in Queen's Vase at Royal Ascot: well beaten last 2 starts, third in listed race at Goodwood: stays 2m: acts on firm going. *P. O'Leary, Ireland*   **88**

CURSORY GLANCE (IRE) 2 b.f. (Mar 14) Taufan (USA) 119 – Honagh Lee (Main Reef 126) [1992 6s 7f] IR 10,500F, 31,000Y: compact filly: third foal: sister to 1990 2-y-o 6f winner Mighty Dragon and half-sister to French 3-y-o 1¼m winner Lagado (by Alzao): dam never ran: always behind in July maidens at Newbury and Yarmouth: sold 1,500 gns Newmarket September Sales. *A. A. Scott*   –

CURTAIN UP (FR) 5 ch.g. Sicyos (USA) 126 – Angelina d'Or (Sun Prince 128) [1991 8d 10m 8f3 8g2 8.3g 8m4 8f 1992 a8g] big, angular gelding: poor mover: on the downgrade: sold 2,800 gns Ascot March Sales. *B. Forsey*   –

CUSHTY 3 b.f. Aragon 118 – Cricklewood Green (Welsh Saint 126) [1991 5g 6m 6m 1992 8f 10g 7f] unfurnished filly: seems of little account. *J. E. Long*   –

CUSTARDORCREAM 5 b.m. Daring March 116 – Bird's Custard 80 (Birdbrook 110) [1991 NR 1992 12m] big, plain mare: second live foal: sister to fairly useful middle-distance winner Silver Owl: dam 5f and 7f winner: soundly beaten in Doncaster claimer on belated debut. *Ronald Thompson*   –

CUTLEAF 3 ch.f. Kris 135 – Catalpa 115 (Reform 132) [1991 NR 1992 10.5f* 9.9d3 11.9s] angular, workmanlike filly: sister to useful middle-distance winners Knifeboard and Kenanga and half-sister to several winners, including Ribblesdale winner Strigida (by Habitat) and 1989 2-y-o 1m winner Tyburn Tree (by High Top): dam and grandam won Ribblesdale Stakes: ran badly after winning Haydock maiden in July: should stay 1½m: sold 20,000 gns Newmarket December Sales. *W. Jarvis*   **81**

CUTTHROAT KID (IRE) 2 b.c. (Mar 23) Last Tycoon 131 – Get Ahead 58 (Silly Season 127) [1992 6f6 6m 6.1g 6m3] IR 13,000Y: medium-sized, sturdy colt: has a round action: brother to 3-y-o 1½m winner Bigwheel Bill and half-brother to several winners, including stayer Sugar Palm (by Gay Fandango) and fairly useful middle-distance handicapper Main Reason (by Main Reef): dam daughter of smart middle-distance stayer Guillotina: blinkered first time and best effort in varied events when third of 17 in nursery at Newmarket in October: should be well suited by further than 6f. *S. G. Norton*   **65**

CUTWATER 3 ch.c. Be My Guest (USA) 126 – Cutlers Corner 111 (Sharpen Up 127) [1991 NR 1992 6d5 8d3] 52,000Y: strong, compact colt: fourth foal: half-brother to 1988 2-y-o 5f winner Sawaik (by Dominion) and useful Irish sprinter, also successful at 7f, Clean Cut (by Formidable): dam 5f winner: twice raced, and similar form in maiden at Redcar and minor event (led until inside last 1f when beaten length by Kristianstad) at Yarmouth in October: sure to improve. *J. H. M. Gosden*   **57 +**

CYNIC 2 ch.f. (Mar 10) Sharpo 132 – Cynomis 82 (Shergar 140) [1992 5d² 5g²] **60** leggy, angular filly: first foal: dam 1¼m winner: second in maidens at Haydock and York (sweating) in May: will be better suited by 6f. *J. W. Watts*

CYPRUS CREEK (IRE) 2 ch.g. (May 3) Red Sunset 120 – Royal Resident 86 **36** (Prince Regent (FR) 129) [1992 6g a7g 7g] IR 4,000Y: leggy, close-coupled gelding: half-brother to several winners in Ireland, all over at least 1m: dam 2m winner: poor maiden: visored final outing. *N. Tinkler*

CYRANO DIAMOND (IRE) 2 b.g. (Mar 28) Cyrano de Bergerac 120 – Rose of **–** The Sea (Diamonds Are Trump (USA) 108) [1992 7.5m] IR 750Y, 4,400 2-y-o: first reported foal: dam hurdles winner in Ireland: always behind in maiden auction at Beverley in September: sold 900 gns Doncaster October Sales. *Ronald Thompson*

CYRILL HENRY (IRE) 3 b.g. Mister Majestic 122 – Stamina 78 (Star Appeal **–** 133) [1991 a6g a7g⁶ 7m⁴ 7.5f⁵ 8.3g 1992 12.1s] sturdy, good-topped gelding: poor plater: stays 7.5f: acts on firm ground. *M. Dods*

CYRUS THE BOLD (IRE) 2 b.c. (May 8) Persian Bold 123 – Etoile Des Galles **73** (Busted 134) [1992 7g 8f³ 8m] 50,000Y: big, lengthy colt, rather unfurnished: has plenty of scope: has a quick action: sixth live foal: brother to smart 7f and 1m winner Llyn Gwynant and half-brother to 2 winners, notably Hazar (by Thatching), at 7f to 8.9f: dam lightly-raced half-sister to dam of Gay Lemur: very edgy, promising third to Dakar Rally in maiden at Doncaster: well below that form in similar event won by Armiger at Newmarket later in September: will stay 1¼m. *B. W. Hills*

CZAR'S WITNESS 2 b.c. (Feb 28) Law Society (USA) 130 – Czar's Bride (USA) **64** p 78 (Northern Dancer (CAN)) [1992 7m⁴ 7m⁶] lengthy, good-quartered colt: brother to a winner in Italy and half-brother to 3 winners in France, from 6f to 1½m: dam middle-distance maiden, out of half-sister to Fanfreluche and Barachois: modest form in maidens at Newmarket and Chester in August: will be well suited by middle distances: has scope, and should do better at 3 yrs. *P. F. I. Cole*

D

DAANIERA (IRE) 2 gr.g. (Mar 17) Standaan (FR) 118 – Right Cash (Right Tack **62** 131) [1992 5s* 6f⁴ 5m⁴ 6g⁵ 6s⁵ 6d⁵ a7g²] IR 6,000F, IR 12,500Y: workmanlike gelding: moderate mover: half-brother to 3 winners, 2 abroad: dam unraced: modest form: won maiden at Hamilton in May: stays 7f: probably acts on any going, including fibresand: blinkered (below form, hanging badly left) third outing. *J. Berry*

DAARIS (USA) 3 ch.c. Diesis 133 – Que Sympatica 108 (Young Generation 129) **67** [1991 6g³ 7g² 7m⁵ 1992 7.5g 7g² 7g³ 7m² 7m* 6m*] small, sturdy colt: moderate performer: won moderately-contested handicaps at Wolverhampton and Yarmouth (apprentices) in midsummer: will prove better at 7f than shorter: acts on good to firm ground: rather headstrong: sold to join C. Tinkler 8,400 gns Newmarket July Sales. *D. Morley*

DABTIYA (IRE) 3 b.f. Shirley Heights 130 – Dabiliya (Vayrann 133) [1991 7s **107** 1992 10g* 10g* 12s² 14s 12d4] first foal: dam unraced half-sister to Darshaan (by Shirley Heights): very useful Irish performer: won maiden at the Curragh in May and listed race at Leopardstown in August: ran well in Irish St Leger and Blandford Stakes at the Curragh in the autumn: stays 1¾m: acts on soft ground. *J. Oxx, Ireland*

DADARISSIME (FR) 3 b.c. Highest Honor (FR) 124 – Toute Cy (Tennyson **115** 119) [1991 9d⁵ 10s⁴ 1992 9g* 10.5s* 11g⁴ 10m 10g 12.5s* 12.5s⁶ 15s* 15.5s] half-brother to very smart French 1988 3-y-o middle-distance stayer Floripedes (by Top Ville) and to a minor winner by Maelstrom Lake: dam, placed over 9f and 1½m in France, is sister to smart French middle-distance stayer Le Mamamouchi: smart French colt: won maiden at Evry and listed event at Longchamp in the spring, another listed event at Deauville in August, then put up best effort when stepped up in trip, landing Group 3 Prix de Lutece at Longchamp in October from Jamshid and Assessor: refused to take any interest in Prix Royal-Oak there later in month, left many lengths at start: suited by a test of stamina: acts on soft ground. *G. Bridgland, France*

DAHLIZ (IRE) 2 gr.c. (Feb 1) Doulab (USA) 115 – Bashush (USA) 86 (Caro 133) **65** [1992 5h² 5d² 6m* 6f⁴ 6d 5g] good-bodied colt: carries condition: has a quick action: first foal: dam 5f (at 2 yrs) and 7f winner, is out of half-sister to high-class 5.5f to 9f winner Believe It, also placed in Kentucky Derby: modest performer: narrowly won maiden at Ayr in July, making most and rallying really well: well below form in nurseries last 2 starts, in blinkers final one: will be better suited by 7f: sold 6,200 gns Newmarket Autumn Sales. *H. Thomson Jones*

DAHYAH (USA) 2 b.c. (May 15) Danzig (USA) – Far (USA) (Forli (ARG)) [1992 **81** p 6g4 7g*] $1,200,000Y: strong, deep-girthed colt: closely related to 2 winners in North America and half-brother to good-class colt Yonder (by Seattle Slew), best at 9f/1¼m: dam, successful at up to 9f, is half-sister to Caerleon and Vision: well-backed favourite, narrowly won maiden at Doncaster in October, rousted along 2f out then staying on really well: will be better suited by 1m +: will improve again. *M. R. Stoute*

DAILY SPORT AUGUST 3 gr.f. Risk Me (FR) 127 – Susie Hall (Gold Rod 129) – [1991 5g6 a6g2 a6g3 a5g6 a6g* 6m 6m 6g a7g a6g a6g a5g 1992 a8g 8g] compact filly: winning plater for J. Berry at 2 yrs: no longer of much account. *M. C. Chapman*

DAILY SPORT DON 2 ro.c. (Apr 21) Risk Me (FR) 127 – Donrae 106 (Don **59** (ITY) 123) [1992 6s6 5.7g5 7d4 7s 6m] 2,800Y: tall, workmanlike colt: brother to 3-y-o Lady Risk Me and half-brother to 3 winners here and abroad, including 7.2f and 12.1f winner Lyn Rae (by Derrylin): dam beat at 2 yrs, winning at 5f: modest maiden: looked difficult ride penultimate start: creditable effort in seller final one: should stay 1m: acts on good to firm and soft ground. *R. Hannon*

DAILYSPORTDUTCH 2 b.f. (Apr 20) Risk Me (FR) 127 – Gold Duchess 53 **55** (Sonnen Gold 121) [1992 5m4 5f*] rather sparely-made filly: has a quick action: third foal: dam 5f winner at 4 yrs: stayed on well to win 7-runner maiden claimer at Hamilton in June: sold 2,200 gns Newmarket Autumn Sales. *P. A. Kelleway*

DAILY SPORT GIRL 3 b.f. Risk Me (FR) 127 – Net Call 108 (Song 132) [1991 **46** 5m5 5d3 5f a5g3 7s3 a7g* a7g5 a7g5 1992 8m a8g 10g 9.7d4 8.3m3 8f6 6.9g2 a7g] lengthy, unfurnished filly: moderate mover: modest plater: trained first 2 starts in 1992 by P. Blockley, next 4 by F. Yardley: stays 8.3f: acts on good to firm ground and on fibresand: blinkered last 2 starts, running creditably first occasion: has joined B. Llewellyn. *R. T. Juckes*

DAILY SPORT'S GIFT 2 b.c. (Apr 20) Risk Me (FR) 127 – Sir Tangs Gift **44** (Runnett 125) [1992 6g4 6m2 7.1f4 a6g 6s] 3,000Y: angular colt: moderate walker and mover: first foal: dam, maiden, stayed 1m: plating-class maiden: well below form in sellers last 2 starts: best effort at 6f: sold 4,000 gns Newmarket Autumn Sales. *J. Berry*

DAISY GIRL 6 b.m. Main Reef 126 – Mellow Girl 88 (Mountain Call 125) **69** [1991 12.4m2 11.9m 10f4 9.9f2 10.1m 10.2m 1992 11.8m* 12.4f* 15m5 12d3 12g* 12m4] sturdy, workmanlike mare: fair handicapper: had a good season, winning at Leicester and Newcastle (idling) in the summer and Kempton (gamely in £8,200 race) in September: probably best at around 1½m nowadays: acts on dead ground, but goes very well on sound surface: tongue tied down. *J. Mackie*

DAISY GREY 4 ro.f. Nordance (USA) – Great Grey Niece 74 (Great Nephew **46** 126) [1991 12m 9m 8f 7g3 8m4 6.9m 10.8g 8m a8g 1992 a8g5 a7g2 a6g4 7d* 7.1g 7d a7g] leggy filly: moderate mover: modest plater: no bid after winning (for first time) at Brighton in April: off course 8 weeks and soundly beaten last 2 starts, in June: effective from 6f to 1m: acts on good to firm and dead ground and on all-weather surfaces: wears blinkers. *A. S. Reid*

DAISY JAMES (IRE) 2 b.f. (Apr 5) Pennine Walk 120 – Shadiyama 58 **41** (Nishapour (FR) 125) [1992 6f 6g 7m2 7d 7g 8s] 3,600Y: sparely-made filly: second foal: dam second over 6f at 2 yrs: poor maiden: stays 7f: below form on a soft surface. *J. M. P. Eustace*

DAJITUS 3 b.c. Damister (USA) 123 – Jilt (ITY) (Bolkonski 134) [1991 NR 1992 **59** 10f 10s 10m6 12d6 11.6m3 16.4m4 16.9d 15.8d] 31,000Y, 10,000Y: lengthy, angular colt: moderate mover: brother to useful 11f and 1½m winner Jack Lang and half-brother to 4 winners in Italy, notably Premio Roma and St Leger Italiano runner-up Jung (by Sexton Blake): dam won 5 races in Italy: modest maiden: well beaten last 2 starts, driven along long way out when visored on final one: stays 16.4f: seems to need a sound surface: wears bandages. *M. J. Heaton-Ellis*

DAJRAAN (IRE) 3 b.c. Shirley Heights 130 – Sugarbird 82 (Star Appeal 133) **112** [1991 8s* 1992 11v* 10.5g2 12g 15d4 15.5d2 15s5] 110,000Y: rangy colt: second foal: half-brother to very useful 1990 2-y-o 7f winner and Poule d'Essai des Poulains third Sapieha (by Petorius): dam 2-y-o 5f winner: very useful French performer: won minor event at Lyon in April and Group 2 Prix Hubert de Chaudenay at Longchamp in July: best efforts in Prix Gladiateur (narrowly beaten by Le Montagnard) and Prix de Lutece there in the autumn: stays 15.5f: yet to race on top-of-the-ground. *A. Fabre, France*

DAKAR RALLY 2 b.c. (Feb 14) Green Desert (USA) 127 – Overdrive 99 (Shirley **74** p
Heights 130) [1992 8f* 8s] strong, good-topped colt: first foal: dam, needed good
test of stamina, from fine staying family: favourite, though carrying plenty of
condition, made extremely promising debut in maiden at Doncaster, always to fore
and keeping on strongly: looked tremendously well but ran poorly in minor event at
Newbury later in autumn: will almost certainly be well suited by 1¼m + : well worth
another chance on a sound surface. *H. R. A. Cecil*

DALALAH 2 br.f. (Feb 24) Doyoun 124 – Balqis (USA) 93 (Advocator) [1992 6m* **73**
6g³ 7m 7g³ 7s⁶] smallish, lengthy, leggy filly: good mover: fourth foal: closely
related to fairly useful stayer Haitham (by Wassl) and 3-y-o 10.2f winner Shahaamh
(by Reference Point) and half-sister to 4-y-o 1m (at 2 yrs) to 1½m winner Libk (by
Kalaglow): dam 2-y-o 5f winner: fair performer: narrowly won maiden at Doncaster
in June: ran well in nurseries last 2 starts: will be better suited to 1m: acts on good
to firm and soft going. *H. Thomson Jones*

DALBY DANCER 8 b.m. Bustiki – Wensum Girl (Ballymoss 136) [1991 14.9m⁴ **57**
14.6m⁴ 16.1m² 13.9g³ 14.9m⁴ 14.6m 14.6g 16.2d³ 13.8m² 16.5da 14g⁶a 14g⁴ 19g² a14g²
a14g³ a16g4] workmanlike mare: moderate mover: modest handicapper: last win
came 23 starts ago, and has since been in frame 15 times: stays well: acts on any
going: has won for apprentice: not seen out after February. *B. A. McMahon*

DALE PARK 6 b.h. Kampala 120 – Coshlea 63 (Red Alert 127) [1991 12g³ 12d –
13d⁶ 12f³ 13f⁵ 1992 a14g 12.4s] leggy, sparely-made horse: has a round action:
seems of little account these days. *N. Tinkler*

DALESIDE 4 gr.g. Full Out (USA) – All Regal (Run The Gantlet (USA)) [1991 –
10f² 11.9g 12m⁴ a14g a14g a12g 1992 17.1d] big, good-topped gelding: rated 68 at best
at 3 yrs: blinkered, well beaten in handicap in April. *T. Fairhurst*

DALEY BRIOCHE 4 b.g. Pharly (FR) 130 – Flaretown 63 (Town Crier 119) –
[1991 7g 11.5m 8g⁶ 7g⁴ 9f 8m 7g 6f⁵ 6g³ 7m⁶ 7g 6s 1992 a7g 5m⁶] sparely-made
gelding: has a round action: rated 53 at 3 yrs: no worthwhile form in 1992. *P. C.
Haslam*

DAL MISS 5 b.m. Dalsaan 125 – Loyal And Regal 51 (Royal And Regal (USA)) –
[1991 6m 8.2g a7g 1992 a7g a7g] workmanlike mare: has round action: no worthwhile form. *R. E. Peacock*

DAL PASCATORE 4 br.g. Noalto 120 – Priors Dean 61 (Monsanto (FR) 121) –
[1991 NR 1992 8.3g 8f 8.9s] lengthy, dipped-backed gelding: no worthwhile form. *F.
J. Yardley*

D'ALTAGNAN 6 ch.g. Dalsaan 125 – Fresh As A Daisy (Stanford 121§) [1991 NR –
1992 a7g a10g⁶] workmanlike gelding: rated 68 in 1990 for R. Hannon: no form in
all-weather handicaps in February: sold to join J. Love 2,000 gns Doncaster March
Sales. *S. G. Payne*

DAMAAZ (IRE) 4 ch.g. Mazaad 106 – Sharpwinds (Tumble Wind (USA)) [1991 –
a7g² a7g⁴ a7g³ a7g⁶ a6g* a7g 6f⁵ a7g 1992 a8g a6g a8g a7g 7d 5.9d 5d a6g] quite
good-topped gelding: has a round action: of little account these days: sold 1,200 gns
Doncaster June Sales. *J. S. Wainwright*

DAMART (USA) 8 b.g. Verbatim (USA) – Ice Wave (USA) (Icecapade (USA)) –
[1991 NR 1992 12.3d 10g] neat gelding: moderate mover: of little account these days.
Miss L. C. Siddall

DAMASK STEEL (IRE) 2 b.g. (Mar 20) Sure Blade (USA) 130 – Seattle Siren –
(USA) 101 (Seattle Slew (USA)) [1992 7s] leggy, quite attractive gelding: fourth live
foal: brother to 1990 2-y-o 6f winner Chimayo and half-brother to Irish 1¼m and
1¾m winner Distant Beat (by Touching Wood) and 3-y-o Sea Clover (by Ela-Mana-
Mou), 7f winner at 2 yrs: dam 6f winner at 2 yrs, is half-sister to very smart
middle-distance winner Pole Position: behind in Salisbury maiden in September,
pulling hard early on, hampered over 2f out and eased: sold 3,100 gns Newmarket
Autumn Sales. *I. A. Balding*

DAM CERTAIN (IRE) 3 b.f. Damister (USA) 123 – Certain Story (Known Fact **59**
(USA) 135) [1991 NR 1992 7f³ 8.2m⁵ 7d a7g⁶ 8.2g⁶ a7g⁴ a6g a7g* a7g* a8g⁵] plain
filly: second foal: half-sister to useful 4-y-o 1¼m to 11.8f winner Pharly Story (by
Pharly): dam unraced daughter of useful sprint winner (later stayed 1m) Epithet:
modest performer: won handicaps at Lingfield and Southwell in November: will
prove at least as effective at 1m as shorter: acts on firm ground and on all-weather
surfaces. *A. W. Denson*

DAME HELENE (USA) 3 b.f. Sir Ivor 135 – Rep's Retton (USA) (J O Tobin –
(USA) 130) [1991 7m 1992 6m 7m 8f 12f6] sturdy, rather dipped-backed filly: no
worthwhile form: last run in June. *P. C. Haslam*

DAMISTRESS 3 b.f. Damister (USA) 123 – Guestimate (FR) (Be My Guest –
(USA) 126) [1991 NR 1992 a8g] 5,200Y: first foal: dam unraced half-sister to Lowther
Stakes winner Kingscote: well beaten in maiden at Southwell: dead. *Miss A. J.
Whitfield*

DAMPIERRE (USA) 4 b.c. Lear Fan (USA) 130 – Danseuse Etoile (USA) 102 **113**
(Buckpasser) [1991 8d3 8s4 10d5 10.5d2 10.5s* 1992 10d2 8g* 8.5d* 8.5d2 8s* 8s6
8.5f4] half-brother to several winners, including smart French 9f and 9.2f winner
Drapeau Tricolore (by Irish River): dam, sister to top-class North American filly La
Prevoyante, won over 1¼m in France and at up to 9f in USA: smart French colt:
progressed well in 1992, winning handicaps at Longchamp in the spring and, after
more than 2 months break, Group 3 Prix Quincey at Deauville in August: below that
form, though not entirely discredited, in Prix du Rond-Point at Longchamp and
Steinlen Handicap at Gulfstream in the autumn: should stay beyond 8.5f: acts on
soft ground, firm effort on firm. *A. Fabre, France*

DANA SPRINGS (IRE) 2 b.f. (Mar 28) Aragon 118 – Dance By Night 84 **58**
(Northfields (USA)) [1992 7g 7d3 8.2s5] 500,000 francs (approx £50,200) Y: small,
leggy filly: half-sister to 3 winners, including very smart French 7f/1m performer
Danseuse du Soir (by Thatching): dam 2-y-o 7f winner: modest maiden: stays 1m:
yet to race on top-of-the-ground. *R. Hannon*

DANCE AND SING (IRE) 2 b.g. (Feb 16) The Noble Player (USA) 126 – **61**
Cherlinoa (FR) (Crystal Palace (FR) 132) [1992 6s 6s 7g] 1,350F, 2,800Y:
workmanlike gelding: has a round action: second foal: dam, French maiden, from
family of Shoot Clear, Sally Brown and Untold: modest maiden: form only on second
start: will stay 7f. *D. L. Williams*

DANCE MAGICAL 2 b.f. (Feb 16) Mashhor Dancer (USA) – Sandi's Gold **41**
(Godswalk (USA) 130) [1992 6g 7g 6s 5.1d] workmanlike filly: first foal: dam
probably of little account: poor maiden: usually gives temperamental display
beforehand. *M. Dixon*

DANCE ON SIXPENCE 4 b.g. Lidhame 109 – Burning Ambition (Troy 137) **60**
[1991 6g 8g 7m5 6g3 6f 7.1m* 7m 7.1m a8g3 a8g 1992 a10g5 7g 7m3 7.1g6 7g5 7f5 8g3
8.1g 7d 6.9v4 7d] rangy gelding: modest handicapper, in-and-out in 1992: effective at
7f and 1m: acts on good to firm and heavy ground: effective visored or not. *H. J.
Collingridge*

DANCER'S LEAP (IRE) 4 ch.f. Salmon Leap (USA) 131 – Villars 84 (Home –
Guard (USA) 129) [1991 NR 1992 11.8g a12g] lengthy filly: fourth foal: dam 1½m
winner: no promise in claimers in July. *J. E. Banks*

DANCE SCENE (IRE) 3 b.g. Dance of Life (USA) – Citissima 96 (Simbir 130) –
[1991 5m 7g 7.1d3 7g* 1992 a8g 8.9g] smallish, strong, lengthy gelding: good mover:
progressive form as a juvenile, but well beaten in handicaps at Southwell (wore
eyeshield) in February and York in May. *D. R. C. Elsworth*

DANCES WITH GOLD 2 b.f. (Mar 11) Glint of Gold 128 – Northern Ballerina **46**
52 (Dance In Time (CAN)) [1992 6m 6s4 7d 7g] 2,200Y: neat filly: fourth foal:
half-sister to 3-y-o Mill Burn and winning 4-y-o sprinter Pretonic (both by
Precocious): dam won sellers at 7f and 8.2f: plating-class maiden: will stay 1m:
possibly suited by soft ground. *M. Johnston*

DANCE TO ORDER (IRE) 2 b.g. (Jan 21) Somethingfabulous (USA) – **69**
Bloomsbarry (USA) (Apalachee (USA) 137) [1992 6.9v 7s6 8.1d2 a7g*] IR 14,500Y:
brother to a winner in USA: dam lightly raced: sire (half-brother to Secretariat) was
fairly useful at up to 9f: fair form: narrowly won maiden at Southwell in December,
holding on well under pressure: will stay 1¼m: acts on dead ground and on
fibresand: may well improve further. *Sir Mark Prescott*

DANCIENNE (FR) 2 b.f. (Apr 19) Groom Dancer (USA) 128 – Termienne (FR) **111**
(Armos) [1992 6s 6s5 7.5g5 8s* 8s2 8s*] third foal: half-sister to French 4-y-o 1¼m
winner Vacation (by Vacarme): dam French 1¼m and 10.5f winner: much improved
late in year, winning minor event at Maisons-Laffitte and Prix des Chenes (by a
length from Dernier Empereur) at Evry and second in Prix des Reservoirs at
Longchamp: will be well suited by 1¼m +: yet to race on top-of-the-ground. *E.
Lellouche, France*

DANCING BEAU (IRE) 3 b.g. Dance of Life (USA) – Kentucky Belle 80 (Glint **58**
of Gold 128) [1991 6f4 7g* 7g4 6.1g5 7f3 8g 1992 a7g 8g3 8m4 8f2 7g a8g3 a8g4 a8g3
a10g5] smallish, sturdy, good-quartered gelding: modest performer and is none too

consistent: better at 1m than shorter: acts on firm ground, probably on equitrack: has worn blinkers and eyeshield. *Mrs L. Piggott*

DANCING BLOOM (IRE) 2 b.f. (Mar 4) Sadler's Wells (USA) 132 – Dancing 94 p Shadow 117 (Dancer's Image (USA)) [1992 6g* 7d²] lengthy filly: has scope: has a long stride: seventh foal: half-sister to smart French 5f and 1m winner River Dancer (by Irish River) and 1986 French 2-y-o 7f winner Entracte (by Henbit): dam, smart 1m to 1¼m performer, is half-sister to Sun Princess and Saddlers' Hall (by Sadler's Wells): heavily-backed favourite, won maiden at Ascot in July in good style, making most: looking very fit, much better form when beaten neck in Group 3 event at Goodwood following month, challenging Love of Silver virtually throughout: open to further improvement and will be better suited by 1¼m. *M. R. Stoute*

DANCING BOAT 3 b.g. Shareef Dancer (USA) 135 – Sauceboat 120 (Connaught 43 130) [1991 NR 1992 8f⁶ 9g 11.8m 12m a8g³ a10g⁵ a10g² a10g] good-topped gelding: eighth foal: brother to fair 1m winner Guapa, closely related to a winner in France by Dance On Time and half-brother to 4 winners, including smart 1m to 11f winner Kind of Hush (by Welsh Pageant) and smart 8.5f and 1¼m winner Dusty Dollar (by Kris): dam won at 6f (at 2 yrs) and stayed 1¼m: sold out of A. Scott's stable 3,500 gns Newmarket July Sales at debut: no worthwhile form next 3 starts for K. Morgan: poor form, including in blinkers, for present trainer: should stay 1½m. *R. F. Johnson Houghton*

DANCING BOY (USA) 3 ch.c. Seattle Dancer (USA) 119 – Clef En Or (USA) 97 (Alydar (USA)) [1991 6f* 6m 6.1m* 6m 1992 6.1g² 6m] sturdy, quite attractive colt: has a fluent action: fairly useful performer: good second to Garah in minor event at Nottingham in April, making most and rallying well: has 3 times been well below form when unable to dominate, tailed off in Haydock listed race in May: worth a try at 7f: not one to trust implicitly. *Mrs J. Cecil*

DANCING DANCER 3 b.f. Niniski (USA) 125 – Verchinina 99 (Star Appeal 45 133) [1991 7d 1992 10m 12g⁴ 14m⁵] unfurnished filly: poor maiden: form only at 1½m: sold to join R. Frost 980 gns Newmarket September Sales. *N. C. Wright*

DANCING DAYS 6 ch.g. Glenstal (USA) 118 – Royal Agnes 71 (Royal Palace – 131) [1991 a12g 13.8d 12.3d 12f 10m³ 12m² 10.8m 12f 10m⁴ 15.8g⁵ a16g 1992 13.6m 13.8g a12g] smallish, workmanlike gelding: poor mover: last win on flat came 29 starts ago, at 3 yrs: soundly beaten in 1992: best form at 1½m: acts on firm and dead ground: effective with or without blinkers or visor: sometimes wanders under pressure: won selling hurdle in November. *J. Parkes*

DANCING DIAMOND (IRE) 2 b.f. (Jan 24) Alzao (USA) 117 – Shay Tien 97 53 (Gunner B 126) [1992 6g 6.1g⁶ 7d] 3,200Y: smallish, close-coupled filly: second foal: dam Irish 7f to 11f winner, is half-sister to smart French miler King James: modest maiden: easily best effort on second start: will prove suited by 1m + . *C. F. Wall*

DANCING DOMINO 2 ch.g. (Mar 22) Primo Dominie 121 – Waltz 75 (Jimmy 45 Reppin 131) [1992 5f³ 5m 5f⁵ 7g 8.3s] 7,200Y: workmanlike gelding: moderate mover: seventh foal: dam, 1m winner, is sister to Joking Apart: poor maiden: no form when dropped to selling company last 2 starts: should stay beyond 5f. *M. H. Easterby*

DANCING GEM 3 b.g. Librate 91 – Opal Lady 64 (Averof 123) [1991 NR 1992 6d – 7g] sixth foal: brother to bad plater Contractors Dream: dam 6f winner: probably of little account. *J. M. Bradley*

DANCING HAZE 2 ch.c. (May 21) Interrex (CAN) – Friendly Miss (Be Friendly – 130) [1992 5.9g 6d] 1,600Y: heavy-bodied colt: half-brother to 1985 Irish 2-y-o 6f winner Tawafan (by London Bells) and a multiple winner in Hong Kong by Noalto: dam 6f winner in Ireland: well beaten in maiden events. *Miss S. E. Hall*

DANCING LEGEND (IRE) 4 b.g. Lyphard's Special (USA) 122 – Princess – § Nabila (USA) (King Pellinore (USA) 127) [1991 12.1s⁶ 10.8m 12.1m 1992 9.2v] big, lengthy gelding: no form and is probably ungenuine. *J. Parkes*

DANCING MISS (IRE) 3 ch.f. Heraldiste (USA) 121 – Tasmania Star (Captain – James 123) [1991 NR 1992 6.9g 8d] sparely-made filly: third foal: dam unraced: well beaten in maidens in September. *P. R. Hedger*

DANCING MOON (IRE) 2 b.f. (Apr 29) Dancing Brave (USA) 140 – Moon's – p Circle (USA) (Irish River (FR) 131) [1992 8d⁶] second foal: closely related to French 3-y-o 1m winner Thunder Star (by Bellypha): dam French 9.1f winner at 4 yrs: 9/1, around 12 lengths sixth of 20 to Lille Hammer in maiden at Yarmouth in October, improving from rear at halfway, unable to quicken again inside final 2f: will stay 1¼m: will improve. *A. A. Scott*

DANCING PET 3 b.f. Dance of Life (USA) – Mummy's Whistler (Mummy's Pet 125) [1991 6m 6.1m 5g 1992 7.5m6 a8g a8s 8.5d3 10g] workmanlike filly: of little account. *W. W. Haigh* –

DANCING PRIZE (IRE) 2 b.f. (Mar 6) Sadler's Wells (USA) 132 – Aim For The Top (USA) 111 (Irish River (FR) 131) [1992 7m6] lightly-made, quite attractive filly: first reported foal: dam 6f (at 2 yrs) to 8.5f winner, from good family: 10/1, over 5 lengths sixth of 12 to Barathea in maiden at Newmarket in October, chasing leaders then keeping on: showed a quick action: will improve. *M. R. Stoute* **70 p**

DANCING SEER 2 b.f. (Apr 18) Lead On Time (USA) 123 – Ile de Danse 76 (Ile de Bourbon (USA) 133) [1992 6.1m6] 50,000Y: leggy, unfurnished filly: first reported foal: dam, French 10.5f winner at 4 yrs, is from family of Bonne Ile and Ile de Nisky (both by Ile de Bourbon): signs of ability in maiden at Nottingham in August: showed a markedly round action: should improve. *M. A. Jarvis* **– p**

DANCING SENSATION (USA) 5 b.m. Faliraki 125 – Sweet Satina (USA) (Crimson Satan) [1991 8g 8m 10m6 8.5m3 8g5 8.1g2 8.3g2 12m 12g 10.2s 1992 10d 10m4 a7g a10g a10g5] big, good-topped mare: fluent mover: poor form: last win came 21 starts ago, at 3 yrs: stays 1¼m: acts on firm going: no improvement in blinkers. *J. Wharton* **37**

DANCING SPIRIT (IRE) 2 br.f. (May 15) Ahonoora 122 – Instinctive Move (USA) (Nijinsky (CAN) 138) [1992 6d3 7g 7d5 7.1s5] 60,000Y: sturdy, lengthy filly: fifth foal: sister to very useful 3-y-o Feminine Wiles, successful at 1m (at 2 yrs) and 1¾m, and half-sister to 2 winners abroad: dam, minor winner in USA, is half-sister to Legal Bid, Law Society and Strike Your Colors: very green, tracked leaders and kept on when third in maiden at Newbury: failed to repeat that form: should be better suited by 7f than 6f. *D. R. C. Elsworth* **72 d**

DANCING STREET 4 ch.f. Scottish Reel 123 – Florence Street (Final Straw 127) [1991 7f3 7f4 9f2 9.2d 9g3 12f5 10m2 10.5m2 10f4 9d4 10g4 1992 12f2 8.1d] tall, leggy, workmanlike filly: carries condition: moderate mover: still a maiden: rated 62 at 3 yrs: sold out of R. Whitaker's stable 3,000 gns Doncaster September Sales after reappearance: tailed off in handicap in November: stays 1½m: acts on firm and dead ground: ran well when visored once at 3 yrs. *T. Craig* **39 +**

DANCING TUDOR 4 b.g. Absalom 128 – String of Beads 63 (Ile de Bourbon (USA) 133) [1991 7v6 10.2f6 10g 14.1f 12f2 11.7f5 13.8m 1992 14.6g 12.3m3 10f 12m5] lengthy gelding: good walker: looked of little account in 1992. *T. H. Caldwell* **–**

DANCING WILD 3 ch.f. Battle Hymn 103 – Peking Dancer 38 (Orbit Dancer (USA)) [1991 6m 7m 1992 8m 8f6 7m5 7.1m5 6f2 6g 6g 6.1g5] close-coupled filly: poor maiden: somewhat headstrong, and at least as effective at 6f as 1m: acts on firm going. *Mrs M. Reveley* **35**

DANCING YEARS (USA) 3 b.f. Fred Astaire (USA) – Resembling (USA) (Nasty And Bold (USA)) [1991 6f5 7m4 7m 1992 12g6 12f4 14g 11.6m4 a12g 11.6g] lengthy, angular filly: shows knee action: modest maiden handicapper: should stay 1¾m: acts on firm going: tried visored. *M. R. Channon* **56**

DANCING ZENA (IRE) 2 b.c. (Apr 15) Dancing Brave (USA) 140 – Princess Zena 96 (Habitat 134) [1992 8s 7.1s] big, heavy-topped colt: moderate mover: tenth living foal: half-brother to several winners here and in France, notably Supreme Leader (by Bustino): dam, 2-y-o 5f winner, is half-sister to dam of Pebbles: soundly beaten in maidens in the autumn: looks sort to do better. *M. A. Jarvis* **– p**

DANDY DESIRE 3 ch.g. Grey Desire 115 – Karsavina 89 (Silly Season 127) [1991 6d 1992 6d5 5g6 8d 6f5 6g 6g5 8m 7g4 7.5m 6d 6d4 5.1s5] workmanlike gelding: poor maiden on balance of form: suited by 6f: probably acts on any going. *B. C. Morgan* **42**

DANGER BABY 2 ch.g. (Mar 31) Bairn (USA) 126 – Swordlestown Miss (USA) (Apalachee (USA) 137) [1992 6g 7m 10g] 5,100Y: unfurnished gelding: sixth foal: half-brother to 3-y-o 8.5f (at 2 yrs) and 11f winner Sword Master and a winner abroad (both by Sayf El Arab): dam Irish 2-y-o 7f winner: poor maiden: off course almost 4 months before final start: may do better. *Bob Jones* **42**

DANGINA 3 b.c. Song 132 – Shere Beauty 83 (Mummy's Pet 125) [1991 6g 7m a8g 1992 8.1g 10d 11g 10f] leggy, shallow-girthed colt: has a round action: of no account. *A. S. Reid* **–**

DANIEL CHALLENGER 4 ch.g. Creetown 123 – Sally Young (Hasty Word 84) [1991 a6g 1992 a7g] seems of little account. *J. P. Smith* **–**

DANNY BLUE (IRE) 2 ch.c. (Mar 31) Bluebird (USA) 125 – Bradan (Salmon Leap (USA) 131) [1992 5f5 6d4 5d3] IR 3,600Y: unfurnished, close-coupled colt: good **63**

walker: first foal: dam ran once: off course 5 months after debut when trained by P. Kelleway: modest form in maidens last 2 starts: will be well suited by further than 6f. *Miss Gay Kelleway*

DANNY BOY   2 b. or br.c. (Apr 23) Damister (USA) 123 – Irish Isle 67 (Realm   **81** p
129) [1992 6g 7m⁴ 7m⁴] 10,500F, 21,000Y: sturdy colt: half-brother to several winners, including useful 3-y-o Irish Memory (by Don't Forget Me) and (at 6f and 7f) useful Benz (by Free State): dam won over 1m: progressive maiden: fourth of 10 in £8,850 event won by Barathea at Newmarket final start: will stay 1m: will win an ordinary maiden. *R. Hannon*

DANROY (USA)   2 b.c. (Mar 16) Sovereign Dancer (USA) – Royal Graustark   **44**
(USA) (Graustark) [1992 8s 7.1s⁶] strong colt: has scope: half-brother to several winners here and in USA, including (at 1m) fair Holtermann (by Mr Prospector) and 1991 2-y-o sprinter Seal Ring (by Known Fact): dam won at up to 7f: backward, poor form when well beaten in maidens at Warwick (disputed lead to straight) and Chepstow (gave trouble stalls) in October: sold 7,600 gns Newmarket Autumn Sales: may do better. *G. Harwood*

DANTE'S VIEW (USA)   4 ch.c. Cox's Ridge (USA) – Only Star (USA)   –
(Nureyev (USA) 131) [1991 7g 9m 10m³ 12d² 12d³ 12g² 1992 12g] first foal: dam French miler: ex-Irish handicapper, fairly useful when trained by J. Oxx as 3-y-o: fair winning novice hurdler in 1991/2 for present trainer: last of 9 in £7,370 race at Ascot in July: stays 1½m: acts on good to firm and dead ground: usually blinkered, wasn't at Ascot. *P. R. Hedger*

DANZA HEIGHTS   6 br.g. Head For Heights 125 – Dankalia (Le Levanstell   **45**
122) [1991 12g* 15.1m* 11.8g⁵ 12.3f⁴ 1992 12.1m⁵ 12.1m* 15.1g⁵ 12.3g² 12m⁶] tall, quite good-topped gelding: has reportedly been hobdayed: has a round action: largely consistent handicapper: easily won at Hamilton in July: looked none too easy a ride final start: effective from 1½m to 15f: acts on firm ground. *Mrs M. Reveley*

DANZARIN (IRE)   4 b.g. Kings Lake (USA) 133 – Sodium's Niece (Northfields   **74**
(USA)) [1991 8g 8d³ 10.1m* 10m⁴ 10m⁴ 10g 8.9g 1992 9d 10g⁶ 10m 10g 9m⁴ 10.3g⁴ 10.1d² 9g] leggy, quite good-topped gelding: fair handicapper: should stay beyond 1¼m: acts on good to firm and dead ground: worth a try in blinkers/visor: sold 7,600 gns Newmarket Autumn Sales. *R. Hannon*

DANZIG LAD (USA)   4 b.g. Ziggy's Boy (USA) – Sexy Ways (USA) (Our Native   **43**
(USA)) [1991 a7g4 a7g6 a8g4 12g6 a7g a10g 1992 a7g4 a8g6 a5g5 a7g4 a7g3 a8g4 5s4 5d6 6f2 6g] smallish, quite good-bodied gelding: has a long stride: poor maiden: bolted to post before good second in amateurs handicap at Redcar: fell approaching straight at Catterick in June and wasn't seen out again: best form at up to 1m: effective with or without visor: sold 900 gns Doncaster November Sales. *M. P. Naughton*

DARAKAH   5 ch.m. Doulab (USA) 115 – Ladytown (English Prince 129) [1991 6g   **67**
8g 10.1g 6g* 8f6 5.8d5 7g 6m6 6m2 8m 7g3 1992 6d6 6v4 6s 7f 7g6 6d 7.6m 6m 7d* 6d 7.6g* 7d6 8s* 7d6] leggy mare: moderate mover: fair handicapper: proved none too consistent at 4 yrs, but in 1992 came out best in close finishes at Goodwood, Lingfield and Bath: suited by 7f/1m: had form on any going, but seemed well suited by some give in the ground at 5 yrs: won for apprentice: in foal to Tragic Role. *C. J. Hill*

DARA LOCH (IRE)   4 b.g. Dara Monarch 128 – Kumari (FR) 78 (Luthier 126)   –
[1991 7g 8d 1992 11g 9.2s] leggy, close-coupled gelding: has a very round action: no form since 2 yrs: sold 920 gns Doncaster October Sales. *Mrs J. R. Ramsden*

DARA MELODY (IRE)   3 b.g. Dara Monarch 128 – Ascensiontide (Ela-Mana-   **48**
Mou 132) [1991 7.5f5 6g5 7m6 8m4 8.2m4 1992 10g 10m5 10g6 11d2] leggy, rather sparsely-made gelding: modest plater: should stay 1½m: acts on good to firm and dead ground: blinkered (ran respectably) last 2 starts at 2 yrs. *J. G. FitzGerald*

DARBONNE (USA)   2 b.c. (Mar 21) Danzig (USA) – Bon Debarras (CAN)   **100**
(Ruritania (USA)) [1992 5.1m* 5f3 6m4 6g3 6m4 7m6] strong, compact colt: closely related to several winners, including fairly useful middle-distance stayer Foreign Asset (by Nijinsky) and 1½m winner Raslaan (by Shareef Dancer) and half-brother to good Canadian gelding Gone To Royalty (by Royal Chocolate): dam never ran: useful performer: won maiden at Bath in May: progressed well during the summer, including when staying-on fourth in Gimcrack Stakes at York (sweating, tongue tied down) in August: didn't get run of race when fair sixth in Somerville Tattersall Stakes at Newmarket over 6 weeks later: will stay at least 1m: yet to race on a soft surface: wears crossed noseband. *G. Harwood*

DARDANELLE 2 ch.f. (Mar 24) Stanford 121§ – Tarte Aux Pommes 75 (Song –
132) [1992 5g 5m 5m] 550F: small, leggy filly: half-sister to 2 winning sprint platers
by Record Token: dam sprinter: no worthwhile form in the spring. *T. Fairhurst*

DARECLIFF (USA) 2 ch.c. (Apr 4) Diesis 133 – Come On Sunshine (USA) (T V   **83**
Lark) [1992 7.1s² 7g³ 8.1s⁵] $50,000Y: rather leggy, close-coupled colt: half-brother
to 2 winners in North America, including smart Mademoiselle Forli (by Forli),
Grade 1 1¼m winner: dam minor winner at 6f: fairly useful maiden: will stay at least
1¼m: acts on soft ground. *R. Hannon*

DARENOT (IRE) 2 b. or br.c. (May 30) Don't Forget Me 127 – Windy Cheyenne   –
(USA) (Tumble Wind (USA)) [1992 5g⁵] 12,500Y: angular, quite attractive colt:
half-brother to 4 winners, 3 successful as 2-y-o's, including useful 1983 6f winner
Keep Tapping (by Tap On Wood): dam won 5 sprints in USA, including stakes event
at 2 yrs: green, fifth in maiden at Newmarket in April: seemed sure to improve: sold
4,000 gns Newmarket Autumn Sales. *C. E. Brittain*

DARE TO DREAM (IRE) 3 b.g. Baillamont (USA) 124 – Tears of Allah (FR)   **57**
(Troy 137) [1991 7g 6.9f 6s 1992 6.9v 7d 10d* 11.6m⁵ 10f⁴ 12m* 14.1m⁴ 12.1g⁵ 14.1d⁴
12f³ 14.6s 10d*] tall, rather leggy gelding: modest mover: modest performer: won at
Nottingham (handicap, for 7-lb claimer) in April, Goodwood (claimer) in June and
Leicester (seller, bought in 4,000 gns) in October: effective from 1¼m (at least on
dead ground) to 1¾m: acts on firm and dead ground: joined R. Akehurst and
promising juvenile hurdler, winner of Grade 1 event at Chepstow in December. *G.
Lewis*

DARING KING 2 b.c. (Feb 16) King of Spain 121 – Annacando 48 (Derrylin 115)   **45**
[1992 5.1g⁶ 5g⁵ 6f a7g⁶ a6g a7g⁴ 8g a6g⁶ 8d] 7,200Y: strong, plain colt: first foal:
dam 2-y-o 6f seller winner suited by 1½m: poor maiden: needs further than 6f, and
stays 1m: visored twice, running creditably though pulling very hard on first
occasion. *D. Sasse*

DARING PAST 2 b.c. (Mar 30) Daring March 116 – Better Buy Baileys 58   **52**
(Sharpo 132) [1992 7g 7g⁵ 6m² 7.5m 7g] 3,600Y: tall colt: first foal: dam placed at 5f
at 2 yrs: modest maiden: stays 7f: acts on good to firm ground. *R. Boss*

DARING TROUBLE 3 b.f. Tremblant 112 – Daring Damsel (Daring March 116)   –
[1991 NR 1992 10s] plain filly: has a round action: first reported foal: dam, daughter
of a fairly useful sprinter, ran once here before winning in Belgium: 25/1, well
beaten in claimer at Salisbury in September. *G. F. H. Charles-Jones*

DARI SOUND (IRE) 4 b.g. Shardari 134 – Bugle Sound 96 (Bustino 136) [1991   **51**
8.5f 12.3d 10d 9.9f⁶ 8m 10m 11m³ 1992 16.2g* 17.1d 13.8d⁶ 16f³ a14g 15.8m³ 16s⁴]
rather leggy gelding: moderate mover: modest handicapper: won seller at Beverley
(no bid) in March: off course 3½ months, creditable fourth in October: stays 17f:
acts on firm and soft ground: tried blinkered earlier in career. *J. G. FitzGerald*

DARIYOUN (USA) 4 b.c. Shahrastani (USA) 135 – Darara 129 (Top Ville 129) **115**
[1991 12d² 12d³ 12g* 12g* 15d² 12.1g² 1992 12d* 14g* 12g* 11g² 12g⁴ 20s³ 15.5s]
first foal: dam won Prix Vermeille and is half-sister to Prix du Jockey-Club winner
Darshaan: smart French colt: won listed race at Longchamp in April when with A. de
Royer-Dupre: competed in Spain on next 4 starts, on one occasion winning Group 1
Gran Premio de Madrid in June: improved form when third to Sought Out in Prix du
Cadran at Longchamp: ran moderately in Prix Royal-Oak there later in October:
effective at 1½m, but evidently suited by test of stamina: acts on soft ground. *C.
Laffon-Parias, France*

DARK AND STORMY 2 b.g. (Mar 15) Aragon 118 – Spanish Chestnut (Philip of   –
Spain 126) [1992 6m 7.1d 6m 6d] 2,000F, IR 4,600Y, 3,100 2-y-o: leggy, unfurnished
gelding: moderate mover: brother to temperamental Dontworryaboutit, a winner in
Malaya, closely related to 4 animals by Tina's Pet, including Yugoslavian winner
Chin The Ref, and half-brother to 2 winners: dam poor plater: of little account:
pulled up after 2f on debut. *M. Dixon*

DARK DEEP DAWN 5 ch.m. Deep Run 119 – Swinging Sovereign (Swing Easy   –
(USA) 126) [1991 NR 1992 12d] third foal: sister to winning chaser Deep Dark Dawn:
dam won NH Flat race and placed over hurdles in Ireland: poor hurdler: tailed off in
Uttoxeter celebrity event in November on flat debut. *John R. Upson*

DARK EYED LADY (IRE) 2 b.f. (Feb 1) Exhibitioner 111 – Tribal Eye 95   **81**
(Tribal Chief 125) [1992 5.3f² 5.1f* 6m⁴ 6f³ 6g] IR 2,500Y: sturdy filly: half-sister to
a winner in Belgium: dam (won 6 times) best at 6f: progressive form in summer
while landing maiden auction at Bath and nursery (made all, wandering inside last)
at Windsor and third in similar event at Newmarket: well beaten in Tattersalls

Tetley Bitter Doncaster Mile—Daros (near side) wears down Tanfith close home

Breeders Stakes at Leopardstown in September: stays 6f well: acts on firm and dead ground. *D. W. P. Arbuthnot*

DARK MIDNIGHT (IRE) 3 br.g. Petorius 117 – Gaelic Jewel 89 (Scottish 47 d
Rifle 127) [1991 5m⁵ 5f² 6f 6f⁶ a8g 1992 a6g³ a7g⁵ 7.1m 10.9d 6m 7g⁶] leggy gelding: modest performer on all-weather tracks: sold out of P. Haslam's stable 1,900 gns Doncaster January Sales and didn't beat a single horse after his return 6 months later: stays 7f. *R. R. Lamb*

DARMSTADT (USA) 2 b. or br.c. (Jan 27) Manila (USA) – Frau Daruma (ARG) 58 p
(Frari (ARG)) [1992 8d] leggy, sparely-made colt: sixth foal: half-brother to several winners, including very progressive 3-y-o 9.9f to 13.9f winner Daru (by Caro) and very useful miler Zelphi (by Conquistador Cielo): dam won Argentinian Oaks: 33/1, around 8 lengths eighth of 19, running green, never able to challenge, to Tomos in maiden at Redcar in October: bandaged near-fore: will improve. *J. H. M. Gosden*

DAROS 3 b.g. Damister (USA) 123 – Tikanova (USA) (Northern Dancer (CAN)) 120
[1991 NR 1992 a6g* a7g² 8g* 10g 10g 10g³ 9f* 12f³ 12f] 6,200 2-y-o: close-coupled, workmanlike gelding: moderate mover: second foal: dam unraced daughter of Cairn Rouge: progressed into very smart performer: trained first 5 starts by Mrs J. Ramsden, winning maiden at Southwell in February and listed race at Doncaster in March: third in Grand Prix de Vichy for J. Hammond in August: subsequently ran in USA, winning Grade 2 event at Del Mar in August and finishing excellent third to Navarone in Oak Tree Invitational at Santa Anita in October: prominent long way in Breeders' Cup Turf final start: stays 1½m: acts on firm ground. *M. Puhich, USA*

DARSHAY (FR) 2 b.f. (Apr 24) Darshaan 133 – So Gay (USA) (Laugh Aloud) 87 p
[1992 7m⁴ 7s 8m⁵] 650,000 francs (approx £65,300) Y: useful-looking, rather unfurnished filly: looks weak: good walker: half-sister to numerous winners, including French 6f (at 2 yrs) to 12.5f winner Tompkins (by Lightning): dam French 1m (at 2 yrs) and 9f winner: progressive maiden: over 7 lengths fifth of 12 to Marillette in May Hill Stakes at Doncaster in September: will stay 1¼m: will probably progress further, and win a maiden. *R. Hannon*

DARSING 2 b.c. (Feb 11) Chief Singer 131 – Alydear (USA) (Alydar (USA)) [1992 38
7g 7g] 5,200Y: big, robust colt: fourth reported foal: half-brother to 3-y-o Factually

207

(by Known Fact), maiden here at 2 yrs later successful in Sweden, and a winner in USA: dam won at around 1m: well beaten in minor event at Kempton and maiden at Lingfield. *M. J. Wilkinson*

DARTINGTON BLAKE   8 b.g. Roscoe Blake 120 – Princess Hot Fire (Hotfoot   –
126) [1991 NR 1992 10g 12m] workmanlike gelding: poor mover: first foal: dam unraced daughter of fairly useful stayer La Foire II: looks of little account. *J. Dooler*

DARUSSALAM   5 ch.m. Tina's Pet 121 – Chinese Falcon 81 (Skymaster 126)   **78**
[1991 a6g 6s 7g 6m 6m* 6f² 6f³ 6d² 6m⁵ 6.9m⁶ 6d² 5.9f² 6f4 7.1g⁶ 6g* 6g 5.1d* 6s⁶ 5d⁴ 1992 5.1m 5.7m 6.1m 6g* 5f 5m⁴ 6m 5g⁶ 5.2g³ 6g* 6d² 6d 6d³ 6g 7g] sparely-made mare: has a round action: fair and largely consistent handicapper: won at Newbury and Kempton in summer: ideally suited by 6f: acts on good to firm ground but goes very well with give: best without blinkers. *R. Lee*

DARU (USA)   3 gr.c. Caro 133 – Frau Daruma (ARG) (Frari (ARG)) [1991 NR **105** p
1992 9.9g* 10m⁶ 12m* 13.9g* 13.9g* 13.3s* 12g²] $150,000Y: close-coupled, workmanlike colt: good walker and mover: fifth foal: half-brother to 13.6f winner Pearl Essence and very useful 7f and 1m winner Zelphi (both by Conquistador Cielo) and to a winner in USA: dam won Argentinian Oaks: progressed extremely well: won maiden at Beverley in March and handicaps at Goodwood in July, York (2 quite valuable events) in late-summer and Newbury in October: best effort, though never travelling well, when second to Turgenev in November Handicap at Doncaster: will prove suited by 1¾m+: acts on good to firm ground and soft: wears a visor: is held up and idles in front: likely to make a smart stayer. *J. H. M. Gosden*

DASHING APRIL   4 b.f. Daring March 116 – Ritruda (USA) 95 (Roi Dagobert
128) [1991 8g⁶ 7.1d³ a7g⁴ 8s⁴ 8g⁶ 10.5g 1992 a7g³ a8g a12g⁶ a13g a12g⁶ a6g⁴ a7g⁴ 7d 7g 8g] leggy, workmanlike filly: moderate mover: still a maiden, and no form for some time. *D. T. Thom*

Racecall Melrose Handicap, York — improving Daru beats Al Karnak and Three Wells

DASHING COLOURS (IRE) 3 b. or br.f. Be My Native (USA) 122 – Near The **100** End (Shirley Heights 130) [1991 5g³ 6g* 6g⁵ 6.3s 1992 6g 7m² 6.3g² 7g 6g* 6g⁵ 6d 6s 7g⁴ 7s*] fourth foal: half-sister to fairly useful Irish 1988 2-y-o 7f winner Dash of Red (by Red Sunset) and a winner in Spain: dam unraced: useful Irish filly: won IR £10,000 event at Leopardstown in August: claimer ridden, fair tenth in Ayr Gold Cup, only start here: best effort when landing listed contest at Leopardstown in November: stays 7f: acts on soft ground: best held up. *Daniel J. Murphy, Ireland*

DASHING LADY 2 b.f. (Feb 5) Marching On 101 – Lady Attiva 72 (Red Regent **–** 123) [1992 5f⁵ 6g] compact filly: first foal: dam won 1¼m seller: no worthwhile form, including in seller: sold 700 gns Doncaster October Sales. *M. Johnston*

DASHWOOD (USA) 5 ch.g. The Minstrel (CAN) 135 – Jane Austen (USA) 76 **–** (Arts And Letters) [1991 NR 1992 a12g a13g] strong gelding: has a round action: seems of little account: sold 600 gns Ascot June Sales. *D. C. Jermy*

DASWAKI (CAN) 4 b.g. Miswaki (USA) 124 – Nice Manners (CAN) (Barachois **91** (CAN)) [1991 6g 8m 7g 10.1m 8m² 8m* 8s* 9m³ 8m* 8m* 9g⁴ 1992 8.1d 8m² 8.1m³ 8f 8.1s 8m 8m 9d⁴ 8g 8s 6.9v a8g³ a8g* a7g* a7g⁴] sturdy gelding: moderate walker: fairly useful handicapper at his best: went through a bad spell but came right back to best late in year at Lingfield, twice running out an emphatic winner: effective at 7f and stays 9f: acts on good to firm and soft ground and on equitrack: blinkered (ran creditably)/visored (well beaten) once each. *R. Hannon*

DAUNT NOT 4 gr.f. Kalaglow 132 – Dare Me 101 (Derring-Do 131) [1991 8g² 8m **–** 1992 8.3g 10m] leggy, workmanlike filly: probably of little account nowadays. *J. White*

DAVAMAL 3 ch.f. Little Wolf 127 – Princess Glory 58 (Prince de Galles 125) **–** [1991 6g 7m 1992 7.1s] plain filly: of little account. *J. M. Bradley*

DAVES CHANCE 2 ch.c. (Feb 6) Hotfoot 126 – Persian Express (Persian Bold **–** 123) [1992 6g 8.5m] 8,000F: workmanlike foal: fourth live foal: half-brother to 3-y-o Sports View (by Mashhor Dancer) and 8.2f (at 2 yrs) and 4-y-o 1½m winner In Truth (by Dreams To Reality): dam poor daughter of half-sister to very smart Tacitus: well beaten in maidens in June and September. *T. Fairhurst*

DAVE'S LASS 3 ch.f. Crever 94 – Monagram 77 (Mon Fetiche 120) [1991 NR **–** 1992 10.2m 10g⁴ 10.2f] lengthy, shallow-girthed filly: half-sister to several winners, including useful 1976 2-y-o 5f winner Japora (by Raffingora) and 1½m winner Chummy's Own (by Sagaro): dam 1m winner: no worthwhile form in maiden and claimers in early-summer. *D. Burchell*

DAVID'S OWN 3 b.g. Petong 126 – Carvery 71 (Milford 119) [1991 5d a6g⁴ 6.1g² **–** 6m 8.1g 7.1m 1992 7g 10d 12.3m] good-bodied gelding: has a quick action: of little account these days: sold 1,300 gns Ascot November Sales. *S. Mellor*

DAVROB 2 b.g. (May 15) Sweet Monday 122 – Glorious Spring 41 (Hittite Glory **56** 125) [1992 7g 7s⁵ 7.6s⁶] sparely-made gelding: moderate walker: second foal: dam poor plater at 2 yrs: form only when fifth of 16 in maiden at Salisbury in September: should stay 1m. *B. Palling*

DAWAAHI (USA) 3 ch.c. Storm Bird (CAN) 134 – Star Mommy (USA) (Pia **90** Star) [1991 NR 1992 7g⁵ 8m* 8f 9d⁴ 9s⁵] $500,000Y: medium-sized, useful-looking colt: half-brother to several winners in North America, notably champion 3-y-o filly of 1985 Mom's Command (by Top Command), winner of 11 races including 1m Acorn Stakes and 1½m CCA Oaks: dam winning sprinter at 3 yrs: fairly useful performer: won maiden at Newmarket in May, hanging left: excellent fourth in Cambridgeshire at Newmarket, staying on strongly from rear: will stay 1¼m: well beaten on firm ground after long lay-off, also tongue strap third start: likely to win more races. *J. H. M. Gosden*

DAWES OF NELSON 7 b. or br.g. Krayyan 117 – Killyhevlin (Green God 128) **56** [1991 6m 6m 5d² 6g 6d² 5s* 5m⁵ 6g⁶ 5.1s⁶ 6.9f 6s⁵ 1992 5g* 6m⁴ 5f 5s 6m³ 5m* 5m* 6g* 5d 6d] workmanlike gelding: has long stride: modest handicapper: won at Sandown in May: at the top of his game in the summer, landing hat-trick at Hamilton (2) and Windsor: effective at 5f, very best effort at 6f: acts on good to firm and soft going. *M. J. Bolton*

DAWN FLIGHT 3 b.g. Precocious 126 – Sea Kestrel 82 (Sea Hawk II 131) [1991 **69** NR 1992 10m⁵ 12.1m³ 11.8g⁴ 13.1f 14d⁶ 12s³ 12v⁵] 16,000Y: strong gelding with scope: sixth reported foal: half-brother to 2 winners by Derrylin, including useful 1987 2-y-o 7f and 1m winner Derry Kestrel and a winner over jumps: dam genuine stayer: fair maiden: stays 1½m: acts on good to firm ground and soft: faced stiff tasks when well below form in blinkers twice. *Lady Herries*

DAWNING STREET (IRE) 4 ch.g. Thatching 131 – Dawn Star 94 (High Line 125) [1991 NR 1992 8g 8g*] well-made gelding: very lightly raced: confirmed promise of reappearance when winning 18-runner handicap at Kempton in May: should stay further: seemed likely to progress further and win again, but didn't reappear: remains in training. *J. L. Dunlop*   **87** p

DAWN'S DELIGHT 14 b.g. Dawn Review 105 – Bird of Passage (Falcon 131) [1991 6v 6m 6g 6g 6m 6g⁶ 7g* 7g 6g 7m 7g 7s⁵ 1992 6v 8.3v² 7g 8d 10g 7d 8d] leggy, workmanlike gelding: moderate mover: a useful handicapper (rated 99) at his best whose 20 wins include 2 Portland Handicaps and a listed event at Doncaster: form in 1992 only when second at Hamilton: stays 8.3f: suited by give in the ground: tried in blinkers and visor. *K. T. Ivory*   **40** d

DAWN SUCCESS 6 br.h. Caerleon (USA) 132 – Dawn Echo (Don (ITY) 123) [1991 a8g³ a8g 8d 8d³ 8g 8.9g² 10.5f 9m 10d 10m a6g a6g a8g 1992 a8g a7g³ a8g⁴ a8g⁴ a12g a12g 8s 10.4m* 10g⁶ 10.1f⁵ 10g 8g 10m 10.5s 7d 7.1g] leggy, close-coupled horse: unreliable handicapper: only success in last 39 starts when dead-heating at York in May: no form last 6 starts, blinkered or visored on 5 of them: effective from 6f to 10.4f: acts on any going: has worn eyeshield on all-weather: has been bandaged: sold to join T. Tate 3,900 gns Doncaster October Sales. *D. W. Chapman*   **61** d

DAYFLOWER (USA) 2 ch.f. (Feb 14) Majestic Light (USA) – Equate (USA) (Raja Baba (USA)) [1992 6m 7m*] $160,000Y: quite attractive filly: first foal: dam, won 3 races in North America, is half-sister to Weldnaas (by Majestic Prince) top-class 8.5f to 1½m performer: reared stalls and refused to race at Doncaster in June: odds on nonetheless, won 10-runner maiden at Newmarket following month, soon chasing leaders after slowish start, leading 3f out and rallying well: looked a useful prospect: sent to spend winter in Dubai. *H. R. A. Cecil*   **90** p

DAYJUZ (IRE) 2 b.c. (Mar 27) Fayruz 116 – Moira My Girl (Henbit (USA) 130) [1992 5s³ 5f⁵ 5g² 5d 5d 5d⁶] IR 7,000F, IR 9,400Y: compact colt: first foal: dam placed over middle distances in Ireland: modest maiden: off course 4 months after third start and well beaten afterwards: will stay 6f: blinkered final start. *F. H. Lee*   **62**

DAY OF HISTORY (IRE) 3 b.f. Shirley Heights 130 – Smeralda (GER) (Dschingis Khan) [1991 NR 1992 8m 10g a12g6 6.9m⁶ 7f 11.6m⁶ 10.2f a10g* 10d³ 12g* 11.9d⁵ 12s* 16s⁶] 12,000Y: leggy, angular filly: sister to Irish maiden Naydo May and half-sister to 4 winners in Germany, including Group winner Soto-Grande (by Kaiseradler): dam won 3 times in Germany and is half-sister to German Oaks winner Slenderella: modest handicapper: won at Lingfield (seller, no bid) in August, Folkestone in September and Goodwood (bumped close home, awarded race) in October: stays 1½m: acts on good to firm and soft ground, and on equitrack. *C. A. Cyzer*   **51**

DAYTONA BEACH (IRE) 2 ch.g. (May 8) Bluebird (USA) 125 – Water Spirit (USA) (Riverman (USA) 131) [1992 5g³ 5.1g² 5f² a6g* 6m²] IR 7,000Y: strong gelding: has scope: third living foal: half-brother to a winner in Italy: dam unraced: progressive form: made all in maiden auction at Southwell, despite saddle slipping: seemed to run lazily when second in claimer at Newcastle later in June: will be well suited by 7f+: worth a try in blinkers. *R. Hollinshead*   **67**

DAZLA 5 b.m. Dublin Taxi – Shahrazad (Young Emperor 133) [1991 a7g 8m a12g 10g 1992 7.1m 8.9m 16.4g 9.7d] close-coupled mare: no longer of much account. *R. Rowe*   **–**

DAZZLE THE CROWD (IRE) 4 b.g. Simply Great (FR) 122 – Katie Roche (Sallust 134) [1991 7g⁵ 6.1m 10d a12g⁶ 1992 a7g³ a10g* a10g* 12d 10m* 10f² a8g⁵ 11.5m⁴ 10m] sturdy gelding: poor mover: modest handicapper: bang in form in the spring, winning at Lingfield (2) and Brighton: not seen out after running moderately in July: probably stays 11.5f: acts on firm ground, and goes well on equitrack: sold 2,600 gns Newmarket Autumn Sales. *C. A. Cyzer*   **61**

DAZZLING BABY 2 b.f. (Mar 22) Bairn (USA) 126 – Jolliffe's Treble (Lochnager 132) [1992 5.1d 5m 5f a5g] 1,100Y: workmanlike filly: fifth foal: half-sister to 1987 2-y-o Barnby Moor (by Raga Navarro), a disqualified 6f winner: dam never ran: of little account. *M. Dods*   **–**

DAZZLING FIRE (IRE) 3 b.f. Bluebird (USA) 125 – Fire Flash 74 (Bustino 136) [1991 7g³ 7g³ 8m⁴ 1992 8s³ 10s³ 12.2g³ 11.7d* 8s⁴] smallish, lengthy filly: good mover: modest performer: narrowly won maiden claimer at Bath in September: suited by middle distances: acts on soft ground, ran moderately on good to firm: races prominently: ran as if something amiss third 3-y-o start and tends to find little: sold to join C. C. Elsey 6,000 gns Newmarket Autumn Sales. *B. W. Hills*   **61**

DEACON BRODIE   2 ch.c. (Feb 23) Primo Dominie 121 – Cardinal Palace 85   –
(Royal Palace 131) [1992 8m 8.5m] 1,900F, 8,600Y: well-grown colt: fifth live foal:
half-brother to 3 winners, including (at 9f) Sharp Order (by Sharpo) and (at 12.4f,
then in USA) Royal Penny (by Thatching): dam won from 9.4f to 1½m: soundly
beaten in maidens in Yorkshire: sold 630 gns Doncaster September Sales. *M. W.
Easterby*

DEAD CALM   2 gr.g. (Mar 23) Another Realm 118 – Truly Bold 76 (Bold Lad   54
(IRE) 133) [1992 5g⁴ 5d⁵ 5g 5f³ 5f² 6.1g³ 5m² 5g² 5g² 5m⁴ 5f² 5g³ 5m⁵ 7m 7g³ 6g 8d
7d] 860F, 1,300Y, 11,000 2-y-o: neat gelding: first foal: dam ran twice at 2 yrs: fair
and consistent plater: stays 7f: acts on firm and dead ground: effective with or
without a visor: has run well when sweating. *C. Tinkler*

DEAR DOCTOR (FR)   5 b.h. Crystal Glitters (USA) 127 – Adele Toumig- **127**
non (Zeddaan 130) [1991 10s² 10g³ 10.5g³ 12d* 12m⁵ 11f² 12g² 12g 1992 10g*
10g* 12g* 10g⁴ 10f* 11f² 12s 12f³]
Contrasting rewards for keeping Suave Dancer and Dear Doctor in training: Fortune frowned on the bigger gamble, smiled on the smaller, as the Arc
winner bowed out after just one run while his year-older stable-companion, in
the same ownership, enjoyed by far his best season and developed into one of
Europe's leading middle-distance horses. Dear Doctor began the latest
season in the shadow of Suave Dancer although he had some good form at
four, notably a win—his only one that year—in the Group 2 Prix Jean de
Chaudenay at Saint-Cloud and seconds in two Grade 1 events at Belmont
Park, the Man o'War Stakes and the Turf Classic. He'd finished fifth of nine to
Topanoora in the Hardwicke Stakes at Royal Ascot. Regarded by his trainer as
a spring and autumn performer, he was brought out very early and was already
the winner of a German Group 3 race, the Grosser Preis der Gelsenkirchener
Wirtschaft, when returned to Britain in April for the similarly-graded T.G.I.
Friday's Gordon Richards EBF Stakes at Sandown, a race he won stylishly
from Red Bishop and Opera House. His regular partner Asmussen was
naturally full of praise on dismounting at Sandown, for Dear Doctor had given
weight all round and had been able to come from behind in a strongly-run
affair. He did add, though, when asked how Suave Dancer had
recently worked—'better than Dear Doctor'—and left no-one in doubt how he
thought they stood, one against the other. As planned, Dear Doctor made

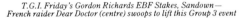

*T.G.I. Friday's Gordon Richards EBF Stakes, Sandown—
French raider Dear Doctor (centre) swoops to lift this Group 3 event*

just one more start before a break. From a range of engagements the near-to-home Prix Jean de Chaudenay three weeks later was selected again. The mile-and-a-half race opened with a surprise as Dear Doctor, not the St Leger winner Toulon, set off in front. And Asmussen called the tune the rest of the way, slowing the tempo before quickening it again in the straight and winning the sprint finish from Vert Amande while odds-on Toulon dropped back to last of six.

Dear Doctor was said to need the race when next seen out in the Bayerisches Zuchtrennen at Munich in August. He ran as if that might be so in coming fourth behind Kooyonga, Zaahi and Perpendicular but it was hard to be sure since, on form, he wasn't expected to beat the winner and he finished only two lengths down. His main objectives lay elsewhere, though; across the Atlantic at Arlington and Belmont Park, while at this stage Suave Dancer was still being aimed at the Arc. The Arlington Million offers a prize that comes closer than most to rivalling the Arc's. One million dollars shared between the first five, with 600,000 dollars (nearly £335,000) to the winner, attracted a very strong, cosmopolitan field in 1992. Most of the twelve runners were well-known on the world stage, not least Sky Classic, Quest For Fame and Golden Pheasant who were leading the North American defence. Current European form was represented by Exit To Nowhere, Second Set, Star of Cozzene and the no-hoper John Rose, in addition to Dear Doctor. On this occasion Dear Doctor came very late. Asmussen had to wait for an opening in the straight, and obtained a run up the inside in the nick of time as Sky Classic and Golden Pheasant were battling it out. Dear Doctor was the fourth European-trained winner in the twelve years of the Million, following Tolomeo, Teleprompter, and Mill Native who won for France in the year the race had to be transferred to Woodbine because of the Arlington fire.

Through winning, Dear Doctor became eligible for a 500,000-dollar bonus if he went on to win the Arc. Bonus apart, he was already under consideration for the race by then as deputy for Suave Dancer who'd just been forced into retirement; and on his current form he deserved the most serious consideration. Before any firm decision about the Arc was taken, he was sent on to Belmont for a second shot at the Man o'War Stakes. He looked to have a better chance than the previous year, but once again foundered on the rock of Solar Splendor, an American horse who beat him three quarters of a length with Spinning third. Apparently thought none the worse for his exertions, Dear Doctor lined up two weeks later at Longchamp showing no sign what-soever of wear. He went out to finish tenth of eighteen to Subotica, beaten around seven and a half lengths in a slowly-run race. It is a measure of his improvement as a five-year-old that that performance could be regarded as disappointing. However, he had a good excuse for finishing so far down the

Prix Jean de Chaudenay, Saint-Cloud—
a Group 2 for Dear Doctor, at the chief expense of Vert Amande

Arlington Million, Arlington—and a Grade 1 for the seasoned traveller

field—he got no sort of run on the inside in the straight, becoming involved in a bumping match with Jolypha, after being held up and still last approaching the final turn. An invitation to compete in the Japan Cup at Tokyo in late-November was a further compliment to Dear Doctor's form. He responded with a fine run. Eight months and many thousands of miles on from his opening victory in Germany, he brought down the curtain on his season with a close third place to the Japanese colt Tokai Teio. Waiting tactics were the order of the day again.

Dear Doctor (FR) (b.h. 1987)	Crystal Glitters (USA) (b 1980)	Blushing Groom (ch 1974)	Red God Runaway Bride
		Tales To Tell (b 1967)	Donut King Fleeting Doll
	Adele Toumignon (b 1971)	Zeddaan (gr 1965)	Grey Sovereign Vareta
		Alvorada (ch 1960)	Beau Prince II Fair Dolly

Report has it that Asmussen will not be retained by M. Chalhoub in 1993. If that is true and there is a change, it will be interesting to see if Dear Doctor is ridden rather less conservatively than has usually been the case. As recently as September the jockey was quoted as saying 'A mile and a quarter is the end of his rope', when the time had long since come to recognize that that simply isn't so. Dear Doctor can be summed up as follows—equally effective at a mile and a quarter and a mile and a half; not beholden to the ground; extremely tough, an outstandingly good traveller, notably consistent; all in all, a credit to his trainer. Dear Doctor, a tall, attractive horse, is also a credit to French breeding, though they let his sire, the good-class mile to mile-and-a-quarter performer Crystal Glitters, join the exodus to Japan the year after Dear Doctor was foaled. Dear Doctor is his sire's best runner so far.

He is also his dam's, but not her only one of account, by any means. Adele Toumignon has produced three other winners from five other runners, the very useful middle-distance stayers Le Mamamouchi (by Tennyson) and Genereux Genie (by General Assembly) among them. One of her non-winners made amends by foaling the 1988 Prix Royal-Oak runner-up Floripides. Adele Toumignon herself managed a small win over nine furlongs. The next two dams were also successful racemares and broodmares, Fair Dolly (Prix de Malleret and Prix de Bagatelle) the better of them on the track; both produced above-average performers, Alvorada the Preis von Europa winner Acacio d'Aguilar. *J. E. Hammond, France*

DEAR PERSON   3 b.f. Rainbow Quest (USA) 134 – Western Star 107 (Alcide 136) [1991 NR 1992 5g⁵ 8g] small filly: ninth living foal: half-sister to several winners, including useful 1m and 1½m winner Startino (by Bustino) and useful 1982 2-y-o 5f winner Star of Taurus (by Mansingh): dam 7f and 1¼m winner, is half-sister to Mr Fluorocarbon: no promise in maidens in August. *J. L. Harris*   –

DEAUVILLE DUCHESS   5 gr.m. Ballad Rock 122 – Miss Deauville (Sovereign Path 125) [1991 NR 1992 10d⁶ 11.6g 16.9d] workmanlike mare: lightly raced and no worthwhile form on flat: tried blinkered. *P. J. Hobbs*   –

DEBACLE (USA)   3 b.c. Raft (USA) 125 – Kuala (USA) (Hawaii) [1991 7m 1992 10m 9.7g* 12d 12d⁵ 10m⁴ 10m] sturdy, attractive colt: good walker: fair performer: won maiden at Folkestone in August: may prove best around 1¼m: acts on good to firm and dead ground. *G. Harwood*   77

DEBJANJO   4 b.g. Critique (USA) 126 – Miss White (FR) (Carwhite 127) [1991 6f⁶ 6m 8m* 8g 11.7g 8m⁵ 8.2f 9.7m 1992 8m 8.3g 10f 8g] tall, leggy gelding: moderate mover: rated 56 at 3 yrs: no longer of much account: sold 900 gns Ascot July Sales. *J. R. Jenkins*   –

DEBORAH SHELLEY   3 b.f. Sweet Monday 122 – Avenmore Star 47 (Comedy Star (USA) 121) [1991 6m 8m 1992 8d 6s] smallish, leggy filly: seems of no account: visored final start. *E. A. Wheeler*   –

DEBOS   2 b.g. (Jan 15) Bustino 136 – Deposit 73 (Thatch (USA) 136) [1992 8.2g³ 8v⁵] fourth foal: half-brother to Ebor winner Deposki (by Niniski): dam second at 6f at 2 yrs, won in West Indies: promising third of 5 in minor event at Nottingham, leading briefly 2f out then keeping on well once headed: still backward, below that form in maiden at Leicester 8 days later in October: claimer ridden: will prove capable of better. *M. R. Stoute*   74 p

DEB'S BALL   6 b.m. Glenstal (USA) 118 – De'b Old Fruit (Levmoss 133) [1991 12d* 13d* 12f² 13.1m² 12.4m* 1992 16.1s⁶ 12m 13.1m⁵ 12f³ 12.1m⁶ 12.4v⁵] quite good-topped mare: modest handicapper: none too consistent: best form at up to 13f: acts on firm and dead ground: ran well when visored once: has flashed tail and idled in front: sometimes very slowly away, and usually set lot to do: won twice over hurdles in August. *D. Moffatt*   59

DEBSY DO (USA)   3 b.f. Dance Bid (USA) 114 – Diablesse (USA) (Dewan (USA)) [1991 6m³ 5.1d² a7g⁶ 7m⁵ 8m a7g³ a7g* 1992 a7g 9.2d⁶ 7g* 7g² 6.1g² 6m³ 7m 5.1m⁶ 7g³ 6f 6s⁴ 7s² a6g³ a7g² a7g* a7g³] good-bodied filly: largely consistent handicapper: won at Catterick in April and Southwell in November: probably best at 6f/7f: acts on good to firm and soft ground and on fibresand: good mount for claimer. *S. G. Norton*   71

DEBT SWAP (USA)   3 ch.g. Manila (USA) – Belle Pensee (USA) (Ribot 142) [1991 NR 1992 10m 10m⁶ 12g⁶ 14.1g⁵ 12m⁵ 11.8d] good-bodied gelding: closely related to 12.2f winner Golden Treasury and half-brother to several other winners, including Gold Cup second Eastern Mystic (by Elocutionist) and high-class 1983 French 2-y-o Treizieme (by The Minstrel): dam, French 1¼m winner, is half-sister to Junius and Gentle Thoughts: fair maiden: suited by 1½m: acts on good to firm ground: bandaged near-hind. *J. H. M. Gosden*   65

DE CHINE   2 b.f. (Apr 2) Kala Shikari 125 – Go Too 78 (Goldhill 125) [1992 5d 5.1s 5f 7d 6m⁴ 6g³ 8.1d 7d] 10,000Y: workmanlike filly: poor mover: half-sister to useful 1980 sprinting 2-y-o Chummy's Special (by Mummy's Pet) and two 2-y-o 5f winners by Dragonara Palace: dam sprinter: modest plater: stays 1m: acts on good to firm and good to soft ground: sold 875 gns Ascot September Sales. *J. S. Moore*   41

DECLASSIFIED (USA)   2 b.g. (Feb 5) Secreto (USA) 128 – Misty Gallore (USA) (Halo (USA)) [1992 7g⁵ 7m² 7g* 8.1g³ 8g²] $60,000Y: tall, angular gelding: half-brother to 7f winner Gaelic Fog (by Irish River), later successful in USA, and a   94 p winner in USA by Mr Prospector: dam high-class winner at up to 1¼m, is half-sister to Minstrella: progressive performer: successful in maiden at Brighton in August: subsequently placed in minor event at Sandown and listed race at Ascot, close up throughout and keeping on really well: will be well suited by 1¼m: likely to keep improving. *L. M. Cumani*

DEDUCE 3 ch.g. Ardross 134 – Miss Maud 57 (Tennyson (FR) 124) [1991 NR 1992 12m⁴ 12m²] 13,000F: big gelding: has a long, rather round stride: second live foal: dam maiden stayed 1¼m: co-favourite, second in maiden at Pontefract in October: will improve again, particularly over further. *G. Wragg* **82** p

DEEPWOOD NANUSKET 6 b.m. Sayf El Arab (USA) 127 – Nanushka 53 (Lochnager 132) [1991 NR 1992 a8g a7g 10d 9.7g 5.3m⁵] smallish, robust mare: poor handicapper nowadays and not seen after May. *M. Madgwick* **30**

DEE RAFT (USA) 2 b. or br.c. (May 18) Raft (USA) 125 – Pharlette (FR) (Pharly (FR) 130) [1992 7.5m²] 16,500Y: quite good-topped colt: half-brother to 4 winners here and in USA, notably Lancashire Oaks winner Pharian (by Diesis): dam unraced: beaten a short head in maiden at Beverley in July, finishing well: showed a markedly round action: looked certain to improve. *B. W. Hills* **75** p

DEER HUNT 3 b.c. Hadeer 118 – Celestial Air 96 (Rheingold 137) [1991 7d 1992 9s* 11.6m² 10m²] good-bodied colt: progressive performer: won median auction contest at Ripon in April: off course 5 months, ran very well when second to Rose Elegance in handicap at Newmarket in September final start: stays 11.6f: acts on good to firm and soft ground: will improve again and win more races. *P. J. Makin* **95** p

DEER MARNY 3 ch.f. Hadeer 118 – Juliette Mariner 52 (Welsh Pageant 132) [1991 NR 1992 8s] neat filly: third foal: half-sister to 2 winning jumpers, notably useful Catch The Cross (by Alias Smith): dam staying maiden: 100/1, always behind in maiden at Pontefract in October. *J. L. Spearing* **–**

DEEVEE 3 b.c. Hallgate 127 – Lady Woodpecker 61 (Tap On Wood 130) [1991 5d 5m 5m 6g 1992 10f² 8d³ 10m³ᵈⁱˢ 10f⁵ 9.7g⁵ 8f² 8.9m⁴ 10d 8m⁴ 10d] close-coupled colt: carries condition: consistent handicapper: ideally needs strong pace at 1m, and stays 1¼m (at least on a sound surface): acts on firm and dead ground: usually slowly away: tends to hang. *C. J. Benstead* **44**

DEFENCELESS 2 ch.f. (Feb 17) Broken Hearted 124 – Injaz (Golden Act (USA)) [1992 5s² 5g² 5g 5g⁶ 5g³ 6m* 6m* 7g 6s] 7,200Y: close-coupled filly: second foal: dam unraced: won nurseries at Windsor and Kempton (making all) shade comfortably in late-summer: better suited by 6f and 7f than 5f: best efforts on a sound surface: sweated profusely fourth outing: sold 10,500 gns Newmarket Autumn Sales. *R. Hannon* **74**

DELAY NO MORE 2 gr.g. (May 15) Nishapour (FR) 125 – Maple Rock (Music Boy 124) [1992 5g⁵ 6d 6d] 1,100F, 5,200Y, 8,000 2-y-o: leggy, close-coupled gelding: second foal: dam unraced: well beaten in maidens. *P. Mitchell* **43**

DEL'S FARGO 3 ch.c. Scottish Reel 123 – Aunt Winnie (Wolver Hollow 126) [1991 7f⁶ a7g 7m 1992 8v 12.2g] rather leggy, close-coupled colt: of little account: visored twice. *J. L. Harris* **–**

DELTA DOWNS 2 b.f. (Mar 19) Deputy Minister (CAN) – Ruthless Rose (USA) (Conquistador Cielo (USA)) [1992 7d³ 7m 6g* 6.5m 7m] tall, lengthy filly, shade unfurnished: first foal: dam twice-raced half-sister to high-class miler Shaadi: sire, best at 2 yrs when champion colt in USA, stayed 1¼m: modest performer: won maiden at Salisbury in August: ran moderately afterwards in nurseries at Doncaster and Newmarket: will prove suited by 7f+: seems unsuited by top-of-the-ground: sold 5,200 gns Doncaster November Sales. *R. Hannon* **67**

DELTA FOXTROT (USA) 3 b.c. Seattle Dancer (USA) 119 – Dame du Nil (FR) (Targowice (USA) 130) [1991 7g 7.1m 10m⁵ 1992 12f⁶ 16m 16.9d 16d] lengthy, well-made colt: good mover: no worthwhile form in 1992: sold to join M. Banks 10,000 gns Newmarket Autumn Sales. *D. W. P. Arbuthnot* **–**

DELVE (IRE) 3 ch.f. Shernazar 131 – Safe Haven (Blakeney 126) [1991 7d⁵ 8m² 1992 10m⁴ 10g* 12f⁴ 11.9g 10g* 10d²] close-coupled, unfurnished filly: sometimes unimpressive in appearance: useful performer: won minor events at Nottingham in May and, showing improved form, Salisbury in August: sweating, good second to King's Loch in listed race at Goodwood in October, though carried head rather awkwardly: best efforts at 1¼m with give in the ground. *J. L. Dunlop* **102**

DEMOCRATIC (USA) 4 ch.c. Miswaki (USA) 124 – Allegra (USA) (Alleged (USA) 138) [1991 8m³ 9m² 8g* 9m 10d⁵ 1992 8g³] sturdy colt: carries condition: fairly useful performer: ran well when third of 24 to High Low in Lincoln Handicap **94**

215

at Doncaster in March: probably stays 9f: acts on good to firm ground and heavy: sold only 1,000 gns Newmarket July Sales. *M. Bell*

DEMOKOS (FR) 7 ch.g. Dom Racine (FR) 121 – Eagletown (FR) (Dictus (FR) 126) [1991 13.8d 14m4 16.5m5 13m a14g 14.1f 12.2m* 12.3f2 12.3f2 12f4 13.8m6 a14g 1992 13.8d5 12.3f2 12.4f3 12.1m5 12.3m 13.8d a12g] lengthy gelding: has long stride: poor handicapper: below form last 3 starts: needs strong pace at 1½m, and stays 2m: acts on firm ground, has seemed unsuited by soft going: has won when sweating: good mount for claimer. *A. P. Stringer* **43**

DEMURRER 2 b.g. (Feb 16) Dominion 123 – Belle Enfant 87 (Beldale Flutter (USA) 130) [1992 7g 7.9s4 7.6s2] 26,000Y: leggy gelding: first foal: dam 1½m winner, is half-sister to Dashing Blade: modest form in frame in maidens at York and Chester in October: will stay 1¼m. *J. G. FitzGerald* **62**

DENIM BLUE 3 ch.c. Mandrake Major 122 – Delphinium 93 (Tin King 126) [1991 6m 7m 6s5 1992 6d6 6.9d 7.1m2 7.1f3 8.5d a8g 8m] quite attractive colt: moderate mover: modest maiden: form at 3 yrs only when placed in handicaps at Edinburgh in June: should stay beyond 7f: acts on firm and soft ground. *C. W. Thornton* **52**

DENSBEN 8 b.g. Silly Prices 110 – Eliza de Rich 57 (Spanish Gold 101) [1991 6d 6s4 6d 7m 6m4 6f3 6g 6g* 7m5 6m 6m4 6g* 6.1m5 6f 6g 7g 1992 6v2 5.9d 6g2 6s 6f* 6g* 6f* 6g2 6m* 6g3 6g 6g3 6d6 6d 6d* 6g3 6v3] smallish, sparely-made gelding: a reformed character who hardly ran a bad race in 1992: successful twice each at Redcar and Pontefract in the summer, and in £13,100 event at York when his form reached a career high in the autumn: ideally suited by 6f: acts on any going: below form when visored earlier in career: good mount for inexperienced rider: has started slowly, and is held up: tough. *Denys Smith* **86**

DENTS DU MIDI (USA) 2 ch.f. (Mar 28) Midyan (USA) 124 – Beverly Hills (FR) (Blakeney 126) [1992 5g 6d] 17,000Y: leggy filly: has a quick action: third foal: half-sister to French 4-y-o 1½m winner Feuilles d'Herbe (by Persian Bold): dam French 9.2f winner: well beaten in maidens at Windsor (slowly away) in July and Kempton (showed up well 3f from moderate draw) in September. *R. W. Armstrong* **–**

DEPOSKI 4 ch.c. Niniski (USA) 125 – Deposit 73 (Thatch (USA) 136) [1991 10m 11.7s4 11.7g* 12g* 13.4d6 16d4 13.9g* 12s4 1992 14g 13.3f 12d6 12m 13.9m 12s6] sparely-made, angular colt: still a fairly useful handicapper, though not so good as at 3 yrs: always close up when sixth of 17 in £60,000 event at Ascot in September final start: best at up to 1¾m: acts on soft ground, probably on firm: usually blinkered/visored these days: has won for 7-lb claimer: sold 40,000 gns Newmarket Autumn Sales. *M. R. Stoute* **90**

DEPRECATOR (USA) 4 ch.c. Topsider (USA) – Deposit (USA) (Mr Prospector (USA)) [1991 7.6d4 7d* 7.1g* 6.9m* 1992 7d 7g* 7f2 7g 7g 7m4 7m* 7.9m2 7d3 8g3 7g2 8g] big, lengthy colt: useful handicapper: successful at Lingfield (minor event) in May and Newmarket (valuable contest, by ½ length from Doulab's Image) in August: ran very well next 3 starts, mulish in preliminaries (more so than usual) and below form final 2: stays 1m: acts on firm and soft ground: usually bandaged behind: active sort: usually held up. *J. H. M. Gosden* **102**

DEPUTY TIM 9 ch.g. Crofter (USA) 124 – Kindle (Firestreak 125) [1991 7m 1992 8d 8d 8.5m 8.2m* 8m6] neat gelding: carries plenty of condition: moderate mover: best effort in 1992 when winning handicap at Nottingham in June: best form at around 1m: acts on any going: best without blinkers. *R. Bastiman* **48**

Coral Sprint Trophy, York—Densben storms clear to crown his excellent season

DERNIER EMPEREUR (USA) 2 ch.f. (Feb 5) Trempolino (USA) 135 – Dear **111** p
Colleen (USA) (In Reality (USA)) [1992 7.5s* 8s²] half-sister to several winners in
North America, one in listed company at 2 yrs: dam won at up to 9f: won 20-runner
newcomers race at Saint-Cloud in October: much better effort when beaten a length
by Dancienne in Prix des Chenes at Evry in November: will stay at least 1¼m: likely
to do better. *A. Fabre, France*

DERRY REEF 5 b.m. Derrylin 115 – Ballyreef (Ballymore 123) [1991 14.6m³ **–**
14.1f⁵ 14.1f² 16m⁴ 12.1g⁵ 12g² 1992 13d⁶] good-topped mare: moderate mover: still a
maiden: sold out of Mrs J. Ramsden's stable 1,700 gns Doncaster January Sales: no
worthwhile form at Hamilton in April: best form at 1½m to 1¾m: acts on firm
ground. *M. Dods*

DESERT CHALLENGER (IRE) 2 b.c. (Feb 1) Sadler's Wells (USA) 132 – **61**
Verily (Known Fact (USA) 135) [1992 8m⁶ 8m] 280,000F, 340,000Y: smallish,
sturdy colt: moderate mover: first foal: dam, French maiden half-sister to smart
French miler River Dancer, out of half-sister to Sun Princess and Saddlers' Hall (by
Sadler's Wells): backward, around 9 lengths sixth of 11, prominent almost 6f, not
knocked about, to Taos in maiden at Doncaster: dropped right away from 2f out at
Newmarket later in September. *A. C. Stewart*

DESERT CHAMP (USA) 3 b.c. Danzig (USA) – Promising Times (USA) **–**
(Olden Times) [1991 NR 1992 6.1d] $550,000F: angular colt: second foal: dam,
half-sister to Grade 1 Manhattan Handicap winner Danger's Hour (stayed 1½m),
ran once at 3 yrs: bandaged off-hind, behind in Nottingham maiden in April, jockey
reporting he thought horse was lame: moved moderately to post. *A. A. Scott*

DESERT DAGGER 3 b.c. Green Desert (USA) 127 – Chasing Moonbeams 99 **70**
(Final Straw 127) [1991 NR 1992 6g³ 5.1m* 6m] 72,000Y: sturdy, useful-looking
colt: second foal: dam 2-y-o 5f winner deteriorated after, is half-sister to stayers Cap
Del Mond and Storm Cloud: fair performer: led close home to win maiden at Bath in
May: struggling over 2f out when stiffish task for Windsor handicap 4 weeks later:
likely to be suited by 7f +: wears tongue strap. *Major W. R. Hern*

DESERT FORCE (IRE) 3 b.c. Lomond (USA) 128 – St Padina 91 (St Paddy **71** d
133) [1991 7m⁶ 8m² 1992 8g 10d² 12f⁴ 10m⁶ 12.3m 8d⁴ 10m 12.2d⁵ a16g⁵] sturdy,
quite attractive colt: has a quick action: fair maiden at best: well below form after
second in handicap at Newbury in April: trained until after fifth start by M.
Moubarak: stays 1¼m: acts on good to firm ground and dead: well beaten in blinkers
once: tongue tied once. *Miss Gay Kelleway*

DESERT GIRL 2 b.f. (May 2) Green Desert (USA) 127 – Upend 120 (Main Reef **– p**
126) [1992 7g] 82,000Y: smallish, sturdy filly: first foal: dam, 1¼m and 1½m winner,
is half-sister to dam of Royal Gait: 13/2 from 5/2 and carrying condition, never better
than midfield in 16-runner minor event at Newbury in September: will improve. *J. R.
Fanshawe*

DESERT LAUGHTER (IRE) 2 ch.g. (Apr 24) Desert of Wind (USA) 83 – **43**
Tickled To Bits (Sweet Revenge 129) [1992 a6g 7f 8g 7g 10g] IR 2,000Y: sturdy
gelding: half-brother to a winner in Norway: dam of little account: sire
middle-distance performer: poor form in maiden events: stays 1¼m: usually slowly
away. *R. Hollinshead*

DESERT MIST 3 gr.f. Sharrood (USA) 124 – Misty Halo 93 (High Top 131) [1991 **54**
7m 8.9d 8s a8g 1992 10f 12f 16f⁵ 11.9f4 15.1m* 15.1f* 15g] big filly: modest
handicapper: won seller (sold out of Sir Mark Prescott's stable 3,700 gns) and
handicap at Edinburgh in July: stays 2m: acts on firm going: blinkered last 5 starts:
tail swisher: has wandered and run in snatches: winning juvenile hurdler. *Denys
Smith*

DESERT NOMAD 2 b.f. (Mar 29) Green Desert (USA) 127 – Pale Gold (FR) **49**
(New Chapter 106) [1992 6g 5d⁶ 6s] 10,000Y: quite good-topped filly: moderate
mover: half-sister to several winners, including (at 1¼m) fairly useful My Tony (by
Be My Guest): dam minor French 6f and 11.5f winner, is half-sister to smart animals
Pale Ale and Polynikis: modest maiden: should be much better suited by 6f than 5f:
slowly away first 2 starts. *S. Dow*

DESERT PEACE (IRE) 3 b.c. Last Tycoon 131 – Broken Wide (Busted 134) **78**
[1991 NR 1992 9.7m² 12.5f³ 10g² 14.1g³ 16m³ 16m*] lengthy colt: third foal:
half-brother to 1½m to 2¼m winner Subsonic (by Be My Guest): dam Irish
middle-distance maiden: fair performer: blinkered, easily won maiden at Lingfield in
August: looked none too keen previous outing: stays well: yet to race on a soft
surface: one paced: sold 20,000 gns Newmarket Autumn Sales. *P. F. I. Cole*

DESERT POWER 3 b.c. Green Desert (USA) 127 – Rivers Maid 83 (Rarity 129) –
[1991 NR 1992 8s] 56,000Y: smallish, good-bodied colt: half-brother to smart 1985
2-y-o Nomination (by Dominion) and several maidens: dam won over 7f at 2 yrs and
is sister to very useful middle-distance performer and good hurdler Decent Fellow:
backward, well beaten in Ripon maiden in April: sold 2,700 gns Newmarket July
Sales. *B. Hanbury*

DESERT SECRET (IRE) 2 b.c. (Feb 20) Sadler's Wells (USA) 132 – **106**
Clandestina (USA) 98 (Secretariat (USA)) [1992 7g⁵ 8f² 8s* 8d4]

Frankly, the latest Royal Lodge winner Desert Secret wasn't one of its
best. He was a maiden going into the race, and was all out to beat a substandard field, the first six of which were covered by barely four lengths; and
nothing achieved subsequently either by himself or by those who followed
him home at Ascot could cast him in a more favourable light. We should say
that Desert Secret is a useful colt, one capable of winning more races outside the very best company. But his standing among his own age-group is
illustrated by his performance in the Racing Post Trophy at Doncaster the
following month, when he was unable to finish within ten lengths of the
winner Armiger.

The twice-raced Desert Secret wasn't most people's idea of the winner
of the Royal Lodge: he was one of three maidens in the ten-runner field, and
started at 12/1 in a market headed rather uneasily by the seven-length
Sandown winner Scottish Peak. At the time all that could usefully be said of
Desert Secret was that his second run, a narrow defeat at the hands of Henry
Cecil's newcomer Dakar Rally in a maiden at Doncaster in September, had
represented a significant improvement on his first, and that, as he still looked
in need of the race at Doncaster, he was pretty much certain to progress
again. Desert Secret looked fully fit in the Royal Lodge for the first time. The
Royal Lodge was run on soft ground, and Desert Secret was given plenty of
time to find his stride at the back of the field as Scottish Peak made the
running closely followed by the exposed Geisway and the Irish challenger
Perfect Imposter, a winner at Galway on his previous outing. As the race took
shape from the home turn Desert Secret knuckled down really well under
pressure, worked his way forward gradually, and, showing none of the slightly
wayward tendencies that had spoiled his finishing effort last time out, stayed
on stoutly to account for Geisway by half a length, with a gap of two and a half
lengths to Lost Soldier, half a length ahead of the Champagne Stakes
runner-up Needle Gun in fourth. Rather surprisingly, Desert Secret was put
in as favourite when the five-day declarations became known for the Racing
Post Trophy. Confidence in his chance weakened through the week as a
substantial gamble built up on Armiger, and on the day he started third

Royal Lodge Stakes, Ascot—Desert Secret (left) and Geisway battle it out

Maktoum Al-Maktoum's "Desert Secret"

favourite at 5/1 along with the May Hill winner Marillette behind Armiger and the Fillies' Mile winner Ivanka. Desert Secret saw his race out gamely but he had his limitations well and truly exposed. He did make some headway under strong pressure into fourth place early in the straight, but that was as near as he got, and he eventually passed the post eleven lengths down, beaten also by Ivanka and the Dewhurst seventh Zind.

Desert Secret (IRE) (b.c. Feb 20, 1990)	Sadler's Wells (USA) (b 1981)	Northern Dancer (b 1961)	Nearctic Natalma
		Fairy Bridge (b 1975)	Bold Reason Special
	Clandestina (USA) (b 1978)	Secretariat (ch 1970)	Bold Ruler Somethingroyal
		My Charmer (b 1969)	Poker Fair Charmer

With his outstanding pedigree—he's by the top-class stallion Sadler's Wells out of a half-sister to Seattle Slew and Lomond—and his good looks, it's no surprise that Desert Secret fetched 800,000 dollars as a yearling at the Saratoga Sales. He's the fourth winner his dam Clandestina has produced, following the mile-and-a-quarter winner Night Secret (by Nijinsky), the mile-and-three-quarter and two-mile winner Bestow (by Shirley Heights) and his own full sister Bineyah, a very useful three-year-old over middle distances in the latest season when she finished in the frame behind User Friendly in

219

both the Irish Oaks and the Yorkshire Oaks. As mentioned, Clandestina, who showed fairly useful form herself over a mile and a quarter, over which distance she won her only race, in Ireland, is a half-sister to Seattle Slew, one of the best horses to have raced in the States. A winner of fourteen of his seventeen races at up to a mile and a half, Seattle Slew was voted champion of his generation in each of his three seasons to race, and was Horse of the Year in his three-year-old season in 1977 when he won five Grade 1 races, including the Kentucky Derby, the Preakness Stakes and the Belmont Stakes, the events which comprise the triple crown. His dam My Charmer, a minor stakes winner at up to a mile, has also foaled three other winners very useful or better, namely the Two Thousand Guineas winner Lomond, the Irish six-furlong and one-mile winner Argosy and the 13,100,000 dollars yearling Seattle Dancer, a very smart winner at a mile and a quarter in Ireland. My Charmer was still very much in demand when offered for sale at the advanced age of eighteen at Keeneland's November Breeding Stock Sale in 1987, fetching an incredible 2,700,000 dollars. *M. R. Stoute*

DESERT SHOT 2 b.c. (May 13) Green Desert (USA) 127 – Out of Shot 116§ **95 p** (Shirley Heights 130) [1992 6f* 6.1g* 7.3s] 175,000Y: unfurnished colt: moderate mover: fourth foal: brother to smart 3-y-o but inconsistent 6f (at 2 yrs) and 7.3f winner Mojave, and half-brother to 1¼m winner Missed Again (by High Top): dam temperamental 1½m winner: fairly useful form: won maiden at Newmarket and minor event at Chester (in impressive style) in August, both in small fields: finished very tired (looked a candidate for a place at one point) in Horris Hill Stakes at Newbury in October: will probably stay 7f: may not be suited by very soft ground: almost certainly capable of good deal better. *M. R. Stoute*

DESERT SPLENDOUR 4 b.c. Green Desert (USA) 127 – Lost Splendour **71** (USA) (Vaguely Noble 140) [1991 9m3 8.9g 7d 9m 8.9m 6m 10.3d 1992 7m2 7g 8g5 7m4 8m 7d 9d 8m] robust colt: impresses in appearance: has a round action: fair form in July and August: well below form after coming fourth at Newcastle: sold to join R. Cambidge 5,800 gns Newmarket Autumn Sales: effective at 7f to 9f: acts on good to firm and dead going. *C. E. Brittain*

DESERT SUN 4 b.c. Green Desert (USA) 127 – Solar 120 (Hotfoot 126) [1991 **111** 8m2 8g6 7g3 7g2 8m* 1992 9g5 8.1g3 8m 10m 12f4 10.5d a8.5f2 a8f3 9f*] strong, lengthy colt: carries condition: impresses in appearance: has a long, fluent action: unreliable performer: below form in Europe after good third in Forte Mile at Sandown in April: left H. Cecil's stable after sixth start: ran in 3 allowance races in USA, winning at Hollywood Park in December: probably stays 1¼m: has won on soft ground, but best efforts on a sound surface. *R. Frankel, USA*

DESERT VENUS 2 b.f. (Feb 10) Green Desert (USA) 127 – Sangala (FR) (Jim **74 p** French (USA)) [1992 6d2 6d3] 48,000F, IR 175,000Y: leggy, quite attractive filly: half-sister to French winners (at 9f and 10.5f) Guard's Gala (by Home Guard) and Gala Smith (by Alias Smith): dam, unraced, from family of Doyoun and Dafayna: placed in maidens at Goodwood and Newmarket in the autumn, on both occasions racing close up and staying on strongly: will be better suited by 7f/1m: may well do better. *B. Hanbury*

DESERT ZONE (USA) 3 ch.c. Affirmed (USA) – Deloram (CAN) (Lord **85 ?** Durham (CAN)) [1991 NR 1992 10d* 10m3 10s5] $120,000Y: rangy colt: fifth reported foal: half-brother to 3 winners, including Canadian 9f stakes winner Smart Lord (by Smarten): dam won sprint maiden at 3 yrs: fairly useful form (winner of maiden) at Brighton on 2 outings in April: sold out of P. Cole's stable only 2,500 gns Newmarket September Sales and well below form in minor event on return: stays 1¼m: acts on good to firm and dead ground. *J. L. Harris*

DESERVE 3 b.c. Green Desert (USA) 127 – Scimitarra 115 (Kris 135) [1991 7m* **77** 1992 8.2d* 10g 8m] angular colt: shows knee action: well-backed favourite, gamely won minor event at Nottingham in April: stiff tasks in competitive minor event at Newbury and Britannia Handicap at Royal Ascot: stays 1m well. *H. R. A. Cecil*

DESIGN WISE 8 b.g. Prince Bee 128 – Wollow Princess (Wollow 132) [1991 8f **–** 8.3f 12f5 11.1s a12g 1992 9.2d] compact gelding: poor handicapper: stays 1½m: probably acts on any going: tried blinkered. *D. Moffatt*

DESIRABLE MISS 2 b.f. (Feb 7) Grey Desire 115 – Miss Realm 86 (Realm 129) **40** [1992 6g 6d 6g6 6m 6.1m 6s4 7d 5d] angular, sparely-made filly: moderate mover: fifth foal: sister to 3-y-o Grey Decision and half-sister to 1989 2-y-o 5f winner Spanish Realm (by King of Spain): dam 2-y-o 5f winner: poor form, including in sellers: stays 6f: acts on soft ground: often blinkered: sold 800 gns Doncaster November Sales. *M. Brittain*

DESIRED GUEST 3 gr.g. Be My Guest (USA) 126 – As You Desire Me 112 **69** (Kalamoun 129) [1991 7m⁵ 1992 7g 6.9d* 10g 10m⁵] sparely-made gelding: landed odds in 3-runner maiden at Carlisle in April: behind in handicap (blinkered and bandaged off-hind) and seller after: should stay 1m: takes strong hold: sold 2,800 gns Newmarket Autumn Sales. *M. R. Stoute*

DEVILRY 2 b.c. (Feb 1) Faustus (USA) 118 – Ancestry (Persepolis (FR) 127) **82** [1992 6g³ 6m* 7d³ 7.9d* 8d] 10,000Y: good-topped colt: has a roundish action: first foal: dam never ran: game and narrow winner of maiden at Windsor in August and nursery at York in September: first modest effort in nursery at Goodwood final start: out-and-out stayer: acts on good to firm and dead ground. *G. Lewis*

DEVIL'S ROCK (USA) 2 ch.c. (Feb 2) Devil's Bag (USA) – Cairn Rouge 127 **110** (Pitcairn 126) [1992 7g⁶ 7.5s* 8g⁴ 9d² a8.5f 8f²] half-brother to 1m winner Roupala (by Vaguely Noble) and useful 6f and 7f winner Aguja (by The Minstrel): dam won Irish 1000 Guineas, Coronation Stakes and Champion Stakes: won minor event at Deauville in August: beaten short neck by Richard of York in 4-runner Prix Saint-Roman at Evry in September: trained by R. Frankel when second in Grade 3 Hoist The Flag Stakes at Hollywood Park in November: will stay 1¼m. *Mme C. Head, France*

DEVIL'S SOUL 4 b.g. Faustus (USA) 118 – Ragged Moon 72 (Raga Navarro **51** § (ITY) 119) [1991 6m 7g 8g⁴ 8s* 8g⁵ 8.3m⁶ 8m⁶ 8m* 7.6g⁶ 10m 1992 10.8v 8m 8s 8m 8g² 11.4f] neat gelding: inconsistent handicapper: reluctant to race/very slowly away first 4 starts in 1992: stays 1m: acts on good to firm and soft going: effective blinkered or not: best left alone. *R. Akehurst*

DEVON DANCER 3 b.f. Shareef Dancer (USA) 135 – Devon Defender 90 **73** (Home Guard (USA) 129) [1991 6m² 7g* 7g 8.1f 1992 8.1s⁴ 10.5d 7.9m⁶ 7.1m² 8.1d⁴ 6m⁶ 6g² 7m⁴ 6d 7s 7s³ 8v⁵] leggy, workmanlike filly: good mover: modest handicapper: effective at 6f and stays 1m: acts on good to firm ground and soft: usually visored: looked unsatisfactory on occasions: sold 8,000 gns Newmarket December Sales. *M. H. Easterby*

DEXTER CHIEF 3 b.g. Elegant Air 119 – Emblazon 91 (Wolver Hollow 126) **65** [1991 NR 1992 8d³ 10v 9m⁵ 10f² 10g⁵] 10,000Y, 39,000Y: tall, leggy gelding: half-brother to several winners, including 6f and 1m winner Taranga (by Music Boy) and 1989 2-y-o 6f winner Walkern Witch (by Dunbeath): dam winner at up to 1½m: modest maiden: stays 1¼m: acts on firm and dead ground: raced very freely when visored: sold to join J. White's stable 10,500 gns Newmarket July Sales. *I. A. Balding*

DHAHRAN 2 b.c. (Apr 22) Mtoto 134 – Fur Hat (Habitat 134) [1992 a7g³ 6m a8g⁴ **57** 8.2d a6g⁴] good-quartered colt: third foal: half-brother to 1¼m winner Wild Sable (by Kris): dam unraced sister to Topsy and half-sister to Teenoso: plating-class maiden: ran creditably blinkered final run: should stay at least 1m: sold 4,000 gns Newmarket Autumn Sales. *P. F. I. Cole*

DIACO 7 b.g. Indian King (USA) 128 – Coral Cave 79 (Ashmore (FR) 125) [1991 **67** 8.2g⁵ 8m³ 8.1g 7.6m* 8f⁵ 8.2f⁵ 8m* 8m 8g* 9.7s 1992 8.1f⁶ 8f³ 8m 8d 8.2d⁴ 8g⁵ 9s 8g a8g⁵] leggy, quite attractive gelding: usually looks very well: inconsistent handicapper: best at around 1m nowadays: acts on firm and dead ground: below best when blinkered: held up. *M. A. Jarvis*

DIAMOND CUT (FR) 4 b.c. Fast Topaze (USA) 128 – Sasetto (FR) (St Paddy **72** 133) [1991 8g 10m 10.2m³ 10.1f⁴ 8.9g³ 11.7m⁵ 1992 10m⁶ 11.9m*] good-topped colt: modest performer: first win on flat when straightforward task in Brighton apprentice event in July: better suited by around 1½m than shorter: acts on firm going. *M. C. Pipe*

DIAMOND INTHE DARK (USA) 4 b.c. Diamond Prospect (USA) – Implicit – (Grundy 137) [1991 6m⁶ 8g⁵ 7g² 7.1m* a8g a8g 1992 7g 7s 7.1g] angular, rather dipped-backed colt: poor handicapper: stays 7f: acts on good to firm ground: ran poorly when blinkered. *C. Tinkler*

DIAMOND LUCY 2 ch.f. (May 19) Midyan (USA) 124 – Bellagio 68 (Busted 134) – [1992 5g] 14,000Y: angular, workmanlike filly: half-sister to 3-y-o Our Man In Havana and fairly useful 7f winner Vilany (both by Never So Bold) and 2 other winners, including useful miler Arany (by Precocious): dam 1¼m winner stayed 1½m: always behind in maiden at Newmarket in May. *W. A. O'Gorman*

DIAMOND POINT 2 b.f. (Feb 21) Kalaglow 132 – Diamond Hill 82 (High Top **64** 131) [1992 a7g² a8g⁴] fifth foal: half-sister to fair 1988 2-y-o 5f winner Crag Hall (by Sharpo) and fair miler Brilliant (by Never So Bold): dam won over 7f and stayed

1½m: beaten a neck in claimer at Southwell: 6/4, dropped away final 2f when poor fourth of 10 in similar event there later in December. *Sir Mark Prescott*

DIAMONDS GALORE (CAN) 7 b.g. Diamond Shoal 130 – Sirona (CAN) **117** (Irish Stronghold (USA)) [1992 7f* 5f* 5m³ 6d⁵] strong, lengthy Canadian sprinter: first foal: dam successful in stakes company at up to 7f: successful, including in stakes company, on 14 occasions, including in 5f £35,000 graded event at Monmouth Park: sweating and tongue tied down, smart performance when 2 lengths third of 11 to Lyric Fantasy in Nunthorpe Stakes at York: well below that form in Laurel Dash after: very speedy, but has won at 7f: acts on firm ground. *Daniel Yella, Canada*

DIAMOND SINGH 5 b.g. Mansingh (USA) 120 – Prime Thought 69 (Primera –
131) [1991 a7g a11g a7g 8h a7g 8m 8m² 1992 8m] sturdy gelding: poor mover: on the downgrade. *S. G. Norton*

DIAMOND WEDDING (USA) 3 b.f. Diamond Shoal 130 – Wedding (USA) **65** (Noholme II) [1991 8.1g 1992 10g⁴ 13.9f⁵ 10.3g³ 10s⁴ 11.8g² 11.6g 11.9d⁶ 10.4s³ 10.3g] lengthy, workmanlike filly: has a scratchy action: disappointing maiden: stays 1½m: acts on soft ground: effective blinkered or not: looked unsatisfactory last 2 starts, and one to be wary of. *N. A. Graham*

DICIEMBRE 3 ch.g. Dominion 123 – Until June (USA) (Be My Guest (USA) 126) –
[1991 7g⁴ 1992 10.2m] good-topped gelding: first foal: dam French 9f winner: twice-raced maiden: never dangerous in May: should stay 1½m. *I. A. Balding*

DICKENS LANE 5 b.g. Caerleon (USA) 132 – Easy Landing 110 (Swing Easy **54** (USA) 126) [1991 8f³ 7g 6f⁴ 6d 6.1g 7g 7.1m* 8.2m 5g 1992 7g 5g 5.1m 6m³ 6.1m 6.1g 6g 5m* 5g³ 5d⁴ 5d 5g⁴ 5s] lengthy, leggy ex-Irish gelding: poor mover: modest handicapper: won at Kempton in August: needs good test at 5f, and stays 1m: probably acts on any going: below form when blinkered. *R. J. Hodges*

DICKINS 2 b.c. (Apr 20) Green Ruby (USA) 104 – Rosie Dickins 59 (Blue **64** Cashmere 129) [1992 6d³ 7v⁵ 7g] angular colt: first foal: dam sprinter: easily best effort in late-season when never-dangerous third of 5 in Leicester minor event. *R. Hollinshead*

DICK WHITTINGTON 3 br.g. King of Spain 121 – Miss Dicky (Lepanto **43** (GER)) [1991 5m 7m⁶ 8.3g 7g 1992 10m 8g⁴ 7g 10d] tall, lengthy gelding: plater: best form at 1m: often has tongue tied down. *C. Tinkler*

DIDYME (USA) 2 b.c. (May 12) Dixieland Band (USA) – Soundings (USA) (Mr **111** Prospector (USA)) [1992 6d* 5.5g* 6s⁵ 7m⁵] smallish, rather leggy colt: second foal: dam, minor winner in USA, is from excellent family: successful in newcomers race and Prix Robert Papin (by a neck from Creaking Board) at Maisons-Laffitte in July: beaten into fifth by Zafonic otherwise, around 3 lengths down in Prix Morny at Deauville in August and around 5 lengths down in Prix de la Salamandre at Longchamp in September: will stay 1m. *Mme C. Head, France*

DIET 6 b.g. Starch Reduced 112 – Highland Rossie 67 (Pablond 93) [1991 6s 6d⁵ 5f **69** 5f³ 6m 6f⁵ 6m* 6d* 6d 6m³ 6.1m 5m 6m 5m 6s 1992 8.3s 5d⁵ 6m* 5f⁴ 6m⁴ 6g 6m² 6.1m 6g³ 7d⁴ 7.1d⁴ 6s² 5d⁵ 6d² 6s⁵] sturdy, good-quartered gelding: carries condition: largely consistent handicapper in 1992, successful at Hamilton: effective from stiff 5f to 7f: acts on any going: goes very well visored, also effective blinkered: sometimes hangs under pressure, but suitable mount for apprentice: front runner. *Miss L. A. Perratt*

DIGGER DOYLE 3 b.g. Cragador 110 – Chaconia Girl (Bay Express 132) [1991 **63** 7d 7m⁵ 6.1m 7m 1992 6m 6m⁶ a7g*] good-bodied gelding: modest performer: won maiden at Southwell in June: stays 7f: acts on good to firm ground and fibresand: ran creditably in visor. *C. N. Allen*

DIG IN THE RIBS (IRE) 2 ch.c. (Apr 19) Digamist (USA) 110 – First Contact **58** 79 (Simbir 130) [1992 7f⁵ 8d⁶ 8v⁶] IR 5,800Y: tall, useful-looking colt: half-brother to 1986 2-y-o 5f seller winner Helens Contact (by Crofter), later a prolific winner in Italy: dam stayed 1m: beaten around 2 lengths when fifth in moderately-run minor event at Doncaster in September: never dangerous but not knocked about in maidens after: looks sort to do better. *R. Hollinshead*

DILI (USA) 2 b.f. (May 12) Chief's Crown (USA) – Untitled 98 (Vaguely Noble – P
140) [1992 8d] half-sister to several winners, including useful 7f to 1¼m winner Jungle Pioneer (by Conquistador Cielo) and a middle-distance winner by Nureyev: dam 1m winner, is half-sister to Dactylographer: very easy to back, shaped really well and much better than midfield position suggests in 20-runner Yarmouth maiden in October, leading travelling strongly to 2f out then not knocked about in the slightest as lack of condition told: bred to stay 1¼m: will improve considerably. *A. C. Stewart*

*Prix de la Porte Maillot, Longchamp—Dilum returns to his best;
Lion Cavern is second, Bog Trotter third*

DILKUSH 3 b.g. Dunbeath (USA) 127 – Good Try 92 (Good Bond 122) [1991 NR   –
1992 a7g⁶ 6.9v 5g a7g 8d a7g] 4,200Y: lengthy, workmanlike gelding: poor walker:
half-brother to many winners, including 5-y-o sprinter Choir Practice (by Chief
Singer) and 1½m winner Castle Heights (by Shirley Heights): dam 2-y-o 5f winner:
no worthwhile form: blinkered final start: sold 1,100 gns Newmarket Autumn Sales.
L. J. Holt

DILUM (USA) 3 br.c. Tasso (USA) – Yanuka 111 (Pitcairn 126) [1991 6d² 6g* **115**
6g* 6g* 6g⁴ 6f³ 1992 8g 8.2g* 7m* 8s 7f⁴ 7m] strong, good-topped colt: good
walker and mover: smart performer: successful in 2-runner minor event at Nottingham and Group 3 event at Longchamp (beat Lion Cavern, who gave 6 lb, by 4
lengths) in June: creditable fourth to Pursuit of Love at Doncaster, easily best effort
in pattern events otherwise in 1992: should prove best at up to 1m: acts on firm
ground, may be unsuited by soft: to join N. Drysdale in USA. *P. F. I. Cole*

DIME BAG 3 ch.f. High Line 125 – Blue Guitar 88 (Cure The Blues (USA)) [1991 **71**
7m⁵ 1992 12m⁶ 11.7s 12.2g* 14m 14.8g⁴ 14d³ a16g* a16g*] lengthy, sparely-made **a87**
filly: has a fluent, round action: fairly useful form: won maiden at Catterick in July
and improved after being stepped up to 2m, leading over 3f out and soon clear to win
handicaps at Lingfield in November: better at 2m than shorter: well beaten on soft
ground. *B. W. Hills*

DIOMAN SHADEED (USA) 3 b.g. Shadeed (USA) 135 – Dimant Rose (USA)   – §
(Tromos 134) [1991 NR 1992 10.5d 10m 8g⁴ 10.1d] strong, useful-looking gelding:
good walker and mover: second foal: dam unraced half-sister to Rainbow Quest,
family also of Warning, Slightly Dangerous and Noblesse: no worthwhile form in
maidens: refused to race final start and subsequently gelded (earlier twice slowly
away). *J. R. Fanshawe*

DIPLOMATIST 2 b.f. (May 25) Dominion 123 – Dame Julian 84 (Blakeney 126) **59** p
[1992 6d 7s⁴] 18,000Y: leggy, quite attractive filly: sister to 3 winners, including
useful 1m to 1¼m performer Fair Dominion, and half-sister to 3 others, including
smart 7f performer Norwich and 2m winner St Ville (both by Top Ville): dam, 1m
winner, is half-sister to good sprinter Daring Boy and very smart Daring March (by
Derring-Do): easily better effort in maidens when one-paced fourth of 14 to
Thawakib at Salisbury in September: will be suited by further than 7f: will improve
again. *I. A. Balding*

DISCO BOY 2 b.c. (Apr 18) Green Ruby (USA) 104 – Sweet And Shiny (Siliconn   **49**
121) [1992 5d a6g⁵ 6d] second live foal: dam of little account: poor form in autumn
maidens: stays 6f. *B. A. McMahon*

DISCORD 6 b.g. Niniski (USA) 125 – Apple Peel 109 (Pall Mall 132) [1991 12.1d   **79**
12d a14g⁴ 1992 12.3g* a12g* 12m*] tall gelding: progressed with each run in first
half of 1992, successful in Wolverhampton claimer and handicaps at Southwell and

223

Kempton: effective at 1½m and stays 13.3f well: acts on good to firm and dead ground and fibresand: effective visored or not. *Lord Huntingdon*

DISKETTE 2 b.f. (Apr 17) Local Suitor (USA) 128 – Last Clear Chance (USA) **70** (Alleged (USA) 138) [1992 5g 6s* 7m6] leggy filly: fourth reported foal: half-sister to 7f winner Bridal Train (by Gorytus) and a winner in Italy by General Assembly: dam ran once: progressive filly: length winner of 16-runner Haydock claimer, running on strongly despite tending to hang left: staying-on sixth of 21 to Wynona in nursery at Newmarket later in September: will be suited by further than 7f: probably acts on any going. *Lord Huntingdon*

DISPUTED CALL (USA) 3 b.c. Alleged (USA) 138 – Tennis Partner (USA) **81** p (Northern Dancer (CAN)) [1991 NR 1992 8g5 10s a12g2 a12g*] $75,000F, 70,000Y: big colt: third foal: half-brother to Irish 7f (at 2 yrs) to 1¼m winner Wingfield (by Devil's Bag): dam unraced sister to Ajdal and half-sister to Formidable and Fabuleux Jane (grandam of Arazi): improved form when stepped up to 1½m at Lingfield, easily winning maiden in December: suited by 1½m: acts on equitrack, well beaten on soft ground: may well progress further. *J. W. Hills*

DISTANT MEMORY 3 gr.g. Don't Forget Me 127 – Canton Silk 108 – (Runnymede 123) [1991 6d6 7m4 6f3 7m 1992 9g 10m4 12g5 10.2g] sparely-made gelding: soundly beaten in 1992: should stay 9f: sold 875 gns Ascot July Sales. *J. W. Hills*

DISTANT SPRING (IRE) 2 br.g. (Mar 23) Dowsing (USA) 124 – Fariha – (Mummy's Pet 125) [1992 7g 6m] 6,800Y: unfurnished gelding: fourth foal: half-brother to 3-y-o Bold Stroke (by Persian Bold), successful at 1m (at 2 yrs) and 1¼m, and a winner in Brazil: dam twice-raced half-sister to smart miler Gwent: behind in maiden auctions at Yarmouth. *G. A. Pritchard-Gordon*

DI STEFANO 4 b.g. Chief Singer 131 – Doree Moisson (FR) 84 (Connaught 130) – [1991 7d 10m4 9s 1992 11.9d] close-coupled gelding: poor maiden: blinkered when running as if something amiss in April: stays 1¼m: possibly best on sound surface. *G. Harwood*

DISTINCT THATCHER (USA) 3 b.g. Stifelius – Clearly Early (USA) (Dis- **102** tinctive (USA)) [1991 6f* 6m* 1992 9g4 8.1g2 8g3] big, lengthy gelding: useful performer: good efforts in spring of 1992 in listed race at Newmarket, minor event at Sandown and Mehl-Mulhens Rennen (ran very well) at Cologne: gives impression should stay 1¼m: acts on firm ground: gelded after final start. *R. Hannon*

DITTISHAM (USA) 2 b.f. (Mar 17) Sir Ivor 135 – Eltisley (USA) 82 (Grey – p Sovereign 128§) [1992 6g6 6d] $37,000F: angular, quite attractive filly: sister to useful 7f winner Applemint and half-sister to several winners here and abroad, including useful sprinter Dare Me (by Derring-Do): dam 2-y-o 5f winner: shaped encouragingly in maidens at Ascot in July and Kempton (not knocked about) 2 months after: will do better, particularly over further. *R. Hannon*

DIVE FOR COVER (USA) 3 b.c. Lear Fan (USA) 130 – Wistoral (USA) **111** (Exceller (USA) 129) [1991 7g* 1992 10.5g3 10m 12g4 12m4 9g 12.5v5 12f5] sturdy, close-coupled colt: sold out of Mrs J. Ramsden's stable 70,000 gns Newmarket Autumn (1991) Sales after winning maiden at Ayr: in frame in listed race at Longchamp, Prix du Lys at Chantilly and Budweiser Irish Derby (best effort, 16 lengths behind St Jovite) at the Curragh: fifth in valuable handicap in USA final start: suited by 1½m: acts on good to firm ground, seemingly not on heavy. *J. E. Hammond, France*

DIVINE GLORY 3 b.f. Valiyar 129 – Mummy's Glory 82 (Mummy's Pet 125) – [1991 NR 1992 6s 10d] 500Y: sturdy filly: fifth foal: half-sister to untrustworthy maiden Tambuli (by Mr Fluorocarbon): dam best at 2 yrs, raced only at 5f: twice raced, and no promise in maiden and seller. *R. Voorspuy*

DIVINE PET 7 br.g. Tina's Pet 121 – Davinia 92 (Gold Form 108) [1991 5g 6g 6d **68** 6g2 5.8d4 6d 7g6 6f* 5.2f* 6g 5.2f3 6g 5d 5.2g6 1992 6g6 6g3 5f3 6d 6m2 6g5 5d 6d6 5.7d*] strong, good-topped gelding: carries plenty of condition: has been hobdayed: has a quick action: modest handicapper: won at Bath in September: should stay 7f: acts on firm and dead going: tough: gets behind. *W. G. R. Wightman*

DIVINE RAIN 2 b.c. (Feb 10) Dowsing (USA) 124 – La Reine de France **51** (Queen's Hussar 124) [1992 6g 6g5 6.9v5 7s] 7,000F, 10,000Y: rangy colt: has scope: moderate mover: sixth foal: half-brother to 3 sprint winners: dam never ran: plating-class maiden: will be better suited by 1m: acts on heavy ground. *J. W. Payne*

DIVING (USA) 4 b.g. Silver Hawk (USA) 123 – Challenging Stage (USA) (Gold **34** + Stage (USA)) [1991 8g 10.8m 9m 1992 13.8d 8.3v5 8.5g] lengthy gelding: poor walker: poor handicapper: seemed to stay 1m and need an easy surface: below form when blinkered once: dead. *Mrs V. A. Aconley*

DIVORCE COURT (IRE)   2 b.c. (Apr 30) Digamist (USA) 110 – Centre Piece   **53 p**
73 (Tompion (USA)) [1992 6d4] 30,000Y: good-bodied colt: half-brother to several winners, notably very smart sprinter Greenland Park (dam of Fitnah) and Coventry Stakes winner Red Sunset (both by Red God): dam ran 4 times at 2 yrs: 5/1, promising 6 lengths fourth of 9 to Bonjour in maiden at Haydock in August, green after slow start then coming through strongly from 1½f out: will improve. *L. M. Cumani*

DIWALI DANCER   2 gr.g. (Mar 12) Petong 126 – Dawn Dance (USA) (Grey   **40 p**
Dawn II 132) [1992 a7g] 5,000F, 9,500Y: half-brother to several winners abroad: dam never ran: 20/1 from 10/1, slowly away and not knocked about when beaten in 12-runner maiden at Lingfield in December: will do better. *A. Bailey*

DIXIELAND MELODY (USA)   2 b.c. (Mar 22) Dixieland Band (USA) –   **77 p**
Celebration Song (USA) (J O Tobin (USA) 130) [1992 7g2 8m*] $100,000Y: good-topped colt: third foal: half-brother to 1990 2-y-o 5f winner Rio Tejo (by Tsunami Slew): dam, in frame at 6f and 1m in Ireland and later placed in USA, is half-sister to Seattle Song: sire smart at up to 9f: confirmed promising second to Emperor Jones in Newmarket maiden when very easily winning Thirsk maiden by 3 lengths from Manaarah later in autumn: has scope, and sure to improve again. *B. Hanbury*

DIZZY DAME   3 b.f. Mummy's Game 120 – Dancing Chimes (London Bells   –
(CAN) 109) [1991 NR 1992 9g 10g 10.2f] 1,400Y: leggy filly: moderate mover: first foal: dam unraced: thrice raced, and poor form in maidens. *M. R. Channon*

DIZZY PENNY   3 b.f. Pennine Walk 120 – Tizzy 79 (Formidable (USA) 125) [1991   **78**
NR 1992 7d2] 21,000Y: good-bodied filly: third living foal: half-sister to fairly useful 1989 2-y-o 5f winner La Galerie (by Glenstal): dam 9f and 1¼m winner: second in newcomers race at Newbury in April: sold only 4,000 gns Newmarket Autumn Sales: sent to USA. *P. F. I. Cole*

DIZZY (USA)   4 gr.f. Golden Act (USA) – Bergluft (GER) (Literat) [1991 8m2   –
8.5m3 10.1g2 9.7m* 8g3 13.8m2 8.1d3 11.1s* 1992 12.1s] rangy, workmanlike filly: rated 80 at 3 yrs: well beaten in handicap in May, only run on flat in 1992: best at around 1¼m: acts on good to firm ground and soft: usually makes running. *P. Monteith*

DJAIS (FR)   3 ch.c. Vacarme (USA) 121 – Dame de Carreau (Targowice (USA) **113**
130) [1991 8g 10g4 10s3 1992 10.5v2 11g* 12d 15d* 15d3 12.5s3 15s] half-brother to 2 winners in France, including tough middle-distance handicapper Sinjar (by Crystal Glitters): dam won 4 races in France between 1¼m and 11f at 4 yrs: smart French performer: won handicap in May and Group 3 Prix Berteux in June, both at Longchamp: best effort when 1¾ lengths third to Modhish in Grand Prix de Deauville Lancel penultimate start: should stay beyond 12.5f: yet to race on top-of-the-ground. *J. Pease, France*

D K DAFFERS (IRE)   2 b.f. (Feb 17) Pennine Walk 120 – Payola (Auction Ring   –
(USA) 123) [1992 7d 8v] IR 2,100F: smallish, quite good-topped filly: third foal: dam unraced: no form in October maidens at Leicester. *B. Smart*

DOC COTTRILL   2 b.g. (Apr 10) Absalom 128 – Bridal Wave (Julio Mariner 127)   **77 p**
[1992 5m 6g 5f4 6d5 7s* 7d3] 6,200F, 6,400Y: unfurnished gelding: moderate mover: second foal: half-brother to a poor maiden: dam unraced half-sister to Cambridgeshire winner Century City: progressive gelding: ¾-length winner of nursery at Redcar: set great deal to do (would have won had run started sooner, and rated accordingly) when third of 21 to So So in similar event at Doncaster later in autumn: will be suited by 1m: has form on firm ground, but best form on soft: has twice reared stalls: should win more races as 3-y-o. *Mrs J. R. Ramsden*

DOCKET (USA)   4 b.f. Robellino (USA) 127 – Allegedly (USA) (Sir Ivor 135)   **53**
[1991 NR 1992 12g4 11.1s2 10f4 10g] fifth foal: sister to 5-y-o 1m to 12.3f winner Prosequendo and half-sister to 2 winners, notably very useful 7-y-o middle-distance stayer Per Quod (by Lyllos): dam unraced half-sister to Alleged: modest maiden: stays 1½m: acts on soft ground: sold 12,000 gns Newmarket December Sales. *B. Hanbury*

DOCKLANDS (USA)   3 b.f. Theatrical 128 – Dockage (USA) (Riverman (USA)   **62 p**
131) [1991 NR 1992 8v4] first foal: dam, out of close relation to Dahlia, won in France over 1m at 2 yrs and 9f (listed race) at 3 yrs: favourite, never able to challenge when 6½ lengths fourth of 10 to Gushing in maiden at Newcastle in November: should improve: has joined H. Pantall, in France. *J. H. M. Gosden*

DOC SPOT   2 b.g. (Apr 13) Doc Marten 104 – Detonate 79 (Derring-Do 131) [1992   **58**
5d 6m a7g⁴ 7.5s³ 7g⁵ 7.5d³ 8m 7d² 8g² 8.3s⁴ 8d] 780F, 1,100Y: good-topped gelding:
seventh foal: dam won at 1¼m: modest performer: will be well suited by middle
distances: acts on soft ground: hung badly right once and not an easy ride but has
run well for 7-lb claimer. *Capt. J. Wilson*

DOCTOOR (USA)   2 ch.c. (Apr 29) Cozzene (USA) – To The Top (USA) (Bold   **74**
Hour) [1992 7g³ 8.2g² 7.9s³] $85,000Y: strong, lengthy colt: ninth foal: half-brother
to 3 winners, notably 6f and 8.5f stakes winner Keep On Top (by Obraztsovy): dam,
stakes placed, winner at 2, 3 and 4 yrs: fair form in maidens: third to Bin Ajwaad at
York final start: will stay 1¼m: tongue tied down second start. *W. Jarvis*

DOCTOR-J (IRE)   2 ch.c. (May 15) Jareer (USA) 115 – Velvet Breeze   **45** p
(Windjammer (USA)) [1992 6g⁶] compact colt: second known foal: dam unraced:
16/1 and burly, never-dangerous sixth of 11 in maiden at Doncaster in November:
will improve. *M. J. Heaton-Ellis*

DOCTOR ROY   4 ch.c. Electric 126 – Pushkar (Northfields (USA)) [1991 8d⁵   **61**
8m* 7g⁶ 7f⁵ 5d⁵ 7m 8.9m⁶ 10f 1992 10.4m 8.5s 7.9d² 8m³ 9.9g 11.9m 13.9g] strong,
angular colt: carries condition: inconsistent handicapper: should stay beyond 1m:
acts on good to firm ground and dead: tends to get on edge, and sometimes pulls
hard: below form for amateur. *N. Bycroft*

DOCTOR'S REMEDY   6 br.g. Doc Marten 104 – Champagne Party (Amber   **40**
Rama (USA) 133) [1991 12f³ 12f⁴ 12.2f* 11f* 12f⁴ 12f⁴ 12.3f⁶ 12.2m⁴ 12.3f 12.2m 12m
1992 12.3g a12g 13.8m⁴ 14.1g 11f⁵ 13.6f 11d³ 9m* 12m 10g⁶ 11.6g³ 11.5g⁵ 11.6g
8.5m⁶] sturdy, rather dipped-backed gelding: carries condition: has a round action:
none too consistent handicapper: won at Redcar in July: effective at 9f to 1½m: acts
on firm and dead ground: seems effective blinkered or not: often soon off bridle, but
suitable mount for claimer. *Mrs J. Jordan*

DODGER DICKINS   5 gr.g. Godswalk (USA) 130 – Sronica (Midsummer Night   **39** §
II 117) [1991 10m* 10d 10m 14m* 18g 14g 14.6m⁴ 14.1f 14.9m⁶ 12.3f 14.1f 11.8m
14.1m⁴ 17.1m² 18m³ a14g 1992 17.1d* 21.6g 17.1m 16m⁵] workmanlike gelding: poor
mover: thoroughly unreliable handicapper: won at Pontefract in April: stays 2¼m:
acts on good to firm and dead ground. *R. Hollinshead*

DODGY   5 b.g. Homing 130 – Beryl's Jewel 86 (Siliconn 121) [1991 7g⁶ 7g 7.6m 8.2f   **65**
7.1m³ 8g* 7d a8g 1992 8f 7f³ 7.6m⁴ 7.6m* 8m* 8g² 7.6d⁴ 7.6g⁵] workmanlike
gelding: poor mover: modest handicapper: won at Lingfield and Newmarket (ladies)
in summer: stays 1m: acts on firm and dead ground: effective blinkered/visored or
not: tail swisher but very game. *S. Dow*

DODGY DANCER   2 b.c. (Jan 29) Shareef Dancer (USA) 135 – Fluctuate 87   **53**
(Sharpen Up 127) [1992 8.2g 8s 10g] close-coupled, angular colt: third live foal:
brother to 1988 2-y-o 6f winner Suhail Dancer, later temperamental, and
half-brother to unreliable middle-distance handicapper Prince Hannibal (by High
Top): dam 5f winner at 2 yrs, is out of close relative of Wassl: bandaged, beaten
around 10 lengths in autumn maidens in the Midlands. *Mrs L. Piggott*

DOESYOUDOES   3 b.f. Bay Express 132 – Captain Bonnie 60 (Captain James   **49**
123) [1991 a6g⁶ 5m² 5g 5.2f³ 5m 5m⁶ 5d³ 6m a6g⁴ a5g³ a6g³ a5g⁶ 1992 a5g* a5g⁵   a**64**
a8g⁶ a5g³ 5g 5v 6g 5g 6m⁶ 5s 5.1g⁵ 5s a5g a5g³ a5g⁵ a5g³ a5g a5g a5g⁴] lengthy,
rather plain filly: inconsistent sprint handicapper: won at Lingfield in January: acts
on equitrack, had form on firm and dead going at 2 yrs: effective visored or not. *D. T.
Thom*

DOGMA   3 b.f. Kabour 80 – Domineering (Dominion 123) [1991 NR 1992 a6g] first   **–**
foal: dam poor maiden: no sign of ability in claimer at Southwell in January, only run.
D. W. Chapman

DOKKHA OYSTON (IRE)   4 b.g. Prince Sabo 123 – I Don't Mind 97 (Swing   **74**
Easy (USA) 126) [1991 6d⁶ 5g 6g² 6g³ 5g* 5.9m⁴ 5.1g⁴ 5f³ 1992 5g⁴ 5.9d* 5m 6d⁴
6s³ 6d 6s² 6s 7.1g*] lengthy gelding: modest handicapper: won at Carlisle (claimer)
in April and Edinburgh in October: stays 7f: probably best with some give in the
ground nowadays: effective blinkered or not: sometimes slowly away: none too
consistent. *J. Berry*

DOLLAR SEEKER (USA)   8 b.h. Buckfinder (USA) – Syrian Song (USA)   **–**
(Damascus (USA)) [1991 NR 1992 18.5d⁶ 15m⁶ 15g⁵ 16.2d 12.1d] compact horse:
moderate mover: on the downgrade on flat: usually blinkered/visored. *A. Bailey*

DOLLAR WINE (IRE)   3 b.g. Alzao (USA) 117 – Captain's Covey (Captain   **46**
James 123) [1991 5m⁴ 5.3m* 6d³ 6m 6.1m⁶ 6g⁵ 6g 6g 6m 8.3s³ 1992 8d 7s³ 8.2g
8.5d⁶ 10m 6g⁵] sturdy gelding: usually takes eye in appearance: little form in 1992:

stays 1m: acts on good to firm and soft ground: below form blinkered/visored. *R. Hannon*

DOLLY MADISON (IRE)   3 b.f. Shirley Heights 130 – Shellshock 110 (Salvo   **58**
129) [1991 7m 1992 11.7d³ 12f⁵ 14d⁶ a12g³] rather leggy, quite good-topped filly: had
a round action: modest maiden: may well have needed test of stamina: acted on firm
and dead going and fibresand: dead. *B. W. Hills*

DOMAIN   4 b.c. Dominion 123 – Prelude 89 (Troy 137) [1991 8g⁶ 10g 10f⁴ 11.7g   **59**
12v 14m 1992 a12g⁵ a14g³ 16.2g³ a14g⁴ a12s] neat, good-bodied colt: has a round   a54
action: moderate walker: disappointing maiden on flat: stays 2m: acts on firm going
and fibresand: effective blinkered on flat. *R. J. Weaver*

DOMES OF SILENCE   2 b.c. (May 23) Vin St Benet 109 – Baby Flo 67 (Porto   **41**
Bello 118) [1992 a6g 5g 6.1d⁴ 5f³ a5g] 1,400Y, 3,000 2-y-o: good-topped colt:
half-brother to 6-y-o 5f winner Banham College (by Tower Walk) and 1986 2-y-o 5f
winner College Wizard (by Neltino), later successful at up to 1¼m in France: dam
sprint plater: poor maiden: may prove best at 5f: acts on firm ground. *J. Berry*

DOMIANA   4 br.f. Primo Dominie 121 – Tatiana 59 (Habitat 134) [1991 6g⁵ 5f⁶ 7m   **28**
7d 5m 5m 6.1m⁴ 5g 6g 6.1m³ 6m⁵ 1992 6v⁵ 6.1d⁶ 7g 6m⁵ 6.1m 8.3m 6.1g 6.1g] leggy
filly: bad maiden: stays 6f: acts on firm and dead ground: sold 1,050 gns Ascot July
Sales. *M. Blanshard*

DOMICKSKY   4 b.g. Dominion 123 – Mumruffin 101 (Mummy's Pet 125) [1991   **79**
7d* 7m³ 8g⁶ 8g* 7.6g* 8m 8g 8.1m 7.9m a7g⁵ a6g 1992 a7g² 8g 7g³ 8s⁵ 8g⁶ 7g 7m²
7.6m³ 7f² 7m³ 8g³ 8m² 8.3g 8d⁶ 7d 8g⁶ 7d 7.6v] good-topped gelding: carries
condition: in good form in handicaps in spring and summer: below best last 6 starts:
effective at 7f/1m: acts on firm and dead going and on equitrack: occasionally pulls
very hard and flashes tail: trained until after twelfth start by M. Ryan, next 5 by R.
Simpson: usually held up. *M. R. Channon*

DOMINANT FORCE   3 b.g. Primo Dominie 121 – Elan's Valley (Welsh Pageant   **63** d
132) [1991 NR 1992 8g 12s 9g⁵ 10m³ 11.9f⁶ 11.6g 10g⁵ 9.7m 8s] 4,100F, 5,200Y:
lengthy, plain gelding: second foal: dam French 8.5f winner: disappointing maiden:
stays 1¼m: below form when blinkered. *R. Hannon*

DOMINANT SERENADE   3 b.g. Dominion 123 – Sing Softly 112 (Luthier 126)   **57**
[1991 6g 7.5f³ 7m³ 7f⁵ 7.1d 1992 a8g⁶ 10d 8d³ 8m 8d 8.2m 8f 12m⁴ 12.2g²] smallish,
good-bodied gelding: maiden handicapper on flat: best efforts last 2 starts (with P.
Harris previously): should stay beyond 1½m: acts on firm and dead ground: below
form when blinkered once: flashes tail: progressive hurdler in the autumn, winning
3 times including gamely at Cheltenham. *M. D. Hammond*

DOMINUET   7 b.m. Dominion 123 – Stepping Gaily 79 (Gay Fandango (USA)   **88**
132) [1991 5g⁴ 5f 6g² 6m 5m* 6g² 5m⁴ 6d 5.1g* 5g⁴ 5g² 6g⁶ 6m³ 5d 6m 1992 5.1d 6g
5m 6d² 6f* 6f² 6g² 5g³ 6g 6g⁶ 6d⁴ 5m 5g] lengthy, quite attractive mare: held her
form well in handicaps in 1992: successful in £11,000 event at York in June: ideally
suited by 6f: acts on firm and dead going: sometimes gives trouble in preliminaries,
and taken down early nowadays: usually held up for a late run. *J. L. Spearing*

DOMOVOY   2 b.f. (Feb 13) Shareef Dancer (USA) 135 – Heavenly Abode (FR)   **55** p
(Habitat 134) [1992 7m⁴] sturdy filly: first foal: dam unraced: in need of race, stayed
on really well when fourth of 7 in maiden at Wolverhampton in June: seemed sure to
improve. *C. E. Brittain*

DOMULLA   2 br.c. (Apr 22) Dominion 123 – Ulla Laing 107 (Mummy's Pet 125)   **68**
[1992 6v² 6d] third reported foal: dam 2-y-o 5f and 6f winner is out of staying mare
Goosie-Gantlet: shaped promisingly when second in maiden at Folkestone: shaped
prominent to 1f out when failing to confirm that run in Yarmouth maiden later in
October. *R. Akehurst*

DOM WAC   4 b.c. Dominion 123 – Noble Wac (USA) (Vaguely Noble 140) [1991   **72**
a8g* a8g⁶ 8g⁴ 8g⁴ 8g 10.1m⁶ 12d² 16.2m* 18.5g³ 14g⁴ 11.4m* 11.9g 12d⁴ 1992 18g⁴
14g⁵ 12.3m⁵ 16m] robust colt: carries condition: shows knee action: modest
handicapper: well below form last 2 starts, not seen out after May: stays 2m: acts on
good to firm ground and dead: won for amateur. *M. Bell*

DONALD STUART   3 gr.c. Sweet Monday 122 – Teminny (Grey Love 103)   **–**
[1991 NR 1992 8d 10.2f] third foal: dam won a 2-runner novice hurdle: twice raced,
and no show in seller and maiden claimer. *M. Tate*

DONIA (USA)   3 ch.f. Graustark (USA) – Katrinka (USA) (Sovereign Dancer (USA))   **70**
[1991 NR 1992 10g⁶ 8.5d⁵ 8f² 10.3g⁴ a12g³ a10g³ a10g²] $37,000Y: big, lengthy,
sparely-made filly: second foal: half-sister to a minor winner in North America: dam
won 5 races at up 1m: fair maiden: best efforts for 7-lb claimer on last 2 starts: stays

1½m: acts on firm and dead ground and equitrack: has joined N. Henderson. *P. F. I. Cole*

DONS-BEST-BOY 4 ch.g. Tickled Pink 114 – Lamdant (Redundant 120) [1991 8g 10g 10g 8g⁶ 8m⁶ 8.2f 1992 a10g] light-framed, plain gelding: poor plater: stays 1m: acts on good to firm ground: below form visored. *J. Pearce* –

DON'T BE SAKI (IRE) 2 b.f. (Feb 8) Tender King 123 – Mar Del Plata 80 (Crowned Prince (USA) 128) [1992 5f 6g³ 7m³ 7.5d 7g 6m⁴ 7g 5.9g⁶ 6m 8.2d] IR 1,600F, 4,600Y: leggy filly: moderate mover: sixth reported living foal: half-sister to 1991 French 2-y-o 6f winner Alzarina (by Alzao) and 2 winners by Julio Mariner, including hurdler Necochea: dam 1m winner: inconsistent maiden: should stay 1m: may be unsuited by a soft surface: ran creditably blinkered, below form visored: sold 1,500 gns Doncaster September Sales. *J. Etherington* 47

DONTBETALKING (IRE) 2 gr.f. (Feb 21) Heraldiste (USA) 121 – Fine Flame (Le Prince 98) [1992 a6g³ 6m 6.1g 6d 6g a7g] workmanlike filly: half-sister to several winners, including 6-y-o sprinter Filicaia (by Sallust) and (at 1½m in Ireland) Fuego Del Amor (by Ahonoora): dam, modest Irish maiden, placed twice at 2 yrs: none too consistent maiden: will stay beyond 6f: best run on dead ground. *J. Wharton* 51

DON'T CRY 4 b.f. Dominion 123 – Black Veil 53 (Blakeney 126) [1991 8s² 8m 10d⁶ a11g 11.9d 9.7s a10g 1992 a12g⁵ a12g⁴ a14g 16.2g⁴ 14.9d³ 14d 16.9g 12.3d 17.5s 12.1s 12.4v⁴] small, lengthy filly: maiden handicapper: stays 14.9f: best form on an easy surface: sometimes finds little: sold out of J. Bethell's stable 4,100 gns Doncaster May Sales after seventh start. *Don Enrico Incisa* 52 d

DONTDRESSFORDINNER 2 b.g. (Apr 24) Tina's Pet 121 – Classic Times 82 (Dominion 123) [1992 7s 6s] leggy gelding: first foal: dam Irish 6f (at 2 yrs) and 1m winner: well beaten in late-season maidens. *D. R. Tucker* –

DON'T DROP BOMBS (USA) 3 ch.g. Fighting Fit (USA) – Promised Star (USA) (Star de Naskra (USA)) [1991 6d⁵ a7g 1992 7g 8.2m³ 8m 8.2d 8m 8s a8g* a8g a8g⁴ a7g²] well-made gelding: was becoming disappointing but much better after being fitted with a visor, winning handicap at Southwell in November: stays 1m: acts on good to firm and dead ground and on fibresand. *A. A. Scott* 48

DONT EMBARRASS ME 3 b.c. King of Spain 121 – Embarrassed 81 (Busted 134) [1991 NR 1992 7m 10m 16.2g 10d 14.6d] 590Y: compact colt: half-brother to 6f winner Don't Annoy Me (by Manado): dam won twice at around 2m: looks of no account. *T. Kersey* –

DON'T FORGET MARIE (IRE) 2 b.f. (Apr 10) Don't Forget Me 127 – My My Marie (Artaius (USA) 129) [1992 7.1d 7m 7m⁵ 9g 7.6v] neat filly: has a round action: half-sister to winners abroad by Salmon Leap and Caerleon: dam lightly-raced daughter of sister to Cheveley Park winner Pasty: modest maiden: probably stays 9f: acts on good to firm ground, soundly beaten on heavy. *R. Hannon* 64

DON'T FORSAKE ME 3 ch.f. Don't Forget Me 127 – Pirate Lass (USA) 90 (Cutlass (USA)) [1991 7m 8m 8m 1992 10m 8.2g⁵ 10m³ 12g 10m* 10.1d 10s⁶ 9.7g⁵ 9d 7d] big, strong, lengthy filly: below form in handicaps after winning at Nottingham in August: stays 1¼m: acts on good to firm ground. *D. Morley* 63

DON'T JUMP (IRE) 2 ch.f. (Feb 17) Entitled 126 – Ruby River (Red God 128§) [1992 5m a6g⁴ 7f⁴ 7g 7s² 7d] 4,800F: lengthy, sparely-made filly: half-sister to 7-y-o 1m to 1¼m winner Knock Knock (by Tap On Wood) and 1988 2-y-o 5f winner Super Zoom (by Ballad Rock): dam once-raced daughter of sister to very smart 1m and 1¼m winner Rymer: easily best effort in modest company when second in maiden at Ayr in September: will be better suited by 1m: evidently suited by soft ground. *M. H. Tompkins* 65

DON'TLIE (IRE) 2 b.f. (Feb 28) Lomond (USA) 128 – Be Discreet (Junius (USA) 124) [1992 5f³ 6g⁴ 7g 7s³ 8s 8g] IR 22,000Y: rather unfurnished filly: has a round action: second foal: half-sister to 1¼m winner Sarabah (by Ela-Mana-Mou): dam won at up to 7f in France: modest maiden: probably stays 1m: acts well on soft ground: sometimes bandaged near-hind: sold 3,400 gns Newmarket Autumn Sales. *G. B. Balding* 62

DON'T MOVE (IRE) 3 ch.f. Soughaan (USA) 111 – Adamantos 92 (Yellow God 129) [1991 a6g 6m a7g a8g 1992 a8g⁵] small, close-coupled filly: seems of little account. *M. H. Tompkins* –

DON TOCINO 2 b.c. (Mar 10) Dominion 123 – Mrs Bacon 82 (Balliol 125) [1992 7g 7s] 21,000Y: strong colt: seventh reported live foal: half-brother to 3-y-o Miss Oasis (by Green Desert), smart sprinter Sizzling Melody (by Song) and 2 winning – p hurdlers: dam 2-y-o 5f winner didn't train on: easily better effort in September maidens when eighth of 16 at Salisbury on second start, fading from 1½f out and beaten around 14 lengths: may do better. *J. L. Dunlop*

DON'T RUN ME OVER   3 b.g. Kafu 120 – Singalong Lass 63 (Bold Lad (IRE)   48
133) [1991 5g 6d 6d 1992 5v⁵ 5g⁶ 5s 5f 5m* 5m 6g² 5g⁴ 5.9f 6g⁵ a5g⁴ 5m 5m 6g 5v⁴ a6g⁵ a5g] neat gelding: plating-class handicapper: won at Beverley in June: stays 6f: twice below form on very firm ground, acts on any other including fibresand: has run creditably for 7-lb claimer: sold 1,400 gns Ascot November Sales. *B. C. Morgan*

DON'T SMILE   3 b.f. Sizzling Melody 117 – Swift To Conquer 87 (Solinus 130)   67
[1991 6g 6g 6f 6f² 6g* 6m 6m³ 6g* 1992 6d² 6g 6d⁴ 6g⁶ 6g 8m² 8.9g* 10.5d 10.5s⁶] leggy, close-coupled filly: has a round action: won claimer at Wolverhampton in July: ideally suited by 1m/9f: acts on good to firm and dead ground: sometimes sweating: suitable mount for claimer. *M. H. Tompkins*

DON'T TELL DICK   2 b.f. (Feb 6) Midyan (USA) 124 – Dawn Redwood 63   –
(Mummy's Pet 125) [1992 5g 5f 6d] 6,800Y: smallish, rather plain filly: half-sister to winning sprinters Daleside Ladybird (by Tolomeo) and Kissagram Queen (by Song): dam 1m winner: no form, in seller final run. *D. R. Laing*

DON'T TELL JEAN   2 br.f. (Mar 19) Petong 126 – Miss Nelski 84 (Most Secret   45 d
119) [1992 5m³ 5h³ 6m 5g 5g 6m 5d a5g] 6,800Y: lengthy filly: sixth foal: half-sister to winning 8-y-o sprinter Ski Captain (by Welsh Captain) and a winner over hurdles: dam 5f winner stayed 7f: regressive maiden: threw jockey in paddock and withdrawn once. *N. Bycroft*

DON'T WORRY (IRE)   3 ch.f. Hatim (USA) 121 – Nadja 77 (Dancer's Image   43
(USA)) [1991 5g⁶ 6m 6g⁴ 7m³ 7g 7.1m 1992 6d 6m 8m² 10g a8g a12g⁶ a10g⁵] workmanlike filly: inconsistent plater: stays 1m: acts on good to firm ground: trained until after fourth start by M. Tompkins. *J. Pearce*

DOODIES POOL (IRE)   2 b.g. (Apr 12) Mazaad 106 – Barncogue (Mon-   53 p
seigneur (USA) 127) [1992 7d 7g⁶] IR 8,000Y: leggy gelding: second foal: dam unraced: bit backward, much better effort in September maidens when around 11 lengths sixth of 9, close up 5f, in maiden at Brighton: should improve again. *G. Lewis*

DOOGAREY   2 b.c. (Feb 18) Lidhame 109 – Good Time Girl 65 (Good Times   33
(ITY)) [1992 6v a7g a8g] 700Y, 7,600 2-y-o: second foal: dam 2-y-o 5f and 6f seller winner: well beaten in maidens at Folkestone and Lingfield. *J. White*

DOOLAR (USA)   5 b.g. Spend A Buck (USA) – Surera (ARG) (Sheet Anchor)   –
[1991 NR 1992 14.1g 14.1m] rather angular, deep-girthed gelding: has a round action: no form in handicaps in 1992: stays 1¼m: acts on firm ground. *P. T. Dalton*

DORAZINE   2 gr.f. (Apr 2) Kalaglow 132 – Doree Moisson (FR) 84 (Connaught   35
130) [1992 5g 5.7d⁶ 6d 8s] 2,600Y: leggy filly: has scope: sixth foal: half-sister to a winner in Italy by Rousillon: dam, 11f winner, is half-sister to Bruni and smart middle-distance winner Royal Blend: poor form in maidens: seems to stay 1m: broke out of stall and withdrawn once: active sort. *C. J. Hill*

DORDOGNE   3 ch.c. Rousillon (USA) 133 – Home Fire 99 (Firestreak 125) [1991   49
6d 7.1s 7m⁴ 8g⁵ 7.6m⁴ 1992 8m 12d 12h³ 14.6g⁴ 14d 14.6g] sturdy colt: on the downgrade: stays 1½m: acts on hard ground: ran well when blinkered: sold 600 gns Newmarket Autumn Sales. *R. Akehurst*

DORKING LAD   10 b.g. Cawston's Clown 113 – High Voltage 82 (Electrify)   49
[1991 6g⁵ 6m² 6g³ 7g⁴ 6m⁴ 6g⁶ 6m⁴ 7g 6s a6g 1992 6g 6.1g 6g⁴ 7g⁶ 7.1s² 7s] lengthy, dipped-backed gelding: has a round action: poor handicapper: stays 7f: not at best on firm going, acts on any other: gets behind. *M. H. Tompkins*

DORMSTON BOYO   2 b.c. (Apr 8) Sula Bula 109 – March At Dawn (Nishapour   –
(FR) 125) [1992 8.2g a8g] third reported foal: dam of little account: no form in maidens. *J. L. Spearing*

DORSET DUKE   5 b.g. Beldale Flutter (USA) 130 – Youthful (FR) (Green   90
Dancer (USA) 132) [1991 a7g* 7m* 7.6d³ 8m⁶ 8d⁴ 7m a7g² a7g 1992 a8g* a8g³ a8g* a8g³ 8g³ 7.9m³ 8f³ 7g] rather leggy, attractive gelding: good mover: fairly useful handicapper: twice successful at Lingfield early in 1992 and good third to Colour Sergeant in Royal Hunt Cup: effective at 1m and probably stays 1¼m: acts on firm and dead ground and all-weather surfaces: effective blinkered or not: sometimes hangs and very slowly away, including final start. *G. Wragg*

DO RUN RUN   3 b.f. Commanche Run 133 – Doobie Do 106 (Derring-Do 131)   75
[1991 NR 1992 7d 6s³ 8s* 7.3g²] sturdy filly: sixth foal: half-sister to 2m winner Gold Tint (by Glint of Gold), 1m winner Zipperti Do (by Precocious) and winners in Norway and Italy: dam, second in Cherry Hinton Stakes, is half-sister to smart

Queen Elizabeth Handicap, Kempton—
Double Blue completes his hat-trick in emphatic fashion

stayer Almeira: lightly raced: 3½-length winner of maiden at Bath before good second in Newbury handicap in early-summer: stays 1m: acts on soft going. *R. Hannon*

DOSSERI 4 b.g. Bellypha 130 – Hants 111 (Exbury 138) [1991 a10g 10.1m² 10g⁶ 1992 10.8v] sturdy gelding: maiden handicapper: should stay 1½m: acts on good to firm ground. *R. J. O'Sullivan* —

DO TELL 2 br.c. (Apr 15) Forzando 122 – Bentinck Hotel 74 (Red God 128§) [1992 6.1d] 17,500F, 12,000Y: half-brother to numerous winners, including 1989 sprinting 2-y-o Shamshoon (by Shareef Dancer), since successful in USA, and 3-y-o 10.3f and 11.7f winner Bentico (by Nordico): dam 2-y-o 5f winner: tailed-off last in maiden auction at Nottingham in August. *T. W. Donnelly* —

DO THE BUSINESS (IRE) 3 b.c. Important Business (USA) – Ehricka Jean (USA) (T V Colony (USA)) [1991 6m⁴ 7m⁵ 6m 5.3f⁵ 6m 7f 7f⁵ a8g 1992 a5g⁵ a5g² a7g⁴ a6g⁴ a6g a6g 5m 7.1m 6.1m 10m⁶ 11.5m⁶] lengthy colt: moderate mover: on the downgrade: stays 7f: acts on all-weather surfaces: below form visored/blinkered. *C. N. Allen* a49

DO THE RIGHT THING 4 ch.f. Busted 134 – Taniokey (Grundy 137) [1991 12m⁶ 10m⁴ 12m* 13.8m 1992 11.9g 11.9f⁵] tall, sparely-made filly: rated 71 at 3 yrs: on the downgrade: should stay beyond 1½m. *J. A. B. Old* —

DOTS DEE 3 ch.f. Librate 91 – Dejote 60 (Bay Express 132) [1991 6g 7m 1992 8s 10d 10f³ 8g a12g a10g] lengthy, rather close-coupled filly: poor plater: stays 1¼m: acts on firm ground. *J. M. Bradley* 28

DOTTEREL (IRE) 4 b.g. Rhoman Rule (USA) – Miysam 60 (Supreme Sovereign 119) [1991 NR 1992 a8s a16g] leggy, sparely-made gelding: seems of little account. *R. G. Brazington* —

DOTTY'S WALKER (FR) 2 b.f. (Mar 3) Double Bed (FR) 121 – Lady Tycoon 67 (No Mercy 126) [1992 5.2s 7d 6d] leggy, rather unfurnished filly: fifth reported foal: half-sister to French 1¼m winner Kala Jane (by Kalaglow) and fairly useful 1¼m and 13.1f winner Tonkawa (by Indian King): dam won at 1¼m: behind in maidens. *C. A. Cyzer* 33

DOUBLE BASS (USA) 2 b. or br.c. (Mar 21) The Minstrel (CAN) 135 – Minstrelete (USA) (Round Table) [1992 7f² 7.1g* 8.2g²] $150,000Y: good-bodied 80 p

230

colt: half-brother to several winners here and abroad, including smart Irish 7f and 9f winner Punctilio (by Forli) and dam of Always Fair: dam, 1m winner, is half-sister to top-class Gay Fandango: progressive colt: always prominent when landing odds by ½ length in maiden at Sandown in July: beaten ½ length by Beneficial in 5-runner minor event at Nottingham 3 months later: races keenly, but will be better suited by 1¼m: sort to progress. *H. R. A. Cecil*

DOUBLE BLUE   3 ch.c. Town And Country 124 – Australia Fair (AUS) (Without   **94** Fear (FR) 128) [1991 NR 1992 5v* 5v* 6d* 5g* 6m² 6f² 6f² 6.3m² 6m 5d 7g³ 6g⁴ 7m* 6d 6s² 6d] 2,000Y: sturdy, workmanlike colt: impresses in appearance: fifth living foal: half-brother to a minor winner in Sweden: dam once-raced daughter of useful Australian middle-distance stayer Chuglin Princess: quite useful performer: had a tremendous season in 1992: successful in Hamilton median auction maiden, handicaps at Pontefract, Kempton and Beverley and minor event at Thirsk: also ran well in several valuable handicaps: best at 6f/7f on a sound surface: most game and consistent: credit to his trainer. *M. Johnston*

DOUBLE ECHO (IRE)   4 br.c. Glow (USA) – Piculet 69 (Morston (FR) 125)   **72** [1991 8g⁶ 9d⁴ 8g 8m 8m² 8m⁵ 6g a10g⁴ a10g a10g* 1992 a10g² 10d* 10d 10.3g²   a81 10.4m⁶ 10.1g³ 8f 8.9g⁴ 8m³ 7.9s⁴ 10.3s 8g a10g* a10g³ a10g] sturdy, compact colt: largely consistent handicapper: successful at Brighton in March and Lingfield in November: effective at 1m, and should stay 1½m: acts on good to firm and soft ground and equitrack: below form when blinkered once: very reluctant to post and ran lack-lustre race final start. *J. D. Bethell*

DOUBLE ENTENDRE   6 br.m. Dominion 123 – Triumphant 90 (Track Spare   **81** 125) [1991 a10g* a8g² 9g* 10m³ 8d 8g⁶ 8f 8.9g³ 8d* 7.9m* 8g 1992 7.9m 8m² 9d³ 8g] leggy mare: moderate mover: fairly useful handicapper: ran well in competitive and valuable events at Newmarket last 2 starts: should prove better suited by 1¼m than shorter: acts on good to firm and soft going: successful for apprentice. *M. Bell*

DOUBLE FEATURE (IRE)   3 ch.g. Exhibitioner 111 – Elmar 87 (Lord Gayle   **59** (USA) 124) [1991 5f³ 5d* 6m⁶ 6m 6m 6g³ 1992 7g³ 6d² 8m 6m⁵ 6.1d⁶ 6m* 6f⁴ 6f 6g³ 6g³ 6s⁴ 6d 6d] angular, workmanlike gelding: modest handicapper: won at Thirsk in July: effective at 6f and 7f: acts on any going: effective visored or not: sold 3,800 gns Newmarket Autumn Sales. *Mrs J. R. Ramsden*

DOUBLE FLUTTER   3 b.f. Beldale Flutter (USA) 130 – Perfect Double 43   **92** (Double Form 130) [1991 8.1d² 7.1d⁵ 1992 9s³ 10f* 10g⁴ 9d³ 10.1g⁶] lengthy, unfurnished filly: moderate mover: progressed with each run in 1992: won minor event at Salisbury in July and would have gone close ridden with more enterprise when third in handicap at Sandown: excellent sixth in listed race won by Red Slippers at Newcastle: should stay beyond 1¼m: acts on any going: held up: should do well at 4 yrs. *M. R. Channon*

DOUBLE LARK   3 b.c. Bairn (USA) 126 – Straffan Girl (Sallust 134) [1991 7m   **46**   d 6.1m⁵ 8g 1992 7g⁵ 8f 6.1g⁴ 7m 6g 8g 6.1d 7g] well-made colt: rated 73 at 2 yrs, has lost his form: stays 6f: below form blinkered. *R. Hollinshead*

DOUBLE SHERRY   3 ch.f. Crofthall 110 – Two's Up (Double Jump 131) [1991   **43** NR 1992 13.1m² 13.6m 11.8m 10.4s⁴ 11v] leggy, lengthy, plain filly: has stringhalt: sixth foal: sister to 1m and 1½m winner Burcroft and half-sister to 10.5f seller winner Bob-Double (by Import): dam never ran: poor plater: stays 1¼m: may need an easy surface. *R. M. Whitaker*

DOUBLE SHIFT   3 b.f. Night Shift (USA) – Laleston 73 (Junius (USA) 124)   **54** [1991 NR 1992 6g² 7f² 6g² 5.1g⁵ a7g] sturdy filly: second foal: half-sister to 5f winner Jess Rebec (by Kala Shikari): dam 5f winner: plating-class maiden: stays 7f: acts on firm ground: trained first 4 starts by R. Dickin. *J. White*

DOUBLE THE STAKES (USA)   3 b.c. Raise A Man (USA) – Je'da Qua (USA)   **43**   d (Fleet Nasrullah) [1991 5m⁵ 5g⁵ 6g 7.5f 7g⁴ 7m 1992 9.2d³ 12.3s³ 9.9m 10f 10g 7.5d⁵] good-topped colt: on the downgrade: stays 1½m: acts on soft going: sold 2,500 gns Doncaster October Sales. *F. H. Lee*

DOUGHMAN   3 b.g. Runnett 125 – Trila Love (Lomond (USA) 128) [1991 6g⁶ 6f   – 1992 8.5g 12d 8h 7f⁶ 8.5d⁶ 9.9m 10f 10m] smallish, lengthy gelding: poor plater: probably stays 8.5f: has form on firm and good ground: below form visored/ blinkered: sold out of J. Etherington's stable 1,500 gns Doncaster June Sales after fourth start. *J. Norton*

DOULABELLA (IRE)   2 ch.f. (Feb 14) Doulab (USA) 115 – Salabella 64 (Sallust   **65** 134) [1992 5.9g* 6m⁵] 60,000Y: smallish, angular filly: fifth foal: half-sister to Irish 3-y-o Dedicated Lady (by Pennine Walk), useful 5f to 6.3f winner at 2 yrs, and 2 other winners at up to 1m: dam, half-sister to Irish St Leger winner M-Lolshan,

Bradford & Bingley Handicap, York —
a big win for the admirable Doulab's Image and apprentice S. Williams;
Deprecator pips Noble Pet (left) for second

stayed 11f: won maiden at Carlisle by a head: strong-finishing fifth of 18 in Pontefract nursery later in autumn: will be suited by 7f +: sold 15,000 gns Newmarket Autumn Sales. *Sir Mark Prescott*

DOULAB'S IMAGE 5 ch.g. Doulab (USA) 115 – Haneena 118 (Habitat 134) **97**
[1991 a8g* a8g6 a8g4 a7g5 a7g* a6g5 7d5 8d2 10g 8m 8.2m3 8m3 10g6 7d a8g a8g 1992 a7g* a8g* a8g a8g6 a7g2 8s5 8d3 7g5 7.5g6 7g* 7d* 7g* 7m2 7.9m* 8m5 7d 8m] smallish, good-bodied gelding: vastly improved and had a tremendous season in handicaps in 1992: successful at Southwell (2) early in year and in summer at Leicester (wasn't blinkered), Wolverhampton, Warwick and York (Bradford & Bingley): best at 7f/1m: acts on good to firm and heavy going and fibresand: usually blinkered: well ridden by claimer S. Williams: held up and suited by strongly-run race: a great credit to his trainer. *J. A. Glover*

DOURAJ (IRE) 3 b.g. Doulab (USA) 115 – Serraj (USA) 57 (Seattle Slew (USA)) **61**
[1991 6m 7m4 7f3 6m 8g 1992 10d 7.1m 7m2 8m4 8d] neat, quite attractive gelding: maiden handicapper: stays 1m: acts on good to firm ground, seemingly not on a soft surface: often sweating: below form when blinkered once. *C. E. Brittain*

DOVALE 4 ch.f. Superlative 118 – Astonishing (Jolly Good 122) [1991 8g3 8g3 **70**
9.9m2 10.1g 1992 11.1m 10.8m2 11.4s* 12d 10.2s3 10s5 10m 9.7v] sturdy, lengthy filly: good mover: below form in handicaps after winning at Sandown in July: stays 11.4f: acts on good to firm and soft ground: below form when blinkered once: sold 6,000 gns Newmarket Autumn Sales. *W. Jarvis*

DOVER PATROL (IRE) 2 b.c. (May 28) Dancing Brave (USA) 140 – **63 p**
Britannia's Rule 108 (Blakeney 126) [1992 7d6 8v3] well-made colt: half-brother to several winners, including useful middle-distance stayers Broken Wave (by Bustino) and Guarde Royale (by Ile de Bourbon): dam Oaks third out of half-sister to Vaguely Noble: modest form in maidens at Leicester in October: has scope, and sure to improve over middle distances. *H. R. A. Cecil*

DOWLAND (USA) 4 b.c. Sovereign Dancer (USA) – Grace Note (FR) 99 (Top **105**
Ville 129) [1991 10g2 13.5g* 11g* 12.3g* 12g4 12g3 14m 14d 1992 10v* 13.4m 10g

9m³ 9m³ 9g³ 10g 10d] leggy, good-topped Irish colt: second foal: closely related to top-class middle-distance colt Belmez (by El Gran Senor): dam, 1¼m winner stayed 1½m, from good family: useful but inconsistent: won Curragh minor event in April: effective at 9f to 13.5f: acts on good to firm and heavy ground: usually forces pace: reportedly broke a blood vessel once in 1992. *M. Kauntze, Ireland*

DOWNLANDS ARIS 2 b.f. (Apr 15) Then Again 126 – Pinaka 69 (Pitcairn 126) –
[1992 5g 5.3f⁶] 760F: half-sister to 3 winners here and abroad, including 7-y-o sprinter R A Express (by Bay Express) and 7f/1m performer Pinctada (by Mummy's Pet): dam 1¼m winner: no form in sellers. *T. J. Naughton*

DOWREYNA 2 br.f. (Mar 7) Dowsing (USA) 124 – Lareyna 98 (Welsh Pageant 53
132) [1992 5g⁶ 7.1g² 7m 6s 6m⁶] smallish, rather sparely-made filly: half-sister to several winners, including 1986 2-y-o 5f winner Ibnalmagith (by Kris) and 13f and 1¾m winner Sure Ground (by Grundy): dam 5f and 6f winner at 2 yrs: went the wrong way after unlucky second in maiden at Edinburgh in July: likely to stay 1m. *M. R. Stoute*

DOYCE 3 b.f. Formidable (USA) 125 – Current Raiser 108 (Filiberto (USA) 123) 60
[1991 8f⁵ 7m⁶ 8.1g 7g⁴ 6m 8.1s* 1992 7.5g* 8.1s² 7.5g⁵ 7.9m 10.3f 10.5g⁵ 10.1f 7.5m 7d 7.1g⁵ 8.1d³] workmanlike filly: inconsistent handicapper: won at Beverley in March: best form at 1m: best on an easy surface: ran creditably when blinkered. *J. Etherington*

DRAFT BOARD 3 b.f. Rainbow Quest (USA) 134 – Selection Board 75 (Welsh 78
Pageant 132) [1991 NR 1992 10.5g⁵ 10.4g⁵ 8d² 6s* 6m⁴ 7v³] tall, leggy filly: good mover: second foal: half-sister to 1m to 11f winner Officer Cadet (by Shernazar): dam twice-raced sister to Teleprompter: landed odds by 8 lengths in maiden at Warwick: ran well later in October in quite valuable handicaps at Newmarket and Redcar: effective at 6f to 7f: acts on good to firm ground and heavy: sometimes bandaged near-hind. *J. H. M. Gosden*

DRAGONMIST (IRE) 2 b.f. (Mar 31) Digamist (USA) 110 – Etage (Ile de 36
Bourbon (USA) 133) [1992 5f 7.1d⁶ 6d 6.1g] 5,800Y: tall filly: second foal: dam won in Germany: poor maiden: should stay 1m: twice slowly away. *G. Lewis*

DRAGON SPIRIT 3 gr.g. Absalom 128 – Fair Eleanor (Saritamer (USA) 130) –
[1991 6g 5d⁶ 5f⁴ 6g⁴ 7g⁴ 7m a8g 1992 9s 7m³ 7.1f⁵ 8g⁶ 10.1f⁵] lengthy gelding: on the downgrade: stays 7f: acts on firm going: below form blinkered: trained first 2 starts by A. Hide: sold to join R. Frost 2,600 gns Newmarket September Sales. *S. P. C. Woods*

DRAGON'S TEETH (IRE) 2 b.c. (Apr 12) Caerleon (USA) 132 – Scots Lass 70 p
79 (Shirley Heights 130) [1992 8m² 8.1d⁴] well-made colt: fluent mover: third foal: half-brother to smart 3-y-o middle-distance stayer Bonny Scot (by Commanche Run) and 10.3f winner Border Guest (by Be My Guest): dam 13f winner: backward and green, shaped promisingly when narrowly beaten by Almamzar in moderately-run maiden at Yarmouth, staying on really well: odds on, failed to confirm that form on softer ground at Haydock later in autumn: well worth another chance. *L. M. Cumani*

DRAMANICE (USA) 2 b.c. (Feb 2) Northern Fling (USA) – Almost Pure (USA) 78
(Barrera (USA)) [1992 6m⁴ 6g⁴] $20,000F, IR 33,000Y: rangy colt: second foal: dam won at up to 7f: sire (by Northern Dancer) 6f to 1¼m winner: similar form in October maidens at Newmarket, behind Serious on second occasion: will be suited by 7f +. *Mrs J. Cecil*

DRAMATIC PASS (IRE) 3 ch.g. Coquelin (USA) 121 – Miss Flirt (Welsh 51
Pageant 132) [1991 8m⁶ 7m 8m 1992 12.3s 10.1s² 10.3f 10.1f⁶ 12m] leggy, rather angular gelding: inconsistent handicapper: stays 1¼m: acts on soft going: below form when blinkered. *Mrs M. Reveley*

DR DEVIOUS (IRE) 3 ch.c. Ahonoora 122 – Rose of Jericho (USA) (Alle- 127
ged (USA) 138) [1991 6d* 6g² 7m* 7g* 7m² 7m* 1992 8g² a10f 12g* 12m² 10.4g⁴ 10d* 12s⁶ 12f⁴ 12f]

To paraphrase: In the beginning was the Derby; and it was good ... Alas, the 'world's premier flat race' has now been taken as a model the world over and isn't what it used to be. It lags some way behind the richest races and depends for its world-wide status nowadays on its glorious tradition. Historically, it has always enjoyed a special position as one of the great attractions in the British sporting year. But there are disturbing signs that the race is also losing its popularity with the sporting public at an alarming rate. There was a particularly sharp fall in the size of the crowd for the latest running, the paid attendance of 21,100 contrasting with 26,300 in 1991, 36,100 in 1990 and an average of over 40,000 in the late-'eighties. The non-paying watchers on the Downs are also much less numerous nowadays. To anyone brought up on the precept that the Derby was an event that brought the country to a standstill, the idea that its status might decline to that of 'just another big race' must seem heretical. But times have changed and that is the way events are heading. In the highly commercialised world of international sport, one dollar, pound, franc or yen smells as good as another, and no event can hope to hold its place nowadays on its traditions. Ambitious new entry proposals put forward in 1990 by United Racecourses, with the support of the Horseracing Advisory Council, would have enabled Epsom to guarantee a total minimum prize money for the Derby of £1,000,000 in 1993, with the winner receiving at least £600,000. The proposal, rejected by the Jockey Club, would have put the Derby once again in the forefront of the world's richest races. United Racecourses also seem to have identified that it no longer makes economic sense to stage its show-piece occasion on a day when most of the nation is at work. The case for moving the great race to a Saturday is well-nigh irresistible and it's time too for a hard look at the rest of the programme at the Derby meeting. There's too much dross for it to be a success nowadays as a four-day, or even a three-day, fixture. A proposal to stage the Derby, Oaks and Coronation Cup on one day would be far too radical to find favour with the powers that be, but action of a similar sort is needed if the prestige of Derby Day is not to be eroded beyond repair.

The latest Derby, sponsored for the ninth year in succession by Ever Ready, was one of the most open for years. The dual Two Thousand Guineas winner Rodrigo de Triano, at 13/2, started the longest-priced Derby favourite since Lavandin at 7/1 in 1956. Nineteen stood their ground (the field was reduced to eighteen when Young Senor refused to enter the stalls) from the original one hundred and fifteen entries made in March, including several who had been highly tried as two-year-olds, having won, or finished close up, in at

Ever Ready Derby, Epsom—the field at Tattenham Corner.
Dr Devious holds third place on the outside of Twist And Turn
and the grey Great Palm; St Jovite has the rails behind the leader

Ever Ready Derby, Epsom—
Dr Devious is a convincing winner from St Jovite and Silver Wisp (left);
Muhtarram takes fourth place

least one major event. Rodrigo de Triano had been the best two-year-old of his year in Britain according to the European Free Handicap, in which he'd been allotted 8-13; Rainbow Corner (8-11 FH), an excellent second to Europe's champion two-year-old Arazi in the Grand Criterium, was sent to Epsom after being narrowly beaten in the Poule d'Essai des Poulains (French Guineas); St Jovite (8-9 FH), winner of the Anglesey Stakes and Futurity Stakes and fourth in the Grand Criterium at two, had been put through his paces before Epsom in the Derrinstown Stud Derby Trial at Leopardstown; Dr Devious (8-4 FH) had won the Dewhurst and been trained as a three-year-old for the Kentucky Derby in which he'd finished seventh of eighteen, staying on having been held up in the rear, a month before Epsom; the Royal Lodge third Twist And Turn (8-2 FH) had won both his races as a three-year-old, the second of them the Chester Vase; and the Racing Post Trophy third Assessor (8-2 FH) had entered the Derby reckoning with a runaway victory in the Lingfield Derby Trial.

Dr Devious had completed his preparation for the Kentucky Derby in the Craven Stakes at Newmarket where, conceding 5 lb, he'd failed by a length and a half to beat another eventual Derby runner Alnasr Alwasheek, who had bounced back to win Britain's most valuable Derby trial, the Dante Stakes at York (from the Dewhurst runner-up Great Palm) after disappointing in the Two Thousand Guineas. Apart from Rodrigo de Triano, the highest-placed horses in the Two Thousand Guineas field sent on to Epsom were Silver Wisp and Muhtarram, fourth and fifth respectively. Dr Devious started second favourite to his stable-companion Rodrigo de Triano at 8/1, with Alnasr Alwasheek, Assessor, Muhtarram and Rainbow Corner at 9/1, Great Palm at 10/1, Silver Wisp at 11/1, Twist And Turn at 12/1, and St Jovite and the Sandown Classic Trial winner Pollen Count on 14/1. Dr Devious ran out a worthy winner, his rider Reid having him well placed from the start and sending him for home in earnest entering the final two furlongs. Pushed out to the line, Dr Devious won by two lengths, keeping on well and never looking likely to be caught. St Jovite was a game second, rallying to get the better of Silver Wisp by a short head after being headed briefly by that horse inside the final furlong; Muhtarram came three and half lengths further back in fourth, with long-time leader Twist And Turn fifth, followed by the 200/1-shot Alflora, Alnasr Alwasheek, Great Palm and Rodrigo de Triano. As is usual in the Derby, most of the leading contenders had been untried at the trip—Twist And Turn and Assessor were the only runners to have won at around a mile and a half—and some of the well-beaten horses went on to show their form at shorter distances, most notably Rodrigo de Triano. On form, it looked a mediocre Derby at the time and by the end of the season little had happened to change that view.

Dr Devious won only one of his six remaining starts. St Jovite reversed the Derby form emphatically in the Budweiser Irish Derby in which Dr Devious—a twelve-length runner-up and all out to hold off Contested Bid —clearly didn't show his best form. Dr Devious was off the course for seven weeks after the Curragh and ran as if he'd be all the better for the outing when fourth to Rodrigo de Triano in the Juddmonte International at York on his return. In the meantime St Jovite had followed up his Irish Derby victory with a runaway victory in the King George VI and Queen Elizabeth Diamond Stakes, reinforcing his claims to be regarded as the best middle-distance horse in Europe. St Jovite started at 7/4-on and Dr Devious at 7/2 when the pair renewed rivalry in the Kerry Group Irish Champion Stakes over a mile

Kerry Group Irish Champion Stakes, Leopardstown—
Dr Devious and St Jovite again, in one of the season's most exciting races

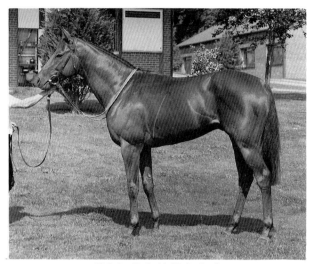

Mr Sydney H. Craig's "Dr Devious"

and a quarter at Leopardstown in September. There were few, if any, more thrilling finishes to a big race all season. Dr Devious and St Jovite produced an epic encounter, battling it out, head to head under strong pressure, for much of the straight, with first one and then the other seeming likely to get the upper hand. St Jovite had rallied to regain a narrow advantage near the finish when he appeared to start hanging left into Dr Devious. Roche stopped riding and the strongly-ridden Dr Devious got back up for a short-head victory. There was a gap of nine lengths to third-placed Alflora who'd finished virtually the same distance behind St Jovite at Epsom. Dr Devious and St Jovite both had hard races, arguably much harder than was ideal with the Prix de l'Arc de Triomphe only three weeks away. But Dr Devious had already proved himself remarkably tough and durable and he gave a very creditable account of himself afterwards in both the Prix de l'Arc (sixth to Subotica, two places behind St Jovite) and the Breeders' Cup Turf at Gulfstream Park (fourth to Fraise, a place ahead of Subotica). Dr Devious was one of four horses invited from Europe for the Japan Cup at the end of November. He rounded off a long season, in which he was raced in five different countries, with a modest tenth; the other Europeans Dear Doctor, User Friendly and Vert Amande came third, sixth and thirteenth behind the Japanese-trained winner Tokai Teio.

Dr Devious will be at stud in Japan in 1993 when he will stand alongside the Kentucky Derby and Breeders' Cup Classic winner Sunday Silence and the Prix de l'Arc winners Tony Bin and Carroll House at Zenya Yoshida's Shadai Farm. The Yoshida family, which completed a deal to buy Dr Devious for stud just before the Breeders' Cup, has a dominant position in Japanese racing with reportedly over three hundred and fifty broodmares. Seldom, if ever, can a Derby winner have changed hands so often as Dr Devious who went through the ring both as a foal (52,000 guineas, Newmarket December) and as a yearling (56,000 guineas, Newmarket Highflyer). He raced in the colours of three different millionaires, starting with Robert Sangster who called him after a nickname once given to Irish vet Demi O'Byrne, who selected Dr Devious for Sangster at the Newmarket Highflyer Sales. Sangster sold the horse towards the end of his two-year-old days to Luciano Gaucci, for whom he won the Dewhurst. Gaucci then parted with him, reportedly for 2,500,000 dollars (around £1,400,000), to the wife of American Sidney Craig who purchased the horse as a sixtieth-birthday present for her husband with the original aim of winning the Kentucky Derby. Dr Devious is only the second horse to contest both the Kentucky Derby and the Derby (Bold Arrangement, second at Churchill Downs and unplaced at Epsom, was the first).

		Lorenzaccio	Klairon
	Ahonoora	(ch 1965)	Phoenissa
	(ch 1975)	Helen Nichols	Martial
Dr Devious (IRE)		(ch 1966)	Quaker Girl
(ch.c. 1989)		Alleged	Hoist The Flag
	Rose of Jericho (USA)	(b 1974)	Princess Pout
	(b 1984)	Rose Red	Northern Dancer
		(ch 1979)	Cambrienne

A striking aspect of Dr Devious' Derby success was that he is by a sprinter; he is the first winner of the race sired by a sprinter since Hard Ridden in 1958. The Derby is a test of stamina, not just because the course itself is a severe one, but also because of the strong pace that is on throughout the race, including the uphill pull from the start to the mile post. A good measure of stamina is therefore essential in a potential Derby winner, and most Derby winners are stoutly bred. Twenty-four of the thirty-three Derby winners between Hard Ridden and Dr Devious were sired by stallions who had won over at least a mile and a half or were out of mares who had been successful at the Derby trip or further. Among these, Larkspur, Relko, Charlottown, Blakeney, Morston, Empery and Reference Point were products of both. Dr Devious' sire Ahonoora, whose final crop of two-year-olds was racing in the latest season, was a thoroughly genuine and consistent racehorse, a good-class five- and six-furlong performer with tremendous initial speed. Ahonoora was from a very speedy family on his dam's side and, not surprisingly, he has proved an influence for speed at stud, the average distance of races won at three years and upwards by his progeny being around seven and a half furlongs. He has sired relatively few winners at a mile and a half or more, the most notable of them before Dr Devious being the Lancashire Oaks winner Park Express and the Blandford Stakes winner Topanoora. Like the dams of Park Express and Topanoora, Dr Devious' dam, the unraced Rose of Jericho, was fairly stoutly bred. She is by the dual Prix de l'Arc winner Alleged, who has been a strong influence for stamina at stud, out of a half-sister to the high-class middle-distance performer Critique, winner of the Cumberland Lodge Stakes and the September Stakes. Dr Devious' grandam, the Northern Dancer mare Rose Red, was a minor winner over six furlongs as a two-year-old in Ireland; she is also a half-sister to the very successful broodmare Cambretta, the dam of Pluralisme (a smart French mile to mile-and-a-quarter performer), Only (a useful six-furlong and one-mile winner), Singletta (a very useful performer best around a mile and a quarter) and Classic Tale (Chester Vase third), as well as Ghislaine, the dam of the Queen Elizabeth II Stakes winner Markofdistinction and the very promising two-year-old Criquette. Earlier generations of the family have produced plenty of good horses. The dam of Dr Devious' great grandam Cambrienne, herself a one-time record-priced yearling, was the Dewhurst winner and Irish Oaks runner-up Torbella III who at stud numbered the Sussex Stakes winner Carlemont and the good-class French stayer Tourangeau among her ten winners. Dr Devious is Rose of Jericho's second foal, following the smart Irish sprinter Archway (by Thatching); she has since produced a filly by Thatching, who died, and a colt and a filly by Sadler's Wells's brother Fairy King. Dr Devious is a quite attractive colt of medium size, and a fluent mover with a quick action. He was just as good at a mile and a quarter as at a mile and a half, and probably acted on any going. It bears repeating that he was superbly tough and genuine. *P. W. Chapple-Hyam*

DREADNOUGHT   12 gr.g. Rugantino 97 – Thwarted (The Ditton 93) [1991 NR   –
1992 10d] leggy gelding: of little account. *R. Hollinshead*

DREAM A BIT   2 b.f. (May 13) Dreams To Reality (USA) 113 – On A Bit 66   **54**
(Mummy's Pet 125) [1992 a5g² 7.1m⁶ a6g⁴ 5g⁶ 6g 7d] smallish filly: has a round
action: half-sister to several winners, including 8.5f winner Wallingfen Lane (by
Lochnager) and fair 9f and 1¼m winner White Sapphire (by Sparkler): dam placed at
up to 9f: poor maiden: should stay 7f: sold 3,100 gns Doncaster October Sales. *J. G.
FitzGerald*

DREAM CARRIER (IRE)   4 b.g. Doulab (USA) 115 – Dream Trader (Auction   **69**
Ring (USA) 122) 7d² 7d² 8m⁶ 7m 7m* 8m² 7f* 7g⁵ 7g² 7.6g* 7g³ 8f 8m 8g⁵
7m 1992 7.6g 8g 7.1m 7g 7g² 8.1m 7.1g² 7.1d* 7f 6.9m⁴ 8.5d⁴ 7d a8g] strong,
close-coupled gelding: carries condition: moderate walker: has a round action:
inconsistent handicapper: won at Sandown in July: effective at 7f to 1m: acts on firm
ground and dead: effective with or without blinkers. *R. Hannon*

DREAMERS DELIGHT   6 b.g. Idiot's Delight 115 – Just Jolly 80 (Jolly Jet 111)   **48** p
[1991 NR 1992 12d*] successful in NH Flat race in 1990/1 and Uttoxeter celebrity
event: stays 1½m: progressive novice hurdler, winning twice later in November. *D.
Nicholson*

DREAMING STAR   7 br.g. Star Appeal 133 – Yea Misty (USA) (Forli (ARG))   –
[1991 NR 1992 18.5g] leggy, close-coupled gelding: poor mover: poor plater. *P. H.
Morris*

DREAM PRINCESS   2 b.f. (Mar 24) Dreams To Reality (USA) 113 – Qualitair   –
Princess (Bay Express 132) [1992 6g a7g⁴] 1,000Y: neat filly: second foal: dam won
over hurdles: no form in poor company: sold 425 gns Ascot July Sales. *J. F. Bottomley*

DREAMS ARE FREE (IRE)   2 b.f. (Apr 24) Caerleon (USA) 132 – Keep The   **67** p
Thought (USA) (Valdez (USA)) [1992 7g] fourth foal: sister to 10.4f and 1½m winner
Llangollen and closely related to a winning selling hurdler by Kings Lake: dam 1m
winner, out of sister to dam of Seattle Slew and Lomond: easy to back, shaped
encouragingly when over 5 lengths eighth of 24 to Fayfa in maiden at Newmarket in
October, prominent long way: will improve. *H. R. A. Cecil*

DREAMS END   4 ch.c. Rainbow Quest (USA) 134 – Be Easy 110 (Be Friendly   **86**
130) [1991 10.2s* 10g 10g* 11.9g⁵ 10.1f⁴ 12s⁶ 1992 12f 10g⁴] sparely-made, quite
attractive colt: fairly useful handicapper: not seen out after fourth in £11,300 race at
Ascot in July: effective at 1¼m to 1½m: acts on any going: sometimes bandaged:
sold only 2,300 gns Newmarket Autumn Sales. *G. Wragg*

DREAMS EYES   4 b.c. Dreams To Reality (USA) 113 – Hairbrush (USA) (Sir   **33**
Gaylord) [1991 6g 7.5g 7g 6m a5g 7m⁵ 8m 6m 6.1m 6m 6m 1992 7.1m 5.9h⁴ 6.1g 8g 5f
6f] leggy, angular colt: has a moderate action: little form in handicaps in 1992: stays
6f: acts on good to firm ground: below form blinkered/visored. *R. Bastiman*

DREAMS TO WOTAN   3 ch.c. Dreams To Reality (USA) 113 – Olga Wagner   –
(ITY) (Sharpen Up 127) [1991 NR 1992 8d 7d] 4,500F: close-coupled colt: has a
round action: third reported foal: half-brother to a winner in Italy by Dance In Time
and to NH Flat race winner Fighter Command (by Milford): dam won 5 races in Italy:
last in maidens: sold 1,000 gns Ascot November Sales. *M. J. Wilkinson*

DREAM SWEET DREAMS (USA)   3 gr. or ro.f. Dahar (USA) 125 – Aronia   –
(USA) (Grey Dawn II 132) [1991 NR 1992 a10g 8m] $17,000F: second foal: half-sister
to a winner in USA: dam unraced daughter of very smart French middle-distance
filly Amazer, a sister to smart middle-distance stayer Sporting Yankee: last in
maiden and claimer: sold 1,150 gns Newmarket September Sales. *B. Hanbury*

DREAM TALK   5 b.h. Dreams To Reality (USA) 113 – Lala 91 (Welsh Saint 126)   **116**
[1991 6.5g² 6.5g* 6s⁴ 6d* 5m⁴ 6d* 6d* 6g 5d³ 6v² 1992 6g* 5m² 6g* 6m* 6.5g³
6s⁵ 5s] leggy, good-topped ex-English horse: smart sprinter nowadays: tough and
had another successful season, winning listed race at Evry, Group 2 race at Rome
and Group 3 event (by 7 lengths in 4-runner race) at Hamburg: placed behind Elbio
at Longchamp and Mr Brooks at Hoppegarten: rare below-par efforts on last 2 starts
in Group 2 contest at Baden-Baden and Prix de l'Abbaye (heavily bandaged and
tongue tied down) at Longchamp: effective at 5f and 6f: acts on any going: blinkered
(ran well) when trained by J. Berry as 3-y-o. *N. Clement, France*

DREAMTIME ECHO   4 b.f. Green Ruby (USA) 104 – Aleda Rose 56 (Char-   –
lottown 127) [1991 5g 6m 6m⁶ 5s⁵ 1992 5g 6.1m 5g⁶ 8f 6m] lengthy filly: bad maiden:
tried blinkered. *J. Balding*

DRESS SENSE (IRE)   3 b.c. Top Ville 129 – Smarten Up 119 (Sharpen Up 127)   **91**
[1991 NR 1992 10g² 9g² 10g* 10.8f* 10.5s⁵ 10g 8m] lengthy colt: fluent mover:

half-brother to several winners, including high-class sprinter Cadeaux Genereux (by Young Generation) and middle-distance stayer Brightner (by Sparkler): dam sprinting half-sister to smart fillies Walk By and Solar: promising colt judged on wins in maiden at Newmarket and minor event at Warwick in June and fifth in quite valuable Haydock handicap in September: failed to confirm that in competitive handicaps last 2 starts: stays 10.8f. *L. M. Cumani*

DRINKS PARTY (IRE)   4 b.f. Camden Town 125 – Holy Water (Monseigneur   **39**
(USA) 127) [1991 10d² 12.3s* 8m 10m⁶ 10.6m³ a11g⁶ 12s³ 11.1d 10.5d 11.8m⁵ 10d³ a11g 1992 12g⁶ 10g⁴ 12m³ 14.6d 10.8s*] compact filly: poor mover: poor handicapper: won selling event (no bid) at Warwick in October: stays 1½m: seems suited by plenty of give in the ground: sold to join M. Charles's stable 2,000 gns Doncaster October Sales. *J. Wharton*

DR LECHTER   2 b.g. (Feb 3) Efisio 120 – Ruby's Chance 71 (Charlottesville 135)   **60**
[1992 5g⁴ 6d] 5,000F, 4,800Y: leggy, angular gelding: half-brother to several winners, including fair 1985 2-y-o 7f winner Hot Gem (by Hot Spark): dam disqualified 1½m winner: came from way back when narrow winner of maiden at Catterick in September: well beaten in nursery at Newmarket following month: should stay at least 6f. *S. M. Hillen*

DROP A CURTSEY   3 b.f. Prince Sabo 123 – Pretty Miss (So Blessed 130) [1991   **–**
NR 1992 a7g a8g⁶ a12g⁴ 10m] angular filly: fifth foal: half-sister to 7f and 1¼m winner Follow The Drum (by Daring March): dam once-raced half-sister to useful 2-y-o Fair Parrot: poor maiden: seems to stay 1½m: sold 680 gns Doncaster September Sales. *J. D. Bethell*

DROUGHT (IRE)   3 b.f. Rainbow Quest (USA) 134 – Short Rations   **69**
(Lorenzaccio 130) [1991 NR 1992 11.4d⁵ 14.1g* 14d² 14.6g] leggy filly: half-sister to several winners, including stayer Patience Camp (by Bustino) and fair 6f and 7f winner Cape Wild (by Bold Lad): dam Italian 2-y-o winner, is half-sister to very smart He Loves Me and Wattlefield: progressed well in second half of 1992, winning claimer at Yarmouth, until well beaten (helped set strong pace) in Wolverhampton handicap: will be suited by 2m +: sold 8,000 gns Newmarket December Sales. *M. R. Stoute*

DRUMDONNA (IRE)   2 b.f. (Apr 20) Drumalis 125 – Decoy Duck 67 (Decoy   **69**
Boy 129) [1992 7.1g³ 7g 7d* 8.1s 8s⁴ 7.6v] IR 7,000Y: rather close-coupled filly: half-sister to 1½m winner Portofino (by Coquelin): dam 2-y-o 6f winner, only season to race: easily best effort when winning maiden at Ayr in August: should stay 1m: acts on dead ground. *J. Berry*

DRUMMER HICKS   3 b. or br.c. Seymour Hicks (FR) 125 – Musical Princess   **81** p
66 (Cavo Doro 124) [1991 8m⁶ 7m 8.1s³ 1992 12.2d⁴ 8.2g 10.3f⁴ 9.2f* 10.1f* 8.9d* 10.3m² 10.3m 8s² 8.9d*] workmanlike colt: has a round action: progressed extremely well in handicaps in 1992, successful at Hamilton, Newcastle and York (2 quite valuable events): effective at around 1m, and bred to stay 1½m: probably acts on any going: races prominently: game, genuine and consistent: a credit to his trainer, and should do well again at 4 yrs. *E. Weymes*

DRUMMER'S DREAM (IRE)   4 b.f. Drumalis 125 – Peaches And Cream (FR)   **38**
(Rusticaro (FR) 124) [1991 6f⁴ 5m 6m 8g 6m a5g 6f 6.1m⁴ 5.3g⁵ a6g⁴ a5g³ a5g³ 1992   a47
a5g⁴ a5g² a6g⁴ a6g⁴ 5g⁴ 7g a5g⁴ 5m⁶ 6.1g a5g* a5g a5g a5g* a6g] small filly: largely consistent performer: won handicaps at Southwell in July and December: effective at 5f and 6f: effective visored or not. *Mrs N. Macauley*

DRUM SERGEANT   5 b.g. Elegant Air 119 – Cala-Vadella 110 (Mummy's Pet   **79**
125) [1991 8m 6m 6g 7.5g⁴ 7.5m² 8d 6g³ 6m 5f⁴ 5f⁶ 5f³ 7g 5m² 5g² 5m³ 5s² 1992 6d 5g² 5g⁵ 5g⁴ 5d* 7.5m 5m³ 5m 5m³ 6f⁵ 5g² 5d⁴ 5.6m* 6.1m* 6g⁶ 6g 5m⁶ 5d 6s*] strong, sturdy gelding: usually looks very well: vastly improved handicapper in 1992: successful at Haydock (first win), Doncaster, Nottingham and York (nowhere near best in seller, no bid): ideally suited by 5f/6f: acts on any going: usually visored/blinkered: often slowly away, and is held up for a late run: tough. *J. Parkes*

DRUM TAPS (USA)   6 b.h. Dixieland Band (USA) – Lavendula Rose 108 **121**
(Le Levanstell 122) [1991 11f 12g² 12f³ 12f* 13.3f* 12g* 12s² 12f 1992 15g* 16.4m* 20f* 15s² 14s³ 20s²]
How on earth could the Derby have fallen to a horse sired by a sprinter? How could the Gold Cup have been won by the son of a stallion whose racing and stud career, admittedly in the United States, have both shown a bias towards speed? Some students of the 'science' of racehorse breeding traditionally answer such seemingly-awkward questions partly by seeking to

credit the stallion with more stamina than he actually displayed on the racecourse. It was pointed out, for example, that Dr Devious' sire Ahonoora was by Lorenzaccio who stayed eleven furlongs. Why do cases such as those of Dr Devious and the Gold Cup winner Drum Taps occasion such surprise? The problem is that most racegoers have only a superficial grasp of breeding principles and are taken in by prejudice and superstition. One of the most prevalent prejudices is that the male elements of a pedigree are more important than the female. The preconception has no rational basis. In so far as it is a science at all, racehorse breeding is a pitifully inexact one. The mating of a sprinter with a stayer may result in anything from one end of the scale to the other; some matings can result in an offspring with more speed or more stamina than either of its parents.

Drum Taps could not be written off as a potential Gold Cup winner. On the one hand, the Northern Dancer stallion Dixieland Band, an American sprinter-miler, wouldn't be an obvious choice for anyone trying to breed a Cup horse. But, on the other hand, the useful Lavendula Rose, the dam of Drum Taps, stayed at least a mile and a half (she came third to Altesse Royale in the Irish Guinness Oaks) and was stoutly bred. Her sire Le Levanstell (a miler) sired two Gold Cup winners, Levmoss and Le Moss, and her unraced dam produced the Goodwood Cup winner Wrekin Rambler. Drum Taps had shown himself a very smart performer at around two miles before the Gold Cup, winning the Coppa d'Oro di Milano at Milan and the Cementone Beaver Henry II Stakes at Sandown, and he looked 'the one to beat' on form in the Gold Cup. Drum Taps had had two of the Gold Cup runners, Arcadian Heights and the 1990 Gold Cup runner-up Tyrone Bridge, behind him in the Henry II Stakes; the French challengers, Mardonius and Turgeon (who had had a tremendous season in 1991), had managed only third and fourth in the Prix Vicomtesse Vigier at Longchamp on their previous outing; and the Aston Park Stakes winner Endoli looked short of Gold Cup-winning standard. The good gallop set by Tyrone Bridge ensured a truly-run Gold Cup in which the field became strung out. The patiently-ridden Drum Taps never looked like being caught after striking the front about a furlong and a half out; kept up to his work, he

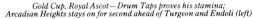

Gold Cup, Royal Ascot—Drum Taps proves his stamina;
Arcadian Heights stays on for second ahead of Turgeon and Endoli (left)

Mr Yoshio Asakawa's "Drum Taps"

beat Arcadian Heights by two lengths with Turgeon three lengths away third, and Endoli fourth.

Drum Taps (USA) (b.h. 1986)	Dixieland Band (USA) (b 1980)	Northern Dancer (b 1961)	Nearctic
			Natalma
		Mississippi Mud (b 1973)	Delta Judge
			Sand Buggy
	Lavendula Rose (b 1968)	Le Levanstell (b 1957)	Le Lavandou
			Stella's Sister
		Inquisitive Rose (b 1952)	Grand Inquisitor
			Rosemary's Queen

Drum Taps wasn't seen out again until the autumn when the best of his three performances came in the Irish St Leger in which he went down by a neck and three quarters of a length to Mashaallah and Snurge, staying on gamely under pressure. Drum Taps came up against France's leading out-and-out stayer Sought Out on his two other starts and was beaten decisively each time, by five lengths in the Prix Kergorlay at Deauville at the end of August, and by four in the Prix du Cadran at Longchamp in October. The good-topped, quite attractive Drum Taps has been fairly versatile so far as distance goes, showing form every bit as good at a mile and a half as a five-year-old as that over staying distances at six; whether he'd be able to do so again now, however, is very doubtful. He probably acts on any going. Splendidly tough and genuine, he stays in training with the Gold Cup again his main target. *Lord Huntingdon*

DRY GIN   9 ch.g. Grundy 137 – Karajinska (USA) (Nijinsky (CAN) 138) [1991 NR   –
1992 a14g 12d] close-coupled, angular gelding: successful over fences in 1992 but of
little account on flat. *M. C. Chapman*

DRY POINT   6 ch.g. Sharpo 132 – X-Data 93 (On Your Mark 125) [1991 7m 6g*   –
6g⁶ 6f⁶ 6g 6f² 7g 6m³ 6m⁵ 6g 1992 7g 6g] strong, angular, workmanlike gelding: has
a round action: fair handicapper (rated 80) at 5 yrs, but none too consistent: not seen
out after April in 1992: suited by 6f and a sound surface: occasionally bandaged. *J. A.
R. Toller*

DR ZEVA   6 b.h. Busted 134 – Dance In Rome 79 (Dance In Time (CAN)) [1991   **34**
a10g* 10d² a12g 10m 10g 10.8m 10m 10.2g 1992 11.9f* 11.5m² 10m a10g 11.9g⁵ 9d   a54   ?
11.5s³ 11.5d a10g a13g² a13g* a12g4] big, deep-girthed horse: poor mover:
inconsistent handicapper: won at Brighton (selling event (no bid)) in July and
Lingfield (for 7-lb claimer, best effort) in December: failed by long way to reproduce
that form 9 days later: stays 13f: acts on any going, including equitrack: below form
when blinkered once. *M. Dixon*

DUBITABLE   3 b.f. Formidable (USA) 125 – Duboff 120 (So Blessed 130) [1991   **53**
6m⁶ 6g4 8m⁵ 7g³ 1992 10.2s4 10m⁵ 11.6m⁵] small, rather sparely-made filly: maiden
handicapper: ran creditably in first half of 1992: stays 11.7f: acts on good to firm and
soft ground: sold 1,550 gns Newmarket December Sales. *H. Candy*

DUBLIN DREAM   3 b.f. Dublin Lad 116 – Warthill Lady 60 (Hittite Glory 125)   –
[1991 6m 5m⁵ 1992 6f 5m⁶] lengthy filly: poor sprint maiden: sold 1,000 gns
Doncaster June Sales. *M. Brittain*

DUBLIN INDEMNITY (USA)   3 b.g. Alphabatim (USA) 126 – Sailongal   **41**
(USA) (Sail On-Sail On) [1991 5g 6m 8d a6g* a7g4 a7g² 1992 a8g* a8g⁵ 10d 8.3s⁶ 8g   a59
6g⁶ 8.2g⁵ 8m⁶ 8f 8g⁶] rangy, good-topped gelding: poor mover: well below form in
modest company after winning Southwell handicap in January: stays 1m well: goes
well on all-weather surfaces: best form blinkered: won selling hurdle in September.
N. A. Callaghan

DUC DE BERRY (USA)   4 ch.c. Chief's Crown (USA) – L'Extravagante (USA)   **84**   d
(Le Fabuleux 133) [1991 10f* 12.3g* 11.9m² 1992 10g 12f 11.4s⁵ 13.1g4 12f⁵ 10s³
10.3v] tall, good-topped colt: rated 97 as 3-y-o: below best in 1992: stays 1½m:
probably acts on any going: blinkered last 2 starts: sometimes has tongue tied down:
hard ride. *G. Harwood*

DUCHESS DE BELFORT   2 b.f. (Apr 11) Belfort (FR) 89 – Perfect Timing 107   **38**
(Comedy Star (USA) 121) [1992 5g 5f4 5.1m4] leggy, sparely-made filly: moderate
mover: first reported foal: dam sprinter: poor form in modest company, not seen out
after July: sold 3,000 gns Doncaster November Sales. *J. Berry*

DUCHESS DIANNE (IRE)   2 b.f. (Apr 6) Tender King 123 – Champers Club   **50**
(Run The Gantlet (USA)) [1992 5v⁵ 5.1d³ 5.1s 6.1m 6.1g 7g⁵ 7g 7d 7d 7s a8g4 a7g] IR
2,100Y: leggy, unfurnished filly: second reported living foal: half-sister to 1½f (at 2
yrs) to 1¼m winner Cuvee Rose (by Lafontaine): dam winning hurdler, placed at
10.1f on flat: modest plater: stays 1m: ran poorly when blinkered once: trained until
after ninth start by R. Holder: sold 800 gns Doncaster November Sales. *P. G.
Murphy*

DUCHESS OF SAVOY (IRE)   4 b.f. Dara Monarch 128 – Shenachie 79 (She-   –
shoon 132) [1991 NR 1992 a14g] good-topped filly: half-sister to a few minor
winners, including Irish 1¼m winner Warning Sound (by Red Alert): dam winning
stayer: bandaged and always behind in poor Southwell maiden in June on debut. *J. E.
Banks*

DUCKINGTON   8 b.g. Bustino 136 – Cribyn 96 (Brigadier Gerard 144) [1991   **72**
7.5g⁶ 6m³ 7m³ 7.5f* 7m² 7.6m4 7g4 7m4 7.1m4 6m 6m 1992 7.5g 7g 7f4 6g³ 7f 7m³]
leggy, close-coupled gelding: has had soft palate operation: fair handicapper: not
seen out after June: probably needs 7f/1m nowadays: goes well on top-of-the-
ground: tough: best held up. *M. H. Easterby*

DUGGAN   5 b.h. Dunbeath (USA) 127 – Silka (ITY) (Lypheor 118) [1991 10g 12f   **57**   d
11.5g⁶ 12f* 11f⁶ 12.3f² 12f* 12.3f4 12m 14.1f⁵ 12.3f9.7s a12g* a13g⁵ 1992 a12g4 12m³
12f³ 12g³ 12m⁵ 12.1s] lengthy, rather sparely-made horse: usually looks well: below
form in handicaps in 1992, and looked somewhat irresolute when blinkered once:
stays 1½m: has gone well on firm ground: sold to join P. Evans 5,200 gns
Newmarket Autumn Sales. *R. J. R. Williams*

DUHARRA (IRE)   4 ch.g. Flash of Steel 120 – Mrs Walmsley 87 (Lorenzaccio   **97**
130) [1991 10d⁶ 11d³ 11m* 12d² 11m² 12g² 14m4 1992 12g³ 16s² 14g* 16s] Irish
gelding: half-brother to a winner in Italy by Welsh Saint and fair 7f to 1¼m winner
Perfect Stranger (by Wolver Hollow): dam raced only at 2 yrs when 6f winner:

consistent handicapper as 3-y-o when trained by J. Oxx: went hurdling with D. Elsworth in 1991/2: not seen out on flat as 4-y-o until August: won minor event at Gowran Park in October by head: effective from 11f to 1¾m: acts on good to firm and dead ground, well below form on soft: blinkered. *D. K. Weld, Ireland*

DUKE OF BUDWORTH 2 b.g. (May 4) Primo Dominie 121 – Supreme **56** Kingdom 85 (Take A Reef 127) [1992 6d 6m³ 7d 6g] leggy, sparely-made gelding: poor mover: second foal: half-brother to plating-class 1991 2-y-o Sakharov (by Bay Express): dam 2-y-o 7.2f winner became temperamental as 4-y-o: plating-class maiden: ran creditably when blinkered in nursery at Newmarket final start: will prove suited by 7f + : best form on a sound surface. *M. H. Tompkins*

DUKE OF DREAMS 2 gr.g. (Jan 19) Efisio 120 – Tame Duchess 71 (Saritamer **46** (USA) 130) [1992 5g⁵ 5d⁵ 5s² 5s⁵ 6d] 1,000F, 11,000Y: strong gelding: third foal: half-brother to a winner in Denmark (by Another Realm): dam maiden stayed 1¼m, is half-sister to smart sprinter Son of Shaka: poor maiden: not seen out after running badly in May: sold 1,650 gns Newmarket July Sales. *Mrs M. Reveley*

DUKE OF EUROLINK 3 b.c. Jupiter Island 126 – Lady Eurolink 55 (Kala **106** p Shikari 125) [1991 8m 8m 1992 10g* 11.6g² 11.9f² 10g* 10m 11.9d* 12m² 12s] rangy, unfurnished colt: progressed really well in 1992: won maiden at Pontefract and £15,000 handicaps at Newmarket and York: very good second to Kasmayo in listed race at Doncaster after: ran poorly on very soft ground in £60,500 handicap at Ascot: stays 1½m: acts on good to firm ground and dead: held up, and has good turn of foot: should do well again at 4 yrs. *L. M. Cumani*

DUKE OF MONMOUTH (USA) 4 b.g. Secreto (USA) 128 – Queen For The **–** Day (USA) (King Emperor (USA)) [1991 10g 11f* 11.6m* 12f⁴ 11.6m⁴ 1992 11.4g] well-made gelding: impressive in appearance: fairly useful (rated 81) 3-y-o for

Eurolink Computer Services Ltd's "Duke of Eurolink"

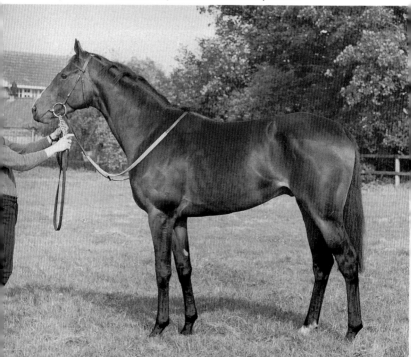

G. Harwood: not knocked about at any stage in Sandown handicap in September, 1992: should stay 1¾m: acts on firm ground: smart hurdler, best form when blinkered, won Triumph Hurdle. *S. E. Sherwood*

DUKE OF PADUCAH (USA)　5 gr.h. Green Dancer (USA) 132 – Flordelisada **104** (USA) (Drone) [1991 9m⁴ 12g 12m⁴ 12g⁴ 15g 1992 12f* 16m 11f] tall, attractive horse: good walker: rated 110 at 4 yrs: had simple task in match at 5 yrs: below best in Goodwood Cup and Grade 2 event at Del Mar after: stays 1½m well: acts on good to firm ground, yet to race on a soft surface. *G. Harwood*

DUKRAME　2 b.f. (Mar 22) Top Ville 129 – Durun 89 (Run The Gantlet (USA))　**65 p** [1992 7d²] 20,000Y: closely related to fair middle-distance stayer Dwadme (by High Top) and half-sister to several winners, including 3-y-o Swiss winner Durunroo (by Sharrood), modest 5f winner here at 2 yrs, and stayer Durbo (by Bustino): dam 1¼m to 1½m winner: 20/1, stayed on well but no chance with winner Urgent Request when second of 20 in maiden at Lingfield in September: should improve, particularly over middle distances. *H. Candy*

DUNE RIVER　3 b.c. Green Desert (USA) 127 – River Spey 96 (Mill Reef (USA)　**71** 141) [1991 7m⁴ 7m 1992 8d² 8s⁴ 10f 7g* 7f² 8g²] big, robust, good-topped colt: good walker: consistent handicapper: won maiden at Catterick in July: suited by 1m: acts on any going: sold to join D. Loder 12,500 gns Newmarket Autumn Sales. *Sir Mark Prescott*

DUNNINGTON　2 ch.f. (Mar 28) Risk Me (FR) 127 – Dutch Girl 78 (Workboy　**–** 123) [1992 5s 5f 5g⁶ 5g⁵] small, leggy, angular filly: sixth foal: half-sister to really tough 5f and 6f winner Golden Flats (by Sonnen Gold): dam, 5f winner, is out of smart sprinter Dutch Gold: little form, including in sellers. *M. W. Easterby*

DUPLICATE　2 b.c. (Mar 25) Then Again 126 – Josilu (Caliban 123) [1992 5m　**47** 7m⁴] 7,200Y: compact colt: half-brother to several minor winners here and abroad, including 1986 2-y-o 5.8f seller winner Josie Smith (by Alias Smith): dam of no account: easily better effort in maidens in first half of 1992 when fourth at Doncaster: seemed likely to improve again. *M. H. Easterby*

DUPLICITY (IRE)　4 b.c. Double Schwartz 128 – Goirtin (Levmoss 133) [1991 **100** 6m³ 6m² 6f* 6m 5g⁶ 5.2m² 6s 5d* 1992 6g⁵ 6g³ 5g⁵ 6g⁵ 6d 6f 6m² 6d] good-topped colt: has a markedly round action: useful sprinter at best: second to Lochsong in Stewards' Cup at Goodwood, best run in 1992: as effective at 5f as 6f: acts on firm and dead ground (stiff task on soft): below form when blinkered and sweating once: sometimes hangs right. *L. J. Holt*

DURNELTOR　4 br.g. Hard Fought 125 – Pounella 91 (Tachypous 128) [1991 6g　**66** 7m⁴ 8g 9g⁵ 8.5m 8g 7d* 7.1g⁵ 8.1s 7.1g⁵ 8m 9s 1992 7m² 7g² 7g⁴ 8f² 7f² 7d³ 8.3d 8f* 7d 8g 8s⁴ 8.1d] leggy, good-topped gelding: modest handicapper: won Brighton claimer in August: effective at 7f to 1m: acts on any going: below form when blinkered once: sold 5,000 gns Newmarket Autumn Sales. *R. Hannon*

DUSKY DUCHESS (IRE)　2 b.f. (May 7) Entitled 126 – June Darling (Junius　**–** (USA) 124) [1992 7s 8d 8.1d] IR 850F, IR 3,200Y: good-topped filly: third foal: half-sister to fair 1990 2-y-o 6f and 7f winner Cal Norma's Lady (by Lyphard's Special): dam never ran: well beaten in maidens. *Miss L. A. Perratt*

DUST D'THRONE (USA)　4 b.g. Bob's Dusty (USA) – Dethroned (USA)　**35** (Grenfall (USA)) [1991 8.2m² 8.2m⁴ 10g 8.1g³ 8m⁶ 1992 8.1g⁴ 10m] quite attractive gelding: has a round action: maiden handicapper: best form at 1m: acts on good to firm ground. *Miss L. C. Siddall*

DUSTY POINT (IRE)　2 b.c. (Feb 26) Reference Point 139 – Noble Dust (USA)　**63** (Dust Commander (USA)) [1992 7g⁵ 7g⁶ 7d⁶ 8.5m 8.2d] 32,000Y: compact, good-bodied colt: fifth foal: half-brother to Irish 1¾m winner Proudfoot and 1989 French 2-y-o 5.5f to 1¼m winner Noble Ballerina (both by Shareef Dancer): dam, unraced, from good family: modest maiden: should be suited by middle distances: possibly unsuited by good to firm ground: took keen hold when running moderately in blinkers final outing. *B. Hanbury*

DUSTY'S DARLING　2 b.f. (Mar 18) Doyoun 124 – Proserpina (FR) (Shafaraz　**– p** (FR) 124) [1992 7g] 10,500Y: first foal: dam French maiden: 33/1, prominent to 2f out when nineteenth of 24 in Newmarket maiden won by Fayfa in October: should do better. *M. A. Jarvis*

DUTCH CZARINA　4 b.f. Prince Sabo 123 – Dutch Princess 70 (Royalty 130)　**45** [1991 10v³ 10g 11.7d⁵ 8s⁶ 8f 1992 a8g a8g⁶ 10m⁵ 10m*] lengthy filly: poor handicapper: made all in apprentice race at Lingfield in June: stays 1¼m: acts on good to firm and heavy going: below form when visored once. *Miss B. Sanders*

DUTCH DANCER (BAR) 2 ch.f. (Mar 24) Bentom (USA) 98 – Calypso Queen —
85 (Laser Light 118) [1992 5g 5m] compact filly: first foal to race here: dam won
over 5f at 2 yrs before export to Barbados: carried head high when well beaten in
September maidens: sold 780 gns Doncaster November Sales, reportedly to
Czechoslovakia. *J. Berry*

DUTCH DEBUTANTE 2 ch.f. (Jan 14) Nicholas Bill 125 – Dutch Princess 70 —
(Royalty 130) [1992 7.1d] compact filly: sixth foal: sister to useful stayer Double
Dutch: dam staying maiden: bit backward, prominent until straight in maiden at
Sandown in July. *Miss B. Sanders*

DUTEST 5 b.h. Aragon 118 – Indian Call 72 (Warpath 113) [1991 NR 1992 12d3] **44** +
leggy, quite attractive horse: rated 70 as 3-y-o for A. Stewart: third in Uttoxeter
celebrity event in November, 1992: stays 1½m: acts on good to firm ground. *M. C.
Pipe*

DUTOSKY 2 b.f. (Feb 2) Doulab (USA) 115 – Butosky 71 (Busted 134) [1992 6m **80**
7g 5.9g5 7s5 7s* 7g] strong, compact filly: sort to carry condition: half-sister to
several winners, including Ebor runner-up Bush Hill (by Beldale Flutter) and 6f (at
2 yrs) and 1m winner Tusky (by Prince Sabo): dam middle-distance half-sister to
very smart sprinter Crews Hill: much improved in nurseries on last 2 starts,
1½-length winner at York in October and fair eighth of 21 to Mhemeanles at
Doncaster: will be suited by 1m: acts on soft ground. *M. J. Camacho*

DUTYFUL 6 b.m. Bold Owl 101 – My Duty 70 (Sea Hawk II 131) [1991 14d 16m —
16.2d5 16m5 16m* 16d3 17.2g2 1992 14d 16.4g 16m] workmanlike mare: seems of
little account nowadays. *M. J. Haynes*

DUTY SERGEANT (IRE) 3 b.g. Pennine Walk 120 – Plainsong (FR) (Amen **57**
(FR)) [1991 5g2 5f* 6m3 6d4 6g4 6d6 5m6 7d 6g 5.7g 1992 6d3 6d 7s 6g 6d 8h6 10f2
8g5 8f 6g3 6d 7g* 8g] smallish, sturdy gelding: poor mover: none too consistent
handicapper: won at Brighton in October: effective at 6f, and seems to stay 1¼m:
acts on firm and dead ground: usually blinkered. *M. P. Muggeridge*

DUVEEN (IRE) 2 b.c. (Apr 8) Tate Gallery (USA) 117 – Wish You Were Here **46**
(USA) (Secretariat (USA)) [1992 5.7d 7s6] IR 9,500Y: good-quartered colt: fifth foal:
closely related to a winner in Sweden by Sadler's Wells: dam 7f and 1¼m winner out
of top-class middle-distance performer Summer Guest: much better effort in
autumn maidens when never-dangerous sixth of 10 at Warwick: will be suited by
1m+: joined M. Bell. *C. R. Nelson*

DYAB (USA) 2 b.c. (Apr 20) Diesis 133 – Petrava (NZ) (Imposing (AUS)) [1992 **85** p
7g 8d*] lengthy colt: has scope: fourth foal: half-brother to 3-y-o 1m winner Muhit
(by El Gran Senor) and 1990 2-y-o 6f winner Jallad (by Blushing Groom): dam won
from 6.5f to 9f in South Africa where champion filly at 3 yrs: won 18-runner maiden
at Leicester in October in good style by 3 lengths from Azzilfi: looked green still,
and should come on again. *P. T. Walwyn*

DYD 4 b.f. Sulaafah (USA) 119 – Wrekin Belle (Dance In Time (CAN)) [1991 8g 9d* —
10.5g 1992 10.8v] rangy filly: rated 75 as 3-y-o: bandaged and well beaten in handicap
in March: stays 9f: acts on dead ground. *F. Jordan*

DYNAVOUR HOUSE 2 ch.f. (Mar 2) Bairn (USA) 126 – Good Natured § (Troy —
137) [1992 6.1m 7m 7d] neat filly: second foal: dam temperamental: seems of little
account. *M. W. Eckley*

E

EAGER DEVA 5 b.h. Lochnager 132 – Deva Rose 80 (Chestergate 111) [1991 5d2 **92** d
5g3 5g* 5f* 5.1g6 5.1g* 5.6m 5f* 5g3 5.1g3 1992 5g 5v 5m* 5m5 5g3 5g 5.2d6 5m 5f6
5m] robust, good-quartered horse: impresses in appearance: good walker and fluent
mover: fairly useful but rather inconsistent handicapper: successful at Pontefract in
May: ideally suited by 5f and a sound surface. *R. Hollinshead*

EAGLE FEATHER (IRE) 4 b.g. Commanche Run 133 – Peacefully (Nonoalco **78**
(USA) 131) [1991 8g5 10g 8g3 1992 10d 10.5g* 10. 1m3 10.5d2 10.5s3] lengthy, angular
gelding: moderate walker: fair performer: won Haydock claimer in July: best efforts
in similar events final 2 starts: should stay 1½m: acts on good to firm and soft
ground: claimed £10,100 final start to race in Scandinavia. *J. L. Dunlop*

EARLY GALES 3 b.f. Precocious 126 – Galesa 90 (Welsh Pageant 132) [1991 NR —
1992 7m a12g] leggy filly: first foal: dam 1½m winner at 3 yrs, ungenuine at 4 yrs:

33/1, well beaten in maidens at Goodwood in May for M. McCormack and Lingfield in December. *J. Pearce*

EARLY SONG 2 b.f. (Feb 18) Precocious 126 – Magic Flute 124 (Tudor Melody 129) [1992 6m 5g 8.5m6 6m] lengthy, unfurnished filly: half-sister to several winners, including useful middle-distance colt Eagling (by Nureyev) and very useful pair Lost Chord (by Busted) and Pamina (by Brigadier Gerard): dam won Cheveley Park Stakes and was very smart at up to 1m: modest maiden: best effort at 8.5f: sold 1,800 gns Newmarket Autumn Sales. *P. T. Walwyn*   **56**

EARLY STAR 3 b.c. Precocious 126 – Staritsa (USA) (Alleged (USA) 138) [1991 7m5 6m 1992 a8g* a8g2 a8g3 a7g* 7g4 6s2 6g6] rather leggy, quite good-topped colt: fair performer: successful at Southwell in claimer in January and £10,800 handicap in March: not seen out after May: effective at 6f under testing conditions, and stays 1m: acts on fibresand and on soft ground. *T. D. Barron*   **70**

EARLY TO RISE 2 b.g. (Mar 11) Don't Forget Me 127 – Foreno (Formidable (USA) 125) [1992 6m6 a8g6 8.2s] 8,000Y: strong, close-coupled gelding: first foal: dam half-sister to smart French sprinter Reasonable: poor maiden: best effort final start. *C. A. Cyzer*   **47**

EAST BARNS (IRE) 4 gr.g. Godswalk (USA) 130 – Rocket Lass (Touch Paper 113) [1991 7.5g5 8.5f 8.2f* 7d6 8m6 8.5m4 9m 11s 8.2f5 8f6 8m 8.3f a8g5 1992 a11g a8g3 a8g a8g3 a8g2 a7g* 7s 8.1d5 a7g4 a7g6 a8g* a8g*] close-coupled gelding: has a quick action: modest performer on the all-weather: won at Southwell in February (off course 7 months afterwards) and twice in December: stays 8.5f well: acts on firm going and fibresand: usually blinkered these days: has run well for amateur/ claimer. *T. D. Barron*   **a60**

EASTER LEE 12 b.g. Idiot's Delight 115 – Stacy Lee 95 (French Beige 127) [1991 NR 1992 17.2f] tall, leggy, lightly-made gelding: fair hunter chaser in 1991/2: looked of no account on first run on flat since 1986. *R. J. Hodges*   **–**

EASTERN GLOW 2 ch.f. (Apr 10) Hadeer 118 – Turtle Dove (Gyr (USA) 131) [1992 7g3 7g 8.2d 7d] small filly: lacks scope: half-sister to numerous winners by Warpath, including middle-distance stayer Path of Peace and fair out-and-out stayer Path's Sister: dam ran once: modest plater: should stay 1m: acts on dead ground. *S. P. C. Woods*   **47**

EASTERN MAGIC 4 b.c. Faustus (USA) 118 – Hithermoor Lass 75 (Red Alert 127) [1991 10g 10m5 10.3m 10.5g 10.3d4 1992 10.8v2 10d a12g4 10m 11.5s 12.5s5] rather leggy colt: fair form in 1992 only on reappearance: stays 10.8f: acts on good to firm ground and heavy going: ran creditably when visored once at 3 yrs. *J. Akehurst*   **70** d

EASTERN MEMORIES (IRE) 2 b.c. (Mar 26) Don't Forget Me 127 – East River (FR) (Arctic Tern (USA) 126) [1992 6g5 7.1g4 8s2 7s3 a7g*] quite attractive colt, rather unfurnished: third living foal: half-brother to 7f seller winner Manhattan River and a sprint winner in USA (both by Gorytus): dam minor French 11f winner: consistent performer: blinkered, won maiden at Lingfield in November: will be better suited by 1¼m: acts on soft going and equitrack, yet to race on top-of-the-ground. *R. Hannon*   **73**

EASTERN PHOEBE 3 ch.f. Pharly (FR) 130 – Damiya (FR) (Direct Flight) [1991 NR 1992 12.3s 12v6] smallish, sturdy filly: third live foal: half-sister to 6-y-o 10.8f to 13f winner/successful jumper Scotoni (by Final Straw) and a winner over hurdles: dam French 10.5f and 1½m winner: well beaten in maiden at Ripon (moved moderately to post) and claimer at Folkestone: sold to join R. Barr 1,200 gns Newmarket Autumn Sales. *A. C. Stewart*   **–**

EASTERN PLEASURE 5 gr.g. Absalom 128 – First Pleasure 73 (Dominion 123) [1991 NR 1992 12m] sturdy gelding: moderate walker: rated 54 on flat as 3-y-o for J. Wharton: burly and stiff task in claimer on first run for 18 months. *M. D. Hammond*   **–**

EASTERN WHISPER (USA) 5 gr.h. Arctic Tern (USA) 126 – Mazyoun (USA) 57 (Blushing Groom (FR) 131) [1991 15.8f2 15g3 1992 11.5m] compact, rather angular horse: moderate mover: rated 64 at 4 yrs when with D. Smith: soundly beaten in claiming handicap in July, 1992: suited by test of stamina: acts on any going: looked unco-operative when visored once at 3 yrs. *A. Moore*   **–**

EASTER TERM 4 b.f. Welsh Term 126 – Silly Woman (Silly Season 127) [1991 12m 8g 1992 9d 10m6] lengthy, good-topped filly: lightly raced and no worthwhile form. *R. J. Holder*   **–**

EASTLEIGH 3 b.c. Efisio 120 – Blue Jane 81 (Blue Cashmere 129) [1991 5d2 5m4 6m5 5m6 5g5 6g4 6m4 6m 5d 6m2 5d4 1992 a6g2 a6g5 a6g* 7g2 8d 6g4 7m4 8m4 8d6]   **67**

8.9g³ 8d⁴ 7.6d* 8g 8.1d⁵ 7g 8g⁶ a7g² 8m⁴ 7d 7s 8v a6g⁶ a7g⁴ a8g*] lengthy, workmanlike colt: modest handicapper: won at Southwell (maiden) in March, Chester in July and Lingfield (claimer) in December: stays 8.9f: possibly unsuited by soft ground, yet to race on firm: has won for 7-lb claimer: has run creditably when sweating. *R. Hollinshead*

EAST LIBERTY (USA) 2 ch.f. (Apr 15) Halo (USA) – Pennsylvania (USA) 83 **86** (Northjet 136) [1992 7.1d* 7.1g³ 7m⁶ 8.1s⁶ 8m⁶] tall, rangy filly: good mover: first foal: dam, maiden, stayed 1¼m, is daughter of Mrs Penny, same family as Hatoof: sire, high class at up to 1½m, twice champion sire in USA: fair performer: won maiden at Sandown in July: best effort when 8 lengths sixth of 12 to Marillette in May Hill Stakes at Doncaster final start, leading briefly 2f out: one paced, and will be well suited by middle distances. *I. A. Balding*

EASY ACCESS (IRE) 2 b.c. (Mar 2) Thatching 131 – Savannah Song (USA) **83** (Riverman (USA) 131) [1992 5g³dis 6m 6m² 6d³ 7m 6g*] 40,000F, 42,000Y: leggy, close-coupled colt: moderate mover: first foal: dam, placed at 1½m in Ireland on only start, is half-sister to Alydar's Best: fairly useful performer: improved form when beating Alyakkh by a short head, pair clear, in maiden at Doncaster in November: should be better suited by 7f than 6f: has worn bandages. *R. Hannon*

EASY DELTA 3 ch.f. Swing Easy (USA) 126 – Songless (Song 132) [1991 6m 5m –
7m 1992 a6g a6g a10g 10g 5m] small filly: moderate mover: no worthwhile form: trained until after third 3-y-o start by C. Holmes. *M. Dixon*

EASY DOES IT 3 b.f. Swing Easy (USA) 126 – Pearl Pet 56 (Mummy's Pet 125) **52** [1991 5m 6m a6g a8g³ a7g 1992 a7g² a7g⁵ a8g⁴ a7g³ a6g³ a7g⁵ 6g* 6d³ 6d⁴ 6d 5.1d⁵] workmanlike filly: poor mover: modest handicapper: sold out of C. C. Elsey's stable 2,000 gns Ascot March Sales after fifth start: made all at Windsor (seller, no bid) in August: ran very well in handicaps last 2 starts: effective at 5f and 6f: acts on dead ground: visored on equitrack. *Mrs A. Knight*

EASY LINE 9 ch.g. Swing Easy (USA) 126 – Impromptu 88 (My Swanee 122) **91** [1991 6g 5m 6g³ 6g⁶ 7m⁵ 7g 8m 7g⁵ 6g* 6m 6f* 5m* 1992 5m⁵ 6m* 6m² 6g⁴ 6m² 6m² 6m⁴ 6m 6g³] tall, lengthy gelding: moderate mover: fairly useful old stager: won Haydock claimer in May: ran well afterwards, mostly in handicaps: ideally suited by 6f: probably not at his best on soft going, acts on any other: tried visored once: bandaged: often hangs, and is best covered up. *P. J. Feilden*

EASY MATCH 6 b.m. Royal Match 117 – Flying Easy (Swing Easy (USA) 126) –
[1991 6f² 7.1m⁶ 7.1m⁵ 1992 a6g³ a8g] big, workmanlike mare: rated 50 at 5 yrs: no form early in 1992: finds 6f too short and should stay 1m: acts on good to firm ground. *C. J. Hill*

EASY OVER (USA) 6 ch.g. Transworld (USA) 121 – Love Bunny (USA) **48** (Exclusive Native (USA)) [1991 13.8d⁵ 12.3s³ 13m³ 11.9d 12.1d⁵ 12.1s⁴ 1992 13.8g³ 12.1s⁵] big, workmanlike gelding: plating-class performer: without a win since 1989: ran creditably in handicaps in the spring, in blinkers last time: stays 1¾m: acts on good to firm and heavy going: sold 5,000 gns Doncaster May Sales. *R. D. E. Woodhouse*

EASY PURCHASE 5 br.h. Swing Easy (USA) 126 – Dauphiness 76 (Supreme **49** Sovereign 119) [1991 a11g⁴ a12g⁴ 12s 12.5g⁶ 11.8m⁶ 1992 11.7d* 11.8m 11.4f⁵ 12d 11.6d⁴] big, angular horse: has a quick action: modest but rather inconsistent handicapper: won at Bath in April: stays 1½m: acts on good to firm and dead ground: tends to carry head high, and has found little off bridle: sold 925 gns Ascot September Sales. *R. J. Holder*

EASY TOUCH 2 b.f. (Mar 19) Bairn (USA) 126 – Lappet (Kampala 120) [1992 5s
5g 6f 6m 7f⁵] 5,000Y: leggy, unfurnished filly: has a round action: first foal: dam twice-raced half-sister to smart 1972 2-y-o filly Silver Birch: soundly beaten in maidens, not seen out after July: blinkered last 2 starts. *M. D. I. Usher*

EATON ROW (USA) 2 b.c. (Mar 11) Alydar (USA) – Royal Entrance (USA) **62** p
(Tim Tam) [1992 7m] leggy colt: brother to 3 minor winners and half-brother to several winners, notably top-class 1979 3-y-o filly in America Davona Dale (by Best Turn): dam won at up to 1m: 20/1 and green, around 16 lengths last of 10, niggled along at halfway, to Barathea in £8,850 event at Newmarket in October: will improve. *P. W. Chapple-Hyam*

EAU D'ESPOIR 3 b.f. Monsanto (FR) 121 – Hopeful Waters 66 (Forlorn River –
124) [1991 5g 5f 6.9m 7m⁶ 7m⁴ 7.1m⁶ 8m 8m⁶ 10m⁵ 1992 a10g⁴ a10g⁶ a10g 12v] smallish filly: no worthwhile form on flat in 1992, not seen out after March: won selling hurdle in November. *J. L. Spearing*

EBAZIYA (IRE) 3 b.f. Darshaan 133 – Ezana (Ela-Mana-Mou 132) [1991 7g³ 7g* **111** 8d² 1992 8v² 10v* 12g⁴ 11d* 12d³ 12d*] second foal: dam, French 11.5f winner, is half-sister to French Group 3 10.5f winner Demia: progressive Irish filly: won listed races at the Curragh in April, Galway in September and Leopardstown in October: best effort when staying-on third in Group 2 Blandford Stakes at the Curragh: would probably have stayed beyond 1½m: raced only with give in the ground: to stud. *J. Oxx, Ireland*

EBONY ISLE 3 gr.f. Grey Desire 115 – Clairwood (Final Straw 127) [1991 NR – 1992 5v 5g 8s⁶ 8.3s 9.2m 8.3f⁵ 8m⁶ 13.1g 12.1g⁴] smallish, stocky filly: third foal: sister to 4-y-o 6f (at 2 yrs) to 11.1f winner Able Lassie: dam highly raced: no worthwhile form: trained first 7 starts by P. Monteith: blinkered final outing, in July. *Miss L. A. Perratt*

ECHO-LOGICAL 3 gr.c. Belfort (FR) 89 – North Pine (Import 127) [1991 5d* **93** 6f³ 5.1m* 5m⁴ 5d² 5g² 1992 5g² 5g 5.1m* 5.1m* 5.1g⁴ 5g* 5m 6d⁵ 6d²] tall, workmanlike colt: fairly useful performer: short-priced favourite, won claimer and minor event at Chepstow and claimer at Ayr (claimed out of J. Berry's stable £15,000) in summer: 33/1, excellent second of 28 to Lochsong in Ayr Gold Cup final start: stays 6f: acts on good to firm and dead ground. *R. Hannon*

ECLIPSING (IRE) 4 b.f. Baillamont (USA) 124 – Exgravity (USA) (Explodent **93** (USA)) [1991 10m 8g² 8g* 8m 8.1m⁵ 8m² 1992 8.1m² 8f 8.1s³ 8s* 8.9g³ 8s* 9d] tall, leggy, lengthy filly: good mover, with a long stride: progressed well in handicaps in 1992, successful at Newbury in July and Ayr (£15,000 event) in September: likely to prove best at 1m: acts on good to firm and soft ground: sometimes has tongue tied down: held up. *R. Charlton*

ECLIPTIC (IRE) 3 b.g. Lomond (USA) 128 – Circulate (High Top 131) [1991 **86** 7m³ 7.5m 7m⁵ 8m 1992 10d* 8.9g* 8m 8m] tall, leggy, lengthy gelding: progressive handicapper in the spring, winning at Newbury and York: well beaten in Britannia Handicap (bandaged behind) at Royal Ascot and £66,200 handicap at Goodwood: stays 1¼m: best efforts on an easy surface: has a turn of foot: has been gelded and sent to race in the Far East. *P. W. Chapple-Hyam*

ECU DE FRANCE (IRE) 2 ch.c. (May 4) Groom Dancer (USA) 128 – Racing **77** Connection (USA) (Sharpen Up 127) [1992 7g⁶ 7d² 7g² 8s⁴] 20,000Y: strong colt: first reported foal: dam, French 11f winner, is half-sister to Lead On Time and Great Commotion: fair maiden: will be suited by a thorough test of stamina. *J. L. Dunlop*

EDEN'S CLOSE 3 ch.g. Green Dancer (USA) 132 – Royal Agreement (USA) **76** (Vaguely Noble 140) [1991 8m⁴ 6m⁶ 1992 10v⁴ 8g⁴ 8.5m⁵ 11.1m* 11.9f³ 12f 11.9d⁵ 11.9f⁵ 10.3m 8.5m³ 9g] rather leggy, angular gelding: fair performer: won maiden at Edinburgh in May: effective at 8.5f and stays 1½m: acts on firm ground, seemingly not on a soft surface: effective visored or not: won novice hurdle at Newbury in October: has been gelded. *M. H. Tompkins*

EDGEAWAY 3 b.f. Ajdal (USA) 130 – Kaweah Maid (General Assembly (USA)) **62** [1991 6m 6.9f² 1992 8s⁴ 10m⁶ 8m² 8d³ 7m* 8d⁴ 7g 8m 10g] rather sparely-made filly: modest performer: 9/4 on, made all in 4-runner maiden at Thirsk in July: well below form in handicaps last 3 starts: suited by 1m: acts on any going: effective visored or not. *J. W. Hills*

EDGE OF DARKNESS 3 br.f. Vaigly Great 127 – Atoka 97 (March Past 124) **62** [1991 NR 1992 8v³ 8s⁴ 10g* 10g⁶ 10.2f³ 10g³ 10.1f² 10d 10.4s* 10.3g] leggy, rather unfurnished filly: seventh foal: sister to 4-y-o Oka Flow and half-sister to 3 winners, including fairly useful 1985 2-y-o 5f winner Oh Boyar (by Young Generation): dam won from 6f to 15f: modest performer: won apprentice claimer at Nottingham in May and selling handicap (sold out of J. Hills's stable 6,000 gns) at York in October: unimpressive in appearance, well beaten final start: worth a try at 1½m: acts on any going. *N. Tinkler*

EDGEWISE 9 b. or br.g. Tanfirion 110 – Regency Girl 89 (Right Boy 137) [1991 – NR 1992 a8g a8g 7f 8f 10g 12.3m 11.5g⁶ 16m] compact gelding: seems of no account nowadays. *D. Morris*

EDIREPUS 4 b.g. Lightning Dealer 103 – Pentland Beauty 49 (Remainder Man **50** 126§) [1991 10g 1992 9g³ 12.4m⁶ 9d 9.2v⁴ 10d³] big, angular gelding: modest performer: should stay 1½m (stiff task when tried): acts on heavy ground. *Mrs M. Reveley*

EDNEGO BAY (IRE) 4 b.g. Hatim (USA) 121 – African Bloom (African Sky **66** 124) [1991 NR 1992 5v⁵ 6.9g 7f⁴ 5.9f³ 6g 6.1d⁵] strong, lengthy gelding: third foal: half-brother to 5-y-o handicapper Falcons Dawn (by Exhibitioner) and plating-class 1988 2-y-o 5f winner Hogans Hero (by Krayyan): dam won twice over 7f in Ireland:

fair performer: blinkered, poor fifth in seller in July: stays 7f: best form on firm ground: effective in a visor. *M. McCormack*

EDUCATED PET 3 gr.g. Petong 126 – School Road 88 (Great Nephew 126) **76**
[1991 5d⁵ 5f⁴ 5f 6f² 6f³ 7g 7m 6g 5d 1992 a6g a6g⁵ a6g* 5s⁵ 5.9d⁴ a5g² 6m⁴ 5s* 5f* 6f* 5f² 5m* 5h4 5.1f⁶ 5s² 5m* 5m 5m 6g 6m⁴ 5g⁵ 6g 6f 6d 6m] sturdy gelding: carries condition: fair handicapper: progressed really well to win at Lingfield, Wolverhampton, Carlisle, Hamilton, Ayr then Newmarket in summer: below form last 4 starts and is now well in at best: stays 6f: acts on any turf going, and on all-weather surfaces: blinkered/visored last 2 starts at 2 yrs: has run well for 7-lb claimer: very tough and game. *M. Johnston*

EFHARISTO 3 b.c. Dominion 123 – Excellent Alibi (USA) (Exceller (USA) 129) **94**
[1991 7g 7.1m⁴ 6s⁶ 1992 a7g 7m² 7g* 8m* 8g² 8m] workmanlike colt: progressive handicapper: successful at Epsom and Royal Ascot (Britannia Handicap, narrowly from Bold Boss and Sharpitor) in June: best effort when neck second to Little Bean in £9,600 contest at Newmarket: never able to challenge in £66,200 contest at Goodwood later in July: will be well suited by 1¼m: acts on good to firm ground. *C. E. Brittain*

EFIZIA 2 b.f. (Apr 11) Efisio 120 – Millie Grey 52 (Grey Ghost 98) [1992 7f 7m² 8g] **51**
400Y: first reported foal: dam, poor on flat, winning hurdler: modest maiden: will probably stay 1¼m. *Mrs M. Reveley*

EFRA 3 b.c. Efisio 120 – Ra Ra (Lord Gayle (USA) 124) [1991 5d 5g⁶ 1992 7s⁵ 6.1d⁵ **65**
6g 7m*ᵈⁱˢ 6m³ 6g 6m⁵ 7d⁴ 6m* 7g 6d 6s⁶] lengthy, good-topped colt: has a round action: fair performer: awarded race (was himself disqualified at Lingfield in May after jockey weighed in light) having been narrowly beaten in maiden at Folkestone in August: stays 7f: acts on good to firm ground and dead: blinkered (tailed off) sixth start: somewhat inconsistent. *R. Hannon*

EGG 2 gr.g. (Mar 19) Another Realm 118 – Slick Chick 89 (Shiny Tenth 120) [1992 **68**
5g³ 5g a7g⁵ a6g⁴ a7g 6s* 6s* 6s² 6s³ 7m 6g⁵ 7g] 1,800F, 2,300Y: leggy, unfurnished gelding: moderate mover: half-brother to 3-y-o Rythmic Style (by Swing Easy), 5f winner at 2 yrs, and several other winners here and abroad, including quite useful 5f to 1¼m winner Basil Boy (by Jimsun): dam stayed 13f: a fair performer since being blinkered: won nurseries at Ripon (selling event, no bid) and Hamilton in late-summer and ran well most starts afterwards: stays 7f, though best form over strongly-run 6f: well suited by soft ground: has won for a 7-lb claimer: usually gets well behind: changed hands 6,400 gns Doncaster November Sales. *T. D. Barron*

EIDOLON 5 b.m. Rousillon (USA) 133 – Eider 80 (Niniski (USA) 125) [1991 5m **–**
8f⁵ 8m 6.1d 10.2g 1992 5.1m] leggy, angular mare: has quick action: of no account. *Mrs N. S. Sharpe*

EID (USA) 3 b.g. Northern Baby (CAN) 127 – Millracer (USA) 79 (Le Fabuleux **76**
133) [1991 8f* 8g⁴ 8g 1992 8.5m² 9.9f⁴ 9.2f³ 12h⁴ 8m²] good-topped gelding: fair

Britannia Handicap, Royal Ascot—a grandstand finish in the driving rain between (right to left) Efharisto, Bold Boss and Sharpitor

performer: should stay beyond 1m: yet to race on soft surface: blinkered (sweating, fair effort)/visored (ran well) once each in 1992: sold to join M. Meade 14,000 gns Newmarket July Sales. *D. Morley*

EIGHTANDAHALF (IRE)　3 b.c. Be My Guest (USA) 126 – Nancy Chere　**75**
(USA) (Gallant Man) [1991 8m 7m 1992 10.3g⁵ 12.1m² 16.2f] good-topped, attractive colt: carries condition: fair maiden: short-headed at Chepstow in May: never travelling well in Queen's Vase at Royal Ascot following month: stays 1½m: possibly unsuited by firm going: sold only 2,200 gns Newmarket Autumn Sales. *P. W. Chapple-Hyam*

EIGHTEENTHIRTYFOUR (IRE)　4 b.c. Ballad Rock 122 – Weavers' Tack　**–**
(Weavers' Hall 122) [1991 8f 10d 10m 1992 12v] leggy, good-topped colt: lightly raced and no worthwhile form. *A. Moore*

EIGHTOFUS　2 b.g. (May 4) Midyan (USA) 124 – Moulin Rapide (USA) (Roberto　**39**
(USA) 131) [1992 5f 6d⁶ 6f⁵ 6m² 5.9f⁴ 6m 6s] 1,200Y, 4,400 2-y-o: rather leggy gelding: moderate walker: third foal: dam, ran once in France, is daughter of Ribblesdale third Fenney Mill: modest plater: ran poorly last 3 starts: should stay 7f: sold 1,300 gns Doncaster September Sales. *G. M. Moore*

EIRAS MOOD　3 b. or br.f. Jalmood (USA) 126 – Pure Perfection (So Blessed　**57**
130) [1991 NR 1992 8.1m⁴ 8f 11.7g 8g² 10g² 10s 8.2g* 8g a10g] small filly: third foal: dam, closely related to Irish 2000 Guineas winner Dara Monarch, showed little worthwhile form: modest performer: trained by R. Dickin first 3 starts: ridden by 7-lb claimer, won selling handicap (no bid) at Nottingham in October: should prove at least as effective at 1¼m as around 1m: below form on soft ground and on equitrack. *B. Palling*

EIRE LEATH-SCEAL　5 b.g. Legend of France (USA) 124 – Killarney Belle　**58**
(USA) (Irish Castle (USA)) [1991 8d⁵ 10g⁶ 10s⁵ 10g 12m⁴ 12f* 12m 12.3g⁵ 11.9m⁴ 12g³ 11.9m² 12f⁴ 12.3f⁵ 11.9g 13.9g 13.1m* 11.9g 11.9d⁵ 12m⁵ 12g⁶ 16.5d 1992 12g⁴ 14.9v 12d⁴ 14g 11.9g³ 12f³ 12m⁶ 11.9f 12.3m³ 10m² 12f² 12f 11.8g 12.3m 12m 15s] small, attractive gelding: usually looks well: bad mover: modest handicapper: formerly tough and genuine, but soundly beaten last 5 starts: effective from 1¼m to 13f: acts on firm and dead going, seems unsuited by heavy: often races up with pace. *M. Brittain*

ELABJER (USA)　3 b.g. Shadeed (USA) 135 – Glamour Girl (FR) (Riverman　**–**
(USA) 131) [1991 NR 1992 7m⁴] compact, attractive colt: half-brother to smart middle-distance stayer Ilium (by Troy): dam, minor French 7f and 9.5f winner, is half-sister to dam of Gold River (by Riverman): fourth of 8 in maiden at York in May: sold to join P. Evans 4,000 gns Newmarket Autumn Sales. *H. Thomson Jones*

ELAINE TULLY (IRE)　4 b.f. Persian Bold 123 – Hanna Alta (FR) (Busted 134)　**80**
[1991 8m⁴ 8g* 8m⁵ 10g³ 10g⁶ 12m⁴ 12d³ 1992 12.5g⁴ 12g³ 8f² 11.9f⁵ 13.1g³ 14g] sturdy filly: fairly useful handicapper: better suited by 1½m/13f than shorter: acts on good to firm and dead ground: suitable mount for lady rider. *M. J. Heaton-Ellis*

ELANMATINA (IRE)　3 ch.f. Burslem 123 – Sally St Clair (Sallust 134) [1991　**75**
6f* 6f² 6.1m⁵ 6m 1992 6v 6d 8d² 8m² 7g⁶ 8g] workmanlike filly: fair handicapper: virtually fell when hampered 2f out final start, in July: ideally needs further than 7f, and should stay beyond 1m: acts on firm and dead ground. *C. F. Wall*

ELBIO　5 b. or br.h. Precocious 126 – Maganyos (HUN) 112 (Pioneer (USA))　**121**
[1991 6m² 5g* 5m* 5m* 6m³ 5g⁵ 1992 5m* 5m⁴ 5f³ 6g⁴ 6.5g⁶ 5m⁴ 6s* 5s³ a6f⁵]
　　Life has been tough at the top for Elbio since he burst onto the sprinting scene in the first half of 1991: eleven starts since he won that year's King's Stand Stakes have brought him just two more wins, both from abroad. Elbio raised hopes of another good season when he set off by winning the Prix de Saint-Georges at Longchamp in May, and to a degree they were fulfilled, in that he mostly ran well afterwards, particularly in top company, and added the Jacobs Goldene Peitsche at Baden-Baden in September to his tally. But the opposition at Longchamp and Baden-Baden was only around the normal standard for a Group 3 sprint in France and a Group 2 in Germany—Dream Talk and Twafeaj finished second respectively—and on all the occasions that Elbio took on the best he found at least two too good for him. The best older sprinters in Britain in the latest season were undoubtedly Sheikh Albadou and Mr Brooks. Elbio never managed to beat either in a series of encounters with one or both until Mr Brooks was struck down in the Breeders' Cup Sprint at

Prix de Saint-Georges, Longchamp—Elbio beats Dream Talk

Gulfstream Park in November, where Elbio came a fair fifth to the American horse Thirty Slews, a place behind Sheikh Albadou. The first of the series, in the King's Stand, went to Sheikh Albadou from Mr Brooks and Elbio; there was little between them at the finish and Elbio looked a shade unlucky, having to be switched for a run. In the July Cup Mr Brooks had the advantage, with Sheikh Albadou third and Elbio, a touch better than the bare result might suggest, fourth. Further clashes saw Mr Brooks and Elbio finish second and fourth respectively to the two-year-old Lyric Fantasy in the Nunthorpe, then first and third in the Prix de l'Abbaye, separated by a margin of approximately two lengths each time.

Elbio remains in training. He won't have Sheikh Albadou or Mr Brooks against him any more, so may well find the going a little easier, although

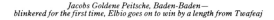

Jacobs Goldene Peitsche, Baden-Baden—
blinkered for the first time, Elbio goes on to win by a length from Twafeaj

Elbio (b. or br.h. 1987)	Precocious (b 1981)	Mummy's Pet (b 1968)	Sing Sing
			Money For Nothing
		Mrs Moss (ch 1969)	Reform
			Golden Plate
	Maganyos (HUN) (br 1980)	Pioneer (b 1971)	Pieces of Eight
			Irish Rule
		Marimba (b 1973)	Indikator
			Marshgate Lass

unless he improves there are still likely to be those around in a normal year who'll come between him and the very top five- and six-furlong prizes. An interesting development in his latest season which could have a bearing on his prospects in the next one was equipping Elbio with blinkers. The experiment, begun in the Goldene Peitsche and extended through the Abbaye to the Breeders' Cup, seems worth persevering with in view of his form in all three races, and in view of the fact that he has in the past looked a difficult ride, tending to hang and find trouble. As yet, there is no hard evidence that they have helped sharpen him up over five furlongs—on the contrary, he took a long time to get going even in testing conditions in the Abbaye, then finished so strongly that he almost snatched second place from Keen Hunter. The good-topped, attractive Elbio acts on any going. There is little to add to the pedigree details supplied in *Racehorses of 1991*. He remains the best of his sire Precocious's offspring, the only one to have won a pattern race. His much-travelled dam Maganyos, a winner in five different European countries, is now producing in New Zealand and in 1989 foaled a filly by Blanco since named Royal Tiara. Maganyos began life in Hungary, where her half-sister Mazurka was rated one of the better two-year-old fillies of her generation. Their grandam Marshgate Lass, a five-furlong seller winner in Britain, produced a Dutch St Leger winner. *P. J. Makin*

EL CORTES (USA) 3 b.c. El Gran Senor (USA) 136 – Millingdale Lillie 119 (Tumble Wind (USA)) [1991 6m* 1992 10.4m 12.3v5] attractive, good-topped colt: chipped knee bone when winning minor event at Ayr (rated 89p) at 2 yrs: tailed off as 3-y-o in Dante Stakes at York and minor event at Chester 5 months later: should stay 1¼m: sold only 2,400 gns Newmarket Autumn Sales, reportedly to stand at stud in Cyprus. *P. W. Chapple-Hyam*
      –

EL DOMINIO 4 b.c. King of Spain 121 – Domicile (Dominion 123) [1991 8s3 8g 9d 11.7g6 10d 8g 8g* 8g6 8s 8g 8g a10g 1992 a10g* a13g* a13g5 a12g2 a12g a12g a16g6 a12g 11.7d 10g a12g4 a10g a12g] close-coupled colt: unreliable handicapper: won twice at Lingfield in January: stays 13f: acts on soft going and equitrack: has worn tongue strap. *K. O. Cunningham-Brown*
      67 d

ELECKYDO 3 ch.f. Electric 126 – Deed 86 (Derring-Do 131) [1991 8d 7g 1992 8v5 10.2d 14.6g 10.2m4 10f3 11.6g5 10m6 10d5 12s4] workmanlike filly: poor maiden handicapper: stays 1½m: acts on any going. *R. J. Hodges*
      47

ELECTROJET 4 b.f. Electric 126 – Shy Talk 93 (Sharpen Up 127) [1991 7g 7m 8.9m 1992 10s 12.1g] stocky filly: moderate mover: of little account nowadays. *A. W. Jones*
      –

ELECTROLYTE 2 b.c. (Mar 18) Electric 126 – This Sensation 48 (Balidar 133) [1992 8s] 3,500Y: tall, good-bodied colt: second foal: half-brother to a winner in Germany: dam maiden sprinter: 33/1 and backward, never a factor in 22-runner maiden at Warwick in October: moved moderately to post. *B. Palling*
      –

ELEGANT ELLIE 2 b.f. (Mar 10) Alleging (USA) 120 – Highly Polished 79 (High Top 131) [1992 7g a7g a8g] 2,100Y: workmanlike filly: half-sister to middle-distance handicapper Star North (by Star Appeal): dam finished fourth at 2 yrs on only start: no worthwhile form in maidens: wore eyeshield last 2 starts. *Mrs L. Piggott*
      –

ELEGANT FRIEND 4 ch.g. Music Boy 124 – Cardinal Palace 85 (Royal Palace 131) [1991 8m 6m6 5.9h* 5g3 5g3 6m5 6m 8d5 8.1d 1992 8g 8m 8f4 8.3g 9g4 10.2s3 8g 9.7v6] leggy, angular gelding: moderate mover: fair handicapper: easily best efforts when in frame: stays 10.2f: acts on any going: retained 2,400 gns Newmarket Autumn Sales. *M. H. Tompkins*
      69

ELEGANT TOUCH 3 b. or br.f. Elegant Air 119 – Teye (Mummy's Pet 125) [1991 5m2 6d4 6f5 7m2 7f2 8m* 8d4 1992 8.5g6 10m3 9.9d6 10m 10g2] leggy, lengthy
      74

filly: fair handicapper: stays 1¼m: acts on good to firm and dead ground: has worn tongue strap: has joined M. Pipe. *M. Moubarak*

ELEGANZA (IRE)   3 b.f. Kings Lake (USA) 133 – Belmont Blue 75 (Kashmir II   **67**
125) [1991 7g 7.5f³ 7g³ 1992 12.3s² 11.7d 11.7s⁶] leggy, close-coupled filly: active
sort: fair maiden: trained by N. Tinkler, best effort when second in handicap at
Ripon: refused to enter stalls later in April: contested handicaps at Bath in
September, better effort when fair sixth, pulling hard early on behind a modest pace:
stays 1½m: acts on soft ground. *S. M. Hillen*

ELEMENTARY   9 b.g. Busted 134 – Santa Vittoria 100 (Ragusa 137) [1991 12d³   **84**
12g 10g 1992 11g* 11.7g* 12g² 10.3g6] strong, quite attractive ex-Irish gelding:
one-time very useful performer/high-class hurdler for J. Bolger: no form for M. Pipe
in 1991/2 season: competed in French Provinces in autumn as 9-y-o, winning 2
amateur races: fairly useful form when sixth in Doncaster minor event: effective
from 1m to 1½m: acts on any going: blinkered early in career. *Paul Green, Jersey*

ELEUSIS (FR)   2 gr.c. (Feb 21) Shernazar 131 – Grande Amie (FR) (Bellypha   **80**
130) [1992 6m⁶ 6m⁴ 7d² 8f³ 8s*] 24,000F, 20,000Y: good-bodied colt: carries condition: good mover: fourth foal: dam French maiden from good family: progressive
performer: won maiden at Bath in September, setting strong gallop and keeping on
well: will stay at least 1¼m: acts on any going: sent to race in Spain. *P. W.
Chapple-Hyam*

ELGIN   3 b.g. Lochnager 132 – Targos Delight (Targowice (USA) 130) [1991 6g 5d   –
7g 7.5f a7g⁵ 7.1m⁴ 6f 8.3g 1992 a10g⁶ a8g⁶ 11.1d⁶ 12.2g⁵ 14.6g 16f] plain,
workmanlike gelding: has a round action: poor maiden: stays 1½m: no improvement
in blinkers: sometimes sweating: headstrong: has joined K. Oliver and won poor
novice hurdle in November. *A. Bailey*

EL GRANDO   2 b.c. (May 9) King of Spain 121 – Easterly Wind 94 (Windjammer   –
(USA)) [1992 7f a7g] colt: moderate mover: seventh foal: half-brother to moderate juvenile 5f winner Northern Trust (by Music Boy) and 1m and 1¼m winner
Shifting Breeze (by Night Shift): dam sprinter: 40/1, always behind in 14-runner
maidens at Salisbury in July and Lingfield in November. *K. O. Cunningham-Brown*

EL GUAPO   2 ch.c. (Apr 19) Stanford 121§ – Puff Pastry 78 (Reform 132) [1992 6f   **44**
6m 5f⁶ 6g³ a7g⁴ 7m⁴ 7f⁶ 7.5d 5g a6g] 1,300Y: big, workmanlike colt: carries
condition: has a round action: fifth live foal: half-brother to 1991 2-y-o 5f winner
Palacegate Gem (by Skyliner) and a prolific winner in Belgium by Daring March:
dam 2-y-o 5f winner: poor maiden: seems suited by 7f: blinkered (well beaten) once:
sold 1,000 gns Newmarket Autumn Sales. *T. Fairhurst*

ELHASNA (USA)   3 b.f. Danzig (USA) – Gold Beauty (USA) (Mr Prospector   **88**
(USA)) [1991 NR 1992 6g* 6g² 6m] well-made filly: has a round action: fourth foal:
sister to brilliant sprinter Dayjur and closely related to Grade 1 9f and 1¼m winner
Maplejinsky (by Nijinsky): dam champion sprinter in USA: fairly useful performer:
won minor event at Leicester in August: struggling when badly hampered in
Newmarket handicap final start: stayed 6f: visits Nashwan. *Major W. R. Hern*

ELHUDHUD   5 ch.h. Habitat 134 – Green Lucia 116 (Green Dancer (USA) 132)   –
[1991 a10g⁴ a12g³ a11g⁶ a10g 10v* 9g⁵ 10.2s⁶ 10f 1992 a12g] leggy, quite
good-topped horse: moderate mover: rated 49 at 4 yrs: off course 10 months, tailed
off in handicap at Southwell in February: stays 1¼m: acts on heavy ground: often
blinkered or visored: hooded once. *D. R. Tucker*

ELISSA   6 ch.m. Tap On Wood 130 – Blakewood 75 (Blakeney 126) [1991 NR 1992   –
a12g a12g 16.2g 17.1m] close-coupled mare: of little account. *G. P. Kelly*

ELITE REG   3 b.g. Electric 126 – Coppice (Pardao 120) [1991 7g 8.1g a8g 1992   **45**
11.6m 13.1m 14.6s³ 12.3d⁴ 14s⁵ 16d 16.1s] good-bodied gelding: plating-class maiden
on flat: stays 14.6f: seemingly suited by a soft surface: blinkered (well beaten) once:
looked unco-operative final start on flat: claimed out of C. Egerton's stable £6,001
first outing over hurdles and, blinkered, progressed really well afterwards for M.
Pipe, winning 3 times. *P. F. I. Cole*

ELIZABETHAN AIR   3 b.f. Elegant Air 119 – Lizabeth Chudleigh (Imperial   **55**
Fling (USA) 116) [1991 7m 8m 7m 1992 a10g³ 8.2g* a8g 8d* 9f⁵ 6.9g⁴ 8.9m² 8d³]   a–
angular filly: modest handicapper: won at Nottingham in April and Leicester in June:
best efforts on last 2 outings, in August: worth another try at 1¼m: acts on good to
firm and dead ground: below form on all-weather surfaces: sold to join A.
Chamberlain 600 gns Newmarket Autumn Sales. *A. N. Lee*

ELIZABETH BAY (USA)   2 b.f. (Apr 10) Mr Prospector (USA) – Life At The **109** p
Top (USA) (Seattle Slew (USA)) [1992 6d* 6.5s*] $1,000,000Y: second foal: dam
high-class filly, stayed 9f, from same family as Bold Forbes, Saratoga Six and

Prix Eclipse, Saint-Cloud—the very promising Elizabeth Bay beats Wixon

Dunbeath: successful in minor event at Chantilly in June and 5-runner Prix Eclipse (by 2 lengths from Wixon) at Saint-Cloud in October: bred to stay 1m: a very promising filly. *A. Fabre, France*

ELIZA WOODING 4 b.f. Faustus (USA) 118 – Red Gloves 83 (Red God 128§) [1991 8m 6m 10g 10.2d⁶ 10.1d 8m⁴ 1992 7.1m a7g a8g³ a7g 10.2m 9.7d⁴ a12g] tall, leggy filly: poor and inconsistent performer: has won one of 22 starts: will stay 1¼m: yet to race on very soft going, acts on any other. *C. J. Hill* **31** a37

ELKHART (USA) 2 br.c. (Mar 28) Gone West (USA) – Elvia (USA) (Roberto (USA) 131) [1992 8.1s² 8m* 8s* 10g] $230,000Y: well-made colt: second foal: dam minor winner at 4 yrs in USA, is daughter of good winner Chain Bracelet: sire (by Mr Prospector) very smart at 1m/9f: fair performer: successful in maiden (struggled to land odds of 5/1 on) at Thirsk and 4-runner minor event (gradually quickening modest pace) at Wolverhampton in September: broke blood vessel when tailed off in Zetland Stakes at Newmarket following month: very much a staying type: sent to G. Jones in USA. *H. R. A. Cecil* **81**

ELLAFITZETTY (IRE) 3 b.f. Ela-Mana-Mou 132 – Etty 81 (Relko 136) [1991 6f⁴ 7d 7m 10m⁵ 1992 14.6g 14.1g 16m⁴ 16.1d*] neat filly: has a quick action: modest performer: won claimer (claimed to join M. Pipe £3,430) at Warwick in July by 12 lengths: suited by a thorough test of stamina: acts on good to firm and dead ground: probably best in blinkers: also hooded once: sold 750 gns Newmarket Autumn Sales. *R. F. Johnson Houghton* **60**

ELLA STREET 5 b.m. King of Spain 121 – More Fun (Malicious) [1991 10m 12f 10g⁶ 1992 10.5g 8g] workmanlike mare: no worthwhile form: sold 1,700 gns Ascot December Sales. *Capt. J. Wilson* **–**

ELLE SHAPED (IRE) 2 b.g. (Apr 18) Treasure Kay 114 – Mamie's Joy (Prince Tenderfoot (USA) 126) [1992 5g⁶ 5.1g* 5m* 5f⁴ 5m 5g⁵ 6v] IR 1,000Y, 11,500 2-y-o: good-quartered gelding: carries condition: moderate mover: second reported foal: half-brother to a temperamental animal: dam lightly raced in Ireland: fairly useful performer: successful in maiden at Chester and 3-runner minor event at Goodwood in May: fourth in Norfolk Stakes following month: off course 8 weeks, well below form in 6f Racecall Gold Trophy at Redcar: speedy: acts on firm ground. *R. Hannon* **87**

EL NIDO 4 ch.g. Adonijah 126 – Seleter (Hotfoot 126) [1991 8s 8f³ 11g* 9m* 12.2m⁶ 1992 10.1s* 12.1g* 12.4s* 12.1s² 11.9d 10.5s 10.3v 12.4v]leggy, workmanlike gelding: has a round action: progressed into fairly useful handicapper on first 4 starts in early-spring, winning twice at Newcastle and once at Edinburgh: no form after near 5-month lay-off: effective from 1¼m to 1½m: easily best efforts with some give in the ground: wears crossed noseband nowadays: is held up. *M. J. Camacho* **74** d

Mr R. E. Sangster's "El Prado"

EL NINO (IRE)   2 b.c. (Apr 20) Fairy King (USA) – Calla (Captain's Gig (USA))   **57**
[1992 6s 6m⁵ 6d³] 4,500F, 2,800Y: smallish, sturdy colt: has quick action: half-brother to 1988 Irish 2-y-o 6f winner Ballyewry (by Prince Tenderfoot) and 2 winners abroad: dam Irish 4-y-o 1¾m winner: modest maiden: claimed to join M. Dixon £6,050 final start: subsequently withdrawn lame at start in late-September: will be better suited by 7f: acts on good to firm ground. *R. Hannon*

EL PRADO (IRE)   3 gr.c. Sadler's Wells (USA) 132 – Lady Capulet (USA) 116   **108**
(Sir Ivor 135) [1991 6g* 6g* 6.3m² 7m* 7m 8s* 1992 10m⁵ 8s 8s] strong, lengthy Irish colt: sort to carry condition: smart performer at 2 yrs: reportedly sprained a joint in March, and not seen out until late-July as 3-y-o: ran in Scottish Classic at Ayr, in Prix Jacques le Marois at Deauville (seventh, best effort in 1992) and Prix du Moulin de Longchamp: should have stayed 1¼m: won on good to firm ground, but easily best effort on soft: tended to race with head high and not an easy ride: reportedly retired to stud in USA. *M. V. O'Brien, Ireland*

EL RABAB (USA)   3 br.f. Roberto (USA) 131 – Brave Raj (USA) (Rajab (USA))   **66**
[1991 6m⁵ 8.1g* 8.1d³ 1992 8m 10g² 11.6m⁵ 12g 11.5m³ 11.8d] sturdy, attractive filly: good mover: fair form: easily best efforts in handicaps in 1992 when placed: stayed 11.6f: acted on good to firm and dead ground: visits Kalaglow. *H. Thomson Jones*

ELSA   3 gr.f. Green Ruby (USA) 104 – Classey (Dubassoff (USA)) [1991 6.1g 6.1m   **45**
7m 8f 1992 8.9v 11g⁶ 10f⁴ 12g 14.6m² 14.6d³ 11.7d⁶ 17.2s] leggy, sparely-made filly: moderate mover: modest plater: stays 14.6f: acts on firm and dead going. *R. J. Holder*

ELSALS   3 b.c. Sizzling Melody 117 – Queen And Country (Town And Country   **74**
124) [1991 NR 1992 6m* 6g 7d 7.1s*] 43,000Y: leggy, workmanlike colt: second foal: dam twice-raced half-sister to Ayr Gold Cup winner Polly's Brother: won maiden at Redcar in August, then showed improved form to land handicap at Chepstow in October when blinkered for the first time: stays 7f well. *H. Thomson Jones*

ELSHARH (IRE)   3 br.c. Sure Blade (USA) 130 – Urjwan (USA) 98 (Seattle Slew   **47 d**
(USA)) [1991 7.5f 7f⁶ 8f 8.2m 8m 1992 a8g³ 12.3s 12g 10g 14.6m⁴] smallish,

close-coupled colt: poor maiden: no form (including when blinkered in seller) after reappearance at Southwell: should be suited by 1¼m + . *J. A. Glover*

ELSKA DIG   2 b.f. (Mar 11) Sayf El Arab (USA) 127 – Galetzky 86 (Radetzky 123)   –
[1992 a6g] 2,700Y: fourth living foal: half-sister to 3-y-o Hazy Prospect (by Hadeer) and 1990 2-y-o 5f winner Good Time Boy (by Good Times): dam won twice at 1m and stayed 1¼m: 12/1 from 5/1, tailed off in 11-runner maiden at Southwell in December. *W. Jarvis*

ELSURIMO (GER)   5 b. or br.h. Surumu (GER) – Elke (GER) (Authi 123) [1991 **101**
16m* 16g* 12f² 9.5g 20d4 15.5d5 1992 12d 16g3 12g3 16g* 16m6 16s4] lengthy German-bred horse: useful performer, winner of German St Leger in 1990: best runs in 1992 over 2m, successful in Hamburg minor event in June: creditable sixth to Further Flight in Goodwood Cup, struggling from before halfway but keeping on dourly final 1f: stays very well: acts on good to firm and soft ground. *B. Schutz, Germany*

EL TARANDA   3 ch.f. Ela-Mana-Mou 132 – Bustara 92 (Busted 134) [1991 8s5   **61**
1992 10d² 9.9m5 12.2d6 12v²] sparely-made filly: consistent maiden: should have stayed 1¾m +: acted on good to firm and heavy ground: visits Warrshan. *G. Wragg*

ELTON LEDGER (IRE)   3 b.g. Cyrano de Bergerac 120 – Princess of Nashua
(Crowned Prince (USA) 128) [1991 5m³ 5m² 6g² 5g4 6g 6f² 6g* 6m² 6m 6g 1992 7s 7.6s 7m] good-topped gelding: fair juvenile for J. Berry: no form in 1992: stays 6f: acts on good to firm ground. *A. A. Scott*

EL VOLADOR   5 br.h. Beldale Flutter (USA) 130 – Pharjoy (FR) 85 (Pharly (FR)   **77**
130) [1991 a10g 8s 9m5 10g 10g² 10.1d a10g a7g* 1992 a7g* a8g² a8g² 8m³ 8d 10m²
12m* 12d 11.9f³ a10g a12g* a12g* a12g*] sturdy, workmanlike horse: poor mover: fairly useful handicapper and had a very good season overall: won at Lingfield and Goodwood in first half of year: withdrawn lame at start in July and off course 4 months: won novice hurdle in November and returned better than ever at Lingfield, winning 3 times in December, in determined fashion last time: effective from 7f to 1½m: goes well on top-of-the-ground and equitrack, mostly below form on dead: best held up: tough. *R. J. O'Sullivan*

ELWAZIR (USA)   3 b. or br.c. The Minstrel (CAN) 135 – Romeo's Coquette   **62**
(USA) (Gallant Romeo (USA)) [1991 6g 1992 6s 7m5 9m4 8m4 8m4 a12g6 8.9g 6.9v] compact colt: fair maiden on his day: below form, including in seller, last 5 starts: stays 9f: acts on good to firm ground: sold out of P. Walwyn's stable 4,000 gns Newmarket July Sales after fifth 3-y-o start. *D. Marks*

EL YASAF (IRE)   4 b.c. Sayf El Arab (USA) 127 – Winsong Melody (Music   **90**
Maestro 119) [1991 5m4 5d* 5m 5d* 5d 5g 6f 5m6 5m5 5.2g 1992 5s5 5g 5m5 6g5 5f5
5g4 5m 5m 6d 5m 5.2s 6s] small, sturdy colt: fairly useful but inconsistent handicapper: trained first 4 starts by G. Eden: flattered when appearing to excel in King's Stand Stakes at Royal Ascot on first of 5 outings for M. Pipe: effective at 5f and 6f: acts on firm and soft ground. *Miss Gay Kelleway*

EMAURA   3 ch.f. Dominion 123 – Klaire 85 (Klairon 131) [1991 5m 5g 1992 8d 6m5   **61**
6m4 8h* 8m³ 8f 8.1d² 8f* 8d4 8d 8s] leggy, sparely-made filly: modest handicapper: trained until after third start by D. Elsworth: game winner at Bath in May and August: below form last 2 starts: best efforts over 1m: acts on hard and dead ground: front runner. *K. O. Cunningham-Brown*

EMBANKMENT (IRE)   2 b.c. (Apr 15) Tate Gallery (USA) 117 – Great Leighs   **81**
87 (Vaigly Great 127) [1992 6g6 6m³ 6s² 7m4 7.3g² 7.9d4 7s³ 7m³] 34,000Y: good-quartered colt: moderate mover: second foal: dam 1m winner, is half-sister to useful 2-y-o 6f winner Ulla Laing: fairly useful and consistent maiden: looked a difficult ride at Salisbury penultimate outing, wandering left and right in front (possibly ground): stays 1m: below best on soft going. *R. Hannon*

EMERALD EARS   3 ch.f. Dublin Lad 116 – Impish Ears 65 (Import 127) [1991   **42**
7.5f 8.3g² 7m6 7m 1992 7d* 7g 7.5m 8f 8g 8g 10g4 10s 10.5s³ 8g a6g a8g] workmanlike filly: modest and inconsistent plater: won at Catterick (no bid) in March: sold out of E. Weymes's stable 1,800 gns Doncaster October Sales after ninth start: well held afterwards: effective from 7f to 10.5f: needs some give in the ground: blinkered twice, running creditably first occasion. *R. J. Hodges*

EMERALD SANDS   2 b.f. (Apr 30) Green Desert (USA) 127 – Bold Flawless   **32**
(USA) 73 (Bold Bidder) [1992 7g 8g] small filly: seventh foal: half-sister to 3-y-o Quest For The Best (by Rainbow Quest) and 3 winners, including useful 1988 2-y-o 6f and 7f winner Life At The Top (by Habitat): dam 1½m winner: poor form, beaten, in maidens at Yarmouth (slowly away) and Leicester. *A. C. Stewart*

EMERALD SUNSET 7 b.g. Red Sunset 120 – Kelly's Curl (Pitskelly 122) [1991 —
NR 1992 16m] modest ex-Irish maiden: no form on flat here: fair handicap hurdler,
winner in October. *A. R. Davison*

EMIGRATOR 3 b.g. Sharrood (USA) 124 – Clicquot 101 (Bold Lad (IRE) 133) —
[1991 NR 1992 7g 6g⁴ 6m] 24,000Y: unfurnished gelding: half-brother to smart
sprinter Premiere Cuvee (by Formidable): dam 5f sprinter: well beaten in maidens
in first half of 1992: trained debut by R. Guest: blinkered final start: sold 640 gns
Newmarket July Sales. *G. Blum*

EMILY ALLAN (IRE) 3 b.f. Shirley Heights 130 – St Louis Sue (FR) 79 —
(Nonoalco (USA) 131) [1991 NR 1992 8d 8d 8d a10g] sparely-made filly: seventh foal:
half-sister to very useful sprinter Whippet (by Sparkler): dam stayed 1¼m: no
worthwhile form. *K. O. Cunningham-Brown*

EMIR ALBADOU (USA) 3 ch.c. Bering 136 – Star Pastures 124 (Northfields 78
(USA)) [1991 NR 1992 7m³ 7.9g² 6.1s² 7d] 90,000Y: well-made colt: fifth foal:
half-brother to 7f winner Turbulent River (by Riverman), fairly useful middle-
distance stayer Lord Justice (by Alleged) and useful Irish 7f to 13f winner Esprit
d'Etoile (by Spectacular Bid): dam won at 6f to 1m, including in stakes company in
USA, and second in 1¼m Sun Chariot Stakes: well below form after placed in
maidens at Newmarket and York in autumn on first 2 starts: stays 1m: seems suited
by a sound surface. *M. R. Stoute*

EMMANDEE 2 br.g. (Apr 13) Mummy's Game 120 – Second Event 86 (Fine 31
Blade (USA) 121) [1992 5f 5g 7.1m⁶ 7.5d 7.5m 8.2d] 1,500F, 2,200F: tall, rather leggy
gelding: half-brother to a winner in Holland: dam 5f to 1½m winner, is out of
half-sister to Irish 2000 Guineas winner Furry Glen: poor maiden: blinkered last 2
starts: should stay 7f. *M. W. Easterby*

EMMA VICTORIA 4 b.f. Dominion 123 – Gwiffina 87 (Welsh Saint 126) [1991 —
10m 7g 10.2g 8.2g³ 10.5m⁵ 10f 10.5d 11d 1992 13.8d 8.2d⁶ a12g 10m 14.6d] leggy filly:
seems of little account. *T. Kersey*

EMPEEKA (USA) 3 b.g. At The Threshold (USA) – Laughing Ruler (USA) —
(Iron Ruler (USA)) [1991 a6g a6g 7g 7f³ 6g a7g² a7g* a7g² 1992 a6g² a7g⁵ 6d a7g³ a77 ?
7d a6g] sturdy gelding: modest performer but inconsistent: creditable third in
Southwell claimer in September on first run for 5 months but ran badly afterwards:
has worn tongue strap: should stay 1m: easily best form on fibresand: hooded
nowadays: usually claimer ridden: sold 2,100 gns Doncaster November Sales. *W. A.
O'Gorman*

EMPEROR ALEXANDER (IRE) 4 b.g. Tender King 123 – Persian Apple 67
(USA) (No Robbery) [1991 10.1m³ 10.2g⁵ a12g⁵ 10m 10g* 11d² 1992 12d 10.3g a12g²
a13g⁵] lengthy, rather unfurnished gelding: good walker: fair performer: not seen
out in 1992 until October: stays 13f: acts on dead ground and all-weather surfaces. *N.
A. Smith*

EMPEROR CHANG (USA) 5 b.g. Wavering Monarch (USA) – Movin Mitzi 36
(USA) (L'Heureux (USA)) [1991 12.3d 12f 10.6g 8.3m 10m 10.5g⁴ 10.5d 1992 a13g
11.9d⁶ 14m⁶ 13m⁶ 14.6g⁴] compact gelding: poor handicapper: stays 1½m: acts on
good to firm ground: below form when blinkered. *R. Hollinshead*

EMPEROR JONES (USA) 2 b.c. (Mar 25) Danzig (USA) – Qui Royalty (USA) 96 p
(Native Royalty (USA)) [1992 7g* 7d³ 7d*] quite attractive colt: eighth foal: brother
to 2 winners, both at 6f at 2 yrs, notably very useful Majlood, closely related to
useful Irish 3-y-o 1m and 1¼m winner Thyer (by Nijinsky) and Bakharoff (by The
Minstrel) and half-brother to 2 winners, including Sum (by Spectacular Bid),
successful at up to 1¼m, including in graded stakes: dam very useful stakes-placed
winner at up to 1m: successful in autumn in maiden at Newmarket and minor event
(by 3½ lengths from Taahhub) at York, forging clear from 2f out: pulled hard and
found little off bridle in Ascot minor event: will stay 1m: tended to carry head bit
high last 2 starts, also wandered final one: possibly capable of better. *J. H. M. Gosden*

EMPERORS WARRIOR 6 ch.g. High Line 125 – Cocoban (Targowice (USA) —
130) [1991 NR 1992 14.1d 14.6s] lengthy gelding: moderate mover: on the downgrade: stays 2m: acts on firm and dead going. *C. D. Broad*

EMPIRE BLUE 9 b.g. Dominion 123 – Bold Blue 82 (Targowice (USA) 130) 72
[1991 NR 1992 10d 12.5g 12.3g² 16m⁴ 14m 16f⁴ 14d⁵ 14g* 16d⁵] workmanlike
gelding: useful handicapper at 7 yrs, not so good nowadays: won at Kempton in
September: best form at up to 1¾m: acts on good to firm and heavy ground:
blinkered early in career: often bandaged. *P. F. I. Cole*

EMPIRE POOL 2 ch.g. (Feb 12) Sharrood (USA) 124 – Reflection 111 (Mill Reef 88
(USA) 141) [1992 6m⁵ 7.1g⁴ 7f* 7g⁵ 8g⁵ 7g] rather leggy, close-coupled colt: has a

fluent, round action: fourth foal: half-brother to 3-y-o 6f winner Ingenuity and ungenuine 7f (at 2 yrs) and 1¼m winner Hall of Mirrors (both by Clever Trick): dam, 2-y-o 7f winner, disappointed as 3-y-o: landed odds in maiden in August: fairly useful form after in £14,700 event at York, Criterium de l'Ouest at Craon and Ascot nursery: will prove better suited by 1m than 7f: acts on firm ground. *Lord Huntingdon*

EMRYS 9 ch.g. Welsh Pageant 132 – Sun Approach 84 (Sun Prince 128) [1991 NR 1992 10.2m 10.2f3 12m] workmanlike gelding: poor handicapper: stays 1½m: acts on any going: won over fences in September. *D. Burchell*   **36**

EN ATTENDANT (FR) 4 ch.g. Bairn (USA) 126 – Vizenia (Vitiges (FR) 132) [1991 7m5 10.1s3 10.1g3 8g* 6g4 7.6m 7d6 10g5 7m3 7m* 7d5 1992 8g 7f 7.5g 7f* 7.5m* 8d 7.9s3 7d4] useful-looking gelding: fairly useful handicapper: won at Doncaster and Beverley (impressively) in September: best at 7f/1m: probably acts on any going: sometimes hangs and finds little: suited by waiting tactics. *B. Hanbury*   **91**

ENAYA 3 br.f. Caerleon (USA) 132 – Ardassine (Ahonoora 122) [1991 6s* 7m2 1992 10.4m4 8m3 7g 10m4 10.3m 8g 7.9s] leggy, lengthy filly: fair but inconsistent performer: appeared to run very well in slowly-run minor event at Newmarket fourth start: better at 1¼m than shorter: acted on good to firm and soft ground: visits Lycius. *R. W. Armstrong*   **77**

ENCHANTED FLYER 5 b.h. Doulab (USA) 115 – Enchanted 116 (Song 132) [1991 9m 10g 12.2g 1992 10d 10g 8.5m 7d] angular, close-coupled horse: poor maiden. *T. W. Donnelly*   **–**

ENCORE UNE FOIS (IRE) 3 b.f. Shirley Heights 130 – Guest Performer 117 (Be My Guest (USA) 126) [1991 8.1g3 8g3 1992 8d4 10.5d3 12.1m6 11.9m* 14.8g* 14.6f 16m] lengthy filly: narrowly won maiden at Haydock and handicap at Newmarket in August: well beaten in handicaps after: should prove as effective at 2m: acts on good to firm ground and dead: ran moderately when sweating profusely once: sometimes wears crossed noseband: sold 21,000 gns Newmarket December Sales. *P. W. Chapple-Hyam*   **84**

ENDEARING VAL 2 ch.f. (Feb 8) Entitled 126 – Corvalent 80 (Busted 134) [1992 8g 8m] sparely-made filly: first foal: dam showed ability only on debut: soundly beaten in autumn maidens at Leicester and Newmarket. *C. N. Allen*   **33**

ENDOLI (USA) 5 b.h. Assert 134 – Grabelst (USA) (Graustark) [1991 14.6s 10d* 14g* 14m5 12m3 12g 12g2 13.9g5 12s5 12m3 16g2 1992 13.3f* 20f4] strong, lengthy horse: good mover: consistent performer: won listed event at Newbury in May by length from Mashaallah: not seen out again after good fourth to Drum Taps in Gold Cup at Royal Ascot following month: effective at around 1½m to 2½m: probably acts on any going. *C. E. Brittain*   **108**

ENERGIC (IRE) 3 b.g. Burslem 123 – Advocada (FR) (Advocator) [1991 5s5 5g 6f 5m 7.5f3 7m 8m6 1992 a8g5 a7g* a7g4 a7g2 a8g6] sparely-made gelding: moderate mover: inconsistent handicapper: won at Southwell in January: not seen out after following month: effective at 7f/1m: acts on firm ground and fibresand: below form when blinkered once: sold 950 gns Newmarket Autumn Sales. *C. N. Allen*   **52**

ENFANT DU PARADIS (IRE) 4 b.f. Shernazar 131 – Fille de L'Orne (FR) (Jim French (USA)) [1991 11m 9m5 10m6 14.6g4 15s* 13d 15.8f6 14.6m2 14.6m3 16.1m 16.9m4 15.1g 13.8m2 13.6d 1992 a14g3 a14g a14g 14.6g4 16.9g 14.6g 14.6m5 15.8g4 14.9g2 14.6g 14.1d4 14.6d6 16d6] small filly: inconsistent staying handicapper: acts on good to firm and soft going: successful twice over hurdles in October. *P. D. Evans*   **41**

ENHARMONIC (USA) 5 ch.h. Diesis 133 – Contralto 100 (Busted 134) [1991 8.5f4 7g 8g* 8g* 8g4 1992 8.1g 8f4 9g2 8g3 8.5f] angular, good-topped horse: very useful performer: ran well in 1992 after reappearance, placed in Group 3 events at Dortmund and Hoppegarten and close seventh in Arlington handicap: stays 9f: yet to race on soft going, acts on any other: headstrong, best held up. *Lord Huntingdon*   **108**

ENKINDLE 5 b.m. Relkino 131 – Nelion 102 (Grey Sovereign 128§) [1991 12.2m5 10.2m 11f5 a12g 17.9f5 16.2f3 16m 18.1m3 1992 17.1m5 16.1m6 18g 13.6f 15.1m] leggy, close-coupled mare: on the downgrade: stays well: acts on firm ground: below form blinkered. *B. W. Murray*   **–**

ENQELAAB (USA) 4 b.g. Chief's Crown (USA) – Affirmatively (USA) (Affirmed (USA)) [1991 11.5m5 1992 12v6 14s3 16g* 20m 14g* 16g3 12g4 12g 16d] strong, close-coupled gelding: maiden when trained here as 3-y-o by M. Stoute: successful in 1992 in Clonmel maiden and minor race at Bellewstown: effective at   **79**

1½m to 2m (stiff task at 2½m in Ascot Stakes): acts on good to firm ground. *M. A. O'Toole, Ireland*

ENTERPRISE LADY (FR)   5 ch.m. Gorytus (USA) 132 – Calder Hall (Grundy   –
137) [1991 11.7g 7g³ 10.1d 8.3g 8f 8.3m 1992 a10g a7g a12g⁵] leggy, lengthy mare: on the downgrade. *M. Williams*

ENVIRONMENT FRIEND   4 gr.c. Cozzene (USA) – Water Woo (USA) 102 **122**
(Tom Rolfe) [1991 8g³ 8m⁵ 10.5g* 12f 10d* 10.4g⁵ 10d² 10m 1992 8.1g 10d⁶ 12m⁵ 10m³] close-coupled, useful-looking colt: top class at best at 3 yrs, won Dante Stakes and Eclipse: took a long time to strike form in 1992 after damaging a lung in the spring but looked more like his old self in Dubai Champion Stakes at Newmarket, staying-on third to Rodrigo de Triano: should have been effective at 1½m: acted on good to firm and dead ground: best held up: retired to Stetchworth Park Stud, Newmarket, fee £4,000 (live foal). *J. R. Fanshawe*

EPISODE ONE   2 br.f. (Mar 17) Vaigly Great 127 – Jaisalmer 97 (Castle Keep   –
121) [1992 6m 6d] 4,000Y: leggy, angular filly: first foal: dam suited by 6f at 2 yrs, only once raced after: well beaten in autumn maidens: sold 700 gns Ascot November Sales. *G. Lewis*

EPSOM DREAM   2 b.f. (Feb 8) Salse (USA) 128 – Miss Derby (USA) (Master   **47**
Derby (USA)) [1992 6d 5m⁴ 7g 7d] leggy, workmanlike filly: has a round action: half-sister to several winners, including 7f winner Orba Gold (by Gold Crest) and 1985 French 2-y-o 6f winner Madame Nureyev (by Nureyev): dam, minor winner in USA, is from very good family: failed to progress after fourth in Beverley maiden in September: blinkered final start: should be suited by further than 5f: sold 3,950 gns Doncaster October Sales. *J. Etherington*

EQUITY CARD (IRE)   4 b.g. King of Clubs 124 – Carntino (Bustino 136) [1991   **71**
10g 12.3g² 1992 14.6g³ 14g 18.1g³ 12g 13.1s 16d⁵] close-coupled gelding: fair but inconsistent handicapper: suited by thorough stamina test: acts on dead ground. *G. A. Pritchard-Gordon*

Mr W. J. Gredley's "Environment Friend"

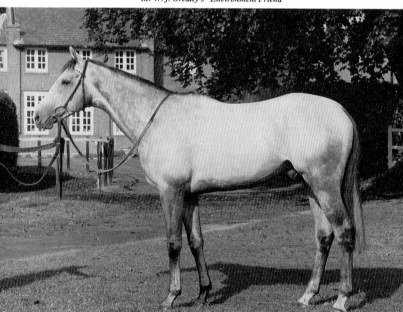

ERDELISTAN (FR) 5 br.h. Lashkari 128 – Eunomia (FR) (Abdos 134) [1991 **117**
10d* 11g* 12g² 10g² 11g⁵ 1992 10v* 11g² 12s* 12d⁶ 11d* 12s³ 10v⁶] very useful
Italian performer: successful at Milan (has gained his last 6 wins there) in listed
races in April and June and, putting up best effort of 1992, Group 3 event in
September beating Half A Tick by a length: ran moderately afterwards: stays 1½m
well: acts on any going. *L. d'Auria, Italy*

EREVNON 5 b.h. Rainbow Quest (USA) 134 – Embryo (Busted 134) [1991 12s –
12.2d⁶ 14.1f² 20g 12g⁶ a12g 1992 a12g a14g⁶ 12.3g⁴ a12g] sturdy horse: rated 62 at 4
yrs: no form in 1992: stayed 1¾m: acted on firm ground, seemed unsuited by soft:
dead. *J. L. Harris*

ERGANA 5 b.m. The Wonder (FR) 129 – Eloura (FR) (Top Ville 129) [1991 10f
10f² 8g⁵ 14.1g 8f 9.7f² 9.7m⁵ 1992 a10g] leggy mare: poor handicapper: stayed 1¼m:
acted on firm ground: dead. *W. Holden*

ERGON 3 ch.f. Stanford 121§ – Heavenly Harmony 47 (Music Boy 124) [1991 a7g **43**
1992 7m³ 6g⁴ 6f⁶ 8.3g] lengthy, good-quartered filly: poor maiden: stays 7f: acts on
good to firm ground: sold 1,400 gns Ascot November Sales. *D. J. S. Cosgrove*

ERICOLIN (IRE) 2 ch.c. (Jan 31) Ahonoora 122 – Pixie Erin 110 (Golden Fleece **79** p
(USA) 133) [1992 7d⁵ 8.1g⁴] 100,000Y: lengthy colt: first foal: dam 7f to 1¼m
winner, is half-sister to smart middle-distance colt Skaramanga, and Star Pastures:
fifth in £8,600 event at Newbury in July: better for race and still green, staying-on
fourth of 6 to Geisway in minor event at Sandown 2 months after: will improve again,
particularly over middle distances, and win a race. *C. E. Brittain*

ERIK ODIN 5 b.g. Nordico (USA) – Assurance (FR) (Timmy Lad 130) [1991 a6g **40**
a6g a6g³ a6g³ a7g a6g* a6g a6g a6g 1992 a6g⁵ 7g a6g a7g] sturdy, lengthy gelding:
poor mover: poor handicapper nowadays: stays 7f and needs further than 5f: has
worn eyeshield: has been bandaged: hard to train. *Mrs L. Piggott*

ERIN'S TOWN 6 b.g. Town And Country 124 – Erin's Hospitality (Go-Tobann)
[1991 NR 1992 12d a12g a16g] smallish, workmanlike gelding: rated 50 as 4-y-o: no
form in handicaps in 1992: should have stayed beyond 1½m: dead. *W. Carter*

ERINY (USA) 3 b.g. Erins Isle 121 – Memorable Girl (USA) (Iron Ruler (USA)) **69**
[1991 7g³ 7.5f 7m³ 8m 8.2m 7m 1992 a8g* 8.9s* a10g⁴ 8.3s⁵ 8f⁵ a8g* a8g³ 8.9m 9s]
leggy, close-coupled gelding: moderate mover: none too consistent handicapper:
won at Southwell (2) and Wolverhampton in between in first half of 1992: should
stay beyond 9f: acts on soft ground and fibresand: below form when blinkered once:
suitable mount for apprentice: sold to join J. Bottomley 8,400 gns Newmarket
Autumn Sales. *S. G. Norton*

ERLEMO 3 b.c. Mummy's Game 120 – Empress Catherine 73 (Welsh Pageant **45**
132) [1991 7.1s 7d 7m 8s³ 8g 7.6m 1992 10d 11.6m 10g 12.1m³ 14g³ 11.6m 12f 12.3m
12d 15.4g² 16g 12s 16.1s] leggy, good-topped colt: moderate mover: inconsistent
maiden: should stay 2m: acts on soft ground: usually blinkered: sold to join W. Clay
4,500 gns Ascot November Sales. *C. J. Benstead*

ERLKING (IRE) 2 b.c. (Mar 30) Fairy King (USA) – Cape of Storms (Fordham **74**
(USA) 117) [1992 6m⁵ 7m 6m⁴ 8.5d² 8d* a7g²] 5,200Y: leggy, close-coupled colt:
fourth foal: dam (well beaten at 2 yrs) out of staying half-sister to top-class sprinter
Sandford Lad: progressive form in nurseries last 3 starts: short-head winner at Bath
in September: good second at Lingfield over 3 months later: will be suited by middle
distances. *Lord Huntingdon*

ERNESTAN 3 ch.c. Stanford 121§ – Lobela 77 (Lorenzaccio 130) [1991 5d* 5m* **93**
5m* 6m* 7g⁴ 1992 8g 7g² 8f² 7f* 8.9d 7s 7g⁵] tall, leggy, lengthy colt: second in
small-field minor events before landing odds in one at Catterick in July: form after
only when fair fifth in Doncaster apprentice handicap: stays 1m: suited by a sound
surface: tends to hang under pressure: sold 23,000 gns Newmarket Autumn Sales.
M. H. Easterby

ERREMA 7 b.m. Workboy 123 – Piethorne 86 (Fine Blade (USA) 121) [1991 NR **50**
1992 10.1s 8d² 8.1g² 8d² 8.5m 9.2d⁴ 8m³ 8.2m 8m⁶ 10.8g 8g⁶] close-coupled mare:
poor handicapper: stayed 1¼m well: acted on good to firm and dead ground: below
form when visored once: sometimes carried head high: in foal. *C. Tinkler*

ERRIS EXPRESS 7 b.g. Bay Express 130 – Royal Home 69 (Royal Palace 131) **51**
[1991 a6g³ a5g* a7g⁴ a7g* a6g* a6g² 5m⁵ 6m⁶ 6d 5m⁵ 5m 5m 5.2f⁶ 1992 a6g⁶ a6g⁶
6d 7g 7.1m 6m 5m² 5.1m² 5g⁴ 5d] good-bodied gelding: carries condition: poor
mover: rated 79 at best in 1991: only plating class nowadays: has won over 7f, but
best form at shorter: acts on firm and dead ground: below form when blinkered
once: trained reappearance by K. Ivory, next 7 starts by J. Moore. *R. Hannon*

ERTLON 2 b.c. (Mar 20) Shareef Dancer (USA) 135 – Sharpina (Sharpen Up 127) 80 p
[1992 7.6s³ 8g⁵] IR 25,000Y: close-coupled colt: brother to 1989 2-y-o 5f winner
Alriyaah and half-brother to 7f and 1¼m winner Paddy Egan (by Tap On Wood): dam
never ran: much better effort at Newmarket in October when keeping-on fifth of 9 to
Shaiba in minor event: will stay 1¼m: may well progress again. *C. E. Brittain*

ESBOOAIN (FR) 3 b.c. Rainbow Quest (USA) 134 – Wind Spring (FR) (Baldric 76
II 131) [1991 7g⁵ 8m⁵ 1992 10d³ 10v⁶ 10.3f⁶ 12g⁵ 12m² 12.2d³ 12v*] rather leggy,
good-topped colt: fair handicapper: won maiden at Folkestone in November: better
at 1½m than shorter: acts on good to firm and heavy ground: sent to Dubai. *L. M.
Cumani*

ESCADARO (USA) 3 b.g. Liloy (FR) 124 – Mlle Chanteuse (USA) (The 42
Minstrel (CAN) 135) [1991 7m 1992 a8g 9.9g 12d⁵ 14.6g⁴ 16.2g 16f³ 15.1m⁴ a14g⁴
13.8f³ a16g⁴] leggy gelding: poor staying maiden: acts on firm going and fibresand:
usually blinkered/visored nowadays. *S. G. Norton*

ESCAPE TALK 5 gr.m. Gabitat 119 – Getaway Girl 63 (Capistrano 120) [1991 27
8g⁴ 8h³ 9.9m³ 10g³ 14.6g 12.2g 11f³ 8f⁶ 12g 12f 1992 a8g 10m⁶ 11f 10f⁵ 10.3g⁴ 12m*
12f³ 12.2g] smallish, close-coupled mare: moderate mover: poor handicapper: won
selling event (no bid) at Beverley in July: effective from around 1¼m to 13.8f: acts
on firm and dead ground: below form when blinkered once: usually soon ridden
along, but genuine. *J. Dooler*

ESPRIT FORT (USA) 3 b.f. Last Tycoon 131 – Spirit of The Wind (USA) (Little 62
Current (USA)) [1991 6m 6.1d³ a8g² a7g a7g⁴ 1992 10.2f⁵ 10s⁴ 9.7m⁴ 12s⁶ 9.7v⁴]
leggy, sparely-made filly: consistent maiden handicapper: effective at 1¼m to 1½m:
acts on any going. *P. W. Chapple-Hyam*

ESSAYEFFSEE 3 b.g. Precocious 126 – Floreal 68 (Formidable (USA) 125) 53
[1991 6g 5g³ 6m⁶ 6m³ 7m³ 7.9g⁵ 7m⁴ 6m 5d 1992 7g 8m³ 9f 8m 8m 9d 11d⁴ 9.2v⁵
8g²] workmanlike gelding: inconsistent maiden: effective at 1m to 11f: acts on good
to firm ground and dead: usually blinkered/bandaged before. *M. H. Easterby*

ESS-PEE-CEE 2 b.f. (Apr 23) Skyliner 117 – Jacqui Joy 63 (Music Boy 124) [1992 – §
5g 7g a5g] smallish, close-coupled filly: moderate mover: second foal: dam best at
5f: no sign of ability and has looked temperamental, twice hanging badly. *W. Clay*

ESTHAL (IRE) 2 b.c. (Feb 17) Kalaglow 132 – Chevrefeuille 87 (Ile de Bourbon 60 p
(USA) 133) [1992 5d² 6d 5s*] 2,900 2-y-o: leggy colt: second foal: dam 12.2f winner
out of Vielle: claimer ridden, readily won maiden at Wolverhampton in September
by length: should prove suited by 6f +. *R. J. Hodges*

ETERNAL 3 ch.f. Kris 135 – Aryenne (FR) (Green Dancer (USA) 132) [1991 –
NR 1992 10.5d] unfurnished filly: has a long stride: moderate walker: fifth foal:
half-sister to Quest For Fame, very useful stayer Silver Rainbow (both by Rainbow
Quest) and 1¼m winner In Orbit (by Habitat): dam, from fine family, won Criterium
des Pouliches and Poule d'Essai des Pouliches: co-favourite and tongue tied down,
pulled hard and led over 7f in maiden at Haydock in September on only start: to stud.
R. Charlton

ETERNAL FLAME 4 br.f. Primo Dominie 121 – Cameroun 106 (African Sky 68
124) [1991 7m* 8.5m* a8g⁴ 8.1m² 7.1m 8g 1992 8m² 7m* 7f 7m² 7m 8f³ 8.5d²
8d² 8m⁶ 9g] lengthy filly: largely consistent handicapper: won at Redcar in June:
effective at 7f to 8.5f: acts on firm and dead ground: suitable mount for apprentice. *J.
W. Hills*

ETIQUETTE 3 b.f. Law Society (USA) 130 – Livry (USA) (Lyphard (USA) 132) 66
[1991 NR 1992 10m⁵ 12d³ 10.5d⁴ 12.1s⁵ a12g²] 50,000Y: leggy, unfurnished filly: first
foal: dam French 11f winner, is half-sister to Defensive Play, also family of Musical
Bliss: fair maiden: will stay beyond 1½m: acts on good to firm and dead ground and
on equitrack. *Lord Huntingdon*

EUPHONIC 2 br.g. (Mar 25) Elegant Air 119 – Monalda (FR) (Claude) [1992 7g 8f 55
8s⁶] rangy gelding: sixth reported living foal: half-brother to 1½m winner Twenty
One Red (by Dunphy) and a winner in Italy by Persian Bold: dam won in Italy and is
half-sister to Italian Derby winner Marracci: plating-class form in maidens: gives
impression will be better suited by 1¼m. *I. A. Balding*

EUPHONIC (USA) 3 ch.f. The Minstrel (CAN) 135 – Razyana (USA) 87 (His 113
Majesty (USA)) [1991 7g* 1992 8g⁴ 8m⁵ 7f 7g* 7g* a7f⁵ 8.5f⁵] big, useful-looking
filly: third foal: closely related to high-class sprinter Danehill (by Danzig), also 7f
winner and third in 2000 Guineas: dam, placed over 7f and 1¼m from 3 starts, is out
of half-sister to Northern Dancer: won listed race at Saint-Cloud in July: good fifth to
Culture Vulture in Poule d'Essai des Pouliches at Longchamp and third to Hydro
Calido in Prix d'Astarte at Deauville: favourite and on toes, soon off bridle in Jersey

Stakes at Royal Ascot: fifth in handicaps in USA on last 2 outings: possibly better at 1m than shorter: possibly unsuited by firm ground: trained by A. Fabre until after penultimate start. *R. Frankel, USA*

EURIDICE (IRE)   3 ch.f. Woodman (USA) 126 – Arctic Kite (North Stoke 130)   **66**
[1991 NR 1992 7g 8g³ 8g³ 9s² 12.2d³ 12.4v³ 9.7v*] IR 42,000Y: angular, useful-looking filly: half-sister to 2 winners in USA: dam minor winner at up to 7f: easily justified favouritism in Folkestone seller (sold 8,000 gns) in November: effective at 9f to 1½m: sometimes edges left. *L. M. Cumani*

EUROBLAKE   5 b.g. Roscoe Blake 120 – Pie Eye 88 (Exbury 138) [1991 a7g³   **70**
a7g* a8g² a7g² 8f 7m⁶ 8m 8f 8d⁶ a6g³ a6g⁶ a8g* a7g⁶ 1992 a8g² a7g³ a8g²   a74
a8g* a8g² a8g⁴ a8g⁴ 7d* 7.5g³ 7.1g* 7.5g⁴ 7g⁴ 8f⁵ 7m* 6.9f³ 7d* 7g² 7g 7m 7f² 8g³
7.1d 7g⁶ 7d⁶] compact, good-quartered gelding: turns off-fore in: splendidly tough and had a good season in handicaps in 1992, successful at Southwell (claimer), Edinburgh and Catterick (3): effective at strongly-run 7f to 8.5f: acts on firm and dead ground and all-weather surfaces: sometimes hung markedly: held up, and ideally suited by a strongly-run race on a turning track: sold 6,000 gns Newmarket Autumn Sales, to Italy. *T. D. Barron*

EURO FESTIVAL   3 ch.c. Precocious 126 – Quisissanno 76 (Be My Guest   **99**
(USA) 126) [1991 5m⁴ 6f* 6m⁵ 6f 7g⁶ 7m 1992 6g³ 6g 6g² 7m⁴ 7.1m* 7g³ 7f⁵ 7.1d³
6g 7.1g* 8m 7.1d³] workmanlike colt: useful handicapper: successful at Sandown in May and (easily best effort) July: failed to reproduce that form, not seen out after July: suited by strongly-run race at 7f, and should stay 1m: acts on good to firm and dead ground: below form when blinkered. *Miss L. C. Siddall*

EUROFLIGHT   3 b.f. Natroun (FR) 128 – Bustling Nelly 94 (Bustino 136) [1991
6g⁴ 7m² 7g⁵ 1992 11.4m 16m⁵ 10.1f³ 11.7d] small, leggy, plain filly: poor maiden: bred to stay well: sold out of B. Hills's stable 2,800 gns Newmarket September Sales after third start. *D. R. Tucker*

EUROLINK THUNDER   2 b.c. (Mar 6) Fairy King (USA) – Prosperous Lady   **89** p
(Prince Tenderfoot (USA) 126) [1992 7g* 7d* 8g⁵] 8,000F: lengthy colt: good mover: first foal: dam unraced: progressive colt: green when comfortably winning maiden at Newbury in August and median auction event at Wolverhampton following month: beaten around 5 lengths by Taos in listed race at Ascot, keeping on unable to challenge: stays 1m: has scope, and should improve further. *J. L. Dunlop*

EUROTWIST   3 b.c. Viking (USA) – Orange Bowl (General Assembly (USA)   **67**
[1991 5f 6m⁵ 5m⁵ a7g⁵ 7f³ 7m⁶ 7m 7m 7m 1992 8s³ 12d* 12.1s* 16.2d² 12d* 12.3m⁶
12.3d 11.9s 12d 12.1v² a12g⁴] small colt: fair handicapper: easily won at Carlisle, Hamilton and Beverley in first half of 1992: best at around 1½m: may well need an easy surface: soundly beaten on fibresand. *T. D. Barron*

EVAHART   2 br.f. (Mar 24) Scottish Reel 123 – Hope And Glory (USA) 87 (Well   –
Decorated (USA)) [1992 5d 5.9g] 5,000F: workmanlike filly: first foal: dam, 2-y-o 6f winner, only season to race, is daughter of half-sister to Legal Bid and Law Society: poor form in northern maidens in autumn. *J. H. Johnson*

EVENING AFFAIR   6 b.m. Red Sunset 120 – Miss Flirt (Welsh Pageant 132)   **31**
[1991 7d 7g 9s 10g 11.8g 10.3d 1992 a10g a12g a10g³ a12g⁶ a12g⁵] lengthy, sparely-made mare: moderate mover: on the downgrade: stays 1¼m: acts on firm going: used to go well blinkered. *W. Holden*

EVENING DRESS   3 ch.f. Night Shift (USA) – Maple Rock (Music Boy 124)   –
[1991 6f 6.1f 7.1m⁴ 7g 8m a7g 1992 8.2m 10m 8.3g 9.7g] compact filly: poor maiden: should stay 1m: below form when visored: sold out of T. Thomson Jones's stable 1,300 gns Doncaster June Sales after reappearance, resold 1,000 gns Ascot November Sales. *I. Campbell*

EVENING SESSION (IRE)   3 ch.g. Burslem 123 – Icefield (Northfields   –
(USA)) [1991 6m 1992 a8g] small, sturdy gelding: twice raced, and no sign of ability. *J. Norton*

EVENING STABLES   3 b.f. Hunter's Delight – Ucando (Sir Nulli 87) [1991 NR   –
1992 8.9s 10f a12g] lengthy filly: first reported living foal: dam unraced: no worthwhile form in modest company. *J. Wharton*

EVENING STAR   6 b.m. Red Sunset 120 – Avereen (Averof 65) [1991 a8g⁶ a8g³   –
a8g 8s 8d a8g³ 8m a8g a8g a8g³ a8g³ a8g a8g 1992 a11g⁶ a8g a8g] leggy mare: on the downgrade. *A. Hide*

EVERGLADES (IRE)   4 b.c. Green Desert (USA) 127 – Glowing With Pride   **84**
114 (Ile de Bourbon (USA) 133) [1991 8s⁴ 7g² 1992 6f 6g 6m 6d⁵ 6.1m* 7m 6g*]
sturdy colt: carries condition: progressed well in autumn after 2½-month lay-off,

successful in big-field handicaps at Nottingham and Doncaster (in good style by 3 lengths): best form at 6f: acts on good to firm ground. *R. Charlton*

EVERGREEN TANGO 2 b.c. (Mar 10) Green Forest (USA) 134 – Bold Tango (FR) (In Fijar (USA) 121) [1992 6.1d3] 14,500Y: workmanlike colt: first foal: dam sister to Fijar Tango: staying-on third of 8 in claimer at Nottingham in July: moved poorly down and not seen out again. *J. Wharton* —

EVERSET (FR) 4 b.c. Green Desert (USA) 127 – Eversince (USA) (Foolish Pleasure (USA)) [1991 7g5 6g2 6g* 7g 6f2 6s 6f 6.1m2 5d a6g* 1992 a6g a8g a8g a6g 5g 5s 6d 6m 6.1d] close-coupled colt: moderate mover: rated 79 at 3 yrs: well beaten in handicaps in first half of 1992: should stay beyond 6f: acts on firm ground and fibresand, seems unsuited by soft. *W. J. Musson* —

EVER SHARP 8 b.g. Sharpo 132 – Blue Jane 81 (Blue Cashmere 129) [1991 NR 1992 5m 5g] big, lengthy gelding: poor mover: on the downgrade. *J. White* —

EVER SO ARTISTIC 5 ch.g. Claude Monet (USA) 121 – Ever So 78 (Mummy's Pet 125) [1991 a5g* a5g3 a5g6 a5g2 a5g* a6g6 5.3f 5m* 5g 5m 5.8d 5.2m a5g a5g a5g4 1992 a5g5 a6g 5.3m 5m6 5m 5m a6g6 a5g5 5.3d a5g a5g a5g] sparely-made gelding: worthwhile form in handicaps in 1992 only when fifth at Lingfield eighth start: best form at 5f: acts on good to firm ground and equitrack: no improvement visored/blinkered: sometimes bandaged behind: has won for apprentice. *P. Howling* a46

EVERSO IRISH 3 b.g. Hatim (USA) 121 – Ever So 78 (Mummy's Pet 125) [1991 7g 7d 7m6 8m3 a7g6 1992 a12g6 12m5 11.8m] leggy gelding: has a round action: rated 58 at 2 yrs: on the downgrade: sold to join P. Evans 1,000 gns Newmarket Autumn Sales. *M. H. Tompkins* —

EVER SO LONELY 3 b.f. Headin' Up – Lonely Dawn (USA) 63 (Plenty Old (USA)) [1991 5m* 5m2 6g 5g6 5d 1992 a5g3 a5g5 5s 5.1d6 5.1d 5.1d* 5d4 5g3 5.1g 5d6 5s] smallish, sparely-made filly: moderate mover: below form after winning Chester claimer in July (soon clear, by 10 lengths): sweated profusely, unruly at stalls final run: best at 5f: acts on good to firm and dead: usually blinkered. *A. Bailey* 56

EVER SO LYRICAL 2 b.c. (Apr 8) Never So Bold 135 – Lyra (Blakeney 126) [1992 6d 7g] 4,300F: second foal: dam won 3 races in Belgium: well beaten in October maidens at Haydock and Doncaster. *P. W. Harris* —

EVERYBODYS TALKING 3 ch.c. Precocious 126 – Abuzz 101 (Absalom 128) [1991 NR 1992 6.9v3 7g4] strong colt: first foal: dam 2-y-o 5f winner later successful at 7.3f: third in maiden at Folkestone: well beaten in Wolverhampton (moved badly to post) minor event later in spring. *C. E. Brittain* 47

EVERY ONE A GEM 5 ch.g. Nicholas Bill 125 – Lady Bequick 81 (Sharpen Up 127) [1991 10f* 10m 10g4 10m* 10m* 10.1m* 10.1f4 10d2 10.1m6 1992 11.5m 10.2f 11.5g5] big, good-bodied gelding: well below best in handicaps in 1992: stays 1¼m: acts on firm and dead ground: ran creditably when blinkered at 4 yrs. *M. Dixon* —

EVE'S TREASURE 2 ch.f. (Mar 12) Bustino 136 – Before Long (Longleat (USA) 109) [1992 10d a8g] 825Y: third foal: half-sister to 3-y-o Not Mistaken (by Sulaafah) and a winner over hurdles: dam never ran: soundly beaten in late-season seller and maiden. *R. Curtis* —

EWALD (IRE) 4 b.g. Green Desert (USA) 127 – Popular Win 103 (Lorenzaccio 130) [1991 7v5 8.2m3 1992 a6g] leggy, quite attractive gelding: trained by J. S. Wilson, well beaten in spring at 3 yrs: good speed over 3f in Southwell claimer in December: bred to stay 7f. *M. Johnston* —

EXARCH (USA) 3 b.c. His Majesty (USA) – Velvet (USA) 69 (Sir Ivor 135) [1991 NR 1992 10s 10.5d 12v6] $35,000Y: strong, rangy colt: first foal: dam, half-sister to U.S. Grade 1 winner Martial Law and Jersey Stakes winner Satin Flower, ran once here at 2 yrs and won once from 10 starts in North America: always behind in autumn maidens, trained first 2 starts by B. Hills. *M. J. Heaton-Ellis* —

EXCELLED (IRE) 3 gr.f. Treasure Kay 114 – Excelling Miss (USA) (Exceller (USA) 129) [1991 5v 6m 1992 6m 7d 6g] light-framed filly: no worthwhile form, including in selling handicap. *B. Gubby* —

EXCELSIS 6 b.h. Shirley Heights 130 – Sacred Ibis (Red God 128§) [1991 12f 10f* 12m* 11.7m 10g 11.9f 1992 12m 9m 11.9g] neat horse: rated 56 as 5-y-o: tailed off in 1992: stays 1½m: acts on firm going: below form when visored once. *J. R. Jenkins* —

EXCESS BAGGAGE (IRE) 2 b.c. (Mar 6) Petorius 117 – Sandra's Choice (Sandy Creek 123) [1992 8m 7g a8g* a8g* a8g5 a7g*] IR 5,800F, 9,400Y: medium-sized, quite attractive colt: second living foal: dam placed over long distances in Ireland: progressive form to win maiden, claimer and nursery at Lingfield late 75 p in year: well suited by 1m: below form on fibresand: may be capable of better. *N. A. Callaghan*

EXCLUSION   3 ch.c. Ballad Rock 122 – Great Exception 84 (Grundy 137) [1991   **82**
6g 1992 8g3] strong, rather angular colt: second foal: dam won over 12.2f and 14.7f:
shaped promisingly when third in maiden at Newmarket in April: looked sure to win
a race, but not seen again. *H. Candy*

EXCLUSIVELY YOURS   2 gr.f. (Apr 8) Shareef Dancer (USA) 135 – Couleur   **69** p
de Rose (Kalaglow 132) [1992 6s* 6v] 4,500F, 3,700Y: compact filly: second foal:
dam unraced daughter of very smart 1980 2-y-o Exclusively Raised: well backed and
green when comfortable 1½-length winner of maiden auction event at Salisbury in
August: much better than thirteenth-of-24 position suggests in Racecall Gold
Trophy at Redcar 2½ months after, slowly away but very good speed to soon lead
and prominent until tiring 1½f out, eased considerably: will prove capable of lot
better. *R. Guest*

EXECUTION ONLY (IRE)   4 b.g. Sure Blade (USA) 130 – Headin' Home 105   **66**
(Habitat 134) [1991 10d 8m3 a8g5 8m4 8d* 10m3 10g4 9d5 7.6d 1992 8s 8d5 10d3
8.9g* 9m2 10m3 10.3f4 10m 10.3m] heavy-topped gelding: in good form in handicaps
in spring, successful at Wolverhampton: below best in second half of 1992: stays
1¼m: acts on good to firm ground and dead: below form when blinkered, effective
visored or not: not easiest of rides: sold 9,500 gns Ascot Junes Sales. *J. W. Watts*

EXECUTIVE FLARE   3 ch.f. Executive Man 119 – Green For Danger 66   –
(Formidable (USA) 125) [1991 6g 7s 7d2 7.5g 6s 6d4 7.5s2 7s 1992 7g a7g5] sturdy
filly: first foal: dam 7f winner, is out of speedy half-sister to dam of Roland Gardens:
ran in Italy at 2 yrs, second twice at Turin: last in maiden at Kempton and apprentice
race at Lingfield in June: withdrawn (injured in paddock) following month: stays
7.5f: acts on soft ground. *D. Sasse*

EXECUTIVE SPIRIT   3 gr.c. Executive Man 119 – Armalou 54 (Ardoon 124)   **64** d
[1991 6g3 6g 6g6 7g4 7.5d5 7s2 6v* 8v4 7s5 6s5 1992 6.1g 7g3 7.6g6 7g a6g5 a7g 8m
7m a7g4 6s 7d 6.9v 6.1s] leggy, angular colt: has a rather round action: poor walker:
fifth foal: half-brother to 1987 2-y-o 6f seller winner Annacando (by Derrylin), later
suited by 1½m: dam, plater, won at 1¼m: won maiden at Turin at 2 yrs: little form
here in 1992: should stay 1m: acts on heavy going and equitrack: below form when
blinkered once: retained 2,800 gns Newmarket Autumn Sales after penultimate
start. *D. Sasse*

EXHIBIT AIR (IRE)   2 b.f. (Apr 28) Exhibitioner 111 – Airy Queen (USA)   **77** ?
(Sadair) [1992 6m 7m6 7f2 8.1d5 7d] IR 6,600Y: good-quartered filly: half-sister to
3-y-o Copy Lane (by Runnett) and several winners, including (at 6f at 2 yrs in
Ireland in 1981) fairly useful Okanango (by Homeric): dam won at 2 yrs and 3 yrs in
Italy: strong-finishing fifth of 16 in Sandown nursery, easily best effort: afterwards
ran poorly in Goodwood nursery: will be suited by middle distances: acts on dead
ground. *R. Hannon*

EXIT TO NOWHERE (USA)   4 b.c. Irish River (FR) 131 – Coup de Folie **122**
(USA) 112 (Halo (USA)) [1991 9d2 9.2m5 6m6 6.5g3 8m6 7d5 8d5 1992 8v* 8g*
9.2d3 8m4 8s* 10f4 8f]

Exit To Nowhere—the French colt who finally got somewhere. The
arguments for and against keeping good racehorses in training as four-year-
olds have been well enough aired of late not to need much in the way of recap-
itulation here. Suffice to say that Exit To Nowhere represents the classic case
for—a colt who realized his potential in the extra year granted him, in so doing
considerably enhancing his stud value while making a significant contribution
to the season. He has now earned a place at his owner's Haras du Fresnay-
le-Buffard and, as a result of his sterling efforts in 1992, can be advertised as a
high-class miler, a Group 1 winner to boot.

Exit To Nowhere, a half-brother to the Two Thousand Guineas second
Machiavellian, went into 1991 a leading Guineas contender along with his
stable-companion Hector Protector. Following a five-length win in the Prix
Thomas Bryon at Saint-Cloud on the last of three outings as a two-year-old
he'd been put in the International Classification on 122, which gave him third
place in the handicap behind Hector Protector and Mujtahid. But he never
made it to the Guineas, and by the end of the year, despite showing very
useful form on most of his seven starts, he was still seeking any sort of win to
add to his Thomas Bryon. He'd been tried at six furlongs to nine furlongs,
looking more a miler than a sprinter (he was outpaced behind Polish Patriot in

the July Cup, and was eventually returned to a mile). Exit To Nowhere's third season opened with a victory in the Prix Edmond Blanc at Saint-Cloud in March. The slim margin of the victory over Zanadiyka probably mattered much less to connections than the fact that the drought had been ended, and the event did prove a turning point in Exit To Nowhere's career. He won his next race as well, the Prix du Muguet on the same course by a length and a half from the 1991 Prix de Diane winner Caerlina, and went to Deauville for the Marois very nearly with a record of four out of four. Whether he would have caught Zoman and Arcangues in the Prix d'Ispahan at Longchamp in May given less to do is a moot point—he made up a deal of ground inside the last two furlongs to close within two lengths, coming from much further back than the first and second—but there is no doubt whatsoever that he would have won the Queen Anne Stakes at Royal Ascot given a trouble-free run. He became boxed in on the inside between two furlongs out and a furlong out; by the time he forced a way through it was just too late, and although he quickened in excellent style and finished best of all, a close fourth behind Lahib, Second Set and Sikeston was his only reward.

Lahib and Sikeston reopposed in the Marois. Second Set was an absentee because of the soft going as was Rodrigo de Triano, but the field remained a strong one and, with fourteen runners, one of the biggest for years. Exit To Nowhere started favourite coupled with his three-year-old half-sister Hydro Calido, a close second to Culture Vulture in the Pouliches in the spring and a clear-cut winner of the Prix d'Astarte over the Deauville mile more recently. In the race, the field stuck together well in the testing conditions behind the pacemaker Hazm, and a rousing finish looked a distinct possibility two furlongs from home as the leaders stretched out towards the centre of the course. At this stage Exit To Nowhere, having been held up, was tucked in going well, poised to make his effort. He made it out wide, showing a sharp turn of foot once past Sikeston, and struck the front a furlong out; once ahead, he ran on strongly and was well on top at the post, a length up on Lahib. The stewards were in action shortly afterwards, for the race had been a rough one. They left the placings unaltered while suspending third-placed Cardoun's jockey for four days. Hatoof, Hydro Calido and Kitwood were the most conspicuous sufferers in all the hurly-burly, the last two particularly so. Exit To

Prix du Haras de Fresnay-le-Buffard Jacques le Marois, Deauville—
left to right, Exit To Nowhere, Lahib and Cardoun

Mr S. S. Niarchos' "Exit To Nowhere"

Nowhere caught Sikeston as he came through, but that horse was weakening at the time and Exit To Nowhere undeniably won on merit.

Exit To Nowhere made two more appearances before retirement. He ran in the Arlington Million instead of the Prix du Moulin and was returned to the States for the Breeders' Cup Mile at Gulfstream Park. The first race showed that he stayed a mile and a quarter and that, although ever since the Thomas Bryon he'd been generally regarded as ideally suited by soft going, he acted well enough on firm, as his run at Royal Ascot confirmed he did. He came late for fourth-of-twelve place behind Dear Doctor, beaten around two and a half lengths. In common with most of the European horses, Exit To Nowhere failed to show his best at Gulfstream Park. In his case, whatever chance he had evaporated when he ran into trouble in midfield on the inside on the tight last bend; he eventually finished eighth of fourteen to the American horse Lure.

			Riverman	Never Bend
Exit To	Irish River (FR)		(b 1969)	River Lady
Nowhere (USA)	(ch 1976)		Irish Star	Klairon
(b.c. 1988)			(b 1960)	Botany Bay
			Halo	Hail To Reason
	Coup de Folie (USA)		(b or br 1969)	Cosmah
	(b 1982)		Raise The Standard	Hoist The Flag
			(b 1978)	Natalma

Remarkably, Machiavellian (by Mr Prospector), Exit To Nowhere and Hydro Calido (by Nureyev) are the first three foals of their dam Coup de Folie, a well-above-average winner at up to a mile and a quarter in France. Details of the pedigree have been set out in previous entries in *Racehorses* on Machiavellian and Exit To Nowhere. Special points of interest to breeders in Exit To Nowhere's pedigree are that he's by a Marois winner who had a good season as a sire in Europe (Brief Truce and Hatoof are also by Irish River) and that the third dam Natalma is the dam of Northern Dancer. At a fee of 40,000 francs (around £4,800) the tall, good-looking Exit To Nowhere—his portrait scarcely does him justice—is likely to appeal to breeders in France. *F. Boutin, France*

EXODUS (IRE) 2 br.c. (Feb 27) Alzao (USA) 117 – Girl On A Swing 79 (High **64** Top 131) [1992 5d⁶ 7g³ 6.1g⁴ 7g] sturdy, compact colt: sixth living foal: closely related to 3-y-o Fragonard (by Pharly), 7f winner at 2 yrs, and half-brother to several winners, including 1¾m winner Dame Elusive (by Blakeney): dam, placed twice at around 7f from 4 starts at 3 yrs, is out of half-sister to Irish Oaks winner Pampalina, dam of Pampapaul: failed to progress after third to Ardkinglass in minor event at Newcastle in June: sold 4,600 gns Newmarket Autumn Sales: stays 7f. *M. H. Easterby*

EXPANSIONIST 3 b.g. Midyan (USA) 124 – Dastina 80 (Derring-Do 131) [1991 **68** 8m 8m a8g 1992 8.9v 10m² 10g 10.1g⁴ 12f* 16.2g* 14.1d* 13.6m*] £mall, close-coupled gelding: has a quick action: had good season in 1992, successful in Thirsk seller (no bid) and claimers at Beverley, Yarmouth and Redcar (claimed to join Mrs J. Ramsden's stable £8,010): best form at 1¾m +: acts on firm and dead going: trained meritorious by A. Hide. *S. P. C. Woods*

EXPLOSIVE SPEED (USA) 4 b.c. Exceller (USA) 129 – Strait Lane (USA) **61** (Chieftain II) [1991 10g 10m 10.8m 10f⁵ 12.3g 1992 10g⁶ 11.1g* 12f* 14.8g] leggy, workmanlike colt: successful in handicaps at Edinburgh in July and Thirsk (sweating) in August: tailed off final start: should prove effective at 1¾m: acts on firm ground. *M. D. Hammond*

EXPO MONDIAL (IRE) 2 b.c. (May 4) Last Tycoon 131 – Hamada (FR) 116 **86** (Habitat 134) [1992 5g 5g⁴ 6f⁴ 6g* 6f² 7g 8m³ 7g] 28,000F, 15,500Y: smallish colt: half-brother to several winners in France, notably sprinter Harifa (by Green Dancer): dam (rated on 2-y-o form when 5f and 6.5f winner in France) later won Group 3 events at 7f and 1m: won 3-runner Yarmouth nursery in July: ran well most starts after, in nursery at Ascot final outing: stays 1m: acts on firm ground. *J. M. P. Eustace*

EXPRESS ACCOUNT 5 b.m. Carr de Naskra (USA) – Miss Audimar (USA) **68** (Mr Leader (USA)) [1991a 12g⁵ 10g⁵ 10f 10m⁵ 10.1f² 11.9m* 12.4m* 10.4m 12f* 12f⁶ 11.9m⁴ 11.4m 12f 12d 10m 1992 12f³ 12d 11.9f⁵] leggy, rather dipped-backed mare: inconsistent handicapper: effective at 1¼m to 1½m: best efforts on top-of-the-ground: ran creditably when blinkered: suitable mount for claimer. *R. J. R. Williams*

EXPRESS GIFT 3 br.g. Bay Express 132 – Annes Gift (Ballymoss 136) [1991 **64** 6m⁴ 6m 1992 7s 6.9d* 8m* 7f 8.1g* 8.9d⁴] angular gelding: in good form in first half of 1992, winning handicaps at Carlisle, Pontefract and Haydock (apprentices): better at 1m than shorter: acts on good to firm and dead ground: good mount for claimer. *Mrs M. Reveley*

EXPRESS MARIECURIE (IRE) 2 ro.f. (Mar 1) Persian Heights 129 – Sweety **72** Grey (Young Emperor 133) [1992 5g⁵ 5m⁵ 7.5d³ 8m² 8g* 6g 8s a7g] IR 9,000Y: good-topped filly: has plenty of scope: good walker: moderate mover: half-sister to winning sprinter Al Trui (by Scottish Rifle) and a winner in France by Workboy: dam ran once: won Warwick nursery in August: ran a good race back at 6f when eighth of 19 in Tattersalls Breeders Stakes at Leopardstown but performed moderately last 2 starts: sold out of P. Chapple-Hyam's stable 6,400 gns Ascot December Sales in between: stays 1m: acts on good to firm and dead ground. *Mrs N. Macauley*

EXPRESS SERVICE 3 b.c. Hotfoot 126 – Avon Belle 75 (Balidar 133) [1991 **78** § 6f 6d² 1992 7g³ 8d² 8m³ 7d² 7d² 7.6s 8.1g⁵] good-bodied colt: bad mover: disappointing maiden: stays 1m: acts on dead ground: below form when blinkered once: carries head high, and temperamental: sold to join W. O'Gorman 3,100 gns Doncaster November Sales. *P. J. Makin*

EXPRESS SIGNMAKER (IRE) 3 b.f. Paean 123 – Moment of Weakness 76 **–** (Pieces of Eight 128) [1991 6g³ 7m 6m 7g³ 8m 1992 8.3g 11.6m 16.1d⁶] angular filly: poor mover: poor plater: sold 640 gns Doncaster September Sales. *J. White*

EZZOUD (IRE) 3 b.c. Last Tycoon 131 – Royal Sister II (Claude) [1991 **120** 7m* 7m 1992 8d² 8.1d* 8g² 8m³ 12m⁵]

Ezzoud wasn't seen out after June but, in the relatively short time that he was around, he had every chance to prove himself. He contested three Group 1 events in the space of six weeks, meeting the very best of his age, and although not up to winning one, he was beaten little more than a length in two of them. The first of those races was the Irish Two Thousand Guineas at the Curragh where he started 5/1 second favourite in a six-runner field dominated by Rodrigo de Triano. Ezzoud hadn't any classic experience or indeed any pattern-race experience, but a short-head defeat when conceding 4 lb to the subsequent Two Thousand Guineas second Lucky Lindy in the Easter Stakes at Kempton and a two-and-a-half-length success in a very strongly-contested graduation event at Sandown gave every encouragement that he would not prove out of his depth. A possible temperament problem, which had manifested itself with a particularly lazy display at Kempton, seemed to have been largely ironed out by the application of blinkers. Ezzoud duly improved on his previous form, reversing placings with Lucky Lindy and holding off the best of the home team, Brief Truce, as well, but the battle for first place went very much as the betting predicted; Ezzoud had no answer to Rodrigo de Triano's turn of foot, though it is easy to forget that there was only a length between them at the line. The first three met again in the St James's Palace Stakes at Royal Ascot and provided the winner. Ezzoud, visored, was again sensibly positioned close to the front and kept on strongly but although Rodrigo de Triano disappointed, Ezzoud was still denied victory as it was Brief Truce, himself blinkered for the first time, who had progressed the better in the month since their last meeting. Ezzoud finished one and a half lengths back in third. Ezzoud's third bid for a Group 1 prize and his final appearance in 1992 was in the Irish Derby, no blinkers or visor fitted, presumably to help him settle over a trip that he wasn't at all sure to stay. This time, however, Ezzoud finished a long way behind the winner. Nothing, of course, was able to get near St Jovite but Ezzoud's fifth of eleven was not a performance of the same order that we'd seen in the Irish Guineas or the St James's Palace.

		Try My Best (b 1975)	Northern Dancer
	Last Tycoon (b 1983)		Sex Appeal
		Mill Princess (b 1977)	Mill Reef
Ezzoud (IRE)			Irish Lass II
(b.c. 1989)		Claude (b 1964)	Hornbeam
	Royal Sister II (b 1977)		Aigue-Vive
		Ribasha (b 1967)	Ribot
			Natasha

Ezzoud certainly shapes as if he should stay a mile and a quarter, and there is sufficient stamina in his pedigree to make one confident of it. Last Tycoon's best other representative in 1992 was the French sprinter Monde Bleu but he has got plenty that stay middle distances and several stayers. Ezzoud's dam Royal Sister II ran in Italy at two, three, four and five years, winning three times as a three-year-old and four times in her final season, but she also had an extended run in Ireland in the second and third of those seasons, winning (when blinkered) over a mile and a quarter and twice being tried at two miles. Easily the best of her previous four foals (the next two are colts by Lomond and Sadler's Wells) was the high-class miler Distant Relative (by Habitat), but this is a family noted mainly for stamina. The grandam Ribasha, a lightly-raced individual who probably needed long distances, is a half-sister to that excellent racehorse and broodmare Natashka; Arkadina, Blood Royal, Gregorian, Truly Bound, Dark Lomond, Gold And Ivory and Mukaddamah all have Natashka as their dam or grandam. *M. R. Stoute*

F

FAAZ (USA) 3 b.c. Fappiano (USA) – Charmie Carmie (USA) (Lyphard (USA) 132) [1991 8f 8f 7m³ 1992 10g⁶ 12d 11.8g 16d⁴ 12s³ 16.1s] good-topped colt: plating-class form: may well prove best short of 2m: acts on good to firm and soft ground: ran creditably blinkered/visored first 3 of last 4 starts: sold 6,400 gns Newmarket Autumn Sales. *A. A. Scott* **49**

FABFER (IRE) 2 b.c. (Feb 2) Mtoto 134 – Snowtop (Thatching 131) [1992 8m **– p** 8.1d] IR 31,000Y: good-topped colt: fluent mover: third foal: half-brother to 3-y-o Climbing High (by Last Tycoon): dam Irish sprinting half-sister to Al Hareb and smart French 9f to 1¼m winner Dr Somerville: bit backward, ran far better than last-but-one position suggests, travelling smoothly long way, in maidens at Doncaster and Haydock in September: sent to Italy: will do better. *P. W. Chapple-Hyam*

FABIUS CUNCTATOR (IRE)   3 b.c. Cyrano de Bergerac 120 – Flower Centre (USA) (Jaipur) [1991 6g 7m 6f 1992 6s] good-bodied colt: no worthwhile form, last seen in May. *B. J. McMath*   –

FABLED ORATOR   7 b.g. Lafontaine (USA) 117 – Brompton Rose 98 (Sun Prince 128) [1991 NR 1992 6g 6g 8m 7m 7g 6g 6.1m 7f 7m⁵ 7d 6m⁴ 6s 7d] strong, lengthy gelding: moderate mover: of little account these days. *P. Howling*   –

FABRIANA   2 b.f. (Apr 27) Northern State (USA) 91 – Fashion Flow (Balidar 133) [1992 6v*] third foal: dam never ran: 33/1, won 11-runner maiden at Folkestone in October by 2½ lengths from Domulla, starting slowly and producing storming run inside final 1f: sure to improve. *T. J. Naughton*   68 p

FABULOUS HOSTESS (USA)   4 ch.f. Fabulous Dancer (USA) 124 – Young Hostess (FR) 110 (Arctic Tern (USA) 126) [1991 10.5g⁵ 8s² 10g* 12s* 12s* 10.5v* 1992 10.5g* 12m⁶ 12.5s* 12d² 10.5s²] first foal: dam won over 9f in France: very useful and consistent French filly: won Group 3 Prix Corrida at Saint-Cloud in April and, despite returning from near 4-month break, Group 2 Ciga Prix de Royallieu at Longchamp in October, getting up close home to beat Good To Dance a nose: ran well in Prix du Conseil de Paris at Longchamp and Prix de Flore at Saint-Cloud later in the autumn: effective from 1¼m to 12.5f: best efforts on an easy surface, and acts on heavy ground. *Mme C. Head, France*   112

FABULOUS WAY   2 br.c. (Apr 6) Fabulous Dancer (USA) 124 – Stylish Sister 66 (Great Nephew 126) [1992 7d] 17,000Y: compact colt: first foal: dam once-raced half-sister to Cesarewitch winner Sir Michael and very speedy 1974 2-y-o Fats Waller: 33/1, prominent nearly 5f but weakened quickly and tailed-off last of 11 in maiden at Yarmouth in August. *M. R. Stoute*   –

FACE NORTH (IRE)   4 b.g. Fayruz 116 – Pink Fondant (Northfields (USA)) [1991 5g 6g 7m 5m 5g 7.6m 5g 6.9s 1992 6s 6m 5g* 5d 5s² 6s 6.1s⁵ a6g²] small, sturdy gelding: moderate mover: modest handicapper: won at Salisbury in August: inconsistent for A. Davison, but ran well for new handler last 2 starts: stays 6.1f: acts on any going. *R. Akehurst*   60

FACE THE FUTURE   3 ch.g. Ahonoora 122 – Chiltern Red (Red God 128§) [1991 NR 1992 6m⁶ 7g 8g³ 6m² 6s] stocky gelding: ninth foal: half-brother to several winners, including very useful 1981 2-y-o sprinter Travel On (by Tachypous) and 1¼m and 1½m winner Min Baladi (by Welsh Pageant): dam poor sister to Red Alert: backward first 3 starts then showed only worthwhile form when short-headed in handicap at Yarmouth in August: will prove as effective at 7f: never able to challenge on soft ground. *P. W. Harris*   60

FACT OR FICTION   6 br.g. Known Fact (USA) 135 – Noble Wac (USA) (Vaguely Noble 140) [1991 a12g* a13g² a12g 8m 12s 12m a12g 1992 a12g⁶] strong,   –

Ciga Prix de Royallieu, Longchamp—
a nose between Fabulous Hostess (No. 3) and Good To Dance, with Spring third

angular gelding: rated 64d at 5 yrs: well beaten in claimer in January, 1992: mostly blinkered or visored nowadays: won novice hurdles early in 1992. *Miss B. Sanders*

FACTUAL (USA) 2 ch.c. (Mar 21) Known Fact (USA) 135 – Mofida 115 (Right **108** p Tack 131) [1992 6g⁴ 6m* 6m³] strong, rangy colt: carries condition: has plenty of scope: good walker: brother to 3-y-o 6f (at 2 yrs) and 1m winner Magnified and half-brother to fairly useful 1990 2-y-o 6f winner Dangora (by Sovereign Dancer) and smart miler Zaizafon (by The Minstrel), herself dam of leading French 2-y-o Zafonic: dam, very tough winner at up to 7f, is grandam of Elmaamul: better for race still, won minor event at Doncaster in September, hanging right and leading over 1f out: excellent 3½ lengths third of 6 to Zieten in Middle Park Stakes at Newmarket following month, staying on well having come off bridle at halfway: will be well suited by 1m: likely to improve further. *B. W. Hills*

FACTUELLE 5 ch.m. Known Fact (USA) 135 – Cayla (Tumble Wind (USA)) **43** [1991 5.3f⁴ 5g² 5m² 5g³ 5d² 5m² 5.2m* 5d 5f³ 5.2f* 5g³ 5m 1992 a5g a6g⁶ a6g⁴ 5s 5s 5d 5.3m³ 5.7m 5g a5g] small, stocky mare: rated 60 at 4 yrs for M. Fetherston-Godley: looked just a poor handicapper in 1992, trained until after penultimate start by D. R. Tucker: effective at 5f and 6f: acts on any going. *C. J. Hill*

FADAKI HAWAKI (USA) 2 b.f. (Mar 4) Vice Regent (CAN) – Vallee Secrete **57** p (USA) (Secretariat (USA)) [1992 6s] $260,000F, $320,000Y: closely related to smart 1990 2-y-o sprinter Mujadil (by Storm Bird) and half-sister to several winners, including useful 1985 2-y-o 5f winner Kombus (by Known Fact) and 3-y-o Mutabahi (by Woodman), 6f winner at 2 yrs now effective at 1¼m: dam French 1m winner from excellent family: 8/1, 8 lengths seventh of 16 to Zarani Sidi Anna in maiden at Newbury in October, held up and unable to quicken: wore bandages behind: will improve. *A. A. Scott*

FAEZ 2 b.c. (Feb 1) Mtoto 134 – Ghanimah 98 (Caerleon (USA) 132) [1992 7s*] **77** p first foal: dam, ran only at 2 yrs, winning at 6f, is half-sister to Marwell: 5/1, won 14-runner maiden at Lingfield in October by 2½ lengths from Marastani, running on well last 2f: will stay 1¼m: will improve. *Major W. R. Hern*

FAIR AMERICAN (USA) 3 ch.c. Mr Prospector (USA) – Win Nona (USA) – (Jacinto) [1991 6m⁵ 7m⁵ 1992 8g 8f 7g] angular colt: moderate mover: no worthwhile form in handicaps in May: should stay 1m: sent to F. Brothers in USA. *M. R. Stoute*

FAIR AVERAGE 4 ch.c. Ahonoora 122 – Fair Head 87 (High Line 125) [1991 **105** 8g* 10.4d⁵ 8.5f² 8g³ 1992 8.1g 8m⁶ 10g² 10m² 10.5d⁵ 12m⁵ 9m⁴ 10g²] workmanlike colt: moderate mover: useful performer: best efforts when in frame, beaten only a short head by Lupescu in listed race at Newmarket final start: effective from 1m to 1¼m: acts on firm and dead ground: sold 37,000 gns Newmarket December Sales. *H. Candy*

FAIR COP (USA) 3 b.c. Al Nasr (FR) 126 – Exclusive Life (USA) (Exclusive **111** Native (USA)) [1991 6g* 6f* 6m* 1992 7f³] compact, good-quartered colt: unbeaten at 2 yrs but suffered pastern injury and was then sent out after Chesham Stakes: returned a year later with bandage on off-hind when 2 lengths third of 12 to Prince Ferdinand in Jersey Stakes at Royal Ascot, always prominent: should stay 1m: seemed sure to win a good race. *P. F. I. Cole*

FAIR CRACK (IRE) 3 b.c. Fairy King (USA) – Have A Flutter (Auction Ring **99** (USA) 123) [1991 5d⁶ 5d³ 5g* 6m⁴ 5.2g⁵ 6m* 5g² 7s* 6g³ 8f 1992 7g⁵ 7g³ 8.5g 10g 7s⁴] small, good-topped colt: usually looks well: has a quick action: useful performer at his best: below form last 3 starts, including in 8.5f Diomed Stakes (mulish beforehand and pretty unsatisfactory in race) at Epsom: should stay 1m: easily best efforts with give in the ground: has worn bandages behind: sold 16,000 gns Newmarket Autumn Sales, reportedly to race in Scandinavia. *R. Hannon*

FAIR DARE 4 b. or br.f. Daring March 116 – Fair Madame 88 (Monseigneur – (USA) 127) [1991 8s⁴ 6g 8g 7f 11g⁴ 10g⁴ 8g* 8f 8m⁴ 10.4m 8.2m 1992 a8g⁵ a8g 8.3d 8m⁵ 10d 8f] leggy filly: moderate mover: poor handicapper, not seen out after June: stays 1m: acts on good to firm ground: sold 740 gns Doncaster November Sales. *C. B. B. Booth*

FAIR ENCHANTRESS 4 b.f. Enchantment 115 – Pts Fairway (Runnymede **58** d 123) [1991 6f 7m 5m³ 5m* 5m⁴ 5m 6m⁵ 5.1d 7m⁴ 1992 5m³ 5.1g 5f⁶ 7.6m³ 7.6m⁴ 7.1s 7.6g 7d a6g] workmanlike, good-quartered filly: keen walker: inconsistent handicapper, easily best efforts when third: effective at 5f and stays 7.6f: acts on good to firm ground: won in blinkers at 3 yrs: tried visored once. *J. A. Bennett*

FAIR FLYER (IRE) 3 b.g. Tilt Up (USA) – Fair Siobahn (Petingo 135) [1991 5m **64** 6d 6m⁴ 7g 8m 7f⁶ 6f³ 6m 6g 7.1m* 1992 7.1g 8.3s 8.1m 10f⁶ 11.1f⁵ 7.1f⁶ 9.2m² 15.1m⁵

15g* 13.1f4 12g* 14.6g5] lengthy, rather sparely-made gelding: modest handicapper: trained until after eighth start by P. Monteith: won at Ayr and Thirsk (easily best effort) in August: ideally suited by 1½m: acts on firm ground: no improvement in blinkers (though successful in them at 2 yrs) or a visor once each in 1992. *M. Johnston*

FAIRFORD 3 br.g. Forzando 122 – Fuddled 74 (Malacate (USA) 131) [1991 6g **59** d 1992 8f5 8.5f2 7.5m4 7m5 a7g4 7.5d4 9.2g] leggy, sparely-made gelding: modest maiden: well beaten last 4 starts, including in seller: should stay beyond 1m: acts on firm going: wore blinkers and eyeshield on fibresand: sold to join L. Barratt 1,250 gns Doncaster November Sales. *J. G. FitzGerald*

FAIRGROUNDPRINCESS 4 ch.f. Kalaglow 132 – Hide Out (Habitat 134) – [199112m6 10.1m 10d 10.9g 16m4 14.6m 12.3g4 12f* 11.8m 11.4m 1992 13.1d4 15g 11g6 12m] close-coupled filly: moderate mover: poor handicapper: stays 1½m: acts on firm ground: often bandaged. *F. H. Lee*

FAIR MAID OF KENT (USA) 2 b.f. (May 2) Diesis 133 – Famed Princess **68** p (USA) (Nashua) [1992 7g 8g*] $300,000Y: lengthy filly: has scope: has a fluent, round action: half-sister to several winners, notably Grade 1 1¼m Swaps Stakes winner Clear Choice (by Raise A Native): dam won 15 races over 5 seasons, including stakes races at 6f to 7f: heavily-backed favourite, narrowly won maiden at Leicester in September, travelling smoothly 5f then running green before buckling down and staying on well to lead post: will stay 1¼m: will improve further. *J. H. M. Gosden*

FAIR REASON (IRE) 4 ch.f. Reasonable (FR) 119 – Fair Colleen (King **48** Emperor (USA)) [1991 NR 1992 6.1d 5m2 6g] smallish, sturdy filly: poor mover: very lightly raced: best effort when second in Sandown claimer in May: fell and had to be put down following month. *D. J. S. Cosgrove*

FAIRSPEAR 3 b.g. Faustus (USA) 118 – Emma's Star (Comedy Star (USA) 121) **43** [19917g 8.1g 8g 7.1s5 7g4 6s3 1992 10.2f 10.2f 10g4] rather unfurnished gelding: only poor form in 1992, not seen after July: stays 1¼m: seems best with some give in the ground: visored twice, including final start: has joined J. White. *L. G. Cottrell*

FAIRYLIKE (CAN) 2 b.f. (Feb 20) Clever Trick (USA) – Lady Inyala (USA) **40** (Apalachee (USA) 137) [1992 6.1m6 6.1s] $103,812Y: good-quartered filly: has a long stride: fourth foal: half-sister to 3 minor winners in USA: dam, placed twice from 9 starts in USA, is half-sister to Bel Bolide, very smart winner at up to 1¼m, including in USA: poor form in maiden at Chepstow and minor event at Bath: sold 620 gns Newmarket Autumn Sales. *P. F. I. Cole*

FAIRY PRINCESS (IRE) 3 b.f. Fairy King (USA) – Sigtrudis (Sigebert 131) – [1991NR 1992 8.1m 10.2f] IR 9,000F, 4,600Y: rather sparely-made filly: half-sister to winners in Italy and Germany and to poor staying maiden Siegerin (by Wolver Hollow), a winner over hurdles: dam, from good German family, was placed at 2 yrs: behind in maidens at Chepstow (reluctant at stalls, rearing several times) and Bath (claiming event) in early-summer. *R. Hollinshead*

FAIRY STORY (IRE) 2 ch.f. (Mar 8) Persian Bold 123 – Certain Story (Known **63** Fact (USA) 135) [1992 5.7f4 5m3 6g2 7g* 6.5m 7.6v5] quite good-topped filly: third foal: half-sister to 4-y-o 1¼m to 11.8f winner Pharly Story (by Pharly): dam unraced daughter of useful 5f and 6f winner Epithet (later stayed 1½m): modest performer: won 13-runner nursery at Lingfield in August: gave impression something amiss in similar event at Doncaster next time: will stay 1m: best efforts on good ground. *J. W. Hills*

FAIRY WISH 2 b.g. (Apr 5) Fairy King (USA) – High Climber 74 (Mandrake – Major 122) [1992 6m] 3,200Y: good-quartered gelding: first foal: dam maiden stayed 7f: backward and very green, always tailed off in maiden at Ripon in July. *C. W. Thornton*

FAIRY WISHER (IRE) 3 b.f. Fairy King (USA) – Valediction 71 (Town Crier **57** 119) [1991 NR 1992 8.5d4 11.9d3 8d3 6m3] close-coupled filly: fourth foal: half-sister to 1987 Irish 2-y-o 6f winner Classic Dilemma (by Sandhurst Prince): dam ungenerous middle-distance staying maiden: modest maiden: needs further than 6f, probably doesn't stay 1½m: sold to join M. Barraclough 4,400 gns Newmarket Autumn Sales. *A. C. Stewart*

FAIT ACCOMPLI (FR) 3 ch.g. Fayruz 116 – Artipiar 106 (Tyrant (USA)) [1991 – 5f6 5m6 7m 5g 5g2 5d 1992 8.1g 8f 12m 8.1d5] neat gelding: no form in 1992: should stay 6f: below best in blinkers, including on reappearance: sold 820 gns Doncaster September Sales. *J. J. O'Neill*

FALCON FLIGHT 6 ch.g. Tampero (FR) – Kemoening 78 (Falcon 131) [1991 – 8m 7m 7m⁴ 8.2d² 8m³ 8.1m 8.2m 1992 a7g] smallish, rather sparely-made gelding: poor mover: modest handicapper (rated 62) at 5 yrs for J. Mackie: progressive winning hurdler in 1991/2: off course over a year, no encouragement in handicap at Lingfield in December. *R. Simpson*

FALCONS DAWN 5 b.g. Exhibitioner 111 – African Bloom (African Sky 124) 57 [1991 8s 7.5f³ 8.2m⁶ 8.2g² 8m⁴ 7.6m³ 8d 7m 10.3d a8g 1992 7m 8f⁴ 8.2m⁵ 10f* 12.2g² 12.3g⁴ 10.9s 10.5d 10.5s³ 8d* 10.3s⁶ 10.3v⁵ 9g⁶ a12g³ a10g⁵ a10g³] leggy, quite good-topped gelding: has a round action: modest performer: trained first 3 starts by M. O'Neill: off course nearly 8 weeks and largely consistent afterwards, winning at Pontefract (ladies) in August and Leicester in October: effective from 1m to 1½m: acts on any going: has been blinkered/visored, not for present trainer: formerly a front runner but held up of late. *A. Bailey*

FALSOOLA 2 b.f. (Apr 12) Kris 135 – Favoridge (USA) 122 (Riva Ridge (USA)) 84 [1992 5g³ 5f* 5m⁵ 6g* 6.5m* 6d⁵] small, compact filly: fifth living foal: half-sister to modest 1m winner Vote In Favour (by General Assembly) and a winner in Holland: dam high-class sprinting 2-y-o later stayed 1m, from excellent family: generally progressive filly: successful in late-summer in maiden at Ripon and nurseries at Newmarket and (after confident ride) Doncaster: ran moderately in listed contest at York (got very upset in stalls then lost action after pulling hard) in October: should stay 7f: edgy type, dismounted at start last 3 outings. *M. R. Stoute*

FAMILY LINE 4 b.g. High Line 125 – Princess Dina 87 (Huntercombe 133) 81 [1991 10g 11d* 16.2g 1992 12.1m² 12.3m 15s] smallish, workmanlike gelding: shows knee action: fairly useful handicapper: second of 4 in moderately-run handicap at Edinburgh: failed to confirm that form: should stay beyond 1½m: acts on good to firm and dead ground: won handicap hurdle in September. *Miss L. A. Perratt*

FAMILY ROSE 3 gr.g. Absalom 128 – Greenhill Lass (Upper Case (USA)) [1991 – 5m 1992 6g] close-coupled gelding: has a round action: no form in spring maidens 13 months apart. *G. H. Eden*

FAMOUS BEAUTY 5 br.m. Vision (USA) – Relfo 124 (Relko 136) [1991 12d 51 16m⁶ 13.8m 12.3g 12.1d³ 12.3d⁴ 12m⁴ 16.2f⁵ 12.3g⁴ 14.1f³ 12f⁵ 14m⁴ 14.6m² 12.1g* 11.9m³ 13.8m⁴ 14g⁴ 16m 12.1d³ 13.6d 12.1s 1992 10.8v³ 12.3v⁴ 14.1d 14.6g⁵ 12m³ 14.1g³ 10.2m 14.1m 12f⁴ 14.6d*] sparely-made mare: consistent handicapper: won at Wolverhampton in July: needs further than 1¼m, and stays 2m: acts on any going: claimer ridden: tough. *R. Hollinshead*

FAMOUS LAD 9 b.g. Bold Lad (IRE) 133 – Famous Band (USA) (Banderilla – (USA) [1991 NR 1992 12d] strong ex-Irish gelding: of no account these days. *R. Lee*

FANCIED 2 b.f. (Jan 28) Dominion 123 – Favourite Girl 82 (Mummy's Pet 125) 62 [1992 5f 5.1d* 5g³] good-quartered filly: has a quick action: first foal: dam 2-y-o 5f winner: modest performer: easily won claimer at Nottingham, leading 2f out and soon clear: respectable third in nursery at Warwick later in July: well worth a try at 6f: acts on dead ground, showed little on firm: may do better. *H. Candy*

FANFAN (IRE) 2 b.f. (Apr 16) Taufan (USA) 119 – Bouffant (High Top 131) [1992 47 5g⁵ 5d 5m³ 6f 6.9h* a7g² 7g⁶ 7g⁴ 7.1s] leggy, good-topped filly: moderate mover: first foal: dam thrice-raced daughter of smart 1m to 1½m winner Lucent, herself daughter of good sprinter Lucasland: modest plater: well-backed favourite, dictated pace at Carlisle (no bid) in June: somewhat in-and-out form afterwards: better suited by 7f than shorter: acts on hard ground and on fibresand: blinkered last 7 starts. *M. H. Easterby*

FANFOLD (IRE) 2 gr.f. (May 24) Siberian Express (USA) 125 – Broken Melody – (Busted 134) [1992 5d 6m 7m a6g] leggy, sparely-made filly: sixth foal: half-sister to 3-y-o 8.3f winner Bold Melody (by Never So Bold) and a winner in Denmark by Valiyar: dam unraced half-sister to very useful middle-distance filly Sing Softly: well beaten in maidens, and in seller on equitrack. *A. W. Denson*

FANGIO 3 b.g. Nordance (USA) – Verily Jane 53 (Royben 125) [1991 NR 1992 7g 84 5v³ 5s.1d* 5s² 5m* 5.7m⁴ 5m³ 5f* 5f* 5g 5.6m] workmanlike gelding: third foal: dam 5f plater here at 2 yrs later winner in Belgium: generally progressive performer: won claimers at Nottingham and Pontefract and handicaps (made all) at Salisbury and Ripon in first half of season: off course 11 weeks before running as if race was needed in 5.6f Portland Handicap at Doncaster: will prove best at 5f: acts on any going: genuine: may be capable of better. *W. G. M. Turner*

FANLIGHT 4 b.c. Beldale Flutter (USA) 130 – Carib Flash (Mill Reef (USA) 141) 57 [1991 8d 10g 14g⁴ 12m⁵ 1992 14.1d³ 18.1g² 17.2s³ 17.2f³ 15.8d 16s 16.5g⁵] neat, quite attractive colt: moderate mover: modest handicapper, still a maiden: stays 2¼m: has form on firm ground, but best runs with give: won juvenile hurdle in 1991/2. *R. Akehurst*

FANNY BURNEY (USA) 3 ch.f. Affirmed (USA) – Forever Waving (USA) –
(Hoist The Flag (USA)) [1991 NR 1992 8s] close-coupled, unfurnished filly: fourth reported foal: half-sister to 1¼m winner Jesters Farewell (by The Minstrel): dam, winner at up to 9f, is half-sister to 1976 champion American 3-y-o filly Revidere: 33/1, slow-starting last of 12 in maiden at Bath in May: sold 680 gns Newmarket Autumn Sales. *P. W. Harris*

FARABOUT 2 b.f. (May 18) Northern Tempest (USA) 120 – Fardella (ITY) –
(Molvedo 137) [1992 5g 5g] leggy filly: good mover: fifth reported foal: half-sister to 1¼m winner Melancolia (by Legend of France): dam minor 11f winner in France: soundly beaten in sellers at Beverley (unseated rider to post and got loose) and Leicester in the spring. *J. P. Leigh*

FARAFASHION 2 b.g. (Mar 28) Farajullah 113 – Welsh Fashion (Welsh Saint –
126) [1992 7g] workmanlike gelding: has a round action: first reported foal: dam unraced: 66/1 and backward, never dangerous or knocked about in maiden at Leicester in July: looked sure to improve. *M. R. Leach*

FARAH 3 b. or br.f. Lead On Time (USA) 123 – Muznah 92 (Royal And Regal –
(USA)) [1991 NR 1992 10.5f4] leggy, lengthy filly: fifth foal: half-sister to 4-y-o 1m and 10.1f winner Jazilah (by Persian Bold) and Irish 1¾m winner Fayafi (by Top Ville): dam 7f and 1m winner seemed to stay 1½m: 33/1, remote fourth of 5 in maiden at Haydock in July: sold to join J. Turner 1,600 gns Newmarket July Sales. *H. Thomson Jones*

FARAT (USA) 4 ch.c. Woodman (USA) 126 – Solac (FR) (Gay Lussac (ITY) 116) **80**
[1991 8.2g2 10m3 12m3 14s2 1992 12g 11.9d 11.9d3 15m* 14s6 13.9g6 16d2 18m3] good-bodied colt: fairly useful handicapper: won £7,000 event at Ayr in July: third in Cesarewitch at Newmarket final start: suited by a test of stamina: acts on good to firm and soft ground: bandaged of late: sometimes edgy: has joined N. Henderson. *J. L. Dunlop*

FARFELU 5 b.h. Lyphard's Special (USA) 122 – Spring Azure 98 (Mountain Call **103**
125) [1991 6g2 6m 6m 5m* 6g6 5m* 5.6m 6m 5d6 6.1s 1992 5m4 5g2 5s 5m6 5m 5m 5m6 6m] robust, good-quartered horse: useful and largely consistent performer: ran well in face of stiff task when seventh in Nunthorpe Stakes at York fifth start: suited by 5f: acts on hard and dead ground, unsuited by soft going: blinkered nowadays. *W. R. Muir*

FARIBOLE (IRE) 3 b.f. Esprit du Nord (USA) 126 – Sandbank (USA) **106**
(Riverman (USA) 131) [1991 6.5g3 7s2 8d 1992 9v3 8g3 8m3 9g3 10d3 10m* 10d4] strong, lengthy filly: second foal: half-sister to French provincial 4-y-o 10.5f to 12.5f winner Glisten (by Glint of Gold): dam won from 1m to 11f in France: useful performer: won minor event at Evry in September: creditable staying-on fourth of 7 to Red Slippers in Sun Chariot Stakes at Newmarket following month: worth a try at 1½m: acts on good to firm and dead ground, probably on heavy. *Edouard Bartholomew, France*

FARLEY (DEN) 2 ch.c. (Feb 10) Prince Mab (FR) 124 – Farandole (DEN) (Gay –
Baron) [1992 7g 7d 6s] leggy, rather angular colt: first reported foal: dam won 3 races in Denmark: always in rear in large fields, in claimer final start. *R. Akehurst*

FARMER JOCK 10 ch.h. Crofter (USA) 124 – Some Dame 72 (Will Somers 114§) **56**
[1991 7f 6s* 5g 6g 6g 6f4 5f 6g6 5m3 5d6 6.1m 1992 7m 6f 6f6 6.1d4 6g4 6g2 7f4 5.7f 6f5 5g] strong, good-bodied horse: carries condition: only a modest handicapper these days: stays 6f: acts on any going: effective with or without blinkers or visor: tends to hang: is held up. *Mrs N. Macauley*

FARMER'S FIRE (IRE) 3 ch.c. Ahonoora 122 – Forlene 108 (Forli (ARG)) –
[1991 7g 7g 1992 14s 11.7d 17.2s] strong, lengthy colt: moderate walker: rated 62 at 2 yrs: no worthwhile form at 3 yrs: tried blinkered. *C. F. Wall*

FARMER'S PET 3 ch.f. Sharrood (USA) 124 – Rectitude 99 (Runnymede 123) **84**
[1991 7m 7d 1992 12g5 14.6g* 16.1m2 14.1m* 14.1d* 16m2 13.9g6 14g5 16m2 14m] angular filly: has a round action: progressed into a fairly useful handicapper: won at Wolverhampton in May then Yarmouth and Redcar in July: ran well when second afterwards: stays 2m: acts on good to firm and dead ground: probably best suited by making the running. *G. A. Pritchard-Gordon*

FARM STREET 5 b.g. Henbit (USA) 130 – Mill Hill (USA) (Riva Ridge (USA)) –
[1991 8d 7g* 7.6d 7f4 8d 8g 7g 1992 8.3m] workmanlike, good-quartered gelding:

moderate mover: rated 81 at best in 1991 for P. Walwyn: bandaged, backward and tailed off in July, 1992: sold 1,700 gns Ascot December Sales. *T. P. McGovern*

FARNDALE   5 gr.g. Vaigly Great 127 – Beloved Mistress 84 (Rarity 129) [1991   **47**
NR 1992 6m 5g⁵ 5m⁴ 5s⁵ 6d] angular gelding: moderate mover: poor maiden
handicapper: stays 6f: acts on good to firm and soft ground. *B. C. Morgan*

FARSI   4 gr.c. Nishapour (FR) 125 – Pot Pourri 97 (Busted 134) [1991 15.3m* 16.2g   **92**
16.2f³ 13.9g⁶ 18m* 16.2f⁴ 16m³ 18m³ 1992 18g 16d⁶ 16g² 18.5g 18f³ 16.5m* 16.1f
16.1g³ 20m² 18m*] close-coupled, good-bodied colt: carries condition: has a quick
action: fairly useful handicapper: successful at Doncaster and Pontefract (Phil Bull
Trophy) in summer: suited by thorough test of stamina: acts on firm ground: has
hung right under pressure, and tends to carry head awkwardly: blinkered nowadays:
consistent. *R. Hollinshead*

FARYAL   3 gr.f. Bellypha 130 – French Cutie (USA) (Vaguely Noble 140) [1991 6.1f   **46**
7g 8.1s 1992 8g 8.2g⁶ 10g⁴ 10d⁵] close-coupled, good-bodied filly: plating-class
maiden: not seen after July: stays 1¼m: acts on soft ground. *J. L. Spearing*

FASCINATION WALTZ   5 b.m. Shy Groom (USA) – Cuckoo Weir (Double   **76**
Jump 131) [1991 6g⁴ 6g 6m 5.1m⁵ 6g 1992 7m 6g⁵ 6f⁵ 6m⁶ 5s⁵ 6d* 6g⁴ 5d⁶ 6d⁴ 6m²
6g] angular, sparely-made mare: fair and largely consistent handicapper: successful
at Lingfield in September: better at 6f than 5f: acts on firm and dead ground:
sometimes has tongue tied down and wears crossed noseband: has run well for an
apprentice: is held up. *D. Shaw*

FASHIONABLE DANCER   2 b.c. (Apr 18) Lomond (USA) 128 – Circulate   **– p**
(High Top 131) [1992 8m] 49,000Y: rather leggy, lengthy colt: second foal: brother to
fairly useful 3-y-o 8.9f and 1¼m winner Ecliptic: dam Irish 1¼m winner, from family
of Nashwan: 50/1 and very green, fifteenth of 17 in maiden at Newmarket in
September, chasing leaders almost 6f and eased: sure to improve. *C. E. Brittain*

FASSADININ   11 ch.g. Condorcet (FR) – Engadina 97 (Alcide 136) [1991 NR 1992   **–**
12g 8.1m] workmanlike ex-Irish handicapper: well beaten in spring on first runs
since 8-y-o, when visored in selling event last time. *W. L. Barker*

Phil Bull Trophy, Pontefract—Farsi takes the race for a second time

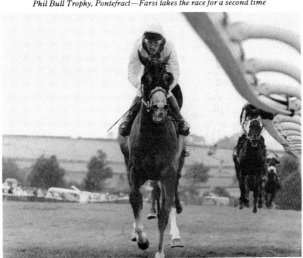

275

FASSFERN (USA) 3 b.c. Alleged (USA) 138 – Comtesse de Loir (FR) 131 (Val **71** §
de Loir 133) [1991 7g⁴ 8m³ 1992 10.3g³ 12.3s* 11.8d⁶ 12.3d 12d] lengthy, workmanlike colt: unreliable handicapper: won at Ripon in April: reportedly had wind ailment
next start: off course over 4 months, tried to pull himself up after 4f at Ripon
(blinkered) then soundly beaten at Goodwood: should be well suited by further than
1½m: acts on good to firm ground and soft: suited by strong handling. *Mrs J. Cecil*

FAST FIESTA 2 ch.f. (Feb 7) Aragon 118 – Pyjama Party 70 (Pyjama Hunt 126) **–**
[1992 7s 7.1s] 950Y: lengthy filly: second foal: dam, 2m winner, is half-sister to a
useful 1½m winner: always behind in maidens at Salisbury (reluctant stalls, slowly
away) and Chepstow (auction event) in September: sold 650 gns Ascot November
Sales. *M. R. Channon*

FAST MANOUVRE (FR) 3 b.g. Fast Topaze (USA) 128 – Cephira (FR) (Abdos **109**
134) [1991 8m⁴ 8m³ 1992 10g* 10.5d³ 12.5s⁵] leggy, angular gelding: impresses in
appearance: has a quick action: useful performer: won £10,000 Ascot maiden in July:
best effort when 2¾ lengths third of 8 to Half A Tick in Group 3 contest at Haydock:
stiff task in Group 2 event at Deauville later in August: should stay 1½m: wears
bandages. *M. Moubarak*

FASTNESS (IRE) 2 gr.c. (Mar 27) Rousillon (USA) 133 – City Fortress (Troy **104**
137) [1992 7.5s* 8g* 8s 8v⁶] tall, leggy colt: second foal: dam French 1¼m and 12.5f
winner: successful in newcomers event at Deauville and listed event at Evry: gave
impression something amiss when well beaten in Grand Criterium at Longchamp,
but returned to form when last of 6, not beaten far, in Prix Thomas Bryon at
Saint-Cloud later in October: will stay beyond 1m: yet to race on top-of-the-ground.
D. Smaga, France

FAST OPERATIVE 5 ch.g. Absalom 128 – Thorganby Victory 82 (Burglar 128) **40**
[1991 NR 1992 8.1m 8.1g 7.6m² 7g⁶ 7.6m] smallish, stocky gelding: has a roundish
action: poor handicapper, still a maiden: favourably drawn when second and failed
to confirm the form: seems to stay 7.6f: acts on any going: tried visored earlier in
career. *K. O. Cunningham-Brown*

FATACK 3 b.c. Kris 135 – Ma Petite Cherie (USA) 93 (Caro 133) [1991 8d 7d 1992 **–**
10s] quite modest form at 2 yrs, none in minor event at Sandown in August, 1992:
should prove better at 1¼m than shorter: sold to join Miss J. Doyle 1,200 gns Newmarket Autumn Sales. *M. R. Stoute*

FATHER DAN (IRE) 3 ch.c. Martin John – Sonia John (Main Reef 126) [1991 **–**
NR 1992 7g 11.1s 10d⁶ 11.1d⁶] IR 850F: plain colt: poor mover: third foal: dam little
worthwhile form in Ireland: no worthwhile form, including in claimers: visored final
start. *D. Moffatt*

FATHER HAYES (USA) 4 ch.g. Stage Door Johnny (USA) – Fleur d'Or (USA) **64**
(Exclusive Native (USA)) [1991 NR 1992 12.1g⁶ 8.5f⁴ a8g 11.4f* 12.4f] lengthy,
good-topped gelding: sixth foal: half-brother to 2 winners in USA, and to fairly
useful Irish 1¼m to 1¾m winner/good jumper Highland Bud (by Northern Baby):
dam 6f winner at 2 yrs: subject of massive gamble and showed improved form to win
handicap at Sandown easily for W. Pearce: tailed off later in June: much better suited
by around 1lf than 1m. *B. Beasley*

FATHERLAND (IRE) 2 b.c. (Feb 27) Sadler's Wells (USA) 132 **– 113** p
Lisadell (USA) 122 (Forli (ARG)) [1992 7g* 7g* 7d* 7s* 7m5]

When Vincent O'Brien retires from training the executive at the
Curragh should name the National Stakes in his honour: Fatherland, his
latest winner, is his fifteenth in all. Fatherland's victory, achieved on merit by
half a length from Maroof, wasn't without its irony, however. The currently
depressed reputation of the National Stakes, for so long Ireland's most
prestigious race for two-year-olds, has coincided with the decline of O'Brien's
stable as a classic force, the irony being that their simultaneous decline began
just as a succession of O'Brien-trained winners of the calibre of Storm Bird, El
Gran Senor and Law Society had helped elevate the National Stakes to Group
1 status in 1984. Fatherland is a very useful youngster, of that we've no doubt,
but like O'Brien's other recent winners El Prado and Classic Fame, he
couldn't hold a candle to Storm Bird or El Gran Senor. Indeed, when really put
to the test, in the Dewhurst Stakes at Newmarket, Fatherland couldn't even
make the frame.

Fatherland lined up at the Curragh in September unbeaten in three
races, the last two over the National Stakes course and distance. After
winning a maiden at Leopardstown in July by two lengths he'd gone on to take

276

the Mitsubishi Electric Tyros Stakes and the Futurity Stakes the following month, showing too much speed for the subsequent one-mile Beresford Stakes winner Frenchpark on the first occasion and then winning by a length and a half again, this time from the British challenger Newton's Law, on the second. For no apparent reason the turnout for the National Stakes was a disappointing one, lacking quality as well as numbers. Only four took Fatherland on, the Railway Stakes winner Ivory Frontier representing the best form of the home-trained contingent while the Lanson Champagne Vintage Stakes winner Maroof provided the only foreign opposition. For the third time in succession Fatherland started at odds on, but this time he had to work hard for victory and very nearly didn't make it at all. The feature of the race was the tremendous confidence with which Fatherland was ridden by his regular jockey Piggott, who still had him plumb last of the five as Maroof, who'd set only a modest gallop, suddenly struck for home with two furlongs to run. Fatherland didn't make any impression initially, but as the finishing line approached, both horse and rider really turned on the style to pass Maroof in the last few strides, the pair finishing three lengths clear of the 14/1-shot Khoraz. Waiting tactics were employed again on Fatherland in the Dewhurst four weeks later but, despite running his best race, he found himself outpaced when Zafonic went for home and eventually finished around five lengths behind the winner in fifth place, just behind the placed horses Inchinor and Firm Pledge. We couldn't help thinking that against such useful rivals seven furlongs on good to firm ground had provided an insufficient test of stamina; the manner in which he was staying on at the finish suggested he'd have been well suited by an extra furlong.

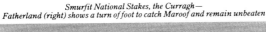

Fatherland (IRE) (b.c. Feb 27, 1990)	Sadler's Wells (USA) (b 1981)	Northern Dancer (b 1961)	Nearctic Natalma
		Fairy Bridge (b 1975)	Bold Reason Special
	Lisadell (USA) (b 1971)	Forli (ch 1963)	Aristophanes Trevisa
		Thong (b 1964)	Nantallah Rough Shod

Fatherland is beautifully bred, having Sadler's Wells as his sire and the Coronation Stakes winner Lisadell as his dam. Lisadell is from a top-class family, the same one as Sadler's Wells, in fact, Lisadell being a full sister to

Smurfit National Stakes, the Curragh—
Fatherland (right) shows a turn of foot to catch Maroof and remain unbeaten

Mrs M. V. O'Brien's "Fatherland"

Sadler's Wells's grandam Special. Special and Lisadell were the first and third foals of the top-class broodmare Thong; the second was the top-class sprinter/miler Thatch, winner of the July Cup and the Sussex Stakes, and Thong went on to produce the disqualified July Cup winner Marinsky and the Irish Derby and St Leger second King Pellinore. Thong, herself, won five races at up to six furlongs, and is a sister to the high-class American performers Ridan, Lt Stevens and Apalachee's dam Moccasin. Lisadell has bred several winners at stud, most notably Fatherland's close relatives Yeats (by Nijinsky), a very useful six-furlong winner in Ireland, and Lisaleen (by Northern Dancer), a fairly useful winner in Ireland at seven furlongs and a mile; she hasn't yet so good a record in that sphere as Special, however, who besides foaling the very useful 1977 Irish two-year-old Fairy Bridge, dam of Sadler's Wells and Tate Gallery, has also bred Nureyev and the good-class American filly Number. Fatherland, a close-coupled, leggy colt, by no means an imposing one, acts on good to firm and soft ground. He never stopped improving in his first season, and the probability is that he'll do even better when he gets the opportunity to tackle a mile or a mile and a quarter. However, Fatherland may not be easy to place. *M. V. O'Brien, Ireland*

FATHOM FIVE (IRE) 3 b.f. Slip Anchor 136 – Sheer Luck 72 (Shergar 140) [1991 NR 1992 10s] leggy, angular filly: first foal: dam 1¼m winner, is half-sister to very smart 1m to 1¼m performer King of Clubs: 6/1, last of 8 in maiden at Newbury in July: moved moderately to post: sold to join M. Williams 4,900 gns Newmarket Autumn Sales. *I. A. Balding*

FAUGERON 3 ch.c. Niniski (USA) 125 – Miss Longchamp 94 (Northfields (USA)) [1991 NR 1992 14m* 14f² 14m⁴ 13.9g 13.9s²] leggy, sparely-made colt: fluent mover: sixth foal: half-brother to several winners, including temperamental but very useful 4-y-o Arcadian Heights (by Shirley Heights), winner at around 1¾m and second in Gold Cup: dam won at 7.2f and 1m at 3 yrs: fairly useful performer: won maiden at Newmarket in May: ran well in minor event at Salisbury and £10,800 handicap at Goodwood next 2 starts: soon driven along in £15,300 handicap and 2-runner minor event (beaten a distance) at York afterwards: sold 11,000 gns Newmarket Autumn Sales: should be suited by 2m: acts on firm ground, possibly not on soft. *G. Wragg*

FAUSTNLUCE LADY 3 b.f. Faustus (USA) 118 – Miss Friendly 72 (Status Seeker) [1991 NR 1992 a7g 7.1g⁵ 10.2g 8.5d⁵ 10.8g 11.7d⁵ 10g a12g⁵ a16g] 2,350 (privately) Y: sturdy, close-coupled filly: moderate walker: seventh foal: dam placed at up to 11f: no worthwhile form, including in visor/blinkers. *G. A. Ham* —

FAWAAYID (USA) 3 b.f. Vaguely Noble 140 – Clara Bow (USA) (Coastal (USA)) [1991 7.8g² 10d* 7s* 9d* 1992 12d⁶ 12f] medium-sized, good-quartered filly: has a powerful, markedly round action: successful in maiden at Listowel and listed events at Leopardstown and the Curragh at 2 yrs: well beaten in Oaks (led 1m) at Epsom and Ribblesdale Stakes at Royal Ascot: should stay 1½m: acted well on a soft surface as 2-y-o. *J. S. Bolger, Ireland* —

FAWZ (IRE) 3 b.f. Green Desert (USA) 127 – Stay Sharpe (USA) (Sharpen Up 127) [1991 NR 1992 10g* 8d³] rather leggy filly: first foal: dam unraced half-sister to dam of Indian Skimmer: won maiden at Brighton, staying on well: creditable third in minor event at Leicester later in autumn: stays 1¼m: sold 32,000 gns Newmarket December Sales: may be capable of better. *R. W. Armstrong*   76

FAY EDEN (IRE) 4 ch.f. Fayruz 116 – Dainty Eden 53 (Orbit 106) [1991 7g⁴ 8s 5g⁵ 6g* 5.1d⁴ 5.7g 6.9m 1992 5s 6v 7g 6g 5.1m 6m⁶ 6.1m 8.1m 5g 6m 7.1s] small, workmanlike filly: moderate mover: rated 60 at 3 yrs: of little account in 1992. *R. J. Hodges* —

FAYFA (IRE) 2 b.f. (Apr 1) Slip Anchor 136 – Eljazzi 92 (Artaius (USA) 129) [1992 7g*] fifth foal: sister to 4-y-o 1½m to 14.6f winner Sarawat and half-sister to Prix de Diane winner Rafha (by Kris), also successful at 6f (at 2 yrs) to 11.5f: dam 2-y-o 7f winner stayed 1¼m, is half-sister to Pitcairn and very smart middle-distance stayer Valley Forge: weak 14/1-shot, won 24-runner maiden at Newmarket in October by 1½ lengths from Stella Mystika, soon close up, leading 2f out and running on very well: sure to improve. *H. R. A. Cecil*   81 p

FAYNAZ 6 ch.h. Tumble Wind (USA) – Ceduna (FR) (Right Tack 131) [1991 7g 6m³ 5.8f 7m⁵ 6m⁶ 7m⁴ 6f 10g 1992 a7g 7g 7f³ 7f⁵ 7m⁵ a10g⁶ a8g⁵ a8g⁶] well-made horse: poor handicapper nowadays: stays 7f: acts on firm going, yet to race on soft: no improvement in blinkers/visor. *W. R. Muir*   47

FAYRE FIND 2 b.f. (Mar 15) Dowsing (USA) 124 – June Fayre (Sagaro 133) [1992 a7g⁴ 7d] sixth foal: half-sister to 4 winners here and abroad, including (from 6f to 9f) plating-class Express Edition (by Comedy Star): dam twice-raced daughter of Pasty, best 2-y-o filly of 1975: no worthwhile form, though signs of ability in claimer at Southwell on debut, in July. *M. H. Tompkins* —

FAY'S SONG (IRE) 4 ch.f. Fayruz 116 – Harp (Ennis 128) [1991 5m⁶ 6d⁴ 6g² 5g 6g³ 5f⁴ 6m 5m² 5g⁴ 5.2g 1992 5f⁵ 6g* 6m⁵ 6g 6d 5g² 7g⁵ 6.1d 6g⁶] compact filly: moderate mover: inconsistent handicapper: won at Lingfield in July: effective at 6f and 7f: probably acts on any going: suitable mount for apprentice. *R. Akehurst*   77

FEELING FOOLISH (IRE) 3 ch.g. Fools Holme (USA) – Felin Geri (Silly Season 127) [1991 6d² 6m³ 8.1g² 8m² 7m⁵ 8.1s⁵ a7g a8g* 1992 a10g³ a8g⁵ a8g⁴ 9s⁵ 11.1m² 12.2m³ 9.2m⁵ 13.8g⁴ 12m³ 15.1f⁶ 12.3s² 10.8s 10d] useful-looking gelding: modest performer: trained until after tenth 3-y-o start by T. Fairhurst: stays 1½m: acts on good to firm, soft ground and on all-weather surfaces: visored when successful: often blinkered, effective without. *B. Forsey*   53 a60

FELAWNAH (USA) 2 ch.f. (Jan 21) Mr Prospector (USA) – Ambassador of Luck (USA) (What Luck (USA)) [1992 6d² 7m⁵] $725,000Y: big, rangy filly: has plenty of scope: fifth known foal: closely related to 2 winners by Alydar, including Grade 3 1m winner Alydavid, and half-sister to 2 winners, notably fairly useful 1988 2-y-o 6f winner Zakhir (by Topsider), later successful in USA: dam, stayed 1m, was champion mare in USA: backward and green, very promising ¾-length second in Blue Seal Stakes at Ascot, held up in last place 4f, then quickening well and keeping on strongly: heavily-backed favourite, though sweating and edgy, similar form when fifth in Group 3 Rockfel Stakes at Newmarket in October: will stay 1m: worth another chance. *H. M. Gosden*   89 p

FELICE'S PET 2 ch.f. (Apr 14) Aragon 118 – Princesse Smile 99 (Balidar 133) [1992 5g 6d⁵] 6,800Y: leggy, sparely-made filly: half-sister to several winners in   47

France, including 1983 2-y-o 7f winner Island Smile (by Ile de Bourbon) and 7f (at 2 yrs) and 1½m winner Shy Gremlin (by Home Guard): dam 7f to 9f winner in Italy, is sister to Bolkonski: poor form in maiden auctions at Windsor and Ayr: will stay 1m: sold 600 gns Newmarket Autumn Sales. *M. H. Tompkins*

FELSINA (IRE)   3 b.f. Slip Anchor 136 – Sepideh (Habitat 134) [1991 NR 1992   –
8m 10m 10d⁵ 12.1g] 12,500F, 20,000Y: ex-French filly: moderate mover: third foal: half-sister to Irish 5f winner Law Gazette (by Law Society): dam, unraced, out of half-sister to Sigy and Sonoma (both by Habitat): blinkered-fifth of 7 in minor event at Saint-Cloud in summer, first sign of ability when trained by M. Zilber: behind in Edinburgh seller 3 months later: seems not to stay 1½m. *W. Storey*

FELT LUCKY (IRE)   2 ch.c. (Jan 18) Coquelin (USA) 121 – Bases Loaded (USA)   **64**
(Northern Dancer (CAN)) [1992 5m 5g⁴ 5m* 6g 6d 5g] IR 4,200Y, 4,300 2-y-o: sturdy colt: carries condition: good mover, with a long stride: half-brother to several winners here and abroad, notably smart middle-distance performer Relief Pitcher (by Welsh Term): dam won at 7f in USA: modest performer: won maiden auction at Beverley in July, quickly over to favoured for rail and making rest: ran moderately in nurseries afterwards, particularly so on last 2 starts: should be better suited by 6f than 5f: possibly requires top-of-the-ground: sold 3,100 gns Newmarket Autumn Sales. *M. R. Channon*

FELUCCA   2 b.f. (Apr 30) Green Desert (USA) 127 – Bloudan (USA) (Damascus   **86** p
(USA)) [1992 6d³ 6m*] good-topped filly: fluent mover: first foal: dam unraced daughter of Chain Store, dam of Al Bahathri: needed race and eased when beaten in Blue Seal Stakes at Ascot: heavily-backed favourite again, won 14-runner maiden at Newmarket in October, soon close up, quickening under 2f out and running on in very good style: should stay 1m: looks sure to improve further, and win more races. *H. R. A. Cecil*

FEMININE WILES (IRE)   3 b.f. Ahonoora 122 – Instinctive Move (USA) **110**
(Nijinsky (CAN) 138) [1991 8.1m⁵ 8m² 8m* 1992 11d² 10g⁶ 10.4g⁴ 12g⁵ 10m* 10d⁶ 10s⁴ 10.1g⁵ 10d² 8.5f3] big, lengthy filly: good mover: very useful performer: looked unsatisfactory early in season (carried head awkwardly and seemed irresolute) but battled on well to win listed race at Newbury in June: held her form well, placed in Sun Chariot Stakes at Newmarket (head behind Red Slippers) and Steinlen Handicap at Gulfstream on last 2 starts: effective at 8.5f and stays 1¼m: probably acts on any going. *P. W. Chapple-Hyam*

FEN DANCE (IRE)   3 b.f. Trojan Fen 118 – Madame Nureyev (USA) (Nureyev   **82**
(USA) 131) [1991 6f⁴ 6.1m² 1992 6.9g³ 7d* 7m² 7m a8g] leggy filly: fairly useful form on her day: easily best efforts when successful in handicap at Leicester in June and second in similar event at Doncaster: hampered several times penultimate start and well beaten 4 months later: should stay 1m. *P. J. Makin*

FENGARI   3 ch.c. Formidable (USA) 125 – Foreseen (Reform 132) [1991 a7g³   **77**
1992 a8g² a10g² a10g* 10d* 12m 10s² 10g 9s] good-quartered colt: fair form at best: won maiden at Lingfield and handicap at Kempton in the spring: best effort when staying-on second in £9,500 handicap at Ascot: well beaten later in autumn, when sweating final start: should be well suited by 1½m: goes well on soft ground: sold 11,200 gns Ascot December Sales. *P. T. Walwyn*

FEN PRINCESS (IRE)   4 b.f. Trojan Fen 118 – Cenerentola (FR) (Caro 133)   **54**
[1991 8g 10g³ 10g² 8.3f6 12.1g 10.4m 12.2g⁵ 1992 8.3v 12g⁵ 14.9d 11.1s 15.8d³ 15.1m* 15.1f² 15.1m* 15.1m4] neat filly: consistent handicapper: twice an easy winner at Edinburgh in midsummer: suited by test of stamina: acts on firm going, seems unsuited by a soft surface: tried visored once at 3 yrs. *P. C. Haslam*

FERDIA (IRE)   3 b.c. Petorius 117 – Kilvarnet 78 (Furry Glen 121) [1991 6g 6g⁶   –
6m 6m⁶ 8.1d 7m a7g* a7g⁵ 1992 a8g² a8g* a8g⁴ 9.9g⁴ 10d 8.2g a8g⁴ a12g⁴] tall, a62 rather leggy colt: modest handicapper: won at Southwell in January, hanging left 2f out: showed he retains ability in December final 2 starts, after 8 months off: suited by 1m: best efforts on fibresand: takes keen hold. *R. Hollinshead*

FERGUS GARBER   2 b.g. (Mar 1) Reesh 117 – Springle 83 (Le Johnstan 123)   –
[1992 6m 7g] 2,300Y: good-topped gelding: third foal: dam 2-y-o 1m winner: carrying condition, little sign of ability in maiden auction at Doncaster and a claimer at Leicester: sold 700 gns Doncaster September Sales. *J. M. Carr*

FERMAIN   3 ch.g. Bustino 136 – Trail of Blues (Cure The Blues (USA)) [1991 NR   –
1992 10g5 11.7d 10g 12v⁵] rather leggy gelding: second foal: dam unraced: well beaten, including in claimers: sold to join A. Barrow 3,400 gns Ascot November Sales. *Lord Huntingdon*

FERMOY (USA) 3 b.f. Irish River (FR) 131 – Victoress (USA) (Conquistador **84**
Cielo (USA)) [1991 6m² 6m³ 1992 10m* 10.1m* 11.9d³] leggy, close-coupled filly:
first foal: dam lightly-raced French 11f winner, is half-sister to Awaasif (dam of Snow
Bride) and several other good winners: fairly useful performer: won 20-runner
maiden at Windsor and 3-runner £7,500 contest at Yarmouth in September: again
well-backed favourite, last of 3 in minor event at York over 3 weeks later: should
have stayed 1½m: acted on good to firm and dead going: visits Groom Dancer. *L. M.
Cumani*

FERN 3 b.f. Shirley Heights 130 – Free Guest 125 (Be My Guest (USA) 126) [1991 **100**
7d³ 8m²ᵈⁱˢ 8d⁴ 1992 10m³ 11.5g⁶ 11.9f* 12g] rather unfurnished, quite attractive
filly: useful form when 5 lengths third to Oumaldaaya in Lupe Stakes at Goodwood
in May: odds on, ran badly in Yarmouth maiden: nowhere near best to win 3-runner
maiden at Brighton in August: acted as pacemaker final start: should have stayed
1½m: easily best efforts on good to firm ground: stud. *L. M. Cumani*

FERN HEIGHTS 5 b.g. Runnett 125 – Jenny's Baubee (Busted 134) [1991 NR –
1992 8.9m⁶ 10d] sturdy gelding: second foal: dam unraced: ex-Irish gelding:
successful over 8.5f as 2-y-o for A. Redmond: little form since. *C. D. Broad*

FERROVIA 3 b.f. Never So Bold 135 – Ouija 104 (Silly Season 127) [1991 6m 7m⁶ **42**
1992 7f 8m⁶ 7g⁵] sparely-made filly: plating-class maiden: stays 1m: blinkered (ran
creditably) final start, in July: sold 6,000 gns Newmarket July Sales. *J. W. Watts*

FERRYCROSTHEMERSEY (IRE) 3 b.f. Red Sunset 120 – Glomach (USA) –
73 (Majestic Light (USA)) [1991 5g 6m 7.5f 5.1g 6m 5m 1992 8s] neat filly: has a
round action: seems of little account. *G. Fleming*

FERRY GIRL (USA) 3 b.f. Ziggy's Boy (USA) – Any Evening (USA) (Banquet –
Table (USA)) [1991 NR 1992 a6g⁶] $20,000Y: second foal: dam minor winner at 6f:
sire (by Danzig) won from 5f to 7f: 10/1 and wearing eyeshield, behind in 9-runner
maiden at Lingfield in February: sold 1,000 gns Ascot May Sales. *D. R. C. Elsworth*

FESTIN 2 br.c. (Mar 2) General Assembly (USA) – Roses Galore (USA) (Stage **66**
Door Johnny) [1992 7.1s⁵ 7g³ 6s 8g⁶ 8.2d⁵ 8d⁵ 7m⁵ 7d a8g³ a7g⁶ a7g] 16,000Y:
sturdy, attractive colt: third foal: half-brother to winners in USA by Cozzene and
Strike Gold: dam showed some ability in USA: fair maiden: sold out of J. Dunlop's
stable 12,000 gns Newmarket Autumn Sales after eighth outing: well below form
last 2 starts: stays 1m well: acts on good to firm and dead ground and on equitrack:
probably best in blinkers. *P. C. Haslam*

FESTIVE CHEER (IRE) 3 b.c. Fayruz 116 – Granny Bunn (Wolver Hollow **86**
126) [1991 6g 5g² 5f* 5m² 6m³ 1992 9g⁵ 6f] strong-quartered colt: rated 98 at 2 yrs:
not so good as at 2 yrs, and form only when fifth in minor event at Tipperary: behind
in Cork And Orrery Stakes at Royal Ascot following month. *T. Stack, Ireland*

FETISH 3 b.f. Dancing Brave (USA) 140 – Bold Fantasy 115 (Bold Lad (IRE) 133) **85**
[1991 6g⁵ 1992 8s* 10.5d² 7.9m* 10g² 9v³] lengthy, deep-girthed filly: moderate
mover: fairly useful performer: successful in maiden at Newcastle and handicap at
York in the spring: off course 5 months, well beaten in minor events last 2 starts:
stayed 10.5f well: acted on good to firm and soft ground: stud. *H. R. A. Cecil*

FETTLE UP 4 ch.g. Lyphard's Special (USA) 122 – Fire Risk (Thatch (USA) 136) –
[1991 10m 12m 1992 16s] neat gelding: lightly raced, and no worthwhile form in
modest company. *J. Wharton*

FIALA (IRE) 4 b.f. Persian Bold 123 – Goody Blake 103 (Blakeney 126) [1991 **87**
8f⁴ 10g 12s² a12g² a13g* 1992 a13g² a14g* a16g⁵] workmanlike filly: has a round
action: fairly useful handicapper: won at Southwell (made all, stayed on strongly) in
January: tailed off final 2f there following month: stays 1¾m well: acts on soft
ground and goes well on all-weather surfaces: joined H. Cecil but didn't reappear. *J.
H. M. Gosden*

FICHU (USA) 4 b.g. Sharpen Up 127 – Mousseline de Soie (FR) (Riverman –
(USA) 131) [1991 NR 1992 10d⁴] sixth foal: half-brother to 3 minor winners abroad:
dam won at up to 9f in USA: unplaced in 2 NH Flat races: fourth in celebrity event at
Wetherby late on. *G. Thorner*

FICTION 3 br.f. Dominion 123 – Sans Blague (USA) 108 (The Minstrel (CAN) –
135) [1991 5.2g³ 5f* 6g 7m 1992 7m 12f² 9f] leggy filly: no form in first half of season
in handicaps and (looking most awkward ride) 2-runner minor event: should stay 7f.
M. P. Naughton

FIELD OF DREAMS 3 b.f. Celestial Storm (USA) 132 – Silka (ITY) (Lypheor –
118) [1991 7g 1992 10g a12g⁴ 14.1g] leggy, unfurnished filly: no worthwhile form. *C.
F. Wall*

FIELD OF HONOUR 4 b.c. Ahonoora 122 – Brickfield Queen (High Top 131) **84**
[1991 7m⁴ 8.5m² 8m* 8g² 8.9m² 7g 1992 7g 8g⁵ 8.1m⁴ 8f 7g 8m 8f 7g* 7d] angular, quite attractive colt: good walker: fairly useful handicapper: won at Brighton in August: never travelling fluently in £50,000 race at Ascot month later: effective from 7f to 9f: best efforts on a sound surface: has edged left: reportedly sent to USA. *L. M. Cumani*

FIELD OF STARS 2 b.c. (Feb 13) Salse (USA) 128 – Marseillaise (Artaius **80** p
(USA) 129) [1992 7m 7g²] 26,000F, 62,000Y: stocky, lengthy colt: second foal: half-brother to disappointing 3-y-o Access Voyager (by Ballad Rock): dam unraced half-sister to Irish 2000 Guineas winner Northern Treasure: burly still, beaten a neck by Dahyah in maiden at Doncaster in October, quickening clear at halfway, wandering closing stages then passed near line: will improve again, and win a similar event. *J. H. M. Gosden*

FIELD OF VISION (IRE) 2 b.g. (Mar 24) Vision (USA) – Bold Meadows 80 **58**
(Persian Bold 123) [1992 5g⁴ 5s⁵ 5.1s 5m⁶ 5m² 5m* 5g 5f⁵ 5g⁴ 5g³] 6,500Y: neat, quite attractive gelding: has a quick action: fourth foal: half-brother to useful Irish 3-y-o 7f (at 2 yrs) to 1½m winner Judicial Field (by Law Society): dam, Irish 6.9f and 1½m winner, half-sister to dam of Kilijaro: sire (brother to Caerleon) won from 8.5f to 1½m (Grade 1 event): modest performer: won 4-runner maiden auction at Hamilton in June: bred to stay beyond 5f, but races very keenly, and may not do so: best form on a sound surface: seems best in blinkers: not one to trust implicitly. *M. Johnston*

FIELDRIDGE 3 ch.c. Rousillon (USA) 133 – Final Thought (Final Straw 127) **91**
[1991 8m² 8.1g³ 1992 10d² 10f² 11.9g 10.2d²] tall, lengthy colt: fairly useful maiden, best effort in handicap at Salisbury second start: off course 2½ months and favourite, well below form when second at Bath final start: should stay beyond 1¼m: easily best effort on firm going: has joined C. Brooks. *C. R. Nelson*

FIERRO 2 b.g. (Mar 29) Miswaki (USA) 124 – Fiesta Libre (USA) (Damascus **62**
(USA) [1992 5g 5m* 6g⁶ 6f 6g] small colt: poor mover: half-brother to several winners in North America: dam 6.5f to 9f winner in North America: modest performer: favourite, won maiden at Leicester in May, quickly away and making all: well beaten afterwards, including in nursery (blinkered, misbehaved beforehand) penultimate start: will stay 6f + . *C. E. Brittain*

FIERY SUN 7 b.g. Sexton Blake 126 – Melanie Jane (Lord Gayle (USA) 124) –
[1991 NR 1992 11g 17.9d 13.8g] sturdy gelding: probably of little account nowadays. *R. E. Barr*

FIGHTER SQUADRON 3 ch.g. Primo Dominie 121 – Formidable Dancer 70 **62**
(Formidable (USA) 125) [1991 6g a7g 5f⁶ 1992 a6g⁵ a5g 5s 5v² 5g a5g² a5g* a5g² 5.1g³ 5g² a6g⁴ a6g³ 5m* 6m³ 6m³ a5g 6m³ a6g⁶ a5g] leggy gelding: consistent handicapper: won at Southwell in May and Pontefract (ridden by 7-lb claimer to lead close home) in July: off course over 3 months, below best twice in December: stays 6f: acts on good to firm and heavy going and on fibresand: usually visored or blinkered nowadays: has hung markedly left. *J. A. Glover*

FIGHTING AJDAL (IRE) 3 b.c. Ajdal (USA) 130 – Ski Sailing (USA) 115 **61**
(Royal Ski (USA)) [1991 NR 1992 7f 10.1d 9s³] compact, good sort: fifth foal: closely related to 11.7f and 1½m winner Shareef Sailor (by Shareef Dancer): dam 7f and 1¼m winner, also second in Lancashire Oaks: form in maidens only when third at Redcar in September: will be suited by return to further. *A. C. Stewart*

FIGHTING BRAVE 5 b.g. Gorytus (USA) 132 – Lady Habitat (Habitat 134) – §
[1991 NR 1992 12m] lengthy gelding: rated 77 at 3 yrs when suited by 1½m and firm ground: sweating and tailed off in handicap in June on first run since: usually blinkered. *N. A. Graham*

FIGHTING TALK (USA) 3 b.g. Fighting Fit (USA) – Nanna's Joy (USA) –
(Tentam (USA)) [1991 NR 1992 11.7s] $7,200Y, resold $10,000Y: strong gelding: fourth foal: dam unraced half-sister to Grade 3 2-y-o winner Darby Fair: 25/1 and very backward, tailed-off last of 11 in maiden at Bath in May. *C. R. Nelson*

FIGHT TO WIN (USA) 4 b.g. Fit To Fight (USA) – Spark of Life (USA) (Key –
To The Mint (USA)) [1991 10m⁴ 12m 12m⁵ 14g 17.2f³ 16m² 16m³ 16.9g⁴ 15.4m³ 1992 18g] sturdy gelding: shows knee action: one paced and still a maiden: rated 65 at 3 yrs when largely consistent: stiffish task, well beaten at Doncaster in March, 1992: stays well: acts on firm going: ran well when blinkered once: winning hurdler in 1991/2. *I. A. Balding*

FILICAIA 6 gr.m. Sallust 134 – Fine Flame (Le Prince 98) [1991 6m 6g 6m² 6f² **66**
5h* 5d 6g⁶ 6m* 6f 6m 6f² 5h³ 5f⁵ 5m⁴ 6m² 6g 1992 6v 6d 5d 6f 6m² 5f³ 6f* 6m² 6m⁴

6m 6g 7m 6g] compact mare: modest handicapper: form in 1992 only when in frame in midsummer, winning at Ripon: effective from stiff 5f to 7f: acts on hard and dead going: earlier in career seemed best in a visor, not visored in 1992: often slowly away, and gets well behind but suitable mount for 7-lb claimer. *Don Enrico Incisa*

FILM LIGHTING GIRL 6 ch.m. Persian Bold 123 – Mey 78 (Canisbay 120) – [1991 NR 1992 12.2d4] leggy, light-framed ex-Irish mare: of little account. *R. J. Weaver*

FINAL ACE 5 ch.g. Sharpo 132 – Palmella (USA) 89 (Grundy 137) [1991 6m 7m – 6m5 8d 8g5 8.2m 8.9m3 10.8m3 10.2m6 9s 10.8g 1992 a14g] robust gelding: rated 56 at 4 yrs when best at around 1¼m on top-of-the-ground: tailed off at Southwell in January, 1992. *Miss S. J. Wilton*

FINAL ACTION 2 ch.f. (Apr 29) Nicholas Bill 125 – Strathclair (Klairon 131) – [1992 6g6 6g 8d] 1,850Y: leggy, sparely-made filly: closely related to winning Irish stayer/hurdler Strathline (by High Line) and half-sister to several other minor winners: dam, placed at up to 7f in Ireland, is half-sister to good sprinter Right Strath: little worthwhile form, including in a seller. *R. M. Whitaker*

FINAL BOUT 4 br.f. Final Straw 127 – Bourton Downs 74 (Philip of Spain 126) – [1991 6g 6d 8f5 6f 6m 1992 7d] small, stocky filly: poor mover: of little account. *Mrs M. Reveley*

FINALDREAM (IRE) 4 b.f. Wassl 125 – Pale Ivory 108 (Silver Shark 129) [1991 – 7m 8g 10g5 12g 10s* 12m2 10g4 12g 1992 12m 10g 9.7g 11.7f5] leggy filly: half-sister to several winners, notably fairly useful Kemago (by Prince Tenderfoot), Group 3 winner over 7f in Ireland: dam effective from 5f to 1m at 2 yrs: ex-Irish handicapper, successful at Ballinrobe at 3 yrs when with D. Gillespie: no form here in summer, mostly in handicaps: stays 1½m: acts on good to firm and soft ground. *A. W. Denson*

FINAL FRONTIER (IRE) 2 b.g. (Apr 22) Common Grounds 118 – Last Gun- **62** boat 50 (Dominion 123) [1992 6g4 5m3 6h2 6m 7g2 9g3 7g] 25,000Y: leggy, workmanlike gelding: rather unfurnished: fifth foal: half-brother to 3 winners, including, at 1½m, 3-y-o Arfey (by Burslem): dam, middle-distance maiden, is half-sister to Oaks-placed Suni and Media Luna: fairly consistent maiden: will stay 1¼m: yet to race on a soft surface. *R. Akehurst*

FINAL SHOT 5 br.m. Dalsaan 125 – Isadora Duncan (Primera 131) [1991 7.6d 7m **65** 6m 6g 6d4 6m2 6d6 6m 6g 6m 6g 7g 1992 6d 7f5 6m5 6m2 6g] small, workmanlike mare: poor mover: fairly useful handicapper (rated 91) at best: run-of-the-mill in 1992: effective at 6f and 7f: acted on firm ground but very best efforts on dead: in foal to Rock City. *M. H. Easterby*

FINALTO 4 ch.c. Kris 135 – Scarcely Blessed 116 (So Blessed 130) [1991 NR 1992 – 12.4m] half-brother to 4 winners, including very useful 6f and 7f winner Breadcrumb (by Final Straw) and irresolute sprinter Pagan Rite (by Formidable): dam sprinting half-sister to Mummy's Pet: 50/1, always behind in Newcastle apprentice maiden in August on belated debut. *R. Hollinshead*

FINAVON 2 b.c. (Mar 20) Soviet Star (USA) 128 – Dunninald 93 (Mill Reef (USA) **70** 141) [1992 6m 6m3 7d4 7f4 8d2 8s4 6m] compact, useful-looking colt: has a quick action: second foal: half-brother to 3-y-o Marvelous Molly (by Shardari): dam 2-y-o 6f winner stayed 8.5f, is out of sister to very smart Joking Apart: fair but inconsistent maiden: suited by 1m: probably acts on any going: effective in a visor or blinkers: sold 14,000 gns Newmarket Autumn Sales. *I. A. Balding*

FINDLAYS CHOICE 3 b.f. Jupiter Island 126 – Truly Blest 75 (So Blessed 130) – [1991 6g5 6.1d 7m2 6m6 7m5 8d5 1992 10m] leggy, angular filly: plating-class maiden at 2 yrs: edgy, tailed off in handicap in May, 1992: should stay 1¼m: acts on good to firm and dead ground. *M. J. Ryan*

FINE AS FIVEPENCE 3 b.f. Sulaafah (USA) 119 – Shes Broke (Busted 134) – [1991 8g 8d 8g 1992 8v a12g4 8.1m5 8d6 8f 10.8g6] sparely-made filly: moderate mover: of little account. *Mrs A. Knight*

FINGERS CROSSED 8 b.m. Touching Wood (USA) 127 – La Pythie (FR) – (Filiberto (USA) 123) [1991 14m 1992 15.1f5] neat, strong mare: poor maiden on flat: modest staying hurdler, won in autumn. *M. D. Hammond*

FINJAN 5 b.h. Thatching 131 – Capricornia (Try My Best (USA) 130) [1991 6g 6g2 **91** 6d5 6m 6m* 6m 6g 6g6 6g3 6m 6d2 6m 1992 6m2 6m* 7m2 5m* 6f* 6.1m 6g6 6g] strong, sturdy horse: keen walker: fairly useful and consistent performer: successful in small fields in early-summer in claimers at Newcastle and Sandown and minor event at Redcar: claimer ridden, good seventh in Great St Wilfrid Stakes (Handicap) at Ripon in August final start: effective from stiff 5f to 7f: acts on firm and dead ground: ran well when visored at 4 yrs: has broken blood vessels, including on reappearance. *M. P. Naughton*

FINMENTAL (IRE) 2 ch.g. (Apr 29) Nordance (USA) – Prima Bella 76 (High **87** Hat 131) [1992 5s⁶ 5g* 6f² 5m*dis 6m³ 6.1d³ 5m* 5m⁴] 8,200Y: workmanlike gelding: good walker: half-brother to several winners here and abroad, including (from 5f to 1½m) No More The Fool (by Jester) and (from 1m to 9f) Monteros Boy (by Crofter): dam stayed well: sire very useful sprinter/miler: fairly useful performer: first past post in maiden at Wolverhampton in May and median auction (disqualified for hampering another runner) and nursery (in good style) at Ayr in summer: best form to date at 5f, though is bred to stay further: probably unsuited by a soft surface: best form in strongly-run races: not seen after July. *A. Bailey*

FINNERAN'S FANTASY 3 b.g. Cree Song 99 – Mab (Morston (FR) 125) [1991 **–** NR 1992 10d 14.1s] 740Y, 2,000 2-y-o: workmanlike gelding: moderate sixth living foal: half-brother to 2 winners abroad: dam placed over 1m on second of 2 starts: showed little in Redcar maiden and Nottingham seller in autumn. *D. Morris*

FIR COPSE 2 b.f. (Mar 8) Aragon 118 – New Pastures (Formidable (USA) 125) **39** [1992 6m 7s 6g] leggy filly: first foal: dam unraced: poor maiden: should stay 7f: gave trouble stalls second start. *P. R. Hedger*

FIREBIRD LAD 4 ch.c. Electric 126 – Arbatina (Sallust 134) [1991 NR 1992 10g] **–** third living foal: half-brother to quite modest handicapper/fair chaser Tinas Lad (by Jellaby): dam poor maiden: burly, always behind in Windsor minor event in July. *R. Curtis*

FIREFIGHTER 3 ch.c. Sharpo 132 – Courtesy Call (Northfields (USA)) [1991 **71** 6f⁵ 1992 a8g³ a8g² a8g² a8g² 8.9s² 8.9v* 12.3s* 12d 8.9s* 10.5g* 12m⁴ a12g² a12g² a64 10.5s⁵ 12.1s⁴ 11v⁶ a12g] compact colt: modest performer: consistent in first half of season, winning claimers at Wolverhampton (2) and Haydock and handicap at Ripon: below best afterwards: effective at 9f and stays 1½m: needs give in the ground on turf, acts on fibresand. *R. Hollinshead*

FIRE IN MY BODY (USA) 2 b.c. (Apr 4) Woodman (USA) 126 – Really **65** p Welcome (USA) (In Reality) [1992 7g 7g a8g³] $30,000F, $115,000Y: leggy, quite attractive colt: first foal: dam, half-sister to a graded-placed winner, won a maiden at about 1m in USA: modest form in maidens: will be well suited by 1¼m +: likely to do better: sent to Italy. *P. W. Chapple-Hyam*

FIRE TOP 7 br.h. Hotfoot 126 – Sirnelta (FR) (Sir Tor) [1991 10g 12g 10.1f* 10g² **100** 10g⁵ 10m³ 10.5f² 10m 10d⁴ 1992 10d⁶ 10d³ 10.1g² 10m² 10d* 10m 10g⁶ 10g 10g⁴] sparely-made horse: usually races really well: useful handicapper: typically gutsy effort when winning very valuable Royal Hong Kong Jockey Club Trophy at Sandown in July by ½ length from Charlo: suited by around 1¼m: acts on any going: sold 31,000 gns Newmarket Autumn Sales: tremendously tough and genuine, usually races up with the pace and should have a good year or 2 in him in USA with S. Schulman. *R. Akehurst*

FIRING LINE (IRE) 3 b. or br.c. Slip Anchor 136 – Red Partridge (Solinus 130) **111** [1991 NR 1992 8s⁴ 9s* 10d² 12g* 10d² 12m⁵] IR 21,000Y: big, lengthy colt: fourth foal: half-brother to winners in Hong Kong and Italy: dam Irish 2-y-o 7.9f winner: very useful performer: successful in minor events at the Curragh in March and May: second to St Jovite in Derby Trial at Leopardstown and to Brief Truce in Gallinule Stakes (best effort) at the Curragh: favourite, soon struggling in straight in Gordon Stakes at Goodwood in July: stays 1½m: possibly unsuited by top-of-the-ground: blinkered/visored last 3 starts. *T. Stack, Ireland*

FIRM FRIEND (IRE) 2 ch.f. (Jan 28) Affirmed (USA) – Chere Amie (FR) (Gay **106** Mecene (USA) 128) [1992 6.5s² 6d* 6.5g* 6.5s³ 8s⁶ 7s⁴] third foal: half-sister to 7.6f and 1¼m winner Green Danube (by Irish River): dam French 1m winner seemed to stay 1¼m: useful performer: successful in minor event at Evry and Criterium d'Evry in September: good fourth of 5 to Kadounor in Criterium de Maisons-Laffitte in November: should stay 1m: yet to race on top-of-the-ground. *D. Smaga, France*

FIRM PLEDGE (USA) 2 b.c. (Apr 11) Affirmed (USA) – Rutledge Place **115** (USA) (Caro 133) [1992 6m* 6g² 7m³ a8.5f]

Those who saw Firm Pledge canter home seven lengths clear in a field of newcomers at Goodwood in May would not have been surprised by a prediction that they had just seen the horse who would finish third in the Dewhurst Stakes at Newmarket in October; those who saw him overturned by Realities when long odds on in a minor event at Windsor on his only start in between might well have been, the more so when Realities' subsequent form showed him to be well below pattern-race standard. Firm Pledge's excellent performance in the Dewhurst served to confirm what was widely touted, that he was the best of his stable's two-year-olds, and although he finished well beaten in the Breeders' Cup Juvenile on his final outing we wouldn't hold that against him.

Firm Pledge's reputation preceded him to Goodwood, where he could hardly have made a more impressive first appearance. Starting a heavily-backed 13/8-favourite, Firm Pledge made just about all the running in a fast time, coming right away from Canaska Star, himself clear in second place, in the final quarter-mile. Royal Ascot went by without Firm Pledge. Sore shins kept him off the course until the middle of August when he had his second race, against the Sandown winner Realities and two no-hopers, in a six-furlong minor event at Windsor. The two market-leaders dominated the finish, but it was Realities, stepping up from five furlongs, who just prevailed in a race that, for the first part, was run at a modest gallop. The absence of a strong gallop probably made the difference between winning and losing for Firm Pledge, but as it was he went down by only a head, putting in a game rally in the dying strides having come off the bridle at halfway. In view of his exciting debut, Firm Pledge's performance at Windsor could be interpreted as being rather disappointing; given the training troubles he'd had in the interim, though, it was a respectable effort against a speedier opponent better suited by the way the race was run, and he showed it wasn't a true reflection of his merit when getting a stronger test of stamina in the Dewhurst. Firm Pledge, who once again looked tremendously well, did better than his position in the market, fifth favourite at 12/1 in a field of eleven, suggested he would. He came out second-best in the three-way battle for second place, a head behind Inchinor and four lengths behind Zafonic, after racing with the leaders from the start. In normal circumstances Firm Pledge should have been suited by the step up to around a mile in his only subsequent race, but, in common with most of the European raiders at Gulfstream Park on Breeders' Cup day at the end of October, he failed to give his running on dirt and eventually trailed home twelfth of the thirteen runners in the Juvenile, having raced prominently to the far turn. Firm Pledge's third place in the Dewhurst leaves no doubt that he was a smart two-year-old, though, and the fact that he had such an interrupted season raises the probability that he is still very much an unexposed horse, certainly over a mile. The likelihood is that we haven't seen the best of him yet.

		Exclusive Native	Raise A Native
	Affirmed (USA)	(ch 1965)	Exclusive
	(ch 1975)	Won't Tell You	Crafty Admiral
Firm Pledge (USA)		(b 1962)	Scarlet Ribbon
(b.c. Apr 11, 1990)		Caro	Fortino II
	Rutledge Place (USA)	(gr 1967)	Chambord
	(b or br 1985)	Bold Place	Bold Bidder
		(b 1969)	Extra Place

Firm Pledge, a strong, lengthy, attractive colt, was bought for 25,000 dollars at Fasig-Tipton's Selected Yearling Sale in July. The sale price is indicative of the low esteem in which the triple crown winner Affirmed is now held as a stallion after his first ten crops had yielded just a handful of Group 1 or Grade 1 winners, though Firm Pledge's owner hasn't any cause for complaint after enjoying plenty of success with the thoroughly genuine Zoman and the Prix Vermeille and Yorkshire Oaks winner Bint Pasha. Firm Pledge is the second foal from his dam, the unraced Rutledge Place, following the 1991 Irish two-year-old five- and six-furlong winner Stellar Empress (by Star de Naskra). Rutledge Place is a half-sister to several winners, of whom the best were the useful French miler Dancing Place and the smart French sprinter Gem Diamond, who suddenly found his form as a five-year-old in France in 1984 when he won four races including the five-furlong Prix du Gros Chene. The second dam Bold Place won nine races, including minor stakes, at up to a mile and is a full sister to the Grade 3 eight-and-a-half-furlong winner Card Table as well as to the dam of the Champion Stakes winner Legal Case. Firm Pledge will stay a mile and a quarter as a three-year-old, and may well get further. A moderate mover, he has raced only on good or good to firm ground on turf. *P. F. I. Cole*

FIRST AFFAIR 2 b.f. (Feb 8) Primo Dominie 121 – Fleeting Affair 98 (Hotfoot 126) [1992 6g 7g⁴ 7g 7.1s] good-bodied filly: good mover: second foal: half-sister to 3-y-o 10.1f and 12.1f winner Trump (by Last Tycoon): dam 1¼m and 1½m winner stayed 2m: form only on second outing: visored in selling nursery final start: will stay 1m: wears bandage off-hind: sold 700 gns Newmarket Autumn Sales. *M. R. Stoute*   **44**

FIRST BID 5 ch.g. Crofthall 110 – Redgrave Design 77 (Nebbiolo 125) [1991 12.3s 11f 9.9g² 9.9f⁵ 11f⁵ 10m² 9.9f² 10.1m 10.5d³ 10m a14g 1992 12f³ 9.9f⁴ 12f² 10f 12s² 11d* 12.2g³ 12d* 12.3m⁴ 11g³ 12m 12m* 11.9s⁴ 12d³] workmanlike gelding: consistent handicapper: successful at Redcar and Beverley (apprentices) in September: effective from 1¼m to 1½m: acts on any going: effective with or without visor or blinkers earlier in career. *R. M. Whitaker*   **65**

FIRST CENTURY (IRE) 3 b.c. Petorius 117 – Parima 72 (Pardao 120) [1991 7d⁴ 6.3s⁴ 8s 1992 7s 10m³ 8.9g 7d⁴ 8g* 8.5d² 8.1d⁶ 8g 10g 7d] good-quartered colt: inconsistent performer: won claimer at Newmarket in June, making most: claimed out of P. Cole's stable £13,258 next start: stays 1¼m: yet to race on firm ground, probably acts on any other: fair effort in blinkers fourth start. *B. R. Millman*   **74 d**

FIRST CRUSADE (FR) 4 b.c. Rainbow Quest (USA) 134 – Saint Osyth 105 (Blakeney 126) [1991 NR 1992 12.1g] lengthy, quite attractive colt: half-brother to useful middle-distance stayer King of Mercia (by Great Nephew): dam won over 1½m: broke down badly in Edinburgh maiden in April. *R. Allan*   **–**

FIRST EXHIBITION 5 b.m. Claude Monet (USA) 121 – All Hail 112 (Alcide 136) [1991 NR 1992 12m 10.5d 12f 18.8m] leggy, sparely-made mare: of little account: sold 600 gns Ascot November Sales. *Mrs A. Knight*   **–**

FIRST FLING (IRE) 3 b.f. Last Tycoon 131 – Flamme d'Amour (Gift Card (FR) 124) [1991 NR 1992 8g⁶ 10.3g² 10.2d a10g⁵ a12g⁴ a10g³] 40,000Y: angular filly: sister to fairly useful 1991 French 3-y-o 1m/1¼m performer L'Amour Fou and half-sister to several winners abroad, including Prix de Diane third Premier Amour (by Salmon Leap): dam, winner over jumps at 3 yrs in France, is out of Gazolina, a smart winner at up to 13.5f: modest maiden: may well stay beyond 1½m: sold out of R. Charlton's stable 5,800 gns Doncaster November Sales after penultimate start: below form (odds on, visored) in December. *Dr J. D. Scargill*   **63**

FIRST FLUSH 6 b.g. Precocious 126 – Rosananti 107 (Blushing Groom (FR) 131) [1991 5m 6m 6m a7g 7m 6f 8.3m 6.9f⁴ 6m⁵ 7.1m 6g 6.1m 7s³ 1992 a5g 8d 6d] sturdy gelding: carries condition: poor walker: inconsistent handicapper: has won 2 of 38 starts: stays 7f: acts on any going: below form when blinkered: wears bandages. *K. T. Ivory*   **–**

FIRST GOLD 3 gr.c. Absalom 128 – Cindys Gold 69 (Sonnen Gold 121) [1991 5m 1992 a5g⁶ a7g⁶ 7g 7g³ 8.2g 6g 6m* 7f⁴ 6g* 6f* 7g 6g⁴ 6m] lengthy colt: fair handicapper: successful twice at Ripon and once at York in summer: best efforts at 6f: acts on firm ground: has won with blinkers and without. *J. Wharton*   **66**

FIRST HEIRESS (IRE) 3 b.f. Last Tycoon 131 – Age of Elegance (Troy 137) [1991 7m 1992 10d⁶ 8.5d 10g] lengthy, lightly-made filly: poor maiden at best: well beaten last 2 starts, in visor on final one, in July. *M. R. Stoute*   **–**

FIRST HOME 5 b.g. Homing 130 – Mill Wind 68 (Blakeney 126) [1991 a10g 1992 a8g a8g] rather leggy gelding: has a quick action: of little account. *Pat Mitchell*   **–**

FIRST OPTION 2 ch.g. (Mar 18) Primo Dominie 121 – Merrywren (Julio Mariner 127) [1992 5m⁵ 5f² 5f² 6m* 5g* 5d* 5.1m⁵ 5g² 5g* 5d²] 6,600Y: close-coupled gelding: third foal: dam won over hurdles: useful plater: successful at Redcar (bought in 3,700 gns) and in claimer at Beverley and non-selling nursery (in good style) at Ayr in August, and at Folkestone (retained 8,600 gns) in September: stays 6f: acts on good to firm ground, but best form on an easy surface. *M. H. Easterby*   **69**

FIRST PLAY 2 b.f. (Feb 14) Primo Dominie 121 – School Concert 80 (Music Boy 124) [1992 5m³ 6m] 8,800F: angular filly: first foal: dam, 6f winner, is sister to high-class French sprinter Kind Music and very useful 5f performer Boy Trumpeter: contested poor maidens at Edinburgh and Doncaster (bandaged behind, dropped right away) in July. *J. Berry*   **46**

FIRST RESERVE 2 ch.c. (May 20) Gabitat 119 – Chinese Princess (Sunny Way 120) [1992 7.5m a7s⁴ a7g 8.5m 10d] rather leggy, workmanlike colt: half-brother to several winners on flat and over jumps, including 1978 2-y-o 1m seller winner Magic Kit (by Namnan) and 7f winner Cunning Plan (by Belfort): dam unraced half-sister to very smart Streetfighter: seems of little account: blinkered last 4 outings: sold 700 gns Doncaster November Sales. *B. S. Rothwell*

FIRST SAPPHIRE   5 b.m. Simply Great (FR) 122 – Yelney 65 (Blakeney 126)   –
[1991 a8g 1992 a12g⁶ a12g] of no account. *W. Jarvis*

FIRST SLICE   2 gr.f. (Apr 8) Primo Dominie 121 – Cottage Pie 106 (Kalamoun   **51**
129) [1992 5m⁵ 5m² 6g⁵] 10,000Y: workmanlike filly: half-sister to 3-y-o Laura (by Never So Bold) and 1986 2-y-o 5f winner Sauce Diable (by Moorestyle): dam, useful staying 2-y-o, is half-sister to Yorkshire Cup winner Riboson: modest maiden, last seen out in July: should be much better suited by 6f than 5f. *J. Berry*

FIRST STAGE   5 b.h. Shareef Dancer (USA) 135 – Bright Landing 78 (Sun   –
Prince 128) [1991 a13g² a12g³ a13g* 12g⁴ 15.5f⁴ 12.5d² a12g³ 12m³ a12g⁶ 1992 a16g] small, sturdy horse: rated 58 at 5 yrs when stayed 1¾m and acted on good to firm and dead ground: soundly beaten in January, 1992: returned to race in Ireland. *J. G. M. O'Shea*

FIRST TRADITION   7 ch.m. Sayyaf 121 – Traditional Miss 90 (Traditionalist   –
(USA) [1991 NR 1992 6m] lengthy, good-bodied mare: poor performer at best: off course 2 years, signs of retaining ability though behind in Folkestone handicap in August, front rank to 2f out: tried blinkered once. *C. J. Hill*

FIRST VEIL   2 b.f. (Jan 30) Primo Dominie 121 – Valika 75 (Valiyar 129) [1992 6g³   **94 p**
6g²] 30,000Y: sturdy, quite attractive filly: has a quick action: first foal: dam, maiden, suited by 1¼m, is half-sister to high-class 5-y-o sprinter Mr Brooks: carrying condition still, 1½ lengths second of 6 to Marina Park in Princess Margaret Stakes at Ascot in July, behind after slowish start, coming off bridle 2f out then staying on well: will probably stay 7f: seemed certain to improve further and win races. *D. R. C. Elsworth*

FIRST VICTORY   6 gr.h. Concorde Hero (USA) 101 – Cestrefeld 94 (Capistrano   –
120) [1991 14m² 12g³ 16. 1m³ 16g⁶ 13.9g⁶ 14.6m³ 12s 16.2d⁶ 12g⁴ 12d 1992 16.4s 16s 13.9m] tall, angular horse: useful handicapper (rated 100) at 5 yrs: shaped as if retaining his ability under unsuitable conditions first 2 starts, but bandaged and rare poor effort in Ebor at York: effective from 1½m to 2m: needed a sound surface: usually came from behind, and was suited by a strong gallop: sold privately to stand at Marsh Benham Stud. *R. Hannon*

FISHKI   6 b.m. Niniski (USA) 125 – Ladyfish 79 (Pampapaul 121) [1991 18.4d 12.1g   **36**
16.2d 15.1s 1992 12.1v⁴] workmanlike, angular mare: only poor form on flat last 2 seasons: fourth in Hamilton handicap in November: stays 15f: has won on firm going, but goes particularly well in the mud: occasionally bandaged behind: won novice chase in November, 1992. *M. D. Hammond*

FISIANNA   3 b.f. Efisio 120 – Jianna 60 (Godswalk (USA) 130) [1991 NR 1992 6s   **47**
6m² 7d] 820F: close-coupled filly: second foal: dam, maiden, stayed 6f: plating-class maiden: easily best effort when second in seller at Leicester, outpaced then staying on well: found little final start: refused to enter stalls later in June: has joined Mrs M. Long. *A. R. Davison*

FIT FOR LIFE (IRE)   4 b.g. Local Suitor (USA) 128 – Strike It Rich (FR)   **40 §**
(Rheingold 137) [1991 a14g 1992 a11g⁶ 14.6g 16.2g³ 21.6g 14.6s 18m] leggy gelding: moderate mover: poor maiden: worthwhile form only when third in spring: tailed off last 2 starts, in autumn: stays 2m: blinkered: one to be wary of: has joined S. Norton. *Mrs N. Macauley*

FITNESS FANATIC   4 b.g. Nishapour (FR) 125 – Bustling Nelly 94 (Bustino   –
136) [1991 10g 10g⁵ 11.9m² 12d⁶ 1992 11.9f⁴ 11.9f 17.2f] rangy, sparely-made gelding: of little account these days. *J. T. Gifford*

FIT ON TIME (USA)   3 ch.c. Lead On Time (USA) 123 – Fitnah 125 (Kris 135)   **71**
[1991 6.1m⁴ 6.9f⁵ 6s⁴ 1992 8m² 8g* 8g² 9d] leggy colt: shows knee action: fair performer: 11/4 on, won 5-runner apprentice maiden at Yarmouth in August: well beaten final start: should stay beyond 1m: below form on extremes of going. *M. R. Stoute*

FIT THE BILL   4 b.g. Nicholas Bill 125 – Golden Windlass 79 (Princely Gift 137)   **46**
[1991 6g² 8d³ 6s² 7d* 9.2d* 7g² 10f 8m 10g 8m 9g 1992 12d⁴ 10d² a7g] lengthy gelding: poor mover: only modest nowadays: effective from 7f to 1½m: acts on soft ground. *C. Tinkler*

FITZCARRALDO (USA)   2 ch.c. (Feb 26) Riverman (USA) 131 – Quest (USA)   **102**
90§ (The Minstrel (CAN) 135) [1992 7f* 7f² 7.1d³ 7m³ 7m³] strong colt: sixth foal:

half-brother to 3-y-o Questing (by Diesis) and 3 winners, including (at 6f here then at 1¼m in Grade 1 company in USA) Bequest (by Sharpen Up) and (at 12.5f) Rozinante (by The Minstrel): dam, 9f and 1¼m winner, is sister to high-class 1983 French 2-y-o Treizieme and half-sister to Gold Cup second Eastern Mystic: useful performer: won 4-runner maiden at Yarmouth in July: third in Solario Stakes at Sandown, Champagne Stakes at Doncaster and Somerville Tattersall Stakes at Newmarket: will be well suited by 1¼m: probably acts on any going. *L. M. Cumani*

FITZROY LAD   2 b.c. (Apr 29) Grey Desire 115 – My-Elane 65 (Welsh Saint 126)   **52**
[1992 7d 7g 7s 7d] 1,900Y: second foal: dam, maiden, stayed 1m: modest maiden: will stay 1m. *M. R. Channon*

FIVE CLUBS (IRE)   2 ch.f. (Feb 10) King of Clubs 124 – Tristan du Cunha   **39**
(USA) (Sir Ivor 135) [1992 5g 6s² 6m⁶ 6m⁶ 7m⁶ 7.1s 6d 10d a7g⁶] IR 1,700F, 500Y: leggy filly: half-sister to Irish 7f and 1m winner Havana Moon (by Ela-Mana-Mou) and 2 winners abroad: dam won over 1¼m in Ireland and is half-sister to very smart stayer Noble Saint: poor and inconsistent maiden: should stay 1¼m. *D. T. Thom*

FIVE ISLANDS   2 b.f. (Mar 22) Bairn (USA) 126 – Melody Park 104 (Music Boy   **62**
124) [1992 a5g* 5g] leggy filly: third foal: sister to 3-y-o 5f performer Creche: dam sprinter: favourite, easily won 5-runner maiden at Lingfield in August: stiff task and ridden by 7-lb claimer, soon towards rear in Newmarket nursery nearly 3 months later: bandaged behind. *P. F. I. Cole*

FIVEOFIVE (IRE)   2 b.f. (Apr 6) Fairy King (USA) – North Hut (Northfields   **60**
(USA)) [1992 5m 7m³ 6g⁴ 5m⁴ 5.3f* 6g 7s 7m 6g⁴] 15,500Y: close-coupled, rather unfurnished filly: half-sister to fairly useful 1990 2-y-o 5f winner The Old Firm (by Hatim) and very smart 1985 2-y-o Dublin Lad (by Dublin Taxi): dam twice-raced daughter of very useful sprinting 2-y-o Whispering II: modest handicapper: blinkered, showed improvement and comfortably won 4-runner nursery at Brighton in August: also blinkered next outing when well beaten for 7-lb claimer: returned to form when creditable fourth at Newmarket: best form at up to 6f: may be suited by a sound surface. *N. A. Callaghan*

FIVESEVENFIVEO   4 ch.f. Enchantment 115 – Miss Times 78 (Major Portion   **77**
129) [1991 5m² 5g* 5f² 5.1d* 5.7g⁴ 5f4 6f* 6m⁶ 6f² 5m⁶ 6g 1992 6d 6.1d 5.1d4 5m* 5g³ 5g² 5.1h* 5.1f³ 5d 5m² 5d 5s 5.1s² 5d 5.2s] close-coupled, good-quartered filly: tends to look dull in coat: has a quick action: fair handicapper: won at Goodwood (apprentices) in May and Bath in June: inconsistent in second half of season: speedy and ideally suited by 5f: acts on any going: has run well for claimer. *R. J. Hodges*

FIVE TO SEVEN (USA)   3 br.c. Little Missouri (USA) – French Galaxy (USA)   **81**
(Majestic Light (USA)) [1991 7.6d² 8.1s² 1992 11.1d³ 12m⁵a12g² 14.1f⁴a12g*a12g*   **a88**
16.2s⁴ 13.1s² 16.2g 15.9s³ 12g a14g²] good-topped colt: has a round action: fairly useful performer: easily won maiden and handicap (ridden by 7-lb claimer) at Southwell within a week in June: stays 2m: acts on fibresand, best turf efforts on soft: front runner. *S. G. Norton*

FLAKEY DOVE   6 b.m. Oats 126 – Shadey Dove 81 (Deadly Nightshade 107)   **–**
[1991 NR 1992 13.3f] workmanlike not-thoroughbred mare: second foal: dam useful hurdler from successful jumping family: useful hurdler: stiff task when behind in Newbury listed race in May on debut on flat. *R. J. Price*

FLAME OF PERSIA (IRE)   2 ch.f. (Mar 14) Persian Heights 129 – Fire Flash   **81 p**
74 (Bustino 136) [1992 7g⁵ 8s* 8s²] IR 10,000Y: fourth foal: half-sister to 3-y-o 11.7f winner Dazzling Fire (by Bluebird) and 2 winners in Austria: dam, never tried beyond 1¼m, is out of smart 7f and 1m performer Dazzling Light, a half-sister to Welsh Pageant: 8-length winner of 17-runner auction event at Tralee in August: well-backed favourite, beaten a neck by Wootton Rivers in 4-runner minor event at Ayr following month, setting only modest pace and keeping on really well when headed: will be suited by 1½m: sure to improve. *M. Kauntze, Ireland*

FLAMING ARROW   4 br.c. Dancing Brave (USA) 140 – Ma Petite Cherie   **95**
(USA) 93 (Caro 133) [1991 10.2m³ 10f* 10g 10m² 1992 10g⁴ 8.9f4 10g² 10.3g² 8f² 9g*
8m² 8g4] compact colt: ran well in varied company most starts before landing odds in Ripon apprentice race in August: rare poor effort in Ascot apprentice race final one: will prove as effective at 1½m as 1m: acts on firm ground, yet to race on a soft surface: suitable mount for amateur. *H. R. A. Cecil*

FLAMING MIRACLE (IRE)   2 b.c. (Apr 11) Vision (USA) – Red Realm   **52 p**
(Realm 129) [1992 8s] 11,000Y: angular colt: half-brother to 3 winners, including 6f/7f performer Petticoat Power (by Petorius) and 1m winner London Standard (by Shack): dam, Irish 8.5f and 9.5f winner, is half-sister to useful stayer/hurdler Old

Dundalk: 20/1 and bit backward, prominent long way when around 11 lengths seventh of 22 in maiden at Warwick in October: moved moderately down: will improve. *P. F. I. Cole*

FLAMINGO ROSE (IRE)   3 ch.f. Antheus (USA) 122 – Tigresse d'Amour   **68**
(USA) 108 (Stage Door Johnny) [1991 a7g4 1992 10m4 11.5d4 14.1m3 14.1d] big, rangy filly: third foal: closely related to useful 1¼m winner Tiger Flower (by Sadler's Wells): dam, French 2-y-o 7f winner, is sister to high-class American middle-distance stayer One On The Aisle: fair maiden: stays 1¾m: acts on good to firm ground: possibly unsuited by a soft surface: bandaged near-hind once. *H. R. A. Cecil*

FLASHELLA (IRE)   2 ch.f. (Apr 11) Legend of France (USA) 124 – Nawara 75   **–**
(Welsh Pageant 132) [1992 7m] IR 550F, 1,800Y: sixth foal: half-sister to good-class 3-y-o miler Alhijaz (by Midyan) and several other winners, including 1¼m to 13f winner Usran (by Valiyar): dam 10.2f winner: prominent to 2f out when behind in maiden auction at Doncaster in June: seemed likely to do better. *T. Fairhurst*

FLASHFEET   2 b.c. (Feb 7) Rousillon (USA) 133 – Miellita 98 (King Emperor   **75 p**
(USA)) [1992 7g2] close-coupled colt: eighth foal: brother to useful 4-y-o 1m to 1¼m winner Flashfoot and half-brother to 2 winners, including (over middle distances) In The Shade (by Bustino): dam 2-y-o 6f winner, stayed at least 1¼m: easy to back, shaped promisingly when beaten ½ length by Pembroke in minor event at Kempton in September, running on well: sure to improve, and win a race or two. *I. A. Balding*

FLASHFOOT   4 ch.c. Rousillon (USA) 133 – Miellita 98 (King Emperor (USA))   **105**
[1991 8g4 9g* 10.4g3 10g2 8g* 8g2 8d 1992 9g3 8.1g5 10m* 8.5g4 8m6 10m6 10.5d5 8d5 9d2] big, lengthy colt: useful performer: won listed event at Goodwood in May by a head from Jura: easily best efforts in listed/pattern company after when in frame in Diomed Stakes at Epsom and listed event in Italy: effective at 1m to 1¼m: acts on good to firm and dead ground: occasionally hangs and carries head high: effective held up or ridden from front. *I. A. Balding*

Mr J. C. Smith's "Flashfoot"

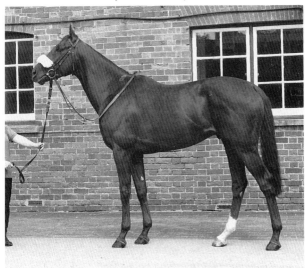

FLASHMAN 2 b.c. (Apr 25) Flash of Steel 120 – Proper Madam 93 (Mummy's **56** p
Pet 125) [1992 6f³ 6.1m⁴ 6s² 5g⁴] well-grown colt: carries condition: sixth living
foal: half-brother to 3 winners, all at sprint distances, including 2 by Milford, and
3-y-o Madam Petoski (by Petoski): dam sprinter: consistent form: fourth in nursery
at Doncaster final start: stays 6f: acts on firm and dead ground: has scope, looks sort
to do better at 3 yrs. *F. H. Lee*

FLASH OF AMBER 2 b.f. (Apr 19) Electric 126 – Orange Silk 68 (Moulton 128) **41**
[1992 5g 6g 7g⁶ 7.5m 7d] £mall filly: eighth foal: closely related to useful
middle-distance performer Bocatower (by Tyrnavos) and half-sister to 3 winners,
including sprinter Bali Sunset (by Balidar): dam placed over 5f and 6f at 2 yrs: poor
plater: should stay 1m + : sold 700 gns Newmarket Autumn Sales. *J. L. Spearing*

FLASH OF JOY 2 b.f. (Apr 12) Lightning Dealer 103 – Joytime (John de Coombe –
122) [1992 5g⁵ 5g 6.1m] sturdy filly: has a roundish action: fourth foal (third to a
thoroughbred stallion): dam ran once: seems of little account. *C. D. Broad*

FLASH OF STRAW (IRE) 3 ch.g. Thatching 131 – Hanna Alta (FR) (Busted **50**
134) [1991 NR 1992 8g 7m 8f⁵ 6g 6m 5m 8d⁶ 10d⁶ 11.7d² 11.9d² 11.5s 11d a 10g² a 12g⁶]
5,000Y: sturdy, good-quartered gelding: poor mover: half-brother to 7-y-o 1¼m to
1½m winner Belmoredean and a winner in Italy (both by Be My Guest) and 4-y-o 1m
winner Elaine Tully (by Persian Bold): dam French 1½m winner out of smart
French 7f winner Hamada: modest handicapper: easily best of last 4 starts when
second at Lingfield: will stay beyond 1½m: acts on dead ground and equitrack,
possibly not on soft: blinkered last 6 starts: sold out of G. Lewis' stable 6,200 gns
Ascot November Sales after penultimate start. *J. Akehurst*

FLASHY'S SON 4 b. or br.g. Balidar 133 – Flashy Looker 92 (Good Bond 122) **68**
[1991 6f⁵ 5.9m⁵ 6m 7f⁵ 1992 6.9f⁶ 7.5g 6.1m 7g² 6m* 7f* 6m* 6m* 7m² 7m⁵] sturdy
gelding: much improved and had excellent season in handicaps in 1992: successful
within 6 weeks in summer at Hamilton, Redcar (amateurs) and apprentice races at
Ripon and Redcar: effective at 6f to 7f: acts on firm ground, yet to race on a soft
surface: sometimes bandaged off-hind: a credit to his trainer. *M. D. Hammond*

FLAT RATE 3 b.f. Prince Sabo 123 – Hellene (Dominion 123) [1991 5.1g⁶ 5m⁵ 6f⁵ –
5.2f⁵ 5f 6m a6g⁴ a7g 1992 a5g⁶ a6g] workmanlike filly: below form early in 1992:
best form at 6f: below form blinkered/visored: sold 720 gns Doncaster March Sales.
W. J. Pearce

FLEETING RAINBOW 3 b.f. Rainbow Quest (USA) 134 – Taplow (Tap On **65**
Wood 130) [1991 7g 1992 10d³ 12.1m⁶] lengthy, quite attractive filly: strong-finishing
third in maiden at Sandown: not seen out again after running moderately later in
May: should have proved effective at 1½m: has been retired. *J. L. Dunlop*

FLETCHINNI (IRE) 3 ch.g. Exhibitioner 111 – All The Same (Cajun 120) [1991 –
5m⁵ 7m 7m 1992 6.9d 10m 10.5d 6s] leggy gelding: poor mover: no worthwhile form:
trained reappearance by M. O'Neill: tried blinkered: collapsed in stalls and had to be
destroyed. *A. Bailey*

FLEUR POWER (IRE) 2 ch.f. (May 10) The Noble Player (USA) 126 – Power **54**
Girl 77 (Tyrant (USA)) [1992 5d 6d³ 6.1m⁵ 7d³ 7s] leggy filly: good mover: sister to
3-y-o Noble Power, 5f winner at 2 yrs, and half-sister to 1987 2-y-o 5f winner
Powerful (by Tumble Wind) and 2 winners abroad: dam won over 5f and 6f:
progressive form, third in median auction at Wolverhampton, until last of 17 in
nursery there: better suited by 7f than less: acts on good to firm and dead ground
(may be unsuited by soft). *B. Palling*

FLIGHT LIEUTENANT (USA) 3 b.c. Marfa (USA) – Lt Golden Girl (USA) **87**
(Lt Stevens) [1991 6d 7s² 1992 8g⁵ 10g⁶ 10d⁶ 10s* 11.4m³ 12f 11g⁵ 13.9g⁵] tall,
lengthy colt: moderate mover: won maiden at Lingfield in May: not discredited in
handicaps 3 of next 4 starts: may prove best at around 1½m: acts on good to firm
ground and soft. *P. Mitchell*

FLIRTING 8 b.m. Free State 125 – Mrs Palmer 88 (Martinmas 128) [1991 9m –
12.2g 12m 1992 a12g] rather plain mare: seems of little account nowadays. *J. Mulhall*

FLITCHAM 5 b.m. Elegant Air 119 – Seldom (Rarity 129) [1991 10.2s 12.4v² 12d⁵
13d* 14m⁶ 14d⁴ 15s³ 1992 a14g a14g] small, close-coupled, angular mare: poor
handicapper: stays 15f: acts on good to firm and heavy ground. *J. R. Bostock*

FLOATING LINE 4 ch.g. Bairn (USA) 126 – County Line 75 (High Line 125) **64**
[1991 8m 9.9m⁵ 9.9f⁶ 8m 1992 10d⁶ 9.9g² 12m⁵ 12m⁶ 10g³ 9.9d* 9f² 9.9g⁵ 12.4v]
leggy, sparely-made gelding: has a round action: largely consistent handicapper:
won at Beverley in July: stays 1½m well: acts on firm and dead ground, seems
unsuited by heavy: sometimes edgy. *P. Wigham*

FLOATING RATE 3 gr.f. Absalom 128 – Dortia (Martinmas 128) [1991 6f a5g6 –
5m3 5m4 5g3 5m 6s 1992 a7g 6s] rather leggy filly: maiden, no form in 1992: should
stay 6f: seems unsuited by soft ground. *J. White*

FLOCKTON'S OWN 6 b.h. Electric 126 – Tree Mallow 71 (Malicious) [1991 NR –
1992 11.9s 11.9d 14m] neat, quite attractive horse: bandaged and never dangerous in
handicaps in spring, first runs since 3 yrs: should stay 1½m: probably acts on any
going: ran well visored as 3-y-o. *Mrs J. R. Ramsden*

FLOODLIGHT (IRE) 2 b.f. (May 2) Exhibitioner 111 – Share The Vision 34
(Vision (USA)) [1992 6f 6.1f4 7d5 7m6 7d a6g] small, sparely-made filly: moderate
mover: first foal: dam unraced: poor maiden: stays 7f: acts on firm and dead ground,
and on equitrack. *R. J. Holder*

FLORAC (IRE) 2 b.f. (Feb 8) Sayf El Arab (USA) 127 – Marton Maid 74 (Silly 54
Season 127) [1992 5m5 5m* 5.2d 6m] IR 4,000F, IR 10,000Y: smallish filly: fifth foal:
sister to 1989 2-y-o 5f winner Megan Blaze and a winner in Italy: dam, inconsistent
maiden, is half-sister to good-class sprinter Haveroid: modest form: won maiden
auction at Warwick in July: not discredited after in Newbury Sales Super Sprint
Trophy and valuable York seller: will stay beyond 6f: sometimes bandaged behind:
retained by trainer 2,500 gns Doncaster November Sales. *M. J. Heaton-Ellis*

FLORAL BOUQUET 3 ch.f. Never So Bold 135 – My Fair Orchid 71 (Roan –
Rocket 128) [1991 6g5 7g6 6m 1992 10d4 12.1s 9f] angular, sparely-made filly: no
form in 1992: seems to stay 7f: tried visored: sold 1,650 gns Doncaster June Sales.
M. J. Camacho

FLOURISHING (IRE) 3 b.f. Trojan Fen 118 – Well Off (Welsh Pageant 132) 85
[1991 7m* 7.1s2 7g4 8m4 7m5 1992 8v2 7.1d2 7.1m2 7g3] small, sparely-made filly:
fair form in minor events, not seen out after June: should have stayed 1¼m: acted on
good to firm and heavy ground: stud. *G. Wragg*

FLOWING (USA) 4 gr.f. El Gran Senor (USA) 136 – Flo Russell (USA) (Round **114**
Table) [1991 7g3 7g3 6m* 5d* 6g2 5d* 5d5 1992 5s3 5m3 5f6 5g* 6g3 5g* 5s5 5s2]
sturdy filly: moderate mover: very useful and consistent Irish sprinter: successful
in Tipperary listed race in July and Group 3 event at Leopardstown in September:
creditable staying-on fifth in Prix de l'Abbaye at Longchamp, beaten just over 3
lengths by Mr Brooks: best form at 5f: acted on any going: reportedly to visit Mr
Prospector. *D. K. Weld, Ireland*

FLUTE (USA) 3 b. or br.f. Woodman (USA) 126 – Popular By Far (USA) (Far 87
North (CAN) 120) [1991 6g4 1992 8v6 7g* 8g2 6f4 6g3 7m] well-made filly: won
maiden at Newmarket in April: fairly useful efforts when in frame in listed race at
Rome and quite valuable handicaps at York and Newmarket: stayed 1m: acted on
firm ground: occasionally slowly away: visits Alzao. *C. E. Brittain*

*Meadow Meats EBF Flying Five, Leopardstown—
the grey Flowing sprints clear of Park Dream (stars) and Poolesta (blinkers)*

FLYAWAY (FR)   7 ch.g. Touching Wood (USA) 127 – Flying Sauce 107 (Sauce   37
Boat (USA)) [1991 NR 1992 12d⁵ 13.8d⁴] lengthy gelding: carries condition: poor
walker and mover: poor handicapper: stays 1¾m: ideally suited by an easy surface:
below form blinkered: has joined R. Emery. *R. J. Weaver*

FLY AWAY SOON (USA)   4 b.g. Lear Fan (USA) 130 – Awenita (Rarity 129)   –
[1991 10g* 12g4 a12g* 12g* 14.6m⁵ 1992 13.3f 10m⁶ 12.1g³ 13.3g] workmanlike,
good-bodied gelding: rated 115 as 3-y-o: well below best in 1992: stays 1½m: best
efforts on good ground (yet to race on a soft surface): sold 11,000 gns Newmarket
Autumn Sales and gelded. *P. F. I. Cole*

FLY FOR GOLD (IRE)   3 b.f. Simply Great (FR) 122 – Golden Pheasant   55
(Henbit (USA) 130) [1991 8g 1992 8.9v 10g² 11g* 11.6m 12.3m² 14.1g 11.8g 9.7g4]
strong, lengthy filly: inconsistent in handicaps after winning Wolverhampton seller
(bought in 5,400 gns) in May: should stay beyond 1½m: acts on good to firm ground:
sometimes bandaged behind: below form for lady rider: won selling hurdle in
November. *D. W. P. Arbuthnot*

FLYING AMY   2 ch.f. (Feb 17) Norwick (USA) 120 – Starky's Pet (Mummy's Pet   40
125) [1992 8d⁶ 8s 10g] 825Y: tall, quite good-topped filly: fifth foal: sister to 3-y-o 7f
(at 2 yrs) and 1¼m winner Liability Order and half-sister to 7f winner Southern Sky
(by Comedy Star): dam behind in 4 starts on flat and over hurdles: soundly beaten in
maidens: bandaged off-hind final start. *R. Curtis*

FLYING BRAVE   4 b.c. Persian Bold 123 – Flying Sauce 107 (Sauce Boat (USA))   109
[1991 7m⁴ 8g 8g* 8g² 8g* 8f4 8s⁶ 1992 8m⁴ 8g 8m 8g² 8g] compact, attractive colt:
has a quick action: very useful performer: easily best runs in 1992 when in frame at
Newbury (Lockinge Stakes) and Hoppegarten (Group 3 race, visored): again
visored, had too much use made of him in Kempton listed race final run: effective at
7f, and should stay at least 1¼m: goes well on a sound surface: sent to C. Moran in
USA. *J. L. Dunlop*

FLYING CONNECTION   4 b.g. Never So Bold 135 – Gunner's Belle 69   –
(Gunner B 126) [1991 10.1g⁶ a11g 12.2m³ 10.1m 1992 12m⁵] rangy gelding: bad
maiden. *W. Clay*

FLYING DOWN TO RIO (IRE)   4 b.c. Try My Best (USA) 130 – Gay France   52
(FR) 91 (Sir Gaylord) [1991 10g 10.1s 8d 7m⁶ 7.6g 10m 1992 7.1g 8d 10m6 9.2d*
10.5m³ 10.5d⁵ 8f4 10g4 8.3m³ 9m⁶ 8g 8g4 8m 10s⁵ 9d⁵ 8.2g] workmanlike colt:
moderate mover: poor handicapper: won selling event (no bid) at Hamilton in May:
stays 1¼m: acts on good to firm and soft ground: below form when blinkered: sold to
join A. Forbes 10,400 gns Doncaster October Sales. *M. P. Naughton*

FLYING GABRIEL   2 b.f. (Mar 25) Gabitat 119 – Flying Easy (Swing Easy   –
(USA) 126) [1992 6g 7g] workmanlike, good-bodied filly: second reported foal:
half-sister to 6-y-o Easy Match (by Royal Match): dam no form: tailed off in maidens.
P. Howling

FLYING HEN   3 b.f. Sizzling Melody 117 – Savahra 82 (Free State 125) [1991 NR   –
1992 6f] 6,000Y: sturdy filly: sixth foal: closely related to 2 winners, notably very
useful 6f to 7f winner Savahra Sound (by Song), and half-sister to 1½m winner
Tesora (by Busted), later successful in USA: dam 11f and 13f winner: bandaged
behind, never dangerous in maiden at Lingfield in May, only run. *W. J. Haggas*

FLYING PETAL   4 gr.f. Petong 126 – Careless Flyer 66 (Malicious) [1991 NR   –
1992 8s 5.7m] good-bodied filly: seems of little account. *C. J. Hill*

FLYING PROMISE   4 ch.c. Stanford 121§ – Impailand (Imperial Fling (USA)   40
116) [1991 a6g5 a5g⁶ 5m³ 5.3f 5s 5m⁶ 5g4 5g² 5g 5m 6g4 6m 7g a6g4 1992 a6g a8g⁵
a6g 6g 5.7m 6d 8.3m³ 8.3d 8.3m 8.3g] strong, lengthy, plain colt: moderate mover:
inconsistent maiden handicapper: stays 8.3f: acts on good to firm ground and
fibresand: below form blinkered. *R. A. Bennett*

FLYING SPEED (USA)   4 b.g. Far North (CAN) 120 – Diatoma (FR) (Diatome   75
132) [1991 8g 10.4m⁶ 1992 14.8f⁵ 10.2f* 10.1f⁵ 10d³ 11d* 12m 10.1d] angular, rather
dipped-backed gelding: shows knee action: won claimers at Bath in July and
Wolverhampton in September: below form last 2 runs: should prove as effective at
1½m: acts on firm and dead ground: won claiming hurdle in December. *M. C. Pipe*

FLYING WIND   3 b.f. Forzando 122 – Handy Dancer 87 (Green God 128) [1991   51
NR 1992 8m 8.5d⁶ 7f³ 6.9g 8f³ 6.1s 6.9v] quite good-topped filly: seventh foal:
half-sister to several winners, including very useful middle-distance performer
Karinga Bay (by Ardross) and 6-y-o 10.1f to 1½m winner Roll A Dollar (by Spin of A
Coin): dam 1¼m winner: plating-class handicapper: well beaten last 2 starts: stays
1m: acts on firm ground: effective blinkered or not. *J. Sutcliffe*

FLYING ZIAD (CAN)   9 ch.g. Ziad (USA) – Flying Souvenir (USA) (Flying   –
Relic 128) [1991 NR 1992 12f6 16.4g] leggy, angular ex-Irish gelding: little worthwhile form in handicaps in 1992: won over fences in August. *R. Curtis*

FLY TO THE END (USA)   2 b.c. (Mar 20) Gulch (USA) – Bold Flora (USA)   60
(Bold Favorite (USA)) [1992 6v5 7s3 7g] $325,000Y: half-brother to several
winners, notably 1989 Grade 1 9f Demoiselle Stakes winner Rootentootenwooten
(by Diesis): dam minor winner at up to 7f: sire (by Mr Prospector) best at up to 1m:
modest form in maidens at Folkestone and Lingfield in October: sweating and well
beaten at Doncaster final run. *A. A. Scott*

FOLIA   3 b.f. Sadler's Wells (USA) 132 – Dunoof 92 (Shirley Heights 130) [1991   83
7m6 1992 10d* 10.2s* 12f 11.9d*] good-topped filly: moderate mover: progressive
form in first half of 1992, successful in maiden at Ripon (hung left for 7-lb claimer)
and handicaps at Bath and York (gamely in £7,700 contest): better at 1½m than
1¼m: best form on an easy surface: stud. *H. R. A. Cecil*

FOLKBOAT   3 b.f. Kalaglow 132 – Boathouse 116 (Habitat 134) [1991 NR 1992 10f   –
12f] leggy, lengthy filly: very good mover: sixth foal: half-sister to fairly useful 10.2f
winner River Patrol (by Rousillon) and smart middle-distance stayer Dry Dock (by
High Line): dam, stayed 1¼m, is half-sister to Bireme and high-class middle-
distance stayer Buoy: no form in maidens at Newbury and Newmarket in first half of
1992. *B. W. Hills*

FOLLINGWORTH GIRL (IRE)   2 ch.f. (Apr 5) Jareer (USA) 115 – Coshlea   –
63 (Red Alert 127) [1992 7g2 7g 7g] 3,000Y: tall, close-coupled, workmanlike filly:
moderate walker: half-sister to 3-y-o Noggings (by Cyrano de Bergerac) and 3
winners, including 5f (at 2 yrs) to 13f winner Dale Park (by Kampala): dam placed
from 11f to 15f: well beaten in late-season maidens at Doncaster. *S. G. Norton*

FOLLOWMEGIRLS   3 b.f. Sparkling Boy 110 – Haddon Anna (Dragonara   57
Palace (USA) 115) [1991 NR 1992 8f 6g* 7.1g3 6f6 6m5 6g6 6m] leggy, lengthy filly:
fourth foal: half-sister to 5f and 6f winner Banbury Flyer (by Mummys Game): dam
unraced: none too consistent in handicaps after winning Pontefract apprentice
maiden (100/1) in July: stays 6f: acts on firm going. *Mrs A. L. M. King*

FOLLY VISION (IRE)   2 b.f. (Mar 6) Vision (USA) – Folle Remont (Prince   58
Tenderfoot (USA) 126) [1992 5.1g5 5g5 6m 5g6 5s2 6m 6d 6.1s4] 9,200Y: small,
compact filly: moderate walker: half-sister to several winners here and abroad,
including smart 6f/7f performer Sylvan Express (by Baptism): dam never ran:
second in Haydock maiden in September: should stay 1m: acts on soft ground. *R.
Hannon*

FONTAINE LADY   5 b.m. Millfontaine 114 – Lady Begorra (Roi Soleil 125)   35
[1991 6.1d3 5d4 5m* 5.2f2 5g4 5f 1992 a5g a6g 6m 5.1m 5g5 6m 6m 6s 6d] leggy mare:
good walker: unreliable handicapper: effective at 5f to 6f: acts on firm and dead
going: effective visored/blinkered. *T. Thomson Jones*

FOOD OF LOVE   4 ch.f. Music Boy 124 – Shortbread 104 (Crisp And Even 116)   80
[1991 5m2 5m* 5m* 5d5 5g2 5g* 5m 1992 5s 5g4 5m6 5m2 5m2 5f4 5m]
close-coupled filly: moderate mover: rated 109 as 3-y-o: not so good in 1992, and
well below form last 3 starts: speedy: best form on a sound surface: below form
when blinkered once: tends to hang left: often bandaged behind. *J. Berry*

FOO FOO (IRE)   4 ch.f. The Noble Player (USA) 126 – Unmistakable 83 (Hello   –
Gorgeous (USA) 128) [1991 6g 8d 6m3 6m5 8.3m 6.9m2 7m6 6m6 1992 7d6 7m 7.1m
7f] workmanlike filly: has markedly round action: on the downgrade. *D. Marks*

FOOLISH HEART (IRE)   2 ch.f. (Feb 18) Fools Holme (USA) – Honorine   90 +
(USA) (Blushing Groom (FR) 131) [1992 7m2 a7g* 7m2 a8g* 7.5d2 8s*] lengthy,
sparely-made filly: fifth foal: half-sister to 4-y-o 1½m winner Must Be Magical (by
Temperence Hill) and fairly useful 9f and 1¼m winner Lord Bertie (by Roberto):
dam placed at 1m in France: progressive colt: won maiden at Southwell in July,
minor event at Lingfield in August and 5-runner Group 3 Premio Dormello (by 2½
lengths) at Milan in October: will be suited by 1½m: probably acts on any going: to
race in Italy. *N. A. Graham*

FOOLISH TOUCH   10 b.g. Hot Spark 126 – Nushka (Tom Fool) [1991 a8g4 a8g3   62
a8g 8s 7g 8.2d4 7.6g5 7m3 7f2 8d* 8d5 8.3m 8g2 7g4 8d 7m 8m 7g2 7d 1992 a7g* a7g
a7g 8g 6d 8d 8g2 7g2 7g3 7g 8m 7f6 8m2 8.3m 7m 8d 8g2 8s 8m5 7d2] workmanlike
gelding: poor walker and mover: inconsistent handicapper: won at Southwell in
January: effective at 6f to 1m: acts on any going, including all-weather: effective
visored or not, below form in blinkers and eyeshield: usually starts slowly and gets
behind, but suitable mount for claimer. *W. J. Musson*

FOOLS ERRAND (IRE) 2 b.g. (Apr 27) Fools Holme (USA) – Zalazula (Lord **73** p
Gayle (USA) 124) [1992 7s 7.6s² 8.2s²] IR 8,500Y, 10,500Y: leggy, close-coupled
gelding: second living foal: half-brother to Irish middle-distance winner Prizegiver
(by What A Guest): dam Irish 1m winner: progressive form in October maidens: no
chance with impressive Revere but battled on well at Nottingham final start: will be
very well suited by 1½m: should win a race. *R. Hannon*

FOREIGN ASSIGNMENT (IRE) 4 b.g. Reasonable (FR) 119 – Lady Pitt **–**
(Pitskelly 122) [1991 8d 7g 7d 8.3g³ 8f* 10g⁵ 9.7m⁵ 8m 1992 a10g 8g 8m 10m] rangy
gelding: moderate walker and mover: rated 53 at 3 yrs: no form in 1992, looking
none too keen final run: acts 1m: acts on firm and dead ground. *J. White*

FORELINO (USA) 3 b.f. Trempolino (USA) 135 – Forelie 88 (Formidable **62** §
(USA) 125) [1991 7g 8.1g 1992 8d 10.5d* 14.1m 10.2g⁵ 8.9d² 10.5d] well-made filly:
none too consistent handicapper: won amateurs event at Haydock in June: refused
to race final start: should have been effective over 1½m +: easily best efforts on
dead ground: has been retired. *J. L. Dunlop*

FORESEE 2 b.c. (Mar 19) Vision (USA) – Sovereign Dona 117 (Sovereign Path **94** p
125) [1992 8s* 7d*] half-brother to useful miler Aventino (by Cure The Blues) and
7f and 1m winner Royal Touch (by Tap On Wood), both later successful in USA,
latter finishing fourth in Breeders' Cup Mile: dam, winner from 6f to 1¼m in Ireland
and France, is half-sister to high-class miler Don: successful in maiden at Tralee in
August and Group 3 Leopardstown Stakes (by a head from Nordic Fox) in October:
may stay beyond 1m. *J. Oxx, Ireland*

FORESHORE (IRE) 2 b.f. (Mar 17) Don't Forget Me 127 – Krismas River **64** p
(Kris 135) [1992 7g²] 14,500Y: third foal: sister to Irish 3-y-o maiden Forgotten
Brief and half-sister to a winner in Italy: dam Irish 1¼m winner: 12/1, stayed on well
when length second of 18 to Azilian in maiden at Doncaster in November: sure to
improve. *A. C. Stewart*

FOREST DEW (USA) 3 b.f. Green Forest (USA) 134 – Faten (USA) (Northern **66** d
Dancer (CAN)) [1991 NR 1992 9.9f² 8.5f* 8m 9.2m⁶ 8m 8m] leggy, unfurnished filly:
has round action: fifth foal: sister to 2 winners in France, both over middle
distances, and half-sister to disqualified 1m winner Black Fighter (by Secretariat):
dam French 1½m winner from family of Be My Guest: won after winning maiden
at Beverley in June: claimed £5,011 final run: stays 1¼m: acts on firm ground: sold
3,800 gns Newmarket December Sales. *M. H. Tompkins*

FOREST FAIRY 3 b.f. Faustus (USA) 118 – Faridetta 107 (Good Bond 122) [1991 **62**
5f² 6f³ 5g⁶ 7m⁴ 1992 6m² 7d⁶ 6d 5m⁴ 5f* a6g 5.1g 6m 5m] leggy, close-coupled,
angular filly: moderate mover: inconsistent handicapper: won at Pontefract in
August: effective at 5f and 6f: acts on firm going. *R. Boss*

FOREST FLYER 2 ch.f. (Mar 24) Indian Forest (USA) 117 – Fine A Leau (USA) **–**
51 (Youth (USA) 135) [1992 5f⁴] 780Y: small, angular filly: moderate walker: first
foal: dam sprinter: fourth in maiden auction at Redcar in May: not seen again. *M.
Brittain*

FOREST LAW (USA) 3 ch.g. Green Forest (USA) 134 – Sierva (ARG) (Super **64** ?
Cavalier 112) [1991 5g³ 1992 6m⁵ 6.9g a8g³] workmanlike gelding: failed to confirm
promise shown in Newmarket maiden on reappearance, and not seen out after June:
should stay 1m: sold 3,300 gns Newmarket September Sales. *P. F. I. Cole*

FOREST SONG 2 b.f. (Mar 13) Forzando 122 – Persian Air (Persian Bold 123) **60**
[1992 7s³ 6d⁶ 7d 7.3s a7g⁵ a7g⁶] smallish, sturdy filly: second foal: dam well beaten:
regressive maiden: should stay 1m: visored final start. *R. Charlton*

FOREST STAR (USA) 3 b.c. Green Forest (USA) 134 – Al Madina (USA) **–**
(Round Table) [1991 NR 1992 12f⁴ 12.2g⁴] well-made colt: sixth foal: half-
brother to middle-distance winners in France by Busted and Sir Ivor: dam ran 3
times at 2 yrs in France: twice raced, and no worthwhile form in northern maidens.
M. Moubarak

FOREST TIGER (USA) 3 ch.c. Green Forest (USA) 134 – Perlee (FR) 122 **91**
(Margouillat (FR) 133) [1991 NR 1992 7g* 8g 7f 7.6m⁵] lengthy, angular colt: has
scope: easy type: sixth foal: half-brother to 3 winners, notably twice-raced Poule
d'Essai des Pouliches winner Pearl Bracelet (by Lyphard): dam French 1m to 1½m
winner: most impressive winner of newcomers race at Doncaster in March: pulled
hard and well beaten after in Craven Stakes (favourite, reportedly suffering blood
disorder), Group 3 event at Newmarket and listed race at Lingfield: wears tongue
strap: needs to settle better. *M. Moubarak*

FOREST WIND (USA)   2 ch.c. (Feb 7) Green Forest (USA) 134 – **111** p
Pompoes (DEN) 117 (Belmont (FR)) [1992 6m* 6g² 6g*]

In company with many of his 1992 stable-companions, the Rokeby Farms
Mill Reef Stakes winner Forest Wind will be racing in America in 1993. His
young trainer couldn't wish for many better three-year-olds with which to
begin his new career in Florida. Without substantial progress, Forest Wind
might well have found his opportunities limited had he remained in training in
Britain, but horses of the ability he showed as a two-year-old, just below the
top class, are comprehensively catered for in the States, and he should win
plenty more races.

Forest Wind made a spectacular first appearance on the racecourse when
he cantered home by ten lengths in a maiden at Goodwood in August. Most of
his nine opponents were either green or backward, or, in several instances,
both, but Forest Wind couldn't have won more impressively, travelling easily
behind the leaders for four furlongs before drawing right away to win as his
rider wished. As it turned out, Forest Wind didn't have much to beat at
Goodwood—those behind him managed only one win, that coming in a seller,
between them in twenty-one starts subsequently—but as expected he proved
well up to the task of taking on the better two-year-olds when he gave the
useful Silver Wizard a race in the BonusPrint Sirenia Stakes at Kempton in
September. Silver Wizard, who was widely considered unlucky not to have
won the Gimcrack Stakes at York on his previous outing, won by two and a
half lengths, as his form entitled him to, but Forest Wind wasn't at all
discredited and comfortably beat another impressive Goodwood winner
Liyakah for second place. Given that the Sirenia Stakes was only Forest
Wind's second race, it wasn't unreasonable to anticipate his improving
further, and in getting the better of a representative field in the Mill Reef at
Newbury later in the month, on his final start, he showed the best form of his
first season. More patient tactics were adopted on Forest Wind on this
occasion—he'd run rather too freely in the initial stages at Kempton—and it's
probably no coincidence that they contributed to his improvement. Dropped
in behind as soon as the stalls opened, Forest Wind still had plenty of distance
to make up on the front-running favourite Marina Park, earlier successful in
the Princess Margaret Stakes and third to Zafonic in the Prix Morny, as he
began his challenge with under two furlongs to run. However, he quickened
really well when put under stronger pressure and, as Marina Park drifted off a
straight line, ran on gamely to take the lead with sixty yards to run. At the line
he had half a length to spare over Marina Park, the pair finishing two lengths
ahead of the useful Sharp Prod with the subsequent Middle Park runner-up
and Racecall Gold Trophy winner Pips Pride in fourth.

Forest Wind is the best runner so far from Green Forest's seventh crop.
Green Forest was a top-class racehorse who won five of his ten races
including the Prix Morny, Prix de la Salamandre and Grand Criterium as a
two-year-old and the Prix Jacques le Marois as a three-year-old. He began
well as a stallion with the pattern-winners Forest Flower and Indian Forest
in his first crop, but, apart from Green Line Express, Made of Gold and

Rokeby Farms Mill Reef Stakes, Newbury—
much improved form from Forest Wind (left) who gets up close home from Marina Park,
with Sharp Prod (noseband) third and Pips Pride (checks) fourth

Ecurie Fustok's "Forest Wind"

	Green Forest (USA) (ch 1979)	Shecky Greene (b 1970)	Noholme II / Lester's Pride
Forest Wind (USA) (ch.c. Feb 7, 1990)		Tell Meno Lies (gr 1971)	The Axe / Filatonga
	Pompoes (DEN) (ch 1977)	Belmont (gr 1967)	Cambremont / Belle de Retz
		Wilhelmina (ch 1970)	Pall Mall / Ziba

Somethingdifferent, has seldom been in the headlines since. Forest Wind's dam Pompoes, a daughter of the smart French two-year-old Belmont, was bred in Denmark and was raced there and in Sweden before continuing her career in France and the United States. Pompoes was an outstanding filly as a two-year-old in Scandinavia, where she won all her seven races, between five and a half and seven furlongs. She was bought by M. Fustok after finishing an excellent second to Aryenne when a 31/1-shot in the Criterium des Pouliches on her final start that year, but, despite holding her form fairly well until she was retired as a four-year-old, never managed to win again. Besides racing in five different countries (she finished well beaten in the One Thousand Guineas on her only start here) Pompoes has also bred winners in three; the best of them apart from Forest Wind are his full brother Centerland, a useful winner at six and seven furlongs, and the French seven-furlong and one-mile winner Three Generations (by Alydar), subsequently a graded stakes-placed winner in the States. Pompoes is a sister to several winners, including

Pompus, a useful winner of four races as a two-year-old in Scandinavia; she's also a daughter of a full sister to Pompous, who won the Prix Eclipse and finished third in the Prix Morny as a two-year-old and second in Ascot's Queen Elizabeth II Stakes at four. Forest Wind, a good-quartered colt, and an excellent mover, may well stay a mile. He has raced only on a sound surface. *M. Moubarak*

FOREVER DIAMONDS 5 ch.g. Good Times (ITY) – Mel Mira 68 (Roi Soleil 82 125) [1991 6d2 8f* 6m3 6m3 6g 7.1m3 11.1s 1992 8d* 8m5 8.3s2 8m2 8.9g* 8s2 10m2 7.9s* 8s] leggy, rather sparely-made gelding: had excellent season and much improved in handicaps in 1992, successful at Ripon and in 2 £7,700 races at York: lethargic in paddock and rare poor effort final start: effective from 1m to 1¼m: acts on any going: twice below form in blinkers: good mount for apprentice: game and consistent: a credit to his trainer. *M. H. Easterby*

FOREVER SHINEING 2 b.f. (Mar 11) Glint of Gold 128 – Patosky 94 62 (Skymaster 126) [1992 7s6 8.9s 8.1g3] good-topped filly: half-sister to several winners, including one-time smart sprinter Crews Hill (by High Top) and 1¾m winner and hurdler Blake's Progress (by Blakeney): dam suited by 7f/1m: best effort when staying-on third in maiden at Edinburgh in October: will be suited by middle distances: may do better. *M. J. Camacho*

FOREVER TWEEKY 3 ch.f. Crever 94 – Joyeuse (Biskrah 121) [1991 NR 1992 – a10g 12g] sixth reported foal by a thoroughbred stallion: dam last on only start: tailed-off last in seller and maiden. *P. R. Hedger*

FORGE 4 ch.g. Formidable (USA) 125 – Red Shoes 74 (Dance In Time (CAN)) – [1991 NR 1992 10g 11.6g] close-coupled, deep-girthed gelding: moderate walker: no worthwhile form. *P. D. Cundell*

FORGE BAY 5 b.g. Buzzards Bay 128§ – Korresia (Derring-Do 131) [1991 a7g – a12g2 a12g 10.8g 8d2 8m5 7.5m 8.3m 10g* 1992 9d] leggy, good-topped gelding: inconsistent handicapper: rated 46 at 4 yrs: effective at 1m to 1½m: acts on good to firm and dead ground. *H. J. Collingridge*

FORGETFUL 3 b.f. Don't Forget Me 127 – Peak Squaw (USA) (Icecapade 50 (USA)) [1991 5.7f5 7.1m6 1992 8m 7g 9g 7f2 10d6 10.2f2 10.2f4 10.8g3 11m2 10m] leggy, workmanlike filly: consistent plater: stays 11f: acts on firm and dead going: raced too freely when blinkered final start: sometimes carries head high: claimed out of R. Hannon's stable £6,854 sixth start. *D. Burchell*

FORLORN DIVER 4 ch.g. Ballacashtal (CAN) – Four Lawns 77 (Forlorn River – 124) [1991 6g 6g 5f 1992 5d 7g 8g5 5.7f 5g] lengthy gelding: on the downgrade. *B. Gubby*

FORMAESTRE (IRE) 2 b.f. (May 10) Formidable (USA) 125 – Maestrette 77 53 (Manado 130) [1992 5g 5.1g* 6g4 5g5 5g 7d 7m6 7m] small, unfurnished filly: fifth reported foal: half-sister to unreliable 8.2f and 1¼m winner God Bless You (by Vision) and 6-y-o middle-distance winner Thimbalina (by Salmon Leap): dam 1m winner: inconsistent in nurseries after winning Nottingham maiden in May: stays 7f: acts on good to firm ground: has joined S. Norton. *M. H. Tompkins*

FORMAL AFFAIR 3 b.f. (Mar 28) Rousillon (USA) 133 – Muznah 92 (Royal 78 And Regal (USA)) [1992 6m3 6f3 7m 6g3 8.2g3 7s* 7s2] 6,200Y: lengthy filly: sixth foal: half-sister to 3-y-o Farah (by Lead On Time), 1m to 10.2f winner Jazilah (by Persian Bold) and Irish 1¾m winner Fayafi (by Top Ville): dam 7f and 1m winner seemed to stay 1½m: much improved on last 2 starts: 4-length winner of nursery at Wolverhampton and second to Cropton in minor event at Warwick: will stay 1¼m: seems well suited by soft ground. *C. A. Cyzer*

FORMALIN 2 ch.g. (Feb 25) Interrex (CAN) – Formula 72 (Reform 132) [1992 – 6m] 2,700Y: half-brother to a winning partner: dam 1m winner: prominent to halfway in maiden auction at Folkestone in August. *W. A. O'Gorman*

FORMAL INVITATION (IRE) 3 ch.c. Be My Guest (USA) 126 – Clarista 60 (USA) 67 (Riva Ridge (USA)) [1991 6d 7m 1992 6.9v 8g 13.1m3 12.1m* 14g 11.6m 12h5 10.2f4 14.6g 16m6 10m 9.7m3 10.8g* 12m5] big colt: tends not to impress in appearance: inconsistent handicapper: won at Chepstow in May and Warwick (seller, bought in 5,400 gns) in August: stays 1½m: acts on good to firm ground: ran fairly well when blinkered once: usually bandaged: joined D. Nicholson. *G. Lewis*

FORMATO UNI (IRE) 2 b.c. (May 11) Mtoto 134 – Martinova 111 (Martinmas 64 p 128) [1992 7m4 7s] IR 15,000Y: close-coupled colt: closely related to 3-y-o 1m winner Salda (by Bustino) and half-brother to 3 winners, notably very useful French sprinter Export Price (by Habitat): dam third in Irish 1000 Guineas, is half-sister to high-class 1¼m performer Lucky Wednesday: better for race, shaped encouragingly in maiden auctions at Lingfield (considerably handled) and Goodwood over 2 months later: will be suited by 1m: will do better. *J. L. Dunlop*

FORMIDABLE FLIGHT   3 ch.f. Formidable (USA) 125 – Gadfly 108 (Le   **109**
Fabuleux 133) [1991 8g³ 8d⁶ 8d 1992 10g* 10m* 9g* 10d 9.3s] 19,000Y: half-sister to numerous winners in France, including Group 3 Prix Fille de l'Air-second Green City (by Green Dancer), and several winners over jumps: dam, French 2-y-o 1m winner, is a half-sister to King Edward VII Stakes winner Bonhomie: very useful French filly: progressed well to win a minor event at Longchamp in May and a listed event and Group 3 Prix Chloe at Evry in midsummer: soundly beaten in pattern events afterwards: stays 1¼m: best form on a sound surface: wears blinkers. *P. Bary, France*

FORMIDABLE LIZ   2 ch.f. (May 12) Formidable (USA) 125 – Areej (Rusticaro   **45**
(FR) 124) [1992 a6g⁶ a7s 6m 6s³ 6d 8.3s] 1,650F, 2,000Y: sturdy filly: moderate mover: half-sister to 2 minor winners in France, one also successful over jumps: dam lightly raced: plater: stays 6f: acts on soft ground and fibresand. *N. Bycroft*

FORM MISTRESS   3 b.f. Formidable (USA) 125 – Proud Miss (USA) (Semi-   **36**
Pro) [1991 5g⁶ 5.1g 5.7f² 6m 1992 8.2m 6g 5g 6g⁶ 5.1s] small, angular filly: poor maiden: stays 6f: acts on firm ground: often visored: sold 1,100 gns Doncaster November Sales. *P. T. Walwyn*

FOR MOG (USA)   3 ch.g. Mogambo (USA) – Forever Command (USA) (Top   **87**
Command (USA)) [1991 7m 1992 12.3s² 12g² 12.1m⁴ 16.2m* 14.5g³ 16d⁴] workmanlike gelding: won £10,600 handicap at Ascot in June: ran well after in Newmarket listed race, St Leger Italiano at Turin and handicap at Newbury: suited by thorough test of stamina: acts on good to firm ground and dead. *C. E. Brittain*

FORM SECRET (IRE)   2 b.f. (May 28) Formidable (USA) 125 – Secret Light-   **–**
ning (USA) 78 (Secretariat (USA)) [1992 5g 7g 5s⁵ 8s] IR 1,200Y: workmanlike filly: has a round action: half-sister to 1987 2-y-o 6f winner Relative Secret (by Great Nephew): dam ran only at 2 yrs, winning at 1m: poor form in maidens. *L. J. Barratt*

FOR REG (IRE)   3 b.c. Theatrical 128 – Swalthee (FR) (Sword Dancer (USA))   **96**
[1991 7d* 1992 10.3m⁵ 8.1g⁴ 8.9d⁴ 10s² 10.3g] short-backed, quite attractive colt: easily best efforts in 1992 when fourth in listed race at Chester and handicap at Leicester, off course over 4 months in between: stays 8.9f: rather headstrong: winner over hurdles in Ireland in December for P. J. Flynn. *A. C. Stewart*

FORT DERRY (IRE)   3 gr.g. Belfort (FR) 89 – Derrygold §§ (Derrylin 115)   **–**
[1991 NR 1992 6m⁴ 8d⁶ 6g⁵ 6.9g 10m] 6,000F: strong, good-topped gelding: fourth foal: brother to untrustworthy plater Doire and half-brother to 1m winner Emsleys Choice (by Windjammer): dam fairly useful 6f and 7f winner at 2 yrs who refused to race last 3 outings on flat, but won over hurdles: no worthwhile form: sold 1,350 gns Doncaster October Sales. *E. J. Alston*

FORTENSKY (USA)   2 b.c. (Feb 7) Blushing Groom (FR) 131 – Casey 119   **82** p
(Caerleon (USA) 132) [1992 6g² 7d³ 7d* 7m⁶] well-made colt: moderate walker: first foal: dam won Park Hill Stakes: progressive colt: comfortably won maiden at Brighton in September: favourite, good sixth of 23, soon niggled along, in nursery at Newmarket following month: will be much better suited by middle distances: should improve further. *L. M. Cumani*

FORTHEMOMENT   2 ch.f. (Feb 24) Formidable (USA) 125 – Forgotten   **39**
Dreams (USA) 82 (Shoemaker 121) [1992 6f⁵ 7g 6g⁶ 7.5m] leggy filly: has scope: has a round action: sister to 1983 2-y-o 6f winner Forelie and half-sister to several winners, including Derby Italiano victor My Top and (at 6f) smart 1986 2-y-o Mountain Memory (both by High Top): dam won 3 races over 2m: poor plater: should stay beyond 6f: ran poorly when blinkered final start: sold 650 gns Doncaster September Sales. *P. Calver*

FOR THE PRESENT   2 b.g. (Feb 14) Then Again 126 – Axe Valley 89 (Royben   **61** p
125) [1992 5f⁴ 6.1m* 5g⁶] 4,000Y: strong, useful-looking gelding: has scope: second foal: half-brother to 3-y-o Shalou (by Forzando), 6f winner at 2 yrs: dam sprinter: gamely won maiden at Nottingham in June: never able to challenge in nursery at York following month: will stay 7f +: likely to do better. *T. D. Barron*

FORT HOPE   3 gr.g. Belfort (FR) 89 – Hopeful Katie 67 (Full of Hope 125) [1991   **§§**
5s⁴ 5m⁴ 6g³ 6m a5g* a6g* a7g 5m a6g a5g⁴ 1992 a5g⁴ a5g⁴ 5d⁵ 5g a5g a5g] leggy, lengthy gelding: most ungenuine and one to avoid. *T. J. Naughton*

FORTHWITH   2 b.f. (Apr 2) Midyan (USA) 124 – Top Society (High Top 131)   **68**
[1992 7s* 7g] leggy, unfurnished filly: first foal: dam unraced: 2½-length winner of

maiden at Salisbury: faded from over 2f out when well beaten in minor event at Newbury later in September. *R. Hannon*

FORTIS PAVIOR (IRE) 2 b.c. (Feb 5) Salt Dome (USA) – Heather Lil 52 (Ballymore 123) [1992 6d 6s³ 7d⁴ 7s] 2,500F, IR 6,000Y: first foal: dam never ran: third in maiden at Newcastle: no comparable form: should stay 1m: bandaged behind penultimate start. *R. M. Whitaker*

FORTROSE (USA) 2 ch.f. (Mar 19) Forty Niner (USA) – Danseur Fabuleux ? (USA) 106 (Northern Dancer (CAN)) [1992 7.5s*] third foal: half-sister to Arazi (by Blushing Groom) and 1989 French 2-y-o 6f winner River Sunset (by Irish River): dam, stayed 1½m, from top-class family: sire top class at up to 1¼m: won 10-runner newcomers event at Saint-Cloud in October by a head: could be anything. *F. Boutin, France*

FORT SHIRLEY (IRE) 3 b.c. Shirley Heights 130 – Brocade 121 (Habitat 134) 59 [1991 NR 1992 10.4d⁴ 14.1g⁵ 12v] rather lightly-made, unfurnished colt: third foal: brother to smart Free At Last, 7f winner at 2 yrs later much better at 1¼m, and half-brother to very promising 2-y-o Barathea (by Sadler's Wells): dam 7f and 1m winner, sister to useful 1982 2-y-o 5f to 7f performer Cause Celebre: quite modest form in maidens at York and Nottingham in October: stays 1¾m: seems unsuited by heavy ground. *M. R. Stoute*

FORTUNE CAY (IRE) 2 b.g. (Feb 4) Treasure Kay 114 – Maellen (River 91 Beauty 105) [1992 5g* 5f² 5m* 6g⁵ 6m] 20,000Y: lengthy gelding: good mover: fifth reported foal: half-brother to 6f (at 2 yrs) to 1½m winner Lifewatch Vision (by Vision), now based in Ireland: dam Irish 1½m winner: successful in good style in maiden at Lingfield in May and minor event at Windsor in June: good fifth of 6 in July Stakes at Newmarket: fair seventh of 8 in Gimcrack Stakes at York: stays 6f: acts on good to firm ground: sold to race abroad. *R. Hannon*

FORTUNE INN 2 ch.f. (Feb 25) Flying Tyke 90 – Habatashie 62 (Habat 127) – [1992 5g] 1,300Y: rather leggy filly: fifth foal: sister to untrustworthy 3-y-o Monti Beppo, 5.3f seller winner at 2 yrs, and 2 other winning platers at up to 7f: dam plating-class maiden: no sign of ability in maiden auction at Beverley in March. *J. S. Wainwright*

FORTUNE STAR (IRE) 3 b.c. Glow (USA) – Lucky For Me 116 (Appiani II 67 128) [1991 NR 1992 10s⁵ 11.8g³ 14s 15.4d* 15.8d] IR 26,000Y: good-topped colt: half-brother to several winners, including very smart stayer Yawa (by Luthier) and very useful 1980 Irish 2-y-o 6f and 1m winner Euclid (by Bellypha): dam middle-distance performer: best form in maidens first 2 starts: landed odds in amateurs maiden at Folkestone in September: stays 15.4f: has raced only on an easy surface: sold 16,500 gns Newmarket Autumn Sales. *J. L. Dunlop*

FORTUNE'S WHEEL (IRE) 4 b.c. Law Society (USA) 130 – North Forland 116 (FR) 99 (Northfields (USA)) [1991 8v² 8v⁴ 12g 10g² 10s² 10s 10v 1992 7.5g² 9.5g* 12g* 10s* 10s* 10.5g⁴ 12m⁵ 10g⁵ 10g⁵] smart French colt: in very good form early in the year, winning a minor and a listed event at Cagnes-sur-Mer in February, Prix Exbury at Saint-Cloud in March and, beating Pistolet Bleu a length, Prix d'Harcourt at Longchamp in April: generally ran well afterwards, 4 lengths fourth to Subotica in Prix Ganay at Longchamp and beaten under 1½ lengths in Group 3 event at Baden-Baden in August final start: stays 1½m: acts on heavy ground, ran moderately on good to firm: has been tried in blinkers. *R. Collet, France*

FORT VALLY 2 gr.f. (Feb 8) Belfort (FR) 89 – Hivally (High Line 125) [1992 5m⁴ 58 5f 7m³ 7.1m⁵ 6m⁵ 8g³ 8f⁵ 7g³ 8.9s⁶] 3,200Y: leggy, lightly-made filly: half-sister to 2 winners in Holland: dam unraced: consistent maiden: stays 9f: probably acts on any going: tends to get on edge, and not easiest of rides. *B. W. Murray*

FORZA AZZURRI (IRE) 3 ch.c. On Your Mark 125 – Miss Legend (USA) 65 d (Bold Legend) [1991 7m a6g a6g 1992 a7g⁵ a7g⁴ a6g a8g³ 7g 6.1d⁴ a5g⁵ 6m 6m a8g⁴ 6m⁶ 7g] angular, close-coupled colt: moderate mover: inconsistent maiden: stays 6f: acts on dead ground and fibresand: usually blinkered. *Mrs N. Macauley*

FOURFORFUN 2 br.c. (Feb 18) Midyan (USA) 124 – Jennyjo 64 (Martinmas 54 128) [1992 7m⁵ 7s⁶ 7.1s] 10,500F, 41,000Y: leggy colt: moderate mover: half-brother to three 2-y-o 5f winners: dam 7f winner: modest form in maidens first 2 starts: soundly beaten final run. *R. Hannon*

FOUROFUS 3 b.g. Wassl 125 – Que Sera 91 (Music Boy 124) [1991 5m 5g⁵ 5s 51 d 1992 5m⁵ 5.7s 5.3f⁵ a5g⁶ 6g 7g] strong, good-quartered gelding: disappointing maiden: should stay 6f: unsuited by soft ground: sold to join W. G. M. Turner 1,300 gns Newmarket September Sales: one to be wary of. *R. Boss*

FOURSINGH 4 br.g. Mansingh (USA) 120 – Maycrest (Imperial Fling (USA) **50** §
116) [1991 12m 7.5f⁶ a7g² 8g 7d 7g⁵ 1992 a7g a8g a8g⁵ a10g³ a10g² a12g 9m a10g 12f⁶
12m] smallish, lengthy, attractive gelding: moderate walker: has a quick action: lost
his form after being placed at Lingfield early in 1992: stays 1¼m: usually blinkered
nowadays: carries head high, and may be irresolute. *C. B. B. Booth*

FOURWALK 8 br.g. Godswalk (USA) 120 – Vaunt (USA) (Hill Rise 127) [1991 6m –
5.8f* 5m⁶ 7m 1992 5g⁶] strong, close-coupled, plain gelding: poor walker: bad
mover: modest handicapper as 7-y-o: below form in March: stays 6f: acts on any
going: below form when visored: sometimes wore tongue strap. *Mrs N. Macauley*

FOX CHAPEL 5 b.g. Formidable (USA) 125 – Hollow Heart 89 (Wolver Hollow **62** §
126) [1991 8d 10g 10s² 10.2m⁴ 11d 10.1f 12d 11.5d 10.3d 1992 8.5g⁴ 10s] good-bodied
gelding: thoroughly unreliable handicapper: effective at 1m to 1¼m: acts on good to
firm and soft ground: below form when visored: retained by trainer 6,100 gns
Doncaster November Sales. *J. G. FitzGerald*

FOXES DIAMOND 4 b.f. Sallust 134 – Rahesh 111 (Raffingora 130) [1991 8d 7.5f **53** d
10f⁶ 8m⁵ 7g⁶ 5m 6m² 7f² 6f³ 7m³ 7m⁴ 6f⁴ 6f⁶ 5f² 6.1m 6g 6m 1992 7d 6d 5.9d³ 5s³
7m 6.9f⁵ 5f 6.1m 5.9h] leggy, angular filly: inconsistent handicapper: effective over
stiff 5f to 7f: probably acts on any going: sometimes blinkered, below form when
visored once: sold 750 gns Doncaster August Sales. *B. Ellison*

FRAAM 3 b.c. Lead On Time (USA) 123 – Majestic Kahala (USA) (Majestic **90**
Prince) [1991 NR 1992 8d* 7d⁵] good-topped colt: half-brother to several winners,
including 1991 3-y-o 5f winner Desert Sport (by Green Desert) and very useful 6f (at
2 yrs) and 12.3f winner Malaak (by The Minstrel): dam good winner at up to 1¼m in
Canada: 1½-length winner of maiden at Goodwood: improved form but finished
lame when fifth of 8 to Lord Chickney in £8,500 contest at Ascot 13 days later in
September. *A. A. Scott*

FRAGONARD (IRE) 3 b.g. Pharly (FR) 130 – Girl On A Swing 79 (High Top –
131) [1991 5d 6g² 7d* 1992 7m] workmanlike gelding: rated 64 at 2 yrs: bandaged
behind in handicap at Newmarket in April: will stay 1¼m: acts on dead ground: sold
to join J. J. O'Neill's stable 2,000 gns Newmarket Autumn Sales. *G. A. Pritchard-
Gordon*

FRAGRANT HACKETTE 3 ch.f. Simply Great (FR) 122 – Martin-Lavell –
News 90 (Song 132) [1991 5m⁴ 5s 1992 5f] poor maiden. *A. Hide*

FRAGRANT HILL 4 b.f. Shirley Heights 130 – English Spring (USA) 116 (Grey **104**
Dawn II 132) [1991 10g* 12m 11.9m 1992 11f* 12d 11.9g⁶ 10m⁵ 8.1d 10d] lengthy,
workmanlike filly: has been hobdayed: moderate walker: easily best efforts in 1992
when winning Newbury handicap in May and good fifth to Ruby Tiger in Group 2
Nassau Stakes at Goodwood: should be suited by 1½m: suited by top-of-the-ground:
below form when blinkered/visored: flashes tail: sold 105,000 gns Newmarket
December Sales. *I. A. Balding*

FRANCIS ANN 4 br.f. Balidar 133 – Supper Party (He Loves Me 120) [1991 a7g **55**
a7g⁶ a7g² a8g⁵ 1992 5s* 6s⁵ 5d 7.1m 6f⁶ 5d² 6s⁸ 5d 6s⁶ 6v] strong, rather
dipped-backed filly: moderate mover: inconsistent sprint handicapper: successful at
Hamilton in seller (no bid) in May and claimer in September: best form on an easy
surface: successful for claimer. *Miss L. A. Perratt*

FRANCISCAN 5 b.g. Godswalk (USA) 130 – Athenian Primrose (Tower Walk –
130) [1991 14m 13d 1992 12.3v⁶ 14.1d 14.6g a14g a12g] well-made gelding: no
worthwhile form on flat in 1992: seems to stay 1¾m: acts on good to firm and dead
ground. *B. Preece*

FRANKIE GOODMAN (IRE) 2 b.c. (Jun 6) Colmore Row 111 – Shukriaa –
(Busted 134) [1992 5.1m] 1,800Y: fourth foal: dam ran twice: always tailed off in
maiden at Bath in May. *J. S. Moore*

FRANKUS 3 b.g. Nicholas Bill 125 – Sigh 75 (Highland Melody 112) [1991 6m 6f⁵ –
7.1s 5.7g 1992 6.9m 8d] leggy gelding: poor maiden: should stay 1m at least: acts
on firm ground. *S. Mellor*

FRASERS HILL (IRE) 2 b.f. (Mar 6) Tate Gallery (USA) 117 – Sybaris 91 –
(Crowned Prince (USA) 128) [1992 5m 6g] IR 15,500Y: small filly: fourth foal:
half-sister to 1988 Irish 2-y-o 7f winner Millennium Queen (by Mendez): dam 2-y-o
5f winner later successful in USA: well beaten in modest company: sold 3,000 gns
Newmarket Autumn Sales. *P. F. I. Cole*

FREAKY DEAKY 5 b.g. Prince Tenderfoot (USA) 126 – Maylands – –
(Windjammer (USA)) [1991 NR 1992 8m 7.1m⁵ 9d] big, good-bodied ex-Irish gelding:

poor form here: probably stayed 1¼m: acted on good to firm ground and dead: ran creditably in blinkers: dead. *N. A. Callaghan*

FRECKENHAM   2 br.f. (Mar 28) Rousillon (USA) 133 – Screenable (USA)   –
(Silent Screen (USA)) [1992 7m 7d 6d a8g] 1,000Y: leggy filly: half-sister to 3-y-o Scottish Ruby (by Scottish Reel), 1½m winner Barrymore (by Robellino), later successful in USA, and a winner in Italy: dam minor winner at around 1m in North America: soundly beaten, including in a seller. *J. E. Banks*

FREDDIE JACK   2 b.c. (May 8) Midyan (USA) 124 – Sule Skerry 78 (Scottish   **33**
Rifle 127) [1992 5.1m a7g a8g6] 17,000Y: smallish, close-coupled colt: eighth foal: half-brother to 1989 2-y-o 5f winner Miss Eurolink (by Touching Wood) and to 3 other winners, all at 1m or more: dam, half-sister to smart fillies Flighting and Bonnie Isle, won twice over 1½m: well beaten in maidens at Chester (off course over 3 months afterwards) and Lingfield. *F. H. Lee*

FREDDIE LLOYD (USA)   3 ch.g. Barrera (USA) – Shredaline (USA) (Shred- **114**
der (USA)) [1991 6m3 5m 5m* 6m3 5m2 6g6 5d2 1992 5v3 6g6 5g* 5.1g2 5m* 5m* 5m* 5m5] robust, good-quartered gelding: carries condition: has a roundish action: had excellent season and vastly improved in 1992: won handicaps at Sandown and York, Group 3 Cara Ballyogan Stakes at Leopardstown and King George Stakes (held Blyton Lad by a neck) at Goodwood: about 2½ lengths fifth of 11 to Lyric Fantasy in Nunthorpe Stakes at York: best at 5f on top-of-the-ground: bandaged off-fore and off-hind once: a credit to his trainer. *N. A. Callaghan*

FREEBYJOVE   2 ch.f. (Mar 22) King Among Kings 60 – London Chimes   –
(London Bells (CAN) 109) [1992 5m 6s 6f 6m 10d a8g] leggy filly: has a round action: fourth foal: dam unraced: well beaten in varied events, including sellers. *P. Butler*

FREE DANCER   2 b.f. (Mar 19) Shareef Dancer (USA) 135 – Free Touch (Kris   **36**
135) [1992 7.1g4 5f5 8.3s] sturdy filly: first foal: dam, unraced, from family of Time Charter: poor maiden: will be suited by middle distances: sold 840 gns Doncaster October Sales. *R. Allan*

FREE EXPRESSION   7 b.m. Kind of Hush 118 – Liberation 63 (Native Prince)   –
[1991 NR 1992 10.2f 10.2m] rangy, sparely-made mare: on the downgrade. *P. Leach*

FREE FLYER (IRE)   3 b.c. Bluebird (USA) 125 – Lassalia (Sallust 134) [1991 **117**
7g4 7.1m* 7m5 7m6 1992 8d2 10s4 9.5s4 10f] well-made colt: good mover: off course 3 months and 33/1, easily best effort when 3½ lengths fourth of 12 to Kooyonga in Coral-Eclipse Stakes at Sandown: beaten under 5 lengths in Grade 2 American Derby and Grade 1 Secretariat Stakes (reportedly not clear run) at Arlington, USA, after: better at 1¼m than 1m: probably acts on any going. *M. Moubarak*

King George Stakes, Goodwood—
Freddie Lloyd (far side) holds on gamely from Blyton Lad (noseband) and Artistic Reef

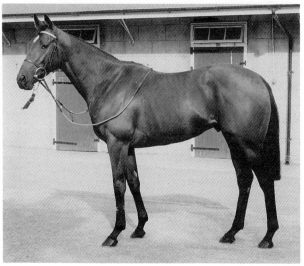

Lord Harrington's "Frenchpark"

FREE MARKET 2 br.g. (Apr 26) Crowning Honors (CAN) – Market Rose 72   –
(Most Secret 119) [1992 5m 6g⁵ 6m] unfurnished gelding: third live foal: dam 2-y-o
7f winner: no form in varied events in the North in first half of 1992. *G. M. Moore*

FREE MINX 6 b.g. Free State 125 – Musical Minx 75 (Jukebox 120) [1991 15.8f⁴   –
16.5g⁶ 12.1f* 13.8m³ 12.1g³ a12g a14g⁴ 1992 a16g 13d] sturdy gelding: well beaten in
1992: stays 15.8f: acts on any going: below form blinkered/visored: sometimes
reluctant at stalls, and refused to race over hurdles in September. *Mrs V. A. Aconley*

FREE MOVER (IRE) 3 br.g. Rousillon (USA) 133 – Free Dance (FR) (Green   79
Dancer (USA) 132) [1991 NR 1992 10m³ 10.2f³ 11.8g* 14.8g] big, unfurnished
gelding: has a long stride: sixth living foal: half-brother to middle-distance winners
by Shirley Heights (2), Known Fact (very useful Free Fact) and Great Nephew: dam
French 8.5f and 9f winner: bought out of R. Hern's stable 5,500 gns Newmarket
Autumn (1991) Sales: won slowly-run maiden at Leicester in July, 1992: seems best
at around 1½m: acts on firm ground. *N. A. Graham*

FREEPHONE (CAN) 3 b.g. Phone Trick (USA) – Flying Aristocrat (USA)   51 d
(Prince John) [1991 6f 5m 6m 1992 7g 10g⁵ 10f³ 9f⁶ 8.5d 8g] good-bodied gelding: on
the downgrade: stays 1¼m: acts on firm ground: often blinkered: sold to join J.
Akehurst's stable 3,500 gns Ascot July Sales. *J. W. Hills*

FREE TRANSFER (IRE) 3 b.c. Dara Monarch 128 – Free Reserve (USA)   73 d
(Tom Rolfe) [1991 6g a7g 8.5f³ 8.9m⁶ a8g a8g⁶ a8g⁶ 1992 10.1s³ 13.9f² 14.8g⁵ 14.1m
a16g⁶ 12m 13.8d 11.5d⁶ a12g] workmanlike colt: carries condition: moderate mover:
good walker: short-head second of 5 in maiden at York in June, staying on well: no
comparable form after, in Southwell claimer final start: stays 1¾m: acts on firm
going: sold to join J. Wainwright 11,500 gns Doncaster November Sales. *P. F. Tulk*

FREEWHEEL (USA) 3 ch.f. Arctic Tern (USA) 126 – Dinner Surprise (USA)   88
(Lyphard (USA) 132) [1991 6.1f* 7m* 1992 7g*] rather leggy, quite attractive filly:

promising 2-y-o: not seen out again in 1992 after landing odds in 3-runner Doncaster minor event in July: will stay 1¼m: sent to USA. *L. M. Cumani*

FRENCH HEIRESS 2 b.f. (Feb 16) Caerleon (USA) 132 – Kereolle (Riverman (USA) 131) [1992 5s5 9,500Y: ninth foal: half-sister to 3-y-o 7f (at 2 yrs) and 11.5f winner Mystery Play (by Sadler's Wells), and to 4 other winners, including very useful stayer Arden (by Ardross): dam second over 6f at 2 yrs in France but mainly disappointing, is half-sister to very good broodmare Miss Manon: 33/1, always outpaced in maiden at Lingfield in September. *C. E. Brittain* –

FRENCH IVY (USA) 5 ch.g. Nodouble (USA) – Lierre (USA) (Gummo (USA) 117) [1991 14d 17.6m4 18f5 15.9m* 1992 18.5g] leggy gelding: rated 90 at 4 yrs: tailed off in Chester Cup in May at 5 yrs: stays well: probably needs a sound surface: ran well when visored at 3 yrs. *Mrs A. L. M. King* –

FRENCHPARK 2 b.c. (Feb 17) Fools Holme (USA) – Piffle 87 (Shirley Heights 130) [1992 5s* 7g2 8d* 10s5] first foal: dam 1½m winner stayed well, is sister to El Conquistador out of half-sister to Mountain Lodge: sire top class at up to 11f in South Africa: successful in 8-runner maiden at Naas and 7-runner Juddmonte EBF Beresford Stakes (by a head, with Wootton Rivers 4½ lengths behind in third) at the Curragh: creditable fifth of 8 to Marchand de Sable in Criterium de Saint-Cloud in November: stays very well: yet to race on top-of-the-ground: to join M. Jarvis. *C. Collins, Ireland* 107

FRENCH REVOLUTION (FR) 3 ch.f. Midyan (USA) 124 – French Beauty (FR) (Jim French (USA)) [1991 a8g5 1992 a8g4 7d4 9.9m 12s] poor maiden. *P. A. Kelleway* –

FRENI 3 b.f. Primo Dominie 121 – F Sharp 83 (Formidable (USA) 125) [1991 5f 5m 5.2g 6m 6m4 5m5 8m5 1992 a10g5 6m 8f 6m] lengthy filly: moderate mover: no form in 1992: has form from 5f to 1m: acts on good to firm ground: blinkered final start. *M. D. I. Usher* –

FRESCADE (USA) 2 b.c. (Apr 9) Green Dancer (USA) 132 – Breeze Me (USA) (Best Turn (USA)) [1992 7g3 8.1g5 10g* 10s] $200,000Y: strong, good-topped colt with lots of scope: has long, round stride: half-brother to French 3-y-o Badawiya (by Miswaki) and Breezing Dixie (by Dixieland Band), successful at up to 9f and placed in graded stakes: dam, unraced, from family of Breeders' Cup Juvenile winner Fly So Free: confirmed earlier promise when length winner of maiden at Nottingham in October but tended to hang running down far side: behind in Group 2 event at Rome in November: should be suited by a thorough test of stamina. *P. F. I. Cole* 75

FRESCOBALDO (USA) 6 b.g. Run The Gantlet (USA) – Voice of The River (USA) (Speak John) [1991 13.8d 13.8g2 12g 13.8m2 15.8f4 12.4m5 12m 12.3m* 12.3f5 12.3f5 12f* 10.9m* 10m6 12m a12g a12g4 1992 a11g2 a12g3 a11g*] leggy, rather sparely-made horse: had a rather round action: modest handicapper: successful at Southwell in January: effective at 11f to 15.8f: acted on firm going and fibresand, unsuited by soft: pulled hard when visored: went very well with forcing tactics: game: dead. *M. P. Naughton* 67

FRET (USA) 2 b.c. (Mar 20) Storm Bird (CAN) 134 – Windy And Mild (USA) (Best Turn (USA)) [1992 6m2 7g* 8s6] $200,000Y: tall, rather leggy, quite attractive colt: good mover: sixth reported foal: half-brother to several winners, notably Billie Osage (by Superbity), successful 15 times, including in minor stakes, at up to 1¼m: dam unraced: progressive colt: landed odds by 4 lengths in maiden at Leicester in July: over 4 lengths sixth of 10 to Desert Secret in Royal Lodge Stakes at Ascot 2½ months later: will stay 1¼m. *P. F. I. Cole* 97

FRIENDLY BRAVE (USA) 2 b.c. (Feb 9) Well Decorated (USA) – Companionship (USA) (Princely Native (USA)) [1992 6m3 6m 7f3 7.1s4 7m5] $57,000Y: good-quartered colt: impresses in appearance: has scope: brother to a minor winner in USA and half-brother to several others, one in minor stakes: dam won at up to 1m, and was placed in graded stakes: sire (by Raja Baba) smart from 6f to 9f: fair maiden: best efforts in frame in 7f races at Newmarket and Sandown (wandered 2f out, demoted from third): will stay 1m: acts on any going. *W. Carter* 76

FRIENDLY CLAIM (IRE) 4 b.g. Petorius 117 – Pitaka (Pitskelly 122) [1991 a6g3 a6g 6g* 6m 7m2 7m 5g4 6m a6g2 a6g* a6g2 1992 a6g4 a6g2] compact gelding: good walker: fairly useful handicapper: stays 7f: acts on good to firm ground and fibresand: suitable mount for a claimer: often set fair bit to do: sent to race in Mauritius. *T. D. Barron* a86

FRIENDLY COAST 6 b.g. Blakeney 126 – Noreena (Nonoalco (USA) 131) [1991 NR 1992 a16g] leggy gelding: rated 53 at 4 yrs: tailed off at Southwell in December: stays 2m: acts on firm going: visored twice. *D. T. Thom* –

FRIENDLY HOUSE (IRE) 3 b.c. Fools Holme (USA) – Perle's Fashion –
(Sallust 134) [1991 NR 1992 10m 12g² a12s⁵ 14.1d⁵] IR 18,000Y: leggy colt: fifth foal:
half-brother to 3 winners, including 1986 Irish 2-y-o 5f winner Snappy Dresser (by
Nishapour) and poor 5-y-o stayer Cost Effective (by Burslem): dam Irish 9f to 1½m
winner: no worthwhile form: blinkered final start. *M. A. Jarvis*

FRIENDLY KNIGHT 2 b.c. (Mar 5) Horage 124 – Be A Dancer (Be Friendly 47
130) [1992 6g 8.3s⁴ 7.1g 8.3v] 1,200Y: strong colt: seventh foal: half-brother to Irish
3-y-o 1½m winner Simply (by Simply Great), 1m winner Persuasius (by Petorius)
and a winner in Norway: dam Irish 7f and 9f winner: poor maiden: stays 1m: acts on
soft ground. *J. S. Haldane*

FRIENDLYPERSUASION (IRE) 4 b.g. Legend of France (USA) 124 – 55
Waladah (Thatch (USA) 136) [1991 10.5m⁵ 10g⁶ 7m 10.5f 10.5d³ 11d* 10.3g 9.7s
a11g⁶ 1992 8s⁴ 8d 10d⁶ 10.5s 12f 8m 10d 8g 8.9g³ 11m⁵ 8g⁴ 8.5m⁵ 10.3g* 8g a8g
a12g] lengthy, angular gelding: moderate mover: inconsistent handicapper: won
Doncaster seller (no bid) in October: better at around 1¼m than shorter, and should
stay 1½m: form only on an easy surface. *R. Hollinshead*

FRIENDLY SMILE 2 b.f. (Apr 5) Vin St Benet 109 – Elfin Smile (Be Friendly 47
130) [1992 6g a6g³] sturdy filly: sixth reported foal: dam little sign of ability: better
effort in maidens when always close-up third at Southwell in December: burly on
debut. *G. H. Eden*

FRIENDLY SONG 4 ch.f. Song 132 – Friendly Jester 90 (Be Friendly 130) [1991 –
5f 5m⁶ 5g² 5f⁵ 5f 5g 1992 a6g] smallish, lengthy filly: poor maiden: blinkered and
well beaten in March: sold 7,000 gns Newmarket December Sales: has been
covered by Timeless Times. *T. Fairhurst*

FRIMLEY PARKSON 8 br.g. Frimley Park 109 – Frimley Grove (Tower Walk 29
130) [1991 5g 5g⁵ 5m 5m⁶ 5m² 6g⁶ 5m⁴ 5m⁴ 5g⁶ 5m³ 5.1d³ 5g² 5g² 5g 5m³ 5m 6f 5f
5m⁶ 5.3g 5g 5m 5.1d 1992 5s 5g⁵ 5.1m 5m⁴ 5m⁵ 4g 6g 5s 5s 5.1s⁶] sturdy, compact
gelding: carries plenty of condition: bad mover: poor sprint handicapper nowadays:
acts on any going: effective with or without blinkers/visor: sometimes has tongue
tied down. *P. Howling*

FRIVOLOUS AIR 2 b.f. (Mar 12) Elegant Air 119 – Luck Penny 87 (Bustino 136) 74
[1992 6s 7m* 8m⁶ 8f] leggy filly: third live foal: dam, winning sprinter improved at 3
yrs, is out of smart sprinter Thrifty Trio: won maiden at Wolverhampton in August:
ran moderately in nursery final start and sold 8,000 gns Newmarket Autumn Sales:
stays 1m. *I. A. Balding*

FROGMARCH (USA) 2 ch.c. (Feb 22) Diesis 133 – La Francaise (USA) (Jim – p
French (USA)) [1992 8v] neat colt: half-brother to 3-y-o 9.7f winner Agincourt Song
(by Al Nasr), 1990 French 7f and 1m winner Laliffe (by Lypheor) and half-brother to
several winners in USA and France: dam, placed in France, is half-sister to Alzao:
outpaced from 3f out when behind in maiden at Leicester in October: will improve.
Major W. R. Hern

FRONTIER FLIGHT (USA) 2 b.c. (Feb 4) Flying Paster (USA) – Sly 85 p
Charmer (USA) (Valdez (USA)) [1992 7g*] $35,000F: lengthy colt: first foal: dam,
unraced as juvenile, won 4 races at up to 1¼m and was minor-stakes placed: sire
high class at up to 1¼m: 6/1 and better for race, won 11-runner maiden at
Wolverhampton in September by 2 lengths from Jackpot Star, making most and
keeping on well: has scope, and sure to improve. *R. Charlton*

FRONT PAGE 5 ch.g. Adonijah 126 – Recent Events (Stanford 121§) [1991 8s* –
9s² 8.5g³ 8g 8.2m 9g 1992 10d 8d 9.7v] workmanlike gelding: carries condition: not
seen out until August and below best in handicaps: stays 9f: acts on any going: below
form when blinkered once: fair handicap hurdler, winner twice in November. *J.
Akehurst*

FROSTY MORNING 2 b.f. (Mar 21) Be My Guest (USA) 126 – Romantic Age – p
(Mill Reef (USA) 141) [1992 6g⁶] leggy filly: first foal: dam Irish 9f winner, is
half-sister to Luth Enchantee (by Be My Guest): 11/1, led 4f when around 15 lengths
sixth of 7 to Rustic Craft in newcomers race at Ascot in October: should improve. *C.
E. Brittain*

FROZEN MINSTREL 8 b.g. Black Minstrel 97 – Arctic Sue (Arctic Slave 116) 54
[1991 NR 1992 16f*] ex-Irish gelding, successful in Thurles novice chase late in 1991
for M. Morris: landed odds by 12 lengths in private sweepstakes at Huntingdon in
May, 1992: stays 2m: acts on firm ground. *J. H. Johnson*

FRUITFUL AFFAIR (IRE) 3 b.f. Taufan (USA) 119 – Lucky Engagement 71 p
(USA) 75 (What Luck (USA)) [1991 6f* 1992 10d⁴] lengthy filly: fourth foal: dam,

maiden, stayed 7f: twice-raced filly: staying-on fourth in claiming handicap at Goodwood in October: can improve again. *T. Thomson Jones*

FULL EXPOSURE   2 gr.f. (Feb 19) Sharpo 132 – Miss Suntan (Bruni 132) [1992   **60**
5g⁶ 7m² a7g 7m⁶] close-coupled, sparely-made filly: fifth foal: sister to 1990 2-y-o 7f winner Miss The Point: dam French 1½m winner from family of Wolver Hollow: modest maiden: will probably stay 1m: best efforts on good to firm ground: headstrong sort: sold 2,000 gns Newmarket September Sales. *W. Jarvis*

FULL QUIVER   7 br.g. Gorytus (USA) 132 – Much Pleasure (Morston (FR) 125)   **53**
[1991 a8g 10.8m 10g³ 1992 12d 10.8d⁶ 10g 11.8m⁵ 11.6g² 11.6g 11.7d⁴ 10g 12g 16s] leggy gelding: moderate mover: inconsistent handicapper, and often finds little: stays 1½m: acts on any going: below form when blinkered once, effective visored or not: sometimes bandaged off-fore/wears tongue strap. *Mrs Barbara Waring*

FULL SIGHT (IRE)   3 b.g. Vision (USA) – Peaches And Cream (FR) (Rusticaro   **51**
(FR) 124) [1991 6m 7m 7m 8m 10.5d³ 1992 13.8g* 14.1g 13.8g⁵] close-coupled gelding: moderate mover: easily won claimer at Catterick in June: behind in handicap and apprentice claimer (visored) after: stays 1¾m: acts on dead ground: sold to join I. Campbell's stable 4,100 gns Newmarket September Sales. *M. H. Tompkins*

FUNDEGHE (USA)   3 b.c. Rainbow Quest (USA) 134 – Les Biches (CAN)   **–**
(Northern Dancer) [1991 NR 1992 12m⁶ a12g⁴ a8g⁶] lightly-made colt: poor mover: sixth foal: half-brother to 1991 Italian 3-y-o 1¼m and 11f winner Svergna (by Commanche Run), 2 winners in France and another in Belgium: dam lightly raced: well beaten in maidens: blinkered except on debut. *J. E. Banks*

FUNNY HILARIOUS (USA)   2 ch.f. (May 28) Sir Ivor 135 – Polestar 77   **52 p**
(Northfields (USA)) [1992 7g] $21,000Y: fourth reported foal: half-sister to 2 winners in North America, including Grade 3 9f turf winner Social Retiree (by Cormorant): dam, 1¼m winner, is sister to Irish 2000 Guineas winner Northern Treasure: never-dangerous eighteenth of 24 in Newmarket maiden in October: should improve. *J. R. Fanshawe*

FUNOON (IRE)   3 ch.f. Kris 135 – Golden Oriole (USA) (Northern Dancer   **74**
(CAN)) [1991 7d⁴ 1992 11.5g³ 12g* 13.1g⁴ 12.3g] tall, angular filly: fair form in maidens first 3 starts, landing odds at Pontefract in July: tailed off in Chester handicap final run: stays 13.1f: sometimes had tongue tied down. *M. R. Stoute*

FURIELLA   4 ch.f. Formidable (USA) 125 – Palmella (USA) 89 (Grundy 137)   **70**
[1991 7f5 a8g⁴ 7h⁶ 6m⁶ 6f² 5m³ 6f* 1992 a6g² a5g a6g⁵ 6d* 6g 6f* 6g² 6g* 6f³ a6g 6m³ 6g 5g² 7g⁶ a6g a6g⁶] stocky filly: poor mover: tough and genuine handicapper: successful at Catterick (2), Ripon and Thirsk (awarded race) in summer: off course nearly 3 months, fair effort at Doncaster (burly), below form at Lingfield 2 weeks later: ideally suited by 6f: acts on firm ground and equitrack, and goes very well with some give (yet to race on heavy ground): tried blinkered: has won for claimer: sold 16,000 gns Newmarket December Sales. *P. C. Haslam*

FURTHER FLIGHT   6 gr.g. Pharly (FR) 130 – Flying Nelly 107 (Nelcius **116**
133) [1991 12m* 12g 15g* 16g* 15g² 15.5m 16m* 12g* 1992 13.9m⁵ 14m⁶ 16m* 15.9g* 18f* 16d* 12s⁶]
This popular stayer joined select company in the latest season, that of The Hero, Isonomy and Brown Jack, the only other horses to have won the Goodwood Cup, the Doncaster Cup and the Ebor Handicap. Further Flight's first major target in the next season will probably be to emulate the first two by winning the Gold Cup, something denied Brown Jack by the gelding-exclusion rule. Further Flight had to miss the Gold Cup in 1992 because of a swelling on a hind leg a couple of days before the event. He wasn't in particularly good form at that time anyway, just a fair effort in the Yorkshire Cup being followed by a disappointing one in a listed race at the Curragh; and after succumbing to a virus which laid the stable low in mid-summer, he arrived at Goodwood at the end of July with half the season gone and nothing to show for it.
In 1980, when Le Moss and Ardross clashed, the Goodwood Cup and the Doncaster Cup produced two of the best finishes of the year between the same two horses. In 1990 it was the same story, the horses this time being Further Flight and Witness Box. At Goodwood Witness Box, who'd won the Northumberland Plate under 9-9 on his previous start, ran prominently in third place while Further Flight was dropped out towards the rear of the field

*Goodwood Cup—a repeat victory for the admirable Further Flight (grey);
Witness Box and Landowner give him a fight*

of twelve in a race run at a sound pace. Three furlongs from home Witness Box was kicked into the lead, soon challenged by the Queen's Vase winner Landowner and Luchiroverte. When Luchiroverte began to flag a furlong and a half out it became clear that Further Flight would be the danger to Sheikh Mohammed's two, especially as the Gold Cup second Arcadian Heights was running moodily. Just as Witness Box began to get the better of Landowner inside the final furlong so Further Flight, head down low as usual, came with a sustained drive on the outside to lead virtually on the line. After this second win in the race, target number-two for Further Flight in 1993 may well be to become the first to win the Goodwood Cup three times. After an easy win

Doncaster Cup—Further Flight and Witness Box again

Jockey Club Cup, Newmarket—much easier this time; Supreme Choice is second

from Landowner in the Lonsdale Stakes at the York August meeting Further Flight started at 15/8 on for the Doncaster Cup, with only Witness Box of his four rivals given a real chance of beating him. Cauthen on Witness Box did his best to steal the race. He set a good gallop, steadied briefly on the top turn, then gradually began to accelerate again so that the outsiders were shaken off. As Further Flight came through virtually on the bridle to challenge under two furlongs out, Witness Box quickened again to open up a lead of a length and a half. But down went Further Flight's head, and under strong driving he gradually reduced Witness Box's advantage, and forced victory on the line, as at Goodwood lowering the course record. Further Flight had a simpler task in the Jockey Club Cup at Newmarket in October, and, as in 1991, he won decisively from his stable-companion Supreme Choice. If he were to win this particular event in the stayers' programme for a third time he would be emulating the 1884 Derby dead-heater St Gatien and the very much more recent High Line.

	Pharly (FR) (ch 1974)	Lyphard (b 1969)	Northern Dancer / Goofed
Further Flight (gr.g. 1986)		Comely (ch 1966)	Boran / Princesse Comnene
	Flying Nelly (gr 1970)	Nelcius (br 1963)	Tenareze / Namagua
		Flying By (gr 1964)	Bleep-Bleep / Japhette

There is little to add to Further Flight's pedigree details set out in *Racehorses of 1991*, as he was the final foal of his Cambridgeshire-winning dam Flying Nelly. A leggy, angular gelding, Further Flight has a round action and is often bandaged behind. He acts on firm and dead ground; while age may well have blunted his speed at a mile and a half anyway, he was never travelling particularly well on soft ground in the St Simon Stakes at Newbury on his final start, a race he won on good in 1991. In our view he'll have no trouble staying two and a half miles. There are a couple of stayers in training whose form is slightly better than Further Flight's, and there are several younger ones more progressive, but this is a racehorse you leave out of calculations at your peril. He has a place in the record-books already, and it's likely he'll add to his achievements in some worthwhile way in 1993. *B. W. Hills*

FUSION 8 b.g. Mill Reef (USA) 141 – Gift Wrapped 116 (Wolver Hollow 126) [1991   –
10g 1992 a12g⁵ a12g⁶ a12g a12g] rangy gelding: on the downgrade. *R. Earnshaw*

FUSION (USA) 3 gr.c. Lyphard's Wish (FR) 124 – French Poem (USA) (Sharpen **72**
Up 127) [1991 NR 1992 8m⁴ 8.1m³ 7d* 7f² 8h³] $25,000Y: workmanlike colt: has a
round action: third foal: closely related to a winner in USA by Al Nasr and
half-brother to fairly useful 7f winner French Senor (by El Gran Senor): dam French
5f winner: consistent performer in first half of 1992: won 4-runner maiden at
Catterick in June: effective at 7f to 1m: acts on firm and dead going: sold 7,400 gns
Newmarket Autumn Sales. *P. F. I. Cole*

FUTURBALLA 2 b.c. (Mar 4) Taufan (USA) 119 – Raja Moulana 75 (Raja Baba **96**
(USA)) [1992 6g* 6s⁵ 7.5d* 7f³ 7.5d4 8.5d* 8d⁵ 9v* 9v³ 10s] 6,000F, 5,800Y, 31,000
2-y-o: lengthy colt: has scope: has a roundish action: second foal: half-brother to
3-y-o Bashamah (by Nashamaa): dam 7f winner: useful colt: successful in maiden at
Goodwood, minor event at Beverley, nursery at Epsom and listed event at Milan:
good third in Rome listed event, but well beaten in Group 2 race there final start:
will stay 1¼m: acts on any going. *J. L. Dunlop*

FUTURES GIFT (IRE) 3 b.g. Try My Best (USA) 130 – Plum Cordial (USA) **55** d
(Proudest Roman (USA)) [1991 5m⁵ 6d⁶ 5f⁶ 6g⁵ 6f³ 7m 7.5f⁶ 7m 8m³ 1992 8s* 10d
9.9g 8m 8m⁶ 8.9g⁵ 12f5 11d 11d 10.3g] smallish gelding: inconsistent handicapper:
won selling event (bought in 7,400 gns) at Ripon in April: seems to stay 1½m: acts
on any going: below form when blinkered once. *A. W. Potts*

FYFIELD FLYER (IRE) 2 ch.g. (Feb 13) Sharrood (USA) 124 – Snowkist **103**
(USA) 77 (The Minstrel (CAN) 135) [1992 6m³ 6m* 6m² 5g² 5d* 5g 5d²] smallish,
lengthy gelding: has a roundish action: first foal: dam 1½m winner, is closely related
to Blue Stag out of very smart French 10.5f winner Snow Day: useful performer:
successful in maiden at Ripon in August and listed race (by 2½ lengths from Lord
Olivier) at Ayr in September: well beaten in Cornwallis Stakes at Ascot, then very
good second to Ansellman in listed event at Doncaster: effective at 5f and 6f: has
form on good to firm ground, but seems well suited by a soft surface: sometimes
takes a strong hold to post: tends to hang right: sent to USA to be trained by M.
Dickinson. *P. W. Chapple-Hyam*

FYLDE FLYER 3 ch.c. Music Boy 124 – Djimbaran Bay (Le Levanstell 122) **109**
[1991 5g⁶ 6m* 7m⁶ 6m³ 6d* 6m* 6m² 6m² 6g² 6m⁴ 6g³ 6m* 6g⁵ 1992 6g* 6m* 6m
6g³ 6f⁴ 6g⁵ 7m⁵ 6g³ 6d 6.1d²] strong, lengthy colt: usually impresses in appearance:
moderate walker: consistent and useful performer, much improved as 3-y-o:
short-head winner of listed races at Doncaster in March and Newmarket (Abernant
Stakes by short head from Case Law): very good second to Montendre in minor
event at Chepstow final start: best efforts at 6f: acts on firm and dead ground: game.
J. Berry

Timeform Harry Rosebery Trophy, Ayr—Fyfield Flyer gets well on top

G

GABBIADINI 5 b.g. Taufan (USA) 119 – Galerida (Silver Shark 129) [1991 8m⁵ **75** d
7d⁵ 7.5f⁵ 7m 8g 7m³ 7.9m 7.1s² 7.1m* 7.6m³ 8d⁴ 8m⁶ a7g a8g² 1992 a7g³ 8g⁶ 7.5m
7m 7m 7g 7d 7.1g⁴ 7g] close-coupled, angular gelding: poor mover: inconsistent, and
only modest handicapper in 1992: stays 8.5f: probably acts on any going: has won in a
visor: sold 4,600 gns Newmarket Autumn Sales. *M. H. Tompkins*

GABESIA 4 b.f. Gabitat 119 – Korresia (Derring-Do 131) [1991 NR 1992 a8g 11.8s –
10g 9s 9.7v] smallish, good-bodied filly: bad mover: sixth foal: dam ran once: no
worthwhile form. *H. J. Collingridge*

GABHADERA 2 ch.f. (Apr 24) Gabitat 119 – Hadera 74 (Northfields (USA)) –
[1992 5d 6m⁶ a6g] compact, good-quartered filly: has a round action: fourth reported
foal (third by Gabitat): dam won from 5f (at 2 yrs) to around 1m: no worthwhile form,
last run in claimer at Lingfield in July. *B. Gubby*

GABIBTI (IRE) 4 ch.f. Dara Monarch 128 – Torriglia (USA) (Nijinsky (CAN) **58**
138) [1991 6f⁴ 6d³ 7g⁵ 6m 6d 5s³ 6g 6f 5g 6.1m 6m 1992 a6g 5g² 5m⁵ 7m⁴ 7m⁵] small,
good-quartered filly: has a quick action: modest handicapper: not seen out after
June: effective from 5f to 7f: acts on any going: sweats. *B. Gubby*

GABR 2 b.c. (Mar 10) Green Desert (USA) 127 – Ardassine (Ahonoora 122) [1992 **83** p
7m² 7d*] compact, useful-looking colt: fourth foal: half-brother to 3-y-o Enaya (by
Caerleon), 6f winner at 2 yrs: dam 1½m winner in Ireland from family of Slip
Anchor: second in maiden at Newmarket before winning similar event at Leicester
later in October in good style: will stay 1¼m: likely to do better. *R. W. Armstrong*

GACHETTE 3 b.g. Lidhame 109 – Renira 60 (Relkino 131) [1991 7g⁶ 7m⁶ 6g 1992 **58**
8g 8g⁵ 8.5d³ 10.3m a10g 8.5d³ 10.2s⁴ 8s⁶ 8d³ 6.9v⁶ 8.2s] strong, workmanlike
gelding: modest maiden: blinkered last 3 starts, running well only on first occasion:
best form at around 1m on dead ground: somewhat headstrong: sold 5,200 gns Ascot
November Sales. *J. Sutcliffe*

GAELGOIR 8 gr.g. Godswalk (USA) 130 – Sagosha (Irish Love 117) [1991 NR –
1992 16.1g 16.9d⁶] medium-sized gelding: rated 54 as 5-y-o: no form on first runs on
flat since: won poor novice handicap hurdle in December. *C. F. C. Jackson*

GAELIC MYTH (USA) 5 b.h. Nijinsky (CAN) 138 – Irish Valley (USA) (Irish **107**
River (FR) 131) [1991 10v³ 8d³ 10d* 10g⁵ 9d² 12g³ 11m² 16s³ 10g³ 11s⁴ 10s³ 1992
10s* 8g 12d* 10v⁵ 12s³ 9m 9m 12f 12g⁵ 12s³ 11g] good-quartered horse: poor mover:
first foal: dam lightly-raced half-sister to Green Dancer (by Nijinsky) and smart
French 1¼m and 1½m winner Ercolano, a good family: useful Irish handicapper:
won twice at Leopardstown in the spring: behind here in Lincoln and Bessborough
Handicaps: effective from 1¼m to 1½m: acts on good to firm (probably not very
firm) going, but goes well with some give and acts on heavy ground. *T. Stack, Ireland*

GAIBULGA 4 b.f. Kris 135 – Dancing Rocks 118 (Green Dancer (USA) 132) [1991 **101** ?
10m* 12g² 11.5g² 12g⁴ 10f* 10.1m* 10m² 1992 9g 10m³ 11.9g 10m 10.1g] big,
lengthy, angular filly: very useful performer at 3 yrs (rated 110): disappointing in
1992, worthwhile form only when under a length third to Flashfoot in listed event at
Goodwood in May, leading until final 1f: tailed-off last afterwards in pattern events
at Haydock (as if something amiss), Goodwood and when blinkered in listed event at
Newcastle: effective from 1¼m to 1½m: acted on firm ground: stud. *G. Wragg*

GAILY DANCE 4 b.f. Monsanto (FR) 121 – Step You Gaily 71 (King's Company –
124) [1991 8.3m 6m 7m 10m 1992 11.9m] sturdy filly: seems of little account. *R. J.
Hodges*

GALACTIC FURY 2 ch.c. (Apr 13) Celestial Storm (USA) 132 – Mother Brown **53**
103 (Candy Cane 125) [1992 6m 6.1m 7g 7m⁵ 8g 8s 10g⁵] 1,500Y: close-coupled,
angular colt: half-brother to several winners, including 1m winner Macarthurs Head
(by Dom Racine): dam genuine handicapper at up to 1¼m: modest maiden: below
form last 2 outings: should stay 1¼m. *B. Stevens*

GALACTIC MISS 3 b.f. Damister (USA) 123 – Galaxie Dust (USA) 86 (Blushing **78**
Groom (FR) 131) [1991 NR 1992 8g⁴ 8f² 8d* 8d² 10s* 9v²] leggy filly: second living
foal: dam 2-y-o 6f winner: fair performer: won maiden at Kempton (sweating) and
minor event (easily) at Leicester in the autumn: stayed 1¼m well: acted on soft
ground: has been retired. *J. L. Dunlop*

GALAXY EXPRESS 4 ch.g. Bay Express 132 – Heaven And Earth (Mid- **41**
summer Night II 117) [1991 6g⁶ 8g 5g 6f 5f 5m⁶ 6m⁵ 6m³ 1992 a5g³ a5g* a5g⁶ 5d 5m
5g* 5s⁶] workmanlike gelding: has a quick, fluent action: won Lingfield maiden in

February and Edinburgh selling handicap (no bid) in July: stays 6f: acts on good to firm and soft ground and on all-weather surfaces: tried visored. *G. H. Eden*

GALEJADE   2 b.f. (Mar 25) Sharrood (USA) 124 – Sans Blague (USA) 108 (The   **58**
Minstrel (CAN) 135) [1992 5g³ 7m⁵ 5.7f³ 6d 7s] 8,400Y: tall, leggy filly: has a
roundish action: seventh foal: half-sister to 3-y-o Fiction (by Dominion), 5f winner
at 2 yrs, very useful 1986 2-y-o 6f and 7.3f winner Nettle (by Kris) and 7-y-o
middle-distance winner Quip (by High Line): dam, suited by 1½m, is half-sister to
very useful middle-distance filly Deadly Serious: modest maiden: will stay at least
1m: below form on soft ground: usually temperamental in preliminaries. *D. Haydn
Jones*

GALLANT EFFORT (IRE)   4 b.c. Thatching 131 – Meeting Adjourned 94   –
(General Assembly (USA)) [1991 a8g⁵ a8g⁵ a7g 8.5m a7g 11.9f⁶ 11.8g 10m³ a10g
1992 12g] tall colt: has a round action: rated 48 at 3 yrs: last in handicap in March,
1992: seems to stay 1½m: acts on good to firm ground: wore eyeshield on the
all-weather: won handicap hurdle in November. *S. Dow*

GALLANT HOPE   10 ch.g. Ahonoora 122 – Amiga Mia 71 (Be Friendly 130)   **61**
[1991 6g 6g 5.8f⁴ 6.1m 5f³ 6m² 5.8d⁶ 5d⁵ 5g³ 5g 6g 6f 5f⁶ 5f³ 5.7f 5.3g⁶ 5.1s 5g 1992
6g⁵ 5.7m 6.1m² 5g⁶ 6d 6d³ 5f 5.1f³ 5.1m⁵ 6d 5.7d⁶ 6.1d] small, stocky gelding:
carries plenty of condition: has been hobdayed: only modest handicapper these
days: last win came 53 starts ago, at 7 yrs: unsuited by soft ground, acts on any
other: blinkered nowadays. *L. G. Cottrell*

GALLANT JACK (IRE)   3 b.g. Flash of Steel 120 – Milveagh 92 (Milesian 125)   **64** d
[1991 7g³ 6g³ 7.1s 7.1m² 8.1g⁶ 1992 9g 8.2g⁵ 10m⁵ 12.1m⁴ 10.2g a12g⁴ 10m 12.3d]
tall, leggy gelding: modest and inconsistent maiden: stays 1½m: acts on good to
firm ground: ran creditably in visor on fibresand: has run well when sweating. *D.
Haydn Jones*

GALLERY ARTIST (IRE)   4 ch.c. Tate Gallery (USA) 117 – Avec L'Amour 75   –
(Realm 129) [1991 a7g³ a6g* 5.1f⁶ 6m⁴ 6f a6g 6g⁵ 5g⁶ 1992 a7g* a7g a6g 6m⁶ a7g⁵ a63
a7g* 7s] small colt: poor mover: modest performer, best on the all-weather tracks:
won seller (edgy, no bid) in May and claimer in September at Southwell: well below
form otherwise: stays 7f: acts on all-weather surfaces: has won for claimer: tried
blinkered earlier in career. *R. Guest*

GALLERY NOTE (IRE)   3 b.f. Tate Gallery (USA) 117 – Thank You Note 73   **51**
(What A Guest 119) [1991 6.1m 6m⁶ 1992 8v a7g⁶ 7g³ 6s⁶] sparely-made filly: has a
quick action: modest maiden: should stay 1m: acts on soft ground: sold 3,700 gns
Newmarket Autumn Sales. *B. W. Hills*

GALLEY GOSSIP   3 b.g. Dunbeath (USA) 127 – Mother Brown 103 (Candy   **53** d
Cane 125) [1991 6g² 6f³ 6m⁴ 1992 8.9s³ 9.2d 8v⁵ 12g⁵ 7g 8.2d⁶ 6f 7g 10d 7.1s 6s a6g]
robust gelding: seems of little account these days: sold out of Mrs J. Ramsden's
stable 2,100 gns Doncaster May Sales after third start: no improvement in a visor. *R.
Brotherton*

GALLOP TO GLORY   2 b.c. (Apr 12) Petong 126 – Merchantmens Girl 58   –
(Klairon 131) [1992 6g 5d] moderate mover: brother to 5-y-o winning sprinter
Barbezieux and half-brother to several other winners: dam placed over 5f: well
beaten in minor event at Windsor and maiden at Lingfield in late-summer. *P.
Mitchell*

GAME GERMAINE   2 b.f. (Jun 1) Mummy's Game 120 – Coppice (Pardao 120)   –
[1992 6m 6s] 4,000Y: leggy filly: half-sister to several winners, including (from 1m
to 10.2f) the fair Madame Bovary (by Ile de Bourbon) and (at 5.1f at 2 yrs in 1986)
Nightdress (by Pyjama Bond): dam second in small 9f race in France: outpaced from
halfway when last in maiden events at Goodwood and Salisbury in August. *B. W.
Hills*

GAN AWRY   5 b.m. Kabour 80 – Wedded Bliss 76 (Relko 136) [1991 NR 1992 a8g]   –
sturdy mare: third foal: sister to 6-y-o Minsk: dam won from 1½m to 2m at 5 yrs +:
won a point in April: never able to get into maiden at Southwell in May. *D. W.
Chapman*

GANESHAYA   3 gr.g. Formidable (USA) 125 – Lammastide 93 (Martinmas 128)   **55**
[1991 6g⁵ 6m* 7m 7m² 6.1g 1992 8d 7m 6d 6.1m³ 6d⁴ 5d² 5g* 5m 5m² 5g* 6f 5m⁵]
sturdy gelding: moderate mover: modest handicapper: improved in the summer,
winning at Doncaster and (apprentice event) Windsor: twice refused to enter stalls
as 3-y-o, including final appearance: best racing close to pace over 5f: acts on good to
firm ground and dead: wears blinkers nowadays: usually has tongue tied down. *M. F.
Barraclough*

GANGLEADER   2 gr.c. (Feb 15) Petong 126 – Good Woman 60 (Good Times   **70**
(ITY)) [1992 5d⁶ 5m² 6.1d 6m 6.1g* 6s³ 6m 6v] 7,400Y: close-coupled, quite attractive colt: second foal: half-brother to 3-y-o Reach Forward (by Reach): dam maiden
probably stayed 6f, is half-sister to smart 1985 2-y-o 5f and 7f winner Moorgate Man:
fair performer: much improved effort when winning 24-runner maiden auction at
Nottingham in September: creditable third in nursery at Folkestone, easily best
subsequent effort (very stiff task in Racecall Gold Trophy last time): will stay 7f:
suited by an easy surface: blinkered last 2 outings. *S. P. C. Woods*

GANT BLEU (FR)   5 ch.g. Crystal Glitters (USA) 127 – Gold Honey (Artaius   **66**
(USA) 129) [1991 8d 7g³ 8f² 8g* 7.5g⁵ 8g² 8f⁵ 7f³ 9m 8f 7m 7f³ 8m 7m 8m³ 8m 1992
8m 8f³ 7.5g 8f³ 7.1f² 6.9h* 7g⁶ 7g* 7m⁶ 7g³ 7.9g* 7f⁵ 7d 7d* 7d 7m] leggy, rather
sparely-made gelding: moderate mover: still not the most reliable handicapper, but
more so than at 4 yrs: successful at Carlisle and Redcar in midsummer, and at York
(claimer) and Newmarket (awarded race on a technicality) in the autumn: ideally
suited by 7f/1m: acts on hard and dead ground: well below form in visor once earlier
in career: often wears crossed noseband: is held up. *R. M. Whitaker*

GARACHICO (USA)   3 b.g. Green Dancer (USA) 132 – Little Lady Luck (USA)   **68**
(Jacinto) [1991 NR 1992 10f 10.2g3 10m³ 12g4 11.6g 9d] $350,000Y: good-topped
gelding: seventh foal: half-brother to 4 winners, including useful 4-y-o sprinter
Chicarica (by The Minstrel) and middle-distance winners by Our Native and
L'Enjoleur: dam 3-y-o 6f winner in North America: fair maiden at best: well beaten
in handicaps last 3 starts, looking a hard ride: stays 1¼m well: acts on good to firm
ground: blinkered except on debut. *G. Harwood*

GARAH   3 b.f. Ajdal (USA) 130 – Abha 117 (Thatching 131) [1991 NR 1992 6m*   **105**
6.1g* 6m* 6m⁴ 5m² 5m⁵ 6g³] smallish, sturdy filly: reportedly split pastern at 2 yrs:
good walker: third foal: dam 5f and 6f winner: useful performer: won maiden and
minor events at Nottingham and Newbury in little over a month in
the spring: easily best efforts in listed races in the autumn when placed behind
Blyton Lad at Newmarket (first run for 4 months) and Doncaster: stays 6f: yet to
race on a soft surface: stays in training. *H. R. A. Cecil*

GARDA'S GOLD   9 b.g. Garda's Revenge (USA) 119 – Mielee (Le Levanstell   **33**
122) [1991 10s 1992 10g³ 11.9f4 10g5] leggy, narrow gelding: moderate mover: poor
handicapper, seen only in midsummer: stays 1½m: acts on good to firm and soft
going: effective with or without visor: tried blinkered: has worn crossed noseband.
R. Dickin

GARDEN DISTRICT   3 b.c. Celestial Storm (USA) 132 – Rose Chanelle (Welsh   **89** p
Pageant 132) [1991 NR 1992 10d² 14.6s* 13.3m* 15.4h* 16.2d² 14m*] 31,000Y:
strong, good-topped colt: has a long stride: second foal: dam unraced granddaughter
of Rose Dubarry: progressive performer: completed hat-trick in small fields in
median auction maiden at Wolverhampton in May and handicaps at Newbury and
Folkestone in June: unlucky not to complete four-timer at Yarmouth in July, finally getting
off the mark again in £10,800 handicap at
Goodwood in July final start, leading 7f out and just holding on: will improve further
back at 2m + : probably best on top-of-the-ground: reportedly suffered foot injury
after final start. *R. Charlton*

GARDEN OF HEAVEN (USA)   3 ch.c. Arctic Tern (USA) 126 – Garden **117** p
of Eden 63 (Exbury 138) [1991 NR 1992 8.5g² 10g² 8.1g* 12s³ 12d*]
   It was dangerous to ignore Clive Brittain's representatives in pattern
races in 1992. One who was ignored, in the betting at least, was Garden of

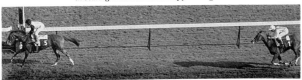

*Prix du Conseil de Paris, Longchamp—Garden of Heaven looks a good prospect
in beating Fabulous Hostess by four lengths*

Heaven who started at 25/1 in a five-runner field for the Cumberland Lodge Stakes at Ascot in September. His latest start had been in another five-runner contest but one of a much less exacting standard, a maiden race at Sandown in July, which he won by a short head at 2/1 on. It had been his third appearance, the others also in maidens for three-year-olds. If the third run in a maiden race catches the eye it is usually with regard to a forthcoming handicap mark. Garden of Heaven, however, never received a mark for handicaps: he was never entered in one, and gave notice that much greater ambitions were realistic when beaten only two and a quarter lengths in the Group 3 Cumberland Lodge. It was a moderately-run race but Garden of Heaven had had to come from the back of the field and looked inexperienced still in doing so, catching Sapience and Bonny Scot but not Opera House and Red Bishop. Garden of Heaven's transformed status was handsomely confirmed in the Group 2 Prix du Conseil de Paris at Longchamp just over three weeks later. In a six-runner field, the recent Prix de Royallieu winner Fabulous Hostess had conditions to suit her but Garden of Heaven brushed her aside by four lengths with those further behind including the 1991 Arc runner-up Magic Night. Michael Roberts was reported to have wanted Garden of Heaven supplemented for the latest Arc, and connections' sights are without question to be set high after their success in the lesser event at Longchamp. Connections were thwarted when Garden of Heaven narrowly failed to get beyond the reserve list for the Breeders' Cup Classic, but will have plenty to look forward to in 1993. This colt has probably not stopped improving yet. A sturdy, attractive individual, Garden of Heaven looks better at a mile and a half than shorter distances and goes well on a soft surface. Sore shins were largely responsible for his late emergence as a horse to be reckoned with in 1992.

		Sea Bird II (ch 1962)	Dan Cupid
	Arctic Tern (USA) (ch 1973)		Sicalade
		Bubbling Beauty (ch 1961)	Hasty Road
Garden of Heaven (USA) (ch.c. 1989)			Almahmoud
		Exbury (ch 1959)	Le Haar
	Garden of Eden (ch 1967)		Greensward
		Mesopotamia (b 1961)	Zarathustra
			Agar's Plough

A 40,000-dollar yearling purchase at Keeneland in July, Garden of Heaven is from a prolific winner-producing family. The third dam Agar's Plough won the Irish Oaks and grandam Mesopotamia was the best two-year-old filly of 1963 and third in the Irish One Thousand Guineas. Garden of Eden, contrastingly, had marked limitations as a racehorse, managing two places in maiden races from seven starts, but she has certainly made up for that at stud. The best of her seven winners prior to Garden of Heaven were Welsh Garden (by Welsh Saint) and Galaxy Libra (by Wolver Hollow). Welsh Garden's aversion to starting stalls prevented her participation in any major races but wins at Mallow, Sligo, Dundalk and Gowran Park, where stalls were not used, were still good enough to establish her as the top two-year-old filly in Ireland in 1975. Sixth of eleven in the Ulster Champion Stakes was the total of Welsh Garden's achievements as a three-year-old but she has done respectably as a broodmare, the dam of Horris Hill winner Celtic Heir and grandam of the useful 1991 colt Volksraad. Galaxy Libra showed useful form at two and three years here but did not fulfil early promise until sent to the United States where he won the eleven-furlong Man o' War Stakes and mile-and-a-half Sunset Handicap, both Grade 1 events on turf, as a five-year-old. *C. E. Brittain*

GARENDARE 3 b.f. Vacarme (USA) 121 – Girouette (USA) (Nodouble (USA)) **105** [1991 9v² 1992 10.5s* 10.5v³ 10.5g⁴ 10.5g* 10.5g 9.3s] leggy, lightly-made filly: first foal: dam unraced half-sister to Gravelines and Grand Pavois: won minor event in February and Prix Cleopatre (in very tight finish with 3 others) in May, both at Saint-Cloud: behind in Prix de Diane at Chantilly and Prix de l'Opera at Longchamp 3½ months later: stays 10.5f: useful. *E. Lellouche, France*

GARNOCK VALLEY 2 b.c. (Feb 12) Dowsing (USA) 124 – Sunley Sinner 93 **73** (Try My Best (USA) 130) [1992 5f³ 6g⁵ 6m² 6m³ 6s] 12,500F, 11,500Y, 37,000 2-y-o: neat colt: second foal: half-brother to 3-y-o 6.9f and 7f winner Morsun (by Aragon): dam 2-y-o 7f winner, is out of very useful filly (at around 1¼m) Sirenivo: fair maiden: off course over 7 weeks, ran moderately in nursery at Ayr final outing: stays 6f: easily best efforts on good to firm ground. *J. Berry*

GARP (FR) 2 b.c. (Mar 19) Lead On Time (USA) 123 – Copy Cat (FR) (King of **60** Macedon 126) [1992 6g⁴ 6m* 7g 8f 7g] 165,000 francs F, 1,500,000 francs (approx £150,600) Y: lengthy colt: third foal: brother to Irish 3-y-o Leading Time, fairly useful 5f winner at 2 yrs: dam French sprinter: modest performer: odds on, narrowly won maiden at Pontefract in July: well beaten in nurseries afterwards: stays 6f. *M. R. Stoute*

GARTH 4 gr.g. Petong 126 – Doppio 62 (Dublin Taxi) [1991 6m 5d 6m² 6m⁶ 6m **74** 1992 6s² 6f⁴ 6d 6m 7d³ 7d⁴ 7d⁴ 8g 7g 7g] sturdy, rather dipped-backed gelding: fair handicapper: mostly ran creditably in 1992 until last 3 starts: effective at 6f and will stay 1m: has form on good to firm ground, but seems best on a soft surface: usually sweats: blinkered (below form) once at 3 yrs: visored nowadays. *P. J. Makin*

GATE OF HEAVEN 2 b.f. (Mar 19) Starry Night (USA) – Halatch (Habat 127) **43** p [1992 6m] 1,000Y: leggy filly: half-sister to 1984 Irish 2-y-o 5f winner Flame Up (by Bustino) and 1988 2-y-o 5f winner Grand Ball (by Rusticaro): dam twice-raced half-sister to Patch: sire (by Northern Dancer) won from 6f to 8.5f: 33/1, backward and bandaged behind, prominent to halfway when thirteenth of 14 in maiden at Newmarket in October. *W. A. O'Gorman*

GAVEKO (USA) 3 b.g. Al Nasr (FR) 126 – Corolina (USA) (Nashua) [1991 NR **–** 1992 8g 12g³ 12.2g] IR 55,000Y: strong, close-coupled gelding: brother to 1991 French provincial 9.5f winner Safeer and smart French filly Bint Alnasr, best at around 1¼m, and half-brother to another winner in France: dam never ran: well beaten in maidens, blinkered on debut: flashes tail: won novice hurdle in November. *J. G. FitzGerald*

GAY GLINT 5 b.g. Glint of Gold 128 – Gay Hellene 111 (Ela-Mana-Mou 132) [1991 **90** § 14m* 16g⁵ 16g 11.9m 14g³ 16.1g* 18m 16.2d² 18m 1992 16g⁵ 14g⁴ 14m* 16.1g 16.2g* 15.9m 16.2g] unfurnished gelding: good mover: fairly useful but thoroughly unreliable handicapper: won at Sandown and Ascot (£11,160 event) in midsummer: stays 16.2f: acts on good to firm and dead ground: usually goes well for S. Cauthen: game enough in a finish. *N. A. Graham*

GAY MING 3 b.f. Gay Meadow 52 – Miss Admington 71 (Double Jump 131) [1991 **50** 6m 7.6d⁵ a7g 1992 8d 10g 10f* a11g⁵ 12f² 14.1g² 14.6g² 13.8f³ 16.2d⁴ 16.1s⁵ 11d³ 14.1s⁴] leggy, lightly-made filly: consistent handicapper: won seller (no bid) at Redcar in May: stays 2m: acts on firm and dead ground: nearly always ridden by 7-lb claimer. *R. Hollinshead*

GAYNOR GOODMAN (IRE) 2 ch.f. (Apr 29) Fayruz 116 – Sassess (Sassafras **42** (FR) 135) [1992 5v 5d³ 5g⁴ 5f⁴ 5f 5h⁴ 5g⁵ 6g 5g 5.3d⁶ 5s] IR 500F: workmanlike filly: has a round action: fifth foal: sister and half-sister to a winner abroad: dam Irish maiden: modest plater: takes keen hold, and may prove best at 5f: acts on firm and dead ground: blinkered twice, running creditably first occasion. *J. S. Moore*

GAYNOR'S BOY (IRE) 3 ch.c. Hatim (USA) 121 – Corista (Tudor Music 131) **–** [1991 NR 1992 10f 8s 12.2d⁵] 5,400Y: close-coupled colt: half-brother to winning Irish stayers Golden Oak (by Tap On Wood) and Gayle Orchestra (by Lord Gayle): dam, winner over 7f at 2 yrs and 1½m at 4 yrs, is sister to Orchestra: no sign of ability. *T. Kersey*

GAY RUFFIAN 6 b.g. Welsh Term 126 – Alcinea (FR) 93 (Sweet Revenge 129) **–** [1991 a12g 17m⁵ 1992 12.1f⁵] lengthy gelding: has a round action: rated 58 at 4 yrs: very lightly raced last 2 seasons, and faced very stiff task in June: stays 17f: acts on top-of-the-ground, and is probably suited by soft: useful winning hurdler in 1991/2: has joined M. Pipe. *D. Burchell*

GDANSK'S HONOUR (USA) 3 b.f. Danzig (USA) – Royal Honoree (USA) **102** (Round Table) [1991 7g³ 7g* 1992 8v* 7d* 8d² 8g 8g² 8g² 8s⁵] Irish filly: has a round action: sister to useful 1988 2-y-o 5f and 6f winner Honoria and half-sister to several winners, including Irish St Leger runner-up Father Rooney (by Val de L'Orne): dam, winner 3 times at up to 6f, is sister to top 1972 French 2-y-o Targowice and half-sister to dam of Manila and Stately Don: useful performer: favourite, successful in minor event at the Curragh and Leopardstown 1000 Guineas Trial in the spring: excellent head second of 7 to Via Borghese in Group 3 contest at the Curragh in August, penultimate start: stays 1m: yet to race on top-of-the-ground: blinkered last 5 outings: consistent. *J. S. Bolger, Ireland*

GEISWAY (CAN) 2 br.c. (Apr 8) Geiger Counter (USA) – Broadway Beauty **105** (USA) (Chompion (USA)) [1992 6m² 6f* 6m⁵ 7g⁴ 7d² 8.1g* 8s²] $103,812Y: leggy, lengthy, useful-looking colt: has scope: half-brother to several winners, including

3-y-o 6f winner Broadway Ruckus (by Bold Ruckus) and the stakes-winning dam of Irish Oaks winner Knight's Baroness: dam minor winner at 2 yrs: sire (by Mr Prospector) minor sprint winning half-brother to Thatch: useful performer: won maiden at Doncaster in May and minor event (quickening well under confident ride) at Sandown in September: much improved form when ½-length second to Desert Secret in Royal Lodge Stakes at Ascot: suited by 1m: acts on any going: genuine. *R. Hannon*

GEMDOUBLEYOU   4 b.f. Magnolia Lad 102 – Amber Windsor 52 (Windjammer (USA)) [1991 NR 1992 a8g 7d 8g 10g 8g 6.9h] close-coupled filly: has a quick action: of little account these days. *F. Jordan* — –

GEMINI BAY   3 b.c. Petong 126 – Deux Etoiles 86 (Bay Express 132) [1991 5s 5g 6s 6m* 6g* 6m* 6g 1992 6d 6g 7.1m 7f 7d 6.9v a6g a7g a7g a6g a6g³] close-coupled colt: fair winner at 2 yrs: no form in 1992 and is one to avoid: nearly always blinkered: has worn tongue strap. *R. Voorspuy* — §

GEMINI FIRE   8 br.g. Mansingh (USA) 120 – Sealady (Seaepic (USA) 100) [1991 5d³ 5g² 5g* 5f 5g* 5m 5d 1992 6f⁵ 5d 6g 5g 5g⁶ 5d 5g] sparely-made gelding: has badly scarred near-quarter: fair performer (rated 83) at 7 yrs (tried in a visor), but well beaten in 1992: wore net muzzle to post on reappearance. *M. P. Naughton* — –

GENAIR (FR)   7 ch.g. General Assembly (USA) – Metair 118 (Laser Light 118) [1991 8.5g 7.5f⁴ 8m 7.5f 8m⁶ 9m³ 8h* 8d 8m⁴ 7.9m⁴ 9f 9m³ 8m⁵ 1992 7.5m² 8f² 8f 8h] big, rather dipped-backed gelding: had soft palate operation: modest handicapper: often got behind and was ideally suited by strongly-run race at around 1m/9f: best efforts on top-of-the-ground: effective blinkered or not: dead. *Mrs M. Reveley* 62

GENERAL BROOKS (IRE)   2 b.g. (Apr 7) Governor General 116 – Choral Park (Music Boy 124) [1992 5d² 5d⁵ 6f 6g⁶³ 5g³ 5d⁶ 5g] IR 1,600F, 8,000Y: robust, angular gelding: carries condition: third foal: half-brother to 2-y-o 5f winners Palacegate Jewel (by Red Sunset) and Warrior Prince (by Prince Sabo): dam poor maiden: poor maiden: better suited by 6f than 5f: sold 700 gns Doncaster November Sales: inconsistent. *J. Berry* 49

GENERAL CHASE   2 ch.f. (Mar 1) Scottish Reel 123 – Make A Signal 76 (Royal Gunner (USA)) [1992 5.1m⁶ 6f 7m⁴ 7m³ 7g 8g* 8d⁴ 8d] 1,500Y: sturdy filly: half-sister to winners abroad by African Sky and Owen Dudley: dam successful stayer (won 2 races) from family of Raise You Ten: modest performer: has improved each time stepped up in distance, winning 20-runner selling nursery (no bid) at Leicester in September: will be better suited by 1¼m +. *R. J. Holder* 63

GENERAL DIXIE (USA)   3 b.g. Dixieland Band (USA) – Bold Example (USA) (Bold Lad (USA)) [1991 NR 1992 10s⁵ 8g⁴] 37,000Y: rangy, useful-looking gelding: closely related to a winner in USA by Northern Baby and half-brother to several winners, including very smart stakes winner at up to 9f (and later dam of Zilzal) French Charmer (by Le Fabuleux), and to the dam of Polish Precedent: dam minor stakes-placed winner at up to 7f: fourth of 16 in maiden at Kempton in May: may well prove suited by return to further: has twice refused to enter stalls, including in June: subsequently gelded: retained by trainer 5,200 gns Doncaster November Sales. *R. Hannon* 77

GENERAL JOHN (IRE)   3 br.g. Cyrano de Bergerac 120 – Hill's Realm (USA) 68 (Key To The Kingdom (USA)) [1991 a7g 1992 a8g* 7g⁵ a6g a8g] strong gelding: shows knee action: fair performer: made all in maiden at Southwell in January: off course 7 months and soundly beaten there last 2 starts late in year: stays 1m: acts on fibresand. *P. C. Haslam* 69

GENERAL LINK   2 b.g. (Apr 22) Governor General 116 – City Link Lass 92 (Double Jump 131) [1992 5m⁵ 6d³ 5d a6g] 9,600Y: angular gelding: half-brother to 3 winners, including 3-y-o 1m winner John Rose (by Tina's Pet) and (at 6f and 7f) Sporting Simon (by Vaigly Great): dam 2-y-o 5f and 6f winner: modest maiden: will be well suited by 7f: acts on dead ground, no form on fibresand. *P. A. Kelleway* 58

GENERALLY   2 b.f. (Apr 16) Governor General 116 – Long Valley 71 (Ribero 126) [1992 6m⁶ 6m 5m 5.2f 5d] 2,500F, 1,000Y: close-coupled, unfurnished filly: half-sister to several winners, including tough 1983 2-y-o 5f winner Who Knows The Game (by John de Coombe): dam showed a little ability at 2 yrs: seems of little account. *Pat Mitchell* 32

GENERAL MOUKTAR   2 ch.c. (Feb 28) Hadeer 118 – Fly The Coop (Kris 135) [1992 8m 10g] 15,000Y: good-topped colt: first foal: dam Irish middle-distance winner: backward, modest form in mid-division of maidens at Newmarket and Nottingham in the autumn: will probably do better. *A. Hide* 50 p

GENEROUS BEN   2 b.g. (Mar 12) Myjinski (USA) – Playtex 72 (Be Friendly   –
130) [1992 a6g 7g] small gelding: lacks scope: moderate mover: third foal: dam
effective from 6f to 1m: no encouragement in seller at Lingfield and maiden at
Brighton in August. *J. Sutcliffe*

GENESIS FOUR   2 b.c. (Mar 31) Dreams To Reality (USA) 113 – Relma (Relko   –
136) [1992 5g 5.1d5 5s 5h a7g a6g a8g6] neat colt: moderate mover: brother to a
winner in Macau and half-brother to several winners abroad: dam won in Italy: no
worthwhile form: wears blinkers. *J. R. Jenkins*

GENIO   2 br.c. (May 3) Glow (USA) – Maxi Girl (My Swanee 122) [1992 7s] big   –
colt: half-brother to several winners, including fair stayer Apache Prince (by Red
Sunset) and a bumpers winner in Ireland: dam, Irish 9f winner, is half-sister to Don:
50/1 and backward, always in rear in 16-runner maiden at Salisbury in September:
showed a round action. *D. Sasse*

GENSERIC (FR)   2 br.c. (Jan 23) Groom Dancer (USA) 128 – Green Rosy (USA)   58
(Green Dancer (USA) 132) [1992 6f5 7g 8m4] 850,000 francs (approx £85,300) Y:
rather leggy colt: has a long stride: third foal: closely related to useful 3-y-o Rose
Indien (by Crystal Glitters), successful at 6f and 7f: dam French 1¼m winner:
worthwhile form only when fourth in maiden at Yarmouth in September, close up
virtually throughout in moderately-run race: will stay 1¼m. *R. W. Armstrong*

GENTLE HERO (USA)   6 ch.g. Hero's Honor (USA) – Tender Camilla 115   76
(Prince Tenderfoot (USA) 126) [1991 5g5 5d6 6g4 7m 6m3 7g* 5g* 6d3 7m3 6d* 6s2   a59 +
6m 7m6 6m 1992 6g 6g 6g 7f 6f4 7g 6m6 6g 7d 6d 6d 6d2 7v 6v a6g a6g5 a7g]
sturdy gelding: blind in right eye: moderate mover: rated 97 as 5-y-o: inconsistent
handicapper in 1992: effective from 5f to 7f: acts on good to firm ground, but best
effort on soft: has hung under pressure: effective visored or not earlier in career,
well beaten in blinkers once in 1992. *M. P. Naughton*

GENTLE MOMENT   2 b.f. (May 13) Teenoso (USA) 135 – Light O'Battle 97   53
(Queen's Hussar 124) [1992 5.7d3 7g a8g] 1,400Y: smallish, angular filly: half-sister
to 10.2f winner Height O'Battle (by Shirley Heights) and fairly useful sprinter
Lobbit (by Habitat): dam winner at 7f from 2 starts at 2 yrs, is sister to Highclere:
modest maiden: best effort on debut: will stay 1m: well beaten on outrack (maiden-
aged behind): sold out of H. Candy's stable 3,600 gns Newmarket Autumn Sales. *G.
Harwood*

GENTLE SECRET (IRE)   3 br.g. Chief Singer 131 – Freeze The Secret (USA)   –
118 (Nearctic) [1991 NR 1992 8d 10s] IR 31,000F, IR 32,000Y: half-brother to several
winners, including 1½m winner Red Secret (by Valiyar) and useful Irish 7f to 8.5f
performer Certain Secret (by Known Fact): dam second in 1000 Guineas and Oaks:
no worthwhile form in maidens at Newbury and Salisbury in the spring: sold 1,000
gns Ascot June Sales. *I. A. Balding*

GENUINE LADY   4 b.f. Lidhame 109 – Responder 70 (Vitiges (FR) 132) [1991   54
8m2 10d 1992 10m5 7g 8g 8m3 8d* 7g 8.1d5 8.2g a8g] leggy filly: fair plater: won
handicap at Brighton (no bid) in September: virtually pulled up final start: effective
at 7f and 1m: acts on good to firm and dead ground: sometimes has tongue tied down.
A. P. Jarvis

GEOFF'S RISK   2 gr.c. (Mar 11) Risk Me (FR) 127 – Dancing Diana 82 (Raga   64
Navarro (ITY) 119) [1992 5.2m5 5m4 5g3 6d3 5g2 5g3 5m 5.1d4] 14,000Y: angular,
good-topped colt: moderate mover: second foal: half-brother to 3-y-o 1m winner
Prince Rodney (by King of Spain): dam 5f (at 2 yrs) to 1m winner: consistent maiden:
in frame in 4 nurseries, blinkered last time: worth another try at 6f: seems suited by
give in the ground: sold 3,800 gns Newmarket Autumn Sales. *G. Lewis*

GEORDIE SONG   2 b.f. (May 19) Dancing Brave (USA) 140 – Itsamaza (USA)   68 p
(Limit To Reason (USA)) [1992 7g] half-sister to several winners, including 1½m
winner Mazano (by Vaguely Noble) and fairly useful 1983 2-y-o 6f winner Jameelapi
(by Blushing Groom): dam, winner at up to 1m, was best at 2 yrs when smart stakes
winner over 7f: 33/1, over 5 lengths seventh of 24 to stable-companion Fayfa in
maiden at Newmarket in October, running on well final 2f: will be very well suited
by middle distances: will improve. *H. R. A. Cecil*

GEORGE AUGUSTUS (USA)   4 b.c. El Gran Senor (USA) 136 – Surely   115
Georgies (Alleged (USA) 138) [1991 7g3 10g2 12g 9g* 10m* 12m* 12m4 10g*
12f 1992 10g* 10g6] rather leggy, quite good-topped colt: very useful performer:
didn't reappear until September, but showed himself as good as ever when winning
a Group 2 event at Frankfurt by 2½ lengths: below best in Group 3 contest won by
Perpendicular at Hoppegarten 2 weeks later: stays 1½m: acts on good to firm and
dead ground: usually wears blinkers. *J. Oxx, Ireland*

GEORGE DILLINGHAM 2 b.c. (May 21) Top Ville 129 – Premier Rose 117 **61** p
(Sharp Edge 123) [1992 7.9s6] angular colt: sixth foal: half-brother to several
winners, including 6-y-o middle-distance winner Opera Ghost (by Caerleon): dam,
sister to useful 7f and 1m filly Shapina, stayed 1m: 25/1 and backward, around 10
lengths last of 6 to Bin Ajwaad in maiden at York in October, driven along early in
straight then fading: should do better. *P. W. Harris*

GEORGE HENRY 3 b.g. Nomination 125 – Majda (USA) (Bustino 136) [1991 **–**
NR 1992 8f 10m] 5,600F, 5,300 2-y-o: poor mover: leggy gelding: poor mover:
dam once-raced half-sister to several winners abroad: remote in maiden at Redcar
and seller at Ripon in midsummer. *T. D. Barron*

GEORGE ROPER 2 b.g. (Apr 26) Hotfoot 126 – Helewise 76 (Dance In Time **70**
(CAN)) [1992 5v* 5.3d2 5s3 6m 7m3 8.5d6 8g5 7s2 7s] 8,000Y: workmanlike
gelding: second foal: half-brother to poor maiden Solway Mist (by Sagaro): dam
2-y-o 1m winner: modest but inconsistent performer: won maiden at Folkestone in
March: good second in 7f nursery at Redcar: stays 1m: acts on good to firm ground,
but is suited by plenty of give: visored last 3 starts. *M. R. Channon*

GERISH (IRE) 3 ch.f. Coquelin (USA) 121 – Esquire Lady (Be My Guest (USA) **–**
126) [1991 NR 1992 8d 8.1d5 10m 11.5m5 10g 10d] 6,000Y: angular filly: has a round
action: third foal: half-sister to 5-y-o 6f winner Tara's Girl (by Touching Wood): dam
won at 1m and 9.5f at 3 yrs in Ireland: well beaten, including in seller. *J. Pearce*

GERMAN LEGEND 2 br.c. (May 26) Faustus (USA) 118 – Fairfields 73 **32**
(Sharpen Up 127) [1992 7.1m 7.1g5] 4,400F, 4,400Y: half-brother to several minor
winners here and abroad: dam 5f winner at 2 yrs later successful in Holland: ridden
by 7-lb claimer, well beaten at Edinburgh in July. *R. R. Lamb*

GERSKI 2 b.f. (May 24) Formidable (USA) 125 – Moorland Lady 74 (Swing Easy **–**
(USA) 126) [1992 6d 6s] lengthy filly: moderate walker: first reported foal: dam 10.6f
winner also successful over jumps: well beaten in seller and maiden claimer at
Goodwood. *R. Hannon*

GESNERA 4 br.f. Rusticaro (FR) 124 – Joie d'Or (FR) (Kashmir II 125) [1991 NR **36**
1992 10.8m6 14.6d 14.6g5 11.8g3 12.1s4 14.1d 12.1s 16s a12g a12g] lengthy filly: has a
roundish action: poor maiden handicapper: stays 14.6f: acts on soft ground: no
improvement in a visor. *K. White*

GET DAILY SPORT 2 b.f. (May 9) Risk Me (FR) 127 – Sendim On Sam 74 **–**
(Lochnager 132) [1992 5g a5g5 5.3f4 a6g 5.2f] IR 550Y: leggy, close-coupled filly:
second foal: dam maiden raced only at 5f, is granddaughter of smart sprinter Dutch
Gold: poor plater: sold 1,000 gns Ascot June Sales. *P. A. Kelleway*

GET SUNDAY SPORT (IRE) 2 gr.c. (Apr 24) Sarab 123 – Queensworthy **–**
(Capistrano 120) [1992 7d 7g] 3,200 2-y-o: half-brother to 6f and 7f winner Reign-
beau (by Runnett) and a winner abroad over jumps: dam once-raced half-sister to
high-class sprinter Typhoon: soundly beaten in maidens at Lingfield in September:
sold 800 gns Newmarket Autumn Sales. *Miss Gay Kelleway*

GHALYOON (USA) 3 b.c. Deputy Minister (CAN) – Foot Stone (USA) (Cyane) **77**
[1991 7g 6m* 6m 1992 5.7s* 6f 6g 7.6s4 8.9d6 8v] sturdy, lengthy colt: poor mover:
fair form: won handicap at Bath in May, leading inside final 1f: sold out of P.
Walwyn's stable 11,000 gns Newmarket Autumn Sales and well beaten in minor
event at Saint-Cloud: needs further than 6f, and will stay at least 1m: won on good to
firm at 2 yrs, but worthwhile form in 1992 only on soft ground. *H. Pantall, France*

GHOSTED HASSLE 3 ch.f. Jester 119 – Little Revenge (Runnymede 123) **–**
[1991 a6g 5d 5m 1992 7f] leggy, close-coupled filly: of little account. *G. F. H.
Charles-Jones*

GHOSTLY GLOW 3 gr.g. Kalaglow 132 – Amerella (Welsh Pageant 132) [1991 **53**
7.1m 7g 6.9f 1992 16m 16.1d4 a12g3 a12g2 14.1m* 16g2 14.6d a16g3 a14g* a14g]
lengthy, lightly-made gelding: fair and largely consistent plater: won at Nottingham
(bought in 4,000 gns) in August and Southwell (claimer) in November: stays 2m:
acts on good to firm ground and all-weather surfaces, seemingly not on dead:
visored nowadays: has gone in snatches and wandered under pressure. *C. C. Elsey*

GHURRAH (IRE) 3 ch.f. Sharpo 132 – Buthayna 85 (Habitat 134) [1991 6s 6m **64** §
6.1m 1992 7g2 7f5 8d 8d2 10g5 10m* 8.3m 8d4 8g2 9g 8s3 10.2d] tall, good-topped
filly: modest handicapper on her day: won at Newmarket in July: stays 1¼m: acts on
firm and soft ground: worth a try in blinkers/visor: has swished tail, found little, and
looked reluctant to race: moody and is not one to trust. *C. J. Benstead*

GHYLLDALE 4 b.f. Sweet Monday 122 – Dreamy Desire 50 (Palm Track 122) **46** §
[1991 8s 10d3 10f* 10g 11m5 8f 10g4 11m2 11.8m3 1992 9.9f 12.3f9f9.2g4 11.9g3 10s*

10m⁶] leggy, angular filly: untrustworthy plater: sweating, easy winner of Redcar selling handicap (no bid) in September: effective from 1¼m to 1½m: acts on any going: usually visored nowadays: ungenuine. *R. Bastiman*

GIBBOT 7 b.g. Taufan (USA) 119 – Gaychimes (Steel Heart 128) [1991 10f⁶ 9s³ – § 8m⁶ 8m⁴ 9g 9d 9.7s 9m 8.3m* 7.6m 8.2f 10g 8g a13g 1992 a8g a10g 9.7g 8g 8g 9d 12f 10d] close-coupled, workmanlike gelding: carries plenty of condition: has a round action: ungenuine, and no form in 1992: sold 900 gns Ascot September Sales. *P. Howling*

GIDDY HEIGHTS (IRE) 3 b.f. Head For Heights 125 – Blaze of Light (Blake- 44 ney 126) [1991 NR 1992 7.5m⁶ a7g⁶ 7.5d³ 7.5d⁵] lengthy, rather plain filly: second foal: dam unraced close relative of Upper Strata: poor maiden: bred to be suited by further: well beaten on fibresand: sold to join R. Stone 580 gns Doncaster October Sales. *J. P. Leigh*

GILBERT'S GIRL 5 b.m. Castle Keep 121 – Traditional Miss 90 (Traditionalist 35 (USA)) [1991 12g 11.9f⁴ 9.7m⁶ 10.2g 1992 a14g⁵ a12g*] leggy, sparely-made mare: poor handicapper: narrowly won at Lingfield in February: stays 1½m: acts on firm and dead ground and on equitrack: has wandered under pressure. *C. J. Hill*

GILDERDALE 10 ch.g. Gunner B 126 – Mertola (Tribal Chief 125) [1991 8g* 86 8m* 10.1f6 10g 8f* 9g² 10m* 1992 9d 8g⁴ 9m⁴ 9m* 8.1f³ 10d 8s⁶ 10m⁴ 8f4 9d³ 8g6 10m⁵ 10d³ a10g*] close-coupled gelding: has quick action: grand old handicapper, winner of 18 races: successful in 1992 at Redcar in June and (first run on equitrack) Lingfield in November: effective from 1m to 1¼m: has form on dead ground, but is particularly well suited by a sound surface: has won for amateur: held up, and ideally suited by a strongly-run race: tough. *J. W. Hills*

GILT THRONE 5 b.g. Thatching 131 – Nikara (FR) (Emerson) [1991 7f⁵ 5m* 6m – 6d 6m⁴ 5d* 5d* 6g* 6d² 1992 6.1s³ 6g] leggy, workmanlike gelding: has round action: very game and useful performer (rated 105) at 4 yrs: not seen out until late-October in 1992 and well below best: effective at 5f and 6f: has won on good to firm ground but best form with some give. *M. H. Tompkins*

GIN AND ORANGE 6 b.g. Mummy's Pet 125 – Amberetta 72 (Supreme Sove- 52 reign 119) [1991 a10g a13g 10.2s 10d 7m 8f 7.6d a12g a14g 1992 10.8d⁴ 10.8g*] rangy gelding: moderate mover: modest performer: won handicap at Warwick in May: needs further than 7f, and stays 10.8f: acts on firm and dead going: has hung left. *J. R. Jenkins*

GINA'S CHOICE 6 b.m. Ile de Bourbon (USA) 133 – Modern Romance (Dance – In Time (CAN)) [1991 8.9m⁴ 8.2m 1992 10.8g] big, rather plain mare: has a round action: of little account these days. *P. A. Pritchard*

GINA'S DELIGHT 4 ch.f. Valiyar 129 – City Swinger (Derrylin 115) [1991 7.5f⁶ – 10.5d a6g 1992 a6g a12g] leggy, good-topped filly: has a quick action: poor plater. *J. R. Jenkins*

GINGER FLOWER 3 ch.f. Niniski (USA) 125 – Monterana 99 (Sallust 134) 60 p [1991 NR 1992 7d² 8.5d² a7g*] rather leggy, close-coupled filly: first foal: dam, 2-y-o 6f and 7f winner who ran only once at 3 yrs, is out of half-sister to Italian Derby winner Ruysdael II: off course long periods between races: won maiden at Lingfield in October, outpaced, and having been 7 lengths behind entering straight: will be very well suited by middle distances: sold to join N. Tinkler 6,200 gns Newmarket December Sales: can progress further. *G. Wragg*

GINNYFASURE (IRE) 2 ch.f. (May 10) Sure Blade (USA) 130 – Ginny Binny 39 p 113 (Ahonoora 122) [1992 5s] 4,900F: second foal: dam won in Italy: 8/1, around 10 lengths seventh of 8 to Wintering in maiden at Folkestone in October: should improve, particularly over further. *D. R. C. Elsworth*

GIORDANO (IRE) 2 br.g. (Apr 15) Cyrano de Bergerac 120 – Kitterland 60 (Rheingold 137) [1992 7m⁶ 7g² 7g] IR 6,200F, IR 4,000Y: rangy gelding: moderate mover: half-brother to a winner in Austria by Wolver Hollow: dam Irish middle-distance winner, is granddaughter of 1968 Irish Oaks winner Celina: modest maiden: will stay 1m. *W. R. Muir*

GIPSY FIDDLER 4 b.g. Bairn (USA) 126 – Miss Cindy 95 (Mansingh (USA) 98 120) [1991 7m⁵ 7f⁶ 7.1f 1992 5d⁵ 5.1g 6g 5.6m] close-coupled gelding: moderate mover: useful but relatively lightly-raced handicapper: fifth in £9,500 event at Haydock in August, but failed to confirm that promise: stays 7f: acts on good to firm and dead ground. *J. J. O'Neill*

GIPSY KING 4 gr.g. Magic Mirror 105 – Sarah Gillian (USA) (Zen (USA)) [1991 – a8g² a8g³ a10g a11g² a10g⁶ a12g⁴ 1992 a12g a10g a16g⁵ 16.2g⁶] leggy, rather sparsely-made gelding: has round action: plating-class maiden: not seen out after March: probably stays 2m: has worn blinkers and eyeshield: carries head awkwardly, and is probably ungenuine. *P. A. Kelleway*

GIRL AT THE GATE   2 b.f. (Apr 12) Formidable (USA) 125 – Ask Mama 83 (Mummy's Pet 125) [1992 6f a7g*] 820F: small, leggy, lightly-made filly: second foal: dam 1¼m winner: easy winner of claimer at Southwell in July, always front rank and quickening clear 2f out: will stay at least 1m. *M. Bell*   53

GIRL NEXT DOOR   2 b.f. (Mar 20) Local Suitor (USA) 128 – Tight Spin (High Top 131) [1992 5g5 5f4 6m4 6d6 5g2 a6g4 5s 6d5 8g a6g5 a6g2 a6g* a7g] workman-like filly: has a round action: first foal: dam once-raced daughter of very useful 5f to 7f winner Petty Purse, herself daughter of very smart sprinter Parsimony: modest performer: sold out of N. Graham's stable 1,150 gns Ascot November Sales after tenth start: won nursery at Southwell in December: ran lack-lustre race when favourite for claimer there 5 days later: stays 6f: has run creditably in a visor. *J. A. Pickering*   51 a58

GIRTON BELLE   2 b.f. (Feb 17) Belfort (FR) 89 – Gay Twenties 70 (Lord Gayle (USA) 124) [1992 a7g a7g] fifth foal: dam stayed 1¼m and was winning hurdler: always behind in maidens at Southwell and Lingfield. *M. D. I. Usher*   –

GIRTON DEGREE   3 b.f. Balliol 125 – Cheb's Honour 70 (Chebs Lad 120) [1991 5d 5.7m 7g5 1992 8d2 7.6m a8g4 7f4] leggy filly: modest plater, not seen out after June: acts on firm and dead ground: visored last 3 starts: trained until after reappearance by R. Hannon: has joined Miss G. Kelleway. *S. Dow*   41

GIVE ALL   6 b.g. Try My Best (USA) 130 – Miss Spencer (Imperial Fling (USA) 116) [1991 NR 1992 12m] good-topped, workmanlike gelding: second foal: half-brother to winning stayer Ejay Haitch (by Be My Native): dam unraced: tailed off in Beverley maiden in May. *B. Richmond*   –

GIVE ME HOPE (IRE)   4 b.f. Be My Native (USA) 122 – Diamond Gig (Pitskelly 122) [1991 10g 12.3d4 a12g a8g6 10.1f 1992 a11g* a12g6 a10g a12g a12g 10.3g 7.1m 8.9s 10.2m] leggy, light-framed filly: inconsistent handicapper: won claimer at Southwell in January: trained first 4 starts by R. Brazington: stays 1½m: acts on soft ground and on fibresand: ran poorly in blinkers: joined R. Price, but wasn't seen after June. *G. H. Yardley*   46 d

GIZLAAN (USA)   3 ch.f. Alydar (USA) – Kamikaze Rick (USA) (Hasty Flyer (USA)) [1991 7f 1992 8g 7d3 6m4 6g6 8.1g5 7g3 6g3 8m 6.9g5] close-coupled, leggy filly: has a round action: modest maiden: blinkered, creditable fifth at Folkestone last time: acts on good to firm and dead ground: tongue tied down (ran fairly well) seventh start: tends to sweat: sold 15,000 gns Newmarket December Sales. *B. Hanbury*   54

GLACIAL MOON (USA)   3 b.f. Arctic Tern (USA) 126 – Hortensia (FR) 119 (Luthier 126) [1991 7d2 1992 10d5 10.2f4 9.9m 10g6] small, sparely-made filly: modest maiden, best effort at 3 yrs on reappearance: subsequently off course nearly 4 months: should stay 1½m: sold 11,000 gns Newmarket December Sales. *B. W. Hills*   62

GLADEER (IRE)   3 ch.f. Hadeer 118 – Really Sharp (Sharpen Up 127) [1991 6g5 6.1m4 1992 7g] angular, workmanlike filly: showed ability at 2 yrs, none in maiden at Kempton in June at 3 yrs. *W. Carter*   –

GLAISDALE (IRE)   3 b.c. Lomond (USA) 128 – Glass Slipper 100 (Relko 136) [1991 7.9m 8m5 1992 12m4 12m* 14f2 16.2g* 16.5g3 14.6g5] good-topped, useful-looking colt: carries condition: fairly useful performer: won maiden at Pontefract in May and 2-runner minor event at Chepstow in July: sold out of H. Cecil's stable 33,000 gns Newmarket Autumn Sales after penultimate start: well beaten final outing: shapes like a thorough stayer. *M. H. Tompkins*   91

GLASGOW   3 b.g. Top Ville 129 – Glasson Lady (GER) 108 (Priamos (GER) 123) [1991 6f3 1992 8g2 8m 7f4 14.1d 8g a8g a14g] quite good-topped gelding: disappointing and unsatisfactory maiden: wore net muzzle and taken very quietly to post first 3 starts: sold out of B. Hills's stable 5,600 gns Newmarket July Sales and gelded: no form last 4 starts, when blinkered in seller final one: resold 1,500 gns Ascot December Sales, to join G. Jones: should be suited by beyond 7f. *E. J. Alston*   64 d

GLASSBLOWER   5 b.g. Shareef Dancer (USA) 135 – Glasson Lady (GER) 108 (Priamos (GER) 123) [1991 8f2 10.1s 10f* 8.5m 8.3m2 7.6m2 10f* 8.9g 1992 8g 10g 11.5f6 7.6m] lengthy gelding: rated 78 at 4 yrs: little form in handicaps in 1992: better suited by 1¼m than 1m: best efforts on top-of-the-ground: has won for apprentice: may be ungenuine. *R. Akehurst*   –

GLASTONDALE   6 b.g. Beldale Flutter (USA) 130 – Glastonbury 73 (Grundy   **38**
137) [1991 11s⁵ 12g⁵ 12d* 11f³ 12g² 12g 12g⁴ 12d 15.8g 12g² 13d³ 12g 1992 10.3g⁶
13.8d* 12.1g³ 12.4s⁵ 12m⁴ 13d⁵] compact gelding: carries condition: moderate
mover: poor handicapper: won at Catterick in March: seems best from 1½m to 1¾m
nowadays: acts on firm and soft going: visored early in career: has won for
apprentice: lacks turn of foot, and goes well forcing pace: sold to join J. Birkett 3,600
gns Doncaster June Sales. *T. D. Barron*

GLENCROFT   8 b.g. Crofter (USA) 124 – Native Fleet (FR) (Fleet Nasrullah)   **–**
[1991 a5g* a6g³ a5g² 5m 5g³ 5.9m 5m⁵ 6m 5h² 5g 5g³ 5m⁶ 5.1s 5m 5s a5g 1992 a5g
a6g⁶ 5f 6m 5m 6.1d] big, strong gelding: has been hobdayed and tubed: prolific
winner but is a shadow of his former self nowadays: best form at 5f: seems to act on
any going: wears blinkers. *D. W. Chapman*

GLENDERRY   10 br.g. Derrylin 115 – Summer Mist 57 (Midsummer Night II   **– §**
117) [1991 NR 1992 8m] neat, strong gelding: poor mover: of little account these
days. *R. Lee*

GLEN ECHO (IRE)   2 b.c. (May 15) Taufan (USA) 119 – Addabub (Manado 130)   **72 p**
[1992 7g⁵] IR 17,500F, 32,000Y: second foal: half-brother to useful 1991 2-y-o 7f
winner Autocracy (by Alzao): dam Irish 1¼m winner also successful over hurdles:
14/1, around 10 lengths fifth of 9 to Catrail in minor event at Newmarket in October,
staying on never dangerous: will improve. *G. Harwood*

GLENELIANE (IRE)   4 b.f. Glenstal (USA) 118 – Sweet Eliane (Birdbrook 110)   **37**
[1991 9.9g⁶ 9.2d⁶ 11g⁴ 8.2f³ 8f⁵ 7m⁶ 1992 7g 6.1g⁴ a6g a7g⁴ 8g 8g 12.1s] lengthy,
good-quartered filly: moderate mover: none too consistent maiden handicapper on
flat: pulled up, reportedly lame, final start, in September: stays 1m: acts on firm
going: often blinkered nowadays: tail flasher: won poor claiming hurdle in August. *J.
L. Harris*

GLENFIELD GRETA   4 ch.f. Gabitat 119 – Glenfield Portion 86 (Mummy's Pet   **61**
125) [1991 6g 6f⁴ 6m⁴ 5f² 5m⁴ 6f³ 6s² 6f⁵ 6m 1992 6v 6d 6f⁵ 6m⁵ 6d 7g² 7.5d² 8g 7g²
7s 7d] small, sturdy filly: none too consistent handicapper: stays 7f: acts on any
going: carries head high. *P. S. Felgate*

GLEN FINNAN   4 ch.f. Ballacashtal (CAN) – Glen Kella Manx 97 (Tickled Pink   **–**
114) [1991 6g 8d 8d⁶ 7.1m 1992 8.9s 8m] compact filly: has a round action: of little
account: trained on reappearance by J. Fox. *M. P. Muggeridge*

GLEN MILLER   2 b.c. (Mar 31) Music Boy 124 – Blakeney Sound (Blakeney   **68**
126) [1992 5m 6.1d⁵ 6g⁵ 6.1d⁵ 5d⁴ 6.1m² 5s² 6m] 9,600Y: close-coupled, workmanlike colt: poor mover: second foal: dam unraced: fair maiden: ran moderately in
Newmarket nursery final start: will prove better at 6f than 5f: acts on good to firm
ground, but may be ideally suited by soft. *J. W. Payne*

GLENSCAR   6 gr.g. Glenstal (USA) 118 – Caranina (USA) (Caro 133) [1991 10.8g²   **43**
10f⁶ 10.8m² 10m 10.8m 9d⁴ 8m³ 8.1g³ 9.7s³ 8f² 10g 8.2m⁴ 7m⁵ 8.3m⁴ 7.1g 1992
10.3g 10.8v 7g² 7m* 7g] angular, sparely-made gelding: poor mover: poor
handicapper: ridden by 7-lb claimer, won at Wolverhampton in August: effective
from 7f to 1¼m: acts on any going: often slowly away, and held up for a late run. *J. L.
Spearing*

GLENSTAL PRINCESS   5 ch.m. Glenstal (USA) 118 – Jessamy Hall 77   **64**
(Crowned Prince (USA) 128) [1991 5d⁶ 6g* 6d² 6g 6g 6m⁶ 7m 1992 5.1m⁵ 6.9f⁴ 6d
7m⁶ 5.1m³ 6f⁴ 6g³ 6.1d³ 5.9f⁴ 7.1m³ 7g 7g³ 10.3m 7s] lengthy mare: modest
handicapper, winner of one of last 30 starts: needs further than 5f and stays 7f: acts
on firm and dead ground: visored (ran creditably) once earlier in career: has run well
for 7-lb claimer: usually goes well at Chester. *R. Hollinshead*

GLENSTAL PRIORY   5 b.m. Glenstal (USA) 118 – Jumbolia (Wolver Hollow   **53**
126) [1991 a10g 10f 12f 14m² 12m⁴ 16.4m* 16m² 16.9m 17.2g a16g⁵ a14g² 1992 a12g⁴   **a40**
18.2g* 16m* 16.4m 17.2s a16g⁴ a14g⁵] small, sparely-made mare: has a quick action:
modest handicapper: off course 6 months, successful at Chepstow (amateurs) and
Nottingham in the summer: stays 2¼m: acts on good to firm going
(found little and finished tired on soft) and all-weather surfaces. *P. F. I. Cole*

GLIDE PATH (USA)   3 ch.c. Stalwart (USA) – Jolly Polka (USA) (Nice Dancer   **86**
(CAN)) [1991 7f7m⁶ 7m³ 7m⁶ 8.3s² 1992 10d² 10f* 11m* 12f 9d⁴ 10.1d² 10g³ 9d 9s⁶]
close-coupled, rather unfurnished colt: usually looks well: has a round action: fairly
useful handicapper: won at Lingfield in May and Redcar (idled) in June: best efforts
when in frame in late-summer: stays 11f: acts on firm going. *J. W. Hills*

GLIMPSE OF HEAVEN   2 b.f. (Apr 16) Vision (USA) – Adriya 94 (Vayrann   **62**
133) [1992 6m 7s⁵ 7.1s⁴ 6s⁶] 4,000Y: unfurnished filly: second foal: half-sister to

Irish 3-y-o 7f winner Adira (by Ballad Rock): dam 7f and 11.7f winner: modest maiden: will stay 1m: acts on soft ground. *D. R. C. Elsworth*

GLINT OF AYR 2 b.f. (Apr 2) Glint of Gold 128 – Iyamski (USA) 86 (Baldski (USA)) [1992 7d] big, workmanlike filly: third foal: half-sister to 1990 5f and 6f winner Ayr Classic (by Local Suitor): dam 7f and 1m winner: 33/1, around 14 lengths ninth of 17 to Rapid Repeat in maiden at Leicester in October: gave trouble when being saddled: looks sort to do better. *W. R. Muir* **39** p

GLISSO (IRE) 2 ch.c. (Apr 12) Digamist (USA) 110 – Gulf Bird 71 (Gulf Pearl 117) [1992 6s⁵ 6d 6v] 37,000Y: smallish, strong colt: has a round action: half-brother to several winners, including useful stayer Saronicos (by Dalsaan) and very useful 5f performer Blue Persian (by Majority Blue): dam 1½m winner: carrying plenty of condition, moved easily into lead 2f out before fading inside last in maiden at Goodwood in October: well beaten both starts afterwards. *L. M. Cumani* **54**

GLODDAETH ISA 2 b.f. (May 5) Sayf El Arab (USA) 127 – Dawn Loch (USA) (Grey Dawn II 132) [1992 6.1m 5m⁶] small filly: moderate mover: second foal: sister to a poor maiden: dam lightly raced, fourth once at 1¾m: no worthwhile form: dead. *J. Berry* **–**

GLORIEUX DANCER (FR) 2 b.c. (Apr 12) Le Glorieux 105 – Teree (FR) (Kaldoun (FR) 122) [1992 5m³ 5.5d² 6d³ 5d* 5.5g⁵ 6s² 8g² 8.5f² a8.3f3] 64,000 francs (approx £6,500) Y: first foal: dam French 2-y-o 5f and 7f winner: won Prix du Bois at Longchamp in July: best other efforts second in Moet & Chandon-Rennen (to ¾-length winner Sharp Prod) at Baden-Baden and Laurel Futurity at Laurel: stays 8.5f: acts on any going. *R. Collet, France* **108**

GLORIOUS ISLAND 2 ch.c. (Apr 21) Jupiter Island 126 – Gloria Maremmana (King Emperor (USA)) [1992 7d 7g⁴ 7g 6m⁴ 6d⁴ 7.6s³] rangy colt: half-brother to several winners, including 7f to 1¼m performer Emperor Hotfoot (by Hotfoot) and 1½m winner Hot Girl (by Hot Grove): dam won at 2 yrs in Italy: modest maiden: bred to be suited by 1m+: acts on good to firm and soft ground. *R. F. Johnson Houghton* **57**

GLOWING DANCER 2 ch.c. (May 8) Glow (USA) – Tuxford Hideaway 102 (Cawston's Clown 113) [1992 5d⁵ 5d 6m⁵ 6d* 6g²] 9,500Y: leggy, useful-looking colt: has scope: third foal: half-brother to useful 3-y-o sprinter Branston Abby (by Risk Me) and fairly useful 1990 2-y-o 6f and 7f winner Big Blow (by Last Tycoon): dam sprinter: sire smart stakes winner at up to 9f: modest performer: won maiden auction at Epsom, rallying well: creditable second of 3 in nursery at Yarmouth later in July: withdrawn at Sandown in August after unseating rider on way to post (something reportedly wrong with tack): stays 6f: acts on good to firm and dead ground: races prominently. *J. R. Jenkins* **62**

GLOWING DARKNESS 7 gr.m. Kalaglow 132 – Guama 89 (Gulf Pearl 117) [1991 NR 1992 12m] IR 30,000Y: lengthy, rather plain mare: sixth living foal: half-sister to winning stayers Powersaver Lad (by Jaazeiro) and Rocas (by Ile de Bourbon): dam 2-y-o 7f winner: tailed off in maiden at Pontefract in September. *J. M. Carr* **–**

GLOWING DEVIL 3 ro.c. Kalaglow 132 – Romantiki (USA) (Giboulee (CAN)) [1991 7m⁵ 8m 1992 9.9g⁶ 12.1m⁶ 11.1f² 12.3f² 15.8m3] tall, leggy, unfurnished colt: modest maiden: ridden with far more enterprise than before when second in handicaps at Hamilton and (ladies event) Ripon in June: stiff task following month: shapes like a stayer. *T. D. Barron* **55**

GLOWING JADE 2 b.f. (Mar 5) Kalaglow 132 – Precious Jade 72 (Northfields (USA)) [1992 6m² 6g²] 8,800Y: tall, long-backed filly: has plenty of scope: half-sister to 3-y-o Jade Mistress and 4 winners, including 1991 Italian 3-y-o 7f winner Precious Dame (also by Damister): dam stayed 1m: modest form in minor event at Windsor (beaten a short head) and median auction maiden at York (travelled best long way) in midsummer: will be very well suited by further: will win a maiden. *M. R. Channon* **65** p

GLOWING MANTLE (IRE) 4 ch.f. Glow (USA) – Dismantle 75 (Aureole 132) [1991 a8g 7g⁶ 12f⁶ 1992 a12g a13g] sparely-made ex-Irish filly: of little account. *R. E. Peacock* **–**

GLOWING PATH 2 b.c. (Apr 20) Kalaglow 132 – Top Tina (High Top 131) [1992 a7g] 1,750Y: third reported foal: dam unraced: 20/1, slowly away and always in rear in 12-runner claimer at Southwell in July. *C. J. Hill* **–**

GLOWING VALUE (IRE) 2 b.c. (Mar 20) Glow (USA) – Party Piece (Thatch (USA) 136) [1992 5s* 5g⁶ 6g³ 6m² 6f³ 7g² 8d⁶ 7d⁶] 6,500Y: leggy, quite good-topped colt: poor walker: third foal: half-brother to 1991 Irish 2-y-o 7f winner Magic **85**

Piece (by Magical Wonder): dam Irish maiden: fairly useful performer: won maiden at Hamilton in May: best effort when short-headed in Chester nursery in August: subsequently tailed off in listed race at Goodwood and minor event at York: stays 7f: best efforts on a sound surface, though has won on soft. *J. Berry*

GLOW OF HOPE   2 b.f. (Apr 19) Prince Sabo 123 – Impailand (Imperial Fling (USA) 116) [1992 5d⁶ 5d⁵ 6m a5g 6d] lengthy, sparely-made filly: third foal: dam never ran: seems of little account. *E. J. Alston*   –

GOAN GIRL   2 gr.f. (Feb 25) Mansingh (USA) 120 – Continental Divide 50 (Sharp Edge 123) [1992 6.1d 5m 7d] sturdy filly: tenth foal: sister to 6-y-o 5f (at 2 yrs) to 8.5f winner Honey Boy Simba: dam poor plater: no form in claimers and a median auction. *P. S. Felgate*   –

GODSALL   5 gr.m. Godswalk (USA) 130 – Sallail (Sallust 134) [1991 a6g a8g 1992 a7g] leggy, sparely-made mare: of little account these days. *Mrs N. Macauley*   –

GODS LAW   11 gr.g. Godswalk (USA) 130 – Fluently (Ragusa 137) [1991 NR 1992 11m 12m 14.1g] leggy, good-topped gelding: carries plenty of condition: probably no longer of any account. *R. Earnshaw*   –

GO EXECUTIVE   4 b.g. Sharpo 132 – Staritsa (USA) (Alleged (USA) 138) [1991 a6g³ 6m 5m 7.6g³ 7m² 8m 6m 7.9g 7g² 7d³ 7m* 8g 1992 a8g⁵ a7g³ 8g 6d 7d 7g* 7g* 8f 7g 7m⁶ 7d 7m] leggy, close-coupled gelding: keen walker: moderate mover: fairly useful handicapper: won at Newmarket in May and Epsom in June, making most: below form afterwards, in blinkers final start: best form at 7f/1m: acts on good to firm and dead ground, and on equitrack: wore eyeshield once: sometimes sweating: sold 10,500 gns Newmarket Autumn Sales since. *C. E. Brittain*   **90**

GO FLIGHTLINE (IRE)   2 ch.f. (Feb 21) Common Grounds 118 – Whilst (Dalsaan 125) [1992 5g² 5d* 5.2g 6d] IR 9,000Y: neat filly: second foal: dam unraced: modest performer: narrowly won maiden at Lingfield: ran moderately in nurseries at Newbury and Newmarket (raced keenly) later in the autumn: should be better suited by 6f than 5f. *M. Bell*   **60**

GOGOLETTE   3 ch.f. All Systems Go 119 – Sarphele Larches (Gay Fandango (USA) 132) [1991 5m 6f 6m 7g⁶ 1992 6.9d] workmanlike filly: probably of little account: sold 720 gns Doncaster June Sales. *M. O'Neill*   –

GOLD BELT (IRE)   3 gr.f. Bellypha 130 – Golden Braid 99 (Glint of Gold 128) [1991 6g⁴ 7f 6m² 6m 7.1m⁴ 1992 8.5m 8.5f 7m² 7g⁴ 8g⁴ 8m 7.1s⁶ 8m a8g 8d a8g a8g*] leggy, lightly-made filly: moderate walker: only plating-class form when in frame, winning apprentice handicap at Southwell in December: stays 1m: acts on good to firm ground and fibresand. *R. Hollinshead*   **44**

GOLD BLADE   3 ch.g. Rousillon (USA) 133 – Sharp Girl (FR) (Sharpman 124) [1991 7g 1992 8g⁶ a7g³ 8m 8s² 8d⁴ a10g² 9.7v a10g⁴ a8g⁴] big, good-topped gelding: modest maiden: changed hands 2,100 gns Newmarket July Sales after reappearance: stays 1¼m: acts on soft ground and equitrack: blinkered last 3 starts. *N. A. Graham*   **64** a68

GOLD DESIRE   2 b.g. (May 2) Grey Desire 115 – Glory Gold 59 (Hittite Glory 125) [1992 5g 6g 8.1d] sparely-made gelding: first foal: dam 6f to 7.5f winner: no worthwhile form: off course over 5 months before final start. *M. Brittain*   –

GOLDEN   5 ch.m. Don 128 – Roll Up (Roll of Honour 130) [1991 16m 16.2f⁶ 1992 18.5g] angular, workmanlike mare: good walker: quite modest handicapper at 3 yrs: backward and soundly beaten in Chester Cup in May, 1992: stays 2m: seems to act on firm and dead going: sold 3,400 gns Newmarket December Sales: has been covered by Superpower. *C. W. C. Elsey*   –

GOLDEN ANCONA   9 ch.g. London Bells (CAN) 109 – Golden Darling 86 (Darling Boy 124) [1991 8v² 8d 7.5g 8m⁵ 10.4d 8.5m a8g⁵ 8d² 8g⁶ 1992 a8g⁵ a8g⁴ a11g 8s 8.3v⁶ 8d 10g 10s⁶ 10.5d 11.1d] close-coupled, lightly-made gelding: poor mover: inconsistent handicapper: last win came 53 starts ago, at 5 yrs: stays 1m: has been blinkered/visored: usually gets behind. *M. Brittain*   **36** a50

GOLDEN BEAU   10 b.g. Crimson Beau 124 – Kantado 93 (Saulingo 122) [1991 8s 10d⁵ 9f⁶ 9.9g⁵ 10g⁴ 10g⁵ 10d⁶ 8g 8.3s⁴ 8.3d⁵ 7f³ 8.1m⁶ 8.3f* 8f 8h 10g 1992 10.3g 8.1g⁶ 9.2d³ 8f 8m a8g⁶ 10f 10m 12.1v] sparely-made, dipped-backed gelding: good mover: inconsistent handicapper these days, winner of one of last 33 starts: stays 9f: acts on any going, except possibly hard: below form when blinkered: effective with or without visor: often gets on edge: has hung badly right and looked none too keen. *A. Harrison*   **24**

GOLDEN CHIP (IRE)   4 ch.g. M Double M (USA) – Kimangao (Garda's Revenge (USA) 119) [1991 7.5g⁵ 10m³ 8.5f³ 10m* 10m 10.5g 10m⁴ 8m² 8f² 8m⁶ 8m² 8m³ 8m⁴ 10.3g³ a8g⁵ a8g* 1992 a8g 8.5g³ 8d⁶ 8s² 8m 8f⁵ 8g² 7.9d* 8m* 7g* 7.5m²]   **81**

7m 7.9m] strong gelding: poor walker: splendidly consistent handicapper: ridden by 5-lb claimer S. Maloney when gamely winning at York and Ayr (2) within a fortnight in July: best at 7f/1m: acts on firm and soft going: often taken down alone: effective held up or ridden from front: tough. *A. P. Stringer*

GOLDEN GUEST 2 ch.f. (Mar 17) Rainbow Quest (USA) 134 – Intimate Guest **73** 110§ (Be My Guest (USA) 126) [1992 6m⁵ 6d² 7.1s⁴] rangy filly: has plenty of scope: good mover: first foal: dam, untrustworthy 6f (at 2 yrs) to 1m winner, is out of very useful 1m/1¼m performer As You Desire Me, a half-sister to Irish Derby and St Leger third Classic Example: fair maiden: looking really well, made most when second to Nicer at Newmarket, rallying well: should stay at least 1m: may not be ideally suited by very soft ground. *Mrs J. Cecil*

GOLDEN GUNNER (IRE) 4 ch.g. Mazaad 106 – Sun Gift (Guillaume Tell – (USA) 121) [1991 10m⁶ 12f* 11m 16.2g⁵ 11.7d⁶ 1992 12s] workmanlike gelding: rated 64 for M. Tompkins at 3 yrs: tailed-off last in Salisbury handicap in September, 1992: won handicap hurdle in October. *M. McCourt*

GOLDEN KLAIR 2 b.f. (Mar 5) Damister (USA) 123 – Woolpack (Golden **41** Fleece (USA) 133) [1992 6m a6g⁵ a6g 6m 8d 8s⁶ 10g a7g* a8g* a7g* a8g*] 7,200F: a78 leggy, workmanlike filly: second foal: dam unraced daughter of Irish 1000 Guineas third and Irish Oaks fourth Klairlone: progressed really well at Southwell towards end of year, winning 2 claimers and 2 nurseries in similar fashion, coming with strong run from off the pace: will stay 1¼m: acts particularly well on fibresand. *C. J. Hill*

GOLDEN MAIN 6 b.g. Glint of Gold 128 – Sea Venture (FR) 98 (Diatome 132) – [1991 NR 1992 14.1g] well-made gelding: tailed off in ladies handicap only run since 3 yrs: stayed 1¾m: acted on good to firm ground: dead. *S. Mellor*

GOLDEN PROPOSAL 3 gr.f. Nomination 125 – Jellygold 95 (Jellaby 124) [1991 **36** 5f 6g² 5m 6m⁴ 7.1m⁵ 7g 1992 6d² 6d 5m 5g 10f⁴ 10s 7d 8g 5s⁶ 5g] leggy, lengthy filly: poor performer: sold out of M. Bell's stable 3,900 gns Newmarket July Sales after fourth 3-y-o start. *M. J. Bolton*

GOLDEN SICKLE (USA) 3 b.g. Amazing Prospect (USA) – Marisickle (USA) **53** (Maris) [1991 a7g⁵ 1992 a6g² a7g⁵ a5g a5g a7g] modest maiden: stays 6f. *W. A. O'Gorman*

GOLDEN TORQUE 5 br.g. Taufan (USA) 119 – Brightelmstone 105 (Prince **69** Regent (FR) 129) [1991 10.2s 8d 8m 8.2d* 8.2g⁵ 8.3d³ 10.1m⁴ 10m 10.1m⁵ 10.5m³ 11.9g* 10.5d* 12d a12g⁴ 1992 10.3g 10d⁴ 12.4s² 8.2m 10.1f 10g² 12m* 12.1g 12.3d*] strong, close-coupled gelding: none too consistent handicapper: won at Thirsk in July and Ripon (bandaged behind) in September: effective from 1¼m to 1½m: acts on good to firm and soft ground: effective with or without a visor earlier in career: ridden by 7-lb claimer in 1992: best held up. *R. Bastiman*

GOLD FORT 2 gr.g. (May 15) Belfort (FR) 89 – Hunting Gold (Sonnen Gold 121) **45** [1992 5m 6d 6g⁶] leggy gelding: first reported foal: dam lightly raced: poor form in maidens in the autumn: will stay 7f. *B. W. Murray*

GOLD JUBILEE 3 b.f. Damister (USA) 123 – Tiny Jubilee 59 (Hard Fought 125) **55** [1991 5g⁵ 5.2g⁴ 6s⁵ 8d 1992 7s² 8.2g 8m⁵ 7d 7g 10.2s 7s a8g] sparely-made filly: moderate mover: modest maiden: stayed 1m: acted on good to firm and soft ground: dead. *P. J. Makin*

GOLDSMITHS' HALL 3 b.c. Glint of Gold 128 – Pipina (USA) 81 (Sir Gaylord) **100** [1991 8.2f⁵ 8m² 1992 12.3s* 12g* 11.5s⁴ 12.3m* 16.2f³ 14.8g 12m³] tall, leggy colt: useful performer: easily made all in small fields for maiden at Wolverhampton and minor events at Thirsk and Ripon in the spring: in frame in Derby Trial at Lingfield, Queen's Vase (below form) at Royal Ascot and minor contest (in July) at Newmarket: well worth another try at 1¾m (saddle slipped and rider unseated at start penultimate outing): acts on good to firm and soft ground: sold 12,500 gns Newmarket December Sales. *G. Wragg*

GOLD SPLASH (USA) 2 ch.f. (Jan 23) Blushing Groom (FR) 131 – **112** p Riviere d'Or (USA) 121 (Lyphard (USA) 132) [1992 6g² 8s⁴ 8s*]

The twice-raced Gold Splash became the first maiden to win the Group 1 Prix Marcel Boussac since Two to Paris beat eleven opponents in 1970, when the race was still known as the Criterium des Pouliches. The Boussac, run at Longchamp in October, is the most important one-mile race for two-year-old fillies in Europe, and currently boasts a formidable reputation as a classic pointer after a run that has seen Triptych, Midway Lady, Miesque, Salsabil,

Prix Marcel Boussac, Longchamp—
a close finish to this usually-informative race;
Gold Splash holds on stoutly from Kindergarten, Love of Silver,
Rouquette and Marillette

Shadayid, Culture Vulture, Hatoof and Caerlina finish either first or second in recent years. Whether the latest renewal will come up to scratch is debatable. With barely six lengths covering the first ten home, and subsequent results suggesting that many of the best fillies, not just those trained in France, were missing from the race, we doubt it.

However Gold Splash turns out, she was a worthy winner on the day. She wasn't entirely unfancied, either, and started at 11/1 in a market dominated by Sheikh Mohammed's coupled pattern-race winners Cox Orange, Kindergarten (the chosen mount of his retained jockey Cauthen) and Marillette, shorter than such as Rouquette, Lorelie and Sissingaya, each of whom had shown useful form when placed behind either Cox Orange in the Prix du Calvados at Deauville or Kindergarten in the Prix d'Aumale at Longchamp. Gold Splash had gone down by a short neck to the subsequent Prix du Petit Couvert winner Wixon, one of the best sprinting fillies in France, in the listed Prix Yacowlef over six furlongs at Deauville in August. After that she was extremely unfortunate by all accounts when fourth to Dancienne, who went on to win the Prix des Chenes, in a minor event over a mile at Maisons-Laffitte in September, finishing with a tremendous rattle after having almost fallen at one stage. Gold Splash was well ridden in the Boussac by Mosse, who'd flown in from Hong Kong to take the ride, and he had her in the front two or three throughout in a race that was contested at a strong gallop for the final six furlongs. Turning into the final straight, just over two furlongs out, Gold Splash was poised in second place behind the 25/1-shot Marviah, narrowly ahead of the Prestige Stakes winner Love of Silver. Striking for home immediately the field had straightened out, Gold Splash saw her race out gamely, proving too strong for the persistent Love of Silver inside the last furlong then holding Kindergarten's late challenge by a short neck, Love of Silver finishing three quarters of a length back in third. Rouquette, who'd taken the home turn in last place, stayed on well for fourth, marginally ahead of the May Hill winner Marillette, who'd met trouble on her run through from the rear. The theory that it had been a substandard Boussac was put to the test by Rouquette, sixth-placed Lorelie and ninth-placed Marviah in the Group 3 Prix de Reservoirs over a mile at Longchamp later in October. They could finish only fourth, fifth and ninth respectively behind Corrazona, Dancienne and Borodislew, who were separated by little more than a neck, in what is usually a much weaker race than the Boussac.

Gold Splash, a small filly, is the first foal of the 1987 Boussac runner-up Riviere d'Or. Besides finishing second to Ashayer at Longchamp, Riviere d'Or won the Prix d'Aumale as a two-year-old then improved in her second season when she won the Prix Vanteaux over an extended nine furlongs and the Prix Saint-Alary over a mile and a quarter, as well as finishing second to Resless Kara in the Prix de Diane. Riviere d'Or is one of two fillies produced by the now-deceased Gold River, winner of the Arc as a four-year-old at odds of 53/1 in 1980. Gold River's starting price reflected the widely-held belief that a mile and a half in top company would be on the sharp side for one who'd won the Prix Royal-Oak and the two-and-a-half-mile Prix du Cadran in the manner of an outstanding stayer; she was the best horse on the day, though, and was at least as effective at a mile and a half as she was over further. Gold River had only three foals besides Riviere d'Or before she died in 1986, all of them by Northern Dancer or one of his sons, namely the smart French middle-distance colt Chercheur d'Or, the Poule d'Essai des Poulains runner-up Goldneyev, and the French mile-and-a-half winner Riviere d'Argent. For the record, Gold River is a daughter of Glaneuse, a half-sister to the One Thousand Guineas winner Gleam and a very good racemare herself as she showed when she won the Gran Premio del Jockey Club in Italy and the Prix Chloe and the Prix de Malleret in France.

Gold Splash (USA) (ch.f. Jan 23, 1990)	Blushing Groom (FR) (ch 1974)	Red God (ch 1954)	Nasrullah
			Spring Run
		Runaway Bride (b 1962)	Wild Risk
			Aimee
	Riviere d'Or (USA) (b 1985)	Lyphard (b 1969)	Northern Dancer
			Goofed
		Gold River (ch 1977)	Riverman
			Glaneuse

In the aftermath of Gold Splash's victory there was some talk that she may be sent over for the One Thousand Guineas. It wouldn't be wise to rule her out of the reckoning given the stable's excellent record in the race—they've won it with Hatoof, Ravinella and Ma Biche in the last ten years—but on what we've seen of her so far it's likely that she'll be better suited by a mile and a quarter. Gold Splash, who has raced only on good or soft ground, needs to make some improvement before she can be considered a genuine classic contender, but, then again, that much can be said about virtually all of her contemporaries. *Mme C. Head, France*

GOLD SURPRISE (IRE) 3 b. or br.g. Petorius 117 – Gold Piece (Golden **50** Fleece (USA) 133) [1991 NR 1992 a8g² 8s² 8v⁵ a8g] IR 38,000Y: smallish, workman-like gelding: moderate mover: first foal: dam unraced half-sister to Greenland Park (dam of Fitnah) and Red Sunset: modest maiden, not seen out until autumn: well beaten last 2 starts: will stay 1¼m: sold 3,600 gns Doncaster November Sales. *J. G. FitzGerald*

GOLD TASSEL 2 b.f. (Apr 26) Glint of Gold 128 – Nastassia (FR) (Noble Decree **68** (USA) 127) [1992 6.1m 7.1d⁴ 8.1s³ 8d 8.2g] small, leggy filly: easy mover: third foal: half-sister to Irish bumpers winner Gilt Dimension (by Dara Monarch): dam placed at up to 9.5f in France: fair maiden: looked to be progressing, but ran badly in Nottingham minor event final start: better suited by 1m than less: acts on soft going. *R. Hannon*

GOLDVEIN (SWE) 4 b.g. Superlative 118 – Follow Me Follow 92 (Wollow 132) **– §** [1991 6.1m² 6m³ 6m³ a6g⁶ a5g 1992 a7g a7g] neat, good-quartered gelding: quite modest maiden at 3 yrs: refused to race final start in 1992, in February: blinkered: has found little, and is not to be trusted. *W. A. O'Gorman*

GONDO 5 br.g. Mansingh (USA) 120 – Secret Valentine 71 (Wollow 132) [1991 **78** a7g 6d³ 6d4 6m* 6m4 6g 6m4 5.1d² 6.1g⁶ 6m4 5m⁶ 6m 6m⁵ 5.1m 5m4 5g* 6g² 5.2g 1992 5g4 6s 5d⁵ 5d² 6g 5m* 6d⁵ 5f4 5g 5f* 6.1d 5d 6g⁵ 5g³ 5m⁶ 5d² 6d4 5s³ 6.1s⁶ 5s 5g] compact gelding: poor mover: consistent handicapper on the whole, successful at Haydock in May and (awarded race on technicality) July: ran moderately last 2 starts: effective at 5f and 6f: acts on firm and soft going: effective with or without visor: effective forcing pace, or held up: below best for claimer in 1992. *E. J. Alston*

GONDOLIER 4 b.g. Slip Anchor 136 – Grimpola (GER) (Windwurf (GER)) [1991 **104** 12g⁵ 12m4 14m* 1992 14g 12.3m³ 16m4 20m* 22.2g² 15.9d 20m] rangy gelding: useful performer: put up thoroughly genuine displays at Royal Ascot when winning Ascot Stakes (made all) and neck second to Romany Rye in Queen Alexandra Stakes: tailed-off last in listed race at York (reportedly returned with irregular heartbeat) then well held in Goodwood Stakes (Handicap) in July: suited by thorough test of stamina: acts on good to firm ground. *H. R. A. Cecil*

GONE BUST (IRE) 3 gr.g. Aragon 118 – Ludovica (Bustino 136) [1991 5g⁴ 5d² 5m 7m a7g 1992 10m⁶] sparely-made gelding: poor maiden: not seen out after May: should stay 7f: acts on dead ground: below form blinkered. *R. F. Johnson Houghton* –

GONE FOR A SONG 2 b.g. (Mar 23) Aragon 118 – Trojan Melody (Troy 137) [1992 5g6] 2,200F, 7,200Y: workmanlike gelding: third foal: dam unraced: last in minor event at Thirsk in April. *M. W. Easterby* –

GONE PROSPECTING (USA) 2 b.c. (Mar 31) Gone West (USA) – Kalista 109 (Bellypha 130) [1992 5g 5v⁶ 6m⁴ 6d³ 5d 6.1m⁵ 8d⁴ 7.1s² 7g] $55,000Y: leggy, workmanlike colt: has a round action: third foal: half-brother to 1m winner Kempinski (by Valiyar) and Irish 1m/9f winner Equal Eloquence (by Top Ville): dam French 1m winner: sire (by Mr Prospector) won from 6f to 9f (Grade 1 event, very smart form): fair performer, easily best effort in nursery seventh outing: suited by 1m: hung right and carried head awkwardly once: sold to race in Trinidad. *R. Hannon* 77

GONE SAVAGE 4 b.g. Nomination 125 – Trwyn Cilan 89 (Import 127) [1991 6g⁶ 5.8m⁴ 5m 5.1g 8g 1992 6g⁴ 6f³ 6g 5f 5s* 5g² 5.2g 5d* 5.6m 5g* 5g³ 5.2s* 5g] strong, good-bodied gelding: carries condition: fairly useful handicapper: successful in 1992 at Sandown (3, including a claimer) and Newbury: effective at 5f to 6f: has form on firm ground but goes particularly well on an easy surface: below form when blinkered once: sometimes bandaged behind. *G. B. Balding* 94

GONG 3 b.f. Bustino 136 – Shannon Princess (Connaught 130) [1991 NR 1992 7d⁶ 10g 10m⁵ 12g² 10d* 10g⁵ 10s 10m 8g] rangy filly: ninth living foal: half-sister to several winners, including very useful middle-distance stayer Waterfield (by Le Moss) and fairly useful 1½m to 19f winner Fitzpatrick (by Oats): dam won over 1m and 1¼m in Ireland: mostly disappointing in handicaps after winning Sandown maiden in July: stays 1½m: acts on good to firm and dead ground: often makes the running. *P. T. Walwyn* 84

GOOD AS GOLD (IRE) 3 ch.f. Glint of Gold 128 – Salote (USA) 109 (Forli (ARG)) [1991 a8g⁴ 1992 a10g⁴ a10g⁶ 8m³] poor handicapper: effective at 1m to 1¼m: acts on equitrack and good to firm ground. *J. L. Spearing* 45

GOODBYE MAGGIE (IRE) 4 b.f. Thatching 131 – Glorious Fate (Northfields (USA)) [1991 a6g 7d² 8m⁶ 8.3g⁵ 8g 7.1d 7d⁴ 6m³ 7g⁶ 7m 6m 6m⁴ a8g 1992 a5g a7g⁵ a7g⁵] compact filly: moderate mover: poor maiden: stays 7f: acts on dead going: usually blinkered nowadays: tends to hang. *M. J. Fetherston-Godley* –

GOODBYE MILLIE 2 b. or br.f. (Mar 15) Sayf El Arab (USA) 127 – Leprechaun Lady 57 (Royal Blend 117) [1992 5.1m⁵ 6g² 6f* 5.1m⁴ 6d 7g 6m a7g⁶ a7g⁴ a8g6] angular filly: first live foal: dam stayer: odds on, won 3-runner maiden at Pontefract: below form at Southwell last 3 outings: probably stays 7f: visored final start. *S. G. Norton* 53

GOODBYE MR MARKS (IRE) 4 b.c. On Your Mark 125 – Ciao (Mandamus 120) [1991 a5g³ 5s² 1992 5m 7.1m] big, workmanlike colt: well beaten in 1992: stays 6f: best efforts on fibresand. *N. Bycroft* –

GOOD FOR A LOAN 5 b.g. Daring March 116 – Game For A Laugh 72 (Martinmas 128) [1991 10g 10m 1992 14.1d⁵ 12g² 11.8d³ 12d* 12m⁴ 14.6m⁶ 11.7d³ 10.5d] well-made gelding: moderate walker and mover: modest handicapper: won (for first time) at Kempton in June: seems to stay 1¾m: acts on good to firm and dead ground: well beaten for amateur, and seems to need a forceful ride. *R. Lee* 68

Ascot Stakes—the extra distance suits Gondolier; he gallops on relentlessly to beat Requested (right) and Crystal Spirit

GOOD FOR THE ROSES 6 b.g. Kampala 120 – Alleyn (Alcide 136) [1991 **52** 8.2d* 8m 1992 8.2m³ 8.2d 9g 8s* 8.2s² a8g⁴ a8g] leggy gelding: has a round action: modest performer: revitalised in handicaps after joining present trainer (with C. Cox previously) winning gamely at Pontefract: best form at 1m but may stay further: acts on any going. *M. McCormack*

GOOD HAND (USA) 6 ch.g. Northjet 136 – Ribonette (USA) (Ribot 142) [1991 **87** 16m⁵ 18.4d 18f⁴ 20g³ 16.1m 20g³ 16.2f³ 17.5m⁵ 18m 1992 16d* 18.5g 18f² 20m⁴ 18.5d⁴ 20m³ 16.2s 15s⁵ 16.1s⁴ 14.6g⁶] close-coupled, sparely-made gelding: fairly useful out-and-out staying handicapper, successful in £7,400 event at Ripon in April: unsuited by soft ground, acts on firm: below form blinkered/visored: not easiest of rides. *J. W. Watts*

GOOD IMAGE 2 b.c. (Apr 7) Farajullah 113 – Fleur de Foret (USA) 61§ (Green **55** Forest (USA) 134) [1992 6m³ 7g⁵ 6.1m² 5.2g³ 5g 6m] small, compact colt: good mover: first foal: dam, sprint maiden, became ungenuine at 3 yrs: inconsistent plater: best effort at 6f. *A. P. Jarvis*

GOODNITEOUT (IRE) 3 b.f. Dance of Life (USA) – Schweppes Forever 112 **79** (Lord Gayle (USA) 124) [1991 6f 7g³ 7d⁴ 1992 7g² 10d² 10.2f³] rather leggy filly: fair maiden: will stay 1½m: acts on dead ground, seems unsuited by firm: sold 8,400 gns Newmarket Autumn Sales. *D. R. C. Elsworth*

GOOD OLD GEORGE (IRE) 3 ch.c. Muscatite 122 – Tolaytala (Be My Guest – (USA) 126) [1991 5s² 5g 7g 6d⁵ 8m 1992 10.2s 10.8s 14.1s] workmanlike colt: no form in 1992. *M. J. Fetherston-Godley*

GOOD REFERENCE (IRE) 3 br.f. Reference Point 139 – Impudent Miss 105 **84** (Persian Bold 123) [1991 7g³ 7f* 7m 7m 1992 8g* 10m⁶ 11.9f6 10f⁴ 8m 10m] lengthy filly: good walker: fairly useful handicapper: awarded race at Newmarket in May: below form last 2 starts: stays 1¼m (stiff task at 11.9f): acts on firm going: sometimes bandaged. *M. Bell*

GOOD TIME BOY 4 b.g. Good Times (ITY) – Galetzky 86 (Radetzky 123) [1991 – 8g 7m⁵ a8g 8g 8.1s a8g 1992 a7g] lengthy, rather angular gelding: on the downgrade: sold 900 gns Doncaster January Sales. *M. Brittain*

GOOD TO DANCE (IRE) 3 b.f. Groom Dancer (USA) 128 – Good To Beat 114 **115** (Hard To Beat 132) [1991 8g⁵ 8d⁵ 10s* 1992 10.5g³ 10g⁶ 10.5g 12.5s² 12f²] won maiden at Deauville as a 2-y-o by 8 lengths: very useful form in 1992, second in Prix de Royallieu at Longchamp (beaten a nose by Fabulous Hostess) and very valuable handicap at Gulfstream Park in the autumn: stays 1½m: acts on any going. *A. Fabre, France*

GOODY FOUR SHOES 4 gr.f. Blazing Saddles (AUS) – Bronzamer 86 (Sari- **49** tamer (USA) 130) [1991 5.1g⁶ 5d⁴ 5.2f⁵ 5m 1992 a6g a6g a6g 5d 5.3m 5.7m 6d 6.1g 6g 5.7f 5g 6s* 5d⁵] leggy, close-coupled filly: poor mover: inconsistent handicapper: won at Folkestone (apprentices) in October: will prove as effective over 7f as 6f: probably acts on any going. *D. R. Tucker*

GOOFALIK (USA) 5 b. or br.h. Lyphard (USA) 132 – Alik (FR) 113 (Targowice **116** (USA) 130) [1991 10g² 8d* 7g³ 9.5f³ 10g* 8d² 10s³ 1992 8v³ 8m 8s⁵ 10g* 10d⁵ 10g³] smallish, good-topped horse: smart and tough French performer: narrowly beat Tel Quel in Group 3 Grand Prix de Vichy in July: below best in Group 3 races at Goodwood and Hoppegarten subsequently: effective at 7f to 1¼m: acts on any going. *J. E. Hammond, France*

GOOGLY 3 ch.f. Sunley Builds 102 – Cheri Berry 87 (Air Trooper 115) [1991 5d **79** 5.7m⁴ 7f 6g 7.1d 6g 6s a6g 1992 7d 9.7g* 9g* 8m 9m³ 10g⁴ 10s² 10s* 12d² 9g² 11.9d* 12g²] leggy filly: moderate mover: had very good season and progressed really well in handicaps: successful at Folkestone, Kempton, Salisbury and Haydock: stays 1½m: acts on good to firm and soft ground: sometimes hangs and carries head awkwardly: a credit to her trainer. *W. G. R. Wightman*

GO ORANGE 2 ch.f. (Jan 16) Norwick (USA) 120 – Langton Herring (Nearly A – Hand 115) [1992 5.1g 5.7f 7.1g 6g 5.9g⁶ 8.2d 6d] lengthy filly: moderate mover: sister to 3-y-o 5f winner Miss Vaxette and 1m (at 2 yrs) and 9f winner San Pier Niceto and half-sister to 2 winners, including useful but untrustworthy Sylvan Breeze (by Sulaafah): dam unraced half-sister to very smart Sylvan Barbarosa: little worthwhile form, including in sellers: tried blinkered/visored: retained 1,050 gns Newmarket Autumn Sales. *J. L. Spearing*

GORINSKY (IRE) 4 ch.g. Gorytus (USA) 132 – Grapette (Nebbiolo 125) [1991 **76** 6m⁴ 6g² 6g 5g a6g² 6g⁴ 6m 6g⁵ 6m² 6.1d a6g² 1992 a5g⁵ a5g² a6g⁴ a6g² 5d⁴ 6g⁴ 6d⁴ 5f⁵ 5m⁵ 6g² 6g³ 6d 6d] sturdy gelding: has a quick action: fair handicapper: effective at 5f and 6f: acts on any ground, including all-weather surfaces: effective blinkered or not: front runner. *J. Berry*

GORODENKA BOY 2 ch.c. (Jan 24) Then Again 126 – Simply Jane (Sharpen Up 127) [1992 5g 5d⁵ 5f⁵ a6g⁵ a5g⁴ a5g] 4,000Y: leggy, close-coupled colt: half-brother to 2 winners, including very speedy Jondebe Boy (by John de Coombe): dam never ran: modest maiden: best efforts on all-weather surfaces: very mulish in preliminaries and withdrawn once. *Mrs J. Jordan* **53**

GORYTUS STAR 6 ch.g. Gorytus (USA) 132 – Bean Siamsa (Solinus 130) [1991 NR 1992 a7g⁵ a6g⁶ a7g⁵ 6v] close-coupled gelding: poor handicapper: stays 7f: acts on equitrack. *D. Haydn Jones* **53**

GO SOUTH 8 b.g. Thatching 131 – Run To The Sun (Run The Gantlet (USA)) [1991 14m 18d³ 18.4d⁴ 14m 20g⁶ 17.2g⁵ 16d² 18.5g* 16.2g⁶ 16.2g⁴ 18m* 16.5d⁴ 1992 16d* 18.5g 20m 15.9m⁵ 16.4s 18.8m⁵ 16s⁵ 20m 16.2s 16g³ 16.2s⁴ 18m 16.5g a16g a16g] sturdy gelding: moderate mover: thoroughly unreliable handicapper: won at Newbury in April: needs good test of stamina: probably acts on any going: below form when visored once, usually blinkered: sometimes drops himself out and takes little interest. *J. R. Jenkins* **76 d**

GO TALLY-HO 4 b.f. Gorytus (USA) 132 – Brush Away (Ahonoora 122) [1991 6f⁵ 6m 12f 6d 8m 8h 7m 1992 8.3v 8d] sparely-made filly: poor maiden: stays 6f: acts on good to firm ground: below form blinkered/visored. *J. J. O'Neill* **–**

GOTCHA (BAR) 3 br.c. Bentom (USA) 98 – Hotcha 70 (Hotfoot 126) [1991 7g⁵ 7.1s* 1992 7m* 8.9g² 8g⁵ 8.9g 8f 10d² 10.1d 8g 8.9d 8m] sturdy, good-quartered colt: mostly disappointing in handicaps after winning minor event at Brighton in April: probably needs further than 1m: acts on good to firm ground and soft: effective blinkered or not: unsatisfactory: has been returned to Barbados. *R. Hannon* **79 §**

GOTT'S DESIRE 6 ch.g. Sweet Monday 122 – Steel Lady 60 (Continuation 120) [1991 7f 7m 9.9f 7m 7.6m² 7.5f³ 7m* 7g 7m 7s⁶ 1992 7g a6g 7f 7f 7f⁵ 7g 7s⁶ 7d] angular gelding: rated 51 at 5 yrs: below form in handicaps in 1992: keen sort, best at around 7f: has gone well on top-of-the-ground: below form visored. *R. Bastiman* **–**

GOVERNOR'S IMP (USA) 3 b.c. Imp Society (USA) – Lady Limbo (USA) (Dance Spell (USA)) [1991 5g³ 5m³ 6g* 6m² 7g² 7g³ 8s⁴ 8s² 10v 1992 8m⁶] lengthy, good-quartered colt: rated 105 at 2 yrs: well beaten in Kempton listed race in May, 1992: best form at 1m: had form on good to firm, but best form on soft: dead. *M. Bell* **–**

GRAB SUNDAY SPORT 2 b.c. (Jan 29) Full Extent (USA) 113 – Siconda 66 (Record Token 128) [1992 5m 5g⁶ 6s 5.3d⁵] 3,900Y, 6,800 2-y-o: workmanlike colt: fifth foal: dam won two 9f sellers: poor maiden: blinkered final start: sold 660 gns Newmarket Autumn Sales. *Miss Gay Kelleway* **–**

GRACE CARD 6 b.g. Ela-Mana-Mou 132 – Val de Grace (FR) (Val de Loir 133) [1991 14.6s 16.2g 21.6f 1992 16.9g6] lengthy, workmanlike gelding: maiden handicapper on flat: not seen out after May: suited by thorough test of stamina: acts on good to firm ground: useful and progressive hurdler, unbeaten in 5 races to end of year. *Mrs M. Reveley* **–**

GRACELAND LADY (IRE) 4 b.f. Kafu 120 – Theda 61 (Mummy's Pet 125) [1991 5m 7g 6m 5d 6f⁵ 5g 1992 8m a6g] tall, leggy filly: poor mover: of little account. *Mrs S. M. Austin* **–**

GRADIENT 2 b.c. (Feb 7) Shirley Heights 130 – Grimpola (GER) (Windwurf (GER)) [1992 8m 8d] lengthy colt: fourth foal: brother to 8.2f (at 2 yrs) and 10.1f winner Golan Heights and closely related to out-and-out staying 4-y-o Gondolier (by Slip Anchor): dam won at 6f and 1m in Germany and stayed 1½m: green and behind in large-field maidens won by Armiger at Newmarket and Dyab at Leicester in late-season: will be suited by 1½m: has scope, and sure to do better. *Mrs J. Cecil* **58 p**

GRANACHE (IRE) 3 br.c. Rousillon (USA) 133 – Mpani 97 (Habitat 134) [1991 NR 1992 11.7s] sturdy colt: third foal: dam 1¼m winner out of Cheshire Oaks and Park Hill winner African Dancer, a good family: tailed off in maiden at Bath in May. *M. R. Channon* **–**

GRAND APPLAUSE (IRE) 2 gr.c. (Apr 21) Mazaad 106 – Standing Ovation (Godswalk (USA) 130) [1992 5.2d⁶ 7d⁶ 8.1s 8m 8s³ 8s⁶] 6,000Y: leggy, angular colt, rather unfurnished: moderate walker and mover: sixth foal: brother to Irish 1¼m winner/winning hurdler Crowded House and half-brother to 1989 2-y-o 7f winner Go Holimarine (by Taufan): dam Irish 1½m winner: fair maiden, easily best effort fourth outing: stays 1m: acts on top-of-the-ground. *R. Simpson* **70**

GRAND AS OWT 2 b.g. (Mar 15) Nomination 125 – Young Diana (Young Generation 129) [1992 7.1m 7d³ 7g 8m⁶] 7,500F, 7,000Y, resold 4,000Y, 1,500 2-y-o: **61**

strong, lengthy gelding: moderate mover: fourth foal: closely related to a plating-class maiden by Dominion and half-brother to 3-y-o True Contender (by Never So Bold): dam unraced half-sister to very smart middle-distance performer Town And Country: form in maidens only when third at Ayr in July. *Denys Smith*

GRAND BAIE 2 b.c. (May 3) Interrex (CAN) – Fuchsia 66 (Hot Spark 126) [1992 –
5f] 1,400F, 650Y, 20,000 2-y-o: stocky colt: third foal: dam maiden suited by 6f: sire (closely related to Secreto) won from 1m to 9.5f: last in maiden auction at Salisbury in June: dead. *S. Dow*

GRAND DANCER (IRE) 2 gr.f. (Mar 5) Fairy King (USA) – Perbury 88 66
(Grisaille 115) [1992 5g 6s* 6f* 6d² 6m⁴ 6g³ 5.2d 5m³ a5s³ 5g⁴ 7s² 8.9s³] IR 5,000F, 6,000Y: close-coupled, unfurnished filly: closely related to 2 winners by Viking, including 7.6f winner Tobago Dancer, and half-sister to 3 winners, including fair 1988 2-y-o 1¼m winner Musafira (by What A Guest): dam 2-y-o 7f winner: consistent performer: made all in sellers at Lingfield and Warwick in May: stays 9f: probably acts on any going: effective with or without blinkers: sold 6,200 gns Newmarket Autumn Sales. *R. J. R. Williams*

GRANDERISE (IRE) 2 b.g. (Jan 15) Digamist (USA) 110 – Miss Morgan –
(Native Prince) [1992 7g] IR 8,200F, 1,000Y: good-topped gelding: half-brother to several winners, including fair middle-distance performer Logamimo (by Lord Gayle), also prolific winner over jumps: dam unraced half-sister to dam of Gay Lemur: backward and always behind in maiden auction at Doncaster in July. *N. Tinkler*

GRAND FELLOW (IRE) 3 br.g. Thatching 131 – Concave (Connaught 130) 59
[1991 6.1m 1992 7s³ 8g 7.6s a7g a8g a7g³ 6g a7g⁴ 7g 8s a8g] angular, close-coupled gelding: moderate mover: inconsistent handicapper: should stay 1m: acts on soft ground and equitrack: usually visored/blinkered: sold to join A. Forte 2,700 gns Doncaster November Sales. *J. D. Bethell*

GRAND GAME 2 b.c. (Feb 15) Mummy's Game 120 – Grand Espoir 50 (Ken- –
mare (FR) 125) [1992 5.1d 5g a5g 7g] 1,500Y: unfurnished colt: first foal: dam stayed 1½m: well beaten in poor company: tried visored. *D. Haydn Jones*

GRAND GUIGNOL (IRE) 4 ch.g. Superlative 118 – Boule de Suif 88 (Major Portion 70
129) [1991 6f a7g² a7g* 7m⁵ 6f 7.6m a7g 7m⁵ 7m* 8g a7g 1992 a7g² a7g² 7g 6s⁵] workmanlike gelding: ran well in Southwell handicaps in early 1992, fairly well on final start (April): stays 7f: acts on good to firm and soft ground and fibresand: suitable mount for claimer: below form blinkered. *G. Wragg*

GRAND HAWK (USA) 4 b.g. Silver Hawk (USA) 123 – Ginger Lass (USA) 114 80
(Elocutionist (USA)) [1991 8m 8f⁴ 7.9m² 1992 10m⁶ 12g⁵ 10m 13.9m] sturdy gelding: below form in handicaps in 1992 after first run: should stay 1½m: acts on good to firm ground: effective blinkered or not: joined M. Pipe and made all in 2 novice hurdles in November. *M. Moubarak*

GRAND HONDA (IRE) 3 b.g. Lomond (USA) 128 – Braneakins (Sallust 134) –
[1991 NR 1992 8g⁴ 10d⁵ 10s] 32,000Y: lengthy gelding: third living foal: closely related to very useful but untrustworthy 1m (at 2 yrs) and 1½m winner Peking Opera (by Sadler's Wells): dam Irish 1½m winner, is half-sister to Park Appeal, Desirable (dam of Shadayid) and Alydaress: well beaten in maidens: sold 4,300 gns Newmarket Autumn Sales. *C. E. Brittain*

GRAND MASTER (IRE) 3 b.c. Sadler's Wells (USA) 132 – Lady's Bridge 97
(USA) 81 (Sir Ivor 135) [1991 7f³ 8m² 8d⁵ 10m² 10v⁴ 1992 12f² 11.7m* 13.1g³ 9d* 8.5d* 9d] big, strong, lengthy colt: moderate mover: had good season in 1992, winning maiden at Bath and handicaps at Sandown and Epsom: effective at 8.5f, and stays 1½m: acts on any going: effective blinkered or not: effective held up or forcing pace: joined N. Drysdale, USA. *P. F. I. Cole*

GRAND PLAISIR (IRE) 3 b.c. Darshaan 133 – Tapage Nocturne (USA) (Irish 111
River (FR) 131) [1991 NR 1992 10s* 11g* 12g] 650,000 francs (approx £64,700) Y: first known foal: dam, placed at 3 yrs in France, is sister to a non-graded stakes winner in USA: lightly-raced French colt: won minor event at Maisons-Laffitte in March and Group 2 Prix Noailles (by 1½ lengths from Modhish) in April: dropped out quickly in straight and virtually pulled up in Prix du Jockey-Club at Chantilly in June: should stay 1½m. *J. C. Cunnington, France*

GRAND PRIX 7 b.h. Formidable (USA) 125 – Mumruffin 101 (Mummy's Pet 125) –
[1991 6g* 6m⁵ 6m 5g⁶ 6g 6f² 6g 6m 1992 6g⁶ 6f 5g⁶ 6m 5.1f] neat, good-bodied horse: moderate mover: rated 91 at 6 yrs: below form in sprint handicaps in 1992: best form on top-of-the-ground: often sweating/edgy: often starts slowly: sold only 2,400 gns Newmarket Autumn Sales. *D. R. C. Elsworth*

GRAND TIME   3 ch.c. Clantime 101 – Panay 77 (Arch Sculptor 123) [1991 5d*   –
5d³ 5f* 5g² 5.7g 5d a7g 1992 a6g⁶ a5g* a6g² 5v 5.1d 5.7f 6g 5.7d 5m 5.1g a5g a5g] a57
neat colt: modest handicapper: won at Southwell in February: not disgraced
penultimate start: stays 6f: acts on firm and dead ground. *C. J. Hill*

GRAND VITESSE (IRE)   3 b.c. Alzao (USA) 117 – Au Revoir 79 (Ballymoss   **82**
136) [1991 6g⁶ 6f⁴ 7f* 1992 10d 8g* 8m⁶ 8g 8m⁴ 8.3g 9d 8s*] smallish, sturdy colt:
fair handicapper: made all at Goodwood in May and October: will prove suited by
further than 1m (burly over 1¼m): acts on any going: well below form when
blinkered once. *R. Hannon*

GRANITE BOY   3 b.c. Music Boy 124 – Jouvencelle 68 (Rusticaro (FR) 124) [1991   **63**
6g 5m 6m⁴ 7g 6m a8g a7g³ a8g³ 1992 a7g⁵ a10g⁴ a10g² a8g*] strong, attractive colt:
consistent performer: not seen out again after easily winning maiden at Lingfield in
March: stays 1¼m: acts on all-weather surfaces: below form blinkered. *P. J. Feilden*

GRANNY MC   5 br.m. Sparkling Boy 110 – Marcus Miss (Marcus Superbus 100)   **60**
[1991 7m⁴ 12.3d 10.3d a6g 6f⁴ 7.1m⁵ 6g 6g² 6d 7.1m 1992 6v 7m⁴ 6f* 7m 5.9h* 6m²
6f³ 6m] big, plain, workmanlike mare: largely consistent handicapper: successful at
Redcar (amateurs) in May and Carlisle in June: effective at 6f to 7f: acts on hard
ground, possibly unsuited by soft surface. *E. J. Alston*

GRAN SENORUM (USA)   2 ch.c. (Jan 20) El Gran Senor (USA) 136 – Sanctum   **71** p
Sanctorum (USA) (Secretariat (USA)) [1992 6g³] smallish, sturdy, quite attractive
colt: eighth foal: half-brother to several winners here and in USA, including 7-y-o
Gulf Palace (by Green Dancer), successful at 1¼m and 1½m: dam, minor winner in
USA, is closely related to a good stakes winner and half-sister to 2 others: 8/1, burly
and green, under 4 lengths third of 8 in maiden at Ascot in late-July, unable to
quicken last 2f: looks sure to improve, particularly over further. *P. F. I. Cole*

GREAT ABSALOM   3 gr.c. Absalom 128 – Sallytude (Tudor Music 131) [1991   –
5f⁵ 5h 7.5f 1992 9.9g³ a12g] leggy colt: no worthwhile form: should stay 1m. *J. S.
Wainwright*

GREAT DIPLOMAT (IRE)   2 b.g. (Apr 15) Simply Great (FR) 122 – Pete's   **68**
Money (USA) (Caucasus (USA) 127) [1992 6g² 6g* 6f⁵] IR 7,000Y: good-topped
gelding: sixth foal: half-brother to 3 winners here and abroad, including 6f/7f
performer Corrin Hill (by Petorius): dam unraced: runner-up in Curragh maiden
before comfortably winning similar event at Fairyhouse in May: beaten 2f out when
creditable fifth of 6 in Chesham Stakes at Royal Ascot following month: will stay 1m.
P. J. Prendergast, Ireland

GREATEST OF ALL (IRE)   4 ch.f. Ela-Mana-Mou 132 – Red Jade 82 (Red   –
God 128§) [1991 8.3m 7m³ 6.9m⁴ 8.9g 8.9m 6m 1992 7f 6m⁵ a10g] tall, leggy, plain
filly: no form in handicaps in 1992: stays 7f: acts on good to firm ground: trained until
after penultimate start by R. Hannon. *D. J. S. Cosgrove*

GREAT HALL   3 gr.g. Hallgate 127 – Lily of France 81 (Monsanto (FR) 121) [1991   **41**
5.7m⁶ 5.3m² 5m 6f⁵ 5m 7g 7g 5.7g a6g⁶ 6s a8g⁵ a7g⁵ 1992 a7g a6g a6g* 6v 7f⁴ 10g 8f a53
7g⁵ 7d 7g⁴ 7.1g⁶ 8d a7g] compact gelding: carries condition: moderate mover:
inconsistent handicapper: won maiden at Lingfield in March: stays 7f: best efforts
on a sound surface or equitrack: often blinkered: below form when visored once:
sold out of W. Wightman's stable 950 gns Ascot March Sales after fourth start. *P. D.
Cundell*

GREAT IMPOSTOR   4 ch.g. Vaigly Great 127 – Lady Waverton (Huntercombe   **50** d
133) [1991 7f 8m³ a10g⁶ 1992 a8g⁶ a8g⁶ 9.7v² 10d 12.3g a10g⁵ 10.2f⁶ 10m² 10.2g
11.5m] close-coupled gelding: poor maiden: sold out of P. Walwyn's stable 4,000 gns
Ascot March Sales (after third start): little form on turf after: stays 1¼m: acts on
good to firm and heavy ground and fibresand: effective blinkered or not. *R. J. Hodges*

GREAT LORD (IRE)   3 b.g. Last Tycoon 131 – Mummy's Favourite 104   **63** §
(Mummy's Pet 125) [1991 6g⁵ 6g⁴ 7m⁵ 7m⁴ 7g⁶ 1992 6f⁶ 6m 6m 8h* 8g³ 10g⁶ 8m
8g⁶] tall, leggy, close-coupled gelding: modest handicapper: won at Carlisle in June:
ideally suited by 1m: acts on hard ground: below form visored: looked ungenuine on
occasions. *J. W. Watts*

GREAT MARQUESS   5 b.h. Touching Wood (USA) 127 – Fruition 89 (Rhein- **106**
gold 137) [1991 14g⁶ 16m 15.9m* 16g² 15g 18m* 14d⁶ 1992 15s⁴ 16g² 22.2g³ 14g²
16s² 20s⁵] close-coupled horse: carries plenty of condition: has quick action: rated
115 (won Doncaster Cup) as 4-y-o for H. Cecil: not so good in 1992, runner-up in
Group 3 race and listed events at Baden-Baden and in well-contested minor event at
Vichy in between: beaten early in straight when 15 lengths third to Romany Rye in
Queen Alexandra Stakes at Royal Ascot: better at around 2m than shorter, and stays
2¼m: probably acts on any going: sometimes blinkered. *J. Pease, France*

GREAT MASHHOR 2 b.g. (Jan 31) Mashhor Dancer (USA) – Celtic Sonata   –
(Music Boy 124) [1992 5g 5g 6f 6f] 3,400Y: angular gelding: has a round action: third
foal: half-brother to 1990 2-y-o 6f winner Gaelic Chief (by Lidhame): dam ran once:
soundly beaten in modest company: visored final start: sold 600 gns Doncaster
August Sales. *J. S. Wainwright*

GREAT MAX (IRE) 3 b. or br.g. Simply Great (FR) 122 – Lockwood Girl 81   **73**
(Prince Tenderfoot (USA) 126) [1991 a7g6 8f 8f5 1992 11.1f 10m* 10d* 11.1f2 11f6
12d2] leggy, lengthy gelding: fair handicapper: won at Nottingham in June and July:
effective at 1¼m to 1½m: acts on firm and dead ground: retained 7,600 gns
Doncaster January Sales, sold to join M. Jarvis' stable 23,000 gns Newmarket September Sales. *Sir Mark Prescott*

GREAT MUSIC 4 ch.g. Music Boy 124 – Amadina 96 (Great Nephew 126) [1991   –
6d 5m 6f 8m 7g 7m 7.5f 6g 1992 a8g] robust gelding: has a round action: on the
downgrade: retained 1,400 gns Doncaster October Sales. *J. S. Wainwright*

GREAT NORTH ROAD 3 ch.g. Night Shift (USA) – Tactless 91 (Romulus 129)   –
[1991 NR 1992 8d6 a12g] 7,000F: half-brother to several winners, including very
useful Padro (by Runnymede), successful at up to 7f: dam won at 1¼m: tailed off in
Carlisle maiden for D. Smith in May and Southwell claimer in November. *Pat
Mitchell*

GREAT ORATION (IRE) 3 b. or br.c. Simply Great (FR) 122 – Spun Gold 106   –
(Thatch (USA) 136) [1991 8m6 8m 1992 12.2g6] rather leggy colt: has a round action:
tailed off in seller in April: should stay middle distances: sold 1,600 gns Doncaster
October Sales. *F. Watson*

GREAT PALM (USA) 3 gr.c. Manila (USA) – Hat Tab Girl (USA) (Al **114**
Hattab (USA)) [1991 6g* 7m2 1992 10.4m2 12g 10g2 10s* 10d6]
    Entering the straight for the Derby, glory beckoned again for owner
Fahd Salman, trainer Paul Cole and jockey Alan Munro. The connections of
Generous were this time represented by Great Palm who, having raced in
third place from well over a mile out, now moved into second, just as Generous had done twelve months earlier. Both colts started among the market
leaders at Epsom having first been propelled into the classic reckoning by
their performances in the Dewhurst Stakes the previous October—Great
Palm finishing runner-up on only his second start—and had one previous run
as a three-year-old. Great Palm's was in the Dante Stakes at York before
which, having been held up in his training by an overreach, he looked in need
of the race but impressed with the physical progress he'd made from two to
three. He caught the eye in the race as well as, having been flat-footed when
Alnasr Alwasheek stepped up the pace three furlongs out, Great Palm was
keeping on very strongly at the death to finish second of seven, a performance
which many considered the most promising Derby trial on the day, and one
of the best all told. On Derby Day, nothing in Great Palm's appearance

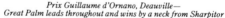

Prix Guillaume d'Ornano, Deauville—
Great Palm leads throughout and wins by a neck from Sharpitor

beforehand or in the way he travelled through three quarters of the race contradicted that view. From the three-furlong marker, however, it all looked very different; whereas Generous had sprinted clear, Great Palm was soon made to look very one paced. He eventually finished eighth of eighteen, beaten about eleven and a half lengths.

It was asking a great deal for Great Palm to be another Generous, of course, but Great Palm's performance against the best of his own generation in the Derby was disappointing. There is the possibility that he did not stay, but the chief reason for his failure is that he was not good enough. On his next two starts, Great Palm restored his reputation somewhat, proving himself a smart colt, notably when winning the eight-runner Prix Guillaume d'Ornano (reduced to the seven-runner Prix Guillaume d'Ornano when Adieu Au Roi dug his toes in as the stalls opened) at Deauville. Fresh from a half-length second to Pollen Count in another Group 2 mile-and-a-quarter race, the Prix Eugene Adam at Saint-Cloud, Great Palm started third favourite behind the St James's Palace runner-up Zaahi with his other opponents including Fast Cure who had finished only a head behind him at Saint-Cloud. With more testing conditions and Munro setting out to make all, Great Palm easily confirmed those placings though he still got home by only a neck, the persistent challenge of Scottish Classic winner Sharpitor requiring a gutsy response after Zaahi had looked the chief danger approaching the final furlong. If his season had ended there we might well once more have been predicting better things from Great Palm. He was given another chance to prove what he was capable of in 1992, however, and failed the test badly; he took up the running before halfway in the Irish Champion Stakes at Leopardstown but was readily left behind in the straight, finishing tailed off.

		⌠Lyphard	⌠Northern Dancer
	⌠Manila (USA)	⟨ (b 1969)	⟨ Goofed
	⟨ (b 1983)	⌊Dona Ysidra	⌊Le Fabuleux
Great Palm (USA)	⟨	(b 1975)	⌠Matriarch
(gr.c. 1989)	⟨	⌠Al Hattab	⌊The Axe II
	⌊Hat Tab Girl (USA)	⟨ (ro 1966)	⌠Abyssinia
	(b 1979)	⌊Desperate Action	⌊Bold Commander
		(b 1971)	⌊Crafty Alice

A return to a mile and a half will probably improve Great Palm's prospects in 1993. A big, rangy colt, he has a smooth long-striding action and acts on both good to firm ground and soft, never having encountered anything more extreme. Great Palm is the sixth foal out of the stakes winner Hat Tab Girl, easily the best of the rest being Black Tie Affair (by Miswaki) who was in his first season at stud in 1992 after four on the racecourse which brought connections over 3,300,000 dollars in prize money. Formerly campaigned as a sprinter, Black Tie Affair stayed a mile and a quarter as a five-year-old, and after winning the Breeders' Cup Classic, his final start, he was named Horse of the Year. *P. F. I. Cole*

GREAT SERVICE 5 ch.g. Vaigly Great 127 – Janlarmar 69 (Habat 127) [1991 10.2s 10f 10.5d² 1992 8.3v 8d 8.3s 12.1g] angular gelding: has a rather round action: no worthwhile form in 1992: stays 11f: acts on heavy ground, below form when blinkered: hard ride. *M. Dods* —

GREAT SPLENDOUR 3 b.f. Pharly (FR) 130 – Lost Splendour (USA) (Vaguely Noble 140) [1991 NR 1992 7d⁵ 8d 8d] well-made filly: half-sister to several winners, including 4-y-o Desert Splendour (by Green Desert), fairly useful 7f winner at 2 yrs, and 1m and 1¼m winner Count Nulin (by Pas de Seul): dam unraced daughter of Roussalka, a half-sister to Oh So Sharp: well beaten in maidens and minor event in autumn: visits Anshan. *C. E. Brittain* —

GREAT STEPS 2 ch.f. (Feb 27) Vaigly Great 127 – Step You Gaily 71 (King's Company 124) [1992 7f² 7s* 7s*] big, lengthy, workmanlike filly: sister to 6-y-o 6f to 1½m winner Vague Dancer and half-sister to several winners here and abroad: dam best at 2 yrs when placed at 8.2f: progressive filly: won maiden at Redcar and 3-runner minor event (by ½ length from Black Mischief, making all) at York in autumn: will be suited by 1m: plenty of scope, and should do well at 3 yrs. *E. Weymes* **88** p

GRECIAN BELLE 3 b.f. Ilium 121 – Bourbon Queen 77 (Ile de Bourbon (USA) 133) [1991 5.1g 7m 7m 1992 10f 9.7d⁶ 7m⁵ 8g³] robust filly: poor maiden: stays 1m: acts on good to firm ground. *D. A. Wilson* **36**

GREEK CHIME (IRE)   3 gr.c. Bellypha 130 – Corinth Canal 77 (Troy 137)   **66**
[1991 8d⁶ 1992 10m 10s⁶ 12g³ 12m* 14g 12m⁶] angular, workmanlike colt: third foal:
half-brother to 12.5f winner Sea War (by Gorytus): dam once-raced sister to Helen
Street: well beaten after gamely winning claimer at Thirsk in September: should
stay 1¾m: acts on good to firm and soft ground: sold 11,500 gns Newmarket Autumn
Sales. *Lord Huntingdon*

GREEK GOLD (IRE)   3 b.g. Rainbow Quest (USA) 134 – Gay Hellene 111   **83**
(Ela-Mana-Mou 132) [1991 NR 1992 10f⁴ 10.5d² 10.3g* 12g⁶ 10s] leggy gelding:
second foal: half-brother to unreliable stayer Gay Glint (by Glint of Gold): dam 1¼m
and 10.5f winner, is daughter of Irish 1000 Guineas winner Gaily: won maiden at
Chester in July: well beaten in quite valuable handicaps after, reportedly lame first
time: should be better suited by 1½m than 1¼m: acts on firm and dead ground: has
been gelded and remains in training. *M. R. Stoute*

GREEK TYCOON (IRE)   3 b.c. Last Tycoon 131 – Praise (FR) 116 (Hard To   **90**
Beat 132) [1991 7f² 1992 11d²] big, lengthy, good-topped colt: twice raced, not seen
out after second in Newbury maiden (swished tail and hung left) in April: seems
lazy: will be suited by further. *P. F. I. Cole*

GREENBANK (USA)   2 b.g. (Mar 15) Trempolino (USA) 135 – Green Boundary   **50** p
(USA) (Robellino (USA) 127) [1992 7s] $61,000Y: leggy, unfurnished gelding:
second foal: dam graded stakes-placed winner at up to 9f: not knocked about once
outpaced last 2f when seventh of 16 in maiden at Salisbury in September: will
improve. *I. A. Balding*

GREEN CHILI   2 ch.f. (Mar 20) Chilibang 120 – Deja Vu (FR) (Be My Guest   **45** p
(USA) 126) [1992 6s] 1,900Y: good-bodied filly: fifth foal: half-sister to 3-y-o 7f to
1¼m winner Jade Vale (by Petorius) and poor 1¾m winner Windward Ariom (by Pas
de Seul): dam won at up to 12.5f in France: burly and never dangerous, swishing tail,
in maiden at Newbury in October: will improve. *J. W. Hills*

GREEN DOLLAR   9 b.g. Tickled Pink 114 – Burglars Girl 63 (Burglar 128) [1991   **96**
6d 6.1m 6f* 6m* 6d² 6m 6d⁶ 6m² 6g 6f⁴ 6m⁴ 6g 5f⁴ 6g* 6m⁴ 1992 5g⁶ 6g* 6g 6g 6g⁶
6d² 6f 6f² 6.1d⁵ 6m 6f⁶ 7m⁶ 6g 6g* 6d 7.1s⁵ 7.6d⁵ 6g⁵ 5d 7m] smallish, strong
gelding: useful handicapper: successful at Newmarket in April and Ripon (Great St
Wilfrid) in August: effective at around 6f to 7f: acts on firm ground and dead: below
form in blinkers and visor, successful for claimer: 5 times a winner at Brighton:
tough and genuine: held up. *E. A. Wheeler*

GREEN FLOWER (USA)   3 b.f. Fappiano (USA) – Ecstacism (USA) (What A   **56**
Pleasure (USA)) [1991 NR 1992 10g 12.2g⁴ 12.2g] $300,000Y: lengthy, sparely-made
filly: sixth foal: sister to 1985 champion U.S. 2-y-o Tasso, runner-up in 1¼m
Hollywood Gold Cup at 4 yrs, 2 animals who achieved little, and half-sister to a

Tote Great St Wilfrid Handicap, Ripon—
Green Dollar settles the issue with a fine burst of speed;
Gorinsky (noseband) takes second

minor winner by Baldski: dam ran a few times: fourth in maiden at Catterick in July: soundly beaten in similar event there following month. *M. R. Stoute*

GREEN KILT 2 b.c. (Apr 21) Green Desert (USA) 127 – Kiliniski 119 (Niniski 77
(USA) 125) [1992 8g⁴ 8.3s³] third foal: dam 1½m winner fourth in Oaks, is out of half-sister to Nureyev: shaped well when fourth of 8 to Pembroke in moderately-run minor event at Newbury: well-backed favourite, found little when well below that form in maiden at Hamilton later in September: possibly unsuited by soft ground. *Lord Huntingdon*

GREEN LANE (IRE) 3 b.c. Green Desert (USA) 127 – Road To The Top 84 93
(Shirley Heights 130) [1991 7g² 1992 8g³ 11.7s* 10g 12g⁴ 13.9g 11.6g* 11.9s* 12d*
12s] lengthy, good-bodied colt: carries plenty of condition: shows knee action: had good season in 1992, winning maiden at Bath and handicaps at Windsor, Haydock and Goodwood: should stay 1¾m: acts on soft going and yet to race on top-of-the-ground: effective blinkered or not: won for claimer: sold 33,000 gns Newmarket Autumn Sales. *R. Charlton*

GREEN LANE (USA) 4 ch.g. Greinton 119 – Memory Lane (USA) 100 (Never 81
Bend (USA)) [1991 10g 12g 11.7g³ 12m⁴ 12m⁴ 17.2g* 16.2m³ 16.2f³ 16f³ 16.2f*
15.9m² 1992 16m 16.5m⁶ 16.2m² 17.2h³ 17.2f⁵ 14.6m 14s⁴ 16.1g² 14.6f⁴ 17.5s 17.2s*]
leggy, close-coupled gelding: good mover: thorough stayer: gamely won handicap at Bath in September: probably acts on any going: below form when blinkered once: sold 20,000 gns Newmarket Autumn Sales. *I. A. Balding*

GREENLET (IRE) 2 b.f. (Apr 6) Green Desert (USA) 127 – Housefull 81 79
(Habitat 134) [1992 5f* 6f² 5m 6g² 6d 6s] sturdy, useful-looking filly: has a quick action: first foal: dam, 1m winner, is closely related to dam of Hot Touch out of 1000 Guineas winner Full Dress II: won maiden at Sandown and second to Ivanka in £8,900 event at Newmarket in June: below form last 4 starts: will stay 7f. *M. R. Stoute*

GREEN MEDINA (IRE) 4 gr.f. Seattle Song (USA) 130 – Bernica (FR) 114 60
(Caro 133) [1991 10d⁵ 10f² 10.1m* 11.9mʷᵒ 1992 10s 12m 11.5m⁶ 10f³ 9d⁵] lengthy filly: has a quick action: moderate walker: rated 84 at 3 yrs: well below form in handicaps in 1992, tried blinkered: stays 1¼m: acts on firm ground. *M. Bell*

GREEN'S BID 2 gr.c. (Apr 4) Siberian Express (USA) 125 – Arianna Aldini 105
(Habitat 134) [1992 6m² 6g* 6m³ 6m² 6g] 6,000F, 13,000Y, 18,000 2-y-o: lengthy, unfurnished colt: fifth foal: half-brother to 6f and 1m winner (later banned from racing on flat) Valid Point (by Valiyar) and fairly useful 6-y-o miler Langtry Lady (by Pas de Seul): dam never ran: first past post in minor event at Kempton (demoted) and £8,400 event at Epsom in spring: much improved when placed in Richmond Stakes at Goodwood and Gimcrack Stakes (beaten ½ length, promoted) at York: ran moderately in Mill Reef Stakes at Newbury final start: will stay 1m. *P. F. I. Cole*

GREEN'S BONHEUR 4 gr.f. Never So Bold 135 – Rectitude 99 (Runnymede –
123) [1991 a6g² a6g³ 8g 8m⁶ 7m a8g a5g 1992 a7g a8g a10g] on the downgrade: below form blinkered/visored. *M. P. Naughton*

GREEN'S CASSATT (USA) 4 ch.f. Apalachee (USA) 137 – Royally Rewarded 56
(USA) (Bold Forbes (USA)) [1991 8s³ 7m⁴ 7.6d 7f⁴ 1992 a10g a7g 7.6g⁶ 8g 7g⁴ 8f*
8.2m* 8.3g³ 9.7m⁶ 8g³ 8g 10g] leggy, angular filly: tough and largely consistent handicapper: successful in August at Thirsk and Nottingham: should prove at least as effective at 1¼m as 1m: acts on any going: held up. *W. M. Brisbourne*

GREEN'S EXHIBIT 3 b.g. Song 132 – Scotch Thistle 73 (Sassafras (FR) 135) –
[1991 6m⁵ 7.1s 6m³ 7g 7f³ 9m 8m a8g 1992 7s⁶ 10f] leggy, close-coupled gelding: moderate mover: poor maiden: should stay 1m: acts on firm ground. *K. O. Cunningham-Brown*

GREEN'S FERNELEY (IRE) 4 gr.c. Taufan (USA) 119 – Rossaldene 79 93 d
(Mummy's Pet 125) [1991 8.2d* 10g⁵ 10.4d⁴ 10d 8m⁴ 8.3m* 11.1m⁴ 8m³ 1992 10d
10d⁵ 10.3g⁶ 10d⁶ 10g 8d² 8g 9d²] leggy colt: fairly useful but none too consistent handicapper: below form after second outing: seems effective from 1m to 11f: acts on good to firm and heavy ground: sometimes bandaged: effective blinkered/visored or not. *R. Charlton*

GREEN SLIPPERS 3 br.f. Green Dancer (USA) 132 – Our Reverie (USA) (J O –
Tobin (USA) 130) [1991 8.9d 1992 12m 12g6] leggy, close-coupled filly: no worthwhile form: middle-distance bred: tried blinkered: may well be ungenuine. *G. Harwood*

GREEN'S SEAGO (USA) 4 ch.g. Fighting Fit (USA) – Ornamental (USA) –
(Triple Crown (USA)) [1991 a7g* a8g a7g² a8g 7d 8m 1992 a8g⁵ 7g a8g] rather sparely-made gelding: easy mover: none too consistent performer: rated 62 at 3 yrs:

effective at 7f to 1m: acts on all-weather surfaces, best turf form on top-of-the-ground: blinkered (well beaten) final start: sometimes hangs. *J. L. Harris*

GREEN'S STUBBS 5 b.g. Ballad Rock 122 – Aventina 83 (Averof 123) [1991 7g 5m 6m 5.8f 5.1m⁴ 6.1d⁵ 5d 6g 6g² 5m⁵ 8f 5.1m 5.7f³ 5.1s 5.1d a6g 1992 6.1d 8g 6m⁴ 7.1m 7f⁵ 10.2m 8f⁵ 6.1g] close-coupled gelding: has a sharp action: poor and inconsistent handicapper: stays 7f: acts on firm and dead ground: below form blinkered/visored. *A. Barrow* —

GREEN'S VAN GOYEN (IRE) 4 b.g. Lyphard's Special (USA) 122 – Maiden Concert (Condorcet (FR)) [1991 8m⁵ 12g⁵ 12m* 12g 11.5g⁶ 1992 12d 14m] workmanlike, lengthy gelding: has a quick action: rated 65 at 3 yrs: below form in spring at 4 yrs: should stay beyond 1½m: acts on good to firm ground: won over hurdles in October. *R. Akehurst* —

GREEN SWORD 2 ch.g. (Jan 21) Sayf El Arab (USA) 127 – Supergreen (Superlative 118) [1992 a6g⁵ 6s 6d] 9,000Y: sturdy gelding: first foal: dam unraced: poor form in maidens and a claimer: blinkered final start. *W. A. O'Gorman* 39

GREEN VOTE 2 bl.f. (Apr 11) Green Ruby (USA) 104 – Miss Poll Flinders (Swing Easy (USA) 126) [1992 5d] leggy filly: second reported foal: dam unraced: went left at start and always behind in maiden at Ripon in April. *M. P. Naughton* —

GREENWICH BAMBI 4 b.f. Music Boy 124 – Coca (Levmoss 133) [1991 8g 8d 10m⁶ 12.3m a10g³ 9.7f⁴ 11.9f² 10g* 11.9g* 12g³ 1992 11.9d⁶ 14.1d 12g 14.1g* 13.6f² 14.1d² 14s³] rather unfurnished filly: won handicap at Yarmouth in June and ran well after: stays 1¾m: probably acts on any going. *W. Carter* 63

GREENWICH CHALLENGE 2 b.c. (Mar 11) Prince Sabo 123 – What A Challenge 70 (Sallust 134) [1992 5g³ 5v⁴ 5s* 5g² 5g³ 5g⁵ 6d⁴ 6m² 6s a6g² a7g⁴] smallish, sturdy colt: poor mover: first foal: dam 2-y-o 6f winner: consistent performer: won maiden at Ripon in April: stays 7f: acts on good to firm and soft ground and on all-weather surfaces: often bandaged behind: retained 4,200 gns Newmarket September Sales. *W. Carter* 77

GREETLAND FOLLY 3 ch.f. Crofthall 110 – Bit of A State 68 (Free State 125) [1991 5m 5f⁵ 6m* 6f² 6d* 6m⁵ 7m 7g 7m³ 6m³ 6m 1992 8g⁵ 7g 7f 8m³ 6.9h⁴ 7m 7m⁶ 7g] neat filly: fair at best as 3-y-o: stays 1m: acts on good to firm ground: effective visored or not: sold 5,200 gns Doncaster November Sales. *R. M. Whitaker* 79 d

GREETLAND GLORY 2 b.f. (Mar 21) Northern State (USA) 91 – Old Silver (Bold Lad (IRE) 133) [1992 5g⁴] sixth foal: half-sister to 3-y-o Trove (by Treasure Kay), 5f and 6f winner at 2 yrs, and 1990 2-y-o 7f seller winner Pilar (by Godswalk): dam placed over 7.9f at 2 yrs in Ireland: last in maiden at Hamilton in July: sold 900 gns Doncaster September Sales. *J. Berry* —

GREETLAND ROCK 4 ch.g. Ballacashtal (CAN) – Zamindara (Crofter (USA) 124) [1991 5m⁴ 5f³ 5g a5g³ a5g* 5d³ 5m³ 5m⁵ 5.1f⁴ 5g⁵ 5.3f³ a5g* 5f³ 5g² 5m⁴ 5m 5g³ 5m⁵ a5g 1992 a5g a6g a5g⁶ a5g 5.3m 5d³ 5g 5.3m 5f 5m 6g 7f 5g] workmanlike gelding: below form in handicaps in 1992: acts on firm ground and fibresand, seems unsuited by heavy: often blinkered nowadays, tried visored. *P. Howling* 42

GREY BUT ROSY (IRE) 3 gr.f. Kafu 120 – Rossaldene 79 (Mummy's Pet 125) [1991 5m 5.1m⁴ 6g⁶ 7g⁶ 6m 1992 10.2s 8f² 7d 8f 8d a10g] leggy filly: moderate mover: poor maiden: stays 1m: acts on firm ground: below form when blinkered: sometimes bandaged behind: trained until after fourth start by D. Elsworth: sold 900 gns Ascot December Sales. *P. M. McEntee* 45

GREY CHARMER (IRE) 3 gr.c. Alzao (USA) 117 – Sashi Woo (Rusticaro (FR) 124) [1991 5m 5d⁵ 5m³ 6f* 5m 6g 6g 6m 1992 5d 6s 6g⁵ 6.9m 6m⁴ 6m 6g³ 6m⁶ 6g* 7g 6d 6s⁴ 7g] close-coupled colt: moderate mover: inconsistent handicapper: won at Salisbury in August: should stay at least 7f: probably acts on any going. *C. James* 56

GREY COMMANDER 4 gr.c. Grey Desire 115 – Melowen 75 (Owen Dudley 121) [1991 10d 8s⁵ 10d⁵ 12.5m⁵ a12g 12d* 13.8g³ 11.1d³ a14g⁶ 15.1s a14g⁵ a12g² a12g 1992 a14g 11.1v⁴ 12.4s⁴ 12g² 13d³ a14g² 12m 12s⁴ a14g a12g* a12g⁵ a12s a12g³ 12.1s³ 13.8d 12.4v] leggy, sparely-made colt: moderate mover: poor handicapper: won at Southwell in July: effective from 1½m to 1¾m: has gone well on a soft surface, acts on fibresand: below form when visored. *M. Brittain* 41

GREY CPHAS 3 gr.g. Grey Desire 115 – Malindi (Mansingh (USA) 120) [1991 NR 1992 6.9v⁶ 8s⁵ 8g⁴ 10m 12s] angular, workmanlike gelding: fourth living foal: half-brother to 10.5f seller winner Lindi's Gold (by Sonnen Gold): dam never ran: no worthwhile form: has joined Mrs S. Williams. *M. McCormack* —

GREY DANCER 4 gr.c. Petong 126 – Infelice (Nishapour (FR) 125) [1991 8g⁵ –
10g a12g⁴ 1992 a10g⁶ a10g⁶] compact colt: poor maiden: stays 1½m: sold 2,500 gns
Ascot March Sales. *J. White*

GREY DECISION 3 gr.c. Grey Desire 115 – Miss Realm 86 (Realm 129) [1991 –
6m 1992 10.1s 7.5m] leggy, close-coupled colt: no form: sold 880 gns Doncaster June
Sales. *M. Brittain*

GREY ILLUSIONS 4 gr.g. Nishapour (FR) 125 – Morica 88 (Moorestyle 137) **41**
[1991 7m 7d⁵ 7.6s⁵ 8.1d⁶ 7m⁶ 7f 1992 6d 7g 7g 9g 8.2g² 8f 8f⁶ 7.6m 8.2m 9s⁶] strong
gelding: moderate walker: inconsistent maiden handicapper: stays 9f: acts on good
to firm ground and soft: below form when blinkered. *L. J. Holt*

GREY POWER 5 gr.m. Wolf Power (SAF) – Periquito (USA) (Olden Times) **64**
[1991 11.5d² 12g³ 14.8s³ 14m 12m 12.1s* 1992 12g 13d⁵ 11.9s 13.1g⁴ 13.1d³ 16.2d³
12m* 12.1s² 12.1v³] good-topped mare: found her form towards end of 1992,
successful in amateurs last time: started at Pontefract and 2 novice hurdles, though pulled up
as if something amiss last time: seems to stay 2m: acts on good to firm and heavy
ground. *Mrs M. Reveley*

GREY PRIDE 2 gr.g. (Mar 8) Bold Owl 101 – Bri-Ette (Brittany) [1992 6f⁵ 5g 5f³ **52**
5g 6s 5d 5d⁵] 5,200Y: leggy gelding: sixth foal: brother to 5f winner Mom Sally and
1988 2-y-o 6f winner Miss Ellie Pea: dam sister to useful sprinter Tinjar:
plating-class sprint maiden: acts on firm and dead ground. *J. Berry*

GREY REALM 4 ch.f. Grey Desire 115 – Miss Realm 86 (Realm 129) [1991 NR –
1992 7m 11f 13.6m] close-coupled, deep-girthed filly: moderate mover: on the
downgrade. *R. E. Barr*

GREY RECORD 4 gr.c. Grey Desire 115 – Record Lady (Record Token 128) **49**
[1991 7d³ 7v³ 7.5g⁴ 10g 9d 8m 9.2s 11.1s⁶ 1992 9.2v² 11.1s⁴] rather angular colt:
shows knee action: ran well in maiden claimers in May: stays 11f: acts on heavy
going: ran moderately on fibresand: sold out of M. Brittain's stable 6,000 gns
Doncaster January Sales, resold 820 gns Doncaster June Sales. *Mrs M. Reveley*

GREY RUNNER 2 gr.f. (Apr 25) Crofthall 110 – Chevet Lady 65 (John de **36**
Coombe 122) [1992 5.1d⁶ 5g⁵ 5.3f³ 5s³ 6m⁴ 6g a6g⁶ a6g] 800Y, resold 650Y:
smallish, leggy filly: second reported foal: dam 8.5f (at 2 yrs) and 1¼m winner: poor
plater: stays 6f: probably acts on any turf going, ran poorly on all-weather tracks. *B.
Palling*

GREY SALUTE (CAN) 9 gr.g. Vice Regent (CAN) – Night Out (USA) (Bustino –
136) [1991 NR 1992 16s] big, heavy-topped gelding: has a round action: on the
downgrade. *J. R. Jenkins*

GREYSTOKE 2 gr.c. (Feb 25) Cozzene (USA) – Sharmood (USA) (Sharpen Up **71**
127) [1992 7.3m³ 7.1d 8m 8d³ 7m] 46,000Y: rather leggy, close-coupled colt: second
foal: dam ran several times in USA: inconsistent maiden: stays 1m: acts on dead
ground: visored last 2 outings: sold 23,000 gns Newmarket Autumn Sales. *Lord
Huntingdon*

GREYSTYLE 2 b.c. (Apr 2) Grey Desire 115 – Riverstyle 63 (River Knight (FR) **38**
118) [1992 5g 5m 6f] tall, plain colt: poor mover: second foal: dam 6f winner: poor
form in maidens in May. *M. Brittain*

GREY WATCH 2 gr.f. (Apr 25) Petong 126 – Royal Custody (Reform 132) [1992 **61**
7f 7d³ 7.1g 7d⁶ a7g a8g] leggy, unfurnished filly: fifth foal: dam unraced half-sister to
several winners, including Ragstone and Castle Moon (dam of Moon Madness,
Lucky Moon and Sheriff's Star): went the wrong way after third in maiden at
Goodwood in August: should be well suited by middle distances: sold out of Lady
Herries' stable 5,000 gns Ascot November Sales after fourth start. *P. Howling*

GRINNELL 2 ch.g. (Apr 16) Gypsy Castle 96 – Rosinka 62 (Raga Navarro (ITY) **62** ?
119) [1992 5m* 5f* 6g 6m³ 6s 6s⁶] 1,150Y, 5,000 2-y-o: sparely-made gelding: third
reported foal: half-brother to ungenuine sprint maiden Always Treasure (by
Lochnager): dam 5f and 6f seller winner at 2 yrs: won maiden at Edinburgh and
nursery at Thirsk in July: appeared to show vastly improved form when third in
Timeform Futurity at Pontefract but failed to confirm it on soft ground: will stay 7f:
well suited by top-of-the-ground. *Denys Smith*

GROGFRYN 2 ch.f. (Apr 4) Nicholas Bill 125 – Connaughts' Trump (Connaught **56**
130) [1992 6g⁴ 8.2d⁶ 7s³ 8.3s⁵] leggy filly: moderate mover: half-sister to Irish 13.5f
winner Gilt Future (by Persian Bold) and 1986 2-y-o 5f and 1m winner Last Dance
(by Last Fandango): dam won 3 races at up to 1½m in Ireland: modest maiden: will
be suited by middle distances. *J. Berry*

GROG (IRE) 3 b.g. Auction Ring (USA) 123 – Any Price (Gunner B 126) [1991 5g **74** 5m 7g5 7g 7f 7g3 7g 8m 10m6 a8g4 a8g* a7g6 1992 a8g2 9.9g* a10g* 10d 9.9f3 8.9s2 8.5d5 10m3 10f2 10g6 9.9m 12g*] strong, compact gelding: carries condition: has a round action: consistent handicapper: successful at Beverley and Lingfield in spring and Salisbury (claimed to join S. Sherwood's stable £11,556) in August: stays 1½m: probably acts on any going, including all-weather surfaces: below form in visor: successful for claimer. *M. R. Channon*

GRONDOLA 5 b.m. Indian King (USA) 128 – Trysting Place (He Loves Me 120) – [1991 8f 1992 9f] leggy, close-coupled mare: on the downgrade. *D. Burchell*

GROOVEY DANCER 3 b.c. Shareef Dancer (USA) 135 – Grove Star (Upper – Case (USA)) [1991 NR 1992 7g 8g] 6,400Y: leggy colt: half-brother to several winners, including very useful Stella Grande (by Record Token), best at up to 1¼m, and fair middle-distance handicapper Wild Hope (by Great Nephew): dam once-raced half-sister to smart Uncle Pokey: tailed off in maiden and (tubed) claimer. *B. J. McMath*

GROUND NUT (IRE) 2 ch.g. (Feb 19) Fools Holme (USA) – Corn Seed 72 **67** (Nicholas Bill 125) [1992 7g 8.1s6 6g5 7s5 7.3s] 2,000Y: workmanlike gelding: first foal: dam maiden stayed 7f: fair maiden: should stay middle distances. *H. Candy*

GROUSE-N-HEATHER 3 gr.f. Grey Desire 115 – Heldigvis 63 (Hot Grove **69** 128) [1991 7m6 7s 1992 12.2m* 12f 13.6f5 12.2g* 13.8g* 12.1g* 12f* 13.6m4] leggy, sparely-made filly: had really good season in 1992, winning claimers at Catterick (3), Hamilton and Pontefract: ideally suited by further than 1½m: acts on firm ground: joined Miss J. Rae. *Mrs M. Reveley*

GROVE DAFFODIL (IRE) 2 ch.f. (Mar 30) Salt Dome (USA) – Tatisha **63 p** (Habitat 134) [1992 7g5 7g3 7g*] IR 1,500Y: angular, good-topped filly: half-sister to 3 winners here and abroad, including (at 1½m and 2¼m) Relkisha (by Relkino) and (at 1m to 1¼m) Shannon Express (by Magic Mirror): dam, French 1m winner, is half-sister to high-class sprinter Green God: sire (by Blushing Groom) sprinter: well-backed favourite following promising third, won maiden auction at Redcar in September by 2 lengths: will be well suited by middle distances: will improve again. *M. H. Tompkins*

GROVE SERENDIPITY (IRE) 4 b.g. Glenstal (USA) 118 – Huppel 83 (Hunt- **55** ercombe 133) [1991 12m a12g* 14g 16m5 12g2 11.5s5 1992 11.7d 13.6f6 11.8g 14s4 14g3 12d 13.8d6] close-coupled, workmanlike gelding: inconsistent handicapper: stays 1¾m: best efforts on a sound surface: often visored: has joined M. Pipe. *A. Hide*

GROWN AT ROWAN 5 b.m. Gabitat 119 – Hallo Rosie 67 (Swing Easy (USA) – 126) [1991 6g 7m6 8f 7.6d 7m3 6m2 6m 6g2 6g4 7g 1992 a8g] rather leggy mare: moderate mover: inconsistent handicapper, rated 66 at 4 yrs: stays 7f: acts on hard ground. *M. Madgwick*

GRUBBY 3 b.f. Green Ruby (USA) 104 – Via Vitae 67 (Palm Track 122) [1991 5m6 **41** 5m 6.1m 5g a6g 1992 a5g2 a5g4 a6g4 5s 5v 5g a5g a8g2 8h3 a7g2 a7g* 8f5 8.9d a7g a53 a7g] workmanlike filly: below form in handicaps after winning maiden at Southwell in July: stays 1m: acts on hard ground and fibresand. *R. Hollinshead*

GRUMPY'S GRAIN (IRE) 2 b.c. (Feb 2) Horage 124 – Godwyn (Yellow God – 129) [1992 6f 7g4] IR 1,700F: good-topped colt: has scope: half-brother to several winners here and in Ireland, including 5-y-o middle-distance handicapper: Princess Roxanne (by Prince Tenderfoot): dam, half-sister to very useful Pianissimo, won over 6f in Ireland: well beaten in Scottish maidens in early-summer. *Miss L. A. Perratt*

GRUNDONIAN 4 b.g. Tina's Pet 121 – Sound Type 92 (Upper Case (USA)) – [1991 10.1d4 10.1m5 10m 16.1g 1992 12s] small, lengthy gelding: good walker: rated 54 at 3 yrs: on the downgrade. *C. A. Horgan*

GUANHUMARA 2 ch.f. (May 2) Caerleon (USA) 132 – Smarten Up 119 (Sharpen – Up 127) [1992 6d 7g 5.1s] neat filly: half-sister to 3-y-o 10.8f winner Dress Sense (by Top Ville) and several winners, including high-class sprinter Cadeaux Genereux (by Young Generation) and middle-distance stayer Brightner (by Sparkler): dam sprinting half-sister to smart fillies Walk By and Solar: well beaten in maiden and minor events: constantly reared stalls second start. *P. T. Walwyn*

GUECA SOLO 4 ch.f. Pharly (FR) 130 – Atitlan (Relko 136) [1991 8g* 10m2 9m3 **84** 7g5 1992 8g3 11.5m3 9m5 10.2s* 11.5m 8g6 9s a10g5 a12g] small, sparely-made filly: moderate walker: has a round action: below form in handicaps after winning at Chepstow in August: should prove as effective at 1½m as 1¼m: has form on good to firm ground, but goes particularly well with some give: trained first 5 starts by H. Cecil: sold 7,800 gns Newmarket December Sales. *D. R. Loder*

GUESSTIMATION (USA)   3 b.g. Known Fact (USA) 135 – Best Guess (USA)   **56**
(Apalachee (USA) 137) [1991 NR 1992 8f 9m3 9.7d6 8d 7m2 7d 7g2 a7g4 a8g a8g2] IR 54,000Y: good-topped gelding: second foal: dam unraced half-sister to numerous winners (only one in stakes race) in North America: modest maiden: easily best efforts in handicaps when in frame: sold out of J. Gosden's stable 5,000 gns Newmarket July Sales after second start: stays 1m: seems not to act on a soft surface. *J. Pearce*

GUEST PLAYER   5 ch.m. Horage 124 – Guestaway (Be My Guest (USA) 126)   **–**
[1991 5m 8f5 10.1s 8g 8m 10.1m 13.1m3 1992 a12g6 11.9d] sparely-made ex-Irish mare: has round action: poor handicapper: stays 13f: acts on good to firm ground and dead: sometimes blinkered. *T. J. Naughton*

GUILLEM (USA)   3 b.f. Nijinsky (CAN) 138 – Miss Manon (FR) (Bon Mot III   **76**
132) [1991 NR 1992 11.4d3] big, lengthy filly: eighth foal: closely related to smart winner at up to 1½m Lydian (by Lyphard) and useful 1¼m winner (best at 1m) Pride of Araby (by Sovereign Dancer) and half-sister to 4 winners, including Ribblesdale winner Ballinderry (by Irish River) and French Derby third Sharpman (by Sharpen Up): dam smart French middle-distance performer: green and tired in last 1f when 7 lengths third of 5 to Mystery Play in minor event at Sandown in August. *H. R. A. Cecil*

GUILTY SECRET (IRE)   3 ch.f. Kris 135 – Miss Toshiba (USA) 113 (Sir Ivor **109**
135) [1991 7m2 7m6 1992 10d4 12f5 12f* 11.9m3 14.6m2 10.9s3 12g6] rangy, rather unfurnished filly: fluent mover: won maiden at Thirsk in August: greatly improved next 2 starts in Yorkshire Oaks (2½ lengths behind User Friendly) and Park Hill Stakes (¾ length behind Niodini) at Doncaster: below best after in listed race at Ayr (sweating) and moderately-run Princess Royal Stakes at Ascot: seems to need at

Mr R. E. Sangster's "Guilty Secret"

least 1½m: acts on firm ground, possibly not on soft: sent to race in Bahrain. *P. W. Chapple-Hyam*

GUISLAINE (FR)   3 br.f. Tropular – Clodette (FR) (Ben Trovato (FR) 128) **115** [1991 6d³ 6g 6g* 7d* 7m³ 7m⁶ 8g* 8d⁴ 1992 8g² 8m³ 10.5g⁴ 10m³ 8g 9f⁵ 8.5f* 8.5f6] smart ex-French performer: in frame in 1992 at Longchamp in Prix de la Grotte, Poule d'Essai des Pouliches (1¼ lengths third to Culture Vulture) and Grand Prix de Paris and at Chantilly in Prix de Diane Hermes (2½ lengths fourth to Jolypha): returned to form when landing Allez France Handicap at Hollywood Park in December: stays 10.5f: acts on firm and dead ground: not blinkered since 2 yrs: trained by P. Bary until after sixth start. *R. Rash, USA*

GUITING GIRL   3 b.f. Primo Dominie 121 – Emily Kent (Royal Palace 131) [1991   – NR 1992 7g 7m 8g6 10.2s] lengthy filly with scope: half-sister to 2 winning jumpers: dam placed over hurdles: no worthwhile form: may prove suited by around 1m. *H. Candy*

GULFLAND   11 ch.g. Gulf Pearl 117 – Sunland Park (Baragoi 115) [1991 12g 12g²   – 12m³ 13d6 12m⁵ 12m⁵ 11.5s 1992 12.3g 14.1g 12.2g] workmanlike, good-bodied gelding: carries condition: moderate mover: poor performer nowadays: stays 1½m: acts on any going. *G. A. Pritchard-Gordon*

GULF PALACE (USA)   7 ch.h. Green Dancer (USA) 132 – Sanctum Sanctorum **94** (USA) (Secretariat (USA)) [1991 12g 12g³ 11.9g* 12m 11.9d² 11g 12d 1992 12g² 14.9v² 14g* 14s5] rangy, well-made horse: moderate mover: fairly useful handicapper: won at Newmarket in April: stayed 14.9f: probably acted on any going: consistent: dead. *R. Akehurst*

GULF SAILOR (IRE)   4 b.c. Darshaan 133 – Grecian Sea (FR) (Homeric 133) **86** [1991 10m⁵ 10s⁴ 1992 8.5f* 10.1g* 12f 10g² 13.9m 10g] good-topped, quite attractive colt: carries condition: fine mover: won Beverley maiden and Yarmouth handicap in spring: form in competitive handicaps after only when second at Ascot: should prove at least as effective at 1½m + as 1¼m: probably acts on any going: sold 12,500 gns Newmarket Autumn Sales, to Italy. *M. R. Stoute*

J. L. Bouchard's "Guislaine"

GULMARG 5 b.g. Gorytus (USA) 132 – Kashmiri Snow 83 (Shirley Heights 130) – [1991 8d 7g 7d 7.6d 7m 1992 a8g a8g5] rangy, attractive gelding: moderate mover: rated 81 at best as 4-y-o: on the downgrade, and not seen out after February, 1992: stays 9f: acts on firm and dead going. *M. H. Tompkins*

GUNMAKER 3 ch.g. Gunner B 126 – Lucky Starkist 57 (Lucky Wednesday 124) – [1991 NR 1992 7v 8.2d 10.2m 7m] smallish gelding: first foal: dam, 5f to 7f winner, is half-sister to Lincoln winner Star of A Gunner (by Gunner B): well beaten, including in seller: sold 1,550 gns Doncaster November Sales. *R. J. Holder*

GUNNER'S DAUGHTER 3 ch.f. Pharly (FR) 130 – Gunner's Belle 69 **73** + (Gunner B 126) [1991 NR 1992 8.1g3 7g4 10.5g6 8g* 8g5 7s] 8,800Y: medium-sized, quite attractive filly: fourth foal: half-sister to 1988 2-y-o 5f winner Gunmaster (by Precocious): dam won from 7f to 1¼m: best effort in maidens when winning at Warwick in August: very stiff tasks after, appearing to run very well when fifth in Newbury minor event: effective with forcing tactics at 1m, and probably stays 1¼m: often bandaged behind: sold 1,000 gns Newmarket December Sales. *H. Candy*

GUN RULE 8 ch.g. Posse (USA) 130 – Brave Lass 114 (Ridan (USA)) [1991 a7g – a7g5 1992 a7g] big, workmanlike gelding: bad mover: on the downgrade. *D. R. Laing*

GUSHING 3 b.f. Formidable (USA) 125 – Piney River 63 (Pharly (FR) 130) [1991 **76** p NR 1992 6s 8v*] compact filly: first foal: dam maiden raced only at 6f and 7f, is out of half-sister to very smart 1973 2-y-o Splashing, dam of Bassenthwaite: not seen out until October, and 2-length winner of maiden at Newmarket in November: sold 9,200 gns Newmarket December Sales: can improve again. *R. Charlton*

GUSSIE FINK-NOTTLE (IRE) 2 b. or br.c. (Apr 30) Treasure Kay 114 – **58** Bright Cecilia (Welsh Saint 126) [1992 6f 5m6 5m2 a6g2 a7g3] IR 4,000F, 8,000Y 2-y-o: leggy, useful-looking colt: third foal: dam lightly raced: modest maiden: odds on, took strong hold, found little on final start: best at sprint distances. *T. D. Barron*

GUSSY MARLOWE 4 b.f. Final Straw 127 – Lady Lorelei 105 (Derring-Do 131) **113** ? [1991 8m3 10g* 10.5m* 8g3 10g4 11.9g 1992 10g 10m 10m 8g* 10m6 10.4g 10d 10d] strong, close-coupled filly: smart performer at best but none too reliable: below par in pattern company after 3½-length win from Lovealoch in Falmouth Stakes at Newmarket: effective at 1m to 10.5f: acts on good to firm ground: effective held up or forcing pace. *C. E. Brittain*

GUSTAVIA (IRE) 2 b.f. (Mar 21) Red Sunset 120 – Vain Deb 66 (Gay Fandango **80** (USA) 132) [1992 7g 7.1g* 7d6] 33,000Y: lengthy, good-topped filly: moderate mover: fourth foal: sister to tough and fairly useful 6-y-o sprinter (won Wokingham) Red Rosein and half-sister to 3-y-o Malcesine (by Auction Ring) and 5-y-o 12.3f (at 3 yrs) to 16.2f winner Vain Prince (by Sandhurst Prince): dam 1m to 9f winner stayed 1¼m: 3½-length winner of maiden at Sandown in September (33/1): very stiff task when tailed-off last in minor event at Newmarket following month: will be better suited by 1m. *R. W. Armstrong*

GUV'NORS GIFT 2 b.f. (Mar 16) Sizzling Melody 117 – La Reine d'Espagne **74** (King of Spain 121) [1992 5g 6g2 6g* 6f* 7d2 6.5m 6d3 6s* 6s] 400Y: leggy, sparely-made filly: first live foal: dam, maiden, stayed 7f: successful in sellers at Folkestone (retained 3,500 gns) and Yarmouth (retained 3,200 gns) in July and nursery at Folkestone in October: best form at 6f: has won on firm ground, but goes particularly well on an easy surface: suitable mount for claimer: sold 1,400 gns Newmarket Autumn Sales. *M. H. Tompkins*

GUV'S JOY (IRE) 2 b.f. (Mar 5) Thatching 131 – Joanne's Joy (Ballymore 123) **72** p [1992 6.1v*] IR 8,000Y: sixth foal: sister to 1m winner Roofing: dam Irish 7f and 1m

Falmouth Stakes, Newmarket—Gussy Marlowe copes well with the return to a mile

winner: won maiden at Chester in October by 3½ lengths from Nutty Brown, travelling best of all to straight then running on strongly: will stay 7f: will improve. *B. W. Hills*

GWEEK (IRE) 2 ch.f. (May 16) Common Grounds 118 – Do We Know (Derrylin **51** 115) [1992 5.1g⁴ 5m³ 7d⁶ 6m] IR 2,600Y: small filly: sixth live foal: half-sister to 3-y-o 1¼m to 1½m winner Bo Knows Best (by Burslem), 9f winner All Greek To Me (by Trojan Fen) and a winner in Spain by Pharly: dam thrice-raced half-sister to high-class 1¼m horse Rarity: plating-class maiden: stiff task final start: will stay 1m: acts on good to firm and dead ground. *P. A. Kelleway*

GYMCRAK CYRANO (IRE) 3 b.f. Cyrano de Bergerac 120 – Sun Gift – (Guillaume Tell (USA) 121) [1991 6d⁶ 6.9m³ 7m² 7.1m* a7g 7.1m³ 9m² 8m⁶ 7.6d⁵ 8.3s 1992 10m 10d] sturdy filly: below form in sellers in August, and looked none too keen final start: stays 9f: acts on good to firm ground: claimed to join Miss L. Plater £2,100 over hurdles in September. *M. H. Easterby*

GYMCRAK PREMIERE 4 ch.g. Primo Dominie 121 – Oraston 115 (Morston **104** (FR) 125) [1991 6g* 7m³ 8m* 9m* 8.2m³ 8m³ 8m² 10g 8m² 8.1m² 1992 7.9m 8f² 10d 10.4d 7m² 7.9m⁵ 8s² 8m 7d⁵ 8g* 8g⁶] lengthy, workmanlike gelding: consistent and useful handicapper: won quite valuable event at Ascot in October by 2 lengths from Shati: best at 7f to 9f: probably acts on any going: visored third start: sometimes swerves markedly: held up. *M. H. Easterby*

GYMCRAK TIGER (IRE) 2 b.g. (Feb 7) Colmore Row 111 – Gossip (Sharp **89** Edge 123) [1992 6g* 6s² 5s⁴ 6d³] 4,400Y: tall, rather leggy, useful-looking gelding: closely related to untrustworthy 3-y-o Bridle Talk and 1984 2-y-o 5f winner Running Edge (both by Runnett), latter successful later in USA, and half-brother to a winner in Malaysia: dam no sign of ability: won maiden auction and excellent second in listed race at Ripon in August: ran moderately after: will stay 7f. *M. H. Easterby*

GYMCRAK TYCOON 3 b.c. Last Tycoon 131 – Brazen Faced 84 (Bold And **73** Free 118) [1991 5m* 5.1f² 6g* 6m⁵ 1992 7g⁶ 6f⁵ 7.5d* 7g⁴ 8m a7g² 7d a6g⁵ a8g⁶ a7g⁵ a6g] leggy, close-coupled colt: fair handicapper: won seller (bought in 5,200 gns) at Beverley in August: stays 7.5f: acts on firm and dead going, and on fibresand: blinkered (well beaten) final start. *M. H. Easterby*

GYPSY CRYSTAL (USA) 2 gr.f. (Apr 20) Flying Saucer 94 – U R Grounded **50** (USA) (Grounded 117) [1992 7g 7m 8m⁴ 8.2d⁶] smallish, leggy filly: half-sister to several minor winners in North America: dam unraced: sire (by Kris) lightly-raced half-brother to very useful Prime Asset: poor maiden: will stay 1¼m: acts on good to firm ground. *R. M. Whitaker*

GYPSY LEGEND 2 b.f. (Feb 1) Legend of France (USA) 124 – Gipsy Scott 87 **41** (Sky Gipsy 117) [1992 5d 5m 6f⁴ 7f⁴ 7m³ 6m⁶ 7g⁴] 1,250F: small, lengthy filly: half-sister to a winner in Scandinavia: dam 2-y-o 5f winner: modest plater: will stay 1m: acts on firm ground: sweated and raced too freely when blinkered once. *W. G. M. Turner*

H

HABEEBITTI NADIA 2 b.f. (Mar 26) Night Shift (USA) – Mrs Feathers 57 – (Pyjama Hunt 126) [1992 7.1s a7g] 14,500F, IR 21,000Y: compact filly: sixth foal: sister to fairly useful 1988 2-y-o 5f to 8.5f winner Nightstalker, later successful in USA: dam maiden: soundly beaten in maiden at Chepstow and claimer at Southwell late in year. *W. J. Haggas*

HABETA (USA) 6 ch.h. Habitat 134 – Prise (Busted 134) [1991 8m* 8m 8m⁴ **71** 8.2d³ 8m² 9m² 9f⁴ 8.9g 8m⁶ 8m 9g⁴ a8g⁶ 1992 8.5g* 8d 8m* 8f⁶ 8.2m² 8m 8m³ 8m⁵ 7m⁶ 7m 8m 8g 8m 8g] quite good-topped horse: carries plenty of condition: modest handicapper: in good form in the spring, winning at Beverley and Pontefract: below form last 5 starts: effective from 1m to 1¼m: acts on any going: best held up for late run, and suited by strongly-run race. *J. W. Watts*

HADAAD (USA) 3 ch.c. Mr Prospector (USA) – Etoile d'Amore (USA) 81 (The **77** Minstrel (CAN) 135) [1991 7g⁶ 6g⁴ 5.9h² 7g* 1992 8.1g⁵ 8.5m* 8.1m 9.9m 8g] good-topped colt: fluent mover: fair performer: won handicap at Beverley in May, always close up: failed to repeat that form and always behind at Newmarket in June final start: stays 8.5f: acts on good to firm ground. *A. A. Scott*

HADEER'S DANCE 2 b.c. (Apr 5) Hadeer 118 – Harvest Dance 79 (Mill Reef **70** p (USA) 141) [1992 6m⁴ 6f⁵ 7m* 7.5d⁶ 8.1d] 10,000Y: angular, workmanlike colt:

moderate mover: first foal: dam, 1¼m winner, is from family of Greenland Park (dam of Fitnah) and Red Sunset: fair performer: well-backed favourite, won maiden auction at Doncaster in June: off course nearly 6 weeks and stiff task, ran well in Sandown nursery final start: suited by 1m: easily best form on dead ground: probably capable of better. *R. W. Armstrong*

HAILSHAM (CAN) 4 b.c. Riverman (USA) 131 – Halo's Princess (CAN) (Halo (USA)) [1991 8m4 10g* 10.5g2 12g* 12f 10d4 12m 1992 10m 12s6 10s] strong, lengthy colt: has a powerful, round action: useful as 3-y-o: no worthwhile form in 1992 in listed races at Goodwood and Milan and (tailed off) Eclipse Stakes at Sandown: stays 1½m: best efforts with give in the ground. *C. E. Brittain* —

HAIRRAISING 2 gr.f. (May 19) Absalom 128 – Haunting 79 (Lord Gayle (USA) 124) [1992 5g4 6g4 5m4 6m5] 5,800Y: leggy, sparely-made filly: half-sister to 3-y-o Invisible Armour (by Precocious) and numerous winners, including 4-y-o 6f to 7.2f winner Panikin (by Red Sunset) and useful 1986 2-y-o 5f and 6f winner Amigo Sucio (by Stanford): dam stayed 1m: poor form, including in seller: should be better suited by 6f than 5f: blinkered (fair effort for 7-lb claimer) third outing. *N. A. Callaghan* **48**

HAITHAM 5 b.h. Wassl 125 – Balqis (USA) 93 (Advocator) [1991 14g5 20g2 16d5 16.1m3 20g* 18m3 16m6 18m 1992 16d 16.2m4 22.2g6 15.9d4 20m 18m3 16d 14d4 16.2g 18m] rather leggy horse: moderate mover: still fairly useful handicapper on his day, but disappointing on the whole in 1992: probably needs 2m+: acts on firm and dead ground: effective ridden from front or held up: has joined R. Buckler. *R. Akehurst* **93 d**

HAITI BELLE 2 b.f. (Jan 12) Belfort (FR) 89 – Haiti Mill 68 (Free State 125) [1992 6m] sturdy, good-topped filly: has scope: third foal: sister to modest 1990 2-y-o 7f winner Nigel's Lucky Girl and half-sister to 3-y-o 7f winner Level Up (by Beveled): dam never ran, is out of sister to Petong: 25/1 and backward, tailed off in 16-runner maiden at Windsor in August: moved moderately down. *M. McCourt* —

HAJAAN 2 gr.f. (May 7) Northern Tempest (USA) 120 – Lucky Amy (Lucky Wednesday 124) [1992 a5g 6m a6g] rather leggy filly: second foal: dam never ran: well beaten in sellers in midsummer. *B. Beasley* —

HAJAIM (IRE) 4 ch.g. Doulab (USA) 115 – Sharrara (CAN) 61 (Blushing Groom (FR) 131) [1991 7d4 8.2m6 7.6d* 10m5 8m5 10g* 11.9g* 10d 1992 11.4s6 12g3 13.9m 13.3g5 12s5 12g] rather leggy, attractive gelding: has a quick action: fairly useful handicapper: effective from 1½m to 1¾m: acts on any going: sometimes sweats: has hung left, and not easiest of rides: blinkered last 2 starts, running creditably first occasion, finding little in November Handicap last time: has been gelded. *C. E. Brittain* **90**

HALESIA (USA) 3 b.f. Chief's Crown (USA) – Hurry Harriet 129 (Yarrah Jr (USA)) [1991 NR 1992 8g4 10g2 10g2 12m4 10s* 12.5s 10.5v*] half-sister to several winners, including French middle-distance colts Dominant (by Lyphard) and Load The Cannons (by Cannonade), latter third in Oak Tree Invitational: dam won Champion Stakes: won minor event at Deauville in August and Group 3 Prix de Fille de l'Air at Saint-Cloud in November, latter from On Credit and Lupescu: stays 1½m: acts on any going. *E. Lellouche, France* **111**

HALF A DOZEN (USA) 2 ch.f. (Feb 12) Saratoga Six (USA) – Exotic Source (USA) 79 (The Minstrel (CAN) 135) [1992 7.1d 7f3 7g 7.9d] $85,000Y: leggy filly: second foal: sister to 3-y-o Saratoga Source, successful at 7f (at 2 yrs) and 1¼m: dam, 1¼m winner, is half-sister to Alydars Best and daughter of sister to Gyr: sire (half-brother to Dunbeath) ran only at 2 yrs when top-class winner at 6f and 1m: modest form when third in maiden at Yarmouth: showed little otherwise: should be better suited by 1¼m: acts on firm ground. *A. A. Scott* **57**

HALF A TICK (USA) 4 b.g. Timeless Moment (USA) – Moon Star Miss (USA) (Star Envoy (USA)) [1991 9m* 10.4d2 12g3 11g5 1992 10g6 10m 12s2 10g* 10.5d* 10s3 11d2 9.7s4 10v6] neat, quite attractive gelding: moderate mover: smart performer: successful in listed race at Milan and Group 3 event at Haydock (by ¾ length from Spartan Shareef) in the summer: in frame afterwards in Group 3 races at Deauville (good third to Corrupt) and Milan (second to Erdelistan) and Prix Dollar at Longchamp: effective from 1¼m to 1½m: acts on firm and soft going, rare modest effort on heavy: has run well when sweating. *P. F. I. Cole* **115**

HALF TERM (USA) 2 b.c. (May 14) Mr Prospector (USA) – Six Months Long (USA) (Northern Dancer (CAN)) [1992 6d*] $825,000Y: brother to American 3-y-o Classic Event, minor winner at 2 yrs, closely related to a winner by Conquistador Cielo and half-brother to several winners, notably Half A Year (by Riverman): dam **89 P**

won twice at up to 1m: co-favourite, won 12-runner maiden at Yarmouth in October most impressively by 5 lengths from Castel Rosselo, bit slowly away, improving from rear over 2f out then quickening clear 1f out: should prove best at up to 1m: looks a very useful prospect and is certain to win more races. *J. H. M. Gosden*

HALHAM TARN (IRE)   2 b.c. (Apr 22) Pennine Walk 120 – Nouniya (Vayrann 133) [1992 7d 8s⁴ 6.9v a8g a8g⁴] strong colt: first foal: dam poor maiden: modest maiden: sold out of P. Walwyn's stable 4,600 gns Newmarket Autumn Sales after third start: will stay 1¼m: best effort on soft ground. *D. R. C. Elsworth*   **57**

HALKOPOUS   6 b.g. Beldale Flutter (USA) 130 – Salamina 106 (Welsh Pageant 132) [1991 10m³ 10.1f⁴ 10g² 11.5d⁴ 10.4m* 10.5f⁴ 12s9m⁶ 10m⁶ 11g* 1992 10g 10.5s² 12s 11s⁵] good-bodied, workmanlike gelding: carries plenty of condition: moderate mover: fairly useful handicapper: didn't reappear until August as 6-y-o, best effort when second to Mr Confusion in quite valuable event at Haydock: should stay 1½m: acts on any going: best visored: progressed into a top-class hurdler, easily winning Fighting Fifth and Bula Hurdle late in year. *M. H. Tompkins*   **93**

HALLEY (USA)   3 b.c. Star de Naskra (USA) – Mumble Peg (General Assembly (USA)) [1991 NR 1992 12g⁶ 10f* 10g] $155,000Y: good-topped colt: poor mover: second foal: half-brother to North American winner Ghost Flower (by Forli): dam unraced half-sister to high-class Little Bonny and smart Noelino: fair form: ridden by 7-lb claimer, won maiden at Ripon in June: well beaten in handicap at Kempton 3 weeks later: pulls hard: sent to race in Dubai. *H. R. A. Cecil*   **76**

HALLMOTE   2 br.c. (Feb 10) Bustino 136 – Inshirah (USA) 90 (Caro 133) [1992 6f 6f a7g] 15,500F, 16,000Y: lengthy, plain colt: second foal: half-brother to 3-y-o Mamzooj (by Shareef Dancer): dam 2-y-o 5f and 7f winner, is granddaughter of leading 1964 2-y-o filly Mira Femme, dam of Femme Elite: no worthwhile form and not seen after July. *J. G. FitzGerald*   **–**

HALLORINA   2 b.f. (Mar 12) Hallgate 127 – Diorina 91 (Manacle 123) [1992 5g 6f⁵ 5.1f 6m* 6.1g* 6m* 6g 6.5m 7.2g] IR 1,150Y: smallish filly: moderate mover: half-sister to 3-y-o Chinaman (by Noalto), winning sprinters by Swing Easy and Air Trooper and 8.3f seller winner Mardior (by Martinmas): dam best at 2 yrs, when 5.3f winner: modest performer: made all in seller (no bid) at Goodwood and nurseries at Chepstow and Goodwood in midsummer: well below best afterwards: better suited by 6f than 5f: yet to race on a soft surface. *W. G. R. Wightman*   **58**

HALLOW FAIR   7 b.g. Wolver Hollow 126 – Fingers (Lord Gayle (USA) 124) [1991 11.7g 12m 14m 10.2g 11.8g* 12g⁵ 1992 11.4f 12d 14.6g] leggy, attractive gelding: seems of little account these days. *C. A. Horgan*   **–**

HALLPLACE   2 ch.c. (May 4) Hallgate 127 – Glory Isle 60 (Hittite Glory 125) [1992 6m⁶ 6.1f⁵ 7g 8g⁶ 8d⁶ 7d² 7.3s⁵] 4,600F, 2,800Y: rangy, workmanlike colt: sixth foal: half-brother to 7f (at 2 yrs) to 1¼m winner Rio Pedras (by Kala Shikari) and a winner in Italy: dam ran only at 3 yrs, winning at 9f: modest maiden: stays 1m: probably acts on heavy ground: visored (ran creditably) fifth outing: sold 6,000 gns Newmarket Autumn Sales. *M. R. Channon*   **58**

HALL'S CREEK (IRE)   3 b.g. Green Desert (USA) 127 – Valois (Lyphard (USA) 132) [1991 NR 1992 6.1s 6d] half-brother to winning hurdler Chateauneuf (by Niniski), fairly useful 7f winner Shannon Cottage (by Shecky Greene) and 1985 2-y-o 7f winner Shannon Vale (by Irish River): dam half-sister to High Top and Camden Town: blinkered, no worthwhile form in maidens at Chepstow and Redcar (bandaged behind) in the autumn. *D. W. P. Arbuthnot*   **–**

HALMANERROR   2 gr.c. (Jun 10) Lochnager 132 – Counter Coup (Busted 134) [1992 a7g] half-brother to Gran Premio d'Italia winner Celio Rufo (by Warpath) and fairly useful hurdler Halmajor (by Mandrake Major): dam lightly raced: 33/1, slowly away when last of 11 in maiden at Southwell. *C. W. C. Elsey*   **–**

HALSTON PRINCE   5 b.g. Petorius 117 – Repicado Rose (USA) (Repicado (CHI)) [1991 10g 8g 8g 1992 8d 10g 8m³ 10.5d 10f* 7m 7.9d] compact, robust gelding: moderate mover: fair performer: claimed out of F. J. Houghton's stable £7,105 after fair effort in blinkers third start: won handicap at Ripon in June: tailed-off last afterwards: stays 1¼m: best efforts on top-of-the-ground: usually races prominently: sold to join B. Mactaggart 2,000 gns Doncaster September Sales. *Mrs J. R. Ramsden*   **65**

HAMADRYAD (IRE)   4 b.c. Fairy King (USA) – Clifden Bottoms (Wolver Hollow 126) [1991 6d⁴ 8m² 8.2f³ 8m³ 6f 7m* 7m⁵ 7s 1992 7g⁶ 8f² 7d² 7f* 7.1f* 7m⁴ 7m⁴ 8g 9d* 10m] leggy colt: impresses in appearance: poor mover: progressed well throughout the season in handicaps: won at Brighton and Haydock in midsummer and at Goodwood (easily best effort, by 5 lengths) in September: effective from 7f to 9f: acts on firm ground, but goes well on dead: sweating (only poor effort) final start: **88**

often wears crossed noseband: often claimer ridden: has idled, and is held up. *W. Carter*

HAMANAKA (USA) 3 b.f. Conquistador Cielo (USA) – Tastefully (USA) (Hail To Reason) [1991 7.1m⁵ 7m 7m⁴ 1992 8s⁵ 10g 8d⁴ 9.7v⁵] tall, leggy, angular filly: modest performer: no worthwhile form in 1992: stays 9.7f: probably acts on any going: ran creditably in visor final start: sold to join M. Hammond 6,200 gns Newmarket Autumn Sales. *J. R. Fanshawe* —

HAMAS (IRE) 3 b. or br.c. Danzig (USA) – Fall Aspen (USA) (Pretense) [1991 NR 1992 7g² 8.1g* 8.1d² 7.1m* 7f 7.9d² 7m⁴ 6g² 8g³ 8s 5m*] lengthy, workmanlike colt: closely related to 3 winners, including 1m to 1¼m winner Northern Aspen (by Northern Dancer) and French 10.5f to 13.5f winner Colorado Dancer (by Shareef Dancer), both smart, and half-brother to several winners: dam smart stakes winner at up to 7f: useful performer: won minor events at Sandown and Chepstow in the spring and listed race (by 2½ lengths from Blyton Lad) at Newmarket in October: useful efforts at 1m but even better form at 5f: acts on good to firm and dead ground, acted as a pacemaker on soft: genuine and consistent: stays in training. *P. T. Walwyn* 109

HAMAYA (USA) 3 br.f. Mr Prospector (USA) – Water Lily (FR) 116 (Riverman (USA) 131) [1991 NR 1992 7m⁴] $750,000Y: seventh foal: closely related to Grade 1 9f winner Talinum (by Alydar) and half-sister to several winners, notably useful but later disappointing 1989 2-y-o 6f winner Gharam (by Green Dancer): dam very useful in France at 2 yrs and Grade 3 handicap winner in USA at 4 yrs: 15/8 favourite, 7 lengths fourth of 10 to 6-length winner Arboretum in maiden at Lingfield in August: should have improved: visits Green Desert. *J. H. M. Gosden* 60

HAMEEM (IRE) 3 b.c. Ajdal (USA) 130 – Colourful (FR) 108 (Gay Mecene (USA) 128) [1991 NR 1992 8d⁴ 8.2d² 7g³ 8g² 7d* 7g 6g 7d] 75,000Y: well-made colt: third foal: half-brother to 9f and 1½m winner Bookcase (by Siberian Express) and 4-y-o 6f and 8.3f winner Ikteshaf (by Green Desert): dam French 2-y-o 5f winner out of high-class French staying 2-y-o First Bloom: fair form: blinkered last 4 starts, winning maiden at Goodwood in August on first, and well beaten in handicaps last 2: probably stays 1m: yet to race on top-of-the-ground: front runner. *A. A. Scott* 71

HAMILTON LADY (IRE) 4 b.f. Zino 127 – Villasanta (Corvaro (USA) 122) [1991 8.1m⁶ 9.2d 16.1m⁶ 1992 a7g a12g⁵ 13d² 16.9g 13f³ 14.1h⁴ 12.1m³ 13f⁴ 12.1g*] lengthy, rather angular filly: inconsistent handicapper: won Hamilton apprentice race in August: effective at 1½m, and should stay well: acts on firm and dead ground. *D. Moffatt* 40

HAMSAH (IRE) 2 b.f. (May 2) Green Desert (USA) 127 – Hayloft (FR) 111 (Tudor Melody 129) [1992 5m² 5f* 5f 5m 5.2g² 5g* 6m⁵ 5m] close-coupled filly: half-sister to Irish 2000 Guineas winner Wassl (by Mill Reef), a winning hurdler and to dam of Queen Mary winner On Tiptoes: dam won 3 races over 5f at 2 yrs: fairly 86

Bentinck Stakes, Newmarket—Hamas looks a useful sprinter in winning this listed race; Blyton Lad (left) narrowly takes second

useful performer: successful in maiden at Salisbury and minor event at Warwick in the summer: best form at 5f: yet to race on a soft surface. *D. R. C. Elsworth*

HAND ON HEART (IRE)   3 b.f. Taufan (USA) 119 – Pichincha 83 (Pharly (FR)   **62**
130) [1991 NR 1992 a8g2 a8g* a8g3 a8g 7g2 8g2 7f* 7.6m* 7.6g 8g3 7d5 6.9g*] IR
7,200F: strong filly: poor mover: half-sister to fairly useful Irish 1¼m winner Peace
Mission (by Dunbeath) and a winner in Italy: dam 5f (at 2 yrs) to 10.6f winner:
modest but well-placed performer: won maiden at Southwell in January, claimer at
Warwick and handicap at Chester (for 7-lb apprentice) in early-summer and another
claimer (claimed by P. Monteith £6,500) at Carlisle in September: should prove best
at up to 1m: acts on firm going (raced on unfavoured part of track on dead) and on
fibresand: mostly consistent. *W. J. Haggas*

HAND PAINTED   8 br.g. Rabdan 129 – Morkulla (SWE) 49 (Royal Park 114)   **61 d**
[1991 a8g2 a8g4 a11g3 a8g3 a10g4 a10g a12g3 9f4 a10g2 10f2 8f2 a8g 9m3 a8g6 11.5m3
11.5m3 11.6m2 10.8m2 a10g5 10g2 10.1s3 a11g* a12g* 1992 a11g* a14g* a14g3 a11g4
a12g 16.2g2 10.8d 12.3g6 17.1m a12g a14g6] leggy gelding: has a round action: won
claimer (claimed out of J. Pearce's stable £6,659) and amateurs event at Southwell
in January: below best afterwards: effective from 1¼m to 1¾m: acts on fibresand
and suited by a sound surface on turf: often bandaged: has put head in air: has won
for claimer and amateur: sold 700 gns Doncaster June Sales. *C. R. Beever*

HANDSOME GENT   3 b.g. Dunbeath (USA) 127 – French Surprise (Hello   **75 d**
Gorgeous (USA) 128) [1991 NR 1992 8g* 10s3 8.3g 8g 10d6 10d2 11v2] lengthy
gelding: first reported foal: dam French maiden: somewhat disappointing performer: won maiden at Warwick in April: only modest form when second in seller and
claimer in the autumn: probably stays 11f: has carried head high: sold to join L.
Lungo 6,400 gns Ascot November Sales. *Lord Huntingdon*

HANDY LASS   3 b.f. Nicholas Bill 125 – Mandrian 103 (Mandamus 120) [1991   **59**
5g 6m 1992 8.9s4 10m* 11.8g3 14.1d] leggy, sparely-made filly: has a long stride:
modest performer: won claimer at Nottingham in June: trained until after next start
by J. Wharton: off course over 2 months, tailed off in handicap in September: stays
11.8f: best effort on good to firm ground, but probably acts on soft: looks headstrong:
sold to join Mrs A. Knight 1,800 gns Doncaster October Sales. *Mrs J. R. Ramsden*

HANG TEN   3 b.c. Kris 135 – Broken Wave 103 (Bustino 136) [1991 NR 1992 10m   **71**
10g6 10g2] smallish, quite attractive colt: split a pastern at 2 yrs: shows knee
action: first foal: dam, 1¼m to 15f winner here and in France, is out of Oaks third
Britannia's Rule, herself daughter of half-sister to Vaguely Noble: well-backed
favourite, form only when 10 lengths second of 7 to Vratislav in weak maiden at
Windsor in July, jockey reporting horse finished lame: sold only 600 gns Newmarket
Autumn Sales. *L. M. Cumani*

HANJESSDAN   4 b.g. Reesh 117 – Palace Travel (High Top 131) [1991 10m 1992   **–**
a8g5 8s6 8v a10g 10m 10.2f 8.9g] robust gelding: seems of little account. *D. Haydn
Jones*

HANLEY'S HANDS (IRE)   3 b.g. Blakeney 126 – Paperwork (Brigadier   **62**
Gerard 144) [1991 NR 1992 10g 7g 8.5f3 11.1m2 11.1g2 12.2d] 6,000F, 6,200Y: small,
stocky gelding: closely related to a maiden by Morston and half-brother to 1m seller
winner City Final (by Final Straw) and 2 winners abroad, one in listed company in
Germany: dam won over 8.5f in France and over hurdles here: modest performer:
well-backed favourite, second in handicaps at Hamilton and Edinburgh in July:
visored, well beaten in claimer in October: much better suited by 11f than shorter.
M. H. Tompkins

HANNAH BROWN (IRE)   4 ch.f. Carlingford Castle 126 – Liebeslied 91 (Dike   **–**
(USA)) [1991 8g 8m 8.5f 1992 a7g a12g] close-coupled, sparely-made filly: seems of
little account. *B. A. McMahon*

HANSOM LAD   9 b.g. Dublin Taxi – Trackalady 96 (Track Spare 125) [1991 a6g2   **–**
a6g a6g4 a5g 6m 5f2 5f 5m 5m 6.1m a8g* 1992 6d] big, good-topped gelding: carries
plenty of condition: rated 65 at 8 yrs on the fibresand at Southwell: burly, never a
threat in handicap in October: suited by sprint distances: has seemed none too
genuine on turf. *W. W. Haigh*

HAPPY SMILE (IRE)   4 b.f. Royal Match 117 – Topping Girl (Sea Hawk II 131)   **95**
[1991 9v 10s3 10v 10m2 10g* 9g 10m4 12g* 11m3 11g5 14g6 12g2 12m3 10.2s2 12g
10g2 12s4 11s6 10g 1992 8d 12d 10g 10m2 9m2 12m* 11m* 12g 9g4 12g3 10g6 12s
10g3 11g5 10d 7g 10g 10g] workmanlike filly: sister to Irish 6f to 1¼m winner Happy
Bride and half-sister to several winners, notably smart Irish middle-distance colt
Topanoora (by Ahonoora): dam never ran: useful Irish handicapper: successful at
the Curragh (ladies race for successive year) and Naas in midsummer: last of 9 in

slowly-run listed race at Newmarket final start: effective from 9f to 1½m: acts on good to firm and soft ground: tough. *F. Dunne, Ireland*

HARCLIFF   3 b.g. Never So Bold 135 – Mrs Danvers 87 (Balidar 133) [1991 NR   **60**
1992 a8g⁴ 10g a7g² a7g³ a7g⁴ a7g a8g] 6,200Y: lengthy, sparely-made gelding: third foal: dam, winner at 2 yrs, best at 5f: modest maiden: showed nothing at 1¼m: acts on equitrack: wears bandages behind. *D. J. S. Cosgrove*

HARD EIGHT   2 b.c. (Mar 3) Primo Dominie 121 – Faisalah (Gay Mecene (USA)   **60 p**
128) [1992 6d] 8,000F, 13,500Y: smallish, sturdy colt: first foal: dam unraced: 33/1 and bit backward, around 8 lengths seventh of 17 to Rain Brother in maiden at Goodwood in September, pushed along at halfway and not knocked about when beaten: will improve. *A. C. Stewart*

HARDLINER   3 b. or br.c. Sizzling Melody 117 – Miss Trilli 89 (Ardoon 124)   **69**
[1991 6f 6m⁵ 6m 6g 1992 6m* 6g 8g] quite good-topped colt: fair performer: won 3-runner minor event at Lingfield in June: off course 11 weeks then well beaten in Newmarket handicap (stiff task) and Leicester claimer: stays 6f: acts on good to firm ground: wore crossed noseband last 4 starts: retained by trainer 1,500 gns Ascot September Sales. *C. F. Wall*

HARD SELL   5 ch.g. Hard Fought 125 – Misoptimist 111 (Blakeney 126) [1991   **–**
a8g⁵ a7g² a7g³ a7g a7g³ 1992 7d a7g a7g] workmanlike gelding: rated 65 at 4 yrs: no form in 1992: stays 1m: acts on firm going and fibresand: wore eyeshield as 4-y-o: often hangs, but has won for apprentice. *J. G. FitzGerald*

HARD TASK   2 b.f. (Feb 4) Formidable (USA) 125 – Myth 89 (Troy 137) [1992   **68**
7g⁴ 7g⁶ 7.1g⁵] 6,400Y: sturdy filly: second foal: half-sister to 4-y-o 1¼m winner Supertop (by High Top): dam middle-distance winner, is out of close relation to Wassl: fair maiden: will be well suited by middle distances. *R. F. Johnson Houghton*

HARD TO FIGURE   6 gr.h. Telsmoss 91 – Count On Me 77 (No Mercy 126)   **101**
[1991 6g 6g³ 7f 5.8d* 6d 5.1g⁴ 5g⁵ 6g⁵ 8f⁵ 6g² 6g 6m² 6g³ 6m³ 6m* 6d⁶ 1992 8d 5g 6g⁶ 6m³ 7g⁵ 5.7f 7d 6m⁴ 6m⁵ 7m³ 6g⁴ 6d² 6g² 6d 7m³ 6m³ 6s*] rather leggy, work-manlike horse: useful and tremendously consistent handicapper: gained deserved reward for numerous good efforts when winning at Lingfield in October: best at 6f/7f: acts on any ground: usually held up: tough. *R. J. Hodges*

HARD TO SNUB   4 b.c. Shardari 134 – Snub (Steel Heart 128) [1991 12g 10m   **–**
1992 9g] rangy colt: seems of little account: sold 1,400 gns Ascot June Sales. *M. Madgwick*

HARITI (IRE)   2 b.f. (Feb 23) Flash of Steel 120 – Abergwrle (Absalom 128)   **45 p**
[1992 5f 8d 7.1s] IR 5,000F, 12,500Y: good-bodied filly: second foal: half-sister to a winner in Italy: dam twice-raced daughter of 1000 Guineas winner Caergwrle: showed signs of ability, considerately handled: probably capable of fair bit better. *D. R. C. Elsworth*

HARLEQUIN GIRL   4 ch.f. Primo Dominie 121 – Song of Gold 85 (Song 132)   **39 d**
[1991 7g 8d⁶ 7g 8.3m 5.3f⁶ 7m⁴ 6f⁴ 6m⁴ 6m² 6m a6g a8g 1992 7m⁵ 8m 7.5m 8.3m 7g 7.6m 6g 7f 8f⁵] workmanlike filly: inconsistent maiden handicapper: stays 7.5f: acts on firm ground: no improvement visored/blinkered. *K. T. Ivory*

HARLESTONE BROOK   2 ch.g. (Mar 9) Jalmood (USA) 126 – Harlestone   **46**
Lake 78 (Riboboy (USA) 124) [1992 7s⁴ a8g] first foal: dam out-and-out stayer: poor form for 7-lb claimer in maidens at Lingfield in the autumn: will be well suited by middle distances at least. *J. L. Dunlop*

HAROLDON (IRE)   3 ch.c. Heraldiste (USA) 121 – Cordon 89 (Morston (FR)   **82**
125) [1991 6d³ 6m² 6m⁴ 1992 8d⁶ 8.5g* 8.1d⁶ 8f 8.5d⁴ 8g 7g] leggy, close-coupled colt: fair handicapper: made all in maiden at Beverley in April: well below form last 2 starts, when sweating first occasion: stays 8.5f: acts on good to firm ground (below form on firm) and dead. *B. Palling*

HARPLEY   5 gr.g. Beldale Flutter (USA) 130 – Jellygold 95 (Jellaby 124) [1991 12g   **–**
13.8f⁴ 12.2m 13.6m⁴ 1992 a14g] sturdy gelding: little worthwhile form on flat, last seen out in January: modest winning hurdler in 1991/2: sold to join M. Castell 2,700 gns Ascot September Sales. *S. E. Kettlewell*

HARPOON LOUIE (USA)   2 b.c. (Mar 23) Eskimo (USA) – Twelfth Pleasure   **84 p**
(USA) (Fappiano (USA)) [1992 6d⁵ 7m² 7.1m* 7s⁵ 7d²] $13,000F, $40,000Y: big, lengthy, well-made colt: has plenty of scope: first foal: dam unraced: sire (by North-ern Dancer) winner at up to 1m: progressive performer: well-backed favourite, won median auction maiden at Edinburgh in July: very much caught eye in York nursery 3 months later then finished excellent second of 21 in similar event at Doncaster: will stay 1m: will continue on the upgrade. *M. H. Easterby*

345

HARRY 2 ch.c. (Mar 3) Risk Me (FR) 127 – Relko's Pride (Relko 136) [1992 7m⁶] **50** p
1,365Y: half-brother to several winners, including 1979 2-y-o 5f winner Welsh Pride
(by Welsh Saint): dam unraced half-sister to Bold Lad: 33/1, over 9 lengths sixth of
16 to True Hero in maiden at Leicester in September, held up and behind then
keeping on final 2f: wore bandages: should improve. *P. A. Kelleway*

HARRY'S COMING 8 b.g. Marching On 101 – Elegant Star 86 (Star Moss 122) **68**
[1991 5g* 5g 5m 6g³ 5m³ 6m 6g* 5d³ 6v⁵ a6g* 5.7m⁵ 6.1m a6g⁵ 5f⁶ 5.1m 1992 6.1d a79
6s 6g 6m 6g⁴ 6h³ 6d² 6g⁴ 6m³ a6g* a7g 6m 6s] leggy, good-topped gelding: fair
handicapper: won at Nottingham and Lingfield in the summer: below form last 2
starts: effective at 6f and 7f: acts on firm and dead going and on equitrack, unsuited
by soft: tried blinkered/visored at 3 yrs: good mount for apprentice. *R. J. Hodges*

HARRY'S GOING 4 b.c. Marching On 101 – Elegant Star 86 (Star Moss 122) –
[1991 6m 8m 6f 1992 a8g] leggy, lengthy colt: no worthwhile form: sold 900 gns
Ascot March Sales. *R. J. Hodges*

HARRY'S JOY 4 b.f. Aragon 118 – Happy Donna 106 (Huntercombe 133) [1991 5d –
7.1m 6m 5d 6m 1992 a6g a7g] leggy, plain filly: of little account. *D. R. Tucker*

HARRY'S LADY (IRE) 4 b.f. Alleging (USA) 120 – Lucky Engagement (USA) –
75 (What Luck (USA)) [1991 8m 10g⁵ 10m 8.2f⁶ 9.2s a8g 1992 8.9m 8.1g 7g 7.6m]
small, leggy filly: no worthwhile form, but has hinted at ability: worth a try over 6f:
usually bandaged: blinkered last 2 starts. *T. Thomson Jones*

HARVEST GIRL (IRE) 3 b.f. Thatching 131 – June Maid 56 (Junius (USA) 124) **104**
[1991 5d² 6m* 5.2g² 5.2f² 6f² 5d² 7.3g⁴ 1992 7m⁴ 8g 6m² 5m⁵ 5m 6g* 5m² 5m⁵
6g] leggy, workmanlike filly: useful performer: won minor event at Kempton: best
effort when neck second to Notley in listed event at Doncaster 4 days later in September: below form afterwards: best at up to 6f: acts on firm and dead ground: tends
to get on toes: sold 76,000 gns Newmarket December Sales. *G. A. Pritchard-Gordon*

HASHAR (IRE) 4 b.c. Darshaan 133 – Hazy Idea 118 (Hethersett 134) [1991 **96**
10g* 12.3g² 9g⁴ 1992 11f⁴ 10.1g* 12f 10.4d⁵ 10m] sturdy, quite-attractive ex-Irish
colt: half-brother to numerous winners, including very smart 1975 2-y-o Hittite
Glory (by Habitat): dam won from 6f to 1¼m: useful performer: won £13,500
handicap at Epsom in June from Fire Top, pair clear: failed to repeat that form:
effective from 1¼m to 1½m: ideally suited by some give in the ground. *D. R. C.
Elsworth*

HASTA LA VISTA 2 b.c. (Apr 21) Superlative 118 – Falcon Berry (FR) (Bustino **48**
136) [1992 5m² 5f a6g a7s 7g 6s⁴ 10.5d⁴] 8,200Y: compact colt: has a round action:
fifth foal: half-brother to middle-distance 6-y-o Beaumond (by Jalmood) and fair
miler Top Berry (by High Top): dam lightly-raced daughter of Cheveley Park
second Red Berry: poor form: best effort at 10.5f: acts on good to firm and dead
ground: blinkered (best effort for some time) penultimate start. *M. W. Easterby*

HASTY AMY 3 b.f. Daring March 116 – Babe In The Wood (Athens Wood 126) –
[1991 6m a6g a7g 1992 12.2g] lengthy, workmanlike filly: of little account. *M. W.
Ellerby*

HASTY SPARK 4 b.g. Shardari 134 – Fire And Ice (FR) (Reliance II 137) [1991 **45**
10m a12g 12.3g 1992 11.8m 10.3g⁵ a12g 10.3g a12g] close-coupled gelding: form only a–
when fifth in Doncaster seller: stays 10.3f. *C. F. Wall*

HATAAL (IRE) 3 ch.f. Hatim (USA) 121 – Tenoria 82 (Mansingh (USA) 120) **32**
[1991 5f⁶ 5g 6d³ 6m 7m⁶ 7f⁶ 7.5f 7m 1992 6.1d 7.5m 8d 8m³ 9.9d³ 9.2m⁵ 8.3f³ 7g⁵
10.9s] unfurnished filly: has a round action: poor, inconsistent plater: should stay
1¼m: acts on good to firm and dead ground: visored last 2 starts. *J. Balding*

HATEEL 6 b.h. Kalaglow 132 – Oatfield 69 (Great Nephew 126) [1991 10g³ 10d* **104**
10g 13.3d³ 12m* 12g⁴ 14g* 12g² 13.3f⁶ 12g⁵ 12s⁶ 1992 10d⁵ 12d 16.2d³dis 16.4m⁴ 12f
14m⁵ 15.9d² 15s 14.6f 10.9s⁴] strong, well-made horse: carries condition: moderate
mover: very useful performer in 1991: best effort at 6 yrs when unlucky third to Al
Mutahm in Sagaro Stakes at Ascot (disqualified for interference) in April: well
below form 5 of last 6 starts and found little when second to Tyrone Bridge in listed
race at York: effective from 1½m to 2m: unsuited by very firm going nowadays, and
best with some give: seems not one to rely on nowadays: sold 16,500 gns Newmarket December Sales. *P. T. Walwyn*

HATOOF (USA) 3 ch.f. Irish River (FR) 131 – Cadeaux d'Amie (USA) 115 **120**
(Lyphard (USA) 132) [1991 8g* 8g² 8d² 1992 7g² 8g* 8m⁶ 8s⁵ 8s³ 9.3s* 10d*]
   The General Accident One Thousand Guineas was a potential sickener
for Walter Swinburn, the preferred jockey for Marling who was contractually

General Accident One Thousand Guineas Stakes, Newmarket—
Hatoof wins a rough race from Marling (noseband), Kenbu (right) and Perfect Circle

obliged to ride Maktoum Al-Maktoum's Hatoof. It still might have been after a lengthy stewards' inquiry, but the order as they passed the post was allowed to stand—Hatoof first, Marling second; the distance between them, a head. The first classic was a nail-biter. Hatoof and Marling shared our vote for pick of the paddock and started 5/1 joint-second favourites, the latter not seen out since an unbeaten two-year-old season which culminated in the Cheveley Park Stakes. Hatoof had been right in the forefront of 1991's two-year-old fillies as well, while giving the impression that a mile might prove on the short side the following season. Given the modest pace and seven-furlong trip, Hatoof's neck second in the Prix Imprudence at Maisons-Laffitte in April, outpaced by Kenbu in the final furlong, was a satisfactory trial. Kenbu was again in opposition at Newmarket where the Fred Darling winner Musicale started 7/2 favourite despite a recent cracked heel. Others in the field included the Marcel Boussac winner and Fred Darling third Culture Vulture and five from the Nell Gwyn Stakes in A-To-Z, Perfect Circle, Soiree, Harvest Girl and Skimble. Unlike several in the fourteen-strong field, Swinburn knew that his mount would have no problems staying the trip. Giving her a superb ride, he positioned Hatoof just off the very conservative early pace which had several pulling for their heads. Mahasin took them along, to be overtaken by Musicale approaching the three-furlong marker with Marling right at the back. Marling could not get a clear run and when Hatoof was produced on the outside two furlongs out Kenbu, on the rails, looked to be her chief danger—Kenbu and her own waywardness, because Hatoof was shortly to start hanging markedly to her left, despite Swinburn's swift change of whip

Ciga Prix de l'Opera, Longchamp—another game performance from Hatoof;
she pips La Favorita in a driving finish, with Ruby Tiger (check cap) third

hand, hampering the beaten Musicale who in turn checked Perfect Circle. That problem resolved, Hatoof wore down Kenbu to lead in the last hundred yards and had a sufficient start to hold Marling's storming finish.

Whether Swinburn would have preferred Marling to Hatoof, we do not know. There was precious little to choose between them on their performances as two-year-olds. Hatoof had been beaten in two of her three starts, but she too could so easily have ended the year with a perfect record. Those defeats, after victory in a newcomers race at Longchamp, were both in photo-finishes when she'd finished best of all, and she was particularly unlucky to go down by the minimum distance to Culture Vulture in the Prix Marcel Boussac after stumbling badly early on then getting hemmed in on the rails. Perhaps Hatoof was due her slice of luck at Newmarket. We concluded our comments in *Racehorses of 1991* by stating that she struck us as 'a likely candidate for the Prix de Diane'. Nothing in Hatoof's Newmarket performance diminished that view but in the meantime Hatoof was to contest the Poule d'Essai des Pouliches. Coupled with her pacemaker Plume Magique, she started 7/4 favourite to complete the double achieved previously only by Imprudence, Miesque and Ravinella. Plans for Hatoof had to be put on hold when she finished only sixth. Plume Magique set a strong pace and Hatoof was sensibly kept second of the nine runners. Nothing else appeared to go right: Hatoof raced freely and failed to handle the turns, had to be given reminders before heading the pacemaker in the straight then was quickly swallowed up. A possible explanation for this tame display was the ground, firmer than at Newmarket or in any of her previous races, but it was also reported that the bit had slipped. Either way, Hatoof was rested and it was another three months, the Prix de Diane long gone, before she was seen out again.

Year in, year out, one must prepare to be disappointed with horses returning from a mid-season break. Thankfully, though, Hatoof was an exception. The first two races of her come-back were the two top mile events in France, the Prix Jacques le Marois at Deauville and the Prix du Moulin de

Maktoum Al-Maktoum's "Hatoof"

Longchamp, in which she finished a never-dangerous fifth of fourteen at Deauville having been at the back of the field for over five furlongs, and an excellent third of ten, ridden with rather less restraint, to All At Sea at Longchamp. Then Hatoof was stepped up in trip and back in the winners enclosure. The Group 2 Ciga Prix de l'Opera at Longchamp on Arc day saw her take on eleven others, including the very smart five-year-olds Ruby Tiger and Leariva, and swoop from the back of the field to challenge a hundred yards from home and beat rank outsider La Favorita half a length, with Ruby Tiger a length back in third. The way in which she was given plenty of time to warm to her task in that strongly-run race over an extended nine furlongs gave every encouragement about her prospects at a mile and a quarter and she was finally given her chance at the trip in the E. P. Taylor Stakes at Woodbine, Canada two weeks later. The 1991 E. P. Taylor was won by the North American-trained Lady Shirl but one has to go back to 1981 to find the next winner of the race that wasn't sent from Europe. Ruby Tiger won in 1990 and was in the field once again. Giving 5 lb as opposed to the 12 lb at Longchamp, Ruby Tiger clearly had a chance to reverse placings with Hatoof, but the result between them was the same, and ten others had to give way as well as Hatoof came with another well-timed challenge in the final furlong to win by a length and a quarter. A strong European showing was completed by Urban Sea in second, Ruby Tiger fourth and Party Cited fifth; Hatoof's performance has to be rated right up with her best.

Hatoof (USA) (ch.f. 1989)	Irish River (FR) (ch 1976)	Riverman (b 1969)	Never Bend
			River Lady
		Irish Star (b 1960)	Klairon
			Botany Bay
	Cadeaux d'Amie (USA) (ch 1984)	Lyphard (b 1969)	Northern Dancer
			Goofed
		Tananarive (b 1970)	Le Fabuleux
			Ten Double

Hatoof's One Thousand Guineas was the first big-race success of 1992 for her sire Irish River, and not the last. His best other runners in Europe were the Prix Jacques le Marois winner Exit To Nowhere and St James's Palace Stakes winner Brief Truce. Both those colts founded their excellent records on performances at a mile but also demonstrated their effectiveness at a mile and a quarter, and a good number of the top-class miler Irish River's earlier successes as a stallion came over middle distances. The dam's side of Hatoof's pedigree also gives grounds for wishing that she had appeared in the Prix de Diane. Her dam's half-sister Mrs Penny won the race in 1980. A superbly tough and genuine filly, Mrs Penny also won the Cheveley Park Stakes at two years, the one-and-a-half-mile Prix Vermeille, and two graded handicaps in the United States as a four-year-old. Her dam Tananarive, a winner of three races at up to a mile and three quarters in France, bred another three winners, including Hatoof's dam Cadeaux d'Amie. A smart two-year-old when she, like Hatoof, contested the Prix d'Aumale (finishing a close third) and Marcel Boussac (running moderately), Cadeaux d'Amie was not quite so good at three when she won only a minor event over a mile and a quarter. Hatoof is a good-topped, attractive filly and an easy mover. One thing much in her favour stepping up in trip was her very relaxed disposition. Whether Hatoof is capable of reproducing her best over even longer distances than a mile and a quarter is questionable, but the good news is that we may still get an opportunity to find out as she is to remain in training. *Mme C. Head, France*

HATTA RIVER (USA) 2 b.c. (Feb 21) Irish River (FR) 131 – Fallacieuse **59** p (Habitat 134) [1992 7g 8d⁴] $17,000F, $75,000Y: good-topped colt: half-brother to fairly useful 1m winner Fecamp (by Nureyev): dam, French 1m winner, is daughter of half-sister to good 1979 Canadian 2-y-o Flightish: over 7 lengths fourth of 16 to Commanche Gold in moderately-run maiden at Kempton in September, gradually outpaced from 2f out: will progress again. *Major W. R. Hern*

HATTA'S MILL 3 b.c. Green Desert (USA) 127 – Mill On The Floss 117 (Mill **100** Reef (USA) 141) [1991 7g² 1992 8d 10.3g* 10m² 8f a11s² 10f³ 11f⁵] good-topped, attractive colt: won £7,100 maiden at Chester: again set pace when 5 lengths second to Jeune in listed race at Goodwood later in May when trained by H. Cecil: placed in allowance races in USA subsequently: may well prove better suited by 1½m: possibly needs a sound surface. *W. Mott, USA*

HATTA SUNSHINE (USA) 2 b.c. (Mar 23) Dixieland Band (USA) – Mountain – p Sunshine (USA) (Vaguely Noble 140) [1992 7d⁶] $130,000Y: lengthy, angular colt: has plenty of scope: ninth foal: half-brother to several winners including Grade 2 Withers Stakes winner Country Pine (by His Majesty), successful at up to 9.5f: dam unraced half-sister to dam of Indian Skimmer: sire smart performer at up to 9f: well-backed 4/1-shot, though burly and green, remote sixth of 7 to Kusamba in minor event at York in September, dropping right away from 2f out: moved poorly down: should do better. *J. H. M. Gosden*

HATTON'S GEM 2 br.f. (May 31) Formidable (USA) 125 – Jewel Chest (Busted 63 p 134) [1992 7g] third living foal: dam once-raced daughter of half-sister to smart sprinter Laser Light: 33/1, around 6 lengths ninth of 24 to Fayfa in maiden at Newmarket in October, staying on from rear: will do better. *J. R. Fanshawe*

HAUNTED WOOD (USA) 2 b.f. (Feb 24) Nijinsky (CAN) 138 – Fairy 67 p Footsteps 123 (Mill Reef (USA) 141) [1992 8.2s⁴] $450,000Y: half-sister to fair 11.7f and 1½m winner Lovely Fairy (by Beldale Flutter) and a winner in France: dam won 1000 Guineas and is half-sister to Light Cavalry: 3/1, 4½ lengths fourth of 14 to Azzilfi in maiden at Nottingham in October, headed just inside final 1f and not knocked about: will improve, particularly over middle distances. *H. R. A. Cecil*

HAUNTING RHAPSODY (USA) 3 ch.f. Count Francescui (USA) – Vitale 57 (Vitiges (FR) 132) [1991 NR 1992 5m² 5f* 5f] $35,000Y: rather leggy filly: half-sister to useful sprinter Haunting Beauty, 1990 2-y-o 5f winner Haunting Obsession and to 2 minor winners in USA, all by Barachois: dam ran once: modest form: 6/4 on, won median auction maiden at Warwick in May: last of 7 in Beverley minor event 11 days later: sold 1,150 gns Newmarket September Sales. *J. Etherington*

HAUT-BRION (IRE) 3 br.g. Alzao (USA) 117 – Romanee Conti (Will Somers 45 114§) [1991 7d 7g 8.1g 1992 10.8g 13d 16.2g 10.1f 12.3m⁴ 12d² 13.8f⁵ 13.8d 12.4v] strong, good-topped gelding: plating-class maiden: trained until after third start by P. Chapple-Hyam: off course 3 months, soundly beaten in handicaps last 2 starts: stays 1½m: acts on good to firm and dead ground: has run in snatches. *W. Storey*

HAVE A NIGHTCAP 3 ch.g. Night Shift (USA) – Final Orders (USA) (Prince 47 John) [1991 7.1m 7g⁶ 8.1m⁶ 1992 8.9v 8m⁶ 8g 7d³ 8f⁴ 8.3m 7f⁵ a7g 8.9d] close-coupled gelding: inconsistent plater: should prove better at 1m than shorter: acts on firm and dead ground, and on fibresand: effective blinkered (when usually edgy) or not: sold out of M. Jarvis' stable 2,500 gns Newmarket July Sales after seventh start: won selling hurdle in October. *J. L. Harris*

HAVEN OF LOVE (IRE) 2 b.f. (May 22) Waajib 121 – Arena 86 (Sallust 134) 47 p [1992 7g] 4,200Y: workmanlike filly: sixth foal: half-sister to 3-y-o Wakil (by Tate Gallery), 1m winner Miss Wassl (by Wassl) and a winner abroad by Cure The Blues: dam lightly raced: 25/1, towards rear of Newmarket maiden won by Fayfa in October, hanging right under pressure. *C. A. Cyzer*

HAVERTON 5 b.g. Carwhite 127 – Rosie Pug (Mummy's Pet 125) [1991 NR 1992 – a10g 10.8g] strong gelding: moderate mover: looks of little account these days: visored final start. *T. Casey*

HAWAII STAR (IRE) 2 b.f. (Mar 29) Dominion 123 – Onika 54 (Great Nephew 51 126) [1992 5d⁵ 5g⁶ 5f 5m⁵ 6h 5.3f⁵] lengthy, good-topped filly: second foal: half-sister to 3-y-o Swale Side (by Sayf El Arab): dam 4-y-o 1m winner: modest maiden: heavily-backed favourite for Brighton seller in August last time: possibly requires some give in the ground. *G. Lewis*

HAWAII STORM (FR) 4 b.g. Plugged Nickle (USA) – Slewvindaloo (USA) 56 (Seattle Slew (USA)) [1991 8.2g 6d 7m 7m 8m 1992 a8g⁵ a7g a7g* a7g⁴ 7.5g⁵ 7g a72 a7g* a7g² a8g² a8g* a7g* 7g³ 7d* 7d 8g a8g⁵ a8g²] leggy gelding: fair handicapper: had a very good season, particularly at Southwell where successful 4 times: also won apprentice race at Salisbury in August: effective at 7f and 1m: acts on good to soft ground and fibresand: usually held up, made all at Salisbury. *Miss A. J. Whitfield*

HAWAIT AL BARR 4 b.f. Green Desert (USA) 127 – Allegedly Blue (USA) 106 **100** (Alleged (USA) 138) [1991 10g² 12f* 11.9m² 12g 14.6m⁵ 13.9m* 16g* 1992 16.2d 16.4m 16.1f4 13.9m 16d4] tall, leggy filly: good mover: useful performer on her day: very good fourth to Witness Box in Northumberland Plate at Newcastle third start, only worthwhile form in 1992: best form at 2m: acts on firm ground. *M. R. Stoute*

HAWA LAYAAM (IRE) 3 ch.g. Kris 135 – Palais Rose (USA) (Northern 74 Dancer (CAN)) [1991 7g 7f⁵ 7m⁶ 8m³ 7m³ 6g 1992 6v⁴ 7g² 7g⁵ 7m* 6g 6f⁴ 7g* 7f 7f⁴] tall gelding: fair performer: made all at Catterick in maiden in May and handicap in July: ridden with more restraint but weakened tamely last 2 starts: needs further than 6f, and stays 1m: acts on good to firm ground (shaped well on heavy): visored last 6 starts: blinkered twice in 1991: somewhat headstrong. *A. A. Scott*

HAWAYAH (IRE) 2 b.f. (Feb 26) Shareef Dancer (USA) 135 – Ghariba 112 **68** (Final Straw 127) [1992 5g³ 5g³ 5.1g⁴ 7m*] sturdy, lengthy filly: first foal: dam, winner of Nell Gwyn Stakes, is half-sister to Braashee, from good family: fair form: made all in maiden at Wolverhampton in June: carried head awkwardly time before: stays 7f: retained 35,000 gns Newmarket July Sales. *B. Hanbury*

HAWAYMYSON (IRE) 2 b.c. (Mar 31) Mazaad 106 – Northern Amber (Shack **57** (USA) 118) [1992 5s 5m 5f 5f³ 5m³ 6m⁶ 5f² 5d] useful-looking colt: fourth foal: half-brother to 4-y-o 5f performer Minizen Music (by Anita's Prince): dam ran several times: modest maiden: trained first 3 starts by A. Stringer: ran respectably at 6f, but gives impression will prove best at 5f: best form on a sound surface. *J. H. Johnson*

HAWKE BAY 2 gr.g. (Mar 24) Bold Owl 101 – Swallow Bay 54 (Penmarric (USA) **38** 111) [1992 5g 5.1s⁵ 6.1g⁵ 6.1f⁶ 5g 7g 6.1m] leggy, close-coupled gelding: first foal: dam 2-y-o 6f seller winner, barely stayed 1¼m: poor plater: should stay beyond 5f: visored final outing: sold 750 gns Ascot September Sales. *D. Haydn Jones*

HAWKISH (USA) 2 b.c. (Feb 24) Silver Hawk (USA) 123 – Dixie Royal (USA) (Inverness – Drive (USA)) [1991 a8g⁵ 1992 9.7v³ 9m] sturdy colt: poor mover: poor maiden, not seen out after May: should stay 1¼m +: probably needs some give in the ground: joined D. Morley. *P. Mitchell*

HAWL (USA) 2 ch.c. (Feb 24) Lyphard (USA) 132 – Madame Secretary (USA) **80** (Secretariat (USA)) [1992 6d 6f³ 7.1g 7.3g⁴ 8.1d 8m* 8s² 7d⁶] robust, good-bodied colt: sort to carry condition: third foal: closely related to useful sprinter/miler Tabdea (by Topsider): dam, successful at up to 9f, is half-sister to Stewards' Cup winner Green Ruby and useful stayer Zero Watt: fair performer: won nursery at Yarmouth in September, staying on strongly to lead line: suited by 1m: probably acts on any going: blinkered (ran moderately) fifth start: tends to sweat: sold 24,000 gns Newmarket Autumn Sales. *A. A. Scott*

HAWWAR (USA) 5 b. or br.g. Lypheor 118 – Berkeley Court 102 (Mummy's Pet – 125) [1991 NR 1992 14.9d 21.6g] rather leggy, quite attractive gelding: good walker: has a fluent, round action: slow maiden, not seen out after April. *Mrs A. L. M. King*

HAZAAF (USA) 3 ch.c. Woodman (USA) 126 – Solo Disco (USA) (Solo Landing **62** (USA)) [1991 NR 1992 8g⁶ 12m⁶ 10m 14.1g 12m² 12f* 12.3m⁵ 14.1d 12s] $275,000Y: workmanlike colt: fifth foal: half-brother to 2 winners in North America: dam winner 5 times at up to 1m in North America and placed in 3 stakes races: modest performer: won handicap at Pontefract in August, always in touch: raced too freely in visor final start: suited by 1½m: acts on firm ground, possibly not on a soft surface: wears crossed noseband: runs in snatches. *A. A. Scott*

HAZAAM (USA) 3 b.c. Blushing Groom (FR) 131 – Sonic Lady (USA) 129 **113** p (Nureyev (USA) 131) [1991 NR 1992 7m* 7.6g* 8m* 8g³ 8g² 7d*]

If a debutant's pedigree such as 'Blushing Groom–Sonic Lady' fails to excite then not much will. Whether the animal in question still excites at the end of its three-year-old season is frequently another matter altogether, but Hazaam is one that does, a colt who has appealed for some time as the sort likely to do better as a four-year-old and whose progressive form in 1992 suggests strongly that he will. We had to wait until May of his three-year-old season for a first glimpse of Sonic Lady's first foal, but in the space of seventeen days Hazaam had justified favouritism in a maiden at York and a well-contested graduation race at Lingfield, held up and then quickening to the front in good style despite looking green. At this stage Hazaam still held entries in the Jersey and St James's Palace Stakes at Royal Ascot. Connections opted for a more patient policy, however, beginning with another minor event, this time at Newbury the week after the Royal meeting, in which Hazaam came with another successful late challenge to beat Kristianstad by three quarters of a length. The next step up the ladder was a listed race at Kempton in September. The form he showed there, and in another Newbury minor event on his next start, was better than that shown on his first three appearances but in being beaten about two lengths in both, first behind Calling Collect, then Tik Fa, Hazaam's merit seemed established at useful, no more. That was a disappointment, but a short-lived one, for on his final start of the

Sheikh Mohammed's "Hazaam"

year Hazaam was upgraded again, to a Group 3 race, and returned to the winner's enclosure. His margin of victory over Prince Ferdinand was just a head and Prince Ferdinand was conceding him 4 lb, but if Hazaam had lost the Supreme Stakes at Goodwood he would have been most unlucky. The two of them were poised to challenge two furlongs out as Swing Low, Storm Dove and Norwich did battle up front, but it was another furlong and a half before Hazaam could be manoeuvred into space, two lengths the deficit he had to make up on Prince Ferdinand. Prince Ferdinand is no shirker in a finish and Hazaam still caught him: a fine effort.

		Red God	Nasrullah
	Blushing Groom (FR)	(ch 1954)	Spring Run
	(ch 1974)	Runaway Bride	Wild Risk
Hazaam (USA)		(b 1962)	Aimee
(b.c. 1989)		Nureyev	Northern Dancer
	Sonic Lady (USA)	(b 1977)	Special
	(b 1983)	Stumped	Owen Anthony
		(b 1977)	Luckhurst

Sonic Lady's emergence in good-class company was a much earlier one than Hazaam's. She was 6/4 favourite for the One Thousand Guineas following wins in the Blue Seal Stakes and Nell Gwyn, was beaten into third in the first classic, but gained handsome recompense in the remainder of that season and then as a four-year-old with victories in the Irish One Thousand Guineas, Coronation Stakes, Child Stakes (twice), Sussex Stakes and Prix du Moulin. It was, perhaps, only her headstrong nature which prevented her from being the complete miler. Sonic Lady's dam Stumped, a granddaughter of the good sprinter Lucasland, was also a winner of the Child Stakes, but produced only two foals at stud. Sonic Lady has had more luck, following Hazaam with the colt Sharman, also by Blushing Groom and unraced at two years, and further colts by Mr Prospector and Nashwan. Hopefully, we will be hearing more of the first two of those in 1993. We should certainly be hearing more of Hazaam. A lengthy, good-looking colt, Hazaam has a moderate, exaggerated action. He is effective at seven furlongs and a mile; and although two of his successes in the summer came on good to firm ground and the evidence can hardly be conclusive for such a lightly-raced individual, there must be a strong possibility that Hazaam's improved showing at Goodwood was in part because the going was on the soft side. *M. R. Stoute*

HAZARD A GUESS (IRE)   2 ch.g. (Feb 27) Digamist (USA) 110 – Guess Who   **47**
76 (Be My Guest (USA) 126) [1992 6d⁶ 5g² 5g⁵ 6g] 3,900Y: tall, leggy gelding: has scope: fifth foal: half-brother to winners in Macau and Hong Kong: dam disqualified 10.4f winner, is daughter of half-sister to Derby second Cavo Doro: poor maiden: should be suited by further than 5f (needed race final start): tended to carry head high time before. *Mrs J. R. Ramsden*

HAZM (USA)   3 b.c. Danzig (USA) – Cold Hearted (USA) (The Axe II 115) [1991   **93**
5m* 6m² 1992 6d² 5.1g³ 6m 6d* 6g 8s 6g 6d* 6d] sturdy colt: impresses in appearance: shows knee action: fairly useful handicapper: won at Epsom in June and (best effort) Haydock in September: well beaten in quite valuable 6f event 2 weeks later: stays 6f (pacemaker over 1m): easily best efforts with give in the ground: rather inconsistent: has been sent to join D. Hayes in Australia. *H. Thomson Jones*

HAZY DAZY   2 b.f. (Apr 21) Faustus (USA) 118 – Mini Myra 49 (Homing 130)   **–**
[1992 5g 5g 6d a6g] 740Y: close-coupled filly: moderate mover: dam 2-y-o 5f seller winner: no worthwhile form, including in sellers. *W. G. M. Turner*

HAZY KAY (IRE)   2 gr.f. (Apr 27) Treasure Kay 114 – Hazy Lady (Habitat 134)   **77**
[1992 5m² 5f⁴] IR 5,000Y: rather unfurnished filly: sixth foal: dam ran once: had a very hard race when 6 lengths second of 5 to Lyric Fantasy in listed National Stakes at Sandown: below that form in Windsor Castle Stakes at Royal Ascot following month: will stay 6f. *P. A. Kelleway*

HAZY PROSPECT   3 b.f. Hadeer 118 – Galetzky 86 (Radetzky 123) [1991 NR   **–**
1992 7d 7m] third foal: half-sister to 1990 2-y-o 5f winner Good Time Boy (by Good Times): dam won twice at 1m and stayed 1¼m: ran as if something amiss in newcomers race at Newbury in April: sweating and on toes, signs of ability, not at all knocked about, in maiden at Goodwood nearly 6 weeks later. *D. R. C. Elsworth*

HAZY SHADES   3 gr.f. General Wade 93 – Gellifawr 80 (Saulingo 122) [1991   **–**
7.1m 1992 10m 7d 5.7d 5.3g⁵ 6s] tall, lengthy filly: moderate mover: no worthwhile form. *J. J. Bridger*

HEAD FOR THE STARS (IRE)   3 b.f. Head For Heights 125 – Star Province   **–**
(Dominion 123) [1991 7.9m⁵ 7s 8d 1992 9f 10d 8m] sparely-made ex-Irish filly: third living foal: sister to Irish 9f winner Cape Shirley: dam unraced half-sister to high-class 6f to 1m winner Star Pastures: seems of little account. *A. P. Stringer*

HEADLESS HEIGHTS   3 b.c. Elegant Air 119 – Littleton Song 73 (Song 132)   **–**
[1991 NR 1992 8f⁵ 9m⁵ 10g⁴ 8.1d 11.6m⁶] strong, workmanlike colt: carries condition: moderate mover: brother to 1990 2-y-o 6f seller winner Shepherd's Song: dam 2-y-o 6f winner: no worthwhile form though did show signs of ability penultimate start. *P. Mitchell*

HEAD TURNER   4 b.f. My Dad Tom (USA) 109 – Top Tina (High Top 131) [1991   **–**
8g² 8m⁶ 8.2f⁴ 10m 7.6g 1992 7m 10.2m 10m 11.9f⁶ 10.8g 12f⁶] sparely-made filly: seems of little account on flat these days: won selling hurdle in September. *C. P. Wildman*

HEAR A NIGHTINGALE   5 br.g. Pitskelly 122 – Calarette 85 (Caliban 123)   **–**
[1991 14.8g 21.6f³ 1992 11.9g⁶ 17.1d] small gelding: has a rather round action: no worthwhile form since 3 yrs, and not seen out after April. *R. J. Hodges*

HEARD IT BEFORE (FR)   7 b.h. Pharly (FR) 130 – Lilac Charm 87 (Bustino   **–**
136) [1991 NR 1992 9.7g 8d] smallish, attractive horse: poor mover: won 6 races at up to 4 yrs: no longer of much account. *R. P. C. Hoad*

HEART BROKEN   2 b.f. (Apr 2) Bustino 136 – Touch My Heart 61 (Steel Heart   **66**
128) [1992 a7g⁴ 5m² 5m² 6.1d⁴ 6.5m⁴ 7m] 7,000Y: sturdy filly: carries condition: half-sister to 4 winners here and abroad, including 1986 2-y-o 5f winner Flaxley (by Godswalk) and Irish 12.8f winner Bally James Duff (by Ballymore): dam placed over 5f at 3 yrs: fair maiden: best effort when fourth in Doncaster nursery penultimate start: ran badly at Newmarket later in September: should stay at least 7f: acts on good to firm and dead ground. *J. G. FitzGerald*

HEARTBURN 4 ch.f. Hard Fought 125 – Sweet And Sour 96 (Sharpen Up 127) –
[1991 7g⁴ 7g 8g 10m a6g a8g 1992 a7g⁵] leggy, sparely-made filly: of little account. *J.
D. Bethell*

HEART FLUTTER 3 gr.g. Beldale Flutter (USA) 130 – Courting Day 90 (Right –
Boy 137) [1991 6m 6g 7m 8m a7g 1992 8m 10g 12f⁵] workmanlike gelding: seems of
little account these days. *A. Smith*

HEART OF DARKNESS 4 br.c. Glint of Gold 128 – Land of Ivory (USA) 109 **102**
(The Minstrel (CAN) 135) [1991 8m² 8m⁶ 9m² 10d² 1992 10d 10g 7.9m 8f 8g
8m^dis 7m⁵ 7d⁴ 7s* 8s* 8g³ 8s] strong, good-bodied colt: useful performer: came to
himself in the autumn and won minor event at Warwick and £7,900 handicap at
Newbury: fair effort in Group 3 race at Saint-Cloud final start: effective from 7f to
1¼m: acts on good to firm and soft ground: probably effective whether blinkered/
visored or not: often sweats: headstrong, and is held up in rear: sold 66,000 gns
Newmarket December Sales. *I. A. Balding*

HEART OF SPAIN 2 b.g. (Apr 18) Aragon 118 – Hearten (Hittite Glory 125) **60**
[1992 6m⁶ 6m⁴ a8g⁴ a8g²] 12,000Y: compact colt: has scope: sixth foal: half-brother
to 3-y-o Spanish Glory (by King of Spain) and 3 winners, including very useful
sprinter Northern Goddess (by Night Shift): dam unraced daughter of smart middle-
distance stayer Nortia: modest maiden: stays 1m: acts on good to firm ground and
equitrack, yet to race on a soft surface. *P. J. Makin*

HEATHER BANK 3 b.g. Nordance (USA) – Miss Rossi (Artaius (USA) 129 **104**
[1991 6f² 5g³ 5m⁴ 5d⁴ 6g* 6g* 6m² 6g³ 6m⁴ 5m⁵ 5d⁵ 1992 6g* 6m⁶ 6f³ 6m⁵ 6m⁴
6d⁵ 5.6m 6d³ 7m 6m*] strong, lengthy, workmanlike gelding: carries condition: an
admirable handicapper who rarely runs a bad race: won quite valuable contests at
Newmarket in April and, making all in good style and again showing improved form,
October: suited by 6f: acts on firm and dead ground: blinkered/visored last 4 starts:
sold 33,000 gns Newmarket Autumn Sales. *J. Berry*

HEATHFIELD (USA) 2 b.c. (Apr 27) Procida (USA) 129 – Mlle Judy (USA) **73**
(Silent Screen (USA)) [1992 5d² 5.2m*] $29,000Y: leggy colt: half-brother to 2
winners by Time To Explode, one placed in graded stakes: dam won 5 races at up to
9f at 3 yrs: much improved effort when winning median auction maiden at Newbury
in May, making virtually all and staying on well: bred to stay at least 1m: seemed
likely to improve again. *P. F. I. Cole*

HEATHYARDS BOY 2 b.c. (Mar 5) Sayf El Arab (USA) 127 – French Cooking **90**
70 (Royal And Regal (USA)) [1992 7d⁶ 8.1d* 7v* 10g⁵] big, strong colt: third foal:
half-brother to 1m winner Parc des Princes (by Anfield): dam 2m winner: fairly
useful form: won moderately-run maiden at Haydock and minor event at Chester in
October: never able to challenge when respectable fifth in Zetland Stakes at
Newmarket: will prove fully effective at 1¼m: yet to race on top-of-the-ground. *R.
Hollinshead*

HEATHYARDS GEM 2 b.f. (Apr 27) Governor General 116 – Quenlyn (Welsh **64**
Pageant 132) [1992 5s³ 5d⁴ 5m⁴ 7m³ 6.1m³ 5g* 5d 6.1g⁴ 6.1s³ 6g] close-coupled,
workmanlike filly: half-sister to 5f winner Roxby Melody (by Song) and a winner in
Belgium by Absalom: dam ran 3 times at 2 yrs: rather inconsistent performer: held
on gamely in maiden at Beverley in August: will stay 7f: acts on soft ground. *R.
Hollinshead*

HEAVEN-LIEGH-GREY 4 gr.f. Grey Desire 115 – North Pine (Import 127) **72**
[1991 6m 5d 5m 5m² 5m* 5.1d⁴ 5g² 5g⁵ 5g 5.6m 5m³ 1992 5f⁵ 5g 5f 5.1m 5g 5.6m
7.1m 7d² 5m 5m² 5m 5.1g² 5s⁶ 5g⁵ a5g] workmanlike filly: fair performer, not so
good as in 1991: has form on soft ground, but very best efforts at 5f on a sound
surface: ran moderately on equitrack: effective blinkered or not, tried visored
earlier in career: has carried head awkwardly. *M. Johnston*

HEAVENLY BODY 2 b.f. (Mar 3) Skyliner 117 – Mature (Welsh Pageant 132) –
[1992 6d 7f] leggy, unfurnished filly: sixth living foal: half-sister to 3 winners here
and abroad, including 1990 2-y-o 6f winner Steam Ahead (by All Systems Go) and
1¼m seller winner Carbo Booster (by Good Times): dam, maiden, ran best race at
7f: well beaten in claimer at Leicester and seller at Redcar in June. *J. W. Watts*

HEAVENLY DREAM 2 ch.f. (Mar 22) Valiyar 129 – Celeste 83 (Sing Sing 134) –
[1992 6g] half-sister to 3-y-o Heavenly Pet (by Petong) and several winners,
including 5f and 7f winner Sharp Celeste (by Sharpen Up): dam stayed at least 6f:
33/1, backward and green, tailed off in 9-runner seller at Yarmouth in June: gave
trouble stalls. *G. Blum*

HEAVENLY RISK 2 gr.c. (Apr 7) Risk Me (FR) 127 – Halo 51 (Godswalk (USA) **76**
130) [1992 6g² 7.1g⁶ 6m* 6g 6s] 4,700F, 1,000Y: rangy colt: fourth foal: half-brother

to fair 3-y-o sprinter Castlerea Lad (by Efisio): dam poor daughter of sister to Thatching: fair performer: won maiden auction at Doncaster in July: faced stiff tasks in nurseries afterwards, running well at Ayr final start: best form at 6f: acts on good to firm and soft ground. *R. Hannon*

HEAVENLY WATERS   3 b.f. Celestial Storm (USA) 132 – Idle Waters 116 (Mill   **64**
Reef(USA) 141) [1991 7g 7m 8g 1992 13.1m 12m 11.6m² 13.1m⁴ 15.8m² 16.1m* 14. 1f²
14.6g* 15.4g4 14.1d⁴ 16m³] workmanlike filly: moderate mover: modest performer:
won maiden at Newcastle in July and handicap at Wolverhampton in September:
suited by good test of stamina: acts on firm going, fair effort on dead: sometimes
bandaged behind: usually set plenty to do. *R. F. Johnson Houghton*

HEAVY ROCK (IRE)   3 ch.f. Ballad Rock 122 – Asian Princess (Native Prince)   **–**
[1991 NR 1992 a8g6 10.1d 13.8g 10.3g] leggy filly: half-sister to several winners,
including Zaahi's dam Alghuzaylah (by Habitat) and very smart French 5.5f to 10.5f
winner Pitasia (by Pitskelly): dam of no account: no form, in seller final start:
trained by R. Marvin on debut. *D. J. S. Cosgrove*

HEAVYWEIGHT (IRE)   3 gr.g. Bellypha 130 – Pennyweight (Troy 137) [1991   **–**
a7g 1992 7g6 8.1g5 11.6g] sturdy gelding: shows knee action: no worthwhile form
though has hinted at a little ability: wore tongue strap final start, in August. *C. A. Horgan*

HEBER SPRING (IRE)   2 br.g. (Mar 22) Cyrano de Bergerac 120 – Naval   **78**
Artiste (Captain's Gig (USA)) [1992 5d 5g² 5.1s³ 5f4 5.1m³ 6s⁴ 5.1d³ 6s²] 3,600Y:
leggy, unfurnished gelding: poor mover: half-brother to several winners, including
sprinters Naval Fan (by Taufan) and Karla's Star (by Kampala): dam Irish 2-y-o 5f
winner: generally progressive form, especially after being gelded (had previously
hung left and carried head awkwardly): best effort when second in nursery at
Newbury, leading final 1f until near line: stays 6f: seems unsuited by top-of-the-
ground, acts on soft: blinkered fifth start. *R. Hannon*

HEBRIDEAN   5 b.g. Norwick (USA) 120 – Pushkar (Northfields (USA)) [1991   **95**
NR 1992 10.8g² 13.3f³ 11.9f4 14g³dis 13.9g 13.3g6 16s*] big, rangy gelding: shows
knee action: half-brother to several winners, including smart middle-distance performer Eradicate (by Tender King): dam never ran: fairly useful performer, unraced
until 1992: on balance of form seems flattered by third in listed event at Newbury
second start: best judged on sixth in £18,200 handicap at Goodwood for 7-lb claimer:
won minor event there later in the autumn: stays 2m: probably acts on any going:
has joined D. Nicholson. *H. Candy*

HEDGEHOG   2 b.f. (Apr 12) Electric 126 – Demderise 80 (Vaigly Great 127)   **–**
[1992 6s] well-grown filly: second foal: half-sister to winning 3-y-o sprinter Sonderise (by Mummy's Game): dam 2-y-o 5f winner, is half-sister to useful sprinter
Alpine Strings: 50/1, green, and in need of run, always behind in maiden at Lingfield
in October. *J. O'Donoghue*

HEIR OF EXCITEMENT   7 b.g. Krayyan 117 – Merry Choice (Yankee Gold   **31**
115) [1991 12d5 11f 12g 11m 10.3m 1992 a12g* a12g4] lengthy gelding: carries plenty
of condition: usually looks well: poor handicapper: narrow winner at Southwell in
February: will stay 1¾m: acts on any going: no improvement in visor/blinkers
earlier in career: has worn a tongue strap. *A. P. Stringer*

HEJRAAN (USA)   2 b.f. (Mar 29) Alydar (USA) – Top Socialite (USA) 117   **73 p**
(Topsider (USA)) [1992 6m4 6d5] $500,000Y: quite attractive filly: good walker:
second foal: half-sister to 3-y-o Allarme Sociale (by Alleged), 8.3f winner at 2 yrs:
dam 5f (at 2 yrs) to 7.3f winner here later won 7 races (including non-graded stakes)
in USA, and is half-sister to Exbourne: progressive form in minor event at
Doncaster (heavily-backed favourite) and Blue Seal Stakes at Ascot (travelled well
4f, carried head high under pressure) in September: will stay 1m: will probably do
better. *M. R. Stoute*

HELAWE   9 ch.g. Last Fandango 125 – Pigmy (Assagai) [1991 a7g* 7f² 7g5 a7g*   **–**
7m* 7m a7g4 7m4 a7g* a7g5 a8g a7g6 1992 a7g 7g 7m] big, lengthy, angular gelding:
good walker: rated 87 on the equitrack at 8 yrs: no worthwhile form in the spring as
9-y-o: stays 7f: best turf form on a sound surface: lazy sort, who needs blinkers: has
won 5 times at Brighton and 4 times at Lingfield: reportedly broke blood vessel once
at 8 yrs. *Sir Mark Prescott*

HELIOPSIS   4 b.g. Shirley Heights 130 – If (FR) (Kashmir II 125) [1991 NR 1992   **50 p**
12.4m 8.3s3 8s 12.1s 13.8d* 15.1d*] good-topped gelding: brother to useful 1m to
1¼m winner Armada, closely related to very useful 7f and 10.5f winner Cameo
Shore (by Mill Reef) and half-brother to 2 winners in France: dam third in Poule
d'Essai des Pouliches: lightly raced and progressive handicapper: successful in

large fields at Catterick and Edinburgh (gamely) in the autumn: will be even better suited by 2m+: acts on dead ground: progressive hurdler as well, winning 2 handicaps in December. *M. D. Hammond*

HELIOS 4 br.g. Blazing Saddles (AUS) – Mary Sunley 62 (Known Fact (USA) 135) **82** [1991 10g 7.6d2 7f* 7m4 7d 7g4 7g 7m5 6f 7g a10g 1992 a7g 7g4 8f3 9m4 8.1s 6m5 7m3 7f* 7m2 6.9m 7g6 7.3g2 7d4] leggy, angular gelding: moderate mover: fairly useful and consistent handicapper: won at Epsom in July: best form at 7f/1m: best on a sound surface: goes particularly well on switchback tracks: usually races prominently. *R. Simpson*

HELLEBORUS 4 b.f. King of Spain 121 – Budget Queen 101 (Good Bond 122) **–** [1991 8g 1992 9m 8.1g] leggy filly: seems of little account. *S. Dow*

HELLO GEORGIE 9 b.g. Hello Gorgeous (USA) 128 – Celina 115 (Crepello **–** 136) [1991 NR 1992 12.1f6] plain, deep-bodied gelding: no sign of ability on flat and untrustworthy over hurdles. *T. Craig*

HELLO HOBSON'S (IRE) 2 b.f. (Mar 18) Fayruz 116 – Castleforbes (Thatch- **67** ing 131) [1992 5m5 6g 5m* 5d3 6g* 6d 6m2] IR 1,000F, 10,000Y: compact, workman-like filly: moderate mover: third foal: half-sister to a useful winner in Czechoslovakia: dam a twin: fair form: won maiden at Folkestone and nursery at Kempton in late-summer, held up both times: effective at 5f and 6f: best form on a sound surface: sold 12,000 gns Newmarket Autumn Sales. *J. Akehurst*

HELLO MY DARLING (IRE) 4 b.c. Law Society (USA) 130 – Helaplane **72** (USA) 68 (Super Concorde (USA) 128) [1991 10m 11.9g5 14s2 16m* 1992 10.8v 14g* 14d 12g] good-bodied colt: fair handicapper: allowed to dictate pace when winning at Sandown: tongue tied down, well below that form later in the spring: stays 2m: best efforts with give in the ground, struggled to land the odds on good to firm. *W. R. Muir*

HELMSLEY PALACE 3 b.f. Dominion 123 – Queen Midas 119 (Glint of Gold **–** 128) [1991 7g5 1992 12m6] workmanlike, rather angular filly: blinkered, raced freely and well beaten in minor event at Beverley in May: should stay at least 1m: sold to join J. White 1,900 gns Newmarket July Sales. *Mrs J. Cecil*

HELVELLYN (USA) 3 b.f. (Feb 13) Gone West (USA) – Accredited (USA) **83 p** (Alleged (USA) 138) [1992 6g5 8.2d* 7d3] $62,000F, $100,000Y: quite attractive filly: fifth reported foal: half-sister to 2 winners in North America, one placed in minor stakes: dam unraced half-sister to smart sprinter Dame Mysterieuse: sire (by Mr Prospector) very smart at 1m/9f: fair form: off course 3 months and 15/2 from 4/1, won 16-runner maiden at Nottingham in August, making all and running on well: readily outpaced when good third to Thawakib in minor event at Ascot following month: will prove suited by 1m+. *H. R. A. Cecil*

HEMINGBY 5 ch.m. Seclude (USA) – Capsville (USA) (Cyane) [1991 7g3 8g4 **–** 11f4 11.1m4 1992 10.3g] quite attractive ex-Irish mare: rated 61 at 4 yrs: burly and behind in amateurs handicap in November, 1992: should stay middle distances: below form when blinkered once. *J. J. O'Neill*

HEMSWORTH LAD (IRE) 3 gr.g. Standaan (FR) 118 – Majestic's Gold **59 d** (Rheingold 137) [1991 6f 6.1m 5s6 1992 6g 5m* 6m 5m5 5g6 5m6 5d] leggy, shallow-girthed gelding: modest handicapper at his best: well below form after leading post at Catterick in May: will stay 6f: acts on good to firm and soft ground: sold 1,250 gns Doncaster October Sales: one to be wary of. *P. Calver*

HENBURY HALL (IRE) 4 gr.g. Bellypha 130 – Rustic Stile (Rusticaro (FR) **66 d** 124) [1991 8g 7.9m* 10m6 1992 8d2 12f2 10f5 10.5g5 9.2m2 8f5 9.2g* 9.2g3 8s] angular, good-topped gelding: moderate walker: fair performer at 3 yrs: nowhere near so good in 1992, and none too consistent to boot: scrambled home in Hamilton seller (bought in 3,200 gns) in July: stays 1¼m: acts on firm and dead ground (possibly not on soft): has carried head high but suitable mount for apprentice: sold to join M. Barraclough 3,600 gns Doncaster September Sales. *Mrs M. Reveley*

HENEQUIN (USA) 2 ch.f. (Jan 29) Woodman (USA) 126 – Miss Henny Penny **57** (USA) (Tom Rolfe) [1992 6m4 6g3 6m5 7d6] $100,000F: lengthy filly, rather un-furnished: has a round action: first foal: dam unraced daughter of sister to Raja Baba and Sauce Boat, family also of A P Indy and Wolfhound: modest maiden: will be suited by 1m+: may prove best on an easy surface: ran creditably in blinkers final start. *J. H. M. Gosden*

HENIU (USA) 3 b.c. Danzig Connection (USA) – Arianne Mon Amour (USA) **66** (Bold Bidder) [1991 NR 1992 a8g4 a12g4 10.5g 10s3 12s 11.8d 9.7v a8g3 a7g*] useful-looking colt: second foal: dam won 2 small races at up to 1m at 2 yrs, and is sister to Belmont Stakes winner Stephan's Odyssey: fair performer: best form in a visor last 2 starts, emphatic winner of handicap at Lingfield in December: best form at up to 1m: acts on soft ground and all-weather surfaces. *Lord Huntingdon*

HE NOSE YOU KNOW (IRE) 2 b.c. (Apr 14) Cyrano de Bergerac 120 – Pleasure Party (Auction Ring (USA) 123) [1992 a5g 6.1m⁶] IR 3,100F, IR 6,100Y, resold 3,600Y: rather leggy colt: first foal: dam ran twice: soundly beaten in claimer at Southwell and maiden (visored) at Nottingham in June: sold 500 gns Ascot July Sales. *C. N. Allen* —

HENPOT (IRE) 4 b.f. Alzao (USA) 117 – Whispered Wishes 87 (High Top 131) [1991 NR 1992 10s* 12.3g] sparely-made filly: moderate mover: first living foal: dam 5f winner at 2 yrs: favourite, easy winner in claimer at Ripon: 2/1 on, soundly beaten in similar event at Wolverhampton (claimed £12,100) later in April: stays 1¼m: acts on soft ground. *H. R. A. Cecil* **68**

HENRY'S FIRST 3 b.g. Aragon 118 – Krafty Kate 73 (Klairon 131) [1991 NR 1992 6d 6m] close-coupled gelding: half-brother to several winners here and abroad, including fairly useful 1982 2-y-o 7f winner Timber Creek (by Hot Grove), later successful at 1½m in Ireland: dam 1¼m winner: no sign of ability in maidens in October. *Miss L. C. Siddall* —

HENRY WILL 8 b.g. Nicholas Bill 125 – Silver Cygnet 71 (My Swanee 122) [1991 5g⁶ 6m 6g 6m 7m⁵ 7g³ 7f 6d² 7m 7f 7m⁶ 6f⁴ 6m 7m 7.1m 7s 8.1s⁴ a6g 1992 a8g a6g 7m 6f³ 6g 6m⁴ 6m 6s 8m 7g⁴ 7s 8s] workmanlike, angular gelding: poor mover: poor handicapper nowadays: last win came 39 starts ago, at 6 yrs: stays 1m: acts on any going: no improvement in blinkers. *T. Fairhurst* **36**

HEPBURN (IRE) 4 b.f. Pitskelly 122 – Bradden 77 (King Emperor (USA)) [1991 7g 8d⁶ 10d 10.1g 10g 8.1s a8g⁵ a10g² a12g a10g a8g] compact filly: rated 51 at 3 yrs: no form in the spring at 4 yrs: stays 1½m: sold out of M. Fetherston-Godley's stable 1,700 gns Ascot February Sales after second start. *R. G. Brazington* —

HERBERTO (USA) 5 b.g. Roberto (USA) 131 – Her Silver (USA) (Herbager 136) [1991 NR 1992 16.2g 12s] close-coupled gelding: rated 80 at 3 yrs for L. Cumani: no form in 1992. *N. Tinkler* —

HERE COMES A STAR 4 b.g. Night Shift (USA) – Rapidus (Sharpen Up 127) [1991 6m 6d 5m³ 5m* 5f 5f⁶ 5m 1992 5g 5g⁵ 6f 5m 5f² 5m* 5g⁴ 5m² 5.1m* 5g³ 6s 5m² 5m⁶ 5m³ 5.1g] sturdy, lengthy gelding: has a round action: generally progressive handicapper: won at Hamilton and Nottingham in the summer: best at around 5f: acts on firm ground, well below form on soft: twice well below form when blinkered: game. *J. M. Carr* **73**

HERETICAL MISS 2 br.f. (Feb 26) Sayf El Arab (USA) 127 – Silent Prayer 58 (Queen's Hussar 124) [1992 6g 7g 8g 6v⁶ 6s⁴ 6g³ 6v a6g³] sparely-made filly: moderate mover: seventh foal: sister to modest maiden Arabian Silence and half-sister to 1988 2-y-o 6f winner Vaigrant Wind (by Vaigly Great): dam won over hurdles: modest maiden: suited by 6f: acts on good ground, ran badly on heavy: blinkered last 4 starts. *R. Hannon* **60**

HER HONOUR 3 b.f. Teenoso (USA) 135 – Burning Ambition (Troy 137) [1991 NR 1992 10.2f* 10s* 12g*] tall, leggy, rather unfurnished filly: second foal: half-sister to 5f (at 2 yrs) and 7.1f winner Dance On Sixpence (by Lidhame): dam well-beaten half-sister to One In A Million: won maiden at Chepstow in June, claimer (claimed out of Lord Huntingdon's stable £15,501) at Salisbury in September and 18-runner handicap (quickening on in good style over 1f out) at Newmarket in October: also won juvenile hurdle in December: very much on the upgrade. *M. C. Pipe* **94 p**

HEROES SASH (USA) 7 b.h. Lypheor 118 – Salish (USA) (Olden Times) [1991 8g 10.1g 8g 9d⁶ 7f⁵ 7g⁶ 7g 7g 1992 8d 8d] useful-looking horse: poor mover: rated 64 at 6 yrs: looked of little account in September, 1992: sold to join J. Thomas 825 gns Ascot November Sales. *A. Moore* —

HEROIC DEED 2 b.c. (Feb 20) Dance of Life (USA) – Ideas And Trends (USA) (Sharpen Up 127) [1992 5m 6s⁵ 6g³ 6m 7g⁵ 7g³ 7.1s 7m] 1,000Y, 8,800 2-y-o: small, sturdy colt: first foal: dam unraced: fair plater: will be suited by 1m +: visored twice (below form), but didn't have clear run): sold 1,200 gns Newmarket Autumn Sales. *M. H. Tompkins* **52**

HERORA (IRE) 3 b.f. Heraldiste (USA) 121 – Kilfenora (Tribal Chief 125) [1991 5g 6g* 5m* 6g⁴ 6g⁴ 1992 7m⁵ 6g 8f⁴ 7s⁵ 6m] small filly: fairly useful form: off course 4 months after finishing 2½ lengths fifth to A-To-Z in Nell Gwyn Stakes at Newmarket, pulling hard in moderately-run race then running on well: failed to reproduce that form (reluctant to post once) and well beaten in handicap at Newmarket final start: should prove best at up to 7f. *N. A. Graham* **95**

HERO'S LIGHT (USA) 3 ch.c. Hero's Honor (USA) – I Love You Baby (USA) **88** (Damascus (USA)) [1991 6m⁵ 7m² 7m* 7d 8d⁴ᵈⁱˢ 9s² 1992 a10g³ 10d 8.1mʷᵒ 8g⁵ **a95** 11.5m³] strong, lengthy, good-quartered colt: fairly useful performer: walked over for minor event at Haydock in May: best effort when third in minor event at Ling-field in April, set plenty to do in moderately-run 3-runner race there in June: probably stays 11.5f: acts on good to firm and soft ground: sold 11,500 gns Newmarket September Sales. *P. F. I. Cole*

HERSHEBAR 2 ch.c. (Apr 13) Stanford 121§ – Sugar Token 66 (Record Token **42** 128) [1992 a5g 5g 5m a6g a6g⁶ a5g⁵ a8g⁶] sturdy colt: first foal: dam won at 6f and 7f (including at 2 yrs): plating-class maiden: stays 6f: blinkered (fair effort) once. *S. R. Bowring*

HE'S A KING (USA) 2 b.c. (Apr 8) Key To The Kingdom (USA) – She's A Jay **67** p (USA) (Honey Jay (USA)) [1992 7m 7m] $19,000Y: close-coupled, quite attractive colt, rather unfurnished: half-brother to 3 minor winners in North America: dam won at up to 1m: sire 9f stakes winner: beaten around 13 lengths at Newmarket in October in maiden won by Placerville and £8,850 event won by Barathea: will be suited by further: will do better. *J. L. Dunlop*

HESTER STANHOPE 3 b.f. Lomond (USA) 128 – Martha Stevens (USA) 102 **61** (Super Concorde (USA) 128) [1991 6g 7g 1992 6d 7g 10f² 10m 10d 11f* 11.5g⁶ 8.9d 10d] sturdy filly: ran moderately after winning handicap at Redcar in August: stays 11f: best efforts on firm ground: sold 8,800 gns Newmarket Autumn Sales. *P. W. Harris*

HIBISCUS IVY (AUS) 4 b.f. Rancher (AUS) – Melodia (AUS) (Sir Tristram – 115) [1991 a7g 6m 1992 a7g4] lengthy filly: no sign of ability. *D. J. S. Cosgrove*

HICKORY BLUE 2 ch.c. (May 13) Clantime 101 – Blueit (FR) 101 (Bold Lad **48** p (IRE) 133) [1992 5f⁵ a5g²] leggy colt: brother to 3-y-o winning sprinter Tino Tere, closely related to fairly useful sprinter Blues Indigo (by Music Boy) and half-brother to 2 other sprinters: dam 2-y-o 5f winner: shaped encouragingly in maidens at Catterick and Southwell: will improve. *S. G. Norton*

HIDDEN FLOWER 3 b.f. Blakeney 126 – Molucella (Connaught 130) [1991 6g – 7g³ 6g 7g 6m 1992 10.2d 14.1m⁶] compact filly: rated 49 at 2 yrs: on the downgrade. *J. D. Roberts*

HIDDEN LAUGHTER (USA) 3 b.f. Kris S (USA) – More Hilarious (USA) **80** (Fast Hilarious (USA)) [1991 7g² 7g* 8m 1992 8f 10f² 13.9g 10m³ 10m] rangy, rather unfurnished filly: fair handicapper: might have proved suited by 1½m: acted on firm going: visits Warrshan. *B. W. Hills*

HIDDEN LIGHT (IRE) 3 ch.c. High Line 125 – Beach Light 89 (Bustino 136) **76** [1991 8m⁶ 1992 12m³ 12m⁴ 14d² 14.8f* 16.2g² 16.1m⁵] leggy, angular colt: has a markedly round action: fair handicapper: sweating, won apprentice maiden at Newmarket in June: ran badly final start: suited by test of stamina: acts on firm and dead going: takes keen hold. *M. A. Jarvis*

HIDEYOSHI (USA) 3 b.c. Devil's Bag (USA) – Fanfreluche (CAN) (Northern **79** Dancer (CAN)) [1991 NR 1992 8g 10m³ 10.1d*] well-made colt: half-brother to numerous winners, notably dual Canadian Horse of the Year L'Enjoleur (by Buckpasser), prolific stakes winner La Voyageuse (by Tentam) and top Canadian 2-y-o Medaille d'Or (by Secretariat): dam Canadian Horse of the Year, successful from 7f to 1½m: similar form in minor events and when landing odds in Epsom maiden in July: may prove better suited by 1½m. *D. R. C. Elsworth*

HIERARCH (USA) 3 ch.c. Diesis 133 – Highclere 129 (Queen's Hussar 124) **86** ? [1991 NR 1992 8d 10s² 11.9f³ 12m⁴ 10g⁵ 12.3s³] lengthy colt: impresses in appearance: half-brother to several winners, including Height of Fashion (by Bustino) and Milford (by Mill Reef): dam won 1000 Guineas and French Oaks: failed to progress after good efforts in quite valuable races at York (ladies contest) and Ascot third and fourth starts: stays 1½m well: acts on firm ground: found nothing final start. *Lord Huntingdon*

HIEROGLYPHIC (IRE) 4 b.c. Darshaan 133 – Sphinx (GER) (Alpenkonig **104** (GER)) [1991 10d³ 12g* 12g* 12.3d* 12m³ 18m⁴ 12d* 14v² 1992 18f³] unfurnished colt: has a round action: rated 120? as 3-y-o when with J. Gosden: looked in fine shape on first run for 9 months and not discredited when around 8 lengths third of 5 to Further Flight in Doncaster Cup in September, 1992, pulling hard long way and not knocked about once held: effective at 1½m on a soft surface, and stays 2¼m: best efforts with give in the ground. *P. W. Chapple-Hyam*

HIGH BACCARAT 3 ch.g. Formidable (USA) 125 – By Surprise 68 (Young **50** Generation 129) [1991 5g⁵ 6m⁶ 7g 7m 1992 7f⁴ 7.1g 10m 8f⁵ 8f⁵ 9.7m 8m⁵ 7.1s] good-topped gelding: inconsistent plater: stays 1m: acts on firm going: usually visored: trained until after penultimate start by C. C. Elsey. *A. J. Chamberlain*

HIGH BEACON 5 ch.g. High Line 125 – Flaming Peace 104 (Queen's Hussar 124) [1991 14.8m⁵ 14m³ 16g⁵ 10d³ 12.1d³ 12g 13.9g⁶ 14s 11g 1992 13.3g 14m 12d⁴ 16s⁶ 14.6g] sturdy, workmanlike gelding: keen walker: easy mover: rated 95 as 4-y-o: no form in 1992: stays 2m: acts on good to firm and dead ground: below form blinkered. *K. C. Bailey* —

HIGHBORN (IRE) 3 b. or br.g. Double Schwartz 128 – High State 72 (Free State 125) [1991 NR 1992 6f 7g 6g⁶ 6d 6.1s 6v⁵] sturdy gelding: third foal: half-brother to 5f and 6f winner Macs Maharanee (by Indian King): dam 9f seller winner: poor plater: should stay 7f. *P. S. Felgate* 41

HIGHBROOK (USA) 4 b.f. Alphabatim (USA) 126 – Tellspot (USA) (Tell (USA)) [1991 10g* 11.9g⁶ 1992 8d 10g 12.2g* 10.1g* 12m 11.9m 10s² 12m* 12m⁵ 12g⁶] lengthy filly: had very good season in handicaps in 1992: successful at Catterick, Yarmouth and Newmarket (£7,400 event): creditable sixth in November Handicap at Doncaster: better at 1½m than 1¼m: acts on good to firm and soft ground: genuine and consistent: held up: trained reappearance by Don Enrico Incisa. *M. H. Tompkins* 86

HIGHCLIFFE JESTER 3 b.g. Jester 119 – Canty Day 87 (Canadel II 126) [1991 NR 1992 7.5d 10m] workmanlike gelding: half-brother to 3 minor winners, including 13f winner Cantycroon (by Crooner): dam 2-y-o 5f winner: last in sellers. *P. Beaumont* —

HIGHEST PRAISE (USA) 9 ch.g. Topsider (USA) – Prides Promise (USA) (Crozier (USA)) [1991 7.6g 7m 7.6d² 7v⁵ 7d³ 7.6m² 7g² 7g* 7g² 7g⁵ 7.6m 7g⁴ 1992 7g] strong, good-bodied gelding: moderate mover: rated 68 in 1991: last-but-one in handicap in November, 1992: stays 7.6f: acts on any going: sometimes finds little: held up. *Miss S. J. Wilton* —

HIGH FINANCE 7 ch.g. Billion (USA) 120 – Miss Plumes 62 (Prince de Galles 125) [1991 NR 1992 a8s⁵ 16.1g 16d a14g] workmanlike gelding: moderate mover: no worthwhile form on flat: won over hurdles in October. *R. J. Weaver* —

HIGH FINISH 2 ch.f. (Apr 18) High Line 125 – Oatfield 69 (Great Nephew 126) [1992 6d 8g⁶] unfurnished filly: sister to 2m winner High Plains, closely related to 3 winners here and abroad, including very useful (at around 1m) Barley Bill (by Nicholas Bill), and half-sister to very useful middle-distance stayer Hateel (by Kalaglow): dam thrice-raced daughter of half-sister to High Line: never able to challenge when in midfield for maidens at Newbury and Leicester: will be suited by 1½m. *H. Candy* 58 p

HIGHFLYING 6 br.g. Shirley Heights 130 – Nomadic Pleasure 91 (Habitat 134) [1991 14g⁵ 16.2g³ 13.9g 13.9g 1992 12f4 14g* 16.1f⁵ 12m] strong, good-bodied gelding: carries plenty of condition: usually impresses in appearance: poor mover: won handicap at Haydock and good fifth in Northumberland Plate at Newcastle in June: not seen out again after below par in £30,000 event at Goodwood month later: effective at 1½m to 2m: acts on firm and dead going (unsuited by very soft): sometimes bandaged. *G. M. Moore* 80

HIGH GRADE 4 b.g. High Top 131 – Bright Sun (Mill Reef (USA) 141) [1991 11.7g 11.7m⁵ 13.1f⁶ 16m 1992 16g⁵ 16.9g] sturdy, lengthy gelding: good walker: poor maiden on flat/winning hurdler: stays 2m: acts on good to firm and dead ground: moody when visored once: tail swisher, and sometimes looks none too keen. *S. Dow* 48 §

HIGH KABOUR 6 b.m. Kabour 80 – High Walk (Tower Walk 130) [1991 NR 1992 a10g⁵ 11.9g] workmanlike mare: fourth living foal: half-sister to modest 1m winner High Port (by Import): dam bad plater: twice raced, and no worthwhile form. *W. G. M. Turner* —

HIGHLAND BATTLE (USA) 3 ch.g. The Minstrel (CAN) 135 – Battle Drum (USA) (Alydar (USA)) [1991 7g 7g 8m 1992 8m³ 10m² 11.6m² 13.1m² 11.7g³ 16d 14.6g 13.8g] close-coupled, sparely-made gelding: has a quick action: good walker: fair maiden: stays 1¾m: acts on good to firm ground: sold 15,500 gns Newmarket Autumn Sales. *I. A. Balding* 68

HIGHLAND DRESS 3 b.c. Lomond (USA) 128 – Colorspin (FR) 118 (High Top 131) [1991 NR 1992 10s* 10g⁴ 10.3g4] 44,000Y: big, good-topped colt: second foal: closely related to high-class 4-y-o middle-distance colt Opera House (by Sadler's Wells): dam Irish Oaks winner, is half-sister to Bella Colora out of Lancashire Oaks winner Reprocolor: won maiden at Newbury on debut in October: appeared to improve considerably in slowly-run listed race at Newmarket but failed to confirm it 103 ?

when heavily-backed favourite for Doncaster minor event, carrying head high and finding little: will stay 1½m: remains in training. *M. R. Stoute*

HIGHLAND FANTASY (USA) 3 b.f. Alleged (USA) 138 – Sheer Fantasy (USA) (Damascus (USA)) [1991 NR 1992 8g⁵ 10g 14.1m* 16m⁴ 14m a14g*] 42,000Y: tall, unfurnished filly: has a round action: half-sister to 3 winners, including 1988 2-y-o 5f and 6f winner Tatouma (by The Minstrel): dam winning daughter of Bold Bikini, dam also of Strike Your Colors, Law Society (by Alleged) and Legal Bid: fairly useful performer: won maiden at Yarmouth in September and handicap at Southwell (blinkered, made all) in November: will prove best with thorough stamina test: has been bandaged behind: sold 31,000 gns Newmarket December Sales. *B. W. Hills*   **81**

HIGHLAND FLAME 3 ch.c. Dunbeath (USA) 127 – Blakesware Saint 74 (Welsh Saint 126) [1991 NR 1992 10d 10g a7g⁵ a8g⁶ a10g³ 11.9g⁶] 3,300Y: plain, good-topped colt: fifth live foal: half-brother to 6f winners Star News (by Tremblant) and Norton Melody (by Absalom): dam 5f winner: poor maiden: seems best at up to 1¼m: best efforts on equitrack: visored final start. *A. N. Lee*   **41**

HIGHLAND HOST 2 b.c. (Apr 1) Be My Guest (USA) 126 – Karietta (Wollow 132) [1992 6s 7g] leggy, workmanlike colt: fourth foal: half-brother to 3-y-o 1¼m winner Sky Train (by Siberian Express) and fair 6f and 7f winner Anna Karietta (by Precocious): dam poor half-sister to Karelia, very useful at up to 1½m: green and never dangerous in maidens at Newbury. *J. L. Dunlop*   **39 p**

HIGHLAND MAGIC (IRE) 4 b.g. Stalker 121 – Magic Picture (Deep Diver 134) [1991 7g² 7d³ 6d 7d⁶ 6g² 6m³ 6g 6g³ 5m 7d 7m⁴ 7g 1992 6d 7g 7g* 6g 7.1m² 7m² a7g 7m 7d³ 7d³ 8s 7d 7d* 7s 7g⁵ 7g*] compact gelding: poor mover: fairly useful but none too consistent handicapper: successful at Kempton (apprentices) in May and York and Doncaster in autumn: effective at 6f and 7f: acts on good to firm and dead ground: sometimes bandaged off-hind. *M. J. Fetherston-Godley*   **81**

HIGHLAND RUBY 4 b.f. Green Ruby (USA) 104 – Highland Rossie 67 (Pablond 93) [1991 6g³ 6g² 7g 6g⁵ 6.9f⁵ 8g 1992 10.8d] workmanlike filly: moderate mover: poor maiden: tailed off in seller in April: should stay 7f: has gone well with give in the ground. *B. A. McMahon*   **–**

HIGH LOW (USA) 4 b.g. Clever Trick (USA) – En Tiempo (USA) (Bold Hour) [1991 7g³ 8m 7f* a8g² 1992 8g* 7d² 8f⁴ 7g 8g 7m 8g 8m] sturdy, quite attractive gelding: good mover: in excellent form in handicaps in first half of 1992: won William Hill Lincoln at Doncaster by 1½ lengths from Mudaffar and in frame at Ascot in Victoria Cup and Royal Hunt Cup: well below par after: effective at 7f to 1m: acts on firm and dead ground: has gone well fresh: game front runner. *W. J. Haggas*   **91**

HIGHLY DECORATED 7 b.g. Sharpo 132 – New Ribbons 79 (Ribero 126) [1991 NR 1992 16f] leggy gelding: poor maiden: stays 1¼m: seemingly needs give in the ground. *Mrs S. J. Smith*   **–**

HIGH MIND (FR) 3 br.c. Highest Honor (FR) 124 – Gondolina (FR) (Vaguely Noble 140) [1991 NR 1992 8g 10.5s⁴ 12m⁶ 14.1d 14s 9.9m 12m⁶ 17.1s 12m] 10,000Y:

William Hill Lincoln Handicap, Doncaster—High Low dominates the near side throughout; in the centre Mudaffar (No. 14) goes past Democratic for second

big, leggy colt: third foal: closely related to French provincial 10.6f winner Nuange Pale (by Kenmare): dam lightly-raced daughter of a French 1m and 9f winner: no worthwhile form: tried blinkered. *Miss L. C. Siddall*

HIGH POST   3 b.g. Lidhame 109 – Touch of Class (FR) 47 (Luthier 126) [1991 6m   **47**
5.7m 6m 6d³ 5.7g 6g a8g 1992 8.9v³ a10g* 10f 10.2f* a8g⁵ 10d 9.7m⁵ 10d a10g 9.7v⁵] smallish gelding: poor mover: plater: successful at Lingfield (awarded race after interference, no bid) in May and Bath (bought in 7,600 gns) in June: better at 1¼m than shorter: acts on firm going and equitrack. *D. Marks*

HIGH PREMIUM   4 b.g. Forzando 122 – High Halo 64 (High Top 131) [1991 5g²   **80**
7g² 7.6d⁵ 6g* 7f* 8.9g⁴ 8m* 8m 9m² 1992 8g⁵ 7.9m 8f] sturdy, good-topped gelding: rated 92 at 3 yrs: shaped encouragingly first 2 starts in 1992 but not seen out again after running moderately in Royal Hunt Cup: best form at 1m/9f: acts on firm going: retained 14,500 gns Newmarket Autumn Sales and gelded. *Mrs J. R. Ramsden*

HIGH PRINCIPLES   3 b.g. Risk Me (FR) 127 – The High Dancer (High Line   **64**
125) [1991 5g² 5d² 5d⁴ 6f⁶ 1992 6d⁵ 5g³ 5m⁶ 5g³ 5f* 5m³ 5.1f³ 6f* 6g⁴ 6g 7g 5g] leggy, close-coupled gelding: good mover: consistent in first of half of 1992, and won Edinburgh maiden and Hamilton handicap: lost his form after: best form at 6f: acts on firm ground and dead: sold 1,500 gns Newmarket Autumn Sales. *J. Berry*

HIGH ROMANCE   2 b. or br.f. (Feb 12) Today And Tomorrow 78 – Nahawand 51   **45**
(High Top 131) [1992 6g⁵ 5d² 5g 5d] lengthy filly: third reported living foal: dam, plater, stayed 7f: failed to progress after second in Edinburgh maiden in August. *D. Moffatt*

HIGH SAVANNAH   4 ch.f. Rousillon (USA) 133 – Stinging Nettle 90 (Sharpen   **68**
Up 127) [1991 12g³ 12m³ 1992 11.9d 10d² 12g 10g 9.7d² a8s² 10g] rangy filly: inconsistent maiden handicapper: stays 1½m: acts on good to firm and dead ground: carries head high. *M. A. Jarvis*

HIGH SEVENS   3 ch.f. Master Willie 129 – Oatfield 69 (Great Nephew 126)   **90**
[1991 6f* 6f² 6g 1992 6m² 6g⁵ 6f³ 7m⁴ 7m 6g⁴] light-framed filly: in good form in first half of 1992, in minor event at Newmarket and £8,100 handicap at Goodwood third and fourth starts: ran moderately last 2: stays 7f: acts on firm ground. *H. Candy*

HIGH SUCCESS   3 gr.c. Petong 126 – Valadon 72 (High Line 125) [1991 NR 1992   **51**
a8g a8g⁵ a8g⁶ a7g a8g² a6g² a8g a7g a8g⁴ a11g⁴] 12,000Y: tall, lengthy colt: third foal: closely related to 1989 2-y-o 7f winner Mogul Prince (by Mansingh) and a winner in Belgium: dam 12.2f winner, is half-sister to smart 6f to 1½m winner Duke of Normandy: maiden handicapper: not seen out after June: stays 1m: acts on all-weather surfaces: below form blinkered/visored. *W. A. O'Gorman*

HIGH SUMMER   2 b.g. (Apr 14) Green Desert (USA) 127 – Beacon Hill 81   **49** p
(Bustino 136) [1992 a8g⁵] fourth living foal: half-brother to 3-y-o Brand (by Shareef Dancer) and winning stayer Rhodes (by Pharly): dam placed over 1¼m from 3 starts, is sister to Height of Fashion, dam of Unfuwain and Nashwan: looked inexperienced in maiden at Lingfield in December, staying on late to finish fifth of 9: should stay beyond 1m: sure to improve. *Lord Huntingdon*

HIGHTOWN-PRINCESS (IRE)   4 gr.f. King Persian 107 – Ambient 68   **37**
(Amber Rama (USA) 133) [1991 7v 6g 8m 6.9m 1992 8.1m 8.9m 12d 7f 7g 7.6m² 8g⁶ 7s] tall, sparely-made filly: poor maiden: form only when visored first time (visored last 3 starts): stays 7.6f: acts on good to firm ground: trained first 6 starts in 1992 by J. Moore. *M. P. Muggeridge*

HIGH TYCOON (IRE)   2 br.c. (May 7) Last Tycoon 131 – Nyama (USA)   **92**
(Pretense) [1992 5.1g² 6m* 6d³ 7g³] 19,000F, 21,000Y: smallish, close-coupled colt: third foal: half-brother to 1990 Irish 2-y-o 5f winner Molly Carter (by Dr Carter): dam won at up to 1m: highly impressive winner of minor event at Ascot in June, probably value for 10 lengths (officially won by 3): well-beaten last of 3 to Silver Wizard in listed race at Newbury following month: left Mrs J. Cecil's stable afterwards, and around a length third in Group 3 Leopardstown Stakes in October: will stay 1m: seems unsuited by good to soft ground. *D. K. Weld, Ireland*

HILLCREST GIRL   3 b.f. Tickled Pink 114 – Miss Pilgrim (Cumshaw 111) [1991   **–**
NR 1992 12.3g] smallish filly: second reported foal: dam won 3m novice hurdle: tailed off in claimer at Wolverhampton in September on belated debut. *T. W. Donnelly*

HILLSDOWN BOY (IRE)   2 ch.c. (Apr 1) Dominion Royale 112 – Lady Mary   **54**
(Sallust 134) [1992 6g 5m 7m 9g a8g³ a8g⁵] IR 720F, 5,200 2-y-o: strong, stocky colt: has a round action: half-brother to winning sprinter Tanfen (by Tanfirion): dam

third over 5f and 9f in Ireland: modest maiden: best efforts in blinkers and eyeshield on all-weather surfaces. *S. Dow*

HILLS OF HOY 6 b.g. Teenoso (USA) 135 – Fairy Tern 109 (Mill Reef (USA) **46** d 141) [1991 9m a 12g 10.2f* 10s 9.7f* 10m 10g 1992 a 10g 10.3g 11.7d3 12g 10.2m 10.2f4 10g 8.9g 11.9g] compact, quite attractive gelding: has been hobdayed: moderate mover: rated 64 at 5 yrs: on the downgrade: stays 1¼m: acts on firm and dead ground: tried blinkered once: joined D. Carey. *K. C. Bailey*

HILLS RACEAID (IRE) 2 ch.f. (Mar 4) Mazaad 106 – Sainthill (St Alphage **60** 119) [1992 5d 5g 5.7m6 5g4 5m4 5d2 5g2] IR 3,400F, 6,000Y: useful-looking filly: eleventh foal: half-sister to 6f and 9f winner Knockglas (by Hardgreen): dam twice-raced sister to top sprinter Sandford Lad: best efforts when second in nursery (for 7-lb claimer) at Wolverhampton and maiden (would have won had rider not dropped hands) at Catterick: will prove best at 5f: best form with give in the ground: blinkered last 4 outings. *J. Berry*

HILLZAH (USA) 4 ch.c. Blushing Groom (FR) 131 – Glamour Girl (ARG) **70** (Mysolo 120) [1991 8g 12d* 11g2 12g 11.9m 12m 11g4 1992 12.3v 11.9s6 11.9f 11d2 11.9s 11.9s] workmanlike colt: moderate walker: poor mover: inconsistent handicapper: stays 1½m well: acts on dead going: sometimes hangs markedly/very slowly away: a hard ride. *R. Bastiman*

HIMLAJ (USA) 7 b.g. Far North (CAN) 120 – Lusaka (USA) (Tom Rolfe) [1991 – NR 1992 12d 12f 11.8g6 14.6g a 16g] workmanlike ex-Irish gelding: has no near-side eye: no worthwhile form on flat here: stays 1½m: probably acts on any going: below form blinkered: won over hurdles in August. *S. Mellor*

HINARI HI FI 7 b.m. Song 132 – Sarah Siddons (Reform 132) [1991 6d 6m 6m 6m6 5h2 5.9m5 7g6 5m5 6g4 5m4 6m3 1992 a 7g a 6g 7m 5m 5m 6.1g 5.9f] sparely-made mare: poor mover: poor handicapper: out of form in first half of 1992: stays 6f: acts on hard and dead going: sold 950 gns Doncaster November Sales. *P. D. Evans*

HINARI VIDEO 7 b.g. Sallust 134 – Little Cynthia 76 (Wolver Hollow 126) [1991 **49** a 6g3 a 6g5 a 5g4 a 5g* a 5g* 5g2 6m 6g 6d 6d a 5g3 5m4 6g4 6f6 6m4 5m5 5m6 5m 5g6 a59 5s 1992 a 5g a 5g3 a 6g3 a 5g4 a 5g5 a 5g* a 5g3 5g 5g 5d 5g 5d2 5f4 6m3 a 5g6 a 5g5 5.1h3 a 5g 5m3 5m3 5g6 6g2 5d4 5g6 5d 6d 5d 5g 6v* a 5g a 6g4 a 5g2] smallish, workmanlike gelding: moderate mover: modest handicapper: successful at Lingfield in March and Hamilton in November: effective at 5f and 6f: acts on good to firm and heavy ground and all-weather surfaces: below form blinkered: remarkably tough. *M. Johnston*

HI NOD 2 b.c. (Mar 19) Valiyar 129 – Vikris (Viking (USA)) [1992 5g 5m4 6g2 7g* **70** 7m3 7g* 7m* 7g* 7.6v3] 1,500Y: leggy colt: progressed well physically: third foal: half-brother to 4-y-o winning sprinter Nordan Raider (by Domynsky): dam lightly-raced half-sister to useful sprinter Westacombe: consistent performer: won seller (bought in 4,400 gns) at Catterick and nurseries at Thirsk (2) and Catterick: will stay 1m: probably acts on any going. *M. J. Camacho*

HINTON HARRY (IRE) 3 b.g. Kafu 120 – Rosy O'Leary (Majetta 115) [1991 – NR 1992 6s 6f 8f 7.6m a 7g a 8g a 12g] IR 5,300F, 5,600Y, 11,000 2-y-o: leggy gelding: seventh living foal: half-brother to 5 winners, including 9f to 1½m winner Gillies Prince (by Furry Glen) and 1m winner Bradman (by Don): dam never ran: seems of little account: blinkered last 2 starts. *S. Mellor*

HIRAM B BIRDBATH 6 b.g. Ragapan 118 – At The King's Side (USA) (Kauai – King) [1991 11.5g 1992 a 7g 11.5m a 14g4] sturdy, workmanlike gelding: no form in 4 runs on flat: tried blinkered: won over fences in October. *J. A. Glover*

HISSMA 3 ch.f. Midyan (USA) 124 – Double Celt 93 (Owen Dudley 121) [1991 **84** 6m* 1992 8f2 8.9g3] medium-sized, quite attractive filly: easily best of 3 runs when second of 5 in handicap at Brighton in May: long odds on in Wolverhampton minor event following month: stays 1m: sold 12,000 gns Newmarket December Sales. *H. R. A. Cecil*

HITCHIN A RIDE 5 b.g. Dublin Taxi – Farmers Daughter (Red Slipper 126) **59** d [1991 6v6 6d 5s 5m 5g 5d 6m 5m 5m 1992 a 5g a 7g5 a 7g 5d2 5.1d 5m5 5g5 5m 8f5 7f 6m 5g 5.3d] good-bodied gelding: has a round action: half-brother to numerous winners here and abroad, including speedy 1979 2-y-o Titauri (by Wishing Star): dam ran only 3 times: successful twice (at 3 yrs) for Mrs P. Doyle in Ireland: not nearly so good in handicaps here: best form at 5f: acts on good to firm and dead ground: below form blinkered/visored. *M. P. Muggeridge*

HI-TECH HONDA (IRE) 3 b.c. Doulab (USA) 115 – Travesty 63 (Reliance II **69** 137) [1991 NR 1992 7g 6g6 7m3 7.1m4 7m2 5m2 5d6 7m 6f2 6m*dis 7g 6m4 7m] IR

362

20,000Y: strong, good-bodied colt: carries condition: sixth foal: half-brother to very useful 5-y-o Case Law (by Ahonoora) and Munawar (by Sharpo), both winning sprinters: dam twice-raced half-sister to numerous winners, including dams of Governor General and Galunpe): none too consistent handicapper: led post in maiden at Folkestone in August, but disqualified for interference: stays 7f: acts on firm ground: below form when blinkered once: sold 4,200 gns Newmarket Autumn Sales. *C. E. Brittain*

HIT THE FAN 3 b. or br.g. Lear Fan (USA) 130 – Embroglio (USA) (Empery **76** (USA) 128) [1991 NR 1992 14s² 14.1d⁴ 10s³] 26,000Y: big, lengthy gelding: has a round action: half-brother to several winners here and abroad, including 1984 2-y-o 6f winner Durayd (by Super Concorde): dam unraced close relation to Noble Decree: not seen out until September, and best run in maidens when third at Leicester: worth a try at 1½m. *R. Charlton*

HIZEEM 6 b.g. Alzao (USA) 117 – Good Member(Mansingh (USA) 120) [1991 8g⁵ **27 §** 1992 7f 7.1m⁶ 7d⁵ 8f 8.3m³ 7g 10g 8.3g⁵ 10d³] small gelding: untrustworthy handicapper: stays 1¼m: acts on firm going: below form blinkered/ran creditably visored. *M. P. Naughton*

HOBEY CAT 2 ch.f. (Mar 28) Interrex (CAN) – T Catty (USA) 62 (Sensitive **44** Prince (USA)) [1992 5g 5.7d⁴ 6d⁶ a6g a8g⁶] workmanlike filly: first foal: dam, maiden, stayed 1½m, is sister to smart performer at around 7f Condrillac: poor form in maidens and a claimer: will probably stay 7f. *D. R. C. Elsworth*

HOB GREEN 3 ch.g. Move Off 112 – Prejudice 83 (Young Generation 129) [1991 **76 p** 6m 8m 6g⁵ 1992 6d 7g 8.2g 8m 8d 6.1m* 7d*ᵈⁱˢ 7m* 7g²] lengthy gelding: has a quick action: no form in handicaps in 1992 until winning at Nottingham in June: progressed extremely well after, successful at Newmarket (2, disqualified first one for jockey claiming wrong allowance) in October and second in apprentice event (idled having led 2f out) at Doncaster: should stay 1m: acts on good to firm ground and dead: best with extreme waiting tactics: has good turn of foot: will do well at 4 yrs, and sure to win more races. *Mrs J. R. Ramsden*

HODGE BECK 2 b.f. (Apr 8) Dowsing (USA) 124 – Lizarra 74 (High Top 131) **–** [1992 5m⁶] leggy filly: third foal: dam raced only at 2 yrs when placed over 6f: around 9 lengths sixth of 15 in claimer at Beverley in May, keeping on under hands and heels: seemed certain to improve. *M. H. Easterby*

HOD-MOD (IRE) 2 b.c. (Mar 14) Digamist (USA) 110 – Sallymiss (Tanfirion **54** 110) [1992 5s⁴ 5.1g³ 6m] 9,800Y: compact colt: first foal: dam Irish 5f winner: in frame in maidens at Hamilton and Chester: ran poorly in maiden auction at Newmarket later in May. *A. Bailey*

HOHNE GARRISON 2 b.g. (Mar 9) Cragador 110 – Chanita (Averof 123) [1992 **38** 6d 5g 7s] 800F, 1,000Y, 2,300 2-y-o: leggy gelding: brother to poor animal Telegraph Touch and half-brother to 6f to 1m winner Merseyside Man (by My Dad Tom): dam unraced: poor form in varied maiden events. *J. White*

HO-JOE (IRE) 2 b.g. (Jan 21) Burslem 123 – Walkyria (Lord Gayle (USA) 124) **58** [1992 6f 6m 7.1m⁴ 7.1m² 7f⁵ 7.5m] 7,000F, 6,200Y: lengthy gelding: fifth foal: half-brother to 1991 2-y-o 5f and 7.6f winner Corals Dream (by Petorius): dam Irish middle-distance winner from family of Slip Anchor: plating-class maiden: ran poorly final start: should be suited by further than 7f: joined J. Carr. *A. Harrison*

HOKEY POKEY (FR) 2 b. or br.f. (May 26) Lead On Time (USA) 123 – Sunclad **48** (FR) (Tennyson (FR) 124) [1992 7m 6s⁶ 6d⁴ 6s] leggy, lengthy filly: half-sister to French 11.5f winner Zinzio (by Zino) and Irish 3-y-o 7f winner Suntan (by Sicyos): dam French 1½m winner: poor maiden: will stay 1m +: bandaged on debut: sold 1,800 gns Newmarket Autumn Sales. *D. Sasse*

HOLD FAST (IRE) 4 b.g. Dara Monarch 128 – No Flight (Nonoalco (USA) 131) **41** [1991 7d⁵ 6g 7m 8.1s a10g 1992 8d 8.2m 7g* 7.1s⁶ 6m 9s] good-topped gelding: good walker: inconsistent handicapper: won at Salisbury in August: should prove as effective at 1m as 7f: sold to join C. Nash's stable 3,200 gns Newmarket Autumn Sales. *H. Candy*

HOLETOWN 3 b.c. Prince Sabo 123 – Cubby Hole (Town And Country 124) **79** [1991 6d 6s² 6m³ 6f* 6m* 5.2f³ 1992 6g 5g 7f² 6m 6g 5d² 6s 7v*] neat colt: has a quick action: inconsistent handicapper: trained until after sixth start (blinkered, not discreted in claimer) by R. Hannon: won at Cologne in November: stays 7f: acts on any going. *A. Lowe, Germany*

HOLIDAY ISLAND 3 ch.g. Good Times (ITY) – Green Island 89 (St Paddy 133) **75** [1991 5d³ 7d⁵ 6m 9m⁴ 8g² 7g⁵ 1992 9.9g² 12.3s 8d* 9g 9m⁶ 11.5m* 10g⁶ 10.1g⁶ 9.9g⁴ 9d 12d⁶] workmanlike colt: fair but inconsistent handicapper: won at Kempton and Lingfield in first half of 1992: best at around 1½m: acts on good to firm ground and dead: joined R. Akehurst. *C. E. Brittain*

HOLLY BROWN 9 br.m. Derrylin 115 – Friday Brown 84 (Murrayfield 119) [1991 NR 1992 12d⁵ 12f] workmanlike mare: has been to stud and had a foal: poor form in handicaps on first runs on flat for 4 seasons: stays 15f: acts on any going. *P. J. Hobbs* –

HOLLY GOLIGHTLY 2 b.f. (Mar 27) Robellino (USA) 127 – Rengaine (FR) (Music Boy 124) [1992 5g² 5.1m* 5f⁶ 6f³ 7m³] workmanlike, good-quartered filly: progressed well physically: third foal: half-sister to 3-y-o Mere Chants (by Kings Lake): dam French 8.5f and 11f winner: improving filly: won maiden at Chester in May: good efforts after in Queen Mary Stakes at Royal Ascot and £8,900 event and moderately-run Sweet Solera Stakes (sweating, never able to challenge Mystic Goddess) at Newmarket: not seen out after August: will stay 1m. *R. Hannon* 83

HOLY WANDERER (USA) 3 b.c. Vaguely Noble 140 – Bronzed Goddess (USA) (Raise A Native) [1991 6m 7f 6g 1992 8.9v⁴ 10d³ 10g 10g⁵ a11g³ a12g* a12g⁵ a12g⁵] compact colt: appeared to show improved form when winning handicap at Southwell: failed to reproduce that later in July, and plating-class handicapper on balance of form: suited by 1½m: acts on fibresand and dead ground: retained 3,800 gns Newmarket Autumn Sales. *D. W. P. Arbuthnot* 64 ?

HOLY ZEAL 6 b.g. Alzao (USA) 117 – Crystal Halo 78 (St Chad 120) [1991 NR 1992 14d⁴ 16m⁵ 11.9d⁵ 13.9m⁶ 13.9g⁵ 13.3g] useful-looking gelding: impresses in appearance: fairly useful handicapper: stayed on well despite not getting best of runs when sixth in Tote Ebor at York, fourth outing and best effort in 1992: pulled up as though something amiss last time: effective at 1½m: acts on firm and dead going: sometimes has tongue tied down/bandaged. *D. W. P. Arbuthnot* 87

HOME AFFAIR 2 b.f. (Mar 18) Petoski 135 – Miranda Julia 73 (Julio Mariner 127) [1992 7g 6g⁶ 7g a5g³ 6m 6g 5g⁴ 6m 5g a7g] 1,600Y: compact filly: third foal: sister to 4-y-o maiden Marine Society and half-sister to 3-y-o Idoni (by Bustino): dam 7f winner: modest maiden: best effort at 5f though bred to stay much further: acts on equitrack: visored 3 times: sold out of D. T. Thom's stable 600 gns Newmarket Autumn Sales before final start. *K. O. Cunningham-Brown* 55

HOME FROM THE HILL (IRE) 2 b.f. (Mar 16) Jareer (USA) 115 – Hill's Realm (USA) 68 (Key To The Kingdom (USA)) [1992 7m 8g* 8f 7m³ 7g] IR 10,000F, 13,000Y: leggy, sparely-made filly: sixth foal: half-sister to 5 winners, including (at 1m) 3-y-o General John (by Cyrano de Bergerac) and (at 9f at 2 yrs in 1990) All The King's Men (by Alzao): dam stayed 6f: gamely won maiden auction at Redcar in August: best effort when third of 21 in nursery at Newmarket: will prove suited by return to further than 7f: possibly unsuited by very firm ground. *M. Bell* 72

HOMEMAKER 2 b.f. (Mar 12) Homeboy 114 – Ganadora (Good Times (ITY)) [1992 5.1s² 6g 6m² 7f* 7m⁵ 5.7m⁴ 7d 7g² 8s] workmanlike filly: third foal: half-sister to 3-y-o Leigh Crofter (by Son of Shaka), successful at 7f (at 2 yrs) and 5.8f: dam unraced: won seller (no bid) at Brighton in June: best subsequent effort when excellent second in non-selling nursery there: should stay 1m: best form on a sound surface. *R. J. Holder* 54

HOMILE 4 b.g. Homing 130 – Rocas 48 (Ile de Bourbon (USA) 133) [1991 8f 8m 10d 8f 9.2m² 8.3m* 7m 1992 8.9g 7m² 8m 8.2d⁵ 8g] leggy, lengthy gelding: poor handicapper: effective at 7f to 9f: acts on good to firm and dead ground: effective blinkered or not. *B. A. McMahon* 49

HOMME DE LOI (IRE) 3 b.c. Law Society (USA) 130 – Our Village (Bally-more 123) [1991 7g² 10m² 10.5s* 10.5s* 9.2s* 10m*] IR 30,000Y: half-brother to several winners, including Middle Park winner Mister Majestic (by Tumble Wind) and 4-y-o 1½m and 1¾m winner Tactical Mission (by Rainbow Quest): dam poor daughter of sister to dam of smart Linda's Fantasy: smart performer: won minor event and listed contest at Saint-Cloud in the spring: progressed really well when successful at Longchamp in Prix de Guiche by ½ length from demoted Calling Collect and Grand Prix de Paris Louis Vuitton by ¾ length from Kitwood: should have stayed 1½m: tended to hang: retired to stud in Normandy for a fee of 25,000 francs (approx £3,000) (Oct 1st). *A. Fabre, France* 120

HONDEGHEM 6 gr.g. Kalaglow 132 – Kajetana (FR) (Caro 133) [1991 NR 1992 16.2m⁵ 12.2g³] tall, lengthy gelding: has long stride: fifth foal: half-brother to 3 winners, including 7-y-o middle-distance stayer K-Brigade (by Brigadier Gerard) and very useful K-Battery (by Gunner B), successful from 7f to 1¼m: dam never ran: won 2 NH Flat races in 1992: around 13 lengths fifth in moderately-run Haydock –

minor event: failed to confirm that when odds on in Catterick maiden later in June.
C. W. C. Elsey

HONEY BOY SIMBA   6 ch.g. Mansingh (USA) 120 – Continental Divide 50   –
(Sharp Edge 123) [1991 8g* 8d⁵ 8m 8m 1992 10.5s 8.5m 8f 9.9f⁶ 8.3f⁵ 10.5g⁴ 8f]
smallish, lengthy gelding: carries condition: poor mover: poor handicapper:
probably stays 1¼m: below form on hard ground, probably acts on any other: usually
visored: sometimes looks moody. *M. J. O'Neill*

HONEY DANCER   8 b.g. Tyrnavos 129 – Hello Honey 105 (Crepello 136) [1991
14m⁴ 18m 1992 a16g 18g 16d 14g⁶] well-made gelding: moderate mover: below form
in handicaps in spring: stays 2¼m: acts on any going: pulled too hard in blinkers.
Miss A. J. Whitfield

HONEY HEATHER (IRE)   3 ch.f. Kris 135 – Heatherfields (Northfields   56
(USA)) [1991 5m³ 6.1d⁴ 6s 1992 6.1m² 7m² 7g 6g³ 7g⁶ a7g² 6d a7g] small filly:
maiden handicapper: stays 7f: acts on good to firm ground and equitrack, possibly
not on a soft surface: sometimes has tongue tied down. *C. F. Wall*

HONEY JUICE   2 b.f. (Apr 23) Bairn (Mill Reef (USA)   33
141) [1992 5.2m 6.1g 7s 6g a7g a8g⁵] 5,000F: compact filly: sister to a winner in Italy
and half-sister to 1991 Irish 2-y-o 6f winner Sing (by Chief Singer): dam ran once:
poor maiden: sold 450 gns Ascot December Sales. *M. J. Fetherston-Godley*

HONEYMOON DAWN   2 b.f. (Feb 23) Dowsing (USA) 124 – Fire And Ice (FR)   32
(Reliance II 137) [1992 5f 6g 5g 6.1v] leggy, unfurnished filly: looks
weak: half-sister to modest 1½m winner Shenestone (by Sharpen Up) and a winner
in Italy by Cure The Blues: dam, little sign of ability in 4 races in France, is out of
sister to St Leger winner Boucher: poor maiden: sold out of R. Whitaker's stable
1,500 gns Doncaster September Sales after third outing. *L. J. Codd*

HONEY SEEKER   3 br.c. Chief Singer 131 – Honey Thief 77 (Burglar 128) [1991   57
NR 1992 5g* 5.7d] 11,000F, 17,000Y: eleventh living foal: half-brother to a winner in
Italy and 3 sprint winners here, notably smart Prince Reymo (by Jimmy Reppin) and
very speedy Silks Venture (by Lochnager): dam 2-y-o 5f winner: well backed when
short-head winner of maiden at Warwick on debut: fair ninth of 19 in Bath handicap
later in autumn: should stay further: may be capable of better. *T. Thomson Jones*

HONEY SNUGFIT   3 ch.f. Music Boy 124 – Buy G's 60 (Blakeney 126) [1991   –
5m⁶ a5g³ 5g⁴ a7g⁴ a7g³ 7.1m³ 7m⁶ 1992 7d] lengthy filly: has scope: moderate
mover: poor maiden: stays 7f: acts on good to firm ground, and on fibresand: below
form when blinkered once. *M. W. Easterby*

HONEY VISION   3 b.f. Vision (USA) – Straw Bonnet (Thatch (USA) 136) [1991   40
5f 7m 6f 8m⁴ 9m 8.2m 8m⁵ 7m⁶ a8g³ a7g² 1992 a6g² a6g⁴ 8m⁵ 10m 7f² 6.9g³ 8.3m⁵   a48
6s] lengthy filly: poor maiden: stays 1m: acts on firm ground and equitrack: below
form when visored: blinkered nowadays. *G. H. Eden*

HONOR AND PRIDE (FR)   2 ro.c. (Feb 23) Highest Honor (FR) 124 – **104**
Indigene (FR) 109 (Hard To Beat 132) [1992 7.5s 8g* 9d³ 8v⁵] 480,000 francs

*Grand Prix de Paris Louis Vuitton, Longchamp—a fourth win from four starts in 1992
for Homme de Loi, who beats Kitwood and Guislaine, but he's not seen out again*

(approx £48,300) Y: half-brother to very useful French 1986 staying 2-y-o Hard Leaf (by Bellypha) and a winner in USA: dam very useful staying 2-y-o: won minor event at Evry in September: around 3 lengths third of 4 to Richard of York in Prix Saint-Roman there later in month: beaten 4 lengths or so when fifth to Mil Foil in Prix Thomas Bryon at Saint-Cloud on final start: stays 9f. *P. Bary, France*

HONORARY GUEST   2 b.f. (Mar 17) Interrex (CAN) – Royal Meeting 44 (Dara   **51** Monarch 128) [1992 6m 8.1s 8g6 7s5 10d2 8g a8g] leggy filly: first reported foal: dam won 1m seller: fair plater: stays 1¼m: acts on soft ground. *D. J. G. Murray-Smith*

HONOUR AND GLORY   2 ch.f. (May 20) Hotfoot 126 – Cheb's Honour 70   **46** (Chebs Lad 120) [1992 6g 7m 7d4 10d 7.6s6] smallish filly: closely related to 3 winners by Firestreak, and half-sister to 3 winners by Balliol, notably smart sprinter Singing Steven: dam placed over 5f at 2 yrs: poor maiden: should stay 1¼m. *Bob Jones*

HOOCHIECOOCHIE MAN (IRE)   2 b.c. (May 12) Taufan (USA) 119 – Regal   **51** p Entrance (Be My Guest (USA) 126) [1992 a8g4] 20,000Y: fourth live foal: half-brother to ungenerous 1989 2-y-o 6f winner Rainbow Bridge (by Godswalk): dam won at 7f in Ireland: showed signs of ability in 9-runner maiden at Lingfield in December, pushed along before halfway and keeping on steadily: sure to improve. *D. W. P. Arbuthnot*

HOOSIE   2 gr.f. (May 9) Niniski (USA) 125 – Hooked Bid (CAN) 76 (Spectacular   **57** p Bid (USA)) [1992 6d 10g3] workmanlike filly: second foal: dam, 1m winner, is daughter of half-sister to Lyphard and Nobiliary: better for race still, staying-on third of 13, beaten over 3 lengths, in maiden at Nottingham in October: behind in Blue Seal Stakes at Ascot previous month: will be suited by 1½m: probably capable of better. *C. E. Brittain*

HOPEFUL BID (IRE)   3 b.g. Auction Ring (USA) 123 – Irish Kick (Wind-   **72** jammer (USA)) [1991 6m 6g6 6f 1992 7g 7m* 7.1m4 7f 7g 8d 7.1g3 7s4 9g] leggy, close-coupled gelding: moderate mover: inconsistent in handicaps after winning maiden at Goodwood in May: may prove best at up to 7f: acts on good to firm ground: effective blinkered or not. *R. Hannon*

HORIZON (IRE)   4 b.g. Red Sunset 120 – Vahila (Relko 136) [1991 10g5 12d 12s4   **48** 10g* 10g* 16.2f4 10.2g* 10.5m* 10.2m 12d6 1992 a12g* a12g* a12g 10.8v 11.7d5   a77 ? 11.6m6 10d 12.3m 12g 12.3d6 12m2 12d2] rangy gelding: moderate mover: easily best efforts in handicaps in 1992 when winning at Southwell (2) in spring: best turf efforts as 4-y-o on last 2 starts: effective from 1¼m to 1½m: acts on good to firm and dead ground and goes well on fibresand: usually forces pace: blinkered nowadays. *T. Thomson Jones*

HORIZONTALE   3 b.f. Night Shift (USA) – Jenny Mere (Brigadier Gerard 144)   **39** [1991 6g 7g 6f6 6m 7m 1992 8.2g 10f 7f4 7m6 6.9g6 7f5] close-coupled filly: poor maiden: should stay 1m: acts on firm going: below form blinkered once. *C. E. Brittain*

HORSERADISH   2 b.g. (Feb 10) Chief Singer 131 – Hot Spice (Hotfoot 126)   **42** [1992 7d 8m 8m] workmanlike gelding: has plenty of scope: good walker: half-brother to 3 winners, including smart 1m to 13.3f winner Sesame (by Derrylin) and middle-distance stayer Turmeric (by Alias Smith): dam never ran: soundly beaten in autumn maidens. *D. Morley*

HOSTILE ACT   7 b.g. Glenstal (USA) 118 – Fandetta (Gay Fandango (USA) 132)   **44** [1991 NR 1992 10g4] good-bodied gelding: poor maiden: first run on flat for 2 seasons when fourth of 19 in Leicester handicap: well worth another try over 1½m (stays 11.5f): acts on good to firm going: bandaged: joined Miss P. Hall. *K. A. Morgan*

HOSTILE WITNESS (IRE)   2 br.c. (Feb 9) Law Society (USA) 130 – No Time   **64** To Dance (Shareef Dancer (USA) 135) [1992 7m3 7d 8d5 7g] IR 14,500Y: leggy, close-coupled colt: first foal: dam unraced granddaughter of Sarah Siddons, dam of Seymour Hicks and Princess Pati: modest form in maidens at Newmarket, Goodwood and Kempton (never placed to challenge under considerate handling) first 3 starts: well beaten in face of stiff task in Ascot nursery after: will stay beyond 1m. *R. Hannon*

HOST (IRE)   3 b.c. Be My Guest (USA) 126 – Take Your Mark (USA) (Round   **89** Table) [1991 NR 1992 10d 10m* 10d4 11.9g5 9g4 10g 9s*] 70,000Y: leggy, lengthy colt: good walker: brother to 2000 Guineas second Charmer, later winner at up to 13.3f, closely related to 3 winners, including 4-y-o 7f and 1½m winner Kimbers (by Lomond), and half-brother to 2 winners: dam lightly-raced half-sister to dam of Leading Counsel: made most when winning maiden at Sandown in June and £11,700 handicap at Newbury in October: should stay 1½m (very stiff task at trip): acts on good to firm ground and soft. *C. E. Brittain*

HOTARIA 2 b.f. (Mar 8) Sizzling Melody 117 – Fair Eleanor (Saritamer (USA) **63** 130) [1992 5m 5f⁴ 5g⁵ 5g² 6d* 6.5m 6s 6m⁶] 4,200Y: lengthy filly: third foal: half-sister to 3-y-o Dragon Spirit (by Absalom) and 1989 2-y-o 7f winner Ardelle Grey (by Ardross): dam poor plater stayed 1m: made all on favoured stand rail in Ripon maiden auction in September: form in nurseries after only when good sixth at Newmarket: best form at 6f: acts on good to firm and dead ground. *R. M. Whitaker*

HOTEL CALIFORNIA (IRE) 2 b.f. (Feb 5) Last Tycoon 131 – Rained Off 83 **58** (Welsh Pageant 132) [1992 6.1m³ 6.1d 6m 6m 7.5m* 8s] IR 29,000Y: leggy, sparely-made filly: first foal: dam middle-distance maiden, is half-sister to Ever Genial out of sister to One Way Street: easily best run when winning selling nursery at Beverley (bought out of J. Hills's stable 6,000 gns) in September: ran moderately in non-selling nursery after: will be suited by middle distances: acts on good to firm ground. *D. W. Chapman*

HOTFOOT HANNAH (IRE) 4 b.f. Anita's Prince 126 – Serendip (Sing Sing **49** 134) [1991 6m 6m⁵ 6.1m 1992 5v² 5g 5d 5d⁵ 5m* 5.1g⁵ 5g 5g*] good-topped filly: moderate mover: sprint handicapper: successful at Folkestone and Wolverhampton in summer: acted on good to firm and heavy ground: sometimes bandaged: dead. *P. S. Felgate*

HOT LAVENDER (CAN) 3 b.f. Shadeed (USA) 135 – Wind Spray 69 (Mill Reef **67** (USA) 141) [1991 5g⁴ 5m³ 1992 5g⁴ 5m 5g⁴ 5.1m² 5m⁴ 5f³ 5d³ 5.1g⁵ 5g⁶] lengthy, workmanlike filly: has a quick action: consistent in handicaps until well below form last 2 starts: acts on firm and dead going: usually has tongue tied down/sweats. *C. F. Wall*

HOT OFF THE PRESS 2 gr.g. (Mar 17) Printafoil – Printbull (Habat 127) **61** d [1992 5g 6f⁴ 6m² 6g³ 7f 6s 7.5m 8.3s³ 7d 7.6s] 4,600F, 2,700Y: small gelding: fourth living foal: half-brother to 8.5f (at 2 yrs) and 11f winner Hard To Name (by Connaught): dam poor half-sister to smart middle-distance stayer Major Green: maiden: easily best effort third outing, poor otherwise: has been tried visored: a hard ride. *R. M. Whitaker*

HOT PROSPECT 3 b.f. Damister (USA) 123 – Smelter 111 (Prominer 125) [1991 **44** NR 1992 8.1d⁵ 8m³ 8m⁵ 10.9s⁴ 10.8s a8g] leggy filly: eighth foal: half-sister to Irish 7f winner Ellaline (by Corvaro) and Irish 1m and 9f winner Northern Vision (by Vision): dam won twice over 7f from 3 starts: poor maiden: stays 10.9f: acts on good to firm and soft ground: below form blinkered: sold to join Mrs P. Russell 2,000 gns Doncaster November Sales. *J. Etherington*

HOT PUNCH 3 ch.g. Dara Monarch 128 – Glebehill 76 (Northfields (USA)) [1991 **42** 5m 5m² 6d 6m⁶ 7.5f 8m 1992 8s 6m 6.1g³ 7.1m⁴ 8m⁵ 8f⁶] sparely-made gelding: poor maiden: stays 1m: acts on good to firm ground. *P. Calver*

HOTSOCKS 2 ch.f. (Apr 11) Hotfoot 126 – Renira 60 (Relkino 131) [1992 6m 7s **34** a7g⁵] 2,100Y: lengthy filly: fourth foal: half-sister to 1990 2-y-o 5f winner Summer Sands (by Mummy's Game): dam poor maiden: poor form in Newmarket seller and all-weather maidens. *Pat Mitchell*

HOT SOUND 3 b.f. Hotfoot 126 – Sound Type 92 (Upper Case (USA)) [1991 NR **–** 1992 8v 8v] 1,600F: seventh foal: half-sister to 9f and 1¼m seller winner Final Sound (by Final Straw) and a winner in Belgium by Busted: dam 7f and 1¼m winner: behind in minor event and seller in April. *B. W. Lunness*

HOT STAR 6 b.g. Hotfoot 126 – La Camargue (Wollow 132) [1991 NR 1992 16.1s⁵ **55** 16.2d²] leggy gelding: has a markedly round action: lightly-raced handicapper: ran well in late-season: stays 2m: best on a soft surface: usually sweats: held up. *G. M. Moore*

HOT STORM 2 b.f. (Apr 28) Celestial Storm (USA) 132 – Canvas Shoe 57 **49 ?** (Hotfoot 126) [1992 7m* 7f⁶ 7g 8.2d 10.5d] compact filly: has a quick action: half-sister to 7f and 8.2f winner Ward One (by Mr Fluorocarbon), a winner abroad and a winner over hurdles: dam 2-y-o 6f seller winner: failed to progress after winning Newcastle claimer in July: retained by trainer 1,700 gns Doncaster August Sales: sold 2,500 gns Doncaster November Sales. *M. J. Camacho*

HOT TIP 3 b.f. Beldale Flutter (USA) 130 – Summer's Darling 63 (Final Straw **–** 127) [1991 7m 8.9m 8.1s 1992 11.1m⁵ 10g] workmanlike filly: poor maiden: should stay at least 1¼m: will be beaten on soft ground: joined J. Eyre. *B. Ellison*

HOULSTON'S WILL 3 ch.f. Nicholas Bill 125 – Falcrello 51 (Falcon 131) [1991 **64** 7m³ 1992 8g 8.3d² 8s³ 10.5d 10.3f 8.2d* 8m 8s* 10s 8v⁴] close-coupled filly: modest

Ladbrokes (Ayr) Silver Cup (Handicap)—
How's Yer Father (far side of the visored Diet) snatches the inaugural Cup
on the line

handicapper: won at Nottingham in August and Ayr (claimer) in September: should prove at least as effective at 1¼m as 1m: seems best with give in the ground: held up: has joined D. Burchell. *Mrs J. R. Ramsden*

HOW'S YER FATHER 6 b.g. Daring March 116 – Dawn Ditty 100 (Song 132) **86** [1991 5m⁶ 5.3f* 6m* 5g 6f² 6d³ 5.1g² 6g² 6.1s* 7g² 6f⁶ 7f³ 7f⁴ 7m 6g 5.1s* 6.1d⁴ 5g² 7d 5d 1992 6d 5.3m⁴ 5.1d³ 6g* 6f⁴ 6.1m* 7g 6m² 7.1f⁵ 5.1f² 6g³ 7g 6d² 6d* 6d 6m 6s⁶] leggy gelding: consistent handicapper: successful at Salisbury and Chepstow in May and £12,400 Silver Cup at Ayr (by a head from Diet) in September: best at sprint distances: acts on any going: sometimes blinkered: ran creditably when sweating/edgy: held up: very tough and consistent. *R. J. Hodges*

HOY-LIEGH-RAG 2 b.c. (Feb 24) Glow (USA) – Wuthering Falls (Wind And **60** Wuthering (USA) 132) [1992 6g 6m² 6.1m² 6m] 5,800F: rather leggy, workman-like colt: has scope: moderate mover: first foal: dam Irish 7f winner, is half-sister to Baronet: easily best efforts in maidens when runner-up at Pontefract and Nottingham: stays 6f: finds little off bridle. *M. Johnston*

HTHAAL (USA) 4 b. or br.g. Caro 133 – Endurable Heights (USA) (Graustark) – [1991 7f³ 7.5m² 11.9m² 1992 13.1m 12.1m 16.2d⁵ 12.1s] big, close-coupled gelding: moderate walker: maiden handicapper: no form in 1992: stays 1½m well: acts on firm going: won poor novice handicap hurdle in November. *L. Lungo*

HUBBERS FAVOURITE 4 ch.f. Anfield 117 – Printafoil (Habat 127) [1991 7g **56** d 10m 12m 10g a12g4 12m⁶ 8.3m 10m 17.1m a12g 1992 7g² a7g a8g² a8g a6g⁶ a7g a10g 7.1s 8m 7s] sturdy filly: poor mover: poor handicapper: effective at 7f to 1½m: best form on all-weather: often visored. *Mrs N. Macauley*

HUDUD (USA) 3 ch.f. Vaguely Noble 140 – Belle Forbes (USA) (Bold Forbes **59** (USA)) [1991 NR 1992 10s⁵ 12v⁵] lengthy filly: first foal: dam, maiden in North America, is half-sister to Lemhi Gold (by Vaguely Noble): twice-raced in maidens: tailed off at Folkestone in November after shaping encouragingly at Newbury previous month: sold 7,000 gns Newmarket December Sales. *A. C. Stewart*

HUESCA 2 gr.f. (May 10) Aragon 118 – Houston Belle 59 (Milford 119) [1992 5v – 5.3d⁶ 5g 6s] 2,000Y: leggy filly: second foal: half-sister to 3-y-o The Grey Texan (by Nishapour): dam maiden stayed 1¼m, won over hurdles: well beaten, including in sellers: blinkered final start: swishes tail, and looks unco-operative. *J. R. Jenkins*

HUFFA (USA) 2 b.g. (Feb 28) Ziggy's Boy (USA) – Science Hill (USA) (Cox's **81** Ridge (USA)) [1992 5d⁵ 5.1g³ 5m⁴] $40,000Y: rather unfurnished gelding: second reported foal: dam unraced: sire (by Danzig) 5f to 7f winner: won maiden at Ripon in April: over 7 lengths fourth of 5 in listed National Stakes at Sandown in May: seemed sure to progress again. *W. J. Haggas*

HUGGING 3 b.f. Beveled (USA) – Pillowing 69 (Good Times (ITY)) [1991 6f4 5g5 **78**
6.1m6 1992 6.9v5 7g6 7s2 8g2 7m4 8.5d* 8m5 7.1g2 8g5 8.1g 8d3 8d] tall filly: good
mover: won maiden at Epsom in June and ran well in handicaps most starts after:
poor effort in Leicester minor event final run: stays 8.5f: seems suited by give in the
ground: ran well when very edgy. *M. McCormack*

HULA BAY (USA) 2 ch.g. (Feb 21) Lord At War (ARG) – Osculate (USA) (Forli **47 p**
(ARG)) [1992 a7g3] $15,000Y, resold $30,000Y: half-brother to several winners
here and in North America, including fairly useful 1983 2-y-o 5f performer Brave
Advance (by Bold Laddie): dam unraced half-sister to Robellino's dam: sire
top-class miler in Argentina later high class from 1m to 1¼m in USA: one paced and
beaten over 8 lengths when third of 4 in maiden at Southwell in July: moved
moderately down. *M. Bell*

HULLO MARY DOLL 3 br.f. Lidhame 109 – Princess Story 64 (Prince de **– §**
Galles 125) [1991 NR 1992 a7g4 8m5 11.6g 8d 8d] leggy filly: moderate mover: tenth
foal: half-sister to several winners, including 6f winner Aquarian Prince (by
Mansingh) and 1¼m and 1½m winner Kiki Star (by Some Hand): dam successful in
sellers at around 1m: no form: most reluctant last 2 starts, blinkered first time. *R.
Ingram*

HUMAM (IRE) 2 ch.c. (Feb 15) Nijinsky (CAN) 138 – Passamaquoddy (USA) **97 p**
(Drone) [1992 6d* 6f* 7g3 7m2] IR 400,000Y: strong, workmanlike colt: fluent
mover: closely related to 3-y-o Tamim (by Topsider), useful sprinter at 2 yrs, and
half-brother to winners by Alydar and Mr Prospector: dam, winner at up to 9f, is
sister to dam of Dancing Brave and Jolypha: most progressive colt: won maiden at
Haydock and Chesham Stakes (by length from Lord President) at Royal Ascot in
June: ran on strongly when second of 10 to Maroof in Lanson Champagne Vintage
Stakes at Goodwood: will be better suited by 1m: strong-galloping type: has plenty
of scope for further progress. *H. Thomson Jones*

HUMBER'S SUPREME (IRE) 2 b.f. (Apr 4) Digamist (USA) 110 – Raise A **–**
Princess (USA) (Raise A Native) [1992 5d5 5f 5g] small, unfurnished filly: half-sister

Maktoum Al-Maktoum's "Humam"

Mr S. S. Niarchos' "Hydro Calido"

to 1986 Irish 2-y-o 6f and 7f winner Native Sal (by Sallust) and 1988 2-y-o 5f seller winner Passage East (by Indian King), later sprint winner in Canada: dam dead-heated over 5f in Ireland at 2 yrs from 3 starts: seems of little account. *B. S. Rothwell*

HUMOUR (IRE) 3 b.f. Sadler's Wells (USA) 132 – Princess Tracy 111 (Ahonoora 122) [1991 7m 1992 8v⁴ 8v⁴ 10.2s³ 13.1m 12.2d⁵ 10f] leggy filly: consistent in maidens and handicaps until final outing: stays 13f: acts on good to firm ground and heavy: ran creditably when blinkered once. *C. F. Wall* **62**

HUNG HING (IRE) 2 b.g. (Jan 30) Cyrano de Bergerac 120 – Turbo Lady (Tumble Wind (USA)) [1992 6g 8s] good-quartered gelding: fifth foal: dam never ran: took strong hold and well beaten in maidens at Thirsk (blinkered) and Newcastle in the autumn: sold 1,300 gns Doncaster November Sales. *J. D. Bethell* **36**

HUNG OVER 6 b.m. Smackover 107 – Passionate 57 (Dragonara Palace (USA) 115) [1991 NR 1992 10g] leggy, lengthy mare: ungenuine maiden: stays 7f: best form on an easy surface: below form blinkered. *R. Champion* **– §**

HUNG PARLIAMENT 2 gr.f. (Feb 28) Sharrood (USA) 124 – Session 80 (Reform 132) [1992 5d⁴ 5d³ 5.1m³ 6f² 7g* 7m 7g³ 6.5m² 7m 6.1s*] 3,000Y: lengthy filly: progressed well physically: fourth foal: half-sister to winners in Italy by Touching Wood and Precocious: dam 7f winner out of half-sister to High Line: progressive and consistent filly: won maiden auction at Yarmouth in July and minor event at Chester in October: will stay 1m: probably acts on any going: sold 30,000 gns Newmarket Autumn Sales. *B. W. Hills* **76**

HUNTED 5 ch.g. Busted 134 – Madam Cody (Hot Spark 126) [1991 16d 1992 17.5s] sturdy gelding: has a quick action: on the downgrade. *A. R. Davison* **–**

HUNTING GROUND 4 b.c. Dancing Brave (USA) 140 – Ack's Secret (USA) (Ack Ack (USA)) [1991 10m² 1992 14.1g² 12.1d⁶ 16.5g a16g a12g5] good-bodied colt: has round action: winning hurdler/lightly-raced maiden on flat: sold out of G. Harwood's stable 5,000 gns Ascot September Sales and well beaten last 4 starts: **79 d**

should prove suited by 2m: acts on good to firm ground: usually has tongue tied down. *R. E. Peacock*

HURRICANE TOKE (IRE) 3 gr.c. Kenmare (FR) 125 – Believer 112 (Blakeney 126) [1991 NR 1992 8g 10m 10.5g 11.8g] workmanlike, good-topped colt: fifth foal: half-brother to fairly useful 1989 2-y-o 5f winner Please Believe Me (by Try My Best): dam won Princess Royal Stakes: no worthwhile form. *A. C. Stewart* —

HUSH BABY (IRE) 2 b.f. (Feb 4) Ballacashtal (CAN) – Kind Lady 56 (Kind of Hush 118) [1992 6.1m 6s⁶ 8.2d⁵ 10.5d⁶ 8d a8g⁴] second foal: half-sister to 3-y-o 7f winner Amadeus Aes (by Dublin Lad): dam 2-y-o 6f seller winner probably stayed 1½m: poor maiden: stays 1m: acts on soft ground: below form when blinkered/visored once. *D. Morris* 48

HUSO 4 ch.g. Sharpo 132 – Husnah (USA) 85 (Caro 133) [1991 6d 8s⁵ 8.5f³ 8.2m* 8.9g* 8g² 8m 8m 9m⁴ 8m⁶ 8.1s a8g 1992 8m 10g 9.2s 8.5m] good-quartered gelding: modest handicapper: little form on flat in 1992: should stay 1¼m: acts on a sound surface: below form when visored once. *P. C. Haslam* —

HYDE'S HAPPY HOUR 2 b.c. (May 31) Primo Dominie 121 – Ixia 91 (I Say 125) [1992 6g 7g 7g³ 7g⁶ 8f] 10,500 2-y-o: good-topped colt: half-brother to several winners, including 6-y-o 1¼m to 13.8f winner Corn Lily (by Aragon) and useful 1m and 1¼m performer Cardinal Flower (by Sharpen Up): dam very game winner at up to 1½m: plating-class form in varied events: never placed to challenge or knocked about in Doncaster nursery final start: should stay 1m. *N. Tinkler* 48

HYDRO CALIDO (USA) 3 b.f. Nureyev (USA) 131 – Coup de Folie (USA) 112 (Halo (USA)) [1991 8g⁴ 1992 7.5v* 8g* 8m² 8g² 8g* 8s 7d 9f⁵] third foal: half-sister to top French 2-y-o of 1989 and 1990 2000 Guineas second Machiavellian (by Mr Prospector) and very smart French 7.5f and 1m winner Exit To Nowhere (by Irish River): dam, out of unraced half-sister to Northern Dancer, successful at up to 1m at 2 yrs in France and 1¼m at 3 yrs: very useful French filly: won minor event at Evry and listed race at Saint-Cloud, and ½-length second to Culture Vulture in Poule d'Essai des Pouliches at Longchamp in the spring: landed Prix d'Astarte at Deauville in August by 1½ lengths from Marble Maiden: best of last 3 starts in Group 1 company (got no run in 1m Prix Jacques le Marois) when fifth in The Matriarch at Hollywood Park in November: stays 1m: acts on good to firm and heavy ground. *F. Boutin, France* 117

HYMN BOOK (IRE) 3 b.f. Darshaan 133 – Divina (GER) (Alpenkonig (GER)) [1991 8.1m⁴ 8.1g 1992 8v³ 11.6m a12g⁵ 10.2f⁶] lengthy, rather lightly-made filly: modest maiden: worth a try at 2m: acts on any turf going: visored and ran poorly on fibresand: sold out of M. Stoute's stable 4,100 gns Newmarket July Sales after third 3-y-o start. *R. J. Manning* 65

HYMNE D'AMOUR (USA) 4 b.f. Dixieland Band (USA) – La Francaise (USA) (Jim French (USA)) [1991 11.6m⁶ 8s 10m 1992 11.6g 10m² 11.8d⁶] smallish, lengthy filly: has quick action: relatively lightly-raced handicapper and form only on last 2 starts: stays 1½m: acts on good to firm and dead ground: won 2 novice hurdles in November. *Miss H. C. Knight* 58

HYNES TORPEDO 2 b.c. (May 13) Today And Tomorrow 78 – Be Cool (Relkino 131) [1992 5f] 700Y: small colt: second foal: dam unraced daughter of half-sister to Derby Italiano winner Appiani II: tailed off in maiden at Ripon in June. *B. Beasley* —

HYPNOTIST 5 b.g. High Top 131 – Tamilian 89 (Tamerlane 128) [1991 9m a8g 8.2m 1992 10d] lengthy, workmanlike gelding: has a round action: won over hurdles in April but on the downgrade on flat. *W. Bentley* —

HY WILMA 2 b.f. (May 4) Jalmood (USA) 126 – Hymettus 103 (Blakeney 126) [1992 5g 6g* 6. 1m⁶ 7d 5g a6g] smallish filly: poor mover: fifth foal: closely related to 3-y-o Indian Quest (by Rainbow Quest): dam won 1½m Galtres Stakes: failed to progress after winning Windsor seller (retained 2,900 gns) in July: bred to be suited by middle distances. *R. J. Hodges* 49 ?

I

IAN'S ACE 2 ch.g. (Mar 29) Aragon 118 – Rose And The Ring (Welsh Pageant 132) [1992 5g 6f⁵ 6v] 7,000Y: good-bodied gelding: half-brother to 3-y-o Supreme Boy (by Superlative) and several winners, including 5f and 1m winner Electric Rose (by Electric) and 1m and 1¼m winner Derryring (by Derrylin): dam ran twice: well beaten in maiden events: off course 5 months before final outing. *B. W. Hills* 38

IBN SINA (USA) 5 b.g. Dr Blum (USA) – Two On One (CAN) (Lord Durham –
(CAN)) [1991 10f 1992 16.5m 16f] angular, well-made gelding: has a round action:
seems of little account nowadays: blinkered final start. *R. O'Leary*

IBRAZ (USA) 2 b.c. (May 11) Cox's Ridge (USA) – Perfect Example (USA) (Far 86
North (CAN) 120) [1992 6g* 7g² 8.1s³] $80,000Y: tall, good-topped colt: has scope:
fifth foal: half-brother to 4 winners, notably 3-y-o Culture Vulture (by Timeless
Moment): dam unraced half-sister to the dam of Polish Precedent, and to French
Charmer, Grade 1 winner at up to 1¼m and later dam of Zilzal: sire good-class miler:
progressive form: won maiden at Yarmouth in July: looking very well, 2 lengths
third to Visto Si Stampi in minor event at Haydock in September: will stay 1¼m: yet
to race on top-of-the-ground: has joined N. Drysdale in USA: may well improve
further. *H. Thomson Jones*

I BROKE THE RULES (IRE) 3 b.f. Montekin 125 – Dar-A-Meter (Dara –
Monarch 128) [1991 6d4 5m4 6m6 6g 7.1d 1992 5v 5.1d 5.1m 5.1m] small, narrow filly:
seems of little account nowadays. *A. J. Chamberlain*

IBSEN 4 b.c. Gorytus (USA) 132 – State of Mind (Mill Reef (USA) 141) [1991 a10g² 60
1992 8.3g³ 8.3g⁵ 11.6g 8m 8.2s] leggy, lengthy colt: modest performer: claimed out
of P. Makin's stable £9,001 on reappearance: heavily bandaged and out of depth in
minor event 3 months later: never near to challenge in handicap next time: will
prove suited by 1¼m +: acts on equitrack. *I. Campbell*

IBTIKAR (USA) 2 b.f. (Mar 8) Private Account (USA) – Anne Campbell (USA) 63
(Never Bend (USA)) [1992 6d⁶ 7d³ 6s] $300,000Y: tall, close-coupled filly:
moderate mover: closely related to high-class Desert Wine (by Damascus),
successful at up to 1¼m and second in Kentucky Derby and Preakness Stakes, and
half-sister to several winners, including useful 7f (at 2 yrs) and 1m winner Arsaan
(by Nureyev): dam minor winner at 3 yrs in USA: sire good-class 9f/1¼m
performer: modest form on first 2 starts, well beaten on very soft ground later in
autumn: will be suited by 1¼m. *P. T. Walwyn*

ICE REBEL 2 br.c. (Mar 3) Robellino (USA) 127 – Ice Chocolate (USA) 73 47
(Icecapade (USA)) [1992 6g⁶ 7d 8d 7.6s⁵] good-bodied colt: first foal: dam 1m and
8.5f winner at 4 yrs, is out of half-sister to dam of Oh So Sharp and Roussalka: poor
maiden: should stay 1¼m. *Miss B. Sanders*

ICE STRIKE (USA) 3 b.c. Eskimo (USA) – Gama Tres (USA) (El Pitirre (USA)) –
[1991 NR 1992 11.7d 12s] $20,000Y: fifth foal: half-brother to a minor sprint winner in
USA by Lucky North: dam dual Grade 1 winner and champion in Mexico, was minor
winner in USA at 4 yrs: no form in maidens at Bath (claimer) and Folkestone in the
autumn. *C. R. Nelson*

ICE WALK 3 gr.f. Kalaglow 132 – Krishnagar (Kris 135) [1991 7d 1992 9.9m 8s⁶] –
tall, lengthy, angular filly: no worthwhile form: will stay 1¼m: sold to join M.
Wilkinson 2,100 gns Newmarket Autumn Sales. *W. Jarvis*

ICTERINA (USA) 2 b.f. (May 15) Secreto (USA) – Sugar And Spice (USA) – p
(Key To The Mint (USA)) [1992 7g] $92,000Y: half-sister to 2 winners in North
America: dam, high-class filly at 3 yrs when successful at up to 1¼m, is half-sister to
Alydar: 11/2 co-favourite from 12/1, though better for race, never on terms after
slow start when well behind in 16-runner minor event at Newbury in September:
evidently thought capable of better. *P. W. Chapple-Hyam*

ICY SOUTH (USA) 2 b. or br.c. (Feb 13) Alleged (USA) 138 – Arctic Eclipse 87
(USA) (Northern Dancer (CAN)) [1992 6m³ 6f³ 7d* 8.1s⁴ 8.1s⁵ 8v4] $140,000Y:
good-bodied colt: has a fluent, round action: first reported foal: dam, won at 7f and
7.5f in France, is half-sister to St Leger fourth Nemain (by Alleged): fairly useful
performer: made all in maiden at Chester in July: good fourth in Gran Criterium at
Milan in October final start: will be suited by middle distances: best form with
plenty of give in the ground. *J. H. M. Gosden*

IDEAL CANDIDATE 3 b.f. Celestial Storm (USA) 132 – Rising Star (St Paddy 80
133) [1991 6g⁵ 8.9d 7m 1992 12g⁴ 10.1m 10f⁶ 10m* a12g³ 11.6g³ a12g* 11.5m* a12g²
a10g² a16g² 14d* 12d4 15.4g* 16d* 16g4] plain filly: poor mover: progressed
really well throughout the season in handicaps: won at Windsor (seller, bought in
3,800 gns) in June, on successive days at Lingfield (claimed out of C. Cyzer's stable
£12,501 second occasion) in July, Sandown in August, and Folkestone and Goodwood (2 days later) in September: stays 2m: acts on good to firm and dead ground,
and on equitrack: tough and genuine. *T. J. Naughton*

IDIR LINN (IRE) 4 b.g. Camden Town 125 – Dippy Girl (Sandford Lad 133) 50
[1991 6v 7g 7g 6m 10g a7g 1992 6g 7g 6m² 6.1m² a6g² a6g⁶ a7g* a7s⁴ 7d 6g³ 6s]
stocky, good-quartered ex-Irish gelding: largely consistent handicapper: won at

Southwell in July: effective at 6f, should stay 1m: acts on good to firm ground (below form for inexperienced riders on a soft surface) and both all-weather tracks: effective blinkered/visored or not: retained 2,200 gns Newmarket Autumn Sales. *D. J. G. Murray-Smith*

I DO CARE   2 ch.c. (Feb 23) Absalom 128 – Oxide (USA) 84 (Our Native (USA)) **40** [1992 5f4 5d3 6m 6m] 7,600F, 10,500Y: compact colt: first foal: half-sister to 4-y-o maiden Marine Society (by Petoski), who stays 1¾m: dam 7f winner: kept on well when third of 5 in maiden at Epsom: prominent over 13f and eased considerably in Queen's Vase at Royal Ascot 13 days later: looked sure to improve: sold to join R. Curtis 5,800 gns Newmarket Autumn Sales. *C. E. Brittain*

IDONI   3 b.c. Bustino 136 – Miranda Julia 73 (Julio Mariner 127) [1991 NR 1992 **79** 10.1g3 16.2f] 10,000F, 25,000Y: small, good-bodied colt: second foal: half-brother to 4-y-o maiden Marine Society (by Petoski), who stays 1¾m: dam 7f winner: kept on well when third of 5 in maiden at Epsom: prominent over 13f and eased considerably in Queen's Vase at Royal Ascot 13 days later: looked sure to improve: sold to join R. Curtis 5,800 gns Newmarket Autumn Sales. *C. E. Brittain*

IDRIS (IRE)   2 b.c. (May 20) Ahonoora 122 – Idara 109 (Top Ville 129) [1992 7d*] **89 p** fifth foal: dam French 11f and 1½m winner: won 7-runner maiden at the Curragh in October by 2½ lengths, apparently quite easily: promising. *J. Oxx, Ireland*

IF IT SUITS   2 b.c. (May 15) Local Suitor (USA) 128 – If (FR) (Kashmir II 125) **–** [1992 6m6] good-quartered colt: half-brother to several winners, including very useful 7f and 10.5f winner Cameo Shore (by Mill Reef) and very useful middle-distance winner Iseo (by Sir Gaylord): dam third in Poule d'Essai des Pouliches: very green, tailed off in 6-runner maiden at Goodwood in June. *R. Akehurst*

IFTAKHAAR (USA)   3 b.c. Private Account (USA) – Old Goat (USA) (Olden **85** Times) [1991 NR 1992 8g 10.3g3 10g3 12g3 12m 12m*] $700,000Y: leggy, well-topped colt: half-brother to several winners in USA, including multiple graded-stakes winner Highland Park (by Raise A Native), best at around 1m: dam Grade 3 sprint winner: sire good-class 9f/1¼m performer: fairly useful performer: wearing crossed noseband, won maiden at Pontefract in October: stays 1½m: yet to race on a soft surface: similar form ridden from the front or held up. *Major W. R. Hern*

IGNITED   2 b.c. (Feb 11) Colmore Row 111 – Flame Up (Bustino 136) [1992 a6g 7m **34** 6s a5g] leggy, sparely-made colt: moderate mover: third foal: dam Irish 2-y-o 5f winner: well beaten in maidens and a nursery: usually bandaged. *Mrs N. Macauley*

IHTIRAZ   2 ch.c. (Feb 25) Soviet Star (USA) 128 – Azyaa 101 (Kris 135) [1992 6g2 **83** 5f 7.1d2 7g* 7m 7v2] good-topped, quite attractive colt: good mover: second foal: dam, 7.5f winner, is granddaughter of Milly Moss: fairly useful performer: barely off bridle to win maiden at Brighton in August: ran well when second in minor event at Chester in October: will stay 1m: acts on heavy going, finished last twice in Group company on top-of-the-ground. *H. Thomson Jones*

IJAB (CAN)   2 b.c. (Mar 7) Ascot Knight (CAN) 130 – Renounce (USA) (Buck- **43** passer) [1992 7d 7s] $100,000Y: good-topped colt: half-brother to several winners, including useful 7f (at 2 yrs) to 9f winner Dowager Empress (by Vice Regent): dam, lightly-raced half-sister to high-class Intrepid Hero, won over 6f and 7f: contested October maidens: form only on debut, never dangerous after taking keen hold: will stay at least 1m. *A. A. Scott*

IKHTIRAA (USA)   2 b.c. (Mar 11) Imperial Falcon (CAN) – True Native (USA) **46 p** (Raise A Native) [1992 8m 6.9v4] $100,000Y: lengthy, angular colt: half-brother to several winners in France and USA, including Carmanetta (by Roberto), successful at 1m at 2 yrs in France, later graded-placed in USA: dam unraced half-sister to the dams of Crystal Glitters and Danzatore: form in autumn maidens only when one-paced fourth at Folkestone: will stay 1¼m. *R. W. Armstrong*

IKHTISAS (USA)   2 gr.f. (Jan 24) Woodman (USA) 126 – Lettre d'Amour (USA) **64** (Caro 133) [1992 6m5 7f 6g5 6m3 7s 7d2] IR 110,000Y: leggy filly: half-sister to useful 7f/1m performer Swordsmith (by Diesis) and a winner in USA: dam unraced daughter of top-class 4.5f to 1m winner Lianga: modest maiden: will stay 1m: acts on good to firm and dead ground: carries head awkwardly: inconsistent, and also appears somewhat ungenuine. *B. Hanbury*

IKTESHAF   4 b.g. Green Desert (USA) 127 – Colourful (FR) 97 (Gay Mecene **87** (USA) 128) [1991 7g 5d4 6.1m 5d3 6f2 6m 6g* 5d5 6.1d3 1992 10.3g 7g4 7f3 8.3m* 7g3 7d 7s2 6s* 6d] compact, attractive gelding: moderate mover: improved performer in 1992 though turned in the odd moderate effort: won handicap in May and minor event in September, both at Hamilton: effective at up to 8.3f: acts on firm and soft ground: below form when blinkered and sweating: sold 20,000 gns Newmarket Autumn Sales. *B. Hanbury*

ILE DE CHYPRE 7 b.h. Ile de Bourbon (USA) 133 – Salamina 106 (Welsh **112** Pageant 132) [1991 NR 1992 10d³ 10g 10m⁴ 8.9m³ 11.1g⁵ 10g] strong, rangy, attractive horse: carries deal of condition: rated 128 at his peak, in 1989: missed 1991 due to foot injury but is still a smart performer: best efforts at 7 yrs in Group 3 event at Ayr (over 4 lengths behind Sharpitor) and £12,300 handicap at York in the summer: best allowed to stride on over 1¼m on top-of-the-ground: sometimes bandaged: has been taken steadily to post: races with head high but game. *G. Harwood*

ILEWIN 5 br.g. Ile de Bourbon (USA) 133 – City Swinger (Derrylin 115) [1991 – a14g 9.7m 8f 1992 11.9d] sturdy gelding: modest winning hurdler in 1991/2: no form on flat. *J. R. Jenkins*

I'LLEAVEITOYOU (IRE) 2 b.g. (Apr 24) Supreme Leader 123 – Bally 74 **65 p** (Balidar 133) [1992 a8g*] IR 3,500Y: fifth foal: half-brother to poor 3-y-o Ballymust (by Muscatite) and sprint winner Balishy (by Shy Groom): dam best effort at 1m: 14/1 and wearing eyeshield, won 9-runner maiden at Lingfield in December, in decisive fashion: sure to progress. *S. Dow*

ILLOGICAL 5 br.m. Ile de Bourbon (USA) 133 – Modern Romance (Dance In – Time (CAN)) [1991 NR 1992 a12g⁵] sturdy, plain mare: bad mover: probably of little account. *J. Wharton*

I'LL RISK IT 2 b.f. (Mar 28) Risk Me (FR) 127 – Gymnopedie (Jaazeiro (USA) – 127) [1992 a6g 6m a6g 5g] 4,000Y: leggy, sparely-made filly: has a round action: second foal: sister to 3-y-o 6f and 7f winner Risk Zone: dam French maiden: soundly beaten in sellers: sold 650 gns Newmarket September Sales. *J. Berry*

ILLUMINATING 3 ch.f. Electric 126 – Jarama (Amber Rama (USA) 133) [1991 – 7m² 8.1g² 1992 10.3g⁴ 11.1d⁵ 8.2d⁶ 8m] workmanlike filly: plating-class maiden: should be suited by further than 1m: best form on a sound surface: rather nervous type: sold 1,700 gns Doncaster June Sales. *Mrs J. R. Ramsden*

ILMENITE 2 gr.f. (Mar 3) Petong 126 – Irenic 64 (Mummy's Pet 125) [1992 5g – 6m 5d] good-topped filly: moderate mover: first foal: dam, maiden seemed suited by 6f, is half-sister to Forzando: no worthwhile form: blinkered final start. *M. A. Jarvis*

IL MORO DI VENEZIA (IRE) 2 b.c. (May 4) Fairy King (USA) – Rosmarita **40** (Sallust 134) [1992 6d 6.1g 6s⁴ 6v] 3,400Y, 7,000 2-y-o: sturdy, close-coupled colt: moderate walker: second foal: dam unraced: poor maiden: will be suited by 7f+: acts on soft ground. *J. L. Dunlop*

I'M A DREAMER (IRE) 2 b.g. (Apr 25) Mister Majestic 122 – Lady Wise (Lord **60** Gayle (USA) 124) [1992 5f⁶ 6g³ 6m 7d³ 6g a8g* a8g²] 3,200Y, 4,600 2-y-o: quite a65 good-topped gelding: half-brother to Irish juvenile 5f winner Before The Storm (by Thatching) and 4-y-o 10.1f winner Lady Baraka (by Shernazar): dam, placed over 8.2f at 2 yrs in Ireland, is half-sister to Middle Park winner Spanish Express: modest performer: won maiden at Southwell in November: suited by 1m: acts on fibresand and an easy surface on turf. *W. W. Haigh*

IMAFIFER (IRE) 2 b.c. (Mar 14) Mazaad 106 – Zareeta (Free State 125) [1992 **38** 5d 5m⁴ 5g 5d⁶ 5g 7g 10d] 4,500Y: sturdy colt: first foal: dam little sign of ability in 4 races: poor maiden: well beaten last 2 starts: blinkered twice, running creditably first occasion. *W. R. Muir*

IMAGINARY (IRE) 2 b.f. (Apr 9) Dancing Brave (USA) 140 – Bold Fantasy 115 **72 p** (Bold Lad (IRE) 133) [1992 7d²] sturdy filly: fluent mover: sister to 2 winners, namely 1991 French 1½m winner Famosa and 1m winner Fetish, and half-sister to several winners here and abroad, notably Lowther Stakes winner Kingscote (by Kings Lake), dam of smart Rainbow Corner: dam Irish 7f winner second in Irish 1000 Guineas: favourite, though better for race, beaten a length by Wild Princess in 16-runner maiden at Leicester in October, soon handy, green and short of room 2f out before finishing strongly: will improve and win races. *H. R. A. Cecil*

IMA RED NECK (USA) 3 b.c. Dixieland Band (USA) – Bright Reply (USA) – (Gleaming (USA)) [1991 NR 1992 9m 10m⁵] stocky colt: eighth foal: closely related to 4-y-o Singing Reply (by The Minstrel) and half-brother to 3 stakes winners in USA: dam ran 3 times: around 8 lengths fifth to Kanvass in maiden at Ripon in July: looked sure to improve again: sold to join J. Moore 6,400 gns Newmarket Autumn Sales. *J. H. M. Gosden*

IMCO DOUBLE (IRE) 4 ch.g. Double Schwartz 128 – Cupids Hill (Sallust 134) – [1991 7g 6d 6s 5m⁶ a6g³ a6g² 6m a5g² a5g* a5g⁵ 1992 a5g² a6g 5s a5g a6g a5g] a64 d close-coupled gelding: modest handicapper: ran well at Southwell on reappearance in August: poorly drawn next time, well below form afterwards: trained until after

374

third start by W. Holden: best at sprint distances: acts on all-weather surfaces, form on turf only on top-of-the-ground. *Pat Mitchell*

I'M CURIOUS   3 b.f. Kirchner 110 – The Dupecat 75 (Javelot 124) [1991 NR 1992 8d 10d 9.7s 8.2g 10.3g a16g] 3,500Y: leggy filly: has a round action: half-sister to several winners, including smart 1982 2-y-o 5f winner Cat O'Nine Tails and fairly useful winner at up to 1¼m Lightning Record (both by Le Johnstan): dam won over 1½m: seems of little account. *R. Thompson*   –

I'M ELECTRIC   6 b.g. Electric 126 – Mouletta (Moulton 128) [1991 NR 1992 8d 7g⁶ 8.1m² 9g³ 10d* 10g* 10g³ 11.4g²] good-quartered gelding: not seen out after 2 yrs until spring, 1992: proved a consistent handicapper: won at Leicester and Pontefract in June: best effort, staying on well closing stages, at Sandown last time: will prove better at 1½m than shorter: acts on good to firm and dead ground. *R. Curtis*   61

IMHOTEP   5 gr.g. Claude Monet (USA) 121 – Miss Melmore (Nishapour (FR) 125) [1991 NR 1992 7g 8g⁴ 8f*] tall, rather angular gelding: has a rather round action: modest and lightly-raced handicapper: gained first win when gamely holding on at Pontefract in August: stays 1m: acts on firm ground. *Mrs M. Reveley*   53

I'M NO FOOL   2 b.g. (Apr 1) Alias Smith (USA) – Duchy 99 (Rheingold 137) [1992 8m] big gelding: has scope: half-brother to 2 winners, including 1m and 8.5f winner Signore Odone (by Milford): dam placed over 1m and 1½m from 3 starts in Ireland: 25/1 and burly, always behind in 11-runner maiden at Thirsk in September: may do better. *M. H. Easterby*   – p

IMPAIR (USA)   2 b.c. (Feb 21) Jade Hunter (USA) – Stitz (USA) (Crimson Satan) [1992 7f³ 7m] $14,000F, $80,000Y: close-coupled colt: closely related to 2 minor winners by Miswaki, one stakes placed, and half-brother to 2 other winners: dam minor sprint winner: sire (by Mr Prospector) best at 4 yrs when Grade 1 9f and 1¼m winner: blinkered both starts, better effort in summer maidens when third of 5 at Brighton, tending to hang left: sold 5,000 gns Newmarket Autumn Sales. *P. F. I. Cole*   70

IMPECCABLE CHARM (USA)   3 b.f. Lyphard (USA) 132 – Island Charm (USA) (Hawaii) [1991 NR 1992 10f² 10.1d⁶ 10d³] smallish filly: fifth living foal: closely related to 7f winner Musical Charm (by The Minstrel) and half-sister to French 1½m winner Honeymooning (by Blushing Groom): dam one of leading sprinters in USA in 1981: fair maiden: stays 1¼m: acts on firm and dead ground: sold 12,500 gns Newmarket December Sales. *J. H. M. Gosden*   65

IMPERIAL BALLET (IRE)   3 b.c. Sadler's Wells (USA) 132 – Amaranda (USA) 115 (Bold Lad (IRE) 133) [1991 7f 1992 10.3m* 10g* 8m⁵] angular, quite attractive colt: useful form: favourite in small fields, easily won maiden at Doncaster (made virtually all) and minor event at Windsor (moved poorly to post, led on bridle over 2f out) in summer: looked a smart performer in the making, but readily outpaced when 7/4 on in moderately-run minor event at Goodwood in August: not certain to stay much beyond 1¼m. *H. R. A. Cecil*   97

IMPERIAL BID (FR)   4 b.g. No Pass No Sale 120 – Tzaritsa (USA) 113 (Young Emperor 133) [1991 6d* 7d 6g 6m 10g⁴ 8.5g⁵ 9m* 8.5g⁵ 9g 8s 1992 6f⁵ 5m³ 5.9h³ 10m 7.1m⁶ 7m 7.1g] leggy, close-coupled ex-Irish gelding: closely related to 7f and 1m winner Norroy (by Northfields) and half-brother to a winner abroad: dam best at 2 yrs, won at up to 1m: trained by C. Collins at 3 yrs when successful at the Curragh and Tramore: fair form here: moved badly to post when well below form final start, first for 2 months: stays 1¼m: acts on hard and dead ground. *Denys Smith*   76

IMPERIAL BRUSH   8 b.g. Sallust 134 – Queen of The Brush (Averof 123) [1991 NR 1992 16d³] leggy, sparely-made gelding: useful hurdler (predominantly for D. Elsworth) at best in 1991/2: very lightly raced on flat nowadays: blinkered, third in celebrity race at Worcester in March: stays 2m: acts on good to firm and soft going. *J. White*   68

IMPERIAL FLIGHT   7 b.g. Pampabird 124 – Queen of Time (Charlottown 127) [1991 NR 1992 12s] strong, good-topped gelding: modest hurdler in 1991/2: very burly on first run on flat since 1989. *J. S. King*   –

IMPERIAL FORTE   2 b.f. (Feb 16) Midyan (USA) 124 – Sunfleet 59 (Red Sunset 120) [1992 7m] first foal: dam maiden seemed suited by 1¼m: 20/1, never a threat in 17-runner claimer at Yarmouth in September. *R. J. R. Williams*   –

IMPRESSIVE LAD   6 b.g. Bold Lad (IRE) 133 – Slow Hands (Pitskelly 122) [1991 NR 1992 8.1m 10.2f³ 9.7g] lengthy ex-Irish gelding: first foal: dam, placed at up to 8.5f in Ireland: poor form (usually blinkered) at 2 yrs when trained by T. Reagan: form in handicaps in the summer only when third at Chepstow. *R. Rowe*   23

375

IMSHI 2 gr.f. (Feb 20) Petong 126 – Lexia 82§ (Sharpo 132) [1992 a5g] first foal: dam irresolute 7f winner: 25/1, little show when last of 10 in Lingfield maiden in November. *D. J. G. Murray-Smith* —

I'M SPECIAL (IRE) 4 ch.f. Lyphard's Special (USA) 122 – Doon Belle (Ardoon 124) [1991 8g² 8.5f⁵ 13d⁴ 8.3f 9.2f 10g⁵ 9.2s⁴ 1992 a12g 11.1s 12f] rather leggy filly: seems of little account these days: no improvement in blinkers/visor: sold 1,000 gns Doncaster June Sales. *A. Harrison* —

I'M YOURS 2 b. or br.f. (Apr 18) Forzando 122 – Welsh Jane 71 (Bold Lad (IRE) 133) [1992 6d5 6g3 6d5 7d] leggy filly: seventh reported foal: half-sister to several winners, including smart miler Only Yours (by Aragon) and smart sprinter Osario (by Kind of Hush): dam (seemed to stay 1m), is out of speedy Abbot's Isle: modest maiden: shaped as though she'd be well suited by 7f, but ran moderately at trip. *R. Hannon* 65

INAN (USA) 3 b.c. El Gran Senor (USA) 136 – Assez Cuite (USA) 114 (Graustark) [1991 8.1g 8m 1992 10.8g⁴ 12.5g⁵ 14.1f² 12.3f³ 11.9d* 10.3m 10g⁴ 10.2s⁶ 10.3s] quite attractive colt: moderate mover with a quick action: fair handicapper: won 3-runner event at Haydock in July: below form afterwards: well worth another try at 1¾m: acts on firm and dead going: blinkered (failed to settle) penultimate start: sold to join R. O'Leary 15,500 gns Newmarket Autumn Sales: may be unsatisfactory. *J. L. Dunlop* 76 d

IN A TIFF (IRE) 3 b.c. Caerleon (USA) 132 – Tifrums 77 (Thatch 85) [1991 7g* 8g⁴ 1992 7d⁵ 9d² 10s* 12g* 12g³ 12d³ 12d 10v] eighth foal: half-brother to 3 winners, most importantly very smart miler Pennine Walk (by Persian Bold): dam Irish juvenile 7f winner: smart Irish colt: won maiden at Tralee at 2 yrs then handicap at Naas and, showing much improved form, Derby Italiano at Rome in May, where made all and held Merzouk by ½ length: off course 11 weeks afterwards and best subsequent effort when about 2 lengths third of 7 to Masad in Gran Premio d'Italia at Milan in September: found to be lame after next start and well held in Premio Roma on heavy: suited by 1½m: yet to race on top-of-the-ground. *D. K. Weld, Ireland* 114

IN A WHIRL (USA) 4 br.f. Island Whirl (USA) – Hurry Marie (USA) (Hurry To Market) [1991 7m 8g 5m 5g⁶ 5m³ 6m⁵ a6g 7s 5m 6.1m a6g² a5g⁴ a7g³ 1992 a5g² a6g⁴ a5g 6d⁴ 7.1g⁴ 6s⁴ 5g 5d³ 6s² 7m 6g⁵ a6g 5.7f] tall, close-coupled filly: plating-class handicapper: only win came 29 starts ago, on debut: ideally suited by 6f: acts on good to firm and soft ground and all-weather surfaces: effective blinkered or not: trained until after eleventh start by D. Chapman. *D. R. Laing* 47 a57

IN CASE (USA) 2 b.c. (Feb 12) Storm Cat (USA) – In Essence (USA) (In Reality) [1992 5m* 5g⁵ 6g⁶ 6m²] $155,000Y: robust, good-quartered, attractive colt: moderate walker: half-brother to several winners, one placed in graded stakes: dam half-sister to dam of Grade 1 8.5f winner Stalwart: sire high-class juvenile: fairly useful performer: narrowly won minor event at Doncaster in June: showed much improved form when short-headed in nursery there in September, rallying gamely: will probably stay 1m: seems well suited by top-of-the-ground. *R. Charlton* 96

INCHCAILLOCH (IRE) 3 b.c. Lomond (USA) 128 – Glowing With Pride 114 (Ile de Bourbon (USA) 133) [1991 7m⁴ 8g³ 1992 10.5s* 12m³ 12m* 11.9d⁶ 11.9s⁶] big, strong, lengthy colt: impresses in appearance: progressive form first 3 starts, winning maiden at Haydock in April and handicap at Newbury in June: ran as if 87 ?

Derby Italiano, Rome—foreign raiders to the fore;
the winner is In A Tiff (No. 6), second is Merzouk (rails), third is Masad (right)

something amiss in handicaps afterwards, off course 3 months in between: should stay beyond 1½m: has worn crossed noseband: may well be suited by forcing tactics: joined J. King. *R. Charlton*

INCHINOR 2 ch.c. (Feb 16) Ahonoora 122 – Inchmurrin 114 (Lomond (USA)) **115** p 128) [1992 6g* 7d* 7m²]

The twice-raced, twice-successful Inchinor carried the greatest hopes of thwarting a daunting foreign challenge in the Dewhurst Stakes at Newmarket in October. Starting third favourite at 13/2 in a market headed by the hugely-impressive Prix de la Salamandre winner Zafonic and the unbeaten Irish colt Fatherland, Inchinor duly led the home defence, but though he managed to hold off Fatherland comfortably enough he still went down by four lengths to Zafonic. Though Inchinor was beaten fairly and squarely, his prospects are far from bleak. The likelihood is that, in spite of running his best race of the season in the Dewhurst, he found the combination of seven furlongs and good to firm ground on the sharp side, and he'll be much better suited by a mile or, probably better still, a mile and a quarter; not only that, he looked much less the finished article at two than did the more-experienced Zafonic. Inchinor may not be the top-class prospect that some imagined after his first two races, but he's a good colt nonetheless, and, with further improvement likely, shouldn't have much difficulty picking up an important race.

Inchinor began his career in Newmarket's Park Lodge Maiden Stakes over six furlongs in August. The rumours before the race suggested it would see a winning debut from Dahyah, a 1,200,000-dollar yearling by Danzig who'd been exciting work-watchers on the Newmarket training grounds and who was heavily backed at 11/10 to the virtual exclusion of the twelve other runners. The risks in taking a short price about a horse making its first appearance in public were highlighted once again as the 12/1-shot Inchinor came back first, a neck in front of Mithl Al Hawa and nearly four lengths in front of third-placed Blues Traveller after staying on really well up the hill to wear down the runner-up near the line. Dahyh finished fourth. By the time Inchinor reappeared in the Personnel Selection Graduation Stakes (formerly the Mornington Stakes) over seven furlongs on dead ground at Ascot the

Personnel Selection Stakes, Ascot—
Inchinor knuckles down to his task and has two lengths to spare over Right Win

Sir Philip Oppenheimer's "Inchinor"

		⎧ Lorenzaccio	⎧ Klairon
	⎧ Ahonoora	⎨ (ch 1965)	⎨ Phoenissa
	⎨ (ch 1975)	⎩ Helen Nichols	⎧ Martial
Inchinor		(ch 1966)	⎨ Quaker Girl
(ch.c. Feb 16, 1990)		⎧ Lomond	⎧ Northern Dancer
	⎨	⎨ (b 1980)	⎨ My Charmer
	⎩ Inchmurrin	⎩ On Show	⎧ Welsh Pageant
	(b 1985)	(br 1978)	⎨ African Dancer

following month, Mithl Al Hawa, Blues Traveller, fifth-placed Brigg Fair and seventh-placed Jobie had all come out and won, and Inchinor made it five with a stylish success over two other promising animals Right Win and Emperor Jones. Soon travelling well, Inchinor, who proved well suited by the stiffer test of stamina, caught a slight bump when the pace began to quicken, but, chased along to lead a furlong out, he ran on pluckily to get the better of Right Win by two lengths, Emperor Jones finishing four lengths back in third. Inchinor was progressing along the right lines and, rather than take the easier option and run him in the Horris Hill Stakes at Newbury, his connections, possibly encouraged by the subsequent victories of Right Win and Emperor Jones in good races at Ascot and York, threw him in at the deep end in the Dewhurst. Inchinor responded with a smart performance, but in common with the nine other runners found himself completely overwhelmed by Zafonic's turn of foot. He battled on in typically game fashion up the hill, though, and came out marginally best in front of Firm Pledge and Sueboog in the three-way battle for second, the trio finishing half a length ahead of Fatherland. It was reported afterwards—not as an excuse—that Inchinor had had a minor set-back before the race.

Inchinor, a small, strong, lengthy colt, is the product of two well-known racehorses: his sire Ahonoora, also responsible for the Derby winner Dr Devious, was a good-class sprinter in the late-'seventies; and his dam Inchmurrin, whose first foal he is, was a speedy two-year-old who went on to show very useful form at a mile and not much worse at a mile and a quarter. Inchmurrin is a daughter of the fairly useful mile-and-a-quarter winner On Show, who also finished second in the mile-and-a-half November Handicap, and is a close relative of the very useful miler Guest Artiste as well as a half-sister to three winners including the very useful 1989 two-year-old six-furlong winner Welney and the fairly useful miler Waterfowl Creek. Inchinor's third dam African Dancer won the Cheshire Oaks and the Park Hill Stakes (a race in which her dam Miba had finished third) and ran placed in the Oaks and Yorkshire Oaks, and has produced several other middle-distance performers at stud besides On Show, including Mpani, Dame Ashfield and Mill Dance. *R. Charlton*

INCOLA 6 b.g. Liboi (USA) 76 – Sdenka (FR) 79 (Habitat 134) [1991 11.7g 12f* 12f 12.2d3 12g6 12m6 11.6m2 11.8m2 1992 12g6 12m 12m 11.6m* 11.6d* 11.8g* 12d* 11.8d] small, angular gelding: modest performer: progressed well while compiling 4-timer in handicaps at Windsor (2, dead-heated second occasion), Leicester and Epsom (apprentices) in the summer: stays 1½m: acts on firm and dead ground: below form when blinkered once at 4 yrs. *H. Candy* **63**

INDERAPUTERI 2 b.f. (Apr 1) Bold Fort 100 – Hello Cuddles 99 (He Loves Me 120) [1992 6m6 6g2 7d3 7m] leggy, angular filly: moderate mover: third reported foal: sister to 6-y-o winning sprinter Samson-Agonistes: dam sprinter: modest maiden: well beaten off favourable mark in Newmarket nursery on final start: stays 7f: bandaged last 3 starts. *Miss Gay Kelleway* **62**

INDIAN DECISION 3 b.c. Wassl 125 – It's Terrific (Vaguely Noble 140) [1991 6f 7g 1992 10.8g5 12d6 14g6] leggy colt: progressive maiden: off course 4 months after reappearance and acquitted himself well in face of very stiff tasks in handicaps: better suited by 1¾m than shorter: sold 3,100 gns Ascot November Sales. *J. L. Dunlop* **70**

INDIAN ENDEAVOUR 3 b.f. Green Desert (USA) 127 – Swanilda (FR) (Habitat 134) [1991 5m4 5m3 5g* 5d2 1992 6.1g5 6m 6d 6m2 6g 6f 6.1m 6s a5g* a5g* a5g* a6g3] sturdy filly: modest handicapper: rather inconsistent during turf season, but in fine form late in year, winning at Lingfield (2) and Southwell: stays 6f: acts on good to firm ground and all-weather surfaces, probably not on a soft surface: blinkered (found conditions against her) once. *R. Guest* **66** a78

INDIAN FLASH (IRE) 2 b.f. (May 26) Chief's Crown (USA) – Sovereign Flash (FR) (Busted 134) [1992 7f3 8.1d4] 17,000Y: good-topped filly: second reported foal: half-sister to 4-y-o Sovereign Niche (by Nishapour), successful over hurdles: dam French middle-distance winner: sire (by Danzig) Grade 1 winner from 6.5f to 1¼m, also placed in 1½m Belmont Stakes: poor form in maidens at Yarmouth and Edinburgh 4 months later: looks sort to do better. *R. Guest* **39** p

INDIAN GUEST 3 b.f. Precocious 126 – Indian Love Song 68 (Be My Guest (USA) 126) [1991 5f 5f5 6d 1992 6d] neat filly: no worthwhile form, visored in handicap in April. *F. H. Lee* **–**

INDIAN HEATHER (IRE) 4 b.f. Indian King (USA) 128 – Yellow Plume (Home Guard (USA) 129) [1991 NR 1992 9m 12m 7.5d] leggy, lengthy, plain filly: poor mover: seventh foal: half-sister to modest 1989 staying 2-y-o Toucan (by King of Clubs): dam winner at around 1m in Ireland: no form, including in sellers: blinkered on debut. *J. Parkes* **–**

INDIAN JACK (IRE) 3 b.c. Bustino 136 – Indian Lily 100 (Indian King (USA) 128) [1991 NR 1992 10.2m2 10f2 11.5d2 10d6] close-coupled, quite attractive colt: first foal: dam 2-y-o 5f winner: fair maiden: stays 11.5f: acts on firm and dead ground. *Major W. R. Hern* **77**

INDIAN MAESTRO 6 b.g. Music Maestro 119 – Indian Wells (Reliance II 137) [1991 NR 1992 10d6 a8g a6g a8g] leggy, angular gelding: quite modest handicapper at 4 yrs for Pat Mitchell: never dangerous in 1992. *Mrs A. Swinbank* **–**

INDIAN MOHAWK (IRE) 4 ch.c. Ahonoora 122 – Joshua's Daughter 61 –
(Joshua 129) [1991 7g 6d 7d 7m 7g 7.1m 6m 1992 8f a10g 9.7s⁵] tall, leggy, rather
shallow-girthed colt: has a round action: trained reappearance by M. Muggeridge:
no worthwhile form but has shown signs of ability: will prove suited by return to
shorter. *D. R. C. Elsworth*

INDIAN QUEST 3 b.c. Rainbow Quest (USA) 134 – Hymettus 103 (Blakeney **68** p
126) [1991 NR 1992 14.1g²] rather lightly-made, workmanlike colt: fourth foal: dam
won 1½m Galtres Stakes: 9/1 from 3/1 and green, neck second of 10 to Neieb in
maiden at Nottingham, soon off bridle but staying on best of all: sold to join N.
Gaselee 15,000 gns Newmarket Autumn Sales: is likely to be well suited by a
thorough test of stamina: won juvenile hurdle in December in good style: will
improve and should win races on the flat as well. *Major W. R. Hern*

INDIAN SECRET (IRE) 2 ch.g. (Apr 2) Indian Forest (USA) 117 – Pendle's **51**
Secret 73 (Le Johnstan 123) [1992 5g 5m³ 5g² 5m 6m] lengthy, useful-looking
gelding: seventh reported foal: half-brother to 3-y-o 6f (seller at 2 yrs) and 8.5f
winner Pride of Pendle (by Grey Desire) and 1986 2-y-o 8.2f winner Rivers Secret
(by Young Man): dam 1¼m winner: modest maiden: trained by P. Calver on debut:
well below form last 2 starts, in midsummer: stays 6f. *B. E. Wilkinson*

INDIAN SLAVE (IRE) 4 ch.c. Commanche Run 133 – Commanche Belle 74 **73**
(Shirley Heights 130) [1991 7m³ 8f² 10f³ 11.1d² 11.5s⁶ 10f³ 12.3g 8h 11.8g 1992 12d
10m⁴ 12m 8f* 8f² 7f* 8m* 8m⁶] leggy colt: fair handicapper: won at Brighton and
Catterick in the summer, and at Doncaster (£16,000 event, by ¾ length from Croft
Valley) in September: easily best form at 7f/1m on top-of-the-ground: suitable
mount for an apprentice. *R. Guest*

INDIAN SOVEREIGN 8 br.g. Indian King (USA) 128 – Sovereign Dona 117 –
(Sovereign Path 125) [1991 NR 1992 10d 8g 7.1m] workmanlike gelding: probably of
little account these days: sold 750 gns Doncaster September Sales. *R. Lee*

INDIAN STYLE (IRE) 3 b.f. Ahonoora 122 – Spirit In The Sky 106 (Tudor **51**
Melody 129) [1991 6f⁴ 1992 6.9g⁴ 7.1m³ 8.1m² 9m² 9.7g 11.9m⁴ 10s] workmanlike
filly: has round action: modest maiden: well below form last 3 starts: should stay
1¼m: makes running/races close up. *R. Guest*

INDIAN TERRITORY 3 ch.g. Dominion 123 – Lady Capilano 87 (Nebbiolo **58**
125) [1991 7m 7g 6d 1992 10.2m⁵ 12g⁵ 11.6m 14.6g⁵ 12.3m⁵ 14.6g³ 14.1d a12g³ a12g a53
a13g⁴] stocky gelding: modest maiden: acts on good to firm ground and
equitrack, possibly not on a soft surface. *D. Haydn Jones*

INDICA (USA) 3 b.f. Green Dancer (USA) 132 – Sweetest Gal (USA) (Honest **35**
Pleasure (USA)) [1991 NR 1992 7.1s⁴ 5.3g⁴ 7d] $80,000Y: lengthy, unfurnished filly:
second foal: dam won maiden at around 7f in USA: poor maiden: highly strung and
possibly none too keen: visits Taufan. *J. H. M. Gosden*

INDIGO BLUE (IRE) 3 ch.f. Bluebird (USA) 125 – Decadence (Vaigly Great **22**
127) [1991 6g 6g 1992 a6g⁶ a5g² a7g] poor maiden, not seen out after March: stays
6f. *N. A. Callaghan*

INDIVISIBLE 6 ch.m. Remainder Man 126§ – Red Ragusa 62 (Homeric 133) –
[1991 10m 12.3f 12f⁶ 10m³ 12.1f⁵ 10.3m⁴ 10m 8.1g 1992 a11g a11g] leggy mare: probably of
little account these days. *R. Hollinshead*

INFANT PROTEGE (USA) 2 b.f. (Apr 4) Theatrical 128 – Realisatrice (USA) **62**
(Raja Baba (USA)) [1992 5.1s 6m⁴ 5m⁵ 5.1f 6g 6g³ 5m² 5g* 6g² 6m⁴] 1,000Y:
smallish, leggy filly: third foal: dam French maiden daughter of King's Stand second
Realty, later the grandam of Ravinella: largely consistent handicapper: won at
Haydock in August: will stay 7f: often ridden by 5-lb claimer: sold 12,000 gns
Newmarket December Sales. *C. E. Brittain*

INFANTRY GLEN 2 gr.g. (Feb 8) Infantry 122 – Rage Glen 67 (Grey Mirage **44**
128) [1992 6d 6g 7s] angular gelding: third reported foal: half-brother to useful 1989
2-y-o 5f and 6f winner Lord Glen and 1¼m and 10.9f winner Master Glen (both by
Rabdan): dam headstrong 8.2f and 1¼m winner also successful over jumps: faded
from 2f out when well beaten in maidens in the autumn: has been gelded. *M. D. I.
Usher*

INFORMATRICE (USA) 2 ch.f. (Mar 5) Trempolino (USA) 135 – Inform- **59** P
atique (USA) (Quack (USA)) [1992 7g*] $80,000Y: rangy, attractive filly: third foal:
closely related to 4-y-o French-trained 1½m winner Sharp Imposter (by Diesis),
formerly fairly useful 7f (at 2 yrs) and 11.8f winner here: dam, second over 11f in
France, is out of very useful 1965 American 2-y-o Silver Bright, also dam of good
animals Banquet Table and State Dinner: odds on, won moderately-run 6-runner

maiden at Yarmouth in July without coming off the bridle: bred to be suited by middle distances: almost certainly capable of considerably better. *H. R. A. Cecil*

INFRASONIC 2 b.c. Dancing Brave (USA) 140 – Infra Green 121 (Laser Light **112** 118) [1992 9d* 10s²] half-brother to several winners, including useful 1m to 2m (in USA) winner Verdance (by Green Dancer), smart 7f and 1m performer Greensmith (by Known Fact) and the dam of Toulon: dam won from 6f to 1½m, including Prix Ganay: won newcomers race at Longchamp by ½ length: beaten a neck by Marchand de Sable in Criterium de Saint-Cloud in November: will be well suited by 1½m: likely to win more races. *A. Fabre, France*

INGENUITY 3 br.f. Clever Trick (USA) – Reflection 111 (Mill Reef (USA) 141) **68** [1991 NR 1992 a6g a6g⁶ a7g⁵ a7g⁵ 6g* 6s 6d* 6s 7g] small filly: third foal: sister to ungenuine 7f (at 2 yrs) and 1¼m winner Hall of Mirrors: dam, 5f to 7f winner at 2 yrs, disappointed as 3-y-o: improved form to win handicaps at Windsor in July and Redcar in October: bred to stay at least 1m, but best form at 6f: probably unsuited by very soft ground. *Lord Huntingdon*

INHERENT MAGIC (IRE) 3 ch.f. Magical Wonder (USA) 125 – Flo Kelly **85** (Florescence 120) [1991 6s⁶ a5g* a6g³ 1992 a6g² a5g³ 5g³ 6v³ 5g* 5.7s 5g² 5f⁴ 5f² 5d² 5m³ 5g* 6d 5.2s⁴ 5g⁶] smallish, sturdy filly: progressed really well in handicaps from January to November, running only one bad race all season: won at Kempton in May and Newmarket (£8,000 contest) in August: best effort at Doncaster final start: stays 6f: acts on any going, including all-weather surfaces: tough and game. *M. McCormack*

INJAKA BOY 3 gr.c. General Wade 93 – Injaka 102 (Right Boy 137) [1991 6g 7m –
6.1m⁵ 6m 1992 a7g⁶ a6g 5s⁶ 5s 5.1d 11g 7f⁶ 5s 5s 6s] leggy, sparely-made colt: seems of little account these days: usually blinkered or visored. *K. White*

INKALA 4 b.f. Kalaglow 132 – Intoxication 73 (Great Nephew 126) [1991 11.8m⁴ –
12m⁴ 14.6m 15.4m⁴ 1992 12.5s 18m] leggy filly: rated 71 at 3 yrs for J. Eustace: soundly beaten in 1992. *W. R. Muir*

INNER CITY (IRE) 3 ch.c. Bob Back (USA) 124 – Heartland 72 (North- **120** p
fields (USA)) [1991 NR 1992 9s² 10g* 10g* 12f³ 10m³ 10g² 9d* 8m* 8g* 7v*]
   The suspension of racing in Hong Kong announced in November came as a blow to those connected with Inner City. For most of the year the shutdown (forced by an outbreak of equine herpes virus) at Sha Tin would have been an irrelevance to them, but Inner City was a revelation in the autumn and would have been bidding for his fifth consecutive win, in the £200,000 Hong Kong Invitation Cup scheduled for mid-December. April 18th is the new date for the race but Inner City will not be making the journey. By the end of the season here Inner City would have looked out of place in any company. Unraced as a two-year-old, he won a maiden at Windsor and a listed race at Rome in May then was placed in the King George V Stakes at Royal Ascot, His Tennents Scottish Classic at Ayr and an £11,000 handicap at Newmarket. His performance in the last-named, where he carried 10-0 and had to give 17 lb to Mamdooh, looked particularly meritorious at the time, but Inner City put that in the shade with the winning sequence that followed. The first three of those successes were in listed races, the fourth in a Group 3; by four lengths on the first two occasions, two and a half on the third and four again on the fourth. The first and last of these clear-cut triumphs were at Milan. The merit of those runs could be debated, but sandwiched between these were two performances at Newmarket which left no room for doubt that Inner City was a good horse. In both the Main Reef Stakes and Ben Marshall Stakes Inner City was a class apart, making smooth headway to take the lead running down into the Dip then, his forward progress punctuated by a swerve to the left, positively bolting clear before being eased near the line. The stronger field was in the moderately-run Ben Marshall for which he was value, conservatively, for at least four lengths ahead of Badawi, who was followed in by seven others all of which had won either a pattern or listed race.
   Sheikh Mohammed had over five hundred horses in training in Europe in 1992 and Inner City has to figure in the top half dozen of them in terms of ratings, ironic for a colt picked up (at the Irish National Yearling Sale) for as small a sum as 37,000 guineas. He had also been through the ring for 17,500 Irish guineas as a foal. Neither his dam Heartland nor grandam Gwendolyn won a race though both were placed, Heartland managing second of five in a

381

Ben Marshall Stakes, Newmarket—
Inner City's turn of foot is too much for Badawi (far side), Swing Low and the rest

mile-and-a-quarter handicap at Nottingham. Gwendolyn, though, is a half-sister to the dam of Royal Lodge Stakes winner Robellino, and both of Heartland's foals prior to Inner City have won races, albeit in minor company; Still Battling (by Hard Fought), a plater here, has gone on to win several times in Macau while Krisvic (by Reach) gained victories in a seven-furlong claimer in the French Provinces at two years and a thirteen-furlong handicap at four. Inner City is from the first crop of Bob Back, who was the only horse to get the better of Pebbles in her four-year-old season, beating her a length and a half in the Prince of Wales's Stakes with another of 1985's outstanding performers, Commanche Run, in third. Bob Back also had fourteen starts in the United States at four to six years, winning one, though his first run there, when second in the Man o' War Stakes, was the best. Bob Back had his second most important winner as a sire half an hour before Inner City's Ben Marshall Stakes when the two-year-old Bob's Return won the listed Zetland Stakes over a mile and a quarter.

Inner City (IRE) (ch.c. 1989)	Bob Back (USA) (br 1981)	Roberto (b 1969)	Hail To Reason Bramalea
		Toter Back (ch 1967)	Carry Back Romantic Miss
	Heartland (ch 1981)	Northfields (ch 1968)	Northern Dancer Little Hut
		Gwendolyn (br 1968)	Bagdad Isobella

Inner City has very useful form at that trip but his best efforts are at up to a mile. He probably acts on any going. An attractive, good-topped colt, Inner City possesses a fine turn of foot that looks sure to win him more races. And if he carries on where he left off, then that looks sure to include a considerably more important prize than those he won in 1992. *L. M. Cumani*

INNOCENT ABROAD (DEN)   2 b.f. (Apr 19) Viking (USA) – Police Girl (FR)   **53**
(Kashmir II 125) [1992 7g 8s 8.9s 8g6] 620F: angular filly: sixth foal: half-sister to 4 winners abroad: dam unraced half-sister to Prix du Jockey-Club winner Policeman: progressive form, in selling nursery at Doncaster last time: will stay beyond 9f. *C. B. B. Booth*

INNOCENT GEORGE 3 b.g. Hallgate 127 – Are You Guilty 83§ (Runnett 125) –
[1991 5d⁶ 5v⁴ 5m 5d 6d² 5m⁶ 6m 5f⁶ a6g 6m 1992 a6g a7g] small gelding: has a round
action: seems of little account these days. *C. B. B. Booth*

IN NO DOUBT 3 b.g. Precocious 126 – Global Lady 94 (Balliol 125) [1991 7g⁴ –
7.5f 6g⁶ 1992 12.1m⁵ 14.1g] good-topped gelding: poor maiden: blinkered, ran
moderately over 1¾m at Edinburgh in June: seems to stay 1½m. *J. J. O'Neill*

INONDER 2 bl. or br.f. (Feb 23) Belfort (FR) 89 – Rainfall 96 (Relko 136) [1992 **31**
6m⁶ 6s 6m 5g 7s] 1,150F: sparely-made filly: half-sister to several maidens: dam
middle-distance stayer: poor maiden: will stay 1m. *M. D. I. Usher*

INOVAR 2 b.c. (Mar 31) Midyan (USA) 124 – Princess Cinders 61 (King of Spain –
121) [1992 6.1d 5d] IR 5,400Y, resold 12,000Y: big, workmanlike colt: poor mover:
first foal: dam maiden, second at 6f, out of half-sister to high-class Moulton and
Freefoot: no worthwhile form. *C. B. B. Booth*

INSEYAB 4 b.f. Persian Bold 123 – Strike Home 82 (Be My Guest (USA) 126) **65**
[1991 8s 7f⁶ 8h² 8g⁶ 7g* 7g³ 8f* 8m* 7f 8f* 8m⁴ 9.2f³ a7g 1992 a7g⁴ a7g a8g⁴ a10g a50
8f⁶ 8.1m³ 7d³ 7f* 8g⁴ 8.1m³ 7g² 7g* 8m*] leggy, close-coupled filly: moderate
walker and mover: modest performer: successful in sellers at Yarmouth (bought in
4,250 gns) and Redcar (no bid) and handicap at Ripon in the summer: effective at 7f
to 9f: acts on hard and dead ground and fibresand: sometimes bandaged behind:
successful when sweating. *P. C. Haslam*

INSIJAAM (USA) 2 ch.f. (Apr 1) Secretariat (USA) – Cadeaux d'Amie (USA) 115 **?**
(Lyphard (USA) 132) [1992 9v*] second foal: half-sister to 1000 Guineas winner
Hatoof (by Irish River): dam, 1m winner at 2 yrs in France won at 1¼m at 3 yrs, is
half-sister to Mrs Penny: won 15-runner newcomers event at Evry in December by
1½ lengths: well bred, and looks promising. *Mme C. Head, France*

INSPECTOR BEN 13 br.g. Bold As Brass 95 – Christmas Gorse (Woodcut 114) –
[1991 NR 1992 16d] winning chaser: tailed off (reportedly finished lame) in celebrity
race in March. *J. P. Smith*

INSTANT AFFAIR (USA) 2 br.f. (Feb 4) Lyphard (USA) 132 – Asiram (USA) **80** p
110 (Sharpen Up 127) [1992 7g* 7m⁴] 18,000Y: smallish, leggy filly: second reported
foal: dam French 2-y-o 7f winner from family of Never Bend and Bold Reason: green
when length winner of 17-runner maiden auction event at Leicester: unimpressive
in appearance when staying-on fourth of 21 in nursery at Newmarket later in
September: will be suited by 1m: will improve further. *P. F. I. Cole*

INSWINGER 6 br.g. Swing Easy (USA) 126 – Cheri Berry 87 (Air Trooper 115) **30**
[1991 a8g² a8g³ a8g² a6g* a10g a5g⁴ a6g² 6f 1991 a5g³ a8g a6g a6g⁵ 1992 a6g⁴ a8g a41
a6g a6g⁴ a5g³ a6g² 6.1m⁵ a6g a5g* 6f⁶ a6g⁴ 6d 5s⁵ a5g⁶ a5g a6g a6g⁴] small,
lengthy, dipped-backed gelding: carries condition: none too consistent handicapper:
won at Southwell in July: effective at 5f to 1m: acts on firm going and all-weather
surfaces: tried blinkered and visored. *W. G. R. Wightman*

INTENT 3 ch.c. Kris 135 – Interval 122 (Habitat 134) [1991 7m⁴ 1992 8s³ 10g*] **78**
compact colt: has a quick action: similar form in maidens, winning at Leicester in
May: stays 1¼m: acts on soft ground: sold 11,000 gns Newmarket July Sales, to race
in Scandinavia. *H. R. A. Cecil*

INTERNAL AFFAIR 4 gr.f. Aragon 118 – Alicia Markova 64 (Habat 127) [1991 **44**
8.9g³ 8.3d* 8m⁵ 8.9m 7g⁵ 8.2m³ a10g 1992 a10g a10g⁶ 7d⁵ 8.1g 7g³ 10m 7f] leggy, a–
rather close-coupled filly: plater: should stay 1¼m: best turf efforts on an easy
surface. *J. Pearce*

IN THE AIR 2 b.f. (Apr 3) Jupiter Island 126 – Hilly 96 (Town Crier 119) [1992 6m –
6d] 2,000Y: close-coupled, rather leggy filly: second foal: dam 2-y-o 6f winner:
always beaten in maiden auction at Newmarket and claimer at Leicester: sold 700
gns Ascot June Sales. *G. A. Pritchard-Gordon*

IN THE GAME (IRE) 3 b.f. Mummy's Game 120 – Carado 82 (Manado 130) **53**
[1991 6f⁵ 6g 7m³ 7m⁵ 7g⁶ 8m 6.1m 6d a7g⁴ 1992 a6g* a6g² 6d a6g⁴ a7g] tall, leggy
filly: won maiden at Lingfield in February: below best in handicaps after next start:
stays 7f: acts on equitrack: sometimes sweats/looks temperamental: races prominently: sold 740 gns Newmarket Autumn Sales. *Miss A. J. Whitfield*

IN THE MONEY (IRE) 3 b.c. Top Ville 129 – Rensaler (USA) (Stop The Music **70**
(USA)) [1991 18.1f 7m 1992 10.3g² 12g³ 11.8d³ a12g⁴ 14.1d⁶ 12.2g² 11.8g⁶ 10.4d²
10.3s 10.3g] leggy colt: none too consistent maiden handicapper: effective at 1¼m to
1½m: acts on dead ground, well below form on fibresand: found little/ducked left
once. *R. Hollinshead*

IN THE PICTURE (IRE) 3 ch.g. Tate Gallery (USA) 117 – Mille Fleurs (USA) **87**
100 (Jacinto) [1991 6g⁴ 7f 8.2f 1992 9.7v* 10d³ 10g* 10g* 11.4m² 10d 10m⁴ 10d⁵]

smallish, quite attractive gelding: progressed well for much of 1992, winning Folke-stone maiden, handicaps at Nottingham and Salisbury and strong-finishing fourth of 18 to Party Cited in £30,000 handicap (got poor run) at Goodwood: gelded after modest effort final start: stays 11.4f: probably acts on any going. *R. Hannon*

IN THE PRINT 4 b.g. Night Shift (USA) – Filwah (High Top 131) [1991 8.2f 1992 7g 10m 10.2f 6.1g] sturdy gelding: has been tubed: seems of little account. *Mrs Barbara Waring* —

IN THE SPOTLIGHT (IRE) 4 b.c. The Noble Player (USA) 126 – On Her Own 80 (Busted 134) [1991 8s 8g 1992 10g 14.6g] good-topped colt: winning hurdler but little show on flat: tried blinkered once. *R. Curtis* —

INTO THE FUTURE 5 b.g. Mummy's Game 120 – Valley Farm 88 (Red God 128§) [1991 8.2d 10.5m6 10m 8m4 10.3m3 9.2f4 9.9f 12m 1992 8.5m 12f 10.1f 15.1m] smallish, good-quartered gelding: no form on flat in 1992: stays 1¼m: acts on firm ground: below form blinkered/visored. *A. P. Stringer* —

INTREPID FORT 3 br.g. Belfort (FR) 89 – Dauntless Flight (Golden Mallard 103) [1991 5g6 5m2 5m3 6m 6f5 5m5 7g 8m 6m 1992 6m 7.5m 9.9m 8.9m 6m 6s 6d a8g5 a7g] workmanlike gelding: poor maiden: no improvement blinkered/visored: changed hands 1,400 gns Doncaster November Sales. *B. W. Murray* —

INTREPIDITY 2 b.f. (Feb 19) Sadler's Wells (USA) 132 – Intrepid Lady (USA) (Bold Ruler) [1992 8v*] closely related to smart sprinter Acushla (by Storm Bird) and half-sister to 3 winners, notably very useful 1m and 1¼m filly Calandra (by Sir Ivor): dam, French 1½m winner, is sister to very smart 1968 American 2-y-o filly Big Advance: 2½-length winner of minor event at Maisons-Laffitte in November: likely to do much better. *A. Fabre, France* **94 P**

INTREPID LASS 5 b.m. Wassl 125 – Risk All 90 (Run The Gantlet (USA)) [1991 NR 1992 14.1d6 17.2s a14g2 16.5g2 14s 16.9d2 17.2s5] tall, leggy mare: moderate mover: maiden handicapper: stays 17f well: acts on dead ground and fibresand: suitable mount for claimer. *H. Candy* **45**

INTRICACY 4 b.f. Formidable (USA) 125 – Baffle 87 (Petingo 135) [1991 8d 10g2 11.7g4 11.5s2 12.3m4 11.7g6 11.5g6 a12g* a14g* a14g2 a16g2 a14g3 1992 a14g a13g6 13.3g3 14m 15.1f4 a14g3 14g4 14d* 16m a16g4 14s2 16.1g 17.5s] sturdy, quite attractive filly: has a quick action: inconsistent handicapper: won (for first time on turf) at Sandown in July: effective from around 1½m to 2m: best efforts with some give in the ground and on all-weather surfaces: below form when blinkered once: sometimes edged left and ran in snatches: reportedly in foal to Reprimand. *C. C. Elsey* **65**

IN TRUTH 4 ch.g. Dreams To Reality (USA) 113 – Persian Express (Persian Bold 123) [1991 10d4 12.3s5 12g* 11.5m 12g 12.3g 10g5 12.4f5 12.1g a12g 1992 a11g3 a12g a14g5 a12g a12g4 12.3m] rangy gelding: moderate mover: poor handicapper nowadays: stays 1½m: best with give in the ground: suited by forcing tactics: sold out of D. Chapman's stable 4,500 gns Doncaster March Sales before final start. *J. P. Leigh* **39**

INVERTIEL 8 b.g. Sparkling Boy 110 – Phyl's Pet (Aberdeen 109) [1991 8s 12g3 11f* 12g 9f* 9m5 8m 1992 12.1v] quite good-topped gelding: easy mover: quite modest handicapper/winning hurdler: soundly beaten in November: probably stays 1½m: well suited by firm going: tends to idle in front and best held up: successful for apprentice. *P. Monteith* —

INVIGILATE 3 ch.c. Viking (USA) – Maria Da Gloria (St Chad 120) [1991 5g6 5d5 8.1g5 8.3g 8m a7g a7g4 1992 a8g4 a7g a7g3 a8g4 a7g2 6m2 6m* 5h2 6g* 5d4 6g4 5g* 6g 6s 6f6 5m] workmanlike colt: moderate mover: modest handicapper: won at Redcar, Catterick and Sandown in first half of 1992: probably best at sprint distances: acts on hard and dead ground (well beaten on soft), and all-weather surfaces: trained until after third start by H. Whiting. *M. P. Naughton* **62**

INVISIBLE ARMOUR 3 gr.g. Precocious 126 – Haunting 79 (Lord Gayle (USA) 124) [1991 6m 1992 11.1m6 8.9d3 11.1f3 13.6f3 a14g2 12.1s] rangy gelding: maiden handicapper: will stay well: acts on firm ground (possibly not on soft) and fibresand. *P. C. Haslam* **45**

INVOCATION 5 ch.g. Kris 135 – Royal Saint (USA) (Crimson Satan) [1991 10g 1992 a10g a7g* a7g* a7g4 7m3 6g 7m6 6d5 a6g6 a7g 7m5 a6g2] big, strong gelding: carries condition: moderate walker: bad mover, dishes near-fore very markedly: fair performer: won claimers at Lingfield in February and March: effective at 6f and should stay 1m: acts on good to firm, dead ground and equitrack: below form blinkered: sometimes bandaged behind: usually races prominently. *A. Moore* **71** a78

IOLITE   2 b. or br.f. (Feb 13) Forzando 122 – Thulium (Mansingh (USA) 120) [1992   **59**
6g 5.9g4 a6g* 6d a6g* a5g*] sturdy filly: moderate mover: first foal: dam a85
lightly-raced sister to Petong: fairly useful performer: took very well to all-weather
racing, winning maiden at Southwell in September and nurseries at Lingfield and
Southwell late in year: stays 6f: well beaten on dead ground. *M. A. Jarvis*

IOMMELLI (IRE)   2 ch.c. (Feb 23) Don't Forget Me 127 – Inner Pearl (Gulf   **88**
Pearl 117) [1992 6m2 6g* 7.3m4 7g6 7g5 8.1d*] 6,800Y: lengthy, good-quartered
colt: half-brother to 2-y-o 5f winners Inner Ring (in France) and Market Gem (both
by Auction Ring): dam won from 4f to 9f in France: won auction event at Epsom in
June and nursery (by neck, showing improved form) at Sandown in August: will stay
1¼m: acts on dead ground. *P. A. Kelleway*

IOTA   3 b. or br.f. Niniski (USA) 125 – Iosifa 108 (Top Ville 129) [1991 7m4 1992   **83**
11.5g5 12.3f3 12d3 10m2 12.2g 14.6s* 16.1s3 15.9s* 16.5g*] smallish, leggy, sparely-
made filly: fluent mover: progressed well in autumn handicaps when stepped up to
long distances, winning at Wolverhampton, Chester and Doncaster: suited by test of
stamina: has form on firm ground, but best efforts with some give. *Mrs J. Cecil*

I PERCEIVE   5 b.g. Vision (USA) – Wavetree (Realm 129) [1991 10.2s 8d 10g 8m3   **71**
7g 10.3d* 1992 10.3g* 10.1s 12g* 11m5 14m2 14g4 12.4f 11.9d* 11.9m 11.9d5 11.9s]
tall, good-bodied gelding: usually looks really well: fair but inconsistent handicapper: successful at Doncaster (ladies) and Thirsk in spring and Haydock in
August: effective at 1¼m to 1¾m: acts on firm and dead ground: below form when
blinkered once: sometimes has tongue tied down: has found nothing: suited by
waiting tactics and strongly-run race. *F. H. Lee*

IPSILANTE   3 b.f. Mansooj 118 – Glint of Victory 96 (Glint of Gold 128) [1991 NR   **44**
1992 a5g2 6d 5g6 a5g a7g 5.1g 5m] lightly-made filly: first foal: dam 1¼m winner
stayed 1½m: claimed out of N. Callaghan's stable in March on debut: best
efforts at 5f: sometimes bandaged: inconsistent: sold 600 gns Newmarket Autumn
Sales. *A. S. Reid*

IREK   3 b.g. Shareef Dancer (USA) 135 – Roussalka 123 (Habitat 134) [1991 NR   **91**
1992 7s* 8.1g* 8m 10.4d 8m3 7d 8g] small, sturdy gelding: impresses in appearance:
fluent mover: closely related to very good sprinter Gayane (by Nureyev) and French
1m winner Summer Impressions (by Lyphard) and half-brother to 1¼m winner High
Altar (by High Line) and smart 1m and 1¼m winner Ristna (by Kris): dam won 7
races at up to 1¼m, and is sister to Our Home and half-sister to Oh So Sharp: looked
promising in spring, winning Lingfield minor event and Sandown handicap: below
best in handicaps other apart from very good third in £20,000 event at Newmarket:
probably best at 1m: acts on good to firm ground and soft: has been gelded. *Lord
Huntingdon*

I REMEMBER YOU (IRE)   2 ch.c. (Mar 23) Don't Forget Me 127 – Non   **71**
Casual 75 (Nonoalco (USA) 131) [1992 7g2 8f] IR 19,000Y: tall, rather lengthy colt:
half-brother to 1m winner Commanding General (by General Assembly), later
successful in USA, and Irish 1m winner Bahama Mama (by Ela-Mana-Mou): dam
2-y-o 5f winner: shaped encouragingly when always-prominent second in maiden at
Ayr in August: dropped away quickly last 2f in similar event at Doncaster following
month: should stay 1m. *F. H. Lee*

IRENE LOCK   4 b.g. Lock And Load (USA) – Porto Irene 73 (Porto Bello 118)   **–**
[1991 NR 1992 11.7f 11.9g] sturdy gelding: no sign of ability. *D. C. Tucker*

IRISH DOMINION   2 b.c. (Mar 13) Dominion 123 – Irish Cookie 80 (Try My   **72 ?**
Best (USA) 130) [1992 7d4 7g6 6m3] compact colt: third foal: half-brother to quite
modest sprinter Bold Cookie (by Never So Bold): dam 6f and 7f winner, best at 4 yrs:
in frame in minor and maiden races in the North: will be suited by return to 7f+.
Miss S. E. Hall

IRISH EMERALD   5 b.g. Taufan (USA) 119 – Gaelic Jewel 89 (Scottish Rifle   **–**
127) [1991 NR 1992 12g] close-coupled, workmanlike gelding: moderate mover:
rated 83 as 3-y-o: never placed to challenge in Newmarket handicap in April, 1992:
should stay 1½m: goes well on soft ground: modest winning hurdler. *G. C. Bravery*

IRISH GROOM   5 b.g. Shy Groom (USA) – Romany Pageant (Welsh Pageant   **43**
132) [1991 10g5 10.2g 10m6 8g5 9.9f6 12m 10.8g 8m 1992 8g4 8m 8.2g 8.9m2 8g*
8.2m2 8.2d3 8.9d] angular gelding: moderate mover: largely consistent in handicaps
in 1992, successful (for first time) at Wolverhampton in July: seems to stay 1¼m:
acts on good to firm ground and dead: effective blinkered or not: suitable mount for
claimer. *J. P. Smith*

IRISH HONEY (IRE)   3 b.f. Last Tycoon 131 – Great Guns 109 (Busted 134)   **43**
[1991 7.1m 8.1g 1992 8.1d3 10g6 12m5 10m3 12g2 12.1s 13.8d] leggy, workmanlike
filly: poor maiden: stays 1½m: may need a sound surface. *B. Hanbury*

IRISH MEMORY 3 b.c. Don't Forget Me 127 – Irish Isle 67 (Realm 129) [1991 **109** 6g* 6g³ 7d* 7m* 7s⁵ 7s² 1992 7d* 8g³ 7v* 8d 8g⁵] quite attractive Irish colt: half-brother to several winners, including useful 6f and 7f winner Benz (by Free State): dam won over 1m: looked good prospect in early-spring, winning Leopardstown minor event, Dermot McCalmont Tetrarch Stakes (by 9 lengths) at the Curragh and 4 lengths third to Alnasr Alwasheek in Craven Stakes at Newmarket: ran moderately final 2 starts in Premio Parioli at Rome and Irish 2000 Guineas at the Curragh: stays 1m: acts on good to firm and heavy ground. *J. S. Bolger, Ireland*

IRISH NATIVE (IRE) 4 b.g. Be My Native (USA) 122 – Irish Bride (Track — Spare 125) [1991 8g⁶ 10g² 8.9m⁶ 11d* a12g³ a14g³ a11g² a12g² a8g a14g⁵ 1992 a12g³ a12g a12g 10.3g a14g a12g] angular gelding: no form in handicaps in 1992: stays 1½m: acts on dead ground: usually blinkered. *C. A. Smith*

IRISH ROOTS (IRE) 2 b.g. (Apr 18) Caerleon (USA) 132 – Gracious Miss (FR) **45** (Gay Mecene (USA) 128) [1992 5d⁴ 6g 7g a7g 7g 8.3s 7d 7.1g a8g a7g* a8g a7g⁶] IR a57 7,600Y: small, rather sparely-made gelding: third foal: half-brother to 3-y-o Bashoofek (by Sadler's Wells): dam French 9f winner, is sister to smart French miler Gay Minstrel and from family of Gold River: modest form: easily best effort to win claimer at Southwell in November: stays 7f: acts on fibresand: visored last 7 starts. *C. Tinkler*

IRISH STAMP (IRE) 3 b.g. Niniski (USA) 125 – Bayazida (Bustino 136) [1991 **82** p NR 1992 11.5d* 12m 14g² 14d4] angular gelding: third foal: closely related to Irish 1½m winner Bayyasa (by Caerleon) and half-brother to Irish 1½m winner Baladiya (by Darshaan): dam in frame at 1½m and 12.5f in France: not seen out until August when gamely winning maiden at Yarmouth for claimer: ran well in handicaps when in frame at Sandown and Haydock: will be well suited by 2m +: should do well at 4 yrs. *J. Pearce*

IRON BARON (IRE) 3 b.c. Sure Blade (USA) 130 – Riverine (FR) (Riverman **58** (USA) 131) [1991 6g 7f⁶ 1992 10.5s³ 10d4 10.4m⁶ a8g³ a11g4 10m³ a12g* 12m* 12m⁵ a14g 10d⁵ 11d³ 10m 13.8g4 12.3s⁵ 12s* 12.2d4 14.1s² a12g³] smallish, close-coupled colt: consistent plater: no bid after winning at Southwell and Doncaster in July and Pontefract in October: effective at 1½m and 1¾m: acts on good to firm, soft ground and fibresand: sometimes hangs left and carries head high. *R. Hollinshead*

IRON KING 6 gr.g. Tender King 123 – Zanskar (Godswalk (USA) 130) [1991 6f4 **74** 5.3f⁵ 5g4 6m² 6f⁶ 6.1d* 6m 5d³ 6g 5m³ 6g 5f 6f 6g³ 6g⁶ 5g* 5m* 5.1s 6.1d 5s4 1992 5s⁶ 5d⁵ 6d 5.3m* 5m⁶ 6f4 6g⁶ 5f² 5.7f4 5m³ 5f⁵ 5m⁶ 6g² 5g* 6.1m 5g4 5d 6d4 5m⁵ 6d 6.1d4 5.2s 5s] sturdy gelding: poor mover: fair handicapper: successful at Brighton in May and Wolverhampton in July: effective from 5f to 7f: acts on firm and dead ground, possibly not soft: effective visored or not, ran moderately when blinkered once: usually gets behind early on but is suitable mount for inexperienced rider: tough. *J. L. Spearing*

IRON MERCHANT (IRE) 2 b.c. (Mar 25) Fayruz 116 – Kinosium (Relkino **83** 131) [1992 5s³ 6m³ 6g² 5g³ 6d* 6m² 6d] 16,000Y: compact colt: moderate mover: third foal: brother to a listed-placed winner in Italy: dam maiden best run at 9.4f: first past post in Windsor minor event (hung left and caused interference) second start and Epsom maiden (made all despite drifting left 1f out) in August: below form in Newmarket nursery final start: should stay 1m: acts on good to firm and dead ground: sold 17,500 gns Newmarket Autumn Sales. *R. Akehurst*

ISABEAU 5 b.m. Law Society (USA) 130 – Elodie (USA) (Shecky Greene (USA)) — [1991 14m 1992 18g] rather sparely-made mare: winning hurdler but little worthwhile form on flat: should stay 1½m. *K. A. Morgan*

ISAIAH 3 gr.c. Bellypha 130 – Judeah 69 (Great Nephew 126) [1991 6f⁵ 6m² 7m4 **94** 6m* 6m* 5d* 1992 6g4 5g4 6g⁵ 5m⁶ 6d 6s² 6.5v4] strong, good-topped colt: carries condition: moderate mover: fairly useful handicapper: should prove suited by 7f: acts on good to firm and soft ground: trained first 4 starts by M. Johnston. *Mrs J. Cecil*

ISDAR (USA) 3 b. or br.c. Known Fact (USA) 135 – Reyah 83 (Young Generation **81** 129) [1991 5m* 6.1m³ 5d⁶ 1992 5v4 5g 6f 5d4 6d] smallish, strong, deep-girthed colt: carries condition: fair but inconsistent handicapper: bred to stay 1m: acts on good to firm and dead ground: sold 11,000 gns Newmarket Autumn Sales: *H. Thomson Jones*

ISLAND BLADE (IRE) 3 b.g. Sure Blade (USA) 130 – Queen's Eyot 79 **52** (Grundy 137) [1991 7m4 8.2f 10m 1992 10m⁶ 11.5m⁵ 12f 12m* 11.6g 12g 11.5s² a14g* a61 a14g⁵] angular gelding: moderate mover: modest handicapper, none too consistent: won at Folkestone in August and, showing improvement, 16-runner event at

Southwell in December, where forged 10 lengths clear: will stay 2m: below form on very firm going, probably acts on any other. *R. Akehurst*

ISLE OF INNISFREE (USA) 3 ch.g. Fit To Fight (USA) – Isle of Success 65 (USA) (Fiddle Isle) [1991 NR 1992 8g 7f² 7m⁴ 8s] $105,000Y: big, good-topped gelding: half-brother to several minor winners in North America and one in South Africa: dam, winner 5 times in North America, is half-sister to Hawaiian Sound and Sonus: persistently hung left when second in Redcar maiden in May: no comparable form, tried blinkered once: should stay beyond 7f: gelded and sent to race in Dubai. *H. R. A. Cecil*

ISOBAR 6 b.g. Another Realm 118 – Lady Eton 106 (Le Dieu d'Or 119) [1991 a14g⁴ – a14g a14g 1992 21.6g a12g 18g 16.5m⁶ 16.2s⁵ 14.6m] close-coupled, leggy gelding: moderate mover: bad handicapper nowadays. *M. C. Chapman*

ISOTONIC 2 ch.f. (Mar 31) Absalom 128 – Melanoura (Imperial Fling (USA) 116) 69 [1992 5d² 5d* 5v* 5g³ 6m 5m³ 5.1g³ 6m⁵ a5s* 6s 5d⁴] sturdy filly: has a round a74 action: second foal: half-sister to Computer Kid (by Alleging), 1991 2-y-o 5f winner here and later successful at 7.5f in Italy: dam ran twice at 2 yrs: modest performer: successful in maiden and minor event at Pontefract in April and nursery at Southwell in August: easily better of last 2 starts when seventh of 10 in Ripon listed race: stays 6f: best efforts on a soft surface: sometimes hangs. *G. M. Moore*

IS SHE QUICK 2 ch.f. (Apr 18) Norwick (USA) 120 – Get Involved 79 (Shiny 46 Tenth 120) [1992 5m 6d⁵ 6.1m 7s] tall filly: moderate mover: eighth foal: half-sister to 1m seller winner Comedy Prince (by Comedy Star) and a winner over hurdles: dam sprinter: failed to progress after staying-on fifth in maiden at Leicester in June: should stay 1m. *Mrs J. C. Dawe*

ISTANBULLU 3 b. or br.c. Jalmood (USA) 126 – Windy Sea 105 (Sea Hawk II – 131) [1991 7d 1992 12g 10g a11g] lengthy colt: poor mover: no worthwhile form: sold 600 gns Ascot July Sales. *M. Bell*

IT BITES (IRE) 2 b.f. (May 17) The Noble Player (USA) 126 – Sea Palace – (Huntercombe 133) [1992 5g 5.7f 5m] leggy, sparely-made filly: sister to 5f performer The Noble Oak and half-sister to a winner in Norway by Sparkling Boy: dam unraced: soundly beaten in maidens and a claimer: has looked reluctant. *A. P. James*

ITHKURNI (USA) 3 b.f. Green Forest (USA) 134 – Queen's Visit (Top – Command (USA)) [1991 6m² 7g⁴ 1992 7g a8g a7g⁶] sturdy, workmanlike filly: rated 59 at 2 yrs: sold out of B. Hanbury's stable 3,200 gns Newmarket July Sales after reappearance and well beaten afterwards: should stay at least 1m. *P. Hayward*

ITQAN (IRE) 4 b.f. Sadler's Wells (USA) 132 – Photo 83 (Blakeney 126) [1991 – 12.2m² 12.2f² 11.9f* 14.8s* 14.6m* 16m² 1992 11.9g 12f 15m³ 13.9m 14.6f] sturdy, good-bodied filly: keen walker: rated 92 as 3-y-o: generally disappointing in handicaps in 1992: stays 2m: acts on any going: sometimes carries head awkwardly/edges right. *B. W. Hills*

IT'S ONLY MONEY 3 b.c. Prince Sabo 123 – Marimba 82 (Music Boy 124) [1991 – 6m 5h² 5d* 5m² 5.1f⁶ 5d 1992 a5g³ a5g⁵ a5g⁶ a5g⁶ a5g³ 5s 5g 5s⁶ 5s 5d] a50 good-topped colt: modest handicapper: form at 3 yrs only on all-weather: speedy: ran well when blinkered, below form when visored once. *T. H. Caldwell*

ITS UNBELIEVABLE 2 ch.g. (Feb 2) Kalaglow 132 – Avon Royale 66 42 (Remainder 106) [1992 8.1s 8s] 2,000Y, 5,100Y 2-y-o: lengthy gelding: half-brother to poor 1983 2-y-o Acer Lad (by Abwah): dam won over 7f and 1m: well beaten in autumn maidens. *J. White*

IVANA (IRE) 3 gr.f. Taufan (USA) 119 – Inanna 105 (Persian Bold 123) [1991 NR 82 d 1992 8g² 7g² 7m³ 8g⁶ 7d² 8v⁶] 35,000F, 78,000Y: tall filly: first foal: dam Irish 6f and 1m winner: went the wrong way after second in Wood Ditton Stakes at Newmarket on debut and seemed irresolute: tried blinkered once. *W. Jarvis*

IVANKA (IRE) 2 b.f. (Mar 5) Dancing Brave (USA) 140 – Diamond Land 113 p (Sparkler 130) [1992 6f* 6g⁵ 8m³ 8s* 8d²]

     Apart from a modest display in the Princess Margaret Stakes at Ascot in July on her second outing, the Fillies' Mile winner and Racing Post Trophy runner-up Ivanka showed herself to be a thoroughly progressive filly, and a very useful one, too, given a good test of stamina. Ivanka is one of four fillies Clive Brittain has in his stable that showed a high level of form as two-year-olds. Unlike her stable-companion Sayyedati though, important middle-distance races will be first on Ivanka's agenda in the coming season, and if she carries on where she left off at two she'll have little difficulty in adding to her tally.

Although Ivanka showed her best form over a mile on soft ground at the end of the season, she was quick enough to win the five-runner Ewar Stud Farm Stakes over six furlongs on firm ground at Newmarket in July on her racecourse debut. For one far from fully wound up and bred so stoutly, her length-and-a-half defeat of the easy Sandown winner Greenlet, with the Queen Mary sixth Holly Golightly a neck back in third, in what was a moderately-run race, was a most auspicious start. She seemed to meet with a set-back when only fifth of six when a well-backed favourite in the Princess Margaret later in the month, but proved her Ascot running to be all wrong when finishing third to the three-length winner Marillette in the May Hill Stakes over a mile at Doncaster in September seven weeks later. Had Ivanka's rider not gone for an optimistic run along the inside rail she would have finished second at least; as it was, she finished strongly from a long way back (she seemed ill at ease on the ground early on) and failed by only a length to catch Self Assured for second. Significantly, perhaps, the ground was very much on the soft side when Ivanka, a poor mover, showed further improvement to win the Fillies' Mile at Ascot later in the month. The field she beat was probably not a strong one—the favourite Iviza still looked singularly green, and one or two of the other fancied runners, none of whom had shown a good level of form, seemed unsuited by the testing ground—but Ivanka won on merit by a length and a half from the Prestige Stakes third Ajfan; and she followed it up with an excellent second to Armiger under near-identical ground conditions in the Racing Post Trophy at Doncaster in October. Ivanka, a supplementary into the race, wasn't able to make any impression on the highly-impressive six-length winner in the final quarter-mile, but she ran on gamely under pressure, relishing the test of stamina, and finished well clear of such useful colts as Zind and Desert Secret, neither of whom could be said to have run below form.

Ivanka's sire Dancing Brave is now in Japan. A brilliant racehorse, winner of the Two Thousand Guineas, Eclipse, King George and Arc besides finishing an unlucky second in the Derby, Dancing Brave didn't make the immediate impact at stud his shareholders had hoped for, and at the time of his sale to the Far East he had sired only one pattern-race winner, the fairly useful 1990 two-year-old Glowing Ardour, successful in the Silken Glider Stakes. In contrast, Ivanka's dam Diamond Land has proved a great success at stud: Ivanka is her sixth foal and fifth winner following the Irish mile-and-

Fillies' Mile, Ascot—Ivanka and Ajfan both stay on

Mr Ali Saeed's "Ivanka"

three-quarter winners Lyndonville (by Top Ville) and Mitsubishi Fax (by King of Clubs), the useful seven-furlong and mile-and-a-quarter winner Pretoria (by Habitat) and the fairly useful Irish five-furlong to seven-furlong winner Keen Cut (by Sharpo), later a winner at around a mile in the States. Diamond Land, who won over thirteen and a half furlongs in Ireland, is from a very stout family. Neither her dam Canaan (who never ran) nor grandam Rustic Bridge won, but they or their descendants have produced numerous winners, particularly over long distances where their number include the St Leger winner Cantelo, the St Leger fourth Oak Ridge, the Chester Cup winner Eric, the Gold Cup runner-up Tyrone Bridge, the Goodwood Cup winner Tug of War, the Park Hill winner Bracey Bridge and the Doncaster Cup winner Biskrah. This is also the family of the Yorkshire Oaks winner Connaught Bridge and the Lancashire Oaks winner Rhein Bridge.

		Dancing Brave (USA) (b 1983)	Lyphard (b 1969)	Northern Dancer
Ivanka (IRE) (b.f. Mar 5, 1990)				Goofed
			Navajo Princess (b 1974)	Olmec
				Drone
		Diamond Land (br 1978)	Sparkler (b 1968)	Hard Tack
				Diamond Spur
			Canaan (br 1966)	Santa Claus
				Rustic Bridge

It hardly needs saying that Ivanka, a rangy, good-topped filly, will be well suited by a mile and a half as a three-year-old; she could well stay a mile and three quarters. Although she has shown herself capable of winning form on firm ground, her prospects of further success in good company will probably be enhanced by soft conditions. She wore protective pads under her shoes in all but her last two races. *C. E. Brittain*

IVANOV (USA) 4 b.c. Nijinsky (CAN) 138 – Fine Spirit (USA) (Secretariat (USA)) [1991 12.3d⁵ 11.8g⁴ 10.5g 16.1g 1992 8m 8s] lengthy colt: no worthwhile form on flat: sold to join J. White's stable 2,300 gns Doncaster May Sales. *P. Mitchell*

IVAN THE TERRIBLE (IRE) 4 ch.g. Siberian Express (USA) 125 – Chrisanthy 81 (So Blessed 130) [1991 8d 7f⁶ 7m 11.5g⁵ 10m* 12g³ 9d 11.1g⁵ a11g 1992 10m 12.3g⁶ 11d] lengthy, workmanlike gelding: fair handicapper at best: no form in 1992: stays 1½m: acts on good to firm and dead ground: below form blinkered once: takes strong hold. *Miss S. J. Wilton*

IVIZA (IRE) 2 b.f. (Apr 6) Sadler's Wells (USA) 132 – Ivy (USA) (Sir Ivor 135) **94** p [1992 7g* 8s³ 8g⁴] 100,000Y: big, rangy filly: has a fluent, rounded action: fifth foal: sister to 1989 2-y-o 7f winner Ivrea, useful over middle distances at 3 yrs, and half-sister to 2 winners, notably very useful Irish 3-y-o 1m (at 2 yrs) and 1½m winner Ivyanna (by Reference Point): dam, placed twice at 2 yrs in USA, is half-sister to Santa Anita Derby winner An Act: won 15-runner maiden at Yarmouth in August: still very green, tending to carry head high, when 4½ lengths third of 8 to Ivanka in Fillies' Mile and over 3 lengths fourth to Taos in listed race at Ascot: will be well suited by further: probably still capable of improvement. *M. R. Stoute*

IVOR'S FLUTTER 3 b.g. Beldale Flutter (USA) 130 – Rich Line (High Line **85** 125) [1991 7.1d 1992 9m⁶ 12g⁴ 11.6m* 11.6m³ 12g² 14d³ 12d⁴ 12g* 13.3s²] leggy, workmanlike gelding: consistent and progressed well in handicaps in 1992: successful at Windsor (hung left) and Ascot (amateurs): very good second to Daru at Newbury final start: effective at 1½m to 1¾m: acts on good to firm ground and soft: usually held up. *D. R. C. Elsworth*

IVORS GUEST 6 b.g. Be My Guest (USA) 126 – Ivor's Date (USA) (Sir Ivor 135) **52** [1991 NR 1992 16d⁵ 12d³ 12g 12m⁴] leggy, quite good-topped gelding: moderate

Mr P. J. P. Gleeson's "Ivory Frontier"

mover: winning hurdler/modest maiden on flat: stays 1½m: acts on dead ground: sometimes looks none too keen. *R. Lee*

IVORS PRINCESS 3 b.f. Mandrake Major 122 – Double Birthday (Cavo Doro 124) [1991 6g⁵ 6f 1992 6m⁴ 8.3f⁶ 7g 10s 8.3s] leggy, workmanlike filly: bad maiden: trained first 3 starts by Mrs M. Reveley before sold 640 gns Doncaster October Sales. *M. Johnston* **39**

IVORY FRONTIER (IRE) 2 ch.c. (Feb 21) Imperial Frontier (USA) 112 – Ivory Home (FR) (Home Guard (USA) 129 [1992 6d* 6g* 6m* 6g⁴ 7s⁴] half-brother to 4 winners, notably very useful Irish 7f (at 2 yrs) to 1¼m winner Upward Trend (by Salmon Leap): dam, unraced, from family of Glad Rags and Gorytus: successful in 15-runner maiden at Leopardstown, 6-runner minor event (by 3½ lengths, first 2 clear) at the Curragh and 6-runner Group 3 John Roarty Memorial Railway Stakes (by a head from Shahik) at the Curragh: over a length fourth of 9, making most, to Pips Pride in Heinz '57' Phoenix Stakes at Leopardstown and 4½ lengths fourth of 5 to Fatherland in Smurfit National Stakes at the Curragh: stays 7f: acts on good to firm ground and dead. *J. S. Bolger, Ireland* **98**

IVORY PALM (USA) 2 b.f. (Mar 4) Sir Ivor 135 – Sunerta (USA) 75 (Roberto (USA) 131) [1992 7.1s*] good-topped filly: has scope: second foal: dam, 7f winner at 2 yrs, is half-sister to Horris Hill winner Super Asset, high-class 8.5f to 1¼m winner Bates Motel and very smart middle-distance winner Hatim: easy to back when winning 12-runner maiden at Chepstow in October by ½ length from Austral Jane, pair well clear, leading over 3f out and staying on strongly: will be suited by middle distances: sure to do better. *J. H. M. Gosden* **75 p**

IVYANNA (IRE) 3 b.f. Reference Point 139 – Ivy (USA) (Sir Ivor 135) [1991 8s* 8d* 1992 12g* 12g 15.5s] very useful Irish filly: made all to beat Armarama a length **112**

Mrs O. White's "Ivyanna"

in Oaks d'Italia at Milan in May: tailed off in Irish Oaks (blinkered, set strong pace) at the Curragh and Prix Royal-Oak at Longchamp over 3 months later: stays 1½m. *J. S. Bolger, Ireland*

IVY BENSON 2 b.f. (Apr 15) Midyan (USA) 124 – Angel Drummer 59 (Dance In –
Time (CAN)) [1992 5f 5.7f⁵] second foal: half-sister to 3-y-o Sure Shot Norman (by Song): dam 2-y-o 7f winner later successful over hurdles: well beaten in Salisbury maiden and median auction event at Bath. *B. W. Hills*

IWAN 4 b.g. Elegant Air 119 – Clouded Vision 74 (So Blessed 130) [1991 10g 10g⁴ – §
12.3d 10g 10.1m⁵ 1992 12m 10f] strong, deep-girthed gelding: no worthwhile form, and has looked most reluctant: stays 1¼m: tried visored/blinkered. *K. A. Morgan*

IYWAAN (IRE) 3 b.c. Sadler's Wells (USA) 132 – Maria Roberta (USA) (Roberto 97
(USA) 131) [1991 7d 8m⁴ 7.9m⁶ 1992 12m* 12g² 10.4m⁴ 16.2f] rangy colt: good mover: looked promising at Newmarket in spring, winning maiden and second of 4 to Allegan in minor event: not seen out again after running as if something amiss in Queen's Vase at Royal Ascot: needs further than 1¼m and should stay beyond 1½m: sold only 5,000 gns Newmarket December Sales. *P. T. Walwyn*

IZITALLWORTHIT 3 b.f. My Dad Tom (USA) 109 – Torlonia 63§ (Royal –
Palace 131) [1991 NR 1992 10m 10g 13.6m 12.3g⁵ 14.1d 16.1s⁴ 18m⁵] small filly: has a round action: seventh reported foal (last 3 by My Dad Tom): dam most ungenuine stayer: moderate fourth in Warwick handicap: probably needs the mud: wears tongue strap. *J. Mackie*

J

JAAZIM 2 ch.c. (Feb 6) Night Shift (USA) – Mesmerize (Mill Reef (USA) 141) 57 p
[1992 6g] $250,000Y: strong, lengthy colt: has scope: half-brother to very smart 1990 2-y-o Mujtahid (by Woodman) and a winner in North America: dam unraced: 6/1 and very green, around 9 lengths ninth of 20 to Serious in Newmarket maiden, struggling halfway and eased running into the Dip: capable of better. *Major W. R. Hern*

JACK BUTTON (IRE) 3 b.g. Kings Lake (USA) 133 – Tallantire (USA) (Ice- 89
capade (USA)) [1991 7m 7.5f⁶ 8m 10m⁴ 1992 12v* 12.3s⁴ 11.6m⁴ 12g 16.2d* 11.9f
16.2d* 18.5d² 16f* 16.2d³ 16.2s* 16m⁶ 18m 16.5g²] good-topped gelding: fairly useful handicapper: progressed well, winning at Folkestone in March, Haydock (twice) and Thirsk in midsummer then at Haydock again in September: suited by a test of stamina: probably acts on any going: unsuccessful when tried in blinkers/visor on 4 occasions, but has run creditably: tough and genuine. *Bob Jones*

JACKPOT STAR 2 ch.c. (Apr 17) Pharly (FR) 130 – Claironcita 97 (Don Carlos) 84
[1992 6g⁶ 7g² 8g⁵ 8m⁴ 7.6s*] 16,000Y: sparely-made, quite attractive colt: half-brother to middle-distance winner Castellita (by Homing) and 7-y-o 7f and 10.5f winner Shabanaz (by Imperial Fling): dam middle-distance winner: fairly useful performer: overcame very slow start to win maiden at Chester in October by 10 lengths: will be better suited by 1¼m: acts on good to firm and soft ground: flashed tail second start. *R. Hannon*

JACKSON FLINT 4 b.c. Nishapour (FR) 125 – Scamperdale 61 (French Beige 78
127) [1991 8g* 12m 13g* 14.1f* 13.9g⁴ 18m² 13.3g* 14.6d² 1992 14.9v⁵ 14g 16g⁴ 14g⁵
13.9m 13.9g⁴] big, strong, lengthy colt: impresses in appearance: shows knee action: not so good a handicapper as at 3 yrs: blinkered last 2 starts, respectable effort when fourth in £8,200 event at York in September: stays 1¾m: best form on a sound surface: has idled in front: best with waiting tactics. *H. Thomson Jones*

JACKSON SQUARE (IRE) 4 b.g. Prince Tenderfoot (USA) 126 – Double –
Habit (Double Form 130) [1991 NR 1992 10g⁶ 11d] strong, lengthy gelding: third foal: half-brother to 6f and 7f winner Too Eager (by Nishapour) and 6f winner King Arbro (by Tumble Wind): dam never ran: no form in maiden and claimer in the autumn. *W. G. M. Turner*

JADE GREEN 3 b.f. Midyan (USA) 124 – Pilley Green 100 (Porto Bello 118) 65
[1991 a7g³ 1992 8g² 10g³ 8.1d a10g a12g*] leggy filly: won claimer at Southwell in November: stays 1½m: acts on fibresand. *P. J. Makin*

JADE MISTRESS 3 b.f. Damister (USA) 123 – Precious Jade 72 (Northfields 51
(USA)) [1991 NR 1992 10g 10g 10m⁵ 11.5g⁵ 10g 10s⁵ 10.1d] lengthy filly: good walker: seventh foal: sister to 4-y-o Italian 7f and 1m winner Precious Dame and half-sister to 3 winners, including 6f and 1m winner Just A Flutter (by Beldale Flutter): dam

stayed 1m: modest maiden: unseated rider and bolted to post before running creditably in apprentice handicap penultimate start: stays 1½m: acts on soft going: blinkered (sweating, well beaten) final outing. *A. Hide*

JADE RUNNER 2 ch.f. (Feb 9) Sylvan Express 117 – Moorgreen 68 (Green God 128) [1992 5.1g4 6m3 6g4 7g 6.1m6 5.2g6 5g 6m 6g a6g] leggy filly: has a smooth action: half-sister to 3 winners over sprint distances: dam placed over 5f: modest plater: may prove best at around 6f: blinkered or visored last 4 starts: sold 1,250 gns Doncaster October Sales. *Mrs N. Macauley* **45**

JADE VALE 3 b.f. Petorius 117 – Deja Vu (FR) (Be My Guest (USA) 126) [1991 NR 1992 7g3 7m* 8m 6g 7m 7g4 8g* 8s3 8m 10.1d*] leggy, unfurnished filly: moderate maiden: fourth foal: half-sister to poor 1¾m winner Windward Ariom (by Pas de Seul): dam winner at up to 12.5f in France from family of Tennyson: fair performer: won maiden at Goodwood in May and claimers at Leicester and Yarmouth (failed to settle, didn't run to best) in the autumn: should prove as effective at 1¼m as shorter: below form on very soft ground, yet to race on firm. *J. W. Hills* **72**

JADIDH 4 b.f. Touching Wood (USA) 127 – Petrol 73 (Troy 137) [1991 14.1m2 1992 a12g] leggy, plain filly: rated 64 in July at 3 yrs for A. Stewart: blinkered, well beaten in maiden at Southwell in March, 1992: dead-heated in handicap hurdle (22f) in October. *Mrs J. C. Dawe* **–**

JADIRAH (USA) 2 b.f. (Apr 2) Deputy Minister (CAN) – Sharmila (FR) (Blakeney 126) [1992 6g5 7d] IR 120,000Y: lengthy, attractive filly: has scope: good walker: third foal: half-sister to 3-y-o 11.9f winner Severine (by Trempolino): dam once-raced half-sister to Petoski: worthwhile form only in maiden at Catterick final start: will be better suited by middle distances. *J. L. Dunlop* **53** p

JAEGER (USA) 5 ch.h. Storm Bird (CAN) 134 – Asoka (USA) (Youth (USA) 135) [1991 8d6 8.5f2 10m6 10m6 10d5 8m6 1992 9.7v6 12g] tall horse: rated 69 at 4 yrs for J. Gosden: no form in the spring at 5 yrs: stays 1m: acts on good to firm ground: ran moderately in blinkers once. *J. R. Jenkins* **–**

JAFETICA 2 gr.f. (May 5) Kalaglow 132 – Rashah 67 (Blakeney 126) [1992 6.1m 6g5 7f6 5g 7s] leggy, unfurnished filly: third foal: half-sister to 3-y-o Christian Warrior (by Primo Dominie): dam probably stayed 1½m: poor maiden: should stay beyond 6f. *D. R. Laing* **42**

JAFFA LINE 4 b.f. High Line 125 – Jacquinta 95 (Habitat 134) [1991 10g2 10.5m5 12m4 12g 12m 14.6m6 1992 10g 13.9m6 16.4m6 12f] useful filly: keen walker: has powerful, round action: stiffish tasks, not discredited though towards rear in Gordon Richards Stakes at Sandown and Yorkshire Cup: always behind in Henry II Stakes at Sandown (slipped entering straight) and Bessborough Handicap at Royal Ascot afterwards: probably stays 1¾m: acts on good to firm and dead ground, yet to race on soft. *D. R. C. Elsworth* **–**

JAGGED EDGE 5 ch.g. Sharpo 132 – Tura (Northfields (USA)) [1991 7d2 6d4 6g 7.1m 7.1d 6g3 6g5 6m 7g 7g3 1992 8m4 9.9g] sturdy gelding: inconsistent handicapper, not seen out after June; only win came 21 starts ago, at 2 yrs: stays 1m: acts on firm and dead ground: has flashed tail: twice below form when blinkered. *R. J. Holder* **43**

JAHAFIL 4 b.c. Rainbow Quest (USA) 134 – River Spey 96 (Mill Reef (USA) 141) [1991 10g3 10g4 12g 11.9g6 12f2 14g* 14.6m 1992 12f* 12.1g2 12m2 12g* 13.4g* 14s] big, rangy, attractive colt: good mover: underwent wind operation in close season and developed into a smart performer after reappearing in June: won listed races at **114**

Fred Archer Stakes, Newmarket—Jahafil makes all and wins going away

Newmarket (by 3 lengths from Shambo) and Chester (by 2½ lengths from Surrealist) and, in between, a Group 3 event at the Curragh by 6 lengths: well-beaten last of 9 in Irish St Leger in September: stays 1¾m: acts on firm ground: usually wears tongue strap and crossed noseband (also blinkered once) at 3 yrs: often sweats: sold 52,000 gns Newmarket December Sales. *Major W. R. Hern*

JAHANGIR (IRE)   3 ch.g. Ballad Rock 122 – Marsh Benham (Dragonara Palace   **84** (USA) 115) [1991 NR 1992 10g 8.1g⁴ 7f² 7m⁴ 8g* 8d* 8m 8s 7d 6d 7v⁵] IR 8,500F, 21,000Y: leggy, workmanlike gelding: half-brother to 3 winners here and abroad by Auction Ring: dam unraced half-sister to smart 1982 Irish 2-y-o sprinter Virginia Deer: fairly useful performer: won maiden at Kempton and handicap at Goodwood in August: below form in handicaps last 3 starts, in blinkers penultimate one: stays 1m: best efforts on an easy surface: has been gelded. *B. Hanbury*

JAIRZINHO (USA)   3 b.c. Robellino 127 – B F'S Sailingal (USA) (Sail   – On-Sail On) [1991 6g⁵ 6m³ 7f* 7m² 8d* 10v² 1992 8d 10g⁵ 7m⁵ 7m 12d⁵] angular, useful-looking colt: useful as 2-y-o: ran poorly in handicaps (including in blinkers twice) in 1992 and not seen after July: suited by 1¼m: probably acts on any going: trained until after fourth start by R. Hannon. *M. R. Channon*

JALCANTO   2 ch.g. (Mar 10) Jalmood (USA) 126 – Bella Canto 82 (Crooner 119)   **64** p [1992 7m³ 8d⁵ 8m] 7,000Y: angular, workmanlike gelding: has scope: half-brother to several winners, including sprinters Erwin Bach (by Tina's Pet) and Dibbinsdale Lass (by Amber Rama): dam won over 1m and 1¼m: modest form in maidens first 2 starts: never placed to challenge under very considerate ride final one: will stay 1¼m: definitely capable of better. *Mrs M. Reveley*

JALDI (IRE)   4 b.f. Nordico (USA) – Havara 82 (African Sky 124) [1991 5f 5g 5.8f   **75** 1992 6s 7g 7.1m* 7m 7.1m* 7f* 7.1f² 7s⁴ 7d 7m²] angular filly: generally progressive handicapper: won at Chepstow (for 7-lb claimer), Sandown and Newmarket in early-summer: ran particularly well in a competitive event at Newmarket (beat everything bar the fast-improving Hob Green) final start: stays 7f: has form on any going, very best efforts on top-of-the-ground: effective blinkered or not, ridden up with pace or held up. *J. Sutcliffe*

JALIB (IRE)   2 b.c. (Jan 27) Lomond (USA) 128 – Crown Godiva 83 (Godswalk   **57** p (USA) 130) [1992 6g⁴] 30,000Y: lengthy colt: fourth foal: brother to French 3-y-o Lacustrine and closely related to 7f and 1m winner Abdicate (by Be My Guest) and Irish 7f winner Cambrina (by El Gran Senor), successful at around 1m in 1992 in USA: dam 1m winner, is half-sister to What A Guest and Dee Stakes winner Infantry: 20/1 and very green, 8 lengths fourth of 9 to Southern Memories in maiden at Doncaster in November, soon pushed along after slow start, late progress: will improve. *C. J. Benstead*

JALLAAF (USA)   2 b.c. (Mar 10) Woodman (USA) 126 – Tenatell (USA) (Clev Er   **76** Tell (USA)) [1992 6f³ 6g³ 6g* 6g² 7g⁶ 7.3s] $260,000Y: tall colt: second reported foal: dam won at 6f: fair performer: won maiden at Brighton in August: should be at least as effective at 7f as 6f: possibly unsuited by soft ground: sent to Dubai. *L. M. Cumani*

JALMUSIQUE   6 ch.g. Jalmood (USA) 126 – Rose Music 86 (Luthier 126) [1991   **92** 8m* 10.2m³ 8m4 8.1m* 8m* 10f² 8.1g⁴ 8f* 8m 1992 10s 8s 8g⁶ 7m² 8m 7.9m 7m] strong, good-bodied gelding: carries condition: has a long stride: had a fine season in 1991: easily best run in 1992 when beaten a head by Sharpalto at Newcastle in May: well beaten last 2 starts: effective from 7f to 1¼m: well suited by top-of-the-ground: below form when visored once: sometimes bandaged behind: usually races up with pace. *M. H. Easterby*

JALORE   3 gr.g. Jalmood (USA) 126 – Lorelene (FR) 97 (Lorenzaccio 130) [1991   **40** NR 1992 6g 6d⁶ 9.2m⁶ 8g 10g 10.8s³ 10d⁴ a14g³ a14g⁵ a14g⁵ a14g] 10,000F, 4,400   a46 2-y-o: lengthy, angular gelding: has a round action: half-brother to several winners, including fairly useful 1m winner Ladrone (by High Top) and 4-y-o 1¼m winner Laburnum (by Glint of Gold): dam won 4 times from 1¼m to 1½m and was second in Ebor: poor form: trained first 3 starts by P. Blockley: suited by 1¾m and may well stay further: acts on soft ground and fibresand. *R. Hollinshead*

JAMAICA BRIDGE   2 b.g. (May 15) Doulab (USA) 115 – Mill Hill (USA) (Riva   **55** p Ridge (USA)) [1992 a7g³] 3,500Y: seventh living foal: half-brother to several winners, including fair miler Farm Street (by Henbit) and winners in Italy by Petoski and Bellypha: dam, placed at up to 9f in France, is half-sister to smart sprinter Peterhof out of half-sister to Mill Reef: third of 6 finishers in maiden at Southwell in November, prominent from start then one pace final furlong when third of 6 finishers: should do better. *J. G. FitzGerald*

JAMAIS BLEU 3 ch.g. Never So Bold 135 – Ahnoora Blue (Ahonoora 122) [1991 –
6m 6g 7m 6s 1992 10.2f] smallish gelding: seems of little account. *T. J. Naughton*

JAMEEL DANCER 3 b.c. Shareef Dancer (USA) 135 – Jameelapi (USA) 94 **58**
(Blushing Groom (FR) 131) [1991 NR 1992 9.7g⁵ 10.1d⁴ 10.2d 7s] fourth foal:
half-brother to 11.6f winner Magical Veil (by Majestic Light) and winning Irish
middle-distance stayer Jameel Ridge (by Cox's Ridge): dam 2-y-o 6f winner: modest
maiden: best effort on debut: seemed to take no interest final start. *M. R. Stoute*

JAMES IS SPECIAL (IRE) 4 b.c. Lyphard's Special (USA) 122 – High –
Explosive (Mount Hagen (FR) 127) [1991 10g 12.5m² 12g* 12d³ 14s³ 12d* 12g³
12.1s³ 13.3g⁵ 1992 12g 11.8d 11.8s a12g] tall, leggy colt: carries condition: poor
mover: rated 66 at 3 yrs: no form in 1992: stays 1¾m: acts on soft ground. *H. J.
Collingridge*

JANAAT 3 b.f. Kris 135 – Triple First 117 (High Top 131) [1991 NR 1992 10.5g³ **74**
12d* 11.9d⁴ 11.4g] 280,000Y: sturdy filly: half-sister to several winners, including
smart middle-distance fillies Third Watch (by Slip Anchor), Three Tails (by
Blakeney), and Maysoon (by Shergar), last-named also placed in 1000 Guineas: dam
won from 5f to 1¼m: fair performer: won maiden at Salisbury in August: good fourth
in £15,100 handicap at York, ran poorly at Sandown 13 days later: will be suited by
1¾m: yet to race on top-of-the-ground. *A. A. Scott*

JANE'S AFFAIR 4 b.f. Alleging (USA) 120 – Blue Jane 81 (Blue Cashmere 129) –
[1991 NR 1992 12m] plain filly: fifth foal: half-sister to one-time useful sprinter Ever
Sharp (by Sharpo): dam 6f winner: pulled up after 3f in Beverley maiden in May. *R.
Thompson*

JANE'S BRAVE BOY 10 b.g. Brave Shot – Jane Merryn (Above Suspicion 127) –
[1991 7f 6f 6g 1992 8.1m 7.1d 8.3s⁵ 7s 6s⁵ 5v] workmanlike gelding: no longer of
much account. *T. Craig*

JANESWOOD (IRE) 4 b.f. Henbit (USA) 130 – Stipa (Silver Shark 129) [1991 –
12.3f⁶ 12f⁶ 12f⁴ 1992 12s⁶ 12m⁶ 12m⁶ 15.1d⁶] sparely-made, angular filly: seems of
little account. *J. Parkes*

JANISKI 9 b.g. Niniski (USA) 125 – Seasurf 106 (Seaepic (USA) 100) [1991 14.8d² **53**
16.4m⁴ 14.9m³ 14m* 16.1m³ 14m 1992 14.9d 17.2s 13.1f⁵ 14.1d 16g* 16d⁶] strong
gelding: has a quick action: modest handicapper: won at Lingfield in September:
stays 2m: acts on firm and dead ground: has run well in blinkers, usually visored: a
difficult ride. *Mrs Barbara Waring*

JAPE (USA) 3 b.c. Alleged (USA) 138 – Northern Blossom (CAN) (Snow Knight **110**
125) [1991 7g² 8g² 10v* 1992 10g⁶ 12.3g² 12g 14.5g* 12g⁵] lengthy, good-quartered
colt: good walker: useful performer: staying-on ¾-length second of 5 to Twist And
Turn in Chester Vase in May: subsequently contested pattern events abroad, easily
best effort when winning St Leger Italiano at Turin in July by 3½ lengths from
Silvernesian: stays 14.5f: acts on heavy going, yet to race on top-of-the-ground. *P. F.
I. Cole*

JARABOSKY 2 ch.g. (Apr 20) Doc Marten 104 – Cutler Heights 62 (Galivanter –
131) [1992 5d⁵ 5m 7f 6.9h⁶] close-coupled gelding: moderate mover: fourth live foal:
half-brother to 9f seller winner Bantel Bowler (by Beverley Boy): dam, winning
plater, stayed 1¾m: well beaten in maiden and sellers, not seen out after June. *M.
W. Ellerby*

JARENA (IRE) 2 b.f. (Mar 17) Jareer (USA) 115 – Coronea (High Line 125) [1992 **68**
5f 5.1h⁵ 5.2s³ 5g* 6m³ 5g] good-topped filly: third reported foal: dam, maiden
stayed 2m, is half-sister to smart middle-distance performer Sabre Dance: fair
performer: won maiden at Warwick in July: easily better effort in nurseries
following month when creditable third of 4 at Kempton: bred to be suited by middle
distances: acts on good to firm and soft ground. *G. Lewis*

JAROMIC 3 b.g. Tina's Pet 121 – Jose Collins 91 (Singing Bede 122) [1991 5m 5m **46** §
6m a5g³ a6g² a5g 1992 a7g a6g a6g⁴ 6m 5m⁴ 5m 5g³ 5.3f 5d 5.3g⁵ 8s] lengthy,
good-bodied gelding: moderate mover: inconsistent maiden: stays 6f: acts on good
to firm ground: no improvement in blinkers: often unruly at stalls: sold 800 gns
Newmarket Autumn Sales: one to be wary of. *P. F. Tulk*

JARRAS 7 b.g. Touching Wood (USA) 127 – Hilary's Hut (Busted 134) [1991 NR **41**
1992 14.1d 14.6g a12g 9d⁶ 10.2f² 10.2g 12m³ a12g⁶ 10.8g] leggy, good-topped gelding:
moderate mover: inconsistent handicapper: seems effective from 1¼m to 1¾m:
best efforts in 1992 on top-of-the-ground: wears blinkers. *C. A. Smith*

JARRETTS WILSHEGAR 3 b.c. Tout Ensemble – Acton Turville 39 (Porto –
Bello 118) [1991 NR 1992 10.2g] sturdy colt: second foal: dam placed once at 6f at 3

yrs and of little account over hurdles: 6/1, tailed-off last of 11 in Chepstow maiden in July. *C. L. Popham*

J'ARRIVE   3 ch.f. Aragon 118 – Balatina 85 (Balidar 133) [1991 NR 1992 6m⁴ 7g   44
7g⁴ 8m⁵ 10s 10.1d⁴ a14g] rangy filly: has a round action: fifth foal: sister to 4-y-o 9.7f seller winner Aragon Court and half-sister to 3 winners, including 1m and 1¼m winner Latin Leep (by Castle Keep): dam sprinter: modest plater: probably stays 1¼m: retained 1,700 gns Ascot November Sales. *J. Pearce*

JARRWAH   4 ch.f. Niniski (USA) 125 – Valiancy 87 (Grundy 137) [1991 8.9g⁴   – §
10.2g 10g 1992 a16g] unfurnished filly: of little account. *J. L. Spearing*

JARZON DANCER   4 br.g. Lidhame 109 – Long Valley 71 (Ribero 126) [1991 7g   –
8m 10g⁴ 10g 8.1s 1992 11.6g 8.2d 8d 16d 12s⁶ 9g] leggy, rather sparely-made gelding: poor mover: seems to stay 1½m and act on soft ground: no improvement in blinkers once. *D. A. Wilson*

JASILU   2 ch.f. (Feb 25) Faustus (USA) 118 – Mosso 81 (Ercolano (USA) 118) [1992   –
a6g 7m⁵ 7.5m] 2,500Y: strong, plain filly: half-sister to 6-y-o 6f to 1m winner Mossy Rose (by King of Spain): dam 2-y-o 5.8f and 6f winner: well beaten in sellers and a maiden auction. *M. W. Easterby*

JASMIN ISLE   2 b.f. (Feb 17) Aragon 118 – Floral 82 (Floribunda 136) [1992 5g 5f   45
a5g⁴ 5.2f² 5.1d⁴ 6m² 6f⁵ 5.3f³ 5m⁶ 5.1d] 5,000Y: close-coupled filly: has a round action: sister to 3-y-o Sea Lord and half-sister to several winners, including 5f (at 2 yrs) to 11f winner Tyrnippy (by Tyrnavos): dam 2-y-o 7f winner: poor plater: better suited by 6f than 5f: acts on good to firm and dead ground: blinkered (finished last) penultimate start: has run creditably for 7-lb claimer: sold 1,050 gns Newmarket Autumn Sales. *Miss Gay Kelleway*

JASOORAH (IRE)   3 b.f. Sadler's Wells (USA) 132 – Fenney Mill 99 (Levmoss   98
133) [1991 8s* 1992 10d⁵ 12s² 11.9d* 12.3v* 12g] tall, useful-looking filly: reportedly fractured pedal bone early in year: progressed well in the autumn, easily winning minor events at York and Chester: well beaten in November Handicap at Doncaster: would have stayed 1¾m: acted on heavy ground: visits Rainbow Quest. *A. C. Stewart*

JATHAAB (IRE)   3 b.g. Ajdal (USA) 130 – Etoile de Nuit (Troy 137) [1991 NR   80
1992 8g⁶ 8.5g³ 8d⁵ 10m] workmanlike, rather angular gelding: first foal: dam twice-raced daughter of close relation to Grand Prix de Paris winner Tennyson: fairly useful form first 2 starts: well beaten afterwards and not seen out after July: should stay 1¼m: sold 4,000 gns Newmarket Autumn Sales. *M. R. Stoute*

JATO   3 b.g. Pharly (FR) 130 – Minsden's Image (Dancer's Image (USA)) [1991 NR   68
1992 9s⁴ 10g 8m⁴ 7m³ 7f] 13,000Y: small, sturdy gelding: fifth foal: half-brother to 1989 Irish 2-y-o 6f winner Janubi (by Chief Singer) and untrustworthy 1m seller winner Native Image (by Try My Best): dam, out of sister to Busted, stayed 2m: fair maiden, not seen after June: stays 9f: acts on good to firm and soft ground: blinkered last 2 starts, running well first occasion: has been gelded. *W. J. Haggas*

JAWAHER (IRE)   3 b.f. Dancing Brave (USA) 140 – High Tern 93 (High Line   60
125) [1991 NR 1992 8g³ 8g² 9.9m² 12s⁴ 14.1g] lengthy, quite attractive filly: has high knee action: third foal: half-sister to 5-y-o 1m to 10.2f winner Sooty Tern (by Wassl): dam, 14.7f and 2m winner, is half-sister to high-class middle-distance stayer High Hawk and to dam of Infamy: modest maiden: stayed 1½m: acted on good to firm and soft ground: visits Old Vic. *R. J. R. Williams*

JAWANI (IRE)   4 b.g. Last Tycoon 131 – Fabled Lady (Bold Lad (IRE) 133) [1991   52
8.2d⁶ 10g 10m 12.3m a16g⁴ a12g³ 1992 a14g⁵ a13g³ a16g* a13g³ a16g² 17.1m* 16.1m
18g] big, rather leggy gelding: modest handicapper: won at Lingfield in January and Pontefract (given enterprising ride) in May: ran moderately afterwards, not seen out after June: stays well: acts on good to firm ground and all-weather surfaces: effective visored or not. *Dr J. D. Scargill*

JAYBEE-JAY   2 b.c. (Mar 18) Reesh 117 – Absurd 60 (Absalom 128) [1992 5g 6m
6m 7m⁵ 7d] leggy colt: third foal: dam 9f winner: well beaten in varied company, including selling: not seen out after July. *M. J. Haynes*

JAZILAH (FR)   4 br.g. Persian Bold 123 – Muznah 92 (Royal And Regal (USA))   69
[1991 8m* 8.9g 9d 7m 7.1m 1992 7g 7s 10.3g 10.1f* 10f* 9.9d² 9m³] rather leggy, good-topped gelding: has round action: trained first 3 starts by M. Naughton: revitalised for present stable, making virtually all at Newcastle (apprentices) and Pontefract in June: ideally suited by 1¼m: acts on firm and dead ground: blinkered (pulled hard) once at 3 yrs: tends to sweat and get on toes: not seen out after July. *Mrs M. Reveley*

JAZITINA 2 ch.f. (Apr 18) Then Again 126 – Tina Rosa (Bustino 136) [1992 5v⁶] –
1,100Y: close-coupled filly: third foal: half-sister to 3-y-o Nomadic Rose (by Nomination): dam poor half-sister to very smart 7f to 1½m winner Saros: never a factor in
7-runner maiden at Folkestone in March: sold 525 gns Ascot June Sales. *M. J.
Haynes*

JAZZ 3 gr.f. Sharrood (USA) 124 – Rainbow's End 83 (My Swallow 134) [1991 7m² **69**
7f² 7m² 1992 6g 10.2d⁵ 10g² 10s] sturdy, quite good-topped filly: fair maiden: easily
best effort as 3-y-o at 1¼m on good ground. *L. M. Cumani*

JDAAYEL 3 b.f. Ajdal (USA) 130 – Vaguely 92 (Bold Lad (IRE) 133) [1991 NR 1992 **101**
7d* 8.1g* 8d* 8g² 8g² 10.5v] sturdy filly: good walker: half-sister to several
winners, notably top-class winner at up to 10.5f Shady Heights (by Shirley Heights)
and useful 1m and 1¼m winner Dimmer (by Kalaglow): dam 1m and 1¼m winner:
useful performer: won maiden at Epsom in August and handicaps at Sandown and
Ascot (£10,000 contest) in September: narrowly-beaten second to Well Beyond in
slowly-run listed race at Ascot and £29,500 handicap at Newmarket in October: led
briefly over 2f out when behind in Group 3 event at Saint-Cloud following month:
stayed 1m: refused to enter stalls on intended debut (may well have been in season):
visits Elmaamul. *A. C. Stewart*

JEETHGAYA (USA) 4 ch.f. Critique (USA) 126 – Born Anew (USA) (Avatar –
(USA)) [1991 12m⁵ 10d a11g 10m³ 9.7f² a12g⁴ 1992 a7g] workmanlike filly: rated 61
at 3 yrs for A. Hide: soundly beaten at Lingfield in February, 1992: may prove suited
by 1¼m: acts on firm going. *B. Smart*

JEFFERSON DAVIS (IRE) 3 b.c. The Noble Player (USA) 126 – Bay Sup- **70**
reme (Martinmas 128) [1991 6m 5m⁵ 6s* a7g³ 1992 a7g* a6g³ 7g³ 7s³ 6.9f* 9f³ 8m
6.9g⁴ 8s] close-coupled, quite good-topped colt: fair handicapper: won at Lingfield
in January for W. Pearce and (after 3-month break) Carlisle claimer in July: below
form last 3 starts: stays 9f: acts on any going, including all-weather surfaces: has run
well for an apprentice: sold 6,800 gns Newmarket Autumn Sales. *B. Beasley*

JELLYROLL BLUES 3 b.f. Tremblant 112 – Daring Ditty (Daring March 116) –
[1991 5m⁶ 6f 8m 1992 7m 11d 6s] sturdy, close-coupled filly: seems of little account.
Mrs M. Reveley

JENDORCET 2 b.f. (Feb 10) Grey Ghost 98 – Jendor 82 (Condorcet (FR)) [1992 **57**
8.5m⁵ 8.1d⁶ 7d] leggy filly: second reported foal: dam 5f (at 2 yrs) and 1m winner,
stayed 1½m: modest maiden: easily best effort on good to firm ground. *T. Fairhurst*

JEREMIAHS BOY 2 gr.g. (May 11) Sulaafah (USA) 119 – Main Chance 63 **54**
(Midsummer Night II 117) [1992 5.1d* 7m] rangy, rather unfurnished gelding: poor
mover: fifth live foal: half-brother to 1984 2-y-o winner Main Star (by Comedy
Star): dam won twice at 11f: 33/1, narrowly won 13-runner maiden at Bath in April:
bit backward, tailed off (something clearly amiss) in apprentice nursery at Lingfield
in August: should stay 1m. *R. J. Hodges*

JERSEY BOB (IRE) 2 ch.c. (Mar 18) Magical Wonder (USA) 125 – Regal **35**
Rhapsody (Owen Dudley 121) [1992 5d 5m 6d a6g 6f 7g⁶] 10,500F, 2,100 2-y-o:
workmanlike colt: second reported foal: dam ran once at 3 yrs in Ireland: poor form
in varied company, including selling: not seen out after July. *J. S. Wainwright*

JERVIA 2 ch.f. (Feb 12) Affirmed (USA) – Jerwah (USA) 94 (Nureyev (USA) 131) **85**
[1992 5m* 5f* 6f⁶ 7g² 8d⁶ 6d⁴ 7d⁴] rather sparely-made filly: moderate walker: first
foal: dam, 7f and 1m winner, is out of half-sister to high-class sprinter Faliraki:
progressed into fairly useful performer: won maiden at Haydock in May and £7,050
event at Beverley in June: good fourth of 21 in Doncaster nursery final outing:
should stay 1m. *J. W. Watts*

JESS REBEC 4 br.f. Kala Shikari 125 – Laleston 73 (Junius (USA) 124) [1991 5m⁴ **54**
5g⁵ 5d 5f⁴ 6.1s 5.7m 5.3f² a5g⁶ 6f⁴ 5.3g³ 5m² 5d 5.1d 6m 1992 5m* 5g³ 5g 5g 5.1s]
smallish, workmanlike filly: moderate mover: modest handicapper: won (for first
time) Warwick handicap in July: well beaten last 3 starts: stays 6f: acts on firm
ground, seemingly not on a soft surface: blinkered (ran poorly) once at 3 yrs. *L. G.
Cottrell*

JESTER'S GEM 3 ch.f. Jester 119 – Tresanna (Treboro (USA) 114) [1991 5g 6m –
7m 7m 8.9m 7m 8m 1992 7g 7g 8f 9.9d⁵] quite good-topped filly: of little account. *B.
W. Murray*

JEST ROSIE 2 b.f. (Apr 14) Jester 119 – Sindur (Rolfe (USA) 77) [1992 6s 7s] –
close-coupled filly: first foal: dam poor on flat and over jumps: soundly beaten in
maidens at Lingfield in October, leading to halfway over 7f. *M. D. I. Usher*

JEUNE 3 ch.c. Kalaglow 132 – Youthful (FR) (Green Dancer (USA) 132) **121**
[1991 6m* 6f² 7d³ 7.3g⁴ 1992 8d³ 8g* 10g³ 10m* 12m² 12g 11.1g* 10d²]

Jeune won two of the spring classic trials, causing a stir because he didn't hold a classic entry. Ironically, the first of those races, the Tetley Bitter Classic Trial at Thirsk which Jeune won by a head, was not reckoned to be a significant trial at the time—the presence of Zaahi in second and My Memoirs in fourth makes good reading now, though—but the second was. The A. R. Dennis Bookmakers Predominate Stakes at Goodwood had Derby hopefuls Young Freeman, Powerful Edge, Viardot, Profusion and Ninja Dancer in the field; Rokeby, who was being aimed at the Belmont Stakes; Beldi, due to contest the Italian Derby; and the promising Cecil-trained Hatta's Mill. Attention was fixed chiefly on the impressive Brighton winner Young Freeman who started 11/8 favourite and was a 12/1-shot for Epsom. That 12/1 was shortly made to look a very mean price indeed with Young Freeman a never-dangerous fourth and Jeune all on his own up front (officially by five lengths) having led virtually on the bridle approaching the two-furlong marker then run right away from the distance.

After that, Jeune was kept to pattern races. Twice, in the King Edward VII Stakes at Royal Ascot and the Select Stakes at Goodwood, he was a strong-finishing second, widely considered to be unlucky. Unlucky to a degree is our assessment because the bad luck he encountered, a poor run up the rails behind Beyton at Royal Ascot and too much ground to make up on the enterprisingly-ridden Knifebox at Goodwood, were largely a result of the restraint exercised by his jockeys in response to Jeune's unwillingness to settle. That tendency further prejudiced his already rather slim chance in the King George VI and Queen Elizabeth Diamond Stakes—he weakened right out of it having gone third on the turn—but Jeune would have been unlucky to have ended the season without a pattern win at all. When it came, the pre-race attention was, as in the Predominate Stakes, directed elsewhere. The Bonus-Print September Stakes at Kempton had an obvious form pick in the Juddmonte International third Seattle Rhyme and, if the betting were to be believed, this was a straightforward task for the 11/8-on shot en route to the Arc de Triomphe. Jeune, at 6/1, was hard to separate in the betting from Red Bishop and Corrupt, with Ile de Chypre completing the field at 16/1. This time it wasn't Jeune's jockey who came under the spotlight. It was Seattle Rhyme who was held up in last, with Jeune, who settled reasonably well despite a very pedestrian early pace, just in front of him. Entering the straight, Jeune was three lengths off the pace, but he'd swept into the lead a furlong later and soon went clear, stretching out in superb style; Seattle Rhyme's effort to keep tabs on him was a laboured one, Red Bishop holding him off for second, and Jeune was again in glorious isolation, the final winning margin three and a half lengths.

Jeune is Youthful's third foal. The first, Dorset Duke (by Beldale Flutter), put up a rather less meritorious performance in the King Edward VII Stakes when a headstrong nature well and truly got the better of him and he finished tailed off. He failed to win that season but did so twice over six

BonusPrint September Stakes, Kempton—
no danger to Jeune from Red Bishop, Seattle Rhyme (blaze) or Corrupt

Sir Robin McAlpine's "Jeune"

		Kalamoun (gr 1970)	Zeddaan
Jeune (ch.c. 1989)	Kalaglow (gr 1978)		Khairunissa
		Rossiter (ch 1970)	Pall Mall
			Sonia
	Youthful (FR) (b 1980)	Green Dancer (b 1972)	Nijinsky
			Green Valley
		First Bloom (b 1969)	Primera
			Flower Dance

furlongs at two years and has since won four handicaps at either seven furlongs or a mile, three of them on the Lingfield equitrack. The two-year-old Beneficial (by Top Ville) won two of his three starts in the latest season, and is followed by fillies by Rainbow Quest and Unfuwain. The racing records of those further back in this family come mainly from France. The second dam First Bloom spreadeagled the opposition on her two appearances as a two-year-old, the second of them in the Prix Thomas Bryon, in such good style in fact that she was rated the best of her age and sex in Europe. She wasn't so good the following season, though she won two races at around nine furlongs, but had pattern/graded successes with First Prayer and Water Lily among her seven winners at stud. Water Lily is the dam of the 1990 Poule d'Essai des Pouliches third Gharam. Jeune's dam Youthful ran at three and four years, thirteen times in all, winning a mile-and-a-half maiden at Longchamp. Like nearly all Kalaglow's best-known progeny, Jeune stays a mile and a half. That good final run of the season came on dead ground, and his best effort at two years (when second in the Mill Reef Stakes) was on firm. A tall, leggy, light-framed colt, Jeune is a fine mover. *G. Wragg*

JEWEL THIEF 2 b.g. (Apr 17) Green Ruby (USA) 104 – Miss Display 47 (Touch **49**
Paper 113) [1992 6g 7s 6s] 2,000Y: compact gelding: second foal: brother to 3-y-o
5f winner Ned's Bonanza: dam, maiden, best at 5f: backward, plating-class form,
always behind, in maidens at Newbury and Salisbury in the autumn. *G. B. Balding*

JEZEBEL MONROE (USA) 3 b.f. Lyphard (USA) 132 – Allicance (USA) 113 **98**
(Alleged (USA) 138) [1991 6g5 1992 10s* 10m2 10m3 11.9g] angular, sparely-made
filly: useful performer: won maiden at Salisbury in April: placed in listed races at
Newbury before running moderately in Lancashire Oaks at Haydock in July: should
stay 1½m: won on soft but best efforts on good to firm ground. *R. Charlton*

JIGGERAK 3 b.f. Belfort (FR) 89 – Errol Emerald 60 (Dom Racine (FR) 121) –
[1991 5s* 6m4 6.1d6 8.3s a6g 1992 7d 8.9v5 5s6 a5g] leggy, workmanlike filly: rated
61 at 2 yrs: no worthwhile form, visored first 3 occasions, in the spring at 3 yrs:
probably needs further than 5f. *S. G. Norton*

JIGSAW BOY 3 ch.c. Homeboy 114 – Chiparia 82 (Song 132) [1991 6g6 6f* 1992 **78**
5.7s3 7m 6m6 6m2 6m6 6g 5.1s* 5.1d 5s*] good-topped colt: fairly useful performer:
best efforts, leading close home, to win handicaps at Chepstow (for R. Holder) and
Leicester in the autumn: effective at 5f on soft ground and should stay 7f: acts on
any going. *P. G. Murphy*

JIHAAD (USA) 2 b.c. (Apr 15) Chief's Crown (USA) – Desirable 119 (Lord Gayle **48**
(USA) 124) [1992 7g 8d 8.1d5] compact, good-bodied colt: third living foal:
half-brother to 1991 2-y-o 7f winner Badie (by Blushing Groom), who became
unsatisfactory in 1992, and to high-class filly Shadayid (by Shadeed): dam 2-y-o 6f
winner placed in 1000 Guineas and at 1¼m, is sister to Nashamaa and half-sister to
Park Appeal and Alydaress: sire top class at 2 and 3 yrs, best at 1¼m: plating-class
form in a minor event and maidens in the autumn. *J. L. Dunlop*

JIM CANTLE 2 ch.c. (Mar 9) Forzando 122 – Mummy's Chick 77 (Mummy's Pet –
125) [1992 7g] leggy, workmanlike colt: third foal: dam 2-y-o 5f winner: 33/1 and
very green, always towards rear after slow start in 16-runner seller at Thirsk in
August: showed high knee action to post. *M. W. Easterby*

JIMLIL 4 b.f. Nicholas Bill 125 – Ozra 63 (Red Alert 127) [1991 8g 9d2 9m 10d4 **79**
10v3 10m2 12f3 8m4 10g4 10m4 11g 1992 8g 12.3v 8.1d* 8.5g3 10m 8.3m 10g 12.1d4]
workmanlike filly: has a round action: fair but inconsistent handicapper nowadays:
effective from a stiff 1m to 1¼m: acts on good to firm and heavy going. *B. Palling*

JIMMY PIP 5 b.g. Creetown 123 – Beth of Houndhill (Filiberto (USA) 123) [1991 –
a8g 7.1m 7m 5s 1992 a11g] leggy gelding: seems temperamental and of little account.
B. A. McMahon

JIM'S WISH (IRE) 4 b.c. Heraldiste (USA) 121 – Fete Champetre 80 (Welsh –
Pageant 132) [1991 8.1s 8.1d 1992 8s 7.1g] workmanlike colt: fair winner (suited by
1m, best on sound surface) at 2 yrs: no worthwhile form on flat since: blinkered on
reappearance. *T. A. K. Cuthbert*

JINGA 7 b.g. Castle Keep 121 – Eldoret 100 (High Top 131) [1991 15.5f5 14d*
16.2g5 14m4 12d4 16.2d* 14s2 14m5 14s3 16m6 1992 14g] lengthy, quite attractive
gelding: rated 75 at 6 yrs: won novice hurdle in autumn 1991: shaped as if retaining
ability only start on flat as 7-y-o (September): stays well: acts on good to firm and
heavy going: raced too freely when blinkered once: has run in snatches. *Lady
Herries*

JINSKY'S JEWEL 4 b.g. Myjinski (USA) – Song of Pride (Goldhills Pride 105) –
[1991 a11g 7m 6.1m 1992 5g 7.1s 6s 10.3g] small, sparely-made gelding: little sign of
ability. *R. Thompson*

JINXY JACK 8 b.g. Random Shot 116 – True Or False (Varano) [1991 NR 1992 18g –
17.5d6] big, rangy gelding: fairly useful performer (rated 94) as a 3-y-o: campaigned
nowadays almost exclusively over jumps and is a fairly useful chaser and smart
hurdler: showed signs he retains ability on the flat in handicaps at Doncaster in the
spring and Ayr in late-summer: stays 2¼m: yet to race on firm ground, probably
acts on any other. *G. Richards*

JITTERBUGGING 3 b.c. Try My Best (USA) 130 – Dancing Sally 100 (Sallust **99**
134) [1991 6d4 7s6 7.3g6 1992 8.1g2 8d4 8g3 8d3 8.8g* 7.5v5] compact, useful-
looking colt: fairly useful performer: in frame in minor event at Sandown and Premio
Parioli at Rome (5¾ lengths behind Alhijaz) for B. Hills first 2 starts: won listed
event at Grosseto, Italy, in August: well worth a try at 1¼m: acts on soft ground. *O.
Pessi, Italy*

JIVE MUSIC 6 b.m. Music Boy 124 – Swift To Conquer 87 (Solinus 130) [1991 **32**
a5g4 a6g 6d6 5d* 5g3 5f2 5f2 5m2 5h 5s5 5g2 5g4 5f 5m6 5m 5f 5g6 5m 5g 5m6 5s

1992 5d⁴ 5d 5f⁵ 5f 5m⁵ 5f a5g 5m³ 5m⁵ 5f 5m 5g] smallish, good-quartered mare: bad mover: inconsistent handicapper, winner of one out of 85 starts: best at 5f: acts on firm and dead going: often blinkered/visored. *N. Bycroft*

JIZYAH 2 b.f. (Apr 6) Green Desert (USA) 127 – Kawkeb (USA) 72 (Vaguely **61** Noble 140) [1992 8d³ 8.1d⁴] compact filly: fourth foal: half-sister to 9f winner Jurz (by Pennine Walk) and fairly useful 7.5f and 10.8f winner Annaf (by Topsider): dam 1¾m winner: in frame in maidens at Goodwood and Haydock (travelling well 2f out, quickly beaten) in the autumn: worth a try at 7f. *H. Thomson Jones*

JOBIE 2 b.c. (Mar 1) Precocious 126 – Lingering 96 (Kind of Hush 118) [1992 6g **70** p 5g*] first foal: dam 2-y-o 5f winner: won maiden at Sandown in September, by 1½ lengths from Ballet, missing break but confidently ridden nonetheless: will stay 6f: should improve further. *W. J. Haggas*

JOCKS JOKER 2 b.g. (May 1) Germont – Kaymay 76 (Maystreak 118) [1992 a6g **35** 5g⁴ 6s a6g³ a5g³ a6g⁵ a5g³] workmanlike gelding: half-brother to winning sprinter a62 Brave Melody (by Heroic Air): dam won at up to 1m: modest maiden: stays 6f: easily best efforts on fibresand. *Capt. J. Wilson*

JODIE BOBS 3 ch.f. Adonijah 126 – Lunaria (USA) (Twist The Axe (USA)) [1991 – 6g 6d 6m 7.5f 5f 1992 a8g] plain filly: of little account. *R. D. E. Woodhouse*

JODY'S GAMBLE 3 b.g. Scorpio (FR) 127 – Forgets Image 87 (Florescence – 120) [1991 NR 1992 8g] leggy gelding: eighth foal: half-brother to 3 winners, including 9f and 13f winner Excavator Lady (by Most Secret): dam, 1m winner, is half-sister to smart Millingdale Lily: pulled up lame in Leicester seller in July: has joined G. Moore. *K. R. Burke*

JOELLISE 2 b.f. (Apr 6) Glint of Gold 128 – Carolside 108 (Music Maestro 119) **35** [1992 7s 6d a5g a6g⁶] 12,500Y: lengthy, rather unfurnished filly: sixth foal: sister to useful but unsatisfactory 6f winner Sure Gold and half-sister to useful 8.5f and 9f winner Eton Lad (by Never So Bold) and 4-y-o 1m winner Little Rousillon (by Rousillon): dam 2-y-o 5f winner didn't progress: poor maiden: best effort in a nursery. *J. Balding*

JOE SUGDEN 8 b.g. Music Boy 124 – Sum Star 67 (Comedy Star (USA) 121) **59** [1991 5d⁵ 5m 6g 5f 6m 5g⁶ 5.7m 6g 5d⁴ 5.2f 5m 5.1m³ 5.2f⁴ 5d³ 5g⁴ 5d 6.1d 5d² a5g⁴ 1992 a6g⁴ 5g 5m⁶ 5g 5m⁶ 5m⁴ 5g³ 5d⁶ 5g 5.2m* 5s² 5s 5.1s⁴ a5g⁴ a6g a5g a6g⁶] tall gelding: moderate mover: sprint handicapper: first win in 40 starts at Yarmouth in September: acts on any going: below form when visored, has run well when blinkered: suitable for apprentice. *P. Howling*

JOHANNA THYME 5 b.m. Reesh 117 – Sea Thyme (Persian Bold 123) [1991 **37** a7g a6g⁶ 7f 5f 5m* 5d⁴ 5.9m* 6g 5.9f 6f 6m² 6s a5g 1992 5d 6m 5m⁴ 6.1m 6g⁴ a5g 6m⁶ a7g] leggy, lengthy mare: poor mover: inconsistent handicapper: effective at 5f and 6f: acts on good to firm and dead ground: sold 440 gns Doncaster November Sales. *R. Bastiman*

JOHANN QUATZ (FR) 3 b.c. Sadler's Wells (USA) 132 – Whakilyric (USA) 113 **115** (Miswaki (USA) 124) [1991 NR 1992 8s* 8g 10.5g* 10.5m* 12g⁴ 10m 10s 12m] robust, sturdy colt: first foal: dam 2-y-o 5.5f and 7f winner probably stayed 1m, not so good at 3 yrs: very useful performer: successful in newcomers race at Saint-Cloud then listed race and Prix Lupin (making all to beat Contested Bid a length) at Longchamp in the spring: 3 lengths fourth of 17 to Polytain in Prix du Jockey-Club Lancia at Chantilly: disappointing afterwards, blinkered on first occasion: effective

Prix Lupin, Longchamp—this French Derby trial goes to Johann Quatz from Contested Bid and Apple Tree (No. 2)

at 1¼m and 1½m: acts on good to firm ground, and has won on soft. *F. Boutin, France*

JOHN O'DREAMS   7 b.g. Indian King (USA) 128 – Mississipi Shuffle 78 (Steel   **45** Heart 128) [1991 6f 6g 6m 6m 1992 6d 5g 5.7g³ 6g 7d 5s⁴ 5.7d³ 6.1m⁶ 5s* 5.1s 6.1s a5g a6g⁶] good-topped gelding: poor walker: moderate mover: poor sprint handicapper nowadays: below par after winning at Warwick in October: acts on soft going, probably on good to firm: below form blinkered: effective with or without visor. *Mrs J. C. Dawe*

JOHN ROSE   3 b.c. Tina's Pet 121 – City Link Lass 92 (Double Jump 131) [1991 **102** 5d⁴ 5m* 6g⁶ 5m 7g² 8.1f³ 8d⁴ 1992 10g 10.3m⁴ 10.5m⁵ 12g 8m² 8g* 10f 8m³ 9m] tall colt: useful performer: won minor event at Brighton in August: good third to Inner City, easily better effort in Newmarket listed races last 2 outings: will prove suited by further than 1m (ran moderately in Derby Italiano over 1½m): acts on firm and dead ground: sweating and edgy last 2 starts: sold 42,000 gns Newmarket December Sales. *P. A. Kelleway*

JOHNS ACT (USA)   2 b.c. (Jan 31) Late Act (USA) – Deluxe Type (USA) (Singh   **79** (USA)) [1992 7m³ 7g³ 8.1d²] $11,000Y: good-topped colt: good mover: third reported foal: half-brother to a winner in USA by Red Ryder: dam winner 3 times at up to 7f at 4 yrs in USA: sire (by Stage Door Johnny) stayed 1½m: best effort in autumn maidens when second of 7 to Blue Blazer at Haydock: will be suited by middle distances: acts on good to firm and dead ground: can win a race. *D. Haydn Jones*

JOHN SHAW (USA)   4 b.c. L'Emigrant (USA) 129 – Ivory Wings (USA) (Sir   **54** Ivor 135) [1991 10ma11g* 10g²11.9g13.8m* 15.9da12g19g³11.9ga12g⁵12.2g 10g 12.3m 12d⁶ 11.9g² 17.9d 14.1d* 14.6s⁵ 12.1g* 15.1d] compact colt: inconsistent handicapper: won at Nottingham and Edinburgh (seller, retained 4,400 gns) in autumn: stays 1¾m: acts on good to firm and dead ground (fair effort on very soft) and on fibresand: sold out of W. Haggas' stable 4,000 gns Doncaster May Sales after third start, trained next 6 by J. Wainwright: has joined R. O'Leary. *C. Tinkler*

JOHNS JOY   7 b.g. Martin John – Saybya (Sallust 134) [1991 10g⁴ 10.8m⁵ 10g   – 10.1s* 8m* 9g⁶ 10g² 8d⁴ 10g⁶ 8g 10m 1992 8g 12v] angular gelding: has a round action: rated 77 at 6 yrs: below form in October, 1992: effective at 1m to 1¼m: probably acts on any going. *D. R. C. Elsworth*

JOHNSTON'S EXPRESS (IRE)   4 b. or br.c. Petorius 117 – Siberian   **64** Princess (Northfields (USA)) [1991 NR 1992 5v 9.2v 8v 7.1m⁴ 7g⁴ 7g³ 5.9f* 7f⁴ 6g 7s³ 6v⁶ a7g² a6g* a5g⁴ a7g* a7g*] strong, good-topped colt: carries condition: first foal: dam never ran: not seen out until 1992: mostly ran well in handicaps, awarded race at Carlisle in July and won 3 times at Southwell late in year: likely to prove best at 6f/7f: acts on firm and soft ground and particularly well on fibresand: has run well for amateur: genuine: may be capable of better still. *E. J. Alston*

JOIE DE PATINA   3 ch.f. Forzando 122 – Joie d'Or (FR) (Kashmir II 125) [1991   – NR 1992 6f 5s⁵ 6g 7.1s] sturdy filly: bad mover: seventh foal: half-sister to 7f/1m performers Joie de Rose and Gurteen Boy (both by Tickled Pink): dam of little account: no sign of ability in maidens: unseated rider (wandered badly and stumbled) on debut. *S. G. Norton*

JOIN THE CLAN   3 ch.f. Clantime 101 – Joint Reward (Netherkelly 112) [1991   **40** NR 1992 8g⁵ 5g⁵ 6.1s 6.1g] 1,400Y: angular filly: second foal: dam showed some ability over jumps: poor maiden: stays 6f. *Mrs N. Macauley*

JOKERS PATCH   5 ch.g. Hotfoot 126 – Rhythmical 69 (Swing Easy (USA) 126)   **50** [1991 12f* 10.8m 12.5d* 16.9m⁵ 14.6g⁴ 12m⁶ 12f 1992 16m 14.1g 16g³ a16g] workmanlike gelding: has a quick action: form as 5-y-o only when never-dangerous third in Lingfield seller: tailed-off last in handicap there 10 weeks later: stays 2m: acts on firm and dead ground: has carried head high and not easiest of rides. *Billy Williams*

JOKIST   9 ro.g. Orchestra 118 – What A Picture 80 (My Swanee 122) [1991 6g 7m³   **64** § 7g* 7m³ 7v 7m* 7f² 7f 7.3m 7g⁶ 7.1m² 7g 1992 7m⁴ 8.5g 8.2m 8m³ a7g 7g⁶ 8g 7s 7s 7d⁶] workmanlike gelding: unreliable handicapper: effective at 6f to 1m: acts on firm and dead ground: below form blinkered. *W. Jarvis*

JOLIS ABSENT   2 b.f. (Mar 21) Primo Dominie 121 – Jolimo 92 (Fortissimo 111)   – [1992 7f 7d 6d 6s] robust filly: half-sister to several winners, including Osric (by Radetzky), successful at 1½m and also a very useful hurdler, and (at 11f) Joli's Girl (by Mansingh): dam won from 1½m to 2¼m: well beaten in maidens and a nursery. *M. J. Ryan*

JOLI'S GREAT 4 ch.f. Vaigly Great 127 – Jolimo 92 (Fortissimo 111) [1991 10d⁴ **55**
7.5g³ 9d² 8g⁴ 8.2m⁴ 9m 10.1f⁶ 8m⁵ 8d 10m 1992 10d³ 11.9m 10d² 11.1s* 10d³ 9g
9.7g³ 10.1d³ 9.7v a12g⁵ a10g] small filly: poor handicapper: won Hamilton maiden
claimer in May: below form last 3 starts: should prove suited by return to further
than 1¼m: has form on good to firm ground, but goes well with give: below form
when visored and blinkered once. *M. J. Ryan*

JOLIZAL 4 ch.f. Good Times (ITY) – New Central 74 (Remainder Man 126§) **36**
[1991 a7g⁵ a7g⁶ 8.2d 8m⁴ 8g 9d 7g³ 8g* 8f² 10m 8f³ 8.2m 1992 8s 10d 8f 8m² 8.2m⁶
8f 8.3g] lengthy filly: poor handicapper: should stay beyond 1m: acts on firm going
and equitrack: below form blinkered. *D. Morris*

JOLTO 3 b.c. Noalto 120 – Joytime (John de Coombe 122) [1991 5g 5m 6m 6f 1992 **48**
8f 7d² 7g* 7d 6.9v⁶ a7g a7g⁴] leggy colt: plating-class form: poor handicapper: won
for claimer at Warwick in August: stays 7f well: suited by an easy surface. *K. O.
Cunningham-Brown*

JOLYPHA (USA) 3 b.f. Lyphard (USA) 132 – Navajo Princess (USA) **123**
(Drone) [1991 NR 1992 8g* 10g² 10.5g* 12m* 12s a10f³]
Having illustrious relatives is no guarantee of success on the race-
course, but Dancing Brave's sister Jolypha must already have fulfilled most
of the hopes entertained for her by her owner-breeder. She didn't emulate
Dancing Brave by winning Europe's richest race the Prix de l'Arc de
Triomphe—she came a fair eighth—but she did win both the Prix de Diane
Hermes and the Prix Vermeille Escada. Acceleration and courage are two of
Jolypha's finest attributes. She produced a fine turn of finishing speed in both
races and didn't flinch in the face of flailing whips as she squeezed through a
narrow gap to get up close home in the Prix Vermeille. She proved herself an
altogether admirable filly who will be a valuable addition to Mr Abdulla's
broodmares when she is retired.
Jolypha wasn't raced as a two-year-old and had only two races before
the Prix de Diane (French Oaks), winning a newcomers race at Saint-Cloud
and finishing a short-head second to Rosefinch in the Prix Saint-Alary at
Longchamp. Six of the runners in the Prix Saint-Alary—including the first
four—were also in the twelve-runner field at Chantilly. They finished in a
different order, Jolypha quickening impressively to win by a length and a short
head from the Prix Saint-Alary seventh and third Sheba Dancer and Verveine. After a break, Jolypha faced nine opponents in the Prix Vermeille at
Longchamp in September, including Verveine and the Prix de Diane sixth and
seventh Urban Sea and Trishyde. But it was a British challenger, the
progressive Cunning, who so nearly denied Jolypha. The Vermeille was run at
a muddling pace and Jolypha was boxed in for much of the straight. By the time
she saw daylight, the handily-placed Cunning had gone on from the
front-running Urban Sea; but Jolypha came through inside the final furlong for
a victory by a head and half a length, with Verveine, Market Booster and

*Prix de Diane Hermes, Chantilly—
Dancing Brave's sister Jolypha wins the French Oaks;
Sheba Dancer and Verveine (No. 13) fill the minor places*

Prix Vermeille Escada, Longchamp—
Jolypha ends Cunning's winning run despite meeting interference;
the photo testifies to the muddling pace

Trishyde also involved with Urban Sea in the photograph for third. Jolypha didn't enjoy the best of runs in the Prix de l'Arc either, taking a hefty bump rounding the final turn and then having anything but a clear passage in the straight. She was running on at the finish, beaten about seven lengths by the winner Subotica; second-placed User Friendly did easily the best of the three-year-old fillies, but Jolypha again finished in front of Verveine (ninth) and Market Booster (sixteenth). Jolypha crowned her three-year-old career with a good third in the Breeders' Cup Classic at Gulfstream Park. Racing on dirt for the first time, she kept on well after losing ground on the last bend, doing best of the European challengers in a race that earned most publicity in Britain for the disappointing run of Rodrigo de Triano. Jolypha was beaten two lengths and half a length by the Belmont Stakes winner A P Indy and the Jockey Club Gold Cup winner Pleasant Tap. It was reported shortly afterwards that Jolypha would continue her racing career as a four-year-old in the United States where she will be trained by Bobby Frankel.

			Northern Dancer	Nearctic
	Lyphard (USA)		(b 1961)	Natalma
	(b 1969)		Goofed	Court Martial
Jolypha (USA)			(ch 1960)	Barra II
(b.f. 1989)			Drone	Sir Gaylord
	Navajo Princess (USA)		(gr 1966)	Cap And Bells
	(b 1974)		Olmec	Pago Pago
			(ch 1966)	Chocolate Beau

The tall, quite attractive Jolypha will eventually join around one hundred and seventy-five broodmares kept by Mr Abdulla's Juddmonte operation which has studs in Britain, Ireland and North America. Whereas Dancing Brave was purchased on behalf of Mr Abdulla as a yearling, Jolypha was home bred, Juddmonte having acquired the dam Navajo Princess the same year Dancing Brave won the Two Thousand Guineas, the Coral-Eclipse, the King George VI and Queen Elizabeth Diamond Stakes and the Prix de l'Arc de Triomphe. Since joining the Juddmonte broodmare band, Navajo Princess, a very smart racemare at up to eight and a half furlongs, has not surprisingly mainly visited Lyphard. She has produced three fillies by him, the fairly useful mile-and-a-quarter winner Balleta (subsequently successful three times in

Mr K. Abdulla's "Jolypha"

the States), Jolypha and an as-yet unnamed foal of 1991. After being barren to Nureyev, Navajo Princess was switched to Europe where she visited Sadler's Wells in 1992. Incidentally, Passamaquoddy, a sister to Navajo Princess, was represented on the racecourse in the latest season by the Chesham Stakes winner Humam. The game and genuine Jolypha should continue to do well in North America. She is effective at a mile and a quarter to a mile and a half, and acts on good to firm and probably on soft going on turf, as well as having shown herself at home on dirt. *A. Fabre, France*

JO N JACK (IRE)   4 ch.g. Gorytus (USA) 132 – Dancing Song 87 (Ridan (USA))   **56** [1991 10m 13.5m 12g⁴ 1992 16d 5s 14g a10g* 9.9m] tall ex-Irish gelding: sixth reported foal: half-brother to 3 winners in Belgium: dam 5f and 6f winner at 3 yrs later successful in Belgium: 33/1 (gambled on off course), first run for present trainer (with Miss Joanna Morgan previously) when winning Lingfield seller (no bid): below that form, sweating profusely, in Beverley handicap later in September: stays 1½m: ran well when blinkered. *R. Ingram*

JONSALAN   2 gr.g. (May 4) Robellino (USA) 127 – Nelly Do Da 78 (Derring-Do   **71** 131) [1992 5m⁴ 5g⁴ 7g⁶ 7g⁶ 8g²] 5,400Y: leggy gelding: has scope: moderate mover: half-brother to several winners, including useful stayer Retouch (by Touching Wood): dam 2-y-o 5.8f winner: much improved effort when second in nursery at Warwick in August, beaten head by Express Mariecurie, starting slowly and driven along in rear 3f out: will be suited by middle distances. *W. Carter*

JOOD (USA)   3 b.f. Nijinsky (CAN) 138 – Kamar (USA) (Key To The Mint (USA))   **87** [1991 7g³ 1992 10g³] tall, quite attractive filly: not seen out after third to User Friendly in maiden at Sandown in April: stud. *M. R. Stoute*

405

JORDYWRATH 2 ch.g. (Mar 8) Efisio 120 – Hedonist 74 (Mandamus 120) [1992 **50**
a5g⁵ 6m³ a6g* 7g a7g⁵ a6g⁴] 2,500Y, 6,400 2-y-o: leggy, lightly-made gelding:
half-brother to several winners, including 1982 2-y-o 5f winner Flinders Range (by
Native Bazaar): dam sprint plater: 6-length winner of seller (retained 6,800 gns) at
Southwell in July: fair effort in nursery final start: should stay 7f: sold to join B.
Palling 475 gns Ascot December Sales. *I. Campbell*

JORROCKS 3 ch.g. Risk Me (FR) 127 – Rosana Park 83 (Music Boy 124) [1991 –
NR 1992 10m 7f 7f⁶ 8f] plain gelding: fourth foal: half-brother to quite modest 5f (at 2
yrs) to 9.7f winner Saysana (by Sayf El Arab) and to plating-class 1½m to 17.6f
winner Angelica Park (by Simply Great): dam 6f winner: no worthwhile form: tried
blinkered. *M. Dixon*

JOSEPH'S WINE (IRE) 3 b.g. Smile (USA) – Femme Gendarme (USA) **46**
(Policeman (FR) 124) [1991 8m 7m 6f 1992 7d 8g 8f* 10s⁵ 9.2s³ 11d*] lengthy
gelding: plating handicapper: no bid when winning at Yarmouth in August and
Redcar in October: effective at around 1m to 11f: probably acts on any going. *R.
Bastiman*

JOSHUA JOHN (IRE) 3 br.g. Nashamaa 113 – Nectareous (Tutankhamen) –
[1991 NR 1992 8.1g⁶ 6f 6s] leggy gelding: closely related to modest and somewhat
unsatisfactory 6f winner Hug (by Ahonoora) and half-brother to fair 1978 2-y-o 5f
winner Storm Crest (by Lord Gayle) and several winners abroad: dam placed 3 times
over 1½m in Ireland: no form in modest company. *B. R. Millman*

JOTRA 2 ch.c. (Apr 16) Clantime 101 – Branston Express (Bay Express 132) [1992 **38**
5g 5s 5d a6g⁵] 3,600Y: third foal: half-brother to 6f winner Waltzing Weazel (by
Nemorino): dam unraced half-sister to useful sprinter Tuxford Hideaway: poor form
in modest company: has been heavily bandaged. *R. M. Whitaker*

JOVIAL KATE (USA) 5 gr.m. Northern Jove (CAN) – Flashy Feet (USA) **43**
(Pretense) [1991 a6g³ a6g² a5g* a6g⁶ a6g⁴ a7g 5m a6g a6g⁴ 1992 a6g⁶ a6g a6g⁴ **a64**
a5g² a6g a6g* a5g 7.5g 5.9d 5m² 5m 5m⁵ 6f⁵ 5g⁵ a6g⁵ a6g² a7g a6g* a7s² 5m 5d a6g
a6g a7g] lengthy, workmanlike mare: good walker: tough handicapper, easily best
on fibresand: sold out of M. Usher's stable 4,600 gns Doncaster January Sales after
fourth start: won at Southwell in February and July: none too consistent on turf:
ideally suited by sprint distances: tried blinkered once: usually bandaged: has
carried head awkwardly. *B. Ellison*

JOVIAL MAN (IRE) 3 b.g. Ela-Mana-Mou 132 – Jovial Josie (USA) (Sea Bird II –
145) [1991 NR 1992 10d 10m 10g 8.9m] IR 6,400Y, 23,000 2-y-o: small, angular
gelding: half-brother to several winners abroad and fairly useful 1991 3-y-o 1m to
13.3f winner Talos (by Taufan): dam poor sister to high-class filly and good broodmare Kittiwake: no worthwhile form. *S. Mellor*

JOYFUL ESCAPADE 2 ch.f. (May 24) Precocious 126 – Mischiefmaker 73 –
(Calpurnius 122) [1992 5g] seventh living foal: half-sister to a winner abroad: dam
1m seller winner at 2 yrs stayed 1¼m: always behind in Lingfield seller in July. *Mrs
N. Macauley*

JOYFUL THOUGHT 3 b.f. Green Desert (USA) 127 – Happy Thought (FR) 57 **41**
(Kauai King) [1991 6m⁴ 6m⁴ 6g 1992 7g 5m 6m⁵ 5m³] quite attractive filly: maiden
handicapper: not seen out after June: headstrong, and best at sprint distances: ran
creditably when blinkered. *Mrs J. R. Ramsden*

JOY OF FREEDOM 2 b. or br.f. (Feb 1) Damister (USA) 123 – Debach Delight **39**
97 (Great Nephew 126) [1992 a8g a8g⁶] 18,000Y: first foal: dam 11f and 1½m winner:
poor in maidens at Lingfield and Southwell late in year: bred to stay beyond 1m.
C. E. Brittain

JOYOFRACING 2 b.c. (Apr 17) Petoski 135 – Lady Bequick 81 (Sharpen Up 127) **93**
[1992 5g³ 5g² 5m* 5d² 5.1g* 5.2d⁴ 6d² 6v] 25,000Y: big, good-quartered colt:
half-brother to several winners, including 3 sprinters (notably useful Joytotheworld
(by Young Generation)) and 3-y-o Cloud of Dust (by Aragon), successful at 6f (at 2
yrs) and 1m: dam ran only at 2 yrs, winning at 5f: won maiden at Windsor and median
auction at Nottingham in early-summer: ran very well next 2 starts after return
from 3-month absence, fourth to Lyric Fantasy in Newbury Sales Super Sprint
Trophy, but soundly beaten in Racecall Gold Trophy at Redcar: stays 6f well: acts on
good to firm and dead ground. *W. A. O'Gorman*

J P MORGAN 4 b. or br.g. Law Society (USA) 130 – Queen of The Brush (Averof **47**
123) [1991 10m⁵ 11m⁴ 11g² 12.4m² 12.3g⁶ 16m² 16.2f⁶ 8.1g⁴ 13.8m⁴ 10.4m 1992 12g
11.1s³ 12.1m³ 16.1m 13.8d⁴ 15.1m⁴ 8.1f³ 8.5s 8.1m 8m⁴ 8g 9.2g 12.1d* 13.1s⁵ 12.1s³
11.8d 12.1g⁴ 12.1v*] leggy, shallow-girthed, angular gelding: somewhat unreliable
handicapper: won at Edinburgh (first win) and Hamilton in autumn: effective at 1m

to 2m: probably acts on any going: below form blinkered, usually visored nowadays: not easiest of rides: won novice hurdle in December. *M. P. Naughton*

JUBAL EARLY (IRE) 3 b.g. The Noble Player (USA) 126 – Miss Galwegian (Sandford Lad 133) [1991 5m³ 6f⁴ 6g⁴ 7s a7g* 7m² 6m² 7g a8g a7g⁶ 1992 12.3s 7g⁵ 5.1d 6m] useful-looking gelding: rated 63 at 2 yrs, lost his form in 1992: stays 7f: acts on good to firm ground and fibresand: blinkered/visored nowadays. *C. N. Allen* —

JUBILATA (USA) 4 ch.f. The Minstrel (CAN) 135 – All Gladness (USA) (Alydar (USA)) [1991 a8g⁶ a7g 6s⁵ 7.5g 7d 7f 8.1g 6g 10.4m² 11m* 10m 1992 12m 12.2g⁵ 12.1s] leggy filly: has a round action: none too consistent handicapper: rated 54 at 3 yrs: should stay 1½m: acts on firm going: below form visored once: has run creditably for lady rider. *M. P. Naughton* —

JUBRAN (USA) 6 b.g. Vaguely Noble 140 – La Vue (USA) (Reviewer (USA)) [1991 9s⁴ 9s⁴ 8.2d 8g* 8m³ 8d³ 7.1g⁴ 7.9m* 7g⁴ 10g² 10g 1992 9d² 10.1m⁴ 9f* 8.9m 8.9g⁵ 8s³ 8s⁶ 9d 10d] quite attractive, close-coupled gelding: fair handicapper: successful at Ripon in August: effective at 7f to 1½m: acts on firm and soft ground: tough. *M. P. Naughton* **73**

JUCEA 3 b.f. Bluebird (USA) 125 – Appleby Park 98 (Bay Express 132) [1991 5m 6s 5g⁶ 1992 6m⁴ 6d a6g² 5d 6m³ 6f⁵ a7g a6g] sturdy, rather angular filly: poor mover: modest handicapper: should prove better at 7f than 6f: acts on good to firm ground and equitrack: seemingly not on a soft surface: ran creditably when blinkered once at 2 yrs. *D. W. P. Arbuthnot* **57**

JUDGE AND JURY 3 br.g. Law Society (USA) 130 – Full of Reason (USA) (Bold Reason) [1991 7f7.1m 7g³ 7g⁵ a8g* 1992 10d³ 10g 11.4m 12m⁵ 13.3m² 13.1m⁵ 11.7d 14.1d 17.2s⁶ 16.1s 14.1s* 12.4v] compact gelding: inconsistent handicapper: won seller (bought in 3,100 gns) at Nottingham in October: stays 1¾m well: acts on good to firm and soft ground and equitrack: ran creditably in blinkers: below best visored: probably ungenuine: sold to join O. Sherwood 6,200 gns Ascot November Sales. *M. J. Fetherston-Godley* **59 §**

JUDGEMENT CALL 5 b.h. Alzao (USA) 117 – Syllabub (Silly Season 127) [1991 5g 6g 6m⁶ 6g 6m 5m 6m³ 6g 7f⁴ 7g 7f² 7g 8f⁶ 6f 1992 a6g 7g⁵ 6m⁴ 6f³ 6d 6m 6f⁵ 7g⁵ 7d 7m³ 6s³ 7d 7d a6g] close-coupled, good-quartered horse: carries condition: has a quick action: none too consistent handicapper nowadays: stays 7f: probably acts on any going: below form when blinkered once: sometimes bandaged. *P. Howling* **63 d**

JUDYS GIRL (IRE) 3 b.f. Simply Great (FR) 122 – Sistina 76 (Charlottown 127) [1991 6d 7m 7m 6m 7.1m 1992 12.2m⁵] leggy, sparely-made filly: of little account. *T. Fairhurst* —

JULFAAR (USA) 5 b.g. Arctic Tern (USA) 126 – Nijit (USA) (Nijinsky (CAN) 138) [1991 10g⁵ 10m⁵ 11.5f⁴ 11.9m⁶ 1992 a12g 12g 12g] rather leggy gelding: moderate walker: has a round action: rated 79 at 4 yrs: no form in 1992: stays 1½m: acts on good to firm ground. *J. Pearce* —

JULIA SABINA 3 b.f. Prince Sabo 123 – Bernice Clare 68 (Skymaster 126) [1991 6m 5d⁶ 6m 6.1m 1992 7m 5m] small, sturdy filly: poor plater: stays 6f. *C. C. Elsey* —

JULIASDARKINVADER 2 br.c. (May 10) Lidhame 109 – Una Donna (GER) (Windwurf (GER)) [1992 7.1d 7m 8s 10d 8v a8g⁴ a8g⁶] lengthy colt: moderate mover: first known foal: dam won over hurdles: modest maiden: stays 1¼m: acts on dead ground and equitrack. *A. Moore* **48** **a55**

JULIET BRAVO 2 b.f. (Apr 11) Glow (USA) – Countess Olivia 80 (Prince Tenderfoot (USA) 126) [1992 5m² 5s⁵ 5m* 5g 6m³ 6g 6m⁶ 6g⁶ 5g 6s] strong, sturdy filly: good mover: seventh foal: half-sister to 3-y-o Black Coral (by Double Schwartz) and 5-y-o 7f winner Coral Flutter (by Beldale Flutter): dam stayed 1¼m: generally disappointing after winning maiden at Ayr in June: stays 6f: easily best efforts on good to firm ground: usually races up with pace: sometimes wears tongue strap. *B. Beasley* **58**, 2,100Y:

JULIETSKI 4 gr.f. Niniski (USA) 125 – Plum Blossom (USA) (Gallant Romeo (USA)) [1991 a10g⁵ 12f³ 12.2m⁶ 15.8f⁴ 12g² 11.7f³ 12f⁴ 1992 13d] small, angular filly: rated 63 as 3-y-o: not seen out on flat after April: should stay beyond 1½m: acts on firm going: successful twice over hurdles in autumn. *M. D. Hammond* —

JULY BRIDE 2 b.f. (Jan 18) Aragon 118 – Ladysave (Stanford 121§) [1992 5d 6f⁶ 6v] leggy filly: fourth foal: half-sister to 2m winner Powersurge (by Electric): dam ran twice: soundly beaten in maidens. *M. J. Haynes* **34**

JUMAIRA SHARK (CAN) 3 b.c. Lyphard (USA) 132 – That's A Kennedy (CAN) (Kennedy Road (CAN)) [1991 NR 1992 10m⁵ 10m* 10g⁵ 10g 10.3m³ 10m³ 8.9d] $550,000Y: sturdy colt: carries condition: brother to 8.5f to 1¼m turf stakes **87**

winner Storm On The Loose, closely related to a stakes-placed winner by Lypheor and half-brother to a winner by Diamond Prospect: dam, twice successful at 3 yrs, is half-sister to No Class, the dam of 4 champions (three 2-y-o's) in Canada: won minor event at Windsor in June: form in handicaps after when third at Doncaster and Newmarket: stays 10.3f: acts on good to firm ground: wears crossed noseband: visored last 3 starts, swishing tail repeatedly in paddock final one. *J. H. M. Gosden*

JUMAIRA STAR (USA) 3 b.c. Blushing Groom (FR) 131 – Disconiz (USA) **64**
(Northern Dancer (CAN)) [1991 NR 1992 8f⁴ 7g⁴ 7m⁶ 7g 6.1g* 7d] $1,050,000Y: sturdy colt: sixth foal: brother to very useful 1987 2-y-o 5f and 6f winner Digamist and fairly useful 1991 3-y-o 1m winner Fly To The Moon and half-brother to minor winners in France and Italy: dam very smart stakes winner at up to 1½m: modest performer: visored first time when winning maiden at Nottingham in September: again visored but never going well on softer ground in Newmarket handicap following month: should stay at least 1m: possibly needs a sound surface: winner in Dubai. *J. H. M. Gosden*

JUMBY BAY 6 b.g. Thatching 131 – Ridge The Times (USA) 78 (Riva Ridge – §
(USA)) [1991 a6g⁴ a7g a7g 1992 a8g] big, rangy gelding: untrustworthy handicapper: effective at 6f to 1m: acts on firm going: twice below form when blinkered: sometimes hangs markedly: sold 2,000 gns Doncaster May Sales. *M. Johnston*

JUNCTION TWENTYTWO 2 ch.g. (Apr 13) Local Suitor (USA) 128 – Polli- **52**
nella 108 (Charlottown 127) [1992 5m 7g 6.1m⁴ 7.1s 8.2d] 2,100Y: big, workmanlike gelding: half-brother to several winners, including 1½m winner Mansfield House (by Swing Easy) and useful 5f to 1m winner Castle Tweed (by Daring March), later successful in USA: dam stayed 1½m: plating-class form in modest company: should stay 1m: visored final run. *C. D. Broad*

JUNE'S LEAR FAN (CAN) 3 b.g. Lear Fan (USA) 130 – Gamba (USA) (Gun –
Bow) [1991 NR 1992 9m a7g⁶ a12g⁴ 10m] good-topped gelding: closely related to very useful French 1¼m and 1½m winner Gamberta (by Roberto) and half-brother to several winners: dam, 5f and 7f winner, is half-sister to good American 1m to 1½m colt State Dinner and high-class 2-y-o Banquet Table: no worthwhile form: trained by G. Harwood on debut. *P. A. Kelleway*

JUNGLE DANCER (IRE) 4 b.g. Sadler's Wells (USA) 132 – Forlene 108 (Forli **95**
(ARG)) [1991 10.1m* 12g³ 11.9g² 11.9g 1992 10m⁵ 16.4s⁴ 14g*¹ 16.2g 15.9m³ 13.9g² 16.2s² 16.2g³ 16.5g²] good-quartered, attractive gelding: looked irresolute in 1991, but useful and consistent handicapper as 4-y-o: gamely won at Sandown in July: effective at 1¾m to 2m: acts on good to firm ground and soft: below form when blinkered/visored: sold 4,000 gns Newmarket Autumn Sales, to race in Italy. *M. R. Stoute*

JUNGLE KNIFE 6 b.g. Kris 135 – Jungle Queen (Twilight Alley 133) [1991 8v* **74**
8d⁴ 10.3d⁵ 1992 8s 9g*] tall, workmanlike gelding: moderate walker and mover: relatively lightly-raced handicapper on flat: not seen out until October, and won Newmarket apprentice event in good style: stays 1¼m: probably needs an easy surface (acts on heavy): held up: very useful hurdler, winner in November. *M. H. Tompkins*

JUNIPER BERRY (IRE) 3 b.f. Last Tycoon 131 – Jackie Berry 97 (Connaught **88**
130) [1991 6d⁵ 1992 8v² 7g* 11.4g² 10m⁵ 8m⁵ 8.9m⁶ 7.1s⁴ 10.2s* 10.9s 12.1d²] lengthy, workmanlike filly: fairly useful performer: won maiden at Newmarket in April and apprentice event at Chepstow in September: good second to Aquamarine in Cheshire Oaks third start: stays 1½m: acts on good to firm and soft ground: tends to sweat: sold 23,000 gns Newmarket December Sales. *P. W. Chapple-Hyam*

JUPITER MOON 3 b.c. Jupiter Island 126 – Troy Moon (Troy 137) [1991 7.1s* **71**
8g 1992 12.1m 12m³ 12f 11.9d a16g⁴ 12m⁴ 14.6g²] stocky colt: carries condition: impresses in appearance: inconsistent handicapper: stays 14.6f: acts on good to firm ground and soft: well below form when blinkered once: sold to join Mrs A. Swinbank 15,500 gns Newmarket September Sales: won over hurdles in October. *C. E. Brittain*

JUPITER RISING 3 b.f. Jupiter Island 126 – Tula Singh 66 (Mansingh (USA) –
120) [1991 NR 1992 6.9g] half-sister to 1984 2-y-o 5f winner Green Spirit (by Dragonara Palace): dam, best at sprint distances, is sister to Petong: behind in maiden at Folkestone in September. *D. W. P. Arbuthnot*

JURA 4 ch.c. Rousillon (USA) 133 – Reuval 102 (Sharpen Up 127) [1991 8.2m² **104**
10g*¹ 10.1f* 10m* 1992 12d 10m² 10m⁴] leggy, rather angular colt: moderate walker and mover: useful performer: in frame in listed races at Goodwood (head second to

Flashfoot) and Kempton in first half of 1992: should stay 1½m: best efforts on top-of-the-ground. *H. R. A. Cecil*

JURIS PRUDENCE (IRE)   4 b. or br.f. Law Society (USA) 130 – Virginia Sham **61** d
(USA) (Sham (USA)) [1991 10.4d⁵ 10d 12m⁶ 10.5g 14m⁴ 15m⁶ 14g 14.1m 10.3d 1992
12f 14.6g³ 14.8f⁴ 14.9g⁵ 18m⁵ 16.9d⁴ 16.9d⁴ 16d] rather leggy, lengthy filly: maiden
handicapper: needs test of stamina: acts on firm and dead ground: below form
blinkered: suitable mount for claimer. *B. A. McMahon*

JURRAN   7 ro.g. Formidable (USA) 125 – Queen's Counsellor 92 (Kalamoun 129) **55** §
[1991 10.1d³ 10d³ 1992 8m³ 9d] strong, lengthy gelding: has a free action: lightly
raced and ungenuine nowadays: stays 1¼m: acts on firm and dead going: ran
moderately in blinkers. *H. Thomson Jones*

JUSTAMANDA   3 b.f. Prince Sabo 123 – Auntie Cyclone (USA) 66 (Dust Com-   –
mander (USA)) [1991 5g 5g 5d⁴ 6m³ 5g* 1992 a5g 5g⁶ 7m 7f] leggy, sparely-made
filly: poor maiden: rated 62 at 2 yrs: no form in 1992: stays 6f. *W. Holden*

JUST A MIRAGE   3 b.f. Green Desert (USA) 127 – Just You Wait (Nonoalco **76**
(USA) 131) [1991 6m³ 1992 7g⁴ 8d³ 8s² 8d⁵] big, leggy, angular filly: off course over
6 months and went wrong way after third of 6 in £9,700 contest at Ascot in April:
stayed 1m: bandaged behind as 3-y-o: visits Machiavellian. *A. A. Scott*

JUST A STEP   6 br.h. Lochnager 132 – My Louise 54 (Manado 130) [1991 7g* 7g⁴ **83** d
7m² 7m² 7m⁵ 7d* 7.1g⁵ 7g 8g 7d 1992 8g 7g* 7s⁶ 8d* 7g 7m⁵ 7g⁶ 7.1s⁶ 7d 7d 7s 7g]
small, sturdy horse: moderate mover: won Thirsk handicap and Carlisle claimer in
spring: lost his form after: effective at 7f to 1m: has form on firm ground, but best
efforts with some give: front runner: changed hands 675 gns Ascot September
Sales. *M. McCormack*

JUST BAILEYS   2 b.f. (Apr 25) Midyan (USA) 124 – Just Precious 77 **42**
(Ela-Mana-Mou 132) [1992 5d³ 5m 5g* 5g⁶ 5.2g 5g 7d 8g 6g] 8,100F, 5,800Y:
sparely-made filly: first foal: dam 7.5f and 1m winner: ran moderately, including in
sellers, after winning maiden at Hamilton in July: best form at 5f: blinkered last 4
starts: wore off-side pricker once: sold 1,800 gns Doncaster November Sales. *M.
Johnston*

JUST BOB   3 b.c. Alleging (USA) 120 – Diami 81 (Swing Easy (USA) 126) [1991 **67**
5g² 5m* 5m² 5f³ 6m³ 5m² 1992 5v 5g 5m 5d* 6.1g* 5m 5m 6d 6s 6.1d]
smallish, leggy colt: moderate mover: modest performer: well below form after
winning amateurs handicap at Hamilton and apprentice claimer at Nottingham in
early-summer: stays 6f: acts on good to firm and dead ground: often slowly away:
usually blinkered nowadays. *S. E. Kettlewell*

JUST CALL ME MADAM (IRE)   3 b.f. Cyrano de Bergerac 120 – Brandywell   –
(Skyliner 117) [1991 NR 1992 a8g] first foal: dam poor Irish maiden: 33/1 and
apprentice ridden at overweight, well-beaten eighth of 11 in Lingfield claimer in
December. *T. Casey*

JUST CRACKER   7 ch.g. Monsanto (FR) 121 – Pertune (Hyperion's Curls) [1991   –
NR 1992 10.2f] second foal: dam poor hurdler: tailed off in Bath seller in June:
improved hurdler in the autumn, winning 3 times: dead. *P. Leach*

JUST FOR KICKS   6 br.g. Saher 115 – Kix 71 (King Emperor (USA)) [1991 9s 8f   –
8m 12.1d 10.9g⁵ 10m 10.5g 1992 8.9s 18.2g 10.9d 10f] rather leggy, sparely-made
ex-Irish gelding: lost his form in 1992: stays 1m: acts on soft going: below form
blinkered. *J. J. O'Neill*

JUST HANNAH   3 b.f. Macmillion 110 – My Charade 79 (Cawston's Clown 113) **63** d
[1991 NR 1992 8d⁶ 8g⁶ 10.2m 10.5d 14.1g] close-coupled, workmanlike filly: second
foal: dam, 5f (at 2 yrs) and 1¾m winner, is half-sister to very useful 6f to 7f
performer Step Ahead: regressive maiden: stays 1m. *Mrs Barbara Waring*

JUST JULIA   3 b.f. Natroun (FR) 128 – Adana (FR) (Green Dancer (USA) 132)   –
[1991 NR 1992 10d 9.9f⁶ 11.5g] leggy, sparely-made filly: fourth foal: half-sister to 7f
(in Italy) and 1m winner Anadax (by Mummy's Game): dam French 9.5f winner: no
worthwhile form in maidens in first half of 1992. *M. R. Channon*

JUST MY BILL   6 ch.g. Nicholas Bill 125 – Misnomer 85 (Milesian 125) [1991 **69**
12.3s* 13d² 12.3d⁶ 11.9g 1992 12g⁴ 11.9s⁵ 16.2d² 14g 16.2d] leggy, rather
sparely-made gelding: modest handicapper: ran poorly last 2 starts: effective at
1½m to 2m: suited by some give in the ground: effective visored or not, below form
when blinkered once: sold out of C. W. C. Elsey's stable 16,500 gns Doncaster May
Sales after third start. *N. Tinkler*

JUST READY (IRE)   4 b.g. Petorius 117 – Lacey Brief (USA) (Roi Dagobert   –
128) [1991 a10g³ a10g a8g⁵ 8g 11.7g 11m⁶ 8f* 7m 8g 1992 11.7d 8m a7g 8.9s 10.2f

409

10m] leggy, workmanlike gelding: has a quick action: rated 51 at 3 yrs: below form, including in sellers, in 1992: probably stays 1¼m: acts on firm going: below form blinkered/visored once. *G. A. Ham*

JUST SPECULATION (IRE) 2 ch.f. (Apr 23) Ahonoora 122 – Rhein Bridge **86** 107 (Rheingold 137) [1992 6d* 6g³ 7.5g² 8d³] strong, compact filly: seventh foal: half-sister to Irish St Leger and Ascot Gold Cup runner-up Tyrone Bridge (by Kings Lake): dam, half-sister to very smart middle-distance filly Connaught Bridge, won Lancashire Oaks: progressive filly: won maiden at Leicester in June: placed after in 2 listed events at Milan and Meadow Meats EBF Killavullan Stakes at Leopardstown: will be better suited by 1¼m. *P. F. I. Cole*

JUST YOU DARE (IRE) 2 b.c. (Apr 3) Common Grounds 118 – Eulalie 85 **62** p (Queen's Hussar 124) [1992 a7g⁴ 7g* 7g⁴] IR 15,000Y: leggy, good-topped colt: has a round action: half-brother to several winners, including (at 7f and 1m) useful Electric Lady (by Electric) and (at 9f and 1¼m) Rattle Along (by Tap On Wood): dam, winner at up to 10.8f, is half-sister to very useful Suni and Honorius: 2½-length winner of maiden at Thirsk in August: got poor run when staying-on fourth of 17 in nursery at Brighton 1½ months after: will stay at least 1m: races keenly: will improve again. *Sir Mark Prescott*

JUVENARA 6 b.g. Young Generation 129 – Sharrara (CAN) 61 (Blushing Groom **42** (FR) 131) [1991 6v 7d⁶ 8f* 8d 8f 7m 7g³ 7d² 7.6s³ 6g 8m³ 8f⁶ 7m⁵ 8.2f 9m 7g 1992 8m 6g 5.7m 7.1m⁴ 7f⁶ 7.1m 6.1g 7f²ᵈⁱˢ 7f² 7d 7g 8d⁵ a10g a6g⁶ a7g²] small, workmanlike gelding: poor walker: inconsistent handicapper: effective at 7f to 1¼m: probably best on a sound surface, and acts on equitrack. *C. J. Hill*

K

KABAYIL 3 b.f. Dancing Brave (USA) 140 – Psylla 96 (Beldale Flutter (USA) 130) **75** [1991 NR 1992 9m⁴ 10.5d⁴ 10f³ 10.5g⁴ 12.3d² 11.4g⁵ 10s⁴ 10d⁴ 10s* 10.3g⁵] angular filly: second foal: half-sister to 1¼m winner Moonjid (by Shirley Heights): dam 9f and 1¼m winner out of half-sister to Kris and Diesis: fair performer: won maiden at Leicester in October: will probably prove better at 1½m than shorter: acts on soft ground: sold to join C. Egerton 17,000 gns Newmarket December Sales. *P. T. Walwyn*

KABCAST 7 b.g. Kabour 80 – Final Cast 50 (Saulingo 122) [1991 5g 5f⁵ 5f⁵ 5g 5g⁶ **57** d 5d⁶ 5s² 5g⁵ 5f³ 5.2m³ 5f² 5.1m* 5f 5f* 5m 5.2f 5g 5m* 5s⁶ 1992 5m 5f⁵ 5f⁴ 5m 5g 5m 5.1d] good-bodied gelding: seemed on the downgrade in 1992, well beaten last 4 starts: best at 5f: acts on any going, but goes particularly well on a sound surface: wears blinkers: often sweats. *D. W. Chapman*

KABERA 4 b.g. Kabour 80 – Boldera 69 (Persian Bold 123) [1991 a7g⁶ 8.3f 5g 6s — a6g⁶ a6g⁵ 1992 a7g⁶ a7g 7.1g 6.1d 5.9d 6g 6g] workmanlike gelding: of little account: sold 1,400 gns Doncaster September Sales. *D. W. Chapman*

KADARI 3 b.f. Commanche Run 133 – Thoughtful 86 (Northfields (USA)) [1991 5g **71** 6f⁶ 7s² 7g² 7f³ 7.5f³ 8.1g* 8m 1992 9.2d² 10.1s³ 12d² 12.1s³ 12f 16f² 14.1g⁴ 9.9d² 12m²ᵈⁱˢ 13.6f² 16.2d* 13.9g 17.9d 17.5s² 17.1s² 15.9s⁶ 16.5g] workmanlike filly: fair handicapper: won at Beverley in August next time: below form last 2 starts: suited by thorough test of stamina: acts on any going: no improvement when visored twice: tail swisher. *A. Harrison*

KADASTROF (FR) 2 ch.c. (Apr 25) Port Etienne (FR) – Kadastra (FR) **78** (Stradavinsky 121) [1992 7s 8v* 7g] angular, well-grown colt: first foal: dam French 11f winner: sire (by Mill Reef) French middle-distance colt: 50/1, won 12-runner maiden at Leicester in October, staying on well: last of 21 in nursery at Doncaster 11 days later: will be well suited by middle distances. *R. Dickin*

KADOUNOR (FR) 2 b.c. (Jan 19) Kaldoun (FR) 122 – Ticarock (FR) (Baly **117** p Rockette 115) [1992 6m* 7g* 8d* 8s 7s*] second foal: closely related to French 3-y-o Kadourock (by Kadrou): dam French 2-y-o 7f winner: progressive French colt: successful in newcomers race at Chantilly, minor event at Evry, Prix La Rochette at Longchamp and, putting up easily best effort, Criterium de Maisons-Laffitte (beat Wixon by 1½ lengths): ran moderately in Grand Criterium at Longchamp, fading from 2f out having taken keen hold: likely to stay 1¼m: may well be capable of better still. *J. Laumain, France*

KAFIOCA (IRE) 2 b.f. (May 1) Fairy King (USA) – Secret Montague (Tumble **48** Wind (USA)) [1992 6g 6m³ 7g² 7m⁶ 7d a8g a7g⁶] IR 42,000F, IR 4,000Y: compact filly: second foal: sister to Irish 1991 2-y-o 5f winner Prudent King: dam Irish 1m winner: largely consistent plater: better suited by 7f than 6f, and will stay 1m: acts on good to firm and dead ground, below form on equitrack: ran creditably in a visor fourth start: sold out of M. Tompkins' stable 3,000 gns Newmarket Autumn Sales after next. *B. J. Meehan*

KAGRAM QUEEN   4 b.f. Prince Ragusa 96 – Arodstown Alice (Sahib 114) [1991   **64**
7g 7f5 10m2 10f 10f2 8.3f3 10g4 8m 1992 8d3 8f 10g* 9f* 10m* 10d] lengthy, dipped-backed filly: useful plater: off course 2 months after rare poor effort (when bandaged near-fore) then completed hat-trick at Ayr, Redcar (both no bid) then Pontefract (bought in 6,600 gns) in the summer: never placed to challenge in non-selling handicap 7 weeks later: should stay 1½m: acts on firm going. *Mrs M. Reveley*

KAHELLAN (FR)   2 b.c. (Feb 15) Fairy King (USA) – Celeste Grimm (Corvaro   **81 p**
(USA) 122) [1992 5.2m4 5g* 5f6] 34,000F, IR 90,000Y: strong, lengthy colt: has plenty of scope: second foal: dam, unraced, from family of Pevero and Romildo: won maiden at Lingfield in May in good style: looking very well, creditable sixth of 9, never able to challenge, to Niche in Norfolk Stakes at Royal Ascot: looked certain to do better, particularly at 6f. *L. M. Cumani*

KAHER (USA)   5 b.g. Our Native (USA) – June Bride (USA) (Riverman (USA)   **78**
131) [1991 12g3 12m3 10.1f5 11.9m5 11.9m 10.2g2 12m4 1992 11.9g2] compact gelding: fair handicapper: ran creditably when beaten a neck at Brighton in March, only outing on flat in 1992: stays 1½m: acts on firm going: takes keen hold. *N. A. Callaghan*

KAHHAL (IRE)   4 gr.f. Doulab (USA) 115 – Queen's Counsellor 92 (Kalamoun   **–**
129) [1991 7g5 8m5 11.7f 1992 10m 10.2f 7g] compact filly: moderate mover: of little account. *Mrs A. Knight*

KAHILI GINGER   2 b.f. (Mar 1) Top Ville 129 – Kamisha (FR) (Lyphard (USA)   **–**
132) [1992 8m] lengthy, sparely-made filly: half-sister to several winners, including (at 1¼m in France) Kamara (by Blushing Groom): dam French 9f winner: 25/1, backward and green, no show in 21-runner maiden at Pontefract in October. *N. A. Graham*

KAISAR (GER)   3 b.c. Shareef Dancer (USA) 135 – Konigsblute (GER) (Cortez   **86**
(GER)) [1991 NR 1992 10.1s* 10.5d3 10m2 12.1g2] small, leggy, close-coupled colt: third known foal: half-brother to winners in Germany by Deep Roots and Ile de Bourbon: dam fairly useful in Germany: fairly useful performer: edgy, won maiden at Newcastle in April: sweating and wearing dropped noseband, easily best efforts

Criterium de Maisons-Laffitte—
easily Kadounor's best effort so far, as he holds the favourite Wixon

when second in minor events at Windsor and Chepstow in midsummer, making most: better suited by 1½m than shorter: sent to race in Dubai. *H. R. A. Cecil*

KAISER WILHELM 3 b.c. Slip Anchor 136 – Kaisersage (FR) (Exbury 138) **87** [1991 NR 1992 10d* 13.3d 14d³ 15.9s² 16.5g³] leggy colt: dam won in Germany: fairly useful performer: won maiden at Leicester in April: better form when placed in handicaps in the autumn: stays 2m: yet to race on top-of-the-ground: one paced. *H. R. A. Cecil*

KAJAANI (IRE) 3 b.c. Simply Great (FR) 122 – Finlandia (FR) (Faraway Son **66** (USA) 130) [1991 8.1g³ 10m² 1992 12s 16m 12d² 11.9f] good-bodied colt: has a long stride: fair maiden: easily best effort in 1992 when second of 4 at Beverley, held up and staying on well: stays 1½m: acts on good to firm and dead ground: blinkered (sweating, well beaten) over 2m: may be unsatisfactory. *P. F. I. Cole*

KALABERRY 4 gr.f. Kalaglow 132 – Moberry 54 (Mossberry 97) [1991 NR 1992 – 12.2g⁴] third foal: half-sister to winning staying hurdler The Lighter Side (by Comedy Star): dam maiden stayed 1m: twice raced in NH Flat races before finishing 30 lengths fourth of 5 in Catterick maiden in June: sold 2,000 gns Doncaster September Sales. *W. W. Haigh*

KALAFLO 3 gr.f. Kalaglow 132 – Turtle Hill 73 (Home Guard (USA) 129) [1991 – NR 1992 10f⁴ 12d⁴] 1,000Y: angular filly: sixth foal: half-sister to a winner in Italy by Ile de Bourbon: dam, 5f winner, is half-sister to high-class 1m to 1¼m performer Gold Rod: well beaten in maidens at Ripon and Beverley (got very upset in stalls, weakened quickly over 2f out) in midsummer: sold 1,150 gns Doncaster November Sales. *P. Calver*

KALAMOSS 3 ch.f. Kalaglow 132 – Moss Pink (USA) (Levmoss 133) [1991 5g 6m – 7g 7m 1992 7.1m 11.7g] small filly: no worthwhile form on flat: bred to stay 1¼m: has shown a little ability over hurdles. *N. R. Mitchell*

KALAR 3 b.g. Kabour 80 – Wind And Reign 55 (Tumble Wind (USA)) [1991 a5g **51** a6g a6g a6g 1992 a8g a7g a5g* a6g a5g 5m 5h⁶ 6g³ 5d³ 5g² 5g⁴ 6f³ 7g² a5g 6m⁵ 7g⁵ 6s⁴ 5s 5s 5g² 5s 5d² a5g] good-bodied gelding: modest handicapper: won at Southwell in January: ran several good races after: retained by trainer 1,200 gns Doncaster March Sales: effective at 5f and 6f: acts on any going, including fibresand: effective blinkered/visored or not. *D. W. Chapman*

KALKO 3 b.c. Kalaglow 132 – Salchow 116 (Niniski (USA) 125) [1991 NR 1992 8g **73 d** 8g⁵ 12g 8.1m⁶ 7.5m* 8g⁶ 8g⁵ 8d 8g] close-coupled colt: second foal: half-brother to 1m winner Carousella (by Rousillon): dam won at 7f (at 2 yrs) and stayed 14.6f: fair form: won maiden at Beverley in June: below form afterwards, including in blinkers final start: well worth another try beyond 1m: acts on good to firm ground: sold to join M. Hammond 5,800 gns Newmarket Autumn Sales. *C. E. Brittain*

KALOKAGATHOS 3 b.c. King of Spain 121 – Kip's Sister (Cawston's Clown – 113) [1991 7g 1992 10m 16m 12s a 12g] workmanlike colt: behind in maidens: visored final start: trained first 3 by C. Cox. *M. McCormack*

KALOOCHI 2 b.c. (Feb 18) Glint of Gold 128 – Eastern House 83 (Habitat 134) **56** [1992 7g 7m* 8.5d 8m 8s 10d⁵ 8g] 6,600Y: small colt: second foal: brother to 1990 2-y-o 7f winner Kashmir Gold: dam won at 7f and 1m: modest form: won seller (no bid) at Newmarket in August: stays 1¼m: acts on good to firm and dead ground: ran well in blinkers last 2 starts: looks a difficult ride: sold 1,100 gns Newmarket Autumn Sales. *R. Hannon*

KAMAATERA (IRE) 2 ch.g. (Feb 9) Night Shift (USA) – La Tuerta 96 (Hot **89** Spark 126) [1992 6f² 5f⁵ 5g* 5m⁵ 6g] 115,000Y: smallish, well-made gelding: fourth foal: half-brother to 3 sprint winners, including Dominio (by Dominion) and La Cabrilla (by Carwhite), latter stayed 1m well: dam sprinting half-sister to Cadeaux Genereux and quite useful stayer Brightner: fairly useful performer: won maiden at Windsor in July: good keeping-on fifth to Millyant in Molecomb Stakes at Good-wood: blinkered, raced on unfavoured part of track in Phoenix Stakes at Leopards-town following month, and run best ignored: should prove ideally suited by further than 5f: may do better. *A. A. Scott*

KANDIYSHA (IRE) 4 b.f. Shahrastani (USA) 135 – Kamisha (FR) (Lyphard – (USA) 132) [1991 14g⁶ 12g⁶ 1992 16.2g] ex-Irish filly: half-sister to 3 winners, including very useful 1985 2-y-o 9f winner Kariya (by Irish River): dam French 1m to 1¼m performer: modest form, though well beaten, at 3 yrs for J. Oxx: well beaten in Beverley seller in March, 1992: has looked irresolute over hurdles. *J. Parkes*

KANDY SECRET (USA) 3 b.g. Secretariat (USA) – Marshua's Rose (USA) **60** (Marshua's Dancer (USA)) [1991 7g 7.1m 8m 1992 10.2m 12g⁶ 10.2g³ 10g* 10m³ 12g⁶ 10.5s] quite attractive gelding: has a quick action: modest performer: visored, won claimer at Sandown in July, looking none too keen then responding well to the whip: ran creditably in blinkers next outing, below form afterwards, particularly so final start: should stay 1½m: acts on good to firm ground: soon off bridle, and best with strong handling: sold to join J. Ffitch-Heyes 3,100 gns Newmarket Autumn Sales: may well be unsatisfactory. *R. Hannon*

KANOOZ (IRE)   4 br.g. Wassl 125 – Countess Candy 106 (Great Nephew 126)   – §
[1991 a8g² a10g² a10g* 10d 10.2s 1992 12g 14.1g 14.1m a12g 16m⁶] workmanlike gelding: rated 62 at 3 yrs: no form and looked irresolute in 1992: blinkered/visored nowadays: won over hurdles (bought in 3,800 gns) in September: sold 1,100 gns Ascot November Sales. *S. Mellor*

KANSK   4 b.c. Top Ville 129 – Kanz (USA) 115 (The Minstrel (CAN) 135) [1991   **97**
11g³ 10.5g* 11.9m* 12.3d³ 1992 10d³ 12g 11.9g⁵ 12d⁴ 12f⁴ 16.1g* 16.2g⁵] good-bodied colt: has a powerful round action: useful and consistent handicapper: comfortable winner of moderately-run race at Newmarket: not seen out after July: seems ideally suited by 2m: acts on firm and dead ground: effective ridden from front or held up. *J. H. M. Gosden*

KANVASS   3 b.c. Shareef Dancer (USA) 135 – Kallista (Zeddaan 130) [1991 NR   **84**
1992 10.3m⁴ 10g 10m* 12.3f² 13.9g 10m 12d⁵ 12g] tall, lengthy colt: good mover: fifth foal: brother to 1991 German 1000 Guineas winner Kazoo and half-brother to a winner in Germany by King of Clubs: dam won from 7f (at 2 yrs) to 9f in Germany: fairly useful performer: claimer ridden, won maiden at Ripon in July: rather inconsistent form in handicaps afterwards: should stay beyond 1½m: acts on firm and dead going: ran moderately (had tongue tied down) fifth start. *J. R. Fanshawe*

KARACHI   2 b.g. (Feb 19) Nishapour (FR) 125 – Lady Dacre 86 (Queen's Hussar   **51** p
124) [1992 6s 6g] leggy gelding: seventh reported foal: dam, placed over 6f at 2 yrs, is sister to Brigadier Gerard: green and never a factor in maidens at Folkestone and Newmarket in October: may well improve again. *C. E. Brittain*

KARAMOJA   3 b.g. Auction Ring (USA) 123 – Cadasi 68 (Persian Bold 123) [1991   **70**
NR 1992 7v* 8d² 9g³ 8d⁵ 8g⁶ 10g 10s³ 10.3g a12g³ a12g⁴] 17,000F, IR 15,000Y: angular gelding: has a rather round action: fourth foal: half-brother to winning Irish sprinter Bold Starlet (by Precocious) and a winner in Italy: dam 2-y-o 6f winner later placed at up to 1m in Ireland, is half-sister to smart Irish sprinter Back Bailey: fair performer: won seller (bought in 7,000 gns) at Wolverhampton in April: stays 1½m: acts on heavy going and fibresand: blinkered last 3 starts: yet to race on top-of-the-ground: lacks turn of foot. *N. A. Graham*

KARAZAN   5 gr.g. Nishapour (FR) 125 – Celestial Path 101 (Godswalk (USA) 130)   –
[1991 8d6 8.5g* 10f⁵ 8g 12f² 11.9g 10.4m⁶ 12d 1992 8g] big, strong gelding: had quick action: one-time fairly useful handicapper: ran moderately in Lincoln Handicap at Doncaster on first start at 5 yrs: seemed best at up to 1¼m: acted on firm and dead ground: had been tried blinkered: tended to carry head high: dead. *J. G. FitzGerald*

KARDELLE   2 b.f. (Apr 4) Kalaglow 132 – Arderelle (FR) 80 (Pharly (FR) 130)   **53** p
[1992 7m] 7,600F: big, workmanlike filly: half-sister to 5f and 6f winner Premier Developer (by Precocious) and French 10.5f winner Ellerton (by Sharpo): dam 1¼m winner out of smart miler Arosa, dam of Arokar: 25/1 and backward, around 13 lengths ninth of 17 to Placerville in maiden at Newmarket, slowly into stride then chasing leaders much of way: showed a light action: will improve. *R. Charlton*

KAREN LOUISE   3 ch.f. Risk Me 127 – Whose Lady (USA) (Master Willie   **69**
129) [1991 7g⁶ 7m² 7.1d³ 6g⁴ 1992 8d 7g 8.3g 7g* 7m⁵ 7d] lengthy, angular filly: moderate mover: easily best effort in 1992 when making all in maiden at Leicester in July: raced too freely for 7-lb claimer final start: should stay 1m: acts on good to firm and dead ground: takes keen hold. *Miss H. C. Knight*

KARIBUNI   2 b.g. (May 9) Alleging (USA) 120 – Crest of Glory (Sallust 134) [1992   –
8m⁶] 1,000Y, 2,000 2-y-o: sturdy gelding: first live foal: dam, ran once at 2 yrs, is daughter of half-sister to Distinctly North: 66/1 and backward, always behind in 10-runner maiden at Thirsk in September. *D. R. Franks*

KARINGA BAY   5 ch.h. Ardross 134 – Handy Dancer 87 (Green God 128) [1991 **113**
10g³ 12g³ 12m⁵ 10g⁴ 10d³ 10g³ 9m 1992 11g⁴ 10m 8f* 10g* 10g] big, strong, close-coupled horse: fluent mover: very useful performer: won at Brighton (straight-forward task in minor event) and Baden-Baden (Group 3 race) in August: stumbled early on and run probably best ignored final start: stays 1½m: acts on good to firm ground, fair effort on dead: has looked a difficult ride, but is game. *G. Lewis*

KARINIYD (IRE)   2 ch.c. (Jun 5) Blushing Groom (FR) 131 – Katiyfa (Auction   **80** p
Ring (USA) 123) [1992 7g*] first foal: dam French 1m and 1¼m winner: odds-on,

won 12-runner maiden at the Curragh in October by a short head: promising. *J. Oxx, Ireland*

KARINSKA   2 b.f. (May 5) Master Willie 129 – Kaiserchronik (GER) (Cortez (GER)) [1992 6f⁵ 7g⁴ 8.2d] angular, workmanlike filly: has a quick action: half-sister to 4 winners in Germany: dam 6f and 10.5f winner in Germany from good family: poor form in claimers and, 2½ months later, a seller: looks a stayer. *Sir Mark Prescott*   **46**

KARNAK   2 b.c. (Apr 30) Shirley Heights 130 – Dokki (USA) (Northern Dancer (CAN)) [1992 8g²] quite attractive colt: first foal: dam unraced half-sister to Slew O' Gold and Coastal: 9/1 and very green, neck second of 9 to Shaiba in minor event at Newmarket in October, running on really strongly up the hill: will improve, particularly over middle distances, and is certain to win races. *R. Charlton*   **88** p

KARUKERA   2 ch.f. (Feb 4) Hallgate 127 – Water Folly (Sharpo 132) [1992 5m² 5g⁵ 5g⁵ 5g] smallish, leggy filly: moderate mover: first foal: dam unraced: modest maiden: will be better suited by 6f. *M. J. Heaton-Ellis*   **53**

KASHAN (IRE)   4 b.g. Darshaan 133 – Kamanika (FR) (Amber Rama (USA) 133) [1991 12g* 12g² 11.5g⁴ 12.5g⁶ 12.5m* 12g³ 15d⁵ 15.5d⁶ 1992 14s⁴ 9d 10.5d 12.1s] leggy, useful-looking gelding: poor mover: half-brother to fair 1m winner Vilanika (by Top Ville) and French 1½m winner Brave Youth (by Youth): dam French 4.5f winner: useful form for A. Fabre at 3 yrs, winning listed race at Deauville: fairly useful winning juvenile hurdler (looked unenthusiastic final start) for N. Henderson in 1991/2, sold out of his stable 11,000 gns Doncaster May Sales after reappearance: off course 5 months and well beaten in the autumn: stays 15.5f: acts on good to firm and dead ground: has been bandaged. *J. M. Bradley*   –

KASHANI (USA)   2 b.c. (Feb 23) Danzig (USA) – Kashan (USA) (Damascus (USA)) [1992 6v*] $625,000Y: brother to a minor winner in North America, closely related to 2 others, notably very smart 1m to 1¼m performer Herat (by Northern Dancer), and half-brother to another: dam won at up to 7f, and was placed in graded stakes: won minor event at Maisons-Laffitte in November by ½ length: sure to do much better at 3 yrs. *A. Fabre, France*   **?**

KASHGAR   3 ch.f. Local Suitor (USA) 128 – Brigata (Brigadier Gerard 144) [1991 NR 1992 a8g a8g a7g a8g 6.9d 5m 6m 6g] 5,200 2-y-o: quite good-topped filly: half-sister to several winners, including useful 1m and 1¼m winner Tafila (by Adonijah) and Irish stayer North Brigade (by Northfields): dam, disappointing maiden, is half-sister to very smart 1½m performer Harmony Hall: of little account. *D. W. Chapman*   –

KASIKCI   3 b.f. Petoski 135 – Top Call 89 (High Top 131) [1991 6m 6g* 7g³ 8m⁵ 10g 1992 8.9g 11s³ 10.1f² 12.3m² 10d⁵ 12.3g⁴ 11.8m² 13.8g³ 12.3s⁴ 12s] rather unfurnished filly: moderate form at best: probably stayed 1½m and acted on any going: broke leg at Pontefract in October. *R. Hollinshead*   **48**

KASISI (IRE)   3 b.f. Bluebird (USA) 125 – Inchmarlo (USA) 99 (Nashua) [1991 7g 1992 10d⁶ 10d 10.4g⁶ 12g*] sturdy filly: good walker: modest form in maidens: made all at Folkestone in September: stays 1½m: acts on dead ground. *A. C. Stewart*   **55** +

KASMAYO   3 b.c. Slip Anchor 136 – Sorbus 121 (Busted 134) [1991 7g² 1992 10g² 11.9d* 12m*] close-coupled, good-topped colt: has a round action: very progressive performer: 28/1 on, not troubled to win 3-runner apprentice maiden at York: given a fine ride by S. Cauthen to make all in 5-runner listed event at Doncaster later in September, beating Duke of Eurolink by 1½ lengths: will stay 1¾m and probably 2m: sure to improve further and win more races. *J. H. M. Gosden*   **109** p

KASSAB   2 b.c. (Feb 25) Caerleon (USA) 132 – Red Comes Up (USA) (Blushing Groom (FR) 131) [1992 7m² 8.1s 8g⁶] 165,000F: workmanlike colt: moderate walker: third known foal: half-brother to 3-y-o 1¼m winner Barahin (by Diesis): dam French maiden sister to Rainbow Quest: fair maiden: didn't really confirm promise shown when rallying short-head second at Newmarket on his debut, but might have been unsuited by the soft ground next time and was set plenty to do in moderately-run minor event at Newbury on final start: will stay at least 1¼m: worth another chance. *J. L. Dunlop*   **76**

KASSBAAN (USA)   2 b.c. (May 2) Alydar (USA) – Ma Biche (USA) 125 (Key To The Kingdom (USA)) [1992 7g²] tall, lengthy colt: sixth foal: half-brother to 2 winners in France, including (at 9f) Bedouin Veil (by Shareef Dancer): dam Cheveley Park and 1000 Guineas winner: weak 8/1-chance and very green, 3½ lengths second of 18 to Tinners Way in maiden at Doncaster in November, keeping on strongly from 2f out: wore bandages behind, and a crossed noseband: will improve and win a maiden at least. *A. A. Scott*   **79** p

KATAKANA (USA) 3 b.f. Diesis 133 – Winds Aloft (USA) (Hoist The Flag **106** (USA)) [1991 6g* 1992 8.1m⁵ 8f³ 8g 10.1m²] leggy, unfurnished filly: fluent mover: promising winner of Newbury maiden at 2 yrs: best effort at 3 yrs when 6¾ lengths third of 7 to Marling in Coronation Stakes at Royal Ascot: ran poorly in Falmouth Stakes at Newmarket in July and 3-runner £7,500 contest (sweating, moved moderately to post) at Yarmouth over 2 months later: should have stayed 1¼m: tended to get on edge, and take keen hold: visits Green Desert. *M. R. Stoute*

KATEB (IRE) 3 ch.c. Pennine Walk 120 – Ridge The Times (USA) 78 (Riva **68** Ridge (USA)) [1991 NR 1992 7.5m⁴ 7f 8f6 8.5f* 7.5m* 10.1f4 8m⁶] 30,000Y: rather leggy colt: fourth foal: half-brother to very useful sprinter Pharaoh's Delight (by Fairy King) and ungenuine 1m winner: Jumby Bay (by Thatching): dam 2-y-o 5f winner: won 2 handicaps within a week at Beverley in June, staying on well from rear: should prove best in strongly-run race at around 1m: acts on firm ground: sold 13,500 gns Newmarket July Sales, and won twice (including at 11f) in Denmark. *R. W. Armstrong*

KATE LABELLE 3 b.f. Teenoso (USA) 135 – Old Kate 110 (Busted 134) [1991 **58** NR 1992 12f³ 10s 12v³] lengthy, sparely-made filly: sixth foal: sister to 6-y-o 1¾m winner Take One and half-sister to several winners, including very useful 11f and 1½m winner Kalakate (by Kalaglow): dam, 9f and 10.2f winner, is sister to very smart soft-ground stayer Old Bill: modest maiden: off course over 5 months after debut: should have stayed 1¾m+: visits Shavian. *G. Wragg*

KATE ROYALE 3 b.f. Beveled (USA) – Silk Lady 97 (Tribal Chief 125) [1991 **49** d 5m⁶ 5g⁵ 5m² 6m⁵ 6m³ 6d² 5f³ 5m 1992 8m a8g⁶ 7m a12g⁶ 11.5g³ 12m² 16g 14.6d 12.3s 10.8s 8.1d] leggy, sparely-made filly: modest plater: claimed out of G. Bravery's stable £4,620 sixth start: stays 1½m: acts on any going: effective blinkered or not: has tended to hang: sold 600 gns Newmarket Autumn Sales. *M. C. Pipe*

KATHS CHOICE 4 b.f. Dunbeath (USA) 127 – Beaufort Star 95 (Great Nephew **30** 126) [1991 5g 6g² 7m 6.9m* 7g4 6.9m 6g 7s 8m a8g 1992 a12g 6g 6g³ 7.1m 6m 9d 9g] lengthy filly: rated 49 at 3 yrs: form in 1992 only when third in apprentice handicap at Yarmouth: stays 7f: acts on good to firm ground: sold 1,600 gns Doncaster November Sales. *H. J. Collingridge*

KATHY FAIR (IRE) 3 b.f. Nicholas Bill 125 – Fair Flutter (Beldale Flutter **42** (USA) 130) [1991 5.7m⁵ 8.1g 7.1m 1992 8g⁵ 11.6m 8.3m⁵ 8g² 8f6 a8g] tall, sparely-made filly: modest plater: should stay beyond 1m, but is headstrong: below form on firm ground: often fractious in preliminaries: one to treat with caution. *R. J. Baker*

Troy Stakes, Doncaster—Kasmayo makes all under Cauthen;
Duke of Eurolink can't reach them

KATIBA (USA)   2 b.f. (Apr 3) Gulch (USA) – Schematic (USA) (Upper Nile   92
(USA)) [1992 6.1m* 6d* 8m 7m⁴] $400,000Y: big, rangy, useful-looking filly: has
plenty of scope: good mover: second foal: half-sister to a winner in North America
by Saratoga Six: dam, successful at up to 7f and placed in graded stakes, is half-sister
to Breeders' Cup sprint winner Very Subtle: sire (by Mr Prospector) won Breeders'
Cup Sprint, third in Belmont Stakes: won maiden at Nottingham and nursery at
Goodwood in August: best effort when over 3 lengths fourth of 7 to Yawl in Rockfel
Stakes at Newmarket, though ran in snatches, tended to hang and once again looked
difficult ride: should stay 1m. *J. L. Dunlop*

KATIE-A (IRE)   3 b.f. Cyrano de Bergerac 120 – Que Tranquila 65 (Dominion   55 §
123) [1991 5f⁴ 1992 5m³ 5f² 5s* 5d⁵ 5m 5g 5g³ 5d⁴ 6.1g 6s 5g] plain, leggy filly:
modest handicapper at her best: won maiden at Beverley in July: best efforts at 5f
with give in the ground: tends to hang: sometimes mulish to post: refused to race
(when visored) penultimate start and reluctant final one: temperamental. *R. M.
Whitaker*

KATIE EILEEN (USA)   2 ch.f. (Jan 5) Bering 136 – Katrina (FR) (Anne's   49
Pretender (USA) 124) [1992 7g 7.1s] 23,000Y: rather leggy filly: third reported foal:
dam French 6.5f to 10.7f winner, is half-sister to good 1984 French 2-y-o stayer
Antartica (by Arctic Tern): shaped well in minor event at Kempton on debut:
soundly beaten in maiden at Chepstow 7 weeks later in the autumn. *R. Hannon*

KATIE'S DREAM (IRE)   3 b.f. Welsh Term 126 – Miss Slip (USA) 107   47
(Coursing) [1991 6g⁴ 6g 6g⁶ 7m⁴ 7m 1992 7g 7.5m* 9f 7d 8f] leggy filly: good mover:
poor performer: won 17-runner seller (bought in 4,200 gns) at Beverley in May:
failed to reproduce that and not seen out after selling event at Ripon (bandaged) in
June: should stay beyond 7.5f: acts on good to firm ground. *P. S. Felgate*

KATY'S LAD   5 b.g. Camden Town 125 – Cathryn's Song (Prince Tenderfoot   74
(USA) 126) [1991 8s 7g³ 10m⁴ 10f 10.8m 10g* 10.8g² 10d* 10.2d⁴ 10.3d⁴ 10.3d 1992
10d* 10.8d* 10.3g⁵ 10g⁴ 10.5g⁴ 12.2g⁵ 10f² 9.9g⁶ 8.9d 10.5d² 10.5s⁴ 10.3s] leggy
gelding: moderate mover: fair handicapper: gained third success at each track
(hasn't won elsewhere) when winning at Pontefract and Warwick in April: stays 11f:
probably acts on any going: best without blinkers: has run well for apprentice: best
when able to dominate. *B. A. McMahon*

KAUSAR (USA)   5 b.h. Vaguely Noble 140 – Kozana 127 (Kris 135) [1991 16g*   63
9v³ 15.9m⁵ 12m⁶ 17.5m⁴ 14g⁶ 1992 16.2s 15s⁶ 16.1s³ 17.1s⁴ 18m 12.4v²] sturdy,
lengthy ex-Irish horse: has round action: modest handicapper: effective at 1½m,
and stays really well: acts on good to firm and heavy ground. *G. M. Moore*

KAWASIR (CAN)   2 b. or br.c. (Mar 2) Gulch (USA) – Madame Treasurer (CAN)   –
(Key To The Mint (USA)) [1992 7d 8s 8.2s] $200,000Y: second foal: dam won 7 races
(2 to 4 yrs) at up to 1m, including in minor stakes: soundly beaten in maidens in the
autumn. *P. T. Walwyn*

KAWWAS   7 b.h. Persian Bold 123 – Tifrums 77 (Thatch (USA) 136) [1991 7f 8m   47
8.1d 8g⁵ 7f⁵ 7m* 7f 7m³ 7s 1992 7d 7.1g² 7m* 7m⁴ 7m⁴ 7f⁴ 7m*] smallish,
attractive horse: poor mover: consistent handicapper: won at Brighton in May and
Kempton in June: stays 7f: seems to need a sound surface: blinkered once earlier in
career: has tended to hang: sold 2,800 gns Ascot June Sales. *W. Holden*

KAYARTIS   3 b.f. Kaytu 112 – Polyartis 78 (Artaius (USA) 129) [1991 7f⁴ 7m⁶   43
8m 1992 9f 12.2g* 13.8f* 12g⁴ 12.2g⁴] sparely-made filly: consistent performer:
narrowly won 2 handicaps at Catterick in July: will stay 2m: acts on firm going: ran
well for lady rider: won novice hurdle (dead ground) in October: game. *Mrs M.
Reveley*

KAY BEEYOU (IRE)   3 b.f. Petorius 117 – Damaslin (Camden Town 125) [1991   –
6m³ 5.7f³ 6f 6g⁶ 6f³ 6s⁴ a8g⁶ 1992 8m⁶ 6.9g] leggy filly: modest maiden: ran badly
last time, in July: best efforts at 6f: acts on any going: bandaged at 3 yrs. *T. Thomson
Jones*

KAYFAAT (USA)   4 b.g. Spend A Buck (USA) – Duped (USA) (On The Sly   –
(USA)) [1991 8m 10g⁵ 14m⁴ 14.1f⁴ 12g 14.6m* 14.6g* 15.9d² 1992 18g 14.6m] leggy,
quite attractive gelding: moderate mover: rated 74 at 3 yrs: winning juvenile
hurdler in 1991/2: ran as if something amiss at Doncaster in March: well below form
at Wolverhampton 3 months later: stays 2m: has won on good to firm, but best
efforts with give in the ground: has been gelded. *M. C. Pipe*

KAYRUZ   4 b.g. Fayruz 116 – Rheinbloom 66 (Rheingold 137) [1991 NR 1992 a6g]   –
half-brother to fairly useful stayer Rhusted (by Busted): dam won over 1½m: 16/1,
well beaten in claimer at Southwell in December. *D. Burchell*

KAY'S DILEMMA (IRE) 4 b.f. Ya Zaman (USA) – Brook's Dilemma 80 **40** (Known Fact (USA) 135) [1991 8g 6.5s 7d a8g a10g 1992 a8g⁴ a8g² a8g* a7g 8.5g 9.5g⁴ 10f⁶ 8.5s] ex-Irish filly: poor form: best effort here when winning Southwell maiden in March: trained until after fifth start by P. Kelleway: afterwards ran in Germany (including over hurdles), reportedly finishing lame last time: stays 1m. *A. Pereira, Germany*

KAYTAK (FR) 5 b.g. Mouktar 129 – Kaythama (Run The Gantlet (USA)) [1991 **72** 14g⁶ 11.5g⁴ 7.6m⁵ 11.5g* 12v⁵ 12m 12d 1992 12g* 12d 12g⁴ 11.4s⁴ 14d] leggy, sparely-made ex-French gelding: fair handicapper: won at Kempton in May: unimpressive in appearance and well beaten final start, in July: should stay beyond 1½m: acts on heavy ground. *J. R. Jenkins*

KAYTURA 3 br.f. Kaytu 112 – Balilyca (Balidar 133) [1991 NR 1992 8g 10g⁶ 10m⁴ – 10m 12.3s] unfurnished filly: fifth living foal: dam plating class: no worthwhile form, and went in snatches in seller final start. *M. H. Tompkins*

KAYVEE 3 gr.g. Kaldoun (FR) 122 – Secret Life (USA) (Elocutionist (USA)) [1991 **96** 5g² 6g² 6m² 7g² 6.9f* 7m⁵ 1992 6m⁴ 6f³ 6f* 6m 7m 6d 6g 7.3g⁴ 7m⁵ 7m] big, close-coupled gelding: carries condition: useful handicapper at his best: third to Red Rosein in Wokingham Handicap at Royal Ascot and won at Salisbury (making virtually all) in June: stays 7.3f: acts on firm going, possibly not at best on a soft surface: blinkered twice, running well second occasion (eighth outing): sometimes wears severe noseband. *G. Harwood*

K-BRIGADE 7 b.h. Brigadier Gerard 144 – Kajetana (FR) (Caro (133)) [1991 **50** 10.1m⁴ 12.4m⁴ 12g⁴ 10.1m² 10.9m⁵ 1992 16.1s⁴ 12.1g² 12.4s³] big, lengthy horse: modest handicapper, last win came 19 starts ago at 3 yrs: stays 2m: possibly not at his best on firm going, acts on any other: ran creditably in blinkers last 2 starts, in April. *C. W. C. Elsey*

KEAMARI 2 ch.f. (May 1) Krayyan 117 – Bonny Music (Music Boy 124) [1992 5g – 5g⁴ 5.3f 6d] neat filly: third reported foal: half-sister to 1988 2-y-o 5f winner Merry Mannequin (by Latest Model): dam ran 3 times: no worthwhile form, including in sellers. *B. Forsey*

KEATING (AUS) 2 ch.g. (Jan 18) Keen 116 – Artistic Princess (AUS) (Luskin **?** Star (AUS)) [1992 6g 7m² 6d] rather unfurnished gelding: first foal: dam Australian sprinter: signs of ability though soundly beaten in maidens at Newmarket (off course 4 months subsequently) and Yarmouth: second in 3-runner private sweepstakes in between: sold 3,700 gns Doncaster November Sales. *Mrs J. Cecil*

KEDGE 2 b.c. (Apr 23) Slip Anchor 136 – Bercheba (Bellypha 130) [1992 7g] rangy **– p** colt: third foal: closely related to 3-y-o 11.9f winner Shirl (by Shirley Heights): dam from good family: 20/1 and backward, ran green, hung left and never a factor in 18-runner maiden at Doncaster in November. *R. F. Johnson Houghton*

KEEN HUNTER (USA) 5 ch.h. Diesis 133 – Love's Reward (Nonoalco (USA) **119** 131) [1991 6g* 5d* 1992 5m⁶ 5s² 5s² 6g²] tall, strong, good-topped horse: smart sprinter: best efforts in 1992 when second in Prix de l'Abbaye (2 lengths behind Mr Brooks) and Prix du Petit Couvert (beaten ¾ length by Wixon) at Longchamp in October: fair effort behind Blyton Lad in listed event at Doncaster following month: very best form at 5f with give in the ground (has won at 6f on good to firm): sometimes bandaged near-fore. *J. H. M. Gosden*

KEEN VISION (IRE) 4 b.g. Vision (USA) – Calvino (Relkino 131) [1991 9d **40** 8.2m² 10d³ 9m 8.2f² 10g² 7m⁵ 8.2f 10m 1992 a12g²] workmanlike gelding: modest maiden on flat, runner-up in handicap at Lingfield in December: stays 1½m: acts on firm ground and equitrack: has put head in air, and tends to find little: fair winning hurdler in 1991/2, including on equitrack. *D. W. P. Arbuthnot*

KEEN WIT 3 gr.f. Kenmare (FR) 125 – Nettle 106 (Kris 135) [1991 NR 1992 a7g⁵ – a8g⁵] first foal: dam 2-y-o 6f and 7.3f winner appeared to stay 1½m, is daughter of Galtres Stakes winner Sans Blague: poor maiden: should stay 1¼m: sold 2,300 gns Ascot March Sales. *Lord Huntingdon*

KEEP BREATHING 2 b.c. (Mar 16) Northern Tempest (USA) 120 – Stolen- – Secret (Burglar 128) [1992 6.9v a7g a7g] brother to 3-y-o Stormbuster and half-brother to 1986 2-y-o 5f seller winner Five Sixes (by Music Maestro): dam closely related to very smart 5f performer Singing Bede: ridden by 7-lb claimer, no worthwhile form in late-season maidens and claimer. *M. H. Tompkins*

KEEP YOUR DISTANCE 2 b.c. (Apr 20) Elegant Air 119 – Normanby Lass **40 p** 100 (Bustino 136) [1992 7g⁵ 8g] 15,500Y: leggy, unfurnished colt: third foal: brother to 3-y-o Miss Debonair: dam 2-y-o 7f winner: backward and green, finished in promising style when fifth in maiden at Thirsk: 5/1 from 10/1, faded from 2f out in maiden auction at Redcar later in August: clearly thought capable of better. *Mrs M. Reveley*

KEEP YOUR WORD   6 ch.m. Castle Keep 121 – So True 116 (So Blessed 130)   **59**
[1991 9s⁵ 10d⁶ 8g³ 10.1g 9d 8d³ 8g* 8g⁴ 7g 8.1m 10g 10.2s 1992 8m 8g² 8s² 8.3m³ 10g³ 9.7m⁵ 9d 9g³ 8d² 8g] tall, sparely-made mare: moderate mover: modest handicapper: effective at 1¼m, but ideally suited by 1m/9f: goes well with some give in the ground, probably not at best on firm: has won for apprentice: sold 1,200 gns Newmarket Autumn Sales. *G. B. Balding*

KELIMUTU   3 br.f. Top Ville 129 – Soemba 86 (General Assembly (USA)) [1991   –
7g 1992 8d 8g⁶ 10.5m⁴ 10.1m 10g 8.9d 10g] leggy filly: no worthwhile form: looked ungenuine before and during race when blinkered final start: sold 9,000 gns Newmarket December Sales. *C. F. Wall*

KELLY MAC   2 b.c. (Feb 5) Precocious 126 – Ridalia 56 (Ridan (USA)) [1992 6g   **72 p**
5g⁴ 5s²] 8,000F, 22,000Y: sturdy, good-quartered colt: has scope: half-brother to fair sprinter Powder Blue (by He Loves Me), 4-y-o 7f winner Tea Dust (by Pennine Walk) and French 9f winner Daring Daphne (by Final Straw): dam showed a little ability: progressive maiden: will stay 6f: likely to improve further and win a race. *N. A. Callaghan*

KELLYS KINGDOM (IRE)   4 b.c. King Persian 107 – Kellys Risc (Pitskelly   –
122) [1991 6m 8m 7g 1992 8d] compact colt: moderate mover: lightly raced since 2 yrs and little worthwhile form. *R. A. Bennett*

KELLY'S KITE   4 br.f. Buzzards Bay 128§ – Bold Kelly 83 (Pitskelly 122) [1991   **42**
10m 8f 6m 6.1m 1992 5f 8m⁴ 7f 8f* 7.6m 8f⁴ 7g 8d 8m⁴ 8g* 9g] compact filly: fairly consistent handicapper: won at Yarmouth (claiming event) in July and Redcar (amateurs) in September: effective at 7f to 1m: acts on firm ground, possibly not on dead: has run well when sweating. *H. J. Collingridge*

KELTIC DANSEUSE (IRE)   2 b.f. (Mar 1) Dance of Life (USA) – Sharp Dres-   **50**
ser (USA) (Sharpen Up 127) [1992 6g 7g³ 7f⁶ 6d] IR 16,000Y: narrow, sparely-made filly: third foal: half-sister to 1m (at 2 yrs) and 4-y-o 1½m winner Rare Detail (by Commanche Run): dam unraced half-sister to Alleging and Nomrood: plating-class maiden: seems flattered by third in moderately-run event at Yarmouth: will stay 1¼m: ridden by 7-lb claimer. *Mrs L. Piggott*

KENBU (FR)   3 gr.f. Kenmare (FR) 125 – Tarlace (FR) (Targowice (USA)** 115
130) [1991 6d² 6g* 6g* 6g² 8d5 1992 7g* 8g³ 8m 7g* 7d³ 8.5f³ 8f² a6f5]
    Two furlongs out it looked as if Kenbu, not Hatoof, might be the French-trained filly to win the One Thousand Guineas; she made smooth headway to join the leaders on the rails then quickened a length or so clear. In the last hundred yards, however, Hatoof managed to reel her back, and Marling eventually got the better of her as well. Kenbu was beaten a head and three quarters of a length, third of fourteen. Supporters of Kenbu would have been in a state of some agitation in the closing stages of all her races in Europe in 1992. Held up in all five, clearly the earliest that she got a view of the front was in the Guineas. Three weeks earlier, she was produced to lead about a hundred and fifty yards out to add the Prix Imprudence at Maisons-Laffitte to wins in a minor event at Saint-Cloud and the Prix de Cabourg at Deauville as a two-year-old. Her most immediate victim in the Imprudence was Hatoof, beaten a neck. That moderately-run seven-furlong contest did little to enlighten on the score of Kenbu's effectiveness at a mile—she had been fifth to Culture Vulture and Hatoof in the Prix Marcel Boussac the previous October—and doubts about whether that was her best trip obviously sur-faced again with the Guineas. A third try at a mile, in the Poule d'Essai des Pouliches, failed to resolve the issue because, although she finished a below-form seventh of nine, Kenbu was beaten only about three and a half lengths and looked short of room on the rails in the final furlong. Anyway, Kenbu's remaining two starts of 1992, after a four-month break, were over seven furlongs. In the listed Prix du Pin at Longchamp she came from the back of a ten-runner field to win by a short neck from Voleris. That was clearly below her Guineas form, but in the Prix de la Foret at the same course three weeks later Kenbu looked back to her best. In this instance, Kenbu indisput-ably did not get the run of the race. Sixth of eight entering the straight, she had to be shuffled through several positions before finally finding daylight inside the final furlong, then managed to reduce a four-length deficit on

Mr T. Wada's "Kenbu"

Wolfhound to just over a length and a half. It seemed a pity at the time that Kenbu did not get the chance to run over six furlongs again in the Breeders' Cup Sprint; she was judged to be last of the seven pre-race entry reserves and, not surprisingly, failed to get a run. However, three outings in the United States at the end of the season included one in a Grade 3 six-furlong race in December in which she finished last of five. Two earlier runs on turf at around a mile had resulted in a creditable two-and-three-quarter-lengths third to Julie La Rousse in a very valuable handicap at Gulfstream Park and a second in an allowance race.

Kenbu (FR) (gr.f. 1989)	Kenmare (FR) (gr 1975)	Kalamoun (gr 1970)	Zeddaan Khairunissa
		Belle of Ireland (ch 1964)	Milesian Belle of The Ball
	Tarlace (FR) (b 1977)	Targowice (b 1970)	Round Table Matriarch
		Alace (b 1961)	Rapace Fair Alycia

A smallish, lengthy filly, Kenbu is by the 1978 Prix Jacques le Marois winner Kenmare, exported from France to Australia in 1988 and champion sire in France in 1988 and 1989. Kenbu's dam Tarlace ran fifteen times in France without success though she showed fair form on occasions. The furthest she was tried over was nine furlongs. Of her four foals prior to Kenbu, three were by Fabulous Dancer and won a race, or races, at around a mile. Her 1990 foal is the Damister filly Lindalace. Tarlace is out of the unraced Alace, another of whose daughters is the dam of Oats. *F. Boutin, France*

KENESHA (IRE) 2 br.f. (Apr 18) Don't Forget Me 127 – Calvino (Relkino 131) [1992 7s] 4,200F: sixth foal: half-sister to 3-y-o Premier Major (by Bluebird), 1987

419

2-y-o 7f winner Y V Tucker (by Valiyar) and temperamental maiden Regal Vine (by Prince Tenderfoot): dam second over 7f at 2 yrs in Ireland: 50/1, always well behind in 14-runner maiden at Lingfield. *S. Dow*

KENNEDYS PRIMA 2 b. or br.f. (Jan 13) Primo Dominie 121 – Double Finesse 97 (Double Jump 131) [1992 6m⁴ 7g⁵ 6m² a6g³ 6g² 6g 5.7d4] angular, workmanlike filly: moderate mover: sister to 3-y-o 7f winner Turtle Beach and half-sister to several winners, including smart 6f to 1m winner Larionov (by Balidar) and 5-y-o July Cup and Prix de l'Abbaye winner Mr Brooks (by Blazing Saddles): dam won at up to 1m: fairly consistent maiden: stays 6f: acts on good to firm and dead ground, below best on fibresand. *A. A. Scott* **65**

KENNINGTON PROTON 2 br.f. (Feb 16) Interrex (CAN) – Supper Party (He Loves Me 120) [1992 6g 7s] leggy, angular filly: fifth foal: half-sister to 3-y-o Chocolate Mint (by Doulab), 5f and 6f winner Francis Ann and a winner abroad (both by Balidar): dam never ran: 66/1, reluctant stalls then always well behind in maidens at Salisbury and Warwick. *J. R. Bosley* **–**

KENSWORTH LADY 2 b.f. (Feb 12) Formidable (USA) 125 – Icefern 88 (Moorestyle 137) [1992 5.1g² 5g 5f² 5g⁶ 6g 5g 6.1g⁴ 6s] 5,200Y: workmanlike filly: first foal: dam sprinter: modest maiden: stays 6f: acts on firm ground: usually gives trouble at the stalls. *M. Blanshard* **55**

KENTUCKY CHICKEN (USA) 3 b.f. Secreto (USA) 128 – Stark Ice (USA) (Icecapade (USA)) [1991 7g 1992 10g 10.5d 12.1m 12g 10m⁵ 10f 14.1g 10g 12m² 14.1m4] angular filly: bad mover: no worthwhile form: blinkered last 6 outings: sold 1,650 gns Doncaster November Sales: has joined D. Swindlehurst. *Miss L. C. Siddall* **–**

KENTUCKY DREAMS 2 b.g. (Feb 27) Dreams To Reality (USA) 113 – Kentucky Tears (USA) (Cougar (CHI)) [1992 5m 7f* 7.5s⁶ 7.5d] small, close-coupled gelding: second reported foal: dam unraced: 14/1, won 20-runner seller (bought in 4,200 gns) at Redcar in June, running on well: well beaten in seller (claimed out of J. Berry's stable £5,751) and nursery (burly) afterwards: stays 7f: acts on firm ground. *Ronald Thompson* **56 d**

KENTUCKY RAIN 3 b.g. Green Ruby (USA) 104 – French Touch 57 (Dieu Soleil 111) [1991 5f⁵ 5f⁵ 5f² 7m⁶ 6f* 7.5f* 7m 1992 8m 6s³ 6.1m² 6d⁶ 7s] modest handicapper: stays 7.5f: acts on any going: sold 4,000 gns Doncaster October Sales. *J. G. FitzGerald* **55**

KENTUCKY STARLET (USA) 3 b.f. Cox's Ridge (USA) – Empress of Canada (CAN) (Accomplish) [1991 6d 7g² 7g 7g² 7g² 8m² 1992 10g 10.8g 11.8d 7f⁶ 6.9g* 7m 6.9m 7g 8.9d] leggy, good-bodied filly: modest handicapper: easily best effort in 1992 when making all at Folkestone in July: stayed 1m: acted on good to firm ground: below form in blinkers. *R. Hannon* **55**

KENYATTA (USA) 3 b.g. Mogambo (USA) – Caranga (USA) (Caro 133) [1991 5g⁴ 5g⁵ 6m⁴ 7d² 7g 7m⁶ 7m 1992 11.1g³ 12f 12g 8.3s⁶ 9g 9d a13g³] leggy, quite attractive gelding: moderate walker: has a round action: form in handicaps since reappearance only on first outing for present trainer (with D. Smith previously) on final start: stays 11.1f: no form in blinkers/visor in 1992, did run well visored at 2 yrs. *A. Moore* **66 d**

KERTALE (IRE) 3 b.g. Soughaan (USA) 111 – Shapely 84 (Parthia 132) [1991 6m⁴ 5m⁵ 5.3f⁴ 5m 5.2f 6m⁵ 7.1m 6m 1992 8f² 7f 8g] smallish, leggy gelding: poor mover: inconsistent plater: well beaten last 2 starts, in midsummer: may well need further than 7f nowadays: acts on firm going. *R. Boss* **48**

KESANTA 2 b.f. (May 6) The Dissident 85 – Nicaline 50 (High Line 125) [1992 6d⁵ 6f⁵ 7g⁶] sparely-made filly: half-sister to winning hurdler Shaston (by Rolfe): dam placed over 1¼m: no worthwhile form, including in sellers: off course nearly 3 months before final start. *W. G. M. Turner* **–**

KETTI 7 br.m. Hotfoot 126 – Nigrel (Sovereign Path 125) [1991 NR 1992 11.6g 8.2d⁶ 8s] smallish, sparely-made mare: fair winning hurdler (stays 3m) in 1991/2: form on flat in 1992 only when not-knocked-about sixth in handicap at Nottingham: will stay beyond 1m: best with plenty of give in the ground: often blinkered. *D. L. Williams* **34**

KEVINSBELLE 4 b.f. Belfort (FR) 89 – Manna Green (Bustino 136) [1991 7g 6m 7m 9.7m 8.3m³ 8f 8.3m⁴ 8g³ 8.2m 8m⁶ a8g⁶ 1992 a7g] light-framed filly: poor walker: rated 48 at 3 yrs: last at Southwell in January, 1992: stays 8.3f: acts on firm going: somewhat headstrong and highly strung. *I. Campbell* **–**

KEY SUSPECT (USA) 3 b.c. Alleged (USA) 138 – Rascal Rascal (USA) (Ack Ack (USA)) [1991 NR 1992 7.1s* 8m³ 7.6s⁶ 7.1s³] sturdy colt: half-brother to **77**

modest 1990 2-y-o 1m winner Alpha Rascal (by Alphabatim) and 2 winners in USA, including a minor stakes winner by Miswaki, and promising 2-y-o Beggarman Thief (by Arctic Tern): dam minor 6f and 2-y-o 8.5f stakes winner: progressive performer: won maiden at Haydock in September: stayed on well when good third in Chepstow handicap having been slowly away final start: will stay 1m: acts on good to firm and soft ground: sold 18,000 gns Newmarket Autumn Sales. *J. H. M. Gosden*

KEY TO MY HEART (IRE)   2 b.c. (Apr 11) Broken Hearted 124 – Originality   **85**
(Godswalk (USA) 130) [1992 5v* 6f* 6g² 6g⁴ 6g 7.9d³ 8.3v² 7g⁶] IR 6,200F, 5,000Y: sturdy, lengthy colt: has scope: moderate mover: fourth foal: dam lightly raced: fairly useful performer: won maiden at Hamilton and median auction event at Thirsk in the spring: ran very well in nurseries final 3 starts: will stay 1¼m: acts on any going. *D. Moffatt*

KHALLOOF (IRE)   3 b.g. Ballad Rock 122 – Tapiola 71 (Tap On Wood 130)   **–**
[1991 7g* 7f³ 6m 1992 10d 8.5m] heavy-topped gelding: good walker: has run poorly in handicaps since finishing third at 2 yrs: stays 7f: acts on firm ground: sold to join D. Smith 2,200 gns Newmarket July Sales: has been gelded. *M. A. Jarvis*

KHANATA (USA)   3 b.f. Riverman (USA) 131 – Kozana 127 (Kris 135) [1991 7g   **108**
7m² 7.8m* 1992 7d³ 8d* 8g⁶ 10m³ 12g⁵] third foal: half-sister to 1¼m winner Khazari (by Shahrastani) and Irish 1¾m and 2m winner Kausar (by Vaguely Noble): dam, French 1m and 1¼m winner third in Arc, is out of Poule d'Essai des Pouliches winner Koblenza: useful performer: won maiden at Dundalk at 2 yrs and listed race at Leopardstown in May at 3 yrs: best effort when staying-on 2 lengths third to Market Booster in Pretty Polly Stakes at the Curragh: weakened over 2f out and well beaten in Irish Oaks final start, in July: stays 1¼m well: acts on good to firm and dead ground. *J. Oxx, Ireland*

KHARAJ   2 b.c. (Apr 11) Midyan (USA) 124 – Queen And Country (Town And   **78**
Country 124) [1992 5g* 5d² 6f²] 40,000Y: small, quite attractive colt: third foal: half-brother to 3-y-o 6f and 7.1f winner Elsals (by Sizzling Melody): dam twice-raced half-sister to Ayr Gold Cup winner Polly's Brother: fair form: won maiden at Newmarket: runner-up in 3-runner minor events at Ascot and (running moderately) Doncaster later in the spring: will stay at least 6f. *A. A. Scott*

KHATTAT (USA)   2 ch.c. (Mar 9) El Gran Senor (USA) 136 – Don't Joke (USA)   **76 p**
(Shecky Greene (USA)) [1992 6g²] $150,000Y: leggy, attractive colt: third reported foal: dam beat at 2 yrs, winning stakes events at 6f and 8.5f: well-backed favourite, 1½ lengths second of 7 to Rustic Craft in newcomers event at Ascot in October, travelling strongly most of way, staying on well when ridden: will stay at least 7f: sure to improve and win a race or two. *J. L. Dunlop*

KHAZAR (USA)   3 b.c. Nureyev (USA) 131 – Kathleen's Girl (USA) (Native   **67**
Charger) [1991 7.1s⁶ 7.1d 7g* 1992 8d 8d 7.6s 7f⁵ 9.2f² 11f* 10g*] leggy, good-topped colt: fair handicapper: won twice at Redcar in midsummer: stays 11f: acts on firm going: has pulled hard: sold 15,000 gns Newmarket July Sales, reportedly to race in Italy. *Sir Mark Prescott*

KHOJOHN   4 ch.g. Chief Singer 131 – Pirate Lass (USA) 90 (Cutlass (USA)) [1991   **–**
a8g² a8g³ a8g⁴ 10.2s² 10f 12.3d 10.6m a11g³ 10m⁶ 7.1g⁶ 10.4m⁴ 1992 16.2g a14g] plain gelding: rated 52 at 3 yrs: no form in 1992: stays 11f: probably best on an easy surface: probably effective visored/blinkered or not: trained by R. Woodhouse first start. *Mrs V. A. Aconley*

KHORAZ (USA)   2 b. or br.c. (Feb 21) The Minstrel (CAN) 135 – Kozana 127   **100 p**
(Kris 135) [1992 6m⁵ 7d² 7s* 7s³] fourth foal: half-brother to 3 winners, including 1¾m and 2m winner Kausar (by Vaguely Noble) and Irish 3-y-o Khanata (by Riverman), successful at 1m and stays 1¼m: dam, French 1m and 1¼m winner third in Arc, is out of Poule d'Essai des Pouliches winner Koblenza: progressive form: successful in maiden at the Curragh in August: 3½ lengths third of 5 to Fatherland in moderately-run National Stakes there following month, keeping on well: will be better suited by 1¼m: likely to continue on the upgrade. *J. Oxx, Ireland*

KHRISMA (USA)   3 ch.f. Kris 135 – Sancta 106 (So Blessed 130) [1991 NR 1992 a10g*   **80**
10.2s⁶ 10.3f³ 10.1m⁵ 10d a10g³ a10g* a10g²] angular filly: sixth foal: closely related to smart 7f (at 2 yrs) and 1¼m winner Carmelite House (by Diesis) and very useful 7f to 10.5f winner Wolsey (by Our Native): dam, winner at 1m and 1¼m, is half-sister to the dam of Kris and Diesis: fairly useful performer: successful at Lingfield in maiden in February and, showing much improved form, handicap in December: stays 10.3f: acts on firm ground and clearly goes very well on equitrack. *Mrs J. Cecil*

KHUBZA   2 b.f. (Apr 8) Green Desert (USA) 127 – Breadcrumb 111 (Final Straw   **48 p**
127) [1992 6s⁶] 98,000Y: third foal: half-sister to useful 1990 2-y-o 5f and 6f winner

Heard A Whisper (by Bellypha): dam 6f and 7f winner from sprinting family: 4/1, over 9 lengths sixth of 14 to Siwaayib in maiden at Leicester in October, fading final 2f: should do better. *H. R. A. Cecil*

KIAWAH 2 ch.f. (Apr 27) Master Willie 129 – Polly Packer 81 (Reform 132) [1992 **51** 7g 8.2d 7g 8g3] small filly: ninth foal: half-sister to several winners, including stayers Upton Park (by High Top) and Regal Reform (by Prince Tenderfoot): dam, second over 7f and 1m, is out of very useful miler Vital Match: easily best effort when strong-finishing third of 20 in selling nursery at Doncaster in October: will be suited by 1½m. *J. R. Fanshawe*

KICKCASHTAL 3 b.g. Ballacashtal (CAN) – Teenager 71 (Never Say Die 137) – [1991 NR 1992 12g4 11.8g 12.3s] angular, workmanlike gelding: half-brother to several winners, including 7.6f to 18.1f winner Creeager (by Creetown) and 1¼m winner Standon Rock (by Mansingh): dam second over 6f at 2 yrs: well beaten in maidens. *B. A. McMahon*

KICK ON MAJESTIC (IRE) 3 b.g. Mister Majestic 122 – Avebury Ring **37** (Auction Ring (USA) 123) [1991 5g4 5.9h3 5g3 7f6 7m2 7g 7m 7f* 7f5 6.9h2 7.5f 1992 a5g5 a8g4 a8g 8.9s4 8s 7g* 6.9d6 7m 7d6 7.1m 8h 7.6g 6f 8g 6.9g 8g] neat gelding: moderate mover: below form in handicaps after winning at Catterick in April: best at 7f: acts on hard ground: effective blinkered or not: below form when visored. *N. Bycroft*

KILCASH (IRE) 4 b.g. Salmon Leap (USA) 131 – Roblanna 85 (Roberto (USA) – 131) [1991 16g2 12m4 14g4 14g2 14s* 12d3 1992 16m] first foal: dam twice-raced Irish 9f winner: ex-Irish performer, rated 77 when successful in Listowel maiden and third in Roscommon handicap as 3-y-o for J. Bolger: well beaten in handicap at Goodwood in May, 1992: stays 1¾m: best efforts on soft ground: effective blinkered or not: twice won over hurdles in October. *P. R. Hedger*

KILDEE LAD 2 b.c. (Apr 15) Presidium 124 – National Time (USA) (Lord Avie **52** (USA)) [1992 5.7f 5g3 5f6 a5g3 6.1s] close-coupled, quite attractive colt: fourth foal: half-brother to plating-class sprinter Meeson Times (by Enchantment): dam ran twice at 2 yrs: modest maiden: should be suited by further than 5f: acts on firm going, ran respectably on fibresand. *A. P. Jones*

KILLICK 4 b.f. Slip Anchor 136 – Enthralment (USA) 78 (Sir Ivor 135) [1991 7g6 **53** 11.5g5 8g 10s6 8g6 1992 10.5m 6d 12f3 11.8g 11.5s4 11.5d a14g6 a8g* a8g* a8g3] leggy, workmanlike filly: won claimer and handicaps at Lingfield in December: seems best at around 1m: acts on any going, including equitrack: out of form when tried blinkered: sometimes wears tongue strap. *R. E. Peacock*

KILLSHANDRA (IRE) 3 b.f. Heraldiste (USA) 121 – Gulistan (Sharpen Up – 127) [1991 NR 1992 7d 10m 11.7m4 14.6g 11.7m4 10d] 4,400Y: leggy, sparely-made filly: half-sister to fair but unreliable 7.6f winner Are You Guilty (by Runnett): dam poor daughter of smart stayer Turf: no worthwhile form, including in seller: needs further than 1¼m. *Mrs Barbara Waring*

KILL THE PLAGUE (USA) 2 ch.g. (May 12) Only Dreamin (USA) – Stephen's – Grad (USA) (Sensitivo) [1992 5f5 6.1g 6m a8g 8d] $3,000Y: good-bodied gelding: half-brother to a winner by Riverman: dam won at up to 9f, including in minor stakes: of no account. *A. P. Jones*

KILLY 3 ch.c. Dominion 123 – Figini 74 (Glint of Gold 128) [1991 6m* 6.1m4 7m4 **77** 7s 1992 8.2d* 10d 8m5 7.9m 7.9s 8m 7g6] sturdy, angular colt: moderate mover: in-and-out form in handicaps after winning Nottingham minor event in April: should stay beyond 1m: acts on good to firm ground and dead: effective blinkered or not, below form visored: retained 7,000 gns Newmarket Autumn Sales after penultimate start. *F. H. Lee*

KILLY'S FILLY 2 b.f. (Feb 27) Lochnager 132 – May Kells (Artaius (USA) 129) **46** [1992 6f2 6d5 7.5m6 8.3s] 1,200Y: rather leggy, workmanlike filly: second foal: half-sister to a temperamental maiden: dam unraced: poor maiden: stays 7.5f: acts on good to firm and dead ground. *J. Berry*

KILMELFORD 3 b.g. Beldale Flutter (USA) 130 – River Aire 82 (Klairon 131) – [1991 6f a6g2 a7g2 7m4 7.3m 7m 1992 6g] compact gelding: modest maiden: not seen out again after running moderately in handicap in April: should be suited by 1m + . *J. A. R. Toller*

KILTROUM (FR) 3 gr.g. Courtroom (FR) 113 – Kiltie (Habat 127) [1991 5g5 5d **62** 5f 6g 7.5f 1992 8g a6g2] sturdy, close-coupled gelding: off course nearly 4 months, easily best effort when second in claimer at Southwell in December: should stay 7f: acts on fibresand: no form visored/blinkered at 2 yrs. *C. Tinkler*

KIMBERLEY BOY   2 b.c. (Feb 20) Mtoto 134 – Diamond House (Habitat 134)   **83** p
[1992 7m 8g 7.6s*] big, lengthy colt: second foal: half-brother to 3-y-o Peacock
Throne (by Persian Bold): dam sister to useful filly Life At The Top (stayed 1¼m):
much improved effort (carrying plenty of condition previously, in stronger company) when winning 5-runner maiden at Chester in October, making all to beat
Fools Errand by 4 lengths: will be suited by middle distances: will improve further.
B. W. Hills

KIMBERLEY PARK   4 b.f. Try My Best (USA) 130 – Georgina Park 88 (Silly   **72**
Season 127) [1991 a8g 7m³ 7g* 7g³ 8m 8.1m⁵ 7s 7m⁴ 7g³ 6.9s² 1992 7g⁴ 7g² 7f 7d⁶
7d 7m⁴ 7v 7g] compact filly: fair handicapper: effective at 7f to 1m: acts on good to
firm and soft ground: effective held up or ridden close to pace. *D. W. P. Arbuthnot*

KIMBERS (IRE)   4 b.c. Lomond (USA) 128 – Take Your Mark (USA) (Round **102** d
Table) [1991 12.1d* 12g⁵ 14g⁵ 1992 12g³ 16.2d 13.3f⁶ 12d 12f 12g 12m] lengthy,
useful-looking colt: good mover: went the wrong way after third in Newmarket
handicap in April: blinkered and looked reluctant final start: stays 1½m: acts on
good to firm and dead ground: sold to join S. Mellor only 3,500 gns Newmarket
Autumn Sales. *C. R. Nelson*

KIMBOLTON KORKER   2 ch.f. (Apr 22) Interrex (CAN) – One Sharper   **54**
(Dublin Taxi) [1992 5.2s 5d⁴ 5d³ 5g⁴ 5m] sparely-made filly: poor walker: third foal:
half-sister to 1988 2-y-o 5f winner Kimbolton Katie (by Aragon): dam twice-raced
half-sister to very smart miler General Vole: modest maiden: stiff task final start:
likely to prove best at 5f: acts on dead ground: bandaged behind last 2 starts. *A. A.
Scott*

KIMS SELECTION (IRE)   3 b.g. Red Sunset 120 – Restless Lady (Sandford   –
Lad 133) [1991 NR 1992 12.2g⁵ 14.1g⁵] IR 8,500F, 6,200Y: workmanlike gelding: fifth
foal: half-brother to 9-y-o Catherines Well (by Ahonoora) and Kali Kopella (by
Ahonoora), both winning sprinters: dam showed little: twice raced and well beaten
in northern maidens. *S. G. Norton*

KINCHENJUNGA   2 b.f. (May 1) Darshaan 133 – Konigsalpen (GER) (Priamos   **67** p
(GER) 123) [1992 8.2g²] close-coupled, quite attractive filly: closely related to very
useful 1m and 1½m winner Konigsberg (by Shirley Heights) and half-brother to 2
winners in USA: dam, winner from 6f to 11f in Germany and USA, is out of German
Oaks second Konigskrone: favourite, made most when 3 lengths second of 7 to
Ajanta in minor event at Nottingham in September: showed a quick action: sure to
improve, and win a staying maiden. *H. R. A. Cecil*

KINDERGARTEN   2 b.f. (Mar 8) Trempolino (USA) 135 – Children's Corner **111** p
(FR) (Top Ville 129) [1992 8g* 8d* 8s²] robust filly: second foal: dam French 1m (at
2 yrs) and 9f winner: successful in newcomers race at Deauville and Prix d'Aumale
at Longchamp (beat Lorelie by 1½ lengths): didn't impress in appearance but ran

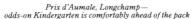

Prix d'Aumale, Longchamp—
odds-on Kindergarten is comfortably ahead of the pack

very well when beaten a short neck by Gold Splash in Prix Marcel Boussac at Longchamp in October, close up 2f out and staying on well: will stay 1¼m: acts on soft going: may well improve further. *A. Fabre, France*

KIND OF CUTE   2 ch.f. (Mar 28) Prince Sabo 123 – So Kind 90 (Kind of Hush 118) [1992 5g 5f 5.7g³ 5m] 1,700F, 8,000Y: lengthy, angular filly: first foal: dam 6f winner probably stayed 7f: ran moderately when sweating final start: will be better suited by 7f. *C. C. Elsey*   **52**

KINDRED CAMEO   3 ch.f. Risk Me (FR) 127 – First Experience 58 (Le Johnstan 123) [1991 5d 1992 6m 5g 5.3m 7m⁴ 8.5d⁵ 10g] compact filly: poor maiden: stays 8.5f: best efforts on a soft surface: sold to join K. Clutterbuck's stable 750 gns Ascot July Sales. *G. Lewis*   **40**

KIND STYLE (IRE)   4 ch.c. Doulab (USA) 115 – Dankalia (Le Levanstell 122) [1991 a8g² a8g³ 8m 9m 8d 10g 10.8m 11.7f⁴ 1992 10.1s 10s 8.5g 8f⁶ 9.9f 7f 7g⁵ 10m⁵ 11d] compact colt: moderate walker and mover: poor maiden: stays 1m: acts on firm going: sold 800 gns Doncaster October Sales: difficult ride. *R. Hollinshead*   –

KINEMA RED (USA)   2 ch.c. (Feb 16) Diesis 133 – Kinema (USA) (Graustark) [1992 7g⁵] second foal: half-brother to 4-y-o 8.1f and 1¼m winner Kinematic (by Sovereign Dancer): dam winner at 1m in USA, is half-sister to dam of Shareef Dancer: 10/1, under 4 lengths fifth of 15 to Abtaal in minor event at Kempton in August, green on turn and running on well final 1f: will improve. *J. H. M. Gosden*   **72** p

KINEMATIC (USA)   4 b.c. Sovereign Dancer (USA) – Kinema (USA) (Graustark) [1991 8.1m* 1992 12d² 10.4m 10.1g³ 10m* 10s² 10.9s⁴ 12g⁵] good-topped colt: has a long, rather round stride: useful handicapper: won at Newmarket in August: effective at 1¼m to 1½m: acts on good to firm and soft ground: suitable mount for inexperienced rider: strong-galloping sort, best ridden up with the pace: sold 37,000 gns Newmarket Autumn Sales. *J. H. M. Gosden*   **96**

KING AL   5 b.h. Indian King (USA) 128 – Impudent Miss 105 (Persian Bold 123) [1991 NR 1992 8m⁵ 7m³ 8m 8m] leggy, lengthy horse: lightly-raced handicapper: heavily bandaged and well below form last 2 starts: best form at around 7f: acts on firm going. *Dr J. D. Scargill*   **88**

KING ATHELSTAN (USA)   4 b.c. Sovereign Dancer (USA) – Wimbledon Star (USA) (Hoist The Flag (USA)) [1991 8m⁴ 10.4m* 9g² 1992 10g] lengthy, good-topped colt: lightly raced but useful (rated 101) at 3 yrs: bandaged behind and tailed-off last in £11,350 handicap at Newmarket in May, only run in 1992: should stay 1½m: acts on good to firm ground. *J. H. M. Gosden*   –

KINGCHIP BOY   3 b.g. Petong 126 – Silk St James (Pas de Seul 133) [1991 5.3m 6s 6m a6g a7g a8g* 1992 9g⁶ 8.2g 8.9g⁶ 8f⁴ 8f* 8.1g* 8g² 8f* 8d 8d a10g⁴ a8g² a8g³] compact gelding: moderate mover: modest handicapper: in excellent form in summer, winning at Yarmouth, Sandown and Brighton: good second at Lingfield in November: suited by 1m: best on a sound surface, acts on equitrack: no improvement in blinkers/visor: wayward in front, and best with waiting tactics. *M. J. Ryan*   **59**

KINGDOM OF SPAIN (USA)   3 b.c. El Gran Senor (USA) 136 – Mystical River (USA) (Riverman (USA) 131) [1991 8m* 8d⁵ 1992 10g⁶] strong, good-bodied colt: won maiden at Doncaster at 2 yrs: reportedly sick with pleurisy next start, and again ran as if something amiss in listed event at Newmarket in May, 1992: one to treat with caution. *H. R. A. Cecil*   –

KING FERDINAND   5 b.g. King of Spain 121 – Gundi 57 (Mummy's Pet 125) [1991 a8g² 8d 7m* a7g³ 1992 a7g a8g⁶ a8g 10.3g 7g] lengthy, workmanlike gelding: moderate mover: rated 68 as 4-y-o: below form in 1992, tried visored once: best efforts at 7f: acts on good to firm ground and fibresand. *D. R. Tucker*   –

KINGFISHER BAY   7 b.h. Try My Best (USA) 130 – Damiya (FR) (Direct Flight) [1991 NR 1992 10m] leggy horse: lightly raced and no form on flat: won over fences in September and October. *J. White*   –

KING HIGH   5 b.g. Shirley Heights 130 – Regal Twin (USA) (Majestic Prince) [1991 NR 1992 a14g⁶] rather leggy, lengthy gelding: carries condition: moderate mover: rated 91 as 3-y-o: well beaten in handicap in January, only run in 1992: stays well: acts on good to firm ground: effective blinkered or not. *A. S. Reid*   – §

KINGLOW (USA)   3 b.c. Sovereign Dancer (USA) – Sconce (USA) (Majestic Light (USA)) [1991 7m⁵ 7m* 1992 8.9g 11.4m* 12f⁵ 11.9d² 11.9m 12g] leggy, quite attractive colt: bad mover: progressed well in handicaps, successful at Sandown in May, until well beaten in quite valuable events last 2 starts: may prove suited by 1¾m: acts on firm and dead going: blinkered last 3 starts. *Mrs J. Cecil*   **83**

KINGMAMBO (USA) 2 b.c. (Feb 19) Mr Prospector (USA) – Miesque (USA) **110**
133 (Nureyev (USA) 131) [1992 6d² 6g* 6g² 6s⁶ 7m² 8s⁵ 8v²] leggy, close-coupled
colt: first foal: dam brilliant miler from good family: won minor event at Maisons-
Laffitte in July: subsequently runner-up in Prix de Cabourg at Deauville, Prix de
la Salamandre at Longchamp (made much of running when beaten 3 lengths by
Zafonic) and Prix Thomas Bryon at Saint-Cloud (beaten ½ length by Mil Foil):
creditable fifth to Tenby in Ciga Grand Criterium at Longchamp: stays 1m: probably
acts on any going: blinkered second and third starts: looks difficult ride. *F. Boutin,
France*

KING OF CHANCE (IRE) 4 b.g. Indian King (USA) 128 – Midnight Chance **82**
(Run The Gantlet (USA)) [1991 6g 7.5g 7g⁶ 8m⁶ 10.1m³ 10.3m⁶ 8m* 8m² 8m² 8m²
1992 8g* 7g² 7d 8f* 8.1m⁴ 8f] angular, good-topped gelding: fair handicapper: won
at Doncaster (ridden by 7-lb claimer) and Thirsk in spring: ran moderately final 2
starts, and not seen out after June: best form at strongly-run 7f or 1m: goes well on a
sound surface. *Mrs J. R. Ramsden*

KING OF MILEEN 6 b.g. Castle Keep 121 – Port Meadow 83 (Runnymede 123) –
[1991 NR 1992 10d 7g 8.1m] lengthy, quite attractive gelding: rated 67 at 4 yrs: below
form in 1992: stays 1¼m: acts on firm ground (shaped well on soft). *D. Shaw*

KING OF NORMANDY (IRE) 3 ch.g. King of Clubs 124 – Miss Deauville **62** d
(Sovereign Path 125) [1991 5g 6d² 7d 8.1m⁵ 8m 6g 7.1s 1992 10g² 10f³ 12m⁴ 11.4d
10f⁶ 12g³ 12.3g 10m a10g⁴] leggy, workmanlike gelding: regressive maiden: seems
to stay 1½m: acts on firm ground and dead: below form blinkered: trained until after
penultimate start by R. Hannon: reluctant, one to treat with caution. *J. Ffitch-Heyes*

KING OLAF (IRE) 3 b.g. Thatching 131 – Regiura (High Top 131) [1991 6m² **101**
1992 7g* 7g* 7f 8f⁵] big, good-topped gelding: shows plenty of knee action:
successful at Newmarket in spring in a maiden and £7,200 contest: well below form
in Jersey Stakes at Royal Ascot and Doncaster minor event 3 months after: should
stay 1m: possibly unsuited by firm ground: sold only 6,000 gns Newmarket Autumn
Sales. *P. W. Chapple-Hyam*

KING OPTIMIST 3 ch.g. King Persian 107 – Misoptimist 111 (Blakeney 126) –
[1991 5d⁵ 5g⁵ 6m⁴ 6m⁶ a6g⁶ 7m⁵ 7.5f 7f 7.5f 6m 10m 1992 8v 7.5m⁶ 10f 8g 12m³
a14g⁶ 10d] tall, plain gelding: poor plater: tried blinkered: won over hurdles in
September. *A. Smith*

KING PARIS (IRE) 2 ch.g. (Apr 27) King of Clubs 124 – Alkis (USA) (Roberto **100**
(USA) 131) [1992 5m* 6m⁴ 7m* 7m* 7.1d² 8d⁵ 8s] well-made gelding: first foal
here: dam, daughter of smart 5f to 1m winner Lady Mere, ran twice before export to
Greece: successful in Haydock maiden in May, nurseries at Newmarket in July and
August: much improved 1½ lengths second of 9 to White Crown in Solario Stakes at
Sandown: under 2 lengths last of 5 in Prix La Rochette at Longchamp and didn't
have best of runs in Royal Lodge Stakes at Ascot: will be suited by 1¼m: has plenty
of form on good to firm ground, but best efforts on dead. *M. Bell*

KING PARROT (IRE) 4 br.g. King of Spain 121 – Red Lory 87 (Bay Express **64**
132) [1991 NR 1992 8.1d a8g* a8g²] leggy, workmanlike gelding: second foal: half-
brother to Bird Bath (by Longleat), plating-class maiden here later successful over
6f in Holland: dam 2-y-o 5f winner: not seen until October: narrow winner of claimer
at Lingfield in December: stays 1m: acts on all-weather surfaces. *Lord Huntingdon*

KINGSDOWN CAVALIER 2 b.c. (May 20) Superlative 118 – Breakaway 98 **60**
(Song 132) [1992 5g⁵ 6m⁴ 6m³ 6g⁶ 8.5d 6m] 9,000F, 6,200Y: close-coupled colt: first
foal: dam 5f winner: modest maiden: stays 6f: usually goes freely to post: sold 3,600
gns Newmarket Autumn Sales. *R. Hannon*

KINGSFOLD PET 3 b.g. Tina's Pet 121 – Bella Lisa (River Chanter 121) [1991 –
NR 1992 7.6m 10.1d³ 10.2g 10m 8.5d⁶] tall, rangy gelding: closely related to winning
hurdler (modest staying maiden on flat) Esport (by Mummy's Game) and half-
brother to several winners, including fairly useful sprinter Kingsfold Trooper (by
King's Troop): dam ran 3 times: no worthwhile form. *M. J. Haynes*

KING'S GUEST (IRE) 3 b.g. Tender King 123 – Saintly Guest (What A Guest **73**
119) [1991 6d a6g 7m⁵ 7m 7d 1992 9.7g³ 10f a12g³ 9.7g² a8g² 8.5d* 9.7m² 9d² 9.7v⁴
a8g³] workmanlike gelding: fair performer: made all in maiden at Beverley in
August: mostly ran well afterwards: stays 9.7f: acts on good to firm ground, dead and
all-weather surfaces: somewhat headstrong and races prominently: has joined G.
Moore. *G. A. Pritchard-Gordon*

KING'S LOCH (IRE) 3 b.c. Salmon Leap (USA) 131 – Regal Beauty (USA) **113**
(Princely Native (USA)) [1991 8.2f* 8.1m* 8d² 8g⁶ 1992 10m 10s⁵ 10d⁴ 10d*] big,
good-bodied colt: moderate walker and mover: easily best effort in 1992 when

2½-length winner from Delve in listed race at Goodwood in October: well held in extremely valuable contest at Deauville and ran badly (found to have irregular heartbeat) previous 2 starts: should stay 1½m: acts on good to firm and dead ground: sold 76,000 gns Newmarket Autumn Sales. *H. R. A. Cecil*

KING'S SHILLING (USA) 5 b.g. Fit To Fight (USA) – Pride's Crossing (USA) (Riva Ridge (USA)) [1991 a10g6 1992 8.2g6 8f] smallish, workmanlike gelding: stays 1¼m: acts on any going. *Mrs S. Oliver* — 47

KING'S SIGNET (USA) 3 ch.c. Nureyev (USA) 131 – Sigy (FR) 132 (Habitat 134) [1991 NR 1992 7d6 6m* 6m* 5d 6d 6g] good-bodied colt: eighth foal: brother to 1989 French 2-y-o 5f winner Company, closely related to high-class French sprinter Sicyos (by Lyphard) and half-brother to very useful 1989 French 2-y-o 5.5f and 6.5f winner Radjhasi (by Raja Baba): dam, brilliantly speedy, won Prix de l'Abbaye as a 2-y-o: impressed in justifying favouritism in maiden at Thirsk and handicap at Yarmouth in September: ran respectably but failed to fulfil that promise in competitive handicaps after: stays 6f: best effort on good to firm ground. *J. H. M. Gosden* — 95

KINGSTON BROWN 2 ch.c. (Apr 8) Chilibang 120 – Smooth Siren (USA) (Sea Bird II 145) [1992 5g6 5f 5d4] 13,000Y: robust, quite attractive colt: closely related to 3-y-o Silky Siren and fairly useful 1985 2-y-o 7f winner Thalassino Asteri (both by Formidable) and half-brother to several winners, including very useful 1¼m winner Sirenivo (by Sir Ivor): dam 6f winner in USA: poor form for J. Berry in maidens in first half of 1992: joined D. Loder afterwards: looked sort to do better. *J. Berry* — 39

KING'S TREASURE (USA) 3 b.g. King of Clubs 124 – Crown Treasure (USA) (Graustark) [1991 8g6 1992 10d 11.7s2 14.6f2 16m6 14g6 14d] big, angular, unfurnished gelding: has a round action: fair maiden: ran poorly in handicap final start: has form on firm ground, but gives impression will prove suited to test of stamina and some give in the ground. *I. A. Balding* — 76

KINGS WATER (IRE) 2 b.c. (Jan 28) Kings Lake (USA) 133 – Alpenwind (Tumble Wind (USA)) [1992 8s] IR 8,000Y: compact colt: second reported foal: dam Irish 9f and 1½m winner: backward in maiden at Warwick in October. *A. P. Jarvis* — –

KING TREVISIO 6 b.g. King of Spain 121 – Gundi 57 (Mummy's Pet 125) [1991 a12g 1992 a8g] workmanlike gelding: poor mover: bad maiden: stays 1m: tried blinkered. *J. L. Harris* — –

KING VICTOR (IRE) 4 br.g. Tender King 123 – Wyn Mipet (Welsh Saint 126) [1991 7m6 6f5m 5m a6g2 5m2 5g 5f 5.1g a5g5 5.1m3 a5g4 6f 5h4 1992 5.1d a5g4 5f a6g 5.9h6] leggy, sparely-made gelding: has a round action: maiden handicapper: stays 6f: acts on hard ground, and fibresand: effective blinkered or not. *R. O'Leary* — 40

KING WILLIAM 7 b.g. Dara Monarch 128 – Norman Delight (USA) (Val de L'Orne (FR) 130) [1991 12g 12f 12m 16.2d3 16.2f* 1992 16.2d 16.2g2 15.8g2 18.2g2] robust gelding: moderate mover: carries condition: formerly an inconsistent handicapper but held his form in early-summer: stays 2¼m: acts on firm and dead ground: won over hurdles in September. *J. L. Spearing* — 35

KINLACEY 5 b.m. Aragon 118 – Mimika 85 (Lorenzaccio 130) [1991 8.5g 9m 8m4 7.5g2 8d 8.2g2 7.1s 6f3 7m 10.5g 8m 9g 7d a7g2 a8g a7g 1992 7.6g* 8g5 a7s* 7d3 7.9g3 a7g4 7d] lengthy, workmanlike mare: good walker: has a long stride: successful in handicaps in summer at Chester (apprentices) and Southwell: below form in autumn: ideally suited by 7f/1m: acts on firm and dead ground, and goes well on fibresand. *B. A. McMahon* — 67

KINNEGAD KID 3 b.f. Formidable (USA) 125 – Recamier 80 (Reform 132) [1991 6m 1992 a6g] IR 15,000Y: third foal: half-sister to a winner in Norway by King of Clubs: dam, 1¼m winner and half-sister to dam of Distant Relative and Ezzoud, is out of half-sister to good broodmare Natashka: well beaten in maiden at Naas at 2 yrs for Ms Joanna Morgan: 33/1, never dangerous in claimer at Southwell late on at 3 yrs. *R. Ingram* — –

KINOKO 4 ch.g. Bairn (USA) 126 – Octavia (Sallust 134) [1991 a8g3 a8g a8g2 a8g2 8.2d3 10d2 11m3 a11g 10.2g2 1992 10g 10d 9.9g 12f4 11.8g* a12g5 12d2 9.9g* 12.3m* 12.3d5 12m3 a14g4 a12g4] lengthy gelding: a reformed handicapper in 1992: successful at Leicester, Beverley and Ripon in the summer: effective from 1¼m to 1½m: acts on firm and dead going: sometimes flashes tail and hangs left but has gone well for a claimer. *K. W. Hogg, Isle of Man* — 59 a42

KINTWYN 2 b.g. (Feb 14) Doulab (USA) 115 – Harriet Emma (USA) (Secretariat (USA)) [1992 5.2d 5.3m6 5g 6.1m2 5.1g5 6m5 6g 5d 5g] 8,400Y: compact gelding: has a quick action: second foal: half-brother to Captain Coll (by Glow), successful in Norway: dam Irish middle-distance winner: modest maiden: effective at 5f and 6f: acts on good to firm and dead ground: often visored. *D. R. Laing* — 55

KIPINI   3 b.f. Roaring Riva 103 – Kivulini (Hotfoot 126) [1991 5g⁴ 6m a5g⁴ 6g 6g   **48**
1992 a7g² a7g⁶ 8s⁶ 7g⁶ 7d² 6g² 6g² 6g 7g 6s 6s] close-coupled filly: moderate
mover: inconsistent maiden: stays 7f: acts on dead ground, and equitrack: below
form blinkered: sold 2,400 gns Newmarket Autumn Sales. *W. J. Musson*

KIRA   2 b.f. (Feb 27) Starry Night (USA) – Irish Limerick 89 (Try My Best (USA)   **36**
130) [1992 6g 8.5m 7s] unfurnished filly: fourth foal: half-sister to modest 5f sprinter
Matching Lines (by Thatching): dam 2-y-o 6f winner: well beaten in maidens in the
North. *Miss L. C. Siddall*

KIRBY OPPORTUNITY   4 ch.f. Mummy's Game 120 – Empress Catherine 73   **59**
(Welsh Pageant 132) [1991 6g³ 6f⁵ 7g⁶ 7g* 7g³ 7d 8m² 7f² 8g² 10.8g 8.2m 7s a8g³
a12g* a12g² 1992 a12g* a12g² a13g* a12g³ a12g⁵ a13g* 11.9g² 10.8d⁵ 12f* 13.8m⁵
12m* 12.3m²] leggy filly: has a high knee action: successful in 3 claimers at
Lingfield, seller (no bid) at Thirsk and claimer at Doncaster in first half of 1992:
claimed to join P. Leach £8,001 after rare below-par effort final start (June): will stay
15f: best turf efforts on a sound surface and goes well on all-weather surfaces: below
form blinkered: goes well for claimer. *J. Pearce*

KIR (IRE)   4 ch.g. M Double M (USA) – Wolver Rose (Wolver Hollow 126) [1991   **–**
a8g² 9m⁵ a10g a12g 1992 15.1m] workmanlike gelding: on the downgrade. *D. R.
Franks*

KIRKBY BELLE   3 b.f. Bay Express 132 – Kirkby 85 (Midsummer Night II 117)   **43**
[1991 5m 5g³ 6g² 7m 1992 7.1m⁴ 9.2m 7d⁴ a8g³ 7g⁴ a8g⁵ 9d] leggy, rather angular
filly: poor maiden: moderate walker: poor maiden: stays 7f. *E. Weymes*

KIRRIEMUIR   4 b.f. Lochnager 132 – Maxine's Here 52 (Copte (FR)) [1991 7d   **51**
1992 8m 7m 6f 6.1m* 6f⁶ a6g 6.1g⁴ 7g* 7g³ 6.9m* 7d 7g a6g] close-coupled,
workmanlike filly: carries condition: modest handicapper: successful in handicaps
at Chepstow, Leicester and Folkestone in the summer: well below form last 3
starts: effective from 6f to 7f: acts on good to firm ground: sometimes hangs. *K. O.
Cunningham-Brown*

KIRSTEN   3 b.f. Kris 135 – Sushila (Petingo 135) [1991 7m³ 1992 10d³ 12g² 14m⁴   **77**
12.2d* 12.2g⁶ 12.4m⁴] angular, useful-looking filly: has a round action: fair performer: won maiden at Catterick in June: last in handicaps following month: should
stay 1¾m: possibly best with give in the ground. *W. Jarvis*

KISMETIM   2 b.c. (Feb 8) Dowsing (USA) 124 – Naufrage (Main Reef 126) [1992   **53**
5.7m³ 5g⁴ 6m⁵ 7g 6s] 8,200Y: lengthy, workmanlike colt: second foal: dam unraced:
poor maiden: should be suited by 7f +: acts on good to firm ground: sold to join B.
Meeham, 4,200 gns Newmarket Autumn Sales. *G. Lewis*

KISSAVOS   6 ch.g. Cure The Blues (USA) – Hairbrush (USA) (Sir Gaylord) [1991   **54**
8d 6m 5.1m* 7m³ 6.1d⁴ 7.6d⁴ 7d⁵ 5.1d² a6g⁵ a7g* a7g² 1992 a7g⁶ a8g* a8g⁶ a7g*   a63
a8g⁶ 6v 8m a7g 8.3d⁴ 7g³ a7s⁶ 6.9m⁴ 7.1s³ 8d 8s³ 6.1d² a6g⁴ a8g⁴ a7g* a7g² a7g⁴]
small, angular gelding: fair performer on the all-weather: won handicaps at Southwell (2) early in year and Lingfield late on: effective from 5f to 1m: acts on good to
firm and heavy going and on all-weather surfaces: has been bandaged behind:
effective blinkered/visored or not. *C. C. Elsey*

KISS IN THE DARK   2 b.f. (Apr 5) Starry Night (USA) – Hasty Sarah 56 (Gone   **55**
Native) [1992 5s³ 5m⁶ 6d 7f² 7g³ 7m⁵ 8m* 8s] plain, angular filly: first foal: dam
won 1¼m sellers: sire (by Northern Dancer) won from 6f to 8.5f: sweating,
improved form when winning nursery at Pontefract in August: ran poorly in similar
event there 1½ months after: will be better suited by 1¼m: best efforts on a sound
surface. *Mrs M. Reveley*

KISU KALI   5 ch.g. Kris 135 – Evita 111 (Reform 132) [1991 11.5g 7m 7g 1992 9.7d]   **–**
big, angular gelding: has a markedly round action: no form on flat for 2 seasons:
stays 1½m: acts on firm ground: modest novice chaser, winner twice. *J. Ffitch-Heyes*

KITAAB (USA)   3 b. or br.c. Trempolino (USA) 135 – Chuckles (USA) (Riverman   **77**
(USA) 131) [1991 NR 1992 8m* 10.5d 8d⁶ 8.5d 10s* 10d⁶] $75,000Y: sturdy,
good-quartered colt: third reported foal: dam once-raced daughter of Kentucky
Oaks third Funny Cat: won maiden at Brighton in April and celebrity race at Ascot in
September: well below form otherwise: stays 1¼m: acts on good to firm and soft
ground. *A. C. Stewart*

KITOTO (IRE)   2 b.c. (Feb 3) Mtoto 134 – Until June (USA) (Be My Guest (USA)   **46** p
126) [1992 8g²] 37,000F: second foal: half-brother to 3-y-o Diciembre (by Dominion):
dam French 9f winner: 20/1, better than twelfth-of-16 position suggests in Lingfield
maiden won by Cropton in September, prominent 5f: sure to improve. *P. F. I. Cole*

Prix Jean Prat, Longchamp—a good finish between Kitwood, Lucky Lindy and Shanghai

KITWOOD (USA) 3 b.c. Nureyev (USA) 131 – Kittywake (USA) (Sea Bird II **119** 145) [1991 7.5d* 1992 9.2s² 9g* 9.2d* 10m² 8s 8s⁵ 9f³] sturdy colt: half-brother to several winners, including top-class filly Miss Oceana (by Alydar) and very smart Larida (by Northern Dancer), latter dam of Coronation Stakes winner Magic of Life: dam high-class winner of 18 races at up to 9f: smart performer: successful in listed race at Evry and Prix Jean Prat (by short neck from Lucky Lindy) at Longchamp: placed afterwards in Grand Prix de Paris at Longchamp (good ¾-length second to Homme de Loi) and Hollywood Derby (third, beaten 1¼ lengths by Paradise Creek): better effort in Group 1 events in between when 6 lengths fifth of 10 to All At Sea in Prix du Moulin de Longchamp: stays 1¼m: acts on any going: to be trained by C. Whittingham. *A. Fabre, France*

KIVETON KABOOZ 4 b.c. Rousillon (USA) 133 – Sea Chant (Julio Mariner **92** 127) [1991 8m⁴ 10g* 12d⁴ 10.6g³ 11.9g³ 12s 12m* 12d² 1992 12g 11.9g 12f⁶ 12m⁶ 13.9m 14.6f² 12m² 14.6g² 14.6g²] good-topped, useful-looking colt: ran well in handicaps most starts in 1992 but tricky ride: effective from 1½m to 1¾m: acts on firm and dead ground: sometimes found little and hung badly: trained by L. Cumani until after seventh start. *J. A. Glover*

KIVETON TYCOON (IRE) 3 b.c. Last Tycoon 131 – Zillionaire (USA) (Vag- **75** uely Noble 140) [1991 NR 1992 12m³ 8f² 10.5d 10f 8g⁴] IR 82,000Y: sturdy, quite attractive colt: half-brother to useful 7f and 10.2f winner Dashing Senor (by El Gran Senor): dam, winner at around 6f in USA at 4 yrs, is out of Cheveley Park and Flying Childers winner Gentle Thoughts: best efforts in maidens first 2 starts: effective at 1m to 1½m: wears blinkers: also fitted with hood final start (looked reluctant), in July: won 2 juvenile hurdles in November in good style. *J. A. Glover*

KLAIROVER 5 b.m. Smackover 107 – Klairove 74 (Averof 123) [1991 5.1m² 6g **50** 5.1g⁵ 6.1s 5f⁴ 6m 1992 7m 5.1m* 6d³ 5g⁴ a6g 5g 5s a6g* a7g³ a6g] big, workman-like mare: poor mover: inconsistent handicapper: won at Chepstow (seller, bought in 3,500 gns) in May and Southwell in November: stays 6f: acts on good to firm and dead ground and on fibresand: sometimes starts slowly. *C. J. Hill*

KLINGON (IRE) 3 b.c. Formidable (USA) 125 – Melbourne Miss (Chaparral **63** (FR) 128) [1991 NR 1992 7g³ 10.1s⁴ 7m a8g⁵ 10.5d⁶ 14.1d⁵ 14.1g⁴ 14.6g³] 28,000F: strong, deep-girthed colt: carries plenty of condition: seventh foal: half-brother to 17f winner Taroudant (by Pharly) and a French 2-y-o winner by Northfields: dam unraced close relation to 15.5f Grand Prix de Paris winner Tennyson: modest maiden: may well prove better suited by 2m: acts on soft ground. *R. Hollinshead*

KLONDIKE (IRE) 2 b.c. (Jun 13) Glint of Gold 128 – Shannon Princess **–** (Connaught 130) [1992 7m³ 7g] strong colt: tenth living foal: half-brother to several winners, including very useful middle-distance stayer Waterfield (by Le Moss) and fairly useful 1½m to 19f winner Fitzpatrick (by Oats): dam won over 1m and 1¼m in Ireland: well beaten in late-season in 3-runner private sweepstakes at Newmarket (swerved violently leaving stalls and reluctant to race) and maiden at Doncaster (visored). *P. T. Walwyn*

KNAYTON LODGER   2 b.f. (Mar 27) Nomination 125 – Corr Lady (Lorenzaccio   **37** 130) [1992 a6g 6f 6.9h⁴ 7.5s a6g] 4,000F, 8,000Y: plain, angular filly: half-sister to several winners here and abroad, including 1m (at 2 yrs) and 9f winner Miami Star (by Miami Springs): dam never ran: poor plater: stays 7f: acts on hard ground: wears blinkers: sometimes flashes tail. *M. W. Easterby*

KNIFEBOX (USA)   4 b.c. Diesis 133 – Matoki (USA) (Hail To Reason) [1991 **118** 10.4d⁶ 10g 8.9g 10.3m³ 10d 10.3d* 10.3d* 10s* 10.5v⁵ 1992 10m⁶ 10.1g⁴ 10g³ 10d* 10s* 9.7s⁶ 10v*] tall, sparely-made colt: has a powerful, round action: much improved in autumn after 3-month lay-off: made all in Group 3 races at Goodwood (gutsy display to hold Jeune), Maisons-Laffitte (beat Steinbeck ¾ length) and Milan (held Funny Baby by 2 lengths): unable to dominate and never going well in Ciga Prix Dollar at Longchamp in between: will prove as effective at 1½m as 1¼m: revels in the mud: ran creditably when wearing crossed noseband and with tongue tied down once, and when sweating. *J. H. M. Gosden*

KNIGHT OF HONOUR   4 ch.g. Touching Wood (USA) 127 – Nobly Born   – (USA) (The Minstrel (CAN) 135) [1991 14g³ 16g⁴ᵈⁱˢ 14.8f⁴ 16.1m² 19m⁶ 1992 17.1d] sturdy, quite attractive gelding: has rather round action: rated 61 at 3 yrs: on the downgrade. *M. Dods*

KNIGHT OF MERCY   6 b.g. Aragon 118 – Little Mercy 90 (No Mercy 126) [1991 **101** 6m 6g⁴ 6g⁴ 6g 6g 7.3m* 7d 7m⁴ 1992 7g 8.1g 8f 7g³ 8m 8m* 7m³ 7.3g 7m 8.1s⁴] strong, good-bodied gelding: carries condition: useful performer: successful in Goodwood claimer before respectable third in York listed race in August: tailed off in Chepstow minor event final run and sold 15,500 gns Newmarket Autumn Sales: effective at 6f to 1m: acts on any going except possibly very soft: slowly away in blinkers: tough. *R. Hannon*

Sheikh Mohammed's "Knifebox"

KNIGHT OF SHALOT (IRE) 2 b.c. (Jan 31) Don't Forget Me 127 – Lady of – Shalott 61 (Kings Lake (USA) 133) [1992 6d] IR 22,000Y: first foal: dam, maiden stayed 1m, is half-sister to Head For Heights: green and not knocked about when last of 11 in maiden at Haydock in June. *P. W. Chapple-Hyam*

KNIGHT PAWN 3 b.g. Uncle Pokey 116 – Lady Carol 42 (Lord Gayle (USA) 124) 58 [1991 NR 1992 8.5f3 10m4 9m6] leggy, good-topped gelding: moderate walker: has a powerful, round action: third reported foal: dam 4-y-o 1m winner: modest maiden: not seen out after July: stays 1¼m. *J. P. Leigh*

KNIGHTS (NZ) 6 br.g. Vice Regal (NZ) – Montrose Lass (AUS) (Gay Gambler – (USA)) [1991 NR 1992 10d6] New Zealand-bred gelding: successful on flat in New Zealand and Australia: first run on flat here, never dangerous in Brighton apprentice event in April: joined C. Broad and won handicap hurdle in November, showing fair form. *Mrs S. Oliver*

KNOBBLEENEEZE 2 ch.g. (Jul 1) Aragon 118 – Proud Miss (USA) (Semi-Pro) 60 [1992 6m 7m 6m2 6.1s6 7.3g5 6s 6m a6g* a7g3 a6g3 a7g4] sturdy gelding: half-brother to 3-y-o Form Mistress (by Formidable) and several winners in USA: dam never ran: modest performer: narrowly won claimer at Lingfield in November, leading close home: stays 7f: acts on top-of-the-ground and all-weather surfaces: visored last 5 starts. *M. R. Channon*

KNOCKAVON 4 b.g. Belfort (FR) 89 – Miss Merlin 79 (Manacle 123) [1991 NR – 1992 8s 8s] leggy, rather sparely-made gelding: rated 75 at 2 yrs: very much on the downgrade. *R. J. Baker*

KNOCK KNOCK 7 ch.g. Tap On Wood 130 – Ruby River (Red God 128§) [1991 95 10g 10g 10.1g* 8m2 11.9m4 9v4 9m* 8.5f2 10m2 10f* 9m 1992 10d6 10m2 10.4m3 11.1m2 10f4 10.8m* 10.4d 10g* 10m* 10g 12s] good-quartered gelding: a grand handicapper who had another good season in 1992: successful in summer at Warwick, Ascot (£11,300 event) and Goodwood (£25,800 Chesterfield Cup, by short head from Pharly Story): ideally suited by around 1¼m on a sound surface: best without blinkers or visor: good mount for inexperienced rider: sometimes finds little, and ideally suited by good gallop and waiting tactics. *I. A. Balding*

Vodac Chesterfield Cup (Handicap), Goodwood—
a short head between Knock Knock (rails) and Pharly Story

KNOCK TO ENTER (USA) 4 b.g. Diesis 133 – Privy (USA) (Tisab (USA)) **87**
[1991 NR 1992 8m⁵ 8m 7m 8s³] rangy gelding: moderate walker: fairly useful
handicapper: stays 1m: acts on good to firm and soft ground: sold to join M. Williams'
stable 11,500 gns Newmarket Autumn Sales. *M. R. Stoute*

KNOWN APPROACH (USA) 2 b.c. (Apr 11) Known Fact (USA) 135 – Low **78**
Approach (Artaius (USA) 129) [1992 7f* 7g² 7m a8g²] 50,000Y: smallish, good-
bodied colt: first foal: dam, showed ability without winning in USA, is half-sister to
Irish 1000 Guineas winner More So: landed odds in maiden at Salisbury in June and
ran creditably in Lanson Champagne Vintage Stakes at Goodwood penultimate
start: stays 1m. *P. F. I. Cole*

KNYAZ 2 b.c. (Apr 15) Governor General 116 – Aleda Rose 56 (Charlottown 127) **34**
[1992 5.1s⁵ 5.1f 7g] 4,000Y: compact colt: half-brother to a winner abroad: dam won
from 7f to 1¼m: poor form in maidens. *L. G. Cottrell*

KOA 2 b.c. (Mar 11) Formidable (USA) 125 – Hawaiian Bloom (USA) 87 (Hawaii) **65**
[1992 6g 7.1s 7m 7s²] leggy, useful-looking colt: moderate mover: first foal: dam
14.7f winner: easily best effort second of 18 in nursery at Leicester in October: will
be better suited by 1m: sometimes bandaged. *M. J. Heaton-Ellis*

KOJIKI 3 gr.c. Niniski (USA) 125 – Goeswell (Roan Rocket 128) [1991 NR 1992 **68**
10m 13.9f³ 12m²] leggy, angular, shallow-girthed colt: third foal: dam in frame over
1¼m: modest maiden: not seen out after July: will be suited by 1½m + . *L. M.
Cumani*

KOOYONGA (IRE) 4 ch.f. Persian Bold 123 – Anjuli (Northfields) (USA)) **125**
[1991 7g* 8g² 8m* 8g* 8m* 8d² 8g 1992 9m⁵ 10m³ 10s* 10g* 10.4g 10d⁴ 10g²]
The Irish had a good year in Britain, winning Group 1 races with St
Jovite, Brief Truce and Kooyonga. The Irish One Thousand Guineas winner
Kooyonga justified the decision to keep her in training with a splendid victory
in the Coral-Eclipse Stakes, becoming only the second filly to win the race
since its inception in 1886. Kooyonga became familiar to British racegoers
as a three-year-old when her victory in the Coronation Stakes—one of the
highlights of Royal Ascot—and her seconds in the One Thousand Guineas
and Queen Elizabeth II Stakes stamped her as an outstandingly game and
consistent filly. She was also first past the post in the Prince of Wales's Stakes
at Royal Ascot on her first outing in Britain as a four-year-old and looked to
have sound credentials in what looked a substandard Eclipse field. The
Eclipse lacked a tip-top performer from among the three-year-olds—there
were only two of that age in the twelve-strong line-up—and bigger dangers to
Kooyonga, who started favourite, included the Prix d'Ispahan first and second
Zoman and Arcangues, and the first two in the Hardwicke Stakes, Rock
Hopper and Sapience. Three of the other runners—Young Buster, Terimon
and Opera House—had passed the post behind Kooyonga at Royal Ascot
two and a half weeks earlier. Persistent rain, which turned the going soft,
appeared to dampen the hopes of some of Kooyonga's supporters. Although
she had proved her ability to stay the Eclipse trip with her performance in the
Prince of Wales's, Kooyonga hadn't been raced on very soft ground before.

Coral-Eclipse Stakes, Sandown—
Kooyonga justifies favouritism in good style against the colts

Her supporters needn't have worried. The patiently-ridden Kooyonga put up probably her best performance, making very smooth headway on the outside to lead over a furlong out. She was soon clear for a comfortable length-and-a-half victory over Opera House, with Sapience the same distance away third; the two three-year-olds, the 33/1-shot Free Flyer and Derby fifth Twist And Turn came next, ahead of Zoman, Rock Hopper and Arcangues.

Kooyonga's Eclipse success was compensation for misfortunes endured by her owner and trainer and those who backed her at Royal Ascot. Kooyonga was demoted to third in the Prince of Wales's Stakes because of careless riding by her regular jockey O'Connor, who failed to take corrective measures to keep her straight in the closing stages, causing interference to third-placed Young Buster. The patrol film showed clearly Kooyonga's brush with Young Buster and confirmed that O'Connor had continued to flourish his whip in his left hand as Kooyonga edged right. Young Buster had no prospects of winning when he was hampered but the stewards had no choice under the now-infamous rule 153 but to place Kooyonga behind Young Buster (a carelessly-ridden horse must be placed behind the horse with which it interfered); the race was awarded to the second horse home Perpendicular with Young Buster promoted to second and Kooyonga placed third. Stewards now have more flexibility when dealing with cases of careless riding than they once had—mandatory disqualification to last place would have been Kooyonga's fate ten years ago—but the Prince of Wales's Stakes was another instance of the injustice that flows from rule 153. Kooyonga was clearly the best horse in the race on the day and it was a travesty that she lost it in the stewards' room. The subject of rule 153 has been covered fully many times in the pages of these Annuals—most recently in the essay on Royal Gait in *Racehorses of 1988*—and we are not going to weary readers by dealing with the issues in detail again. Suffice to repeat that damage will continue to be done to the integrity of racing by cases like that of Kooyonga until rule 153 makes a clear distinction between consideration of the equity of the result, and the disciplining of jockeys for breaching the rule. They are two quite different matters which should be dealt with separately. When interference takes place, the stewards should first and foremost have to consider whether the interference altered the placings of the horses involved. Transgressions by jockeys in their riding should be dealt with by penalties that fall upon them, and them alone, by

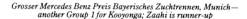

Grosser Mercedes Benz Preis Bayerisches Zuchtrennen, Munich— another Group 1 for Kooyonga; Zaahi is runner-up

Mitsuo Haga's "Kooyonga"

fines or suspensions appropriate to the nature and the iniquity of the offences. As the rule stands, the stewards at Royal Ascot could not discipline her jockey for careless riding—he received a six-day suspension—without disqualifying Kooyonga. Yet that action deprived the innocent owner of Kooyonga—and backers of the horse—of their just rewards. Had the interference between Kooyonga and Young Buster been deemed accidental, the stewards would have left the Prince of Wales's placings unaltered, as they have the discretion to do in cases involving accidental interference which does not improve a horse's placing (we should think few would argue that the interference between Kooyonga and Young Buster cost Young Buster a winning chance though it probably cost him second; justice would be served in a case like this by Young Buster's connections being compensated from the winner's purse for the difference between second and third prize money, in this instance about £12,000).

Kooyonga was returned to Britain in August for the Juddmonte International at York, having in the meantime added another Group 1 race to her record, the Grosser Mercedes Benz Preis Bayerisches Zuchtrennen at Munich in which she beat the St James's Palace runner-up Zaahi and the promoted Prince of Wales's winner Perpendicular by three quarters of a length and a length and a quarter, with the widely-travelled Dear Doctor a very close fourth. Unfortunately, Kooyonga ran badly at York, being virtually pulled up from two furlongs out. It was a performance totally out of character and her trainer took the admirable step of making a statement the next day to explain her poor run. She was found to be in season after the Juddmonte

International. Ireland has a rule that requires trainers to notify anything that might explain the poor running of a horse; the information is then published in the *Racing Calendar*. A similar rule was recommended to the Jockey Club in the latest season after a study of the effectiveness of the system in Ireland by Jockey Club officials. Kooyonga's training in the autumn was geared to having her at her peak for the Japan Cup in late-November which was said to have been the long-term objective of her four-year-old campaign. But she ran well below her best in two races at Leopardstown—the Irish Champion Stakes (reportedly returning with a 'tied-up shoulder muscle') and a four-runner minor event (starting odds on)—and she earned a Tokyo invitation only as a reserve.

Kooyonga (IRE) (ch.f. 1988)	Persian Bold (br 1975)	Bold Lad (b 1964)	Bold Ruler
			Barn Pride
		Relkarunner (b or br 1968)	Relko
			Running Blue
	Anjuli (ch 1978)	Northfields (ch 1968)	Northern Dancer
			Little Hut
		Katricia (ch 1968)	Skymaster
			Anxious Call

As readers of *Racehorses of 1991* will know, we thought it most unlikely that Kooyonga would stay a mile and a half, the distance of the Japan Cup. There is much more speed than stamina on the distaff side of her pedigree. Kooyonga's unraced dam Anjuli is a daughter of a sprinter and a half-sister to the Two Thousand Guineas winner Roland Gardens; Anjuli's two previous winners, the useful Hatton Gardens (by Auction Ring) and the Cheveley Park third Jaljuli (by Jalmood), both showed their best form at six and seven furlongs. The good-topped Kooyonga, a really good walker who showed a markedly round action in her faster paces, was effective at a mile to a mile and a quarter. She acted on good to firm and on soft ground and could produce a fine turn of foot when held up, as she showed in the Eclipse. Kooyonga has been retired to stud. The plan, at the time of writing, is that she visits Belmont Stakes and Breeders' Cup Classic winner A P Indy. *M. Kauntze, Ireland*

KOVALEVSKIA 7 ch.m. Ardross 134 – Fiordiligi 109 (Tudor Melody 129) [1991 a13g⁶a13g³a12g⁶ 12g 12g 12f 11.8m 1992 a14g³a16g⁶a13g² 14.1d2 1.6g⁶ 11.5da13g⁶] a38 small, sparely-made mare: unreliable handicapper: stays 1¾m: possibly unsuited by firm going, acts on any other: suitable mount for amateur. *D. A. Wilson*   –

KRAYYAN DAWN 2 ch.c. (May 1) Krayyan 117 – Tana Mist 71 (Homeboy 114) [1992 6s 6.1g 6m 8.2d 6s 6g] workmanlike colt: second known foal: half-brother to 3-y-o Mastamist (by Tickled Pink): dam 2-y-o 5f winner stayed 1¼m: of little account. *R. Voorspuy*   –

KREISCHIM (IRE) 4 b.g. Kreisler – Chimela (Ela-Mana-Mou 132) [1991 7d⁴ 7g 8m⁶ 8g 8.3g 6m 5m 5.3f 6m a10g 8g 1992 a7g⁵ a8g a10g a12g] angular, workman-like gelding: has a round action: very much on the downgrade. *M. Madgwick*   –

KRISFIELD 7 b. or br.g. Anfield 117 – Kristallina 86 (Homeric 133) [1991 a7g a7g² 7f² 7.1d² 6g 8g³ 8.3m⁴ 8.3m⁴ a8g a7g 1992 a10g] lengthy gelding: rated 53 at 6 yrs: poor mover: on the downgrade. *T. P. McGovern*   –

KRISTIANSTAD 3 b.c. Kris 135 – Our Home 115 (Habitat 134) [1991 7d² 1992 **101** 7.9f* 8m² 7.9d⁶ 8d*] angular, quite attractive colt: moderate mover: promising in first half of 1992, winning maiden at York and beaten ¾ length by Hazaam in Newbury minor event: sustained back injury next start and not at best to win Yarmouth minor event 3½ months after: stays 1m. *Mrs J. Cecil*

KRISTIS GIRL 5 ch.m. Ballacashtal (CAN) – Fleur d'Amour 85 (Murrayfield **53** 119) [1991 5d 6d 6.1d 6v 6g⁴ a6g² a6g 7.6m a7g⁵ 6g 6g³ 6.1d 7g⁵ a8g* a7g⁴ a8g⁴ 1992 a8g⁶ a8g⁴ a7g⁵] plain, angular mare: moderate mover: modest handicapper: not seen out after February: stays 7f: has form on good to firm ground, but probably best with give: acts on all-weather surfaces: sold 1,100 gns Doncaster August Sales. *D. Haydn Jones*

KRONPRINZ (IRE) 4 b.g. Local Suitor (USA) 128 – Kaiserchronik (GER) (Cortez (GER)) [1991 a8g 10g 12.2g⁵ 1992 a12g a12g a7g] leggy gelding: has a round action: no worthwhile form on flat for 2 years: should stay 1¼m: below form blinkered: has appeared none too resolute over hurdles, successful in 1991/2. *M. C. Chapman*   –

434

KRYPTOS (USA) 2 b.f. (Feb 22) Chief's Crown (USA) – Sea Basque (USA) **66** p
(Seattle Slew (USA)) [1992 7g 8.1d³] $100,000Y: second foal: dam 3-y-o allowance
winner at up to 1m in USA, also second in Grade 1 Matron Stakes, is half-sister to
good-class and versatile Grade 1 winner Bounding Basque: sire champion 2-y-o colt
also top class at 3 yrs: much better effort in autumn when strong-finishing third of 7
to Blue Blazer in maiden at Haydock: stays 1m: should improve. *Lord Huntingdon*

KUMMEL KING 4 b.g. Absalom 128 – Louise 71 (Royal Palace 131) [1991 6f² **64**
7m³ 6m⁴ 7g⁵ 6g⁴ 7m⁵ 5h⁵ 6m⁶ 8m 1992 6.9f* 7.5g⁴ 7.1f² 7f⁵ 8.3g 8g² 8m⁴ 7s⁵ a8g
a7g] compact gelding: improved handicapper for new stable, successful at Carlisle in
May: below form last 2 starts: effective from 7f to 1m: acts on any going: tried
blinkered once: usually races prominently. *E. J. Alston*

KUSAMBA (USA) 2 ch.c. (Feb 24) Nureyev (USA) 131 – Alliance (USA) 113 **89** p
(Alleged (USA) 138) [1992 7d* 7.3s⁵] rather leggy, close-coupled, quite attractive
colt: fluent mover: sixth foal: brother to very useful 5-y-o 1½m performer Matador
and French provincial middle-distance winner Beauté Dangereuse and closely
related to 3-y-o 1¼m winner Jezebel Monroe (by Lyphard): dam, French 10.5f
winner who stayed 1½m, is half-sister to Blushing Groom: won minor event at York
in September, running on really well to beat Black Dragon by ½ length, pair clear:
never able to challenge when over 8 lengths fifth of 11 to Beggarman Thief in
Vodafone Horris Hill Stakes at Newbury following month: will be better suited by
1m: should improve. *R. Charlton*

KUT-EL-AMARA 3 b.g. Teenoso (USA) 135 – Kajetana (FR) (Caro 133) [1991 **–**
NR 1992 10.3g] workmanlike gelding: seventh foal: half-brother to 3 winners on flat,
including very useful 7f to 1¼m winner K-Battery (by Gunner B) and modest 1m
and 1¼m winner K-Brigade (by Brigadier Gerard), and to NH Flat race winner
Hondeghem (by Kalaglow): dam never ran: reluctant at stalls and no promise in
maiden at Doncaster in March: sold 925 gns Ascot September Sales. *C. W. C. Elsey*

KYRENIA GAME 2 br.f. (Apr 26) Mummy's Game 120 – Kyrenia Sunset (CYP) **62**
(Lucky Look (CYP)) [1992 5g⁶ 6g² 6m 7m* 7d³ 8.5d⁵ 7d* 7m] sparely-made filly:
third living foal: dam unraced Cypriot-bred: modest performer: soon ridden along in
rear when winning strongly-run nurseries at Lingfield (apprentices) in August and
Goodwood (swerved left finish) in September: will stay 1¼m: acts on good to firm
and dead ground: not an easy ride. *P. Mitchell*

L

LA BAMBA 6 br.g. Laxton 105 – Rimamba 82 (Ribocco 129) [1991 7m 7f⁴ 7m* 7g³ **79**
7g⁶ 7f² 7m* 7m² 7g² 7m 7g³ 7d* 1992 7g⁵ 7m³ 7f 7f⁶ 7.1g 7g⁶ 7f 8g 7d* 8m 7v 7g⁴]
leggy gelding: fair handicapper: won at Redcar in October: effective at 7f and 1m:
acts on firm and dead ground (below form on heavy): usually slowly away: held up
and has turn of foot. *G. A. Pritchard-Gordon*

LA BELLE VIE 6 b.m. Indian King (USA) 128 – Engage (Whistling Wind 123) **72**
[1991 7f² 6d⁵ 8g⁴ 7m³ 7f⁶ 7.1g 8m³ 7m 7s 6.1d* a7g 1992 5.7m⁵ 7.1m 7.1m*
7m⁵] workmanlike, good-quartered mare: moderate mover: fair handicapper: won
amateurs event at Chepstow in June: effective from 6f to 1m: acted on firm and dead
ground: suitable mount for apprentice: in foal to Never So Bold. *R. J. Baker*

LA BONITA (IRE) 2 gr.f. (Mar 12) Common Grounds 118 – Catherine Linton **54**
(USA) (High Echelon) [1992 a7g 7f 7.5d⁶ 6d⁴ a6g² 6d² 6.1v] 7,800Y: compact filly:
half-sister to several winners here and abroad, including 10.5f winner For Sure For
Sure (by Northfields) and Irish middle-distance performer Imposing (by Hello
Gorgeous): dam, unraced, from family of Malinowski, Gielgud, Try My Best and El
Gran Senor: modest maiden: stays 6f: acts on equitrack and dead ground, well
beaten on heavy: blinkered or visored last 4 starts: sold 4,600 gns Doncaster
October Sales. *J. Berry*

LABUDD (USA) 2 ch.c. (Apr 8) Deputy Minister (CAN) – Delightful Vie (USA) **73** p
(Barbs Delight) [1992 7g³] $200,000F: good-topped colt: half-brother to several
winners, notably prolific stakes winner at up to 1¼m Sefa's Beauty (by Lt Stevens):
dam ran 5 times: sire champion 2-y-o, later stayed 1¼m: refused to enter stalls on
intended debut: weak 12/1-chance and carrying plenty of condition, 6 lengths third of
18 to stable-companion Tinners Way in maiden at Doncaster in November, staying
on well: will be suited by middle distances: sure to improve. *J. H. M. Gosden*

LABURNUM 4 gr.g. Glint of Gold 128 – Lorelene (FR) 97 (Lorenzaccio 130) **88**
[1991 10.4g⁶ 10g* 10d³ 1992 10m² 10g² 12g² 12s 12m 12g] big, lengthy, angular

gelding: fairly useful handicapper: ran well when second: well beaten last 3 starts, trained until after penultimate one by L. Cumani: will stay 1¾m: best form on a sound surface: held up. *Mrs J. R. Ramsden*

LA CALDERONA 2 br.f. (Apr 26) King of Spain 121 – Lizabeth Chudleigh –
(Imperial Fling (USA) 116) [1992 5g] 6,400Y: good-topped filly: fifth foal: sister to modest (but later unreliable) 1988 2-y-o 6f winner Syrus P Turntable and half-sister to useful Irish 8.5f to 1¼m winner Jonjas Chudleigh (by Aragon) and 1m and 8.2f winner Elizabethan Air (by Elegant Air): dam never ran: 11/2, outpaced throughout in 8-runner maiden auction at Windsor in August: sold 1,700 gns Doncaster November Sales. *A. A. Scott*

LACERTA (IRE) 2 b.f. (Feb 27) Thatching 131 – Cup Defender (USA) 45 60
(Topsider (USA)) [1992 6m*] IR 30,000Y: leggy, unfurnished filly: has scope: first foal: dam 1¼m winner, is out of sister to Effervescing, high class at up to 1½m: favourite, narrowly won maiden at Newbury in May, responding well after travelling comfortably: seemed sure to improve but didn't reappear. *P. W. Chapple-Hyam*

LA CHANCE 2 b.c. (Feb 11) Lafontaine (USA) 117 – Lucky Omen 99 (Queen's 77 p
Hussar 124) [1992 7.1g³] 28,000Y: strong, rangy colt: has plenty of scope: brother to 4-y-o 1¼m winner Latour and smart 6f and 9.2f winner Lapierre and half-brother to several winners, including very useful sprinter Lucky Hunter (by Huntercombe): dam 2-y-o 5f and 6f winner: 16/1, backward and green, length third of 8 to Double Bass in maiden at Sandown in July, pushed along 3f then staying on well not knocked about: will stay 1m: looked sure to improve. *C. E. Brittain*

LACOTTE (IRE) 2 b.c. (Mar 29) Sadler's Wells (USA) 132 – La Dame du Lac 76 p
(USA) (Round Table) [1992 7g²] compact, useful-looking colt: brother to Irish 3-y-o Miznah, fairly useful 6f winner at 2 yrs, closely related to 5 winners, including useful 1990 Irish 2-y-o 6f to 7f winner Nazoo (by Nijinsky), and half-brother to a stakes-placed winner by Exceller: dam, unraced, from very good family: 4/1 and bit backward, 5 lengths second of 7, clear, to Lord President in maiden at Newmarket in July, travelling well and keeping on strongly not knocked about: showed a fluent action: looked an absolutely sure-fire winner of a similar event at least, but wasn't seen again. *J. H. M. Gosden*

LA COUSINE 3 b.f. R B Chesne 123 – Princess Lieven (Royal Palace 131) [1991 –
7g 1992 8g³ 8g⁶] leggy, unfurnished filly: no worthwhile form at Newmarket, in maiden and Challenge Whip in May: bred to stay 1¼m. *C. E. Brittain*

L'ACQUESIANA 4 ch.f. Crofthall 110 – Well Connected (Bold And Free 118) 33
[1991 10g 10.2m a12g³ a8g⁵ a12g 8.5f⁶ 8.2m 10g 10g 7.6m⁵ a8g³] lengthy filly: poor mover: ran only in July, form only when visored last 2 starts: should stay 1¼m. *D. Shaw*

LA DAMA BONITA (USA) 3 ch.f. El Gran Senor (USA) 136 – Marie 87
d'Argonne (FR) (Jefferson 129) [1991 6.1f⁴ 6f² 5.1g* 7.3g⁶ 1992 7.9m⁵ 7m² 6g 7m⁵ 7d 7.3g* 6m] lengthy, sparely-made filly: fairly useful performer on her day: won handicap at Newbury in September: needs further than 6f and will stay 1m: best efforts on a sound surface. *D. W. P. Arbuthnot*

LA DELITZIA (USA) 2 ch.f. (Feb 28) Diesis 133 – Hotel Street (USA) 93 58 p
(Alleged (USA) 138) [1992 7f⁵ 10g 8v²] tall, close-coupled filly: third foal: sister to 1991 2-y-o 7f winner Providence and half-sister to 7f (at 2 yrs) and 11f winner Widyan (by Fappiano): dam lightly-raced 1½m winner, is half-sister to stakes winners Royal And Regal and Regal And Royal: 20/1, best effort in maidens when 15 lengths second of 11 to Pistol River at Leicester in October, off bridle by halfway then keeping on well: will stay 1½m: should prove capable of better. *P. F. I. Cole*

LADY ADARE (IRE) 2 b.f. (Mar 7) Jareer (USA) 115 – Dane Valley (Simbir 130) –
[1992 5f 5g 7.5m 8.3s] 1,000Y: leggy, sparely-made filly: half-sister to 3-y-o Orchid Valley (by Cyrano de Bergerac) and several winners, including 1987 2-y-o 1m winner Valley of Danuata (by Taufan): dam ran once: no worthwhile form. *J. J. O'Neill*

LADY ALL STAR (USA) 2 ch.f. (Feb 12) The Minstrel (CAN) 135 – All –
Gladness (USA) (Alydar (USA)) [1992 7d] $85,000Y: third foal: sister to 11f seller winner Jubilata and half-sister to 3-y-o Muktaar (by Polish Navy): dam, unplaced from 6 starts, is out of prolific stakes winner (twice in Grade 3 6f event) Gladiolus: 20/1, little promise in 20-runner maiden at Lingfield in September. *A. A. Scott*

LADY ARABELLA 2 b.f. (May 2) Sayf El Arab (USA) 127 – Wollow Maid 73 41
(Wollow 132) [1992 7d 7g] 6,200Y: rather leggy, workmanlike filly: fifth foal: half-sister to 3-y-o winning miler Super Summit (by Superlative) and fair sprinter

Pinnacle Point (by Lochnager): dam, 1¼m winner, refused to race once: 33/1, well beaten in big fields of maidens at Leicester and Newmarket in October. *J. Pearce*

LADY ARGENT (IRE) 2 gr.f. (Apr 10) Exactly Sharp (USA) 121 – Shalara (Dancer's Image (USA)) [1992 6f 6.1g⁶ 7d 10.5d a8g] IR 6,200Y: leggy filly: half-sister to several winners, including (at 1m and 9f in France) useful Shayzari (by Nishapour) and (at 6f in Ireland) Majesterium (by Red Regent): dam unraced half-sister to very useful miler Shasavaan: no worthwhile form, including in sellers. *A. P. Jarvis* —

LADY BARAKA (IRE) 4 b.f. Shernazar 131 – Lady Wise (Lord Gayle (USA) 124) [1991 10g⁴ 10g² 10.1m* 10m⁶ 11.5f 10m³ a11g 1992 a8g⁶ a10g⁵ 9.7v 9.7g⁴ 9.2d 10m] small filly: moderate mover: poor handicapper, trained first 4 starts by I. Campbell, and not seen out after June: should stay beyond 1¼m: acts on good to firm ground: has run creditably when sweating. *Miss Gay Kelleway* 37

LADY BUCHAN 3 b.f. Elegant Air 119 – Regain 86 (Relko 136) [1991 NR 1992 10m 10m³ 8f² 7g] 11,000F, 860,000 francs (approx £86,000) Y: tall, angular filly: sixth foal: half-sister to several winners, including 6-y-o stayer White River (by Pharly) and 4-y-o miler Wild And Loose (by Precocious): dam 1½m winner: fair form: placed in maidens at Sandown and Yarmouth in June: stiff task and dull in coat, moved moderately to post and never travelling well in £11,600 handicap following month: bred to stay middle distances: sold to join N. Tinkler 9,800 gns Newmarket December Sales. *Mrs J. Cecil* 71

LADY BUNTING 5 b.m. Well Decorated (USA) – Lady's Flag (USA) (Fifth Marine (USA)) [1991 6s 7d 7g 8m³ 8.3m 8f² 8f* 9.7f 9.7s 1992 9m 7f 9.7g] leggy mare: rated 48 at 4 yrs: tailed off in midsummer in 1992: best form at 7f/1m on top-of-the-ground: tried blinkered once. *R. Voorspuy* —

LADY DEBRA DARLEY 3 b.f. Damister (USA) 123 – Song Grove 61 (Song 132) [1991 NR 1992 7m² 8.5d² 7f* 7g³ 7m* 7g 7s⁵ 8d⁵ 7d² 8d*] 16,000F: good-topped filly: half-sister to several winners, including 4-y-o sprinter Sir Harry Hardman (by Doulab) and 5-y-o Sir Arthur Hobbs (by Lyphard's Special), fairly useful juvenile sprinter, now stays 1m: dam 4-y-o 5.8f winner in Ireland: fairly useful performer: won minor event at Salisbury and handicap at Doncaster in midsummer and minor event (best effort) at Leicester in October: stays 8.5f: acts on any going: consistent: sent to race in Macau. *R. Hannon* 92

LADY DOMINION 3 b.f. Dominion 123 – Blakeney Belle (Blakeney 126) [1991 NR 1992 10.3g⁵] sturdy filly: half-sister to several winners, including Rocamadour (by Royal Match), smart at up to 1¾m here, and fairly useful Irish 1½m winner Forever Lonely (by Manado): dam poor half-sister to Daring Boy and Daring March: 25/1 and burly, showed signs of ability in 6-runner maiden at Chester in August: sold 5,000 gns Newmarket December Sales. *A. Bailey* —

LADY DONOGHUE (USA) 3 b.f. Lyphard's Wish (FR) 124 – It's High Time 69 (High Line 125) [1991 NR 1992 9s⁶ 12m 8v] 5,000Y: angular, workmanlike filly: second foal: half-sister to minor sprint winner in USA, Sizzle 'Em (by Indian King): dam won over 1½m at 4 yrs: no worthwhile form in maidens. *Mrs M. Reveley* —

LADY DUNDEE (USA) 3 b.f. Northern Baby (CAN) 127 – Add Mint (USA) (Vigors (USA)) [1991 a8g 1992 10.5d⁴ 12m⁴ a12g² 11.5g³ 12.3d 12g⁵ 10s³ 10d* 10v⁵ a10g² a10g*] workmanlike filly: fair performer: won maiden at Redcar in October and handicap at Lingfield in December: stays 1½m: acts on soft ground and equitrack, probably on good to firm: changed hands 20,000 gns Newmarket December Sales. *Mrs J. Cecil* 68

LADY ELECTRIC 6 b.m. Electric 126 – Romping (Sir Gaylord) [1991 NR 1992 14.1d* 12.1s³ 17.2s²] workmanlike mare: consistent handicapper: won at Nottingham in April: not seen out after May: stays 17.2f: acts on good to firm and soft ground, seemed unsuited by very firm at 4 yrs. *R. J. Hodges* 47

LADY GAIL 2 ch.f. (Jan 21) Sharrood (USA) 124 – Martian Princess 90 (Cure The Blues (USA)) [1992 7g 8.1g²] 6,000Y: sparely-made filly: first foal: dam, maiden, stayed 1m: fair form: reluctant at stalls before being beaten a neck by Seama in maiden at Edinburgh in October, leading under 3f out until close home: stays 8.1f: may well improve again. *J. L. Spearing* 65

LADY GHISLAINE (FR) 5 b.m. Lydian (FR) 120 – Planeze (FR) (Faraway Son (USA) 130) [1991 NR 1992 8m a8g] workmanlike, plain mare: has a round action: no worthwhile form on flat: won selling hurdle (sold to join J. White 2,500 gns) in December. *A. S. Reid* —

LADY HONDA (IRE) 2 ch.f. (May 4) Adonijah 126 – Wolverhants 79 (Wolver Hollow 126) [1992 5.2d] 17,000Y: leggy, unfurnished filly: sister to one-time useful —

4-y-o 6f (at 2 yrs) and 8.5f winner Sylva Honda, closely related to fair stayer Break-out (by High Line) and half-sister to several winners here and abroad: dam, second over 6f on both starts, is half-sister to dam of very smart middle-distance winner King's Island: 50/1, soon tailed off in 11-runner Newbury Sales Super Sprint Trophy in July. *C. E. Brittain*

LADY KHADIJA 6 b.m. Nicholas Bill 125 – Chenkynowa 48 (Connaught 130) – [1991 NR 1992 a7g] lightly raced and no sign of ability. *G. P. Kelly*

LADY LACEY 5 b.m. Kampala 120 – Cecily (Prince Regent (FR) 129) [1991 7g 8g 55 8m 8d4 9s3 8m 8g2 10g 9s 8g 10.5d 8d* 1992 9d 8d 8g* 8g3 8.9g3 7f 8.3g 8d3 8g 10m3 10s3 10g2 9d4 10.2s2 9s 10.2d3 12.1s6 10.3g4 a10g4 a12g3] rather lightly-made, quite attractive mare: moderate mover: largely consistent handicapper: won at Wolver-hampton in April: effective from 1m to 1¼m: acts on any going: visored nowadays: suitable mount for inexperienced rider: usually set plenty to do: tough. *G. B. Balding*

LADY LAWN 2 ch.f. (Apr 14) Gabitat 119 – Joara (FR) (Radetzky 123) [1992 5d 7f – 5g] leggy, rather plain filly: first foal: dam very lightly raced on flat but winning hurdler, is sister to very useful but most unreliable stayer Petrizzo: no form in maiden and sellers in first half of season. *J. M. Carr*

LADY LYDIA 3 b. or br.f. Ela-Mana-Mou 132 – Sumaya (USA) §§ (Seattle Slew 52 (USA)) [1991 8.9d6 8s 1992 11.1d* 11.8d] workmanlike, rather unfurnished filly: has rather round action: modest form: won maiden at Hamilton, making all and staying on strongly: ran badly in handicap at Leicester later in April: may well stay 1¾m. *M. A. Jarvis*

LADY MARRIOTT 4 b.f. Niniski (USA) 125 – Braconda 86 (So Blessed 130) – [1991 10m4 1992 10g6 10.2s5 10g] lengthy filly: modest maiden: never able to challenge in 2 minor events and Brighton handicap in 1992: stud. *L. M. Cumani*

LADY OF LETTERS 3 ro.f. Primo Dominie 121 – Teacher's Game 64 (Mummy's 36 Game 120) [1991 5g4 5g3 5d 6.1s5 6m4 7m5 6m 6m a7g 1992 a8g4 a8g2 a8g a8g 7d 7d 7m] small, workmanlike filly: has quick action: poor maiden: soundly beaten last 5 starts and not seen out after June: should prove as effective at 7f as 1m: suited by a sound surface: showed nothing in visor once at 2 yrs. *T. Thomson Jones*

LADY OF SARDINIA (BEL) 3 b.f. Efisio 120 – Lady of The Manor 78 (Astec 67 128) [1991 7m4 7f 8.2m* 8g3 1992 10d 9g 9m2 10g 10g 10.1f4 8g 9.7g2 8v* 8v] leggy, close-coupled filly: inconsistent performer: runner-up here in handicap at Sandown in June and seller at Folkestone in September for J. Payne: subsequently won claimer at Saint-Cloud in November: stays 9.7f: acts on good to firm and heavy ground. *J.-P. Gallorini, France*

LADY OF SHADOWS 2 ch.f. (Feb 14) Ballacashtal (CAN) – Little Madam 66 43 (Habat 127) [1992 6m 6g 5f6 6m6 5g 6m6 6f3 5.3f2 6m a6g a6g5 a8g a6g] compact filly: fourth foal: half-sister to 1988 2-y-o 5f seller winner Alo' Niko (by Mansingh): dam won twice over 5f: poor maiden: stays 6f: acts on firm ground: has worn blinkers, visor and eyeshield: rather inconsistent. *S. Dow*

LADY OF THE FEN 4 b.f. Myjinski (USA) – Flying Glory (Flying Mercury) – § [1991 7m 5m5 a5g* 6m 7g 5.1f a5g2 a5g2 5f a5g6 a5g a5g a5g2 1992 a5g a5g a5g a6g6 a60 § a5g* 5m a5g 5m5 5m] leggy filly: has a quick action: inconsistent handicapper: won at Southwell in March: reluctant to race from halfway when tailed off final start, in July: suited by 5f: no improvement in blinkers or a visor: flashes tail and carries head high: sold 3,000 gns Newmarket September Sales: not one to trust. *Mrs N. Macauley*

LADY POLY 4 b.f. Dunbeath (USA) 127 – First Temptation (USA) (Mr Leader – (USA)) [1991 a7g4 10f 11.5m 8.5m3 10m6 11.5s4 10g5 a10g 1992 a10g 11.9d 15.4g 16g6 11.5s] small, leggy filly: winning selling hurdler in 1991/2: still a maiden on flat: may stay 1¾m: acts on good to firm ground: tried blinkered: sold to join R. Stone 900 gns Ascot November Sales. *Miss B. Sanders*

LADY RANDOLPH 3 b.f. Elegant Air 119 – Cara Rose (Rheingold 137) [1991 6g – 7g4 7f5 7f 8.2m 8.3g5 10.5d 1992 8s 8v 10g 8g] sturdy, compact filly: no longer of much account. *I. Campbell*

LADY REEM (USA) 3 b.f. Al Nasr (FR) 126 – Lorn Lady (Lorenzaccio 130) – [1991 NR 1992 9.9g 6m] leggy, sparely-made filly: moderate walker: ninth foal: half-sister to several winners, notably Prix de Diane winner Lady In Silver (by Silver Hawk): dam Irish 8.5f winner from very good family: well beaten in maidens at Beverley (co-favourite) and Brighton in the spring: sold 2,400 gns Ascot September Sales. *M. Moubarak*

LADY RELKO 2 b.f. (May 10) Sizzling Melody 117 – Rosalka (ITY) (Relko 136) **45**
[1992 5d 6f³ 6m 6g⁴ 7m] 2,000Y: leggy, sparely-made filly: moderate mover: half-
sister to several winners, including fair 5f performer Bella Rossi (by Mummy's Pet)
and French 7f and 1m winner John Hawkwood (by Irish River): dam won 4 times in
Italy: plating-class maiden: better suited by 7f than 6f: acts well on good to firm
ground. *R. Voorspuy*

LADY RISK ME 3 gr.f. Risk Me (FR) 127 – Donrae 106 (Don (ITY) 123) [1991 –
a7g 7m 1992 a7g 8f a10g] leggy, shallow-girthed filly: of little account: trained by K.
Wingrove on reappearance. *J. R. Bostock*

LADY ROXANNE 3 br.f. Cyrano de Bergerac 120 – Red Lory 87 (Bay Express **65**
132) [1991 5m 1992 6g² a7g³ 7.1d⁵ 6d 7g] leggy, sparely-made filly: has a quick
action: modest maiden: shapes as if stays 7f: has raced freely and drifted left:
claimer ridden. *Lord Huntingdon*

LADY SABO 3 br.f. Prince Sabo 123 – Nice Lady 65 (Connaught 130) [1991 5m³ **69**
5d⁴ 5f* 6m 6g 6m³ 6.1m⁵ 1992 5g⁶ 5g 6m* 7g 7f³ 5.7h* 5d⁵ 6g⁶ 6f⁵ 6g³ 6d³ 6f 6s a53 +
a7g a8g⁴] smallish, leggy filly: fair performer: won claimers at Goodwood in May and
Bath in June: below form last 4 starts, final 3 for an apprentice: stays 7f: acts on any
going except perhaps soft: sometimes bandaged behind. *G. Lewis*

LADY'S MANTLE (USA) 8 ch.m. Sunny Clime (USA) – Alchemilla (USA) **46**
(Quadrangle) [1991 5d 5g 5g 5f⁴ 5f* 5g 5g⁶ 5f* 5.2m² 5f⁴ 5m* 5f⁶ 5f² 5.2f⁴ 5m 1992
5g 5g 6g 5m⁴ 5f 5m⁶ 5f⁶ a5g*] good-bodied mare: was usually dull in coat: moderate
mover: plating-class handicapper: returned to form when making all in Southwell
apprentice event in July: speedy: had form on dead going, but went particularly well
on top-of-the-ground and fibresand: tried in blinkers and visor earlier in career:
often wore crossed noseband: died soon after final win. *R. Bastiman*

LADY SNOOBLE 5 b.m. King of Clubs 124 – Ides of March 87 (Mummy's Pet –
125) [1991 NR 1992 7g a7g a7g] small, sturdy mare: of little account. *K. O. Cunningham-Brown*

LADY ST LAWRENCE (USA) 3 ch.f. Bering 136 – Lady Norcliffe (USA) **56**
(Norcliffe (CAN)) [1991 8.2m⁶ 8.9d 8.1s³ a8g 1992 12v² 12.3s 12.2g* 12g*]
workmanlike filly: easy mover: modest performer: blinkered, won seller (bought in
6,200 gns) at Catterick and claimer (claimed £6,650) at Thirsk in the spring: will
stay at least 1¾m: acts on heavy ground: game. *Sir Mark Prescott*

LADY WESTGATE 8 b.m. Welsh Chanter 124 – Church Bay 76 (Reliance II –
137) [1991 17.1m 16.2g 14.8m⁴ 12.1d 16.2g⁶ 16.2d² 16.4m 14.6m⁵ 1992 14.9d 16.2d
17.2s 18.2g a16g6 16.4m⁵ 12.1s⁶ 15.4g 17.2s a12g] leggy, rather plain mare: has won 2
of 33 starts: poor staying handicapper at best nowadays: acts on firm and dead going:
tried visored once. *G. B. Balding*

LA FAVORITA (FR) 3 b.f. Nikos 124 – Didia Clara (Sea Break 129) [1991 8s 8d⁴ **115**
8v⁴ 8v⁴ 8v* 1992 10s* 10.5g⁶ 10m⁵ 8s³ 8s* 10s 9.3s² 8.5f] half-sister to French
11.5f winner Calimala (by Son of Silver) and useful French middle-distance stayer
Sudaka (by Garde Royale): dam French 6.5f to 1½m winner: very useful French
filly: won handicap at Evry in March and listed race at Deauville in August: easily
best effort when ½-length second to Hatoof in Prix de l'Opera at Longchamp: last of
11 in very valuable handicap at Gulfstream Park final outing: stays 1¼m: acts on soft
going. *E. Lellouche, France*

LAFKADIO 5 b.g. Gay Mecene (USA) 128 – Lakonia (Kris 135) [1991 a14g* **44**
a14g* a12g⁵ a14g² a14g³ 13.8d⁴ 17m³ 21.6f* 16.2f* 18g⁴ 20g 16.5m* 16.5g³ 16f⁴
1992 16.2d 15.9g 18.2m⁴ 17.1s a14g a14g⁴] smallish, good-bodied gelding: poor
mover: only a poor handicapper in 1992: best form with really good test of stamina:
acts on firm and dead ground and on fibresand: usually blinkered. *M. C. Chapman*

LAGEN 2 b.g. (Jan 31) Local Suitor (USA) 128 – Lagta 75 (Kris 135) [1992 6g⁶ 7f⁵] **51**
stocky gelding: second foal: dam 1½m and 1¾m winner: modest form in maidens at
Newmarket in June: looked a bit backward and seemed likely to do better. *C. E.
Brittain*

LAGGARD'S QUEST 3 br.c. Daring March 116 – Doubtful Request (Cheveley –
Lad 105) [1991 7.1s 1992 a5g 5.1g 5.1m 6g] sturdy colt: seems of little account. *C. D.
Broad*

LAHIB (USA) 4 b.c. Riverman (USA) 131 – Lady Cutlass (USA) (Cutlass **129**
(USA)) [1991 8g² 8g* 1992 9g⁶ 8m² 8m* 8s² 8s* 10m²]
     The phrase 'better late than never' rings all too true for Lahib. Training
troubles kept him off the racecourse as a two-year-old and severely restricted

Queen Anne Stakes, Royal Ascot—
Lahib (striped cap) rallies to snatch a well-contested race from Second Set,
Sikeston and the almost-hidden Exit To Nowhere

his appearances at three: he had a trapped testicle removed at two after persistent lameness was traced to his being a rig, and he was side-lined for most of his second season with damaged soft tissue in a knee. Lahib made up for lost time in the latest season and developed into a top-class performer, one of the best around at a mile to a mile and a quarter. After a considerate introduction in the Earl of Sefton Stakes at Newmarket, Lahib finished an excellent second to Selkirk in a strong field for the Lockinge Stakes at Newbury in May. He was then sent to Royal Ascot where notwithstanding his inexperience—he'd run only four times, gaining his only victory in a Newmarket maiden—he had a sound chance on his Lockinge form in the Queen Anne Stakes. Lahib received weight from the penalized Group 1 winners Second Set and Sikeston and also from Rudimentary and Goofalik who had been successful in Group 2 pattern races. Lahib rallied splendidly, after being one of the first to come under pressure, to win by a head and half a length from Second Set and Sikeston. French-trained Exit To Nowhere, only a short head further back in fourth, would have won the Queen Anne with a trouble-free run, and Lahib couldn't confirm Royal Ascot placings when the pair met again in the Prix Jacques le Marois at Deauville in August. On much more testing going—the ground had been on the firm side at Royal Ascot—Lahib couldn't match Exit To Nowhere over the final furlong, going down by a length but confirming in the process that he was still on the upgrade.

The Queen Elizabeth II Stakes, centrepiece of the Festival of British Racing programme at Ascot in September, was the next target for Lahib. When it was introduced in 1987, the Festival of British Racing enjoyed magnificent publicity. Some labelled it 'Britain's Breeders Cup' and it was welcomed on all sides. There is always a novelty factor with any sumptuous new event, however, and the omens for long-term success seem less favourable now. The quality of horses attracted to the day's programme—which includes four pattern races—remains high but the size of the crowd has never reached the level that the organisers anticipated and can be said to have become disappointing, allowing for indifferent weather some years. The day's official attendance in 1992 was 15,202, over 2,000 down on 1991 and comparing with 25,619 for the inaugural Festival. One of the drawbacks of the Festival is that, with the Prix de l'Arc only a week away, it cannot stage a big middle-distance event. The milers as a group don't enjoy the same high profile as the mile-and-a-half horses who receive the lion's share of the media attention each season. The Queen Elizabeth II Stakes drew an excellent field and could fairly be billed as a European championship. It attracted Marling, Selkirk (the 1991 winner) and Second Set, the first three in the Sussex Stakes, Britain's other all-aged Group 1 event over a mile. Also in the line-up were All At Sea and Brief Truce, first and second in the Group 1 Prix du Moulin de Longchamp earlier in the month. Unfortunately, the race was marred by scrimmaging and interference around the home turn and in the straight, in which Selkirk was a notable sufferer. Lahib was prominent from the start, as his pacemaker Hamas and the enigmatic 1991 Two Thousand Guineas winner Mystiko set a testing gallop. Lahib took over more than two furlongs out and kept on very well to hold off Brief Truce by two lengths with Selkirk, who would have finished at least second with a clear run, a length and a half further away in third; All At Sea, Second Set and Mystiko secured the prize money for fourth, fifth and sixth. Lahib couldn't have had a better ride than Carson gave him in the Queen Elizabeth II Stakes or in his final race the Dubai Champion Stakes at Newmarket where he went down by a neck to Rodrigo de Triano who had missed the Queen Elizabeth because of the soft ground. Carson drove Lahib into the lead entering the Dip at Newmarket and kept him going strongly all the way to the line; but he couldn't hold off Rodrigo de Triano, brought with a sweetly-timed run by another notable veteran, Piggott. Fifty-year-old Willie Carson retains all his zest and vigour but he didn't enjoy so much of the limelight as usual in the latest season when the championship was dominated by Roberts and Eddery. Carson still reached the hundred-winner mark in a season for the twenty-first time in his career and confirmed that he has no intention of retiring yet.

The big, rangy Lahib is an imposing individual who invariably took the eye in the paddock. He is a good mover, too. His North American-based sire the Poule d'Essai des Poulains (French Guineas) winner Riverman has proved an admirable stallion and is still going strong. He was also represented most notably in Europe in the latest season by All At Sea. Lahib's dam Lady Cutlass, a winner at five to seven furlongs in North America, is a half-sister to General Store, the grandam of the Irish One Thousand Guineas and Coronation Stakes winner Al Bahathri. Al Bahathri provided Hamdan Al-Maktoum with his first classic winner and Lady Cutlass was acquired privately for the owner's Shadwell Stud in the same year. Lady Cutlass has now produced five winners from six foals of racing age, the best of them before Lahib being Maceo (by Nodouble), who showed very useful form in the States at around a mile, and Sajjaya (by Blushing Groom), a game and useful miler handled by Lahib's trainer. Lady Cutlass' three-year-old Alhaajib, a brother to Sajjaya, ended the latest season still a maiden. Lady Cutlass is a half-sister to ten

Queen Elizabeth II Stakes, Ascot—Lahib responds well to Carson's riding,
chased by Brief Truce, Selkirk (right), All At Sea (rails) and Second Set

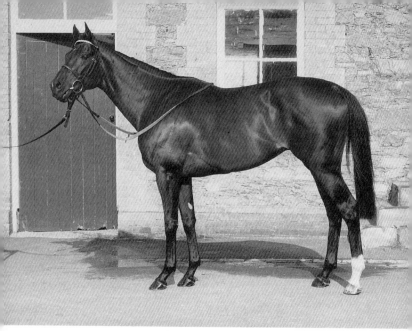

Hamdan Al-Maktoum's "Lahib"

		Never Bend	Nasrullah
	Riverman (USA)	(b 1960)	Lalun
	(b 1969)	River Lady	Prince John
Lahib (USA)		(b 1963)	Nile Lily
(b.c. 1988)		Cutlass	Damascus
	Lady Cutlass (USA)	(b 1970)	Generals Sister
	(b 1978)	Generals Sister	Count Fleet
		(b 1960)	Cigar Maid

winners in all, notably to the Vanity Handicap and Del Mar Oaks winner Commissary and to General Holme who showed high-class form at up to ten and a half furlongs in France. The game and genuine Lahib stayed a mile and a quarter and acted on good to firm and soft ground. He has been retired to stud and will stand at Derrinstown in County Kildare at a fee of IR 6,000 guineas with the October 1st concession. *J. L. Dunlop*

LAHOOB (USA) 3 b.c. Miswaki (USA) 124 – Sure Locked (USA) (Lyphard (USA) 132) [1991 NR 1992 7.9g 8.3s* 7d 8s* 8.9d² 7.1s] $185,000Y: strong-quartered, quite attractive colt: poor mover: first foal: dam listed winner at 1m as 3-y-o in France, is half-sister to Sure Blade: fair performer: changed hands 10,500 gns Newmarket July (1992) Sales: won maiden at Hamilton and handicap at Salisbury in September: very good second in £9,400 handicap at York, edging left: needs further than 7f, and stays 8.9f well: yet to race on top-of-the-ground, though gives impression probably well suited by a soft surface: has tongue tied down: bandaged behind first 3 starts. *B. Hanbury*   **73**

LAID BACK BEN 2 ch.c. (Jun 11) Starch Reduced 112 – Mrs Dumbfounded (Adropejo 114) [1992 6v a6g] eighth foal: half-brother to 8.2f winner Baker's Double   **–**

442

(by Rapid River): dam bad plater: no promise in maidens at Hamilton and Lingfield in November. *B. Palling*

L'AIGLE D'OR (USA)   2 ch.c. (Mar 5) Believe It (USA) – Thirst For Gold   **73** (USA) (Mr Prospector (USA)) [1992 6m² 7d] IR 36,000Y: lengthy, good-topped colt: has plenty of scope: closely related to a winner in USA by Valid Appeal and half-brother to a winner by Pleasant Colony: dam minor winner at up to 9f: sire (by In Reality) good-class 5½f to 9f winner: promising second to very easy winner High Tycoon in minor event at Ascot in June: favourite, went freely down, got well worked up in stalls then wasn't knocked about in Salisbury maiden following month: should stay 7f: worth another chance. *G. Lewis*

LAILATI (USA)   2 ch.f. (Mar 21) Mr Prospector (USA) – Carduel (USA) (Buck-   **53** p passer) [1992 6g5] close-coupled, unfurnished filly: seventh live foal: half-sister to 3-y-o 1m winner Asaasy and smart 6f (at 2 yrs) to 1m winner Always Fair (both by Danzig): dam, winner at up to 1m, is half-sister to smart Irish 1m/1¼m performer Punctilio, family of Gay Fandango: 11/1, under 10 lengths fifth of 9 to Lost Soldier in minor event at Newmarket in August, outpaced over 2f out: will improve, particularly over 1m. *M. R. Stoute*

LAJADHAL (FR)   3 gr.c. Bellypha 130 – Rose d'Amour (USA) (Lines of Power   – (USA)) [1991 NR 1992 a12g a12g5] first living foal: dam French 3-y-o 1m winner out of Kentucky Oaks winner Nancy Jr, also the dam of several smart performers including middle-distance filly Joli Vert and 7f/1m winner Rapide Pied: bought out of B. Hanbury's stable 3,400 gns Newmarket July (1992) Sales and well beaten in claimer and maiden at Lingfield. *J. A. Bennett*

LA JOYA (USA)   3 b.f. Affirmed (USA) – Watership (USA) (Foolish Pleasure   – (USA)) [1991 NR 1992 10.2h³ 9.7d³ 11.9f³ 15.4d5] good-bodied filly: first foal: dam not placed from 9 starts in USA: well beaten in maidens. *G. Harwood*

LAKAB (USA)   2 ch.f. (Mar 1) Manila (USA) – River Lullaby (USA) (Riverman   **63** (USA) 131) [1992 6m5 7g³ 7s] $150,000Y: quite attractive filly: second reported foal: half-sister to 3-y-o Berceau (by Alleged), successful in 1½m Prix de Royaumont: dam Irish 2-y-o 6f winner later stayed middle distances, is daughter of smart stakes winner (at up to 1¼m) Aladancer: sire (by Lyphard) won Breeders' Cup Turf: similar form in maidens at Ascot (well backed but green) in June and Yarmouth in August: ran moderately at Salisbury following month: will be very well suited by middle distances: may do better. *H. Thomson Jones*

LAKE DOMINION   3 b.g. Primo Dominie 121 – Piney Lake 54 (Sassafras (FR)   **70** d 135) [1991 6d 6d³ 6m³ 7g4 1992 10d5 8f4 8d³ 8g5 8.3g 8d5] close-coupled, quite good-topped gelding: modest maiden: stays 1¼m: yet to race on very soft ground, probably acts on any other: blinkered twice, running creditably first occasion: sold 10,500 gns Newmarket Autumn Sales and gelded. *P. W. Harris*

LAKE PLEASANT (IRE)   2 b.f. (Mar 16) Elegant Air 119 – Laugharne (Known   **90** Fact (USA) 135) [1992 6g* 6g³ 7d] 77,000Y: leggy, close-coupled filly: has a quick action: third foal: half-sister to fairly useful 3-y-o sprinter Power Lake (by Form-idable): dam once-raced daughter of Boathouse, a half-sister to Bireme and Buoy: fairly useful performer: won maiden at Newmarket: very good third of 6 to Marina Park in Princess Margaret Stakes at Ascot later in July, staying on well: looked sure to improve further, but ran badly in Group 3 event at Goodwood month later: should stay at least 7f. *R. Hannon*

LAKE POOPO (IRE)   2 b.f. (May 11) Persian Heights 129 – Bolivia (GER)   **51** p (Windwurf (GER)) [1992 7g 7m] tall, leggy filly: has scope: fourth foal: half-sister to fairly useful 1991 2-y-o 6f and 7f winner Cochabamba (by Thatching) and 2 other winners, including 1990 2-y-o 7f winner Mystic Crystal (by Caerleon): dam useful winner at 2 yrs in Germany: bit backward still, never better than mid-division in 17-runner maiden at Newmarket in October: may do better. *B. W. Hills*

LAKE PRINCESS (IRE)   2 b.f. (May 2) Kings Lake (USA) 133 – Nigel's Star   **38** (Ashmore (FR) 125) [1992 6m 6g6 7m 8s] 2,000Y: leggy, unfurnished filly: fourth foal: half-sister to a winner in Belgium by Magical Wonder: dam ran twice: poor maiden. *S. Dow*

LA KERMESSE (USA)   3 gr.f. Storm Bird (CAN) 134 – La Koumia (FR) 119   **58** (Kaldoun (FR) 122) [1991 NR 1992 8d 8g 7f³ 7f³ 7g* 8g5 7g5 7g] $130,000F: close-coupled filly: second foal: closely related to Irish maiden Le Jongleur (by The Minstrel): dam very useful 5.5f (at 2 yrs) to 1¼m winner at 2 and 3 yrs in France, later Grade 1 winner in USA: modest form: won maiden at Catterick in July: stayed 1m: acted on firm ground: often slowly away: visits Saumarez. *J. H. M. Gosden*

LA MADRIGAL 2 ch.f. (Apr 16) Music Boy 124 – Prosperous Gal (Good Times 50 (ITY)) [1992 5m⁵ a5g⁵ 5s² 5.1d 6g] strong, lengthy filly: has scope: second foal: dam ran twice: poor maiden: will stay 6f: best effort on soft ground. *J. Wharton*

LAMARSH (IRE) 4 ch.c. Be My Guest (USA) 126 – Annabella 88 (Habitat 134) – [1991 7d² 8f* 8g⁵ 8g* 7g 8m 1992 7g] stocky colt: rated 86 when game handicapper at 3 yrs: stayed 1m: acted on firm and dead ground: wore severe bridle as 3-y-o: reportedly suffered heart attack on the gallops in April: dead. *J. H. M. Gosden*

LAMASTRE 3 b.f. Jalmood (USA) 126 – Daring Lass 87 (Bold Lad (IRE) 133) – [1991 5g* 5f⁴ 5.8d³ 6g 1992 8m 8d 7m 8m 10m 8.3m 6g] smallish filly: has a quick action: won a seller on her debut, but no form in 1992 and not seen out after July: seems rather headstrong, but bred to stay 1¼m: tends to hang: has joined C. Weedon. *R. J. Hodges*

LAMBSON 5 b.g. Petorius 117 – Julie Be Quick (USA) (Selari) [1991 10f 10f 8m⁴ – 10m 10.2g 12g 1992 10s] leggy gelding: moderate mover: untrustworthy and no worthwhile form on flat for long time: won over hurdles in April. *R. M. Whitaker*

LA MENORQUINA (USA) 2 b.f. (Mar 10) Woodman (USA) 126 – Hail The 65 Lady (USA) (Hail The Pirates (USA) 126) [1992 6m⁶ 7d² 6s] $80,000Y: quite good-topped filly: third reported foal: dam won at up to 1¼m: best effort in maidens when second at Redcar (bandaged behind), soon towards rear, every chance over 2f out then one pace: will stay at least 1m: acts on dead ground: well below best on very soft: may be capable of better. *L. M. Cumani*

LAMORE RITORNA 3 br.f. Lidhame 109 – Arbor Lane 70 (Wolverlife 115) 50 [1991 7.1m⁵ 7g 1992 8d⁵ 10g 8.5d a8g² a7g³ a7g⁴ 8.3d* 8f 7d 10d 8d 8d] leggy filly: modest performer: won claimer at Windsor in July: below form afterwards: stays 1m: acts on dead going and equitrack: retained 600 gns Newmarket Autumn Sales. *K. O. Cunningham-Brown*

L'AMOUR PRECIEUX 3 b.g. Precocious 126 – La Mortola (Bold Lad (IRE) – 133) [1991 5m 6d 5m⁴ 1992 a8g 7d 7g 7g 8m] workmanlike gelding: poor form: should stay 1m: tubed on last 2 starts. *M. W. Easterby*

LAMSONETTI 2 b.f. (Mar 24) Never So Bold 135 – Orient 106 (Bay Express 42 p 132) [1992 6s⁴ 5d 5v⁴] 34,000Y: lengthy, quite good-topped filly: second foal: half-sister to Irish 3-y-o 5f winner Arcade (by Rousillon): dam sprinter: poor form in maidens: best effort last time despite being virtually tailed off from flag start: stays 6f: yet to race on a sound surface: gave trouble to post (showed nothing) second start: should prove capable of better. *R. M. Whitaker*

LAMU LADY (IRE) 2 b.f. (Feb 25) Lomond (USA) 128 – Noble Mark 120 (On 70 p Your Mark 125) [1992 6m⁴ 6d⁴ 7d*] useful-looking filly: closely related to several winners, including good miler The Noble Player (by The Minstrel) and useful 1987 2-y-o 5f and 7f winner Border Guard (by Nureyev), and half-sister to several winners, including over middle distances: dam very smart sprinter: fair form: off course 7 weeks, won maiden at Catterick in October, running on strongly to lead last strides: will be suited by 1m +: will improve further. *P. W. Chapple-Hyam*

LANCASTER PILOT 2 ch.g. (Feb 14) Crofthall 110 – Spinner 59 (Blue 57 Cashmere 129) [1992 5f 7m⁴ 6f² 7s⁵] workmanlike gelding: poor mover: brother to unreliable 6-y-o Resolute Bay, one-time fairly useful 5f to 7f handicapper, and half-brother to 3 winners, including 3-y-o Young Valentine (by Bairn), successful at 5f at 2 yrs: dam sprinter: modest maiden: stays 7f: probably acts on any going. *R. M. Whitaker*

LANDED GENTRY (USA) 3 b.c. Vaguely Noble 140 – Phydilla (FR) 126 65 (Lyphard (USA) 132) [1991 7g 8g 1992 11d⁶ 12.5g 12.5g² a12s⁴ 16.9d 14.1g³ 13.8g⁶ 16.1s] good-bodied colt: has a round action: fair maiden on flat: will stay 2m: may be unsuited by a soft surface: sold to join C. Broad 6,200 gns Newmarket Autumn Sales and won novice hurdle in November. *P. W. Chapple-Hyam*

LAND O'LAKES (IRE) 2 b.c. (Feb 26) Kings Lake (USA) 133 – Amboselli 73 67 (Raga Navarro (ITY) 119) [1992 6v² a7g³ a7g²] half-brother to several winners, a60 including fairly useful 3-y-o Mrs Fisher (by Salmon Leap): dam placed over 5f at 2 yrs: fair form in maidens late in season at Folkestone (beaten a short head) and Southwell: stays 7f. *Sir Mark Prescott*

LANDOWNER (IRE) 3 b.c.c. Kris 135 – Laluche (USA) 100 (Alleged (USA) 138) 111 [1991 7m⁴ 1992 8g 10d⁵ 12.1g* 11.6g* 12m* 16.2f* 12m 15d⁶ 16m³ 15.9g² 15s⁶ 16g] strong colt: carries condition: fluent mover: smart performer: won maiden at Edinburgh in April, handicaps at Windsor and Goodwood in May and Queen's Vase (by 6 lengths from Belgran) at Royal Ascot: well beaten in Irish Derby next start: creditable sixth in Group 2 event at Longchamp then put up best efforts, despite being rather edgy in the preliminaries, behind Further Flight in both Goodwood Cup (sweating, beaten 1½ lengths) and listed race at York: tongue tied down, sweating freely and headstrong to post, ran as if something amiss final start: suited by test of stamina: acts on firm and dead ground. *J. H. M. Gosden*

LANDRAIL (USA) 2 ch.f. (Apr 10) Storm Bird (CAN) 134 – Vaguely Sensitive (USA) (Sensitive Prince (USA)) [1992 5.7d²] $95,000Y: third foal: dam twice-raced half-sister to Indian Skimmer (by Storm Bird): 11/2 from 7/2, 2 lengths second of 9 to Pluck in maiden at Bath in September, green and pushed along early, then staying on well: will improve, particularly given greater test of stamina. *B. W. Hills*   **59** p

LANGTONIAN 3 br.g. Primo Dominie 121 – Yankee Special 60 (Bold Lad (IRE) 133) [1991 6f³ 6d* 6m² 6m² 6d⁴ 6m 1992 6.1g 6f 6f 6f⁶ 6m² 5g⁴ 5g⁴ 5d⁵ 5d 5s³ 5s² 5d 5g⁶] sturdy gelding: carries condition: good walker: fair winner at 2 yrs: nowhere near so good in 1992 and looked wayward: stays 6f: acts on good to firm ground and soft: blinkered last 9 starts: not one to trust. *J. Berry*   **59** §

LANGTRY LADY 6 b.m. Pas de Seul 133 – Arianna Aldini (Habitat 134) [1991 a8g² 8d 7m 7.6d² 7m 8f⁴ 8m* 7s² 8.5f³ 7.6m⁵ 7.6m⁵ 8m² 8d² 8d³ 7.6d³ 8g 1992 8.5g² 8d 9d⁴ 7.6g⁵ 8g⁶ 8f³ 8.1g⁴ 7f⁶ 8.1d 8g 8.1g⁵ 9d* 7s⁶] leggy, sparely-made mare: fairly useful handicapper: dropped to claiming company when comfortable winner at Kempton in September: effective from 7f to 9f: acts on any going: visored last 3 starts: has run well for claimer: below form for amateur: has carried head high: consistent. *M. J. Ryan*   **84**

LANGUEDOC 5 b.h. Rousillon (USA) 133 – Can Can Girl 69 (Gay Fandango (USA) 132) [1991 a6g⁴ a5g* a5g² a6g⁴ 5d 5m⁴ 5m³ 5f 5g 5f 7g³ 7m² 7m 6g³ 7g 8.1s* a6g² a8g* a8g⁴ 1992 a7g⁶ 8g 7g⁶ 6d⁶ 7g 7m⁵ 6m⁶ 8.1f 7f⁶ 7s 6d³ 5s⁵ 7d] tall,   **65**

Sheikh Mohammed's "Landowner"

attractive horse: modest handicapper: best from 6f to 1m: acts on good to firm and soft ground, and on all-weather surfaces: ran moderately when blinkered once earlier in career: has carried head high. *M. P. Naughton*

LANKRIDGE 2 b.c. (May 16) Alzao (USA) 117 – Free Dance (FR) (Green Dancer **50** p (USA) 132) [1992 7m] close-coupled, workmanlike colt: half-brother to 3-y-o 11.8f winner Free Mover (by Rousillon) and 4 other winners, all at 1¼m + : dam French 8.5f and 9f winner: 33/1, slowly into stride and well behind last 2f in 12-runner maiden at Newmarket in October: should do better. *Major W. R. Hern*

LAPIAFFE 8 b.g. Piaffer (USA) 113 – Laval (Cheval 117) [1991 16m2 17.1d* – 17.2g4 17.2f 1992 13.8m 15.1d] rather sparely-made gelding: moderate mover: rated 41 at 7 yrs: well beaten in 1992, trained first start by R. Hodges: acts on good to firm and dead ground: won poor claiming chase in December. *A. Harrison*

LAP OF LUXURY 3 gr.f. Sharrood (USA) 124 – Lap of Honour 100 (Final Straw **90** 127) [1991 NR 1992 8f3 8.2m* 8.3g6 8g* 8g* 8m2 8g5] sparely-made filly: moderate mover: second foal: half-sister to useful 6f winner La Stupenda (by Chief Singer): dam useful 6f and 7f winner out of half-sister to Oaks second Vielle: progressed into a fairly useful performer: won maiden at Nottingham in August and handicaps at Kempton and Newbury (£15,100 contest) in September: ran well in valuable handicaps at Newmarket last 2 starts: stays 1m well: yet to race on a soft surface: consistent. *W. Jarvis*

LA POSADA 2 b.f. (Feb 27) Procida (USA) 129 – Chepstow Vale (USA) 97 (Key **48** p To The Mint (USA)) [1992 7.1s6] leggy, unfurnished filly: fourth foal: half-sister to fair 4-y-o Brown Fairy (by Northern Baby), winner at up to 7.5f and effective at 1¼m: dam 2-y-o 5f and 6f winner stayed 1m: 12/1, 12 lengths sixth of 12 to Ivory Palm in maiden at Chepstow in October, slowly away and late headway past beaten rivals: refused to enter stalls 11 days later: should improve. *R. Hannon*

LA RAPTOTTE 5 b.m. Alzao (USA) 117 – Maypole Hie (Bold Lad (IRE) 133) – [1991 a7g4 a8g3 10.8g 10.8g 12.2d6 12s 8.9g 1992 10.8g 8m5] angular mare: no worthwhile form on flat since 3 yrs: modest hurdler, winner in October. *M. J. Charles*

LARA'S BABY (IRE) 4 ch.f. Valiyar 129 – Tapiola 71 (Tap On Wood 130) [1991 **68** 10g 8m3 8g4 8.5m 11.7m 12.1s5 a12g* 1992 a12g* a11g2 a12g* a12g2 10.3g] sturdy filly: moderate mover: fair performer: won 2 claimers early in the year for R. Akehurst at Southwell: off course 6 months, faded from 2f out at Chester final start: better at 1½m than shorter: acts on good to firm and soft ground, and on fibresand: won selling handicap hurdle later in August. *N. Tinkler*

LARA'S IDEA 4 b.f. Primo Dominie 121 – Lara's Song (USA) (Russian Bank **112** (USA)) [1991 8g* 8s* 8v3 12g4 10g* 11g* 10g5 10s* 10v* 10v2 1992 10v3 10s3 10g3 10d* 12d3 11.9m6 10g* 10d2 12s6] smallish, lengthy Italian filly: moderate mover: very useful performer: won Group 3 race at Milan in June and listed race at Rome in September: ran well when placed behind Mashaallah in 1½m Gran Premio di Milano and Oumaldaaya in 1¼m Group 2 race at Rome: poor sixth in Yorkshire Oaks and Group 1 event at Milan: effective from 1¼m to 1½m: goes well on a yielding surface, probably not on good to firm: has been blinkered (was at York). *L. Camici, Italy*

LA REINE ROUGE (IRE) 4 ch.f. Red Sunset 120 – Free Rein (Sagaro 133) **48** [1991 a12g 1992 a10g2 a12g3 10.5s6 a12g* a12g2] smallish filly: poor handicapper: apprentice ridden, won (for first time) at Lingfield in May: stays 1½m: acts on all-weather surfaces: sold 2,100 gns Newmarket Autumn Sales. *P. J. Makin*

LARK RISE (USA) 4 ch.g. The Minstrel (CAN) 135 – Glowing Prospect (USA) – (Mr Prospector (USA)) [1991 9g5 8g 8d3 10.2s* 1992 12d] angular gelding: has a long, round stride: rated 68 in first half of 1991 then sold out of I. Balding's stable 15,000 gns Newmarket Autumn (1991) Sales: no show in Kempton handicap in April: stays 1¼m: acts on soft going. *C. Weedon*

LARN FORT 2 gr.g. (Mar 22) Belfort (FR) 89 – Larnem 43 (Meldrum 112) [1992 **49** 5m 6s3 8d a7g3] tall, leggy gelding: looks weak: first reported foal: dam 7f to 11.5f winner probably stayed 13f: poor maiden: should stay 1m. *T. Fairhurst*

LARRIKIN (USA) 3 b.f. Slew O' Gold (USA) – For The Flag (USA) 66 (Forli **85** p (ARG)) [1991 NR 1992 10g4 10.4g* 12g] tall, leggy, unfurnished filly: sixth reported foal: half-sister to 4 winners of at least fairly useful ability, including smart 1¼m winner On The Staff (by Master Willie): dam, from good family, maiden here later 1m winner in USA: sire top-class 9f to 1½m performer: fairly useful form: won maiden at York in September, leading over 1f out and battling on bravely: never travelling well in November Handicap at Doncaster: will prove well suited by 1½m: lightly raced and is open to improvement. *Lord Huntingdon*

LASCAR (USA) 4 ch.g. Riverman (USA) 131 – Meteoric 102 (High Line 125) **47**
[1991 NR 1992 10d⁴ 10.1d⁵ 11.8m⁵ 14.6s 12d⁶] sturdy gelding: first foal: dam 6f
winner, is half-sister to very useful sprinter Fine Edge: unraced when sold out of J.
Gosden's stable 4,800 gns Newmarket Autumn (1991) Sales: poor maiden: should
stay 1¾m: acts on good to firm and dead ground, well beaten on soft. *G. Thorner*

LAST APPEARANCE 3 b.f. Slip Anchor 136 – Thespian 76 (Ile de Bourbon   –
(USA) 133) [1991 7g 1992 7.6g⁵ 8m] close-coupled filly: no worthwhile form: sold
1,100 gns Newmarket July Sales. *M. Bell*

LAST CONQUEST (IRE) 3 b.g. Slip Anchor 136 – Migiyas 87 (Kings Lake **64**
(USA) 133) [1991 8s 8.1d⁵ 10m⁶ 8.1s 1992 11.6m 13.1m⁴ 14g* 14.1f³ 16.2d³] good-
topped gelding: good mover: modest and consistent handicapper: ridden by 7-lb
claimer, won at Goodwood in June: stays 2m: acts on firm and dead ground: sold to
join J. Joseph 2,500 gns Newmarket September Sales. *P. F. I. Cole*

LAST EMBRACE (IRE) 3 b.f. Shernazar 131 – Melodramatic 112 (Tudor **86** p
Melody 129) [1991 NR 1992 10m* 12g* 11.9d] 8,000Y: smallish, workmanlike filly:
sister to plating-class 1½m winner Showmanship and useful Irish 8.5f (at 2 yrs) to
1¾m winner Opinionated, closely related to 2 winners by Bustino, including 1½m
winner Overcall, and half-sister to several winners, including smart miler Crown
Witness (by Crowned Prince): dam won at 7f and 9f: fairly useful form: won maiden
at Pontefract and £7,300 handicap at Newbury in the summer: again held up, unable
to get into moderately-run £15,100 handicap at York in September: stays 1½m: may
well be capable of better. *Lord Huntingdon*

LAST EXIT 3 b.f. Dominion 123 – Nepula 105 (Nebbiolo 125) [1991 6g* 6d* 6f³ **80**
6g⁶ 6.3s⁴ 1992 7g³ 8.1d 6m⁵] workmanlike filly: fairly useful performer: should
prove better at 1m (tailed off in listed race in August) than shorter: acts on any
going: sold 11,000 gns Newmarket December Sales. *W. Jarvis*

LAST OF MOHICANS 4 b.g. Warpath 113 – Gemima Tenderfoot (Prince   –
Tenderfoot (USA) 126) [1991 NR 1992 14.1m⁴] smallish, workmanlike gelding: sixth
foal (all by Warpath): brother to 3 poor animals: dam never ran: 66/1, no promise in
5-runner Yarmouth claimer in July: sold 2,200 gns Ascot September Sales, resold
975 gns Ascot November Sales. *C. Weedon*

LAST ORDERS (USA) 3 b. or br.f. Temperence Hill (USA) – Tyrants Escape   –
(Tyrant (USA)) [1991 6m 8.1g 6.1f 6d 1992 9m 10.2f⁶ 11.5g] leggy, sparely-made filly:
no worthwhile form at 3 yrs, trained until after penultimate start by R. Hannon:
blinkered, bolted to post and tailed off in 11.5f Yarmouth handicap: sold 700 gns
Ascot July Sales. *P. Mitchell*

LA STRAVAGANZA 4 b.f. Slip Anchor 136 – St Isadora (Lyphard (USA) 132)   –
[1991 8d⁴ 10f⁴ 11.5f 1992 11.9d 10.8s] leggy, unfurnished filly: rated 68 at 3 yrs for W.
Jarvis: no worthwhile form in autumn, 1992, though shaped as if retaining ability on
reappearance: stays 1¼m: has joined B. Baugh. *L. J. Codd*

LAST STRAW 4 b.g. Blushing Scribe (USA) 107 – Straw Reef 64 (Final Straw **41**
127) [1991 7g 7g⁶ 7m 1992 a6g 5.1d² 5g³ 5d⁶ 5d 5m³ 5.1g 5g² 5m³ 6g⁶ 5g² 5m² 5f³ 5d
5s⁶ 5d a5g a6g⁶] leggy gelding: maiden handicapper: should stay 6f: acts on firm and
soft ground: effective blinkered or not: has wandered under pressure, but runs well
for 7-lb claimer: below form when sweating. *A. W. Jones*

LAST TYPHOON 2 b. or br.f. (Apr 23) Dowsing (USA) 124 – Song Grove 61   –
(Song 132) [1992 5d⁶ 5m 5g] 4,000Y: leggy, close-coupled filly: half-sister to several
winners, including 5-y-o Sir Arthur Hobbs (by Lyphard's Special) and useful 4-y-o
sprinter Sir Harry Hardman (by Doulab): dam 4-y-o 5.8f winner in Ireland: well
beaten, not knocked about, in maidens at Haydock in May and Wolverhampton in
June: fell halfway in similar event in between. *E. H. Owen jun*

LATEST FLAME (IRE) 2 b. or br.f. (Mar 29) Last Tycoon 131 – Vagrant Maid **66**
(USA) 85 (Honest Pleasure (USA)) [1992 6.1m² 6m⁶ 7m 8.1s⁴ 7g² 7.5m* 7m]
9,000Y: tall, rather leggy filly: fourth foal: half-sister to 1987 2-y-o 6f winner Votsala
(by Tap On Wood) and French middle-distance winner Wayfaring (by Be My Guest):
dam 12.2f winner: fair performer: favourite, won maiden auction at Beverley in
September, staying on well: will stay beyond 1m: acts on good to firm and soft
ground: consistent. *M. R. Channon*

LATIN LEADER 2 b.c. (Apr 10) Primo Dominie 121 – Ravaro 96 (Raga Navarro **67**
(ITY) 119) [1992 5d 6g* 8f⁶ 8.2d⁴] 16,500Y: workmanlike colt: has scope: third foal:
half-brother to 1990 2-y-o 1m winner Character (by Never So Bold), later Grade 2
winner in USA: dam Irish stayer, also useful hurdler: off course over 4½ months,
won maiden at Thirsk in August: subsequently ran creditably in nurseries: worth a

try at 7f: acts on firm and dead going: sold to join W. Jarvis 21,000 gns Newmarket Autumn Sales. *Mrs J. R. Ramsden*

LATIN MASS 4 ch.f. Music Boy 124 – Omnia 80 (Hill Clown (USA)) [1991 5g 5f a5g5 6f5 7g6 7m3 7.1d 7g 6m 7m 8f 6m 1992 7.1m] workmanlike filly: has quick action: still a maiden, and tailed off in handicap in June. *A. Barrow* —

LATIN QUARTET 4 b.g. Chief Singer 131 – Pampas Miss (USA) (Pronto) [1991 8v* 9d4 10m* a11g2 1992 10.3g] strong gelding: poor mover: rated 58 for W. Haggas at 3 yrs: blinkered, well beaten in ladies event in March, 1992: should stay 1½m: acts on good to firm ground and heavy: has joined K. Burke. *L. J. Codd* —

LATOSKY 4 br.g. Teenoso (USA) 135 – Patosky 94 (Skymaster 126) [1991 8v3 8d4 8f3 10m 1992 10s] good-topped gelding: no worthwhile form for a long time. *J. Norton*

LATOUR 4 b.g. Lafontaine (USA) 117 – Lucky Omen 99 (Queen's Hussar 124) [1991 10v* 12d2 12g2 14g6 13.9g 10m 1992 10.8v6 10m5 12d4 11.9g 12d 12g 11.9d3 12g 12s 10g2 12s] rather leggy, quite attractive gelding: unreliable handicapper: well beaten when blinkered final start: should prove better at 1½m + than shorter: acts on good to firm and heavy going: sold to join Mrs A. Swinbank 9,800 gns Newmarket Autumn Sales. *C. E. Brittain* **70 d**

LATVIAN 5 gr.g. Rousillon (USA) 133 – Lorelene (FR) 97 (Lorenzaccio 130) [1991 11f3 12.2f* 12f2 11.9g3 13.1m3 16.1m 1992 15.8d4 12.4f2 11.1m3 12.1g* 12.3f4 12.2g 15.1d] lengthy gelding: moderate walker: fair handicapper: made all at Edinburgh in July: should prove effective beyond 1½m: acts on firm ground, rare recent effort on dead: carries head high. *R. Allan* **70**

LAUGHING FALCON 3 b.f. Bellypha 130 – Falcon Berry (FR) (Bustino 136) [1991 7m 6s 1992 8g 10m 10g 8f 11.4d] small, leggy filly: moderate mover: poor form at best: blinkered/visored last 2 starts: sold 3,800 gns Newmarket July Sales: stud. *J. L. Dunlop* —

LAUGHSOME 3 b.f. Be My Guest (USA) 126 – Laughing Girl 110 (Sassafras (FR) 135) [1991 NR 1992 10m2 10.5f3 10.1g4 9g* 10d] lengthy filly: tenth foal: half-sister to several winners, including smart but untrustworthy 6f to 11f winner Percy's Lass (by Blakeney) and good 1m to 11.3f winner Braiswick (by King of Spain): dam, fourth in Oaks, is half-sister to Furioso (dam of Teenoso) and Favoletta: fair form: 7/4 on, easy winner of 4-runner maiden at Redcar in August: well beaten in handicap there 2 months later: stayed 1¼m: acted on firm ground: visits Mtoto. *J. H. M. Gosden* **76**

LAUGHTON LADY 3 ch.f. Crofthall 110 – No Illusion 48 (Grey Mirage 128) [1991 6g a5g 7.5f 1992 a12g 14.1g2 14.1g3 14.6g3 16m4 11.5g 14.6d4 10m3 12.3s] leggy, sparely-made filly: modest plater: was effective from 1¼m to 1¾m: acted on good to firm and dead ground: blinkered final 2 starts: collapsed and died at Wolverhampton in September. *Mrs N. Macauley* **41**

LAUNDRY MAID 3 b. or br.f. Forzando 122 – Spin Dry (High Top 131) [1991 5g 7f6 6s3 1992 7g3 7.1g* 7g3 7f4 6m4 7m] quite attractive filly: has a quick action: fairly useful performer: made all in maiden at Chepstow in July: ran well in handicaps next 3 starts, including for 7-lb claimer: effective at 6f and 7f: acts on firm ground, easily best 2-y-o effort on soft. *H. Candy* **89**

LAURA 3 gr.f. Never So Bold 135 – Cottage Pie 106 (Kalamoun 129) [1991 NR 1992 7m2] 19,000Y: leggy, lengthy, unfurnished filly: half-sister to useful 1986 2-y-o 5f winner Sauce Diable (by Moorestyle): dam useful staying 2-y-o, is half-sister to Yorkshire Cup winner Riboson: 9/1, bit backward and green, 1½ lengths second of 7 to Robingo in maiden at Yarmouth after none too clear a run: carried head high: withdrawn lame later in June and not seen again. *H. Thomson Jones* **65**

LAUREL DELIGHT 2 ch.f. (Apr 14) Presidium 124 – Foudroyer (Artaius (USA) 129) [1992 5g* 5f 6m2 5g6 5g3 5g* 5d4] 7,000Y: workmanlike filly: good mover: half-sister to 2 winning sprinters by Petong, notably very useful 3-y-o Paris House: dam twice-raced daughter of half-sister to smart animals Lighted Glory and Torus: progressed into fair performer: won maiden at Warwick in May and nursery at Wolverhampton (clear throughout) in September: ran well, around 8 lengths fourth of 5, behind Fyfield Flyer in listed race at Ayr: very speedy, and will prove best at 5f. *J. Berry* **72 p**

LAUREL ETOILE 2 b.f. (May 8) Taufan (USA) 119 – Last Star (Comedy Star (USA) 121) [1992 7.1m 7m5 7.1f3 7.5d 8g 7d] 6,200Y: close-coupled filly: first foal: dam twice-raced sister to smart stayer Another Sam and useful sprinter Middleton Sam: consistent plater: stays 1m: acts on firm and dead ground: sold 1,700 gns Doncaster October Sales. *J. Berry* **40**

LAUREL KING 2 ch.g. (May 1) Mansingh (USA) 120 – Boa (Mandrake Major **46** 122) [1992 6g a7g³ 6m 7d] 10,500Y: quite good-topped gelding: fourth foal: brother to 3 winners, all at sprint distances: dam lightly-raced half-sister to useful stayers Frog and Ophite: poor form: best effort when blinkered second start: probably a sprinter: sold 1,500 gns Doncaster October Sales. *J. Berry*

LAUREL QUEEN (IRE) 4 ch.f. Viking (USA) – Prima Bella 76 (High Hat 131) **75** [1991 7g* 7m⁴ 7m* 7m³ 8.2m* 8h² 6.9m⁵ a8g 8m⁵ 8.1g* 7m* 8.2m 7d² 8m* 8.1s 1992 7.5g² 8.3d⁴ 8.5g* 8d⁴ 7m 6.9h* 8.1m* 7g* 8g* 8m 8g² 7d* 7m* 8m 7d] neat filly: fair performer, progressive: successful in claimers at Beverley, Carlisle, Edinburgh and Ayr (3), before gaining sixteenth win of career and putting up best effort when landing handicap at Newcastle in August: effective from 7f to 8.5f: acts on hard and dead ground: has hung: tremendously tough. *J. Berry*

LAW COMMISSION 2 ch.c. (Feb 27) Ela-Mana-Mou 132 – Adjala 89 (North- **99 p** fields (USA)) [1992 6m⁵ 7g 6d³ 7s² 7m* 6v⁴] IR 23,000Y: smallish, sturdy colt: second foal: brother to a winner in Germany: dam 2-y-o 5f winner, only season to race, is daughter of useful half-sister to dam of Blushing Groom: progressive form: ridden by 7-lb claimer, won 23-runner nursery at Newmarket in October: fourth of 24 to Pips Pride in Racecall Gold Trophy at Redcar 12 days later, soon off bridle but keeping on well on unfavoured stand side: will stay 1m: acts on good to firm and heavy ground: probably capable of better still. *D. R. C. Elsworth*

LAW FACULTY (IRE) 3 b.g. Law Society (USA) 130 – Ask The Wind 106 (Run – The Gantlet (USA)) [1991 8s⁵ 8d³ 1992 12.5d 10.3g⁶ 14.6g 12.3s] leggy ex-Irish gelding: half-brother to 3 winners in Ireland, notably 1988 2-y-o 7f/1m winner and very useful middle-distance performer Phantom Breeze (by Vision), later success- ful in 3 graded events on turf in USA: dam winner at 7f to 1¼m in Ireland and France, suited by 1½m: modest form in maidens at 2 yrs for D. Weld, none as 3-y-o: middle-distance bred: trained reappearance by P. Aspell: tried in blinkers and a visor. *G. A. Ham*

LAWNSWOOD GOLD (IRE) 4 b.g. Godswalk (USA) 130 – Octet (Octavo – (USA) 115) [1991 12.5m 8m³ 12m 1992 8.2g] sturdy gelding: good mover: rated 59p at 3 yrs for R. Hollinshead: in mid-division in selling handicap at Nottingham in October, 1992, giving impression he needs further than 1m nowadays: sold 880 gns Doncaster November Sales. *B. A. McMahon*

LAWNSWOOD JUNIOR 5 gr.g. Bairn (USA) 126 – Easymede 85 (Runnymede **67** 123) [1991 a10g³ a10g³ 10.8g 12.2m a12g 10.3d⁶ 1992 10.8g 8.1m* 8f* 8f³ 8.1m² 8f 8.1f* 8.3g² 7.1d² 8g 8.5m² 8s³ 8d⁵ 7.1g² 8.1d* 10.3g] workmanlike gelding: moderate mover: consistent handicapper: progressed through the season: no bid after winning selling events at Edinburgh and Carlisle in May: successful in handicaps in July and November, both at Edinburgh: ideally suited by 1m to 1¼m: acts on firm and soft ground: below form when blinkered once at 4 yrs: has run well when visored, didn't wear them in 1992. *J. L. Spearing*

LAWNSWOOD PRINCE (IRE) 3 b.g. Anita's Prince 126 – La Croisette **47** (Nishapour (FR) 125) [1991 5d 5d 5m 5m 5g² 5m 5m³ 5m⁴ 5.7g 1992 5m 5.1m⁵ 5f⁵ 5m 5f³ 6.9h⁴ 7.1m⁴ 6.9d 8f 5s] sturdy gelding: inconsistent maiden: stays 7f: acts on hard ground: blinkered once (ran poorly) at 2 yrs. *J. L. Spearing*

LAWNSWOOD QUAY 2 ch.c. (May 24) Bairn (USA) 126 – Miss Quay (Quay- **37** side 124) [1992 7m 7d a7s⁵] leggy, angular, close-coupled colt: ninth foal: half- brother to 14.7f winner Milford Quay (by Milford): dam fairly useful staying hurdler: poor form, including in seller at Southwell: will stay 1¼m: sold 3,100 gns Doncaster August Sales. *J. Berry*

LAXEY FLYER 2 gr.f. (Mar 2) Belfort (FR) 89 – Kisses For Kate (Gold Song **31** 112) [1992 5g⁶ 5m 6g 7d] 700Y: sturdy filly: first foal: dam won in Denmark: poor plater. *J. Berry*

LAZY HILL 5 b.m. Kabour 80 – Hilly's Daughter (Hillandale 125) [1991 a6g a8g 6f **26** 8m 5m 6g 6m a5g 1992 a5g⁵] strong, close-coupled mare: third foal: dam bad maiden: of little account: tried blinkered. *D. W. Chapman*

LAZY RHYTHM (USA) 6 gr.g. Drone – Ritual Dance 84 (Godswalk (USA) 130) **55** [1991 7.1g 6g 8.3m 7m 5.1d 5s⁶ 1992 8.3v 8.1g* 8.3s* 8.2g 8.1g] lengthy gelding: carries condition: has been pin-fired: modest handicapper: claimer ridden, won 2 at Edinburgh (seller, bought in 2,000 gns) and Hamilton in the spring: below form in midsummer: should prove as effective at 1¼m as around 1m: acts on soft going, possibly unsuited by firm. *R. Akehurst*

LEADING ROLE 8 ch.g. Rolfe (USA) 77 – Paravant (Parthia 132) [1991 NR 1992 – 15.8d] neat gelding: modest hurdler: well beaten in handicap at Catterick in October on first outing on flat since 1986. *A. Harrison*

LEAD NOTE (USA)   2 ch.f. (Feb 27) Nijinsky (CAN) 138 – I Will Follow (USA)   **62 P**
117 (Herbager 136) [1992 8.1s*] leggy, unfurnished filly: has scope: half-sister to 2
winners by Blushing Groom, notably Rainbow Quest: dam, smart middle-distance
winner, is half-sister to dam of Warning and is daughter of Oaks second Where You
Lead and granddaughter of Oaks winner Noblesse: 2/1 on and bit green, made a
debut full of promise in moderately-run 5-runner maiden at Haydock in October,
travelling well, leading on bit 2f out and gradually drawing 3 lengths clear of
Solartica, not at all hard ridden: will be well suited by middle distances: certain to go
on to much better things. *H. R. A. Cecil*

LEAD THE DANCE   3 b.c. Lead On Time (USA) 123 – Maiyaasah 75 (Kris 135)   **102**
[1991 6m2 6f* 6s2 7m2 7m4 1992 8.2g2 8f* 7.9d3 8g4 7.9m] tall, quite attractive colt:
useful performer: won 3-runner minor event at Newcastle in June and might well
have won strongly-contested minor event at York in July but for saddle slipping
(eventually beaten 2½ lengths by Susurration): got bad run in ladies race at Ascot
then well beaten in £25,600 handicap at York last 2 starts: stays 1m: acts on any
going: probably best held up. *H. R. A. Cecil*

LEAGUE LEADER (IRE)   2 b.c. (Mar 31) Shirley Heights 130 – Happy Kin   **76 p**
(USA) (Bold Hitter (USA)) [1992 8m5 8d4] medium-sized, quite attractive colt: good
mover: half-brother to several winners here and abroad, including William Hill
Futurity winner Emmson (by Ela-Mana-Mou), later stayed 1½m: dam won from 6f
to 8.5f in USA: similar form in maidens at Newmarket and Leicester in the autumn:
likely to make up into a fairly useful middle-distance stayer. *M. R. Stoute*

LEAP IN THE DARK (IRE)   3 br.c. Shadeed (USA) 135 – Star Guide (FR)   **66**
(Targowice (USA) 130) [1991 8.1m2 8m* 1992 10d 12m5 10m3 12.3m 10d 8g5] big,
lengthy colt: easy mover: fair handicapper: best at up to 1¼m: acts on good to firm
ground: sold to join Miss L. Siddall 8,400 gns Newmarket Autumn Sales. *J. L.
Dunlop*

LEARIVA (USA)   5 ch.m. Irish River (FR) 131 – Leandra (FR) 125 (Luthier 126)   **112**
[1991 10v* 10g6 10.5g 8g* 8m6 9d 10s* 10f 1992 8m 9.2d 9.3s5 10d4 8s3 8v3] strong,
rangy French mare: smart performer: seventh of 10 to Selkirk in Lockinge Stakes at
Newbury in spring: off course 4 months before running at least fairly well in Prix de
l'Opera at Longchamp, Budweiser International at Laurel, and a Group 3 race at
Saint-Cloud in the autumn: well below form final start: ideally suited by around
1¼m with give in the ground. *D. Smaga, France*

LEAR KING (USA)   2 b.c. (May 8) Lear Fan (USA) 130 – Our Tina Marie (USA)   **64 P**
(Nijinsky (CAN) 138) [1992 6g6] $38,000Y: big, rangy colt with plenty of scope:
half-brother to 3 winners in USA, one graded-stakes placed: dam never ran: 33/1,
6½ lengths sixth of 20 to Serious in maiden at Newmarket in October, slowly away,
switched to far side and really catching the eye in the closing stages not knocked
about in the slightest: looks capable of considerably better and will win races. *G.
Harwood*

LEARMONT (USA)   2 b.c. (Mar 18) Lear Fan (USA) 130 – Wistoral (USA)   **– P**
(Exceller (USA) 129) [1992 6g] 1,150,000 francs (approx £115,500) Y: rangy, attractive colt, with plenty of scope: brother to 1991 2-y-o 7f winner and Irish Derby fourth
Dive For Cover and half-brother to a winner in USA at up to 1¼m: dam sprint
winner at 4 yrs: well-backed favourite though very green, beaten around 11 lengths
in mid-division of maiden at Newmarket in October, eased considerably once held 2f
out: looks capable of a good deal better. *J. H. M. Gosden*

LEAVE A KISS   2 ch.f. (Feb 19) King of Clubs 124 – Farewell Song (USA) 80   **60**
(The Minstrel (CAN) 135) [1992 5.1h4 7.5m4 7g4 7g] small, compact filly: first foal:
dam 1m winner: progressive form first 3 starts in the summer: last of 14 in nursery
at Catterick in September, dropping out quickly in straight: will stay middle
distances: sold 2,300 gns Newmarket Autumn Sales. *I. A. Balding*

LEAVE IT TO LIB   5 b.m. Tender King 123 – Nuit de Vin (Nebbiolo 125) [1991   **65**
7g4 8m4 7m5 7h4 8g3 a7g5 7.6g2 8f* 8.1m* 7m5 8f* 8d 8m 1992 7f4 8.1m4 8.1m5
7g* 7m* 7f4 7m 7m 7g 7s 7d] small, sparely-made mare: modest handicapper: won
twice at Catterick in July: below form last 5 starts: effective at 7f/1m: best on a
sound surface: goes well on turning track: usually ridden by 7-lb claimer J. Tate. *P.
Calver*

LE BARON PERCHE (FR)   3 b.c. Vayrann 133 – Dayira (Sparkler 130) [1991   **68**
6m 7f4 7f* 8g 1992 10g6 10.5g 10f6 12d2 12f5] sturdy colt: fair handicapper: stays
1½m: acts on firm and dead ground. *C. James*

LE CHIC   6 b.g. Kabour 80 – Boom Shanty 66 (Dragonara Palace (USA) 115) [1991   **58**
5f 5d2 5d2 5m* 5d 5m2 5m4 5g 5m 5.2f 5g 5g 1992 5g 6f 5d 5.2m4 6d 5d 5.1g 5d5 a5g*

a5g⁵ a5g²] strong, workmanlike gelding: modest handicapper: won at Southwell in November: best form at 5f: acts on firm and dead going, and on fibresand: tried blinkered once in 1989: sometimes doesn't find much: not one to trust. *D. W. Chapman*

LECH (USA) 4 b.c. Danzig (USA) – Wedding Reception (USA) (Round Table) **107** [1991 NR 1992 8f⁶ 8.5g⁴ 8f⁵ 8.9d⁴ 8m² 7.5v*] strong, round-barrelled colt: sort to carry condition: sixth foal: closely related to 2 winners by Nijinsky, including 1989 U.S. 2-y-o Grade 3 8.5f winner Savina, and half-brother to a winner by Believe It: dam 3-y-o 1m winner: ex-American colt, successful in 4 of his 8 starts as 3-y-o, notably Grade 3 events at Belmont (8.5f) and Saratoga (9f): didn't show that form in 1992 (left D. Donk's stable after third start), but encouraging efforts in frame in listed races at York (heavily bandaged) and Evry before easily winning similar event in Florence in October: probably stays 1¼m: acts on any going. *Mrs L. Piggott*

LE CORSAIRE (USA) 4 br.c. Nureyev (USA) 131 – Little Bonny 126 (Bonne **100** Noel 115) [1991 10m² 12g* 12.3g² 16.2g³ 12g* 12g³ 1992 14s* 13.3f⁵ 16.2m³ 16m 13.3g] strong, deep-girthed colt: useful performer: won minor event at Salisbury in April: ran well in Newbury listed event and well-contested Haydock minor event in May: off course over 2 months, well held in Goodwood Cup, then £18,200 handicap at Newbury 7 weeks later: stays 2m: acts on firm and soft ground: found less than seemed likely under pressure on occasions at 3 yrs: sent to Dubai. *L. M. Cumani*

LE COUTEAU 2 br.c. (Apr 17) Dowsing (USA) 124 – Razor Blade 65 (Sharp Edge **57** 123) [1992 5g 5g⁵ 6f² 6.1g³ 7m 7m² 7d⁵ 6.1s] 22,000F, 24,000Y: compact colt: eighth foal: half-brother to several winners here and abroad, including sprinter Keen Edge (by Good Times): dam 2-y-o 5f and 7f winner: modest maiden: stays 7f: best form on a sound surface: has run creditably for an apprentice: has joined W. Haggas. *D. W. P. Arbuthnot*

LEE ARTISTE 4 b.f. Tate Gallery (USA) 117 – Mirkan Honey 83 (Ballymore **95** 123) [1991 7.3g⁴ 8g 6m* 7.6g² 7g⁵ 6s 1992 6m⁶ 6f² 7s 8.1s³] smallish, compact filly: shows knee action: moderate walker: useful performer at her best: creditable second in well-contested minor event at Thirsk in May: subsequently below form in similar contests after near 5-month break: stays 7.6f: acts on good to firm and dead ground, unsuited by soft. *P. F. I. Cole*

LEGAL ARTIST (IRE) 2 b.c. (Apr 8) Tate Gallery (USA) 117 – Dowdstown **47** Miss (Wolver Hollow 126) [1992 7m 7s a8g] 15,000F, 12,000Y: fourth living foal: half-brother to 2 minor winners in North America: dam (half-sister to Strong Gale and from family of Star Appeal) won at up to 1½m in USA: poor maiden: better suited by 1m than 7f. *N. A. Graham*

LEGAL DANCER 2 b.c. (Mar 5) Belfort (FR) 89 – Isle Maree (Star Appeal 133) **35** [1992 5g 7m 6.1d 7g⁵] 4,200F, 7,400Y: quite attractive, unfurnished colt: first foal: dam unraced: poor form in varied company, including selling: best efforts at 7f: not seen out after July. *R. J. R. Williams*

LEGAL EMBRACE (CAN) 3 ch.f. Legal Bid (USA) 120 – Tina Rosa (CAN) **73** (Hans II) [1991 6.9f³ 1992 10m⁴ 10m* 11.9d³ 10f³] leggy, sparely-made filly: fair form: 11/8 on, won minor event at Nottingham in June: creditable third in £7,700 handicap at York and minor event at Salisbury (looked to race too freely) in July: stays 1½m: acts on firm ground and dead. *J. R. Fanshawe*

LEGAL RISK 2 b.f. (Apr 29) Risk Me (FR) 127 – Loyal And Regal 51 (Royal And **59** Regal (USA)) [1992 6.1d 6.1m⁴ 5.1m 5.7d³ 6s⁶ 6d 6s] leggy filly: sixth reported foal: half-sister to 3 winners, including modest 1m and 1¼m winner Cool Run (by Deep Run) and fair sprinter Tax Roy (by Dublin Taxi): dam winning selling hurdler: modest maiden: blinkered, not entirely discredited, though edged left, penultimate start: stays 6f: acts on good to firm and dead ground. *D. Haydn Jones*

LEGAL VIEW (USA) 4 b.c. Riverman (USA) 131 – Dictina (FR) (Dictus (FR) **95** 126) [1991 10d² 9g* 11g 192g 8.9f² 10.4d] close-coupled, quite attractive colt: has a quick action: good walker: lightly raced, but useful handicapper: best effort when just failing to catch Lucky Guest in £8,460 race at York in June: heavily-backed favourite but always behind in Magnet Cup there in July: may well prove best at up to 1¼m: acts on firm and dead ground: sold only 2,000 gns Newmarket Autumn Sales, reportedly to Italy. *L. M. Cumani*

LEGAL WIN (USA) 4 ch.c. Arctic Tern (USA) 126 – Banker's Favorite (USA) **–** (Lyphard (USA) 132) [1991 10.2s⁵ 10.8d 11.7s⁵ 13.1f* 16m 14.1g² 14.1g 1992 16.9g] sturdy, quite attractive colt: rated 55 at 3 yrs for M. Bell: blinkered, reluctant to race when tailed off on reappearance in May: should stay 2m: acts on firm going: usually visored: sold to join M. Usher 1,500 gns Ascot November Sales: best left alone. *F. Jordan*

LEGENDARY HERO   2 b.g. (Apr 5) Legend of France (USA) 124 – Ana   **53**
Gabriella (USA) (Master Derby (USA)) [1992 5d⁶ 5g³ 5f⁴ 6g 6m⁵ 5s 7d⁴] 9,200Y:
compact gelding: fifth reported foal: half-brother to 3 winners, including 4-y-o
sprinter Adwick Park (by Blazing Saddles) and 7f and 1m winner Burkan (by Star
Appeal): dam ran once: modest maiden: best form at 7f: acts on dead ground: ran
creditably in visor fifth start, moderately in blinkers next time: has looked a difficult
ride: sold 1,300 gns Doncaster October Sales. *T. D. Barron*

LEGENDARY (IRE)   3 b.c. Sadler's Wells (USA) 132 – Godzilla 106 (Gyr (USA)   **65**
131) [1991 7g³ 1992 9.9g³ 12g⁴ 10.2d 8m* 8g] good-quartered colt: fair handicapper
on his day: won at Ayr in June, wandering under pressure before staying on well to
lead close home: soundly beaten otherwise apart from reappearance: will stay 1¼m:
best effort on good to firm ground: sold 4,200 gns Newmarket Autumn Sales: has
looked ungenuine and is not one to trust implicitly. *P. W. Chapple-Hyam*

LEGEND DULAC (IRE)   3 b.c. Legend of France (USA) 124 – Westerlake   **59**
(Blakeney 126) [1991 6g 1992 8m a7g⁵ 8g* 8.2d* 7f⁶ 8d 8.2s] leggy colt: modest
performer: easily best efforts to win seller (no bid) at Leicester and handicap at
Nottingham in July, making most: will stay 1¼m: acts on dead ground: headstrong,
wears net muzzle these days, and is taken down early. *J. L. Harris*

LEGION OF HONOUR   4 b.c. Ahonoora 122 – Shehana (USA) 86 (The Min-   **72**
strel (CAN) 135) [1991 8m³ 10.5g³ 12g³ 12m* 1992 12m⁵ 11.9m] lengthy colt: has
round action: fair handicapper: bandaged near-hind, creditable fifth at Goodwood:
looking in fine shape, well beaten in £12,500 event at York later in summer: stays
1½m: acts on good to firm ground: lacks turn of foot: sold 5,000 gns Newmarket
Autumn Sales. *W. Jarvis*

LEGITIM   3 br.g. Move Off 112 – Eliza de Rich 57 (Spanish Gold 101) [1991 5f 6m⁴   **32**
7m 1992 12.1s⁶ 9f 6m³ 6f³ 6g 7g 6m⁵] leggy, rather angular gelding: has a quick
action: poor maiden: will stay 7f. *J. M. Jefferson*

LEGUARD EXPRESS (IRE)   4 b.c. Double Schwartz 128 – All Moss 66   **–**
(Prince Tenderfoot (USA) 126) [1991 7g³ 8f⁶ 8g³ 7g 8d⁵ 8.2g 8g 8m 8d 1992 12.1s
16s] good-topped colt: rated 63 early on at 3 yrs: no worthwhile form last 5 starts,
including in blinkers once. *O. O'Neill*

LEIF THE LUCKY (USA)   3 ch.c. Lemhi Gold (USA) 123 – Corvine (USA)   **73**
(Crow (FR) 134) [1991 8g⁴ 1992 10m 7.9g⁴ 8d² 9s* 8m] rather leggy, short-backed
colt: fair form: 7/4 on, won maiden at Redcar in September: ran moderately in
Newmarket handicap 3 weeks later: unlikely to stay much beyond 9f: possibly
unsuited by top-of-the-ground: formerly headstrong. *W. Jarvis*

LEIGH CROFTER   3 ch.g. Son of Shaka 119 – Ganadora (Good Times (ITY))   **65**
[1991 5g⁶ 5m⁶ 6d⁴ 6g² 7g 6g 7m* 7m⁶ 1992 8.9v⁶ 7g⁵ 5.7m² 6m 6g⁶ 5.7g⁵ 6f⁴ 7.1s
6s 7s] workmanlike gelding: inconsistent performer: trained until after penultimate
start by R. Holder: stays 7f: acts on good to firm ground: blinkered 7 of last 8 starts:
has run well for 7-lb claimer. *P. G. Murphy*

LEMON'S MILL (USA)   3 b.f. Roberto (USA) 131 – Mill Queen 86 (Mill Reef   **80**
(USA) 141) [1991 NR 1992 12g* 11.4m⁴ 14f³ 12g³ 12d⁵] big, workmanlike filly: sixth
foal: half-sister to 7f winner Miller's Tale (by Nureyev) and 1½m winner Golden
Mill (by Mr Prospector): dam won over 7f and 9f: fairly useful form: very edgy, won
maiden at Newmarket in May: ran creditably in frame in minor event and handicaps:
will probably stay 2m: acts on firm ground, below form on dead: sold 13,500 gns
Newmarket December Sales. *J. H. M. Gosden*

LE MONTAGNARD (FR)   4 b.c. Saint Cyrien (FR) 128 – La Montagnaise   **107**
(Carmarthen (FR) 130) [1991 10d⁴ 10g³ 12g³ 12g* 12g³ 11.5g³ 12m³ 10.5d⁶
12g* 12g² 12g 1992 12g³ 11g⁴ 12d³ 15.5g* 12.5d³ 15.5d* 20s⁶] half-brother to 3
minor winners in France: dam 2-y-o 6.7f winner in French Provinces: useful and
consistent French colt: successful as 4-y-o in listed race in June and Group 3 Prix
Gladiateur (beat Dajraan by short head) in September, both at Longchamp: effective
from 1½m to 2m, stiff task and far from disgraced in Prix du Cadran over 2½m: acts
on dead ground. *G. Henrot, France*

LEONADIS POLK   3 ch.g. Hadeer 118 – Brokelsby Anne 69 (Dunphy 124) [1991   **55**
5f⁵ 5m⁶ 6d³ 6m⁴ 6g 6m⁴ 6m⁴ 8.3s⁴ 1992 8.2g 8m⁵ 11m a8g⁵ 8m 12g⁵] tall,
workmanlike gelding: moderate mover: plating-class performer: trained until after
fourth start by W. Pearce: stays 8.3f: acts on any going: no improvement in blinkers/
visor: looks a difficult ride. *J. H. Johnson*

LEONARDO 3 br.g. Sulaafah (USA) 119 – Satina 83 (Pall Mall 132) [1991 NR 1992 –
10g] leggy, light-framed gelding: eleventh foal: half-brother to several winners,
including quite useful 1980 2-y-o 5f winner Jiva (by Mummy's Pet) and 1¾m winner
Chetinkaya (by Ragstone): dam, placed at up to 1m, is daughter of Irish 1000
Guineas winner Black Satin: 50/1 and steadily to post, tailed-off last of 7 in £10,000
maiden at Ascot in July. *P. R. Hedger*

LER CRU (IRE) 3 b.c. Lafontaine (USA) 117 – Kirsova (Absalom 128) [1991 7m⁵ **64**
8d 1992 10g 8m⁶ 10m 10.1d⁶ 7.6m* 7.1d a7g³ 8m 8m 6g 7d 7g³ 7g] strong-quartered,
deep-bodied colt: inconsistent handicapper: won at Lingfield in June: effective at
7.6f and stays 1¼m: acts on good to firm ground, seemingly not on a soft surface:
seems effective blinkered or not: sold to join J. Ffitch-Heyes 5,200 gns Newmarket
Autumn Sales. *C. E. Brittain*

LES AMIS 5 b.m. Alzao (USA) 117 – Les Sylphides (FR) (Kashmir II 125) [1991 **38**
10d⁵ 8m³ 8m* 9m⁴ 8g 8.1g 8m⁵ 8.2m⁴ 8g⁵ 8d a8g³ 1992 a7g³ a10g⁴ a8g⁶ a8g 8.2m
8.9m⁵] sturdy, workmanlike mare: poor handicapper: below form on turf in June
after 5-month lay-off: stays 1¼m: acts on good to firm and dead ground and on
all-weather surfaces: has run well when blinkered. *M. J. Ryan*

LE SAULE D'OR 5 br.m. Sonnen Gold 121 – Richesse (FR) (Faraway Son (USA) –
130) [1991 10.8m 10d a7g 8m⁵ 8.2g 10g 8.1g 9.7m⁴ 9.7g 1992 10.2f⁵ 11f 8.2d⁵ 8m]
leggy, sparely-made mare: inconsistent handicapper, winner of one of 26 starts:
stays 1¼m: often blinkered earlier in career. *A. P. James*

LES ETOILES (IRE) 2 b.f. (Feb 9) Siberian Express (USA) 125 – Sugar Walls –
(USA) 110 (Lyphard (USA) 132) [1992 6f⁵] rather unfurnished filly: second foal: dam
French 2-y-o stayed 1m, only season to run: 10/1, bit backward and green,
tailed-off last of 5 in £8,900 event at Newmarket in June, fading quickly from 2f out:
wore a tongue strap. *M. Moubarak*

L'ETE (IRE) 4 b.f. Kafu 120 – Miss Merryweather (Sexton Blake 126) [1991 6v⁶ **53**
5d 5g 6d 5g 5m 5m⁶ 5d 1992 5g⁴ 5f 5f 6m] good-quartered, workmanlike filly:
modest handicapper at best nowadays: reared in stables and fell final outing, in June:
best form over 5f: acts on firm ground: sold 1,000 gns Newmarket Autumn Sales. *P.
Mitchell*

LE TEMERAIRE 6 b.h. Top Ville 129 – La Mirande (FR) (Le Fabuleux 133) **70**
[1991 NR 1992 a12g³ a12g³ a11g* a12g² a12g³ a12g⁶ a13g⁴ 12g] leggy horse: fair
handicapper: won claimer at Southwell in February: not seen on flat after April:
should stay 1¾m: acts on good to firm and heavy ground, and on fibresand: won
novice chase in October. *N. Tinkler*

LETSBEONESTABOUTIT 6 b.g. Petong 126 – My Bushbaby 100 (Hul A Hul **90** d
124) [1991 6d⁴ 6g 6s 6m³ 6m 5.8d² 6m⁵ 6d 6d 6f 7m 6m³ 6g* 6m⁴ 6m³ 6g 6d 1992
6g³ 6m 7g 6d 6f 7m 6f³ 6g³ 5g 6m 6.1m 6g] tall, strong gelding: poor mover: fairly
useful but inconsistent handicapper, not so good as at 5 yrs: acts on firm and dead
and (unsuited by very soft) ground: visored earlier in career, seems effective
blinkered or not: has joined G. Lewis. *Mrs N. Macauley*

LET'S GET LOST 3 ch.c. Chief Singer 131 – Lost In France 80 (Northfields **76**
(USA)) [1991 7.1m³ 8m² 1992 10.1d² 10.3g² 10m 12g³ a12g⁴ 8.9d5] lengthy colt: fair
maiden: below best last 2 starts: stays 1½m: acts on good to firm and dead ground:
has been bandaged. *W. J. Haggas*

LET'S GO LOCHY 6 b.m. Lochnager 132 – Happy Donna 106 (Huntercombe –
133) [1991 5.1g 10g² 5d 6g] good-bodied mare: poor walker: lightly raced and no
worthwhile form: caught eye in handicaps in the spring, never placed to challenge,
tenderly handled, but wasn't seen again. *C. J. Hill*

LETS GO SABO 4 ch.g. Prince Sabo 123 – Run For Her Life 75 (Runnymede **46** d
123) [1991 NR 1992 a5g* a6g a5g 6f a5g] angular, robust gelding: carries plenty of
condition: sixth foal: half-brother to fair 1985 2-y-o 6f winner Seclusive (by Good
Times): dam won at 1¼m: made all in maiden at Southwell in January: no show in
handicaps afterwards: sold 1,800 gns Doncaster June Sales. *D. W. Chapman*

LETTERMORE 2 b.f. (Jun 6) Elegant Air 119 – Midnight's Reward 84 (Night **44**
Shift (USA)) [1992 5m 6g² 7g 7m 7.5m 10.5d] leggy filly: first foal: dam 2-y-o 5f
winner: modest plater: form only at 6f: visored (tailed off) final start: tends to hang.
R. M. Whitaker

LETTS GREEN (IRE) 4 ch.g. Exhibitioner 111 – Cress (Crepello 136) [1991 –
10v⁴ 10.8g 10g 12.2m 11.5m⁴ 11.5d³ 14g 9.7s² 10g 9m 1992 12s 12v] strong, compact
gelding: has a markedly round action: still a maiden, and no worthwhile form for long
time. *M. J. Haynes*

LEVEL UP 3 ch.f. Beveled (USA) – Haiti Mill 68 (Free State 125) [1991 5d^6 5d^5 **53**
a8g^3 a8g^4 1992 a7g* a7g^3 a7g 8g] plating-class handicapper: won at Lingfield in
January: trained until after penultimate start by R. Guest: stiff task on first run for 6
months, most reluctant to post and showed nothing in ladies race in September: will
prove better suited by 1m than shorter: has run creditably for claimer. *C. D. Broad*

LEXUS (IRE) 4 b.g. Gorytus (USA) 132 – Pepi Image (USA) 111 (National) [1991 **43**
8f^5 10.4g 10.2m^4 10g^3 11.5s a16g 1992 10.2m^5 8.2m 7.6m^5 10.3m^5] good-bodied
gelding: still a maiden: creditable strong-finishing fifth of 24 in Doncaster handicap
in September final start: effective from 1m to 1¼m: acts on firm going. *R. J. R.
Williams*

L'HERMINE 3 b.c. Slip Anchor 136 – Mondialite (FR) (Habitat 134) [1991 7f 7m **100**
7m* 1992 8d4 10g^5 11.5s 12m^6 8m^3 8.3g^3 8f^2 8m] leggy, workmanlike colt: has a
round action: useful performer: good second to Tik Fa in minor event at Doncaster:
ran moderately in Newmarket listed race later in the autumn: stays 1m: acts on firm
and dead ground: effective blinkered or not: often makes the running. *H. Candy*

LIABILITY ORDER 3 b.g. Norwick (USA) 120 – Starky's Pet (Mummy's Pet **68**
125) [1991 7g 7m 8m^6 8d^3 a7g* a8g^5 1992 9s 11.8d^4 10m^2 10m 12d^6 10g* 10.3m^5
10.5d^4 10.3g^6 10.1d^3] big, lengthy gelding: moderate mover: fair handicapper: won at
Leicester in July, swishing tail: ran creditably in claimers last 3 starts: best at
around 1¼m: acts on good to firm and dead ground, and on equitrack: blinkered once
at 2 yrs: has run creditably when sweating: sold to join M. Hammond 8,200 gns
Newmarket September Sales and won juvenile hurdle (soft ground) in December. *R.
Boss*

LIBBY-J 2 b.f. (Feb 20) Faustus (USA) 118 – Lismore 61 (Relkino 131) [1992 5m 5f **–**
a7g 7g] sparely-made filly: has a round action: third reported foal: dam, maiden,
stayed 1¾m: no worthwhile form in sellers: should be suited by 1m+. *M. W.
Easterby*

LIBERTY GLEN 3 b.f. Glenstal (USA) 118 – Liberation 63 (Native Prince) [1991 **–**
NR 1992 6g^6 7m^6 6g 6.9g] 800F: sparely-made filly: half-sister to several winners,
including 1986 2-y-o 5f winner Bastillia (by Derrylin): dam twice-raced half-sister to
good sprinter Tudor Grey: no worthwhile form: trained first 3 starts by B. Ellison. *J.
L. Eyre*

LIBK 4 b.c. Kalaglow 132 – Balqis (USA) 93 (Advocator) [1991 12d 11.5m* 11.9m* **96**
11.9m* 14g^4 14.6m 12m^3 1992 12g 12.3m^4 12d 12f 12g* 11.9m 12m^2 12m] strong,
well-made colt: carries condition: impresses in appearance: has a quick action:
useful handicapper, unreliable in 1992: won £7,370 race at Ascot in July: effective at
1½m to 1¾m (should stay 2m): suited by a sound surface. *H. Thomson Jones*

LIBRA LEGEND (USA) 3 ch.c. Believe It (USA) – Posslq (USA) (Cyane) **56** d
[1991 7m 7f^4 7m 6g 1992 a8g^4 7d^4 7m 7g 7m^6 7f^3 6.1g 9.7d] lengthy, good-topped
colt: inconsistent handicapper: stays 1m: acts on firm and dead ground: sold 750 gns
Newmarket Autumn Sales. *C. E. Brittain*

LICORNE 2 b.f. (Feb 25) Sadler's Wells (USA) 132 – Catawba 98 (Mill Reef **67** p
(USA) 141) [1992 8d4] first foal: dam 1¼m winner stayed 1½m, is daughter of
Ribblesdale winner Catalpa: 8/1, shaped well when fourth of 20 in maiden at Yar-
mouth in late-season, leading 2f out but no extra final 1f and beaten 3½ lengths by
Lille Hammer: will be well suited by middle distances: will improve and win a
maiden. *H. R. A. Cecil*

LIDANZIA 4 br.f. Lidhame 109 – Lady Antonia 66 (Owen Anthony 102) [1991 8m **39**
8.2m 10g 8m^6 8.1s^2 10g^4 12.1g^5 1992 10.5s^3 12m^6 14m 16.2g^5 18.2m] leggy,
sparely-made filly: moderate mover: poor handicapper: pulled up (reportedly lame)
final run, in June: stays 2m: has form on firm ground, but goes well with give. *R. J.
Holder*

LIDA'S DELIGHT (IRE) 2 b.c. (Apr 8) Double Schwartz 128 – Villars 84 **–** p
(Home Guard (USA) 129) [1992 6g] IR 2,000F, IR 1,600Y: plain, workmanlike colt:
sixth foal: dam 1½m winner: backward, bandaged and green, behind in maiden at
Thirsk in August: showed round action: should improve. *M. W. Easterby*

LIDOMA (IRE) 2 ch.f. (Apr 2) Dominion 123 – Live Ammo 94 (Home Guard **48**
(USA) 129) [1992 6g 7f^4 7g^6 8s^5 a8g] leggy filly: seventh foal: half-sister to 3
winners here and abroad, including smart sprinter Powder Keg (by Tap On Wood):
dam 2-y-o 6f winner: plating-class maiden: stays 1m: acts on any going except
perhaps fibresand: sold out of J. Dunlop's stable 6,800 gns after penultimate start.
M. C. Pipe

LIFE AFTER DEATH 4 b.g. Lucky Wednesday 124 – Hitravelscene (Man- **–**
singh (USA) 120) [1991 NR 1992 7d] sparely-made, dipped-backed gelding: fourth

living foal: brother to poor winning 7-y-o sprinter B Grade and to a thoroughly temperamental animal: dam poor plater: well behind in maiden race at Catterick in October, only run on flat. *J. Balding*

LIFE'S A BREEZE 3 b.c. Aragon 118 – Zahira (What A Guest 119) [1991 NR 46 1992 a6g⁴ a7g² a6g³ 6.9v 5.1d² 7s⁵ 5.7s 6m 5.3f⁴ 5s 5.7d 6g⁵ a6g a8g a7g] 6,400F, 5,200Y: close-coupled colt: poor mover: first foal: dam never ran: inconsistent maiden: stays 6f: acts on dead ground. *M. R. Channon*

LIFETIME FAME 3 b.c. Sayf El Arab (USA) 127 – Hot Momma 81 (Free State 71 125) [1991 6g⁶ 6d 7m 1992 7g 6f* 6m⁵ 6.1m⁵ 6m⁶ a6g⁵ 6f³ 5g³ 6m] leggy, quite attractive colt: modest handicapper: won maiden at Lingfield in May: stays 7f: acts on firm ground: effective blinkered or not: sold 10,000 gns Newmarket Autumn Sales. *J. W. Payne*

LIFETIMES AMBITION 4 br.c. Hotfoot 126 – Consistent Queen 55 (Queen's – Hussar 124) [1991 8s 10g9.2d⁵9.2m⁴a8g⁵ 12m³ 10.6g 11.1g³ 12d³ 11.8m* 1992 a12g a13g⁶ a16g⁴ a13g a16g 14.6g 18.2g 14.1d] compact colt: has a quick action: below form in handicaps in first half of 1992: should stay beyond 1½m: acts on good to firm ground and soft: looked temperamental when blinkered. *T. Casey*

LIFEWATCH VISION 5 b.h. Vision (USA) – Maellen (River Beauty 105) [1991 108 8d⁶ 8f* 8f² 8g⁵ 8d* 12f* 8m⁴ 10m⁵ 8.9g³ 12s 8m³ 8d² 9m 1992 9g* 10d 10g⁵ 9s⁵ 10g⁴ 12.3g³] angular, workmanlike ex-English horse: has a round action: very useful handicapper, raced here at 4 yrs for M. Johnston: successful at Fairyhouse in May, 1992: effective at 1m to 1½m: acts on firm and dead ground: best form without blinkers than with. *D. K. Weld, Ireland*

LIFFEY RIVER (USA) 4 ch.c. Irish River (FR) 131 – Close Comfort (USA) 67 (Far North (CAN) 120) [1991 7g⁶ 6f⁶ 5m² 6g 5m* 5f⁵ 5m 6.1m 1992 6v 6.1d 6g 5m⁵ 5m⁴ 6m* 6g 7g 6f* 6m⁴ a6g³ 6m 6g 5m²] compact colt: poor mover: successful in summer in Folkestone seller (bought in 4,100 gns) and Brighton handicap: almost certainly flattered when second in Pontefract claimer final run: ideally suited by 6f on top-of-the-ground: often wears tongue strap: sometimes bandaged/hangs: sold 7,400 gns Newmarket Autumn Sales. *Mrs L. Piggott*

LIFFORD (USA) 3 ch.c. Shahrastani (USA) 135 – Liffey Lass (USA) 95 (Irish – River (FR) 131) [1991 NR 1992 10m⁶ 11.4d 11.8g] good-topped colt: third foal: half-brother to Irish 2-y-o 6f and 7f winner Isle of Glass (by Affirmed) and a winner in USA by Relaunch: dam 2-y-o 7f winner out of half-sister to high-class colts Home Guard and Boone's Cabin: no worthwhile form: had tongue tied down: dead. *M. R. Stoute*

LIFT AND LOAD (USA) 5 b.g. Lyphard's Wish (FR) 124 – Dorit (USA) 99 (Damascus (USA)) [1991 12s⁴ 10s 12g⁵ 12s³ 12g* 12m 12g⁶ 11.9m³ 12g⁵ 13.9g 12m* 13.3m 12s³ 12m 12d⁵ 1992 12g³ 12d 14g³ 11.9g 13.3g 12s² 12g 12g] lengthy, good-quartered gelding: moderate mover: useful but none too consistent handicapper in 1992: best run when second to Quick Ransom in £60,000 Krug Trophy at Ascot: effective at 1½m to 1¾m: goes very well with some give (yet to race on heavy): sometimes sweats/wanders: lazy, but game. *R. Hannon*

LIFT BOY (USA) 3 b.g. Fighting Fit (USA) – Pressure Seat (USA) (Ginistrelli 48 (USA) 117) [1991 5d 5m⁵ 6d 6m 6g 6m 6.1d⁶ 1992 8s 5m 6m a7g² 5h³ 6g* 5m⁴ 6g⁴ 6m 6s² 6s a8g³ a6g² a7g] small, sturdy gelding: poor handicapper: won 2-runner maiden at Catterick in July: trained until after tenth start by D. Smith: stays 7f: acts on good to firm and soft ground and on all-weather surfaces: twice visored, running creditably first occasion. *A. Moore*

LIGHT HAND 6 b.m. Star Appeal 133 – No Cards 109 (No Mercy 126) [1991 74 a12g⁴ 10.6g³ 10g* 10.2g³ 10.5m³ 10.9m² 1992 10.5g³ 10g² 10m⁶ 10.5g* 10.5s² 10.5d* 10.5d* 10v⁴ 12g] leggy, workmanlike mare: moderate mover: fair handicapper: successful 3 times at Haydock (2 apprentice events and claimer) in second half of 1992: effective at 1¼m to 1½m: probably suited by some give: below form blinkered/visored: held up: consistent. *M. H. Tompkins*

LIGHTNING DECISION 4 b.g. Lightning Dealer 103 – Tintern Abbey (Star – Appeal 133) [1991 NR 1992 6f 10.3g a8s 7.1s 6m 6.1m 6s] leggy gelding: moderate walker: fifth foal: dam unraced: no worthwhile form. *J. P. Smith*

LIGHTNING SPARK 3 b.f. Electric 126 – Hot Money 50 (Mummy's Pet 125) – [1991 NR 1992 8.5f⁵ 8m 10.5g 8m 9.9d⁴ 12.2g 8g] 4,000Y: tall, leggy, workmanlike filly: half-sister to several winners here and abroad, including 5f winner Robrob (by Mansingh): dam 6f winner: poor maiden: probably stayed 1¼m: dead. *M. Avison*

EBF Timeform Charity Day Stakes, York—newcomers Lindon Lime and Marillette

LIGHT-OF-THE-LOCH 4 b.f. Lightning Dealer 103 – Balmenoch (Queen's **–**
Hussar 124) [1991 6g⁶ 7m 7g 6d a8g 10.5d⁶ 1992 a12g 12.3s 12s] leggy filly: of little
account. *A. W. Potts*

LIGHT THE BAY 2 ch.f. (May 5) Presidium 124 – Light The Way 72 (Nicholas **38**
Bill 125) [1992 6f³ 7g 6m] close-coupled filly: second foal: dam won 8.2f seller: well
beaten after last of 3 in Pontefract maiden: tried blinkered. *Mrs V. A. Aconley*

LIHBAB 9 ch.g. Ballad Rock 122 – Sovereign Bloom (Florescence 120) [1991 NR **–**
1992 8s 8.1d] rangy gelding: on the downgrade. *J. M. Bradley*

LIJAAM (IRE) 2 ch.c. (May 16) Persian Bold 123 – Etoile de Nuit (Troy 137) **64 p**
[1992 7g⁶] second foal: half-brother to 3-y-o Jathaab (by Ajdal): dam twice-raced
daughter of close relative of Grand Prix de Paris winner Tennyson: 16/1, green and
burly, stayed on well when around 3 lengths sixth of 18 to Azilian in maiden at
Doncaster in November: sure to improve. *A. A. Scott*

LILLAH DARAK (USA) 4 ch.g. Shadeed (USA) 135 – Foreign Courier (USA) **69**
(Sir Ivor 135) [1991 NR 1992 7m 5m*] neat gelding: fifth foal: half-brother to 1989
2-y-o 5f winner Kissogram Girl and to Green Desert (both by Danzig): dam unraced
half-sister to top-class filly Althea: bought out of M. Stoute's stable 2,400 gns
Newmarket Autumn (1991) Sales: twice raced: 33/1 and bandaged, much better
effort when winning maiden at Beverley in May by ¾ length: looked capable of
better. *P. D. Evans*

LILLE HAMMER 2 b.f. (Apr 4) Sadler's Wells (USA) 132 – Smeralda (GER) **76 p**
(Dschingis Khan) [1992 8d*] half-sister to several winners here and in Germany,
including 3-y-o 1¼m and 1½m winner Day of History (by Shirley Heights) and
Group-winner Soto-Grande (by Kaiseradler): dam won 3 times in Germany and is
half-sister to German Oaks winner Slenderella: 10/1, won 20-runner maiden at
Yarmouth in late-season by a short head from Tochar Ban, leading over 1f out: will
be very well suited by middle distances: sure to improve. *L. M. Cumani*

LILY MORETON 3 ch.f. Morston (FR) 125 – Dominant 86 (Behistoun 131) **–**
[1991 NR 1992 9.7d⁴ 10s 12v 14.1s] leggy filly: sister to 2 winners, notably useful
middle-distance stayer Mubarak of Kuwait, and half-sister to several winners: dam,
1½m winner, is half-sister to Dominion: well beaten, including in seller: sold 680
gns Doncaster November Sales. *M. J. Heaton-Ellis*

LIME STREET LIL 4 br.f. Precocious 126 – Merchantmens Girl 58 (Klairon **30** 131) [1991 6d 7g 6.1m 6m 7g 1992 5m⁶ 10g 7d² 6g² 7.6m 8g 7f] strong, lengthy filly: moderate mover: well beaten after second in July handicaps: effective at 6f/7f: form only with give in the ground: below form visored. *D. A. Wilson*

LINCOLN IMP (USA) 2 b.c. (May 1) Imp Society (USA) – Full of Questions **59** (USA) (Nain Bleu (FR)) [1992 5m 6g⁵ 6s 6g⁴ 7d] $15,000Y: robust, good-quartered colt: has scope: has a roundish action: third reported foal: dam unraced: modest form in varied events: stays 6f: tends to get stirred up. *A. Moore*

LINCSTONE BOY (IRE) 4 b.g. Reach 122 – Babylon (Hello Gorgeous (USA) **56** 128) [1991 6m⁵ 5m 5f 8f a5g 6f 5g 5g 5s⁴ 5s³ a5g 1992 5.1g² 5f⁶ 5.2g⁴ a5g³ 5d* 5g 5.2m 5s 5s³ 5.1g⁶ 5s² a5g⁶ a5g a5g⁴ a5g³] tall, plain gelding: modest handicapper: formerly untrustworthy but much more reliable in 1992: won at Ripon in September: races mainly at around 5f: acts on good to firm and soft ground and on fibresand: has carried head high, and not easiest of rides: trained first 2 starts by W. Pearce/B. Beasley. *S. R. Bowring*

LINDEMAN 3 b.g. Reach 122 – Montana Moss (Levmoss 133) [1991 7m⁶ a8g³ **45** a7g a8g 1992 a8g⁵ a10g 6.9v 9.7g 10g 8f² 8.5d⁴ 9m 8.5d⁶] good-bodied gelding: poor maiden: should stay 1¼m: best effort on dead ground. *S. Dow*

LINDERHOF (USA) 2 ch.c. (Feb 18) Lyphard (USA) 132 – Royal Weekend – (USA) (Secretariat (USA)) [1992 6g] angular, workmanlike colt: first reported foal: dam winner at around 1m at 2 yrs and placed in Grade 2 event, is granddaughter of champion Canadian 2-y-o Queen Louie: behind in maiden at Goodwood in June: seemed likely to improve. *M. R. Stoute*

LINDON LIME (USA) 2 br.c. (Feb 23) Green Dancer (USA) 132 – White **102** p Reason (USA) (Hail To Reason) [1992 6f* 7m* 8s⁶] $55,000Y: rangy colt: shade unfurnished: fluent mover: half-brother to several winners here and in North America, including 1½m winner Wayak (by Forli) and useful 1988 2-y-o 6f winner here Wonder Dancer (by Raise A Native): dam twice-raced sister to top-class 1973 French 2-y-o filly Hippodamia: favourite when successful in maiden at York and minor event at Chester (by 5 lengths) in June: around 10 lengths sixth of 11, soon off bridle, stayed on late, to Tenby in Grand Criterium at Longchamp over 3 months after: will be well suited by 1¼m+: looks sure to improve again, and win more races. *P. F. I. Cole*

LINE DRUMMER (USA) 4 ch.g. Topsider (USA) – Samarta Dancer (USA) **79** (Marshua's Dancer (USA)) [1991 7m a12g⁶ a12g 1992 a12g³ a10g 14.6g² 11.9d 12g² 18.5g³ 11f² 10f⁴ 20m 16.2m³ 16.1f⁶ 14.6m² 12f⁴ 11.9m] close-coupled gelding: moderate mover: versatile and largely consistent handicapper: effective at 1¼m to 2¼m: acts on firm ground: below form in eyeshield and blinkers: usually bandaged: below best for amateur. *P. A. Kelleway*

LINE ENGAGED (USA) 4 b.c. Phone Trick (USA) – Quick Nurse (USA) (Dr – Fager) [1991 5m⁶ 5m 1992 6m 5m 10f⁵ 8f³] lengthy, angular colt: has a quick action: rated 108 as 2-y-o: no worthwhile form in 1992, visored once: effective at 5f and 6f: acts on good to firm ground and dead. *P. T. Walwyn*

LINE OF KINGS 3 b.g. Local Suitor (USA) 128 – Royal Nugget (USA) 104§ (Mr – Prospector (USA)) [1991 NR 1992 12.3s³ 12g⁶] sturdy, lengthy gelding: good mover: second foal: half-brother to fairly useful 1½m winner Niani (by Niniski): dam placed from 6f to 1m but very disappointing at 3 yrs: no worthwhile form in maidens: dead. *D. Morley*

LINGDALE LASS 3 gr.f. Petong 126 – Our Mother 95 (Bold Lad (IRE) 133) – [1991 5g⁶ 5f 5f³ 5m 5d² 6.9m 6d* 6d⁶ 1992 10f 8f 11g⁵ 6m⁵ 7.1s 6m] small, leggy filly: rated 60 at 2 yrs: well beaten, including in sellers, in 1992: stays 6f: best efforts on a soft surface: below form visored/blinkered: sometimes looked ungenuine: trained until after fourth 3-y-o start by Mrs M. Reveley. *M. W. Eckley*

LINNGA (IRE) 3 b.f. Shardari 134 – Lisana 97 (Alleged (USA) 138) [1991 NR **112** 1992 10.5s* 10.5g* 12g* 13.5s⁴ 12m] second foal: half-brother to useful Liyoun, now a useful middle-distance staying handicapper in France: dam, 1½m winner, is half-sister to top-class French 1½m performers Acamas, Akarad and Akiyda: smart French filly: progressed well, winning a minor event at Saint-Cloud, a listed event at Longchamp and Group 3 Prix de Minerve (beat Urban Sea a neck) at Evry: ran well in Prix de Pomone at Deauville, not discredited in Prix Vermeille at Longchamp afterwards: stays 13.5f: acts on soft going. *A. de Royer Dupre, France*

LINPAC EXPRESS 3 b.g. Siberian Express (USA) 125 – North Page (FR) 81 **66** d (Northfields (USA)) [1991 NR 1992 8g 10.1s³ 10.1s⁴ 14.1g a12g 10.1m 17.5s 10d⁵] rather leggy, quite attractive gelding: moderate mover: half-brother to several

Doonside Cup, Ayr—soft-ground specialist Linpac West gains a well-deserved listed win, from Percy's Girl and Guilty Secret (No. 4)

winners, including useful 6-y-o 8.2f to 11.9f winner Linpac West (by Posse): dam placed at up to 10.6f: disappointing maiden: below form blinkered: carries head high: sold to join P. Dalton 3,000 gns Doncaster October Sales and gelded. *C. W. C. Elsey*

LINPAC WEST   6 b.h. Posse (USA) 130 – North Page (FR) 81 (Northfields **109** (USA)) [1991 8d⁴ 10.4d² 11d* 10g 12d² 1992 8g⁵ 12d⁴ 11.9g* 10d 10.9s* 10.4s² 12s] lengthy, angular horse: poor mover: very useful and consistent performer: won York handicap in May and listed Doonside Cup (from Percy's Girl) at Ayr in September: rare modest effort in St Simon Stakes at Newbury final run: suited by middle distances: best on an easy surface, and goes well in the mud: sometimes edges under pressure, but game. *C. W. C. Elsey*

LION CAVERN (USA)   3 ch.c. Mr Prospector (USA) – Secrettame (USA) (Secretariat (USA)) [1991 6g* 6g² 6g³ 6m² 7.3g* 1992 7d* 8g³ 7m² 6.5g 8s⁶ 7d⁴] good- **117** topped, angular colt: has a quick action: smart performer: led post to beat River Falls in Group 3 Greenham Stakes at Newbury in April: subsequently in frame at Longchamp in Poule d'Essai des Poulains (best effort to be length third to Shanghai), Prix de la Porte Maillot (went down by 4 lengths to Dilum) and Prix de la Foret (5¾ lengths behind Wolfhound): stays 1m: yet to race on very firm ground, acts on any other: sent to W. Mott in USA. *A. Fabre, France*

LISALEE (IRE)   4 b.f. Montekin 125 – Ivy Holme (Silly Season 127) [1991 8m 8m — 9.9f 12.1m 1992 12f 13.8d⁵ 12.1m 15.8g⁶] workmanlike filly: moderate mover: on the downgrade. *J. Parkes*

Singer & Friedlander Greenham Stakes, Newbury—
Lion Cavern (left) gets up on the line from River Falls

LITERARY CRITIC (IRE)   3 b.c. Taufan (USA) 119 – Beaume (FR) (Faraway   45
Son (USA) 130) [1991 NR 1992 a8g⁴ 10g⁶ 10s] 9,800Y: angular colt: brother to Irish
5f to 1m winner Erin Dale and 1987 2-y-o 7f winner Be My Fan: dam unraced
granddaughter of Sweet Solera: well beaten after fourth in Southwell maiden in
September: blinkered final start: sold to join A. Chamberlain's stable 3,100 gns
Newmarket Autumn Sales. *J. A. R. Toller*

LITHO BOLD FLASHER   3 b.g. Bold Owl 101 – Flash O' Night (Patch 129)   –
[1991 6m 8.1m a8g⁶ a8g⁵ 1992 12d 12.1d³ 13.8g 12.1s] sturdy gelding: poor maiden:
trained until after second 3-y-o start by W. Pearce. *Capt. J. Wilson*

LITMORE DANCER   4 br.f. Mashhor Dancer (USA) – Daring Charm (Daring   43
March 116) [1991 7g² 6s⁶ 7.1d⁵ 7g 7f 6.1m 8m⁵ 6.9f a8g* a7g² 1992 a8g a8g a8g⁶ 5d
8.9g 8f 8g 8d a7g a7g³] lengthy, angular filly: has a round action: inconsistent
handicapper: effective at 7f to 1m: acts on firm and dead ground and all-weather
surfaces: sold out of J. Bethell's stable 4,000 gns Doncaster May Sales after third
start. *J. M. Bradley*

LITTLE BANG   4 ch.f. Bustino 136 – Live Ammo 94 (Home Guard (USA) 129)   –
[1991 7g² 8f³ 8.3m 7d⁴ 7f⁵ 9.7g 1992 10.2f 11.9f] lengthy, sparely-made filly: maiden
plater: stays 1m: acts on firm and dead going. *K. Bishop*

LITTLE BEAN   3 b.c. Ajdal (USA) 130 – Sassalya (Sassafras (FR) 135) [1991 NR   99 p
1992 8m² 8g* 8m 8g* 8m* 7.9m 7d²] leggy, attractive colt: half-brother to several
winners, including very useful middle-distance stayer Chauve Souris (by Beldale
Flutter) and smart 7f performer Sally Rous (by Rousillon): dam useful Irish 7f and
1¼m winner: split a pastern at 2 yrs: progressed really well in 1992, winning Yarmouth maiden and handicaps at Newmarket (£9,600 race) and Goodwood (Schweppes Golden Mile in good style by 2 lengths from Mudaffar): very good second of 21 to
Sharpalto in valuable Festival Handicap at Ascot final run: stays 1m: acts on good to
firm ground and dead: held up, and has good turn of foot: sure to do well at 4 yrs. *G.
Wragg*

LITTLE BIG   5 b.g. Indian King (USA) 128 – Route Royale (Roi Soleil 125) [1991   43
8.3g 8m 10.2s 9.7s 1992 a10g⁵ a12g 10.8f⁶ 14.6g* 22.2g] well-made gelding: poor
nowadays: won selling handicap (bought in 3,400 gns) at Wolverhampton: out of
depth in Queen Alexandra Stakes at Royal Ascot later in June: stays 1¾m well: acts
on any going: ran well in blinkers: won selling hurdle in October. *C. D. Broad*

LITTLEDALE (USA)   6 b.g. Lypheon 128 – Smeralda 105 (Grey Sovereign   50 d
128§) [1991 NR 1992 a10g² a12g a10g 10g 10d 10g] lengthy gelding: untrustworthy
handicapper nowadays: reluctant to race and pulled up once in 1992: stays 1¼m:
acts on good to firm ground and equitrack. *D. J. G. Murray-Smith*

LITTLE IVOR   3 b.g. Kings Lake (USA) 133 – Ange Gris (USA) (Grey Dawn II   38
132) [1991 7s 7f² 7f⁵ 7m 8m 7m 1992 8.1m 10f 10g⁵ 8f 12.2g³ 11g² 9m] sparely-made
gelding: has a round action: maiden handicapper: needs further than 9f, and should
stay beyond 1½m: below form visored. *Denys Smith*

LITTLE MISS POLLY   4 ch.f. Pharly (FR) 130 – Polly Packer 81 (Reform 132)   –
[1991 NR 1992 a7g a8g 12.3g] 1,600Y, resold 2,400Y: small filly: seventh foal:
half-sister to winning stayers Upton Park (by High Top), Regal Reform (by Prince

Schweppes Golden Mile (Handicap), Goodwood—
Little Bean, having missed all the trouble, shows a striking turn of foot

Tenderfoot) and Sun Street (by Ile de Bourbon): dam daughter of very useful miler Vital Match, was second over 7f and 1m: no form, pulled up lame final run. *C. J. Hill*

LITTLE NOD 3 ch.c. Domynsky 110 – Vikris (Viking (USA)) [1991 7m 8m⁵ 8.1s⁴ a7g⁶ a8g⁴ 1992 a8g² a7g² a7g² 7v³ 5.1d⁶ 8m 6g 8f 8.3g a7g² 6g⁴ 6s a7g⁶] lengthy, quite good-topped colt: maiden, best on all-weather: stays 1m: acts on soft ground, and all-weather surfaces: claimed out of M. Camacho's stable £4,125 third start. *J. White* **42** a62

LITTLE OSBORNE (IRE) 2 b.f. (Apr 27) Glow (USA) – Joma Kaanem (Double Form 130) [1992 6g] IR 13,000Y: angular, workmanlike filly: fifth foal: sister to modest 1991 3-y-o miler Killinghall and half-sister to fair miler Fenjaan (by Trojan Fen), Irish 3-y-o 1¼m to 1½m winner Jomel Amou (by Ela-Mana-Mou) and a minor winner by Taufan: dam ran once: bandaged behind and in need of race when tailed off in maiden at Newmarket in August: showed a quick action. *M. Bell* –

LITTLE PARK 3 b.f. Cragador 110 – Liberated Girl (Free State 125) [1991 7m 8s 1992 7m⁵ 7.1f⁴ 8f⁵ 9s a7g] sparely-made filly: little form: trained by G. Pritchard-Gordon until after third start. *C. N. Williams* –

LITTLE RED HEN 7 ch.m. Henbit (USA) 130 – Torriglia (USA) (Nijinsky (CAN) 138) [1991 7v⁶ 12v 11m 16g 14g 14g 12m 1992 a11g⁴ a8g a11g⁵ a12g] ex-Irish mare: probably of little account. *O. O'Neill* –

LITTLE ROUSILLON 4 b.c. Rousillon (USA) 133 – Carolside 108 (Music Maestro 119) [1991 7m 8f³ 7g⁵ 7g⁵ 9.2s² 1992 8d 8s* 8g³ 8m⁵ 10f 8.3g 8.9d] sturdy, lengthy, attractive colt: good mover: successful in Salisbury handicap in May: well below form in second half of 1992, blinkered final run: should stay 1¼m: acts on good to firm and soft ground: sometimes wears tongue strap. *A. C. Stewart* **69**

LITTLE SABOTEUR 3 ch.f. Prince Sabo 123 – Shoot To Win (FR) (Rabdan 129) [1991 5m⁴ 6m² 6g³ 6.1m⁴ 5d⁴ 5s* a6g⁴ 1992 5d⁵ 6f 6g 5g² 5g² 5.3d⁴ 5g* a5g² a5g² a6g⁴] useful-looking filly: fair handicapper: won at Edinburgh in October: best form at 5f: acts on soft going and all-weather surfaces: probably effective blinkered or not: consistent: retained 3,300 gns Ascot November Sales. *P. J. Makin* **72**

LITTLETON LULLABY 7 ch.m. Milford 119 – Littleton Song 73 (Song 132) [1991 NR 1992 10d 11.6d⁵ 12m 11.9g] smallish, good-quartered mare: moderate mover: no form in handicaps in summer: stays 1¼m: often bandaged off-hind. *E. A. Wheeler* –

LITTLE TOO MUCH (IRE) 2 b.c. (Feb 17) Storm Bird (CAN) 134 – Begonia (USA) (Plugged Nickle (USA)) [1992 6g⁵ 6g* 6f² 7m⁵ 7d* 7.1d⁵] 155,000Y: tall, well-made colt: has a fluent action: second reported foal: dam (ran in USA) daughter of Dahlia, dam also of Dahar, Wajd (by Northern Dancer) and Rivlia: fair performer: won minor events at Pontefract in June and Salisbury in August: good efforts in Group 3 events at Goodwood and Sandown (beaten under 7 lengths by White Crown in Solario Stakes) fourth and final runs: should stay 1m: acts on firm and dead ground: looked nervous and carried head high on occasions but not final start: consistent. *G. Harwood* **88**

LITTLEWICK (IRE) 3 b.f. Green Desert (USA) 127 – Loralane 86 (Habitat 134) [1991 NR 1992 8d³ 8s³ 10.3g a8g] workmanlike filly: seventh foal: half-sister to 4 winners, including fair 1m and 1½m winner Casamurrae (by Be My Guest) and useful miler Diggers Rest (by Mr Prospector): dam, 7f winner, is half-sister to On The House: not seen out until September: poor maiden: should stay beyond 1m: sold 8,200 gns Newmarket December Sales. *G. Wragg* **49**

LIU LIU SAN (IRE) 4 ch.f. Bairn (USA) 126 – The Saltings (FR) (Morston (FR) 125) [1991 7g a10g a13g 1992 7g 7f 9.7g⁴ 11.9d] good-topped filly: moderate mover: bad maiden. *P. Butler* –

LIVE AND LET FLY 3 gr.g. Import 127 – Glendyne 58 (Precipice Wood 123) [1991 NR 1992 6m] close-coupled gelding: second reported foal: dam best at 1½m on flat, won over hurdles and fences: tailed off in claimer at Redcar in April. *S. E. Kettlewell* –

LIYAKAH (USA) 2 ch.f. (Feb 1) Ogygian (USA) – Propositioning (USA) (Mr Prospector (USA)) [1992 6m* 6g³ 6d] $375,000Y: well-grown filly: has plenty of scope: half-sister to good-class 1990 American 2-y-o Deposit Ticket (by Northern Baby), successful at up to 7f: dam French 7f/1m winner: sire (by Damascus) high class, best at up to 1m: green when winning July maiden at Goodwood and over 4 lengths third of 6 to Silver Wizard in listed race at Kempton over 5 weeks later: pulled hard and found little off bridle when below-form seventh of 8 in moderately-run listed event at York: will stay 7f. *Major W. R. Hern* **88**

LIZZIE DRIPPIN (CAN) 3 b. or br.f. Artichoke (USA) – Adieu (FR) (Tompion – (USA)) [1991 6m 6g 6m a7g a8g6 1992 a8g2 a10g3 10d a8g6 a12g] plating-class a46 maiden: off course 7½ months and no form last 2 starts: stays 1¼m: acts on all-weather surfaces: below form blinkered. *M. D. I. Usher*

LLOYDS DREAM 3 b.g. Lidhame 109 – Christnes Lady (Roman Warrior 132) – [1991 NR 1992 8d 9d 12s] workmanlike gelding: second foal: dam pulled up in 2 novice hurdles: soundly beaten in autumn maidens and claimer. *D. Shaw*

LOBILIO (USA) 3 b.c. Robellino (USA) 127 – Nabila (USA) 58 (Foolish Pleasure **87** (USA)) [1991 8d 1992 12m 10g5 12m2 12g 12m3 10g3 13.9g 10.1d2 10g 12s2 10.4d*] well-made colt: placed in varied company in 1992, also finished behind in the Derby: not at best to win maiden at York (drifted left) in October: effective at 1¼m to 1½m: acts on good to firm ground and soft: usually makes running. *C. E. Brittain*

LOBINDA 3 b.f. Shareef Dancer (USA) 135 – Lobbino 72 (Bustino 136) [1991 7g **80** 8.5f* 8.1d* 9s5 1992 8d 12f* 13.3m4 16d6 14g6] stocky filly: best effort in handicaps in 1992 when winning at Salisbury in June: mulish at start and below form final one: needed at least 1½m: acted on firm and dead going: retired. *J. L. Dunlop*

LOCAL DEALER 4 ch.g. Scottish Reel 123 – Green Pool 39 (Whistlefield 118) – [1991 6g 7.5g 8f a7g 1992 10d] workmanlike gelding: seems of little account nowadays. *J. F. Bottomley*

LOCAL HEROINE 2 ch.f. (Mar 12) Clantime 101 – Hollia 72 (Touch Boy 109) **65** [1992 5s2 5d 5.1m* 6s6 5m6] sturdy filly: has a quick action: first foal: dam 2-y-o 5f winner: first run for almost 4 months when winning maiden at Chester in August: stiff task next time, creditable sixth in nursery at Newmarket final run: should stay 6f. *J. Berry*

LOCH CLAIR (IRE) 3 b.f. Lomond (USA) 128 – Burghclere 86 (Busted 134) – [1991 7m5 8s4 1992 14.1d6] lengthy, sparely-made filly: thrice-raced maiden: not seen out in 1992 until October, and stiff task at Redcar: looks like an out-and-out stayer: may do better. *Mrs J. Cecil*

LOCH MERE 2 b.f. (Apr 28) Lochnager 132 – Errema 71 (Workboy 123) [1992 7f] – 1,100Y: first foal: dam 9f winner: behind in seller at Redcar in June. *C. Tinkler*

LOCHORE 2 b.c. (Mar 19) Nordico (USA) – Hound Song 84 (Jukebox 120) [1992 **63** 5v 5m5 5.3m3 6m3 6m 6f2 8.1d6 8.5d 8f a8g5 a8g a7g] small colt: poor mover: sixth a53 foal: half-brother to a winner in Austria by Daring March: dam sprinter: inconsistent maiden: stays 1m well: acts on good to firm and dead ground and equitrack: no improvement in blinkers. *R. Ingram*

LOCH PATRICK 2 b.g. (Mar 17) Beveled (USA) – Daisy Loch (Lochnager 132) **40** p [1992 5g6] good-topped gelding: has scope: fourth foal: dam poor plater: never dangerous in maiden at Lingfield in May: showed a round action. *L. J. Holt*

LOCHSONG 4 b.f. Song 132 – Peckitts Well 96 (Lochnager 132) [1991 7f2 **111** p 6m* 7g* 1992 6v3 6g* 6f4 6m* 5.6m* 6d* 6d2]
The Stewards' Cup, the Portland, the Ayr Gold Cup—one after the other, three of the season's big sprint handicaps fell to Lochsong, a tough and genuine four-year-old filly who was still improving when put by after finishing a length-and-a-half second to Wolfhound in the Diadem Stakes at Ascot on her pattern-race debut. The sprint treble had never been achieved before. The key to it was unflagging improvement which kept Lochsong ahead of the handicapper. Overall, from April to September, she made a phenomenal amount of progress from a low mark which derived from a short-head win in an apprentice event at Newbury on the last of three outings in 1991. Following an encouraging return at Pontefract she started a heavily-backed favourite for a competitive handicap at York in May and, receiving weight from nearly all her opponents, justified the confidence in decisive fashion. The Wokingham at Royal Ascot came next. Although it was feared that the firm ground would count against her there, she finished a good fourth of twenty-nine to Red Rosein, showing fine speed up the middle of the track to lead by about two lengths approaching halfway and keeping on well when headed. She was the only one among the first eight home not drawn on the far side, so, no more than two lengths down on the winner, she probably ran even better than the bare result would suggest.
Either way, Lochsong was clearly still on the upgrade. Yet very few can have been prepared for all that followed at Goodwood, Doncaster and Ayr, as she defied the efforts of, in total, seventy-seven opponents to lower her

461

*William Hill Stewards' Cup, Goodwood—Lochsong hangs on from Duplicity (No. 7);
on the far side of Duplicity are Consigliere and Heather Bank (noseband),
then come Hard To Figure (No. 12), Master Planner (No. 18),
Double Blue (No. 17) and Tbab (No. 6)*

colours. She faced twenty-nine at Goodwood. The Stewards' Cup is usually
hotly contested; the latest was no exception, and attracted a quality field by
today's standards (nowadays horses rated above 115 are excluded, though this
will change from 1993 when £50,000 handicaps will be open), with top-weight
Notley attempting to follow up his previous year's win. Lochsong and Notley
raced on opposite sides of the course, Lochsong soon prominent in a group of
ten near-side, travelling comfortably, then quickening ahead over two
furlongs out. Inside the last she was driven along to go two lengths clear and
needed to be ridden out to hold on by half a length from Duplicity. The
Bunbury Cup winner Consigliere did best of the far-side runners, coming
third, while Notley, one of several over there who found himself short of
room, came thirteenth. A 6-lb rise in the official ratings as a result of this
performance did not prevent Lochsong's starting a clear favourite for the
Portland, and in the end she left the strong impression that she was value for
rather more than the neck verdict over Venture Capitalist, tending to idle and
needing to be driven out again after she had cruised along in front against the
stand rail almost from the start and quickened a couple of lengths clear going

Tote-Portland Handicap, Doncaster—Lochsong is pressed by Venture Capitalist

Ladbrokes (Ayr) Gold Cup (Handicap) — it's a procession as Lochsong completes the treble; Echo-Logical takes second ahead of the visored Heather Bank

into the final furlong. That in mind, and considering how she was improving physically as well, another good run was to be anticipated in the Ayr Gold Cup. There were two important points to consider, though. First, a jockey change — Carson, whose enterprising handling had played no small part in her development, was claimed to ride elsewhere, being replaced by the stable's 7-lb claimer Arrowsmith. Secondly, she was drawn twenty-eight of twenty-

Mr J. C. Smith's "Lochsong"

eight. Because of the draw she was opposed in the market on the day, having been ante-post favourite. Her supporters need not have worried for she turned the race into a procession after a smart break, sprinting clear soon after halfway. Although she tired a little and started to come back to the field towards the finish, she was never challenged; the closest the runner-up Echo-Logical managed to get was two lengths. Lochsong in full flow in the Ayr Gold Cup was one of the season's most striking sights. She found a repeat beyond her in the Group 3 Diadem Stakes the following week but, while unable to dominate, she showed up from the start and held the advantage approaching the final furlong before Wolfhound outpaced her. Lochsong remains in training with a pattern-race programme in view. This last run, undoubtedly her best so far, makes the venture seem well worth undertaking.

Lochsong was nearly sent for the Prix de l'Abbaye de Longchamp instead of the Diadem. Her style of racing gives the impression that she will be fully effective over five furlongs, and it is to be hoped she is tried over the distance in future. The dam Peckitts Well was equally effective at five and six, a winner over both distances as a two-year-old and a three-year-old. Lochsong is Peckitts Well's only runner to date. The next two dams were also sprinters, Grey Shoes much the better one. Great Grey Niece has proved the better at stud, however; among her other successful produce is Peckitts Well's half-brother, the veteran sprinter Absolution.

Lochsong (b.f. 1988)	Song (b 1966)	Sing Sing (b 1957)	Tudor Minstrel
			Agin The Law
		Intent (gr 1952)	Vilmorin
			Under Canvas
	Peckitts Well (b 1982)	Lochnager (br 1972)	Dumbarnie
			Miss Barbara
		Great Grey Niece (gr 1976)	Great Nephew
			Grey Shoes

Lochsong, who filled out into a strong, lengthy filly, never fails to impress in the paddock. Reportedly she is not an easy subject to train, has bad joints and is intermittently lame. Connections, therefore, hoped for good ground or easier whenever she ran. Nevertheless, the form-book says she acts on any going; as a point of interest, the Wokingham was decided on firm and both the Stewards' Cup and the Portland on good to firm. *I. A. Balding*

LOCK KEEPER (USA)   6 b.g. Riverman (USA) 131 – Jamila (Sir Gaylord) [1991   **68**
10.8m a7g* a8g* a7g² 8m³ 8.3s a8g 7m 8.2m a8g 1992 a7g a7g⁵ a8g⁴ a8g² a8g³ a8g*] stocky, attractive gelding: moderate walker: fair handicapper: improved form to win claimer at Southwell in December: stays 1m well: acts on good to firm ground and fibresand, possibly not soft: won over hurdles in August. *J. Mackie*

LODESTAR (IRE)   4 b.c. Rainbow Quest (USA) 134 – Air Distingue (USA) 120   –
(Sir Ivor 135) [1991 10d³ 10m* 12g 1992 10.5d] big, good-topped colt: has a markedly round action: rated 81 at 3 yrs: well below form in Haydock claimer in September, 1992: should be much better at 1½m than 1¼m: acts on good to firm and dead ground: disappointing over hurdles, broke blood vessel in November. *N. Tinkler*

LODGING   5 ch.g. Longleat (USA) 109 – Mollified 67 (Lombard (GER) 126) [1991   –
10f 10f a12g⁵ 10g 12.3d 11s 12f⁵ 12.3f* 12g³ 12f 12m⁵ 14.1f 12f 1992 9.9m a12g] smallish, workmanlike gelding: no form in 1992: stays 1½m: suited by sound surface (below form on hard ground): visored or blinkered nowadays: has hung left. *B. Ellison*

LOFT BOY   9 b.g. Cawston's Clown 113 – Burglar Tip 73 (Burglar 128) [1991 6g³   **61**
5m³ 6g 5.1g⁴ 5g³ 5g⁴ 6g 6f 5.2f² 5m 6m 5g 1992 5g 5.7f 5.6m 5f⁵ 5m⁵ 5m 5s³ 6s] sturdy gelding: moderate mover: sprint handicapper: acts on any going: usually blinkered/visored: occasionally bandaged off-hind: tough. *J. D. Bethell*

LOFTY DEED (USA)   2 b.c. (Apr 4) Shadeed (USA) 135 – Soar Aloft (USA)   **46**
(Avatar (USA)) [1992 6f⁶ 7m 7m 7g² 7.1f² 7m³ 8.5d 8d] $57,000Y: well-made colt: moderate walker: half-brother to several winners, including Soaring Princess (by Sensitive Prince), runner-up in Grade 1 9f race at 2 yrs: dam half-sister to Ferdinand (by Nijinsky): easily best efforts when placed in 2 sellers and apprentice nursery: should be well suited by 1m +: acts on firm ground, possibly unsuited by dead: ran too freely when blinkered once: sold 5,200 gns Newmarket Autumn Sales. *Sir Mark Prescott*

LOGAN'S LUCK (USA) 2 b.c. (Mar 22) Believe It (USA) – Fancy Wings (USA) **78** p
(Wing Out (USA)) [1992 6m⁵ 5v*] $32,000Y: compact colt: fourth reported foal:
half-brother to Irish 6f and 7f winner Side Winger (by Topsider): dam won at up to
1¼m and was placed in graded stakes: sire good 5.5f to 9f winner and third in
Kentucky Derby: very green, staying-on fifth to Felucca in maiden at Newmarket:
favourite, didn't have to repeat that form to win maiden at Redcar later in October,
leading in final 1f: bred to stay 1m: capable of better. *M. R. Stoute*

LOGARITHM 4 b.f. King of Spain 121 – Hearten (Hittite Glory 125) [1991 8g 8g –
8m 8g 7g a11g 1992 12.3g] rangy filly: no worthwhile form. *P. J. Makin*

LOKI (IRE) 4 ch.g. Thatching 131 – Sigym (Lord Gayle (USA) 124) [1991 8g³ 9m **86**
11.5m 8.5m⁴ᵈⁱˢ 8m 8g² 7.1g² 8m⁶ 8s³ 8m² 10.2g³ 8g 10g² 12.1s² 10.3d² 10d* 1992
9.7g 11.7d a12g⁶ 12d² 10g⁴ 12d 10.1f* 10d² 10g* 10.1d* 10.2s* 10m* 10.3v4] strong
gelding: sometimes dull in coat: fluent mover: had tremendous season in handicaps
in 1992, successful at Epsom (2, one a claimer), Kempton (apprentices), Chepstow
and Newmarket (apprentices): effective at 1¼m to 1½m: probably acts on any
going: ran well in blinkers at 3 yrs: held up: a credit to his trainer. *G. Lewis*

LOLA WANTS 2 br.f. (May 9) Lidhame 109 – Plain Tree 71 (Wolver Hollow 126) **49**
[1992 6.1d 7g 6s³] 3,600Y: tall, leggy filly: half-sister to 3 winners here and abroad,
including 7-y-o sprinter Plain Fact (by Known Fact) and 1¼m winner/successful
hurdler Arbor Vitae (by Dominion): dam, 7f winner, is half-sister to good French
middle-distance stayer Djakao: poor form in maidens: will be better suited by 1m. *C.
F. Wall*

LOMBARD OCEAN 3 ch.g. Ballacashtal (CAN) – Realm Gift 75 (Realm 129) **68** d
[1991 5f 5g* 6m⁵ 5m⁴ 6m* 7g 6g² 5d 1992 7g 6s³ 6d 6m⁵ 5f⁵ 5f³ 6f³ 6m⁶ 5g⁶ 10.5d
8s 8.2g a12g] tall, workmanlike gelding: moderate mover: disappointing in 1992:
stays 6f: acts on any going: trained until after ninth start by M. O'Neill. *A. Bailey*

LOMBARD SHIPS 5 ch.m. Orchestra 118 – Tina's Star (Simbir 130) [1991 7.5f **59** d
8f* 8m 8.1m³ 8f² 8g 1992 a8g 7g* 7g 8d⁴ 8f⁶ 8.1g⁵ 8g⁴ 8.3g⁵] sparely-made mare:
has a quick action: inconsistent handicapper: won at Thirsk in April: stays 1m: acts
on any going. *M. O'Neill*

LOMITAS 4 ch.c. Niniski (USA) 125 – La Colorada (Surumu (GER)) [1991 8.5f* **121**
11g* 12g² 12g* 12m* 12g* 1992 12d* 11g² 11m* 12g⁵] top-class German colt, winner of 9 of his 12 races: successful in Group 2 contests in 1992 at Cologne (Gerling
Preis) in May and Hamburg (gave Captain Horatius 8 lb more than w-f-a and a
comfortable 4-length beating in Idee Hansa-Preis) in June: well below best when
fifth of 6 in Group 1 event at Dusseldorf in July: stays 1½m: acts on good to firm and
dead ground: has proved very awkward at stalls, refusing to enter them once as
3-y-o: sent to USA to be trained by R. McAnally. *A. Wohler, Germany*

LONELY LASS 6 b.m. Headin' Up – Lonely Dawn (USA) 63 (Plenty Old (USA)) **40**
[1991 a5g² 5g 5d⁵ 5.1g⁵ a5g⁴ 5m 1992 a5g⁶ a7g a6g 5g⁵ 5f⁵ 5g 6g 5g⁵ 5g⁵ 5g4]
lengthy, rather sparely-made mare: poor mover: maiden handicapper: stays 6f: acts
on any going, including fibresand: below form blinkered once: trained until after
third start by L. Barratt. *A. W. Jones*

LONESOME DOVE (IRE) 4 br.f. Fast Topaze (USA) 128 – Magic In The Air –
(USA) (Home Guard (USA) 129) [1991 8g³ 9m⁵ 8m³ 10g⁶ 12d 1992 a8g 6g 6.9v
a10g] 10,000Y: second foal: dam French maiden, stayed 8.5f: ex-Irish filly, with G.
Connolly at 3 yrs (rated 71): soon outpaced all starts in 1992: best form at 1m: acts on
good to firm ground. *J. White*

LONESOME TRAIN (USA) 3 ch.g. Crafty Prospector (USA) – Alaki Miss **52**
(USA) (Olden Times) [1991 6m² 7f 7f 7m 1992 7d 8.2g 8f³ 8g 8m⁵ 12v4] sturdy
gelding: has a round action: plating-class handicapper: stays 1½m: acts on any
going: effective visored or not: sold out of J. Gosden's stable 4,200 gns Ascot July
Sales after penultimate start: won over hurdles in August and September. *C.
Weedon*

LONG FURLONG 4 b.g. Castle Keep 121 – Myrtlegrove (Scottish Rifle 127) **57**
[1991 12s 7g 8m 12.2g 10d 12f⁵ a10g 10m* 10g* 9.7f* 10m 9.7s² 1992 11.1v⁵ 12.1g⁶
10m³ 10.2m 9.7g² 10m⁴ 10g⁴] leggy gelding: none too consistent handicapper in
1992: ideally suited by 1¼m: probably acts on any going: below form blinkered:
sometimes finds little, carries head high, and not easiest of rides: trained until after
penultimate start by R. Akehurst. *M. C. Pipe*

LONG LANE LADY 6 ch.m. Longleat (USA) 109 – Teresa Way 66 (Great White **46**
Way (USA)) [1991 a5g⁶ 6g⁴ 6d* 6g 6g⁵ 6.1m² 6d a6g 1992 6g 6.1d⁵ 6m⁵ 7g² a7g³ 7g
7.1s 7d a7g] lengthy, good-quartered mare: inconsistent handicapper: effective at

6f/7f: acts on good to firm and dead ground and fibresand: often has tongue tied down. *J. Mackie*

LONG LAST 3 b.f. Kabour 80 – Final Cast 50 (Saulingo 122) [1991 NR 1992 5g 5s a5g a5g] workmanlike filly: fourth foal: sister to 5f performer Kabcast and 6f winner Miss Kive: dam, 5f winner at 4 yrs, stayed 7f: little worthwhile form, including in sellers. *D. W. Chapman* —

LONGLIFE (IRE) 2 b.c. (Apr 26) Simply Great (FR) 122 – Petrolea Girl (Connaught 130) [1992 a6g 7m³ 7g 10d] IR 3,600F, IR 7,000Y: first reported foal: dam placed over hurdles in Ireland: plater: stays 1¼m: acts on good to firm ground: ran creditably in visor final run: sold 880 gns Newmarket Autumn Sales. *M. H. Tompkins* 37

LONG SILENCE (USA) 3 b.f. Alleged (USA) 138 – Mystical Mood (USA) (Roberto (USA) 131) [1991 NR 1992 10m 10s⁴ 12.3s* 11.9d²] unfurnished filly: moderate mover: sixth foal: sister to smart Irish 7f to 1¼m winner Fair Judgment and half-sister to very useful 1m (at 2 yrs) to 2m winner Orpheus (by The Minstrel) and a winner in North America: dam successful at up to 6f and smart at 2 yrs: not seen out until August, but progressed with every run: 8-length winner of slowly-run maiden at Ripon before running-on second in moderately-run handicap at Haydock: will be well suited by stiffer test of stamina: will improve further at 4 yrs. *Mrs J. Cecil* 85 p

LONSOM LASS 4 ch.f. Headin' Up – Lonely Dawn (USA) 63 (Plenty Old (USA)) [1991 5f 6f* 5.2m⁶ 5.1s 1992 5g 5.1g 5d 5g] lengthy, shallow-girthed filly: rated 73 at 3 yrs: no form in handicaps in summer in 1992: stays 6f: best efforts on top-of-the-ground. *L. J. Barratt* —

LOOKATMYFOOT 2 ch.f. (May 4) Banner Bob 86 – Zilliant (Private Account (USA)) [1992 6g] leggy filly: first foal: dam unplaced from 6 starts in North America: last in seller at Windsor in July. *J. Sutcliffe* —

LOOKINGFORARAINBOW (IRE) 4 ch.g. Godswalk (USA) 130 – Bridget Folly (Crofter (USA) 124) [1991 6f 6m 5m³ 5m⁵ 5d² 9.7m² 9f* 8m 9m⁵ 10.5d⁶ 9g 1992 10.8v⁵ 14.1d² 14.1d³ 16.2d 14.1g* 14.1g⁴ 14.6m⁴ 14.1d³ 14.8g a10g³ a10g* a8g² a14g*] close-coupled gelding: fair handicapper: won at Nottingham in May, Lingfield in November and Southwell in December: effective at 1¼m and stays 1¾m: acts on firm and dead ground and all-weather surfaces: travels strongly through his races but has found little under pressure and seems best with waiting tactics. *Bob Jones* 70

LOOK WHO'S HERE (IRE) 2 b.g. (Feb 17) Heraldiste (USA) 121 – House Call (Artaius (USA) 129) [1992 6.1m⁴ 6m³ 6s⁴ 6g² 6d* 6d⁶ 6v] 1,600F, 2,100Y, 4,600 2-y-o: workmanlike gelding: good mover: first foal: dam Irish maiden sister to very useful Day Is Done: easily best effort when winning Haydock nursery in September: held up and never able to challenge in moderately-run listed event at York (pulled hard) and Racecall Gold Trophy at Redcar after: will be better suited by 7f+: acts well on a soft surface. *B. A. McMahon* 90

LOOSE ZEUS (USA) 3 b.g. Double Zeus (USA) – Dareing Driver (USA) (Sadair) [1991 7.5f 8.1g 8m 1992 a8g 7g 6m 6m³ 6.1g⁵ 7f 5f² 6m 5d⁴ 5g⁶] good-topped gelding: moderate mover: plating-class maiden: best efforts over stiff 5f: acts on firm and dead ground: below form blinkered: goes well with tongue tied down: sold 2,600 gns Newmarket Autumn Sales. *C. F. Wall* 55

LOOTING (USA) 6 b. or br.g. Pirate's Bounty (USA) – Bank Examiner (USA) (Buckfinder (USA)) [1991 6g 6d⁶ 6g 6g 6.1s 6g⁶ 6m⁴ 7s 6g 6g 1992 6g 7m a7g a7g 7s a6g⁶ a7g⁴ a6g a7g⁵ a7g²] good-bodied gelding: poor handicapper: stays 7f: acts on good to firm going and on equitrack, possibly unsuited by soft. *M. D. I. Usher* 41

LORD ADVOCATE 4 br.g. Law Society (USA) 130 – Kereolle (Riverman (USA) 131) [1991 9f5 11.1d³ 13.8g a12g a12g³ a13g a10g* 1992 a10g a14g⁶ a12g* a12g² a12g a14g² a12g 12.1s 13d 13m 12.3f 12.2g² a12g 11.1m² 10.9d² 12f5 15.1d⁴ 12.4v 11.1d³ a12g a16g² a14g⁴ a12g] workmanlike gelding: very poor mover: unreliable handicapper: stays 2m: acts on firm and dead ground and all-weather surfaces: effective blinkered/visored or not: sometimes forces pace: changed hands 920 gns Doncaster November Sales. *M. P. Naughton* 47 §

LORD ALFIE 3 ch.c. Beveled (USA) – Fair Nic (Romancero 100) [1991 7g 6f 1992 8m] tall, leggy colt: thrice raced, and no worthwhile form. *R. J. Hodges* —

LORD BELMONTE (IRE) 3 b.g. Cyrano de Bergerac 120 – Noble Nancy (Royal And Regal (USA)) [1991 7f 7m 8d 1992 9.7v 7s 8f 10f 8.3m 5d] leggy, angular gelding: seems of little account: sold 1,300 gns Ascot July Sales. *C. A. Cyzer* —

LORD CHICKNEY (USA) 3 b.c. Chief's Crown (USA) – Chic Shirine (USA) **97**
(Mr Prospector (USA)) [1991 NR 1992 7d* 8m⁶] quite good-topped colt: has
reportedly been freeze fired: first foal: dam Grade 1 8.5f winner at 3 yrs out of Grade
1 1m winner Too Chic: not seen out until September when 2-length winner from
Talb of £8,500 contest at Ascot: failed to fulfil that promise when co-favourite in
Newmarket listed race 9 days after: should be suited by 1m: may be capable of better
back on an easy surface. *J. H. M. Gosden*

LORD CHIEF JUSTICE 2 b.c. (Jan 26) Alleging (USA) 120 – Ring of Pearl **32**
(Auction Ring (USA) 123) [1992 7m 7d] 3,400F, 29,000Y: workmanlike colt: third
foal: half-brother to 3-y-o Miss Shadowfax (by Absalom), 5f winner at 2 yrs, and 1990
2-y-o 6f seller winner Blazing Pearl (by Blazing Saddles): dam ran 3 times at 2 yrs:
never a factor in large-field maidens at Kempton and Lingfield: sold 2,400 gns
Newmarket Autumn Sales. *J. L. Dunlop*

LORD FUTURE (IRE) 4 ch.g. The Noble Player (USA) 126 – Little Spinner 57 –
(Tachypous 128) [1991 a8g³ a10g a8g4 10g⁵ 11.1s² 13d³ 12m 17.1m 13.8m 1992 14.1d
14.1m] leggy gelding: has a round action: still a maiden, and no form in 1992: stays
13f: acts on soft ground. *A. W. Potts*

LORD HASTIE (USA) 4 b.g. Affirmed (USA) – Sheika (USA) (Minnesota Mac) **83**
[1991 10.2s* 10d⁶ 11.9g 11.9d* 1992 a12g* 12g 11.9s² 11.9d4 12.3m² 11.9d4 14.6m³
14m* 13.9m 16.2d4 18m] tall, rather leggy gelding: fair handicapper: blinkered,
edged noticeably left when winning 3-runner race at Haydock in August: best
efforts from 1½m to 14.6f: acts on good to firm and soft ground, and on fibresand:
successful for apprentice but not an easy ride and will prove best with strong
handling: sometimes wears near-side pricker. *S. G. Norton*

LORD HIGH ADMIRAL (CAN) 4 b.c. Bering 136 – Baltic Sea (CAN) (Danzig **73**
(USA) [1991 8s 7g4 7f4 1992 6d 6.1d² 6g³ 6g² 6g 7d] tall, leggy colt: impresses in
appearance: ran well when placed in handicaps in 1992 for R. Hannon: first run for
present trainer and for 4 months, shaped better than sixteenth-of-19 position
suggests in 7f York handicap, weakening quickly final 1f: may prove ideally suited by
6f: acts on firm and dead ground. *C. G. Cox*

LORD LAMBSON 3 b.g. Today And Tomorrow 78 – Sum Star 67 (Comedy Star –
(USA) 121) [1991 NR 1992 7.5g 6f⁶ 6m⁶ 6.1m4 6f⁵ 7.5g 6f 6d 8.1g4] 4,400Y: tall
gelding: moderate mover: fifth foal: half-brother to 2 winners, including 8-y-o
sprinter Joe Sugden (by Music Boy): dam won 5 times from 5f to 1m at 5 yrs: no
worthwhile form. *R. M. Whitaker*

LORD LEITRIM (IRE) 3 b.c. Nordico (USA) – Brave Louise 76 (Brave Shot) **44**
[1991 7m a7g a8g³ 1992 6m 9.7g⁶ 9g 8d³ 8g 10m 8.3m a8g² 8g a6g⁶ 10d a8g] leggy,
lightly-made colt: impresses in appearance: poor mover: poor maiden: best efforts
at 1m: acts on dead ground, and all-weather surfaces. *N. A. Callaghan*

LORD MAGESTER (FR) 5 ch.g. Magesterial (USA) 116 – Lady Zia (FR) (Sir –
Tor (FR)) [1991 a6g 1992 5f³ 5f 7g 6m] big, lengthy, good-quartered gelding: still a
maiden, and well below form in first half of 1992: should stay beyond 5f: acts on firm
going, seems unsuited by soft. *Mrs M. Reveley*

LORD NASKRA (USA) 3 b.g. Naskra (USA) – Corvallis (USA) (Sir Ivor 135) **61**
[1991 NR 1992 a7g⁵ a6g³ a6g* 8g a6g a6g a8g] $9,000Y: first foal: dam unraced: won
claimer at Southwell in June: off course 4 months and ran poorly afterwards: should
stay beyond 6f: usually very slowly away. *W. A. O'Gorman*

LORD NEPTUNE 3 gr.g. Petong 126 – Odile (Green Dancer (USA) 132) [1991 –
6.1m⁶ 6g³ 1992 7g 8f 7f 10g 10g 9.7v a8g a6g⁵] angular gelding: rated 58 at 2 yrs: no
form in 1992: should stay 1m: sold out of M. Jarvis' stable 900 gns Newmarket
Autumn Sales after fourth start. *J. R. Jenkins*

LORD NITROGEN (USA) 2 b. or br.c. (Feb 17) Greinton 119 – Jibber Jabber **63** p
(USA) (Jacinto) [1992 8d⁶] 11,000Y: leggy, unfurnished colt: half-brother to 3
winners abroad, notably dual Grade 3 winner Lawyer Talk (by Alleged): dam
unraced close relative of Boldnesian: 14/1 and backward, 9½ lengths sixth of 18 in
maiden at Leicester in October, keeping on having been outpaced over 2f out:
showed a round action: will improve. *M. Bell*

LORD OBERON (IRE) 4 b.g. Fairy King (USA) – Vaguely Jade (Corvaro **66**
(USA) 122) [1991 7.6g 10g 8.2g* 9m⁵ 8g² 8f 10m² 8.2m* 8m* 7.9m4 8g 1992 8g 8d
9m 8f4 8g³ 7.6m³ 7m 9.7m4 8g⁵ 8s⁶ 8d 9s] angular, lengthy gelding: moderate
mover: none too consistent handicapper: effective at 1m to 1¼m: acts on good to
firm and soft ground: below form blinkered once: has joined J. Akehurst. *R. J.
O'Sullivan*

LORD OF THE FIELD 5 b.h. Jalmood (USA) 126 – Star Face (African Sky 124) **97** +
[1991NR 1992 9d 10g] good-topped, attractive horse: easy mover: rated 115 as 3-y-o:
reportedly suffered a fractured fibia in May, 1991: still retains plenty of ability
judged on runs at Newmarket in October in Cambridgeshire and slowly-run listed
race won by Lupescu: should stay 1½m: yet to race on very soft going, probably acts
on any other. *J. A. R. Toller*

LORD OLIVIER (IRE) 2 b.c. (Apr 22) The Noble Player (USA) 126 – Burkina **95**
(African Sky 124) [1992 5.1g⁴ 5f* 5m2 5g⁴ 5f* 5m4 5g3 5d2 5m2 5g6] IR 4,300F,
11,000Y: strong colt: poor mover: second foal: dam Irish 2-y-o 5f winner, is
granddaughter of Ribblesdale winner French Fern, dam of Gold Cup winner
Shangamuzo: quite useful performer: won maiden at Thirsk in May and claimer at
Ripon in August: ran very well after when second in listed race at Ayr and nursery at
Newmarket: stiff task final outing: acts on firm and dead ground: consistent. *W.
Jarvis*

LORD PRESIDENT (USA) 2 br.c. (Feb 22) Danzig Connection (USA) – A **90** p
Surprise (USA) (Bold Bidder) [1992 5d3 6f2 7g* 7m5] $100,000Y: robust, good-
quartered colt: has scope: fourth reported foal: half-brother to 2 minor winners by
Relaunch: dam maiden in USA: sire won Belmont Stakes: second in Chesham
Stakes at Royal Ascot before impressive 5-length winner of maiden at Newmarket
(made all) following month: heavily-backed favourite, modest fifth in Laurent
Perrier Champagne Stakes at Doncaster, edging left last 2f and one pace: will be
better suited to 1m. *P. F. I. Cole*

LORD'S FINAL 5 ch.g. Royal Match 117 – White Cone (Celtic Cone 116) [1991 **37**
10.8g 1992 10m 8.1m3 8.1m3 8.1g⁴ 7g] close-coupled gelding: ran well when placed
in handicaps in 1992: may prove ideally suited to 1¼m: acts on good to firm ground.
C. R. Barwell

LORD VIVIENNE (IRE) 3 b.g. Don't Forget Me 127 – Lady Vivienne (Golden **79** d
Fleece (USA) 133) [1991 a8g* a8g* 1992 12m6 10m 8g⁴ 8g3 7f* 7d 7g* 7f9d3 7d 8.9d
8g 7g a8g] lengthy gelding: fair performer at best: generally well below form after
winning Newmarket claimer (bandaged) and seller (hung left in front and swished
tail, sold out of P. Cole's stable 7,000 gns) in August: probably stays 9f (slipped up
over 1¼m): acts on firm and dead going and all-weather surfaces: below form
blinkered: sometimes has tongue tied down: one to have reservations about. *R. C.
Spicer*

LORELIE (FR) 2 ch.f. (Jan 14) Ti King (FR) 121 – Royal Flirt (FR) (Pharly (FR) **106**
130) [1992 7.5g* 8d2 8s6 8s5 8f] 40,000 francs (approx £4,000) Y: first foal: dam
French 1¼m and 1½m winner: useful French filly: won minor event at Deauville in
August: runner-up to Kindergarten in Prix d'Aumale at Longchamp: creditable fifth
on Corrazona in Prix des Reservoirs also at Longchamp: seventh of 10 in Miesque
Stakes at Hollywood Park in November: will stay 1¼m: acts on soft going. *F.
Boutin, France*

LORICA D'OR 5 ch.g. Hotfoot 126 – Dayana (Burglar 128) [1991 NR 1992 a14g –
8d5 a10g] lengthy, leggy, angular gelding: sixth foal: half-brother to a winner in
Belgium: dam ran once: no worthwhile form. *P. F. Tulk*

LORINS GOLD 2 ch.g. (Mar 13) Rich Charlie 117 – Woolcana 71 (Some Hand **56** p
119) [1992 5.1f 6g 5g⁴] 3,000Y: close-coupled, workmanlike gelding: eighth foal:
half-brother to 4 winners, including modest 7f winner Pullover (by Windjammer)
and 1990 2-y-o 6f winner Ageetee (by Tina's Pet): dam 5f winner: still on backward
side, best effort in maidens when around 4 lengths fourth of 8 at Windsor in August,
showing up well 4f: speedy: may well do better. *Andrew Turnell*

LOST MOMENT 8 b.m. Hotfoot 126 – Elizabeth Howard 68 (Sharpen Up 127) –
[1991 NR 1992 5s a8g] of little account: sold 900 gns Ascot December Sales. *H. J.
Collingridge*

LOST REPUTATION (IRE) 3 b.f. Law Society (USA) 130 – Reputation **93**
(Tower Walk 130) [1991 NR 1992 7d* 7.1d3 10.3g5 10.3v* 14.6g*] 13,000Y: leggy
filly: first foal: dam maiden stayed 1½m, is from family of Nonoalco: won newcomers
race at Newbury in April and handicap at Chester and minor event at Doncaster
(made all) in autumn: stays 14.6f: goes very well on heavy ground: sold 31,000 gns
Newmarket December Sales. *B. W. Hills*

LOST SOLDIER (USA) 2 b.c. (Apr 19) Danzig (USA) – Lady Winborne (USA) **100**
(Secretariat (USA)) [1992 6f* 6g* 8s3 7m] $500,000F: rangy, good sort: moderate
walker: half-brother to several winners including Al Maymoon, successful over 6f at
2 yrs in 1985, and Al Mamoon (both by Believe It), useful sprinter in Britain and very
smart at around 1m in USA: dam, half-sister to Allez France, won over 9f in Ireland

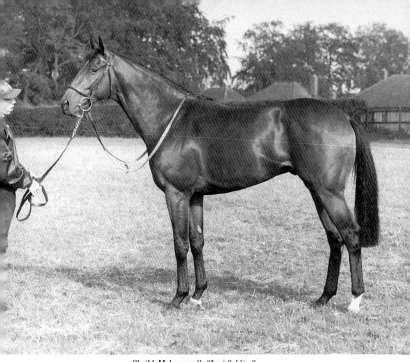

Sheikh Mohammed's "Lost Soldier"

from 2 starts: comfortable winner of maiden at Yarmouth and minor event at Newmarket in August: good third, beaten 3 lengths, to Desert Secret in Royal Lodge Stakes at Ascot: no danger from halfway when creditable tenth of 11 in Dewhurst Stakes at Newmarket: stays 1m: acts on any going. *L. M. Cumani*

LOTS OF LUCK 9 gr.m. Neltino 97 – Safe Passage (Charlottown 127) [1991 **71** a11g* a12g* 10g 11.8g 9g 10.3d 1992 10.3g⁵ 10.5d² 12.3f⁴ 9.7h* 10d⁵ 9.9m* 8g* 10.5d 10.3g²] smallish, workmanlike mare: moderate mover: had a good season in handicaps in 1992, successful in amateurs race at Folkestone and ladies events at Beverley and Newbury: unlucky second in Doncaster ladies race final run: effective from 1m to 1½m: acts on any going and all-weather surfaces: ran creditably when blinkered: ridden by Mrs L. Pearce. *J. Pearce*

LOUDEST WHISPER 4 b.g. Reach 122 – Dancela 74 (Ela-Mana-Mou 132) **56 d** [1991 8d 10.1f³ 8m 1992 a8g⁶ a10g³ a12g² 10.8d 8.9g 8m 14.6m 8g 10.8g] tall, angular gelding: inconsistent maiden handicapper: stays 1½m: acts on firm ground and fibresand: ran well when visored once, poorly when blinkered once: joined Miss S. Wilton. *K. S. Bridgwater*

LOUISVILLE BELLE (IRE) 3 ch.f. Ahonoora 122 – Lomond Fairy (Lomond **71** (USA) 128) [1991 7d 1992 8d 6s 7.1m⁴ 7.1m⁵ 8m³ 7g⁵ 7g* 7d 8d] small, sturdy filly: fair handicapper: well below form after winning at Newbury (edged right) in August: effective at 7f to 1m: suited by a sound surface (yet to race on very firm ground): usually bandaged behind. *M. D. I. Usher*

LOUVRE (FR) 2 b.c. (May 5) Persian Bold 123 – Pride of Paris (Troy 137) [1992 **62 p** 6s² 7.1s³] 42,000Y: rather leggy colt: second foal: dam once-raced half-sister to smart miler Gwent: modest form in autumn maidens at Newcastle (caught post) and Chepstow: will be suited by middle distances. *Mrs J. Cecil*

LOVEALOCH (IRE)   4 b.f. Lomond (USA) 128 – Civility 108 (Shirley Heights **106** 130) [1991 8g* 12m² 8g² 8.2m 9m* 10v³ 8d⁵ 1992 8.1g⁴ 8.1m³ 8m 8g² 10.1g 8m⁴ 9m] good-topped filly: useful performer at best, fourth in Group 2 Forte Mile at Sandown and second (to Gussy Marlowe) in Falmouth Stakes at Newmarket: below par, mostly in listed events, otherwise in 1992: effective at 1m to 1¼m: acts on good to firm ground and heavy: races with tongue tied down: sold 34,000 gns Newmarket December Sales. *M. Bell*

LOVE IN THE MIST (USA)   2 ch.f. (Feb 6) Primo Dominie 121 – Sleeping **59** p Beauty 87 (Mill Reef (USA) 141) [1992 6m² 6s⁶] sturdy, quite attractive filly: has a quick action: first foal: dam, 1m winner, is half-sister to Galtres Stakes winners Deadly Serious and Sans Blague: promising head second in maiden at Newbury in May: faded final 1f as lack of condition told when over 7 lengths sixth of 16 in similar event there over 5 months after: will do better. *I. A. Balding*

LOVE JAZZ (USA)   3 b.c. State Dinner (USA) – Snow Lover (USA) (Knightly **84** Sport (USA)) [1991 5m 6f* 7.5f⁵ 7m* 7m* 7g 7m³ 7f⁶ 7m 1992 6s* 8.1g 7m 5.9h* 6f⁴ 7.6d⁴ 6m⁴ 6g⁴ 6f 6d⁴ 7d³ 7v² 6vdis] leggy, short-backed colt: fair handicapper: won claimers at Haydock in April and Carlisle in June: best form at 6f or 7f: acts on any going: sometimes sweats. *T. D. Barron*

LOVE LEGEND   7 ch.g. Glint of Gold 128 – Sweet Emma 108 (Welsh Saint 126) **89** d [1991 a5g³ a6g⁴ 5d⁶ 5g 5d² 5g⁴ 6m² 5m 5m⁴ 6g 6g 5.6m 6m 6g⁵ 5m² 6m 5.2g 5d⁵ 1992 5.2d 5g 5.1m* 5m 6d³ 6f 6.1d 7g 5d 6d 6.1s³ a6g a6g⁴] smallish, sparely-made gelding: poor walker: has a quick action: fair sprint handicapper: won at Chester in May: below that form after next start: acts on firm and dead ground: best efforts in 1992 when blinkered: successful for apprentice. *D. W. P. Arbuthnot*

LOVELY BIRD (USA)   2 ch.f. (Mar 20) Arctic Tern (USA) 126 – Swift Gal **60** p (USA) (Little Current (USA)) [1992 6d³ 6.1s²] second reported foal: half-sister to a minor winner in USA: dam minor winner at around 7f, is from family of Tom Rolfe and Chieftain: placed in October in maiden at Goodwood and minor event (led until close home when beaten ¾ length by Hung Parliament) at Chester: will improve again, particularly at 7f+. *M. Bell*

LOVE OF SILVER (USA)   2 ch.f. (Feb 25) Arctic Tern (USA) 126 – **110** Silver Clover (USA) (Secretariat (USA)) [1992 6g* 7m⁴ 7d* 8s³ a8.5f]

Love of Silver came out best of the three British-trained fillies in the Prix Marcel Boussac at Longchamp in October. Starting a little under 7/1, she finished a short neck and three quarters of a length behind Gold Splash and Kindergarten, seeing the distance out well but losing second in the last half-furlong after pressing the winner closely for most of the straight. Love of Silver's third place in the Boussac represented an improvement on her three previous efforts as a two-year-old. The signs were favourable beforehand —not only did she look exceptionally well, but her form had progressed significantly each time she'd set foot on the racecourse and her running in each of her races over seven furlongs had indicated that a mile would suit her extremely well. Love of Silver also benefited from a sound tactical ride in a well-run race at Longchamp. Connections seemed to have realized after her performance in the Sweet Solera Stakes at Newmarket on her second outing, where she was caught flat-footed in a moderately-run race before running on well into fourth, that she would be best ridden up with the leaders. Roberts rode Love of Silver in her last three races, and he was seen to particularly good advantage on her when they made all the running to win the Butlins Southcoast World Prestige Stakes (formerly the Waterford Candelabra) at Goodwood at the end of August. With nobody else willing to go on, Roberts dictated the pace, quickened the gallop gradually in the last three furlongs and kept his mount running strongly and straight to hold the Virginia Water Maiden winner Dancing Bloom and the subsequent Fillies' Mile runner-up Ajfan by a neck and a length and a half. The Prestige Stakes win was Love of Silver's second of the season following a simple one at the expense of two poor opponents in a maiden at Haydock in July. Further success eluded her by some way when she was sent to Gulfstream Park in Florida for the Breeders' Cup Juvenile Fillies. Conditions at Gulfstream Park were vastly different from anything she'd encountered on a racecourse in Britain—notably the dirt

Butlins Southcoast World Prestige Stakes, Goodwood—
a game front-running display from Love of Silver,
who meets a sustained challenge from Dancing Bloom

surface—and like most of the other European raiders Love of Silver wasn't able to give her true running, eventually finishing tenth of the twelve runners. On the pick of her form, there's little doubt that Love of Silver is one of the best staying fillies of her age.

Love of Silver (USA) (ch.f. Feb 25, 1990)	Arctic Tern (USA) (ch 1973)	Sea Bird II (ch 1962)	Dan Cupid
			Sicalade
		Bubbling Beauty (ch 1961)	Hasty Road
			Almahmoud
	Silver Clover (USA) (gr 1981)	Secretariat (ch 1970)	Bold Ruler
			Somethingroyal
		Clover Lane (gr 1967)	Tudor Way
			Grass Shack

The tall, attractive Love of Silver was bought at Keeneland's July Yearling Sale for 100,000 dollars. She's a daughter of the high-class middle-distance performer Arctic Tern out of the Secretariat mare Silver Clover, a winner of three races at up to nine furlongs in North America as a four-year-old in 1985. Love of Silver is Silver Clover's second foal; her third, a filly by Afleet, was withdrawn at a late stage from the latest July Sale. Silver Clover's dam Clover Lane has produced six other winners, most of them run-of-the-mill, of whom only the minor stakes winner Cricket Club, successful at up to seven furlongs and later the dam of a Grade 3-winning miler, and Dragon Slayer, a winner of eighteen of his one hundred and twenty-four races, are worthy of mention. Clover Lane won seven races herself, and showed some of the best two-year-old form in the United States in 1969 when she won four races, notably the Mademoiselle Stakes over five and a half furlongs and the Arlington Washington Lassie Stakes over six and a half. Her dam Grass Shack never ran, but foaled plenty of winners and is also the third dam of the top-class colt Deputy Minister, the champion North American two-year-old in 1981 when he was also named 'Horse of the Year' in Canada. Love of Silver will be well suited by middle distances as a three-year-old. Her best form has

Mr Ali Saeed's "Love of Silver"

been shown on a soft surface, but she's a good mover who handled good to firm ground perfectly well in the Sweet Solera. *C. E. Brittain*

LOVE RETURNED   5 b.m. Taufan (USA) 119 – Miss Loving 89 (Northfields **81** (USA)) [1991 5g* 6d 5f 5.1d⁶ 5.1g 5.1g² 6m* 5m 6f⁶ 5.6m³ 6m 6g³ 5.1g* 1992 5g³ 5d a**84** 5m* 5g⁴ 5m³ 5g⁵ 5.6m⁶ 6d 5d⁴ 5.1d 5m⁴ 6v⁴ a5g* a6g] lengthy mare: moderate mover: fairly useful performer: won at Lingfield (claimer) in May and Southwell in November: barely stays 6f: acts on any going: usually finds little off bridle and held up: not easiest of rides. *W. Jarvis*

LOVISTE BAY   3 b.f. Mummy's Game 120 – Miss Maina (Thatching 131) [1991 5g – 6m a8g 1992 12m 8f] neat filly: seems of little account. *J. Ffitch-Heyes*

LOWAWATHA   4 b.g. Dancing Brave (USA) 140 – Shorthouse 102 (Habitat 134) – [1991 11.8g⁶ 12.5m³ 10.3d 1992 14.1d 9g] good-topped gelding: has high knee action: rated 61 at 3 yrs for H. Cecil: tongue tied down, well beaten in handicaps in 1992: should stay beyond 1½m: acts on good to firm ground. *D. Morris*

LOWLANDS BOY   3 b.c. Claude Monet (USA) 121 – Aquarian Star (Cavo Doro – 124) [1991 5m 6d 7.5f* 7m⁵ 6m 7g 1992 7g 8d⁴ 8.9g 8m a7g 7g 6.9f⁵ 8.3s a7g 11d] tall, workmanlike colt: has a round action: on the downgrade: sold 1,200 gns Doncaster October Sales. *T. Fairhurst*

LOWRIANNA (IRE)   2 b.f. (May 18) Cyrano de Bergerac 120 – Tallow Hill **50** (Dunphy 124) [1992 5.1m 5g* 6g 5.7m² 5.1m 6.1s 5s 7s] 5,600Y: leggy filly: second foal: sister to 1991 2-y-o 5.9f and 7f winner Talberno Boy: dam unraced half-sister to Cheveley Park winner Pass The Peace: should prove suited by 7f: acts on good to firm ground, seems unsuited by soft. *D. Haydn Jones*

LT WELSH (USA)   2 b.c. (May 8) Silver Hawk (USA) 123 – Lake Ivor (USA) (Sir **66** Ivor 135) [1992 7m³ 7d⁵ 7g⁵] $105,000Y: leggy, attractive colt: has scope: half-

472

brother to 5 minor winners in North America: dam unraced half-sister to useful Irish 2-y-o's Nazoo and Lake Como and from good family: fair form in quite useful maiden company: will be better suited by 1m. *I. A. Balding*

LUCAYAN TREASURE 2 b.c. (Feb 22) Absalom 128 – Cindys Gold 69 (Sonnen **75** Gold 121) [1992 5d a6g a5g*] 15,000Y: good-topped colt: third reported foal: brother to 3-y-o 6f winner First Gold: dam, plater, stayed 7f, is out of sister to Petong: always behind in maidens for J. Berry: improved form in a visor to win at Lingfield in November after a 5½-month break: will stay 6f: acts on equitrack. *D. R. Loder*

LUCEDEO 8 gr.g. Godswalk (USA) 130 – Lucy Limelight 98 (Hot Spark 126) **84** [1991 5g 5g 5m 5g² 6g⁵ 5m² 5g⁴ 6m 5m* 5m⁶ 6g 6m² 5.6m 6m 5f 5m 5.2g 5d⁶ 1992 5g 5m 5f² 5g⁶ 5f*ᵈⁱˢ 5.2d⁵ 5m 5.6m 5d 5.6m 5m 6m 6g] sturdy, compact gelding: carries condition: in-and-out form in handicaps in 1992: won at Haydock in July, but disqualified after failing a dope test: effective at 5f and 6f: best form on sound surface: won form when blinkered once: excellent mount for inexperienced rider: usually slowly away, and held up: very tough. *J. L. Spearing*

LUCHIROVERTE (IRE) 4 b.c. Slip Anchor 136 – Green Lucia 116 (Green **115** Dancer (USA) 132) [1991 11g⁶ 12.3d² 10g² 12m⁴ 12m 14.6m⁴ 1992 12g* 12g² 13.9m⁴ 16.4m⁵ 12f³ 12g² 16m⁵] lengthy, useful-looking colt: impresses in appearance: good walker and mover: smart and consistent performer: won Doncaster Shield in March: in frame in pattern company after, in Hardwicke Stakes (3½ lengths behind Rock Hopper) and Princess of Wales's Stakes (beaten 3 lengths by Saddlers' Hall) last 2 occasions: ran as if failing to stay in Goodwood Cup final start: stays 1¾m: acts on firm ground and dead. *C. E. Brittain*

LUCKIFOSOME 2 ch.f. (Apr 13) Smackover 107 – Spark Out (Sparkler 130) **45** [1992 5g⁴ 5s* 5g³ 5g⁴ 5g 6s⁶] leggy filly: first foal: dam probably of little account: poor performer: won maiden at Wolverhampton in April: good sixth in Ayr nursery: stays 5f: acts well on soft ground. *P. D. Evans*

LUCKNAM DREAMER 4 b.g. Macmillion 110 – River Damsel (Forlorn River **67** 124) [1991 7f³ 8d⁵ 8d 7d² 7m* 7g² 7.6g 1992 8s 8g⁵ 7.6g⁴ 7g 8d] tall, leggy gelding: fair performer: well beaten in handicaps last 2 starts: stays 1m: acts on good to firm ground and dead. *Mrs Barbara Waring*

LUCKNAM STYLE 4 b.g. Macmillion 110 – Mrs Currie 74 (He Loves Me 120) **37** [1991 6f⁶ 1992 8s 7f 7.6g 7d 6.1s a6g a7g⁶ a7g⁵ a8g⁶] leggy, sparely-made gelding: poor handicapper nowadays: stays 1m. *Mrs Barbara Waring*

LUCKY BARNES 5 b.g. Lucky Wednesday 124 – Hutton Barns 92 (Saintly Song **27** 128) [1991 NR 1992 8.3v 10.8d 9.2d 8.3m⁵ 11.9f 7.1m 7.6g 9.7d⁵] workmanlike gelding: moderate mover: inconsistent handicapper: stays 9.7f: acts on firm and dead ground: blinkered/visored: trained until after fifth start by P. Blockley. *F. J. Yardley*

LUCKY BLUE 5 b.g. Blue Cashmere 129 – Cooling 89 (Tycoon II) [1991 6g 1992 – a6g a6g a6g] workmanlike gelding: poor handicapper nowadays: stays 6f: acts on firm going: below form visored/blinkered: has joined R. Hodges. *J. C. Fox*

LUCKY GUEST 5 bl.h. Be My Guest (USA) 126 – Gay Fantasy (Troy 137) [1991 **95** 8g 8d 8g 8d 10m³ 10.8m* 9.5g* 10v 1992 10d 10g⁵ 10f 4.8.9f* 10.3f² 10.4d 10m⁶ 8.9m⁵ 9d 8g4] tall, attractive horse: impresses in appearance: has quick action: useful handicapper: won £8,400 event at York in June: good fourth to Inner City in Newmarket listed race final run: best at 1m to around 1¼m: acts on firm and dead ground: well below form when blinkered once: sometimes finds little: gets on edge and usually attended by 2 handlers: remains in training. *J. L. Dunlop*

LUCKY LINDY (IRE) 3 b.c. Trojan Fen 118 – Excruciating (CAN) (Bold **118** Forbes (USA)) [1991 7f⁴ 7g² 6.3s² 1992 8d* 8g² 8g 4 9.2d² 10m⁵ 10.3m⁵ 10d 8s⁴ 8.5s*]

The latest Two Thousand Guineas had a 50/1 runner-up in Lucky Lindy, from the same stable that sent out the 50/1-winner Mon Fils in 1973. Lucky Lindy was the apparently least-fancied of three Hannon runners, behind 20/1-shots River Falls and Swing Low. That pair had won important prizes as two-year-olds while Lucky Lindy had come within a head of winning the Goffs Premier Challenge Race, ending that season, however, still a maiden. Lucky Lindy's position in the pecking order was unchanged going into the Guineas even though he won his trial and the other two had both been beaten in theirs. Filling the minor places in the Greenham Stakes represented considerably better form than Lucky Lindy's win in Kempton's BonusPrint

Easter Stakes. Or so it appeared at the time. A one-and-a-half-length second of sixteen to Rodrigo de Triano showed that Lucky Lindy had been underestimated, and the Easter Stakes third Silver Wisp was only about a length further behind in fourth. Lucky Lindy's was a very genuine performance though not one that ever threatened to upstage Rodrigo de Triano; he was under strong pressure to keep in touch from before the three-furlong marker and responded willingly, finally emerging best in the battle for second close home. Two weeks later, in the Irish Two Thousand Guineas at the Curragh, Lucky Lindy had the chance to prove that that was no fluke, little chance though, realistically, of reversing form with Rodrigo de Triano. For our money, even though his margin of defeat was doubled and he had to settle for fourth—the Easter Stakes second, Ezzoud, also finished second here—Lucky Lindy ran every bit as well at the Curragh as he had at Newmarket, his reduced standing explained by the progress of his rivals. That was pretty well the story of Lucky Lindy's season. Nowadays the Guineas do not play much part in the end-of-season standings of the top three-year-olds and Lucky Lindy could not improve on those two performances in May. He put up several other smart efforts in the months that followed, notably when a narrowly-beaten second to Kitwood in the Prix Jean Prat at Longchamp, but it was October and the Grosser Preis von Dusseldorf, in which he finished two and a half lengths clear of Irish Source, before Lucky Lindy won again.

One legitimate disappointment with Lucky Lindy's season was that he failed to show he stays a mile and a quarter: on several occasions we thought he would be suited by it. However, he has now had three runs at the trip—in the Prince of Wales's Stakes at Royal Ascot, a £13,000 contest at Doncaster and the Select Stakes at Goodwood—putting up only a fair effort on the first occasion and some way below his best on the others. The first two of those races coming on top-of-the-ground suggested that underfoot conditions might well have been the explanation, but at Goodwood the going was good to soft. A factual summary of Lucky Lindy's racing record is that he stays nine furlongs and has put up his best efforts on an easy surface. He ran fairly well in blinkers on his penultimate start when fourth to Arazi in the Prix du Rond-Point.

The efforts of Lucky Lindy have come much too late to boost the fortunes of Queen Anne Stakes winner Trojan Fen at stud; he was exported to India in 1989 and died in 1992. The nearest Lucky Lindy's dam Excruciating came to winning in four outings in Irish middle-distance maidens was ten and three quarter lengths. Three of her four previous foals failed to make much of an impression either, but it's not surprising that Richard Hannon bought

BonusPrint Easter Stakes, Kempton—Lucky Lindy (No. 6), Ezzoud and Silver Wisp (No. 3)

			Troy	Petingo
	Trojan Fen		(b 1976)	La Milo
	(b 1981)		Fenella	Thatch
Lucky Lindy (IRE)			(b 1975)	Abanilla
(b.c. 1989)			Bold Forbes	Irish Castle
	Excruciating (CAN)		(b 1973)	Comely Nell
	(b 1979)		Crucial Decision	Damascus
			(ch 1974)	Slapton Sands

Lucky Lindy (for 21,000 Irish guineas) as a yearling, for the one that did win
was the useful Hard Act (by Hard Fought) whom Hannon trained to win four
races carrying the same colours, including a seven-furlong Irish listed
contest. After Trojan Fen, Excruciating visited Prince Rupert, Al Hareb and
Gadabout. The grandam Crucial Decision was well related, being a half-sister
to that good-class but idiosyncratic colt Riboboy and the smart French filly
Sea Sands, but her own experience of the racecourse and the paddocks was
incomplete; having shown fairly useful form as a two-year-old, she was pulled
up in the Musidora Stakes on her only appearance at three and had just two
foals. *R. Hannon*

LUCKY MILL 2 b.f. (Mar 8) Midyan (USA) 124 – Frasquita (Song 132) [1992 5d **50**
5g⁴ 5m] 13,500Y: good-topped filly: has scope: moderate mover: second foal: dam
unraced sister to smart sprinter Jester: easily best effort in maidens when fourth of
6 at York in May: off course over 4 months after. *F. H. Lee*

LUCKY NOIRE 4 b.f. Aragon 118 – Noire Small (USA) (Elocutionist (USA)) **69**
[1991 8m³ 10.1g 10m⁵ 8g⁴ 7.6d³ 9.7s 8f* 8.3m³ 8.3g* 7m 8.3m* 8m³ 8.1m 8g 1992
a7g⁶ 9d 7g⁴ 8m 8.1m 8.1m⁴ 8.3g 7.6m* 7f⁵ 7.6m 7d⁵ 8d³ 8g 9s³ 9.7v 9g 8v* 9.7v*]
good-topped filly: modest handicapper: won at Lingfield in July and Newcastle
(claiming event) and Folkestone in November: effective from 7f to 9f: acts on any
going: sometimes bandaged/wears net muzzle: rather headstrong but successful for
claimer: held up. *G. Harwood*

LUCKY OWL 2 ch.f. (May 24) Indian Forest (USA) 117 – Heldigvis 63 (Hot **41**
Grove 128) [1992 5s 6d 6f 5f⁵ 7m 7.1g² 7.1f* 7g⁵ 7g⁶ 7.5m 7d] small, sparely-made
filly: lacks scope: moderate walker: fourth foal: half-sister to 3-y-o 12.1f to 13.8f
winner Grouse-N-Heather (by Grey Desire): dam 2-y-o 7f and 1m winner: plater:
won 4-runner race at Edinburgh in July: well beaten last 2 starts: stays 7f: acts on
firm ground: sometimes gives trouble stalls. *Miss L. A. Perratt*

LUCKY PARKES 2 b.f. (Mar 12) Full Extent (USA) 113 – Summerhill Spruce 70 **89** p
(Windjammer (USA)) [1992 5d* 5g* 5.1g* 5f⁵ 5m² 5m*] lengthy, workmanlike filly:

Ripon Horn Blower Stakes—Lucky Parkes (No. 3) improves to beat Ansellman

progressed well physically: good walker: second living foal: half-sister to a winner in Holland by Jupiter Island: dam 6f winner: progressed with every run: successful in 2 minor events at Catterick and Lily Agnes Stakes (ran lazily) at Chester in early season and in competitive minor event (by neck from Ansellman) at Ripon in August: speedy front runner: tends to edge left but is thoroughly genuine. *J. Berry*

LUCY DANCER (IRE) 4 ch.f. No Pass No Sale 120 – Daoulas (Thatching 131) **55**
[1991 6g3 6m6 5s3 5g 5.1g 5f5 a5g a7g a8g 1992 5s 5d3 5.1d 5f2 5.1m4 5.1g 5m2 5g6 5m] compact filly: poor mover: inconsistent handicapper: effective at 5f and 6f: acts on any going: effective visored or not: sold 920 gns Doncaster September Sales. *C. G. Cox*

LUGHNASA 2 b.f. (Apr 29) Lochnager 132 – Lardana 65 (Burglar 128) [1992 5g] –
1,500Y: sister to modest sprinter The Mechanic and half-sister to 2 winners, including 1990 2-y-o 5f and 6f winner Access Holidays (by Faustus): dam 9f winner: burly and very green in median auction maiden at Windsor in August: withdrawn lame at start following month. *J. J. Bridger*

LUKS AKURA 4 b.g. Dominion 123 – Pacificus (USA) 65 (Northern Dancer) **49**
[1991 a8g3 a10g5 12.3s 8.2f4 8f4 8g* 7g 8m2 7g3 8d6 8g 8f 8m3 1992 a10g a8g5 a10g6 a10g 10.1s4 10d 13.8m 12f* 13f* 15.1m6 12f4 12g3 12.4f6 12.1m2 16.2s4 12f2 12f 14g 12.1s 13.8d5 12g] small, sturdy gelding: successful in summer handicaps at Carlisle and Hamilton: stays 13f: probably acts on any going: below form blinkered, visored nowadays: not easiest of rides but successful for claimer: front runner: tough but unreliable. *M. Johnston*

LUMBERJACK (USA) 8 b.g. Big Spruce (USA) – Snip (Shantung 132) [1991 **60**
NR 1992 13d6] close-coupled gelding: rated 83 + as 5-y-o: still retains ability judged on sixth in handicap at Hamilton in May: stays 13f: acts on any going: won over fences in October and November: sold to join C. Egerton 21,000 gns Doncaster November Sales. *J. G. FitzGerald*

LUNA BID 9 b.g. Auction Ring (USA) 123 – Moonscape 87 (Ribero 126) [1991 6m **65**
6g5 6g3 6g4 6d* 6.1m3 6g4 6m 6d4 6m 6g 6g 6m 6g 6d3 6m6 7g 7g4 7d 1992 6d 6s2 6s 6g2 6f 6.1m3 6g 6.1m 6g6 6d5 6m5 6g* 6m 6g 6m 6d 6.1m 6.1d] good-topped gelding: carries plenty of condition: turns fore-feet in markedly: poor mover: inconsistent handicapper: won at Yarmouth in July: best form at 6f: has form on good to firm ground, but seems ideally suited by some give: has reportedly broken blood vessels: usually gets behind. *M. Blanshard*

LUNAGRAPHE (USA) 4 ch.f. Time For A Change (USA) – Lightship (USA) –
(Majestic Light (USA)) [1991 11g 10.7g 9s6 8v 1992 a10g 8.5f a7g a7g a8g4 a12g] $100,000Y: leggy, sparely-made ex-French filly: first foal: dam unraced half-sister to high-class 7f to 9f winner in USA Polish Navy: ran 4 times in France (including in Provinces) for F. Boutin: no worthwhile form here, including in handicaps: looks headstrong. *Bob Jones*

LUNAR RISK 2 b.c. (Feb 15) Risk Me (FR) 127 – Moonlight Princess 49 (Alias **54**
Smith (USA)) [1992 7g 8s6 8d] 7,000Y: good-bodied colt: first foal: dam 10.8f seller winner: plating-class form in maidens at Bath and Leicester final 2 starts: may well stay beyond 1m. *W. R. Muir*

L'UOMO CLASSICS 5 b.g. Indian King (USA) 128 – Sperrin Mist 83 (Camden **66**
Town 125) [1991 8.2m3 8d5 1992 10m6 11.5m3 10s* 11.4g 12s5] big, good-topped gelding: keen walker: moderate mover: modest handicapper: won at Salisbury in September: stays 1½m: acts on good to firm ground and soft: worth a try in blinkers/ visor. *R. Rowe*

LUPESCU 4 ch.f. Dixieland Band (USA) – Keep Me Posted (USA) (Stage Door **102**
Johnny) [1991 10m* 10g* 10.5v3] lengthy, good-topped filly: has a fluent, rather round action: good walker: led post when short-head winner from Fair Average of slowly-run listed event at Newmarket in October, first run for present trainer: good third of 11 to Halesia in Group 3 Prix Fille de l'Air at Saint-Cloud following month: will stay 1½m. *D. R. Loder*

LUST OF LOVE 6 b.m. Sallust 134 – Aridje 79 (Mummy's Pet 125) [1991 7m* –
7f* 7m 7m4 7g 7m 1992 7f 7m] leggy, rather sparely-made mare: poor walker and mover: rated 66 at 5 yrs: below form in 1992: stays 7f: has gone well on top-of-the-ground: ran moderately when blinkered once: sold 1,500 gns Doncaster August Sales. *Mrs V. A. Aconley*

LUSTY LAD 7 b.g. Decoy Boy 129 – Gluhwein (Ballymoss 136) [1991 NR 1992 –
a13g] rather sparely-made gelding: modest handicapper as 3-y-o: lightly raced since and long way below his best: stays 7f: acts on firm going: hooded once at 4 yrs: winning hurdler (has reportedly broke blood vessel). *M. J. Haynes*

476

LUTHIOR (FR) 6 gr.g. Carwhite 127 – Luthiana (FR) (Luthier 126) [1991 12g 9m — 1992 a12g] leggy ex-French gelding: moderate walker: has a rather round action: no form on flat in last 2 seasons: stays 1½m: acts on good to firm and dead ground. *Mrs M. E. Long*

LUZUM 8 ch.g. Touching Wood (USA) 127 – Velvet Habit 89 (Habitat 134) [1991 **69 d** a8g4 a8g 9s 8f4 7m 1992 a7g4 a8g a7g 7g] small, sturdy gelding: moderate mover: very much on the downgrade. *J. A. Glover*

LYCIAN MOON 3 b.f. Norwick (USA) 120 – Brigannie Moon (Brigadier Gerard — 144) [1991 NR 1992 10d 10.2f5 11.7d] unfurnished filly: third living foal: dam unraced twin: no worthwhile form: sold out of J. Dunlop's stable 925 gns Ascot July Sales after second start. *Mrs J. C. Dawe*

LYFORD CAY (IRE) 2 gr.c. (Apr 25) Waajib 121 – Island Goddess (Godswalk **78 p** (USA) 130) [1992 8.1s2 7s2 7s*] 16,000Y: good-topped colt: fluent mover: second foal: dam, from family of Juliette Marny and Julio Mariner, ran once at 2 yrs in Ireland: promising second, caught near line, in maidens before justifying favouritism by 1½ lengths in York auction event, confidently ridden: should stay 1¼m: should improve. *P. W. Chapple-Hyam*

LYNDON'S LINNET 4 b.g. Prince Sabo 123 – Miss Rossi (Artaius (USA) 129) **60** [1991 10.8g 6f2 6g2 5m* 6m3 5m5 6g4 6g6 6m a6g 1992 5g3 6.1m 5.1g a6g 5g6] lengthy, plain gelding: modest sprint handicapper: acts on firm ground, yet to race on a soft surface: below form when blinkered penultimate start. *R. Ingram*

LYN'S RETURN (IRE) 3 b.c. Nordico (USA) – Salmas (FR) (Right Royal V **63** 135) [1991 7d3 7g 8m3 9m 8.9m 8m 1992 8s5 8.2d5 10g* 12g5 12g* 12g5 12m5 8.5d3 8g2 10g6 8m6 8f 11d4 10d* 13.8g2 10.5d5 12s4 11v5] small colt: modest performer: won seller (bought in 4,400 gns) at Nottingham in April and claimers at Goodwood in May and September: stays 1¾m: acts on good to firm and dead ground: ran creditably for apprentice. *R. Simpson*

LYPHANTASTIC (USA) 3 b.c. Lyphard's Wish (FR) 124 – Tango Five Juliet **85 p** (USA) (Fappiano (USA)) [1991 NR 1992 9.7m* 12f*] second foal: half-brother to North American winner Dance To The Band (by Key To The Mint): dam unraced: won maiden at Folkestone and handicap (made all, by 3½ lengths) at Salisbury in June: stays 1½m: remains in training. *M. R. Stoute*

LYPHARD'S SONG (IRE) 4 b.f. Lyphard's Special (USA) 122 – Supreme **35** Song (Supreme Sovereign 119) [1991 12m4 12g4 10m 15.8g 15.1s 1992 15.1f5 18.8m4 16m6 16m] long-backed filly: inconsistent staying handicapper: acts on firm ground: below form when blinkered. *N. A. Graham*

LYPH (USA) 6 b.g. Lypheor 118 – Scottish Lass (Scotland) [1991 NR 1992 a10g4] — good-quartered gelding: well beaten twice for J. Gosden at 3 yrs: never-nearer fourth in maiden claimer at Lingfield in December, 1992. *P. R. Hedger*

LYRIC FANTASY (IRE) 2 b.f. (Jan 30) Tate Gallery (USA) 117 – Flying **115** Melody (Auction Ring (USA) 123) [1992 5m* 5m* 5f* 5.2d* 5m* 6m2]
More than any other horse it seemed, Lyric Fantasy kept the headline writers busy in 1992. Her name was rarely off the front page from the time she won the Queen Mary Stakes at Royal Ascot by the widest margin for twenty-one years to the time her unraced four-year-old half-sister was sold in bizarre circumstances at Goffs in December. She was the first two-year-old to win the Nunthorpe Stakes for thirty-six years, and became the third-highest-priced two-year-old in training when sold for 340,000 guineas at the Newmarket December Sales in front of the biggest crowd seen at Park Paddocks all year. While Lyric Fantasy—five victories from six starts, including also in the Newbury Sales Super Sprint Trophy, the race she was bought with a view to winning—wasn't the brilliant filly the Press built her up to be, her contribution to the season was undeniably immense. For many racing enthusiasts she lit up the summer, and whatever direction her three-year-old career takes—and it's asking an awful lot for her to do as well again—her achievements at two have already ensured her place in racing folklore.

Lyric Fantasy first burst into the view of the wider racing public when she stormed away with the Queen Mary Stakes at Royal Ascot in June on her third start of the season. However, if her half-length defeat of previous winners Ancestral Dancer and Sheila's Secret in a minor event on a Monday evening at Windsor in April had passed virtually without comment, her six-length slamming of the newcomer Hazy Kay (with Ancestral Dancer another length behind in third) in a fast time in the listed Winalot National Stakes at another night meeting at Sandown in May hadn't, and she was the subject of a gamble for the Queen Mary, eventually starting favourite at 11/8 having been available at 9/4 in the morning. Lyric Fantasy rewarded her supporters with a marvellous performance. Soon blazing the trail after a smart break, she set such a gallop that it was all her rivals could do by halfway to keep themselves in touch, and from that point she was devastating: requiring virtually no assistance from her rider Roberts, who later claimed he'd never gone so fast, she powered further and further clear until she was allowed to ease down in the last fifty yards to win in tremendous style. Left trailing at least six and a quarter lengths (it was officially given as five) behind were ten previous winners, headed by Mystic Goddess and Toocando, who just over two weeks later made a good race of it with Sayyedati in the Cherry Hinton at Newmarket; ten lengths back in fourth came the subsequent Princess Margaret winner Marina Park. While praise was lavished upon Lyric Fantasy's performance—even the normally guarded Tony Morris, writing in the *Racing Post*, called it 'quite the most impressive thing I have ever seen accomplished by a two-year-old'—too much was made of it, as well of the fact that she became the first youngster to crack a minute over Ascot's stiff five furlongs. Her track record was one of four that were established the same afternoon, which, if nothing else, indicates that conditions were ideal for the setting of fast times. The actual *time value* of Lyric Fantasy's victory, the only credible assessment of the merit of her performance on the clock, arrived at after quantifying and then compensating for the effects of such factors as track and weather conditions, weight-for-age, race distance and standard times, was a hardly-exceptional 103.

Four weeks later Lyric Fantasy ran clean away with the recently-inaugurated Newbury Sales Super Sprint Trophy, worth almost £60,000 to the winner. The 'Super Sprint' was devised by Lyric Fantasy's then-owner Lord Carnarvon in the wake of the huge interest aroused amongst owners and trainers by the sales-related concept of the Racecall Gold Trophy at Redcar. Unlike the Redcar race, which is open to any two-year-old and is run over six furlongs at the end of the season, the 'Super Sprint' is run over an extended five furlongs in July and is confined to those two-year-olds who were sold as yearlings at selected sales for 30,000 guineas or less. The initial running of the race in 1991 proved a great success with a good field and an exciting finish which went the way of the subsequent Flying Childers winner Paris House. The number of runners might have been on the disappointing side again in 1992—only eleven went to post—but there was no call for the skills of the

Queen Mary Stakes, Royal Ascot—
a breathtaking display by Lyric Fantasy, who wins by five lengths in record time

Newbury Sales Super Sprint, Newbury—5/2 on, and another one-sided affair

judge on this occasion: Lyric Fantasy, who had been bought on behalf of Newbury racecourse chairman Carnarvon for 12,500 guineas, cantered home with six lengths to spare. Starting a heavily-backed 5/2-on shot in spite of the well-publicized fear of her trainer that she wasn't likely to be suited by the good to soft ground—she'd raced only on good to firm or firm ground to that point—Lyric Fantasy showed that dead ground didn't inconvenience her in the slightest with another dazzling front-running performance. Having started less sharply than usual—she'd been the first to be loaded, and had been in the stalls a rather long time—Lyric Fantasy was soon showing her opponents a distant pair of heels and had all bar the top-weight Joyofracing off the bridle after a couple of furlongs. Keeping up the gallop in tremendous fashion, Lyric Fantasy had Joyofracing stone cold as well soon after halfway, and by the time Aradanza and Lyric Fantasy's stable-companion Princely Favour had come through to fill the minor placings, the filly had started pulling up with the race well and truly won.

The next stop on Lyric Fantasy's agenda, as it had been for Paris House, was a crack at her elders in the Keeneland Nunthorpe Stakes at York in August. In a quote given to the *Racing Post* after her win in the 'Super Sprint', Paris House's trainer Berry, drawing on his own experience, said that he couldn't see how Lyric Fantasy could be beaten at York. Paris House, of course, had finished a highly creditable second to Sheikh Albadou in 1991, giving best to the subsequent Breeders' Cup Sprint winner only in the last sixty yards after a bold attempt to become the first of his age since Ennis in 1956 to be successful. Lyric Fantasy's prospects of going one better than Paris House were very good. Her form was superior, she had less weight to carry, notwithstanding the small amount of overweight Roberts would have to put up, and, most importantly of all, perhaps, she didn't have Sheikh Albadou to contend with. With Paris House, whose form had been rather in-and-out in the intervening year, third-placed Blyton Lad and fifth-placed Elbio surviving from the 1991 running, the principal dangers to Lyric Fantasy seemed to be her five-year-old stable-companion Mr Brooks, who'd finished ahead of Sheikh Albadou, Elbio (fourth) and Paris House (fifth) when successful in the July Cup, and the progressive three-year-old Freddie Lloyd, who'd beaten Blyton Lad narrowly in the King George Stakes at Goodwood earlier in August for his third win on the trot. In the paddock the small, sturdy, good-quartered Lyric Fantasy—so tiny as a yearling, apparently, that she frequently got stuck under the horsewalker at the stable where she was reared—looked no match for the bigger, more powerful older sprinters, but both she and the jockey, who managed to ride at 7-8, 4 lb less than his usual minimum, responded bravely to the challenge. Lyric Fantasy didn't try to run her rivals off their feet in the manner that saw Paris House fail gallantly the year before, but kept company with the Canadian challenger Diamonds Galore a length and a half behind the pace-setting Freddie Lloyd until beginning her forward move at halfway. When pushed into the lead with a furlong and a half to run Lyric Fantasy quickened immediately and, without being subjected to maximum pressure, ran on strongly to hold the late challenge of Mr Brooks comfortably by half a length, Diamonds Galore staying on to finish a length and a half behind in third. Lyric Fantasy's Nunthorpe victory was one of the highlights in a magnificent season for her remarkable trainer Hannon, who dominated the trainers' championship, and for Roberts, who became champion for the first time in Britain after a very successful career in South Africa.

479

Hannon's large and busy stable not only produced more winners than any other—one hundred and forty-seven in all during the turf season—but also finished ahead of the established top stables in first-prize-money earnings. The winners came thick and fast too for the indefatigable Roberts who, from a record-breaking 1,068 rides, became only the second jockey to score a double century of winners in a flat season since the era of Gordon Richards. Roberts' total of two hundred and six winners was three short of the figure achieved by Eddery in 1990.

Lyric Fantasy's tremendous run of success in the summer seemed to persuade many commentators that she was one of the outstanding racehorses of all time. She was constantly referred to as the 'modern-day Mumtaz Mahal', and many within the sport went on record as saying that she was the fastest filly they'd ever seen. We are unable to rate her quite so highly. While her wide-margin victories against her own age-group in the National Stakes, Queen Mary Stakes and 'Super Sprint' were undoubtedly impressive to the eye, and do indeed represent a high level of merit not surpassed by any other British-trained two-year-old over the distance all year, they don't, even if a generous allowance is made for the ease with which she won each of those races, represent the outstanding level of achievement that her many support-ers would have us believe. The most conclusive proof that Lyric Fantasy wasn't a brilliant sprinting two-year-old was provided, paradoxically, by the result of the Nunthorpe, the race which to many seemed to seal her claim to greatness. The fact that Lyric Fantasy became the first two-year-old filly to win the Nunthorpe since its inception in 1922 and only the fourth two-year-old in all, following also High Treason in 1953 and My Beau in 1954, might put her achievement into a historical perspective, but it tells us little about the ability she needed to show to win the race. She was favoured to the tune of approximately 6 lb (ignoring the sex allowance) or two lengths by the official weight-for-age scale and strictly on that basis comes out a worse horse at the weights than Mr Brooks, Diamonds Galore, Elbio and Freddie Lloyd; and she emerged only a 7-lb better horse than the eased-up Paris House, and only a 10-lb better horse than Farfelu, no-one's idea of a top-class sprinter. There's no disputing that Lyric Fantasy was a very good filly over five furlongs as a two-year-old, good enough certainly to be considered at least on a par with the best sprinting two-year-old fillies in recent years, but even at her best, she can't be rated the outstanding youngster that her public relations machine, official and unofficial, constantly made out.

The immediate talk after the Nunthorpe was that Lyric Fantasy would be sent to France for the Prix de l'Abbaye at Longchamp on Arc day, but in the event she was supplemented into the Cheveley Park at Newmarket at the end of September to set up an eagerly-awaited clash with the Cherry Hinton and Moyglare Stud Stakes winner Sayyedati. Lyric Fantasy, chosen by Roberts in preference to Sayyedati whom he had partnered to both pattern-race victories, was given top billing in the build-up to the race, but it was Sayyedati who stole the glory after making all the running for a comprehen-sive and fully-deserved victory. Lyric Fantasy, who didn't look nearly so well in herself as earlier in the season, being dull and patchy over her quarters, was ridden in much the same fashion as had served her well in the Nunthorpe, and tracked Sayyedati as the 9/4 second favourite—Lyric Fantasy started at 2/1-on, in spite of stamina worries on her first attempt at six furlongs—set a modest pace until quickening the gallop approaching halfway. Such tactics could reasonably have been expected to favour Lyric Fantasy rather than the stoutly-bred Sayyedati, but it was Lyric Fantasy who came off the bridle first as Sayyedati kept increasing the pace in front, and despite fighting on well to get within a length at the furlong-pole she had no more to offer in the last hundred and fifty yards as Sayyedati stretched her lead to two lengths at the line. In that she looked second-best from halfway Lyric Fantasy's perform-ance was a disappointing one, but the result—the Flying Childers winner Poker Chip was a length and a half back in third, the only other runner Anonymous well back in fourth—doesn't discredit her, and we can't believe that she failed to stay the sixth furlong or ran much below her best. Hannon suggested afterwards that she might have fared better had she made the running, but we don't feel that different tactics would have significantly

Keeneland Nunthorpe Stakes, York—a pat down the neck for Lyric Fantasy as she beats her elders; Mr Brooks (blaze) is second, the Canadian challenger Diamonds Galore (right) is third

altered the result. The better filly won on the day, and Roberts probably hinted as much when, in one of his post-race comments, he revealed that 'Sayyedati is the best filly I have sat on with a view to next year's classics'.

Lyric Fantasy is from the third crop of the Northern Dancer stallion Tate Gallery, who died in 1990 in transit from Coolmore Stud to Heathrow from where he was due to be flown to take up stallion duties in Japan. Tate Gallery spent his life very much in the shadow of his older brother Sadler's Wells, both on the racecourse and in his short time at stud. Although capable of smart form as a racehorse, as he showed when winning the National Stakes at the Curragh as a two-year-old, Tate Gallery proved something of a morning glory and wasn't raced again after trailing home last of fifteen in Dancing Brave's Two Thousand Guineas. Though he's had the odd good runner at stud, he's not hit the heights as a stallion, either. Strangely enough, given that the vast majority of Sadler's Wells's numerous high-class representatives have needed at least a mile and a quarter to show their form, Tate Gallery's only pattern winners have come at sprint distances: besides Lyric Fantasy, he's also the sire of the 1991 King George Stakes winner Title Roll. Perhaps it's not altogether surprising that Lyric Fantasy turned out to be a sprinter, though; the three mares on the bottom line of her pedigree were all best over five or six furlongs, and her great grandam Peggy West was a half-sister to the legendary Pappa Fourway. Lyric Fantasy's dam Flying Melody, who is now in the ownership of the Al-Maktoum family, was a useful performer on the racetrack in France. She looked a smart prospect when she won her only race as a two-year-old, but any classic pretensions she had were destroyed when she could finish only a remote fourth in the seven-furlong Prix Imprudence early the following season, after which she spent most of her time in sprints, eventually winning a race for gentleman riders over six and a half furlongs at Evry. Lyric Fantasy is her sixth foal (she's since had a colt by Al Hareb, sold for 33,000 guineas at the recent Houghton Yearling Sales) and third winner, following the fair northern sprinter Mere Melody (by Dunphy) and the exported Flying Monarch (by Tender King), who has found the competition much less demanding in Italy after failing to win in selling company over here. Although one of the grandam Whispering Star's half-sisters threw the high-class miler Mr Fluorocarbon and the Cornwallis winner Western Jewel, and Whispering Star herself foaled the very useful racemare and broodmare Pearl Star as well as the very useful miler Portese, this isn't a top-class family by any means, and even with her racing record it's rather surprising that Lyric Fantasy should have fetched 340,000 guineas when sold at Tattersalls just two years after she went through the same sale ring for only 3,300 guineas as a foal. In what was a bizarre postscript to her own sale, Lyric Fantasy's unbroken four-year-old half-sister Fantasy To Reality (by Jester) was apparently sold for IR 92,000 guineas at Goffs Bloodstock Sales at Kill in December just a week after vanishing in mysterious fashion from the farm in Surrey where she had been boarded since her arrival from Ireland two months previously. At the time of writing the circumstances surrounding her disappearance from the farm in Surrey are being investigated by the local constabulary, and the issue of the filly's ownership has been taken to the High Court in Dublin.

Lyric Fantasy (IRE) (b.f. Jan 30, 1990)	Tate Gallery (USA) (b 1983)	Northern Dancer (b 1961)	Nearctic
			Natalma
		Fairy Bridge (b 1975)	Bold Reason
			Special
	Flying Melody (b 1979)	Auction Ring (b 1972)	Bold Bidder
			Hooplah
		Whispering Star (ch 1963)	Sound Track
			Peggy West

Following Lyric Fantasy's sale to an international consortium of businessmen, she has been returned to Hannon's stable and will reportedly be prepared for the One Thousand Guineas. Her connections have little to lose and much to gain from adopting such an attacking policy, but her classic prospects don't look good. Lyric Fantasy's main assets as a two-year-old were her precocity and her tremendous early pace, and although she got the sixth furlong well enough in the Cheveley Park she didn't finish the race in the manner of one who'd be suited by seven furlongs, let alone a mile. And being on the small size as well, with six races behind her already, there seems no reason why she should make the more-than-normal improvement required to force her way into contenton. It would be for the undoubted good of racing if she does—and here's hoping—but it may be that her best days are already behind her. *R. Hannon*

LYS (IRE) 2 ch.f. (Mar 31) Don't Forget Me 127 – Lycia (Targowice (USA) 130) **67**
[1992 6g 6m* 6d 7m] IR 45,000Y: smallish, leggy filly: half-sister to Irish 7f to 1¼m winner Rare Chic (by Henbit): dam won at up to 9f in Ireland: ran moderately in nurseries after winning 4-runner minor event at Lingfield in August: should stay 1m. *C. E. Brittain*

LYSIRRA (USA) 3 ch.f. Lyphard (USA) 132 – Hopespringsforever (USA) 82 (Mr –
Prospector (USA)) [1991 7g 1992 7g 8g] lengthy, good-topped filly: thrice raced, and poor form in maidens: not seen out after May: visits Anshan. *B. W. Hills*

M

MAAMUR (USA) 4 gr.g. Robellino (USA) 127 – Tiger Trap (USA) 80 (Al Hattab **71**
(USA)) [1991 10.2s² 11g² 12g 1992 a12g* 12.3v³ 16.2s⁵ 12g²a14g³] big, good-bodied gelding: carries condition: fluent mover: fair handicapper: straightforward task in Southwell maiden in March: should prove as effective at 2m as 1½m: yet to race on top-of-the-ground: progressive winning hurdler. *D. Burchell*

MAASTRICHT 2 b.g. (Apr 22) Common Grounds 118 – Awatef (Ela-Mana-Mou **68**
132) [1992 8m 8.2s a7g] 11,000Y: workmanlike gelding: moderate mover: third foal: half-brother to 3-y-o Italian 1m winner Daja (by Doulab), 7f winner here at 2 yrs: dam poor French maiden from good family: best effort in autumn maiden at Newmarket on debut: soundly beaten at Nottingham and in Southwell claimer, where helped set too strong a pace. *W. J. Haggas*

MABAADI (USA) 2 b. or br.c. (Mar 25) Kris S (USA) – Faultless Too (USA) –
(Tudor Grey 119) [1992 7g] $65,000Y: seventh foal: half-brother to 5 winners, including Grade 2 9f winner Faultless Ensign (by Blue Ensign): dam sprint winner in USA at 3 and 4 yrs: sire minor stakes winner at up to 9f, making a better sire: 10/1 and backward, last of 14 in maiden at Doncaster in October. *M. A. Jarvis*

MA BELLA LUNA 3 b.f. Jalmood (USA) 126 – Macarte (FR) (Gift Card (FR) **76**
124) [1991 7g⁵ 8.1g⁴ 1992 8d* 8.9d³ 8m³ 10.3g] sturdy filly: fair form: made all in

median auction maiden at Carlisle in April: ran well when placed in handicaps: will prove better at 1¼m (had been off course 3 months, and was hampered, when tried) than shorter: acts on good to firm and dead ground. *J. L. Dunlop*

MABONNE   3 b.f. King of Spain 121 – Monsarah 63 (Monsanto (FR) 121) [1991 6s   **51** 6d4 6f3 1992 6m6 7g 6.9m 7g3 7.6m 7m 7.1s a7g] leggy filly: good walker: modest maiden: inconsistent in handicaps in 1992: acts on firm going: below form when blinkered/visored last 3 starts: sold 1,600 gns Newmarket Autumn Sales. *J. L. Dunlop*

MABTHUL (USA)   4 b.g. Northern Baby (CAN) 127 – Persuadable (USA) (What   **– §** A Pleasure (USA)) [1991 7g 10f 10.6m 1992 10d 12.3g 8.3g] big, rangy gelding: no form since 2 yrs: tried blinkered once: has joined K. Bailey: not one to trust. *M. J. Heaton-Ellis*

MACFARLANE   4 br.g. Kala Shikari 125 – Tarvie 101 (Swing Easy (USA) 126)   **74** [1991 6m3 5d* 6g 5.1d 5g4 6m 5d 6.1d2 5.2g5 5g4 1992 5.2d2 5g3 5.1m 6d6 6m 5s4 5.2s] stocky, lengthy gelding: poor mover: fair handicapper: off course over 3½ months and blinkered, well beaten final start: stays 6f: best efforts on dead ground: has worn tongue strap: hung markedly left once at 4 yrs. *M. J. Fetherston-Godley*

MACK THE KNIFE   3 b.c. Kris 135 – The Dancer (FR) 122 (Green Dancer **112** (USA) 132) [1991 6m2 7g* 7.1m4 8d2 8g2 1992 9g 12.3g3 11.6g* 14.6m5 12.1d* 12s4] strong, close-coupled colt: has a round action: very useful performer: made most to win minor events at Windsor in August and Chepstow in October: made best efforts when 10½ lengths fifth of 7 to User Friendly in St Leger at Doncaster (led till 3f out and eased) and 3 lengths fourth of 8 to Up Anchor in St Simon Stakes at Newbury: not certain to stay beyond 14.6f: acts on good to firm and soft ground: genuine. *Major W. R. Hern*

MAC RAMBLER   5 b.g. Hotfoot 126 – Arkengarthdale (Sweet Story 122) [1991   **30** 8g4 10.2s 10d a11g6 10.5d 13.8m 1992 13d 10.5g4 12.3d3] poor handicapper and still a maiden: retained 4,700 gns Doncaster March Sales before reappearance: stays 1½m: acts on dead ground. *N. Bycroft*

MACROBIAN   8 b.g. Bay Express 132 – White Domino 67 (Sharpen Up 127)   **98** [1991 5m 5g 6f6 6d6 6.1g3 6m2 6g* 6g2 1992 5d3 5m2 6f1] good-bodied gelding: has had operation for soft palate: useful and consistent handicapper: narrowly beaten in quite valuable events at York in May and in June: effective at 5f and 6f: best on a sound surface: tried visored and blinkered earlier in career: game front runner. *M. H. Easterby*

MAC'S FIGHTER   7 ch.h. Hard Fought 125 – Geoffrey's Sister (Sparkler 130)   **82** [1991 6g5 7m 6g 6g 7m 7m 6m 8g a7g4 a8g4 a6g* 1992 a8g4 a7g2 a8g3 a7g3 a6g2   **a89** 6g 7g6 6m3] compact horse: moderate mover: only a fairly useful handicapper nowadays: generally ran consistently in 1992: effective from 6f to 1m: possibly unsuited by soft going, acts on any other: often blinkered or visored: not seen after May and has joined R. O'Sullivan. *W. A. O'Gorman*

MAC'S PRINCESS (USA)   4 b.f. Sovereign Dancer (USA) – Jungle Princess   **62** (USA) (Jungle Road) [1991 a7g2 a8g3 7m 8g2 8m 9g a8g3 a8g2 a7g a8g3 1992 a8g4 a8g2 a8g2 a8g6 a7g3 a7g2] smallish, workmanlike filly: modest handicapper, still a maiden: better at 1m than shorter nowadays: goes well on fibresand: rather an awkward ride: not seen after February: has been covered by Damister. *W. A. O'Gorman*

MAC THE LAD   3 ch.g. Rabdan 129 – Halkissimo 61 (Khalkis 127) [1991 NR 1992   **–** 8f] small, sparely-made gelding: half-brother to winners including useful 1989 2-y-o 5f to 1m winner Champagne Gold (by Bairn), fair middle-distance handicapper Mac's Delight (by Scottish Rifle) and several winning jumpers: dam best at around 1m: 20/1, soon tailed off as if something amiss in maiden at Thirsk in May: has been gelded. *Denys Smith*

MAC TOMB   2 b.c. (May 3) Valiyar 129 – Elaine Ann 66 (Garda's Revenge (USA)   **–** 119) [1992 6m 6m 7m 6m] 500 (privately) Y: small colt: fourth foal: dam 6f winner: seems of little account. *K. O. Cunningham-Brown*

MADAGANS GREY   4 gr.g. Carwhite 127 – Cheri Berry 87 (Air Trooper 115)   **75 §** [1991 8d5 a12g3 16g 16.2g4 14.8m5 13.9g 16d* 16.5m5 1992 14g 14.6m 10m5 8g a7g] leggy gelding: moderate mover: untrustworthy handicapper: form in 1992 only when fifth: stays 2m: acts on good to firm and dead ground: no improvement in blinkers: sometimes wears crossed noseband: has found little: retained 3,700 gns Doncaster October Sales. *R. Boss*

MADAM CAPRICE   2 b.f. (May 17) Salse (USA) 128 – Maiden Pool 85 (Sharpen   **54** Up 127) [1992 7m 7f4 8d] 20,000Y: quite attractive filly: half-sister to several winners, including very useful sprinter Rich Charlie (by Absalom) and 3-y-o Walking On Water (by Celestial Storm), 6f winner at 2 yrs: dam 5f winner: modest maiden: worth a try at 6f. *R. Guest*

MADAM CYN'S RISK 2 b.f. (Feb 27) Risk Me (FR) 127 – Very Special Lady 78 **46** (Mummy's Game 120) [1992 5g⁴ a5g² 6f³ a6g⁴ 6m⁴ 7m⁴ 7m³ 7g* 8.1d 8g 6g] 1,500Y: small, sparely-made filly: moderate mover: first foal: dam 5f winner at 2 yrs: modest plater: retained 4,500 gns after winning at Catterick in August: well below form afterwards: will stay 1m: acts on good to firm ground: blinkered once (ran respectably): has run well for 7-lb claimer: sold 1,500 gns Newmarket Autumn Sales. *N. A. Callaghan*

MADAME CRESSON 2 b.f. (May 3) Petong 126 – Sunley Stars (Sallust 134) – [1992 5d 5g] 7,200Y: neat filly: first foal: dam poor daughter of sister to Runnett: no worthwhile form in the spring, in seller (blinkered, very geed up) last time. *G. A. Pritchard-Gordon*

MADAM PETOSKI 3 b.f. Petoski 135 – Proper Madam 93 (Mummy's Pet 125) **49** [1991 5.1g² 6g 5g² 5.2f 6.1m 5.1g⁵ 1992 5d 5m³ 6f] leggy, close-coupled filly: modest maiden: should stay 6f: wore blinkers and eyeshield final start in 1991: usually on toes, twice bolted to post (before finishing last) and is highly strung. *F. H. Lee*

MADELEINE'S DREAM (USA) 2 b. or br.f. (May 27) Theatrical 128 – **105** p L'Attrayante (FR) 123 (Tyrant (USA)) [1992 8g* 8v*] sister to Irish 3-y-o 1½m winner Miss Lenora and half-sister to 2 winners over middle distances in France: dam won from 5.5f (at 2 yrs) to 1¼m in Europe, including Poule d'Essai des Pouliches and Irish 1000 Guineas, then won 4 races in the States: won maiden at Compeigne in November and listed Prix Herbager (by ¾ length) at Maisons-Laffitte in December: will stay 1¼m: promising. *F. Boutin, France*

MAD MARCH HARE 2 ch.c. (Mar 26) Jester 119 – Maleiha 78 (Martinmas 128) – [1992 5.1h 5.7g 6.1m] 780Y: sturdy colt: second foal: dam, headstrong maiden, stayed 7f: soundly beaten, including in seller. *D. R. Tucker*

MAD MILITANT (IRE) 3 b.c. Vision (USA) – Ullapool (Dominion 123) [1991 7f **84** 7m* 8.1f 6.3s 7.6d³ 8.3s 1992 a8g* a8g* a8g* 10d 8.1s³ 12.3g⁴ 9.9f 10.5g* 12.3f⁶ 12.3g* 11.9s³ 11.9d 12g⁴ 15.9s⁵] compact colt: has quick action: fairly useful performer: won 3 claimers at Southwell early in the year and handicaps at Haydock and Chester in the summer: should stay 1¾m: well below form on firm going but acts on any other, including fibresand. *R. Hollinshead*

MAD MYTTON 2 b.g. (Feb 17) Crowning Honors (CAN) – Vynz Girl 82 (Tower **57** Walk 130) [1992 5s² 6m 7g 7m⁴ 7g 7d⁶ 6s] 8,800Y: leggy, quite good-topped gelding: has a round action: fifth foal: half-brother to 3 winners here and abroad, including 4-y-o Broom Isle (by Damister), successful at 7f (at 2 yrs) and 14.9f: dam 1½m winner: modest maiden: often travels well most of way before finding little off bridle: well worth another try at 6f: blinkered twice, not discredited first occasion, raced on unfavoured part of track final start. *A. Bailey*

MAELKAR (FR) 8 b.g. Maelstrom Lake 118 – Karabice (Karabas 132) [1991 NR – 1992 13.1s] workmanlike ex-Irish gelding: moderate walker: very useful hurdler at best here, winning 3m handicap at Ascot in April: 14/1 from 33/1, found slowly-run amateurs event at Ayr in September an insufficient test of stamina. *J. J. O'Neill*

M A EL-SAHN 2 b.c. (May 12) Presidium 124 – Hoonah (FR) (Luthier 126) [1992 **57** 5s 6.1v⁵ a5g a6g⁶] lengthy, unfurnished colt: fourth foal: half-brother to temperamental 1m and 1¼m winner Mohammed El-Sahn (by Trojan Fen): dam, grand-daughter of 1000 Guineas winner Honeylight, won 3 times at around 1½m in France: modest maiden: will stay 1m: below best on equitrack. *R. Hannon*

MAESTROSO (IRE) 3 b.c. Mister Majestic 122 – That's Easy (Swing Easy **68** (USA) 126) [1991 6m* 6g 6g⁶ 6m⁶ 6m 1992 10d⁶ 10.2d⁴ 11.6g³ 10.1d⁴ 11.6m⁵ 12m* 11.6m⁴ 11.8g⁴ 14.1d⁶ 14d⁵] sturdy colt: consistent handicapper: won at Pontefract in July: worth a try at 2m: acts on good to firm and dead ground: effective blinkered or not. *R. F. Johnson Houghton*

MAGADEER (USA) 3 b.f. Mogambo (USA) – Star Silhouette (USA) (Dancer's **68** Profile (USA)) [1991 6m³ 7m⁴ 6.9f² 1992 10g⁶ 10.1m 10s⁵ a12g⁵ 12m³ 10d² 10s⁴ 8v³ a13g] leggy, useful-looking filly: fair maiden: stays 1½m: probably acts on any turf going, below best on equitrack: retained 3,100 gns Ascot November Sales. *J. L. Dunlop*

MAGDALENE HEIGHTS 4 ch.g. All Systems Go 119 – Carreg-Wennol – (Dublin Taxi) [1991 8h 11m 12.2m⁵ 17.9f 1992 13.6m] lightly-made gelding: headstrong, and no worthwhile form: dead. *D. R. Franks*

MAGDALENE (IRE)   4 b.f. Runnett 125 – Grattan Princess (Tumble Wind   –
(USA)) [1991 5m a8g 1992 8.5g 5s] plain, angular filly: no worthwhile form. *T. Fairhurst*

MAGGIE SIDDONS   4 b.f. Night Shift (USA) – Sarah Siddons (Reform 132)   **80**
[1991 8g 8g 9d 7d² 5.7m* 5.7m* 6g* 8f² 6m 7d⁴ 6m 8g 1992 8g 7d 6g⁴] good-topped filly: carries condition: has a round action: fairly useful handicapper: showed promise when fourth at Lingfield in May, but didn't reappear: may prove ideally suited by 7f/1m: probably acts on any going. *C. J. Hill*

MAGGIES LAD   4 b.g. Red Johnnie 100 – Busted Love (Busted 134) [1991 a7g   –
a7g 6g⁶ 8s³ 11f³ 11g 8g* 8s⁵ 12.1d² 1992 18g] workmanlike gelding: poor mover: rated 58 at 3 yrs for T. Fairhurst: well beaten at Doncaster in March, 1992: effective from 1m to 1½m: acts on any going: effective with or without blinkers or visor: good mount for a claimer. *L. J. Codd*

MAGICAL QUEEN (IRE)   2 ch.f. (Feb 18) Magical Wonder (USA) 125 – Lough   **68**
Graney (Sallust 134) [1992 7m⁴ 7f² 8.1s²] IR 15,000Y: leggy, unfurnished filly: has a roundish action: sixth foal: sister to Irish 3-y-o 8.5f and 1½m winner Accell and half-sister to Irish 7f winner Indian Lagoon (by Indian King) and 1988 2-y-o 6f winner Safwah (by Ahonoora): dam, Irish 1½m winner, is half-sister to Tap On Wood: fair maiden: flashed tail and one paced closing stages at Chepstow last time: will stay middle distances: acts on firm and soft ground. *M. Moubarak*

MAGICAL RETREAT (USA)   2 b.f. (Feb 18) Sir Ivor 135 – Known Charter 96   **56** p
(Known Fact (USA) 135) [1992 7g 6v³] first foal: dam 2-y-o 6f winner later stayed 10.8f, is half-sister to Time Charter out of very useful sister to Nicholas Bill and Centroline: strong-finishing third at Folkestone in November: will be well suited by middle distances: likely to improve further. *C. A. Cyzer*

MAGICATION   2 b.f. (Mar 18) Nomination 125 – Gundreda 93 (Gunner B 126)   **64**
[1992 5f² 6m² 6g⁵ 7g 7m] small, sturdy filly: third living foal: dam 8.2f and 1¼m winner: modest maiden: off course over 2 months, first moderate effort on final start: will stay 1m: sold 4,700 gns Doncaster November Sales. *C. E. Brittain*

MAGIC FAN (IRE)   2 b.g. (Apr 19) Taufan (USA) 119 – Magic Gold (Sallust 134)   **40**
[1992 6.1d 7m 7s] IR 14,000F, 15,000Y: small, sturdy gelding: first foal: dam Irish 1¼m winner: form only in maiden at Leicester on good to firm ground. *P. W. Harris*

MAGIC NIGHT (FR)   4 b.f. Le Nain Jaune (FR) 121 – Pin Up Babe   **122**
(Prominer 125) [1991 7g⁵ 8d4 10g⁴ 10.5d² 12d* 10m² 12m* 12d² 12f² 1992 9.2d 12m³ 12d² 13.5s* 12m* 12s 12d⁵]

  Magic Night's season fizzled out like a damp squib, in sharp contrast to the previous one which had seen her go on from a victory in the Prix Vermeille to finish a good second in both the Prix de l'Arc de Triomphe and the Japan Cup. A rare lack-lustre performance behind Garden of Heaven when

*Prix de Pomone, Deauville—Magic Night lands the odds
from Sought Out and Always Friendly in this race for fillies*

Prix Foy Escada, Longchamp—
Magic Night squeezes through on the rails to get up from Subotica (No. 2) and Tel Quel

100/30 on for the Prix du Conseil de Paris in mid-October, which put paid to another Japan Cup bid, came hard on the heels of a frustrating two and a half minutes for her connections and all her backers in her second tilt at the Arc. Magic Night might just as well have remained in her stable. She's a sound stayer, well suited by a strong gallop at a mile and a half, yet was held up in a slowly-run race; in consequence, she was left badly placed when the pace quickened going into the final turn. Things then went from bad to worse as, in attempting to improve from a back-five position, she was so badly checked two furlongs out that any chance of making the first ten behind Subotica went by the board. Her regular jockey Badel was replaced by Asmussen afterwards.

Magic Night looked to have a good chance in the Arc provided she was at her best, and started second favourite at 9/2 in the field of eighteen. She'd run Suave Dancer to two lengths in similar conditions the previous year and, having clearly been trained for the race again, she looked to be approaching her peak at just the right time. Magic Night was given five races up to her second Arc and won her last two, the Prix de Pomone at Deauville in August and the Prix Foy Escada at Longchamp in September. She ran well in defeat once stepped up to a more suitable distance after being started off in the Prix d'Ispahan on the last day in May, finishing third to Pistolet Bleu in the Grand Prix d'Evry and second to the same colt in the Grand Prix de Saint-Cloud. Pistolet Bleu beat her by two lengths at Evry and by five at Saint-Cloud, but on the latter occasion Magic Night ran on past Subotica and Saganeca for a clear second place. Second, third and fourth at Saint-Cloud met again when completing their Arc preparation in the Foy. In the meantime Magic Night had won the Pomone. The Pomone—a Group 2 race of nearly a mile and three quarters confined to fillies and mares, and in 1992 run on soft going—might have been framed for Magic Night. She impressed enormously. Held up in a truly-run affair (the designated pacemaker couldn't keep up with Cecil's Miss Plum who led to two furlongs out), Magic Night swooped on Sought Out and Always Friendly in the last furlong and won by a length and a short neck. The Foy was a different test altogether. All three Arc trials on the day's card were slowly-run, the Foy notably so. Tel Quel set a crawl of a pace to the three other runners as far as the straight on the firmish ground, and turned it into a two-furlong sprint between himself, Subotica and Magic Night, with Magic Night hemmed in by the colts. In the nick of time, Magic Night got half an opening on the inside as Tel Quel began to tire and drift off the rail; showing great resolution she forced her way to the front near the finish.

		Pharly	Lyphard
	Le Nain Jaune (FR)	(ch 1974)	Comely
	(ch 1979)	Lady Berry	Violon d'Ingres
Magic Night (FR)		(ch 1970)	Moss Rose II
(b.f. 1988)		Prominer	Beau Sabreur
	Pin Up Babe	(ch 1962)	Snob Hill
	(b 1972)	Mini Skirt	Kythnos
		(br 1967)	Modern Lady

Gameness and consistency have been big features of Magic Night's career. It would seem very unlikely that the buffeting she received in the Arc sapped any of her enthusiasm. She has been well described as 'all heart'. As must be widely known by now she's no oil painting, to put it mildly; just sparely made and on the small side. She's unfashionably bred, too, by a staying sire who even after her performances as a three-year-old was covering in France at the equivalent of less than £1,000 (non-thoroughbreds at much less than half that), out of a mare who was knocked down at auction, carrying Magic Night, for approximately £250. The dam and grandam were minor winners, Pin Up Babe in France and Mini Skirt in Ireland, while the third dam Modern Lady, unraced, is a half-sister to the 1965 Musidora Stakes winner Arctic Melody. *P. H. Demercastel, France*

MAGIC ORB 2 b.f. (Mar 20) Primo Dominie 121 – Tricky 66 (Song 132) [1992 5g⁴ 5.1g⁶ 5m⁶ 5d* 5g 5s⁶] 16,500Y: small, sparely-made filly: moderate mover: third foal: half-sister to 3-y-o 1¾m winner Witches Coven (by Sharrood): dam poor sister to smart sprinter Jester: modest performer: apprentice ridden at overweight, easily best effort when winning nursery at Wolverhampton in August from 7 lb out of the handicap: will stay 6f. *J. L. Spearing*   **60**

MAGIC PEARL 2 gr.f. (Mar 20) Belfort (FR) 89 – Oyster Gray 61 (Tanfirion 110) [1992 5g 5s² 5.1m² 5f² 5f 5m⁵ 5.1m³ 5d⁵ 6d⁴ 5s² 6.1s⁶] 1,500Y: leggy, angular filly: second known foal: dam maiden best at up to 6f: inconsistent maiden: best efforts at 5f: acts on any going. *E. J. Alston*   **68**

MAGIC PENNY 3 b.f. Sharrood (USA) 124 – Bluebell 103 (Town Crier 119) [1991 NR 1992 7g a8g⁶] rangy filly: moderate walker and mover: eighth foal: half-sister to several winners, including fair 1m winner Mountain Bluebird (by Clever Trick) and modest 9f and 1¼m winner Speedwell (by Grundy): dam, out of half-sister to Queen's Hussar, ran only at 2 yrs when 6f and 7.3f winner: behind in maidens at Kempton (wandered under pressure) and Lingfield (apprentices) in June: sold 1,300 gns Newmarket Autumn Sales. *C. A. Cyzer*   **–**

MAGIC RING (IRE) 3 b.c. Green Desert (USA) 127 – Emaline (FR) 105 (Empery (USA) 128) [1991 5g* 5g*dis 5m* 5d³ 5d* 1992 7d] strong-quartered, deep-girthed colt: rated 115 as a juvenile, beaten just over a length when third in the Prix de l'Abbaye de Longchamp, then winning Cornwallis Stakes at Ascot, in October: in need of race and very much on toes, refused to settle when last in Greenham Stakes at Newbury in April and wasn't seen again: will stay 6f: stays in training. *P. F. I. Cole*   **105**

MAGIC SECRET 4 b.g. Local Suitor (USA) 128 – Meissarah (USA) (Silver Hawk (USA) 123) [1991 10g² 10g⁶ 10g³ 10.1g⁸ 8.9g 10.3m 10d² 8d 10.3d a12g² a12g* 1992 a11g³ a12g² a13g* 12.3m 16.1g⁴ 13.1g* 16.2g 12.1g⁶ 13.6m⁵] workmanlike gelding: carries condition: has a round action: fair handicapper: won at Lingfield in January and Ayr in July: respectable fifth in Redcar claimer (claimed to join P. Bevan £8,005) final start: effective at 1½m, and probably stays 2m: best turf form with give in the ground and acts on all-weather surfaces: has run well when blinkered. *P. C. Haslam*   **74**

MAGIC STEPS 3 b.f. Nomination 125 – Magic Tower 76 (Tower Walk 130) [1991 5.1m* 5.2f* 1992 7g 8d 6.1s] sturdy filly: won nursery at Newbury in August, 1991: off course over a year and no worthwhile form in 1992: should stay 1m. *C. E. Brittain*   **–**

MAGIC STREET 2 ch.f. (Apr 11) Magical Wonder (USA) 125 – Pushkinia (FR) 95 (Pharly (FR) 130) [1992 6g³ 6d³ 6g] good-quartered filly: third foal: half-sister to winners in USA (at 1m) and France: dam French 2-y-o 7f winner from good family: modest maiden: ran only in the summer: will stay 1m. *M. Moubarak*   **63**

MAGIQUE ROND POINT (USA) 2 b.f. (Feb 14) Greinton 119 – Petit Rond Point (USA) (Round Table) [1992 6g³ 7m* 8s⁶] $23,000F, $7,000Y: medium-sized, attractive filly: half-sister to several winners, including 7f and 1m winner Miss Tatting and 1990 2-y-o 6f winner Too Conspicuous (both by Miswaki): dam, un-   **89**

placed in 6 starts, is half-sister to dam of Lyphard's Wish: progressive form: heavily-backed favourite, most impressive winner of maiden at Goodwood in July, showing excellent turn of foot: around 7 lengths sixth of 8 to Ivanka in Fillies' Mile at Ascot 2 months later, close up turning for home then one pace: bred to stay 1¼m. *H. R. A. Cecil*

MAGIRIKA (IRE)   2 br.g. (Apr 23) Magical Wonder (USA) 125 – Minarika (FR)   **40**
(Djakao (FR) 124) [1992 5m5 6m6 5m] compact gelding: half-brother to smart French miler Turkish Ruler and French middle-distance winner Rising Wind (both by In Fijar): dam dead-heated in small 9f race in France: poor form in varied events, including a claimer at Wolverhampton in August last time. *M. Moubarak*

MAGNETIC POINT (USA)   3 ch.f. Bering 136 – Nonoalca (FR) 120 (Nonoalco   **60**
(USA) 131) [1991 7d 1992 10d 8f4 8g4 9f 8m5 10g2 8.1d3 8f3 10f5 9s 10m a12g a7g] big, rangy filly: plating-class maiden: effective from 1m to 1¼m: acts on firm and dead ground, possibly not on soft or equitrack: has shown form when sweating and edgy: wears a crossed noseband: lacks a turn of foot. *A. A. Scott*

MAGNETIC PRINCE   3 b.g. Tina's Pet 121 – Miss Magnetism (Baptism 119)   **–**
[1991 6f6 6m 6g3 6m 7g 8.2m 10.5d 1992 8.9v 11g 8g 10m] workmanlike gelding: of little account these days. *G. Blum*

MAGNIFICENT   3 b.g. Damister (USA) 123 – Tantalizing Song (CAN) (The   **69**
Minstrel (CAN) 135) [1991 7g 6m* 1992 7d* 8.1s* 8.1m 7g 8d 9g4 10.5d] leggy, lengthy gelding: moderate mover: fair handicapper: narrowly successful for 7-lb claimer at Brighton and Haydock in April: should stay 1¼m (beaten long way from home when tried): has won on good to firm ground, but best form on a soft surface: blinkered last 2 starts, running creditably first occasion. *M. A. Jarvis*

MAGNIFICENT STAR (USA)   4 b.f. Silver Hawk (USA) 123 – Gulanar (Val   **–**
de Loir 133) [1991 7g5 8m3 10d* 12m5 12g2 11.9g* 12m5 1992 13.5s 11.9m 14.6m] big, good-bodied filly: moderate walker: powerful mover with a round action: very smart filly (rated 122) at 3 yrs when game winner of Yorkshire Oaks: off course for 11 months and well beaten in pattern company in the autumn as 4-y-o: should stay beyond 1½m: best form with give in the ground and on a galloping track. *M. Moubarak*

MAGNIFIED (USA)   3 br.g. Known Fact (USA) 135 – Mofida 115 (Right Tack   **98**
131) [1991 6g3 6m* 5g5 1992 8g2 8g* 8m6 7.9m] leggy, useful-looking gelding: good walker: useful perfomer: won handicap at Leicester in May: creditable efforts in valuable handicaps at Goodwood and York in the summer: likely to stay beyond 1m: sent to Hong Kong. *B. W. Hills*

MAGSOOD   7 ch.g. Mill Reef (USA) 141 – Shark Song 103 (Song 132) [1991 12f   **48**
1992 14m4 16.5m4 16.2m 17.2f6] lengthy, good-looking gelding: moderate mover: seems only poor these days: needs a thorough test of stamina: acts on firm going, probably unsuited by soft: has won in blinkers: not seen after July. *S. Mellor*

MAHAASIN   4 b.f. Bellypha 130 – Dame Ashfield 90 (Grundy 137) [1991 10m5   **–**
10m5 12s 1992 12.3g 12.3m 13.8m 10.5d 12f6 10m] leggy filly: moderate mover: rated 70 at 3 yrs for A. Stewart: no worthwhile form in 1992: blinkered (ran poorly) once at 3 yrs. *L. J. Codd*

MAHAIRY (USA)   3 b.c. Theatrical 128 – Papamiento (USA) (Blade (USA))   **69** d
[1991 7d 1992 10.5d6 10m6 11.6g6 12f3 14.1g 12.3d 11.5s] tall, close-coupled, attractive colt: has a long, round stride: modest form: well beaten last 3 outings, blinkered/visored on last 2: stays 1½m: acts on firm and dead going. *A. A. Scott*

MAHASIN (USA)   3 b.f. Danzig (USA) – Icing 112 (Prince Tenderfoot (USA)   **90**
126) [1991 6g2 1992 8g 8m* 7d* 8f6 7m5] big, good-topped filly: has a very powerful, round action: reportedly suffered fetlock injury and operated on after bout of colic at 2 yrs: fairly useful performer: made all in maiden at Kempton in May and minor event (14/1 on) at Leicester in June: creditable fifth in listed race at Goodwood in July: stayed 1m: acted on good to firm ground (behind, facing stiff task, in Coronation Stakes on firm), didn't have to be anywhere near best on dead: used to get very much on edge (particularly at stalls) but somewhat calmer towards end of career: visits Mujtahid. *J. L. Dunlop*

MAHFIL   4 b.g. Head For Heights 125 – Polavera (FR) (Versailles II) [1991 10.1s5   **75**
12m2 12g4 11.9g* 11.8g4 10m2 10.5d 1992 12m 11.5m* 10f3 12d* 12m 12g2] lengthy gelding: very consistent handicapper: won at Lingfield in May and Epsom in July: effective from 1¼m to 1½m: acts on firm and dead ground: has edged left. *R. Akehurst*

MAHOGANY LIGHT (USA)   2 b.c. (Mar 2) Woodman (USA) 126 – Antique   **74**
Lamp (USA) (Seattle Slew (USA)) [1992 7m 8.5m3 8d4 8m] $360,000Y: strong,

good-topped colt: moderate mover: first foal: dam, third twice from 10 starts in North America, is daughter of top French 2-y-o Theia, family of Phardante: fair maiden judged on close fourth of 19 at Redcar, close up throughout and keeping on well: failed by long way to confirm the improvement back on faster ground at Pontefract later in October: will stay 1¼m: blinkered second outing: sold 32,000 gns Newmarket Autumn Sales. *G. Harwood*

MAHONG 4 gr.g. Petong 126 – Balearica 90 (Bustino 136) [1991 a7g* 7.6g 8g 8m⁶ **61** 9s⁶ 8.1s* 1992 11.6g 10.3m 10g* 10g³] leggy gelding: modest performer: won claiming handicap at Nottingham in September: will prove at least as effective at 1½m as shorter: goes well with give in the ground and acts on soft. *Mrs H. Parrott*

MAHOOL (USA) 3 b.c. Alydar (USA) – Tax Dodge (USA) (Seattle Slew (USA)) **–** [1991 8m⁵ 7m* 1992 10.5d⁶] tall colt: rated 87 at 2 yrs: ran as though race was needed when sixth in handicap at Haydock in May, leading to over 2f out, not knocked about afterwards: should stay 1¼m. *A. A. Scott*

MAHRAJAN 8 b.h. Dominion 123 – Dame Julian 84 (Blakeney 126) [1991 12g 12m **66** 11.7g⁴ 11.7m* 11.7m 11.6m³ 14g 12g* 11.8g⁴ 12d⁵ 1992 12d 14d⁶ 12g⁶ 12d³ 11.6m⁵ 11.6g* 11.6d³ 11.6g 11.6g 14g 12d] rangy horse: poor mover: modest performer: won handicap at Windsor (fourth win over course and distance) in July: well below form last 4 starts: stays 1½m: acts on any going: flashed tail and looked none too keen once at 7 yrs: usually held up. *C. J. Benstead*

MAHSUL (IRE) 4 b.c. Ela-Mana-Mou 132 – Afrah (USA) 85 (Our Native **68** (USA)) [1991 6m⁴ 6d⁵ 6g⁶ 6g 7m* 7g² 8m⁶ 1992 7g 8.1d⁴ 8m 7f⁵ 8g⁴ 8f* 8d⁶ 8m 10m* 10m² 10d³ 12g 11.4g⁴ 10d] good-bodied colt: bad mover: fair handicapper: won at Salisbury and Windsor in midsummer: should prove as effective at 1½m as shorter: has form on dead going, but best efforts on top-of-the-ground: is held up: none too consistent. *C. J. Benstead*

MAHZOOZ 3 ch.g. Crystal Glitters (USA) 127 – Gandoorah 90 (Record Token **–** 128) [1991 6m⁵ 7g⁵ 7m 6s⁶ 1992 7m 8.5d 6f 6g] lengthy, good-topped gelding: good mover: no worthwhile form in 1992: should stay 1m: possibly unsuited by soft ground: blinkered final outing. *M. Moubarak*

MAID OF ICE 3 b.f. Siberian Express (USA) 125 – Kalorama (FR) 102 (Bold Lad **–** (IRE) 133) [1991 7m 8s 1992 8d⁴ 10m] leggy, lengthy filly: seems of little account. *Dr J. D. Scargill*

MAID WELCOME 5 br.m. Mummy's Pet 125 – Carolynchristensen 58 (Sweet **75 d** Revenge 129) [1991 a5g⁵ a6g³ a5g³ a5g⁴ a5g⁶ 5.3f² 5f* 5g 5f 5m a5g* 5m³ 6m² 5m 5m⁴ 5m 5.1g² 5d a5g a6g³ 1992 a5g a5g* a5g⁵ 5g 5.2g⁵ 5.1f a5g a6g] sturdy mare: has a round action: fair performer: won Southwell claimer in February: well beaten on turf and when returned to Southwell after over 3-month break: effective at 5f and 6f: suited by top-of-the-ground (acts on hard) and all-weather surfaces: blinkered nowadays: suitable mount for apprentice. *Mrs N. Macauley*

MAIN BID (IRE) 3 b.g. Auction Ring (USA) 123 – Annabella 88 (Habitat 134) **92** [1991 7m⁵ 7g* 1992 8f³ 8m 7.9m] strong, workmanlike gelding: wearing tongue strap, fairly useful form when third in handicap at Newmarket: well held in valuable handicaps at Goodwood and (wore crossed noseband, edgy) York in the summer: stays 1m: acts on firm going. *M. Moubarak*

MAINLY ME 3 b.f. Huntingdale 132 – Mainmast 63 (Bustino 136) [1991 6m² 6g³ **70 d** 7m⁵ 6s⁶ 6m³ 6m² 1992 7g² 10g⁶ 7.6g⁴ 7m² 8.5d 8g³ 7f² 10g 7d 8g 7g] workmanlike filly: modest maiden, inconsistent in 1992: stays 1m (saddle slipped second attempt at 1¼m): below form on extremes of going: trained until after third start by Mrs J. Cecil: sold 2,300 gns Doncaster November Sales. *P. T. Walwyn*

MAI PEN RAI 4 ch.g. All Systems Go 119 – Jersey Maid 82 (On Your Mark 125) **–** [1991 9d 11.7g 10g 7g 10.1d 8m² 7g 8.1s* 9.9f⁴ 8s 8f 10.5m² 10m⁵ 8g 8.2m 8d a7g 1992 a11g a10g a12g a10g⁵ 11.7d 10.8g] sparely-made, angular gelding: rated 57 at 3 yrs: seemed of little account in 1992. *C. J. Hill*

MAJAL (IRE) 3 b.g. Caerleon (USA) 132 – Park Special (Relkino 131) [1991 6g⁵ **78** 7m² 7.5f* 7g³ 7m 1992 9.9g³ 8.1g 8.5m 10.1m² 10m⁵ 8m³ 8.1d⁴ 10s² 12d⁶ 10.5d⁴ 8.1d⁴] good-bodied gelding: impresses in appearance: moderate walker: fair handicapper in the summer: below form in claimers last 2 starts, claimed to join J. Wainwright £10,561 after being tenderly handled on final one: probably stays 1½m: acts on any going. *B. Hanbury*

MAJBOOR (IRE) 3 b.c. Wassl 125 – Mashteen (USA) (Majestic Prince) [1991 6g **88** 1992 8d³ 8g* 10m² 8g 7g² 7g 8d 8d] good sort: carries condition: fairly useful form on his day: made all in maiden at Warwick in April: below form in handicaps last 3 starts: should prove suited by return to 1¼m: acts on good to firm and dead ground: sold 12,000 gns Newmarket Autumn Sales. *P. T. Walwyn*

MAJED (IRE)   4 b.c. Wolverlife 115 – Martin Place (Martinmas 128) [1991 11.1d³   **81** p
11.5m⁴ 11.7m a12g² 12m⁵ 10g² 11.5s* a12g² 1992 a12g⁵ 9.7v* 8.3d* 10m⁴ 8.5g³ 10g
8.3g⁵ 10f 10.5d⁵ 10.3g³ 10.5d* 10.4s* 10m⁵ 10v*] useful-looking colt: good walker: a
fairly useful performer who had a fine season: won at Folkestone (claimer) and
Hamilton in the spring for N. Callaghan, claimed £10,000 eighth start: yet to run
moderately for new connections, winning handicaps at Haydock (amateurs), York
and Redcar in the autumn followed by 2 novice hurdles late in the year: has form
from 1m to 1½m, very best effort at around 1¼m: acts on good to firm and heavy
ground: tried blinkered once at 3 yrs: is held up: has won for both amateur and
apprentice: genuine and very consistent. *Mrs M. Reveley*

MAJESTIC HAWK (USA)   2 br.c. (Feb 9) Silver Hawk (USA) 123 – Rose of   **91**
The Sea (USA) 115 (The Minstrel (CAN) 135) [1992 6f⁴ 6g⁴ 7m 8.1s 8.1s⁴] strong,
good-quartered colt: usually impresses in appearance: good mover: second foal:
half-brother to a winner abroad by Siberian Express: dam French sprinter: fairly
useful performer: easy winner of Ripon maiden in June: beaten 4 lengths or so in
Group 3 events at Newmarket and Goodwood in July: below best on soft ground last
2 starts, blinkered final one: best form at 6f but probably stays 7f: acts on firm
ground. *M. Moubarak*

MAJESTIC IMAGE   6 ch.m. Niniski (USA) 125 – Regal Twin (USA) 77   **86**
(Majestic Prince) [1991 a11g² a14g* 14d* 14m* 16d* 13.9g 1992 16.4s² 16.2g 14s*
18m] workmanlike, rather angular mare: has a rather round action: fairly useful
handicapper: easy winner at Sandown in August: rare modest efforts when unplaced, never a factor in Cesarewitch last time: should stay beyond 2m: acts on good
to firm, but goes extremely well on a soft surface: usually ridden by D. Harrison.
Lord Huntingdon

MAJESTIC MELODY   4 ch.f. Crooner 119 – Royal Birthday (St Paddy 133)   –
[1991 7g⁴ 7.6s 8g 7g 1992 7f 11.8g 9d] sparely-made filly: rated 52 at 3 yrs: no
worthwhile form in 1992 and showed signs of temperament. *W. Carter*

MAJESTIC SINCLAIR (IRE)   3 b.c. Mister Majestic 122 – Katie's Delight   **58**
(Relko 136) [1991 6d 1992 7.9g⁶ 7g³ 8s⁵ 10d⁵ a12g⁴ a12g²] useful-looking colt:
modest maiden: stays 1½m: acts on fibresand: ran creditably in blinkers final start.
R. Hollinshead

MAJI   3 b.f. Shareef Dancer (USA) 135 – Majoritat (GER) (Konigsstuhl (GER)   **70**
[1991 7g 1992 10d² 10m² 10f² 11.1f³ 14.1f⁵ 11g⁴ 12.2g* 12.3g³ 12g 13.8g³ 11.5s 15.8d]
compact filly: fair and largely consistent performer: edgy, won maiden at Catterick
in August: stayed 13.8f: acted on firm and dead going, seemingly not on soft: visits
Robellino. *D. Morley*

MAJJRA (USA)   3 b.c. Danzig (USA) – Private Colors (USA) (Private Account   **77**
(USA)) [1991 NR 1992 8g 8.1d* 10.3m] well-made colt: has a round action: second
foal: dam, successful 3 times in minor company at up to 1m in North America, is
sister to champion filly Personal Ensign and high-class Personal Flag: fair form:
narrowly won moderately-run 5-runner maiden at Haydock, travelling well behind
leader, green then keeping on strongly to lead close home: tailed off in handicap at
Doncaster later in July: stays 1m well: easily best effort on a soft surface. *J. H. M.
Gosden*

MAJOR BUGLER (IRE)   3 b.c. Thatching 131 – Bugle Sound 96 (Bustino 136)   **85**
[1991 7g⁶ 7g³ 7d³ 1992 8d⁶ 8s³ 8f⁶ 10s⁴ 10.2s² 11.4g 10s* 12g⁶] big, workmanlike
colt: fairly useful performer: won £9,500 handicap at Ascot in September: should
prove better at 1½m than shorter: acts on soft ground, well below form on firm:
largely consistent: fairly useful form in juvenile hurdles, winning in November. *G.
B. Balding*

MAJORITY HOLDING   7 b.g. Mandrake Major 122 – Kirkby 85 (Midsummer   –
Night II 117) [1991 12.5g 1992 9g] lengthy, rather dipped-backed gelding: seems of
little account these days. *M. J. Wilkinson*

MAJORITY (IRE)   2 b.c. (Mar 26) Dancing Brave (USA) 140 – Majoritat (GER)   **73** p
(Konigsstuhl (GER)) [1992 7g³] sturdy, angular colt: second known foal: half-
brother to 3-y-o 12.2f winner Maji (by Shareef Dancer): dam German bred: well-
backed 9/4-shot, though carrying plenty of condition, ran green when over 3 lengths
third of 13 to Dahyah in maiden at Doncaster in October: will stay middle distances:
sure to improve. *B. W. Hills*

MAJOR IVOR   7 ch.g. Mandrake Major 122 – Double Birthday (Cavo Doro 124)   **60**
[1991 8m 9m⁶ 10m 1992 11m 9f³ 8.2g 8f² 8f³] big, workmanlike gelding: carries

condition: modest performer: consistent efforts when placed in handicaps in mid-summer: stays 9f: nearly always races on a sound surface, ran creditably on dead ground once in 1989. *Mrs M. Reveley*

MAJOR MOUSE 4 ch.g. All Systems Go 119 – Tzu-Hsi (Songedor 116) [1991 **78** 5m² 5g⁴ 5f³ 6m⁶ 6m³ 7f² 6.9f* 7.5f⁶ 8m² 7m³ 8m 1992 7.5m* 8f⁵ 7.5g* 8f* 8.9m 8s 7.5m] strong, compact gelding: won at Beverley (twice) and Ripon in first half of season: off course over 2 months and no show on last 3 starts: should stay beyond 1m: acts on firm going: is held up: goes well for A. Culhane. *W. W. Haigh*

MAJOR RISK 3 ch.g. Risk Me (FR) 127 – Brampton Grace 80 (Tachypous 128) **44** §
[1991 6g⁶ a8g 1992 a10g⁵ a10g 12.2g³ 11g a12g 11.8g⁵ 12f⁴ a16g 15.4d⁴] tall, leggy gelding: untrustworthy plater: stays 1½m: possibly unsuited by firm ground: tried blinkered: carries head high: sold to join P. Bevan 4,000 gns Newmarket Autumn Sales. *P. A. Kelleway*

MAJOR'S LAW (IRE) 3 b.c. Law Society (USA) 130 – Maryinsky (USA) **75** (Northern Dancer) [1991 7m² 7m 7m 8m 6.1d* 1992 7g 10d 8.1g⁶ 12.3g³ 12d² 12f 10m⁶ 12d 11.5m² 14d 10.3v²] compact, good-bodied colt: fair but inconsistent handicapper: should stay beyond 1½m: acts on good to firm and heavy ground: sometimes sweating: sold to join I. Campbell 16,500 gns Newmarket Autumn Sales. *C. E. Brittain*

MAJOR TRIUMPH (IRE) 2 ch.f. (Feb 14) Hatim (USA) 121 – Hetty Green **64** (Bay Express 132) [1992 a7g² a7g² a7g³] IR 2,500Y: second live foal: half-sister to 1989 Irish 2-y-o 6f winner Cohete (by Sallust): dam Irish middle-distance winner: fair form when second in maidens at Southwell, but ran moderately when 6/4 favourite at Lingfield: will stay 1¼m. *G. C. Bravery*

MAJOR YAASI (USA) 2 b.c. (Apr 24) Arctic Tern (USA) 126 – Dimant Rose **67** p (USA) (Tromos 134) [1992 7s⁴ 10g²] strong colt: has scope: third foal: half-brother to ungenuine 3-y-o Dioman Shadeed (by Shadeed): dam unraced half-sister to Rainbow Quest, family also of Warning and Slightly Dangerous: backward still, stayed on strongly when second of 13 in maiden at Nottingham in October: will stay at least 1½m: will improve again. *J. R. Fanshawe*

MAKE IT HAPPEN (IRE) 2 b.c. (Jan 29) Fayruz 116 – Genzyme Gene 38 **53** (Riboboy (USA) 124) [1992 5s³ 5g 5m² 5m* 5m³ 5g 6s⁵ 7s a7g] 15,000Y: medium-sized colt: fourth foal: half-brother to 2 winners abroad: dam, plater, stayed 1¼m: plating-class form: narrowly won 5-runner maiden at Edinburgh in June: stays 6f: best form on top-of-the-ground: effective with or without blinkers: sold 3,600 gns Doncaster November Sales, reportedly to Czechoslovakia. *J. Berry*

MAKEMEASTAR (IRE) 4 ch.f. Horage 124 – Sally St Clair (Sallust 134) [1991 **–** 8g 1992 a8g] compact filly: rated 61 when winning at Southwell as 2-y-o: no form either start since. *M. J. Ryan*

MAKE ME PROUD (IRE) 3 b.f. Be My Native (USA) 122 – Miami Life (Miami **–** Springs 121) [1991 6f 7g 7g 1992 10d a12g⁵ a12g⁵ a12s⁶ 16g⁵] leggy, unfurnished filly: looked of little account in 1992: sold to join W. Bentley 2,000 gns Newmarket Autumn Sales. *R. W. Armstrong*

MAKE MINE A DOUBLE 2 ch.g. (Mar 30) Sharpo 132 – My Fair Orchid 71 **55** (Roan Rocket 128) [1992 5s 5m³ 5f* 6f⁴ 5g⁴ 6g 6s] strong gelding: fifth foal: half-brother to 3-y-o Floral Bouquet (by Never So Bold) and fair 7f winner Oriental Splendour (by Runnett): dam, plater, showed form only at 5f: modest form: won maiden at Ripon in June: form only at 5f: acts on firm ground: visored (raced freely) final start: retained 1,600 gns Doncaster September Sales. *Miss S. E. Hall*

MAKEMINEMUSIC 3 ch.g. Music Boy 124 – Ultra Vires 87 (High Line 125) **–** [1991 5d⁶ 6d 5f² 6g 5m³ 6g 7m 1992 8.1f 6g 8s] leggy gelding: plating-class maiden at 2 yrs: sold out of Mrs M. Reveley's stable 1,500 gns Doncaster June (1992) Sales and no form, when visored in claimer last time. *F. Watson*

MAKE OR MAR 8 b. or br.m. Daring March 116 – Martelli 70 (Pitskelly 122) **44** [1991 NR 1992 6f⁶ 5.9h⁵ a5g 6g⁴ 6.1d 5f⁶] sparely-made mare: rated 81 at 5 yrs for J. Jenkins: went to stud and had a foal: poor form in varied company in the summer at 8 yrs: stays 6f: acts on firm going. *B. Ellison*

MALAIA (IRE) 2 b.f. (Apr 23) Commanche Run 133 – Spartan Helen (Troy 137) **50** p [1992 8s⁵] fourth foal: half-sister to useful 3-y-o 8.9f and 1¼m winer Spartan Shareef (by Shareef Dancer): dam unraced daughter of staying half-sister to Blakeney and Morston: 14/1 and backward, around 10 lengths fifth of 12 to Star Manager in maiden at Bath in September, green entering straight and no impression: will improve. *M. J. Heaton-Ellis*

MALCESINE (IRE) 3 b.f. Auction Ring (USA) 123 – Vain Deb 66 (Gay Fan- **45** dango (USA) 132) [1991 NR 1992 a8g⁴ a8g a8g⁴ 7.5g³ 7g⁴ 6.9d⁴ 7.1m² 7.6g 8f 8.9d 6s⁵ 7g 7.1g⁶ 6s] IR 13,000Y: leggy filly: third foal: half-sister to useful 6-y-o sprint- er Red Rosein (by Red Sunset) and 5-y-o 12.3f to 16.2f winner Vain Prince (by Sandhurst Prince): dam 1m to 9f winner stayed 1¼m: plating-class maiden: ran creditably only once in last 7 starts: should stay 1m: acts on good to firm and soft ground, no form on fibresand: well beaten in a visor once. *Capt. J. Wilson*

MALEDETTO (IRE) 3 b.c. Double Schwartz 128 – Croglin Water (Monsanto **103** (FR) 121) [1991 5v* 5v* 5g* 5m⁶ 6g³ 6m² 1992 5s* 6g² 5m² 6f 5g² 6g 6g 6g] close-coupled, quite attractive colt: has a quick action: useful performer: won minor event at Leopardstown in March: good second in Group 3 events at the Curragh and at Leopardstown (length behind Freddie Lloyd) next 2 starts: well below form, including in Cork And Orrery Stakes at Royal Ascot, 4 of last 5 starts: acts on good to firm and heavy ground. *J. S. Bolger, Ireland*

MALENOIR (USA) 4 b.g. Solford (USA) 127 – Viewed (USA) (Alydar (USA)) **62** [1991 a11g²a12g²12d⁶11.6m⁶a12g16m12.1sa13ga12g1992a14ga16g²a14g²a16g* a14g 13.8g* 17.1m³ 13d a14g 14.6g a12g a14g² a16g² a16g*] leggy, quite attractive gelding: modest handicapper: won at Southwell and Catterick (first run for 10 weeks) in the spring: trained until after ninth start (May) by W. Pearce and off course 5 months afterwards: returned to form late in year, winning at Southwell (for apprentice) in December: stays 17f: acts on good to firm ground (possibly not on dead) and all-weather surfaces: usually visored nowadays: below form in blinkers. *R. C. Spicer*

MALIGNED (IRE) 3 b.f. Alzao (USA) 117 – Place Royale (Pall Mall 132) [1991 **–** NR 1992 10g 10.1d⁴ 11.9m³ 12g 14.1d]32,000F, IR 14,000Y, resold 3,500Y: workman- like filly: half-sister to several winners, including Scruples (by Windjammer), a leading colt at 3 yrs in Belgium and subsequently a smart middle-distance winner in USA: dam Irish 2m winner: no worthwhile form, though showed signs of a little ability when in frame in maidens: sold 2,500 gns Newmarket September Sales. *J. R. Fanshawe*

MALUNAR 7 gr.g. Mummy's Pet 125 – Tranquility Base 112 (Roan Rocket 128) **62** [1991 5m 6f6 6f* 7g⁵ 7m² 7.1g⁴ 6.1g² 1992 6v³ 6d 6v⁶ 6s³ 7f² 7f] close-coupled gelding: carries plenty of condition: modest handicapper: off course 2½ months, bandaged and well beaten final start: effective at 6f and 7f: probably acts on any going: no improvement in blinkers/visor: has run well for apprentice: sold 1,400 gns Newmarket Autumn Sales. *M. H. Tompkins*

MALZETA (IRE) 2 b.f. (Apr 18) Alzao (USA) 117 – Place of Honour (Be My **49** Guest (USA) 126) [1992 6m 6d 7m 7g 6s] 32,000Y: smallish filly: lacks scope: has a fluent, round action: fifth foal: half-sister to a winner in Italy and Irish 7f winner Nouschka (by Ahonoora): dam, Irish middle-distance winner, from family of Captain James and Nikoli: modest maiden: ran as if something amiss on fourth start and no show last time: should be better suited by 7f than 6f. *M. J. Heaton-Ellis*

MAMALAMA 4 ch.f. Nishapour (FR) 125 – Gauloise 93 (Welsh Pageant 132) **35** [1991 7g 8m³ 10g³ 12d⁴ 11.7m 10g⁵ 14.1f³ 12f³ 16m³ 15.4f⁴ 17.2g 1992 10m 11.8m 12m³ 14.6g⁴ 10m⁶ 11.9f 11.5m] leggy, angular filly: still a maiden after 25 starts: needs further than 1¼m, and stays 2m: acts on firm and dead ground: has joined J. Bridger. *L. J. Holt*

MAMDOOH 3 b.g. Green Desert (USA) 127 – Shore Line 107 (High Line 125) **100** [1991 NR 1992 10m* 10g* 10.1m 10m 12m] robust, attractive gelding: impresses in appearance: good mover: half-brother to 2 winners, including 1½m winner South Shore (by Caerleon): dam 7f winner also fourth in Oaks, is sister to Park Hill winner Quay Line: useful performer at best: won maiden and £11,200 handicap at Newmarket in August: ran poorly next start, not given hard race in handicaps at Newmarket afterwards: should stay 1½m: yet to race on a soft surface: gelded and sent to join D. Hayes in Australia. *A. C. Stewart*

MAMMA'S TOO 3 b.f. Skyliner 117 – Maple Syrup 89 (Charlottown 127) [1991 **91** 5f* 5m² 5m⁴ 5.1m* 5g* 5m² 5.2f* 5f² 6g* 5d⁴ 1992 6s² 5g⁴ 5m 5d* 6m 5m* 5d² 7g² 8m 8d⁶ 7m⁵ 6g] leggy filly: fairly useful performer: won claimer at Wolver- hampton and handicap at Redcar in the summer: claimed out of J. Berry's stable £15,000 seventh start: best at around 7f: acts on firm ground, probably on dead: has flashed tail under pressure: sold abroad 18,500 gns Newmarket Autumn Sales. *M. Bell*

MAM'ZELLE ANGOT 2 b.f. (Jan 29) Balidar 133 – Ragirl (Ragusa 137) [1992 **60** 6f³ 6g³ 6s² 7m² 6m⁵ 7.3s⁴] tall, unfurnished filly: half-sister to several winners, including very speedy 1974 2-y-o Fats Waller (by Sing Sing) and middle-distance stayer The Prudent Prince (by Grundy): dam never ran: modest form in varied company: will stay 1m + : probably acts on any going: wears bandages behind: sold 10,500 gns Newmarket Autumn Sales. *M. R. Stoute*

MAMZOOJ (IRE)   3 br.f. Shareef Dancer (USA) 135 – Inshirah (USA) 90 (Caro 133) [1991 NR 1992 8d] first foal: dam 2-y-o 5f and 7f winner, is granddaughter of leading 1964 2-y-o filly Mira Femme: 9/1, behind in 21-runner maiden at Warwick in April: sold 1,500 gns Newmarket December Sales. *H. Thomson Jones*   –

MANAARAH (USA)   2 ch.f. (Apr 1) Slew O' Gold (USA) – Edgewater (USA)   **66** (Verbatim (USA)) [1992 7g 8m2 8.1d2 10g*] $47,000F, $60,000Y: leggy, unfurnished filly: good mover: third foal: dam won at up to 9f: sire top-class middle-distance colt: fair form in maidens: idled when winning at Nottingham in October: will stay 1½m. *A. A. Scott*

MANADEL   2 b.f. (Mar 15) Governor General 116 – Manabel 73 (Manado 130)   – [1992 6f a5g a6g] 720Y: lengthy filly: first foal: dam effective from 5f to 9f: no form in plating-class company: blinkered last 2 starts. *S. R. Bowring*

MANAIR (IRE)   3 b.c. Elegant Air 119 – Romantic Overture (USA) 73 (Stop The   – Music (USA)) [1991 NR 1992 10v 10g] lengthy colt: first known foal: dam 6f winner at 2 yrs, lightly raced: visored, well beaten in maiden at Pontefract and seller at Nottingham in the spring: sold to join W. Clay 2,000 gns Ascot June Sales. *A. C. Stewart*

MANAOLANA   4 b.f. Castle Keep 121 – Ladysave (Stanford 121§) [1991 10.2s6   – 11f4 10m2 13d 1992 a10g 11.9d 9.7g a10g] big, heavy-bodied filly: rated 45 at 3 yrs: seems of little account these days. *A. Moore*

MANBAA (IRE)   3 ch.f. Doulab (USA) 115 – Dayajeer 85 (Shirley Heights 130)   **45** [1991 7m* 8.3s 1992 9s 8d 7f6 8m5] sturdy, lengthy filly: showed she retains some ability in handicaps last 2 outings: should stay 1m: possibly needs a sound surface: sold 5,800 gns Newmarket July Sales, probably to Scandinavia. *H. Thomson Jones*

MANDALAY PRINCE   8 b.g. Nishapour (FR) 125 – Ops (Welsh Saint 126)   – § [1991 16s5 18d5 18f 1992 17.1d5 17.1m 12d] lengthy, well-made gelding: has a round action: poor out-and-out staying handicapper: acts on firm and dead going: tried in blinkers and visor: untrustworthy hurdler, winner of 3 novice events in August but showed no enthusiasm in the autumn: sold 1,000 gns Ascot November Sales. *J. G. M. O'Shea*

MAN FROM ELDORADO (USA)   4 b.c. Mr Prospector (USA) – Promising   **116** Girl (USA) (Youth (USA) 135) [1991 10g2 10g* 1992 8g5 12d 10m 9f*] big, lengthy colt: has long stride: very useful performer: way below form in listed events and John Porter Stakes for G. Harwood in the spring: running on lasix, narrowly won 4-runner Grade 2 handicap at Hollywood Park in July from Bold Russian and Golden Pheasant: stays 1¼m: acts on firm ground: often sweats: has worn a dropped noseband. *N. Drysdale, USA*

MANGO MANILA   7 b.h. Martinmas 128 – Trigamy 112 (Tribal Chief 125) [1991   **91** 7g3 6g 7v2 7g5 7.1s* 6g2 7g2 8m6 7d 6m 7d4 1992 8g6 7g* 7d3 7g4 7g 7.3g] robust horse: bad mover: fairly useful handicapper: well backed, impressive winner of £7,900 event at Newmarket in April: good third in Victoria Cup at Ascot: off course for fairly lengthy periods before each of last 2 starts, and well below form: effective from a stiff 6f to 1m: acts on good to firm ground, but goes very well with some give (acts on heavy going): usually wears crossed noseband: best held up. *C. A. Horgan*

MANGROVE MIST (IRE)   4 b.f. Nishapour (FR) 125 – Antiguan Cove (Mill   – Reef (USA) 141) [1991 13.8m 15g2 12.1d3 16.1m5 1992 12.1s 17.5s] lengthy filly: rated 46 at 3 yrs: tailed off in handicaps in September: better at 2m than shorter: acts on good to firm and dead ground. *P. Monteith*

MANILA BAY (USA)   2 b.c. (Feb 11) Manila (USA) – Betty Money (USA) (Our   **70** p Native (USA)) [1992 6m4 7d2 7g6] $65,000Y: big, lengthy, rather unfurnished colt: has scope: moderate mover: third reported foal: half-brother to winning French sprinter Miss Manila (by Liloy): dam won 11 races in North America at up to 9f and was graded stakes-placed: sire (by Lyphard) won Breeders' Cup Turf: fair form, looking one paced, in minor event at Newbury and maidens at Ayr and Newmarket in the summer: will probably stay 1¼m: well backed all starts: will do better in time. *M. Bell*

MAN OF THE SEASON (USA)   3 ch.g. Naked Sky (USA) – Kizzie (USA)   **63** (Naskra (USA)) [1991 6m3 5m4 5f 6g a6g a5g5 a5g 1992 7v2 7g3 8m] compact gelding: moderate mover: useful plater: broke down final start, in May: should stay

1m: acts on heavy ground and equitrack (ran moderately on fibresand): blinkered twice at 2 yrs. *J. Akehurst*

MANON LESCAUT 2 b.f. (Apr 18) Then Again 126 – Rather Warm 103 (Tribal **56** Chief 125) [1992 6f 6g 7g6 8.2d 8s2] 7,000Y: good-topped filly: has scope: moderate mover: seventh foal: half-sister to several winners, including 1991 2-y-o 6f winner Prince Emilio (by Prince Sabo) and 6-y-o 1¼m and 10.4f winner Woodurather (by Touching Wood): dam won at up to 7.6f at 2 yrs: ridden by 7-lb claimer, improved form when second of 18 in nursery at Warwick, always prominent then staying on well: will stay 1¼m: easily best effort on soft ground. *A. P. Jarvis*

MANOR ADVENTURE 2 ch.f. (Mar 20) Smackover 107 – Klairove 74 (Averof **66** 123) [1992 5g 5d4 5m2 5g5 5g3 6.1d3 5s 6m 5g5] 5,000Y: good-bodied filly: good mover: fourth foal: sister to 5.1f and 6f winner Klairover and half-sister to useful 3-y-o sprint winner Bunty Boo (by Noalto): dam 1m seller winner also successful over hurdles, is out of half-sister to high-class stayer Proverb: fair maiden: ran well from stiffish mark in Newmarket nurseries last 2 outings: stays 6f: acts on good to firm and dead ground. *B. A. McMahon*

MANSARD (IRE) 2 br.g. (May 13) Thatching 131 – Near The End (Shirley **64** Heights 130) [1992 6g 6s3 6d 6.1v] IR 10,000F: smallish, good-bodied gelding: half-brother to 3 winners, including Irish 3-y-o 6f and 7f winner Dashing Colours (by Be My Native): dam unraced: fair maiden: well beaten when visored final start: has raced only on an easy surface. *J. H. M. Gosden*

MANSBER (IRE) 3 b.g. Mansooj 118 – Our Bernie (Continuation 120) [1991 5d **50** d 6m5 5m6 5m 5g 6m5 6g 1992 7s 6g 6f5 7m2 6.1g6 8g 8f 5d4 6m 12g 12m 9.7s] compact gelding: has a poor action: poor form: stays 1m: acts on good to firm ground, probably on dead: blinkered twice, but no improvement. *Pat Mitchell*

MANSE KEY GOLD 5 ch.m. Vaigly Great 127 – Carafran (Stanford 121§) [1991 – 8g 7.5g 8.2d 8.2d 8m 10d 8m* 8.2m 8m5 8m 10.8g 1992 a8g6 16.2g6] compact mare: rated 39 at 4 yrs: sold out of R. Bastiman's stable 1,200 gns Doncaster March Sales: no worthwhile form in the summer. *J. Dooler*

MANSOOREE (USA) 2 ch.c. (Apr 9) Nureyev (USA) 131 – Lady Norcliffe **48** (USA) (Norcliffe (CAN)) [1992 5f 6f6 5d3 7m] 86,000Y: sturdy, good-bodied colt: easy mover: fifth foal: half-brother to 3-y-o 1½m winner Lady St Lawrence (by Bering) and 1989 Irish 2-y-o 5f and 7f winner Shagudine (by Shadeed): dam good winner at up to 11f: plating-class form in midsummer: well beaten final start: sold 1,500 gns Newmarket Autumn Sales. *A. A. Scott*

MANTLEPIECE (IRE) 2 ch.f. (Apr 8) Common Grounds 118 – Piney Pass – (Persian Bold 123) [1992 5g6 5g] 4,000Y: neat filly: fifth foal: half-sister to 4 winners, including 3-y-o Pass The Key (by Treasure Kay), successful at 7f at 2 yrs, and 4-y-o 5f to 7f winner Allinson's Mate (by Fayruz): dam Irish 2-y-o 8.5f winner: no worthwhile form: sold 6,000 gns Ascot May Sales. *T. D. Barron*

MANULEADER 3 b.g. King of Spain 121 – Balnerino 68 (Rolfe (USA) 77) [1991 **60** 5g 5g3 5d2 a5g2 6m2 7f4 6m 1992 7.1g 5g4 6d 6m6 6f4 7g6 a6g a6g4 6g* 6g2 5d 6f 7g] strong gelding: modest performer: trained until after fifth start by W. Pearce: won handicap at Thirsk in August: well beaten last 3 starts: stays 7f: acts on firm and dead ground: often blinkered/visored: sold to join J. Norton 1,000 gns Doncaster October Sales: inconsistent and may well be temperamental. *B. Beasley*

MANULIFE 3 b.g. King of Spain 121 – Try G'S (Hotfoot 126) [1991 6m3 6g 5f3 **65** d 6m2 6f5 7m 1992 8.3s3 9m 8.3f2 8.1d3 8.5d6 8.1g6 10m 8.3g 8g 6.9g6] quite good-topped gelding: has a quick action: inconsistent maiden: trained until after third outing by W. Pearce: stays 8.3f: acts on any going: visored (below form) last 3 starts: sold to join R. Brotherton 2,500 gns Doncaster October Sales. *B. Beasley*

MANX MONARCH 2 ch.f. (Feb 26) Dara Monarch 128 – Solemn Occasion **57** (USA) (Secreto (USA) 128) [1992 a7g5 8.2d5 7f4 8.5m 6d3 6g] close-coupled, work-manlike filly: poor mover: first foal: dam twice-raced (at 2 yrs) half-sister to very useful miler Soprano: modest form: stays 8.2f: acts on firm and dead ground. *R. Hollinshead*

MANY A QUEST (USA) 3 b.c. Riverman (USA) 131 – Call The Queen (USA) **82** (Hail To Reason) [1991 NR 1992 8m3 8f* 8m3 9g5 10m] $150,000Y: quite good-topped, attractive colt: eleventh foal: brother to 1m winner River Rhine, half-brother to ungenuine Empshott (by Graustark) and several winners, including 1985 2-y-o 6f winner Shehana (by The Minstrel): dam 6f-winning daughter of champion 2-y-o filly Queen Empress: fairly useful performer: won 2-runner maiden at Ripon in August: best efforts in handicaps at Doncaster and Newbury next 2 starts: stays 9f: yet to race on a soft surface: reportedly sent to USA. *L. M. Cumani*

MANZOOR SAYADAN (USA)   4 b.g. Shahrastani (USA) 135 – Icing 112   **71**
(Prince Tenderfoot (USA) 126) [1991 10.4m² 10g⁴ 14.6d⁴ 1992 14m⁴ 16.2m⁴ 16.4s³
14g² 14d⁶] good-bodied gelding: poor mover: very consistent handicapper but still a
maiden: stays at least 2m: acts on good to firm and soft ground: raced only in midsummer in 1992. *R. Simpson*

MAOUJOUD   4 b.g. Green Desert (USA) 127 – Anne Stuart (FR) (Bolkonski 134)   **–**
[1991 NR 1992 8.3g a10g 9.7v] big, rangy gelding: fourth foal: half-brother to very
useful 1¼m winner Anvari (by Persian Bold) and useful 1988 2-y-o 1m winner Star
Shareef (by Shareef Dancer): dam French 1m winner, is half-sister to good French
colt Arokar: no sign of ability. *R. P. C. Hoad*

MAPLE BAY (IRE)   3 b.c. Bold Arrangement 111 – Cannon Boy (USA) (Canon-   **70**
ero II (USA)) [1991 7g 1992 8d 8g⁴ 8g 9g 10d² 10.1d⁵ a12g⁴ a12g³] fair maiden:
probably stays 1½m: acts on dead ground: sold out of P. Makin's stable 6,000 gns
Ascot November Sales after sixth start. *K. White*

MAP OF STARS (USA)   2 b.c. (Feb 28) Danzig (USA) – Luminaire (USA) (Al   **77** p
Hattab (USA)) [1992 6m²] $400,000Y: unfurnished colt: fourth foal: dam Grade 2 9f
and 9.5f winner at 4 yrs in USA: well-backed 5/4-on shot and bandaged near-fore, 5
lengths second of 6 to Revelation in valuable maiden at York in August, outpaced
final 2f: showed a round action: should improve. *M. R. Stoute*

MARAADY (USA)   3 b.g. Alydar (USA) – Ma Petite Jolie (USA) 80 (Northern   **–**
Dancer (CAN)) [1991 NR 1992 8g 10s] second reported foal: dam 7f winner, is
half-sister to top-class North American filly Gorgeous Song and champion 1983
American 2-y-o Devil's Bag: behind in maidens at Newmarket and Salisbury in
April: sold to join G. Enright 3,100 gns Newmarket July Sales and gelded. *M. R.
Stoute*

MARABELLA STAR (USA)   3 b.c. Imp Society (USA) – Percentage (USA)   **96**
(Vaguely Noble 140) [1991 6.1m* 6g³ 7m* 1992 7m⁴ 8.1m⁵ 8.5d* 8m 8.5f 8.5f a8f⁶
8.5f⁶ a6f] leggy, quite good-topped colt: useful handicapper: comfortably best effort
when winning £10,600 contest at Epsom in June: trained by H. Cecil first 4 starts:
unplaced in allowance races and Grade 3 handicap in USA: stays 8.5f: acts on good to
firm ground and dead. *D. Combs, USA*

MARABOU (USA)   3 ch.f. Roberto (USA) 131 – Last Feather (USA) 120   **62**
(Vaguely Noble 140) [1991 NR 1992 10g⁵ 12.2g³] leggy, workmanlike filly: half-sister
to 3 winners, including fairly useful 1m winner Contessa (by Blushing Groom) and
Irish 1¼m winner Limber Dancer (by Nijinsky): dam 7.3f and 10.5f winner third in
Oaks: 3/1 on but green, held up then every chance in straight when third in 7-runner
maiden at Catterick in July. *L. M. Cumani*

MARADONNA (USA)   3 b.g. Alleged (USA) 138 – Kiss 88 (Habitat 134) [1991   **64**
NR 1992 10d 12g⁴ 14.1g⁴] strong, lengthy gelding: sixth reported foal: half-brother
to several winners, notably useful middle-distance stayer Crack (by High Line) and
smart 11.5f to 14.6f winner Casey (by Caerleon): dam sprinting half-sister to very
useful stayer Meistersinger: modest form: fourth in claimer at Newmarket in
August, eventually staying on well: had looked sure to improve over further, but
weakened closing stages at Carlisle 10 days later. *L. M. Cumani*

MARANDISA   5 ch.m. Pharly (FR) 130 – Marissiya (Nishapour (FR) 125) [1991   **37**
a11ga12ga12g8m12d515.1g³12.2m³12.1g1992 11m 12f8f10.5d12.3f³13.8f²12m6]
leggy, close-coupled mare: poor handicapper: stays 15f: acts on firm ground: tongue
tied down final start. *M. P. Naughton*

MARASTANI (USA)   2 ch.g. (Apr 3) Shahrastani (USA) 135 – Marianna's Girl   **89** ?
(USA) (Dewan (USA)) [1992 8d² 7g³ 6.9v² 7s²] $25,000Y: lengthy gelding: has
scope: first foal: dam, U.S. Grade 3 winner at around 1m at 3 yrs, is half-sister to 2
other graded-stakes winners: fairly useful performer: 4 lengths third of 8 to Right
Win in £8,900 event at Ascot, headed 2f out: well below that form in maidens at
Folkestone and Lingfield (raced in usually unfavoured centre of track) afterwards:
will stay beyond 1m: possibly requires sound surface. *G. Harwood*

MARATHIA   2 ch.f. (May 28) Blushing Scribe (USA) 107 – Nonpareil (FR) 92   **40** p
(Pharly (FR) 130) [1992 7g] 1,000Y: fifth foal (all by Blushing Scribe): sister to 1989
2-y-o 5.8f winner Access Leisure and fair 1988 2-y-o 5f winner Mister Lawson: dam
best at 2 yrs: 33/1, always behind in 24-runner maiden at Newmarket in October. *S.
P. C. Woods*

MARBLE MAIDEN   3 ch.f. Lead On Time (USA) 123 – Lastcomer (USA) 100   **117**
(Kris 135) [1991 NR 1992 8s² 8d* 8v² 8g² 8d* 8g* 8g² 9.5f⁴ 9d* 10f⁵] second foal:
half-sister to fair Greendale (by Green Desert), placed 3 times at around 1m: dam 6f
(at 2 yrs) and 1¼m winner, is out of half-sister to Gorytus: developed into a smart

filly, winning minor event at Saint-Cloud, listed race at Longchamp, Prix de Sandringham at Chantilly (by a neck from Hydro Calido) and All Along Stakes at Laurel (beat Wedding Ring 2¾ lengths): 4½ lengths fifth to Super Staff in Yellow Ribbon Invitational at Santa Anita on final outing: stayed 1¼m: appeared to act on any going: consistent: visits Forty Niner. *A. Fabre, France*

MARCHAM (IRE)   4 b.c. Sadler's Wells (USA) 132 – Dazzling Light 116 (Silly Season 127) [1991 8g4 8m5 1992 8g 10d] lengthy, workmanlike colt: rated 100 when fourth in listed event in March, 1991: clearly difficult to train, and no form either start in spring at 4 yrs: should stay at least 1¼m: sold 20,000 gns Newmarket December Sales: stud in Czechoslovakia. *B. W. Hills*   –

MARCHAND DE SABLE (USA)   2 b. or br.c. (May 7) Theatrical 128 – Mercantile (FR) (Kenmare (FR) 125) [1992 7g2 7d2 7s3 8d2 9d2 10s*] 320,000 francs (approx £32,100) Y: second foal: dam French 9f to 1½m winner, is daughter of very useful Mercurial, a half-sister to Prix Vermeille winner Haltilala: progressive colt: runner-up in Prix La Rochette and Prix de Conde at Longchamp in autumn before winning Criterium de Saint-Cloud in November by a neck from Infrasonic: suited by a test of stamina: acts on soft ground, yet to race on good to firm. *E. Lellouche, France*   **113**

MARCH BIRD   7 ch.g. Dalsaan 125 – Late Swallow (My Swallow 134) [1991 NR 1992 8g] strong, lengthy gelding: moderate mover: rated 81 as a 5-y-o when won Schweppes Golden Mile at Goodwood (bandaged) final start: backward, well beaten at Kempton in May, 1992: stays 1m well: acts on firm and dead going: sometimes bandaged and sweating. *J. Sutcliffe*   –

MARCHMAN   7 b.g. Daring March 116 – Saltation 111 (Sallust 134) [1991 11.7g6 10m4 12g3 10.2g 1992 11.5f2 11.8m6 12f*] big, strong, good-topped gelding: carries condition: modest performer: bandaged, won 19-runner amateurs handicap at Salisbury in June: needs a strongly-run 1¼m and stays 1¾m: acts on firm going. *J. S. King*   **59**

MARCHWELL LAD   2 ch.c. (Mar 30) Marching On 101 – Wellington Bear (Dragonara Palace (USA)) 115) [1992 6g* 5d5 5m 6g4 6g 5g] 8,000 2-y-o: leggy, close-coupled colt: sixth foal: half-brother to 3-y-o Capital Lad (by Dublin Lad) and 1989 2-y-o 7f winner Freddie's Star (by Tina's Pet): dam never ran: fair form when winning maiden at Goodwood and when over 5 lengths fifth of 6 to Marina Park in listed event at Sandown: no comparable form, off handy marks in nurseries at Kempton (pulled hard, final start for M. Channon) and Redcar (wore crossed   **73**

Criterium de Saint-Cloud—a close finish to this late-season Group 1 event between Marchand de Sable, Infrasonic and Arinthod

noseband) on last 2 starts: stays 6f: never travelling well on good to firm ground. *Mrs M. Reveley*

MARCO CLAUDIO (IRE)   2 br.c. (Feb 13) Standaan (FR) 118 – Mandy Girl   – p (Manado 130) [1992 7f] IR 6,200F, 7,200Y: half-brother to 1988 2-y-o 5f winner Incendiary Blonde (by Glenstal) and 2 other winners abroad: dam ran a few times in Ireland: 20/1, held up and always behind in 10-runner maiden at Yarmouth in August: should do better. *P. A. Kelleway*

MARCO MAGNIFICO (USA)   2 b. or br.c. (Mar 31) Bering 136 – Viscosity   **88** p (USA) (Sir Ivor 135) [1992 7g⁶ 7g² 8m³] 66,000Y: leggy colt: half-brother to 4 winners in USA: dam, from good family, won 3 races in USA: progressive maiden: under 3 lengths third of 19 to Bashayer at Newmarket in October, joining leaders over 2f out and staying on well: will be suited by further: capable of further improvement and will win races. *B. W. Hills*

MARCUS BRODY (USA)   4 ch.c. Palace Music (USA) 129 – Guilty Miss **105** (USA) (Mr Redoy (USA)) [1991 10g² 11.5g⁵ 12g² 12g³ 12.5g⁶ 12s⁴ 12g⁴ 12s⁶ 1992 12g 13.3f 12g⁴ 12d 10g² 12d 12.4m* 10d 10d* 10d³ 12.1d⁵ 10g*] lengthy, quite good-topped colt: has a quick action: useful performer: usually contested pattern/listed races: straightforward tasks when winning apprentice maiden at Newcastle in August and minor events at Nottingham in the autumn: effective from 1¼m to 1½m: acts on good to firm and soft ground: tried blinkered (well beaten) once: wears bandages. *P. A. Kelleway*

MARDESSA   4 b.f. Ardross 134 – Marquessa d'Howfen 93 (Pitcairn 126) [1991   **66** d 10d* 10d² 12m⁵ 10.2m³ 10.6m* 11m* 11.9m 10.2g⁴ 10.9g³ 10.1m² 11.9g³ 10.3m 10.9m 11.9g 10.3d 1992 10.3g 10s⁶ 10m³ 10.5m⁶ 11.9d³ 10.3m 10.5d⁵ 10.5d² 10.3s 10.3g⁵] workmanlike filly: inconsistent handicapper: shaped promisingly on several occasions in 1992 but proved frustrating to follow: effective from 1¼m to 1½m: acts on firm and dead ground: held up: has won for apprentice. *F. H. Lee*

MARDIOR   4 b.f. Martinmas 128 – Diorina 91 (Manacle 123) [1991 7m 8d 12f⁵ 10f   **34** 1992 a10g³ a13g⁶ a10g⁶ 10m 8.3m* 9.7d³ 8f 10.8s a10g] leggy filly: poor form: won (for first time) selling handicap at Windsor (no bid) in June: effective at 1m, and will probably stay 1½m: acts on good to firm and dead ground: effective blinkered or not. *W. G. R. Wightman*

MARDONIUS   6 b.h. Persian Bold 123 – Dominica (GER) (Zank) [1991 12g² **107** 14.5s* 16m⁴ 1992 15.5s 15.5g³ 20f⁵] big, workmanlike horse: useful French stayer at best: narrowly beaten behind Commendable in Group 2 Prix Vicomtesse Vigier at Longchamp: swishing tail, given reminder long way from home and always behind in Gold Cup at Royal Ascot following month: stays very well: acts on good to firm and soft going, possibly unsuited by firm: usually blinkered. *A. Fabre, France*

MARGARET'S GIFT   2 ch.f. (Jan 31) Beveled (USA) – Persiandale (Persian   **69** Bold 123) [1992 5g⁴ 5.1m⁵ 5g² 5f² 5d* 5.9f³ 5g⁴ 6d] 6,000Y: compact filly: has a quick action: second foal: half-sister to 1990 2-y-o 5f winner Satalite Boy (by Blazing Saddles): dam unraced: fair performer: won maiden auction at Beverley in July: first poor effort on final start: probably better suited by 6f than 5f: acts on firm and dead ground. *J. Berry*

MARGS GIRL   5 b.m. Claude Monet (USA) 121 – Aquarian Star (Cavo Doro 124)   **54** [1991 a11g 10.2s* 10s* 10f 10.4d 12.3g² 12g⁶ 12d² 12m⁵ 12.2f² 12f³ 12f² 11.9g⁶ 12.3f 12g 1992 a12g² a12g⁵ 12.1g⁵ 10.8d³ 11m³ 10.3m 10s 10.5d] leggy mare: poor mover: modest handicapper: swishing tail and edgy, below form facing stiff task in Haydock claimer final start: effective from 1¼m to 1½m: acts on any going, including fibre-sand: lacks turn of foot. *T. Fairhurst*

MARIA CAPPUCCINI   4 ch.f. Siberian Express (USA) 125 – Mary Martin (Be   **53** My Guest (USA) 126) [1991 5d 6g 7.3d 6s⁵ 7m³ 6.9f 7g⁴ 5.7f 8g 1992 6d⁶ 5m* 6m 7f⁴ 5g 6g 5g] rather sparely-made filly: good mover: modest handicapper: won at Lingfield in July: below form last 3 starts: effective from 5f to 7f: acts on firm ground: below form when sweating and edgy: ran well when blinkered once: has looked none too easy a ride: covered by Anshan. *K. O. Cunningham-Brown*

MARIAN EVANS   5 b.m. Dominion 123 – Kindjal 84 (Kris 135) [1991 8.2m 1992   – 11.1m 8.3f⁶ 15.1m] sturdy mare: has markedly round action: seems of little account nowadays. *T. Craig*

MARIBELLA   2 b.f. (Feb 7) Robellino (USA) 127 – Infanta Maria 82 (King of   **62** ? Spain 121) [1992 5m 5f* 6.1d* 7m 6s] 3,600Y: unfurnished filly: second foal: dam, 5f performer, is daughter of half-sister to smart Pearlescent: modest performer: ridden by 7-lb claimer, won maiden auction at Redcar and claimer at Nottingham in midsummer: subsequently ran moderately in seller at Newmarket and, 2 months later, nursery at Folkestone: better suited by 6f than 5f: acts on firm and dead ground: has worn bandages: sold 2,600 gns Doncaster November Sales. *P. F. I. Cole*

MARIETTE LARKIN   3 b.f. Elegant Air 119 – Straw Boater 89 (Thatch (USA)   **54** 136) [1991 7.1d 1992 8g 7m 7f⁴ 6d 8.2d 8g 8s 5.1s 6.1s⁶] workmanlike, good-quartered filly: inconsistent maiden: should be suited by 1m + : acts on any going: has tongue tied down. *G. B. Balding*

MARIGNAN (USA)   3 ch.c. Blushing Groom (FR) 131 – Madelia 127 (Caro 133) **117** [1991 NR 1992 11g* 10m⁵ 12g² 12m⁶ 12m⁵] ninth foal: half-brother to several winners, notably Dante Stakes winner Claude Monet (by Affirmed) and smart 7f winner Magdalena (by Northern Dancer): dam, half-sister to Mount Hagen and Monsanto, won all her 4 starts, including Poule d'Essai des Pouliches and Prix de Diane: very useful French performer: won newcomers race at Longchamp in April: best effort in pattern events when 1½ lengths second of 17 to Polytain in Prix du Jockey-Club at Chantilly, finishing very strongly despite hanging markedly: off course 11 weeks (after Irish Derby) and burly, fair fifth of 8 to Songlines in moderately-run Prix Niel at Longchamp, soon off bridle and keeping on steadily: stays 1½m well: may prove best with give in the ground. *A. Fabre, France*

MARILLETTE (USA)   2 b.f. (Feb 14) Diesis 133 – Stormette (USA) **107** (Assert 134) [1992 6f² 7m* 7g* 7m³ 7m* 7g⁵ 8m* 8s⁵ 8d]
    That Marillette's form should have progressed so far as it did in a demanding nine-race season is testimony to the skills of John Gosden and his staff at Stanley House Stables. Until she came home ninth of ten in the Racing Post Trophy at Doncaster in October, Marillette's record, which included a clear-cut victory in the Group 3 May Hill Stakes, had been one of almost constant improvement and by the end of the season there were few better staying two-year-old fillies around. In the beginning temperament threatened to get the better of Marillette. She delayed the start for several minutes before finishing a promising second to Lindon Lime at York in June on her first appearance when, having been unruly in the paddock and the canter to post, she had to be walked from the three-furlong pole; she again gave trouble before disposing of modest opposition in her next two races at Wolver-hampton and Chester. But by the time Marillette defied top weight in a fifteen-runner nursery contested by nine other winners at Goodwood in August for her third win of the year, stepping up significantly on anything she'd achieved previously, her behaviour had improved considerably and, apart from a minor relapse before the May Hill, when she was slightly wilful when being mounted, it remained far more settled. By now, Marillette was really thriving, and after another fine effort under top weight in the valuable Eglinton Nursery over seven furlongs at the York August meeting she came up with her best performance yet when put over a mile for the first time in the May Hill at Doncaster in September. Marillette started second-favourite at Doncaster behind Sheikh Mohammed's other representative Self Assured, attempting to give Henry Cecil his eighth winner in the race in eleven years and the chosen mount of retained jockey Cauthen, but she proved much too strong for her market rival and the ten others in the last half-mile. Held up as usual, well off the strong pace, Marillette began her run from just over three furlongs out, quickened past Self Assured to the front with more than a furlong to run and then stayed on resolutely to win by three lengths, the subsequent Fillies' Mile winner Ivanka finishing a length behind in third. Marillette, who was guilty of causing some interference when making her run, was herself a victim when beaten less than two lengths into fifth behind Gold Splash in the Prix Marcel Boussac at Longchamp in October; with a clear run she'd most likely have given the winner a close race. Marillette can be forgiven her poor effort in the Racing Post Trophy, her ninth race in a little over four months; paddock inspection beforehand revealed that she looked past her best for the season and she ended up trailing throughout.
    At 475,000 dollars from the Selected Session of the Keeneland July Sale, Marillette was easily the most expensive yearling sold at public auction in 1991 from the sixth crop of the top-class Diesis, sire of such as Diminuendo, Elmaamul and Keen Hunter. Much of Marillette's appeal, however, must have stemmed from the female side of her pedigree, for she's from a family whose members have regularly attracted seven-figure bids at the major North Amer-

May Hill Stakes, Doncaster—Marillette develops into a very useful filly;
Self Assured (rails) holds Ivanka for second

ican sales and who, on the whole, have done very well in Europe. Marillette's grandam South Ocean must be one of the best-known broodmares in the American Stud Book. Chief amongst her eight winners, all of whom are by Northern Dancer or one of his descendants, is Storm Bird. The remaining seven include Storm Bird's full sister Northernette, winner of the nine-furlong Canadian Oaks and dam of the smart 1984 Irish two-year-old seven-furlong and one-mile winner Gold Crest as well as the American Grade 1 mile-and-a-quarter winner Scoot; the good Canadian miler Ocean's Answer, also the dam of the smart sprinter Al Zawbaah and several winners besides; the one-time world-record yearling purchase Ballydoyle; and the 1992 first-season stallion Northern State who, like Ballydoyle, is a full brother to Storm Bird and was a winner as a two-year-old in Ireland. Marillette's dam Stormette, a daughter of the stamina-influencing Assert, won over a mile and a half on the first of her two starts in Ireland; South Ocean, incidentally, won the Canadian Oaks and was then rated the best of her sex as a three-year-old in Canada.

Marillette (USA) (b.f. Feb 14, 1990)	Diesis (ch 1980)	Sharpen Up (ch 1969)	Atan
			Rocchetta
		Doubly Sure (b 1971)	Reliance II
			Soft Angels
	Stormette (USA) (b 1984)	Assert (b 1979)	Be My Guest
			Irish Bird
		South Ocean (b 1967)	New Providence
			Shining Sun

The medium-sized, quite attractive Marillette was much better suited by a mile than shorter as a two-year-old, and most probably will require at least a mile and a quarter to be seen to best advantage from now on. While she possesses the scope to train on, it may well be significant that her trainer, who's usually very patient with his youngsters, raced her so frequently as a two-year-old. Marillette has her share of temperament, but it should be stressed that, apart from at Newmarket on her fourth outing, where she pulled hard and flashed her tail, she raced very genuinely. Marillette, who won only for Pat Eddery, probably acts on any going. *J. H. M. Gosden*

MARILYN (IRE) 3 ch.f. Kings Lake (USA) 133 – Welshwyn 113 (Welsh Saint **72** 126) [1991 5g 6f 6g³ 1992 8s⁴ 7v² 8s⁴ 9g 9d 14g² 14g³ 12g² 13g* 12s⁵ 12s² 13.1s⁶ 12d 11d⁶] IR 34,000Y: quite attractive filly: sixth foal: sister to fair sprinter Rayhaan: dam sprinter: fair Irish performer: dead-heated in amateurs maiden at Fairyhouse in August: below form (including in amateurs event at Ayr) afterwards: stays 1¾m: acts on heavy ground: sold IR 8,000 gns Goffs October Sales. *M. Kauntze, Ireland*

MARINA PARK   2 b.f. (Apr 6) Local Suitor (USA) 128 – Mary Martin (Be **105**
My Guest (USA) 126) [1992 5m² 5g* 5f⁴ 5d* 6g* 6s³ 6g²]

Up-and-coming Middleham trainer Mark Johnston had easily his most
successful season in 1992 when he sent out fifty-three winners and landed his
first pattern-race victory when Marina Park won the Princess Margaret
Stakes at Ascot in July. Marina Park had the best form of any two-year-old filly
trained in the North. She won three of her seven races over five and six
furlongs and never once finished out of the frame, all the while displaying an
admirable enthusiasm for racing.

Marina Park rose from humble beginnings. Her first appearance, in a
maiden at Redcar in April, saw her beaten a length by Bonus Point in what
proved to be a very run-of-the-mill affair. Marina Park never looked back from
that point, and almost two months later, after winning a maiden at York's May
meeting, she lined up as the North's representative in the Queen Mary Stakes
at Royal Ascot. Marina Park ran a fine race to finish fourth of thirteen to Lyric
Fantasy, showing that her participation hadn't been over-optimistic, and after
beating Joyofracing by two lengths in the listed Wharf Dragon Stakes at
Sandown in July she was sent back to Ascot for the Princess Margaret. Marina
Park started second favourite in a field of six behind the once-raced Ivanka,
successful in a minor event at Newmarket earlier in the month. Ivanka didn't
give her running at Ascot, and Marina Park, proving well suited by the step up
to six furlongs, took full advantage, putting her experience to good use to
make all the running and beat First Veil by a length and a half. The Princess
Margaret Stakes has occasionally been won by a smart filly, but creditably
though Marina Park ran in her subsequent races she wasn't able to add to her
tally. She finished third to Zafonic (who showed better form in his later
victories in the Prix de la Salamandre and Dewhurst Stakes) in the Prix Morny
at Deauville in August on ground much softer than she'd encountered before;
and in the Mill Reef Stakes at Newbury in September, in which she started a
well-backed 5/4 favourite, she was caught close home by the half-length
winner Forest Wind after attempting to make all.

Marina Park is a daughter of the exported stallion Local Suitor, a high-
class racehorse as a two-year-old when he won the Mill Reef Stakes and
finished a close third in the Dewhurst but a disappointment subsequently,
both on his only start as a three-year-old and in his time at stud. In contrast,
Marina Park's dam Mary Martin has turned out to be a success at stud; Marina
Park is her fourth foal following the 1989 two-year-old six-furlong winner
Pacific Gem (by Valiyar), the five-furlong winner Maria Cappuccini (by
Siberian Express) and, most recently, her full brother Boy Martin, a winner
over six furlongs in the latest season. Mary Martin, who never ran, is a
half-sister to the very smart sprinters Greenland Park (herself the dam of the

Princess Margaret Stakes, Ascot—
Marina Park runs on well to win from First Veil (right) and Lake Pleasant

high-class French middle-distance performer Fitnah) and Red Sunset. Her dam Centre Piece was lightly raced while her grandam Table Rose, a four-furlong winner in the States, was a half-sister to the dam of the good five-furlong colt Amber Rama as well as the French Derby second Timmy My Boy; Table Rose was also a half-sister to the grandam of the recent Poule d'Essai des Poulains winner Fast Topaze.

Marina Park (b.f. Apr 6, 1990)	Local Suitor (USA) (b 1982)	Blushing Groom (ch 1974)	Red God
			Runaway Bride
		Home Love (b 1976)	Vaguely Noble
			Homespun
	Mary Martin (ch 1983)	Be My Guest (ch 1974)	Northern Dancer
			What A Treat
		Centre Piece (b 1970)	Tompion
			Table Rose

Marina Park is reportedly being trained for the One Thousand Guineas. Her record as a two-year-old, progressive though it was, suggests she's got plenty to find to be good enough to win the race, even if she stays the mile, which isn't certain. By our reckoning, Marina Park will be most profitably campaigned over sprint distances, where the competition is also not likely to be so strong. A poor mover, the sturdy Marina Park acts on any going. *M. Johnston*

MARINE DIVER 6 b.g. Pas de Seul 133 – Marine Life (Deep Diver 134) [1991 **74** 10g⁴ 8.2g 8d² a10g⁵ 9m⁴ 12m⁴ 8g* 7g³ 8m⁶ 8g³ 8d 8g² 1992 8s 8.1m² 8.1g* 8f⁶ 10d 8m 7.1s² 8m⁶ 8d³ 9d 8s 8g] quite attractive gelding: carries condition: good walker: formerly an untrustworthy handicapper, but generally much better in 1992: best at up to 1¼m: acts on any going, but tailed off on equitrack: sometimes wears severe bridle: a difficult ride. *B. R. Millman*

MARINE SOCIETY 4 b.g. Petoski 135 – Miranda Julia 73 (Julio Mariner 127) **74** d [1991 12d 12.1g⁵ 12g² 12s⁵ a14g 1992 14d² 16m 14m⁵ 14.6m³ 14g 14.6g⁴ 12d⁵ 14.6s 12.5s³ 10.2d] well-made colt: grand walker: still a maiden, and inconsistent in handicaps in 1992: better at 1½m/1¾m than shorter: acts on good to firm and soft ground: effective visored or not: sold out of P. Walwyn's stable 8,200 gns Newmarket September Sales after seventh start. *R. Lee*

MARIONETTA (USA) 3 b.f. Nijinsky (CAN) 138 – Mariella (USA) 106 (Rob- **63** erto (USA) 131) [1991 NR 1992 12f² 11.5d⁵] tall, unfurnished filly: easy mover: third foal: sister to middle-distance maiden Ballet Russe: dam middle-distance winning daughter of Monade: form only when second in 5-runner maiden at Thirsk: looked none too keen at Yarmouth later in August: visits Kefaah. *L. M. Cumani*

MARITIME LADY (USA) 3 b.f. Polish Navy (USA) – Quixotic Lady (USA) **58** (Quadratic (USA)) [1991 6g⁶ 1992 8g⁵ 7g³ 7g⁶ 7g] sturdy filly: modest maiden: better suited by 1m than shorter. *M. R. Stoute*

MARIUS (IRE) 2 b.c. (Apr 14) Cyrano de Bergerac 120 – Nesreen (The Parson **80** 119) [1992 5g⁶ 7m 7.5d* 8m 9g* 8.9s⁴ 7.6s*] IR 4,300Y: sturdy colt: has a quick action: sixth foal: dam Irish 1¾m and 2m winner, also won over hurdles: fair performer: won maiden auction at Beverley in August and nurseries at Sandown and Lingfield in the autumn: will stay at least 1¼m: ran poorly on good to firm ground, acts on soft: usually bandaged behind. *B. W. Hills*

MARJONS BOY 5 ch.g. Enchantment 115 – Nevilles Cross (USA) 67 (Nodouble **29** § (USA)) [1991 8g 8v 8f³ 8m² 8m⁶ 8m 8d⁶ 8g 8m³ 10.1f⁴ 9m a10g⁶ a10g 1992 10d 10d 10.8g 9f² 9.9g 8.9m 11d⁵ 10.1g⁵ 8g 11.6g 11.9g] big, angular gelding: moderate mover: most inconsistent handicapper, winner of one of last 35 starts: stays 1¼m: acts on firm and dead ground: often blinkered or visored: sometimes wears tongue strap: has looked reluctant and is one to be wary of. *C. D. Broad*

MARKET BOOSTER (USA) 3 b.f. Green Dancer (USA) 132 – Final **117** Figure (USA) (Super Concorde (USA) 128) [1991 7g⁴ 6m³ 6m⁵ 7d² 7g⁵ 1992 7v* 8g² 10m* 12g² 12s* 12s]

It was a speculative but by no means hopeless investment to supplement Market Booster for the Prix de l'Arc de Triomphe. In the event, the connections' £30,000 had to be written off, Market Booster never getting in a blow, but she had looked to be progressing so well up to that point that the opportunity to run her in the Arc was one they felt they could not forego.

The latest evidence of that progress, from the Prix Vermeille over course and distance three weeks earlier, however, was largely circumstantial. The muddling pace made the Vermeille an unsatisfactory contest which didn't leave us much wiser about the limit of Market Booster's capabilities as she stayed on from the rear to be fifth of ten to Jolypha, beaten about three quarters of a length after her task had been made harder still by a lack of room on the rails. A creditable effort, but was this form she could improve on? Her previous five runs of 1992, all at the Curragh, indicated that it would be unwise to say no. Market Booster had begun the season with fairly useful two-year-old form, kept to listed or pattern races after winning a maiden at Galway on her debut, and earned a place in the Irish One Thousand Guineas when she made all in the four-runner Athasi Stakes, a listed race on heavy going at the Curragh. She started at 20/1 in the Guineas. Only bad luck in running could have beaten Marling that day but Market Booster was best of the rest, leading until the furlong marker and keeping on strongly to be beaten just a length as the favourite idled.

Second in the Guineas put Market Booster at the forefront of the Irish three-year-old fillies, and she stayed there through the season. The Guineas sixth Khanata took her on again in the Irish Independent Newspapers Pretty Polly Stakes over a quarter of a mile further the following month and was again put in her place. The toughest opposition to Market Booster came from the five-year-old Ruby Tiger, bidding to repeat her success in the race twelve months earlier, and it was a thorough test she provided; Ruby Tiger had a clear lead most of the way up the straight but Market Booster stuck to her task well to win by a length. Market Booster had been second favourite to Ruby Tiger, and an English challenger again was preferred to her in the betting when she lined up for the Irish Oaks two weeks later. User Friendly was understandably odds on. The odds in running, however, were very different. Two furlongs out Market Booster, at User Friendly's shoulder and seemingly travelling much the better, was poised to upset the rankings and if she didn't then Arrikala, also in close pursuit, surely would. But User Friendly

Irish Independent Newspapers Pretty Polly Stakes, the Curragh —
Market Booster keeps the prize at home by a length from the grey Ruby Tiger

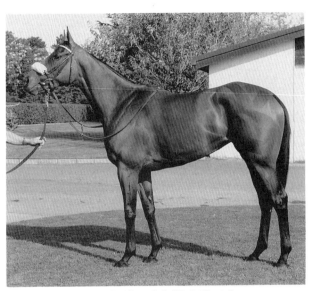

Moyglare Stud Farms Ltd's "Market Booster"

still had a neck advantage at the line; Market Booster kept on strongly when put under pressure but could never get quite on terms. She had every chance, unlike Arrikala who finished half a length back in third. To concede Arrikala 7 lb, as Market Booster had to in the Meld Stakes over course and distance six weeks later, looked a stiff task. In the event, Arrikala failed to give anything like her Irish Oaks running but that takes nothing away from Market Booster whose three-length victory over Dabtiya was another improved effort before connections cast their net further afield.

Market Booster (USA) (b.f. 1989)	Green Dancer (USA) (b 1972)	Nijinsky (b 1967)	Northern Dancer Flaming Page
		Green Valley (b 1967)	Val de Loir Sly Pola
	Final Figure (USA) (b 1980)	Super Concorde (b 1975)	Bold Reasoning Prime Abord
		Sphere (b 1970)	Round Table Gal I Love

After the Meld Stakes, it was announced by her owner-breeders that Market Booster would remain in training as a four-year-old. Her record so far indicates that she is suited by middle distances, and acts on good to firm ground and heavy, never having raced on firm. She wore blinkers on her final start at two years, but showed no signs of needing them at three. Market Booster is a medium-sized, attractive filly, a good walker, by Suave Dancer's sire Green Dancer. Her dam Final Figure has had two previous winners in Ireland from four foals, namely the eight-and-a-half-furlong winner Work That Way (by Czaravich) and the very useful mile-and-a-quarter and eleven-furlong winner Spending Record (by Topsider) who has since gone on to win in the United States. The third dam Gal I Love has a good enough record at stud, her winners including the dam of Mashaallah, in whose entry further details of this successful family can be found, but her daughter Sphere rather let the side down, failing to get any winners at all. Final Figure, the fifth of her eight foals, showed fair form in Irish maidens as a two-year-old and tried her luck in North America at three. *D. K. Weld, Ireland*

MARKET TRADER 3 ch.f. Viking (USA) – Magelka 77 (Relkino 131) [1991 a6g –
1992 10.8g 14.1m] small filly: behind in sellers. *M. F. Barraclough*

MARK'S CLUB (IRE) 2 b.g. (Feb 11) The Noble Player (USA) 126 – Never 62
Home 57 (Home Guard (USA) 129) [1992 6g 6s 6m³ 7d* 7s a7g³] IR 4,600Y: smallish, sparely-made gelding: good mover: fourth reported foal: dam poor half-sister to very useful 1969 2-y-o Sayes: modest form: ridden by 7-lb claimer when winning claimer (claimed out of B. Hills's stable £5,200) at Catterick: ran moderately afterwards: will be at least as effective at 1m: acts on good to firm and dead ground. *T. D. Barron*

MARLIN DANCER 7 b.g. Niniski (USA) 125 – Mullet 75 (Star Appeal 133) –
[1991 NR 1992 17.1d] workmanlike, angular gelding: has a round action: poor form on flat: useful hurdler, winner of handicap (2½f) in December. *Miss B. Sanders*

MARLING (IRE) 3 b.f. Lomond (USA) 128 – Marwell 133 (Habitat 134) **124**
[1991 5g* 5m* 5g* 6m* 1992 8g² 8g* 8f* 8m* 8s a9f5]
Fears that she would not stay a mile proved groundless. Fears that she would not train on proved groundless. There was no better miler of her sex in Europe than Marling. Before the One Thousand Guineas, however, all that the racing public had to go on was her pedigree and performances in 1991; she had not appeared in any of the classic trials, a minor joint injury ruling out a run in the Nell Gwyn Stakes although she would probably have been an absentee in any case. Our assessment at the end of her two-year-old season was that Marling's chances of staying a mile were better than even. The doubts on breeding centered on her dam Marwell who had failed in the Guineas (having won over an extended seven furlongs in the Fred Darling Stakes) before showing outstanding form as a sprinter. That breeding, of course, hardly fixed a limit on Marling's merit. Neither did her performances as a two-year-old. She had had four races at up to six furlongs and won all of them, including the Queen Mary Stakes at Royal Ascot and Cheveley Park Stakes at Newmarket, showing the turn of foot of a high-class racehorse and a tendency to idle in front that further whetted the appetite as to what she might achieve when fully extended. Looking in tremendous condition, as was nearly always the case, Marling started 5/1 co-second favourite in a field of

Goffs Irish One Thousand Guineas, the Curragh—
Marling gains compensation, as Market Booster can't match her finishing burst

Coronation Stakes, Royal Ascot—Marling and Culture Vulture draw clear

fourteen for the Guineas. Her performance answered all the doubters and still left the promise of better to come—but she was beaten. Two furlongs out Hatoof had already ranged up alongside the leaders but Marling had only two stragglers behind her and a wall of horses in front. Marling was switched to the rails behind Kenbu, then to Kenbu's outside and outside Hatoof, before launching a tremendous challenge in the last hundred yards, a challenge that took her almost level with Hatoof by the line, but not quite. The consensus, with which we concur, was that Marling was an unlucky loser.

There are plenty of opportunities to make amends, and Marling was well up to it. Just over three weeks after Newmarket there is the Goffs Irish One Thousand Guineas at the Curragh. With Hatoof and Kenbu having run in the French version six days earlier and Perfect Circle in the Musidora Stakes, one

Sussex Stakes, Goodwood—
facing defeat by Selkirk, Marling stages a tremendous fight-back;
Second Set and Sheikh Albadou come next

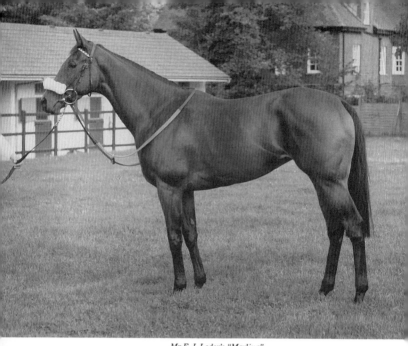

Mr E. J. Loder's "Marling"

had to look to the home team for a danger to Marling and none was apparent although Bezelle, who had beaten Norwich a neck in the Gladness Stakes on her first start for nine months, was surprisingly well backed at 7/2. The next shortest price in a nine-runner field was Khanata at 10/1. Those who had supported Marling down to 5/4 on were duly rewarded but not before suffering an unsettling case of deja vu approaching the two-furlong marker when Marling was hemmed in, seventh of nine. She edged her way out shortly after, however, and quickened to the front a furlong out, earlier than ideal but never looking in danger of defeat before finishing a length to the good over Market Booster. The Pouliches winner Culture Vulture remained a threat to Marling's supremacy among the fillies at a mile and it was not long before the issue was resolved in Marling's favour. There was little between the two on form but no doubt in the betting as to which would emerge on top in the Coronation Stakes at Royal Ascot, Marling sent off at 11/8 on, Culture Vulture 9/2 and the five other runners largely ignored. It was an absorbing match, the market leaders ridden for a turn of foot and keeping each other company off the pace as the field swung into the straight, whereupon Culture Vulture was directed towards a run up the rails and Marling switched to the outside. They were together again before the furlong marker and Marling always had the advantage though Culture Vulture battled on determinedly to keep the margin down to three quarters of a length, the rest very much in a race of their own.

Five previous winners of the Irish One Thousand Guineas had gone on to victory in the Coronation Stakes, all in the last twelve years, and four Coronation Stakes winners (Winkipop in 1910, Olein 1939, Humble Duty 1970 and Sonic Lady 1986) in the present century won the Sussex Stakes. Only Sonic Lady had won all three, and now Marling attempted to do the same. Thourios, some way off the best, was the sole representative of the three-year-old colts but the collection of six older horses in the latest Sussex Stakes could hardly have been any stronger. The 1991 winner Second Set was joined by the top miler of 1991 Selkirk; the leading sprinter Sheikh Albadou; the evergreen Sikeston; Forte Mile winner Rudimentary; and Breeders' Cup Mile third Star of Cozzene, now trained in France. No filly took the field against Marling who again started favourite, at 11/10. This was a race that promised much and produced even more, possibly the most stirring finish of the British season. Thourios set a furious pace, with Rudimentary a couple of lengths behind him and Marling another five back, at the head of the pursuers. Marling got to the leaders approaching the final furlong but was joined by Selkirk, apparently going the better, almost as soon as she had done so. This time she had to pull out all the stops. The result was in doubt until the very last stride but it was Marling, responding superbly to Eddery's driving finish, who had her head in front again thirty yards out and still held the advantage at the line as Selkirk came again. Second Set had been slightly checked in his run, Sheikh Albadou rather more so, before finishing third and fourth, beaten three quarters of a length and two.

The Sussex Stakes was the zenith of Marling's career. At this stage, with a little more luck at Newmarket hers would still have been an unbeaten record, but, after a two-month break, her last two appearances on a race-course brought clear-cut defeats. Bad luck in running played its part in her fifth-of-fourteen placing in the Breeders' Cup Distaff on dirt at Gulfstream Park—she had to be switched after running out of room on the inside going into the final turn—but it would be stretching things to suggest that Marling might have caught the four-length winner Paseana there and, five weeks earlier, she never looked like being concerned in the finish of the Queen Elizabeth II Stakes at Ascot once the field had come into the straight. It was reported that Marling had looked as good as ever on the gallops before and after Ascot. The scale of her defeat in a very strong field there probably owed a good deal to the soft ground—though she was also very edgy and got into a muck sweat beforehand—and her effort at Gulfstream Park showed that Marling was still capable of very smart form when her illustrious career came to a close.

		Northern Dancer (b 1961)	Nearctic
Marling (IRE) (b.f. 1989)	Lomond (USA) (b 1980)		Natalma
		My Charmer (b 1969)	Poker
			Fair Charmer
	Marwell (b 1978)	Habitat (b 1966)	Sir Gaylord
			Little Hut
		Lady Seymour (b 1972)	Tudor Melody
			My Game

Marling is a lengthy filly, though one lacking in substance compared to most of her rivals at Goodwood and Ascot, and a good walker who has a quick action in her faster paces. She acted on firm going. One suggestion that cropped up frequently in the first half of the season was that Marling might be returned to sprinting, like her dam. How she would have coped in the July Cup or the Haydock Park Sprint Cup is only speculation; in hindsight it is obviously easier to conclude that the decision to go for the Sussex Stakes was the right one. The way she kept finding more at Goodwood, as well as her overall record, leave no doubt that Marling stayed a mile really well. Marwell was put back to sprinting immediately after the One Thousand Guineas and won the King's Stand Stakes, July Cup and Abbaye. Her four foals prior to Marling include the good-class colt Caerwent (by Caerleon) who showed his effectiveness at both five furlongs and a mile with seconds in the Irish Two Thousand Guineas and, promoted from third, the Abbaye. This family has featured prominently in many previous editions of *Racehorses* but the issue of stamina potential continues to intrigue. This will be more than ever the case with Marwell's next two foals who are colts by Sadler's Wells. Her 1992 foal is another colt, by Royal Academy. It was reported that Marling will start her stud career with a visit to Riverman. *G. Wragg*

Lanson Champagne Vintage Stakes, Goodwood—Maroof is punched clear of Humam

MAROOF (USA) 2 b.c. (Apr 12) Danzig (USA) – Dish Dash 118 (Bustino 136) **107**
[1992 5m* 6g² 7m* 7s²] compact, useful-looking colt: seventh foal: closely related
to 3-y-o 1¼m winner Mayaasa (by Lyphard) and a winner in France and half-brother
to useful 1986 2-y-o 7f winner Arrasas (by Irish River): dam won Ribblesdale
Stakes: won maiden at Lingfield in June, then Lanson Champagne Vintage Stakes at
Goodwood in July (beat Humam by 1½ lengths): ½-length second of 5 to Fatherland
in National Stakes at the Curragh over 7 weeks later, making most, initially at a
modest pace, and running on well: will stay at least 1m: very progressive but
fractured off-fore cannon bone and wasn't seen out again (said to have made a good
recovery and will be in training in 1993). *R. W. Armstrong*

MAROWINS 3 ch.g. Sweet Monday 122 – Top Cover (High Top 131) [1991 5f⁶ **49**
6m⁴ a7g³ a7g⁴ 7m 8m 8.1g 10.5d 1992 10.5m 8.9s 9f² 10g³ 10g⁴ 10.9d⁵ 11g⁴ 12.1s³
10.5d 12.2d⁵ 9.2v³] robust gelding: has a quick action: largely consistent maiden
handicapper: ideally needs further than 9f, and stays 1½m: probably acts on any
going: below form when visored at 2 yrs. *E. J. Alston*

MARPATANN (IRE) 3 b.c. Vision (USA) – Eimkar (Junius (USA) 124) [1991
7m⁶ 8d 1992 8d 12g 10m 16.1d a12g] quite attractive ex-Irish colt: first foal: dam
unraced half-sister to high-class French miler Daring Display: of little account. *A. S.
Reid*

MARROS MILL 2 ch.f. (Apr 16) Glint of Gold 128 – Springwell 73 (Miami **60**
Springs 121) [1992 7m⁵ 8m³ 8d] good-topped filly: third foal: half-sister to 3-y-o
Chill Wind (by Siberian Express) and a winner in Sweden by Primo Dominie: dam
10.2f winner: modest maiden: will be well suited by middle distances. *M. Bell*

MARTINA 4 b.f. Tina's Pet 121 – Tin Tessa 87 (Martinmas 128) [1991 a6g⁴ 6g³ **71**
6m 6d² 6d 6g² 7m⁵ 7g 1992 5g² 5m³ 5f² 5f* 5m² 5.1f⁴ 5g³ 7.6v 7g] workmanlike
filly: fair handicapper: bang in form in the summer, winning at York: off course over
3 months, below form in October last 2 starts, though shaped as if retaining her
ability: best at up to 6f: acts on firm and dead ground. *J. Wharton*

MARTINI EXECUTIVE 4 b.c. King of Spain 121 – Wigeon 80 (Divine Gift 127) **66**
[1991 a6g⁴ a8g³ a8g⁴ 9m 8m 9m 9m a8g a10g 1992 a8g* a8g* a8g² a8g³ 7.5g⁶ 8s 8f⁵ **a83**
8.3m² 8m² 9d³ 8m⁴ 7f 8g³ 8s⁶ 8d] lengthy, workmanlike colt: poor mover: reportedly cured from his tendency to break blood vessels at 3 yrs and showed himself a
fairly useful performer on the all-weather, winning at Lingfield and Southwell in
January: consistent handicapper on turf for the remainder of the season (well beaten
on both occasions when not blinkered), trained until after penultimate start by W.
Pearce/B. Beasley: will stay 1¼m: acts on any going: seems to need blinkers: good
mount for an apprentice: tough: sold to join B. Wilkinson 6,000 gns Doncaster
November Sales. *C. B. B. Booth*

MARTINI'S COURIER 5 br.g. Lucky Wednesday 124 – Be My Sweet 78 **– §**
(Galivanter 131) [1991 12f 8.1g⁵ 10g³ 8m 1992 a8g] leggy gelding: turns off-fore in:

508

rated 41 at 4 yrs: well beaten in February, 1992: sold 680 gns Doncaster June Sales: one to leave alone. *R. E. Barr*

MARTINOSKY 6 b.g. Martinmas 128 – Bewitched 63 (African Sky 124) [1991 6m **66** 6g³ 6g⁶ 6g³ 5f² 7m 5.3g⁵ 5g⁶ 5.1s 6.1d³ 7g 7g 1992 7m⁵ 5g* 7.1m⁵ 5m² 6f² 6.1g* 5m⁴ 6f⁵ 6g 6d 5s³ 6g⁵ 7g 5d 6.1d⁶] big gelding: good walker: fair handicapper: won at Lingfield in May and Chepstow in July: suited by 6f/7f: acts on any going: effective blinkered earlier in career but well beaten when tried in 1992: has run creditably for amateur. *W. G. R. Wightman*

MART LAGACHE (FR) 4 b.g. Crofter (USA) 124 – Match Point (Hotfoot 126) **–** [1991 a7g 8m a7g⁶ a8g a12g 1992 a8g] big, workmanlike gelding: moderate mover: no worthwhile form. *D. W. Chapman*

MARVELOUS MOLLY 3 b.f. Shardari 134 – Dunninald 93 (Mill Reef (USA) **–** 141) [1991 6f 7g⁴ 8.1g 1992 10f 8h⁴ 9.7g⁴ 8.1d 7f⁵ 7d] smallish, leggy filly: no worthwhile form in 1992, in blinkers once: bred to be suited by 1m +: takes keen hold: sold 1,800 gns Newmarket Autumn Sales. *I. A. Balding*

MARWELL MITZI 2 b.f. (Apr 22) Interrex (CAN) – Lily of France 81 (Mon- **50** santo (FR) 121) [1992 5f⁶ 5d 5.3f⁴ 6g⁵ 6v⁵ 6s⁵ 6v a6g⁵ a7g⁴] compact filly: fourth foal: half-sister to 3-y-o 6f winner Great Hall (by Hallgate): dam sprinter: modest maiden: stays 6f: acts on any going. *W. G. R. Wightman*

MARYLAND WILLIE 5 b.g. Master Willie 129 – Maryland Cookie (USA) 101 **49** (Bold Hour) [1991 NR 1992 10f³ 12m² 16f5] angular, workmanlike gelding: rated 89 at 3 yrs for D. Elsworth: only poor form in early-summer at 5 yrs, including in claimers: should stay 2m: acts on firm and dead going: wears bandages: sold 840 gns Newmarket July Sales. *N. A. Callaghan*

MARY MACBLAIN 3 b.f. Damister (USA) 123 – Tzarina (USA) (Gallant Romeo **45** (USA)) [1991 5m⁵ 5g a6g 7g 7m 8.1s 1992 10f⁶ 12.2g⁶ 7m² 8g⁴ 7g³ 8m 8.3s³ 7d] plain, shallow-girthed filly: has a round action: plating-class maiden: stays 8.3f: acts on good to firm and soft ground: hangs left, and has worn near-side pricker. *J. L. Harris*

MARZOCCO 4 ch.g. Formidable (USA) 125 – Top Heights (High Top 131) [1991 **58** 7g 10g 10g 7m* 8.2g⁶ 8g 10g 6.9f⁶ 8m 1992 a8g³ a8g 10d⁵ 8m* 10m 8m⁵ 9g² 10m² 10m 10m⁵ 8m 8d] good-topped gelding: moderate mover: inconsistent handicapper: won at Brighton in April: effective from 1m to 1¼m: acts on good to firm ground and equitrack: below best in blinkers twice: has swished tail: a difficult ride. *J. Ffitch-Heyes*

MASAD (IRE) 3 b.c. Sadler's Wells (USA) 132 – Marmolada (Sassafras **119** p (FR) 135) [1991 7d⁶ 7m² 1992 11g* 12g³ 10m* 10.4g⁵ 12d* 10m⁶]

The weekend trip to Italy has become a popular option for British-trained horses, increasing prestige and financial rewards being added to the lure of black type. Drum Taps, Mashaallah, Alhijaz, Sikeston, Oumaldaaya and Silvernisian were among those to gain important successes in Italy in 1992. Another was Masad. This three-year-old won for the first time in the Premio Conte Felice Scheibler, a race without pattern or listed status, at Rome in May and won connections over £100,000 in the process. The race was for Italian breds—Masad (who carries the IRE suffix) qualifying for his Italian owner/breeders apparently thanks to his swift removal to Italy after birth—and featured several breeders bonuses to supplement the already substantial first prize of nearly £70,000. Add to that reward the distance of the race, eleven furlongs, and the ease with which he won it, and this was a most satisfactory trial for the Derby Italiano at the same course three weeks later. His second place in the Houghton Stakes at Newmarket the previous October was, perhaps, more persuasive evidence to the racing public here that Masad might well have the necessary class. A thirteen-strong field for the Derby Italiano included six British-trained colts, one French, one Irish and one who had been trained in Ireland until after his latest start. The shuffling of ownership that is a customary prelude to this race saw a half-share sold in the Dermot Weld-trained In A Tiff, and a swift return when In A Tiff held the fast finish of Boutin's Merzouk with the less experienced Masad, who had held every chance in the final furlong, beaten about three quarters of a length in third.

The Derby Italiano form might not carry much weight in the overall assessment of European pattern performers, but improvement was a persist-

Mrs G. Zanocchio's "Masad"

Masad (IRE) (b.c. 1989)	Sadler's Wells (USA) (b 1981)	Northern Dancer (b 1961)	Nearctic Natalma
		Fairy Bridge (b 1975)	Bold Reason Special
	Marmolada (b 1977)	Sassafras (b 1967)	Sheshoon Ruta
		Mobola (b 1969)	Mincio Waltzing Matilda

ent feature of Masad's season and he went on to prove himself a smart animal. After he had brushed aside useful opposition, quickening in sparkling fashion after a sedate early gallop, in a minor event at Newmarket in July, Masad was kept to Group 1 events. He was again pitted against In A Tiff in the Gran Premio d'Italia at Milan in September, and turned the tables convincingly, travelling strongly just behind the leaders before being switched wide two furlongs out and driven out to catch Modhish as well in the last fifty yards. It was not one of the strongest Group 1 contests of 1992—although Modhish had beaten Snurge at Deauville on his previous start—but that criticism cannot be levelled at the International at York or the Champion Stakes at Newmarket. Masad was unable to quicken with the principals and finished out of the frame in both of those races, but he wasn't beaten far—seven lengths at York and about four and three quarters at Newmarket. It is likely that Masad will prove better at one and a half miles as a four-year-old, and probable that he will be an even better racehorse. A strong, good-topped colt with a fluent action, Masad has yet to race on extremes of going but acts on good to firm and dead.

510

Masad's dam Marmolada made a big impact in a far less exalted period for Italian racing, one dogged by stories of doping, race fixing and illegal betting. She won at two, three and four years, thirteen times in all, with her best season coming at three years in 1980 when she won eight of her ten starts, including the eleven-furlong Oaks d'Italia and one-and-a-quarter-mile Premio Lydia Tesio by an aggregate of sixteen lengths. Marmolada's third season included setting an Italian record for one mile. Her dam, Mobola, won four times over sprint distances in France but apart from her grandam Waltzing Matilda's half-brother Roan Rocket, good winners are thin on the ground in Marmolada's pedigree, and her own producing record prior to Masad was an uninspiring one. Her offspring by Ela-Mana-Mou, Teenoso, Wassl and Caerleon all failed to win a race. Masad was retained for 210,000 guineas at the Highflyer Sales, since when Marmolada has thrown a 1990 colt by Law Society (sent to Italy) and a 1992 filly by Doyoun. *L. M. Cumani*

MASAI MARA (USA) 4 ch.g. Mogambo (USA) – Forever Command (USA) – (Top Command (USA)) [1991 7m 10g⁵ 9m² 10m* 10.6g² 10g* 10m 14.1m* 13.9g 12.3f* 12m 16m⁵ 12m² 12m 1992 12.3m] tall, useful-looking gelding: carries condition: fairly useful handicapper (rated 89) at 3 yrs: found conditions too sharp at Ripon in August at 4 yrs: needs stiff test of stamina at 1½m, and should prove ideally suited by 1¾m + : acts on firm ground: soon off bridle, and edges right: worth a try in blinkers: will prove best with strong handling: usually awkward at stalls: sold 3,200 gns Doncaster November Sales and has joined J. Ffitch-Heyes. *P. C. Haslam*

MASAKEN 4 ch.f. Doulab (USA) 115 – Amalee 57 (Troy 137) [1991 7g 1992 5m a5g 8m] workmanlike filly: seems of little account. *T. Kersey*

MASHAAER (USA) 3 b.f. Shadeed (USA) 135 – Princess Sucree (USA) **62** (Roberto (USA) 131) [1991 6g³ 1992 7g⁵ 7m³ 7g 6.9g³ 8d] lengthy, angular filly: inconsistent maiden: likely to stay 1m: acts on good to firm ground, possibly not on a soft surface: sold 16,000 gns Newmarket December Sales. *R. W. Armstrong*

MASHAALLAH (USA) 4 b.c. Nijinsky (CAN) 138 – Homespun (USA) **123** (Round Table) [1991 10m⁶ 10.2m* 11.9m* 1992 10g* 13.3f² 12d* 12d* 12g³ 12.5g² 12g⁶ 12s* 14s* 12s 12d]

The Irish St Leger attracted its strongest field since the race was controversially thrown open to four-year-olds and upwards in 1983. Detractors might say that that does not mean a great deal. However, the field in 1992 was undeniably a good one, strong in the older-horse department which comprised, in betting order, the 11/4 favourite Mashaallah, Drum Taps, Snurge, Rock Hopper, Jahafil and Vintage Crop. The favourite, known to be suited by the prevailing soft going and confidently expected to stay the trip, was one of the most improved horses in training. When Rock Hopper won the Yorkshire Cup back in May, Mashaallah, a good-bodied colt who looked the part, had still to make his mark outside handicap company; he remedied that shortly afterwards by finishing second to Endoli in the Aston Park Stakes at

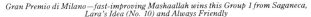

Gran Premio di Milano—fast-improving Mashaallah wins this Group 1 from Saganeca, Lara's Idea (No. 10) and Always Friendly

Grosser Preis von Baden, Baden-Baden—
all four finishers, Mashaallah, Platini, almost-hidden Sapience and Hondo Mondo

Newbury and beating Glity for the Prix de la Porte de Madrid at Longchamp. And when Drum Taps won the Gold Cup back in June, Mashaallah had still to make his mark outside listed company; again, he soon did so, beating Saganeca for the Gran Premio di Milano. Between the Gran Premio di Milano and the Irish St Leger, Mashaallah made four more starts and won on the last of them, picking up his second Group 1 race on the Continent in the Grosser Preis von Baden at Baden-Baden in the first week in September, a race in which he had Sapience around three lengths back in third place, with the leading German three-year-old Platini in second. The three defeats over this period lost him no caste, although he was coming to look increasingly like a horse who needed a good gallop to be shown to advantage at a mile and a half. He was being highly tried when third to Saddlers' Hall in the Princess of Wales's Stakes at Newmarket on the first occasion, and also, in hindsight, when a neck runner-up to Vert Amande giving him 7 lb in the Prix Maurice de Nieuil at Maisons-Laffitte on the second; on the third, he became involved in a sprint finish in the Aral-Pokal at Gelsenkirchen and came out worst of six, although beaten only two lengths by the winner Tel Quel.

Snurge, just touched off at Gelsenkirchen, proved Mashaallah's most dangerous opponent at the Curragh. The pair of them dominated the race the length of the straight but were attended in a close finish by Drum Taps. A strong gallop set by the pacemaker Tropicarr and Jahafil had the nine runners spread out twenty-five lengths after a couple of furlongs. Mashaallah was settled in third, some way behind the leaders yet clear of the rest. As the field began to come back together with five furlongs to go Mashaallah improved past Tropicarr, and before long he moved comfortably past Jahafil, too, showing the way into the straight to Snurge, Drum Taps and Rock Hopper. Mashaallah gamely made the rest. He was pressed hard by Snurge, part-

512

icularly in the last two furlongs, and needed to be driven out to stay a neck up. The older horses filled the first five places; after the strong-finishing Vintage Crop in fifth there came a clear gap to the three-year-old fillies Arrikala and Dabtiya. While Snurge maybe wasn't in quite the same form as when he took third place in the Prix de l'Arc de Triomphe in 1990, the result of the Irish St Leger gave the improving Mashaallah a fair each-way chance in the latest Arc, his next engagement, as long as the race developed into a searching test, which seemed very likely when the ground came up soft. Not so. For once they dawdled early on, and when the race developed into a sprint from the turn Mashaallah, who had been given an unenterprising ride for so stout a stayer, was bang in trouble, outpaced. From being a prominent sixth, he eventually dropped down to eleventh of eighteen, and was beaten around eight lengths by Subotica. A bold bid by connections for compensation two weeks later in the Rothmans International at Woodbine in Canada came to nothing. Made favourite, he finished a below-form eleventh of fourteen to the subsequently-disqualified Wiorno, fading in the closing stages although again beaten only about eight lengths.

Mashaallah (USA) (b.c. 1988)	Nijinsky (CAN) (b 1967)	Northern Dancer (b 1961)	Nearctic
			Natalma
		Flaming Page (b 1959)	Bull Page
			Flaring Top
	Homespun (USA) (b 1969)	Round Table (b 1954)	Princequillo
			Knight's Daughter
		Gal I Love (ch 1959)	Nasrullah
			Gallita

Mashaallah was bought as a yearling for 525,000 dollars at Keeneland. He didn't reach the racecourse until the age of three, and appeared only three times that season because he became an early victim of the coughing that ran through the stable. He went down after a very impressive win in a handicap at York in the summer, at a time when he was looking a likely candidate for the Ebor. On his return as a four-year-old he again won very impressively in handicap company, at Newmarket, and had been showing enough at home to warrant entry in the Coronation Cup and Hardwicke Stakes; in the end he took a different route towards the top. Mashaallah's half-brother Sarangani Bay (by Manila) raced as a two-year-old in Britain in the latest season, showing modest form in maidens which he should be able to improve upon given the chance to tackle longer distances. Back in the United States, Mashaallah has a number of well-known relatives. His dam, a minor winner there, has produced seven other winners so far, including the graded stakes performers Sportin' Life and Folk Art by Mashaallah's sire Nijinsky. An unraced mare out of the same dam is Home Love, the dam of the Mill Reef Stakes winner Local Suitor and the Prix Jean Prat winner Local Talent. The unraced grandam Gal I Love is a sister to the champion American two-year-old Nadir and is maternal great-grandam of the Champion Stakes winner of 1979 Northern Baby and the smart Irish three-year-old Market Booster.

Jefferson Smurfit Memorial Irish St Leger, the Curragh — Mashaallah's third Group 1 he keeps Snurge, Drum Taps and Rock Hopper behind

Whither Mashaallah now? Connections are most likely to continue to look for suitable openings at a mile and a half or a mile and three quarters and hope that a little more improvement is forthcoming. No doubt further trips overseas will be on the agenda, particularly as, while he has some form on firm going, he has shown himself so well suited by soft. On his performance in Ireland Mashaallah is worth a trial over a longer distance, but that option seems less likely to be taken up, and then only if he is found wanting at a mile and a half. Wherever he goes, it's a pound to a penny that this admirable colt will continue to do credit to all concerned with him. *J. H. M. Gosden*

MASHAIR (USA)   2 b.f. (Mar 26) Diesis 133 – Lucky Lucky Lucky (USA)   **62** p
(Chieftain II) [1992 7m] tall, leggy, lengthy filly: fourth foal: half-sister to 3-y-o Alsaarm, 7f winner at 2 yrs, and 1990 2-y-o 6f and 7f winner Aimaam (both by Danzig): dam, high-class filly successful from 7f to 9f, won Kentucky Oaks: 25/1 and green, 8 lengths eighth of 12 to Barathea in maiden at Newmarket in October, slowly away and outpaced, modest late headway: will stay 1¼m: showed a round action: will improve. *J. L. Dunlop*

MASHAKEL (USA)   3 b.c. Sovereign Dancer (USA) – Rivermande (FR) (River-   **79**
man (USA) 131) [1991 NR 1992 7g⁵ 7m 10m* 9m³ 9m 10m⁴ 11.4d⁶] $160,000Y: useful-looking colt: moderate mover: seventh reported foal: half-brother to 3 winners, notably fairly useful 1984 2-y-o 5f performer Sharp Ascent (by Sharpen Up), a Grade 3 8.5f winner at 3 yrs in USA: dam very useful winner at around 1m in France: fair performer: won claimer at Newmarket in May: well below form in similar event (claimed £10,552 to race in Scandinavia) at Sandown in July: stays 1¼m: acts on good to firm ground: below form in blinkers second start: usually bandaged. *B. Hanbury*

MASH THE TEA (IRE)   3 b.g. Mazaad 106 – Tassie (Lochnager 132) [1991 NR   –
1992 6d 10g 8.5f 10m] IR 1,600F: sturdy gelding: sixth foal: half-brother to Irish 1m and 8.5f winner Noora Beag (by Ahonoora): dam ran once in Ireland: no worthwhile form, including in a visor. *H. J. Collingridge*

MASNUN (USA)   7 gr.g. Nureyev (USA) 131 – Careless Kitten (USA) (Caro 133)   **84**
[1991 6s 7g 6g 6m 7g³ 7.6m⁵ 6m 5g 6g³ 6f⁵ 6g* 6g 6m* 7g 6m 6m³ 1992 5g 6g 6m⁵ 6g 6f³ 5g⁵ 6m 6g 6d] sturdy gelding: fairly useful handicapper on his day: effective at 6f and 7f: has form on any going, but particularly effective on a sound surface: often on toes: has hung right, and been reluctant to post. *R. J. O'Sullivan*

MASRUR (USA)   3 b.c. Mt Livermore (USA) – Presto Youth (USA) (Youth   **61**
(USA) 135) [1991 NR 1992 8g 7g 7f⁵ 7d⁴ 6m² 6m 7d*] $30,000Y, resold $92,000Y: smallish, rather leggy colt: fifth foal: half-brother to a minor winner by Lear Fan: dam, lightly raced, from family of Jalmood: sire good class over 6f/7f (also won over 1m): modest form: won 3-runner maiden at Warwick in July: stays 7f: acts on firm and dead ground: hung left and looked none too keen once: sold to join D. Marks 5,600 gns Newmarket July Sales. *R. W. Armstrong*

MASSIBA (IRE)   3 b.f. Shareef Dancer (USA) 135 – Massorah (FR) 108 (Habitat   **90**
134) [1991 NR 1992 10.1s⁵ 8s³ 8g⁴ 6m* 6g³ 6m* 6g* 6g⁵ 6g 6d⁵ 6m 5.2s] good-quartered filly: fourth foal: sister to French 1m winner Mashoura and French 7.5f and 1m winner Monaiya: dam French sprinter: fairly useful performer: won maiden at Pontefract in May: claimed out of B. Hanbury's stable £21,053 next start: impressively made all in handicaps at Windsor and Haydock in midsummer: rather inconsistent afterwards and looked a difficult ride, tending to hang: best at sprint distances: below form on soft going, acts on any other: flashes tail. *M. J. Heaton-Ellis*

MASTAMIST   3 ch.g. Tickled Pink 114 – Tana Mist 71 (Homeboy 114) [1991 NR   **43**
1992 7s 8d 6m 6.9m 7.6m⁴ 8f² 8d⁵ 9d] plain gelding: poor mover: first known foal: dam 2-y-o 5f winner stayed 1¼m: poor maiden: worth another try beyond 1m: acts on firm going: blinkered last 5 starts. *R. Voorspuy*

MASTER COPY (IRE)   3 b.c. Bluebird (USA) 125 – Music of The Night (USA)   **48**
(Blushing Groom (FR) 131) [1991 7g 7.5f⁶ 1992 8g 10m³ 12.2g⁵ 10g 10g³ 9f 10.5g⁵ 10d* 10s] compact colt: inconsistent handicapper: won at Ayr in August: stays 1¼m: acts on dead ground, never travelling well on firm: usually blinkered or visored: may be temperamental: sold 3,700 gns Doncaster November Sales, reportedly to Czechoslovakia. *C. B. B. Booth*

MASTER D DEE   4 gr.g. Absalom 128 – Elizabeth Howard 68 (Sharpen Up 127)   –
[1991 NR 1992 10d⁶ 8g] lengthy gelding: third foal: dam middle-distance winner: no sign of ability: has joined H. Collingridge. *P. W. Harris*

MASTER FIDDLER 2 b.c. (Apr 6) Teenoso (USA) 135 – Musical Princess 66 **52**
(Cavo Doro 124) [1992 6f 7d 8m⁵ 8.5m⁴ 8s⁶ 8.1g] lengthy colt: moderate mover:
fourth foal: half-brother to 3-y-o 8.9f to 10.1f winner Drummer Hicks (by Seymour
Hicks) and 1m to 1½m winner Oh Danny Boy (by Rabdan): dam won 4 times, at
1½m and 2m, at 5 yrs: plating-class form in maidens: first moderate effort when
failing to handle bend at Edinburgh final start: will stay beyond 1m: probably acts on
any going. *E. Weymes*

MASTER FOODBROKER (IRE) 4 br.g. Simply Great (FR) 122 – Silver **86** §
Mantle 70 (Bustino 136) [1991 12g* 12m⁴ 14s 1992 20m⁴ 14s 14g] workmanlike
gelding: fairly useful handicapper on his day: reluctant to race last 2 starts, in
blinkers first occasion: stays 2½m: acts on good to firm ground: sold to join W.
Musson 2,600 gns Newmarket Autumn Sales: one to treat with caution. *D. R. C.
Elsworth*

MASTER HYDE (USA) 3 gr.c. Trempolino (USA) 135 – Sandspur (USA) (Al **62**
Hattab (USA)) [1991 6s⁶ 7.1s⁶ 6m⁶ 6g⁵ 1992 7.6s⁶ 10f⁶ 7.5m 7f⁴ 6m³ a6g 6m 6g² a7g
a6g³ a7g*] leggy, workmanlike colt: inconsistent, but 2 good efforts on Lingfield
equitrack late in year, strong run to lead close home in handicap: stays 7f well: acts
on soft ground and equitrack, probably on good to firm: no improvement in
blinkers/visor. *P. Mitchell*

MASTER LINE 11 ch.h. High Line 125 – Fair Winter 111 (Set Fair 129) [1991 –
10.8m⁵ 12g² a12g a14g 1992 11.7d⁶ 11.8g³ 11.4f 14.1m] small, sparely-made horse:
has a sharp action: no longer of much account. *H. Candy*

MASTER OF PASSION 3 b.c. Primo Dominie 121 – Crime of Passion 115 **92**
(Dragonara Palace (USA) 115) [1991 5g* 5m 6m* 6m³ 1992 7g 7.1d 6f 6g 5m⁶ 5m⁶
5.2g] lengthy, angular colt: has a quick action: fairly useful form on his day: may
prove best at 6f: acts on good to firm ground: behind in blinkers once: visored last 2
starts, running creditably first occasion. *J. M. P. Eustace*

MASTER OFTHE HOUSE 6 b.g. Kind of Hush 118 – Miss Racine (Dom –
Racine (FR) 121) [1991 7d 9f² 1992 a8g⁵ 8d] sturdy gelding: poor mover: still a
maiden on flat and well held in the spring: seems to stay 9f: acts on any going: has
been tried in blinkers and visor: has sweated: modest winning hurdler in 1991/2,
including in May. *M. D. Hammond*

MASTER OF THE ROCK 3 b.c. Alzao (USA) 117 – Come True (FR) (Nasram **62**
II 125) [1991 NR 1992 8g 10f 10m 11.6g 12f 8s⁴ 8d 11.8s⁶] sturdy colt: has a long,
round action: half-brother to several winners, including useful 1m to 1¼m winner
Spanish Dancer (by Gay Fandango) and 7f winner Cosmic Princess (by Fairy King),
latter successful in small race at around 9f in France: dam Irish 1½m winner:
inconsistent maiden: stays 1¼m: probably acts on any going: blinkered (ran poorly)
fifth start: sold to join Mrs P. Barker 8,200 gns Newmarket Autumn Sales and won
selling hurdle (bought in 5,000 gns) in December. *P. J. Makin*

MASTER PEACE (FR) 2 b.c. (Mar 25) Irish River (FR) 131 – Melite (USA) **107**
(Caro 133) [1992 6d⁴ 6s² 6g² 7s* 8s] third foal: brother to French 3-y-o Malmed:
dam ran 6 times: put up useful effort in Challenge d'Or Piaget at Deauville, winning
by 2½ lengths: beaten a neck by Kingmambo in minor event at Maisons-Laffitte
previous month: well beaten in Grand Criterium at Longchamp on final outing:
should be better suited by 1m than less: has raced only on a soft surface. *J. C.
Cunnington, France*

MASTER PECKITT 2 b.g. (May 14) Tinoco 80 – Pretty Soon 75 (Tina's Pet –
121) [1992 5g 7d 5v] small, angular gelding: first foal: dam 7f winner, possibly
became ungenuine: no worthwhile form. *S. E. Kettlewell*

MASTER PLAN (FR) 6 b.g. Carwhite 127 – Manene (FR) (Tapioca II 123) [1991 **22**
10.2s 8g 8.5f⁶ 8.3s 8f 10.5g 1992 8.3v 13d 8.1g 8.3s 16.2m 8.1m 8.3m⁵ 8.3g³ 8g 10g
8g] compact gelding: moderate mover: of little account nowadays. *D. L. Williams*

MASTER PLANNER 3 b.g. Night Shift (USA) – Shaky Puddin (Ragstone 128) **102**
[1991 6g* 6d³ 6g 6m² 6f² 6m 5g⁵ 1992 a7g 6g² 6g* 6m³ 6f⁵ 6f 7.1d⁴ 6g* 6s 6m⁶ 6g⁶
6g 6g 7d 6.5s⁶] leggy, close-coupled, angular gelding: useful handicapper: won at
Newmarket in May and (£7,800 event) July, then landed £13,100 contest at York (by
a length from Stack Rock) in August: suited by 6f: acts on firm ground: used to hang
left: makes running/races prominently. *C. A. Cyzer*

MASTER POKEY 8 br.g. Uncle Pokey 116 – September Fire (Firestreak 125) –
[1991 5d 6s 6d 7m 6m⁴ 7g⁶ 6m⁵ 6d² 6g 7g 5.6m 6m 1992 7g 7s 6d 7g] sturdy,
good-quartered gelding: carries plenty of condition: rated 85 at 7 yrs: no form in
1992: ideally suited by 6f: probably not at his best on very soft going: acts on any

515

other: often heavily bandaged in front: had tongue tied down on reappearance: tends to give trouble at stalls: not seen out after May. *M. W. Easterby*

MASTER'S CROWN (USA) 4 ch.g. Chief's Crown (USA) – Mastoora (USA) **43**
69 (Raise A Native) [1991 NR 1992 12g⁴ 11.9f a14g⁵ 11.5m² a12g⁴ 12m 18m4] tall, workmanlike gelding: first foal: dam ran once: sold out of M. Stoute's stable 3,300 gns Newmarket Autumn (1991) Sales: poor form in varied company: will prove best at up to 2m: has run creditably for amateur, and when sweating: won over hurdles in October. *M. C. Chapman*

MASTER SHIKARI 3 b.g. Kala Shikari 125 – La Bambola 95 (Be Friendly 130) **47**
[1991 5v³ 5m 7d a7g 1992 8.9s 7g 8m³ a8g] lengthy gelding: form in 1992 only when third in seller at Brighton: stays 1m: acts on good to firm ground: joined N. Tinkler and won over hurdles afterwards. *J. E. Banks*

MASTER SINCLAIR (IRE) 2 b.c. (May 9) Mister Majestic 122 – Pichincha 83 **55**
(Pharly (FR) 130) [1992 5g⁴ 7m 6g⁵ 6.1d⁶ 5f⁴ 6g* 6m 6d⁶ 7s⁵ a7g* a7g² a7g⁵ a8g³] a66
IR 4,000Y: leggy, close-coupled colt: half-brother to 3-y-o 6.9f to 1m winner Hand On Heart (by Taufan), fairly useful Irish 1¼m winner Peace Mission (by Dunbeath) and a winner in Italy: dam 5f (at 2 yrs) to 10.6f winner: fair handicapper: ridden by 7-lb claimer, came from long way back to win nurseries at Catterick in August and Southwell in November: probably stays 1m: acts well on easy surface and fibresand: often starts slowly, and is well served by an end-to-end gallop. *R. Hollinshead*

MATADOR (USA) 5 ch.h. Nureyev (USA) 131 – Alliance (USA) 113 (Alleged **106**
(USA) 138) [1991 16g⁴ 16g⁵ 14g² 16.2m³ 12s 1992 12.5g* 12.3m* 12f³ 11.9g* 12m 12g³ 12.5s* 10s⁶ 12g] leggy horse: has a long, fluent stride: progressed into a useful performer: won handicaps at Warwick and Chester in the spring, Old Newton Cup at Haydock (by neck from Quick Ransom) in July and a listed race at Saint-Cloud in October: trained until after then by R. Charlton: suited by 1½m or more: acted on any going: formerly held up, but raced in touch in 1992: really game, genuine and consistent: stud in Venezuela. *D. Smaga, France*

MATARIS 2 b.f. (Feb 23) Shirley Heights 130 – Psylla 96 (Beldale Flutter (USA) **66**
130) [1992 6g⁴ 7g⁴ 7s⁴] close-coupled filly: third foal: sister to 1¼m winner Moonjid and half-sister to 3-y-o 1¼m winner Kabayil (by Dancing Brave): dam 9f and 1¼m winner, is out of half-sister to Kris and Diesis: fair form in maidens and a minor event: will be better suited by middle distances: yet to race on top-of-the-ground. *P. T. Walwyn*

MATCHING GREEN 3 b.f. Green Ruby (USA) 104 – Accuracy 83 (Gunner B **70**
126) [1991 7g⁶ 7d 1992 10s* 12d 12d³ 10s³ 11.7s 12.1s³ 11.8s] lengthy filly: moderate

Old Newton Cup (Handicap), Haydock —
Matador, Quick Ransom (No. 9) and Secret Society give of their best

walker: fair performer: won maiden at Salisbury in April: likely to stay 1¾m: raced only on a soft surface in 1992: visored last 2 starts, running creditably first occasion: not an easy ride. *G. B. Balding*

MATHAAYL (USA) 3 br.f. Shadeed (USA) 135 – Manal (FR) 74 (Luthier 126) **78** [1991 6g² 7m⁵ 1992 6m* 6g⁴ 6m³ 7m³ 10g* 10g⁵ 8d² 7m] big, well-made filly: good walker: fair performer: won maiden at Brighton in April and slowly-run 3-runner handicap at Redcar in August: good second in quite valuable handicap at Ascot in September: might have proved best at around 1m: acted on good to firm and dead ground: blinkered last 5 starts: sometimes found little off bridle: visits Lahib. *H. Thomson Jones*

MATHAL (USA) 3 b.c. Storm Bird (CAN) 134 – Bare Essence (USA) (Youth **59** (USA) 135) [1991 8d 1992 8g⁵ 10d 10g] lengthy colt: moderate mover: modest form on reappearance: disappointing subsequently (should stay 1¼m) and not seen after July: sold 1,700 gns Newmarket September Sales. *M. R. Stoute*

MATRON OF HONOR 2 ch.f. (May 17) Hadeer 118 – Che Gambe (USA) **51** (Lyphard (USA) 132) [1992 6g⁶ 7m] lengthy, angular filly: second foal: sister to 3-y-o Walk That Walk, 5f winner at 2 yrs: dam won in USA at 6f: plating-class form in minor event at Newmarket (outpaced virtually throughout) and claimer at Yarmouth in late-summer: sold 600 gns Newmarket Autumn Sales. *N. C. Wright*

MATTHEW DAVID 2 ch.c. (May 31) Indian Forest (USA) 117 – Mazurkanova **42** 51 (Song 132) [1992 5s⁵ 5g 5m 6d a6g* a5g* a7g⁵ 6g 5d a6g] small, sparely-made a51 colt: has a roundish action: second foal: dam won over stayed 7.5f: inconsistent performer: won 2 sellers at Southwell in June: no comparable form: stays 6f: acts well on fibresand. *M. Brittain*

MATTS BOY 4 b.g. Runnett 125 – Thatchville 65 (Thatch (USA) 136) [1991 7v* **–** 7m 7g⁵ 8m* 8.9m 8f 1992 8.5g 8s 8d⁶ 8f 9m⁵ 9f⁴ 8s] good-topped, attractive gelding: poor mover: rated 77 at 3 yrs: below form in 1992: stays 1m: acts on good to firm ground and heavy: visored (stiff task, well beaten) last time. *Miss S. E. Hall*

MAUSER 2 b.c. (Apr 9) Chilibang 120 – Macarte (FR) (Gift Card (FR) 124) [1992 **– p** 6d] good-quartered colt: seventh foal: half-brother to 3-y-o 1m winner Ma Bella Luna (by Jalmood), 6f winner Mariano (by Aragon) and 1m (at 2 yrs) and 9f winner Marasol (by Siberian Express): dam minor French 1m and 9f winner: 33/1 and very much in need of race, lost plenty of ground at start, recovered well by halfway before being eased right up when unable to sustain run in 17-runner maiden at Goodwood in September: will do better. *J. L. Dunlop*

MAWAYED (USA) 2 br.c. (Mar 19) Blushing Groom (FR) 131 – Thaidah (CAN) **74** 105 (Vice Regent (CAN)) [1992 6g 5.7f² 6g³ 6m] close-coupled, quite good-topped colt: has quick action: first foal: dam 5f (at 2 ys) to 7f winner, is half-sister to top-class American filly Glorious Song and champion 1983 American 2-y-o Devil's Bag: fair form when placed: well backed, ran poorly in Doncaster nursery final outing: stays 6f: active type, tends to get on edge. *P. T. Walwyn*

MAYAASA (USA) 3 br.f. Lyphard (USA) 132 – Dish Dash 118 (Bustino 136) **70** [1991 NR 1992 8d 9g³ 10g 9.7d⁵ 10s 12g 10g* 9.7v] lengthy filly: sixth foal: closely related to useful 2-y-o Maroof (by Danzig) and a winner in France, and half-sister to useful 1986 2-y-o 7f winner Arrasas (by Irish River): dam won Ribblesdale Stakes: fair form: 33/1, won 19-runner handicap at Brighton in September: stayed 1¼m well: probably needed a sound surface: visits Lahib. *R. W. Armstrong*

MAYBE GOLD 2 ch.c. (Apr 14) Vaigly Great 127 – Hurry On Honey 76 (Be **60** Friendly 130) [1992 6f* 6g 5g* 5g⁵ 6g⁴ 7.3g 6s 6s] 4,800Y: leggy, unfurnished colt: third reported foal: half-brother to a winner in Jersey: dam, placed here at 2 yrs, later won 6 races in Jersey: modest performer: won maiden auction at Salisbury in May and nursery at Folkestone in July: ran moderately last 3 starts: stays 6f (pulled too hard over slowly-run 7f): seems unsuited by soft surface: wears bandages behind. *D. W. P. Arbuthnot*

MAY HILLS LEGACY (IRE) 3 b.f. Be My Guest (USA) 126 – May Hill 124 **68** (Hill Clown (USA)) [1991 6g* 8g 1992 7m 7m 8.1d⁵ 6.9g² 7f 7d 10.5s 8g] small, angular filly: inconsistent handicapper: bred to stay beyond 7f: well below form on a soft surface, never placed to challenge on firm: bandaged last 7 starts. *D. W. P. Arbuthnot*

MAYLES LASS 3 b.f. Absalom 128 – Gosforth Lady 73 (Linacre 133) [1991 5d **–** 5.7m 6g 6m 6f 1992 7f 5.3f⁶ 9m] close-coupled filly: moderate mover: of little account. *J. J. Bridger*

MAYO MAN (IRE)   3 ch.g. Master Willie 129 – Kuwaiti 77 (Home Guard (USA)   –
129) [1991 6g 7g 6m 1992 12.3s 12.3s⁴ 12d⁶ 13.8d] angular gelding: seems of little
account. *Mrs M. Reveley*

MAY SQUARE (IRE)   4 ch.g. Nicholas Bill 125 – Casa Rosada (Known Fact   52
(USA) 135) [1991 10.2m 8.2g* 8.2f 8.2f³ 9.7m² 1992 10m⁴ a10g² 10.5d 8m 8g⁶ a8g   a57
a13g] angular, workmanlike gelding: has been operated on for soft palate: modest
performer: sold out of K. Bailey's stable 5,000 gns Ascot June Sales before reappearance: effective from 1m to 1¼m: acts on firm ground and equitrack. *Mrs A.
Knight*

MAZIN   4 b.c. Faustus (USA) 118 – Polly Oligant (Prince Tenderfoot (USA) 126)   –
[1991 6.9s 10m 8.3m 1992 a8g 10g a10g] sturdy colt: of little account: sold 850 gns
Ascot July Sales. *C. J. Benstead*

M'BEBE   2 b. or br.c. (May 7) Mtoto 134 – Canton Silk 108 (Runnymede 123) [1992   50 p
7m] half-brother to 3-y-o Distant Memory (by Don't Forget Me) and several
winners, including very smart 7f and 1m filly Brocade (by Habitat) and useful 1¼m
winner Organza (by High Top): dam 5f performer: 33/1, around 9 lengths seventh of
16 to True Hero in maiden at Leicester in September, held up in rear after slow
start, staying on final 1f: will improve. *B. W. Hills*

MBULWA   6 ch.g. Be My Guest (USA) 126 – Bundu (FR) 88 (Habitat 134) [1991   61
NR 1992 7m 6g⁴ 8.5s 8.1m² 10.1m* 8g* 10g* 7m 12m 7.9s⁶ 10.3s] smallish, sturdy
gelding: rated 88 at best as 3-y-o for G. Wragg: not seen out again until 1992: won
handicaps at Newcastle, Ayr (claimer) and Ripon in the summer: ideally suited by
1m to 1¼m (raced too freely over 1½m): acts on firm going, fair effort on soft:
blinkered on reappearance: often mulish at stalls. *S. E. Kettlewell*

MCA BELOW THE LINE   4 ch.g. Lucky Wednesday 124 – Delayed Action 113   63
(Jolly Jet 111) [1991 7g* 8.5f² 8.3m 7f* 7m⁵ 8d 7m³ a8g⁴ 1992 a7g³ a8g² 7d² 7g² 7m²
a7g² 7m³ 8f 7f³ 7.1m* 7f⁶ 7.5g⁵] dipped-backed gelding: poor mover: modest
performer: very consistent first 7 starts for W. Pearce: well below best afterwards,
including when sold out of B. Beasley's stable 5,000 gns after winning Edinburgh
seller (in July): stays 8.5f: acts on firm going and all-weather surfaces: usually
blinkered. *W. L. Barker*

MCNAB (IRE)   3 b.g. Treasure Kay 114 – Finlarrig (Thatching 131) [1991 NR   –
1992 7d 7.1s] IR 8,500F, 16,500Y: has round action: second living foal: half-brother
to 1988 2-y-o 7f winner Thrintoft (by Sandhurst Prince): dam Irish maiden: bought
1,000 gns Ascot May (1992) Sales: no sign of ability on flat. *C. P. Wildman*

MDM RACER (IRE)   2 b.g. (Apr 20) Reasonable (FR) 119 – Giddy Lyn (USA)   53
(Relko 136) [1992 5g⁶ 5.1s 6m 6m 5f⁶ a5g⁶ 5m⁵ 5s⁶ 5d 5d] IR 5,000Y: compact
gelding: carries condition: poor mover: half-brother to several minor winners here
and abroad, including 1988 2-y-o sprinter Supersingle Lady (by Kafu): dam won at up
to 7f in USA: fair plater: ran poorly last 2 starts: should stay 6f: acts on any going. *J.
Berry*

MEADMORE MAGIC   2 ch.f. (Apr 22) Mansingh (USA) 120 – Suzannah's Song   68
(Song 132) [1992 5.1m² 5.2f⁴ a5g* 5g* 5m⁵] smallish, lengthy filly: moderate
mover: third reported foal: dam unraced: modest form in midsummer: made all in
maiden at Southwell and nursery at York: speedy: yet to race on a soft surface. *J. L.
Harris*

MEADOW VIEW (IRE)   2 b.f. (Apr 5) Red Sunset 120 – South Meadow (Prince   –
Tenderfoot (USA) 126) [1992 5v 5g a6g] 2,900Y: compact filly: first foal: dam Irish
middle-distance winner: looks of little account. *C. J. Hill*

MEANT TO BE   2 b.f. (Mar 2) Morston (FR) 125 – Lady Gerardina 82 (Levmoss   42
133) [1992 7s⁵ 8d] eighth live foal: half-sister to a winner in South Africa: dam,
half-sister to high-class miler Saintly Song, won over 6f and 1½m: poor form in
maidens at York (auction, kept on) and Yarmouth in October: will stay 1¼m. *H. J.
Collingridge*

MEAVY   2 b. or br.f. (May 8) Kalaglow 132 – Feather Flower 74 (Relkino 131) [1992   63 p
7g] 14,500Y: fourth foal: sister to 3-y-o 14.1f winner Betelgeuse and 4-y-o 7f (at 2
yrs) and 10.6f winner Corcina and half-sister to a winner in Brazil: dam placed at
1¼m here before winning at 11.8f in France, is closely related to very smart
middle-distance stayer Relay Race: 33/1, around 6 lengths tenth of 24 to Fayfa in
maiden at Newmarket in October, late progress never dangerous: will improve. *W.
Jarvis*

MECONOPSIS   2 b.f. (Apr 29) Presidium 124 – Silk Lady 97 (Tribal Chief 125)   41
[1992 5g³ 5m⁴ 5g 7s 7d a5g] 3,500F: leggy filly: half-sister to 3-y-o Kate Royale (by
Beveled) and numerous winners, including sprinter Mzeff (by Ahonoora) and 5f to 7f

winner Mister Colin (by Lord Gayle): dam won three 5f races at 2 yrs: poor maiden: should stay 7f. *T. Fairhurst*

MEDAILLE D'OR 4 ch.c. Primo Dominie 121 – Alezan Dore 82 (Mountain Call **107** 125) [1991 6g3 6m2 5s* 5d6 5m* 5.1g* 5g6 5g 5m 1992 6d3 5s 6f* 5m3 6f 5s* 6s 5m 5m5 5m] good-topped, lengthy colt: good walker: poor mover: useful performer: won Thirsk minor event in May and listed event at Sandown (by head from Tbab) in July: respectable effort in Nunthorpe Stakes at York eighth start: effective at 5f and 6f: probably acts on any going: usually visored: has hung, and takes keen hold: often edgy. *J. W. Payne*

MEDBOURNE (IRE) 3 b.f. Alzao (USA) 117 – Dress In Spring 63 (Northfields **33** § (USA)) [1991 6g 6m5 a6g 7g a7g a8g a8g 1992 a8g a8g6 8d4 7d5 8f 12.2g5 10g 12.3g 12.3s a12g] smallish, good-topped filly: has round action: poor plater: stays 1m: acts on dead ground: twice reluctant to race at 3 yrs when blinkered: one to be wary of. *J. L. Harris*

MEDIA MESSENGER 3 b.g. Hadeer 118 – Willow Court (USA) (Little Current – (USA)) [1991 6g5 8m 8.1d3 1992 12.2d 8g 9.2v a8g] close-coupled gelding: modest maiden at 2 yrs for C. Brittain, best effort final start: not seen out until October and no form as 3-y-o. *Denys Smith*

MEDIA STAR 7 ch.m. Star Appeal 133 – Linduna (Derring-Do 131) [1991 12g4 – 13.8f 13.6g* 16.5m 14.6m* 14.1f4 16m 14.6m 14.1m 13.8m 13.6d 1992 13.8g5 13.8m 12.3f 14.6m 13.8g4 16.1g 12s6] leggy, angular mare: has a round action: poor and inconsistent handicapper: stays 2m: acts on firm and dead going: usually bandaged. *T. Kersey*

MEDIATOR 3 b.g. Valiyar 129 – Blushing Cousin (Great Nephew 126) [1991 a7g5 – a8g4 1992 10m6 16g5 12v] well-made gelding: plating-class form: sold out of P. Cole's stable 2,200 gns Ascot March Sales before reappearance: stays 2m: seems not to act on heavy going: blinkered and wore tongue strap (ran creditably) on reappearance. *A. Moore*

MEDLAND (IRE) 2 ch.c. (Feb 8) Imperial Frontier (USA) 112 – Miami Dancer **58** 55 (Miami Springs 121) [1992 6.9v a8g5 a7g2 a7g5 a8g] IR 6,900F, 3,000Y: fourth foal: half-brother to 1m and 9f winner Hazy Dancer (by Hays): dam won 1¼m seller: modest maiden: will stay 1m: acts on equitrack. *A. W. Denson*

MEESONS (IRE) 2 ch.f. (Jan 20) Salt Dome (USA) – Buzzing Around (Prince **53** p Bee 128) [1992 6g4] IR 7,000F, IR 2,000Y: lengthy filly: second foal: dam Irish 7f winner from family of Time Charter and Nicholas Bill: 25/1, 9 lengths fourth of 11 to Easy Access in maiden at Doncaster in November, held up and keeping on from 2f out: will stay 7f: will improve. *C. B. B. Booth*

MEESON TIMES 4 b.f. Enchantment 115 – National Time (USA) (Lord Avie – (USA)) [1991 6f6 7m 7m6 7g4 7g 6.9f2 8.2m 7m 6g5 6m 6m5 6m6 5s* a6g6 a5g2 a5g* a63 1992 a5g3 a5g* a5g3 a6g* a5g5 a6g3 5g 5s 5m 6d 5s a5g6 a5g a6g] sturdy, compact filly: has round action: modest handicapper, best on the all-weather: won at Southwell and Lingfield early in the year: off course 5 months and form afterwards only on twelfth start: effective from 5f to 7f: acts on any going, including all-weather surfaces: twice below form when visored. *B. Ellison*

MEGAN'S FLIGHT 7 ch.m. Welsh Pageant 132 – Escape Me Never 75 (Run – The Gantlet (USA)) [1991 NR 1992 a16g 13m 16.5m5 18.8m 14.1d 12g] leggy, workmanlike mare: seems of little account nowadays. *T. H. Caldwell*

MELISIO 2 b.f. (Apr 11) Efisio 120 – Lady Eton 106 (Le Dieu d'Or 119) [1992 5.1f – a6g5 a6g 7.1s5] 1,000Y: half-sister to 1988 2-y-o 6f and 7f seller winner Isobar (by Another Realm) and 1982 2-y-o 5f winner Paddock Princess (by Dragonara Palace): dam 2-y-o 5f and 6f winner: no worthwhile form. *C. P. Wildman*

MELLABY (USA) 4 ch.c. Nureyev (USA) 131 – Hitting Irish (USA) (Irish Ruler **99** (USA)) [1991 8s* 8g2 8g6 10.1m* 10g5 10.3d5 1992 12.3m2 10.1g5 12g 12f5 10s 10m 10s5] rangy, quite attractive colt: useful performer: well below form in handicaps last 2 starts (in visor first occasion) having been used as a pacemaker previous 3 outings: stays 1½m: acts on firm ground, has won on soft. *M. R. Stoute*

MELLOTTIE 7 b. or br.g. Meldrum 112 – Lottie Lehmann 69 (Goldhill 125) **112** p [1991 10.2m* 8g* 10f2 8g4 8.9g 8.9g4 8m2 9m* 1992 8.9m 8m2 8m* 9d 9m*] Mellottie's star has risen with his stable's. Having begun his career in a National Hunt Flat race at Market Rasen, he has progressed to the point where he can hold his own against colts as good as Rainbow Corner and Calling Collect. Already the winner of eight handicaps from marks of 62 to 98, he made a successful transition to listed company at the end of a season in which Mary Reveley's dual-purpose yard doubled its previous best total of flat winners. In a competitive renewal of the Baring International Darley Stakes at Newmarket in October, Mellottie started a well-backed 7/2 shot in a field of eleven which included four pattern-race winners, and he put up the best performance of his career to date. The firmish ground and sound pace suited him ideally, and, having been dropped out as usual, going well, he quickened to join issue entering the final furlong and forged ahead under pressure to beat Rainbow Corner a length. It was a run which suggests he's well worth his place in pattern company in 1993, although his trainer's characteristically modest post-race comment was 'I knew he was on song, but I thought he'd be outclassed'.

No trainer is currently more successful under both codes than Mrs Reveley, and during the same week as Mellottie won at Newmarket she was voted jumps trainer of the year by the racing Press. Few horses better illustrate her talent for getting the best out of her charges than Mellottie: his unorthodox route to listed-race success was achieved with a combination of patience and shrewd placement. Bred by the trainer, he was gelded as a foal and didn't make his debut until he was four, winning both the bumpers he contested before trouncing a modest bunch at Newcastle on his hurdling debut. After a slightly disappointing second when he jumped none too fluently in a similar event a month later, he was put away for the winter and not seen out again over obstacles. He gained his first flat success the following May and progressed relentlessly throughout 1990, winning three more handicaps before finishing an excellent second in Risen Moon's Cambridgeshire on his final outing. Twelve months later he won the Cambridgeshire, just getting the better of High Premium. Things didn't go so smoothly for Mellottie in the spring of 1992: he went down with a virus, then threw a splint, and it wasn't until the York Ebor meeting that he made his reappearance, finishing an encouraging seventh in the Andy Capp Handicap. Having shaped well again at Newcastle ten days later, he was sent to Doncaster on Leger day for the Coalite Handicap, a race he'd used as a stepping-stone to Newmarket the year before, and went one better under a confident ride from his regular partner Lowe. It was an excellent Cambridgeshire trial, and, though a 5-lb penalty brought his weight up to 9-12, Mellottie was installed the 8/1 clear favourite for the first leg of the autumn double. In the following three weeks he was deposed at the head of the market by another seven-year-old trying to win the race for the second time, Rambo's Hall. In the event, the weather turned against Mellottie. Almost an inch of rain fell the night before, and the going, which had been on the firm side for the first three days of the meeting, became dead. Mellottie produced a respectable effort from a mark two stone higher

Coalite Handicap, Doncaster—Mellottie (centre) is better than ever;
he picks up another valuable handicap cleverly from Double Entendre (right)
and Double Echo

Baring International Darley Stakes, Newmarket—
Mellottie's listed win, with Rainbow Corner (No. 2) and Calling Collect the chief victims

than two years before, particularly as he didn't get the run of the race, being knocked back to last after scrimmaging three furlongs out. However, the sharp turn of foot that characterised his best efforts was missing as he finished eighth of thirty to the favourite.

Mellottie's dam Lottie Lehmann was a contributor to the yard's early success. A winner on the flat at two and three, Lottie Lehmann had spells with Hills, Callaghan, Rohan and Etherington before being bought for 2,100 guineas at Doncaster November Sales 1979. In her first season for Mrs Reveley she was placed to win two of her four novice hurdles; she showed consistent form, racing for four more seasons over jumps, winning seven times in all and, like her first foal Mellottie, proving particularly effective on top-of-the-ground. Sadly, Mellottie excepted, her career at stud hasn't been so successful. Her second foal, Lehmans Lot (by Oats), ran only once, finishing second in a Perth bumper. Lottie Lehmann wasn't covered in 1987, and in the succeeding four years aborted early twice, produced a dead foal and slipped a foal. On a happier note, Lehmans Lot's first offspring, a filly by Move Off, was born in April 1992.

		Meldrum (br 1966)	Hard Sauce (br 1948)	Ardan
				Saucy Bella
Mellottie (b. or br.g. 1985)			Ruffino (ch 1960)	Como
				Rufina
		Lottie Lehmann (br 1976)	Goldhill (br 1961)	Le Dieu d'Or
				Gilded Rose
			Sing High (b 1962)	Sound Track
				Singing Lady

Mellottie is a good-topped gelding who carries plenty of condition; he has the build of one who would have had a future over jumps had it been necessary to persevere with him in that sphere. As it is, he probably goes in search of a pattern-race win, something narrowly missed by fellow National Hunt Flat race winner Morley Street in the Doncaster Cup in 1991. The very genuine and most consistent Mellottie is effective at a mile to a mile and a quarter, and suited by a sound surface. *Mrs M. Reveley*

MELODIC DRIVE   2 b. or br.g. (May 23) Sizzling Melody 117 – Gleneagle 91   **30** (Swing Easy (USA) 126) [1992 6.1d 6.1m] lengthy, workmanlike gelding: has scope: half-brother to winners abroad by Sayf El Arab and Coquelin: dam 5f and 6f winner: always behind in maidens at Nottingham in the summer. *P. S. Felgate*

MELODIC HABIT   5 b.m. Muscatite 122 – Magyar Melody (Prince Tenderfoot   **38** (USA) 126) [1991 a8g 7.1s⁵ 8f 1992 8g 7m 8m⁵ 7.1m 10d 7m 6.1d² 5.7f 6g 6.1m 7s] leggy, sparely-made ex-Irish mare: poor handicapper: a winner once in 28 tries: stays 1m: acts on good to firm and dead ground: below form when blinkered. *Mrs A. Knight*

MELODY ANNE   3 ch.f. Clantime 101 – Louisa Anne 73 (Mummy's Pet 125)   **–** [1991 5m⁶ 5s⁴ 5g⁶ 5m 1992 5m 7.1m 5h⁵ 6m⁶ 5g] leggy, unfurnished filly: of little account. *J. S. Haldane*

521

MELODY MOUNTAIN (IRE)   3 b.f. Ardross 134 – Seattle Serenade (USA) 82   –
(Seattle Slew (USA)) [1991 NR 1992 10.1g⁵ 11.4d⁵ 9.9m] 500Y: smallish, plain filly:
third foal: half-sister to 11.7f and 13.1f winner Serenader (by Ela-Mana-Mou): dam
second over 6f on 2-y-o debut then last both subsequent starts: little sign of ability
after debut. *C. E. Brittain*

MELODYS DAUGHTER   2 b.f. (Jan 25) Sizzling Melody 117 – Dancing   **60**
Daughter 79 (Dance In Time (CAN)) [1992 5m 5d⁶ 5.7d⁶ 5d³ 5g* 5g⁵] lengthy filly:
has a moderate action: fourth live foal: half-sister to milers Take Two (by Jupiter
Island) and Handsome Hotfoot (by Hotfoot): dam 13.4f winner: modest performer:
comfortably best effort when gamely making most to win Newmarket nursery in
October: will stay 6f: blinkered last 3 starts, very fractious in preliminaries first
occasion. *R. F. Johnson Houghton*

MELODY'S HONOUR   8 b. or br.m. Unknown Melody 70 – Honour Girl (Hon-   –
our Bound 109) [1991 8g 1992 10d] smallish, angular non-thoroughbred mare: twice
raced and tailed off in modest company. *J. Dooler*

MELOS MODUS (IRE)   2 b.g. (May 22) Nordico (USA) – Pollination 100   –
(Pentotal) [1992 a6g⁶] third foal (all by Nordico): brother to 1991 Irish 2-y-o 7f
winner Nordic Beat: dam Irish 2-y-o 7f winner, is out of half-sister to Hard Fought:
10/1 from 4/1 and wearing eyeshield, well beaten in maiden at Lingfield in
November, slowly away and soon behind: subsequently gelded. *Mrs L. Piggott*

MELPOMENE (USA)   4 b.f. Lear Fan (USA) 130 – Melodrama 102 (Busted 134)   **103**
[1991 7.3d* 7.3f⁵ 8.1m⁴ 8d³ 8d⁶ 1992 8.1d² 8d* 9.3s] lengthy, good-topped filly: has
a round action: useful performer: not seen out until August when second to Amwag
in listed race at Sandown: won similar event at Milan by 8 lengths: ran well, beaten
under 6 lengths, though towards rear in Prix de l'Opera at Longchamp later in the
autumn: well worth a try at 1¼m: acts on any going. *Lord Huntingdon*

MEL'S ROSE   7 ch.g. Anfield 117 – Ragtime Rose (Ragstone 128) [1991 7g² 7.1g⁶   **64**
7g 8m 8f² 7m⁴ 8m³ 7g 1992 7g⁶ 7g] tall gelding: has a quick action: modest
handicapper: form in 1992 only when sixth at Newmarket (apprentices) in June: off
course 4½ months afterwards: best form at 7f/1m: acts on firm and dead going: tried
blinkered once. *Dr J. D. Scargill*

MELTONBY   3 ch.f. Sayf El Arab (USA) 127 – Superlife (USA) 64 (Super Con-   **47**
corde (USA) 128) [1991 5m⁶ a6g³ 6d* 6.9m* 7g² 7.5f³ 7m 6m 7g 7m⁴ 7.1m⁵ a6g*   a61
a7g² a8g* 1992 a8g⁵ a7g³ a8g* a8g² a8g² a8g² a8g⁵ 8m⁵ 7f⁵ 10m⁴ 8g⁵] leggy,
close-coupled filly: moderate mover: modest performer winter 1991/2, making all in
claimer at Southwell in January for J. Hetherton: trained fifth start only by C. W. C.
Elsey: only fair plater returned to turf: should stay 1¼m: acts on good to firm and
dead ground, and on fibresand: good mount for 7-lb claimer: not seen out after July:
genuine: has joined C. Tinkler. *N. Tinkler*

MEMPHIS TOES (FR)   5 b.g. Vayrann 133 – Popsicle Toes (Nureyev (USA)   –
131) [1991 NR 1992 16.2g⁵] first foal: dam unraced daughter of half-sister to 1000
Guineas winner Mrs McArdy: beaten over 15 lengths in claimer at Beverley in
August. *K. S. Bridgwater*

MEMSAHB   3 b.f. Prince Sabo 123 – Hyatti 74 (Habitat 134) [1991 5m³ 5g* 5m*   **76**
5m* 5g 1992 5g 5f⁵ 5s* 5d 6d⁵ 6g] leggy, good-topped filly: moderate walker: fair
form on her day: won 4-runner handicap at Beverley in July: probably suited by 5f:
probably acts on any going. *J. Berry*

MEMU (USA)   3 b. or br.f. Tsunami Slew (USA) – Ahrex (USA) (Dr Fager) [1991   –
5g* 6f⁴ 5.2f⁶ 6.1m* 7d 1992 6g] leggy, lengthy filly: won maiden and nursery (made
all in good style) as 2-y-o: last in handicap in April and not seen again: should stay 7f:
acts on top-of-the-ground, possibly not on dead: tends to sweat. *D. R. C. Elsworth*

MENA   2 b.f. (Apr 23) Blakeney 126 – Martin-Lavell Mail (Dominion 123) [1992 6f   **58**
6m 6f² 7d⁶ 7g⁴ 8d³] 1,000Y: sparely-made filly: third foal: half-sister to 3-y-o Pharly
Dancer (by Pharly) and a winner abroad by Petorius: dam unraced: modest maiden:
will be well suited by 1¼m +: acts on firm and dead ground. *J. W. Payne*

MENAGHI   5 br.m. Tina's Pet 121 – Alidante 65 (Sahib 114) [1991 NR 1992 13.1s]   –
leggy, close-coupled, lightly-made mare: fourth live foal: dam plating-class maiden
at 2 yrs: no sign of ability for J. Upson in novice hurdles/chases in 1991/2: 200/1,
never a factor in amateurs event at Ayr in September. *R. Thompson*

MENTALASANYTHIN   3 b.g. Ballacashtal (CAN) – Lafrowda 71 (Crimson   **64**
Beau 124) [1991 7m 7s⁵ 6d* 7g 7m 6f 8m⁶ 6g² 8.3s* 6s* 1992 7.1s 6g 6d 6s 7s 10.3v⁶
a12g⁴ a12g³] sturdy gelding: progressive juvenile (rated 85), easily best efforts on
soft ground: didn't reappear until September and not nearly so good as 3-y-o. *A.
Bailey*

MEQDAAM (USA)   5 b.h. Storm Bird (CAN) 134 – Nobiliare (USA) (Vaguely   –
Noble 140) [1991 NR 1992 10d 10.8g] workmanlike horse: fifth foal: brother to top-
class 1¼m winner Indian Skimmer and half-brother to a winner in USA by Tentam:
dam unraced daughter of half-sister to Dark Mirage, 1968 champion 3-y-o filly in
USA: sold out of M. Stoute's stable 2,600 gns Newmarket November (1990) Sales:
33/1 and backward, showed little in Kempton listed event and Warwick maiden in
the spring. *R. Akehurst*

MERCHANT HOUSE (IRE)   4 ch.g. Salmon Leap (USA) 131 – Persian Polly   –
99 (Persian Bold 123) [1991 8d 7m 1992 a8g³ a7g] first sign of ability when 10 lengths
third of 14 in claimer at Southwell in February: bred to stay further: has joined M.
Pipe. *W. Holden*

MERCHANT OF VENICE   4 b.g. Precocious 126 – Silka (ITY) (Lypheor 118)   –
[1991 a8g² a10g* 10d 12m⁶ 13m² 13f² 13d³ a12g* 12.4f³ 16.1g⁵ 13.8m 1992 a12g 17.1d
12h⁵] good-topped gelding: rated 67 at best on all-weather at 3 yrs for W. Pearce:
won over hurdles in 1991/2 but well beaten in handicaps on flat as 4-y-o: stayed 13f:
acted on firm ground: often blinkered: dead. *M. H. Tompkins*

MERCH FACH (IRE)   2 b.f. (May 2) Jareer (USA) 115 – Finely Feathered   32
(Prince Tenderfoot (USA) 126) [1992 5g⁵ 6.1m 5.7f⁴ 7s] 600F: angular, workmanlike
filly: has scope: has a round action: half-sister to Irish 1¼m winner Sunshine Seal
(by Horage): dam Irish maiden: poor maiden: should stay 1m + : tailed off on soft
ground. *J. D. Roberts*

MERE CHANTS   3 b.f. Kings Lake (USA) 133 – Rengaine (FR) (Music Boy 124)   62 d
[1991 5d⁵ 5.7m⁶ 7g² 7g⁵ 1992 8g⁴ 8.1d 8m 10d 7d a7g] leggy, lengthy filly: moderate
mover: no worthwhile form after reappearance in a maiden, in July: trained until
after fourth start by D. Elsworth. *C. Weedon*

MERITRE (IRE)   2 ch.f. (Mar 18) Thatching 131 – Dance of The Nile 59 (Quiet   44
Fling (USA) 124) [1992 6g 8.1s 7d] big, lengthy filly: has a roundish action: fourth
foal: dam won over hurdles: poor form, well beaten, in maidens: will be suited by
middle distances. *R. J. Holder*

MERLINS WISH (USA)   3 ch.g. Yukon (USA) – Dear Guinevere (USA)   83
(Fearless Knight) [1991 6g 6g⁶ 6m 6m* 7d⁵ 1992 8m⁴ 7g 7g⁵ 8m 7.1d 8g² 8m⁴ 7d²
8m 8g] quite attractive gelding: good mover: fairly useful handicapper: probably
better suited by 1m than shorter: acts on good to firm and dead ground. *R. Hannon*

MERLS PEARL   3 b.f. Aragon 118 – Thrice Nightly (Gallant Romeo (USA)) [1991   40
7m 8m 7g a6g 1992 8m 16.1s 10d³ 10.3g] leggy filly: worthwhile form in 1992 only
when blinkered in sellers last 2 starts: unlikely to stay 2m: acts on dead ground. *J. A.
Glover*

MERRYHILL KERRY (IRE)   2 b.f. (Jan 16) Tate Gallery (USA) 117 – Stony   30
Ground (Relko 136) [1992 a5g⁶ 6m 7g 8.2d 7d] IR 4,000Y: moderate mover:
half-sister to several winners here and abroad, including 1983 2-y-o 7f winner Green
Mist (by Derrylin) and 1m winner and useful hurdler Bank View (by Crofter): dam
Irish 1½m winner: poor plater. *J. L. Harris*

MERRYHILL MADAM   3 b.f. Prince Sabo 123 – Western Line (High Line 125)   62
[1991 6g 6.1m² 6.1f³ 7g 1992 6.1m⁶ a8g a7g² a8g a8g² a7g] tall, leggy filly: modest
maiden: stays 1m: acts on fibresand: fair effort when visored: sweating and reluctant
stalls, reared start on reappearance. *J. L. Harris*

MERRYHILL MAID (IRE)   4 ch.f. M Double M (USA) – Piazza Navona   68
(Upper Case (USA)) [1991 6g⁵ 6g* 6m⁴ 6g 6d 5m² 6m⁶ 6s⁵ 8m 6f 6.1m 6m* 6m 6g
7g 1992 6d 6g⁴ a5g 6g 6g 7f 6.1g 7d] leggy, angular filly: poor walker: moderate
mover: little worthwhile form in handicaps after fourth at Newmarket in April: best
form at 6f: acts on good to firm and dead ground: visored (soundly beaten) once at 3
yrs. *J. L. Harris*

MERRY MARIGOLD   6 b.m. Sonnen Gold 121 – Manna Green (Bustino 136)   57 d
[1991 10d⁴ 10.8m 8f⁵ 10.1s⁶ 12ga12g* 10.2g² 12g 12.1d² 10g² 1992 a12g 12.5g² 11.7d⁴
12g 10.2m a12g⁴ 14.9f³ 14.9g³] lengthy, workmanlike mare: has a rather round
action: none too consistent handicapper: seems effective from 1½m to 15f: acts on
any going: often bandaged. *J. D. Roberts*

MERRY MERMAID   2 ch.f. (Apr 29) Bairn (USA) 126 – Manna Green (Bustino   53
136) [1992 7f 6g³ 7m² 7f⁴ 7g² 7.5m² 8.2d² 10.5d] tall, leggy, unfurnished filly:
half-sister to several winners, including 9f claimer winner Taxi Man (by Dublin
Taxi) and 3-y-o Luvly Jubly (by Belfort), 5f winner at 2 yrs: dam ran twice: plater:
suited by a test of stamina: acts on firm and dead ground. *J. F. Bottomley*

MERSEYSIDE MAN 6 b.g. My Dad Tom (USA) 109 – Chanita (Averof 123) **54**
[1991 a8g⁴ a8g a10g 7m 1992 a8g² a8g⁴ a10g² a10g* a10g⁴ a10g] lengthy, workmanlike gelding: poor mover: modest handicapper: ridden by 7-lb claimer, won at
Lingfield in February: effective from 1m to 1¼m: acts on firm going and equitrack:
tried blinkered once, usually visored: has been slowly away: not seen out after
March. *Dr J. D. Scargill*

MERTOLA'S PET 6 b.m. Tickled Pink 114 – Mertola (Tribal Chief 125) [1991 –
5.8f5 5f* 5g² 5g5 5.2g 5.1m* 5.6m 1992 5m 5g] small, quite good-quartered mare:
rated 81 at 5 yrs when very speedy handicapper: collapsed and died after finishing in
midfield at Epsom in June: best at 5f: acted well on top-of-the-ground. *L. G. Cottrell*

MERTON MILL 5 b.m. Dominion 123 – Brookfield Miss 73 (Welsh Pageant 132) **66**
[1991 12g 10g 10g 10m 10d 12f5 12g³ 14g5 14.1g* 14.1f* 16m* 14.1f² 14.1m 17.2g³
16.5d 1992 14.1d 16.2d 16.9g³ 16.1m³ 14.1m 16.5m* 17.2f² 14.1g6 17.9d* 16d5 16d⁴
16s] workmanlike mare: usually looks very well: moderate mover: fair but somewhat inconsistent handicapper: won at Doncaster in June and Ripon in September:
stays 2¼m: acts on firm and soft ground: usually blinkered nowadays: has gone in
snatches, and found little. *D. Morley*

MESAAFI (IRE) 3 b.f. Slip Anchor 136 – Nijinsky Sentiment (USA) 86 (Nijinsky –
(CAN) 138) [1991 6g* 7d² 8m 1992 7m⁴] quite attractive filly: has a round action: fair
performer at 2 yrs, when second to Musicale in Prestige Stakes at Goodwood:
looking very well but wearing net muzzle and very much on toes, tailed-off last of 4
when favourite for minor event at Yarmouth in July as 3-y-o, taking very strong
hold: bred to stay at least 1m: possibly unsuited by top-of-the-ground: visits Old Vic.
Major W. R. Hern

MESLEH 5 b.h. Alleged (USA) 138 – Forlene 108 (Forli (ARG)) [1991 10.8g* 1992 **109** p
10s² 10d*] strong, lengthy horse: moderate mover: very lightly raced but improving
handicapper: first run for over 4 months when winning £8,025 event at Newbury in
August in good style from Vallance, ridden along firmly over 3f out, then quickening
well to lead 1f out and still full of running at the finish: gives strong impression will
prove suited by give in the ground: will improve again, particularly when stepped up
to 1½m, and should win more races. *J. H. M. Gosden*

METAL BOYS 5 b.g. Krayyan 117 – Idle Gossip (Runnett 125) [1991 5g6 5g 6g **86**
5g³ 5m5 5m⁴ 5.9m6 5m⁴ 5.2g5 5f* 5m* 5.2f 5m* 5g 5m⁴ 5m* 1992 5m² 5g* 5d6
5m³ 5f² 5g 5.1g² 5g 5.1s5 5m 5d5 5m 5m 5g] good-bodied gelding: poor mover: fairly
useful handicapper: ridden by 7-lb claimer, won at Pontefract in July: best at 5f: acts
on firm and soft ground: races prominently. *R. Hollinshead*

METTERNICH 7 b.g. Habitat 134 – Sarah Siddons (FR) 122 (Le Levanstell 122) **64**
[1991 9v5 1992 9.7v³ 10d⁴ 10s³ 9.7g* 8d* 9.7v] heavy-topped gelding: modest
performer: won claimers at Folkestone and Carlisle in the spring: weak in market,
always behind in handicap at Folkestone on first outing for 5½ months: stays 1¼m:
acts on heavy ground: usually races up with pace: game. *M. H. Tompkins*

MEXICAN DANCER 3 b.f. Dance of Life (USA) – Mexican Two Step (Gay **51**
Fandango (USA) 132) [1991 5d³ 6m6 6g⁴ 6f6 6m 1992 10.2d 6m⁴ 7g 6f 7g³ 8.3g⁴
8.9d⁴ 10m 7s5 8.2g⁴ 8g*] sparely-made filly: moderate mover: modest performer:
trained until after penultimate start by R. Holder: won selling handicap at Doncaster
(no bid) in November: should stay 1¼m: acts on soft going: well beaten in blinkers
once. *P. G. Murphy*

MEZAAJ (USA) 4 br.g. Shadeed (USA) 135 – Honor To Her (USA) (Sir Ivor 135) –
[1991 12m5 10.2s⁴ 10g6 12.3g 1992 10d] small, sturdy gelding: moderate mover:
seems of little account. *B. Preece*

MHEMEANLES 2 br.g. (Mar 13) Jalmood (USA) 126 – Folle Idee (USA) **88** p
(Foolish Pleasure (USA)) [1992 6f5 6f* 7d³ 7g 7.9d6 7g 8.9s* 7g*] compact gelding:
has a round action: first foal: dam unraced: progressed into a fairly useful performer:
won maiden at Redcar in June, claimer at York in October and, putting up best effort,
21-runner nursery at Doncaster in November: effective from 7f to 9f: acts on firm
and soft ground. *M. H. Easterby*

MIAMI BANKER 6 ch.g. Miami Springs 121 – Banking Coyne 76 (Deep Diver – §
134) [1991 6g 5s⁴ 5.1d 5g 5m 5d 5g 1992 5g 5.2d 5d 5m5 5g 5.2d 5d 5.1s 5.1s] strong,
lengthy gelding: moderate mover: unreliable sprint handicapper last 2 seasons:
usually blinkered/visored nowadays: trained first 3 starts by W. Muir. *P. Howling*

MIAMI SANDS (IRE) 2 b.f. (Feb 17) Ela-Mana-Mou 132 – Madame du Barry **87**
(FR) (Wollow 132) [1992 7s* 7s²] fifth foal: half-sister to 7f and 1¼m winner Monte
Bre (by Henbit) and a multiple winner in USA: dam French maiden half-sister to
Prix Royal-Oak winner Mersey: won maiden at Roscommon in September by 3

lengths: 1½ lengths second of 8 to Asema in C L Weld Park Stakes at the Curragh later in month: will stay at least 1¼m. *J. Oxx, Ireland*

MICHAELA MIA (USA)   2 b.f. (Feb 11) Great Charmer (USA) – Tres Agreable   **71** p
(FR) (Luthier 126) [1992 8d³] $20,000Y: half-sister to St Leger winner Michelozzo (by Northern Baby) and useful middle-distance stayer Micheletti (by Critique): dam, half-sister to Prix Royal-Oak winner El Cuite, won over 10.5f at 4 yrs in France: sire, modest form, is closely related to Lomond and Seattle Dancer and a half-brother to Seattle Slew: 33/1, 2 lengths third of 20 to Lille Hammer in maiden at Yarmouth in October, keeping on well from mid-division: will be extremely well suited by middle distances: will improve and win a maiden. *D. R. Loder*

MICHELOZZO (USA)   6 b.h. Northern Baby (CAN) 127 – Tres Agreable (FR)   **109**
(Luthier 126) [1991 12g⁴ 15.5g 15s* 15.5d⁴ 12v² 13.5g* 1992 12g 12g⁶ 15.5s⁶ 12.1g* 13.3g⁴ 15s³] finely-made, attractive horse: poor mover: won 1989 St Leger for H. Cecil, but is not so good nowadays: straightforward task on first start for present trainer (had been with J. Hammond in France) when successful in Chepstow apprentice race: best effort in 1992 when 9 lengths third to Sought Out in Prix Kergorlay at Deauville in August: best form given test of stamina with plenty of give in the ground. *R. Hannon*

MICK'S TYCOON (IRE)   4 b.g. Last Tycoon 131 – Ladytown (English Prince   –
129) [1991 8d 11g 12.8g⁴ 12m 12m³ 12d³ 14g⁴ 1992 11.9g] leggy gelding: fourth foal: half-brother to 5-y-o miler Darakah (by Doulab): dam, Irish 1¼m winner, is half-sister to Irish St Leger winner M-Lolshan: ex-Irish maiden, trained at 3 yrs by E. O'Grady: visored, well held in Brighton selling handicap in August, 1992: stays 1½m: acts on good to firm ground: often blinkered in Ireland: visored, won 2 selling handicap hurdles late in the year. *M. C. Pipe*

MIDARIDA (IRE)   2 b.f. (Feb 18) Taufan (USA) 119 – Jamie's Girl (Captain   **43**
James 123) [1992 6m⁵ 6f³ 7g 7d a6g] 7,200Y: small, quite attractive filly: moderate mover: fourth foal: half-sister to 1990 2-y-o 6f winner Daazam (by Mazaad) and 1m and 1¼m winner By Choice (by Sallust): dam unraced: poor maiden: sold out of R. J. R. Williams' stable 1,400 gns Ascot July Sales after third outing, resold 725 gns Ascot November Sales. *B. Forsey*

MIDDAY SHOW (USA)   5 b.h. Roberto (USA) 131 – Worlds Fair (USA) (Our   –
Hero (USA)) [1991 14.6s 12.5d⁵ 10f* 10.1f 11.7m 1992 11.9d 11.9m 11.5f a12g 12d] well-made horse: ex-Irish performer: rated 71 when successful at 4 yrs: no form on flat since: stays 1¾m: won novice selling hurdle in September. *J. R. Jenkins*

MIDGET GEM   2 ch.c. (Feb 16) Midyan (USA) 124 – Nafla (FR) (Arctic Tern   –
(USA) 126) [1992 5g 6m 6d] 10,500F, 7,000Y, resold 6,400Y: leggy colt: third foal: dam French 7f to 1¼m winner, is granddaughter of Park Hill winner Cursorial: no worthwhile form, trained first 2 starts by Miss L. Siddall. *N. A. Graham*

MIDHISH   2 b.c. (Mar 27) Green Desert (USA) 127 – Swanilda (FR) (Habitat 134)   **68** p
[1992 6m⁵] 76,000Y: big, good-bodied colt: has plenty of scope: brother to winning 3-y-o sprinter Indian Endeavour and half-brother to several winners, including useful stayer Arizelos (by Shirley Heights) and 1¼m winner Ephemeral (by Shernazar): dam won over 1m in France, and is half-sister to Super Dan, very useful up to 9f: carrying plenty of condition, highly promising fifth of 9, beaten around 2 lengths, to Power of Polly in minor event at York in May: seemed sure to improve considerably, but wasn't seen again. *B. Hanbury*

MIDNIGHT AIR (USA)   3 br.f. Green Dancer (USA) 132 – Evening Air (USA)   **104**
(J O Tobin (USA) 130) [1991 7g² 7f* 8m* 8d*ᵈⁱˢ 1992 7m 11.4g⁴ 11.9m 10.1g³ 8m² 8g⁴] tall, lengthy, sparely-made filly: good mover: won May Hill Stakes and first past post in Fillies' Mile at Ascot as 2-y-o: best efforts in 1992 when placed in listed events, length second to Perfect Circle at Doncaster: best form at up to 1¼m: acts on good to firm and dead ground: sold 270,000 gns Newmarket December Sales. *H. R. A. Cecil*

MIDNIGHT GALAXY   3 b.g. Natroun (FR) 128 – Sister Jinks 88 (Irish Love   –
117) [1991 8m 7d 1992 9.7v 12g] tall, leggy gelding: shows knee action: seems of little account: sold 875 gns Ascot June Sales. *A. N. Lee*

MIDNIGHT HEIGHTS   2 b.f. (Mar 2) Persian Heights 129 – Midnight Music   **59**
(Midsummer Night II 117) [1992 7g 6d] 16,500 2-y-o: workmanlike filly: eighth foal: half-sister to very useful 7f (at 2 yrs) and 1¼m winner Galitzin and modest stayer Hellbrun (both by Hotfoot) and a winner in Scandinavia by Radetzky: dam of little account: modest form in minor events at Kempton (very green) and Ascot (sweating) in September: should stay 1¼m. *J. W. Payne*

MIDNIGHT LASS   4 b.f. Today And Tomorrow 78 – Capel Lass (The Brianstan   –
128) [1991 6v⁵ 5g 5.1f 5m³ 5d⁵ a5g 5m 1992 5g 5f⁴ 5m⁶] leggy filly: moderate mover:
seems of little account. *W. J. Pearce*

MIDNIGHT MISCHIEF   2 b.f. (Feb 7) Bairn (USA) 126 – Secret Valentine 71   –
(Wollow 132) [1992 7f⁴] third foal: half-sister to 5-y-o 5f and 6f winner Gondo (by
Mansingh): dam 6f to 1m winner: 16/1, soundly-beaten fourth of 5 in maiden at
Yarmouth in June. *M. J. Ryan*

MIDWINTER DREAM   2 b.c. (Mar 29) Midyan (USA) 124 – Pennies To   **85** p
Pounds 80 (Ile de Bourbon (USA) 133) [1992 5.2d 6g² 6d 7g 6m*] rangy, quite
attractive colt: has scope: excellent walker: fluent mover: fourth foal: half-brother
to modest 7f winner Platinum Disc (by Song): dam 8.5f winner out of sprinting
half-sister to Mummy's Pet: progressive colt: in excellent shape, showed much
improved form when impressive winner of 18-runner nursery at Pontefract in
October, always travelling well and quickening to lead 1f out: should prove as
effective at 7f: easily best effort on good to firm ground: looks sort to do well at 3
yrs. *D. R. C. Elsworth*

MIDYAN BLUE (IRE)   2 ch.c. (Mar 28) Midyan (USA) 124 – Jarretiere 78 (Star   **65**
Appeal 133) [1992 7m 7g² 7s] IR 4,000Y: sparely-made colt: shows plenty of knee
action: second foal: dam maiden stayed 1m: easily best effort in maidens when
staying-on second of 18 at Redcar in autumn: will stay 1m. *J. M. P. Eustace*

MIDYANZIE   3 b.f. Midyan (USA) 124 – Golden October 62 (Young Generation   –
129) [1991 NR 1992 a8g⁶ a6g⁵ a8g] 850Y: fourth foal: dam won over 6f: no
worthwhile form. *C. Holmes*

MIGHTY GLOW   8 gr.g. Kalaglow 132 – Faridetta 107 (Good Bond 122) [1991   – §
a14g a14g a16g² a14g a13g 14m 12m 12.1d 12.3d 1992 16f4 13.6f] leggy, workmanlike
gelding: moderate mover: rated 45 at 7 yrs when thoroughly unreliable staying
handicapper: sold 4,500 gns Doncaster March Sales: dead. *J. H. Johnson*

MIGHTY MISS MAGPIE (IRE)   2 b.f. (Apr 19) Red Sunset 120 – Carcajou   **54**
(High Top 131) [1992 5.1s⁴ 6m 6m³ 7f³ 7m⁴ a7g* 7g 8d 6g³ 7d 7d 7.6v⁴]
sparely-made filly: sister to very useful 1m to 11f winner Sunset Boulevard and
half-sister to several winners here and abroad, including 10.2f winner Springwell
(by Miami Springs): dam lightly-raced daughter of very useful stayer Wolverine:
inconsistent plater: won 15-runner contest (no bid) at Southwell in August: sold
2,500 gns Newmarket Autumn Sales: will stay 1¼m: acts on any going: visored (ran
creditably) ninth start. *M. R. Channon*

MIGHTY WRATH   2 b. or br.c. (Feb 23) Robellino (USA) 127 – Gravad Lax 82   **54** p
(Home Guard (USA) 129) [1992 6m] 1,000Y: sturdy, quite stiff living foal:
dam, second over 5f at 2 yrs, is half-sister to 1000 Guineas winner Enstone Spark:
50/1 and in need of race, around 12 lengths ninth of 14 to Felucca in maiden at
Newmarket in October, outpaced from halfway: will improve. *I. Campbell*

MILAGRO   3 br.f. King of Spain 121 – Milva 56 (Jellaby 124) [1991 5g 6g² 7g⁵ 6f³   **84**
6m* 6m⁵ 6.1m³ 1992 6g 6m* 6m⁵ 6g⁴ 6m 6g 6d] robust filly: fairly useful 6f
handicapper: won at Goodwood in May: acts on firm ground, possibly not on a soft
surface: consistent. *R. Hannon*

MILANESE   3 b.f. Elegant Air 119 – Embroideress 80 (Stanford 121§) [1991 7g⁴   **80** d
1992 10d⁴ 8.1d² 8f* 9.9m* 10.1f² 9.9d⁶ 10.1m⁶ 10g³ 10g 11.5m⁵ 10d 11v³ a12g]
lengthy, plain filly: inconsistent handicapper: won at Thirsk (maiden) in May and
Beverley in June: stays 1¼m: best effort on firm going: carries head high, and
difficult ride: sold 8,200 gns Newmarket December Sales. *D. Morley*

MILAN FAIR   8 b.g. Mill Reef (USA) 141 – Fairweather Friend (USA) (Forli   –
(ARG)) [1991 NR 1992 a6g a10g] lengthy gelding: on the downgrade. *D. L. Williams*

MILBANK CHALLENGER   2 gr.g. (Jan 13) Belfort (FR) 89 – Princess   **54**
Sharpenup 63 (Lochnager 132) [1992 6g 6m⁴ 5f³ 6d 5g⁶ 6m] 3,000Y: workmanlike
gelding: fourth foal: brother to 3 winners, including fair sprinter Sharp Anne
and 1m winner My Concordia: dam third over 5f at 2 yrs, only start: plating-class
maiden: should be as effective at 6f as 5f: ran creditably when blinkered once. *M. H.
Easterby*

MIL FOIL (FR)   2 b.c. (Jan 30) Mille Balles (FR) 124 – Balsamine (Gosport 117) **111** p
[1992 7g* 8v*] third foal: half-brother to 2 winners in France, including 3-y-o 9f
winner Bugle (by Comrade In Arms): dam French 6.5f and 1m winner: successful in
minor event at Compiegne and Prix Thomas Bryon (by ½ length from Kingmambo)
at Saint-Cloud in October: will stay 1¼m: likely to do better. *J. Pease, France*

MILITARY EXPERT 3 ch.c. Superlative 118 – Times 55 (Junius (USA) 124) **63**
[1991 6.9m 6g 7m a6g 7m³ 7.5f 7g* 7m* 7.6d² 1992 6m³ 8m 8.1d 7g 7g⁴ 8m 7g³ a7g⁶ a49 +
9g² 9d 8.2g² 8.1d² a8g³] workmanlike colt: poor mover: modest handicapper: may
well be better suited by 1¼m: acts on good to firm and dead ground: blinkered last 3
starts: suitable mount for 7-lb claimer: sold 6,800 gns Doncaster November Sales.
Capt. J. Wilson

MILITARY FASHION 6 ch.h. Mill Reef (USA) 141 – Smarten Up 119 (Sharpen **103**
Up 127) [1991 9m³ 8g⁶ 1992 8.1g⁶ 7.9m⁵ 8.9m²] tall, good-topped horse: moderate
walker: poor mover: suffered hairline fracture of cannon bone in 1990: useful
performer: creditable efforts in Group 2 Forte Mile at Sandown and quite valuable
handicap at York: very good second to Badawi in competitive York handicap in
August on first run for over 3 months: stays 9f well: acts on good to firm ground:
sold 20,000 gns Newmarket December Sales, reportedly to Greece. *L. M. Cumani*

MILITARY HONOUR 7 b.g. Shirley Heights 130 – Princess Tiara 111 (Crown- –
ed Prince (USA) 128) [1991 16s 16.2g² 1992 17.1d] lengthy, attractive gelding: poor
mover: poor nowadays: stays 2m: acts on soft going: effective blinkered or not: won
poor novice chase in November. *M. W. Easterby*

MILIYEL 3 ch.f. Rousillon (USA) 133 – Amalee 57 (Troy 137) [1991 6m⁶ 1992 7g **53**
8.3s² 9.2m³ 10m² 15.1m² 12.1m⁴ 12.1g² 15g² 9.2g⁵ 12.1d⁵ 10.9s⁶ 11.1d²] good-
bodied, workmanlike filly: plating class on balance of form: stays well: yet to race on
firm going, probably acts on any other: claimed out of B. Hanbury's stable £6,010
third start: sometimes carries head high. *P. Monteith*

MILLADOR 3 b.f. Glint of Gold 128 – Tsar's Bride (Song 132) [1991 6m 7.5f⁵ 6.1f –
7m 1992 10.8g 16.2d³ a12g⁵ a12g³] big, good-topped filly: poor maiden on Flat: stays
1½m: probably acts on both all-weather surfaces: won over hurdles in August and
October. *M. H. Tompkins*

MILL BURN 3 ch.g. Precocious 126 – Northern Ballerina 52 (Dance In Time **42**
(CAN)) [1991 7m 8m 1992 a8g³ 7.5g 8.2g a8g⁵ a8g] lengthy gelding: has markedly
round action: poor maiden: worth a try over 1¼m: sold 700 gns Doncaster June
Sales. *I. Campbell*

MILLEFIORI 3 b.f. Battle Hymn 103 – Lane Patrol (Hopton Lane 70) [1991 NR –
1992 5s 7v a7g] small, close-coupled filly: first foal: dam of no account: seems of
little account. *K. S. Bridgwater*

MILLFIT (USA) 3 b.f. Blushing Groom (FR) 131 – Musique Royale (USA) **62**
(Northern Dancer (CAN)) [1991 6f⁴ 8f⁶ 7g³ 1992 9.2d 7g* 8.3s 7m⁴ 8g⁴ 7f] leggy
filly: modest handicapper: won at Wolverhampton in April for claimer: should stay
1m. *B. Hanbury*

MILLIE (USA) 4 ch.f. Master Willie 129 – La Zonga (USA) (Run The Gantlet –
(USA)) [1991 10.1g 10f⁵ 11.7g 10m* 10m³ 12g³ 10.5g³ 12f³ 1992 12m 10f 17.1s]
sparely-made filly: moderate mover: rated 64 at 3 yrs: no form in handicaps in 1992:
should stay beyond 1½m: acts on firm going: sold out of J. Jenkins' stable 1,300 gns
Doncaster May Sales before reappearance. *G. Fleming*

MILLIONAIRE'S ROW 5 b.h. Niniski (USA) 125 – One In A Million 125 –
(Rarity 129) [1991 NR 1992 12m] rangy, angular horse: had a rather round action:
rated 86+ as 3-y-o: bandaged, in midfield in £30,000 handicap at Goodwood, only
run after: stayed 1½m: acted on hard ground: carried head high: dead. *H. R. A. Cecil*

MILLION IN MIND (IRE) 3 ch.g. Lomond (USA) 128 – Klairhore 116 (Klairon **90**
131) [1991 NR 1992 9g 10.1g* 12d* 11.9d 12m³ 12m⁴] big, lengthy gelding: split hind
pastern at 2 yrs: good mover: brother to fair 1987 2-y-o 6f winner Always Alone and
half-brother to numerous winners, notably Irish Heart (by Steel Heart), useful
winner at up to 1¼m at 2 yrs here later stakes winner in USA: dam in frame in Irish
1000 Guineas and Irish Oaks: looked promising when winning Yarmouth maiden and
Newbury minor event in summer: ran fairly well in handicaps last 2 starts: would be
suited by further than 1½m: front runner. *Mrs J. Cecil*

MILLROUS 4 b.f. Rousillon (USA) 133 – Brookfield Miss 73 (Welsh Pageant 132) **44**
[1991 12.2g⁴ 14.1m³ 12m 9.7g 8.2m⁴ 1992 10g 9.7s⁶ 10.1d²] tall, leggy, angular filly:
poor maiden: stays 1½m: acts on good to firm and dead ground: sometimes carries
head high: joined M. Pipe and won selling hurdle in December. *R. Guest*

MILLSOLIN (IRE) 4 b.g. Millfontaine 114 – Isolin (Saulingo 122) [1991 8.2d⁵ **80**
8m⁶ 10g 8d 7m⁴ 1992 6.9g⁶ 7.6m⁵ 7g 5m⁴ 6d 7g* 7d* 7m* 8g] leggy, workmanlike
gelding: has a round action: progressed dramatically for present stable in autumn
(previously with A. Davison), winning large-field handicaps at Wolverhampton,
Kempton and Newmarket (heavily-backed favourite): easy to back when last of 18 in
£29,500 Newmarket handicap final run: should prove suited by 1m: acts on good to

firm and dead ground: has hung and wandered under pressure: sometimes sweating. *R. Akehurst*

MILLYANT 2 ch.f. (Mar 20) Primo Dominie 121 – Jubilee Song 71 (Song 132) **97** p [1992 5g* 5m* 5m⁵] 18,000Y: strong, long-backed filly: carries condition: eighth living foal: half-sister to several winners, including good 5f performer Prince Sabo (by Young Generation) and 3-y-o Swellegant (by Midyan), 5f winner at 2 yrs: dam 5f winner: won maiden auction at Windsor and Philip Cornes Molecomb Stakes (by length from Palacegate Episode) at Goodwood in July: bumped 2f out when below-par fifth of 7 in Flying Childers Stakes at Doncaster: speedy: bandaged behind last 2 starts. *R. Guest*

MILLY BLACK (IRE) 4 b.f. Double Schwartz 128 – Milly Lass (FR) 85 (Bold **42** Lad (USA)) [1991 7g³ 10.1d² 10m 10g 9s 10.8g² 11m⁵ 11.8m 8d 1992 a12g 16.2g 16f⁶ a14g² a14g a12g⁴] close-coupled filly: inconsistent maiden: stays 1¾m: acts on good to firm and dead ground and fibresand: ran well blinkered: hung badly for claimer: sold to join J. Akehurst 1,050 gns Ascot September Sales. *J. L. Harris*

MILLYROUS (IRE) 3 b.f. Rousillon (USA) 133 – What A Pity 97 (Blakeney 126) **42** [1991 NR 1992 6g⁵ a8g a7g⁴ a7g⁵] 16,500Y: lightly-made filly: poor mover: fourth foal: half-sister to 2 winners in Italy, including Junk Bond (by Last Tycoon), fairly useful 6f and 7f winner at 2 yrs here: dam lightly-raced 7f winner from sprinting family: poor maiden: stays 7f: sold 1,350 gns Newmarket September Sales. *R. Guest*

MILNGAVIE (IRE) 2 ch.g. (May 22) Pharly (FR) 130 – Wig And Gown **55** (Mandamus 120) [1992 6f⁵ 6g* 7m⁶ 8f 6s 8s] 3,600Y: close-coupled gelding: has a round action: half-brother to numerous winners, including useful stayers Halsbury (by Exbury) and Drumhead (by High Line) and useful 1976 2-y-o 6f winner Freight Forwarder (by Calpurnius), later successful jumper: dam unraced: won maiden auction at Pontefract in July: below that form last 3 starts, giving impression something amiss final 2: should be well suited by middle distances: has been gelded. *M. Johnston*

MILS MIJ 7 br.g. Slim Jim 112 – Katie Grey 60 (Pongee 106) [1991 NR 1992 12f⁵] – smallish, sturdy gelding: useful hurdler: lightly raced on flat nowadays: stays 2¼m: acts on good to firm and heavy going. *T. A. K. Cuthbert*

MILTON ROOMS (IRE) 3 ch.c. Where To Dance (USA) – Raga Rine (Raga **45** Navarro (ITY) 119) [1991 6g⁶ 1992 6.1d 7m 8.3s³ a7g 8.1d³ 9.2s 8g 8s³ 10.3g] good-bodied colt: poor maiden: likely to stay 1¼m: acts on soft ground: usually blinkered: has joined D. Garraton: headstrong. *C. B. B. Booth*

MILZIG (USA) 3 b.c. Ziggy's Boy (USA) – Legume (USA) (Northern Baby **99** (CAN) 127) [1991 7g⁵ 7.1m⁵ 8.1g² 8m³ 8m⁴ 1992 10.1g² 10d* 12m² 12m⁴ 12g⁴ 11.5g² 10s³ 10g] strong colt: has a quick action: won maiden at Kempton in June: ran well all starts after (including in Group 3 Gordon Stakes at Goodwood fourth start) apart from final run: effective at 1¼m, and should stay beyond 1½m: acts on good to firm and soft ground. *D. R. C. Elsworth*

MIM 2 ch.f. (May 5) Midyan (USA) 124 – Klaire 85 (Klairon 131) [1992 7g 7g 7g] **39** angular filly: half-sister to several winners, including smart sprinter Young Hal (by Young Generation), 5-y-o 5f (at 2 yrs) to 7.2f winner Norton Challenger (by Absalom) and 3-y-o 1m winner Emaura: dam, 2-y-o 7f winner, is half-sister to high-class stayer Proverb: never a factor in big-field minor events at Kempton and Newbury and maiden at Doncaster late in season. *G. B. Balding*

MIMIQUE 3 b.c. Sadler's Wells (USA) 132 – Millieme 107 (Mill Reef (USA) 141) **82** [1991 8d⁴ 7d² 1992 9.9g² 10d* 11.9s² 12d⁶] good-topped, attractive colt: good walker and mover: ran well in handicaps after winning Ripon maiden in September: stays 1½m: takes strong hold: carries head high: forces pace: sent to race in Dubai. *H. R. A. Cecil*

MIMIQUE (GER) 2 b.f. (Feb 28) Local Suitor (USA) 128 – Mode Classique (FR) – (Top Ville 129) [1992 6m] rangy filly: has scope: second foal: dam French 1½m winner: faded from 2f out and not knocked about when in midfield in 15-runner maiden at Newbury in June: seemed sure to improve. *C. E. Brittain*

MINDOMICA 3 b.f. Dominion 123 – Nordica 99 (Northfields (USA)) [1991 6f² **57** 7g² 7g* 1992 8.1s 7m 10.1m⁴ 9f⁴ 10.1f 9m⁴ 9.9m 8f⁵ 8d 7m] tall, leggy filly: inconsistent handicapper: may prove best short of 1¼m: best on a sound surface: below form visored once. *M. Bell*

MIND THE ROOF (IRE) 2 b.f. (Feb 19) Thatching 131 – Thunderflash 83 **62** (Runnett 125) [1992 6m⁶ 6m 7g³] IR 6,000Y: leggy, lengthy, angular filly: first foal: dam 7f winner: best effort in second half of 1992 when over 2 lengths third of 17 in maiden auction at Leicester: will stay 1m. *D. R. C. Elsworth*

MING BLUE 3 ch.f. Primo Dominie 121 – Burnt Amber (Balidar 133) [1991 6m⁴   –
7g 7.6d⁴ 1992 8g 7g 10g] strong filly: poor maiden: should stay 1m: acts on good to
firm and dead ground: below form blinkered: sold 950 gns Newmarket Autumn
Sales. *P. J. Makin*

MINGUS (USA) 5 b.g. The Minstrel (CAN) 135 – Sylph (USA) 110 (Alleged   **60**
(USA) 138) [1991 11.9g⁴ 12m 12g 12.1d 1992 10.3g 10d 12.4s⁶ 16.2m⁴ 13.8m³ 12f²
12.3g³ 12.2g² 12m² 10.3m³ 10.5g² 12.1d² 10.3m² 8s 10.3s⁵ a14g³ a14g²] compact,
heavy-topped gelding: has long stride: consistent handicapper, but last win 22 starts
ago, at 3 yrs: stays 1¾m: acts on firm and dead ground and on fibresand: below form
blinkered once: tends to hang but suitable mount for apprentice: sold out of Mrs J.
Ramsden's stable 7,600 gns Newmarket Autumn Sales before last 2 starts. *R. F.
Fisher*

MINI FETE (FR) 3 br.f. Un Desperado (FR) 125 – Minifa (FR) (Pharly (FR) 130)   – §
[1991 NR 1992 8m⁵ 7m 10d] tall, leggy filly: has a round action: dam
successful 3 times at 2 yrs in French Provinces and once at 3 yrs, from 4.2f to 7.7f:
ungenuine maiden: tried blinkered. *J. Parkes*

MINIZEN MUSIC (IRE) 4 b.g. Anita's Prince 126 – Northern Amber (Shack   **38** §
(USA) 118) [1991 5s⁵ 6d⁵ 5f 6m 6g⁶ 5m 5m* 5m 5s² 6d⁵ 6g³ 5m² 6m³ 6f³ 5f 5m 6f⁶
5m 6m 6g 5d 1992 a7g a6g 5s⁴ 6v⁵ 6d⁴ 5g 5s⁴ 5g 6f 6d 5m a6g 6.1m 5g⁵ 7m 6f a7s 5d²
5d 5g 5d] leggy, sparely-made gelding: poor mover: thoroughly inconsistent handicapper: effective at 5f and 6f: acts on any going: below form blinkered. *M. Brittain*

MINOAN LIGHT (IRE) 3 b.g. Trojan Fen 118 – Ashton Amber (On Your Mark   –
125) [1991 a6g⁵ a8g 1992 6.9g 9g 10m] good-bodied gelding: no worthwhile form:
tried blinkered: sold 2,800 gns Ascot June Sales. *M. Brittain*

MINSHAAR 2 b.f. (Feb 12) Jalmood (USA) 126 – Meissarah (USA) (Silver Hawk   **68**
(USA) 123) [1992 5m³ 5f⁴ 5g* 5g* 5.7m⁵ 5g⁵ 5g] lengthy filly: has a round action:
third foal: closely related to 3-y-o Agwa and 4-y-o 8.2f (at 2 yrs) to 13f winner Magic
Secret (both by Local Suitor): dam never ran: won seller (sold out of B. Hanbury's
stable 5,600 gns) at Wolverhampton and nursery at Warwick in July: below best in
nurseries after: should stay 1m: best form on an easy surface. *K. S. Bridgwater*

MINSK 6 ch.m. Kabour 80 – Wedded Bliss 76 (Relko 136) [1991 5f 5g⁶ 5g⁶ 5h 5g   –
1992 5.9f⁶ 5lf⁶ 7.1m 5g 6s⁶] workmanlike mare: no worthwhile form. *T. Craig*

MINSTER MAN (IRE) 2 b.c. (Feb 4) Jareer (USA) 115 – Walk In The Forest   **44**
(Bold Lad (IRE) 133) [1992 5d⁵ 5m 6d 5m 6m 8g] IR 1,800Y, 1,400 2-y-o: useful-
looking colt: moderate walker: third foal: dam unraced: poor form in varied events:
stays 6f: acts on good to firm and dead ground: ran creditably blinkered once: sold
1,100 gns Doncaster November Sales. *B. S. Rothwell*

MINT ADDITION 3 b.f. Tate Gallery (USA) 117 – Nana's Girl 109 (Tin Whistle   –
128) [1991 5m 5m⁴ 6g² 5.3m⁴ 1992 6m 5.1d a7g 10m] sparely-made filly: has a quick
action: plating-class maiden: no form in 1992: bred to stay 1m+: trained until after
second start by R. Hannon: sold 5,200 gns Newmarket December Sales. *K. O.
Cunningham-Brown*

MINTEEN 2 b. or br.f. (Apr 13) Teenoso (USA) 135 – English Mint 66 (Jalmood   –
(USA) 126) [1992 8.2d] compact filly: first foal: dam disappointing maiden stayed 1m:
66/1 and extremely green when last of 16 in maiden at Nottingham in August, soon
tailed off. *J. White*

MIRAMEDE 4 b.f. Norwick (USA) 120 – Mrewa (Runnymede 123) [1991 6.9f   –
5.3g⁴ 5.1g 1992 5g 5.1m 5m 6.1g] lengthy filly: no form in 1992. *R. J. Hodges*

MIRAMICHI BAY 2 b.g. (Apr 27) Daring March 116 – Eyry 85 (Falcon 131)   –
[1992 5g 8g 8m 7.5m] 3,200Y: leggy gelding: half-brother to several winners here
and abroad, including 7f winner Coraki (by Crofter): dam 2-y-o 5f winner: well
beaten in maidens: mulish at stalls then whipped left and unseated apprentice as
race began second start: blinkered next outing: sold 600 gns Doncaster November
Sales. *Mrs V. A. Aconley*

MISAKO TOGO (USA) 3 b.f. Theatrical 128 – Eastland (USA) 110 (Exceller   **104**
(USA) 129) [1991 7g² 7m³ 7g³ 7m* 8d* 8.5s 1992 7d⁴ 10s* 12g 11d* 8g⁴ 8s 10d*
7g⁶] Irish filly: successful as 3-y-o in minor event at Gowran Park in May and listed
races at the Curragh in June and October: needs further than 7f, should stay 1½m:
acts on good to firm and soft ground. *D. K. Weld, Ireland*

MISBELIEF 2 b. or br.f. (Mar 26) Shirley Heights 130 – Misguided 106 (Homing   **64**
130) [1992 7m 7s⁴ 8d] 19,000Y: sixth foal: closely related to 3-y-o California
Dreamin (by Slip Anchor) and fairly useful 1987 2-y-o 5f and 7f winner Kajar (by
Persian Bold): dam sprinting half-sister to smart 6f and 1m winner Missed Blessing:

best effort in maidens when staying-on fourth of 17 at Redcar in September: should be suited by 1m + . *J. R. Fanshawe*

MISDEMEANOURS GIRL (IRE) 4 b.f. Fairy King (USA) – Dar-A-Meter **70** (Dara Monarch 128) [1991 a7g⁶ a7g⁵ a6g⁵ a6g³ a5g³ a5g² 5f⁵ 5g³ 5.8m⁵ 5m³ 5m² a49 + 5m² 5.1d³ 6d² a6g³ 5g* 5f³ 5f 5.1m 5m⁴ 6.1m 1992 a5g a6g a5g a6g a6g* a5g 5g* 5.2d 5g⁴ 5.1d⁵ 5g⁶ 6f 5d* 5.7g² 5.6m⁶ 6f⁴ 5g⁵ 5d² 6d 5m⁴ 6d] small, lengthy, sparely-made filly: moderate mover: largely consistent handicapper: won at Lingfield and Beverley (2) in first half of 1992: effective at 5f to 6f: acts on firm and dead going and on equitrack: usually claimer ridden: tough. *M. R. Channon*

MISIL (USA) 4 ro.c. Miswaki (USA) 124 – April Edge (The Axe II 115) [1991 8s* **120** 8v* 8g* 8d* 8v² 8v* 1992 8v⁴ 8d 9g* 8s* 8s 8s⁴ 8s³ 10v*] very smart Italian performer: successful in minor event at Milan in May, Premio Emilio Turati (for second year running, by 7 lengths from Judge Decision and Sikeston) at Milan the following month and Group 1 Premio Roma (by 5½ lengths from Alhijaz) at Rome in November: bit below his best in between in Prix Jacques le Marois (eighth) at Deauville, Prix du Moulin de Longchamp (5 lengths fourth to All At Sea) and Premio Vittorio di Capua (6 lengths third to Alhijaz) at Milan: stays 1¼m: goes well on heavy going. *V. Caruso, Italy*

MISLEMANI (IRE) 2 b.c. (Apr 21) Kris 135 – Meis El-Reem 124 (Auction Ring – p (USA) 123) [1992 7g] sturdy, rather close-coupled colt: third foal: brother to 8.2f winner Cartel: dam 5f to 1m winner: 5/1 and green, never able to challenge when twelfth of 18 in maiden at Newbury in August: showed quick action: should do better. *M. R. Stoute*

MISSA BREVIS (USA) 2 b.f. (Apr 21) Miswaki (USA) 124 – Miss Tusculum **66** (USA) (Boldnesian) [1992 5.9g³ 7s 6d²] $230,000F: sparely-made filly: half-sister to several winners, including Breeders' Cup Turf winner Miss Alleged (by Alleged) and Nancy's Champion (by Northern Jove), stakes winner at up to 9f: dam unraced: improved effort (blinkered previously) when 3½ lengths second of 21 to Specified in maiden at Redcar in October, staying on well: should prove better suited by 7f than 6f: possibly unsuited by very soft ground. *J. W. Watts*

MISSAL (IRE) 3 b.f. Alzao (USA) 117 – Priors Mistress 71 (Sallust 134) [1991 – 5g⁵ 6g 6f 9m 6g 6m 6.9f 7.6m 1992 6m 7d 8f 6g] small filly: poor mover: poor plater: bred to stay 1m: sometimes blinkered. *Pat Mitchell*

MISS ARAGON 4 b.f. Aragon 118 – Lavenham Blue (Streetfighter 120) [1991 6d **50** 6m⁶ 6f 10g 6m⁴ 6s⁴ a6g³ 1992 a7g 6m* 5.9f⁵ 6g⁴ 6m³ 6s² 6d 5g² 6.1g 5s⁴ 5s 6d³] rangy filly: good mover: in-and-out form in handicaps after winning (for first time) at Ripon in July: effective at 5f to 6f: acts on good to firm ground and heavy, possibly unsuited by firm: suitable mount for claimer. *Miss L. C. Siddall*

MISS BELL RINGER 4 b.f. Belfort (FR) 89 – Immatation (FR) 67 (Polyfoto **33** 124) [1991 5f⁶ 6g 5m 6m* 1992 a6g a6g a6g⁶ 5d 5.3m 6.1m 7g 6.9d⁵ a6g] workmanlike, good-quartered filly: poor handicapper: stays 7f: acts on good to firm and dead ground. *C. J. Hill*

MISS BLUEBIRD (IRE) 3 b.f. Bluebird (USA) 125 – Welsh Dancer 94 (Welsh **88** Saint 126) [1991 5m² 6m³ 6g⁴ 7m 7s 1992 10m⁶ 8f⁴ 6h* 6m* 7m 6g] tall, lengthy filly: fairly useful performer: easily best efforts in 1992 when winning minor events at Folkestone and Lingfield in the summer: stiff tasks last 2 starts: effective at 6f and 7f: acts on hard ground, possibly unsuited by soft: blinkered last 4 starts: bandaged last 2: sold 35,000 gns Newmarket December Sales. *P. A. Kelleway*

MISS BRIDGE (IRE) 2 ch.f. (Mar 20) Common Grounds 118 – Stop The **33** Cavalry (Relko 136) [1992 6f 6g 7m 8s] IR 2,200Y, resold 7,200Y: small, lengthy filly: sixth foal: half-sister to 3-y-o Super Sarena (by Taufan), fair staying maiden at 2 yrs, and winners abroad by Auction Ring and Try My Best: dam never ran: poor maiden: should stay at least 1m. *M. Bell*

MISS BRIGHTSIDE 4 ch.f. Crofthall 110 – Fidget (Workboy 123) [1991 5m³ **36** 6d⁴ 6g² 6f³ 7f⁵ 6f 6.1m⁵ 6m 6m⁵ 1992 7d 5g 6.1d 6g⁵ 7m² 5m a5g³ 6.1g² 6.1d⁶ 6f⁶ 6.1g 5d⁴ a6g] leggy filly: inconsistent maiden: effective from 5f to 7f: acts on firm and dead ground and on fibresand. *A. Smith*

MISS BROUGHTON 4 b.f. Never So Bold 135 – Yelney 65 (Blakeney 126) – [1991 a7g⁵ a6g⁶ 6s⁴ 6d* 7g 6g 7g⁶ 9d 8d 8d a8g 1992 a10g⁵ a10g] workmanlike filly: inconsistent handicapper, not seen out after January: best effort at 6f on dead ground: usually soon behind. *W. J. Musson*

MISS CALCULATE 4 ch.f. Mummy's Game 120 – Antique Bloom 101 (Sterling – Bay (SWE)) [1991 7m 1992 a6g² a6g² a6g³ 6s⁵ 6d 6d a6g² a6g*] lengthy, angular a67 filly: has a moderate action: fair form at Southwell early and late in year: just got up in claimer in December: best form at 6f/7f: acts on fibresand: effective blinkered or not. *Capt. J. Wilson*

MISS COOKIE 4 ch.f. Nicholas Bill 125 – Maryland Cookie (USA) 101 (Bold Hour) [1991 7f² 7m³ 8g² 7d⁵ 6.9f⁴ 7g³ 5d 1992 10.8d 7g⁶ 8.3g a7g 8g] sparely-made filly: below form in 1992, pulled up having broken down final start: stayed 1m: acted on firm ground: below form blinkered: headstrong and looked difficult ride: dead. *M. C. Pipe* —

MISS CRESTA 3 b.f. Master Willie 129 – Sweet Snow (USA) (Lyphard (USA) 132) [1991 7f⁴ 7m⁵ 1992 7g 8m 8.2d] small filly: rated 67 at 2 yrs: on the downgrade: should stay at least 1m: sold 1,100 gns Newmarket Autumn Sales. *H. Candy* —

MISS DEBONAIR 3 gr.f. Elegant Air 119 – Normanby Lass 100 (Bustino 136) [1991 7m 6m⁴ 1992 6.1d⁶ 7m] leggy, quite good-topped filly: poor maiden: not seen out after April: should be suited by 7f + . *D. Morley* —

MISS DELIVERY 2 bl.f. (Apr 29) Durandal 114 – Paphidia (Mansingh (USA) 120) [1992 6m⁴ 5d a6g a7g⁶] neat filly: first foal: dam poor maiden: poor form in varied events. *P. Howling* 36

MISS DOODY 3 b.f. Gorytus (USA) 132 – Kittycatoo Katango (USA) (Verbatim (USA)) [1991 6d⁶ 6m 6g 6d⁶ 6m* 6m⁴ 6g³ 7g 6g² 6m* 6g 7m 1992 8d 7g³ 9g² 7.9m 10f 8f⁴ 9m 11.6m 10.2f² 10m* 11.5m] smallish, sturdy filly: moderate mover: inconsistent handicapper: reluctant early on when successful in seller (bought in 5,400 gns) at Ripon in July: stays 1¼m: acts on firm ground: visored: jinked markedly left once at 3 yrs: sometimes slowly away. *M. R. Channon* 63

MISSED FLIGHT 2 b.c. (Mar 21) Dominion 123 – Loveskate (USA) 78 (Overskate (CAN)) [1992 7d 8.2s³] 7,000F, 31,000Y: second foal: dam, 15.8f winner, is closely related to high-class middle-distance performer Raft: much better effort in October maidens when running-on 3 lengths third of 14 to Azzilfi at Nottingham: will be suited by middle distances. *C. F. Wall* 75 p

MISSED THE BOAT (IRE) 2 b.g. (May 5) Cyrano de Bergerac 120 – Lady Portobello (Porto Bello 118) [1992 5f 5m⁴ 5g⁵ 6g² 7g 7d⁶ 7d a6g³] IR 4,600Y, 9,000 2-y-o: rather leggy gelding: third foal: dam, maiden, best effort at 7f: modest maiden: will prove better suited by 1m: acts on dead ground and fibresand: found little off bridle when visored once. *T. D. Barron* 54

MISS FASCINATION 2 b.f. (Jan 20) Damister (USA) 123 – Tantalizing Song (CAN) (The Minstrel (CAN) 135) [1992 7g³ 7g⁴ a8g³] sturdy filly: moderate mover: fourth foal: sister to 3-y-o 6f (at 2 yrs) to 8.1f winner Magnificent: dam ran 5 times in North America: fair maiden: easily best effort on first outing: will be better suited by 1¼m. *M. A. Jarvis* 68

MISS FAYRUZ (IRE) 2 b.f. (May 8) Fayruz 116 – Susan's Blues (Cure The Blues (USA)) [1992 6g⁵ 6h⁵ 7g* 7f 6g⁴ 6m 7m 8g] leggy filly: second foal: dam placed at 9f in Ireland: poor performer: won seller (retained 3,000 gns) at Yarmouth in July: should stay 1m: acts on good to firm ground: sometimes bandaged. *Mrs L. Piggott* 52

MISS FITNESS 2 ch.f. (Apr 12) Hallgate 127 – Lady Woodpecker 61 (Tap On Wood 130) [1992 6g a6g 6m⁵ 7g⁴ 6m 6s] rather sparely-made filly: third foal: sister to 3-y-o Dee Vee and half-sister to a winner in Italy: dam, maiden, stayed 5f: poor form in claimers and sellers: visored last 2 starts. *Dr J. D. Scargill* —

MISS FOXTROT 4 b.f. Bustino 136 – Java Jive 63 (Hotfoot 126) [1991 8m² 10m³ 12m* 1992 12f] compact, quite attractive filly: rated 71 at 3 yrs: found little in handicap in June, first run for a year: stayed 1½m: in foal to Aragon. *J. L. Dunlop* —

MISS GORGEOUS (IRE) 2 b.f. (Mar 3) Damister (USA) 123 – Rocket Alert 110 (Red Alert 127) [1992 a5g⁵ a5g² a6g* a8g⁴] 25,000Y: fourth foal: sister to 6f and 7f winner Rejoice and half-sister to useful 1¼m and 10.6f winner Ardlui (by Lomond): dam 5f to 7f winner: modest form: won maiden at Southwell in December, strong run to lead closing stages: no impression final 2f in nursery there 2 weeks later: stays 6f well. *W. A. O'Gorman* 64

MISS GROSSE NEZ (IRE) 3 b.f. Cyrano de Bergerac 120 – Fait Dodo (On Your Mark 125) [1991 5m 6d 5m⁴ 5f³ 5m³ 6f 5m 1992 6f 7g 7d 8m] sparely-made filly: moderate mover: rated 50 at 2 yrs: on the downgrade. *C. W. Thornton* —

MISS HAGGIS 3 b.f. Scottish Reel 123 – Bambolona 108 (Bustino 136) [1991 NR 1992 8m 8.9g* 10m⁵ 8m* 7g* 8m⁵ 7m⁶ 8.1d 6g] 7,800F, 11,000Y: big, strong, rangy filly: second foal: sister to 4-y-o 1¼m and 10.8f winner Scottish Bambi: dam 2-y-o 6f winner: progressed well for much of 1992, winning Wolverhampton minor event, handicaps at Wolverhampton and Newmarket (£11,600 contest) and sixth in 86

Goodwood listed race: well below form final start: should prove as effective at 6f as 1m: acts on good to firm ground: held up, and has idled. *R. Boss*

MISS HYDE (USA)   3 br.f. Procida (USA) 129 – Little Niece 79 (Great Nephew   **54** 126) [1991 6g2 6m6 8m 1992 10.1s3 10d a8g3 10.5m* 10.5g6 12.3f6 10f a12g5 11g] rather leggy filly: below form after winning apprentice handicap at Haydock in May: stays 10.5f: acts on good to firm ground: usually visored, blinkered final start: usually races up with pace: won over hurdles in November. *J. A. Glover*

MISSISSIPI MAID   2 b.f. (Mar 7) All Systems Go 119 – Coins And Art (USA)   **47** (Mississipian (USA)) [1992 5g 6m3 a6g4] sparely-made filly: sixth foal: half-sister to several winners, including 6-y-o 1½m winner Present Times (by Sayf El Arab) and 1987 2-y-o 7f winner Valued Collection (by Valiyar): dam never ran: similar form when in frame in claimers at Pontefract and Lingfield in autumn: stays 6f: acts on good to firm ground and equitrack. *W. G. M. Turner*

MISSISSIPPI BEAT (USA)   5 b.g. Dixieland Band (USA) – Jungle Dance   – (USA) (Graustark) [1991 a14g4 14.6s 15g 14.6g a14g3 a14g a16g5 a16g6 1992 a14g4   a43 a12g2 a12g* a12g a14g4 a12g4 a12g 12f] lengthy, dipped-backed gelding: moderate mover: poor handicapper: won maiden at Lingfield in January: effective at 1½m and should stay 2m: acts on firm and dead going, and all-weather surfaces: successful for claimer: swishes tail: sometimes visored: sold to join D. Nolan 1,650 gns Doncaster November Sales. *M. P. Naughton*

MISSISSIPPI QUEEN   3 b.f. Nishapour (FR) 125 – Honey Pot 111 (Hotfoot   – 126) [1991 a8g a8g 1992 a10g a7g6 7.5m 6m 7d] leggy, angular filly: poor plater: stays 7f: looks a hard ride: sold out of R. J. R. Williams' stable 900 gns Doncaster January Sales after second start. *Mrs N. Macauley*

MISS KINGFISHER (USA)   3 b.f. Temperence Hill (USA) – Glory Street   – (USA) (The Pruner (USA)) [1991 6f6 6m5 7g 6d 1992 a6g 7.5g5 10d 9f 8.5f5] leggy filly: moderate mover: poor maiden: stays 7.5f: below form blinkered once. *S. G. Norton*

MISS KNIGHT   5 ch.m. Longleat (USA) 109 – Ethel Knight (Thatch (USA) 136)   **39** [1991 a7g6 a7g2 a7g3 a7g 7d 6d2 a7g 6g 8g 7m 6d* 7g3 6.1m5 6g 8.2m 1992 a7g a7g6 8.3v3 6d5 8.1g 8d 8.1m6 8.3g 8.3s6] smallish, compact mare: carries condition: moderate walker: inconsistent handicapper: effective at 6f to 1m: acts on any going: often slowly away: sometimes unruly in preliminaries. *R. Bastiman*

MISS LIMELIGHT   3 ch.f. Crofthall 110 – Floral Light 74 (Florescence 120)   – [1991 NR 1992 6m4 a8g 6m] leggy filly: eleventh foal: dam placed over 5f and 6f: no sign of ability. *A. Smith*

MISS MAGENTA (IRE)   4 b.f. Tate Gallery (USA) 117 – Crimson Crown (Lord   **36** Gayle (USA) 124) [1991 a8g5 a7g a6g5 6m 5f 7g 7d5 6f 6g 6m 7s 1992 6.9g5 7m3 7g 7f6 8m 8g6 8.3m4 8g2 8g3 8f 7d 8.9d6] leggy, sparely-made filly: poor mover: largely consistent maiden handicapper: may well prove suited by 1¼m: best on a sound surface. *R. Thompson*

MISS MARIGOLD   3 b.f. Norwick (USA) 120 – Kiki Star 59 (Some Hand 119)   – [1991 NR 1992 16.9d6 10.2d 10s6] workmanlike filly: second foal: dam won sellers at 1¼m and 1½m: well beaten in maidens and claimer: reluctant to race once. *R. J. Hodges*

MISS MOODY   6 ch.m. Jalmood (USA) 126 – Ice Galaxie (USA) (Icecapade   **36** (USA)) [1991 6v 7m 7.1g 6.1m4 1992 a6g5] workmanlike, good-quartered mare: poor maiden: should stay 7f + : acts on good to firm and soft going and on fibresand. *J. M. Bradley*

MISS MOVIE WORLD   3 b.f. Slim Jim 112 – Regal Artist 72 (Breakspear II)   **62** [1991 6m 7.5f 7.1m 5f6 5m5 5g 1992 5v 5m 8f a7g5 5d* a7g3 6f4 6g2 a7s 6g2 a6g* 6f2 5d6 5m2] sturdy filly: modest handicapper: won at Wolverhampton in July and Lingfield in August: improved form when second at Doncaster and Newmarket after: best form at up to 6f: acts on dead ground and all-weather surfaces, and goes well on top-of-the-ground: often apprentice ridden. *N. Bycroft*

MISS NARNIA   3 b.f. Viking (USA) – Nagalia 80 (Lochnager 132) [1991 6g5 5f5   – 5g4 7m 8g a6g a6g4 1992 a6g5 a7g4 6m5 5g 6f] sparely-made filly: poor maiden: stays 7f: below form blinkered: sold 820 gns Doncaster September Sales. *M. Dods*

MISS NOSEY PARKER (IRE)   3 b. or br.f. Cyrano de Bergerac 120 – Renzola   **99** (Dragonara Palace (USA) 115) [1991 5v 5s* 5.2g3 5g2 5.2f3 5m* 5g2 5m* 1992 6d* 5m3 5s5 5d 5m4 5m4 6g] small, sturdy filly: poor mover: useful performer: made all in minor event at Kempton in April: easily best runs after when in frame in £17,900

Ascot handicap and listed races at Newmarket: effective at 5f and 6f: acts on good to firm and dead going: sold 34,000 gns Newmarket December Sales. *R. Hannon*

MISS OASIS   3 b.f. Green Desert (USA) 127 – Mrs Bacon 82 (Balliol 125) [1991 6m⁶ 1992 6m] rather sparely-made filly: twice raced, well below debut form in Lingfield maiden in July. *P. J. Makin*   –

MISS OFFIE   2 b.f. (Mar 28) Presidium 124 – Off The Mark (On Your Mark 125)   **38** [1992 7d 6s a8g a7g] tenth foal: dam French 1m winner: well beaten in maidens and a nursery, never dangerous. *R. Hollinshead*

MISS ORIENT   3 b.f. Damister (USA) 123 – Brown Maid (URU) (Admirals   – Launch 118) [1991 NR 1992 a7g²] second known foal: dam bred in Uruguay: 10 lengths second in maiden at Lingfield in February: reportedly finished very lame on off-fore. *W. A. O'Gorman*

MISS OTTER (IRE)   2 br.f. (May 10) Magical Wonder (USA) 125 – Otterhill 67   **35** (Brigadier Gerard 144) [1992 5d 6m 5g 6d] IR 4,000F, IR 2,800Y: leggy, close-coupled filly: half-sister to 3 winners here and in Ireland, including useful miler Ottergayle (by Lord Gayle): dam daughter of very smart 2-y-o Lowna: poor maiden: sold 700 gns Newmarket Autumn Sales. *G. A. Pritchard-Gordon*

MISS PARKES   3 ch.f. Mummy's Game 120 – Bonne Baiser 88 (Most Secret 119)   **46** [1991 7m⁴ 6m² 7m 1992 7d³ 7g⁶ 7.5m⁴ 9.2d⁶ 9.9f 7.1m³ 8.1f⁴ 6m² 7.1m³ 8m⁵] leggy, lengthy filly: fair plater: stays 1m: acts on firm ground and dead: below form blinkered final start. *J. Berry*

MISS PIGLET (IRE)   2 ch.f. (Apr 4) Double Schwartz 128 – Miss Bagatelle 70   – (Mummy's Pet 125) [1992 6m a6g a8g] IR 500F, IR 2,000Y: plain filly: second foal: dam, placed over 5f here at 2 yrs when somewhat temperamental, won at 6f at 3 yrs in Ireland: well beaten, including in a seller. *R. Ingram*

MISS PIMPERNEL   2 b.f. (Mar 19) Blakeney 126 – New Edition 72 (Great   **62** Nephew 126) [1992 7m⁶ 7d 7d⁴] workmanlike filly: has scope: third foal: half-sister to 7f winner Arabian King (by Sayf El Arab) and 3-y-o Never Late (by Never So Bold): dam, 2-y-o 5f winner, appeared to stay 7f: similar form when in first 6 in October maidens at Newmarket and Catterick: well below form other run: will be suited by 1m + . *B. Hanbury*

MISS PINOCCHIO   5 b.m. Noalto 120 – Floral 82 (Floribunda 136) [1991 7g 8g   – 1992 6d] angular mare: on the downgrade. *R. R. Lamb*

MISS PIN UP   3 gr.f. Kalaglow 132 – Allander Girl (Miralgo 130) [1991 5g 6g⁵ 6g⁶   **73** 6d 7m² 7m 7g 7f 6m⁵ 8m 1992 12v 8.9v 9.7g² 8m 10f⁴ 14.1g* 16f⁶ 14.6m* 14.1g* 14g* 14m⁵ 12m* 13.9g 14g⁴ 14g⁴ 14d⁶] leggy, sparely-made filly: had excellent season in handicaps in 1992, sucessful at Nottingham (2), Doncaster, Sandown and Kempton, twice in apprentice events: effective from 1½m to 1¾m: acts on good to firm ground: below best blinkered: usually ridden by D. Biggs. *Pat Mitchell*

MISS PLUM   3 b.f. Ardross 134 – Heaven High (High Line 125) [1991 7g³ 1992   **86** 12g* 11.5d⁴ 13.1g* 13.5s 14m 16g⁵] leggy, close-coupled filly: good mover: made most to win maiden at Beverley in April and minor event at Bath in July: easily best other effort when fair fifth in moderately-run listed race at Newmarket: should stay beyond 13f: best efforts on good ground: trained until after fourth start by H. Cecil. *D. R. Loder*

MISS PRECOCIOUS   4 b.f. Precocious 126 – Hissy Missy 70 (Bold Lad (IRE)   **37** d 133) [1991 10d 1992 7d 6.9g 8g 5f⁴ 5g³ 5f6 5m⁵ 6.1g 5s 6s 5.1g] workmanlike filly: has a round action: maiden handicapper: seems best at sprint distances: acts on firm ground: visored nowadays: has hung badly left. *D. Shaw*

MISS RIBBONS   2 b.f. (Mar 13) Nomination 125 – New Ribbons 79 (Ribero 126)   **45** [1992 5g 6m 7g 9g 10g⁵ 7.6s⁴] 2,100Y: small, leggy filly: half-sister to three 2-y-o winners and a winner in Italy: dam 1½m winner: poor performer: seems to stay 1¼m: acts on soft ground: races freely. *Pat Mitchell*

MISS RITA   3 ch.f. Master Willie 129 – Florita 86 (Lord Gayle (USA) 124) [1991   **63** 6g³ 1992 10.2d4] sparely-made filly: twice-raced maiden: fourth at Bath in September: seemed likely to improve: sold 840 gns Newmarket December Sales. *C. F. Wall*

MISS SARAHSUE   6 br.m. Van Der Linden (FR) – Blakesware Dancer 68   – (Dance In Time (CAN)) [1991 9.7s 10m 1992 11.5m⁶ 11.9f 11.9m] lengthy mare: of little account in 1992: dead. *J. E. Long*

MISS SARAJANE   8 b.m. Skyliner 117 – Taffeta 72 (Shantung 132) [1991 a8g*   **50** a8g 8s 8g³ 8d⁶ 8.2d 9m² 8m³ 8m* 8.1m⁶ 8f² 9f 8.2m⁴ 9m 8m⁵ 9g a8g 1992 8g a8g* 8.2m⁵ 10.3m⁶ 8g⁴ 9g 8g 8s] leggy, workmanlike mare: good mover: modest handicapper: won at Southwell in August: effective at 1m to 1¼m: probably unsuited by soft surface nowadays, acts on any other. *R. Hollinshead*

MISS SHADOWFAX   3 ch.f. Absalom 128 – Ring of Pearl (Auction Ring (USA)   –
123) [1991 5g⁶ 5m 6g⁶ a5g⁵ 5m* 5m² 5m³ 5g* 5. 1f 5.7g 6g 1992 5.1g⁶ 5.3f⁶ 6.1m 5s]
compact filly: rated 62 at 2 yrs: well below form in handicaps in 1992: best form at 5f:
acts on good to firm ground: sold 1,200 gns Doncaster November Sales. *C. N. Allen*

MISS SHUN LEE   3 b.f. All Systems Go 119 – Belle of Stars 58 (Beldale Flutter   –
(USA) 130) [1991 NR 1992 7g] workmanlike filly: first foal: dam poor plater: last in
Warwick claimer in April: sold 900 gns Ascot June Sales. *D. R. Tucker*

MISS SIHAM (IRE)   3 ch.f. Green Forest (USA) 134 – Miss Derby (USA)   44
(Master Derby (USA)) [1991 5m⁶ 5m5 5g* 5m⁵ 5m³ 6g⁶ 5.1f5 6m⁴ 5m² 5d 1992 5g
6m 5f 5.1g 5m⁴ 5m⁶ 6m² 6f³ a5g⁶ 5d 5d] sturdy filly: moderate mover: poor
handicapper: stays 6f: acts on firm ground. *J. Balding*

MISS VAXETTE   3 b.f. Norwick (USA) 120 – Langton Herring (Nearly A Hand   78
115) [1991 6d⁴ 5d⁴ 5f³ 5.3m* 5m⁴ 5m* 5g 5m² 6g⁶ 5m 1992 5m⁴ 5s³ 5g³ 5f* 5m⁵
5d³ 5d* 5s⁵ 5m 5.3d² 5s 5.1d³ 5s] compact filly: fair handicapper: successful at
Edinburgh (2) in summer: best form at around 5f: probably unsuited by very soft
ground, acts on any other: suitable mount for claimer. *J. L. Spearing*

MISS WHITTINGHAM (IRE)   2 b.f. (Mar 8) Fayruz 116 – Windini (Wind-   41
jammer (USA)) [1992 5m⁴ 5g 5.1m³ a5g 5g⁶ 5g⁶ 5d⁵ 5s] IR 18,000Y: compact,
good-bodied filly: moderate mover: second foal: sister to Irish 3-y-o 6f winner
Faydini: dam unraced: poor maiden: will prove best at 5f: acts on good to firm and
soft ground: ran creditably visored, below form blinkered: sometimes hangs left:
sold 1,300 gns Doncaster September Sales. *J. Berry*

MISS WITCH   4 gr.f. High Line 125 – Magic Spell (FR) (Dancer's Image (USA))   52
[1991 8.9g⁵ 11.7m⁶ 12.5m⁴ 12.3g³ 12g² 1992 11.8m³ 12f 10.2f 12m² 11.6g³ 12g⁶ 12s]
leggy, lengthy filly: has round action: maiden handicapper: worth a try beyond 1½m:
acts on good to firm ground: front runner. *H. Candy*

MISSY-S (IRE)   3 b.f. Sarab 123 – Monaco Lady 83 (Manado 130) [1991 6g 5m⁶   51
6m⁴ 6f⁴ 7g 7m 1992 8.2g 7d² a7g⁴ a8g* 9.7h² a8g³ 8.1d⁴ 10g⁵ 8.9d³ 9s a10g] leggy,
rather sparely-made filly: moderate mover: modest handicapper: won apprentice
maiden at Lingfield in June: stays 9.7f: acts on hard and dead ground, and on
all-weather surfaces: suitable mount for inexperienced rider. *G. A. Pritchard-Gordon*

MISTER BLAKE   2 b.g. (Mar 23) Damister (USA) 123 – Larive 80 (Blakeney   55
126) [1992 5g 6g⁵ a6g⁶ 6m² a6g² 7g 7d⁶ a6g⁵ a6g a8g² a8g⁴ a7g* a7g³ a7g* a8g²]   a74 ?
2,900Y: compact gelding: good mover: fourth foal: dam 1½m winner stayed 2m: fair
performer: inconsistent early on but in good form late in season, winning 2
nurseries at Southwell: will stay further than 1m: acts on good to firm ground, and
on fibresand: hampered when visored: goes well in blinkers though has won
without. *W. A. O'Gorman*

MISTERIOSO   3 b.f. Forzando 122 – Ragged Moon 72 (Raga Navarro (ITY) 119)   100
[1991 5m³ 6g* 6m* 1992 8m⁴ 8.5g² 7f 8g⁵ 7m 6d 8g⁵] rather leggy, lengthy filly:
in-and-out form in pattern/listed events in 1992: best efforts when in frame at
Kempton and Epsom (Diomed Stakes): stays 8.5f: acts on good to firm ground
(possibly unsuited by firm): below form visored once: trained until after fourth start
by D. Elsworth. *Lord Huntingdon*

MISTER JOLSON   3 br.g. Latest Model 115 – Impromptu 88 (My Swanee 122)   63   p
[1991 6f 5g 1992 5.1g⁴ 5.1m* 5.7d⁴ 5.3d³ 5d²] sturdy gelding: progressive sprint
handicapper: won at Bath in August: very good second at Goodwood in October: acts
on good to firm and dead ground: held up: should win more races. *R. J. Hodges*

MISTER LAWSON   6 ch.g. Blushing Scribe (USA) 107 – Nonpareil (FR) 92   –
(Pharly (FR) 130) [1991 NR 1992 a7g a12g⁶ a10g] close-coupled gelding: fairly useful
as 2-y-o (best form at 5f on top-of-the-ground) but nowhere near so good nowadays.
B. Forsey

MISTER ODDY   6 b.g. Dubassoff (USA) – Somerford Glory 44 (Hittite Glory   –
125) [1991 NR 1992 11.8d 12.1s] leggy, workmanlike gelding: poor maiden on flat:
stays 7f: acts on heavy going. *J. S. King*

MISTERTOPOGIGO (IRE)   2 b.c. (Feb 19) Thatching 131 – Decadence   78   p
(Vaigly Great 127) [1992 5m* 5.1g* 5m 5g²] 3,000F, 7,000Y: strong, lengthy colt:
has scope: moderate walker: second foal: half-brother to 3-y-o Indigo Blue (by
Bluebird): dam sister to Hallgate: won maiden at Newcastle in June and median
auction event at Chepstow in July: ran poorly next start but very well when head

second of 9 (led until close home) in Haydock nursery: likely to make quite useful sprinter. *B. Beasley*

MISTIC GLEN (IRE)   3 b.f. Mister Majestic 122 – Northern Glen (Northfields (USA)) [1991 NR 1992 13.8g 12.1g] IR 2,500F: lengthy, workmanlike filly: half-sister to several winners, including Irish listed-placed sprinter Wolverglen (by Wolverlife): dam unraced half-sister to very useful 1971 2-y-o 5f winner Pert Lassie: not seen out until September, and behind in claimer and seller in North. *J. Parkes*   –

MIST OF THE MARSH (USA)   3 b.f. Seattle Slew (USA) – Shywing (USA) (Wing Out (USA)) [1991 NR 1992 8m 8g 8.2d6 10s 11.8g 12s3] $325,000Y: strong, lengthy filly: has a round action: first foal: dam successful in 5 stakes races (over 6½f and 1m) at 3 and 4 yrs: poor maiden: stayed 1½m: acted on soft ground: visits Formidable. *J. H. M. Gosden*   47

MISTRESS MINX   3 b.f. Faustus (USA) 118 – Arctic Jewel (Mandamus 120) [1991 NR 1992 10.5g 7d] leggy filly: moderate mover: half-sister to several winners, including 10.5f winner Tudor Diamond (by Henry The Seventh): dam unraced half-sister to high-class German horse Luciano: tailed off in August maidens. *L. J. Codd*   –

MISTY GODDESS (IRE)   4 gr.f. Godswalk (USA) 130 – Silent Sail (Aglojo 119) [1991 7g 8.2m 8f3 8m4 a10g 1992 a10g a11g 10.8d2 12g4 10g* 10.5g6 10.2f* 10.8g* 10s4 10m2] sturdy filly: consistent performer: successful in 1992 in sellers at Leicester (no bid), Chepstow (bought in 10,000 gns) and Warwick (bought in 7,200 gns): badly struck into final run: stays 10.8f: acts on firm and dead going: excellent mount for apprentice. *M. A. Jarvis*   62

MISTY JENNI (IRE)   2 b.f. (Mar 10) Night Shift (USA) – Mousil 84 (Moulton 128) [1992 6d 6g* 6g6] 1,600F, 1,600Y: good-topped filly: fifth foal: half-sister to a minor winner under both codes in France: dam, 1¼m winner, is half-sister to 1000 Guineas winner Full Dress II: 33/1-winner of minor event at Folkestone, making all on stand rail: poor sixth of 7 in minor event there later in September. *R. Akehurst*   64

MISTY NIGHT   4 gr.f. Grey Desire 115 – Maha (Northfields (USA)) [1991 12f3 15g6 11.1d 15s 15g5 12.1d 1992 9.2v] small, workmanlike filly: on the downgrade. *P. Monteith*   –

MISTY SILKS   2 b.f. (Mar 12) Scottish Reel 123 – Silk St James (Pas de Seul 133) [1992 6d 7d 8d] smallish, stocky filly: first reported foal: dam unraced: poor form in maidens: will probably stay 1¼m. *M. J. Ryan*   53

MISTY VIEW   3 gr.f. Absalom 128 – Long View 68 (Persian Bold 123) [1991 6m3 6g6 a7g2 a7g3 7g* 8m4 7g3 7m5 7.6m 1992 10g6 10f* 10f* 10m2 10m 10.1d6 12d] sturdy filly: fair handicapper: won at Sandown and Salisbury in June: should prove effective at 1½m: acts on firm and dead ground: suitable mount for claimer: game: sold to join J. White 13,000 gns Newmarket Autumn Sales. *M. A. Jarvis*   71

MISUNDERSTANDING (IRE)   3 b.g. Wolverlife 115 – Wallpark Princess (Balidar 133) [1991 5m3 6g 6m3 7m* 7g* 7m5 8m* 7d 1992 7g 7s3 7g3 8.9g6 7.1m3 7.5v] lengthy gelding: has a roundish action: fairly useful handicapper: effective at 7f/1m: acts on good to firm ground and soft: sold out of Mrs J. Ramsden's stable 14,000 gns Newmarket July Sales after fifth start to race in Italy, behind in listed race final outing. *B. Agriformi, Italy*   84

MITHI AL GAMAR (USA)   2 ch.f. (Feb 11) Blushing Groom (FR) 131 – Raahia (CAN) 91 (Vice Regent (CAN)) [1992 6g] small filly: second foal: half-sister to 3-y-o Tlaad (by Mr Prospector): dam 2-y-o 6f winner stayed 7f: green and very easy to back, never able to challenge when around 9 lengths eighth of 20 in maiden at Newmarket in October: should improve. *M. R. Stoute*   53 p

MITHL AL HAWA   2 b.f. (Mar 2) Salse (USA) 128 – Moon Drop 103 (Dominion 123) [1992 6g2 6d* 6d2 6v] smallish, sturdy filly: first foal: dam sprinter: progressed well in autumn, comfortable winner of Kempton maiden and ¾-length second to Rain Brother in York listed race, until never dangerous on heavy ground in Racecall Gold Trophy at Redcar: will stay 7f: has worn bandage near-hind. *J. R. Fanshawe*   99

MITSUBISHI CENTRE (IRE)   3 gr.f. Thatching 131 – Checkers (Habat 127) [1991 7g 8g 6.3m6 6m6 1992 8g] IR 17,000Y: fourth foal: half-sister to Larnaca (by Shernazar) and Mitsubishi Video (by Doulab), both successful at about 1m in Ireland, the former a useful hurdler: dam placed over 1m in Ireland: no worthwhile form at 2 yrs (tried blinkered) in Ireland for J. Oxx: tailed off in selling handicap in November. *A. P. Stringer*   –

MITSUBISHI VIDEO (IRE)   4 gr.f. Doulab (USA) 115 – Checkers (Habat 127) [1991 7.8g* 7g2 7g3 9.5m5 8.5g 8m 7m 7.5d4 10g 1992 a6g 5s6 7g 7f 8g6] workmanlike filly: third foal: half-sister to Irish 1m winner Larnaca (by Shernazar): dam, placed over 1m in Ireland: fair ex-Irish handicapper, won at Dundalk at 3 yrs for J. Oxx: little form here in 1992: stays 1m: acts on dead ground: below form blinkered: trained first start by A. Stringer. *Dr J. D. Scargill*

MITTENOSKI PET 3 b.f. Petoski 135 – Runabay (Run The Gantlet (USA)) – [1991 NR 1992 9g a12g⁵ 10.2f] 500Y: unfurnished filly: fourth foal: half-sister to a winning jumper in France: dam French maiden: no form in maidens and seller. *T. J. Naughton*

MIZAAYA 3 ch.c. Riverman (USA) 131 – Exclusive Order (USA) (Exclusive **96 +** Native (USA)) [1991 7.1d 1992 8g* 8d 7m* 7m* 8.5g 7f 8m] useful-looking colt: moderate mover: won maiden at Doncaster and handicaps at Chester and York (£19,400 contest) in spring: no other form at 3 yrs, twice running badly in pattern events but travelled well until badly hampered over 1f out in £66,200 Goodwood handicap final run (July): stays 1m: acts on good to firm ground: remains in training. *M. R. Stoute*

MIZNAH 3 b.f. Sadler's Wells (USA) 132 – La Dame du Lac (USA) (Round **102** Table) [1991 6.3m² 6m* 7m 7s² 1992 7m 7g³ 7s² 6s⁶] smallish, quite attractive filly: has a round action: useful performer: off course 3 months after contesting Nell Gwyn Stakes at Newmarket first start: best efforts after when placed in listed races at Leopardstown and the Curragh: will stay 1m: acts on good to firm and soft ground. *J. S. Bolger, Ireland*

MIZORAM (USA) 3 ch.c. Miswaki (USA) 124 – Ask Me How (USA) (Secretariat **80** (USA)) [1991 NR 1992 7g 8f* 7m* 8.5d² 8m] $49,000F: workmanlike, good-quartered colt: fifth reported foal: brother to U.S. winner Questioning, closely related to French 9f winner Gano (by Gold Crest) and half-brother to a minor winner in USA: dam successful at up to 7f at 3 and 4 yrs: claimer ridden when winning maiden at Doncaster in May and handicap at Lingfield (well-backed favourite) in June: effective at 7f and 8.5f: acts on firm and dead going: sent to race in Dubai. *H. R. A. Cecil*

MIZYAN (IRE) 4 b.g. Melyno 130 – Maid of Erin (USA) (Irish River (FR) 131) **65** [1991 8d⁵ 8g 8m⁶ 10m² 10g³ 12.4m⁶ 10g³ 10g⁴ 12m 12.1s 10.3d⁴ 1992 10d⁴ a12g² a12g* 11.5d⁴] tall, leggy gelding: has a round action: in good form in handicaps in 1992, gaining first win at Southwell in July: effective at 1¼m to 1½m: acts on good to firm ground, dead and fibresand. *J. E. Banks*

Norwest Holst Trophy (Handicap), York—
Mizaaya (blaze) defies a penalty and considerable trouble, and gets up from Sky Hunter

MMA INTERNATIONAL (IRE) 3 ch.g. Milk of The Barley 115 – Serena –
Maria 63 (Dublin Taxi) [1991 NR 1992 8g 10s 8.5d] 8,000Y: close-coupled gelding:
second foal: brother to 5f to 7f winner Waad: dam won 6f seller: no form: sold 1,200
gns Ascot July Sales. *B. R. Millman*

MODEL NURSE 5 b.m. Exhibitioner 111 – Majestic Nurse 80 (On Your Mark **35**
125) [1991 a10g⁴ a8g a8g 7d⁵ a10g 1992 a8g⁴ a8g a8g³ a10g a8g] close-coupled mare:
has a quick action: poor handicapper: stays 1¼m: acts on hard and dead ground and
all-weather surfaces: below form when visored once. *Mrs A. Knight*

MODERN ART (IRE) 4 b.g. Tate Gallery 115 – Fair Flutter (Beldale –
Flutter (USA) 130) [1991 9g³ 7g³ 1992 a8g 10.2f 8.3m] stocky gelding: first foal: dam
unraced: ex-Irish gelding: rated 75 in maidens when trained as 3-y-o by V. O'Brien:
well held, including in seller, in summer as 4-y-o: stays 9f: sold 950 gns Ascot
November Sales. *R. Akehurst*

MODERN DANCE (USA) 3 b.f. Nureyev (USA) 131 – Remedia (USA) (Dr –
Fager) [1991 NR 1992 8d] quite good-topped filly: closely related to a winner in USA
by Nijinsky and half-sister to several winners, including very smart 7f and 1m
winner Lord Florey and Grade 1 1m winner Too Chic (both by Blushing Groom):
dam, winner at up to 1m, is daughter of Oaks winner Monade, grandam of Prima
Voce and Sadeem: close up 5f then weakened quickly in maiden at Kempton in
September: visits Kefaah. *L. M. Cumani*

MODERNISE (USA) 3 ch.c. Known Fact (USA) 135 – Modena (USA) (Roberto **115**
(USA) 131) [1991 7g² 7m* 1992 10g² 8.9g⁴ 8.1m³ 8g⁶ 8.5g* 9f⁶] useful-looking colt:
good walker: useful form here, in frame in competitive handicaps in spring when
trained by R. Charlton: won Grade 3 handicap at Bay Meadows in September and ran
extremely well to be beaten 1½ lengths when sixth in Grade 1 Hollywood Derby 3
months later: stays 1¼m: acts on firm ground. *R. Frankel, USA*

MODEST HOPE (USA) 5 b.g. Blushing Groom (FR) 131 – Key Dancer (USA) **58**
(Nijinsky (CAN) 138) [1991 14.6s 9s 9g 8.2d⁵ 9s 8.2g 10.2g 8.2m 10g⁶ 10.3g² 1992
10d⁵ 9.7g⁵ 12f⁶ 8m 10m* 9.7v³ a12g* a12g³] big, rather angular gelding: poor
mover: modest form: ran well in handicaps for new stable (previously with G. Eden)
after 5-month lay-off, winning for apprentice at Pontefract and Southwell: effective
at 1¼m to 1½m: acts on any going, including fibresand: sometimes bandaged
behind. *R. C. Spicer*

MODESTO (USA) 4 b.g. Al Nasr (FR) 126 – Modena (USA) (Roberto (USA) 131) **69**
[1991 7g* 10.5m 10.1m⁴ 10s* 10m⁶ 10m 9m 10.2s⁶ 8.1d a10g 1992 a10g⁴ a10g* a10g³ **a74**
a10g² a10g* a10g* a8g⁴ a12g* a10g* a12g³ 12d 10d 10.3g* 11.5m⁴ a12g³ 11.7d 10.2s]
rather unfurnished gelding: consistent and had excellent season in handicaps in
1992, successful at Lingfield (5) and Chester: effective at 1¼m to 1½m: needs a
sound surface on turf, and goes very well on equitrack: successful when blinkered at
3 yrs: good mount for apprentice: sometimes bandaged: genuine front runner. *K. O.
Cunningham-Brown*

MODHISH (IRE) 3 b.c. Sadler's Wells (USA) 132 – Arctique Royale 114 (Royal **117**
And Regal (USA)) [1991 8v⁴ 8v⁴ 1992 12d* 11g² 12g⁵ 12g⁵ 12s³ 12.5s* 12d²] closely

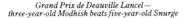

Grand Prix de Deauville Lancel—
three-year-old Modhish beats five-year-old Snurge

Gardner Merchant Hungerford Stakes, Newbury—
Mojave (diamonds on sleeves) comes from last to first
to upset the odds-on Pursuit of Love (light colours, left)

related to a minor French 1m and 1¼m winner by Be My Guest and half-brother to 3 winners in France, notably smart 1m (at 2 yrs) and 10.5f winner Truly Special (by Caerleon): dam, Irish 1000 Guineas winner, is half-sister to dam of Ardross: won minor event at Saint-Cloud in March and Grand Prix de Deauville Lancel (by 1½ lengths from Snurge) in August: creditable ¾-length second of 7 to Masad in Gran Premio d'Italia at Milan final start: should stay 1¾m: acts on soft going, yet to race on top-of-the-ground. *A. Fabre, France*

MODI (USA) 2 b.f. (Feb 6) Deputy Minister (CAN) – Katie Cochran (USA) (Roberto (USA) 131) [1992 7g⁵ 7d²] $40,000Y: unfurnished filly: seventh foal: sister to useful 1990 3-y-o 6f (at 2 yrs) to 1½m winner Curia Regis and a minor winner in USA and half-sister to 2 winners: dam winner at around 6f, is half-sister to Oaks third Ludham: sire, top class at up to 1¼m, has made fine start at stud: similar form, staying on, in minor event won by Athens Belle at Kempton and maiden at Brighton won by Fortensky in September: will be suited by middle distances. *Lord Huntingdon*   **66 p**

MOFADOR (GER) 8 br.h. Esclavo (FR) – Mantilla (GER) (Frontal 122) [1991 7g 8d⁴ 8d 7.5f⁴ 8m² 8m² 8.3d* 8d* 8d 7.9m 7.5f 8.2m 8.1s 1992 a8g 8.3d⁶ 8s 8f 8.3f³ 8f⁶ 8m 8d] lengthy, round-barrelled horse: impresses in appearance: rated 71 at best at 7 yrs: below form in handicaps in 1992: stays 1m: acts on firm ground, dead and fibresand: sold 2,300 gns Newmarket Autumn Sales. *F. H. Lee*   **49**

MOGWAI (IRE) 3 b.c. Alzao (USA) 117 – Maltese Pet 74 (Dragonara Palace (USA) 115) [1991 5d 7m⁴ 7m 6g* 6m⁴ 6g 6s 1992 8d 6g⁵ 6g³ 7m³ 7g⁵ 7g⁶ 6.1m⁴ 6.1d 6.9v a6g⁵ a6g a7g⁴] smallish, strong colt: modest handicapper: effective at 6f and 7f: unsuited by a soft surface: acts on equitrack: seems best in blinkers nowadays. *R. F. Johnson Houghton*   **64**

MOHANA 3 br.f. Mashhor Dancer (USA) – The Ranee (Royal Palace 131) [1991 7f 7m 8.9d 1992 11.6m 12g²] leggy, rather plain filly: modest maiden on flat (rated 65 at 2 yrs): claimed £4,521 after good second in claimer at Newbury in June: should stay well: progressed into fairly useful juvenile hurdler for M. Pipe, winning 6 times by end of the season. *J. L. Dunlop*   **59 +**

MOHICAN BRAVE (IRE) 2 ch.c. (Apr 14) Salt Dome (USA) – Mrs Tittlemouse (Nonoalco (USA) 131) [1992 6f 5g a7g* 7.5d² 7f 8m] 6,100F, 3,000Y, 11,500 2-y-o: tall, close-coupled colt: fifth foal: half-brother to 3-y-o 7f seller winner Rock Song (by Ballad Rock) and 1990 2-y-o 7f winner Carnbrea Cuddy and 1m winner Solo   **61**

Court (both by King of Clubs): dam unraced half-sister to high-class miler Bairn: sire (by Blushing Groom) sprinter: easily best efforts when winning maiden at Southwell (wore eyeshield, veered markedly right) in June and second (despite carrying head high) in auction event at Beverley following month: tailed-off last in Pontefract nursery final run: should stay at least 1m: unsuited by top-of-the-ground. *J. G. FitzGerald*

MOHICAN GIRL 4 b.f. Dancing Brave (USA) 140 – Unsuspected 95 (Above **112** Suspicion 127) [1991 10d* 10d2 11.9m4 11.4m* 12d 10d* 1992 10g5 8.5g5 10m* 10m3] workmanlike filly: smart performer: ran well in 1992, winning listed race at Kempton in June and very good 3¼ lengths third of 7 to Ruby Tiger in Nassau Stakes at Goodwood in August: effective at 1¼m to 1½m: acts on good to firm ground and dead. *J. R. Fanshawe*

MOJAVE 3 b.c. Green Desert (USA) 127 – Out of Shot 116§ (Shirley Heights 130) **112** [1991 6s* 7g3 7m2 1992 7m2 7.1g 7.3d* 8s 8g] useful-looking, rather angular colt: 16/1-winner of Gardner Merchant Hungerford Stakes at Newbury in August, beating Pursuit of Love by 2 lengths, having been last 2f out: no comparable form at 3 yrs: best with testing conditions at around 7f, and should prove effective at 1m: remains in training. *M. R. Stoute*

MOLLY SPLASH 5 b.m. Dunbeath (USA) 127 – Nelly Do Da 78 (Derring-Do **55** 131) [1991 8f 10d 10s3 10m6 10s3 10g 10s 7.6m6 12.3g5 9.7g5 1992 9.7v4 10d 10.8d* 12.3g3 a12g 10g5 11.9f5 10g 9.7d* 10m2 10m6 11.6g2 10g5 10.8g2 9.7m 12.3s3] small, compact mare: poor mover: consistent selling handicapper: no bid when successful at Warwick and Folkestone: effective at 1¼m to 1½m: acts on any going: suitable mount for lady rider: retained by trainer 6,200 gns Newmarket Autumn Sales. *C. A. Cyzer*

MOLTEN COPPER (IRE) 3 ch.g. Pennine Walk 120 – Danger Signal 106 (Red – God 128§) [1991 5g5 5m2 a7g 5f a6g* 7g4 7.9g* 8m 7m 1992 7g 8s 8.2g a8g a11g 10m] sturdy, good-topped gelding: good walker and mover: rated 70 at 2 yrs: no form in handicaps 1992: best form at 1m on an easy surface: below form blinkered. *M. W. Easterby*

MOMENT OF TRUTH 8 b.g. Known Fact (USA) 135 – Chieftain Girl (USA) **37** (Chieftain II) [1991 15.1m5 1992 16.1s 15g3 17.5d5 17.5s] close-coupled, good-topped gelding: good mover: very lightly-raced handicapper on flat: stays well: acts on good to firm and dead ground: winner over hurdles in August and fences in October. *P. Monteith*

MONAAFIS 3 b.c. Kris 135 – Mangayah (USA) 115 (Spectacular Bid (USA)) [1991 – 8g 1992 10v] twice raced, and no sign of ability: sold 1,000 gns Newmarket July Sales. *A. A. Scott*

MONARDA 5 ch.g. Pharly (FR) 130 – Emaline (FR) 105 (Empery (USA) 128) **74** [1991 12d 14g 12m* 11.5m* 11.5m4 12.2d4 12m 11.7f* 1992 12m4 11.9f* a12g* 12h4 a77 13.1g* 13.1f3 12d 12d] leggy, close-coupled gelding: has a round action: fair handicapper: successful at Brighton, Lingfield and Bath in first half of 1992: will stay 1¾m + : yet to race on very soft going, acts on any other, including equitrack. *P. F. I. Cole*

MONASTIC FLIGHT (IRE) 2 ch.g. (May 7) Carmelite House (USA) 118 – **49** Short Stay (Be My Guest (USA) 126) [1992 6m 7g3 7m 7m] leggy, unfurnished gelding: second live foal: half-brother to a winner in Sweden: dam, Irish maiden, stayed middle distances: well beaten apart from third in seller at Catterick in August: pulled hard in blinkers final outing. *B. S. Rothwell*

MONAZITE 2 b.c. (Feb 28) Damister (USA) 123 – Princely Maid 71 (King's **44** p Troop 118) [1992 7g] half-brother to several winners, including Forzando (by Formidable), good performer at up to 8.5f here and in USA, and fairly useful sprinter Zanoni (by Mummy's Pet): dam 5f winner at 2 yrs: burly and never a threat in maiden at Doncaster in November: should do better. *M. A. Jarvis*

MONDAY AT THREE 2 ch.c. (Mar 12) Absalom 128 – Angel's Sing (Mansingh – (USA) 120) [1992 5.7f6 7.1s] 3,200F, 5,000Y: neat colt: first foal: dam unraced: well beaten in maiden and maiden auction (visored). *B. R. Millman*

MONDE BLEU 4 b.c. Last Tycoon 131 – Make Plans (USA) (Go Marching **118** (USA)) [1991 6v 7s5 8g5 7g 8g5 7g2 6g* 7g2 1992 6g2 5g* 5d* 5f 6.5g2 6d2 7d5] strong, good-topped French colt: half-brother to several winners, notably high-class sprinter on his day Sayf El Arab (by Drone): dam lightly-raced daughter of smart 9f stakes winner Sister Antoine: improved performer in 1992: successful in Palace House Stakes at Newmarket (from Paris House) and Prix Gros-Chene at Chantilly (by a length from Showbrook): good second in Group 3 races at Hoppegarten (beat-

Palace House Stakes, Newmarket — French raider Monde Bleu beats Paris House

en ½ length by Mr Brooks) and Maisons-Laffitte (went down by ½ length to Central City): best efforts at up to 6.5f: best form with give in the ground. *A. Fabre, France*

MONDOVA (IRE) 3 b.f. Lomond (USA) 128 – Padova (USA) (Forli (ARG)) [1991 NR 1992 7m⁴ a8g⁴ a8g 11d] IR 20,000Y: good-bodied filly: moderate mover: sister to Irish 1m winner Lake Magic and half-sister to several winners, including fair 6f (at 2 yrs) and 1½m winner Saba Nejo (by Malacate): dam placed at 1½m: of little account. *F. H. Lee*

MONDRAGON 2 b.c. (Apr 30) Niniski (USA) 125 – La Lutine 95 (My Swallow 134) [1992 7g² 7g 7s³ 7g] leggy, unfurnished colt: third foal: half-brother to smart sprinters Montendre and Mon Tresor (both by Longleat): dam 5f and 7f winner at 2 yrs later successful at up to 10.2f: shaped promisingly last 2 starts in maiden auction at York and nursery at Doncaster (looked likely to be concerned in finish over 1f out but got no sort of run) in autumn: will be extremely well suited by middle distances: acts on soft ground: certain to do better and one to follow at 3 yrs. *Mrs M. Reveley* **74** p

MONET MONET MONET 2 ch.f. (Mar 23) Claude Monet (USA) 121 – Delta Wind 72 (Tumble Wind (USA)) [1992 5g 6g⁴ 6m³ 5.2g⁵ 5g 6g] sparely-made filly: third foal: dam best at 2 yrs: plater: will be suited by 7f+: acts on good to firm ground. *W. Carter* **46**

MONET ORDER 2 ch.f. (Apr 8) Claude Monet (USA) 121 – Surely Great 75 (Vaigly Great 127) [1992 5g 6g 6g 6f⁶] unfurnished filly: first foal: dam, untrustworthy maiden, stayed 7f: well beaten in minor events and seller. *J. R. Jenkins* –

MONEY SPINNER (USA) 3 b.f. Teenoso (USA) 135 – Silver Dollar 106 (Shirley Heights 130) [1991 7m 1992 a8g* 10.2s 11.6m] lengthy filly: tailed off in handicaps after winning poor Southwell maiden in February: should stay beyond 1m: sold 11,000 gns Newmarket December Sales. *Lord Huntingdon* **61**

MONIAIVE 3 b.g. Son of Shaka 119 – Lady Bounty 82 (Hotfoot 126) [1991 NR 1992 a6g 6m 7g 10d] 700F: compact gelding: third foal: dam best at 2 yrs when placed at up to 1m: no promise, including in sellers. *W. Clay* –

MONOROSE 3 b.f. Nomination 125 – Phoenix Rose 85 (Frankincense 120) [1991 6g 6g 5.7f² 6m³ 7m⁴ 7g 1992 7g⁴ 8m a11g 10.2f⁶ a12g² 14.6g 11m³ a14g 14.6d] **46**

lengthy filly: poor plater: stays 1½m: acts on firm going and fibresand: usually visored: may be temperamental. *D. Haydn Jones*

MONSCOMA (IRE) 4 b.c. Montelimar (USA) 122 – Scoma (Lord Gayle (USA) 124) [1991 7m 7.6d 1992 7d 10.8s³ a6g a12g a10g5] sturdy colt: on the downgrade: sold out of A. Davison's stable 1,050 gns Ascot May Sales after reappearance. *R. Ingram* –

MONSIEUR DUPONT (IRE) 2 b.c. (Feb 26) Alzao (USA) 117 – Katie Koo 82 (Persian Bold 123) [1992 7g 8.1d] 35,000F, 135,000Y: small, good-bodied colt: fourth foal: half-brother to 1987 Irish 2-y-o 6f and 7f winner Hakari (by Glenstal) and 1m and 1¼m winner Lady Philippa (by Taufan): dam won at 11.7f and 13.1f: behind in Kempton minor event and Haydock maiden in September: looks sort to do better. *B. W. Hills* **50 p**

MONTAGNE 3 br.f. Midyan (USA) 124 – La Masse (High Top 131) [1991 NR 1992 8g6 8s 7d 10g 9.7m³ 10s] 24,000Y: good-topped filly: has quick action: half-sister to winners in France by Carwhite and Electric: dam French middle-distance winner: poor handicapper: stays 9.7f: sold to join S. Coathup's stable 2,500 gns Newmarket Autumn Sales. *H. Candy* **49**

MONTANA D'OR 2 b.f. (May 9) Crooner 119 – Ijazah (Touching Wood (USA) 127) [1992 6m 7m 5g] close-coupled, sparely-made filly: first foal: dam, lightly raced and little sign of ability, is out of half-sister to Suni and Media Luna, both placed in Oaks: soundly beaten in claimer and sellers. *R. Curtis* –

MONTE BRE 6 ch.g. Henbit (USA) 130 – Madame du Barry (FR) (Wollow 132) [1991 9s 8.1d 1992 9.7v 10m 7m³ 7m 7f* a7g 7m6 8f] lengthy, workmanlike ex-Irish gelding: moderate walker and mover: poor handicapper: won Brighton claimer in July: reportedly broke blood vessel final start: seems ideally suited by 7f: acts on any going. *R. Akehurst* **53**

MONTENDRE 5 b.g. Longleat (USA) 109 – La Lutine 95 (My Swallow 134) [1991 6d² 6g 6m³ 5g³ 6g³ 6s* 5m4 6s² 6d4 1992 6g6 7.1d4 6m6 6f5 6s* 7m4 6g 6d³ 6.1d* 6g4] leggy gelding: fluent mover: very useful, tough and consistent performer: successful in Newbury listed race in July (from Notley) and well-contested minor event at Chepstow in October: good third in Group 3 event at Ascot (to Wolfhound), then fourth in Doncaster listed race: effective at 5f to 7f: has form on firm ground, and goes well on a soft surface. *M. McCormack* **112**

MONTI BEPPO 3 ch.f. Flying Tyke 90 – Habatashie 62 (Habat 127) [1991 5g6 5m² 5.3f* 5m6 5.2g6 5m 7m 1992 a6g4 6s a7g 7.1d 7g] good-bodied filly: poor performer: stays 6f: acts on firm ground, and fibresand: not one to trust. *L. J. Barratt* **47 §**

MONTONE (IRE) 2 b.c. (Feb 10) Pennine Walk 120 – Aztec Princess (Indian King (USA) 128) [1992 6g* 5d³ 7s] IR 7,000F, IR 9,000Y: quite good-topped colt: first foal: dam unraced half-sister to Indian Ridge: failed to progress after winning Hamilton maiden auction in July: should be suited by further than 6f. *C. B. B. Booth* **58**

MONTPELIER 4 b.g. Bustino 136 – Leg Glance 87 (Home Guard (USA) 129) [1991 8d* 8.9m* 11g³ 1992 8g 11f³ 10d 10g³ 10g* 9d² 9s 8g] tall, leggy gelding: fairly useful handicapper: in very good form in autumn, winning £18,200 event at Newbury and second to Rambo's Hall in Cambridgeshire: effective from 9f to 11f: acts on good to firm and dead ground, seems unsuited by very soft: held up, and has **90**

Hackwood Stakes, Newbury—Montendre accounts for Notley and other useful sprinters

turn of foot: sold 36,000 gns Newmarket Autumn Sales after penultimate run: to race in Sweden. *Lord Huntingdon*

MONTRAVE 3 ch.g. Netherkelly 112 – Streakella 79 (Firestreak 125) [1991 NR 1992 8.3f] fourth living foal: half-brother to 1988 2-y-o 5f winner Princess Way and a winning hurdler (both by Mr Fluorocarbon): dam 2-y-o 5f winner: tailed-off last in Hamilton maiden claimer in July, only run. *P. Monteith* —

MOODIESBURN (IRE) 2 b.f. (Feb 20) Red Sunset 120 – Acquire 105 (Burglar 128) [1992 5.3d* 5g² 5.1g⁴ 5f 5g³ 5d] 5,000Y: sturdy filly: sister to 3-y-o 6f winner Coolaba Prince and half-sister to several winners, including smart 5f performer Chellaston Park (by Record Token): dam won twice over 5f at 2 yrs: modest performer: won minor event at Brighton in April: modest effort in nursery final run: acts on firm and dead ground: has joined T. Craig. *A. Bailey* 62

MOONA (USA) 4 b.f. Lear Fan (USA) 130 – Dance Empress (USA) (Empery (USA) 128) [1991 7m 7.1d² 6.9m⁶ a7g* 7.1m 1992 8d 7m] leggy, close-coupled filly: rated 73 at 3 yrs: no form in claimers in first half of 1992: stays 7f: best form on an easy surface: sold 1,900 gns Doncaster June Sales. *G. M. Moore* —

MOON CARNIVAL 2 b.f. (Feb 7) Be My Guest (USA) 126 – Castle Moon 79 (Kalamoun 129) [1992 7m 7g⁵ 8m] leggy, unfurnished filly: sister to fair maiden Moon Festival and half-sister to several winners, notably Sheriff's Star (by Posse), Moon Madness (by Vitiges) and Lucky Moon (by Touching Wood): dam, 1m to 13f winner, is sister to Castle Keep and half-sister to Ragstone: modest form in big-field maidens in second half of 1992: will be suited by middle distances. *Lady Herries* 65 p

MOONLIGHT ECLIPSE 2 ch.c. (May 7) Jupiter Island 126 – Moonlight Bay 53 (Palm Track 122) [1992 8v] leggy, lengthy colt: fourth reported foal (previous 3 by Sweet Monday): dam won 1m seller: tailed off in Leicester maiden in October. *E. J. Alston* —

MOONLIGHT QUEST 4 gr.c. Nishapour (FR) 125 – Arabian Rose (USA) (Lyphard (USA) 132) [1991 8m⁵ 10.1g⁵ 10.5g² 12g* 13.3g 12d⁶ 1992 10m 10.3g⁴ 12m² 11.8d* 14m] close-coupled, workmanlike colt: carries condition: fair handicapper: won at Leicester: not seen again after disappointing later in June: should prove as effective at 1¾m as 1½m: acts on good to firm and dead ground. *B. Hanbury* 80

MOONLIGHT SHIFT 6 ch.g. Night Shift (USA) – Rana (Welsh Pageant 132) [1991 NR 1992 10g 11.9d 16.2d] leggy, quite good-topped gelding: bad maiden: stays 1½m: acts on firm going. *W. Clay* —

MOON OVER MIAMI 2 ch.f. (May 5) Beveled (USA) – Run Amber Run (Run The Gantlet (USA)) [1992 5.1s* 6g² 6d⁴ 6s⁵] 4,000Y: neat filly: moderate mover: half-sister to 4-y-o 1¼m winner Quick Ransom (by Hostage) and a winner in USA by Somethingfabulous: dam, minor winner in USA, is half-sister to Irish 2000 Guineas second Mr John: won maiden auction at Bath in May: off course nearly 4 months after and ran well in nurseries at Ascot and Newbury last 2 starts: will probably stay 1m. *C. James* 78

MOON RISK 3 ch.f. Risk Me (FR) 127 – Squires Girl (Spanish Gold 101) [1991 8g 1992 9m⁵] workmanlike filly: twice-raced maiden: fifth at Ripon in July. *R. M. Whitaker* 62

MOONSHINE DANCER 2 b.g. (May 17) Northern State (USA) 91 – Double Birthday (Cavo Doro 124) [1992 5f 6g 7m 7.1m³ 7f 8m] 8,600Y: sturdy, workmanlike gelding: fifth reported foal: half-brother to 5f (at 2 yrs) and 1m winner Major Ivor (by Mandrake Major): dam ran once: well beaten apart from when third in maiden auction at Edinburgh in July: should stay 1m. *Mrs M. Reveley* 48

MOON SPIN 3 b.f. Night Shift (USA) – Hors Serie (USA) (Vaguely Noble 140) [1991 6g 8m⁶ 7.1d 7g² 1992 8.2g³ 10f 11.7f* 10s⁶ 11.9g⁴ 11.7d a10g] leggy, good-topped filly: modest handicapper: won at Bath in August: best efforts at around 1½m: acts on firm ground, possibly not on a soft surface. *Major W. R. Hern* 70

MOON STRIKE (FR) 2 b. or br.c. (Apr 15) Strike Gold (USA) – Lady Lamia (USA) (Secreto (USA) 128) [1992 6d³] 20,000Y: first foal: dam unraced: sire 6f/7f performer: co-favourite, 9 lengths third of 12 in maiden at Yarmouth in October, unable to quicken final 2f: will probably stay 1m: should improve. *W. A. O'Gorman* 62 p

MOONSTRUCK BARD 2 b.g. (Apr 2) Blushing Scribe (USA) 107 – Smitten 72 (Run The Gantlet (USA)) [1992 5d 5m 7m⁶ 6g 7.5m 8.9s 7s⁵ a6g a8g² a8g³ a7g* a8g*] 820Y: workmanlike gelding: sixth foal: brother to 1½m seller winner The Healy and 1¼m winner Auto Connection: dam ran only at 2 yrs when placed at 6f and 7f: fair form: trained first 2 starts by A. Hide: came to himself late in the season, best efforts when winning 2 claimers at Southwell: finds 6f too sharp, and stays 1m: 62 a69 acts on soft ground and all-weather surfaces: no form when blinkered fourth start. *S. P. C. Woods*

MOON WATCH 2 ch.f. (Mar 17) Night Shift (USA) – Moonscape 87 (Ribero 126) **64** [1992 6d² 6m⁵ 6g⁶ 7s] good-topped filly: moderate mover: closely related to 1½m winner Caithness Cloud (by Lomond) and half-sister to several winners, including very useful middle-distance stayer Lemhill (by He Loves Me) and one-time useful 6f winner Luna Bid (by Auction Ring): dam staying half-sister to Derby fourths Moon Mountain and Great Wall: failed to progress after promising second in Leicester maiden in June: prominent long way in Wolverhampton nursery final start: should be much better suited by 7f than 6f: acts on dead ground. *J. R. Fanshawe*

MOORISH 2 b.c. (Feb 9) Dominion 123 – Remoosh (Glint of Gold 128) [1992 7s* **88** 7g 8s⁴] good-topped colt: second foal: brother to 3-y-o Paradise Way, 6f winner at 2 yrs: dam poor half-sister to high-class 1985 2-y-o 5f and 6f winner Nomination (by Dominion): 3½-length winner of maiden at Salisbury in September: easily better effort in minor events following month when very good 3 lengths fourth of 8 to Arusha at Newbury: bred to stay beyond 1m: races keenly. *P. F. I. Cole*

MOOR LODGE (USA) 3 b.g. Hero's Honor (USA) – Prospector's Star (USA) **66** (Mr Prospector USA) [1991 5g 6g 7m⁵ 7m 8m² 8.3s 1992 12.1s² 12f* 12g 11.4d4 11.8g⁴ 16.2d⁵] leggy gelding: modest handicapper: won at Beverley in June: should stay beyond 1½m: probably acts on any going: sometimes hangs right: won over hurdles in August and September (2). *M. H. Tompkins*

MOOTAWEL (USA) 3 b.c. Northern Baby (CAN) 127 – Elk's Ellie (USA) **74** (Vaguely Noble USA) [1991 7g⁴ 1992 10g³ 11.9m⁴ 14d* 16.4s⁵ 14.8g⁵ 14d 13.3s] tall, close-coupled colt: fair handicapper: won at Kempton in June: should stay 2m: acts on good to firm and dead ground: sometimes sweating: retained by trainer 20,000 gns Newmarket July Sales after fourth start. *H. Thomson Jones*

MOOT POINT (USA) 4 b.c. Sharpen Up 127 – Gaelic Logic (USA) (Bold **48** + Reason) [1991 8.3m⁵ 15.4m* 1992 12d 14.1d 14.6g 14.1g a14g* 14.6g⁵ 12s⁶ 12d² a63 a16g³] lengthy colt: inconsistent handicapper: won at Southwell in July: stays 15.4f: acts on good to firm and dead ground and on fibresand: blinkered last 5 starts. *J. R. Jenkins*

MORCINDA 6 ch.g. Ballacashtal (CAN) – Montelimar 108 (Wolver Hollow 126) – [1991 6f 5d 5g⁵ 8s⁶ 7g* 7m² 8.1m⁵ 1992 9.2g 10d⁵ 8s 10d⁵] strong, lengthy gelding: poor mover: poor handicapper: stays 1¼m: acts on good to firm and dead going: ran fairly well when visored once. *P. Monteith*

MORE ICE 6 b.m. Runnett 125 – Spoons (Orchestra 118) [1991 NR 1992 a8g] – leggy ex-Irish mare: little sign of ability here. *C. Weedon*

MOREIRWEN 5 b. or br.m. Bold Owl 101 – Neophyte II (Never Say Die 137) – § [1991 a10g 9s 11.5m a12g 12g⁵ 11.5m 11.6m⁴ 11.9f* 1992 10m 12m] tailed off in handicaps in summer: stays 1½m: acts on firm ground: reluctant to race once at 4 yrs. *J. O'Donoghue*

MORE LARKS (IRE) 4 b. or br.g. Godswalk (USA) 130 – Charmeuse (Cut – Above 130) [1991 8g 5g⁵ 7m⁶ a5g⁴ a7g³ 5.1d a5g a5g 1992 7.1m a6g 10.3g] strong, compact gelding: poor performer. *M. B. James*

MORE THAN LOVE 2 b.f. (Mar 16) Nomination 125 – Chasten (Manacle 123) **38** [1992 7m 6m 6.1g 10d] 3,600Y: workmanlike filly: half-sister to several winners here and abroad, including modest sprinter Tyrian Belle (by Enchantment): dam never ran: poor form, including in a seller. *P. A. Kelleway*

MORGANNWG (IRE) 4 b. or br.f. Simply Great (FR) 122 – Kitty's Sister **78** (Bustino 136) [1991 7.9m³ 8.1m³ 7.1d* 8m 7f* 7.1f⁶ 8d 6.1s⁶ 1992 6f 6.1m⁴ 7.1g⁶ 7f] strong, angular filly: fairly useful but inconsistent handicapper: respectable sixth in listed event at Haydock in June: effective at 6f/7f: acts on firm and dead ground: somewhat headstrong, and sometimes awkward after bolting to start last appearance (September): taken early to post: often slowly away: joined J. White. *R. Dickin*

MORGANS ACE 3 ch.c. Morgans Choice 85 – Adjals Ace (London Glory 104) – § [1991 NR 1992 10s 10.2m 7d 12s 11.7d] good-quartered colt: fifth foal: dam non-thoroughbred, very lightly-raced novice hurdler: seems ungenuine and of little account. *B. R. Millman*

MORJINSKI DANCER 3 b.f. Myjinski (USA) – Morley (Hotfoot 126) [1991 NR 1992 7v 7g 10f] lengthy filly: first foal: dam ran once and refused to enter stalls once: looks of little account: sold 700 gns Ascot July Sales. *R. Simpson*

MORLEY STREET   8 ch.g. Deep Run 119 – High Board (High Line 125) [1991 **101**   +
15.9g⁴ 18m² 1992 16.5g*] big, angular, good-topped gelding: fluent mover: top class
but unreliable hurdler: lightly raced but very useful on flat (rated 111 + in 1991):
impressive 3½-length winner of minor event at Doncaster in October: stays 2¼m:
acts on good to firm ground: capable of better. *G. B. Balding*

MORNING NEWS (IRE)   2 b.c. (Apr 19) Cyrano de Bergerac 120 – Elle Et Lui   **49**
84 (Dike (USA)) [1992 5.1m 6f 7g⁵ a6g⁵ 6m 6m] IR 4,100F: small colt: half-brother to
a winner in Italy: dam disappointing daughter of Queen Mary winner Grizel: poor
maiden: stays 6f: below form visored once: sold 850 gns Newmarket September
Sales. *M. H. Tompkins*

MOROCCO (IRE)   3 b.g. Cyrano de Bergerac 120 – Lightning Laser 68 (Mon-   **77**
seigneur (USA) 127) [1991 5g 5d5 5.7m* 6g 6s 1992 6d 6s⁶ 6m 7.3g³ 7m* 8f² 7g⁴
7.1g² 7d² 7s] small, workmanlike gelding: moderate mover: fair handicapper: won at
Warwick in June: probably stays 1m: acts on any going: below form blinkered once:
carries head high. *R. Charlton*

MORPICK   5 ro.g. Morston (FR) 125 – Pickwood Sue 74 (Right Boy 137) [1991   **54**
a5g⁵ a6g* a6g⁶ a5g⁶ a6g* 1992 a7g a6g a6g a7g a7g a7g⁴ a6g³ 5.1d 5f² 6g² 5m²
6.1m² a5g⁴ 7m⁶ a6g² 6m] plain, close-coupled gelding: poor walker: consistent
handicapper: best at 5f and 6f: acts on firm and dead ground, and fibresand: usually
visored/blinkered: goes well for claimer. *J. P. Leigh*

MORSUN   3 b.g. Aragon 118 – Sunley Blossom 93 (Try My Best (USA) 130) [1991 7f   **77**
8m² 10m⁴ 1992 6.9g² 7.5m² 7m* 8.9g 7f³ 6.9h* 7g² 8m⁴ 7f³ 7.5m 7m 8g³] close-
coupled, rather angular gelding: fair handicapper: successful at Lingfield (apprentices, awarded race) in May and Folkestone in June: effective at 7f to 1m: acts on
hard going: usually blinkered: sold 12,500 gns Newmarket Autumn Sales. *D. Morley*

MOSCATOP (IRE)   2 ch.c. (Feb 16) Waajib 121 – Tagik (Targowice (USA) 130)   **51**
[1992 5g⁵ 5.1g³ 6m 6.1m] 9,500F, 7,200Y: sparely-made colt: good mover: half-
brother to 3-y-o 8.5f winner Cappahoosh (by Salmon Leap) and several winners,
including (at 1m and 8.5f in Ireland) Miss Retlaw (by Kampala): dam, winner in Italy,
is half-sister to high-class sprinter Green God: poor maiden: should be better suited
by 6f than 5f: sold 700 gns Newmarket Autumn Sales. *R. Hollinshead*

MOSCOW SEA (USA)   2 b.c. (Mar 24) Chief's Crown (USA) – How High The   **79** p
Moon (USA) (Majestic Light (USA)) [1992 8m³] $240,000Y: leggy, attractive colt:
third foal: dam, winner at 7f, is half-sister to Quick As Lightning: shaped
promisingly when 1½ lengths third of 21 to Bob's Return in maiden at Pontefract in
October, running wide home turn and staying on really well: will be well suited by
middle distances: sure to do better, and win a race. *H. R. A. Cecil*

MOSS PAGEANT   2 b.g. (Feb 21) Then Again 126 – Water Pageant 58 (Welsh   –
Pageant 132) [1992 6m 6d] 9,600F, 7,000Y, 10,000 2-y-o: good-topped gelding:
half-brother to several winners, including 1991 2-y-o 6f winner Baileys By Name (by
Nomination) and middle-distance stayer Sanchi Steeple (by Niniski): dam middle-
distance maiden: well beaten in large-field maidens at Ripon. *Mrs P. A. Barker*

MOSSY ROSE   6 b.m. King of Spain 121 – Mosso 81 (Ercolano (USA) 118) [1991   **59**
a7g⁴ a6g³ 6v* 6g 6.1m 6.1d 1992 a6g³ a7g⁴ 8d* 8s³ 7m² 7d⁴ 8g⁴ 7.6g 8s⁵] strong,
good-bodied mare: poor mover: modest handicapper: won at Pontefract in April:
should prove better suited by 1m than 7f: acts on any going and all-weather surfaces.
Lord Huntingdon

MOST EMINENT   2 b.c. (Apr 5) Superlative 118 – Loup de Mer 86 (Wolver   **67**
Hollow 126) [1992 5d⁵ 6s* 6s⁴] 4,400Y: leggy colt: half-brother to modest 7f to 8.3f
winner Shadow Boxer, later successabroad, and another winner abroad (both by
Absalom): dam stayed 1m: well backed when winning maiden at Lingfield: edged left
when good fourth of 18 in nursery at Newbury later in October: will be better suited
by 7f + . *P. W. Harris*

MOST INTERESTING   7 b.m. Music Boy 124 – Quick Glance (Oats 126) [1991   –
NR 1992 10.5d] rather angular mare: has a long stride: very lightly raced nowadays,
behind in June. *G. H. Jones*

MOST SURPRISING (IRE)   3 b.g. Runnett 125 – Blue Elver (Kings Lake   **54**
(USA) 133) [1991 5m³ 5f* 5g 6m⁴ 1992 6f² 6f⁶ 7g² 7g] lengthy gelding: modest
handicapper: off course 2½ months before running moderately final start: ideally
suited by 7f: acts on firm going: sometimes hangs: sold to join P. Evans' stable 2,700
gns Doncaster September Sales. *R. M. Whitaker*

MOTHERS DAY MAGIC   6 ch.m. Kabour 80 – Gay Walk 67 (Farm Walk 111)   –
[1991 13.8f⁶ 13.8f⁶ 18m⁵ 1992 16.2g] sparely-made, angular mare: poor mover: of
little account. *J. Dooler*

544

MOTLEY   4 br.f. Rainbow Quest (USA) 134 – Sans Blague (USA) 108 (The   –
Minstrel (CAN) 135) [1991 10g⁶ 1992 12g⁶ 11.1s⁶ 9.2d] angular, workmanlike filly:
seems of little account. *W. G. M. Turner*

MOUCHEZ LE NEZ (IRE)   2 b.f. (Mar 17) Cyrano de Bergerac 120 – Gale   **41**
Force Seven (Strong Gale 116) [1992 6g 5f 6g 5g 7d] 7,500Y: sturdy, lengthy filly:
moderate mover: first foal: dam unraced: poor maiden: blinkered final run: sold 750
gns Newmarket Autumn Sales. *J. Akehurst*

MOUGINS (IRE)   3 ch.c. Ela-Mana-Mou 132 – Western Goddess 95 (Red God   **94**
128§) [1991 7.1s² 7g* 8v⁴ 1992 7g⁴ 7.6g² 8m 8m 8.3g4] big, lengthy colt: good
walker: useful performer: went left leaving stalls and unseated rider penultimate
run: will stay 1¼m: acts on heavy going: sold 12,500 gns Newmarket Autumn Sales.
D. R. C. Elsworth

MOUJEEB (USA)   2 b.c. (Apr 24) Riverman (USA) 131 – Capricorn Belle 115   **70**
(Nonoalco (USA) 131) [1992 7.1g 8s³ 8m] lengthy, workmanlike colt: moderate
mover: third foal: half-brother to 3-y-o Yazaly and 7f winner Desert Dirham (both by
Blushing Groom): dam won from 6f (at 2 yrs) to 9f (in USA): best effort in autumn
maidens when over 3 lengths third of 22 at Warwick: will stay beyond 1m: possibly
suited by soft ground. *M. R. Stoute*

MOUMAYAZ (USA)   2 b.c. (Apr 19) Nureyev (USA) 131 – Foreign Courier   **95**
(USA) (Sir Ivor 135) [1992 6g4 5d* 5g5] seventh foal: closely related to 3 winners,
all at sprint distances, by Danzig, notably Green Desert, and half-brother to 5f
winner Lillah Darak (by Shadeed): dam unraced half-sister to top-class filly Althea:
won 6-runner minor event at Tipperary in July by 2½ lengths: excellent fifth of 9 to
Flowing in Meadow Meats EBF Flying Five at Leopardstown nearly 2 months later:
better form at 5f than 6f. *J. S. Bolger, Ireland*

MOUNTAIN HIGH (FR)   2 b.g. (Apr 8) Lashkari 128 – Lady River (FR) (Sir   **67**
Gaylord) [1992 8f⁵ 8s⁵ 8d] 68,000Y: angular, useful-looking gelding: half-brother to
numerous winners in France, including middle-distance performers Satin River (by
Satingo) and Tonaccio (by Fabulous Dancer), former also successful just short of
2½m: dam showed only a little ability in France: similar form when fifth in maidens
at Doncaster and Newcastle in September: ran moderately final start: will stay
1½m. *J. G. FitzGerald*

MOUNTAIN KINGDOM (USA)   8 b.h. Exceller (USA) 129 – Star In The   –
North (USA) 94 (Northern Dancer (CAN) [1991 12s² 12g4 12g² 14g5 12m5 16g5 15g6
18m 1992 13.9m 16.2m⁶] lengthy, quite attractive horse: good-class performer at
best: sold out of D. Elsworth's stable 12,000 gns Doncaster March Sales before well
held in Yorkshire Cup and Haydock minor event in May: effective at 1½m to 2m: has
won on heavy going, but best form on a sound surface: tailed off when blinkered:
sometimes bandaged behind. *N. Tinkler*

MOUNTAIN RETREAT   6 br.g. Top Ville 129 – Tarrystone (So Blessed 130)   –
[1991 NR 1992 13.1g⁶] rather leggy, useful-looking gelding: rated 69 as 3-y-o:
tailed-off last in Bath handicap in July, 1992: stays 1¾m: acts on firm ground: won
over hurdles in October. *G. A. Ham*

MOUNTAIN SPRING   2 b.c. (Apr 3) Myjinski (USA) – Flying Glory (Flying   –
Mercury) [1992 6m a5g] brother to winning sprinter Lady of The Fen and half-
brother to 2 winners, one abroad: dam unraced: well beaten in maidens at Newmarket (burly) and Lingfield (slowly away) late in season. *M. D. I. Usher*

MOUNTAIN WILLOW   2 b.f. (Feb 28) Doyoun 124 – Mountain Lodge 120   **67 p**
(Blakeney 126) [1992 8.1d³ 8v⁴ 7g] lengthy filly: fourth foal: half-sister to 3-y-o Tree
Frog (by Lomond), 4-y-o 12.5f winner Uluru (by Kris) and 1¼m winner Turbine
Blade (by Kings Lake): dam won Cesarewitch and Irish St Leger: in frame in
maidens at Haydock and Leicester in October: well beaten in Doncaster maiden
final outing: will be suited by middle distances. *Lord Huntingdon*

MOUNT HELENA   3 b.f. Danzig (USA) – Helen Street 123 (Troy 137) [1991   –
6.1m* 1992 10g4 7g] strong, good-quartered filly: has scarred fore-joints: moderate
mover: most promising 2-y-o (rated 82P): well beaten in first half of 1992 in
4-runner minor event at Nottingham and £11,600 handicap at Newmarket: visits
Woodman. *H. R. A. Cecil*

MOUNT NELSON   6 ch.g. Morston (FR) 125 – Doogali 93 (Doon 124) [1991 NR   –
1992 14d 14s 16.2s] tall gelding: has a roundish action: bandaged and no form in
handicaps in 1992: stays 2m well: acts on firm ground. *D. W. P. Arbuthnot*

MOUNT ROSE   2 ch.c. (May 5) Blushing Groom (FR) 131 – Outstandingly (USA)   **69 p**
(Exclusive Native (USA)) [1992 8g] quite attractive colt: third foal: half-brother to
3-y-o 1¼m winner Avice Caro (by Caro) and a winner in USA by Seattle Slew: dam

won from 5.5f to 9f, including in Breeders' Cup Juvenile Fillies and 4 other graded events: backward and green, soon last of 9 in Newmarket minor event in October, beaten under 9 lengths and not knocked about: will improve. *L. M. Cumani*

MOUSSAHIM (USA) 2 ch.c. (Apr 2) Riverman (USA) 131 – Abeesh (USA) 77 **62** (Nijinsky (CAN) 138) [1992 8s⁵ 7v⁵ 7v³] workmanlike colt: third known foal: half-brother to 1989 2-y-o 7f winner Tickle Touch (by Stop The Music) and fair 1990 Irish 2-y-o 6f winner Beloved Visitor (by Miswaki): dam lightly-raced middle-distance maiden: similar form in late-season maidens: will stay beyond 1m. *M. R. Stoute*

MOVE A MINUTE (USA) 3 br.c. Al Nasr (FR) 126 – Call Me Goddess (USA) **78** (Prince John) [1991 NR 1992 8.1g² 8m⁶] $30,000Y: sturdy, angular colt: tenth reported foal: half-brother to several winners, notably very smart French 7.5f to 10.5f winner Smuggly and very useful 7f and 11f winner Asl (both by Caro): dam stakes-placed winner at up to 1m out of CCA Oaks winner Marshua: twice raced, and easily better effort when staying on and beaten short head by Garden of Heaven in 5-runner maiden at Sandown: will be better suited by 1¼m. *D. R. C. Elsworth*

MOVE SMARTLY (IRE) 2 b.c. (Mar 19) Smarten (USA) – Key Maneuver **65** (USA) (Key To Content (USA)) [1992 7g⁵ 8.1d⁶ 7s⁶ 7d 7g⁵] IR 24,000Y: sturdy, workmanlike colt: moderate walker: second foal: dam ran 4 times in North America: sire high class over middle distances: modest maiden: will be suited by middle distances: best runs on good ground. *F. H. Lee*

MOVING FORCE 5 b.g. Muscatite 122 – Saint Simbir 82 (Simbir 130) [1991 7m **35** 5.8f 7g 6d 6g 5.7m 7g 7.6m⁵ 8g⁴ 6.9f 8g 1992 7m⁶ 9m 7.1m⁵ 9.7g 9.7d² 10f⁵ 11.6g 8g 10.8g⁶ 12.3s] leggy, sparely-made gelding: none too consistent handicapper: stays 11f: acts on firm and dead ground. *E. A. Wheeler*

MOVING IMAGE (IRE) 2 b.f. (Apr 30) Nordico (USA) – Aunty Eileen **63** (Ahonoora 122) [1992 5d 5g² 5m² 5d* 6d³ 6g 5g 5s a6g⁶ a6g a7g] IR 17,000Y: leggy, unfurnished filly: third foal: half-sister to 3-y-o Ambitious Venture (by Gorytus), 6f winner at 2 yrs: dam, unraced, from family of Mtoto: regressive form in nurseries after winning maiden at Redcar in July: stays 6f: acts on good to firm and dead ground: sometimes bandaged behind: trained until after eighth start by M. Bell. *H. J. Collingridge*

MOVING OUT 4 b.c. Slip Anchor 136 – New Generation 91 (Young Generation **78** 129) [1991 14f³ 16.2g² 14s* a14g³ 16.5d a16g* 1992 16d² 16d⁵ 14.9d* 18.5g 12.1f³ 16.2s² 16.1g6 14.9g⁴ 16.1g 17.5s4] sturdy colt: poor mover: modest handicapper: made all at Warwick in April: suited by test of stamina/soft surface: also acts on fibresand: sold to join Miss H. Knight's stable 37,000 gns Newmarket Autumn Sales. *Sir Mark Prescott*

MOW WAAL (USA) 2 ch.f. (Apr 20) Shadeed (USA) 135 – Bambee T T (USA) **54** p (Better Bee) [1992 7g] angular filly: half-sister to several winners, notably high-class 1¼m performer Ascot Knight (by Danzig) and champion Canadian turf horse Bounding Away (by Vice Regent): dam won twice at up to 1m: 33/1 and ridden by 7-lb claimer, slowly away and never placed to challenge in maiden at Newmarket in October. *M. R. Stoute*

MR BROOKS 5 b.h. Blazing Saddles (AUS) – Double Finesse 97 (Double **125** Jump 131) [1991 6v² 7d* 6g² 5m* 7g* 8g⁶ 6d² 1992 5s* 6m² 5f² 6g* 6.5g* 5m² 6d² 5s* a6f]

This should have been an optimistic account of a very tough sprinter's late flowering. Instead, it must begin by reporting his demise at Gulfstream Park in October as a consequence of his breaking his off-fore on the last bend in the Breeders' Cup Sprint. Only a short while before, Mr Brooks had consolidated his position among Europe's best by adding the Ciga Prix de l'Abbaye de Longchamp to the July Cup, and connections were looking forward to another campaign in 1993. Alas, although as top sprinters go he couldn't be counted exceptional, he was the type of horse who will be missed more than most.

Mr Brooks had been around for a long time before he made top grade. He didn't establish himself fully until he won the latest July Cup at Newmarket three weeks after dividing Sheikh Albadou and Elbio in a closely-contested King's Stand Stakes at Royal Ascot. Those were his first two races for Hannon's stable. He was formerly based in Ireland, first with Connolly and then, when Connolly decided to train in Macau mid-way through 1991, with Bolger. Connolly prepared Mr Brooks for the classics, but turned him to sprinting after he finished last in Quest For Fame's Derby. In 1991 the horse won three Group 3 races in Ireland and carried his good form over into the spring of 1992 when he won a listed race at Tipperary and finished second to Shalford, en-route to Hannon, in the Duke of York Stakes at York. Despite his excellent start to the season, there were those with better credentials in the July Cup, the year's first Group 1 sprint. The betting suggested a close race between Sheikh Albadou, who'd been making his reappearance at Royal Ascot, and Shalford, who'd gone on from York to win the Cork And Orrery Stakes. Also much shorter than Mr Brooks were Elbio and the three-year-olds Wolfhound and Pursuit of Love. The long-shots Paris House and Tbab completed a field that lacked possible contenders in Marling, Keen Hunter and the French pair Monde Bleu and Lion Cavern. The race was a dramatic one, particularly in the last furlong and a half where positions changed rapidly as the pacesetters Shalford and Tbab cracked. The pair set a strong pace and some of the riders were content to bide their time, notably Mr Brooks's rider Piggott, nine times a previous winner of the July Cup. Mr Brooks raced comfortably in last place and remained there until launching a smooth run down the outside with about two furlongs left. At this point Sheikh Albadou looked poised for victory but, although he took a clear advantage when shaken up, Mr Brooks reached his heels entering the final furlong and edged ahead less than a hundred yards from the finish. The outside proved the best place to be. Some scrimmaging occurred as things tightened up, involving twice-hampered Pursuit of Love who, once he finally found room, finished so strongly inside Sheikh Albadou that he took second and would have been in front in another thirty yards. The first three crossed the line almost as one, a length and a half in front of Elbio who met minor interference two furlongs out but was beaten on merit, well clear of the rest.

If there have been better July Cup winners than Mr Brooks, not one of them could have beaten his consistency in the time remaining to him. He made another three appearances before the Abbaye, winning the Group 3 Grosser Preis von Berlin at Hoppegarten by half a length from Monde Bleu and finishing second in the Nunthorpe and the Haydock Park Sprint Cup. The Nunthorpe underlined his chance in the Abbaye, for he coped well with the return to five furlongs on top-of-the-ground and battled on very gamely in the last two furlongs to run Lyric Fantasy to half a length at weights which favour the two-year-olds. At Haydock he and Sheikh Albadou had the finish to themselves in what was probably the best sprint of the season in Europe; Sheikh Albadou crossed him under pressure but the better horse won on the day, by two and a half lengths. Both Sheikh Albadou and Lyric Fantasy gave the Abbaye a miss. In their absence Mr Brooks was sent off a shade of odds on

July Cup, Newmarket—one of the most exciting sprints of the season;
Mr Brooks challenges on the outside of Sheikh Albadou as the unlucky Pursuit of Love
goes for the gap on the rails; Elbio is fourth

*Ciga Prix de l'Abbaye de Longchamp—another good run from the tough Mr Brooks;
he is on top of Keen Hunter and Elbio from two furlongs out*

against the previous year's winner Keen Hunter, Elbio, Twafeaj and the
two-year-old Peperonata from Britain, the Irish fillies Flowing and Bezelle,
Bold N'Flashy from Canada and the single home challenger Dream Talk: a
field rather lacking strength in depth. The race was run at a cut-throat pace on
soft ground and placed a greater emphasis on stamina than usual. All the
runners were hard at work by halfway after Bold N' Flashy and Dream Talk
had jumped out smartly and shown tremendous initial speed. Mr Brooks had
to fight his way up from the mid-division under pressure, but once at the head
of affairs he never looked like being overtaken, even though he shied at the
advertising hoardings in a similar way to Dayjur two years previously. He
kept on very strongly to win by two lengths and a neck, the result going to
form with Keen Hunter second and Elbio third.

Mr Brooks (b.h. 1987)	Blazing Saddles (AUS) (br 1974)	Todman (ch 1954)	Star Kingdom / Oceana
		Lady Simone (br 1969)	Wilkes / Day Tripper
	Double Finesse (b 1975)	Double Jump (ch 1962)	Rustam / Fair Bid
		Horus Blue (b 1970)	Golden Horus / Real Blue

    Mr Brooks's form-lines read rather better than his blood-lines. His sire
Blazing Saddles was returned to Australia, where he'd been a good two-year-
old, after five seasons at stud in Europe. Mr Brooks is by some way the pick of
Blazing Saddles' runners over here. The dam Double Finesse won three races
at up to a mile, two of them as a four-year-old when carrying to Balidar. The
resulting offspring, Larionov, proved to be her best winner—he showed smart
form at around a mile—until Mr Brooks came along. In between came five
other foals, all winners, three of them, Admirals All (by Julio Mariner) and
Marimba and Our Music (both by Music Boy), successful. Two foals by Primo
Dominie followed Mr Brooks—another winner in Turtle Bush and the
two-year-old of 1992 Kennedys Prima. The next dam Horus Blue, a maiden,
became disappointing as a three-year-old. She was out of a winner in
Germany, Real Blue, whose half-sister Lalibela won the 1967 Cheveley Park
Stakes. In no respect is this a Derby pedigree; the main encouragement for
running at Epsom, we suspect, lay elsewhere in his good fifth in the Irish Two
Thousand Guineas. Mr Brooks was visored at Epsom. He later won in Ireland
when so equipped, but ran without all through the latest season. That he was
ever tried visored is no slur on Mr Brooks; over and again he underlined his
toughness and reliability. *R. Hannon*

MR BUTCH   2 b.c. (Mar 20) Aragon 118 – Kittycatoo Katango (USA) (Verbatim   **65**
(USA)) [1992 5g 6m3 6g3 7m2 6g3 7g 7d5 6m* 6d2 6s4 6m] good-quartered colt:
moderate mover: third foal: half-brother to 3-y-o Miss Doody (by Gorytus),
successful at 6f (at 2 yrs) and 1¼m: dam won in Italy: 3½-length winner of claimer
at Pontefract in September: good efforts in nurseries next 2 starts, well below-form
favourite at Pontefract final one: best form at 6f: acts on good to firm and soft
ground. *M. R. Channon*

MR CONFUSION (IRE)   4 b.c. Kafu 120 – Mrs Foodbroker (Home Guard   **97** p
(USA) 129) [1991 8d2 8m5 7.6m4 8d3 8.1m4 1992 10.3g* 10d* 10g* 10.4d* 10.5s*]

John Smith's Magnet Cup (Handicap), York—
apprentice-ridden Mr Confusion wins on merit from Tell No Lies and Steerforth (right),
and although demoted on the day is reinstated later

workmanlike colt: has a long stride: good walker: unbeaten and one of most improved handicappers in training in 1992: successful at Doncaster, Nottingham, Pontefract, York (John Smith's Magnet Cup, drifted left and demoted after beating Tell No Lies a length, but later reinstated after appeal) and Haydock (£11,350 race): stays 1¼m: suited by some give in the ground: usually ridden by 7-lb claimer O. Pears: held up, and idles in front: a credit to his trainer. *S. G. Norton*

MR COPYFORCE 2 gr.c. (Jan 26) Sharrood (USA) 124 – Cappuccilli 111 (Loren- **50**
zaccio 130) [1992 7.1s 7g⁴ 7d 8d a8g⁶] 17,000Y: lengthy colt: half-brother to several
winners, including (at 7f) useful 1983 2-y-o Falstaff (by Town And Country) and (at
6f) 1984 2-y-o Vie Parisienne (by Homing): dam staying 2-y-o didn't train on: poor
maiden: ran creditably on equitrack final outing: stays 1m. *Miss B. Sanders*

MR CUBE (IRE) 2 ch.c. (Jan 24) Tate Gallery (USA) 117 – Truly Thankful **53**
(CAN) (Graustark) [1992 7m² 6.1g 6s 7.3s a6g² a6g³ a6g³ a8g*] IR 10,000Y: sturdy **a61**
colt: first foal: dam unraced: modest performer: decisive winner of maiden at Lingfield in December: stays 1m: acts on all-weather surfaces, below form (including in
blinkers) on soft ground: not an easy ride. *P. F. I. Cole*

MR DINGLE 2 ch.g. (Mar 29) Music Boy 124 – Toot Toot 59 (Alias Smith (USA)) **50**
[1992 5g³ 5s a6g] strong, sprint type: first foal: dam 1½m and 13.1f winner: off
course 4 months after promising third in early-season maiden at Lingfield: showed
nothing at Southwell final outing. *W. J. Haggas*

MR ELK 3 gr.g. Bellypha 130 – Shuteye 91 (Shirley Heights 130) [1991 7m 7.1m⁵ **37**
7m 1992 14.6g 14.1f⁵ 13.8g³ 16f 15.1m³ 15.1m] angular gelding: poor handicapper:
stays 15f: acts on good to firm ground (tailed off on firm): blinkered last 2 outings,
running well first time. *Mrs M. Reveley*

MR FLOOD (USA) 3 gr.c. Al Nasr (FR) 126 – Flood (USA) (Riverman (USA) **89**
131) [1991 6d⁴ 1992 8s² 8g² 10.2m² 12f* 12g] close-coupled, deep-girthed colt: fairly
useful performer: landed odds in 3-runner maiden at Carlisle in May: not seen out
after last in Newmarket handicap following month: stays 1½m: acts on any going:
sold 6,800 gns Newmarket Autumn Sales. *Mrs J. Cecil*

MR GENEAOLOGY (USA) 2 b.c. (Feb 23) Procida (USA) 129 – Que Mona **61** (USA) (Ribot 142) [1992 7g4 7.5d 7g6 8.1g5] 5,200 2-y-o: leggy, angular colt: half-brother to several winners, notably very smart Prima Voce (by Elocutionist), suited by 1¼m+: dam, 4-y-o 6f winner, is daughter of Oaks winner Monade, family also of Sadeem: visored first time and best effort in maiden when staying-on fifth at Edinburgh in October: looks a stayer. *J. L. Spearing*

MR KEWMILL 9 b.g. Homing 130 – Muninga 108 (St Alphage 119) [1991 NR – § 1992 10s] close-coupled gelding: has a round action: unreliable handicapper: probably best short of 1¼m: below form blinkered, usually visored. *J. A. Bennett*

MR MARTINI (IRE) 2 b.c. (May 15) Pennine Walk 120 – Arab Art (Artaius **96** (USA) 129) [1992 5.7f* 5f 6m3 7m2 6g*] IR 8,400Y: smallish colt: moderate mover: half-brother to 2 winners, including Irish middle-distance stayer Orembo (by Tap On Wood): dam Irish maiden: progressive colt: successful in maiden auction at Bath in June and valuable Tattersalls Breeders Stakes at Leopardstown in September: ran well when placed in nurseries at Lingfield and Newmarket: will stay 1m: blinkered last 3 outings. *C. E. Brittain*

MR NEVERMIND (IRE) 2 b.g. (Apr 6) The Noble Player (USA) 126 – Salacia **58** 93 (Seaepic (USA) 100) [1992 5d 5g 6m2 5g4 5m 6g6 7g 6m4 6m2 7g*] IR 4,500Y: well-grown, useful-looking gelding: keen walker: half-brother to 3-y-o Louisa Scarlett (by Cyrano de Bergerac), fair 5f to 7f winner at 2 yrs, 1¼m winner Red Hill Girl (by Riboboy) and a winner in Malaysia: dam disqualified 7f winner at 2 yrs: modest performer: improved on last 2 outings, ¾-length winner of nursery at Brighton in September: should stay 1m: acts on good to firm ground: blinkered last 3 starts: sometimes slowly away. *G. Lewis*

MR NEWS (IRE) 3 b.c. Trojan Fen 118 – Princess Biddy 86 (Sun Prince 128) – § [1991 a6g 7g6 a7g6 8m5 8.1g3 8m 1992 12.3s5 12.3s 11.1m 12.2g6 10m6 11.1g4 9f 12g4 13.6m 12m 13.8g 12.2d6] close-coupled colt: poor mover: reluctant maiden on flat and one to avoid: no improvement when blinkered/visored: trained until after penultimate start (sold 1,050 gns Doncaster October Sales) by W. Pearce/B. Beasley: won seller and claimer over hurdles, before being claimed £6,101 probably to go to Scandinavia. *S. E. Kettlewell*

MR OPTIMISTIC 5 ch.g. King Persian 107 – Saybya (Sallust 134) [1991 NR 1992 – 17.5s] leggy gelding: well beaten in handicap in September, first run on flat for 3 years: won 2½m hurdle in April. *J. J. O'Neill*

MR POPPLETON 3 ch.c. Ballacashtal (CAN) – Greenstead Lady 67 (Great **56** Nephew 126) [1991 NR 1992 8.2d4 12g3 12m2 14g5 13.1m6 14m6 15.4g] big colt: moderate mover: second foal: dam 1½m and 1¾m winner: modest maiden: ran badly in handicap final start: stays 1¾m: acts on good to firm ground: sometimes bandaged. *D. W. P. Arbuthnot*

MRS BARTON (IRE) 4 gr.f. Faustus (USA) 118 – Phar Lapa 59 (Grundy 137) **67** [1991 10g 12d* 16.2m4 13.8f* 14.1f2 13.1f2 16.1m* 16.2f2 15.9d4 1992 14g 16.1f 18.8m6 14.9g 16d6 14.1d2 15.8d* 14.6g5] small filly: good mover: modest performer, good form in autumn, and won handicap at Catterick: suited by test of stamina: acts on firm and dead going: effective blinkered or not: tough and genuine: sold 11,000 gns Newmarket Autumn Sales. *B. W. Hills*

MRS CLAYPOOL 4 br.f. Petong 126 – Rare Legend 69 (Rarity 129) [1991 8.2m – a12g 8.1s 12g6 1992 10.8g] smallish, sparely-made filly: poor maiden: stays 1m: acts on fibresand. *M. A. Jarvis*

MRS DAWSON 2 gr.f. (Feb 1) Sharrood (USA) 124 – Faraway Grey 99 (Absalom **52** 128) [1992 5d 5d6 7d3 7g4 8m 8g a8g5] 13,000Y: leggy filly: second foal: half-sister to poor maiden Glad To Be Grey (by Song): dam 2-y-o 5f winner stayed 1m: poor form: should stay 1m: acts on dead ground: below form when visored once: usually slowly away: inconsistent. *Dr J. D. Scargill*

MRS FISHER (IRE) 3 b.f. Salmon Leap (USA) 131 – Amboselli 73 (Raga Nav- **94** arro (ITY) 119) [1991 a7g2 7m* 7m2 7g* 7m* 8.1m2 1992 7f* 7g2 7.1g* 7m3 8.1d6 7d*] leggy, lengthy filly: quite useful performer: won minor events at Redcar and Chepstow in early-summer and apprentice race at Ascot in September: creditable third to Storm Dove in listed race at Goodwood: should prove effective at 1m: acts on firm and dead going: consistent. *Sir Mark Prescott*

MRS JAWLEYFORD (USA) 4 b.f. Dixieland Band (USA) – Did She Agree – (USA) (Restless Native) [1991 NR 1992 16s5] angular filly: has round action: half-sister to several winners in USA, notably graded-stakes winner at up to 9f Restless Thief (by No Robbery): dam never ran: bandaged, well beaten in Goodwood minor event in October: winning hurdler. *C. Smith*

MRS JEKYLL (IRE) 2 ch.f. (Mar 3) Sure Blade (USA) 130 – Grey Walls 86 50
(Habitat 134) [1992 6m 7d⁵ 7.1g³ a8g] leggy, lengthy filly: first foal: dam 2-y-o 6f
winner, is half-sister to high-class middle-distance performer Pelerin: modest form:
will stay 1m: blinkered (well beaten) on equitrack final start. *C. F. Wall*

MR SMILEY 5 b.g. Pharly (FR) 130 – Yelming 76 (Thatch (USA) 136) [1991 7f 6d   –
6f⁵ 1992 7.1s 5.3d a7g] small, deep-girthed gelding: little worthwhile form: tried
blinkered. *R. J. Baker*

MRS MOUSE 4 ch.f. Formidable (USA) 125 – Mary Mary Mouse (USA) (Valdez   –
(USA)) [1991 NR 1992 10d 11d] lengthy filly: second foal: half-sister to 1½m winner
Standing Room Only (by Stalwart): dam unraced from family of Legal Bid and Law
Society: twice raced and tailed off in claimers. *N. A. Twiston-Davies*

MR SNUGGS (IRE) 3 b.c. Nordico (USA) – Kilboy Concorde (African Sky 124)   –
[1991 NR 1992 a8g² a8g⁵] seventh foal: half-brother to Irish 1m winner Father Phil
(by Kampala): dam poor Irish maiden: poor form in claimers at Southwell: sold out of
M. Tompkins' stable 700 gns Ascot February Sales after debut, resold 1,300 gns
Ascot November Sales. *B. J. McMath*

MR SUNNY 3 b.g. Revolutionary (USA) – Paddy's Widow (Paddy Boy 101) [1991   –
NR 1992 9.9g⁴ 10d 12m] big gelding: first reported foal: dam unraced: no sign of
ability in maidens. *P. Beaumont*

MRS WEST (USA) 2 b.f. (Mar 28) Gone West (USA) – Mrs Hat (Sharpen Up 86
127) [1992 6g 6m* 7m⁵ 6s 7.5d* 8s⁵] leggy filly: half-sister to 3 winners by Hagley,
including modest sprinter Golden Cap: dam, winner at around 6f in North America,
is granddaughter of Glad Rags II: sire (by Mr Prospector) very smart winner at 1m
and 9f: won minor event at Warwick in June and listed race (by a short neck from
Foolish Heart) at Milan in September: easily best other effort when around 5
lengths fifth of 8 to Mystic Goddess in moderately-run Sweet Solera Stakes at
Newmarket: should stay 1m: acts on good to firm and dead ground, unsuited by very
soft. *J. L. Dunlop*

MR TATE (IRE) 3 ch.g. Tate Gallery (USA) 117 – Free Wheeler (Prince 64
Tenderfoot (USA) 126) [1991 5d 5g⁶ 7d 7g 1992 8.1d⁶ 8f² 8.5d⁵ 9d² 9.7m 8g 9g⁴] IR
8,000Y: sturdy gelding: closely related to a winner in Malaysia by Be My Guest and
half-brother to 4 winners abroad including Let Freedom Ring (by Tap On Wood),
1986 Irish 2-y-o 1¼m winner: dam unraced half-sister to dam of Niniski: trained by
J. Coogan in Ireland at 2 yrs: modest form in handicaps here: should be suited by
1¼m: acts on firm and dead ground: suitable mount for apprentice. *R. Akehurst*

MR TAYLOR 7 b.g. Martinmas 128 – Miss Reliant 65 (Reliance II 137) [1991 16m 36
16.5m⁶ 1992 18g³ 22.2g⁵ 18.2g 20m] leggy, angular gelding: poor mover: none too
reliable handicapper: stays 2¼m: yet to race on soft going, acts on any other. *H. J.
Collingridge*

MR VINCENT 2 ch.g. (Apr 28) Nishapour (FR) 125 – Brush Away (Ahonoora 67
122) [1992 6g³ 6.1d² 7g⁶ 6d] 3,000F, 1,500Y: workmanlike gelding: fourth foal:
half-brother to 3 winners, including 1990 2-y-o 5f winner Go Tally-Ho (by Gorytus)
and useful Irish performer Takwim (by Taufan), successful at up to 7f: dam unraced
half-sister to useful stayer Princess Genista: failed to progress after second in
maiden auction at Nottingham in August: should stay 1m. *G. Lewis*

MR WELLRIGHT 2 b.c. (May 10) War Hero 116 – Trinity Bug (Bonne Noel 115)   –
[1992 7m] 950F: second reported foal: dam winning Irish hurdler: always well
behind in seller at Wolverhampton in June. *A. P. James*

MR WISHING WELL 6 ch.g. Dunbeath (USA) 127 – Little Change 70 (Grundy 58
137) [1991 10m 10.1g 9d a8g⁴ 10s a8g 12s* 11.8g a11g* 12.3g⁶ 12m 12d 11.5s a12g*
a12g* a12g⁵ 1992 a11g² a14g a10g² a11g a12g a12g⁵ a12g² a12g a12g² 10d⁶ a12g
12.2g 10.5g 10s a12g² a12g* a12g a12g] quick-ground gelding: none too consistent
handicapper in 1992: sold out of R. J. R. Williams' stable 2,800 gns Newmarket
Autumn Sales after fourteenth start: ran really well next 2 outings, winning at
Southwell: stays 1½m: acts on good to firm and soft ground, and on all-weather
surfaces: below form when visored and for amateur: has won for apprentice. *S. Dow*

MR ZIEGFELD (USA) 3 b.g. Fred Astaire (USA) – I Assume (USA) (Young 60
Emperor 133) [1991 7m⁴ 7g 8.3g* 8d² 1992 a10g⁵ 10d 11.8d⁵ 12g* 13.1m 12m³
12.3m⁶ 12g 12.1s] strong, lengthy gelding: inconsistent handicapper: won claimer at
Kempton in May: stays 1½m: acts on good to firm and dead ground: sold to join R.
Baker's stable 10,000 gns Newmarket Autumn Sales. *Sir Mark Prescott*

MU-ARRIK 4 b. or br.c. Aragon 118 – Maravilla 73 (Mandrake Major 122) [1991 55
7m 8g⁶ 7.5m 7f³ 7m 7m 6f⁴ 6f⁴ 7m 6.9f 1992 5g 6s 7g 7m⁶ 6d² 7m² 7f² 7d 6d⁴ 6.9d
6f³ 7d 6m 6.1m³ a6g a8g] sparely-made colt: has a quick action: maiden handicapper:

effective at 6f and 7f: acts on firm and dead going: visored once: sold out of D. Wilson's stable 5,800 gns Newmarket Autumn Sales. *J. S. Wainwright*

MUBIN (IRE) 4 b.g. Wassl 125 – Mashteen (USA) (Majestic Prince) [1991 7g 10g³ 10m² 12.1g 11.6m⁶ 11.9g² 10m³ 12g 10m³ 1992 12d 14g 10.8g] strong gelding: has a round action: rated 77 as 3-y-o: below form in handicaps in 1992: best form at 1½m: acts on good to firm ground: sometimes takes strong hold. *C. C. Elsey* —

MUCH SOUGHT AFTER 3 b.g. Adonijah 126 – Lady Clementine 68 (He 81 Loves Me 120) [1991 7g 7m 8m⁶ 8m⁴ 1992 8.2g² 8m⁴ 8f² 10g² 12.3g* 12.3d 12m³ 12s³ 12d 12g] close-coupled gelding: fair handicapper: won at Ripon in August: better at 1½m than shorter: acts on any going: sometimes bandaged behind. *D. Morley*

MUDAFFAR (IRE) 4 b.c. Simply Great (FR) 122 – Baleen (Lochnager 132) 94 [1991 7s² 8s* 10g 8.1m³ 10m 8m* 8m³ 8m² 9g³ 1992 8g² 8d 8g² 7.9m 8f 8.1s² 8m² 8.9m 8s⁶ 9d] small colt: moderate mover: rather in-and-out form in handicaps in 1992, second 4 times, including in Lincoln at Doncaster (to High Low) and in valuable Schweppes Golden Mile at Goodwood (to Little Bean): suited by strongly-run race at 1m, and should stay 1¼m: acts on good to firm and soft ground: set lot to do. *R. W. Armstrong*

MUDDY LANE 4 b.g. Ilium 121 – Monstrosa 70 (Monsanto (FR) 121) [1991 12f 7g 10.2d* 8g 10g 10g 1992 10.8v⁴ 14.1d 11.7d] smallish, sturdy gelding: poor handi-capper: stays 1¼m: acts on heavy ground: below form blinkered once: sometimes troublesome at stalls. *B. R. Millman* —

MUDGEE 2 b.f. (Mar 9) Nishapour (FR) 125 – Bold Duchess 78 (Persian Bold 44 123) [1992 5d⁶ a6g⁶] 500F: lengthy, useful-looking filly: second foal: half-sister to 3-y-o Certain Lady (by Absalom), 5f winner at 2 yrs now best at 7f: dam 1m winner: poor form in late-year maidens in December. *T. D. Barron*

MUFID (USA) 3 ch.c. Woodman (USA) 126 – Princess Laika (USA) (Blushing Groom (FR) 131) [1991 NR 1992 6m⁶ 6f³] $425,000Y: small, quite attractive colt: fifth foal: half-brother to 2 minor winners in North America: dam placed 4 times from 13 starts: better effort in maidens when sixth at Newmarket: not seen out after June: should stay 1m: sold 2,200 gns Newmarket Autumn Sales. *Major W. R. Hern* —

MUGHAL PRINCESS (IRE) 2 b.f. (Mar 14) Pennine Walk 120 – Astania 52 p (GER) (Arratos (FR)) [1992 7g⁴ 7f³] IR 7,000Y: lengthy filly: half-sister to several winners, including 10.2f and 1½m winner Northants (by Northern Baby): dam Irish 13f winner, is half-sister to dam of leading German middle-distance colt Alpenkonig: shaped promisingly in Catterick seller and maiden auction (stayed on well never dangerous after slow start) at Thirsk in July: will be suited by 1m: should improve again. *Mrs J. R. Ramsden*

MUHARIB (USA) 3 b. or br.c. Far North (CAN) 120 – Rachael Tennessee (USA) (Matsadoon (USA)) [1991 6d³ 7.3g³ 7g* 1992 10.3m] useful-looking colt: moderate mover: rated 97 at 2 yrs: bandaged near-fore, last in listed race at Chester in May at 3 yrs: should be well suited by 1m + : joined C. Brittain. *N. A. Callaghan* —

MUHAYAA (USA) 3 b.c. Danzig (USA) – La Basque (USA) (Jean-Pierre) [1991 93 NR 1992 8g* 10d³ 10d⁴ 8f⁶] $600,000Y: leggy, good-topped colt with scope: fluent mover: half-brother to numerous winners in North America, including good miler El Basco (by Vigors) and top middle-distance colt Bounding Basque (by Grey Dawn): dam minor winner at 3 yrs, is half-sister to champion 2-y-o filly Heavenly Cause (by Grey Dawn): won newcomers event at Newmarket in April and good third in £8,000 handicap at Newbury 4 months later: below form in minor events after: stays 1¼m. *A. A. Scott*

MUHIT (USA) 3 b.f. El Gran Senor (USA) 136 – Petrava (NZ) (Imposing (AUS)) 79 [1991 6m⁵ 1992 8g* 8f⁵ 7d² 10s⁵ 8m* 7s³ 8d 8g³ 7g] lengthy filly: has a long stride: fair but none too consistent: successful at Kempton in maiden in May and handicap in August: should have stayed 1¼m: acted on good to firm and soft ground: visits Cadeaux Genereux. *P. T. Walwyn*

MUHTARRAM (USA) 3 b.c. Alleged (USA) 138 – Ballet de France (USA) 117 101 (Northern Dancer (CAN)) [1991 7m* 7m* 1992 8g⁴ 8g⁵ 12g⁴]
The twenty-two seasons 1970-1991 saw Two Thousand Guineas runners provide seven winners of the Derby and nearly one third of the placed horses. With Rodrigo de Triano thought at first an unlikely runner, the Derby contes-tant that attracted most attention after the latest Guineas was Muhtarram. He actually finished fifth at Newmarket, one place and half a length behind another intended Derby runner Silver Wisp, but if any performance could

catch the eye behind Lester Piggott's thirtieth British classic victory, it was this one. Drawn next to the rails and held up, Muhtarram was last of the sixteen runners three furlongs out. He had already suffered interference before that point and did so again afterwards, short of room with Carson unable to provide his usual vigorous encouragement until inside the final furlong whereupon Muhtarram ran on in good style, eventually beaten about two and a half lengths and leaving the impression that he could have gone close for second. Two days later Muhtarram was disputing the Derby favouritism. A couple of wins in minor company at two years and a fourth in the Craven Stakes had been Muhtarram's only other racecourse appearances. That comparative inexperience and his breeding, as well as his effort in the Guineas, suggested that he would continue to progress, particularly over middle distances. A knock on his near-fore shortly before the Dante meant that the first chance he had to prove it would be in the Derby. This time there were no excuses on grounds of bad luck in running. Muhtarram was soon well positioned just behind the leaders, fifth into the straight, but he couldn't quicken with those in front, or indeed with Silver Wisp who deprived him of that Derby placing; Muhtarram finished fourth, five and a half lengths behind Dr Devious. He had not fulfilled all the hopes that could be held for him after the Guineas, but what was really disappointing was that he didn't race again. The nearest he got was when declared for the Eclipse and withdrawn following overnight rain.

The record of his sire Alleged provided strong encouragement that Muhtarram would prove suited by middle distances but doubts could be conjured up by that of his dam. Trained by David O'Brien for Robert Sangster, Ballet de France won a six-furlong maiden before being put into pattern events for her remaining two starts at two years, finishing towards the rear in the Moyglare Stud Stakes then winning a Group 3 over seven furlongs at Phoenix Park. As a three-year-old she was seen out only twice, beaten at 5/4 on in a minor event and fourteenth of twenty-three in the Irish One Thousand Guineas. One does not have to search far in her family, however, to find a middle-distance performer of distinction; a half-brother is the high-class St Hilarion. Their grandam Alyne Que, incidentally, is a close relation to Exclusive Native. Muhtarram is the third foal and first winner out of Ballet de France who was sold for 1,275,000 dollars at Keeneland in 1985 in foal to Alleged. Muhtarram made 650,000 dollars at the Keeneland July Selected Yearling Sale and is followed by two colts sent to the Keeneland September Yearling Sales. A son of Gulch went unsold at 40,000 dollars in 1991 but a Gone West colt made 150,000 dollars twelve months later.

Muhtarram (USA) (b.c. 1989)	Alleged (USA) (b 1974)	Hoist The Flag (b 1968)	Tom Rolfe
			Wavy Navy
		Princess Pout (b 1966)	Prince John
			Determined Lady
	Ballet de France (USA) (b 1981)	Northern Dancer (b 1961)	Nearctic
			Natalma
		Fabulous Native (ch 1974)	Le Fabuleux
			Alyne Que

An angular, good-bodied colt who carried plenty of condition on all his appearances in 1992, Muhtarram has a short action that connections feel strongly is best suited to a sound surface. We are equally confident that he will prove best over middle distances. *J. H. M. Gosden*

MUHTASHIM (IRE) 2 b.c. (Feb 2) Caerleon (USA) 132 – Baccalaureate 109 (Crowned Prince (USA) 128) [1992 7g] IR 270,000Y: sixth foal: brother to smart Irish 6f and 7f performer Corwyn Bay and closely related to modest 1¼m winner Trois Vallees (by Ile de Bourbon): dam, 7f and 1m winner, out of smart sprinter Bas Bleu: heavily-backed favourite, soon niggled along and never able to challenge in maiden at Doncaster in November: has scope, and will improve over 1m + . *J. L. Dunlop*   – p

MUIRFIELD VILLAGE 6 b.g. Lomond (USA) 128 – Ukelele (USA) (Riva Ridge (USA)) [1991 9s⁶ 10m 10.1s⁴ 10m 11.5g² 14m⁵ 11.5g 12g³ 12.1d 11.5m⁴ 12s 10m⁶ 1992 11.5f] good-bodied gelding: poor performer: not seen out after May: seems to stay 1¾m: acts on good to firm and soft going: none too genuine. *S. Dow*   – §

MUIR STATION (USA)   4 b.c. Darby Creek Road (USA) – Donna Inez (USA) **101**
(Herbager 136) [1991 14g⁵ 14g* 14m³ 12m³ 14d⁴ 16d⁴ 16s⁴ 12s⁵ 12.3g* 16s 1992
16d⁴ 12v* 16g⁴ 14m* 22.2g⁴ 12g 16s⁶] useful but inconsistent performer: successful
by wide margins in 1992 in minor events at Tipperary and Leopardstown:
well-beaten fourth in Queen Alexandra Stakes at Royal Ascot: stays 2m: acts on
good to firm and heavy ground: usually blinkered. *J. S. Bolger, Ireland*

MUIZENBERG   5 b.g. Mashhor Dancer (USA) – Allotria 86 (Red God 128§)   **73**
[1991 10.4d⁵ 11.5m² 10d 13.4d³ 12.3g² 1992 10.2m* 15.9m³ 12.3g² 11.9d⁴ 12.3g²]
good-topped gelding: carries condition: good walker: fair handicapper: successful at
Chepstow in June: effective at 1¼m to 2m (at least in moderately-run race): suited
by a sound surface: consistent: has swished tail, wandered and found little: won over
hurdles in October. *J. A. C. Edwards*

MUJAAZAFAH (USA)   2 br.c. (Apr 30) Mr Prospector (USA) – Cope of   **74** p
Flowers (USA) (Tom Rolfe) [1992 7g² 8d³] $175,000Y: good-topped colt: has quick
action: third foal: dam graded stakes placed-winner at up to 9f: shaped really well
when second in maiden at Newbury: similar form when close third of 19 in similar
event at Redcar 2 months after, again taking plenty of time to hit top pace: will stay
beyond 1m: will do better. *J. H. M. Gosden*

MUJADIL (USA)   4 b.c. Storm Bird (CAN) 134 – Vallee Secrete (USA)
(Secretariat (USA)) [1991 6s 5m 6s⁵ 5m 1992 6d] quite attractive colt: poor walker:
moderate mover: won Cornwallis Stakes at 2 yrs (rated 119): soundly-beaten last of
8 in minor event at Kempton in April, and not seen out again: stayed 6f: acted on
good to firm ground: retired to Rathasker Stud, Co Kildare, fee IR £2,000 (Oct 1st).
R. W. Armstrong

MUJAWAB   2 b.c. (Mar 26) Night Shift (USA) – False Front 85 (Bustino 136)   **55** p
[1992 7s 6.1v⁶] 43,000F, 70,000Y: angular, good-bodied colt: second live foal: dam
11.7f winner, is granddaughter of Irish 1000 Guineas winner Lacquer, family also of
Bright Finish and Shining Finish: similar form, showing up well to 2f out, in maidens
at Salisbury and Chester in autumn: may do better. *H. Thomson Jones*

MUJID (IRE)   3 gr.c. Kalaglow 132 – Ibtidaar (USA) 90 (Danzig (USA)) [1991 8f³   **71**
8.1s⁶ 1992 9.7v² 9.7g 10.3f² 12d⁴ 12h* 12.1s] sturdy colt: has a quick action: modest
handicapper: gamely won at Carlisle in June: ran poorly 4 months after: stays 1½m:
suited by top-of-the-ground. *H. Thomson Jones*

MUKADDAMAH (USA)   4 b.c. Storm Bird (CAN) 134 – Tash (USA) (Never   **99**
Bend (USA)) [1991 7g² 8g⁵ 7g⁴ 8g* 10.4g⁶ 8m² 8d 1992 8.1g 8m 8g⁴ 9m] tall, rather
leggy colt: has a long stride: has had soft palate operation: rated 125 at best at 3 yrs:
well below best in 1992, and was particularly disappointing final run: stays 1m:
probably acts on any going: sometimes carries head rather high: tends to sweat: has
joined T. Skiffington in USA. *P. T. Walwyn*

MUKHAMEDOV   2 b.c. (Mar 4) Robellino (USA) 127 – Gold Bracelet § (Golden   **94**
Fleece (USA) 133) [1992 7g⁶ 7.1d* 7.1d 7m⁴ 8g³ 8d] 34,000Y: lengthy, good-topped
colt: has plenty of scope: moderate mover: second foal: dam ungenuine half-sister to
top-class sprinter Thatching out of very smart sprinter Abella: useful colt: won
maiden at Sandown in July: ran well in pattern and listed events last 3 starts, eighth
of 10 to Armiger in Racing Post Trophy at Doncaster: will be better suited by 1¼m:
acts on good to firm and dead ground: trained first 4 starts by H. Cecil. *D. R. Loder*

MUKTAAR (USA)   3 b.c. Polish Navy (USA) – All Gladness (USA) (Alydar   –
(USA)) [1991 NR 1992 8g 10m 8m] $325,000Y: rangy colt: moderate mover: second
foal: half-brother to 11f seller winner Jubilata (by The Minstrel): dam, unplaced from
6 starts, is out of prolific stakes winner Gladiolus (twice in Grade 3 6f event): sire,
high class at 2 yrs and 3 yrs, stayed 1¼m: easily best effort in first half of 1992 in
minor event at Windsor second start: wears crossed noseband. *J. R. Fanshawe*

MULCIBER   4 b.g. Head For Heights 125 – Quisissanno 76 (Be My Guest (USA)   **76**
126) [1991 9s⁵ 7m² 7g² 8g³ 8g⁵ 1992 9d 9g 8m³ 7.6m³ 8f 8s 9g a8g⁴ a10g* a10g²
a10g*] leggy gelding: fair performer: improved form when stepped up in trip late in
season, winning 2 handicaps at Lingfield and rather unlucky in between: suited by
1¼m: acts on firm ground and equitrack, not on soft: occasionally carries head
awkwardly: below form blinkered. *G. Harwood*

MULLED ALE (IRE)   2 b.f. (Mar 13) Flash of Steel 120 – Bru Ri (FR) (Sir Gay-   –
lord) [1992 8d] 30,000F, 7,200Y: half-sister to several winners here and abroad,
including very useful 1987 2-y-o 6f and 7f winner Acajou (by Tap On Wood): dam ran
twice at 2 yrs in Ireland: no promise in Yarmouth maiden in October. *C. F. Wall*

MULL HOUSE   5 b.g. Local Suitor (USA) 128 – Foudre 76 (Petingo 135) [1991   **78**
13.3d⁶ 12g 14g⁶ 12f⁵ 13.9g 16m³ 16.2g 1992 14d 16m² 14m² 20m 17.2h² 16.1g² 16s*

14.6m* 16.1m* 14.8g⁶ 18f⁵ 18m] strong, rangy gelding: has a markedly round action: had an excellent season in 1992, successful in handicaps at Newbury, Doncaster and Newmarket and good last of 5 in Doncaster Cup: suited by test of stamina: probably acts on any going: often sweating: below form blinkered once. *F. J. O'Mahony*

MULLITOVER 2 ch.c. (May 3) Interrex (CAN) – Atlantic Air (Air Trooper 115) 81 p
[1992 7d² 7s* 7.3s] close-coupled, workmanlike colt: third live foal: half-brother to 1990 2-y-o 5f winner Domino Dancing (by Lidhame) and a winner in Belgium: dam won in Italy: sire (closely related to Secreto) won from 1m to 9.5f: 3-length winner of maiden at Warwick, racing keenly: brought to race on unfavoured part of track when well beaten in Newbury nursery later in October: will stay 1m: should do better. *M. J. Heaton-Ellis*

MUMMY'S BREW 3 b.f. Mummy's Game 120 – Tea-Pot 77 (Ragstone 128) –
[1991 NR 1992 a7g⁴ 6.9f³ 7f⁵ 8m 9.2s] 3,000Y: leggy, unfurnished filly: fifth foal: half-sister to 7-y-o middle-distance winner (stays 2m) One For The Pot (by Nicholas Bill) and a winning hurdler: dam out-and-out stayer: no worthwhile form in maidens and handicaps. *B. Beasley*

MUMMY'S EMERALD 4 ch.f. Mummy's Game 120 – Emerald Eagle 78 –
(Sandy Creek 123) [1991 7m 7m⁵ 7d³ 7g* 7m 7d³ 7m 7d 1992 a8g 7d] leggy filly: has rather round action: rated 76 at 4 yrs: well beaten in spring of 1992, including in seller: stays 7f: acts on good to firm ground and dead: sold 1,200 gns Ascot May Sales. *N. Tinkler*

MUMMYS ROCKET 3 ch.f. Mummy's Game 120 – Rockery (FR) 101 (Roan 41
Rocket 128) [1991 6g 5f 7m⁵ 8m 1992 8s 10.1s⁶ 8f⁵ 8f³ 7.1m⁴ 8g 8.1g² 10.3g 8m²] sturdy, lengthy filly: consistent plater: stays 1m: acts on firm ground, well beaten on soft: effective blinkered or not: sometimes bandaged. *M. O'Neill*

MUNDAY DEAN 4 ch.g. Kind of Hush 118 – Nancy Brig 63 (Brigadier Gerard a72
144) [1991 a8g³ a7g⁴ 8g⁶ 10m⁴ 10.9g 12.1g⁶ 12g* 12.1d 1992 a12g⁴ a12g* 12d 11.9m 12g a12g] good-quartered gelding: has a markedly round action: well beaten since winning Lingfield handicap in March: should stay 1¾m: acts on equitrack, seems unsuited by dead ground: has won for claimer: trained until after penultimate start by D. Arbuthnot. *R. J. O'Sullivan*

MUNNASIB (FR) 2 ch.c. (Mar 7) Highest Honor (FR) 124 – Parole Et Musique ?
(USA) (Nureyev (USA) 131) [1992 7m*] 460,000 francs (approx £46,200) Y: leggy colt: first foal: dam French 4-y-o 8.8f winner, is sister to Lead On Time and Great Commotion: ½-length winner from Keating of 3-runner private sweepstakes at Newmarket in October. *A. A. Scott*

MURAADI ANA (IRE) 2 b. or br.g. (Mar 3) Jareer (USA) 115 – Romany 60
Pageant (Welsh Pageant 132) [1992 6g 6m⁶ 7g 7f³ 8m⁴ 7m² 7d] IR 19,000F, 21,000Y: useful-looking gelding, rather leggy: closely related to useful 7f and 8.5f winner Laurie's Warrior (by Viking) and a half-brother to 2 winners by Red Sunset and 1m winner Irish Groom (by Shy Groom): dam never ran: easily best efforts third in Yarmouth maiden and second in nursery at Thirsk: should stay 1m: acts on good to firm ground: took keen hold when blinkered last 2 starts: tends to carry head awkwardly: has been gelded. *A. A. Scott*

MURASIL (USA) 3 b.c. Diesis 133 – Minstinguette (USA) (Boldnesian) [1991 7g 64 d
7g⁶ 7g⁴ 1992 10d 10.8g⁴ 10m⁴ 9.7g 11.9f⁶ 8m 7g 6d 9.2v] well-made colt: good walker and mover: went wrong way as 3-y-o, and sold out of R. Hern's stable 5,600 gns Newmarket September Sales after sixth start: best efforts at around 1¼m on a sound surface. *M. P. Naughton*

MURMURING 6 b.m. Kind of Hush 118 – Beryl's Jewel 86 (Siliconn 121) [1991 –
a6g³ a5g⁴ a6g² a6g² a7g³ a6g³ a7g⁴ a7g³ a7g³ 7m 7g⁴ 6g⁴ a6g² 5m a5g⁵ a6g* a6g² a61
1992 a6g² a6g⁴ a6g a7g⁴ a6g* a7g a6g⁵ a6g] angular mare: good walker: has a quick action: won handicap at Lingfield in February: not seen out after March: stays 7f: acts on hard ground and all-weather surfaces. *S. Dow*

MURPHY'S HOPE (IRE) 2 b.c. (May 14) Common Grounds 118 – Legs And 66
Things 92 (Three Legs 128) [1992 7.1s 6.9v 6g³] IR 14,500Y: leggy colt: half-brother to 1987 2-y-o 1m winner Coquillage (by Coquelin): dam, Irish 6f winner, is half-sister to smart sprinter Royal Captive and very useful stayers Melody Rock and Lawrence T: easily best effort in autumn maidens when third at Doncaster: should stay beyond 6f. *M. J. Heaton-Ellis*

MURRAY'S MAZDA (IRE) 3 ch.g. M Double M (USA) – Lamya 73 (Hittite 62
Glory 125) [1991 5f³ 6g² 5f⁵ 6d⁶ 5f⁵ 1992 5s⁴ 5g⁴ 5.9f² 6f* 5m² 5.9h⁶ 6m⁴ 5d 5g] leggy gelding: modest performer: won seller (no bid) at Hamilton in June: ran poorly last 3 outings: stays 6f: seems to act on any going. *J. Berry*

MUSCADINE 5 b.m. Muscatite 122 – Bee Hawk 87 (Sea Hawk II 131) [1991 NR 1992 13.1g⁵] leggy, lengthy mare: seems of little account. *A. J. Chamberlain* —

MUSE 5 ch.g. High Line 125 – Thoughtful 86 (Northfields (USA)) [1991 12s* 16g³ 12m 16.2g² 16.2d⁴ 18m⁶ 1992 16d 16.2s⁵ 18m] leggy gelding: has a rather round action: fair handicapper at best: well suited by test of stamina: probably acts on any going: suited by forcing tactics: smart and very genuine hurdler, winner of Grade 2 event at Ascot in November. *D. R. C. Elsworth* —

MUSHY BOFF 4 ch.f. Tina's Pet 121 – Rely On Guy 73 (Reliance II 137) [1991 5d 6m 7g 5.1d² 5g⁶ 7d² 8f 6.1s⁵ 7f 6g 6.1d 8d 1992 a7g a7g⁴ a7g* a7g⁴ a7g 8d 7g a7g³ a6g⁶ a8g] sturdy filly: poor mover: poor handicapper: won at Southwell in February: stays 7f: goes well on fibresand and a soft surface. *C. J. Hill* 51

MUSICALE (USA) 3 ch.f. The Minstrel (CAN) 135 – Gossiping (USA) (Chati (USA)) [1991 6m* 7g* 6m* 7d* 7m* 1992 7.3d* 8g 8s⁴] close-coupled, quite attractive filly: has a fluent, round action: most promising at 2 yrs, unbeaten, including in Cherry Hinton Stakes and Rockfel Stakes at Newmarket: looked ill at ease on ground when landing odds in Fred Darling Stakes at Newbury by a length from Wiedniu on reappearance: cracked a heel before modest run when favourite in 1000 Guineas at Newmarket later in April and off course over 4 months after: fair fifth (promoted) of 6 in Group 3 event at the Curragh: should have been well suited by 1m. *H. R. A. Cecil* 109

MUSICAL LYRICS 4 b.f. Song 132 – Spanish Ribbon (Pieces of Eight 128) [1991 8g 5f⁶ 7g 6g² 6g 6m 1992 7g 8f 8.3g a7g] small, sparely-made filly: poor plater: best effort at 6f. *Mrs J. G. Retter* —

MUSICAL PHONE 2 b.g. (Mar 8) Music Boy 124 – Kaleidophone 73 (Kalaglow 132) [1992 6m 6.1d⁴ 5m³ 8.1d 5s 6d] 6,400Y: leggy colt: moderate mover: first foal: dam 1m winner: poor maiden: needs further than 5f, and stays 1m: acts on good to firm and dead ground: races keenly. *J. P. Leigh* 54

MUSICAL PROSPECT (USA) 2 b.f. (Apr 4) Tank's Prospect (USA) – Belle Et Deluree (USA) (The Minstrel (CAN) 135) [1992 5.2g² 5f² 6g⁵ 6f² 6d⁶ 5g 7s] heavy-topped filly: moderate walker: first foal: dam, French 1m (at 2 yrs) and 1¼m winner, is closely related to Cheveley Park second Dancing Tribute: sire (by Mr Prospector) won Preakness Stakes: modest maiden: blinkered and well below form last 2 outings: should be better suited by 1m: acts on firm ground, possibly unsuited by soft: sold 4,400 gns Newmarket Autumn Sales. *R. Hannon* 60

MUSICAL TIMES 2 b.f. (Feb 8) Sylvan Express 117 – Musical Piece 91 (Song 132) [1992 5g⁶ 5s 5m³ 6d a5g a6g a6g] leggy filly: poor mover: half-sister to several winners here and abroad, including two 6f seller winners: dam best at sprint distances: modest maiden: below form last 4 starts, in blinkers last time: should stay 6f: may be suited by top-of-the-ground. *Mrs N. Macauley* 54

MUSIC DANCER 3 b.g. Music Boy 124 – Stepping Gaily 79 (Gay Fandango (USA) 132) [1991 6g⁶ 5g³ 1992 5v² 5g³ 6d* 6m⁵ 6.1m 5m³ 6g 6d² 6d⁴ 6s² 6.9v] leggy, close-coupled gelding: modest handicapper: won maiden at Hamilton in May: stays 6f: probably best on a soft surface: races prominently: sold out of J. Berry's stable 6,400 gns Newmarket Autumn Sales before final start. *R. J. Hodges* 61

MUSIC IN MY LIFE (IRE) 3 b.f. Law Society (USA) 130 – Music And Dance (USA) (Northern Dancer (CAN)) [1991 7.1d 6s⁵ 1992 8g⁴ 7.5m² 8m⁴ 10g 7g] compact, good-quartered filly: has a quick action: modest maiden: pulled up lame final start: stays 1m: acts on good to firm ground. *W. Jarvis* 59

MUSKET SHOT 4 br.g. Zambrano – Now You Know (Scottish Rifle 127) [1991 7m 8.3m⁴ 10m 8g 8.2m 1992 8.3m 15.1g⁶] leggy gelding: no worthwhile form: tried blinkered. *V. Thompson* —

MUSTAHIL (IRE) 3 gr.g. Sure Blade (USA) 130 – Zumurrudah (USA) 82 (Spectacular Bid (USA)) [1991 7f 8.2f 8.5f* 8g 7d 1992 6v 7.6s 13.1m⁶ 12.1m⁴ 14.1g 8h² 7.1f³ 8f⁶ 8g² 8f 8f 7d] small, good-topped gelding: carries condition: modest handicapper: effective at 1m to 1½m: acts on firm going, below form on a soft surface: blinkered 3 times, running well first time. *R. J. Hodges* 68

MUSTAKIM (IRE) 2 ch.c. (Feb 6) Persian Bold 123 – Majestic Amber (USA) (Majestic Light (USA)) [1992 6s³] 40,000F, IR 95,000Y: fourth foal: half-brother to a winner in Belgium by Plugged Nickle and Irish 1m and 9f winner Majestic Guest (by Be My Guest): dam won at up to 7f, including in stakes: always prominent when 4 lengths third of 13 in maiden at Folkestone in October: will stay 1m: will improve. *R. W. Armstrong* 57 p

MUST BE MAGICAL (USA) 4 ch.g. Temperence Hill (USA) – Honorine – (USA) (Blushing Groom (FR) 131) [1991 NR 1992 8.5m 10.5d 13f⁴ 8f 7.6g 8m⁶ a12g* a39 11.8g a12g* a12g 12.1s 12.5s 10m] leggy gelding: form in 1992 only when winning 2 handicaps at Southwell in the summer: stays 1½m: blinkered/visored nowadays: forces pace: sold 2,200 gns Doncaster November Sales. *F. H. Lee*

MUSVAL 3 ch.f. Music Boy 124 – Marie's Valentine (Piaffer (USA) 113) [1991 5g⁴   **49** 5.2g 1992 5.1m⁶ 5f³ 5g⁴ 5g⁵ 5d 5g] lengthy, unfurnished filly: modest maiden: raced only at 5f: acted on firm ground: to stud. *R. Hannon*

MUTABAHI (CAN) 3 b. or br.c. Woodman (USA) 126 – Vallee Secrete (USA)   **93** (Secretariat (USA)) [1991 6d⁴ 6g* 7.1m⁶ 1992 7g⁶ 8.9g 8m⁵ 8f⁴ 7g⁶ 8m⁶ 10m³] small, sturdy colt: carries condition: fairly useful handicapper: not seen again after narrowly-beaten third of 18 to Party Cited in £30,600 event at Goodwood in July: better at 1¼m than shorter: acts on good to firm ground: lazy, and well worth a try in blinkers/visor: consistent. *R. W. Armstrong*

MUTAKALLAM (USA) 2 b.c. (Feb 13) Fappiano (USA) – Stark Drama (USA)   **65** (Graustark) [1992 7m⁴ 7d 8m³] $550,000Y: rangy, good-topped colt: has plenty of scope: fluent mover: brother to 2 winners in USA, notably Grade 1 1m Acorn Stakes winner Aptostar, and half-brother to 2 winners: dam graded stakes-placed winner at up to 1¼m: sire (by Mr Prospector) good-class winner from 5f to 9f: failed to progress as anticipated in maidens after promising fourth at Kempton in August: should stay 1m. *H. Thomson Jones*

MUZO (USA) 5 b.g. Irish River (FR) 131 – Dance Flower (CAN) (Northern – Dancer (CAN)) [1991 10s 1992 11.8d 10.2f 10.2f⁶ 10.2g a12g 9.7d] strong, well-made gelding: very much on the downgrade: sold 1,100 gns Ascot September Sales. *J. M. Bradley*

MY ABBEY 3 b.f. Hadeer 118 – Rose Barton (Pas de Seul 133) [1991 5s² 5m* 5d³   **66** d 5m⁵ 5g 5d² 5d³ 5.1m* 5g 1992 6.1g³ 5m 5m⁵ 7.6d a5g] leggy, rather close-coupled filly: well below form in handicaps after third in May: best form at 5f: acts on good to firm ground: ran creditably when visored. *E. J. Alston*

MY ALIBI (IRE) 4 ch.g. Hatim (USA) 121 – Serriyya 53 (Tap On Wood 130)   **46** [1991 10d 8m⁴ 8.3m 8f 8m⁴ 10g 8m 1992 a7g 10.1f⁴ 9.7m] workmanlike gelding: inconsistent handicapper: probably stays 1¼m: acts on firm going: usually blinkered: has carried head high: trained first start by W. Carter. *S. Dow*

MYASHA (USA) 3 b.g. Imp Society (USA) – Mauna Loa (USA) (Hawaii) [1991   **67** 5g⁴ 5d⁵ 5g⁶ 5g³ 5m⁴ 5.2f a5g² a5g³ 1992 a6g* a7g⁵ 7g² 5m a7g³ 7f³ 6g 6g⁵] neat gelding: in-and-out form in varied company after winning maiden at Lingfield in January: stays 7f: acts on equitrack: below form blinkered: wears eyeshield on all-weather: usually bandaged behind. *Mrs L. Piggott*

MY BALLYBOY 2 ch.g. (Apr 19) Ballacashtal (CAN) – Pink N' Perky (Tickled   **57** Pink 114) [1992 5g 7m 7d 10g⁵ 7.6s⁵ 6v² a7g a8g] 3,200Y: compact gelding: third foal: half-brother to 3-y-o Battle of Britain (by Beveled), 5f and 6f winner at 2 yrs: dam poor maiden: modest maiden: should prove effective over at least 1m: easily best effort on heavy ground, ran poorly on fibresand: often blinkered: races keenly. *A. Bailey*

MY BEST VALENTINE 2 b.c. (Feb 14) Try My Best (USA) 130 – Pas de Calais   **59** (Pas de Seul 133) [1992 6m³ 6d³ 6.9v] 5,800Y: compact colt: second foal: dam unraced: shaped encouragingly when third in maiden auctions at Folkestone and Ripon in autumn: finished well beaten on heavy ground in Folkestone maiden: should be better suited by 7f than 6f. *P. W. Harris*

MY BONUS 2 b.f. (May 5) Cyrano de Bergerac 120 – Dress In Spring 63   **79** (Northfields (USA)) [1992 5m* 5g⁴ 5m² 5m² 5.1g² 5g* 5g² 5g³ 5d⁵ 6d] 1,900Y: rather unfurnished filly: third foal: half-sister to 3-y-o Medbourne (by Alzao): dam 6f and 7f winner: consistent performer: successful in maiden auction at Pontefract in May and nursery at Leicester in July: should stay 6f: acts on good to firm and dead ground: ran creditably for claimer: sometimes bandaged behind. *D. J. S. Cosgrove*

MY BOY BUSTER 3 b.c. Kind of Hush 118 – Happy Donna 106 (Huntercombe – 133) [1991 6m 1992 7d 10m 8f] rather sparely-made colt: no form and may well be ungenuine. *C. J. Hill*

MY CHERRYWELL 2 br.f. (May 18) Kirchner 110 – Cherrywood Blessin (Good   **58** Times (ITY)) [1992 5d⁴ 6m⁶ 5g⁴] sparely-made filly: first foal: dam never ran: best effort in summer maidens when close fourth of 9 at Beverley final start. *Mrs V. A. Aconley*

MY CHIARA 6 b.m. Ardross 134 – My Tootsie 88 (Tap On Wood 130) [1991 10g **73**
15.5f³ 12g 12m* 12g⁶ 12f² 12m³ 12d² 11.5d 12f³ 12f⁴ 12m³ 13.9g 12f 12.2m⁴ 12.1g 12f⁵
1992 14.6m 18.5d* 20m 15.9m 16.2d* 16.5g4] leggy, quite good-topped mare: fair
handicapper: wide-margin winner on dead ground at Chester in July and Haydock in
October: mostly below form otherwise: stays 2¼m: has form on firm ground, but
clearly needs an easy surface nowadays: below form visored once: tough. *P. J. Bevan*

MY CZECH MATE 3 ch.g. Risk Me (FR) 127 – Legal Sound 85 (Legal Eagle –
126) [1991 5g⁶ 5g⁴ 8m 6g⁶ 5m 1992 6f⁵ 6g⁵ 8f 7g] good-bodied gelding: moderate
mover: poor handicapper: stays 6f: best effort on good ground: sold 600 gns Ascot
July Sales. *R. Hannon*

MY DESIRE 4 ch.f. Grey Desire 115 – Another Move 69 (Farm Walk 111) [1991 **75**
13.8g² 12.3g³ 12.4f* 16.2f² 17.9f* 16.2f* 16m⁶ 1992 16.1m 15.1f³ 16.2s* 16.2d* 16.2g
15.9m] leggy, shallow-girthed filly: improved handicapper when successful at
Beverley (2) in July: well beaten on faster ground after: stays well: has won on firm
but clearly well suited by soft ground: usually held up, has hung, and not easiest of
rides: won novice hurdle in November. *Mrs M. Reveley*

MY DUCATS (IRE) 4 b.f. Red Sunset 120 – Saulonika 94 (Saulingo 122) [1991 –
8.2g⁴ 6m 5.2m 6m 6.1d 1992 6f 8.3m] sturdy, workmanlike filly: no worthwhile form:
tried blinkered. *T. Casey*

MYFONTAINE 5 b.h. Persepolis (FR) 127 – Mortefontaine (FR) (Polic 126) **74**
[1991 10.8g* 10.8m* 11.7g² 11d⁵ 10s 11.6m⁵ 11.5g⁴ 10.5d 9.7f 11.5s⁶ 1992 10.8v*
10m* 10g³ 10f 11.6g 10.1m 9d] leggy horse: fair handicapper: goes well in spring,
successful at Warwick and Newmarket as 5-y-o: off course over 3 months and well
below form last 3 starts (blinkered final one): effective at 1¼m to 1½m: acts on good
to firm and heavy ground. *K. T. Ivory*

MY FOXY LADY 2 b.f. (Mar 1) Jalmood (USA) 126 – La Petite Noblesse 105 –
(Thatching 131) [1992 5.7f⁵ 5s⁴ 6s a6g] leggy filly: first foal: dam easy-ground
sprinter: no worthwhile form. *D. Haydn Jones*

MY GIRL FRIDAY 3 b.f. Scorpio (FR) 127 – Nikancy 76 (Castlenik 107) [1991 –
a6g 1992 11s⁴ 11.8g] lengthy, workmanlike filly: no worthwhile form. *W. Clay*

MY GODSON 2 br.c. (Feb 15) Valiyar 129 – Blessit 79 (So Blessed 130) [1992 5s⁵ **57**
5m⁶ 6d 5f³ a5g 5g* 5g⁴ 6d⁴ 6s⁶ 5g] sturdy colt: third reported foal: brother to 3-y-o
Anna Manana, winner in Scandinavia: dam sprinter: won seller (no bid) at Catterick in July and ran well most starts after: stays 6f: acts on dead ground: usually
blinkered: trained first 4 outings by W. Pearce. *B. Beasley*

MY GRAIN 3 ch.f. Ballacashtal (CAN) – Sequoia 87 (Sassafras (FR) 135) [1991 6d **42**
8m 1992 12.3s⁴ 8d⁵ 8m 6f⁴ 10m 6d⁵ 7.1s⁵ 8m] workmanlike filly: moderate mover:
poor plater: best efforts at 6f: acts on firm going: retained 1,100 gns Newmarket
September Sales after seventh start, resold 1,200 gns Doncaster October Sales and
850 gns Ascot November Sales. *R. Hollinshead*

MY HARVINSKI 2 b.c. (Mar 15) Myjinski (USA) – Autumn Harvest (Martinmas **62**
128) [1992 7g 6d⁶ 7d⁴ 8s] leggy, unfurnished colt: half-brother to 1984 2-y-o 5f
winner Jackie Blair (by Rupert Bear): dam of no account: similar form, not knocked
about unduly, in maidens at Goodwood and Brighton second and third starts:
showed little on very soft ground in Warwick nursery after: should be much better
suited by 1m. *P. W. Chapple-Hyam*

MY JERSEY PEARL (IRE) 3 b.f. Cyrano de Bergerac 120 – Blessingtonia 79 –
(So Blessed 130) [1991 5g* 6m³ 6g⁶ 6f³ 6f⁴ 6m 6.1m 7d 1992 7g 6.9d 8m 7m 10g 8g
8m 6.9g 8s] close-coupled filly: of little account these days: sold 650 gns Newmarket
Autumn Sales. *Don Enrico Incisa*

MYKINDOFMUSIC 3 b.f. Petong 126 – Harmonious Sound (Auction Ring **49** §
(USA) 123) [1991 a5g⁶ 5g* 5g⁵ 5f⁶ a6g⁴ 5m³ 5.3m⁴ a5g 1992 a5g² a5g³ a8g² a8g²
10g] smallish, lengthy filly: temperamental handicapper: not seen again after
showing nothing in seller in April: stays 1m: acts on good to firm ground and
equitrack: often blinkered: sold 1,000 gns Newmarket July Sales. *M. J. Haynes*

MY LINDIANNE 5 gr.m. Alias Smith (USA) – Lindrick Passion (Silly Season –
127) [1991 NR 1992 10.3g 10d] first foal: dam poor animal: probably of little account.
J. Dooler

MY MEMOIRS 3 b.c. Don't Forget Me 127 – Julip 99 (Track Spare 125) **122**
[1991 6.1g* 7m* 7g⁶ 7m² 7m 1992 8g³ 8g⁴ 10.3m* a12g² a9f]
  My Memoirs came close to providing a second win in three years for
Europe in the mile-and-a-half Belmont Stakes, following Go And Go's magni-

ficent effort. Had he won he would have caused a surprise, for he started at 18/1, and, although improving, he wasn't regarded as being among the top European three-year-olds at the time. My Memoirs ran his best race in Britain when stepped up to a mile and a quarter in the Dee Stakes at Chester in May, recording his first win since picking up a minor event at York on his second start as a two-year-old, six outings back. He hadn't made the International Classification, and seemed fairly well exposed by the end of his two-year-old days. My Memoirs appeared twice in the spring before being sent to Chester—in the Doncaster Mile, where he was beaten just over a length and a half into third place behind the future Del Mar Invitational Derby winner Daros, and in the Thirsk Classic Trial, where he finished fourth, nearly eight lengths behind Jeune after being outpaced from halfway. At Chester My Memoirs ran as though a mile and a quarter had become a minimum for him. He stayed on remarkably strongly under pressure and headed Profusion on the post. The runner-up had run lazily in front and it was he who received most of the encouraging write-ups, but in giving him 4 lb My Memoirs was clearly progressing. Shortly afterwards he was sold to a partnership in America who decided to supplement him for 50,000 dollars to their oldest classic.

There were four principal American contenders for the eleven-runner Belmont Stakes. Having won the last six of his seven starts, the 11/10 favourite was A P Indy who had been withdrawn from the Kentucky Derby after suffering a quarter crack, and had also missed the Preakness Stakes before returning with an impressive win thirteen days earlier in the Grade 2 Peter Pan Stakes at Belmont. Second choice at just under 4/1 was the Preakness winner Pine Bluff, ahead of 9/2-shot Casual Lies, who'd finished third at Pimlico and second in the Kentucky Derby. The only other to start at under 20/1 was the Prix Hocquart-fourth Cristofori. The Belmont, on dirt, was run at a good pace. As Agincourt and Casual Lies set the gallop down the back stretch, Pine Bluff tracked them two lengths behind, ahead of A P Indy and then My Memoirs, both of whom were racing against the inside rail. Belmont has a long sweeping home turn and as Pine Bluff made his challenge, so A P Indy came wide for a clear run while My Memoirs, who had lost his position towards the end of the back stretch and been switched, began to run on again but about three lengths adrift. On straightening up with about three hundred and fifty yards to go, Pine Bluff hit the front only to be challenged immediately by A P Indy; after a good tussle, A P Indy steadily pulled ahead in the last seventy-five yards and while it never looked as if My Memoirs would win, he stayed on strongly to snatch second from Pine Bluff close home and reduced the winning margin to three quarters of a length. The remainder, headed by Cristofori, were thirteen lengths and upwards adrift. The official time was the joint-second fastest in the history of the race, equalling that of Easy Goer in 1989 and two seconds behind the astonishing time set by Secretariat in 1973.

While A P Indy went on to lay his claim to Horse of the Year honours in the Breeders' Cup Classic, all did not go well for the placed horses. Pine Bluff tore a ligament on his near-fore during a workout at Belmont on June 22nd and was retired to stud. My Memoirs reappeared under the care of Mark Hennig in the Jim Dandy Stakes at Saratoga in August, having been transferred from Hannon's stable. Sent off the 9/5 favourite in a field of eight he ran a dismal race, beaten more than twenty-five lengths. He was afterwards found to have a throat infection, and although Hennig reported at the time that he was hopeful his colt would make the Travers Stakes line-up, My Memoirs wasn't seen out again after sustaining an injury at exercise. At the time of writing efforts are being made to find him a position at stud.

My Memoirs is the eighth foal of his dam, the only other of much consequence being the first, the London Bells colt Patriarch. A useful and genuine performer, he completed the Royal Hunt Cup-Bunbury Cup double as a four-year-old and won pattern races on the Continent in each of the next two seasons. The dam's only other winner was the Irish middle-distance performer Fiestal, who was by Last Fandango. Julip showed her best form as a two-year-old when twice a winner over seven furlongs, but she performed well enough in handicaps the following season to suggest she stayed a mile

My Memoirs (b.c. 1989)	Don't Forget Me (b 1984)	Ahonoora (ch 1975)	Lorenzaccio
			Helen Nichols
		African Doll (b 1978)	African Sky
			Mithril
	Julip (b 1977)	Track Spare (b 1963)	Sound Track
			Rosy Myth
		Jacine (ch 1957)	Owen Tudor
			Weighbridge

and a half. She was herself a half-sister to three useful or better two-year-olds including Tiepolo who earned a rating of 121 in 1966. The grandam Jacine was only modest but one of her half-sisters, Libra, produced the St Leger winners Ribocco and Ribero, while another, Gloria Nicky, was the top two-year-old filly of 1954 and her half-brother, Edmundo, was one of the top two-year-olds the following season. Dual Two Thousand Guineas winner Don't Forget Me has made a satisfactory start at stud. My Memoirs is easily his biggest earner but he's had plenty of winners including the useful Irish Memory, who won the Tetrarch Stakes, and the listed-winner Well Beyond. Don't Forget Me was tried beyond a mile only once, and that when possibly unsuited by restraining tactics and dead ground in the Champion Stakes, but he's already got several horses who stay at least a mile and a quarter. My Memoirs was clearly a staying type and, on racecourse evidence, would have had little difficulty getting a mile and three quarters. He would have found no suitable opportunities over a mile and a half and more on dirt, however, because the Americans have squeezed all their important races into the confines of six furlongs and a mile and a quarter. *M. Hennig, USA*

MY MISS MOLLY (IRE) 2 ch.f. (Mar 10) Entitled 126 – Marine Life (Deep Diver 134) [1992 7g⁶ 6.1m⁵ 6m a8g] tall, unfurnished filly: moderate mover: closely related to 6-y-o 1m to 1¼m performer Marine Diver (by Pas de Seul) and French 1m to 10.5f winner Mouhareb (by Northfields): dam, 6f winner in Ireland, is half-sister to high-class 1m to 1½m performer Dickens Hill: no worthwhile form, including in sellers: should stay at least 7f. *Miss Gay Kelleway* –

MY MOODY GIRL (IRE) 3 b.f. Alzao (USA) 117 – Young Grace (Young Emperor 133) [1991 6.1d 6.1g 7f 1992 8s 7v] compact filly: no worthwhile form. *C. R. Barwell* –

MY NOMINEE 4 b.c. Nomination 125 – Salala 83 (Connaught 130) [1991 8g 8g⁴ 7f⁵ 7f* 7g 1992 7m 8f] workmanlike, angular colt: rated 68 at 3 yrs: below form in first half of 1992: probably stays 1m: acts on firm ground: sold 1,450 gns Doncaster September Sales. *S. E. Kettlewell* –

MY PATRIARCH 2 ch.c. (Mar 25) Be My Guest (USA) 126 – Early Rising (USA) (Grey Dawn II 132) [1992 6g⁴ 6d⁵ 8f 7g⁶] lengthy, good-topped colt: fluent mover: sixth foal: closely related to useful sprinter Silver Singing (by Topsider) and half-brother to 3-y-o 1¼m winner Spectacular Dawn (by Spectacular Bid) and a winner in USA: dam, minor winner in USA at about 1m, is out of half-sister to top-class Key To The Mint: shaped with promise in maidens before much-improved sixth of 16 to Brigante di Cielo in nursery at Ascot in October, keeping on well: will be better suited by 1¼m: probably unsuited by a soft surface: has plenty of scope, and should do well at 3 yrs. *J. L. Dunlop* 77 p

MYPETO 3 ro.c. Petong 126 – Mycenae Cherry 69 (Troy 137) [1991 NR 1992 10d 12.2m 8m 10f] workmanlike colt: first foal: dam 10.2f winner appeared to stay 2m, is daughter of Cherry Hinton: no promise in maiden and claiming events: visored once: sold 980 gns Doncaster June Sales. *P. Calver* –

MY RUBY RING 5 b.m. Blushing Scribe (USA) 107 – Bells of St Martin 89 (Martinmas 128) [1991 8f⁴ 8f 7f 7.1g 8m 6.1s² 7m⁴ 6m⁴ 6f* 6m 6g 6m² 6g² 5.1d 1992 6.1d⁴ 5.3m⁶ 6f* 6f 6.1m 6.1m 6m⁵ 6m³ 6m⁵ 6m³ 6m⁵ a6g² a7g⁶ 6m³ 6.1g* 6s³ 6d* 6d⁵ 6.1s] leggy, angular mare: moderate mover: consistent handicapper: successful in 1992 at Salisbury (apprentices), Nottingham and Haydock: effective from 5f to 7f: probably acts on any going on turf and goes well on equitrack: often bandaged: sometimes awkward at stalls: good mount for claimer: very tough. *D. R. Laing* 59

MY SENOR 3 b.g. Jalmood (USA) 126 – San Marguerite 80 (Blakeney 126) [1991 5m 7m 7m 7g 8m 1992 9.7g⁴ 12.5g³ 10f 14g 11.6m 11.9m⁵ 10d] compact gelding: poor maiden on flat: should stay beyond 12.5f: possibly best on an easy surface: fair juvenile hurdler, winner twice. *M. Madgwick* 46 d

560

MYSILV 2 ch.f. (Apr 17) Bustino 136 – Miss By Miles 91 (Milesian 125) [1992 6m **62 p**
7g] 4,000Y: leggy filly: sister to useful 1¼m and 1½m winner Buzzbomb and
half-sister to several winners, including (at 6f and 1m) smart Missed Blessing (by So
Blessed): dam game miler: much better effort in maidens at Newmarket in October
on final run when making most and beaten around 7 lengths by Fayfa: will be suited
by middle distances: sure to improve. *C. F. Wall*

MY SISTER LUCY 2 b.f. (Mar 6) Farajullah 113 – Woven Gold (No Lute (FR) **–**
129) [1992 8g 8.1d 10g] plain filly: first foal: dam ran twice at 2 yrs: soundly beaten in
maidens. *A. P. Jarvis*

MY SOVEREIGN (USA) 3 b.f. Sovereign Dancer (USA) – Copper Creek 78 **74**
(Habitat 134) [1991 5.2g⁶ 6m⁴ 1992 5g* 5g³ 5f 5g⁴ 6m 5g 5s³ 5.1d² 6.1s] good-bodied
filly: usually impresses in appearance: inconsistent in handicaps after winning
minor event at Thirsk in April: should be effective at 6f: best form with some give in
the ground: below form when visored: trained first 6 starts by J. Fanshawe: sold
8,800 gns Newmarket December Sales. *R. Hannon*

MYSTERIOUS MAID (USA) 5 ch.m. L'Emigrant (USA) 129 – Body Heat **57**
(USA) (Sir Ivor 135) [1991 10.1g 11.5m⁶ 10g³ 12.3d* 11.5g⁵ 11.8g* 12g⁴ a12g² a14g⁶
1992 12g 11.9d 10.8d 9.9m 11.8g⁴ 12v] lengthy, rather angular mare: below form in
handicaps in 1992: best form at 1½m: acts on firm and dead ground and equitrack:
successful for lady. *J. Pearce*

MYSTERIOUS WAYS (FR) 2 b.c. (Apr 7) Common Grounds 118 – Polaregina **64**
(FR) (Rex Magna (FR)) [1992 5m² 6g 5f² 5.1m 5d² 5g⁵] rather leggy, quite attractive
colt: has a quick action: fifth known foal: half-brother to Irish 7f winner Slip And
Slide (by Pennine Walk) and 2 winners in France: dam unraced daughter of Sly Pola:
modest performer: should stay 6f: acts on firm and dead ground: well below form
with tongue strap once. *Mrs J. Cecil*

MYSTERY BAND (USA) 6 b.h. Dixieland Band (USA) – Lindaria (USA) (Sea **–**
Bird II 145) [1991 a11g a11g* a12g³ a12g² a14g⁶ a12g² a12g² a14g⁴ 10d a12g⁴ a12g
1992 16.1s] big, angular horse: poor walker and mover: on the downgrade. *Mrs S. J.
Smith*

MYSTERY CARGO (USA) 4 b.c. Storm Bird (CAN) 134 – Verset Holiday **–**
(USA) (Ribots Holiday (USA)) [1991 8g 7m 5s 5d⁴ 6m⁵ 5g* 5m⁵ 6g 5d 7d 1992 5m]
leggy, quite good-topped colt: rated 55 as 3-y-o: below form in May, 1992: headstrong, and best form at up to 6f: acts on good to firm ground and dead: not one to
trust implicitly. *J. Sutcliffe*

MYSTERY LAD (IRE) 3 b.c. Ela-Mana-Mou 132 – Bold Miss (Bold Lad (IRE) **58**
133) [1991 8s 8m 8m 8.3s a8g a8g² 1992 12g 11.6m 15.1m* 13.8g² 11.5g*] workmanlike colt: poor mover: modest performer: won claimers at Edinburgh and
Yarmouth in first half of 1992: stays 15f: acts on good to firm ground and equitrack:
usually blinkered/bandaged: front runner. *N. A. Callaghan*

MYSTERY PLAY (IRE) 3 b.f. Sadler's Wells (USA) 132 – Kereolle (Riverman **100**
(USA) 131) [1991 7g* 8d² 7m² 1992 10g³ 10m³ 11.9g 11.4d* 10.1g⁴ 10d⁵] leggy
filly: useful performer: won minor event at Sandown in August: ran creditably after
behind Red Slippers in listed event at Newcastle and Sun Chariot Stakes at Newmarket: should have beeen suited by 1½m: acted on good to firm and dead ground:
visits Diesis. *B. W. Hills*

MYSTIC CRYSTAL (IRE) 4 b.f. Caerleon (USA) 132 – Bolivia (GER) (Wind- **77**
wurf (GER)) [1991 8g² a12g⁴ 8g 7s⁴ 8m⁶ 8g a7g⁵ a7g³ 1992 a8g² a8g⁴] leggy, rather
sparely-made filly: fair handicapper: not seen out after running poorly in February
(visored): effective at 7f, and should stay 1¼m: acts on dead ground: successful for
apprentice: effective blinkered or not. *W. A. O'Gorman*

MYSTIC GODDESS (USA) 2 ch.f. (Feb 20) Storm Bird (CAN) 134 – Rose **94**
Goddess (Sassafras (FR) 135) [1992 6g* 5f² 6g³ 7m* 8s 7m³] useful-looking filly:
has a quick action: half-sister to 3-y-o 7f winner Native Idol (by Diesis) and several
other winners, including (at 6f to 1m at 2 yrs in 1986) smart Sanam (by Golden Act):
dam unraced daughter of half-sister to Caro: fairly useful filly: successful in maiden
at Leicester in May and moderately-run Sweet Solera Stakes (by ½ length from
Reine de Neige, making all and battling on well) at Newmarket in August: placed in
Queen Mary Stakes at Royal Ascot (found trip too sharp), Hillsdown Cherry Hinton
Stakes (had tongue tied down) at Newmarket and Rockfel Stakes (wore special
bridle, beaten under 3 lengths by Yawl) at Newmarket: sweated freely before
running moderately in Fillies' Mile at Ascot: takes keen hold and may prove suited
by 7f: acts on firm ground. *M. R. Stoute*

MYSTIC MEMORY 3 b. or br.f. Ela-Mana-Mou 132 – Mountain Memory 109 **64**
(High Top 131) [1991 7f 1992 12.2g² a12g³ 16f*] quite good-topped filly: similar form
in maidens: won maiden claimer (claimed to join Mrs M. Reveley's stable £9,600) at
Redcar in August: stays 2m: acts on firm going, ran moderately on fibresand. *Sir
Mark Prescott*

MYSTIC PANTHER 4 b.g. Sulaafah (USA) 119 – Aljaw 66 (Touching Wood **53**
(USA) 127) [1991 7d³ 7g⁶ 8.3m⁴ 9.7f 10g 5.1g⁵ 1992 6d 8d 8.3g⁶ 10g 10.2f4 10.2f³ 9.7d
11m] smallish gelding: modest maiden: stayed 1¼m: acted on firm ground and dead:
tried blinkered: dead. *R. J. Holder*

MYSTIKO (USA) 4 gr.c. Secreto (USA) 128 – Caracciola (FR) (Zeddaan 130) –
[1991 7m* 8g* 12f 8g 6f4 7m* 1992 8m⁵ 8d⁶ 8s⁶ 7m] sturdy, angular colt: has a
quick action: front runner, rated 124 at his best: successful 3 times at Newmarket as
3-y-o, notably in 2000 Guineas: below form elsewhere in last 2 seasons, particularly
so in pattern company in 1992, and was also well beaten at Newmarket final start:
best form at 7f/1m on a sound surface: tended to sweat and get on toes: taken last
and quietly to post: retired to Barton Stud, Bury St Edmunds, fee £4,000 (Oct 1st).
C. E. Brittain

MY SWAN SONG 7 b.g. Soul Singer 97 – Palmaria (Be Friendly 130) [1991 12.3g **37**
1992 14.1d* 14.6g³ 16m⁴ 16.9d 12.5s4] close-coupled gelding: poor mover: poor
handicapper: won at Nottingham in July: suited by test of stamina: seems to act on
any going: below form blinkered. *J. P. Smith*

MY THREE GIRLS (IRE) 4 b.f. Tumble Wind (USA) – Winter Harvest –
(Grundy 137) [1991 8m 8g 7m 8.2m 1992 a8g] angular, leggy, sparely-made filly:
seems of little account. *H. J. Collingridge*

MY TURN NEXT 4 b.f. King of Spain 121 – Its My Turn 80 (Palm Track 122) –
[1991 8g 9d 6m 8g 10g 8g 1992 16.2g 8.3v 11.8g4 16.2g 10.5g 17.9d] lengthy, angular
filly: no worthwhile form in 1992: stays 1m: acts on firm ground: headstrong. *K. W.
Hogg, Isle of Man*

MZURI SANDS 2 ch.f. (May 6) Sayf El Arab (USA) 127 – Mzuri Sana (Hello –
Gorgeous (USA) 128) [1992 7d 8m] close-coupled, leggy, angular filly: second foal:
dam poor half-sister to good Irish miler Celestial Bounty: behind in Redcar seller
and maiden at Pontefract in October: sold 1,100 gns Doncaster November Sales. *M.
J. Camacho*

N

NAAWY 2 b.c. (Mar 31) Reference Point 139 – Strike Home 82 (Be My Guest **68**
(USA) 126) [1992 8.2g 8d⁵ 7g] small colt: poor mover: third foal: half-brother to
3-y-o Aneeda (by Rainbow Quest) and modest 7f and 1m winner Inseyab (by Persian
Bold): dam, 11.7f winner, is half-sister to Ballad Rock: fair maiden: one paced, and
will be suited by middle distances. *M. R. Stoute*

NA-AYIM (IRE) 2 b.f. (Feb 23) Shirley Heights 130 – Christabelle (USA) **68** p
(Northern Dancer (CAN)) [1992 6m*] 170,000Y: good-topped filly: second foal: dam
daughter of Where You Lead, dam also of Slightly Dangerous and grandam of
Rainbow Quest, Warning and Scenic: weak 10/1-shot, won 15-runner maiden at
Newbury in June by a short head from White Shadow, headway 2f out and running on
under vigorous ride to lead post: wore bandage off-hind: moved moderately to post:
seemed sure to improve. *A. A. Scott*

NABJELSEDR 2 b.c. (Apr 28) Never So Bold 135 – Klewraye (Lord Gayle (USA) **82** p
124) [1992 6d4 6s* 7g] 42,000Y: leggy colt: half-brother to 5 winners here and
abroad, including 6f winner Caffarelli (by Mummy's Pet) and 1¼m and 11.7f winner
High I Kew (by High Top): dam Irish 2-y-o 7f winner: progressive form: favourite,
won maiden at Goodwood in October, staying on strongly from unpromising position
2f out: creditable tenth of 21 in nursery at Doncaster following month: will stay 1m:
probably capable of more improvement. *C. J. Benstead*

NAEL (IRE) 3 b.c. Never So Bold 135 – Night Encounter (Right Tack 131) [1991 –
6f 1992 7g 8g] useful-looking colt: no form: broke leg final start and had to be put
down. *C. J. Benstead*

NAFUTH (USA) 2 b. or br.c. (Mar 26) Nureyev (USA) 131 – Costly Array (USA) **86**
(Riverman (USA) 131) [1992 6s² 6m² 6g²] $500,000Y: leggy, workmanlike colt:
good mover: third foal: dam graded stakes-placed winner at up to 7f: fairly useful

maiden: best effort when beaten 1½ lengths by Felucca at Newmarket second start: will be at least as effective at 7f: possibly suited by top-of-the-ground. *P. T. Walwyn*

NAGEM 9 b.m. Headin' Up – Eleonora 70 (Falcon 131) [1991 5d 6m 5.1m⁶ 6g 6.1d 5.1d 7.6g 6m 1992 6g 6m] strong, lengthy mare: has run tubed: poor mover: no longer of much account: sold 630 gns Doncaster September Sales. *L. J. Barratt* –

NAGIDA 3 b.f. Skyliner 117 – Kept In Style 49 (Castle Keep 121) [1991 NR 1992 5m³ 6g² 5m² 5m 6m* 5.7g⁴ 6d* 6g*dis 6g⁶ 6m³ 6m² 5g] strong filly: carries condition: moderate mover: first foal: dam winning hurdler but maiden on flat, suited by around 1¾m: fairly useful performer: first past the post in maiden at Lingfield and in handicaps at Newbury and Yarmouth (disqualified for apprentice jockey's careless riding) in the summer: probably needs further than 5f, and should stay 7f: acts on good to firm and dead ground: consistent. *J. A. R. Toller* 84

NAHLATI (IRE) 2 b.f. (May 30) Mtoto 134 – Formido 61 (Formidable (USA) 125) [1992 6g 7m⁶ 5g⁵] leggy filly: fourth foal: half-sister to 1991 2-y-o 5f winner Medoso (by Never So Bold) and modest 1989 2-y-o 7f winner Tasarly (by Miller's Mate): dam, 7f winner, is granddaughter of 1000 Guineas winner Fleet: modest form in maidens: will be well suited by 1m+: should prove capable of better. *C. E. Brittain* 56 p

NAIF (USA) 2 b.c. (Feb 5) Storm Bird (CAN) 134 – Benguela (USA) 76 (Little Current (USA)) [1992 6m³] $300,000Y: tall colt: has scope: first foal: dam (out of half-sister to Allez France) was placed at 6f here at 2 yrs and later successful twice as 4-y-o in USA, and is a half-sister to Al Manoom, a useful sprinter here and very smart at around 1m in USA: 10/1, 4 lengths third of 14 to Felucca in maiden at Newmarket in October, soon travelling strongly and keeping on well after getting bit outpaced 2f out: constantly on toes beforehand: will stay 1m: will improve, and win races as 3-y-o. *L. M. Cumani* 79 p

NAJARAN (USA) 2 ch.c. (Feb 11) Storm Cat (USA) – Still Waving (USA) (Star Spangled (USA)) [1992 6f⁴ 7g] $135,000Y: big, lengthy colt: first reported foal: dam won 5 races in North America: sire (by Storm Bird) high-class 2-y-o: beaten around 14 lengths in maidens at Newmarket in June and Doncaster (not knocked about) in October: will do better. *M. R. Stoute* 49 p

NAJEB (USA) 3 b.c. Chief's Crown (USA) – Modiste (USA) (Sir Ivor 135) [1991 8m³ 6m* 7m 1992 7g⁵ 10.5g 7g 8.5d 8f 7.9g] smallish colt: looked a fair performer at 2 yrs: showed little at 3 yrs, blinkered penultimate start: bred to stay 1¼m: sold to join P. Evans 1,300 gns Newmarket Autumn Sales. *B. Hanbury* –

NAKORA BISTRAYA (USA) 5 b.m. Robellino (USA) 127 – Calypsa (USA) 83 (The Minstrel (CAN) 135) [1991 8v⁶ 9s⁵ 10.3d 10d² a10g 1992 10.3g] close-coupled mare: has a markedly round action: rated 73 at 4 yrs: bit backward, held up and never a threat in apprentice event at Doncaster in March: stayed 1¼m: went very well with plenty of give in the ground: sold in foal to Prince Sabo 8,400 gns Newmarket December Sales. *G. A. Pritchard-Gordon*

NAKUPITA (IRE) 3 ch.f. Formidable (USA) 125 – Bassita (Bustino 136) [1991 NR 1992 8.2m²] strong, lengthy filly: second foal: dam unraced daughter of La Dolce, dam also of Pebbles: 10/3 and in need of race, very green when 3½ lengths second of 7 to Lap of Luxury in maiden at Nottingham in August, looking well beaten 2f out then staying on strongly: should improve. *A. C. Stewart* 44 p

NANCY (IRE) 2 b.f. (Apr 23) Vision (USA) – Splendidly Gay 80 (Lord Gayle (USA) 124) [1992 5g 6.1m 7g⁴ 7g 8.3s 7d⁵ a7g⁵] IR 1,400Y: smallish, plain filly: third living foal: half-sister to Irish 1½m winner Thatch Island (by Burslem): dam, 10.1f and 1¾m winner, is half-sister to very useful miler Tack On: plating-class maiden: should be better suited by 1m: acts on dead ground. *C. W. C. Elsey* 48

NANNY MARGARET (IRE) 2 b.f. (Apr 30) Prince Rupert (FR) 121 – Ferjima's Gem (USA) (Wajima (USA)) [1992 8m 8.1s⁴ 8d a8g a8g⁴ a8g⁴] IR 2,000F, IR 2,000Y: big, lengthy, good-topped filly: half-sister to champion Venezuelan performer The Iron (by Iron Ruler): dam unraced: modest maiden: should stay 1¼m: blinkered last 3 starts. *P. A. Kelleway* 50

NASEEM ELBARR (USA) 4 ch.c. The Minstrel (CAN) 135 – Doubling Time (USA) 117 (Timeless Moment (USA)) [1991 NR 1992 12.1g⁴ 12m² 13.3g⁵ 14.1m⁵ 14.6d⁴ 16.2d² 17.9d⁴] quite good-topped colt: shows knee action: third reported foal: half-brother to useful miler Timely (by Kings Lake), later successful in North America: dam stayed 1¼m well: consistent handicapper: one paced, stays 2¼m: acts on good to firm and dead ground: takes keen hold. *A. C. Stewart* 70

NASEER (USA) 3 b.g. Hero's Honor (USA) – Sweet Delilah (USA) (Super Concorde (USA) 128) [1991 7m 8.2f 8m 1992 7.6s 10m² 10m* 10f⁶ 12m² 11.6m⁶ 62

14.1m3 12.1m 12g a12g a10g4 a12g] strong, lengthy gelding: inconsistent handicapper: awarded race at Leicester in May: stays 1¾m: acts on good to firm ground: blinkered last 3 starts, running creditably once: has run well for 7-lb claimer. *N. A. Callaghan*

NASHOON (IRE) 3 b.c. Nashamaa 113 – Nistona (Will Somers 114§) [1991 6g5 – § 7f 6m 1992 8m 6g6] leggy colt: has been tubed: probably ungenuine, and looked of little account in 1992: has joined T. Kersey. *Miss L. C. Siddall*

NASHVILLE BLUES (IRE) 3 ch.f. Try My Best (USA) 130 – Requena (Dom **94** Racine (FR) 121) [1991 6g3 7g3 1992 8m2 7g* 7.9m2 7d3 8m2 8m 8m* 8g5] leggy, angular filly: progressive handicapper: first past post at Warwick in May, Ascot (£11,700 1m contest, demoted for interference) in June and Doncaster in September: seemingly best effort when around 3½ lengths fifth to Well Beyond in slowly-run listed race at Ascot: better at 1m than shorter: acts on good to firm and dead ground: tongue tied down last 2 starts. *J. W. Hills*

NASSEER 3 br.g. Top Ville 129 – Ibtihaj (USA) 97 (Raja Baba (USA)) [1991 8s – 1992 7g 8d] small, sturdy gelding: no worthwhile form at Newmarket in April for A. Stewart (sold 4,200 gns Newmarket July Sales) and Goodwood in September: resold 1,350 gns Newmarket Autumn Sales. *P. Mitchell*

NASSMA (IRE) 2 b.f. (Feb 25) Sadler's Wells (USA) 132 – Pretoria 100 (Habitat **61** p 134) [1992 7g4] smallish filly, rather unfurnished: first foal: dam 7f (at 2 yrs) and 1¼m winner: 16/1, around 6 lengths fourth of 13 to Dahyah in maiden at Doncaster in October, green and niggled along at halfway then keeping on well: sure to improve. *J. R. Fanshawe*

NATASHA NORTH 2 ch.f. (Apr 5) Northern State (USA) 91 – Pilley Green 100 **36** (Porto Bello 118) [1992 7g 7g 6s] 3,000Y: good-quartered filly: half-sister to 3-y-o Jade Green (by Midyan) and several winners, including 7.2f and 1m winner Bold Pillager (by Formidable): dam best at 6f: poor maiden. *T. Casey*

NATCHEZ TRACE 3 b.f. Commanche Run 133 – Lighted Lamp (USA) (Sir – Gaylord) [1991 NR 1992 10g4] leggy, unfurnished filly: half-sister to numerous winners, including smart French 7f to 1½m performer Lighted Glory (by Nijinsky) and smart middle-distance stayer Torus (by Ribero): dam half-sister to Crocket: 11/1 and backward, well-beaten last of 4 to Anne Bonny in minor event at Sandown in September: stud. *J. L. Dunlop*

NATIONAL EMBLEM (FR) 3 b.c. Sadler's Wells (USA) 132 – Kaliopa (FR) **60** (Zeddaan 130) [1991 10m* 1992 10d 10g3 11.6g4 12.1m5 11.7s] workmanlike colt: shows high knee action: modest handicapper: 4 months off, well beaten at Bath final start: probably stays 1½m: sold 3,400 gns Newmarket Autumn Sales: not one to trust. *P. F. I. Cole*

NATIVE CHIEFTAN 3 b.c. Trojan Fen 118 – Habituee (Habitat 134) [1991 5m **84** d 6g 7m 7m2 7g* 7d 1992 7d 7g4 7g a8g4 a10g a8g5] close-coupled colt: fairly useful performer on his day: not seen out until October and still bit backward, best effort when fourth in apprentice handicap at Doncaster: failed to fulfil that promise: should stay 1m: possibly unsuited by a soft surface. *R. Hannon*

NATIVE CROWN (IRE) 4 b.g. Be My Native (USA) 122 – Crystal Halo 78 (St **65** d Chad 120) [1991 9m6 1992 12.1g5 11.1m4 17.5d 16.1g 12.1s] leggy, rather sparely-made gelding: moderate mover: worthwhile form on flat only on reappearance: trained until after second start by Miss L. Perratt: blinkered final outing: won handicap hurdle in November. *Mrs S. C. Bradburne*

NATIVE IDOL (USA) 3 b.c. Diesis 133 – Rose Goddess (Sassafras (FR) 135) **76** [1991 NR 1992 a7g* a7g6 8d 7g* 7f] smallish, close-coupled colt: moderate mover: fifth foal: half-brother to 2 juvenile winners, notably smart 1986 6f to 1m winner Sanam (by Golden Act), and to 5-y-o 1m to 9.2f winner Avishayes (by Al Nasr): dam unraced daughter of half-sister to Caro: fair performer: won maiden at Southwell in February and apprentice handicap at Newmarket: hampered halfway and run best ignored final start, later in June: should stay 1m: below form on dead ground. *J. R. Fanshawe*

NATIVE LASS (IRE) 3 ch.f. Be My Native (USA) 122 – Fun Frolic (Sexton – Blake 126) [1991 5g 5m5 6g 5m 1992 a6g 10.1s] workmanlike filly: has a markedly round action: seems of little account. *J. Balding*

NATIVE MAGIC 6 ch.m. Be My Native (USA) 122 – Tuyenu 77 (Welsh Pageant **69** 132) [1991 12d6 13.9g4 14.6m 14s 15.8g* 13.6d4 14g 1992 a12g a14g 14.1g2 a– 14.1f4 17.9d] sparely-made, angular mare: fair handicapper: best efforts in 1992 when in frame: stays 2m: yet to show her best form on a soft surface, acts on any other: effective blinkered or not: none too consistent. *R. W. Armstrong*

NATIVE TRIO (USA)   2 b.c. (Jan 28) Our Native (USA) – Ransomed Captive   **65**
(USA) (Mr Leader (USA)) [1992 7.5m⁵ 7g⁵ 7d] $52,000Y: medium-sized, quite
attractive colt, rather unfurnished: first foal: dam won at up to 9f, including in
Grade 2 8.5f event: sire won from 5.5f to 9f: fair maiden: will stay beyond 1m. *P. W.
Harris*

NATIVE WORTH   2 b.g. (Apr 5) Uncle Pokey 116 – Jenavia (Krayyan 117) [1992   **34**
5g 8m 7.5m 7g] 2,000Y: good-topped gelding: first foal: dam of little account: poor
form, well beaten, in varied events: went freely to post, then unseated rider stalls,
before second start. *J. M. Jefferson*

NATRAL EXCHANGE (IRE)   3 b.c. Natroun (FR) 128 – Aladja (Mill Reef   **55**
(USA) 141) [1991 7f 7g⁶ 10m³ 1992 12.2d³ 11.7d 13.8g² 18.2m³ 15.8m² 15g] smallish,
lengthy colt: has a round action: modest maiden: stays 2¼m: acts on good to firm
ground: blinkered (below best, hung persistently) third 3-y-o start: visored
afterwards, including when successful 3 times over hurdles in September: sold
3,000 gns Newmarket Autumn Sales. *J. W. Hills*

NAUGHTY CHARLOTTE   2 ch.f. (Mar 12) Farajullah 113 – Miss Sanur   **35**
(Mummy's Pet 125) [1992 5.3f⁴ 5.2g 5g 7m] light-framed filly: first foal: dam unraced: poor form in sellers and maidens. *A. P. Jarvis*

NAVARESQUE   7 b.m. Raga Navarro (ITY) 119 – Esquinade 84 (Silly Season   **42**
127) [1991 7g 7.1d 7.1g⁵ 8g* 8.1g⁶ 8.3g 7g 6.9f* 7f 8g 6g⁶ 6.9f² 7g 1992 7.1m⁶ 8f⁶
7.1f⁵ 7d⁵ 8f² 6.9m⁵ 7d] leggy, angular mare: has a round action: poor handicapper:
effective from 7f to 9f: acts on firm and dead going. *R. J. Hodges*

NAWAAYA (USA)   2 b.f. (Jan 27) Fappiano (USA) – Skeeb (USA) 94 (Topsider
(USA)) [1992 6d] lengthy filly: third foal: closely related to 5f and 6f winner La
Masaas (by Miswaki): dam, 2-y-o 6f winner, is sister to million-dollar earner North
Sider: 14/1, very slowly away and always behind in maiden at Newmarket in
October: showed a moderate action. *A. A. Scott*

NAWWAR   8 ch.h. Thatching 131 – Priceless Pin (Saint Crespin III 132) [1991 6s⁴   **54**
7m 6g 6g⁴ 7m³ 7g⁴ 1992 6d 7m⁶ 7g⁶ 7.1s 8d⁵] strong, close-coupled horse: modest
handicapper: last win came 25 starts ago, at 5 yrs: effective from 6f to 1m: acts on
good to firm and dead going: often gets behind. *C. J. Benstead*

NAZARE BLUE   5 b.g. Absalom 128 – Top Stream 87 (Highland Melody 112)   **39**
[1991 7.6g 6g 7.1g 5m⁵ 6.1s³ 6m* 6g 6g³ 6.1m⁵ 1992 a7g a8g 7g⁴ 6f 6d⁶ 8.1m 7f⁵ 6.1g
7g 11.8g] big, rather angular gelding: poor handicapper: has won one of 36 starts:
stays 7f: acts on any going: has run creditably when visored. *Mrs Barbara Waring*

NBAAT (USA)   3 ch.c. El Gran Senor (USA) 136 – Antartica (FR) 124 (Arctic   **65**
Tern (USA) 126) [1991 NR 1992 7m⁴ 6m³ 6m³ 7m⁵ 6m⁴ 6d² 7.1s] neat colt: has a
round action: first foal: dam French miler: fair maiden: will stay 1m: acts on good to
firm and dead ground, tailed off on soft. *C. J. Benstead*

NECTAR COLLECTOR   3 b.c. Natroun (FR) 128 – Mirkan Honey 83 (Bally-   **62 d**
more 123) [1991 6f⁴ 8m² 1992 8g 9g⁵ 10f² 10m a12g⁶ 10s 9.7m] close-coupled colt:
has a round action: no worthwhile form, including in blinkers final start, after
finishing second in handicap at Lingfield in May: should be suited by further than
1¼m: acts on firm going: sold 2,600 gns Newmarket Autumn Sales. *C. F. Wall*

NEDAARAH   2 b.f. (Mar 27) Reference Point 139 – Shining Eyes (USA) (Mr   **43**
Prospector (USA)) [1992 7m 8g] workmanlike filly: moderate mover: first foal: dam
unraced daughter of high-class French miler Phydilla, a half-sister to Observation
Post: poor form in maidens at Newmarket (badly hampered 2f out, eased) in July and
Leicester in September: sold to join C. C. Elsey 1,500 gns Doncaster November
Sales. *A. A. Scott*

NED'S BONANZA   3 b.g. Green Ruby (USA) 104 – Miss Display 47 (Touch   **69**
Paper 113) [1991 5d² 5m² 5m* 5m⁴ 5f² 5g³ 5m³ 6g 1992 5g⁵ 5g³ 5m³ 5m⁴ 5m* 5d
5m 5g 5m 5m 5m] workmanlike, quite good-topped gelding: fair handicapper:
trained until after reappearance by R. Whitaker: consistent early in season: wandered under pressure when winning at Doncaster in June: no worthwhile form, stiffish
tasks, afterwards: may well prove best at 5f: acts on good to firm ground: has run
well when sweating and edgy: has been gelded. *M. Dods*

NEEDLE GUN (IRE)   2 b. or br.c. (Mar 6) Sure Blade (USA) 130 – Lucayan   **99 p**
Princess 111 (High Line 125) [1992 6m² 7m² 8m 8s⁴] looking really well colt: looks
weak: third foal: half-brother to 4-y-o 1m winner Celia Brady (by Last Tycoon): dam
2-y-o 7f winner stayed 1½m: looking really well on first run since mid-June, 1½
lengths second of 9 to Petardia in Champagne Stakes at Doncaster, staying on from
rear: gave trouble in paddock before showing similar form when fourth of 10 to

Saeed Manana's "Needle Gun"

Desert Secret in Royal Lodge Stakes at Ascot later in September, drifting right and one pace final 2f: will be better suited by 1¼m: likely to do better. *C. E. Brittain*

NEEDWOOD MUPPET 5 b.g. Rolfe (USA) 77 – Sea Dart 55 (Air Trooper 115) **58** [1991 12g 12m² 1992 16.1s* 14.6g³ 16.9g⁴ 14.6s³ 16.2d 16s³] angular gelding: consistent handicapper: won at Newcastle in March: suited by a thorough test of stamina: acts on soft ground. *B. C. Morgan*

NEEDWOOD NUGGET 2 ch.c. (Apr 12) Rolfe (USA) 77 – Needwood Nut 70 – (Royben 125) [1992 6g] close-coupled colt: first foal: dam 6f winner: 33/1 and backward, showed nothing in 11-runner maiden at Doncaster in November. *B. C. Morgan*

NEEDWOOD POPPY 4 b.f. Rolfe (USA) 77 – Needwood Nap (Some Hand 119) **29** [1991 10.5d 10m 11.1s 1992 11.1v³ 13d 12.4s 12.3s 12.1v] compact filly: has a quick action: form in handicaps only on reappearance: stays 11f: acts on heavy ground. *B. C. Morgan*

NEGATIVE PLEDGE (USA) 3 b.f. Alleged (USA) 138 – Laredo Lass (USA) – (Bold Ruler) [1991 NR 1992 8f⁵ a12g⁵] rather unfurnished filly: seventh reported living foal: half-sister to several winners, notably Grade 1 8.5f La Canada Stakes winner Mitterand (by Hold Your Peace): dam winning sprinter in North America: little promise in maidens at Pontefract and Southwell (bandaged behind) in mid-summer. *J. H. M. Gosden*

NEGATORY (USA) 5 ch.g. Secreto (USA) 128 – Negation (USA) (Mongo) [1991 – a14g a8g⁵ 15.9g⁵ 11m 12m* 17.1m 16.5m⁶ 10.3d a14g 1992 a14g] big, workmanlike gelding: carries condition: bad mover: rated 66 at 4 yrs solely on strength of win at

Pontefract: had won 2 novice hurdles prior to finishing well beaten at Southwell in January: stays 1½m: acts on good to firm ground. *M. C. Chapman*

NEIEB (USA) 3 b.f. Alleged (USA) 138 – Victoria Star (CAN) (Northern Dancer **64** (CAN)) [1991 8g⁵ 8.1d⁵ 1992 11.5d³ 12.4m³ 12g 9.9m 14.6s² 14.1g* 12.1v⁵] leggy, good-topped filly: has a quick action: half-sister to numerous winners, including fairly useful 1988 2-y-o 5f and 6f winner Stellaria (by Roberto): dam minor 2-y-o winner out of Canadian Oaks winner Solometeor: modest performer: narrowly won maiden at Nottingham in October: will be better suited by 2m: acts on good to firm and soft ground. *B. Hanbury*

NEITHER NOR 3 ch.f. Norwick (USA) 120 – Leap In Time (Dance In Time **63** (CAN)) [1991 5.7f⁶ 6d² 6f⁶ 1992 6s³ 7g³ 6m⁶ 6.1s* 7.6s 7.1s] quite good-topped filly: has knee action: fair form: won maiden at Chepstow in September: ran poorly, facing stiff tasks, in handicaps following month, refusing to settle when blinkered final start: should stay 7f: best efforts on a soft surface. *R. J. Holder*

NELLIE DEAN 3 ch.f. Song 132 – Pubby 73 (Doctor Wall 107) [1991 5m² 5s⁴ **53** 5m³ 1992 a7g² a7g² 7m 5g a7g 7d* a8g² a7g] close-coupled, sparely-made filly: modest form: gamely made all in maiden at Catterick in October: stays 1m: yet to race on firm ground, probably acts on any other, including fibresand: effective blinkered or not: changed hands 1,600 gns Newmarket Autumn Sales. *J. A. R. Toller*

NELLIE HEN 2 b.f. (May 6) Vaigly Great 127 – Janlarmar 69 (Habat 127) [1992 **–** 7s 6d] 1,400F, 2,000Y: leggy, useful-looking filly: sister to 5f (at 2 yrs) and 1m winner Great Service and 6f seller winner Crimpsall: dam 6f seller winner: last in maidens at Ayr and Haydock in the autumn. *A. Bailey*

NELLIE'S GAMBLE 2 b.f. (Feb 28) Mummy's Game 120 – Harmonious Sound **57** (Auction Ring (USA) 123) [1992 5g⁵ 5g 5m 6.1g⁴ a6g⁶ 5f⁶ 7d* 8g 8.3v⁴] 2,600Y: leggy, close-coupled filly: sister to plating-class sprint maiden Powerful Pierre and half-sister to 6-y-o 1½m to 2m winner Puff Puff (by All Systems Go) and 3-y-o Mykindofmusic (by Petong), 5f winner at 2 yrs: dam unraced: modest form: won 30-runner seller at Redcar (no bid) in October, staying on strongly: excellent fourth, apprentice ridden, in nursery at Hamilton following month: better suited by 1m than shorter: well suited by a soft surface: well held when blinkered twice. *A. P. Stringer*

NELTEGRITY 3 b.g. Neltino 97 – Integrity 108 (Reform 132) [1991 6f 7m 8.1g **61** 10.5d⁵ 7.6d² 7m 7d 1992 10v 9.2m* 10.5g 10.3m⁴ 8m² 8.2d² 10g⁴ 10.5d] close-coupled, quite good-topped gelding: moderate mover: modest performer: won claimer at Hamilton in May: ran well in a visor all 3 outings in July, below form when facing stiff task in Haydock claimer 2 months later: stays 10.5f: acts on good to firm and dead ground: mostly claimer ridden: won novice hurdle in November. *T. H. Caldwell*

NEMEA (USA) 2 b.f. (Apr 4) The Minstrel (CAN) 135 – Donna Inez (USA) **97** (Herbager 136) [1992 6f⁴ 7m² 8m 8s] $100,000Y: close-coupled, quite attractive filly, rather leggy: good walker: half-sister to several winners, including Irish 3-y-o 1m (at 2 yrs) and 1½m winner Bryan Station and useful Irish 4-y-o stayer Muir Station (both by Darby Creek Road) and useful 1m (at 2 yrs) and 1¼m winner Topsider Man (by Riverman): dam, half-sister to Ferdinand, won 4 races at up to 9f: showed considerable improvement when 7 lengths seventh of 11, never dangerous, in Prix Marcel Boussac at Longchamp in October on dirt start: strong-finishing second at Chester 2 months previously: will be well suited by 1¼m + : evidently acts well on soft ground. *J. R. Fanshawe*

NEMIR 3 b.c. Rainbow Quest (USA) 134 – Orange Hill 75 (High Top 131) [1991 NR **77** 1992 14s⁴ 14.1m² 14.1d² 14.1g³] angular colt: second foal: dam won Cesarewitch: fair maiden: found little when below form at Nottingham final start: should be suited by test of stamina: acts on good to firm and dead ground: wears bandages. *J. H. M. Gosden*

NEO-CLASSICAL 3 b.f. Primo Dominie 121 – Musical Sally (USA) (The **–** Minstrel (CAN) 135) [1991 6d³ 6g² 6m² 7g* 1992 7m] rangy, unfurnished filly: rated 72 at 2 yrs: off course 10 months, led 5f when last of 15 in handicap at Newmarket in April: better form at 7f than 6f. *B. W. Hills*

NEOLOGIST 6 b. or br.g. Bold Owl 101 – Neophyte II (Never Say Die 137) [1991 **–** NR 1992 14s⁶] angular, plain gelding: brother to poor 1½m winning plater Moreirwen and half-brother to winners over jumps: dam never ran: 66/1, bit backward and very green, soon tailed off in 6-runner minor event at Salisbury in April. *J. O'Donoghue*

NEPTUNE'S PET 4 b.c. Tina's Pet 121 – Abalone (Abwah 118) [1991 8g 7m **85** 7.1g⁴ 8m³ 9.7m* 9m⁴ 10g³ 9g 9m 8s 9m⁵ 7.1m 10m² 8.9m* 8f* 9m* 10f² 8.5d

8.1g* 8g 8m] tall, workmanlike colt: has a long stride: fairly useful handicapper: had a very good season, winning at Wolverhampton, Bath and Goodwood (£7,600 event) in the summer and at Sandown in September: effective from 1m to 1¼m: acts on firm ground, seems unsuited by soft surface: was out of form when tried blinkered once: genuine. *G. Lewis*

NEROLI   4 b.f. Nishapour (FR) 125 – Norska 67 (Northfields (USA)) [1991 9g 8f   – §
7.1s³ 7f³ 7.1m⁶ 10f 7.6g⁵ 8m 1992 a8g a6g 10d 7g] lengthy, angular filly: rated 78 at 3
yrs for R. Hannon: no form in 1992. *A. P. Jones*

NESSUN DORMA   2 b.c. (Jun 7) Night Shift (USA) – Scala di Seta 85 (Shantung   73
132) [1992 7d⁴ 7m⁴ 7s²] quite good-topped colt: has scope: has a moderate action:
half-brother to several winners, including high-class Italian 5f to 1½m winner Stone
(by Moulton) and fair stayer Rothko (by Ile de Bourbon): dam 1½m winner: fair
maiden: odds on in maiden at Warwick final start, setting slow pace: will be well
suited by further. *G. Wragg*

NEST   3 ch.f. Sharpo 132 – Sanctuary (Welsh Pageant 132) [1991 6f 5m⁶ 1992 6d   65
6d⁵ a8g 6g² 7.1s² 8g² 8s² 9g] angular filly: fair maiden: best efforts when second in
1m handicaps at Newbury (ladies) and Goodwood: well worth a try at 1¼m: acts on
soft ground. *Lord Huntingdon*

NEVADA MIX   8 gr.h. Alias Smith (USA) – Northern Empress 80 (Northfields   42
(USA)) [1991 6g 6m a7g 7m 6.1d 6g 6f* 6f 6m² 8d 6g 1992 7.1g⁶ 5.9d 6f 6f⁶ 5f² 6m⁶
5.9h⁴ 6g] strong, stocky horse: poor mover: inconsistent handicapper: effective at
up to 7f: acts on any going: below form in blinkers earlier in career: sold 860 gns
Doncaster November Sales. *Miss L. A. Perratt*

NEVER A CARE (USA)   3 b.f. Roberto (USA) 131 – Imperturbable Lady (CAN)   86
(Northern Dancer (CAN)) [1991 7.1d* 1992 8d² 10m⁴ 10g³] rangy filly: fairly useful
performer: in frame in £9,700 contest at Ascot and Lupe Stakes at Goodwood in the
spring, and a minor event at Salisbury in August: stayed 1¼m: acted on good to firm
and dead ground: to stud. *B. W. Hills*

NEVER IN THE RED   4 b.g. Wattlefield 117 – Swing Gently 78 (Swing Easy   91
(USA) 126) [1991 5s³ 5m³ 5m 5m² 5g³ 5m³ 1992 5.1m⁴ 5g 5g 5g² 5g² 5m³ 5d 5.1g⁵
5d³ 5d 5s⁴] leggy, lengthy gelding: last win came 21 starts ago at 2 yrs, but is nonetheless a fairly useful handicapper: speedy: acts on any going: best blinkered/
visored. *J. Berry*

NEVER IN TOUCH   2 b.f. (Apr 30) Never So Bold 135 – Yelney 65 (Blakeney   –
126) [1992 5d⁵ 5.1d 5g 5m⁵ a6g 7f] 1,000Y: leggy, lengthy, sparely-made filly: poor
mover: sister to 6f winner Miss Broughton and half-sister to 3 winners, including
6-y-o (from 6f to 1m) Crosby (by Music Boy) and middle-distance stayer Golden
Heights (by Shirley Heights): dam 1½m winner out of Cheshire Oaks winner Yelda:
no worthwhile form: blinkered penultimate start. *M. Brittain*

NEVER LATE   3 b.f. Never So Bold 135 – New Edition 72 (Great Nephew 126)   48
[1991 5d⁴ 5m⁶ 5m³ 5g² 5.1g³ 6m 5f² 5m³ 1992 6g 5m⁶ 8.1f 6g³ 5f⁶] rather leggy filly:
good walker: plating-class maiden: only time visored, best effort of 1992 when third
of 4 in handicap at Catterick in July: best form at 5f: acts on firm going: blinkered
(ran creditably) last 2 starts at 2 yrs: sold 1,000 gns Newmarket September Sales.
M. H. Easterby

NEVER SO BRAVE   2 ch.g. (May 14) Never So Bold 135 – Another Move 69   46
(Farm Walk 111) [1992 8.5m⁶ 8s 8d] 1,100Y: lengthy, rather unfurnished gelding:
sixth foal: half-brother to 5f and 7f winner Ela-Yianni-Mou (by Anfield) and winning
middle-distance stayers by Grey Desire and Nicholas Bill: dam, 1½m winner, is
sister to very useful middle-distance stayer Move Off: poor form in maidens,
including an auction, in the autumn: shapes like a thorough stayer. *Miss S. E. Hall*

NEVER SO LOST   2 ch.c. (Feb 23) Never So Bold 135 – Lost In France 80   66
(Northfields (USA)) [1992 5g⁶ 7m] lengthy, workmanlike colt: has scope: second
foal: half-brother to 3-y-o Let's Get Lost (by Chief Singer): dam (showed ability only
on debut) is half-sister to top-class French and American middle-distance
performer Perrault: easily better effort in Newmarket May maiden on first outing:
off course nearly 3 months afterwards. *B. W. Hills*

NEVER SO SURE   4 br.g. Never So Bold 135 – Amerella (Welsh Pageant 132)   99
[1991 6g* 6g² 6m² 6g⁶ 6d 1992 5g³ 5d² 5.9d² 7.6g 5m⁶ 7m⁶ a6g* 6.1d* 6g³ 7m 6d³
6g* 5.6m 6d 5s² 6d] workmanlike gelding: moderate mover: progressed into a
useful handicapper in 1992: claimed out of Mrs J. Ramsden's stable £10,800 third
start: won at Lingfield and Chester in midsummer, and at York (£15,600 event, from
Bertie Wooster) in September: best at 6f: acts on good to firm and soft ground, and
on equitrack: visored last 5 starts, blinkered previous 4: has won for 7-lb claimer:

usually held up: tough and consistent: retained 12,000 gns Doncaster September Sales then sold to Scandinavia for 26,000 gns Doncaster November Sales. *A. Bailey*

NEVISKIA (USA) 3 ch.f. Arctic Tern (USA) 126 – Water Dance (USA) 85 – (Nijinsky (CAN) 138) [1991 NR 1992 10f] $72,000Y: leggy, sparely-made filly: sixth reported foal: half-sister to winners in North America by Mr Prospector and Sensitive Prince: dam 1m winner here later successful 15 times in USA, is half-sister to Little Current and the dam of Nabeel Dancer: 50/1, never dangerous after slow start in maiden at Newbury in May. *C. F. Wall*

NEWARK ANTIQUEFAIR 4 b.g. Rolfe (USA) 77 – Sea Dart 55 (Air Trooper – 115) [1991 12g 13.8m³ 11.8m⁶ 15.1s 1992 12.1s 13.8m 16.2g⁶ 14.1m 15.8m⁵ 16.2d 17.5d] small, angular gelding: inconsistent handicapper: stays 2m: acts on good to firm ground. *B. C. Morgan*

NEW BEGINNING 9 b. or br.h. Persian Bold 123 – Bumble-Bee (High Line – 125) [1991 12.1d 5g 6f 6m 6f 8.3f⁵ 8m 12.1s 8.1s 1992 12.1m 8.1f⁶ 7.1d 7g 8.1d] leggy, lengthy horse: of little account nowadays. *J. S. Haldane*

NEWBURY COAT 2 b.g. (Mar 16) Chilibang 120 – Deanta In Eirinn (Red Sunset 66 120) [1992 6g 6g⁶ 5d² 5m⁵] smallish, sturdy gelding: first foal: dam ran once: fair maiden: easily best efforts at 5f but shapes as if will prove at least as effective at 6f. *M. McCormack*

NEW CAPRICORN (USA) 2 ch.c. (Feb 11) Green Forest (USA) 134 – Size Six 86 ? (USA) (Caerleon (USA) 132) [1992 6m* 6m 7d* 7.3s] $57,000Y: sturdy, quite attractive colt: second reported foal: dam unraced daughter of Bitty Girl: fair performer: awarded 11-runner minor event at Kempton in May: narrowly won 4-runner similar event at York in July, rallying in very game fashion: off course over 3 months and bit backward, well beaten in Horris Hill Stakes at Newbury: will probably stay 1m. *M. A. Jarvis*

NEWGATESKY 2 ch.f. (Mar 10) Domynsky 110 – Streets Ahead 67 (Ovid 95) – [1992 5m 6f 7g 6m 8.3s] close-coupled, sparely-made filly: half-sister to 7f winner Bills Ahead, middle-distance stayer Running Money and a winner abroad (all by Billion): dam won from 6f to 1½m: no worthwile form in varied events, including sellers: blinkered penultimate start. *B. W. Murray*

NEW HALEN 11 br.g. Dikusa 94 – Miss Pear (Breakspear II) [1991 NR 1992 – 12.1g⁶] rather leggy, close-coupled gelding: twice raced on flat: last in apprentice event at Chepstow in July: fairly useful chaser, finished lame in August. *A. P. James*

NEWINGTON BUTTS (IRE) 2 br.f. (Mar 14) Dowsing (USA) 124 – Cloud 59 Nine 97 (Skymaster 126) [1992 5.3m 6g⁴ 6d⁶ 7d 6v] 15,000Y: small, close-coupled filly: half-sister to 3 winners, including useful 7f/1m performer Sky Cloud (by Formidable): dam won from 5f to 1¼m: modest maiden: best effort (for claimer) on third start: should stay at least 7f. *R. Akehurst*

NEWINSKY 2 b.c. (Mar 3) King of Spain 121 – Gentle Stream 55 (Sandy Creek 48 123) [1992 5f 6g⁴ 7m 6g 6m] 1,300F, 4,300Y, 5,400 2-y-o: smallish, leggy colt: fourth foal: half-brother to a minor winner abroad: dam Irish 11.2f and 1½m winner: plating-class maiden: well beaten last 3 starts (visored first 2 occasions), including in a seller: stays 6f. *C. Tinkler*

NEW KID IN TOWN 2 br.g. (Mar 22) Sayf El Arab (USA) 127 – Davill 83 40 (Record Token 128) [1992 7g 6m 6s⁵ 7d] IR 1,700F, 6,400Y: compact gelding: first reported foal: dam sprinter: poor maiden: should stay 7f: visored (soundly beaten) in seller final start: sold 1,200 gns Newmarket Autumn Sales. *N. Tinkler*

NEW MEXICO 8 br.g. Free State 125 – Trigamy 112 (Tribal Chief 125) [1991 NR – 1992 10d 10g] sturdy gelding: carries plenty of condition: moderate mover: rated 86 at 6 yrs when severed tendon after line on final start: never a threat in large fields at Nottingham in April. *D. Morley*

NEW QUEST 2 b.g. (Apr 23) Elegant Air 119 – Sharp Jose (USA) (Sharpen Up 71 127) [1992 7d⁵ 7s⁴] 21,000Y: leggy gelding: fourth foal: half-brother to 3-y-o Sharp Dance (by Dance of Life) and 4-y-o 9f winner Sharp Dream (by Dominion): dam won at up to 9f in USA: bandaged behind, better effort when fourth of 10 in maiden at Warwick in October: will stay 1m +: sold 3,900 gns Newmarket Autumn Sales. *P. F. I. Cole*

NEW RHYTHM 2 b.g. (Mar 23) Presidium 124 – Serranilla 64 (Tap On Wood – 130) [1992 5g 6g] 1,500Y: close-coupled gelding: first foal: dam maiden stayed 9f: no form in maidens at Windsor (auction) in August and Doncaster in November. *G. H. Eden*

NEWTON POINT   3 b.g. Blakeney 126 – Assertive (USA) (Assert 134) [1991   **75**
a7g⁵ 7m⁶ 8.2f 1992 12.3s 12m⁴ 12g³ 13.9f* 13.6f³ 16.4g* 14d³ 16d⁵ 14.8g] workmanlike, good-bodied gelding: fair performer: won maiden at York and handicap at
Folkestone in midsummer: rare modest effort final start: effective at 1¾m/2m: acts
on firm and dead ground: effective whether blinkered or not: consistent: won over
hurdles at Cheltenham in October. *G. A. Pritchard-Gordon*

NEWTON'S LAW (IRE)   2 b. or br.c. (Jan 12) Law Society (USA) 130 – Cato-   **98**
petl (USA) (Northern Dancer (CAN)) [1992 7g⁴ 7d² 7m 7s* 8d⁶] 43,000F: good-
topped colt: fifth foal: brother to Irish middle-distance winner Dliadore: dam
unraced sister to Secreto: useful performer: easy pillar-to-post winner of maiden at
Salisbury in September: ran well when second to Fatherland in Futurity Stakes
at the Curragh and when sixth to impressive Armiger in Racing Post Trophy at
Doncaster: will stay beyond 1m: acts on soft ground, well beaten on good to firm. *P.
W. Chapple-Hyam*

NEW YEARS EVE   3 b.g. Ballacashtal (CAN) – Almadena 73 (Dairialatan 111)   **–**
[1991 NR 1992 10m] 2,500 (privately) Y: leggy gelding: half-brother to 3 winners,
including useful 1½m winner Kalmadene (by Kalaglow) and very useful 6f and 7f
winner Scarrowmanwick (by Tickled Pink): dam placed on debut at 2 yrs: 10/1 and
burly, always behind in 10-runner claimer at Nottingham in June, not knocked about:
sold 1,200 gns Newmarket Autumn Sales. *P. J. Makin*

NIANI (IRE)   4 ch.f. Niniski (USA) 125 – Royal Nugget (USA) 104 (Mr Pros-   **–**
pector (USA)) [1991 10g⁴ 12m* 10m² 1992 12g 11.9g 13.3g] lengthy filly: rated 92 in
summer at 3 yrs: no form in handicaps in 1992: visits Never So Bold. *J. L. Dunlop*

NIBBS POINT (IRE)   4 ch.f. Sure Blade (USA) 130 – Fanny's Cove 89 (Mill   **98**
Reef (USA) 141) [1991 10m² 10m* 11.9g* 14.6m² 12s² 12d⁶ 1992 13.9m 15.9g⁴
14.6m] smallish, lengthy, sparely-made filly: often unimpressive in appearance:
useful performer: off course 3 months, returned to form when fourth to Further
Flight in listed race at York in August: well beaten in Park Hill Stakes at Doncaster
following month: effective from 1½m to 2m: acted on good to firm and soft ground:
to stud. *L. M. Cumani*

NICEA (IRE)   2 b. or br.f. (Mar 2) Dominion 123 – Nishila (USA) 90 (Green   **90** p
Dancer (USA) 132) [1992 7d*] first foal: dam 1m winner, is daughter of smart 5f to
1m winner Nasseem: weak in market, won 17-runner maiden at the Curragh in
October by 2½ lengths: promising. *J. Oxx, Ireland*

NICELY THANKS (USA)   3 b.c. Great Charmer (USA) – Laque de Chine   **66**
(USA) (Lord Avie (USA)) [1991 5g² 6m 6m 8m 8m* 8m² 1992 7.5g² 9s⁵ 8d⁶
8.5m⁴ 8m 9.9g² 9.9m⁶ 10.1f³ 10g 10.1m³ 11.8g⁵ 13.8g 10s² 9d] strong, good-
quartered gelding: carries condition: modest handicapper: stays 11.8f: acts on any
going: has run well for 7-lb claimer: usually set a lot to do: sold 5,800 gns Newmarket Autumn Sales. *T. D. Barron*

NICE PICTURE (IRE)   4 b.c. Kings Lake (USA) 133 – Nana Mana Mou (Ela-   **–**
Mana-Mou 132) [1991 a10g a10g 12m 1992 12f 18.8m] sturdy, dipped-backed colt:
poor mover: still a maiden, and well beaten in handicaps in the summer. *R.
Champion*

NICER (IRE)   2 gr.f. (Mar 19) Pennine Walk 120 – Everything Nice 107   **84**
(Sovereign Path 125) [1992 7m⁵ 7g² 7s⁵ 6d* 7.3s⁴] 10,500F, 27,000Y: leggy filly:
half-sister to 3-y-o 7f winner Be My Everything (by Be My Guest) and several
winners abroad: dam won from 5f (at 2 yrs) to 10.5f: fairly useful form: won maiden
at Newmarket in October: ran well when fourth of 8 to Criquette in listed event at
Newbury 3 weeks later: will stay 1m: acts on soft ground. *B. W. Hills*

NICHE   2 ch.f. (Apr 5) Risk Me (FR) 127 – Cubby Hole (Town And Country   **100**
124) [1992 5m* 5g* 5f* 6g⁴ 5m³ 6m* 5m⁶]
    Lyric Fantasy's owner Lord Carnarvon was fortunate enough to have a
second two-year-old filly to make her mark in pattern company. Niche wasn't
in the same class as her illustrious stable-companion but she won four of her
seven starts including the Norfolk Stakes and the Lowther Stakes. The leggy,
angular Niche looked out of place in the paddock against a good-looking bunch
of colts at Royal Ascot but she followed up earlier successes at Windsor and
Newmarket with a vastly-improved performance, racing close up all the way
and holding the renewed challenge of the favourite Silver Wizard by a head.
Niche confirmed herself a useful sprinting two-year-old when finishing in the
frame in the Cherry Hinton Stakes and the Molecomb Stakes on her next two
starts, penalised 5 lb in each of those Group 3 events for her Norfolk Stakes

Lowther Stakes, York—Niche is an easy winner from Shamisen;
the favourite Toocando (right) goes lame

victory. She started second favourite in a substandard field for the Lowther Stakes at York where her task was made easier by the favourite Toocando's suffering a knee injury during the race. Niche made all and won by four lengths from Shamisen with Toocando in third. Judged on the style of her victory at York—she was extending her advantage at the line—and on her subsequent below-par effort in the Flying Childers Stakes at Doncaster, Niche was better at six furlongs than five by the end of the season.

		Sharpo	Sharpen Up
	Risk Me (FR)	(ch 1977)	Moiety Bird
	(ch 1984)	Run The Risk	Run The Gantlet
Niche		(b 1976)	Siliciana
(ch.f. Apr 5, 1990)		Town And Country	Town Crier
	Cubby Hole	(b 1974)	First Huntress
	(ch 1984)	Hiding Place	Doutelle
		(ch 1963)	Jojo

Niche's sire Risk Me was a mile- to mile-and-a-quarter performer and her dam the poor maiden Cubby Hole, a half-sister to Gold Cup winner Little Wolf, was placed at two miles. Speed, however, is Niche's strong suit as it is with Cubby Hole's first foal and three-year-old Holetown (by Prince Sabo) who was successful twice at six furlongs as a two-year-old and placed over five and seven in the latest season. A product of her owner's Highclere Stud, Niche was knocked down to her trainer for 7,600 guineas as a yearling at the Newmarket December Sales. Niche's sire Risk Me had made a modest start at stud and Niche had an unfashionable maternal grandsire in Town And Country; but her dam is a half-sister to another very smart stayer in Smuggler and to the Horris Hill winner Disguise among the nine winners bred by the Nell Gwyn winner Hiding Place. Hiding Place is also the grandam of Sheikh Albadou in whose commentary further details of the family can be found. Niche, a fluent mover, acts well on top-of-the-ground and has yet to race on a soft surface. *R. Hannon*

NICHODOULA 2 gr.f. (Mar 5) Doulab (USA) 115 – Nicholas Grey 100 (Track –
Spare 125) [1992 6v] 40,000Y: half-sister to several winners, including high-class middle-distance colt Terimon (by Bustino) and quite useful but unreliable 6f winner Butsova (by Formidable): dam, 2-y-o 5f to 7f winner, second in Oaks d'Italia: 5/1, well-beaten ninth of 11 in Folkestone maiden in October, fading from halfway and eased right up. *Sir Mark Prescott*

NICHOLAS MARK 8 ch.g. Gunner B 126 – Bargain Line 68 (Porto Bello 118) –
[1991 NR 1992 14m 15.8d] close-coupled gelding: poor walker: has a quick action: tough and genuine front-running handicapper (rated 75) as 6-y-o for R. Whitaker: won over hurdles in March before finishing well beaten in handicaps: effective at 1½m and unlikely to stay stiff 2m: best form on a sound surface: has run creditably for lady rider. *J. G. FitzGerald*

NICHOLAS STAR 3 ch.g. Nicholas Bill 125 – Jumra (Thatch (USA) 136) [1991 –
NR 1992 8s 7f 7d] 500Y: small, leggy gelding: second foal: half-brother to 1990 2-y-o

1m seller winner Sharp Glow (by Reach): dam never ran: looks of little account. *R. E. Peacock*

NICK-ELA-NOO (IRE)   3 ch.f. Ela-Mana-Mou 132 – Dewan's Niece (USA)   – (Dewan (USA)) [1991 NR 1992 7g] unfurnished filly: second foal: dam minor winner in USA, is closely related to dam of Emmson: 12/1 and backward, always behind in 15-runner maiden at Kempton in June. *R. Hannon*

NICKI-J (IRE)   2 b. or br.f. (May 4) Jareer (USA) 115 – Velinowski (Malinowski   **64** (USA) 123) [1992 5d 5.1s* 6g* 6m] 3,600Y: close-coupled, useful-looking filly: fourth foal: half-sister to 6f (at 2 yrs) to 10.2f winner Tendresse (by Tender King): dam unraced half-sister to smart Lord Helpus, successful from 5f to 1½m: was progressing really well, winning seller (retained 3,800 gns) at Bath and claimer (staying on strongly) at Leicester in May: gave impression something badly amiss in Lingfield nursery in July: better suited by 6f than 5f. *R. Hannon*

NICKY MYGIRL   2 b.f. (Mar 19) Chief Singer 131 – Aquarula 88 (Dominion 123)   **46** [1992 5s 5g4 5d2 5m3 5g* 5g] 1,050Y: leggy, lightly-made filly: fourth foal: half-sister to winning middle-distance handicapper To Be Fair (by Adonijah): dam 2-y-o 5f and 6f winner, is half-sister to 2 useful or better 2-y-o winners: plating-class form: made virtually all in maiden auction at Haydock in June, keeping on gamely: outpaced throughout when facing stiff task in York nursery following month: will stay 6f: evidently suited by some give in the ground. *M. Brittain*

NICO MIKE   2 ch.c. (Mar 31) Trempolino (USA) 135 – Farewell Letter (USA)   **77** p (Arts And Letters) [1992 6.1g3 7s2 6.9v*] 10,500Y: unfurnished colt: half-brother to several winners, notably useful stayer Parting Moment (by The Minstrel): dam very smart over middle distances: progressive form: won maiden at Folkestone in October, travelling well most of way then staying on well to lead near line: likely to be well suited by middle distances: yet to race on top-of-the-ground: reportedly sold privately to join M. Jarvis: likely to improve again. *P. W. Chapple-Hyam*

NIDOMI   5 ch.g. Dominion 123 – Nicholas Grey 100 (Track Spare 125) [1991 12f   – 1992 12g] leggy, good-topped gelding: moderate mover: generally competes as a hurdler these days and well beaten on flat since 3 yrs: should stay middle distances. *G. P. Enright*

NIFTY FIFTY (IRE)   3 b.f. Runnett 125 – Swift Verdict 89 (My Swallow 134)   **81** [1991 5g2 5g* 5s5 5m* 5f* 5g4 6m2 6f5 1992 5m 5m 5m 5.6m 7g2 7d] leggy, quite good-topped filly: not nearly so effective as at 2 yrs, worthwhile form only when second in a handicap at Redcar: stays 7f, at least when conditions aren't testing: easily best form (at 2 yrs) on top-of-the-ground: tongue tied down fourth 3-y-o start: has run well when sweating. *J. Berry*

NIGALS FRIEND   3 ch.g. Sharpo 132 – No Cards 109 (No Mercy 126) [1991   **58** 6.1g5 5.7m2 6m3 6g 5d6 5.7g6 1992 5s2 5g 7d 6.1m 5d a6g] tall, leggy gelding: moderate mover: modest maiden: no worthwhile form, including in a visor, after reappearance: stays 6f: acts on good to firm and soft ground. *D. Haydn Jones*

NIGELSCHINAPALACE   3 b.g. Comrade In Arms 123 – Ergo 82 (Song 132)   **39** [1991 NR 1992 10.3g 8s3 8.9v] 1,500Y, 2,200 2-y-o: leggy gelding: half-brother to several winners here and abroad, including useful Irish 2-y-o Up And At 'Em (by Forzando): dam 5f winner at 2 yrs: form in the spring only when third in seller at Wolverhampton: may prove best short of 1m: blinkered last 2 starts. *Miss S. J. Wilton*

NIGELS LADY   3 ch.f. Ra Nova 83 – Curzon House 73 (Green God 128) [1991 NR   – 1992 a7g] fourth reported foal: dam sprint plater: 33/1, slowly away and always behind in claimer at Lingfield in October. *M. C. Pipe*

NIGELS PROSPECT   2 b.c. (May 12) Allen's Prospect (USA) – Shortning   **48** Bread 83 (Blakeney 126) [1992 5g 5m5 6.1d a6g a8g6] 3,800Y: leggy colt: first foal: dam stayer: looks just a plater: stays 1m. *D. Haydn Jones*

NIGHT ASSET   3 b.g. Night Shift (USA) – Fine Asset (Hot Spark 126) [1991 5g5   **60** 5g4 6g 5g6 5m 5.7g5 6g* 1992 6d 6g2 5.7m3 7g6 6d2 6.1m3 6.1m 6s] strong, sprint type: carries condition: moderate mover: modest handicapper: off course 3 months and behind last 2 starts: stays 6f: acts on good to firm and dead ground: wears blinkers. *G. Lewis*

NIGHT CLUBBING (IRE)   3 b.c. Dance of Life (USA) – Tigeen (Habitat 134)   **79** [1991 6m6 7g4 7d2 6d* 7g4 6m4 6g4 6g4 8d5 1992 6d3 6g 6g 5s 6s 8g a10g5] IR 5,800Y: half-brother to several winners, including useful sprinter Alkaaseh and 7f and 1¼m winner Mardood (both by Ela-Mana-Mou): dam, won twice over 5f in Ireland, is sister to Bitty Girl and Hot Spark: ex-Irish colt: fair form for N. Meade, running best race on reappearance: shaped quite promisingly in Lingfield handicap on first run for new trainer, final start: should stay 1¼m: acts on good to firm and dead ground: has been blinkered. *R. Akehurst*

NIGHT CLUB (GER) 8 ch.g. Esclavo (FR) – Nightlife (GER) (Priamos (GER) **33** 123) [1991 a7g 7.5f⁴ 1992 8.5s⁶ a8g⁵] tall gelding: poor maiden: stays 8.5f: acts on any ground: has run creditably when blinkered. *J. P. Smith*

NIGHT EDITION 2 b.c. (Jun 14) Night Shift (USA) – New Chant (CAN) (New **48** p Providence) [1992 7m 7g 7g 6.9v] robust colt: good mover: half-brother to several winners here and abroad, including modest 14.5f winner Sierra Star (by Mill Reef): dam 2-y-o 6f winner, is half-sister to Canadian colt Giboulee: poor form, well beaten, in maidens: looks sort to do better. *S. Dow*

NIGHT GOWN 3 b.f. Night Shift (USA) – Mossage 75 (Ballymoss 136) [1991 NR **41** 1992 8m⁵ 6m 6m a7g⁵ a8g 5.3g³ 6s] lengthy, angular, workmanlike filly: third reported foal: sister to quite modest 6f winner Whisper The Wind and half-sister to fairly useful 1987 2-y-o 5f winner Tower Glades (by Tower Walk): dam stayed 1½m: inconsistent maiden: has form at 7f but may prove better at shorter: well beaten on soft ground: made most when blinkered/visored last 4 starts: wears bandages: sold 1,800 gns Newmarket Autumn Sales. *Miss Gay Kelleway*

NIGHT MANOEUVRES 3 b.c. Night Shift (USA) – Rattle Along 80 (Tap On **111** Wood 130) [1991 6d² 6g* 1992 7.1d* 6g² 7.3d³ 8g²] round-barrelled, very powerful colt: carries condition: moderate mover: consistent and very useful performer: won listed race at Haydock in May by length from Night Jar: ran well subsequently in £7,800 handicap at Newmarket, Hungerford Stakes (hung right when 2½ lengths third to Mojave) at Newbury and listed event (2 lengths second of 9 to Calling Collect, best effort) at Kempton: stays 1m: acts on dead ground, yet to race on top-of-the-ground: sold 50,000 gns Newmarket Autumn Sales to race in Italy. *H. Candy*

NIGHTMARE LADY 2 b.f. (Mar 14) Celestial Storm (USA) 132 – Presentable – 60 (Sharpen Up 127) [1992 6m 6s] 1,450F, 400Y: sparely-made filly: half-sister to several winners, including 9f and 1¼m winner Blakesware Gold (by Vaigly Great) and 1985 2-y-o 1m winner Centrepoint (by Reform): dam, placed over 1½m, is half-sister to Gimcrack winner Wishing Star: green, well beaten in seller at Yarmouth and maiden at Lingfield in the autumn. *W. Holden*

NIGHT MELODY (IRE) 2 br.c. (Mar 8) Night Shift (USA) – Quaver 86 (Song **86** 132) [1992 5g⁴ 5.1d² 5.3m* 6m⁴ 5m* 6g³ 5m² 6m* 5m* 5m* 5m³ 5d* 6g³ 5d⁵] 23,000F, 41,000Y: sturdy, close-coupled colt: active sort: third foal: brother to 1989 2-y-o 5f winner Key Shift: dam sprinter from good sprinting family: tremendously consistent performer: won maiden at Brighton and minor events (never more than 8 runners) at Newcastle, Catterick, Thirsk (day later), Doncaster and Salisbury between May and August: equally effective at 5f and 6f: acts on good to firm and dead ground: usually has tongue tied down nowadays. *R. Hannon*

NIGHT TRANSACTION 5 ch.m. Tina's Pet 121 – Beech Tree 67 (Fighting **59** Ship 121) [1991 7.6g 9g⁶ 8m* 8.1g 10g⁴ 7m 9s 8.2m² 8d⁵ a8g³ a7g⁵ 1992 a10g 8g 8m a8g⁶ 9m⁴ 8f* 8.5s⁵ 8g³ 7f⁵ 7.6m* 8g 8m* 8g] stocky mare: modest handicapper: won at Redcar (ladies event, for second successive year) and Lingfield (apprentices) in the summer, and Yarmouth in September: effective from around 1m to 1¼m: acts on firm and soft ground and on fibresand: effective blinkered or not at 4 yrs: usually claimer ridden. *A. Hide*

NIJMEGEN 4 b.g. Niniski (USA) 125 – Petty Purse 115 (Petingo 135) [1991 NR **78** 1992 12.2g⁵ 9m³ 14.8g³ 14d* 16.2g² 12g] good-bodied gelding: progressed into a fair handicapper: dictated pace when successful at Haydock in October: stays 2m: acts on dead ground: won handicap hurdle in December. *J. G. FitzGerald*

NIKATINO 6 b.m. Bustino 136 – Latakia 80 (Morston (FR) 125) [1991 NR 1992 **52** 14.1g⁵ 17.2f² 16.5m³] leggy, rather sparely-made mare: has a round action: modest handicapper: ran creditably all 3 starts, in June: stays 17f: acts on hard ground. *Dr J. D. Scargill*

NIKITAS 7 b.g. Touching Wood (USA) 127 – Hi There 89 (High Top 131) [1991 – 16g 14.8m⁴ 14g 14m⁵ 14g* 13.4d⁵ 14m³ 14.6m 1992 14.1d⁵ 16.2d 14g] good-topped gelding: rated 64 at 6 yrs: no worthwhile form in 1992, last seen out in June: stays 2m: acts on any going: best when allowed to dominate: bandaged near-fore nowadays: fairly useful hurdler, successful 4 times in the autumn. *Miss A. J. Whitfield*

NIKITRIA 2 b.f. (May 3) Robellino (USA) 127 – Hi There 89 (High Top 131) [1992 **36** 6s 6g] 2,100Y: plain filly: half-sister to middle-distance stayer Nikitas (by Touching Wood) and a winner in Macau: dam, half-sister to Pas de Seul, won over 5f at 2 yrs:

backward, poor form in maidens at Leicester and Doncaster in the autumn. *Miss A. J. Whitfield*

NIKKI DOW   6 b.g. Tanfirion 110 – Amboselli 73 (Raga Navarro (ITY) 119) [1991   –
6v 6g 5m⁶ 7.1g 6g 5.1g 1992 6.1m] small, angular gelding: poor mover: looks of little
account these days. *P. Howling*

NIKKI NOO NOO   2 b.f. (Mar 18) Precocious 126 – Miss Caro Star 76§ (Rusti-   **58**
caro (FR) 124) [1992 5g⁶ 5.1h⁶ 5g² 6m 5.3f* 5d⁴ a6g a5g] 3,500Y: good-topped filly:
moderate mover: first foal: dam 2-y-o 5f winner became temperamental and lost her
form: modest performer: made virtually all in seller (no bid) at Brighton in August,
running on strongly: off course 3 months, below form on all-weather: should prove
effective at 6f: acts on firm ground, fair effort on dead. *C. J. Hill*

NIKOLAYEVICH   5 b.g. Niniski (USA) 125 – Rexana (Relko 136) [1991 NR 1992   –
17.2s] strong, workmanlike gelding: no sign of ability. *D. C. Jermy*

NILE DELTA (IRE)   3 b.c. Green Desert (USA) 127 – Tolmi 122 (Great   **75**
Nephew 126) [1991 NR 1992 8m* 8m2] sturdy, heavy-topped colt: sixth foal: half-
brother to a winner abroad by Niniski: dam 1000 Guineas second out of outstanding
broodmare Stilvi: 6/4 on, won 5-runner maiden at Redcar in July: 11/4 on, narrowly
beaten in 4-runner handicap there 16 days later, leading 2f out until close home. *H. R. A. Cecil*

NIMBLE DEER   3 ch.f. Hadeer 118 – Nibelunga (Miami Springs 121) [1991 7m²   **66**
6.1m 6m⁶ 1992 7g³ 8g 7g] big, lengthy filly: just a fair performer on balance of form,
seemingly flattered by her sixth in Cheveley Park Stakes: best effort in 1992 when
third in a maiden auction at Thirsk: well beaten in 1000 Guineas in May and £11,600
handicap at Newmarket in July: should stay 1m: sold 3,400 gns Newmarket September Sales. *N. C. Wright*

NINA'S CHOCOLATES (USA)   3 b.f. Alleged (USA) 138 – Shark's Jaws   **73**
(USA) (Mitey Prince (USA)) [1991 NR 1992 12g³ 10.4m³ 12.5m⁴ 14m] $60,000F,
$15,000Y: lengthy, workmanlike filly: moderate walker: easy mover: half-sister to
prolific North American winners Raja's Shark (by Raja Baba) and Wyetown (by Al
Hattab): dam successful 11 times at up to 1¼m at 3 and 4 yrs, including in stakes
company: fair maiden: stiffish task, led 9f when soundly beaten in £10,800 handicap
at Goodwood final start, in July: should prove better at 1½m than shorter. *C. E. Brittain*

NINJA DANCER (USA)   3 b.c. Miswaki (USA) 124 – Professional Dance (USA) **101**
(Nijinsky (CAN) 138) [1991 6g⁴ 7.1s* 7m 8d* 8g⁵ 1992 9g 10m⁵ 12g 7.6m⁶ 10s²]
rangy colt: usually looks well: useful performer: ran creditably when 6 lengths fifth
of 9 to Jeune in listed event at Goodwood and when second to Mining Tycoon in
minor event at Leopardstown: tailed off in the Derby and Lingfield listed event:
much better suited by 1¼m than 7f: acts on good to firm ground and soft: sometimes
has tongue tied down: trained until after penultimate start by Mrs J. Cecil. *D. K. Weld, Ireland*

NIODINI (USA)   3 b.f. Nijinsky (CAN) 138 – Home Thoughts (USA) (Tom Rolfe) **110**
[1991 6g³ 7g² 7f* 8v⁵ 1992 10d² 11.5d² 10m² 12f² 11.9g* 11.9m⁴ 14.6m⁵ 15s 12s⁵]
well-made filly: good mover very useful performer: won Lancashire Oaks at
Haydock in July (by 1½ lengths from Armarama) and Park Hill Stakes (by ¾ length
from Guilty Secret) at Doncaster in September: in frame in Ribblesdale Stakes at
Royal Ascot and Yorkshire Oaks (3 lengths fourth to User Friendly) fourth and sixth
outings and ran fairly well in St Simon Stakes at Newbury final one: stayed 14.6f:
best efforts on a sound surface: effective visored or not: genuine and consistent:
visits Private Account. *M. R. Stoute*

NIP   4 br.f. Bay Express 132 – Broken Accent (Busted 134) [1991 11g⁶ 10.1s 1992   –
a14g] workmanlike filly: no worthwhile form, not seen out after June. *A. S. Reid*

NIPOTINA   6 b.m. Simply Great (FR) 122 – Mothers Girl (Huntercombe 133)   **42** d
[1991 a12g³ a12g³ 12d³ 12f 12f 12f5 12g 16.2g⁶ 12m⁵ 10.1d4 15.8g² 17.2f4 16m²a12g⁵
16m³ 11m³ 16.9m² 1992 12f* 10.5m⁵ 16.2g 14.6m⁶ 12f 12.3d 12m 12.5s 13.8d 11.8s
12d⁵ a12g a12g a12g] small, sturdy mare: moderate mover: poor handicapper: little
form after winning at Beverley in May: effective at 1½m, and stays long distances:
acts on hard and dead going: often claimer ridden. *R. Hollinshead*

NISHARA   4 br.f. Nishapour (FR) 125 – Sardara 106 (Alcide 136) [1991 NR 1992   –
16.2g 10s 8d 12.2g 9.2s] lengthy, workmanlike filly: poor mover: half-sister to Irish
2000 Guineas winner Dara Monarch (by Realm) and fair miler Kazarow (by Blue
Cashmere): dam staying half-sister to St Leger winner Intermezzo: no worthwhile
form. *N. Bycroft*

NISHIKI (USA) 3 b.f. Brogan (USA) 110 – A Honey Belle (USA) (Son Ange (USA)) [1991 NR 1992 9.9g] sparely-made, angular filly: sixth reported foal: half-sister to 4 winners in North America: dam unraced half-sister to smart 1981 graded 6f and 8.5f winner Apalachee Honey: always behind in maiden at Beverley in March: joined R. Whitaker. *J. A. Glover* –

NITEOWLADY 2 b.f. (Apr 14) Dreams To Reality (USA) 113 – Palace Pet (Dragonara Palace (USA) 115) [1992 5g⁵ 5m a6g³ 6f⁶] 3,800Y: sparely-made filly: moderate walker and mover: fifth reported foal: dam ran once: poor form in maiden auctions and sellers: stays 6f: blinkered final start. *S. G. Norton* 40

NITOUCHE 2 ch.f. (Feb 10) Scottish Reel 123 – Loredana 64 (Grange Melody) [1992 5g* 6f⁶ 6g 5g⁴ 6d 6d⁶] lengthy filly: progressed physically: moderate mover: third foal: dam 7f and 1m winner: won maiden auction at Thirsk in May: best effort in nurseries after when fourth at Wolverhampton: probably stays 6f: hung on firm ground (off course 3 months after). *Pat Mitchell* 64

NOBBY 6 b.g. Dalsaan 125 – Parkeen Princess (He Loves Me 120) [1991 8.2m 1992 9.9g 12f] workmanlike gelding: has a round action: lightly raced and no form since 3 yrs. *T. Fairhurst* –

NOBBY BARNES 3 b.g. Nordance (USA) – Loving Doll 72 (Godswalk (USA) 130) [1991 6f 5g⁶ 7m⁴ 6.1m 1992 6g a11g a8g⁵ a7g² a8g² a8s³ 7g³ a7g⁶ 7d⁵ 7d⁵ 7.6s⁵ 9s⁵ 10.3g 9.7v³ a7g⁶ a8g* a8g²] neat gelding: has a round action: modest handicapper: sold out of R. Armstrong's stable 4,100 gns Newmarket September Sales after eighth start: won amateurs contest at Southwell in December: stays 9f: acts on heavy ground and on all-weather surfaces. *D. A. Wilson* 62

NOBLE CAUSE (IRE) 3 b.g. Reasonable (FR) 119 – Luan Causca 70 (Pampapaul 121) [1991 5g 5m³ 6g⁶ a6g³ a7g³ 7g⁵ 6g 6g⁵ 8m⁵ 1992 8.5f 8m 6m⁵ 6g] leggy, sparely-made gelding: rated 62 at 2 yrs: below form in 1992: stays 1m: acts on good to firm ground and fibresand: sold 1,500 gns Newmarket September Sales. *R. Earnshaw* –

NOBLE FELLOW 5 b.g. The Noble Player (USA) 126 – Fravelot (Javelot 124) [1991 NR 1992 a12g 14.6g] close-coupled gelding: has a round action: on the downgrade: trained reappearance by B. McMath. *J. P. Smith* –

NOBLE MEASURE (IRE) 2 ch.g. (Mar 19) Lord Avie (USA) – Measuring 104 (Moorestyle 137) [1992 a6g] 15,500F, 31,000Y: first living foal: dam 2-y-o 5f winner, is half-sister to top 1978 2-y-o filly Devon Ditty, later good winner at up to 9f in USA: tailed-off last of 10 in maiden at Southwell in June: sold 680 gns Doncaster August Sales. *Sir Mark Prescott* –

NOBLE PET 3 gr.g. Petong 126 – Barbary Court (Grundy 137) [1991 5m 6g² 6f² 6g 1992 6s⁴ 6f² 7g² 7.1d* 7.9m³ 7.1s 7d] sturdy gelding: quite useful handicapper: won £7,300 contest at Sandown in July and excellent third in £25,600 event at York in August: got poor run last 2 starts: stays 1m: acts on any going: held up, and has good turn of foot: consistent. *P. J. Makin* 93

A. F. Budge Park Hill Stakes, Doncaster—
Niodini (right) stays on strongly under the whip to hold off Guilty Secret
and Anna of Saxony (left)

NOBLE POWER (IRE)   3 ch.c. The Noble Player (USA) 126 – Power Girl 77   **69**
(Tyrant (USA)) [1991 5m² 5g* 5m³ 6d⁵ 1992 6.1m⁶ 6d 6m⁶ 5m⁵ 5d⁵ 5s 5.1s 5s⁵ 5.1d
5.1s³ a6g³ a6g*] leggy colt: fair handicapper: back to form last 4 starts, winning at
Lingfield in November: stays 6f: acts on good to firm and dead ground and on
equitrack. *B. Palling*

NOBLE RISK   2 b.c. (Apr 29) Risk Me (FR) 127 – Nativity (USA) (Native Royalty   **62** p
(USA)) [1992 7m] big, lengthy, workmanlike colt: half-brother to several winners,
including useful 6f and 7f winner Native Charmer (by Gay Fandango), later successful at up to 9f in USA, and 1¼m winner Fearless Native (by Final Straw): dam
lightly-raced 2-y-o 5f winner: backward and green, behind in £8,850 event won by
Barathea at Newmarket in October, held up and not knocked about when beaten:
will improve. *R. Hannon*

NOBLE SINGER   3 ch.f. Vaguely Noble 140 – Shark Song 103 (Song 132) [1991   **59**
7m² 8s⁶ a8g⁴ a8g² a8g² 1992 a10g* a10g²] consistent performer: won maiden at
Lingfield in January: not seen after following month: stays 1¼m: best form on
equitrack: joined H. Thomson Jones. *H. Thomson Jones*

NOBLE VIENNA (USA)   3 ch.c. Vaguely Noble 140 – Native Lovin (USA) (Ex-   **62**
clusive Native (USA)) [1991 10m 8d a7g 1992 12.3s 12m 12.3f⁵ 10.3m² 10d] sturdy
colt: moderate mover: worthwhile form only when second in Chester claimer: stays
10.3f: sold 2,000 gns Newmarket September Sales. *R. Hollinshead*

NOCATCHIM   3 b.g. Shardari 134 – Solar 120 (Hotfoot 126) [1991 7m 6f 1992 8d   **54**
9.9m 8.2d⁵ 10.2d⁵ a10g] good-topped gelding: modest maiden: well beaten final run:
well worth a try at 1½m: sold 12,500 gns Newmarket Autumn Sales. *B. W. Hills*

NO COMEBACKS   4 b.f. Last Tycoon 131 – Dead End (Bold Lad (IRE) 133)   **61**
[1991 7g³ 6f² 6m⁴ a8g⁶ 7.1m 11m 9s 10.4m 8.2m* 6m² 8d 1992 8f 10.5d 8f³ 8.9m⁴
7.6g³ 8f³ 7f 10.5g³ 10.3m³ 12.3d⁶ 9.2s* 9.9m* 10.5d 9d* 10m 10.3s⁴ 10.3g a8g² a12g
a8g] leggy filly: modest handicapper: successful in autumn at Hamilton, Beverley
and Redcar: effective at 1m, and stays 1½m (at least in moderately-run race): acts
on any going: below form blinkered once: carries head high and best with strong
handling: is held up. *E. J. Alston*

NO CREDIBILITY   10 ch.g. Ahonoora 122 – Karlaine 86 (Tutankhamen) [1991   **– §**
NR 1992 16.2g] sturdy gelding: ungenuine. *B. Richmond*

NOCTURNAL REVERIE (USA)   5 b.m. Assert 134 – Grey Dream 101   **–**
(Auction Ring (USA) 123) [1991 a12g⁶ a14g a12g⁵ a12g* a13g⁶ a12g⁴ 16.2g 12f 10.1d⁶
12g a16g 1992 a13g⁶] leggy mare: moderate mover: inconsistent handicapper: stays
1¾m: acts on good to firm and dead ground: effective blinkered or not. *T. J.
Naughton*

NO DECISION   5 br.g. King of Spain 121 – Really Fine VII (Urami 100) [1991 NR   **–**
1992 8d 8d a8g⁴ a8g² a7g⁴ a8g² 8s] heavy-topped gelding: has rather round action: a56
modest handicapper: better at 1m than shorter: best efforts on fibresand: best
blinkered: often slowly away. *M. W. Easterby*

NOEL (IRE)   3 b.g. Fairy King (USA) – Glenardina (Furry Glen 121) [1991 7m   **54**
7.6d³ 1992 7s 9g a11g² 10d 10.3g²] tall gelding: regressive maiden: second in seller   a65
final run: should stay 1½m: acts on fibresand: sold 7,400 gns Newmarket Autumn
Sales. *G. A. Pritchard-Gordon*

NO EXTRAS (IRE)   2 b.g. (Mar 9) Efisio 120 – Parkland Rose (Sweet Candy   **64**
(VEN)) [1992 5m 6g 5h⁵ 6g² 6g* 6m³ 6.1s³ 6m³ 7s⁶ 6v³] 900F, 2,600Y, 12,000
2-y-o: leggy gelding: first living foal: dam, ran twice, from family of Greenland Park,
Fitnah and Red Sunset: won seller (retained 5,250 gns) at Leicester in July: ran well
in nurseries most starts after: should prove as effective at 7f as 6f: probably acts on
any going: below form when blinkered once. *J. Sutcliffe*

NOGGINGS (IRE)   3 b.g. Cyrano de Bergerac 120 – Coshlea 63 (Red Alert 127)   **–**
[1991 5d 5g 5d³ 6m 7f⁶ 7m² 7f³ 7.9g 1992 7s 8m⁵] compact gelding: rated 59 at 2 yrs:
well below form in 1992: should be suited by 1m: acts on firm ground: ran creditably
when blinkered once. *N. Tinkler*

NO ISLANDS   3 ch.f. Lomond (USA) 128 – Land Line (High Line 125) [1991 NR   **–**
1992 12g] 20,000Y: lengthy filly: first living foal: dam unraced sister to Park Hill
winner Quay Line: always behind in Folkestone maiden in April, only run: sold in
foal to Robellino 5,800 gns Newmarket December Sales. *M. R. Stoute*

NOMADIC FIRE   2 b. or br.g. (Mar 17) Sharrood (USA) 124 – Flaming Peace 104   **45** p
(Queen's Hussar 124) [1992 6m 8.2s 7g] 7,200Y: leggy, close-coupled gelding: half-
brother to numerous winners, including 2 middle-distance winners by High Line
and 3-y-o Billy Blazer (by Nicholas Bill), successful at 6f (at 2 yrs) and 10.9f: dam

2-y-o 7f winner: behind in seller at Newmarket and maidens (when giving impression capable of better) at Nottingham and Doncaster in autumn: will be suited by middle distances: will improve. *D. Morley*

NOMADIC ROSE 3 b.f. Nomination 125 – Tina Rosa (Bustino 136) [1991 5.2g 6f⁵ 7f 1992 7s 10m 10m⁴ 10d] sturdy filly: poor maiden on flat: claimed out of B. Hills's stable £3,001 third start: stays 1¼m: won selling hurdle and juvenile hurdle in the autumn. *T. J. Naughton* **41**

NOMINATOR 2 b.c. (Apr 14) Nomination 125 – Najariya (Northfields (USA)) [1992 5g² 5d² 5g² 6f 5f² 6f* 6.1d² 5m³ 5m² 5.9f² 6f* 5m³ 6m* 6s³ 8d² 7m* 7.3s⁴ 6v] 5,200Y: close-coupled, workmanlike colt: carries condition: second foal: dam unraced: progressed throughout 1992, having been on the go from opening day of turf season: successful in small-field minor events at Pontefract (in Timeform Futurity on second occasion) and Redcar and listed Somerville Tattersall Stakes (beat Urgent Request a neck) at Newmarket: rare below-par run on heavy ground in Racecall Gold Trophy at Redcar final start: suited by 7f/1m: acts on firm and soft ground: tough, consistent and thoroughly genuine: a credit to his stable. *R. Hollinshead* **107**

NOMINEE PRINCE 3 b.g. Nomination 125 – Be Royal 97 (Royal Palm 131) [1991 6s 6s 1992 7g 8m 8d 7f] plain gelding: poor plater: tried visored once. *R. Guest* **–**

NONANNO 3 b.g. Noalto 120 – Fortune's Fancy (Workboy 123) [1991 6m⁶ 6g 1992 8f 6m 6g³] big, plain gelding: no worthwhile form. *A. J. Chamberlain* **–**

NONCOMMITAL 5 b.h. Mummy's Pet 125 – Shadow Play (Busted 134) [1991 8g⁶ 10.2m 8g⁵ 7m 8.2m 8m 9.2s 1992 14.6g² 15.1m⁶] good-topped horse: poor plater: form only at 1¾m. *J. Mackie* **41**

NOORA'S ROSE (NZ) 3 br.f. Ahonoora 122 – Tristihill (NZ) (Sir Tristram 115) [1991 NR 1992 8d 8v] lengthy filly: third foal: dam unraced: not seen out until October, and no form in minor event and maiden. *G. Harwood* **–**

NO QUARTER GIVEN 7 b.g. Don 128 – Maggie Mine 85 (Native Prince) [1991 6s 5g 5f³ 5m⁴ 6g 6d 6g³ 5.1g³ 5g³ 5m⁴ a5g² a5g⁴ 5.2f* 5.1m 5m⁵ 6m 1992 5s⁶ 5s* 5s* 5d⁵ 5m a5g 5.7f⁵ 5g² 6g⁴ 5g⁴] rangy, well-made gelding: carries plenty of condition: fair handicapper: successful in April at Wolverhampton and Newcastle: effective at 5f to 6f: acts on any going: good mount for apprentice. *P. S. Felgate* **73**

NORDAN RAIDER 4 ch.f. Domynsky 110 – Vikris (Viking (USA)) [1991 9g 8m⁶ 10.5d 8m 1992 7d² 6m* 6f² 6m² 6d* 6d⁵ 6.1s*] leggy, lengthy filly: impresses in appearance: no form in first season to race at 3 yrs, but progressed really well in handicaps in 1992: successful in 2 apprentice events at Ayr and Haydock, and at Chester (held Crystal Jack by neck, pair well clear): active sort, best at up to 7f: acts on any going: held up: game: should have another good season in sprint handicaps at 5 yrs. *M. J. Camacho* **66 p**

NORDANSK 3 ch.g. Nordance (USA) – Free On Board 73 (Free State 125) [1991 6m⁶ 6g⁴ 5m 7m 1992 7f⁵ 6m 8g 7g 6s 9.7v⁴] workmanlike gelding: poor maiden: stays 9.7f: acts on any going: has joined M. Madgwick. *L. J. Holt* **42**

NORDIC BRAVE 6 b.h. Indian King (USA) 128 – Belle Viking (FR) (Riverman (USA) 131) [1991 6s⁵ 6s 6d* 6m 7g 6m 6m 7m⁴ 6m 7g² 6d* 7m 6d 6d 6m 6g 6m 7g 7m* 8d 7m 7m⁵ 7d 1992 8g⁵ 6d* 7g 6g 7f* 7g 6f 7m² 7g 6g³ 7m] leggy, lightly-made, angular horse: moderate mover: inconsistent handicapper: successful at Kempton **78**

Timeform Futurity, Pontefract—thirteenth start of the season for Nominator, who leads Fyfield Flyer from early in the straight

and Doncaster in spring: suited by 6f/7f: probably acts on any going: successful for apprentice, and when sweating: front runner. *M. Brittain*

NORDIC BRIEF (IRE)   3 b.c. Nordico (USA) – Bold And Brief (Bold Lad (IRE) **105** 133) [1991 5g* 7m² 7g² 6m⁶ 6m⁶ 7m² 1992 10d³ 7f⁶ 8g² 9g² 8g4] good-topped colt: useful and consistent performer: best effort when 4 lengths third of 6 to Brief Truce in Gallinule Stakes at the Curragh: ran respectably in Jersey Stakes at Royal Ascot and listed races at the Curragh, Leopardstown and Fairyhouse last 4 starts: better at 1¼m than shorter: acts on good to firm ground and dead: usually blinkered. *J. S. Bolger, Ireland*

NORDIC FOX (IRE)   2 b.c. (Mar 14) Nordico (USA) – La Meilleure 86 (Lord   **92** Gayle (USA) 124) [1992 5d² 6s³ 6g4 6s² 6g* 7d²] IR 20,000Y: first foal: dam Irish 7f and 1m winner, from family of Double Form and Scimitarra: really found his form in October, winning maiden at Punchestown, nursery at Naas and running second to Foresee in Leopardstown Stakes: will stay 1m: has raced only on an easy surface. *J. S. Bolger, Ireland*

NORDIC SPIRIT (IRE)   2 b.c. (Apr 16) Nordico (USA) – Persian Goddess   – (Persian Bold 123) [1992 5m 7s] IR 16,000F, 11,000Y: leggy colt: second foal: dam unraced: no form in maidens at Windsor and Warwick, off course 5 months in between: sold 800 gns Ascot December Sales. *C. F. Wall*

NORDOORA (IRE)   3 b.f. Fayruz 116 – African Cousin (Kampala 120) [1991 NR   **42** 1992 6m³ 5g³ 5g 5m 5d 6s³ a6g a5g] IR 1,800Y: angular, plain filly: poor mover: first foal: dam fair Irish 2-y-o 5f and 6f winner: poor handicapper: stays 6f: acts on good to firm and soft ground, below form on fibresand. *J. L. Harris*

NO RESERVATIONS (IRE)   2 b.f. (Mar 8) Commanche Run 133 – Light Link   **87** 99 (Tudor Music 131) [1992 5g² 6f* 6g³ 7.5d⁵ 6g* 6f4 7g² 6.5m 7m² 7g³ 7.3s³] IR 1,400Y: workmanlike filly: half-sister to several winners, including very useful sprinters Hamada (by Hot Spark) and Sanu (by Steel Heart) and Irish middle-distance winner French Chain (by Ile de Bourbon): dam won over 5f and 6f at 2 yrs: fairly useful performer: successful in Salisbury maiden auction in May and nursery at Ascot in July: good third in Newbury listed race won by Criquette final start: will stay 1m: probably acts on any going: genuine and consistent. *R. F. Johnson Houghton*

NORFOLK HERO   2 b.c. (Apr 3) Elegant Air 119 – Caviar Blini 80 (What A   **73** p Guest 119) [1992 6m³ 6s*] 15,500Y: quite attractive colt: first foal: dam, 2-y-o 5f winner, is out of sister to top-class sprinter Deep Diver and half-sister to Irish 2000 Guineas winner King's Company: favourite, confirmed promising debut in Ascot minor event when winning maiden at Newbury in July by 2 lengths, always prominent: should stay 1m: seemed sure to improve again. *D. J. G. Murray-Smith*

NORFOLKIEV (FR)   6 b.g. In Fijar (USA) 121 – Touraille (FR) (Jim French   **67** (USA)) [1991 6m³ 6m4 6v 6g⁵ 7f³ 7.6m 6g 1992 7.5g4 6d 7f* 7f4 7d a7g* 7m²] good-bodied gelding: moderate mover: fair handicapper: won at Brighton (apprentices) in June and Lingfield (£8,000 event) in July: effective at 6f/7f: acts on hard ground and equitrack, unsuited by dead: sometimes has tongue tied down: races prominently. *M. Moubarak*

NORFOLK LASS   4 b.f. Blakeney 126 – Balgreggan (Hallez (FR) 131) [1991   – 12m⁶ 11.8m 14.1f⁵ 14.1f⁵ 16m 1992 a14g a12g] angular, plain filly: has a round action: no worthwhile form: sold 1,000 gns Ascot June Sales. *M. C. Pipe*

NORFOLK THATCH   6 b.g. Thatching 131 – Pellarosa (Crepello 136) [1991   **36** 8.9g 8g4 1992 8g 8.9g 8.2m⁶ 7.5d] sturdy gelding: poor handicapper: may well prove suited by 1¼m: acts on good to firm ground: sometimes hangs markedly. *K. S. Bridgwater*

NORLING (IRE)   2 ch.g. (Apr 20) Nashamaa 113 – Now Then (Sandford Lad 133)   **63** [1992 5g* 6m⁵ 5g4 7m 7d] IR 3,800Y: sturdy gelding: fourth foal: half-brother to 1½m winner Salubrious (by Sallust): dam, half-sister to Record Run, placed in Ireland from 7f to 1¼m: well backed when winning seller (no bid) at Newcastle in August for B. Beasley: ran well in nurseries third and fourth starts: gives impression may prove ideally suited by 6f: acts on good to firm ground. *N. Tinkler*

NORMANTON PARK   2 b.c. (Apr 13) Nomination 125 – Conway Bay 74 (Sari-   **75** p tamer (USA) [1992 6m* 5m⁶] 31,000Y: lengthy, quite attractive colt: half-brother to 4 winners at up to 8.2f, all moderate at best: dam placed over 5f at 2 yrs, appeared not to train on: won maiden at Newmarket in July, making all: looked particularly well when 10½ lengths sixth of 7 to Sabre Rattler in listed race at York month later, never able to challenge: will do better, particularly back over 6f: sold to join M. Heaton-Ellis 9,200 gns Doncaster November Sales. *R. Hannon*

NORMAN WARRIOR 3 gr.g. Petong 126 – Petulengra 98 (Mummy's Pet 125) **52**
[1991 7m 7d 1992 8d* 8g 8m 8f⁶ 10m 8g] leggy gelding: in-and-out form in handicaps
after winning Leicester seller (bought in 4,200 gns) in June: stays 1m: acts on dead
ground. *D. Morris*

NORSTANO 2 ch.c. (Mar 16) Stanford 121§ – Norapa 91 (Ahonoora 122) [1992 **60**
5s* 5g 6m⁵ 5f⁶ 6g⁴ 5m 5g² 5d⁶] compact colt: first foal: dam 2-y-o 6f winner: in-and-
out form after winning maiden at Haydock in April: ran very well in nursery at
Redcar penultimate start: probably stays 6f: acts well on soft going: blinkered last 4
starts: sold 6,600 gns Newmarket Autumn Sales. *M. H. Easterby*

NORTHANTS 6 b.g. Northern Baby (CAN) 127 – Astania (GER) (Arratos (FR)) **51**
[1991 NR 1992 16.1s⁵ 13d⁴ 16.1m⁴ 15.8d² 15.9m⁴ 15.8m] sturdy gelding: carries
condition: staying handicapper: used to be blinkered and ungenuine but not in 1992:
will be suited by 2m +: acts on any going: bandaged: not easiest of rides. *W. Storey*

NORTH ARDAR 2 b.c. (Jan 8) Ardar 87 – Langwaite (Seaepic (USA) 100) [1992 **47**
7d⁵ 7v⁴ a8g⁶ a7g⁴] close-coupled colt: first reported foal: dam unraced: plating-
class form in varied events: looks a stayer. *M. Johnston*

NORTH CALL 2 b.f. (Apr 28) Northern State (USA) 91 – Calling High (USA) 88 **–**
(Mountain Call 125) [1992 6d 7g] workmanlike filly: half-sister to several winners,
including middle-distance handicapper Common Farm (by Tachypous) and 1981
Irish 2-y-o 5f winner Swansea Bay (by Moulton): dam 2-y-o 6f winner: backward,
well beaten in October maidens at Newmarket and Doncaster. *G. H. Eden*

NORTHERN BIRD 2 ch.f. (Mar 2) Interrex (CAN) – Partridge Brook 109 **82**
(Birdbrook 110) [1992 5g⁴ 5g* 6f³ 5.7m* 6m⁴ 6s 6d⁴ 6v] 5,200Y: close-coupled filly:
half-sister to several winners, including 1990 2-y-o 6f winner Swingaway Lady (by
Nomination) and 1m to 1½m winner Topsoil (by Relkino): dam won from 5f to 1¼m:
sire (closely related to Secreto) smart 1m to 9.5f winner: progressed well: won
Sandown maiden auction in May, nursery at Bath (first run for 3 months) in August
and fourth in Lowther Stakes at York penultimate run: will stay 7f: acts on firm and
dead ground (twice well beaten on very soft): wears bandages: effective held up or
ridden from front. *B. W. Hills*

NORTHERN BLADE (IRE) 3 b.c. Sure Blade (USA) 130 – Secala (USA) **–**
(Secretariat (USA)) [1991 7d⁶ 8.1g⁵ 8m 7g⁶ 1992 8g 10g 11g 8m] leggy, workmanlike
colt: has a round action: no form in 1992: stays 1m: sold 1,800 gns Ascot June Sales.
R. Hollinshead

NORTHERN BLUFF 2 b.g. (Jan 31) Precocious 126 – Mainmast 63 (Bustino **56**
136) [1992 5m⁴ 6g 5s³ 6d] 10,000Y: big, useful-looking gelding: has plenty of scope:
has a round action: second foal: half-brother to 3-y-o Mainly Me (by Huntingdale):
dam, twice-raced, from family of Bireme and Buoy: easily best effort in maidens
when third at Haydock: ran badly at Ayr later in September: should stay beyond 5f. *J. W. Watts*

NORTHERN BRED (IRE) 2 b.c. (Feb 21) Alzao (USA) 117 – Good Relations **74 p**
(Be My Guest (USA) 126) [1992 7m⁶ 6g] IR 43,000Y: smallish, sturdy colt: fourth
foal: half-brother to 1990 2-y-o 7f winner Affair of Honour (by Ahonoora) and 1m
winner Tacoma Heights (by Taufan): dam Irish 7f and 1½m winner, is half-sister to
Montekin: better effort at Newmarket when sixth in £8,850 event, outpaced from 2f
out: soon chased along in maiden later in October: will be better suited by 1m: sure
to improve. *L. M. Cumani*

NORTHERN CHIEF 2 b.c. (Feb 6) Chief Singer 131 – Pacific Gull (USA) 67 **62**
(Storm Bird (CAN) 134) [1992 6m 6g 7d⁶ 7d⁶ 8.3v*] 5,800F, 5,600Y: quite attractive
colt: moderate mover: first foal: dam 8.5f winner: much improved effort when
winning nursery at Hamilton in November: will be suited by middle distances: acts
on heavy going. *M. H. Easterby*

NORTHERN CONQUEROR (IRE) 4 ch.g. Mazaad 106 – Gaylom (Lord **56 d**
Gayle (USA) 124) [1991 a5g⁵ a7g⁴ 10.1s⁴ 10g* 8.5m⁴ 10g* 10m⁶ a10g⁶ 7.6m⁶ 10.1f
10g a10g 1992 a13g 8.5g⁶ 10f 11.9f⁶ 8.1g 8.9g³ 10.1f 8d 10.1d 8d 9s 9.7v² a8g] small,
lightly-made gelding: easy mover: inconsistent handicapper nowadays: better at
1¼m than shorter: acts on good to firm ground and heavy: below form in visor,
blinkers and eyeshield. *T. J. Naughton*

NORTHERN CRYSTAL 4 b.c. Crystal Glitters (USA) 127 – North Cliff (FR) **114**
(Green Dancer (USA) 132) [1991 10d⁵ 8g* 10g² 1992 9g* 10.5g* 10d⁵ 8s*ᵈⁱˢ 8s*]
very useful French colt: had a good season, first past post in 4 of his 5 starts, minor
event at Compiegne and listed race at Strasbourg in May, another listed event at
Maisons-Laffitte (disqualified after a positive dope test) in October and Group 3 Prix

Perth at Saint-Cloud (by a neck from Voleris) in November: stays 10.5f: acts on soft going. *A. Fabre, France*

NORTHERN EMPEROR (IRE)   3 b.g. The Noble Player (USA) 126 – Stad-   –
eras (Windjammer (USA)) [1991 6m 7m 8m 7m 1992 14.1f⁶ 10.3m⁶ 7d 5.9f⁶] leggy
gelding: poor handicapper: seems to stay 7f: acts on firm and dead ground. *M. H. Easterby*

NORTHERN FLYER   4 ch.g. Bairn (USA) 126 – Fly The World (USA) 74   –
(Empery (USA) 128) [1991 7g⁴ 7m 10d* a10g² 10g⁶ 10m³ 12g⁵ 11g a12g a10g⁶ a12g⁵
1992 a11g] rather sparely-made gelding: rated 74d at 3 yrs: pulled up lame in
Southwell claimer in February: should stay 1½m: acts on good to firm ground and
dead: headstrong sort. *M. C. Chapman*

NORTHERN GALLERY (IRE)   4 ch.g. Tate Gallery (USA) 117 – Cliona (FR)   –
(Ballymore 123) [1991 8m 6g 8f 6m 1992 10g a10g] leggy, good-topped gelding: poor
plater: bred to stay beyond 6f: below form blinkered and in eyeshield. *W. J. Musson*

NORTHERN GRADUATE (USA)   3 b.g. Northrop (USA) – Lady Blackfoot   68
108 (Prince Tenderfoot (USA) 126) [1991 6m 6m⁶ 6.1d 1992 7.1m² 8.1f² 8.3m* 8m*
8f² 10.1m* 9.2s 11v⁴] useful-looking gelding: consistent and progressed well for
much of 1992: successful in maiden at Hamilton and handicaps at Doncaster and
Newcastle: below form on soft ground last 2 starts: should prove as effective at
1½m as 1¼m: goes well on top-of-the-ground: well beaten when visored once at 2
yrs. *Mrs M. Reveley*

NORTHERN JUDY (IRE)   2 ch.f. (May 14) Jareer (USA) 115 – Robin Red   40
Breast 74 (Red Alert 127) [1992 6m 6d 8.1d] 2,000Y: tall, leggy filly: fourth known
foal: half-sister to 5f winner Pious Bird (by Tender King): dam 2-y-o 5f winner: poor
form in maidens: carried head awkwardly, hung left and looked ungenuine final
outing. *R. Hollinshead*

NORTHERN KINGDOM (USA)   3 b.g. Graustark – Wonder Mar (USA) (Fire   70
Dancer (USA)) [1991 NR 1992 10.3g⁵ 12.1g³ a12g* 11.9f² 11.9d⁴ 12.1g² 13.8g⁴]
$30,000F, $50,000Y: sturdy gelding: second reported foal: half-brother to U.S. 4-y-o
Hail To Baba (by El Baba): dam 1m and 8.5f stakes winner: won maiden at Southwell
in May and ran well in handicaps most starts after: stays 13.8f: acts on firm going,
possibly not on a soft surface: visored (looked none too keen) penultimate start. *S. G. Norton*

NORTHERN LION   9 br.g. Northfields (USA) – Pride of Kilcarn 74 (Klairon   –
131) [1991 a12g 10.6g 12m 1992 10.3g] leggy ex-Irish gelding: bad handicapper: won
over fences in May. *R. Thompson*

NORTHERN NATION   4 b.g. Nomination 125 – Ballagarrow Girl 66 (North   –
Stoke 130) [1991 5m 5g 7m 8g 8.9g 7g⁵ 6.9s⁴ a6g 7m⁵ 6m⁵ 1992 8.9g 8.2d] workmanlike, good-quartered gelding: bad mover: rated 48 at 3 yrs: seems on the downgrade
on flat: best form at sprint distances: acts on good to firm ground and soft: below
form visored: carries head high: second over hurdles in October. *W. Clay*

NORTHERN PRINTER   7 ch.g. Baptism 119 – Stradey Lynn 57 (Derrylin 115)   56
[1991 NR 1992 8g 7g 8g⁵ 8g 7.5m⁵] sturdy gelding: poor mover: seems on the
downgrade: sold 1,000 gns Doncaster October Sales. *M. J. O'Neill*

NORTHERN RAINBOW   4 b.g. Rainbow Quest (USA) 134 – Safe House 81§   80
(Lyphard (USA) 132) [1991 8s 12g⁶ 10.4d⁴ 8g⁵ 1992 8g² 7m⁵] lengthy gelding: still a
maiden: improved form on first run for over a year when second in Newmarket
handicap: failed to confirm that in similar company later in June, and not seen out
again: stays 1¼m: acts on good to firm and soft ground: ran creditably blinkered
once: sold to join I. Campbell's stable 2,000 gns Newmarket September Sales. *P. F. I. Cole*

NORTHERN SPARK   4 b.g. Trojan Fen 118 – Heavenly Spark (Habitat 134)   59
[1991 9m 6m⁶ 6m* 7m* 6m² 7f⁶ 6m⁵ 7d 7m 1992 6f 6d⁴ 7f 7f⁵ 6m⁴ 6m⁶ 8m 7g⁵ 7m]
leggy gelding: has a round action: inconsistent handicapper: stays 7f: acts on firm
going, hampered on heavy: below form blinkered once. *C. W. Thornton*

NORTHERN TRIAL (USA)   4 b.g. Far North (CAN) 120 – Make An Attempt   53 §
(USA) (Nashua) [1991 8g⁴ 10s³ 10.2f³ 10g 11.7m² 10g⁶ 10f² 10g² 1992 8f 10g⁵ 8.9g⁶]
sturdy gelding: rated 86 at best at 3 yrs: untrustworthy and well below form in 1992:
probably stays 1½m: acts on good to firm and soft going: below form blinkered once:
sold to join R. Curtis' stable 1,550 gns Ascot September Sales. *C. R. Nelson*

NORTHERN VISION   5 b.g. Vision (USA) – Smelter 111 (Prominer 125) [1991   –
8v 9d 10v 8g⁴ 8g⁶ 10m⁴ 10g 8g 9g 9.5m⁶ 1992 a12g a7g⁶ a6g 10.8d 8.9g] angular
gelding: seventh foal: half-brother to Irish 7f winner Ellaine (by Corvaro): dam won

John of Gaunt Stakes, Haydock—a late surge from the grey Norton Challenger sees him home narrowly from Powerful Edge (No. 10)

twice over 7f from 3 starts: successful in handicaps in Ireland at 2 and 3 yrs for D. Weld: no worthwhile form here in spring of 1992: stays 1¼m: mostly blinkered: sold 4,000 gns Doncaster May Sales. *P. A. Blockley*

NORTH ESK (USA)   3 ch.g. Apalachee (USA) 137 – Six Dozen (USA) (What A Pleasure (USA)) [1991 6m* 6m⁴ 6g 1992 8.5m 8f 8m 10g 10m³ 8m] good-topped gelding: fair handicapper: stays 1¼m: acts on good to firm ground: edgy sort: joined D. Smith and well beaten over hurdles before sold 3,000 gns Newmarket Autumn Sales. *J. W. Watts*   **74**

NORTH FLYER   3 b.g. Norwick (USA) 120 – Minuetto 59 (Roan Rocket 128) [1991 5f 5m² 5m 5h⁴ 8g 7m 1992 a6g⁶ a6g 8.9s⁵ 12.3s⁵ 10g⁴ 6m⁶ 8.2m 5.9h⁵ a7g³ 6g 8.2d a8g³ a8g a8g⁴] smallish, rather leggy gelding: modest maiden: stays 1m: acts on hard ground and fibresand: sold out of B. McMahon's stable 1,800 gns Doncaster October Sales after twelfth start. *D. Burchell*   **45 a49**

NORTH OF WATFORD   7 ch.h. Jasmine Star 113 – Wallie Girl (Right Tack 131) [1991 a5g⁴ a5g⁵ 5f⁶ 5f 5g⁶ 6f 6f 5d³ 1992 5m 5f 5m² 5g* 5m⁵ 5m⁶ 5d³] lengthy, good-quartered horse: moderate walker and mover: poor handicapper: successful at Leicester in July: best at 5f or 6f: acts on good to firm and dead ground. *M. P. Naughton*   **49**

NORTH RUSSIA (CAN)   3 ch.g. Bering 136 – Supreme Excellence (USA) (Providential 118) [1991 NR 1992 9m² 10.2g* 10g² 8.9g] $275,000Y: good-topped gelding: first foal: dam, half-sister to Golden Pheasant, won 7 races, including stakes events at 1m and 8.5f (2): comfortably landed odds in maiden at Chepstow and good second to Pabouche in Windsor minor event: visored and tongue tied down, well below-form last of 7 in handicap at York later in summer: stays 1¼m: has been gelded. *J. H. M. Gosden*   **88**

NORTH-WEST ONE (IRE)   4 b.g. Camden Town 125 – Shahrazad (Young Emperor 133) [1991 7.6m 7g a12g 1992 a8g a10g⁴ a12g⁴ 16.2d] workmanlike gelding: moderate mover: poor handicapper: probably stays 1½m: acts on equitrack. *H. J. Collingridge*   **30**

NORTON CHALLENGER   5 gr.h. Absalom 128 – Klaire 85 (Klairon 131) [1991 6d* 7g² 6g 7.2g² 6m 7g* 7m 7g³ 6d³ 1992 6g⁴ 7g² 7.1d⁶ 7.1g* 7.9d⁴ 7m 6g 7d] rangy, good-topped horse: good walker and mover: very useful at best: successful in   **105**

Sheikh Mohammed's "Norwich"

Haydock listed race in June: way below form last 3 starts: effective at 6f to 1m: goes well with give in the ground (acts on heavy going): sometimes bandaged: usually visored nowadays: has joined Mrs M. Reveley. *M. H. Easterby*

NORWICH 5 b.h. Top Ville 129 – Dame Julian 84 (Blakeney 126) [1991 NR 1992 **111** 7v² 6m 7.3d 7f⁵ 7s* 7d⁶ 7m⁶] big, useful-looking horse: very useful performer at best: 4-length winner of listed event at the Curragh in September: much better effort after in pattern company on final run when creditable effort behind Selkirk at Newmarket: ideally suited by 7f: acts on any going: usually front runner: goes freely to post. *B. W. Hills*

NORWICK STAR 4 b.f. Norwick (USA) 120 – Gentle Star 77 (Comedy Star –
(USA) 121) [1991 9f 12.2g 13d⁵ 8f⁵ 16m a12g 10m 1992 a13g] rather angular filly: good mover: may prove best short of 1½m: acts on firm going: below form in visor, blinkers and eyeshield: sold 1,650 gns Ascot February Sales. *Mrs M. E. Long*

NO SUBMISSION (USA) 6 b.h. Melyno 130 – Creeping Kate (USA) (Stop The **85**
Music (USA)) [1991 10g* 10g* 10f³ 10g 10d⁶ 1992 10s 10d² 8.9f⁵ 10d 10.4d a8g⁶ a12g] tall, leggy, quite attractive horse: poor mover: fairly useful handicapper at his best: well below form for most of 1992 and sold out of C. Nelson's stable only 3,100 gns Newmarket Autumn Sales after fifth start: stays 1¼m: acts on any going: sometimes on edge: front runner. *D. W. Chapman*

NOTABLE EXCEPTION 3 b.g. Top Ville 129 – Shorthouse 102 (Habitat 134) **53**
[1991 7g 8m 8m 1992 10.2d² 12m⁵ 14.1g 16f³ 12.1s 12.2d³ 11.1d⁴] lengthy gelding: modest performer: stays 2m, at least in moderately-run race: acts on firm and dead

ground: trained until after fourth start by J. Hills, fifth by S. Kettlewell: won juvenile hurdle in November. *Mrs M. Reveley*

NOT ALL BLISS 4 ch.f. Kabour 80 – Wedded Bliss 76 (Relko 136) [1991 NR 1992 10d] sister to several moderate animals: dam won from 1½m to 2m at 5 and 6 yrs: tailed off in celebrity event at Wetherby in November. *G. P. Kelly* —

NOTANOTHERONE (IRE) 4 b.g. Mazaad 106 – Maltese Pet 74 (Dragonara Palace (USA) 115) [1991 a7g a7g⁴ a6g 6f⁵ 6d⁵ 7m 1992 a6g 8g] leggy, close-coupled gelding: rated 49 at 3 yrs: soundly beaten in spring of 1992: stays 7f: acts on hard and dead ground and equitrack: below form blinkered once, often visored: trained first run by J. Long: sold 1,600 gns Ascot June Sales. *J. L. Harris* —

NOTEABILITY 2 ch.f. (Apr 20) Sayf El Arab (USA) 127 – Last Note (Welsh Pageant 132) [1992 7m⁶ 6f⁴ 6m 6g⁵ 7g⁵ 6d 7d] 8,400Y: compact, good-bodied filly: has a quick action: first foal: dam, fourth over 1½m on only start, is out of half-sister to very useful stayer Fortissimo: poor maiden: stays 7f: well below form when blinkered once: sold 1,200 gns Ascot November Sales. *J. Berry* 42

NOT EARSAY 2 ch.f. (Feb 27) Sayyaf 121 – Chubby Ears (Burglar 128) [1992 5g 5f⁴ 6g⁵] half-sister to a winner in Spain: dam ran twice: no worthwhile form. *E. Weymes* —

NOTED STRAIN (IRE) 4 b.g. Gorytus (USA) 132 – Almuadiyeh 69 (Thatching 131) [1991 10g⁴ 10g⁴ 10m⁴ 10m⁵ 10m³ 10.4m⁵ 10d⁵ a14g⁵ a11g⁴ a10g⁵ 1992 10d⁴ 11.9d³ 12.3s 12.1g² a12g* a12g³] good-topped gelding: modest performer: returned to form late in season and won claimer at Southwell: stays 1½m: acts on good to firm and dead ground and on fibresand: ran moderately in visor third start: has had tongue tied down. *P. J. Makin* 52 a57

NOT GORDONS 3 b.c. All Systems Go 119 – Lady Abernant 90 (Abwah 118) [1991 7m 7m 8.3g 1992 8f⁶ 16.1m³] angular, quite good-topped colt: no worthwhile form. *J. H. Johnson* —

NOTHING DOING (IRE) 3 b.g. Sarab 123 – Spoons (Orchestra 118) [1991 NR 1992 10f² 11.4d 10g⁴ 10m⁵ 12s 10m 9.2v²] IR 6,400F, 6,000Y: sturdy gelding: fifth foal: dam unraced: plating-class handicapper: may prove best short of 1¼m: possibly suited by a sound surface: trained by W. Haggas first 3 starts. *W. J. Musson* 52

NOT IN DOUBT (USA) 3 b.c. Tom Rolfe – Trillionaire (USA) 111 (Vaguely Noble 140) [1991 7m 1992 10d⁶ 12.1m* 14f* 14f³ 13.3d⁴ 14.6f 16m⁵ 14m²] close-coupled, unfurnished colt: fairly useful performer: won maiden at Chepstow in May and minor event at Salisbury in June: ran well when blinkered in handicaps last 2 starts, particularly when second at Newmarket: should be suited by test of stamina: acts on firm ground. *H. Candy* 95

NOTLEY 5 b.g. Formidable (USA) 125 – Riviere Bleue (Riverman (USA) 131) [1991 5g 6m⁴ 6m⁴ 5.1g* 6g* 5m* 5m² 6d⁵ 1992 6g² 5s⁴ 6s² 6m 6s 6g 5m* 6.1d³ 6g⁶] sturdy gelding: very useful sprinter but none too consistent in 1992: blinkered first time when winning Doncaster listed race (for second successive season, by a 110

Doncaster Bloodstock Sales Scarbrough Stakes, Doncaster—
only win of the season for Notley (left); he produces a very useful performance
to beat Harvest Girl and Blyton Lad

neck from Harvest Girl) in September: below form in blinkers final run: effective at 5f and 6f: acts on good to firm and soft ground: sometimes edged left but suitable mount for claimer: sent to USA. *R. Hannon*

NOTRELLA (IRE) 3 b.f. Trojan Fen 118 – Recline 70 (Wollow 132) [1991 NR 1992 8.1g4] 1,000F: plain filly: fifth foal: half-sister to 2-y-o sprint winners Yuffrouw Ann (by Tyrnavos) and City Code (by Try My Best) and to 7f winner Princess Silca Key (by Grundy): dam placed over 5f at 2 yrs: well-beaten fourth in claimer at Haydock in August: moved poorly down. *Miss L. A. Perratt* –

NOT SO GENEROUS (IRE) 2 b.f. Fayruz 116 – Ribero's Overture 72 (Ribero 126) [1992 5v3 5g6 5.1s4 5.3f* 5m* 5.1d2 5g3] 1,500Y: leggy, close-coupled filly: has a round action: half-sister to winning hurdler/chaser Sawdust Jack and a winner in Belgium (both by Rarity): dam placed over 5f and 7f at 2 yrs, is sister to Lingfield Oaks Trial winner Riboreen: easily best efforts when winning sellers at Brighton (no bid) and Wolverhampton (retained 3,000 gns) in early-summer: has raced only at 5f: evidently well suited by top-of-the-ground. *W. G. M. Turner* 53

NOT YET 8 b.g. Connaught 130 – Ritratto (Pinturischio 116) [1991 9m 10g5 10d 9.9f 9m 10m4 10.5m5 8m4 8h3 9.9f5 10g* 8.2m 8m 1992 13.8d6 12.1g4 10g 12f5 10m4 9.9f2 12.1f4 12h4 12.1m2 11.1m4 a 12g2 a 12s5 12.2g6 a 12g3 10s 12.1g5] small gelding: carries condition: bad mover: poor handicapper: stays 1½m: acts on fibresand and probably on any turf going: usually held up. *E. Weymes* 45

NOUSHY 4 ch.f. Ahonoora 122 – Bolkonskina (Balidar 133) [1991 7m 6m 10g6 8m5 1992 a 11g3 8s4 10.8d 10g 9.9f 10.8g] small, workmanlike filly: poor maiden: stays 1m: acts on good to firm and soft going: below form visored. *K. S. Bridgwater* 33

NOW BOARDING 5 b.m. Blazing Saddles (AUS) – Strictly Swing 89 (Swing Easy (USA) 126) [1991 7.1d 8m 7m 1992 8d 7g 7m 7.1m 10.2f2 10m3 10.2f* 10m3 11.7f6] lengthy mare: poor handicapper: won at Bath (apprentices) in July: stays 1¼m: acts on hard and dead going. *R. J. Hodges* 39

NOYAN 2 ch.c. (Jan 14) Northern Baby (CAN) 127 – Istiska (FR) (Irish River (FR) 131) [1992 a 7g2 a 7g* 7f* 7g* 7.9d 8d5] 9,000F: rangy, useful-looking colt: fifth foal: closely related to a winning 2-y-o stayer in France by Cresta Rider and half-brother to a winning jumper there and American 3-y-o Zurich (by Private Account), smart performer at 2 yrs: dam French maiden: progressive colt: won maiden at Southwell in July and nurseries at Brighton and York (£12,100 event), rallied splendidly to short head No Reservations in August: visored first time, excellent fifth of 10 to Armiger in Racing Post Trophy at Doncaster: better at 1m than shorter: acts on firm and dead ground: likeable type. *M. Bell* 96

NUCLEAR EXPRESS 5 b.g. Martinmas 128 – Halka (Daring March 116) [1991 5f 5f5 6m4 5g a 8g 1992 5.1m 6g6 8.1m 5d3 6.1d4 5.7f2 6g 6m2] leggy, workmanlike gelding: turns fore-feet in: modest handicapper: stays 6f: acts on firm and dead going: below form blinkered: tends to hang and carry head high: sold out of D. Wintle's stable 3,400 gns Ascot May Sales after first run. *R. Lee* 62

NUEZ 3 b.c. Shareef Dancer (USA) 135 – Nuas (GER) (Aspros (GER)) [1991 NR 1992 10.8g*] compact colt: first foal: dam smart at 2 and 3 yrs in Germany, successful at up to 1¼m in Group/listed company: won maiden at Warwick in April on debut by 2 lengths from Hebridean: seemed sure to improve but suffered hairline fracture of the cannon bone. *C. E. Brittain* 85

NUN THE WISER (IRE) 3 b.f. Commanche Run 133 – Welsh Abbey (Caerleon (USA) 132) [1991 7f 7.5f 7m 8.9d 1992 7v 10d 8d] leggy, sparely-made filly: moderate mover: no form in sellers in 1992. *B. A. McMahon* –

NUR (USA) 3 ch.f. Diesis 133 – Shicklah (USA) 106 (The Minstrel (CAN) 135) [1991 5m* 5m 5.1m3 6g* 6.1m 1992 6.1g 6g5 5.1g] sturdy, lengthy filly: rated 74 at 2 yrs: no form in 1992: stayed 6f: acted on good to firm ground: visits Mujtahid. *H. Thomson Jones* –

NURYANDRA 2 b.f. (Mar 7) Reference Point 139 – Nuryana 107 (Nureyev (USA) 131) [1992 5g2 6m* 6f3 7.1g2 7d4] quite attractive filly: second foal: half-sister to 3-y-o Mystic Park (by Rainbow Quest), 8.1f winner at 2 yrs: dam 1m winner, is out of half-sister to 1000 Guineas winner On The House: landed odds in maiden at Lingfield in May: ran creditably after, third of 6 in Chesham Stakes at Royal Ascot and fourth of 6, beaten around 10 lengths, to Yawl in minor event at Newmarket on first run for 2½ months: will be better suited by 1m. *G. Wragg* 86

NU SHAN (IRE) 2 b.g. (Feb 23) Shareef Dancer (USA) 135 – Nutria (GER) (Tratteggio 123) [1992 7g5 7m5 7d6 9g] good-bodied gelding: half-brother to numerous winners in Germany, including good 2-y-o Nuas: dam won 2 races in Germany: 62

584

modest maiden: visored, found little off bridle and hung left in nursery final outing: should stay beyond 7f: has been gelded. *M. R. Stoute*

NUTACRE 7 b.m. Julio Mariner 127 – Misacre 66 (St Alphage 119) [1991 NR 1992 9g⁶ 17.9d] rangy, workmanlike mare: seems of little account. *G. P. Kelly*   –

NUT BUSH 2 ch.c. (Apr 30) Aragon 118 – Divissima 62 (Music Boy 124) [1992 6m 5m⁵ 6g⁶ 5m² 7m⁶ 6m⁵ 6m a6g* a6g² a6g⁴] 3,500F, 5,400Y: compact colt: somewhat unfurnished: second live foal: dam 6f winner, is half-sister to very useful 1978 2-y-o sprinter Eyelet: fair performer: made all in claimer at Lingfield in November: subsequently sold out of N. Callaghan's stable 2,500 gns Doncaster November Sales: ran creditably afterwards: stays 6f: acts on top-of-the-ground, well suited by all-weather: has run creditably in blinkers. *M. J. Heaton-Ellis*   **50** a67

NUTMEG LASS 3 br.f. Shanekite (USA) – Indian Flower 87 (Mansingh (USA) 120) [1991 NR 1992 10.1d a8g] 4,800Y: second foal: dam 5f winner at 2 and 3 yrs here, later successful 8 times in USA: sire smart sprinter: always behind in claimers at Yarmouth and Lingfield. *B. J. McMath*   –

NUTTY BROWN 2 b.g. (Mar 3) Primitive Rising (USA) 113 – Nuthill (Derrylin 115) [1992 5m² a6g³ a7g³ 7.5d 6g⁶ 6s² 6.1v² a7g⁶] rather unfurnished gelding: third reported foal: dam lightly raced and no form: fair performer: runner-up in nursery at York and maiden at Chester in October: should be at least as effective at 7f as 6f: well suited by plenty of give in the ground, below best on fibresand: well below form when blinkered once. *S. G. Norton*   **69** a55

NYMPH ERRANT 2 b.f. (Jan 20) Be My Guest (USA) 126 – Shirley Superstar 94 (Shirley Heights 130) [1992 a7g⁶] 25,000Y: first foal: dam lightly-raced 7f winner (at 2 yrs), is daughter of very useful (at up to 1¾m) Odeon: 6/1, showed some promise when remote sixth in maiden at Southwell in December: should be suited by 1m + : sure to improve. *P. J. Makin*   – p

O

OAK APPLE (USA) 3 ch.f. Theatrical 128 – Virginia Hills (USA) (Tom Rolfe) [1991 7m⁵ 6.1m² 8.1g⁵ 7m 7g⁵ 1992 7g⁴ a8g 12.2d² 12f² 9.9m⁶ 11.5s*] leggy, close-coupled filly: fair performer: soon pushed along but stayed on well final 2f when winning handicap at Lingfield in October: well worth a try over further than 1½m: acts on any going: has worn bandages. *B. Hanbury*   **67**

OAKMEAD (IRE) 2 b.f. (Apr 5) Lomond (USA) 128 – Amazer (USA) 122 (Vaguely Noble 140) [1992 8.2s⁶] 16,000Y: half-sister to 2 winners in France, notably Delighter (by Lypheor), successful at up to 12.5f and also successful in USA: dam won at up to 12.5f in France and USA, and is sister to Sporting Yankee: 13/2 from 7/2, 14 lengths sixth of 14 to Revere in maiden at Nottingham in October, somewhat detached in rear at halfway then keeping on: will be suited by middle distances: will improve. *P. W. Chapple-Hyam*   **51** p

OARE SPARROW 2 b.f. (Feb 6) Night Shift (USA) – Portvasco 90 (Sharpo 132) [1992 6m⁵ 6d⁴ 7d⁴ 7s] strong, good-bodied filly: has scope: first foal: dam 6f winner: fair maiden: should stay 7f: flashed tail second start. *P. T. Walwyn*   **64**

OBELISKI 6 b.g. Aragon 118 – Pasha's Dream (Tarboosh (USA)) [1991 10d⁴ a11g a14g 14g a14g² a14g²⁴ a14g 11.1v⁶] leggy, angular gelding: has a round action: plating-class handicapper: easily best effort on flat in 1992 when second at Southwell in January: stays 1¾m: goes very well on soft going: blinkered, won claiming chase (claimed by Claes Bjorling £9,560) in October. *P. C. Haslam*   **48**

OBSIDIAN GREY 5 gr.h. Lyphard's Special (USA) 122 – Marcrest (On Your Mark 125) [1991 a5g² a7g* 1992 a7g⁶ a8g 8s 7.5g² 8m⁴ 8.9g] sparely-made horse: modest handicapper: best efforts in 1992 when in frame: stays 1m: acts on good to firm ground and fibresand: not seen out after May. *B. A. McMahon*   **62**

OCARA (USA) 2 b. or br.f. (May 2) Danzig Connection (USA) – Relevant (USA) (Hold Your Peace (USA)) [1992 6g] smallish, light-framed filly: fourth foal: half-sister to 3 minor winners in USA: dam won maiden at around 1m at 2 yrs: sire won Belmont Stakes: 13/2, around 12 lengths eighth of 13 to Inchinor in maiden at Newmarket in August, chasing leaders over 4f then fading and not knocked about: showed a round action: sure to improve: has joined D. Loder. *H. R. A. Cecil*   **58** p

OCEAN LAD 9 b.g. Windjammer (USA) – Elixir 99 (Hard Tack 111§) [1991 NR 1992 14.9v] plain, good-bodied gelding: poor mover: 250/1 and very stiff task on first run on flat since 6 yrs, tailed off in Warwick handicap in March: poor hurdler, successful in 1990/1. *A. J. Chamberlain*

OCO ROYAL   3 b.c. Tinoco 80 – Queen's Royale 80 (Tobrouk (FR)) [1991 6g 6g 7g³ 7g 8m 10m² 8m 1992 12v⁵ 10d4 11.7d⁵ 11.5m 11.7g⁵] leggy, quite attractive colt: modest maiden: should stay 1½m: acts on good to firm and dead ground: usually blinkered on flat, wasn't when winning over hurdles in August. *J. Ffitch-Heyes*   –

OCTOBER BREW (USA)   2 ch.c. (Mar 25) Seattle Dancer (USA) 119 – Princess Fager (USA) (Dr Fager) [1992 7f 7d 8m] $55,000Y: lengthy, good-topped colt: has scope: half-brother to several winners here and in USA: dam won twice over sprint distances in USA at 3 yrs: progressive maiden: sweating, stayed on well from 2f out for seventh of 17 behind Armiger at Newmarket, final and easily best effort: likely to continue on the upgrade. *G. Lewis*   69 p

ODOEN (USA)   3 b.g. Capitol South (USA) – Charbon Risque (USA) (Bold Reason) [1991 6m 1992 7d 8d 9.7g 10g 11g 8.3m] smallish, workmanlike gelding: moderate mover: of little account. *M. R. Channon*   –

O'DONNELL'S FOLLY   3 b.g. Beveled (USA) – Silk Imp 72 (Imperial Fling (USA) 116) [1991 6m 7m4 7s 7d⁵ 7g² 7m 1992 8g³ 6g] leggy, quite good-topped gelding: modest maiden: gambled-on favourite, creditable third in Newmarket claimer in May: died of heart attack at Pontefract nearly 2 months later: was effective at 7f and 1m. *A. Bailey*   50

OEIGHTNINEEIGHT (USA)   3 b.f. Phone Trick (USA) – Kazankina 107 (Malinowski (USA) 123) [1991 NR 1992 a6g³] $57,000Y: fourth reported foal: sister to U.S. winner Deceptive Operator and half-sister to 2 minor winners by Wavering Monarch: dam Irish 1m and 1¼m winner later successful in USA, including in 2 stakes races: sire top-class sprinter, has made very good start at stud: third in maiden at Lingfield in February, very slowly away: dead. *D. R. C. Elsworth*   42

OFFAS IMAGE   4 ch.g. Norwick (USA) 120 – Eridantini (Indigenous 121) [1991 NR 1992 a7g] half-brother to several winners, notably prolific sprint winner Offa's Mead (by Rathlin) and useful sprinter Perfect Timing (by Comedy Star): dam never ran: 33/1 and ridden by apprentice, well beaten in 15-runner claimer at Lingfield in December. *J. M. Bradley*   –

OFFICER CADET   5 b.g. Shernazar 131 – Selection Board 75 (Welsh Pageant 132) [1991 10g 10.4d 10g² 10g² 10d 10.2g² 11.8g² 14m4 14m 1992 16m 16s] close-coupled gelding: moderate mover: rated 57 at 4 yrs: winning hurdler in 1991/2 but no worthwhile form on flat in handicaps in May and October: effective from 1¼m to 1¾m: acts on good to firm ground, but ideally suited by some give: wandered markedly when blinkered: has hung left: sold to join D. Wilson 6,000 gns Ascot December Sales. *R. Curtis*   –

OH SO HANDY   4 b.g. Nearly A Hand 115 – Geordie Lass 58 (Bleep-Bleep 134) [1991 NR 1992 10.3g 11.6g] unfurnished gelding: half-brother to 1980 2-y-o 5f winner Mull of Kintyre (by Murrayfield): dam barely stayed 5f: tailed off in amateurs race and seller in the summer. *R. Curtis*   –

OH SO RISKY   5 b.g. Kris 135 – Expediency (USA) (Vaguely Noble 140) [1991 10g³ 12g 1992 12d6] tall, close-coupled gelding: very smart hurdler, second in 1992 Champion Hurdle: fairly lightly raced on flat, and put up best effort when around 15 lengths sixth of 11 to Saddlers' Hall in John Porter Stakes at Newbury in April, running on having been last entering straight: stays 1½m: acts on good to firm and dead ground: has worn dropped noseband: has been gelded. *D. R. C. Elsworth*   96

OH SO ROSY   3 gr.f. Lomond (USA) 128 – Red Rose Bowl (Dragonara Palace (USA) 115) [1991 6.1m 1992 6m² 6g] close-coupled filly: best effort when second in maiden at Brighton in April: would have stayed 7f: dead. *P. F. I. Cole*   64

OKA FLOW   4 b.c. Vaigly Great 127 – Atoka 97 (March Past 124) [1991 9g6 10d 10g6 a8g³ a11g4 1992 a8g6 a12g 11.1v] leggy, angular colt: has a quick action: rated 49 as 3-y-o for J. Fanshawe: tailed off in spring in 1992: stays 1m: wears blinkers: sold to join Mrs L. Jewell 1,200 gns Doncaster May Sales: not one to trust. *P. A. Blockley*   – §

OKAKU   5 b.g. Be My Guest (USA) 126 – Be My Darling 82 (Windjammer (USA)) [1991 a8g 7g 1992 5f5] strong, good-topped gelding: seems of little account and may well be ungenuine: sold 2,300 gns Ascot July Sales. *D. Burchell*   –

OKAZ (USA)   7 b.g. Temperence Hill (USA) – She Is Gorgeous (USA) (Drop Volley) [1991 NR 1992 10.3g] lengthy gelding: very lightly raced and no worthwhile form on flat. *J. S. Moore*   –

OK BERTIE 2 b.c. (Mar 24) Interrex (CAN) – Rockery 91 (Track Spare 125) **66**
[1992 5g⁵ 7m⁴ 7s 6m 6v] sturdy colt: half-brother to 3-y-o Mummys Rocket (by
Mummy's Game) and 2 winners by Blakeney, including fair 1½m and 2m winner
Rough Stones: dam 2-y-o 6f winner: fair maiden: well beaten when very stiff task in
Racecall Gold Trophy final start: better suited by 7f than 5f: seems suited by
top-of-the-ground. *D. Morris*

OK GUV 2 gr.g. (Mar 20) Governor General 116 – Debbie Do 90 (Absalom 128) –
[1992 5m] 5,200Y: robust gelding: first foal: dam sprinter: blinkered, last of 10 in
seller at Wolverhampton in June. *J. Balding*

O K KEALY 2 gr.c. (May 10) Absalom 128 – Constanza 94 (Sun Prince 128) [1992 – p
7g] 1,500F, 1,100Y: plain colt: half-brother to middle-distance winner Toscana (by
Town And Country) and winners abroad by Sallust and Henbit: dam won over 1½m
from 2 starts: 66/1 and carrying condition, always behind in 18-runner maiden
auction at Redcar in September. *J. M. Carr*

OK RECORDS 5 b.g. Cure The Blues (USA) – Last Clear Chance (USA) –
(Alleged (USA) 138) [1991 NR 1992 12.1s] angular, lightly-made gelding: seems of
little account. *O. O'Neill*

OLD COMRADES 5 ch.g. Music Boy 124 – Miss Candine 66 (King Emperor **58**
(USA)) [1991 5g⁵ 5.8f 5.1m 8.1d 8.1g 8m⁴ 8f⁶ 8f² 8f⁵ 8g* 7g⁴ 6.9f* 6.9s⁴ 1992
7g³ 6g³ 7m 6.1m⁶ 7f³ 8f* 6.9d 8f⁴ 7g⁴ 7d² 8d⁴ 7s⁶ 6.9v² 6.9v³] workmanlike,
good-quartered gelding: poor mover: consistent handicapper: won at Brighton in
July: effective from 6f to 1m: acts on any going: sometimes sweating. *L. G. Cottrell*

OLD FOX (FR) 3 b.g. In Fijar (USA) 121 – Warning Bell 88 (Bustino 136) [1991 –
NR 1992 10g a7g a7g 7d a10g a7g] 170,000 francs (approx £16,800) 2-y-o: plain
gelding: first foal: dam, out of half-sister to top 1981 2-y-o filly Circus Ring, ran 4
times at 3 yrs, winning once over 1¼m: no form. *D. Sasse*

OLD GLORY 4 ch.g. Valiyar 128 – Old Kate 110 (Busted 134) [1991 10d 8.5f⁴ –
7.1m² 7g* 1992 7.6g 8s 10.2d] smallish, sturdy gelding: rated 67p at 3 yrs for G.
Wragg: no form in handicaps in 1992: stays 7f: has joined M. Saunders. *R. J. Holder*

OLD PEG 4 b.f. Reach 122 – Lizarra 74 (High Top 131) [1991 8d 7v² 7g⁶ 8d 1992 –
10.5d] rather angular filly: rated 55 at 3 yrs: modest winning hurdler in 1991/2: still a
maiden on flat, and well beaten in amateurs handicap at Haydock in June: will stay
beyond 7f: acts on heavy going: sold to join R. Manning 4,200 gns Newmarket
September Sales. *M. H. Easterby*

OLD SPECKLED HEN 4 ch.f. The Noble Player (USA) 126 – Making Tracks –
79 (Sagaro 133) [1991 a7g⁵ a8g* a10g² a10g⁵ 10g 8.2f 10m* 9.7f³ 10.8m a8g 1992
10.2g] leggy, rather sparely-made filly: rated 55 (on the all-weather) at 3 yrs for M.
Fetherston-Godley: last of 16 in handicap in July, 1992: stays 1¼m: acts on firm
ground and equitrack. *T. Casey*

OLEJ (USA) 3 b.c. Danzig Connection (USA) – Smarted (USA) (Smarten (USA)) –
[1991 8.2f 7g 1992 11.7s 16s] smallish colt: poor maiden: off course over 5 months
between starts in 1992: should stay middle distances: sold 1,150 gns Ascot November Sales. *Lord Huntingdon*

OLETTE 3 b.f. Rousillon (USA) 133 – Royal Loft 105 (Homing 130) [1991 7m³ **91**
6.1m* 1992 7g⁴ 8m* 7g 7f* 7d⁴ 8g⁶ 7d² 8g*] rather leggy, plain filly: fluent mover:
progressed into a fairly useful performer: made all in handicaps at Doncaster and
Brighton in the summer: clearly best efforts in apprentice races at Ascot last 2
starts, leading 4f out when successful: effective at 7f/1m: acts on any going:
blinkered (fair effort at the time) on reappearance: tends to take keen hold and carry
head high: sent to race in USA. *G. Wragg*

OLICANA (IRE) 2 ch.g. (Mar 13) Persian Bold 123 – Maniusha 87 (Sallust 134) **50** p
[1992 7f 8.2g 8v] IR 31,000Y: angular, workmanlike colt: has a free, rather round
action: half-brother to 3 winners abroad, one over jumps: dam 10.2f and 1½m
winner, is out of half-sister to Lord Gayle: probably capable of better than he's
shown in minor event at Doncaster (when very green) and maidens at Nottingham
(never placed to challenge) and Leicester (on very heavy ground) in the autumn:
will be suited by 1¼m: has joined J. Hanson. *B. W. Hills*

OLIFANTSFONTEIN 4 b.g. Thatching 131 – Taplow (Tap On Wood 130) [1991 **80**
6f* 6d² 5m 7d 6g 5m 1992 6d 5d* 5g* 5.1d² 6g 5g⁵ 6d 5s³ 5g* 5m 5.2g⁴ 5d⁵ 5d 5d
5g] lengthy, angular gelding: fairly useful handicapper: won at Kempton and
Sandown (2): well below par last 3 starts: best form at 5f: acts on firm and soft
ground: effective blinkered or not: has run creditably when sweating: speedy. *R.
Simpson*

OLIVADI (IRE)   2 b.c. (Mar 16) Prince Rupert (FR) 121 – So Stylish 77 (Great   **62**
Nephew 126) [1992 6g⁶ 8g⁶] 18,500Y: smallish, stocky colt: second foal: half-brother
to 1991 2-y-o 7f winner Well Appointed (by Petorius): dam, maiden suited by 1½m,
is half-sister to Cesarewitch winner Sir Michael: modest form, not knocked about,
in auction event at York in July: well-backed favourite though still carrying plenty of
condition, well below that form at Redcar 7 weeks later. *L. M. Cumani*

OLLIVER DUCKETT   3 b.g. Bustino 136 – Tatiana 59 (Habitat 134) [1991 NR   –
1992 9f⁴ 10f⁵ 10d] 7,200Y: lengthy gelding: second foal: half-brother to poor sprint
maiden Domiana (by Primo Dominie): dam maiden stayed 1m, is out of half-sister to
Derby second Cavo Doro: no worthwhile form in maidens, off course 4 months
before final one. *P. Calver*

OLYMPIC RUN   2 b.f. (Feb 7) Salse (USA) 128 – Figini 74 (Glint of Gold 128)   **56**
[1992 7.1d⁴ 7m 8.1s⁵ 7s] 20,000Y: smallish, good-bodied filly: second foal: half-
sister to 3-y-o 6f (at 2 yrs) and 8.2f winner Killy (by Dominion): dam lightly-raced
half-sister to high-class middle-distance colt Electric: modest form in maidens first
3 starts, each time giving impression capable of better: well beaten in 18-runner
nursery at Leicester final start. *J. L. Dunlop*

OMBRE DARME (IRE)   2 b.g. (Mar 25) Vacarme (USA) 121 – Just A Shadow   **54**
(Laser Light 118) [1992 5g 6m 6f² 6d 7f² 7g 8g] IR 8,600F, 6,200Y, 10,000 2-y-o:
strong, lengthy gelding: half-brother to modest miler Overpower (by Try My Best)
and a winner in Italy by Head For Heights: dam fair Irish 5f performer: modest
maiden: best efforts when runner-up in sellers at Warwick and Brighton: suited by
7f: acts on firm ground: blinkered last 5 starts: sold 3,400 gns Newmarket Autumn
Sales. *J. W. Payne*

OMIDJOY (IRE)   2 ch.f. (Mar 6) Nishapour (FR) 125 – Fancy Finish 67 (Final   **68**
Straw 127) [1992 6.1m 8.2d 8g² 8.5m³] IR 5,000Y: smallish, sparely-made filly:
second living foal: dam should have been suited by 7f or 1m: much improved efforts
in maidens at Leicester and Beverley last 2 starts: stays 8.5f: acts on good to firm
ground. *S. P. C. Woods*

OMORSI   5 b.m. Prince Tenderfoot (USA) 126 – Her Name Was Lola (Pitskelly   –
122) [1991 a 12g a 13g 12f 12f³ 12d 12g 16.2d⁶ 14.1f⁶ 16m⁶ 1992 12d] leggy mare: poor
maiden. *J. White*

ONCILLA   3 b.f. Sure Blade (USA) 130 – 'tis A Kitten (USA) (Tisab (USA)) [1991   –
NR 1992 10m 10.4g] lengthy, plain filly: moderate walker: fifth foal: half-sister to 7f
winners Catundra (by Far North) and Elemis (by Sir Ivor) and a winner in USA: dam
winner at up to 9f, from good family: readily outpaced in 8-runner maidens at
Newmarket and York (swished tail repeatedly in paddock) in late-summer: sold
3,600 gns Newmarket December Sales. *A. C. Stewart*

ONE DOLLAR MORE   4 b.c. Gabitat 119 – Burglars Girl 63 (Burglar 128) [1991   –
8g 7d 6.1m 1992 7m⁶ 10g] workmanlike colt: no worthwhile form in midsummer, in
Windsor seller (wore near-side pricker) last time: sold 450 gns Ascot September
Sales. *B. Gubby*

ONE FOR THE BOYS   5 ch.g. Superlative 118 – Contenance (GER) (Luciano)   –
[1991 NR 1992 12.3m a 12g 16.2d] sturdy gelding: rated 50 at 3 yrs: well beaten in
handicaps in 1992, pulling up lame final start: probably stayed 1¾m: acted on good to
firm ground: dead. *Capt. J. Wilson*

ONE FOR THE CHIEF   4 b.g. Chief Singer 131 – Action Belle (Auction Ring   –
(USA) 123) [1991 12.3s 12m 16m 16.2g 1992 16.2g 14.1d 21.6g] sturdy gelding: moderate mover: no form since 2 yrs, including in seller and in a visor. *R. M. Whitaker*

ONE FOR THE POT   7 ch.g. Nicholas Bill 125 – Tea-Pot 77 (Ragstone 128)   –
[1991 13d* 18.4d⁶ 14g³ 13.4d⁴ 11.9g⁴ 11.9d³ 16.5d 1992 12.3v] strong, short-backed
gelding: rated 71 at 6 yrs for Mrs J. Ramsden: sold 15,000 gns Doncaster March
Sales: never dangerous and not knocked about in handicap in April: stays 2m: acts
on any going, but particularly well on easy surface: held up, has turn of foot, and
suited by strong gallop: has won for apprentice. *M. P. Naughton*

ONE FOR TONDY   2 b.f. (Mar 16) Local Suitor (USA) 128 – Transcendence   –
(USA) 71 (Sham (USA)) [1992 6m] 1,300F: heavy-topped filly: second foal: half-
sister to a winner in Germany: dam 11f and 12.3f winner: backward, gave trouble
stalls, well behind throughout in maiden at Ripon in August. *N. Bycroft*

ONE MAGIC MOMENT (IRE)   4 b.f. Thatching 131 – Debutante 78 (Silly   **47**
Season 127) [1991 6g 1992 a 8g a 8g a 6g* a 6g a 7s 6m a 6g⁴ a 6g⁵ a 7g⁵ 8d a 7g] big,
workmanlike filly: turns fore-feet markedly: moderate mover: inconsistent handicapper: won at Southwell in July: best at up to 7f: acts on all-weather surfaces and

good to firm ground: sold to join Mrs F. White 2,100 gns Newmarket Autumn Sales. *C. A. Cyzer*

ONE MORE POUND   2 b.g. (Jun 2) Northern State (USA) 91 – Malise (Royal   –
Palace 131) [1992 a8g a8g] half-brother to 3-y-o Husthwaite Hills (by Efisio) and
1984 2-y-o 5f winner Esilam (by Frimley Park): dam ran twice: well beaten in
maidens at Lingfield. *M. D. I. Usher*

ONE OFF THE RAIL (USA)   2 b.c. (Feb 19) Rampage (USA) – Catty Queen   65
(USA) (Tom Cat) [1992 a8g6 a8g3 a8g2 a8g2] $6,500Y, resold $11,500Y: half-brother
to a minor winner by Drop Your Drawers: dam ran once: sire best at around 9f: fair
form in maidens at Lingfield: stays 1m well. *A. Moore*

ONE OF THE LADS   10 ch.g. Decent Fellow 114 – Medford Lady (Kabale 103)   –
[1991 NR 1992 8f 11.5m 7m 18.2g 10f] plain gelding: third foal: dam never ran: of little
account. *B. R. Cambidge*

ONE VOICE (USA)   3 ch.c. (Apr 8) Affirmed (USA) – Elk's Ellie (USA) (Vagu-   43
ely Noble 140) [1992 7d 8v 7g] $18,000Y: tall, close-coupled, angular colt: has a
round action: half-brother to 2 winners by Northern Baby, including 3-y-o 1¾m
winner Mootawel, and a winner in France at 1m: dam minor winner in North
America from good family: poor form in maidens: will be better suited by middle
distances. *Sir Mark Prescott*

ONEWITHWHITEPAW   2 ch.g. (Jan 27) Vaigly Great 127 – Aunt Blue 75 (Blue   –
Refrain 121) [1992 5s 6.1d4 6m] 2,200F, 14,000Y: robust gelding: first foal: dam
lightly-raced maiden, herself twice over 7f at 2 yrs, is half-sister to very smart Sauceboat and daughter of good 1¼m filly Cranberry Sauce: no worthwhile form, in
blinkers last time: sold to join G. Jones 800 gns Doncaster September Sales. *A.
Bailey*

ON GOLDEN POND (IRE)   2 b.f. (Apr 6) Bluebird (USA) 125 – Art Age   62 p
(Artaius (USA) 129) [1992 7s] IR 30,000Y: strong, lengthy filly: first foal: dam
unraced: 20/1, around 10 lengths eleventh of 19 to Rockover in maiden auction at
Goodwood in October, fading from 2f out: will improve. *P. F. I. Cole*

ONLY A ROSE   3 br.f. Glint of Gold 128 – No More Rosies 74 (Warpath 113) [1991   –
NR 1992 9m 12d5 12.4m5 14.1g 14.6s] 2,500F: leggy, close-coupled filly: second foal:
half-sister to juvenile 7f winner/winning hurdler Beachy Head (by Damister): dam
1¼m winner from 2 starts, is half-sister to Derby third Mount Athos and smart
sprinter John Splendid: has shown signs of a little ability: should prove suited by
1¾m: won juvenile hurdles in November. *C. W. Thornton*

ONLY ROYALE (IRE)   3 b.f. Caerleon (USA) 132 – Etoile de Paris 116 108 p
(Crowned Prince (USA) 128) [1991 NR 1992 8.1m* 10m* 10s* 10d* 10g2 12v*] IR
54,000Y: good-topped filly: seventh foal: half-sister to fair 1990 Irish 2-y-o 6f winner
Green Lightning (by Green Desert) and 11f winner The Soviet (by Nureyev): dam
Irish 6f and 7f winner is half-sister to high-class 1m to 1½m performer Northern
Treasure: highly progressive performer: successful in maiden at Edinburgh in May,
2 handicaps at Newbury in midsummer, a £9,300 contest at Milan in September and
a listed event there by 5 lengths in November: 1½ lengths second to Plan Ahead in
handicap at Ascot: stays 1½m: acts on good to firm and heavy ground. *L. M. Cumani*

ON REQUEST (IRE)   2 ch.f. (Mar 10) Be My Guest (USA) 126 – Welcome   53
Break (Wollow 132) [1992 6m 8.1s 8g4 8.2d] leggy filly: seventh foal: sister to smart
6f to 1¼m winner Invited Guest, later a good winner in USA: dam unraced half-
sister to Interval and daughter of Cambridgeshire winner Intermission: modest
maiden: shapes like a stayer. *I. A. Balding*

ON THE EDGE   4 b.c. Vaigly Great 127 – Final Request 63 (Sharp Edge 123)   75
[1991 a5g* a5g* a6g2 a6g2 a7g5 6f4 5m2 5g 5f 6f3 5m3 1992 a5g2 a5g3 a6g5 a5g 6g6 a79
5m3 5m4 5m 6d 5s6 6d] quite attractive colt: fair handicapper: usually ran creditably, but below form on a soft surface last 3 starts: should prove at least as effective
at 6f as 5f: best on top-of-the-ground or on fibresand: yet to race on equitrack: has
worn tongue strap: rather fractious sort: sold 1,600 gns Doncaster November Sales.
T. D. Barron

ON THE HOP (IRE)   3 b.f. Milk of The Barley 115 – Rapid Rhythm 63 (Free   –
State 125) [1991 5m6 1992 7.5m 6f] leggy, close-coupled filly: seems of little
account. *A. P. Stringer*

ON THE RAMPAGE   3 b.f. Midyan (USA) 124 – Rampage 93 (Busted 134) [1991   –
NR 1992 10d 7f 10.2f 8g 10.1g] small, sparely-made filly: half-sister to several
winners, including 1½m winner Rambo Castle (by Castle Keep) and French 11.7f
winner Catalogue (by Auction Ring): dam, out of half-sister to 1000 Guineas winner

Full Dress II, won from 11f to 1¾m: no worthwhile form, including in blinkers once: trained first 3 starts by R. Hannon: sold 450 gns Ascot July Sales. *P. Mitchell*

ON TIPTOES   4 b.f. Shareef Dancer (USA) 135 – Pennyweight (Troy 137) [1991 6m³ 5m 5.2m* 5m* 1992 5m 5m] big, good-bodied filly: easy mover: useful performer (rated 107) at 3 yrs when gained last win in listed race at Newmarket: fair eighth of 14 under 10-0 in handicap at York on reappearance: always struggling in Temple Stakes at Sandown later in May: best at 5f: yet to race on a soft surface: sweating and edgy (ran moderately) once. *J. P. Leigh*   **97**

ON Y VA (USA)   5 ch.m. Victorious (USA) – Golden Moony (Northfields (USA)) [1991 7d³ 7.6g⁴ a7g⁵ 7g² 8.2d⁴ 7v* 8g 7m 7s² 6.9s* a10g a7g a8g⁵ a7g² 1992 a7g* a7g⁶ 8s³ 8g⁴ 7g 7f a7g 7m 7.1g⁴ 7g³ a7s⁵ a7g² a7g³] sparely-made, angular mare: modest handicapper: won at Southwell in January: effective at 7f/1m: best with give in the ground or on all-weather surfaces. *R. J. R. Williams*   **67 a63**

OOZLEM (IRE)   3 b.c. Burslem 123 – Fingers (Lord Gayle (USA) 124) [1991 7g 7g 1992 12g 10s⁶ 11.8g 12d] workmanlike colt: poor maiden. *C. A. Horgan*   **–**

OPEN AGENDA (IRE)   3 b.c. Ajdal (USA) 130 – Metair 118 (Laser Light 118) [1991 NR 1992 7g⁴ 7m] lengthy colt with scope: ninth foal: half-brother to several winners, including 1m winner Connue (by Known Fact) and useful sprinters Meteoric (by High Line) and Fine Edge (by Sharpen Up): dam game sprinter: tenderly handled when fourth in newcomers race at Doncaster: sweating, led briefly over 2f out, faltered and eased as if something amiss in York maiden later in the spring: sold 3,100 gns Newmarket July Sales. *B. W. Hills*   **62**

OPENING OVERTURE (USA)   6 b.m. At The Threshold (USA) – Rhine Queen (FR) (Rheingold 137) [1991 NR 1992 a12g] big, angular, unfurnished mare: has a long stride: soon struggling in handicap at Southwell in February, first run on flat since 3 yrs: sold to join C. Beever 1,300 gns Doncaster May Sales. *C. N. Allen*   **–**

OPERA GHOST   6 b.h. Caerleon (USA) 132 – Premier Rose 117 (Sharp Edge 123) [1991 11.9d⁴ 1992 11.9g⁶ 12d⁴ 11.9d² 12d* 12g³ 11.9m* 12g⁶ 12s 12m⁶] close-coupled, quite good-topped horse: carries plenty of condition: fairly useful handicapper: won at Newbury and York (very strongly-run £12,500 race) in the summer: should stay beyond 1½m: acts on firm and dead ground (got poor run on soft): well suited by strongly-run race: has run well when sweating: game and genuine, and most consistent. *P. W. Harris*   **91**

OPERA HOUSE   4 b.c. Sadler's Wells (USA) 132 – Colorspin (FR) 118 (High Top 131) [1991 10m* 10g² 12g⁴ 1992 10g³ 10g* 10m* 10m⁶ 10s² 12g³ 12s*]   **125**

Held up by an injury to a pastern as a three-year-old, Opera House put in his first full season in 1992 and turned out to be pretty much the colt he'd promised to be when, as a very well-bred youngster, he'd thrashed his field in a back-end maiden at Leicester on his debut. He won three pattern races in 1992, the Tattersalls Rogers Gold Cup at the Curragh, the Brigadier Gerard Stakes at Sandown and the Hoover Cumberland Lodge Stakes at Ascot, and ran into a place on the two occasions on which he was stepped up to Group 1, in the Coral-Eclipse and the King George VI and Queen Elizabeth Diamond Stakes. It is an indication of his ability and his consistency that a six-length defeat into sixth-of-eleven place behind Kooyonga when favourite for the Prince of Wales's Stakes at Royal Ascot can be counted his only remotely disappointing performance.

Although by Sadler's Wells out of the Irish Oaks winner Colorspin, Opera House was put back to a mile and a quarter to start with and was kept there until after the Eclipse. In truth, there seemed no pressing reason to go up again in distance as the season began to unfold. He was soon off the mark in the Tattersalls Rogers Gold Cup, confirming a very promising return against Dear Doctor in the Gordon Richards Stakes at Sandown, and before the end of May he had the Brigadier Gerard Stakes in the bag as well. This form demanded he be taken seriously for the Eclipse. In receipt of 3 lb, he'd got the better of hardened campaigner Zoman in a desperate finish in Ireland, wearing him down on the post as they came well clear of the rest; at Sandown, he'd beaten Wiorno and Young Buster convincingly in a tactical three-runner race. There was the matter of his defeat behind Kooyonga at Royal Ascot to consider, of course, as well as the soft ground; however, he had, perhaps, been ridden a shade too conservatively at Royal Ascot, and it was a fact that he'd been forced wide on the home turn. On Eclipse day, Opera House showed that soft ground is no handicap to him by finishing a length-and-a-half second of twelve to Kooyonga. At the same time, the winner made him look a grade short of top class. Opera House came to take the lead from Arcangues over a furlong out, but was soon outpaced by the filly.

Opera House could scarcely have faced a much tougher test on his return to a mile and a half than in the King George, and it wasn't seriously anticipated that any improvement brought about by the longer distance would be enough to swing the outcome his way. St Jovite beat him even more convincingly than Kooyonga had. Nevertheless Opera House finished a creditable third, only half a length behind his stable-companion Saddlers' Hall, keeping on as well as he could, having been shaken off by St Jovite early in the straight. He found the opposition in the Cumberland Lodge Stakes less exacting when returned to course and distance in the autumn on his next outing. Sapience, Red Bishop and the three-year-olds Bonny Scot and Garden of Heaven provided it, Red Bishop in particular expected to go well on his first start at a mile and a half. Opera House won by a length and a half from Red Bishop, who was eased near the finish, after a sustained duel in the straight. Opera House took the lead two and a half furlongs out, lost it for a few strides around the furlong marker, then battled back to get clearly on top in the last hundred yards. Red Bishop was receiving 5 lb, and the winner's performance was a high-class one, a point underlined by the third home Garden of Heaven when that lightly-raced colt won the Prix du Conseil de Paris next time out. Opera House was also due to have another run, but he failed to meet his engagement in the Turf Classic at Belmont.

Opera House's family is a strong one. Colorspin was one of the easiest winners imaginable of the Irish Oaks, while her half-sister, the One Thousand Guineas third Bella Colora, is the dam of Stagecraft who won the Prince of

Tattersalls Rogers Gold Cup, the Curragh—Opera House (right) just wears down Zoman

Hoover Cumberland Lodge Stakes, Ascot—
another battling performance from Opera House;
he holds off Red Bishop and Garden of Heaven (right)

	Sadler's Wells (USA) (b 1981)	Northern Dancer (b 1961)	Nearctic Natalma
Opera House (b.c. 1988)		Fairy Bridge (b 1975)	Bold Reason Special
	Colorspin (FR) (b 1983)	High Top (b 1969)	Derring-Do Camenae
		Reprocolor (ch 1976)	Jimmy Reppin Blue Queen

Wales's Stakes as well as the Brigadier Gerard Stakes in 1991. Opera House is Colorspin's first foal. The second, Highland Dress (by Lomond), has had even less racing than Opera House at the same stage but has shown very useful form. Opera House, a leggy, quite attractive colt, is a good walker with a fluent action in his faster paces. He is equally effective at a mile and a quarter and a mile and a half, and on soft and good to firm going. He will win more races, even if the very best are out of reach. *M. R. Stoute*

OPTICAL (IRE) 3 b.g. Vision (USA) – Sussita (On Your Mark 125) [1991 NR **77**
1992 a8g⁴ a8g⁶ 7d 5v³ 8s 6d² 5m* 5g* 5f* 5m⁴] 8,000F, 5,300Y: small, sturdy
gelding: half-brother to Irish 7f winner Sussed Out (by Dara Monarch) and a winner

592

in Belgium: dam won over 5f at 3 yrs in Ireland: fair performer: trained first 2 starts by H. Whiting: won 4-runner maiden at Hamilton in May and handicaps at Catterick and Sandown (apprentices, quickened well) in June: ran creditably in £17,900 handicap at Ascot week later, having got well behind early on: seems suited by sound surface at 5f. *M. P. Naughton*

ORATEL FLYER   5 gr.h. Kirchner 110 – Hyperion Princess (Dragonara Palace   **27** (USA) 115) [1991 5f 5m2 5m 5d4 5d 5f 5m 5.3g a6g a5g a5g5 a6g6 1992 a6g 6f5 5m4 5m 5m4 5.1f] close-coupled, rather angular horse: moderate mover: maiden handicapper: stays 6f: acts on firm going: below form blinkered once, usually visored nowadays. *R. Thompson*

ORBA GOLD (USA)   4 br.f. Gold Crest (USA) 120 – Miss Derby (USA) (Master   – Derby (USA)) [1991 7v4 6d a7g* a7g2 a7g4 1992 a7g a8g] lengthy, rather angular filly: keen walker: moderate mover: rated 67 at 3 yrs: well beaten in January, 1992: stays 7f: acts on fibresand: often bandaged. *R. J. Manning*

ORCHANDA   4 b.f. Pennine Walk 120 – My Fair Orchid 71 (Roan Rocket 128)   – [1991 7v4 8g 8h2 10.5g 11m 9.2s 1992 a8g a13g 8.5m] neat filly: bad mover: bad maiden: should stay 1¼m: acts on any going: wore net muzzle final start: sold 725 gns Ascot June Sales. *Mrs A. Knight*

ORCHARD BAY   3 ch.f. Formidable (USA) 125 – Green Pool 39 (Whistlefield   **46** d 118) [1991 5d5 5d2 5f 5f3 5m* 5m3 6m2 5g5 6d 7f4 7f 5.7g a7g 1992 7v 5.1d3 7.1m 5.7h2 7f6 6f5 5.7f 7d6 5.7d 6g 6s] compact filly: poor plater: best form at up to 6f: acts on dead and hard ground: below form visored. *D. R. Tucker*

ORCHARD QUEEN (IRE)   2 ch.f. (Mar 4) The Noble Player (USA) 126 –   – Galaxy Scorpio (Saritamer (USA) 130) [1992 5.1m] IR 2,500Y, 6,600 2-y-o: half-sister to several winners, including 2-y-o 5f winners Do I Know You (by Kafu) and Micdan (by Exhibitioner): dam unraced daughter of sister to Abergwaun: always behind in maiden at Bath in May. *J. White*

ORCHID VALLEY (IRE)   3 b.f. Cyrano de Bergerac 120 – Dane Valley (Simbir   – 130) [1991 7m 1992 5.1m] close-coupled filly: twice raced, and no worthwhile form in maidens. *R. M. Whitaker*

ORIBI   3 b.f. Top Ville 129 – Regent's Fawn (CAN) (Vice Regent (CAN)) [1991 NR   **59** 1992 12.1m5 12d6] lengthy filly: third foal: half-sister to useful middle-distance stayer Regent's Folly (by Touching Wood) and quite modest 1¼m winner Fallow Deer (by Jalmoud): dam, maiden, suited by 1½m: green, showed ability in maidens at Chepstow (bandaged) and Salisbury 2 months after: visits Mtoto. *P. F. I. Cole*

ORIENT AIR   4 b.f. Prince Sabo 123 – Chinese Falcon 81 (Skymaster 126) [1991   **60** 5f2 5m5 5f 5f 6f 7m* 7m 7m 8m 7m 1992 a6g* a6g3 a5g 6d5 7g 5.9d 6g 6f 5d* 5g] big, a68 lengthy filly: none too consistent handicapper: won at Southwell in February and Catterick (first run for 5 months) in October: stays 7f: acts on firm and dead going, and on fibresand: below form visored, usually blinkered: sometimes slowly away: has hung and flashed tail but suitable mount for claimer. *T. D. Barron*

ORIENTAL PRINCESS   2 b.f. (Apr 10) Reesh 117 – Eastern Romance 73   – (Sahib 114) [1992 6m4 a6g 7g] leggy, rather sparely-made filly: half-sister to several winners, most short of 1m: dam 2-y-o 6f seller winner: soundly beaten in minor event and maidens: bolted before start final run. *Mrs S. Oliver*

ORIENTAL SONG   3 ch.f. Battle Hymn 103 – Miss Kung Fu 70 (Caliban 123)   – [1991 NR 1992 a7g 8g6 5g 5s 6m a5g] workmanlike filly: fifth reported foal: half-sister to 2 winners in Malaysia: dam won 7f seller: no worthwhile form, including in blinkers. *K. S. Bridgwater*

ORIENTEER   3 b.g. Reference Point 139 – Optimistic Lass (USA) 117 (Mr   – Prospector (USA)) [1991 NR 1992 12g] good-topped gelding: fourth foal: half-brother to high-class sprinter/miler Golden Opinion (by Slew O' Gold): dam won Musidora and Nassau Stakes: tailed-off last of 8 in Newmarket maiden in May, only run: sold to join Mrs A. Swinbank's stable 3,400 gns Newmarket July Sales. *L. M. Cumani*

ORMSBY (IRE)   3 b.c. Ela-Mana-Mou 132 – Saving Mercy 101 (Lord Gayle **109** (USA) 124) [1991 NR 1992 8s* 10g* 12m] 58,000Y: fourth reported foal: half-brother to quite modest Irish 1¼m and 9f-placed Ballinafagh (by Kings Lake) and fair 7f-placed Missing You (by Ahonoora): dam won Lincoln Handicap and stayed 1¼m: useful Irish performer: won minor event at Naas and listed race (by length from Andros Bay) at the Curragh in spring: not seen out again after never-dangerous seventh of 11, beaten over 20 lengths, in Irish Derby at the Curragh in June: stays 1¼m: may be capable of better. *D. K. Weld, Ireland*

ORPEN (IRE) 4 gr.g. Caerleon (USA) 132 – Caring (Crowned Prince (USA) 128) – [1991 8g⁶ a12g⁵ 1992 a7g⁶] thrice raced and modest ex-Irish maiden: not seen again on flat after blinkered in Southwell claimer in January: stays 1m: joined C. Cowley. *W. A. O'Gorman*

ORTHORHOMBUS 3 b.c. Aragon 118 – Honeybeta 105 (Habitat 134) [1991 5m3 99 5m* 5g² 5.2g⁴ 6m⁴ 6.1m² 6.1s³ 1992 6d⁵ 6g 6f* 6g 6f* 6m 6s⁵ 6m 6g 5d⁵ 5.6m 8d 7m] strong, workmanlike colt: useful handicapper: won at Newbury (apprentice ridden) in May and York (£24,000 William Hill Golden Spurs Trophy, by a neck from Double Blue) in June: ideally suited by 6f: acts on firm and dead ground: has run creditably visored but mostly blinkered: inconsistent. *G. Lewis*

OSCARS QUEST 2 b.g. (Jan 29) Nomination 125 – Northern Pleasure (North- 44 fields (USA)) [1992 5s⁶ 5f⁴ 5m² 6f 5m⁵ 5g] 3,700F, IR 4,000Y: small, heavy-topped gelding: moderate mover: first foal: dam unraced: went the wrong way after second in Edinburgh maiden in May: should be better suited by 6f than 5f: sold 740 gns Doncaster September Sales. *J. Berry*

OSCILANTE 4 b.g. Swing Easy (USA) 126 – Lillylee Lady (USA) (Shecky – Greene (USA)) [1991 8g 7m 10m 8.3m 1992 7d 5.7d 6g 8s] leggy, lengthy gelding: moderate mover: no worthwhile form. *R. Akehurst*

OSGATHORPE 5 ch.g. Dunbeath (USA) 127 – Darlingka 77 (Darling Boy 124) – [1991 10d 10d³ 10.9g⁵ 12g 1992 a8g⁶ a8g a10g] big, good-bodied gelding: rated 47 on flat at 4 yrs: successful over hurdles in August but mostly disappointed afterwards and sold out of G. Richards' stable 3,400 gns before reappearance: stays 1¼m: acts on firm and dead ground: tried blinkered once. *M. D. I. Usher*

OSSIE 3 b.c. Nicholas Bill 125 – Ozra 63 (Red Alert 127) [1991 6f 8.1g 8m 1992 a5g³ 40 a7g a6g⁵ a7g 10s⁶ a12g] close-coupled colt: fluent mover: poor form. *B. Palling*

OTHELLO 3 br.c. Ahonoora 122 – Cent Fleurs (USA) (Nijinsky (CAN) 138) [1991 – NR 1992 a8g⁴] lengthy, unfurnished colt: 52,000Y: first foal: dam, ran once, is daughter of half-sister to Mill Reef: bit backward, signs of only a little ability in weak maiden at Lingfield in December: moved moderately: may do better. *W. Carter*

OTHER ONE 2 ch.f. (Mar 17) Hadeer 118 – Penny In My Shoe (USA) (Sir Ivor 60 135) [1992 5g* 6g⁶] leggy filly: poor mover: half-sister to a winner in USA by Believe It: dam half-sister to Gorytus out of 1000 Guineas winner Glad Rags II: green when 1½-length winner of maiden at Doncaster in March: always last in 6-runner listed race at Kempton over 5 months after. *N. C. Wright*

OTTER BUSH 3 b.g. Daring March 116 – Rhythmical 69 (Swing Easy (USA) 126) – [1991 NR 1992 8g 7.6m 10f a12g 10m] close-coupled, good-topped gelding: third foal: half-brother to unreliable 1¼m to 12.5f winner Jokers Patch (by Hotfoot): dam, maiden plater, stayed 7f: seems of little account. *G. Blum*

OUBECK 2 b.f. (Apr 6) Mummy's Game 120 – School Road 88 (Great Nephew 56 p 126) [1992 5.9g 7s⁶ 6d] 7,800F: good-topped filly: moderate mover: sister to 1990

William Hill Golden Spurs Trophy (Handicap), York—
little between the blinkered Orthorhombus and Double Blue on Timeform Charity Day;
the 22nd Timeform Charity Day raised £141,742, mostly for Cancer charities

Hamdan Al-Maktoum's "Oumaldaaya"

2-y-o 6f winner Penny Mint and half-sister to 4 winners, including 1988 2-y-o 5f winner Gleeful (by Sayf El Arab) and 3-y-o sprinter Educated Pet (by Petong): dam, 6f and 7f winner at 4 yrs, is sister to smart miler Saher: shaped promisingly when over 7 lengths seventh of 21 to Specified in maiden at Redcar in October, good speed to dispute lead to over 1f out then not hard ridden: burly and green previous month: has scope, and looks sort to do better at 3 yrs. *E. Weymes*

OUMALDAAYA (USA) 3 b.f. Nureyev (USA) 131 – Histoire (FR) (Riverman **111** (USA) 131) [1991 6.1f⁵ 7m² 7g* 1992 7.3d⁵ 8g⁴ 10m* 10.5g 10m⁴ 10s⁴ 10d*] quite attractive filly: good walker and mover: very useful performer: won Lupe Stakes at Goodwood (by 3 lengths from Niodini) in May and Premio Lydia Tesio (beat Lara's Idea ¾ length) at Milan in September: ran creditably in between, in Prix de Diane Hermes at Chantilly, Nassau Stakes (took very strong hold) at Goodwood and Prix de la Nonette at Deauville: stayed 1¼m: acted on good to firm ground and soft: blinkered fifth and sixth starts: front runner: visits Nashwan. *J. L. Dunlop*

OUR AISLING 4 b.f. Blakeney 126 – Mrs Cullumbine 60 (Silly Season 127) [1991 **82** 9s³ 12m² 14f* 13.8m* 14g³ 13.8g* 16f* 16.2f⁴ 16m⁴ 14m 1992 16d² 18.5g⁶ 18f⁵ 15.8d* 15.9m* 16.1g 15.9m* 16.2g⁶] lengthy, angular filly: fair handicapper: successful in summer at Catterick and Chester (2): suited by test of stamina: acts on any going: good mount for claimer: goes really well on a turning track. *S. G. Norton*

OUR AMBER 5 gr.m. Kabour 80 – Amber Vale 98 (Warpath 113) [1991 a6g⁶ a12g **–** 1992 a7g a5g³ a6g 8.1g 5.9h a5g⁵ a6g a5g⁴ 8.1g 6g 6m] workmanlike mare: little a24 worthwhile form in handicaps, tried blinkered once: should stay beyond 5f. *D. W. Chapman*

OUR EDDIE 3 ch.g. Gabitat 119 – Ragusa Girl (Morston (FR) 125) [1991 7m 7g **–** 1992 6g 7m⁶ 7.6m a7g⁵ 8.5d 8.3m 7.6m⁶] leggy, sparely-made gelding: shows knee a56 action: poor maiden: should stay 1m: acts on fibresand: below form visored, often blinkered. *B. Gubby*

OUR EILEEN   3 b.f. Claude Monet (USA) 121 – Have Form (Haveroid 122) [1991   –
NR 1992 7g 6.1d 5g a7g] leggy, angular filly: third foal: half-sister to 5f and 6f winner
Shikari's Son (by Kala Shikari): dam, poor performer, stayed 7f: well beaten in
maidens and handicap: should be suited by 7f + . *B. Smart*

OUR EMMA   3 b.f. Precocious 126 – Miller's Daughter (Mill Reef (USA) 141)   –
[1991 7m⁶ 6g⁴ 6.1m 1992 7g 7m 7g 6g] small, sparely-made filly: soundly beaten in
1992: tried visored. *Mrs Barbara Waring*

OUR JOEY   3 br.g. Daring March 116 – Poppy's Pride (Uncle Pokey 116) [1991 NR   –
1992 12.3m³ a12s⁶ 10d] tall, unfurnished gelding: first foal: dam unraced: no sign of
ability. *J. Wharton*

OUR JOHN   3 b.c. Ballacashtal (CAN) – Ballyreef (Ballymore 123) [1991 5m 5.9h⁴   51
5d⁴ 6g⁴ 5f⁴ 6f 8m a8g⁵ 1992 7v 5g 5m⁵ 6.1g 6m* 6f² 6m⁴ 7g⁵ 6s] good-topped colt:
has a round action: mainly consistent performer: won seller at Hamilton in July:
stays 7f: suited by a sound surface: below form when visored. *Ronald Thompson*

OUR MAN IN HAVANA   3 ch.g. Never So Bold 135 – Bellagio 68 (Busted 134)   –
[1991 a7g⁴ 1992 8d 6.1g a8g⁵] lengthy gelding: has a round action: no form: sold out
of P. Cole's stable 3,300 gns Newmarket Autumn Sales before final outing. *Mrs A.
Swinbank*

OUR MICA   2 gr.g. (Jan 18) Belfort (FR) 89 – Aristata (Habitat 134) [1992 5v³ 5m   48
6d 5g* 5g 5f⁴ 6g⁴ 5g⁵ 5d] 8,400Y: leggy gelding: good walker: moderate mover:
fourth reported foal: half-brother to a winner abroad: dam never ran: somewhat
in-and-out form after winning Haydock seller (no bid) in July and not an easy ride:
should stay 6f: probably acts on any going: usually blinkered. *J. Berry*

OUR NIKKI   2 gr.f. (Mar 26) Absalom 128 – Whisper Gently 91 (Pitskelly 122)   –
[1992 5g 6m 6f] 2,500Y: leggy, sparely-made filly: poor walker: half-sister to 1m
winners Spanish Whisper (by Aragon) and Mascalls Lady (by Nicholas Bill): dam
Irish 9.5f to 1½m winner: seems of little account. *G. Blum*

OUR OCCASION   3 b.c. Sizzling Melody 117 – Skiddaw (USA) (Grey Dawn II   84 d
132) [1991 6d⁴ 6d³ 1992 7.1f* 8m³ 8m 8f 8m* 7g⁴ 7g 8d 8m⁶ 7d] leggy colt: fair form
at best: won maiden at Sandown in June and claimer at Newmarket (easily best
effort, claimed £13,300 out of R. Hannon's stable) in August: below form in
handicaps after: stays 1m: acts on firm going: sometimes wore tongue strap and
crossed noseband: carries head high and none too keen: sold 10,000 gns Newmarket
Autumn Sales. *W. J. Musson*

OUR PAUL   2 b.g. (Mar 7) Dubassoff (USA) – Lady Liza 69 (Air Trooper 115)   –
[1992 6f] 500F: leggy gelding: first foal: dam stayed 1¼m: always well behind,
hanging right, in seller at Ripon in June. *B. W. Murray*

OUR PRICE   2 b.g. (May 19) Silly Prices 110 – Eliza de Rich 57 (Spanish Gold 101)   –
[1992 5g 6f 7f] 1,800Y: small, leggy gelding: fourth reported foal: brother to winning
sprinter Densben and half-brother to 3-y-o Legitim (by Move Off): dam winning
miler: soundly beaten in auctions and seller. *G. M. Moore*

OUR RITA   3 b.f. Hallgate 127 – Ma Pierrette 77 (Cawston's Clown 113) [1991 NR   78
1992 5g⁴ 6f⁴ 6m* 6f² 6f* 6f⁴ 8.1d 5g* 6m⁵ 7m 6s³ 6v*] leggy, lengthy filly: bad
mover: half-sister to 6f (at 2 yrs) and 1m winner Millfields Lady and a winner in Italy
(both by Sayf El Arab), and to 1987 2-y-o 5f winner My Home (by Homing): dam won
from 5f to 1¼m: progressed well in handicaps in 1992, winning at Leicester (seller,
no bid), Thirsk, Sandown (claimed out of P. Kelleway's stable £9,000 in claimer) and
Newcastle: ideally suited by 6f: acts on any going. *Dr J. D. Scargill*

OUR SHADEE (USA)   2 b.c. (Jun 17) Shadeed (USA) 135 – Nuppence 79   57
(Reform 132) [1992 6f 5m² 6m 5m⁶ 6m⁵ 5d² 5g] 4,000Y: lengthy colt: half-brother to
very useful sprinter Posada (by Homing) and fairly useful 1985 2-y-o 6f winner
Mihaarb (by Formidable), later successful at up to 1m in France: dam, second twice
over 5f, is half-sister to Mummy's Pet: modest maiden: ran moderately in
Newmarket nursery final run: stays 6f: acts on good to firm and dead ground: races
keenly. *K. T. Ivory*

OUR SLIMBRIDGE   4 b. or br.g. Top Ville 129 – Bird Point (USA) 87 (Alleged   –
(USA) 138) [1991 10.8d 12f 12.2m⁴ 12.5m³ 12.2m⁴ 11g³ 12m 8.2f 11.8g 12.3g³ 10m⁴
1992 10.8v 11.8d] plain, rather leggy gelding: moderate mover: rated 56 at 3 yrs:
below form in handicaps in 1992: should stay beyond 1½m: acts on good to firm
ground: won over hurdles in October and November. *C. N. Williams*

OUR TOPSIE   5 b.m. My Dad Tom (USA) 109 – Tops 73 (Club House 110) [1991   40
6d⁶ 7g 6g 8m 6g 8.2m 1992 a10g⁶ a10g³ a12g⁶ a10g a10g⁵ 10s² 9s 12v] workmanlike   a26

mare: poor maiden: stays 1¼m: acts on equitrack, form on turf only with some give in the ground: well beaten in blinkers once. *F. J. O'Mahony*

OUT OF ACES 2 b.f. (Mar 20) Relkino 131 – Gambling Wren 53 (Knave To Play 79) [1992 5f² 5g 5d] sparely-made filly: second reported living foal: dam 4-y-o 1½m winner stayed well and also won over hurdles: easily best effort when strong-finishing second in claimer at Ripon in August: outpaced after: needs further than 5f. *Mrs V. A. Aconley* — **38**

OUT OF HOURS 2 br.f. (Mar 9) Lochnager 132 – Tempt Providence 56 (Tina's Pet 121) [1992 5g] first foal: dam maiden best at 2 yrs, stayed 6f: always behind in maiden at Windsor in July. *Dr J. D. Scargill* — **–**

OUT OF STOCK 9 gr. or ro.g. Neltino 97 – Millingdale 65 (Tumble Wind (USA)) [1991 14d³ 14g 1992 12.1s] leggy gelding: poor maiden: stays 1¾m: acts on firm and dead ground: below form blinkered. *R. J. Hodges* — **–**

OUTSET (IRE) 2 ch.c. (Apr 25) Persian Bold 123 – It's Now Or Never 78 (High Line 125) [1992 8s² 8d] 10,000Y: leggy colt: second living foal: dam 1¼m winner, is out of half-sister to top-class sprinter Set Fair: better effort in maidens when staying on at Bath: pulled hard and outpaced from 2f out at Leicester later in autumn: should be suited by 1¼m. *H. Candy* — **63**

OVERPOWER 8 b.g. Try My Best (USA) 130 – Just A Shadow (Laser Light 118) [1991 8m² 8h³ 9d² 8.5f⁴ 10g 8g² 10m² 10.5g² 8.9g 10.5f³ 10.1f⁶ 10.5g⁵ 8m⁵ 10.1s a10g 1992 8.5m* 8m* 8f² 9m⁵ 8h³ 10.5g³ 9.9m 10f³ 10.5d⁶ 10.5s 9d⁵] workmanlike gelding: carries condition: largely consistent in 1992: successful in Beverley apprentice handicap and Pontefract claimer in May: effective at 1m to 1¼m: best form on a sound surface: below form visored once: held up. *M. H. Tompkins* — **68**

OVER SHARP 3 b.f. Beveled (USA) – Over Beyond 78 (Bold Lad (IRE) 133) [1991 5g³ 5g⁵ 5m² 5m 5m 6m 1992 6g] leggy filly: has a quick action: modest plater: should stay at least 7f: acts on good to firm ground. *J. White* — **–**

OVER THE CLIFFS (IRE) 2 b. or br.f. (Feb 8) Bluebird (USA) 125 – Nonnita 71 (Welsh Saint 126) [1992 5.7f] IR 3,000F, IR 3,400Y: good-bodied filly: fourth foal: half-sister to 1988 2-y-o 6f winner Nicely Placed (by Tumble Wind) and a winner in Macau: dam 6f winner: well behind after 1f in maiden at Bath in August. *J. A. Bennett* — **–**

OVER THE DEC 2 b.f. (Apr 6) Smackover 107 – Condec (Swing Easy (USA) 126) [1992 5g⁴ 5m 6g 5s⁵ 5.1m³ 5g⁶ 5g⁴ 5m] 980Y: leggy, sparely-made filly: poor mover: fourth foal: dam no sign of ability either start: moderate plater: best form at 5f on easy surface: sold 480 gns Doncaster October Sales. *B. A. McMahon* — **38**

OWNER'S DREAM (USA) 3 b.g. Northern Baby (CAN) 127 – Glim (USA) (Damascus (USA)) [1991 7d⁴ 7m² 8.1g³ 7d 1992 9.9g 7f⁶ 7f* 7f* 7g 7.1g³ 7m²] compact gelding: good mover: fair handicapper: won at Brighton (maiden) and York in first half of 1992: effective at 7f to 1m: acts on firm going: somewhat headstrong: effective held up or ridden from front: game. *B. Hanbury* — **78**

OXRIB 2 b.g. (Mar 27) Anita's Prince 126 – Queen Caroline 86 (Ragusa 137) [1992 6g⁶ 6m 7m⁶ 6m 7.1g] 3,800F, 2,000Y: good-topped gelding: has a round action: half-brother to several winners here and in Italy, including winning sprinter Brave Prince (by Scorpio): dam placed over 6f at 2 yrs: poor maiden: stays 6f. *J. Berry* — **32**

OYSTON'S LIFE 3 b.g. Be My Guest (USA) 126 – I Don't Mind 97 (Swing Easy (USA) 126) [1991 6m⁶ 6g 5m* 6m⁵ 7m⁶ 7g 1992 6d 5.9d 8.1d 7.1m⁴ 7.1f² 8.3m 7g 6.9f³ 6f³ 6g³ 8.1g⁶ 6s 7g] useful-looking gelding: good walker: modest handicapper: effective at 6f and 7f: best efforts on a sound surface: twice below form when blinkered, including final start: sold 1,800 gns Doncaster October Sales. *J. Berry* — **52**

P

PAAJIB (IRE) 2 b.g. (Mar 5) Waajib 121 – Parkeen Princess (He Loves Me 120) [1992 5m 6f 6f³ 6g 6g⁶ 7g] 9,800F, 13,000Y: leggy, sparely-made gelding: fifth foal: half-brother to 4 winners, including (at 8.2f and 9f) Transitional (by Dalsaan) and 1991 2-y-o 10f winner Strange Knight (by Gorytus): dam never ran: modest maiden: off course nearly 2 months and well below form last 3 starts. *C. Tinkler* — **54**

PABOUCHE (USA) 3 b.c. Roberto (USA) 131 – Lady's Slipper (AUS) (Dancer's Image (USA)) [1991 8m* 1992 11d³ 10d⁴ 13.9g⁴ 10g* 10.1m] strong, good sort: has a short, quick action: fairly useful performer: off course over 3 months, won minor event at Windsor in August, making all and running on strongly, swerving left inside — **90**

final 1f: well below form in handicap month later: stays 11f (ran as if something amiss over 13.9f): acts on good to firm and dead ground. *H. R. A. Cecil*

PACE E SALUTE   3 ch.f. King Luthier 113 – Sagareina (Sagaro 133) [1991 6m 6m⁶ 6g 6m 1992 a8g⁵ a8g 8s 6m] small, workmanlike filly: good mover: poor plater: soundly beaten last 3 starts, in a visor on final one, in May: should stay at least 1m. *S. Dow*   –

PADDY CHALK   6 gr.h. Tina's Pet 121 – Guiletta 63 (Runnymede 123) [1991 6g 6g 6g⁶ 6g 5d 6g 1992 5g 6d³ 6s 6g 6m² 6m* 5.1f² 5g⁶ 5m* 5.6m⁵] leggy, workmanlike horse: fairly useful handicapper: won at Windsor and Goodwood in the summer: stays 6f: probably acts on any going: wears bandages. *L. J. Holt*   83

PADINA TOP   3 b.f. Top Ville 129 – Zahiah 90 (So Blessed 130) [1991 NR 1992 a7g] leggy filly: half-sister to fairly useful 1984 2-y-o 5f winner Rahash (by Song) and Irish 2-y-o 5f and 6f winner Pas du Tout (by Pas de Seul): dam 2-y-o 6f winner: tailed off in maiden at Southwell in June: dead. *C. Smith*   –

PAGEBOY   3 b.c. Tina's Pet 121 – Edwins' Princess 75 (Owen Dudley 121) [1991 6g 7m 6g² 6m* 7g 6m² 6m⁴ 7m 1992 7g 6s⁵ 6g² 7m³ 6m 6g² 6f³ 5g⁴ 5d³ 6f 6s] small, sturdy colt: moderate mover: fairly useful handicapper: blinkered, ran creditably twice over 7f in July: off course over 8 weeks and no blinkers, well beaten last 2 starts: stays 6f (fair effort at 7f): fair effort on extremes of going, at very best on good and dead. *P. C. Haslam*   83

PAINT THE LILY   4 ch.f. Claude Monet (USA) 121 – Screen Goddess 65 (Caliban 123) [1991 a8g* a8g⁵ a8g⁵ a10g 10f⁴ 12.2g* 11m 10.2d 10.1d a12g a13g 1992 11.9d 8d a10g] leggy filly: seems of little account these days. *D. C. Jermy*   –

PAINT THE WIND (IRE)   2 b.f. (Feb 27) Fayruz 116 – Pink Fondant (Northfields (USA)) [1992 7g³ 6m 5g³ 6g³ 5g² 5g* 6d³ 6d a6g a7g] IR 8,000Y: second foal: sister to winning sprinter Face North: dam ran twice at 2 yrs: won nursery at Tipperary in August: sold out of T. Stack's stable 2,700 gns Newmarket Autumn Sales after eighth start: well held at Southwell last 2: stays 6f: acts on dead ground: blinkered last 4 starts, running creditably first occasion. *R. F. Fisher*   68 ?
a–

PAIR OF JACKS (IRE)   2 ch.c. (Mar 5) Music Boy 124 – Lobbino 72 (Bustino 136) [1992 6f⁴ 5m⁴ 5g 6m⁶ 6m² 6g* 6g] strong, lengthy colt: has scope: third foal: half-brother to 3-y-o 1½m winner Lobinda (by Shareef Dancer), also successful twice at around 1m at 2 yrs: dam, maiden should have stayed middle distances, is out of sister to Highclere: fair form: stayed on strongly to win nursery at Kempton: appeared to be improving, but struggling by halfway at Newmarket later in August: will be well suited by 7f + . *W. R. Muir*   70

PALACEGATE EPISODE (IRE)   2 b.f. (May 27) Drumalis 125 – Pasadena Lady (Captain James 123) [1992 5v* 5s* 5d² 5m² 5.2g* 5g*] leggy, lengthy filly: fluent mover: third foal: sister to fairly useful 3-y-o 5f performer Another Episode and half-sister to 4-y-o 5f winner Sports Post Lady (by M Double M): dam never ran: useful performer: wide-margin winner early in season of maiden at Warwick and minor event at Ripon: best effort when easy 5-length winner of listed St Hugh's Stakes at Newbury: only narrowly landed odds of 5/2 on in £7,600 event at York in September: very speedy: yet to race on very firm ground, acts on any other. *J. Berry*   94

PALACEGATE GIRL   2 ch.f. (Mar 22) Music Boy 124 – Long Girl (Longleat (USA) 109) [1992 5d⁴ a5g] 5,400Y: first foal: dam won 3 races (one listed) in Belgium: modest form in maiden auction at Edinburgh in November, close up throughout: failed to confirm that in maiden at Southwell. *J. Berry*   57

PALACEGATE GOLD (IRE)   3 b.c. Sarab 123 – Habilite 94 (Habitat 134) [1991 5f⁴ 5m 6g* 7m 6m² 6f⁴ a6g* 6g³ 5m 6g 1992 6v 7v 5v⁵ 5.1d 5s² 5.7s⁴ 5m⁵ 6m⁴ 7f 6m⁵ 8g 5.3f⁴ 6g 6g³ 6s] sturdy colt: has a quick action: none too consistent plater: ideally suited by 6f: probably acts on any going, including equitrack: sometimes blinkered, including when successful. *R. J. Hodges*   48

PALACEGATE KING   3 ch.g. King Among Kings 60 – Market Blues (Porto Bello 118) [1991 6m 7m³ 7m³ 7f⁴ 6f 5s⁵ 1992 a6g* a7g* a7g* a7g³ a7g⁴ 7d⁴ 6d³ 5g⁶ 6m⁵ a8g 6f⁶ 7g a7g] sparely-made gelding: modest performer: won handicaps then claimer at Southwell in January: well beaten last 4 starts: effective at 6f/7f: acts on soft ground and on fibresand: ran moderately when blinkered once: has made all or most when successful: game: sold to join A. Whillans 2,000 gns Doncaster October Sales and won juvenile claiming hurdle in December. *J. Berry*   68 d

PALACEGATE PRINCE   2 br.c. (Feb 20) King of Spain 121 – Malindi (Mansingh (USA) 120) [1992 5m⁵ 5g³ a6g* 6f* 6.1m⁵ 6m² 6m⁴ 7g⁴ 7m a6g⁶ 6m 7.1g] 7,200Y: compact colt: has quick action: fifth living foal: half-brother to 10.5f seller winner Lindi's Gold (by Sonnen Gold): dam never ran: modest form: made all   58 or most when easy winner of seller (retained 3,600 gns) at Southwell and claimer at Hamilton in June: ideally suited by 6f: acts on firm ground (yet to race on a soft surface) and fibresand: below best when blinkered twice: sold 1,800 gns Doncaster October Sales. *J. Berry*

PALACEGATE QUEEN (IRE) 3 br.f. Milk of The Barley 115 – Up And At It 72 (Tamerlane 128) [1991 5f 6d6 1992 7.1m5] workmanlike filly: well beaten in northern maidens. *J. Berry*

 –

PALACEGATE RACING 3 b. or br.g. Belfort (FR) 89 – Call Me Kate 72 (Firestreak 125) [1991 5g 5m4 5m2 5f6 6.1m2 a6g2 a6g* 6m2 6g 6g* a6g2 1992 a6g3 a6g* a5g4 a6g6 6s 5s5 a5g* a6g* 5g a6g a6g2 a6g6 6m] close-coupled gelding: fair performer on the all-weather: won claimer at Southwell in January and handicaps at Southwell and Lingfield in June: no worthwhile form on turf in 1992: stays 6f: tends to wander: sold 2,400 gns Doncaster October Sales. *J. Berry*

 a71

PALACEGATE SUNSET 2 gr.c. (May 4) Skyliner 117 – Grey Morley 78 (Pongee 106) [1992 6.1d6 6.1d5 a7g2 a7s 7d 8.3s* 10.5d2 8g 8.3v] 3,200Y: tall, quite good-topped colt: good walker: has a round action: fifth reported foal: half-brother to 6f winner Grey Tudor (by Import): dam placed at 5f at 2 yrs, won over hurdles: fair plater: won nursery (no bid) at Hamilton in September: stays 10.5f: yet to race on top-of-the-ground, acts on soft going and on fibresand. *J. Berry*

 58

PALACEGATE TOUCH 2 gr.g. (Feb 7) Petong 126 – Dancing Chimes (London Bells (CAN) 109) [1992 6.1d 6m* 6d* 6d* 6d] 2,400Y: good-topped gelding: second foal: half-brother to 3-y-o Dizzy Dame (by Mummy's Game): dam unraced: fair performer: won seller at Yarmouth (bought in 6,750 gns) and nurseries at Haydock and (week later, on really well despite hanging left), Newmarket: stiff task in listed event at York later in the autumn: stays 6f: acts on dead ground, needed to show only modest form to win on good to firm: slowly away first 3 starts: tends to race with head high. *J. Berry*

 78

PALACE PAGEANT (USA) 2 b.c. (May 7) Nijinsky (CAN) 138 – Crown Treasure (USA) (Graustark) [1992 8d* 8.1d2 7g5] strong, good-topped colt: has plenty of scope: half-brother to numerous winners, including Diamond Shoal and Glint of Gold (both by Mill Reef) and useful 5-y-o stayer/hurdler Crystal Spirit (by Kris): dam very useful at 2 yrs in USA when winner at 5f: fairly useful form: won maiden at Goodwood in September: creditable efforts in minor event at Haydock (still not fully wound up, set modest pace and kept on well) and £8,900 contest at Ascot: capable of better at middle distances. *I. A. Balding*

 93 p

PALEY PRINCE (USA) 6 b.h. Tilt Up (USA) – Apalachee Princess (USA) (Apalachee (USA) 137) [1991 a6f6 a6f a6f 5f4 5f3 a5f 5d 5f 8.5f 8.5g5 1992 6f5.1f 5g 5g 5m 5.6m 5f3 5.2g 5d 5m a5g3 5d 5m3 a5g3] strong-quartered, lengthy horse: rated 106 here as 4-y-o: raced in USA at 5 yrs: just a fair handicapper in 1992: creditable efforts when third: stays 6f: acts on top-of-the-ground and equitrack: has been bandaged. *M. D. I. Usher*

 80

PALLIUM (IRE) 4 b.c. Try My Best (USA) 130 – Jungle Gardenia (Nonoalco (USA) 131) [1991 5s 5g3 5g3 5g3 5m* 5m3 5m2 5g 5m* 5g 6m 1992 5d3 5m 5m4 6d 5g5 5g 5g5 5m 5g4 5m* 5d3 5m 6m] good-bodied colt: moderate mover: fair handicapper: won at Beverley in September: should stay 6f: acts on firm and dead ground: not so good in a visor: has hung: inconsistent. *M. P. Naughton*

 75

PALMAS PRIDE 5 b.g. Dalsaan 125 – Sabirone (FR) (Iron Duke (FR) 122) [1991 NR 1992 8g 8g 8s] sturdy gelding: seems of little account these days. *M. D. Hammond*

 –

PALM CHAT 2 ch.f. (Feb 5) General Holme (USA) 128 – Lady Chatterley (USA) (Roberto (USA) 131) [1992 5f3 5d3 6g* 6g3 7m6] smallish, sturdy filly: has a quick action: first foal: dam 1m winner, is daughter of Grade 1 9f Monmouth Oaks winner Sharp Belle, an excellent family: modest performer: won maiden at Ayr in July, quickening well: fair efforts in nurseries at Windsor and Thirsk afterwards: should stay 1m: carried head awkwardly first 3 starts: sent to Dubai. *L. M. Cumani*

 57

PALM HOUSE 7 ch.g. Coquelin (USA) 121 – Kew Gift (Faraway Son (USA) 130) [1991 12g 1992 13.1g6] lengthy, angular gelding: good mover: lightly raced and no worthwhile form on flat: fair hurdler, winner 4 times in the autumn: has joined W. Storey. *G. Richards*

 –

PALOMELLE (FR) 3 b.f. Moulin 103 – Pacific Drive (FR) (Kenmare (FR) 125) [1991 6g 6g* 5.5g5 7.5g 9g* 8g 8v2 8s* 1992 9.2g6 9g 10d2 10d* 12m 9.3s6] medium-sized filly: third foal: half-sister to French 8.5f and 11f winner Palata (by Darly): dam French 1m winner: improved to win Group 3 Prix de Psyche at Deauville in August: beaten only 3½ lengths and far from disgraced afterwards at

 112

Longchamp in both Prix Vermeille (seventh of 10 behind Jolypha) and Prix de l'Opera (sixth of 12 behind Hatoof): stays 1½m: acts on soft going. *A. Spanu, France*

PAMAR 2 b.c. (Apr 18) Shareef Dancer (USA) 135 – Helen's Dream (Troy 137) [1992 6m⁵ 7g⁵ 7f⁵] 25,000Y: leggy, quite attractive colt: sixth foal: half-brother to fairly useful 1¼m winner Helens Dreamgirl (by Caerleon): dam, unraced, from family of Gorytus: plating-class form in the summer in minor events at Ascot and Chester and maiden (prominent 5f, not at all knocked about when beaten) at Yarmouth: will stay at least 1m: probably capable of fair bit better. *C. E. Brittain*   42 p

PAMZIG (USA) 2 b.f. (Jan 27) Danzig (USA) – Burst of Colors (USA) (Crimson Satan) [1992 7g*] rangy, good-topped filly: has scope: third foal: half-sister to Fappaburst (by Fappiano), dual graded winner at 7f: dam won at up to 1¼m: heavily-backed favourite, won 14-runner maiden at Doncaster in October by a length, clear, from Tajhiz, tracking leaders until going on over 1f out then running on really well despite looking green: will stay 1m: sure to improve. *B. W. Hills*   76 p

PANATHINAIKOS (USA) 7 b.g. Nodouble (USA) – Faisana (ARG) (Yata Nahuel) [1991 NR 1992 a16g] sparely-made, angular gelding: has a long stride: first run on flat since 3 yrs, well beaten in Lingfield handicap: tried visored: won maiden hurdle on equitrack in 1991/2. *G. A. Ham*   –

PANCHELLITA (USA) 3 b.f. Pancho Villa (USA) – Counselor's Pride (USA) (Good Counsel (USA)) [1991 6g² 6m* 7d³ 1992 7.9m 6m 6g 6m 6g⁴ 6f 6g 5.1d 5s] big, workmanlike filly: trained until after reappearance by D. Smith: form in 1992 only when blinkered, fourth at Brighton in August: should stay 7f: below form on a soft surface. *J. Sutcliffe*   57

PANIC BUTTON (IRE) 2 br.f. (Feb 4) Simply Great (FR) 122 – Hysteria (Prince Bee 128) [1992 5d² 6f⁵ 7m⁶ 7g] leggy filly: second foal: closely related to 3-y-o Rowandene (by Wassl): dam unraced daughter of German 7f to 9f winner Kallista, dam of German 1000 Guineas winner Kazoo and daughter of good German mare Kandia: modest maiden: failed to progress, off course lengthy periods before each of last 2 starts: should be suited by 7f. *M. H. Easterby*   48

PANICO 5 b.g. Superlative 118 – Ex Dancer (USA) (Executioner (USA)) [1991 8.1g⁶ 9g⁶ 9m 1992 10.3g⁴ 10.5g] strong gelding: poor handicapper and still a maiden on flat since 4 yrs: probably stays 1¼m: acts on firm and dead going: effective visored or not: has been edgy, mulish at stalls and put head in air: sold 1,400 gns Doncaster September Sales. *Miss S. E. Hall*   –

PANIKIN 4 gr.g. Red Sunset 120 – Haunting 79 (Lord Gayle (USA) 124) [1991 7m⁵ 7.2m* 7.6d³ 6m* 8m⁵ 6g 6g 6m 1992 5g² 6g 6f 7m² 7m³ 7m 6g 6d⁵ 6.1s 5g a6g³ a7g² a6g*] leggy, close-coupled gelding: useful handicapper: winner at Lingfield in December: ideally suited by 6f/7f: acts on good to firm and soft ground and on all-weather surfaces: has run well for an apprentice: held up: consistent. *J. Wharton*   95

PANTHER (IRE) 2 ch.c. (Apr 6) Primo Dominie 121 – High Profile (High Top 131) [1992 6g³ 6g⁵ 6g⁶ 7g 7g 6d² 6d 6s] 6,000Y: leggy, rather angular colt: first foal: dam unraced half-sister to Middle Park winner Mattaboy: fair maiden: ran moderately in nurseries last 2 starts: should be well suited by further than 6f: best effort on dead ground. *C. W. C. Elsey*   67

PANT LLIN 6 b.g. Mummy's Pet 125 – Goosie-Gantlet 63 (Run The Gantlet (USA)) [1991 NR 1992 10.3g 11.9d] good-quartered gelding: good walker: fair winner at 2 yrs: no worthwhile form in the spring on first runs on flat since 1989: winning (1991/2) hurdler but is ungenuine. *F. Jordan*   –

PAPA WESTRAY 3 b.g. Scottish Reel 123 – Bronze Princess 72 (Hul A Hul 124) [1991 6m 6m 5f³ 6m 1992 a7g a7g⁴ a8g*] strong gelding: poor mover: progressive form: claimer ridden, best effort to win 9-runner handicap at Southwell in February: stays 1m: has been gelded. *T. D. Barron*   58

PAPER CLIP 3 b.f. Jalmood (USA) 126 – Westonepaperchase (USA) 71 (Accipiter (USA)) [1991 7g 7g² 8d⁴ a8g² a8g² a8g* 1992 11.6g⁵ 12d 11f 10.3m 11.8g 10s 12s⁴ 15.8d⁶ 14.1s] small, sturdy filly: rated 66 at 2 yrs: no worthwhile form in 1992: blinkered sixth start: tongue tied down penultimate one: sold to join J. Cresswell 1,600 gns Doncaster November Sales. *J. D. Bethell*   –

PAPER CRAFT 5 b.g. Formidable (USA) 125 – Civility 108 (Shirley Heights 130) [1991 NR 1992 a10g³ a12g² 10s⁴ 10.8d a12g³ 12f⁴ 8m 9.2m 10g⁴ 8.3m⁵] heavy-topped gelding: carries condition: none too consistent performer: effective from 1¼m to 1½m: goes well on all-weather surfaces and soft ground: has hung, and not easiest of rides: usually visored or blinkered. *M. Johnston*   55

PAPER DANCE 4 b.g. Mashhor Dancer (USA) – April Days 75 (Silly Season **64**
127) [1991 10.2g* 10g³ 12d 10g² 10.2g 11.8m 1992 12g⁵ 14.1d 16.9g⁵ 14.1g 17.2f*
17.2f³ 13.1g²] rangy, shallow-girthed gelding: turns off-fore out: stays mover:
modest handicapper: won at Bath in June: stays well: best form on a sound surface:
has given trouble in preliminaries: effective held up or ridden from front: not seen
out after July. *R. J. Holder*

PAPER DAYS 2 b.c. (Mar 26) Teenoso (USA) 135 – April Days 75 (Silly Season **45 p**
127) [1992 7g 7m 8s] lengthy, useful-looking colt: brother to modest maiden Trying
Days and half-brother to several winners here and abroad, including (at 10.2f to
2m+) 4-y-o Paper Dance (by Mashhor Dancer): dam 10.4f winner, is out of Oaks
second Maina: plating-class form in maidens: given considerate ride when bit
backward on first run for 8 weeks on final start: has joined P. Murphy: looks sort to
do better. *R. J. Holder*

PARADISE FORUM 3 ch.f. Prince Sabo 123 – Sovereign Love 75 (He Loves **63 d**
Me 120) [1991 5g⁴ 5g⁶ 5m³ 5.1f* 5m³ 5m² 5d³ 1992 6d 5m 7.1m 7d 6m³ 7g⁶ 5g 6g
5d⁴ 7d 10g] sparely-made filly: sweating and edgy, modest form in 1992 only when
third in handicap at Windsor in June: stays 6f: acts on firm and dead ground: well
beaten when visored once. *C. A. Horgan*

PARADISE NAVY 3 b.c. Slip Anchor 136 – Ivory Waltz (USA) (Sir Ivor 135) **81**
[1991 NR 1992 11d 14m² 12g 16.2f 12f⁶] close-coupled, quite attractive colt:
half-brother to a winner in USA by Golden Fleece and to 2 winners in Scandinavia:
dam unraced half-sister to General Assembly: fairly useful form when keeping-on
second of 6 in maiden at Newmarket in May, having set a modest pace: no chance in
the Derby, well beaten in Queen's Vase (prominent long way in strongly-run race)
at Royal Ascot, and weakened tamely final 3f in Newmarket maiden in June: stays
1¾m: has joined N. Wright. *C. E. Brittain*

PAR DE LUXE 5 b.m. Superlative 118 – Parbold 54 (Sassafras (FR) 135) [1991 **–**
7d⁶ 7.5g 10f 5m² 6d⁴ 5m 8f⁵ 7m⁶ 5g 6.1m³ 6m 6m 1992 7d⁵ 5g 5g 6g] workmanlike
mare: moderate mover: looked of little account in the spring: sold to join C. W. C.
Elsey 1,500 gns Doncaster October Sales. *B. W. Murray*

PARFAIT AMOUR 3 ch.f. Clantime 101 – Chablisse 69 (Radetzky 123) [1991 **73**
6m³ 6g³ 5.9h* 6m 1992 6m² 7m³ 6g 6d 6m 6d 7.1g 7g] lengthy, sparely-made filly:
tends to look dull in coat: fair form in handicaps when placed in July, unlucky for 7-lb
claimer on reappearance: disappointing afterwards, in a visor last time: may prove
best at around 6f: acts on hard ground. *R. M. Whitaker*

PARIS HOUSE 3 gr.c. Petong 126 – Foudroyer (Artaius (USA) 129) [1991 5d* **110**
5d* 5m* 5g* 5m² 5.2g* 5g² 5m* 5d 1992 5s* 5d 5f 6g⁵ 5m 5m⁶ 5m] leggy, lengthy
colt: smart performer: won listed race at Haydock by a length from Stack Rock and
second to Monde Bleu in Palace House Stakes at Newmarket in the spring: easily
best effort afterwards when creditable 5 lengths sixth of 11 to Lyric Fantasy in
Nunthorpe Stakes at York: best at 5f: acts on good to firm and soft ground: visored
(well beaten in latest event) final start: tends to wander. *J. Berry*

PARISIAN EXPRESS (FR) 4 gr.f. Siberian Express (USA) 125 – Parisana **–**
(FR) (Gift Card (FR) 124) [1991 8f⁶ 8.2d 12m 8d* 10g³ 8.3m 8f 8.1s 1992 a8g] tall,
lengthy filly: rated 48 at best at 3 yrs: ran poorly in February, 1992: unlikely to stay
beyond 1¼m: acts on dead ground: covered by Slip Anchor. *K. O. Cunningham-
Brown*

PARISIENNE KING (USA) 3 b.g. Key To The Kingdom (USA) – Paris Dawn **–**
(USA) (Mr Redoy (USA)) [1991 6f⁶ 5m⁵ 7g 6g 1992 7.5g 6g 5f 5g 6g a7g a12g] leggy,
close-coupled gelding: looks of little account these days: sold out of F. Lee's stable
720 gns Doncaster September Sales after sixth start. *R. F. Marvin*

PARISIEN SINGER 3 br.f. Chief Singer 131 – Parisana (FR) (Gift Card (FR) **–**
124) [1991 5d⁵ 5m* 5.2f⁶ 1992 6m⁴ 6f 7f] leggy, rather unfurnished filly: has a quick
action: rated 69 at 2 yrs: no worthwhile form in 1992: bred to stay 1m: sold 5,400 gns
Newmarket December Sales. *I. A. Balding*

PARIS OF TROY 4 b.c. Trojan Fen 118 – Little Loch Broom 60 (Reform 132) **–**
[1991 10d⁴ 10g⁵ 9m 9m⁴ 12d⁴ 8m⁶ 10m* 10.5d⁵ 1992 14m 12g⁶ 14.6g] leggy, quite
attractive colt: has a long, round action: rated 75d at 3 yrs: no form in 1992: best
form at around 1¼m: acts on good to firm and dead ground: useful front-running
hurdler, winner 3 times in the autumn. *N. A. Twiston-Davies*

PARK DANCE 2 b.f. (Jan 7) Dance of Life (USA) – Chellaston Park 117 (Record **49**
Token 128) [1992 5g 6.1m⁶] 8,600Y: smallish, lengthy filly: fourth foal: half-sister to
2 winners, including fairly useful 1990 2-y-o 5f winner Fiorentia (by Final Straw):

dam sprinter: plating-class form in mid-division in maiden auctions in midsummer. *W. Jarvis*

PARK DREAM (IRE)   3 b.f. Ahonoora 122 – Summer Dreams (CAN) (Victoria **110** Park) [1991 6m* 6g⁵ 1992 7v 7m* 6g* 6g* 5g²] 36,000Y: half-sister to several winners, including 1983 2-y-o 5.5f stakes winner Deputy General (by Vice Regent): dam lightly-raced 2-y-o winner at around 5f from good family: progressed really well in 1992 to win handicaps at the Curragh and Leopardstown and Group 3 Phoenix Sprint Stakes (beat Poolesta by 1½ lengths) in August: creditable second to Flowing in Group 3 Meadow Meats EBF Flying Five at Leopardstown final run: best form at 5f and 6f. *J. S. Bolger, Ireland*

PARKING BAY   5 b.g. Bay Express 132 – Sophie Avenue (Guillaume Tell (USA)   – 121) [1991 10.3m² 10.5g* 12d⁵ 1992 10m 10m a8g⁶] tall, good-topped gelding: modest handicapper: rated 77 at 4 yrs: no worthwhile form in 1992, not seen out until late on: stays 10.2f: acts on firm going: suitable mount for inexperienced rider. *G. A. Pritchard-Gordon*

PARLEMO (IRE)   3 b.c. Dance of Life (USA) – Crannog (Habitat 134) [1991 7d   **66** a7g* a7g⁴ 1992 a7g 7d³ 8d⁶ 9g 8.5d²] workmanlike, rather dipped-backed colt: fair handicapper: form in 1992 only on dead ground, best effort when blinkered-second in £10,600 event at Epsom in June: shapes as if will be better suited by 1¼m: acts on dead ground and on equitrack. *J. D. Bethell*

PARLIAMENT PIECE   6 ch.g. Burslem 123 – Sallywell (Manado 130) [1991   **96** 8m³ 8g 7m* 7f* 7g 8g² 7g⁴ 7.1f⁴ 1992 7.6g* 7.9m⁶ 7g⁵ 8f 7m⁶ 8m 7m 8m⁴] big, lengthy gelding: poor mover: useful handicapper: won £14,000 event at Chester in April when trained by R. Whitaker: ridden by 7-lb claimer on second run for new stable, returned to form when fourth in valuable event at Doncaster in September (clear 3f out): suited by 7f/1m: acts on firm ground: effective visored or not: usually races up with pace. *Mrs M. Reveley*

PARR (IRE)   4 b.g. Salmon Leap (USA) 131 – Mums 88 (Mummy's Pet 125) [1991   – 7m² 8f 1992 10g 8m 8.2g 8m 10g] lengthy, workmanlike gelding: good walker: still a maiden and no worthwhile form in 1992: worth a try in blinkers: has tongue tied down: has worn near-side pricker: sold 1,500 gns Doncaster September Sales. *J. Mackie*

PARTING MOMENT (USA)   5 ch.h. The Minstrel (CAN) 135 – Farewell **104** d Letter (USA) (Arts And Letters) [1991 14m³ 16.2s⁴ 14m* 16m⁴ 22.2m³ 16.1m 15s² 16g⁶ 1992 12d³ 16.2d⁵ 13.4m³ 12g⁵ 14m² 15.9d³ 16m 13.9m 13.3g] rather leggy, attractive horse: good walker: has round action: generally in good form first 6 starts in 1992 in group and listed company: subsequently well beaten in Goodwood Cup, Ebor Handicap and £18,200 handicap (visored, headed and quickly beaten 3f out) at Newbury: effective at 1½m, and stays extremely well: probably acts on any going: effective ridden from front or held up: sold 34,000 gns Newmarket December Sales. *I. A. Balding*

PARTY CITED (USA)   3 b.f. Alleged (USA) 138 – Dream Play (USA) (Blushing **110** Groom (FR) 131) [1991 7g 8m 8d³ 7m 1992 10g⁴ 10g⁵ 8m* 10g* 10m* 10g² 10d³ 10d⁵] lengthy, sparely-made filly: good mover: progressed into a very useful performer: trained until after second start by P. Kelleway: won minor events at Kempton and Windsor then £30,600 handicap at Goodwood (by head from Wild Fire) in midsummer: creditable efforts in Group 3 contest at Goodwood (2½ lengths

Leslie And Godwin Spitfire Stakes (Handicap), Goodwood—
the greatly-improved Party Cited hangs on well in a tight race;
her closest challengers turn out to be Wild Fire (No. 13) and Mutabahi (striped cap, wide)

behind Knifebox) and E P Taylor Stakes at Woodbine (5 lengths behind Hatoof) last 2 starts: suited by 1¼m: acts on good to firm and dead ground. *D. R. C. Elsworth*

PARTY TREAT (IRE)   4 ch.f. Millfontaine 114 – Party Dancer (Be My Guest   – §
(USA) 126) [1991 6g 6g 7g 6g 6m 5m 6f⁶ 5f 7g 8f 1992 6g 5s 5s 5.1g] workmanlike filly: of little account these days: ran tubed last time. *D. Marks*

PASS THE KEY (IRE)   3 b.g. Treasure Kay 114 – Piney Pass (Persian Bold   –
123) [1991 6d 6m⁶ 7s* 7m³ 1992 12g⁴ 8.3s⁵] strong gelding: off course 10 months and well beaten in claimers in May: should stay 1m + : has form on good to firm and soft ground. *N. Tinkler*

PATER NOSTER (USA)   3 b.c. Stately Don (USA) 122 – Sainera (USA) 89   **102**
(Stop The Music (USA)) [1991 6s* 1992 7m* 7f] rather leggy, quite attractive colt: has a fluent, round action: useful form: won 4-runner minor event at Leicester by 4 lengths from Mojave, leading well over 1f out and nudged clear: not discredited when 6½ lengths eighth of 12 to Prince Ferdinand in Jersey Stakes at Royal Ascot following month, never able to challenge: will stay 1m. *Mrs J. Cecil*

PATIENCE PLEASE   3 br.f. King of Spain 121 – Navarino Bay 102 (Averof 123)   **59**
[1991 NR 1992 7f³ 6f² 7m* 6g 6f² 7m* a7g² 7d 6.9g² 8g⁴ 7d] leggy filly: fifth foal: half-sister to a winner over hurdles: dam won over 5f at 2 yrs and stayed 1½m: consistent performer: won ladies maiden at Doncaster and claimer at Redcar in the summer: best effort when fourth in amateurs handicap at Redcar: suited by 1m: acts on firm ground and fibresand, well below form (including on only time tried blinkered) on dead. *M. H. Easterby*

PATONG BEACH   2 ch.f. (Mar 17) Infantry 122 – Winter Resort (Miami Springs   **60**
121) [1992 5f⁶ 5g⁶ a6g 6g a8g⁴ a7g] rather leggy, short-backed filly: third reported foal: half-sister to 3-y-o Stormy Winter (by Reasonable), sprint winner in Macau where renamed Ground Commander, and 6f winner Masella (by Aragon): dam unraced: modest maiden: suited by 1m: acts on equitrack: ran poorly on fibresand: not discredited in blinkers final outing. *J. W. Hills*

PAT POINDESTRES   2 b.f. (Apr 8) Interrex (CAN) – Glen Kella Manx 97   **55** ?
(Tickled Pink 114) [1992 5.7f⁴ 5g⁴ 6g⁶ a6g* a6g⁶ 5.1d a6g a5g] small filly: third foal: dam 5f and 6f winner stayed 7f: modest performer: sold out of M. Muggeridge's stable 5,800 gns after winning seller at Lingfield in September: ran poorly last 3 starts: better suited by 6f than 5f: acts on equitrack: one to treat with caution. *M. Dixon*

PATRICIAN MAGICIAN   3 b. or br.c. Lord Ballina (AUS) – Singing Witch 71   **70** d
(Sing Sing 134) [1991 5d² 6f* 6g 7d a6g³ a7g³ 1992 a6g² a7g² a7g6 a7g⁴ a10g² a8g⁴ a8g⁴ a8g³ a6g²] leggy colt: modest performer on the all-weather between January and March, easily best effort first start: effective at 6f and probably stays 1¼m: has run well for 7-lb claimer. *R. J. R. Williams*

PATROCLUS   7 b.g. Tyrnavos 129 – Athenia Princess 80 (Athens Wood 126)   **48**
[1991 18d⁶ 16m³ 16.2g³ 20g 16.2g⁴ 17.2f* 16g⁴ 1992 18g 16d 21.6g* 17.2s⁴ 18g* 20m 18.2m⁵] workmanlike gelding: has a round action: formerly ungenuine and a very difficult ride, much better in 1992: won at Pontefract in April and June, leading closing stages: needs a thorough test of stamina: probably acts on any going: tried blinkered once: has been bandaged. *R. Voorspuy*

PATROL   3 b.c. Shirley Heights 130 – Tender Loving Care 105 (Final Straw 127)   –
[1991 NR 1992 10m⁶ 11.5d 14s⁶] good-topped, attractive colt: moderate mover: good walker: second foal: half-brother to 1990 2-y-o 7f winner Noble Destiny (by Dancing Brave): dam 2-y-o 7f winner, is half-sister to useful 2-y-o's Satinette and Silk Pyjamas: well beaten in maidens, though showed signs of a little ability: visored final start: sold to join J. H. Johnson 7,200 gns Newmarket Autumn Sales. *M. R. Stoute*

PATSY GRIMES   2 b.f. (Apr 3) Beveled (USA) – Blue Angel (Lord Gayle (USA)   **62**
124) [1992 6v⁴ a7g² a8g³ a7g²] second reported foal: dam never ran: modest maiden: stays 1m well: acts on equitrack. *M. P. Muggeridge*

PAULINUS   4 b.g. Nomination 125 – New Ribbons 79 (Ribero 126) [1991 8s⁶ 8d⁵   –
9f⁴ 12.4m 10.1m 9m 10.3d 1992 a16g⁶ a12g] workmanlike gelding: of little account. *Denys Smith*

PAVERS GOOD SHOES   4 b.f. Good Times (ITY) – Windy Sea 105 (Sea Hawk   –
II 131) [1991 a7g⁵ a8g⁶ 12f⁵ 10.6m 9m 10.4m 8m 1992 7m a8g] lengthy, angular filly: seems of little account these days: sold 1,400 gns Doncaster June Sales. *M. Brittain*

PAVONIS   3 b.c. Kalaglow 132 – Snub (Steel Heart 128) [1991 8m² 1992 10.8g³   **80**
12g² 14.6f*] leggy colt: fairly useful form: 11/10 on, won 3-runner maiden at Don-

caster in May by 5 lengths, making all: stays 14.6f: sold only 2,800 gns Newmarket Autumn Sales. *H. R. A. Cecil*

PAY HOMAGE   4 ch.g. Primo Dominie 121 – Embraceable Slew (USA) (Seattle   **96** Slew (USA)) [1991 9s² 8g 9m² 8g4 10.6g 8.5f* 7.6g² 8m² 8.3m³ 7g4 7.6m² 9m* 9m 1992 8d 8g4 8.1m* 8.9f³ 8f 8.1s⁵ 8g4 9m³ 8.9m 8m 8g4] angular, workmanlike gelding: moderate walker: useful handicapper: won Whitsun Cup at Sandown in May: should stay 1¼m: has form on soft ground, but best efforts on a sound surface: blinkered once at 2 yrs, visored (ran creditably) final start: has won for apprentice: has hung right: is held up. *I. A. Balding*

PEACE FORMULA (IRE)   3 ch.g. Thatching 131 – Greatest Pleasure (Be My   **50** Guest (USA) 126) [1991 5g 7g⁵ 8m 6m³ 7s 7g a6g³ a7g⁵ 1992 a8g a7g³ 9d 8d] rather unfurnished gelding: modest maiden: off course over 7 months, well beaten in handicaps in October last 2 starts: should stay 1m: acts on good to firm and soft ground, and on fibresand: has run moderately for 7-lb claimer: sold to join M. Tate 3,000 gns Newmarket Autumn Sales. *R. Hollinshead*

PEACEFUL AIR   2 b.f. (Mar 4) Hadeer 118 – Rose Barton (Pas de Seul 133)   **70** [1992 5d6 6g² 5m4 7.1m* 6g³] 4,600Y: workmanlike filly: second foal: sister to 3-y-o My Abbey, 5f winner at 2 yrs: dam unraced daughter of sister to Blue Cashmere: won maiden auction at Edinburgh in July: stayed 7.1f: acted on good to firm ground: dead. *E. Weymes*

PEACEFULL REPLY (USA)   2 b.c. (Feb 28) Hold Your Peace (USA) – Drone   **66** Answer (USA) (Drone) [1992 6m6 6d 6g² 5.9g² 7s 6s 6m] $26,000Y: close-coupled, good-topped colt: poor mover: second foal: dam placed third once from .10 starts in North America: sire high-class stakes winner at 6f and 9f also third in Kentucky Derby: fair maiden: best efforts when second, keeping on willingly both times: poorly drawn in Pontefract nursery final start: should stay 7f: seems unsuited by a soft surface. *F. H. Lee*

PEACE KING   6 ch.g. Adonijah 126 – Flaming Peace (USA) 64 (Lyphard (USA)   – 132) [1991 12.2d 1992 11.5m4 16.4g] strong, chunky gelding: good walker and fluent mover: rated 79 at 4 yrs: no form since: stays 13.3f: acts on hard ground: tempera- mental hurdler, successful in September: sold 4,400 gns Newmarket Autumn Sales. *G. Harwood*

PEACOCK FEATHER   4 b.f. Bustino 136 – Wide of The Mark 91 (Gulf Pearl   – 117) [1991 10m6 15.3m5 12d 1992 14.6g 16.9g] leggy filly: no worthwhile form on flat. *K. R. Burke*

PEACOCK THRONE   3 b.g. Persian Bold 123 – Diamond House (Habitat 134)   – [1991 NR 1992 10d 12m] sturdy gelding: first foal: dam sister to useful filly Life At The Top (stayed 1¼m): well beaten in maidens at Ripon and Pontefract in September: sold 2,600 gns Newmarket Autumn Sales. *Mrs J. R. Ramsden*

PEAK DISTRICT   6 b.g. Beldale Flutter (USA) 130 – Grand Teton 64 (Bustino   **57** 136) [1991 10d4 a14g5 a12g 1992 16.2g* 17.1d a16g² a14g a16g] small, lengthy a43 gelding: bad mover: modest performer: fit from the jumps, easily best effort on flat for long time when narrowly winning maiden at Beverley in March: stays well: acts on good to firm ground and dead: modest hurdler, won conditional jockeys handicap in September. *K. S. Bridgwater*

PEAK FITNESS   2 b.g. (Mar 1) Adonijah 126 – Ravens Peak (High Top 131)   **37** [1992 5d6 5m a6g6 a7g6 a7g 10.5d] leggy, sparely-made gelding: moderate mover: second foal: half-brother to inconsistent plater Ravenshurst (by Bustino): dam lightly-raced half-sister to very useful 1981 staying 2-y-o Ashenden: poor plater: dead. *J. A. Glover*

PEARL ANGEL   3 ch.f. Superlative 118 – More Or Less 64 (Morston (FR) 125) **101** [1991 6g4 7g* 7m4 1992 8g 12d³ 12f 11.9m5 12g] sturdy filly: useful performer: 10½ lengths seventh of 14 to Hatoof in 1000 Guineas at Newmarket and 23½ lengths third of 7 to User Friendly in the Oaks at Epsom: easily best effort in pattern events afterwards when fair fifth in Yorkshire Oaks: stays 1½m: acts on dead going, fair effort on good to firm: usually held up in rear: has joined D. Loder. *Miss B. Sanders*

PEARL RANSOM   5 ch.m. Durandal 114 – Seed Pearl (Ben Novus 109) [1991 9g   **44** 1992 a8g³ 6g5 6.9d 10g 8d4 9.7m 12d] leggy non-thoroughbred mare: poor maiden: better at 1m than shorter: acts on dead ground and equitrack. *W. G. R. Wightman*

PEARLY MIST (IRE)   2 b.f. (Apr 30) Persian Heights 129 – Silent Movie   **58** p (Shirley Heights 130) [1992 7g 8g²] lengthy, angular filly: has a round action: first foal: half-sister to one-time fairly useful 7f winner Runun (by Sharpo): dam poor half-sister to very smart 7f to 1¼m performer Noalto: 12/1, 4 lengths second of 10 to

Brightside in maiden at Leicester in September, disputing lead and keeping on well: strong-galloping sort, likely to stay beyond 1m: will improve again. *C. E. Brittain*

PEARLY WHITE   3 b.f. Petong 126 – White's Pet (Mummy's Pet 125) [1991 5d – 5.7m 6f³ 7m⁶ 6m³ 1992 6g 6m 6g] lengthy filly: rated 57 at 2 yrs: no form in 1992, hanging and looking none too keen on reappearance: visored final outing: sold to join H. Manners 550 gns Ascot July Sales: one to treat with caution. *G. B. Balding*

PEATSWOOD   4 ch.c. Rolfe (USA) 77 – Cathy Jane 86 (Lauso) [1991 NR 1992 – p 16.2g 16.9d⁵] smallish, leggy colt: half-brother to several winners, including 6f to 1¼m winner Hot That (by Hot Spark) and fair stayer Jamesmead (by Import): dam stayed extremely well: twice raced on flat and signs of ability only when staying-on fifth in maiden at Wolverhampton: has progressed into a fairly useful hurdler, winner of handicap in November. *M. R. Channon*

PEEDIE PEAT   2 gr.c. (Apr 12) Petong 126 – White's Pet (Mummy's Pet 125)   54 [1992 5g² 5g³ 7s] 10,000Y: big, strong, lengthy colt: has plenty of scope: very good walker: third foal: brother to 3-y-o Pearly White and to 1990 2-y-o 1m winner Encore Au Bon: dam never ran: modest form in maiden auctions at Edinburgh in April and Hamilton (heavily-backed favourite) in August: hung under pressure, dropped quickly away and eased in similar event at York over 7 weeks later: will stay 1m. *J. J. O'Neill*

PEERAGE PRINCE   3 b.g. Thatching 131 – Belle Viking (FR) (Riverman (USA)   73 131) [1991 6m 6g⁵ 5m 6.1m⁴ 6g* 6m² 5d 1992 7s 6g 6g 6g 7d⁶ 6.1m⁴ 6m 6g 6g² 7g 7m 7.6s 5.1g* 6g a5g³ a5g² a5g*] compact gelding: poor mover: fair handicapper: won at Nottingham and (best effort) Southwell in the autumn: stays 6f: may well be best on a sound surface on turf, acts on fibresand: has looked a tricky ride: much more reliable since being blinkered. *Pat Mitchell*

PEGGY MAINWARING   3 b.f. Petong 126 – Bertrade 75 (Homeboy 114) [1991   45 5m 5g 5m⁶ 6g⁶ 5d 1992 5s³ 6s 6g 8f⁴ 8.9s 7f] smallish, sparely-made filly: moderate mover: inconsistent maiden: blinkered, ran poorly in seller final start, in June: stays 1m: acts on any going: sweating (ran creditably, for 7-lb claimer) fourth start. *R. J. Holder*

PELARGONIA   3 ch.f. Primo Dominie 121 – Pellinora (USA) (King Pellinore   80 (USA) 127) [1991 6g 1992 8m² 8g² 8.2d* 8g³] lengthy, quite attractive filly: moderate mover: fairly useful performer: raced only in the summer and best effort on reappearance: easily justified favouritism in maiden at Nottingham: should stay 1¼m: best effort on good to firm, has won on dead: ran creditably for apprentice: sold 22,000 gns Newmarket December Sales. *R. Charlton*

PELDER (IRE)   2 b.c. Be My Guest (USA) 126 – Sheer Audacity (Troy 137) 113 [1992 7s² 6v³ 7g* 7.5g* 8v³ 8v*] IR 10,500F, IR 7,000Y: second foal: half-brother to a poor animal: dam placed in Italy, is closely related to very useful middle-distance filly Miss Petard: progressive Italian colt: won minor event at Milan and listed race at Turin in early-summer: off course 2½ months before next start and greatly improved effort to beat Right Win by 3½ lengths with rest well strung out in Gran Criterium at Milan in October: should stay 1½m: yet to race on top-of-the-ground, clearly goes extremely well on heavy. *L. d'Auria, Italy*

PELORUS   7 b.g. High Top 131 – St Isabel (Saint Crespin III 132) [1991 9s⁶ 10.1s   86 8m⁴ 10g² 10m* 1992 8g 10g* 8f 10d 10m³ 11.5g² 8g 10g² 10m] leggy gelding: usually looks well: consistent and fairly useful performer: won claimer at Goodwood in June: ideally suited by 1¼m to 1½m: probably acts on any going: has won for an apprentice: usually mounted on track: has started slowly, and is usually held up. *D. R. C. Elsworth*

PEMBROKE (USA)   2 b.c. (Jan 30) Gone West (USA) – College Bold (USA)   93 p (Boldnesian) [1992 7g* 8g*] $160,000F: sturdy, useful-looking colt: eleventh foal: half-brother to high-class 9f to 1½m winner Nasty And Bold (by Naskra) and multiple Grade 2 winner Told (by Tell) as well as several minor winners: dam unplaced: sire very smart at 1m/9f at 3 yrs: carrying condition, won minor event at Kempton, idling in front: odds on, followed up in similar event at Newbury 2 weeks later in September, quickening well to beat The Informer by 1½ lengths: should stay 1¼m: will make up into a useful colt at least. *J. H. M. Gosden*

PENANDO   4 b.g. Dreams To Reality (USA) 113 – Pendona 72 (Blue Cashmere   – 129) [1991 a6g 6.1m 6g 6m a6g a7g a5g 1992 7g 8g a7g⁶] smallish, workmanlike gelding: has a round action: seems of little account these days. *O. O'Neill*

PENANG STAR (IRE)   2 ch.g. (Mar 29) Jareer (USA) 115 – Nozet (Nishapour   69 (FR) 125) [1992 5m³ 6.1d² a6g* 6f⁵] 8,600F, 12,500Y: close-coupled, workmanlike gelding: has scope: moderate mover: second foal: dam French 9f winner: progressive form: favourite, won 5-runner maiden auction at Southwell in July, leading under 2f out and running on well: virtually pulled up in nursery at Pontefract following month, giving impression something amiss: will stay 7f. *W. A. O'Gorman*

PENDOR DANCER 9 b.g. Piaffer (USA) 113 – Bounding (Forlorn River 124) 55 d
[1991 5g 5.3f6 5g6 5m 5d4 5g 5d 5g6 5m 5m4 5g6 5m 5.1d a5g* a5g2 a5g5 1992 a5g5 a5g4 a5g 5.3m2 5.7m 5.1m2 5.7f 5.1m 5g a5g6 a6g a5g a5g5 a6g a5g5] lengthy gelding: poor sprint handicapper: has won one of last 36 starts: acts on any going: effective with or without blinkers or visor: sometimes wears crossed noseband: usually sweats. *B. Forsey*

PENNINE LAD (IRE) 2 ch.g. (Apr 24) Pennine Walk 120 – Dominica (GER) –
(Zank) [1992 5m a7g 7d] IR 3,200Y: quite attractive gelding: brother to Irish 1¼m winner Pivotal Walk, closely related to 2 winners, notably useful French stayer Mardonius (by Persian Bold), and half-brother to several winners: dam won at 9f and 1½m in Ireland: no worthwhile form though showed signs of a little ability in maiden events in midsummer. *B. Gubby*

PENNINE STAR (IRE) 4 b.f. Pennine Walk 120 – Sterna Regina 102 (Royal 68
And Regal (USA)) [1991 NR 1992 10s2 10m5 12f 10.5g5 12.2g 11.9d4 12m5 11.8d*] sturdy filly: poor mover: fair handicapper: best effort when 5-length winner of 22-runner race at Leicester in October, leading over 2f out and soon clear: effective from 1¼m to 1½m: ran as if something amiss on firm ground, best effort on dead: in foal. *C. W. C. Elsey*

PENNY HAGEN (IRE) 2 b.f. (May 5) Pennine Walk 120 – High Explosive 45
(Mount Hagen (FR) 127) [1992 5g 5d3 5m 6m 6g2 6.1m4 6s2 7.5m6] IR 1,600Y: well-grown, lengthy filly: has scope: moderate mover: half-sister to several winners, including quite useful sprinter Myra's Special (by Pitskelly) and 6f and 9f winner Ultra Light (by Superlative): dam poor staying maiden: modest plater: stays 7.5f: acts on good to firm and soft ground. *M. Johnston*

PENNY DROPS 3 b.f. Sharpo 132 – Darine 114 (Nonoalco (USA) 131) [1991 5g5 73
5g5 6m2 5m 6g 7m6 6.1m a7g 1992 6d* 7d4 7s* 8.2s* 7g2 a10g5] leggy filly: has a very round action: fair performer: in good form in big fields in the autumn, leading inside final 1f to win handicaps at Haydock (claimer), Newbury (apprentices) and Nottingham: bit below best final start, on equitrack: should prove effective beyond 8.2f: goes well on soft ground. *Lord Huntingdon*

PENNY HASSET 4 b.f. Lochnager 132 – Bad Payer 72 (Tanfirion 110) [1991 5m 72
6f5 5f5 7.5f 6m6 5f 5f 1992 5s* 5s2 5g* 5.9d* 6g4 5d* 5m* 5f2 5g* 6s5 5m 5d3 6d 5s] strong, lengthy filly: consistent handicapper: successful between March and July at Wolverhampton, Catterick (apprentices), Carlisle (2), Edinburgh and Hamilton (both apprentices): well below form final 2 starts: effective at 5f and 6f: acts on any going: usually races prominently: very tough and genuine. *M. W. Easterby*

PENNY ORCHID (IRE) 3 b.f. Taufan (USA) 119 – Honest Penny (USA) – §
(Honest Pleasure (USA)) [1991 6g 6g* 6m3 6m 1992 8.2d4 7m 8g 8.9d 8s] tall, leggy, unfurnished filly: moderate mover: fair winner at 2 yrs: behind in 1992 (including for W. Pearce), looking most reluctant early on in claimer final start: should be suited by 7f +: blinkered last 2 starts. *B. Beasley*

PEPERONATA (IRE) 2 b.f. (Feb 24) Cyrano de Bergerac 120 – Good Game 71 91
(Mummy's Game 120) [1992 5d* 5g2 5g4 5m4 5s] 8,600Y: strong, compact filly: first foal: dam, maiden, form only at 5f: fairly useful performer: won maiden at Ripon in April: left N. Tinkler's stable after next start and put up best effort when fourth to Poker Chip in Flying Childers Stakes at Doncaster in September: not discredited in face of very stiff task in Prix de l'Abbaye de Longchamp following month: speedy: acts on good to firm and soft ground. *B. W. Hills*

PERCY'S GIRL (IRE) 4 b.f. Blakeney 126 – Laughing Girl 110 (Sassafras (FR) 103
135) [1991 10.3m* 10m* 12d5 1992 10d 11.9g5 10d3 12m5 11.9m2 10.9s2 12m4 12g5] smallish, useful-looking filly: has a fluent, rather round action: useful and consistent performer: ran well in handicap, listed and pattern company in 1992, fifth to Cunning in Princess Royal Stakes at Ascot final start: probably ideally suited by 1½m: acted on good to firm and soft ground: visits Doyoun. *G. Wragg*

PERDITION (IRE) 2 b.f. (Mar 29) Red Sunset 120 – Free Rein (Sagaro 133) 60
[1992 5s 6f2 6d2 6m2 7m 6m5] 2,700Y: leggy, workmanlike filly: sister to 3 winners, including one-time 1m winner 7-y-o Sunset Reins Free and 1¼m winner Ice Magic: dam, unraced, from family of Troy: modest maiden: trained on debut by W. Pearce: ran creditably in 2 nurseries at Newmarket in the autumn: will stay 1m: acts on good to firm and dead ground. *J. W. Hills*

Reference Point Sceptre Stakes, Doncaster—
Perfect Circle (No. 5) returns to form against Midnight Air

PERFECT CIRCLE   3 b.f. Caerleon (USA) 132 – Fair Salinia 125 (Petingo 135) **114**
[1991 6g² 7g* 8d 1992 7m² 8g⁴ 10.4g² 12d 8m* 10d⁶ 7m⁵] lengthy, workmanlike
filly: tends not to take the eye in appearance: smart performer: won listed race at
Doncaster in September by a length from Midnight Air: in frame in Nell Gwyn
Stakes and 1000 Guineas (best effort, got poor run, about 1¼ lengths behind Hatoof)
at Newmarket and Musidora Stakes at York: ran badly in Oaks and some way below
best in Sun Chariot and Challenge Stakes at Newmarket in the autumn: best effort
at 1m, stays 10.4f at least in slowly-run race: probably needs a sound surface: has a
good turn of foot: sold 240,000 gns Newmarket December Sales. *M. R. Stoute*

PERFECT HALO (USA)   2 ch.c. (Mar 20) Halo (USA) – Inscrutable Lady   **97 p**
(USA) (Exclusive Native (USA)) [1992 6m* 6f*] $180,000Y: tall, rather unfurnished
colt: has scope: half-brother to a winner in North America and French 1991 3-y-o
1¼m winner Enigmatic (by Green Dancer): dam won at around 6f: sire high class at
up to 1½m: promising juvenile: won minor event at Newbury and 3-runner £12,000
event (by a length from Little Too Much) at Salisbury in June: will stay at least 1m:
looked a useful prospect and well worth his place in pattern company, but wasn't
seen again. *P. F. I. Cole*

PERFECT IMPOSTER (IRE)   2 b.c. (Apr 4) Persian Bold 123 – Tifrums 77   **82 p**
(Thatch (USA) 136) [1992 7m* 7g* 8s] sturdy, quite attractive colt: brother to
good-class miler Pennine Walk and 7-y-o 6f and 7f winner Kawwas and half-brother
to Italian Derby winner In A Tiff (by Caerleon): dam Irish 2-y-o 7f winner: fairly
useful form: won maiden at the Curragh in June and 3-runner minor event at Galway
4 weeks later: ran creditably when around 13 lengths eighth of 10 to Desert Secret in
Royal Lodge Stakes at Ascot in September: stays 1m: acts on good to firm and soft
ground. *J. S. Bolger, Ireland*

PERFECT LIGHT   3 b.c. Salmon Leap (USA) 131 – Sheer Gold 92 (Yankee Gold   –
115) [1991 8m 8.1g 8.1d 1992 11.8d 12m 16m 12.3m] big, workmanlike colt: no
worthwhile form in 1992: bred to be suited by middle distances but may well be too
headstrong to do so. *Mrs S. J. Smith*

PERFECTLY ENTITLED (IRE)   2 ch.f. (Feb 8) Entitled 126 – Little Red   –
Hut (Habitat 134) [1992 6m a5g] IR 5,800Y: fourth live foal: dam lightly-raced

half-sister to smart middle-distance colt Red Regent: soundly beaten in seller at Newmarket and maiden at Southwell in the autumn. *J. Pearce*

PERFECT PASSION 2 b.f. (May 1) Clantime 101 – Charming View 62 (Work- **58** boy 123) [1992 5d⁶ 5m⁵ 5f⁵ 5.2s⁶ 5m 5g⁶ 5.1s⁶ 5s⁴ 6v] 500Y: lengthy, unfurnished filly: moderate mover: first foal: dam, plater, stayed 1¼m: modest maiden: best effort in Molecomb Stakes at Goodwood (sweating) on fifth outing: should stay 6f: acts on firm and soft ground. *J. J. Bridger*

PERFECT SET (IRE) 2 b.f. (Feb 18) Red Sunset 120 – Feshang 74 (Artaius **45** (USA) 129) [1992 8.1s 8g 7s] IR 9,000Y: leggy, angular filly: fourth foal: half-sister to a winner in Italy by Persian Bold: dam once-raced half-sister to very useful sprinter Welshwyn: plating-class form on good ground. *M. R. Channon*

PERFORATE 3 b.g. Teenoso (USA) 135 – Bag Lady 86 (Be My Guest (USA) **58** 126) [1991 a7g⁴ 7s⁴ 7m 8g 8.3s a8g 1992 a12g* 12d² 14.6g⁵ 11.1m³ a12g⁴ 14.1g⁵ a16g² 16.1s 18m⁶] sturdy gelding: poor walker: moderate mover: generally consistent: won claimer at Lingfield in April: off course over 11 weeks and showed little in handicaps last 2 starts: stays 2m: acts on good to firm and dead ground, and on equitrack: effective blinkered or not: usually bandaged behind: sold to join R. Baker 6,000 gns Newmarket Autumn Sales. *Sir Mark Prescott*

PERIGORD (IRE) 2 br.g. (Feb 11) Cyrano de Bergerac 120 – Recline 70 **54** (Wollow 132) [1992 5g 5.7f 5m⁶ 5s⁵ 5d] 15,500F, 9,600Y: leggy, quite attractive gelding: sixth foal: half-brother to 3-y-o Notrella (by Trojan Fen) and 3 winners, including 2-y-o sprint winners Yuffrouw Ann (by Tyrnavos) and City Code (by Try My Best): dam, placed over 5f at 2 yrs, is half-sister to very speedy 1980 2-y-o Labista: plating-class maiden: should stay 6f: acts on soft ground: looks headstrong: trained first 3 outings by W. Muir. *M. H. Easterby*

PERO 2 b.c. (Mar 12) Reference Point 139 – Pelf (USA) 79 (Al Nasr (FR) 126) **– p** [1992 7m] second foal: half-brother to 3-y-o Zaire (by Riverman): dam, 7f winner in Italy, from good family: 20/1, around 12 lengths ninth of 16 to True Hero in maiden at Leicester in September, green over 2f out and unable to make any headway: will improve. *B. W. Hills*

PERPENDICULAR 4 b.c. Shirley Heights 130 – Pris (Priamos (GER) 123) **119** [1991 10s* 10.5g³ 10g* 1992 10g⁴ 10m* 10g³ 10s⁴ 10d⁴ 10g*] good-topped colt: moderate mover: consistent and smart performer: successful in 1992 in Prince of Wales's Stakes (beaten 1½ lengths on merit by demoted Kooyonga) at Royal Ascot in June and Group 3 event (made all when holding Arastou by 1½ lengths) at Hoppegarten in October: good third behind Kooyonga in Group 1 event at Munich, bit below best when fourth in between in Group 3 races won by Corrupt at Deauville and Knifebox at Goodwood: will prove at least as effective at 1½m as 1¼m: acts on good to firm and soft ground: tail swisher, but genuine. *H. R. A. Cecil*

PER QUOD (USA) 7 b.g. Lyllos (FR) – Allegedly (USA) (Sir Ivor 135) [1991 **100** 15s* 13.4d* 14g⁴ 20g 12g⁴ 13.4m⁵ 15.5m 15s⁴ 16g 1992 12g⁶ 15g⁴ 11.9g 14d⁵] leggy, workmanlike gelding: usually looks very well: has a quick, round action: useful performer nowadays: ran creditably when fourth to Drum Taps in Group 3 event at Milan and (heavily bandaged, stiffish task) when seventh in Old Newton Cup at Haydock 10 weeks later: probably better at 1¾m than shorter nowadays: not as his best on firm ground, goes very well on a soft surface: tough and genuine: has joined N. Henderson. *B. Hanbury*

PERSIAN ANTHEM (IRE) 3 ch.f. Persian Bold 123 – Northern Anthem **–** (Northfields (USA)) [1991 NR 1992 a8g 5g] sparely-made filly: second foal: dam unraced half-sister to Unite: little sign of ability in maidens at Southwell and Edinburgh in the spring: sold 1,000 gns Newmarket December Sales. *G. Wragg*

PERSIAN BRAVE (IRE) 2 b.c. (Feb 13) Persian Heights 129 – Commanche **84** Belle 74 (Shirley Heights 130) [1992 7g² 7d* 7m* 7g⁶] 27,000F, IR 34,000Y: rangy colt: third reported foal: half-brother to 7f and 1m winner Indian Slave (by Commanche Run): dam middle-distance maiden half-sister to Band and Zimbalon: fairly useful performer: made all in minor events at Redcar and Newcastle in July: creditable 4¾ lengths sixth in £14,700 event at York following month, never able to challenge: will be better suited by 1m. *M. Bell*

PERSIAN BUD (IRE) 4 b. or br.c. Persian Bold 123 – Awakening Rose (Le **–** Levanstell 122) [1991 10.1m 10.5g⁶ 12s 1992 10.8f a7g⁵ 9m⁶ 8f⁶ 8.3g] well-made colt: inconsistent maiden: stays 9f: acts on firesand and good to firm ground. *J. R. Bosley*

PERSIAN CHARMER (IRE) 2 b.c. (Feb 13) Persian Heights 129 – Merlins **71** Charm (USA) 113 (Bold Bidder) [1992 7g³ 8g² 7s³] 14,500Y: tall, good-topped colt: has rather ungainly action: half-brother to 3 winners, including 1989 2-y-o 7f winner

Native Guile (by Lomond) and 8.5f winner Island Charm (by Golden Fleece): dam won Jersey Stakes: fair form in 2 maidens at Ayr and a maiden auction at Redcar: stays 1m well: yet to race on top-of-the-ground: tends to race keenly: looked green off bridle last 2 starts. *Miss L. A. Perratt*

PERSIAN CHIMES (IRE) 2 b.g. (Mar 15) Persian Heights 129 – Ring The Changes 72 (Auction Ring (USA) 123) [1992 6s] 42,000Y: leggy gelding: half-brother to 3 winners here and in USA, including useful 6f and 7f winner Bell Tower (by Lyphard's Wish): dam 5f winner at 3 yrs: 14/1, soundly beaten in 14-runner maiden at Lingfield in October: moved moderately to post. *G. A. Pritchard-Gordon* —

PERSIAN DYNASTY 8 br.h. Persian Bold 123 – Parez 67 (Pardao 120) [1991 8m² 9m⁶ 7.1m⁴ 8.2f³ 8.1d³ 8.1g* 8f⁵ 8.2m 10m⁶ 8.2f⁶ 1992 8d 8g⁶ 8.9g² 7.1m³ 8.1m] small horse: poor handicapper: ran creditably penultimate start, but gives impression suited by 9f/1¼m nowadays: acts on firm and dead going: suitable mount for claimer. *J. M. Bradley* 45

PERSIAN FANTASY 3 br.f. Persian Bold 123 – Gay Fantasy (Troy 137) [1991 7g⁴ 7.1m³ 8f⁴ 7d 1992 10.2d 9.9f² 12f* 12f* 14.8g² 14d² 16g²] leggy, lightly-made filly: usually looks well: has a round action: fairly useful performer: favourite in small fields, won handicaps at Thirsk and Carlisle in July: very good second in moderately-run listed race won by Specificity at Newmarket final start: stayed 2m: acted on firm and dead going: has been retired. *J. L. Dunlop* 94

PERSIAN FLEECE 3 ch.f. Bold Arrangement 111 – Microcosme 100 (Golden Fleece (USA) 133) [1991 5g 7.1d 1992 9.2g² 10m³ 10g² 12m⁴ 10.9s* 10.5d⁶ a16g⁶] sparely-made filly: moderate mover: fairly useful plater: sold out of Mrs M. Reveley's stable 8,000 gns after winning at Ayr in September, leading 3f out and staying on strongly: below form afterwards: needs a strong pace at 1¼m and stays 1½m: best effort on soft ground. *A. Bailey* 54

PERSIAN FOUNTAIN (IRE) 2 ch.f. (Apr 26) Persian Heights 129 – Misty Lady (Habitat 134) [1992 6d 7m⁶ 7.5d* 7g] IR 2,800Y: angular filly: closely related to 1989 Irish 2-y-o 1m winner Albakht (by Persian Bold), and half-sister to 3 winners 60

Prince of Wales's Stakes, Royal Ascot—
Kooyonga's jockey celebrates too soon, for the filly is demoted in favour of Perpendicular;
blinkered Young Buster takes third ahead of the grey Terimon

abroad: dam Irish 7f winner from good sprinting family: easily best effort when winning strongly-run auction event at Beverley in July, given plenty to do: last of 14 in £12,100 nursery at York 5 weeks later: stays 7.5f: acts on dead ground. *B. S. Rothwell*

PERSIAN GUSHER (IRE) 2 gr.g. (Apr 17) King Persian 107 – Magnanimous 65 (Runnymede 123) [1992 5d 6m 6d a6g2 6s a7g2 a7g*] IR 1,500F, 3,600Y: leggy a71 gelding: half-brother to several winners here and abroad, including fair 1984 2-y-o 5f and 7f winner Ernie Bilko (by Raga Navarro) and fairly useful 1986 2-y-o 6f winner Able Saint (by Welsh Saint): dam ran only at 5f: fair performer on all-weather: won maiden at Lingfield in December: stays 7f: well below form on soft ground: has worn eyeshield. *S. Dow*

PERSIAN HOUSE 5 ch.g. Persian Bold 123 – Sarissa 105 (Reform 132) [1991 52 11.9d 14.6m 1992 8.3m4 9.9g] big, good-topped gelding: rated 73 at 3 yrs: staying-on fourth in handicap at Hamilton, clearly better effort in June, 1992: stays 1½m+: acts on good to firm and dead ground: winning hurdler (1991/2), won novice chase in October. *J. M. Jefferson*

PERSIAN LION 3 br.c. Reesh 117 – Parijoun (Manado 130) [1991 6.1g6 7.1d 1992 – 11.1d] leggy colt: no worthwhile form, in claimer on reappearance in November: bought 2,500 gns Doncaster August (1992) Sales. *F. Watson*

PERSIAN MELODY (IRE) 2 b.f. (Feb 17) Persian Heights 129 – Whist 51 Awhile (Caerleon (USA) 132) [1992 5g 5d 6d5 6m] 1,000F: leggy filly with scope: second foal: half-sister to 3-y-o Qualitair Memory (by Don't Forget Me): dam unraced half-sister to very useful 1983 2-y-o Mahogany: ridden by 7-lb claimer, easily best effort when fifth in maiden at Goodwood in October: well beaten in 29-runner seller at Newmarket 13 days later: will be suited by 7f+: may well be unsuited by top-of-the-ground: sold 1,500 gns Newmarket Autumn Sales. *D. R. C. Elsworth*

PERSIAN NOBLE 2 ch.c. (May 8) Persian Heights 129 – Charmina (FR) – (Nonoalco (USA) 131) [1992 5.1d 6m] workmanlike colt: half-brother to several winners here and abroad, including 6f winner Floral Charms (by Shecky Greene): dam, French 8.2f winner, from family of Dahlia: bit backward, soundly beaten in maiden at Bath in April and seller (coltish, badly drawn) at Lingfield in July. *C. J. Hill*

PERSIAN REVIVAL (FR) 2 gr.c. (Mar 15) Wassl 125 – Une Florentine (FR) 90 (Pharly (FR) 130) [1992 6m3 6m 6f* 7m 7.1d 5g5 7m6 6d5 6v 7g2] 1,100F, 4,800Y: good-topped colt: has scope: shows keen action: half-brother to useful stayer Top of The World (by Top Ville) and a winner in France: dam French 5.5f and 9f winner, is half-sister to high-class French 1m to 1¼m performer Un Desperado: fairly useful performer: won maiden at Haydock in July: ran well in Racecall Gold Trophy at Redcar and 21-runner nursery at Doncaster last 2 starts: finds 5f too sharp, and will stay 1m: acts on any going: has run the odd moderate race. *B. A. McMahon*

PERSIAN SATAN (IRE) 4 b.f. King Persian 107 – Irish Myth (St Paddy 133) – [1991 7m 1992 a7g a12g] angular filly: of little account: dead. *C. J. Hill*

PERSIANSKY (IRE) 2 b.g. (Feb 28) Persian Bold 123 – Astra Adastra (Mount 67 Hagen (FR) 127) [1992 7g3 7g 6.1m5 8.1d3 8m2 8m4 8.3s2 7.6s5] IR 31,000Y: lengthy, rather leggy gelding: has scope: good mover, with a long stride: half-brother to several winners, including fairly useful Baraz (by Busted), at 1½m, and Precious Air (by Precocious), from 5f (at 2 yrs) to 1m: dam Irish 2-y-o 5f winner, is half-sister to Ballad Rock: fair performer: in frame in maidens and nurseries: very slowly away and seemed reluctant to race when tailed off at Chester final start: stays 1m: probably acts on any going: usually has tongue tied down nowadays: usually races keenly: tends to be fractious in preliminaries. *B. Hanbury*

PERSIAN STAR (FR) 2 ch.f. (Mar 28) Village Star (FR) 131 – Usherette (FR) – (Persian Bold 123) [1992 8.2g a8g] ex-French filly: second foal: half-sister to French 3-y-o Pebble Mill (by Moulin), 1m winner at 2 yrs: dam never ran: no form in maiden at Amiens when trained by A. Fabre and well beaten at Lingfield in December. *K. O. Cunningham-Brown*

PERSIAN TRAVELLER (IRE) 2 b.c. (Apr 20) Persian Bold 123 – Something 60 Swift (Rarity 129) [1992 6m 7m a6g4 a7s* a7g3 7g* 7g 8s] 1,900Y: sparely-made colt: second foal: half-brother to Irish 9f and 1¼m winner Vistage (by Prince Tenderfoot): dam unraced: modest form: won sellers at Southwell (by 10 lengths, no bid) and Thirsk (sold out of C. Allen's stable 6,200 gns) in August: ran moderately in non-selling nurseries afterwards: should stay 1m: acts on fibresand: suitable mount for a 7-lb claimer: sold to join T. Fairhurst 2,900 gns Doncaster November Sales. *Mrs J. R. Ramsden*

PERSONAL HAZARD   3 ch.g. Risk Me (FR) 127 – Princess Lily 65 (Blakeney   **71**
126) [1991 5m⁶ 6g⁴ 7m² 7m³ 7m* 7m 7m 7.6d⁶ 1992 7g 8d³ 8.9g] quite good-topped
gelding: fair handicapper: form in the spring only when third of 7, making most, at
Carlisle: stays 1m: acts on good to firm ground and dead: visored final start at 2 yrs:
won novice hurdle in December. *M. H. Easterby*

PERSONIMUS   2 b.c. (Mar 14) Ballacashtal (CAN) – Sea Charm 70 (Julio   **43**
Mariner 127) [1992 8.1d a7g] 9,400Y: good-topped colt: has scope: brother to
one-time fair sprinter Profilic and half-brother to a winner in Italy: dam, third over
13f from 4 starts, is half-sister to high-class middle-distance stayer Mistigri and
useful stayer Tanaka: green when blinkered in late-season maidens at Haydock and
Southwell: looks sort to need time and longer distances. *Capt. J. Wilson*

PERSPICACITY   5 b.m. Petorius 117 – Grattan Princess (Tumble Wind (USA))   **–**
[1991 NR 1992 8f 7.1m⁵ 8.1f⁵ 7d 10g] sturdy mare: no worthwhile form in 1992,
including in sellers. *M. Dods*

PERSUASIUS (IRE)   4 b.g. Petorius 117 – Be A Dancer (Be Friendly 130) [1991   **58**
5d⁶ 8m 7g² 8f⁵ 8.5f 9.2f⁵ 10.3d 1992 a8g³ 13m 8f* 6.9h² 8f⁶] leggy gelding: modest
handicapper: trained until after second start by W. Pearce: blinkered and in good
form next 2 outings, gaining first win when making all at Thirsk: seemed to sulk
when unable to dominate on final start, in August: effective at 7f/1m: acts on hard
ground: twice refused to enter stalls in 1991: sold to join M. Smith 4,800 gns
Doncaster November Sales. *B. Beasley*

PERSUASIVE   5 b.m. Sharpo 132 – Queen's Eyot 79 (Grundy 137) [1991 11s³   **59**
15m⁴ 15.1s 1992 13d 13d* 12.1v] lengthy, rather sparely-made mare: has a round
action: modest handicapper: won at Hamilton in May: well beaten there 5½ months
later: appears to stay 15f: acts on any going: fairly useful hurdler, won 2 handicaps in
November. *Miss L. A. Perratt*

PESIDANAMICH (IRE)   4 b.g. Mummy's Treasure 84 – Bay Supreme   **45**   +
(Martinans 128) [1991 a7g³ 7g a7g* a7g* a7g² a6g³ a7g* a7g² 7g³ 6m 7m 7m 7m a6g   **a72**
a6g² 1992 a7g³ a7g⁵ a7g³ a7g² a6g² 7d⁵ 7d 7g a6g⁴ a7g³ a7g a6g²] sturdy gelding:
poor mover: fair handicapper, best on the all-weather: sold out of T. Barron's stable
4,600 gns Doncaster May Sales after sixth start: better at 7f than 6f: acts on any
going: best in blinkers: usually a front runner. *J. P. Leigh*

PETAL GIRL   3 ch.f. Caerleon (USA) 132 – Amazer (Mincio 127) [1991 7f² 7m⁴   **96**
1992 7g² 7.6g² 10m⁵ 8.1g* 8m* 8.1d³ 8m⁴ 7g] leggy, lightly-made filly: has a quick
action: useful and consistent performer: narrowly successful in maiden at Chepstow
and slowly-run minor event at Newmarket in July: ran very well in listed races at
Sandown and Doncaster (5 lengths behind Perfect Circle) next 2 starts, moderately
at Naas final one: stayed 1m well: acted on good to firm and dead ground: to stud. *R. Hannon*

PETANK (IRE)   4 ch.c. Double Schwartz 128 – Hay Knot (Main Reef 126) [1991   **–**
a7g⁶ 6g 6.1m 1992 a5g⁶ a7g⁶ a5g] lengthy, dipped-backed colt: of little account. *Pat Mitchell*

PETARDIA   2 b.c. (Feb 15) Petong 126 – What A Pet (Mummy's Pet 125) **108**
[1992 5f* 6m* 6m 7m* 7m⁶]
   It's a measure of the calibre of animal that Petardia beat in the Coventry
Stakes at Royal Ascot and the Laurent-Perrier Champagne Stakes at Doncaster—a double last achieved by Sure Blade in 1985—that he should run
right up to his best form in the Dewhurst Stakes at Newmarket in October and
still finish seven lengths off the winner Zafonic. Petardia was never the
remotest threat in sixth, checked slightly as he began to make ground with
two furlongs to run. In normal circumstances the winner of the Coventry, and
more particularly the Champagne Stakes, is entitled to be regarded as one of
the best of his generation, but every now and again the standard of certain
events within the pattern falls well below the level expected, and Petardia was
able to carry a 3-lb penalty to victory in what wasn't, after the withdrawal of
the likely favourite White Crown on account of the good to firm ground, a
strong renewal of the Champagne. In a race run at a strong pace, Petardia was
ridden in his usual manner, given plenty of time to find his stride, and came
full of running as the leaders dropped away with two furlongs to run before
quickening clear, despite tending to idle, to account for the subsequent Royal
Lodge fourth Needle Gun by a length and a half, the Solario Stakes third
Fitzcarraldo finishing a neck behind in third. Petardia's performance con-

Coventry Stakes, Royal Ascot—the year's first big test for two-year-olds goes to Petardia (noseband), from So Factual (right) and Pips Pride

firmed that he'd put behind him whatever had ailed him in the Gimcrack at York in August—his connections reported that he'd jumped a path early on and had then led with the 'wrong' leg—where he'd finished last of the eight runners behind Splendent. Petardia had started a well-backed favourite at York to follow up his short-head victory over So Factual in the Coventry and his five-length slamming of four modest opponents in a maiden at Doncaster in May. The Coventry is the first major test of the season for two-year-olds and has been contested by the last two Derby winners, but we'd be most surprised if the latest running contained a third. By the end of the season it had become evident that Petardia wasn't the best horse in the field—that distinction fell to third-placed Pips Pride, runner-up in the Middle Park and successful in the Racecall Gold Trophy—but on the day he produced just enough to emerge best of the eight who passed the two-furlong marker almost in a line. The determination that Petardia showed to short-head So Factual at Ascot wasn't quite so evident later in the season, and we were left with the impression, in

Laurent-Perrier Champagne Stakes, Doncaster—first and third, Petardia and Fitzcarraldo

the Dewhurst in particular, in which he found little when eventually getting a clear run, that he might be a little short on resolution.

		Mansingh	Jaipur
	Petong	(b 1969)	Tutasi
	(gr 1980)	Iridium	Linacre
Petardia		(br 1969)	Tula Melody
(b.c. Feb 15, 1990)		Mummy's Pet	Sing Sing
	What A Pet	(b 1968)	Money For Nothing
	(b 1981)	Moben	Counsel
		(gr 1967)	Chysanthia

Petardia is a good-topped, attractive colt who must have been an impressive yearling: he was sold for 125,000 guineas at Newmarket October Sales, an extraordinary sum for a son of Petong, a stallion whose yearlings seldom change hands for five figures, let alone six. Petardia has an unexceptional pedigree. Petong, a top-class sprint handicapper who won the Vernon's Sprint Cup on the final start of his career, has had only a handful of winners of any real significance among his first six crops, while Petardia's dam What A Pet, a winner over a mile in France, has bred only one other winner, the modest French dual-purpose performer Bourrasque (by What A Guest), from three previous foals. However, What A Pet is a full sister to the very useful French and British five-furlong to one-mile performer Teacher's Pet; Petardia's second dam, Moben, a minor winner at seven furlongs from just three outings, is a half-sister to the high-class stayer Grey Baron and the dam of the Triumph Hurdle winner Baron Blakeney; and the third dam Chysanthia is a daughter of the brilliantly speedy Abelia.
We don't anticipate Petardia's taking a hand in the classics; on his Dewhurst form he has a lot to find in the Guineas, and he's unlikely to be tried over further than a mile. A fluent mover, who has raced so far only on top-of-the-ground, Petardia possesses a useful turn of foot but tends to idle in front. *G. Wragg*

PETASTRA 3 b.f. Petoski 135 – Star Face (African Sky 124) [1991 7m4 8.1d 8m4 1992 7f 10.3f 8.2g] workmanlike filly: moderate mover: no worthwhile form in handicaps in late-spring: bred to stay 1¼m. *Mrs J. R. Ramsden* —

PETAURISTA 3 b.f. Petong 126 – Lydia Rose 68 (Mummy's Pet 125) [1991 5m6 6m 6d 1992 a6g6 5v 6m] sturdy filly: no worthwhile form in the spring. *M. Johnston* —

PETAVIOUS 7 b.g. Mummy's Pet 125 – Pencuik Jewel (Petingo 135) [1991 9s* 10.8m4 12m2 12g4 11.5g 12g4 11.8m* 12m* 10.2g4 1992 12g2 12m* a12g3 11.5d a12g] leggy gelding: moderate mover: fair handicapper: in good form in the spring, successful at Beverley: well held last 2 starts after 5½-month break: stays 1½m: acts on good to firm and soft ground, and on fibresand: suitable mount for apprentice. *Lady Herries* 70

PETERED OUT 2 b. or br.g. (Mar 30) Nomination 125 – Fading (Pharly (FR) 130) [1992 5m2 5f5 a5g a7g4] first foal: dam, unraced, from good family: plating-class maiden: beaten a short head in 5-runner race at Edinburgh: stays 7f. *T. D. Barron* 41

PETER MARTIN TWO 3 b.g. Farajullah 113 – Transonic 60 (Continuation 120) [1991 NR 1992 11.1s] 7,00Y, 700 2-y-o: second foal: dam sprinter: 50/1, led 7f, soon outpaced and eased, in 20-runner claimer at Hamilton in September: has joined J. Gillen. *T. Craig* —

PETER PUMPKIN 4 b.g. Tickled Pink 114 – Wild Pumpkin (Auction Ring (USA) 123) [1991 a8g5 a5g a6g5 a8g3 10f 7f5 8d4 8f 7g 1992 9d] workmanlike gelding: poor mover: rated 35 at 3 yrs when rather temperamental: bandaged, well beaten in April: stays 1m: acts on firm and dead going, and on equitrack: often blinkered: races freely: pulled up lame over hurdles in September. *R. Voorspuy* —

PETERSFORD GIRL (IRE) 2 b.f. (Apr 28) Taufan (USA) 119 – Engage (Whistling Wind 123) [1992 6g2] leggy filly: sister to useful 3-y-o 5f and 6f winner Taufan Blu and half-sister to several winners, including useful sprinter African Lady (by African Sky) and (at 9f in Ireland) Cluster of Diamond (by Ballad Rock): dam won from 5f to 1m in Ireland: 33/1, beaten ½ length by Blues Traveller in 20-runner maiden at Newbury in September, travelling well, quickening to lead inside last but caught close home: should win an ordinary maiden. *Miss Jacqueline S. Doyle* 79 p

PETIOLE 2 b.f. (Feb 10) Petong 126 – Crystal Gael 79 (Sparkler 130) [1992 6m⁶ –
6g 6d 6d 8s] angular filly: half-sister to several minor winners: dam 2-y-o 1m winner:
soundly beaten, including when blinkered in a seller. *W. R. Muir*

PETITE BELLE 3 b.f. Legend of France (USA) 124 – Bishah (USA) 86 (Balzac –
(USA)) [1991 6m⁵ 7m 8.5f⁵ 7g 8.9m⁵ 1992 10m 10g⁵ 12m⁶ a12g a12g a12g a12g]
small, good-bodied filly: poor maiden: no form at 3 yrs. *R. M. Whitaker*

PETITE-D-ARGENT 3 b.f. Noalto 120 – Honey To Spare 63 (Track Spare 125) 91
[1991 5h⁴ 5g² 5m⁵ 6m² 5m² 5.1f³ 5m⁵ 6m* 1992 6d² 6m⁴ 6m² 7d*] compact filly:
moderate mover: fairly useful handicapper: won £7,100 event at Epsom in June: will
prove best at up to 7f: acts on good to firm and dead ground: ran well in visor at 2 yrs:
tends to hang under pressure: reportedly suffered hairline fracture of near-fore in
August. *Miss L. A. Perratt*

PETITE EPAULETTE 2 ch.f. (Feb 1) Night Shift (USA) – Note Book 94 70
(Mummy's Pet 125) [1992 5f* 5f⁵ 6f³ 6f⁴ 5.2g⁶ 5s⁶] close-coupled, sparely-made
filly: first foal: dam 6f winner, is half-sister to smart miler Long Row out of Irish
1000 Guineas winner Front Row: consistent performer: won maiden at Thirsk in
May: will be well suited by return to 6f: probably acts on any going: sold 17,000 gns
Newmarket December Sales. *W. Jarvis*

PETITE JESS 2 b.f. (Apr 30) Nomination 125 – Khadine 79 (Astec 128) [1992 6f⁴ 45
7m⁴] 3,100 2-y-o: half-sister to a winner abroad by Night Shift: dam required good
test of stamina: plating-class form in maidens at Epsom and Redcar (auction event)
in the summer: will be well suited by middle distances. *W. Carter*

PETITE LASS 2 b.f. (Jan 25) Lidhame 109 – Titian Beauty (Auction Ring (USA) 43
123) [1992 5v³ 5.3d⁵ 5g* 5f 5g⁶] smallish, leggy filly: first foal: dam poor daughter of
sister to top-class sprinter Deep Diver and half-sister to Irish 2000 Guineas winner
King's Company: poor form: dropped in class, won seller at Wolverhampton (no bid)
in April: may prove best at 5f: not seen after July. *W. Carter*

PETITE LOUIE 2 gr.f. (Mar 14) Chilibang 120 – Sisola (USA) (Coastal (USA)) 45
[1992 6d 7m⁶ 8g] 3,100F, 23,000Y: leggy filly: second foal: closely related to a
winner in Italy by Forzando: dam, winner in Italy, is half-sister to Environment
Friend: poor form in maidens: best effort second start: off course over 2 months and
in need of race, raced too freely final outing: stays 7f. *W. Carter*

PETITE SONNERIE 3 b.f. Persian Bold 123 – Hiding 84 (So Blessed 130) [1991 78
7g⁶ 6g⁶ 6f⁶ 7f⁴ 6s² 7m 1992 8d² 7g² 7d⁵ 7.1g³ 8.5f² 8.5f* 8.5f² 8.5f²] big,
good-topped filly: fair form in Britain for G. Lewis: sent to USA after fourth start,
and won maiden at Bay Meadows in October: effective at 7f and 1m: acts on any
going. *W. Greenman, USA*

PETITESSE 4 gr.f. Petong 126 – Foudroyer (Artaius (USA) 129) [1991 6m⁶ 5s² 48
6g 6g 6g⁶ 6f⁶ 5d⁵ 5g* 5d* 5f* 5s² 5.1m 5m 5.3f⁵ 1992 5d⁶ 6d 5f 5g 5.1g⁶ 5m² 5f4 6g
5.1m⁶ 6m⁶ 5g] small, dipped-backed filly: inconsistent handicapper: stays 6f: acts on
any going: tried blinkered earlier in career: has been mounted on track and often
mulish to post. *G. Blum*

PETITE VINO 2 b.f. (Feb 24) Petoski 135 – El Vino (Habitat 134) [1992 5g 6f 5d 42
5m⁶ 5m 6g 6m⁴ 6f⁶ 7d 5g 8d 6.9v a8g⁶ a8g] 400Y: leggy filly: modest mover: first
foal: dam ran twice: poor performer: stays 1m: no improvement in blinkers: has run
well for 7-lb claimer. *J. J. Bridger*

PETIT LOUP (USA) 3 b.c. Danzig (USA) – Bambee T T (USA) (Better Bee) 121
[1991 8g⁶ 10d⁶ 1992 9v² 9g³ 10g* 10g* 11g* 12g* 12m² 12s] good-topped colt:
eighth foal: brother to high-class 1¼m winner Ascot Knight, closely related to 2
winners by Vice Regent, notably champion Canadian grass horse Bounding Away,
and half-brother to a winner by Nodouble: very smart performer: won minor events
at Evry and Longchamp, then 2 Group 1 contests at San Sebastian, Spain, all in the
summer: beaten a nose by Songlines in Prix Niel at Longchamp, penultimate start,
eventually staying on strongly: chased leaders 1¼m when twelfth of 18 in Prix de
l'Arc de Triomphe there on final outing: stays 1½m: best form on a sound surface.
Mme C. Head, France

PETIVARA 5 b.m. Petong 126 – Avahra 108 (Sahib 114) [1991 7m 7.6s⁶ a7g² a7g –
9m³ 8.9m a8g 1992 7g 8f] leggy, workmanlike mare: seems of little account these
days. *S. Dow*

PETMER 5 b.g. Tina's Pet 121 – Merency 75 (Meldrum 112) [1991 9d⁵ 10.2g⁵ –
10.2d* 10g 1992 12g 10g 10m 10d⁵] tall, leggy gelding: rated 53 at 4 yrs: no
worthwhile form in 1992: should stay 1½m: acts on firm and dead ground: joined R.
Curtis in the autumn and won claiming hurdle in October: has shown signs of being
irresolute. *G. B. Balding*

PETO 3 b.c. Petoski 135 – Rimosa's Pet 109 (Petingo 135) [1991 NR 1992 10v* **107**
10m* 11s* 12m 10d* 10g5] sturdy colt: sixth living foal: half-brother to 3 winners,
including very smart 6f winner and 1000 Guineas second Kerrera (by Diesis) and
very useful performer at up to 1m Rock City (by Ballad Rock): dam 6f to 10.5f
winner: very useful performer: won maiden at Pontefract and minor events at
Windsor and Wolverhampton in the spring, then dead-heated with Adam Smith in
£9,150 event at Newbury in July: favourite, below best in King Edward VII Stakes at
Royal Ascot and listed race at Windsor on other outings: should stay 1½m: best
efforts on an easy surface. H. R. A. Cecil

PETONELLA JILL 2 br.f. (May 4) Petong 126 – Crackerjill 37 (Sparkler 130) **45**
[1992 5.2s 6.1m5 6d] leggy, unfurnished filly: has scope: good walker: third reported
foal: half-sister to useful 3-y-o sprinter Arabellajill (by Aragon): dam stayed 1m:
poor form in maidens: looks to need time. R. Hannon

PETONICA (IRE) 3 b.f. Petoski 135 – Ivoronica 89 (Targowice (USA) 130) –
[1991 7g2 7m6 1992 8s] lengthy filly: promising second on debut: split a pastern next
start and well beaten in maiden (bit backward) on belated reappearance, in October:
should stay 1m. M. H. Tompkins

PETONY (IRE) 4 b.f. Petorius 117 – Norme (FR) (Dark Tiger) [1991 7m5 6f5 –
5m6 7g 5m4 5f 5d 6.1m 5s 1992 a12g 5s] leggy filly: rated 43 at best at 3 yrs: no form
in 1992: stays 7f: acts on firm going: blinkered (soundly beaten) once at 3 yrs: tail
swisher: sold 900 gns Ascot March Sales. C. W. C. Elsey

PETOSKI'S CHOICE 4 b.f. Petoski 135 – Elegida 93 (Habitat 134) [1991 8g 8f6 –
8.3d4 7m4 8m* 1992 9d 8.1d] strong filly: moderate walker: rated 69 at 3 yrs:
backward, no worthwhile form in spring, 1992: should prove suited by 1m + : acts on
good to firm ground, seems unsuited by a soft surface: has wandered badly. M. J.
Ryan

PETRACO (IRE) 4 b.c. Petorius 117 – Merrie Moira (Bold Lad (IRE) 133) [1991 **77**
6d5 5m 6g* 6m* 7g 6g 6g 5m3 6m 5d6 6m4 5g 1992 6g5 5.1m3 5m 6g4 6f 8f6 6g 5m3
5d 5.2g 6d 6s3 5s* 6g 6d 6d 7d] workmanlike colt: has a quick action: rather
inconsistent handicapper: won at Haydock in September: effective at 5f and 6f: acts
on any going: effective blinkered or not: has hung right. L. J. Codd

PETROPOWER (IRE) 4 b.g. Petorius 117 – Gay Honey (Busted 134) [1991 6d –
6f5 a5g 6m 6f 9.9f 7m4 6f a6g 1992 a8g3 8s 6d] lengthy, rather angular gelding: a55
moderate mover: modest handicapper at best: soundly beaten last 2 starts, in the
spring: stays 1m: acts on firm going and fibresand: tried blinkered: sold 900 gns
Doncaster May Sales. M. O'Neill

PETTICOAT POWER 6 b.m. Petorius 117 – Red Realm (Realm 129) [1991 7m5 –
8.2g3 8.1g3 7f 8.3m 8m5 7s2 8g5 7g 6.9s3 1992 a8g5 8.2m 8.1g] workmanlike,
sparely-made mare: modest handicapper at best: off course 4½ months, well beaten
last 2 starts, including in a visor, in midsummer: effective from 6f to 1m: probably
acts on any going: suitable mount for inexperienced rider: sometimes bandaged.
Mrs Barbara Waring

PETTY CASH 3 b.f. Midyan (USA) 124 – Money Supply (Brigadier Gerard 144) –
[1991 6.9f a8g 1992 10d 14.1f 11.5g 7g 12.3g] close-coupled, sparely-made filly: looks
of little account: sold 620 gns Doncaster September Sales. Dr J. D. Scargill

PFAFF'S CELLAR 2 ch.f. (Apr 1) Krayyan 117 – Lysithea 63 (Imperial Fling –
(USA) 116) [1992 5.1d 5g6 5.1s 5f 5.3f] leggy, lengthy filly: first foal: dam 6f seller
winner later placed several times over jumps: well beaten in sellers in the spring:
blinkered on debut. W. G. M. Turner

PFALZ 4 b.f. Pharly (FR) 130 – Leipzig 107 (Relkino 131) [1991 8m* 8m* 8g 1992 **101**
7g 8.5g3 10m5] leggy filly: useful performer: best effort when staying-on third to
Zaahi in Diomed Stakes at Epsom: tongue tied down, led at modest pace to over 2f
out when creditable fifth of 6 in Kempton listed event later in June: seemed to stay
1¼m, at least in moderately-run race: acted on good to firm ground: in foal to
Warning. M. R. Stoute

PHARAMINEUX 6 ch.g. Pharly (FR) 130 – Miss Longchamp 94 (Northfields **79**
(USA)) [1991 14g2 14d2 16.2g2 14m* 16.2m5 11.5d* 14s 12m* 12s 1992 11.9f*]
strong, workmanlike gelding: has a quick action: tough and consistent handicapper
as a 5-y-o: returned better than ever, winning by a short head at Brighton in June,
tenderly handled to lead close home: best from 1½m to 1¾m: acts on firm and dead
ground, unsuited by soft: blinkered once earlier in career: successful 4 times at
Sandown: has turn of foot: looked sure to progress but wasn't seen out again. R.
Akehurst

PHARAOH'S DANCER 5 b.g. Fairy King (USA) – Marie Louise 86 (King **78** Emperor (USA)) [1991 9s 8m 8.3m⁶ 8g⁵ 7g³ 8g 7m⁵ 7g² 1992 6d5 6v* 7g⁵ 6g* 6s* 5m 6g 6f 5s 7.6g⁶ 5s³ 5.1d 5s 6v] good-topped gelding: has round action: fairly useful handicapper at his best: only one worthwhile piece of form (when third) after winning at Pontefract, Thirsk and Hamilton in the spring: trained until after tenth start by E. Wheeler: has form on good to firm ground, but ideally suited by 6f and an easy surface. *R. Simpson*

PHARGOLD (IRE) 3 ch.g. Phardante (FR) 120 – Mallee (Malinowski (USA) – 123) [1991 5g 6g 6f a8g 1992 12f4 11.1m⁶ a14g] sturdy gelding: of little account on flat: winner over hurdles in August: sold out of P. Haslam's stable 1,200 gns Doncaster September Sales. *R. J. Weaver*

PHARLANDER (IRE) 3 br.g. Phardante (FR) 120 – Moll Flanders (ITY) **42** (Maestrale (USA)) [1991 6g4 7g 7f4 7m² 8m 1992 12.3s 12d³ 12f3 16f4] workmanlike gelding: plating-class maiden, not seen out after June: blinkered, in frame in handicaps last 3 starts: stays 2m: acts on firm and dead going: visored once at 2 yrs. *M. H. Easterby*

PHARLY DANCER 3 b.c. Pharly (FR) 130 – Martin-Lavell Mail (Dominion 123) – [1991 6d 1992 10.5d5] leggy, angular colt: has a round action: 50/1 on first run for 12 months, keeping-on fifth in maiden at Haydock in June. *W. W. Haigh*

PHARLY STORY 4 b.c. Pharly (FR) 130 – Certain Story (Known Fact (USA) **100** 135) [1991 8d4 7g² 6m³ 10m* 11.8m* 1992 10m 13.4m5 11.5m* 12f 11.9g6 10.3g* 10m² 10s* 10.2s³ 10g] lengthy, rather dipped-backed colt: useful performer: won amateur events at Lingfield, Doncaster and Sandown in the summer: ran very well when second to Knock Knock in £25,800 Chesterfield Cup at Goodwood, but moderately last 2 starts: effective from 1¼m to 13.4f: has won on soft going, but best efforts on top-of-the-ground: usually wears crossed noseband. *M. C. Pipe*

PHIL-BLAKE 5 br.g. Blakeney 126 – Philogyny 94 (Philip of Spain 126) [1991 10f **39** 11.7g 12m 14.8m 9d 12d 10g 1992 a7g 10.3g² 9m³ 10g4 10.8f3 8.9d 9.7m 12s5] leggy, workmanlike gelding: largely consistent handicapper, still a maiden: stays 11f: acts on any going: sometimes wears crossed noseband: suitable mount for lady rider: poor winning hurdler in 1990/1. *S. Mellor*

PHILGUN 3 b.g. K-Battery 108 – Andalucia 57 (Rheingold 137) [1991 6m 6g 7m **65** 7m 8.3g4 1992 9s* 9.2d* 10.1s4 10.5d5 11.1m* 11.1f4 10.1f 10.3m 12.3f3 12.3m 11.8g3 10.9s³ 11.9s5 12.1v⁶] leggy, close-coupled gelding: fair performer: won handicap at Hamilton and claimers at Newcastle and Edinburgh in the spring: ran creditably later in season: stays 1½m: has form on firm ground, but goes particularly well on soft: often apprentice ridden. *C. W. C. Elsey*

PHILIDOR 3 b.c. Forzando 122 – Philgwyn 66 (Milford 119) [1991 6f2 6m5 7g* **89** 1992 6g 8f* 8m 8m 8m* 7.9m4 8s] smallish, strong colt: fairly useful handicapper: won at Newbury in May and Goodwood (£7,600 contest) in July: very good fourth in £25,000 contest at York, staying on strongly from towards rear: suited by good pace at 1m, and should stay further: acts on firm going, seemingly not on soft. *J. M. P. Eustace*

PHIL-MAN 3 b.c. Tina's Pet 121 – Pakpao 77 (Mansingh (USA) 120) [1991 7s **45** 7.5f2 7m² 7m³ 7.5f⁶ 7m4 6f 6m a7g 1992 a6g 7.5g⁶ 8s 8h² 8g 7.1m² 8m⁶ 8f 8g 6.9g3 8s 10s 8s 8.1g3] workmanlike colt: inconsistent maiden: may prove best at 1m on a sound surface: sold 720 gns Doncaster November Sales. *T. Fairhurst*

PHILOSTRA 4 b.f. Final Straw 127 – Philogyny 94 (Philip of Spain 126) [1991 NR – 1992 8m] sixth foal: half-sister to 5-y-o Phil-Blake (by Blakeney), 7-y-o 1m winner Sporting Wednesday (by Martinmas) and 1¼m winner The Footman (by Hotfoot): dam won 5 sprints: bandaged, well beaten in Brighton maiden. *Andrew Turnell*

PHINEAS T BARNUM (IRE) 4 b.c. Godswalk (USA) 130 – Circus Lady – (High Top 131) [1991 6m³ a8g 1992 6d 8m] sturdy colt: no worthwhile form, though has shown signs of a little ability: sold 1,700 gns Doncaster September Sales. *J. J. O'Neill*

PHROSE 2 b.c. (Jan 23) Pharly (FR) 130 – Rose Chanelle (Welsh Pageant 132) **67** p [1992 8d6 10g² 10g] smallish colt: third foal: half-brother to progressive 3-y-o stayer Garden District (by Celestial Storm): dam unraced granddaughter of Rose Dubarry: bandaged off-hind, second in a maiden at Nottingham in October, running on strongly, despite hanging left, from an unpromising position over 2f out: very stiff task when well beaten in listed event at Newmarket 12 days later: capable of improvement over 1½m + . *R. Hannon*

PHYLIEL (USA) 3 ch.f. Lyphard (USA) 132 – Alydariel (USA) (Alydar (USA)) – [1991 6m* 6m³ 1992 8d6 6f] rather unfurnished filly: rated 82 on debut: tailed off on reappearance in April and soon outpaced in £24,600 handicap (bandaged off-hind, sweating) at York in June: bred to stay 1m. *M. R. Stoute*

PICA 3 ch.f. Diesis 133 – Barada (USA) (Damascus (USA)) [1991 8m² 8.5f² 8.9d² 1992 12.5g* 14d 14m⁵ 12g² 16.5g] useful-looking filly: fairly useful performer: off course 4½ months after winning handicap at Warwick in May: good efforts in 2 Newmarket handicaps in October but didn't look so well when below form at Doncaster week later: should have stayed 2m: never raced on soft going, probably acted on any other: visits Salse. *H. R. A. Cecil* **84**

PICK AND CHOOSE 4 br.f. Nomination 125 – Plum Bold 83 (Be My Guest (USA) 126) [1991 a8g 5s⁶ 6m 5g⁶ a5g 7.5m 1992 a7g] close-coupled filly: moderate walker: seems of little account these days: sold 820 gns Doncaster January Sales. *J. P. Leigh* **–**

PICKLES 4 b.g. Petoski 135 – Kashmiri Snow 83 (Shirley Heights 130) [1991 11g 8d 9m 8g⁵ 6.9f 1992 a10g 8f³ 8m 7g* 7g² 7f 7d] rangy, quite attractive gelding: modest handicapper: made all at Ayr in July: best at 7f/1m: acts on firm ground, ran respectably on dead: has worn crossed/dropped noseband: has drifted markedly left: raced too freely for amateur once: sold to R. Lee 10,000 gns Newmarket Autumn Sales. *P. C. Haslam* **56**

PICKUPADAILYSPORT 2 b.c. (Mar 3) Bairn 125 – Bold Gift 61 (Persian Bold 123) [1992 6m 7f⁴ 6g⁴ 7g⁴ 8d] 3,000Y, 5,200 2-y-o: good-topped colt: has scope: fifth foal: half-brother to 1991 2-y-o 7f winner Try To Be Good (by Crofthall) and 7f and 1m winner Mrs Gates (by Good Times): dam, ran only at 2 yrs, stayed 7f: modest maiden: should stay 1m: never able to challenge for 7-lb claimer final start. *Miss Gay Kelleway* **52**

PIE HATCH (IRE) 3 b.f. Huntingdale 132 – Small Is Beautiful (Condorcet (FR)) [1991 8s a8g a7g 1992 10f 12g⁶ 11.1m³ 12f* a12g³ a12g* a12g⁴ 11.9g⁵] leggy filly: plating-class handicapper: won at Pontefract (seller, bought in 3,800 gns) and Southwell in the summer: below form afterwards: stays 1½m: acts on firm ground. *Sir Mark Prescott* **50**

PIGALLE WONDER 4 br.c. Chief Singer 131 – Hi-Tech Girl 93 (Homeboy 114) [1991 6g 7m 6g 7m 6g⁶ 7g 5.1m 6f² 5f² 6g⁴ 5g 5g a5g⁶ 1992 a7g⁶ 6v 5m 7g² 7.6m 7m 6.9m³ 6d 7d a7g⁵ a6g a6g³ a6g* a7g*] chunky colt: good walker: moderate mover: modest form: sold out of W. Holden's stable 1,950 gns Ascot March Sales: one-time inconsistent maiden but was in really good form late in year, winning 2 handicaps at Lingfield: stays 7f: acts on firm ground and equitrack: often blinkered. *R. J. O'Sullivan* **57**

PILAR 4 gr.f. Godswalk (USA) 130 – Old Silver (Bold Lad (IRE) 133) [1991 7d⁴ 6g 7g 8f² 8m 7m⁶ 8.9m 8f 1992 a7g a8g⁴ a7g a8g 7m] neat filly: poor mover: inconsistent handicapper: off course 3½ months, well beaten final start, in June: best form at 1m: acts on firm ground and fibresand: tried blinkered once. *Mrs N. Macauley* **44**

PILGRIM BAY (IRE) 2 b.g. (Feb 6) Treasure Kay 114 – Lala 91 (Welsh Saint 126) [1992 5s⁵ 5g⁵ a5g³ 5f⁴ 5g* 5g⁶ 6s⁵ 6m] 14,500Y: leggy, workmanlike gelding: fourth foal: half-brother to smart French sprinter Dream Talk (by Dreams To Reality): dam, 2-y-o 6f winner stayed 7f, is out of half-sister to Cajun: modest performer: won median auction maiden at Hamilton in August: ran well in nurseries next 2 starts, moderately final one: stays 6f: best form on an easy surface: free-running type. *J. Berry* **62**

PIMSBOY 5 b.g. Tender King 123 – Hitopah (Bustino 136) [1991 a11g⁶ 8g² 8d 7.5g² 7.5f³ 8m 10d 8.3g² 8.3m⁵ 7m 8.3m² 8f³ 7m* 8.5f 7g 1992 7.5g 8s⁴ 7g² 7g 7.5m a7g 8.3m² 7.1m⁶ 7g 7g 7.5d⁶ 7.5g⁴] rather angular gelding: poor mover: inconsistent handicapper: trained until after ninth start by P. Blockley: effective from 7f to 1m: acts on any going: usually blinkered nowadays: ran respectably when visored: has swished tail, and looked none too easy a ride. *F. J. Yardley* **55 d**

PIMS CLASSIC 4 gr.g. Absalom 128 – Musical Maiden 76 (Record Token 128) [1991 a6g* 6m 7m 8g a7g a8g 1992 a7g⁵ a10g⁶ a7g⁵ a12g³ a12g⁴ 11.9g⁵ 10.8d 10m⁵ 8m a12g² 12.3d⁵ 10g a16g] well-made gelding: good mover: modest handicapper: sold out of W. Haggas's stable 4,200 gns Doncaster May Sales after eighth start: effective from 1m to 1½m: acts on fibresand: bolted for inexperienced rider and withdrawn once in spring. *J. L. Harris* **52**

PIMS GUNNER (IRE) 4 b.g. Montelimar (USA) 122 – My Sweetie (Bleep-Bleep 134) [1991 10.1s 8.5m 10.1f⁵ 11m* 12m⁴ 1992 a13g⁶] lengthy gelding: has a round action: rated 68 at 3 yrs: winning hurdler in 1991/2 but never dangerous in claimer at Lingfield in March: should stay 1½m: acts on firm going. *D. Burchell* **–**

PINECONE PETER 5 ch.g. Kings Lake (USA) 133 – Cornish Heroine (USA) 101 (Cornish Prince) [1991 12f 1992 10g⁶] leggy, angular gelding: poor mover: rated 59 at 3 yrs: winning hurdler in 1990/1 but no form since, in seller at Pontefract in June: needs further than 9f, and stays 11f well: has hung right: retained by trainer 2,000 gns Ascot June Sales. *O. Brennan*   –

PINE GLEN PEPPER 4 ch.g. Aragon 118 – The Ranee (Royal Palace 131) [1991 6f⁴ 6m 7.6g 8.5m 10g 8f 6m 8m 1992 7m 5m 5m⁶ 6.1g⁶ 6.9d 8.3m⁶] leggy gelding: bad maiden: inconsistent, and one to avoid: tried blinkered/visored. *J. Akehurst*   25 §

PINE RIDGE LAD (IRE) 2 gr.g. (Mar 11) Taufan (USA) 119 – Rosserk (Roan Rocket 128) [1992 5m 5s² 5f a7g 7g⁴ 7f³ 7.5d 5m* 5g 6d 6m] IR 14,000F, 9,000Y: good-topped gelding: has a roundish action: half-brother to 1989 2-y-o 6f winner Wild Dancer (by Gorytus): dam, lightly-raced Irish maiden, is sister to very speedy dam of Ballad Rock: inconsistent performer: trained first 3 starts by W. Pearce: narrowly won maiden at Beverley in August: best runs at 5f: acts on firm and soft ground: sometimes edgy in preliminaries: has been gelded. *M. Johnston*   61

PINETO 2 b.g. (Feb 28) Dominsky 110 – North Pine (Import 127) [1992 6f] 24,000Y: heavy-topped gelding: fourth foal: half-brother to fairly useful 3-y-o sprinter Echo-Logical (by Belfort) and 2 other winners at 5f, including one-time fairly useful Heaven-Liegh-Grey (by Grey Desire): dam poor half-sister to top-class sprinter Lochnager: 12/1, tailed off in 10-runner maiden at Ripon in June: moved moderately to post: sold to join S. Hillen 600 gns Newmarket Autumn Sales. *J. Berry*   –

PING PONG 4 br.f. Petong 126 – Conway Bay 74 (Saritamer (USA) 130) [1991 a7g⁴ a7g⁴ a6g 7.5g a6g⁶ a6g 1992 a6g a7g a7g] compact filly: moderate mover: seems of little account these days. *T. Fairhurst*   –

PINK CITY 2 br.g. (Apr 8) Green Ruby (USA) 104 – Hitravelscene (Mansingh (USA) 120) [1992 a8g] 1,400Y: half-brother to winning sprinter B Grade (by Lucky Wednesday): dam poor plater: 50/1, tailed off in 10-runner claimer at Southwell in December. *J. Balding*   –

PINKERTON'S SILVER 2 gr.c. (Apr 24) Northern State (USA) 91 – Real Silver 85 (Silly Season 127) [1992 5d⁴ 5m⁴ 6g 7f⁵ 6s 8.2d³ 7d] 3,800Y: leggy, angular colt: second foal: half-brother to a winner abroad: dam 6f (at 2 yrs) and 7f winner: poor efforts in sellers at Nottingham and Redcar last 2 starts: suited by 1m: acts on firm and dead going: blinkered last 4 outings. *M. H. Easterby*   43

PINK GIN 5 ch.g. Tickled Pink 114 – Carrapateira (Gunner B 126) [1991 NR 1992 16.2g³ 21.6g] good-topped gelding: modest performer: sweating, good third in maiden at Beverley in March: ran poorly in handicap at Pontefract following month: stays 2m: acts on good to firm and soft ground: sold to join M. Hammond 24,000 gns Doncaster May Sales: won 2 novice chases in November. *Miss S. E. Hall*   55

PINKJINSKI (IRE) 3 b.g. Petoski 135 – Winterlude (Wollow 132) [1991 6g 8.2f 8m 8g 1992 10.8g 11.7d 13.1f] quite attractive gelding: seems of little account these days: sold out of R. Hannon's stable 2,800 gns Ascot June Sales after second 3-y-o start. *D. Burchell*   –

PINK'N BLACK (IRE) 3 b.f. Double Schwartz 128 – Miss Pinkerton (Above Suspicion 127) [1991 5g 5m 5m 7m 6f* 6m² 5g³ 6f* 6.1m 1992 6.1g 6m 7f 6m³ 6f 6g⁴ 6m 6g 6s a6g a6g⁶] smallish, sparely-made filly: moderate mover: inconsistent plater nowadays: suited by sprint distances: acts on firm ground: has won for 7-lb claimer. *G. Blum*   44

PINK ORCHID 2 gr.f. (Apr 25) Another Realm 118 – Country-Inn (Town And Country 124) [1992 6d 7.1s] leggy filly: first reported foal: dam unraced: well beaten in maidens at Kempton and Chepstow in the autumn. *M. P. Muggeridge*   –

PIPE OPENER 4 b.f. Prince Sabo 123 – Bold Polly 67 (Bold Lad (IRE) 133) [1991 7d³ 7.1d 8m⁴ 8.1m 8s 1992 5.9f⁴ 6m 6d 5.9f 6g] close-coupled filly: disappointing maiden: sold 1,300 gns Newmarket December Sales. *J. L. Spearing*   56 d

PIPERS REEL 2 ch.f. (Feb 10) Palace Music (USA) 129 – Fair Country 89 (Town And Country 124) [1992 6m³ 7s a6g² a8g* a7g] sparely-made filly: first known foal: dam 7f and 1m winner later placed in USA: modest form: favourite, decisive winner of weak Southwell maiden late in year: will stay 1¼m: acts on all-weather surfaces. *Lord Huntingdon*   58

PIPER'S SON 6 b.g. Sagaro 133 – Lovely Laura (Lauso) [1991 NR 1992 14s² 16.2m] workmanlike gelding: half-brother to 4 winning jumpers, including fairly useful chaser Laundryman (by Celtic Cone): dam placed over 6f in France at 2 yrs: fair hurdler in 1991/2, best effort when stepped up to 25f in March: bandaged, ½-   90 ?

length second of 6 to Le Corsaire in Salisbury minor event on flat debut: well beaten in well-contested Haydock minor event in May: should stay 2m. *M. Bradstock*

PIPPAS SONG 3 b.f. Reference Point 139 – Dancing Rocks 118 (Green Dancer –
(USA) 132) [1991 NR 1992 a11g³ 16m⁵ a12g* a12g² 12.3g⁶ 11.7s 11.8d] lengthy, a75
workmanlike filly: sixth foal: half-sister to 4-y-o 1¼m winner Gai Bulga, 10.4f
winner Kirpan (both by Kris) and fairly useful 1m winner Gale Yaka (by Habitat):
dam won Nassau Stakes: fair performer on the all-weather: visored, won 5-runner
maiden at Lingfield in July: easily best effort in handicaps when second at
Southwell: shapes like a stayer: best efforts on turf on good ground: also visored
fourth and sixth outings, blinkered final one: sold 17,000 gns Newmarket December
Sales. *G. Wragg*

PIPPIN PARK (USA) 3 b.f. Our Native (USA) – Oxslip 106 (Owen Dudley 121) 77
[1991 NR 1992 10g³ 10d⁶ 10.2f⁴ 8m⁵ 8d⁵ 8d* 8s 10.3g*] angular, useful-looking filly:
good walker: sixth foal: sister to two 1¼m winners, including Sliprail, and
half-sister to quite useful 1¼m and 1¾m winner Sixslip and very useful Irish 1m
winner Thornberry (both by Diesis): dam 7f to 13f winner, is half-sister to very
useful stayer Kambalda: fair form: tongue tied down, won apprentice maiden at
Leicester in October: sold out of H. Candy's stable 17,000 gns Newmarket Autumn
Sales: best effort when landing ladies handicap at Doncaster next outing: will
probably stay 1½m: acts on any going except, seemingly, very soft. *M. Bell*

PIP'S OPTIMIST 3 b.g. Primo Dominie 121 – Great Optimist 55 (Great Nephew –
126) [1991 a8g 1992 12g 11d a12g⁶ a10g⁶] looks of little account. *P. J. Feilden*

PIPS PRIDE 2 ch.c. (Apr 9) Efisio 120 – Elkie Brooks 82 (Relkino 131) **115**
[1992 5d* 5d* 6m³ 6g³ 6m⁵ 6g* 6g⁴ 6m² 6v*]
The Racecall Gold Trophy at Redcar has quickly established itself as a
welcome distraction from the humdrum end-of-season fare. The conditions
deliberately set out to favour the progeny of the less popular stallions (the
weight each runner carries is determined by the median yearling selling price
of its sire) but each of the four runnings has still been won by one of the
season's leading two-year-olds. The latest winner Pip's Pride, who won three
of his eight other races and also ran second in the Middle Park Stakes, is
probably the best yet. On the form he'd shown in the Middle Park three weeks
previously Pips Pride had an outstanding chance at the weights at Redcar,
but, in a field of twenty-four, he started second favourite behind the filly Star
Family Friend, largely because of the latter's proven ability to act on the
prevailing ground. The race was run in pouring rain with several parts of the
track under water, but despite the murky conditions, which made for poor
visibility, there was no mistaking Pips Pride's superiority. Ridden by
McKeown, a late deputy for Dettori, Pips Pride went to the front on the far
side of the track after a furlong and a half, had all his rivals off the bridle at
halfway, and, though coming back to his field close home, held on readily
enough to win by a length and a half from his stable-companion Revelation
with Young Ern a neck behind in third, the trio finishing well clear of some

Heinz 57 Phoenix Stakes, Leopardstown—
Pips Pride (light colours) holds on from Shahik (blaze) and Darbonne (noseband)

very tired rivals. Conditions were so bad, in fact, that the remainder of the meeting was abandoned.

The £88,000 Pips Pride earned at Redcar took his prize money for the season past £200,000, a phenomenal amount for a two-year-old. Most of the rest had come from his half-length defeat of Shahik in the Heinz 57 Phoenix Stakes at Leopardstown in August. Pips Pride was a surprise winner of the Phoenix Stakes. He'd won his first two races, a maiden at Kempton and a minor event at Ascot, and had then run a good third to Petardia in the Coventry Stakes at Royal Ascot, but seemed to have his limitations exposed when able to finish no better than third to Wharf in the July Stakes at Newmarket or fifth of six to his stable-companion Son Pardo in the Richmond Stakes at Goodwood. One interesting characteristic of Hannon's two-year-olds is that their form often starts to pick up again just as their improvement seems to have come to a halt, and Pips Pride was another to do so when improving to the tune of 10 lb or so at Leopardstown. Pips Pride's task was made easier by the draw, which effectively eliminated the three runners (including Son Pardo) who stayed on the far side, but he did well all the same to defeat the quintet who raced on his side of the course. Benefiting from an enterprising ride, Pips Pride was close up throughout and ran on strongly in the final two furlongs to keep Shahik at bay with the Richmond fourth Darbonne a neck behind in third. The 4-lb penalty that Pip's Pride picked up for his victory at Leopardstown meant that he had it all to do in the Mill Reef Stakes at Newbury in September, conceding weight to such as Marina Park and Forest Wind, and he ran as well as could be expected to finish fourth to Forest Wind. Pips Pride improved again, nearly causing an upset in the process, when second to Zieten in the Middle Park Stakes at Newmarket in October; kicked into a clear lead soon after halfway, Pips Pride still held the lead entering the last furlong but was unable to hold off Zieten in the last sixty yards and went down by a length. Any suggestion that Pips Pride was flattered by his finishing position at Newmarket—for a while it looked like he'd stolen a winning march in what wasn't a truly-run race—were swiftly dispelled by his display in the Racecall Gold Trophy.

Pips Pride, a 3,800-guinea foal, went through the ring twice more as a yearling, eventually being sold for 15,000 guineas at Doncaster's October Sales little more than five weeks after he'd fetched only 3,200 guineas at the St Leger Sales. His sire Efisio was a very smart performer who held his form tremendously well throughout a twenty-six-race career. Efisio won all four of his races as a two-year-old, including the Horris Hill Stakes, and also managed to win a pattern event at either seven furlongs or a mile in each of the next three seasons. Pips Pride and Young Ern are easily the best runners from his

Racecall Gold Trophy, Redcar—Pips Pride defies the conditions; stable-companion Revelation (left) takes second ahead of Young Ern

second crop; his first, rather extraordinarily, was headed by the 1991 Racecall Gold Trophy winner Casteddu, since successful in the Beeswing Stakes at Newcastle. Efisio's first crop also included Pip's Pride's brother Sunday's Hill, a fairly useful performer from six furlongs, over which distance he won twice as a two-year-old, to a mile. As well as Pips Pride and Sunday's Hill, the dam Elkie Brooks has produced the 1988 two-year-old six-furlong winner Dolly Bevan (by Another Realm) from two other foals of racing age; her fifth foal, also by Efisio, will be in training in 1993. Elkie Brooks ended up a maiden, but was a fair performer on her day, finishing second over six furlongs as a two-year-old and running near enough to her form at three to suggest she stayed a mile and a quarter. Her dam Cresset, a six-furlong winner as a two-year-old, wasn't much of a success at stud, foaling only one winner, but Cresset's dam Quoff, a fairly useful miler, bred six winners including the useful staying two-year-old Ashendene, later a useful jumper, and the middle-distance stayer Quality Blake.

		Formidable		Forli
	Efisio	(b 1975)		Native Partner
	(b 1982)	Eldoret		High Top
Pips Pride		(b 1976)		Bamburi
(ch.c. Apr 9, 1990)		Relkino		Relko
	Elkie Brooks	(b 1973)		Pugnacity
	(b 1981)	Cresset		Henry The Seventh
		(b 1972)		Quoff

The angular, good-topped Pips Pride was better suited by six furlongs than five furlongs as a two-year-old and gave the impression on several occasions before his final two starts that he might have been better suited by seven. Until the Middle Park it would probably have been concluded that Pips Pride was suited by an easy surface, but the probability now is that he acts on any going. Pips Pride is likely to train on well, but unless he makes significant improvement he'll find winning races much more difficult in his second season. *R. Hannon*

PIPS PROMISE   3 b.g. Doc Marten 104 – Little Muff (Potent Councillor 98)   –
[1991 NR 1992 8f a12g] rather leggy, plain gelding: first reported foal: dam, non-thoroughbred, tailed off on only start: no sign of ability in midsummer maidens. *J. M. Jefferson*

PIQUANT   5 b. or br.g. Sharpo 132 – Asnoura (MOR) (Asandre (FR)) [1991 7v 6g3   **90**
6m* 8f2 7.6m* 7.3m2 8g 7g 1992 6d 7d6 8g2 8.1m* 7f3 8f* 8g2 8.1d4 8m 8d 8m]
small, stocky gelding: carries condition: fairly useful performer: held his form really well in handicaps through the summer, winning at Haydock and Newcastle: below form last 3 starts, not completely discredited last time: seems best at 1m nowadays: acts on any going: tried visored earlier in career: has swished tail: effective held up or ridden from front. *Lord Huntingdon*

PIRATES GOLD (IRE)   2 ch.c. (Mar 20) Vaigly Great 127 – Hemline 77   **65**
(Sharpo 132) [1992 5g6 5.1d 5m3 5d 5m 5d2] 30,000Y: smallish colt: easy mover: first foal: dam, 7f winner stayed 1m, is out of useful 1½m winner Ma Femme, a half-sister to Acclimatise: modest maiden: should prove better suited by 6f: acts on good to firm and dead ground: sold 7,000 gns Newmarket Autumn Sales. *M. J. Heaton-Ellis*

PISTOLET BLEU (IRE)   4 b.c. Top Ville 129 – Pampa Bella (FR) 115 **133**
(Armos) [1991 11g* 12d* 12m2 12d3 12g5 1992 10s2 10.5g2 12m* 12d*]
For the second year in succession the Wildenstein team went into the Prix de l'Arc de Triomphe without its number-one colt. Epervier Bleu, runner-up to Saumarez in 1990, had had to be retired after winning the Grand Prix de Saint-Cloud mid-way through the following season; then Pistolet Bleu, who'd deputized so well for his stable-companion in the Arc of 1991 by coming third to Suave Dancer, had to be retired after winning the latest Grand Prix de Saint-Cloud. There is no doubt that on their respective performances at Saint-Cloud, Pistolet Bleu was the more sorely missed at Longchamp. If Epervier Bleu had been impressive in beating Rock Hopper by three lengths in his race, that was nothing compared to Pistolet Bleu, who put up a stunning performance to beat Magic Night by five lengths with Subotica half as far again adrift in third. The Grand Prix de Saint-Cloud has long been one of

*Grand Prix de Saint-Cloud—a memorable finale from Pistolet Bleu;
he leaves Magic Night and Subotica trailing*

France's top middle-distance events, although nowadays it has to compete for entries with some powerful counter-attractions, particularly in Britain, and the classic generation tends to be drawn elsewhere. It is the big race of the season for Saint-Cloud, a course which seems shabbily treated in being allotted only one other Group 1 race (for two-year-olds) compared with Longchamp's allotment of eighteen. There is usually a strong challenge from abroad for the Grand Prix, and in the 'eighties British stables collected with Glint of Gold, Diamond Shoal, Teenoso, Moon Madness and Sheriffs Star, while the Germans did so with Acatenango. French-trained horses had the stage to themselves in 1992, but the race was little the worse for that as a test of merit. Seven went to post, mostly old rivals well used to competing in the top flight: Subotica, Pistolet Bleu and Magic Night supported by Saganeca, Danae de Brule and Pistolet Bleu's stable-companions Art Bleu and pacemaker L'Oiseau Bleu Roi. The pacemaker did his job well before giving way on the home turn to Danae de Brule who led them into the straight tracked by Subotica, an unlucky fourth in the Coronation Cup, with Pistolet Bleu tucked in on the rail next to Art Bleu, ahead of Saganeca and Magic Night who'd both been held up in touch. Danae de Brule couldn't hold her place for long. As she and Art Bleu began to weaken, the race momentarily promised to be close between the other four. But over two furlongs out Pistolet Bleu slipped through on Subotica's inside and quickened into a lead of four or five lengths. He did it so easily. Hard-ridden Subotica could find no more, and Magic Night ran into second place as Saganeca was left standing.

Pistolet Bleu remained an Arc candidate until September, when it was announced that he'd knocked himself and damaged a tendon earlier in the month, and would, therefore, be retired forthwith. A pity, for that was certainly some performance at Saint-Cloud, even allowing for the tendency of softish ground to exaggerate superiority. Things had been going much to plan up to then. He'd been brought along nicely, coming second in the Prix d'Harcourt and the Prix Ganay (a neck behind Subotica) in the spring before winning the Grand Prix d'Evry, three weeks away from what turned out to be his final appearance, comfortably by half a length and one and a half lengths from Art Bleu and Magic Night. Had he been able to run in the Arc he would almost certainly have started favourite.

Pistolet Bleu (IRE) (b.c. 1988)	Top Ville (b 1976)	High Top (b 1969)	Derring-Do Camenae
		Sega Ville (b 1968)	Charlottesville La Sega
	Pampa Bella (FR) (ch 1981)	Armos (ch 1967)	Mossborough Ardelle
		Kendie (b 1963)	Klairon Amagalla

Pistolet Bleu has been retired to the Haras d'Etreham, where he'll stand alongside his sire the Prix du Jockey-Club winner Top Ville at a fee of 70,000 francs (around £8,300). Comfortably his successful sire's best runner so far, he was typical of Top Ville's stock in that he was well suited by the longest distance he tackled, in his case a mile and a half. The dam Pampa Bella was a good-class racemare in France. Never tried beyond ten and a half furlongs,

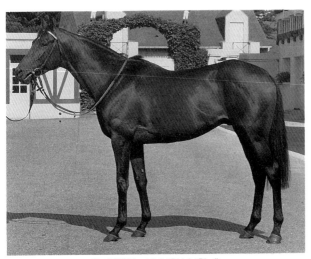

Daniel Wildenstein's "Pistolet Bleu"

over which distance she won the Prix Penelope in testing conditions, she finished third in the Prix Saint-Alary and the Prix de Diane. She has had three other foals to reach racing age by other sires, but Pistolet Bleu, her second produce, is her only runner to date. In contrast, nine of her dam Kendie's foals won a race of some description, including over jumps; both Kendie and her dam Amagalla were minor winners in France. Pistolet Bleu, an attractive colt, was at one time regarded as suited by plenty of give in the ground; and that was probably true on the occasions when the ground helped to provide him with a stiffer test of stamina than he might otherwise have had. However, he handled good to firm on the two occasions he encountered it, in the Grand Prix d'Evry and against Subotica in the Prix Niel in 1991. He was genuine and consistent. *E. Lellouche, France*

PISTOL (IRE) 2 ch.c. (May 9) Glenstal (USA) 118 – First Wind (Windjammer **71** (USA)) [1992 5g² 5.1d⁵ 7d³ 7m² 7g⁵ 6g⁴ 6s⁵ a6g⁵] IR 12,500F, IR 22,000Y: workmanlike, good-topped colt: has scope: closely related to Irish 7f and 1¼m winner Causa Sau (by Try My Best) and half-brother to 2 winners in Ireland: dam unraced half-sister to sprinters Rollahead and Glenturret: consistent form until running poorly when blinkered on equitrack final start: will be better suited by 1m: acts on good to firm and dead ground. *P. F. I. Cole*

PISTOL RIVER (IRE) 2 b.c. (Feb 24) Simply Great (FR) 122 – Pampala (Bold **94** p Lad (IRE) 133) [1992 7g 7s² 8v*] 18,500F, 34,000Y: small, angular colt: moderate walker: half-brother to 2 winners, notably very useful 1m to 1½m performer Noble Patriarch (by Alzao): dam Irish maiden: progressive colt: 15-length winner of maiden at Leicester in late-October, forging clear from 2f out: will stay 1½m: acts on heavy ground. *R. Hannon*

PISTOLS AT DAWN (USA) 2 b.c. (Mar 18) Al Nasr (FR) 126 – Cannon Run **63** p (USA) (Cannonade (USA)) [1992 6m 8.1s 7d⁵ 8.2d³] IR 22,000Y: leggy, attractive colt: first foal: dam, Irish 11f winner, is out of half-sister to Northern Dancer:

consistent form until improved third of 20 to Boldville Bash in nursery at Nottingham in September: will stay 1½m: will improve again. *R. Hannon*

PISTON (IRE) 2 b.c. (Feb 23) Common Grounds 118 – Domino's Nurse 104   **81**
(Dom Racine (FR) 121) [1992 7m⁶ 7g² 7.1g³ 6s⁵ 7m²] 38,000Y: good-topped colt: has scope: second foal: half-brother to Irish 3-y-o 1¼m winner Domino's Ring (by Auction Ring): dam Irish 7f (at 2 yrs) and 1¼m winner, later successful in USA: made most when placed in varied events, caught line by Law Commission in 23-runner nursery at Newmarket final run: should stay 1m: probably unsuited by soft ground: races very keenly: can win a race. *B. Hanbury*

PITCH BLACK (IRE) 3 br.g. Be My Native (USA) 122 – Turbina (Tudor   **–**
Melody 129) [1991 6m⁵ 8m 5m⁴ 1992 6m 7g] leggy gelding: rated 56 at 2 yrs: no form in first half of 1992: should stay at least 1m: acts on good to firm ground. *M. W. Easterby*

PIT PONY 8 b.g. Hittite Glory 125 – Watch Lady (Home Guard (USA) 129) [1991   **–**
NR 1992 13.1s] small, stocky gelding: moderate mover: of little account on flat. *Miss L. A. Perratt*

PIZZA CONNECTION 2 b.c. (Apr 17) Chilibang 120 – Glen Na Smole 86   **89**
(Ballymore 123) [1992 6.1d* 6d² 6.1m* 6g² 6g² 5d² 6v 6s] 6,000F, 7,200 2-y-o: rangy, attractive colt: has scope: moderate walker and mover: fifth foal: half-brother to Irish 3-y-o 1m winner Queens Glen (by Kings Lake) and a winner in Italy: dam 7f performer: successful in maiden and nursery at Nottingham in summer: ran well all starts after, including in 2 listed races at Rome, apart from when always behind in Racecall Gold Trophy at Redcar: will stay 7f: best form on an easy surface: sometimes slowly away. *J. L. Dunlop*

PLACE MAT 3 b.f. Bustino 136 – Anzeige (GER) (Soderini 123) [1991 NR 1992   **–**
10.1g 12d] 1,200 3-y-o: workmanlike filly: half-sister to several winners, including useful 7f winner Flower Bowl (by Homing) and 1¼m to 1¾m winner Beebob (by Norwick): dam German 1m winner out of a German Oaks runner-up: well beaten in maidens: dead. *Dr J. D. Scargill*

PLACERVILLE (USA) 2 b.c. (May 31) Mr Prospector (USA) – Classy Cathy   **90 p**
(USA) (Private Account (USA)) [1992 7m*] $400,000Y: tall, good sort: good walker: third foal: dam, high-class filly, won at up to 11f: heavily-backed favourite and made most encouraging debut when winning 17-runner maiden at Newmarket in October by 1½ lengths from Storm Canyon, soon disputing lead, going on 2f out and running on really strongly: will stay 1m: wore bandages and scratched to post: very highly regarded, and will go on to better things. *H. R. A. Cecil*

PLACID LADY (IRE) 3 b.f. Runnett 125 – Break of Day (On Your Mark 125)   **– §**
[1991 6.1m 5g 1992 6g⁵ 6m 7g 10f 8m 8f] lengthy, plain filly: moderate mover: of little account and probably temperamental to boot. *W. Carter*

PLAIN FACT 7 b.g. Known Fact (USA) 135 – Plain Tree 71 (Wolver Hollow 126)   **91**
[1991 5m² 7d 5f* 5m* 5.9m³ 5m* 6g 5m⁵ 5.6m 5d⁶ 5d a6g* a6g* a6g² 1992 6d³ 5s² 5.3m* 5g⁵ 5f* 6d 5m* 5f² 5m* 5g⁴ 6g 6f² 6g 5.1g 5.6m 5d³ 5g] compact, workmanlike gelding: splendidly tough and had excellent season in 1992: successful in handicap at Brighton and claimers at Redcar (claimed out of Sir Mark Prescott's stable £8,259), Edinburgh and Wolverhampton (claimed out of A. Harrison's stable £13,751): effective at 5f and probably stays 7f: acts on any going: sometimes hangs right. *J. W. Hills*

PLAN AHEAD 3 ch.f. King of Clubs 124 – Calametta (Oats 126) [1991 6m 5.3g⁵   **81**
6g² 6g³ 6g² 6g 1992 7g⁴ 8.2d* 8g* 7.6s* 7g³ 8.5d* 10f² 10m⁴ 11.4d* 11.6g³ 9.7m* 9s* 10g* 11s³] small, sparely-made filly: progressed really well and had a tremendous season in 1992: successful in claimer at Nottingham, handicaps at Warwick (apprentices) and Lingfield, claimers at Epsom and Sandown and handicaps at Folkestone, Goodwood (another apprentices) and Ascot (£8,500 event): effective at around 1m to 11.6f: acts on any going: excellent mount for claimer: usually ridden with waiting tactics: tough, game and consistent: sold 32,000 gns Newmarket Autumn Sales. *G. Lewis*

PLANETARY ASPECT (USA) 2 b. or br.c. (Mar 31) Risen Star (USA) –   **98 p**
Santiki 116 (Be My Guest (USA) 126) [1992 8m² 8s⁵] close-coupled, good-topped colt: has plenty of scope: second reported foal: dam, middle-distance performer, later successful in USA, is half-sister to Derby third Shearwalk: sire (by Secretariat) won Preakness and Belmont Stakes: shaped most promisingly behind Taos in Doncaster maiden: excellent fifth of 10, keeping on and beaten under 4 lengths, to Desert Secret in Royal Lodge Stakes at Ascot later in September: will be suited by middle distances: sure to improve again, and win races. *P. W. Chapple-Hyam*

PLAN MORE ACTION (IRE) 3 ch.g. Doulab (USA) 115 – Numidia (Sallust 134) [1991 a7g 1992 a6g] IR 14,000F, IR 6,000Y: twice raced, and tailed off in maidens. *J. Akehurst* —

PLATINI (GER) 3 ch.c. Surumu (GER) – Prairie Darling (Stanford 121§) [1991 7s* 8g* 8v2 1992 7.5s* 8.5s* 8g* 12s4 12g* 12g* 12s2 12g2] German-bred colt: the top German-trained 3-y-o of 1992, successful in listed events at Dusseldorf and Krefeld, Mehl-Mulhens Rennen at Cologne (awarded race after being beaten short head by Alhijaz), Group 1 event at Dusseldorf (by a head from Snurge) and Group 3 race at Hoppegarten (beat Beyton 4 lengths): runner-up in Group 1 events afterwards, to Mashaallah in Grosser Preis Von Baden and Apple Tree in Geno Europa Preis at Cologne: favourite, came up unfavoured centre of course when only fourth in German Derby at Hamburg on other start: stays 1½m: acts on heavy going: reportedly stays in training. *B. Schutz, Germany* 119

PLATINUM VENTURE 2 ch.g. (Apr 14) Legend of France (USA) 124 – Ceramic (USA) (Raja Baba (USA)) [1992 6m6 5d6 7m5 7d 8f 7m] leggy gelding: third foal: half-brother to 3-y-o Sebosan (by Prince Sabo), 5f winner at 2 yrs, and a winner in Sweden: dam (ran once in Ireland) is granddaughter of top-class 4.5f to 9f winner Furl Sail: modest maiden: well beaten in nurseries last 2 outings: stays 7f: acts on good to firm ground: trained by A. Hide on debut. *S. P. C. Woods* 59

PLAYFUL JULIET (CAN) 4 b.f. Assert 134 – Running Around (USA) (What A Pleasure (USA)) [1991 NR 1992 12.3g6 8f 12.2g2 14.1m] close-coupled, good-topped filly: fifth foal: half-sister to 1m winner Tamono Dancer (by Northern Dancer): dam, winner at up to 9f in USA, is half-sister to high-class Full Out, successful at up to 1m: refused to enter stalls once and sold out of B. Hanbury's stable 7,800 gns Newmarket July Sales at 3 yrs: no worthwhile form in first half of 1992. *B. R. Cambidge* —

PLAYFUL POET 5 ch.g. The Noble Player (USA) 126 – Phamond 61 (Pharly (FR) 130) [1991 6s6 5g 6m 5d5 5g 5m* 5.1m 5g 1992 6d 5g4 5d2 5m* 5g] deep-girthed, strong-quartered gelding: moderate mover: won handicap at Ayr: was effective at 5f and 6f: acted on good to firm and dead ground: front runner: dead. *M. H. Easterby* 70

PLAY HEVER GOLF 2 b.g. (Feb 17) Alleging (USA) 120 – Sweet Rosina 61 (Sweet Revenge 129) [1992 6g5 6m6 5g2 6v5 a7g4 a6g2] leggy gelding: half-brother to several winners here and abroad, including stayer Infeb and middle-distance performer Taylors Realm (both by Another Realm): dam in frame over 5f and 6f: fair maiden: stays 7f: stiff task on top-of-the-ground, acts on all-weather surfaces. *T. J. Naughton* 55 a66

PLAY THE BLUES 5 gr.m. Cure The Blues (USA) – Casual Pleasure (USA) (What A Pleasure (USA)) [1991 8f 1992 9.7d] leggy, sparely-made mare: has a round action: very lightly raced on flat and no form for 3 seasons: stays 1m: won over fences in August. *R. G. Frost* —

PLAY WITH ME (IRE) 2 b. or br.f. (Mar 8) Alzao (USA) 117 – Strike It Rich (FR) (Rheingold 137) [1992 7d6 7d4] strong, compact filly: fifth foal: half-sister to 2 winners, including useful 1m to 1½m winner Lady Bentley (by Bellypha): dam Irish 9f and 1¼m winner, is half-sister to smart stayer Yawa: first run for 3 months and easily better effort in maidens when over 3 lengths fourth of 17 to Rapid Repeat at Leicester in October, staying on strongly to finish well clear of rest on stand side: will improve, particularly given stiffer test of stamina. *J. L. Dunlop* 62 p

PLEASE PLEASE ME (IRE) 4 b.f. Tender King 123 – Tacama 64 (Daring Display (USA) 129) [1991 5m5 7d5 6m a7g 7f 6m2 6.9m4 5m 8f5 9m 8g 6.1d a8g 1992 a8g 7m 8.2g3 8.1m6 8f 8.3m 10.2f5 9.7d 8f3 10s a8g] smallish, sparely-made filly: still a maiden on flat, and rather inconsistent: effective at 1m to 1¼m: acts on firm ground: tried blinkered once: sometimes slowly away: won claiming hurdle in September. *K. O. Cunningham-Brown* 33

PLEASE SAY YES (IRE) 2 b.c. (Jun 4) Nordance (USA) – That's Swiss (Thatching 131) [1992 7g] IR 16,000Y: angular colt: half-brother to 7f winner Victoria Road (by Runnett) and a winner in Hong Kong: dam ran once at 4 yrs in Ireland: green, lost place quickly 2f out in maiden auction at Leicester in September: should improve. *C. N. Allen* – p

PLEASURE AHEAD 5 b.g. Taufan (USA) 119 – Nan's Mill (Milford 119) [1991 a7g6 a6g5 a7g5 a8g2 7d4 8f2 7m 7f3 7g6 7m a10g5 a12g4 a10g4 a12g3 1992 a11g a10g* a10g* a10g4 a10g3 11.8g4 11.4fa12g6 9.7d3 a16g 11.9ga12g4 a16g3 a13g5 a12g6 a14g] leggy, close-coupled gelding: poor mover: successful in maiden and claimer (claimed out of M. Channon's stable £4,250) at Lingfield in February: well below – a53 d

Flying Childers Stakes, Doncaster—Poker Chip at 33/1;
Saint Express (right) beats Satank by a short head for second

form for long time: effective from 1¼m to 1½m: acts on hard and dead ground, best form on equitrack. *M. Dixon*

PLEASURE QUEST 3 b.f. Efisio 120 – Eagle's Quest 62 (Legal Eagle 126) [1991 5g 6f⁶ 6g 1992 a6g 8.2s⁶ a8g] leggy, close-coupled filly: no worthwhile form. *D. W. P. Arbuthnot* —

PLEASURING 3 ch.f. Good Times (ITY) – Gliding 94 (Tudor Melody 129) [1991 6g⁵ 6f 5.1g⁴ 1992 6m⁵ 7d 7d³ 6.1s⁶ 6.1g⁶] workmanlike filly: poor maiden: stays 6f: acts on good to firm ground. *M. McCormack* — 56 d

PLECTRUM 4 b.f. Adonijah 126 – Cymbal 80 (Ribero 126) [1991 10.4g a12g² a10g⁴ 1992 a12g² a12g² a12g a12g 12.3v a12g] rather leggy, unfurnished filly: poor handicapper: stays 1½m: acts on equitrack: below form blinkered once. *J. L. Spearing* — 48

PLUCK 2 b.f. (May 6) Never So Bold 135 – Tahilla 112 (Moorestyle 137) [1992 6g² 5.7d* 6.1g⁶] leggy, unfurnished filly: moderate mover: second foal: dam suited by 1m: confirmed debut promise when landing odds in maiden at Bath in September by 2 lengths: ran badly when odds on for median auction event at Nottingham. *R. Charlton* — 72

PLUM FIRST 2 b.c. (Mar 15) Nomination 125 – Plum Bold 83 (Be My Guest (USA) 126) [1992 5g 5v⁶ 5.1d² 5g³ 5g⁵ a6g³ 6f* 5g⁴ 6g² 7f⁶ 5g⁶ 6m³ 5m²] 620Y: lengthy, workmanlike colt: has a round action: half-brother to 3 winners here and in Ireland, all at up to 1m: dam 6f winner: made virtually all to win seller (no bid) at Thirsk in June: ran well after when in frame in nurseries and a valuable York seller: effective at 5f and 6f: acts on firm and dead ground: effective with or without blinkers: tough and genuine. *N. Bycroft* — 63

POCKET PIECE (USA) 2 ch.f. (Apr 25) Diesis 133 – Secret Asset (USA) (Graustark) [1992 6g⁶] leggy filly: half-sister to several winners here and in USA, notably Warrshan, Razeen (both by Northern Dancer) and Assatis (by Topsider): dam unraced daughter of champion 2-y-o filly Numbered Account, dam also of Private Account: 14/1, one pace from 2f out when around 7 lengths sixth of 20 to Blues Traveller in maiden at Newbury in September: will improve, particularly over further. *M. R. Stoute* — 60 p

POCO PIERNA (IRE) 2 ch.f. (Apr 6) Ahonoora 122 – Flaunting 73 (Kings Lake (USA) 133) [1992 5g 6s 6g² 6g 7f⁵ 8.1d 8.5d] 6,800Y: unfurnished filly: moderate mover: second foal: sister to 3-y-o Breathless: dam 1¼m winner, is half-sister to smart 5f to 7f winner Hadeer, a good family: second in seller at Yarmouth in June: should stay 1m: sold 1,050 gns Ascot September Sales. *W. Carter* — 46

PODRIDA 6 gr.m. Persepolis (FR) 127 – Pot Pourri 97 (Busted 134) [1991 14m 1992 11.9m 14.9d 16.4g³ 16.4m³] good-bodied mare: carries condition: moderate — 48

mover: poor handicapper nowadays: thorough stayer: acts on firm going: sometimes heavily bandaged. *R. J. O'Sullivan*

POETIC LIGHT 4 b.f. Ardross 134 – Sheer Gold 92 (Yankee Gold 115) [1991 10.5g 1992 16f5] strong, lengthy filly: twice raced and no form. *Mrs S. J. Smith* –

POETS COVE 4 b.g. Bay Express 132 – Miss Milton (Young Christopher 119) [1991 6f3 5m5 5g 5f6 5m 5.2m 1992 5m6 6m6 6d* 6f2 5.2d4 6m 6g 6d] compact non-thoroughbred gelding: good walker: has quick action: useful handicapper at best: successful at Epsom in June: lost his form in second half of 1992: ideally suited by 6f: acts on firm and dead ground: below form blinkered once. *M. McCormack* 85

POINCIANA 3 b.c. Big Spruce (USA) – Andrushka (USA) (Giboulee (CAN)) [1991 6f 7.1m4 1992 11d5 12m2 12m 12g2 11.9d6 14m] good-topped colt: fair handicapper: should be suited by 2m: acts on good to firm and dead ground. *R. Hannon* 75

POINT THE WAY (IRE) 2 b.f. (Apr 4) Reference Point 139 – Tender Loving Care 105 (Final Straw 127) [1992 7g3] third foal: closely related to 3-y-o Patrol (by Shirley Heights) and half-sister to 1990 2-y-o 7f winner Noble Destiny (by Dancing Brave): dam 2-y-o 7f winner, is half-sister to useful 2-y-o's Satinette and Silk Pyjamas: 13/2, shaped promisingly when 2½ lengths third of 18 to Azilian in maiden at Doncaster in November, staying on well: will improve over further. *M. R. Stoute* 60 p

POKER CHIP 2 ch.f. (Jan 16) Bluebird (USA) 125 – Timely Raise (USA) (Raise A Man (USA)) [1992 5g3 5.2s* 6s 5m* 6m3] strong, lengthy filly: first known foal: dam, miler successful 6 times in North America, is sister to very useful middle-distance stayer Primitive Rising: won Newbury maiden in July and 6-runner Flying Childers Stakes (strong run to lead close home and beat Saint Express by ¾ length when 33/1) at Doncaster in September: excellent 3½ lengths third of 4, came under serious threat, to Sayyedati in Tattersalls Cheveley Park Stakes at Newmarket: broke pelvis subsequently, but will be back in training as 3-y-o: stays 6f: easily best form on good to firm ground. *I. A. Balding* 106

POKEY'S PRIDE 9 b.g. Uncle Pokey 116 – Strawberry Ice (Arctic Storm 134) [1991 NR 1992 14.6s 14.6g] leggy, quite attractive gelding: moderate mover: tailed off in handicaps in 1992: effective at 1½m to 2m: acts on any going. *J. R. Bostock* –

POLANIE (CAN) 2 ch.f. (Feb 8) Danzig Connection (USA) – Sister Shu (USA) (Nashua) [1992 6d6 6d 7g] $170,000F: sturdy sort: sister to very useful American colt Shudanz, successful at up to 1¼m at 3 yrs in 1991, closely related to very useful sprinter/miler Nordance (by Danzig) and half-sister to several winners, including dam of very useful sprinter/7f performer Nicholas (by Danzig): dam, placed in USA, very well bred: modest form in Newmarket maidens in October: slowly away first 2 starts, still bit backward when beaten around 6 lengths by Fayfa final one: sure to do better, particularly over further. *L. M. Cumani* 63 p

POLAR MOON 2 b.f. (Apr 11) Damister (USA) 123 – Almitra (Targowice (USA) 130) [1992 5.1m4 6g2] 5,800Y: tall, leggy, unfurnished filly: half-sister to 7f winner Armaiti (by Sayf El Arab) and fairly useful 5f winner Bay Hero (by Bay Express): dam Irish 9f winner out of smart 7f to 1¼m winner Donna Cressida: shaped promisingly in maidens at Chester in May: has joined I. Balding. *B. A. McMahon* 56

POLAR STORM (IRE) 2 b.f. (Feb 24) Law Society (USA) 130 – Arctic Winter (CAN) (Briartic (CAN)) [1992 6g4 6m* 5m 6g 6s] 15,000Y: rangy filly: has scope: fourth foal: half-sister to very useful sprinter Polar Bird (by Thatching): dam unraced sister to very smart Son of Briartic, successful in 1¼m Queen's Plate: gamely made most when winning maiden at Goodwood in June: never able to reach challenging position in nurseries: will be better suited by 1m. *Lady Herries* 64

POLEDEN (USA) 2 b.c. (May 6) Danzig (USA) – Paradise (FR) (Brigadier Gerard 144) [1992 6g 6g a7g* a7g2] $825,000Y: leggy colt: half-brother to very useful 1987 French 2-y-o 6f and 8.5f winner Antiqua (by Lypheor): dam, daughter of outstanding Italian filly Orsa Maggiore, won over 1m and 10.5f in France and was later successful in USA: showed marked improvement on last 2 starts, making all in maiden and second in nursery on all-weather at Southwell: suited by 7f: reluctant to go down second start. *A. A. Scott* 72

POLISH BLUE (USA) 3 b.c. Danzig (USA) – Office Wife (USA) (Secretariat (USA)) [1991 7m4 1992 8d 8g2 10.5d* 10.4m* 10.4f2 10m 8.9d3 12m3 10d6] good-bodied colt: useful performer: won maiden at Haydock and minor event at York in May: best efforts after in listed races at York on fifth and seventh outings: may prove best at around 1¼m: acts on firm ground and dead: dropped himself out early on once and ran as if something amiss once. *M. R. Stoute* 103

POLISTATIC 5 br.m. Free State 125 – Polyandrist 92 (Polic 126) [1991 11.7g 10.1g 12m3 12f4 12g* 11m* 12s4 12m2 12f 11.8g3 11.8m 11.5s3 1992 11.9g3 12g 14.1g 42

10d 11.6d² 14.6g² 14s² 14.1d³ 12s] smallish mare: poor handicapper: should prove suited by 2m: acts on any going. *C. A. Horgan*

POLITY PRINCE   2 b.g. (Jan 21) Dominion 123 – Chiming Melody 71 (Cure The   **59** Blues (USA)) [1992 5v⁴ 5s* 6m] quite good-topped gelding: first foal: dam 1m winner: won maiden at Lingfield in April: not seen again after well beaten in Kempton minor event following month. *L. J. Holt*

POLLEN COUNT (USA)   3 b.c. Diesis 133 – Apalachee Honey (USA) **115** (Apalachee (USA) 137) [1991 7g³ 1992 8d* 10g* 12g 10m 10g* 9.7s 10m]
    Pollen Count's season began excellently, ended poorly and had a distinctly patchy middle. He was a horse of considerable promise in the spring. With racecourse experience amounting to two runs—one at two years then victory in what turned out to be a very strong minor event at Kempton—he lined up for the Group 3 Thresher Classic Trial at Sandown against colts such as Bonny Scot, Assessor and Aljadeer who were already in the reckoning for the Derby. Inexperience proved no bar, though, and Pollen Count emerged the winner by a head in a gripping duel with Aljadeer, the pair five lengths clear. Whether the verdict would still have gone his way had Aljadeer not been checked in his run then jumped a path is obviously open to doubt, but there was nothing to criticise in Pollen Count's terrifically game effort. With the promise of further improvement from such a lightly-raced individual, he would have been firmly in the Derby picture but for sustaining a cut to his near-hind during the race at Sandown. Still, even if Pollen Count failed to make the field at Epsom, the best from him was surely still to come.
    Unfortunately, it did not quite turn out that way. Pollen Count did make it to Epsom, a 14/1-shot who looked tremendously well, but having raced prominently for a mile he dropped out quickly and finished sixteenth of eighteen. His next three runs were in France, largely it seems in an attempt to find some give in the ground. Conditions, however, were faster than ideal in the Grand Prix de Paris at Longchamp and, though not beaten far, Pollen Count was soon found one paced in the straight and managed only seventh of ten. That was a lot better performance than in the Derby, of course, and in the Prix Eugene Adam at Saint-Cloud sixteen days later he produced another. The Derby eighth Great Palm started favourite in the absence of any outstanding candidate among the home team and he and Pollen Count swung into the straight first and second. Pollen Count and Cauthen had set out to make all but had only a length's advantage leaving the turn, the dangers queueing up. Pollen Count's response to the challenge, though, was tenacity itself; he kept finding more and, Great Palm and Fast Cure now the only threats, refused to relinquish the lead, eventually keeping them at bay by half

Thresher Classic Trial, Sandown—Pollen Count (left) and Aljadeer come clear

Prix Eugene Adam, Saint-Cloud—Pollen Count makes all;
he is pressed by Great Palm, Fast Cure (No. 3) and Non Partisan

a length and a head. That was the last we saw of Pollen Count on song. After a lay-off of nearly three months he reappeared in the Prix Dollar at Longchamp and was last of eight having set a strong early pace. The competition in the Dollar was a lot stronger than in the Eugene Adam. That was also a sound enough reason for defeat in the Champion Stakes at Newmarket two weeks later, but not for the scale of his defeat; Pollen Count again failed to beat any home, moving none too comfortably as he passed the post tailed off.

Pollen Count (USA) (b.c. 1989)	Diesis (ch 1980)	Sharpen Up (ch 1969)	Atan
			Rocchetta
		Doubly Sure (b 1971)	Reliance II
			Soft Angels
	Apalachee Honey (USA) (b or br 1979)	Apalachee (b 1971)	Round Table
			Moccasin
		Elisa Honey (gr 1971)	Abe's Hope
			Mohduma

The leggy, good-topped Pollen Count was a 225,000-dollar purchase from the Keeneland July Selected Yearling Sale. His dam Apalachee Honey had winners with both her previous foals, the fairly useful 1987 two-year-old seven-furlong winner Le Miel (by Lyphard) and the minor North American winner Active Account (by Private Account). Le Miel seemed to stay a mile and a half here at three years and has gone on to win several times in North America. Apalachee's star has only sparkled occasionally since his unbeaten two-year-old season but Pollen Count's dam Apalachee Honey was a good advert. She was among the best two-year-olds of her sex in 1981 when her wins included the Grade 1 six-furlong Sorority Stakes then the eight-and-a-half-furlong Alcibiades Stakes. Take away that season, however, and this family has little to crow about. Apalachee Honey managed just two minor successes as a three-year-old and the only other achievements to catch the eye—apart from two graded-race triumphs in the Dominican Republic by one of Apalachee Honey's half-brothers—are the third dam Mohduma's also being third dam to Our Native and a half-sister to the 1950 Travers Stakes winner Lights Up.

The most striking impression one has of Pollen Count on the racecourse is left by his extremely powerful, round action. One cannot help but think that some give in the ground will suit him best, and the form-book tends to support that view. As for his trip; well, one run in the Derby hardly proves that Pollen Count does not stay a mile and a half. His breeding does not increase confidence in his staying but he's a really strong galloper, best with plenty of use made of him when at a mile and a quarter. *J. H. M. Gosden*

POLLY LEACH 2 b.f. (Feb 28) Pollerton 115 – Come On Gracie (Hardiran) [1992 **32** 6.1m 7.1d] workmanlike filly: first reported foal: dam poor plater on flat was quite a useful hurdler: well beaten in maidens in early-summer. *B. R. Millman*

POLONEZ PRIMA 5 ch.g. Thatching 131 – Taiga 69 (Northfields (USA)) [1991 **92** 10g⁶ 8g 9.9f³ 10.1m³ 7g* 8.1g* 7.9g⁵ 7.1f² 8m 9m 8m³ 8g² 1992 10.1g⁶ 10g 8m⁴ 8g² 7m* 8m³ 7m* 7.6d² 7m 8m] good-bodied gelding: carries plenty of condition nowadays: fairly useful handicapper: successful at Newmarket and Chester (£9,900 race) and ran well most other starts: seems suited by 7f/1m: acts on firm and dead ground: below best when sweating twice: good mount for apprentice: held up. *J. E. Banks*

POLYPLATE 4 b.f. Song 132 – Countless Countess 65 (Morston (FR) 125) [1991 **–** 12.3s 12.2m 10.1f 11.7g 1992 a12g 16.2g⁵ 16.2d] leggy, quite attractive filly: poor maiden on flat: probably stayed 2m: tried blinkered: won selling hurdle in May: dead. *M. J. Ryan*

POLYROLL 6 b.h. Kampala 120 – Hail To Feathers (USA) (Hail To All) [1991 a8g **–** 1992 a8g] big, lengthy horse: moderate mover: on the downgrade: sold 1,050 gns Ascot February Sales. *M. R. Channon*

POLY SNIP 3 b.f. Executive Man 119 – Wild Jewel (Great Heron (USA) 127) [1991 **–** NR 1992 7g⁵ 7m] leggy, sparely-made filly: poor mover: seventh reported foal: half-sister to fair sprinter Singing Star (by Crooner): dam never ran: soon outpaced in maidens in May. *Miss B. Sanders*

POLYTAIN (FR) 3 ch.c. Bikala 134 – Paulistana (USA) (Pretense) [1991 **120** NR 1992 9v* 10.5g* 10m³ 12g* 12m 12s]

No need to dwell on the latest Prix du Jockey-Club Lancia. The race turned out every bit as ordinary as seemed possible when the second horse Marignan and third Contested Bid were trounced by St Jovite in the Irish Derby next time, and ultimately none of the seventeen runners could be counted among the season's star performers. The winner Polytain finished stone-cold last in both his subsequent races, the Prix Niel and the Prix de l'Arc de Triomphe. His is, nevertheless, a remarkable story, the stuff of which small owners' dreams are made. Polytain first appeared on the racetrack in March, representing Boutin's stable far away from the classic scene in a claimer at Maisons-Laffitte. He won the race but didn't return home, for he was claimed for the sum of 205,099 francs, equivalent to £21,188 then, and was sent to join the much smaller-scale operation of his present trainer. In the next ten weeks he ran another twice, beating minor opposition at Saint-Cloud before finishing a close third to Break Bread in the Group 3 Prix La Force at Longchamp. His Longchamp run represented greatly improved form; all the same, supplementing him for the Prix du Jockey-Club seemed optimistic and he started among the outsiders at Chantilly at around 36/1.

Even beforehand there was a suspicion that the Jockey-Club field was substandard. Although French classic-trial form was very well represented,

Prix du Jockey-Club Lancia, Chantilly—
Polytain wins decisively from Marignan (No. 15) and Contested Bid

Mme B. Houillion's "Polytain"

only Silver Kite of the thirteen who'd run as two-year-olds had made the International Classification, while the overseas challenge consisted of Binkhaldoun and Jape. Nearly all the home starters, including the filly Paix Blanche, had taken part in the trials; Apple Tree (Prix Greffulhe), the unbeaten Grand Plaisir (Prix Noailles), Johann Quatz (Prix Lupin) and Adieu Au Roi (Prix Hocquart), besides Break Bread, had won one. The French sporting media favoured Johann Quatz or Apple Tree as the probable winner; none of the forty-one country-wide press and radio-station tipsters featured in the morning's *Paris-Turf* table forecast Polytain to finish in the first six. It was at a late stage before Polytain moved into the first six in the race. While Jape set just a fair pace, Polytain was held up among the backmarkers, not asked for any sort of effort until straightening up for home about three furlongs out where he was eased away from the inside. When really sent about his business a furlong later he made ground quickly through the bunched field and sprinted clear, looking home and dried. Marignan and Contested Bid, who'd also been ridden from behind, chased hard, particularly Marignan out wide, but Polytain kept on well to stay a length and a half up by the line. Of the two media fancies, Johann Quatz did the better, finishing fourth; Apple Tree, one of six runners supplied by Fabre, finished seventh, a place behind Binkhaldoun.

No question that Polytain was other than a deserving winner, although Johann Quatz had a slightly-unlucky run and Grand Plaisir went lame. Indeed, apart from tending to edge right he was quite impressive, and he looked a far better colt than his subsequent performances would suggest. When Polytain was next seen out three months later, preparing for the Prix de l'Arc de Triomphe in the Prix Niel, he failed to improve appreciably from towards the back of the field as the pace quickened, and was eased once clearly held. Marignan, Contested Bid, Johann Quatz and Apple Tree all beat him; they themselves were beaten by Songlines and Petit Loup, and did not go on to the Arc. Polytain, said by his jockey Lanfranco Dettori to have needed the run badly in the Niel, went on to start at 37/1 for the Arc. He failed to take the eye in the paddock and turned in a poor performance. Having failed to quicken before the home turn, he had no chance from well over two furlongs out and was virtually pulled up. According to Dettori again, the colt got battered about at the back of the field and was winded. There might be something in the excuses offered; nevertheless it is hard to avoid the conclusion that Polytain's racing merit is a long way behind that shown by his sire Bikala, winner of the Prix du Jockey-Club and close second to Gold River in the Arc in 1981.

Polytain (FR) (ch.c. 1989)	Bikala (b 1978)	Kalamoun (gr 1970)	Zeddaan Khairunissa
		Irish Bird (b or br 1970)	Sea Bird II Irish Lass II
	Paulistana (USA) (ch 1980)	Pretense (b or br 1963)	Endeavour II Imitation
		Near Me Now (b or br 1967)	Nearctic Tempted

The suffix shows Polytain was bred in France, so his former owner qualified for some slight compensation for losing him in the claimer by way of the winning breeder's prize in the Prix du Jockey-Club. The dam Paulistana had been passed on at the Deauville Sales at the end of 1989, the year Polytain was foaled, in foal again to Bikala. Sent to Britain, she came to public notice shortly after Polytain's victory when she was listed in the Doncaster Summer Sales catalogue, due to be sold with her Indian Forest foal at foot by order of the York sheriff's officer. She never came under the hammer though, presumably because of her sudden increase in value. As a broodmare Paulistana had had some success before Polytain came along, three of her four previous foals having won races. Her first Palibella (by Bellman) won in Spain; her second Paulivayra (by Vayrann) and third Palavera (by Bikala) in France, the last-named showing quite useful form at up to a mile. *A. Spanu, France*

POLY VISION (IRE)   2 b.c. (May 2) Vision (USA) – Beechwood (USA) (Blushing Groom (FR) 131) [1992 7f⁴ 7.1s⁶ 7.5d³ 7g³ 7m⁴ a6g² 8.1d a8g⁵ 8g⁴ 8f 7.5m⁵ a8g] **58**
IR 2,000Y: angular colt: third foal: half-brother to staying plater Marjorie Wood (by Dreams To Reality) and Irish 3-y-o Blushing Blue (by Bluebird): dam French 10.8f winner: modest form in varied events, including a selling nursery: stays 1m: acts on good to firm and dead ground and on equitrack: below best in blinkers/visor last 2 starts: tends to sweat: sold to join M. Tate 1,700 gns Doncaster November Sales. *M. R. Channon*

POMPION (USA)   3 b. or br.c. Mr Prospector (USA) – Midnight Pumpkin (USA) **72**
(Pretense) [1991 NR 1992 8g 10m⁴ 10m⁶ 10.5d³ 10s] $1,050,000Y: big, workmanlike colt: seventh foal: brother to Preakness Stakes winner Tank's Prospect and half-brother to 2 winners in USA: dam won 3 races at up to 9f: similar form in maidens until tailed off on soft ground: will stay 1½m: sometimes bandaged near-fore. *J. H. M. Gosden*

PONDERED BID   8 b. or br.g. Auction Ring (USA) 123 – Ponca (Jim French **37**
(USA)) [1991 14d³ 12d 16.5m 14d 14g* 14.6m⁴ 1992 a14g a14g⁶ a12g a13g a14g 14.1d 14.1d 14m 14.1g⁴ 14.1m 14.1m² 16.5m 14.1d⁶ 14d 12m a12g] angular gelding: poor mover: inconsistent staying handicapper: acts on good to firm and dead ground: has run well for apprentice: has been blinkered and worn eyeshield: often bandaged. *Pat Mitchell*

PONDERING   2 br.c. (Apr 3) Another Realm 118 – Fishpond 71 (Homing 130) **56**
[1992 6g 6m⁵ 6m⁵ a6g 5g 8g 8g⁴ 8d 10d³ a8g³ a8g] 1,050F, 2,000Y, 6,400 2-y-o: sturdy colt: has a round action: second foal: dam won over hurdles and stayed well on flat: modest maiden: stays 1¼m well: visored fifth start and wore blinkers and eyeshield on all-weather. *S. Dow*

PONDS   2 b.f. (Feb 15) Slip Anchor 136 – Pomade 79 (Luthier 126) [1992 8d] fifth   –
foal: sister to 3-y-o middle-distance stayer Spikenard and half-sister to fair 1m
winner Face Up (by Top Ville) and winning hurdler Pomatum (by General
Assembly): dam disqualified 9f winner on sole outing: showed up to halfway when
last of 20 in maiden at Yarmouth in October. *Mrs J. Cecil*

PONSARDIN   3 b.c. Petoski 135 – Premiere Cuvee 109 (Formidable (USA) 125)   85
[1991 6m⁴ 5m* 1992 6d* 6g 6m² 6m⁴ a7g² 7f³ a6g³ 6s⁴] smallish, stocky colt: fairly
useful handicapper: won at Brighton in March: stays 7f: acts on good to firm and
dead ground, and equitrack: ran moderately blinkered once: sold 16,500 gns
Newmarket Autumn Sales. *Sir Mark Prescott*

PONTE CERVO   3 b.g. Hadeer 118 – Pontevecchio Due 87 (Welsh Pageant 132)   –
[1991 5g 5g⁶ 6m 1992 6.9d] leggy gelding: no worthwhile form: bred to stay 1m. *G.
Richards*

PONTENUOVO   7 b.g. Kafu 120 – Black Gnat (Typhoon 125) [1991 8g 8d 7.6m   –
8g³ 8d 8m² 7.9g* 8g 7d 7m 8g⁴ 1992 8.1m] rangy gelding: has a rather round action:
rated 107 as 6-y-o: shaped as if retained plenty of ability in Whitsun Cup (Handicap)
at Sandown in May, but not seen out again: suited by 7f/1m and a sound surface: goes
very well at Ascot: genuine: front runner. *D. R. C. Elsworth*

PONTEVECCHIO MODA   2 b.f. (Apr 23) Jalmood (USA) 126 – Pontevecchio   64
Due 87 (Welsh Pageant 132) [1992 5f⁴ 5.7f² 6d⁶ 7m* 7d² 7.3s*] 1,600Y: sparely-
made filly: shows knee action: fourth foal: half-sister to very useful hurdler Coulton
(by Final Straw): dam 6f (at 2 yrs) to 8.5f winner: consistent performer: narrowly
won maiden auction at Yarmouth (for 5-lb claimer, drifting left) and nursery at
Newbury (rallied in fine style) in autumn: should be well suited by 1¼m: acts on any
going: sold 6,000 gns Newmarket Autumn Sales. *D. R. C. Elsworth*

POPPET PLUME   2 b.f. (Apr 7) Governor General 116 – Sparkling Hock (Hot   38 ?
Spark 126) [1992 5g⁵ 5d⁴ 6g 5g 6s] small, sturdy filly: first foal: dam ran once at 3
yrs: poor maiden: should be better suited by 6f than 5f. *G. M. Moore*

POPPY CHARM   5 b.m. Star Appeal 133 – Pop Music (FR) (Val de Loir 133)   –
[1991 9.7s 1992 12m⁵ 14.1m⁶] sparely-made mare: poor handicapper: stays 1¾m:
acts on any going. *R. Curtis*

POPPYLAND   2 b.f. (May 17) Blakeney 126 – Sunderland (Dancer's Image   –
(USA)) [1992 7g] neat filly: sixth foal: half-sister to 3-y-o 7f and 7.1f winner Ships
Lantern (by Kalaglow), fair 1986 2-y-o 7f winner Sannox Bay (by Shirley Heights)
and a winner in Italy by Ardross: dam 2-y-o 5f and 6f winner in Ireland: well beaten
in maiden at Doncaster in October: sold 1,200 gns Newmarket Autumn Sales. *C. F.
Wall*

POP TO STANS   3 b.g. Gold Crest (USA) 120 – Lady of Camelot (FR) (Bolkonski   71 §
134) [1991 5g² 5g* 5m⁴ 6.1m³ a6g³ 6g 1992 a6g* a6g² a7g² a7g* a7g* a7g⁴ a6g³ a7g   a75 §
7g⁶ 6d³ 6m* 6d⁴ 6m³ 6f⁴ 6g a7g⁵ a7g] leggy, good-topped gelding: fair performer at
best: won 3 claimers at Southwell early in 1992 and another at Redcar (claimed out
of T. Barron's stable £8,503 afterwards) in April: lightly raced after June and done
form: stays 7f: acts on good to firm ground and dead, goes well on fibresand:
sometimes looks reluctant. *J. Pearce*

PORICK   4 b.g. Marching On 101 – Natina-May 59 (Mandrake Major 122) [1991 8d   41
9.9f 12g 1992 a8g⁶ a11g⁴ a8g⁶ a12g] leggy, close-coupled gelding: poor form: tried
blinkered and visored. *J. C. Haynes*

PORTICO (USA)   3 ch.c. El Gran Senor (USA) 136 – Thorough 115 (Thatch   107
(USA) 136) [1991 7s* 1992 7d* 8g⁶ 8m⁴ 7m⁵ 8g⁵] Irish colt: failed to progress as
anticipated after winning Leopardstown 2000 Guineas Trial in April by a neck from
Brief Truce: easily best effort in pattern events after when fourth to Sikeston in Sea
World International Stakes at the Curragh: ran in San Sebastian, Spain, final run:
stays 1m: acts on good to firm and soft ground. *M. V. O'Brien, Ireland*

PORT IN A STORM   3 b.c. Blakeney 126 – Crusader's Dream 88 (St Paddy 133)   54
[1991 7m⁴ 1992 9s 10g 8.3m² 10m² 12g6 11.8g 12s⁵ 10.3g⁴] workmanlike colt:
modest maiden: sold to join N. Tinkler 8,400 gns Newmarket Autumn Sales: should
stay 1½m: acts on good to firm ground. *W. Jarvis*

PORT LUCAYA   2 ch.c. (Mar 6) Sharpo 132 – Sister Sophie (USA) (Effervescing   98
(USA)) [1992 5g³ 6m* 6f³ 6g* 6d² 7m 6s 7m⁵ 7.3s³] 29,000Y: close-coupled colt:
moderate mover: third reported foal: half-brother to a winner in USA: dam, 1¼m
winner in USA, is half-sister to Diminuendo: useful performer: successful in maiden
at Goodwood in June and minor event (on disqualification) at Windsor in July:
blinkered when good third, beaten 5 lengths, to Beggarman Thief in Group 3 Horris

Hill Stakes at Newbury final start: stays 7.3f: possibly unsuited by very firm ground, probably acts on any other: effective blinkered or not. *R. Hannon*

PORTRAIT GALLERY (IRE) 2 b.c. (Feb 16) Sadler's Wells (USA) 132 – Lady Capulet (USA) 116 (Sir Ivor 135) [1992 7s*] 190,000Y: brother to smart 1991 2-y-o 6f to 1m winner El Prado and half-brother to high-class 1m winner Entitled (by Mill Reef), also second in Phoenix Champion Stakes: dam won Irish 1000 Guineas: won 15-runner maiden at the Curragh in November by ½ length: promising. *M. V. O'Brien, Ireland* **81 p**

PORTREE 3 b.f. Slip Anchor 136 – Rynechra 102 (Blakeney 126) [1991 7g² 1992 10m⁴ 10m⁴ 9.9m⁴ 12.2d² 10s⁶] leggy filly: modest maiden: will stay beyond 1½m: acts on good to firm and dead ground. *H. R. A. Cecil* **66**

PORT SUNLIGHT (IRE) 4 ch.g. Tate Gallery (USA) 117 – Nana's Girl 109 (Tin Whistle 128) [1991 10g 10g⁴ 11.7g⁵ 11.5m³ 12g⁶ 11.7m 10m² 10m³ 9m* 10d⁵ 8.9m 9g 1992 10d⁴ 8.1d³ 9m*] strong, workmanlike gelding: carries condition: has a quick action: fairly useful handicapper: not seen out after winning at Goodwood in May: effective at 9f to 1½m: acts on good to firm ground and soft. *R. Hannon* **84**

POSITIVE ASPECT 3 ch.f. Jalmood (USA) 126 – Miss Bunty 70 (Song 132) [1991 6m 8m⁵ 8s 1992 10d 10g 11.5g² 12g⁶ 10m⁴ 10.8s] rather sparely-made filly: has a roundish action: poor handicapper: better at 1½m than shorter: acts on good to firm ground, seemingly not on soft: changed hands 700 gns Ascot July Sales after second start. *J. Pearce* **44**

POSSESSIVE DANCER 4 b.f. Shareef Dancer (USA) 135 – Possessive (Posse (USA) 130) [1991 8g* 9d* 12g* 12m* 11.9g⁵ 12m 1992 12g] tall, workmanlike filly: rated 118 at 3 yrs, gaining final win in Irish Oaks at the Curragh: below form after that in Group 1 events, and not seen again after well-beaten last of 9 in Jockey Club Stakes at Newmarket in May: best form at 1½m: acts on good to firm ground and dead: stud. *A. A. Scott* **–**

POSSESSIVE LADY 5 ch.m. Dara Monarch 128 – Possessive (Posse (USA) 130) [1991 8m⁵ 9m³ 1992 10g 9g 8m] leggy, lightly-made mare: rated 52 as 4-y-o: no form in handicaps in 1992: should have stayed 1¼m: acted on firm going: reportedly in foal to Shareef Dancer. *M. Bell* **–**

POSTAGE STAMP 5 ch.g. The Noble Player (USA) 126 – Takealetter (Wolver Hollow 126) [1991 12m³ 12m⁴ 16.2g* 20g 15.8g⁶ 14s⁴ 16.1g² 15.9m⁴ 16.2g 18m⁵ 1992 a16g² 16m] rangy, good-topped gelding: good walker: has rather round action: fair handicapper: not seen out on flat after May: won over hurdles later in month: stays well: acts on firm and dead ground: suitable mount for apprentice. *J. Pearce* **68**

POST IMPRESSIONIST (IRE) 3 b.f. Ahonoora 122 – Roblanna 85 (Roberto (USA) 131) [1991 7m 7g 1992 8g⁵ 11.7g⁶ 11.8g⁴ a16g] leggy filly: modest maiden handicapper: stays 11.8f: sold 5,000 gns Newmarket December Sales. *B. W. Hills* **63**

POT HUNTING 3 b.g. Rainbow Quest (USA) 134 – Pot Pourri 97 (Busted 134) [1991 NR 1992 12m 16m] good-bodied gelding: half-brother to several winners, including 4-y-o Farsi (by Nishapour) and 6-y-o Podrida (by Persepolis), both stayers: dam stayer and half-sister to very smart middle-distance stayer Almiranta: twice raced: backward and soon pushed along in maidens at Beverley and Nottingham in June: sold to join D. Greig 2,600 gns Doncaster November Sales. *W. Jarvis* **–**

POWERFUL EDGE 3 ch.g. Primo Dominie 121 – Sharp Castan 101 (Sharpen Up 127) [1991 6m⁴ 6f* 1992 10d³ 10m 7.1g²] leggy, attractive gelding: lightly raced but useful performer: best effort when collared close home by Norton Challenger in listed race at Haydock in June: may prove best at 7f/1m: acts on firm and dead going. *I. A. Balding* **94**

POWER LAKE 3 br.c. Formidable (USA) 125 – Laugharne (Known Fact (USA) 135) [1991 5m* 5m³ 6d² 5m² 5g* 5g 5m² 5.3g* 6m⁴ 5d³ 1992 6m 5g* 6.1g³ 5g⁵ 5.2g 5m] small, robust colt: has a quick action: useful performer: won minor event at Folkestone in April: off course 4 months before well beaten last 2 outings: should prove best at 5f: has form on dead ground, but very best efforts on good to firm: appears best with a tongue strap: sold to Italy 10,500 gns Newmarket Autumn Sales. *R. Hannon* **93**

POWER OF POLLY (USA) 2 br.c. (May 8) Green Dancer (USA) 132 – Polly Daniels (USA) 110 (Clever Trick (USA)) [1992 5g* 6m* 5g³ 7.5g³ 7.5g 6g⁵ 8d] $50,000Y: smallish, leggy, useful-looking colt: third foal: half-brother to 3-y-o Polly Proceeds (by Procida), 5f winner at 2 yrs: dam useful sprinter: successful in a maiden at Sandown and minor event at York in spring: raced in Italy afterwards, finishing third in listed events at Rome and Milan: better suited by 6f than 5f. *P. F. I. Cole* **84**

POYLE AMBER 3 ch.f. Sharrood (USA) 124 – Hithermoor Lass 75 (Red Alert   –
127) [1991 NR 1992 6.1g 10g a7g6 a7g] sturdy filly: fifth reported foal: half-sister to
1990 2-y-o 7f winner Eastern Magic (by Faustus), very useful sprinter Poyle George
(by Sharpo) and a winner in Belgium by Final Straw: dam placed from 5f to 7f, is out
of poor sister to smart handicapper Idiot's Delight: soundly beaten in varied
company. *M. Blanshard*

PRAIRIE GROVE 2 b.c. (Mar 14) Primo Dominie 121 – Fairy Fans (Petingo   52
135) [1992 6g 7m 6.1d] 19,000Y: leggy, unfurnished colt: ninth foal: half-brother to 3
winners here and abroad, including very useful miler Protection (by Thatch): dam,
unraced, from family of Connaught: similar form in maidens at Newmarket and
maiden auction at Nottingham: will be suited by 1m. *R. Hannon*

PRAKASH (IRE) 2 b.g. (Mar 26) Shernazar 131 – Shomoose (Habitat 134) [1992   – p
8d 8m] smallish, good-bodied gelding: first foal: dam unraced: backward and green,
never troubled leaders in large-field maidens at Leicester and Pontefract in
October. *C. E. Brittain*

PRAWN CRACKER (IRE) 2 ch.f. (May 11) Common Grounds 118 – El Zaana
(Priamos (GER) 123) [1992 5s4 5g 5m a6g 6g] 1,900Y: small, short-backed, leggy
filly: good mover: second foal: dam, no form, including when distant second over
2m, is half-sister to 2 stayers out of a stayer: no worthwhile form, including in
sellers: tried visored: sold out of C. Tinkler's stable 740 gns Doncaster June Sales
after third outing. *J. L. Eyre*

PREAMBLE 3 b.f. Baillamont (USA) 124 – Luth Celtique (FR) (Thatch (USA)   37
136) [1991 6f5 7m 1992 5s5 7g 7g 6.9d 7m 7d 8.2m 8m 10.5s4 6s4 8v2] tall, leggy,
plain filly: poor plater: effective at 6f to 10.5f: best efforts on soft going: sold to join
S. Chadwick 3,200 gns Doncaster November Sales. *Mrs J. R. Ramsden*

PRECENTOR 6 ro.g. Music Boy 124 – La Magna 104 (Runnymede 123) [1991 6g5   65
5.8f3 6f5 5f3 6m* 5.7f2 5m* 5m3 6.1d4 a6g a6g2 a7g6 1992 5g* 5.1g4 6d 5m 5s4 6.1s]
strong, close-coupled gelding: moderate mover: fair handicapper: successful at
Beverley in August: effective at 5f and 6f: probably acts on any going: sometimes
wears tongue strap: has hung left and idled in front: effective blinkered or not. *J. D.
Bethell*

PRECIOUS AIR (IRE) 4 ch.f. Precocious 126 – Astra Adastra (Mount Hagen   57
(FR) 127) [1991 7m2 7m* 7g6 7m 7d4 6.9f5 6m a7g6 a6g 1992 a7g a6g5 a8g a6g5 8m   a51
10m 8.3m2 8f* 8g5 8d* 7g 6.1d 6.9v a8g3 a10g4 a8g6] rather sparely-made filly:
moderate mover: modest form: won Bath seller (bought in 3,000 gns) in August and
Brighton handicap in September: below form afterwards: better at around 1m than
shorter, and should stay further: acts on good to firm and dead going (below form on
all-weather): sometimes carries head awkwardly: below form visored. *A. Moore*

PRECIOUS HENRY 3 b.g. Myjinski (USA) – Friendly Glen (Furry Glen 121)   –
[1991 NR 1992 10m] good-bodied gelding: third foal: half-brother to winning jumper
Armagret (by Mandrake Major): dam, winning chaser, ran 3 times on flat: showed
nothing in maiden at Ripon in July, only run: sold 3,200 gns Doncaster November
Sales. *B. E. Wilkinson*

PRECIOUS WONDER 3 b.c. Precocious 126 – B M Wonder (Junius (USA)   65
124) [1991 6g 6.9f 7m6 1992 6.9v2 7d3 8d 7.6s 6.9v* 7g 6.9v2 a6g5 a7g] workmanlike
colt: has round action: fair handicapper: won at Folkestone in October: below form
on all-weather: best efforts at around 7f on heavy going. *P. Butler*

PRECUSSION 2 b.g. (May 16) Dominion 123 – Cymbal 80 (Ribero 126) [1992   62
6.1g a7g a8g*] 8,400Y: brother to a poor maiden and half-brother to 3-y-o Gamelan
(by Music Boy), 7f winner at 2 yrs, and 2 other winners, including 1¼m winner Beau
Mirage (by Homing): dam, half-sister to smart performers Band and Zimbalon, won
3 times over middle distances from only 5 starts: modest performer: improved for
step-up in trip, winning maiden at Southwell in November, coming from behind in
strongly-run race: looks a staying type. *R. W. Armstrong*

PREDESTINE 7 b.g. Bold Owl 101 – Combe Grove Lady (Simbir 130) [1991 8g   53
1992 11.9g 10.8g2 12g5 10g 12m 10m6 11.6g] small, leggy gelding: modest handicapper: stays 1½m: suited by give in the ground: bandaged nowadays. *D. Morris*

PREDICTABLE 6 ch.g. Music Boy 124 – Piccadilly Etta 76 (Floribunda 136)   –
[1991 a8g* a8g* a8g* a7g* 8s a7g3 7m 8f6 8.1d a10g4 8g a7g 1992 a8g6 a8g5 a8g   a67
a7g* a7g3 a7g a7g 7g a7g4 7.6v a10g6 a8g6 a8g a8g] lengthy, angular gelding:
moderate mover: made all in Lingfield handicap in February: out of form late in year,
including in blinkers: effective at 7f to 1m: acts on good to firm and soft going and
all-weather surfaces: has gone well for claimer: effective with or without visor. *Mrs
A. Knight*

PREFABRICATE (FR)   6 b.g. Kings Lake (USA) 133 – Celtic Assembly (USA)   –
95 (Secretariat (USA)) [1991 9s 10d 8m 9.9m 1992 12.3f] workmanlike gelding: on
the downgrade: sold 1,150 gns Ascot November Sales. *J. L. Harris*

PREMIER BLUES (FR)   2 b.f. (Mar 9) Law Society (USA) 130 – Etoile   35
d'Ocean (USA) (Northern Dancer (CAN)) [1992 6d 6m 8d] 3,000F, 10,000Y: third
foal: dam French maiden from good family: backward and well beaten in maidens and
a seller. *R. J. R. Williams*

PREMIER DANCE   5 ch.g. Bairn (USA) 126 – Gigiolina (King Emperor (USA))   44 d
[1991 a7g a7g³ a10g* 10.2s² 10d 10g 10.8g³ 10.2g³ 12g a10g³ 8.9g⁵ 10g 10.5d³ a10g⁴   a51 d
a10g 1992 a10g* 10.8v 10.8g⁵ 10.8f² 10.2m⁶ 10.2m³ a8g⁴ a10g 10.3m a12g⁴ 11.5s a12g
a10g a10g²] compact gelding: has quick action: poor performer: successful in
handicap at Lingfield in January: in-and-out form afterwards: probably stays 1½m:
probably acts on any going: effective with or without blinkers: visored (out of form)
once. *D. Haydn Jones*

PREMIER ENVELOPE (IRE)   3 b.c. King Persian 107 – Kellys Risc   –
(Pitskelly 122) [1991 5d² 5g5 5d4 5g² 5m4 5m6 a5g² a5g² 5m* 5m4 5.1m5 5m 1992
5v 6m⁶ a7g 6m 6m] neat colt: moderate mover: rated 56 at 2 yrs: well below form
in 1992: stays 6f: acts on good to firm and dead ground, and on fibresand: ran
moderately in blinkers. *N. Tinkler*

PREMIER LEAGUE (IRE)   2 gr.c. (Mar 21) Don't Forget Me 127 – Kilmara   46 p
(USA) 78 (Caro 133) [1992 8v⁶] 12,500Y: tall colt: first foal: dam, raced twice at 2 yrs,
is daughter of very smart French 1m/1¼m performer Kilmona: 33/1, backward and
green, weakened under pressure from 2f out when beaten around 15 lengths in
12-runner maiden at Leicester in October: will improve. *J. E. Banks*

PREMIER MAJOR (IRE)   3 b.g. Bluebird (USA) 125 – Calvino (Relkino 131)   41
[1991 7m 6m 8m⁵ 1992 8.2g 8m 8m⁴ 8m⁵] close-coupled gelding: poor maiden: acts
on firm to firm ground: joined S. Kettlewell. *B. Beasley*

PREMIER PRINCE   6 b.g. King of Spain 121 – Domicile (Dominion 123) [1991   57
8d 7.6g 7.1m 7g* 7v³ 7.1g 7.1s⁴ 7f* 8g⁵ 7m* 8m 7m⁵ 7g⁶ 1992 6s 7g 7.1m⁶ 7g*
7.6m² a7g⁵ 7.6m⁵] strong, workmanlike gelding: modest handicapper: won at
Goodwood (for second successive year) in June: ideally suited by around 7f: acts on
any turf going and equitrack. *L. G. Cottrell*

PREMIER PRINCESS   6 b.m. Hard Fought 125 – Manntika 77 (Kalamoun 129)   45
[1991 13.8g 17.2g⁴ 1992 21.6g² 14.6g⁶ 19m* 16.2d⁵ 16.1g 16d] workmanlike mare:
well below form after winning handicap at Redcar in August: suited by thorough test
of stamina: acts on good to firm and dead going: not easiest of rides. *G. A. Ham*

PREMIER VENUES   4 b.g. Gorytus (USA) 132 – Tarnished Image 88   –
(Targowice (USA) 130) [1991 7f⁵ 7f⁴ 7g⁶ 7f 7m⁴ 10f⁵ 12.1f* 12f⁶ 1992 12f 13.8m 10g
10f⁶ 12.1m⁶] leggy, sparely-made gelding: rated 50 at 3 yrs: below form in first half
of 1992: stays 1½m: acts on firm ground: tends to carry head high. *S. G. Norton*

PREMIUM   2 ch.c. (Feb 3) Dominion 123 – Primulette 82 (Mummy's Pet 125)   64
[1992 6m⁵ 6m* 7m 7.3g⁵ 7g 7m⁴ 7m³] 31,000Y: angular colt: poor mover: first foal:
dam 5f (at 2 yrs) and 1m winner: won maiden at Ripon in July: back to form in
nurseries last 2 starts, equal-third of 23 when bandaged near-hind at Newmarket:
sold 5,800 gns Newmarket Autumn Sales: stays 7f: blinkered last 3 starts. *W. J.
Haggas*

PRENONAMOSS   4 b.g. Precocious 126 – Nonabella 82 (Nonoalco (USA) 131)   87
[1991 5.8m* 6d² 8m 7g² 6m³ 5d 6m 1992 5.2d⁶ 6f³ 6f 7d⁵ a7g 7.1m 6g⁴ 7.1s⁴ 6d⁶ 7m⁴
7d² 7g] lengthy, rather angular gelding: generally ran well without winning in
competitive handicaps in 1992: effective at 6f and 7f: acts on firm and dead ground:
below form when blinkered: usually bandaged behind: held up. *D. W. P. Arbuthnot*

PREPARE (IRE)   4 b.f. Millfontaine 114 – Get Ready 91 (On Your Mark 125)   37
[1991 6m⁴ 7g⁵ 6g⁴ 5.1d⁵ 5.7g 5.1f⁵ 5m⁴ 7f 7m* 7.1m 8g 7g 1992 7g⁶ 8.9g⁵ 7.1m
7.5g 6.1m 7f⁶ 7m⁴ 7d 6.1g⁶] rather leggy filly: in-and-out form in handicaps in 1992:
effective at 7f, and seems to stay 9f: acts on firm ground and dead: sold 1,100 gns
Doncaster November Sales. *R. J. Holder*

PREPONDERANCE (IRE)   2 br.f. (Mar 6) Cyrano de Bergerac 120 –   85
Mitsubishi Style (Try My Best (USA) 130) [1992 5d* 5m⁴ 5g] leggy, workmanlike
filly: third foal: dam Irish maiden, third over 1m: 4-length winner of maiden at
Tipperary in July: 9/1, ran well when around 4 lengths fourth of 11 to Millyant in
Philip Cornes Molecomb Stakes at Goodwood but last of 9 in Meadow Meats EBF
Flying Five at Leopardstown 6 weeks after: will be suited by 6f+. *J. G. Burns,
Ireland*

PRESENT TIMES 6 b.g. Sayf El Arab (USA) 127 – Coins And Art (USA) 33
(Mississipian (USA) 131) [1991 12d⁶ 12f 1992 a12g* a12g³ 11.9g] close-coupled,
deep-girthed gelding: poor handicapper: won (for first time) at Lingfield in February: not seen out after following month: stays 1½m: acts on good to firm ground
and equitrack. *A. Moore*

PRESQUE NOIR 4 br.c. Latest Model 115 – Orlaith 68 (Final Straw 127) [1991 54
8g 6m 8d³ 7g² 7m 7f 9m 8.1d 9g² 10.3d⁵ 1992 10d 10d⁵] good-bodied colt: moderate
mover: maiden handicapper: stays 1¼m: acts on firm and dead ground. *H. Candy*

PRESS GALLERY 2 ch.c. (Feb. 20) Carmelite House (USA) 118 – Mixed 74
Applause (USA) 101 (Nijinsky (CAN) 138) [1992 7m⁵ 7m⁵ 7d³ 7.3s] good-topped
colt: has scope: sixth live foal: closely related to 3 winners by Kris, notably
high-class miler Shavian, and half-brother to 2 winners, notably Paean (by Bustino):
dam won at up to 7f at 2 yrs: similar form in maidens first 3 starts before outclassed
in Group 3 Horris Hill Stakes at Newbury: will be well suited by middle distances:
capable of winning an ordinary race. *Mrs J. Cecil*

PRESS THE BELL 2 b. or br.g. (Mar 21) Belfort (FR) 89 – Northern Empress 60
80 (Northfields (USA)) [1992 5g³ 5g³,5m⁴ 5m* 5m 5g 5s] useful-looking gelding:
has a quick action: seventh reported living foal: half-brother to 3 winners here
and in Belgium, including (at 6f and 7f) Nevada Mix (by Alias Smith) and (at 8.2f)
Bold Mac (by Comedy Star): dam ran 3 times: below form in nurseries after making
all in 5-runner Edinburgh maiden in July: speedy, and will prove best over sharp 5f:
seems unsuited by soft ground: tends to swish tail and hang, and may not be genuine. *J. Berry*

PRESSURE OFF 2 gr.c. (Apr 30) Petong 126 – Arch Sculptress 85 (Arch 33
Sculptor 123) [1992 5f⁴ 5f 5.9g] 3,500F, 10,000Y: rather leggy colt: sixth foal:
half-brother to 3 winners, including 5f and 6f winner Psalm (by Song) and 1m to
1¼m performer San Roque (by Aragon): dam, soft-ground sprinter, is half-sister to
smart French middle-distance colt El Famoso: well beaten in maidens: trained by A.
Stringer on debut. *J. H. Johnson*

PRESTON GUILD (IRE) 2 b.g. (Apr 12) Mazaad 106 – Dying Craft (Thatching 50
131) [1992 5g³ 6s⁴ 5.9f⁵ 8f 8s⁴] IR 8,000F, IR 8,200Y, 21,000 2-y-o: sturdy, compact
gelding: second living foal: half-brother to Irish 3-y-o 7f and 8.5f winner Thatching
Craft (by Alzao): dam Irish maiden: poor form in maidens first 3 starts for J. Berry:
improved after, fourth to Boldville Bash in Pontefract nursery: will be better suited
by 1¼m: best form on soft going. *Miss S. E. Hall*

PRETONIC 4 b.f. Precocious 126 – Northern Ballerina 52 (Dance In Time 63
(CAN)) [1991 7f 6m* 6d* 6g 5d a6g³ a6g⁴ a7g 1992 6v⁶ 6.1d 6g³ 6f³ 6m 6f² 5.9h³ 6f a72
6m 6.1d³ 5.9f³ 5g³ 5g 5m* 7s⁵ 5s² 6d⁶ 6.1s 5v² a6g* a6g* a6g² a6g*] workmanlike
filly: poor mover: fair handicapper: stood up to a busy season, winning Beverley
seller (no bid) in September and a claimer and 2 handicaps at Southwell late in year:
effective from 5f to 7f: acts on any going: blinkered (ran creditably) once: has run
well when sweating: game and genuine. *M. Johnston*

PRETTY AVERAGE 2 b.f. (Feb 4) Skyliner 117 – Marock Morley 59 (Most 35
Secret 119) [1992 5d 5.9g 5g] 1,250F: stocky filly: seventh foal: half-sister to 3
winners, including modest 1990 3-y-o 7f winner Vintage Type (by Import): dam won
over 5f at 5 yrs: poor maiden. *T. Craig*

PRETTY SURE 2 b.f. (May 2) Gabitat 119 – Its For Sure 63 (Ardoon 124) [1992 –
5d] small filly: fifth foal: dam lightly-raced 5f performer: tailed off in maiden at
Kempton in April. *B. Gubby*

PRETZEL (IRE) 2 b.c. (May 11) Cataldi 123 – Cheerleader 90 (Floribunda 136) 44
[1992 5g 5m 6s⁶ a6g² a6g² a5g² 5g⁴ a7g⁶] IR 4,700Y: neat colt: moderate mover:
half-brother to modest 1990 2-y-o 5f to 7f winner Panama Pete and 1¼m winner
Another Wish (both by Horage) and several winners in Italy: dam 2-y-o 5.1f winner
later successful in Italy, is out of half-sister to On Your Mark: plater: seemed ideally
suited by 6f: often visored: dead. *N. Tinkler*

PREVENE (IRE) 2 b.c. (Mar 14) Alzao (USA) 117 – Assya (Double Form 130) 83
[1992 7g² 7f* 7d³ 8.1s⁶ 10g] 40,000Y: strong colt: has scope: fourth foal: dam
unraced granddaughter of Never Too Late: won maiden at Newmarket in June: ran
well in listed race there over 1¼m, but gave impression ideally suited by shorter:
acts on firm and dead ground. *P. F. I. Cole*

PRICELESS FANTASY 5 ch.m. Dunbeath (USA) 127 – Linda's Fantasy 108 –
(Raga Navarro (ITY) 119) [1991 a11g 10f 10m 11.7g⁵ 10m 10f⁶ 12g 10g⁶ 10.1g⁴ 10.2f³
10.2g 10.8g* 12f⁵ 9.7s* a12g 1992 a11g a8g⁵ a10g a13g⁴ a10g 10.3g] small, lengthy

mare: good walker: has a round action: rated 53 at 4 yrs: little worthwhile form in spring of 1992: stays 1½m: probably acts on any going. *Pat Mitchell*

PRICELESS HOLLY   4 b.g. Silly Prices 110 – Holly Doon (Doon 124) [1991 NR 1992 7g 8m] angular, workmanlike gelding: moderate mover: lightly raced, and no sign of ability. *M. Avison*   –

PRICELESS PET   3 b.f. Tina's Pet 121 – Spring Lane 85 (Forlorn River 124) [1991 5g 6m 1992 10.2h4] leggy filly: has a round action: looks of little account: sold 700 gns Ascot July Sales. *J. J. Bridger*   –

PRICE RUMPUS (IRE)   2 b.c. (May 5) Salt Dome (USA) – Royal Rumpus (Prince Tenderfoot (USA) 126) [1992 5g6 5.1g] IR 32,000Y: leggy colt: first foal: dam lightly-raced half-sister to Second Set: sire (by Blushing Groom) sprinter: last in minor event and maiden (reportedly broke blood vessel) in spring. *J. Berry*   41

PRIDE OF BRITAIN (CAN)   3 ch.f. Linkage (USA) – Witches Alibhai (USA) (Your Alibhai) [1991 6g 5.7f7.1d 1992 10g4 10f 10.2f5 a12g* a12g2 12.3m4 12s2 12v*] leggy filly: modest handicapper: won at Lingfield (claimer ridden) in June and Folkestone (amateurs event) in October: should stay beyond 1½m: acts on any going, including equitrack: sometimes pulls hard. *L. G. Cottrell*   56

PRIDE OF PENDLE   3 ro.f. Grey Desire 115 – Pendle's Secret 73 (Le Johnstan 123) [1991 6d 6m6 6.1m 6m* 6f 7g 1992 8m 8m 10f 8.5s3 8.5d* 9m2 8f 8m5 8s 8.5m 8g] leggy, angular filly: modest handicapper: won ladies event at Beverley in July: below form last 2 starts: stays 9f: below form on very firm ground, acts on any other: joined B. Wilkinson. *P. Calver*   51

PRIDE'S DESIRE   2 gr.f. (Feb 26) Grey Desire 115 – Lindrake's Pride (Mandrake Major 122) [1992 5d4 5f6] leggy, shallow-girthed filly: fourth foal: half-sister to 1990 2-y-o 7.5f winner Darika Lad (by Belfort): dam never ran: failed to confirm debut promise and hung left from halfway in maiden at Thirsk in June. *T. D. Barron*   41

PRIDIAN (IRE)   3 ch.c. Ahonoora 122 – Priddy Blue (Blue Cashmere 129) [1991 6s4 1992 7.5g2 6d 7g* 7m] leggy colt: fair performer: made all in maiden at Catterick in April: broke leg following month: should have stayed 1m: possibly needed a sound surface: dead. *G. Wragg*   71

PRIMA AURORA   4 br.f. Primo Dominie 121 – Alumia (Great Nephew 126) [1991 6m 6.1m 6.1m6 8d 1992 8g] useful-looking filly: good walker: poor hurdler: no form on flat. *C. P. E. Brooks*   –

PRIMA SINFONIA   2 b.f. (Feb 3) Fairy King (USA) – Bourbon Queen 77 (Ile de Bourbon (USA) 133) [1992 7g4] 10,000Y: second foal: dam placed over 7.6f at 2 yrs later showed ability over hurdles: backed at long odds, always prominent when over 2 lengths fourth of 17 to Instant Affair in maiden auction at Leicester in September: will be better suited by 1m: should improve. *S. M. Hillen*   64 p

PRIME MOVER   4 b.g. Mummy's Game 120 – Feast-Rite (Reform 132) [1991 6m2 6g 1992 a6g5 8v3 8d3 5d3 8.1m a8g3] tall gelding: sold out of Sir Mark Prescott's stable 3,800 gns Ascot February Sales before first run in 1992: fair handicapper: stays 1m: acts on good to firm and dead ground and on all-weather surfaces: sometimes slowly away. *D. Burchell*   66

PRIME PAINTER   2 b.c. (Apr 29) Robellino (USA) 127 – Sharp Lady 70 (Sharpen Up 127) [1992 6m6 6g2 7m5 7.1m2 a7g6 5.9g 8.5m 8.3s] 5,000Y: close-coupled colt: has a long stride: half-brother to 1¼m winner Spoiled Brat and 5f and 1m winner Good N'Sharp (both by Mummy's Pet): dam won five 6f races: modest maiden: off course 2 months and ran moderately last 3 starts: will be better suited by 1¼m: acts on good to firm ground, possibly unsuited by very soft. *R. F. Fisher*   51

PRIMERA BALLERINA   4 ch.f. Primo Dominie 121 – Yankee Special 60 (Bold Lad (IRE) 133) [1991 6.1m5 7g 1992 10.8d 8f6 8.9s 10m 11.9f 10.8g4 10.8g4] long-backed filly: poor maiden: stays 11f. *J. R. Bosley*   38

PRIMINO (FR)   7 b.g. Zino 127 – Primula (FR) (Petingo 135) [1991 NR 1992 8d6] seventh foal: half-brother to 6 winners, including Prix Morny winner (later second in Poule d'Essai des Pouliches) Sakura Reiko (by Kenmare) and smart winner at up to 10.5f Dom d'Albignac: dam useful French miler: useful performer at 3 yrs in France when trained by A. Fabre, successful 3 times at around 1m, including in a listed event: poor form over hurdles for T. Tate in 1992 before never-dangerous sixth in Carlisle claimer in May. *J. J. O'Neill*   –

PRIMITIVE GIFT   2 b.f. (May 24) Primitive Rising (USA) 113 – Annes Gift 38 p (Ballymoss 136) [1992 8.3s 6v5] half-sister to 1982 2-y-o 5f seller winner Leandros (by Lepanto), 3-y-o 6.9f to 8.1f winner Express Gift (by Bay Express) and 2 winners abroad: dam of no account: poor form, never reaching leaders, in maidens at Hamilton in autumn: will probably do better back over further. *Mrs M. Reveley*

PRIMOCELLE   2 br.f. (Apr 15) Primo Dominie 121 – Jouvencelle 68 (Rusticaro   **54** p
(FR) 124) [1992 6g⁵] workmanlike filly: fourth foal: closely related to fair 9f winner Land Afar (by Dominion) and half-sister to 3-y-o Granite Boy (by Music Boy) and 1½m winner Valiant Warrior (by Valiyar): dam maiden at up to 14.7f: backward and green, never able to challenge when 5 lengths fifth of 12 in maiden at Salisbury in August: should improve over further: retained by trainer 1,400 gns Newmarket Autumn Sales. *H. Candy*

PRIMO FIGLIO   2 b.c. (Apr 7) Assert 134 – Prima Domina (FR) 89 (Dominion   **68**
123) [1992 6g³ 6m 6.1g² 7s⁴ 6v*] 4,200Y: smallish, lengthy colt: first foal: dam sprinting sister to Primo Dominie: consistent form in maidens: short-head winner at Folkestone in November: will be well suited by 1m: acts on heavy going. *R. Hannon*

PRIMO PAGEANT   3 b.c. Primo Dominie 121 – Tribal Pageant 73 (Welsh   **–**
Pageant 132) [1991 NR 1992 7m 8f⁶ a12g⁶ 8m] big, strong colt: first foal: dam 11f winner, is half-sister to smart 1984 2-y-o Brave Bambino out of speedy half-sister to high-class sprinter Runnett: no worthwhile form, and looked a hard ride when blinkered final start: should prove best short of 1½m: sold 2,600 gns Doncaster September Sales. *M. J. Camacho*

PRIMO PRINCE   2 b.c. (Apr 18) Primo Dominie 121 – Pellinora (USA) (King   **–**
Pellinore (USA) 127) [1992 5g 6s] 15,000F, 8,200Y: smallish, lengthy colt: has scope: good walker: moderate mover: seventh foal: brother to 3-y-o 8.3f winner Pelargonia and half-brother to 1m (at 2 yrs) and 1¼m winner Prince Russanor (by Rousillon) and fairly useful 1½m winner Peleus (by Irish River): dam once-raced half-sister to Park Hill winner I Want To Be, an excellent family: no show in auction event at Newmarket and seller at Lingfield in May: sold 1,650 gns Newmarket September Sales. *P. F. I. Cole*

PRIMULA BAIRN   2 b.f. (Mar 21) Bairn (USA) 126 – Miss Primula 81 (Dominion   **62**
123) [1992 5m⁴ 5f² 5g³ 6d] workmanlike filly: moderate mover: third foal: dam sprinter: modest form in maidens first 3 starts: should stay 6f: possibly unsuited by dead ground. *Mrs J. R. Ramsden*

PRINCE BELFORT   4 b.g. Belfort (FR) 89 – Princess Sharpenup 63 (Loch-   **71**
nager 132) [1991 6d 5g 6g⁴ 5f² 5m* 5m⁶ 5f 5m³ 6g 1992 6f 5f³ 5f⁶ 5f* 5s⁶ 5m⁴ 5f* 5f⁴ 6m 5m 5m 5s⁶ 5d 5d⁶] leggy, workmanlike gelding: successful in handicaps at Hamilton and Catterick (apprentices) in early-summer: below form after: should prove best at 5f: goes well on top-of-the-ground: not discredited when visored: sometimes hangs. *M. P. Naughton*

PRINCE FERDINAND   3 b.c. King of Spain 121 – Greensward Blaze 50 **116**
(Sagaro 133) [1991 5m* 5f² 6m* 6m⁵ 6g³ 6m² 6m² 6g² 1992 6g* 7g* 6m* 7f* 7f² 6g⁵ 7f² 7d² 7m4]

'Bloodstock breeding', wrote Sir Charles Leicester in 1957, 'is not an exact science, but a question of averages.' In terms of racing merit, the mating of King of Spain with Greensward Blaze in 1987 and 1988 has come up with an average which is the product of extremes: the first foal is the poor Prosport, who has so far failed to win a race or reach a place, and the second is the smart Prince Ferdinand, the winner of six races and placed in all but three of his other eleven. Prince Ferdinand has exceeded expectations in no small measure since being bought for 4,000 guineas at the Doncaster St Leger Yearling Sales. His efforts as a two-year-old included a second prize of £34,900 in the Racecall Gold Trophy and the highlight of his three-year-old season was a win at Royal Ascot. Twelve lined up for the Jersey Stakes, including two who had contested a classic in the Poule d'Essai des Pouliches fifth Euphonic and the European Free Handicap winner and Two Thousand Guineas third Pursuit of Love, along with the race's usual quota of less exposed three-year-olds. The Irish pair Nordic Brief and Reported helped cut out the early pace with Fair Cop, who had not been seen out since winning the previous year's Chesham Stakes, Prince Ferdinand waited with in mid-division. One and a half furlongs out his rider's confidence looked fully justified, Prince Ferdinand still virtually on the bridle and the rest under vigorous pressure, and so it proved with Reid driving him out to head Pursuit of Love a hundred yards out and win

Jersey Stakes, Royal Ascot—
Prince Ferdinand proves himself equally effective at seven furlongs,
in winning from Pursuit of Love (white sock) and Fair Cop (left)

by half a length, with Fair Cop third and Reported fourth. The winning time
was one of four track records set on the day.

The Jersey Stakes, with entry conditions that rule out those who have
won a Group 1 or Group 2 event and provide an 8-lb and 5-lb penalty for the
winners of Group 3 and listed races, often throws up a surprise winner, but
Prince Ferdinand was not one of them. He had been performing well above his
pedigree a long time before that. His two-year-old form had been very useful
and it was clear as early as his first appearance of the season that he was an
improved horse. That race, a £6,000 contest at Thirsk in April, saw Prince
Ferdinand well backed and an impressive winner; he followed up at 5/2 on in a
similar event at Wolverhampton one month later and then put up a performance which put him bang in line for the Jersey, despite earning a penalty, with
a two-length and three-and-a-half-length beating of Central City and Wilde
Rufo in the listed Sandy Lane Stakes at Haydock. On each occasion, as at
Royal Ascot, Prince Ferdinand had travelled sweetly with waiting tactics. He
failed to win again after the Jersey Stakes but his record and reputation
suffered little. Fifth in the Phoenix Sprint Stakes at Leopardstown in August,
when reportedly wrong in his blood, was disappointing, and fourth in the
Challenge Stakes at Newmarket on his final start was a below-form effort, but
Prince Ferdinand's three other runs rank with his best. With a little more luck
in running he might well have beaten Toussaud in the Criterion Stakes at
Newmarket on the first of them. The improving Pursuit of Love beat him two
lengths in the Kiveton Park Stakes at Doncaster and it was second again for
Prince Ferdinand in the Supreme Stakes at Goodwood, Hazaam denying him
in the dying strides.

Prince Ferdinand (b.c. 1989)	King of Spain (br 1976)	Philip of Spain (b 1969)	Tudor Melody
			Lerida
		Sovereign Sails (b 1962)	Sovereign Path
			Red Sails
	Greensward Blaze (ch 1979)	Sagaro (ch 1971)	Espresso
			Zambara
		Urugano (ch 1960)	Buisson Ardent
			The Tempest V

Greensward Blaze had three foals prior to Prosport and Prince Ferdinand and they, too, gave little indication that she was capable of throwing a

pattern-race winner, although one, by Crofter, won races in Hong Kong. Nor was Greensward Blaze much of a racehorse herself, the winner of a one-mile seller at Bath as a three-year-old, but her dam Urugano showed pretty useful form in winning six races from two to four years at up to a mile and a quarter. Prince Ferdinand's sire, the good-class sprinter King of Spain who died in 1989, was a long way removed from the top flight of stallions but has had several other noteworthy progeny, including the Sun Chariot and E. P. Taylor Stakes winner Braiswick.

The lengthy, angular Prince Ferdinand impresses in condition as well as with his consistency and genuine nature. He is a credit to his trainer who had gained earlier Royal Ascot victories with Horage in the Coventry and St James's Palace Stakes and Night of Wind in the Queen Mary. Prince Ferdinand is a good walker and moderate mover, effective on firm and dead going. He has never run on soft. The form Prince Ferdinand showed over seven furlongs in the Jersey Stakes and afterwards is marginally better than that of his win in the six-furlong Sandy Lane Stakes, but then again he didn't have much chance to prove himself at six furlongs in the second half of the season. He is reportedly to do most of his racing over six furlongs in 1993. *M. McCormack*

PRINCE HANNIBAL 5 b.h. High Top 131 – Fluctuate 87 (Sharpen Up 127) 80 §
[1991 12.2d⁴ 12d⁴ 12g³ 11.5m* 12.1d* 11.9m* 11.5g⁴ 11.9m* 11.6m⁴ 12m² 13.3m 12m 1992 10m 12g⁴ 12m⁵ 11.9f³ 10m² 10g⁶ 11.9f² 12d⁶] rangy horse: rather in-and-out form in handicaps in 1992: stays 1½m: acts on firm and dead ground: sometimes bandaged off-hind: usually well up: sometimes swishes tail: finds little: not one to trust. *J. L. Dunlop*

PRINCE JAKATOM 5 ch.g. Ballad Rock 122 – Ballysnip (Ballymore 123) [1991 —
7g 8m 8d⁵ 8d 10.5f⁶ 11.5g 8.1s⁵ 1992 9.7g] lengthy, good-quartered gelding: poor mover: rated 68 at 4 yrs: on the downgrade: sold to join J. Thomas 1,000 gns Ascot June Sales. *D. W. P. Arbuthnot*

PRINCELY FAVOUR (IRE) 2 b.c. (May 10) Anita's Prince 126 – Kiss The 79
Bride (Sweet Revenge 129) [1992 5g⁴ 5d² 5.2d³ 6f⁴ 6s² 6g 6s* 6m] 800F, 3,000Y: lengthy, quite good-topped colt: good walker: fourth foal (third by Anita's Prince): dam Irish sprinter: fair performer: made all in maiden at Lingfield in October: excellent third in Newbury Sales Super Sprint Trophy on third start: stays 6f: has form on good to firm ground but seems ideally suited by soft. *R. Hannon*

PRINCE LYPHARD 6 ch.g. Lyphard's Special (USA) 122 – Devoted 96 (Roan —
Rocket 128) [1991 14g 1992 10d 12.3g⁵ 11.5f] lengthy gelding: third reported foal: half-brother to 2 winners by Song, including 1985 2-y-o 5.1f winner Cupid's Song: dam, half-sister to Devon Ditty, won over 8.5f and 1¼m: ex-Irish performer (trained by A. Redmond), successful twice as 2-y-o: little form on flat after: should have stayed 1½m: acted on heavy going: dead. *R. Akehurst*

PRINCE MANKI 2 b.c. (Feb 17) Risk Me (FR) 127 – Egnoussa 76 (Swing Easy 54
(USA) 126) [1992 5m⁶ 5h² a5g* 6g 5g 5.1d] 1,800Y: rather sparely-made colt: seventh foal: half-brother to 6f winner Fiorini and a winner in Italy (both by Formidable): dam, 7f winner, half-sister to very smart Devon Ditty: below form, including in seller, after winning maiden at Southwell in August: should stay 6f: sold 3,600 gns Newmarket Autumn Sales. *R. Hannon*

PRINCE MERCURY 3 ch.g. Sharrood (USA) 124 – Princess Zita 90 (Manado 84
130) [1991 7g7.1s⁴7d 1992 10g 14.6s² 13.9f⁴ 16.4g² 15g⁴ 16.1g³ 16.9d* 16.1s* 16.2g⁴ 15.9s⁴] big, good-topped gelding: has a round action: much improved handicapper in second half of 1992: won at Wolverhampton (by 8 lengths, despite wandering markedly) and Newcastle (very comfortably): stays well: goes well on a soft surface: not discredited when blinkered once: probably suited by waiting tactics: sold 35,000 gns Newmarket Autumn Sales. *J. L. Dunlop*

PRINCE OF DARKNESS (IRE) 3 b.c. Shadeed (USA) 135 – Intensive (USA) 64
(Sir Wiggle (USA)) [1991 NR 1992 8g⁴ a7g⁴ 9m* 8.1g 8.9m⁵ 7g] big, strong, well-made colt: half-brother to 3 winners abroad, including Grade 3 winner Intensive Command (by Dust Commander): dam never ran: below form in handicaps after winning Lingfield maiden in June: takes keen hold, and may prove best at up to 9f: may be unsatisfactory. *Sir Mark Prescott*

PRINCE OF MUSIC (USA) 2 b.c. (Feb 5) Tasso (USA) – Singing Rockett —
(USA) (Key To The Kingdom (USA)) [1992 8.1s] $30,000Y: half-brother to 2 winners in North America, including High Rockett (by Highland Park), successful at

up to 9f: dam won at up to 9f: sire (best as 2-y-o) stayed 1¼m: struggling by halfway in maiden at Chepstow in August. *P. F. I. Cole*

PRINCE OF SOUL   2 ch.c. (Mar 29) Faustus (USA) 118 – Casa Rosada (Known   –
Fact (USA) 135) [1992 a7g a7g] 2,500Y, 5,000F, 3,200 2-y-o: third foal: half-brother
to 1m winner May Square (by Nicholas Bill): dam, no form, is daughter of Nell Gwyn
winner Evita: 33/1, never threatened in maidens at Southwell and Lingfield. *Pat
Mitchell*

PRINCE OF THE SEA (IRE)   4 gr.c. Double Schwartz 128 – Baracuda (FR)   –
(Zeddaan 130) [1991 6d* 6m* 7g 1992 7d 8g 7.1d5 6m 6d 7.1s 7d] leggy, close-
coupled colt: very much on the downgrade: sold 2,000 gns Newmarket Autumn
Sales. *D. W. P. Arbuthnot*

PRINCE PERICLES (IRE)   3 b.c. Nordico (USA) – Countess Eileen 111   **63**
(Sassafras (FR) 135) [1991 7g5 7d 1992 12m 12g5 8s5 10m] sturdy, useful-looking
colt: good shaper: modest maiden: off course 5 months before well beaten in
handicaps last 2 starts: should stay beyond 1½m: acts on good to firm ground: sold
IR 6,400 gns Goffs October Sales. *H. Candy*

PRINCE POLINO (USA)   3 b.c. Trempolino (USA) 135 – Casting Call (USA)   **109**
(Stage Door Johnny (USA)) [1991 8m4 8d3 1992 10s2 10s* 12g3 12g 10d3 10g2]
$100,000Y: ninth reported foal: half-brother to several winners in North America,
notably Laurel Futurity winner Cast Party (by Caro): dam unraced: won minor
event at Longchamp in April: placed in Prix Hocquart and Prix du Prince d'Orange
(6 lengths second of 5 to Arcangues) at same course third and final starts: stays
1½m: acts on soft going. *P. Bary, France*

PRINCE RODNEY   3 gr.g. King of Spain 121 – Dancing Diana 82 (Raga Navarro   **63**
(ITY) 119) [1991 5s5 6m3 5g3 7g6 6m 6m 1992 6g2 8m4 7g 8m 8g* 8f*] rather
sparely-made gelding: moderate mover: modest performer: not seen again after
winning claimers at Newmarket and Salisbury in May: stays 1m: acts on firm
ground: below best when visored once. *R. Hannon*

PRINCE ROONEY (IRE)   4 b.c. Dayeem (USA) – Fourth Degree (Oats 126)   **58**
[1991 7v2 7d5 7f6 8m4 7m 7.6d 7g3 8d2 8.3m 7m5 1992 8.3g* 7.1s* 9.7s 7d a7g5]
close-coupled colt: has a round action: sold out of M. Pipe's stable 1,200 gns Ascot
June Sales, rejoining present trainer: well beaten after winning sellers at Windsor
(no bid) and Chepstow (retained 4,000 gns) in autumn: stays 8.5f: seems to act on
any going, except firm: sometimes bandaged: suitable mount for claimer. *P. Butler*

PRINCE RUSSANOR   4 b.g. Rousillon (USA) 133 – Pellinora (USA) (King   **107**
Pellinore (USA) 127) [1991 10d* 10g3 12g 1992 10d 10g 10.3m3] lengthy, rather
angular gelding: had quick action: useful at best: best effort in 1992 when 2½
lengths third of 5 to Young Buster in £13,000 event at Doncaster: should have
stayed 1½m: acted on good to firm and dead ground: dead. *J. L. Dunlop*

PRINCE SOBUR   6 b.g. Jalmood (USA) 126 – Ultra Vires 87 (High Line 125)   **64**
[1991 16g 16g2 16m3 16.2g 16.5m2 22.2m 16g2 17.5m3 16.2g 16.2d 1992 18g 16d2 14d
13.3g2 14g2 16.4s6 14.6d2 16s2 14.1g*] rangy gelding: moderate mover: consistent
handicapper: not seen again after winning at Yarmouth in July: effective at 13.3f and
stays well: acts on good to firm and heavy ground: sold 1,250 gns Newmarket
Autumn Sales. *M. Blanshard*

PRINCE SONGLINE   2 b.g. (Apr 25) Prince Sabo 123 – Question Mark 83   **– p**
(High Line 125) [1992 5.1g6] 8,400Y: good-bodied gelding: half-brother to several
winners here and abroad, including (over middle distances) Taiga (by Northfields)
and The Betsy (by Imperial Fling): dam, winner twice at 1½m, is sister to Park Hill
winner Quay Line: soon struggling in maiden at Nottingham in June: looked sort to
do better. *R. Boss*

PRINCESS ANNIE   3 br.f. Prince Sabo 123 – Elaine Ann 66 (Garda's Revenge   –
(USA) 119) [1991 5g 6f 6m 5.2f4 5f 1992 6m 7f] leggy filly: poor plater: should stay 6f:
sold 500 gns Newmarket July Sales. *G. Blum*

PRINCESS BORGHESE (USA)   2 b.f. (Feb 10) Nijinsky (CAN) 138 – Molly   **68 P**
Moon (FR) (Kalamoun 129) [1992 8m6] tall, attractive filly: sixth foal: closely related
to disqualified 1988 2-y-o 1m winner Moonfish (by Northern Baby) and half-sister to
French 6f to 9.3f winner Exgravity (by Explodent): dam ran 4 times in USA:
favourite, but green, most promising sixth of 19, beaten around 9 lengths, to
Bashayer in 19-runner maiden at Newmarket in October, soon recovering from slow
start, making smooth progress 3f out then not at all knocked about when beaten:
moved fluently to post: has plenty of scope, and looks type to do considerably better
at 3 yrs: should have no difficulty winning a race. *H. R. A. Cecil*

PRINCESS DECHTRA (IRE)   3 b.f. Bellypha 130 – Moretta (Artaius (USA)   –
129) [1991 6.1d⁴ 6d³ 1992 8v 6.1d] good-topped filly: poor mover: rated 65 at 2 yrs:
soundly beaten in April: should be very well suited by 7f + . *R. Hollinshead*

PRINCESS ERMYN   3 b.f. Shernazar 131 – Trois Vallees 77 (Ile de Bourbon   –
(USA) 133) [1991 NR 1992 10s 10.1d⁶ 12g⁶] tall, rangy filly: has a round action: third
living foal: dam 1¼m winner: no worthwhile form in maidens: should prove suited
by 1½m + . *M. Dixon*

PRINCESS EUROLINK   4 gr.f. Be My Guest (USA) 126 – Sweety Grey   –
(Young Emperor 133) [1991 8.3f⁵ 7m⁶ 8m 1992 a8g] leggy filly: no worthwhile form.
G. P. Enright

PRINCESS EVITA (FR)   3 b.f. Kings Lake (USA) 133 – Very Bissy (BRZ)   33
(Harken (URU)) [1991 7g 1992 8g 10g 10f³ 11.5g⁵ a14g 14.1m 12s] sparely-made filly:
moderate mover: poor maiden: stays 11.5f: acts on firm ground. *R. Guest*

PRINCESS HAIFA (USA)   2 b.f. (Mar 2) Mr Prospector (USA) – South Sea   63 p
Dancer (USA) (Northern Dancer (CAN)) [1992 7g] $650,000Y: leggy filly: fourth
foal: sister to 11.9f winner Sijjaal and half-sister to 7f and 8.5f winner Island Wedding
(by Blushing Groom): dam won at up to 9f at 4 and 5 yrs, and is sister to Storm Bird
and Northernette (dam of Gold Crest): 20/1, held up and never placed to challenge in
24-runner maiden at Newmarket won by Fayfa in October: sure to do better. *M. R.
Stoute*

PRINCESS JESTINA (IRE)   4 b.f. Jester 119 – Royal Aunt (Martinmas 128)   –
[1991 5d⁶ a5g⁵ 5g 8m³ 8f 8g a8g 7g 6g* 6m⁴ 7g⁵ 6f⁴ 7m 6f 1992 a6g⁵ a6g 8s 7g 8f 5.7f
5.1s] leggy, sparely-made filly: very much on the downgrade. *G. H. Yardley*

PRINCESS JO   3 b.f. Prince of Peace 109 – Avec Amour 69 (Jolly Jet 111) [1991   –
NR 1992 a12g] fifth foal: sister to 5-y-o Mahatmacoat: dam winning hurdler: 40/1, no
sign of ability in maiden at Lingfield in December. *Mrs A. Knight*

PRINCESS KRIS   2 b.f. (Mar 13) Kris 135 – As You Desire Me 112 (Kalamoun   61 p
129) [1992 7d⁵] angular, plain filly, rather lightly made: seventh foal: half-sister to
several winners, including 3-y-o 6.9f winner Desired Guest and useful but
untrustworthy 6f to 1m winner Intimate Guest (both by Be My Guest): dam, won 3
times at around 1m in France, from good family: 4/1, around 6 lengths fifth of 16 to
Wild Princess in maiden at Leicester in October, hanging right and tiring inside last
1f: will improve. *M. R. Stoute*

PRINCESS MAXINE (IRE)   3 b.f. Horage 124 – Sallywell (Manado 130) [1991   57
5g 7g³ 6f 7m 8.3g 1992 10.5s 8.3s² 6.9d² 7g³ 8m* 8g² 8g⁴ 7d⁵] leggy filly: consistent
in 1992, and won maiden claimer at Ayr (drifted left) in July: ideally suited by 1m:
acts on good to firm and soft ground. *Miss L. A. Perratt*

PRINCESS MOODYSHOE   4 ch.f. Jalmood (USA) 126 – Royal Shoe (Hotfoot   72
126) [1991 11.7f* 12m* 14.1m⁵ 1992 16.2m⁵ 10.2f² a12g* 11.5g³ 11.7d*] plain filly:
has a round action: fair performer: comfortably won Lingfield claimer in July and
handicap at Bath in September: seems effective from 1¼m to 2m: acts on firm and
dead ground and on equitrack: consistent. *M. C. Pipe*

PRINCESS NEBIA   2 br.f. (Apr 18) King of Spain 121 – Nebiha 85 (Nebbiolo 125)   –
[1992 6h 7g 7m] 1,000F, 2,800Y: plain, leggy filly: fourth living foal: half-sister to a
winning hurdler: dam 1½m winner: no form, including in a seller. *B. J. McMath*

PRINCESS OBERON (IRE)   2 b. or br.f. (Jan 20) Fairy King (USA) – Flash of   69
Gold 78 (Pardao 120) [1992 5g³ 6m³ 5m* 5f⁴] IR 4,000F, IR 11,000Y: leggy,
useful-looking filly: half-sister to several winners, including 1980 Irish 2-y-o 6f
winner Corkstone Ace (by Mon Fils): dam 2-y-o 6f winner: favourite, made all in
maiden at Sandown in May, beating Hamsah by 2 lengths: respectable fourth of 7 in
£7,050 event at Beverley following month: should be as effective at 6f as 5f. *M. Bell*

PRINCESS OF ALAR   2 b.f. (Apr 27) Bold Owl 101 – Krafty Kate 73 (Klairon   –
131) [1992 5.1g 6m 7d 6g] 1,000Y: smallish filly: half-sister to 4 winners here and
abroad, including 8.3f seller winner Queen Kate (by Queen's Hussar) and 1978 2-y-o
6f seller winner Knife Edge (by Sharpen Up): dam 1¼m winner: well beaten in
maiden and sellers: looked none too enthusiastic with blinkered final outing. *B.
Palling*

PRINCESS OF ORANGE   3 ch.f. Master Willie 129 – Outward's Gal (Ashmore   54 d
(FR) 125) [1991 6g⁵ 7g⁶ 8.1g⁶ 9m³ 8g a8g 1992 10d⁴ 10.2d⁶ 11g² 12m 10g⁶ 10.8g²
a10g⁶ 10m 10m 12.3s⁶ 10.8s⁶ 14.1s] leggy filly: unreliable plater: stays 12.3f: acts on
good to firm ground and soft: trained until after eighth start by C. C. Elsey. *W. M.
Brisbourne*

PRINCESS PROUDFOOT 3 b.f. Hotfoot 126 – Farandella 86 (English Prince – 129) [1991 7f 1992 10g] workmanlike filly: twice raced, and no sign of ability. *Miss L. C. Siddall*

PRINCESS ROXANNE 5 b.m. Prince Tenderfoot (USA) 126 – Godwyn 57 (Yellow God 129) [1991 a11g³ a14g a12g² a10g² a10g⁶ a8g³ a10g⁶ 8d² 9f² 10.4d⁶ a62 8.2m⁶ 8m 10.5g³ 10.3m* 10.3m⁶ 10.5f⁴ 10.5g 10m⁴ 10.3d* 10.3d 9.7s a10g* a10g³ a10g⁵ 1992 a10g* a10g³ 10.3g³ 9d³ 10.5s⁵ a12g³ 10m⁴ 10.5g 11.1f* 10g² 10.3m⁴] lengthy mare: carries condition nowadays: moderate walker: poor mover: modest handicapper: successful at Lingfield in January and Hamilton in July: effective at 1m to 1½m: acts on firm and dead going and all-weather surfaces: effective with or without blinkers: successful for apprentice: tough: sold 4,000 gns Doncaster September Sales. *A. Bailey*

PRINCESS TAMAR 3 gr.f. Absalom 128 – Alkion (Fordham (USA) 117) [1991 – 5s⁶ 5m⁶ 7m 7.5f 1992 12.3s 10f] sturdy filly: bad maiden: stays 7.5f. *P. C. Haslam*

PRINCESS TARA 4 br.f. Prince Sabo 123 – La Magna 104 (Runnymede 123) – [1991 6g 6d 6g⁴ 8m* 7m³ 8m³ 8g 7.6m 7d 1992 6m⁵ 6d 8g] workmanlike, good-quartered filly: modest handicapper at best: not seen out after June: effective at 7f and 1m: best form on a sound surface: reportedly in foal to Risk Me. *G. Lewis*

PRINCESS TATEUM (IRE) 2 b.f. (Apr 28) Tate Gallery (USA) 117 – Church 63 Mountain 83 (Furry Glen 121) [1992 7g⁵ 7d³ 7d³] 5,200F: sparely-made filly: half-sister to 1985 2-y-o 6f winner Mac's Flyer (by Godswalk) and a winner in Italy: dam won over 6f at 2 yrs, but failed to train on: similar form when third in maidens at Redcar and Catterick in June: will be better suited by 1m. *M. R. Channon*

PRINCIPAL PLAYER (USA) 2 br.g. (Apr 28) Chief Singer 131 – Harp Strings 59 (FR) 109 (Luthier 126) [1992 5d³ 5v⁴ 5v⁴ 5m⁴ 6m⁶ 6m³ 6f² 6f⁴ 5d 5g⁴ 6d⁶] 4,800Y: leggy, rather angular gelding: moderate mover: half-brother to 3 winners here and abroad, including fairly useful 2-y-o 6f winner Gentle Persuasion (by Bustino) and fair 10.1f winner Full Orchestra (by Shirley Heights): dam useful at up to 9f: modest maiden: will stay 7f: has form on heavy ground, but best efforts on firm: tends to hang, and looks a tricky ride: trained until after eighth start by W. Bentley. *P. Monteith*

PRINT FINISHER 6 ch.m. Mandrake Major 122 – Chubby Ears (Burglar 128) – § [1991 NR 1992 a5g 6f] workmanlike mare: moderate walker: seems of little account nowadays, and probably temperamental. *Bob Jones*

PRIOK 9 b.g. Monsanto (FR) 121 – Aracara (Prince Tenderfoot (USA) 126) [1991 – NR 1992 a8g 12d] leggy, lengthy gelding: no promise in handicaps in summer: stays 1¼m: seems to act on any going. *W. G. R. Wightman*

PRIVATE BANK (USA) 3 b.c. Private Account (USA) – Lady Ice (CAN) (Vice 63 Regent (CAN)) [1991 7m 8.1s 1992 9.7g³ 10.1d³ 12m⁵ 12.4v] good-topped colt: modest maiden: tried blinkered last 2 starts: stays 9.7f. *A. C. Stewart*

PRIVATE LINER 2 b.c. (Apr 18) Skyliner 117 – Private Sue 61 (Brigadier 40 § Gerard 144) [1992 5m 5m 5f⁶ 5m 7f a6g² a6g] 400F, 780Y: tall, leggy colt: third foal: dam poor maiden: poor and ungenuine plater: stays 6f: tends to hang/carry head high: tried blinkered: one to have severe reservations about: sold 1,000 gns Doncaster October Sales. *Ronald Thompson*

PRIVATE PRACTICE 3 gr.f. Kalaglow 132 – Lady Gaylass (USA) (Sir Gaylord) – [1991 NR 1992 10.2g⁶ 10f⁵ 10.1d 10g 12v] big, lengthy filly: sister to fair 1½m winner Topglow and half-sister to 3 middle-distance winners: dam winner at up to 1m in France, is out of half-sister to Blakeney and Morston: little form: injured when unseated rider and bolted on intended debut: sold 820 gns Doncaster November Sales. *M. J. Heaton-Ellis*

PROBATION 3 b.c. Nomination 125 – Ballagarrow Girl 66 (North Stoke 130) – [1991 5m 5m 1992 8d 10.2d] leggy colt: fifth foal: poor maiden: should stay 1m. *B. R. Millman*

PROCADA 2 b.g. (May 5) Damister (USA) 123 – Smelter 111 (Prominer 125) 42 p [1992 6m⁶ 7s⁶] rangy gelding: brother to 3-y-o Hot Prospect and half-brother to 2 winners, including Irish 7f winner Ellaine (by Corvaro): dam won twice over 7f from 3 starts: poor form in maidens at Pontefract and York (auction event, stayed on late behind Lyford Cay) in autumn: will stay 1m +: has scope, and should do better. *J. Etherington*

PROFILIC 7 b.h. Ballacashtal (CAN) – Sea Charm 70 (Julio Mariner 127) [1991 6d 79 d 6m 6g² 6m 6m* 6g 6m 7.1g⁶ 6g 6m* 7.6m 7g 6f⁵ 6g 7m 6g 1992 6d² 6g 6g 6f⁵ 6f 6g⁴ 6.1d⁴ 6g⁶ 6m³ 7.1m⁵ 7m⁴ 6s⁶ 7d 7.5m⁶ 8d 7d 6g] big, strong, lengthy horse: usually looks very well: has a long, round stride: inconsistent handicapper: best form at strongly-run 6f: acts on any going: below form blinkered: usually gets behind. *Capt. J. Wilson*

PROFIT A PRENDRE   8 b.g. Tina's Pet 121 – Brave Ballard (Derring-Do 131)   **58**
[1991 a6g 5g 7m 8g 7m 6f* 7.1d* 7m⁶ 8.1g⁶ 9m 8m 7m² 7m 7m³ 8d⁴ 6.1d 6.9s 1992 5g 7g 6f⁵ 7.1m³ 8f 7.1f³ 7g² 6d² 6.9d* 7f² 7m 6m⁶ 7.6m⁴ 7d] big, lengthy gelding: has round action: formerly inconsistent but held his form well in handicaps in 1992: successful at Folkestone in July: effective at 6f to 1m: acts on any going: sometimes hangs/carries head high, but goes well for claimer/amateur: sometimes bandaged: has won 4 times at Redcar. *D. A. Wilson*

PROFIT STREAM   3 ch.g. Adonijah 126 – River Reem (USA) (Irish River (FR)   –
131) [1991 7m 6m⁶ 5g a7g a6g⁵ 1992 a7g⁴ 7d 7v] smallish, workmanlike gelding: poor mover: poor maiden: should stay 1m: acts on good to firm ground and dead: sold 1,000 gns Doncaster June Sales. *M. W. Easterby*

PROFUSION   3 b.c. Rainbow Quest (USA) 134 – Pauvresse (FR) (Home Guard **104** (USA) 129) [1991 7g* 7g⁴ 1992 10d* 10.3m² 10m⁶ 10g² 12m* 12.1g³ 12g] good-bodied colt: useful performer in first half of 1992: won minor event at Nottingham and £9,000 contest at Ascot (bandaged near-hind): also ran very well when placed in Dee Stakes at Chester (short-headed by My Memoirs), listed race at Rome (beaten a nose by Inner City) and £14,100 contest at Chepstow: off course 4 months before soundly beaten in November Handicap at Doncaster: better at 1½m than shorter: acts on good to firm ground and dead: may prove suited by waiting tactics. *P. F. I. Cole*

PROSEQUENDO (USA)   5 b.g. Robellino (USA) 127 – Allegedly (USA) (Sir   **72**
Ivor 135) [1991 8d³ a8g* 10.1f 10g³ 1992 12.3g* a12g* 14m³ 12m² 14m² 14g⁵ 14.1g⁴ 12g* 14s⁵ 12g⁴ 14.1d] tall, leggy, quite good-topped gelding: has quick action: successful in claimers at Wolverhampton and Lingfield in spring and Folkestone handicap in August: effective from 1½m to 1¾m: acts on good to firm and soft ground and equitrack: consistent: fair hurdler, successful twice late in year. *M. Dixon*

PROSPECT OF WHITBY   6 ch.m. True Song 95 – Looking For Gold (Gold-   –
fella 80) [1991 NR 1992 a12g] first foal: dam selling hurdler: no sign of ability over hurdles and tailed off in claimer at Southwell on flat debut. *P. A. Pritchard*

PROUD BRIGADIER (IRE)   4 b.g. Auction Ring (USA) 123 – Naughty One   **55**
Gerard (Brigadier Gerard 144) [1991 8f⁵ 5m 6m⁴ 7m⁶ 7f 6d 6g⁴ 6m⁵ 7m⁴ 7f² 6m 6g* 6m a6g³ a7g⁴ 1992 a6g⁵ 7m 6.1m⁴ 6f³ 6.1g⁵ 6f² 6d 6m⁵ 6g² 6s² 6.9v³] lengthy, sparely-made gelding: poor mover: consistent handicapper: effective at 6f to 7f: acts on firm and heavy going and equitrack: suitable mount for an apprentice. *W. Carter*

PROUD MOMENT (BAR)   2 b.f. (Jan 20) Bentom (USA) 98 – Proud Perform-   –
ance 71 (Owen Anthony 102) [1992 7g 5.1s] leggy filly: first known foal: dam went to Barbados in 1978: green, slowly away and always behind in minor events at New-bury and Bath in September. *R. Hannon*

PROVE IT'S GOLD   3 b.f. Alleging (USA) 120 – Goldyke 63 (Bustino 136) [1991   –
NR 1992 a8g⁴ 10g a8g⁵ 10f⁵] sturdy, lengthy filly: third known foal: half-sister to hurdlers Run Fast For Gold (by Deep Run) and As Good As Gold (by Oats): dam winning hurdler/chaser: no worthwhile form: sold 1,600 gns Ascot July Sales. *T. M. Jones*

PTOLEMY (FR)   5 gr.g. Persepolis (FR) 127 – Rivoltade (USA) (Sir Ivor 135)   –
[1991 NR 1992 11.8s⁴ 22.2g 12.1g⁵ 14.9g] 7,000 3-y-o: workmanlike gelding: moderate walker: third foal: half-brother to smart but temperamental French middle-distance stayer Rachmaninov (by Brustolon): dam unraced half-sister to top-class 1m to 1½m filly Riverqueen: little worthwhile form on flat. *Miss H. C. Knight*

PUBLIC APPEAL   3 b.g. Law Society (USA) 130 – Vacherin (USA) (Green   –
Dancer (USA) 132) [1991 7g⁵ 8s⁵ 8.1d⁴ 10m³ 1992 12s] leggy, quite good-topped gelding: good walker: rated 69 at 2 yrs: tailed off in maiden in October, 1992: should stay 1½m: acts on good to firm ground: best run when blinkered: sold to join S. Leadbetter 1,500 gns Doncaster November Sales. *P. F. I. Cole*

PUBLIC WAY (IRE)   2 b.g. (Apr 21) Common Grounds 118 – Kilpeacon (Flores-   **55**
cence 120) [1992 5s⁴ 5d³ 6d 7g 7s⁴ 8s 7d 7d* 8.3v⁵] IR 3,600Y: small, leggy gelding: half-brother to several winners, including 3-y-o Mighty-Q, 5f seller winner as 2 yrs, and Irish 1½m winner Tracy's Sundown (both by Red Sunset): dam won from 5f to 7f in Ireland: modest performer: second run in 2 days when winning selling nursery

at Catterick in October: probably stays 1m: seems well suited by a soft surface: suitable mount for claimer. *N. Chamberlain*

PUENTA AGUILA 2 gr.g. (Mar 17) Belfort (FR) 89 – Sarah's Venture 70 **52** (Averof 123) [1992 5s³ 5g] 6,200F, 6,600Y: leggy gelding: second foal: dam middle-distance winner: third in maiden at Ripon in April: well beaten in maiden auction at Thirsk following month: dead. *M. W. Easterby*

PUFF PUFF 6 b.m. All Systems Go 119 – Harmonious Sound (Auction Ring **47** (USA) 123) [1991 a12g⁴ a12g² 12f* 12f³ a16g* 14f⁴ 14m³ 15.4f 16m⁴ a16g⁶ 1992 11.5m⁶ 12d 11.9f⁵ 11.5m⁴ 16.4g⁴ 14d] rather leggy mare: moderate mover: poor handicapper: effective from 1½m to 2m: acts on firm going and equitrack, seems unsuited by a soft surface. *Miss B. Sanders*

PUFFY 5 ch.g. Wolverlife 115 – Eskaroon (Artaius (USA) 129) [1991 8s 7.5f⁶ 7m² **47 §** 8h⁴ 7.5g⁶ 8m² 7.1g 10.5d 1992 10.1s⁶ 8d⁴ 7.5m 10m² 8f 7.1g] leggy, rather sparely-made gelding: poor mover: temperamental handicapper: acts on any going: sometimes blinkered/visored. *M. Dods*

PUGET DANCER (USA) 2 b.f. (Mar 18) Seattle Dancer (USA) 119 – Basin **62** (USA) (Tom Rolfe) [1992 8g³ 7s] $22,000F, $25,000Y: workmanlike filly: half-sister to several minor winners: dam lightly-raced half-sister to 5 stakes winners, including Belmont Stakes and Kentucky Derby third Dike: encouraging third in maiden at Leicester: bandaged off-hind and failed to confirm that run in similar event at Redcar later in September. *M. Bell*

PURBECK CENTENARY 2 b.c. (Jan 28) Lidhame 109 – Double Stitch 74 **41** (Wolver Hollow 126) [1992 5g 5.1s 5g 6d 6s 5.1d] 1,100Y: leggy colt: poor mover: fifth foal: half-brother to 3-y-o 5f winner Absolutely Nuts (by Absalom): dam 8.2f winner: poor plater. *M. R. Channon*

PURCHASED BY PHONE (IRE) 2 b.f. (Feb 10) Wolverlife 115 – Gerise **48** (Nishapour (FR) 125) [1992 5d* 5m* 5g* 5d³ 5g] IR 1,850Y: tall, unfurnished filly: moderate mover: second foal: dam Irish 1½m winner at 3 yrs also won over hurdles: successful in claimers in first half of 1992 at Hamilton (for apprentice, claimed out of D. Moffatt's stable £5,505) and Beverley (2, fortunate to be awarded race final one, claimed out of P. Haslam's stable £9,001): ran moderately after: should stay 6f: retained 5,000 gns Doncaster August Sales. *J. S. Wainwright*

PURE BLISS 5 b.m. Idiot's Delight 115 – Julie Emma (Farm Walk 111) [1991 6m **–** 6g 7f a7g 1992 a10g] lengthy mare: little worthwhile form. *R. J. Hodges*

PURE FORMALITY 3 b.f. Forzando 122 – Sharp Celine (Sharpo 132) [1991 6d* **84 ?** 1992 6d³ 6m⁴ 7.3g 8d 7s] workmanlike filly: ran poorly in handicaps after fourth in Newbury minor event in May: should be suited by further than 6f: acts on dead ground: blinkered final start. *D. R. C. Elsworth*

PURE MADNESS (USA) 2 b.c. (Apr 1) Northern Prospect (USA) – Icy **53** Oddsmaker (USA) (Icecapade (USA)) [1992 6.1m⁵ 5m⁴ 5.1m⁴ 6m] 34,000Y: well-grown colt: has scope: third reported foal: half-brother to a winner in USA by Naskra: dam minor sprint winner at 2 yrs: wore tongue strap when staying-on fourth in maiden at Chester: looked to be progressing, but showed little in nursery after: should be well suited by further than 6f. *Dr J. D. Scargill*

PURE MISK 2 b.f. (Apr 12) Rainbow Quest (USA) 134 – Miller's Creek (USA) 62 **55 p** (Star de Naskra (USA)) [1992 7m] 64,000Y: fourth foal: half-sister to 3-y-o Sandro (by Niniski) and 6f (at 2 yrs) to 10.2f winner Stone Mill (by Caerleon): dam maiden suited by 1m, is out of half-sister to top Canadian colt Giboulee: soon outpaced in maiden at Newmarket in July. *B. Hanbury*

PURITAN (CAN) 3 b.c. Alleged (USA) 138 – Conform (CAN) (Blushing Groom **82** (FR) 131) [1991 NR 1992 14.1d² 11.7g* 12f² 16d³ 16.1g⁴ 16d³ 16.1s⁶ 18m*] quite good-topped colt: second foal: half-brother to 1991 U.S. 3-y-o sprint maiden winner Fifty Mile System (by Saratoga Six): dam group-placed winner from 9f to 10.5f in France at 3 and 4 yrs, later stakes winner in USA: consistent handicapper: won at Bath (maiden) in July and Pontefract in October: suited by a thorough test of stamina: acts on firm going, seems unsuited by very soft: sold to join N. Tinkler's stable 25,000 gns Newmarket Autumn Sales. *G. Harwood*

PURSUIT OF LOVE 3 b.c. Groom Dancer (USA) 128 – Dance Quest (FR) **124** 117 (Green Dancer (USA) 132) [1991 6g³ 7m* 7m⁴ 1992 7g* 8g³ 8m² 7f² 6g² 6.5g* 7.3d² 7f* 7d⁶]

    This Pursuit of Love at least has won its place at stud. Fourth in the Dewhurst Stakes just fifteen days after his win in a Newmarket maiden as a

European Free Handicap, Newmarket—Pursuit of Love is well on top

two-year-old, Pursuit of Love remained a standard-bearer for Henry Cecil and Lord Howard de Walden virtually throughout his second season. Only once did he finish out of the places in nine starts as a three-year-old, contesting some of the top pattern races at six furlongs, seven furlongs and a mile. He gained three victories: in the European Free Handicap, the Prix Maurice de Gheest and the Kiveton Park Stakes. Pursuit of Love carried bottom weight in the European Free Handicap at Newmarket in April—although the range was only from 9-1 up to the 9-7 carried by the French colt Steinbeck and Goffs Million winner Fair Crack—but put up a performance impressive enough to place him in the forefront of contenders for the Two Thousand Guineas. Looking as if the race was sure to bring him on, Pursuit of Love looked the winner a long way out and was soon well in command once sent on at the two-furlong marker, not having to be hard ridden to maintain a two-length advantage over the dead-heaters Steinbeck and Wilde Rufo. Pursuit of Love again had his head in front going into the Dip thirteen days later in the Guineas, but in the stronger company he could not match Rodrigo de Triano, losing out to Lucky Lindy as well close home in finishing third of sixteen, beaten two lengths.

It was early-August and Deauville four outings later before Pursuit of Love was winning again. In the interim he went down conceding 5 lb at 13/8 on to Torrey Canyon in the listed Heron Stakes at Kempton. That wasn't a bad effort compared to his Guineas form and his next two starts saw him start a short-priced favourite at Deauville: he ran a most genuine race to be beaten half a length by Prince Ferdinand in the Jersey Stakes at Royal Ascot then took on the best sprinters around in the July Cup at Newmarket. A 13/2-chance looking in exceptional condition, Pursuit of Love went under by just a

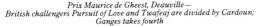

Prix Maurice de Gheest, Deauville—
British challengers Pursuit of Love and Twafeaj are divided by Cardoun;
Ganges takes fourth

647

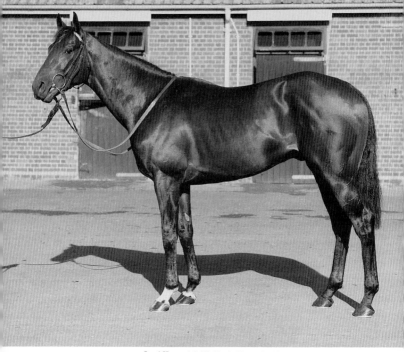

Lord Howard de Walden's "Pursuit of Love"

head to Mr Brooks—beating Sheikh Albadou, Elbio, Paris House, Wolfhound, Shalford and Tbab—and was unlucky at that. True, he had to be pushed along from an early stage, leaving the clear impression that six furlongs was a minimum trip, but he met trouble in running at two points after halfway before being switched to mount a tremendous late challenge on the rails. The Group 2 Maurice de Gheest twelve days later contained only Elbio apart from Pursuit of Love from the July Cup field, a far from daunting challenge from the home team, and a reproduction of the July Cup form saw Pursuit of Love come home a length and a half in front of Cardoun, pushed out, no mishaps ever seeming likely as he raced in the front rank on the rails throughout.

Game, genuine and consistent was an irresistible tag for Pursuit of Love at this stage, after his sixth start in three and a half months. He was kept on the go, his record on the score of consistency suffering somewhat when a beaten favourite at short odds in the Hungerford Stakes at Newbury and Prix de la Foret at Longchamp, both on dead ground. However, sandwiched between those two modest efforts was his career best. The Kiveton Park Stakes at the Doncaster St Leger meeting attracted ten runners, including, in betting order, the progressive filly Storm Dove, who had won a listed race by seven lengths last time out; the Prix de la Porte Maillot winner Dilum; Prince Ferdinand; and the previous year's Kiveton Park winner Bog Trotter. Pursuit of Love looked to have a far from straightforward task at the weights but that wasn't the way it went in the race; he was set alight approaching the two-furlong marker to take over from Bog Trotter, then forged clear in the final furlong to register a two-length victory over Prince Ferdinand, who received 3 lb.

		Blushing Groom	Red God
	Groom Dancer (USA)	(ch 1974)	Runaway Bride
	(b 1984)	Featherhill	Lyphard
Pursuit of Love		(b 1978)	Lady Berry
(b.c. 1989)		Green Dancer	Nijinsky
	Dance Quest (FR)	(b 1972)	Green Valley
	(b 1981)	Polyponder	Barbizon
		(ch 1974)	Second Thought

Pursuit of Love will be standing at the Plantation Stud, Newmarket, at a fee of £5,000 (1st October terms). A strong, good-topped colt, he invariably impressed in appearance on the racecourse, and, though he was a moderate mover in his slower paces, he caught the eye with his powerful action at full stretch. Pursuit of Love is from the first crop of Groom Dancer, a colt who disappointed in the Derby and Arc de Triomphe in 1987 but whose five other completed starts (he unseated his rider after clipping an opponent's heels on one) that year, between a mile and ten and a half furlongs, all resulted in victories, establishing him as a high-class performer with an excellent turn of foot. The dam's side of Pursuit of Love's pedigree was described in the last two years' *Racehorses*, as his year-older half-sister is the Prix du Gros-Chene, Prix de Ris-Orangis and Prix de Seine-et-Oise winner Divine Danse. Both the dam Dance Quest and grandam Polyponder were smart sprinters as well. Pursuit of Love is Dance Quest's fourth foal; the next three are all by Kris. Pursuit of Love can be described as effective at six furlongs to a mile, although his best effort was at seven furlongs; he acted on firm going, seemingly not on a soft surface. *H. R. A. Cecil*

PUSEY STREET BOY 5 ch.g. Vaigly Great 127 – Pusey Street 96 (Native **43** Bazaar 122) [1991 10.2s 8g a7g a10g⁵ 1992 a8g 10.2m² 10.2g⁴ 10g³ 10s⁴ a10g⁵ a12g a13g] leggy, lengthy, dipped-backed gelding: has been tubed: poor handicapper: stays 11.5f: acts on any going. *J. R. Bosley*

PYARE SQUARE 3 b.g. Reference Point 139 – Land of Ivory (USA) 109 (The **71 §** Minstrel (CAN) 135) [1991 7f⁵ 1992 11d 10s² 8.9g 9f² 9.9m⁴ 12f³ 11.7m³] sturdy gelding: modest maiden: found little last 2 starts: stays 1½m: probably acts on any going: seems effective blinkered or not: probably unsatisfactory. *I. A. Balding*

PYRAMIS PRINCE (IRE) 2 b.c. (May 23) Fairy King (USA) – Midnight Patrol (Ashmore (FR) 125) [1992 7d] 5,200Y: lengthy colt: closely related to 1988 2-y-o 7.5f winner Punta Baluarte (by Viking) and half-brother to 6f winner Viceroy Jester (by Jester): dam placed over 1¼m in Ireland: tailed off in maiden at Salisbury in July: moved poorly down. *M. R. Channon*

PYRRHIC DANCE 2 b.c. (Feb 19) Sovereign Dancer (USA) – Cherubim (USA) **60 p** (Steward) [1992 7m 7d 6d⁵] 31,000F, 20,000Y: lengthy, quite attractive colt: poor mover: half-brother to 3 winners in USA: dam, minor winner, is half-sister to Diamond Prospect: sire useful at up to 1½m in France at 4 yrs: similar form in October maidens: will stay 1m: should do better. *J. W. Hills*

PYTCHLEY DAWN 2 b.f. (May 1) Welsh Captain 113 – Cawston's Arms (Caw- **45** ston's Clown 113) [1992 a6g a7g⁶] third foal: dam never ran: poor form in claimers at Southwell. *D. Morris*

PYTCHLEY NIGHT 5 b.g. Red Sunset 120 – Lili Bengam (Welsh Saint 126) **68 +** [1991 a8g² a8g* a10g a8g⁵ a8g³ 8d 7m 7.6m³ 7g 7f⁵ 8.2m 7g* a7g⁴ a7g* a8g a7g* a95 1992 a7g* a8g* 8g 7g4] lengthy, quite good-topped gelding: best on all-weather, and successful in handicaps at Lingfield in February and March (£10,800 race): none too consistent on turf: not seen out after April: best at 7f/1m: acts on firm going and all-weather surfaces, unsuited by dead ground: keen sort. *D. Morris*

Q

QAFFAL (USA) 2 b.c. (Feb 17) Seattle Dancer (USA) 119 – Samalex 110 **75** (Ela-Mana-Mou 132) [1992 7.5m* 7f⁶ 8.2d] 1,000,000 francs (approx £100,400) Y: finely-made, rather attractive colt, shade unfurnished: fourth foal: half-brother to French 1m and 11f winner Septieme Art (by Bering): dam, French 9f (at 2 yrs) and 11f winner stayed 1½m, is granddaughter of top-class American filly Bayou: fair form: narrowly won maiden at Beverley in July, travelling smoothly then running on well: creditable efforts in minor event at Doncaster (set slow pace, outspeeded) and nursery at Nottingham in September: will stay beyond 1m: acts on firm and dead ground. *D. Morley*

Q-EIGHT (IRE)   4 b.c. Vision (USA) – Warning Sound (Red Alert 127) [1991 7s 9m 11.1g² 12m² 11m² 10.2s 13.3g 1992 14.6d 14.1d 12f 12m] workmanlike colt: has a round action: seems of little account these days. *A. P. Jarvis*   –

QUADRANT   3 b.g. Shirley Heights 130 – Sextant 98 (Star Appeal 133) [1991 NR 1992 8g 10s a12g* 12m⁵ 14m a16g²] good-bodied gelding: seventh foal: half-brother to 7f winner Pilot (by Kris) and a winner in Italy by Brigadier Gerard: dam won twice at around 1¼m and is out of smart Fluke, a half-sister to Bireme and Buoy: fair performer: won maiden at Lingfield in September: blinkered, best effort in handicaps when second there following month: stays 2m: best efforts on equitrack. *B. W. Hills*   77

QUADRIREME   3 b.c. Rousillon (USA) 133 – Bireme 127 (Grundy 137) [1991 7m 1992 12m 10m⁴ 11.7m² 11.8g 12g* 11.6g⁵ 14g] leggy, quite attractive colt: fair performer: held up (made most previous 3 starts) and led inside final 1f when winning handicap at Kempton in August: never able to challenge in handicaps afterwards: stays 1½m well: acts on good to firm ground: carries head high: sold to join J. Old 27,000 gns Newmarket Autumn Sales. *Major W. R. Hern*   78

QUALITAIR AVIATOR   6 b.g. Valiyar 129 – Comtec Princess 73 (Gulf Pearl 117) [1991 a13g* a13g⁴ a14g 12.1g 12m a16g* a14g a16g 1992 a14g*] close-coupled, workmanlike gelding: moderate mover: fair but inconsistent handicapper on all-weather surfaces: returned to form when winning at Southwell in January by 5 lengths: stays 2m: no form on turf for a long time. *J. F. Bottomley*   a80

QUALITAIR BLAZER   5 ch.m. Blazing Saddles (AUS) – Midfirna (Midsummer Night II 117) [1991 a14g⁴ a12g⁴ a14g⁵ a11g⁴ 9.9m a12g* 14g a11g² a12g⁴ a12g² a14g⁴ a11g³ a14g² a13g² 1992 a12g* a14g³ a13g³ a12g⁴] compact mare: modest handicapper on the all-weather: won at Southwell in January: not seen out after February: effective from 11f to 1¾m: twice below form when visored: no form on turf for a long time. *J. R. Jenkins*   a53

QUALITAIR FLYER   10 b.g. Kampala 120 – Ziobia 78 (Tribal Chief 125) [1991 8.2d a7g a8g⁴ a8g a11g⁶ a11g² 11m a12g³ 1992 a11g* a12g⁴ a10g⁶ a12g] small, lengthy gelding: has a round action: unreliable handicapper: won at Southwell in January: below form in the spring: seems to stay 1½m: acts on any turf going and fibresand: has worn blinkers and a visor: tends to hang and is a difficult ride: sold 1,000 gns Doncaster June Sales. *J. F. Bottomley*   31 §

QUALITAIR IDOL   3 b.f. Dreams To Reality (USA) 113 – Village Idol 74 (Blakeney 126) [1991 NR 1992 a7g² a10g a8g⁶ 8.3s⁴ a7g 8g 8.3m³ 10d] 4,000F, 1,900Y: workmanlike filly: half-sister to several winners here and abroad, including 7f seller winner Sporting Idol (by Mummy's Game): dam stayed 1½m: inconsistent maiden: should prove best at 1m + : yet to race on firm ground, probably acts on any other: no improvement in a visor: sold 1,300 gns Doncaster October Sales. *J. F. Bottomley*   49 d

QUALITAIR MEMORY   3 ch.g. Don't Forget Me 127 – Whist Awhile (Caerleon (USA) 132) [1991 5m a7g³ 1992 8.5f⁴ 9f 9.9d² 11.1m a12g 9.7v] leggy, unfurnished gelding: untrustworthy handicapper: edgy, best effort when second at Beverley: soundly beaten afterwards, visored and reluctant to race after 4f at Southwell: subsequently sold out of J. Bottomley's stable 1,050 gns Ascot July Sales: will stay beyond 1¼m: best with give in the ground: easy winner of selling hurdle in December. *J. Akehurst*   36 §

QUALITAIR PROMISE   4 ch.f. Reach 122 – Maputo Princess (Raga Navarro (ITY) 119) [1991 10m 10f 9.9m 1992 17.1m] sparely-made filly: had a round action: of little account: dead. *G. M. Moore*   –

QUALITAIR REALITY   4 b.f. Dreams To Reality (USA) 113 – Blushing Nurse (Saritamer (USA) 130) [1991 6f 7m 5m⁶ 5.1m 5m 8f 1992 7f] small filly: poor mover: of little account: sold 1,500 gns Ascot June Sales. *M. F. Barraclough*   –

QUALITAIR RHYTHM (IRE)   4 b.f. Drumalis 125 – Abbe's Realm (Realm 129) [1991 10m a8g⁵ 7.9g⁴ 8g 10.5d⁵ a6g³ 1992 a7g² a8g⁵ a8g⁴ a8g* 8s³ 11.8g* a8g⁵ a7g a7g 12.5* 12.1s² a16g* a12g⁵] leggy, close-coupled filly: poor mover: moderate handicapper: trained first 2 starts by J. Hetherton, next one by W. Haigh: won maiden at Southwell in March and handicaps at Leicester in May and Warwick (very easily for 7-lb claimer) and Southwell in the autumn: effective at 1½m and stays 2m: 63 possibly needs an easy surface on turf, acts on all-weather surfaces: successful blinkered or not. *I. Campbell*

QUALITAIR SOUND (IRE)   4 b.g. Mazaad 106 – A Nice Alert (Red Alert 127)   –
[1991 8s 8.2d³ 8g 9m⁵ 12g⁶ 10g⁵ 8m 8g⁵ 8m⁶ 10g 8.9g 8d 1992 a12g² 10.3m a12g⁶ a58
10m 12g] compact, workmanlike gelding: has a round action: maiden handicapper on flat: well below form last 2 starts: stays 1½m: acts on good to firm and heavy ground and on fibresand: useful hurdler, winner in December. *J. F. Bottomley*

QUALITAIR SWEETIE   5 ch.g. Sweet Monday 122 – Right Abella 74 (Right   –
Boy 137) a11g a12g⁵ a14g 1992 a11g a13g⁵] workmanlike gelding: rated 59 at 3 yrs, twice below form when blinkered: no worthwhile form since: should stay 1¾m: acts on good to firm going: sold 700 gns Doncaster June Sales, resold 660 gns Doncaster September Sales and now with T. Rollingson. *J. F. Bottomley*

QUANTITY SURVEYOR   3 b.c. Aragon 118 – Quaranta 83 (Hotfoot 126) [1991   63
NR 1992 a7g a7g a7g* 8.3s* 9g] leggy colt: has a markedly round action: half-brother to several winners, including Cambridgeshire winner Quinlan Terry (by Welsh Pageant), also successful at 1½m, and modest 4-y-o 7f and 1m winner Quinzii Martin (by Song): dam 2-y-o 5f winner, is half-sister to smart 5f to 7f performer Quy: fair form: won maiden at Southwell in July and claimer at Hamilton in September, staying on: should stay 9f: acts on soft ground and fibresand. *Sir Mark Prescott*

QUARRINGTON HILL   3 b.g. Mansingh (USA) 120 – Stonebow Lady 52   –
(Windjammer (USA)) [1991 NR 1992 7d³ 7g 11d] 920F, 2,600Y: leggy gelding: brother to a plating-class sprint maiden and half-brother to several poor animals: dam second over 1m and 9f, is half-sister to dam of Petong (by Mansingh): tailed off in Warwick maiden and Wolverhampton claimers. *K. S. Bridgwater*

QUATRE FEMME   5 b.m. Petorius 117 – Irish Kick (Windjammer (USA)) [1991   54
6m² 5g⁶ 6f 6g³ 5m⁵ 5f4 6f³ 6m⁵ 7m 6m 1992 5d 6g 5d a6g² a6g a6g³] leggy, angular mare: largely consistent handicapper at 4 yrs: form in 1992 only when placed late in year: should stay 7f: acts on firm going and fibresand: has edged left. *M. Johnston*

QUATTRO   2 b.c. (Apr 8) Robellino (USA) 127 – Load Line (High Line 125) [1992   39
a7g a8g⁴ a8g] 10,000F, 10,000Y: first foal: dam, never ran, is sister to Park Hill winner Quay Line: poor maiden: one paced and will stay middle distances. *R. W. Armstrong*

QUAVER (USA)   2 b.f. (Jan 20) The Minstrel (CAN) 135 – Que Sympatica 108   69 p
(Young Generation 129) [1992 6s⁴] 170,000Y: compact, useful-looking filly: second foal: half-sister to 3-y-o 6f and 7f winner Daaris (by Diesis): dam 6f to 1m winner also winner in Italy, is out of sister to Park Hill winner Quay Line: 7/1, promising fourth of 16 to Zarani Sidi Anna in maiden at Newbury in October, losing many lengths at start, making smooth headway halfway then staying on to finish 3½ lengths down: sure to improve, and win a similar event at least. *J. H. M. Gosden*

QUEEN CANUTE (IRE)   3 ch.f. Ahonoora 122 – Rising Tide 101 (Red Alert   –
127) [1991 NR 1992 5.1g 5g 6.1g 6m⁶] IR 25,000Y: workmanlike filly: half-sister to fairly useful Irish sprinter Northern Tide (by North Pole) and winners in France and Malaysia: dam 2-y-o 5f winner didn't train on: well beaten in maidens: retained 820 gns Doncaster October Sales after third start. *F. H. Lee*

QUEEN CAROLINE (USA)   3 b.f. Chief's Crown (USA) – Fager's Glory   67
(USA) (Mr Prospector (USA)) [1991 NR 1992 10.5d³ 9.9f4 8f³ 8.2d³ 10.3g³ 10g³] $350,000Y: leggy, useful-looking filly: shows knee action: poor mover: half-sister to several winners, including 7f winner Rahaam (by Secreto) and very useful 1986 2-y-o 7f and 7.5f winner Glory Forever (by Forever Lasting), later third in French 2000 Guineas: dam never ran: consistent maiden: best effort, for 5-lb claimer, at Chester (edged left, demoted from second for interference) penultimate start: took good hold, found little final one: stayed 10.5f: acted on firm and dead ground: visits Reprimand. *H. R. A. Cecil*

QUEEN LEONOR (IRE)   3 b.f. Caerleon (USA) 132 – Pudibunda (Bold Lad   72 p
(IRE) 133) [1991 NR 1992 10s²] IR 150,000Y: third foal: half-sister to Irish 4-y-o 7f (at 2 yrs) and 1¼m winner Thin Ice (by Try My Best) and a winner in Italy by Salmon Leap: dam unraced half-sister to smart middle-distance performers Icelandic and Snow: weak 11/1, 1½ lengths second of 14 to Kabayil in maiden at Leicester in October: will stay 1½m: should improve. *J. H. M. Gosden*

QUEEN OF DREAMS   4 ch.f. Ti King (FR) 121 – Humeur de Reve (USA) (Lord   37
Avie (USA)) [1991 a10g⁶ a10g⁴ 12v 1992 a10g a7g² a7g⁶ a8g⁶ a8g³ 8m 8m⁴ 8.2m 6.9m] good-topped filly: poor handicapper, still a maiden: stays 1m: acts on good to firm ground and all-weather surfaces. *Dr J. D. Scargill*

Blue Seal Stakes, Ascot—newcomers Queen's View and Felawnah

QUEEN OF PENDONA 3 b.f. King of Spain 121 – Pendona 72 (Blue Cashmere – §
129) [1991 5.3f 6m 5s² 7m 6m 5m 6g 6s⁵ a6g a7g 1992 a8g 12.2d⁵ 8.2d 11.1s] smallish,
leggy filly: moderate mover: bad maiden and ungenuine: often blinkered, once
visored: sometimes edgy. *D. Moffatt*

QUEEN OF SHANNON (IRE) 4 b.f. Nordico (USA) – Raj Kumari (Vitiges 76
(FR) 132) [1991 7m 8d⁶ 7f⁶ a7g³ 1992 7g* 7f² 8.3g⁵ 7s* 8g⁴ 8m 7g] quite good-
topped, angular filly: has reportedly been operated on 3 times for wind problems: off
course over a year but returned as a fair handicapper: won at Yarmouth in July and
Salisbury in September: ran moderately last 2 starts: acts on any going: best at 7f/1m: acts on any
going: has been bandaged: much more tractable these days. *D. Morris*

QUEEN OF THE DALES 3 b.f. Beldale Flutter (USA) 130 – Perang's Niece –
82 (High Award 119) [1991 NR 1992 12.2d 11v] rangy, workmanlike filly: fourth foal:
dam stayed 1m: backward, behind in maiden at Catterick and claimer at Redcar in
the autumn. *G. M. Moore*

QUEEN OF THE QUORN 2 b.f. (Mar 3) Governor General 116 – Alumia 45
(Great Nephew 126) [1992 6m⁵ 6m 6g⁴ a6g⁴] workmanlike filly: eighth foal: dam
unplaced 3 times at 2 yrs: poor maiden: should stay 7f: acts on good to firm ground
and on fibresand: reared stalls second start. *G. M. Moore*

QUEENS CONSUL (IRE) 2 gr.f. (Mar 8) Kalaglow 132 – Queens Connection 49
(Bay Express 132) [1992 7d⁵ 7g] IR 750Y: leggy, lightly-made filly: second foal: dam
ran 3 times at 2 yrs: beaten around 14 lengths in minor event at York and maiden at
Doncaster in October. *B. S. Rothwell*

QUEENS CONTRACTOR 2 b.g. (Mar 7) Formidable (USA) 125 – Salazie 87 57
(Ile de Bourbon (USA) 133) [1992 7m 6g⁶ 7g³] 5,800Y: lengthy colt: second foal:
half-brother to a winner in Austria: dam, 1m winner at 2 yrs, is out of half-sister to
Final Straw and Achieved: bandaged behind, similar form in maidens at Salisbury
(wore crossed noseband) and Brighton: should prove better suited by 7f than 6f. *M.
J. Heaton-Ellis*

QUEEN'S TICKLE 3 b.f. Tickled Pink 114 – Queens Pearl (Queen's Hussar **51**
124) [1991 6m* 6g 5.7g² 5d 1992 5s 6g 6m 6d⁵ 6.1m³ 7m 8m] workmanlike filly: poor
handicapper: best efforts at 6f on top-of-the-ground: often bandaged near-hind:
effective blinkered or not. *A. P. Jarvis*

QUEENS TOUR 7 b.h. Sweet Monday 122 – On Tour 60 (Queen's Hussar 124) **37** d
[1991 12s 13d 13d 13m³ 12m⁶ 11.9m⁵ 13d⁴ 13d 13.1m⁶ 10.5d a14g 1992 10.8d⁴ 12.3g⁴
12.1s⁶ 9.2d⁵ 10.1f⁴ 10g⁴ a12g 12m 10.5g 12.3d a12g 12.1s⁵ 12s³ 15.8d⁵] small,
lightly-made horse: poor walker and mover: poor handicapper: effective at 1¼m and
seems to stay 2m: acts on any ground: retained 1,700 gns Doncaster May Sales, sold
1,500 gns Doncaster October Sales. *M. Brittain*

QUEEN'S VIEW (FR) 2 b.f. (Apr 6) Lomond (USA) 128 – Mill Path (Mill Reef **99** p
(USA) 141) [1992 6d* 7m²] quite attractive filly: first foal: dam, ran once, from
family of Teenoso: 10/1, comfortably won Blue Seal Stakes at Ascot in September by
¾ length from Felawnah: looking really well, ran on strongly when beaten ¾ length
by Yawl in 7-runner Rockfel Stakes at Newmarket following month: will be suited by
1m +: sure to better, and win more races. *L. M. Cumani*

QUEEN WARRIOR 3 b.f. Daring March 116 – Princess Zenobia 72 (Record **71** d
Token 128) [1991 NR 1992 7d⁴ 8g* 7m² 8m² 8m a7g³ 8g 8d] tall, leggy,
sparely-made filly: third foal: dam 10.2f and 11.7f winner: landed odds in 3-runner
Newmarket Challenge Whip and ran well when second in maidens at York and
Kempton later in May: went the wrong way after: should prove better suited by
1¼m: acts on good to firm ground. *P. T. Walwyn*

QUESSONG 2 gr.c. (Apr 21) Petong 126 – Marquessa d'Howfen 93 (Pitcairn 126) **30**
[1992 6m 6d 8.1d] lengthy colt: moderate mover: sixth foal: half-brother to 4-y-o
middle-distance winner Mardessa (by Ardross): dam 2-y-o 7f winner: poor form in
maidens: blinkered on debut. *F. H. Lee*

QUEST FOR THE BEST 3 b.f. Rainbow Quest (USA) 134 – Bold Flawless **– p**
(USA) 73 (Bold Bidder) [1991 NR 1992 7.9g⁵] leggy filly: sixth foal: half-sister to 3
winners, including useful 1988 2-y-o 6f and 7f winner Life At The Top (by Habitat)
and 1990 2-y-o 5f and 6f winner Bold Double (by Never So Bold): dam 1½m winner:
very easy to back and bit backward, outpaced from over 2f out when well-beaten
fifth of 8 in moderately-run maiden at York in September: should improve. *A. C.
Stewart*

QUESTING (USA) 3 ch.c. Diesis 133 – Quest (USA) 90§ (The Minstrel (CAN) **–**
135) [1991 7g 1992 8m⁶ 9s] stocky colt: no worthwhile form in maidens: bred to stay
1¼m. *J. H. M. Gosden*

QUESTION OF DEGREE 6 b.h. Known Fact (USA) 135 – Bernice Clare 68 **41**
(Skymaster 126) [1991 8d 8d 8m 10m 8.2f⁶ 1992 a8g³ a7g a7g* a7g⁵] small,
deep-girthed horse: moderate walker: poor handicapper nowadays: blinkered, won
at Southwell in January: not seen out after following month: stays 1m: acts on firm
going and fibresand. *N. Tinkler*

QUESTION OF HONOR 4 b.g. Legend of France (USA) 124 – Snow Goose **–**
(Santa Claus 133) [1991 12s 12.2g 1992 10d] close-coupled gelding: very much on the
downgrade. *A. W. Jones*

QUICK RANSOM 4 ch.g. Hostage (USA) – Run Amber Run (Run The **93**
Gantlet (USA)) [1991 a10g* a10g a10g³ 10d* 12g³ 12.3d⁶ 12g³ 12m 12d³
a12g⁵ a14g³ 1992 11.9d* 14g³ 11.5m² 12d² 16.1f 11.9g² 11.9d* 12m⁵ 13.9m*
12s* 18m]
Few other four-year-old geldings running off a mark of between seventy
and ninety can have achieved so much as this fellow. His entry in the Doncaster November Sales catalogue summed up his career thus: 'Quick Ransom
won six races, £170,033, at three and four years to date including Tote Ebor
Handicap, York, £72,714, and Krug Trophy Handicap, Ascot, £60,466, also
placed 12 times including second in Northern Dancer Handicap, Epsom, Old
Newton Cup, Haydock Park, and Royal Sussex Handicap, Goodwood'. Most of
that came in the latest season, the two big-handicap victories one after the
other in August and September. Despite his success he remains on a handy
mark, but nobody was prepared to go as far as his 70,000 guineas reserve at
the Sales (bidding closed at 61,000 guineas), so he'll be back in training at
Kingsley House stables in 1993.
Quick Ransom had been having an excellent season even before he ran in
the Ebor. He'd won handicaps at Haydock and York and had been knocking at

the door in better ones, notably when beaten in photo-finishes at Epsom and Haydock. Considering the form he'd been in, he looked to have a fair chance in a hotly-contested Ebor, but not quite so fair at the weights as Castoret or Brier Creek on their running together last time out in the Tote Gold Trophy at Goodwood in July, where Quick Ransom had come a creditable fifth. Quick Ransom's regular jockey McKeown had been mildly criticized for going too soon there—he'd pressed ahead three furlongs from home—but while it was true that the usual tactics were to hold Quick Ransom up, pressing ahead three furlongs from home had paid off at York the time before. And McKeown produced the perfect reply in the Ebor, giving his mount an enterprising ride which resulted in avoiding all the trouble behind. Having shot out of the stalls Quick Ransom was allowed to take up a position just behind the leaders, and he kept it until pushed along to make a challenge over three furlongs out. Passing the two-furlong marker he took the lead, and he went up by around two lengths before some of the others, notably Brier Creek, began to get back at him. Challenged persistently in the closing stages, he held on very gamely in a finish that saw less than two lengths covering the first seven. Quick Ransom confirmed Ebor placings with Whitechapel (fourth), Castoret (seventh) and Deposki (eighth) at Ascot, with different tactics on different ground. Possibly because of the soft ground, he was held up. Most of the seventeen runners were in contention turning for home, and we had another very close finish, Quick Ransom producing a storming run on the outside from an unpromising position to get up virtually on the line from Lift And Load and Whitechapel. Maybe that should have been it for the season. He cut little ice in the Cesarewitch under a 4-lb penalty, being unable to make any impression in the last three furlongs and never looking likely to come higher than his ninth-of-twenty-four place behind the eight-length winner Vintage Crop, having been held up to get the trip.

It might be, of course, that Quick Ransom doesn't stay two and a quarter miles, but it seems a bit harsh to judge him on the one run at the end of a hard season, as well as a bit hasty in view of the way he shaped when around four lengths seventh of thirteen to Witness Box in the Northumberland Plate on his only other outing beyond a mile and three quarters. For what it's worth at this stage of his career, his pedigree doesn't exactly shout stamina although both grandsires are strong influences. His sire Hostage won the Grade 1 Arkansas Derby over nine furlongs and lesser races over shorter. On the

Tote Ebor (Handicap), York—less than two lengths between the first seven as Quick Ransom (rails) holds on from Brier Creek (star on cap) and Steerforth (in between)

*Krug Trophy (Handicap), Ascot—another big prize for Quick Ransom,
who gets up on the line from Lift And Load (centre) and Ebor fourth Whitechapel*

	Hostage (USA) (b 1979)	Nijinsky (b 1967)	Northern Dancer / Flaming Page
Quick Ransom (ch.g. 1988)		Entente (b 1971)	Val de Loir / Her Honor
	Run Amber Run (b 1979)	Run The Gantlet (b 1968)	Tom Rolfe / First Feather
		Ashton Amber (ch 1975)	On Your Mark / Ashton Jane

distaff side, the grandam Ashton Amber is a twice-raced half-sister to the Jersey Stakes and Stewards' Cup winner Red Alert, out of a winning two-year-old who appeared not to train on. Ashton Amber's best produce is the 1986 Irish Two Thousand Guineas runner-up Mr John. The rather-slower Run Amber Run got off the mark as a five-year-old in a one-mile maiden in the USA. Quick Ransom is her second foal and second winner, following a minor one in the USA called Fabulous Run (by Somethingfabulous). The two-year-old of 1992 Moon Over Miami (by Beveled) is her third. The leggy, lengthy Quick Ransom never impresses going to post—but what of it? He acts on any going. A tougher, more genuine and consistent handicapper would be hard to find. *M. Johnston*

QUICK SILVER BOY 2 gr.c. (Apr 7) Kalaglow 132 – Safidar 83 (Roan Rocket 128) [1992 5g 5.2m 6.1m² 7g 6.1d] 1,000Y: tall, leggy, close-coupled colt: half-brother to 1988 2-y-o 8.2f winner El Dalsad (by Dalsaan) and a winner in Yugoslavia: dam 1m winner: easily best effort in maidens when short-head second at Nottingham in June: should stay 1m: possibly unsuited by dead ground. *D. Burchell* **58**

QUICK STEEL 4 b.g. Alleging (USA) 120 – Illiney Girl 66 (Lochnager 132) [1991 7m 7f 7.1g 6g* 6.1m⁴ 7s* 6.9s⁶ 1992 7g⁵ 7g³ 6g⁶ 7g² 6d 6s⁴] sparely-made gelding: largely consistent handicapper: effective at 6f to 7f: acts on good to firm ground and soft: effective blinkered or not. *T. P. McGovern* **55**

QUICK VICTORY 2 b.f. (Mar 8) Sharpo 132 – In Triumph (USA) (Hoist The Flag (USA)) [1992 6m 5m] small, rather leggy filly: seventh foal: half-sister to Irish 3-y-o 1m winner Command 'N Control (by Hadeer) and 4 winners, including 7.5f stakes winner Tomalu (by Accipiter) and 8.2f winner Lava Falls (by Riverman): dam ran 4 times: no promise in sellers at York and Beverley: sold 1,300 gns Doncaster November Sales. *P. C. Haslam* **–**

QUIETLY IMPRESSIVE (IRE)   4 b.f. Taufan (USA) 119 – Way Ahead 81   **47**
(Sovereign Path 125) [1991 7d⁵ 9s² 8.2d⁵ 8m* 8d⁵ 8.5m 8d³ 10g⁶ 8m* 8.9m* 8.3m⁶
9m 8g³ 8.1d² 8g⁴ 1992 8s 8s⁵ 8s⁴ 8m 8.2g 8f⁵ 12m⁴ 12g 10.1d⁴ 10g] leggy,
sparely-made filly: moderate mover: rated 66 at 3 yrs: only poor form in handicaps in
1992: effective from 1m to 1½m (at least in moderately-run race): acts on good to
firm ground and soft: usually wears tongue strap nowadays: ran creditably when
blinkered once: sold to join Mrs P. Sly 2,400 gns Newmarket Autumn Sales. *M. Bell*

QUIET MISS   3 b.f. Kind of Hush 118 – Miss Acrow (Comedy Star (USA) 121)   –
[1991 8.9d a8g⁴ a8g³ a7g* a7g* 1992 a8g⁴ a8g⁵ 10.5g 8m 7.6m 7.6s] lengthy filly:
rated 73 at 2 yrs: no form on turf on flat in 1992: should stay at least 1m: trained until
after second start by D. Elsworth: successful over hurdles in August and October.
Mrs A. Knight

QUIET RIOT   10 b.g. Hotfoot 126 – Tuyenu 77 (Welsh Pageant 132) [1991 NR   –
1992 10g 8f 13.8d³ 12f 11.9f 11.6g⁶] strong, good-topped gelding: has a round action:
on the downgrade. *J. White*

QUIET VICTORY   5 b.m. Never So Bold 135 – Les Saintes (Kris 135) [1991   **50**
8.3g³ 5m² 8g² 6f³ 8.3g 7f 7g³ 7g 6s a8g⁴ a10g 1992 7f³ 8m⁵ 7d⁴ 7m* 6.1m⁶ 7g 7g⁵
7f⁶ 7g 7g 8g 6m 7s] workmanlike mare: below form, including in seller, after
winning Doncaster handicap in June: effective at 6f to 1m: acts on firm and dead
ground: below form visored once, usually blinkered nowadays. *Miss L. C. Siddall*

QUINSIGIMOND   2 ch.f. (Feb 20) Formidable (USA) 125 – Quillotern (USA)   **71**
(Arctic Tern (USA) 126) [1992 7f² 7s⁵ 7s⁵ 7d⁵ 6s² 6g³] 26,000Y: good-topped filly:
has plenty of scope: first foal: dam well-beaten half-sister to Leap Lively (dam of
Forest Flower): improved effort when beaten a neck, staying on well, in maiden at
Leicester on penultimate start: modest form otherwise: will stay 1m: probably acts
on any going: retained 8,000 gns Newmarket Autumn Sales. *Sir Mark Prescott*

QUINTA (IRE)   4 b.g. Truculent (USA) – Feliscoa (FR) (Royal Ascot) [1991 NR   –
1992 8m] lengthy gelding: moderate walker: seems of little account. *G. P. Kelly*

QUINTA ROYALE   5 b.g. Sayyaf 121 – Royal Holly (Royal Buck) [1991 8m⁵ 8.2f³   **58**
11.8g⁴ 9.7m* 11.5g 12f 1992 a8g a11g 8f⁴ 8.9s 9m⁶ 7f² 7d⁶] strong, lengthy gelding:
moderate mover: ran with credit most starts in amateur handicaps in 1992, and
unlucky when beaten head at Redcar in August, rider losing irons final 1f: needs
strongly-run race at 7f, and effective at 1¼m: acts well on firm going, possibly not
on soft: successful when blinkered: trained first 2 starts by J. Jenkins. *W. G. M.
Turner*

QUINZII MARTIN   4 b.g. Song 132 – Quaranta 83 (Hotfoot 126) [1991 a6g⁴ 5g⁴   **55**
5f³ 6h³ 5.1d 5m⁴ 8m 6m³ 5.7f 7m a6g a8g⁵ 1992 a11g² a10g³ a8g* a7g³ a7g⁴ 7g 7m
a7g* 7.1m a7g a8g a8g³ a7g⁵ a6g⁵ a7g a8g a7g a7g² a8g] strong, good-bodied
gelding: has a quick action: won handicaps at Lingfield in February and Southwell in
May: effective from 6f to 11f: acts on hard ground and all-weather surfaces: effective
visored or not: below form when blinkered. *D. Haydn Jones*

QUIP   7 ch.g. High Line 125 – Sans Blague (USA) 108 (The Minstrel (CAN) 135)   **30**
[1991 12g 12g³ 12.3d⁵ 11s⁴ 12f² 12.3f⁵ 15.1m³ 12f² 12m² 1992 12f⁶ 14m 16.2g 12f⁵
13.6f⁴ 11d⁴ 15.1m 12m⁴ 12m⁵ 12g] leggy gelding: carries condition: has a long stride:
poor handicapper: effective at 11f to 15f: probably acts on any going: best without
visor. *M. P. Naughton*

QUIXOTIC   3 gr.c. Bellypha 130 – Pushy 112 (Sharpen Up 127) [1991 NR 1992 8g   **51**
8g⁵ 7d³ 7.1s⁵ 8s] strong colt: poor mover: half-brother to several winners, including
smart 6f and 7.3f winner Bluebook (by Secretariat) and fairly useful 1984 2-y-o 6f
winner Eye Drop (by Irish River): dam, raced only at 2 yrs when winner of 4 races,
including Queen Mary, is daughter of outstanding broodmare Mrs Moss: sign of
ability in maidens only when third at Goodwood: sold 2,300 gns Ascot November
Sales. *P. W. Harris*

R

RAAWI   4 b.g. Be My Guest (USA) 126 – Fast Motion 86 (Midsummer Night II 117)   – §
[1991 11d³ 10g⁶ 10g 10g⁴ 8.1g 12g⁴ 10m⁵ 7.1m⁴ 8.2m 10m⁵ 1992 10.3g] tall gelding:
untrustworthy handicapper (rated 51) for R. Boss at 3 yrs: well beaten in ladies
event in March, 1992: probably stays 11f: blinkered final start at 3 yrs: has hung
badly and carried head high: has joined J. Glover. *J. Norton*

RAAYA 3 b.f. Be My Guest (USA) 126 – Fast Motion 86 (Midsummer Night II 117) **40**
[1991 NR 1992 a8g³ a7g a8g³] sister to untrustworthy 4-y-o Raawi, high-class
middle-distance colt Raami and Scandinavian winner Razeen and closely related to
fair 1½m winner Alanood (by Northfields): dam 2-y-o 6f winner: ridden by 5-lb
claimer, poor form in maidens at Southwell in February: weakened quickly closing
stages all starts, when blinkered and favourite last time. *W. A. O'Gorman*

RABBIT'S FOOT 4 b.f. Touching Wood (USA) 127 – Royal Custody (Reform **–**
132) [1991 a12g 12s 10g 11.8g 10.2g 10m 10m² 10g 10m 1992 12h⁶] small, lightly-made
filly: poor maiden (rated 45) at 3 yrs for Lady Herries: tailed off on only outing in
1992, in June: should stay 1½m+: acts on good to firm and soft ground: tried
blinkered once. *R. J. O'Sullivan*

RABSHA (IRE) 4 b.f. Taufan (USA) 119 – Serraj (USA) 57 (Seattle Slew (USA)) **–**
[1991 11d* 10m 16.2g 12s 1992 13.1s] big, lengthy filly: shows knee action: rated 64 at
3 yrs for B. Hanbury: burly, well beaten in amateurs event at Ayr in September: won
selling hurdle in October for D. McCune. *Denys Smith*

RACE TO TIME (IRE) 4 b.g. Runnett 125 – Plunket's Choice (Home Guard **–**
(USA) 129) [1991 a8g* a10g 8g* 8m 10d⁵ 8d² 8m a10g⁶ 1992 a12g] leggy, quite
attractive gelding: rated 58 at 3 yrs: pulled up at Lingfield in March: best form at 1m:
below form on top-of-the-ground: dead. *R. Akehurst*

RACHELLY 2 b.f. (Feb 4) Faustus (USA) 118 – Linda's Design (Persian Bold **–**
123) [1992 7m] fourth foal: half-sister to a winner in Sweden: dam soundly-beaten
daughter of half-sister to very smart animals Prominent and Dominion: always
behind from moderate draw in 12-runner seller at Lingfield in June. *A. R. Davison*

RACING RASKAL 5 b.g. Dunphy 124 – Raskaska (Aureole 132) [1991 12m **34**
14.6m⁵ 17.9f⁶ 15.1g⁴ 13.8m⁴ a16g³ a14g⁶ 1992 16.2g⁶ 13.8m* 13m³ 13f² 15.8g³
15.1m⁵ 15.1f⁴ 15.1d²] smallish gelding: poor mover: largely consistent handicapper:
won at Catterick in May: stayed long distances: acted on firm and dead going: dead.
Capt. J. Wilson

RACING TELEGRAPH 2 b.c. (Feb 5) Claude Monet (USA) 121 – Near Enough **73**
(English Prince 129) [1992 6d⁴ 5g² 6m⁴ 5d³ 6m* 6m] 420Y: well-grown, rather
leggy colt: second foal: dam fourth once at 1½m: fair performer: fairly consistent
before winning maiden auction at Yarmouth in September: stiffish task in Newmarket nursery final start, and wasn't entirely discredited: worth a try over further:
yet to race on extremes of going: suitable mount for an apprentice. *J. Pearce*

RAD 2 b.g. (May 11) Valiyar 129 – Phlox 101 (Floriana 106) [1992 7d 6.1g⁵ 6m] **53**
workmanlike gelding: half-brother to several winners here and abroad, including
Indian Flower (by Mansingh), fairly useful 5f winner here later successful at up to 7f
in USA: dam won 4 times over 5f: modest maiden: will stay 7f. *S. P. C. Woods*

RADAR KNIGHT 4 b.c. Beldale Flutter (USA) 130 – Eurynome (Be My Guest **–**
(USA) 126) [1991 8f 10g 10m 12f⁶ 14d 14.1g* 13.8g⁴ 14.6m⁴ 17.2g 1992 16m⁵ 16.4m]
leggy, lengthy colt: moderate mover: rated 43 at 3 yrs: no form in August, 1992:
stays 1¾m: acts on firm going. *R. A. Bennett*

RADIO CAROLINE 4 b.g. All Systems Go 119 – Caroline Lamb 74 (Hotfoot **–**
126) [1991 8.2f 8g⁶ 9.2d 11g* 8.5f⁴ 12m³ 10f⁶ 9m² 8m 12.2g⁶ 1992 8d 8g 8g⁵ 10.8f]
close-coupled, rather sparely-made gelding: rated 56 at 2 yrs: little form in spring in
1992: probably needs further than 1m but unlikely to stay beyond 1½m: acts on firm
and dead going: effective visored or not: blinkered last 2 starts. *M. Tate*

R A EXPRESS 7 b.g. Bay Express 132 – Pinaka 69 (Pitcairn 126) [1991 5f 5g 5m⁴ **34**
6.1m 5.1m 5m 5g 1992 5s 5s 5d a5g 5g 5m 5.1d⁵ 6m⁴ 5m] good-topped gelding: has
shown signs of stringhalt: poor mover: last win came 27 starts ago at 5 yrs when
best form at 5f on a soft surface: blinkered, form in 1992 only when fourth in Ripon
apprentice handicap. *B. A. McMahon*

RAFAH 3 b.f. Dominion 123 – Lys River 119 (Lyphard (USA) 132) [1991 NR **73**
1992 8g* 7.1m² 8m 8.1g³ 7g² 7d² 8.1g 8d⁴] sturdy filly: moderate mover: seventh
foal: half-sister to 4 winners, including 2m winner Tirwadda (by Troy) and fairly
useful 1m winner My Shafy (by Rousillon): dam French middle-distance filly: fair
performer: won maiden at Warwick in May: none too consistent afterwards, good
fourth in minor event at Leicester: should prove ideally suited by 1m+: acts on good
to firm and dead ground: sold 5,800 gns Newmarket Autumn Sales. *B. Hanbury*

RAGAMUFFIN ROMEO 3 b.g. Niniski (USA) 125 – Interviewme (USA) **–**
(Olden Times) [1991 7.1d a8g³ 1992 12m] lengthy gelding: promising third in maiden
at Lingfield for C. Brittain at 2 yrs: 50/1, led 6f when beaten 15 lengths in similar
event at Newmarket in April: should stay beyond 1m. *N. C. Wright*

RAGAZZO (IRE) 2 b.g. (Apr 29) Runnett 125 – Redecorate (USA) (Hatchet Man –
(USA)) [1992 7g] IR 5,500Y: fourth foal: half-brother to a winner in USA and
plating-class 1990 2-y-o Miss Sunpuss (both by Gato Del Sol): dam won at up to 7f:
66/1, last of 18 in maiden auction at Redcar in September. *N. Tinkler*

RAGE 5 ch.g. Final Straw 127 – Nasty Niece (CAN) (Great Nephew 126) [1991 –
11.9g 1992 11.1m5 7.1d 7.1g] rangy gelding: good mover: trained by M. H. Easterby,
rated 65 at 3 yrs: blinkered, well beaten in handicaps in 1992: has joined D. Nolan. *T.
Craig*

RAGGERTY (IRE) 2 b.c. (May 20) Prince Rupert (FR) 121 – Princess Martina 46
64 (English Prince 129) [1992 a6g 6.9h 8f] IR 4,400F, IR 5,000Y, resold 5,600Y:
workmanlike colt: half-brother to 1987 2-y-o 6f and 7f winner Beamsley (by Kafu)
and winning sprinter Torius (by Petorius): dam 15.8f winner: off course 2½ months,
worthwhile form only when eleventh of 13, never in contention, in maiden at
Doncaster in September on final start: will stay 1¼m. *J. Berry*

RAGING THUNDER 2 b.g. (Feb 12) Taufan (USA) 119 – Nasty Niece (CAN) 57
(Great Nephew 126) [1992 6g 6f2 6h4 7d 6d 7m] 17,000F, 32,000Y: quite attractive
colt: half-brother to several winners, including fairly useful 1m to 1¼m winner
Penelope Strawbery (by Anfield) and 1988 2-y-o 6f winner Specialised Boy (by
Mummy's Game), useful winner at 7f to 9f in Italy in 1990: dam won over 7f at 2 yrs
in Canada: modest maiden: creditable eighth of 23, never a factor, to Law
Commission in nursery at Newmarket final start: well worth a try over 1m +: ran
poorly when blinkered penultimate outing. *G. Lewis*

RAGTIME 5 b.g. Pas de Seul 133 – Boldella (Bold Lad (IRE) 133) [1991 9s6 1992 36
17.1d2 1.6g5 16.9g] neat, strong gelding: good walker: winning (1991/2) hurdler: poor
maiden on flat: form in 1992 only when fifth at Pontefract: stays extreme distances:
not seen after May. *A. S. Reid*

RAG TIME BELLE 6 ch.m. Raga Navarro (ITY) 119 – Betbellof 65 (Averof 123) 34
[1991 NR 1992 10.3g 7m* 8g 7f 8.9s 8.1m] sparely-made mare: inconsistent
performer: led post in handicap at Redcar in April: well below that form afterwards:
should stay 1m: acts on good to firm ground: sometimes sweating: modest winning
chaser for G. Charles-Jones. *M. W. Eckley*

RAGTIME SONG 3 b.c. Dunbeath (USA) 127 – Kelowna (USA) (Master Derby –
(USA)) [1991 7m 7g 7.1s 7.6m 1992 10f] good-bodied colt: no worthwhile form. *R.
Akehurst*

RAHEENA (USA) 3 b.f. Lyphard (USA) 132 – Hard Knocker (USA) (Raja Baba 69
(USA)) [1991 NR 1992 8g3 10.5g 12.3s2 12m2 12s5 12.4v] $225,000Y: smallish,
sturdy filly: second foal: dam unraced half-sister to dam of Local Talent and Local
Suitor: fair maiden: worth a try at 1¾m: acts on good to firm and soft going, well
beaten in handicap on heavy. *J. H. M. Gosden*

RAHIF 4 b.c. Shirley Heights 130 – Vaguely 92 (Bold Lad (IRE) 133) [1991 8.1m2 64
1992 10f 11g3 8m2 8g6] well-made, lightly-raced colt: rated 85 at 3 yrs for R.
Armstrong: modest form in 1992: may well prove best at up to 1m: acts on good to
firm ground: wore crossed noseband first 2 starts, set too strong a pace final one, in
August. *Mrs M. Reveley*

RAHON (IRE) 2 ch.f. (May 7) Ahonoora 122 – Carillon Miss (USA) (The 53
Minstrel (CAN) 135) [1992 5g2 5f5 5.7g6 5g5 6v2 5v*] IR 19,000Y: neat filly: fifth
known foal: half-sister to French 3-y-o 6.5f and 1m winner Campanology (by
Ahonoora) and a winner in USA by Nishapour: dam unraced close relation of Try My
Best and El Gran Senor: modest form for P. Chapple-Hyam: stiff task, creditable
fifth of 6 in nursery at Redcar final start here: subsequently won maiden race at
Rome: will be well suited by 6f. *O. Pessi, Italy*

RAINBOW CORNER 3 b.c. Rainbow Quest (USA) 134 – Kingscote 118 **118**
(Kings Lake (USA) 133) [1991 8m* 8m2 8d2 1992 8g* 8g2 12g 9g2 9m2 10g3]
    As a three-year-old, Rainbow Corner came within a short neck of win-
ning a classic but still did not come up to expectations. As the judge's distance
suggests, that classic was in France; the Poule d'Essai des Poulains. In
Arazi's absence, Rainbow Corner looked the obvious choice. Arazi had put
him in the shade as a two-year-old, giving him a comprehensive beating into
second in the Grand Criterium but, him aside, there weren't any better
prospects around in France for 1992 and Rainbow Corner had won his
reappearance race, the Prix de Fontainebleau. The next four home in the
Fontainebleau (Highest Ody, Judge Decision, Bakari and Take Risks) all
reopposed in the Poulains and Highest Ody in particular had a chance, on

Prix de Fontainebleau, Longchamp—
Rainbow Corner wins by a neck from Highest Ody

paper at least, of reversing the form of the Fontainebleau in which Rainbow Corner had beaten him by a neck. Rainbow Corner, though, was an even-money favourite and disposed of that quartet readily, without, however, being able to contain the late burst conjured up by Shanghai. As well as defeat, Eddery suffered a four-day suspension for careless riding after he'd switched Rainbow Corner sharply left off the rails.

The jockey, quoted afterwards about Rainbow Corner's Derby prospects, said that he doubted whether he would stay beyond a mile. But the Derby was Rainbow Corner's next appearance. For us, there was little in Rainbow Corner's style of running to say that he would not stay further, and plenty in the record of his sire Rainbow Quest and his progeny to suggest that he would. His appearance at Epsom was a chance well worth taking but one could be forgiven for thinking differently when Rainbow Corner trailed in eleventh of eighteen. He tended to run in snatches and was beaten quickly in the straight, a performance we found hard to attribute solely to the trip. At the end of the season, the explanation that springs to mind most readily is, purely and simply, that he wasn't good enough. Rainbow Corner's three races after Epsom, none above Group 3 standard, all brought defeats. The first two were at nine furlongs, the third at a mile and a quarter, and they brought a change in trainer as well as trip when, after a length-and-a-half beating by Steinbeck at level weights in the Prix Daphnis at Evry, Rainbow Corner was transferred from Fabre to Cecil. When reappearing in a listed race at Newmarket nearly three months later, Rainbow Corner ran well but not well enough to get the better of the seven-year-old handicapper Mellottie. In a similar event there two weeks later, the extra furlong failed to see a reproduction of that form but, with a slow early pace, it was hardly given a chance to; Rainbow Corner took time to respond but ran on well up the hill, being beaten only a short head and a head by Lupescu and Fair Average. He will be racing in the United States as a four-year-old with R. Frankel.

Rainbow Corner (b.c. 1989)	Rainbow Quest (USA) (b 1981)	Blushing Groom (ch 1974)	Red God
			Runaway Bride
		I Will Follow (b 1975)	Where You Lead
	Kingscote (b 1983)	Kings Lake (b 1978)	Nijinsky
			Fish-Bar
		Bold Fantasy (b 1974)	Bold Lad
			Ribot's Fantasy

Rainbow Quest has quickly established himself as a pronounced influence for stamina, but the dam's side of Rainbow Corner's pedigree is, in that respect, far less convincing. His dam Kingscote wanted little for class, winning the Lowther Stakes and coming second in the Cheveley Park, but she was unable to show that she stayed any further than six furlongs, appearing only once as a three-year-old. Her dam Bold Fantasy was lightly raced as well but had a much better run at three years, coming second in the Irish One Thousand Guineas and Cork and Orrery Stakes. *H. R. A. Cecil*

RAINBOW FLEET 4 b.f. Nomination 125 – Olderfleet 59 (Steel Heart 128) **61**
[1991 5s 5g 5.3f⁴ 7m 6.9m 6m⁵ 1992 6g² 6m* 6g 6d⁶ 6m* 6.1d] strong, workman-like filly: modest performer: won handicaps at Goodwood in June and Yarmouth (gamely) in September: modest run in ladies race final start: stays 6f: acts on firm and dead going. *D. Marks*

RAINBOW STRIPES 5 ch.g. Rainbow Quest (USA) 134 – Pampas Miss (USA) –
(Pronto) [1991 15.8g 1992 18m 15.1d] big gelding: rated 60 at 3 yrs: seems of little account these days. *B. S. Rothwell*

RAIN BROTHER (USA) 2 b.c. (May 23) Lear Fan (USA) 130 – Ritualism **106**
(USA) (Exclusive Native (USA)) [1992 7g³ 6d* 6g* 6d* 8v⁶] rather sparely-made colt: seventh foal: half-brother to 4 winners in USA, 2 of them minor stakes placed: dam unraced half-sister to Grade 1 winner Acaroid: progressed into a useful performer: successful in maiden at Goodwood and minor event at Folkestone in September: looking really well, won 9-runner listed race at York following month by ¾ length from Mithl Al Hawa, making all, initially at modest pace, and running on well from 2f out: ran moderately in Gran Criterium at Milan 15 days later: should prove as effective at 1m as 6f: acts on dead going, yet to race on top-of-the-ground. *P. W. Chapple-Hyam*

RAIN-N-SUN 6 gr.g. Warpath 113 – Sun Noddy (Tom Noddy 104) [1991 NR 1992 –
a16g] lengthy, angular, plain gelding: well beaten on flat: visored only start at 4 yrs: won novice claiming hurdle in October. *J. L. Harris*

RAIN RIDER 3 b.c. Fools Holme (USA) – Moon Parade 73 (Welsh Pageant 132) **111**
[1991 8g 1992 10d² 14.1m* 14f* 14.8g* 14d* 14.6m] tall, lengthy, useful-looking colt with plenty of scope: did well physically: long-striding, and fluent mover: smart performer: successful in summer in small fields in maiden at Yarmouth, minor event at Salisbury, then listed races at Newmarket (received 5 lb, caught Bonny Scot close home to win by ½ length) and, after 7-week break, Goodwood, where joined issue with Allegan (who received 4 lb) 2f out and won by a head: looking very well, soon

March Stakes, Goodwood—Rain Rider (No. 1) gives 4 lb to Allegan

Mrs E. M. H. Ogden White's "Rain Rider"

under pressure in straight in St Leger at Doncaster 2 weeks later, but found little
and eased to finish last of 7: suited by test of stamina: acts on firm and dead ground:
sold to race in Saudi Arabia. *J. L. Dunlop*

RAINRIDGE   3 b.c. Rainbow Quest (USA) 134 – Beveridge (USA) 86 (Spectac-   **86**
ular Bid (USA)) [1991 8m⁴ 8.1d² 1992 10m 10.5d⁵ 10f* 11.5m* 11.5g³] well-made,
good-quartered colt: good mover: fairly useful form: set pace when winning maiden
at Brighton in May and 3-runner minor event at Lingfield in June: off course 3
months and stiff task, last of 3 in similar contest there: stays 11.5f: best efforts on
top-of-the-ground, ran promisingly on dead final start at 2 yrs: blinkered second
3-y-o start, visored afterwards: carries head high: tends to sweat and get on edge:
sold only 1,300 gns Newmarket Autumn Sales. *J. L. Dunlop*

RAIN SPLASH   2 gr.f. (Feb 16) Petong 126 – Bargouzine 67 (Hotfoot 126) [1992   **74**
5d⁴ 5g* 6m 6g⁴ 6g⁴ 6m² 6d⁵ 7m] 8,400Y: leggy, sparely-made filly: has a quick
action: fourth foal: half-sister to ungenuine D'Yquem (by Formidable): dam, stayed
1m, is half-sister to useful sprinter As Friendly: fair performer: won maiden at
Newmarket in May: rather inconsistent afterwards: should stay 7f: acts on top-of-
the-ground and dead: sold 6,500 gns Newmarket Autumn Sales. *R. Hannon*

RAITH PC   3 ch.g. Aragon 118 – All Fine (Fine Blade (USA) 121) [1991 7d 1992   **–**
12.2g] big, close-coupled gelding: off course over a year, behind in maiden at
Catterick (headstrong) in August. *G. Richards*

RAJAI (IRE)   3 br.c. Last Tycoon 131 – Flame of Tara 124 (Artaius (USA) 129)   **83** §
[1991 8.2m² 1992 8d⁵ 10d² 12g⁴ 12.1m* 13.1m³ 14.6g* 12d⁵ 11.9s⁴ 10s⁵] tall,
attractive colt: fair walker: fair form: consistent, and won a maiden at Chepstow
and a handicap at Wolverhampton in midsummer, but twice looked wayward,
repeatedly hanging in behind leaders on fifth start, finding little under pressure on
seventh: stays 14.6f well: acts on good to firm and soft ground: blinkered last 6
starts, running poorly for amateur final one: exported to race in Dubai. *J. L. Dunlop*

RAJANPOUR (USA) 7 ch.h. Riverman (USA) 131 – Rajpoura 118 (Kashmir II **35** §
125) [1991 14d 18d* 16.5m 16.2g* 16m* 20g 16.5m 1992 18g 16.2m 14.8g 15.8d a16g3
a16g] angular, sturdy horse: carries condition: poor mover: thoroughly unreliable
handicapper: stays long distances: acts on good to firm going: effective blinkered or
not. *R. Curtis*

RAJAYA (USA) 4 b.c. Nureyev (USA) 131 – Don't Sulk (USA) 115 (Graustark) –
[1991 10m4 10d3 12.5m 11m 1992 a11g4 a14g] sturdy, quite attractive colt: rated 55 at
3 yrs for A. Scott: blinkered, well beaten at Southwell in January: stayed 1¼m: acted
on good to firm and dead ground: dead. *R. O'Leary*

RAKIS (IRE) 2 b. or br.c. (May 12) Alzao (USA) 117 – Bristle 96 (Thatch (USA) **90**
136) [1992 7g 6s5 7.1s* 8g3] 46,000Y: third foal: half-brother to 3-y-o Big Leap (by
Auction Ring), successful from 6f (at 2 yrs) to 1m: dam Irish 2-y-o 8.5f winner stayed
1½m: progressive form: won maiden at Chepstow in October by 6 lengths, making
all: best effort when third in minor event at Newmarket 10 days later, rallying well:
will stay 1¼m: yet to race on top-of-the-ground. *C. J. Benstead*

RAMAAS (USA) 3 b.c. Danzig (USA) – Milliardare (USA) (Alydar (USA)) [1991 –
6d 1992 7g] sturdy colt: appeared in Racehorses of 1991 under the name Shaam
(USA): no worthwhile form in maidens. *A. A. Scott*

RAMBLE (USA) 5 ch.m. Highland Park (USA) – Hill Pleasure (USA) (What A **37**
Pleasure (USA)) [1991 12s5 12s 9g6 16g 12d3 13v 1992 a12g5 a12g6 11.9g3 11.9m]
sister to 2 winners in USA and half-sister to a stakes-placed winner by Doonesbury:
dam French 3-y-o 7f winner: placed 4 times (from 11f to 15.5f) from 12 outings in
France: sold out of A. Fabre's stable 4,600 gns Newmarket December (1991) Sales:
competed here in the spring, form only when third in claimer at Brighton: stays
15.5f: acts on good to firm and dead ground. *J. A. B. Old*

RAMBO'S HALL 7 b.g. Crofthall 110 – Murton Crags 81 (No Argument **110**
107) [1991 NR 1992 10.5g2 6m5 10.5d* 10.5s* 8d* 9d* 8g4]
  Rambo's Hall crowned a magnificent come-back with a second impressive success in the William Hill Cambridgeshire at Newmarket, joining
Hackler's Pride, Christmas Daisy, Sterope, Prince de Galles and Baronet as
dual winners of the race since its inception in 1839. Rambo's Hall was a really
progressive four-year-old who, after winning the Cambridgeshire by six
lengths and finishing second in a listed race, was sold for 100,000 dollars to
race in the States. However, he did not take to it at all and after a 1990 season
which amounted to one third-place finish from four starts he was bought back
for only a quarter of that sum. A bad case of warts then delayed his return to
this country, and a damaged tendon prevented him from appearing on a
racecourse during 1991. When Rambo's Hall did return to the track it appeared
as if connections didn't believe him capable of recapturing all his old ability,
because he was competing in claimers. However, the quite valuable Juddmonte series had been targeted and after a promising reappearance and a
sharpener over an inadequate trip, he returned to the winner's enclosure with
an easy success at Haydock in August. A month later he won the £11,000 final
at the same course, though he didn't find so much as seemed likely after
hitting the front and, in the end, held on by a length from Light Hand. A bit of
comic opera followed. Jockey Nicholls dismounted shortly after the post
saying he feared the horse was lame. The stewards initially didn't believe him,
and handed out a fine of £75 on the grounds he was trying to avert potential
claims, but later they changed their minds after hearing the result of a
veterinary examination. Trainer Glover, meanwhile, went to post a friendly
claim of £25,000, but mistakenly put a congratulatory letter from the sponsors
into the box instead of his bid, an oversight which, when no other claims were
received, saved connections around £6,000 in deductions! Rambo's Hall had
much more to do in the Hoover Handicap at Ascot later in September, but
showed no ill effects from Haydock, quickening away from Croft Valley with
the remaining eleven runners strung out behind, and on the strength of that
victory he looked the pick of the weights for the Cambridgeshire. After
overnight rain had softened the ground appreciably, he was sent off the 9/2
favourite in a typically competitive thirty-strong field. Confidently ridden, he
quickened to lead over a furlong out and the result was never in doubt;
galloping on really strongly he beat Montpelier Boy by two and a half lengths,
giving his trainer a third winner in the race from as many starters, for Glover

Hoover Handicap, Ascot—Rambo's Hall comes bang into Cambridgeshire reckoning; Croft Valley (centre) and Marine Diver chase him home

had also saddled Balthus in 1987. As in 1989, Rambo's Hall went on from the Cambridgeshire to show improvement in defeat back at Newmarket, on this occasion when battling on, just over a length behind Cambrian, under top weight in the valuable Ladbroke Autumn Handicap.

Rambo's Hall (b.g. 1985)	Crofthall (ch 1977)	Native Bazaar (ch 1968)	Indigenous
			Fair Exchange
		Woodland Promise (b 1972)	Philemon
			Sister Willow
	Murton Crags (b 1969)	No Argument (b 1960)	Narrator
			Persuader
		Platter (b 1963)	Hornbeam
			Legal Fare

Rambo's Hall is hardly bred in the purple and is comfortably the best of Murton Crags's offspring, though she did also throw three winning fillies including the fairly useful Dragonlea (by Dragonara Palace) who beat Teleprompter a short head in the Andy Capp Handicap before herself producing three minor winners in the States. Murton Crags, whose dam never ran, was a fairly consistent handicapper in the mid-'seventies winning seven times over

William Hill Cambridgeshire Handicap, Newmarket—
Rambo's Hall wins for a second time, justifying heavy support by two and a half lengths; then come Montpelier Boy (rails), Double Entendre, Dawaahi, Cru Exceptionnel, Revif, Barford Lad and Mellottie

middle distances. Although Rambo's Hall's best effort was at a mile, he'll be just as effective back at nine furlongs and a mile and a quarter. Depending on the ground and the handicapper's view of him next autumn, he should give a good account in his bid to become the first horse to win the Cambridgeshire three times. Rambo's Hall was effective on good to firm ground in his younger years, but all of his best form has been with some give and he is very effective on a soft surface. Game and genuine, he's a credit to his trainer. *J. A. Glover*

RAMI (USA) 5 br.h. Riverman (USA) 131 – Ancient Regime (USA) 123 (Olden **109** Times) [1991 7g* 6m3 8g2 7g 7.3f3 7m 7g5 1992 7g* 8m3 7.3d4 7s6] leggy, close-coupled, quite attractive horse: has a quick action: useful performer: trained here as 4-y-o by P. Walwyn: won Group 3 event at Tipperary at 5 yrs: ran well in frame in Group 2 race at the Curragh (2 lengths third to Sikeston) and Hungerford Stakes at Newbury later in the summer: well below form in listed event at the Curragh in September: effective at 7f and 1m: acts on firm and dead ground: ran respectably when visored final start at 4 yrs, blinkered at 5 yrs. *D. K. Weld, Ireland*

RAMIYA 2 b.f. (Mar 30) Dancing Brave (USA) 140 – Nouvelle Star (AUS) (Luskin **69** p Star (AUS)) [1992 7g5] fourth foal: half-sister to 7f winner Sariah (by Kris): dam won from 5f to 8.2f in Australia and was champion older filly at 4 yrs: 10/1, 5 lengths fifth of 24 to Fayfa in maiden at Newmarket in October, travelling smoothly halfway, eased once beaten: will improve. *Major W. R. Hern*

RAMPAL (IRE) 3 b.g. Dancing Brave (USA) 140 – Zinzara (USA) 119 (Stage **63** Door Johnny) [1991 NR 1992 15.8m4 11.5d 10d3 10g5 9.7v6] lengthy, angular gelding: fourth foal: half-brother to useful 1½m winner Zinsky and very useful 4-y-o stayer Romany Rye (both by Nijinsky): dam 6f and 1¼m winner: modest maiden: will be well suited by return to 1½m+: visored (tailed off, hanging left throughout) on debut: sold to join D. Wintle 8,000 gns Newmarket Autumn Sales. *G. Wragg*

RANCHO MIRAGE 5 ch.g. Superlative 118 – Que Sera 91 (Music Boy 124) – [1991 5g 6m 6m2 6g5 6v 6m3 6m a6g a6g5 a6g 1992 a5g a8g] robust, sprint type: one-time fair handicapper: has lost his form: sold only 950 gns Doncaster January Sales. *Mrs N. Macauley*

RANDAMA 5 b.m. Akarad (FR) 130 – Ramanouche (FR) 122 (Riverman (USA) – 131) [1991 NR 1992 a14g] unfurnished mare: rated 77 at 3 yrs for M. Stoute: tailed off in Southwell handicap on New Year's Day: should stay well: acts on good to firm ground: won selling handicap hurdle (finished lame) in May: has joined P. Rich. *D. J. Wintle*

RANDYBAY 7 b.g. Bay Express 132 – Kiara (Great Nephew 126) [1991 NR 1992 – 8m 10g 12.2g] angular, workmanlike gelding: moderate mover: sixth foal: dam of little account: seems of little account. *J. Mackie*

RANEEN ALWATAR 2 b.f. (Mar 12) Sadler's Wells (USA) 132 – Samya's **60** p Flame 97 (Artaius (USA) 129) [1992 7g] attractive filly: first foal: dam 9f and 1¼m winner, is sister to Flame of Tara (herself dam of Salsabil, by Sadler's Wells, and Marju) and half-sister to the dam of Kneller and Great Marquess: 16/1, around 7 lengths fourteenth of 24 to Fayfa in maiden at Newmarket in October, racing freely until fading from 2f out: will improve. *L. M. Cumani*

RANGER (FR) 2 b.c. (Feb 6) Un Desperado (FR) 125 – Reine Caroline (FR) 117 **111** (Pharly (FR) 130) [1992 7g* 7d* 7s6 9d3 10s4 8v3] 90,000 francs (approx £9,000) Y: half-brother to French sprint winner Rubini (by Nikos): dam French sprinting 2-y-o: successful in newcomers race at Saint-Cloud in July and listed event at Deauville in August: very useful form last 3 starts, placed in Prix de Conde at Longchamp, Criterium de Saint-Cloud and Prix des Chenes (over a length third to Dancienne) at Evry: stays 1¼m: has raced only on an easy surface. *P. H. Demercastel, France*

RANGE RIDER (IRE) 2 b.c. (Mar 21) Bold Arrangement 111 – Top Fille (FR) **71** (Top Ville 129) [1992 7f6 7.1d5 8.1s 7d2 6g 7g 6.1v3 7g 9v5] strong, good-topped colt: has scope: moderate walker: second foal: half-brother to German 3-y-o 8.5f winner Top Lake (by Kings Lake): dam French 9f winner: fair form in varied events: best of last 5 runs when around 7 lengths last of 5 in listed race at Evry in November: needs further than 6f (even on heavy ground) and is bred to be well suited by 1¼m: best efforts on a soft surface: below best when twice tried in blinkers. *C. E. Brittain*

RANUNCULUS 2 ch.g. (Mar 5) Music Boy 124 – Preziosa 74 (Homing 130) **60** p [1992 7g 8s 6d] close-coupled, good-bodied gelding: carries condition: first foal: dam 1½m winner: progressive form: took strong hold first 2 starts: should prove as effective at 7f/1m as shorter: may well improve further. *J. Berry*

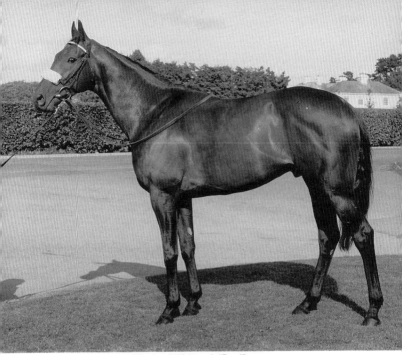

Hamdan Al-Maktoum's "Rami"

RAPID LAD 14 b.g. Rapid River 127 – Seacona (Espresso 122) [1991 10d 10.8m **29** 10f6 10m2 9.9g 9.9f3 1992 10d 10.8d 9.9m 10m3 10f4 10f6] compact gelding: good mover: tough and grand old handicapper, rated 75 in his heyday: won 14 of his 122 starts, the last 12 successes all at Beverley where he has a race named in his honour: best at 1¼m: needed top-of-the-ground: had worn blinkers, but not for long time: held up and best in strongly-run race: was particularly well handled by D. Nicholls: has been retired. *J. L. Spearing*

RAPID MOVER 5 ch.g. Final Straw 127 – Larive 80 (Blakeney 126) [1991 9s 8.3f **32** 15.1g 1992 8.3f4 8.1m6 8.1f 12.1m3 12.1m] workmanlike gelding: poor handicapper, and still a maiden: stays 1½m: acts on good to firm ground: tried visored/blinkered: has joined D. Nolan. *T. Craig*

RAPID REPEAT (IRE) 2 b.f. (Mar 4) Exactly Sharp (USA) 121 – Silver Echo **70** p (Caerleon (USA) 132) [1992 6g4 7d*] IR 27,000Y: leggy, attractive filly: fluent mover: first foal: dam unraced half-sister to Irish 2000 Guineas third Prince Echo: off course 3 months but favourite, won 17-runner maiden at Leicester in October by 2½ lengths from Ikhtisas, chasing leaders, leading over 1f out and running on strongly: will be at least as effective at 1m: will improve. *Mrs J. Cecil*

RAPID ROSIE 4 ch.f. Noalto 120 – Cora 53 (Current Coin 118) [1991 8m 8g 7g **–** 10.1d 8.3g 8.1g 8.1s6 8.3m 10m 1992 10g 9.7d 8.3m 10d 11.9g 9.7g a10g] plain, sparely-made filly: of little account: tried visored. *D. R. Laing*

RAPID SUCCESS (USA) 2 ch.c. (Mar 23) Sort (USA) – Golden Rhyme 87 **82** (Dom Racine (FR) 121) [1992 6g* 7d3 8.1g6] $23,500Y: rangy, rather angular colt: good walker: fourth living foal: closely related to 3-y-o Seattle Rhyme (by Seattle

Dancer), very smart 6f and 1m winner at 2 yrs, and half-brother to 7f to 1m winner Malhamdale (by Dixieland Band): dam 7f winner: sire (by Nijinsky) unraced close relative of Nureyev: fair form: won maiden at Ascot in July in good style: failed to progress as anticipated, finding little off bridle both starts in fairly useful company. *D. R. C. Elsworth*

RAPPORTEUR (USA) 6 b.g. His Majesty (USA) – Sweet Rapport (USA) **69** (Round Table) [1991 a12g² a10g* a10g* 10g 10m 10.1f 10d⁴ 10g 11.7m⁴ 10s⁵ 9f⁶ **a88** 11.5g* 10m* a10g³ a12g a10g² a10g² 1992 a10g* a12g* a10g³ a10g² 11.5g 12d⁴ 10s 12g³ 9.7v² a10g a12g a10g] leggy, angular gelding: largely consistent handicapper: successful on 13 occasions at Lingfield (10 times on equitrack), including early in the year, and hasn't won elsewhere: effective from 1¼m to 1½m: easily best form on equitrack: often bandaged: has won for apprentice: goes very well for W. Newnes: tough and genuine. *C. C. Elsey*

RAP UP FAST (USA) 3 b.g. Eskimo (USA) – Naomi's Flash (USA) (Ray Jeter – (USA)) [1991 6m 7m 8.1m 1992 9.2d 11g 10s 12.2g] leggy, lengthy gelding: no form in handicaps in 1992: stays 8.1f: well-beaten third in claiming hurdle (claimed to join N. Waggott £2,700) in September. *C. W. Thornton*

RARE DETAIL (IRE) 4 ch.f. Commanche Run 133 – Sharp Dresser (USA) **74** (Sharpen Up 127) [1991 12v* 11.7g² 12g* 12d⁴ 11.8g² 12.1s⁶ 11.8m³ 10.3d 1992 12d² 12.5g⁶ 12g⁴ 11.8d 12d⁵ 12g 16d⁴] leggy, lengthy filly: moderate mover: inconsistent handicapper, trained first 5 starts by Mrs L. Piggott: should stay beyond 1½m: acts on good to firm and heavy going and on equitrack: sold to join M. McMillan 5,600 gns Newmarket Autumn Sales. *D. R. C. Elsworth*

RARE OCCURANCE 2 b.c. (May 7) Damister (USA) 123 – Superior Quality 67 – (Star Appeal 133) [1992 7g 7m 8s] 1,000F, 3,800 2-y-o: big, lengthy, workmanlike colt: has scope: half-brother to a winner in Belgium: dam unraced: no worthwhile form in maidens. *M. J. Charles*

RARFY'S DREAM 4 b.c. Dreams To Reality (USA) 113 – Elbandary (Shirley – Heights 130) [1991 6f⁵ 8.3d⁵ 6s 7.1s 8f⁵ 7f 10m 1992 a10g 10d 11.8g⁶ 10m] sturdy colt: seems of little account on flat these days: winning hurdler (on both all-weather tracks) in 1991/2. *J. E. Banks*

RASAN 5 ch.h. Dominion 123 – Raffle 82 (Balidar 133) [1991 7g 7g⁵ 7.6m 7.9g – 7.6m² 1992 7g⁴] good-bodied horse: carries condition: moderate mover: rated 94 in 1991 when second at Lingfield: bit backward, weakened quickly 2f out when fourth in minor event there in May, 1992: stays 7.6f: goes well on firm going: sold 4,000 gns Newmarket December Sales. *R. W. Armstrong*

RASCO 3 gr.g. Natroun (FR) 128 – Kabylia (FR) (Dancer's Image (USA)) [1991 8m – 6.1m 7m² 7g 7d 1992 10g 8f 7m 8f] leggy, lengthy gelding: no worthwhile form in 1992, in a visor third start: sold 1,250 gns Doncaster June Sales. *J. Etherington*

RASHITA 5 b.m. Alzao (USA) 117 – Apapa Port 80 (My Swanee 122) [1991 11.5g – 10.2g 1992 10.1g⁶ 14.9g 14.1f] lengthy mare: seems of little account these days. *G. H. Eden*

RAVECINO 3 ch.f. Ballacashtal (CAN) – Lemelasor 75 (Town Crier 119) [1991 **33** 5f⁵ 5m* 5m⁵ 6m 6f 6f 7m 7.1m 1992 7.1m 6.9h³ 7.1m⁵ 6f 7.1d 6.9g] rather plain filly: inconsistent plater: better at 7f than shorter: acts on hard ground: apprentice ridden in 1992. *J. S. Haldane*

RAVEN RUNNER (USA) 3 b.f. Storm Bird (CAN) 134 – Simple Taste (USA) **79** 93 (Sharpen Up 127) [1991 7g² 7d³ 1992 8m⁵ 7g⁴ 6m* 8g* 8.5f 8.5g³] lengthy, angular filly: split pastern at 2 yrs: fair form: 6/5 on, easily best effort for I. Balding in 1992 when winning maiden at Lingfield in June by 7 lengths, making all: sent to USA and won allowance race at Belmont in July: stays 1m: acts on good to firm and dead ground. *R. O'Connell, USA*

RAWAAN (FR) 5 b.g. Labus (FR) – Rose Ness (Charlottesville 135) [1991 13.8f – 1992 10.1s] tall ex-French gelding: won maiden at Bordeaux at 3 yrs when trained by A. de Royer-Dupre: well beaten on flat here, when burly in March: probably stays 1¾m: fair winning hurdler, including in May, runner-up but finishing lame later same month. *N. Tinkler*

RAW HEALTH 2 b.c. (Mar 24) Sizzling Melody 117 – Upholder (Young – Generation 129) [1992 5m] 2,400F, 1,500Y: lengthy colt: second foal: dam ran 3 times: 10/1, always behind and not knocked about in 14-runner maiden at Windsor in April: sold 500 gns Ascot November Sales. *M. J. Heaton-Ellis*

RAYS MEAD 4 gr.f. Tremblant 112 – Free Range 78 (Birdbrook 110) [1991 5m⁶ **51** 5.1m³ 6g⁵ 5.3f⁴ 5m² 6.1m⁵ 5.3g² 1992 5d 5.3m 5m⁵ 5g 5m* 5f³ 5m² 5g³ 5m⁴ 5.3d] leggy filly: modest performer: won (for first time) handicap at Warwick in June: held her form well afterwards until, after 7-week break, final start: seems best at 5f: acts on firm going. *L. J. Holt*

RAZAROO (USA)   2 b.g. (Apr 27) Buckaroo (USA) – Mislop (USA) (Our Hero   **66** (USA)) [1992 5f⁵ 6g³ 7g⁴ 7.9d 7s] $25,000Y, resold $16,500Y, resold 10,000Y: good-topped, useful-looking gelding: carries condition: brother to a winner in USA at up to 9f in 1991 and half-brother to 2 winners in Peru: dam half-sister to Spend A Buck (by Buckaroo): sire high-class 1m and 9f stakes winner: fair performer: won median auction maiden at Beverley in May: ran creditably in frame in minor events, and when visored in a nursery final start: should stay 1m: probably acts on any going: tends to get edgy: has been gelded. *J. Etherington*

REACH FOR GLORY   3 b.g. Reach 122 – Carlton Glory (Blakeney 126) [1991   **60** 5f⁵ 5g⁴ 6d⁵ 7.5f⁴ 7.5f⁴ 7m³ 7.5f³ 8.3g⁶ 10.5d 1992 8s 12.3s 10f² 12f² 11.1m* 12h⁵ 12f³ 10.9s² 10s 12s 12.2d 14.1s⁵ a14g⁴ a12g] small gelding: modest performer: won handicap at Edinburgh in June: ran moderately last 4 starts: stays 1½m: acts on any going: tried visored once at 2 yrs: has run in snatches, and tends to hang right. *R. M. Whitaker*

REACH FORWARD   3 b.f. Reach 122 – Good Woman 60 (Good Times (ITY))   **–** [1991 5g⁴ 5m 5m⁵ 6.1s⁶ 6g⁵ a7g 1992 5.1d 5.1m] smallish, leggy filly: rated 41 at 2 yrs: no form in sellers in the spring: best form at 5f: sometimes sweating and edgy. *R. J. Holder*

REACH ME NOT (IRE)   3 ch.f. Reach 122 – Injaz (Golden Act (USA)) [1991 a8g   **–** 1992 a6g⁶ a8g⁵] well beaten in early-season maidens at Lingfield: has joined Mrs N. Sharpe. *C. Holmes*

READY TO DRAW (IRE)   3 ch.c. On Your Mark 125 – Mitsubishi Art (Cure   **62** The Blues (USA)) [1991 5d⁶ 5g³ 5m⁵ 6m* 6g² 6d⁴ 6.9m⁴ a6g⁴ a6g⁵ 7f 8m a6g⁵ 1992 a7g² a7g⁵ a7g² 8.9v² 8v² 10d* 12g² 11g⁵ 9.2s⁴ 10.9s³ 11.1s⁵ 10.5s* 11d] sparely-made, angular colt: bad mover: useful plater: no bid when successful at Ripon (edgy, ridden by 7-lb claimer) in April and Haydock in October: effective from 9f to 1½m: best turf efforts on an easy surface, also acts on fibresand. *Ronald Thompson*

REALITIES (USA)   2 ch.c. (Apr 23) Cozzene (USA) – Alquizar (USA) (Star de   **94** Naskra (USA)) [1992 5g* 6g* 5m⁵ 6g² 5g⁵] $11,000F, $40,000Y: strong, good-quartered, workmanlike colt: fluent mover: third foal: dam won at up to 7f in North America: sire high-class 1m/9f performer, improved with age: useful performer: won maiden at Sandown in July and 4-runner minor event (not finding much off bridle) at Windsor in August: sweated up then got very upset in stalls prior to running moderately at York third outing: ran well when second in minor event at Folkestone and staying-on fifth to Up And At 'Em in Cornwallis Stakes at Ascot: ideally needs further than 5f, and is worth a try at 7f. *G. Harwood*

REALLY HONEST   11 b.g. He Loves Me 120 – Whitethorn (Gulf Pearl 117)   **–** [1991 NR 1992 8m] tall gelding: good mover: fair front-running handicapper at 5 yrs: bandaged on first run on flat since 1987 (modest hurdler in 1991/2), always behind, not knocked about, in Pontefract claimer in May: blinkered (pulled hard) once. *M. W. Easterby*

REAL STUNNER   5 ch.m. Chief Singer 131 – Real Party 68 (Realm 129) [1991   **69** a5g 5d⁴ 5m⁴ 5g 5g² 5g* 5d⁵ 6g 5m⁵ 5f² 5f² 5.6m 6m 5d⁴ 1992 5d⁵ 5m⁵ 5m⁴ 5f⁴ 5f³ 6f⁵ 5f² 6g⁴] big, strong, close-coupled mare: moderate mover: fair handicapper: had generally been running creditably until finishing poor last of 4 at Catterick in July: effective at 5f and 6f: acts on firm and dead ground: below form when visored once earlier in career. *M. P. Naughton*

REASONS FOR LOVE (IRE)   2 ch.f. (Apr 3) Common Grounds 118 – Fodens   **71** Eve 80 (Dike (USA)) [1992 5d³ 5.9g³ 7s⁴ 7s 7d 8g*] 15,500Y: smallish, close-coupled filly: has a roundish action: half-sister to several winners, including 5-y-o (at 5f to 7.1f) Night Jar (by Night Shift) and (at 1m) Lopski (by Niniski): dam 2-y-o 5f winner: fair performer: much improved effort when winning 20-runner selling nursery (no bid) at Doncaster in October, leading over 3f out, soon clear and running on well: suited by 1m: best form on a sound surface: sold 6,400 gns Doncaster November Sales, reportedly to Czechoslovakia. *J. J. O'Neill*

REBEL CALL   3 b.g. Never So Bold 135 – Supper Time 71 (Shantung 132) [1991   **90** § NR 1992 7g² 8d² 10g² 10.4m⁵ 10.1g⁵ 10f⁶] 33,000F, IR 130,000Y: tall, good-bodied gelding: half-brother to several winners, including smart middle-distance stayer Rakaposhi King (by Bustino): dam lightly-raced 1½m winner: capable of fairly useful form, but is unreliable: soon pushed along when second in newcomers race at

Doncaster, maiden at Newbury and minor event at Newmarket: ran moderately afterwards, taking little interest and carrying head high fifth start and not seen out after June: should stay 1½m: sold 12,000 gns Newmarket Autumn Sales. *R. Hannon*

RECEPTIONIST 3 b.f. Reference Point 139 – Ever Genial 117 (Brigadier **84** Gerard 144) [1991 a8g2 1992 a12g3 12.5f2 11.8g3 14.1f* 16d* 16.2s3 18.2m* 16m] good-bodied filly: moderate mover: progressed into a fairly useful performer: won maiden at Yarmouth in July then handicaps, leading over 1f out, at Newbury in August and Yarmouth in September: first moderate run when tailed off at Newmarket: suited by test of stamina: probably acts on firm and dead ground. *H. R. A. Cecil*

RECIPDICO MIST (IRE) 2 ch.f. (Apr 24) Digamist (USA) 110 – Repicado – Rose (USA) (Repicado (CHI)) [1992 5g6 6f5 6m 6s 6v] 6,000F, 3,000Y: sparely-made filly: seventh foal: half-sister to several winners, including 5-y-o 7f to 1¼m winner Halston Prince (by Petorius): dam placed in USA: no worthwhile form in maidens and a nursery: blinkered final start: sold 525 gns Ascot November Sales. *T. J. Naughton*

RECIT D'ARGENT 2 b.c. (May 7) Legend of France (USA) 124 – Shiny Penny **47** 70 (Glint of Gold 128) [1992 5m 5m 6m 5.7d5] 400Y: angular, sparely-made colt: first foal: dam, maiden, probably stayed 1¾m: plating-class maiden: best effort final start: will be suited by middle distances: acts on dead ground. *C. James*

RECORDING CONTRACT 4 b.g. Song 132 – Port Na Blath (On Your Mark – 125) [1991 8m 7m4 6d 7.5g6 9s6 10g 1992 10v 8v] ex-Irish gelding: first foal: dam won over 6f from 2 starts on flat in Ireland: maiden handicapper (rated 74 at 3 yrs, well below form in 1992), with B. Kelly in Ireland until before final start: won selling hurdle (sold 5,000 gns, probably to Scandinavia) in December. *J. Parkes*

RECORD LOVER (IRE) 2 b.c. (Apr 29) Alzao (USA) 117 – Spun Gold 106 **56** (Thatch (USA) 136) [1992 6s4 7s] IR 34,000Y: leggy colt: second foal: half-brother to 3-y-o Great Oration (by Simply Great): dam 7f (at 2 yrs) and 12.2f winner: modest form in maidens at Lingfield in October: should stay middle distances: has joined Lord Huntingdon. *J. H. M. Gosden*

RED ADMIRAL 2 ch.g. (Feb 10) Formidable (USA) 125 – Dancing Meg (USA) **48** 113 (Marshua's Dancer (USA)) [1992 6g 6g a6g3 a6g5] 20,000Y: heavy-topped, workmanlike gelding: half-brother to 2 winners, including useful 6f performer Flower Girl (by Pharly), later successful in USA: dam won at 6f and 1m at 2 yrs and later stayed 1½m: poor maiden: will stay 7f: acts on all-weather surfaces. *P. C. Haslam*

RED AND GOLD (NZ) 9 ch.g. Redolent II (AUS) – Lady Hamilton (NZ) (The – Admiral 114) [1991 NR 1992 a8g] New Zealand-bred gelding: 100/1, tailed-off last of 14 in claimer at Southwell in February. *Mrs S. Oliver*

RED ARCHER 3 ro.g. Gorytus (USA) 132 – Carose (Caro 133) [1991 a7g6 1992 **69** § 8g 7g4 8g3 7.1f2 8h5] lengthy, rather unfurnished gelding: fair form when neck second of 5 in maiden at Sandown in June, but found little after leading on bridle 1½f out: should stay 1m: acts on firm going: blinkered (sweating and on toes) last 3 starts: sold 2,800 gns Newmarket Autumn Sales: not one to trust. *P. J. Makin*

RED BALLET 2 gr.f. (Mar 10) Siberian Express (USA) 125 – Kabylia (FR) **52** (Dancer's Image (USA)) [1992 6m4 6.1m 6g 7g* 6f2 5g 6s 6m a8g] 3,500Y: leggy, unfurnished filly: half-sister to 3-y-o Rasco (by Natroun) and half-sister to several winners here and abroad, including 6f (at 2 yrs) and 1m winner Schhh You-Know-Who (by Longleat): dam, useful French sprinting 2-y-o, is sister to Godswalk: inconsistent performer: made all in seller (no bid) at Yarmouth in July: best effort when second in similar event there, caught post having been long way clear: ran poorly afterwards: best form at 6f: acts on firm ground: blinkered last 6 outings: active sort. *Mrs N. Macauley*

RED BISHOP (USA) 4 b. or br.c. Silver Hawk (USA) 123 – La Rouquine (Silly **118** Season 127) [1991 10.5g* 10d* 12g5 1992 10d* 10g2 11.1g2 12s2 12s2 10v] well-made colt: smart performer: successful in listed race at Kempton in April: second in pattern races in Britain at Sandown (bandaged near-hind, subsequently off course 4½ months after finishing 1½ lengths behind Dear Doctor), Kempton (went down by 3½ lengths to Jeune) and Ascot where soon pushed along and tended to hang before improving to have every chance 1½f out behind Opera House (beaten 1½ lengths) in Cumberland Lodge Stakes: again beaten 1½ lengths, by Silvernesian, in Group 1 Gran Premio del Jockey Club at Milan in October: stays 1½m: acts on soft going, yet to race on top-of-the-ground: well beaten when tried in blinkers in Group 1 race at Rome final start. *J. H. M. Gosden*

RED BOMBER   4 b.c. Law Society (USA) 130 – Elodie (USA) (Shecky Greene   –
(USA)) [1991 a12g 1992 a10g a10g] second foal: brother to winning hurdler Isabeau:
dam 11f and 1½m winner: no worthwhile form at Lingfield in February. *K. O.
Cunningham-Brown*

RED CENT   2 b.c. (Mar 23) Jalmood (USA) 126 – String of Beads 63 (Ile de   58 §
Bourbon (USA) 133) [1992 7.5d² 7.5m 7g² 8m⁵ 7m 8.2d 10.5d] good-topped colt:
third foal: half-brother to 3-y-o 11f to 1½m winner Salu (by Ardross): dam (of doubtful temperament) stayed 2m, is half-sister to very smart 1983 2-y-o Creag-An-Sgor:
modest form on his day: ran creditably in nursery fourth start, moderately in similar
events (including when blinkered) afterwards: sold 5,200 gns Doncaster November
Sales: stays 1m: races keenly: has carried head awkwardly, probably isn't genuine. *J.
Etherington*

RED DOLLAR   7 ch.g. Tachypous 128 – Burglars Girl 63 (Burglar 128) [1991   41
1992 a8g a12g³ a12g 11.9m 10m a12g] rangy, workmanlike gelding: good mover:
rated 76 at 3 yrs: lightly raced and form since only when third at Lingfield in
February: stays 1½m: acts on good to firm and soft going: possibly best in visor:
hooded on reappearance: not seen after May. *B. Gubby*

REDENHAM (USA)   2 ch.c. (Mar 27) Sir Ivor 135 – Norette (Northfields   95 p
(USA)) [1992 6m² 7.3m* 8d] $47,000Y: strong colt: good mover: brother to useful
stayer Ivory Fields and half-brother to several winners abroad: dam, Irish 9f winner,
is sister to Ribblesdale winner Nanticious and Stewards' Cup winner Repetitious:
progressive form: created very favourable impression on debut, and long odds on,
won 5-runner minor event at Newbury in June in good style by 5 lengths: bit
backward and green still, 16 lengths seventh of 10 to Armiger in Racing Post Trophy
at Doncaster 4 months later, never dangerous: will be suited by middle distances:
has further improvement in him. *R. Hannon*

RED FAN (IRE)   2 b.g. (Mar 4) Taufan (USA) 119 – The Woman In Red 68 (Red   –
Regent 123) [1992 7d⁶] 18,500F, 20,000Y: sturdy gelding: has scope: third foal:
half-brother to 3-y-o 7.6f winner Scarlatine (by Alzao) and a winner in Italy: dam,
second at 1m at 2 yrs, is half-sister to 2 good Italian performers: 10/1, well-beaten
last of 6 in moderately-run Redcar minor event won by Persian Brave in July, slowly
away, running green in rear and readily outpaced from 2f out: looked sort to do
better but wasn't seen again. *J. W. Watts*

RED FOR DANGER   3 b.g. Formidable (USA) 125 – Red Shoes 74 (Dance In   – §
Time (CAN)) [1991 7d 6g* 6d⁴ 7f⁵ 8m 8f 8g 1992 a10g 9.7g 8m 10m⁶] close-coupled,
workmanlike gelding: moderate mover: no worthwhile form in 1992, collapsed and
died after final start: best form at 7f on firm ground: often blinkered or visored:
tended to sweat: trained on reappearance by M. Dixon. *A. Moore*

RED INK   3 ch.g. Blushing Scribe (USA) 107 – Pink Robber (USA) 85 (No   53
Robbery) [1991 5g⁴ 6g³ 5.3f 6g 1992 6m 8f⁵ 7g 8m² 8d a8g] rather unfurnished
gelding: has a markedly round action: maiden plater: worth a try beyond 1m: acts on
firm ground, possibly not on a soft surface: blinkered (soundly beaten) final 2-y-o
start: trained until after penultimate start by J. Sutcliffe. *J. R. Jenkins*

REDISHAM   3 ch.c. Persian Bold 123 – Barsham 94 (Be My Guest (USA) 126)   80
[1991 7m⁵ 8m* 8g 1992 7g 8g* 9m²] leggy, lengthy colt: fairly useful form: off
course 3 months, won handicap at Kempton: best effort when second in handicap at
Redcar (hung left but kept on under pressure) later in July: should stay 1¼m: wears
a tongue strap. *J. H. M. Gosden*

RED JACK (IRE)   3 b.g. Red Sunset 120 – Rockeater 94 (Roan Rocket 128) [1991   60 d
7g 7.8m 1992 6.5v⁶ 8f 9m 8.3g 6.9m⁶ 7g 8.2g a7g] 4,500F, IR 5,400Y: neat gelding:
half-brother to 2 winners, including fair 5f (at 2 yrs) to 1¼m winner Black Sophie
(by Moorestyle), and to dam of Italian 1000 Guineas winner Arranvanna: dam stayed
11f: best effort in Irish maidens for N. Meade on reappearance: form here only in 6.9f
handicap at Folkestone: blinkered last 2 starts: won selling hurdle in November. *J.
Akehurst*

RED JAM JAR   7 ch.g. Windjammer (USA) – Macaw 85 (Narrator 127) [1991 NR   –
1992 10g 12.3m⁵ 12f⁶ 11g] good-bodied gelding: moderate mover: poor handicapper,
has won only once on flat: stays 1½m: acts on firm and dead going: has worn tongue
strap, bandages and crossed noseband: tends to carry head high and may be
irresolute: won novice hurdle at Worcester in September. *J. Mackie*

RED KAY TU   3 ch.g. Kaytu 112 – Red Penny (Red Alert 127) [1991 6.1m⁵ 1992   –
10.8g] small, lengthy gelding: no form, tailed-off last in seller at Warwick in July. *F.
Jordan*

Wokingham Handicap, Royal Ascot—
33/1-shot Red Rosein wins from the favourite Double Blue and Kayvee;
behind them are Lochsong (No. 23), So Rhythmical (No. 30),
Sylvan Breeze (No. 15) and Windpower

RED KITE 3 ch.g. Bluebird (USA) 125 – Affirmation (FR) (Affirmed (USA)) [1991   **67**
5m 5g³ 5d 7g 6g³ 6m 7d³ 1992 8d² 8.3s* 10.3f 9m 8m² 8f² a8g³ 8m³ 8m⁴ 8.3g³ 8d
8d] smallish, workmanlike gelding: moderate mover: fair handicapper: won at
Hamilton in May: rare poor efforts last 2 starts: suited by 1m: acts on any going on
turf, probably on fibresand: has run well for 7-lb claimer. *M. Bell*

RED LEADER (IRE) 2 b.c. (May 16) Vision (USA) – Try My Rosie 93 (Try My   **69**
Best (USA) 130) [1992 5d³ 5.1f⁵ 5.7m² 5m³ 5.2g⁴ 5g 5s⁴ 6g* 6v*] IR 3,800Y, 10,000
2-y-o: small colt: first foal: dam Irish 2-y-o 6f winner: fair peformer: ridden by 7-lb
claimer, won nurseries at Newmarket and Folkestone late in the season: better
suited by 6f than 5f: probably acts on any going, but best form on heavy: ran
respectably in blinkers once. *P. F. I. Cole*

RED-MICHELLE 3 ch.f. Jalmood (USA) 126 – Northern Dynasty 65 (Breeders   **–**
Dream 116) [1991 NR 1992 10d 10m 7m 10.2d] deep-girthed filly: sixth reported live
foal: half-sister to 4-y-o 1¼m winner Sarah-Clare (by Reach) and to 3 other winners,
including fair middle-distance performers Southern Dynasty (by Gunner B) and
6-y-o Western Dynasty (by Hotfoot): dam 1m winner: behind in maidens and minor
event: pulled up lame final start: dead. *E. A. Wheeler*

RED MIRAGE (IRE) 3 ch.f. Red Sunset 120 – Dusty Highway (High Top 131)   **–**
[1991 NR 1992 6g 7f 9.7g] IR 3,000F, 6,600Y: close-coupled filly: second foal:
half-sister to 4-y-o 1m winner Will He Or Won't He (by The Noble Player): dam
unraced: well beaten in maidens and a claimer. *M. McCormack*

REDNET 5 b.m. Tender King 123 – Red For Go (Tanfirion 110) [1991 a6g⁵ 1992   **56**
5m 5f 5m⁴ 5.1g* 5g⁵ 5m] tall, good-topped mare: moderate mover: modest handicapper: favourably drawn when narrowly winning at Nottingham: below that form
later in June, when bandaged and on toes final occasion: effective at 5f and 6f: acts on
good to firm ground: blinkered (below form) on reappearance: has worn tongue
strap. *P. D. Evans*

RED RED WINE 2 b.c. (Apr 26) Domynsky 110 – Hunslet 72 (Comedy Star   **–**
(USA) 121) [1992 5d 5m] workmanlike colt: has scope: fourth foal: dam 7.2f winner,
is sister to useful 1m and 1¼m winner and smart jumper Starfen: always behind in
maiden at Ripon and seller at Beverley in the spring: sold 720 gns Doncaster June
Sales. *M. H. Easterby*

670

RED RIVER BOY   9 b.g. Latest Model 115 – Count On Me 77 (No Mercy 126)   –
[1991 a7g* a6g⁴ a7g a5g³ a5g 7g 9g 1992 5.1f 7g] lengthy gelding: carries plenty of
condition: seems of little account these days. *R. J. Hodges*

RED RONNIE   2 ch.f. (Mar 2) Faustus (USA) 118 – Lady of Leisure 75 (Record   –
Run 127) [1992 5g 5.1d] 1,000Y: leggy, short-backed filly: third foal: dam won twice
over 5f, including as 2-y-o: bit backward, not much sign of ability in northern sellers
in the spring. *J. Berry*

RED ROSEIN   6 b.m. Red Sunset 120 – Vain Deb 66 (Gay Fandango (USA) 132)   **97**
[1991 6d 6d 7g 6g⁶ 6m 7.1m⁶ 7f⁵ 6g* 6g* 6f* 6m* 6.1m* 6m 6f* 6g 6m 6g 7m 6.1d
1992 6d 6g 6f⁴ 6f³ 6d³ 6f* 6d⁶ 6m* 6.1d 6m 6.1m⁵ 6g³ 6g⁴ 6g 6d 6d] leggy,
workmanlike mare: has a quick action: improved further at 6 yrs and developed into
useful handicapper: first past the post at Thirsk (edged left, demoted), Royal Ascot
(Wokingham Stakes, by ¾ length from Double Blue) and Ripon in the summer: good
fourth to Rose Indien in listed race at Newmarket but well below form afterwards:
suited by 6f and a sound surface: below form when blinkered earlier in career:
usually bandaged off-hind: usually slowly away, and is held up: tough. *Capt. J. Wilson*

RED RUSSIAN   2 b.c. (Mar 26) Myjinski (USA) – Dame du Moulin 81 (Shiny   –
Tenth 120) [1992 6g 7g 6m] 1,250Y: neat colt: fourth foal: dam, 2-y-o 7f winner, is
half-sister to useful middle-distance fillies Rollrights and Rollfast: no worthwhile
form, including when blinkered, in the summer. *B. J. McMath*

RED SLIPPERS (USA)   3 ch.f. Nureyev (USA) 131 – Morning Devotion (USA)   **111**
102 (Affirmed (USA)) [1991 6g² 7d* 8d 1992 7m⁶ 7m⁴ 10.1g* 10d* 12f] lengthy filly:
has a quick action: came to herself and proved a smart performer in the autumn,
winning listed event at Newcastle and Sun Chariot Stakes (favourite, beat Feminine
Wiles by a head) at Newmarket: behind in £79,800 handicap at Gulfstream Park in
November: stayed 1¼m: acted on dead ground, probably on good to firm: visits
Alleged. *L. M. Cumani*

RED SOMBRERO   3 ch.g. Aragon 118 – Hat Hill (Roan Rocket 128) [1991 5m³   **54**
5g³ 6g⁶ 5.8d⁴ 6.1g² 6.1s⁴ 5.7f³ 7f 6g 1992 6g⁵ 7d⁵ 8h 6g 7m³ 7f 8.3g² 7.1s⁴ 9d
a8g] sturdy, close-coupled gelding: fair plater: stays 8.3f: acts on good to firm
ground: well beaten in a visor fourth start: sold out of G. Cottrell's stable 2,000 gns
(privately) Ascot November Sales after ninth start. *R. Brotherton*

RED SPARKY   4 b.f. Green Ruby (USA) 104 – Electrified 67 (Gunner B 126)   –
[1991 NR 1992 a10g a8g⁶ a12g] medium-sized filly: of little account. *W. J. Pearce*

Cheveley Park Stud Sun Chariot Stakes, Newmarket—
it's close between Red Slippers (rails) and Feminine Wiles

REDSTELLA (USA) 3 ch.c. Theatrical 128 – Orange Squash 78 (Red God 128§) **60** p
[1991 NR 1992 12f³ 15.9g⁶] good-topped colt: sixth reported foal: half-brother to
3 winners, notably very useful 1½m and 1¾m winner Prime Assett (by Welsh
Pageant), later successful in USA: dam won 3 times at around 1m: staying-on third
of 5 in maiden at Thirsk, having been held up taking a good hold: still bit backward,
no chance in listed race later in August: should improve. *R. M. Whitaker*

RED TEMPEST (IRE) 4 b.g. Red Sunset 120 – Msida (Majority Blue 126) –
[1991 11d⁴ 11d 11g⁶ 15g 10m⁶ 9.2d⁴ 10m 1992 13d 8d 9.2d] compact gelding: of little
account. *L. Lungo*

RED VERONA 3 ch.f. Ballacashtal (CAN) – Chicory (Vaigly Great 127) [1991 **40**
5m² 6m 5.1m 6g 1992 6v 5.1d 7g 6d 6g 6g 5.1g⁶ 5.1m³ 6g 6g 5g] workmanlike filly:
poor maiden: should stay 7f: acts on good to firm ground: not discredited in blinkers
once: sometimes sweating and on toes. *E. A. Wheeler*

RED WHIRLWIND 2 b.c. (Apr 24) Shadeed (USA) 135 – Red Red Rose (USA) –
90 (Blushing Groom (FR) 131) [1992 7g] fourth foal: closely related to Irish 3-y-o
1½m winner Green Glen (by Green Dancer): dam 1m winner: 9/1, well beaten in
minor event at Kempton in August, eased once held. *M. R. Stoute*

REEL OF TULLOCH (IRE) 3 b.g. Salmon Leap (USA) 131 – Miss Sandman **61**
86 (Manacle 123) [1991 7g* 1992 7g 8.1s⁶ 9.9m 8f 9.9m² 10f⁶ 10f³ 11.9d 9.2g⁴ 9.2g*
10s 9.9m 10s 11.1s² 10.8s 8.2g] rangy gelding: none too consistent performer: won
seller (bought in 6,000 gns) at Hamilton in August: stays 1¼m: possibly needs a
sound surface: blinkered twice, finding little first occasion, unsuited by conditions
on second: may well be suited by waiting tactics: sold 8,000 gns Newmarket
Autumn Sales. *P. C. Haslam*

REFLECTING (IRE) 3 b.c. Ahonoora 122 – Shining Water 111 (Kalaglow 132) **72**
[1991 NR 1992 8f³ 10d 8f³ 8m² 10m³ 10d³ a10g a10g⁴] moderate walker:
first foal: half-brother to 2-y-o Tenby (by Caerleon): dam 2-y-o 6f and 7f winner later
second in 14.6f Park Hill Stakes, is daughter of smart stayer Idle Waters: fair
maiden: worth a try at 1½m: acts on firm and dead ground, fair effort on equitrack:
retained 14,500 gns Newmarket Autumn Sales. *J. H. M. Gosden*

REFUGIO 2 b.c. (Mar 1) Reference Point 139 – Fatah Flare (USA) 121 (Alydar **56** p
(USA)) [1992 7g⁴] fourth foal: half-brother to fairly useful 7f winner Mata Cara (by
Storm Bird) and quite useful 1989 2-y-o 6f winner Fire And Shade (by Shadeed): dam
6f (at 2 yrs) and 10.5f winner, is from excellent family: favourite but backward, 13
lengths fourth of 18 to Tinners Way in maiden at Doncaster in November, prominent
over 5f: will improve. *H. R. A. Cecil*

REGAL AURA (IRE) 2 ch.g. (Feb 27) Glow (USA) – Dignified Air (FR) 70 **84**
(Wolver Hollow 126) [1992 6m 7g* 7m² 7.5d³ 7m 7g 7.6s³] 110,000 francs (approx
£11,000) Y: big, workmanlike gelding: has scope: fluent mover: fifth foal: dam, 4-y-o
6f winner, is out of half-sister to very smart Joking Apart: fairly useful performer:
made all in maiden at Wolverhampton in June: returned to best, despite being
hampered inside last, when third in nursery at Lingfield in October: will stay 1¼m:
acts on good to firm and soft ground. *G. Harwood*

REGAL CHIMES 3 gr.c. Another Realm 118 – London Cries (FR) (Bellman **87**
(FR) 123) [1991 5d² 5d² 5g² 5d³ 5m 5.2g⁶ 5g³ 5g³ 5f* 5m² 6m 5g⁵ 1992 5g⁴ 5.1g]
leggy, useful-looking colt: fairly useful performer: creditable fourth in Folkestone
minor event: last of 8 in £7,000 Chester handicap later in the spring: best at 5f: acts
well on firm ground. *B. A. McMahon*

REGAL LOVER (IRE) 3 b.c. Alzao (USA) 117 – King's Chase (King's Leap 111) **74**
[1991 7m⁶ 7m³ 1992 8g 8g 12m 11.6g² 11.1m* 12.4m² 12.3f³ 14d⁵ 14.1d 11.8d]
good-topped colt: fair handicapper: won at Hamilton in July: well below form last 3
starts, visored first 2 occasions: stays 1½m well: acts on good to firm ground,
probably not on a soft surface: wears tongue strap: sold 8,000 gns Newmarket
Autumn Sales. *M. Bell*

REGAL RACER 3 b.g. Elegant Air 119 – Cantico 58 (Green Dancer (USA) 132) **79**
[1991 7d⁴ 6m 1992 6s* 7f⁶ 6g² 6f⁵ 7.1d 10g³ 10m] leggy gelding: fair form at his best:
won maiden at Salisbury in April: below best last 4 outings: should prove effective at
1¼m: best efforts with some give in the ground, and acts on soft: keen sort, tends to
sweat and get on edge: not seen after August. *D. R. C. Elsworth*

REGAL ROMPER (IRE) 4 b.c. Tender King 123 – Fruit of Passion (High Top –
131) [1991 a8g⁶ 7g 6d³ 6m 6g 5g 1992 7g 10.5g] rather leggy, good-topped colt: has a
round action: rated 36 at 3 yrs for F. Lee: last in big fields in the summer as 4-y-o:
best form at 6f on an easy surface: blinkered (soundly beaten) once at 3 yrs: won
over hurdles (seller) in October. *Mrs S. J. Smith*

REGAL SCINTILLA 3 b.f. King of Spain 121 – Trwyn Cilan 89 (Import 127) 93
[1991 5d⁶ 5m² 5.2d⁴ 5d* 5g⁵ 5g⁴ 5.2f⁴ 5m* 1992 5m 5d⁶ 5m 5m 5.2g⁶ 5d 5m 5g⁵
5.2s] good-topped filly: good walker: capable of fairly useful form: contested French
pattern events for J. Hammond first 2 starts in 1992 before returning to 2-y-o
trainer: speedy: acts on good to firm and dead ground, seemingly not on soft: visored
last 2 starts, running very well first occasion. *G. B. Balding*

REGALSETT 2 b.c. (Mar 6) Blakeney 126 – Sleepline Princess 86 (Royal Palace 78
131) [1992 6s⁵ 6.1m* 7d⁴ 7g⁵ 7g³ 7s] smallish, sturdy colt: moderate walker: sixth
foal: half-brother to several winners at up to 1m, including Sleepline Royale (by
Buzzards Bay) and Sleepline Palace (by Homing): dam won over 6f at 2 yrs: fair
performer: won maiden at Nottingham in August by 5 lengths: good staying-on third
of 17 in nursery at Brighton: will be suited by further: acts on good to firm ground,
soundly beaten on soft ground. *R. Hannon*

REGAL TIGER 7 gr.g. On Your Mark 125 – Regal Doll (Sovereign Path 125)   –
[1991 NR 1992 a6g 5v⁴ a7g 5s a7g 5m] leggy, angular, sparely-made gelding: no
worthwhile form, and has looked reluctant. *Mrs J. C. Dawe*

REGENT LAD 8 b.g. Prince Regent (FR) 129 – Red Laser 95 (Red God 128§) 70
[1991 8s 7.5g⁴ 7m 7.5f² 7.5f² 8m* 8.2g³ 8g 7.9m⁵ 7.5f³ 8m³ 8.9g 8f⁴ 8m 8.5f 1992 8f
8.9f⁶ 8g⁶ 7f 8g] leggy gelding: good walker: fair handicapper, though not so good as
at 7 yrs: probably best short of 1¼m: acts on any going except possibly heavy: best
without blinkers: best with extreme waiting tactics in strongly-run race: won novice
hurdle in October. *Miss L. C. Siddall*

REGENT'S FOLLY (IRE) 4 ch.f. Touching Wood (USA) 127 – Regent's Fawn 99
(CAN) 72 (Vice Regent (CAN)) [1991 10g³ 9m 12g³ 14.6m⁵ 1992 14g 13.4m⁴ 12d
12f²] strong, good-bodied filly: carries condition: useful performer: ran well in 1992
when fourth to Saddlers' Hall in Ormonde Stakes at Chester and second of 20 to
Spinning in strongly-run Bessborough Handicap at Royal Ascot: stays 14.6f: acts
well on firm ground, probably unsuited by dead: often sweats. *W. Jarvis*

REGENT'S LADY 2 b.f. (Mar 4) Interrex (CAN) – Anjonic 56 (Le Levanstell 53
122) [1992 5.1m* 5.1d⁶ 6m² 6g⁵ 5g] angular, workmanlike filly: half-sister to several
winners, including 1m winner Sul-El-Au (by Tachypous) and fairly useful 2-y-o 5f
winners Silk Lady (by Tribal Chief) and Snow Card (by Imperial Fling): dam poor
maiden: modest performer: made all in 5-runner seller (bought in 3,800 gns) at
Nottingham in June: better suited by 6f than 5f: best form on top-of-the-ground: gets
taken down early. *C. James*

REILTON 5 b.g. Cure The Blues (USA) – Chanson de Paris (USA) (The Minstrel 53
(CAN) 135) [1991 7s 10g 1992 12f³ 7g⁵ 8.5s⁴ 8m 10g³ 9f² 7.5d 11g 9.9m] smallish,
sturdy ex-Irish gelding: second foal: dam unraced: still a maiden on flat: well beaten
on last 3 starts: stays 9f: acts on firm and soft ground: sometimes blinkered in
Ireland, not here: tongue tied down last 4 starts: won over hurdles in October: sold
to join A. Forbes 2,600 gns Doncaster November Sales. *J. Parkes*

REINA 4 b.f. Homeboy 114 – Sun Queen 76 (Lucky Sovereign 122) [1991 6m⁶ 6.1m 24
1992 8m 6g a7g a8g 7.1m⁴ 6.1g⁵ a7g⁶ 6g] small, lengthy filly: poor form at best and
still a maiden: stays 7f: acts on good to firm ground: blinkered last 4 starts. *J. D.
Bethell*

REINE DE NEIGE 2 b.f. (May 5) Kris 135 – Don't Rush (USA) 93 (Alleged 87 ?
(USA) 138) [1992 7m² 7m² 8.2d²] tall, close-coupled filly: has a round action: first
foal: dam 1½m winner, is half-sister to 1984 champion Canadian 3-y-o Key To The
Moon out of champion Canadian filly Kamar: fairly useful performer: heavily-backed
second favourite after promising debut, beaten ½ length by Mystic Goddess in
moderately-run Sweet Solera Stakes at Newmarket, soon recovering from slow
start and staying on well from 2f out: on toes, sweating and troublesome stalls,
below form in maiden at Nottingham later in August, not handling bend then staying
on under pressure from 2f out: will require middle distances: acts on good to firm
ground. *A. A. Scott*

REKLAW 5 b.g. Hard Fought 125 – Rubina Park 64 (Ashmore (FR) 125) [1991 NR 35
1992 10d⁴ 10.5m 12m 10d⁴ 8.9d⁴ 8g a8g³] angular, sparely-made gelding: shows
plenty of knee action: poor maiden: stays 1¼m: acts on dead ground and fibresand:
effective in blinkers. *M. D. Hammond*

RELATIVELY RISKY 3 ch.f. Risk Me (FR) 127 – Skelton 70 (Derrylin 115) 42
[1991 5g 5m 5f 7m 1992 8m³ 7g] lengthy, unfurnished filly: form only when third in
claimer at Newmarket in July. *J. Wharton*

REMANY 3 gr.f. Bellypha 130 – Moonscape 87 (Ribero 126) [1991 7m 7m 1992 8f² 66
8.9d 8.9d⁵ 9.9m* 10m⁶ 10d⁵] tall, sparely-made filly: has a roundish action: fair

form: won maiden at Beverley in September: better at 1¼m than shorter, and will stay 1½m: acts on good to firm ground, fair efforts on dead. *J. R. Fanshawe*

REMEMBER THE ALAMO   6 b.g. Scorpio (FR) 127 – Chelsea Charmer   –
(Ballymore 123) [1991 NR 1992 9.2v] leggy gelding: poor novice hurdler: first run on flat since 4 yrs, soundly beaten in maiden claimer at Hamilton in April: sold 1,050 gns Ascot June Sales. *J. J. O'Neill*

REMEMBER THE NIGHT   2 b.c. (Apr 20) Petong 126 – Free On Board 73   –
(Free State 125) [1992 5.1g] third foal: half-brother to 3-y-o Nordansk (by Nordance): dam stayed 1¼m: 50/1, unruly and very backward, always behind in 9-runner maiden at Nottingham in June. *J. Balding*

REMEMBRANCE DAY (IRE)   2 ch.c. (Feb 17) The Noble Player (USA) 126 –   **44**
Blackeye (Busted 134) [1992 5g 6g 7f⁶ 8d] IR 10,000F, 14,500Y: good-topped colt: good walker: moderate mover: fifth foal: half-brother to 2 winners abroad: dam unraced half-sister to Triple First, dam of Oaks-placed Maysoon and Three Tails: poor maiden: off course almost 4 months, well beaten final start: should stay 1m: sold 10,000 gns Newmarket Autumn Sales. *R. Hannon*

REMWOOD GIRL   6 b.m. Remainder Man 126§ – Aliwood Girl 64§ (Broxted   **35**
120) [1991 9s 8.1g 10m* 12m⁴ 10.1s 1992 8g 12m a12s⁴ 12.3g³ 11d⁶ a12g] small, plain mare: carries condition: moderate mover: poor performer: stays 12.3f: acts on good to firm and dead ground, well beaten on all-weather surfaces. *K. S. Bridgwater*

RENTA KID   3 b.f. Swing Easy (USA) 126 – Dewberry 68 (Bay Express 132) [1991   –
6m 5d³ 5.7m³ 5f* 5m⁵ a6g 1992 8.3g] leggy, workmanlike filly: plating-class form at 2 yrs for R. Boss: soundly beaten in seller in August, 1992: should stay at least 6f: acts on firm ground. *P. J. Hobbs*

REPLEDGE (IRE)   3 b.c. Alleged (USA) 138 – Repetitious 103 (Northfields   **67** ?
(USA)) [1991 8.1m⁴ 8.1s² 1992 10d⁴ 10.5s⁶] lengthy colt: progressive form in frame in minor event and maidens: 5/4 on but blinkered on first run for over 5 months, ran badly in Haydock seller in October: should be suited by 1½m: sold 820 gns Doncaster November Sales. *P. F. I. Cole*

REPLICATE   4 ch.f. Vaigly Great 127 – Remould 83 (Reform 132) [1991 7m⁵ 7f   –
8d⁵ 8m² 10g 8m⁶ 8.2m³ 8.1s 8m⁴ a10g 1992 a8g a8g a8g] smallish, lengthy, sparely-made filly: shows quick action: rated 60 at 3 yrs: soundly beaten in 1992: stays 1m: possibly best on a sound surface: sold 800 gns Doncaster March Sales. *M. J. Charles*

REPORTED (IRE)   3 ch.c. Heraldiste (USA) 121 – Peach Melba 96 (So Blessed   **106**
130) [1991 6g 7g⁴ 6m⁵ 7m* 8g⁵ 1992 7v* 10v² 10d⁴ 10g⁴ 7f⁴ 8g³ 8.3g² 7m* 7f] IR 3,000Y: good-topped, workmanlike colt: half-brother to fair 1983 2-y-o 5f winner Llandwyn (by Jaazeiro) and a winner in Australia: dam 2-y-o 5f winner: useful performer: won handicap at the Curragh in April: trained until after fifth start by V. Bowens, in Ireland: marginally best effort when landing listed race at York in August, given enterprising ride, soon well clear, and holding off Consigliere by 2 lengths: best form at 7f/1m: acts on any going. *M. J. Heaton-Ellis*

REQUESTED   5 b.g. Rainbow Quest 134 – Melody Hour 105 (Sing Sing   **77**
134) [1991 10.1s⁵ 14g³ a12g⁴ 14m² 13.3d⁴ 16.2m 14.1f⁴ 14f* 14g⁶ 14m⁵ 16.2d* 1992 16m⁵ 20m² 16.1f 16.2g² 16.1m² 14s 16.2s⁶ 18m] leggy, sparely-made gelding: poor mover: fair handicapper: runner-up 3 times in 1992, including behind Gondolier in Ascot Stakes: tailed off 2 of last 3 starts: effective from 2m to 2½m: acts on any going: has found little under pressure: has won when blinkered and for apprentice. *R. Akehurst*

RESHIFT   4 b.f. Night Shift (USA) – Repoussee (Jimmy Reppin 131) [1991 7d* 6g   –
6d* 7d* 7d 1992 6g] angular, good-topped filly: moderate mover: a game performer when rated 94 at 3 yrs: off course 10 months, never travelling particularly well when seventh of 9 in Doncaster listed event in March: should prove best short of 1m: goes well on dead ground: keen sort: usually apprentice ridden: sold only 2,800 gns Newmarket December Sales. *M. Bell*

RESIST THE FORCE (USA)   2 br.c. (Mar 16) Shadeed (USA) 135 – Countess   **78** p
Tully 112 (Hotfoot 126) [1992 6s 6g²] $37,000F, $32,000Y: smallish, sturdy colt: sixth foal: half-brother to fairly useful 10.5f winner Honeychurch (by Bering) and useful 1988 French 2-y-o 1m winner Russian Countess (by Nureyev): dam useful winner at 8.5f and 1¼m in Ireland, later successful in USA: off course 3½ months and 33/1, 1½ lengths second of 20 to Serious in maiden at Newmarket, responding to pressure to lead inside final 1f, outpaced close home: will stay 1m: will improve and win a maiden. *C. A. Cyzer*

RESOLUTE BAY   6 b.g. Crofthall 110 – Spinner 59 (Blue Cashmere 129) [1991   **80** §
5g 7m 6g³ 6m³ 6m 7m² 7m 6.1g* 6m⁶ 7.1m² 7.9g 7.6m 7m⁵ 7.3m⁵ 6g 7m⁵ 6m 1992

6g 6f³ 6f 8f⁴ 7.1f⁵ 7g⁶ 7m⁴ 6m⁵ 6g] lengthy gelding: has a rather round action: capable of fairly useful form, but is an unreliable handicapper: has won once in last 35 starts: stays 7f: suited by a sound surface: effective visored/blinkered or not: retained 2,500 gns Doncaster October Sales. *R. M. Whitaker*

RESOLUTION TIME   2 ch.g. (Apr 13) Presidium 124 – Miss Times 78 (Major   **30** Portion 129) [1992 6f 6d 8m] 2,100Y: small, close-coupled gelding: half-brother to 3 winners by Enchantment, all at sprint distances: dam 6f seller winner at 2 yrs, is out of half-sister to very smart sprinter Runnymede: soundly beaten in maidens: lame at start and withdrawn from Edinburgh stalls in July: subsequently off course 4 months before final start, when tried in blinkers: sold 800 gns Doncaster.November Sales. *Mrs V. A. Aconley*

RESOUNDING SUCCESS (IRE)   3 b.f. Law Society (USA) 130 – Dawn Echo   **82** (Don (ITY) 123) [1991 6m⁴ 1992 10.4m² 9m³ 12.5g* 11.7d a12g] tall, leggy filly: fairly useful performer on her day: 11/4 on, set fair bit to do when winning moderately-run 5-runner maiden at Warwick in July by a short head, running nowhere near best: off course leaving periods before finishing well beaten afterwards, as if something amiss last time: probably stays 12.5f: sold 16,000 gns Newmarket December Sales. *B. W. Hills*

RESPECTABLE JONES   6 ch.g. Tina's Pet 121 – Jonesee 64 (Dublin Taxi)   **72** [1991 a5g² a5g² a6g² a7g* 5d 5g⁶ 6s 6g 6g 5g 6m² 6g 5.7m³ 6.1m 5m 5f² 6m 6d 5.1s⁴   a84 6.1d 5g⁵ a6g² a6g* 1992 a6g³ a7g* 6d 5.7m⁶ 6m 6d* 7f⁶ 5.1f 6s a5g² a6g* a6g*] leggy, lengthy gelding: fairly useful handicapper on equitrack: won at Lingfield in January and Warwick (easily best turf effort in 1992) in July for G. Balding, and 2 claimers back at Lingfield in December on first runs (had been claimed for £8,089) for new stable: effective at sprint distances and, at least on equitrack, 7f: acts on any going: effective visored or not: good mount for inexperienced rider: game. *R. Hollinshead*

RESPLENDENT   3 b.f. Sharrood (USA) 124 – Damaska (USA) (Damascus   **72** (USA)) [1991 7m⁴ 7d⁴ 1992 10g⁶ 10g⁵ 11.5g* 12m 14d] rangy, rather plain filly: fair form: easy winner of handicap at Yarmouth in July: failed to confirm that form: stays 11.5f: tongue tied down last 6 starts: sweating (raced freely, below form) second 3-y-o start: sold 2,200 gns Newmarket Autumn Sales. *N. C. Wright*

RESTART   2 b.g. (Jan 27) Then Again 126 – Rising Star (St Paddy 133) [1992 6m   **44** 7g 8.2s] 9,800F: fair sort: half-brother to 3-y-o 1¼m to 2m winner Ideal Candidate (by Celestial Storm) and several winners abroad: dam temperamental half-sister to very useful Riot Act and Laurentian Hills: poor form: tailed off final start: will stay middle distances. *Lord Huntingdon*

RESTITUTION   2 ch.c. (Apr 30) Hadeer 118 – Rest 70 (Dance In Time (CAN))   **53** [1992 7m 7s⁵] angular colt: fourth foal: half-brother to 1989 2-y-o 5f seller winner Premier Girl (by Petong): dam 1½m winner: bit backward still, around 12 lengths fifth of 10 to Mullitover in maiden at Warwick in October, outpaced 3f out: will stay 1m +: sold 6,400 gns Newmarket Autumn Sales. *J. R. Fanshawe*

RESTLESS MINSTREL (USA)   3 b.c. The Minstrel (CAN) 135 – Dismasted   **63** (USA) (Restless Native) [1991 NR 1992 10d⁵ 12m³ 11.1m² 11.1f⁶] sturdy colt: first foal: dam won 14 races at up to 13f, including Grade 1 1¼m event: modest maiden: co-favourite, made most when well below form in handicap final outing, in June: stays 1½m: sold to join J. Banks 4,700 gns Newmarket September Sales. *L. M. Cumani*

RESTLESS NIECE   4 b.f. Uncle Pokey 116 – Lucille Astik (Meldrum 112) [1991   **–** 6g 6d a8g 1992 a7g a10g⁵ a12g a8g² a8g] strong, workmanlike filly: no worthwhile form though has shown signs of a little ability: should stay beyond 1m: not seen after March. *T. D. Barron*

RESTORE   9 ch.g. Habitat 134 – Never So Lovely 87 (Realm 129) [1991 5m* 7g   **55** d 6m⁴ 6d⁵ 6f⁵ 6f* 7.1m² 7m 6m⁶ 7d 7g 6.9s 1992 5s 5.3m⁵ 6s 6f² 6f⁴ 6g⁵ 6m⁵ 7f⁴ 7g] useful-looking gelding: hobdayed twice: inconsistent handicapper: best form at 6f on a sound surface: normally blinkered or visored: often on edge: best with strong handling. *R. Voorspuy*

RESTRAINT   2 b.f. (Feb 4) Bustino 136 – Queens Message 93 (Town Crier 119)   **–** [1992 7g] 900Y: angular, quite attractive filly: half-sister to several winners here and abroad, including 6f (at 2 yrs) and 1m winner Mahogany Run (by Sonnen Gold): dam speedy 2-y-o: 33/1, around 18 lengths eleventh of 14 to Pamzig in maiden at Doncaster in October, soon off bridle. *P. Calver*

RETENDER (USA)   3 br.g. Storm Bird (CAN) 134 – Dandy Bury (FR) (Exbury   **78** 138) [1991 NR 1992 7g⁵ 8.2g³ 7g³ 9f⁴ 10.1f* 11g² 9g 10d 10.3g] $70,000F: useful-

Moorestyle Convivial Maiden Stakes, York—Revelation confirms his debut promise

looking gelding: half-brother to several winners, including 1989 Irish 2-y-o 6f winner Artistic Idea (by Kris) and smart French (7.5f and 1¼m) and U.S. winner Daily Busy (by Trepan): dam placed over middle distances in France: fair form: won claimer at Yarmouth in August: easily best effort in handicaps afterwards when unlucky second at Redcar: sold out of L. Cumani's stable 15,000 gns Newmarket Autumn Sales: behind in ladies event on only run for new stable: worth a try at 1½m: acts on firm ground: often bandaged behind. *Mrs J. R. Ramsden*

RETOUCH 6 b.h. Touching Wood (USA) 127 – Nelly Do Da 78 (Derring-Do 131) **91**
[1991 16g 16g² 16g* 20g⁶ 16.1m⁶ 20g² 15.9g² 16.2g⁵ 1992 11.5m⁵ 14g 20m⁵ 18m²]
workmanlike, rather sparely-made horse: good mover: fairly useful handicapper: suited by thorough test of stamina: acts on good to firm and dead going: sold to join J. Harris 12,000 gns Newmarket Autumn Sales. *P. F. I. Cole*

REVEL 4 ch.g. Sharpo 132 – Waltz 75 (Jimmy Reppin 131) [1991 6m² 5f³ 6m² 6f 7m —
6g 9.2s 1992 7.1g 5.9d 5d] compact gelding: rated 67d at 3 yrs: no form in handicaps in 1992: stays 6f: acts on good to firm ground: tried blinkered: sold to join T. Gibson 1,500 gns Doncaster June Sales. *L. Lungo*

REVELATION (IRE) 2 b.c. (Feb 10) Thatching 131 – Angelus Chimes 80 **111**
(Northfields (USA)) [1992 7m 6m* 7g⁴ 6v²] IR 14,000Y: good-topped colt: moderate mover: half-brother to winners abroad by High Top and Persepolis: dam Irish 4-y-o 1½m winner: progressive at 2 yrs: confirmed promise of debut (rider and trainer fined £400 each for not running horse on merits) when winning valuable York maiden by 5 lengths in August: hung final 2f next outing and subsequently off course nearly 8 weeks: put up easily best effort when 1½ lengths second of 24 to Pips Pride in Racecall Gold Trophy at Redcar in October, struggling to go pace then staying on strongly from 2f out: will stay 1m: best effort on heavy ground, has won on good to firm: may do better. *R. Hannon*

REVERE (IRE) 2 b.c. (Apr 1) Dancing Brave (USA) 140 – Bint Pasha (USA) 126 **85** p
(Affirmed (USA)) [1992 8.2s*] first foal: dam won Yorkshire Oaks and Prix Ver-meille: 7/4 favourite, created very favourable impression when winning 13-runner maiden at Nottingham in October by 6 lengths from Fools Errand, tracking pace, roused along to lead over 1f out, drawing clear final 100 yds: will be very well suited by 1½m: an interesting prospect, certain to win more races. *P. F. I. Cole*

REVIF (FR) 4 gr.c. Kenmare (FR) 125 – Reverente (FR) (Riverman (USA) 131) **109**
[1991 8d⁴ 10.6g² 11.8g² 12s 1992 10s* 10d* 8.9g⁶ 9d⁶ 10g⁶ 10.5v*] tall, quite leggy, good-topped colt: impresses in appearance: improved into a useful performer: very impressive winner of handicaps at Ripon and Kempton in April: off course over 4 months but remained in good form, finishing sixth in Cambridgeshire and a slowly-run listed race at Newmarket, then landing listed contest at Saint-Cloud in November: effective at 9f and stays 11.8f: goes well on any surface, backward on only run on good to firm: sold 110,000 gns Newmarket December Sales, reportedly to race in Saudi Arabia. *A. C. Stewart*

REVOKE (USA) 5 ro.m. Riverman (USA) 131 – Queens Only (USA) (Marshua's **45**
Dancer (USA)) [1991 8g 7f 10.8g 8.2m⁵ 7g² 8d 1992 8m a8g 8.1m⁵ 8.1m 7g⁵] small, sparely-made mare: moderate mover: still a maiden, and form in handicaps in 1992

676

only when fifth: effective at 7f and 1m: acts on good to firm going: not seen after July. *C. J. Hill*

REXY BOY 5 b.g. Dunbeath (USA) 127 – Coca (Levmoss 133) [1991 13.8d 8.2d 33 12.3d 12m⁶ 11.1s³ 13d³ 12.1m* 10m⁶ 12.1f² 12m⁴ 12.1g 1992 13.8g⁶ 12m 12m 15.8d⁵ 16.5m⁴ 15.8g* 15.8m⁶ 16m³ 15.1f³ 16.2m⁶ 15.8d] good-bodied gelding: carries condition: moderate mover: poor handicapper: won at Catterick in July, allowed to dominate: stays 2m: probably acts on any going: has worn crossed noseband: tried blinkered and visored: won novice handicap hurdles in September and December. *W. L. Barker*

REZA 4 gr.g. Superlative 118 – Moon Charter 45 (Runnymede 123) [1991 NR 1992 – 8.3g⁴ 8f a7g 9.2g 8s a7g] sturdy gelding: no worthwhile form since 2 yrs: tried blinkered: refused to race over hurdles once. *J. L. Eyre*

RHETT'S CHOICE 2 b.f. (Mar 23) Beveled (USA) – Return To Tara (Homing 67 130) [1992 6m³ 5m* 5g² 6.1g³ 5m] 3,400Y: rather leggy filly: third foal: sister to fair 3-y-o sprinter Cranfield Comet: dam well beaten: fair form: won maiden auction at Ripon in July: ran well in nursery at Redcar and 4-runner minor event at Chester, soundly beaten after slow start in Newcastle nursery following month: probably better suited by 6f than 5f. *J. Berry*

RHYTHMIC DANCER 4 b.g. Music Boy 124 – Stepping Gaily 79 (Gay 82 Fandango (USA) 132) [1991 5d³ 6m⁶ 6m 5.1g³ 5g 5.2m 1992 5g 6m 5g⁴ 5m⁶ 5g a5g*] leggy, close-coupled gelding: fair handicapper: off course 4 months, easy winner at Lingfield late in year: speedy: acts on firm and dead going: headstrong. *J. L. Spearing*

RHYTHMIC ECHO 3 b.g. Sizzling Melody 117 – Calling High (USA) 88 (Mountain Call 125) [1991 6g⁶ 6m⁴ 5f⁵ 1992 a8g a7g⁶ 8s] tall, unfurnished gelding: no worthwhile form in claimers (on equitrack) and seller in the spring: should stay beyond 6f. *P. Howling*

RIBBOLD 2 b.c. (Mar 12) Bustino 136 – Water Woo (USA) 102 (Tom Rolfe) [1992 – p 6m] 78,000Y: sturdy, useful-looking colt: half-brother to several winners here and abroad, notably 4-y-o Environment Friend (by Cozzene): dam, French 2-y-o 6f winner, is daughter of Waterloo: 12/1 and green, well-beaten seventh of 8 in minor event won by Perfect Halo at Newbury in June, dropping away, not knocked about, from 2f out: seemed likely to improve. *C. E. Brittain*

RIBBONWOOD (USA) 2 b.f. (Mar 8) Diesis 133 – Ribbon (USA) (His Majesty 91 (USA)) [1992 6f² 6d* 7d⁴] unfurnished filly with scope: has round action: half-sister to several winners here and in USA, including Preakness and Belmont Stakes winner Risen Star (by Secretariat) and useful 9f and 1½m winner Silk Braid (by Danzig): dam prolific winner from 6f to 11f at 3 yrs in USA: fairly useful performer: heavily-backed 6/5-chance, won 16-runner maiden at Newbury in August, moving like a winner all way and striding clear last furlong: 11/8 favourite but sweating and on toes, 1¾ lengths fourth of 7 to Love of Silver in Group 3 event at Goodwood 2 weeks later, always prominent and keeping on final 1f: will be better suited by 1¼m. *J. H. M. Gosden*

Prix Le Fabuleux, Saint-Cloud—Revif picks up a listed race

RIBHI (USA) 2 b.c. (Apr 30) Riverman (USA) 131 – Antartica (FR) 124 (Arctic **84**
Tern (USA) 126) [1992 6g³ 6.1m* 7s² 7s4] leggy, quite attractive colt: second foal:
half-brother to 3-y-o Nbaat (by El Gran Senor): dam French miler: fairly useful
performer: won maiden at Nottingham in September: very good second in nursery
(unseated rider at start) at York following month, missing break, coming through
well over 1f out but getting no run thereafter: came from long way back when
respectable fourth in similar event at Leicester in October: will stay at least 1m: acts
on good to firm and soft ground. *D. Morley*

RICHARD OF YORK 2 b.c. (Feb 22) Rainbow Quest (USA) 134 – Triple First **111** p
117 (High Top 131) [1992 8s* 9d*] 380,000Y: half-brother to several winners,
including Oaks third Three Tails (by Blakeney), 1000 Guineas and Oaks-placed
Maysoon (by Shergar) and Ribblesdale winner Third Watch (by Slip Anchor): dam
won from 5f to 1¼m: won newcomers race at Longchamp: followed up in Group 2
Prix Saint-Roman (by a short neck from Devil's Rock) at Evry later in September: a
promising young stayer who should make his presence felt in 1993. *A. Fabre, France*

RICH HEIRESS (IRE) 3 b.f. Last Tycoon 131 – Lamya (USA) (Alydar (USA)) **49**
[1991 NR 1992 a12g⁶ a8g²] first foal: dam ran twice: backward, better effort in
Lingfield maidens in December when distant second: stays 1m. *A. Moore*

RICH MIDAS (IRE) 2 ch.f. (Jan 24) Salt Dome (USA) – Raging Storm (Horage **59**
124) [1992 5m³ 5d 5g⁵ a5g⁴ 6g 5g³ 5m 6s* 6d] IR 16,500Y: sparely-made filly: first
foal: dam Irish 2-y-o 8.5f winner: modest performer: ridden by 7-lb claimer, showed
improved form (beaten in sellers previous 2 starts) when winning claimer at
Goodwood in October: better suited by 6f than 5f: acts on soft going: sold 3,100 gns
Newmarket Autumn Sales. *G. Lewis*

RICHMOND (IRE) 4 ch.g. Hatim (USA) 121 – On The Road (On Your Mark **59**
125) [1991 7d 8s 8.2d⁴ a8g⁶ 8.3d* 8m³ 9.2d⁵ 8.3s⁵ 8f 8.1g⁴ 8m 1992 9m⁵ 8g⁵ 7.5d³
9.2g² 9g] sturdy gelding: moderate mover: modest handicapper: has won one of 26
starts: trained first 2 starts by S. Norton, next 2 (ran well in sellers) by B. Beasley:
well beaten at Redcar nearly 6 weeks later: stays 9f: acts on good to firm and soft
ground: usually visored/blinkered, not last time: won novice hurdle in November.
N. Tinkler

RICH PICKINGS 3 b.f. Dominion 123 – Miss By Miles 91 (Milesian 125) [1991 **39**
5m 6g 1992 10g⁵ 11g 10g⁶ 8m 16.1d³ 14.1g⁶ 16g⁴ 15.4d] sparely-made filly: inconsistent plater: better at 2m than shorter: acts on dead going: sold out of C. Cyzer's

Prix Saint-Roman, Evry—
promising young stayer Richard of York beats Devil's Rock in a four-runner race

stable 4,800 gns Newmarket September Sales after seventh 3-y-o start: won selling hurdle (bought in 5,000 gns) in November. *D. R. Tucker*

RIENROE (IRE)   3 b.f. Caerleon (USA) 132 – Flying Bid 71 (Auction Ring (USA)   56
123) [1991 NR 1992 7m² 10m 9m4] tall filly: sixth foal: closely related to modest 7f
winner Vision of India (by Vision) and half-sister to 3 winners, including useful Irish
2-y-o 5f and 6f winner Flutter Away (by Lomond) and 1½m winner Rawah (by
Northern Baby): dam Irish 1¼m winner: modest maiden: stiff task when last at
Newcastle final start, in July: stays 1¼m. *N. A. Graham*

RIFLEBIRD (IRE)   2 b.f. (May 18) Runnett 125 – Sacred Ibis (Red God 128§)   –
[1992 7m] IR 10,000Y: leggy filly: half-sister to several winners, including useful 5f
to 1m winner Cremation (by Ashmore) and 1985 2-y-o 5f winner Sugarbird (by Star
Appeal), latter dam of Horris Hill winner Sapieha: dam, sister to very useful 1969
2-y-o Red Velvet, looked a short runner: 10/1, tailed off in 14-runner seller at
Newmarket in August: showed a round action: sold 2,800 gns Newmarket Autumn
Sales. *M. Bell*

RIGHT WILL PREVAIL   2 ch.c. (Mar 23) Bairn (USA) 126 – Catherines Well   –
99 (Junius (USA) 124) [1992 5g 5m 5.7d] 20,000Y: good-quartered, useful-looking
colt: second living foal: dam sprinter: no worthwhile form in maiden events, off
course 3 months before final start: sold 1,100 gns Newmarket Autumn Sales. *G.
Lewis*

RIGHT WIN (IRE)   2 br.c. (May 2) Law Society (USA) 130 – Popular Win 103   106
(Lorenzaccio 130) [1992 6f² 6g* 7d² 7m 7d² 7g* 8v²] IR 6,000F, IR 10,000Y:
lengthy, workmanlike colt: moderate mover: half-brother to several winners here
and abroad, including (at 6f at 2 yrs in 1988) Coq du Nord (by Coquelin) and (at 7f to
9.5f in Ireland) Popular Glen (by Glenstal): dam 5f and 7f winner out of Musidora
winner Jakomima: progressed into a useful performer: won maiden at Newmarket in
July and £8,900 event at Ascot in October, quickening clear entering final furlong:
confirmed that form when 3½ lengths second of 14 to Pelder in Gran Criterium at
Milan 15 days later: stays 1m: suited by an easy surface. *R. Hannon*

RIMOUSKI   4 b.c. Sure Blade (USA) 130 – Rimosa's Pet 109 (Petingo 135) [1991   –
10d 11.7m³ 12.2f³ 9.9f 10m 14.6g⁵ 1992 12.5s 6.1d] quite attractive colt: has a
markedly round action: rated 57 at 3 yrs for M. Stoute: well beaten in October, 1992:
best form at around 1½m: has had tongue tied down: visored (below form) once. *B.
R. Cambidge*

RINGLAND (USA)   4 b.c. Gate Dancer (USA) – Tinnitus (USA) (Restless Wind)   84
[1991 10.4g 10g³ 1992 a7g* a8g² a6g⁶ a7g³ 7s 7.5m³ 6f² 7m* 7f* 7g 7m 7m a7g³
7d⁵ a8g³] strong, compact colt: carries condition: moderate mover: fairly useful
performer: on the go from start of year and very tough: won maiden claimer at
Southwell in January, claimer at Redcar and handicap at York in June: effective from
6f to 1m: acts on firm and dead ground and all-weather surfaces, seems unsuited by
very soft going: sold out of P. Haslam's stable 12,000 gns Doncaster September
Sales after thirteenth start: won novice hurdle in October. *D. Moffatt*

RINGLET (USA)   2 b.f. (Feb 6) Secreto (USA) 128 – Double Lock 104 (Home   – p
Guard (USA) 129) [1992 7g] $200,000F: lengthy, good-topped filly: has plenty of
scope: closely related to French 1m winner Sure Locked (by Lyphard) and
half-sister to several winners, including top-class miler Sure Blade (by Kris) and
useful miler Sure Sharp (by Sharpen Up): dam 1¼m winner: 8/1 and backward,
around 16 lengths eighth of 16 to Sueboog in minor event at Newbury in September,
slowly away and considerably handled throughout: looks sort to do better. *B. W.
Hills*

RING TOM (IRE)   2 ch.c. (Feb 25) Ahonoora 122 – Crimson Royale 84 (High   44
Line 125) [1992 5d 6.1g 6g 7d 7s] IR 2,200Y: long-backed, workmanlike colt: fifth
foal: brother to 4-y-o Come On Dancer and half-brother to Irish juvenile hurdle
winner Loose Ends (by Persian Bold): dam, 1¼m to 11.7f winner, is sister to very
smart 1¼m horse Crimson Beau: poor form in varied events including selling: will
probably stay 1m: yet to race on top-of-the-ground. *M. W. Easterby*

RINJA (USA)   5 b.h. Robellino (USA) 127 – Dijla 82 (Hittite Glory 125) [1991 8g4   83
10m² 12g* 10g 14.9m* 13.9g 14g² 13.3m 1992 11.9g² 12f] strong, lengthy horse:
carries plenty of condition: moderate mover: usually impresses in appearance: tough and
genuine handicapper at 4 yrs: ran well on reappearance at York in May, below best
in Bessborough Handicap at Royal Ascot 5 weeks later: effective from 1½m to
1¾m: acts on good to firm ground: often bandaged behind: sold only 4,600 gns
Newmarket Autumn Sales. *D. W. P. Arbuthnot*

RIO TRUSKY 3 b.g. Ballacashtal (CAN) – Polly's Song 65 (Song 132) [1991 5m **36**
6m⁵ 6g⁵ 8d 1992 7d⁶ 5m 6g 7m⁵ 9m 9.7h⁵ 8.1d 8f⁶ a7g a8g⁶] tall, leggy gelding: poor
maiden: stays 7f: acts on dead going and equitrack, probably on hard: twice slowly
away, when blinkered and reluctant stalls on first occasion: tends to sweat and get
on toes. *M. D. I. Usher*

RIPSNORTER (IRE) 3 ch.c. Rousillon (USA) 133 – Formulate 119 (Reform **63**
132) [1991 8m 7.1d5 7g² 1992 10d 9.7g 11.1s⁵ 8.2g⁴ 7d³ 8h 8.2d* 8g 9s] big, strong
colt: modest form at best: won handicap at Nottingham in July on last start for Sir
Mark Prescott: soundly beaten afterwards: seems best at up to 1m, and with waiting
tactics: probably unsuited by hard ground. *J. A. Bennett*

RISE OVER 6 ch.m. Smackover 107 – Stewart's Rise 52 (Good Bond 122) [1991 **–**
8m* 1992 8.2s] big mare: has a round action: rated 45 at 5 yrs: off course over 17
months, shaped as if still retains ability at Nottingham in October: stays 1m: acts on
good to firm ground: sometimes sweats. *P. D. Evans*

RISE UP SINGING 4 ch.g. Noalto 120 – Incarnadine 67 (Hot Spark 126) [1991 **73**
8m 8g⁴ 8g* 8m* 8m⁴ 7f 10.5f 1992 8g 8d 8.3g² 7g 8g 8g 7m* 7m 8m 7d 8m 7g]
strong, lengthy gelding: carries condition: moderate mover: inconsistent handicapper: claimed out of R. Hannon's stable £9,555 third start: won at Newmarket in
July: effective at 7f/1m: acts on any going, except apparently heavy: best in blinkers:
twice below form when sweating: not one to trust. *W. J. Musson*

RISING TEMPO (IRE) 4 b.g. Lomond (USA) 128 – May Hill 124 (Hill Clown **64**
(USA)) [1991 a7g² 7d a8g* a7g* 10g⁶ a7g³ 8m a10g⁶ a7g 11.5g 1992 a10g³ a12g⁴ 8d⁶
10g⁴ 12g 10m* 11.8d⁵ 10f² 10m² 12d⁴ 10f² 11.5m² 10g² 13.9g³ 11.4g 13.3g 9.7v]
sturdy, heavy-topped gelding: modest handicapper: won at Sandown in May: below
form last 3 starts: effective from 1¼m to 1¾m: acts on good to firm ground and
equitrack, unsuited by a soft surface: has run well for lady rider, though tends to
hang and has swished tail: has joined B. Baugh. *C. A. Cyzer*

RISK A LITTLE 2 ch.f. (Apr 10) Risk Me (FR) 127 – Lightning Legend 71 (Lord **37**
Gayle (USA) 124) [1992 5d 6g⁶ 5g 5g⁵] 1,700Y: lengthy, sparely-made filly: second
foal: dam 2-y-o 7f winner: poor plater, not seen out after July. *M. J. Heaton-Ellis*

RISK MASTER 3 b.c. Risk Me (FR) 127 – Trigamy 112 (Tribal Chief 125) [1991 **87**
6f 7g 6d⁴ 1992 7m 6g³ 7.3g* 8g 7g 8d* 10s⁴ 11s] lengthy, angular colt: fairly useful
handicapper: won at Newbury (made all) in June and Goodwood (detached in rear
early on) in September: stays 1¼m: may well be suited by give in the ground. *C. A.
Horgan*

RISK ME'S GIRL 2 b.f. (Feb 5) Risk Me (FR) 127 – Miss Serlby 65 (Runnett **79**
125) [1992 5g* 5.1g² 5g* 5.2d 5.2g³ 6m⁵ 6s⁶ 5m] 3,400Y: sturdy, good-quartered
filly: has a round action: fourth foal: dam maiden best at 5f: fairly useful performer:
won maiden at Sandown and minor event (impressively) at Windsor in the spring:
ran really well in Lowther Stakes at York (fifth to Niche) and £9,200 event at Ripon
(not beaten far) in August: had run creditably in blinkers fifth outing, but ran badly in
them final 2 starts: got upset in stalls and withdrawn final intended race: suited by
6f: acts on good to firm and soft ground: sold 10,000 gns Newmarket Autumn Sales.
R. Hannon

RISK PROOF 2 b.c. (Mar 15) Risk Me (FR) 127 – Queen's Piper 99 (Song 132) **56**
[1992 5g⁶ 5g 6d* 7d 6d a6g⁶ a8g] 7,200Y: angular colt: first foal: dam sprinter: no
comparable form after winning seller at Goodwood (sold out of G. Lewis' stable
6,500 gns) in August: stays 6f. *K. O. Cunningham-Brown*

RISK THE WITCH 2 b.f. (Apr 7) Risk Me (FR) 127 – Singing Witch 71 (Sing **–**
Sing 134) [1992 6.1s⁵] half-sister to several winners, including 6-y-o sprinter
Cantoris (by Song) and 1985 2-y-o 1m winner My Ton Ton (by Good Times): dam
half-sister to smart sprinter Vilgora: soundly-beaten fifth of 6 in minor event at
Chester in October. *D. J. S. Cosgrove*

RISKY NUMBER 2 ch.c. (Mar 17) Risk Me (FR) 127 – Out of Harmony 79 (Song **50**
132) [1992 5d 5.1f 6m² 7m⁴ 6m³ 6d 6g⁵ 5g⁶ a6g a6g* a6g²] 4,100Y: workmanlike **a57**
colt: moderate mover: second foal: dam 2-y-o 5f winner stayed 6f: made all in
claimer at Lingfield in October: retained 650 gns Newmarket Autumn Sales: headed
line in another claimer there in November: needs further than 5f and stays 7f: well
suited by equitrack: sold 1,400 gns Ascot November Sales. *J. S. Moore*

RISKY ROSIE 2 ch.f. (Apr 8) Risk Me (FR) 127 – Star Rose (FR) (Star Appeal **–**
133) [1992 5.1s 5.3f] 2,100Y: small, plain filly: poor mover: first reported foal: dam
useful French middle-distance filly: tailed off in maiden auction and seller in May. *R.
Voorspuy*

RISK ZONE 3 b.g. Risk Me (FR) 127 – Gymnopedie (Jaazeiro (USA) 127) [1991 **73**
5g⁶ 6g⁵ 6g a7g 1992 6v² 7d 6s⁶ 6g* 7f* 6g² 7d 6m 6g² 7g 7f³ 7.6g³ 7m 8m] sturdy
gelding: fair handicapper: won at Windsor and Salisbury in May: creditable efforts
most starts after but (trainer reported horse resents being crowded) has looked
reluctant on other occasions: better at 7f than 6f, and should stay 1m: best efforts on
a sound surface: usually blinkered or visored: sold 6,400 gns Newmarket Autumn
Sales. *R. Hannon*

RISPOTO 2 b.f. (May 17) Mtoto 134 – River Spey 96 (Mill Reef (USA) 141) [1992 **56**
7g 7d] unfurnished filly: fourth foal: half-sister to 3-y-o 7f winner Dune River (by
Green Desert) and very useful 7f (at 2 yrs) to 1¾m winner Jahafil (by Rainbow
Quest): dam 2-y-o 7.3f winner later stayed middle distances, is out of sister to very
smart Joking Apart: never able to challenge when around 7 lengths seventh of 16
in maiden at Lingfield in September: well beaten in similar event at Leicester
following month. *Sir Mark Prescott*

RISTON LADY (IRE) 2 b.f. (Feb 13) Salt Dome (USA) – Trompe d'Oeil 75 **66**
(Longleat (USA) 109) [1992 5s 5s² 5d⁴ 5f⁵ 5.1m² 5.1g* 5g² 5m² 5.1m*] IR 1,200Y:
small filly: second foal: first foal: dam won here at 1m at 2 yrs and at 9.9f at 3 yrs in
Ireland: sire (by Blushing Groom) smart sprinter: consistent performer: won at
Chester in maiden in July and nursery (made all) in August: speedy: ran creditably
when blinkered once. *B. S. Rothwell*

RISZARD (USA) 3 ch.c. Danzig Connection (USA) – Tendresse (USA) (Secre- **97**
tariat (USA)) [1991 6m* 6m 1992 10d² 8d³ 10g⁴ 14g³] workmanlike colt: failed to
progress after head second to Top Register in £9,500 contest (swished tail) at
Ascot: fair efforts in listed race and minor events last 3 starts: should stay 1½m:
acts on good to firm and dead ground: wandered badly and demoted once. *J. S.
Bolger, Ireland*

RIVAL BID (USA) 4 b.g. Cannonade (USA) – Love Triangle (USA) (Nodouble **72**
(USA)) [1991 7f³ 10.2m⁴ 10m³ 9.7m² 10m 8m⁵ 12g⁶ 1992 10.1g³ 10.1f⁵ 10m* 10g²
8.9d* 9.9m² 10m] workmanlike, close-coupled gelding: fair handicapper: successful
at Lingfield (first win) and Wolverhampton in summer: tailed off in apprentice race
final start: should stay 1½m: acts on good to firm (below form on firm) ground and
dead: mount for apprentice: usually held up. *M. A. Jarvis*

RIVE-JUMELLE (IRE) 4 b.f. M Double M (USA) – Riverwave (USA) (River- **70** d
man(USA)131)[1991 10d 10m² 10m* 10.6m² 10.1f⁵ 11.7d³ 11.5g³ 10m* 10.5m⁶ 11m³
9.9f⁶ 10g* 10m² 1992 10.3g⁴ 10m³ 10.4m 10.1g⁵ 10.1g³ 10m⁵ 10g 10.1d⁵ 10g 10m³
10m³] lengthy, sparely-made filly: moderate mover: rated 78 at 3 yrs: below form in
handicaps in 1992: best at 1¼m on a sound surface: joined J. Jenkins. *M. Bell*

RIVER ANCHOR 3 b.f. Slip Anchor 136 – Tuloma (USA) (Irish River (FR) 131) **69**
[1991 NR 1992 8d 10g 12s* 13.3s] 14,000Y: lengthy filly: second foal: dam unraced:
best effort on first run for 5 months when winning maiden at Folkestone: well
beaten in Newbury handicap later in October: should stay beyond 1½m: sold 15,000
gns Newmarket December Sales. *R. Charlton*

RIVER BOYNE (USA) 2 ch.c. (Apr 21) Irish River (FR) 131 – Bethamane **80** p
(USA) (Wajima (USA)) [1992 8g4] stocky colt: half-brother to several winners,
including (at 1½m) Betony (by Majestic Light) and (in bumpers in Ireland) Merino
Waltz (by Nijinsky): dam unraced half-sister to smart 6f (at 2 yrs) to 10.6f winner
Wassl Touch from excellent family: 14/1 and green, shaped well when 3¾ lengths
fourth of 9 to Shaiba in minor event at Newmarket in October, running on strongly
up the hill: will improve, and win a maiden at least. *G. Harwood*

RIVER CHASE (USA) 4 ch.f. Salmon Leap (USA) 131 – Amboselli 73 (Raga **–**
Navarro (ITY) 119) [1991 a8g* 8g* 8f³ 8g³ 8m* 7.1m⁴ 1992 a7g⁴] big, lengthy filly:
rated 61 on turf as 3-y-o: below form in February: stays 1m: acts on firm ground. *Pat
Mitchell*

RIVER DEFENCES (USA) 3 b.c. Riverman (USA) 131 – Durtal 121 (Lyphard **102** §
(USA) 132) [1991 7m⁵ 1992 8d* 12.3g⁵ 8m⁵ 10g³ 8v] tall, attractive colt: good
walker: most promising when winning Newbury maiden in April by 4 lengths: off
course 5 months after disappointing (refused to settle) in Chester Vase: looked
unsatisfactory next 2 starts, and tailed off in Group 2 event in Italy final one. *P. W.
Chapple-Hyam*

RIVER DELTA (USA) 2 b.f. (Mar 22) Riverman (USA) 131 – Godetia (USA) 119 **91** +
(Sir Ivor 135) [1992 8.1d*] leggy, attractive filly: half-sister to several winners here
and in USA, including (at 1½m) Shout And Sing (by The Minstrel): dam won Irish
1000 Guineas and Oaks: highly impressive 8-length winner of maiden at Haydock in
September: broke hind leg on gallops in October: dead. *R. Charlton*

RIVER FALLS 3 b.c. Aragon 118 – More Fizz (Morston (FR) 125) [1991 6g² 6m* **110** d
6g² 6g* 7m² 6m³ 1992 7d² 8g 8m 7f⁶ 8m* 7.3d 8g 7f⁶ 8g⁶] rangy, good sort:
impresses in appearance: smart 2-y-o and looked set for successful season in 1992
after very good second to Lion Cavern in Greenham Stakes at Newbury, headed
post: proved disappointing, winning only minor event at Goodwood in August:
should have proved fully effective at 1m, but headstrong sort: acted on good to firm
ground and dead: below form blinkered once: often made the running: tended to
wander to his left: retired to Ballyhane Stud, Co. Carlow, fee IR £1,250 (Oct 1st). *R.
Hannon*

RIVER FIRE (IRE) 2 br.f. (Jan 21) Petong 126 – River Maiden (FR) 86 –
(Riverman (USA) 131) [1992 a7g 6g] leggy filly: moderate mover: fourth foal: dam 7f
winner: no form in maidens. *J. Berry*

RIVER HAWK 3 b.g. Local Suitor (USA) 128 – Larive 80 (Blakeney 126) [1991 –
NR 1992 9.7m⁶ 12g 11.6g 11.7d] angular gelding: has a round action: third foal: dam
1½m winner stayed 2m: no worthwhile form. *R. F. Johnson Houghton*

RIVER ISLAND (USA) 4 b.g. Spend A Buck (USA) – Promising Risk (USA) –
(Exclusive Native (USA)) [1991 10d* 10f³ 11.8g⁵ 10.8d³ 12.1d⁴ 1992 12d] quite
attractive gelding: rated 83d at 3 yrs for P. Cole: no promise in April, 1992: should
stay 1½m: reportedly had wind operation: won novice hurdle in December. *J. A. B.
Old*

RIVER NORTH (IRE) 2 ch.c. (Apr 16) Lomond (USA) 128 – Petillante (USA) **61** p
(Riverman (USA) 131) [1992 6.9v³] 21,000Y: third foal: half-brother to 1m winner
Ante Up (by Sharpen Up): dam won at up to 9f: never able to challenge when under 3
lengths third of 11 in maiden at Folkestone in October: sold 7,000 gns Newmarket
Autumn Sales. *M. R. Stoute*

RIVER NYMPH (USA) 3 b.f. Riverman (USA) 131 – Fourteen (Bellypha 130) **114**
[1991 8g² 1992 10.5v* 10.5g 10m³ 10.5m³ 10d⁴ 10s* 12m 12.5s 10.5v] fourth
reported foal: dam unraced daughter of useful French 10.5f winner Valderna, a
half-sister to Durtal and Detroit: won minor event at Saint-Cloud in March and Prix
de la Nonette at Deauville (by a length from Trishyde) in August: behind in Prix
Vermeille next time and ran moderately last 2 starts: stays 1¼m: best effort on soft
ground. *J. de Roualle, France*

RIVER REFUGE 2 gr.c. (Feb 6) Belfort (FR) 89 – Rhodabourne (Aragon 118) **48** p
[1992 5d] 700F, 2,000Y, 7,000 2-y-o: first foal: dam lightly raced as 2-y-o: 33/1,
around 5 lengths ninth of 19 in maiden at Lingfield in September, good progress
from over 1f out: sure to improve. *J. A. R. Toller*

RIVER WAY (IRE) 4 b.f. Soughaan (USA) 111 – Eccentric Lady (London Bells –
(CAN) 109) [1991 NR 1992 a7g] compact filly: little worthwhile form. *C. J. Hill*

RIVET 3 gr.g. Superlative 118 – Moon Charter 45 (Runnymede 123) [1991 5m 1992 –
5s 6s⁵ 7g 7d 5.1m⁵] small gelding: poor plater: best effort over 6f on soft ground. *M.
Blanshard*

RIVIERA RAINBOW 4 b.g. Rainbow Quest (USA) 134 – Miss Beaulieu 106 – §
(Northfields (USA)) [1991 10g⁵ 8m² 8f² 8m 8m 8m⁵ 8.1m⁵ 1992 a10g⁴ a8g² a10g* a70 §
10d] smallish, sturdy gelding: unreliable performer: won apprentice maiden at Lingfield in March: not seen again after soundly beaten following month: stays 1¼m:
acts on firm ground and all-weather surfaces: tried in blinkers, visor, and eyeshield.
D. R. C. Elsworth

RIVIERA SCENE 9 gr.g. Mummy's Pet 125 – Pariscene 86 (Dragonara Palace –
(USA) 115) [1991 NR 1992 7.6m] tall gelding: on the downgrade. *P. J. Makin*

RIVIERA VISTA 3 b.c. Shirley Heights 130 – Miss Beaulieu 106 (Northfields **89** d
(USA)) [1991 7f⁴ 7g² 1992 8m* 8m⁴ 10m⁴ 9d 10g 8m⁶ 7g 12.1s] rangy, angular colt:
moderate mover: landed odds in Yarmouth maiden in July and ran well in Newmarket handicaps next 2 starts: went wrong way after: should prove better at 1¼m
than shorter: tried blinkered: sold 14,000 gns Newmarket Autumn Sales. *G. Wragg*

RIVIERE ACTOR (USA) 2 b.c. (Mar 19) Theatrical 128 – Riviere Salee (FR) **66** p
(Luthier 126) [1992 7m⁶ 8.2g⁶] $13,000Y: tall, leggy, lightly-made colt: half-brother
to several winners here and in France, including very useful 8.5f and 1¼m winner
Azayim (by Be My Guest): dam lightly-raced sister to good-class 1973 French
2-y-o stayer Riverton and half-sister to high-class 1972 French 2-y-o 7f and 1m
winner Robertino: shaped promisingly in maidens at Newmarket and Nottingham,
particularly catching eye on first run for 2 months when tenderly handled behind
Bagalino: will do better, particularly over middle distances. *J. L. Dunlop*

RIYADH LIGHTS 7 b.g. Formidable (USA) 125 – Rivers Maid 83 (Rarity 129) **34** §
[1991 12m 13m⁶ 18g² 17.1d³ 22.2m 16.2d a16g⁶ 1992 a16g a13g⁴ a16g³] compact
gelding: moderate mover: unsatisfactory maiden handicapper: best efforts with
good test of stamina: sometimes blinkered/bandaged behind. *M. D. I. Usher*

ROADRUNNER 2 ch.g. (May 2) Sunley Builds 102 – Derraleena 61 (Derrylin –
115) [1992 6g] 700Y: rather sparely-made gelding: first foal: dam, maiden, suited by
6f: slowly away and always behind in maiden at Newbury in September. *W. G. R.
Wightman*

ROAD TO AU BON (USA) 4 b.g. Strawberry Road (AUS) 128 – Village Lady –
(USA) (Crimson Satan) [1991 8m⁵ 11.5g⁵ 10g 1992 10.2s 10.2d] lengthy gelding:
moderate walker: lightly raced and no worthwhile form: bred to stay 1¼m: tried
blinkered once. *R. J. Baker*

ROARING BREEZE 3 ch.f. Roaring Riva 103 – Tree Breeze 111 (Farm Walk –
111) [1991 6m³ 5.9h⁶ 6.1m 7m 1992 10g 7g⁶] leggy, sparely-made filly: poor maiden:
seems to stay 7f: sold 1,000 gns Doncaster September Sales. *Miss S. E. Hall*

ROAR ON TOUR 3 b.g. Dunbeath (USA) 127 – Tickled Trout 70 (Red Alert 127) **62**
[1991 5m⁴ 7m⁵ 8.1g⁶ 8m⁶ 7g* 1992 7f 8m³ 7d 8s 8.2s] good-bodied gelding: no
form in handicaps in 1992 after second start: best effort at 1m: acts on good to firm
ground: has gone well visored: tongue tied down once: has been gelded. *M. H.
Easterby*

ROBENKO (USA) 3 b.c. Roberto (USA) 131 – Kendra Road (USA) (Kennedy **74**
Road (CAN)) [1991 NR 1992 10m 13.9g³ 14.1m²] $350,000Y: strong colt: fifth foal:
half-brother to a graded stakes-placed winner by Top Command: dam showed a little
ability in USA at 3 yrs: thrice raced, and easily best effort when third of 4 in minor
event at York in May: not seen out after June: should stay 1¾m + . *C. E. Brittain*

ROBERTO'S GAL 3 b.f. Roberto (USA) 131 – Grafitti Gal (USA) (Pronto) [1991 **58**
7g 6s⁴ 8m 1992 9g 12g 11.9f² 10.1d⁶ 10g] close-coupled filly: has a quick action:
modest maiden: best effort at 1½m: acts on firm ground: below form visored: sold
1,900 gns Newmarket Autumn Sales. *N. C. Wright*

ROBERT THOMAS (IRE) 3 ch.g. Coquelin (USA) 121 – Douschkina 86 –
(Dubassoff (USA)) [1991 NR 1992 10.5s 10.5d 8f] 3,000£: unfurnished gelding: fifth
reported foal: brother to 1m winner Swift Romance: dam 6f winner on only start at 2
yrs but no form at 3 yrs: well beaten in maidens: sold 2,000 gns Doncaster June
Sales. *M. O'Neill*

ROBERTY LEA 4 b.c. Alleging (USA) 120 – Rosy Lee (FR) (Le Haar 126) [1991 **73**
a8g⁶ a8g* a8g⁶ a8g⁴ 10d 12.3s² 12m 12m* 12g⁴ 11m⁶ 12g² 12d* 11.9m⁶ 14g³ 13.9g²
16.2g 16m 13.3g 1992 12g 11.9g 12.3m⁶ 12d³ 12d] close-coupled colt: well below form
in handicaps in 1992 apart from when third at Epsom in June: effective at
1½m/1¾m: probably best with some give in the ground (acts on soft):
below form blinkered once: sometimes sweating. *T. Fairhurst*

ROBIN DES PINS (USA) 4 b.c. Nureyev (USA) 131 – Rare Mint (USA) (Key **113**
To The Mint (USA)) [1991 10d² 8g⁴ 7.5g* 7d 9g² 8s⁴ 8v⁶ 1992 7s² 7g** 7d* 7m 8g²
8.5s⁵ 8s⁶] sixth reported foal: brother to useful French 1989 2-y-o 6.5f winner Robin
des Bois, closely related to good-class French 1m (at 2 yrs) to 1½m winner Mystery
Rays and 1¾m winner Dragon's Blood (both by Nijinsky) and half-brother to a
useful winner in France: dam unplaced daughter of half-sister to dams of Be My
Guest and Golden Fleece: improved French colt: followed up win in Longchamp
listed race when making all in Group 3 Prix du Palais-Royal there in May, holding on
narrowly from Zanadiyka and Tertian: best subsequent effort when second in Group
3 race at Cologne: effective at 7f to 9f: possibly unsuited by top-of-the-ground, acts
on any other. *F. Boutin, France*

ROBINGO (IRE) 3 b.c. Bob Back (USA) 124 – Mill's Girl (Le Levanstell 122) **88**
[1991 8f⁴ 1992 7m* 8f⁵ 7.6d⁵ 8.1d² 10g⁴ 12g⁵ 10m 12g* 11s*] close-coupled colt:
fairly useful handicapper: won at Yarmouth (maiden) in June and Ascot (£7,600
event) and Newbury in October: stays 1½m: acts on any going: blinkered last 3
starts: sold to join M. Pipe's stable 26,000 gns Newmarket Autumn Sales. *C. E.
Brittain*

ROBINS FIND (IRE) 4 b.g. Reasonable (FR) 119 – Skyway 76 (Skymaster 126) –
[1991 9g⁶ 11.9g⁶ 12.2m⁴ a14g 1992 a14g] workmanlike gelding: poor maiden: stays
1½m: wears severe noseband: sold to join R. Frost 1,000 gns Doncaster May Sales.
J. R. FitzGerald

ROBIX (IRE) 2 b.c. (Jan 11) Glenstal (USA) 118 – Pocket (Tumble Wind (USA)) **63**
[1992 5s⁶ 5m 6f 6g² 6s⁶ 7d 7.1g] 8,000F, 24,000Y: workmanlike colt: fourth foal:

dam never ran: ran moderately after second in maiden at Hamilton in August: blinkered final start: should stay 7f. *J. Berry*

ROBLEU 2 b.g. (Feb 19) Robellino (USA) 127 – Blue Flower (FR) (Carwhite 127)   – p
[1992 6g] 15,500F, 27,000Y: close-coupled gelding: first foal: dam French 8.2f and 9f winner also placed over jumps: 33/1, always towards rear in Newmarket maiden in October. *G. Harwood*

ROCALITY 3 b.f. Dreams To Reality (USA) 113 – Rocas 48 (Ile de Bourbon   **76**
(USA) 133) [1991 5m 6m 6f 7.1m3 7g* 7m3 7m* 1992 10.2d 7.9m3 8f* 7d4 8.9d 7d* 8.1g 8s] leggy filly: in-and-out form in handicaps in 1992: won at Brighton in May and Epsom in August: stays 1m (bit backward over 10.2f): acts on firm and dead ground, tailed off on soft: tends to hang badly. *R. Hannon*

ROCA MURADA (IRE) 3 br.g. Cyrano de Bergerac 120 – Keppols (Furry Glen   **64**
121) [1991 6g4 8m 7d 1992 9g 10.1m6 10m4 7g3 7g* 8g2 7f3 7g* 7g3 8m 7d 7d2 7d4 7g6] tall, close-coupled gelding: modest handicapper: won at Leicester in July and Yarmouth in August: best at 7f/1m on an easy surface: efffective visored or not. *M. J. Ryan*

ROCKALONG 7 ch.m. Native Bazaar 122 – Rockery 91 (Track Spare 125) [1991   –
NR 1992 a8g a8g a6g5] neat mare: bad maiden. *M. J. Charles*

ROCKAWHILE (IRE) 3 b.f. Dancing Brave (USA) 140 – Melody (USA) (Lord   **97**
Gayle (USA) 124) [1991 NR 1992 8v* 8.9g* 10.3v 10.3g*] 50,000Y: sturdy, lengthy filly: moderate mover: half-sister to several winners, including 1988 2-y-o 6f winner Creole (by Sadler's Wells) and smart 7f filly Guest Performer (by Be My Guest): dam Irish 7f to 1½m winner: won minor events at Wolverhampton (2) in April and Doncaster (gamely) in November: off course 6 months before finishing in mid-division in handicap at Chester: stays 1¼m: yet to race on top-of-the-ground: stays in training. *H. R. A. Cecil*

ROCK BAND (IRE) 3 b.c. Ballad Rock 122 – Bobs (Warpath 113) [1991 NR 1992   **59**
6m 6s 5.1m4 5m3 6g2 7g6 7g6 8g a10g] IR 38,000Y: leggy, quite attractive colt: first foal: dam poor half-sister to very useful middle-distance performers Donello and Juggernaut: modest maiden: best short of 1m: acts on good to firm ground: has worn net muzzle: sold to join T. Jones's stable 6,400 gns Newmarket September Sales. *L. M. Cumani*

ROCKBOURNE 3 b.f. Midyan (USA) 124 – River Music (Riverman (USA) 131)   **57**
[1991 5g2 5.2g 5.3m3 5m5 7m 1992 6m 8f6 8f 7d5 7d2 8g4 8d 6g*] tall, light-framed filly: modest handicapper: won selling event (no bid) at Brighton in September: effective at 6f to 1m: acts on dead ground, fair effort on firm: trained until after fifth start by D. Elsworth: sold 2,500 gns Ascot November Sales: has joined Mrs J. Cecil. *W. G. M. Turner*

ROCKET TO THE MOON (IRE) 2 b.c. (Apr 10) Common Grounds 118 –   **87**
Randolina (Wolver Hollow 126) [1992 5.2m2 5m5 5.1f3 5.9g* 7g6 6.1g3 6v 7g3] 7,200Y: leggy, sparely-made colt: fourth foal: half-brother to 1989 2-y-o 5f winner My Croft (by Crofter): dam half-sister to useful Irish 7f and 1m winner Final Moment: consistent performer: won maiden at Carlisle in September: very good third of 21 in nursery at Doncaster final start: stays 7f: easily best effort on good ground. *P. W. Chapple-Hyam*

ROCK HARD 3 ch.g. Ballad Rock 122 – Norska 67 (Northfields (USA)) [1991 7g   **65** d
1992 9.9g4 11.1d4 12.5g] good-topped gelding: has a quick action: modest maiden: not seen out after May: probably stays 11f: sold to join W. Price's stable 5,600 gns Newmarket July Sales and gelded. *W. Jarvis*

ROCK HOPPER 5 b.h. Shareef Dancer (USA) 135 – Cormorant Wood 130 **124**
(Home Guard (USA) 129) [1991 12g* 12g* 12m3 12m* 12m2 12m* 12m3 12g2 12f 1992 12g5 13.9m* 12g2 12f* 10s 12g5 13.3g3 14s4]
  Another year on the road saw Rock Hopper advance his total of pattern-race victories from five to six, in the Yorkshire Cup, then to seven, in the Hardwicke Stakes. Seven is a handsome total, as are career earnings topping £500,000, especially for a horse prevented from running after May as a three-year-old by a hairline fracture of a cannon bone. Yet a Group 1 prize eluded him to the end. On the form-book beforehand Rock Hopper got his best chance of such a prize in the Irish St Leger on what turned out to be his final appearance, but though he ran respectably for fourth place behind Mashaallah there, he came closer to winning one, as in the previous season, in the Coronation Cup. Beaten half a length and a neck behind In The Groove and

Terimon in 1991, he improved a place when around the same distance behind his stable-companion Saddlers' Hall in 1992. Rock Hopper's other starts in Group 1 in 1992 went unrewarded—entirely predictably in respect of the King George VI and Queen Elizabeth Diamond Stakes, less so in the Coral-Eclipse. Reproducing somewhere near his best brought only fifth place, some seven lengths adrift of St Jovite, in the former; while in the latter he finished only seventh to Kooyonga, beaten around five lengths, failing to muster the pace to challenge. He was tried visored in the Eclipse; he'd finished a creditable third to Generous in blinkers in the King George of 1991.

The races for the Yorkshire Cup and the Hardwicke Stakes each featured a tactical battle between Pat Eddery on Rock Hopper and Ray Cochrane on Sapience. Eddery, riding a horse who hadn't run well first time up and was making his debut at a mile and three quarters, gave a memorable performance in a very slowly-run affair at York. Sapience dictated to the seven others at a dawdle until stepping up the pace coming into the straight, at which stage Rock Hopper brought up the rear having been restrained in the last two from the start. As Sapience continued to quicken, so that he had most of the field in trouble, Eddery kept remarkably cool, spending time to pick a way through towards the inside and, without flustering his mount, getting there plenty soon enough to be able to switch between Sapience and Luchiroverte inside the last furlong and win a shade cleverly. Rock Hopper was made to work much harder at Royal Ascot. On that occasion his pacemaker Mellaby set a sound gallop and was about five lengths clear passing halfway, tracked by Sapience with Rock Hopper held up in touch. There were only five runners. Mellaby, Sapience, Rock Hopper, Luchiroverte, Runyon, was the order in which they turned into the straight, where Rock Hopper was being chased along looking in danger of a reverse. Rock Hopper looked in even more danger when Sapience quickened to the front a furlong and a half out and his head

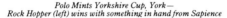

Polo Mints Yorkshire Cup, York —
Rock Hopper (left) wins with something in hand from Sapience

Hardwicke Stakes, Royal Ascot—Rock Hopper and Sapience again;
Rock Hopper is made to pull out all the stops

began to come up as he was subjected to stronger pressure. However, he began to challenge a furlong out, and after a protracted struggle he got up by a short head. Twelve months back, things had been equally tight at the finish of the previous Hardwicke Stakes. On that occasion Rock Hopper had just failed to catch Topanoora, but had been awarded the race after the stewards spotted interference early in the straight.

		Northern Dancer (b 1961)	Nearctic
Rock Hopper (b.h. 1987)	Shareef Dancer (USA) (b 1980)		Natalma
		Sweet Alliance (b 1974)	Sir Ivor
			Mrs Peterkin
	Cormorant Wood (b 1980)	Home Guard (br 1969)	Forli
			Stay At Home
		Quarry Wood (b 1968)	Super Sam
			Phrygia

Rock Hopper, a well-made horse with a quick, fluent action who almost invariably impressed in appearance, has been retired to the Meddler Stud, Newmarket, and will begin at a fee of £3,000 (live foal). Both his sire and dam were Group 1 winners, Shareef Dancer in the Irish Sweeps Derby (in which he beat Teenoso and Caerleon), Cormorant Wood in the Dubai Champion Stakes as a three-year-old and the Benson and Hedges Gold Cup as a four-year-old. Cormorant Wood had stamina limitations, but she was out of a staying mare and in addition to Rock Hopper has produced a real staying type in Cliveden Gail (by Law Society) who won twice in Ireland in the latest season. Rock Hopper seemed equally effective at a mile and a half and a mile and three quarters. One of his biggest assets was a turn of foot, and that, plus a tendency to wander under pressure, meant that the right way to ride him was to hold him up for a late run. A sound surface suited him ideally, although his performance on soft going in the Irish St Leger was, as we said, a respectable one. His overall record is that of a high-class, tough and consistent animal. *M. R. Stoute*

ROCK LEGEND 4 ch.c. Legend of France (USA) 124 – Two Rock 70 (Mill Reef –
(USA) 141) [1991 7g 10g⁴ 7g⁶ 8.9g⁵ 6s³ 7m⁵ 10g⁵ 11.6m* 12g² 11.5g³ 11.8g⁵ 12.1d
1992 12g⁶ 12g 10g 12d 11.5d] sturdy colt: rated 66 at 3 yrs: below form in handicaps in
1992: should stay beyond 1½m: acts on good to firm ground and soft: sometimes has
tongue tied down. *D. Shaw*

ROCK OPERA (IRE) 4 ch.g. Ballad Rock 122 – Time For Romance (Cure The **61**
Blues (USA)) [1991 5m³ 5m⁶ 6f² 1992 5f⁴ 5g* 5g³ 6f⁴ 6g⁵ 5d 5m 6d 5d² 5s⁴ 6v³ a5g
a6g³] quite good-topped gelding: modest handicapper: won at Catterick in July: may
well prove suited by 7f: acts on any going. *M. P. Naughton*

ROCKOVER 2 b.c. (May 30) Tate Gallery (USA) 117 – Goosie-Gantlet 63 (Run **78** p
The Gantlet (USA)) [1992 5.2m 7f⁵ 7g³ 7d² 7g² 7s*] 7,000Y: smallish colt: moderate walker: has quick action: half-brother to numerous winners, including useful
1984 2-y-o sprinter Ulla Laing (by Mummy's Pet) and 1¼m winner Great Saling (by
Vaigly Great): dam staying daughter of very useful Goosie: progressive colt: gamely
made most in maiden auction at Goodwood in October: will be better suited by
1¼m: best run on soft ground. *R. Hannon*

ROCKRIDGE 5 b.g. Chief Singer 131 – Croda Rossa (ITY) (Grey Sovereign –
128§) [1991 12s 10.8m 1992 8g] rather leggy, attractive gelding: on the downgrade.
K. S. Bridgwater

ROCK SONG (IRE) 3 ch.g. Ballad Rock 122 – Mrs Tittlemouse (Nonoalco **52**
(USA) 131) [1991 6d 6m 6m 7m 6g 7m⁴ 1992 7d 7g⁶ 7f* 6g⁵ 7m 8.3m 8f] tall, rather
leggy gelding: easy mover: inconsistent plater: bought in 5,000 gns when winning at
Warwick in June: pulled up (broke blood vessel) final run (August): stays 7f: acts on
firm ground: effective blinkered or not: sold 2,100 gns Doncaster November Sales.
P. F. I. Cole

ROCK SYMPHONY 2 ch.c. (Mar 11) Ballad Rock 122 – Shamasiya (FR) **89**
(Vayrann 133) [1992 5g 5g⁴ 5f² 5g*] 15,500F, 16,000Y: strong colt: moderate mover:
first foal: dam French middle-distance winner: much improved when making all
against favoured far end in £7,050 event at Beverley in June: not seen out again:
possibly suited by an easy surface. *A. A. Scott*

ROCK THE BOAT 2 b.f. (Apr 28) Slip Anchor 136 – Rimosa's Pet 109 (Petingo **49** p
135) [1992 6g⁵ 6m⁴] rather unfurnished filly: seventh living foal: half-sister to
several winners, notably Kerrera (by Diesis), Rock City (by Ballad Rock) and 3-y-o
1¼m and 11f winner Peto (by Petoski): dam 6f to 10.5f winner: similar form when
beaten around 8 lengths in minor event at Windsor and maiden at Doncaster in July,
not knocked about when unable to quicken last 2f: will be suited by 1¼m: will
improve further. *R. Hannon*

ROCKY BAY 3 ch.f. Bold Owl 101 – Overseas 48 (Sea Hawk II 131) [1991 5m 5g **51** d
6m 6g 6g² 6f² a7g² a6g⁵ 7g⁵ 7m 1992 a6g⁶ 8s* 8.9v 8f⁵ 6g⁴ 7g 7.1s a8g] neat filly:
has a quick action: below form after winning seller at Wolverhampton (no bid) in
April: stays 1m: best effort on soft ground. *D. Haydn Jones*

ROCKY WATERS (USA) 3 b. or br.g. Rocky Marriage (USA) 95 – Running **93**
Melody 86 (Rheingold 137) [1991 5f² 6f* 5g⁶ 6m 6m⁶ 1992 7f* 7g 8m 7d* 7m* 6s⁶]
leggy, lightly-made gelding: has a roundish action: fairly useful handicapper: won at
Lingfield in May and Epsom and Goodwood (£8,100 event) in July: stiff task and not
disgraced in Group 2 event at Baden-Baden final start: stays 7f: acts on firm and
dead ground: tends to sweat: front runner. *G. Lewis*

ROCQUAINE BAY 5 b.m. Morston (FR) 125 – Queen's Royale 80 (Tobrouk **46**
(FR)) [1991 7m 8g⁵ 8.3m 10m² 10g⁵ 8g 9.2s⁵ 1992 10.8d 12d4 10m² 12f* 14s 11.9g²
12g² 12s] leggy mare: poor handicapper: won at Salisbury in July: better suited by
1½m than shorter: suited by a sound surface nowadays. *M. J. Bolton*

ROCTON NORTH (IRE) 4 ch.g. Ballad Rock 122 – Northern Scene 78 **94**
(Habitat 134) [1991 6g² 6d³ 8m² 7g* 8m³ 7m³ 8m⁶ 7m* 1992 7.9m 8.5g 7f³ 7m 7m⁵
7.9m 7f² 7d 7m⁶] compact gelding: often looks dull in coat: poor mover: useful
handicapper, in-and-out form in 1992: best form at 7f/1m on a sound surface: goes
well blinkered: sold 10,500 gns Newmarket Autumn Sales. *R. Hannon*

RODMARTON 5 br.g. Durandal 114 – Soulieana 58 (Manado 130) [1991 a12g –
1992 a11g] no worthwhile form. *A. P. Jarvis*

RODRIGO DE TRIANO (USA) 3 ch.c. El Gran Senor (USA) 136 – Hot **130**
Princess 101 (Hot Spark 126) [1991 6g* 6g* 7f* 7m* 6m* 1992 7d⁴ 8g* 8g*
12g 8m⁴ 10.4g* 10m* a10f]

Top two-year-olds that train on to win classics had been thought an
endangered species in recent times. But the latest season provided some

General Accident Two Thousand Guineas Stakes, Newmarket—
Rodrigo de Triano (spotted cap) bursts through to win impressively from
Lucky Lindy (right), Pursuit of Love and Silver Wisp (extreme left);
then come Muhtarram (striped cap) and Tertian

splendid advertisements for the so-called 'old-fashioned style' of preparing possible classic contenders by running them in races designed to test the best two-year-olds. The Dewhurst winner won the Derby (for the second successive year), the first two in the Prix Marcel Boussac won the Poule d'Essai des Pouliches and the One Thousand Guineas (by a head from the Cheveley Park winner), and the Two Thousand Guineas went to the Champagne Stakes and Middle Park winner who had been unbeaten in five races as a two-year-old. The fashionable theory that competing in the cut and thrust of pattern races as a two-year-old damages a horse's classic potential should now be consigned to the dustbin where it belongs. In a normal year, it takes an outstanding horse—a Shadeed, a Dancing Brave or a Nashwan—to overcome relative inexperience to win the Two Thousand Guineas, for example. When the Guineas races are run the turf season is barely six weeks old and, other things being equal, the later-developing backward types have not had time to make the necessary improvement to beat their more experienced counterparts. Of course, there are always exceptions, but there's justification in the maxim that the Two Thousand and One Thousand Guineas are won by animals that have been good two-year-olds, and as often as not by a colt or filly that has been among the best half-dozen of his or her generation.

Rodrigo de Triano's victories in the Laurent-Perrier Champagne Stakes and the Newgate Stud Middle Park on his last two outings as a two-year-old earned him second place in the International Classification, 8 lb below the outstanding French-trained champion Arazi. With Arazi aimed at the Kentucky Derby, Rodrigo de Triano looked a worthy winter favourite for the General Accident Two Thousand Guineas. Rodrigo de Triano's prospects didn't look quite so bright after a relatively modest effort behind the Horris Hill winner Lion Cavern in the Greenham, a traditional Guineas trial at Newbury in April. Rodrigo de Triano encountered a soft surface for the first time at Newbury which almost certainly played a part in his downfall. But he also looked beforehand as if the race would do him good and his trainer predicted confidently that Rodrigo de Triano would do himself full justice at Newmarket. With the horse's regular rider Carson claimed for the 25/1-shot Muhtarram, Piggott was booked to ride Rodrigo de Triano in the Guineas and partnered him beforehand in a gallop at Manton in which he reportedly worked much better than the Craven Stakes runner-up Dr Devious who, like Arazi, was being trained for the Kentucky Derby. The absence of Arazi, Dr Devious (who had won the Dewhurst), and the likes of Seattle Rhyme (Racing Post Trophy) and El Prado (National Stakes) left Rodrigo de Triano, who recovered from an eleventh-hour heel injury to take his place in the field, as the only Group 1 winner in a substandard-looking sixteen-runner field. Alnasr Alwasheek, conqueror of Dr Devious in the Craven, started favourite for the Guineas at 5/2 with the European Free Handicap winner Pursuit of Love (9/2) also preferred to Rodrigo de Triano (6/1). French-trained 8/1-shot Cardoun, successful in the Criterium de Maisons-Laffitte as a two-year-old and the Prix Djebel on his reappearance, was the only other runner to start at odds shorter than 12/1. The Guineas field split into two groups and Rodrigo de Triano was waited with last of those on the stand side. He missed some scrimmaging, which involved Muhtarram, Alnasr Alwasheek and others, as he came with a smooth run to collar Pursuit of Love inside the final furlong and quicken away for a length-and-a-half victory over the staying-on 50/1-shot Lucky Lindy. Pursuit of Love kept on for third, half a length further back, with Silver Wisp and unlucky-in-running Muhtarram close behind; Alnasr Alwasheek came home ninth, and Cardoun twelfth.

Rodrigo de Triano's Two Thousand Guineas victory provided his owner Robert Sangster with his first English classic winner since Rodrigo de Triano's sire El Gran Senor won the same race in 1984. Sangster's racing strength nowadays is mainly centred on the superbly-appointed training complex at Manton where Peter Chapple-Hyam, assistant to the previous incumbent at Manton, Barry Hills, took over when negotiations for Hills to purchase Manton fell through in the winter of 1990/91. Chapple-Hyam who'd been looking at the possibility of training in Australia, has been a revelation since taking over at Manton, the magnificent achievements of Rodrigo de Triano and Derby winner Dr Devious putting him firmly on the map after only two seasons as a trainer. Chapple-Hyam wasn't born when Rodrigo de Triano's jockey Lester Piggott rode the first of his Two Thousand Guineas winners Crepello. Since then Piggott has won the race on Sir Ivor, Nijinsky and Shadeed; Rodrigo de Triano's success took his total of English classic victories to thirty. Piggott's unexpected return to riding in 1990, after retiring from the saddle in 1986 to take up training and then serving time in prison for tax offences, was one of the most amazing sporting comebacks of recent times. He remains extremely popular with the racing public and his association with Rodrigo de Triano in the latest season provided some of the most striking images of the flat-racing year.

Rodrigo de Triano went on to complete the Anglo-Irish Two Thousand Guineas double, only the fourth horse to do so, following Right Tack in 1969, Don't Forget Me in 1987 and Tirol in 1990. Four other Two Thousand Guineas winners—High Top, Nebbiolo, To-Agori-Mou and Lomond—have attempted the double and failed at the Curragh. Lucky Lindy was the only member of the Guineas field to take on Rodrigo de Triano in the Irish equivalent for which there were only six runners. Rodrigo de Triano won in similar style to

Airlie/Coolmore Irish Two Thousand Guineas, the Curragh—
Rodrigo de Triano impresses again; Lucky Lindy is fourth this time,
beaten by the blinkered Ezzoud and Brief Truce

Juddmonte International Stakes, York —
Rodrigo de Triano gets the trip well under a supremely confident ride;
All At Sea is a good second, followed in by Seattle Rhyme (rails) and Dr Devious

Newmarket, producing a fine last-to-first run to land the odds a shade comfortably by a length from Ezzoud with Brief Truce third ahead of Lucky Lindy. Where now with Rodrigo de Triano? Piggott made plain his view that Rodrigo de Triano wouldn't get much further than a mile, and at first connections reportedly pencilled in the St James's Palace Stakes at Royal Ascot for the colt's next race. But there was a change of heart and Rodrigo de Triano took his chance in a very open-looking Ever Ready Derby, for which he started 13/2 favourite, just ahead of Dr Devious. Although he was by no means certain to stay the Derby trip, Rodrigo de Triano wasn't, in truth, given much opportunity to prove his stamina one way or the other in the Derby. Piggott seemed to accept a long way out that Rodrigo de Triano wasn't going to be involved in the finish; the horse was neither placed to challenge nor knocked about, running on past stragglers in the closing stages to finish ninth after being in an impossible position at Tattenham Corner. It was a puzzling performance, allowing that Rodrigo de Triano had sweated up uncharacteristically and become more on edge than usual in the preliminaries. Piggott reported that Rodrigo de Triano hadn't handled the track. There were obvious excuses for Rodrigo de Triano's defeat in the St James's Palace Stakes on his next outing thirteen days later. He didn't look at his best physically and Piggott gave him too much to do, anchoring him at the back in a slowly-run race with the result that he faced a well-nigh impossible task soon after the pace quickened sharply approaching the final straight. After swinging very wide into the straight, Rodrigo de Triano made up a lot of ground in the centre of the track and looked for a moment as if he might win. But his efforts took their toll and he finished fourth behind Brief Truce, Zaahi and Ezzoud, one place in front of the disappointing Arazi.

Rodrigo de Triano was given a break after Royal Ascot and, after being withdrawn from his next intended objective, the Prix Jacques le Marois over a mile at Deauville in August, because of heavy ground, he was switched to the Juddmonte International at York. 'If Rodrigo can finish in the first three, he will go for the Prix du Moulin,' said his trainer. In a strong field, the very

690

Dubai Champion Stakes, Newmarket—
perfect timing from Piggott once more, and Lahib is beaten a neck

confidently-ridden Rodrigo de Triano exceeded most expectations, storming through in a race run at a true gallop to win impressively by a length—idling after taking the lead—from the Oaks runner-up All At Sea, with Seattle Rhyme third and Dr Devious fourth. The York crowd gave Piggott and Rodrigo de Triano a rousing reception, probably the most enthusiastic given to any winner in Britain all season. Piggott produced another virtuoso performance on Rodrigo de Triano in the Dubai Champion Stakes at Newmarket in October which became the next target after soft going ruled him out of the Moulin and the Queen Elizabeth II Stakes at Ascot. After being an uncertain runner at Newmarket because of a recurrence of a thrown splint, the bandaged Rodrigo de Triano was ridden with coolness and impeccable judgement by Piggott who stalked his main rival Carson on the Queen Elizabeth II Stakes winner Lahib until producing a perfectly-timed challenge to lead about a hundred yards out. After travelling strongly on the bridle from the start, Rodrigo de Triano needed only to be ridden with hands and heels and won a shade cheekily by a neck, the first two finishing three lengths clear of the rest headed by Environment Friend.

The Champion Stakes was Rodrigo de Triano's fourth Group 1 victory of the season and the success prompted his owner—who used to be criticised for under-racing some of his top-class colts—to send him to the Breeders' Cup at Gulfstream Park for a crack at North America's best. Rodrigo de Triano ran in the Breeders' Cup Classic on dirt in preference to the Breeders' Cup Mile on turf, but he finished last of fourteen runners, virtually tailed off. Swinburn was a last-minute replacement for Piggott, injured when the July Cup winner Mr Brooks took a fatal fall in the Breeders' Cup Sprint. Rodrigo de Triano's magnificent racing career therefore ended on a low note. But his defeat at Gulfstream Park on an unfamiliar surface in unfamiliar climatic conditions shouldn't be allowed to detract from his earlier achievements. He was a top-class performer at a mile to a mile and a quarter, described by Piggott as 'up there with the best I've ridden'. 'He has all the attributes,' said Piggott, 'including speed—so you can go along easily all the way—and a very good finish.' Rodrigo de Triano's first class turn of foot was a formidable weapon. A

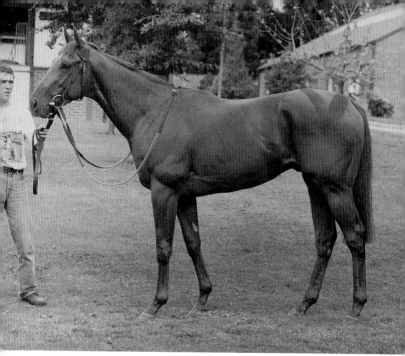

Mr R. E. Sangster's "Rodrigo de Triano"

tendency to idle once he'd hit the front, however, meant that his finishing effort had to be saved as late as possible, with the result that he probably didn't always show the full measure of his superiority over those he ran against. Horses whose most telling weapon is a turn of foot are, generally speaking, always more likely to be favoured by top-of-the-ground conditions, which place emphasis on finishing speed, than by soft which put the accent on stamina; the quick-actioned Rodrigo de Triano showed his best form on a sound surface and acted on firm going.

Rodrigo de Triano (USA) (ch.c. 1989)	El Gran Senor (USA) (b 1981)	Northern Dancer (b 1961)	Nearctic
			Natalma
		Sex Appeal (ch 1970)	Buckpasser
			Best In Show
	Hot Princess (ch 1980)	Hot Spark (ch 1972)	Habitat
			Garvey Girl
		Aspara (gr 1972)	Crimson Satan
			Courtside

Rodrigo de Triano, angular but quite good-topped in appearance, was sold for a reported 6,200,000 dollars (around £3,750,000) before the Breeders' Cup and will be at stud in Japan in 1993. It is understood that plans had been quite well advanced for Rodrigo de Triano to be syndicated to stand at Coolmore and his sale illustrates how different the commercial bloodstock market is nowadays from the days in the 'seventies and early-'eighties when Mr Sangster's racing empire was at its height. Rodrigo de Triano would have

692

been regarded as far too attractive a stud proposition to have found his way to Japan in those days. He had much in common with his sire El Gran Senor, a very genuine racehorse with a superb turn of foot who developed quickly and was able to shine in the major two-year-old races before training on to win classics. El Gran Senor has had fertility problems and his first few crops averaged only around twenty-five named foals—he has had more in his most recent crops—but that hasn't stopped him making a name for himself as a sire. He has had a high ratio of stakes winners to runners and is also the sire of the King George VI and Queen Elizabeth Stakes winner Belmez. The average distance of races won at three years and upwards by the progeny of El Gran Senor is about nine and a half furlongs; the Queen's Vase runner-up Belgran and the fair handicapper Inan were his only winners at eleven furlongs or further in the latest turf season in Britain. The stamina doubts about Rodrigo de Triano before the Derby also reflected the predominance of speed on the distaff side of his pedigree. His dam Hot Princess, a fairly useful winner at up to seven furlongs in Ireland and afterwards successful twice at eight and a half furlongs and once at nine in the United States, is a product of two sprinters. Her sire Hot Spark showed his form only at five furlongs and her dam the modest maiden Aspara did nearly all her racing over the minimum trip. The much-travelled Hot Princess, incidentally, has been repatriated to Ireland from New Zealand where she produced colts by Danzatore and Sir Tristram in 1990 and 1991; now in foal to Sadler's Wells, Hot Princess had one living foal before Rodrigo de Triano, the Assert colt Cedrela who won a seven-furlong maiden event at Brighton as a two-year-old before being sold for 17,500 guineas at the Newmarket Autumn Sales for export to Malaysia where he has also been successful. *P. W. Chapple-Hyam*

ROGER RABBIT (FR)   3 b.g. Rusticaro (FR) 124 – Bustelda (FR) (Busted 134)   **43**
[1991 7g 5s a7g⁶ 1992 9.2d⁴ 10d⁵ 8.2g⁴ 8.2g 8f 10g 14.1g⁵] sturdy gelding: poor performer: stays 1¾m: acts on soft ground: ran poorly when blinkered once: sold 2,600 gns Newmarket September Sales. *R. Boss*

ROGER THE BUTLER (IRE)   2 ch.c. (Jan 30) Ahonoora 122 – Indian Jubilee   **97**
81 (Indian King (USA) 128) [1992 5g 7g⁴ 7m² 6d² 6s* 5g² 5d⁴] 39,000Y: strong, lengthy colt: moderate mover: first foal: dam sprinter: useful performer: not at best to win maiden at Newcastle in September: excellent second to Up And At 'Em in Cornwallis Stakes at Ascot next outing, and not discredited in Doncaster listed race after: best at 6f or testing 5f: acts on soft going. *M. Bell*

ROKEBY   3 b.c. Lomond (USA) 128 – Rose Bowl (USA) 131 (Habitat 134) [1991 **110**
6d⁵ 6m* 6g³ 6m² 7d* 8m² 8d³ 8s 1992 a10g² a9g³ 10m] smallish, sturdy, rather dipped-backed colt: moderate mover: useful performer: best efforts when placed in minor event at Lingfield (bandaged off-fore) and Grade 1 Wood Memorial Stakes at Aqueduct: not seen again after running poorly when blinkered in listed race at Goodwood in May: should prove suited by 1¼m+: acts on good to firm and soft ground. *I. A. Balding*

ROLL A DOLLAR   6 b.g. Spin of A Coin 88 – Handy Dancer 87 (Green God 128)   **90**
[1991 12g 12g 13.9g² 1992 10g 12g³ 13.3g 12m] tall, workmanlike gelding: good mover: below form in handicaps after third in £8,200 race at Kempton in September: effective at 1½m to 2m: acts on firm going, probably unsuited by soft. *D. R. C. Elsworth*

ROLLING THE BONES (USA)   3 b.c. Green Dancer (USA) 132 – Davelle's   **74**
Bid (USA) (Bold Bidder) [1991 NR 1992 8g 10d⁵ 11.7s⁵ 10m 14d⁴ 14.1f² 14g 16.2g² 17.5d* 16.1g⁵ 16d 15.8d 15.1d] $20,000Y: lengthy colt: half-brother to several winners, including fairly useful 5f (at 2 yrs) to 1m winner Hills Bid (by Temperence Hill), later successful in USA: dam never ran: well below form after winning handicap at Ayr in August: suited by test of stamina: acts on firm and dead going: below form when blinkered once: claimed out of J. Fanshawe's stable £12,060 eighth start. *M. P. Naughton*

ROLY WALLACE   3 b.g. Primo Dominie 121 – Ethel Knight (Thatch (USA) 136)   **63** §
[1991 6g⁶ 6f² 5m² 6g 5.7m³ 6f² 6f* 6m⁶ 7m 6f 7f 5m 6m 6m⁴ 1992 7d 7g 10g³ 10m³ 10f⁴ 9.9m⁵ 8f* 8.9d 8m⁴ 8m 9g 8.2g] neat gelding: poor mover: well below form after winning claiming handicap (ran in snatches) at Salisbury in June: stays 1¼m: acts on firm ground: effective in blinkers or not: moody, one to treat with caution. *K. T. Ivory*

ROMALITO 2 b.g. (Mar 26) Robellino (USA) 127 – Princess Zita 90 (Manado 130) **62**
[1992 7d 7m⁴ 8g⁴ 8.2d 8d 10g⁶] 10,500Y: good-topped gelding: has a markedly round
action: fifth foal: half-brother to 3-y-o 17f winner Prince Mercury (by Sharrood),
1½m seller winner Bourbon Prince (by Star Appeal) and a winner in Brazil: dam, 7f
winner, is out of half-sister to smart stayer Karadar: modest maiden: should prove
better suited by 1½m: acts on good to firm ground. *M. Blanshard*

ROMANCE (IRE) 3 b.f. Alzao (USA) 117 – Kilistrano (Capistrano 120) [1991 NR –
1992 7g⁶ 10m 9.7g 8.9d 10.2d] IR 10,000F, IR 18,000Y: small filly: half-sister to
several winners, including 1983 Irish 2-y-o 7f winner Malistrano (by Malinowski),
subsequently a useful hurdler, and 1½m seller winner Stray No More (by Ballymore): dam Irish 2-y-o 5f winner: no worthwhile form: sold 1,000 gns Doncaster
November Sales. *M. J. Heaton-Ellis*

ROMANIAN (IRE) 4 ch.c. Sallust 134 – Cailin d'Oir (Roi Soleil 125) [1991 8f² **47**
10d 8f³ 8m² 8g 9.7m³ 12f⁴ 10m 1992 11.9d 11.9m 11.9f³ 17.2f⁴ 14.1m³ 12v⁶ a16g²]
compact colt: often ran creditably, but sometimes looked none too resolute: stays
2m: best efforts on top-of-the-ground: trained until after fifth start by A. Davison. *R.
Akehurst*

ROMANSH 3 b.c. Shernazar 131 – Romara 105 (Bold Lad (IRE) 133) [1991 7m **73**
8m⁵ 1992 12.2d* 12.3s³ 10d² 10.2d³ 10s² 10s⁶] tall, leggy, angular colt: has a quick
action: fair handicapper: won maiden at Catterick in March: rare poor effort in celebrity race at Ascot final start after 2½-month lay-off: effective at 1¼m and 1½m: acts
on soft ground: consistent: sold to join Miss J. Doyle 5,000 gns Newmarket Autumn
Sales. *G. Wragg*

ROMANY RYE 4 ch.c. Nijinsky (CAN) 138 – Zinzara (USA) 119 (Stage Door **102**
Johnny) [1991 12m³ 12m⁴ 14m² 14.6f² 13.9m* 15m* 13.9m² 16g³ 1992 14s³ 16.2m*
22.2g*] big, lengthy colt: carries condition: easy mover: consistent stayer: won
well-contested Haydock minor event in May and Queen Alexandra Stakes at Royal
Ascot (by neck from Gondolier, pair clear) in June, both after tremendous last 2f
battle: progressing well, but not seen out again and sold only 8,000 gns Newmarket
Autumn Sales: stays extremely well: ran creditably on soft ground, but best form on
a sound surface: held up. *G. Wragg*

ROMEO OSCAR 2 b.c. (Apr 24) Bairn (USA) 126 – Supreme Rose 95 (Frimley **60**
Park 109) [1992 6g⁶ 5v² a5g] smallish, angular colt: first foal: dam sprinter: modest
maiden: off course over 3 months before easily best effort when second at Redcar in
October, staying on well: sold out of B. Hills's stable 7,400 gns Newmarket Autumn
Sales: again slowly away on final start: will stay 6f: acts on heavy ground. *J. S.
Wainwright*

ROMOLA NIJINSKY 4 b.f. Bustino 136 – Verchinina 99 (Star Appeal 133) [1991 –
7m⁵ 7g⁴ 10g⁵ 11.9m 8g⁵ 1992 a13g 10.2f 8.3m 8.9g] workmanlike filly: moderate
mover: rated 88 early as 3-y-o: well below best in 1992, including in sellers: stays
1¼m: won selling hurdle in September. *P. D. Evans*

ROMOOSH 3 b.f. Formidable (USA) 125 – Missed Blessing 115 (So Blessed 130) **69**
[1991 NR 1992 8g⁵ 9.9g* 11.9m 8g] 26,000Y: sturdy filly: moderate mover: fifth foal:
half-sister to fair 11.7f winner Lake Mission (by Blakeney) and fair 7f and 1m winner
Reality (by Known Fact): dam 6f and 1m winner: trained by N. Callaghan on debut in
May: improved to win 4-runner maiden at Beverley in August: no chance in listed
race at York and well held in handicap at Kempton after: stays 1¼m: sold to rejoin N.
Callaghan 7,600 gns Newmarket Autumn Sales. *C. E. Brittain*

ROSA WHY (IRE) 3 b.f. Damister (USA) 123 – Fallen Rose (Busted 134) [1991 **69**
6g 6m⁴ 7m² 8.2m⁶ a7g 1992 a8g³ a8g* a8g* a10g*] rather finely-made, quite
attractive filly: in fine form to win maiden and handicaps at Lingfield, but not seen
out after February: better suited by 1¼m than shorter: goes very well on equitrack.
W. Jarvis

ROSCOMMON JOE (IRE) 2 b.c. (Apr 12) Simply Great (FR) 122 – Kilvarnet **41**
78 (Furry Glen 121) [1992 7d 7g 6m] rangy colt: has plenty of scope: second foal:
half-brother to 3-y-o 7f (at 2 yrs) and 1m winner Ferdia (by Petorius): dam 5f (at 2
yrs) and 7.6f winner: backward and behind in maidens at Ayr (ran wide into
straight), Newcastle and Pontefract (hit rail and hung right in early stages) in
second half of season: broke out of stalls and withdrawn once. *J. J. O'Neill*

ROSE ALTO 4 ch.f. Adonijah 126 – Rose Music 86 (Luthier 126) [1991 8m⁶ 10g⁴ **90**
9.9m* 10g 10m 1992 10f* 10d 10m 10g⁴ 11.5m* 10g³ 12g⁵] leggy, rather close-
coupled filly: fairly useful handicapper: successful at Redcar (gamely in Zetland
Gold Cup) in May and Yarmouth in September: good fifth in November Handicap

at Doncaster: effective at 1¼m to 1½m: best efforts on a sound surface. *J. R. Fanshawe*

ROSEATE LODGE   6 b.g. Habitat 134 – Elegant Tern (USA) 102 (Sea Bird II   **80**
145) [1991 8g² 8d² 8g⁶ 8m⁴ 8g 10g 8.9g⁶ 8.1m⁶ 9m 1992 a5g² 8g 8d² 8g³ 9m⁶ 8f 8m
8m² 8.3g² 9d² 9d⁵ 8s⁴ 9d] compact, workmanlike gelding: fair handicapper: very
hard to win with nowadays: stays 9f: acts on any going: held up: sold to join K.
Burke's stable 11,000 gns Newmarket Autumn Sales. *R. W. Armstrong*

ROSE CUT (USA)   5 ch.g. Diesis 133 – Sweet Ramblin Rose (USA) (Turn-To)   **38**
[1991 12d 14.1f⁶ 1992 9m 11.5m³ 10g] bad maiden: stays 11.5f: acts on good to firm
ground: blinkered last 2 starts: sold 1,200 gns Ascot November Sales. *D. J. S. Cosgrove*

ROSE EDGE   3 b.c. Kris 135 – Butterfly Rose (USA) (Iron Ruler (USA)) [1991 NR   –
1992 8g 10f 8g] 20,000Y: good-bodied colt: half-brother to winners in Italy and
Norway: dam leading filly in Norway: no form in maidens and claimer. *J. W. Hills*

ROSE ELEGANCE   3 ch.f. Bairn (USA) 126 – Shapina 105 (Sharp Edge 123)   **83**
[1991 7.1d⁴ 1992 8g³ 8f* 8m⁶ 8g³dis 8d⁵ 10m*] tall, leggy filly: progressed well in
1992: won maiden at Brighton in June and handicap (reported to be bleeding
internally afterwards) at Newmarket in September: ideally suited by 1¼m and a
sound surface. *W. R. Muir*

ROSEFINCH (USA)   3 ch.f. Blushing Groom (FR) 131 – Oh So Sharp 131 (Kris **117**
135) [1991 NR 1992 10s² 10g* 10g* 10.5g⁵ 12g³ 9.3s 10f⁶] third foal: half-sister to
very useful Shaima (by Shareef Dancer), successful over 7.3f and 8.9f here then
1½m in USA, and to Irish 1m winner Ben Alisky (by Dunbeath), subsequently
successful in Hong Kong: dam 1000 Guineas, Oaks and St Leger winner: successful
at Longchamp in minor event and Prix Saint-Alary (beat Jolypha short head) in May:
best subsequent efforts when over 2½ lengths fifth to Jolypha in Prix de Diane at
Chantilly and over 4½ lengths sixth to Super Staff in Yellow Ribbon Invitational at

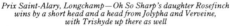

*Prix Saint-Alary, Longchamp—Oh So Sharp's daughter Rosefinch
wins by a short head and a head from Jolypha and Verveine,
with Trishyde up there as well*

Santa Anita: needed further than 9f but bit below best over 1½m: smart: visits Sadler's Wells. *A. Fabre, France*

ROSE FLYER (IRE)   2 b.f. (Mar 18) Nordico (USA) – String of Straw (Thatch-   **37** ing 131) [1992 6g a6g 7m a5g⁶ a5g 7m a7g⁴ a8g⁵] robust filly: fourth foal: dam unraced: poor maiden: best form at 1m: seems none too easy ride. *M. C. Chapman*

ROSE GEM (IRE)   3 b.f. Taufan (USA) 119 – Mombones (Lord Gayle (USA) 124)   **62** [1991 6g 6m³ 7m 1992 7.5m² 7.1m⁴ 7.1m* 8f⁵ 7.1m* 7g* 7g 7g] rather leggy filly: modest performer: made all in maiden claimer at Edinburgh and handicaps at Edinburgh and Ayr in summer: probably ideally suited by 7f: acts on firm ground: takes keen hold: sold 3,600 gns Doncaster September Sales. *P. C. Haslam*

ROSE GLEN   6 b.m. Lochnager 132 – Phoenix Rose 85 (Frankincense 120) [1991   **65** a8g 7d⁶ 7m 8m⁵ 10.6g⁴ 9m* 10.3d* 10.5m² 10.9g* 10.9m* 10.5g⁵ 10.5f 10m³ 9m 10.3d³ 9g 1992 10.3g 8.3d² 9m 10.3g³ 8.9g⁴ 10f* 10.3m* 10.5g⁵ 12.3g* 10.1f 10.3s] big, workmanlike mare: has a rather round action: modest claimer/handicapper: successful in summer at Redcar and Chester (2): effective at 9f to 1½m: acts on firm and dead ground: effective with or without blinkers or visor: successful for amateur: tough and genuine. *A. Bailey*

ROSE INDIEN (FR)   3 br.f. Crystal Glitters (USA) 127 – Green Rosy (USA)   **108** (Green Dancer (USA) 132) [1991 6.1f² 6m* 7m* 1992 7.3d⁶ 7f² 7g 6m* 6g 6g* 6d⁶] leggy, lengthy filly: off course 2½ months after disappointing sixth in Fred Darling Stakes at Newbury but in good form in second half of 1992: successful in good style at Newmarket in handicap and listed race (best effort to beat Hamas 2½ lengths, always front rank on far rail): below form in Group 3 event at Ascot final start: should prove as effective at 7f as 6f: well below form on a soft surface. *M. Moubarak*

ROSE NOBLE (USA)   2 b.f. (Feb 22) Vaguely Noble 140 – La Papagena (Habi-   **– p** tat 134) [1992 8d] second live foal: dam unraced daughter of very smart 5f to 1m winner Magic Flute: 10/1, shaped lot better than tenth-of-20 position suggests to Lille Hammer in Yarmouth maiden in October, prominent to under 2f out and not knocked about in slightest, beaten around 17 lengths: capable of fair bit better. *W. Jarvis*

ROSE OF MACMILLION   3 b.f. Macmillion 110 – Tic-On-Rose (Celtic Cone   **60** 116) [1991 6f 7m 1992 10d 10f 16m⁵ 16.9d] rangy filly: has a round action: modest maiden: tailed off final start: appears to stay 2m. *Mrs Barbara Waring*

ROSE OF MAN   2 b.f. (Mar 30) Bold Owl 101 – Lake Superior 49 (Right Tack 131)   **36** [1992 7g 7m 8.5m 8m 8.3v] 1,400F: good-bodied filly: sixth living foal: half-sister to 1m to 10.7f winner Four For Uncle (by Uncle Pokey) and a winner abroad: dam winning plater: well beaten in varied company, including selling: sold out of J. Berry's stable 1,000 gns Doncaster September Sales after third outing. *D. Moffatt*

ROSES HAVE THORNS   5 ch.m. Ela-Mana-Mou 132 – Cienaga (Tarboosh   **47** (USA)) [1991 10d² 10g 10d 10.4m 10.2g⁵ 10m 12m³ 11.5f⁴ 11m⁵ 11.8m⁵ 12m 12m² 10.3g⁵ 1992 10.3g 11.5d⁵] leggy, rather shallow-girthed mare: poor handicapper: stays 1½m: acts on firm and dead ground: effective visored or not: has joined D. Wintle. *D. Morris*

ROSGILL   6 ch.g. Mill Reef (USA) 141 – Speedy Rose (On Your Mark 125) [1991   **65 +** a13g³a13g³ 11.5m² 12v* 11.5s* 12.2d² 14m 14s 12d² 16m 12d 1992 12d⁵ 11.9f⁶ 12m⁶] angular gelding: rated 76 at 5 yrs: below form in handicaps in first half of 1992: effective at 1½m to 2m: has form on any going, but particularly well suited by give: sometimes carries head high but suitable mount for inexperienced rider: fair hurdler, now with M. Tompkins. *P. Mitchell*

ROSIE O'REILLY (IRE)   2 b.f. (May 11) Dominion Royale 112 – Bay Supreme   **–** (Martinmas 128) [1992 5g] 3,000Y: fifth foal: half-sister to 4 winners, including 3-y-o Jefferson Davis (by The Noble Player), successful at 6f (at 2 yrs) and 7f, and 6f/7f performer Pesidanamich (by Mummy's Treasure): dam unraced: always behind in maiden auction at Haydock in June. *E. J. Alston*

ROSIE'S GOLD   2 b.f. (Mar 21) Glint of Gold 128 – New Central 74 (Remainder   **37** Man 126§) [1992 a7g a8g⁶] third foal: half-sister to 3-y-o Kashmir Rose (by Local Suitor) and 1m winner Jolizal (by Good Times): dam 6f to 1m winner: poor form in maidens at Lingfield late in season. *D. Morris*

ROSIETOES (USA)   4 b.f. Master Willie 129 – Desrose 74 (Godswalk (USA)   **46** 130) [1991 7m³ 8g² 8.3m 7m² 9d 8m 1992 8g 8.1m 7.1m⁶ 8.3m⁵ 10s 9g] leggy, angular filly: rated 67 at 3 yrs: below form in handicaps in 1992: stays 1m: acts on good to firm ground. *L. G. Cottrell*

ROSINA MAE 3 b.f. Rousillon (USA) 133 – Dame Ashfield 90 (Grundy 137) [1991 **75**
NR 1992 8m⁶ 10d 10.2f² 11.9m² 14.1m⁴ 16m* 14m⁴] leggy, sparely-made filly: fourth
foal: sister to fair 2-y-o 6f and 7f winner Dame Rousara and half-sister to winning
hurdler Valiant Dash (by Valiyar): dam 1½m winner out of Cheshire Oaks and Park
Hill winner African Dancer: consistent form in maidens before winner and good
fourth in Newmarket handicaps in October: will stay beyond 2m: probably acts on
firm and dead going. *Lord Huntingdon*

ROSMARINO 2 br.g. (Mar 16) Persian Bold 123 – No More Rosies 74 (Warpath **47**
113) [1992 7s 8.3s⁶ 8d] 27,000F: tall, rather leggy gelding: third foal: half-brother to
7f (at 2 yrs) winner Beachy Head (by Damister) and 3-y-o Only A Rose (by Glint of
Gold): dam 1¼m winner from 2 starts, is half-sister to Derby third Mount Athos and
smart sprinter John Splendid: form in autumn maidens only when never-dangerous
sixth at Hamilton: still looked green and burly on final start. *C. W. Thornton*

ROSSANITA (IRE) 4 b.f. Anita's Prince 126 – Chanrossa (High Top 131) [1991 **–**
6s³ 6f 5.9h⁴ 7g 6f 6f 8.2m 8m 1992 8v] lengthy, workmanlike filly: carries condition:
moderate mover: no worthwhile form: tried blinkered. *N. Bycroft*

ROSSCOYNE 2 b.f. (Feb 15) Ardross 134 – Banking Coyne 76 (Deep Diver 134) **–**
[1992 6d] compact filly: sixth known foal: half-sister to 5f performer Miami Banker
(by Miami Springs) and 1m seller winner Greek Banker (by Avgerinos): dam best at
5f: 50/1, backward and bandaged behind, slowly away and always behind in maiden at
Kempton in September. *W. R. Muir*

ROSS GRAHAM 4 gr.g. Macmillion 110 – Play It Sam (Mandamus 120) [1991 8m **–**
12g 14.6d³ 1992 12d 14.1d 16s 14.6g⁶] lengthy, leggy gelding: no worthwhile form in
1992: should stay beyond 1¾m: acts on dead ground. *Mrs Barbara Waring*

ROSTAND (IRE) 2 gr.c. (Mar 28) Cyrano de Bergerac 120 – Farmers Daughter **–**
(Red Slipper 126) [1992 5m] IR 10,000F, 15,500Y: lengthy colt: has scope: closely
related to a winner by Ballad Rock and half-brother to several winners here and
abroad, including speedy 1979 2-y-o Titavri (by Wishing Star): dam ran 3 times:
always behind in 11-runner maiden at Windsor in June: sold 1,100 gns Newmarket
Autumn Sales. *L. J. Holt*

ROSTANDS HERO (IRE) 3 b.g. Cyrano de Bergerac 120 – Miel (Pall Mall **–**
132) [1991 5m 8m 8d 1992 7s a8g] smallish, good-bodied gelding: poor mover: bad
maiden: tried in blinkers and visor. *H. J. Collingridge*

ROSTOVOL 7 b.g. Vaigly Great 127 – Emerin 85 (King Emperor (USA)) [1991 **– §**
NR 1992 8.1g 8.1m] leggy gelding: moderate mover: untrustworthy handicapper:
stays 1m: probably acts on any going: below form blinkered/visored. *D. R. Franks*

ROUCELLIST BAY 4 ch.g. Rousillon (USA) 133 – Cellist (USA) (Bagdad) [1991 **–**
12.2m 13.8f⁵ 1992 12h⁶ 12.1m] leggy, plain gelding: no sign of ability. *V. Thompson*

ROUGH GUESS (IRE) 2 br.f. (Apr 22) Believe It (USA) – Fenny Rough 114 **52**
(Home Guard (USA) 129) [1992 5.1s² 6m⁶ 6.1d 8f 8.3s] IR 6,000Y: small, workmanlike filly: fourth foal: half-sister to a winner in Italy by Sharpen Up: dam 5f to 7f
winner later successful in USA: sire 5.5f to 9f winner: off course 3 months after
second in maiden auction at Bath and showed little after return: visored final outing:
sold 700 gns Ascot November Sales. *Lord Huntingdon*

ROUND BY THE RIVER 3 b.f. Superlative 118 – Marie Galante 73 (Shirley **63**
Heights 130) [1991 5m 7m⁵ 5g⁶ 1992 7f 7m* 8m⁵ 7.5d* 8m² 8m] close-coupled
filly: modest performer: successful in maiden at Newcastle in May and claimer at
Beverley in July: stays 1m: acts on good to firm and dead (badly hampered on firm).
W. W. Haigh

ROUQUETTE 2 b. or br.f. (Apr 25) Rousillon (USA) 133 – Zamayem (Sadler's **108**
Wells (USA) 132) [1992 5.5g⁴ 6s* 5.5g³ 7s² 8s⁴ 8s⁴] 4,100Y: small, good-bodied
filly: first foal: dam, unraced, from family of Full Dress II: progressive filly: narrowly
won minor event at Maisons-Laffitte in July: in frame after in Prix Robert-Papin at
Maisons-Laffitte, 5-runner Prix du Calvados at Deauville and Prix Marcel Boussac
(under 2 lengths fourth to Gold Splash) and Prix des Reservoirs at Longchamp: will
stay 1¼m: has raced only on an easy surface. *Mme M. Bollack-Badel, France*

ROUSILLA 2 b.f. (Feb 15) Rousillon (USA) 133 – Secret Life (USA) (Elocutionist **–**
(USA)) [1992 7g] 7,500Y: lengthy, workmanlike filly: third foal: half-sister to 3-y-o
Kayvee (by Kaldoun), successful at 6f and (at 2 yrs) 6.9f: dam French 1m winner:
always behind in maiden auction at Yarmouth in July. *K. T. Ivory*

ROUSILLON TO BE 5 b.g. Rousillon (USA) 133 – Triple Bar 71 (Jimmy Reppin **–**
131) [1991 a11g a12g⁶ 1992 12d 17.2f] big, leggy gelding: successful over hurdles in

1991/2 but on the downgrade on flat: stays 1½m: has joined D. McCarthy. *Miss B. Sanders*

ROUSITTO   4 ch.g. Rousillon (USA) 133 – Helenetta 97 (Troy 137) [1991 8d³ 8s⁶   **73**
10.1s* 8g³ 8.2m 10.1g⁴ 9m 1992 8g⁴ 10s³ 9.9g⁴ 10.4m 12.3f* 11.6g⁶ 11.9s³ 11.8d 12d
12g] tall, angular gelding: moderate mover: modest handicapper: won at Ripon in
June: below form last 3 starts: should stay beyond 1½m: acts on any going: tends to
carry head rather awkwardly, and held up. *R. Hollinshead*

ROUTING   4 b.g. Rousillon (USA) 133 – Tura (Northfields (USA)) [1991 6f⁶ 10f*   **60**
10g⁴ 9m⁶ 8g³ 9m⁵ 8.1m³ 9.2f 1992 8.5m⁶ 8f⁴ 8f⁵ 8.1m* 8m⁴ 10m⁴ 8.1f² 7.5g⁶
8.5m] angular gelding: modest handicapper: won at Edinburgh in June: effective at
1m to 1¼m: acts on firm ground and dead: has found little, carried head awkwardly,
and been somewhat headstrong. *M. D. Hammond*

ROUWI (IRE)   2 b.f. (Apr 30) Stalker 121 – Rohana (Roan Rocket 128) [1992 5g⁶   –
6s] neat filly: sixth reported living foal: half-sister to a winner in Italy by Tumble
Wind: dam unraced: daughter of good middle-distance filly Parthian Glance: bandaged near-hind, well beaten in minor event and seller in spring. *N. A. Callaghan*

ROWANDENE (IRE)   3 gr.g. Wassl 125 – Hysteria (Prince Bee 128) [1991 5g⁶   –
1992 7d 8v 12g] leggy gelding: no form in 1992: should prove suited by at least 7f. *M.
H. Easterby*

ROWAN EMPIRE   3 gr.f. Elegant Air 119 – Hallo Rosie 67 (Swing Easy (USA)   –
126) [1991 NR 1992 8f 12g 14g] 8,200Y: workmanlike filly: third reported foal: half-
sister to 5f winner Spot On Annie (by Miami Springs) and 7f winner Grown At
Rowan (by Gabitat): dam won 5f seller: no worthwhile form in maidens: unruly start,
got loose, first intended start: trained debut by M. Madgwick. *C. G. O'Donovan,
Ireland*

ROW REE   4 b.c. Ore 116 – A'Dhahirah (Beldale Flutter (USA) 130) [1991 NR 1992   **65**
12m* 20m a16g] strong, lengthy colt: first foal: dam unraced half-sister to smart 7f
to 1¼m performer Beau Sher: successful in 2 NH Flat races and Beverley maiden in
spring: well beaten in handicaps after, off course 4½ months before final run: stays
1½m. *P. J. Hobbs*

ROXY MUSIC (IRE)   3 b.f. Song 132 – Roxy Hart (High Top 131) [1991 5m 5m⁴   **47**
a5g⁴ 7m⁴ a7g² 7.1m* 9m⁶ 7m⁵ 1992 7a 8g a8g 8g⁶ 8f 6g² 7g a7g 6s 7s] compact filly:
inconsistent handicapper: stays 7f: acts on good to firm ground: effective blinkered
or not: trained until after fifth start by G. Pritchard-Gordon: sold 14,500 gns Newmarket December Sales. *K. O. Cunningham-Brown*

ROXY RIVER   3 ch.f. Ardross 134 – Royal Yacht (USA) 65 (Riverman (USA) 131)   –
[1991 NR 1992 10.2d⁶ 10s⁴ 10d] 1,800F: leggy filly: fourth foal: half-sister to winners
abroad: dam placed at 7f, from family of high-class Traffic: no worthwhile form,
including in seller. *R. Hannon*

ROYAL ACCLAIM   7 ch.g. Tender King 123 – Glimmer 58 (Hot Spark 126)   **46 d**
[1991 7.6g 8d* 8g 8g⁶ 7.6m⁴ 8f 10.1f⁵ 8f⁴ 8m a12g⁶ 1992 a8g⁵ a10g a7g³ 8s² 10d⁴
10.8d 10.8g 10.8f⁵ a8g a10g a8g⁴] sturdy gelding: carries condition: inconsistent
handicapper: stays 1m: probably acts on any going: usually blinkered or visored:
often races with head high and seems none too resolute. *J. M. Bradley*

ROYAL BEAR   10 gr.g. Rupert Bear 105 – Queens Leap 54 (King's Leap 111)   –
[1991 NR 1992 5.1m a5g 5m 5d] rangy gelding: poor sprint handicapper: acts on any
going: ran poorly when blinkered. *J. M. Bradley*

ROYAL BOROUGH   7 b.g. Bustino 136 – Lady R B (USA) (Gun Shot) [1991 12s   –
12m 12.3g 11.9m 12d 1992 12.1g 12.3m⁵] attractive gelding: has a quick action:
modest handicapper nowadays, no worthwhile form in last 2 seasons: not seen out
after May: best form at 1½m: best runs on good ground: takes keen hold, and held
up. *M. P. Naughton*

ROYAL CIRCUS   3 b.g. Kris 135 – Circus Ring 122 (High Top 131) [1991 6f 8m   –
1992 10d 12d 10f 6.9m 7f] workmanlike gelding: no worthwhile form: tried blinkered:
sold 625 gns Ascot July Sales. *P. W. Harris*

ROYAL COMEDIAN   3 gr.f. Jester 119 – Royal Huntress (Royal Avenue 123)   **58**
[1991 NR 1992 8.3s² 10d⁴ 10s] leggy filly: eighth reported foal: half-sister to 1½m
winner Royal Craftsman (by Workboy): dam winning hurdler: not seen out until
September, modest form in maidens at Hamilton and Redcar: tailed off final start:
should prove better at 1¼m than shorter: unseated rider leaving paddock and
injured herself second intended outing. *B. W. Murray*

ROYAL COURSE   7 ch.g. On Your Mark 125 – Debnic 86 (Counsel 118) [1991 NR   – §
1992 a8g] lengthy, plain gelding: moderate mover: of little account. *B. Ellison*

ROYAL DARTMOUTH (USA) 7 ch.g. Czaravich (USA) – Blushing Emy 57
(USA) (Blushing Groom (FR) 131) [1991 7g⁵ 10m 8d⁶ 7.1m³ 8.5m² 8g 8g⁴ 8.3g³ 8f
1992 8s 8.1m* 7d² 8g⁵ 7f³ 8.3g⁵ 8d 9d 8s 10.2d⁶ 7s² 6.1s] tall, lengthy gelding:
somewhat in-and-out form in handicaps after winning at Chepstow in June: best at
7f/1m: acts on any going: usually bandaged: occasionally slowly away/finds little:
suitable mount for apprentice. *B. R. Millman*

ROYAL DEED (USA) 2 ch.f. (Apr 13) Shadeed (USA) 135 – Twilight Crown 76
(USA) (Roberto (USA) 131) [1992 5.1d 5g 5.3f⁵ 7m 6g⁴ 6.5m 5.1s² 6s³ 5g*]
$38,000Y: close-coupled filly: third foal: half-sister to a minor winner in North
America by Spectacular Bid: dam ran 3 times: in good form last 3 outings (previously
inconsistent, and had seemed of unsatisfactory temperament) and won nursery at
Doncaster in November by 3 lengths: takes keen hold, and is probably a sprinter:
often edgy: sold out G. Lewis' stable 1,400 gns Ascot June Sales after third outing. *P.
M. McEntee*

ROYAL DIVA 2 ch.f. (Jan 5) Chief Singer 131 – Rustle of Silk 67 (General 71
Assembly (USA)) [1992 6f⁶ 6g* 6s³ 7m 7s⁶] leggy, workmanlike filly: fourth foal:
half-sister to 6f winner Craven (by Thatching): dam lightly-raced half-sister to very
smart middle-distance horse Kirtling and daughter of Irish 1000 Guineas second
Silky: made all in maiden at Redcar in August: below form in nurseries last 2 starts:
should stay 1m: bandaged behind penultimate start. *Miss S. E. Hall*

ROYAL EXECUTIVE (IRE) 2 b.g. (Mar 12) Waajib 121 – Royal Episode (Royal –
Match 117) [1992 7g] IR 9,000F, IR 8,000Y: small, sturdy gelding: first foal: dam
Irish 6f and 7f winner: well beaten in maiden at Doncaster in October: showed a
quick action. *C. E. Brittain*

ROYAL FLEX (USA) 2 b.f. (Mar 28) Majestic Light (USA) – Expressive Dance 57
(USA) (Riva Ridge (USA)) [1992 6g² 6m³ 7g³ 6m⁵ 7m] $315,000Y: unfurnished filly:
has scope: has a round action: half-sister to 6 winners, including Chief Honcho (by
Chief's Crown), successful at up to 11f, including graded company: dam won 12 races
at up to 9f, including 3 Grade 3 events: sire top-class 8.5f to 1½m performer: modest
maiden: will be better suited by 1m: bandaged near-hind first 2 starts. *Mrs L. Piggott*

ROYAL FOLLY (IRE) 2 br.f. (Apr 5) Fools Holme (USA) – Royal Wolff (Prince 53
Tenderfoot (USA) 126) [1992 5g³ 5g³ 5m³ 6g*] IR 1,000Y: plain filly: fourth foal:
half-sister to 3-y-o Blue Is True (by Bluebird) and a winner in Macau: dam Irish
sprinter: won maiden auction at Pontefract in June: dead. *C. W. C. Elsey*

ROYAL GIRL 5 b.m. Kafu 120 – Royal Aunt (Martinmas 128) [1991 8d 1992 7m 63
7m²dis 7.5m 6f* 7g⁶ 6m* 7f 7s 7s] angular mare: moderate mover: successful in
summer at Ripon in maiden and seller: below best on soft ground last 2 starts:
effective at 6f to 7f: acts on firm ground: hung badly left once and disqualified. *Miss
S. E. Hall*

ROYAL GLINT 3 b.f. Glint of Gold 128 – Princess Matilda 110 (Habitat 134) –
[1991NR 1992 7d 10d 9.7m 10f 6.9g 8.3d 15.4d² 16.1s] 25,000Y: smallish, leggy filly:
eighth foal: sister to Kalgoorlie, a modest performer here later successful in Italy,
closely related to 1988 2-y-o 1m winner Mired (by Mill Reef) and half-sister to 2
winners: dam, 7f winner at 3 yrs, is half-sister to St Leger winner Bruni: poor form
at best: well beaten when blinkered: trained first 6 starts by I. Balding. *M. J.
Heaton-Ellis*

ROYAL INTERVAL 2 ch.g. (Mar 24) Interrex (CAN) – Sister Rosarii (USA) 65
(Properantes (USA)) [1992 5f⁶ 6m⁴ 7g³ 6s⁴] strong, lengthy gelding: sixth foal:
half-brother to 1988 2-y-o 5f seller winner Another Sigwells (by Ballacashtal): dam
never ran: best form on third outing, having been off course almost 4 months: will be
better suited by 1m: possibly suited by an easy surface. *W. G. M. Turner*

ROYAL LIASON (IRE) 2 b.f. (Mar 19) Prince Rupert (FR) 121 – Sinful Secret –
(Hello Gorgeous (USA) 128) [1992 5m] leggy filly: first foal: dam poor plater:
brought down 2f out in maiden at Haydock and broke a leg: dead. *C. W. C. Elsey*

ROYAL MEADOW (IRE) 2 b. or br.g. (May 6) Auction Ring (USA) 123 – 51
Princess of Nashua (Crowned Prince (USA) 128) [1992 7.1m⁴ 7d⁵] 20,000Y: good-
topped gelding: closely related to 1990 2-y-o sprinter It's All Academic (by Mazaad)
and half-brother to 3 winners here and abroad, including 3-y-o Elton Ledger (by
Cyrano de Bergerac), successful at 6f at 2 yrs: dam unraced: easily better effort in
July when over 4 lengths fourth of 7 in median auction maiden at Edinburgh: sold
1,100 gns Newmarket Autumn Sales. *J. Berry*

ROYAL OPERA STAR 3 b.g. King Among Kings 60 – Rojael (Mansingh (USA) –
120) [1991 6g 1992 8.3g 10.2m a12g 16m] small gelding: no worthwhile form: sold 700
gns Ascot December Sales. *J. R. Bosley*

Vodafone Nassau Stakes, Goodwood—
a close race between two admirable fillies, the grey Ruby Tiger and All At Sea

ROYAL PRINT (IRE) 3 ch.g. Kings Lake (USA) 133 – Reprint 99 (Kampala – 120) [1991 7m 7m⁵ 1992 8g 8f 10m 8g⁶ 7g] sturdy gelding: winning hurdler but poor maiden on flat: should stay 1¼m: tried blinkered. *W. R. Muir*

ROYAL REBEKA 2 gr.f. (Apr 18) Grey Desire 115 – Warthill Girl 70 (Anfield – 117) [1992 7g⁶] leggy, sparely-made, angular filly: first foal: dam 2-y-o 6f winner: tailed off in minor event at Newcastle in June. *M. Brittain*

ROYAL ROLLER (IRE) 2 b.c. (Feb 12) Dara Monarch 128 – Tumble Dale 88§ **72** (Tumble Wind (USA)) [1992 6m² 7m³ 7.1d⁶ 7d⁵ 8d⁴ 7s] IR 5,400F, 5,000 2-y-o: useful-looking colt: third foal: half-brother to 3-y-o Strong Suit (by King of Clubs), fairly useful 6f and 7f winner at 2 yrs: dam ungenuine sprint maiden here at 2 yrs, won in USA at 3 yrs: beaten around 9 lengths when sixth of 9 in Solario Stakes at Sandown, running on when hampered 1½f out: no comparable form, carrying head high and looking difficult ride last 2 starts: stays 7f: has run well for 7-lb claimer: has had tongue tied down. *C. N. Allen*

ROYAL SEATON 3 b.c. Blakeney 126 – Aldbury Girl 79 (Galivanter 131) [1991 **88** 5s* 6m 7g⁴ 7.9g⁴ 7d⁴ 6g 1992 11d⁵ 12g 8m⁶ 10.1d* 10d 10g⁴ 12m⁵ 10s⁵ 12g⁵ 9s²] close-coupled colt: fairly useful handicapper: won £7,000 event at Epsom in June: ran creditably in quite valuable events last 3 starts: effective at 9f to 1½m: goes well with some give in the ground (acts on soft), well beaten on good to firm: held up. *B. R. Millman*

ROYAL SULTAN 3 b.g. Destroyer 105 – Hopeful Subject 81 (Mandamus 120) – [1991 7g 8.1s 1992 12.3f⁴ 8m 11d] strong gelding: no form, including in seller: bred to stay beyond 1m. *Denys Smith*

ROYAL VERSE (FR) 5 b.h. Recitation (USA) 124 – Sauce Royale (Royal Palace **27** 131) [1991 12s 11.5m 10.1f⁶ a12g 8f 1992 11.5m 12g 14.1d 13.8d a12g a12g⁴ a12g] good-topped horse: very much on the downgrade. *R. Curtis*

RUANO 2 gr.c. (Jan 13) Belfort (FR) 89 – Lady Ever-So-Sure 80 (Malicious) [1992 **51** 6g a7g⁵ a6g a7g⁵ a7g⁵] 6,800Y: neat, quite attractive colt: has a quick action: third foal: dam won from 6f to 1½m, mostly in sellers: modest maiden: stays 7f: acts on equitrack. *S. P. C. Woods*

RUBICON WATCH 3 b. or br.f. Green Ruby (USA) 104 – Watch Lady (Home – Guard (USA) 129) [1991 NR 1992 8.1d] lengthy filly: half-sister to 1983 2-y-o 5f winner Magdolin Place (by Dublin Taxi) and winning hurdler Pit Pony (by Hittite Glory): dam ran twice: showed nothing in claimer at Chepstow in October on belated debut. *C. R. Barwell*

RUBIDIAN 2 ch.c. (Mar 22) Primo Dominie 121 – Red Tapsi (Tap On Wood 130) **44**
[1992 7m 8.2g 7s a8g] lengthy, good-topped colt: has plenty of scope: first foal: dam,
maiden second over 1½m in Ireland, is out of sister to Bustino: poor form in
maidens: backward first 3 starts: needs time. *Sir Mark Prescott*

RUBY COOPER 2 br.f. (May 5) Green Ruby (USA) 104 – Redcross Miss 64 **50**
(Tower Walk 130) [1992 5g3 5.1d* 5g* 5m4 6g 7m 6d] lengthy filly: moderate
mover: second living foal: dam middle-distance maiden: won sellers at Nottingham
(retained 3,400 gns) and Leicester (no bid) in April: off course 3 months and below
form last 2 starts: should stay beyond 5f: acts on dead ground. *J. Wharton*

RUBY TIGER 5 gr.m. Ahonoora 122 – Hayati 94 (Hotfoot 126) [1991 9m3 10v5 **119**
11m* 10g* 10g* 1992 11g3 10m2 10m* 10.4g 9.5f2 9.3s3 10d4] workmanlike mare:
moderate walker: game, consistent and smart performer: successful in 1992 in
Group 2 Nassau Stakes at Goodwood for second year in succession, holding All At
Sea by a neck: placed after in Grade 1 Beverly D Stakes at Arlington (1½ lengths
second to Kostroma) and Ciga Prix de l'Opera (beaten 1½ lengths by Hatoof) at
Longchamp: fourth to Hatoof in Grade 2 event at Woodbine last time: rare modest
effort in International Stakes at York: effective at 1¼m to 1½m: acts any going: a
credit to her trainer. *P. F. I. Cole*

RUDDA CASS 8 b.g. Rapid River 127 – Glaven (Blakeney 126) [1991 NR 1992 11g **33**
9.9m6 8g 10m] smallish, workmanlike gelding: poor handicapper: should stay 1¾m:
acts on firm and dead ground: below form blinkered. *Mrs V. A. Aconley*

RUDIMENTARY (USA) 4 b.c. Nureyev (USA) 131 – Doubly Sure 59 **118**
(Reliance II 137) [1991 10g2 10.1f* 10f3 10m3 8m* 8g4 1992 8d* 8.1g* 8m3 8m6
8m 8d3 8s2]

This imposing half-brother to leading sire Kris always had a place at
stud, but whether he could gain the racecourse qualifications ordinarily
required of a likely stallion here was for some time open to question. His
listed win in the Main Reef Stakes at Newmarket as a three-year-old might
just have been enough to get him there, but he made sure by running well
against the top milers as a four-year-old. Rudimentary, a powerful galloper
with a round action, described by his trainer as 'all arms and legs' as a three-
year-old, left his three-year-old form behind on his reappearance with an
impressive performance under 10-0 on softish ground in the Ladbrokes Spring
Handicap at Newbury in April. While not the race it used to be in its heyday as
the Newbury Spring Cup, the Spring Handicap is usually well contested still.
The latest certainly seemed so beforehand, and yet Rudimentary ran right
away from his eighteen opponents in the last furlong and a half to win by seven
lengths. That was Rudimentary's first and last appearance in a handicap. Two

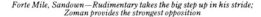

Forte Mile, Sandown—Rudimentary takes the big step up in his stride;
Zoman provides the strongest opposition

Lord Howard de Walden's "Rudimentary"

weeks later he won the Group 2 Forte Mile at Sandown with something in hand by a length and a half from Zoman, who was conceding only 4 lb, thereby earning an extended run in big mile races. That extended run—in the Lockinge Stakes, Queen Anne Stakes, Sussex Stakes, Celebration Mile and, finally, the Premio Vittorio di Capua at Milan—showed him consistently around 10 lb behind the best. Selkirk, Lahib and Marling all beat him on merit whenever they met, Selkirk three times, Lahib twice. There were no more victories for Rudimentary after the Forte Mile but there were, to embellish the stud card, third places behind Selkirk in the Lockinge and Celebration Mile and second place behind Alhijaz in the Vittorio di Capua. Despite his good form through the summer, there was a feeling that Rudimentary would be better, and get back on the winning track, when the weather broke. However, on dead ground in the Celebration Mile, Selkirk (and Steinbeck) came from behind to catch him; and it was a similar story on soft ground at Milan, where Rudimentary again forced the pace only to be caught by Alhijaz.

Rudimentary (USA) (b.c. 1988)	Nureyev (USA) (b 1977)	Northern Dancer (b 1961)	Nearctic
			Natalma
		Special (b 1969)	Forli
			Thong
	Doubly Sure (b 1971)	Reliance II (b 1962)	Tantieme
			Relance III
		Soft Angels (ch 1963)	Crepello
			Sweet Angel

Rudimentary's retirement means there are now six sons of Doubly Sure at stud—Kris, Diesis and Keen (all by Sharpen Up), Presidium (by

General Assembly) and Doubletour (by Lyphard) being the others. The unraced Doubletour is due to have his first runners in the next season. Doubly Sure died in 1991, leaving behind a filly foal by Danzig, since named Pevna, who, with any luck, could also be racing in the next season. Lord Howard de Walden has had relatively little luck with Doubly Sure's fillies. Escrime (by Lyphard) showed quite useful form at up to a mile and a quarter, but she is the only one to have reached the racecourse so far; two of them died before reaching racing age. *H. R. A. Cecil*

RUE DE REMARQUE 4 ch.f. The Noble Player (USA) 126 – Carolynchrist- – ensen 58 (Sweet Revenge 129) [1991 7g 1992 6.1d 7g 7f] compact filly: poor mover: no worthwhile form. *M. J. Haynes*

RUHR (IRE) 3 b.g. Flash of Steel 120 – Astral Way (Hotfoot 126) [1991 5g4 5g2 **89** 7g4 7m* 8.1f6 7m4 1992 8g6 7g6 7g3] strong, lengthy gelding: carries condition: rated 109 at 2 yrs: below form in 1992, off course 6 months after first run (reportedly swallowed tongue): should stay 1m: acts on good to firm ground: blinkered final start (ran well) at 2 yrs and throughout in 1992: one to have reservations about: has been gelded. *B. W. Hills*

RULED BY FASHION 2 b.f. (May 4) Governor General 116 – Fashion Lover – 70 (Shiny Tenth 120) [1992 6.1g] 1,000Y: workmanlike filly: fifth foal: half-sister to a winner in Malaysia: dam 1m seller winner: dropped out rapidly soon after halfway in seller at Nottingham in May. *J. Balding*

RULLY 3 ch.g. Rousillon (USA) 133 – Hysterical 68 (High Top 131) [1991 7.1s3 – 7.1m 7.6d* 10g6 1992 8.1d6] strong, well-made gelding: rated 75 at 2 yrs: always last in £7,600 handicap in August, only run in 1992: stays 1¼m: yet to race on firm going, probably acts on any other: retained 5,500 gns Newmarket Autumn Sales. *C. E. Brittain*

RUMBELOW 3 b.c. Welsh Captain 113 – Romana 72 (Roman Warrior 132) [1991 – 6d6 7m2 1992 7g 8.9s 10.1g6] leggy colt: below form in 1992: should stay 1m. *J. R. Jenkins*

RUMBLED AGAIN (IRE) 3 b.g. Head For Heights 125 – Gentle Rhythm 67 – (Ballad Rock 122) [1991 5f 1992 a6g] good-bodied gelding: twice raced, and no worthwhile form. *T. D. Barron*

RUMPUS (IRE) 2 b.f. (Jan 28) Kahyasi 130 – Helietta 78 (Tyrnavos 129) [1992 **97** p 7d2] lengthy filly: second foal: dam 9f and 1¼m winner, is half-sister to Oaks second Vielle: 8/1, bandaged and very green, shaped promisingly when beaten 6 lengths by Yawl in minor event at Newmarket in October, travelling comfortably most of way then keeping on under considerate ride: will improve, particularly over middle distances, and win a race or two. *L. M. Cumani*

RUM TEMPEST 2 b.c. (Apr 12) Northern Tempest (USA) 120 – Rum Year – (Quorum 126) [1992 6g 6g] 2,600Y: leggy colt: half-brother to several winners here and abroad, including 7.5f and 1¼m winner Just The Ticket (by Faraway Times) and 1984 2-y-o 5f winner Runager (by Lochnager): dam placed over hurdles: no promise in auction races at Haydock and Ripon in August. *C. Tinkler*

RUN BY JOVE (USA) 9 gr.g. Northern Jove (CAN) – Running Eagle (USA) – (Bald Eagle 119) [1991 NR 1992 10m] workmanlike, close-coupled gelding: on the downgrade. *J. White*

RUN DON'T FLY (USA) 6 b.h. Lear Fan (USA) 130 – Gantlette (Run The – Gantlet (USA)) [1991 10g* 12g* 1992 13.3f 10g 10d a10g] sturdy, quite attractive horse: carries condition: rated 115 at best: soundly beaten in varied company last 3 starts, blinkered final one: effective at 1¼m to 1½m: acts on firm going: changed hands with 4,500 gns Newmarket Autumn Sales after third start. *P. F. I. Cole*

RUN FAST FOR GOLD 5 ch.m. Deep Run 119 – Goldyke 63 (Bustino 136) – [1991 NR 1992 16d] second known foal: dam maiden, suited by 1½m, later won over hurdles and fences: tailed off in celebrity event at Worcester in March on debut. *G. B. Balding*

RUN FREE 7 b.g. Julio Mariner 127 – Lucky Appeal 36 (Star Appeal 133) [1991 – NR 1992 9.7v 12g 12g 12d] smallish, leggy gelding: on the downgrade. *Pat Mitchell*

RUN HIGH 9 b.g. Thatch (USA) 136 – Fleet Noble (USA) (Vaguely Noble 140) **57** [1991 12f 1992 12g 14g 12m3 14m5 12f4] strong gelding: moderate mover: modest handicapper: not seen out after June: needs at least 1½m and stays 2m: acts on any going. *P. Mitchell*

RUNNEL 3 b.c. Runnett 125 – Ariadne 79 (Bustino 136) [1991 5s 5.3m³ 6g³ a7g² – a7g⁵ 7m* 7m⁵ 7g 8m 7m³ 6m⁶ 7m a7g⁵ a6g a6g* a6g² a7g* a8g² 1992 a6g⁴ a7g* a70 a8g³ a6g⁵] small, strong-quartered colt: good walker: best at Southwell, successful in claimer: found nil there late in January and not seen out again: best form at 7f: below form blinkered: front runner. *D. W. Chapman*

RUNNETT DANCER (IRE) 2 b.c. (Feb 5) Runnett 125 – Chinafield 52 – (Northfields (USA)) [1992 5d] IR 7,000F, 10,500Y: compact colt: half-brother to 3-y-o China Bright (by Sarab), winning sprinter Duck Flight (by Decoy Boy) and a winner abroad: dam poor maiden: behind in maiden auction at Kempton in April: sold 3,000 gns Newmarket July Sales. *M. R. Stoute*

RUNNING GLIMPSE (IRE) 4 br.f. Runnett 125 – One Last Glimpse 73 **78** (Relko 136) [1991 6g* 5g 5m 6m 6m 1992 6m² 5m⁴ 7m³ 6d* 7g 6m* 6g 5d² 6d⁴ 6g] smallish filly: consistent handicapper: successful at Epsom and Newmarket (gamely) in July: effective at 5f to 6f: acts on good to firm and dead ground: tends to carry head awkwardly: races prominently. *Miss B. Sanders*

RUN ON REBEL (IRE) 2 b.c. (Mar 31) Prince Rupert (FR) 121 – Rebecca's – Song (Artaius (USA) 129) [1992 5g 5.3m 6m] 22,000Y: neat colt: half-brother to winners in Macau and Italy: dam French 1m to 9f winner: no form, blinkered in seller final run: sold 700 gns Newmarket September Sales. *P. F. I. Cole*

RUNRIG (IRE) 2 b.f. (May 5) Jalmood (USA) 126 – Bluethroat 95 (Ballymore **57** 123) [1992 6g² 6f³ 7d⁵ 7.5m² 7g⁶ 6m] IR 2,000Y: leggy filly: fourth living foal: half-sister to 1989 2-y-o 6f and 1m winner Simply Blue (by Simply Great): dam successful over 6f and 8.2f here at 2 yrs and at 1½m at 3 yrs in Ireland: none too consistent maiden: will be well suited by 1m+: best efforts on top-of-the-ground. *Miss L. A. Perratt*

RUNYON (IRE) 4 b.c. Sadler's Wells (USA) 132 – Deadly Serious (USA) 113 **113** (Queen's Hussar 124) [1991 9v* 9g* 10g* 10g² 11.9g4 1992 10g⁴ 12f⁴ 10.5d² 10s³ 10s] big, lengthy colt: has a round action: smart ex-Irish colt: best run in 1992 when second to Wiorno in Group 3 La Coupe at Longchamp: performed respectably (including in Hardwicke Stakes) most other starts: effective at 1¼m to 1½m: best form on an easy surface (acts on heavy ground): trained until after third run by T. Stack. *J. E. Hammond, France*

RUPPLES 5 b.g. Muscatite 122 – Miss Annie 73 (Scottish Rifle 127) [1991 7d³ 9s – 8m² 7.6g 8f 8g 7.1d 8.3g 14.1m⁶ 8m 1992 a8g] leggy, workmanlike gelding: poor handicapper: stays 1m: acts on good to firm ground: below form visored, usually blinkered. *M. C. Chapman*

RURAL LAD 3 b.g. Town And Country 124 – French Plait (Thatching 131) [1991 **64** NR 1992 6d³ 5g² 7s⁶ 8f 6g⁴ 10m³ 7d 6.9v* a8g⁵] rather unfurnished gelding: first foal: dam, out of a 2m winner, was seemingly of little account: modest performer: claimed out of Mrs J. Ramsden's stable £6,010 in 1¼m seller: won handicap at Folkestone in November: effective at 7f and stays 1¼m: acts on good to firm and heavy ground, fair effort on fibresand. *R. C. Spicer*

RUSHALONG 2 ch.c. (Feb 21) Rousillon (USA) 133 – Mousquetade (Moulton **34** 128) [1992 7m 6g 6m] 2,500F, 3,000Y: useful-looking colt: half-brother to 8.2f and 16.5f winner Shtaifeh (by Welsh Pageant): dam, from very good staying family, never ran: poor maiden. *R. D. E. Woodhouse*

RUSHANES 5 ch.g. Millfontaine 114 – Saulonika 94 (Saulingo 122) [1991 a6g² **59** a7g 5g5 6d5 6f a5g 5.3g³ 5m⁴ 5.1s² 5.1d5 a6g* a5g⁶ a6g⁴ a6g⁴ a6g⁴ 1992 a5g a6g⁵ **a62** a6g a6g² a5g⁴ a5g* a6g⁵ a6g³ a6g³ 5v* 5s⁴ a5g⁶] small, sturdy gelding: poor mover: shows traces of stringhalt: modest handicapper: won at Lingfield and Warwick (claimer) in spring: effective at 5f and 6f: acts on any going and all-weather surfaces: suitable mount for amateur: has run poorly when sweating and edgy, including final start after almost 9-month break. *T. Casey*

RUSHEEN NA CORRA (IRE) 3 b.f. Burslem 123 – Ivy Holme (Silly Season – 127) [1991 NR 1992 10.9s] strong, lengthy filly: fourth foal: half-sister to 4-y-o Lisalee (by Montekin) and a winner in Italy (by Mansingh): dam race once: looked of no account in seller at Ayr in September. *J. J. O'Neill*

RUSHLUAN 8 gr.g. Kalaglow 132 – Labista 116 (Crowned Prince (USA) 128) **49** [1991 12f⁴ 1992 9.7v 10.8d 12.3g³ 16.9g 12m⁶] leggy, good-topped gelding: has a quick action: poor handicapper: should stay beyond 1½m: acts on firm going, probably unsuited by soft surface: ran creditably in visor. *R. J. Hodges*

RUSSET WAY 2 b.f. (May 31) Blushing Scribe (USA) 107 – Orchard Road 74 **34** (Camden Town 125) [1992 a6g⁵ 5.2f³] light-framed filly: sixth foal: dam placed at up to 7f at 2 yrs, only season to race: poor form in sellers at Southwell and Yarmouth in June: should stay 1m. *Mrs N. Macauley*

RUSSIAN VISION 3 b.g. Petoski 135 – Visible Form 99 (Formidable (USA) 70 d 125) [1991 NR 1992 10m 10g 10.2m4 12d5 11.6m 12.3m2 11.6g 10m4 14.1d4 12v] 22,000Y: well-made gelding: good mover: fourth foal: half-brother to 8.2f and 1¼m winner Living Image (by Taufan) and 1989 2-y-o 6f winner Azeb (by Young Generation): dam 6f and 1¼m winner out of half-sister to very smart stayer Raise You Ten: modest maiden: should stay 1¾m: acts on good to firm ground, seemingly not on a soft surface: ran creditably when blinkered: visored once on soft ground. *A. A. Scott*

RUSSIA POBEDA (USA) 2 b.f. (Apr 20) Danzig Connection (USA) – Arianne 57 Mon Amour (USA) (Bold Bidder) [1992 7g2 7f 7g 8m6] rangy filly: has scope: third foal: sister to 3-y-o 7f winner Heniu: dam won 2 small races at up to 1m at 2 yrs, and is sister to Belmont Stakes winner Stephan's Odyssey (by Danzig): failed to progress after second in maiden at Yarmouth in July: should stay 1m: bandaged behind. *Mrs L. Piggott*

RUSSIA WITH LOVE 2 ro.f. (Mar 11) Siberian Express (USA) 125 – Late 49 Matinee 84 (Red Sunset 120) [1992 6m3 5s4 6m 5g] compact filly: first foal: dam 2-y-o 6f winner: poor form: tongue tied down, not entirely discredited in Newmarket nursery final run: best form at 5f: probably acts on any going. *J. D. Bethell*

RUSTAKA (USA) 3 b.f. Riverman (USA) 131 – Katsura (USA) (Northern 68 Dancer (CAN)) [1991 7m 1992 7d2 10s] leggy filly: thrice-raced maiden: second in 4-runner race at Epsom in August: tailed off at Leicester 2 months after: bred to stay further than 7f: has joined H. Pantall, France. *B. W. Hills*

RUSTIC CRAFT (IRE) 2 ch.c. (Mar 8) Thatching 131 – Western Goddess 95 79 p (Red God 128§) [1992 6g*] rangy colt: has plenty of scope: half-brother to several winners, including 3-y-o Mougins (by Ela-Mana-Mou), useful 7f winner at 2 yrs, and useful miler Hollywood Party (by Be My Guest): dam Irish sprinting half-sister to very smart 1975 2-y-o Western Jewel and Mr Fluorocarbon, from family of Lyric Fantasy: 12/1 and green, won 7-runner newcomers event at Ascot in October by 1½ lengths from Khattat, chased along after slow start and staying on strongly from 2f out: sure to improve. *D. R. C. Elsworth*

RUSTIC HUNTER (IRE) 4 gr.g. Rusticaro (FR) 124 – Huntress (Hunter- – combe 133) [1991 NR 1992 a8g] IR 2,700F, 5,500Y: half-brother to 1984 2-y-o 6f winner Caernarvon Boy (by Wolverlife) and 2 winners in Belgium: dam never ran: no sign of ability in Southwell maiden in March on debut. *C. J. Hill*

RUSTY RAJA 2 gr.g. (Apr 4) Mansingh (USA) 120 – Rust Free 58 (Free State – 125) [1992 6m6 5g 5g 7g] 38,000Y: workmanlike gelding: fifth foal: brother to a winner in Hong Kong and half-brother to 3 winners, including sprinter Snowgirl (by Mazaad) and 1989 2-y-o 7f winner Glazerite (by Dunphy), later effective at middle distances: dam maiden stayed 1¼m, is half-sister to Petong (by Mansingh): little form in varied events: blinkered and looked difficult ride final start: sold 1,100 gns Doncaster October Sales. *R. Hannon*

RUSTY REEL 2 ch.g. (May 5) Scottish Reel 123 – Blakeney Heights (Blakeney 63 126) [1992 7g 6g3 7d5 8m5] leggy gelding: first foal: dam unraced: modest maiden: stays 1m: acts on good to firm and dead ground: has scope, and may do better. *C. E. Brittain*

RUSTYSIDE 5 b.m. Rustingo 94 – Deriside (Saucy Kit 76) [1991 NR 1992 10.2f – 11.9m 16.2g] ex-Irish mare: first foal: dam unraced: always behind in claimer and apprentice maiden in July. *C. T. Nash*

RUTBAH 3 b.f. Shareef Dancer (USA) 135 – Aldhabyih 86 (General Assembly 55 d (USA)) [1991 NR 1992 9.7g4 10d6 8d 12.2d] rangy filly: third living foal: half-sister to fairly useful 1988 2-y-o 6f and 7f winner Alhathaf (by Tap On Wood): dam 2-y-o 5f winner stayed 7f, is half-sister to Kafu and smart 7f to 1¼m winner Moomba Masquerade: regressive maiden. *A. C. Stewart*

RUTH'S GAMBLE 4 b.g. Kabour 83 – Hilly's Daughter (Hillandale 125) [1991 56 6f3 7g4 7g3 6m5 7g4 6g 6f2 6f3 7g 6m 1992 a7g5 8.2m 8g5 7.1d 8g* 7s6 8s 7d 7d] lengthy gelding: inconsistent handicapper: won at Carlisle in September: stays 1m: acts on any going: below form when blinkered: sold to join Mrs L. Jewell 4,000 gns Newmarket Autumn Sales. *D. W. Chapman*

RYEWATER DREAM 4 b.f. Touching Wood (USA) 127 – Facetious 88 50 (Malicious) [1991 10m 12m 10f 11.7f* 12m5 17.2g a12g 1992 14.1m5 10.2f 10.2f6 8.3m4 7f3 7.6m 8d 6.1g] smallish, workmanlike filly: none too consistent handicapper:

effective from 7f to 1½m: acts on firm going: seemed to sulk when blinkered final start: front runner. *R. J. Hodges*

RYTHMIC RASCAL 2 ch.g. (May 6) Grey Desire 115 – Tango Lady (Gorytus 30 (USA) 132) [1992 5g a6g 6m⁵ 6g] small, close-coupled gelding: first foal: dam unraced daughter of half-sister to disqualified Irish Oaks winner Sorbus: poor plater: retained by trainer 460 gns Doncaster June Sales. *M. Brittain*

RYTHMIC STYLE 3 b.f. Swing Easy (USA) 126 – Slick Chick 89 (Shiny Tenth – 120) [1991 5g 5f* 5m 1992 a7g a7g] poor performer: not seen out after January: best run at 5f. *T. D. Barron*

S

SAAFEND 4 b.f. Sayf El Arab (USA) 127 – Gilt Star 92 (Star Appeal 133) [1991 6d³ 76 7g³ 6g 7g 8m* 8m² 7f⁴ 7m⁶ 7s⁵ 7.6g 9g 1992 6d 8m² 8g 8m* 8m 8.3g⁴ 8.3g⁴ 8g 8g³ 8m* 7g] sparely-made filly: fair handicapper: successful at Goodwood in May and Newmarket (valuable event) in October: effective at 7f and 1m: probably acts on any going: blinkered (well below form) once at 3 yrs: has been bandaged off-hind: below best for apprentice. *J. Sutcliffe*

SABO'S EXPRESS 2 b.c. (Mar 11) Prince Sabo 123 – Lady Farrier (Sheshoon 63 132) [1992 6m 6.1d² 7g* 8g³ 8s⁴ 8s] 5,400F: workmanlike colt: moderate mover: third reported foal: dam unraced: modest form: made all in claimer at Leicester in August: ran creditably, though hung left and looked ungenerous, penultimate start: needs further than 6f and stays 1m: acts on soft ground: best form on good ground: blinkered last 2 outings: sold 5,600 gns Newmarket Autumn Sales. *R. Hannon*

SABO SONG 2 ch.f. (Jan 14) Prince Sabo 123 – Nice Lady 65 (Connaught 130) 67 [1992 5m* 5m²] 900F: workmanlike filly: third foal: sister to winning 3-y-o sprinter Lady Sabo and half-sister to a winner in Italy: dam lightly-raced maiden second over 9.4f: fair form in the spring: won 4-runner maiden at Edinburgh: looked green still and tended to hang left, behind easy winner Night Melody in 4-runner minor event at Newcastle 11 days later. *R. Allan*

SABOTAGE (FR) 6 ch.h. Kris 135 – Subject To Change (USA) (Buckpasser) 89 [1991 8m² 8g 8d 1992 8g 8.1s⁶ 8g³ 8d] leggy, quite good-topped, attractive horse: good mover: fairly useful handicapper: easily best effort in 1992 when fourth (promoted) in Ascot apprentice event in July: stays 9f: seems best on a sound surface: ran creditably when visored once at 4 yrs: usually bandaged behind. *M. R. Stoute*

SABOTEUR 8 ch.g. Pyjama Hunt 126 – Frondia 76 (Parthia 132) [1991 7m* 7m 36 7f⁶ 7m 1992 7f 7g 7m⁴] lengthy, dipped-backed gelding: bad mover: inconsistent handicapper: best form at 7f on a sound surface: blinkered once at 3 yrs. *W. J. Musson*

SABO THE HERO 2 ch.c. (Mar 7) Prince Sabo 123 – Daima (Dominion 123) 55 [1992 6d 5d⁴ 6v³] 22,000Y: leggy, lengthy colt: first foal: dam unraced: modest form in maidens in the autumn: has raced only on a soft surface. *Sir Mark Prescott*

SABRE RATTLER 2 ch.c. (Apr 14) Beveled (USA) – Casbah Girl 79 (Native 100 Bazaar 122) [1992 5g³ 5v² 5.2d* 5g* 6m² 5f 5g² 5m 5m* 6s⁴ 5m] rather leggy, plain colt: second foal: half-brother to 3-y-o Cashtal Queen (by Ballacashtal), 6f sellers winner at 2 yrs: dam 6f and 7f winner: useful sprinter: won maiden at Newbury and minor event at Folkestone in April and, showing improved form, listed race at York in August: fair effort in £9,200 event at Ripon 12 days later: best effort at 5f on good to firm ground, far from discredited at 6f on soft: blinkered (raced freely) once: occasionally swishes tail. *J. Berry*

SABZY 3 ch.f. Seymour Hicks (FR) 125 – Golnessa (Lombard (GER) 126) [1991 – NR 1992 8.9v 10.5s 7.5m] plain filly: second foal: dam, out of a 1m winner, showed little worthwhile form: well beaten in claimer and maidens in the spring. *P. D. Evans*

SADDLEHOME (USA) 3 b.g. Aragon 118 – Kesarini (USA) 87 (Singh (USA)) 77 [1991 6g 5g² 5f³ 5m³ 5m⁵ 5g³ 1992 6d² 6m⁴ 7m⁴ 5m⁴ 6g* 6f⁶ 6g⁵ 5m² 5m⁴ 5m 6d⁵ 6.1s⁵ 6g a5g⁵] leggy, short-backed gelding: fair performer: made all in apprentice maiden at Pontefract in June: at least as effective at 5f as 6f: seems unsuited by firm going, acts on good to firm and soft: below form visored once: sold out of R. Whitaker's stable 7,200 gns Doncaster November Sales after penultimate run: bolted prior to final start. *Dr J. D. Scargill*

SADDLERS' HALL (IRE)   4 b.c. Sadler's Wells (USA) 132 – Sunny **126**
Valley (Val de Loir 133) [1991 10g* 10.5g2 12g* 12m6 11.9g2 14.6m2 12g 1992
12d* 13.4m* 12g* 12g* 12g2 12s 12d5]

The two colts who fought out the St Leger of 1991 had contrasting seasons as four-year-olds. While Toulon went backwards, Saddlers' Hall trained
on so well that he was sent for the King George VI and Queen Elizabeth
Diamond Stakes in July aiming for a fifth straight win and priced at only 7/2
against achieving it. Both colts were campaigned over middle distances,
where the money is. Readers of *Racehorses of 1991* will know well enough that
we expected neither of them to be seen to best advantage at such distances,
and we went so far as to say that Saddlers' Hall would be chasing shadows in
top mile-and-a-half company. Toulon's lack of success could be ascribed to the
nature of the programme he was given, though that is almost certainly not the
whole story. On the other hand, Saddlers' Hall might be held to have done
more than enough to confute *Racehorses'* assessment of him, in the first
instance by winning the John Porter Stakes by ten lengths and the Ormonde
Stakes by ten lengths, then in the second by taking the Group 1 Coronation
Cup, even though the opposition at Newbury and Chester wasn't all that hot.
However, we still think that he was essentially a staying type, not quite in the
top bracket at a mile and a half, and in support cite his performances behind St
Jovite in the King George and behind Subotica, an unlucky fourth at Epsom, in
the Prix de l'Arc de Triomphe.

Subotica made up a two-pronged French challenge for the Coronation
Cup along with the filly Saganeca. His recent neck defeat of Pistolet Bleu in
the Prix Ganay put him in with a major chance, but Saddlers' Hall started
favourite at 5/4 after his runaway wins at Newbury, where Shambo chased him
home, and at Chester, where Arcadian Heights did. All nine in the Epsom field
had been in good recent public form except for the seasonal debutant
Terimon, who in any case had a splendid record both first time up and over the
course. It was hard to rule out any of them apart from Rock Hopper's
pacemaker Mellaby and, perhaps, the second filly Always Friendly; you
certainly couldn't rule out the latest Yorkshire Cup winner Rock Hopper, or
Sapience and Snurge, the second and third at York. And in the event most of
the runners proved closely matched. The race developed into a rough one
after Mellaby had taken them along at a strong pace, with a good deal of
scrimmaging over the last two and a half furlongs. Very well served by

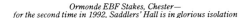

Ormonde EBF Stakes, Chester—
for the second time in 1992, Saddlers' Hall is in glorious isolation

Hanson Coronation Cup, Epsom—
Saddlers' Hall has to work a good deal harder to hold off Rock Hopper

Swinburn, Saddlers' Hall avoided most of the trouble and ran out a thoroughly workmanlike winner. Swinburn made a crucial move early in the straight, where, having been poised in fourth place behind Snurge, Sapience and Terimon, he drove his mount along on the outside, catching Subotica's jockey Jarnet, having his first ride at Epsom, napping. Saddlers' Hall's sustained challenge got him the lead with over two furlongs to go, and although he began to edge slightly left on the camber as he struck the front, tightening up those on the inside, he galloped on strongly under firm driving to win by three quarters of a length and the same from Rock Hopper and Terimon. The inevitable stewards inquiry into possible interference found, after long deliberation, that firstly, Terimon had interfered with Sapience and that subsequently Saddlers' Hall had also interfered with Sapience whose jockey had to snatch up. This in turn caused interference to Subotica whose jockey also had to snatch up. The stewards considered all the interference to have been accidental and that no horse had improved its placing thereby, so the placings remained unaltered. But strong-finishing Subotica, who failed by only a neck to overhaul Terimon after having a desperate run, would surely have gone close to winning given a clear passage.

The Coronation Cup provided confirmation that Saddlers' Hall had improved from three to four, though he hadn't, apparently, improved by as much as the more liberal interpretations of his two previous performances, particularly that at Chester where Arcadian Heights hardly got him off the bridle, would suggest. He went on to confirm his superiority over Rock

Princess of Wales's Stakes, Newmarket—
a fourth consecutive pattern victory for Saddlers' Hall

Hopper, Sapience and Terimon in the King George VI and Queen Elizabeth Diamond Stakes seven weeks later, having in the meantime shown his continued well-being by landing the odds in good style from Luchiroverte, Mashaallah and Always Friendly in a four-runner Princess of Wales's Stakes at Newmarket. In the King George, Saddlers' Hall ran right up to his best to finish second to St Jovite but had his limitations exposed, not only by an above-average classic winner but by Opera House and Sapience with whom he fought a long battle before just getting on top in the closing stages, six lengths behind the winner. He had had to be chivvied along well before the half-mile marker, as a result of St Jovite's stepping up the slow gallop. The Prix de l'Arc de Triomphe, Saddlers' Hall's next race, took most people by surprise by also being run at a slow pace. When the sprint developed in the short straight Saddlers' Hall couldn't hold his place just behind the leaders and he eventually finished in the last six. On his final appearance Saddlers' Hall had a more suitable test in the Rothmans International in Canada and ran a much better race without reaching his best. He made late ground to come fifth of fourteen, three and a half lengths behind the French-trained Wiorno who was subsequently demoted in favour of Snurge.

			Northern Dancer (b 1961)	Nearctic
Saddlers' Hall (IRE) (b.c. 1988)	Sadler's Wells (USA) (b 1981)			Natalma
			Fairy Bridge (b 1975)	Bold Reason
				Special
	Sunny Valley (b 1972)		Val de Loir (b 1959)	Vieux Manoir
				Vali II
			Sunland (ch 1965)	Charlottesville
				Sunny Gulf

Saddlers' Hall has been retired to the Cheveley Park Stud in Newmarket, at a fee of £7,500 with the October 1st concession. His career statistics stood at six wins and four seconds from fifteen starts, and earnings of £423,974. One of his two wins as a three-year-old came in the King Edward VII Stakes at Royal Ascot, by six lengths after he'd made most of the running; he finished sixth to Generous in the King George VI and Queen Elizabeth Diamond Stakes that season. A late foal, he ran just once (in the autumn) as a two-year-old. As has been written many times, Saddlers' Hall is a handsome colt, strong and lengthy, with a handsome pedigree. His sire needs no introduction, his dam scarcely any since she had previously produced Sun Princess (by English Prince), winner of the Oaks and the St Leger and second in the Prix de l'Arc de Triomphe. As well as handsomely bred, Saddlers' Hall is stoutly bred. Sunny Valley was a useful winner at up to a mile and a half, by the French Derby winner Val de Loir out of the staying Sunland, and staying types predominate in the family. However, Sun Prince (out of Sunland's half-sister Costa Sola) won the Coventry Stakes and St James's Palace Stakes; Then Again (out of Sunny Valley's half-sister New Light) was a good miler; and River Dancer (out of Saddlers' Hall's half-sister Dancing Shadow) finished third in the French Guineas. *M. R. Stoute*

SADLER'S WAY 3 b.c. Sadler's Wells (USA) 132 – Sophisticated Lady (FR) (Habitat 134) [1991 8g 6s 1992 8.1g⁶ 8g⁶ 12m² 12f 12.1m² 14.1d* 14s 14d] tall, leggy colt: fair performer at best: ran in snatches when winning maiden at Nottingham in July, edging left but battling on well: ran badly in handicaps afterwards: best at 1¾m than shorter: acts on good to firm and dead ground: tends to hang and carry head high: sold to join M. Barraclough 1,900 gns Newmarket Autumn Sales. *G. Lewis* **74**

SAFA 4 b.f. Shirley Heights 130 – Beveridge (USA) 86 (Spectacular Bid (USA)) [1991 10f² 10d 1992 8g² 10g⁵ 11.9f² 9g] good-topped filly: very good walker: fairly useful performer: beaten length in 9-finisher £10,600 lady riders event at York, not for first time finding little off bridle: behind in Group 3 event at Dortmund later in June: effective from 1m to 1½m: acted on firm ground, possibly unsuited by a soft surface: tail swisher: visits Sadler's Wells. *A. A. Scott* **87**

SAFARI PARK 3 ch.f. Absalom 128 – Nyeri 104 (Saint Crespin III 132) [1991 6g⁶ 6m 6.1m 1992 9s a12g 7m 8.2d⁴] smallish, workmanlike filly: poor maiden: stays 8.2f: best efforts on an easy surface: has looked headstrong. *B. S. Rothwell* **–**

SAFE BID 2 b.f. (Mar 28) Sure Blade (USA) 130 – Princess Biddy 86 (Sun Prince 128) [1992 5s⁵ 6g a5g] IR 2,000Y: smallish filly: half-sister to several winners, **44**

including 1986 2-y-o 6f winner Hydraulic Power (by Northfields) and 6f winner Fawley's Girl (by He Loves Me): dam stayed 7f, is half-sister to Royalty, Double Jump and Sunyboy: failed to progress after fifth in maiden at Haydock: fractious stalls and tongue tied down second run. *R. Hollinshead*

SAFE TO SAY 2 b.f. (Feb 10) Sayf El Arab (USA) 127 – Maravilla 73 (Mandrake – Major 122) [1992 5.1g 5f] 6,200Y: sturdy, workmanlike filly: third foal: half-sister to 1991 2-y-o sprint winner Sultry Singer (by Sizzling Melody): dam, maiden stayed 1m, is half-sister to useful miler Deadly Nightshade: backward, well beaten in the spring, in seller at Beverley last time: dead. *Mrs J. R. Ramsden*

SAFETY IN NUMBERS 2 b.g. (Feb 6) Slip Anchor 136 – Winter Queen 60   **49** p (Welsh Pageant 132) [1992 8.1d⁵ 7d 7v⁶] 16,000Y: tall gelding: has scope: fifth living foal: half-brother to very useful 1m and 1¼m winner Main Objective (by Main Reef): dam won over 13f at 4 yrs in Ireland: poor form, considerably handled, in late-season maidens: will be suited by 1m + : backward first 2 starts and looks sort to do better. *Mrs J. R. Ramsden*

SAFETY (USA) 5 b.g. Topsider (USA) – Flare Pass (USA) (Buckpasser) [1991   **52** 9s 12.5d 1992 a10g⁶ a12g a16g*] lengthy gelding: moderate mover: won over fences in August and handicap at Lingfield late in year: stays 2m: often blinkered. *J. White*

SAFFAAH (USA) 5 ch.g. Secreto (USA) 128 – Somebody Noble (USA) (Vaguely   **77** Noble 140) [1991 10.8g² 12m⁵ 14g⁴ 12v² 12.2d 1992 12g³ 14.9v³ 11.9s* 12g²] strong, round-barrelled gelding: fair performer, better than ever for new stable in the spring, winning at Haydock: not seen out on flat after very good length second at Salisbury in May: headstrong, and likely to prove ideally suited by around 1½m: acts on heavy ground: tongue tied down nowadays: races prominently. *W. R. Muir*

SAFIR (USA) 2 b.c. (Mar 21) Slew O' Gold (USA) – Icing 112 (Prince Tenderfoot   **67** (USA) 126) [1992 7f⁴ 7m 8m³ 8.5m² 10g³] $700,000Y: close-coupled colt: half-brother to several winners, including fairly useful 3-y-o Mahasin (by Danzig), successful at 7f and 1m, William Hill Futurity winner Al Hareb (by El Gran Senor) and smart French 9f to 1¼m winner Dr Somerville (by Chief's Crown): dam won from 5f to 1m at 2 yrs, including Fillies Mile: sire top class at up to 1½m: fair maiden: will stay 1½m: yet to race on a soft surface. *J. L. Dunlop*

SAGA BLUE 2 ch.f. (Mar 21) Legend of France (USA) 124 – Meme Chose (USA)   – (On-And-On) [1992 a7g] half-sister to several winners, including Australian graded winner Red Coral (by Red God), dam of useful sprinter Tarib: dam unraced: 25/1, tailed off throughout in 9-runner maiden at Southwell in July. *Bob Jones*

SAGAMAN (GER) 6 b.g. Solo Dancer (GER) – Scholastika (GER) (Alpenkonig   **54** (GER)) [1991 18s* 16g 16s 22.2m⁶ 18.8f² 11.4m³ 14m⁶ 16.2d 1992 18.1g⁵ 16m 18f⁴ 18g⁵] angular gelding: modest handicapper: out-and-out stayer: probably acts on any going: ran poorly when visored, also tried blinkered: joined K. Burke, and won handicap hurdle at Cheltenham in October despite reportedly suffering quite a serious injury. *L. J. Codd*

SAGANECA (USA) 4 b.f. Sagace (FR) 135 – Haglette (USA) (Hagley (USA))   **120** [1991 10g⁵ 9d² 10.5g⁵ 12g 10g² 10g⁴ 12m³ 12m⁴ 12.5d* 12g 1992 12g⁴ 12g⁵ 12g⁶ 12d² 12d⁴ 12m⁴ 12s⁵ 12s] smallish, leggy filly: moderate mover: very smart French performer: mainly ran creditably in Group 1 company in 1992, best effort when staying-on 3¾ lengths fifth of 18 to Subotica in moderately-run Prix de l'Arc de Triomphe at Longchamp in October: ran poorly in Italy 2 weeks later: ¾-length second to Mashaallah in Gran Premio di Milano earlier: better suited by 1½m than 1¼m: acts on good to firm and soft ground: retained 800,000 francs at Goffs Arc de Triomphe Sale. *A. Spanu, France*

SAGEBRUSH ROLLER 4 br.g. Sharpo 132 – Sunita (Owen Dudley 121) [1991   **78** 7v* 8s² 7g⁵ 7m² 7.1g⁴ 7g 8d 7m 1992 7s² 7d 7.6g⁴ 8.1g² 8.1g² 8m 8s⁵ 8s² 8s⁴ 7d³ 7.6v* 7g⁵] rangy gelding: consistent handicapper in 1992: won at Chester in October: poor efforts only in valuable events: suited by strongly-run 1m: yet to race on firm going, acts on any other: has run well for apprentice: effective visored or not: held up: has hung under pressure and found little. *J. W. Watts*

SAHARA SHIELD 3 ch.c. Alydar (USA) – El Fabulous (FR) 111 (Fabulous   **63** Dancer (USA) 124) [1991 NR 1992 8g 10g⁴ 12f² 12g 10f] useful-looking colt: second foal: half-brother to 1991 French provincial 1½m winner Exemina (by Slip Anchor): dam French 1m (at 2 yrs) and 10.5f winner: modest maiden: flattered third start: well beaten afterwards: should prove better at 1½m than shorter: sold to join W. G. M. Turner 5,200 gns Ascot July Sales. *A. A. Scott*

SAHARA STAR 3 b. or br.f. Green Desert (USA) 127 – Vaigly Star 118 (Star   – Appeal 133) [1991 5g* 5g* 6g³ 1992 5g] useful-looking filly: has a quick action: won

Molecomb Stakes at Goodwood and third (finding little off bridle) in Lowther Stakes at York as 2-y-o: first run for over 10 months, very stiff task and struggling by halfway in £9,100 handicap at York in July: should prove as effective at 6f as 5f. *M. R. Stoute*

SAHEL (IRE)   4 b.g. Green Desert (USA) 127 – Fremanche (FR) (Jim French   **93** (USA)) [1991 7g³ 1992 6.1d³ 7m² 7f² 8g* 8g⁴ 7m] angular, good-topped gelding: fairly useful handicapper: gelded after second start: successful at Newmarket and would have gone close with clear run in £10,770 Ascot race in July: better than twelfth-of-22 position suggests at Newmarket after 3-month absence, tenderly handled once held: much better suited by 1m than shorter: acts on firm and dead ground: is held up. *J. H. M. Gosden*

SAIF AL ADIL (IRE)   3 b.g. Reference Point 139 – Hardihostess 104 (Be My   **52** Guest (USA) 126) [1991 7g 7f 1992 11.1d² 12d⁶ 12.1s⁵ 12g³ 10.5g⁴ 12m² a12g 12f⁴ 14.1f³ 14.1g 16.9d 14.1m⁶ 10.8s] sturdy, lengthy gelding: moderate mover: none too consistent maiden: stays 1¾m: acts on firm and dead ground: no form in blinkers twice: sold out of B. Hanbury's stable 7,000 gns Newmarket July Sales after seventh start. *K. T. Ivory*

SAIFAN   3 ch.g. Beveled (USA) – Superfrost 49 (Tickled Pink 114) [1991 5d⁶ 5m³   **60** 5m³ 5.2f 5m 6m⁴ 6s³ 1992 7m 6.1m 8m* 8s 8.2g 7d³] tall, close-coupled, angular gelding: has a round action: inconsistent handicapper: won seller (bought in 3,600 gns) at Yarmouth in September: effective at 7f and 1m: acts on good to firm and soft ground: blinkered last 4 starts. *D. Morris*

SAILOR BOY   6 b.g. Main Reef 126 – Main Sail 104 (Blakeney 126) [1991 17.1m   **47** d 13.1m⁵ 13.1f⁴ 14.8s⁵ 11.7f³ 14s⁶ a13g² a16g a13g³ 1992 a12g a13g² 11.9d 17.1d 18.1g 13.8d 14.1m⁵] smallish gelding: easy mover: no form after being claimed out of R. Akehurst's stable £5,000 on second start: turned in moody performance last time, in July: best left alone. *A. S. Reid*

SAINT BENE'T (IRE)   4 b.g. Glenstal (USA) 118 – Basilea (FR) (Frere Basile   **58** d (FR) 129) [1991 8.2f³ 11.1d⁴ 11.1d² 11.5m 12.1g 12.1s 1992 a12g 16.2g 9.2v* 10s 10.5s 12g 9.2d 9.2m 8.1m 8f] workmanlike gelding: unreliable performer: form in 1992 only when 8-length winner of maiden claimer at Hamilton in April: stays 11f: acts on any going: often races freely: no improvement in blinkers: sold to join K. Wingrove 3,200 gns Doncaster June Sales: won over hurdles in August. *P. C. Haslam*

SAINT CIEL (USA)   4 b.c. Skywalker (USA) – Holy Tobin (USA) 83 (J O Tobin   **72** (USA) 130) [1991 8s³ 10f* 12d 9.9m³ 10.1d* 10.5m⁵ 10.5f² 10.3m 10.5g* 1992 12.3v⁵ 10.8d 12f 10.3g³] rather leggy, quite attractive colt: has a round action: fair handicapper: returned to form when close third in Doncaster ladies race in November on first run for almost 6 months: stays 1¼m: acts on any going: twice below form in blinkers at 3 yrs. *F. Jordan*

SAINTED SUE   2 ch.f. (Apr 24) Aragon 118 – Nosey 96 (Nebbiolo 125) [1992 7g   **–** 6m 6g 7.1g] 1,100Y: leggy, lightly-made filly: moderate mover: third foal: half-sister to winning hurdler Fierce (by Carwhite): dam Irish 2-y-o 5f and 6f winner: well beaten in claimers and sellers. *J. S. Haldane*

SAINT EXPRESS   2 ch.g. (Apr 15) Clantime 101 – Redgrave Design 77   **103** p (Nebbiolo 125) [1992 5m* 5g² 6m* 5.2d⁶ 6f² 5m² 5m²] 16,000Y: smallish, lengthy gelding: fifth foal: brother to 3-y-o Syke Lane and half-brother to 1987 2-y-o 5f winner Arroganza and 5-y-o 11f and 1½m winner First Bid (both by Crofthall): dam 2-y-o 5f winner: progressive performer: won maiden at Ripon in May and minor event at Doncaster in June: improved in leaps and bounds on last 3 starts, ¾-length second to Poker Chip in Flying Childers Stakes at Doncaster on final one: stays 6f: acts on firm ground, ran much better than position suggests on dead: game and genuine. *R. M. Whitaker*

SAINT SYSTEMS   6 b.m. Uncle Pokey 116 – Fire Mountain 87 (Dragonara   **47** Palace (USA) 115) [1991 a5g⁵ 5.3f 6g 6m 5.8f a5g 5d⁶ 5.1g⁶ 5m 5.7m² 5m⁵ 5m² 5d³ 5m⁴ 5m⁴ 5.7f⁵ 5.3g² 5m 1992 5g 5.1g 5.1h² 6.1d] angular, sparely-made mare: poor handicapper: last win came 24 starts ago, at 4 yrs: form in 1992 only when caught post in 3-runner race at Bath in June: effective at 5f and 6f: acts on hard and dead going: below form in blinkers: has won for apprentice. *C. J. Hill*

SAINT VENDING   4 br.c. Grey Desire 115 – Girdle Ness 56 (Pitskelly 122)   **46** [1991 12s⁵ 1992 12.3g 8.3s⁴] sparely-made colt: has a round action: very lightly raced, plating-class performer: staying-on fourth in handicap at Hamilton in May: should be effective over further than 1m: acts on soft ground, possibly unsuited by firm: blinkered once at 3 yrs: sold 400 gns Doncaster June Sales. *M. Brittain*

SAJA (USA) 2 b.f. (Mar 29) Ferdinand (USA) – Summer Silence (USA) (Stop The **56** Music (USA)) [1992 6m⁴ 7d⁶] workmanlike filly: has scope: third foal: dam, 7f winner in USA, is out of sister to Mill Reef: sire (by Nijinsky) won Kentucky Derby, Horse of The Year at 4 yrs and best at 1¼m: modest form in maidens at Yarmouth and, wearing tongue grip, Redcar (not clear run) in the autumn: will probably be better suited by 1¼m. *H. Thomson Jones*

SAKBAH (USA) 3 b.f. Al Nasr (FR) 126 – Delray Dancer (USA) (Chateaugay) – [1991 NR 1992 9.9f⁵ 14.1m³ 10m⁵] $22,000Y: sparely-made filly: half-sister to numerous winners, including outstanding American chaser Zaccio (by Lorenzaccio) and Acomb Stakes winner Kohayalan (by Mr Prospector): dam unraced daughter of half-sister to dam of Arts And Letters: no worthwhile form in maidens then claimer: should prove suited by 1½m + : sold 2,600 gns Newmarket July Sales. *J. R. Fanshawe*

SAKHAROV 3 b.g. Bay Express 132 – Supreme Kingdom 85 (Take A Reef 127) **43** [1991 5f⁵ 5g⁶ 7g 6m 1992 5s 7d⁵ 6s a6g⁴] leggy, unfurnished gelding: poor maiden: stays 7f: acts on dead ground. *M. A. Jarvis*

SALADAN KNIGHT 7 b.g. Dalsaan 125 – Exciting Times (Windjammer (USA)) – [1991 a6g³ 5g 7.5f⁶ 6g 1992 a7g⁶ a7g² a6g³ a6g⁴ a6g⁴ a6g² 6d 5d 5m a7g] lengthy, a64 good-topped gelding: moderate mover: modest handicapper on the all-weather: won apprentice handicap at Southwell in February: well beaten last 4 starts: stays 7f: blinkered nowadays, also wears eyeshield on all-weather: once visored (raced alone): has gone well for 7-lb claimer, though tends to wander: sold 1,600 gns Doncaster August Sales. *J. G. FitzGerald*

SALAR'S SPIRIT 6 ch.g. Salmon Leap (USA) 131 – Indigine (USA) (Raise A – Native) [1991 NR 1992 8.3d 10m] robust gelding: no form on flat: poor hurdler. *W. G. M. Turner*

SALATIN (USA) 2 b.c. (Mar 4) Seattle Dancer (USA) 119 – Ivory Wings (USA) **96** p (Sir Ivor 135) [1992 6m⁴ 7g* 7g²] 275,000Y: lengthy colt: good mover: fifth foal: half-brother to 4-y-o 11f to 1¾m winner John Shaw (by L'Emigrant) and French 1¼m to 11f winner Wings of Wishes (by Alydar): dam French 1¼m and 1½m winner later successful in USA, is out of high-class mare and broodmare Kittiwake: progressive form: won 4-runner maiden at Ascot in July, leading over 2f out and running on strongly: looking very well, very free to post and took good hold in race when head second of 8 to Woodchat in £14,700 contest at York following month, leading just inside final 1f until close home: will stay at least 1m: will improve again. *P. T. Walwyn*

SALBUS 2 b.c. (Apr 16) Salse (USA) 128 – Busca (USA) 49 (Mr Prospector (USA)) **47** p [1992 7d] good-bodied colt: third living foal: half-brother to 3-y-o Banish (by Don't Forget Me) and 4-y-o 1¼m and 1½m winner Abingdon Flyer (by Pennine Walk): dam (stayed 9.4f) is out of Kentucky Oaks winner Bag of Tunes: 9/1 and backward, 15 lengths eleventh of 15 to Gabr in maiden at Leicester in October, held up after slow start, not knocked about when beaten: sold 4,200 gns Ascot December Sales. *G. Harwood*

SALBYNG 4 b.c. Night Shift (USA) – Hsian (Shantung 132) [1991 8.2d* a8g* **66** 8.2m³ 8g* a8g⁶ 8m 10.2g² 10f⁴ 11.4m⁴ 12g 8g⁶ 10.3d 1992 9d⁵ 8d² 8s 8m⁴ 9g⁶ 8.3g* 8.2d² 8d³ 9d³ 8s² 10.2d] strong colt: carries condition: usually looks well: moderate mover: consistent handicapper: gamely won at Windsor in August on first run since having soft palate operation: modest effort only on final start: effective at 1m, and probably stays 11.4f: acts on firm and soft going: has run fairly well for apprentice. *J. W. Hills*

SALDA 3 b.g. Bustino 136 – Martinova 111 (Martinmas 128) [1991 8m⁵ 7m 7s 1992 **76** 7g⁴ 7g⁴ 8m⁵ 8.1d* 7.9m 10.1m 8s* 7.9s] big, lengthy gelding: moderate walker: fair form: short-head winner of handicaps at Haydock in August and Newcastle (set modest pace) in September: should stay 1¼m: best on a soft surface: twice withdrawn lame in 1992. *R. M. Whitaker*

SALIK (IRE) 2 b. or br.c. (Mar 16) Doyoun 124 – Safe Home 94 (Home Guard – (USA) 129) [1992 6d] IR 8,200F, 380,000 francs (approx 38,200) Y: lengthy colt: fourth foal: half-brother to Irish 3-y-o 1m winner Home Counties (by Ela-Mana-Mou) and a winner in Italy by Shardari: dam, best at 2 yrs when 5f winner in Ireland, is half-sister to very useful sprinter Touch Paper out of half-sister to Blue Wind: 14/1, visored and burly, last of 9 throughout in maiden at Haydock in August, swishing tail and not responding to early reminders: sold 1,200 gns Newmarket Autumn Sales. *P. T. Walwyn*

SALINGER 4 b.g. Rousillon (USA) 133 – Scholastika (GER) (Alpenkonig (GER)) **49**
[1991 NR 1992 8.1g 7g 10.8g³ 8d 10s⁴ 10.8s] angular, workmanlike gelding: inconsistent handicapper, still a maiden: effective from 1m to 1¼m: acts on soft ground. *J. W. Hills*

SALISONG 3 gr.c. Song 132 – Sylvanecte (FR) 70 (Silver Shark 129) [1991 7m³ **69**
7g* 1992 8d 6d 5.7s² 7f 6d⁶ 7d* 7g⁵ 8d 8g 7.1s⁶] rangy colt: fair handicapper: ridden by 7-lb claimer, won claimer at Salisbury in August, leading inside final 1f: below form last 3 starts (in blinkers twice), including in ladies race: stays 7f well: best efforts with give in the ground, and acts on soft: sold 5,400 gns Newmarket Autumn Sales. *P. F. I. Cole*

SALLY FAST 3 ch.f. Legend of France (USA) 124 – Strip Fast 71 (Virginia Boy **43**
106) [1991 NR 1992 8s⁶ 8m 7.1g⁶ 7g 8.3m* 7d 8.3g 8.9d 8d] small filly: sixth foal: half-sister to winners abroad by Noalto and Ahonoora: dam won 4 races from 1m to 10.2f, one at 9 yrs: inconsistent performer: dropped in class, won 17-runner seller at Windsor in August by a short head: ran poorly last 3 starts, blinkered last time: should stay beyond 1m: acts on good to firm going: usually claimer ridden: sold privately 1,450 gns Doncaster October Sales. *B. Palling*

SALLY FAY (IRE) 4 b.f. Fayruz 116 – Trust Sally 65 (Sallust 134) [1991 6m⁵ **33**
5m⁶ 6d² 5f 7g³ 6d² 6g⁶ 6m* 6m⁵ 6g⁵ 7m⁶ 7g a6g 1992 8.5g 8d 8m 8.9g⁶ 8f 8.9m 9g³ 10.1m 11d] leggy, workmanlike filly: moderate mover: inconsistent handicapper: seems to stay 9f: acts on good to firm and dead ground, ran poorly on fibresand. *T. Kersey*

SALLY FORTH 6 b.g. Sallust 134 – Sally Knox (Busted 134) [1991 NR 1992 10d –
10g 9.7g] angular, deep-girthed gelding: still a maiden, and no promise in handicaps in 1992. *J. R. Bostock*

SALLY SAAD 4 gr.f. Green Desert (USA) 127 – Biding 97 (Habat 127) [1991 7g –
7g⁴ 7f³ 6f⁵ 6.1m 1992 6.1m] leggy, angular filly: has a quick action: poor maiden at 3 yrs for B. Hanbury: burly, tailed off in handicap in June, 1992: stays 7f: acts on firm ground. *D. J. S. Cosgrove*

SALLY'S SON 6 b.g. Beldale Flutter (USA) 130 – Sally Chase 101 (Sallust 134) –
[1991 a5g³ a6g* a6g⁵ a6g² a7g* a6g² 5m 7f⁶ 5m 5m⁶ 6m 6m⁵ 5.2f⁵ 7g a6g⁵ a6g 1992 a82 d
a7g³ a6g* a6g* a5g² a7g² a7g⁴ a6g² a7g² 7g a6g⁵ a7g⁴ a7g² a7g a7g⁴ a7g⁶]
strong, good-bodied gelding: carries plenty of condition: moderate walker: best on the all-weather, and won 2 handicaps at Lingfield in January: off course 4 months after ninth outing and below best after: none too consistent on turf: effective from 5f to 7f: acts on firm ground and all-weather surfaces: effective with or without blinkers or visor: usually held up: claimer ridden. *W. A. O'Gorman*

SALLY TADPOLE 3 b.f. Jester 119 – Sorata (FR) (Sodium 128) [1991 5g² 1992 –
6d⁴ 6s] leggy, close-coupled filly: off course a year and backward, last of 4 in maiden at Newcastle and seventh of 8 in apprentice race at Ripon in the spring. *N. Tinkler*

SALMAN (USA) 6 b.g. Nain Bleu (FR) – H M S Pellinore (USA) (King Pellinore **49**
(USA) 127) [1991 10s² 10s³ 10.4d 8.9g 10m 9m⁶ 9m⁴ 10m 10m⁶ 1992 a8g 10d a12g
10.3m* 9.9m⁵ a8g⁵] strong, good-topped gelding: has had soft palate operation: modest performer: first run for over 3 months and best effort in 1992 when 7-length winner of apprentice handicap at Chester in August, allowed to dominate: stays 1¼m: acts on any going: has edged right: headstrong: sometimes has tongue tied down: none too genuine. *S. G. Norton*

SALMON DANCER (IRE) 3 b.c. Salmon Leap (USA) 131 – Welsh Walk –
(Welsh Saint 126) [1991 6m 7g 8.1g 8.2m 8m 1992 10.8g 10g 11g 11.8g 7.1s 10d] leggy, lengthy colt: seems of little account: sold 950 gns Doncaster November Sales. *M. F. Barraclough*

SALT N VINEGAR (IRE) 2 ch.c. (Mar 17) Salt Dome (USA) – Karissima 90 –
(Kalamoun 129) [1992 5g 5g² 8d] IR 2,600Y, 16,500 2-y-o: small colt: half-brother to winners in Italy by Cure The Blues and Ela-Mana-Mou: dam 2-y-o 7f winner: no worthwhile form in maidens. *Ronald Thompson*

SALU 3 br.f. Ardross 134 – String of Beads 63 (Ile de Bourbon (USA) 133) [1991 **60**
7g² 8.9d 1992 12.2d² 12d³ 14.6g 11m⁶ 12.2g⁴ 12d³ 12f² 12f² 12g* 12g⁶ 12m³ 11.8m³
12m⁶ 11.1s* 11v* 11.1d*] sparely-made filly: modest performer: successful in second half of season in claimers at Thirsk, Hamilton, Redcar and Edinburgh: stays 1½m well: acts on any going: visored/blinkered: has twice hung left when in front. *J. Etherington*

SALUTING WALTER (USA) 4 b.c. Verbatim (USA) – Stage Hour (USA) –
(Stage Director (USA)) [1991 8m⁶ 8g³ 9m³ 10m² 10.6g² 10m³ 8d* 8m 9d⁶ 7.6g³
8.9m⁴ 8m 9g³ 7d⁶ 1992 7g 10g] leggy, good-topped colt: rated 80 at best as 3-y-o for

M. Ryan: backward and below form at 4 yrs: stays 1¼m: acts on good to firm ground and dead: occasionally sweating. *I. Campbell*

SALVATORE GIULIANO 2 ch.c. (Mar 8) Superlative 118 – Bonny Bright   **49** p
Eyes 58 (Rarity 129) [1992 6s⁶] 3,300F, 4,600Y: strong, compact colt: third foal: dam lightly raced: 25/1, and carrying condition, around 7 lengths sixth of 7 to Nabjelsedr in maiden at Goodwood in October, steadily outpaced from 2f out: reluctant stalls: looks sort to do better. *S. M. Hillen*

SAMAIN (USA) 5 ch.m. Caerleon (USA) 132 – Samarta Dancer (USA)   **51**
(Marshua's Dancer (USA)) [1991 6d 7f⁴ 6m 9m⁵ 10m 11.5s⁵ 8.1g⁵ 10g⁶ 10m 1992 13d⁴ 10g⁵ a12g 12m* 16.1m* 18g⁴ 14.1m³ 12f* 16.2d² 14d⁴ 12f²] tall, leggy mare: very consistent handicapper: won twice at Pontefract, and at Newcastle in between, in first half of season: not seen out after running really well in August (had operation for twisted gut): effective from 1½m to 2m: acts on dead going, but goes very well on top-of-the-ground: below form when visored once: game. *J. A. Glover*

SAMANTHAS JOY 2 b.f. (Mar 13) Marching On 101 – Sister Racine 58 (Dom   **47**
Racine (FR) 121) [1992 5g⁵ 5m⁶ a5g² a5g a5s² 6s a6g⁵ 7d⁵ a6g4] leggy, lengthy filly: moderate walker: poor mover: second reported foal: dam, maiden plater, is out of useful miler Geoffrey's Sister: a consistent plater on last 5 starts: effective from 5f to 7f: acts on soft ground and all-weather surfaces. *T. Fairhurst*

SAMJAMALIFRAN 3 b.f. Blakeney 126 – Royal Shoe (Hotfoot 126) [1991 10m   **–**
1992 12g⁶ 7d a7g 10.8s] small filly: has a round action: seems of little account. *M. C. Pipe*

SAMMY SLEW (USA) 3 br.g. Tsunami Slew (USA) – Big Sparkle (USA) (The   **58**
Big Boss (USA)) [1991 6m⁵ 6g⁵ 1992 6d⁶ 6g 7m⁶ 6f⁴ 7m⁴ 5m 6d⁶ 5v⁵ a5g⁵] lengthy gelding: modest maiden: left S. Norton and off course 4 months after sixth start: effective at 6f/7f: acts on firm going: no form once each in visor/blinkers. *C. Parker*

SAMSOLOM 4 b.g. Absalom 128 – Norfolk Serenade 83 (Blakeney 126) [1991 5f⁴   **64**
5m² 6m³ 6f 5d⁴ 5g² 5m³ 6s⁶ 6m 5f 1992 5g 5m⁴ 5f⁶ 5f⁵ 5m 6m 5.6m⁵ 5d 8m 5m³ 5m a6g³ a5g⁴ a6g⁴ a6g³ a6g⁵] strong, good-quartered gelding: has round action: none too consistent handicapper: best at up to 6f: acts on any going, except seemingly soft: below form visored/blinkered (also tongue tied down) once: sometimes hangs left, and has found little. *J. Balding*

SAMSON-AGONISTES 6 b.h. Bold Fort 100 – Hello Cuddles 99 (He Loves   **83**
Me 120) [1991 5m* 5f* 5f⁶ 5g⁵ 5m 1992 5m² 5f* 5g 6.1d* 5g² 5.1f⁵ 5m* 5m 5m* 5s 5m⁶] leggy horse: poor mover: fairly useful handicapper: had a really good season, successful at Warwick and Nottingham (not at best to win seller, no bid) in the summer and at Thirsk and Pontefract (third win there) in September: best at 5f: acts on firm and dead going: goes well for 7-lb claimer S. Sanders: front runner. *B. A. McMahon*

SAM THE MAN 5 b.g. Aragon 118 – First Temptation (USA) 67 (Mr Leader   **–**
(USA)) [1991 10v* 8.3g 1992 7m 10f 10.2m 11.9d] rather sparely-made gelding: rated 56 at 4 yrs: no promise in handicaps in 1992. *J. Ffitch-Heyes*

SAMURAI GOLD (USA) 4 b.c. Golden Act (USA) – Taipan's Lady (USA)   **58** d
(Bold Hour) [1991 5d 8g 6g⁶ 6m 5g⁵ 5m⁴ 6g⁵ 6m 5f 6g⁴ a10g³ a10g⁵ 1992 a10g² a10g² a12g² 12d 10g³ 10m² 10.2m* 10d 10m⁵ 10d 10.1d 12m 10.5d 12v] rather leggy colt: modest handicapper at his best: won at Chepstow in June: well beaten last 5 starts: sold out of P. Walwyn's stable 5,600 gns after second of them: effective from 1¼m to 1½m: acts on firm ground and on equitrack: has form on dead ground, not in 1992: has worn blinkers, usually visored nowadays: sometimes edgy: takes keen hold: below form for amateur. *C. James*

SANAWI 5 b.g. Glenstal (USA) 118 – Russeting 76 (Mummy's Pet 125) [1991 NR   **51**
1992 8f⁵ 8.9s⁴ 8.2g⁴ 10f⁵ 8.9m³ 8f⁴ 8f⁶ 8.9g* 10.5g 10.3m⁵ 8.9d³ 8g 12g] strong, attractive gelding: poor mover: consistent handicapper: won apprentice claimer at Wolverhampton in July: was effective from 1m to 1¼m: acted on any going: good mount for inexperienced rider: won selling hurdle in October: dead. *P. D. Evans*

SAND CASTLE 11 ch.g. Tap On Wood 130 – Pacific Sands (Sandford Lad 133)   **–**
[1991 NR 1992 a16g a16g⁵ a16g a13g⁵ 9d] compact, well-made gelding: of little account these days. *P. Howling*

SANDCASTLE CITY 3 b.g. Formidable (USA) 125 – Sandstream 72 (Sandford   **44**
Lad 133) [1991 5g³ 5d⁴ 5g² 5d* 5g* 5.2g 6.1g⁶ 6g 1992 6g 6f 6m 7m⁵ 6m 6d 8m 7d⁴ 7g 6.1m] well-made, sturdy gelding: moderate mover: inconsistent performer: may prove best at 6f: acts on good to firm and dead ground: no improvement in blinkers. *R. Hannon*

SANDMOOR DENIM 5 b.g. Red Sunset 120 – Holernzaye 93 (Sallust 134) **62**
[1991 a8g⁵ a7g 6d 8d 10m 7f* 8.2d⁶ 8m* 7f a7g³ 8.2m³ 7m³ 8.2f⁴ 7m² 7m² 7m³ 8m²
a8g⁶ 1992 a7g⁴ a7g a7g² a7g⁴ 8s 6v 7m⁵ 8.5m⁵ 7f⁵ 10d⁵ a8g* a7g* a7g⁴ 8m³ a8g*
7.9d³ a7g² a7g² 7.5g* 7f 7.5m⁵ a5g a7g⁵ a7g⁴ a7g⁶ a7g⁵] close-coupled gelding:
very tough and genuine handicapper: had excellent season in 1992, showing remarkable consistency, and successful at Southwell (3) and Beverley in the summer:
effective at 7f and 1m: acts on firm and dead ground and on all-weather surfaces:
below form when blinkered earlier in career: sometimes slowly away: thrives on
racing and tends not to be at best after a lay-off. *S. R. Bowring*

SANDMOOR SATIN 2 b.f. (Mar 16) Music Boy 124 – Fall About 68 (Comedy –
Star (USA)) [1992 5f⁵ 8m 7d] 7,000Y: leggy filly: first foal: dam, 1½m winner at 4
yrs: no worthwhile form, including in a seller: sold 600 gns Doncaster October
Sales. *M. H. Easterby*

SANDRO 3 b.g. Niniski (USA) 125 – Miller's Creek (USA) 62 (Star de Naskra **55**
(USA)) [1991 7g 8m 1992 12s 13.1m⁵ 16.2g 11.5m² 12m 12g⁴ 11.7d] leggy gelding:
inconsistent maiden: stays 13f: best efforts on top-of-the-ground: below form in
blinkers last 2 starts: sold out of J. Fanshawe's stable 7,000 gns Newmarket
September Sales after first of them: won novice hurdle in September. *R. J. Baker*

SANDSWIFT 2 b.f. (Jun 3) Elegant Air 119 – Swiftsand 65 (Sharpen Up 127) **50**
[1992 5g⁶ 6d 8s] tall filly: has scope: third living foal: dam, raced only at 3 yrs,
half-sister to St Leger second Zilos: modest form first 2 starts: blinkered, soundly
beaten final one: should stay 1m: sold 600 gns Ascot November Sales. *R. F. Johnson
Houghton*

SAND TABLE 3 b. or br.g. Green Desert (USA) 127 – Keyboard 88 (High Top **86**
131) [1991 NR 1992 a7g* a7g³ 7m⁵ 8.1m⁶ 7.3g³ 9d 8m⁴] good-bodied gelding: fourth
foal: half-brother to fair 1989 2-y-o 6f winner Nice Day (by Shirley Heights), later
placed over 1¼m: dam 2-y-o 7.6f winner disappointing at 3 yrs, is half-sister to very
useful middle-distance winner Galveston: fairly useful performer: won maiden at
Lingfield in January: good efforts in frame in handicaps at Newbury and Newmarket
in autumn: promises to stay 9f (fair effort in Cambridgeshire when tried): acts on
good to firm ground, probably on dead: visored (ran moderately) once: sold to join J.
Sutcliffe 28,000 gns Newmarket Autumn Sales and gelded. *Lord Huntingdon*

SANFOYT (USA) 3 br.c. Foyt (USA) – Kiku San (USA) (Bushido (USA)) [1991 –
NR 1992 a7g] $3,600Y: workmanlike colt: fifth reported foal: brother to North
American winner Raise N San and half-brother to 3 minor winners: dam won stakes
races from 6f to 8.3f: sire stakes-placed brother to Alydar: 33/1 and blinkered,
beaten 14 lengths in maiden at Southwell in June: well behind after slow start then
some late headway: moved moderately to post. *Mrs N. Macauley*

SAN ROQUE 7 b.g. Aragon 118 – Arch Sculptress 85 (Arch Sculptor 123) [1991 –
a10g a13g⁶ a10g³ a12g 10.2s 9g 8m 8f 12f⁴ 8f 12g 9d 10s 12g 10m 10s⁴ 12s 1992 10m
10f 11.9f] sturdy, close-coupled gelding: has a quick action: rated 56 over 1m/1¼m at
5 yrs: no longer looks of much account. *S. Woodman*

SANTANA LADY (IRE) 3 b.f. Blakeney 126 – Santalina (Relko 136) [1991 7d⁶ **72**
a7g⁵ 1992 8d 10s⁵ 8.3m* 10g* 10d⁵ 12g 10.2s⁴ 9g³] rather leggy filly: fair
handicapper: always close up when winning twice at Windsor in the summer, in an
apprentice contest second occasion: should stay beyond 1¼m: acts on good to firm
ground, probably on soft. *M. J. Heaton-Ellis*

SANTARAY 6 ch.g. Formidable (USA) 125 – Stockingful (Santa Claus 133) [1991 **54**
14.6s 10.8g⁵ 8.1d 1992 11.1v² 10.8d] big, strong, rangy gelding: fair winning hurdler
in 1991/2: shaped promisingly when second in apprentice handicap at Hamilton in
April: well below form at Warwick 19 days later: should stay 1½m: has worn crossed
noseband and had tongue tied down: has been gelded. *J. Mackie*

SANTAREM (USA) 4 b.f. El Gran Senor (USA) 136 – Une Amazone (USA) **71**
(Youth (USA) 135) [1991 NR 1992 14.8f² 14.1g⁴ 14.1f³] heavy-topped filly: fourth
reported foal: half-sister to 3 winners, including smart stayer Al Maheb (by Riverman): dam unraced half-sister to Prix Royal-Oak winner Henri Le Balafre: shaped
encouragingly on belated debut when second in apprentice maiden at Newmarket:
bandaged, failed to confirm that run in Yarmouth maidens later in midsummer. *W. J.
Haggas*

SANTI SANA 4 b.f. Formidable (USA) 125 – Eldoret 100 (High Top 131) [1991 **68**
7g⁶ 7d* 8m⁶ 8.1d 1992 8g 8.1f² 9m³ 7d² 7g⁴ 8.2d 8g 8.2s] strong, stocky filly: fair
handicapper: stays 1m: acts on firm and dead ground: effective blinkered or not:
usually races to the fore: ran moderately last 3 starts: sold 18,000 gns Newmarket
December Sales. *Lady Herries*

SAPIENCE 6 ch.h. Niniski (USA) 125 – Claretta (USA) 82 (Roberto (USA) 131) **124**
[1991 12m 12m⁶ 12m⁵ 12.5m 10.9m⁶ 1992 12g* 13.9m² 12g 12f² 10s³ 12g⁴ 13.3g² 12s³
12s⁵ 12s] useful-looking, rather angular horse: carries condition: good mover: very
smart performer at his best: 40/1, won Jockey Club Stakes at Newmarket in April by
3 lengths from Luchiroverte, allowed to dictate modest pace under excellent ride
from R. Cochrane: ran well when second in Yorkshire Cup and Hardwicke Stakes (to
Rock Hopper both times), third in Eclipse (3 lengths behind Kooyonga) and 7
lengths fourth to St Jovite in King George VI and Queen Elizabeth Diamond Stakes:
some way below form after, best effort when third to Mashaallah in Group 1 race at
Baden-Baden: effective from 1¼m (at least when conditions are testing) to 1¾m:
acts on any going: has hung: effective visored or not: blinkered once at 5 yrs: trained
by J. FitzGerald in 1991. *D. R. C. Elsworth*

SAPPHIRINE 5 b.m. Trojan Fen 118 – By Surprise 68 (Young Generation 129) **73**
[1991 8.5g² 7m⁶ 8m⁶ 8m⁴ 10m 12.3f 10m 12f² 12m 9m 12g* 1992 12.3m³ 12f3 15.1f*
12f 14.1d 10.9d 12f³ 12.2g* 11.9m²] lengthy mare: moderate mover: fair handicapper:
successful at Edinburgh in June: in good form in August, winning at Catterick before
going down narrowly in very strongly-run £12,500 race at York when ridden by 7-lb
claimer: effective from 1½m to 15f: best form on a sound surface: below form when
blinkered once. *R. M. Whitaker*

SARA ANNE (IRE) 3 b.f. Sarab 123 – Frans Cap (Captain James 123) [1991 5m⁴ **–**
5m⁴ 5f⁶ 5m² 6m 5g* 5m² 5m³ 6g 6.1m⁴ 1992 a5g³ a5g 6.1m⁵ 7.6g 5g] leggy, rather
sparely-made filly: had a round action: inconsistent handicapper: stayed 6f: acted on
good to firm ground: trained first 3 starts by L. Codd: dead. *W. M. Brisbourne*

SARAH-CLARE 4 b.f. Reach 122 – Northern Dynasty 65 (Breeders Dream 116) **57**
[1991 8f 8d 11.5f 10g³ 10g² 11.5m 10g* 10g 10m⁶ 10g 10.3d 11.5s 1992 9.9g* 10m³
11.6m 10g* 10m 10g⁵ 10.1d⁴ 9.7g 10s² 9.7v³ 9.7v⁵ a10g⁶] rangy filly: moderate
mover: modest handicapper: won at Beverley and Sandown (apprentices) in
midsummer: stays 1¼m: best form with give in the ground, though only fair efforts
on heavy. *R. Akehurst*

SARAH HEIGHTS 2 b.f. (Apr 16) Sayyaf 121 – Temple Heights 72 (Shirley **54**
Heights 130) [1992 6d 7g 6v⁶] angular, close-coupled filly: third foal: half-sister to a
winning hurdler: dam 2m winner out of game stayer Hardirondo: modest maiden:
best effort on debut: should stay at least 1m. *Miss L. C. Siddall*

SARANGANI BAY (USA) 2 b.c. (May 31) Manila (USA) – Homespun (USA) **80** p
(Round Table) [1992 6m⁵ 6g³ 6d³] $90,000 2-y-o: strong, lengthy colt: has plenty of
scope: half-brother to several winners, including 4-y-o Irish St Leger winner Mashaallah and graded-stakes performers Folk Art and Sportin' Life (all by Nijinsky):
dam minor winner: sire won Breeders' Cup Turf: fair form in maidens: made much
of running at Newbury and Redcar on last 2 starts: strong-galloping sort, type to be
better suited by middle distances. *P. W. Chapple-Hyam*

General Accident Jockey Club Stakes, Newmarket—
Sapience's first run since changing stables; those he beats include (from left to right)
Toulon, Always Friendly, Rock Hopper and Luchiroverte

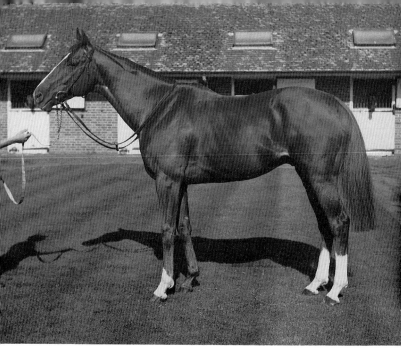

Mr W. H. O'Gorman's "Sapience"

SARASWATI 2 b.f. (Feb 12) Mansingh (USA) 120 – French Bugle 71 (Bleep- **55** d
Bleep 134) [1992 5.2s⁴ 5f⁵ 5g 5g 5.1d] leggy, shallow-girthed filly: sister to
ungenuine 7f winner Cor de Chasse, closely related to Norfolk Stakes winner
Petillante (by Petong) and half-sister to several winners, including useful sprinter
Piencourt (by Averof): dam won at 1m: regressive form in maidens and a nursery:
should stay at least 6f: acts on firm and soft ground. *P. J. Makin*

SARATOGA SOURCE (USA) 3 ch.f. Saratoga Six (USA) – Exotic Source **106**
(USA) 79 (The Minstrel (CAN) 135) [1991 7g* 7m³ 7g* 8.5s⁶ 1992 10m* 12d⁴ 9g²
10.5g² 8m] sturdy, useful-looking filly: useful performer: won listed race at Newbury in May: best efforts when second in Group 3 events in France (to Formidable
Flight) and Germany: needs further than 1m, and stays 10.5f (well-beaten fourth in
Oaks): acts on good to firm ground, well beaten on soft in Grade 3 event in USA at 2
yrs. *I. A. Balding*

SARAWAT 4 b.g. Slip Anchor 136 – Eljazzi 92 (Artaius (USA) 129) [1991 12m² **86**
12m* 12g² 12m³ 13.8m* 1992 11.9m 14.6f 15s³ 16d³ 14.6g*] smallish, workmanlike
gelding: has a moderate, round action: fairly useful handicapper: gradually came to
hand in the autumn, leading 3f out and running on well to win at Doncaster: effective
from 1½m to 15f: acts on good to firm and soft ground. *Mrs M. Reveley*

SARCITA 4 b.f. Primo Dominie 121 – Zinzi (Song 132) [1991 6m 6m⁴ 5g⁴ 5m* 6m³ –
5m 5g* 6f* 5g² 5.6m* 6m* 5d² 5m⁴ 1992 6g] lengthy, good-topped filly: carries
condition: one of the most improved perfomers in training at 3 yrs, winning Portland
Handicap and Ayr Gold Cup: backward, last of 8 in listed race at Lingfield in May:
effective at 5f and 6f: acted on firm and dead ground: blinkered (below form) once:
tough and genuine: in foal to Cadeaux Genereux. *D. R. C. Elsworth*

717

SAREEN EXPRESS (IRE) 4 gr.g. Siberian Express (USA) 125 – Three **43** Waves (Cure The Blues (USA)) [1991 7g 1992 a6g a7g³ a8g⁴ a8g³ a10g⁴ a8g⁵ a7g⁶ a52 a10g a8g* a7g⁴ a8g³ a8g⁵ 8.2m³ 8.1m⁶ 8m² 8.1g⁵ 8g 8.2m 7.1s³ 10g 8s 8s a8g* a8g⁶] lengthy, plain gelding: none too consistent handicapper: won at Lingfield in May and November: suited by testing 7f and 1m: acts on good to firm and soft ground, and on all-weather surfaces: often used to be blinkered, but not nowadays: usually claimer ridden. *Mrs J. C. Dawe*

SARENA LADY (IRE) 2 b.f. (Apr 30) Auction Ring (USA) 123 – Parima (Par- **55** p dao 120) [1992 5f²] 9,000Y: unfurnished filly: sister to smart 7f to 1¼m performer Trucidator and half-sister to 3 winners here and abroad, including fairly useful 1983 2-y-o 6f winner Rusticello (by Rusticaro): dam won in Norway: 5/2 and bandaged, beaten a length in a maiden at Salisbury in July, leading at halfway and keeping on well when headed: moved moderately down: seemed sure to improve. *P. F. I. Cole*

SARSTA GRAI 4 b.f. Blakeney 126 – Horton Line 89 (High Line 125) [1991 8.2f² **56** 8f⁶ 12.2m 12.3g 12f* 12f³ 12m a14g² 1992 12f⁴ 16.2g 12m* 12.3f⁵] lengthy, workmanlike filly: modest handicapper: won at Beverley, battling on well: failed to reproduce that in ladies event at Ripon later in June: stayed 1½m: acted on firm going, unsuited by heavy: in foal to Domynsky. *M. H. Easterby*

SARTIGILA 3 b.f. Efisio 120 – Ichnusa 83 (Day Express 132) [1991 5m 1992 6.9v⁴ **60** 6d⁴ 6g⁴ 5g⁴ 5s⁵] good-topped filly: moderate mover: progressive form: best effort when fifth in handicap at Leicester on second run after a 5-month lay-off: will be suited by return to 6f: acts on soft ground: sold 2,800 gns Newmarket Autumn Sales. *J. W. Payne*

SARUK (IRE) 3 br.f. Tate Gallery (USA) 117 – Lovely Kate 104 (Le Levanstell **–** 122) [1991 6s 7g a7g 1992 a6g a8g a6g a5g⁶ 5.3m 5.1d] small filly: of little account. *J. J. Bridger*

SARUM 6 b.g. Tina's Pet 121 – Contessa (HUN) (Peleid 125) [1991 a7g a10g⁵ **52** a10g⁴ a8g* a10g³ a8g² a7g² a7g² 7m³ 7g³ a7g⁴ a7g⁵ 1992 a7g² a8g³ a8g³ a8g* a8g* a64 a8g* a7g² a7g³ 8m⁵ 8s a8g² 7m a8g⁵ a7g⁶] tall, leggy, rather narrow gelding: poor mover: consistent handicapper in spring, successful 3 times (including apprentice event) at Lingfield: below form last 2 starts after lengthy absence: effective at 6f to 1m: acts on good to firm ground and equitrack, possibly not on soft: has run well for apprentice. *C. P. Wildman*

SARWAN (IRE) 4 ch.g. Shernazar 131 – Sellasia (FR) (Dankaro (FR) 131) [1991 **–** 11m⁶ 10g² 12.8g* 12g* 1992 12g 11.9s] workmanlike ex-Irish gelding: poor mover: sixth foal: half-brother to fairly useful 7f to 1½m performer Simjour (by Adonijah) and fair 1¼m winner Samanpour (by Nishapour): dam, granddaughter of top French filly Apollonia, was placed over 10.5f in France: successful in claimers at Roscommon and Wexford in summer at 3 yrs for J. Oxx: no form here, running as if something badly amiss final start, in April: withdrawn lame in November: stays 12.8f. *A. P. Stringer*

SASEEDO (USA) 2 ch.c. (Mar 31) Afleet (CAN) – Barbara's Moment (USA) **74** (Super Moment (USA)) [1992 5m 5s⁴ 5d* 5g² a7g⁵] 28,000Y: close-coupled colt: first foal: dam won 5 races in USA and was graded stakes-placed at 11f: sire (by Mr Prospector) won from 6f to 9f and was Horse of the Year in Canada: won maiden at Catterick and not at all discredited after slow starts in nurseries at Newmarket and Lingfield after: bred to stay at least 1m, but has plenty of pace and shapes as if worth a try at 6f: acts on dead ground. *W. A. O'Gorman*

SASPARELLA 3 ch.f. Sharpo 132 – Palmella (USA) 89 (Grundy 137) [1991 5m* **69** 5g 6g 6m 1992 8.2d² 10.2s 8d 7f 6m² 5m⁶] workmanlike, sparely-made filly: fair performer: moderate mover: off course nearly 3 months and blinkered, ran creditably in handicaps at Yarmouth and Newmarket last 2 starts: effective from 5f to 1m: acts on good to firm and dead ground: sold 5,400 gns Newmarket Autumn Sales. *W. Jarvis*

SASSAMOUSE 2 b.f. (Feb 22) Bairn (USA) 126 – Westminster Waltz (Dance In **48** Time (CAN)) [1992 6m 7.1g⁴ 7g] 1,600Y: leggy filly: second foal: half-sister to 1991 2-y-o 7f winner Juldee (by Cragador): dam twice-raced daughter of half-sister to Busted: plating-class maiden: will be suited by 1m+ : ran creditably for 7-lb claimer on debut. *R. Guest*

SASSIVER (USA) 2 b.c. (Feb 24) Riverman (USA) 131 – Sassabunda 108 (Sassa- **45** p fras (FR) 135) [1992 8.2s 7g] half-brother to several winners, including useful 1m to 10.2f winner Habitassa (by Habitat) and quite useful 1983 2-y-o 1m and 9f winner Sassagrass (by Thatch): dam short-head second in Irish Oaks: never dangerous in maidens at Nottingham and Doncaster in the autumn: will be better suited by middle distances: sold to join R. Hollinshead 11,000 gns Ascot December Sales. *R. Charlton*

SASSY LASSY (IRE)   4 b.f. Taufan (USA) 119 – Miss Reasoning (USA) (Bold –
Reasoning (USA)) [1991 6m⁵ 6g³ 7g* 7g⁴ 7.1m 8m 8d⁵ 1992 a8g] leggy, close-
coupled filly: rated 64 at 3 yrs for Lord Huntingdon: well below form in claimer at
Southwell in January: should prove better at 1m than shorter: possibly needs an
easy surface: has run well for 7-lb claimer. *D. Burchell*

SASTAGO (USA)   3 b.c. Skywalker (USA) – Sastarda (CHI) (Iram (ARG)) [1991   **82**
8m* 1992 10d⁶ 12.3g* 12d 12f⁵ 11.9d² 12.3g 11.5m] angular, workmanlike colt: fairly
useful handicapper on his day: won £7,100 handicap at Chester in May: better at
1½m than shorter: best efforts in 1992 on an easy surface: seems best when able to
set the pace: sold 21,000 gns Newmarket Autumn Sales. *J. H. M. Gosden*

SATANK (USA)   2 b.c. (Feb 9) Victory Stride (USA) – Iron Franco (USA)   **103** p
(Barrera (USA)) [1992 5g³ 5f* 5g⁵ 5g² 5m³] $3,500Y, $42,000 2-y-o: strong,
lengthy colt: has plenty of scope: good walker: has a quick action: fourth reported
foal: dam minor winner at up to 7f: sire (by Northern Dancer) minor 6f winner:
progressive form: made all in Windsor Castle Stakes at Royal Ascot: placed in listed
race at York and Flying Childers Stakes (caught close home) at Doncaster in
September: worth a try at 6f: yet to race on a soft surface: tends to wander under
pressure: sure to win more races. *J. W. Watts*

SATIN DANCER   2 b.g. (Apr 5) Rousillon (USA) 133 – Sequin Lady (Star Appeal   **81**
133) [1992 7m* 8d² 7g 7d] 2,000Y: strong gelding: third foal: dam, unraced, from
family of Juliette Marny and Julio Mariner: fair performer: gambled-on co-favourite,
won moderately-run 19-runner maiden auction at Lingfield in July: off course over 2
months, good second of 17 in nursery at Goodwood, looking likely winner from 1f out
but caught post: below that form afterwards, though ran better than position
suggests each time: will stay beyond 1m. *G. Harwood*

SATIN LOVER   4 ch.g. Tina's Pet 121 – Canoodle 66 (Warpath 113) [1991 12s⁴ 7g   **95**
12d 12m 16g 14.1m* 16.1g* 14m² 14.6m* 16.5d² 1992 16d³ 14g² 16m² 16.1f³ 13.9m
14.6f⁶] workmanlike gelding: useful handicapper: ran very well in 1992, particularly
when close third to Witness Box in Northumberland Plate at Newcastle on first start
for new stable (trained previously by R. Akehurst) until below par on last 2 outings:
effective from 1¾m to 2m: acts on firm and dead ground: tends to idle in front, and
will prove best with strong handling: most promising novice hurdler, unbeaten in
his 5 starts up to the end of the year. *N. Tinkler*

SATZ (USA)   2 ch.f. (Mar 4) The Minstrel (CAN) 135 – Sateen (USA) (Round   **50**
Table) [1992 5m³ 6d⁴] sturdy filly: seventh foal: sister to 1988 2-y-o 7f winner
Angelic Note and half-sister to 5 winners, notably smart 7f/1m performer Satin
Flower (by Shadeed) and Grade 1 1¼m winner Martial Law (by Mr Leader): dam
won two 6f races: favourite, poor form in maidens at Haydock and Leicester (edgy,
found little after pulling hard) in late-spring: bred to stay at least 1m: sent to C.
Clement in USA. *J. H. M. Gosden*

SAUVIGNON (IRE)   4 b.f. Alzao (USA) 117 – Romanee Conti (Will Somers   **42**
114§) [1991 8d³ 8.1s³ 7g⁴ 7g² 6.9s⁵ 1992 a7g* a8g a8g 9d 9.9m 8m⁴] sturdy, good-
topped filly: moderate mover: rated 63 at 3 yrs for L. Cumani: only plating-class in
1992, winning maiden at Lingfield in February: stays 1m: acts on soft ground and
equitrack: sold to join C. Broad 1,650 gns Ascot December Sales. *R. Guest*

SAVALARO   3 b.f. Tinoco 80 – Miss Shifter (Realm 129) [1991 a5g⁴ 5.3m² 5.3f³   **53**
5.3g⁴ 5m a6g a6g⁵ 1992 6g⁴ 5.3m⁶ 5.1d* 5f 5.3f³ 5m 5.1m³ 5m⁶ 5.3f² 6g² 5g⁵ 5.3d 6g

Windsor Castle Stakes, Ascot—northern challenger Satank (noseband) makes all

Coral 1st Sunday Race, Doncaster—Savoyard's good day of 1992;
he comes between Gymcrak Premiere and Panikin (rails) to lead virtually on the line

a6g3] sparely-made filly: modest performer: made all in seller (no bid) at Bath in April: ran moderately last 2 starts, in blinkers last time: best at 5f or an easy 6f: acts on firm and dead ground. *J. Ffitch-Heyes*

SAVANGA (USA) 4 b.g. Secreto (USA) 128 – Sun Sprite (USA) (Graustark) [1991 10.2s 8f3 7m 7.5f* 8f 8g6 7.5f3 8f 7d 8f 1992 8.3g 8f 8f 7d 7f] smallish, lengthy gelding: rated 55 at 3 yrs, no form in 1992: should stay 1¼m: acts on firm going: often visored, also tried blinkered: tongue tied down last time. *M. McCormack* –

SAVASH (USA) 3 b.g. Arctic Tern (USA) 126 – Princess Iman (USA) (Seattle Slew (USA)) [1991 7m3 8m4 7s 1992 10g 8.1g2 8m6 9d] leggy, attractive gelding: moderate mover: fair maiden: well below form in handicaps last 2 starts: should stay 1¼m: blinkered (well beaten in Goffs Million) final start at 2 yrs. *M. Moubarak* 77

SAVILLE WAY 5 ch.g. Gorytus (USA) 132 – Claretta (USA) 82 (Roberto (USA) 131) [1991 10.8g 10g5 9.9m4 13d 10m* 10m2 12.1g 10m 1992 a12g6 a12g] strong, workmanlike gelding: rated 33 at 4 yrs: well beaten in 1992: dead. *W. J. Musson* –

SAVINGS BANK 2 b.c. (Apr 5) Shernazar 131 – Yen (AUS) (Biscay (AUS)) [1992 6m 6d4 6.1m3 7d 6m] useful-looking colt: fifth foal: half-brother to 1991 2-y-o 5f winner Wistful (by Glint of Gold) and a winner in Australia: dam ran without success in Australia: modest maiden: ran poorly last 2 outings, off course 3 months and burly when in rear in seller at Newmarket last time: should be well suited by further than 6f: sold 6,400 gns Newmarket Autumn Sales. *G. A. Pritchard-Gordon* 50

SAVINIEN (IRE) 3 b.g. Cyrano de Bergerac 120 – Golden Tears (Rheingold 137) [1991 NR 1992 a6g5 a5g6 a6g6 6g a6g a6g] 4,000F: rather leggy, close-coupled gelding: fourth foal: dam unraced: no worthwhile form. *P. J. Feilden* –

SAVOYARD 4 b.c. Sayf El Arab (USA) 127 – Ballad Island 83 (Ballad Rock 122) [1991 7g* 6d2 7g* 7g 7m* 7f4 7d 7m6 1992 7d 7.9m 7.1g4 7m* 8.1d5 7m 7.9g5 7g3] angular, good-topped colt: poor mover: useful performer on his day: won £10,000 handicap at Doncaster in July by short head from Gymcrak Premiere: easily best subsequent effort when third in minor event there in October: should stay 1m: acts on good to firm and dead ground: seems best in blinkers these days: sometimes bandaged: sold 11,500 gns Newmarket Autumn Sales. *M. A. Jarvis* 99 ?

720

SAXON LAD (USA) 6 b.g. Lear Fan (USA) 130 – Presto Youth (USA) (Youth (USA) 135) [1991 10f4 10f3 7m6 1992 10.2f 7.6m5 8g] tall, leggy gelding: has a poor action: of little account these days. *G. P. Enright*   –

SAXON MAGIC 2 ch.f. (Feb 27) Faustus (USA) 118 – Wessex Kingdom 68 (Vaigly Great 127) [1992 6.1d5 6.1m3] 5,000Y: leggy, lengthy filly: moderate mover: second live foal: half-sister to 1990 2-y-o 6f winner Majestic Gambler (by Enchantment): dam 5f winner: modest form on favoured rail in maidens at Nottingham in the summer. *J. A. Bennett*   **51**

SAYANT 7 b.g. Sayyaf 121 – Bodnant (Welsh Pageant 132) [1991 NR 1992 10s 8.5g 8m] stocky gelding: moderate mover: probably of little account these days. *W. Clay*   –

SAYH 3 b.c. Bluebird (USA) 125 – Relfo 124 (Relko 136) [1991 NR 1992 10m* 12g3 11.8s* 12f 10g 11.9d 12m] IR 55,000Y: lengthy, good-topped colt: poor mover: half-brother to several winners, including fair 1988 2-y-o 7.5f winner Pericot (by Persian Bold) and Irish 1000 Guineas fourth Lady of The House (by Habitat): dam won Ribblesdale Stakes and second in Prix Vermeille: fairly useful form when winning maiden at Newmarket in April and minor event at Leicester in June: no worthwhile form in handicaps afterwards: needs further than 1¼m, and should stay 1¾m: acts on good to firm and soft ground: sold to join J. White 9,000 gns Ascot November Sales: won over hurdles in December. *M. A. Jarvis*   **87**

SAYSANA 5 b.m. Sayf El Arab (USA) 127 – Rosana Park 83 (Music Boy 124) [1991 a7g 8f 10m 7f6 6f4 6g6 9.7m* 10f 9.7g 9.7s 1992 a8g 9.7g 5.3m 6f 9m a10g] leggy, quite good-topped mare: rated 41 at 4 yrs: no worthwhile form in 1992. *A. Moore*   –

SAY SUNPAK 2 b.f. (Apr 24) Sayf El Arab (USA) 127 – Melindra 83 (Gold Form 108) [1992 5g 5m5] 6,600Y: smallish, sturdy filly: fourth living foal: sister to 2-y-o 5f winners The Irish Sheikh and Jennie's Gem and half-sister to 5f winner Mia Scintilla (by Blazing Saddles): dam sprinter: no worthwhile form in the spring. *Mrs V. A. Aconley*   –

SAYYEDATI 2 b.f. (Jan 26) Shadeed (USA) 135 – Dubian 120 (High Line 125) [1992 6m2 6g* 7s* 6m*]   **116** p

At a time when barely an optimistic word was heard from the ranks of the country's racehorse trainers, Clive Brittain declared in an autumn television interview that he had no less than *eight* two-year-old fillies of exceptional merit at his Carlburg stables! Brittain's unfailing optimism hasn't always survived the difficult transition from training ground to racecourse, but the racecourse test was his greatest ally in the latest season as Sueboog, Ivanka, Love of Silver and Sayyedati all turned in one or more very useful performances. Exactly how Brittain will play such an enviable hand—and who's to say now that there aren't four more?—remains to be seen, but he shouldn't have any difficulty in finding suitable opportunities for Sayyedati, clearly the best of

Moyglare Stud Stakes, the Curragh—Sayyedati (right) beats Bright Generation

the bunch on the evidence of her victory over the previously-unbeaten Lyric Fantasy in the Tattersalls Cheveley Park Stakes at Newmarket in September. Sayyedati looks certain to carry the stable's main hopes in the One Thousand Guineas, and she is the filly who, at this stage, looks sure to take the world of beating.

The only occasion on which Sayyedati was beaten in four outings as a two-year-old came when she went down by two lengths to the one-time Guineas favourite Sumoto in the Halifax Maiden Stakes at Ascot in June. Sayyedati was unfortunate to come up against such a useful opponent first time out, but while Sumoto was subsequently kept off the course by a sprained hock, Sayyedati never looked back, and less than three weeks later she took on and beat the second and the third in the Queen Mary, Mystic Goddess and Toocando, the Norfolk Stakes winner Niche, the Acorn Stakes winner Anonymous and two others in the Hillsdown Cherry Hinton Stakes at Newmarket in July. Starting 6/4 favourite, Sayyedati ran out a more comfortable winner than her margin of half a length and a neck over Toocando and Mystic Goddess would imply; after making impressive headway from the rear of the field at halfway, she idled once she got to the front with two furlongs to go and allowed Toocando and Mystic Goddess to get within a length after Niche, who was conceding 5 lb all round, had dropped away. Sayyedati was clearly going the right way, and after a two-month break (she hadn't been entered for the Lowther Stakes at the York August meeting) she started a short-priced favourite for the Group 1 Moyglare Stud Stakes at the Curragh in September. The decision to increase the distance of the race from six furlongs to seven furlongs in 1992 was instrumental in bringing about an attractive clash between Sayyedati and the unbeaten Bright Generation, but did little to boost the overall quality of the field; only Ancestral Dancer, a winner of two listed races in Italy and fourth to Maroof in the Lanson Champagne Vintage Stakes, and the subsequently-withdrawn Asema, winner of the Killavullen Stakes, amongst the other declared runners had anything resembling reasonable pattern-race form. Sayyedati maintained her improvement to take the £82,000 first prize by a length and a half and the same from Bright Generation and the Irish-trained newcomer Alouette, quickening on with over a furlong to run and being kept up to her work in the soft ground. She didn't look entirely at ease in the testing conditions, though, and her trainer was quick to suggest after the race that she would leave that form behind back on firmer ground.

On more than one occasion during the season Brittain took to comparing Sayyedati with his 1984 One Thousand Guineas winner Pebbles. The two fillies aren't physically alike—in her racing days Pebbles was sparely made, while Sayyedati is rangy and attractive with plenty of scope—but the com-

Tattersalls Cheveley Park Stakes, Newmarket—
Lyric Fantasy (right) loses her unbeaten record
and Sayyedati becomes a short-priced favourite for the One Thousand Guineas

parison has some validity, particularly in respect of their ability (at least that shown at two) and temperament. Pebbles was a high-mettled filly who tended to get on her toes before her races and had her stable companion Come On The Blues to accompany her to the racecourse. Sayyedati also tends to be a bit edgy, though not to quite the same degree that Pebbles ever was, and she, too, was provided with a travelling companion for the flight to the Curragh. Pebbles and Sayyedati also both had their final race as a two-year-old in the Cheveley Park Stakes. But whereas Pebbles wasn't quite good enough to win, going down by a neck to Prickle, Sayyedati went one better in a race that was billed as a showdown between her and the unbeaten Lyric Fantasy, who on her previous outing had beaten most of the best older sprinters in Europe to become the first two-year-old for thirty-six years to win the Nunthorpe. Such were the reputations of Sayyedati and Lyric Fantasy that only Anonymous, who'd finished out of the frame in both her races since the Cherry Hinton, and the surprise Flying Childers winner Poker Chip stood their ground, making the four-runner field the smallest since Corejada beat two others in 1949. The clash between Sayyedati and Lyric Fantasy provided plenty of speculative copy in the Press, much of which centred upon how the race would be run. Would Lyric Fantasy, whose stamina over six furlongs was unproven, run from the front in the same aggressive manner that had demolished her rivals in the Queen Mary and the Newbury Super Sales Sprint over five furlongs? Or would Sayyedati, now she was back at six furlongs on good to firm ground, throw down the gauntlet and put Lyric Fantasy's suspect stamina to the test? Of all the possible permutations, few envisaged that Sayyedati, second favourite at 5/2 behind the 2/1-on shot Lyric Fantasy, would actually take the four runners along at a modest gallop for the first two and a half furlongs. Such tactics should supposedly have favoured Lyric Fantasy; but contrary to expectations it was she who came under pressure first as Sayyedati kept increasing the pace and the contest entered its final quarter. Although Lyric Fantasy got to within a length with around a furlong to go, Sayyedati never looked like being caught, and under Swinburn, deputizing for Roberts who'd chosen to ride Lyric Fantasy, she passed the post two lengths in front, Poker Chip finishing a length and a half behind Lyric Fantasy in third with Anonymous six lengths back in fourth. Lyric Fantasy probably wasn't at her very best—she didn't take the eye beforehand in the manner she had earlier in the season, while Sayyedati looked extremely well—but we don't doubt that the better filly won, and needed to put up a smart performance to do so.

		Nijinsky	Northern Dancer
	Shadeed (USA)	(b 1967)	Flaming Page
	(b 1982)	Continual	Damascus
Sayyedati		(b or br 1976)	Continuation
(b.f. Jan 26, 1990)		High Line	High Hat
	Dubian	(ch 1966)	Time Call
	(b 1982)	Melodina	Tudor Melody
		(br 1968)	Rose of Medina

Oddly, for a filly who heads the market for the One Thousand Guineas, Sayyedati's pedigree is one that will also be familiar to followers of the jumping game; her dam Dubian, whose second foal she is following her full sister Shihama, a winner over six furlongs in 1990, is a half-sister to the triple Champion Hurdler See You Then. Dubian was a very smart racehorse at her best, successful in four of her eleven starts. She won her only race as a two-year-old, the seven-furlong Stable Stud and Farm Stakes at Newbury, then came into her own the following season when she finished third in the Oaks and Irish Oaks besides winning a mile-and-a-quarter minor event at Yarmouth; as a four-year-old she won the Group 3 Royal Whip Stakes over a mile and a quarter and the Group 1 Premio Lydia Tesio over a mile and a half either side of a creditable fourth in the Phoenix Champion Stakes. Dubian is a half-sister to numerous winners besides See You Then (who had useful form over middle distances in Ireland before being sent hurdling), notably Milverton, a useful winner at seven furlongs in Ireland and third in the ten-and-a-half-furlong Mecca-Dante Stakes, and Polar Run, a useful winner over seven furlongs as a two-year-old who stayed well enough to finish third in the Queen's Vase over two miles the following season. Their dam Melodina was a

723

Mr Mohamed Obaida's "Sayyedati"

very speedy two-year-old who won the Seaton Delaval Stakes when it was still run over five furlongs and finished third in the Cheveley Park; she wasn't short on stamina, either, and later ran into a place in the Ribblesdale Stakes over a mile and a half. Melodina is a daughter of the One Thousand Guineas fourth and Oaks third Rose of Medina and a half-sister to the Irish Oaks winner Celina as well as grandam of the high-class miler Sure Blade and the Craven Stakes runner-up Sure Sharp. There's plenty of stamina in this particular branch of the family; Rose of Medina was also a half-sister to the Irish St Leger winner Ommeyad. Sayyedati should have little trouble in staying beyond a mile on breeding, although several other daughters of Shadeed haven't stayed so well as was expected—notably Shadayid. However, connections will start 1993 with high hopes of Sayyedati over a mile. She has both the pedigree and the build of a filly who will train on well, and we look forward to seeing her again as a three-year-old. *C. E. Brittain*

SAY YOU WILL   8 b.g. Riboboy (USA) 124 – Polita 86 (Constable 119) [1991 a7g⁴ a7g a7g⁴ 7d 7g 7f⁵ 7.6g³ 7m⁶ 7g⁴ 7f² a7g⁶ 7f 7m 7.1m 7g⁶ a8g² a8g⁶ 1992 a7g a6g³ a5g⁶ a6g a7g³ a7g⁵ 8.1g 7m 7.1f 7m 7f³ 6g⁶] robust gelding: carries condition: has a quick action: poor handicapper: last win came 32 starts ago, at 6 yrs: stays 1m: possibly unsuited by soft going nowadays, acts on any other: has worn blinkers, usually visored: has looked unenthusiastic. *M. P. Naughton*   **30 a40**

SCALA MILANO   3 b.f. Music Boy 124 – Song Book 85 (Saintly Song 128) [1991 6.1f 6m⁶ 5g⁵ 1992 6g* 6f 5d⁶ 7g 6g] leggy filly: has a quick action: modest form at best: won 3-runner maiden at Yarmouth in July: faced some stiff tasks afterwards, but soundly beaten in selling handicap (wore net muzzle) final start: will prove best at sprint distances. *K. T. Ivory*   **58**

724

SCALES OF JUSTICE 6 br.m. Final Straw 127 – Foiled Again 110 (Bold Lad **73** (IRE) 133) [1991 8g 9m 8g 9d 7m 7.3m⁴ 8m* 8m* 8g* a10g 1992 8.3g 8g 8g 9d 8.1d* 8m 8g a10g⁶ a10g⁴] big, rangy mare: won claimer at Chepstow (for apprentice) in October: below best otherwise in 1992: effective from 1m to 1¼m: acts on firm and dead ground, possibly unsuited by equitrack: held up. *J. W. Hills*

SCALP 'EM (IRE) 4 b.g. Commanche Run 133 – Supremely Royal (Crowned **30** Prince (USA) 128) [1991 16.9g⁶ 15m 12.3g⁶ 15.9d⁶ 15.1s 1992 15g 17.5d 17.9d a16g³ 17.1s⁶] rangy gelding: has round action: worthwhile form only when third in poor race at Southwell in September: stays 2m. *F. H. Lee*

SCANDALMONGER (USA) 3 b.c. Foolish Pleasure (USA) – Queen Vega **82** (USA) (Te Vega) [1991 7m 7m⁶ 1992 7m³ 8.1m* 10g³ 10m 9d 8m] lengthy, useful-looking colt: fluent mover: fairly useful form: won maiden at Chepstow in May: better efforts in good-class handicaps at Newmarket and Goodwood in July: travelling well when badly hampered final start: stays 1¼m: acts on good to firm ground, well below form on dead. *B. W. Hills*

SCARABEN 4 b.g. Dunbeath (USA) 127 – Varushka 74 (Sharpen Up 127) [1991 **–** 7.6s³ 7m³ 7.9g³ 7.1g⁴ 7m 1992 7d 10s³ 9.2v] strong, lengthy gelding: has a quick action: modest maiden handicapper: no worthwhile form in 1992: stays 1¼m: acts on good to firm and soft ground. *H. J. Collingridge*

SCARLATINE (IRE) 3 b.f. Alzao (USA) 117 – The Woman In Red 68 (Red **81** Regent 123) [1991 6m⁴ 6.3s 1992 6d² 8d 7.6g* 8f 7.6v] good-bodied filly: fairly useful form: won maiden at Chester: wandered under pressure when well beaten at Newbury later in May: off course 5 months and below form afterwards: should stay 1m: may well need give in the ground: sold 3,500 gns Newmarket Autumn Sales. *J. H. M. Gosden*

SCARLET PRINCESS 4 b.f. Daring March 116 – Noble Mistress 80 (Lord **48** Gayle (USA) 124) [1991 6m 5g 8m 6g 6d* 5d 6m 1992 7g 6g 6f 8.1m 6.1d* 6.1g³ 6f 7g 6.1g] smallish, leggy filly: inconsistent handicapper: form in 1992 only in July, winning at Nottingham: stays 6.1f: suited by give in the ground. *R. J. Hodges*

SCENIC DANCER 4 b.g. Shareef Dancer (USA) 135 – Bridestones 92 (Jan **55** Ekels 122) [1991 9d 10g* 10.1f 12g 11.7m* 12g⁶ 12f⁶ 10.3m 10.3d 1992 10m 10d 10d 11.4f⁴ 12m 10m⁵ 10m* 11.9f⁶ 10.1d 12g] small, compact gelding: inconsistent handicapper: won at Brighton in July: stays 1½m: acts on firm ground, seems unsuited by a soft surface: has worn blinkers, effective visored or not: has worn a bandage on off-hind: often slowly away: retained by trainer 2,300 gns Ascot December Sales: has been gelded. *A. Hide*

SCENIC REEF (IRE) 2 ch.f. (Apr 4) King of Clubs 124 – Northern Scene 78 **52** (Habitat 134) [1992 5d 5m 6m² 6m 6m³ 6f⁴] 3,600Y: small, angular filly: moderate mover: half-sister to several winners, including 4-y-o Rocton North (by Ballad Rock), fairly useful winner at 6f (at 2 yrs) and 7f: dam Irish 2-y-o 5f winner: modest form, including in claiming events: will be much better suited by 7f/1m. *J. M. P. Eustace*

SCENT OF BATTLE 4 ch.c. Rousillon (USA) 133 – Light O'Battle 97 (Queen's **46** Hussar 124) [1991 10v² 10g 10g⁵ 10g 8.3m 9.7m 10m 1992 12g⁵ 16.4g⁵ 14d² 16.4m] strong, lengthy colt: moderate mover: poor maiden: ran well when second in handicap at Sandown in July: should prove effective at 2m: best efforts on yielding surface, and acts on heavy ground. *M. J. Haynes*

SCHERZO IMPROMPTU 3 ch.f. Music Boy 124 – Law And Impulse 104 **–** (Roan Rocket 128) [1991 NR 1992 7m 8f] 8,400Y: strong filly: half-sister to several winners, including very useful sprinter Governor General (by Dominion), very useful 1m winner Power Take Off (by Aragon) and 10.2f winner Cross-Bench (by Sharpo): dam 2-y-o 5f winner: showed nothing in maidens on flat, then refused to enter stalls at Beverley in May: joined G. Cottrell, pulled up once over hurdles and sold 4,100 gns Newmarket December Sales. *T. Fairhurst*

SCHILLACHI (IRE) 4 b.c. Flash of Steel 120 – Chalfont Mo 66 (Mummy's Pet **–** 125) [1991 12.1g a12g 1992 10.8g] good-bodied colt: tailed off in maidens: tried blinkered. *B. A. McMahon*

SCHOOL OF SCIENCE 2 b.c. (Mar 14) Then Again 126 – Girl's Brigade **–** (Brigadier Gerard 144) [1992 5g⁵ 5.1s⁶ 5.3f 6m a7g] workmanlike colt: poor mover: third foal: half-brother to a winner in Italy by Song: dam, dead-heated over 7f at 2 yrs in Ireland and stayed 1¼m, is from family of Connaught: no worthwhile form. *M. B. James*

SCHWANTZ 4 b.g. Exhibitioner 111 – Hardirondo 93 (Hardicanute 130) [1991 a8g 9m⁶ 11.8m 1992 12.2g] strong, good-bodied gelding: seems of little account. *W. T. Kemp*

SCIACCA 5 ch.m. Dalsaan 125 – Hill of Howth (Sassafras (FR) 135) [1991 6v⁵ 7f 8f — 28 10.8m 10m a7g³ a8g² 10m⁴ 8m⁵ a11g⁴ a8g⁶ 10g⁵ 8.9g 10m⁴ 1992 a7g³ a10g 7g 10m⁶ 11.5m 9.7d²] small, lengthy ex-Irish mare: inconsistent, and still a maiden on flat after 23 starts: stays 11f: acts on good to firm and dead ground: sold out of S. Mellor's stable 1,650 gns Doncaster May Sales after third start: won over hurdles in July and August. *C. Weedon*

SCOFFERA 2 b.f. (Mar 2) Scottish Reel 123 – Single Bid 68 (Auction Ring (USA) 48 123) [1992 6g 6m 6m 6d 7.5m 8g a7g a8g² a7g³] 3,600Y: good-topped filly: has a round action: fourth foal: half-sister to 3-y-o Prime Bid (by Primo Dominie), 1m and 1¼m winner Bid For Elegance (by Nordance) and a winner abroad: dam ran only at sprint distances: poor maiden: will be better suited by 1¼m: acts on good to firm ground and fibresand. *N. Tinkler*

SCORCHED AIR 2 b.f. (Jan 22) Elegant Air 119 – Misfire 56 (Gunner B 126) 66 p [1992 7s⁶ 6.9v³] 15,500Y: third foal: half-sister to Irish 7f (at 2 yrs) and 1¼m winner Synergy (by Dominion) and a winner in Italy: dam, 1½m seller winner, is half-sister to Fred Darling winner Littlefield: similar form in maiden auction at Goodwood and maiden at Folkestone in October: will be much better suited by 1¼m. *J. W. Hills*

SCORCHER (IRE) 2 b.g. (Jan 18) Glow (USA) – Go Feather Go (USA) (Go 52 Marching (USA)) [1992 6f 7m 7g] 16,000Y: smallish, good-bodied gelding: closely related to 1991 Irish 2-y-o 6f winner Flora Macleod (by Lomond) and half-brother to numerous winners, including (at 7f and 1m in Ireland) useful The Caretaker (by Caerleon) and sprinter Feather's Lad (by Sandford Lad): dam Irish 2-y-o 5f winner: modest form in fair maiden company: will stay 1m: may do better. *C. E. Brittain*

SCORED AGAIN 2 b.g. (Feb 10) Music Boy 124 – Thorner Lane 86 (Tina's Pet 54 121) [1992 5m³ 5g² 5m 5s⁶] 22,000Y: lengthy, good sort: first foal: dam sprinter: modest maiden: acts on good to firm ground, fair effort on soft. *R. M. Whitaker*

SCORTON (IRE) 3 gr.g. Standaan (FR) 118 – Shanty (Sea Hawk II 131) [1991 — 6.1m⁶ 1992 7f5 12f 6g⁶] leggy, workmanlike gelding: sold out of Miss S. Hall's stable 1,700 gns Doncaster May Sales before reappearance: no worthwhile form: refused to enter stalls once at 3 yrs: resold 1,700 gns Ascot November Sales. *M. Dods*

SCOSSA (USA) 4 ch.f. Shadeed (USA) 135 – Scythe 84 (Sharpen Up 127) [1991 — 7d 8.5f⁵ 10m³ 10m⁶ 10.1f⁴ 10f² 8.9m⁵ 10g³ 9.7f 10.1s⁴ 1992 9d] tall, leggy ex-French filly: has round action: rated 52 at 3 yrs for J. Toller: well beaten in apprentice handicap at Kempton in April at 4 yrs: unlikely to stay much beyond 1¼m: acts on firm ground: headstrong: has carried head high. *J. L. Spearing*

SCOTONI 6 ch.g. Final Straw 127 – Damiya (FR) (Direct Flight) [1991 a10g³ 51 a10g⁵ a12g* a12g* a13g² a12g⁵ 12d² 12f 7.6m⁴ 11.5m⁶ 7.6m 11.5g a12g a8g⁵ a13g* a12g 1992 10.3g 12m³ 12g³] close-coupled, rather sparely-made gelding: modest handicapper: off course 4½ months, ran well when placed in August: stays 13f: acts on firm and dead going and goes well on equitrack: below form when blinkered once: good mount for apprentice: won novice chase in October. *R. J. O'Sullivan*

SCOTS LAW 5 b.g. Law Society (USA) 130 – Tweedling (USA) (Sir Ivor 135) 45 [1991 a7g³ a8g a7g³ a7g⁵ 7d 8f a7g* a7g 6g 7.6m⁴ a7g a6g a7g a8g⁵ a7g 1992 a10g a8g a7g⁶ a7g³ a8g*] leggy, quite attractive gelding: poor handicapper: made all at Lingfield late in year: stays 1m: acts on good to firm ground and equitrack: blinkered once earlier in career: has carried head awkwardly, appearing rather ungenerous: seems best with forcing tactics. *R. J. O'Sullivan*

SCOTSMAN (IRE) 2 b.c. (Mar 7) Lomond (USA) 128 – Catina 102 (Nureyev 81 p (USA) 131) [1992 8m³] IR 110,000Y: angular, unfurnished colt: looks weak: first foal: dam, Irish 2-y-o 6f winner suited by 1m, is half-sister to Italian 1000 Guineas winner Rosananti and good English and German performer Claddagh: 12/1, over 7 lengths third of 17 to Armiger in maiden at Newmarket in September, prominent and staying on final 2f: showed a quick action: sure to improve. *P. F. I. Cole*

SCOTTISH BALL 3 b.f. Ardross 134 – Dance In Time 79 (Dance In Time — (CAN) [1991 NR 1992 10m⁵] smallish, sturdy filly: seventh foal: half-sister to 3 winners, including 6-y-o middle-distance performer Dr Zeva (by Busted): dam raced only at 2 yrs, winning at 6f: 8/1, 11 lengths fifth of 20 to Vanroy in claimer at Windsor in July, showing inexperience on turn then staying on steadily: should be suited by further. *Sir Mark Prescott*

SCOTTISH BAMBI 4 ch.g. Scottish Reel 123 – Bambolona 108 (Bustino 136) 75 [1991 7g² 10.2g⁵ 7m⁴ᵈⁱˢ 7g² 8.1d 7g 1992 7g⁴ 8g 10g* 10.8f* 10f⁵ 10m⁴ 10g* 10s⁵

10m] rangy, workmanlike gelding: has a round action: consistent handicapper: won at Windsor and Warwick in May and at Leicester (gamely) in August: unsuited by slow pace last 2 starts: will prove at least as effective at 1½m as shorter: acts on firm and dead ground: good mount for claimer. *R. Hannon*

SCOTTISH PARK 3 ch.f. Scottish Reel 123 – Moss Agate (Alias Smith (USA)) **68** [1991 5m 6.1m⁴ 6.1f 7g² 7d 1992 7.5g⁴ 7.5m* 7f⁴ 7g² 9.9g a7g⁵ 7d⁴ 8v a8g] sturdy, lengthy filly: in-and-out form after winning maiden at Beverley in May: should stay at least 1m (ran as if something amiss over 9.9f): acts on firm and dead going, below form on fibresand: usually claimer ridden. *J. P. Leigh*

SCOTTISH PEAK (IRE) 2 ch.c. (Apr 10) Lomond (USA) 128 – Road To The **91** p Top 84 (Shirley Heights 130) [1992 7.1s* 8s] sturdy, angular colt: fifth foal: half-brother to fairly useful 3-y-o middle-distance winner Green Lane (IRE) (by Green Desert) and fairly useful 1988 2-y-o 6f winner Road To Reason (by Known Fact), later stayed 1¼m: dam 1¼m winner, from good family: 3/1 though carrying condition, won 8-runner maiden at Sandown in July by 7 lengths, leading under 2f out and staying on really well final 150 yds: favourite, last of 10 in Royal Lodge Stakes at Ascot over 2½ months later, leading 6f: will stay at least 1¼m: yet to race on a sound surface: probably capable of better. *Lord Huntingdon*

SCOTTISH RUBY 3 ch.g. Scottish Reel 123 – Screenable (USA) (Silent Screen – (USA)) [1991 6m⁵ 6d⁵ 6m 5.9h⁴ 6m⁶ 7d 1992 7f 7g 8m] close-coupled, angular gelding: poor mover: of little account. *C. Tinkler*

SCOTTISH TEMPTRESS 2 ch.f. (Mar 22) Northern Tempest (USA) 120 – Scotch Rocket 60 (Roan Rocket 128) [1992 a6g 8.1d] smallish, workmanlike filly: third reported foal: sister to 6f winner Degree of Force and half-sister to a winner in Malaysia: dam 7f winner: backward, soundly beaten in maidens at Southwell and Haydock in September: sold 760 gns Doncaster October Sales. *J. P. Leigh*

SCOTTISH TINA 4 b.f. Scottish Reel 123 – Tina's Melody 80 (Tina's Pet 121) – [1991 8f⁶ 7g 1992 a6g] leggy, plain filly: no worthwhile form. *A. Moore*

SCOTTISH WEDDING 2 b.f. (Mar 8) Scottish Reel 123 – Pearl Wedding 86 – (Gulf Pearl 117) [1992 8m] 2,200F, 2,800Y: half-sister to several winners, including Cambridgeshire winner Century City (by High Top): dam 1¼m and 1½m winner: 100/1, last of 21 in maiden at Pontefract in October. *J. Balding*

SCRAVELS SARAN (IRE) 4 b.f. Nishapour (FR) 125 – Persian Royale 94 – § (Persian Bold 123) [1991 7m 7m 7s⁶ 5.1f 7m 7s 1992 a7g a10g] angular filly: no worthwhile form since 2 yrs: tried blinkered once: flashes tail. *Dr J. D. Scargill*

SCREECH 2 b.f. (May 4) Daring March 116 – Songless (Song 132) [1992 5m⁴ 5h³ **45** 5g a6g] 725Y: sturdy filly: moderate mover: fourth foal: dam unraced: modest plater: off course 2½ months after falling third start then towards rear of Lingfield claimer in October. *C. James*

SCRIBE (IRE) 2 b.c. (Feb 4) Sadler's Wells (USA) 132 – Northern Script (USA) **107** p 95 (Arts And Letters) [1992 7g² 7g² 7s* 8d²] brother to useful 1m/1¼m performer Northern Hal and half-brother to Irish 1m (at 2 yrs) and 1¼m winner Caerless Writing (by Caerleon): dam miler: won maiden at the Curragh in August: much improved effort when beaten a head by Frenchpark in Juddmonte Beresford Stakes at the Curragh in October: will be better suited by 1¼m. *J. S. Bolger, Ireland*

SCRUTINEER (USA) 3 b.c. Danzig Connection (USA) – Script Approval **94** (USA) (Silent Screen (USA)) [1991 8g⁵ 1992 10f³ 10m² 10.1g* 11.5m² 10g* 10m⁵ 11.9m³ 10.5s 10.3v] robust colt: good mover with a powerful action: won maiden at Epsom and handicap (made all) at Kempton in midsummer: ran next 2 starts in £30,600 handicap at Goodwood and £12,000 handicap won by Opera Ghost (sent clear 3½f out in very strongly-run race, looked assured winner but tired final 1f) at York: stays 1½m: acts on good to firm ground, soundly beaten on a soft surface: game: has joined D. Nicholson. *J. H. M. Gosden*

SCULLER (USA) 2 b.c. (May 9) Riverman (USA) 131 – Nimble Folly (USA) **77** p (Cyane) [1992 7m 8s*] close-coupled colt: good walker: ninth foal: half-brother to 3-y-o 6f (at 2 yrs) to 10.4f winner Skimble (by Lyphard) and several other winners, including useful 1989 sprinting 2-y-o Old Alliance and good American juvenile Contredance (both by Danzig): dam unraced: off course over 2 months but well-backed 11/4-shot, won 22-runner maiden at Warwick in October, making most from halfway and coming clear from 2f out: will prove better suited by 1¼m: will improve. *H. R. A. Cecil*

SCULTORE (USA) 3 b.g. Leo Castelli (USA) – Glamorous Nell (USA) (Dis- – tinctive (USA)) [1991 8m 1992 10s⁶ 10g 16.1d⁵] deep-girthed, plain gelding: no worthwhile form, though has shown signs of a little ability: not seen after July 1. *M. R. Channon*

SCUSI 2 ch.c. (Mar 29) Kris 135 – Dance Quest (FR) 117 (Green Dancer (USA) 132) [1992 6m⁶ 6m⁶] strong, angular, good sort: has a free, round action: fourth living foal: brother to smart French sprinter Divine Danse and half-brother to good-class 3-y-o Pursuit of Love (by Groom Dancer), successful at 6.5f and 7f: dam smart French sprinting half-sister to Noblequest out of a good sprinter/miler: very green, pulled hard early on in minor event at Doncaster and never placed to challenge or knocked about: seemed sure to improve considerably, but only sixth in maiden at Newmarket in October: will stay 7f: yet to race on an easy surface: almost certainly capable of better. *W. Jarvis* **67** p

SCU'S LADY (IRE) 4 b.f. Mazaad 106 – Lydja 75 (Hethersett 134) [1991 6d⁶ 6f 10f 12d 9.9f a8g⁴ 1992 7d 8.3v] small, sturdy filly: no form since 2 yrs: tried blinkered: sold to join M. Barraclough 1,500 gns Doncaster August Sales. *A. Smith* –

SEA-AYR (IRE) 2 ch.f. (Apr 11) Magical Wonder (USA) 125 – Kunuz (Ela-Mana-Mou 132) [1992 5g 5m⁴ 5f⁶ 6m⁵ 6g⁵ 5f⁴] IR 3,000Y: small filly: first foal: dam ran twice: poor maiden, not seen after July: will be better suited by 7f: tends to hang, and looks a hard ride. *Miss L. A. Perratt* **41**

SEA BARON 2 ch.c. (Apr 14) Dominion 123 – Mai Pussy 91 (Realm 129) [1992 6g 6s⁴ 7m 6s 7g 5g⁵ 6s²] 5,200F, 9,200Y: quite good-topped colt: has a round action: closely related to fairly useful 3-y-o 8.3f winner Bold Boss (by Nomination) and half-brother to several winners, including smart 7f/1¼m performer Beau Sher (by Ile de Bourbon) and fair middle-distance handicapper Samhaan (by Niniski): dam stayed 6f: fair maiden: should be suited by further than 6f: acts on soft ground: ran creditably when sweating once. *M. Blanshard* **66**

SEA CLOUD (USA) 3 b.f. African Sky 124 – Candle In The Wind 90 (Thatching 131) [1991 6f 6f5 6.1m 6g 1992 7s 10g5 5.1m 5.1m 7m² 7m⁵ 7f⁶] big, close-coupled filly: inconsistent maiden: best effort at 7f: no form when blinkered once: sold 3,700 gns Newmarket July Sales. *M. Blanshard* **47**

SEA CLOVER (IRE) 3 b.f. Ela-Mana-Mou 132 – Seattle Siren (USA) 101 (Seattle Slew (USA)) [1991 7m⁵ 7.3g⁵ 1992 10.2s 10g³] leggy, unfurnished filly: has a roundish action: fair form at 2 yrs: below form in 1992, though showed some ability final start: visits Never So Bold. *Major W. R. Hern*

SEA CRUSADER 3 b.g. Formidable (USA) 125 – Historical Fact 78 (Reform 132) [1991 5g 6d 6g⁶ 7g 7m⁶ 5.1m 5f* 5m⁶ 5d 1992 6v 5m⁶ 6g 8f 6g³ 5d⁴ 6m 5m 5.7f⁶ 6g] compact gelding: poor mover: inconsistent plater: stays 6f: acts on firm going: no improvement in blinkers: has shown his form when sweating and on toes. *M. Blanshard* **45**

SEA-DEER 3 ch.g. Hadeer 118 – Hi-Tech Girl 93 (Homeboy 114) [1991 NR 1992 7f⁵ 6m⁶ 6m⁴ 6m⁴ 5.3f³] 20,000F, IR 15,000Y: strong gelding: second foal: half-brother to 4-y-o 6f and 7f winner Pigalle Wonder (by Chief Singer): dam 2-y-o 5f winner suited by 6f: modest maiden: favourite, looked unlucky when narrowly-beaten third in handicap at Brighton in August, staying on well after being chopped for room on the inside at halfway: stays 6f well: looked capable of better. *L. J. Holt* **64** p

SEA DEVIL 6 gr.g. Absalom 128 – Miss Poinciana 78 (Averof 123) [1991 6m 6m⁵ 6g 6m* 6.1d 6s* 7d 1992 6v⁴ 6s* 6g² 6g 6f² 6g 6d 6d⁴ 6m 7v⁴] lengthy, heavy-topped gelding: carries plenty of condition: moderate mover: fairly useful handicapper: won at Ripon in April: suited by 6f/7f: has form on firm ground, but goes particularly well with give: has drifted right: is held up. *M. J. Camacho* **82**

SEA DUNE 3 b.f. Jupiter Island 126 – Song God 96 (Red God 128§) [1991 6g⁶ 1992 8d³ 7g* 7f²] workmanlike filly: fair form: odds on, won 13-runner maiden at War-wick very easily: good second in handicap at Lingfield later in May: stays 1m: acts on firm and dead ground: sold 2,400 gns Newmarket December Sales and sent to Czechoslovakia. *R. Charlton* **77**

SEA EXHIBITION (IRE) 2 b.f. (Apr 19) Tate Gallery (USA) 117 – Energie Solaire (USA) (Alleged (USA) 138) [1992 5d 5g 5d² 5g³ 5m 5g⁶ 7g⁴ 7m⁵ 8d³ 7s 6m⁶ 8g⁵] 6,200Y: leggy, workmanlike filly: has a round action: fourth foal: half-sister to 3-y-o Stos (by Bluebird) and winners in France and Italy: dam unraced daughter of Solar, a half-sister to Try My Best and El Gran Senor: modest maiden: ran credit-ably in sellers last 2 starts: stays 1m: acts on good to firm and dead ground (below form on soft): sometimes sweats: sold 5,600 gns Newmarket Autumn Sales. *M. Blanshard* **61**

SEA GAZER (IRE) 2 ch.c. (Feb 17) Magical Wonder (USA) 125 – Apapa Port 80 (My Swanee 122) [1992 5f* 5m³ 5d* 6d* 6v⁵] IR 10,000Y: lengthy, workmanlike **97** p colt: half-brother to 2 winners in Ireland (at 6f and 9f) and one in Malaysia: dam 5f mudlark: very progressive performer: won maiden at Catterick in July, then nursery at Haydock and minor event (best effort despite not handling turn) at Catterick in October: not at all discredited fifth of 24 in Racecall Gold Trophy at Redcar 10 days later, including fifth of 24 in Racecall Gold Trophy at Redcar 10 days especially considering raced on unfavoured stand rail: probably acts on any going: looks a very useful sprinter in the making and will win more races in 1993. *T. D. Barron*

SEA GODDESS   4 b.f. Slip Anchor 136 – Elysian 94 (Northfields (USA)) [1991   **94**
10.8m³ 1992 10d² 12g 11.9d² 14m* 13.3g* 11.9f* 11.9g 11.9m⁶ 14.6f] lengthy, good-topped filly: fairly useful handicapper: made all at Haydock, Newbury and York (£10,600 ladies event, the Queen Mother's Cup) in early-summer: below form afterwards, including in Group 3 and listed company: likely to stay 2m: acts on firm and dead ground. *W. Jarvis*

SEAGULL HOLLOW (IRE)   3 b.g. Taufan (USA) 119 – Marthe Meynet   –
(Welsh Pageant 132) [1991 6g* 6g³ 7d³ 1992 7m 9g⁵] tall, leggy, close-coupled gelding: modest winner at 2 yrs but not seen out after June: no worthwhile form in £19,400 handicap (visored, front rank 4f) at York in May and apprentice race at Ripon in August: should be better suited by 7f than 6f: won juvenile hurdles at back-end of year. *M. H. Easterby*

SEAL INDIGO (IRE)   4 b.f. Glenstal (USA) 118 – Simply Gorgeous (Hello   **89**
Gorgeous (USA) 128) [1991 10g 10.2m⁵ 12g* 12m³ 11.7d4 10.2d³ 12f* 10.5f* 10m³ 12.1s* 1992 12g⁵ 12.3m⁶ 12f4 12f 11.9d² 12d² 12m4 11.9m4 12m* 12s 10g 11s4] workmanlike filly: moderate mover: fairly useful handicapper: well handled by Pat Eddery when idling winner at Doncaster in September: ideally suited by 1½m: acted on firm and soft ground: seemed suited by waiting tactics: consistent: to stud. *R. Hannon*

SEA LORD   3 b.g. Aragon 118 – Floral 82 (Floribunda 136) [1991 7m 6m 1992 7.5g⁶   –
9.2v 10m 8d 8.5f³ 8f 12.3d a12g 9.9g 8.1g⁵ 10m⁶ 12m] strong gelding: inconsistent plater: better at 1¼m than shorter: acts on firm going: often apprentice ridden. *K. W. Hogg, Isle of Man*

SEAMA (USA)   2 ch.f. (Mar 8) Affirmed (USA) – Isticanna (USA) 96 (Far North   **70** p
(CAN) 120) [1992 8.5m² 8.1g*] lengthy, unfurnished filly: first foal: dam, 2-y-o 5f

Queen Mother's Cup, York—
Sea Goddess is one of thirteen winners in 1992 for Lydia Pearce, a record for a lady amateur

and 6f winner, is granddaughter of top-class Mesopotamia: won maiden at Edinburgh in October, green then responding well to lead close home: will be suited by further: will improve. *Sir Mark Prescott*

SEAMERE   9 b.g. Crofter (USA) 124 – Whistling Waltz (Whistler 129) [1991 5.9m   **85**
5m 5m* 5m* 5f* 5g* 5m2 5g2 1992 5d6 5.6m3 5d 5g 5m 5s 5.1d 5m] workmanlike, deep-bodied gelding: carries plenty of condition: moderate mover: fairly useful handicapper on his day: suited by 5f on top-of-the-ground: tried in visor: usually blinkered nowadays, not last 3 starts: was an excellent mount for apprentice, usually ridden by J. Lowe in 1992: has idled. *B. R. Cambidge*

SEAN'S DELIGHT   2 ch.f. (Apr 2) Superlative 118 – Josephine Gibney (High   –
Top 131) [1992 6g6 7g 6.1m 8m] smallish, close-coupled filly: fourth foal: sister to 5f (at 2 yrs) to 1m winner Super One: dam winner in Italy from family of high-class sprinter Green God: well behind throughout, including in sellers: sold 600 gns Doncaster November Sales. *J. M. Carr*

SEAN'S SCHOLAR (USA)   5 b.m. Kris S (USA) – Nalees Scholar (USA)   **51**
(Nalees Man (USA)) [1991 10m* 12f2 12m 1992 14g4 16d5 14d 10d3 10m3 8.3m6 10f4] sparely-made, lengthy mare: modest handicapper: effective from 1¼m to 1¾m: acts on firm and dead ground: suitable mount for claimer. *C. N. Allen*

SEA PADDY   4 b.g. Reach 122 – Sea Thyme (Persian Bold 123) [1991 8d 7.5f 8g   **55**
8d4 9.9f* 9.2d3 9m 10m 8m 9.7f5 9.9f 10m 1992 12g* 12m3 13m* 14.1m4 14.1m6 a12g2 12.1s 15.1d a14g] leggy, close-coupled gelding: won seller at Pontefract (bought in 4,000 gns) and handicap at Hamilton in the spring: well beaten last 3 starts: stays 1¾m: acts on firm going and fibresand: usually ridden by 7-lb claimer H. Bastiman. *R. Bastiman*

SEA PET   3 b.f. Dubassoff (USA) – Palace Pet (Dragonara Palace (USA) 115) [1991   –
NR 1992 14.1m 15.4d] leggy filly: has a round action: fourth reported foal: dam ran once: behind in maidens in September: sold to join J. Birkett 4,500 gns Doncaster October Sales. *Miss Gay Kelleway*

SEA PLANE   3 gr.c. Nishapour (FR) 125 – Pirogue 99 (Reliance II 137) [1991 8m   **69**
1992 12.5f4 11.7g2 16m2 14s 15.4g5 14.1g6] leggy, sparely-made colt: modest maiden: best efforts when second, though looked most unco-operative second occasion: blinkered subsequently: stays 2m: acts on good to firm ground, seemingly not on soft: sold 11,000 gns Newmarket Autumn Sales. *Major W. R. Hern*

SEA PRODIGY   3 b.g. Precocious 126 – Aunt Judy (Great Nephew 126) [1991 7d   **51**
6m 6g2 6m 1992 8.2g 7g6 7.1m 6m 6.9h6 7g6] workmanlike gelding: inconsistent maiden, not seen after July: should stay 1m: best efforts on good ground: may well be unsatisfactory. *M. Blanshard*

SEARCHING STAR   4 b.f. Rainbow Quest (USA) 134 – Little White Star (Mill   –
Reef (USA) 141) [1991 7m 8m a11g5 11.7m3 10g4 14.1m 12.1d 1992 a10g a12g a12g 12g6] close-coupled filly: moderate mover: rated 56 at 3 yrs: no form in 1992: worth another try beyond 1½m: acts on good to firm ground and fibresand: has worn eyeshield. *P. A. Kelleway*

SEARCY   4 b.g. Good Times (ITY) – Fee 111 (Mandamus 120) [1991 12g3 12g   –
13.1m5 12.3m 12g4 16.2f4 16.9g5 1992 a14g6] workmanlike gelding: good mover: rated 48 at 3 yrs for F. J. Houghton: hooded, tailed off at Southwell in January: probably stays 17f: possibly best on an easy surface: often blinkered: has joined Miss S. Wilton. *D. Burchell*

SEASIDE MINSTREL   4 ch.g. Song 132 – Blackpool Belle 70 (The Brianstan   **60**
128) [1991 8g 8.3m 7m2 8f4 8m2 8f6 8g 1992 7m 8f2 8g2 8.9d 8d* 12.1s] leggy gelding: worthwhile form in 1992 only in 1m selling events, winning at Bath getting up close home (trained until after then by C. J. Hill) in September: stays 1m: acts on firm and dead going (below form on fibresand): tried visored/blinkered earlier in career. *R. J. Manning*

SEA SIREN   2 gr.f. (May 14) Slip Anchor 136 – Seriema 72 (Petingo 135) [1992   **61** p
7g6] 25,000Y: closely related to 3-y-o Shesadelight and very smart 1¼m and 1½m winner Infamy (both by Shirley Heights) and half-sister to 2 winners, including (at 7f in Ireland) Lady Regent (by Wolver Hollow): dam, best at 1m, is half-sister to good staying filly High Hawk (dam of In The Wings): 7/1, over 5 lengths sixth of 16 to Cropton in maiden at Lingfield in September, tracking leaders stand side and keeping on well: sure to improve over further. *H. Candy*

SEASONAL SPLENDOUR (IRE)   2 b.f. (Mar 9) Prince Rupert (FR) 121 –   **73**
Snoozy Time 65 (Cavo Doro 124) [1992 a5g2 6s2 6g 7d 7m] 13,500F, 8,000Y: workmanlike filly: half-sister to several winners here and abroad, including fairly useful miler Dream of Fame (by Petorius): dam 2-y-o 5f winner, is half-sister to

smart performers Grey Desire and The Dunce: fair maiden: best effort when never-nearer eighth of 21 in Newmarket nursery won by Wynona in September on fifth start: withdrawn on veterinary advice nearly 2 weeks later: will be better suited by 1m. *C. A. Cyzer*

SEASON'S STAR 2 b.f. (Apr 3) Nomination 125 – Tosara 84 (Main Reef 126) **48** p [1992 7d 7s] angular filly: second foal: sister to 8.1f winner Dibloom: dam 1¼m winner, is half-sister to smart French stayer Chawn: better for race, beaten 9 lengths or more in maidens at Lingfield and Redcar in September: retained by trainer 2,000 gns Newmarket Autumn Sales. *H. Candy*

SEA STRAND 2 b.f. (Apr 29) Last Tycoon 131 – Sandstream 72 (Sandford Lad **47** 133) [1992 5m 6.1m 6m⁵ 6d⁵ 6m 5g 5s] 2,200Y: has a quick action: half-sister to several winners here and abroad, including 3-y-o Sandcastle City (by Formidable), 5f winner at 2 yrs: dam 2-y-o 6f winner, is half-sister to Manado: poor form, including in sellers: worth a try at 7f: sold 2,200 gns Newmarket Autumn Sales. *M. Blanshard*

SEA SYRAH (IRE) 2 b.c. (May 20) Last Tycoon 131 – Wineglass (Wolver – Hollow 126) [1992 7g 7g] 10,500Y: sturdy, angular colt: closely related to a maiden by Try My Best and half-brother to fairly useful 1985 2-y-o 7f winner Anbaal (by Thatch), later successful over middle distances in USA, and Italian St Leger second Bodoni Condensed (by Caerleon): dam once-raced half-sister to smart stayers Frascati and The Admiral: soundly beaten in maidens at Brighton and Lingfield: sold 4,200 gns Newmarket Autumn Sales. *M. Blanshard*

SEATON DELAVAL (USA) 2 b.c. (Apr 11) Seattle Dancer (USA) 119 – Brass **113** p Needles (USA) (Twice Worthy (USA)) [1992 8d* 8d³ 8s⁴] $220,000Y: fourth known foal: half-brother to 2 minor winners in North America: dam, won at up to 9f, from family of very smart middle-distance performer Spruce Needles: progressive form: won newcomers event at Deauville in the summer: 1½ lengths third of 5 to Kadounor in Prix La Rochette and 5 lengths fourth of 11 to Tenby in Grand Criterium, both at Longchamp: will be better suited by 1¼m: yet to race on a sound surface. *A. Fabre, France*

SEATTLE RHYME (USA) 3 ch.c. Seattle Dancer (USA) 119 – Golden Rhyme **120** 87 (Dom Racine (FR) 121) [1991 6m* 7.1m² 8m* 8d³ 8g* 1992 8.9d² 10.4g³ 11.1g³

Mrs H. J. Senn's "Seattle Rhyme"

12s 10m] strong, angular colt: impresses in appearance: has long, fluent stride: leading British 2-y-o of 1991, third to Arazi in Grand Criterium and winner of Racing Post Trophy, but suffered foot injury in the spring: best effort at 3 yrs in Juddmonte International at York (4 lengths third to Rodrigo de Triano): had 2 races in Britain afterwards, in September Stakes at Kempton (odds-on third to Jeune) and Champion Stakes at Newmarket (6½ lengths eighth of 10 to Rodrigo de Triano): chased leaders, weakened quickly 2f out in Prix de l'Arc de Triomphe at Longchamp penultimate outing: best 3-y-o form at around 1¼m: acts on good to firm and good to soft ground. *D. R. C. Elsworth*

SEA VIKING 2 b.g. (Feb 20) Glenstal (USA) 118 – Timid Bride (USA) 76 – (Blushing Groom (FR) 131) [1992 8s] 13,000Y: workmanlike gelding: fourth foal: brother to fair 1989 2-y-o 6f and 7f winner Kerama: dam 10.4f winner: 33/1 and backward, never a factor in 22-runner maiden at Warwick in October: sold 4,000 gns Newmarket Autumn Sales. *M. Blanshard*

SEBOSAN 3 b.g. Prince Sabo 123 – Ceramic (USA) (Raja Baba (USA)) [1991 5m2 **73** 5g* 6d3 6g 6f3 6m 6g 1992 7s2 8s6 10s6 7f* 7.1d] sturdy gelding: trained until after third start by A. Hide: fair form to win handicap at Yarmouth in June: nothing similar in 1992: stays 7f: best effort on firm going: blinkered last 2 outings: has been gelded. *S. P. C. Woods*

SECOND ADVENTURE 4 br.g. Another Realm 118 – Friendly Miss (Be – Friendly 130) [1991 a6g2 a7g4 a6g2 a5g3 6g6 7m 1992 a7g5 a7g6] plating-class maiden: blinkered, well held in handicaps at Lingfield early in the year: should be suited by further than 6f: visored last 3 outings at 3 yrs. *D. J. G. Murray-Smith*

SECOND CALL 3 ch.f. Kind of Hush 118 – Matinata (Dike (USA)) [1991 NR 1992 **67** 10s4 10f 8d* 10d6 10g5 11.4g 11.7s5 10.2d*] 6,400Y: sturdy, plain filly: has a round action: sister to 1¼m to 11.5f winner Early Call and half-sister to 3 winners, including 1985 2-y-o 6f seller winner Lydia Languish (by Hotfoot): dam ran once: fair performer: won maiden at Wolverhampton in July and handicap (always close up, quickened clear over 3f out and just held on) at Chepstow in October: stays 1¼m: well beaten on firm ground: sold to join G. Harwood 18,000 gns Newmarket Autumn Sales and won novice hurdle in December. *H. Candy*

SECOND CHANCE (IRE) 2 ch.c. (Mar 28) Digamist (USA) 110 – Flash Donna **72** (USA) 70 (Well Decorated (USA)) [1992 5g4 5d 5g 5m3 5d 5g* 5g4 5g4 6d2 5g 5.2g5 5.1d2 6s3 5g3] 4,800Y: sparely-made colt: shows knee action: third foal: half-brother to 3-y-o Norwegian winner Orynac (by Cyrano de Bergerac): dam modest maiden at 2 yrs well beaten as 3-y-o: fair performer: won maiden at Folkestone in July, making virtually all: ran well in nurseries last 3 starts: acts on good to firm ground, but best form on easy surface: wore a visor (which slipped) fifth start, run best ignored. *P. Mitchell*

SECOND COLOURS (USA) 2 b. or br.c. (Apr 22) Timeless Moment (USA) – **68** Ruffled Silk (USA) (Our Hero (USA)) [1992 5m 5g6 6m* 5.7f2 6.1f2 5.1m2 6m* 5m* 5m5 5.7m3 7d5 6m6 6m5 a6g] $37,000Y: strong, compact, sprinting type: carries condition: brother to a minor winner in USA and half-brother to another: dam second once from 3 starts in North America: fair performer: successful at Hamilton in maiden in May, then claimer and nursery (under 10-0, making most in moderately-run race) on successive days in July: ran moderately last 4 starts: stays 6f: has done most of his racing on top-of-the-ground: not discredited when visored once. *P. S. Felgate*

SECOND SET (IRE) 4 b.c. Alzao (USA) 117 – Merriment (USA) (Go **127** Marching (USA)) [1991 7g* 8.2m* 8g2 8g* 8d4 8g 1992 8m2 8m3 10f 8s5 7m3]
    It's a reflection on the depressed state of the bloodstock market in Britain that no place could be found at stud for a game and high-class racehorse like Second Set. Although he didn't win a race as a four-year-old— to add to his successes at three which included the Sussex Stakes—Second Set showed himself as good as ever when placed in the Queen Anne Stakes at Royal Ascot (beaten a head by Lahib who received 6 lb) and the Sussex Stakes at Goodwood (beaten a head and three quarters of a length by Marling and Selkirk). He didn't do quite so well afterwards, however, finishing down the field in both the Arlington Million (over a mile and a quarter) and the Queen Elizabeth II Stakes (on unsuitably soft ground) and running below form when third to Selkirk in the Challenge Stakes on his final outing. He is to continue his racing career in the United States where he should do well as a five-year-old. Incidentally, when Second Set ran on bute in the Breeders' Cup Mile

Mr R. L. Duchossois' "Second Set"

as a three-year-old it was not, as stated in *Racehorses of 1991*, because he'd broken blood vessels in the past. We are reliably informed that Second Set was always sound in this capacity and are happy to set the record straight.

Second Set (IRE) (b.c. 1988)	Alzao (USA) (b 1980)	Lyphard (b 1969)	Northern Dancer
			Goofed
		Lady Rebecca (b 1971)	Sir Ivor
			Pocahontas II
	Merriment (USA) (b 1975)	Go Marching (b 1965)	Princequillo
			Leallah
		Tiddlywinks (b 1963)	Court Martial
			Banri An Oir

There is hardly anything to add to the pedigree details that appeared in the essay on Second Set in *Racehorses of 1991* except to say that his sire the Coolmore-based Alzao had another fairly good season. The dam Merriment, a quite useful but lightly-raced maiden in France, is a sister to the high-class French miler Brinkmanship. The smallish, deep-girthed, quite attractive Second Set has shown his best form at a mile on a sound surface. *L. M. Cumani*

SECRAGE (USA) 2 b.f. (Mar 4) Secreto (USA) 128 – Wayage (USA) (Mr **104** Prospector (USA)) [1992 5s* 5g* 6s⁴ 6g² 6g* 6s² 8s] $17,000Y: smallish, angular filly: second foal: closely related to 1991 2-y-o 7f winner Minstrel's Age (by The Minstrel): dam French maiden daughter of smart French mare Waya, later top class at up to 1½m in USA: useful Italian filly: won twice at Rome in May, in listed race on second occasion: landed Prix de Cabourg at Deauville on first outing in France: ¾-length second to Zafonic in Prix Morny there later in August: fair seventh of 11, beaten around 5 lengths, behind Gold Splash in Prix Marcel Boussac at Longchamp 6 weeks later: stays 1m: has raced only on an easy surface: has joined R. Charlton. *F. Brogi, Italy*

SECRETARY OF STATE 6 b.g. Alzao (USA) 117 – Colonial Line (USA) **61** + (Plenty Old (USA)) [1991 NR 1992 10d⁵ 9d 8g 10f*] strong, workmanlike gelding: carries condition: good mover: rated 97 in first half of 1990 season: bandaged, didn't have to be anywhere near best to win 4-runner apprentice event at Brighton in May by 4 lengths: effective at around 1m to 1¼m: acts on firm going. *P. F. I. Cole*

SECRET ASSIGNMENT (USA) 2 ch.g. (Jan 8) Naevus (USA) – Swedish Ivy **67** p (USA) (Northjet 136) [1992 6g 7s³ a8g²] $30,000Y: leggy gelding: has a round action: third foal: dam unraced: sire (by Mr Prospector) best at 1m/9f: progressive maiden: second at Lingfield in November: will be better suited by 1¼m: should improve again. *C. A. Cyzer*

SECRET FANTASY (IRE) 2 b.f. (Apr 3) Taufan (USA) 119 – Thank One's **45** p Stars (Alzao (USA) 117) [1992 6.1d 6d 7m⁵] 10,000Y: small filly: has a round action: first foal: dam unraced: staying-on fifth in claimer at Yarmouth in September, final and easily best effort: will be better suited by 1m: may well progress further. *C. F. Wall*

SECRET FORMULA 2 b.g. (Jan 30) Sulaafah (USA) 119 – Bidula (Manacle 123) **42** [1992 6f 6d 7d] 700Y: leggy gelding: looks weak: half-brother to several winners here and abroad, including (at 5f at 2 yrs in 1990) Sulastar (by Sulaafah): dam never ran: well beaten in the summer: gives impression needs time. *G. B. Balding*

SECRET HAUNT (USA) 4 ch.c. Secreto (USA) 128 – Royal Suite (USA) **111** (Herbager 136) [1991 8.2m* 12g² 1992 10g 12g* 11d⁵] strong, good-bodied colt: moderate performer: smart performer, lightly raced: not discredited in Group 3 event at Sandown in April: won Group 2 race at Rome following month: off course 3½ months, below form in Group 3 contest at Milan in September: stayed 1½m: acted on good to firm ground: has been retired to the French National Stud. *L. M. Cumani*

SECRET KIN (IRE) 3 gr.c. Montekin 125 – Secret Lady (The Go-Between 129) – [1991 NR 1992 6m 10g] IR 2,200F: smallish, workmanlike colt: second living foal: dam lightly-raced sister to smart sprinter Vorvados: tailed off in maiden and apprentice claimer in May: sold 700 gns Doncaster June Sales. *O. Brennan*

SECRET PICNIC (USA) 3 b.c. Secreto (USA) 128 – Slew's Picnic (USA) – (Seattle Slew (USA)) [1991 NR 1992 11d 10.5s⁶ 6g] $21,000Y: strong, lengthy colt: fifth reported foal: half-brother to 2 minor winners in North America: dam unraced: signs of ability (keen hold, no extra final 2f) in maidens at Newbury and Haydock: finished last at Salisbury later in May. *B. Hanbury*

SECRET SOCIETY 5 b. or br.h. Law Society (USA) 130 – Shaara (FR) (Sanctus **88** II 132) [1991 10g 12.3g* 12m⁴ 13.9g 11.9m* 12s 12m 12d 1992 12f³ 11.9g³ 12m 12m⁵ 12s⁴] big, deep-girthed horse: moderate walker: has a rather round action: fairly useful handicapper: ran well when third to Matador in Old Newton Cup at Haydock in July on second outing and when fourth of 17 to Quick Ransom in £60,000 Krug Trophy at Ascot in September: will probably stay 1¾m: acts on firm and soft going: blinkered at Ascot: is held up. *M. J. Camacho*

Premio Ellington, Rome—Secret Haunt (near side) gets the better of Kohinoor

SECRET TALE   2 b.f. (May 8) Faustus (USA) 118 – No Can Tell (USA) (Clev Er   –
Tell (USA)) [1992 5g 5g 6m⁵ 6m 5.2f⁶ 6m⁶ 7g] 1,800Y: workmanlike filly: has a
round action: third foal: sister to a winner in Hungary and half-sister to 1990 2-y-o 5f
winner Anonoalto (by Noalto): dam, maiden, out of half-sister to dam of Dibidale:
seems of little account: sold 660 gns Newmarket September Sales. *G. Blum*

SECRET THING (USA)   3 b.c. Secreto (USA) 128 – Nothing Sweeter (USA) **100**
(Darby Creek Road (USA)) [1991 5g³ 6.1m² 7d² 8s⁴ 6v 1992 8g 7d* 8d⁵ 7g⁵ 7.1m³
6g⁵ 8.8g 7.5v 8v⁴ 6s] compact colt: shows high knee action: useful performer: won
maiden at Brighton in April: raced in Italy for most of rest of season, best effort
when around 6 lengths fourth to Stubass in Group 2 event at Rome in November:
better suited by 1m than shorter: has form on good to firm ground, best efforts on
soft and heavy. *C. E. Brittain*

SECRET TREATY (IRE)   3 b.f. Commanche Run 133 – Pass The Secret (CAN) **56**
(King's Bishop (USA)) [1991 NR 1992 10m³ 7f² a8s⁵ 8g⁵ 10.3m 9g 10.5s a12g a8g³]
lengthy, unfurnished filly: second reported living foal: dam unraced half-sister
to 2 North American stakes winners, notably 1980 Grade 1 2-y-o winner Trumpets
Blare: modest maiden: better at around 1¼m than 1m: below form on soft ground
and all-weather surfaces: sold out of P. Chapple-Hyam's stable 4,400 gns Newmarket December Sales before final outing. *R. J. Manning*

SECRET TURN (USA)   6 b.g. Secreto (USA) 128 – Changing (USA) (Forli   –
(ARG)) [1991 NR 1992 8s] lengthy gelding: carries condition: ran 3 times at 3 yrs for
P. Cole: in need of race in handicap at Bath in September: bred to stay 1½m, was too
intractable at 3 yrs: acts on good to firm ground: has shown ability over jumps.
Andrew Turnell

SEDGY MEAD   4 b.g. Myjinski (USA) – Miss Monroe 73 (Comedy Star (USA)   –
121) [1991 NR 1992 12d 17.2s] strong gelding: no form since 2 yrs: sold 1,350 gns
Ascot June Sales. *P. J. Jones*

SEDGY'S SISTER   2 b.f. (Mar 6) Myjinski (USA) – Miss Monroe 73 (Comedy **46**
Star (USA) 121) [1992 5g⁵ 6m⁶] leggy, unfurnished filly: third foal: dam, maiden,
stayed 1¼m: poor form, beaten around 5 lengths, in maidens at Sandown and
Newbury in the spring: bred to be suited by 1m + . *P. J. Jones*

SEEKIN CASH (USA)   3 b.g. Our Native (USA) – Tis Eloquent (USA) (Caro **78**
133) [1991 NR 1992 10d² 11.9m² 14.1d³ 16.1m²] $15,000F: tall gelding: has a round,
free action: fourth reported foal: half-brother to 2 winners in North America: dam
unraced: fair maiden: well below form in 3-runner contest at Newcastle final start, in
July: takes keen hold, but probably stays 1¾m: acts on good to firm and dead
ground. *J. W. Watts*

SEEK THE PEARL   2 b.f. (Apr 12) Rainbow Quest (USA) 134 – Made of Pearl **48**
(USA) (Nureyev (USA) 131) [1992 7g 8d] leggy filly: second known foal: half-sister
to 3-y-o 1½m winner Cultured (by Saint Cyrien): dam French 7f and 1m winner:
never a factor in large fields in minor event at Kempton and maiden at Redcar in the
autumn: has joined J. Fanshawe. *M. R. Stoute*

SEEMENOMORE   3 b.f. Seymour Hicks (FR) 125 – Tuneful Queen (Queen's   –
Hussar 124) [1991 NR 1992 7.1s 6.1s] 1,500 2-y-o: plain filly: moderate mover: fifth
foal: dam ran twice in Ireland: last in well-contested minor event then maiden (tailed
off) at Chepstow in the autumn. *R. J. Price*

SEE NOW   7 ch.g. Tumble Wind (USA) – Rosie O'Grady (Barrons Court) [1991   –
9.9m 1992 17.2f⁶] lengthy gelding: no worthwhile form on flat since 3 yrs: won
selling handicap hurdle in August. *Mrs A. Knight*

SEE THE LIGHT   5 b.m. Relkino 131 – Sun Worshipper (Sun Prince 128) [1991   –
NR 1992 16.2g⁵ 13.8m] lengthy, rather sparely-made mare: no worthwhile form on
flat: winning hurdler in 1990/1. *Mrs V. A. Aconley*

SEE US THERE (IRE)   2 b.c. (Mar 5) Vision (USA) – Fastidious (Guillaume **31**
Tell (USA) 121) [1992 6m⁵ 7g 6d 6d] compact colt: fourth foal: half-brother to 3
winners, including 1989 2-y-o Irish 1m winner Fastbit (by Henbit): dam never ran:
poor maiden: should stay 1m. *J. Berry*

SEE YOU JIMMY   2 ch.c. (Apr 7) Stanford 121§ – Lucky Pauline (Lucky   –
Wednesday 124) [1992 5m] 1,000Y: big, lengthy colt: second foal: dam once-raced
daughter of soft-ground sprinter Swakara: 25/1, backward and green, always outpaced in 14-runner maiden at Ripon in May. *Ronald Thompson*

SEFIO   2 ch.g. (Mar 7) Efisio 120 – Moonlight Fling (Imperial Fling (USA) 116) **44**
[1992 5.1d 5.1d³ a6g⁵ 6m⁶ 6s] 7,000Y: close-coupled gelding: fourth foal: dam
unraced: off course over 2 months, form only when over 7 lengths third of 6 in

claimer at Nottingham in July: blinkered or visored last 2 starts: should be better suited by 6f than 5f: looks a hard ride: sold 650 gns Newmarket September Sales. *J. Berry*

SEHAILAH 2 b.f. (Apr 29) Mtoto 134 – Fabulous Rina (FR) (Fabulous Dancer **70** (USA) 124) [1992 7m³ 8.2d³ 8m 7g⁴] 12,500Y: lengthy filly: has a round action: third foal: dam, French 1¼m and 10.5f winner, is closely related to smart French middle-distance performer Lys River: consistent form in varied events, including May Hill Stakes at Doncaster and mixed-age event at Newmarket on last 2 starts: very much a staying type: acts on good to firm and dead ground. *Mrs L. Piggott*

SELAAH 5 b.g. Rainbow Quest (USA) 134 – Marwell 133 (Habitat 134) [1991 8d 8g **89** 7.6m 8m 8g* 8d⁵ 8g 1992 7.6g⁶ 7.9m 10g⁶ 10g⁴ 10g⁵] leggy, sparely-made gelding: fairly useful handicapper: effective from 1m to 1¼m: acts on firm ground, possibly unsuited by dead: is held up: had seemed best with strong handling, but best efforts in 1992 for apprentice: acts on good to firm and dead ground. *M. R. Stoute*

SELAGINELLA 3 ch.f. Pharly (FR) 130 – Smagiada (Young Generation 129) **49 ?** [1991 7g⁶ 1992 8m 8f² 8f⁵ a7g⁶ 10g 10.1g² 8.3m a10g 10d 8.9d 8m] sparely-made filly: modest plater: better at 1¼m than shorter: acts on firm going, seemingly not on a soft surface: often claimer ridden: has flashed tail. *M. R. Channon*

SELDOM IN 6 ch.g. Mummy's Game 120 – Pinzamber (Pinicola 113) [1991 **45** a14g⁶ 14d⁴ 16.2g⁵ 13.8g³ 16.5m³ a14g³ 14.6g⁶ 16.2f³ 16.5g 19m* a18g³ 17.9f 1992 16.9g* 14m³ 18g 18.8m 14.6g³ 19m⁵ 16.9d] leggy, lengthy gelding: inconsistent handicapper: won at Wolverhampton in May: out-and-out stayer: acts on firm and dead ground: has won when sweating: not one to trust. *J. Wharton*

SELECTABLE 2 b.f. (Mar 30) Nomination 125 – Persian Case (Upper Case **34** (USA)) [1992 5.3d 6m⁵] 3,200Y: neat filly: half-sister to 3 winners, including Persian Soldier (by Henbit), successful at 7f (at 2 yrs) and 1½m: dam French 2-y-o 7.8f winner: poor form, well beaten, in minor event at Brighton and maiden at Lingfield in the spring. *M. D. I. Usher*

SELF ASSURED (IRE) 2 ch.f. (Mar 23) Ahonoora 122 – Impudent Miss 105 **97 ?** (Persian Bold 123) [1992 7f² 7f* 7g³ 8m² 7d³] 100,000Y: rather leggy, angular filly: fifth foal: half-sister to 3-y-o Good Reference (by Reference Point), successful at 7f (at 2 yrs) and 1m, and 5-y-o 6f and 7.6f winner King Al (by Indian King): dam, Irish 2-y-o 5f to 1m winner, is half-sister to very smart sprinter Sayyaf: fairly useful performer: well-backed favourite, won maiden at Yarmouth in July: best effort when 3 lengths second to Marillette in May Hill Stakes at Doncaster: looked past best and ran moderately when favourite for Newmarket minor event in October: lacks a turn of foot, and will stay beyond 1m. *H. R. A. Cecil*

SELF EXPRESSION 4 b.g. Homing 130 – Subtlety (Grundy 137) [1991 8s 8g **75** 8.2m 9m² 10d 8.5f* 8g* 10g⁴ 8.9g 8.9g 10.3m* 10d 1992 9d⁶ 8g 10f8.1f⁵ 8.1g⁵ 9.9m⁶ 8.3g 8m⁴ 8g 12g 10.3g] leggy gelding: poor mover: unreliable handicapper: stays 1¼m: acts on firm ground, possibly unsuited by a soft surface: no improvement in blinkers/visor: carries head high and tends to hang but has won for inexperienced rider: sold out of I. Balding's stable 7,800 gns Newmarket Autumn Sales after penultimate start. *Mrs J. R. Ramsden*

SELFISH LADY 2 ch.f. (Mar 3) Sayf El Arab (USA) 127 – Snow Tree 86 (Welsh **–** Pageant 132) [1992 6s] small, angular filly: fourth foal: half-sister to 3-y-o Stopher (by Lidhame): dam middle-distance winner out of half-sister to smart stayer Celtic Cone: 20/1 and green, showed nothing in 14-runner maiden at Lingfield in October. *J. L. Spearing*

SELKIRK (USA) 4 ch.c. Sharpen Up 127 – Annie Edge 118 (Nebbiolo 125) **129** [1991 8g² 11.5g³ 10g³ 8m⁴ 8g* 8d* 1992 8m* 9.2d⁶ 8m² 8d* 8s³ 7m* 8f⁵] The top prizes eluded Selkirk as a four-year-old but he retires with plenty to recommend him as a stallion. He was a high-class miler with a fine turn of foot and has both the looks and the pedigree to match his ability. A big colt, who had been rather on the leg as a three-year-old, Selkirk made up into quite a handsome individual in the latest season though he still retained a rather leggy appearance. He was superbly turned out for all his races as a four-year-old and always cut a dash on the way to the start, his long-striding, easy action making him an impressive horse to watch in his faster paces. Selkirk's sire Sharpen Up, who had to be put down in March, was a splendid stallion, and Selkirk's dam Annie Edge was a good-class racemare. Selkirk takes up duties at Lanwades Stud, Newmarket in 1993 when he will stand at a fee of £8,000 (1st October concession).

Juddmonte Lockinge Stakes, Newbury—Selkirk storms clear

Selkirk's career as a racehorse took off following an operation after his fourth outing as a three-year-old to ease discomfort found to have been caused by an undescended testicle. He went on to produce two impressive winning performances—the second of them in the Group 1 Queen Elizabeth II Stakes at Ascot—and ended that season almost universally regarded as the best miler in training in Europe, albeit in an ordinary year. A leg injury prevented Selkirk's completing his three-year-old programme in the Challenge Stakes and the Breeders' Cup Mile, but he got his chance in both races as a four-year-old. He made a breathtaking reappearance in the Juddmonte Lockinge Stakes at Newbury in mid-May, disposing of a strong field—which included most of the top older milers still in training—in a manner which suggested it would take a tip-top three-year-old to beat him. After travelling fluently from the start and pulling over his field two furlongs out Selkirk drew away to win comfortably from Lahib, who received 5 lb. Selkirk was off the course for two months after disappointing on his next start, in the Prix d'Ispahan at Longchamp after which he was found to be coughing. A slight injury in training to his off-fore then interrupted his preparation further for

Beefeater Gin Celebration Mile, Goodwood—
Selkirk has few problems catching Rudimentary;
for the record, Steinbeck eventually grabs second

the Sussex Stakes at Goodwood—'I would have liked another week before the race', his trainer warned in advance. Selkirk overcame his problems to give a magnificent performance in the Sussex, his duel over the last two furlongs with the three-year-old filly Marling providing one of the abiding memories of the season. The Sussex Stakes was run at a tremendous gallop. Selkirk looked sure to win when taking a narrow lead inside the final furlong, but Marling forced her head in front again close home and held on in a photo-finish, with the previous year's winner Second Set staying on strongly three quarters of a length behind in third.

Compensation for Selkirk was forthcoming over the Sussex Stakes course and distance a month later in the Beefeater Gin Celebration Mile in which, confidently ridden, he landed the odds with plenty in hand from French-trained Steinbeck and the Sussex Stakes seventh Rudimentary. Selkirk started 5/4 favourite in a field of nine to stage a repeat success in the Queen Elizabeth II Stakes at Ascot in September when Marling, who hadn't been out since the Sussex Stakes and was encountering soft going for the first time in her career, was again among the opposition. Three of the other leading contenders had shown high-class form on soft: All At Sea and Brief Truce when first and second in the Prix du Moulin earlier in the month, and Lahib when runner-up in the Prix Jacques le Marois. Scrimmaging in the home straight spoiled a good race in which Selkirk, who didn't get a run until too late, managed only third to Lahib and Brief Truce. With a clear passage Selkirk would certainly have finished second and, though it's hard to state he'd have won, there wouldn't have been anything like three and a half lengths between him and Lahib. The Queen Elizabeth II Stakes confirmed that Selkirk was on a par with the best milers in Europe and he arrived at Gulfstream Park at the end of October as one of Britain's main hopes on the prestigious Breeders' Cup programme. Selkirk had limbered up for the Breeders' Cup Mile in the Challenge Stakes at Newmarket, where he had given his regular jockey Cochrane an armchair ride, showing a fine turn of finishing speed and demonstrating in the process his effectiveness at seven furlongs. Concern about the long-striding Selkirk's proving fully effective around the tight turns at Gulfstream Park was expressed beforehand, but whether that accounted for his below-par effort is a moot point, and not of a lot of concern now. Suffice to record that Selkirk didn't give his running, finishing fifth, two lengths and two places behind Brief Truce, to the American-trained three-year-old Lure after being well placed on the final turn.

As described earlier, Selkirk's dam Annie Edge was a good-class race-mare, winner of the Kiveton Park Stakes and placed in several pattern races including the Irish One Thousand Guineas. She was sold for 330,000 guineas to George Strawbridge at the end of her three-year-old days and continued racing in the States, gaining her most important victories as a four-year-old in two graded races on turf, the New York Handicap over a mile and a quarter at Belmont Park and the Riggs Handicap over an extended mile at Pimlico. Annie Edge's pedigree isn't so distinguished as her racing record—she

Challenge Stakes, Newmarket—Selkirk's last run in Britain

Mr George Strawbridge's "Selkirk"

		Atan	Native Dancer
	Sharpen Up	(ch 1961)	Mixed Marriage
	(ch 1969)	Rocchetta	Rockefella
Selkirk (USA)		(ch 1961)	Chambiges
(ch.c. 1988)		Nebbiolo	Yellow God
	Annie Edge	(ch 1974)	Novara
	(ch 1980)	Friendly Court	Be Friendly
		(ch 1971)	No Court

fetched only IR 6,800 guineas as a yearling—but she has done well at stud so far. All three of her foals to reach the racecourse have won. Her first, the fair handicapper Casual Flash, had a strikingly-different racing character from his year-younger full brother Selkirk; Casual Flash stayed well and gained both his wins over two miles. Annie Edge's third foal, the headstrong and somewhat highly-strung Vailmont (a daughter of the Sharpen Up stallion Diesis) was also in training at Kingsclere in the latest season; she's a fairly useful sprinter at her best and won twice in 1992. Selkirk ran well in the Grand Criterium on the second of two outings as a two-year-old and was regarded initially as a Derby candidate. He reverted to a mile after being beaten into third in the Lingfield Derby Trial and another Derby trial, the Predominate Stakes. Selkirk acted on good to firm and soft ground. He was a credit to his trainer who described him after the Challenge Stakes as 'the best I have trained since Mill Reef'. *I. A. Balding*

SELLAFIELD (IRE)   2 ch.c. (Mar 26) Salt Dome (USA) – Bombalurina (Pharly   **48** p
(FR) 130) [1992 7g] IR 2,200Y, 4,600 2-y-o: leggy colt: half-brother to winning Irish sprinter Outgoing (by Exhibitioner): dam unraced: 50/1 and bit backward, soon close up after slow start and raced keenly 5f in 17-runner maiden auction at Leicester

in September: showed a round action: sold 4,800 gns Newmarket Autumn Sales: should do better. *W. R. Muir*

SELVOLE 2 b.f. (Feb 28) Midyan (USA) 124 – Sharrara (CAN) 61 (Blushing **46** Groom (FR) 131) [1992 5f 5m 6f 5m5 5m4 5f* 5d4 6s3 6s 6g 7d] 4,000F, 5,400Y: leggy filly: fifth foal: half-sister to 3 winners here and abroad, including 6f/1m performer Juvenara (by Young Generation) and 7f (at 2 yrs) to 11.9f winner Hajaim (by Doulab): dam, lightly-raced maiden, stayed 1¼m: modest plater: made all in 5-runner claimer at Edinburgh in July: should stay 7f: acts on any going: no improvement in a visor: keen sort: tends to drift right. *Miss L. A. Perratt*

SEMILLON 2 b.c. (Apr 20) Rousillon (USA) 133 – Simova (USA) (Vaguely Noble **74** 140) [1992 7d3 7g2 7s2 6.9v* 7s] well-made colt: good mover: second foal: brother to 3-y-o 11.9f winner Simonov: dam, French maiden, is out of half-sister to Jalmood: fair performer: hung left, carried head high and looked ungenuine when second: blinkered subsequently, winning maiden at Folkestone narrowly but cosily, then soundly beaten when facing stiff task in nursery at Leicester: will stay 1m: yet to race on top-of-the-ground: sent to France. *G. Harwood*

SENECA REEF (IRE) 4 b. or br.f. Simply Great (FR) 122 – Inesdela (Wolver **84** d Hollow 126) [1991 6v 7g 1992 6f 6m3 6f 6f 5.2g6 5s 7.3g 7d] good-bodied ex-Irish filly: has a quick action: first foal: dam never ran: trained by L. Browne in Ireland at 3 yrs: disappointing here, easily best run when third in handicap at Kempton in May: stays 6f: acts on good to firm ground: visored/blinkered last 3 starts: sold 8,000 gns Newmarket December Sales. *I. A. Balding*

SENNON COVE 3 ch.f. All Systems Go 119 – L'Irondelle (On Your Mark 125) **–** [1991 NR 1992 7g 7d 7g 7g a7g a8g] workmanlike filly: third foal: sister to bad plater Little Conker: dam never ran: no sign of ability, including in a seller. *M. J. Charles*

SENOR L'AMOUR 2 b.g. (Feb 19) King of Spain 121 – Encore L'Amour (USA) § **–** (Monteverdi 129) [1992 5m] 2,000Y: good-bodied gelding: second foal: dam no form and was temperamental: 33/1 and carrying plenty of condition, soon tailed off in 8-runner maiden auction at Warwick in July. *Andrew Turnell*

SENSABO 2 ch.f. (Feb 22) Prince Sabo 123 – Gas Only 63 (Northfields (USA)) **32** [1992 5v 5f 6m 5m4] 4,000F, 2,200Y: good-bodied filly: third foal: half-sister to 1987 2-y-o 6f winner Glowing Report (by Kalaglow): dam 9f and 1¼m winner: poor fourth of 5 in maiden at Edinburgh in July. *Miss L. A. Perratt*

SENSE OF HUMOUR 2 b.f. (May 13) Dowsing (USA) 124 – Travel On 111 **49** (Tachypous 128) [1992 7d 7s 6g5] 11,000Y: workmanlike filly: fifth live foal: half-sister to a minor winner in Denmark: dam won Cherry Hinton Stakes: around 10 lengths fifth of 11 to Easy Access at Doncaster in November, easily best effort in maidens: should stay 7f. *J. W. Payne*

SEQUESTRATOR 9 b.g. African Sky 124 – Miss Redmarshall 80 (Most Secret **–** 119) [1991 7f 8.9m 1992 7.6g 8.9g] small, light-framed gelding: of little account these days. *P. D. Evans*

SERAPHIM (FR) 3 b.f. Lashkari 128 – Sassika (GER) (Arratos (FR)) [1991 NR **48** 1992 13.8f* a14g4 12.1s6 16.1s 11d5 12.1g3] lengthy, sparely-made filly: sixth foal: half-sister to fair 1991 3-y-o 10.6f winner Shoka (by Kaldoun) and 11f winner Harmonical (by Lyphard's Wish): dam, from good German family, won in Germany: bought out of M. Stoute's stable 2,900 gns Newmarket July (1992) Sales: fair plater: won at Catterick (no bid) in July: should stay 2m: acts on any going. *T. D. Barron*

SEREN QUEST 2 b.f. (Mar 31) Rainbow Quest (USA) 134 – Serenesse (Habat **54** 127) [1992 7.1d6 7g] leggy filly: fourth live foal: half-sister to 1¼m winner Towny Boy (by Camden Town): dam listed winner in Italy: backward for maidens at Sandown (seemingly much better effort, moderately-run event) and Yarmouth in the summer: bred to be suited by middle distances. *A. W. Denson*

SERGEANT MERYLL 8 b.g. Marching On 101 – Mistress Meryll 61 (Tower **34** Walk 130) [1991 a7g2 a8g a8g4 a7g6 10.1s 7.6g 7g4 8.1d5 7.6d 7v6 7.6s2 7.1g2 8.3m 8g5 7g 7g a8g 1992 a7g 9.7v 7d2 7g 8g a7g5 a7g 7g 8.1g] sturdy, quite attractive gelding: moderate mover: inconsistent handicapper: last win 28 starts ago at 6 yrs: stays 1m: acts on fibresand, and best form on an easy surface on turf: tried visored earlier in career. *P. Howling*

SERIOUS 2 b.c. (Feb 10) Shadeed (USA) 135 – Azallya (FR) (Habitat 134) [1992 **82** p 6g*] lengthy, quite good-topped colt: second foal: closely related to 3-y-o Bayadere (by Green Dancer): dam French 8.3f winner, is half-sister to a smart French middle-distance winner out of another: 14/1, burly and green, won 20-runner maiden at Newmarket in October by 1½ lengths from Resist The Force, chased along vigorously by halfway, then making tremendous progress once meeting the rising ground: will stay at least 1m: sure to improve. *M. R. Stoute*

SERIOUS ACTION   3 b.g. Slip Anchor 136 – Silly Woman (Silly Season 127)   –
[1991 NR 1992 a8g⁵ 8g 6.9d⁶ a8g a8g a10g] 110,000Y: rather leggy, good-bodied gelding: fifth live foal: half-brother to poor maiden Easter Term (by Welsh Term), useful 6f to 1m winner Serious Trouble (by Good Times) and smart 1985 2-y-o 5f and 7f winner Moorgate Man (by Remainder Man): dam unraced: no worthwhile form. *Sir Mark Prescott*

SERIOUS HURRY   4 ch.g. Forzando 122 – Lady Bequick 81 (Sharpen Up 127)   57
[1991 a5g* 5.3f³ 5f 1992 a5g a7g a5g a6g 5g² 5g³ 5m³ 5f⁴ 5g² a5g⁴ 5.3d⁵ a5g³ a5g² a5g⁴ a5g³] strong, heavy-topped gelding: carries plenty of condition: has a quick action: modest handicapper: best at 5f: acts on firm ground and equitrack, seems unsuited to a soft surface: usually blinkered nowadays: usually forces pace: sold out of Sir Mark Prescott's stable 4,200 gns Newmarket Autumn Sales after eleventh start. *C. C. Elsey*

SERIOUS RESULT   2 b.f. (May 8) Jester 119 – Little Revenge (Runnymede   38
123) [1992 6g⁶ 5.1s⁴ 6v] 400F: leggy, sparely-made filly: fifth foal: sister to 3-y-o Ghosted Hassle: dam unraced: never-dangerous fourth of 11 in minor event at Bath in September, only indication of merit. *R. Akehurst*

SERIOUS TIME   4 ch.g. Good Times (ITY) – Milva 56 (Jellaby 124) [1991 a8g⁶   51
a8g⁴ a7g 8.9g⁴ 1992 10d a10g² 8m⁶ 10f³ 11.9f² a14g*] leggy gelding: consistent handicapper: first past post in selling handicap at Lingfield (edged right and demoted) in May and poor Southwell maiden (tired last 1f and held on by short head) in June: will prove best at up to 1¾m: acts on firm ground and all-weather surfaces: sold to join T. Cunningham 7,600 gns Ascot July Sales. *Sir Mark Prescott*

SERLBY CONNECTION   7 ch.g. Crofthall 110 – Well Connected (Bold And   –
Free 118) [1991 NR 1992 8m 8.2g 8.2m] big, lengthy gelding: carries plenty of condition: rated 55 as 5-y-o: bandaged, no promise in 1992: stays 1m: acts on any going: not an easy ride. *S. R. Bowring*

SEROTINA (IRE)   2 b.f. (Feb 23) Mtoto 134 – Northshiel 85 (Northfields   – p
(USA)) [1992 7g] 64,000Y: rather unfurnished filly: second foal: half-sister to 3-y-o 9f winner Boloardo (by Persian Bold): dam, 2-y-o 7f winner, is closely related to Waajib out of useful middle-distance filly Coryana: 25/1, beaten around 15 lengths when tenth of 15 in maiden at Yarmouth in August, pulling hard 4f then fading: moved moderately to post: should improve. *W. Jarvis*

SERRANT (USA)   4 b.g. Bering 136 – Saison (USA) 90 (L'Enjoleur (CAN)) [1991   118 p
11m* 10d* 12.1g³ 1992 10.5v⁶ 10g* 10g* 11m* 11g* 12g*] French gelding: fourth living foal: dam, out of half-sister to Hula Dancer, 7f winner on 3 starts here and later stakes winner in USA: improved into a smart performer, winning handicap at Longchamp, and listed races at Maisons-Laffitte, Longchamp (by 1½ lengths from Glity), Clairefontaine-Deauville and Bordeaux, last-named by 6 lengths in September: stays 1½m: acts on good to firm and good to soft going. *A. Fabre, France*

SETTA   2 ch.f. (May 24) Fast Topaze (USA) 128 – Kantado 93 (Saulingo 122) [1992   55 p
8f⁶] tall, leggy, quite good-topped filly: half-sister to several winners, notably In Excess (by Siberian Express), 6f and 7f winner here later top class at 1m/1¼m in USA: dam raced mainly at 5f: 12/1 and in need of race, around 6 lengths sixth of 13 to Dakar Rally in maiden at Doncaster in September, chasing leaders and keeping on not knocked about: sure to improve. *M. Moubarak*

SET TABLE (USA)   3 gr.c. Caro 133 – Room For The Sauce (USA) (Sauce Boat   83
(USA)) [1991 NR 1992 8g² 10.3g⁴ 9m² 8.5d⁶ 8m 8m 7f 7g* 7d] $250,000Y: leggy, workmanlike colt: second foal: dam, 2-y-o winner in North America, is half-sister to high-class U.S. graded winner Badger Land: fairly useful form at best: won maiden at Catterick in September: below form previous 4 starts (in valuable handicaps on 3 occasions) and again (took strong hold) on final one: stays 1¼m: seems best on a sound surface: visored/blinkered last 3 starts. *J. H. M. Gosden*

SET THE FASHION   3 br.g. Green Desert (USA) 127 – Prelude 89 (Troy 137)   54
[1991 NR 1992 a8g⁵ a10g⁴] second foal: half-brother to modest maiden (winning hurdler) Domain (by Dominion): dam stayer: again visored, keeping-on fourth at Lingfield, much better effort in maidens in the spring: likely to stay 1½m. *Lord Huntingdon*

SET UP   4 b.g. Sarab 123 – Gitee (FR) (Carwhite 127) [1991 a8g³ a7g 8f 7m⁶ 7.1m   –
6.1m⁶ 1992 8m 10g 10.2f] well-made gelding: rated 42 at 3 yrs: no form in 1992. *D. Burchell*

SEVERINE (USA) 3 b.f. Trempolino (USA) 135 – Sharmila (FR) (Blakeney 126)   **65**
[1991 6g 7f³ 6.3s 7g 1992 8m 10m³ 12f² 11.9f* 12m³ 13.8d] close-coupled, attractive
filly: fair handicapper: won at Brighton in August, leading 2½f out: burly, weakened
quickly 3f out at Catterick final start: suited by 1½m + : acted on firm ground, might
of been unsuited by a soft surface: retired to stud. *J. L. Dunlop*

SEVINCH 2 b.f. (Mar 5) Dunbeath (USA) 127 – Serdarli (Miami Springs 121)   **–**
[1992 7g 7g 7m⁴] tall, angular filly: second foal: dam placed at 1½m and over
hurdles: seems of little account: sold 720 gns Doncaster September Sales. *M. W.
Easterby*

SEXY MOVER 5 ch.g. Coquelin (USA) 121 – Princess Sinna (Sun Prince 128)   **35**
[1991 12m 8h 1992 16.1m 15.1m² 15.8g 15.8m* 16m² 12.2g] leggy gelding: poor
handicapper: won at Catterick in July: better at around 2m than shorter: acts on
good to firm ground: visored earlier in career: won handicap hurdle (dead ground) in
November. *W. Storey*

SHABANAZ 7 b.g. Imperial Fling (USA) 116 – Claironcita 97 (Don Carlos) [1991   **81**
NR 1992 a7g² a8g⁴ a8g⁶ 10.3g² 10s 8.5m⁴ 10.5s*] rangy, angular gelding: good
mover: fair handicapper: claimer ridden, quickened very well to lead close home
having been short of room 2f out in competitive event at Haydock in October:
effective from 7f to 10.5f: acts on firm and soft ground and fibresand: visored (well
below form) once: has run well in blinkers. *S. G. Norton*

SHADANZA (IRE) 3 b.c. Shardari 134 – Amanzi 94 (African Sky 124) [1991 NR   **53**
1992 10m³ 12.3s⁶ 12m⁵ 13.8g⁵ 11.1s³ 10.4s] IR 3,800Y: rather leggy colt: has a round
action: third living foal: half-brother to 4-y-o winning hurdler Captain My Captain
(by Flash of Steel): dam, Irish 2-y-o 5f winner, is half-sister to very useful sprinter
Touch Paper out of half-sister to Blue Wind: inconsistent maiden: ran poorly in
selling handicap final start: should be suited by at least 1½m: yet to race on firm
ground, probably acts on any other. *A. P. Stringer*

SHADAYLOU (IRE) 3 ch.f. Standaan (FR) 118 – Grande Madame 64 (Mon-   **–**
seigneur (USA) 127) [1991 7g⁴ 7d³ 7m⁴ 7g 6m⁴ 1992 a6g 6d 5g 8.3m⁴ 8.1g 9.2g 10d
12.1s 10.9s] leggy, sparely-made filly: seemed of little account: dead. *Miss L. A.
Perratt*

SHADES OF CROFT 2 b.c. (Apr 28) Alleging (USA) 120 – Peta 93 (Petingo   **46**
135) [1992 5.2d 5g 6m 6g⁵ a7g² a6g³ a7g* 7.1s a6g 8s] sturdy, leggy colt: sixth
living foal: half-brother to fairly useful 2-y-o 6f winner Addenbroke (by Relkino):
dam 2-y-o 6f winner: poor form: gamely made all in seller at Southwell (no bid) in
July: soundly beaten afterwards, racing very keenly early on final start: suited by 7f:
acts on fibresand, possibly unsuited by soft ground. *M. D. I. Usher*

SHADES OF JADE 4 gr.f. General Wade 93 – Gellifawr 80 (Saulingo 122) [1991   **57**
5f 6f⁵ 5s⁶ 5d² 5f⁴ 5.3f⁵ 5m 5m² 5d 5g 5.1m⁵ 5g 5d⁶ 5f 1992 5f 5m 5g³ 5m* 5m* 5.1f
5m³ 5m³ 5f⁶ 5m 6d a5g] rangy filly: has a very round action: modest handicapper: in
good form in midsummer and won twice at Lingfield: well below form last 3 starts:
very speedy: acts on good to firm ground and dead. *J. J. Bridger*

SHADIDEEN (USA) 4 ch.g. Shadeed (USA) 135 – Allegretta 101 (Lombard   **63**
(GER) 126) [1991 8g 10g 9m 11.7f³ 1992 10.5d 12.1f* 10m⁵ 12.1m⁴ 15.1m 13.1g² 13f²]
leggy, close-coupled, angular gelding: consistent handicapper: ran only in midsummer, winning amateurs stakes at Hamilton: ideally suited by 1½m/13f: acts on
firm going, seems unsuited by soft surface. *Miss L. A. Perratt*

SHADOW BIRD 5 b.m. Martinmas 128 – In The Shade 89 (Bustino 136) [1991   **59**
12d 12m³ 12m⁵ 12g 10.1m⁴ 11.5m² 12g² 11.5f⁶ 10m⁴ 11m 12m* 12d* 12f 1992 12g
11.8d² 11.4f 12f5 11.8g³ 10.9d⁴ 11.5g*¹ 12.3d* 12m⁵ 12g³] leggy, workmanlike mare:
poor mover: modest handicapper: won at Yarmouth and Wolverhampton in August:
best at around 1½m: acts on firm and dead ground: effective blinkered or not: has
won for amateur. *G. A. Pritchard-Gordon*

SHADOW JURY 2 ch.c. (Mar 6) Doulab (USA) 115 – Texita 65 (Young   **72**
Generation 129) [1992 5g² 5g* 5d³ 5m² 5f* 5m* 6d³ 5m* 6m³ 5d⁶ 6g³ 5m⁶ 5g 6s
6m] 8,400Y: rather leggy, useful-looking colt: has a quick action: second foal:
half-brother to 3-y-o Forbourne (by Forzando): dam ran 3 times here at 2 yrs, later
winner in Norway: largely consistent between March and mid-August, winning 2
sellers (retained 8,200 gns then 8,400 gns) at Beverley, a claimer (claimed out of
Mrs M. Reveley's stable £12,869) at Edinburgh and a median auction event
(awarded race) at Ayr: left J. Wainwright's stable after penultimate start: effective at
5f and 6f: acts on good to firm and dead ground: unseated rider in stalls tenth start:
visored last 5 starts, running poorly on last 3 occasions. *C. Tinkler*

SHADOWLAND (IRE)   4 ch.g. Be My Native (USA) 122 – Sunland Park   –
(Baragoi 115) [1991 12g 12m² 13.8m⁴ 13.6g⁵ 11.5g 1992 a12g⁴ 14.6g 14.6g] strong
gelding: poor maiden: sold out of G. Pritchard-Gordon's stable 1,200 gns Ascot
March Sales after reappearance: stays 13.6f: acts on good to firm ground. *M. J.
Charles*

SHADOWS OF SILVER   4 gr.f. Carwhite 127 – Mimika 85 (Lorenzaccio 130)   69 p
[1991 NR 1992 12m*] big, leggy filly: half-sister to 3 winners, including 5-y-o
7f/1m performer Kinlacey (by Aragon) and modest stayer San Carlos Bay (by Hittite
Glory): dam 2-y-o 5f winner: won a NH Flat race in 1991/2: 3/1 after promising debut,
won moderate 10-runner maiden at Pontefract in September, leading 4f out and
keeping on willingly: will prove as effective back at 1¾m: may well improve further.
B. A. McMahon

SHAFAYIF   3 ch.f. Ela-Mana-Mou 132 – Rare Roberta (USA) 118 (Roberto (USA)   43
131) [1991 6.1m 8m 1992 8f⁵ 8d 14.6g⁶ 12f³ 10m⁵ 8g 10s³] lengthy filly: moderate
walker: inconsistent plater: sold out of B. Hanbury's stable 2,100 gns Newmarket
July Sales after fifth start: won selling event over hurdles in August: gambled-on
favourite, good third at Redcar in September: stays 15f: acts on good to firm and soft
ground: sold 1,350 gns Ascot November Sales. *I. Campbell*

SHAFFAAF (USA)   4 b.g. Shadeed (USA) 135 – Refill 88 (Mill Reef (USA) 141)   73
[1991 10m 10.6g⁵ 10d 11.7m 10m 10m 11.9g 9m 1992 a12g⁴ 12.3v 10g* 9g² 8.9g² 8.1g²
7d* 8s⁵ 10.5d³ 7.9s² 8s² 9s⁴] strong, good-bodied gelding: looked one to be wary of
at 3 yrs but a most consistent handicapper in 1992: won at Windsor (seller, bought in
3,200 gns) in July and Goodwood (amateurs) in October: effective from 7f to 10.8f:
acts on soft going: effective visored/blinkered or not: suitable mount for apprentice:
best with waiting tactics. *P. D. Evans*

SHAFFIC (FR)   5 b.g. Auction Ring (USA) 123 – Tavella (FR) (Petingo 135) [1991   –
NR 1992 10.3m] rather angular, leggy gelding: has a long stride: rated 78 for D.
Elsworth as 3-y-o: modest novice hurdler in 1991/2: burly, never placed to challenge
in handicap at Doncaster in September. *M. D. Hammond*

SHAHAAMH (IRE)   3 b.f. Reference Point 139 – Balqis (USA) 93 (Advocator)   85
[1991 NR 1992 10.5f² 10d5 10.2f* 14.6m 11.9d² 12.3v3] lengthy filly: third foal:
closely related to useful 5-y-o stayer Haitham (by Wassl) and half-sister to useful
4-y-o middle-distance stayer Libk (by Kalaglow): dam 2-y-o 5f and 6f winner, is
half-sister to dam of Hollywood Derby winner Slew The Dragon: fairly useful
performer: made all in maiden (swished tail) at Bath in August: somewhat flattered
by 10 lengths seventh to Niodini in Park Hill Stakes at Doncaster: stayed 14.6f:
acted on firm and dead ground, soundly beaten on heavy: visits Polish Precedent. *H.
Thomson Jones*

SHAHDJAT (IRE)   4 ch.f. Vayrann 133 – Shahdiza (USA) (Blushing Groom (FR)   55
131) [1991 12g* 12m* 16s³ 1992 13.3g 10f⁶ 16s 12m 14g 16d 18m 16s⁵] lengthy, rather
sparely-made ex-Irish filly: poor mover: second foal: dam 1m (at 2 yrs) and 13.1f
winner: useful performer in 1991 for J. Oxx: backed at long odds, first worthwhile
form on flat here when fifth in Nottingham handicap: stays 2m: acts on good to firm
and soft ground: won novice hurdle in November. *K. C. Bailey*

SHAHIK (USA)   2 b.c. (Feb 28) Spectacular Bid (USA) – Sham Street (USA) 100
(Sham (USA)) [1992 5d* 6m² 5g³ 6g² 6s⁴ 6g²] $105,000Y: fourth foal: half-brother
to 2 winners in North America, including stakes winner Queen's Gray Bee (by
Drone), successful at up to 1¼m: dam won 4 races at up to 1¼m: won maiden at
Leopardstown in April: much improved after, running best race (though flashed tail)
when ¾-length second to Pips Pride in Heinz 57 Phoenix Stakes at same course on
fourth outing: will probably be better suited by 7f. *K. Prendergast, Ireland*

SHAIBA (USA)   2 ch.c. (Mar 17) Alysheba (USA) – Stage Luck (USA) (Stage   90 p
Door Johnny) [1992 7g² 8g*] $550,000Y: leggy, lengthy colt: has scope: half-brother
to several winners, notably champion American 2-y-o and 3-y-o (won fillies triple
crown) filly Open Mind (by Deputy Minister): dam won 6 races in USA: sire
top-class middle-distance colt: attended by 2 handlers, 9/4 on after promising debut,
won 9-runner minor event at Newmarket in October by a neck from Karnak, pushed
along to lead over 1f out when running lazily: will stay 1¼m: likely to do better. *M. R.
Stoute*

SHAIEEF (IRE)   4 gr.f. Shareef Dancer (USA) 135 – Shaiyneen (Kalamoun 129)   66
[1991 9.5m⁵ 7m⁶ 7g⁶ 8g 8g 8g² 10g⁴ 10s 7g 11d 10g 1992 a8g a12g 8m* 8m* 8g*
10.1f⁶] small, leggy ex-Irish filly: has quick, moderate action: fourth living foal: half-
sister to fairly useful 1¼m winner Shaynoor (by Niniski): dam, French provincial 7f
and 9f winner, is half-sister to Shergar and Shernazar: trained in Ireland at 3 yrs by
F. Dunne: consistent performer: led inside final 1f when successful in handicaps at

Ripon, Thirsk (apprentices) and Yarmouth within 16 days in July: effective from truly-run 1m, to 1¼m: acted on good to firm ground: usually blinkered at 3 yrs: in foal to Keen. *R. J. R. Williams*

SHAKELA (USA)   3 ch.f. Alydar (USA) – Jellatina (Fortino II 120) [1991 6f 1992   **54** 10.4m⁵ 8.1m³ 11.1f 9g² 12.8g 9g⁶ 8.5g 10g] tall, sparely-made filly: no worthwhile form here for B. Hanbury and sold 29,000 gns Newmarket July Sales after third start: second of 4 in a maiden at Tranmore in August: stays 9f: blinkered last 2 starts. *J. C. Hayden, Ireland*

SHAKE TOWN (USA)   4 b.g. Caro 133 – All Dance (USA) (Northern Dancer   **–** (CAN)) [1991 10m 12g 8.1d³ 7m⁴ 7f 7m² 7f⁶ 7m⁴ 8g³ 7g* 7m⁵ 7m* 6.9f⁴ 7g* 1992 a8g 8g 6.9m⁶ 7g 8g] good-bodied gelding: moderate mover: fair handicapper (rated 80) at 3 yrs: below form in 1992, though showed signs of retaining ability in visor last 3 starts: effective at 7f/1m: acts on firm and dead going: has won for 7-lb claimer, but tends to hang left and should prove best with strong handling: usually held up: sold 5,000 gns Ascot December Sales. *M. H. Tompkins*

SHAKINSKI   3 gr.f. Niniski (USA) 125 – Shakana 91 (Grundy 137) [1991 5.2g 6g   **–** 7m⁶ 8s a8g⁵ 1992 11.5g a11g* 11.5g 12g 11.8g a16g* 17.2s a14g³ a16g⁵] leggy, work-   a67 manlike filly: has a quick action: no form on turf in 1992: successful in handicaps at Southwell in June and September (visored): stays 2m: acts on fibresand. *M. J. Ryan*

SHAKREEN (USA)   3 b.f. Alleged (USA) 138 – My Sister 101 (Nonoalco (USA)   **67** 131) [1991 7g 8f² 7.1s³ 1992 8d 8f² 6.9g⁵ 8g² 10m⁵ 7m⁵ 7g] tall, workmanlike filly: has a round action: fair maiden: probably stays 1¼m: probably acts on any going. *Mrs L. Piggott*

SHALABIA   3 ch.f. Fast Topaze (USA) 128 – Mangala (USA) (Sharpen Up 127)   **84** [1991 leggy, sparely-made filly: moderate mover: second foal: half-sister to French 1m winner Barraq (by Crystal Glitters): dam French 7f and 1m winner out of sister to Majestic Prince and Crowned Prince: bandaged all round, fairly useful form in maidens at Newmarket in April and Chepstow in July: will probably stay 1m. *M. Moubarak*

SHALAKO   2 b.c. (Mar 19) Nomination 125 – Straffan Girl (Sallust 134) [1992   **–** 6.1m] fourth foal: brother to fair 5f winner Bit of A Lark and half-brother to 3-y-o Double Lark (by Bairn) and 1988 2-y-o 6f winner My Audrees (by Auction Ring): dam unraced: 25/1 and burly, slowly away, ran green and never a factor in 8-runner maiden at Nottingham in September. *R. Hollinshead*

SHALFORD (IRE)   4 ch.c. Thatching 131 – Enigma 87 (Ahonoora 122) **124** § [1991 8g⁶ 7g³ 8g 6d* 6m 7g 7.3f⁴ 6f⁵ 6s* 7m⁴ 1992 7g* 7.1d⁵ 6m* 6f* 6g 6d⁴ 6d]

Shalford's form went to pieces after Royal Ascot. A five-length win in the Cork And Orrery Stakes preceded by a three-and-a-half-length win in the Duke of York Stakes put him in line for the sprint championship, but he was subsequently well beaten in the July Cup, the Haydock Park Sprint Cup and the Diadem Stakes. Consistency had never been a strong point of Shalford's, and before York he had disappointed in a listed race at Haydock, following a five-length win in a similar event at Leicester on his seasonal debut. When he was good he was very good, when he was bad he was horrid! What to make of him, we don't know. Varied excuses were advanced for his poor performances, some of which were perfectly plausible, but on his final appearance in the Diadem Stakes, very lethargic beforehand as he had been in the July Cup, he simply looked as if he had had enough of the game and dropped himself out once put under pressure. He won't be racing in 1993. He was bought for stud before Royal Ascot and will stand alternate seasons in Ireland and Australia, beginning at the Kilsheelin Stud, Co. Tipperary, a branch of the Coolmore operation, at a fee of IR 3,500 guineas with the October 1st concession.

When Shalford was good he was very good, that's true. His defeat of his future stable-companion Mr Brooks at York was really impressive. He went clear of his eight opponents from two furlongs out and the jockey eased up in the closing stages. The dependable Amigo Menor, beaten five lengths into third place there, was beaten the same distance into second in the Cork And Orrery Stakes, in which Shalford started favourite at 3/1 in a field of seventeen. Shalford made virtually all the running on this occasion, travelling strongly on the far side, and won a non-vintage renewal unchallenged. From there, it was all downhill. Royal Ascot tactics were tried again at Newmarket,

Duke of York Stakes, York—
Shalford has three and a half lengths to spare over Mr Brooks (right)

but he surrendered the lead tamely after four furlongs and was beaten a dozen lengths behind Mr Brooks; reportedly he returned distressed. At Haydock, where he finished fourth to Sheikh Albadou in the best sprint race of the season, he led for going on for five furlongs before the winner and Mr Brooks swept by on either side of him. Shalford had won the Diadem Stakes in spectacular fashion as a three-year-old with a much-improved display. In similar conditions to that day, he had only to reproduce his York or his Royal Ascot running to be virtually assured of winning the race for a second time. However, he beat a retreat two furlongs out and was eased.

Shalford (IRE) (ch.c. 1988)	Thatching (b 1975)	Thatch (b 1970)	Forli / Thong
		Abella (ch 1968)	Abernant / Darrica
	Enigma (b 1983)	Ahonoora (ch 1975)	Lorenzaccio / Helen Nichols
		Princess Ru (b 1962)	Princely Gift / Chiru

Shalford's sire Thatching also won the Duke of York and the Cork And Orrery as a four-year-old, and he went on to win the July Cup the same season. Blinkers improved him out of all recognition. In view of that, it would have

Cork And Orrery Stakes, Ascot—Shalford at his best

been interesting to have seen what difference blinkers or a visor made to Shalford once he'd lost his form. Shalford, a strong, close-coupled colt, impressive in appearance, showed his best form at six furlongs but was also highly effective at seven; he acted on any going. His dam Enigma was a sprinter, and so, too, were Enigma's best-known recent relatives, her sister the Ballyogan and Phoenix Stakes winner Princess Tracy and half-sister the Sandown National Stakes winner Trasi Girl. Enigma's second foal Bletchley Park (by Caerleon) showed useful form at up to seven furlongs as a three-year-old in the latest season. Her third, a sister to Shalford called Corn Circle, is in training with Heaton-Ellis. *R. Hannon*

SHALHOLME 2 ch.f. (Apr 8) Fools Holme (USA) – Shalati (FR) (High Line 125) [1992 7s 5.7d] leggy filly: first reported foal: dam French 3-y-o 1m winner: always behind in maidens and Salisbury and Bath. *R. J. Holder* –

SHALL WE RUN 3 b.f. Hotfoot 126 – Sirnelta (FR) (Sir Tor) [1991 5m³ 5.2d 5.1g⁵ 6m⁶ 1992 8g] leggy, rather sparely-made filly: off course a year and bit backward, outpaced halfway when tailed off in handicap in July: should be suited by 7f +. *R. F. Johnson Houghton*

SHALOU 3 b.c. Forzando 122 – Axe Valley 89 (Royben 125) [1991 7m 6m* 6g 1992 8.3m⁴ 8f 8g 8d 8g] smallish, lengthy colt: inconsistent plater: easily best effort in 1992 when never-nearer fourth at Windsor in August: should stay 1¼m. *R. J. Hodges* — 49

SHAMAM (USA) 2 ch.c. (Apr 18) Shadeed (USA) 135 – Goodbye Shelley (FR) 116 (Home Guard (USA) 129) [1992 6s³ 7m² 7d⁴ 7.3g* 7g⁴] unfurnished colt: sixth foal: half-brother to 1990 2-y-o 7f winner Aghniyah (by Lyphard) and a winner in USA by Halo: dam, won from 7f to (Prix Marcel Boussac) 1m, is half-sister to Heighlin: fair form: comfortably won slowly-run nursery at Newbury in September, showing good turn of foot 1f out and never challenged: travelled strongly long way when creditable fourth in nursery at Ascot following month: will stay 1m: acts on good to firm and soft ground. *P. T. Walwyn* — 78

SHAMBO 5 b.h. Lafontaine (USA) 117 – Lucky Appeal 36 (Star Appeal 133) [1991 16g* 16g* 16.2s² 14g² 15.5m³ 20g 15.9m³ 16g³ 13.9g⁴ 16m³ 15.5d² 14v 1992 12d² 16.2d³ 12f⁵ 12f² 11.9g 13.3g* 15s⁵ 16d³ 12s] strong, quite attractive horse: usually impresses in appearance: moderate mover: very useful performer on his day: won slowly-run Ibn Bey Geoffrey Freer Stakes at Newbury in August by ½ length from Sapience: well below form in pattern company afterwards: had earlier been runner-up in John Porter Stakes at Newbury and listed race won by Jahafil at Newmarket: needs a test of stamina at 1½m and stays 2m: acts on any going. *C. E. Brittain* — 110

SHAMEEM (USA) 3 ch.f. Nureyev (USA) 131 – Just One More Time (USA) 65 (Raise A Native) [1991 NR 1992 10d 10.1g⁴ 12d] leggy filly: twelfth reported foal: closely related to a minor winner in North America and half-sister to several winners, notably Lucky Lucky Lucky (by Chieftain), a leading filly at both 2 and 3

Ibn Bey Geoffrey Freer Stakes, Newbury —
a slowly-run race sees Shambo (left) come from behind to break a losing sequence of fifteen and win his first pattern event

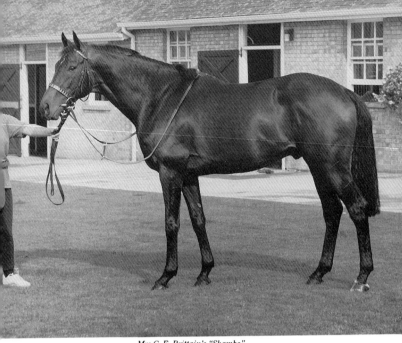

Mrs C. E. Brittain's "Shambo"

yrs in USA: dam won 3 of 7 races and twice stakes placed: fair form in 1¼m maidens: off course 2½ months, well beaten at Salisbury in August. *M. R. Stoute*

SHAMGAAN (USA)   2 b. or br.c. (May 31) Nureyev (USA) 131 – Fine Spirit **58** p (USA) (Secretariat (USA)) [1992 7g] $600,000Y: leggy colt: third foal: closely related to 2 colts by Nijinsky, including lightly-raced 4-y-o Ivanov: dam third in Breeders' Cup Juvenile Fillies and 7f stakes winner at 3 yrs: 13/2 and green, beaten around 9 lengths in minor event at Kempton in August, travelling keenly tracking leaders 5f, weakening and eased final 1f: seemed likely to improve. *M. R. Stoute*

SHAMISEN   2 ch.f. (May 3) Diesis 133 – Contralto 100 (Busted 134) [1992 7f* **86** 7g⁵ 6m²] 46,000Y: rangy filly: sister to one-time smart 6f (at 2 yrs) to 1m winner Enharmonic, closely related to very useful miler Soprano (by Kris) and half-sister to several winners, including 4-y-o miler Talent (by Clever Trick): dam, 2-y-o 6f and 7f winner, is closely related to smart Rhyme Royal: fairly useful performer: won 5-runner maiden at Yarmouth in June: improved form when 4 lengths second of 6 to Niche in Lowther Stakes at York, outpaced over 2f out then staying on: will prove better suited to 1m: yet to race on a soft surface. *C. E. Brittain*

SHAMROCK DANCER (IRE)   2 b.f. (Apr 9) Dance of Life (USA) – Practical   – 95 (Ballymore 123) [1992 7.1s 7d] IR 2,000Y: workmanlike filly: half-sister to several winners, including 3-y-o 1m (at 2 yrs) and 10.1f winner Shrewd Partner (by Ahonoora) and (at 7f in Ireland) Pot of Gold (by Rainbow Quest): dam Irish 9f and 1¼m winner, is well related: well beaten in maidens at Chepstow (flashed tail) and Brighton in September. *R. J. Baker*

SHAMSHOM AL ARAB (IRE)   4 gr.c. Glenstal (USA) 118 – Love Locket **41** (Levmoss 133) [1991 7f⁵ 10m⁴ 10g 9m 1992 a10g 10d 8.9m 9.7g* 12d³ 11.9g³ 10g] lengthy, angular colt: plating-class handicapper: won (for first time) at Folkestone in July: effective at strongly-run 1¼m and should stay beyond 1½m: yet to race on soft ground, has form on any other: below form in blinkers: held up and ideally suited by strongly-run event: has jinked S. Norton. *W. Carter*

SHANAKEE   5 b.g. Wassl 125 – Sheeog 80 (Reform 132) [1991 NR 1992 a6g a8g]   –
medium-sized gelding: on the downgrade. *K. S. Bridgwater*

SHANGHAI (USA)   3 b.c. Procida (USA) 129 – Korveya (USA) 116 **119**
(Riverman (USA) 131) [1991 5.5g² 6d* 6g⁵ 1992 8s⁵ 6g⁵ 8d* 8g* 9.2d³ 8s 8s⁵ 9f4]

For the second year running the Dubai Poule d'Essai des Poulains was won by a son of Korveya, Shanghai in the footsteps of his close relation Hector Protector. Watch out for her Nijinsky three-year-old Gioconda in 1993! It would be quite an achievement for Boutin to send out the as-yet unraced Gioconda to win a classic but, then again, Shanghai was hardly among the front-runners for the Poulains twelve months ago. After winning a six-runner maiden at Chantilly in June by four lengths, Shanghai was last of five in the Prix Cabourg at Deauville two months later and leg problems meant that he was not seen out again. Three runs before the Poulains in 1992 didn't mark him out as a classic winner although he won the Prix Montenica, a listed race at Maisons-Laffitte, in good style on the third of them. Shanghai was sent off at about 12/1 in the Poulains the following month, his trainer afterwards explaining that the most he could realistically hope for was a place. He should know what it takes to win the race having sent out L'Emigrant in 1983, Blushing John in 1988 and Linamix in 1990, as well as Hector Protector. An excellent turn of foot saw Shanghai add his name to the roll of honour. Held up last of nine early on, avoiding the trouble near at hand when Lion Cavern stumbled badly, Shanghai was still there leaving the final turn. He had begun to creep closer two furlongs out, where the sole British challenger Zaahi took up the running, then unleashed a rare turn of speed which wiped out a deficit of at least three lengths in the space of a furlong, bursting through on the rails to lead a hundred yards out in an effort which saw him home by a short neck from Rainbow Corner. Third and fourth, beaten another three quarters of a length and a length, were Lion Cavern and Zaahi.

Surprisingly, Shanghai did not win another race. He was off the course for over three months between running in the Prix Jean Prat and Prix du Moulin, both at Longchamp, easily the better of those efforts being his narrowly-beaten third of five to Kitwood in the Prix Jean Prat when he had to come from last in a very slowly-run race. A trip to Milan for the Premio Vittorio di Capua saw him trail in a distant fifth of six and it was November 22nd and the Hollywood Derby before Shanghai once again revealed the form he'd shown in May; with two lengths separating the first eight, Shanghai finished fourth to Paradise Creek, a place and a head behind Kitwood.

Shanghai is by Procida who won the Hollywood Derby, as well as the Prix de la Foret, in 1984. He stood for 5,000 dollars in Kentucky in 1992 when his other best known representative was probably the Prix de la Foret runner-up

Dubai Poule d'Essai des Poulains, Longchamp —
Shanghai's rare turn of foot denies Rainbow Corner and (No. 4) Lion Cavern

Mr S. S. Niarchos' "Shanghai"

Shanghai (USA)
(b.c. 1989)

	Procida (USA) (b or br 1981)	Mr Prospector (b 1970)	Raise A Native / Gold Digger
		With Distinction (b 1973)	Distinctive / Carrie's Rough
	Korveya (USA) (ch 1982)	Riverman (b 1969)	Never Bend / River Lady
		Konafa (b 1973)	Damascus / Royal Statute

Silicon Bavaria. Both sire and dam raced in the colours of Shanghai's owner-breeder Stavros Niarchos but Korveya changed hands late in 1989 and now belongs to Gerald Leigh. Her 1991 foal Dexter (by Green Dancer) failed to reach his reserve at 575,000 dollars at the latest Keeneland July Selected Yearling Sale. Korveya's successes with Hector Protector and Shanghai, her second and third foals, have both come via Mr Prospector stallions as Hector Protector was by Woodman. Korveya, winner of the nine-furlong Prix Chloe, is a half-sister to the high-class sprinter Proskona who was by Mr Prospector. Their dam Konafa, a 66/1-second in the One Thousand Guineas, is a half-sister to Akureyri and Awaasif and is out of a sister to the dam of Brief Truce. *F. Boutin, France*

SHANNON EXPRESS 5 gr.g. Magic Mirror 105 – Tatisha (Habitat 134) [1991 a8g2 a8g* a8g4 10.2g 8g6 9.7f* 10f 9.7m2 9.7g 1992 a8g a8g a8g6] leggy, angular, plain gelding: rated 72 on all-weather at 4 yrs: well below form at Southwell in 1992: effective from 1m to 11f: acts on firm going, unsuited by dead: ran well when blinkered: trained reappearance by M. Hammond. *E. J. Alston* –

SHANNON KING (IRE) 4 ch.g. Boyne Valley 107 – Miss Royal (King's Company 124) [1991 NR 1992 10d] half-brother to fair sprinter Royal Fan (by Taufan): dam unraced: tailed off in celebrity event at Wetherby in November. *J. G. FitzGerald* –

749

SHANTI FLYER (IRE)   3 b.f. Mister Majestic 122 – Dominia (Derring-Do 131)   –
[1991 7m 8g⁶ 8s⁵ 1992 10.1s 14.1g 14.1g³ 14.1g⁶ 14.1f³ 16m] quite attractive filly: has
quick action: plating-class form: trained until after second outing in 1992 by A. Hide:
stays 1¾m: blinkered last 2 starts, running creditably first occasion: sold 1,900 gns
Newmarket September Sales. *S. P. C. Woods*

SHAPELY DEB   3 gr.f. Beveled (USA) – Rustling 68 (Rusticaro (FR) 124) [1991   –
6m 6.1g⁶ 6m⁶ 7f 6g a8g a6g 1992 8s 8f 7.1m] leggy, sparely-made filly: poor form at 2
yrs, none in first half of 1992: should stay beyond 6f: blinkered first 2 starts at 2 yrs,
wore eyeshield final one. *D. R. Laing*

SHAPING UP (USA)   3 b.f. Storm Bird (CAN) 134 – Manicure Kit (USA) (J O
Tobin (USA) 130) [1991 6g² 7g⁶ 5.7f* 7m 1992 7m 8.3g 7s] quite attractive filly: good
walker: progressive form at 2 yrs: towards rear in 1992 in handicaps at Goodwood
(£8,100 event), Windsor (headstrong) and Salisbury: should stay 1m: acts on firm
going, never travelling well on soft: blinkered final start each season, running
creditably at 2 yrs: sold 8,400 gns Newmarket December Sales. *I. A. Balding*

SHARDRA   3 b.f. Sharrood (USA) 124 – Dragonist 82 (Dragonara Palace (USA)   44
115) [1991 NR 1992 10f³ 15.1m⁵ 9.2g³ a10g⁴ 8g⁴] leggy filly: fifth foal: half-sister to
useful sprinter Come On Chase Me (by Sharpo) and middle-distance winners by
Ardross and Homing: dam winning sprinter: poor maiden: sold out of M. Camacho's
stable 2,700 gns Doncaster August Sales after penultimate start: fair fourth in
Leicester claimer in September: stays 9.2f: races prominently: refused to enter
stalls final appearance. *M. F. Barraclough*

SHARE A MOMENT (CAN)   2 b.g. (Mar 6) Timeless Moment (USA) – Silver   68 p
Slippers (USA) (Silver Series (USA)) [1992 7g⁶ 7g⁴ 7.5m⁶ 7g] $25,000Y: sturdy,
good-quartered gelding: sort to carry condition: fourth reported foal: half-brother to
3 winners in North America: dam, third once from 4 starts in USA, is daughter of
Oaks third Ludham: sire very smart at up to 1m: fair form in varied events:
creditable seventh in Leicester nursery final outing, never getting into race: will be
well suited by at least 1m: may well prove capable of better. *M. R. Stoute*

SHAREEF STAR   4 b.g. Shareef Dancer (USA) 135 – Ultra Vires 87 (High Line   –
125) [1991 10g 13.1f 1992 14.1d 18.1g⁶] leggy gelding: no worthwhile form on flat:
modest winning hurdler in 1991/2. *M. Blanshard*

SHAREEK (USA)   2 b.c. (May 12) Alysheba (USA) – All Rainbows (USA) (Bold   75 p
Hour) [1992 7d² 7m²] leggy colt: has scope: moderate mover: eleventh foal: half-
brother to several winners, notably champion 3-y-o filly (won Kentucky Derby)
Winning Colors (by Caro): dam, half-sister to champion filly Chris Evert, won three
8.5f stakes races: sire top-class middle-distance colt: runner-up in maidens at
Yarmouth, travelling smoothly both times and staying on well: will be well suited by
1¼m: sure to win races. *M. R. Stoute*

SHARE HOLDER   4 b.f. Shareef Dancer (USA) 135 – Silver Dollar 106 (Shirley   32
Heights 130) [1991 NR 1992 8.5f 7m⁵ 6f 6h⁵ 9.7g 8g⁶ a7s 7.6m 10.1d 9.7g² 16g 10.2s]
leggy, plain filly: first foal: dam 6f winner at 2 yrs but rather disappointing at 3 yrs
(should have stayed 1½m): poor and inconsistent maiden: stays 1¼m: often
bandaged. *Miss Gay Kelleway*

SHAR EMBLEM   4 b. or br.f. Shardari 134 – Lady's Flag (USA) (Fifth Marine   52
(USA)) [1991 11.5f 10.1f⁶ 12g⁴ a12g⁵ a13g a16g* a13g⁵ 1992 a16g⁵ a16g⁴ 12f⁵ 20m
15.4h² 18.2g] lengthy, rather sparely-made filly: moderate mover: modest handicapper: sold to join B. Forsey 4,200 gns Ascot July Sales: stays 2m: acts on firm
ground and equitrack, yet to race on a soft surface. *S. Dow*

SHARISA   2 b.f. (May 7) Bairn (USA) 126 – Kissimmee (FR) (Petingo 135) [1992   41
5f⁶ 5m⁵ 5.1m⁵] 1,000F: leggy, sparely-made filly: half-sister to several winners here
and abroad, including fairly useful 1991 2-y-o 5f winner Bit-A-Magic (by Beveled)
and fair 1990 2-y-o 7f winner Recalde (by King of Spain): dam placed at 1½m in
French Provinces: poor form in maiden and sellers: sold 900 gns Doncaster June
Sales and won over 5f and 6f in Belgium. *J. Berry*

SHARJAH (USA)   2 b.c. (Apr 17) Nijinsky (CAN) 138 – Office Wife (USA)   92 p
(Secretariat (USA)) [1992 8.1s* 8.1d³ 10g³] $475,000Y: rangy colt: has scope: fourth
foal: closely related to useful 3-y-o winner at about 1¼m Polish Blue (by Danzig)
and Irish 1½m and 13f winner Green Marine (by Green Dancer) and half-brother to
a winner in North America: dam winning (and graded-placed) half-sister to Golden
Fleece: fairly useful performer: won minor event at Sandown in August: ran very
well when over 3 lengths third of 9 to Bob's Return in listed race at Newmarket in
October, final start: will be well suited by 1½m: likely to do better. *M. A. Jarvis*

SHARLING   3 gr.f. Sharrood (USA) 124 – Mrs Darling 70 (Mummy's Pet 125)   **71**
[1991 7m⁶ 7m⁶ 5g a7g 1992 6m⁴ 6.1g* 6m 6d 5.1g³ 7g 6.1g] rather leggy, lengthy
filly: fair handicapper: won at Chester in May: behind last 2 starts: will prove better
at 6f than 5f: best efforts on good ground: sold 3,100 gns Newmarket Autumn Sales.
J. H. M. Gosden

SHARPALTO   5 br.g. Noalto 120 – Sharp Venita 84 (Sharp Edge 123) [1991 8g⁶ **103**
6g⁴ 7m⁴ 7m⁴ 8.2g 6m⁶ 7m⁴ 7g³ 7.1s³ 7g 7g 8m 7d 7m* 7m 7.6d* 8g 1992 8g 7g⁵ 7s*
7d 7f³ 7m* 7f⁵ 7m⁴ 7m² 7m⁶ 7d⁴ 8m⁶ 7s* 7d* 8m⁴] workmanlike gelding:
progressed into a useful handicapper for new trainer: won twice at Newcastle in the
spring but in the form of his life in the autumn, following up success at Ayr with
most impressive 3½-length win from Little Bean in £50,000 Festival Handicap at
Ascot: effective at 7f and 1m: acts on good to firm and soft ground (creditable efforts
at the time on firm): sometimes slowly away: held up and has excellent turn of foot:
effective blinkered or not: suitable mount for 7-lb claimer: sold 52,000 gns
Newmarket Autumn Sales. *Mrs M. Reveley*

SHARP AS YOU LIKE   3 ch.g. Risk Me (FR) 127 – Debutina Park 87 (Averof   –
123) [1991 5f⁴ 5.1m⁴ 5f⁵ 7g 5d 5d 8m 1992 10d 7.5m a5g⁴ 5m] lengthy gelding: poor
mover: rated 59 at 2 yrs: no form in 1992: has been tried in blinkers/visor: sold 1,350
gns Doncaster June Sales. *J. Etherington*

SHARP DANCE   3 b.f. Dance of Life (USA) – Sharp Jose (USA) (Sharpen Up 127)   **41**
[1991 7g 1992 10s 7d³ 8m⁴ 9.7g 7g 8d⁶ a8g⁵ a10g] unfurnished filly: has a long stride:
inconsistent maiden: somewhat headstrong, seems best at 7f/1m: acts on good to
firm and dead ground. *B. Smart*

SHARP DREAM   4 ch.f. Dominion 123 – Sharp Jose (USA) (Sharpen Up 127)   **76**
[1991 9g* 9g⁶ 8d 11.7g 1992 10g 10d⁶ 8.1d⁵ 9g* 8g⁴ 10m 9s] tall, useful-looking filly:
has rather round action: won maiden at Longchamp as 3-y-o when trained by J.
Pease: fair handicapper: flattered when fifth in minor event at Sandown in August:
just got up at Kempton (apprentices) in September: stayed 1¼m: acted on good to
firm and dead ground, ran moderately on soft: sold in foal to Nicholas 7,000 gns
Newmarket December Sales. *B. Smart*

SHARP FAIRY   4 ch.f. Sharpo 132 – Flying Fairy 79 (Bustino 136) [1991 NR 1992   –
5g 8.3s 9s] smallish, short-legged filly: poor mover: first foal: dam, twice-raced
maiden, is daughter of 1000 Guineas winner Fairy Footsteps: no show in maidens in
the autumn. *A. Bailey*

SHARP GAZELLE   2 ch.f. (May 7) Beveled (USA) – Shadha 57 (Shirley Heights   **57**
130) [1992 5.7m* 6g⁵ 5.7m 7.3s] 800Y: leggy filly: fourth foal: half-sister to 3-y-o
Vellandrucha (by Cragador) and a winner in Italy: dam ran twice at 2 yrs: plating-
class form: backed at long odds, narrowly won maiden auction at Bath in July, off
bridle at halfway, leading close home: stiff tasks in nurseries, struggling long way
from home at Newbury last time: should stay 7f. *B. Smart*

SHARP IMP   2 b.c. (Apr 22) Sharpo 132 – Implore 71 (Ile de Bourbon (USA) 133)   –
[1992 5m 5m 6d⁶] 3,600Y: workmanlike colt: first foal: dam, maiden, stayed 1¼m, is
half-sister to high-class milers Achieved and Final Straw: soundly beaten in maiden
events in midsummer. *J. Sutcliffe*

Festival Handicap, Ascot—Little Bean and nineteen others are routed by Sharpalto

Tennents Scottish Classic, Ayr—from left to right;
Inner City, Sharpitor, Alflora and Ile de Chypre

SHARP ISSUE (USA)   4 ch.g. Diesis 133 – Concentrate (USA) (Broadway Forli   –
(USA)) [1991 11m 12m 10.2m a12g a14g 12m a12g a14g⁶ a16g 1992 a12g] big, lengthy
gelding: has a markedly round action: second foal: dam unraced: no sign of ability:
tried blinkered. *M. C. Chapman*

SHARPITOR (IRE)   3 b.c. Montelimar (USA) 122 – Flaxen Hair (Thatch (USA) **113**
136) [1991 7g³ 7.5f* 7m* 1992 8.1g³ 8.1m* 8m³ 10d³ 10m* 10s²] sturdy, close-
coupled colt: improved virtually with every start of his career: won £18,300
handicap at Haydock in May and Group 3 event (held Alflora by a neck) at Ayr in
July: neck second of 7 to Great Palm in Prix Guillaume d'Ornano at Deauville in
August: very useful form on good to firm and soft ground: has good
turn of foot: visored last 2 starts: game: sent to race in Saudi Arabia. *W. Jarvis*

SHARP N' SMOOTH   5 ch.h. Sharpo 132 – Winning Look 71 (Relko 136) [1991   **76**
a7g⁶ 8s⁴ 6s⁶ 7m³ 8d⁴ 8.2m* 8.5m 8g 7m⁶ 7g 8m⁵ 8.1m* 7d⁶ 1992 8d³ 7d⁴ 8g² 8s⁴]
close-coupled horse: poor mover: fair handicapper: in frame in 3 valuable races in
the spring: off course 5½ months, fair fourth in £7,900 event at Newbury in October: better suited by 1m than shorter: acts on good to firm and soft ground: has run
well for apprentice. *R. Hannon*

SHARP PRINCE   3 ch.c. Sharpo 132 – Jungle Queen (Twilight Alley 133) [1991   **89**
7.1d* 1992 8d 8g³ 8.9g] big, useful-looking colt: fairly useful performer: first past
post in close finish to handicap at Newmarket, but demoted to third for interference:
front rank 7f when well beaten in competitive York handicap later in May: stays 1m:
joined P. Cole but didn't appear for him and was sold to join S. Kettlewell for only
3,000 gns Newmarket Autumn Sales. *H. R. A. Cecil*

SHARP PROD (USA)   2 ch.c. (May 12) Sharpo 132 – Gentle Persuasion **110**
95 (Bustino 136) [1992 5.2m³ 5d* 5m* 6m* 6f* 6s* 6g³ 7.3s]

The Queen had an 'annus horribilis', as she described it, and the successes of her racehorses made headlines that were more agreeable than most
that featured her family in 1992. The Queen's racing fortunes have been in
decline for many years—she was leading owner twice in the 'fifties—but she
had one of her most successful years for some time in 1992, her best of all as
an owner/breeder in terms of races won. Colour Sergeant provided her with a

Moet & Chandon-Rennen, Baden-Baden—a fifth win for Sharp Prod

Royal Ascot success in the Royal Hunt Cup, and another fairly valuable handicap victory on Diamond Day at Ascot in July; Top Register won the White Rose Stakes at Ascot in April; the fairly useful Piquant held his form well in handicaps through the summer, winning at Haydock and Newcastle; the improved Whitechapel won three handicaps in the spring; and the front-running Talent also chalked up three victories. All were trained by Lord Huntingdon as was the Queen's most prolific scorer, the genuine and progressive two-year-old Sharp Prod.

The Queen hasn't won a pattern race in Britain since Height of Fashion's victory in the Princess of Wales's Stakes in 1982, but Sharp Prod won in listed and pattern company abroad and was also a good third in the Group 2 Mill Reef Stakes at Newbury in October, keeping on well to be beaten only half a length and two by Forest Wind and Marina Park. Sharp Prod won five in a row before the Mill Reef, most recently the Group 2 Moet & Chandon-Rennen at Baden-Baden in September, when he beat the French-trained Glorieux Dancer by three quarters of a length with the Richmond Stakes winner Son Pardo fourth. Sharp Prod's winning run started in a maiden race at Epsom in June, continued later in the same month in a minor event at Windsor, and was completed by successes in a nursery at Lingfield and the Criterium de Bequet at Bordeaux, both in July.

Sharp Prod (USA) (ch.c. May 12, 1990)	Sharpo (ch 1977)	Sharpen Up (ch 1969)	Atan	Rocchetta
		Moiety Bird (ch 1971)	Falcon	Gaska
	Gentle Persuasion (ch 1984)	Bustino (b 1971)	Busted	Ship Yard
		Harp Strings (br 1978)	Luthier	Gilding

The rather leggy Sharp Prod, who is a moderate mover, is the second foal and second winner—following the modest sprinter Prompting (by Primo Dominie)—of the quite useful Gentle Persuasion, who gained her only victory in the Kingsclere Stakes at Newbury on her racecourse debut and afterwards made the frame in the Princess Margaret Stakes and the Rockfel Stakes. Gentle Persuasion, by St Leger winner Bustino out of the useful Harp Strings who stayed nine furlongs, was suited by a mile as a three-year-old. Sharp Prod failed to confirm an impression that he'd be effective at longer distances than six furlongs when well beaten in the Horris Hill Stakes on his final start. He acts on any going. *Lord Huntingdon*

SHARP REVIEW (IRE) 4 b.g. Sharpen Up 127 – Pleasant Review (USA) (The **94** Minstrel (CAN) 135) [1991 10g² 8f³ 1992 10s⁴ 7g* 8.5g³ 9g* 7g³ 8s 8s 8d] robust Irish gelding: third foal: dam (ran once in Ireland at 2 yrs) winner at up to 1¼m in USA at 3 yrs: successful in 1992 in maiden at Fairyhouse and handicap at

Joseph Sebag's "Sheba Dancer"

Leopardstown and good third in Curragh handicap: well beaten last 3 starts, pacemaker twice including in Queen Elizabeth II Stakes: stays 9f: best efforts on good ground: has been gelded. *D. K. Weld, Ireland*

SHARP THISTLE 6 b.m. Sharpo 132 – Marphousha (FR) (Shirley Heights 130) **45**
[1991 NR 1992 9.7v a10g⁴] leggy, light-framed mare: moderate mover: rated 69 as 4-y-o: only modest nowadays: stays 1½m: probably acts on any going. *W. J. Musson*

SHARPTINO 3 ch.c. Bustino 136 – Sharper Still (Sharpen Up 127) [1991 NR 1992 **63**
7f² 7.1f³ 6m² a7g] smallish colt: sixth foal: half-brother to several winners, including very useful 1991 3-y-o Jimmy Barnie (by Local Suitor), sprint winner at 2 yrs: dam never ran: placed in maidens in early-summer: well beaten in Lingfield handicap in December: will prove suited by 7f +. *R. Akehurst*

SHARP TO OBLIGE 5 ch.g. Dublin Taxi – Please Oblige (Le Levanstell 122) **–**
[1991 NR 1992 a8g] rather angular gelding: rated 54 when placed in maidens at 3 yrs: visored, last in handicap at Southwell in January: should stay 1¼m. *R. M. Whitaker*

SHARP TOP 4 b.f. Sharpo 132 – Two High 89 (High Top 131) [1991 5f⁴ 6.9m 11d **62**
10.1s⁵ a12g³ 1992 a12g³ a12g⁵ a12g⁶ 10.1s² 11.9d* 10d⁵ 13d³ 11.8m 12d² 12g⁵ **a39**
14.1m² 14.1g³ 12d² a12s 16.4m* 14.1d 15.4g³ 12.1s 12s² 12v* 11.5d a12g] tall, leggy filly: modest handicapper: won at Brighton in April and at Folkestone in August (apprentices) and October (claiming event): best with testing conditions at 1½m, and stays 2m: acts on good to firm and heavy ground and on equitrack, seemingly not on fibresand: tough: won novice hurdle in November. *M. J. Ryan*

754

SHARQUIN 5 b.h. Indian King (USA) 128 – Lady of The Land 75 (Wollow 132) **35**
[1991a11g 10.2s⁶ 10s 10m³ 10f⁴ 10d 10m³ 12g² 10m⁵ 12m 10.1m³9.9f 12f10g⁴ 12.3m²
10.1m⁴ 11m⁴ 10.5m 9m 1992 12g⁶ 10d 9.9g 11m⁴ 9.9m⁵ 10.5m² 9f⁶ 10d 11f⁶ 10.3m⁶
10.1m⁵ 12m⁴ 11f 10.5g 11g⁵ 10.1m] close-coupled horse: carries plenty of condition:
inconsistent handicapper, without a win for 37 starts: stays 1½m: best on a sound
surface: has run creditably blinkered, below form visored once. *M. Brittain*

SHARRIBA 3 gr.f. Sharrood (USA) 124 – Alsiba 68 (Northfields (USA)) [1991 –
7.1s³ 7g⁴ 7.1m² 7.1s² 7.1d² 1992 8m 8.5d⁴ 10s 12d⁵ 10.1d⁶] tall, rather leggy filly:
modest maiden at best: stays 8.5f: acts on good to firm and soft ground: sold to join
G. Humphrey 3,200 gns Newmarket Autumn Sales. *D. R. C. Elsworth*

SHARRO 2 gr.g. (Mar 2) Sharrood (USA) 124 – Sarah Gillian (USA) (Zen (USA)) **68**
[1992 5g⁶ 5g 5m³ 5g⁵ 7f³ 7g 8m⁶ a8g³ a8g⁵ a8g] leggy, close-coupled gelding: fourth a58
foal: half-brother to 3-y-o 1¼m winner Slight Risk (by Risk Me): dam well beaten:
modest maiden: suited by a test of stamina: below best on all-weather surfaces:
blinkered final start. *P. A. Kelleway*

SHATI (IRE) 3 b. or br.c. Last Tycoon 131 – Shurooq (USA) 94 (Affirmed (USA)) **95**
[1991 6f³ 5f* 5.3g² 6m² 1992 6s⁴ 6.1g⁴ 5g³ 7.3g5 8m 8g 7m² 7.3g⁵ 8g² 8d²] leggy,
useful-looking colt: useful handicapper, generally consistent: second in £9,200
event at Ascot (to Gymcrak Premiere) and minor event at Yarmouth last 2 starts:
better at 1m than shorter: probably acts on any going. *H. Thomson Jones*

SHAURNI GIRL 4 ch.f. Precocious 126 – Crockfords Green 73 (Roan Rocket –
128) [1991 a8g² a12g a12g⁵ 1992 a10g] rated 53 late on at 3 yrs: well beaten in
handicap at Lingfield in January: stays 1m. *R. V. King*

SHAWINIGA 6 b.m. Lyphard's Wish (FR) 124 – Shining Bright (USA) (Bold **37**
Bidder) [1991 8.2d 12m 5m⁵ 8.2f² 7.1d³ 8.1m⁴ 10m⁴ 7m 8f⁵ 8m⁵ 8m⁴ 1992 12.2g 9d⁴]
sparely-made mare: consistent handicapper at 5 yrs: not seen out until September
1992, creditable fourth at Redcar: stays 1¼m: acts on any going. *L. Lungo*

SHAWWAL (USA) 5 b. or br.h. Shirley Heights 130 – Lady of Camelot (FR) –
(Bolkonski 134) [1991 13.8m 11.1s 1992 14.1d] lengthy, workmanlike horse: has a
quick action: no worthwhile form on flat since 3 yrs: winning selling hurdler in
1991/2. *R. O'Leary*

SHAYNA MAIDEL 3 ch.f. Scottish Reel 123 – Revisit 86 (Busted 134) [1991 7m **39**
7m a8g 1992 11.1m⁶ 8m 12.3d² 15.1g³ 12.3m³ 12m⁶ 12.1s⁴] sturdy filly: poor maiden:
below best last 2 starts: stays 15f: acts on good to firm and dead ground: sold to join
Miss H. Knight 900 gns Ascot December Sales. *M. Bell*

SHEBA DANCER (FR) 3 b.f. Fabulous Dancer (USA) 124 – Elisheba 104 **117**
(Nonoalco (USA) 131) [1991 8v³ 1992 8s* 8v* 9.2g* 10g 10.5g² 10s² 9d³] 134,000
francs Y: half-sister to several winners in France, notably useful 7f winner Elisharp
(by Sharpman): dam lightly-raced 2-y-o 6f winner, out of half-sister to Glad Rags:
smart French filly: successful early in season in minor event at Evry, listed race at
Saint-Cloud and Group 3 Prix Vanteaux at Longchamp: placed afterwards in Prix de
Diane at Chantilly (best effort, length second to Jolypha), very valuable restricted
race at Deauville (to Urban Sea) and All Along Stakes at Laurel (over 5 lengths third
to Marble Maiden): stays 10.5f: acts on heavy going. *E. Lellouche, France*

SHEBL (USA) 2 b.c. (Feb 26) Green Desert (USA) 127 – Christmas Bonus **89**
(USA) (Key To The Mint (USA)) [1992 6d² 6m 7g* 7m³ 7.1d 8.1g² 7d⁴ 9v³ 10g⁴]
$350,000Y: leggy colt: has scope: good mover: half-brother to 1986 2-y-o 7f winner
Yaqut (by Northern Dancer) and 2 winners in North America, notably Santa Anita
Oaks-placed Bright Candles (by El Gran Senor): dam, useful winner at up to 1m, is
out of half-sister to dam of Alydar: fairly useful performer: won maiden at Wolverhampton in July: ran creditably in frame in listed races at Milan and Newmarket last
2 starts: suited by a good test of stamina: probably acts on any going: visored (ran
poorly) fifth outing: none too consistent. *M. R. Stoute*

SHECANGOSAH 3 b.f. Sulaafah (USA) 119 – Hagen's Bargain 62§ (Mount –
Hagen (FR) 127) [1991 NR 1992 10.2f 10g 7m 7g] unfurnished filly: third living foal:
dam 2-y-o 5f seller winner who probably stayed 9f: little sign of ability, including in
sellers. *R. J. Hodges*

SHEDAD (USA) 4 ch.g. Diesis 133 – Love's Reward (Nonoalco (USA) 131) [1991 **48**
8.2d⁵ 6m 6m 6d³ 5f⁵ 6g 6m⁶ 5g 5s² a5g6 a5g⁶ a7g⁴ 1992 a7g a7g* a6g⁶ a7g³ a7g⁴
a6g³] rangy gelding: has a round action: plating-class handicapper: won maiden
claimer at Southwell in January: stays 7f: probably acts on any turf going, also on
fibresand: headstrong: blinkered once earlier in career: sent to race in Mauritius. *T.
D. Barron*

SHEER ECSTASY 2 b.c. (Mar 17) Sure Blade (USA) 130 – Height of Passion **46** (Shirley Heights 130) [1992 7g 8.1s 8d a8g] 25,000Y: lengthy colt: poor mover: fourth foal: half-brother to very useful middle-distance stayer Warm Feeling (by Kalaglow) and a winner in Germany: dam ran 3 times: poor form, well beaten, in maidens: sold out of R. Charlton's stable 1,000 gns Ascot September Sales after second outing: ran far too freely in blinkers next time. *P. M. McEntee*

SHEIKH ALBADOU 4 b.c. Green Desert (USA) 127 – Sanctuary (Welsh **128** Pageant 132) [1991 6f* 7g² 6g* 7g⁴ 5g* 6f² 5d² a6f* 1992 5f* 6g³ 8m⁴ 6d* a7f² a6f⁴]

The scale of European involvement in races in North America has done much to further the cause of international racing. Much more, it has to be said, than the scale of North American involvement in races in Europe, or anywhere else for that matter. North American trainers have provided only ten runners in major flat races in Europe in the past four years. The Irish Two Thousand Guineas winner Fourstars Allstar has been the only North-American-trained winner in that period, though the Canadian sprinter Zadracarta came within a short head of victory in the 1989 Prix de l'Abbaye de Longchamp. The presence of North-American based sprinters in the Nunthorpe in the past three years—Mr Nickerson in 1990, Klassy Briefcase in 1991 and Diamonds Galore in 1992—has been very welcome but has owed a good deal to the behind-the-scenes efforts of race sponsors Keeneland. The seemingly-encouraging trend of 1991, when Fourstars Allstar, Irish Linnet (Irish One Thousand), Klassy Briefcase, Forty Niner Days (Queen Elizabeth II Stakes), El Senor (Prix de l'Arc) and Fire The Groom (Prix de l'Opera) ran in Europe, wasn't continued in the latest season when Bold N'Flashy (Prix de l'Abbaye) was the only other North American-trained challenger, though Fourstars Allstar was for a long time an intended runner in the Queen Elizabeth II Stakes. There are, of course, good reasons why many fewer American-based horses take on the Europeans in their own backyard than vice-versa—among them the level of prize money, the fact that most of America's top races are run on dirt, and that certain medications used in North America are not permitted in Europe—but if American horses started running over here in numbers which were on a par with Europeans' participation in North America's top races, evaluating and comparing American and European form each year could be done with more confidence.

Take the latest Breeders' Cup, for example, for which European stables provided no fewer than twenty-one runners. For only the second time in the nine-year history of the Breeders' Cup, the European challenge failed to yield a single winner. Strong on quality as well as quantity, the European team was virtually whitewashed, only Irish-trained Brief Truce and French-trained Jolypha reaching a place, in the Mile and Classic respectively. Home advantage will always give the Americans the edge in the Breeders' Cup, as will weight of numbers, but the Europeans faced added difficulties in 1992 when the Breeders' Cup meeting was staged at Gulfstream Park in Florida. Long journeys aren't so big a hurdle nowadays but the unaccustomed heat and humidity of Florida, and to a lesser extent the unusually tricky Gulfstream Park circuit, almost certainly contributed to the downfall of some of Europe's best. The Europeans also came away empty-handed when the Breeders' Cup meeting was staged at Gulfstream Park in 1989; the climate seems partic-

King's Stand Stakes, Ascot—little more than a length separates the first seven, with Sheikh Albadou (second right) a half-length winner

*Haydock Park Sprint Cup—the best sprint performance of 1992,
as Sheikh Albadou beats Mr Brooks and the rest*

ularly hostile for horses used to Europe. Some American opinion would have it that the 1992 Breeders' Cup results proved conclusively the supremacy of their horses. Perhaps they did—on home ground in conditions unfriendly to the visitors. The form of the American horses seemed to stand up reasonably well with fancied horses winning or going close, except in the Sprint, and it's hard to argue that the programme provided anything less than a fair test on the day for them. But, so far as the Europeans were concerned, it would be dangerous to take a single day's results out of context. As usual nowadays, European-trained horses did well over the year in North America, particularly on the turf, and the Europeans need feel no inferiority judged on the overall performance of their raiders. A European version of the Breeders' Cup is being mooted and, if it comes to fruition, it will be a great spectacle to see some of North America's best put to the test each year at Longchamp or Ascot.

The European challenge on Breeders' Cup day is no longer largely restricted to the two races on grass, as it was in the 'eighties when Lashkari and Pebbles won the Breeders' Cup Turf and Last Tycoon and Miesque (twice) won the Breeders' Cup Mile. In the 'nineties, In The Wings and Miss Alleged have continued Europe's fine record in the Turf, and Royal Academy has won the Mile, but there have been victories too on the dirt for Arazi (Breeders' Cup Juvenile) and Sheikh Albadou (Breeders' Cup Sprint). Sheikh Albadou's programme as a four-year-old was mapped out with one eye on another crack at the Breeders' Cup Sprint which he won comfortably at Churchill Downs in 1991. Sheikh Albadou was the only European-trained runner in the Breeders' Cup Sprint on that occasion, but in the latest edition he was joined by the July Cup and Prix de l'Abbaye winner Mr Brooks and the good-class Elbio, both also trained in Britain. Sadly, Mr Brooks suffered a fatal fall but both Sheikh Albadou (fourth) and Elbio (fifth) ran fair races behind the American five-year-old Thirty Slews. Sheikh Albadou had appeared to run an excellent trial for the Breeders' Cup in the seven-furlong Grade 1 Vosburgh Stakes at Belmont Park in early-October when second, beaten three quarters of a length, to the high-class Rubiano. Sheikh Albadou started second favourite behind Rubiano at Gulfstream Park but, running on bute for the first time in his life because of the 'fast' dirt surface at Gulfstream Park, he never held out hopes in the closing stages of repeating his 1991 victory, though he finished closer to third-placed Rubiano than at Belmont Park.

Sheikh Albadou's four-year-old career established him as the best sprinter on this side of the Atlantic. He returned to action, bandaged behind but looking in tremendous shape, at Royal Ascot where he won a non-vintage King's Stand Stakes; quickening to lead approaching the distance, Sheikh Albadou always looked likely to hold on and won by half a length from Mr Brooks, with about two lengths covering the first seven home. Sheikh Albadou met Mr Brooks on his two other outings in sprinting company in Europe, in the July Cup and the Haydock Park Sprint Cup. Mr Brooks turned the tables at Newmarket where the pair were separated by the three-year-old Pursuit of Love in a photo-finish, the smooth-travelling Sheikh Albadou looking likely to score impressively for a long way but being caught in the final fifty or sixty yards after challenging and taking a decisive-looking lead entering the final furlong. Sheikh Albadou beat Mr Brooks decisively by two and a half lengths at Haydock in his last race in Europe, surviving a stewards' inquiry after crossing Mr Brooks when veering right after taking the lead. The first two were well clear of third- and fourth-placed Wolfhound and Shalford, the winner giving by our reckoning the best performance seen in a sprint all year in Europe.

Sheikh Albadou (b.c. 1988)	Green Desert (USA) (b 1983)	Danzig (b 1977)	Northern Dancer
			Pas de Nom
		Foreign Courier (b 1979)	Sir Ivor
			Courtly Dee
	Sanctuary (ch 1979)	Welsh Pageant (b 1966)	Tudor Melody
			Picture Light
		Hiding Place (ch 1963)	Doutelle
			Jojo

Sheikh Albadou was an impressive individual as a three-year-old—strong and good-bodied, a typical sprinting type—but he developed into a horse of even more substance, rippling with muscle, with another year on him. He had seemed not to stay much beyond six furlongs at three but saw out the mile of the Sussex Stakes as a four-year-old, coming about three lengths fourth to Marling after taking a hefty bump from Selkirk over a furlong out. Sheikh Albadou's pedigree was dealt with fully in *Racehorses of 1991*. His sire Green Desert was runner-up in the Two Thousand Guineas but gained his finest victories over sprint distances, winning the July Cup and the Sprint Cup at Haydock. Sheikh Albadou's unraced dam Sanctuary, whose third winner he is, is a daughter of the Nell Gwyn winner Hiding Place, dam of nine winners including those genuine and consistent stayers Smuggler and Little Wolf. Sheikh Albadou's great grandam Jojo also had an outstanding breeding record, producing the Sussex Stakes winner Queen's Hussar among other good winners. Sheikh Albadou, who acted on firm and dead ground, was thoroughly genuine. He should prove popular as a stallion when he starts his new career at the Gainsborough Stud in Kentucky in 1993. *A. A. Scott*

SHEILA'S SECRET (IRE)   2 b.f. (Jan 17) Bluebird (USA) 125 – Exemplary 106   **92**
(Sovereign Lord 120) [1992 5s 5d* 5m3 5d3 5f6 5m2 6m4 5g* 6g5 5g* 5m* 5g]
10,000Y: quite good-topped filly: has a quick action: half-sister to numerous winners here and abroad, including (at 6f and 1¼m) Run For Ever (by Runnett): dam best at 5f: fairly useful performer: had a very good season, winning maiden at Kempton in April and nurseries at Redcar, Sandown and at Newmarket (by 2 lengths from Lord Olivier, showing improved form) in early-autumn: below form in Cornwallis Stakes at Ascot in October: best form at 5f: acts on firm and dead ground: blinkered (ran creditably) sixth start: sometimes bandaged behind. *W. Carter*

SHE LOOKS ON HIGH (USA)   3 b.f. Secreto (USA) 128 – Life's Light (USA)   **71**
(Mjestic Light (USA)) [1991 NR 1992 7d5 7g4] big, lengthy filly: second foal: dam

won 8 races, including minor stakes, at up to 9f at 4 and 5 yrs: fair form in maidens at Newmarket and Newbury in April: will be well suited by 1m+: seemed likely to improve again. *B. Hanbury*

SHEMAKA (IRE)   2 b.f. (Mar 21) Nishapour (FR) 125 – Shashna (Blakeney 126) **111** p [1992 8g4 8s* 9d*] third foal: half-sister to 2 winners in France: dam twice-raced half-sister to Grand Prix de Saint-Cloud winner Shakapour and to dam of Shahrastani: progressive filly: won minor event at Deauville in August and Prix de Conde (by ¾ length from Marchand de Sable) at Longchamp in October: will stay 1½m. *A. de Royer-Dupre, France*

SHENTIT (FR)   4 b.f. Shirley Heights 130 – Porte Des Lilas (FR) (Sharpman   – 124) [1991 12m 14.1m6 17.1m* 18.1m* 17.2g 1992 18.1g 16.1g 16.5g 14.6s6 16d] big, rangy filly: rated 77 at 3 yrs, but reportedly suffered an injury when brought down final start: no worthwhile form in 1992: stays 2¼m: acts on good to firm ground: blinkered last 2 starts: sold 6,400 gns Newmarket December Sales. *J. L. Dunlop*

SHERIFFMUIR   3 b.c. Shirley Heights 130 – Tartan Pimpernel 109 (Blakeney   **99** 126) [1991 NR 1992 12m* 12f* 12m4 12m6] rangy colt with scope: half-brother to several winners, including 4-y-o 1m winner Colour Sergeant (by Green Desert), fairly useful 1983 2-y-o 7f winner Elusive (by Little Current) and useful juvenile hurdler Hopscotch (by Dominion): dam, half-sister to Dunfermline, won May Hill and Galtres Stakes: useful performer: impressive winner of maiden at Beverley and minor event at Doncaster in June: best effort when 3¼ lengths fourth of 6 to Spring in minor event at Newmarket, wandering under pressure: unsuited by slowly-run race later in July, and would have been well suited by further: raced only on top-of-the-ground: swished tail last 2 starts: has reportedly been retired. *L. M. Cumani*

SHERINGA   3 b.f. Tout Ensemble – Liza Paul 66 (Ron 103) [1991 7.1s3 1992 10s3   **76** 10.2m6 10s 12d2 12s* 12d3] workmanlike filly: fair handicapper: won at Salisbury in September by 5 lengths, held up, leading over 2f out and soon clear: ran creditably at Goodwood 8 days later: better at 1½m than shorter: acts on soft ground, below best on good to firm. *G. B. Balding*

SHERRAA (USA)   3 ch.f. Polish Navy (USA) – Ambry (USA) (Gallant Man)   **48** [1991 NR 1992 12m5 11.9f5] $70,000Y: lengthy, sparely-made filly: eighth foal: half-sister to 5 winners, including 1987 2-y-o 1m winner Church Lyric (by Stop The Music), later successful in USA, and good American 2-y-o filly Wonders Delight (by Icecapade): dam won small race and is half-sister to Hollywood Derby winner Poleax: form in maidens in May only when staying-on fifth at Beverley on debut: sold 5,000 gns Newmarket July Sales. *M. A. Jarvis*

SHE'S A BREEZE   2 ch.f. (Mar 21) Crofthall 110 – Firdale Flyer (The Go-   **35** Between 129) [1992 a5g 6d6 a6g 8d] 1,000Y: lengthy, narrow filly: sister to a winner in Macau: dam, poor maiden, ran only at 5f: poor maiden: stays 6f. *A. Smith*

SHESADELIGHT   3 b.f. Shirley Heights 130 – Seriema 72 (Petingo 135) [1991   **67** NR 1992 10s 12g4 14.1f2 16m2 16.9d2 14.1m] 220,000Y: rangy, rather unfurnished filly: sister to very smart 1¼m and 1½m winner Infamy and half-sister to 2 winners: dam, best at 1m, is half-sister to good staying filly High Hawk, the dam of In The Wings: fair maiden: stayed 2m, at least on a sound surface: acted on firm ground, probably on dead: blinkered last 2 starts: retired. *J. L. Dunlop*

SHE'S PLEASED (USA)   3 b.f. Storm Bird (CAN) 134 – Mohair (FR) (Blue   **79** Tom 127) [1991 6g* 1992 7.3g 8m 8.1g3 8d4 10d4 9s] leggy, lengthy filly: fair form: ran well in frame in handicaps then minor event: never dangerous in £11,700 handicap at Newbury final start: stayed 1¼m: acted on dead ground: to stud. *L. M. Cumani*

SHE'S SPECIAL   3 ch.f. Superlative 118 – Royal Agnes 71 (Royal Palace 131)   **69** [1991 5m4 5g 6g a5g4 5m3 5m3 5d* 5m3 5s2 6d3 7m 6g2 6f 5m6 5g2 5d5 6m 1992 6v 8.1s5 7s2 7f 6m3 7d2] strong, lengthy filly: has a round action: fair performer: second in moderately-run handicap at Newcastle in April and claimer (below best, claimed £11,699) at Epsom in June: will prove best at up to 7f: acts on good and soft ground: visored all starts in 1992, also blinkered at 2 yrs. *Miss L. A. Perratt*

SHIKARI KID   5 b.g. Kala Shikari 125 – Muffet 75 (Matador 131) [1991 10.2s2   – 11s2 13d 10m 10.3d a11g 12f6 12f3 11.1s4 1992 a14g] smallish gelding: has a round action: rated 42 at 4 yrs: claimed out of S. Norton's stable £3,449 over hurdles: well beaten at Southwell later in March: stays 1½m: acts on firm going, but ideally suited by very soft: has been visored or blinkered but not nowadays: not one to trust implicitly. *P. A. Blockley*

759

SHIKARI'S SON 5 br.g. Kala Shikari 125 – Have Form (Haveroid 122) [1991 6g   **74**
6g 5.8f⁶ 5m⁶ 5f 6m 6g 1992 6g 7m 6f² 6f* 6f* 6d³ 6m* 6f* 5d 5d] tall, leggy gelding:
fair handicapper: in very good form in the summer, winning 4 times at Brighton:
effective at 5f and 6f: acts on hard and dead ground. *J. White*

SHILLELAGH BAY (IRE) 2 b.c. (Mar 24) Nordico (USA) – Adorable   **46**
Princess 91 (Royal Palace 131) [1992 6d 7s⁵] IR 15,000F: smallish, good-bodied colt:
brother to poor 4-y-o F-Troop and Irish 6f (at 2 yrs) to 1½m winner Nordic Surprise
and half-brother to a winner in Hong Kong: dam Irish 1½m winner at 4 yrs, from
family of Double Schwartz: poor form when well beaten in maidens at Haydock and
Lingfield in October. *P. W. Harris*

SHIMMER 3 br.f. Bustino 136 – Light Duty 113 (Queen's Hussar 124) [1991 NR   **55**
1992 8m 10d4 10d³ 9g⁶ 10m] lengthy, workmanlike filly: half-sister to 5 winners,
including useful 1985 2-y-o 7f winner Laughter (by Shirley Heights) and Paradise
Bay (by Mill Reef), very useful performer at up to 1½m: dam, very useful over
middle distances, is sister to Highclere: modest maiden: led 2½f out but flashed tail
and weakened inside last when sixth in handicap at Redcar: well beaten final start:
bred to stay 1½m, but is rather headstrong. *Lord Huntingdon*

SHINING BRIGHT 3 b.f. Rainbow Quest (USA) 134 – Bourbon Girl 116 (Ile de   **98**
Bourbon (USA) 133) [1991 8d² 8d³ 1992 10g* 12d5] tall, leggy, unfurnished filly: first
foal: dam 2-y-o 7f winner also second in Oaks and Irish Oaks: 10/9 on, won 9-runner
minor event at Longchamp in April: 20/1, 27½ lengths fifth of 7 to User Friendly in
Oaks at Epsom, dropping back to last 3f out but keeping on: bred to be suited by
1½m: has joined R. McAnally in USA. *A. Fabre, France*

SHINING JEWEL 5 b.h. Exhibitioner 111 – Vaguely Jade (Corvaro (USA) 122)   **71**
[1991 a8g⁴ a10g⁴ a8g² a7g⁶ 8d 8.5g⁶ 7m⁴ 8d³ 8m 8f* 8.2m⁶ 8m 1992 7g 8m⁶ a8g⁴
8m⁵ 9d* 10.1f³ 8m* 10.1g 8g⁴ 8m³ 7f* 7g⁴ 8m⁵ 8d³ 7s 9g] strong, lengthy horse:
usually looks well: moderate mover: fair handicapper: held his form between May
and September, winning at Kempton (for lady rider) and twice at Yarmouth: below
par in apprentice races last 2 starts: effective from 7f to 1¼m: acts on hard and dead
ground: not easiest of rides. *Mrs L. Piggott*

SHINING WOOD 4 b.f. Touching Wood (USA) 127 – Nihad 76 (Alleged (USA)   **41** d
138) [1991 12f5 10m² a11g² 12m⁶ 10.2d a10g a12g³ a13g 1992 a12g⁴ a13g5 a14g³ 14.6g
13.8d 9.2v 9.9f a12g] rather leggy, workmanlike filly: has a round action: still a
maiden and no worthwhile form after third outing, on first 3 starts trained by A.
Reid: stays 1¾m: acts on good to firm ground, and on fibresand: tried blinkered. *J. S.
Wainwright*

SHINTILLO (IRE) 2 b.c. (May 2) Lomond (USA) 128 – Supremely Royal   **86** p
(Crowned Prince (USA) 128) [1992 8m 8m 7v*] 32,000Y: big, lengthy colt: has
plenty of scope: fluent mover: brother to 3-y-o Citiqueen, successful from 1m (at 2
yrs) to 12.6f, closely related to 6f and 10.2f winner Royal Invitation (by Be My
Guest) and half-brother to several winners, including stayer Elegant Monarch (by
Ardross) and very smart 6f to 1m winner Capricorn Belle (by Nonoalco): dam poor
maiden from top American family: heavily-backed odds-on chance, confirmed the
considerable promise shown on 2 occasions at Newmarket when very easy 6-length
winner of maiden at Newcastle in November: still has plenty of improvement in him,
and is an interesting middle-distance prospect. *L. M. Cumani*

SHIPS LANTERN 3 b.f. Kalaglow 132 – Sunderland (Dancer's Image (USA))   **89**
[1991 7g 1992 7g* 7.1d* 8.1m⁶ 8m³ 8g⁶ 7.1s² 8d] tall, sparely-made filly: fairly
useful performer: won median auction maiden at Thirsk and minor event at
Haydock in the spring: ran creditably afterwards until well beaten in £10,000
handicap at Ascot last time: may prove best at up to 1m: acts on good to firm and soft
ground: sometimes on toes: sold 20,000 gns Newmarket December Sales. *C. F. Wall*

SHIRL 3 b.f. Shirley Heights 130 – Bercheba (Bellypha 130) [1991 8m 8m a8g   **41**
1992 a8g 11.8g 11.9g* 12.1s] sturdy, lengthy filly: poor form: sold out of W. Haggas'
stable 2,200 gns Ascot February Sales after reappearance: won apprentice selling
handicap (no bid) at Brighton in August: stays 1½m: well beaten on soft ground. *G.
F. H. Charles-Jones*

SHIRLEY ANN 9 ch.m. Buckskin (FR) 133 – Doone Gate (Arctic Slave 116)   **–**
[1991 NR 1992 a8g 12g³ 14.1d] close-coupled mare: unreliable hurdler (stays 2½m):
thrice raced on flat and well beaten. *R. J. Weaver*

SHIRLEY ROSE 2 b.f. (Feb 19) Shirley Heights 130 – Corley Moor 97 (Habitat   **54**
134) [1992 7g5 7g] sixth foal: closely related to 8.2f winner Corley Boy (by Elegant
Air) and half-sister to fairly useful 1987 2-y-o 6f winner Topsy Moor (by High Top):

dam 2-y-o 5f winner: modest form in maidens at Doncaster and Newmarket in October: will stay 1m. *M. Johnston*

SHIRLEY'S TRAIN (USA) 3 br.g. Malinowski (USA) 123 – Tiger Trap (USA) **72** 80 (Al Hattab (USA)) [1991 NR 1992 8d 8g⁵ a8g* 9m⁵ 8.3g 8m 8m 10.3g] leggy, attractive gelding: brother to very useful 1m/9f winner Wood Dancer (by Malinowski) and half-brother to fair 1m/9f performer False Start and 4-y-o 1½m winner Maamur (both by Robellino): dam 2-y-o 6f winner: fair performer: won maiden at Southwell in May: well below form in handicaps (including in a visor) then seller (got poor run when every chance 1f out) last 4 starts: should stay 1¼m: acts on good to firm ground and fibresand. *Lord Huntingdon*

SHIRLEY VALENTINE 3 br.f. Shirley Heights 130 – Slightly Dangerous **104** (USA) 122 (Roberto (USA) 131) [1991 8s² 1992 10g² 10d² 11.9g⁴ 11.8g* 11.9m³ 14.6m⁴] close-coupled filly: useful performer: won maiden at Leicester in rather workmanlike style at 5/2 on in July: easily best efforts when fourth in Lancashire Oaks at Haydock and Park Hill Stakes at Doncaster, beaten 4½ lengths by Niodini on both occasions: hung left fifth outing: should have stayed 2m: acted on good to firm ground, shaped well on debut on soft: retired to stud. *H. R. A. Cecil*

SHIRO 2 b.c. (Apr 18) Fabulous Dancer (USA) 124 – Miss Shirley (FR) 76 (Shirley **90 p** Heights 130) [1992 6m 6.1d* 6.1s* 6m* 6d³] leggy, good-topped colt: third foal: half-brother to 3-y-o 14.6f to 16.1f winner Child Star (by Bellypha) and a winner in Hong Kong: dam 1½m winner, is half-sister to high-class French miler Mendez: progressive colt: won maiden at Nottingham in July and nurseries at Chepstow in August and Leicester (particularly impressive, showing smart turn of foot) in September: fine third of 12 in nursery at Ascot 10 days later, travelling strongly long way under top weight: will stay 7f: probably acts on any going: twice slowly away: likely to progress further and do well in 1993. *R. J. R. Williams*

SHOCKING TIMES 3 b.f. Skyliner 117 – Mashin Time 73 (Palm Track 122) **54 §** [1991 7g⁵ 6m² 6g 1992 a6g² a5g⁴ a7g⁴ a6g⁵ 5f⁶ 5.1m² 7f²] sparely-made, close-coupled filly: plating-class inconsistent maiden: temperamental, and refused to enter stalls twice after final start: stays 6f: acts on good to firm ground and equitrack: one to be wary of. *R. Simpson*

SHOEHORN 5 br.g. Prince Tenderfoot (USA) 126 – Relkalim 102 (Relko 136) **56 d** [1991 NR 1992 10.8d³ 10m² 10g 11.8g⁵ 10g⁴ 10g³ 10.5d 8g⁵ 11d⁵] sturdy, lengthy gelding: has a quick action: modest form for M. Pipe, trained by him until after seventh start: better at 1¼m than 1m: acts on firm and dead going: below form in blinkers twice: often wears crossed noseband: has been bandaged: claimed to join D. Turner £2,001 final start and won handicap hurdle later in September. *R. E. Peacock*

SHOMBERG (IRE) 2 b.c. (Apr 22) Pennine Walk 120 – Northern Chance 78 **41** (Northfields (USA)) [1992 6g 7d 5v⁶] 22,000F, IR 25,000Y: lengthy colt: shows knee action: half-brother to 4 winners, including fair 1987 2-y-o 5f winner Toshair Flyer (by Ballad Rock) and Irish 1¼m and 11f winner Northern Pet (by Petorius): dam 1m winner: poor form in maiden events: should stay 1m: acts on heavy going, yet to race on top-of-the-ground. *P. Calver*

SHOOFE (USA) 4 ch.g. L'Emigrant (USA) 129 – Bid For Manners (USA) (Raise **74** A Bid (USA)) [1991 8d 10d 10g 10d 12.3g² 11.5m⁴ 16.9g* 16.9m⁶ 16m* 16m 15.9d* 1992 14.9v⁴ 16d⁴ 16d 14g⁶ 15.9m⁶ 18.8m³ 16.5g³ 16.1g⁶ 14.1d⁶] good-topped gelding: fair handicapper: below best last 2 starts, in visor final time: suited by good test of stamina: acts on good to firm and dead ground: fair hurdler. *D. Morley*

SHOOTING LODGE (IRE) 4 b.c. High Line 125 – Heather Croft 79 (Kala **57** Shikari 125) [1991 11.7g⁶ 15.3m² 14m² 13g² 13.8f² 1992 16.2g² 14m] good-topped colt: modest handicapper, still a maiden: dyed-in-the-wool stayer: acts on good to firm ground. *J. R. Jenkins*

SHOTLEY AGAIN 2 b.c. (Apr 17) Then Again 126 – Sweet Candice 71 (African **35** Sky 124) [1992 5f⁵ 7f 5d 6s] 2,500F, 5,000Y 5,000V 2-y-o: has a round action: half-brother to 1¼m seller winner Fast Market (by Petong) and 1987 2-y-o 5.8f winner Almetise (by Mummy's Game): dam, 5f winner, is half-sister to good French 1½m performer Odisea: poor form, including in a seller. *N. Bycroft*

SHOT STOPPER 4 gr.f. Bellypha 130 – Ideal Home 104 (Home Guard (USA) **–** 129) [1991 8g⁵ 8d 8g² 7.1g 10g³ 10m³ 7m³ 7f⁵ 8g 1992 8g⁶ 8.1m 8m⁶] close-coupled, rather leggy filly: good mover: somewhat inconsistent maiden at 3 yrs: out of depth in listed events then never dangerous in apprentice handicap in first half of 1992: stays 1¼m: acts on firm going, possibly unsuited by dead: looked irresolute when blinkered once. *M. J. Heaton-Ellis*

SHOWACA 4 b.g. Show-A-Leg 107 – Elsaca (Ela-Mana-Mou 132) [1991 a6g a5g3 – a7g a5g 7d6 8s2 8f a8g 8m 1992 a14g] leggy gelding: rated 34 at 3 yrs: soundly beaten in January: stays 1m: acts on soft going, probably not on firm: blinkered (never placed to challenge) once: sold to join F. Gibson 1,850 gns Doncaster September Sales. *R. F. Marvin*

SHOWBROOK (IRE) 3 gr.c. Exhibitioner 111 – Aldern Stream 102 (Godswalk **116** (USA) 130) [1991 6g2 6f* 6g5 6m* 5.5g2 6g2 6m* 6f* a8.5f 1992 8g 5d2 6s] compact, sprint type: good mover: very useful performer: trained by R. Hannon as 2-y-o, when wins included July Stakes at Newmarket and Mill Reef Stakes at Newbury: easily best effort in French pattern events in 1992 when beaten a length by Monde Bleu in Prix du Gros-Chene at Chantilly in June: stays 6f: ran poorly on soft ground final start, acts on any other: tried blinkered on dirt in USA final start at 2 yrs. *N. Clement, France*

SHOW FAITH (IRE) 2 ch.c. (May 6) Exhibitioner 111 – Keep The Faith 86 **73** p (Furry Glen 121) [1992 6m4 5g3 6d5 7.3s2] IR 7,000Y, 18,000 2-y-o: leggy colt: second foal: dam Irish 1¼m winner later successful in North America: fair maiden: bit backward, beaten a head in a nursery at Newbury in October, held up, leading 1f out, just caught: will stay 1m: acts on soft ground. *R. Hannon*

SHOWGI (USA) 3 ch.c. Topsider (USA) – Shoag (USA) (Affirmed (USA)) [1991 **87** 6g3 6m4 7m* 7d 1992 7m3 8.1g4 8.5d 8f2 8g 10g 7d] close-coupled, useful-looking colt: carries condition: moderate mover: fairly useful performer: in frame in hand-icaps, hanging left when first put under pressure before rallying strongly when beaten head at Newcastle: stays 1m: acts on firm going, probably unsuited by a soft surface: blinkered final outing: sweating (ran moderately) fifth start. *J. R. Fanshawe*

SHREWD GIRL (USA) 4 b.f. Sagace (FR) 135 – Hydahs (USA) (Chieftain II) **42** [1991 10g6 10f2 1992 14.6g 10.8g 10f 9d 10.2f5 8m3 10.8g5] leggy filly: shows round action: poor maiden nowadays: should stay 1½m: acts on firm ground: sold to join T. Cunningham 2,700 gns Ascot July Sales, resold 3,200 gns Doncaster November Sales. *B. W. Hills*

SHREWD IDEA 2 b.c. (Apr 20) Alleged (USA) 138 – Domludge (USA) (Lyphard **91** (USA) 132) [1992 7g3 8g* 8.1s2 8g* 9d4] lengthy filly: moderate walker: third foal: dam lightly-raced half-sister to Mrs Penny and dam of Hatoof: fairly useful performer: won maiden at Gowran Park in August and nursery there in October: excellent second, keeping on gamely, in minor event at Haydock in between: will stay 1¼m: acts well on soft going, yet to race on top-of-the-ground. *M. Kauntze, Ireland*

SHREWD PARTNER (IRE) 3 br.c. Ahonoora 122 – Practical 95 (Ballymore **85** 123) [1991 7m6 8s* 7d5 8g 1992 8.5d 10m2 10f5 10g3 10d4 10.1d* 8d3 11s6] workmanlike colt: has a round action: fairly useful handicapper: won at Epsom in September: ran creditably at 1m but is ideally suited by further: only fair effort on firm ground, acts on any other: sold 28,000 gns Newmarket Autumn Sales. *D. R. C. Elsworth*

SHROPSHIRE BLUE 2 gr.f. (Apr 4) Risk Me (FR) 127 – Six Ashes (Bruni 132) – [1992 6.1m 5g] neat filly: has a round action: fourth foal: half-sister to 3-y-o Casting Shadows (by Chief Singer): dam unraced: bit backward, well beaten in maidens at Chepstow and Warwick in midsummer. *R. Dickin*

SHUAILAAN (USA) 3 ch.c. Roberto (USA) 131 – Lassie's Lady (USA) **122** (Alydar (USA)) [1991 7m* 1992 10g2 8.3g* 10g* 14.6m4 10m4]

The form which saw Shuailaan make the frame in User Friendly's St Leger and Rodrigo de Triano's Champion Stakes entitles him to inclusion among the top dozen or so three-year-olds of 1992. What distinguished him from other good-class performers, though, was his lack of pattern-race success, something which must be linked to the fortunes of his stable in general. Alec Stewart had a season he's probably glad is behind him, with his lowest total of winners for eight years and a losing spell which stretched ninety days. The yard was hit by a virus in early-summer, forcing a complete shut-down, and Shuailaan, a late-developing type described by stable-jockey Roberts as the 'nicest prospect' he'd ridden in 1991, had limited opportunity to fulfil his potential. Despite having already taken on some of the best, he remains something of an unknown quantity.

Having beaten Masad in the Houghton Stakes on his only start at two, the well-bred Shuailaan, a 750,000-dollar yearling, was made a short-priced favourite to put himself into the classic picture on his reappearance, in the

Sheikh Ahmed Al-Maktoum's "Shuailaan"

ten-furlong Newmarket Stakes at the Guineas meeting. A two-length beating by Captain Horatius at levels was somewhat disappointing, but considering his inexperience and the fact that the stable's runners were already beginning to show signs that all wasn't well, Shuailaan was by no means disgraced. Side-lined with the rest of the string, he wasn't seen out again until contesting a Windsor graduation event on August 10th. Sweating quite freely, he made hard work of landing the odds there, but he was stepping down to a mile, and the steady early pace put the emphasis firmly on speed, and he gave the strong impression he'd do much better returned to further. That was confirmed back at Windsor over an extra couple of furlongs later in the month, when he accounted for Adam Smith and the smart Knifebox (who went on to win three Group 3 events) in the listed Winter Hill Stakes, shaping as though there was further improvement in him given a still stiffer test of stamina. A step up to a mile and a half seemed the most likely option, the dam's side of Shuailaan's pedigree casting doubt on his staying much further; but, with a small field expected for the St Leger, Stewart allowed him to go forward to Doncaster. The venture was rewarded with a tremendous effort from Shuailaan. Ridden to get the trip, which in hindsight weren't ideal tactics given the steady early pace, he was last of the seven when the tempo quickened turning for home, then stayed on well inside the final quarter-mile, failing by only a neck and three quarters of a length to peg back the placed horses Sonus and Bonny Scot. Shuailaan surpassed even that effort on his final start of the season in the Champion Stakes, while giving the impression the return to ten furlongs wasn't entirely in his favour. He couldn't quicken with the likes of Rodrigo de Triano and Lahib when the tempo increased, but did keep on well

763

under pressure up the hill to finish around three and a half lengths fourth of ten.

Shuailaan (USA) (ch.c. 1989)	Roberto (USA) (b 1969)	Hail To Reason (br 1958)	Turn-To Nothirdchance
		Bramalea (b 1959)	Nashua Rarelea
	Lassie's Lady (USA) (b 1981)	Alydar (ch 1975)	Raise A Native Sweet Tooth
		Lassie Dear (b 1974)	Buckpasser Gay Missile

A tall, leggy, useful-looking colt, Shuailaan is the third foal of Lassie's Lady, the better of the preceding two being Bite The Bullet (by Spectacular Bid), successful in the States at up to seven furlongs, including in a Grade 2 event in his first season. The second dam, Lassie Dear, a very useful stakes winner at two, has been a notable success at stud; two of her most recent sons are the useful 1987 two-year-old Al Mufti (like Shuailaan, by Roberto, who later stayed a mile and a half, and the good three-year-old Wolfhound (by Nureyev). Lassie Dear's second foal was Weekend Surprise, the dam of the top-class American performers Summer Squall and A P Indy, winners of the 1990 Preakness and 1992 Belmont respectively. Shuailaan's optimum trip may well turn out to be a mile and a half. A really good mover, he has raced only on a sound surface to date. If, as reported, he remains in training, he is one to keep a close eye on; on his form at three alone he shouldn't be difficult to place to win that first pattern race, and could well go on from there. *A. C. Stewart*

SHU FLY (NZ)   8 ch.g. Tom's Shu (USA) – Alycone (NZ) (Philoctetes 111) [1991 9g⁴ 1992 8g⁵ 8.9g] workmanlike gelding: useful 2m hurdler in 1991/2: lightly raced on flat: should stay 9f: has joined C. Broad. *Mrs S. Oliver*   –

SHUJAN (USA)   3 b.c. Diesis 133 – Linda's Magic (USA) 114 (Far North (CAN) 120) [1991 6d* 1992 8d 7.9d⁴] good-topped colt: off course 2½ months, form in handicaps in 1992 only when fourth at York (dull in coat, still green) in July: should be better suited by 1¼m: seems rather lazy: sold 6,000 gns Newmarket December Sales. *R. W. Armstrong*   –

SHYLOU   3 b.f. Petoski 135 – Lady of The Land 75 (Wollow 132) [1991 5g⁶ 6g⁶ 7f 1992 7g] sparely-made filly: seems of little account: sold 440 gns Newmarket July Sales. *J. W. Hills*   –

SHY MAIDEN (IRE)   4 br.f. Shy Groom (USA) – Relda 67 (Relko 136) [1991 10m⁵ 1992 a12g] 5,200Y: ex-Irish filly: fourth foal: sister to a winner in Macau: dam disappointing half-sister to very smart middle-distance performers Jolly Good and Roscoe Blake: won auction event at Down Royal at 2 yrs: no form here. *C. Weedon*   –

SHYNON   2 gr.g. (Jan 30) Nishapour (FR) 125 – Sunset Ray 74 (Hotfoot 126) [1992 5d⁴ 5g 7g 8.5d⁴ 9g⁶ 8s 8.3v³] 4,900F, 2,200Y: smallish, plain gelding: half-brother to 1½m winner Miss Adventure (by Adonijah): dam won from 1m to 2m: modest maiden: largely consistent in nurseries last 4 starts, including for 7-lb claimer: will be well suited by middle distances: has raced only on an easy surface. *M. H. Tompkins*   56

SHY ROMANCE   2 ch.f. (Feb 19) Shy Groom (USA) – Waveguide 76 (Double Form 130) [1992 5g a5g⁶ 5m⁴ 5g 5g 5s a6g] 600F: lengthy filly: third foal: half-sister to 3-y-o Waveband (by Thatching): dam, placed at 5f at 2 yrs, is out of half-sister to Centro, dam of Nicholas Bill and Centrocon (dam of Time Charter): poor form in varied events, including a seller: blinkered (pulled hard, finished last) fourth start: flashes tail: trained on second start by R. Hollinshead: sold 550 gns Ascot December Sales. *P. M. McEntee*   43

SIANEMA   4 ro.f. Persian Bold 123 – Seriema 72 (Petingo 135) [1991 8g 8m⁵ 8g³ a10g a10g 1992 a10g⁴] leggy filly: rated 69 in spring at 3 yrs: last of 4 in handicap at Lingfield in January: should be suited by 1¼m: sold 13,000 gns Newmarket December Sales. *D. R. Laing*   –

SIAN WYN   2 ch.f. (Mar 30) Hotfoot 126 – Curzon House 73 (Green God 128) [1992 5.7f⁶ a6g 7s 6.1v] sparely-made filly: fifth reported foal: dam sprint plater: poor form in maidens and a minor event: off course 10 weeks before penultimate start and should stay 7f: probably acts on any going. *K. R. Burke*   45

SIBERIAN KING   3 b.g. Siberian Express (USA) 125 – Fallen Angel 88 (Quiet Fling (USA) 124) [1991 5d 5d 6g⁴ 7.5f 7.5f 1992 12g] tall, lengthy, dipped-backed gelding: probably of little account these days. *A. Smith*   –

764

SIBERIAN SWING 3 gr.f. Siberian Express (USA) 125 – Swing Is Back – (Busted 134) [1991 6m 1992 10.2g] leggy, angular filly: tailed off in maidens: refused to enter stalls later in July. *J. D. Roberts*

SICILY OAK 2 b.f. (Apr 14) Ballacashtal (CAN) – Martyrdom (USA) (Exceller 53 (USA) 129) [1992 5.1g³ 5m² 6g 5g³ 6d] 550Y: leggy, angular filly: has round action: third foal: dam unraced: modest maiden: should be better suited by 6f than 5f: acts on good to firm ground, possibly not on dead. *D. McCain*

SIDDINGTON LODGE (IRE) 4 b.g. Wassl 125 – Eloquent Charm (USA) – (Private Account (USA)) [1991 8g 10g 1992 10.2f] small, sparely-made gelding: seems of little account. *A. J. Chamberlain*

SIDE BAR 2 b.g. (Mar 28) Mummy's Game 120 – Joli's Girl 79 (Mansingh (USA) 51 120) [1992 7g 6g 7m 6.9v⁵] 21,000Y: angular, unfurnished gelding: has a round action: second foal: half-brother to useful 6f (at 2 yrs) and 1m winner Joli's Princess (by Prince Sabo): dam 9f winner stayed 1½m: well beaten in maidens: improved effort at Folkestone final start: acts on heavy ground. *M. J. Ryan*

SIDNEY SMITH (IRE) 4 ch.g. Tate Gallery (USA) 117 – Miss Anna § (King's – Company 124) [1991 10d 9s⁴ 11.8g 8.3m⁶ 7m² 1992 a8g] IR 45,000Y: lengthy, sparely-made gelding: moderate mover: rated 54 on final start at 3 yrs for J. Gosden: tailed off in amateurs handicap at Southwell in February: may prove ideally suited by 1m/1¼m: best effort when visored. *E. H. Owen jun*

SIE AMATO (IRE) 3 ch.g. Soughaan (USA) 111 – Wolviston (Wolverlife 115) 57 [1991 7m a6g³ a7g* 7m a7g⁴ a7g a7g 1992 8s 8.3s a8g* a7g³ a8g a8g⁴ 10g² 8.9m³ 10d² 10s² 11.8g 9.9m 10.5s] sparely-made gelding: fairly consistent handicapper between mid-May and late-August, winning at Southwell: ran moderately last 2 starts: stays 1¼m: acts on good to firm and soft ground and on fibresand: usually races up with pace. *Capt. J. Wilson*

SIESTA KEY 7 b.g. Glint of Gold 128 – Petite Hester 85 (Wollow 132) [1991 16m² – 14.6m³ 1992 16.1g] leggy, quite good-topped gelding: moderate mover: rated 79 at 6 yrs for M. Johnston: bandaged, tailed off in August, 1992: stays 2m: acts on firm going. *T. Kersey*

SIFTON'S PRIDE (CAN) 4 b.f. Majesty's Prince (USA) – Original Script – (CAN) (Codex (USA)) [1991 11.4m⁴ 12m² 10g 1992 18.2m] big, leggy, lengthy filly: rated 63 + at 3 yrs: tailed off in handicap in June, 1992: should stay beyond 1½m: acts on good to firm ground: has joined P. Kelleway. *G. Harwood*

SIGAMA (USA) 6 ch.g. Stop The Music (USA) – Lady Speedwell (USA) 84 (Secretariat (USA)) [1991 5m³ 5g 5g³ 5f² 5f 5g⁴ 5m⁴ 5m 5m 5m² 5g 5m² 5m* 5.2f⁶ 5d 1992 5d 5m² 5f² 5m⁵ 5g³ 5m² 5f* 5g² 5m 5d 5m⁵ 5g] sturdy, dipped-backed gelding: has a quick action: fairly useful handicapper: won at Epsom in August: best on a sound surface: has been tried in blinkers/visor/hood, not successfully and not in 1992: usually apprentice ridden: very speedy. *F. H. Lee*

SIGNOR SASSIE (USA) 4 ch.c. The Minstrel (CAN) 135 – Sahsie (USA) (Forli 51 (ARG)) [1991 10g² 10m⁶ 12m³ 1992 14.6g⁴ 16.2g⁴ 14.6g] lengthy, heavy-topped colt: good mover: modest maiden, not so good as when with G. Harwood at 3 yrs: off course 7 months and in need of race final start: probably stays 2m: acts on good to firm ground: has had tongue tied down: winning hurdler in 1991/2. *N. Tinkler*

SIKESTON (USA) 6 b.h. Lear Fan (USA) 130 – Small Timer (USA) 123 (Lyphard (USA) 132) [1991 10g² 10.5g⁴ 10v* 9m⁶ 8g* 8g⁴ 8m 8d 8v* 8v² 10v* 1992 10s 8.1g 10g* 8s³ 8m³ 8m* 8m⁵ 8s]

The tough and game Sikeston, now retired, won only once in Britain in a long career—in the Queen Anne Stakes at Royal Ascot in 1991—but the best

Premio Presidente della Repubblica, Rome—right to left, Sikeston, Sillery and Lara's Idea

Sea World International Stakes, the Curragh—
the last of eleven pattern-race successes for Sikeston

of his performances at home in the latest season confirmed that, as in the previous seasons, he wasn't far behind the best milers and he goes to stud having been in the International Classifications in five successive seasons. He finished a close third to Lahib and Second Set in the Queen Anne and a creditable fifth, beaten less than three lengths by the winner Marling, in the Sussex Stakes. It had long been the belief that Sikeston needed some give in the ground—nearly all his best performances had been in the mud—but both the Queen Anne and the Sussex were run on a different surface, proving that, no matter how long a horse has been around, it's unwise to think there's nothing new to learn about him. Sikeston largely made his reputation abroad, particularly in Italy where he won at least one Group 1 event in each of his five seasons to race. Italian pattern races aren't usually so strongly contested as those in Britain and France, and Sikeston's Group 1 victories there came in the Gran Criterium at two, the Premio Parioli (Italian Two Thousand Guineas), the Premio Presidente della Repubblica (twice), the Premio Vittorio di Capua (twice) and the Premio Roma. He won the latest Premio Presidente della Repubblica at Rome in May by half a length from the good French four-year-old Sillery. Sikeston also ran in Ireland—where he won the Sea World International Stakes at the Curragh in June from Sure Sharp and Rami—and in France in the latest season. His moderate effort in the Prix Jacques le Marois at Deauville in August turned out to be his last run. He will be at stud in Italy in 1993.

Sikeston (USA) (b.h. 1986)	Lear Fan (USA) (b 1981)		Roberto (b 1969)		Hail To Reason
					Bramalea
			Wac (b 1969)		Lt Stevens
					Belthazar
	Small Timer (USA) (b 1980)		Lyphard (b 1969)		Northern Dancer
					Goofed
			Watch Fob (b or br 1965)		Tompion
					Pet Child

The robust, heavy-topped Sikeston usually carried plenty of condition even when race-fit. He was effective at a mile to a mile and a quarter and acted on good to firm and heavy going. He is by the Gainesway stallion Lear Fan,

Luciano Gaucci's "Sikeston"

who is building a good record at stud, out of an unraced daughter of the tough
Watch Fob, a very useful stakes winner at around a mile who won eleven of
her fifty-six starts. *C. E. Brittain*

SILCA-CISA 3 ch.f. Hallgate 127 – Princess Silca Key 61 (Grundy 137) [1991   **93**
5.1g² 5g² 5m³ 5g* 1992 5g² 6g² 6m 5m* 5m⁴ 6d 5m 5d²] angular, sparely-made
filly: moderate mover with quick action: fairly useful performer: best effort to win
handicap at Goodwood in July: stiff tasks in 5f listed events (ran creditably) and Ayr
Gold Cup next 3 starts: below form in 4-runner minor event final one: stays 6f: acts
on good to firm ground. *M. R. Channon*

SILENT EXPRESSION 2 gr.f. (Apr 29) Siberian Express (USA) 125 – Silent   **63**
Sun 90 (Blakeney 126) [1992 6m* 6m 7m³ 7s 7d] rangy, rather unfurnished filly:
moderate mover: fifth foal: half-sister to 1989 2-y-o 6f to 1m winner Closed Shop
(by Auction Ring): dam won over 1¼m here and 1m in France: won seller (retained
7,000 gns) at Doncaster in June: creditable third in nursery at Yarmouth only other
worthwhile form: stays 7f: possibly unsuited by a soft surface. *D. Morris*

SILENT PRINCE 2 b.c. (May 8) Prince Sabo 123 – Queensbury Star 76   **42**
(Wishing Star 117) [1992 5g 6g⁵ 7d a7g] leggy, angular colt: fifth foal: half-brother to
6-y-o 7f winner Vuchterbacher and 1989 2-y-o 6f and 7f winner Beehive Boy (both
by Longleat): dam won over 6f at 2 yrs but no form after: poor maiden: withdrawn
once after giving trouble stalls: should stay 7f. *Miss B. Sanders*

SILICA (USA) 3 ch.f. Mr Prospector (USA) – Skillful Joy (USA) (Nodouble   **62**
(USA)) [1991 7m² 7g 1992 8d⁴ 6.9g 6.9d⁴ 7f⁴ 7g² 7f² 6g*] angular filly: has a
quick, round action: modest performer: 5/4 on, won 5-runner maiden at Brighton in
August: ideally needed further than 6f: probably acted on firm ground and dead:
visits Rock Hopper. *J. H. M. Gosden*

SILICON BAVARIA (FR) 5 br.m. Procida (USA) 129 – Siliciana 113 (Silly   **115**
Season 127) [1991 6g⁵ 6d⁴ 6.5g⁶ 6g² 6d³ 7d⁶ 7s* 6v⁴ 1992 5m 7d⁵ 6d³ 6.5g⁴ 6s⁴ 6d³

Ciga Prix Dollar, Longchamp—Sillery beats the 1991 winner Wiorno (right) and Corrupt

7d² 6d² a7f] very useful French mare: winner of 2 pattern races in her career, including Group 3 event at Milan at 4 yrs: ran creditably most outings in 1992, best effort when neck second to Wolfhound in Prix de la Foret at Longchamp in October: 3 lengths runner-up to Glen Kate in Laurel Dash later in month: effective at 6f and 7f: acts on soft ground. *R. Collet, France*

SILK DEGREES 6 gr.g. Dunbeath (USA) 127 – Bustling Nelly 94 (Bustino 136) [1991 16m² 15g* 15g⁵ 13g⁴ 16.1m⁶ 15.8g 1992 14.1d⁵] rather plain gelding: lightly-raced handicapper on flat (rated 50 at 5 yrs): fairly useful winning hurdler in 1991/2: encouraging fifth of 7 at Redcar in July, but didn't reappear: stays 2m well: acts on good to firm ground: has worn near-side pricker. *W. Storey* —

SILK DYNASTY 6 b.g. Prince Tenderfoot (USA) 126 – Mountain Chase (Mount Hagen (FR) 127) [1991 NR 1992 10d] small gelding: moderate mover: on the downgrade. *R. Hollinshead* —

SILKEN WORDS (USA) 3 b.f. Alleged (USA) 138 – Tie A Bow (USA) (Dance Spell (USA)) [1991 6f 7f⁶ 7m³ 8g 1992 10.2s 10g 14.6g 11.9f⁵ 14.6g⁴ 16g² 17.2s a16g⁴ a16g²] good-topped filly: has a round action: largely consistent maiden handicapper: stays 2m: acts on equitrack, possibly best on a sound surface on turf: suitable mount for apprentice. *W. R. Muir* 59 a55

SILKY HEIGHTS (IRE) 2 b.f. (Mar 17) Head For Heights 125 – Silk Trade (Auction Ring (USA) 123) [1992 6m⁵ 7g 7g 7g] 9,000 2-y-o: lengthy, workmanlike filly: half-sister to 3-y-o Buddy (by Double Schwartz), successful from 5f (at 2 yrs) to 1m, and 2 other winners, including 1985 2-y-o 6f winner Synthetic (by Reform): dam unraced daughter of half-sister to Troy: modest form, including in a nursery: will do better, particularly over further. *M. J. Camacho* 53 p

SILKY SIREN 3 b.f. Formidable (USA) 125 – Smooth Siren (USA) (Sea Bird II 145) [1991 NR 1992 7d⁴ 8f⁶ 10g 8f⁵ 7g⁵ 10d 7g² 7m⁶ 6s] sturdy filly: sister to fairly useful 1985 2-y-o 7f winner Thalassino Asteri and half-sister to several winners, including very useful 1¼m winner Sirenivo (by Sir Ivor): dam 6f winner in USA: modest performer: blinkered first time, comfortably best effort when short-head second of 18 in handicap at Kempton, always prominent: again wore blinkers afterwards: stays 1m: has joined M. Pipe. *E. A. Wheeler* 57

SILLARS STALKER (IRE) 4 b.g. Stalker 121 – Mittens (Run The Gantlet (USA)) [1991 10d³ 12.3s³ 14g 12d² 11.8g 1992 11.1v* 13d* 14.1d² 17.1m² 16.1g⁴ 17.5s* 17.1s⁵] workmanlike gelding: moderate walker: progressive handicapper: won at Hamilton (twice, including apprentices) in April and at Ayr (tended to hang under pressure) in September: effective at 11f when conditions are testing, and 55 stays really well: acts on good to firm ground, goes particularly well on a soft surface: tried visored and blinkered, not in 1992: usually held up for late run: progressed into a fairly useful hurdler, winning 3 handicaps by the end of the year. *Mrs J. R. Ramsden*

SILLERY (USA)   4 b.c. Blushing Groom (FR) 131 – Silvermine (FR) 124 **122** (Bellypha 130) [1991 9.2g⁶ 9d* 9.2m* 10d² 8g 8m⁴ 10s² 9f 1992 8g* 10g² 10s² 10d* 9.7s* 10d²]

Sillery's victory in the Prix Dollar on Ciga weekend at Longchamp was a family affair: the colt was bred by Alec Head, owned by his wife Ghislaine, trained by daughter Criquette and ridden by son Freddie. French racegoers are familiar with the combination, and the same connections were also involved with Sillery's dam the Poule d'Essai des Pouliches winner Silvermine who was by the Heads' top-class miler Bellypha out of their very useful seven-and-a-half- to nine-furlong winner Sevres. Sillery had won listed races at Saint-Cloud and Longchamp, and the Prix Dollar was his second pattern race success following the Prix Jean Prat at Longchamp as a three-year-old when, among other creditable performances, he also ran Subotica close in the Grand Prix de Paris. Sillery and Wiorno were the only home-trained runners in the Prix Dollar and they finished first and second, Sillery winning a shade cleverly by a length after being held up. Corrupt, who had won the Prix Gontaut-Biron at Deauville in August from Sillery, did best of the six British challengers, beaten a length and a half by Wiorno. British-trained horses denied Sillery in the Premio Presidente della Repubblica at Rome in May (beaten half a length by Sikeston) and in the Budweiser International at Laurel in October (beaten a head by Zoman when runner-up for the second successive year).

Mme A. Head's "Sillery"

Sillery (USA) (b.c. 1988)	Blushing Groom (FR) (ch 1974)	Red God (ch 1954)	Nasrullah
			Spring Run
		Runaway Bride (b 1962)	Wild Risk
			Aimee
	Silvermine (FR) (b 1982)	Bellypha (gr 1976)	Lyphard
			Belga
		Sevres (b 1974)	Riverman
			Saratoga II

The big, leggy, attractive Sillery has been retired to the Head family's Haras du Quesnay in Normandy where he will stand in 1993 at a fee of 50,000 francs (about £6,000) with the October 1st concession. His sire Blushing Groom, now deceased, had a brilliant career as a stallion and Sillery should be popular with French breeders, especially as the distaff side of Sillery's pedigree is further distinguished by Silvermine's being a half-sister to the Grand Criterium winner Saint Cyrien. The consistent Sillery was effective at a mile and a quarter, and showed his form on going ranging from good to firm to soft. *Mme C. Head, France*

SILLY HABIT (USA)   6 b.m. Assert 134 – Habitassa 100 (Habitat 134) [1991   –
16.2g³ 21.6f² 1992 a10g a14g a16g] workmanlike mare: moderate mover: rated 47 at
2 yrs: on the downgrade: stays 2¼m: acts on firm and dead ground. *H. J. Collingridge*

SILLY SALLY   2 ch.f. (Mar 8) Music Boy 124 – Carpadia (Icecapade (USA)) [1992   –
5s⁴ 5.1d 5g⁵ 5.1s 6f] 400F: leggy, unfurnished filly: third foal: half-sister to 3-y-o
Tancred Grange (by Prince Sabo), successful at 6f (at 2 yrs) and 1m: dam placed
once at 3 yrs in France: no worthwhile form, including in sellers, in the spring:
looked temperamental final start. *W. G. M. Turner*

SILLY'S BROTHER   6 ch.g. Longleat (USA) 109 – Scilly Isles 54 (Silly Season   –
127) [1991 a8g a7g* a7g⁶ a6g* a6g* a6g³ 7d³ 6m a5g⁴ a5g a6g⁶ a6g 7m 8.1s a7g a6g⁵
1992 a7g⁶] heavy-topped gelding: carried plenty of condition: rated 63d at 5 yrs: well
held in handicap at Southwell in January: best form at 6f: acted on good to firm and
heavy going and on fibresand: blinkered once: dead. *N. Bycroft*

SILVER ANCONA   8 b.g. Tanfirion 110 – Wild Romance 96 (Pirate King 129)   – §
[1991 NR 1992 11.9g⁵ 11.9d] sparely-made gelding: blinkered, no worthwhile form
(reluctant to race) at Brighton in the spring, first runs on flat since 3 yrs: temperamental hurdler. *J. O'Donoghue*

SILVER CANNON (USA)   10 gr.g. Lot O'Gold (USA) – So High (USA) (Sea   –
Bird II 145) [1991 a10g 1992 10d] seems of little account on flat these days: winning
chaser in 1991/2 but one to treat with caution. *R. Voorspuy*

SILVER CONCORD   4 gr.c. Absalom 128 – Boarding House 73 (Shack (USA)   –
118) [1991 7g 6g 8m 7g⁴ 7m³ 7m² 7m 7g 1992 a7g 11f] workmanlike colt: maiden,
rated 52 at 3 yrs: no form in 1992: should stay 1m: acts on good to firm ground,
seems unsuited by soft: hung badly when blinkered once at 3 yrs: sold 1,650 gns
Doncaster October Sales. *G. M. Moore*

SILVERDALE (USA)   2 ch.c. (Mar 30) Silver Hawk (USA) 123 – Norene's   **89** p
Nemesis (CAN) (King Emperor (USA)) [1992 8m2] $120,000Y: leggy colt: has
scope: third reported foal: half-brother to a minor winner in North America: dam
won at up to 7f: 15/2, bandaged behind and bit green, promising 2½ lengths second
to Bashayer in 19-runner maiden at Newmarket in October, soon close up travelling
strongly and keeping on well not knocked about: moved fluently down: sure to
improve, and win a race or two. *J. H. M. Gosden*

SILVER GROOM (IRE)   2 gr.c. (Apr 16) Shy Groom (USA) – Rustic Lawn   **58**
(Rusticaro (FR) 124) [1992 6g 6g⁵ 6g⁵ 7g⁶ 7g 6.1g 8d] smallish, angular colt: first
foal: dam unraced: modest maiden: should be suited by 1m: yet to race on top-of-the-
ground: has run creditably for a claimer. *A. P. Jarvis*

SILVER HAZE   8 gr.g. Absalom 128 – Chance Belle 85 (Foggy Bell 108) [1991   **61**
NR 1992 7m 8.3f* 10.1f³ 8m 8.3m⁴] workmanlike, good-bodied gelding: carries
plenty of condition: has a round action: rated 92 as 4-y-o and subsequently successful in Switzerland before returning here: only modest nowadays: failed to repeat
form of handicap win at Hamilton in June: effective from 8.3f to 1¼m: acts on any
going: has found little: modest chaser, winner twice in August: has joined J. Wade.
W. A. Stephenson

SILVER HELLO   6 gr.g. Nishapour (FR) 125 – Si (Ragusa 137) [1991 NR 1992   **63**
12.1f²] rather leggy, quite good-topped gelding: good mover: rated 78 on flat in 1989:
second of 6 in amateurs event at Hamilton in June, 1992: stays 1½m: acts on firm
going, possibly unsuited by heavy: fair chaser and won handicap in September, ran
as if something amiss following month. *Miss L. A. Perratt*

SILVER KING (FR)   6 ch.g. Son of Silver 123 – Lakara (USA) (Le Fabuleux 133)   **76**
[1991 NR 1992 16d*] ex-French gelding: second foal: half-brother to French 1¼m
winner Fairlane (by Fabulous Dancer): dam won at around 11f in France: successful
over 1½m on flat at 3 yrs when trained by M. Papoin: smart juvenile hurdler in
1989/90: first run on flat since when winning celebrity race at Worcester in March:
stays 2m. *M. C. Pipe*

SILVERLOCKS   2 gr.f. (Apr 5) Sharrood (USA) 124 – Philgwyn 66 (Milford 119)   **88**
[1992 6g⁴ 6m² 7m* 7g 6s* 6s] 7,200Y: angular, sparely-made filly: moderate
mover: second foal: half-sister to 3-y-o Philidor (by Forzando), successful at 7f (at 2
yrs) and 1m: dam maiden stayed 7f, is half-sister to very smart sprinter Primo
Dominie: fairly useful performer: simple task to win maiden auction at Redcar in
August: easily best effort when landing Ayr nursery following month: will stay 1m:
acts on good to firm ground, but is clearly well suited by soft. *Miss S. E. Hall*

SILVERNESIAN (USA)   3 b. or br.c. Alleging (USA) 138 – Loot (USA) **119**
(Boldnesian) [1991 8g⁶ 1992 11d⁴ 12s² 11.9m* 14.5g² 15.9g⁵ 12d⁴ 14m⁴ 12s*] tall
colt: made great progress and developed into a smart performer: won maiden at
Haydock in May: only subsequent run here when 10 lengths fifth of 7 to Further
Flight in listed race at York: best effort when landing Group 1 event at Milan in
October, making all to beat Red Bishop by 1½ lengths: should prove as effective at
2m as 1½m: acts on good to firm and soft ground: remains in training. *J. L. Dunlop*

SILVER SAMURAI   3 b.c. Alleging (USA) 120 – Be My Lady (Be My Guest   **71**
(USA) 126) [1991 5f⁴ 8m⁴ 6m³ 7d⁴ a7g⁴ a8g⁶ 1992 a8g* a8g³ a8g⁴ a8g² 9s² 8.2d²
12g³ 10m⁴ 10g³ 10m³ 10g* 11.8g² 10g² 12f³ 10.3g* 13.6m³ 12m² 11.8m⁴ 10.5d³
a12g² a12g⁶ a12g³] smallish colt: has a quick action: consistent and tough
performer: won claimers at Southwell in January, and at Nottingham and Chester in
summer: claimed out of R. Hollinshead's stable £8,302 after nineteeth start: stays
13.6f: acts on any going: successful for claimer. *Mrs V. A. Aconley*

SILVER'S GIRL   7 b.m. Sweet Monday 122 – Persian Silver 61 (Cash And   **–**
Courage 116) [1991 NR 1992 12.1v] plain mare: rated 58 as 4-y-o when stayed 1¼m
and needed give in the ground: tailed off in handicap at Hamilton in November: tried
blinkered once. *D. Moffatt*

SILVER STANDARD   2 b.g. (Mar 27) Jupiter Island 126 – One Half Silver   **48**
(CAN) (Plugged Nickle (USA)) [1992 6d 5s 5d] 3,500Y: sturdy, close-coupled
gelding: first foal: dam unraced half-sister to Prix Minerve winner Gamberta:
carrying condition, poor form in maidens in the autumn: probably requires much
further. *J. W. Watts*

SILVER STONE BOY   4 gr.c. Another Realm 118 – Elkie Brooks 82 (Relkino   **42** d
131) [1991 5f 6f⁴ 5m⁴ 5g 1992 5g 7s⁵ 6.1d 7m 6s 8.3m] workmanlike, good-quartered
colt: inconsistent maiden handicapper: stays 7f: acts on soft ground: not seen after
May. *W. J. Pearce*

SILVER WISP (USA)   3 b.c. Silver Hawk (USA) 123 – La Ninouchka **123**
(USA) (Bombay Duck (USA)) [1991 6d⁵ 7d* 7g* 7f* 1992 8d³ 8g⁴ 12g³ 12.1g*
12g]
    At the start of the season, 33/1, at least, was available against both Geoff
Lewis training fifty winners or the Derby winner in 1992. The first bet,
concerning fifty-four nominated horses, was landed on October 13th and
reportedly provided the stable with a £90,000 windfall to add to the £100,000
from a similar bet to train forty winners in 1991. Lewis failed to send out the
Derby winner but that bet wasn't such a bad one, either: Silver Wisp finished
third of eighteen, a considerable improvement on the fortunes of the trainer's
first Derby runner, Yawa, who was badly hampered and unseated his rider
on the descent to Tattenham Corner in 1983. At the same stage in the 1992
running, Silver Wisp's prospects also looked none too bright. He was in
twelfth and had been off the bridle from an early stage but, taken to the outside approaching the three-furlong marker, Silver Wisp launched a storming
challenge that took him into second entering the final furlong. Dr Devious had
gone beyond recall, however, and, hanging left, Silver Wisp eventually lost
out to St Jovite as well. Three days later, another Epsom trainer, Brooke

Sanders, sent out the Oaks third Pearl Angel. The last Epsom-trained classic winner was the 1969 John Sutcliffe-trained Two Thousand Guineas winner Right Tack, ridden by Lewis, and their last Derby winner Walter Nightingall's Straight Deal in 1943. Silver Wisp was an 11/1-chance at Epsom having also made the frame in the Guineas, again beaten about two lengths. He'd shaped like a middle-distance performer at Newmarket, and one with a deal of promise on what was only his second start since completing a hat-trick the previous summer. Silver Wisp's season after the Derby, however, was predominantly one of frustration and disappointment. He was efficient enough in landing odds of 7/4 on in the Welsh Brewers Premier Stakes at Chepstow in July but various minor physical problems prevented his participation in more important events. The Irish Derby, Grand Prix de Saint-Cloud and Great Voltigeur Stakes all went by without him in the summer and having been declared at the overnight stage for the September Stakes, Silver Wisp was found lame at evening stables, an injury which also ruled out any possibility of his making the field for the Japan Cup. The one major race that he was able to compete in after Epsom was the King George VI and Queen Elizabeth Diamond Stakes, but the competition he provided was disappointing; having pulled hard, Silver Wisp never looked like getting in a blow. Let's hope that 1993 sees many more opportunities for Silver Wisp to show his ability; he's got plenty of it and was progressing really well before those physical problems intervened.

Silver Wisp (USA) (b.c. 1989)	Silver Hawk (USA) (b 1979)	Roberto (b 1969)	Hail To Reason
			Bramalea
		Gris Vitesse (gr 1966)	Amerigo
			Matchiche II
	La Ninouchka (USA) (ch 1978)	Bombay Duck (b 1972)	Nashua
			Egret
		Astro Lady (ch 1970)	Skymaster
			Arawak

A stocky, deep-girthed colt who carries plenty of condition, Silver Wisp has yet to race on soft ground but won on firm and dead as a two-year-old. A 28,000-dollar foal and 65,000-dollar yearling, he comes from the second liaison between Silver Hawk and La Ninouchka. The first produced the two-year-older Mutual Destiny who was last seen towards the rear in a gentlemen riders race at Lisieux in August. He has gained just one success, also in the French Provinces, in a handicap over an extended one and a half miles in 1991. Both Silver Hawk and his sire Roberto were, of course, like Silver Wisp, concerned in the finish of the Two Thousand Guineas and Derby, but the merits of the maternal grandsire Bombay Duck require some research. Succinctly described in the *Racing Update 1992 Sire Handbook* as 'of little account as a sire, for a long time', Bombay Duck showed very smart form in the United States in winning seven of his twenty-three starts, five at two years followed by stakes victories over six furlongs at three years and eight-and-a-half at four. Before her visits to Silver Hawk, La Ninouchka threw two foals, including the four-time winner Zooming Star (by Star Gallant). La Ninouchka was a winner, once at three years and twice at four years, and one of eight out of the unraced Astro Lady. The most noteworthy of the rest appears to be Fight For U whose efforts earned him the description 'champion imported older horse in Puerto Rico', but the third dam and some of her progeny should mean more to racegoers here. Arawak was third in both the Irish and Yorkshire Oaks and her foals include the Chester Vase winner Kaytu and smart miler Spring In Deepsea. *G. Lewis*

SILVER WIZARD (USA) 2 b.c. (Mar 9) Silver Hawk (USA) 123 – **112** Cherie's Hope (USA) (Flying Paster (USA)) [1992 5g* 5f* 5f2 6d* 6m3 6g* 6m4]

While Silver Wizard's first season was highly satisfactory in that he won four of his seven races, it was also frustrating for his connections in that he should have won one of the three pattern races he lost. The winner of his first two races, a maiden at Newmarket and a minor event at Salisbury, the latter in good style by five lengths, Silver Wizard was narrowly denied an early-season hat-trick in the Norfolk Stakes at Royal Ascot in June by a vastly-improved

BonusPrint Sirenia Stakes, Kempton—an emphatic success for Silver Wizard

performance from the 9/1-shot Niche, a filly to whom he was conceding 5 lb. Silver Wizard, who would have won with a little further to travel, never ran at five furlongs again. After getting back to winning ways with a convincing, if narrow, defeat of Port Lucaya in the listed Newbury Rose Bowl Stakes in July, Silver Wizard started second favourite behind the Coventry Stakes winner Petardia in the Gimcrack Stakes at York in August but found all the trouble going and went down by a head to Splendent. The view that Silver Wizard would have run out a comfortable winner of the Gimcrack with a clear run—he was eventually moved down to third for causing interference to Green's Bid—was given plenty of credence when he won the BonusPrint Sirenia Stakes at Kempton in September very easily by two and a half lengths from the subsequent Mill Reef winner Forest Wind. Silver Wizard won so impressively at Kempton that he started at odds on to follow up in the Middle Park Stakes at Newmarket in October, but he ruined his chance by running too freely, both to post and then to halfway in the race, and eventually finished fourth of the six runners behind Zieten. As things turned out Silver Wizard would have needed to improve upon his Kempton form to have beaten Zieten, but such was the ease with which he won there that it was all the more disappointing that he didn't allow himself the chance at Newmarket to show what he could do. If Silver Wizard returns to form as a three-year-old—and being a strong, good-topped colt, he looks the sort to do so—he shouldn't have to wait too long for his first win in pattern company; the Cork and Orrery Stakes or the seven-furlong Jersey Stakes would seem likely objectives at the Royal meeting.

		Silver Hawk (USA) (b 1979)	Roberto (b 1969)	Hail To Reason / Bramalea
Silver Wizard (USA) (b.c. Mar 9, 1990)			Gris Vitesse (gr 1966)	Amerigo / Matchiche II
		Cherie's Hope (USA) (b 1983)	Flying Paster (b 1976)	Gummo / Procne
			Hill Pleasure (ch 1978)	What A Pleasure / Hill River

Silver Wizard is by the Derby- and Irish Derby-placed Silver Hawk out of the unraced Flying Paster mare Cherie's Hope. There's not much to dwell upon on the female side of Silver Wizard's pedigree: his grandam Hill Pleasure, a minor seven-furlong winner in France, is the only one of the first four dams on the bottom line to have seen the racecourse. All four have had some success at stud, though, producing plenty of winners between them, the best being Hill River's half-brother L'Heureux, a good winner at up to a mile

Mrs Shirley Robins' "Silver Wizard"

and a half; Hill Pleasure's full brother Honest Moment, a winner of five races and one-time six-furlong turf course record-holder at Belmont Park; and half-sister Python, a useful two-year-old in the States in 1985 when she was placed in a couple of Graded events at around a mile. Silver Wizard, a 30,000-dollar buy from Keeneland's September Yearling Sale, is Cherie's Hope's third foal; both the previous two have won, one of them, Game Hope (by Game Dancer), successful at up to nine furlongs. Silver Wizard himself is much better suited by six furlongs than five furlongs, and is well worth a try over seven. He has yet to race on very soft going, but acts on any other. *G. Lewis*

SILVIES STAR   2 ch.f. (Apr 5) Myjinski (USA) – When I Dream (Sparkler 130)   **32**
[1992 7m 8.2d 7g] stocky filly: has round action: third reported foal: half-sister to 1m winner Eric's Pet (by Petong): dam poor maiden: poor form in maidens. *C. D. Broad*

SIMMERING   2 b.f. (Mar 2) Mas Media – Barely Hot (Bold Lad (IRE) 133) [1992   **84**
5g 5.1g* 5.1g⁵ 5g 6m² 6.1m² 6g* 6g* 6s⁵] 3,800Y: leggy, useful-looking filly, somewhat lightly made: good mover: sixth foal: half-sister to ungenerous 1989 2-y-o 5f seller winner Or Nor (by Cure The Blues) and winners in Italy and Scandinavia: dam, placed over 5f in Ireland, is half-sister to Trojan Fen and Kashi Lagoon: fairly useful performer: won maiden at Nottingham in April, then auction contest at Haydock and minor event at Windsor (also easily) in August: ran moderately in Ayr listed race final start: should stay 7f: acts on good to firm ground, possibly unsuited by soft: sold to go to Norway. *G. Wragg*

SIMMIE'S SPECIAL   4 b.f. Precocious 126 – Zalatia 97 (Music Boy 124) [1991   **65**
5g² 5g* 6m⁵ 5m⁴ 5m⁴ 5m⁶ 5f² 5.1g 5d³ 5d³ 1992 6d 5d⁶ 5f 5g³ 5f⁴ 5f³ 5d 5m³ 5f⁴

5.1m⁴ 6m 5m³ 5s⁵ a5g] angular filly: consistent handicapper but hard to win with: should prove best at 5f: probably acts on any going: carries head awkwardly, and tends to hang. *R. Hollinshead*

SIMON ELLIS (IRE)   3 ch.g. Magical Wonder (USA) 125 – Rose In Time (Hello   **49** Gorgeous (USA) 128) [1991 5g⁴ 6g 5.3f 7m 6m 7g a8g⁶ 1992 a7g a10g 7v⁵ 8m 8f⁴ 10.2f 7m⁴ 10f⁴ 8f³ 8g 9.7s a8g a10g²] leggy, sparely-made gelding: inconsistent maiden plater: should prove effective at 1¼m: acts on firm ground: ran creditably in a visor. *D. R. Laing*

SIMONOV   3 br.c. Rousillon (USA) 133 – Simova (USA) (Vaguely Noble 140)   **80** [1991 8m 1992 11.7s⁶ 11.9f* 12f 10m³ 11.9f⁴ 10d⁴ 12d²] lengthy colt: fairly useful but inconsistent performer: won maiden at Brighton in May: clearly best efforts in handicaps when placed at Lingfield (and beaten head by Thamestar) Doncaster: stays 1½m: acts on firm and dead going: has carried head high under pressure: usually makes the running: sold 27,000 gns Newmarket Autumn Sales, reportedly to race in USA. *G. Harwood*

SIMPLE SOUND (IRE)   3 b.c. Simply Great (FR) 122 – Warning Sound (Red   **– p** Alert 127) [1991 6d* 7.5g³ 8v⁵ 1992 7g⁶ 7g⁶ 7f⁵ 6m⁵] workmanlike colt: fourth foal: half-brother to Irish 1¼m winner Second Guess (by Ela-Mana-Mou) and 5f (at 2 yrs) and 1m winner Remthat Naser (by Sharpo): dam Irish 5f to 1¼m winner: won maiden at the Curragh for C. Collins then third and fifth (to Alhijaz) in listed races at Florence and Rome for S. Saggiomo as 2-y-o (rated 81): raced over an inadequate trip in 1992, not seen after Lingfield (very stiff task and blinkered, slowly away and always last in minor event) in July: will do better in handicaps when granted 1¼m. *M. A. Jarvis*

SIMPLY AMISS   2 b.f. (Mar 14) Simply Great (FR) 122 – Squire's Daughter (Bay   **64** Express 132) [1992 5g⁶ 6m* 6g* 6.1g⁶ 6g 6s 7s⁶] IR 10,500Y: compact filly: half-sister to 5-y-o miler Stylish Gent (by Vitiges): dam French 2-y-o 5.5f winner: modest form: won seller at Warwick (bought in 6,200 gns) and claimer at Haydock in midsummer: stiff task, not discredited in nursery at Wolverhampton on final outing: will stay 1m: acts on good to firm and soft ground. *Sir Mark Prescott*

SIMPLY A STAR (IRE)   2 ch.g. (Mar 10) Simply Great (FR) 122 – Burren Star   **–** (Hardgreen (USA) 122) [1992 6f 6g⁶ 7g] IR 11,500Y: leggy, workmanlike gelding: shade unfurnished: third foal: dam Irish maiden: no worthwhile form: sold 680 gns Doncaster September Sales. *M. W. Easterby*

SIMPLY CANDY (IRE)   4 b.f. Simply Great (FR) 122 – What A Candy (USA)   **–** (Key To The Mint (USA)) [1991 7d⁵ 7m² 10m⁵ 11g² 7d⁶ 9m 9s³ 1992 a8g³ a11g² a10g   **a42** 9.2v⁴ 10g⁶ 8f a12g] lengthy ex-Irish filly: has round action: fourth foal: half-sister to 5f winner Fine A Leau (by Youth) and Irish 1¼m and 11f winner Lyphard's Candy (by Lyphard's Wish): dam useful French 2-y-o 7f winner, later successful at up to 9f in USA: still a maiden, and tailed off, including in seller, last 3 starts: stays 11f: acts on good to firm and heavy ground: ran fairly well when visored once: covered by Dunbeath. *A. P. Stringer*

SIMPLY FINESSE   2 b.g. (Feb 28) Simply Great (FR) 122 – Spring In Rome   **64** (USA) (Forli (ARG)) [1992 6m⁴ 5m⁴ 5g³ 6m² 6g 7g⁴] 4,600F, 9,400Y, 14,000 2-y-o: leggy, angular gelding: moderate mover: closely related to useful 1¼m winner Cherry Hill (by Shirley Heights) and half-brother to several winners here and abroad, including fair 1¾m winner Caetani (by Busted): dam onced-raced granddaughter of champion American filly Cicada: modest maiden: stays 7f: yet to race on a soft surface: has been gelded. *R. Akehurst*

SIMPLY GEORGE   3 b.g. Simply Great (FR) 122 – Grand Occasion 63 (Great   **56** Nephew 126) [1991 5m⁵ 7g² 7g* 7g⁴ 7m⁶ 8m³ 9m* 8g 1992 9.9g⁶ 13.1m 14.1g 11.9f⁴ 10m 9.7m] leggy, angular gelding: moderate performer: probably stays 1½m: acts on good to firm ground: takes good hold: blinkered (well beaten) final start: has joined J. White. *R. Boss*

SIMPLY-H (IRE)   3 b.g. Simply Great (FR) 122 – Coupe d'Hebe 87 (Ile de   **78** Bourbon (USA) 133) [1991 5g² 5m⁴ 7g² 7m⁶ 1992 11.8d* 11.6m* 13.1m* 14.9f² 12f 13.3d 12m⁶ 11.9m⁵ 12d⁶ 11.7s² 12m² 11.9s³ 12.2d* 12d] small, lightly-made gelding: usually impresses in condition: easy mover: fair handicapper: ridden by 7-lb claimer, successful at Leicester, Windsor and Bath in the spring then at Catterick (claimer) in October: stays 13.1f well: acts on good to firm and soft ground: tough: sold 16,500 gns Newmarket Autumn Sales. *M. Bell*

SIMPLY SOOTY   2 gr.f. (Jan 20) Absalom 128 – Classical Vintage 80 (Stradavin-   **77** sky 121) [1992 5.2d³ 5d² 5g² 5.2g³ 6g² 5.2s⁵ 5g* 6s³ 5.1s* 5g] lengthy, good-topped filly: fourth foal: sister to 4-y-o 6f and 7f winner Abso and half-sister to a winner in

Belgium: dam 2-y-o 5f winner: progressed into a fairly useful performer: wide-margin winner of median auction at Windsor and minor event at Bath: ran respectably in face of stiff task in Cornwallis Stakes at Ascot later in the autumn: seems suited by 5f: has raced only on an easy surface. *B. R. Millman*

SIMPLY SUPERB 2 ch.g. (Feb 5) Superlative 118 – Coral Princess (Imperial **36 p**
Fling (USA) 116) [1992 6m 8g 6d 6.1g] 5,000F, 6,200Y: strong, good-quartered gelding: third foal: half-brother to a winner in Austria: dam won in Norway: not knocked about in large fields when towards rear in maiden auctions and a seller: looks sort to do better. *M. W. Easterby*

SINCLAIR LAD (IRE) 4 ch.c. Muscatite 122 – Kitty Frisk 64 (Prince Tender- **70**
foot (USA) 126) [1991 9s³ 8.2d⁵ 10.4d⁶ 8m³ 11m⁴ 9g⁴ 7.6g⁴ 10f⁵ 10g* 11m⁶ 8m 1992 12f 10m 9f 9.9g⁵ 12f³ 11f² 10g⁶ 10.3m* 10m* 11f4 9.9g³ 10g⁶ 11g* 10g² 9.9m⁴ 9g³ 10d] leggy, quite good-topped colt: poor mover: fair handicapper: held his form really well between June and September, winning at Doncaster, Pontefract and Redcar: effective from 9f to 11f: best form on a sound surface: visored (stiff task) once at 3 yrs: has run in snatches, and best held up in strongly-run race: sold 8,000 gns Doncaster October Sales. *R. Hollinshead*

SING ANOTHER 3 ch.f. Chief Singer 131 – Another Move 69 (Farm Walk 111) **–**
[1991 6m 7m 8m 1992 11g⁶ 16f5] lengthy, angular filly: no worthwhile form and seems headstrong: sold 720 gns Doncaster September Sales. *Mrs M. Reveley*

SING AS WE GO 2 b.f. (Feb 9) Music Boy 124 – Song To Singo 63 (Master Sing **36**
109) [1992 6f⁵ 5d 5d] leggy filly: third foal: dam, plater, seemed to stay 1m: poor maiden: will be better off in sellers/claimers. *Bob Jones*

SINGER ON THE ROOF 2 b.f. (Jan 24) Chief Singer 131 – On The Tiles **55**
(Thatch (USA) 136) [1992 8.1s⁶ 7g] first foal: dam, from family of Blushing Groom, ran 3 times at 3 yrs in Ireland, winning a 1¼m maiden: modest form in maiden at Chepstow (not knocked about) and minor event at Newbury in the autumn: may do better. *I. A. Balding*

SINGERS IMAGE 3 br.g. Chief Singer 131 – Little White Lies 78 (Runnett 125) **63**
[1991 5g 6d 6d 6g⁵ 7f 7.3m 1992 7f 8d 8g⁶ 8f* 8f⁶ 9g 8s 8.1d⁶ 8g4] workmanlike gelding: easy mover: modest handicapper: won at Salisbury in July, wandering under pressure: should stay beyond 1m: acts on firm ground, fair effort on soft: effective visored or not. *G. B. Balding*

SINGING DETECTIVE 5 gr.g. Absalom 128 – Smoke Creek 67 (Habitat 134) **–**
[1991 a14g a8g 8g 10m⁴ a12g 11.8g 1992 10d 16f³ 12m 12f] rangy gelding: moderate mover: has a round action: still a maiden and no form in 1992: stays 1¾m: acts on any going: tried blinkered: has joined P. McEntee. *R. Curtis*

SINGING GOLD 6 b.g. Gold Claim 90 – Gellifawr 80 (Saulingo 122) [1991 NR **–**
1992 a7g] sturdy gelding: moderate mover: rated 38 as 4-y-o: blinkered, always behind in Lingfield claimer in October, first run on flat since: stays 1m: acts on firm going: usually visored. *P. F. Tulk*

SINGING MISTRESS 2 b.f. (May 5) Primo Dominie 121 – Cantico 58 (Green **–**
Dancer (USA) 132) [1992 6s] unfurnished filly: fourth foal: half-sister to fair 7f winner Dauntess (by Formidable) and 3-y-o 6f winner (probably stays 1¼m) Regal Racer (by Elegant Air): dam staying maiden, half-sister to very smart 1m to 1½m filly Calderina, same family as Mystiko: 33/1, pushed along with plenty to do at halfway and never dangerous in 16-runner maiden at Newbury in October: sold 750 gns Newmarket Autumn Sales. *D. R. C. Elsworth*

SINGING REPLY (USA) 4 b.f. The Minstrel (CAN) 135 – Bright Reply (USA) **36**
(Gleaming (USA)) [1991 8m 10g⁴ 12.3d² 12.2g³ 12.2m⁵ a12g 1992 11.9g⁶ 12g 10.8g 11.8m 11.5m⁵ 18g⁶ 18.2g 12.5s² a12g a16g a12g] leggy, sparely-made filly: rated 67 at 3 yrs for J. Gosden: poor and inconsistent in 1992: stays 1½m: best with give in the ground. *D. Marks*

SINGING SARAH 4 b.f. Mansingh (USA) 120 – Fressingfield (Riboboy (USA) **–**
124) [1991 7g 11.7m 10.2f 5.1m 1992 7.1s] workmanlike filly: of little account. *J. D. Roberts*

SINGING STAR 6 b.g. Crooner 119 – Wild Jewel (Great Heron (USA) 127) [1991 **81**
5f⁵ 5m* 5g⁵ 5f* 5f 5m³ 5g 5m⁵ 5m 5f⁴ 5m 1992 5m 5m 5f⁴ 5m 5m] close-coupled gelding: carries plenty of condition: fairly useful performer: off course 4 months after third start: shaped as if retaining his ability final one: worth another try over 6f: best on top-of-the-ground: often slowly away: has worn blinkers, but not when successful: sometimes bandaged. *J. Balding*

SING THE BLUES   8 b.g. Blue Cashmere 129 – Pulcini 61 (Quartette 106) [1991   –
16.5m 1992 a16g⁵ a16g⁵] big, lengthy gelding: seems of little account on flat these
days: has won 7 races over hurdles on the equitrack, but none since January, 1991.
C. J. Benstead

SINGULAR RUN   6 b.g. Trojan Fen 118 – Needy (High Top 131) [1991 NR 1992   –
a14g 9d] lengthy, workmanlike gelding: rated 84 at 3 yrs for P. Cole: well beaten in
handicaps at Southwell (blinkered) and Kempton in the spring: stayed 1½m: acted
on firm going, possibly unsuited by soft: dead. *Mrs J. C. Dawe*

SIOLFOR (USA)   3 b.g. Alleged (USA) 138 – Hester Bateman (USA) (Codex   –
(USA)) [1991 NR 1992 8.3d 8s 8.5g 14.1g⁵] $15,000Y: leggy gelding: fourth foal:
brother to Irish 9f winner Alterezza: dam unraced: soundly beaten in maidens and
claimer: apprentice ridden, some promise when fifth in handicap at Nottingham in
June: sold 1,100 gns Doncaster November Sales. *Mrs J. R. Ramsden*

SIOUX PERFICK   3 b.f. Blakeney 126 – Siouxsie 90 (Warpath 113) [1991 6g⁴ 7m   –
7m 1992 12.3s 15.1m 14.6d] smallish, workmanlike filly: of little account: sold 750
gns Doncaster November Sales. *C. W. Thornton*

SIR ARTHUR HOBBS   5 b.g. Lyphard's Special (USA) 122 – Song Grove 61   64
(Song 132) [1991 6d 6s a7g 6g 8m 8.1m² 8g* 8.1m* 8.2f 8g⁶ 6d 6.1m² a8g²
1992 a6g⁴ 7.5g 8d 7f* 8.2g 7m* 7.1f⁴ 8.1g⁴ 7g³ 7.1m² 8.1g⁴ 6d 7s 6d 7s] strong
gelding: moderate mover: none too consistent handicapper: successful at Doncaster
(apprentices) in May and Ayr in June: well below form last 4 starts: effective from 6f
to 1m: acts on firm and dead ground and fibresand: has been blinkered (refused to
enter stalls) and visored: held up, and suited by strongly-run race: sold 2,300 gns
Newmarket Autumn Sales. *F. H. Lee*

SIR BOUDLE (IRE)   3 b.c. Double Schwartz 128 – Marqueterie (USA) (Well   83
Decorated (USA)) [1991 5m 6m⁴ 6d* 1992 6g⁵ 7g³ 7g 6g⁴ 7m 7f 7.3g 6s] compact
colt: has a quick action: fairly useful handicapper on his day: below form (including
in a visor once) after good fourth in £10,600 handicap at Ascot in July, hanging right
then staying on very well: stays 7f: best efforts on an easy surface: sold 13,500 gns
Newmarket Autumn Sales. *C. R. Nelson*

SIR CRUSTY   10 br.g. Gunner B 126 – Brazen 83 (Cash And Courage 116) [1991   –
NR 1992 14.9v⁶] sturdy, deep-bodied gelding: carries plenty of condition: very
lightly raced on flat of late and no worthwhile form since 1988: fairly useful winning
hurdler. *O. O'Neill*

SIR DANCELOT (USA)   4 b.g. Far North (CAN) 120 – Princess Morvi (USA)   –
(Graustark) [1991 11.7m² 12f³ 12m⁵ 13.1f 12.1g⁶ 9m 1992 a16g] big gelding: rated 77
on debut at 3 yrs: probably of little account these days. *R. Simpson*

SIR EDWARD HENRY (IRE)   2 b.c. (Jan 31) Taufan (USA) 119 – Finessing   –
(Indian King (USA) 128) [1992 8.2s 7g] IR 5,600F, IR 27,000Y: rangy colt: first foal:
dam ran several times: well beaten in maidens at Nottingham (slowly away) and
Doncaster in the autumn. *F. H. Lee*

SIR GEORGE CHUFFY (IRE)   4 b.g. Welsh Term 126 – Grand Legacy 56   –
(Relko 136) [1991 10g³ 10.5m³ 10.4g 13.1m 8d 1992 10d] leggy, good-topped gelding:
rated 75 at 3 yrs: well beaten on reappearance, in April: needs further than 1m, and
should stay 1½m: acts on good to firm ground: sold 3,400 gns Doncaster September
Sales. *F. H. Lee*

SIR HARRY HARDMAN   4 b.c. Doulab (USA) 115 – Song Grove 61 (Song 132)   101
[1991 6m⁵ 5g² 6g⁴ 5m 5m⁵ 5g 5g⁴ 5m⁵ 1992 6m³ 5s³ 5g⁵ 6f³ 6f 5s⁴ 6g 6g 6d 7m 7g
6.1s²] strong, good-quartered colt: carries condition: impresses in appearance:
moderate mover: useful performer at best: ran well when in frame in first half of
season, including in 3 listed events: form afterwards only when second of 3 in
slowly-run minor event at Nottingham in October: best at 5f/6f: acts on firm and soft
ground: often blinkered/visored, not last 4 starts: has hung markedly left. *F. H. Lee*

SIR JOEY (USA)   3 ch.c. Honest Pleasure (USA) – Sougoli (Realm 129) [1991 NR   71
1992 10g⁵ 7d 8g 6s² 5.1s* 6.1s³] $3,500F: workmanlike colt: fourth foal: half-
brother to a minor winner in North America by Mr Justice: dam, Irish 2-y-o 5f
winner unplaced on 9 starts in North America, is half-sister to tough sprint
handicapper Gods Solution out of a half-sister to high-class French horse Full of
Hope: fair form: won handicap at Chepstow in October in fine style for R. Holder:
fair effort in similar event final start: stays 6f: goes well on soft ground: may be
capable of better. *P. G. Murphy*

SIR MARK SYKES (IRE)   3 b.g. Reference Point 139 – American Winter   84
(USA) 78 (Lyphard (USA) 132) [1991 NR 1992 8d 10g⁴ 8d* 8.1m] 16,000Y: good-
topped gelding: moderate mover: fourth foal: half-brother to 1m winner American

Hero (by Persian Bold) and 1988 Irish 2-y-o 1m winner Classic Pleasure (by Shirley Heights): dam, 7f winner, is out of half-sister to top-class filly and broodmare Fanfreluche: fairly useful performer: won maiden at Carlisle by 8 lengths, always close up and running on well: never able to challenge in £18,300 handicap at Haydock 16 days later in May: seems to need testing conditions at 1m, and should prove effective back at 1¼m. *J. R. Fanshawe*

SIRMOOR (IRE) 3 b.c. Try My Best (USA) 130 – Muted Song (Artaius (USA) 129) [1991 6g 1992 7g5 7g 8f 7s 8d 8g5 a6g4 a7g a7g] close-coupled colt: poor mover: none too consistent maiden: stays 1m. *R. Hannon* **57**

SIR NORMAN HOLT (IRE) 3 b.c. Ela-Mana-Mou 132 – Ploy 87 (Posse (USA) 130) [1991 8m6 7g 1992 8.2d5 10g 8f6 10.3f 11m5 11.1f* 13.1m 10d6 9d 8m* 10s6 11d 8.2g3 8g a8g2 a7g*] good-topped colt: none too consistent handicapper: successful in 1992 at Hamilton, Pontefract (seller, bought in 5,400 gns) and Lingfield: effective setting pace at 7f/1m, and stays 11f: acts on firm ground, seemingly not on a soft surface: blinkered or visored nowadays: goes well with forcing tactics. *F. H. Lee* **63**

SIR OLIVER (IRE) 3 b.g. Auction Ring (USA) 123 – Eurorose (Busted 134) [1991 6d3 1992 8.1g 7g2 8m 6.9m5 7.6m4 8m 7g4 8d 10.2s5 9.7g6 8d] good-topped gelding: has round action: inconsistent maiden handicapper: should stay 1m: acts on good to firm ground. *R. J. Hodges* **65**

SIR PAGEANT 3 b.g. Pharly (FR) 130 – National Dress 64 (Welsh Pageant 132) [1991 a8g2 1992 12g4 11.7d4 12m3 12s6 a16g] sturdy colt: has a round action: modest maiden: stays 1½m: acts on good to firm and dead ground, possibly unsuited by very soft: sold out of P. Cole's stable 12,500 gns Newmarket Autumn Sales. *K. S. Bridgwater* **64**

SIR TASKER 4 b.c. Lidhame 109 – Susie's Baby (Balidar 133) [1991 5s 5.8m 8m6 7m4 7g 7g5 7f4 7m 6m 6m2 5g3 6.1m 5d* 5g 5s a6g6 a5g* a5g a5g2 1992 a5g* a5g a5g* a5g* a5g* a5g 5g 5m* 5.1m 5f3 5g 5f 5m a5g a5g a5g a6g6] compact, quite attractive colt: fair handicapper: successful at Southwell and Lingfield (3) early in the year and at Redcar (for 7-lb claimer) in April: well held after 4-month break last 5 starts: speedy: acts on firm and dead ground and all-weather surfaces: good round a turn: usually runs well on equitrack. *J. L. Harris* **72**
a75

SIRTELIMAR (IRE) 3 b.c. Montelimar (USA) 122 – Sajanjal (Dance In Time (CAN)) [1991 7m 1992 10m4 12g 8.2g 10.2g a8g* 8.9m 10d3 11.5s a8g3] tall colt: shows knee action: inconsistent performer: made all in maiden at Southwell in July: trained until after next outing by Bob Jones: best efforts at 1m on fibresand: tongue tied down last 2 starts. *R. C. Spicer* **59**
a69

SIR THOMAS BEECHAM 2 b.g. (Apr 16) Daring March 116 – Balinese 86 (Balidar 133) [1992 7g 7s 8m] leggy, unfurnished gelding: fifth foal: brother to 5f winner Bally Brave and a winner in Belgium and half-brother to 1m winner Trembalino (by Tremblant): dam suited by 7f: modest form, never a factor, in maidens in the autumn. *S. Dow* **52**

SIR VIDAR (IRE) 3 b.c. Caerleon (USA) 132 – Very Charming (USA) (Vaguely Noble 140) [1991 8s4 8.1d4 1992 a11g 14.1g a16g] big colt: moderate mover: modest maiden at 2 yrs: soundly beaten in 1992: blinkered, collapsed and died at Southwell in September: should have been suited by further than 1m. *M. Bell* –

SISON (IRE) 2 b.g. (Mar 18) Vacarme (USA) 121 – Silent Sail (Aglojo 119) [1992 5d4 5g*] 8,000Y: compact gelding: half-brother to 4 winners here and abroad, including (at 1m) fair Russell Creek (by Sandy Creek) and (at 5.3f) Jellabia (by Pal's Passage): dam Irish 1¼m winner, is half-sister to Jellaby: 2½-length winner of maiden at Thirsk in April. *R. M. Whitaker* **66**

SISSINGAYA (USA) 2 ch.f. (Apr 6) Bering 136 – Sissy's Time (USA) (Villamor (USA)) [1992 7g* 7s3 8d4 8s] half-sister to 2 minor winners in North America: dam very useful winner of 11 races at up to 7f: 4-length winner of newcomers race at Evry: in frame after in Prix du Calvados at Deauville (beaten 2¾ lengths by Cox Orange) and Prix d'Aumale at Longchamp (over 2 lengths behind Kindergarten): beaten around 5 lengths when creditable eighth of 11 to Gold Splash in Prix Marcel Boussac at Longchamp: will be better suited by 1¼m: yet to race on top-of-the-ground. *F. Boutin, France* **102**

SISTADARI 4 b.f. Shardari 134 – Sistabelle (Bellypha 130) [1991 10m3 9g2 10m3 7m2 1992 8g 8m] angular filly: fair maiden: rated 84 at 3 yrs: below form in handicaps in summer at 4 yrs: stays 1¼m: acts on good to firm ground: sold 21,000 gns Newmarket December Sales: covered by Warning. *L. M. Cumani* –

SIT ALKUL (USA) 2 br.f. (Feb 10) Mr Prospector (USA) – Lypatia (FR) **73 p** (Lyphard (USA) 132) [1992 7g⁴] $950,000Y: sister to Middle Park winner and 2000 Guineas second Lycius and half-sister to several winners, including Akabir (by Riverman), winner in France then in graded company at 9.5f and 1½m in North America: dam French 6.5f winner: 12/1, prominent throughout when over 3 lengths fourth of 24 to Fayfa in maiden at Newmarket in October: will improve. *M. R. Stoute*

SIWAAYIB 2 b.f. (Jan 13) Green Desert (USA) 127 – Ma Petite Cherie (USA) 93 **72 p** (Caro 133) [1992 6s*] third foal: half-sister to 3-y-o Fatack (by Kris) and 4-y-o 9f and 1¼m winner Flaming Arrow (by Dancing Brave): dam, French 1m (at 2 yrs) to 1¼m winner: justified favouritism by a neck in 14-runner maiden at Leicester in October, progress 2f out and running on well to collar Quinsigimond close home: will improve, particularly at 1m. *A. A. Scott*

SIXOFUS (IRE) 4 b. or br.g. Glenstal (USA) 118 – Grace Darling (USA) **–** (Vaguely Noble 140) [1991 6v² 6d⁶ 5m⁵ 5.1g³ 6f² 5f 7g² 6m³ 6f⁵ 8m* 8m 9.7s 1992 10m 8.3m 8f a6g] leggy, rather angular gelding: has a quick action: rated 58 at 3 yrs: below form in 1992, including in sellers: stays 1m: acts on good to firm ground and dead. *W. G. M. Turner*

SIZZLING AFFAIR 3 b.c. Sizzling Melody 117 – Vivchar 80 (Huntercombe 133) **–** [1991 6.1g⁵ 7g 6f 1992 6m 6f 8f] workmanlike colt: has a round action: poor maiden: probably stays 7f. *T. Casey*

SIZZLING ROSE 3 b.f. Sizzling Melody 117 – Garnette Rose 74 (Floribunda **34** 136) [1991 5m 5g³ 6g⁴ 6g⁵ 5s³ 5g² 6m 7m a6g 1992 a8g 8s 8m 5.1f⁴] leggy, sparely-made filly: moderate mover: poor maiden: stays 6f: best form with some give in the ground: sold 550 gns Ascot July Sales. *W. Carter*

SIZZLING SAGA (IRE) 4 b. or br.c. Horage 124 – Alsazia (FR) (Bolkonski **98** 134) [1991 5g³ 6f² 6d* 6m⁵ 6f* 6m* 6m* 6g² 6.5s* 6s⁴ 6d⁶ 5m 1992 7.1g 6f 6f* 6s 6d⁶ 6.1d⁴ a5g] strong, sturdy colt: poor mover: useful but none too consistent sprinter: 7-length winner of Haydock claimer in July: best effort after when creditable last of 4 to Montendre in well-contested Chepstow minor event: better at around 6f than 5f: acts on any going: trained until after sixth start by J. Berry: front runner. *J. Wharton*

SIZZLING SARAH 3 b.f. Sizzling Melody 117 – Gundreda 93 (Gunner B 126) **–** [1991 NR 1992 6.1d a12g 9.9f] 1,800F, 2,500Y: leggy filly: second living foal: dam 8.2f and 1¼m winner: last in maidens: visored final start. *Bob Jones*

SIZZLING THOUGHTS 3 b.g. Sizzling Melody 117 – Palace Guest (Be My **–** Guest (USA) 126) [1991 NR 1992 10s 10s⁵ 8f 8m] 3,500F: good-topped gelding: has been hobdayed: fourth foal: brother to a winner in Sweden and half-brother to a winner in Sweden: dam, winner in Sweden, is half-sister to smart middle-distance performer Palace Gold: no sign of ability: sold 600 gns Ascot July Sales. *G. Lewis*

SKI CAPTAIN 8 b.g. Welsh Captain 113 – Miss Nelski 84 (Most Secret 119) [1991 **55** 5g 5m 5m 5g⁴ 5g 5m* 5f 5g 5g* 5m³ 5.2g 5m⁶ 5m 5g³ 5.1m 5m² 5g 5.1s 5g a5g 1992 a5g³ a5g 5g 5d² 5g 5m 5m 5g 5m² 5.2g* 5.2f³ 5m 5.2m⁶] strong, workmanlike gelding: usually looks well: moderate mover: 5f handicapper: made all at Yarmouth in July: acts on any going: has run well when blinkered or visored, but hasn't worn them since 1987: successful for apprentice: tough. *P. Howling*

SKIMBLE (USA) 3 ch.f. Lyphard (USA) 132 – Nimble Folly (USA) (Cyane) **95** [1991 6m* 1992 7m 8g 10.4m* 8.1m 8.5f* 8.5f* 9f2] attractive, good-topped filly: useful performer here in spring: won minor event at York and ran in much better company otherwise, refusing to settle in 1000 Guineas second start: stays 10.4f: left H. Cecil for USA after fourth start, winning 2 non-graded stakes races in the autumn. *R. Frankel, USA*

SKIMMER HAWK 3 b.g. Buzzards Bay 128§ – Song To Singo 63 (Master Sing **– p** 109) [1991 NR 1992 12.3g 11.7d 12.2d 11.5d] strong gelding: third foal: dam 2-y-o 5f winner seemed to stay 1m: no worthwhile form but showed signs of ability in handicap final start. *Bob Jones*

SKIPPER TO BILGE 5 b.g. Night Shift (USA) – Upper Deck 115 (Sun Prince **72** 128) [1991 8g⁵ 8v 8d⁴* 7m 7g 7.6d* 7.6s⁴ 7s* 7d 1992 8.3d 8.5g⁵ 8g⁴ 8g* 7g⁵ a7g* 8s³ 8.1d 7g] lengthy gelding: none too consistent performer: won claimers at Goodwood in June and Southwell in September: probably stays 1¼m: goes very well with some give in the ground (acts on heavy going) and on fibresand: races up with pace: suitable mount for apprentice: sold 7,000 gns Newmarket Autumn Sales. *M. A. Jarvis*

SKIP TRACER 4 b.g. Balliol 125 – Song To Singo 63 (Master Sing 109) [1991 7f⁴ –
8g 7f⁵ 10m 8m 8m 1992 a7g⁶ a10g 7d] close-coupled, angular gelding: poor maiden:
blinkered final start: sold 1,500 gns Ascot May Sales. *K. T. Ivory*

SKISURF 6 b.g. Niniski (USA) 125 – Seasurf 106 (Seaepic (USA) 100) [1991 NR 58
1992 16m 14.1g² 17.2f⁴ 18.8m² 16s³ 20m 14.1f] close-coupled, workmanlike gelding:
modest handicapper: dyed-in-the-wool stayer: probably acts on any going: suitable
mount for claimer. *C. E. Brittain*

SKULLCAP 2 b.g. (Feb 3) Sharrood (USA) 124 – Falaka 83 (Sparkler 130) [1992 60
6m⁶ 6m⁵ 6m* 6m 7g⁴ 7.1s⁶ 5g⁵ a6g²] angular gelding, somewhat unfurnished: third
reported foal: dam 7f and 1m winner: consistent performer: won seller (sold out of
D. Morley's stable 5,750 gns) at Yarmouth in July: should stay 1m: acts on good to
firm and soft ground, and on equitrack. *T. J. Naughton*

SKY BURST 2 ch.f. (Apr 8) Gunner B 126 – Sky Bonnet 72 (Sky Gipsy 117) [1992 –
6d 7.1s 7g] smallish filly: half-sister to 8.2f seller winner Frisco (by Absalom) and a
winner in Hong Kong: dam 1m and 1¼m winner: soundly beaten in maidens. *L. G.
Cottrell*

SKY CAT 8 b.g. Skyliner 117 – Spring Kitten (Pitcairn 126) [1991 12m 8g² 9m² 41
7m* 7f⁶ 8.2g⁴ 7m⁵ 8.2m 8.3f² 8f 1992 8m 7g 9m⁴ 8.1f³ 8f 8.3g⁶] leggy, good-topped
gelding: poor handicapper: stays 9f: probably acts on any going: effective blinkered/
visored or not: often sweats: sometimes finds little, and best with extreme waiting
tactics. *C. Tinkler*

SKY HUNTER (USA) 3 b. or br.c. Star de Naskra (USA) – Hunt The Thimble 90
(USA) 86 (Turn And Count (USA)) [1991 7m² 7g⁴ 8m⁵ 1992 8g⁶ 8d* 8.2d³ 7g* 7m²
7.1m] tall, quite good-topped colt: fairly useful performer: won maiden at Brighton
in March and £7,400 handicap (visored and edgy) at Newmarket in May: not seen
out again after running moderately in May: stays 1m: acts on good to firm ground
and dead: none too easy ride. *R. Hannon*

SKY RECORD 3 b.g. Skyliner 117 – On The Record 72 (Record Token 128) [1991 –
NR 1992 6m] 480Y: first foal: dam sprinter best treated with caution: soon behind in
maiden at Redcar in August: sold to join D. Moffatt 2,400 gns Doncaster November
Sales. *Miss S. E. Hall*

SKY TRAIN (IRE) 3 gr.f. Siberian Express (USA) 125 – Karietta (Wollow 132) 65
[1991 7m 7f³ 7m⁵ 1992 10.2m³ 10m⁴ 10.8m⁴ 10f* 10m 11.7d 10g⁵ 9.7v] lengthy,
sparely-made filly: below form in handicaps after winning at Brighton in July: stays
10.8f: acts on firm going, seemingly not on a soft surface: tends to sweat: sold 7,000
gns Newmarket Autumn Sales. *J. L. Dunlop*

SKY WISH 2 b.g. (Apr 10) Skyliner 117 – On The Record 72 (Record Token 128) 57
[1992 5g 5m 7f² 6d 7.5m³] 620Y: angular gelding: second foal: brother to 3-y-o Sky
Record: dam sprinter best treated with caution: best effort in maiden auctions when
staying-on third of 18 at Beverley in September: will be better suited by 1m. *Miss S.
E. Hall*

SLADES HILL 5 b.h. Lochnager 132 – Mephisto Waltz 98 (Dancer's Image 62
(USA)) [1991 6g 6d 5f 6f 5f⁵ 5g⁵ 6g 6d 1992 a5g⁶ 5g* 5m⁶] small, good-quartered
horse: moderate mover: modest handicapper: won at Thirsk in April but not seen
again after that month: may prove ideally suited by 6f: acts on firm going: ran fairly
well when visored, too free in blinkers. *T. D. Barron*

SLANDERINTHESTRAND (IRE) 3 b. or br.g. Millfontaine 114 – Eccentric 38
Lady (London Bells (CAN) 109) [1991 6d 7m 7g⁵ 6m 1992 8g 8m⁵ 10f⁵ 10m⁵ 8.5d]
good-topped gelding: modest plater: stays 1¼m: acts on good to firm ground: stiff
task when visored once. *M. J. Haynes*

SLEEPLINE FANTASY 7 ch.g. Buzzards Bay 128§ – Sleepline Princess 86 –
(Royal Palace 131) [1991 a7g* 7f* 7g² 7m 8g 8m* 8f 8m 1992 7.5g] leggy, sparely-
made gelding: none too consistent handicapper, rated 74 at 3 yrs: effective at 7f to
1m: acts on any going. *M. R. Channon*

SLIGHT RISK 3 b.f. Risk Me (FR) 127 – Sarah Gillian (USA) (Zen (USA)) [1991 –
5v⁶ 5m³ 6g⁶ 7g² 7g⁵ 7m⁴ 7m 9m 7d a8g 1992 a10g* a10g* a10g² 12v a10g² a10g⁶ 10d a72 ?
a7g a10g a12g² a12g⁵ a12g³] tall, leggy filly: has a quick action: modest performer:
won claimer and handicap (made all) at Lingfield early in year: appeared to run best
race when second over 1½m on same course in November: stays 1½m: best form on
equitrack, seems not to act on heavy ground: wears eyecover. *P. A. Kelleway*

SLIP-A-SNIP 5 b.m. Wolverlife 115 – Stramenta (Thatching 131) [1991 5d³ 5g⁴ 62 d
5g 5m⁵ 5d* 5.2f 5f 5m⁴ 5g 5.2g a5g³ a5g³ 1992 a5g⁴ a5g⁵ 5.3m 5d⁴ 5.3m 5g 7g³ 5.7f⁵
6g 6.9m] lengthy, sparely-made mare: poor mover: inconsistent handicapper: best

at sprint distances: yet to race on very soft going, acts on any other: successful for claimer: has found little off bridle: sold 1,250 gns Ascot November Sales. *G. B. Balding*

SLIVOVITZ 2 b.c. (Apr 7) Petoski 135 – Hiding 84 (So Blessed 130) [1992 7s⁶ 7g⁶] 4,000F, 4,000Y: quite attractive, unfurnished colt: brother to 7f (at 2 yrs) and 10.1f winner Evading and half-brother to sprint winners by Formidable and Pas de Seul: dam 2-y-o 5f winner from family of Bassenthwaite: shaped promisingly in Salisbury maiden in September but off bridle soon after halfway when beaten around 13 lengths in similar event at Doncaster following month. *M. J. Heaton-Ellis* **61**

SLUMBER THYME (IRE) 3 ch.f. Burslem 123 – Chive (St Chad 120) [1991 7g 7m 1992 5g 8m⁴ 8m 8m⁶] neat filly: poor maiden: has given impression will prove suited by 1¼m. *J. G. FitzGerald* **40**

SLY PROSPECT (USA) 4 ch.g. Barachois (CAN) – Miss Sly (USA) (Diamond Prospect (USA) 126) [1991 7f⁴ 8g³ 7f⁴ 8m 7f* 7.5f 7m⁵ 1992 8f 7.5g⁶ 7.1m 7g 14.6d] strong, lengthy gelding: has a light action: rated 73 at 3 yrs for J. Etherington: way below best in handicaps in 1992: stays 1m: acts on firm going: often blinkered, below form visored. *K. White* **–**

SMARGINATO (IRE) 2 gr.c. (May 14) Simply Great (FR) 122 – Aldern Stream 102 (Godswalk (USA) 130) [1992 6.1d⁶ 7d 6.1g²] IR 36,000Y: rather unfurnished colt: sixth foal: half-brother to French 3-y-o Showbrook (by Exhibitioner), useful sprinter here at 2 yrs, and 1988 Irish 2-y-o 7f winner Alpine Spring (by Head For Heights): dam won over 5f and 7f: easily best effort when staying-on second to Snowy River in median auction at Nottingham in September: will stay 1m: should improve. *J. L. Dunlop* **73 p**

SMART DAISY 2 b.f. (Mar 22) Elegant Air 119 – Michaelmas 72 (Silly Season 127) [1992 7m 7s⁵ 8s³] leggy, lengthy filly: seventh foal: half-sister to 7f seller winner Coldwater Canyon (by Dominion) and modest 1984 2-y-o 1m winner Rowanberry (by Great Nephew): dam thrice-raced half-sister to high-class miler Martinmas: modest form in maidens last 2 starts: will be well suited by 1¼m. *I. A. Balding* **53**

SMARTIE LEE 5 ch.m. Dominion 123 – Nosy Parker (FR) (Kashmir II 125) [1991 12s² 17.2f 12m² 11.9f² 14m a12g a16g³ 1992 10g 16m⁴ 14s 14.1d a16g] small, close-coupled mare: keen walker: poor handicapper: stays 2m: acts on any going, including equitrack: ran creditably blinkered once. *P. F. I. Cole* **50**

SMART TEACHER (USA) 2 b. or br.c. (Apr 1) Smarten (USA) – Finality (USA) (In Reality) [1992 6g 6.1d 6g] $55,000Y: leggy, unfurnished colt: looks weak: half-brother to 2 winners in North America, one stakes placed: dam won at up to 7f at 2 yrs and 3 yrs: sire high-class middle-distance colt: soundly beaten in maidens, after swerving and unseating rider leaving stalls on debut. *P. W. Harris* **–**

SMILES AHEAD 4 ch.g. Primo Dominie 121 – Baby's Smile 68 (Shirley Heights 130) [1991 12.2g² 10m⁶ 12m² 12g³ 12.2m² 13.8m³ 12.2g² 12.3g 12.1d* 12g* 12.3g 1992 11.6g 11.9s⁶ 11.9s] lengthy gelding: rated 72 at 3 yrs: below form in handicaps in 1992: stays 13.8f: acts on firm ground, but particularly well suited by an easy surface: takes keen hold, often wears net muzzle and taken to post alone: won over hurdles in November. *P. J. Bevan* **–**

SMILINGATSTRANGERS 4 b.f. Macmillion 110 – My Charade 79 (Cawston's Clown 113) [1991 NR 1992 14.1d 14.1m 18.2m² 18.8m* 16.5g* 19m⁴ 16.1g⁵ 16d 16d² 16.2d⁵ 18m⁵ 16.5g] small, rather sparely-made filly: won handicaps at Warwick and Doncaster in July and generally in good form after, excellent fifth in Cesarewitch: suited by thorough test of stamina: acts on good to firm and dead ground: effective visored or not. *Mrs Barbara Waring* **58 +**

SMILING CHIEF (IRE) 4 ch.g. Montelimar (USA) 122 – Victa 79 (Northfields (USA)) [1991 10g³ 10g⁶ a12g 12g a12g 1992 a10g² a12g² 14m⁵ 11.4f² 12m 11.5m³ 14.6d a12g³ 10d* a10g* 11.5g 9d] big, lengthy gelding: below par after winning Salisbury claimer (first win) and Lingfield handicap in August: effective at 1¼m to 1½m: acts on firm and dead going and equitrack: joined R. Hodges and won novice handicap hurdle in November. *C. A. Cyzer* **66**

SMILING SUN (IRE) 4 ch.g. Thatching 131 – Charites (Red God 128§) [1991 8g³ 8g³ 8m 7g⁵ 7d 7m² 7g³ 1992 a7g] sturdy gelding: poor walker and mover: inconsistent handicapper: rated 91 at 3 yrs: effective at 7f/1m: acts on good to firm and dead ground and equitrack: below form blinkered once. *W. A. O'Gorman* **–**

SMITH N'ALLAN 2 b.c. (Mar 26) Tina's Pet 121 – Mertola (Tribal Chief 125) [1992 6m 6d] 6,200Y: half-brother to several winners, including 10-y-o (from 7f to 1¼m) Gilderdale (by Gunner B) and sprinter Mertola's Pet (by Tickled Pink): dam **56**

ran once: beaten over 5 lengths when in midfield of maiden auction at Yarmouth in September: always behind in Redcar maiden following month. *Bob Jones*

SMITH'S PEAK   8 ro.g. Alias Smith (USA) – Sacred Mountain 74 (St Paddy 133)   – [1991 10m 9m* 10m³ 11.7g⁵ 12g 10g 9m³ 8g⁴ 10m³ a12g a10g⁴ 1992 a10g⁴ a12g⁵] workmanlike gelding: rated 56 at 7 yrs: blinkered and below form in handicaps in spring: stays 1¼m: acts on good to firm ground. *R. J. O'Sullivan*

SMOCKING   2 ch.f. (Apr 4) Night Shift (USA) – Sue Grundy 104 (Grundy 137)   – p [1992 6s] third foal: dam, 7f (at 2 yrs) and 1¼m winner, is granddaughter of 1000 Guineas winner Full Dress II: 33/1, prominent to halfway in maiden at Leicester in October: will improve. *G. Wragg*

SMOKE   6 gr.m. Rusticaro (FR) 124 – Fire-Screen 92 (Roan Rocket 128) [1991   **46** 16.2g 12m 12g 9.9m⁶ 12m* 12.3d² 12f4 12.3f6 12f² 12f* 12.3f* 1992 13.8d 12g 9.9g³ 9.9m⁶ 12f² 13m⁵ 10.5d 9.9d² 9.9d⁴ 12m² 12d] good-topped mare: poor mover: largely consistent handicapper: rare poor effort final start and sold 2,500 gns Doncaster September Sales: better at around 1½m than shorter: acts on any going, but goes very well on firm: best without blinkers. *J. Parkes*

SMUDGEMUPUM   3 b.c. Green Ruby (USA) 104 – Cloudless Sky 67 (He Loves   **45** d Me 120) [1991 NR 1992 a7g⁶ a8g⁶ a8g 7d 10m 6g* 6g 5g⁵ 7m 6g 7.1g 6g a7g] 1,100Y: sparely-made colt: first foal: dam miler: way below form after winning apprentice selling handicap (no bid) at Windsor in July: best effort at 6f: very stiff task when visored once: sold 825 gns Ascot November Sales. *Miss B. Sanders*

SNAADEE (USA)   5 br.h. Danzig (USA) – Somfas (USA) (What A Pleasure **114** (USA)) [1991 7m* 7g* 7g⁴ 5m⁶ 6d* 1992 6m⁴ 6d⁶ 5m*] strong, good-topped horse: carries condition: retired to stud in Australia after putting up best effort when 14/1-winner of UB Group Temple Stakes at Sandown, making all to beat Blyton Lad by 2 lengths: raced with little zest and gave impression none too resolute previous 2 runs in Abernant Stakes at Newmarket (most reluctant to go to post) and minor event at Kempton: effective up to 7f: acted on good to firm and dead ground: sometimes wore crossed noseband. *M. R. Stoute*

SNAPPY'S BOY JOSH   3 b.g. Hotfoot 126 – September Snap 46 (Music Boy   – 124) [1991 7f 7g 1992 10m 10g 10g] big gelding: no sign of ability. *P. J. Feilden*

SNICKERSNEE   4 b.g. Kris 135 – Cat Girl (USA) (Grey Dawn II 132) [1991 12m⁶   – 12m 11.5g* 12m 1992 12m 11.6g 12d 11.5m] big, strong, rangy gelding: rated 72 at 3 yrs: tailed off in handicaps in 1992: blinkered final start: stays 11.5f: sold 2,800 gns Ascot November Sales. *M. Dixon*

SNO MARQUE   4 ch.g. Carwhite 127 – Hyacine 43 (High Line 125) [1991 7v   – 10m³ 12d⁴ 14g 11m* 10g² 11.5m³ 1992 9.7v] close-coupled gelding: rated 61 at 3 yrs: blinkered and always behind in Folkestone seller in November, 1992: should stay beyond 1½m: acts on good to firm and dead ground: below form when visored once. *A. S. Reid*

SNOOKER TABLE   9 b.g. Ballymore 123 – Northern Twilight (English Prince   – 129) [1991 NR 1992 12.3g] workmanlike gelding: on the downgrade. *T. B. Hallett*

UB Group Temple Stakes, Sandown—Snaadee puts his best foot forward on his final start

SNO SERENADE 6 b.g. Song 132 – When The Saints (Bay Express 132) [1991 –
10.2m 7m 7.1m 10.1f 8.3d⁶ 8.9m 8g⁴ a6g 1992 a8g 7g 7s a8g a8g a8g⁶] tall, leggy,
quite attractive gelding: has a quick action: on the downgrade. *M. Dods*

SNOW BLIZZARD 4 gr.c. Petong 126 – Southern Dynasty 81 (Gunner B 126) **61**
[1991 10g 7g 10m 10g 9.7m* 10g³ 12f⁴ 11.5s 1992 12m* 12d 12h* 11.9g⁶ 12v a12g*
a12g³] big, workmanlike colt: modest handicapper: won at Folkestone (2) and
Lingfield in 1992: stays 1½m: seems to need a sound surface: sometimes wears
tongue strap. *S. Dow*

SNOW BOARD 3 gr.g. Niniski (USA) 125 – Troja (Troy 137) [1991 7s 8.1g 1992 **65** p
10d 14.1g³ 16d*] workmanlike gelding: lightly raced and improved with each run in
1992: still green when narrowly winning handicap at Nottingham in September,
finishing with a flourish to lead close home: will prove suited by thorough test of
stamina: off course 3½ months and changed hands 8,000 gns Newmarket
September Sales after second start: should improve further. *B. W. Hills*

SNOWGIRL (IRE) 4 gr.f. Mazaad 106 – Rust Free 58 (Free State 125) [1991 6g³ **68**
5g* 5m* 5d³ 5m³ 5m⁶ 5m⁴ 6s* 6m³ 6m³ 5d⁵ 6g 1992 5s⁶ 6g 6d 6m 7.6v]
good-topped filly: has a quick action: rated 82 at 3 yrs: below form in handicaps in
1992: stays 6f: acts on good to firm ground and soft: usually forces pace: has joined
Mrs E. Slack. *J. Berry*

SNOWY RIVER (FR) 2 ch.c. (Apr 10) Ti King (FR) 121 – River Goddess (USA) **83**
(Northern Dancer (CAN)) [1992 6g³ 7g² 6m* 6. 1g* 6m] 4,100F, 7,800Y: strong colt:
fourth foal: half-brother to 3-y-o French winner Dick Tracy (by Top Ville), successful from 6f (at 2 yrs) to 11f: dam unraced sister to Woodstream and half-sister to
Jaazeiro: comfortably made all in maiden auction at Folkestone in August and
median auction at Nottingham in September: dropped out quickly when headed and
finished last of 17 in Newmarket nursery final start: stays 7f: possibly needs to
dominate. *Dr J. D. Scargill*

SNUG SURPRISE 2 b.f. (Mar 26) Elegant Air 119 – Persevering 95 (Blakeney – §
126) [1992 a6g 7g 7g 10.5d] 2,000F, 3,400Y: close-coupled, workmanlike filly: sister
to 3-y-o Elegant Solution, 7.1f winner at 2 yrs, and half-sister to several winners,
including fairly useful sprinter Fair Test (by Fair Season) and (at 1¼m) Winoski (by
Petoski): dam winner 4 times at up to 2m, is out of half-sister to very smart
middle-distance stayer Petty Officer: soundly beaten, including in sellers: looked
very hard ride when blinkered final start: seems ungenuine. *J. S. Wainwright*

SNURGE 5 ch.h. Ela-Mana-Mou 132 – Finlandia (FR) (Faraway Son (USA) **122**
130) [1991 13.3d* 12g* 12.5m* 12d 12s³ 14v* 1992 13.9m³ 12g 12d⁵ 12g² 12g²
12.5s² 14s² 12d* 14s⁶]
   The Rothmans International at Woodbine in October provided a very
valuable, though arguably fortunate, victory for the itinerant Snurge. After
being beaten half a length by French-trained Wiorno, Snurge was promoted
after Wiorno was found to have hampered third-placed Ghazi (an appeal
against the decision of the Woodbine stewards by Wiorno's connections was
turned down some time afterwards); Saddlers' Hall, Beyton, Mashaallah and
Spinning were the other European challengers further down the field. The
1990 St Leger winner Snurge has been seen only three times on a British
racecourse in the last two seasons. He ran in the Yorkshire Cup, in which he
came a good third to Rock Hopper, and the Coronation Cup in the latest
season before being sent on his travels again. In all, he ran in five other
countries—Canada, France, Germany, Ireland and Italy—and finished second
in four good races before the Rothmans International. He was beaten a head in
two Group 1 events in Germany, by German-trained Platini at Dusseldorf in
July and by French-trained Tel Quel in the Aral-Pokal at Gelsenkirchen-Horst
in August; then came a length-and-a-half defeat by Modhish in the Grand Prix
de Deauville and a neck defeat by Mashaallah in the Irish St Leger; he ran one
of his best races when staying on strongly at the Curragh (Drum Taps, Rock
Hopper and Vintage Crop were third, fourth and fifth).
   The pedigree of the big, strong, lengthy Snurge isn't of great relevance
for the time being, since he's to continue racing. His dam Finlandia showed
little sign of ability but is a half-sister to several winners including the Irish
Derby third Master Guy and the very useful French middle-distance filly
Musique Royale. Finlandia is also the dam of the Irish Oaks fourth Faraway
Pastures (by Northfields) and the useful miler Suomi (by Tate Gallery), a

Rothmans International, Woodbine—
Wiorno is the winner on merit but not after the stewards inquiry;
another big prize goes to Snurge

Snurge (ch.h. 1987)	Ela-Mana-Mou (b 1976)	Pitcairn (b 1971)	Petingo Border Bounty
		Rose Bertin (ch 1970)	High Hat Wide Awake
	Finlandia (FR) (b 1977)	Faraway Son (b 1967)	Ambiopoise Locust Time
		Musical II (ch 1961)	Prince Chevalier Musidora

winner in the United States in the latest season. Snurge is effective at a mile and a half to a mile and three quarters and will probably stay further. He has a high knee action but has shown good-class form on going ranging from good to firm to heavy. Although he sometimes shows some reluctance to enter the stalls, Snurge is thoroughly tough and genuine. *P. F. I. Cole*

SOAKING 2 b.g. (Mar 3) Dowsing (USA) 124 – Moaning Low 85 (Burglar 128) **68** [1992 6m 6s² 6m* 6s] 10,000F, 12,000Y: strong, useful-looking gelding: half-brother to several minor winners here and abroad: dam 6f winner at 3 yrs: won seller (sold out of B. Hills's stable 8,500 gns) at Newmarket: below-form favourite in Newbury nursery later in October: will stay 7f: acts on good to firm and soft ground: swished tail second start. *G. Lewis*

SOBA GUEST (IRE) 3 ch.g. Be My Guest (USA) 126 – Brazilian Princess 66 **69** (Absalom 128) [1991 5g³ 5m² 5s⁵ 7d 5f* 5m⁶ 5m⁴ 5d* 1992 5d 5.1g⁶ 6d⁵ 5.7f 6m⁴ 7g³ 6f* a5g³ 6m³ 6d 5s 6s 6.1d 5v* a6g a5g⁴] smallish gelding: inconsistent handicapper: no bid after making all in sellers at Thirsk (ladies) in August and Hamilton in November: stays 6f: acts on any turf going, and on fibresand: sometimes bandaged or plastered near-hind. *J. Berry*

SO BEGUILING (USA) 3 b. or br.f. Woodman (USA) 126 – Clint's Sec (USA) **–** (Secretariat (USA)) [1991 6.1d⁵ 7m⁶ 7m* 7.9g 8f 8.2m 1992 8.9s 8g 16.1d 10g 8f] smallish, close-coupled filly: no promise in 1992: seems to stay 1m: acts on good to firm ground: tailed off when visored once. *Mrs A. L. M. King*

SOBERING THOUGHTS 6 ch.g. Be My Guest (USA) 126 – Soba 127 (Most **42** Secret 119) [1991 a6g a8g a7g⁴ a5g² a5g* a6g* 5g⁴ 7.5g 7g⁶ a7g⁵ a7g⁴ a5g* 6m⁶ a5g⁶ a5g³ a5g a6g 1992 a7g a7g 5g³ 5s a5g³ a5g³ a6g⁴ 5g⁵ a5g² 5d] big, plain gelding: moderate mover: largely consistent handicapper: effective at 5f to 7f: goes well on all-weather surfaces, possibly unsuited by soft ground: usually blinkered nowadays. *D. W. Chapman*

SOBER LAD (IRE) 2 gr.g. (Mar 21) Cyrano de Bergerac 120 – Renzola 74 d (Dragonara Palace (USA) 115) [1992 5d* 5g* 5g⁵ 5f 6m 6.1g 5s] 28,000Y: leggy, close-coupled gelding: has scope: third foal: brother to useful 3-y-o sprinter Miss Nosey Parker: dam never ran: well below form after making all in maiden at Leopardstown and minor event at Thirsk in spring: may well prove best at 5f: acts on dead ground: below form blinkered once. *J. Berry*

SOCIAL VISION (IRE) 2 b.g. (May 14) Parliament 117 – Elegant Miss (Prince – Tenderfoot (USA) 126) [1992 7d] IR 1,450F: fourth foal: dam Irish maiden: visored and always behind in seller at Redcar in October. *M. Avison*

SOCIETY GOWN (USA) 2 br.c. (Apr 19) Imp Society (USA) – Black Gown 48 (USA) (Groton) [1992 a7g⁶ 7.1g⁴ 7g⁴ 8g 7.5m 6g] $8,000Y: sturdy, angular colt: moderate mover: half-brother to minor winners in North America by Silent Screen and Text: dam minor sprint winner: sire best at 4 yrs when graded winner between 8.5f and 1¼m: poor maiden: should be suited by 1m: possibly unsuited by top-of-the-ground: below form blinkered once: sold 1,500 gns Newmarket Autumn Sales. *T. D. Barron*

SOCIETY LADY (USA) 2 ch.f. (Mar 30) Mr Prospector (USA) – La Voyageuse 75 (CAN) (Tentam (USA)) [1992 6m⁴ 7g² 8m 7d⁴] $200,000Y: big, lengthy filly: has plenty of scope: has a powerful, round action: sister to a minor winner and half-sister to several others, including useful French 1987 2-y-o 5.5f winner Kentucky Slew (by Seattle Slew), later successful in USA: dam, champion Canadian filly, is daughter of top racemare and broodmare Fanfreluche: clear second of 19 to Athens Belle in minor event at Kempton: fair effort in May Hill Stakes at Doncaster next outing, but never dangerous after slow start (got upset in stalls) in Ascot minor event: should be as effective at 1m as 7f. *A. A. Scott*

SOCKEM 5 b.g. Nordico (USA) – Floating Petal 90 (Wollow 132) [1991 a7g 7f 8m – 7m 8g³ 7g 7m 8f³ 7g 1992 7d a8g 8m] compact, rather sparely-made gelding: moderate mover: very much on the downgrade. *C. N. Williams*

SOCKS AND SHARES 3 ch.c. Shardari 134 – Lady Tippins (USA) (Star de 63 d Naskra (USA)) [1991 7g 6.1m⁴ 7g 1992 10g 10f³ 10.1m 10g 11.6g 14.9g 14.1f⁵ 12g 10d³ 10s] rather leggy, close-coupled colt: moderate walker and mover: fair at best: below form in 1992: should stay beyond 1¼m: below form blinkered: sold 6,200 gns Newmarket Autumn Sales. *P. W. Harris*

SODA POPINSKI (USA) 4 b.c. Sir Ivor 135 – Four Runs (USA) (Reviewer – (USA)) [1991 12g⁵ 10.4m 1992 a12g⁵ 8d] quite attractive colt: won over hurdles in February but poor maiden on flat nowadays: sold 1,900 gns Doncaster June Sales. *I. Campbell*

SO FACTUAL (USA) 2 br.c. (Mar 4) Known Fact (USA) 135 – Sookera (USA) 99 ? 117 (Roberto (USA) 131) [1992 6m⁶ 6m² 6d²] strong, attractive colt: half-brother to French 3-y-o 1¼m winner Soothfast (by Riverman) and several other winners, including Irish 7f to 1m winner Field Dancer (by Northfields) and 1988 2-y-o 5f winner Krameria (by Kris): dam won Cheveley Park Stakes but never ran again: comfortably won median auction at Folkestone before vastly improved effort when beaten a short head by Petardia in Coventry Stakes at Royal Ascot: burly and way below that form in minor event at Leicester, first run for 4 months: should stay 1m. *G. Harwood*

SOFT NOTE (IRE) 3 b.g. Dance of Life (USA) – Sharp Dresser (USA) (Sharpen – Up 127) [1991 NR 1992 10.2m 13.8g⁵ 8f⁶ 13.8f⁶ 10d] IR 82,000Y: angular gelding: good walker: second foal: half-brother to 4-y-o Rare Detail (by Commanche Run), successful at 1m (at 2 yrs) and 1½m: dam unraced half-sister to Alleging and Nomrood: no form, visored in seller final start: bandaged behind: sold 1,600 gns Newmarket September Sales. *M. Bell*

SOFT VERGES 4 b. or br.f. Another Realm 118 – Sharp Celeste 81 (Sharpen Up – 127) [1991 NR 1992 10g 12f 16g⁶] lengthy filly: third reported foal: sister to plating-class 1989 2-y-o 7.5f winner Haslingden Boy and half-sister to 7f and 1m winner Bleu Celeste (by Rabdan): dam 5f and 7f winner: no sign of ability. *W. Carter*

SO GREAT 3 ch.g. Simply Great (FR) 122 – Chrisanthy 81 (So Blessed 130) [1991 – NR 1992 a8g⁵ a8g⁶] 8,600F: fifth reported foal: brother to a maiden and half-brother to 7f (at 2 yrs) and 1¼m winner Ivan The Terrible (by Siberian Express) and 2 other winners: dam 2-y-o 5f winner failed to train on: well beaten in claimer and maiden at Southwell in January: sold 850 gns Doncaster January Sales. *W. W. Haigh*

SOHAIL (USA) 9 ch.g. Topsider (USA) – Your Nuts (USA) (Creme Dela Creme) – [1991 a13g 1992 10m] good-topped gelding: only poor nowadays: stays 1½m: acts on any going: effective with or without blinkers. *J. White*

SOIREE (IRE) 3 b.f. Sadler's Wells (USA) 132 – Seminar 113 (Don (ITY) 123) **100**
[1991 6m³ 7m* 7m⁶ 7.3g* 1992 7m³ 8g 8f 8s² 8m² 10g] rather leggy, quite attractive filly: has a round action: promising 2-y-o but failed to progress as anticipated in
1992: placed in Group 3 races at Newmarket (short of room when 1¾ lengths third
to A-To-Z) and the Curragh (2 lengths behind Cloud of Dust) and listed event at
Newmarket: below form in 1000 Guineas and Coronation Stakes in between: should
prove best at middle distances: acts on good to firm and soft ground. *B. W. Hills*

SOLAR STAR (USA) 3 b.f. Lear Fan (USA) 130 – Lajna 88 (Be My Guest (USA) –
126) [1991 6m* 6g* 6m⁵ 1992 10m⁶ 7g⁶] leggy, rather unfurnished filly: rated 93
when successful at 2 yrs: off course about a year, below best in listed races at
Newbury and Leopardstown in 1992: should stay 1¼m. *M. Bell*

SOLARTICA (USA) 2 b. or br.f. (May 29) Halo (USA) – Telescopica (ARG) **56**
(Table Play) [1992 7g⁶ 8g⁵ 8.1s²] $60,000Y: unfurnished filly: second reported foal
in USA: half-sister to 8.5f stakes winner Ms Aerosmith (by Skywalker): dam
Argentinian sister to Grade 3 1¼m winner Telefonico: best effort in maidens when
3 lengths second of 5 to Lead Note at Haydock in October: will be better suited by
1¼m: found little off bridle second start. *J. R. Fanshawe*

SOLDIERS BAY 2 b.g. (Feb 9) Robellino (USA) 127 – Yankee Special 60 (Bold **66 p**
Lad (IRE) 133) [1992 5m³ 5m³ 6g⁴ 6d⁴ 7m⁵] 5,200Y: small gelding: fourth foal:
half-brother to disappointing 3-y-o Langtonian (by Primo Dominie), 6f winner at 2
yrs: dam plating-class maiden: fair maiden: set plenty to do when running-on fifth in
nursery at Yarmouth: will be suited by 1m +: acts on good to firm and dead ground:
likely to improve further. *Lord Huntingdon*

SOLE CONTROL 4 b.f. Jupiter Island 126 – Maureen Mhor 70 (Taj Dewan 128) –
[1991 12.2d³ 14.8f³ 12g 1992 14.1d] angular filly: no worthwhile form. *H. Candy*

SOLEIL DANCER (IRE) 4 b.g. Fairy King (USA) – Cooliney Dancer (Dan- **89 d**
cer's Image (USA)) [1991 8s* 8d* 7m² 8g 7.6g⁴ 6s 7g⁶ 8.1d 1992 8g⁴ 7m² 7g⁶ 8.1d⁶
7m³] lengthy, good-quartered gelding: good walker: useful at best, went wrong way
in 1992 and looked somewhat irresolute on last 2 outings: stays 1m: acts on good to
firm ground and soft: trained first 4 starts by M. McCormack: hurdling with D. M.
Grissell. *N. Tinkler*

SOLEIL D'OR 2 gr.c. (Mar 16) Standaan (FR) 118 – My Ginny 83 (Palestine 133) **37**
[1992 5g 5m 5m] 10,000Y, 21,000Y: sturdy colt: good walker and mover: half-brother
to numerous winners, including 1979 2-y-o 5f winner Auntie Bessy (by No Mercy)
and stayer/hurdler Mariner's Dream (by Julio Mariner): dam 2-y-o 6f winner: poor
form in varied company, including selling: blinkered last 2 starts: sold 1,200 gns
Ascot July Sales. *M. McCormack*

SOLEIL RAYON (IRE) 2 b.c. (Mar 6) Fayruz 116 – Trust Sally 65 (Sallust 134) **53**
[1992 6g² 6m⁴ 6s 6m⁶ a6g⁵ a7g⁴ a8g⁵] IR 8,200F, 28,000Y: strong, useful-looking
colt: good walker: brother to 6f winner Sally Fay, closely related to modest 1987
2-y-o 5f winner Marley Supalite (by Jester) and half-brother to 2 winners, including
6f winner Reasonable Kid (by Reasonable): dam won 5f seller: failed to progress
after second in maiden at Goodwood: off course over 4 months (trained until after
then by M. McCormack) after fourth start. *T. D. Barron*

SOLEMN MELODY 5 b.g. Jalmood (USA) 126 – Garganey (USA) (Quack –
(USA)) [1991 7.1m 1992 a8g] big, angular gelding: no sign of ability. *A. Barrow*

SOLID (IRE) 4 b.g. Glenstal (USA) 118 – Reine de Chypre (FR) (Habitat 134) **50**
[1991 8.2d 8.2m 8.3g* a8g³ 8d⁴ 1992 8s* 8.3d⁵ 9g 10g 9.7s³] leggy gelding: in-and-
out form after winning handicap at Wolverhampton in March: stays 1¼m: acts on
soft ground and fibresand: ran moderately when visored once: joined D. Cosgrove. *J.
R. Jenkins*

SOLID STEEL (IRE) 4 b.c. Flash of Steel 120 – Bonny Brae (Cure The Blues –
(USA)) [1991 a10g³ a8g³ a10g 12g² 11.9g³ 11.9m 14m³ 12m⁶ 12f⁶ 1992 10da12g 11.9f
11.6g 11.9g] tall colt: has a round action: poor maiden nowadays on flat: stays 1¾m:
acts on firm going: below form in eyeshield/visor: won 3 selling hurdles in autumn.
A. Moore

SOLO CHARTER 2 b.c. (Feb 20) Chief Singer 131 – Royal Agreement (USA) **46 p**
(Vaguely Noble 140) [1992 6s 6g] 3,000Y: big, rather leggy colt: has a markedly
round action: sixth foal: half-brother to 3-y-o 11.1f winner Eden's Close (by Green
Dancer): dam went at up to 9f in USA: backward and never dangerous in maidens at
Folkestone and Newmarket in October: should do better over 1¼m +. *M. H.
Tompkins*

SOLOMAN SPRINGS (USA) 2 ch.c. (Feb 21) Wajima (USA) – Malilla (CHI) **66**
(Prologo) [1992 a7g² a7g² 8.1d² 10g⁴] tall, rangy colt: has scope: moderate walker:

third foal: brother to a winner in North America at up to 7f at 2 yrs: dam Chilean-bred: sire top class from 9f to 1½m: fair maiden: consistent until final start: should stay well. *S. G. Norton*

SOLOMON'S DANCER (USA)   2 b. or br.c. (Feb 4) Al Nasr (FR) 126 –   **64 p**
Infinite Wisdom (USA) (Sassafras (FR) 135) [1992 7g⁶ 7g⁴] good-topped colt: second reported foal: dam, minor sprint winner at 3 yrs, is half-sister to smart 7f stakes winner Strike Gold: still bit backward, much better effort in late-season maidens when under 3 lengths fourth of 18 to Azilian at Doncaster: should stay 1m: has scope, and should do better. *W. W. Haigh*

SOL ROUGE (IRE)   3 ch.f. Red Sunset 120 – Grace de Bois (Tap On Wood 130)   **–**
[1991 NR 1992 a10g⁶ a7g] 2,000Y: small filly: second foal: half-sister to poor maiden Petite Melusine (by Fairy King): dam minor winner in France at around 9f: no sign of ability. *R. Thompson*

SOLSTICE   3 br.g. Supreme Leader 123 – Legal Miss 79 (Comedy Star (USA) 121)   **–**
[1991 NR 1992 9.2m⁴ 8.3f⁵ 12.1g³] workmanlike gelding: first reported foal: dam 5f and 7f winner: poor maiden. *Mrs M. Reveley*

SOMEONE BRAVE   4 b.g. Commanche Run 133 – Someone Special 105 (Habitat   **–**
134) [1991 12d 11.7m⁴ 14m 11.7g 8m 1992 11.6g 14.1g] smallish, sparely-made gelding: moderate walker: rated 63 at 3 yrs: no show on flat in 1992: stays 11.7f: yet to race on soft ground, probably acts on any other: won over hurdles in August. *Bob Jones*

SOMNIFERE (USA)   2 ch.f. (Apr 11) Nijinsky (CAN) 138 – Shoot A Line 127   **63 p**
(High Line 125) [1992 6g⁵ 7s⁵] leggy, sparely-made filly: lacks scope: fifth reported foal: closely related to very useful 1989 2-y-o 6f winner Line of Thunder (by Storm Bird), also winner over 7f and stayed 1¼m though not so good at 3 yrs, and disappointing 1987 2-y-o 7f winner Pamusi (by Mr Prospector): dam won Irish Oaks and second in Ascot Gold Cup: much better effort in autumn on final run when around 6 lengths fifth of 8 to Cropton in Warwick minor event: will be well suited by middle distances: will improve. *P. W. Chapple-Hyam*

SONALTO   6 br.g. Noalto 120 – Sanandrea (Upper Case (USA)) [1991 NR 1992 9m   **–**
8f 18.2g 18.5d 10m 10g] leggy, lengthy gelding: very much on the downgrade. *D. L. Williams*

SONDERISE   3 br.c. Mummy's Game 120 – Demderise 80 (Vaigly Great 127)   **68**
[1991 6g 6m 6m 5m² 5m⁶ 5.1m 5d⁴ 5d* 1992 6v² 6d 6g 6d* 6m⁶ 6d 5m 6.1s 6g 5g a6g] lengthy colt: inconsistent handicapper: won at Haydock in May: effective at 5f to 6f: best on an easy surface, and acts on heavy. *N. Tinkler*

SONG IN YOUR HEART   2 b.c. (May 20) Sizzling Melody 117 – Honeybuzzard   **–**
(FR) (Sea Hawk II 131) [1992 6m 7g 5g] 6,000Y, 4,200 2-y-o: tall, short-backed colt: half-brother to several winners, including fairly useful 1m to 1½m winner Misaaff (by Mummy's Pet): dam Irish 1¼m winner: little form in maidens: visored final outing. *A. Harrison*

SONGLINES (FR)   3 b.c. High Top 131 – Aborigine 117 (Riverman (USA) 131) **121**
[1991 8s³ 1992 9g* 10.5g⁶ 12d* 12g* 12.5g³ 12m*] good-topped, attractive French colt: third foal: half-brother to French 9f winner Embers (by Fabulous Dancer) and Aboriginal (by Kalaglow), successful at 1m (at 2 yrs) to 17f winner also in France: dam French 9f (at 2 yrs) and 1½m winner: improved to win minor event at Evry, listed event at Longchamp, Prix du Lys at Chantilly and Prix Niel at Longchamp, in last-named making running and battling on gamely to hold off Petit Loup by a nose: third to Vert Amande in Prix Maurice de Nieuil at Maisons-Laffitte over 7 weeks earlier: stays 12.5f: acts on good to firm ground: genuine. *E. Bartholomew, France*

SONIC SIGNAL   6 b. or br.m. Trojan Fen 118 – Danger Signal 106 (Red God   **42**
128§) [1991 10v⁵ a12g 10s 10m 11.5m⁶ 11.6m³ 14.1f² 15.4f² 16.2d 15.8g² 14.6m³ a16g 1992 16d 14.9d⁴ 18.1g⁴ 14.1g 16.5m² 18.2m 14.9g⁶] small, sparely-made mare: inconsistent handicapper: stays 2¼m: acts on any going: effective visored or not. *M. J. Haynes*

SON OF PEARL (IRE)   4 b.g. Reasonable (FR) 119 – Moving Pearl (Gulf Pearl   **–**
117) [1991 NR 1992 7g] stocky gelding: fourth foal: dam unraced: tailed off in Wolverhampton claimer in July. *O. Brennan*

SON OF SHARP SHOT (IRE)   2 b. or br.c. (Apr 9) Sharp Shot 82 – Gay   **69**
Fantasy (Troy 137) [1992 7g 7.1g⁶ 7s] leggy, quite attractive colt: fifth foal: half-brother to useful 5-y-o 8.9f to 10.8f winner Lucky Guest (by Be My Guest) and 3 other winners, including 1½m winner Persian Fantasy (by Persian Bold): dam unraced half-sister to very useful middle-distance filly Miss Petard: sire 6f and 1m winner: best effort in autumn maidens when over 6 lengths sixth of 13 at Sandown: will be suited by 1m +: possibly unsuited by soft ground. *J. L. Dunlop*

Scottish Equitable Richmond Stakes, Goodwood—Son Pardo holds off Canaska Star

SON PARDO 2 b.c. (Mar 1) Petong 126 – Flitteriss Park 62§ (Beldale **107**
Flutter (USA) 130) [1992 5g⁵ 6f* 6f* 6g* 6m* 6g 6m⁵ 6s⁴ 6v⁶]
    Son Pardo's official assessment as the seventh-best two-year-old in
Europe—on a mark of 117 in the International Classification—should raise a
few eyebrows. He failed to progress after a much improved effort in the
Scottish Equitable Richmond Stakes at Goodwood on his fifth start and looks
considerably flattered. The Richmond is a prestigious event—a Group 2
pattern race—but even at the time it looked unlikely to prove a great pointer
to the remaining big two-year-old races. Son Pardo had won his last three
races, a Newbury maiden, a minor event at Doncaster and the listed Cock of
the North Stakes at Haydock where he beat the odds-on Windsor Castle
Stakes third Colyan gamely by a head. Son Pardo started at 7/1 in a field of six
for the Richmond in which Darbonne's Norfolk Stakes third, Canaska Star's
July Stakes second and Pip's Pride's Coventry Stakes and July Stakes thirds
all looked better form than anything he'd achieved. Son Pardo disputed the
lead with Darbonne in the early stages but, enterprisingly ridden, he showed
in front before halfway and ran on strongly under the whip to hold off Canaska
Star by a length with Green's Bid third and Darbonne fourth. Penalized 5 lb for
his Richmond success, Son Pardo managed only fifth in the Scottish Equitable
Gimcrack at York the following month; Green's Bid and Darbonne were
among those who finished in front of him. The Gimcrack was just one of four
defeats for Son Pardo after Goodwood: his running in the Heinz 57 Phoenix
Stakes at Leopardstown is best ignored because he was one of those
disadvantaged by racing on the far side, but he finished only fourth to Sharp
Prod in the Moet & Chandon-Rennen at Baden-Baden and sixth (starting at
25/1) in the Racecall Gold Trophy at Redcar.

		Mansingh	Jaipur
	Petong	(b 1969)	Tutasi
	(gr 1980)	Iridium	Linacre
Son Pardo		(gr 1969)	Tula Melody
(b.c. Mar 1, 1990)		Beldale Flutter	Accipiter
	Flitteriss Park	(b 1978)	Flitter Flutter
	(b 1984)	Geopelia	Raffingora
		(b 1974)	Little Bird

    Whatever else he achieves, Son Pardo has already proved a bargain. He
cost 17,500 guineas as a yearling at the Newmarket October Sales. His sire
the Vernons Sprint Cup winner Petong, whose fee in 1993 is £3,000, is also
the sire of the speedy Paris House and the latest Coventry and Champagne

Stakes winner Petardia. Son Pardo is the first foal of the ungenuine Flitteriss Park who gained her only victory when making all in a handicap over a mile at Redcar as a three-year-old. Son Pardo's grandam, the useful Geopelia, was a tough and genuine sprinter; his great grandam Little Bird gained her only victory over five furlongs as a two-year-old. The rather leggy, good-quartered Son Pardo is a quick-actioned colt; he has yet to race beyond sprint distances and has shown his best form on a sound surface. He's a tail swisher but never flinched under pressure in the Richmond, keeping on gamely. *R. Hannon*

SONUS (IRE)   3 b.c. Sadler's Wells (USA) 132 – Sound of Success (USA) **120** (Successor) [1991 8m³ 8m* 1992 10g* 12m⁴ 11.9g² 14.6m² 12m²]

Fourteen years after the first, and a year and a half after her death, the broodmare Sound of Success was represented by her second British classic runner-up in Sonus. The first was Hawaiian Sound, the colt on which Willie Shoemaker lost out to Shirley Heights in photo-finishes for both the Derby, in which he led until the dying strides, and Irish Derby. Sonus' second in the latest St Leger was, in truth, a performance of a clearly lower order as well as a much more comprehensive defeat; at no point did he look capable of holding User Friendly, although he briefly got his head in front two and a half furlongs out having been ridden close to the pace from the off. The difference between them at the post was three and a half lengths. Hawaiian Sound won the Benson and Hedges Gold Cup (now the Juddmonte International) as a three-year-old and the nine-furlong Earl of Sefton Stakes on his reappearance the following season. While the good-topped Sonus is the sort to come on with time, his winning tally to date boasts just a Leicester maiden (at two years) and a Newbury minor event. That Newbury success, catching the useful Fair

Sheikh Mohammed's "Sonus"

Average close home on his reappearance in June, was over one and a quarter miles but it is hard to envisage Sonus returning successfully to that sort of distance now, as Hawaiian Sound did, unless he is campaigned below pattern-race class. Runs in three pattern races after Newbury showed Sonus to good effect with a test of stamina, then one in a listed contest on his final start showed that he needed it. The highlights were the Great Voltigeur Stakes and the St Leger. Before that Sonus had stayed on from towards the rear to be fourth of twelve in the King Edward VII Stakes. Alflora had been third at Royal Ascot and Bonny Scot sixth, a finishing order that was turned on its head when the three met again in the Voltigeur, Sonus being outpaced from the furlong marker by Bonny Scot and beaten a length and a half, and reversed again between Bonny Scot and Sonus in the St Leger where Bonny Scot was a neck behind in third. Sonus' part in these form reversals can be attributed to improvement with age, experience and distance. The importance of this last factor was underlined by his defeat at 11/10 on in the listed Godolphin Stakes over a mile and a half at Newmarket in October. Carrying none of the penalties, Sonus was fully entitled to those odds on his St Leger form but, in an eight-runner field, his jockey was the first to show signs of unease. Sonus' eventual one-and-a-half-length second to Zinaad was well below his best form but a lot better than had seemed likely when the whip was produced well over three furlongs out.

		Northern Dancer	Nearctic
	Sadler's Wells (USA)	(b 1961)	Natalma
	(b 1981)	Fairy Bridge	Bold Reason
Sonus (IRE)		(b 1975)	Special
(b.c. 1989)		Successor	Bold Ruler
	Sound of Success (USA)	(b 1964)	Misty Thorn
	(ch 1969)	Belle Musique	Tudor Minstrel
		(b 1963)	Bellesoeur

Seven of Sound of Success' ten other living foals saw the racecourse and all were winners, the most notable being the very useful mile-and-a-half winner Rapids (by Head of The River) and the American stakes winners Lullaby (by Hawaiian Sound's sire Hawaii) and Charming Ballerina (by Caerleon, the last of whom also won twice here as a two-year-old. Sound of Success, contrastingly, ran only twice, unplaced on both occasions, and was covered as a three-year-old, but she was a granddaughter of a good two-year-old winner and broodmare in Bellesoeur. *J. H. M. Gosden*

SOOJAMA (IRE)   2 b.c. (May 6) Mansooj 118 – Pyjama Game 56 (Cavo Doro   **44**
124) [1992 7m 7d 8d 6s] IR 3,000F, 7,200Y: rather leggy colt: half-brother to winners in Germany and Belgium: dam, placed at up to 2m, is half-sister to Grey Desire: little worthwhile form in varied events. *R. Voorspuy*

SOOTY SWIFT (IRE)   2 br.f. (Mar 28) Akarad (FR) 130 – Swift And Sure (USA)   **80 p**
98 (Valdez (USA)) [1992 7g⁴ 6m* 5g] leggy filly: moderate walker, has a long stride: third foal: half-sister to modest 1990 3-y-o maiden Reliant (by Shirley Heights), placed at up to 1¾m: dam 5f and 10.5f winner: comfortably made all in maiden at Yarmouth in September: always struggling for pace but not at all discredited when eighth of 13 to Up And At 'Em in Cornwallis Stakes at Ascot following month: will stay 1¼m. *C. E. Brittain*

SOOTY TERN   5 br.h. Wassl 125 – High Tern 93 (High Line 125) [1991 12.5d⁶   **57**
10.8m 9m* 9f² a8g 11m⁴ 10.2d 8.9m³ 1992 a8g⁵ a8g* a8g* 10.3g 8d 8d⁴ 8g² 9f⁴ 9g⁵   a66
8.2g* 10.8m³ 8.1m² 8.3m² 8f⁶ 8.2d] compact horse: won claimers at Lingfield and Southwell in February and handicap at Nottingham in June: effective at 1m to 1¼m: acts on firm and dead ground, goes particularly well on all-weather surfaces: races prominently. *J. M. Bradley*

SOPHIE'S BOY   2 ch.g. (May 5) Hard Fought 125 – Mrs Hubbard 73 (Silly   **46**
Season 127) [1992 6f⁵ a7g⁵ 6m³ a7g 7g] rather leggy gelding: fourth reported foal: dam stayed 1½m: poor maiden: will stay 1m: acts on firm ground. *M. H. Easterby*

SOPHISTICATED AIR   2 b.f. (Apr 8) Elegant Air 119 – Blubella 86 (Balidar   **60**
133) [1992 5f² 5.7f³ 5.7d²] leggy, lengthy filly: third living foal: half-sister to 3-y-o Cumbrian Classic (by Glint of Gold): dam sprinter: modest maiden: will be better suited by 1m: acts on firm and dead ground. *I. A. Balding*

SORAYAH'S PET 2 b.c. (Mar 25) Petoski 135 – Sorayah 89 (Persian Bold 123) **51**
[1992 7f 7v a7g a7g] 9,400Y: second foal: half-brother to 3-y-o Queensberry Rules
(by Vaguely Noble), a winner abroad: dam sprinter here later won at up to 11f in
USA: plating-class maiden: bred to stay at least 1m. *Sir Mark Prescott*

SO RHYTHMICAL 8 b.g. Dance In Time (CAN) – So Lyrical 68 (So Blessed **83**
130) [1991 5g* 6m 5g6 6d 5g4 5.6m 5.2f 7m 6m5 7g 1992 5.2d3 7d 6g2 6m2 6f5
6.1d 6m2 6m* 6d* 6g3 6d 5g6 6m] sturdy gelding: carries condition: consistent
handicapper in 1992, successful at Newmarket and Goodwood (£12,100 event) in
August: effective at up to 7f: acts on any going: usually bandaged off-hind: often
sweats: sometimes slowly away/drifts right: held up. *G. H. Eden*

SO SAUCY 2 b.f. (Mar 13) Teenoso (USA) 135 – Saucy Bird (Henbit (USA) 130) **38**
[1992 6g 7d 8.2g6] leggy, lengthy filly: second foal: dam (ran twice at 2 yrs) is
granddaughter of sister to Ribocco and Ribero: poor maiden: should stay 1m. *C. E.
Brittain*

SO SMUG (USA) 3 b. or br.f. Nureyev (USA) 131 – Smuggly (USA) 121 (Caro **70**
133) [1991 6g3 1992 7.9f3 8m4 9m2 8g* 8.1g5 10s6] leggy, good-topped filly:
seemed to idle when landing odds in maiden at Thirsk in August: form in handicaps
after only when good fifth at Sandown: should stay 1¼m: acts on firm going,
possibly not on soft: visored last 2 starts. *J. H. M. Gosden*

SO SO 2 ch.f. (Mar 23) Then Again 126 – Swinging Gold 80 (Swing Easy (USA) **84**
126) [1992 5g2 5g6 5.9f2 6g* 7s3 7s4 7d*] rangy, angular filly: has scope: third foal:
half-sister to 1990 2-y-o 5f winner Spinechiller (by Grey Ghost): dam sprinter: fair
performer: won maiden at Newcastle in June and nursery (by short head from
Harpoon Louie, showing improved form) at Doncaster in October: suited by 7f: best
form on a soft surface. *T. D. Barron*

SO SUPERB 3 b.g. Superlative 118 – Top And Tail (USA) 81 (Tilt Up (USA)) **71** d
[1991 6g 6m 6g 1992 6d 6d 5s2 5m2 5m3 5.7m4 6m5 7g 6m2 6.1g 6d3] good-quartered
gelding: inconsistent sprint maiden: acts on good to firm and soft ground: best
blinkered or visored: has looked unco-operative: sold to join M. Dods's stable 1,800
gns Newmarket Autumn Sales. *J. L. Dunlop*

SOUGHAAN'S PRIDE (IRE) 4 gr.f. Soughaan (USA) 111 – Divine Apsara –
(Godswalk (USA) 130) [1991 a7g a7g 8g 8.3m4 8.3m 11.6m6 9.7f 1992 a12g] leggy,
sparely-made filly: has a round action: poor maiden: stays 1m: sold 725 gns Ascot
March Sales. *R. A. Bennett*

SOUGHT OUT (IRE) 4 b.f. Rainbow Quest (USA) 134 – Edinburgh 117 **119**
(Charlottown 127) [1991 10g2 11.3d4 14.1f* 12g3 14.6m 15d* 14v5 1992 16g*
11.9g5 13.5s2 15s* 20s* 15.5s3]
The Prix du Cadran, the French equivalent of the Gold Cup which is now
run in October, was won convincingly by the ex-English filly Sought Out who
made great strides as a four-year-old. Transferred from Stoute's yard after
developing into a useful staying three-year-old, Sought Out arrived at
Longchamp already established as the best out-and-out stayer in France.
Receiving weight, she'd beaten the Gold Cup winner Drum Taps by five
lengths, with the rest strung out, in the Prix Kergorlay at Deauville in August
on her most recent outing. Sought Out romped home again in the Cadran,
making all to beat Drum Taps by four this time, meeting him on terms 7 lb
worse than at Deauville; Dariyoun, from whom Sought Out had won the Prix

Ciga Prix du Cadran, Longchamp—
Sought Out follows up her win in the Prix de Lutece
at the same meeting twelve months earlier

Lord Weinstock's "Sought Out"

de Lutece on the same card twelve months earlier, came third, with the Goodwood Cup and Doncaster Cup runner-up Witness Box fourth. Sought Out again had Witness Box and Dariyoun behind in the Prix Royal-Oak three weeks later but, starting odds on, she was below her best and managed only third to the British-trained three-year-old Assessor. Sought Out, who put up another good performance when runner-up to Magic Night in the Prix de Pomone at Deauville in August, also ran in Germany and Britain in the latest season. She won the Oleander-Rennen, a Group 3 event at Baden-Baden, on her reappearance in May, but she didn't make the frame when sent for the Lancashire Oaks in July, running as though a mile and a half on good ground wasn't enough of a test of stamina. Sought Out needs further than a mile and a half nowadays and stays really well. She's best forcing the pace and, although she has won on firm ground, seems ideally suited by testing conditions which place more emphasis on stamina. She's a tail swisher but runs her races out in genuine fashion. Don't underestimate her if she's sent over for the Gold Cup.

			Blushing Groom	Red God
Sought Out (IRE) (b.f. 1988)	Rainbow Quest (USA) (b 1981)		(ch 1974)	Runaway Bride
		I Will Follow	Herbager
		(b 1975)	Where You Lead
	Edinburgh (b 1974)	Charlottown	Charlottesville
		(b 1963)	Meld
		Queen's Castle	Sovereign Path
		(gr 1969)	Country House

The rather leggy Sought Out is by the much-sought-after Rainbow Quest, sire already of a Derby winner in Quest For Fame and an Arc winner in Saumarez. Sought Out's dam Edinburgh, a smart performer at around a mile as a two-year-old who later showed she stayed ten and a half furlongs, has bred several other winners, all fillies, including the St Simon Stakes third Queen Helen (by Troy), the French mile-and-a-quarter and mile-and-a-half winner Greektown (by Ela-Mana-Mou), the fairly useful Castle Peak (by Darshaan), a winner over a mile and a half, and Scots Lass (by Shirley Heights) the dam of St Leger third Bonny Scot. Sought Out's grandam Queen's Castle was a winning half-sister to Reform. *J. E. Hammond, France*

SOUL DREAM (USA)   2 br.f. (Jun 10) Alleged (USA) 138 – Normia 104   – p
(Northfields (USA)) [1992 7g⁵] leggy filly: fifth foal: half-sister to French 1m winner Metamorphose (by Lord Avie) and a winner in USA by Roberto: dam, French 2-y-o 1m winner, is closely related to smart American horse Regal Bearing, successful at up to 1½m, out of half-sister to top French horses Grey Dawn II and Right Away: green and faded last 1f when fifth of 6 in maiden at Yarmouth in July: seemed sure to do better. *Mrs J. Cecil*

SOUL EMPEROR   2 b. or br.c. (May 4) Our Native (USA) – Dance Empress   67
(USA) (Empery (USA)) 128) [1992 8m⁵ 8.1d* 9v] leggy, workmanlike colt: has a round action: sixth foal: half-brother to winners at up to 1m by Lear Fan and The Bart: dam 6f winner: favourite, ½-length winner of maiden at Haydock in September: well beaten in listed race at Milan following month: should stay 1¼m. *M. Bell*

SOUL INTENT   4 b.f. Lochnager 132 – Tricky 66 (Song 132) [1991 7g 6f 1992   –
5.9f] workmanlike filly: little sign of ability: sold 1,000 gns Doncaster June Sales. *W. Bentley*

SOUL TRADER   3 b.f. Faustus (USA) 118 – Hot Case 92 (Upper Case (USA))   –
[1991 6g⁵ 6f 6.1f 1992 10m⁴ 9.7m a10g] good-bodied filly: rated 61 at 2 yrs: no worthwhile form in 1992: should stay 7f+: blinkered last 2 starts: sold 880 gns Newmarket Autumn Sales. *B. W. Hills*

SOUNDS RISKY   2 b.f. (Mar 2) Risk Me (FR) 127 – Sound Type 92 (Upper Case   31
(USA)) [1992 6f 5h⁴ a5g a6g³ a6g² a7s³ 6m a6g 7s a7g] 4,400F: small, angular filly: has a round action: half-sister to 9f and 1¼m seller winner Final Sound (by Final Straw) and a winner in Belgium by Busted: dam 7f and 1¼m winner: poor maiden: stays 7f: looked thoroughly ill at ease on hard ground. *Miss S. J. Wilton*

SOURCE OF LIGHT   3 b.g. Rainbow Quest (USA) 134 – De Stael (USA) 93   99
(Nijinsky (CAN) 138) [1991 NR 1992 10.2m* 11s² 12f* 11.9f³ 10m⁶] leggy, good-topped gelding: good mover: second foal: dam 2-y-o 6f winner, is sister to Quiet Fling and Peacetime: looked most promising colt when winning maiden at Bath in May and King George V Stakes (Handicap) at Royal Ascot (by 2½ lengths from Wild Fire), quickening in good style each time: failed to progress, finding little next start and hanging badly right when fair sixth in £30,600 handicap at Goodwood: stays 1½m: suited by top-of-the-ground: a difficult ride: has been gelded. *R. Charlton*

SOUSON (IRE)   4 b.g. Soughaan (USA) 111 – Down The Line 74 (Brigadier   45 +
Gerard 144) [1991 NR 1992 12.2g³ 15.8m] tall gelding: lightly raced on flat nowadays, but still shows ability: acts on firm ground: best at up to 1½m. *M. W. Easterby*

SOUTARI   4 br.g. Scorpio (FR) 127 – Sousocks (Soueida 111) [1991 11.7g 12m   –
a12g⁵ a11g 11.7m 1992 a10g a12g] good-bodied gelding: no worthwhile form: tried blinkered. *M. McCormack*

King George V Stakes (Handicap), Ascot—
Source of Light leads home Wild Fire and Inner City

SOUTHAMPTON 2 b.g. (Mar 19) Ballacashtal (CAN) – Petingo Gold 69   **32**
(Pitskelly 122) [1992 5g 6m 6m 7g] plain gelding: first foal: dam maiden, best at 2
yrs, stayed 6f: always behind in varied events, including sellers: blinkered final
outing. *G. B. Balding*

SOUTH CROSS (USA) 7 ch.g. Valdez (USA) – Blue Cross Nurse (USA)   –
(Needles) [1991 NR 1992 15.8d] well-made gelding: moderate mover: rated 69 as
3-y-o: soundly beaten in handicap in June, 1992: stays 1¼m: possibly unsuited by
soft going. *G. M. Moore*

SOUTHERN MEMORIES (IRE) 2 b.c. (Mar 19) Don't Forget Me 127 – Our   **80**
Pet 64 (Mummy's Pet 125) [1992 7d⁴ 7m⁶ 7s 7d⁵ 6g*] lengthy colt: has scope: first
foal: dam 2-y-o 1m winner: much improved effort when 2-length winner of maiden at
Doncaster in November: will stay 1m: possibly unsuited by very soft ground. *R.
Hannon*

SOUTH SEA 3 ch.c. Dunbeath (USA) 127 – Silent Pearl (USA) (Silent Screen   **78**
(USA)) [1991 8s 7g 8d* 8g 1992 9g³ 10s⁴] big, lengthy colt: fair maiden: carried head
awkwardly final run: should stay 1¼m: sold 17,000 gns Newmarket Autumn Sales.
L. M. Cumani

SOUTHWOLD AIR 3 b.c. Elegant Air 119 – Habutai 70 (Habitat 134) [1991 7g   **68**
1992 8g 8f⁴ 7f* 8f⁴ 8g⁶ 6g³ 7g 7.6g 6d] good-bodied colt: modest handicapper: won
at Salisbury in June: well below form last 3 starts and sold 8,000 gns Newmarket
Autumn Sales: stays 1m: acts on firm going: sometimes looks reluctant, and worth a
try in blinkers/visor. *J. L. Dunlop*

SOVEREIGN GRACE (IRE) 3 gr.f. Standaan (FR) 118 – Gay Nocturne 63   **81** +
(Lord Gayle (USA) 124) [1991 NR 1992 7g⁴ 5g* 5m] small, lengthy filly: half-sister
to several winners, including Irish 8.5f to 1¼m winner Welsh Flyer (by Welsh
Saint): dam twice-raced daughter of very useful sprinter Pianissimo: thrice-raced
Irish filly: 7-length winner of maiden at Tipperary in August, making all: very stiff
task and not disgraced in listed event at Doncaster 3 weeks after: will probably
prove best at sprint distances. *J. G. Burns, Ireland*

SOVEREIGN HEIGHTS 4 b.g. Elegant Air 119 – Blubella 86 (Balidar 133)   –
[1991 NR 1992 7.6m 9m⁴] sturdy gelding: thrice raced on flat and no worthwhile
form. *M. R. Channon*

SOVEREIGN NICHE (IRE) 4 gr.g. Nishapour (FR) 125 – Sovereign Flash   **44**
(FR) (Busted 134) [1991 6g 7.5g 8m⁵ 10.2f³ 12g⁵ 10g 12g⁵ 1992 13.8g⁴ 12m 10.5d⁴
10m⁵ 11.8s a8g] sturdy, lengthy gelding: maiden handicapper: probably needs a test
of stamina nowadays: acts on firm and dead going: sold out of N. Miller's stable
5,800 gns Doncaster August Sales, rejoining 3-y-o trainer: won selling hurdle in
November. *Mrs J. R. Ramsden*

SOVEREIGN PAGE (USA) 3 ch.g. Caro 133 – Tashinsky (USA) (Nijinsky   **81**
(CAN) 138) [1991 6m 1992 10m⁵ 10g⁵ 11.1f* 11.6g⁴ 10m² 10d 12d 10g⁶ 10m⁴ 10v] tall,
rather leggy gelding: good walker and mover: fair handicapper: won maiden at
Hamilton in June: effective at 1¼m and 1½m: needs a sound surface: effective
blinkered or not: has been gelded. *B. Hanbury*

SOVEREIGN ROCK (IRE) 3 ch.g. Ballad Rock 122 – Sweet Accord (Balidar   **84**
133) [1991 5m 5m 6.1m 6m 7d² 1992 7g⁶ 6v* 7m⁶ 7f⁴ 7f⁵ 7g² 7f 8.3g 7g* 6f 7.6s*
7.1s²] compact gelding: good walker: moderate mover: fair handicapper: successful
in 1992 at Warwick, Kempton and Lingfield: should stay 1m: best with give in the
ground (acts on heavy): ran well when blinkered once as 2-y-o: sold 18,500 gns
Newmarket Autumn Sales. *R. Hannon*

SOVIET EXPRESS 2 br.c. (Feb 23) Siberian Express (USA) 125 – Our Shirley   **60**
84 (Shirley Heights 130) [1992 7m 6m*] 5,400Y, 7,200 2-y-o: half-brother to 2
winners in France, including 3-y-o 1m winner Carry The Fire (by Lead On Time),
and winning hurdler Clos du Bois (by High Top): dam, 1¼m winner, is half-sister to
smart Miner's Lamp: head winner of seller (bought in 7,200 gns) at Folkestone in
August: may improve again. *P. F. I. Cole*

SOVIET SECRET 2 b.c. (Apr 5) Soviet Star (USA) 128 – Secretive (FR)   **65** p
(Secretariat (USA)) [1992 6s*] 60,000Y: tall, quite attractive colt: half-brother to
several winners in France, notably good-class 7f (at 2 yrs) to 9.2f winner Secret
Form (by Formidable): dam ran once: favourite but very green, won 5-runner
maiden at York in October by 3 lengths from Flashman, leading 1½f out: wore
bandages, and had tongue tied down: sure to improve. *B. Hanbury*

SPACE CAMP 3 ch.c. Kalaglow 132 – Base Camp 80 (Derring-Do 131) [1991 NR   –
1992 10s⁶ 10.2m] 11,500Y: tall, leggy colt: half-brother to several winners, including
stayer Revisit (by Busted) and useful performer at up to 1¼m Crampon (by Shirley

Berkeley Stakes (Handicap), Ascot—
20/1-shot Spaniards Close carries 9-7 to victory over Ashtina

Heights): dam won 3 times over 1¼m: always behind in maidens in May. *R. J. Hodges*

SPANIARDS CLOSE   4 b.g. King of Spain 121 – Avon Belle 75 (Balidar 133) **110** [1991 6d⁴ 6m² 6m⁴ 6d* 5.7g³ 5d* 5g* 5d² 5.2g³ 5d* 1992 6g 6f⁵ 5d* 5g² 6g⁵] lengthy, workmanlike gelding: very useful performer: off course over 4 months before improved efforts when winner and second (to Ashtina) in quite valuable Ascot handicaps: went with little zest in Doncaster listed race final run: should prove as effective at 6f as 5f: has form on firm ground, but best efforts with some give: held up, and has good turn of foot. *P. J. Makin*

SPANISH EXPRESS   3 br.g. King of Spain 121 – Pour Moi 73 (Bay Express **45** 132) [1991 5m⁵ 5f⁵ 5g⁵ 5d² 6g⁵ 1992 6d 5g 7f 8.2g 7.5m³ 8f⁴ 7g³ 7f* 8f a7g*] a66 gelding: modest performer: successful in claimers at Catterick in July and Southwell in August: acts on firm and dead ground, and on fibresand: below form visored once. *R. Boss*

SPANISH GLORY   3 b.f. King of Spain 121 – Hearten (Hittite Glory 125) [1991 **53** 6g 7d 1992 7s 8s 8f³ 8m⁵ 8f³ 7d³ 6.9g⁴ 8d 8s] leggy, workmanlike filly: modest maiden: stays 1m: best efforts on a sound surface: below form blinkered/visored: trained until after sixth start by I. Balding: sold 1,200 gns Newmarket December Sales. *K. O. Cunningham-Brown*

SPANISH GRANDEE (USA)   4 b.g. El Gran Senor (USA) 136 – Stealthy Lady **79** d (USA) (USA) 130) [1991 8g⁴ 10m 8g² 8m* 7.1g² 8m 8f 1992 7f² 10.1g 7g 10.2s 6.9v] sparely-made gelding: poor mover: fair handicapper: well below par in 1992 after first run: should prove better suited by 1m + than 7f: acts on firm ground: sometimes bandaged behind. *P. W. Chapple-Hyam*

SPANISH LOVE   6 b.m. Precocious 126 – San Marguerite 80 (Blakeney 126) **47** [1991 8g⁴ a7g 8.3m⁵ 6.9m* a7g 1992 7.1m 8g⁵ 6.9d³ 6.9m 7.1s* 7d 7s³] close-coupled, workmanlike mare: modest handicapper: won at Chepstow in August: effective from 7f to 9f: probably acts on any going: successful for claimer. *C. G. Cox*

SPANISH MINER (USA)   3 b.c. Northern Prospect (USA) – Bo Bolero (USA) **89** d (Chieftain II) [1991 6d 7.1d² 8.2g⁵ a7g* a7g³ 1992 7m² 7g 8g 7.1d 7.1d⁶ 8m⁵] compact colt: fairly useful performer at best: well below form in 1992 after first run: should stay 1m: acts on good to firm and dead ground: below form blinkered once: sold 4,100 gns Newmarket September Sales. *A. A. Scott*

SPANISH ONE 2 b. or br.g. (Apr 30) Lochnager 132 – Spanish Infanta 56 (King – of Spain 121) [1992 6g] smallish gelding: first foal: dam 1m seller winner stayed 1½m: always behind in seller at Leicester in July. *P. S. Felgate*

SPANISH PERFORMER 3 br.f. King of Spain 121 – Dauphiness 76 (Supreme 47 Sovereign 119) [1991 5f⁶ 5f² 6g³ 5m² 5f⁴ 6g 1992 6m² 5m 6m 8.1f* 6.9h² 7g 10g 8.1m⁶ 7m⁴ 8m 8m] leggy, workmanlike filly: moderate walker and mover: inconsistent performer: won maiden claimer at Edinburgh in June: stays 1m: acts on hard ground, yet to race on soft surface: ran moderately when blinkered. *T. Fairhurst*

SPANISH REALM 5 b.m. King of Spain 121 – Miss Realm 86 (Realm 129) [1991 36 5g a6g⁵ 5.1m a5g⁶ a6g⁶ 6m* 6m 7g 7m 1992 a7g 6d 6v 5m⁵ a6g 6g⁶ 6m 7.1d³ 7s] small, sparely-made mare: moderate mover: inconsistent handicapper: stays 7f: acts on firm and dead going: tends to hang: well beaten when blinkered. *M. Brittain*

SPANISH SAHARA (IRE) 2 b.c. (May 16) Sadler's Wells (USA) 132 – Melody 62 p (USA) (Lord Gayle (USA) 124) [1992 8m] lengthy, angular colt: brother to 1988 2-y-o 6f winner Creole, closely related to 3 winners, including smart 7f filly Guest Performer (by Be My Guest), and half-brother to 3 winners, including 3-y-o 1m and 8.9f winner Rockawhile (by Dancing Brave): dam Irish 7f to 1½m winner: bandaged and in need of race, never dangerous in maiden at Newmarket in October: moved moderately down: will do better. *P. W. Chapple-Hyam*

SPANISH STORM (IRE) 3 b.g. King of Spain 121 – Storm Crest 80 (Lord 98 Gayle (USA) 124) [1991 5s² 5d* 5g³ 6g* 6g 7g³ 7m* 7m³ 7g⁵ 1992 7d⁶ 8m⁵ 6f³ 5s 6s 7m] lengthy, useful-looking gelding: good walker: moderate mover: well below form after excellent third to Shalford in Cork And Orrery Stakes at Royal Ascot in June: ran as if something amiss in handicap final run: best effort at 6f: acts on firm ground and probably on dead: trained until after second start by A. Hide: has been gelded. *S. P. C. Woods*

SPANISH THREAD 2 b.f. (Mar 25) King of Spain 121 – Persian Tapestry 70 49 (Tap On Wood 130) [1992 5g 5g a6g⁴ 5f³ 5m⁵ 5.2g] 2,100Y: sparely-made filly: moderate walker: first foal: dam 1¼m winner: went wrong way after third in Pontefract maiden: sold 600 gns Ascot September Sales. *G. A. Pritchard-Gordon*

SPANISH TOWER 2 b.g. (Apr 18) Aragon 118 – Kilttaley 74 (Tower Walk 130) 34 [1992 5g 5s⁶ 5m 5.1d⁶ a6g] sturdy gelding: has a round action: fourth foal: half-brother to 3-y-o 6f seller winner Ceatharlach (by Sayf El Arab): dam stayed 1m: poor form, including in sellers: should stay 6f: blinkered last 2 starts, running creditably first time: sold 850 gns Doncaster November Sales. *P. G. Murphy*

SPANISH VERDICT 5 b.g. King of Spain 121 – Counsel's Verdict (Firestreak 73 125) [1991 8g 8m³ 7h³ 7f 8d⁶ 8m² 7d⁴ 8f* 7f³ 7.5f³ 8m⁵ 8f⁶ 8h⁶ 8.5f 7m 1992 7d⁶ 7.5g 7m² 8f³ 7f 8f² 8f* 8h* 8.3m* 7g³ 8f² 10g⁵ 7m 8m 7.5m⁴ 7s* 7d⁶ 8m 7v⁶] sturdy, good-quartered gelding: has a round action: consistent handicapper: successful in 1992 at Carlisle (2), Hamilton and Redcar: effective from 7f to 1¼m (at least in moderately-run race): acts on any going: effective visored or not: effective ridden from front or held up: genuine and really tough. *Denys Smith*

SPANISH WHISPER 5 b.g. Aragon 118 – Whisper Gently 91 (Pitskelly 122) 35 [1991 a10g a10g⁴ 10.2s⁴ 12m⁶ 8.2d 8m² 9.7s⁴ 10m 7m⁶ 1992 a12g a12g⁴ 8.9s² 7.1m 8f 10g 12.2g³ a14g] compact gelding: moderate mover: inconsistent handicapper: needs further than 7f, and stays 1½m: acts on good to firm and soft going: ran moderately in blinkers: tends to hang under pressure but suitable mount for amateur. *J. R. Bostock*

SPAREATHOUGHT 3 b.f. Alleging (USA) 120 – Spare Wheel 67 (Track Spare – 125) [1991 NR 1992 7v⁶ 8g 6m 5.1m] leggy, angular filly: third foal: half-sister to 1m (at 2 yrs) and 6f winner Pacific Rim (by Absalom): dam 1½m seller winner also successful over hurdles: well beaten in sellers and claimers. *C. N. Allen*

SPARK (IRE) 2 ch.f. (Apr 21) Flash of Steel 120 – Sperrin Mist 83 (Camden 74 Town 125) [1992 5f³ 6m* 6g⁵ 6f³] IR 2,200Y: tall, leggy filly: shows knee action: fourth foal: half-sister to 2 winners, including 1988 5f 2-y-o winner Pastoral Jem (by Horage): dam 2-y-o 5f winner: made all in maiden auction at Yarmouth in June: never a factor but excellent fifth of 7 to Sayyedati when 100/1-chance in Hillsdown Cherry Hinton Stakes at Newmarket: creditable close last of 3 to Nominator in minor event at Redcar after: should stay 1m: tended to wander on firm ground: has sweated. *C. W. C. Elsey*

SPARKLER GEBE 6 b.g. Be My Native (USA) 122 – Siliferous (Sandy Creek 47 123) [1991 NR 1992 11.9g* 11.9d⁵ a12g 14.1g² 16m⁵] tall, leggy gelding: poor handicapper: won at Brighton in March: effective from 1½m to 2m: acts on good to firm and dead ground: ran creditably blinkered last 2 starts: won over hurdles in October. *R. J. O'Sullivan*

SPARKLING SKIES 3 b. or br.f. Skyliner 117 – Sparkling Ears 61 (Sparkler 130) [1991 NR 1992 7g^5 9g^4] stocky filly: moderate walker: fifth foal: dam maiden stayed 1¼m: seems of little account. *E. Weymes*   –

SPARKLING VISION 3 b.f. Vision (USA) – Amina 80 (Brigadier Gerard 144) [1991 6d^4 7m^5 7m 1992 9.2v 12d^5 12.1m^3 14.1g] smallish, sparely-made filly: poor handicapper: pulled up final start: stays 1½m: acts on good to firm ground: often blinkered. *Mrs M. Reveley*   41

SPARKY'S GIRL 2 ch.f. (Mar 23) Doulab (USA) 115 – Romantic Overture (USA) 73 (Stop The Music (USA)) [1992 5.7d] 550 2-y-o: second foal: dam 2-y-o 6f winner: tailed off in maiden at Bath in September. *R. J. Baker*   –

SPARKY'S SONG 2 b. or br.f. (Mar 24) Electric 126 – Daring Ditty (Daring March 116) [1992 6m 5g 6s^3 8d 7d] unfurnished filly: second foal: half-sister to 3-y-o Jellyroll Blues (by Tremblant): dam twice-raced daughter of useful sprinter Dawn Ditty: poor maiden: stays 1m: acts on soft ground. *J. W. Hills*   44

SPARTAN SHAREEF (IRE) 3 b.c. Shareef Dancer (USA) 135 – Spartan Helen (Troy 137) [1991 8m 1992 8d^5 9g^5 10g* 11.5s^6 12g 10.3m^4 10.5d^2 8.9d* 9.7s^5 10g^5] strong colt: easy mover: smart performer: won minor event at Newmarket in April and listed race (beat Badawi 3 lengths) at York in September: best effort in between when second to Half A Tick in Group 3 event at Haydock: below form in Prix Dollar at Longchamp and Newmarket listed race last 2 starts: stays 10.5f: acts on good to firm and dead ground. *C. E. Brittain*   113

SPEAKER'S HOUSE (USA) 3 b.c. Lear Fan (USA) 130 – Bring Me Flowers (FR) (Dancer's Image (USA)) [1991 5m* 7d* 1992 8f* 8.9d* 8m^3] strong, workmanlike colt: has a short action: useful performer: showed excellent turn of foot to win handicap at Newmarket in June (first run for a year) and 3-runner median auction contest (beat-odds on Seattle Rhyme by 1½ lengths) at York in July: creditable third in Group 2 contest in Turkey later in month: stays 9f: acts on firm and dead going: held up. *P. F. I. Cole*   106

SPECIAL DAWN (IRE) 2 ch.g. (Feb 16) Be My Guest (USA) 126 – Dawn Star 94 (High Line 125) [1992 7s] fifth foal: half-brother to 6f winner Dawn Storm (by Runnett) and 4-y-o 7f (at 2 yrs) and 1m winner Dawning Street (by Thatching): dam 1¼m winner and 11f winner, is half-sister to useful Domynsky: green, bumped halfway and no progress final 2f when beaten 15 lengths in maiden at Salisbury in September: will improve. *J. L. Dunlop*   52 p

SPECIALIST DREAM (IRE) 3 b.g. Irish River (FR) 131 – Confiture (USA) (Empery (USA) 128) [1991 6g 6g 1992 7m^4 a8g 8h^5 8g^5 8.2m 7g^6] angular gelding: poor maiden: stays 1m: acts on hard ground. *L. J. Codd*   41

SPECIAL ONE 2 b.f. (Apr 9) Aragon 118 – Special Guest 67 (Be My Guest (USA) 126) [1992 5m^5 5.1g^3 5g* 6g^2] quite attractive filly: good mover: third foal: closely related to 1990 2-y-o 5f winner Northern Host (by Petorius): dam 2-y-o 7f winner   66 p

Reference Point Strensall Stakes, York — Spartan Shareef runs on too strongly for Badawi

stayed 9f: progressive filly: won Wolverhampton maiden in July: good second in nursery at Windsor following month: should stay 7f: should improve. *J. W. Hills*

SPECIAL RISK (IRE) 2 br.g. (Feb 26) Simply Great (FR) 122 – Ahonita 90   **52** (Ahonoora 122) [1992 6m 6.1m² 6h⁶ 6g⁴ 7d⁴] 5,400F, 11,000Y: small, leggy gelding: first foal: dam best at 5f, won at 2 yrs, is daughter of good-class 1¼m winner in Italy: second in median auction at Nottingham in June: should stay 1m. *M. Bell*

SPECIFICITY (USA) 4 b.f. Alleged (USA) 138 – Mandera (USA) 112 (Vaguely   **98** Noble 140) [1991 10.5g³ 12.2g* 12s³ 1992 12g 13.3g⁴ 18m² 16g*] leggy filly: lightly raced: not seen out in 1992 until September, but improved with each run: second to Vintage Crop in Tote Cesarewitch at Newmarket before making all in listed race there, beating Persian Fantasy by 4 lengths: suited by a test of stamina: acts on soft going and good to firm: bandaged behind and sweating first 2 starts. *J. H. M. Gosden*

SPECIFIED (USA) 2 ch.c. (May 2) Known Fact (USA) 135 – Scierpan (USA) 86   **86** p (Sharpen Up 127) [1992 6d* 6g²] sturdy, compact colt: has a short, scratchy action: second foal: half-brother to 3-y-o 8.9f winner Cachou (by Roberto): dam placed at 5f and 6f at 2 yrs, is daughter of Solartic, smart winner at up to 1m and second in 9f Canadian Oaks: impressive 3½-length winner of maiden at Redcar, quickening clear under 2f out: heavily-backed odds-on shot, similar form when beaten a length by Wathik in 5-runner minor event at Doncaster later in October, still green and drifting left 1f out: should stay 1m: sure to do better. *J. H. M. Gosden*

SPECTACLE JIM 3 b.g. Mummy's Game 120 – Welsh Blossom 100 (Welsh   – Saint 126) [1991 6s a5g a6g⁴ 1992 a7g 7m⁵ 6d⁵ 6g 5f] leggy gelding: poor maiden: stays 6f: acts on dead ground: stiff task when blinkered. *J. O'Donoghue*

SPECTACULAR DAWN 3 gr.f. Spectacular Bid (USA) – Early Rising (USA)   **81** (Grey Dawn II 132) [1991 7.1m⁶ 7m⁴ 1992 8d 10g⁶ 10f* 10.2m 10m* 9.9d* 12d⁵ 13.1f² 11.7s³] leggy filly: progressed well in handicaps in 1992: won at Lingfield (2) and Beverley: stays 13.1f: probably acts on any going: races prominently: joined N. Henderson. *J. L. Dunlop*

SPEED OIL 3 br.c. Java Tiger 79 – Maydrum 50 (Meldrum 112) [1991 8.3g⁵ 6d   **50** 1992 5s 7v⁴ 10d⁵ 10.1g 8m⁵ 11.1s⁶ 8g³] workmanlike colt: poor maiden: may prove best at up to 1m: probably acts on good to firm and heavy ground: ran well visored final start. *R. Bastiman*

SPEEDO MOVEMENT 3 ch.f. Scottish Reel 123 – Third Movement 75 (Music   **59** Boy 124) [1991 6m⁶ 6.1f8.1g⁷g 1992 10s⁴ a12g 11.8g⁵ 12.5g⁴ 12.3d² 11.8g² 12m 12m⁴ 14.6g⁴] angular filly: has a quick action: modest maiden: stays 14.6f well: suited by give in the ground. *B. A. McMahon*

SPEEDY BEAUTY 3 b.f. Rousillon (USA) 133 – Rye Tops 97 (Ile de Bourbon   **42** (USA) 133) [1991 NR 1992 8.1d⁴ 11g⁴ 10g] big, plain filly: moderate mover: third foal: half-sister to 11f winner Wassifa (by Sure Blade): dam 10.5f winner stayed 1½m, is sister to Most Welcome and daughter of Topsy, smart winner at up to 1¼m: similar form when fourth in maiden and seller: tailed off in seller final run in June: stays 11f: sold 5,400 gns Newmarket July Sales. *B. Hanbury*

SPEEDY CLASSIC (USA) 3 br.g. Storm Cat (USA) – Shadows Lengthen 73   **67** d (Star Appeal 133) [1991 NR 1992 6s⁴ 6m⁴ 7.5m⁵ 6d a6g 7g 6s⁴ 7d a6g a8g a10g] workmanlike gelding: has round action: fourth foal: dam (ran only at 2 yrs) showed modest form in 3 starts at up to 1m, is half-sister to Bedtime: sire one of leading U.S. 2-y-o's of 1985: modest maiden: best effort on debut: should stay further than 6f: trained first 5 starts by C. Tinkler, next 3 by B. Hills. *M. J. Heaton-Ellis*

SPEEDY SIOUX 3 ch.f. Mandrake Major 122 – Sioux Be It (Warpath 113) [1991   **56** d 6m 7m 1992 7g 8.3s⁶ 10m² 10g⁵ 10m⁴ 10.9s⁵ 12.3s] lengthy, sparely-made filly: moderate mover: first foal: dam NH Flat race winner: plater: should stay 1½m: acts on good to firm ground, seemingly not on soft: won over hurdles in October: sold to join S. Chadwick 2,500 gns Doncaster November Sales. *C. W. Thornton*

SPELL OF THE YUKON (USA) 3 ro.f. Spectacular Bid (USA) – Winter   **63** Words (USA) (Northern Dancer (CAN)) [1991 5g² 5d* 5m³ 6g* 6g 6g⁴ 1992 6m 5.2m⁵ 5g⁴ 5d³] compact, quite attractive filly: rated 81 at 2 yrs but fractured knee on final outing: well below form in 1992: stays 6f: acts on dead ground: tends to be slowly away: sold 8,400 gns Newmarket December Sales. *I. A. Balding*

SPENCER'S REVENGE 3 ch.g. Bay Express 132 – Armour of Light (Hot   **76** Spark 126) [1991 NR 1992 7g⁶ a8s* 7d³ 7v a7g²] sturdy gelding: first foal: dam poor maiden: generally progressive form: won maiden at Southwell in August and excellent second in handicap at Lingfield final start: stays 1m: acts on dead ground and all-weather surfaces, seems unsuited by heavy going. *Lord Huntingdon*

*Bessborough Stakes (Handicap), Ascot—Spinning belies his reputation;
the closest pursuers are Regent's Folly (second right) and Matador (white face)*

SPENDER 3 b. or br.g. Last Tycoon 131 – Lady Hester (Native Prince) [1991 NR **42**
1992 8g 8g 7d⁵ 6.1s a7g⁶ a7g³] 8,800Y: small, well-made gelding: half-brother to
several winners, including smart French 1m and 9f performer L'Irresponsable (by
Ile de Bourbon) and 2-y-o 5f winner Aunt Hester (by Caerleon): dam Irish 5f and 6f
winner, is granddaughter of excellent broodmare Zanzara: best effort in handicap on
final outing: should stay 1m. *P. W. Harris*

SPENMAX (IRE) 2 br.g. (Apr 23) Cyrano de Bergerac 120 – Lady Elka (Lord **–**
Gayle (USA) 124) [1992 5.1s 6f 5m⁶] 2,800 2-y-o: leggy, plain gelding: poor mover:
third living foal: brother to a winner abroad: dam unraced: poor form in maiden
auctions and a claimer. *W. G. M. Turner*

SPICE AND SUGAR 2 ch.f. (Mar 4) Chilibang 120 – Pretty Miss (So Blessed **49** p
130) [1992 6s*] smallish filly: sixth foal: half-sister to 3-y-o Drop A Curtsey (by
Prince Sabo) and 7f and 1¼m winner Follow The Drum (by Daring March): dam
once-raced half-sister to useful 2-y-o Fair Parrot: 10/1, better for race and green,
won 5-runner maiden at Newcastle in September by a short head from Louvre, short
of room from 2f out but running on well to lead line: will improve. *J. D. Bethell*

SPICY AFFAIR 2 gr.f. (Mar 17) Chilibang 120 – Boarding House 73 (Shack **45**
(USA) 118) [1992 5f³ 6d 5.7d] 3,300F, 8,200Y: rather leggy filly: fourth foal: half-
sister to a winner in Malaysia: dam best at 5f: best effort in maiden auction at
Salisbury on debut: dead. *Dr J. D. Scargill*

SPIKENARD 3 b.f. Slip Anchor 136 – Pomade 79 (Luthier 126) [1991 7f 8.1g³ **89** ?
1992 9.9f* 12.5m³ 14.1g* 13.3d* 13.9g 14d⁴ 14m 16.5g] workmanlike filly: in
excellent form in first half of 1992, winning Beverley maiden, Nottingham minor
event and handicap at Newbury: lost her form in second half of season: should stay
2m: acts on firm and dead ground: sold 16,000 gns Newmarket December Sales. *P.
T. Walwyn*

SPINAYAB 3 b.f. King of Spain 121 – Pallomere 85 (Blue Cashmere 129) [1991 7g **–**
1992 8f 7.1g 8.3m 7d] tall filly: no worthwhile form. *E. A. Wheeler*

SPINNING 5 b. or br.g. Glint of Gold 128 – Strathspey 105 (Jimmy Reppin 131) **110**
[1991 10v⁶ 10.4m⁴ 12g³ 12g² 13.3f² 12m⁶ 10.9m² 12g⁴ 16.5m* 14.6d 1992 12g⁵ 13.3f

*Tote Gold Trophy Stakes (Handicap), Goodwood—
the first of two wins for Spinning (noseband) at the meeting*

12g² 12f* 10.3f³ 12m* 12m* 13.4g³ 11f³ 12d] tall, useful-looking gelding: good walker: easy mover: formerly a most difficult ride (kept hanging), but much better in 1992: won Bessborough Handicap at Royal Ascot, Tote Gold Trophy at Goodwood and Goodwood listed event (by 1½ lengths from Jahafil, who gave 5 lb), last 2 in space of 3 days: ran well when third to Solar Splendor in Man o' War Stakes at Belmont penultimate run: effective at 1½m to 2m: acts on firm going, seems unsuited by a soft surface: has run creditably in blinkers, but didn't wear them in 1992: occasionally wears net muzzle. *I. A. Balding*

SPIRIT SAM 7 ch.h. Music Boy 124 – Kalia (Wollow 132) [1991 9.7m a8g 1992 12f 9.7h⁶ 12f] robust horse: moderate mover: seems of little account. *P. J. Feilden* —

SPITZABIT 8 br.g. Pitskelly 122 – Marsabit (Martinmas 128) [1991 NR 1992 5s] leggy gelding: moderate mover: on the downgrade. *Pat Mitchell* —

SPLASH OF SALT (IRE) 2 b.f. (Feb 24) Salt Dome (USA) – Indian Splash 94 (Prince Tenderfoot (USA) 126) [1992 6d 6m 6m⁴ 6g² a7g³ a6g*] 8,600Y: good-topped, quite attractive filly: has a quick action: fourth foal: dam Irish 2-y-o 6f winner is half-sister to Long Pond: sire smart sprinter: modest performer: won claimer at Southwell late in year: best form at 6f: retained 4,000 gns Newmarket Autumn Sales after fourth start. *W. J. Haggas* **63**

SPLENDENT (USA) 2 ch.c. (Feb 28) Shadeed (USA) 135 – Sticky Habit 79 (Habitat 134) [1992 5g³ 6g* 6f* 6g⁵ 6m* 7m³ 8s] 120,000Y: lengthy, strong-quartered colt: has plenty of scope: half-brother to several winners, including very useful 6f to 8.5f winner Aim For The Top (by Irish River) and 7f winner Surmise (by Alleged): dam, from good family, won at 1m and 1¼m: successful in 3-runner minor events at York and Thirsk in summer before much improved effort to land Scottish Equitable Gimcrack Stakes (by ½ length from unlucky-in-running Silver Wizard) at York in August: creditable third of 6 to Zafonic in Prix de la Salamandre at Longchamp but ran moderately in Grand Criterium at Longchamp after: strong-galloping sort, should stay 1m: possibly requires top-of-the-ground. *P. F. I. Cole* **108**

SPLICE 3 ch.f. Sharpo 132 – Soluce 98 (Junius (USA) 124) [1991 5d⁴ 5m² 5m* 5m* 6f⁶ 5m* 5d 1992 6g 6g⁴ 6m* 6f⁶ 6f⁴ 7m 8.1d⁴ 8m 6m* 6m⁶] rather leggy filly: useful performer: claimer ridden, quickened well to win handicaps at Newmarket in May (£19,000 event) and October: effective at 6f, and probably at 1m: acts on good to firm and dead ground: nervy type: held up. *J. R. Fanshawe* **96**

SPLIT SECOND 3 b.g. Damister (USA) 123 – Moment In Time 91 (Without Fear (FR) 128) [1991 7m 6m 8.1s 1992 12.3s⁶ 14.6g 13.8g⁶] leggy, rather angular gelding: no form on flat: tried visored: claimed to join Mrs V. A. Aconley's stable £2,000 final start in June: subsequently placed over hurdles. *J. W. Watts* —

Scottish Equitable Gimcrack Stakes, York—from right to left and in finishing order;
Splendent, Silver Wizard and Green's Bid

SPONTANEOUS (IRE) 3 b.f. Bluebird (USA) 125 – Cairnfold (USA) 68 (Never –
Bend (USA)) [1991 NR 1992 11.7d⁶ 8f] 18,500Y: sturdy, lengthy filly: good walker:
half-sister to several winners, including Irish 8.5f and 9f winner Azaris (by
Northfields), later successful in USA: dam, 11.7f winner, is half-sister to dam of
Cheshire Oaks winner Malaak and Canadian Grade 1 winner Crowning Honors: no
worthwhile form in maiden and claimer in spring: sold to join W. Clay's stable 1,300
gns Ascot June Sales. *R. Charlton*

SPOOF 5 b.m. Precocious 126 – Thimblerigger 62 (Sharpen Up 127) [1991 10.2s –
12g⁴ 13.8g⁶ 12m⁶ 16m² 15.9m 1992 16.2g] workmanlike mare: poor handicapper:
probably best short of 2m: acted on good to firm ground and dead: below form
blinkered once: dead. *M. D. Hammond*

SPORADES (USA) 3 ro.f. Vaguely Noble 140 – Stresa (Mill Reef (USA) 141) **117**
[1991 NR 1992 8v² 8g⁴ 8.5m* 8d* 9.3s⁴ 10.5s* 9f⁶] tall, close-coupled filly: eighth
reported foal: half-sister to several winners, notably Arlington Million winner Mill
Native (by Exclusive Native) and high-class 1m and 9f winner French Stress (by
Sham): dam French 1¼m winner: progressed into a smart performer: successful in
minor event and listed race at Longchamp and Group 3 Prix de Flore at Saint-Cloud,
last-named by short neck from Fabulous Hostess in October: also ran well when 1½
lengths fourth to Hatoof in Prix de l'Opera at Longchamp fifth outing and 4½
lengths sixth behind Flawlessly in Grade 1 The Matriarch at Hollywood Park:
should stay 1½m: acts on any going. *A. Fabre, France*

SPORTING MISSILE (USA) 2 ch.f. (Jan 24) The Minstrel (CAN) 135 – **43**
Sporting Ack (USA) (Ack Ack (USA)) [1992 a7g a8g⁴] first foal: dam stakes-winning
miler: fourth in end-of-year maiden at Lingfield (bandaged near-hind). *J. H. M.
Gosden*

SPORTING SPIRIT 2 br.g. (Apr 9) Dunbeath (USA) 127 – Silent Plea 43 (Star **54**
Appeal 133) [1992 5g⁵ 5d* 6s 5d 7s 7s 5g] first foal: dam, plater, stayed 6f: no
comparable form after winning Edinburgh maiden in August: should be suited by
further than 5f. *D. W. Chapman*

SPORTING WEDNESDAY 7 b.g. Martinmas 128 – Philogyny 94 (Philip of – §
Spain 126) [1991 a10g 8f 10.1s 8.1d 7m 1992 7.1m] leggy gelding: one to avoid, tailed
off in amateurs handicap only run in 1992: stays 1m: acts on firm going: tailed off
when blinkered once. *J. S. Moore*

SPORTING WEEKEND (FR) 5 br.g. Vayrann 133 – Danesta (USA) (Majes- –
tic Prince) [1991 NR 1992 10m 11.5f 8f 9m] leggy gelding: fifth foal: half-brother to
winners in France by Brigadier Gerard and Nice Havrais: dam ran twice at 3 yrs:
won over 7f and 9f at 2 yrs in Italy for present trainer, and placed at up to 10.5f there
at 3 yrs: no form here, hampered and rider unseated in amateurs event final run:
sometimes wears tongue strap and crossed noseband. *D. Sasse*

SPORTS POST LADY (IRE) 4 ch.f. M Double M (USA) – Pasadena Lady **47**
(Captain James 123) [1991 a5g² 5d 6g 5m* 5f³ 5m* 5g⁴ 5.2f⁶ 5.1m² 5.1m 5g 5.1d 5.1g a56
a5g* 1992 a6g a6g a5g² a5g 5.3m 5.1d 5.7f 6g 5m 5m⁶ 5.1m a6g] angular,
sparely-made filly: inconsistent handicapper: best form at 5f: acts on firm going,
probably not on dead. *C. J. Hill*

SPORTS VIEW 3 b.g. Mashhor Dancer (USA) – Persian Express (Persian Bold **59**
123) [1991 6f 8g⁶ 7g⁵ 1992 10d 10d 12.5g² 13.1m 12m⁴ 10.2s⁶ 16.1s² 16s²] compact
gelding: maiden handicapper: unlucky final start: well suited by test of stamina: best
efforts on an easy surface: trained until after penultimate start by R. Holder. *P. G.
Murphy*

SPOTLAND LASS 2 ch.f. (Apr 19) Risk Me (FR) 127 – Golden Machine 68 –
(Glint of Gold 128) [1992 5g 5v] 1,000Y: first foal: dam, maiden, stayed 7f: well
beaten in seller and maiden in spring. *W. G. M. Turner*

SPOT THE DOVE 3 b.f. Riberetto 107 – Grey Dove (Grey Love 103) [1991 NR –
1992 8.9g³ 8g 7d⁶ 8.9g] workmanlike, unfurnished filly: non-thoroughbred:
half-sister to 14.8f winner Celtic Dove (by Celtic Cone): dam useful over hurdles at
up to 2½m: no worthwhile form: should be well suited by 1¼m +. *R. J. Price*

SPOT THE EARLYBIRD (USA) 3 ch.c. Mertzon (USA) – Cornered (USA) –
(Bold Commander (USA)) [1991 5f⁴ 5g³ 5m² 5d⁴ 5m⁴ 5m 5m⁴ 5m⁵ 7g 1992 7g 9.2v]
small, sturdy colt: sprint maiden: rated 58 at 2 yrs: well beaten in spring of 1992:
easily best form on a sound surface: below form when visored/blinkered once. *N.
Tinkler*

SPRAY OF ORCHIDS 3 ch.f. Pennine Walk 120 – Mana (GER) (Windwurf **57**
(GER)) [1991 5f⁵ 5f⁴ 6d 6.9m² 7.5f 7m 7.5f⁴ 7m⁶ 7.1m² 1992 a7g⁵ 8.5f⁴ a8g³ a11g²
a12g³ 10m² 10m² 10g* 10s* 10.3m 10.5d³ 11.8s 12.1v] lengthy filly: modest

handicapper: successful at Ripon (2, no bid in seller first time) in August: best turf form at around 1¼m: acts on any turf going, and on fibresand: below form blinkered once: held up. *J. Etherington*

SPRING   3 b.f. Sadler's Wells (USA) 132 – Gull Nook 120 (Mill Reef (USA) 141) **112** [1991 NR 1992 10f⁶ 12f* 12m* 12.5s³ 12s² 14s*] good-topped, attractive filly: second foal: sister to 1991 3-y-o 12.2f winner Tanz: dam ran 4 times, winning over 10.5f and 1½m (Ribblesdale Stakes), and is out of half-sister to Shirley Heights: held up when successful at Newmarket in maiden in June and minor event in July: very useful performances when about 2 lengths third of 12 to Fabulous Hostess in Prix de Royallieu at Longchamp and length second of 8 to Up Anchor in St Simon Stakes at Newbury: didn't have to be at best to win Group 3 race at Rome in November: stays 1¾m: acts on soft going: remains in training. *J. L. Dunlop*

SPRING FLYER (IRE)   2 b.f. (Feb 27) Waajib 121 – Late Swallow (My Swallow **60** 134) [1992 5d a7g* a7g³] 19,000Y: leggy, rather sparely-made filly: half-sister to several winners, including one-time very useful sprinter A Prayer For Wings (by Godswalk) and fair miler March Bird (by Dalsaan): dam never ran: always behind in maiden at Haydock in May when trained by M. O'Neill: off course around 7 months before winning Southwell maiden and third in nursery there: will stay 1m. *A. Bailey*

SPRING FORWARD   8 b.h. Double Form 130 – Forward Princess (USA)   – § (Forward Pass) [1991 14m 21.6f 18.4d 17.6m 15s⁴ 16m* 15.1m⁶ 19m 15.9m a14g 1992 12d⁵ 16.4g a16g] small, leggy horse: unreliable staying handicapper: acts on any going: sometimes blinkered, usually visored nowadays: tends to get behind. *R. E. Peacock*

SPRING HIGH   5 b.m. Miami Springs 121 – High Voltage 82 (Electrify) [1991 6m **63** 10f 10.1d 7g 8m 8f² 6.9f² a7g² 7m⁶ 6m⁶ 7s a7g⁴ a8g⁴ 1992 a5g* 5m⁵ 5f² 5m³ 5m⁶ a66 5.2m³ 7d³ 6g* a5g² 5.2f* 5.1f* 6f* 6d⁴ 5.2m² 6m] tall, leggy, lengthy mare: had an excellent year in handicaps in 1992, successful at Southwell (seller, no bid), Yarmouth (3) and Bath: best form at up to 7f: acts on firm and dead going and goes well on fibresand, seems unsuited by soft: best blinkered: a credit to her trainer. *K. T. Ivory*

SPRING PLAY   8 ch.g. Hard Fought 125 – Spring Snow (Reliance II 137) [1991 NR 1992 14.8f] deep-bodied gelding: half-brother to several winners, including stakes-placed American performer Dilmoun (by Kalamoun): dam French 15f winner: no promise over jumps or (blinkered) on flat in June. *J. Akehurst*

SPRING SAINT   3 ch.c. Midyan (USA) 124 – Lady of Chalon (USA) (Young   – Emperor 133) [1991 7g⁵ 1992 8.2d⁴ 8.2m⁶ 9.7m] close-coupled colt: no worthwhile form. *M. J. Heaton-Ellis*

SPRING SIXPENCE   2 br.f. (Apr 25) Dowsing (USA) 124 – Little Change 70 **55** (Grundy 137) [1992 6.1d 6m⁶ 6.9v⁶] 13,500Y: sixth foal: half-sister to 3 winners here and abroad, including 1m to 1½m winner Forfun (by Jalmood), successful in 1992 over 7f and 9f in Australia: dam, from good family, best at 2 yrs when placed over 5f: staying-on sixth of 16 in maiden auction at Yarmouth second start: never a factor in maiden at Folkestone later in autumn: should be suited by 7f+: possibly unsuited by soft ground. *J. R. Fanshawe*

SPRING SUNRISE   2 b.f. (Apr 7) Robellino (USA) 127 – Saniette (Crystal **59** Palace (FR) 132) [1992 5g⁴ 6s² 5g⁴ 6g* 6.5m³ 7m] IR 480Y, 6,000 2-y-o: tall, lengthy filly: fifth foal: half-sister to 13.1f winner Shoe Tapper (by Song) and 2 winners abroad: dam, ran once in France, is daughter of French Oaks fourth Shoeless: won maiden auction at Catterick in July and nursery at Salisbury in August: not discredited in big-field nurseries after: will be better suited by 1m: probably acts on any going: bandaged behind final run. *M. Blanshard*

SPRINGS WELCOME   6 b.m. Blakeney 126 – Tomfoolery 73 (Silly Season **69** 127) [1991 16g⁶ 14d 11.5g* 11.9m⁶ a16g³ 12g a10g* 10m⁴ 14s⁵ 12d² 12g⁵ 12d 1992 a14g⁵ 9d a12g³ 11.4s² 15.9d⁵ a12g⁴ 12m⁴ a16g³ 10.1g] workmanlike mare: ran well in handicaps most starts in 1992: stays 2m: acts on good to firm and soft going and all-weather surfaces: successful for claimer: sometimes gives impression worth a try in blinkers/visor. *C. A. Cyzer*

SPRING TERN (USA)   4 ch.c. Arctic Tern (USA) 126 – Date (USA) (What Luck   – (USA)) [1991 9d 10g 12g 10m⁶ 12m* 12f³ a11g⁴ 1992 a12g 16.2g 12g] sturdy colt: has a quick action: rated 60 at 3 yrs: out of form in 1992: stays 1½m: best efforts on top-of-the-ground: wears blinkers. *R. O'Leary*

SPRING TO ACTION   2 b.c. (May 3) Shareef Dancer (USA) 135 – Light Duty **74** p 113 (Queen's Hussar 124) [1992 8d² 8m⁶] rangy colt: good walker: half-brother to several winners, including useful 1985 2-y-o Laughter (by Shirley Heights) and

Paradise Bay (by Mill Reef), very useful at up to 1½m: dam middle-distance performer, is sister to Highclere: progressive form in big-field September maidens at Kempton (second to Commanche Gold) and Newmarket (sixth to Armiger): will be suited by middle distances: has plenty of scope, and will do better. *I. A. Balding*

SPRING TO THE TOP   5 b.g. Thatching 131 – Queen of The Brush (Averof 51 123) [1991 10m 8d 8f⁴ 8g* 7g 8g² 9g⁶ 1992 8d 7g 8d 8m⁴ 10.3m⁶ 10g 9d] rather leggy gelding: has a round action: somewhat disappointing in handicaps in 1992: should prove better suited by 1¼m than 1m: best efforts on a sound surface: sold to join C. Nash's stable 3,400 gns Newmarket Autumn Sales. *J. W. Payne*

SQUIRE YORK   2 b.c. (Apr 17) Bairn (USA) 126 – Alice Parry (Kampala 120) 55 p [1992 a6g²] third foal: dam poor daughter of 1½m winner: 25/1, second of 8 in maiden at Lingfield in December, staying on under hands and heels after slow start: will stay at least 1m: should improve. *J. L. Spearing*

SRIVIJAYA   5 b.h. Kris 135 – Princess Pati 124 (Top Ville 129) [1991 9f³ 10.6g – 9m* 8s* 7d² 7m⁴ a8g 1992 8g 7d] good-bodied horse: moderate mover: modest handicapper, rated 76 at 4 yrs: always behind in March, 1992: effective at 7f to 12.5f: acts on good to firm and soft going: below form blinkered: joined Mrs M. Reveley and won several hurdles in April. *Mrs J. Jordan*

STACK ROCK   5 b.m. Ballad Rock 122 – One Better 77 (Nebbiolo 125) [1991 97 10.8m 6m² 7m² 7.1g³ 6g² 7g² 6g* 5g⁶ 6g⁵ 7m⁴ 6m* 6m* 1992 6g⁴ 5.2d* 5s² 6m⁵ 7.1g³ 6f 7m 5d 6g² 6g⁶ 5.6m 6d 5g] robust mare: poor walker and mover: useful sprinter: successful in Newbury handicap and placed in listed contests in spring: good second to Master Planner in £13,100 handicap at York in August: ideally suited by 5f or 6f: has form on good to firm but is well suited by some give: below form visored once: suitable mount for claimer: often forces pace: tough and genuine. *E. J. Alston*

STAGE ARTIST   2 ch.f. (Mar 15) Chief Singer 131 – Trila Love (Lomond (USA) 36 128) [1992 8m 7s 10d 6g] big, good-topped filly: has scope: second foal: half-sister to 3-y-o Doughman (by Runnett): dam unraced half-sister to Doncaster Cup second Bourbon Boy: well beaten in maidens and a seller: sold 1,600 gns Doncaster November Sales. *J. Etherington*

STAG NIGHT   3 ch.g. Good Times (ITY) – Deer Forest (Huntercombe 133) [1991 – 5f⁴ 6g² 7m² 6m⁶ 7m 1992 7g 8s⁵ 8s 8v 9.2d 10.9s] strong, workmanlike gelding: poor mover: poor plater at 2 yrs (rated 51): no worthwhile form in 1992: best form at up to 7f: acts on good to firm ground: below form visored: sold out of C. Tinkler's stable 1,500 gns Doncaster June Sales after penultimate run. *A. W. Potts*

STAIRWAY TO HEAVEN (IRE)   4 b.f. Godswalk (USA) 130 – Cathryn's 63 Song (Prince Tenderfoot (USA) 126) [1991 a7g² 8.2m³ 7g⁶ 6d³ 6.9m² 7g⁴ 8f³ 7m⁶ a– 8m* 8m* 8.3f6 a8g a7g 1992 7.1f5 8.2d4 8m6 8.2m 8g2 7.5d4 8g* 8s3 8s 8s a8g a8g] angular, sparely-made filly: moderate mover: none too consistent handicapper: won at Thirsk in August: better over 1m than shorter, and should prove as effective over 1¼m: acts on any going: blinkered nowadays: has been reluctant at stalls and hung badly left, but has run well for apprentice. *T. D. Barron*

STALLED (IRE)   2 b.c. (Apr 11) Glenstal (USA) 118 – Chauffeuse 76 (Gay 64 Fandango (USA) 132) [1992 7g⁵ a7g⁵ a8g³] IR 5,200Y, resold 12,000Y: half-brother a58 to a couple of poor animals: dam 5f winner at 2 yrs on only start, is out of half-sister to high-class sprinters Boone's Cabin and Home Guard: modest maiden: best effort on debut (November): stays 1m. *P. T. Walwyn*

ST ALZINA (IRE)   2 b.c. (May 21) Alzao (USA) 117 – St Padina 91 (St Paddy 133) [1992 6s 5v] 10,000Y: smallish, leggy filly: half-brother to several winners, including (at 2m) fair Invasion (by Kings Lake) and (at 1¼m) useful Double Lock (by Home Guard): dam, half-sister to Irish Oaks winner Celina, won at 1m: soundly beaten in October maidens. *G. H. Eden*

STAMSHAW   3 ch.f. Noalto 120 – Saint Motunde 84 (Tyrant (USA)) [1991 NR 49 1992 6m 6.1m 7g⁴ 6.9g 5m a5g a5g⁶ a6g⁵ a6g⁴ a6g⁴] workmanlike filly: fifth reported foal: half-sister to sprinters Saint Navarro (by Raga Navarro) and Hannah's Boy (by Smackover): dam best at 2 yrs, later won at 6f to 1m: poor maiden: should stay 7f: acts on fibresand: sold 800 gns Doncaster October Sales. *B. A. McMahon*

STAND AT EASE   7 b.g. The Brianstan 128 – Plush 75 (Lombard (GER) 126) 35 [1991 12m 8f6 12m 8h* 9m⁶ 8s³ 8g⁵ 8.3f⁴ 8f 1992 5.9d⁵ 8.1m 8f³ 8f⁴ 8.1m⁴ 8h⁴ 9d⁶ 8.1m⁴ 9m³] workmanlike gelding: carries condition: inconsistent handicapper: stays 1m: acts on any going. *W. Storey*

STANFORD AVENUE 2 ch.f. (Feb 8) Stanford 121§ – Bourienne 58 –
(Bolkonski 134) [1992 5.1s 6f] 1,400Y: angular filly: fifth foal: dam 1m and 9f seller
winner: well beaten in maiden auctions in May. *B. Forsey*

STANI (USA) 3 b.c. Shahrastani (USA) 135 – Shelf Talker (USA) (Tatan (ARG)) **84**
[1991 7m* 1992 8.9g 12m6 9d6 7g* 7.1s 8m*] strong colt: has a round action: won
handicaps at Newmarket and Pontefract (dead-heated) in autumn: stays 1m: acts on
good to firm and dead ground (seems not to act on very soft): tends to get on edge. *B.
Hanbury*

STAPLEFORD LADY 4 ch.f. Bairn (USA) 126 – Marie Galante (FR) (King of –
The Castle (USA)) [1991 12f 14g5 12d4 12f4 a12g2 12m3 1992 10.8g] leggy, angular
filly: poor plater: should stay well: acts on dead ground. *R. J. Manning*

STAPLEFORD LASS 2 b.f. (Mar 21) Bairn (USA) 126 – Idabella (FR) **53**
(Carwhite 127) [1992 5.1g5 6f3 a6g6 7.5m 10.5d*] third foal: dam French 9f winner:
best effort when 20/1-winner of selling nursery (no bid) at Haydock in October,
running on well despite carrying head awkwardly: will stay well: acts well on a soft
surface. *S. P. C. Woods*

STAPLETON (IRE) 3 b.c. Dance of Life (USA) – Flying Anna (Roan Rocket **77**
128) [1991 6f5 6m2 6m2 1992 10d4 10m* 11m4 13.1m2 12f4 12m2 10.5d 14.6g] strong,
lengthy colt: won handicap at Pontefract in May: good second twice afterwards:
should stay beyond 13f: acts on good to firm ground: below form when blinkered
once: may prove best with strong handling. *J. W. Watts*

STAR CATCH 3 b.g. Skyliner 117 – Let Slip 77 (Busted 134) [1991 NR 1992 12.3f] –
4,000F: leggy gelding: half-brother to several winners, including fairly useful
middle-distance performer Petite Rosanna (by Ile de Bourbon): dam showed some
ability at 2 yrs: tailed off in Ripon apprentice maiden in June, only run on flat. *W.
Carter*

STARCHY COVE 5 br.m. Starch Reduced 112 – Rosey Covert (Sahib 114) [1991 –
6m3 5f 5g 5.9f6 5.1m a5g 1992 6g 5.1m 5g a6g4 6m6] leggy mare: poor handicapper
nowadays: stays 6f: acts on fibresand, probably best on turf on top-of-the-ground. *B.
R. Cambidge*

STAR CONNECTION 4 b.f. Faustus (USA) 118 – Emerald Rocket 69 (Green **68**
God 128) [1991 8.2d4 8.5f4 7m5 1992 8s6 8d3 8g* 7f6 10f6 8f4 8g] strong, lengthy
filly: carries plenty of condition: poor mover: consistent handicapper: first success
when winning Thirsk Hunt Cup in spring: not seen out after August: best form at
1m: has form on firm ground, but goes very well with some give (acts on soft going):
ran moderately when blinkered once. *R. M. Whitaker*

STARDUST EXPRESS 2 b.g. (Apr 2) Sylvan Express 117 – Sancilia (Dalsaan **56**
125) [1992 5g2 5g5 5d4 5m 5m4 5m3 5d5 5g 7.5m 6g4 a6g4] 1,100F,
4,500Y: tall gelding: progressed well physically: has a quick action: second foal: dam
sprint maiden: won claimer at Lingfield in October: good fourth in similar event
there following month: stays 6f: acts on good to firm and dead ground: races keenly:
looks well suited to all-weather racing. *M. Johnston*

STAR FAMILY FRIEND (IRE) 2 ch.f. (May 10) Double Schwartz 128 – **92**
Jane's Idea (Ballad Rock 122) [1992 5d* 5m* 5f 6s* 6s3 6v] medium-sized, lengthy
filly: moderate mover: second foal: dam Irish 2-y-o 6f winner, is daughter of half-
sister to very useful Irish middle-distance filly Santa Roseanna: successful in
maiden at Haydock and minor event at Pontefract in May and listed event in good
style at Ripon in August: never dangerous on heavy ground in Racecall Gold Trophy
(favourite) at Redcar: better suited by 6f than 5f: ran creditably on firm ground, but
best efforts on a soft surface. *M. H. Tompkins*

STAR GODDESS (USA) 3 ch.f. Northern Jove (CAN) – Sonseri 95 (Prince **80**
Tenderfoot (USA) 126) [1991 NR 1992 7d 7g* 8m 7.1s6] sturdy, quite attractive filly:
sixth foal: dam, 5f and 6f winner who stayed 1m, is half-sister to very useful 6f to 1m
winner Apres Demain: below form in minor events after winning Kempton maiden
in June. *M. R. Channon*

STARLIGHT FLYER 5 b.g. In Fijar (USA) 121 – Nareen (USA) (The Minstrel **99**
(CAN) 135) [1991 6s 7m 8m* 8.2m2 8g* 8d* 8.1g3 7.9g 8.1m 8m 1992 10d2 10m4
8.1s* 8g5 8.1d3 8.5f] good-bodied gelding: carries condition: moderate mover: in
good form in minor event and handicaps here in 1992, comfortable winner of £10,500
race at Sandown in July: ran at Arlington final outing: effective at 1m to 1¼m: best
efforts with give in the ground: usually blinkered nowadays, wasn't first run when
losing race due to swerving markedly right close home: joined N. Tinkler. *M.
Moubarak*

STARLIGHT ROSE (IRE) 2 b.f. (Mar 8) Broken Hearted 124 – Star Province **51**
(Dominion 123) [1992 7d 7g 7d] IR 1,100Y: leggy filly: fourth foal: half-sister to Irish
9f winner Cape Shirley (by Head For Heights): dam unraced half-sister to Star
Pastures: poor maiden: will stay 1m. *C. A. Horgan*

STARLIGHT WONDER 6 ch.m. Star Appeal 133 – My Lady Muriel (USA) **–**
(Visible (USA)) [1991 9g⁴ 14.1m⁹ a8g⁵ 12.1g 13.8g 12m] lengthy,
sparely-made mare: on the downgrade. *R. E. Barr*

STAR MANAGER (USA) 2 b.c. (Feb 12) Lyphard (USA) 132 – Angel Clare **76** p
(FR) (Mill Reef (USA) 141) [1992 8s* 8g] $25,000Y: close-coupled, useful-looking
colt: brother to a minor winner in North America and half-brother to another: dam
won at up to 9f: 6-length winner of maiden at Bath in September, making all and
easily coming clear from 2f out: beaten around 10 lengths by Taos in listed race at
Ascot following month but not at all discredited: sure to do better. *P. F. I. Cole*

STAR MINSTREL (IRE) 2 b.g. (Mar 16) Farajullah 113 – Hot Sauce (Hot **59**
Spark 126) [1992 5g 6.1d 6m² 6g⁴ 6m] IR 1,750F, 2,600 2-y-o: quite good-topped
gelding: has a round action: first foal: dam ran twice over hurdles: modest maiden:
will be suited by 1m: acts on good to firm ground. *M. McCormack*

STAR OF CHINA 2 b.f. (Feb 24) Celestial Storm (USA) 132 – Golden Panda 77 **?**
(Music Boy 124) [1992 8d³ 8d⁴ 8s*] 2,700Y: sturdy, workmanlike filly: first foal:
dam 8.2f winner: similar form in big-field maidens at Kempton and Redcar in autumn
for C. C. Elsey: won seller at Saint-Cloud afterwards (blinkered): will be better
suited by 1¼m. *W. J. S. Cargeeg, France*

STAR OF COZZENE (USA) 4 br.c. Cozzene (USA) – Star Gem (Pia Star) **119**
[1991 a9f* a9f³ a9s* a9f⁵ a8.5f* 8.5f⁴ a8.5d² 8.5f⁴ 8.5s* 8f* 8g³ 1992 8g² 8m⁶
8s⁴ 8s⁴ 10f] lengthy colt: carries condition: second foal: half-brother to Livermore
Lil (by Mt Livermore), minor stakes winner in USA: dam very tough and prolific
winner in USA at up to 9f: trained by D. Wayne Lukas, tough and consistent
performer in USA as 3-y-o, successful 6 times, and also third in Breeders' Cup Mile
at Churchill Downs: best efforts in Europe on third and fourth starts, staying on well
in Sussex Stakes (4¾ lengths sixth of 8 to Marling) at Goodwood and Prix Jacques le
Marois (around 1½ lengths behind Exit To Nowhere) at Deauville: below par in
Deauville Group 3 race and Arlington Million last 2 outings: should prove as
effective at 1¼m as 1m: acts on good to firm and soft ground. *F. Boutin, France*

STAR OF GDANSK (USA) 4 ch.c. Danzig Connection (USA) – Star Empress **113**
(USA) (Young Emperor 133) [1991 7g* 8g² 8g² 12f³ 12g³ 8g⁶ 8m* 8d⁴ 8d 10m⁵ a10f]
1992 9g⁴ 10g³ 8m] big, lengthy colt: very useful performer: ran respectably first 2
starts in Earl of Sefton Stakes at Newmarket and Tattersalls Rogers Gold Cup at the
Curragh (6 lengths third to Opera House): not seen again after well held in Queen
Anne Stakes at Royal Ascot, edging left under pressure: stays 1¼m (well-beaten
third in both Derby and Irish Derby): acts on firm ground, seems unsuited by a soft
surface: blinkered last 2 starts. *J. S. Bolger, Ireland*

STAR PLAYER 6 ch.h. Simply Great (FR) 122 – Star Girl (Sovereign Gleam 117) **88**
[1991 14.6s² 16.2g* 16m* 18.4d⁴ 20g⁴ 16.1m 14.8s⁴ 14s* 18m 16g⁵ 1992 14g⁴ 18.5g
16m³ 16.1f 18.5d³ 16.2g 13.9m⁵ 14.6f 16s²] close-coupled horse: fairly useful
handicapper: best run in 1992 when fifth in Tote Ebor at York: effective from 1¾m
to 2½m: acts on good to firm and soft ground, seems unsuited by firm: held up, and
has turn of foot. *R. J. Baker*

STAR QUEST 5 b.h. Rainbow Quest (USA) 134 – Sarah Siddons (FR) 122 (Le **79** ?
Levanstell 122) [1991 10.8d² 14g⁵ 12m² 12s 12d 1992 14.6g* 16d* 16g⁶ 16m 13.9m]
lengthy horse: has round action: well below form in handicaps after winning at
Doncaster (maiden) and Kempton in spring: stays 2m: acts on good to firm and dead
ground: suited by strong handling. *J. R. Jenkins*

STAR RAGE (IRE) 2 b.c. (Mar 5) Horage 124 – Star Bound (Crowned Prince **52**
(USA) 128) [1992 8.2s a7g a8g] IR 900F, 4,400Y: seventh foal: dam Irish 7f to 9f
winner: poor form in late-season maidens. *J. Wharton*

STATAJACK (IRE) 4 b.g. King of Clubs 124 – Statira 103 (Skymaster 126) **78**
[1991 a8g* 9s² 8.9m³ 9g 1992 10m 12d 12m⁵ 8.3g⁶ 10s³ 12d* 10.2s² 12d³
12.1s* 12g] leggy, sparely-made gelding: ran well in handicaps most starts in 1992,
successful at Epsom (amateurs) and Chepstow in second half of season: effective
from 9f to 1½m: well suited by a soft surface: effective blinkered or not: held up. *D.
R. C. Elsworth*

STATE DANCER (USA) 5 b.h. El Gran Senor (USA) 136 – Bimbo Sue (USA) **96**
(Our Michael (USA)) [1991 8g³ 8m* 8g³ 8g⁵ 7m 8g⁶ 7.9m² 8g 1992 8g² 8d 8g 8g*

8f* 8m³ 8m³] angular, lengthy horse: poor mover: useful handicapper: suffered with virus and off course around 3 months after second start but returned in really good form: successful at Ascot (apprentices) and Pontefract: stays 1m: acts on firm ground: effective ridden from front or held up: tough, genuine and consistent. *M. Moubarak*

STATE FLYER 4 ch.g. Flying Tyke 90 – Sunshine State (Roi Soleil 125) [1991 66 §
7m 8m⁵ 9m 10d 7g³ 6m² 6d* 6g² 7f³ 8.1g⁶ 7g⁶ 7m 7m 1992 7s⁴ 7m 8.3s⁶ 7f⁶ 7m⁵ 6g² 5d⁵ 6g* 6m 6m⁶ 7d⁶ 7f 6d 7d 6.1s] tall, leggy gelding: unreliable handicapper: successful at Doncaster in July: effective at 5f to 7f: acts on good to firm ground and soft: usually visored nowadays: often ridden by claimer: often soon off bridle, and wanders under pressure: has found little and been very slowly away. *C. B. B. Booth*

STATE GOVERNOR 4 ch.g. Song 132 – Brazilian Beauty (Busted 134) [1991 60 d
8.3d 6m³ 5m⁴ 5.1m² 7m² 7m² a8g* 8f³ a7g a8g⁴ 1992 a7g² a8g a8g a7g⁵ a7g a6g⁶ a6g a8g⁶ a6g a7s 6s 8g 6d 8g] lengthy gelding: lost his form in second half of 1992: stays 1m: acts on firm ground and fibresand: sometimes bandaged: retained 1,150 gns Doncaster October Sales. *D. W. Chapman*

STATELY RUN (USA) 2 b.g. (Mar 15) Stately Don (USA) 122 – Run Tulle Run –
(USA) (Tom Tulle (USA)) [1992 5g] 3,000Y: leggy, plain gelding: fourth known foal: half-brother to 2 winners in USA: dam won 7 races at up to 9f from 3 yrs to 5 yrs: unseated rider at start before behind in maiden at Leicester in April: sold 700 gns Doncaster June Sales. *M. Brittain*

STATE OF AFFAIRS 5 b.g. Free State 125 – Trigamy 112 (Tribal Chief 125) 44
[1991 10.8g³ 10m 10g 10g 1992 7g 8.2d 7d³ 8m⁶ 8g 6.9v4] sturdy gelding: moderate mover: none too consistent handicapper: should prove ideally suited by 1m: acts on any going: sometimes bandaged: headstrong. *C. A. Horgan*

ST ATHANS LAD 7 b.g. Crooner 119 – Greasby Girl (John Splendid 116) [1991 41
NR 1992 14.1g 10.2m⁵ 10.2g] strong, workmanlike gelding: poor handicapper: easily best run in first half of 1992 when blinkered only time: stays 1¼m: acts on good to firm ground: successful 4 times over fences after. *R. Curtis*

STATIA (IRE) 4 b.f. Slip Anchor 136 – Antilla 87 (Averof 123) [1991 10g 10.2g⁶ 31
12g⁴ 12g 12.1s 12s² 1992 a12g 9.2v 12g 12m⁹.9g⁶ 11f 10f 12.3m⁴ 13.8g 10.5d 10.3g] leggy, attractive filly: bad maiden: stays 1¼m: acts on firm ground. *Don Enrico Incisa*

STATION EXPRESS (IRE) 4 b.g. Rusticaro (FR) 124 – Vallee d'O (FR) 49 d
(Polyfoto 124) [1991 8m 8m 8f 8.9g 10m 8m 1992 a7g 7d⁴ 6d⁶ 8.1g³ 8d 8g 8.1m⁵ 8f 8g 7f⁴ a7g 8.3s 7s] smallish gelding: on the downgrade: trained first run by R. Hollinshead: won poor novice selling hurdle in November. *B. Ellison*

STAUNCH FRIEND (USA) 4 b.g. Secreto (USA) 128 – Staunch Lady (USA) 77 +
(Staunchness) [1991 8v* 8m³ 10s² 10m 10g³ 12g⁶ 1992 13.1s³ 16s³] $175,000Y: workmanlike gelding: half-brother to numerous winners in USA, including minor stakes winner (second in Grade 1 event at 2 yrs) Sunny Bay (by Northern Bay): dam 2-y-o 5f winner from 4 starts: ex-Irish gelding: won maiden at Leopardstown at 3 yrs (rated 88): bought out of J. Oxx's stable 32,000 gns Newmarket Autumn (1991) Sales: ran respectably in autumn in amateurs event at Ayr and minor event won by Hebridean at Goodwood: stays 2m: suited by some give in the ground: well beaten when blinkered once: very smart hurdler, winner 3 times later in year. *M. H. Tompkins*

STAY AWAKE 6 ch.g. Anfield 117 – Djimbaran Bay (Le Levanstell 122) [1991 8d –
8.2d² 8m⁶ 10m 1992 8g] rangy gelding: has been hobdayed: poor handicapper on flat: should stay 1¼m: acts on any going: winning hurdler/chaser. *J. J. O'Neill*

STAY GREAT 2 ch.c. (Feb 22) Vaigly Great 127 – Alice Hill 78 (Persian Bold –
123) [1992 5s 5.1d 6s 7f] 1,000Y: leggy, close-coupled colt: second foal: dam 2-y-o 5.3f winner didn't train on: little form, mostly in sellers: sold 440 gns Ascot June Sales. *W. Carter*

STAY WITH ME BABY 2 ch.f. (Mar 18) Nicholas Bill 125 – Uranus (Manacle 62
123) [1992 6m⁵ 6s⁶ 7d⁵ 8.2g⁵ 6.9v4] 1,550Y: close-coupled filly, rather unfurnished: half-sister to several winners, including smart 7f and 1m winner Tellurano (by Guillaume Tell) and very useful (at up to 9f here and in USA) Bruiser (by Persian Bold): dam won twice over 5f at 2 yrs in Ireland: modest maiden: will be suited by middle distances: probably acts on any going. *D. R. C. Elsworth*

STEADING 2 ch.f. (Apr 28) Master Willie 129 – Stedham 84 (Jaazeiro (USA) 127) 52
[1992 5.7f³ 7d] 700F: small, angular filly: third foal: half-sister to 3-y-o Songster (by Song), 7f winner at 2 yrs: dam 2-y-o 6f winner: third of 5 in median auction at Bath in

August: well beaten in maiden at Leicester 2 months after and sold 2,200 gns Newmarket Autumn Sales. *H. Candy*

STEAL A MARCH 2 b.g. (Mar 22) Pennine Walk 120 – November Sky (Martinmas 128) [1992 5m 7g⁶ 8m 7.5m] quite good-topped gelding: fifth foal: half-brother to a winner in Scandinavia by Touching Wood: dam, Irish 1½m winner, is half-sister to very smart 1981 French 2-y-o sprinter Maelstrom Lake: poor form in maidens and selling nursery, but caught eye on occasions: should stay 1¼m: should do better. *M. W. Easterby* **38 p**

STEAMBURD 2 b.f. (Apr 27) Dowsing (USA) 124 – No Control 82 (Bustino 136) [1992 8v] leggy, angular filly: second reported foal: dam 9f and 12.2f winner: virtually bolted to post for claimer before tailed off last in Leicester maiden in October: sold 800 gns Ascot November Sales. *J. A. Glover* **–**

STEEL MIRROR 3 b.c. Slip Anchor 136 – I'll Try 71 (Try My Best (USA) 130) [1991 7d⁴ 1992 10m 10d⁵] tall, leggy colt: has fluent, round action: shaped promisingly on debut but well beaten in maidens in April, 1992. *Mrs J. Cecil* **–**

STEERFORTH (IRE) 4 b.c. Lomond (USA) 128 – Waffles 100 (Wollow 132) [1991 8m 10m* 10g⁶ 1992 8.1m 10d⁵ 10.4d³ 13.9m³ 12m³] strong, useful-looking colt: good mover: ran well all starts in 1992, mostly in highly competitive handicaps, and unlucky not to win a race: third in Magnet Cup (top weight) and Tote Ebor Handicap (beaten under a length behind Quick Ransom) at York and listed race (under 2 lengths behind Zinaad) at Newmarket: likely to prove ideally suited by 1½m +: acts on good to firm and dead ground: held up. *A. C. Stewart* **110**

STEINBECK (USA) 3 b.c. Mr Prospector (USA) – Femme Elite (USA) 124 (Northjet 136) [1991 5m* 5g² 5.5g³ 8m* 1992 7g² 8g 8s² 9g* 8d² 10s² 10m 9f⁶] small, attractive colt: smart performer: won Prix Daphnis at Evry in July by 1½ lengths from Rainbow Corner: second in European Free Handicap (sweating) at Newmarket, Prix de la Jonchere at Saint-Cloud, Beefeater Gin Celebration Mile at Goodwood and La Coupe de Maisons-Laffitte (beaten ¾ length by Knifebox): well below form in 2000 Guineas at Newmarket, but ran well in Champion Stakes there penultimate start: stays 1¼m: acts on good to firm ground and soft: joined N. Drysdale. *A. Fabre, France* **119**

STE-JEN (IRE) 3 b.g. Stalker 121 – Bellinor (Le Levanstell 122) [1991 NR 1992 a12g⁵ a12s³] 7,200Y, 8,000 2-y-o: half-brother to several winners in Malaysia: dam Irish 1m and 1½m winner: twice raced, and easily better effort in Southwell maidens when third: still green there, and should improve again: subsequently won over hurdles. *G. M. Moore* **61 p**

Prix Daphnis, Evry—
Steinbeck from the favourite Rainbow Corner (No. 2) and Italian-trained Stubass

STELBY 8 ch.h. Stetchworth (USA) 98 – Little Trilby 107 (Tyrant (USA)) [1991 **58** d
8.5f⁴ 7m² 7h² 6m 6m 7m 8m 1992 8.5m⁴ 7m⁶ 6m 7m 9.9d⁴ 8g⁶ 9m] small horse:
good mover: only poor handicapper nowadays: best form at up to 8.5f on a sound
surface. *O. Brennan*

ST ELIAS (USA) 2 ch.c. (Apr 3) Temperence Hill (USA) – Vast Domain (CAN) **80** p
(Vice Regent (CAN)) [1992 7s*] third known foal: half-brother to 1991 French 2-y-o
7f winner Americarr (by Carr de Naskra): dam, graded-stakes placed at 2 yrs, won at
up to 1¼m: sire won Belmont Stakes: favourite, won 8-runner maiden at
Fairyhouse in September by 2 lengths: sure to go on to better things. *J. S. Bolger,
Ireland*

STELLA MYSTIKA (USA) 2 ch.f. (Feb 26) Diesis 133 – Share The Fantasy **77** p
(USA) (Exclusive Native (USA)) [1992 7g²] tall, leggy filly: fifth foal: half-sister to
useful 3-y-o miler Wesaam (by Riverman): dam smart winner at up to 7f at 2 yrs: 9/1
and green, 1½ lengths second of 24 to Fayfa in maiden at Newmarket in October,
taking time to find stride then staying on: sort to improve a lot at 3 yrs, and will win a
race. *L. M. Cumani*

STEPANOV (USA) 2 br.c. (Mar 20) Nureyev (USA) 131 – Sigy (FR) 132 **84** p
(Habitat 134) [1992 5s³ 5d* 5d⁵] strong colt: brother to 3 animals, 2 of them
winners, including 3-y-o 6f winner King's Signet, closely related to high-class
sprinter Sicyos (by Lyphard) and half-brother to very useful 1987 French 2-y-o 5.5f
and 6.5f winner Radjhasi (by Raja Baba), later successful at 1m: dam, brilliantly
speedy, won Prix de l'Abbaye as a 2-y-o: long odds on following promising debut,
very easy 2½-length winner of maiden at Catterick: progressed again when over 5
lengths fifth of 10 to Ansellman in listed race at Doncaster later in October: wore a
tongue strap first 2 starts: sure to improve further. *J. H. M. Gosden*

STEPHANENTSE 2 gr.f. (Apr 14) Another Realm 118 – Stephandre 94 **53**
(Derring-Do 131) [1992 7g 8.5m 8.1d⁶] 720F: leggy, sparely-made filly: sixth foal:
half-sister to modest 1m (at 2 yrs) to 12.3f winner Final Step (by Final Straw) and
modest sprinter Stephalotus (by Coded Scrap): dam won from 5f to 1¼m: never
dangerous in autumn maidens: best effort at Haydock on final start: should stay
1¼m. *W. W. Haigh*

STEP ON IT 2 ch.f. (Apr 14) Music Boy 124 – Quick As A Wink (Glint of Gold 128) **30**
[1992 5d 5d 5.7d] lengthy filly: first foal: dam unraced: poor maiden: tailed off final
start. *C. P. Wildman*

STEPPE CLOSER 2 gr.f. (Mar 29) Nishapour (FR) 125 – Red Shoes 74 (Dance **46**
In Time (CAN)) [1992 8s 7s⁶ a8g] lengthy filly: third foal: half-sister to ungenuine
3-y-o Red For Danger (by Formidable), 6f winner at 2 yrs: dam stayed 1½m, is out of
Oaks and St Leger winner Dunfermline: poor form in late-season maidens. *Lord
Huntingdon*

STEPPEY LANE 7 b.m. Tachypous 128 – Alpine Alice 94 (Abwah 118) [1991 **71**
a14g* a14g* a14g³ 13.8d* 14m* 16m⁶ 1992 a14g³ a14g* 13.8d³ 16d4 18.5g] leggy,
workmanlike mare: has a round action: fair handicapper: won at Southwell in March:
not seen out after May: probably stays 2m: acts on any going and fibresand:
sometimes mounted on track and taken down early. *W. W. Haigh*

STEPPIN HIGH 2 gr.g. (Jan 8) Siberian Express (USA) 125 – Moogie 103 **56**
(Young Generation 129) [1992 5f⁶ 5g⁵ 7m 6g³ 7d⁶] 13,000Y: lengthy gelding: has
scope: first foal: dam 2-y-o 6f winner suited by 9f at 3 yrs: modest maiden: should
stay 1m: possibly unsuited by dead ground. *Lord Huntingdon*

STERLING BUCK (USA) 5 b.g. Buckfinder (USA) – Aged (USA) (Olden –
Times) [1991 a10g 12f 7m 10g 9d 10.1m 1992 16.9d] leggy, close-coupled gelding: has
a round action: placed over hurdles but seems of little account on flat. *G. H. Yardley*

STERLING PRINCESS 2 b. or br.f. (Feb 26) Sayf El Arab (USA) 127 – Make **41**
Or Mar 84 (Daring March 116) [1992 5m⁶ 6m 5.2f⁵ 6g⁶ 5.3f³ a6g] leggy filly: poor
mover: first foal: dam 5f performer: form only when blinkered first of 2 occasions, in
seller penultimate run. *J. R. Jenkins*

STERLING PROSPECT 3 b.g. Cyrano de Bergerac 120 – Akka (Malacate **§§**
(USA) 131) [1991 5.8d⁵ 6g 7m 7.1m* 7d 7m 1992 10d 10g] leggy gelding: rated 69 at 2
yrs: virtually refused to race in 1992: stays 7f: acts on good to firm going: below form
in visor and blinkers: must be avoided. *W. Carter*

STEVEN'S DREAM (IRE) 2 ch.f. (Apr 8) Heraldiste (USA) 121 – Battle **37**
Queen 85 (Kind of Hush 118) [1992 6d³ 5s 6m 5s a6g] 825Y: leggy filly: first foal:
dam best at 6f or 7f: no comparable form after third in maiden claimer at Hamilton:
should stay 7f. *J. White*

STEVIE'S WONDER (IRE) 2 ch.g. (Mar 26) Don't Forget Me 127 – Azurai 80   59
(Dance In Time (CAN)) [1992 6g 6.1m 7g 8g⁵ 8g 8.2d a8g³] 10,000Y: sturdy gelding:
second foal: half-brother to 1990 2-y-o 5f and 6f winner Time For The Blues (by
Wassl): dam 10.2f winner, is half-sister to Wollow: modest maiden: best efforts at
1m: usually wears a tongue strap: below form blinkered once: changed hands 575
gns Ascot September Sales. *W. Carter*

STINGER 3 ch.c. Midyan (USA) 124 – Copt Hall Princess 70 (Crowned Prince   –
(USA) 128) [1991 7d² 7.1s 7m 7f⁴ 7d 1992 10f⁵ 10.1m 9m] strong, angular colt:
disappointing maiden, and has looked rather irresolute: should stay further than 7f:
sold 3,100 gns Newmarket July Sales. *C. R. Nelson*

STING IN THE TAIL 3 b.f. Scorpio (FR) 127 – Polola 42 (Aragon 118) [1991 NR   –
1992 10.1d a8g] rather unfurnished filly: has scope: first foal: dam ran 3 times at 2
yrs, third once at 5f: no sign of ability: trained by G. Lewis on debut: blinkered final
run. *P. R. Hedger*

STINGRAY CITY (USA) 3 b.g. Raft (USA) 125 – Out of This World 76 (High   67
Top 131) [1991 6f 6d² 7m³ 7.5f³ 8m 7.9g 8m 1992 12f⁴ 11.1m² 12h² 13.8f² 16f² 12g²
15.1d* 14.6d² 17.5s⁶ 16d²] good-topped gelding: has a quick action: consistent
handicapper: easily landed odds in seller at Edinburgh in August: stays well: acts on
any going: effective visored/blinkered or not. *J. Etherington*

STITCHCOMBE 2 b.c. (Feb 10) Night Shift (USA) – Ranya's Pet (Busted 134)   71
[1992 7g² 6m⁴ 8s²] 34,000F, IR 50,000Y: stocky colt: type to carry condition:
second foal: grandam unraced granddaughter of Irish 1000 Guineas winner Royal
Danseuse: best effort in autumn maidens at Warwick final start: should be better
suited by 1¼m: sold 14,500 gns Newmarket Autumn Sales. *P. W. Chapple-Hyam*

STITCHED UP (IRE) 3 ch.c. Ahonoora 122 – Needlewoman 73 (Moorestyle   63
137) [1991 NR 1992 7f⁶ 8d⁶ 7g⁴ 6s² 6.1d] 70,000Y: angular, quite attractive colt:
second foal: dam maiden best at 9f and 1¼m: modest maiden: ran moderately in
ladies handicap final run: sold only 3,100 gns Newmarket Autumn Sales: may prove
suited by 1m: acts on soft ground. *P. W. Chapple-Hyam*

ST JAMES'S ANTIGUA (IRE) 3 b.f. Law Society (USA) 130 – Thunderflash   75 +
(FR) (Northfields (USA)) [1991 7m³ 7m 1992 8.3d* 11.4g⁵] lengthy, good-topped
filly: has a quick action: comfortably won maiden at Hamilton in April: lost touch
only final 1f and eased when last of 5 in Cheshire Oaks following month: probably
stays 11.4f: seemed capable of better, but not seen out again. *W. J. Haggas*

ST JOVITE (USA) 3 b.c. Pleasant Colony (USA) – Northern Sunset 135
(Northfields (USA)) [1991 7m* 6.3m* 8g* 8d⁴ 1992 7v⁴ 10d* 12g² 12m* 12g*
10d² 12s⁴]

Pursuing a fighting policy with an outstanding racehorse has its risks.
St Jovite's defeats in the Irish Champion Stakes and the Prix de l'Arc de
Triomphe on his last two starts eroded the sky-high reputation he had earned
in the summer with outstanding performances in the Budweiser Irish Derby
(which he won by twelve lengths) and the King George VI and Queen
Elizabeth Diamond Stakes (which he won by six). Expectations were raised to
the highest pitch by his victories at the Curragh and Ascot. So complete in
every respect was St Jovite's demolition of the opposition that confident talk
that he might end the season bracketed with the 'middle-distance greats' of
the post-war era didn't seem out of place. Alas, St Jovite's subsequent record
led to some tempering of that view. But it was, nonetheless, a surprise that he
secured only three votes—including that of Timeform—in the end-of-season
Racehorse of the Year award decided by a twenty-six-strong selection panel
drawn from the racing Press. User Friendly topped the poll with fifteen votes,
eight more than Rodrigo de Triano; that splendid handicapper Lochsong was
the only other to receive a vote. Judged solely on the *quality* of the big-race
victories achieved by User Friendly, Rodrigo de Triano and St Jovite, there's
no doubt which horse possessed the greatest racing merit. The marvellous
achievements of User Friendly and Rodrigo de Triano rightly captured the

Budweiser Irish Derby, the Curragh—St Jovite reverses the Derby form in style

*King George VI and Queen Elizabeth Diamond Stakes, Ascot—
St Jovite begins to stretch his rivals on the home turn . . . . .*

racing public's imagination; each won four Group 1 races during the season showing exemplary toughness and reliability, as well as high-class form. But St Jovite's clear-cut victories in the Irish Derby and the King George marked him unmistakably as a colt superior to the general run of classic winners, something that couldn't be claimed for any other three-year-old in training in Europe in 1992—not the way we read the form-book, anyway.

St Jovite showed good form as a two-year-old, proving well suited by a test of stamina on his last two starts, winning the Panasonic Smurfit EBF Futurity Stakes over a mile at the Curragh and coming a highly creditable fourth to Arazi in the Grand Criterium over the same trip. The round-actioned St Jovite was galloping on strongly at the end of both races and looked sure to develop into a force over a mile and a quarter or, better still, a mile and a half as a three-year-old. A tall, attractive colt with plenty of scope, he looked just the type to train on. St Jovite had impressed with his enthusiasm, too, racing with plenty of zest. According to his trainer—whose stable has done much to bolster Irish prestige following the steady decline of Ballydoyle—St Jovite was slow to come to himself as a three-year-old. 'He was desperately hard to train in the early part of the season,' Bolger said. 'He wasn't eating well and on work days I would scratch my head wondering whether I should gallop him or leave him alone . . . No horse I have ever had has made me think so much.' St Jovite was a soundly-beaten fourth when odds on for the Gladness Stakes over seven furlongs on heavy ground at the Curragh on his reappearance in April. He had one more outing before the Ever Ready Derby, gaining a workmanlike victory in the Derrinstown Stud Derby Trial at Leopardstown over a mile and a quarter, a much more suitable trip, again starting odds on. 'He improved almost every day after that, particularly so after we galloped him again at Leopardstown,' Bolger told us, 'but, as it was, Epsom came just too soon.' St Jovite's Derby credentials were quite strong and, truth to tell, his prospects were generally underestimated in an open race. He was available at 25/1 on the Saturday before and still represented good value at his starting price of 14/1. Ridden along from the start to take up a prominent position from an inside draw, St Jovite rallied gamely after looking chopped for speed early in the straight to snatch second place from Silver Wisp, two lengths behind the winner Dr Devious. St Jovite proved very well suited by the Derby trip; his strong-galloping style was in evidence, as was his round action which is often taken as a sign that a horse is best served by some give in the ground. As we have said before, however, the knowledge of how a horse moves is interesting

. . . . . and proves a class apart

and can be profitable, but it is a common misconception that all round-actioned types are favoured by soft going. Each season provides enough examples of exceptions to this generally-held theory to show that it's not safe to assume anything about a horse's going requirements from its action. Take St Jovite for example . . .

The going was firmer than at Epsom when St Jovite and Dr Devious met again in the Budweiser Irish Derby at the Curragh at the end of June. Derby winners have an excellent record in the Irish Derby—only two, Teenoso and Quest For Fame, had failed to complete the double from the nine who had contested the race in the previous fifteen years. Dr Devious started at 5/4 on, St Jovite at 7/2. St Jovite reversed the Derby form to some tune, looking a different horse under the changed conditions. Always handy in a very strongly-run race—his stable ran two pacemakers—St Jovite provided one of the most exhilarating exhibitions of the European season as he stretched away from his field, galloping on relentlessly, after looking an assured winner from the moment Roche sent him into a clear lead soon after rounding the home turn. How strong a gallop was set in the Irish Derby can be judged partly from the fact that the officially-recorded electrical time 2m 25.6sec—which looked too fast by around a second and a half—was three seconds inside Tambourine II's time record for the race, set in 1962. It goes without saying that St Jovite's performance easily surpassed anything he had achieved before, even allowing for Dr Devious' being below his best. There were three other horses in the field who had been placed in a classic—the Prix du Jockey-Club third Contested Bid finished thirteen lengths behind St Jovite in third, the Irish Two Thousand Guineas runner-up Ezzoud was beaten nearly seventeen lengths into fifth, just ahead of the Prix du Jockey-Club runner-up Marignan in sixth. St Jovite's margin of victory—twelve lengths—was the widest officially recorded in the Irish Derby since it became a major international race in 1962, when its value was boosted significantly for the first time by major sponsorship. Shahrastani and Assert were both officially returned eight-length winners; Santa Claus, Troy, Shergar and Old Vic won by four.

St Jovite showed himself a very fine mile-and-a-half horse indeed on Irish Derby day, in our view clearly the best in Europe over the distance at that time. But there's nothing like a second victory to allay any suggestion that the first may have flattered, and St Jovite went on to put up another sparkling show on a sound surface in the King George VI and Queen Elizabeth Diamond Stakes at Ascot at the end of July. His participation was in some doubt for a time because of injuries received when he was struck into behind at the Curragh. But his trainer warned British racegoers on the day: 'Remember the St Jovite you saw at Epsom no longer exists. He is a totally different horse now and I am happy he's as good as he was at the Curragh.' St Jovite was without his regular jockey Roche at Ascot. Roche's solicitor had been successful before the Irish Derby in persuading the Irish stewards to postpone the hearing of an appeal against a fifteen-day suspension imposed on Roche for allegedly striking another rider with his whip in a race at Naas.

Without the initial postponement—granted, according to the Turf Club, to allow Roche's legal advisors more time—the ban would have been in force for the Irish Derby. The connections of St Jovite had said before the Irish Derby that they would be 'reluctant' to run the horse if Roche was unable to ride. Roche lost the appeal when it was heard but then had a long-running battle with the Turf Club in the High Court in Dublin. The High Court granted an interim injunction temporarily lifting the ban and enabling Roche to resume riding the day before the Irish Oaks (in which he partnered the Bolger-trained Ivyanna); but when the full case was heard—taking three days—Roche failed to obtain an injunction restraining the Turf Club from applying the ban. The failure to obtain that injunction resulted in Roche's serving the rest of his suspension in a period that included the King George VI and Queen Elizabeth Stakes. St Jovite was ridden at Ascot by Craine who made the most of the opportunity. He took St Jovite into the lead early on when none of the other jockeys seemed prepared to make the running and gradually stepped up the pace before sending St Jovite for home in earnest with more than half a mile to run. Given a slap rounding the home turn, St Jovite kept on with gusto, eating up the ground and, as at the Curragh, never looking likely to be caught after stamping his authority on the race a good way from the finish. The winning distance over the high-class four-year-old Saddlers' Hall, whose impressive winning sequence had included the Coronation Cup and the Princess of Wales's Stakes, equalled the six-length victory margins in the race of Dahlia and Mill Reef, which have been surpassed only by Generous, who won by seven. The Coral-Eclipse runner-up Opera House took third, half a length behind Saddlers' Hall, with the Eclipse third Sapience fourth, just in front of the tough five-year-old Rock Hopper, runner-up to Saddlers' Hall in the Coronation Cup; the two other three-year-olds in the field, the Derby third Silver Wisp and the progressive Jeune, filled the last two places in an eight-strong field that, taken as a whole, was of second rank for a King George. That said, St Jovite, who started at 5/4 on, disposed of those that turned up in a manner which could have left no good judge in any doubt that his was another tip-top performance. On a strict interpretation of the form-book there was little to choose between St Jovite's King George performance and his runaway victory in the Irish Derby. Both were right out of the top drawer.

St Jovite's next intended appearance was in the Juddmonte International at York in August. But, with the Prix de l'Arc de Triomphe in mind, connections eventually decided that the International 'might be one too many'. St Jovite had one race between the King George and the Prix de l'Arc, the Kerry Group Irish Champion Stakes at Leopardstown in September. St Jovite started at 7/4 on in an eight-strong field that also included Dr Devious and the Coral-Eclipse winner Kooyonga. Back to a mile and a quarter, going left-handed and on more yielding ground than at the Curragh and Ascot, St Jovite wasn't the champion he had been in the summer. He was never able to shake off Dr Devious and went down by a short head after a dogged, drawn-out battle in the final straight. It could be argued that St Jovite was unfortunate—Roche stopped riding near the finish after the hanging St Jovite had taken a narrow lead—but it was clear that he would have to step up considerably on this running to win an Arc. St Jovite reversed the Irish Champion Stakes form with Dr Devious at Longchamp but, on soft going, he was again below his best. The Derby winners finished fourth and sixth behind the French-trained four-year-old Subotica, St Jovite racing with the leaders all the way and hanging when he came off the bridle in the straight. St Jovite went down with a respiratory infection after the Prix de l'Arc and missed the Breeders' Cup at Gulfstream Park at the end of October. He'd been announced as a probable runner in the Breeders' Cup Classic over a mile and a quarter on dirt. Latest news at the time of writing is that St Jovite is likely to start his four-year-old career in the United States where, if he adapts well to racing on dirt, he will spend the year aimed at the big events before possibly being returned for another crack at the Prix de l'Arc. A successful campaign on dirt would make him an even more desirable commercial proposition for stud in North America. We wish him well.

St Jovite's sire Pleasant Colony, a grandson of Ribot, was America's champion three-year-old in 1981 when he won the Kentucky Derby and the

Preakness Stakes. He's been an influence for stamina at stud, though not many of his offspring have been raced in Europe. St Jovite was his only runner in Britain and Ireland in the latest season. St Jovite, who takes his name from a Canadian ski resort, was bred by his owner from a tough but modest ex-Irish racemare Northern Sunset who has proved a rare bargain since being bought at the Newmarket December Sales as a three-year-old for 10,500 guineas. Northern Sunset ran sixteen times on the flat, winning over six and seven furlongs, and was fifth over hurdles at Tralee on her final start. St Jovite is the sixth winner bred by Northern Sunset. Her offspring also include two notably durable graded stakes winners at a mile to a mile and a quarter in North America, Salem Drive and Lac Ouimet, each of whom was still running in good company at up to seven years old, and the very smart and consistent French middle-distance performer Norberto (by Roberto), runner-up in four pattern races including the Grand Prix de Paris. Salem Drive (by Darby Creek Road) won twelve races in North America, including the Stars and Stripes Handicap and the Bougainvillea Handicap, both Grade 2, and was also successful in Japan. Lac Ouimet, a full brother to St Jovite, also won twelve times in North

St Jovite (USA) (b.c. 1989)	Pleasant Colony (USA) (b 1978)	His Majesty (b 1968)	Ribot / Flower Bowl
		Sun Colony (b 1968)	Sunrise Flight / Colonia
	Northern Sunset (ch 1977)	Northfields (ch 1968)	Northern Dancer / Little Hut
		Moss Greine (b 1964)	Ballymoss / Blaith Na Greine

Mrs Virginia Kraft Payson's "St Jovite"

America, a record which included five Grade 2 races, the Jim Dandy Stakes, the Excelsior Handicap (which he won twice), the Nassau County Handicap and the Fayette Handicap. Salem Drive and Lac Ouimet now stand in Lexington, Kentucky, at the stud of St Jovite's owner Mrs Virginia Kraft Payson. Mrs Payson says she was attracted to the dam Northern Sunset because 'she had raced over hurdles in Ireland and there was proven toughness in her background, qualities which are often lacking in the speed-minded United States'. Northern Sunset's dam Moss Greine won over a mile as a two-year-old in Ireland but became disappointing—placed at up to a mile and a half—after starting off in useful company as a three-year-old. St Jovite's great grandam Blaith Na Greine won only as a two-year-old but bred two good-class horses, the Lonsdale Produce Stakes winner Prince of Greine and the Two Thousand Guineas third Time Greine. Blaith Na Greine was a half-sister to the One Thousand Guineas and Oaks winner Godiva and the Irish triple crown winner Windsor Slipper. *J. S. Bolger, Ireland*

ST NINIAN   6 ch.h. Ardross 134 – Caergwrle 115 (Crepello 136) [1991 8d² 8g* **104**
8d* 8g 8.1g⁶ 8m³ 8.9g² 9m 8g³ 1992 8g⁴ 7.9m⁴ 8.1m⁵ 8f⁵ 7.9d⁵ 8.1d* 8g⁵ 10g³ 10d⁴ 10g⁴] useful-looking horse: usually looks really well: useful and consistent performer: won £7,600 handicap at Haydock in August from Badawi and ran well in listed races at Kempton and Goodwood after: effective from 1m to 1¼m: acts on any going: sometimes bandaged near-hind: effective held up or ridden from front: game and genuine. *M. H. Easterby*

STOCKAIR   6 ch.g. Air Trooper 115 – Fair Nic (Romancero 100) [1991 NR 1992   **–**
a6g] leggy, light-framed gelding: seems on the downgrade. *R. J. Hodges*

STOCKTINA   5 ch.m. Tina's Pet 121 – Mrewa (Runnymede 123) [1991 5.1m³ 5f²   **42**
5g² 5d³ 6g⁵ 5m a5g 5f⁶ 5.3g* 5g² 5m 5.1d³ 1992 5s 5.3m 5f 5m 5g⁴ 5g² 5d⁴ 5g⁴ 5.3d 5s⁴ 5.1g 5s] smallish mare: ran with credit most starts in handicaps in 1992 but hard to win with: well worth another try at 6f: probably acts on any going: twice below form when blinkered. *R. J. Hodges*

STONE FLAKE (USA)   6 ch.g. Diesis 133 – Wyandra (So Blessed 130) [1991   **–**
NR 1992 a7g a14g⁵ a14g] neat gelding: one-time useful performer: no form on flat in January, 1992, trained first start by P. Hobbs and blinkered final one: fair winning hurdler in 1991/2. *P. A. Kelleway*

John Mallinson Stakes (Limited Handicap), Haydock —
a driving finish, with St Ninian getting the better of Badawi (near side) and Starlight Flyer

STONELEIGH ABBEY (IRE) 4 b.g. Sallust 134 – Yellow Creek (Sandy – Creek 123) [1991 a6g⁶ 6g⁴ 6m 8d a6g a8g 1992 7d 10.5d] sturdy gelding: carries condition: poor performer nowadays: trained first run in 1992 by D. Moffatt. *B. R. Cambidge*

STONEWALL JACKSON (IRE) 3 b.c. Treasure Kay 114 – What A Friend 67 (What A Guest 119) [1991 5g⁴ 5s² 1992 5g* 5m⁴] good-topped colt: won maiden at Edinburgh and good fourth in Catterick handicap in spring: seemed likely to improve further over 6f. *W. J. Pearce*

STOPROVERITATE 3 ch.f. Scorpio (FR) 127 – Luscinia 73 (Sing Sing 134) 53 [1991 5f 7m 7.5f⁵ 8.3g 7m⁴ 7m 6s² 5s³ a6g 1992 7g 8.3d⁵ 7s⁴ 8d² 8m⁶ 9.9g 8f⁵ 8.1f⁶ 9.2g⁶ 6.9g* 8s* 8s 8v³] workmanlike filly: modest handicapper: won claimers at Carlisle and Newcastle in September: stays 1m: acts on good to firm ground and heavy: not discredited when visored once. *S. G. Norton*

STORITHS (IRE) 2 b.c. (Mar 22) Double Schwartz 128 – Atlantic Dream (USA) 85 (Muscovite (USA) 105) [1992 6m* 6d² 6d³ 6m] IR 10,000Y: lengthy, attractive colt: first reported foal: dam Irish 2-y-o 6f winner: progressive form, winning maiden at Ripon in July and a nursery at Haydock and Newmarket, until final run when moderately drawn and getting poor run in Pontefract nursery: will be better suited by 7f: sometimes drifted right. *J. W. Watts*

STORMBUSTER 3 b.g. Northern Tempest (USA) 120 – Stolen-Secret (Burglar 44 128) [1991 6g 6m 5m⁴ 5m 1992 5.1d³ 5m 6.1m 6.1g 5g⁶ 6g⁴ 5s 6d 5s 5v] leggy, lengthy gelding: moderate mover: poor maiden: stays 6f: acts on good to firm and dead ground: sold 950 gns Ascot December Sales. *P. S. Felgate*

STORM CANYON (IRE) 2 ch.c. (Jan 22) Storm Bird (CAN) 134 – Diamond 99 p Field (USA) 71 (Mr Prospector (USA)) [1992 7m² 7m²] good-topped, attractive colt: first foal: dam, placed over 5f at 2 yrs from 2 starts, is half-sister to once-raced Mashhor Dancer (by Northern Dancer) out of sister to Observer Gold Cup winner Take Your Place and top-class middle-distance filly Drum Top, dam of Topsider (also by Northern Dancer): shaped most promisingly when beaten 1½ lengths by Placerville in maiden at Newmarket, running on well, not knocked about, having reared stalls: heavily-backed favourite, pulled well clear of rest when beaten a neck by Barathea in Houghton Stakes there later in October, running on strongly despite carrying head bit high: will stay 1m: tongue tied down and taken steadily to post last time: certain to improve and win races. *J. H. M. Gosden*

STORM CROSSING (USA) 3 ch.c. Storm Bird (CAN) 134 – Ala Mahlik 116 97 (Ahonoora 122) [1991 7d⁶ 1992 12.5f* 12m² 13.9m 12m²] big, workmanlike colt: has a free, round action: won maiden at Warwick in June and did really well when second, staying on strongly from rear, in handicaps at Goodwood and (beaten head) Newmarket: should stay beyond 1½m (favourite when in mid-division for Ebor Handicap at York): acts on firm and dead going: sent to Saudi Arabia. *G. Harwood*

STORM DOVE (USA) 3 b.f. Storm Bird (CAN) 134 – Daeltown (FR) 117 108 (Dictus (FR) 126) [1991 7s⁶ 6g* 6f³ 6g³ 1992 6.1m⁴ 7m* 7f³ 7d⁴ 8.5f²] leggy, lengthy, quite attractive filly: good mover: progressed extremely well in first half of 1992, most impressive winner of handicap at Lingfield and listed race (beat Susurration 7 lengths) at Goodwood: didn't go on as anticipated, creditable efforts when placed in Group 3 event at Doncaster (third to Pursuit of Love) and allowance race at Gulfstream Park: effective at 7f to 1m: seems best on top-of-the-ground: tail swisher: joined R. Frankel in USA. *R. Charlton*

STORM DRUM 3 ch.g. Celestial Storm (USA) 132 – Bushti Music 63 (Bustino 56 136) [1991 a7g a8g 1992 10d⁶ 9.7g 13.1m 14.1g⁶ 12f* 11.9f³ 10d⁴ 11.8m⁶] tall, quite good-topped gelding: won claimer at Epsom in July and ran creditably after: should stay beyond 1½m: acts on firm and dead going: has looked none too keen: sold 6,200 gns Newmarket Autumn Sales. *P. J. Makin*

STORM DUST 3 b.g. Celestial Storm (USA) 132 – Mary Sunley 62 (Known Fact 70 (USA) 135) [1991 NR 1992 10g 10m⁶ 10s⁵ 11.6m⁴ 12d* 12m* 11.9f³ 12d 14d] 16,000F: angular, close-coupled gelding: good mover: second foal: half-brother to 7f winner Helios (by Blazing Saddles): dam maiden suited by 1¼m, is half-sister to Roseate Tern and Ibn Bey: below best after winning minor event at Beverley and apprentice claimer at Newmarket in July: should stay beyond 1½m: acts on good to firm and dead going: promising hurdler. *J. R. Fanshawe*

STORM GAUGE (USA) 3 ch.f. Arctic Tern (USA) 126 – Got A Cold (USA) – (Drone) [1991 NR 1992 11.5d⁶] workmanlike filly: fourth foal: half-sister to North American winners by Fit To Fight and Raja Baba: dam, minor winner, is half-sister to smart Irish 6f and 7f winner It's Freezing, later a graded winner in USA: showed signs of a little ability in maiden at Yarmouth in August on belated debut: sold 4,800 gns Newmarket December Sales. *Mrs J. Cecil*

STORM GAYLE (IRE) 3 b.f. Sadler's Wells (USA) 132 – Princess Gayle 107 –
(Lord Gayle (USA) 124) [1991 NR 1992 12f³ 11.1f⁴ 12.4m⁴ 12.1s] 31,000Y: sturdy, good-topped filly: half-sister to 4 winners here and abroad, including stayer Halcanor (by Irish River): dam, half-sister to smart sprinter Ubedizzy and Middle Park winner Cajun, won over sprint distances: no worthwhile form but showed signs of ability in maidens and handicap. *M. Johnston*

STORM MELODY (USA) 3 b.g. Storm Cat (USA) – Celebration Song (USA) 87 ?
(J O Tobin (USA) 130) [1991 5f* 5g* 5m⁴ 6m 5g⁵ 1992 5m 6g 5g⁴] angular, good-topped gelding: reportedly hobdayed after final start at 2 yrs: went the wrong way in 1992: bred to stay beyond 5f: acts on firm ground. *A. A. Scott*

STORMSWEPT (USA) 3 b.f. Storm Bird (CAN) 134 – Kanmary (FR) 117 –
(Kenmare (FR) 125) [1991 5d³ 5m² 5g⁴ 5.1d* 5s⁴ 6.1m⁵ 7g⁵ 1992 6v⁵ 7g 8m 6m 6s 8.9d 9.9m] smallish filly: rated 74 at 2 yrs: below form in 1992: stays 6f: acts on good to firm ground: below form when blinkered: sold out of P. Chapple-Hyam's stable 6,000 gns Newmarket July Sales after second start. *M. Brittain*

STORM VENTURE (IRE) 2 b.c. (Mar 1) Taufan (USA) 119 – Crimson Crest 62
(Pampapaul 121) [1992 6f⁴ 6f² 6d² 7g 6d6 7.3s] 7,500F, 13,500Y: strong, lengthy colt: fourth reported foal: half-brother to poor 4-y-o Abu Nasser (by Burslem): dam modest Irish sprint maiden: modest maiden: should stay 7f: acts on firm and dead ground: trained by W. Pearce/B. Beasley first 4 starts: sometimes wears tongue strap. *W. Jarvis*

STORMY HEIGHTS 2 b. or br.f. (Feb 12) Golden Heights 82 – Brown Taw 66 55
(Whistlefield 118) [1992 5v² 5v⁵ 5.3m⁴ 5f³ a6g² 5.1m* 6g 5.1m6] lengthy filly: first reported foal: dam won 5f seller: modest performer: won maiden at Chester in June: stays 6f: acts on firm ground and fibresand. *J. R. Jenkins*

STORMY PRAISE (USA) 8 ch.g. Storm Bird (CAN) 134 – Prayers'n Promises 32
(USA) (Foolish Pleasure (USA)) [1991 a6g a6g 8.2s* 8m 8f a8g 9.7s 1992 9.7v 8.3v4 8.1g] lengthy, angular gelding: inconsistent handicapper nowadays: effective at 6f to 1m: probably acts on any going: below form in hood and blinkers: headstrong and not an easy ride. *W. G. M. Turner*

STORMY'S MAD 8 ch.g. Royal Match 117 – Copped (Tumble Wind (USA)) [1991 –
NR 1992 10.3g] strong, plain ex-Irish gelding: probably of little account. *G. Fleming*

ST PATRICK'S DAY 4 ch.g. Night Shift (USA) – Princess Lieven (Royal Palace 66 ?
131) [1991 10.1f³ 10.3m 8m 8d6 8m⁵ 9.7s* 1992 10m 8.5m² 10m⁵ 10g] leggy, rather sparely-made gelding: very good mover: rated 73 at 3 yrs: went wrong way in 1992, and not seen on flat after running as if something amiss in June: stays 1¼m: acts on good to firm ground and soft: often slowly away: refused to race once at 3 yrs: joined A. Turnell. *C. E. Brittain*

ST PIRAN'S LASS 3 br.f. Sulaafah (USA) 119 – Aljaw 66 (Touching Wood (USA) –
127) [1991 NR 1992 5v 8m 12.1m 10g] leggy, short-backed filly: second foal: sister to poor 4-y-o Mystic Panther: dam ran 3 times at 3 yrs, seeming to stay 1¼m: no worthwhile form. *R. J. Holder*

STRADBROKE 5 b.g. Fairy King (USA) – Mattira (FR) (Rheffic (FR) 129) [1991 – §
10.8d 8m³ 12.5d 8f⁵ 12g 8h⁴ 8.9m 1992 10.8d 16.2d 10.5m a14g³] big, strong, lengthy gelding: has been tubed: moderate mover: ungenuine maiden: stays 1¼m: acts on good to firm ground: ran creditably when blinkered: has refused to race. *M. B. James*

STRANGERSINTHENITE 3 ch.c. Legend of France (USA) 124 – Angail 89 –
(Northfields (USA)) [1991 6d 6g³ 6m6 7.9g 6g 1992 6.9d a8g⁵ a8s 8m 10m 8s 10.3g] small, sturdy colt: has a round action: on the downgrade. *J. S. Wainwright*

STRATAGEM 2 ch.g. (Feb 10) Jalmood (USA) 126 – Strathoykel 94 (Aberdeen –
109) [1992 a7g] brother to fairly useful Bocas Rose, successful at 5f and 5.3f at 2 yrs and later effective at 1m, and half-brother to 2 winners, including (at 6f at 2 yrs in 1985) useful Bambolona: dam best at sprint distances: always struggling in Southwell claimer late in year. *Sir Mark Prescott*

STRATFORD LADY 3 b.f. Touching Wood (USA) 127 – Hawks Nest 66 47 d
(Moulton 128) [1991 6m 7g 1992 a8g 8s⁴ 12.2g² 10g 12.2m⁴ a12g⁵ 11.8g 12m⁴ 10m 10d² 11d6 a12g] compact filly: untrustworthy plater: stays 1½m: acts on good to firm and soft ground: below form visored, effective blinkered or not. *J. A. Glover*

STRATHCARRON 3 ch.g. Adonijah 126 – Marypark 93 (Charlottown 127) [1991 –
NR 1992 10.4d] workmanlike gelding: has stringhalt: closely related to 1989 2-y-o 1m winner Advie Bridge (by High Line), later suited by 1½m, and half-brother to

several winners, 3 at least fairly useful, including middle-distance colt Loch Seaforth (by Tyrnavos): dam well suited by long distances: burly and green, soundly beaten in maiden at York in October. *W. Jarvis*

STRAT'S LEGACY 5 b.g. Chukaroo 103 – State Romance 67 (Free State 125) **51**
[1991 10.8m⁶ 8m* 8f 8.2m 8f⁵ 10f² 10.2m⁶ 10g 1992 a12g* a10g a12g3 10g* 10.2d⁴ a12g⁵ a12g² a12g²] small, light-framed gelding: modest handicapper: successful after lengthy absences at Lingfield in January and Brighton (ladies) in August: effective from 1m to 1½m: acts on firm and dead ground and equitrack. *D. W. P. Arbuthnot*

STRAW THATCH 3 b.g. Thatching 131 – Lashing (USA) 98 (Storm Bird (CAN) **72**
134) [1991 6g 8m 7.9m⁵ 8g 1992 6.9d* 8m² 7.5g3 7f⁶ 7g² 7g² 8f³ 10m 10g 10.1m 9.2s⁵] strong, workmanlike gelding: won maiden at Carlisle in May and largely consistent in handicaps after: suited by 1m: yet to race on heavy ground, probably acts on any other: swishes tail: joined R. Allan. *M. Johnston*

STREET REBEL (CAN) 4 b.c. Robellino (USA) 127 – Street Ballet (USA) **110**
(Nijinsky (CAN) 138) [1991 8v² 7d³ 8g* 8g⁵ 8g³ 10g* 10m⁶ 9g4 1992 7v³ 10v⁴ 6g* 6f 6g³ 8g⁶ 6g⁴ 7s⁴ 6s² 7s²] tall, good-quartered Irish colt: very useful performer: successful in Greenlands Stakes at the Curragh in May by ½ length from Maledetto: in frame after in Group 3 event and listed races at Leopardstown and the Curragh: mid-division in Cork And Orrery Stakes at Royal Ascot: best at 6f or 7f on an easy surface: effective with or without blinkers: consistent. *N. Meade, Ireland*

STRENGTH IN DEPTH (IRE) 4 b. or br.f. Strong Gale 116 – Second Service **43**
(Red Regent 123) [1991 7m 12.1s 1992 8.3s⁵ 8.1m 9.9g 13.8d] leggy, workmanlike filly: went the wrong way in first half of 1992 and sold 1,700 gns Doncaster June Sales: stays 1m: acts on soft ground. *M. Johnston*

STREPHON (IRE) 2 b.g. (Apr 28) Fairy King (USA) – Madame Fair (Monseigneur (USA) 127) [1992 5g 6g 6g 6m 7.5m 10.5d⁵ a8g⁶] IR 7,000Y: leggy gelding: **50**
third foal: half-brother to fair 4-y-o 9f and 1¼m winner Virkon Venture (by Auction Ring): dam, Irish 1½m winner, is sister to useful Irish middle-distance stayer Maiden Fair: poor maiden: best run when fifth in selling nursery at Haydock: will stay well: acts on good to soft ground: ran respectably visored once: sold 1,400 gns Newmarket Autumn Sales after sixth start. *M. H. Tompkins*

STRICTLY PERSONAL (USA) 2 b. or br.c. (Mar 12) Secreto (USA) 128 – **71 p**
Tash (USA) (Never Bend (USA)) [1992 a7g³ a8g² a8g*] $210,000Y: eighth foal: closely related to very smart but inconsistent miler Mukaddamah and minor stakes winner Contempt (both by Storm Bird) and half-brother to several other winners: dam won twice over 6f at 2 yrs: shaped promisingly in Lingfield maidens before winning one in December by 3 lengths: will stay 1¼m: should improve further. *J. H. M. Gosden*

STRIDING EDGE 7 ch.g. Viking (USA) – Kospia (King Emperor (USA)) [1991 **–**
NR 1992 10m 10m] compact ex-Irish gelding: no form on flat for long time: won over hurdles/fences in August and October. *J. R. Jenkins*

STRIKE-A-POSE 2 ch.f. (Mar 30) Blushing Scribe (USA) 107 – My Bushbaby **53**
100 (Hul A Hul 124) [1992 5d 6g4 7m* 7g³ 7g* 7m 8m 7m⁴ 7g] tall, leggy, sparelymade filly: moderate mover: half-sister to several winners, including fairly useful 6-y-o sprinter Letsbeonestaboutit (by Petong): dam, half-sister to 1974 2-y-o sprinter Panomark, won over 5f at 2 yrs: well-backed favourite when winning sellers at Lingfield (no bid) and Wolverhampton (retained 3,200 gns) in early-summer: stays 1m: acts on good to firm ground: gets on edge: sold 2,800 gns Doncaster November Sales. *C. N. Williams*

STRIKING DISTANCE 5 ch.g. Never So Bold 135 – Gallatin Valley (USA) **–**
(Apalachee (USA) 137) [1991 10d 11.5m⁴ 12g4 1992 a12g² 11.9m] tall gelding: rated 50 at 4 yrs: soundly beaten in spring, 1992: stays 1½m: acts on good to firm ground. *J. Ffitch-Heyes*

STRIKING IMAGE (IRE) 3 ch.f. Flash of Steel 120 – Sister Sala (Double-U- **69**
Jay 120) [1991 7m⁶ 7m³ 7.1d 1992 10d 10.2s 11.6m 11.6m* 10s⁵ 11.6g4 12s⁵ 10.2d] good-bodied, workmanlike filly: fair handicapper: won at Windsor in August, making most but carrying head rather high: stays 1½m: acts on good to firm and soft ground. *R. Hannon*

STRIP CARTOON (IRE) 4 ch.g. Tate Gallery (USA) 117 – Reveal (Pitskelly **55**
122) [1991 5m 6d 6.9f a11g a8g a5g 5m⁵ 5f4 5g⁵ 5d⁴ 5m⁵ 6m a5g a5g 1992 a7g4 a6g* a6g a6g⁵ a7g⁵ 5s² 5g³ 6.1d* 5g a7g⁶ a6g* 6.1d a6g² 6g³ a6g 6f⁵ a7g⁴ 7g 6m⁶ 6.1m⁵ 7s⁴ 6d 6.1s4 a6g⁶ a6g a6g⁵] smallish, workmanlike gelding: very tough handicapper, successful in 1992 at Southwell (2, first a claimer) and Nottingham:

Prix Ganay, Longchamp—
Suave Dancer and Pistolet Bleu head the betting, but Subotica takes the spoils

effective from 5f to 7f: goes well on an easy surface and fibresand: below form visored once: usually blinkered nowadays: suitable mount for claimer. *S. R. Bowring*

STROIKA (IRE) 2 ch.f. (May 1) Shy Groom (USA) – Pam Story (Sallust 134) [1992 6m 7d⁶ 6.1m a6g* 7g⁶ a6g a6g] IR 2,000F: workmanlike filly: fifth foal: half-sister to 1989 2-y-o 5f winner Midsummer Breeze (by Tumble Wind): dam second over 5f at 4 yrs in Ireland: won seller (retained 5,200 gns) at Lingfield in August but no comparable form: stays 6f: sold 425 gns Ascot November Sales. *C. James* **54**

STRONG SUIT (IRE) 3 b.c. King of Clubs 124 – Tumble Dale 88§ (Tumble Wind (USA)) [1991 6g⁵ 6g² 7.1s⁴ 7g* 7f⁶ 6f* 7m 6g 1992 8.1g 8.1m 8m³ 8.1s⁴ 7m⁵ 7m⁵ 8.1g] workmanlike colt: fairly useful handicapper: well below form when blinkered final start: should stay beyond 1m: acts on firm ground: sold 7,200 gns Newmarket Autumn Sales. *R. Hannon* **86**

STUBASS (IRE) 3 b.c. Alzao (USA) 117 – St Louisan 109 (St Chad 120) [1991 6g⁵ 6g* 7g² 7.5g⁴ 8s² 8v³ 8s 8v⁴ 1992 7.5v² 7.5g* 8v* 8g* 8d* 9g³ 8s⁴ 8v*] very useful Italian colt: half-brother to winners here and abroad, including 6f to 1m winner Nazeem (by Auction Ring) and French middle-distance winner Vale of Tears (by Val de L'Orne): dam useful over 5f at 2 yrs: successful in minor events at Milan (2), listed races at Rome and Milan and Group 2 Premio Ribot at Rome, last-named by ½ length from Prospective Ruler: 1½ lengths third to Steinbeck in Prix Daphnis at Evry on sixth outing: stays 9f: acts on heavy going, yet to race on a firm surface: has joined L. Cumani. *A. Botti, Italy* **112**

STYLISH DUTCH 3 ch.f. Risk Me (FR) 127 – Dutch Gold 117 (Goldhill 125) [1991 6g 6m⁵ 1992 5s 5g] close-coupled filly: no worthwhile form: sold 700 gns Doncaster August Sales. *M. W. Easterby* **–**

STYLISH GENT 5 br.g. Vitiges (FR) 132 – Squire's Daughter (Bay Express 132) [1991 7.5v 6.5g 7m⁵ 8m* 8.3m* 8m* 7.6m³ 8g 8m 1992 8g 8.3m 10.5g 7.9d⁵ 10.3m] strong, lengthy gelding: rated 74 at 4 yrs: no form in first half of 1992: stays 9f: acts on good to firm ground and dead: below form blinkered/visored: claimed to join J. Birkett when second over hurdles in August. *N. Tinkler* **–**

STYLISH ROSE (IRE) 2 b.f. (May 3) Don't Forget Me 127 – Cottage Style 65 (Thatch (USA) 136) [1992 5v⁵ 8.1d³] fifth foal: dam, winner twice at 1½m, is daughter of half-sister to Lorenzaccio: easily better effort in late-season maidens when third to Ansillo at Edinburgh: should stay 1¼m. *W. A. Stephenson* **55**

SUAVE DANCER (USA) 4 b.c. Green Dancer (USA) 132 – Suavite **117** (USA) (Alleged (USA) 138) [1991 10g* 10.5d* 10.5d² 12m* 12g² 10d* 12d* 1992 10.5g³]

A leg injury kept the Prix de l'Arc winner Suave Dancer out of action after he'd finished a disappointing third to Subotica and Pistolet Bleu in the Prix Ganay on his reappearance. He'd been an outstanding three-year-old—winner of the Prix du Jockey-Club and the Irish Champion Stakes as well as the Arc—and his four-year-old career had been eagerly anticipated. It was a good bet that the major studs would have been falling over themselves to secure Suave Dancer as a stallion had his owner decided to retire him at that point. Twelve months on, Suave Dancer was secured to stand at the National Stud at Newmarket—reportedly after his owner, who has retained a half share, rejected a higher offer from Japan—and will start his new career at the very reasonable fee of £12,000 with the October 1st concession. With lesser racehorses commanding similar or higher fees, Suave Dancer seems sure to prove attractive to a wide range of breeders. He quickly filled with fifty-five mares in 1993 and should have every chance of proving himself as a stallion. Let's hope he lives up to expectations!

		Nijinsky	Northern Dancer
	Green Dancer (USA)	(b 1967)	Flaming Page
Suave	(b 1972)	Green Valley	Val de Loir
Dancer (USA)		(b or br 1967)	Sly Pola
(b.c. 1988)		Alleged	Hoist The Flag
	Suavite (USA)	(b 1974)	Princess Pout
	(b 1981)	Guinevere's Folly	Round Table
		(b 1976)	Lodge

Suave Dancer has the looks and pedigree to match his racing merit. A good-looking individual, and a very good mover, he's by the successful Nijinsky stallion Green Dancer out of a graded-placed daughter of the even more successful Alleged. *Racehorses of 1991* contains full details of Suave Dancer's pedigree. *J. E. Hammond, France*

SUBOTICA (FR) 4 b.c. Pampabird 124 – Terre de Feu (FR) (Busted 134) **131** [1991 11g² 12d² 12m² 10d* 10g⁵ 12m* 1992 10.5g* 12g⁴ 12d³ 12m² 12s* 12f⁵]

Racing's precarious relationship with British television was highlighted when live coverage of Europe's richest race, the Ciga Prix de l'Arc de Triomphe, was dropped by Channel 4 in favour of an Italian football match. The move underlined the simple truth that racing isn't, in television terms, 'an audience winner'. The Italian football is understood to have attracted an average of 2.5 million viewers, compared to the previous year's average of 1.6 million for live coverage of the Prix de l'Arc. Perversely, Channel 4 had an audience of 2.4 million for its coverage of the latest Arc in a recorded highlights programme, though this was surely the result of holding the football audience. The French racing authorities are said to be 'determined', in the

Ciga Prix de l'Arc de Triomphe, Longchamp—
Subotica gets the better of a gripping duel with User Friendly;
they are followed in by Vert Amande, St Jovite, Saganeca (No. 8) and Dr Devious

interests of the day's sponsors, to secure the return of live coverage of Prix de l'Arc day on British television in 1993. But the success or failure of their efforts may well depend on what else is available to Channel 4. It is thought unlikely, for contractual reasons, that either of the BBC channels would be offered coverage of the 1993 Arc; ITV dropped racing long ago and Sky Sports don't touch it. Although racing's greatest occasion the Grand National still attracts the biggest television audience for any annual sporting event—over sixteen million viewers in 1992—most televised racing in Britain looks vulnerable. The debacle over the live showing of the Prix de l'Arc is a warning that racing will have to work hard to maintain its prominence on television.

The latest Prix de l'Arc attracted, as usual, the strongest field, judged on quality in depth, assembled for a middle-distance race in Europe during the season. The nine three-year-olds among the eighteen runners included the winners of the Derby (Dr Devious), the Irish Derby and King George VI and Queen Elizabeth Stakes (St Jovite), the Prix du Jockey-Club (Polytain), the Oaks, Irish Oaks, Yorkshire Oaks and St Leger (User Friendly) and the Prix de Diane and Prix Vermeille (Jolypha). The nine older horses included the previous year's Prix Vermeille winner and Arc runner-up Magic Night, the Coronation Cup winner Saddlers' Hall, the Grosser Preis von Baden and Irish St Leger winner Mashaallah, the Arlington Million winner Dear Doctor and the Prix Ganay winner Subotica. Subotica won the Prix Ganay at Longchamp in May gamely from two other four-year-olds Pistolet Bleu and Suave Dancer, who were the most notable absentees from the Prix de l'Arc field. Suave Dancer, successful in the previous year's Arc after a fine season which included a clear-cut victory in the Prix du Jockey-Club (from Subotica), wasn't seen out after the Ganay; the injured Pistolet Bleu, third in Suave Dancer's Arc, had looked the main French hope after beating Magic Night and Subotica by five lengths and two and a half in the Grand Prix de Saint-Cloud in July. Pistolet Bleu was to have had his final warm-up race in the Prix Foy at Long-champ three weeks before the Arc; Magic Night won that race, a slowly-run affair, from Subotica who was having his first run since the Grand Prix de Saint-Cloud and gave the impression he'd come on for the outing.

On balance the Prix de l'Arc winners of our experience have had a slight edge in merit over their counterparts in the King George VI and Queen Elizabeth Stakes, the other great test in Europe of the comparative merits of top-class middle-distance horses from different generations and different countries. But that wasn't so in the latest season. The Prix de l'Arc is not without its drawbacks. It is run late in the season, arguably a shade too late for most horses that have featured for the classics and then the top prizes in the summer, and a big field increases the risk of some of the runners meeting with interference. The modest early gallop—a rare occurrence in an Arc—contributed to the latest Arc's proving a less than satisfactory test. The Arc, of course, is never won by a bad horse, but Subotica, who got the better of the favourite User Friendly after a tremendous duel in the home straight, wasn't the best horse in the Arc field and, putting his performance into perspective, he ranks among the lower-rated Arc winners. Everything went right for him at Longchamp where he was one of those who got the run of a muddling race. Proven in the mud, he was sensibly ridden by the French champion jockey Jarnet who immediately took up a forward position and had Subotica ideally positioned when the tempo quickened; the riders of some of the fancied runners who were held up—among them Jolypha, Dear Doctor and Magic Night—met a good deal of trouble when they tried to launch their finishing efforts. Subotica steadily wore down User Friendly to win by a neck with St Jovite (who was unsuited by the ground) and Dr Devious the best-placed of the other fancied horses in fourth and sixth. The field was more massed at the finish than might have been expected given the prevailing soft ground, and for us the proximity of the French-trained outsiders Vert Amande and Saganeca in third and fifth holds the form down.

If there was an element of good luck in Subotica's Prix de l'Arc victory, then he certainly suffered a slice of the other kind on his only appearance in Britain. Subotica was the main sufferer in a rough race for the Coronation Cup at Epsom in June. Jarnet was caught napping on this occasion as the main home-trained hope Saddlers' Hall was dashed up on the outside over two

O. Lecerf's "Subotica"

furlongs out; badly hampered and pocketed soon afterwards as Terimon's rider switched his mount for a run, Subotica couldn't be extricated until far too late. Subotica stayed on strongly in fourth, beaten about a length and a half by the winner Saddlers' Hall, and would have gone very close, to say the least, with a clear run. Subotica's only other race outside France was the Breeders' Cup Turf at Gulfstream Park on his final appearance when he ran some way below his Prix de l'Arc form, finishing fifth to the American outsider Fraise, one place behind Dr Devious and two behind the 1990 Derby winner Quest For Fame who showed something like his best American form.

		Pampabird (b 1979)	Pampapaul (b 1974)	Yellow God
Subotica (FR) (b.c. 1988)				Pampalina
			Wood Grouse (ch 1967)	Celtic Ash
				French Bird
		Terre de Feu (FR) (b 1983)	Busted (b 1963)	Crepello
				Sans Le Sou
			Ludivine (b 1973)	Luthier
				Tita

The big, lengthy Subotica has been retired to the Haras de Mezeray in Normandy where he will stand at a fee of 60,000 francs (about £7,200) in 1993 with the October 1st concession. Tough and genuine as Subotica was, his unfashionable pedigree reduces his likely appeal for commercial breeders. His sire Pampabird was a good-class miler but has sired none of similar merit to Subotica; he has had another Prix du Jockey-Club runner-up in Ghost Buster's, a colt who, however, had no other form to compare with his effort at Chantilly. Subotica is more stoutly bred on his dam's side than on his sire's—his grandsire Pampapaul and his great grandsire Yellow God were both milers—and full details of the distaff side of his pedigree can be found in *Racehorses of 1991*. Subotica's dam Terre de Feu, a daughter of Busted, won at up to a mile and a quarter in France and is out of a half-sister to Margouillat, a top-class middle-distance colt who was third in the 1974 Prix de l'Arc. Subotica is Terre de Feu's first foal and only winner to date (her fourth foal, by Rainbow Quest, made 500,000 francs at the Deauville August Yearling Sales); Terre de Feu is a half-sister to several winners, the best of them a useful middle-distance handicapper in France called Force de Frappe. Subotica stayed a mile and a half well and acted on good to firm and soft going. *A. Fabre, France*

SUBSONIC (IRE)   4 b.c. Be My Guest (USA) 126 – Broken Wide (Busted 134)   **83 p**
[1991 10d⁶ 12f 14g* 12.3d* 14m³ 16.1m* 16m* 18m* 16.5d 1992 16d 16d³ 16m 14g²] big, good-bodied colt: usually impresses in appearance: has a round action: progressive staying handicapper at 3 yrs, successful 5 times: failed to win in 1992, but shaped encouragingly most starts: first run for 3½ months (finished lame previous outing) when beaten a neck over inadequate trip at Kempton in September: will prove suited by 2m+: acts on dead ground, and goes very well on top-of-the-ground: rather lazy, idles in front, and usually held up: capable of better, and should win a good staying handicap at 5 yrs provided all remains well with him. *J. L. Dunlop*

SUDANOR (IRE)   3 b.c. Khartoum (USA) – Alencon (Northfields (USA)) [1991   **63 d**
7d³ 1992 8g³ 10v 7d⁵ 7m⁴ 8.1g 7g⁵ 6.9m 7d 8g 10.2d] rangy colt: disappointing maiden: stays 1m: acts on good to firm and dead ground: below form when blinkered: has joined R. Millman. *M. J. Heaton-Ellis*

SUDBURY (IRE)   2 b.f. (May 3) Auction Ring (USA) 123 – Confiture (USA)   **69**
(Empery (USA) 128) [1992 6s* 6g³ 7s 8s*] IR 3,000Y: workmanlike filly: has a quick action: second reported foal: dam French 1m and 1¼m winner: successful in maiden auction at Hamilton in May and nursery (much improved form) at Warwick in October: off course 4 months after second start: will be suited by 1¼m: acts well on soft ground: sold 5,000 gns Newmarket Autumn Sales. *M. H. Tompkins*

SUDDEN SPIN   2 b.g. (Apr 5) Doulab (USA) 115 – Lightning Legacy (USA) 78   **43**
(Super Concorde (USA) 128) [1992 6g 7s⁶ 8.1d] 8,000Y: leggy, good-topped gelding: fifth foal: half-brother to useful 1¼m to 11f winner Black Monday (by Busted) and 5-y-o 1¾m to 2½m winner Cabochon (by Jalmood): dam, maiden, stayed 1m: poor form in maidens: should stay at least 1m. *J. Berry*

SUEBOOG (IRE)   2 b.f. (Apr 1) Darshaan 133 – Nordica 99 (Northfields **109 p**
(USA)) [1992 7g* 7m⁴]

    It might be imagined a foolhardy venture to supplement a once-raced filly whom her trainer had at one time considered to be 'too big, and too slow a learner, to be trained as a two-year-old', at a cost of £12,500 into the Dewhurst Stakes. The race was widely considered to be easy pickings for the French-trained colt Zafonic, and no filly had won the race since Torbella III thirty-five years before. As things turned out, Sueboog, the filly in question, finished fourth of the eleven runners, losing her owner in the region of £5,000 on the gamble. However, those bare facts of the matter don't reflect the credit due to Sueboog for an excellent effort in the face of a difficult task on what was only her second appearance on the racecourse, or how close she came to rewarding her connections' judgement. The 14/1-chance Sueboog ran a cracking race, and had she finished half a length closer to the four-length winner Zafonic she'd have come second, in the process earning more than enough to cover her supplementary fee. Sueboog's fourth place was all the more meritorious when one considers that she had had less racing experience than any of the ten other runners, and that that initial education, a bloodless victory over modest opposition in the Jock Collier Memorial Stakes at Newbury in September, had hardly taught her much about racing. Sueboog took the race to the others from the start, making the running travelling strongly for around four furlongs, then held her ground well as Zafonic went clear, losing out only narrowly to Inchinor and Firm Pledge in a three-way photo for second. Connections are unlikely to mind about the cost of substituting her at Newmarket, for the fact remains that they have unearthed a really useful prospect for the coming season, one more than capable of paying for her keep.

At 56,000 guineas from Newmarket's Highflyer Sales, Sueboog was one of the more expensive yearlings by Darshaan to be sold at auction in 1991. Darshaan's influence in Britain has diminished since his owner and chief supporter the Aga Khan concentrated all his racing interests in France and Ireland in the wake of the Aliysa affair, but his reputation as a stallion with a high winner-to-runner ratio, a strong influence for stamina to boot, is as solid as ever. While Sueboog's dam Nordica stayed a mile and a quarter, she showed better form and gained all her victories at shorter distances, winning three races at a mile when trained here by Alec Stewart before being moved to Ireland where she scored over six furlongs. Sueboog is Nordica's third foal; the first, Manhal (by Sure Blade) never ran, while the second, Mindomica (by Dominion) won over seven furlongs as a two-year-old in 1991 and ran mainly at a mile to a mile and a quarter in the latest season. Sueboog's grandam Princess Arabella, the dam of two winners besides Nordica, including the Irish one-mile winner Casla, raced only at seven furlongs, over which distance she won a maiden at Redcar. Her next dam Fair Arabella, a winner at up to a mile in the States, also produced five other winners, notably the One Thousand Guineas second and Oaks and Irish Oaks winner Fair Salinia and the useful eight-and-a-half-furlong (in the States) and mile-and-a-quarter winner Rambo Dancer. Fair Salinia is the dam of the Ebor third Horn Dance and the latest One Thousand Guineas fourth Perfect Circle; her own grandam, Locust Time, incidentally, is also the dam of the top-class French miler Faraway Son and the very smart French middle-distance performer Liloy, as well as being the ancestress of the good-class and more recent duo Lyphard's Wish and Baillamont.

Sueboog (IRE) (b.f. Apr 1, 1990)	Darshaan (br 1981)	Shirley Heights (b 1975)	Mill Reef Hardiemma
		Delsy (br 1972)	Abdos Kelty
	Nordica (ch 1983)	Northfields (ch 1968)	Northern Dancer Little Hut
		Princess Arabella (b 1978)	Crowned Prince Fair Arabella

Although Sueboog's sire and dam stayed middle distances there must be slight reservations as to whether she will be effective at a mile and a half (her trainer, in a pre-Dewhurst quote, revealed that she'd not been sent to France for the Prix Marcel Boussac because she'd become too stirred up in a preparatory gallop). Whatever her ideal distance turns out to be, the tall, good-bodied Sueboog is probably a filly of whom we have yet to see the best. So far, she has raced only on good or good to firm ground. *C. E. Brittain*

SUEMAX (IRE) 4 ch.f. Soughaan (USA) 111 – Cousin Clare (Pontifex (USA))   –
[1991 NR 1992 8m 10.2f] workmanlike filly: eighth reported foal: half-sister to 3 winners, including 7-y-o sprint handicapper Dee And Em (by Crofter): dam unraced: twice raced and no worthwhile form, including in seller. *R. J. Hodges*

SUEZ CANAL (IRE) 3 b.g. Commanche Run 133 – Sphinx (GER) (Alpenkonig   74 §
(GER)) [1991 7g⁴ 7.1s 1992 10g² 12.1d² 12.3m² 13.1m* 13.1g² 16f² 16.2d² 13.9g 13.6m⁶] leggy, lengthy, angular gelding: landed odds in match for maiden at Ayr in June: not discredited most starts after but didn't impress with attitude: stays 2m: acts on firm and dead going: ran well when blinkered, below form visored: joined F. Jordan. *P. W. Chapple-Hyam*

SUGAR LOAF (IRE) 3 b.f. Head For Heights 125 – Casa Rosada (Known Fact   –
(USA) 135) [1991 NR 1992 8.5g 10g 10f] leggy, lengthy, angular filly: second foal: half-sister to 8.2f winner May Square (by Nicholas Bill): dam poor daughter of Nell Gwyn winner Evita: no worthwhile form, blinkered and showed signs of temperament final run: sold to join D. Bell's stable 1,100 gns Ascot June Sales. *N. A. Graham*

SUGEMAR 6 ch.g. Young Generation 129 – Jade Ring 92 (Auction Ring (USA)   64
123) [1991 7m⁶ 7m* 8g 7m³ a8g⁴ 8f⁶ 8m 1992 7g 8m 7m² 7m* 7f² 7m³ 8g 7g² 7m⁶ 7.6d a8g³ a7g⁵ a8g a8g a8g] big, strong gelding: poor walker and mover: won handicap at Yarmouth in June but in-and-out form in second half of 1992: effective at 7f to 1¼m: acts on any going: usually races prominently: sold out of J. Toller's stable 1,900 gns Newmarket Autumn Sales after tenth start. *M. C. Chapman*

SUI GENERIS (IRE) 2 ch.f. (Apr 17) Doulab (USA) 115 – Markon (On Your   43
Mark 125) [1992 5.2g 5m⁵ 5d] IR 3,000F, IR 2,000Y: rather sparely-made filly:

half-sister to useful 1984 Irish 2-y-o 7f winner Stramar (by Orchestra), 7f to 1m winner One To Mark (by He Loves Me) and a winner in Italy: dam unraced daughter of half-sister to Humble Duty: poor maiden. *C. G. Cox*

SUITABILITY (IRE)   2 b.f. (May 7) Local Suitor (USA) 128 – Amina 80 (Brig-   **38** adier Gerard 144) [1992 5f⁴ 6g⁵ 6.9h³ 6s] close-coupled filly: has a round action: half-sister to several winners, including 7f/1m performer Salmino (by Salmon Leap): dam 1¼m winner, is sister to Lancashire Oaks winner Princess Eboli: poor form in sellers: probably stays 7f: not discredited in visor penultimate start: sold 600 gns Doncaster September Sales. *P. C. Haslam*

SUIVEZ   2 b.c. (Mar 13) Persian Bold 123 – Butterfly Kiss 69 (Beldale Flutter   **77** ? (USA) 130) [1992 7.3m² 6f⁴] 30,000F, 86,000Y: tall colt: has scope: first foal: dam 1½m winner: shaped well when second in minor event at Newbury in June: well-beaten favourite in 5-runner maiden at Yarmouth 1½ months after: should stay at least 1m. *C. E. Brittain*

SUIVEZ MOI   8 ch.g. Pas de Seul 133 – Reparata (Jukebox 120) [1991 a14g a16g   **34** a14g 1992 14.1d 21.6g³] small, light-framed gelding: poor mover: poor handicapper: needs long distances: acts on any going except possibly heavy: raced too freely when visored: genuine. *C. N. Allen*

SUKEY TAWDRY   6 gr.m. Wassl 125 – Jenny Diver (USA) (Hatchet Man (USA))   – [1991 10s⁴ 12g 1992 10m 11.6g] leggy mare: of little account nowadays. *R. A. Bennett*

SULAAH ROSE   3 b.f. Sula Bula 109 – Dusky Damsel 68 (Sahib 114) [1991 8m   – 1992 12.2g 10m 7d] leggy filly: no worthwhile form. *Mrs J. Jordan*

SULLI BOY (NOR)   7 b.g. Sparkling Boy 110 – Lady Sullivan (Pitcairn 126)   – [1991 10.1g 8g⁶ 1992 11.6g 12g 10g] sturdy, dipped-backed gelding: winner 8 times in Scandinavia, including twice over 1m in 1989: no worthwhile form in varied events on flat here: third over hurdles in October. *Miss B. Sanders*

SULLY'S CHOICE (USA)   11 b.g. King Pellinore (USA) 127 – Salute The   **51** Coates (USA) (Solar Salute (USA)) [1991 6f 5m⁶ 6f⁶ 6f⁵ 6m* 6m* 6f² 6f 6f 6m⁶ 6g 6f* 6g² 5m 6m 7.1m 5s a5g³ a6g 1992 a5g⁶ a6g⁶ a5g³ a5g² 5g⁵ 5g 6d⁴ 6g 6f* 6g⁵ 6m³ 6g⁶ 6g⁴] small, sturdy gelding: carries plenty of condition: modest sprint handicapper: won at Thirsk in June: acts on any going: below form when visored: effective with or without blinkers: suitable mount for apprentice: front runner: tough. *D. W. Chapman*

SULTAN'S SON   6 b.g. Kings Lake (USA) 133 – Get Ahead 58 (Silly Season 127)   – [1991 12g 12s⁵ 11d 1992 12f 12d⁶ 12f⁵] strong, good-bodied gelding: has a round action: well beaten on flat in last 2 seasons: best form at 1½m: acts on firm ground: in frame over hurdles in autumn. *John R. Upson*

SULUK (USA)   7 b.h. Lypheor 118 – Cheerful Heart (Petingo 135) [1991 a12g   – 11.8g 12m⁶ a12g⁵ a14g* a16g 1992 14g² 16.1s a12g⁴ a14g a16g⁵ a16g⁴ a16g] a51 dipped-backed, good-quartered horse: carries condition: modest handicapper, best at Southwell: best at 1¾m: acts well on fibresand (on which also prolific winning hurdler): suitable mount for claimer: usually forces pace: tough and genuine. *R. Hollinshead*

SUMMER CRUISE   3 b.g. Slip Anchor 136 – Enthralment (USA) 78 (Sir Ivor   **74** d 135) [1991 7m³ 1992 10d³ 11.9m³ 9.7g⁶ 10g⁵ 9.7v] good-bodied gelding: moderate mover: on the downgrade: sold out of H. Cecil's stable 7,800 gns Newmarket July Sales after second start. *A. N. Lee*

SUMMER EXPRESS   3 gr.g. Bay Express 132 – Bit O' May (Mummy's Pet 125)   **62** [1991 NR 1992 a6g* a6g* a7g⁴ 6v⁶ 5.1d a5g⁶ a6g²] 1,200Y: leggy, shallow-girthed gelding: first foal: dam poor daughter of half-sister to Oaks runner-up Mabel: won maiden and claimer at Lingfield in February: easily best subsequent effort on last day of year: should stay 7f. *J. L. Spearing*

SUMMER FLOWER   2 b.f. (Jan 29) Nomination 125 – Hedda Garbler 67 (Strad-   **51** p avinsky 121) [1992 6s⁴] 1,300Y: lengthy filly: first foal: dam, maiden, stayed 1m: 10/1 and green, shaped well when under 7 lengths fourth of 14 to Princely Favour in maiden at Lingfield in October, keeping on under tender handling: showed a round action: will improve. *B. W. Hills*

SUMMER PAGEANT   2 b.f. (May 26) Chief's Crown (USA) – Troyanos (Troy   **65** 137) [1992 7m³ 7g] leggy, unfurnished filly: fourth foal: dam unraced half-sister to Sun Princess and Saddlers' Hall: stayed on well when over 4 lengths third of 19 in maiden at Kempton in August: raced freely in front rank to 2f out then dropped right away in similar event there following month. *J. R. Fanshawe*

SUMMER READING (USA) 3 b.f. Alleged (USA) 138 – Sharp Belle (USA) – p
(Native Charger) [1991 NR 1992 10d⁵] quite attractive filly: sixth foal: half-sister to
winners in USA by Sauce Boat and Clever Trick: dam won 10 races in USA at up to
1¼m, including Grade 1 Monmouth Oaks: one pace last 2f when 9½ lengths fifth of
8 in maiden at Brighton in September: moved moderately to post: should improve.
L. M. Cumani

SUMMER SANDS 4 ch.f. Mummy's Game 120 – Renira 60 (Relkino 131) [1991 –
6m 5s 8m 6g⁵ 7g⁴ 7d⁴ 6.9m³ 5d³ 7m² 7d³ 7f 8g 1992 a7g a10g 6d] lengthy filly: on
the downgrade. *J. L. Harris*

SUMMERS DREAM 2 b.f. (Mar 25) Dreams To Reality (USA) 113 – Well 41
Connected (Bold And Free 118) [1992 5m⁶ 5g⁴ 6f⁴ 6m⁵ a6g⁴ a6g⁶ 6.1m 8.2d⁴ 10.5d
8v] 3,300Y: angular, workmanlike filly: moderate mover: half-sister to 7f to 1m
winner Serlby Connection (by Crofthall) and 5f and 6f seller winner My Topic (by
Mansingh): dam poor maiden: poor plater: doesn't stay 10.5f, and worth a try at 7f:
acts on firm and dead ground: below form when visored once. *B. Richmond*

SUMMIT FEVER (IRE) 2 ch.f. (Feb 1) Persian Heights 129 – Seminar 113 –
(Don (ITY) 123) [1992 6d⁶ 7s] 32,000Y: rather unfurnished filly: half-sister to
numerous winners, including 1981 2-y-o 6f winner Solaboy (by The Minstrel) and
3-y-o Soiree (by Sadler's Wells), 7f winner at 2 yrs: dam, half-sister to Boldboy, very
useful over 5f at 2 yrs and won at 1m at 3 yrs in USA: poor form in maidens at
Leicester and Salisbury (dropped right away) 3 months later: sold 10,000 gns
Newmarket December Sales. *P. F. I. Cole*

SUMMONED BY BELLS 3 ch.f. Stanford 121§ – Mephisto Waltz 98 (Dancer's –
Image (USA)) [1991 5m⁴ 5g 6d 1992 6d] workmanlike filly: regressive maiden:
sprint bred: possibly doesn't have ideal attitude. *M. Johnston*

SUMOTO 2 b.f. (Jan 13) Mtoto 134 – Soemba 86 (General Assembly (USA)) **101** p
[1992 6m*]

It must be a worry to those who backed Sumoto to win the One Thousand
Guineas after her impressive defeat of Sayyedati in the Halifax Maiden Fillies
Stakes at Ascot in June that she wasn't seen out again on account of spraining
a hock. But the news, so far as we understand it, is that she's made a full
recovery. The result of the Halifax Maiden, in which Sumoto beat Sayyedati
by two lengths, the pair finishing eight lengths clear of six others, shouldn't
be taken as a literal guide to their respective merits: it is maiden-race form,
after all, and Sayyedati was more highly tried subsequently, notably when she

EBF Halifax Maiden Fillies Stakes, Ascot—
an early favourite for the One Thousand Guineas, but Sumoto is not seen out again

won the Cheveley Park Stakes from Lyric Fantasy at Newmarket in October. The strong probability is, though, that Sumoto is a much better filly than her one piece of public form shows: she was all the rage at Ascot, a heavily-backed 11/10-on favourite, and won smoothly under a confident ride. Sayyedati fully deserves her position at the head of the Guineas market on what she achieved afterwards, but if one of the less-exposed fillies is to shake up the established order then Sumoto could be the one. She left her rider Swinburn in no doubt whatsoever about her ability—upon dismounting he was reported to have said he'd '. . . just ridden the next Marling'.

It augurs well for Sumoto that she was able to show sufficient speed to win over six furlongs on good to firm ground in the June of her first season, for she's a daughter of the top-class middle-distance colt Mtoto, a late-developing son of Busted who didn't come into his own until his fourth year when he won the Brigadier Gerard Stakes, the Prince of Wales's Stakes and the Coral-Eclipse, the last-named at the expense of Reference Point and Triptych. In fact, Sumoto was the only two-year-old from Mtoto's first crop to win over six furlongs; the four other winners all needed time and a longer distance. Sumoto, a third foal, is a half-sister to the useful seven-furlong and one-mile winner Sumonda (by Lomond). Their dam Soemba won over nine furlongs and is a daughter of the seven-furlong and eleven-furlong winner Seven Seas, half-sister to the smart seven-furlong to mile-and-a-quarter winner Fluellen. Seven Seas's dam Ya Ya was a fair stayer and is a half-sister to the Park Hill winner African Dancer. This is the same family, incidentally, as the stable's good two-year-old colt Inchinor.

Sumoto (b.f. Jan 13, 1990)	Mtoto (b 1983)	Busted (b 1963)	Crepello
			Sans Le Sou
		Amazer (b 1967)	Mincio
			Alzara
	Soemba (b 1983)	General Assembly (ch 1976)	Secretariat
			Exclusive Dancer
		Seven Seas (b 1978)	Riverman
			Ya Ya

Sumoto, quite an attractive filly though still unfurnished at two, a good walker, will be well suited by a mile; her breeding suggests that she'll have little difficulty in staying a mile and a quarter, but in view of the speed that she showed at Ascot her connections may not be in a hurry to try her at the distance. That's all for the future. Let's hope her reappearance proves to have been well worth waiting for. *G. Wragg*

SUNBEAM CHARLIE 2 ch.g. (Apr 19) Krisinsky (USA) – Bright Favor (Sparkler 130) [1992 8s 6.9v⁵ 8v] tall gelding: first reported foal: dam stayed 1½m: well beaten in maidens. *A. Moore*   **38**

SUNDAY'S HILL 3 b.c. Efisio 120 – Elkie Brooks 82 (Relkino 131) [1991 6.1g 6g² 6m* 6g* 6m⁴ 7.3g 1992 6d⁴ 6m5 6m* 6g 6s 6g 6g 6d³ 6d 8.1s²] good-bodied colt: carries condition: has a markedly round action: useful handicapper: won at Newbury in June: stays 1m: acts on good to firm and soft ground: effective visored or not. *M. Blanshard*   **97**

SUNDERLAND ECHO 3 br.g. Daring March 116 – Incarnadine 67 (Hot Spark 126) [1991 6g 7g⁴ 6g 8m 1992 10.3f5 12.1s* 10s* 10.5s 10m2 12.4v*] good-bodied, workmanlike gelding: off course 3½ months after first run in 1992 but in excellent form in handicaps in autumn: successful at Hamilton, Redcar and Newcastle (much improved form to win 17-runner contest by 10 lengths): best effort at 1½m: acts on good to firm ground, but goes particularly well on soft: takes keen hold, and held up: should win more races. *Mrs M. Reveley*   **74** p

SUN ECLIPSE (IRE) 3 ch.f. Palace Music (USA) 129 – Sun Breiz (FR) (Boran) [1991 7m 7d 1992 9.7v 10d] lengthy, unfurnished filly: no worthwhile form: blinkered once. *M. McCormack*   **–**

SUN GLORY (IRE) 3 b.f. Glow (USA) – Sun Bed (Habitat 134) [1991 a8g a7g 1992 a10g a10g⁴ a10g] neat filly: little sign of ability. *W. Jarvis*   **–**

SUN GREBE (IRE) 2 b.f. (Feb 18) Arctic Tern (USA) 126 – Bronzewing 103 (Beldale Flutter (USA) 130) [1992 7g 7.1g] leggy filly: first foal: dam 6f and 1m winner: much better effort in autumn maidens on final run when around 9 lengths eighth of 12, never a threat, at Sandown: may do better. *J. L. Dunlop*   **55** p

SUNLEY SILKS 3 b. or br.f. Formidable (USA) 125 – Brown Velvet 68 **80** ?
(Mansingh (USA) 120) [1991 NR 1992 7d⁴ 7g³ 5.1g* 7s a7g⁵ a8g] workmanlike filly:
poor mover: fifth foal: half-sister to French 7f and 1m winner Bartizan and 6f winner
Berkeley Hill Boy (both by Castle Keep): dam, possibly short runner, is half-sister
to smart Stumped, dam of Sonic Lady: third in maiden at Newmarket in April: off
course 3 months and well below that form after, but won similar event at Bath: stays
7f. *M. R. Channon*

SUNLEY SPARKLE 4 b.f. Sunley Builds 102 – Royal Darwin 69 (Royal Palm **45**
131) [1991 a6g* 8g 7m⁴ 6g⁴ 7m³ 7m* 7.6d⁵ a7g⁴ 6m⁵ a7g 7m⁴ 7g⁶ 8.1s 8.2m 1992
a8g 6f 6m 8g 7g 8d⁵ 8d² 8.2g] leggy, rather sparely-made filly: poor handicapper:
should stay beyond 1m: acts on good to firm and dead going and on equitrack. *D. R.
Gandolfo*

SUNNYSIDE ROCK (IRE) 4 ch.g. Ballad Rock 122 – Havana Moon (Ela- **–**
Mana-Mou 132) [1991 6g⁴ 6d³ 6m 7m² 7.1g 10.5d 8.1m 1992 8f a8s 8.2d 6g]
workmanlike gelding: seems on the downgrade: sold 700 gns Doncaster September
Sales. *J. Etherington*

SUNNYVIEW LAD 2 b.g. (Feb 18) Kabour 80 – Magic Mover (Julio Mariner **–**
127) [1992 6g⁵ a6g] workmanlike gelding: second foal: dam, poor maiden, from
family of So Blessed and Lucasland: not beaten far in slowly-run minor event at
Doncaster in October: well beaten in Lingfield claimer following month. *P. C.
Haslam*

SUN OF SPRING 2 b.c. (Mar 17) Green Desert (USA) 127 – Unsuspected 95 **65** p
(Above Suspicion 127) [1992 7m 8v³] medium-sized, sturdy colt: half-brother to
several winners, notably Sally Brown (by Posse) and Untold (by Final Straw): dam
won 8 times from 1m to 1¾m: pushed along after slow start and not at all knocked
about from halfway when eighth of 10 in £8,850 event at Newmarket: favourite,
below that form and never travelling particularly well in maiden at Leicester (moved
poorly to post) later in October: worth another chance. *M. R. Stoute*

SUNRAYS (IRE) 3 br.f. Vision (USA) – Daybreaker (Thatching 131) [1991 6m⁴ **–**
8m 6s a7g 1992 a8g⁶ 9.2v 10d 6g] leggy filly: poor maiden: best efforts over 6f: sold
850 gns Ascot May Sales. *C. W. C. Elsey*

SUNRISE MORNING (USA) 2 b.f. (Jun 5) El Gran Senor (USA) 136 – Glori- **77** p
ous Morning (USA) (Graustark) [1992 7s³] $28,000Y: small, angular, sparely-made
filly: fifth foal: half-sister to a minor winner by Little Current: dam unraced sister to
3 graded winners, including top 3-y-o filly Tempest Queen: 7/2, 3 lengths last of 3 to
Great Steps in minor event at York in October, no extra close home: will improve. *P.
W. Chapple-Hyam*

SUN SEEKER (IRE) 3 b.c. Rainbow Quest (USA) 134 – Sun Princess 130 **95** +
(English Prince 129) [1991 NR 1992 10d³ 12g* 12m] leggy, good sort: good mover:
fourth foal: half-brother to high-class 7f to 1¼m winner Prince of Dance (by Sadler's
Wells) and 1¼m winner Ruby Setting (by Gorytus): dam won Oaks and St Leger,
and is half-sister to Saddlers' Hall: progressive colt: comfortably won maiden at
Salisbury in May: looking very well, prominent until entering straight and far from
disgraced when tenth of 12 in King Edward VII Stakes at Royal Ascot: will stay
further: sent to France. *M. R. Stoute*

SUNSET REINS FREE 7 b.g. Red Sunset 120 – Free Rein (Sagaro 133) [1991 **37**
a8g 8.5f⁴ 10m⁵ 10.5m 12m² 1992 8s⁶ 10d 13d 8.9s⁵ 10.5d⁴ 12h²] big, good-bodied
gelding: carries plenty of condition: moderate mover: poor handicapper: not seen
out on flat after June: sold 6,000 gns Doncaster June Sales: stays 1½m: probably
acts on any going: effective visored or not: suitable mount for amateur. *E. J. Alston*

SUNSET STREET (IRE) 4 b.g. Bellypha 130 – Sunset Reef (Mill Reef (USA) **62**
141) [1991 a10g⁶ 8g 11g⁴ 6d 8.5m 8g⁵ 6g 10d 8.1d 1992 a8g² a8g⁵ 6m 6.9m⁵ 7g² a7g²
7d 9.7m a8g² a8g] lengthy, workmanlike gelding: has a quick action: modest
handicapper: stays 1m: acts on good to firm ground and equitrack: below form in
eyeshield/blinkered/visored. *S. Dow*

SUNSHINE IN RAMSEY 2 ch.f. (May 5) Hard Fought 125 – Pashmina 68 **40**
(Blue Cashmere 129) [1992 5f⁵ 5m⁶ 6f 7f 6.9h⁵ 6m⁴ 6g 7d] small, lightly-made filly:
first live foal: dam 5f winner: moderate plater: best form at 6f: acts on firm ground,
possibly unsuited by dead: blinkered last 3 starts: sold 520 gns Doncaster October
Sales. *T. Fairhurst*

SUNTARA (IRE) 2 b.f. (Apr 26) Sure Blade (USA) 130 – First Act (Sadler's **69**
Wells (USA) 132) [1992 7g² 7g² 7d²] sturdy, lengthy filly: first foal: dam unraced
daughter of Arkadina (dam also of Dark Lomond) from very good family: promising
second of 16 to Sueboog in minor event at Newbury in September on debut: didn't

progress as anticipated, beaten head at Catterick final run: will be suited by 1m. *B. W. Hills*

SUNWIND 6 b.g. Windjammer (USA) – Mrewa (Runnymede 123) [1991 a10g 1992   **30** a6g a10g4 a8g4 a7g] stocky gelding: maiden handicapper: stays 1¼m: acts on firm and dead going. *David Heath*

SUPER BEAUTY 3 b.f. Capricorn Line 111 – Super Lady (Averof 123) [1991 5m   **47** 7m5 1992 8s5 8f3 8f 11.4d 10g] smallish, sturdy filly: poor maiden: sold 750 gns to join Miss S. Waterman Ascot July Sales. *G. B. Balding*

SUPER BENZ 6 ch.g. Hello Gorgeous (USA) 128 – Investiture 62 (Welsh   **75** Pageant 132) [1991 a6g* a6g6 6d 7g3 7m4 7m 8d3 6d 7g2 7.5f4 7g* 7m6 7m* 7g a7g*   a89 1992 a7g6 a6g* 7g 7.5m 7f 7f2 7m 7g 7m5 7d 7.5m 7d 7d 7g3 7v a6g] leggy, lengthy gelding: has a roundish action: tough and genuine handicapper: effective at 6f to 1m: acts on firm and dead going and on fibresand (won at Southwell early in year): effective visored or not: successful for apprentice: front runner. *T. Fairhurst*

SUPER BLUES 5 b.m. Welsh Captain 113 – Pitskelly Blues (Pitskelly 122) [1991   **61** d NR 1992 12.2g3 12.1g3 11.1f3 12.3m 12.3g 12m] big, workmanlike mare: moderate mover: third foal: dam poor maiden: well below form after third in 11f Edinburgh maiden: stays 1½m: acts on firm ground. *T. D. Barron*

SUPERBRAVE 6 b.h. Superlative 118 – Tribal Feast 100 (Tribal Chief 125) [1991   **78** 5g6 6m 5m 6m6 5m5 5g 6m3 5m4 6g4 1992 6m3 7m* 7g5 7m 7d5 7.3g 6s5] strong, lengthy horse: ran well in handicaps for most of 1992, winning quite valuable event at Newcastle in June: well below form last 2 outings, in seller final one, and sold only 600 gns Newmarket Autumn Sales: best form at 7f: acts on firm and dead ground: below form when visored once: sometimes bandaged. *W. Jarvis*

SUPER CHARGE 3 b.g. Superlative 118 – Daisy Warwick (USA) 91 (Ribot 142)   – [1991 5g 6m 7f 6m 1992 10f a12g 10g 6.9g] good-topped gelding: seems of little account nowadays. *M. W. Ellerby*

SUPER ELEGANT 2 b.c. (Mar 30) Elegant Air 119 – Catulle (Roan Rocket 128)   – [1992 8d] 5,600Y: good-topped colt: fourth living foal: dam unraced half-sister to Gold Cup winner Shangamuzo: well beaten in maiden at Leicester in October: showed knee action. *M. J. Fetherston-Godley*

SUPERENSIS 2 ch.c. (Mar 18) Sayf El Arab (USA) 127 – Superlife (USA) 64   **51** (Super Concorde (USA) 128) [1992 5g 6f6 5.7m4 5g5 6m2 6m 7.1s 8g] 2,500F, 7,200Y: good-topped colt: second foal: brother to 3-y-o Meltonby, successful from 6f to 1m, including at 2 yrs: dam maiden suited by 7f: little show, including in selling nurseries, after second in Brighton claimer in July: best form at 6f: effective blinkered or not. *W. R. Muir*

SUPER FLYER (IRE) 3 b.g. Fayruz 116 – Flying Beauty (Super Concorde   **42** (USA) 128) [1991 a6g3 7f 1992 8.3g 8f6 8d] leggy, angular gelding: poor maiden: seems to stay 1m: possibly unsuited by soft surface: sold out of C. Weedon's stable 950 gns Ascot March Sales before first run in 1992. *Mrs A. Knight*

SUPER HEIGHTS 4 b.g. Superlative 118 – Shadha 57 (Shirley Heights 130)   **58** d [1991 8g 8g 10.2g 6f* 6g 6m 7d 5.7m5 6m6 6m3 6m6 5.7f4 6g5 6m a6g5 a7g5 a7g3 a7g a6g* 1992 a6g* a6g5 a7g a6g2 a6g6 a6g a6g 6.1g a6g 7g 10.3g] useful-looking gelding: poor mover: unreliable handicapper: won at Lingfield in January: stays 7f: acts on firm and dead going and all-weather surfaces: sometimes blinkered: often gets behind: sold out of Miss A. Whitfield's stable 920 gns Newmarket Autumn Sales after penultimate run. *D. L. Williams*

SUPERLATIVEMAXIMUS (IRE) 4 ch.g. Superlative 118 – Samra 62   **50** (Welsh Saint 126) [1991 NR 1992 6.1d a5g3 5m4 a5g5] strong, heavy-topped gelding: fourth foal: dam lightly-raced Irish maiden: poor maiden: should stay 6f. *J. A. Bennett*

SUPER MARCO 3 b.c. Superlative 118 – Sterlonia 96 (Sterling Bay (SWE))   – [1991 5g 5.9h2 5m 5g6 5f 1992 7d 7g 10d 7.5m a7g 7m 7d 7g] close-coupled, good-quartered colt: on the downgrade: sold 1,150 gns Doncaster September Sales. *W. W. Haigh*

SUPER MORNING 6 b.h. Martinmas 128 – Super Lady (Averof 123) [1991   **50** a10g* a10g* a10g2 a10g6 a10g5 9g 10.8m 10.8m* 8.1d4 8.1g5 10g6 8.3g5 8f3 9g3 10.3m* 10m 10.5d 8g2 a10g6 a8g3 a10g3 1992 10.8d 10m 10d 10d4 9g6 9.7m 10m] tall, good-bodied horse: carries condition: poor handicapper: sold out of G. Balding's stable 3,000 gns Ascot July Sales after fourth start: effective from 1m to 10.8f: acts on any going: effective blinkered/visored or not. *J. Pearce*

SUPEROO 6 b.g. Superlative 118 – Shirleen (Daring Display (USA) 129) [1991   **77** 8.5m 8g 7m2 8g5 7.9g3 7m2 7m 1992 7g 7g 7g 7f* 8f 7g4 8m 7m 7f6 7m6] big, workmanlike gelding: carries plenty of condition: has a rather round action: won Salisbury handicap in June and ran well in competitive events most starts after: ideally suited by strongly-run 7f: acts on firm going: held up. *J. Sutcliffe*

SUPER RITCHART 4 b.g. Starch Reduced 112 – Karousa Girl (Rouser 118) – [1991 12.1g⁴ 16.2s² 11.8m 12.1g⁴ 16.1g 12.1d 17.2g 1992 17.5s 12s] strong gelding: seems on the downgrade on flat: won weak handicap hurdle in November. *B. Palling*

SUPER ROCKY 3 b.g. Clantime 101 – Starproof 46 (Comedy Star (USA) 121) 76 [1991 5m² 5f* 5m² 5f* 6m² 5m⁴ 1992 5v 5m⁴ 5m² 5m² 5m² 5f⁶ 5m³ 5g 5f² 5m³ 5m⁶ 5m⁶ 5m 5m 5s 6g 5d] compact, rather leggy gelding: fair handicapper: well below best last 3 starts: best over sharp 5f: has gone well on top-of-the-ground: tends to hang left: suitable mount for 7-lb claimer. *R. Bastiman*

SUPER SALLY 5 ch.m. Superlative 118 – Sally Chase 101 (Sallust 134) [1991 7m⁵ 102 8.1d² 7g⁵ 10.3d⁶ a8g* a8g² a8g* a10g* 1992 a8g* a8g³ a10g³ a8g* a8g² a8g* a8g² a 8g] strong mare: not seen out until October, 1991: in tremendous form very early in season, successful at Southwell (2) and Lingfield and excellent second in £10,800 event at Lingfield penultimate start: third favourite, ran lack-lustre race in Lincoln Handicap at Doncaster, and not seen out again: effective at 1m to 1¼m: acts on dead ground and all-weather surfaces: usually held up, and well ridden by D. Biggs: game and genuine. *M. J. Ryan*

SUPER SARENA (IRE) 3 b.f. Taufan (USA) 119 – Stop The Cavalry (Relko 65 136) [1991 6m³ 6m 7d³ 8m³ 8d⁵ 1992 10.4g⁵ 10g⁴ 11.9m² 14m 16m³ 14s⁵] lengthy, rather angular filly: has a quick action: rated 87 at 2 yrs: not so good in 1992, and still a maiden: stays 1¾m: acts on good to firm and dead ground: trained until after first start by D. Elsworth. *R. Simpson*

SUPER SCENARIO 2 ch.c. (May 10) Superlative 118 – Sporting Empress – (Busted 134) [1992 5f⁴ 6g 5d] 1,250F, IR 4,000Y: sturdy, compact colt: half-brother to several winners, including useful middle-distance stayer Corbadge (by Tap On Wood): dam ran once: looks of little account over sprint distances. *E. J. Alston*

SUPER SERENADE 3 b.c. Beldale Flutter (USA) 130 – Super Melody 72 (Song 70 132) [1991 5.1g⁴ 7m⁶ 1992 6g⁴ 7m³ 7.1m 7f² 7d² a7g* 7m⁶ 7g 7.3g 7g⁶ 7.1s a7g² a79 a7g³] angular colt: fair handicapper: won maiden at Lingfield in July: best efforts last 2 starts: should stay 1m: acts on firm ground and equitrack: often sweating. *G. B. Balding*

SUPER SEVE (IRE) 2 ch.c. (Apr 22) Superlative 118 – Sally Chase 101 (Sallust 65 134) [1992 a5g* 6d⁴ 5g a5s⁴ 6d 6m⁶ a6g] 5,200F, 5,000Y: strong, sturdy colt: carries condition: fifth foal: brother to 5-y-o 1m and 1¼m winner Super Sally and half-brother to 2 winners, including 6-y-o 6f/7f performer Sally's Son (by Beldale Flutter): dam sprinter, ran only at 2 yrs: won Southwell maiden in May but went wrong way in second half of 1992: stays 6f: best form on fibresand and on dead ground on turf. *J. Berry*

SUPER-SUB 3 b.f. Formidable (USA) 125 – Charlton Athletic (Bustino 136) 40 [1991 5g⁶ a6g⁴ 6m 6g 7m² 7m² a8g⁶ a7g³ a8g⁵ 1992 a8g⁵ a7g³ a10g 7.5m³ 6m a8g 7m 8g a6g] small, sturdy filly: moderate mover: maiden plater: stays 1m: acts on good to firm ground and equitrack: below form blinkered once: sold 8,500 gns Ascot February Sales, resold 1,500 gns Doncaster March Sales: trained until after third start by M. Fetherston-Godley. *G. Fleming*

SUPER SUMMIT 3 ch.c. Superlative 118 – Wollow Maid 73 (Wollow 132) [1991 76 7d 7m 6.1m 8m 1992 8.5m⁶ 8.2g² 7.5m⁵ 10d 8.1g³ 8m⁴ 8.1d* 8m* a8g* a10g⁴ a8g*] compact colt: had good season in 1992, winning claiming events at Edinburgh (maiden), Newcastle, Lingfield and Southwell: stays 8.5f: acts on good to firm ground and soft and all-weather surfaces. *J. Pearce*

SUPER TED 5 ch.g. Superlative 118 – Gandoorah 90 (Record Token 128) [1991 – NR 1992 6d 8.5g 8g] lengthy gelding: no worthwhile form. *W. J. Musson*

SUPERTOP 4 b. or br.g. High Top 131 – Myth 89 (Troy 137) [1991 10g⁴ 10.1m 58 10.2m 10f⁴ 1992 10.3g⁵ 10d² 9.9g* 10g³ 10g² 10.2m⁴ 10.3m⁴ 10g 10g* 10s⁵] leggy, workmanlike gelding: has a round action: consistent handicapper: successful at Beverley in April and Leicester in September: will stay 1½m: acts on firm and dead ground: below form for apprentice. *P. W. Harris*

SUPPER WITH SUSIE 2 b.f. (Feb 7) Dominion 123 – Legendary Dancer 90 – (Shareef Dancer (USA) 135) [1992 7d 7s] 10,000Y: leggy, sparely-made filly: first foal: dam 1½m winner, from family of Wassl: always behind in autumn maidens at Lingfield and Goodwood. *T. J. Naughton*

Morven Stud Ltd's "Supreme Choice"

SUPREME BOY 3 ch.c. Superlative 118 – Rose And The Ring (Welsh Pageant 132) [1991 6f 6f 7g⁴ 7g 1992 7.5g 7f³] angular, workmanlike colt: modest maiden: not seen out after May: will stay 1m: acts on firm going. *P. W. Harris*   **58**

SUPREME CHOICE (USA) 4 b.c. Sovereign Dancer (USA) – Editor's Choice (USA) (Sir Ivor 135) [1991 8g⁶ a11g* 11.9m³ 13.3g* 14g² 15.9g* 18m⁴ 16m² 1992 16.2d² 16.4m 15s 13.3g 16d² 18m] strong, lengthy colt: very useful stayer (rated 114) in 1991: didn't progress as anticipated from 3 to 4 yrs but not discredited when second to Al Mutahm in Sagaro Stakes at Ascot and to Further Flight in Jockey Club Cup at Newmarket: suited by test of stamina (will stay 2½m): acts on good to firm and dead ground. *B. W. Hills*   **103**

SUPREME COURT 5 b.g. Yashgan 126 – My Natalie 64 (Rheingold 137) [1991 9m 7.5f 1992 11.1m³ 8g⁵ 9f] lengthy, sparely-made gelding: seems of little account. *M. Dods*   **–**

SUPREME DESIRE 4 gr.f. Grey Desire 115 – Fire Mountain 87 (Dragonara Palace (USA) 115) [1991 5m² 6f a7g 5m 5f 5h 6.1m 6g 8m 1992 5m 5f² 5m⁵ 5m 6m³ 5g⁴ 6g² 6g⁵ 5g* 5s 5d*] leggy, shallow-girthed filly: consistent handicapper: successful in autumn at Carlisle (first win) and Edinburgh: effective at 5f and 6f: acts on firm and dead ground, seemingly not soft. *A. Smith*   **55**

SUPREME MASTER 2 b.c. (Feb 9) Primo Dominie 121 – French Surprise (Hello Gorgeous (USA) 128) [1992 7m 7g 7m] 2,400Y: good-topped colt: second reported foal: half-brother to 3-y-o 1m winner Handsome Gent (by Dunbeath): dam unraced: shaped encouragingly when seventh of 17 in maiden auction at Leicester: always behind in similar event there later in September: looks sort to do better. *R. Hannon*   **53** p

SUPREME OPTIMIST 8 b.g. Absalom 128 – Cachucha (Gay Fandango (USA) –
132) [1991 a7g 5m 7m 5g 7d a6g a6g⁶ a6g⁴ 1992 a6g 6g 5s 7s] small, workmanlike
gelding: poor mover: of little account nowadays. *R. E. Peacock*

SUPREME SOVIET 2 ch.c. (Apr 14) Presidium 124 – Sylvan Song (Song 132) 49
[1992 5d⁶ 5g⁶ 7g 7d a7g] 1,000Y: unfurnished colt: first foal: dam poor sister to very
useful Shark Song, successful at up to 9f, and to dam of Prince Sabo: poor maiden:
will stay 1m. *J. S. Haldane*

SURAGON 2 ch.c. (Feb 22) Superlative 118 – Blue Rag 70 (Ragusa 137) [1992 –
5g⁶] 8,200F, 28,000Y: big, lengthy colt: half-brother to several winners, including
fair sprinter Blubella (by Balidar) and to dam of useful sprinter Almost Blue: dam 9f
winner: green, soon well outpaced in 6-runner £7,600 event at York in September:
should do better. *J. Wharton*

SURE HAVEN (IRE) 3 b.g. Sure Blade (USA) 130 – Tea House 107 (Sassafras 75
(FR) 135) [1991 7.1s 8.1m² 1992 12g² 12.5g⁴ a12g* 12.1s 12g a14g⁶] strong, rangy
gelding: poor mover: won maiden at Southwell in May: off course 5 months (gelded)
and below form in handicaps after: should stay 1¾m + . *Sir Mark Prescott*

SURE LORD (IRE) 3 ch.c. Sure Blade (USA) 130 – Lady Graustark (USA) 73
(Graustark) [1991 7.1s⁵ 7m³ 6.9f⁴ 7g³ 1992 7g 6m³ 5.7m² 6m² 6m⁵ 6g* 6d 7m]
workmanlike colt: moderate mover: well below form after winning handicap at
Brighton in August: stays 6f: acts on good to firm ground: below form when visored
once. *W. R. Muir*

SURELY GIFTED (IRE) 3 b.c. Sure Blade (USA) 130 – Gift Wrapped 116 –
(Wolver Hollow 126) [1991 8.1d⁶ a8g⁶ 1992 10d 11.6g 13.1m] lengthy, angular,
unfurnished colt: poor maiden on most form: sold 1,300 gns Ascot June Sales. *W. R.
Muir*

SURE PRIDE (USA) 4 b.g. Bates Motel (USA) – Coquelicot (CAN) (L'Enjoleur –
(CAN)) [1991 8g 10d 13g³ 16.2m⁶ a12g⁴ 14. 1f 15.4m⁶ 1992 12v] big gelding: has a long
stride: rated 66 at best at 3 yrs: on the downgrade. *A. Moore*

SURE RIGHT (IRE) 2 b.c. (Apr 9) Sure Blade (USA) 130 – Crown Witness 95 45
(Crowned Prince (USA) 128) [1992 8s 7.1s⁴ 8.2s] 15,000F: lengthy, unfurnished
colt: half-brother to fairly useful 1990 2-y-o 7f winner Trojan Crown (by Trojan Fen)
and 9f and 10.6f winner Oral Evidence (by Rusticaro): dam miler: poor form in
autumn maidens: will stay 1¼m. *J. W. Hills*

SURE RISK 2 b.f. (Feb 2) Risk Me (FR) 127 – Spinney Hill (Dominion 123) [1992 46 d
5g³ 5.1g a5g⁴ 5g⁶ a7g 6s] 24,000F, 12,000Y: tall, unfurnished filly: first foal: dam
poor close relative of prolific winner Misty Halo: went wrong way after third in
Sandown maiden auction: trained first 5 starts by R. Hannon: one to avoid. *M. W.
Easterby*

SURE SHARP (USA) 5 b.h. Sharpen Up 127 – Double Lock 104 (Home Guard 109
(USA) 129) [1991 10m 8d³ 8m² 8m² 8g* 8m* 9m⁵ 1992 9g* 10g 8m² 7m² 8g³ 8s⁶

*Earl of Sefton EBF Stakes, Newmarket—
one and a half lengths separate Sure Sharp from Adam Smith*

9m[5]] big, good-topped horse: has a fluent, round action: very useful performer: game winner of Earl of Sefton Stakes at Newmarket in April by 1½ lengths from Adam Smith: ran well most starts after, placed in pattern company at the Curragh (2) and Newcastle: should prove at least as effective at 1¼m as 7f: acts on good to firm ground, seemingly unsuited by soft: sometimes edges right and carries head awkwardly but has run respectably for lady rider. *B. W. Hills*

SURE SHOT NORMAN 3 b.c. Song 132 – Angel Drummer 59 (Dance In Time (CAN)) [1991 6g 5d 5m[5] 6g 1992 6s 7m 8g[2] 8g[6] 6g[3] 7g[3] 7m 7g 8.2s[4]] good-topped colt: good walker: moderate mover: none too consistent plater: sold to join G. H. Jones 1,000 gns Ascot November Sales: may prove ideally suited by 7f/1m: possibly needs an easy surface. *J. Sutcliffe* **44**

SURE TO WIN (IRE) 3 ch.g. Sure Blade (USA) 130 – Mahabba (USA) 74 (Elocutionist (USA)) [1991 5g* 5m[6] 7g 8f 8f[2] a8g[2] 1992 a7g[6] a10g[3] a8g[2] 9s[4] 8m[3] 8d] lengthy gelding: modest handicapper: not seen out after June: stays 1¼m: acts on firm ground and all-weather surfaces: effective blinkered or not: trained first 3 starts by A. Bailey. *D. Morris* **56**

SURF 3 ch.c. Sharpen Up 127 – Ebbing Tide (USA) (His Majesty (USA)) [1991 7g[2] 1992 10f* 10.3f[3] 12m] good-topped colt: has a rather round action: won maiden at Newbury and good third of 4 to Binkhaldoun in minor event at Doncaster in May: not seen out again after running as if something amiss in King Edward VII Stakes at Royal Ascot: should stay 1½m. *Mrs J. Cecil* **95**

SURF BOAT 3 ch.f. Master Willie 129 – Wave Dancer 76 (Dance In Time (CAN)) [1991 7m 8m 1992 12d[4] 14s[3] 13.8g[6] 12v[2] a12g] medium-sized, unfurnished filly: modest maiden: stays 1¾m: acts on heavy going: sometimes bandaged: found little third start: sold to join N. Tinkler's stable 5,600 gns Newmarket December Sales. *B. W. Hills* **65**

Howard Kaskel's "Surrealist"

SURPRISE OFFER 2 b.g. (Apr 20) Superlative 118 – Vexed Voter (Pontifex 94 (USA)) [1992 5d 5g³ 5f² 5.2d⁵ 5.7d* 5.3d* 5g³ 5d³] 6,200F, 7,600Y: sturdy, good-quartered gelding: moderate walker: good mover: brother to a winner in Malaysia and half-brother to several winners, including useful Italian sprinter Manoftheyear (by Sayf El Arab): dam useful 5f winner in Ireland: progressive sprinter: won maiden (made all, by 8 lengths) at Bath and minor event (not blinkered and below best) at Brighton in September: very good third to Up And At 'Em in Cornwallis Stakes at Ascot and to Ansellman in listed race at Doncaster: best in blinkers: has been gelded. *R. Hannon*

SURPRISE PARTNER 2 ch.c. (May 7) Local Suitor (USA) 128 – Test Case 90 46 (Busted 134) [1992 5d 5g 7f³] leggy colt: first foal: dam lightly-raced 1m winner probably stayed 1½m: third in seller at Redcar in June: dead. *M. Johnston*

SURPRISE SURPRISE 2 b.f. (Mar 1) Robellino (USA) 127 – Fair And Wise 75 67 p (High Line 125) [1992 7.1s*] 4,400Y: small, sturdy filly: third foal: half-sister to 7f and 1m winner Venus Observed and 1¼m seller winner Musical Note (both by Sharpo): dam suited to 1¾m: 5-length winner of maiden auction at Chepstow in September, soon clear 2f out: refused to enter stalls before Newmarket nursery following month. *H. Candy*

SURREALIST (IRE) 4 b.c. Tate Gallery (USA) 117 – Natuschka (Authi 123) 108 [1991 10m* 12m* 12m* 12s4 1992 12g⁶ 12f⁵ 12m³ 13.4g2 12m] strong colt: fluent mover: very useful performer: best runs in 1992 when placed in listed races at Goodwood (to Spinning) and Chester (to Jahafil): beaten when badly hampered 1f out in Newmarket listed race final run: should prove better suited by 1¾m than shorter: probably acts on any going. *B. W. Hills*

SURREY DANCER 4 b.g. Shareef Dancer (USA) 135 – Juliette Marny 123 77 (Blakeney 126) [1991 12g² 12.3d⁵ 10g* 10.1m³ 10d³ 10.9m 10d 8.9m 10.3d² 9g 1992 8.5g⁵ 10s4 10d* 10m* 10.4m 10.1f² 10f⁶ 10.1d* 9d* 9d 10.5d⁶ 9s³] leggy gelding: usually impresses in appearance: poor mover: had good season in handicaps in 1992, successful at Leicester, Pontefract (gamely), Yarmouth and Goodwood (amateurs): should prove as effective at around 1m as 1¼m: probably acts on any going: effective blinkered or not: usually held up. *B. Hanbury*

SURREY RACING 4 b.g. Electric 126 – Garnette Rose 74 (Floribunda 136) 76 [1991 6f* 7g* 7g³ 7m³ 7g 1992 7g 6g 7g² 6d 7f 7f² 7g* 5.7f* 6.9m* 6.9m² 7.6d⁶ 7d 7d 7g*] neat gelding: has a round action: had a good season in 1992, successful in Wolverhampton claimer, Bath seller (no bid) and handicaps at Folkestone and

Richmond-Brissac Trophy (Handicap), Goodwood—
fourth win of the season for Surrey Dancer, in this amateur riders event

Newmarket: effective from 5.7f to 7f, and will stay 1m: has form on dead ground, but best efforts on a sound surface: held up. *G. Lewis*

SUSANNA'S SECRET 5 b.h. Superlative 118 – Queens Welcome 60 (Northfields (USA)) [1991 6s 7m⁵ 7m² 7m 7m 7.6m 7g 7m 7m 7g* 7m⁶ 7g 1992 7g 7m⁵ 7.1m 7f⁵ 7g 7f² 7g 7g 7g 7s] strong, close-coupled horse: keen walker: has a quick action: inconsistent handicapper: better at 7f than 6f: best form on a sound surface: ran fairly well when blinkered: has joined S. Norton. *W. Carter* **48**

SUSIE CREAMCHEESE 5 b.m. Netherkelly 112 – Melfio Miss 40 (Town Crier 119) [1991 NR 1992 8f 12f4] leggy mare: fifth foal: half-sister to a winner in Belgium by Music Boy: dam plater stayed 7f: twice raced, and no worthwhile form: sold 1,800 gns Doncaster August Sales. *E. J. Alston* **–**

SUSQUEHANNA DAYS (USA) 2 b.f. (Apr 17) Chief's Crown (USA) – Gliding By (USA) (Tom Rolfe) [1992 7g³ 8.1d4] leggy, unfurnished filly: moderate mover: half-sister to several winners, notably Clare Bridge (by Little Current) and Song of Sixpence (by The Minstrel): dam 6f winner on only start, is closely related to top-class Key To The Mint and half-sister to Horse of the Year Fort Marcy: green and niggled along before halfway when over 8 lengths third of 16 to Sueboog in minor event at Newbury: off bridle 3f out when well beaten in maiden at Haydock later in September: will stay middle distances. *I. A. Balding* **55**

SUSURRATION (USA) 5 b.m. Erins Isle 121 – Grease 125 (Filiberto (USA) 123) [1991 10s⁴ 7g² 7.6m³ 9g² 9v* 8m* 8g² 8m⁶ 7g² 9m* 8v* 9f 1992 7g³ 8.1m* 8.5g 7.9d* 7m² 10d³ 8v] tall, angular mare: very useful and consistent performer: won listed race at Sandown in May (by short head from Cloud of Dust) and well-contested minor event at York in July: fair efforts in Goodwood listed race and Sun Chariot Stakes at Newmarket next 2 starts, but rare poor effort in Group 3 race at Milan final run: best form at 7f to 9f: acts on good to firm and heavy ground: successful for lady: has seemed ill at ease on undulating track: tough and genuine. *J. H. M. Gosden* **109**

SUZIE SUE (IRE) 3 ch.f. Ore 116 – Bridal Blush 74 (Coquelin (USA) 121) [1991 7m 1992 6s 10.5d 11.6m 11.6g a14g] lengthy filly: no worthwhile form: sold 600 gns Newmarket Autumn Sales. *D. W. P. Arbuthnot* **–**

SWAGMAN (USA) 5 ch.g. Graustark – Mawgrit (USA) (Hoist The Flag (USA)) [1991 a12g a14g⁴ a12g a12g⁴ a12g² 1992 a12g³ a12g⁶ a14g] sparely-made gelding: good mover: rated 47 at 4 yrs: seems on the downgrade. *B. Richmond* **41**

United Breweries Fillies Stakes, Sandown—
Susurration and Cloud of Dust are separated by the minimum distance

Monks Cross Stakes, York—
Susurration beats Hamas (striped cap), Lead The Dance and Norton Challenger

SWALE SIDE 3 b.g. Sayf El Arab (USA) 127 – Onika 54 (Great Nephew 126) –
[1991 a6g⁶ a7g 1992 a5g] poor maiden: should stay 7f. *Mrs M. Reveley*

SWALLOWCLIFFE 3 b.f. Caerleon (USA) 132 – La Tuerta 96 (Hot Spark 126) 74
[1991 5d⁶ 6g* 6m 1992 7.9m 7d 7g 10m 8.3g 8g³ 8.1g 8d⁶] unfurnished filly: good
mover: fair handicapper: stays 1m: best visored: sold 27,000 gns Newmarket
December Sales. *P. T. Walwyn*

SWAN HEIGHTS 3 b.f. Shirley Heights 130 – Swan Ann 84 (My Swanee 122) 70
[1991 NR 1992 10m 12g⁵ 11.7g⁴ 11.5g⁴ 14.6g 9.7m⁶ 12s* 11.8d⁴ 11.8s*] 40,000Y:
leggy, rather unfurnished filly: moderate mover: half-sister to several winners,
including very smart sprinter Primo Dominie (by Dominion) and Salisbury 2000
Guineas Trial winner Poyle Crusher (by Sweet Revenge): dam 6f winner: modest
handicapper: 5-length winner at Folkestone and Leicester in October: stays 1½m:
goes well on soft ground: sold 30,000 gns Newmarket December Sales. *J. R.
Fanshawe*

SWANK GILBERT 6 b.g. Balliol 125 – Song To Singo 63 (Master Sing 109) –
[1991 NR 1992 9.2g 8.3g 7.1d 12.1g] workmanlike gelding: of little account nowadays.
T. A. K. Cuthbert

SWAN STAR 3 br.f. Petong 126 – Lewista (Mandrake Major 122) [1991 5g 6g 6g⁴ –
6d 6f⁴ 6m 6g 1992 7d 8g 7m⁵] tall, leggy filly: on the downgrade. *G. Blum*

SWEET BLOOM 4 br.f. Durandal 114 – Soulieana 58 (Manado 130) [1991 NR –
1992 8.1d 10.3g] sparely-made filly: first foal: dam, maiden, raced only at 2 yrs:
lightly raced and no worthwhile form. *A. P. Jarvis*

SWEET BUBBLES (IRE) 4 ch.f. Dominion 123 – Regal Decoy (Troy 137) 48
[1991 a12g* a10g a12g² a12g² a14g³ 11.5m⁵ a12g* 1992 a12g⁶ a12g⁴ a12g⁵ a14g]

angular filly: poor mover: poor handicapper: stayed 1¾m: acted on all-weather surfaces: dead. *C. A. Cyzer*

SWEET DISORDER (IRE) 2 br.f. (Apr 22) Never So Bold 135 – Mists of   **62**
Avalon (USA) 76 (Nureyev (USA) 131) [1992 5d 5g 6m² 7m² 7.1m⁵ 7m 6m 7s³ 7g]
3,400Y: leggy, sparely-made filly: third foal: dam 2-y-o 1m winner successful at 7f at
3 yrs in France: modest maiden: ran well in nurseries last 3 starts: stays 7f: acts on
good to firm and soft going. *G. A. Pritchard-Gordon*

SWEETINGS SCAMPY (IRE) 2 b.f. (May 16) Taufan (USA) 119 – Renda 103   **44**
(Gulf Pearl 117) [1992 5f² 5g 6g⁴ 6m 5s 7d] IR 4,500Y: leggy, sparely-made filly:
half-sister to several winners abroad and in Ireland, including middle-distance
stayers Ranald (by Rusticaro) and Ranulph (by Lord Gayle): dam won from 1m to 11f:
failed to progress after second in maiden auction at Redcar: should stay 1m. *M. H.
Easterby*

SWEET JAFFA 3 b.f. Never So Bold 135 – Spinelle 88§ (Great Nephew 126)   **73** **§**
[1991 NR 1992 7d* 7d 8.1g⁴ 7.6s] 12,000F, 41,000Y: workmanlike, good-bodied filly:
second foal: sister to Irish maiden Ever So Bold: dam, 1½m winner, disappointing
daughter of Jacinth: won maiden at Salisbury in August: twice ran as if something
amiss in handicaps after: stays 1m: sold 27,000 gns Newmarket December Sales:
not one to trust. *Major W. R. Hern*

SWEET LIPS 3 ch.f. Vaigly Great 127 – Kenton's Girl 86 (Record Token 128)   **46**
[1991 5f⁴ 1992 7.1m*] sturdy, workmanlike filly: twice raced: won maiden at
Edinburgh in May: seemed likely to improve further. *J. G. FitzGerald*

SWEET MIGNONETTE 4 b.f. Tina's Pet 121 – Ixia 91 (I Say 125) [1991 a11g 8g   **60**
10g 12g⁵ a10g 1992 9m* 8.5m³ 9f* 8.3m* 10g³ 8.3g* 10s] lengthy, rather sparely-
made filly: moderate mover: progressed extremely well in handicaps in 1992 for new
trainer (with G. Pritchard-Gordon at 3 yrs): successful at Redcar (2, including ladies
event) and Hamilton: well beaten on first run on a soft surface in £10,400 event at
Ayr: should prove effective at 1½m: goes very well on a sound surface. *Mrs M.
Reveley*

SWEET 'N' LOW 5 b.g. Kampala 120 – Karin Maria 86 (Double Jump 131) [1991   **–** **§**
a8g⁶ a8g⁴ a10g a10g⁵ 1992 a11g⁵ a12g] angular, rather sparely-made gelding:
untrustworthy maiden: stays 1¼m: ran fairly well visored, below form blinkered. *P.
J. Feilden*

SWEET NOBLE (IRE) 3 ch.g. The Noble Player (USA) 126 – Penny Candy   **–**
(Tamerlane 128) [1991 8m 7m 7.6d³ 1992 9.9f⁶ a12g 12m] sturdy, close-coupled
gelding: poor maiden: stays 7.6f. *J. G. FitzGerald*

SWEET POPPY 2 b.f. (Feb 13) Governor General 116 – Chryseis (Anax 120)   **34**
[1992 5m 5d⁵ 5m⁵ 6g⁵ a7g] 1,350Y, 1,500 2-y-o: smallish, lengthy filly: has a round
action: fourth foal: little worthwhile form. *J. S. Wainwright*

SWEET QUEST 3 ch.f. Rainbow Quest (USA) 134 – Sweet Soprano 80 (High   **75**
Line 125) [1991 NR 1992 10d* 11.8s] lengthy, unfurnished filly: fourth foal:
half-sister to 1990 2-y-o 7f winner Leitrim Pride (by Law Society): dam, 7f and 11f
winner, is out of half-sister to Royal Hive and Attica Meli: twice-raced filly: won
maiden at Redcar: tailed off in handicap there later in October: should stay 1½m. *H.
R. A. Cecil*

SWEET REQUEST 4 b.c. Rainbow Quest (USA) 134 – Attica Meli 125 (Primera   **44**
131) [1991 1g 14m³ 10.5g⁵ 16.2d 13.3g 1992 12d 14.1d 18.1g 13.8m 14.1g³ 14.1m³
14.1m⁶ 12.3m² 12f⁵] tall, leggy colt: moderate mover: none too consistent
handicapper: effective from 1½m to 1¾m: acts on good to firm ground: below form
blinkered: has occasionally swished tail and wandered under pressure. *J. R. Bostock*

SWEET REVIVAL 4 b.f. Claude Monet (USA) 121 – Semperflorens (Don 128)   **37**
[1991 8g 12.3f 12f 10.4m 1992 8f² 10.8s⁵ a12g² a12g⁵ a12g⁶] tall filly: poor
handicapper: stays 1½m: acts on firm ground and fibresand, fair run on soft. *J. A.
Glover*

SWEET ROMEO 2 ch.g. (May 1) Local Suitor (USA) 128 – Ladoucette 102   **67**
(Bustino 136) [1992 6g⁶ 7m* 7.5d⁴ 6f⁶ 6g] IR 2,000Y: useful-looking gelding:
progressed well physically: half-brother to several winners, including Irish middle-
distance stayer Les Dancelles (by Pas de Seul): dam, Irish mare, stayed well: made
most when winning maiden at Ayr in June: first home on far side when good sixth in
nursery at Newmarket but last of 19 in Tattersalls Breeders Stakes at Leopardstown 6 weeks after: will be well suited by 1m+: acts on good to firm and dead
ground. *M. Johnston*

SWELLEGANT 3 b.f. Midyan (USA) 124 – Jubilee Song 71 (Song 132) [1991 6f² – 6m 5g* 1992 5g⁵ 5g] sturdy, well-made filly: good walker and mover: rated 84 at 2 yrs: stays ran poorly in spring at 3 yrs: stays 6f: usually bandaged behind. *W. J. Haggas*

SWELL TIME (IRE) 4 b.f. Sadler's Wells (USA) 132 – Amata (USA) (Nodouble 30 (USA)) [1991 9m 12f 11.7g 12.4m 18.1m 1992 a7g⁶ 10m⁴ 8.9m a12g³ a12g³ a12g⁶ a12s³] small filly: poor handicapper: should prove ideally suited by 1¾m +: acts on good to firm ground and fibresand: tongue tied down last 2 starts: sometimes bandaged behind. *C. N. Allen*

SWIFTLET (IRE) 2 ch.f. (Mar 13) Sure Blade (USA) 130 – Tapaculo 94 (Tap On 45 Wood 130) [1992 5g² 5m 6m⁶ a6g 7d 6m a6g] IR 2,700Y: small, good-topped filly: second foal: dam 2-y-o 7f winner, is half-sister to high-class middle-distance stayer High Hawk, dam of In The Wings: failed to progress after second in maiden auction at Pontefract, tried blinkered final start: should stay beyond 5f: sold out of M. Bell's stable 3,200 gns Newmarket July Sales after third start. *D. J. S. Cosgrove*

SWIFT REVENGE 2 ch.f. (Mar 13) Precocious 126 – Carolynchristensen 58 35 (Sweet Revenge 129) [1992 6m 7s⁶ 7.1s a7g] smallish, good-bodied filly: fourth foal: closely related to modest sprinter Maid Welcome (by Mummy's Pet) and half-sister to 3-y-o Canadian Capers (by Ballacashtal), successful at 5.7f (at 2 yrs) and 7.6f: dam won from 5f to 9.4f: poor maiden. *M. R. Channon*

SWIFT ROMANCE (IRE) 4 ch.g. Coquelin (USA) 121 – Douschkina 86 65 (Dubassoff (USA)) [1991 7g 8g* 8g 7.6g⁵ 10.1m 8m 5.7m² 7.1g⁵ 7g 6f 7.1m³ 7.6g 8.9m 9g⁶ 1992 8.1g³ 8.2m⁴ 8.3g 9d 8g 8s 8m] leggy, workmanlike gelding: moderate walker: inconsistent handicapper: should prove suited by 9f +: best efforts on sound surface: takes good hold. *B. R. Millman*

SWIFT SILVER 5 gr.g. Bairn (USA) 126 – Asmalwi 61 (Averof 123) [1991 a10g³ 62 10g 10.1d* 11.7g³ 10m⁵ 11.1d²9g 10.3d² 1992 10d² 12g³ 10m⁶ 10g 10g² 10.9d* 11.6g* 11.6g⁴ 9g 12s⁵] leggy, sparely-made gelding: has round action: modest handicapper: won at Ayr (amateurs) in July and Windsor in August: stays 1½m: acts on good to firm and dead ground: sometimes bandaged/hangs left. *W. J. Musson*

SWIFT SPRING (FR) 2 b.f. (Jan 24) Bluebird (USA) 125 – Schezerade (USA) 50 p (Tom Rolfe) [1992 8.1s³] 33,000Y: leggy, workmanlike filly: first foal: dam French 10.5f and 1½m winner, is closely related to April Run: bandaged off-fore and green, one pace from 3f out when 5½ lengths third of 5 to Lead Note in maiden at Haydock in October: will do better. *P. F. I. Cole*

SWIFT STREAM 4 ch.f. Chief Singer 131 – Sandstream 72 (Sandford Lad 133) – [1991 6m 5g⁶ 7g² 8m 8g⁶ 1992 7d 7g] tall, lengthy, dipped-backed filly: rated 58 at 3 yrs: on the downgrade. *A. Barrow*

SWIFT SWORD 4 gr.g. Sayf El Arab (USA) 127 – Lydiate 77 (Tower Walk 130) – [1991 8d⁴ 8g⁴ 8m* 8m 10f* 12g⁴ 13.9g 11.9g⁵ 10.9m³ 1992 10d⁴ 12g⁶] good-topped gelding: moderate walker and mover: useful handicapper: should have proved better suited by 1½m than shorter: never raced on soft ground, appeared to act on any other: lazy sort, who needed plenty of driving: dead. *Mrs M. Reveley*

SWINGING LADY 4 ch.f. Ballacashtal (CAN) – Parabems 72 (Swing Easy – (USA) 126) [1991 6f⁴ 6g⁶ 7m 5f⁴ 7f² 6f⁵ 7f³ a8g⁵ a7g 1992 a7g² a7g 8g⁵ a6g² a6g* a63 6.1d a6g² a6g a6g* 5m⁵ 5g 5m 6d a6g⁵ a6g⁴ a6g⁵] big, leggy, sparely-made filly: modest handicapper: successful in 1992 at Southwell (2), first in an apprentice maiden: effective from 6f to 7f: acts on firm ground and fibresand: has run well for claimer: sometimes bandaged behind. *W. W. Haigh*

SWINGING TICH 3 b.f. Swing Easy (USA) 126 – Little Tich (Great Nephew 53 126) [1991 NR 1992 5f² 6g³ 7g 6m³ 6g 6m 6.1g³ 8s 8d 6s⁵ a6g⁶ a6g³ a6g² a7g a7g] 600Y: leggy, rather plain filly: first living foal: dam, an unraced twin, is half-sister to very useful 1¼m winner Sirenivo: maiden handicapper: stays 6f (stiff tasks at 1m): acts on any going. *B. A. McMahon*

SWING LOW 3 ch.c. Swing Easy (USA) 126 – Little Tich (Great Nephew 126) 111 [1991 5g⁶ 6m* 6.1s* 6m* 6g* 7s* 1992 7d³ 8g 7d³ 8g³ 6s*] angular, leggy colt: has a quick action: very useful performer: third in Greenham Stakes at Newbury, Supreme Stakes at Goodwood and listed race at Newmarket: best effort to win Group 3 event at Rome in November by 2½ lengths from Arranvanna: off course 5 months after 2000 Guineas at Newmarket, where prominent 6f and beaten 6¾ lengths: seems ideally suited by 6f or 7f: acts on good to firm and soft ground. *R. Hannon*

SWING LUCKY 7 b.g. Swing Easy (USA) 126 – Bounding (Forlorn River 124) – [1991 NR 1992 6v⁶ 8s] big, workmanlike gelding: moderate mover: on the downgrade. *K. T. Ivory*

SWING O'THE KILT 3 b.f. Hotfoot 126 – La Piccolina 85 (Tudor Rhythm 112) –
[1991 5m 6f a6g 7m a7g 1992 a8g⁶] small filly: of no account. *P. Calver*

SWISS MOUNTAIN 2 b. or br.f. (May 30) Formidable (USA) 125 – Helvetique 50
(FR) (Val de Loir 133) [1992 7s 7g⁶ 8s 6d 6v4] lengthy filly: has a round action:
half-sister to several winners, including smart stayer Harly (by Pharly): dam won
twice at around 1¼m in France: poor maiden: should be suited by 1m+: acts on
heavy ground. *D. R. Laing*

SWORD MASTER 3 b.g. Sayf El Arab (USA) 127 – Swordlestown Miss (USA) 82
(Apalachee (USA) 137) [1991 7m 7f² 8m³ 8g* 10g⁵ 1992 10.5d 10f 8g4 10g⁵ 11.5m*
11.5g⁶ 11.7d² 10.5d² 10.5s² 10m4 10v⁶] strong, workmanlike gelding: carries
condition: fair handicapper: won at Lingfield in August: good second 3 times
subsequently: better at around 1½m than shorter: acts on good to firm ground and
soft: has run well for inexperienced rider. *Bob Jones*

SWYNFORD FLYER 3 b.f. Valiyar 129 – Qualitairess 49 (Kampala 120) [1991 –
NR 1992 a7g a8g⁶ 8g] 2,100Y: plain, good-topped filly: second foal: dam 1m winner:
no worthwhile form. *J. F. Bottomley*

SYBARITIC SAM (IRE) 3 b.c. Tate Gallery (USA) 117 – My Natalie 64 56
(Rheingold 137) [1991 7f 7m 8.1d⁵ a8g* a8g4 1992 7m 8.1g 12m⁵ 11.6m 9.7g4] useful-
looking colt: has a quick action: modest handicapper: should have stayed 1½m:
dead. *N. A. Callaghan*

SYBILLIN 6 b.g. Henbit (USA) 130 – Tea House 107 (Sassafras (FR) 135) [1991 –
a11g² 10m* 10.1m⁶ 10.3m4 8m² 1992 8.2s] compact gelding: has a quick action:
lightly-raced handicapper on flat: always behind in October: keen sort, best at 1m to
1¼m: acts on good to firm ground: smart hurdler, top-class novice chaser. *J. G.
FitzGerald*

SYKE LANE 3 b.f. Clantime 101 – Redgrave Design 77 (Nebbiolo 125) [1991 5m³ 35
5m 6d³ 6g 7g² 7.1m 8m 1992 7.5g 10d 8g 7.1m4 7d⁵ 8g⁵ 6g⁶ 6.9g³ 8s4 8s 6s] small,
sparely-made filly: poor plater: stays 1m: acts on soft ground. *R. M. Whitaker*

SYLVA HONDA 4 ch.c. Adonijah 126 – Wolverhants 79 (Wolver Hollow 126) 106
[1991 7g⁶ 7g 8.5f* 7g 7.6g³ 7.3f⁶ 7m 9m 1992 7g 7.9m² 8.5g⁶ 7.3d 8d 7f 8m] leggy,
lengthy colt: has good form in spring, sixth in Diomed Stakes at Epsom, but subsequently off course 2½ months and lost his form: stays 8.5f: yet to race on very soft
ground, acts on any other: has gone well at Epsom: game front runner. *C. E. Brittain*

SYLVAN BREEZE 4 b.c. Sulaafah (USA) 119 – Langton Herring (Nearly A 84 d
Hand 115) [1991 8g 6m4 6g 6g³ 6m 6d 7g⁶ 1992 6f³ 5g 6f⁶ 6h² 5g 6m² 5f⁵ 6m 5.2g⁵
a5g 5m 6m a7g⁵ a7g] sturdy, good-quartered colt: has a round action: unreliable
maiden handicapper: bred to stay beyond 6f, but headstrong: acts on firm ground:
ran creditably when blinkered/visored: tends to hang and a hard ride. *P. Mitchell*

SYLVANIA (IRE) 2 b.c. (Apr 23) Thatching 131 – Salvationist (Mill Reef (USA) 71
141) [1992 8.2g4 7s 8v²] 8,400F, 54,000Y: quite attractive colt: half-brother to
several winners, including fair 1m to 13.3f winner Failiq (by Bustino) and fairly
useful 10.6f winner Sartorius (by Henbit): dam, French 11f and 11.5f winner, is out of
half-sister to Lorenzaccio: fair form in autumn maidens: will be better suited by
1¼m: acts on heavy ground. *R. Hannon*

SYLVAN (IRE) 3 b. or br.f. Taufan (USA) 119 – Unspoiled (Tina's Pet 121) [1991 83
5g³ 6m² 6g* 6m* 6m 6m² 7m 1992 7g 8g 8.1g² 8m⁵ 7.6s³ 8.9d³ 8m 7g] fair
performer: has a markedly round action: fair handicapper: will stay 1¼m: acts on
soft ground. *C. F. Wall*

SYLVAN SABRE (IRE) 3 b.g. Flash of Steel 120 – Flute (FR) (Luthier 126) 82 d
[1991 5d* 5m² 6g* 6g 6d² 7f³ 6m⁵ 8s 7.3g⁵ 1992 7.5s 6g 7.1d 7g 6g4 6g 7.6d³ 7d 8m
6s4 6.9v] good-bodied, close-coupled colt: has a markedly round action: inconsistent handicapper: effective at 6f and probably stays 1m: acts on any going: twice
blinkered, running well first time only: not to be trusted. *P. Mitchell*

SYLVAN STARLIGHT 2 b. or br.f. (Apr 6) Sylvan Express 117 – Kakisa 81 60
(Forlorn River 124) [1992 a6g² 6f³ 6v² 5d²] 4,000Y: lengthy, unfurnished filly: has
scope: fourth foal: half-sister to sprint winners Lake Mistassiu, Fenton Lake and
Darling Miss Daisy (all by Tina's Pet): dam 5f and 6f winner: modest maiden: stays
6f: acts on heavy ground and fibresand. *Sir Mark Prescott*

SYMMETRICAL 3 ch.c. Kris 135 – Flawless Image (USA) 109 (The Minstrel –
(CAN) 135) [1991 7d 1992 10g] angular colt: twice raced: well beaten in minor event
at Windsor, first run for over 8 months: sold 2,100 gns Ascot November Sales. *B. W.
Hills*

SYSTEMATIC   3 b.c. All Systems Go 119 – Greyburn 85 (Saintly Song 128) [1991   **63**
5g⁶ 5g⁶ 6.1g⁴ 7g³ 7d⁶ 1992 8d⁵ 8.2g 8d 10.2m³ 8.5d* 8g⁴ 8.1d⁵] good-topped colt:
moderate mover: modest handicapper: won claimer at Epsom in July: not seen again
after that month: stays 1¼m: acts on good to firm and dead ground: sold to join T.
Caldwell 5,800 gns Newmarket Autumn Sales. *R. Hannon*

T

TAAHHUB (IRE)   2 b.c. (Mar 31) Nordico (USA) – Undiscovered (Tap On Wood   **83**   p
130) [1992 7g* 7d²] 14,500F, 78,000Y: first foal: dam Irish maiden: won maiden at
Lingfield in September: looked green still when 3½ lengths second to Emperor
Jones in minor event at York over 3 weeks later: will stay 1m: will improve again. *B.
W. Hills*

TABKIR (USA)   2 b. or br.c. (Feb 11) Storm Cat (USA) – Taruma (USA) (In   **51**
Reality) [1992 6g 7d] 250,000Y: angular colt: fourth foal: dam French maiden: sire
(by Storm Bird) high-class juvenile: behind in maidens at Newmarket and Leicester
(took drawn hold) over 6 weeks later. *J. L. Dunlop*

TACHYON PARK   10 b.h. Frimley Park 109 – Frimley's Alana 73 (Lear Jet 123)   **–**
[1991 5g 5m⁶ 5f⁶ 5.2m⁵ 5.2f³ 5f⁵ 5m³ 5f⁵ 5f⁴ 5.7f 5.2f³ 5g⁵ 5m⁶ a6g a5g⁵ a5g a6g⁵
a6g 1992 a5g 5g 5f 5m⁶ 7.1m 5m 5.1m 5g 6m] strong, good-quartered horse: no
worthwhile form in 1992 and last win came 42 starts ago, in 1989: usually blinkered/
visored. *P. Howling*

TACIT MAC (USA)   3 b.c. Tasso (USA) – Third And Ten (USA) (Pass Catcher   **59**   p
(USA)) [1991 NR 1992 a8g*] 5,800 2-y-o: fifth foal: half-brother to several minor
winners in America: dam minor stakes winner at 1m: 3/1, won 6-runner maiden at
Southwell in December, pushed along firmly to draw 1½ lengths clear of Believe In
Me inside last furlong: will improve. *W. A. O'Gorman*

TACITURN (USA)   2 ch.f. (Apr 8) Tasso (USA) – Angling (USA) (Angle Light   **32**
(USA)) [1992 a8g a8g⁶] $45,000Y: fourth foal: half-sister to 1990 6f and 7f winner
Hokusai (by Fighting Fit), later smart at around 9f and also creditable seventh in
Derby: dam ran twice: sire won Breeders' Cup Juvenile and stayed 1¼m: poor form
in maidens late in the year. *Sir Mark Prescott*

TACTICAL MISSION (IRE)   4 b.g. Rainbow Quest (USA) 134 – Our Village   **68**
(Ballymore 123) [1991 10g 12d3 12g² 12d² 12da12g* 14g 12d 1992 17.1d³ 16d⁶ 16.2m³   a78
a14g*] lengthy, angular gelding: moderate mover: fair handicapper: won at
Southwell (2 out of 2 there) in May: acts on good to firm and dead ground,
best form on fibresand: won novice hurdle in December. *J. Akehurst*

TADORA (IRE)   3 gr.g. Tate Gallery (USA) 117 – Silbadora 67 (Don (ITY) 123)   **58**
[1991 6d⁶ 6s⁵ 5m⁴ 6g 6m 5.7g 1992 a8g³ a10g 7d 7m 7f⁴ 8g⁶ 8f 7g* 7g 6.9m a7g a10g
7g a8g* a8g² a8g] tall gelding: moderate mover: inconsistent handicapper: won at
Lingfield in July and November: stays 1m: acts on equitrack, below form on a soft
surface. *C. J. Benstead*

TAFFY JONES   13 br.g. Welsh Pageant 132 – Shallow Stream 100 (Reliance II   **–**
137) [1991 10.8m 1992 13.1g⁵] big gelding: carries plenty of condition: moderate
chaser: no longer of much account on flat. *M. McCormack*

TAFRAH (IRE)   3 b.f. Sadler's Wells (USA) 132 – Minnie Hauk (USA) 100 (Sir   **71**
Ivor 135) [1991 NR 1992 7d 10d 10s* 12g] 620,000Y: tall, attractive filly: closely
related to very useful 6f to 1m performer Aviance (by Northfields), later dam of
Chimes of Freedom, and half-sister to a winner in USA by Kings Lake: dam, winner
at 7f and 1m, is sister to Malinowski and Gielgud, and half-sister to the dam of El
Gran Senor: only worthwhile form when winning maiden at Newbury in July, leading
over 3f out: edgy, tailed off in £7,300 handicap there 4 weeks later: stayed 1¼m:
possibly best with plenty of give in the ground: visits Diesis. *Major W. R. Hern*

TAFSIR   3 b.f. Doulab (USA) 115 – Sit Elnaas (USA) 82 (Sir Ivor 135) [1991 NR   **61**   d
1992 8g⁵ 8.9g² 11.5m⁴ 12d⁴ 10s 8.9d] sturdy filly: first foal: dam, staying maiden,
granddaughter of Juliette Marny: plating-class maiden: best efforts first 2 starts,
tailed off final 2: sold 2,000 gns Newmarket Autumn Sales. *H. Thomson Jones*

TAGETES   3 br.f. Chief Singer 131 – Sandford Lady 116 (Will Somers 114§) [1991   **55**   d
5g⁶ 1992 6d 5g³ 6m³ 6.1g 6m 6g] rather leggy filly: poor mover: modest maiden:
below form after second outing: blinkered, well beaten in selling handicap final
start, in July: stays 6f: acts on good to firm ground: claimer ridden: *J. Pearce*

TAHASUN (IRE) 2 b.c. (Feb 3) Shareef Dancer (USA) 135 – Narjis (USA) 87   **68**
(Blushing Groom (FR) 131) [1992 5.1m⁶ 5.9f³ 5.1h*] strong, lengthy colt: carries
condition: has a quick action: first foal: dam, 2-y-o 5f winner, is half-sister to 3 useful
or better winners at up to 1m out of smart 6f to 7f stakes winner Mashteen:
progressive form: won maiden at Bath in June, running on well: should be suited by
6f + : sold 5,200 gns Newmarket Autumn Sales. *H. Thomson Jones*

TAHDEED (USA) 2 ch.c. (Apr 25) Shadeed (USA) 135 – Widaad (USA) 109 (Mr   **86**
Prospector (USA)) [1992 5v* 5v* 5g* 6m] leggy, useful-looking colt: had a long
stride: fourth foal: half-brother to a winner in USA: dam won Queen Mary Stakes:
fairly useful performer: won maiden, minor event and listed contest at the Curragh
in the spring: well-backed co-favourite, modest seventh in Coventry Stakes at Royal
Ascot: should have stayed 6f: dead. *J. S. Bolger, Ireland*

TAHDID 2 b.f. (May 2) Mtoto 134 – Yaqut (USA) 77 (Northern Dancer (CAN))   **60 p**
[1992 7g 7.1s³] sturdy, quite attractive filly: second foal: dam 2-y-o 7f winner from
family of Alydar: much better effort when keeping-on third in maiden at Chepstow in
October, not knocked about: will be better suited by 1m + : will improve again. *P. T.
Walwyn*

TAHITIAN 3 b.g. Precocious 126 – Pacificus (USA) 65 (Northern Dancer (CAN))   **70 p**
[1991 7m 7g⁶ 1992 8g 9.9g 10d 7f 8m⁵ 8d 8g² 8f⁵ 10.1f² 10d 8.3g 8m* 8m² 8m* 8m²]
well-made gelding: has a fluent, round action: fair handicapper: found his form
late-on in the season, winning twice at Pontefract and finishing very good second of
23 to Cambrian at Newmarket: best form at 1m, but should prove as effective at
1¼m: best form on top-of-the-ground: best form without blinkers, though twice ran
second in them in mid-season: should do well at 4 yrs. *Mrs J. R. Ramsden*

TAJARIB (IRE) 2 gr.f. (May 28) Last Tycoon 131 – Turkish Treasure (USA) 111   **52**
(Sir Ivor 135) [1992 6m³ 6g⁴ 5.9g⁴ 7g 7.6s] leggy, unfurnished filly: half-sister to
several winners, including smart The Miller (by Mill Reef), successful from 7f to
13f, and useful Irish juveniles Magic Mirror (by Nureyev) and Treasure Trove (by
The Minstrel): dam won over 6f and 1m at 2 yrs: modest maiden: will be better suited
by 1m: sold 5,200 gns Newmarket Autumn Sales. *J. L. Dunlop*

TAJDID (IRE) 2 ch.c. (Mar 18) Caerleon (USA) 132 – Tarib 108 (Habitat 134)   **62**
[1992 6m⁴ 7g³ 7g 8.2d 8s] strong, good-topped colt: good mover: third foal: dam
sprinter: modest maiden: blinkered first time, respectable eighth in nursery at
Pontefract in October final start: may prove best at 7f: acts on good to firm ground,
probably on soft. *H. Thomson Jones*

TAJDIF (USA) 2 br.c. (Apr 23) Storm Cat (USA) – Hankow Willow (USA) (No   **85**
Robbery) [1992 5.1g 6g* 6f* 7g 6d4 6s] $130,000Y: quite good-topped colt:
moderate mover: half-brother to several minor winners in USA: dam minor winner
at up to 7f: sire high-class 2-y-o, Grade 1 8.5f winner: fairly useful performer:
successful in good style in maiden at Yarmouth and nursery at Newmarket in the
summer: should stay 7f (something seemed amiss when tried): acts on firm and
dead ground. *D. Morley*

Colmans of Norwich Nursery, Newmarket—Tajdif is a comfortable winner

TAJFEHN (USA)   3 ch.f. Chief's Crown (USA) – Capay (USA) (Sir Ivor 135)   –
[1991 NR 1992 10.5f⁵ 12f⁵] sturdy filly: moderate mover: third foal: half-sister to a winner by Storm Bird: dam minor winner from good family: bit backward, last in maidens at Haydock and Thirsk in the summer: sold 8,800 gns Newmarket December Sales. *B. Hanbury*

TAJHIZ (USA)   2 b.c. (May 6) Woodman (USA) 126 – Princess Ivor (USA) (Sir   **79 p**
Ivor 135) [1992 7g²] $400,000Y: close-coupled colt: half-brother to Irish 1¼m winner Princess Dixieland (by Dixieland Band) and 4 minor winners in North America: dam, winner of 7 races at up to 9f, including in stakes company, is from good family: 5/1, burly and green, length second of 14 to Pamzig in maiden at Doncaster in October, breaking smartly and keeping on well to pull clear of the remainder: sure to improve, and win races. *J. H. M. Gosden*

TAJIGREY   3 gr.f. Grey Desire 115 – Taj Singh 77 (Mansingh (USA) 120) [1991   **85**
6d 1992 8v⁶ 9s 10d 7g 7g³ 8m* 7.6m⁶ 10s 9.8g* 11.8s* 12.5v4 12v* 10v3] big, lengthy filly: modest performer here when often apprentice ridden: well beaten for B. Lunness first 3 starts: won handicap at Bath in July on third of 4 outings for R. Curtis: had a break and went to France, showing much better form and winning 3 minor events in the Provinces in the autumn: stays 1½m: has won on good to firm ground but clearly well suited by plenty of give. *Guy Le Guern, France*

TAKE BY STORM (IRE)   3 b.c. Bluebird (USA) 125 – Laurel Express 76 (Bay   **76**
Express 132) [1991 NR 1992 a7g³ a8g* a12s* 13.9g 10.9s² 11.9s] 11,000Y: leggy, lengthy colt: fourth foal: dam second over 7f from 2 starts: fair performer: won maiden and handicap at Southwell in the summer: easily best effort afterwards when good second in moderately-run race at Ayr: stays 1½m, but should prove as effective at 1¼m: acts on soft going and fibresand, yet to race on top-of-the-ground. *G. M. Moore*

TAKE ISSUE   7 b.g. Absalom 128 – Abstract 73 (French Beige 127) [1991 11.5g   **33 §**
1992 a16g³] well-made gelding: lightly-raced handicapper nowadays on flat: stays 2m: acts on any going: ran poorly when blinkered as 5-y-o: fairly useful winning hurdler in 1991/2. *R. M. Flower*

TAKE IT IN CASH   3 ch.f. Ballacashtal (CAN) – Soft Secret (Most Secret 119)   **54**
[1991 7d 1992 8g 10s 5.1g 5s³ 6.1s² 5d4] strong, lengthy filly: fourth reported foal: sister to fairly useful 4-y-o sprinter Ballasecret: dam maiden in Belgium: modest maiden: best efforts when placed in handicaps at Leicester and Nottingham within 3 days in October: probably better at 6f than 5f: yet to race on top-of-the-ground. *R. Dickin*

TAKENHALL   7 b.g. Pitskelly 122 – Great Dora (Great Nephew 126) [1991 7m⁵   **74**
7g⁴ 7m³ 8g 7.9m² 7g* 8m³ 8g⁶ 7g* 7m³ 8d⁶ 7d 8g⁵ 7g 1992 7d 8g 8.1m 7f 7g⁴ 7f4 8g 8m⁴ 7d* 8m 8g⁵ 8g⁵ 8m 7g*] lengthy, workmanlike gelding: moderate mover: fair handicapper, though still runs the odd moderate race: won at York (for third year running) in September and Doncaster (apprentices) in October: best form at 7f/1m: acts on firm and dead going: tried in blinkers earlier in career: usually gets behind, and not an easy ride. *M. J. Fetherston-Godley*

TAKE ONE   6 b.h. Teenoso (USA) 135 – Old Kate 110 (Busted 134) [1991 a12g⁴   –
a13g 16g 14m⁵ 12s⁶ 11.5g 1992 17.1d 9.9g 13.1m 12.4f] lengthy, robust horse: carries plenty of condition: poor mover: no worthwhile form since 4 yrs, tailed off in blinkers final start. *R. R. Lamb*

TAKE RISKS (FR)   3 gr.c. Highest Honor (FR) 124 – Baino Bluff (Be My Guest   **116**
(USA) 126) [1991 9s³ 1992 8s* 8g⁵ 8g⁶ 8s* 8s* 8s 8s 8s] very useful French colt: first foal: dam French mile winner: won maiden race at Saint-Cloud in March and 2 mid-season pattern races, at Saint-Cloud (Prix de la Jonchere by a length from Steinbeck) and Maisons-Laffitte (beat Metal Storm a neck in Prix Messidor): below form subsequently in Prix Jacques le Marois at Deauville, Prix du Moulin de Longchamp and Prix Perth at Saint-Cloud: stays 1m: acts on soft going. *J. Lesbordes, France*

TAKE THE MICK   2 b.g. (Apr 5) Hello Sunshine 90 – Avenmore Star 47   –
(Comedy Star (USA) 121) [1992 5m 6m 7d 8s] workmanlike gelding: second foal: half-brother to 3-y-o Deborah Shelley (by Sweet Monday): dam sprint maiden: no worthwhile form in minor event and maidens. *E. A. Wheeler*

TAKE TWO   4 b.g. Jupiter Island 126 – Dancing Daughter 79 (Dance In Time   **77**
(CAN)) [1991 8.2m² 8.2g* 8m4 10.5m⁶ 10.5f 8.1s 8m 1992 8g 8.3g*] workmanlike gelding: fair handicapper: disappointing last 4 starts (including in blinkers) at 3 yrs for F. J. Houghton: well backed and returned to form when winning 20-runner

claimer at Windsor in May, leading close home: stays 8.3f: acts on good to firm ground: winning juvenile hurdler, including later in May. *J. White*

TAKE YOUR PARTNER (IRE)   2 b.f. (Jan 8) Dance of Life (USA) – Kentucky   **49** Belle 80 (Glint of Gold 128) [1992 5g 5d⁴ 6s³ 7.1g³ 7m⁴ 7g² 6m 7.1g⁵ 6g] small, sturdy filly: second foal: sister to 3-y-o Dancing Beau, 7f winner at 2 yrs: dam twice-raced daughter of half-sister to Wollow: sire (by Nijinsky) high class on turf at middle distances: poor form, including in sellers: largely consistent: will be suited by 1m + : acts on good to firm and soft ground: has run well when sweating. *M. Johnston*

TALATON FLYER   6 b.g. Kala Shikari 125 – Pertune (Hyperion's Curls) [1991   – NR 1992 8.9s⁶ 12f] leggy, lengthy gelding: modest hurdler: no worthwhile form on flat. *P. J. Hobbs*

TALB (USA)   3 b. or br.c. Caro 133 – Go March (USA) (Go Marching (USA)) [1991   **97** NR 1992 7g³ 8g* 8f³ 7d² 7s² 6m 6g] $215,000Y: close-coupled colt: half-brother to several winners, including Grade 1 9f Hollywood Oaks winner Tango Dancer (by Unconscious) and 1989 Irish 2-y-o 6f winner Saratoga World (by Saratoga Six): dam successful 5 times at 3 yrs, notably in 9f Del Mar Oaks: useful performer: off course 4½ months, won maiden at Newmarket in August: best form when placed in minor events at Doncaster, Ascot and Warwick: blinkered, fair effort in listed race at Doncaster final start: stays 1m: acts on any going: has joined T. Skiffington in USA. *J. L. Dunlop*

TALENTED   2 b.f. (Mar 17) Bustino 136 – Triple Reef (Mill Reef (USA) 141)   **63**   p [1992 8.2s⁴] 52,000Y: half-sister to 3 winners, including one-time useful middle-distance stayer Trifolio (by Touching Wood): dam unraced daughter of smart middle-distance filly Triple First and half-sister to Three Tails and Maysoon: 7/1, 8½ lengths fourth of 14 to Revere in maiden at Nottingham in October, keeping on steadily: will be very well suited by 1½m + : will improve. *J. L. Dunlop*

TALENTED TING (IRE)   3 ch.g. Hatim (USA) 121 – An Tig Gaelige (Thatch   **82** (USA) 136) [1991 5f⁴ 7.5f⁴ 8m³ 7g⁴ 8.3s⁶ a7g² a7g 1992 8.5m 7f 8m* 9f³ 9.2m* 10g* 11f³ 10g* a10g⁶ a10g²] strong, lengthy gelding: good walker: fairly useful handicapper: successful, twice in apprentice contests, at Ripon, Hamilton, Ayr and Redcar in the summer: effective at 1¼m and should stay 1½m: acts on any going: game. *P. C. Haslam*

TALENT (USA)   4 b.g. Clever Trick (USA) – Contralto 100 (Busted 134) [1991   **89** 8d⁵ 8d 7g² 7f² 7.1m² 8m⁴ 1992 7g* 8f* 7.1f⁴ 9m² 8f* 8g 8s⁶] smallish gelding: has a quick action: fairly useful handicapper: in excellent form in the summer, winning at Goodwood (claimer), Brighton and Bath: well below form at Newbury in the autumn: effective from 7f to 9f: acts on firm ground: visored in 1992: front runner. *Lord Huntingdon*

TALES OF WISDOM   3 br.f. Rousillon (USA) 133 – New Generation 91 (Young   **63** Generation 129) [1991 7g 7d a7g 1992 10.1f⁴ 12.3m* 11.5g² a12s² a12g⁴ 12g 12s] big,   a70 strong, plain filly: modest handicapper: won at Ripon in July: cocked jaw over 1f out at Southwell fourth start, and ran poorly, including in blinkers, afterwards: should stay beyond 1½m: acts on firm ground and on fibresand: sold 13,000 gns Newmarket Autumn Sales. *Sir Mark Prescott*

TALISH   4 br.g. Persian Bold 123 – Baheejah (Northfields (USA)) [1991 7v⁶ 12m³   **48**   d 11m⁵ 12.3g* 12f⁴ 11.5m³ 12f a12g a12g 1992 a11g⁶ 12g 13.8g 11m 12f⁵ 12f 12m⁵ 12.3f 8.3m 7.1m² 7d 8m 8.1f] smallish, quite good-topped gelding: inconsistent handicapper: has won one of 24 starts: effective from 7f to 1½m: acts on good to firm ground, possibly not on dead: no improvement in blinkers/visor: sold 2,000 gns Doncaster August Sales. *T. D. Barron*

TALLINO   2 b.f. (Apr 6) Robellino (USA) 127 – Labista 116 (Crowned Prince   **?** (USA) 128) [1992 6.1d 5d³ 6s* 6d³ 7s⁴ 7v⁶] 7,000Y: compact filly: half-sister to 3-y-o Brambleberry (by Sharrood) and several winners, including 1m winner Poniard (by Kris) and middle-distance winner Rushluan (by Kalaglow): dam speedy 2-y-o, appeared not to train on: third in Wolverhampton maiden in August for C. C. Elsey: won seller at Saint-Cloud following month: stays 7f. *W. J. S. Cargeeg, France*

TAMARPOUR (USA)   5 b.g. Sir Ivor 135 – Tarsila (High Top 131) [1991 16.2m²   **74** 16.1m* 18m 1992 18g³ 18.5g⁴ 16m⁶ 20m⁶] strong, lengthy gelding: fair handicapper: best effort in 1992 when fourth in Chester Cup: fair never-dangerous sixth in Ascot Stakes last time: stays 2½m: acts on good to firm ground: has run well when sweating and on edge: seems effective visored or not: sometimes wears crossed noseband: has been bandaged: has gone in snatches. *M. C. Pipe*

TAMASHA   3 b.f. Hotfoot 126 – Polonaise (Takawalk II 125) [1991 6s 6d 8m 7d⁵
1992 a8g a8g⁵ 7d 8g 10d 6s] leggy filly: has a quick action: quite modest maiden at 2
yrs for J. Shaw: no form in 1992: bred to stay middle distances. *C. J. Hill*   –

TAMIM (USA)   3 gr.c. Topsider (USA) – Passamaquoddy (USA) (Drone) [1991   88
5m* 5m⁵ 6m* 6m³ 5m* 5g* 1992 5s⁶ 6f⁴ 6g 6.1m 7g⁴ 7.9s⁵ 7.6v] lengthy colt: good
walker: has a quick action: fairly useful handicapper: stays 1m: acts on firm and soft
ground, seemingly not on heavy: blinkered twice, running creditably second
occasion: racing in Dubai. *H. Thomson Jones*

TANAGOME (USA)   2 gr.g. (Mar 19) Procida (USA) 129 – Tasha Two (USA)   70
(Cougar (CHI)) [1992 5g⁴ 5s³ 6f⁶ a7g³ 5.9g² 7.6s⁴ a5g* a6g⁵] 15,000Y: close-
coupled gelding: has a roundish action: third reported foal: dam twice-raced sister to
Gato Del Sol and half-sister to Tersa: fair form: clear-cut winner of maiden at Southwell late in year: stays 6f: best form on fibresand: effective visored or not, below
form in blinkers once. *S. G. Norton*

TANANA   3 b.f. Teenoso (USA) 135 – La Nureyeva (USA) (Nureyev (USA) 131)   –
[1991 8.1g⁴ 8.9m 8m⁵ 7d 1992 7d a12g⁴ a7g⁶ 8.9d] lengthy, light-framed filly:
plating-class maiden: rated 52 at 2 yrs, little worthwhile form in 1992: may prove
better suited by 1¼m: blinkered on reappearance: sold 920 gns Doncaster October
Sales. *J. G. FitzGerald*

TANCRED GRANGE   3 ch.g. Prince Sabo 123 – Carpadia (Icecapade (USA))   61 d
[1991 6m⁶ 6g* 7g³ 6m⁵ 7g² 8.9m 8g 7d 1992 9m 8m⁶ 10g⁵ 8f* 9f 8g 8s⁵ a12g a8g]
strong, lengthy gelding: moderate walker: modest handicapper: won apprentice
event at Carlisle in July: ran moderately afterwards, including in a visor: probably
stays 1¼m: acts on firm ground: sometimes carries head awkwardly: sold out of
Miss S. Hall's stable 6,100 gns Doncaster October Sales after seventh start. *B.
Preece*

TANEGRUS   4 b.g. Dunbeath (USA) 127 – Tanagrea (Blakeney 126) [1991 9g 7g   –
7d⁴ 7m² 5.1m⁴ 7f³ 7g⁴ 1992 a8g] compact, good-quartered gelding: good mover:
rated 72 at 3 yrs: wearing eyeshield, helped set strong pace when well beaten in
handicap at Lingfield in January: needs further than 5f, and stays 7f: acts on firm and
dead ground: sold 2,400 gns Ascot July Sales. *D. R. C. Elsworth*

TANFITH (CAN)   5 b.h. Chief's Crown (USA) – Foxy Olympia (USA) (Stage   100
Door Johnny) [1991 7.6d 1992 a10g* 8g² 8g³ 10m⁵] rather sparely-made horse:
useful performer: 7-length winner of minor event at Lingfield in March: ran well in
better company later in the spring, including when head second to Daros in listed
event at Doncaster: effective from 1m to 1¼m: acts on good to firm ground and
equitrack. *J. E. Banks*

TANGO TIME   4 ch.g. Music Boy 124 – Liberty Tree 96 (Dominion 123) [1991 6m   58 +
7g 8g 6v² 6s* 5.1f* 5s* 5g² 5g³ 5f² 1992 5m* 6f 5.1d² 6m] strong gelding: bad
mover and withdrawn lame at start once: rated 84 at 3 yrs: didn't have to be
anywhere near best to win Sandown claimer (claimed out of R. Hannon's stable
£10,702) in May: well beaten afterwards, in seller last time: effective at 5f and 6f:
acts on any going. *N. Tinkler*

TANODA   6 b.m. Tyrnavos 129 – Anoda (FR) (Amber Rama (USA) 133) [1991 12g*   50
12.4v³ 12.3s⁶ 10.1g⁶ 12g 10d* 10.2g⁵ 10d⁵ 10.9g² 12.1g 10.5d⁴ 10.3d⁶ 12.1s a12g 1992   a–
10.3g³ 10.8v 10.5s² 10d⁶ 11.8g² a12g⁵ 12.4f⁵ 11.8g⁵ 10g² 12.1d³ 10s⁶ 10.5s] leggy
mare: poor mover: largely consistent handicapper, though proving hard to win with:
effective from 1¼m to 1½m: acts on firm and soft ground, ran moderately on
fibresand: tends to edge left, and has hung badly. *M. Brittain*

TAOS (IRE)   2 b.c. (Mar 16) Sadler's Wells (USA) 132 – Tenea (Reform 132)   100 P
[1992 8m* 8.1d* 8g*]
    Among the two-year-olds who showed winning form outside pattern
company in 1992, John Gosden's progressive colt Taos appeals more than
most as one to follow closely in the coming season. A beautifully-bred colt, by
Sadler's Wells out of a once-raced daughter of the outstanding broodmare
Stilvi, the thrice-raced, thrice-successful Taos is stabled with one of the finest
trainers in the country, and he has already shown himself capable of useful
form without any attempt having been made to get to the bottom of him. Taos
looks set to reap the benefit of patient handling when he takes on stronger
company as a three-year-old.
    There was plenty to like about Taos's initial effort, in an eleven-runner
maiden race over a mile at Doncaster's St Leger meeting in September,
where, despite looking far from fully wound up, he came home a length and a

Autumn Stakes, Ascot—Taos continues very much on the upgrade, quickening clear from Declassified (right); Iviza finished fourth

half ahead of the subsequent Royal Lodge fifth Planetary Aspect after being ridden for a turn of foot in a moderately-run race. Two weeks later, in another falsely-run race, Taos found little difficulty in disposing of the previous winners Palace Pageant and Sharjah by two lengths and a head in a disappointing three-horse turnout for the Stanley Leisure Organisation Dream Mile at Haydock. The race served to confirm that Taos possessed a useful turn of speed for a staying two-year-old, and could handle good to soft ground as capably as he could good to firm. It was his third and final appearance, when an impressive winner from eight well-regarded rivals in the listed Autumn Stakes, again over a mile, at Ascot in October, which staked his claim to consideration as a classic candidate. Any doubts that Taos would be unable to produce his turn of foot at the conclusion of a truly-run and more strongly-contested race were swept aside, as, from a position five or six lengths back on the turn for home, he stormed past the long-time leader Iviza entering the final furlong and won by three lengths. Form lines through the runner-up Declassified, an improving colt who'd chased home the Royal Lodge runner-up Geisway under similar conditions at Sandown on his previous start, and third Mukhamedov, fourth in the Laurent Perrier Champagne Stakes on his previous outing, suggest that Taos would have been worthy of a place in pattern company. The more important colts' races will certainly be on his agenda in 1993.

	Sadler's Wells (USA) (b 1981)	Northern Dancer (b 1961)	Nearctic / Natalma
		Fairy Bridge (b 1975)	Bold Reason / Special
Taos (IRE) (b.c. Mar 16, 1990)			
	Tenea (b 1979)	Reform (b 1964)	Pall Mall / Country House
		Stilvi (b 1969)	Derring-Do / Djerella

Taos, a sturdy, attractive colt, if slightly dipped-backed, will be well suited by middle distances. Neither of Tenea's other winning foals, Gold

Discovery and Gold Necklace (both by Golden Fleece), ran beyond a mile, and her own dam Stilvi was a sprinter (a good one, too, successful in five races, including the Duke of York Stakes and the King George Stakes) but there's plenty of stamina in the family. Sadler's Wells is a strong middle-distance influence, as is Taos' maternal grandsire Reform; all of Stilvi's best-known sons have stayed at least a mile, and some of them, such as the Irish Derby winner Tyrnavos, the Land of Burns winner Taxiarchos and the useful Tanaos, were very well suited by a mile and a quarter and more. Whatever his distance, Taos will continue his improvement into his second season. We fancy much more will be heard of him! *J. H. M. Gosden*

TAPESTRY DANCER 4 b.g. Lidhame 109 – Royal Bat 69 (Crowned Prince **33** (USA) 128) [1991 8d 7g 9m 10g 8g 7g² 6g⁴ 6.9m² 7g 7m 6m a8g 1992 a10g a7g⁵ 7d⁴ 8v 9m a8g 10.2f] close-coupled gelding: inconsistent maiden on flat: stays 1m: acts on good to firm and dead ground, and on equitrack: has worn tongue strap: won selling hurdle in September. *M. J. Haynes*

TAPIS ROUGE (IRE) 3 ch.c. Irish River (FR) 131 – Marie Noelle (FR) 114 **104** (Brigadier Gerard 144) [1991 NR 1992 11d* 11.5s² 10d* 11.5g* 12m⁶ 10d³] tall, angular colt: has a round action: brother to French provincial 9.5f winner Leocadia and half-brother to Prix Marcel Boussac winner Mary Linoa (by L'Emigrant): dam French 2-y-o 7.5f winner later won 3 races at up to 1¼m in USA: useful and consistent performer: won maiden at Newbury in April and minor events at Nottingham in August and Lingfield in September: stays 1½m: acts on good to firm and soft ground: sent to race in Dubai. *H. R. A. Cecil*

TARA'S DELIGHT 5 b.m. Dunbeath (USA) 127 – Tickton Bridge (Grundy 137) **61** d [1991 10f3 9.7s 8.9m* 8.9g* 9m⁴ 9s* a10g² a8g⁴ a10g² 1992 a10g³ a8g* a8g* a8g² a8g⁵ a10g³ a7g² 7m⁶ a8g a8g* a6g a7g a8g⁵ a8g] deep-girthed mare: consistent handicapper early in the year: won claimers at Southwell and Lingfield in January: trained until after fourth start by M. Ryan: some way below best when successful at Lingfield in June: effective from 1m to 11f: probably acts on any going: below best when blinkered once earlier in career: has worn tongue strap: has won for apprentice. *W. A. O'Gorman*

TARA'S GIRL 5 b.m. Touching Wood (USA) 127 – Esquire Lady (Be My Guest – (USA) 126) [1991 6g⁵ 6.1s⁴ 7m² 7g 7.6m² 6g* 7m 7d 1992 8d 8g 5.7m 6.9f 7f 8.2m 8g] small mare: rated 72 at 4 yrs: no form in 1992, trained until after fifth start by P. Blockley, next one by J. Yardley: effective from 6f to 1m: acts on good to firm and soft going: effective with or without blinkers or visor. *R. T. Juckes*

TARDA 5 ch.m. Absalom 128 – Ixia 91 (I Say 125) [1991 9f 10m 8g* 9f* 10m⁴ 9.2f² **56** 9.9f3 1992 11m⁶ 10.4m⁴ 9m⁴ 10f3 9d⁴ 8.3m² 9m* 10g⁴ 10g] angular, shallow-girthed mare: has a round action: consistent handicapper: won at Newcastle (apprentices) in July: effective at 1m, and should stay 11f: acts on firm ground: is held up: found little once at 5 yrs. *Mrs M. Reveley*

TARGET LINE 2 b.g. (May 12) Skyliner 117 – Tree Breeze 111 (Farm Walk 111) – [1992 7d 6f] 1,400Y: lengthy gelding: sixth reported living foal: dam won 9 times at up to 2¼m and was fairly useful staying hurdler: bit backward at least, tailed-off last in maidens at Chester and Pontefract in the summer. *D. McCain*

TARGET TIME 2 b.f. (May 1) Faustus (USA) 118 – Alicia Markova 64 (Habat – 127) [1992 6g⁶ 6s 8.1d 8.1s⁵] 975Y: leggy filly: has a round action: sister to 3-y-o Copper Trader and half-sister to several winners, including 1987 2-y-o 6f winner Markstyle (by Moorestyle) and 4-y-o 8.3f winner Internal Affair (by Aragon): dam, half-sister to Music Maestro, Saulingo and Outer Circle, ran 3 times at 2 yrs: little sign of ability in varied company at Haydock, blinkered last time. *D. McCain*

TARGET ZERO (USA) 2 ch.c. (Apr 3) Star de Naskra (USA) – Clouhalo (USA) – (Halo (USA)) [1992 5s 7g] $11,500Y: useful-looking colt: third foal: half-brother to a minor winner in USA: dam won at up to 9f: well-beaten last in minor event at Pontefract and maiden at Doncaster in the autumn. *M. J. Heaton-Ellis*

TARMON (IRE) 4 ch.g. Whistling Deer 117 – Royal Performance 57 (Klairon – 131) [1991 10g 10.2d 10.2g3 9.7m² 11.5m* 11.9m5 11.8m 11.7f5 9.7m 1992 14.1d 12.5s] workmanlike gelding: moderate mover: fair plater (rated 52) at 3 yrs: winning selling hurdler in 1991/2: tailed off in non-selling handicaps on flat in 1992: stays 11.5f: acts on good to firm ground: usually blinkered. *A. Barrow*

TARNSIDE ROSAL 2 b.f. (Apr 11) Mummy's Game 120 – Alison Rose 58 **68** (Jaazeiro (USA) 127) [1992 5d* 5m⁵ 6f⁵ 6m* 6f3 7g⁴ 6d⁵ 6m3] leggy filly: third living foal: sister to 1989 2-y-o 6f winner Tarnside Club and half-sister to 1m winner

Turbo Rose (by Taufan): dam lightly raced at 2 yrs, is out of half-sister to Runnett: fair performer: successful in good style in poor maiden at Carlisle in April and nursery at Newcastle in July: stays 7f: acts on good to firm (fair efforts on firm) and dead ground. *J. Etherington*

TAROOB (IRE) 3 ch.f. Roberto (USA) 131 – Tobira Celeste (USA) (Ribot 142) **62** [1991 8.2m² 8.9d* 1992 12m⁶ 14s 14.6g 14.1d⁵ 16.1s] leggy filly: modest handicapper: faced stiff tasks until creditable fifth of 20 at Nottingham: stayed 1¾m: acted on good to firm and dead ground: visits Kris. *J. L. Dunlop*

TAROUDANT 5 b.g. Pharly (FR) 130 – Melbourne Miss (Chaparral (FR) 128) **–** [1991 a11g² a12g a12g4 16.2g² 17m* 18d² 18.4d³ 18f 16.2d4 18m 1992 18g6] rangy gelding: has long stride: rated 74 at 4 yrs: shaped as if retaining all his ability at Doncaster in March: suited by good test of stamina: acts on any going except perhaps very firm. *R. J. Holder*

TARTAR'S BOW 5 b.g. Gorytus (USA) 132 – Sweet Eliane (Birdbrook 110) **–** [1991 8g6 10.5d 1992 8g6 8.1m 10.2m] lengthy, quite attractive gelding: plating-class handicapper: not seen out after June: stays 1m: best form on a sound surface: tried blinkered earlier in career. *R. J. Holder*

TARTOUKA 2 ch.f. (May 2) Vaigly Great 127 – Mrs Mainwaring (FR) 64 (Home **50** Guard (USA) 129) [1992 5.2g⁵ 6m 7s 7m⁶ 6s] tall, workmanlike filly: has a round action: first live foal: dam, maiden, stayed 10.6f: plating-class maiden: stays 7f: acts on good to firm and soft ground: sold 650 gns Ascot November Sales. *G. Lewis*

TARWIYA (IRE) 3 b.f. Dominion 123 – Touraya (Tap On Wood 130) [1991 6g² **103** 6g² 6g² 5m³ 5g* 7g* 6m² 7d* 1992 7v⁴ 8g³ 8m⁵ 8g⁵ 8s³ 7s³ 6s] first foal: dam lightly-raced French 1m winner from good family: useful Irish performer: ran consistently well after finishing 2 lengths third to Marling in Irish 1000 Guineas at the Curragh, until final outing: needs further than 6f and should stay beyond 1m: acts on good to firm and soft ground: effective blinkered or not. *J. Oxx, Ireland*

TASSAGH BRIDGE (IRE) 2 b.f. (Apr 28) Double Schwartz 128 – Kasarose **–** (Owen Dudley 121) [1992 6v] first reported foal: dam little sign of ability and temperamental at 2 yrs: 25/1, always behind when last of 9 in maiden at Folkestone in November. *J. W. Payne*

TATE DANCER (IRE) 3 b.c. Tate Gallery (USA) 117 – Namatanga (USA) **79** (Foolish Pleasure (USA)) [1991 6m⁵ 5m² 6m³ 6m² 5m* 6g 1992 5g6 7f³ 7g4 7f³ 7.1d a6g4 a6g* 6f³ 6m] leggy, sparely-made colt: moderate walker: fair handicapper: comfortable winner at Lingfield in July: likely to prove best at up to 7f: acts on firm ground and all-weather surfaces: makes running/races prominently: has run well when sweating: consistent: sold 18,000 gns Newmarket Autumn Sales. *R. W. Armstrong*

TATE EXPRESS (IRE) 3 b.c. Tate Gallery (USA) 117 – Maryville Bick (Mala- **–** cate (USA) 131) [1991 6m 7.5f4 7.5f6 1992 8.5g 8m] leggy, narrow colt: no form in 1992, blinkered when tailed off in 1m seller in May: bred to stay middle distances. *N. A. Graham*

TATHIR (CAN) 4 ch.c. Blushing Groom (FR) 131 – Great Verdict (USA) (Le **50** d Fabuleux 133) [1991 NR 1992 12.3f6 11g4 8m³ 8f5 7.6m 12.4m] good-topped colt: sixth foal: half-brother to 2 winners in USA, and French 11.7f to 2m winner Popular Decision (by Riverman): dam French 1½m winner: plating-class maiden: blinkered, tailed off final start: should stay beyond 1m: wears bandages: sold to join D. Jermy 1,050 gns Newmarket September Sales. *D. Morley*

TAUBER 8 b.g. Taufan (USA) 119 – Our Bernie (Continuation 120) [1991 a5g* **66** a6g* 6d 6g 6g 6g 5m² 5g 5g 5.2f 5g 6m 6m 6g 6d 7m 6m 5s* a6g a5g4 a6g6 1992 a6g 5s4 6g5 5f³ 5m* 5g6 5f 5m³ 6m* 6g² 6m 5.6m 7m 6d 6m a5g4 a5g] rather leggy gelding: has a markedly round action: fair handicapper: a regular at Lingfield, gaining his eleventh win there (and seventh on turf) in May: also successful at Kempton in June but generally below form last 7 starts: effective at 5f and stays 1m: acts on any going, including equitrack: good mount for inexperienced rider. *Pat Mitchell*

TAUFAN BLU (IRE) 3 b.f. Taufan (USA) 119 – Engage (Whistling Wind 123) **95** [1991 6m⁵ 5g² 1992 6d4 6g³ 5.7s⁵ 5m* 5m* 6m³ 6s4 6m 7m4 5.6m 6d 6s³ 5s] tall, leggy filly: useful and largely consistent performer: won maiden at Newcastle in March and handicaps at Newcastle (£7,200 contest) in May and Ascot (£17,900 event) in June: ran fairly well in Ayr Gold Cup and listed race at the Curragh eleventh and twelfth starts but clearly looked reluctant final one: stays 7f: acts on good to firm and soft ground: usually blinkered nowadays: tends to hang and sometimes slowly away. *M. Johnston*

TAUNTING (IRE) 4 b.g. Taufan (USA) 119 – Dancing Decoy 78 (Troy 137) **59**
[1991 8d 8g 9.5m 1992 8s² 10d³ 10s⁶ 10.8g 11.1m 10.5g⁵ 8.1m² 8g 8.9m 8.1d 10.3g⁶ 8g
a10g* a10g³] leggy, lightly-made gelding: moderate mover: inconsistent ex-Irish
handicapper: second foal: brother to Irish 11f winner Catch Twenty Two: dam placed
at 1m and 1¼m: bought out of J. Oxx's stable 2,400 gns Newmarket Autumn (1991)
Sales: narrowly won apprentice event at Lingfield in December: stays 1¼m: acts on
any going: tried blinkered earlier in career. *M. Blanshard*

TAURIAN PRINCESS 3 b.f. Electric 126 – Facetious 88 (Malicious) [1991 NR –
1992 8d a12g 12m⁶] 5,000F, 3,200Y: strong, lengthy filly: half-sister to several
winners here and abroad, including 4-y-o 11.7f winner Ryewater Dream (by
Touching Wood) and fairly useful 1982 2-y-o 5f winner Bottesford Boy (by Record
Token): dam disappointing maiden: no form in maidens and a claimer: sold to join W.
Clay 1,700 gns Newmarket July Sales and won claiming hurdle in December. *A. N.
Lee*

TAUZIO (IRE) 4 b.g. Taufan (USA) 119 – Ziobia 78 (Tribal Chief 125) [1991 NR –
1992 8m 12m 12.3g 11d] lengthy, good-topped gelding: fifth living foal: brother to
fairly useful 1987 2-y-o 5f and 6f winner Greens Masterpiece, later successful in
Italy, and half-brother to 2 winners, including one-time fairly useful but unreliable 6f
to 11f winner Qualitair Flyer (by Kampala): dam placed at up to 7f: seems of little
account. *J. Mackie*

TAWAFIJ (USA) 3 ch.c. Diesis 133 – Dancing Brownie (USA) (Nijinsky (CAN) **70**
138) [1991 6m⁵ 1992 8.2d²] good-topped, attractive colt: carrying plenty of condition
on first run for 10 months, reportedly cracked cannon bone when ¾-length second
of 5 to Deserve in minor event at Nottingham in April: sold only 6,400 gns Newmarket Autumn Sales. *H. Thomson Jones*

TAWAJJAH 2 b.c. (Mar 9) Midyan (USA) 124 – River Music (Riverman (USA) **61**
131) [1992 6s⁶ 6v³] IR 76,000Y: sixth living foal: brother to 3-y-o 6f winner Rockbourne and half-brother to useful sprint winner Time Machine (by Connaught) and
useful 1m and 9.1f winner Young Jazz (by Young Generation): dam won over 5f from
3 starts at 2 yrs in Ireland: favourite, 6 lengths third of 11 to Fabriana, better effort in
October maidens at Folkestone: will stay 7f: sold 11,500 gns Newmarket Autumn
Sales. *P. T. Walwyn*

TA WARDLE 8 ch.g. Import 127 – Zephyr Lady 59 (Windjammer (USA)) [1991 –
18d 16m 13d⁶ 12s⁴ 10.5g 1992 a16g] tall, leggy gelding: of little account nowadays:
sold 875 gns Ascot November Sales. *M. Williams*

TAX AVOIDANCE (IRE) 2 b.f. (Feb 2) Mister Majestic 122 – Reparata (Juke- –
box 120) [1992 6m 5m] IR 300F: good-quartered filly: poor mover: half-sister to
several winners, including stayer Suivez Moi (by Pas de Seul): dam Irish 6f winner:
soundly beaten in seller and maiden at Windsor in June. *S. Dow*

TAYISH 2 ch.c. Chilibang 120 – More Fizz (Morston (FR) 125) [1992 5d **42**
5f³ 5.3f⁵ 7g 6m] 16,500F, 50,000Y: leggy, close-coupled colt: third foal: half-brother
to 3-y-o River Falls (by Aragon), very useful at 6f/1m and fair 6f and 7f winner Fizz
Time (by Good Times): dam French 9.2f winner from family of Zeddaan: poor
maiden: no form in blinkers last 2 starts: should stay 6f: tends to hang right: sold 920
gns Newmarket Autumn Sales. *T. Thomson Jones*

TAYLOR QUIGLEY (USA) 3 b.c. Taylor's Falls (USA) – Heather's Turn **92** d
(USA) (Turn To Mars (USA)) [1991 6g² 6f* 6g² 7.1m⁵ 6.3s³ 7v⁶ 1992 7g 10g⁴ 8m
a7g²] leggy, quite attractive colt: fairly useful form when seventh of 9 in European
Free Handicap at Newmarket on reappearance, best effort in 1992: blinkered last 2
starts, well held on equitrack in June: stays 7f: easily best form with some give in
the ground, acts on heavy. *C. N. Allen*

TAYLORS PRINCE 5 ch.g. Sandhurst Prince 128 – Maiden's Dance (Hotfoot **64**
126) [1991 8s 7g 8m² 9m* 9m 8.3d⁴ 10.1g* 9m³ 10.1m³ 10.1m⁶ 11.5m⁵ 10.1f 10.5g
10m 11.5s⁴ 1992 10d³ 10d 12g³ 12f* 12d⁴ 12f² 10.1g² 10f⁴ 12g³ 12s⁴ 12g⁴ 11.5d] leggy,
lengthy, angular gelding: moderate mover: reformed handicapper and largely
consistent in 1992: won at Doncaster in May: stays 1½m: acts on any going: has run
creditably in a visor (didn't wear one in 1992): has hung right: below par for amateur.
H. J. Collingridge

TBAB (IRE) 4 b.c. Thatching 131 – Madam Loving 99 (Vaigly Great 127) [1991 **106** ?
7d⁴ 6s* 6g 6m² 6s 6m 1992 5g⁵ 6f 5s² 6g 6m 6d 6d 5g 5m⁶] useful-looking colt: good
mover: useful performer: ran easily best race of 1992 when head second to Medaille
d'Or in listed event at Sandown in July: not discredited (in blinkers first occasion) in
quite valuable handicaps at Ascot and listed race at Newmarket last 3 starts: stays

6f: acts on good to firm ground but goes well on soft: had tongue tied down (well beaten) once at 3 yrs. *C. E. Brittain*

TEA DUST (IRE) 4 b.f. Pennine Walk 120 – Ridalia 56 (Ridan (USA)) [1991 7g **66** 8m² 7d² 8g² 7d³ 6.1m³ 8.2m² 8g 1992 7m* 7g⁴ 7m⁶] good-topped filly: fair form: wore off-side brush pricker, won (for first time) handicap at Lingfield in May: effective at 7f and 1m: best efforts on a sound surface: not seen out after June: sold 5,200 gns Newmarket December Sales. *P. J. Makin*

TEANARCO (IRE) 4 b.f. Kafu 120 – Lady Kasbah (Lord Gayle (USA) 124) [1991 **67** 7m 8.5m 5.8d 6d 5.7m⁶ 7g⁶ 6g⁵ 6f 6m* 6m 6.1d 7g 1992 6v 6s 6f² 6g⁴ 5.7f⁶ 7.1f² 6.9d⁴ 7f* 7m⁴ 7s 7s³ 6d⁵ 7g] leggy filly: fair handicapper: given strong ride by M. Roberts when winning at Salisbury in July: effective at 6f/7f: acts on any going: tried blinkered/visored earlier in career: sometimes sweats. *R. J. Holder*

TEDDY'S PLAY (USA) 3 b.c. Theatrical 128 – Stricly (ARG) (Dancing Moss **82** 113) [1991 7g⁵ 7d 8g⁴ 1992 a12g² 14g² 16.2f⁵ 14.9m* 13.9g⁴] leggy, useful-looking colt: has a round action: progressive performer: 11/4 on, won maiden at Warwick in July: good fourth of 15 to Daru in £15,300 handicap at York following month: suited by test of stamina: acts on firm going, and on fibresand: may be capable of further improvement. *J. W. Hills*

TEE-EMM 2 b.c. (May 31) Lidhame 109 – Tower Glades 90 (Tower Walk 130) **41** [1992 5g a5g⁵ a5g 5h⁶ 5g 5.2g a6g a6g* a6g] good-topped, plain colt: first foal: dam a**64** 2-y-o 5f winner: looked a poor plater prior to winning maiden at Lingfield in December at 50/1, making all: weakening when badly hampered in nursery at Southwell week later: stays 6f: easily best effort on equitrack. *P. Howling*

TEE GEE JAY 2 b.f. (Mar 25) Northern Tempest (USA) 120 – Immaculate Girl **63** 67 (Habat 127) [1992 5g 5g⁴ 6d* 6m 6m³ 7g² 7.1s] big, workmanlike filly: poor mover: fourth foal: half-sister to a winner in Italy: dam maiden should have stayed 1¼m: modest performer: won claimer at Leicester in June, coming with strong burst to lead entering last then drifting right: blinkered/visored, ran creditably last 3 starts: should stay 1m: usually bandaged behind. *C. N. Williams*

TEEJAYEM (IRE) 2 b. or br.f. (Feb 27) Mansooj 118 – Farriers Slipper (Prince **–** Tenderfoot (USA) 126) [1992 8m] lengthy, angular filly: first reported foal: dam unraced: 50/1 and backward, tailed off from 3f out in moderately-run maiden at Yarmouth in September: showed a round action. *M. C. Chapman*

TEEN JAY 2 b.c. (Feb 11) Teenoso (USA) 135 – Spoilt Again 91 (Mummy's Pet **–** 125) [1992 8v] lengthy colt: first foal: dam, 9f and 1¼m winner, is out of Park Hill winner Reload, a half-sister to 1000 Guineas winner Full Dress II: 11/1 and bit backward, tailed-off last but one in 12-runner maiden at Leicester in October. *G. Wragg*

TEES GAZETTE GIRL 3 b.f. Kalaglow 132 – Shadiliya 90 (Red Alert 127) **42** [1991 7g 8m 1992 10.3g 12.3s 9f 11g* 11.1m⁴ 13.6f4] tall, lengthy filly: poor form: won very strongly-run apprentice handicap at Redcar in July, having been some 30 lengths behind on home turn: will probably stay 1¾m: only fair efforts on top-of-the-ground, well beaten on soft: claimer ridden. *Mrs M. Reveley*

TEJANO GOLD (USA) 2 ch.c. (May 18) Tejano (USA) – Nelli Forli (USA) **49** (Broadway Forli (USA)) [1992 7s⁵ 7s] $10,000Y: leggy, unfurnished colt: fifth foal: half-brother to 2 minor winners in USA: dam unraced half-sister to Coventry winner Lake City: sire high-class 6f to 1m winner at 2 yrs: around 12 lengths fifth of 6 to Anaxagoras in maiden at Warwick, running wide bend, unable to sustain run: always well behind in similar event at Lingfield later in October: has joined P. Cole. *J. M. P. Eustace*

TELEGRAPHIC 3 gr.g. Petong 126 – Duck Soup 55 (Decoy Boy 129) [1991 NR **–** 1992 a6g³ a7g a7g³ 10m] angular gelding: bad mover: seventh foal: half-brother to several winners, including fairly useful 1985 2-y-o sprinter Crete Cargo (by King of Spain) and 1½m winner Joseph (by Rolfe): dam 7f winner from 3 starts: poor maiden: trained on debut by W. O'Gorman: off course nearly 4 months, tailed off at Lingfield in June final start: should stay 1m: sold 1,150 gns Newmarket July Sales. *M. Bell*

TELEPHONIC (USA) 2 b.g. (Apr 6) Phone Trick (USA) – Sound of Summer **34** p (USA) (Drone) [1992 a6g] $110,000Y: half-brother to several winners, including fair 1½m winner Naswara (by Al Nasr): dam winner at up to 9f, including in graded company: sire top-class sprinter: 16/1, missed break and looked green when never a factor in maiden at Southwell in December: should improve. *Sir Mark Prescott*

TELEPHUS 3 b.g. Efisio 120 – Mrs Bizz (Status Seeker) [1991 NR 1992 8.3g **53** 10m* 12s 11.5d] 5,800F, 2,200Y: compact gelding: fifth reported living foal:

half-brother to Irish 6f and 1m winner Shirley Bizzy (by Welsh Saint) and 2 maidens (one ungenuine) by Lord Gayle: dam Irish 1m and 9f winner: form only when well-backed winner of seller (bought in 6,500 gns) at Leicester in September, in rear 3f out, staying on strongly despite edging right: well below that form in handicaps on a soft surface: should prove suited by 1½m. *B. J. McMath*

TEL E THON 5 b.g. Ela-Mana-Mou 132 – Costa Rossa (ITY) (Welsh Pageant 132) [1991 16m* 16g⁶ 16m 1992 a12g 12.1g⁴ 12f] leggy ex-Irish gelding: fourth foal: dam, useful winner in Italy, is half-sister to Italian Derby winner Cerreto: easily best effort in 1991 when winning maiden at Wexford for J. Oxx: flattered when never-dangerous fourth of 6 in Chepstow apprentice race: tailed off in claimer later in July: stays 2m: acts on good to firm ground: usually blinkered, not in 1992: won over hurdles in August and (visored) September. *P. J. Jones* —

TELLGAS 3 ch.g. Precocious 126 – Gas Only 63 (Northfields (USA)) [1991 NR 1992 5.9f5 5.9f³ 8h²] 4,800Y, 1,700 2-y-o: sturdy, short-backed gelding: moderate mover: third foal: half-brother to 1987 2-y-o 6f winner Glowing Report (by Kalaglow): dam won over 9f and 1¼m, is half-sister to dam of Sarab: plating-class form at Carlisle in early-summer: probably stayed 1m: dead. *W. Storey* **55**

TELL MAMA 2 b.f. (Mar 4) Never So Bold 135 – Mums 88 (Mummy's Pet 125) [1992 6d] angular, workmanlike filly: fourth foal: dam ran only at 2 yrs, winning at 5f: 50/1 and bandaged near-hind, ran very green and not knocked about in 17-runner maiden at Goodwood in September: moved poorly down: sold 1,000 gns Newmarket Autumn Sales. *H. Candy* —

TELL NO LIES 5 b.m. High Line 125 – No Cards 109 (No Mercy 126) [1991 10g 10.1m2 10g⁴ 10.1m* 10g³ 10m* 8.9g* 8d 10.4m5 1992 9m² 8f 10.4d² 10m³ 12.3f* 11.9m 10.5s⁴ 10s* 12s] lengthy, rather angular mare: useful handicapper, better than ever in 1992: won at Ripon in August and Ayr (£10,400 event, by a short head) in September: probably needs beyond 1m these days, and stays 1½m: acts on firm and soft ground: held up and has good turn of foot, but idles in front: largely consistent. *M. H. Easterby* **96**

TEL QUEL (FR) 4 br.c. Akarad (FR) 130 – Best Girl 108 (Birdbrook 110) [1991 **123** 9.2g² 9d⁴ 10d³ 9d* 10d* 10m* 1992 9.2d⁵ 10m 10g² 12g* 12m³ 12f⁴ 10f 12g⁶] tall,

Sheikh Mohammed's "Tel Quel"

leggy colt: has a long, round stride: good-class performer: won Group 1 Aral-Pokal at Gelsenkirchen-Horst in August by a head from Snurge: not discredited in very slowly-run Prix Foy Escada at Longchamp (¾-length third to Magic Night) and Grade 1 Turf Classic at Belmont Park (4½ lengths fourth to Sky Classic) in the autumn: effective from 1¼m to 1½m: acts on firm and dead ground: trained until after penultimate start by A. Fabre in France. *C. Whittingham, USA*

TEMPELHOF (IRE) 3 b.c. Alzao (USA) 117 – Konigin Kate (GER) (Authi 123) **68**
[1991 8m 8.1d⁶ 8m 1992 10m 10m* 10.5g² 12g³ 15.4g6] sturdy, quite attractive colt: good mover: fair handicapper: gamely made all at Goodwood in June: led 1¼m and weakened over 2f out when well beaten at Folkestone final start: may prove best at up to 1½m: acts on good to firm ground: has run well for apprentice: sold to join Miss J. Doyle 15,000 gns Newmarket Autumn Sales. *J. W. Hills*

TEMPERING 6 b.g. Kris 135 – Mixed Applause (USA) 101 (Nijinsky (CAN) 138) **45**
[1991 a12g* a11g* a11g* a10g a11g* a8g a11g 8m⁶ 10f4 12g⁶ 9f³ 8m⁵ 9s4 11s⁶ 10.9g³ a76
10f⁶ 12m 12.3f⁶ 11m4 16m a12g³ a14g² a11g* a8g⁶ a12g4 1992 a12g* a10g4 a14g³
10.5s 9f⁵ 8.3m⁶ a12g⁶ 10g⁵ 12.1g 12.1d a12g⁵ 8g⁵ a12g⁶ a14g² a12g³ a12g⁵ a12g*
a8g4 a12g*] strong, good-bodied gelding: fair handicapper: easily best efforts at Southwell where successful 9 times, including in February and twice in claimers in December: best from 1½m to 1¾m: suited by fibresand, yet to show form on equitrack: probably acts on any turf going: has often sweated: usually a front runner: tough. *D. W. Chapman*

TEMPESTA ROSSA (IRE) 2 ch.f. (Mar 26) Persian Heights 129 – Red Jade –
82 (Red Gold 128§) [1992 7s 7g 5.1s] 33,000Y: neat filly: good mover: half-sister to several winners here and abroad, including fairly useful sprinter Hinari Televideo (by Caerleon) and useful winner at around 7f Mahogany (by Tap On Wood): dam 2-y-o 5f winner: bit backward, well beaten in maiden at Salisbury and minor events at Newbury and Bath in September: may do better. *B. W. Hills*

TEMPLE FORTUNE (USA) 3 br.f. Ziggy's Boy (USA) – Our Feast (USA) **74**
(Banquet Table (USA)) [1991 5g4 5.2g² 5g4 5.1g⁶ 5.7g 1992 5.1m³ 5g 5g* 5g² 5m 6g4
6d* 6d 5.2s] sturdy filly: fair handicapper: trained first 2 starts by D. Elsworth: won at Folkestone (maiden) in July and Epsom in September: ran moderately at Haydock (reluctant stalls) and Newbury afterwards: stays 6f: best efforts on good/dead ground: seems best without blinkers. *R. Hannon*

TEMPLE HILL 2 br.f. (Jan 22) Another Realm 118 – Gay Patricia 63 (Gay –
Fandango (USA) 132) [1992 a8g] 500F: first reported foal: dam stayed 7f: 33/1, slowly away and always behind in maiden at Southwell in November. *J. M. Carr*

TEMPLE ISLAND (IRE) 4 ch.f. Salmon Leap (USA) 131 – Sainthill (St –
Alphage 119) [1991 10d⁶ a11g⁶ a12g 1992 9g 17.2s 10g 13.8d] sturdy filly: no form, including when blinkered in sellers: sold 900 gns Ascot November Sales. *P. J. Makin*

TEMPLE KNIGHT 3 b.g. Never So Bold 135 – Nelly Do Da 78 (Derring-Do 131) **73**
[1991 NR 1992 10s4 14.1m4 11.4d a16g⁵ 12g² 12g* 15.4g 12m*] 6,600Y: sparely-made gelding: moderate mover: eighth foal: half-brother to several winners, including fairly useful 6-y-o 7f (at 2 yrs) to 2½m winner Retouch (by Touching Wood): dam 2-y-o 5.8f winner: fair performer: won claimers at Newmarket in August and October: should stay beyond 1½m: acts on good to firm and soft ground: tailed off (over 2m) on equitrack. *C. A. Cyzer*

TENAYESTELIGN 4 gr.f. Bellypha 130 – Opale 117 (Busted 134) [1991 NR **53 d**
1992 a10g a12g4 a12g² a16g³ 10d 10d a12g⁵ a10g 9.7m 12s] workmanlike filly: turns fore-feet out: poor mover: modest form at best: out of sorts after placed at Lingfield in February: worth a try at 1¾m: acts on dead ground and equitrack: usually races prominently. *D. Marks*

TENBY 2 b.c. (Jan 21) Caerleon (USA) 132 – Shining Water 111 (Kalaglow **125 p**
132) [1992 7m* 7d* 8s*]
Seldom has an owner monopolised the top races for two-year-olds as Khalid Abdulla did in 1992. His green, pink and white colours were carried to success in the Prix Morny, Prix de la Salamandre and Dewhurst by Zafonic, the Grand Criterium by Tenby and the Racing Post Trophy by Armiger in a run of dominance not known since 1934 when the present Aga Khan's grandfather had ownership of four of the top six colts in the Free Handicap including the top three of Gimcrack and Middle Park winner Bahram, Coventry and Dewhurst winner Hairan and Ham Stakes and Windsor Castle winner Theft. Abdulla's nearly-identical achievement of having three of the

Washington Singer Stakes, Newbury —
Tenby draws right away from Right Win and Civil Law

top four is all the more remarkable when one considers that the horse population as well as the number of owners has increased significantly in the intervening period, and that the scope of the Free Handicap was expanded in 1980 to include the best of the two-year-olds trained in France, Germany and Italy; indeed, the nearest any owner has come to it in the last thirty years was when Carlo d'Alessio's Wollow and Take Your Place were officially rated first and third in 1975 and when Mr J. R. Mullion's Hardicanute and Prominer occupied two of the top four places in 1964. Abdulla, who also had another pattern-winning two-year-old in 1992 in the July Stakes winner Wharf, will no doubt be hoping that his three first-rate two-year-olds go on to do as well as those of the Aga Khan's in 1935: between them they won the Two Thousand Guineas, Derby, St Leger, St James's Palace Stakes, Greenham Stakes, Jersey Stakes and Sussex Stakes!

Until his stable-companion Armiger ran away with the Racing Post Trophy, Tenby was all the rage in the ante-post exchanges for the Derby after establishing his credentials with a convincing two-and-a-half-length defeat of Blush Rambler and Basim in the Group 1 Grand Criterium at Longchamp in October. Tenby's performance was a high-class one, certainly one of the best from a Criterium winner in recent years and undoubtedly good enough to merit his recognition as a leading candidate for top middle-distance honours. In complete contrast to the two winners of the Criterium who preceded him, Arazi and Hector Protector, both of whom had good form at sprint distances going into the race and ended their racing careers best at a mile, Tenby will need a mile and a half or more and a strong pace to be seen to best advantage as a three-year-old. His no-frills style, evident in his pillar-to-post victory in the seven-furlong Washington Singer Stakes at Newbury on the second of his two previous appearances, was exemplified in the Criterium, where, in a race run at an end-to-end gallop on soft ground, he needed virtually all of the mile to stamp his authority on a strong field. Initially ridden close to the pace, set first by the Prix La Rochette winner Kadounor and then by the six-length Anglesey Stakes winner Basim, Tenby was sent to the front as the field

Ciga Grand Criterium, Longchamp — Tenby puts himself bang in the Derby picture;
Blush Rambler (near side) and Basim are in pursuit

approached the final bend into the short straight. For the next furlong or so, Tenby, who looked in magnificent condition, incidentally, succeeded only in maintaining a narrow advantage, but the longer the race went on the stronger and more impressive he became, and, in the final hundred yards, Tenby stretched clear in excellent style. The progressive young stayer Blush Rambler, a runaway winner of the listed Stardom Stakes at Goodwood on his previous outing, kept on strongly to snatch second bang on the line from the tiring Basim as the French, seeing their most prestigious two-year-old race go abroad for only the fifth time since the war, failed to fill any of the three places. Tenby's margin of victory over such a useful field—among those with good form who finished in a long line behind Basim were Kingmambo, Splendent and Canaska Star (second, third and fourth respectively in the Prix de la Salamandre), the Challenge d'Or Piaget winner Master Peace, the Rochette third Seaton Delaval, and the three-length Evry listed race winner Fastness, most much more experienced than he—augurs extremely well. Cecil suggested afterwards that Tenby might run again in the Racing Post Trophy three weeks later but Armiger did duty instead. Had he met Armiger at Doncaster what a race that might have been!

Tenby was sent to Longchamp the winner of both his previous races. His reputation was such that he was confidently expected to make a winning debut in the Selsey Maiden Stakes over seven furlongs at Goodwood in July. In beating Pistol by six lengths, Tenby, a well-made, good-quartered colt, easily the pick of the paddock, couldn't have been any more impressive, but with horses like Aberdeen Heather and Friendly Brave fairly close up it was evident that he hadn't beaten much of consequence and would need to achieve a great deal more to justify his sudden instalment at the head of the betting for the Two Thousand Guineas and Derby. That Tenby was a youngster of considerable ability became fully evident just two weeks later when he accounted for Right Win and Civil Law by four lengths and six in the Washington Singer Stakes at Newbury in August. The Washington Singer Stakes nearly always attracts a small field and is frequently won by a good horse—Rodrigo de Triano and Prince of Dance are amongst its recent winners—and Tenby added his name to its roll of honour with an admirable display of strong front running. Ridden to make it a severe test of stamina in the softish ground—it had been good to firm when he won at Goodwood—Tenby took the field along at a good gallop, gradually got the better of the persistent Right Win, a useful animal under the conditions, and then stayed on with great enthusiasm to draw clear.

Tenby (b.c. Jan 21, 1990)	Caerleon (USA) (b 1980)	Nijinsky (b 1967)	Northern Dancer
			Flaming Page
		Foreseer (b or br 1969)	Round Table
			Regal Gleam
	Shining Water (b 1984)	Kalaglow (gr 1978)	Kalamoun
			Rossitor
		Idle Waters (b 1975)	Mill Reef
			Midsummertime

If further evidence were needed that Tenby's future lies over middle distances then one had to look no further than his breeding: his sire Caerleon was top class at a mile and a half, over which distance he won the Prix du Jockey-Club by three lengths; his dam Shining Water ran a fine second in the Park Hill over the St Leger distance, and there is an abundance of other strong stamina influences close up in the pedigree. In common with Caerleon, who won the Anglesey Stakes as a two-year-old, Shining Water was also forward enough to win a pattern event at two, the Solario Stakes over Sandown's stiff seven furlongs. She took time to come to herself as a three-year-old, but returned to her best when chasing home Trampship in the Park Hill, after which Mr Abdulla purchased her privately for Juddmonte Farm's band of broodmares. Shining Water, whose second foal Tenby is, following the three-year-old Reflecting by Ahonoora, is a daughter of the top-class middle-distance colt Kalaglow out of the smart stayer Idle Waters. Idle Waters was a thoroughly game and genuine racemare who won three of her seventeen races, improving no end as a three-year-old when besides going one better than her daughter in the Park Hill she was placed in the Cumberland Lodge Stakes and the Princess Royal Stakes at Ascot over a mile and a half. Idle Waters has proved an overwhelming influence for stamina at stud, for she's bred a hatful of stayers including the useful fillies Heavenly Waters and Secret Waters. Tenby's third dam Midsummertime, an unraced daughter of a winning half-sister to the 1963 Two Thousand Guineas and King Edward VII Stakes winner Only For Life, threw several winners besides Idle Waters, though none of any great account, and is the foundation mare of the High Canfold Stud, from whose owners Tenby's dam Shining Water was acquired. *H. R. A. Cecil.*

TENDER LOOK (IRE) 3 b.f. Prince Tenderfoot (USA) 126 – Piercing Glances (Patch 129) [1991 7f 1992 8.9v 12g⁵ 8d] leggy, sparely-made filly: seems of little account: sold 620 gns Newmarket July Sales. *A. N. Lee* —

TENDER MOMENT (IRE) 4 b.f. Caerleon (USA) 132 – Cannon Boy (USA) (Canonero II (USA)) [1991 7m⁶ 8m⁵ a10g⁵ 1992 8s 8m⁶ 7g* 7d⁵ 7m² 7f 7m 7m³ 7g² 7s 7.3g 6.9v a7g] leggy, sparely-made filly: moderate mover: fair handicapper: flattered when 7-length winner (drew clear on stand rail) at Warwick in April: better judged on placed efforts in August: no form afterwards: best efforts at 7f: acts on good to firm and dead ground. *C. E. Brittain* **68**

TENDER MONARCH (IRE) 3 br.c. Tender King 123 – Loving Cup 93 (He Loves Me 120) [1991 5m³ 5f 5f 5g⁶ a5g 5m 7m 5g 6m 1992 6m 8g 9.9d⁶] sparely-made colt: moderate mover: poor performer: no form in 1992: sometimes blinkered or visored: may be temperamental. *P. J. Bevan* —

TENDER REACH 4 b.f. Reach 122 – Betty's Bid (Auction Ring (USA) 123) [1991 10d a7g 7f a8g⁵ 9.9f⁶ 1992 a12g] small filly: seems of little account. *R. Voorspuy* —

TENDRESSE (IRE) 4 b.f. Tender King 123 – Velinowski (Malinowski (USA) 123) [1991 7g 7g* 7g 8f 7m* 7m² 8m* 8.9m³ 8m⁴ 8g 8m 8g 8d² 1992 9d 8m 7g 8m 8f⁴ 8g⁵ 8f 8m² 10.2s* 10g⁴ 10.8s² a8g* a8g⁶] workmanlike filly: modest form: rejoined present trainer after seventh start (with D. R. Tucker previously) and impressive winner of apprentice handicaps at Bath and Southwell in the autumn: seemed well treated after both successes, but didn't confirm the form and may be unsuited by turning out again quickly: stays 11f: acts on firm and soft ground, and on fibresand. *C. J. Hill* **51**

TEN HIGH (IRE) 3 b.f. Leap High (USA) – Another Decade (Daring Display (USA) 129) [1991 6m 8.1g 7m 1992 7m 7.1m⁶ 10.3m 7.9g⁶ 8m 10.3g a12g] sparely-made filly: inconsistent maiden: trained until after second start by B. Ellison: stays 10.3f: acts on good to firm ground: no form in blinkers. *J. Dooler* —

TEN TO SIX 2 b.f. (Mar 18) Night Shift (USA) – Nigel's Dream (Pyjama Hunt 126) [1992 6f² 6f* 6s] 6,200Y: good-topped filly: third reported foal: half-sister to a winner in Italy by Kalaglow: dam ran once here then sent to Belgium: favourite, won minor event at York in June, front rank throughout and finishing strongly: tailed-off last of 11 in nursery there 4 months later: will stay 1m. *E. Weymes* **66**

TEQUILA GOLD 4 b.g. Green Ruby (USA) 104 – Diamante 83 (Sparkler 130) [1991 10d 9d² 8.2f 10.6g 10m⁴ 1992 7d 11.1v 8.1g⁴] rather angular gelding: moderate mover: poor maiden handicapper: stayed 9f: best runs on an easy surface: tried visored once: dead. *J. J. O'Neill* **38**

TEQUILA TWIST (IRE) 2 br.f. (Feb 24) Midyan (USA) 124 – Mexican Two Step (Gay Fandango (USA) 132) [1992 5g 5g⁶ 6.1m] IR 15,000Y: quite attractive filly: moderate mover: eighth foal: half-sister to several winners, including (at 1m) 3-y-o Mexican Dancer (by Dance of Life) and useful middle-distance performer Busted Rock (by Busted): dam fairly useful 2-y-o 6f winner: soundly beaten in maiden events in the summer: dead. *A. A. Scott* —

TERIMON 6 gr.h. Bustino 136 – Nicholas Grey 100 (Track Spare 125) [1991 9m* **120** 12m² 10g³ 10d⁵ 12m⁴ 10.4g* 10m 12f 1992 12g³ 10m⁴ 10s 12g⁶ 10.4g] good-topped horse: good walker: has a rather round action: twice winner of Earl of Sefton Stakes and gained most important success when landing Juddmonte International at 5 yrs: put up good-class efforts in 1992 when in frame in Coronation Cup at Epsom (1½ lengths third to Saddlers' Hall) and Prince of Wales's Stakes at Royal Ascot (3 lengths fourth behind demoted Kooyonga) well below form in Group 1 company afterwards: effective from a strongly-run 9f to 1½m: best on a sound surface: below

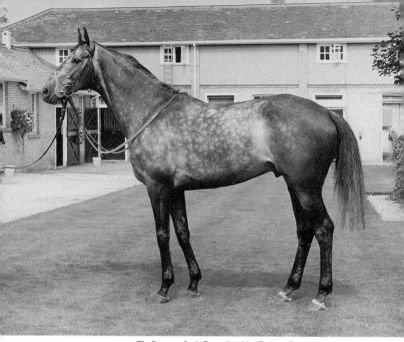

The Dowager Lady Beaverbrook's "Terimon"

form when blinkered once: retired to Barton Stud, Bury St Edmunds, fee £2,000 (Oct 1st). *C. E. Brittain*

TERNIMUS (USA) 5 ch.h. Arctic Tern (USA) 126 – Lustrious (USA) (Delaware – Chief (USA)) [1991 12d 12f2 14m6 12d 11.9m 12f 12.3f 1992 12.3d 12.3s] leggy, quite attractive horse: moderate mover: rated 70d at 4 yrs: no longer worth a rating: stays 1¾m: acts on any going: twice below form when blinkered. *B. Preece*

TERRHARS (IRE) 4 b.c. Anita's Prince 126 – Clodianus (Bay Express 132) **100** [1991 5d2 5m6 5g2 5.8m 5g3 5m4 6m5 5g* 5m3 5g5 5.2g* 5g 5.2f4 5.1m 5d4 5.2g* 5g* 1992 5g6 5g2 6g6 5g 6f 5s6 5.2d3 5.6m 5d5 5g] leggy colt: useful and consistent performer: nearly always has to carry big weights in handicaps: ran moderately in listed race sixth outing: effective at 5f and 6f: below form on soft ground once, acts on any other: usually taken alone to post: below form when sweating once at 3 yrs: tough and genuine. *R. Hannon*

TERTIAN (USA) 3 b.c. Danzig (USA) – Tertiary (USA) (Vaguely Noble 140) **110** [1991 8g* 7m* 7v2 1992 8g6 7d3 6.5g 6d a7f] big, strong, good-bodied colt: shows plenty of knee action: very useful performer: good efforts when 4 lengths sixth of 11 to Rodrigo de Triano in 2000 Guineas at Newmarket (wandering under pressure) and narrowly-beaten third in Prix du Palais-Royal at Longchamp in May: hampered in Prix Maurice de Gheest at Deauville in August and below form in Group 3 event at Maisons-Laffitte following month: beaten in stakes handicap in Florida in October: probably needs further than 6f and stays 1m: acts on good to firm and heavy ground: now with R. Frankel in USA. *A. Fabre, France*

TESLEMI (USA) 3 b.f. Ogygian (USA) – Martha Queen (USA) (Nijinsky (CAN) **73** d 138) [1991 NR 1992 8s* 8d4 11m 10m6 8g 9g 8d 10d4] $40,000Y: workmanlike filly: first foal: dam, placed at 4 and 5 yrs in USA, is sister to champion grass mare De La

Rose and Grade 1 1¼m winner Upper Nile, and is out of sister to dam of Sea Pigeon: sire, best at up to 1m (won over 9f), was high class: fair performer at best: won apprentice maiden at Newcastle in April: no worthwhile form after next outing (flattered final one): sold out of B. Hanbury's stable 6,800 gns Newmarket July Sales after fourth start: should stay beyond 1m: acts on soft going, seems unsuited by top-of-the-ground. *A. J. Maxwell, Ireland*

TETRADONNA (IRE)   4 b.f. Teenoso (USA) 135 – Miss Bali Beach 88   **95** (Nonoalco (USA) 131) [1991 7m² 8g 10.5g⁶ 10g⁴ 10.4m³ 10g 1992 10m⁴ 10g³ 12f³ 16m 10.2s⁴ 16s⁴] rangy filly: has a long stride: disappointed after debut as 3-y-o for D. Elsworth, including in blinkers once: still a maiden, but held her form for new stable until encountering soft ground last 2 starts: worth a try at 1¾m (running creditably until tired markedly over 1f out in 2m Goodwood Cup fourth outing): acts on firm ground. *R. Hannon*

TEXAN CLAMOUR (FR)   4 b.g. Vacarme (USA) 121 – Texan Maid (FR) (Tar-   **–** gowice (USA) 130) [1991 a7g³ 8g⁶ 8g² 8f* 9m² 10g⁴ 8m⁴ 10.3d 1992 a10g⁵ 8m 10.3g⁵] small gelding: rated 66 at 3 yrs for R. Hannon: little worthwhile form in 1992: stays 9f: acts on firm going: tried blinkered: sometimes bandaged off-hind. *J. S. Moore*

TEXAN TYCOON   4 b.g. Last Tycoon 131 – High Move (High Top 131) [1991 8g⁴   **75** 10g⁴ 13m² 12m⁶ 12m³ 12g⁴ 12g 14g⁵ 10s⁴ 1992 10m 10.1f³ 8g 11.9d* 12d* 12g] sturdy, good-quartered ex-Irish gelding: seventh foal: half-brother to modest 1986 2-y-o 5f winner Miss Sunday Sport (by Sharpo): dam poor maiden: trained by N. Meade as 3-y-o: fair handicapper: well backed when winning for 7-lb claimer at Brighton and Goodwood (jinked left in last 1f and idled) in the autumn: shapes as if will be better suited by 1¾m: acts on firm and dead ground: tried blinkered earlier in career. *R. Akehurst*

TEXAS COWGIRL (IRE)   2 ch.f. (May 10) Salt Dome (USA) – Cloven Dancer   **56** (USA) (Hurok (USA)) [1992 6m 6m² 6g 6s² 6v] IR 4,000Y: sparely-made filly: fourth foal: half-sister to 3-y-o 7f winner Boursin (by Taufan) and 1989 Irish 2-y-o 7f winner Bop Shop (by Prince Tenderfoot): dam Irish 1m winner: sire sprinter: modest maiden: runner-up in seller at Yarmouth and nursery at Folkestone: stays 6f: acts on good to firm and soft ground: seems inconsistent. *G. A. Pritchard-Gordon*

THAKAWAH   3 br.g. Green Desert (USA) 127 – Index To Forli (USA) (Forli   **72** (ARG)) [1991 NR 1992 8d 10.8g 7.5m³ 9.9g 16f* 14.6m³ 16.2s³] rangy gelding: fourth foal: half-brother to a winner in Italy by Sadler's Wells: dam French 10.5f winner, is half-sister to Alydar's Best: fair performer: won handicap at Ripon in June: below best in moderately-run apprentice event (when 2/1 on) and handicap at Beverley (finished very tired) afterwards: stays 2m: probably best on a sound surface: sold to join J. Old 14,000 gns Newmarket July Sales and gelded. *R. W. Armstrong*

THALEROS   2 b.c. (Apr 1) Green Desert (USA) 127 – Graecia Magna (USA) 109   **82 p** (Private Account (USA)) [1992 7m 7m³] big, strong, lengthy colt: has plenty of scope: fourth foal: brother to smart 3-y-o Thourios, best at up to 1m, and half-brother to unreliable 1991 3-y-o maiden Aellopous and useful middle-distance performer Akamantis (both by Kris): dam won at 7f and 1½m: looking very well, though better for race still, over 7 lengths third of 10 to Barathea in £8,850 event at Newmarket, travelling comfortably, keeping well: coltish on debut: will stay 1m: will do better. *G. Harwood*

THAMES GLOW   3 gr.f. Kalaglow 132 – Thamesfield Lady (Stanford 121§) [1991   **69** NR 1992 7m⁵ 8g² 6.9g* 8s⁶ 8.1d] rangy filly: first foal: dam, reluctant to race on only start, out of a 1¼m winning close relation to Mandrake Major: fair performer: odds on, won maiden at Folkestone in September: below form for 7-lb claimer in handicap and claimer (sweating, bandaged all round) following month: should stay beyond 1m: may be unsuited by a soft surface. *D. R. C. Elsworth*

THAMESTAR (IRE)   3 b.g. Al Nasr (FR) 126 – Star River (FR) (Riverman   **81** (USA) 131) [1991 NR 1992 8d⁴ 8g² 9f* 10s 10g 10.5s⁵ 12d* 12g] 52,000Y: leggy, angular gelding: fifth foal: half-brother to 7f winner Saraa-Ree and French 1m winner Sir Bruce (both by Caro): dam, winner at up to around 9f in France, is sister to top-class Irish River: fair form: won at Redcar (maiden) in May and Doncaster (handicap, got up on line under superb ride from L. Piggott) in October: sold out of J. Dunlop's stable 18,500 gns Newmarket Autumn Sales: behind in November Handicap at Doncaster: better suited by 1½m than shorter: probably acts on any going. *M. Bell*

THATCHENNE   7 b.m. Thatching 131 – Enterprisor (Artaius (USA) 129) [1991   **–** 6m* 7m 6g² 8.2d 6g* 6g 5.7m⁴ 7m⁵ 6.1m 10.3d 1992 a7g] leggy, lengthy mare: rated 53 at 6 yrs: claimed out of M. Eckley's stable £4,011 in January over hurdles: well beaten on flat following month: stays 7f: acts on firm ground: usually blinkered or visored. *P. R. Hedger*

THAWAKIB (IRE)   2 b.f. (Feb 15) Sadler's Wells (USA) 132 – Tobira Celeste **100** p (USA) (Ribot 142) [1992 6g⁵ 7s* 7d*] 260,000Y: compact filly: closely related to a winner by Lyphard and half-sister to several winners, including Celestial Storm (by Roberto): dam winner at up to 9f in France: very progressive form: won maiden at Salisbury: heavily-backed favourite, followed up in 8-runner minor event at Ascot later in September, leading 1½f out and battling on well to beat Criquette a length, pair well clear: will stay at least 1m: clearly effective in soft conditions, yet to race on top-of-the-ground: tends to carry head rather high: will improve again. *J. L. Dunlop*

THE ATHELING (IRE)   2 b.c. (Mar 1) Taufan (USA) 119 – Shady Glade (Sun **54** Prince 128) [1992 5g⁴ 5g⁵ 6d 6v a7g⁴ a8g] 12,500Y: angular, good-bodied colt: has scope: half-brother to 1988 2-y-o 5f winner Finnair Finesse (by Camden Town): dam lightly raced in Ireland: modest maiden: off course almost 6 months after second start: should stay 7f: yet to race on top-of-the-ground, fair effort on heavy. *M. H. Tompkins*

THE AUCTION BIDDER   5 b.h. Auction Ring (USA) 123 – Stepping Gaily 79 – (Gay Fandango (USA) 132) [1991 6d⁵ 6g² 7g 6m³ 6m 6m⁶ 6m⁴ 6g 7m 7s 1992 6g 6g⁶ 6g 6g 6.1s 6g 6g] robust, sprint type: carries condition: good mover: rated 97 at best at 4 yrs: no worthwhile form in 1992: stays 6f: acts on good to firm and soft going: has hung right. *R. Hollinshead*

THE BETHANIAN   2 b.c. (May 15) Absalom 128 – Jose Collins 91 (Singing Bede **54** 122) [1992 5m² 5m³] 3,000Y, 26,000 2-y-o: lengthy colt: sixth live foal: half-brother to 3-y-o Jaromic (by Tina's Pet) and a winner in Italy: dam best at 5f: placed in maiden auctions at Warwick and Redcar (bandaged behind) in July, on both occasions caught close home having looked the likely winner for a long way: taken down early and steadily: speedy. *W. R. Muir*

THE CAN CAN MAN   5 b.g. Daring March 116 – Dawn Ditty 100 (Song 132) **68** d [1991 6s³ 7m* 8m⁶ 7g* 7.6m 8g 7m 8g 7.1m³ 7m² 8f³ 7d 7g 7d 1992 6v 7g 7m⁵ 7f⁵ 8.1g⁵ 7m 7f] big, rangy gelding: turns fore-feet in: inconsistent handicapper and nowhere near so good as at 4 yrs: best efforts at 7f/1m: probably acts on any going: probably best allowed to stride on: has hung: sometimes awkward at stalls, refusing to enter them once: joined G. Fleming after final start, in June, but didn't reappear. *M. Johnston*

THE COUNTRY DANCER   2 br.f. (Apr 2) Mashhor Dancer (USA) – Slip The – Ferret 109 (Klairon 131) [1992 6.1g] 1,100Y: half-sister to 3-y-o Broughpark Azalea (by Song), Irish middle-distance winner Fly The Loop (by Kris) and a winner in Italy: dam very useful at up to 1m: 33/1, bandaged and green, last but one in 24-runner maiden auction at Nottingham in September: sold 925 gns Ascot November Sales. *Mrs L. Piggott*

Kensington Palace Graduation Stakes, Ascot—
Thawakib (right) and Criquette draw right away

THE CUCKOO'S NEST   4 b.c. Precocious 126 – Troy Moon (Troy 137) [1991   –
a8g 7s* 8g⁴ 7m⁶ 7g 7.2m³ 7m² 7g³ 7g 7g³ 8m 7.6m⁶ 1992 6.9m 7d 6m 8g a7g a7g]
close-coupled colt: rated 74 at 3 yrs: little form in 1992: sold out of C. Brittain's
stable 6,600 gns Newmarket September Sales after second start: stays 1m: acts on
good to firm and soft ground: no form in blinkers: wore eyeshield on all-weather. *M.
Williams*

THE CUT   2 ch.f. (Feb 2) Sharpo 132 – Penultimate (Final Straw 127) [1992 5s 5.1d   –
5f a7g] 2,000Y: small filly: first foal: dam once-raced daughter of very useful stayer
Wolverene: no worthwhile form: trained first 3 starts by M. Johnston and off course
7 months afterwards. *C. B. B. Booth*

THE DANDY DON (IRE)   3 ch.g. On Your Mark 125 – Balacco 70 (Balidar 133)   55
[1991 5m 6m6 1992 8.3d⁴ 8.3s³ 8.5m 8.2g³ 11.1m 11.1m⁵ 8. 1g² 8.3g³ 8m² 9.2s⁶ 8g]
modest maiden handicapper: stays 8.3f: acts on good to firm and soft ground: no
form when visored once, nor for inexperienced rider twice. *Denys Smith*

THE DEVIL'S MUSIC   8 ch.g. Music Boy 124 – Obergurgl 69 (Warpath 113)   41 d
[1991 6d 6m6 6m 6m 5.9m² 6g⁴ 6g³ 6m6 7m² 7m 1992 7d³ 8d 8.1g 7f 6.9f] robust
gelding: carries plenty of condition: turns fore-feet out: shows a quick action: poor
handicapper nowadays: last win came 27 starts ago, at 6 yrs: not seen out after
May in 1992: ran creditably on reappearance: not knocked about next 2 starts, well
beaten afterwards: stays 7f: not at best on soft going, acts on any other: no improvement in blinkers/visor. *Mrs J. R. Ramsden*

THE DOMINANT GENE   3 gr.c. Dominion 123 – Judy's Dowry 80 (Dragonara   34
Palace (USA) 115) [1991 5d 5g 5g 1992 8v 9.7g 10f5 8f² 10d a10g] leggy colt: has a
round action: poor plater: should prove suited by further than 1m: acts on firm going:
blinkered (soundly beaten) final start. *J. R. Jenkins*

THE DREAM MAKER (IRE)   3 b.f. Cyrano de Bergerac 120 – Bermuda   –
Princess (Lord Gayle (USA) 124) [1991 5m⁵ 5h⁵ 6m 7.5f 1992 5g 6m 5m⁶ a7g⁶   a50
a8g a5g⁴ a6g³ a5g* 5m⁵ 5d⁶ 6.1g a6g⁴ a6g⁵ a7g a5g] plain, angular filly: modest
performer: won apprentice handicap at Southwell in August: stays 6f: easily best
form on fibresand. *Mrs N. Macauley*

THE EXECUTOR   2 ch.g. (Feb 1) Vaigly Great 127 – Fee 111 (Mandamus 120)   68
[1992 6g 7m⁶ 7g 8.1s³ 8d⁵] lengthy gelding: half-brother to several winners, including fair stayer Franchise (by Warpath) and (at 11.5f) ungenuine Bawbee (by Dunbeath): dam 1¼m performer from stoutly-bred family: fair maiden: likely to stay
well: acts on good to firm ground: tends to carry head awkwardly: strong-galloping sort. *R.
F. Johnson Houghton*

THE FED   2 ch.g. (May 4) Clantime 101 – Hyde Princess 75 (Touch Paper 113)   63 ?
[1992 5.1g³ 5d² 5g³] small, strong gelding: first foal: dam sprinter: modest maiden:
will stay 6f: not seen out after July. *R. M. Whitaker*

THE GOLDEN SPORT   2 ch.g. (Mar 26) Risk Me (FR) 127 – Golden Guilder 69   –
(Sonnen Gold 121) [1992 5g 7d 6s 10d] small gelding: second foal: dam sprinter:
soundly beaten in varied events, including when blinkered, and after pulling hard in
1¼m seller: sold 1,000 gns Newmarket Autumn Sales. *G. Lewis*

THE GOLD SOUK (IRE)   2 b.c. (Apr 24) Wassl 125 – Gaelic Jewel 89 (Scottish   57
Rifle 127) [1992 7g⁶ 7f³ 7g⁵ 8g³ 8.2d 7d²] leggy, angular colt: fifth foal: half-brother
to 3-y-o Dark Midnight (by Petorius) and 5-y-o Irish Emerald (by Taufan), one-time
fair 1¼m handicapper: dam 1¼m winner, is daughter of very useful miler Red Ruby,
a half-sister to Laser Light: fair plater: unlucky second of 19 in nursery at Catterick,
slowly away, stumbling early on and long way behind on home turn: should be well
suited by further than 7f: yet to race on very soft ground, acts on any other: sold
6,200 gns Newmarket Autumn Sales. *J. L. Dunlop*

THE GOOFER   5 b.g. Be My Native (USA) 122 – Siliferous (Sandy Creek 123)   77
[1991 12.2d5 10s6 12.3d⁴ 12m 11.5s⁴ 12.5g⁵ 1992 10v³ 9v* 10.3g] tall gelding: has a
round action: fair performer: not seen out in 1992 until late-October, 6-length
winner of 3-runner Newcastle minor event: stiff task week later: effective from 9f to
1½m: very well suited by a soft surface. *A. P. Stringer*

THE GORROCK   3 b.g. Petoski 135 – Aquarula 88 (Dominion 123) [1991 5g 7g⁶   –
8m³ 8s 1992 13m 16.9d] IR 9,400Y: ex-Irish gelding: third foal: half-brother to 1½m
winner To Be Fair (by Adonijah): dam 2-y-o 5f and 6f winner: trained until after reappearance by P. Prendergast: soundly beaten at Wolverhampton in August on first
start for over 3 months: bred to stay 1¼m+: tried in blinkers. *A. J. Chamberlain*

THE GREY TEXAN   3 gr.c. Nishapour (FR) 125 – Houston Belle 59 (Milford   –
119) [1991 NR 1992 10m 16m] leggy, close-coupled colt: first foal: dam maiden stayed

1¼m, won over hurdles: always behind in maidens at Windsor (moved moderately to post) and Lingfield in August. *Miss B. Sanders*

THE HUYTON LADY 4 ch.f. Brotherly (USA) 80 – The Huyton Girls 67 – (Master Sing 109) [1991 7.1m 5g 5d 1992 a6g] stocky filly: of little account. *M. B. James*

THE INFORMER (USA) 2 b.c. (Feb 25) Slew O' Gold (USA) – Comicus (USA) 87 (Northern Jove (CAN)) [1992 5m³ 6m³ 7g² 8g² 7m³ 5g] $100,000Y: good-bodied colt: first foal: dam, minor winner at around 6f at 4 yrs in USA (had been placed in France at 3 yrs), is half-sister to Prix Saint Alary winner and Prix de Diane second Smuggly: sire top-class 9f to 1½m performer: off course during the summer but returned a fairly useful performer: ran excellent race when around 6 lengths seventh of 13 to Up And At 'Em in Cornwallis Stakes at Ascot: stays 1m: yet to race on a soft surface: strong-galloping sort: sure to win a race. *P. F. I. Cole*

THE INSTITUTE BOY 2 b.c. (Apr 5) Fairy King (USA) – To Oneiro 69 60 (Absalom 128) [1992 5f³ 5.1f⁶ 6g³ 6.1d 5.2g 6m a6g³ 5s 5d³ 5g⁶ a5g³] 6,400Y: smallish, strong colt: poor mover: fifth foal: brother to modest sprinter Athenian King and half-brother to 3-y-o Resa Girl (by Legend of France) and a winner in Norway: dam 5f and 6f winner: inconsistent maiden: in frame in varied races, including a seller on equitrack: stays 6f: acts on firm and dead ground: effective with or without blinkers: retained 3,500 gns Doncaster October Sales. *K. R. Burke*

THE JONES BOY (FR) 5 b.g. Top Ville 129 – Rythmique (CAN) (The Minstrel – (CAN) 135) [1991 NR 1992 11.8s⁶ 14.6g] lengthy, rather angular gelding: poor walker: rated 76 at 3 yrs for D. Burchell: well beaten in June, 1992, in selling handicap last time: sold 2,000 gns Ascot July Sales. *G. H. Jones*

THE KARAOKE KING 3 b.c. Sayf El Arab (USA) 127 – Lady Warninglid 66 (Ela-Mana-Mou 132) [1991 7m 8g⁵ 8.9m² 1992 11.6g⁶ 12.1m² 11.5m³ 11.9f 11.5m* 10d 11.9f⁴ 14.1g⁵ 10g⁶ 11.8g 12.2g³ 12v³ 10.3g a12g* a12g⁶] sturdy colt: moderate walker: good mover: modest performer: won amateurs maiden at Yarmouth in July and handicap at Lingfield in November: needs further than 1¼m and stays 1¾m: acts on firm ground and equitrack, probably on heavy: blinkered last 5 starts. *R. Hannon*

THE LAST EMPRESS (IRE) 4 b.f. Last Tycoon 131 – Beijing (USA) 89 61 (Northjet 136) [1991 13.1f 11m³ 14.6g³ 16.2g* 16m* 16.2f⁵ 17.2g⁴ 1992 11.5f⁴ 13.8d* 16g* 13.9g a16g a16g] workmanlike filly: moderate mover: modest form: straight-forward tasks when easily winning sellers at Catterick (bought in 10,600 gns) in June and Lingfield (sold out of P. Cole's stable 8,200 gns) in August: well beaten afterwards: better at around 2m than shorter: acts on good to firm and dead going. *A. S. Reid*

THE LAST WASHER (IRE) 3 b.g. Mazaad 106 – Gigo Jive (Jukebox 120) – [1991 7m⁶ 7g 7m 8m 1992 10.5d 7.1s] deep-bodied gelding: carries condition: seems of little account these days: sold out of M. Tompkins' stable 1,200 gns Newmarket September Sales after reappearance. *R. J. Baker*

THE LIQUIDISER 5 ch.g. Connaught 130 – Frivolity 70 (Varano) [1991 12s⁶ – 10d 12.5d 1992 a12g] quite good-topped ex-Irish gelding: fairly useful at 3 yrs: no form here, off course 14 months before Southwell handicap in July. *R. Hollinshead*

THE LITTLE FERRET 2 ch.c. (Feb 2) Scottish Reel 123 – Third Movement 80 p 75 (Music Boy 124) [1992 6s²] 13,000F, 9,400Y: leggy colt: brother to 3-y-o Speedo Movement and half-brother to 11f winner Pleasure Flight (by Jalmood) and a winner in Italy: dam, maiden, stayed 7f: 10/1 and green, ¾-length second of 16 to Zarani Sidi Anna in maiden at Newbury in October, never far away and keeping on well: will stay 7f + : sure to improve. *R. Hannon*

THE LOON 2 b.c. (Feb 24) Local Suitor (USA) 128 – Trojan Desert 97 (Troy 137) – [1992 6g 5d 5g 8.3s] 2,600Y: workmanlike colt: first foal: dam 7f winner later won in USA: no worthwhile form, including in a selling nursery: sold 600 gns Doncaster October Sales. *J. J. O'Neill*

THEMEDA 3 b.f. Sure Blade (USA) 130 – Choire Mhor 100 (Dominion 123) [1991 69 NR 1992 10d⁴ 10.2m⁵ a11g* 12f⁴ 14g⁵ 12g 14d] 38,000Y: sturdy filly: carries condition: moderate mover: second foal: dam (ran only at 2 yrs) triple 6f winner, is granddaughter of very useful 6f and 1¼m winner Sleat, grandam of Reprimand and Wiorno: fair performer: easily won maiden at Southwell in June: off course nearly 2 months, tailed off last 2 outings: stays 1¾m: acts on firm and dead ground, and on fibresand. *C. R. Nelson*

THE METROPOLE (IRE) 3 ch.g. Where To Dance (USA) – Mother Flutter – 62 (Gulf Pearl 117) [1991 5s⁶ 6d⁴ 7m² 7f⁵ 8.3g 7m 7g 1992 10.5d 7m 8.5s 10.3g 10f

16.2d⁶] neat gelding: fair plater at best at 2 yrs (ran poorly in blinkers once): no longer seems of much account: wore net muzzle last 4 starts. *A. W. Potts*

THE NEW GIRL 3 b.f. Primo Dominie 121 – Try The Duchess 99 (Try My Best (USA) 130) [1991 5.1m 5m⁵ 5d² 5f² 6m 5.7g³ 1992 6f² 6m² 7g 6g 6.1s 6s 6m⁴ a7g] lengthy, sparely-made filly: modest maiden: suited by 6f: acts on any going: well beaten in a visor once: usually unruly at stalls: sold 5,000 gns Newmarket December Sales. *C. C. Elsey*   **60** d

THE NOBLE OAK (IRE) 4 ch.g. The Noble Player (USA) 126 – Sea Palace (Huntercombe 133) [1991 11.7g 12m 10.6g 10.2d 7d 6m* 6m* 5.7m⁶ 1992 a5g a6g⁶ a5g a6g 6v 5g² 5g² 5m³ 5f 5.1m⁶ 5g* 5g* 5m³ 5.1d³ 5d² 5m³ 5.1m 5d⁵ 5m 5d 6.1d] small, strong, close-coupled gelding: fair handicapper between April and August: won at Goodwood and Wolverhampton in June: very speedy, but sometimes slowly away: acts on firm and dead going: usually blinkered nowadays. *M. McCormack*   **65**

THE OIL BARON 6 gr.g. Absalom 128 – Ruby's Chance 71 (Charlottesville 135) [1991 10v 12m 1992 11.5m] leggy gelding: no longer of much account. *R. P. C. Hoad*   **–**

THE OLD CHAPEL 3 b.c. Lomond (USA) 128 – Chapel Cottage 117 (Homing 130) [1991 6g 6d 6d⁶ 1992 8g 6d* 6s* 6.1g⁶ 7m 6f 7m 6d] leggy, good-topped colt: poor mover: fairly useful from best: won maiden at Pontefract and apprentice race at Ripon in April: below form afterwards, not seen out after August: should prove best at sprint distances: form only on a soft surface. *B. A. McMahon*   **88**

THE ORDINARY GIRL (IRE) 2 b.f. (Apr 29) Millfontaine 114 – Saulonika 94 (Saulingo 122) [1992 5g² 5.1s⁵ a6g³ a5g⁵] neat filly: has a round action: seventh reported foal: sister to sprinters Aughfad and Rushanes: dam 2-y-o 5f winner: modest maiden: stays 6f: acts on equitrack, below form on soft ground: bit below best in visor final start. *T. Casey*   **53**

THE POWER OF ONE 3 b.g. Bellypha 130 – Biding 97 (Habat 127) [1991 7g 6.9f³ 1992 8d⁶ 8.1g² 8.5d 8m 10m 9d] lengthy, rather dipped-backed gelding: fair form: strong-finishing second in £10,800 handicap at Sandown in April: disappointing in good handicaps afterwards: stays 8.1f. *R. Simpson*   **76** ?

THE PREMIER EXPRES 2 gr.c. (May 17) Siberian Express (USA) 125 – Home And Away (Home Guard (USA) 129) [1992 6g⁴ 7.1m³ 5g 7d³ 7.6s] 8,000Y: lengthy, quite good-topped colt: half-brother to several winners here and abroad, including 1984 2-y-o 7f winner Top of The League (by High Top): dam unraced half-sister to high-class American middle-distance performer Galaxy Libra: modest maiden: trained until after third start by B. Beasley then off course nearly 3 months: dropped to seller and best effort when third of 30 at Redcar, nearest finish: will be suited by 1m: acts on dead ground. *C. B. B. Booth*   **53**

THE PRUSSIAN (USA) 6 b.h. Danzig (USA) – Miss Secretariat (USA) (Secretariat (USA)) [1991 10g⁴ 1992 a12g] compact, rather angular horse: moderate mover: useful handicapper in 1990: lightly raced since and probably no longer of much account. *K. G. Wingrove*   **–**

THE RIGHT TIME 7 b.g. King of Spain 121 – Noddy Time 97 (Gratitude 130) [1991 6g 5g⁴ 5m⁵ 6f³ 6g 6d⁵ 6m⁶ 5g² 5f⁵ 6m 5f² a5g 5f* 5f 5f² 5g 6m 5m⁶ 5s 1992 6d 5s⁵ 5g 5d 5m² 5f³ 5f⁴ 5m 5m² 5m² 6m 5m⁴ 5g 5d³ 5d² 5g 5m³ 5s⁶ 6s 5g³ 5v⁶] robust gelding: poor handicapper: has won one of last 54 starts: best at 5f: acts on any going: blinkered. *J. Parkes*   **46**

THE ROVER'S 2 b.c. (Mar 21) Adonijah 126 – Woodrush 70 (Mummy's Pet 125) [1992 5s 5m 7m] 1,400F, 1,500Y: well-grown, lengthy, leggy colt: has a round action, sixth foal: half-brother to 1987 2-y-o 5f winner Quick Or Be Damned (by Mandrake Major): dam sprint plater: soundly beaten in maiden and sellers: sold 850 gns Doncaster September Sales. *Ronald Thompson*   **–**

THE SEER 2 b.c. (Feb 9) Robellino (USA) 127 – Serration (Kris 135) [1992 5g² 6f³ 6m³ 8.5m* 8d 7.6v*] 11,500Y: workmanlike colt: shows knee action: first live foal: dam lightly-raced maiden, fourth at 9f in France: fairly useful performer: won maiden at Beverley in September then showed much improved form when beating Anaxagoras by a head in nursery at Chester following month: will be well suited by middle distances: probably acts on any going. *B. W. Hills*   **86**

THE SHANAHAN BAY 7 b.h. Hays 120 – Tanala Bay (Sterling Bay (SWE)) [1991 5d 5g 5g⁴ 5m 5g a5g⁵ 5m⁵ 5g 5d 5g⁶ a6g a7g³ a8g a6g² a6g 1992 a6g a6g⁴ a7g a5g 6d a5g² a6g⁵ a6g³ a5g² a5g⁵ a6g] angular horse: poor mover: inconsistent handicapper: was effective from 5f to 7f: acted on any going and all-weather surfaces: usually blinkered or visored: tended to carry head high: went well with forcing tactics: dead. *Mrs N. Macauley*   **56**

THE SHARP BIDDER (IRE) 2 b.c. (Apr 21) Auction Ring (USA) 123 – My **81**
Destiny (USA) 97 (L'Enjoleur (CAN)) [1992 5g 5g⁵ 5m⁴ 5m² 6g* 6f² 6g⁵ 6m³ 5m
6m] IR 1,000Y: strong, workmanlike colt: carries condition: moderate mover:
half-brother to a winner in France by In Fijar: dam 2-y-o 7f winner: fairly useful
performer: won maiden auction at Leicester in July: best efforts when placed in
minor events at Thirsk and Doncaster: ran moderately in 3 Newmarket nurseries
(including when sweating) otherwise: best form at 6f: inconsistent. *R. Hollinshead*

THE SQUARE CENTRE (USA) 4 ro.c. Topsider (USA) – Shindy (USA) –
(Roberto (USA) 131) [1991 5g 6m⁴ 7m³ 7g⁶ 8g 1992 a7g⁶ a7g 9.7v] fourth reported
foal: half-brother to 3 minor winners in USA: dam thrice raced in USA and
successful at up to 9f: ex-Irish maiden, in frame at the Curragh and Fairyhouse
when trained by D. Weld as 3-y-o, blinkered last 2 starts: no worthwhile form in
claimers here: stays 7f: acts on good to firm ground. *P. Burgoyne*

THE STRID (IRE) 2 ch.f. (Mar 20) Persian Bold 123 – Riverine (FR) (Riverman **53** p
(USA) 131) [1992 7m] 320,000 francs (approx £32,100) Y: half-sister to several
winners here and abroad, including quite useful 1986 2-y-o 6f winner Lucayan
Knight (by Dominion) and 3-y-o 1½m winner Iron Baron (by Sure Blade): dam
French 1¼m winner: 20/1 and green, 11 lengths seventh of 14 to Magique Rond
Point in maiden at Goodwood in July, held up and never placed to challenge or
knocked about: looked sure to do better. *J. H. M. Gosden*

THE TEFLON DON 3 b.c. Myjinski (USA) – Greta's Song (Faraway Times –
(USA) 123) [1991 NR 1992 7f⁶ 5g] sturdy colt: first foal: dam no form on flat or over
hurdles: tailed-off last in maidens at Brighton (showed a quick action) and Warwick
in August. *R. Brotherton*

THE TITAN GHOST 3 ch.c. Nicholas Bill 125 – Holloway Wonder 93 (Swing **57** d
Easy (USA) 126) [1991 7d 1992 10.3g 8.2d⁴ 11.8d² 10.5d⁶ 11.9m⁶ 12s⁵ 10d 8.2g] big,
strong, rangy colt: carries condition: modest maiden: no form after finishing in
frame in April: stays 11.8f: possibly needs a soft surface: usually sweating: sold to
join S. Coathup 1,950 gns Doncaster October Sales. *B. A. McMahon*

THEWAARI (USA) 3 b.f. Eskimo (USA) – Flying Jester (USA) (Winged T) **68**
[1991 6g³ 6d 6.1d 1992 10d 6m³ 6.9m* 7.5m² 8f⁴ 7m* 7m⁶ 7m 8m 7g* 8g 7g³ 7s]
good-topped filly: impresses in appearance: good walker: fair handicapper: won at
Folkestone, Doncaster and Redcar in the summer: should prove effective at 1m:
probably unsuited by a soft surface: visored once at 2 yrs: twice below form in ladies
contests. *A. A. Scott*

THE WEND 2 b. or br.f. (Apr 15) Nomination 125 – Martini Time 90 (Ardoon 124) **42**
[1992 5g 5g⁴ 5g 5g⁴ 6g³ a6g³ 7.1s 6g 6m] small, angular filly: half-sister to several
winners here and abroad, including 5f performer Anytime Anywhere (by Daring
March): dam raced only at 2 yrs, when tough and genuine 5f performer: poor
maiden: ran poorly in nurseries (including a seller) last 3 starts: stays 6f. *D. T. Thom*

THE WHERE WITHAL 2 b.c. (Feb 27) Glint of Gold 128 – Bourgeonette 81 **62**
(Mummy's Pet 125) [1992 7s 8d 8m a8g] 12,500Y: leggy, unfurnished colt: has
scope: good mover: sixth foal: closely related to 5f to 7f winner Wantage Park (by
Pas de Seul) and half-brother to 3 winners, including middle-distance performer
Silks Domino (by Dominion): dam 1m and 1¼m winner: modest maiden: will stay
1¼m: well beaten on equitrack. *Sir Mark Prescott*

THE YOMPER (FR) 10 ch.g. Arctic Tern (USA) 126 – Grundylee (FR) (Grundy –
137) [1991 10.1g 11.5m 13.8f³ 11.5g 12v 1992 12g 11.4f⁶ 10g 10m] sturdy gelding: of
little account these days. *R. Curtis*

THIMBALINA 6 ch.m. Salmon Leap (USA) 131 – Maestrette 77 (Manado 130) **41**
[1991 12s 12d⁴ 12f* 12f² 12g⁵ 12.2f⁴ 12m² 12f³ 11.8m 16.2f⁵ 10.5g 1992 10d 12m 12f
12h² 10d* 10g³ 9.9m⁵ 12f 12d⁴ 12s³ 12.2g 12v 11.5d] leggy, lightly-made mare:
moderate walker: landed gamble in amateurs handicap at Salisbury in July: effective
from 1¼m to 1½m: not at best on very soft ground, acts on any other: races keenly:
has edged badly right. *D. A. Wilson*

THINKING TWICE (USA) 3 ch.c. Kris 135 – Good Thinking (USA) (Raja **69**
Baba (USA)) [1991 6d⁶ 6f 1992 6.9v* 8d 8d³ 8.5m³ 8m 8.3g³ 8g* 8.3g 9g] strong,
compact colt: has a quick action: fair form: won maiden at Folkestone in March:
mostly ran creditably in handicaps, but behind last 2 starts: should be suited by
further than 1m: acts on good to firm and heavy ground: sold 13,000 gns Newmarket
Autumn Sales. *P. W. Harris*

THIN RED LINE 8 b. or br.g. Brigadier Gerard 144 – Golden Keep 77 (Worden **45**
II 129) [1991 10f⁴ 12d⁴ 10m 12f 10.1g³ 11.5m⁴ 12g⁴ 10g³ 10m³ 10f² 10.1f³ 10f⁶ 10g⁶
10.1s² 10.3d 1992 10.8d⁵ 11.7d² 10m⁶ 10f⁴ 11.4f 11.9d⁴] leggy gelding: poor

handicapper nowadays: last win came 22 starts ago, in 1990: stays 1½m: acts on any going: usually visored: often sweating and edgy. *J. R. Jenkins*

THISONESFORALICE   4 b.g. Lochnager 132 – Bamdoro 54 (Cavo Doro 124) 51
[1991 NR 1992 7g⁵ 6s⁴ 8.3m⁶ 8m 8.1f⁵ 8.3g 9.2s² 9.9m 9.2v⁶ a8g] leggy gelding: inconsistent handicapper: stays 9f: best efforts on soft going: trained until after third outing by W. Pearce: well beaten in a visor. *A. Harrison*

THOMAS LENG   7 ch.g. Homing 130 – Fast Asleep (Hotfoot 126) [1991 a11g⁵   –
10.2s 9g 10.2s⁴ 10d* 10g* 10.4d⁴ 12.3d² 12g 12.4m³ 12.3g³ 11.8g⁶ 13g² 12.1m⁵
10.9m⁶ 1992 12.3m 11.8m⁴ 11.8d] leggy, rather sparely-made gelding: moderate mover: not so good as at 6 yrs (rated 69) in handicaps: effective from 1¼m to 13f: acts on good to firm ground, and has gone particularly well with give: has worn blinkers and visor, not in 1992: often bandaged: has been gelded. *M. Brittain*

THORNFIELD BOY   6 b.g. Homeboy 114 – Pink Blues 103 (Tickled Pink 114)   –
[1991 6g 6g 6m 1992 6g 6m 6g 5m⁴ 8f 6d 6g 6d] workmanlike, good-bodied gelding: carries condition: rated 103 as 3-y-o: a shadow of former self nowadays. *R. J. Holder*

THORNTON GATE   3 b.g. Hallgate 127 – Lola Black (FR) (Relkino 131) [1991 73
5m² 5m 5m 7f* 7m⁵ 6g⁵ 8m⁶ 7m 1992 7g 7f 8.5f² 7.1f⁴ 8f* 7g* 7.1d* 7g 7g 7d] leggy gelding: moderate mover: fair handicapper: apprentice ridden, won at Thirsk, Ayr and Edinburgh (best effort) in the summer: well below form afterwards: effective from 7f to 8.5f: acts on firm and dead going: seems best in blinkers/visor: takes good hold and is a front runner. *M. H. Easterby*

THOR POWER (IRE)   3 b.c. Auction Ring (USA) 123 – Kitty's Sister (Bustino 49
136) [1991 7g⁴ 6s 6d a7g⁶ a7g a8g 1992 12v³ 12.3s⁶ 12.3s² 12d⁴ 12. 1s⁴ 12.3m³ 15.8m⁴ a14g³ 17.9d³ 16.9d³ 12s] sturdy, lengthy colt: consistent maiden: suited by test of stamina: acts on good to firm and heavy going, and on all-weather: twice below form in a visor: has run creditably for 7-lb claimer: lacks turn of foot. *D. T. Thom*

THOURIOS   3 b.c. Green Desert (USA) 127 – Graecia Magna (USA) 109 (Private **117**
Account (USA)) [1991 7g* 7g⁵ 7m³ 8g 1992 8g 12g 10m 7.6m* 8m 6s² 6d⁵ 7m²]

Mr A. Christodoulou's "Thourios"

big, good-topped colt: carries condition: good walker: has a round action: smart performer: short-head winner of listed event at Lingfield in July: second to Twafeaj (beaten short head) in Prix de Meautry at Deauville in August and Challenge Stakes at Newmarket (best effort, ridden with more restraint than usual, when 2½ lengths behind Selkirk) in October: effective at 6f to 7.6f: acts on good to firm and soft ground: effective blinkered/visored or not: sweating (ran moderately) penultimate start: game. *G. Harwood*

THOUSLA ROCK (IRE)   3 ch.c. Thatching 131 – Resooka (Godswalk (USA) 130) [1991 6g 6f* 5.8d² 6m² 1992 7g 6g] quite good-topped colt: usually looks really well: has a round action: fairly useful form: not seen out until late-October and well held, though not at all discredited in listed event at Doncaster last time: stays 6f. *P. W. Chapple-Hyam*   **81 +**

THREE AND A HALF   3 b.g. Nearly A Hand 115 – Miss Comedy 56 (Comedy Star (USA) 121) [1991 NR 1992 10m 10g 10f] good-topped gelding: first foal: dam maiden plater on flat and well beaten over hurdles: no worthwhile form in maiden and (visored) sellers. *Miss L. Bower*   **–**

THREE LAKES   8 b.g. Stanford 121§ – Boundary 90 (Ballymoss 136) [1991 NR 1992 16d⁶] ex-Irish gelding: modest winning selling hurdler in January: well beaten in celebrity race in March. *S. G. Griffiths*   **–**

THREE LUCKY (IRE)   4 ch.f. Final Straw 127 – Some Dame 72 (Will Somers 114§) [1991 6.1m 6m³ 1992 5v 6f 6f⁵ 5m⁴ 5.2m⁴ 6f⁶ a5g 8.1d] compact filly: inconsistent handicapper: stays 6f: acts on firm ground. *M. D. I. Usher*   **36**

THREEOFUS   2 gr.g. (Apr 3) Robellino (USA) 127 – Teacher's Game 64 (Mummy's Game 120) [1992 5d 5g 6f] 8,200Y: good-topped gelding: second foal: half-brother to 3-y-o Lady of Letters (by Primo Dominie): dam sprint maiden close relative of Teacher's Pet: little worthwhile form in maiden events in the spring. *K. T. Ivory*   **–**

THREEPENCE   3 b.g. Sharpo 132 – Penny Blessing 112 (So Blessed 130) [1991 5v* 6g³ 5m 7m³ 6.1s⁵ 6m⁴ 1992 5g² 6d* 6g 6m³ 6f³ 7m 7g 7.1s 6d 6s³ 5d⁴ 7s* a7g*] sturdy gelding: moderate mover: fairly useful performer at his best: won minor event at Warwick in April and returned from below-par spell to land claimers at Chester and Lingfield (below form) in October: stays 7f: acts on good to firm and heavy ground: takes keen hold: effective blinkered or not: sold 8,200 gns Newmarket Autumn Sales. *J. Berry*   **89**

THREE WELLS   3 b.c. Sadler's Wells (USA) 132 – Spring Triple (USA) (Spring Double) [1991 7g⁵ 7g⁵ 8.1d² 1992 10d⁵ 11.7s⁴ 11.9f² 14g⁴ 14.6m* 14.1d² 14m³ 13.9g³ 16.2s 18m] close-coupled, useful-looking colt: moderate mover: useful handicapper: won at Wolverhampton in June: best efforts on form next 3 starts, but hung left and carried head awkwardly when third to Daru in £15,000 event at York: well beaten last 2 outings, when visored in Cesarewitch final one: should stay 2m: acts on firm and dead going: seems not to have ideal attitude: sold 20,000 gns Newmarket Autumn Sales. *J. L. Dunlop*   **96**

THRESHFIELD (USA)   6 b.h. Northern Prospect (USA) – French Cutie (USA) (Vaguely Noble 140) [1991 a7g 10.8d⁶ 7g 8m 7f* 6g 8.1g* 8m* 7s³ 1992 9.7v] tall, quite good-topped horse: rated 72 at 5 yrs: never near to challenge in handicap in November: better at 7f/1m than shorter: probably acts on any going: sometimes bandaged behind: takes keen hold and usually wears crossed noseband. *B. J. Curley*   **–**

THRIE-NA-HELAH (IRE)   3 b.f. Tender King 123 – Lady Bidder (Auction Ring (USA) 123) [1991 6g 6g³ 6m⁴ 6m* 7f² 6g* 6f 7m² 1992 6g 6.1g⁶ 7.9m 7m 6m² 7m² 7.6m⁶ 6g² 7m⁶ 6g 6s 5m] lengthy filly: moderate mover: fair handicapper: ran well fifth to eighth starts: effective from 6f to 7.6f: acts on firm ground, badly hampered on soft: seems effective visored or not: usually races prominently: sold 3,000 gns Newmarket Autumn Sales. *R. M. Whitaker*   **70**

THRILL   4 ch.f. Good Times (ITY) – Naughty Party (Parthia 132) [1991 10m a11g³ a12g a12g⁶ 12.3g 11m 1992 a12g] stocky filly: carries condition: good walker: rated 45 at 3 yrs: well beaten in February, 1992: stays 11f: no improvement in visor and blinkers. *K. G. Wingrove*   **–**

THROW AWAY LINE   3 bl.f. Petorius 117 – Corsage (FR) (Nureyev (USA) 131) [1991 5f 5f⁴ 1992 5g 6m 7d² 8m⁴ 7m 8m³ 6f⁵ 7m² 6m 8m⁶ 6.9g⁵ 7g] tall, leggy, close-coupled filly: largely consistent maiden plater: sold out of J. Etherington's stable 1,700 gns Doncaster June Sales after fifth start: stays 1m: acts on good to firm and dead ground: stiff task in a visor (looked none too keen) final start. *R. E. Barr*   **45**

THUNDERBIRD ONE (USA)   3 b.c. Star de Naskra (USA) – Grande Couture (USA) (Miswaki (USA) 124) [1991 NR 1992 8d 8g 10.2f* 10.3m³ a12g* 9.9m 10f³   **59**

10g³ 12.2g⁵ 12.3d⁴ 9.9m 10.5d 10.3g a12g⁶ a12g* a12g⁶ a12g⁵] $50,000Y: leggy, close-coupled colt: first foal: dam French 3-y-o 1m winner, successful in minor event in USA at 4 yrs: sire champion sprinter, stayed 9f: modest performer: won claimers at Bath and Southwell (claimed out of C. Nelson's stable £7,757) in the summer, and at Southwell again in December: effective over stiff 1¼m, and stays 1½m: acts on firm and dead ground, and on fibresand: has run well for amateur. *Denys Smith*

THUNDER BUG (USA)   4 ch.f. Secreto (USA) 128 – Followeveryrainbow   –
(USA) (Mehmet (USA)) [1991 12.2g⁵ 8g⁴ 8m⁵ 10.1f³ 8.3f² 9s⁵ 9.7g* 10.3d 1992 10d 10m 14g⁶ 14.1g⁶ a12g 12.3f 13.6f] leggy, close-coupled filly: rated 64 at 3 yrs: scant promise in 1992: stays 1¼m. *A. P. James*

THUNDERING   7 b.g. Persian Bold 123 – Am Stretchin' (USA) (Ambiorix II 130)   **33**
[1991 8g⁶ 9f 8.9g 12.3g 1992 a10g² 8f 8.9s* 9m 12h³ 8.5d³ 10.3g³ 10f⁴ 10g 8.9d] lengthy gelding: has a round action: none too consistent performer: won Wolver-hampton amateurs race in May: effective from around 1m to 1½m: acts on any going: tried blinkered once: has run well when sweating. *A. W. Jones*

THUNDER RIVER (IRE)   2 ch.c. (Apr 11) Thatching 131 – In For More (Don   **54** p
128) [1992 7g] IR 13,000F, 260,000 francs (approx £26,100) Y: first foal: dam unraced half-sister to useful 1978 Irish 2-y-o Just A Game, later stakes winner in USA: 25/1, around 7 lengths seventh of 18 to Azilian in maiden at Doncaster in November, slowly away and behind, stayed on well: will improve. *M. J. Heaton-Ellis*

THURSLEY   3 ch.g. Pharly (FR) 130 – Russian Waltz (USA) 75 (Czaravich   **44**
(USA)) [1991 6f 6g³ 6g² 6g* 7g a7g⁵ 1992 a8g a10g⁴ 7.5g⁴ 6m] big, workmanlike gelding: moderate mover: plating-class performer: stays 7.5f: sold 2,600 gns Ascot June Sales. *H. J. Collingridge*

THYER (USA)   3 b.c. Nijinsky (CAN) 138 – Qui Royalty (USA) (Native Royalty   **105**
(USA)) [1991 8d* 1992 a10g* 9g³ a10f 12m 8g² 8s* 8s³] tall, rangy colt: has a long stride: useful performer: won minor event at Lingfield in April (by 2½ lengths from Rokeby) and listed race at Tralee in August: creditable third to Twist And Turn in listed race at Newmarket in April: soon struggling in Kentucky Derby following start: stays 1¼m: acts on soft going and on equitrack: effective blinkered or not: below form when sweating and edgy: sent to race in Germany. *J. S. Bolger, Ireland*

TIARUM   10 b.g. Tiran (HUN) – Contessa (HUN) (Peleid 125) [1991 NR 1992 10m]   –
poor hurdler/chaser (stays 21f): seems of little account on flat: sold 1,250 gns Ascot December Sales. *G. A. Ham*

TIBBY HEAD (IRE)   4 b.g. Lyphard's Special (USA) 122 – Deer Park (FR)   –
(Faraway Son (USA) 130) [1991 7m 10g 11.5m 8g³ 7.1m 1992 10g 8m 8f] tall, angular gelding: rated 54 as 3-y-o: on the downgrade. *J. Mackie*

TICKERTY'S GIFT   2 b.c. (May 3) Formidable (USA) 125 – Handy Dancer 87   **69** p
(Green God 128) [1992 6d 6g⁴ 7d⁵] good-topped colt: eighth foal: closely related to 3-y-o Flying Wind (by Forzando) and half-brother to several winners, including useful middle-distance performers Karinga Bay (by Ardross) and Roll A Dollar (by Spin of A Coin): dam 1¼m winner: similar form, keeping on well, in autumn maidens at Newbury and Leicester final 2 starts: will be suited by 1m+: will improve. *R. Hannon*

TICKHAM VIXEN (IRE)   4 b.f. Heraldiste (USA) 121 – Camden Dancer (Cam-   **37**
den Town 125) [1991 NR 1992 a8g a7g 8.3g⁶ 6.1g 8.1f⁴ 6m 7.1s³ 6.1g] workmanlike filly: maiden handicapper: needed further than 6f, and would have been worth a try over 1¼m: best efforts on an easy surface: dead. *J. D. Bethell*

TIDAL RIVER   3 gr.f. Absalom 128 – Ebb And Flo 82 (Forlorn River 124) [1991   –
5d⁴ 7f⁴ 8.1s 1992 10.1s⁶ 8.3s 10d] lengthy filly: moderate mover: bad maiden. *Denys Smith*

TIFFANY GEM (IRE)   3 ch.f. Caerleon (USA) 132 – Lady Habitat (Habitat 134)   –
[1991 NR 1992 8v 10g⁴ 10d a16g⁵ a13g⁶] 32,000Y: sturdy, workmanlike filly: closely related to 11.7f winner Fighting Brave (by Gorytus) and half-sister to several winners, including fairly useful middle-distance stayer The Gaelcharn (by Prince Bee): dam won 4 times in Italy: no worthwhile form, including in a visor. *Lord Huntingdon*

TIFFANY'S CASE (IRE)   3 ro. or gr.f. Thatching 131 – Spindle Berry 92   **65**
(Dance In Time (CAN)) [1991 6m⁵ 7.1m 7g 1992 8.2g⁶ 8.1g 8g* 8g* 8.9m⁶ 8d² 8g⁴ 8d⁵ 10d⁵] lengthy, good-topped filly: consistent handicapper: won at Wolverhamp-ton (swished tail) and Leicester in July: effective at 1m to 1¼m: acts on dead ground: sometimes hangs left, and held up. *C. A. Horgan*

TIGANI   6 b.h. Good Times (ITY) – She Who Dares (Bellypha 130) [1991 6d² 6g³   **63**
5m 5g 1992 a6g a5g⁴ a6g⁶ a5g 5g 5.1d 5.9d 6m⁴ 6.1m 5d 6g 5m⁴ 5m 5m⁵ 5d⁶ 5s]
big, good-topped horse: carries condition: rated 112 at his best at 4 yrs: a shadow
of former self nowadays: effective at 5f and 6f: probably acts on any going: effective visored/blinkered or not: sold 5,000 gns Doncaster November Sales. *D. W.
Chapman*

TIGER CLAW (USA)   6 b.g. Diamond Shoal 130 – Tiger Scout (USA) 86 (Silent   **59 d**
Screen (USA)) [1991 10f³ 10s⁴ 12f⁴ 10m² 9g² 9m² 10d 10.2d 10g⁴ 10f⁴ 11.9g 10.2s²
9.7f⁶ 9.7s⁵ 1992 10d² 11.9m³ 10m³ 9m³ 9g 10.2m² 11.9f³ 11.9f⁵ 10d² 10m³ 10f³ 10g
9d⁵] good-bodied gelding: placed numerous times in 1992 but generally disappointing: stays 1½m: probably acts on any going: below form when visored, has run
creditably blinkered: suitable mount for amateur. *R. J. Hodges*

TIGER SHOOT   5 b.g. Indian King (USA) 128 – Grand Occasion 63 (Great   **53**
Nephew 126) [1991 10g* 11.5g² 8m⁴ 9m² 8m 10m⁶ 12m 1992 10g⁵ 11.1m⁵ a12g⁶
11.6m⁴ 8.1g⁶ a10g³ 10.1d³ 12.3d⁴ 9d⁶ 10s*] close-coupled, workmanlike gelding:
consistent handicapper: won at Lingfield in October: stays 1½m: acts on good to
firm and soft ground: usually has tongue tied down: effective visored or not: trained
until after second start by P. Feilden. *D. J. S. Cosgrove*

TIGERSPIKE (IRE)   2 ch.g. (Feb 20) Mazaad 106 – Skimmer 86 (Skymaster   **35**
126) [1992 5d⁶ 5.2m 6f] IR 3,000F, 4,000Y: strong, compact gelding: moderate
walker: poor mover: half-brother to several winners abroad or in Ireland: dam 2-y-o
5.9f winner: poor maiden. *M. McCormack*

TIK FA (USA)   3 b.c. Timeless Moment (USA) – How Fortunate (USA) (What   **108**
Luck (USA)) [1991 7d⁴ 8.1f² 8g² 9s⁵ 1992 10d³ 10m² 12m³ 8g 8f* 8g* 8s 9m] quite
good-topped colt: visored and improved performer in autumn: showed good turn of
foot to win minor events at Doncaster and Newbury (by 2½ lengths from Hazaam):
creditable seventh of 11 to Arazi in Group 2 event at Longchamp: below that form in
Newmarket listed race final start: best at around 1m: probably acts on any going. *B.
Hanbury*

TILDEN PARK   6 b.m. Bustineto – Moycarkey (Raise You Ten 125) [1991 NR   **–**
1992 12.2g⁶] lengthy ex-Irish mare: fifth foal: dam unraced: won selling chase in
April but behind on debut on flat here: dead. *P. J. Bevan*

TILT TECH FLYER   7 b.g. Windjammer (USA) – Queen Kate 52 (Queen's   **–**
Hussar 124) [1991 10d 1992 8.2s] big, leggy, sparely-made gelding: on the downgrade on flat.*J. Akehurst*

TIMBER TOPPER   2 ch.g. (Mar 12) Crowning Honors (CAN) – Clairwood   **–**
(Final Straw 127) [1992 7m 7d 7d] 4,000Y: tall, lengthy gelding: fourth foal: half-
brother to 6f (at 2 yrs) to 11.1f winner Able Lassie (by Grey Desire): dam lightly
raced: soundly beaten, including in a seller. *Mrs M. Reveley*

TIME FOR A FLUTTER   3 b.f. Beldale Flutter (USA) 130 – Time Warp 63   **63**
(Town And Country 124) [1991 NR 1992 11.6g⁴ 12g³ 10s⁴] leggy filly: shows marked
knee action: first foal: dam staying maiden: modest maiden: better at 1½m than
1¼m. *D. R. C. Elsworth*

TIME HONORED (USA)   2 b.c. (May 15) Time For A Change (USA) – La   **49 p**
Paqueline (FR) (Sassafras (FR) 135) [1992 7d 7m 7s] $30,000Y: unfurnished colt:
good mover: half-brother to several winners, notably high-class 1982 French 2-y-o
5f to 7f winner Deep Roots (by Dom Racine): dam twice-raced (in France) daughter
of very useful sprinting 2-y-o Etari, dam also of very useful middle-distance stayer
Queribus: sire (by Damascus) won from 7f to 9f: shaped better than positions
suggest in maidens at Yarmouth and Salisbury last 2 starts in September, fading
quickly closing stages: probably capable of better. *Sir Mark Prescott*

TIME LAPSE   3 ch.f. The Noble Player (USA) 126 – Low Line 66 (High Line 125)   **62**
[1991 a6g² 6m* 6m³ 8m⁶ 8f⁴ 1992 7g a7g⁶ 8d³ 8d 8g⁴] sparely-made filly: moderate
mover: modest handicapper: will prove better suited to 1¼m: acts on firm and dead
ground: sometimes hangs. *P. J. Makin*

TIMES ARE HARD   8 b.g. Bay Express 132 – Raffinrula 75 (Raffingora 130)   **38**
[1991 9s⁴ 8m a10g⁵ 8m a7g² 10.3d 1992 10.8g a7g 8.9s³ a8g² 8f² a8g⁵] close-coupled   a41
gelding: poor handicapper: effective at 1m to 1¼m: probably acts on any turf going
and on equitrack: ran creditably when visored. *C. A. Smith*

TIME'S ARROW (IRE)   2 b.g. (Feb 12) Wolverlife 115 – Arachosia (Persian   **86 p**
Bold 123) [1992 a6g* a6g* 6f⁵ 7g*] 1,700F, 3,500 2-y-o: workmanlike gelding: has a
quick action: third foal: brother to 3-y-o Confound: dam ran once at 3 yrs in Ireland:
progressive gelding: successful in 1992 in seller (bought in 6,500 gns) at Southwell,

claimer at Lingfield and nursery (gamely by a neck) at Leicester: will stay 1m: sort to keep improving. *G. C. Bravery*

TIME TO RUN   3 b.f. Green Desert (USA) 127 – Dare Me 101 (Derring-Do 131) [1991 NR 1992 6g] half-sister to several winners, including good sprinter Forty-second Street (by Sharpen Up) and moderate 2m winner Scolt Head (by Troy): dam won three 5f races from 5 starts: 33/1, never able to challenge in listed event at Doncaster in November: sold 6,500 gns Newmarket December Sales. *Major W. R. Hern*   –

TIMOTHY CASEY   2 b.c. (Apr 20) Hadeer 118 – William's Bird (USA) 104 (Master Willie 129) [1992 6g⁴ 7g] good-topped colt: has plenty of scope: first foal: dam 5f and 7f winner at 2 yrs, ran only once at 3 yrs: similar form at Newmarket in early-summer maiden and listed event (around 13 lengths last of 7 to Ardkinglass): seemed sure to improve, but not seen again. *N. C. Wright*   **73**

TIMURID (FR)   3 b.c. Persian Bold 123 – Kumari (FR) 78 (Luthier 126) [1991 7m 8m⁶ 1992 10d 12d 10.3f 8.9g* 9f* 10g² 10.3m⁶ 12.3g 10.3m] tall, useful-looking colt: moderate mover: fair handicapper: won at Wolverhampton and Redcar within a week in June: best form at up to 1¼m: possibly needs a sound surface: sold to join M. Bell's stable 14,000 gns Newmarket Autumn Sales. *J. L. Dunlop*   **75**

TINA MEENA LISA   3 b.f. Kala Shikari 125 – Miss Speak Easy (USA) (Sea Bird II 145) [1991 5g 5g 5.1m 1992 5s 8.9s⁵ 12.3d 8.9g⁴ 8.9m 10.3m 8.9d 8.3s⁴] sparely-made filly: has a quick action: poor maiden: stays 8.9f: possibly needs some give in the ground. *E. H. Owen jun*   **38**

TINA'S ANGEL   5 b.m. Martinmas 128 – Tina's Magic (Carnival Night) [1991 NR 1992 7d 6f 8.9s] leggy, sparely-made mare: no worthwhile form. *J. C. Fox*   –

TINA'S GAME   4 ch.f. Mummy's Game 120 – Mantina (Bustino 136) [1991 NR 1992 a7g 9g⁴ 12.4m 9.2s 12.1s] leggy, lengthy filly: fourth foal: half-sister to fairly useful 7f and 1m winner Yearsley (by Anfield): dam never ran: worthwhile form only on second start. *A. P. Stringer*   **25**

TINAS LASS   3 b.f. Dreams To Reality (USA) 113 – Arbatina (Sallust 134) [1991 NR 1992 NR] half-sister to quite modest middle-distance winner (also successful over hurdles/fences) Tinas Lad (by Jellaby): dam of little account: showed nothing in claimer at Kempton in September. *R. Curtis*   –

TINDARI (FR)   4 ch.g. Vacarme (USA) 121 – Yseult (FR) (Olantengy (FR) 122) [1991 7.5f 8m 1992 11.1d⁵] small, good-bodied gelding: no worthwhile form in northern claimers on flat but has shown signs of ability: won weak maiden hurdle in December. *J. M. Jefferson*   –

TINKERS FAIRY   3 b.f. Myjinski (USA) – Anatolian Elf (Hittite Glory 125) [1991 NR 1992 7.1g 7g] 1,800Y: leggy, angular filly: moderate mover: fifth foal: half-sister to 2-y-o 5.8f winner Tinkins Wood (by Vin St Benet) and a winner in Italy: dam poor plater: little promise in July maidens. *D. T. Thom*   –

TINKOSUMTIN   6 b.m. Taufan (USA) 119 – Stapelea (FR) (Faraway Son (USA) 130) [1991 NR 1992 11.8s 8m⁶ 10g 7.6m 7g] sturdy mare: moderate mover: related to minor winners in Ireland at up to 1m: dam Irish maiden: no form in 1992. *P. Burgoyne*   –

TINNERS WAY (USA)   2 ch.c. (May 25) Secretariat (USA) – Devon Diva (USA) (The Minstrel (CAN) 135) [1992 7g*] rangy colt: fourth foal: half-brother to   **88** P

Flanders Maiden Stakes (Div. 1), Doncaster—
from the final crop of Secretariat, the promising Tinners Way beats Kassbaan in good style

smart 3-y-o sprinter Western Approach (by Gone West) and 6f (at 2 yrs) and 7f winner Daki (by Miswaki): dam 9f winner at 4 yrs in USA, is daughter of Devon Ditty: second favourite but in need of race, won 18-runner maiden at Doncaster in November in really good style by 3½ lengths from Kassbaan, soon close up after slow start, leading before halfway and staying on strongly: will be suited by 1¼m: has scope, and sure to improve a lot at 3 yrs. *J. H. M. Gosden*

TINO TERE   3 ch.g. Clantime 101 – Blueit (FR) 101 (Bold Lad (IRE) 133) [1991   **83**
5d2 5m* 5d2 5g3 5m2 5m* 5m2 5m2 5.2f2 5d6 1992 5.2d5 5.1g 5m4 5m4 5s 5d a5g2]
close-coupled, quite attractive gelding: good walker: rated 94 at 2 yrs: had a disappointing season at 3 yrs, but ran respectably for 7-lb claimer in handicap at Southwell: will prove best at 5f: acts on firm and dead ground and on fibresand: blinkered third outing. *J. Berry*

TINSASHE (IRE)   2 br.f. (Mar 3) Sayf El Arab (USA) 127 – Rheinbloom 66   **44** p
(Rheingold 137) [1992 8d] lengthy filly: half-sister to 3-y-o Early Bloom (by Superlative), fairly useful middle-distance stayer Rhusted (by Busted) and a winner in USA: dam 1½m winner, is half-sister to high-class Gold Rod: better for race, past pace to over 2f out when around 10 lengths seventh of 16 in maiden at Kempton in September: will improve. *M. Moubarak*

TINSTONE   2 b.f. (Mar 22) Nishapour (FR) 125 – Tino-Ella 73 (Bustino 136)   **36**
[1992 8.2d 7d] leggy filly: first foal: dam 1¼m winner out of half-sister to Teenoso: well beaten in maiden and claimer in autumn. *J. A. Glover*

TIOGA (IRE)   2 b.c. (Feb 25) Taufan (USA) 119 – Brave Ivy 68 (Decoy Boy 129)   –
[1992 8m] 9,200F, IR 42,000Y: angular colt: fourth live foal: half-brother to 1989 2-y-o 5f winner Najat (by Tender King) and a winner in Belgium: dam placed here at 5f at 2 yrs, later won in Italy: backward, pulled up in maiden at Doncaster in September, after progress to dispute lead under 2f out: dead. *R. Hannon*

TIOMAN ISLAND   2 gr.c. (Apr 30) Midyan (USA) 124 – Catch The Sun   **90**
(Kalaglow 132) [1992 5m2 6.1m* 7d2 7f* 7.1d4] 19,000Y: tall, rather unfurnished colt: moderate mover: second foal: dam unraced: progressive colt: won median auction event at Nottingham in June and 2-runner minor event at Newmarket (by 3½ lengths from Fitzcarraldo) in August: staying-on fourth of 9 to White Crown in Solario Stakes at Sandown: will be better suited by 1m: acts on firm and dead ground. *P. F. I. Cole*

TIP IT IN   3 gr.g. Le Solaret (FR) – Alidante 65 (Sahib 114) [1991 NR 1992 5s6 6m6   –
8f2 10m 10g6] 480Y: small, dipped-backed gelding: moderate mover: fifth living foal: half-brother to a prolific winner in Yugoslavia by Imperial Fling: dam ran only at 2 yrs, suited by 1m: no worthwhile form on flat: won selling handicap hurdle in December. *A. Smith*

TIPPERARY AZUL (IRE)   4 b.g. Godswalk (USA) 130 – Kilboy Concorde   –
(African Sky 124) [1991 9g5 12d4 8m5 1992 a8g a10g a12g4 16d 10.8d] leggy ex-Irish gelding: half-brother to Irish 1m winner Father Phil (by Kampala) and a winner in Hong Kong by Ballymore: dam little form in Ireland: modest form at 3 yrs (twice blinkered) for J. Bolger: poor form at best here: visored and soundly beaten in seller final run: probably stays 1½m. *M. H. Tompkins*

TIPPLING (USA)   5 b.m. Full Out (USA) – Lady Mellody (USA) (Beat Inflation   **29**
(USA)) [1991 5m 5m3 6s3 6g a5g 6m3 6m 7.1m 6.1m 1992 5f 5.1m5 6d 5m6 6.1g] smallish, sturdy mare: moderate mover: poor handicapper here: stays 6f: acts on good to firm and soft going. *P. Burgoyne*

TISSISAT (USA)   3 ch.g. Green Forest (USA) 134 – Expansive 111 (Exbury 138)   **87**
[1991 NR 1992 8f* 8f2 8.9d2 10m 8.3g] good-bodied gelding: half-brother to several winners, including 1½m winners Chesnut Tree (by Shadeed), Salient (by High Top) and Trying For Gold (by Northern Baby): dam won Ribblesdale Stakes: won maiden at Salisbury and ran well when second in handicaps later in June: well below form after: should be suited by 1¼m +: acts on firm and dead ground. *I. A. Balding*

TITIAN GIRL   3 ch.f. Faustus (USA) 118 – Redhead 66 (Hotfoot 126) [1991 5m 6d   –
7m 8.3g 1992 10d 12.3s 14.6d 11.8m 10.5s5 10.3g] sparely-made filly: of little account. *Miss L. C. Siddall*

TITLED GIRL (IRE)   2 b.f. (May 15) Alzao (USA) 117 – Sweet Goodbye   **46**
(Petorius 117) [1992 7d a8g a8g5 a8g] IR 10,500Y: workmanlike filly: first foal: dam unraced: form only on debut. *P. F. I. Cole*

TITLE ROLL (IRE)   4 ch.f. Tate Gallery (USA) 117 – Tough Lady 91 (Bay   **107**
Express 132) [1991 7g2 8g4 5m5 5f2 5d2 5m* 5g 1992 5s2 6g4 5m4 5g4 5m4] angular, workmanlike filly: moderate mover: useful Irish performer: won King George Stakes at Goodwood in 1991 and put up best effort as 4-y-o in same race when under

2 lengths fourth to Freddie Lloyd on final start, best of those near stand rail: effective from 5f to 7f: acts on good to firm and soft ground: below form when blinkered once: sold 50,000 gns Newmarket December Sales. *T. Stack, Ireland*

TLAAD (USA) 3 ch.f. Mr Prospector (USA) – Raahia (CAN) 91 (Vice Regent (CAN)) [1991 NR 1992 7d 7g3] lengthy filly: first foal: dam 2-y-o 6f winner, third in Nell Gwyn Stakes at 3 yrs: not seen out again after 8½ lengths third in maiden at Catterick in April. *M. R. Stoute* —

TOCHAR BAN (USA) 2 b.f. (Mar 22) Assert 134 – Guest Night 109 (Sir Ivor 135) [1992 8d2] $29,000Y: half-sister to several winners, including fairly useful 1987 2-y-o 5f and 6f winner Isticanna (by Far North) and fair 1979 2-y-o 7f winner Downderry (by English Prince): dam, daughter of top-class Mesopotamia, won over 7f and 9f: 14/1, shaped promisingly when short-headed by Lille Hammer in maiden at Yarmouth in October, switched right over 1f out and staying on really strongly: will be very well suited by middle distances: will improve and win a race. *D. R. C. Elsworth* — 76 p

TODDEN 2 b.c. (Apr 18) Aragon 118 – Marguerite Gerard 78 (Rheingold 137) [1992 7m 6d 7g] close-coupled, unfurnished colt: fourth foal: half-brother to 1m winner Strike A Chord (by Song), quite modest 1986 2-y-o Tap The Baton (by Music Maestro) and a winner in Italy: dam won over 1¼m and stayed 13f: well beaten in autumn maidens at Leicester and Redcar before never placed to challenge in mixed-age event at Newmarket. *C. F. Wall* — 46

TOFF SUNDAE 2 b.g. (Apr 28) Risk Me (FR) 127 – Rose Sundae 62 (Dominion 123) [1992 5d 5d3 5g2 5.1s 5s* a6g 6m4 6g] 8,000F, 3,000Y: smallish, leggy gelding: poor mover: first living foal: dam 2-y-o 5f winner: none too consistent performer: retained 2,000 gns after winning seller at Wolverhampton in May: sold out of G. Lewis' stable 1,750 gns Ascot June Sales before final start: has been gelded. *P. M. McEntee* — 49

TOLEDO QUEEN (IRE) 2 gr.f. (Feb 21) El Gran Senor (USA) 136 – Grey Dream 101 (Auction Ring (USA) 123) [1992 6.1m3 5f 7s*] lengthy filly, rather unfurnished: has a roundish action: second living foal: half-sister to 1½m winner Nocturnal Reverie (by Assert): dam useful 5f and 6f winner in Ireland at 2 yrs later placed in stakes in USA: odds on, short-head winner of maiden at Ayr in September: late headway but always towards rear when beaten 11 lengths in Queen Mary Stakes at Royal Ascot: will stay 1m. *P. W. Chapple-Hyam* — 65 p

TOLLS CHOICE (IRE) 3 ch.g. Sun Valley 103 – Creativity (Creative Plan (USA)) [1991 5m 5g5 5f 8m2 8m5 8m 1992 8s* 9.9g6 a12g] leggy, unfurnished gelding: well below form after winning handicap at Ripon in April, and not seen out after June: best form at 1m on soft ground. *M. W. Easterby* — 66

TOMAHAWK 5 ch.g. Be My Guest (USA) 126 – Siouan 78 (So Blessed 130) [1991 15.9g6 13.9g5 12d 1992 12s] leggy, quite good-topped gelding: moderate mover: modest handicapper: rated 72 at 4 yrs: stays 1¾m. *R. J. Holder* —

TOMASHENKO 3 ch.c. Efisio 120 – Stockingful (Santa Claus 133) [1991 NR 1992 10.3g5 10m6 11.8g6 10g 8g] deep-girthed colt: half-brother to several winners, including useful stayer Wesley (by High Top): dam once-raced half-sister to smart miler Richboy: poor maiden: seems to stay 1m. *J. Mackie* —

TOMMY TEMPEST 3 ch.g. Northern Tempest (USA) 120 – Silently Yours (USA) 53 (Silent Screen (USA)) [1991 NR 1992 7g 6m6 7d 5m2 5m 5g5 5.2m5 5.3g2 5d3 5.1s2 a5g5 a5g a5g2] 3,200Y: angular gelding: second foal: dam 2-y-o 5f seller winner: modest but quite consistent maiden: easily best efforts at around 5f: acts on good to firm and soft ground and on equitrack: ran creditably in blinkers final start. *K. R. Burke* — 51 a44

TOMOS 2 b.c. (Mar 5) Sure Blade (USA) 130 – Princess Genista 108 (Ile de Bourbon (USA) 133) [1992 7m 8d*] tall, leggy colt: looks weak: first foal: dam 1m (at 2 yrs) and 8.5f winner stayed 15f, is out of half-sister to Old Country: green when winning maiden at Redcar in October, staying on strongly to lead close home: will be well suited by further: will improve further. *D. Morley* — 75 p

TOM PARKER 2 b.g. (Mar 12) Today And Tomorrow 78 – Winding Street (Pitskelly 122) [1992 6s a7g] 1,050Y: workmanlike gelding: first foal: dam poor maiden: always behind in maidens at Lingfield. *P. Howling* —

TOM PIPER 2 b.g. (Apr 29) Music Boy 124 – Run For Love 70 (Runnett 125) [1992 5d 5.1g5 5.1g* 5.1g6] tall, close-coupled gelding: first foal: dam best at 2 yrs seemed to little account as 3-y-o: easily best run when making all against favoured stand rail in maiden at Nottingham in June: well-beaten last in median auction event following month. *J. Berry* — 59

TOM'S APACHE 3 br.g. Sula Bula 109 – Tom's Nap Hand (Some Hand 119) **46**
[1991 6m⁶ 7f 7g 1992 7m 7f⁴ 8h 8.1g⁴ 8f 7g⁴ 7g 7.6s] leggy gelding: inconsistent
maiden: should stay beyond 7f: acts on firm going: not discredited when visored,
below form blinkered. *Billy Williams*

TOM THE TANK 2 b.c. (May 16) Skyliner 117 – Mistral Magic (Crofter (USA) –
124) [1992 8.9s 8m] 1,000Y: good-topped colt: has a markedly round action: second
foal: dam lightly-raced daughter of Ribblesdale third Hunting Cap: burly and always
behind in claimer at York and maiden at Pontefract in October. *N. Tinkler*

TONGUE TIED 4 br.f. Petong 126 – Tight (Lochnager 132) [1991 5g⁵ 5f* 5m 6g **70**
6f³ 5m² 5h*dis 5m 5m 5m* 1992 6g⁶ 5m* 5f* 5f⁶ 5.2m² 5g] rather leggy,
close-coupled filly: in excellent form in handicaps in spring, winning at Newmarket
and Redcar: not seen out again after modest run in July: should prove as effective at
6f as 5f: acts on hard ground, yet to race on a soft surface: occasionally slowly away.
J. Wharton

TONKAWA 7 b.g. Indian King (USA) 128 – Lady Tycoon 67 (No Mercy 126) [1991 –
NR 1992 11.7d 14d] big, robust gelding: good mover: on the downgrade. *J. M. Bradley*

TONY SAN (IRE) 3 b.c. Pennine Walk 120 – Millers Lady (Mill Reef (USA) 141) **85**
[1991 6m 8m⁶ 7m 1992 10.4m³ 10g 7.5v⁵] small, quite attractive colt: has a quick
action: fairly useful performer: third in graduation race at York in May: raced in Italy
afterwards, and showed some ability there: should prove better at around 1¼m than
shorter: acts on good to firm ground. *C. E. Brittain*

TONY'S MIST 2 b.c. (Apr 19) Digamist (USA) 110 – Tinas Image (He Loves Me **50**
120) [1992 5m⁵ 6m⁶ 6s a8g⁵] close-coupled, unfurnished colt: good walker: third
foal: half-brother to Irish 8.5f and 9f winner Tony's Delight (by Krayyan): dam
showed little ability: poor maiden: stays 6f. *R. Hannon*

TOOCANDO (IRE) 2 b.f. (Apr 27) Nordance (USA) – Romantic Air 62 (He **94**
Loves Me 120) [1992 5g* 5g* 5f³ 6g² 6m³] IR 2,000Y: small, leggy filly: has a quick
action: fourth foal: dam ran 3 times at 2 yrs, showing best form at 1m: progressed
really well first 4 starts, impressive winner of Beverley minor event and Newmarket auction (flashed tail) in spring and placed in Queen Mary Stakes at Royal
Ascot and Hillsdown Cherry Hinton Stakes (stayed on strongly behind Sayyedati
having had to be switched) at Newmarket: not seen out again after below-par third
(finished lame) of 6 in Lowther Stakes at York: should stay 1m. *C. N. Allen*

TOO EAGER 6 b.g. Nishapour (FR) 125 – Double Habit (Double Form 130) [1991 –
8s 7d⁷ 6s* 6d² 6m 8d⁵ 7m 1992 8g 7d 7g 6v 7m] lengthy, dipped-backed gelding:
none too consistent handicapper: rated 70 at 5 yrs: stays 7f: best form on an easy
surface: best blinkered: sold 600 gns Doncaster June Sales. *M. W. Easterby*

TOOLEY'S BOY 3 b.g. Adonijah 126 – Marita 76 (Great Nephew 126) [1991 6g⁴ –
6f 7m 8m 8g 1992 10m⁵ 12g⁶] small gelding: moderate mover: poor maiden: should
be well suited by further than 6f. *Mrs Barbara Waring*

TOP CEES 2 b.c. (May 21) Shirley Heights 130 – Sing Softly 112 (Luthier 126) **58** p
[1992 6g] fifth live foal: half-brother to 3-y-o winning hurdler Dominant Serenade
(by Dominion): dam 6f winner at 2 yrs later very useful over middle distances: 50/1,
one pace from 2f out when around 10 lengths tenth of 20 in maiden at Newbury in
September: will improve. *P. W. Harris*

TOPCLIFFE 5 b.m. Top Ville 129 – Sandford Lady 116 (Will Somers 114§) [1991 **39**
10g 10g 11m³ 9.9f⁵ 10.9m³ 16m 12f⁶ 11m⁵ 13.8m⁵ 12m* 12.4m² 1992 17.1d⁶ 16.2g⁴
16.5m⁵ 16.2s 13.6m] leggy, lightly-made mare: moderate mover: poor handicapper:
effective at 1½m to 17f: acts on firm and dead going: below form blinkered once,
usually visored nowadays. *Mrs V. A. Aconley*

TOPHARD 6 b.g. Lyphard's Special (USA) 122 – Tomard (Thatching 131) [1991 –
NR 1992 11.8g 14.9g 14.6g] leggy, workmanlike gelding: seems of little account. *R.
Lee*

TOP IT ALL 4 b.g. Song 132 – National Dress 64 (Welsh Pageant 132) [1991 a12g⁴ –
12.3s 14.1f⁶ 16m 1992 a13g] heavy-bodied gelding: poor maiden on flat: stays 1½m.
M. J. Ryan

TOP ONE 7 ch.g. Sallust 134 – Light Diamond (Florescence 120) [1991 6f² 7.6d **58**
1992 a8g 8g 6g 8m* 8.2g a8g a7g] close-coupled gelding: form in 1992 only when **a–**
landing gamble by 6 lengths in selling handicap (no bid) at Yarmouth in June: stays
1m: acts on any going on turf, seemingly unsuited by fibresand: often bandaged. *C. J.
Hill*

TOP PET (IRE) 2 br.g. (Feb 17) Petong 126 – Pounelta 91 (Tachypous 128) [1992 **87**
7d⁶ 5f* 6g⁴ 6g 6d² 7v⁶] leggy, rather unfurnished gelding: third foal: half-brother to

3-y-o Top Song (by Noalto) and untrustworthy 6f (at 2 yrs) and 7f winner Durneltor (by Hard Fought): dam 2-y-o 7f winner, probably stayed 1½m, is half-sister to Dead Certain: won maiden at Salisbury in July after swerving at stalls: easily best effort when second in nursery at Ascot: should be as effective at 7f as 6f: acts on firm and dead ground, well below best on heavy: none too easy ride. *R. Hannon*

TOP PRIZE　4 b.c. High Top 131 – Raffle 82 (Balidar 133) [1991 a12g 1992 a12g5 12g6 15.1d5 13.8g 16d 15.8d] lengthy colt: on the downgrade: sold 1,250 gns Doncaster October Sales. *M. Brittain*　–

TOP RANK　2 b.c. (Mar 9) Law Society (USA) 130 – On The Top (High Top 131) [1992 7s4 8g2] 2,300Y: leggy, angular colt: third foal: dam unraced half-sister to Double Schwartz: encouraging fourth in maiden at Salisbury: better effort beaten around 8 lengths, never able to challenge, by Taos in listed race at Ascot later in autumn: will stay 1½m: can win a race. *J. S. Moore*　78

TOP REGISTER (USA)　3 b.c. Dixieland Band (USA) – Contralto 100 (Busted 134) [1991 8g2 1992 10d* 10.4m6 10.5d 8.9m] strong, rather angular colt: won £9,500 contest at Ascot in April: best effort when 9 lengths sixth of 7 in Dante Stakes at York: off course 3 months after and soundly beaten in Group 3 contest and £12,300 handicap: gave impression should stay 1½m: yet to race on extremes of going. *Lord Huntingdon*　98

TOP ROYAL　3 br.c. High Top 131 – Maria Isabella (FR) (Young Generation 129) [1991 7.1s 7m5 1992 8m6 8.2g 10f* 11.9f* 11.9f2 14g3 12d* 12d2 11.9d3 14m] good-bodied colt: fairly useful handicapper: had good season in 1992, successful at Brighton (2) and Goodwood: best at 1½m to 1¾m: acts on firm and dead going: wore tongue strap last 4 starts: tough and consistent: sold 52,000 gns Newmarket Autumn Sales. *J. L. Dunlop*　86

TOP SCALE　6 b.g. Tower Walk 130 – Singing High 87 (Julio Mariner 127) [1991 9f9.9g* 8.2d 11m3 10m3 9f* 9f 8h2 8.5f2 9m2 8m 1992 9.9g 8f 10f2 9d 8f4 11f2 10.1m5 12m4] strong, good-topped gelding: poor handicapper: effective at 1m to 11f: suited by a sound surface: suitable mount for inexperienced rider: effective with or without visor and blinkers: won over hurdles in August: sold to join K. Bailey 18,000 gns Doncaster November Sales. *W. W. Haigh*　39

TOP SIRE　3 b.g. Elegant Air 119 – Encore L'Amour (USA) § (Monteverdi 129) [1991 NR 1992 8m 8g4 8m] 15,500F, 10,500Y: smallish, lengthy, heavy-bodied gelding: first foal: dam temperamental granddaughter of top-class 4.5f to 1m winner Lianga: tailed off, including in seller: sold 1,200 gns Newmarket Autumn Sales. *J. H. M. Gosden*　–

TOP SONG　3 br.f. Noalto 120 – Pounelta 91 (Tachypous 128) [1991 6f 7.1m 7f2 1992 7g4 8f2 7.1g4 7f4] tall filly: moderate mover: modest maiden: withdrawn lame fourth intended appearance before virtually pulled up (reportedly lame) final run, in July: gives impression should stay 1¼m: acts on firm going. *R. Hannon*　70

TOP SPIN　3 b.c. Niniski (USA) 125 – Spin (High Top 131) [1991 7d 7g 8.1g6 8f* 7s 1992 12m6 14d* 14d2 13.3s5] small, leggy, quite attractive colt: good walker: fairly useful handicapper: won at Kempton in September: will be well suited by 2m: acts on firm and dead ground: sold to join J. Jenkins' stable 52,000 gns Newmarket Autumn Sales. *Major W. R. Hern*　92

TOP TABLE　3 b.f. Shirley Heights 130 – Lora's Guest 99 (Be My Guest (USA) 126) [1991 NR 1992 10g 12f2 12.2d4 12s5 12.4m3 a14g 14g 16d] 27,000Y: small filly: moderate mover: first foal: dam, 7f winner and stayed 1m, is sister to 1000 Guineas winner On The House: modest maiden: well below form last 3 starts, visored last 2: stays 1½m: acts on firm and dead going: sold 10,000 gns Newmarket December Sales. *M. R. Stoute*　65

TOP VILLAIN　6 b.g. Top Ville – Swan Ann 84 (My Swanee 122) [1991 12f5 10m 10m* a11g* 10.6g5 a12g2 10m a11g3 8.9g 10m 1992 10.3m2 9.9g2 12m5 9.9m a10g5] rangy gelding: formerly unreliable handicapper: gives impression will prove ideally suited by around 1¼m: effective blinkered or not: ran fairly well for amateur. *B. S. Rothwell*　41

TORCHON　4 b.c. High Top 131 – Cecilia Bianchi (FR) (Petingo 135) [1991 8g 104 § 10g* 12g* 11.9g* 11.9g 12m3 12m6 10m 0d* 13.3f4 12g* 12f6 12.1g4 12m6] lengthy colt: disappointed after landing odds in minor events at Pontefract (fortunate) in April and Beverley in June, finding nothing off bridle in Goodwood listed event final start: ideally suited by 1½m/13f: acts on firm and dead ground: sold 36,000 gns Newmarket Autumn Sales, reportedly to go jumping in USA with G. Oxley. *G. Wragg*

TORKABAR (USA) 7 ch.h. Vaguely Noble 140 – Tarsila (High Top 131) [1991 §§
NR 1992 a12g] medium-sized, sparely-made horse: moderate mover: ungenuine
maiden: often refuses to race. *G. A. Ham*

TORREY CANYON (USA) 3 b. or br.c. Gone West (USA) – Tovalop (USA) 113
(Northern Dancer (CAN)) [1991 7g* 7g* 8d4 1992 8g 10.3m3 8m* 10.4f3] tall,
attractive colt: very useful performer: 2½-length winner from Pursuit of Love of
listed race at Kempton in May: not seen here again after well below par, ridden
along 4f out and tending to hang, in listed race at York following month: best form at
1m (made most when visored second start): acts on good to firm and dead ground:
reportedly sent to race in Saudi Arabia. *R. Charlton*

TORWADA 9 b.g. Troy 137 – Miss By Miles 91 (Milesian 125) [1991 11.8g 9.7s 51
1992 16.2d4] strong, stocky gelding: good mover: extremely lightly raced on flat
nowadays: heavily-backed favourite in amateurs handicap at Haydock in May: stays
2m: acts on good to firm ground, and has gone very well with plenty of give: fairly
useful hurdler in 1990/1. *B. J. Curley*

TOSHIBA COMET 5 b.g. Noalto 120 – Silk Lady 97 (Tribal Chief 125) [1991 75 d
a6g* a6g* a6g* a6g4 6g5 6m5 6f* 6m2 6f 6g 6m 6g4 6.1d a6g5 a6g3 1992 a6g6 a7g4
a6g* a6g* a7g2 a6g4 6d6 6v2 7g 6m 5d 7.6m a6g 6d 6s6 a6g5 a7g a6g a6g3] strong,
sturdy gelding: moderate walker: successful in handicaps at Lingfield and Southwell
in February but well below form after eighth outing: stays 7f: acts on any going,
including all-weather surfaces: sometimes wears tongue strap: usually blinkered,
tried visored and in eyeshield: trained until after penultimate start by W. Pearce/B.
Beasley. *Pat Mitchell*

TOSHIBA COMET TOO (IRE) 4 ch.g. Gorytus (USA) 132 – No Jargon (Nono- –
alco (USA) 131) [1991 8m a8g 11m 8d a10g6 a12g 12g2 a8g] big, close-coupled
gelding: little worthwhile form: tried blinkered: sold 1,250 gns Doncaster March
Sales. *W. J. Pearce*

TOSS THE DICE 3 ch.g. Risk Me (FR) 127 – Curfew 76 (Midsummer Night II 56
117) [1991 8m5 1992 10.5s5 10g 8d4 8.9g5 8.3g3 6.9g4 10m 8s 6s6 7d 6v2] strong,
lengthy gelding: has a quick action: modest handicapper: best at up to 1m: acts on
heavy ground: twice well beaten when blinkered: has joined M. Tompkins. *M. A.
Jarvis*

TOTALLY UNIQUE (USA) 2 b.c. (Feb 25) Al Nasr (FR) 126 – Heavenly Halo 67
(USA) (Halo (USA)) [1992 5g2 5g3 6m4 7g3 7d] $45,000Y: compact colt: has a quick
action: second reported foal: dam minor winner at 9f at 2 yrs, is daughter of
champion American filly Heavenly Cause: best effort when third of 5 to Marillette in
minor event at Chester in July: well below form in Ayr maiden 6 weeks after: will be
better suited by 1¼m: possibly unsuited by dead ground. *M. Bell*

TOTAL TRUTH 2 br.f. (Apr 5) Reesh 117 – Token of Truth (Record Token 128) –
[1992 5.1d4 5g 6m] small, leggy, angular filly: third live foal: sister to fair 3-y-o
winning sprinter Truthful Image: dam granddaughter of Cry of Truth, best 2-y-o filly
of 1974: plater: not seen after June: should stay 6f. *J. White*

TOUCH WOOD (USA) 6 b.g. Touching Wood (USA) 127 – B A Poundstretcher 82 61
(Laser Light 118) [1991 8m 10f* 10m 9.9g3 10d 9.9f4 10.2g6 9.9f3 12m2 9.9f* 10.1m
12f6 9.9f2 9m3 9m* 10m 1992 10s 9.9g 9.9m* 10m5 10.1f6 9.9d5 9.9d3 9.9m2 11f5
10g3 10.1m4 12m 10m 10.3g a12g5] sturdy gelding: carries condition: good mover:
modest handicapper: won at Beverley (seventh win there) in May: effective at 9f to
1½m: acts on soft ground, goes particularly well on a sound surface: usually held up,
and goes well in strongly-run race: tough. *T. D. Barron*

TOUCHING STAR 7 b.g. Touching Wood (USA) 127 – Beaufort Star 95 (Great –
Nephew 126) [1991 NR 1992 12m6 17.2f] leggy, good-topped gelding: has a quick
action: on the downgrade. *P. J. Hobbs*

TOUCHING TIMES 4 b.g. Touching Wood (USA) 127 – Pagan Deity 88 –
(Brigadier Gerard 144) [1991 12s* 12.3s4 12m4 14f5 12.2m 11.7g3 12.4m3 12.3g
13.6m* 12m4 1992 a16g 13.1g5 15g 17.5s] angular, sparely-made gelding: rated 58 at
3 yrs: on the downgrade nowadays: sold out of G. Pritchard-Gordon's stable 3,000
gns Doncaster January Sales. *T. Craig*

TOUCH N' GLOW 2 b.f. (Apr 26) Petong 126 – Glow Again 78 (The Brianstan §§
128) [1992 6g 6f6 7g2 7g 7m6 7g3 8g] close-coupled, sparely-made filly: second foal:
dam 2-y-o 5f and 6f winner: plater: thoroughly temperamental (twice refused to
race): stays 7f: trained first 2 starts by R. Hannon, claimed out of J. Spearing's stable
£5,010 on third. *N. Tinkler*

TOUCH OF WHITE 6 ch.m. Song 132 – Cayla (Tumble Wind (USA)) [1991 5g 77
5g 5g 5m 1992 5.2d4 5d 5g 5.1m2 5g6 5.2d] big, useful-looking mare: none too

consistent 5f handicapper: acts on good to firm and dead ground: effective blinkered or not: sometimes hangs markedly left, and none too easy ride. *J. E. Banks*

TOUCH PAPER (USA) 3 br.g. Majestic Light (USA) – Mitey Lively (USA) **78**
(Olden Times) [1991 7g 6m 7m² 1992 10.3g* 12.3g² 10.3m 10m⁶ 12m 12g] sturdy, lengthy gelding: has a fluent action: won maiden at Doncaster in spring: shaped very well on first run for over 4 months in handicap at Doncaster third start but failed to fulfil that promise: should be better at 1½m than shorter: acts on good to firm ground: blinkered final start: has been gelded. *B. W. Hills*

TOUCH SILVER 2 ch.g. (May 2) Local Suitor (USA) 128 – Octavia Girl 104 **62** §
(Octavo (USA) 115) [1992 5g* 6m 6m 6m 6d] unfurnished gelding: fifth foal: closely related to fairly useful 7f and 1m winner Festival Mood (by Jalmood) and half-brother to 1m (at 2 yrs) to 15f winner Lofty Lady (by Head For Heights): dam 2-y-o 6f winner later stayed 1m: went wrong way after winning minor event at Doncaster in March: should stay 6f: gets on edge: seems best left alone. *B. W. Hills*

TOULON 4 b.c. Top Ville 129 – Green Rock (FR) (Mill Reef (USA) 141) [1991 **117**
10.5d³ 12.3d* 12.5g* 14.6m* 12d⁴ 1992 12g³ 12g⁶ 12m⁴ 12v⁴] tall, rangy colt: powerful galloper, with a long stride: high-class performer at 3 yrs, St Leger winner: well below that form in 1992, best effort when 4½ lengths third to Sapience in Jockey Club Stakes at Newmarket in May: needs a strongly-run race at 1½m, and should prove best at 1¾m+: acts on good to firm and dead ground: seemed unsuited by firm, and by track at Epsom: to be trained by R. Frankel in USA. *A. Fabre, France*

TOUR LEADER (NZ) 3 ch.c. Nassipour (USA) 95 – Colleen (NZ) (Karyar) **60**
[1991 NR 1992 12m⁴ 11.1m³ 12m⁵ 11.6g⁴ 12m⁶] sturdy, workmanlike New Zealand-bred colt: sire 1½m and 1¾m winner here later very successful (4 victories, including Rothmans International) in North America: modest maiden: will be well suited by 1¾m+. *T. D. Barron*

TOUSSAUD (USA) 3 b. or br.f. El Gran Senor (USA) 136 – Image of Reality **110**
(USA) (In Reality) [1991 6f² 1992 6g* 6.1m* 7f* 7.6m² 7m³ 9f⁴] quite good-topped filly: progressed really well in 1992, successful in maiden at Yarmouth, minor event at Nottingham and Group 3 event at Newmarket (by ¾ length from Prince Ferdinand) in June: short-head second to Thourios in listed contest at Lingfield: beaten just over a length in Grade 1 contest at Keeneland in October, final start and first for nearly 3 months: stays 9f: acts on firm ground: joined R. Frankel in USA. *J. H. M. Gosden*

TOWER OF IVORY (IRE) 2 b.f. (Apr 30) Cyrano de Bergerac 120 – Merta **–**
(USA) (Jaipur) [1992 7f⁵] IR 9,500Y: half-sister to several winners, including fairly useful sprinter Elegida (by Habitat) and middle-distance winner Yellow Jersey (by Levmoss): dam useful 6f winner in Ireland: tailed off in 5-runner maiden at Yarmouth in June. *W. A. O'Gorman*

Van Geest Criterion Stakes, Newmarket—
Toussaud holds the unlucky-in-running Prince Ferdinand (left), and Casteddu

TOWN FLOWER 3 b.f. Top Ville 129 – Dance Flower (CAN) (Northern Dancer   –
(CAN)) [1991 NR 1992 8.5g6] compact filly: third foal: half-sister to 7f and 1m winner
Peru (by Conquistador Cielo) and 10.6f winner Muzo (by Irish River): dam 6f to 1m
winner in USA out of half-sister to The Minstrel (by Northern Dancer): green when
beaten 12 lengths in maiden at Beverley in April: visits Mtoto. *L. M. Cumani*

TRACHELIUM 2 b.f. (Feb 12) Formidable (USA) 125 – Penny Blessing 112 (So   **65**
Blessed 130) [1992 7d 7s3 6d] 15,000Y: lengthy, rather unfurnished filly: sister to
modest 7f winner Quick Profit and quite moderate 9f and 1¼m winner Tizzy and
half-sister to several winners, including 1988 2-y-o 5f winner Song of Hope (by
Chief Singer): dam best at 2 yrs, when 5f winner: easily best effort in autumn when
third of 17 in maiden at Redcar, leading until inside last 1f: should stay 1m. *J. Hanson*

TRADERS DREAM 3 b.g. Superlative 118 – Divine Thought 102 (Javelot 124)   **63** d
[1991 6g 6m 7m 1992 7f3 7.5m3 10f3 9.7g5 8g 8s] good-topped gelding: modest
maiden: below form after second start: should stay 1m: acts on firm ground. *T.
Thomson Jones*

TRADITION 3 b.f. Last Tycoon 131 – Consolation 95 (Troy 137) [1991 7m4 8m3   **87** ?
1992 10m4 11.4g3 10g5 10.2d 12g] angular, quite attractive filly: good walker and
mover: beaten only about a length by Aquamarine in 5-runner Cheshire Oaks on
second start, easily best effort: should be better suited to 1½m: sold 15,500 gns
Newmarket December Sales. *Major W. R. Hern*

TRAFALGAR BOY (USA) 3 b.c. Stalwart (USA) – Emy's A Natural (USA)   **86**
(Coastal (USA)) [1991 6g5 8m3 8.1d* 8.3s5 1992 8d* 10.5d4 8.9g3 8.1d2 8m 8m 8s4
8s] workmanlike colt: fairly useful handicapper: won at Carlisle in April: below form
last 4 starts, blinkered final one: stays 9f: seems best on an easy surface. *J.
Etherington*

TRAINEE (USA) 3 b.f. Danzig Connection (USA) – Rosette (USA) (Military   –
Plume) [1991 7d 1992 7g 7g a8g 10g 10d] leggy filly: no worthwhile form: sold 920
gns Newmarket September Sales. *W. J. Haggas*

TRAMPOLI (USA) 3 b. or br.f. Trempolino (USA) 135 – Luth de Saron 118 **111**
(Luthier 126) [1991 NR 1992 10g 10.5g* 10g5 12m2 13.5s5 10g* 9f3] sixth foal:
half-sister to 4 winners in France, notably very smart 11f and 1½m winner Luth
Dancer (by Blushing Groom): dam smart at around 1¼m: very useful French filly:
successful in Group 3 Prix Penelope at Saint-Cloud in April: good second to
Trishyde in Prix de Malleret at Longchamp in June and fair fifth to Magic Night in
Prix de Pomone at Deauville (trained by A. Fabre): subsequently raced in USA,
winning handicap by 6 lengths and finishing good third in Grade 1 event at
Keeneland: appears to stay 13.5f: acts on firm going. *C. Clement, USA*

TRAPEZIUM 2 b.f. (Apr 2) Soviet Star 128 – Glancing 113 (Grundy 137)   **60** p
[1992 6g5] sturdy filly: good walker: sixth foal: half-sister to Irish 3-y-o 1½m winner
Looking Brill (by Sadler's Wells) and 4 winners here and abroad, including (at 6f and
7f) fair Inshad (by Indian King) and (at 1¼m) fairly useful Hidden Cove (by Slip
Anchor): dam 2-y-o 5f and 6f winner, is half-sister to Bassenthwaite: 4/1 and green,
around 6 lengths fifth of 20 to Serious in Newmarket maiden in October, not given
hard time when unable to quicken 2f out: will stay 7f+: will improve. *L. M. Cumani*

TRATTORIA (USA) 3 b.f. Alphabatim (USA) 126 – Falabella (Steel Heart 128)   –
[1991 5m* 5m4 7m4 7.5f 7.6d 1992 8f5] leggy, sparely-made filly: moderate walker
and mover: rated 62 at 2 yrs: well below form only run in 1992, in June: should stay
1m: acts on good to firm ground. *J. Sutcliffe*

TRAVELLING LAD 2 b.c. (Mar 21) Local Suitor (USA) 128 – Clymene 86   **42**
(Vitiges (FR) 132) [1992 a7g a7g5 7m4] IR 8,000Y: strong, good-topped colt: has
scope: has a roundish action: fourth foal: half-brother to Irish 3-y-o Jane Morgan (by
Adonijah): dam, 7f winner at 2 yrs on only start, is half-sister to useful 6f and 7f
winner Saluzzo and daughter of staying half-sister to smart Harmony Hall: showed
signs of ability in maidens at Southwell first 2 starts: tailed off in Newcastle minor
event in July. *B. Beasley*

TRAVELLING LIGHT 6 b.g. Electric 126 – La Levantina (Le Levanstell 122)   –
[1991 NR 1992 11.9s 16d6 14g] good-topped gelding: moderate mover: rated 95 as
4-y-o: lightly raced and well below form subsequently: best with good test of
stamina and a soft surface. *Mrs J. R. Ramsden*

TRAVEL TOKEN 4 b.g. Tina's Pet 121 – Guiletta 63 (Runnymede 123) [1991 6s   –
6g5 6m4 1992 8s 6.1d 6g] smallish, lengthy gelding: has a very round action: on the
downgrade. *L. J. Holt*

TREASURE BEACH 3 ch.g. Dublin Lad 116 – Melowen 75 (Owen Dudley 121)   **35**
[1991 NR 1992 7g 7.5g 9s 10g 8m 10f 7.5m6 8m] leggy gelding: has a fluent, round

action: third foal: half-brother to 1½m seller winner Grey Commander (by Grey Desire) and temperamental Sunny Jorvick (by Mansingh): dam 6f and 7f winner stayed 1m, is out of close relation to outstanding sprinter Floribunda: little worthwhile form: should stay beyond 7.5f: sold to join K. Linton's stable 1,200 gns Doncaster June Sales. *M. Brittain*

TREASURE COURT   5 b.g. Mummy's Treasure 84 – Julia Too 93 (Golden   –
Horus 123) [1991 NR 1992 a12g 7.1m 7.1s] tall, rather close-coupled gelding: seems of little account. *P. Burgoyne*

TREASURE TIME (IRE)   3 b.f. Treasure Kay 114 – Dowcester 63 (Habitat   **63**
134) [1991 6m 6f 6.1f⁶ 5f² 6m 1992 6d³ 5g² 6m³ 6m* 5.1f² 7m⁵ 5.3f* 6g a5g] strong-quartered, workmanlike filly: modest handicapper: won at Hamilton (maiden) in June and Brighton in August: best at 5f/6f: acts on firm ground, showed little on equitrack. *J. White*

TREBLE LASS   2 b.f. (Feb 11) Damister (USA) 123 – Stock Hill Lass 87 (Air   –
Trooper 115) [1992 6v] first reported foal: dam stayed 1m: soundly beaten in maiden at Hamilton in November. *M. Johnston*

TREE FROG (IRE)   3 b.f. Lomond (USA) 128 – Mountain Lodge 120 (Blakeney   –
126) [1991 7d 1992 10.3g⁶ 12s 14.6g] stoutly, lengthy filly: little promise in 1992, visored and tailed-off favourite final start: bred to stay middle distances: swishes tail, and may well be ungenuine. *Lord Huntingdon*

TREE OWL   3 b.g. Bold Owl 101 – Jennie's Darling (The Brianstan 128) [1991 5g⁶   –
5g 7m 7f 1992 7g] sparely-made gelding: poor plater. *M. W. Ellerby*

TREMENDISTO   2 b.c. (Apr 2) Petoski 135 – Misty Halo 93 (High Top 131)   **40** p
[1992 8.1d⁶] 2,000Y: strong colt: fourth foal: half-brother to 3-y-o winning stayer/hurdler Desert Mist (by Sharrood) and 1¼m to 1¾m winner Rock Face (by Ballad Rock): dam prolific winner at 1m to 2¼m: 25/1 and in need of race, 14 lengths sixth of 10, travelling smoothly long way after slow start and not knocked about when beaten, in maiden at Haydock in September: showed a round action: will improve. *Capt. J. Wilson*

TREMENDOUS (USA)   4 b.g. Spectacular Bid (USA) – Returned Conqueror   –
(USA) (Danzig (USA)) [1991 NR 1992 12m 11.1m⁶ 12.2g⁵] big gelding: has shown a round action: first foal: dam unraced: no worthwhile form on flat. *J. Norton*

TREMOLANDO (USA)   2 ch.c. (Apr 23) Trempolino (USA) 135 – Alia 112 (Sun   **86** p
Prince 128) [1992 8s³] lengthy colt: sixth live foal: closely related to fair 11.9f winner Scimitarlia (by Diesis) and half-brother to fair 1986 middle-distance winner Apply (by Kings Lake): dam won 5 races from 1¼m to 1½m: 9/1, green and in need of race, pushed along soon after halfway when 1½ lengths third of 8 to Arusha in minor event at Newbury in October: will improve, particularly over further. *R. Charlton*

TRENDY AUCTIONEER (IRE)   4 b.g. Mazaad 106 – Trendy Princess   **37**
(Prince Tenderfoot (USA) 126) [1991 8m* 8.2m a8g 7g 8f 8.2m 10m 10d² 1992 a12g 10m 8.3g 10g 10m³ 10.2f² 10g⁶ 10.8g a10g] sturdy gelding: inconsistent handicapper: stays 1¼m: acts on firm ground and dead: goes well blinkered/visored: has run well for apprentice: trained until after penultimate start by M. Pipe: sold to join Mrs L. Jewell 1,800 gns Ascot November Sales. *J. S. Moore*

TRENTESIMO (IRE)   2 ch.g. (Feb 28) Imperial Frontier (USA) 112 – Be   **73**
Nimble (Wattlefield 117) [1992 5s⁵ 5m⁶ 5h* 6g² a6g 5m* 5g³ 5.3d³ 5g] 15,000Y: small, stocky gelding: good mover: first foal: dam, Irish 7f winner, is half-sister to Carol's Treasure: modest performer: made all or most when winning maiden at Carlisle and claimer at Pontefract in summer: stays 6f: acts on hard and dead ground (ran moderately on equitrack). *J. Berry*

TREPIDATION (IRE)   2 b.g. (Feb 6) Cyrano de Bergerac 120 – Shenley Lass   **57**
(Prince Tenderfoot (USA) 126) [1992 5g 5g⁶ 6m 6g 5g 8d 8s 10d* 8g] IR 4,800F: good-bodied gelding: has a round action: first foal: dam Irish maiden: wearing brush pricker, best effort when leading line in seller at Leicester in October: not discredited in selling nursery at Doncaster after: stays well: acts on dead ground: below form blinkered, visored last 2 starts: sold 6,000 gns Newmarket Autumn Sales. *M. J. Fetherston-Godley*

TRESARIA (IRE)   2 b.f. (Apr 25) Taufan (USA) 119 – Tres Bien (Pitskelly 122)   **36**
[1992 7.1d 7m 6m] 2,000Y: leggy filly: fifth foal: half-sister to modest 1¼m winner Persian Lord (by Persian Bold): dam showed only a little ability in USA: no promise, including in a seller. *P. Howling*

873

TRESILIAN OWL 4 b.c. Bold Owl 101 – High Lee 71 (Will Hays (USA)) [1991 NR 1992 10.2f 10g 11.6g] leggy colt: fourth foal: half-brother to a winning hurdler by Roman Warrior: dam selling hurdler: no worthwhile form in sellers. *R. J. Hodges* —

TRETS 2 b.f. (May 30) Risk Me (FR) 127 – French Spirit (FR) (Esprit du Nord (USA) 126) [1992 8.1d⁵ 8d 7.1g² 8v⁴] 625Y: leggy, workmanlike filly: first foal: dam unraced: modest maiden: should be at least as effective at 1m as 7f: sold 1,300 gns Newmarket Autumn Sales. *P. A. Kelleway* **55**

TREVORSNINEPOINTS 2 ch.f. (Apr 24) Jester 119 – Miss Merlin 79 (Manacle 123) [1992 6d² 5m* 6f² 5.2f* 5g² 5g⁶ 7m 5s⁵ 6m⁴ 6g] 1,000Y: lightly-made filly: moderate mover: half-sister to several winners, including 1990 2-y-o 5f winner Knockavon (by Belfort) and fairly useful sprinter Lyndseylee (by Swing Easy): dam won twice at 6f: successful in sellers at Redcar (no bid) and Yarmouth (bought out of N. Tinkler's stable 5,500 gns) in June: stays 6f: best form on a sound surface. *M. J. Ryan* **56**

TREVVEETHAN (IRE) 3 ch.g. On Your Mark 125 – Carrick Slaney (Red God 128§) [1991 5m 7m 1992 a7g a8g] workmanlike gelding: no worthwhile form. *J. Balding* —

TRIAL TIMES (USA) 3 ch.c. Court Trial (USA) – Vany (USA) (Lord Vancouver (CAN)) [1991 7g² a7g⁴ a7g* 7g⁵ 8m³ 1992 7g 8g² 10g³ 7f³ 8g6 a8g* a8g²] compact colt: carries condition: has a quick action: consistent handicapper: returned from 4-month lay-off with best 3-y-o effort to win claimer at Lingfield in November: effective at 7f, and probably stays 1¼m: acts on firm ground and goes well on all-weather surfaces. *W. A. O'Gorman* **77**

TRIANGLEPOINT (IRE) 2 b.f. (Mar 25) Auction Ring (USA) 123 – Tapestry (Tap On Wood 130) [1992 6m 7g⁵ 7s] 5,000Y: good-topped, workmanlike filly: has a round action: second foal: dam unraced: best effort in autumn maidens fifth of 18 at Redcar: should stay 1m: possibly unsuited by soft ground. *G. A. Pritchard-Gordon* **55**

TRICKY VERA (IRE) 3 ch.f. Pennine Walk 120 – Madam Loving 99 (Vaigly Great 127) [1991 5m⁶ 1992 a8g] lengthy, sparely-made filly: well beaten in 6-runner £8,000 event at Epsom in June at 2 yrs: retained by trainer 650 gns Ascot March Sales then last of 11 in claimer at Lingfield in December, 1992. *T. J. Naughton* —

TRICOTRIC 5 br.m. Electric 126 – Orpheline 76 (Thatch (USA) 136) [1991 12.4v* 12d² 13d⁴ 15m⁶ 12.1g 16.2d 1992 14d 12s] lengthy, good-topped mare: rated 42 at 4 yrs: seems on the downgrade: stays 13f: used to go well with plenty of give in the ground. *G. M. Moore* —

TRICYCLE (IRE) 3 b.g. Phardante (FR) 120 – Push Bike (Ballad Rock 122) [1991 8m 8m⁶ 8.1m 1992 12.3s 14.1f* 16f 16.2d⁴] good-topped gelding: ran poorly after winning (hung markedly right) handicap at Redcar in May: shapes like a stayer: acts on firm going, seemingly not on a soft surface: not seen out after July. *J. W. Watts* **38**

TRIENNIUM (USA) 3 ch.c. Vaguely Noble 140 – Triple Tipple (USA) 111 (Raise A Cup (USA)) [1991 NR 1992 8d³ 10.5d³ 10g⁴ 10.5g² 11.8s] $55,000Y: rangy, rather unfurnished colt: second reported foal: half-brother to useful 1m winner Triode (by Sharpen Up): dam, 7f to 1m winner later stakes winner in USA, is out of half-sister to very useful middle-distance filly Trillionaire: fairly useful maiden: tailed off in handicap final run: should stay 1½m: acts on dead ground. *L. M. Cumani* **80**

TRIFOLIO 5 b.h. Touching Wood (USA) 127 – Triple Reef (Mill Reef (USA) 141) [1991 NR 1992 14m] rangy, attractive horse: good mover, rated 99 as 3-y-o: burly but shaped as if retains ability in Sandown handicap in June, only subsequent run: best with test of stamina: acts on firm and dead ground. *N. J. Henderson* —

TRI MY WAY (IRE) 2 ch.f. (Feb 1) It's The One (USA) – Jetting Ways (USA) (Tri Jet (USA)) [1992 6g 7.1m 6g⁶ 7d] 700F, 6,000 2-y-o: rather leggy filly: sister to 2 minor winners in USA and half-sister to another: dam won at 1m in USA: poor maiden. *R. R. Lamb* **30**

TRING PARK 6 b.g. Niniski (USA) 125 – Habanna 107 (Habitat 134) [1991 11.4m 17.2g 1992 11.9f 18.2g] big, leggy gelding: on the downgrade. *R. Curtis* —

TRINITY HALL 2 b.f. (May 3) Hallgate 127 – Trigamy 112 (Tribal Chief 125) [1992 5g 6s 6v³] angular filly: half-sister to 3-y-o 7.3f and 1m winner Risk Master (by Risk Me) and many other winners, including (at 7f to 1¼m) New Mexico (by Free State) and (at 7f) 7-y-o Mango Manila (by Martinmas): dam 5f performer: much improved effort in maidens when strong-finishing third at Folkestone in October: should be better suited by 7f. *C. A. Horgan* **50**

TRIOMING 6 b.g. Homing 130 – Third Generation 58 (Decoy Boy 129) [1991 NR 1992 6f 5m 7.6m 5d⁵ a5g³ 5.2g² 5g⁶ 6d] compact gelding: moderate mover: second reported foal: dam sprint maiden: poor handicapper: should prove suited by further than 5f: acts on fibresand: below form when blinkered once. *A. P. Jones* **40**

TRIPLE 2 b.c. (Feb 27) Caerleon (USA) 132 – Three Stars 93 (Star Appeal 133) [1992 7g² 8d] leggy colt: third live foal: half-brother to French 1½m winner Star of Dance (by Sadler's Wells): dam 1½m winner from staying family: beaten ½ length by Cropton in maiden at Lingfield in September: ran moderately when favourite in similar event at Leicester month after: should stay middle distances. *B. W. Hills* **78**

TRIPLE TOP 7 b.g. High Top 131 – Dalmally 89 (Sharpen Up 127) [1991 NR 1992 11.8d 16s] good-bodied gelding: on the downgrade. *K. White* **–**

TRIPLE TROUBLE 3 br.c. Nomination 125 – Be Malicious (Malicious) [1991 6f 7m 7g 1992 8.2g 10d 7f⁶ 7.1d] workmanlike colt: poor mover: poor handicapper: seems to stay 7f. *H. J. Collingridge* **–**

TRIPPIANO 2 b.c. (Jan 22) Fappiano (USA) – Hence (USA) (Mr Prospector (USA)) [1992 7.1g² 8m] rangy colt: has a long stride: fourth foal: dam 7f winner: sire (by Mr Prospector) 6f to 9f stakes winner: well-backed favourite, stayed on really well when beaten 3½ lengths by Gustavia in maiden at Sandown: green still when one-paced ninth of 19 to Bashayer in similar event at Newmarket later in autumn: will stay beyond 1m: has scope, and sort to do better at 3 yrs. *H. R. A. Cecil* **77 p**

TRISHYDE (USA) 3 ch.f. Nureyev (USA) 131 – Rose du Boele (FR) (Rheffic (FR) 129) [1991 NR 1992 10s* 10g⁴ 10.5g 12m* 10s² 12m⁶ 9.3s 12f⁶ 9f² 12g³] 105,000Y: fifth reported foal: sister to useful French 7f and 9f winner Idefix, closely related to French provincial 11f winner Le Streghe (by Lyphard) and half-sister to useful 2-y-o 7f and 1m winner Spirits Dancing (by Melyno): dam unraced granddaughter of La Lagune: smart performer: won new-comers race in April and Prix de Malleret (by ½ length from Trampoli) in June, both at Longchamp: ran well most outings afterwards, including when sixth in Prix Vermeille (beaten a length) at Longchamp and Breeders' Cup Turf (beaten 5½ lengths) at Gulfstream Park and placed at Hollywood Park in handicap and Hollywood Turf Cup (1¼ lengths third to subsequently-demoted Fraise): effective at 9f and stays 1½m: acts on any going: usually held up off pace: reportedly to be trained by C. Speckert in USA. *F. Boutin, France* **116**

TROJAN ENVOY 4 br.g. Trojan Fen 118 – Gold Maid (FR) (Green Dancer (USA) 132) [1991 10d 8s 10m 14f⁴ 14f⁴ 14g 16.2g 14.6m 14.1m 1992 21.6g⁴ 17.2s 16.4g⁶ 16.4m⁶] sturdy, close-coupled gelding: inconsistent handicapper: suited by test of stamina: acts on firm going: sold to join Mrs R. Henderson 1,800 gns Newmarket September Sales. *W. Carter* **34**

TROJAN LANCER 6 b.h. Trojan Fen 118 – Dunster's Cream 51 (Sharpen Up 127) [1991 12m⁵ 12g⁵ 12m⁴ 12m* 11.8g⁵ 11.8g² 12g³ 12d 1992 12m⁴ 12.4f⁴ 10g 14.6m⁴ **61**

Prix de Malleret, Longchamp—Trishyde accounts for Trampoli

16.1m[4] 14g 12d] sturdy, close-coupled horse: carries condition: moderate walker and mover: modest handicapper: stays 14.6f: ideally suited by top-of-the-ground: held up. *Dr J. D. Scargill*

TRONCHETTO (IRE) 3 b.g. Shernazar 131 – Idle Days 80 (Hittite Glory 125) 55 [1991 8g[5] 8.1d a7g 1992 8.9s 12d* 12.1m[4]] strong, workmanlike gelding: has a round action: modest handicapper: won at Carlisle in May: not seen after that month: will stay further: acts on good to firm and dead ground: sold to join J. J. O'Neill's stable 9,400 gns Ascot June Sales. *Sir Mark Prescott*

TROON 2 gr.c. (Apr 23) Beveled (USA) – Cestrefeld 94 (Capistrano 120) [1992 85 5m[4] 6m[6] 5.3f* 5g[2] 6g[4] 5.3d[2] 5d 5g[4]] 6,600Y: leggy, narrow colt: half-brother to several winners here and in West Indies, notably useful 6-y-o middle-distance stayer First Victory (by Concorde Hero): dam, 5f and 6f winner at 2 yrs, is half-sister to Young Generation: won maiden at Brighton in August and ran well all starts after, in Doncaster listed race and Newmarket nursery last 2: should prove suited by 6f/7f: acts on firm and dead ground: bandaged. *Mrs L. Piggott*

TROOPING (IRE) 3 b.c. Auction Ring (USA) 123 – Tunguska 76 (Busted 134) 82 [1991 6d[6] 1992 8g 8g[3] 9m 8m[4] 8f* 7m[3] 8d[2] 8d[5] 8d[4] 9d 8m 8g] good-bodied colt: has a round action: fair handicapper: landed odds in maiden at Pontefract in June: well below form last 3 starts: stays 1m: acts on firm and dead ground. *G. Harwood*

TROPICAL 2 b.f. (Jan 11) Green Desert (USA) 127 – Bermuda Classic 98 (Double 98 Form 130) [1992 6g* 6m* 6m[3] 5g* 6g[6] 6s[4]] second foal: half-sister to 3-y-o Virginia Cottage (by Lomond): dam Irish 2-y-o 5f and 6f winner stayed 1m: successful in maiden (dead-heated) and minor event at Leopardstown and in 8-runner Shernazar EBF Curragh Stakes (by 2½ lengths from Bint Albadou) at the Curragh: fair fourth of 6 in listed race at the Curragh final start, in August: stays 6f: ran moderately when blinkered fifth outing. *D. K. Weld, Ireland*

TROPICAL MIST (FR) 12 b. or br.g. Faraway Son (USA) 130 – Tropical Cream – (USA) (Creme Dela Creme) [1991 NR 1992 14.6g] modest chaser nowadays (stays 3m): tailed off only run on flat in 1992. *G. A. Ham*

TROPICAL TIA (IRE) 2 b.f. (Mar 31) Camden Town 125 – Serena Maria 63 40 § (Dublin Taxi) [1992 6m 5h 5g[3] 5m[5] 5.2g 6d] 4,000 2-y-o: leggy, narrow filly: poor mover: third foal: half-sister to 5f to 7f winner Waad and 3-y-o Mma International (both by Milk of The Barley): dam won 6f seller: poor plater: sometimes wears a tongue strap: unseated rider at start on fifth run: one to treat with caution. *R. Voorspuy*

TROPICAL WATERS (USA) 2 b.f. (Feb 21) Green Forest (USA) 134 – North- 68 p ern Premier (USA) 117 (Northern Baby (CAN) 127) [1992 6.1d[2] 6f[2]] leggy, sparely-made filly: second foal: dam French 6.5f (at 2 yrs) to 1m winner, including in 2 Group 3 events: similar form when second in maidens at Nottingham and Yarmouth (pulled hard when beaten 4 lengths by Lost Soldier): should stay 7f. *M. Moubarak*

TROUPE 4 b.g. Sadler's Wells (USA) 132 – Lovelight 112 (Bleep-Bleep 134) [1991 74 7g[3] 7.6d* 8m 10m[6] 10g 8.9g[5] 8.9g 8m[2] 9m 9g 1992 8d[5] 7.6g 7s[4] 7v] lengthy gelding: in-and-out form in handicaps in 1992: absent over 5 months after second outing, tailed off final start: effective from around 1m to 1¼m: acts on good to firm ground and soft: tends to get on edge: found little when blinkered: held up: sold 8,400 gns Newmarket Autumn Sales. *B. W. Hills*

TROVE 3 b.g. Treasure Kay 114 – Old Silver (Bold Lad (IRE) 133) [1991 5m* 6m* 82 d 6m[5] 6m[4] 1992 5g[4] 6m 6m a6g a7g 10.4s[5] a10g] leggy gelding: capable of fairly useful form but went wrong way in 1992: stays 6f: below form blinkered once: sold out of Mrs N. Macauley's stable 2,900 gns Doncaster November Sales before final start. *M. J. Heaton-Ellis*

TROY BOY 2 b. or br.c. (May 7) Wassl 125 – Petrol 73 (Troy 137) [1992 8.2g] – 4,300Y: fifth foal: half-brother to 3 winners, including 1m and 9f winner Zammah (by Jalmood), later winner in USA, and 2m winner Dhakrah (by Touching Wood): dam won at 1m and stayed 1¼m: very mulish at stalls before soundly beaten in maiden at Nottingham in September. *R. Hannon*

TRUBEN (USA) 3 ch.f. Arctic Tern (USA) 126 – Cadbury Hill (USA) (Northern 85 Baby (CAN) 127) [1991 6.1m[5] 1992 12g* 12.3m* 12.5m[2] 12.3g[4] 11.9d 12g[4] 12g] lengthy, sturdy filly: good mover: fairly useful handicapper: won at Folkestone (maiden) in April and Ripon in May: creditable fourth at Newmarket in October, penultimate start: will stay beyond 1½m: acts on good to firm ground: trained until after fifth start by H. Cecil. *D. R. Loder*

TRUE CONTENDER 3 b.f. Never So Bold 135 – Young Diana (Young Generation 129) [1991 NR 1992 a8g a12g] 6,200Y: sturdy filly: third foal: half-sister to plating-class middle-distance maiden Sansool (by Dominion): dam unraced half-sister to very smart middle-distance horse Town And Country: last in apprentice maiden at Lingfield: pulled up at same course after: dead. *C. A. Cyzer* —

TRUE HERO (USA) 2 b.c. (Apr 16) The Minstrel (CAN) 135 – Badge of Courage (USA) (Well Decorated (USA)) [1992 7m* 7g4] $450,000Y: strong colt: has .•round action: fourth foal: half-brother to 1990 Irish 2-y-o 7f and 1m winner Patently Clear (by Miswaki), later successful in USA: dam unraced half-sister to Known Fact, Tentam and dam of Gone West and Lion Cavern: landed odds by neck in 16-runner maiden at Leicester in September, heading Roger The Butler close home: one-paced fourth of 8 to Right Win in £8,900 event at Ascot following month: will stay 1¼m: has scope, and should improve again. *J. H. M. Gosden* **87 p**

TRUE MOOD 3 b.f. Jalmood (USA) 126 – Madam Muffin 77 (Sparkler 130) [1991 6s a8g a8g 1992 a10g] no worthwhile form: sold 675 gns Ascot February Sales. *J. D. Bethell* —

TRUE PRECISION 2 b.f. (Apr 21) Presidium 124 – Madam Muffin 77 (Sparkler 130) [1992 5m2 5d4 5d5 6v] small, sturdy filly: poor mover: dam sprinter: off course 3 months after fourth of 6 to Marina Park in listed event at Sandown (very fractious preliminaries, taken early to post) in July and well below form on return: should stay 6f: bandaged. *J. D. Bethell* **71 ?**

TRUE STORY (IRE) 2 b. or br.c. (Jun 16) Reasonable (FR) 119 – Doctor's Choice 116 (Petingo 135) [1992 6g 6d6 6m* 6.1g2 6g* 7g6 6.1s4 6s] 2,000 (privately) Y: lengthy, useful-looking colt: good walker: half-brother to 1m winner Prescription (by Cure The Blues) and fairly useful 1981 2-y-o 1m winner Twist Home (by Homeric): dam smart French 2-y-o 1m winner: successful at Windsor in seller (no bid) in June and nursery in August: ran well in nurseries next 2 runs, raced on unfavoured side of track when blinkered final outing: refused to enter stalls once after and sold 3,200 gns Newmarket Autumn Sales: should stay 1m: probably acts on any going. *R. Hannon* **63**

TRUE TOUCH 3 gr.g. Grey Ghost 98 – La Raine 93 (Majority Blue 126) [1991 NR 1992 a8g 5m 6f 5g4 6g] rather unfurnished gelding: brother to 5f winner Grey Tan and half-brother to 2 winners, one over 5f and the other over fences: dam a 2-y-o 5f winner, seemed later to need further: little worthwhile form: sold 1,600 gns Doncaster September Sales. *T. D. Barron* **39**

TRUMP 3 b.g. Last Tycoon 131 – Fleeting Affair 98 (Hotfoot 126) [1991 NR 1992 a8g5 a8g3 a8g2 10.1s* 12.1s*] sturdy gelding: first foal: dam, 1¼m and 1½m winner stayed 2m, is sister to leading 1991/2 novice hurdler Flown: not seen on flat after winning handicaps at Newcastle and Hamilton in spring: stays 1½m: sold out of Sir Mark Prescott's stable 16,000 gns Ascot May Sales after fourth start: seems rather lazy: broke out of stalls once. *C. Parker* **56**

TRUMPET 3 ch.c. Dominion 123 – Soprano 112 (Kris 135) [1991 6f6 7f4 7g 1992 10.2d5 12m* 12f6 11.4d3] angular colt: consistent in 1992: won claimers at Goodwood in May and Newbury in June: claimed to join J. O'Shea £18,875 final run: will stay beyond 1½m: acts on firm and dead ground: usually held up. *Lord Huntingdon* **71**

TRUNDLEY WOOD 2 b.f. (Jan 28) Wassl 125 – Tharwat (USA) 83 (Topsider (USA)) [1992 5g5 6g6 a7g2 a6g5 7g5 7m* 7m] unfurnished filly: first foal: dam 6f (at 2 yrs) and 1m winner: modest performer: won nursery at Yarmouth in September: ran badly final outing: will stay 1m: acts on good to firm ground and fibresand. *G. A. Pritchard-Gordon* **66**

TRUNK CALL (USA) 3 b. or br.g. Phone Trick (USA) – Sabreline (USA) (Lines of Power (USA)) [1991 NR 1992 9g $50,000Y: plain gelding: second foal: dam once-raced half-sister to Preakness Stakes second Play On: showed nothing in maiden at Kempton in May: sold 1,250 gns Newmarket July Sales. *Mrs J. Cecil* —

TRUTHFUL IMAGE 3 b.f. Reesh 117 – Token of Truth (Record Token 128) [1991 5m2 6m2 6f 5m4 a5g3 7f 6m4 5m3 5d2 5.7g* 1992 6d5 6d5 5m* 5.7s 5m3 6m4 6m4 5.7m* 5.7g 6g* 5g 6d 6m 5d5 5.1d 5g a7g a6g5] good-topped filly: moderate mover: fairly useful handicapper: successful in 1992 at Windsor, Bath and Yarmouth: ideally suited by 6f: best on a sound surface: well below form in visor once, normally blinkered. *M. J. Ryan* **81**

TRY LEGUARD (IRE) 3 gr.c. Try My Best (USA) 130 – Crown Coral (Main Reef 126) [1991 5v2 5d* 5d2 5g2 6g3 6g 5d 1992 a6g4 a7g2 a7g3 a7g* a8g4 a7g5 7g 7g* 8d 7g5 7m4 7f 7.1g 7f 6.9m3 8g] close-coupled colt: moderate mover: generally **81 d**

below form after winning handicaps at Lingfield and Thirsk in spring: best form at 7f: acts on dead ground and equitrack: usually races prominently: trained until after penultimate start by W. Carter. *J. S. Moore*

TRY N' FLY (IRE) 2 b.g. (Mar 10) Carmelite House (USA) 118 – Gruntled – (Grundy 137) [1992 7g] IR 4,000Y: half-brother to modest Irish maiden Enthusiastic (by Ela-Mana-Mou): dam, possibly stayed 2m, is out of smart middle-distance stayer Guillotina, dam of Princess Royal winner One Way Street: very green and always well behind in maiden at Ayr in August. *Miss L. A. Perratt*

TSAR ALEXIS (USA) 4 br.c. Topsider (USA) – Evening Silk (USA) (Damascus – (USA)) [1991 6m 7m⁶ 10.2f a8g² 8.1m a16g 1992 8s a8g⁶ a10g⁶] quite attractive colt: has a quick action: rated 66 at 3 yrs: on the downgrade. *C. L. Popham*

TSUNAMI 4 b.c. Niniski (USA) 125 – Seasurf 106 (Seaepic (USA) 100) [1991 – 10.8g⁴ 12m 14m⁵ 10.4g³ 14.1f² 16m 1992 14g 14m 14m] tall, leggy, sparely-made colt: poor mover: rated 80 at 3 yrs: on the downgrade and sold to join Mrs J. Read 2,000 gns Newmarket Autumn Sales. *C. E. Brittain*

TTYFRAN 2 b.c. (Apr 9) Petong 126 – So It Goes 73 (Free State 125) [1992 5d 62 7m⁶ 6m² 7d⁵ 7g³ 7g] 13,000Y: stocky colt: first foal: dam, 2-y-o 6f winner, is half-sister to smart Italian 5f to 1m winner Melbury Lad: modest maiden: should stay 1m: seems unsuited by dead ground. *F. H. Lee*

TUDELA 2 ch.f. (Apr 7) Aragon 118 – Divine Penny 65 (Divine Gift 127) [1992 5g³ 39 5.1s 6g 7d] 1,000Y: sparely-made filly: moderate mover: eighth reported foal: half-sister to 1¼m and 1½m winner Divine Charger (by Treboro) and modest stayer Pour Encourager (by Kind of Hush): dam, placed in sellers at up to 1¼m, later won 5 times in Hong Kong: well beaten after third in seller at Wolverhampton in April: sold out of M. Haynes's stable 1,100 gns Ascot June Sales after penultimate run. *Mrs A. Knight*

TUDOR DA SAMBA 3 b.g. Sizzling Melody 117 – La Belle Princesse 85 (Royal 57 Match 117) [1991 6f⁵ 8g⁶ 8m 1992 10d 11.5g³ 12f⁶ 12g⁵ 14.1d 15.8d⁴] leggy gelding: moderate mover: maiden handicapper: seems suited by 2m: acts on dead ground: sold to join M. Pipe's stable 2,200 gns Newmarket Autumn Sales and won selling hurdle in December. *J. R. Fanshawe*

TUDORGATEWAY 4 b.g. Martinmas 128 – Shikra (Sea Hawk II 131) [1991 6f 57 6d⁶ 6.9s³ 6m* 7.6g⁶ 7.1m 8m a6g² 1992 a7g⁵ a8g a6g⁵ a7g] stocky, deep-girthed gelding: none too consistent handicapper: rated 65 at 3 yrs: not seen after February: should stay 1m: acts on good to firm and soft ground: effective visored or not: reluctant to race once, and probably one to be wary of: sold 700 gns Ascot February Sales. *M. H. Tompkins*

TUDOR ISLAND 3 b.c. Jupiter Island 126 – Catherine Howard 68 (Tower Walk 77 ? 130) [1991 8m 8m 1992 12d³ 11.8g² 10s³ 12m³ 16m 12m 10s a12g⁶] unfurnished colt: easily best run in handicaps in 1992 when blinkered for only time, on fourth start: should stay 1¾m: acts on good to firm ground. *C. E. Brittain*

TULAPET 3 gr.f. Mansingh (USA) 120 – Iridium 78 (Linacre 133) [1991 6m 6m 42 d 1992 6g³ 6m 6f⁶ 7d 10m 6.9h³ 6g 6.9g 8.1d a10g a7g a10g] angular, workmanlike filly: worthwhile form only when visored third in handicap at Folkestone: stays 7f: acts on hard ground: tailed off last 3 starts, when wearing blinkers and eyeshield. *S. Dow*

TULFARRIS 5 b. or br.g. Glenstal (USA) 118 – Trusted Maiden (Busted 134) – [1991 a7g³ a7g⁴ 6s a8g³ 6g 7m 9.2s a8g 1992 12.3d] big, workmanlike gelding: moderate walker and mover: poor maiden: stays 1m: acts on dead going and fibresand: below form visored. *M. D. Hammond*

TUMBLING (USA) 4 b.c. Irish River (FR) 131 – Trephine (FR) (Viceregal 37 (CAN)) [1991 8g 8s 10d 10d⁵ 1992 14.6g 12.1g 10.1s⁵ 5s³ 5d⁴] sturdy, good-bodied ex-French colt: fourth foal: half-brother to Prix de l'Arc de Triomphe winner Trempolino (by Sharpen Up): dam useful winner at up to 1¼m in France, and later successful in USA: fair form as 3-y-o for Mme C. Head: poor form here: stays 1¼m: acts on good ground. *R. Allan*

TUNBRIDGE WELLS (IRE) 3 b.c. Sadler's Wells (USA) 132 – Tenea 94 p (Reform 132) [1991 8m 1992 10d⁴ 10.4d⁵ 10s² 10.3g²] strong, good-bodied colt: off course nearly 6 months after first run in 1992: improved with each start on return, tongue tied down when rallying second in minor event at Doncaster final start: will prove better suited by 1½m: acts on soft ground: sure to win a race at 4 yrs. *J. H. M. Gosden*

TURBULENT RIVER (USA) 4 b. or br.c. Riverman (USA) 131 – Star – Pastures 124 (Northfields (USA)) [1991 8d 7f* 8g 7m 7.6g 7g 1992 7g 8v] lengthy

William Hill November Handicap, Doncaster—
a sixth training success in the race for the Gosden family as Turgenev holds Daru

colt: poor mover: rated 71 at 3 yrs: well below form in sellers in spring of 1992: should stay 1m: sold 1,500 gns Ascot May Sales. *N. Tinkler*

TURF DANCER 5 b.m. Anfield 117 – Cachucha (Gay Fandango (USA) 132) [1991 **35** 11s 10d 11f 10.6g 12.1d 10g⁶ 11.1s⁴ 9.2d 10.9g⁴ 12.1m 1992 12m²] leggy, workmanlike mare: maiden handicapper: stays 1½m: acts on good to firm and soft ground. *P. C. Haslam*

TURFMANS VISION 2 b.c. (Apr 30) Vision (USA) – Persian Alexandra **51** (Persian Bold 123) [1992 a7g 7d⁴ 7g 8.2d 7d] 6,000F, 6,000Y: leggy, unfurnished colt: fourth foal: half-brother to Italian 3-y-o 1¼m Group 3 winner Taff's Acre (by Dance of Life), successful there and in Ireland (at 7f) at 2 yrs: dam, Irish 2-y-o 7f winner, is half-sister to Windsor Castle winner Sea Falcon: modest maiden: should stay 1¼m: acts on dead ground. *R. Hollinshead*

TURGENEV (IRE) 3 b.c. Sadler's Wells (USA) 132 – Tilia (ITY) (Dschingis **103** p Khan) [1991 NR 1992 10g 10g² 10.5d* 12f 14g⁴ 12g² 14d⁴ 11.9s* 12g*] strong, deep-bodied colt: has a fluent, round action: half-brother to Italian Derby winner Tommy Way (by Thatch) and a winner in Italy by Fordham: dam won in Italy: progressed really well in 1992: successful at Haydock in maiden and handicap, and in 25-runner November Handicap at Doncaster in good style by 1½ lengths from stable-companion Daru: should stay beyond 1½m: probably acts on any going: hung left once: held up, and has good turn of foot: will have another good season at 4 yrs. *J. H. M. Gosden*

TURGEON (USA) 6 gr.h. Caro 133 – Reiko (FR) (Targowice (USA) 130) [1991 **111** 14.5s² 15.5m* 12m 15g* 14d* 15.5d* 14v³ 1992 15.5g⁴ 20f³ 15s⁶] good-topped, rather leggy horse: rated 119 and had tremendous season in 1991: creditable efforts on first 2 starts at 6 yrs in Prix Vicomtesse Vigier at Longchamp (2½ lengths behind Commendable) and Gold Cup at Royal Ascot (beaten 5 lengths by Drum Taps): not seen out again after well beaten in Prix Kergorlay at Deauville: effective at around 1¾m to 2½m: acts on any going: below form when blinkered once: held up. *J. Pease, France*

TURNING HEADS 3 b.f. King Among Kings 60 – Jacinda (Thatching 131) [1991 – NR 1992 a8g a8g a8g 10f 9.9f] sparely-made filly: first foal: dam ran once at 3 yrs: of little account. *Capt. J. Wilson*

TURRET GATES 3 ch.c. Ahonoora 122 – Cape Race (USA) 88 (Northern **68** Dancer (CAN)) [1991 NR 1992 8g 7g⁵ 7m⁶ 7g² 7f* 7g] leggy, workmanlike colt:

half-brother to several winners, including useful 1m to 1¼m winner Raiwand (by Tap On Wood) and useful 1981 2-y-o 5f and 7f winner Final Strike (by Artaius): dam 1m winner, is half-sister to very smart colts Lord Gayle and Never Return: modest performer: won maiden at Thirsk in August: should stay 1m: acts on firm going. *J. A. R. Toller*

TURTLE BEACH 3 ch.c. Primo Dominie 121 – Double Finesse 97 (Double **69** Jump 131) [1991 6d⁴ 1992 7g⁵ 7s⁵ a8g² a7g* a8g⁵] good-topped colt: modest peformer: won maiden at Southwell in June: not seen out after following month: stays 1m: retained 9,000 gns Ascot June Sales, sold to join C. C. Elsey's stable 4,200 gns Newmarket Autumn Sales. *A. A. Scott*

TURTLE POWER 2 ch.g. (May 15) May Be This Time 74 – Miss Chianti – (Royben 125) [1992 7g] sparely-made gelding: sixth reported foal: half-brother to winning stayer/hurdler Between The Sheets (by Crooner): dam poor sprint plater: late progress but never-dangerous ninth of 18 in maiden at Doncaster in November. *T. Thomson Jones*

TUSCAN DAWN 2 ch.g. (Mar 21) Clantime 101 – Excavator Lady 65 (Most **66** Secret 119) [1992 5d⁴ 5m³ 5.1g² 5m² 5g 5g⁴ 5s] 6,800Y: leggy, lengthy gelding: moderate mover: fourth foal: dam stayed 1¾m on flat and won selling hurdles: fair performer: won maiden auction at Kempton in April: speedy: probably acts on any going. *J. Berry*

TUSKY 4 ch.g. Prince Sabo 123 – Butosky 71 (Busted 134) [1991 8d 6g 1992 7g **84** d 10s⁵ 8s* 7d 8.1m³ 8.1g 7m³ 7m 7.9g² 8s 8s⁵ 7s] tall, good-topped gelding: moderate walker: poor mover: in-and-out form after winning Newcastle handicap in April: effective at strongly-run 7f, to 1¼m: probably acts on any going: effective visored or not: has been very troublesome at stalls: usually forces pace: sold to join G. Moore 8,400 gns Doncaster November Sales. *M. J. Camacho*

TWAFEAJ (USA) 3 b.f. Topsider (USA) – Billy Sue's Rib (USA) (Al Hattab **110** (USA)) [1991 5g² 5m² 6m* 6m⁴ 6m² 6m* 6m⁴ 1992 8d 8g⁴ 6.5g³ 6s* 6s² 6d⁴ 5s] strong, good-bodied filly: good walker and mover: very useful performer: won Prix de Meautry at Deauville in August by short head from Thourios: in frame in Falmouth Stakes at Newmarket, Prix Maurice de Gheest at Deauville (2 lengths third to Pursuit of Love), Group 2 contest at Baden-Baden (went down by a length to Elbio) and Diadem Stakes at Ascot (beaten 3½ lengths by Wolfhound): best efforts at around 6f: acts on good to firm ground and soft. *B. Hanbury*

TWICE AS MUCH 3 ch.f. Tremblant 112 – Two Diamonds (Double Jump 131) – [1991 NR 1992 10.1d 10g 10d⁶] workmanlike filly: third foal: dam of no account: takes after her mother. *D. A. Wilson*

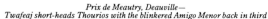

Prix de Meautry, Deauville—
Twafeaj short-heads Thourios with the blinkered Amigo Menor back in third

Dalham Chester Vase, Chester—to the sponsors the spoils;
Twist And Turn holds Jape (left) and Mack The Knife

TWICE THE GROOM (IRE)   2 b.c. (Mar 21) Digamist (USA) 110 – Monaco   **70**
Lady 83 (Manado 130) [1992 6m³ 6g²] 8,000Y: tall, rather leggy colt: fourth foal:
half-brother to 3-y-o 1m winner Missy-S (by Sarab), 1¼m seller winner Uniroyal
Windway (by Runnett), also successful in France, and a winner in Macau: dam
second twice over 1m: similar form in minor event at Kempton and maiden at
Goodwood: should stay 1m: not seen out after early-June. *P. Mitchell*

TWILIGHT FALLS   7 ch.g. Day Is Done 115 – Grattan Princess (Tumble Wind   **53**
(USA) [1991 7d 6m⁴ a6g⁵ 8m 6m⁵ 6.1m* 1992 a6g 6d* 5.9d³ 5m 6d 6d 6.1s]
medium-sized, good-topped gelding: carries plenty of condition: poor mover: landed
gamble (for third time) in selling handicap (bought in 4,800 gns) at Pontefract in
April: below form last 4 starts after returning from 5-month lay-off: should stay 7f:
acts on good to firm and dead going: often troublesome at stalls. *M. J. Camacho*

TWILIGHT SECRET   3 b.f. Vaigly Great 127 – Kristal Air 76 (Kris 135) [1991   **67**
7m⁶ 1992 8d5 8g² 7f³ 8g 8.1g 9s⁴ 10.3s a10g⁴ a10g* a10g²] workmanlike filly: fair
performer: won apprentice handicap at Lingfield in November, leading over 4f out:
stays 1¼m: acts on soft going and equitrack, seemingly not on firm. *J. W. Hills*

TWIST AND TURN   3 ch.c. Groom Dancer (USA) 128 – Twyla 101 (Habitat 134) **116**
[1991 7m³ 7f* 8.1m* 8d³ 1992 9g* 12.3g* 12g⁵ 10s⁵ 10.3m² 8.9d⁶] good-topped colt:
fluent mover: smart and consistent performer: won listed Feilden Stakes at
Newmarket (by head from Young Senor) and Group 3 Dalham Chester Vase (by ¾
length from Jape) in spring: better efforts when fifth in Derby (made most, beaten 8
lengths by Dr Devious) at Epsom and Eclipse Stakes at Sandown (beaten 4 lengths
by Kooyonga): rare poor effort in York listed race final start: effective at 1¼m and
1½m: acts on any going: genuine: sent to B. Schutz in Germany. *H. R. A. Cecil*

TWITCHER   2 b.f. (Mar 19) Dowsing (USA) 124 – Frontal Attack (Pitskelly 122)   **–**
[1992 5.1d 5g 6d 6d] 500Y: sturdy, workmanlike filly: second foal: dam unraced: little
worthwhile form, including in sellers. *G. Blum*

TWO AND SIXPENCE (USA)   3 b.f. Chief's Crown (USA) – Candelight   **74**
Service (USA) (Blushing Groom (FR) 131) [1991 7m 1992 10.3g 12.1m⁵ 16.9d*
18.2m³ 17.2s² 15.9s] lengthy filly: shows a high knee action: progressive form in
1992, winning Wolverhampton maiden in August, until running as if something
amiss in Chester handicap final start: well suited by thorough test of stamina: acts
on good to firm and soft ground. *B. W. Hills*

TWO BIRDS   3 b.f. Prince Sabo 123 – Particular Miss 70 (Luthier 126) [1991 5m   **–**
6m⁵ 7g 1992 7g 6g 8.3m 7d 7d 8g] leggy, workmanlike filly: on the downgrade and
sold 500 gns Ascot September Sales. *C. A. Horgan*

TWO LEFT FEET   5 b.g. Petorius 117 – Whitstar 93 (Whitstead 125) [1991 8d² **106**
8d 10d⁵ 7.6d 8d⁶ 8g 8g 1992 8g 10d* 8d 8s³ 10.3g 8.1g³ 8g 8d* 8s* 7.1s³ 8d 8.1s* 8g⁶
7s³ 8v²] tall, lengthy gelding: good walker: poor mover: useful performer:
successful in Brighton apprentice event, handicaps at Salisbury and Ripon and
minor event at Chepstow (from Sunday's Hill): best at 7f/1m with give in the ground

(goes extremely well on heavy): occasionally carries head rather awkwardly: held up. *Sir Mark Prescott*

TWO LUMPS 2 b.g. (Apr 4) Nomination 125 – Tea-Pot 77 (Ragstone 128) [1992 **58** 8s⁴ 6.9v] leggy gelding: sixth foal: half-brother to middle-distance winner One For The Pot (by Nicholas Bill) and winning hurdler Mr Dormouse (by Comedy Star): dam out-and-out stayer: shaped encouragingly when fourth in maiden at Bath in September: below that form but not knocked about once held in similar event at Folkestone following month. *I. A. Balding*

TWO MOVES IN FRONT (IRE) 2 ch.c. (Feb 19) Ballad Rock 122 – Kentucky **70** Wildcat 64 (Be My Guest (USA) 126) [1992 5g 5g* 6g⁵ 5m⁴ 5m* 6g⁴ 6m⁴ 6m⁴ 5g* 5d⁵] 6,000Y: strong, workmanlike colt: has plenty of scope: first foal: dam, maiden, stayed 2m: none too consistent performer: won maiden auction at Edinburgh in April and auction events at Hamilton in July and Carlisle in September: best form at 5f on a sound surface. *J. Berry*

TWO TIMES TWELVE (IRE) 2 ch.g. (Apr 25) Mansooj 118 – Tacama 64 **65** (Daring Display (USA) 129) [1992 5d³ 5s⁴ 5g³ 5g² 5f⁴ 5g² 5g² 5g2] IR 5,400F, 5,800Y: workmanlike gelding, rather unfurnished: half-brother to several winners, including fair 1988 2-y-o 6f winner Eezepeeze (by Alzao): dam, plater, half-sister to useful stayer Drishaune: modest maiden: speedy: best form in blinkers: sold 2,000 gns Newmarket Autumn Sales. *J. Berry*

TYCHONIC 2 b.c. (Mar 23) Last Tycoon 131 – Metair 118 (Laser Light 118) [1992 **66 p** 6m⁵ 6m*] useful-looking colt: half-brother to several winners, including useful sprinters Meteoric (by High Line) and Fine Edge (by Sharpen Up): dam game sprinter: bandaged behind, shaped really promisingly in well-contested maiden at York in May: not seen again until September when comfortably landing the odds by ¾ length in Pontefract maiden, always going well but green: will stay 7f: sort to do better and should win more races. *B. W. Hills*

TY HIGH (IRE) 4 b.f. High Line 125 – Lady Tycoon 67 (No Mercy 126) [1991 NR **–** 1992 7m⁵ 7m⁴ 6.9h⁵] leggy, useful-looking filly: fourth foal: half-sister to fairly useful 1¼m and 13f winner Tonkawa (by Indian King) and French 1¼m winner Kala Jane (by Kalaglow): dam won at 1¼m: shaped with promise on belated debut when staying-on fifth of 16 in Redcar maiden in April: never pace to challenge after, not knocked about in Carlisle claimer final run (June): will be suited by further. *T. D. Barron*

TYKEYVOR (IRE) 2 b.c. (May 1) Last Tycoon 131 – Ivoronica 89 (Targowice **86 p** (USA) 130) [1992 6m 7f* 7m 6g³] quite good-topped colt: half-brother to several winners, including one-time useful 5f and 6f winner Lochonica (by Lochnager) and sprinter Diamond Appeal (by Star Appeal): dam 2-y-o 5f winner: progressive colt: won minor event at Doncaster in September: never able to challenge in listed Somerville Tattersall Stakes at Newmarket: stayed on well when third to Wathik in minor event at Doncaster: will be better suited by 1m: has scope, and should improve. *M. H. Tompkins*

TYLERS WOOD 7 br.g. Homing 130 – Beryl's Jewel 86 (Siliconn 121) [1991 a7g **–** a7g 1992 a7g 6m 6d 5m⁵] smallish, compact gelding: poor handicapper: stays 6f: yet to race on soft going, acts on any other. *S. Dow*

TYNRON DOON 3 b.g. Cragador 110 – Bel Esprit (Sagaro 133) [1991 5f 7m 6m² **63 ?** 6f 6.9h⁵ 7g⁴ 7m 7.1m³ 1992 8.3v* 8v* 12.3g⁵ 6.1d] lengthy, sparely-made gelding: showed little after winning sellers at Hamilton (no bid) and Pontefract (sold out of J. Berry's stable 6,000 gns) in April: bandaged penultimate run and off course 4 months after: should stay beyond 1m: best form on soft going: has run well blinkered. *D. J. Wintle*

TYRIAN 5 b.m. Elegant Air 119 – Character Builder 92 (African Sky 124) [1991 a7g **–** 8.3g 10g⁴ 1992 8.1d] lengthy mare: moderate mover: poor handicapper: stays 1¼m: acts on firm going: ran well when blinkered. *R. J. Baker*

TYRIAN PURPLE (IRE) 4 b.c. Wassl 125 – Sabrine (Mount Hagen (FR) 127) **66** [1991 10.2s 12.2d⁴ 12g 14f 8.2m 8.5m 8d 8.2f 8g³ 8f² a8g* 8m³ 8m³ 8m 8m 1992 a8g a8g a8g³ 8d* 8g 8g 8f⁶ a8g* a7g* 8.2d² 7.6g² 8m² 7.5m* 8f² 7.5g² 8.5m] leggy, angular colt: had a good season in handicaps in 1992, successful at Warwick, Southwell (2) and Beverley: ideally suited by 7f/1m: acts on firm and dead ground and fibresand: usually ridden by 7-lb claimer M. Humphries: sometimes wears tongue strap: front runner: sold 7,000 gns Newmarket Autumn Sales. *R. Hollinshead*

TYRNIPPY 6 b.g. Tyrnavos 129 – Floral 82 (Floribunda 136) [1991 a11g* a12g⁴ **–** a12g 11s a11g³ 1992 a12g] smallish, sparely-made gelding: moderate mover: rated 58

Foster's Silver Cup Stakes, York — Tyrone Bridge forges clear of Hateel

at 5 yrs: seems on the downgrade and sold 880 gns Doncaster June Sales. *M. Brittain*

TYRONE BRIDGE 6 b.g. Kings Lake (USA) 133 – Rhein Bridge 107 (Rheingold **106** 137) [1991 NR 1992 16.4m³ 20f⁶ 15.9d* 16m 15.9g³ 16g⁴] close-coupled, angular gelding: useful stayer: best efforts in 1992 in Henry II Stakes at Sandown (third to Drum Taps) and listed races at York, successful by 4 lengths (from Hateel) in July and third (to Further Flight) in Lonsdale Stakes: off course 2½ months before below-par run in Newmarket listed race final outing: best with good test of stamina: acts on good to firm and heavy ground: effective blinkered or not: tough. *M. C. Pipe*

TYRONE FLYER 3 b.c. Celestial Storm (USA) 132 – Dance A Jig (Dance In **53** Time (CAN)) [1991 8m⁴ 7g 7.1s a8g⁴ a8g 1992 10d³ 8g 8f⁶ 8g³ 10m⁶ a7g* 7s² 7d² 7d **a62** a6g⁶ a7g³] leggy colt: modest performer: trained first 3 starts by G. Eden, next 3 by M. Pipe, on final one winning apprentice handicap at Southwell in September: ran well when placed after: best short of 1m: acts on soft going and fibresand (below best on equitrack): takes good hold: has joined R. Rowe. *Miss Gay Kelleway*

TYRONE TURBO (USA) 3 ch.c. Premiership (USA) – My Go Go (USA) **–** (Santiago Road) [1991 5m 5g 5m⁵ 6.1m 1992 5m 5m] sparely-made colt: moderate walker and mover: headstrong maiden: suited by sharp 5f. *J. Akehurst*

U

UCCELLO 3 br.c. Efisio 120 – Silver Berry (Lorenzaccio 130) [1991 5m³ 6m 5g³ **72** 5m² 5m 1992 5s* 5g 5.3f² 6d³ 6m 5.7m³ 7.1g] lengthy colt: fair but none too consistent handicapper: won maiden at Wolverhampton in March: not seen out after July: stays 6f: acts on any going. *L. J. Holt*

UGLY 6 b.g. Cleon 92 – Lammas (Manicou) [1991 NR 1992 10.2f 14.1g] sturdy, **–** plain gelding: third foal: dam poor hurdler/chaser: no form in 2 outings over hurdles: always behind in seller at Bath and claimer at Yarmouth in midsummer. *R. P. C. Hoad*

UKAM'S LADY 2 ch.f. (Apr 28) Risk Me (FR) 127 – Deep Lady 78 (Deep Diver **38** § 134) [1992 5g 5s² 5g a7g 6m] 2,900F, 3,600Y: sturdy, lengthy filly: half-sister to 1986 2-y-o 6f winner Green's Herring (by Mansingh) and 1984 2-y-o 6f winner/fair hurdler Ballyarry (by Balliol): dam 2-y-o 5f winner: poor maiden: looked ungenuine when visored in seller final start, in July: should stay 6f: one to be wary of. *R. Hannon*

ULLADULLA 3 b.c. Dominion 123 – Ulla Laing 107 (Mummy's Pet 125) [1991 NR **65**
1992 6.1g⁴ 6s a8g³ a7g³ a8g⁴] leggy colt: third foal: brother to lightly-raced maiden
Milly-Mandy: dam 2-y-o 5f and 6f winner out of staying mare Goosie-Gantlet: fair
maiden: best form at 1m: acts on equitrack. *R. Akehurst*

ULLSWATER 6 b.g. Wassl 125 – Dignified Air (FR) 70 (Wolver Hollow 126) **–**
[1991 NR 1992 a12g] first foal: dam, 6f winner, is out of half-sister to Joking Apart:
tailed off in maiden at Southwell in March: poor hurdler, won handicap in August. *A.
S. Reid*

ULTRAKAY (IRE) 2 b.c. (Apr 28) Treasure Kay 114 – Ultra (Stanford 121§) **35**
[1992 5.9g 8.3s 8m] IR 8,000Y: angular colt: fourth foal: half-brother to 6f to 1m
winner Sure Victory (by Stalker): dam maiden: soundly beaten in maidens: has
joined J. Haynes. *J. Berry*

ULURU (IRE) 4 b.g. Kris 135 – Mountain Lodge 120 (Blakeney 126) [1991 10g² **80**
13.9m² 14.8g³ 15m² 12.3d* 1992 12g 14g⁶ 14g 11.9d⁵ 11.9d⁶] quite attractive colt:
has markedly round action: useful performer (rated 100) at 3 yrs: well below form in
1992 and not seen out after August: will prove suited by 2m +: best effort on a soft
surface: sold to join C. Nash 5,800 gns Newmarket Autumn Sales. *Mrs J. R. Ramsden*

UM ALGOWAIN (USA) 2 ch.c. (Feb 5) Lyphard (USA) 132 – Moonlight **68** p
Serenade (FR) (Dictus (FR) 126) [1992 7s³] $325,000Y: sixth foal: closely related to
useful 1988 French 2-y-o 7f winner Corviglia (by Cresta Rider) and half-brother to 2
winners in France: dam French 1½m winner: 10/1, 4 lengths third of 14 to Faez in
maiden at Lingfield in October, staying on well in small group on far side: will
improve. *M. R. Stoute*

UMBRIA 3 ch.f. Master Willie 129 – Gay Shadow 99 (Northfields (USA)) [1991 7f **40**
6m 1992 10g 7g 6g³] light-framed filly: poor form: claimed out of C. James's stable
£6,000 on reappearance: repeatedly hampered when gambled on next start: best
effort when third of 23 in handicap at Thirsk in August, making most far side: stays
6f. *M. P. Naughton*

UMBUBUZI (USA) 2 ch.c. (Mar 1) Timeless Native (USA) – Making Rounds **70**
(USA) (Dr Blum (USA)) [1992 5m⁵ 6f³ 6g 6g* 7g⁶ 7g* 7d 7s 7d] $24,000Y: sparely-
made colt: not a good walker: first foal: dam minor winner in North America:
sire won from 5f to 9f, very smart at 4 yrs: fair performer: won nurseries at Ayr and
Newcastle in the summer: should stay 1m: unsuited by a soft surface: lazy sort, and
needs plenty of driving, but game. *F. H. Lee*

UME RIVER (IRE) 2 b.g. (May 25) Nordance (USA) – So Delighted (Main Reef **57**
126) [1992 6g 7.5d⁴ 8g 7.5m⁵ 8d] IR 1,000Y: leggy, workmanlike gelding: has a round
action: second foal: dam Irish maiden from family of Guillotina: modest maiden: ran
respectably in a visor final start: looks a thorough stayer. *M. H. Tompkins*

UMHAMBI 2 br.f. (Apr 12) Dowsing (USA) 124 – Global Lady 94 (Balliol 125) **59**
[1992 6g 7s⁴ 7g] 3,100Y: good-bodied filly: second foal: half-sister to 3-y-o In No
Doubt (by Precocious): dam won from 6f (at 2 yrs) to 7.6f: off course 5 months,
modest form in late-season maidens at Lingfield and Doncaster: retained 2,600 gns
Newmarket Autumn Sales. *B. W. Hills*

UNASSUMING 4 ch.g. Vaigly Great 127 – Petard 112 (Mummy's Pet 125) [1991 **–**
8s* 8d⁴ 12f* 10.6m 12g 10g 10m² 9m³ 10m 8m⁶ 8m 10m³ 10m⁶ 1992 a14g 10.3g a12g]
workmanlike gelding: rated 47 at 3 yrs when stayed 1½m and acted on any going: no
worthwhile form in 1992: sold out of J. Wainwright's stable 1,500 gns Doncaster
March Sales after second start. *J. A. Pickering*

UNCERTAIN 4 ch.c. Noalto 120 – Paridance (Doudance 99) [1991 8g 1992 8.2d **–**
11.7d] rather leggy colt: no worthwhile form. *D. Haydn Jones*

UNCLE ERNIE 7 b.g. Uncle Pokey 116 – Ladyfold 60 (Never Dwell 89) [1991 **51** +
a11g⁶ 1992 10d*] leggy, workmanlike gelding: has a round action: very smart
chaser, very lightly raced on flat: favourite, won celebrity minor event at Wetherby
in November: acts on any going. *J. G. FitzGerald*

UNDER THE BRIDGE 3 b.c. Ajdal (USA) 130 – Connaught Bridge 124 **72** d
(Connaught 130) [1991 NR 1992 6g⁶ 6m⁵ 6m² 7g 8.1g⁵ 6m³ a7g⁴ 10d] close-coupled
colt: seventh living foal: half-brother to several winners, including 1½m
winner Wassl Reef (by Mill Reef): dam won Nassau Stakes and Yorkshire Oaks:
disappointing maiden: failed to confirm promise of second at Lingfield in July:
should prove best at 1m +: acts on good to firm ground: blinkered last 2 starts,
showing some ability on equitrack: sold 11,000 gns Newmarket Autumn Sales. *P. W.
Harris*

UNFINISHEDBUSINESS 2 ch.g. (Mar 9) All Systems Go 119 – My Willow 80
(Tap On Wood 130) [1992 6.1d] sparely-made gelding: first reported foal: dam 13.8f
winner stayed 2¼m: green, around 14 lengths seventh of 14 to Shiro in maiden at
Nottingham in July, held up after slow start, modest progress under considerate
ride. *T. J. Naughton*
 –

UNFORGIVING MINUTE 3 b.c. Bellypha 130 – Kindjal 84 (Kris 135) [1991 7g
7m3 1992 8g3 10g2 10m4 10s2 10.4g2 10.5d* 10d* 10v2] quite attractive colt: has a
round action: fairly useful performer: won maiden at Haydock and handicap at
Redcar in the autumn: well worth a try at 1½m: best efforts with give in the ground
and acts on heavy: ran creditably for a claimer once: game and consistent. *P. W.
Harris*
 89

UNIFICATION (IRE) 3 ch.f. Double Schwartz 128 – Hydro Princess (Pitskelly
122) [1991 NR 1992 8m] workmanlike filly: second foal: dam, placed twice (over 5f)
at 2 yrs and once (over 1m) at 3 yrs in Ireland, is half-sister to useful Irish sprinter
Pitmarie: 33/1 and bit backward, soon struggling and only modest late headway in
15-runner minor event at Kempton in June: moved moderately to post. *R. Akehurst*
 –

UNINVITED 5 b.m. Be My Guest (USA) 126 – Fai La Bella (USA) 85 (Fifth
Marine (USA)) [1991 a8g a8g4 a13g 10v 9s 8m 1992 a12g2 a12g] leggy, angular mare:
winning selling hurdler in 1991/2: worthwhile form on flat since 3 yrs only when
second in handicap at Southwell in January: stays 1½m. *A. Glover*
 36

UNIQUE TRIBUTE 3 b.g. Celestial Storm (USA) 132 – Fearless Felon (USA)
(Bailjumper (USA)) [1991 NR 1992 11.9f6 a8s 16m4] plain, good-topped gelding: third
foal: half-brother to modest 7f and 1m winner Vanishing Spirit (by Crofter): dam
never ran: 33/1, first form in maidens when 7½ lengths fourth of 11 to Desert Peace
at Lingfield in August: burly previously: sold 1,500 gns Newmarket Autumn Sales.
C. A. Cyzer
 66

UNITED COLOURS 2 b.c. (May 16) Midyan (USA) 124 – Two High 89 (High
Top 131) [1992 7g] 25,000Y: leggy, unfurnished colt: fifth living foal: half-brother to
5 winners, 3 of them over middle distances: dam won 4 times over 1½m: weak
12/1-shot, green and on toes, over 16 lengths seventh of 9 to Shebl in maiden at
Wolverhampton in July, travelling comfortably 4f then eased when beaten: sold
3,600 gns Newmarket Autumn Sales. *L. M. Cumani*
 –

UNITED KINGDOM (USA) 3 b.f. Danzig (USA) – Unite 126 (Kris 135) [1991
NR 1992 10g2 10g* 10m3 8m3 11g4 8g* 8v4] well-made filly: first foal: dam, successful over 1m then in Oaks and Irish Oaks: useful performer: impressive winner of a
maiden at Newmarket in midsummer: left H. Cecil after fourth start: won minor
event at Toulouse and (best effort) fourth of 9 in listed event at Maisons-
Laffitte in the autumn: effective at 1m and stayed 11f: acted on good to firm and
heavy ground: rather mulish to post last 2 outings here: visits Lear Fan. *H. Pantall,
France*
 93

UNIVERSAL (FR) 2 b.f. (Feb 10) Village Star (FR) 131 – Sudden Star (Grundy
137) [1992 9d5 8m 8s a7g] ex-French filly: fifth foal (previous 4 by Moulin): dam poor
maiden: no worthwhile form: trained by A. Fabre first 3 starts. *K. O. Cunningham-
Brown*
 –

UNPAID MEMBER 8 b.g. Moorestyle 137 – Sunningdale Queen 88 (Gay
Fandango (USA) 132) [1991 NR 1992 a16g3 a14g2 a14g* a12g5 a14g] smallish,
workmanlike gelding: has a round action: won 4-runner handicap at Southwell in
February: soundly beaten afterwards, off course 6 months in between: stays 1¾m:
acts on dead going and fibresand: goes well for claimer. *J. Wharton*
 50

UN SOUVERAIN 4 b.g. Kenmare (FR) 125 – Serenita (FR) (Lyphard (USA)
132) [1991 8f 8d 12m a11g 1992 a12g 15.8m] leggy gelding: poor mover: successful
over hurdles (2½m) in July but no sign of ability on flat. *W. Bentley*
 –

UNVEILED 4 ch.f. Sayf El Arab (USA) 127 – Collegian 90 (Stanford 121§) [1991
7d* 6m* 8g 5.8m 6g3 5g3 6d 6s4 5.7m3 7.1g6 7m* 6f3 7.1m 5.1m 5g 7m 1992 5v 5d
7g 5.7m 5f4 6m5 7f 5.7g6 5.7f3 6g2 6g5 5s 5.7d 6s 6.1d] sturdy, good-quartered filly:
moderate mover: modest handicapper: ideally needs further than 5f, and stays 7f:
probably acts on any going. *R. J. Hodges*
 64

UP ALL NIGHT 3 b.f. Green Desert (USA) 127 – Vielle 123 (Ribero 126) [1991
7g4 1992 8g4 a8g5 8m 8.3d6 10m3 10g6 11.7d3 11.1s4] smallish, sturdy, attractive
filly: poor maiden: should prove suited by 1½m+: acts on good to firm ground and
soft: below form on fibresand: joined R. Curtis. *J. W. Hills*
 43

UP ANCHOR (IRE) 3 b.f. Slip Anchor 136 – Pageantry 83 (Welsh Pageant 132)
[1991 6g6 8.1g2 8.2m* 1992 10d4 10.2d* 12g3 12.5m* 12g4 12s* 12v3] rangy,
attractive filly: has a round action: won handicap at Bath in April and minor event at
 114

Castrol St Simon Stakes, Newbury—25/1-shot Up Anchor stays on really gamely to beat Spring, Zinaad (left) and Mack The Knife

Warwick in June: 25/1, improved form to win St Simon Stakes at Newbury in October, gamely making virtually all to beat Spring a length: only fair third in listed event at Milan following month: will stay beyond 1½m: has won on good to firm ground, but best effort on soft. *P. F. I. Cole*

UP AND AT 'EM 2 b.c. (May 21) Forzando 122 – Ergo 82 (Song 132) [1992 6g³ **106** p
5g* 5d* 6.3s² 5g⁴ 6s* 5g*] 6,500Y, 6,400 2-y-o: medium-sized, quite good-topped colt: closely related to a minor winner in France by Formidable and half-brother to several winners, including 1982 2-y-o 5f winner Henceforth (by Full of Hope): dam 5f winner at 2 yrs: progressive Irish colt: successful in maiden at Tipperary and minor event (by 2½ lengths from Basim) at Leopardstown in August, listed race at the Curragh in September and Cornwallis Stakes (most impressively by 2½ lengths from Roger The Butler) at Ascot in October: ran well when over 2 lengths fourth to Flowing in Meadow Meats EBF Flying Five at Leopardstown: speedy, and best efforts at 5f on good ground: sure to improve further. *J. G. Coogan, Ireland*

UPPANCE 4 b.f. Kabour 80 – Final Cast 50 (Saulingo 122) [1991 NR 1992 a7g a7g **33**
a8g 5s 5g⁶ 5g 6g 5m 5.1m 5g³ 6g 5d⁴ 5m] workmanlike, angular filly: poor mover: third foal: sister to sprint handicap winners Kabcast and Miss Kive: dam, winner over 5f at 4 yrs, stayed 7f: poor handicapper: best form at 5f: acts on dead ground: sold 2,000 gns Doncaster August Sales after tenth start. *T. Craig*

Cornwallis Stakes, Ascot—Irish raider Up And At 'Em looks a smart sprinter in the making

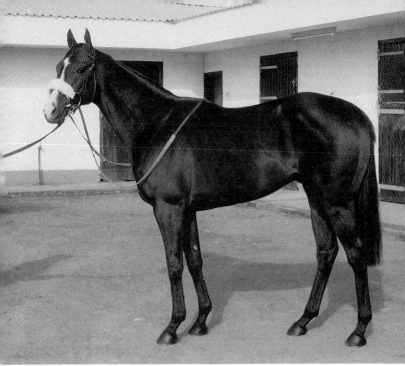

Mrs A. Hughes's "Up And At 'Em"

UPPER HOUSE   3 b.c. Shirley Heights 130 – On The House (FR) 125 (Be My   **69**
Guest (USA) 126) [1991 8f 8m⁶ 1992 a12g* 12m* 14d 11.6g⁶ 13.8g* 16m 12.2d²]   a78
close-coupled, attractive colt: fluent mover: fair but none too consistent performer:
won maiden at Southwell in July and claimers at Newmarket in August and Catterick
in September: stays 13.8f: acts on good to firm ground and fibresand: has looked
lazy, and visored first 4 starts: sold to join M. Heaton-Ellis 21,000 gns Newmarket
Autumn Sales. *G. Wragg*

UPPER MOUNT CLAIR   2 b.f. (Feb 6) Ela-Mana-Mou 132 – Sun Street 73 (Ile   **73** p
de Bourbon (USA) 133) [1992 8m⁴] smallish, leggy filly: first reported foal: dam
out-and-out stayer: 25/1 and bit backward, over 7 lengths fourth of 19, close up
throughout and leading briefly over 2f out, to Bashayer in maiden at Newmarket in
October: sure to do better. *C. E. Brittain*

UP THE PUNJAB   3 br.f. Daring March 116 – Hunza Water 70 (Relko 136) [1991   **50** d
6m⁶ 5m 7s² 7g³ 6f⁶ 7.1m⁴ 8m* 8f² 8.2m² 8d⁶ 8m⁴ a7g 1992 a8g³ a7g³ a7g⁶ a8g*   a62 d
a8g³ 8.9s 8m* 8.3g⁴ 8d a8g⁴ 8.5d⁴ 8g 8f 10g 8.3g a8g a8g⁴ a10g⁶ a8g] lengthy,
dipped-backed filly: has a round action: modest performer: won claimer at Lingfield
and seller (no bid) at Brighton in spring: below form in second half of 1992: best form
at 1m: best efforts on top-of-the-ground and all-weather surfaces: suitable mount for
inexperienced rider: sometimes bandaged near-hind: trained first 11 starts by S.
Dow. *A. Moore*

UPTHORPE GIRL   3 ch.f. Ballacashtal (CAN) – Zamindara (Crofter (USA) 124)   **–**
[1991 NR 1992 6.1d 6f⁶] rather leggy filly: second foal: sister to 4-y-o 5f winner

Greetland Rock: dam poor maiden stayed 1m: twice raced, and no worthwhile form in seller and claimer in July. *A. P. Jarvis*

URARAGSKAL 3 br.f. Kala Shikari 125 – Seragsbee (Sagaro 133) [1991 5s⁶ 6m 7s 7f a5g 1992 a10g] sturdy, plain filly: well beaten in varied events. *J. Akehurst*

URBAN SEA (USA) 3 ch.f. Miswaki (USA) 124 – Allegretta 101 (Lombard **117** (GER) 126) [1991 7d² 8s* 7d⁴ 1992 7g 8g⁶ 8d³ 10d* 10.5g⁶ 12g² 10s* 12m³ 10d² 10f] 280,000 francs (approx £28,000) Y: leggy, angular filly: moderate walker: fifth foal: half-sister to 12.1f winner Shadideen (by Shadeed) and 2 winners in France, including 1989 2-y-o 9f and 1¼m winner Irish Allegre (by Irish River): dam 2-y-o 1m and 9f winner, stayed 1½m: won listed race at Longchamp in May and extremely valuable Piaget d'Or at Deauville in August: improved form in Prix Vermeille (just over ½-length third to Jolypha) at Longchamp and E P Taylor Stakes (1¼ lengths second behind Hatoof) at Woodbine: last of 9 in Yellow Ribbon Invitational at Santa Anita final outing: effective at 1¼m and 1½m: acts on good to firm and soft ground: changed hands 3,000,000 francs (approx £365,000) Goffs Arc de Triomphe Sale. *J. Lesbordes, France*

URGENT REQUEST (IRE) 2 gr.c. (Feb 15) Rainbow Quest (USA) 134 – **103** Oscura (USA) 82 (Caro 133) [1992 7d²* 7m² 7.3s⁶] tall, leggy, unfurnished colt: has scope: good mover, with a long stride: fourth foal: half-brother to French 3-y-o Mettlesome (by Lomond), 1m (at 2 yrs) and 9f winner, and 1990 2-y-o 5.8f winner Kembla (by Known Fact): dam, 1m winner, is half-sister to champion grass horse Johnny D: impressive winner of maiden at Lingfield in September: favourite following month when beaten a neck by Nominator in Somerville Tattersall Stakes at Newmarket and modest sixth in Horris Hill Stakes at Newbury: will be better suited by 1m: bandaged first 2 starts: free-running sort: worth another chance back on a sound surface. *B. W. Hills*

URRY URRY URRY 2 b.f. (Mar 10) Never So Bold 135 – Gwiffina 87 (Welsh **85** Saint 126) [1992 6g* 6g⁴ 6s] well-grown, close-coupled filly: has an easy action: fourth foal: half-sister to 5-y-o 7f winner Creselly (by Superlative): dam 2-y-o 6f winner stayed 7f, didn't train on: won median auction maiden at York: beaten 5 lengths by Marina Park in Princess Margaret Stakes at Ascot later in July: never travelling well in listed event at Ripon following month: seems unsuited by soft ground. *M. J. Camacho*

URSHI-JADE 4 b.f. Pennine Walk 120 – Treeline 59 (High Top 131) [1991 8d 8m⁵ 10.2m 1992 7d 8g 8.9g⁶ 7m 10.5g 11d 10g] leggy, lengthy filly: poor mover: no worthwhile form. *K. White*

USA DOLLAR 5 b.h. Gabitat 119 – Burglars Girl 63 (Burglar 128) [1991 7g 8m **58** § 8d⁶ 8g 10g⁵ 8m 10g 8g³ 8.9g 8d 8m² 8g³ 8g 1992 a8g⁶ a8g³ a8g² a8g⁵ 7.5g 7d 8m a72 § 8.1m 8.5g⁴ a8g* 8g⁵ a7g² 8m a10g⁵] big, strong horse: untrustworthy handicapper: best efforts in 1992 on equitrack, winning amateurs race in June: should stay beyond 1m: acts on good to firm ground and equitrack: has worn hood and visor, but usually blinkered nowadays: usually sweating: a difficult ride, and has failed to go through with effort. *B. Gubby*

USAIDIT 3 b.c. Commanche Run 133 – Smurfiusa (USA) (Sharpen Up 127) [1991 **72** 7m² 7g⁴ 1992 9s 7.6s⁴ 8m 10m² 9.7g² 12d³ 10.2d³ 10m] leggy, angular colt: fair maiden: stays 1½m: yet to race on very firm going, probably acts on any other: ran well when blinkered once. *W. Carter*

USER FRIENDLY 3 b.f. Slip Anchor 136 – Rostova 91 (Blakeney 126) **128** [1991 NR 1992 10g* 11.5d* 12d* 12g* 11.9m* 14.6m* 12s² 12f⁶]

It's a case of where to begin with the outstandingly tough and genuine User Friendly. She was arguably the best filly in Europe in 1992 and became widely regarded as one of the best British-trained middle-distance fillies of recent times, even before her excellent second in the Prix de l'Arc de Triomphe. Six races, six victories, was the record she took to Longchamp where she started favourite in the strongest field assembled all year for a middle-distance race in Europe. Four of User Friendly's victories were in Group 1 races—she became only the third filly to land the Oaks, Irish Oaks and Yorkshire Oaks treble and only the seventh Oaks winner this century to go on to success in the St Leger. Perhaps, in the final analysis, she didn't quite measure up to her immediate predecessors among those who have completed the Oaks-St Leger double—Dunfermline, Sun Princess and Oh So Sharp—but she earned a special place in the affections of the racing public and it came as

Gold Seal Oaks, Epsom—User Friendly stays on resolutely to beat All At Sea, with Pearl Angel fully twenty lengths back in third

no surprise to see her walk away with the end-of-season Racehorse of the Year award decided by a selection panel drawn from the racing Press.

User Friendly failed to reach her reserve—reportedly 25,000 guineas— at the Newmarket October Yearling Sales in 1990 and didn't see a racecourse as a two-year-old. According to her trainer, she was so backward and showed so little when first put into training as a three-year-old that she was sent home. 'I must say they did a magnificent job with her,' Brittain told us in a *Timeform Interview.* 'She came back in, got back on to her feed and I've never seen a filly improve like it. I've never seen *any horse* improve like she has.' User Friendly started at 25/1 on her debut in a Sandown maiden towards the end of April and immediately stamped herself as a useful middle-distance filly in the making. She took the eye in the paddock, a filly of size and scope, and drew clear, driven out, to win in clear-cut fashion despite being slowly away and running green. Brittain explained in his *Timeform Interview* that User Friendly's owner-breeder Bill Gredley had bred her 'to run at Epsom: he said you could breed a Derby or an Oaks winner by breeding from two horses that won at Epsom' (User Friendly's dam Rostova made all in the Grand Metropolitan Handicap the same year her sire Slip Anchor ran his Derby field into the ground). Everything went smoothly with User Friendly up to Epsom. She followed in her sire's footsteps by completing her preparation at Lingfield where the mile-and-a-half course (1m3f106yds to be precise) bears a quite close resemblance to the Derby and Oaks course and is a good testing ground for Epsom classic contenders. User Friendly had only four opponents in the Daily Star Oaks Trial and, starting favourite, she took the lead early in the straight, after being waited with, and kept on well to beat Niodini by two and a half lengths with the others well beaten off. And so to Epsom where the field of seven for the Gold Seal Oaks was the smallest since Fifinella completed the Derby-Oaks double in a war-time substitute at Newmarket seventy-six years before. User Friendly, the pick of the paddock, started third favourite behind the first and second in the Tattersalls Musidora Stakes, All At Sea and the close One Thousand Guineas fourth Perfect Circle. The Musidora had promised to be the most revealing of the Oaks trials but turned into a sprint with All At Sea getting the better of Perfect Circle by a length with User Friendly's stable-companion Armarama—reportedly regarded much inferior to User Friendly at home—a length further back in third. There was an Oaks challenger from Ireland, Fawaayid representing the Bolger stable who had been successful with Jet Ski Lady the previous year, and one from France, Shining Bright. User Friendly won the race fairly and squarely, stalking the front-running Fawaayid from the start and galloping on relentlessly after being sent on over three furlongs out. All At Sea, who travelled like a winner for much of the way, kept up a game challenge until inside the final furlong but the hard-ridden User Friendly won going away by three and a half lengths; All At Sea had pulled twenty lengths clear of the long-priced third Pearl Angel at the line. User Friendly's win gave her jockey George Duffield a first classic winner; he went on to pass the hundred-winner mark for the season after several near misses in a long career.

There was some talk that User Friendly would next go for the Budweiser Irish Derby—in which the 1990 Oaks winner Salsabil had beaten the colts—but in the end connections decided on the easier and more conventional option of the Kildangan Stud Irish Oaks. Unite, in 1987, had been the last filly to win the Oaks and Irish Oaks outright. In the interim, Diminuendo had dead-heated at the Curragh after winning at Epsom, and Aliysa and Jet Ski Lady had both been beaten. The so-called Aliysa saga, incidentally, apparently reached its conclusion in the latest season when her owner the Aga Khan, who has fought a long legal battle to have her reinstated following her disqualification in the 1989 Oaks, had his appeal to challenge the Jockey Club

Kildangan Stud Irish Oaks, the Curragh—User Friendly holds Market Booster with the unlucky Arrikala (checked cap) searching in vain for a clear run

Aston Upthorpe Yorkshire Oaks, York — having looked beaten early in the straight, User Friendly storms back to beat Bineyah (right), Guilty Secret and the blinkered Niodini

through judicial review dismissed; three Appeal Court judges were unanimous that the Jockey Club wasn't susceptible to judicial review in this particular case and said it was unlikely that the Aga would be granted leave to appeal to the House of Lords. Both Aliysa and Jet Ski Lady failed fairly narrowly in the Irish Oaks, finishing second to progressive fillies who hadn't run in the Oaks. None of those behind User Friendly at Epsom took her on again at the Curragh where she was odds on. She won, but not with the ease the betting predicted, and may well have been fortunate to win at all, the unconsidered Arrikala looking a most unlucky loser after being unable to get a run. The going at the Curragh wasn't so yielding as at Epsom and User Friendly's performance suggested she might prove ideally suited by some give in the ground, although she had been side-lined for a time after the Oaks with a leg injury. As at Epsom, she took up the running early in the home straight and stayed on gamely under pressure. But she couldn't shake off her closest pursuers and was all out to hold off the Irish One Thousand Guineas runner-up Market Booster by a neck with Arrikala, full of running, half a length back in third.

Talk about User Friendly's going requirements dominated the build-up to the Coalite St Leger after she maintained her unbeaten record with an uninspiring victory on firmish ground in the Aston Upthorpe Yorkshire Oaks. Odds-on User Friendly started slowly, after a lengthy delay because of trouble with the stalls, and had to be bustled along some way from home; her jockey, tugging at the right rein, had a difficult job preventing her from edging left as she challenged on the outside but she steadily forged clear for a two-and-a-half-length victory over the Irish Oaks fourth Bineyah, with Guilty Secret and Niodini close up. User Friendly's connections paid £25,000 at the supplementary entry deadline a week before the St Leger, but the filly's participation in the final classic remained in doubt until the morning of the race. Clerk of the course John Sanderson defended his decision to water the Doncaster track copiously as the ground dried out, saying 'we are not doing it just for one horse, we don't want any horse to go away from this meeting jarred up'. There's no doubt that User Friendly wouldn't have been risked on very firm ground with her principal autumn target the Prix de l'Arc de

Triomphe only three weeks away. User Friendly's trainer said on the Thursday: 'If the race had been today then User Friendly would not have run. We have paid the supplementary entry fee but we think we have a filly good enough to win the Arc, and the money doesn't come into it. We just don't want to risk jarring her up.' With the going also on the firm side at Longchamp, the option of switching User Friendly to the Prix Vermeille the same weekend was ruled out. 'She is fine at the moment and her work has been excellent. She doesn't really need to run again before the Arc,' said Brittain. The St Leger would have been much the poorer for User Friendly's absence. Another of the main protagonists, the March Stakes runner-up Allegan, was pulled out on the day of the race because of the going, leaving six colts to take on User Friendly, including the first three in the Great Voltigeur Stakes, Bonny Scot, Sonus and Assessor, and the March Stakes winner Rain Rider. User Friendly dispelled any doubts about her ability to handle top-of-the-ground conditions, putting her rivals firmly in their place with a telling burst when asked for her effort two furlongs out. She soon had the race in safe keeping and ran on strongly to win by three and a half lengths and a neck from Sonus and Bonny Scot, form which represented a return to her best. Could User Friendly now go on to success in Europe's most valuable race the Prix de l'Arc de Triomphe? No winner of the Leger has completed the double in the same season. Nijinsky is the example most often quoted by those who claim that there is a supposed 'St Leger hoodoo' in the Arc, but his narrow defeat at Longchamp resulted from a combination of factors not all of which were connected with his having run in the St Leger. In fact, the record of St Leger winners in the Arc is fairly good, given that the Arc almost always takes more winning. Of the ten St Leger winners between Nijinsky and User Friendly who had gone on to run next in the Arc, five had reached the frame at Longchamp including both fillies among them, Dunfermline, who came fourth to St Leger runner-up Alleged in 1977, and Sun Princess, who was second in 1983 to All Along, the last filly to win the Arc. User Friendly ran a fine race in the Arc, Duffield—unfairly criticised in some quarters afterwards—having her close up from the start and sending her into the lead once the field was in line for home. User Friendly kept on in her usual game fashion but couldn't quite hold off the French four-year-old Subotica after a sustained duel in the straight. User Friendly went down by a neck, running at least as well as she'd ever done. The early pace in the Arc was sedate by the normal standards of the race and post-race criticism of User

Coalite St Leger Stakes, Doncaster—
User Friendly remains unbeaten and is well in command of Sonus (rails) and Bonny Scot

Friendly's rider centred on the fact that he should have made more use of the filly's stamina by sending her on much further out. User Friendly's approachable trainer, who enjoyed a magnificent season, countered the criticism in typical style: 'Everybody's got the right to criticise. But if George had let her go, and she'd been beaten, people would have come up with the argument that nobody makes the running in the Arc and would have asked why he hadn't held her up. You're talking about being beaten a neck, and beating the best in Europe. And they criticise the jockey!' User Friendly was kept in training for the Japan Cup at Tokyo at the end of November—a race her stable had won in 1986 with Jupiter Island—but she could finish only sixth, fading in the straight, possibly feeling the effects of a long season. Connections immediately announced that User Friendly stays in training as a four-year-old when the plan is to concentrate on the big races at a mile and a quarter (including the Eclipse) to a mile and a half (including the King George and the Arc). We'd have reservations about User Friendly's proving equally as effective at a mile and a quarter as she is at a mile and a half and upwards. She's by no means a one-pacer but stamina is undoubtedly her strongest suit and a really good middle-distance horse with pace would most probably have the edge on her at a mile and a quarter. And there's also the question of whether she'll train on. Neither Dunfermline nor Sun Princess recaptured her top-class three-year-old form as a four-year-old, and the records show that not many classic-winning fillies kept in training succeed in enhancing their reputations. Let's hope the admirable User Friendly proves an exception.

Members of the Horserace Writers' Association voted User Friendly's breeder 'owner of the year', one of a number of well-deserved end-of-season honours for the achievements of User Friendly and for the adventurous approach of her owner and trainer. Unfortunately, Mr Gredley, frustrated by the level of prize money and by the Government's apparently ambivalent attitude to racing's economic problems, received a bad press when he called for an owners' boycott of a nondescript day's racing in November (perhaps he could have made his point more effectively by withdrawing User Friendly from the St Leger when the eyes of the racing world were focussed on his filly). Keeping a grip on reality is seemingly impossible for some involved in racing. Mr Gredley's call—withdrawn after he yielded to Jockey Club pressure—coincided with a public furore over the threatened closure of over half the nation's coal mines. With the country in the deepest recession for a generation, prize money in racing is hardly likely to be of great concern to the Government. The Government receives the biggest slice taken from betting turnover on horse racing in the four hundred million pounds that it raises from the betting tax. Mr Gredley called for the Government to put more of this money back into racing so that prize money could be raised. The level of prize money is one of the reasons given for the announced 'twenty-four per cent reduction' in the number of horses Britain's leading owner Sheikh Mohammed will have in training on the flat in Britain in 1993. He started 1992 with around three hundred and fifty horses in training in Britain, around one hundred and forty in France, fifty or so in the United States and around forty in Ireland; in 1993 he will expand further in France and the United States and will also have horses in training in Germany. Sheikh Mohammed gave a rare interview on the *Panorama* TV programme which examined the effects of the recession on racing. He also voiced disquiet about the impending effects of the European Community VAT laws which, from January 1st 1993, were due to lead, among other things, to bloodstock sold in Britain being subject to 17.5% VAT, compared to special rates of 2.7% in Ireland and 5.5% in France. The Government's reply that it would be 'politically unacceptable' to levy a lower rate on bloodstock than on any other commodity was a polite way of saying that it couldn't be seen to be arranging for one of the richest men in the world to pay less tax on his hobby. Nevertheless, the VAT situation did result in Britain's major sales company Tattersalls announcing that it would be moving its most prestigious yearling sale to Ireland in 1993. In what was interpreted as a statement about the effects of VAT on their racing empires, Sheikh Mohammed and the rest of the Al-Maktoum family didn't buy in 1992 at the Tattersalls Houghton Yearling Sales at which the average price of yearlings was down by over forty-four per cent on 1991 prices. Prices were

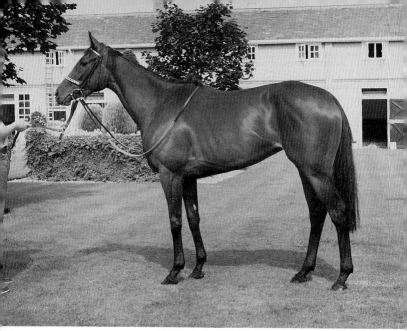

Mr W. J. Gredley's "User Friendly"

down by forty-nine per cent at Tattersalls October Yearling Sales as the yearling market suffered a dramatic slump on the scale of that of 1974, which followed the devastating impact of the virtual quadrupling of the price of crude oil by the major oil-producing states. Racing adjusted to the situation then and it will have to trim its sails to suit the wind again. A steady hand on the tiller is needed in rough water and it is hoped that the British Horseracing Board, which is due to come into being on April 1st 1993, will be able to provide the right leadership. It is more democratic and representative than the Jockey Club, which will stand it in good stead with the Government; but it has to be said that it faces a well-nigh impossible task if it is expected to obtain special protection against the chill winds of recession for racing.

User Friendly (b.f. 1989)	Slip Anchor (b 1982)	Shirley Heights (b 1975)	Mill Reef / Hardiemma
		Sayonara (b 1965)	Birkhahn / Suleika
	Rostova (br 1981)	Blakeney (b 1966)	Hethersett / Windmill Girl
		Poppy Day (b 1968)	Soleil II / Red Poppy

The rangy User Friendly usually looks a picture before her races, has a phlegmatic temperament and is usually a straightforward ride; she's a moderate mover and sometimes displays an unusually high head carriage in her races, providing a good illustration of the folly of automatically labelling all horses that show that tendency as ungenerous. User Friendly is British-bred, by the Plantation Stud stallion Slip Anchor whose fee for 1993 is £12,500 (1st

894

October concession), out of a mare who descends from one of the most famous families at Mr H. J. Joel's Childwick Bury Stud. Mr Joel, who died in March aged ninety-seven, did extremely well with the descendants of his war-time One Thousand Guineas winner Picture Play. One of her daughters, Queen of Light, became the grandam of Two Thousand Guineas and Derby winner Royal Palace and the great grandam of One Thousand Guineas winner Fairy Footsteps and St Leger winner Light Cavalry. Another of Picture Play's daughters, the Yorkshire Oaks runner-up Red Shoes, produced a Yorkshire Oaks winner in West Side Story, who came very close to providing Mr Joel with victory in the 1962 Oaks. West Side Story's sister Red Poppy is the great grandam of User Friendly. Twice-raced Red Poppy bred nothing of note herself and User Friendly's grandam Poppy Day was weeded out of the Childwick Bury Stud after showing only fair form, in the frame in maiden events at Windsor and Yarmouth as a two-year-old and failing to train on. Poppy Day bred several winners, including the fairly useful middle-distance stayer Judd who was subsequently only fair but her 1981 Blakeney filly—User Friendly's dam Rostova—made only 2,000 guineas as a yearling when she was purchased by User Friendly's owner. Rostova didn't race at two but showed fairly useful form at three and four, winning three times at a mile and a half and once at a mile and three quarters. User Friendly is the third foal out of Rostova, and her first winner. Rostova's first two foals—an unnamed filly by Dominion and a once-raced Never So Bold colt Berlin Breakout—are both dead but there are two offspring by Slip Anchor following on, the unraced filly Peaches Polly (who'll be a three-year-old in 1993) and a two-year-old colt. *C. E. Brittain*

USHAK   4 b. or br.g. Baby Turk 120 – Persian Carpet (FR) (Kalamoun 129) [1991   –
10.1g 11.6m³ a12g 12g 1992 10.8d 12g] leggy gelding: soundly beaten in handicaps in spring at 3 yrs: blinkered final start: stays 11.6f: acts on good to firm ground: joined J. Webber. *H. Candy*

USHBA (FR)   4 b.f. Head For Heights 125 – Uruguay (GER) 69 (Thatch (USA)   60
136) [1991 8g 7g 7g² 6m* 6s 1992 7g 6g 7g⁵ 6f* 6m 6s] compact filly: moderate walker: well backed when winning handicap at Pontefract in August: no comparable form in 1992: effective at 6f and 7f: goes well on top-of-the-ground, seems unsuited by soft surface: very slowly away when visored final start: often bandaged behind. *C. G. Cox*

USTKA   3 b.f. Lomond (USA) 128 – Krakow 85 (Malinowski (USA) 123) [1991 NR   60
1992 8g 7f* 7m⁵ 7m³] 40,000F: sparely-made filly: moderate mover: fifth foal: closely related to useful 4-y-o 1¼m winner Adam Smith and smart 10.1f to 15.5f winner Braashee (both by Sadler's Wells), and half-sister to Nell Gwyn winner/1000 Guineas fourth Ghariba (by Final Straw): dam, from good family, won at 7f: won maiden at Lingfield in May: bandaged behind, not seen after creditable third in Warwick handicap in June: should prove suited by further than 7f: acts on firm ground. *M. R. Stoute*

UTAMARO   3 b.f. Reference Point 139 – Cerise Bouquet 75 (Mummy's Pet 125)   –
[1991 NR 1992 10s 14.1d] 170,000Y: strong, lengthy filly: second foal: half-sister to Irish 7f winner Bourree (by Nordance): dam, 2-y-o 5f winner later placed in USA, is half-sister to Ibn Bey and Roseate Tern: no worthwhile form in maidens, off course 5 months in between starts. *B. W. Hills*

V

VADO VIA   4 b.f. Ardross 134 – Brigado 87 (Brigadier Gerard 144) [1991 11f²   –
12m⁴ 10.6g 16.2m⁵ 12g* 12m⁶ 11.8g⁵ 1992 11.8s⁴] leggy, workmanlike filly: rated 56 on her day at 3 yrs when with Mrs J. Ramsden: well matched against another try over 1¾m: acts on any going: progressed into fairly useful hurdler late in the year, winning 4 handicaps on easy ground. *D. J. Wintle*

VAGRANCY   3 br.f. Dancing Brave (USA) 140 – Trampship 110 (High Line 125)   64
[1991 NR 1992 8g 10f³ 10.2d a10g³] sturdy, lengthy filly: has a quick action: first foal: dam 1½m and 14.6f (Park Hill Stakes) winner from good family: fair maiden: bred to

be suited by at least 1½m: acts on firm ground and equitrack: well beaten on dead ground after lengthy lay-off: has joined H. Pantall, France. *B. W. Hills*

VAGUE DANCER   6 b.g. Vaigly Great 127 – Step You Gaily 71 (King's Company   **74**
124) [1991 8s² 8v 10d* 10.2m² 12m⁶ 10.6g³ 10g* 12g* 15g³ 10m³ 10.3m³ 10.9m⁴
9m³ 1992 8g 10s 9.9g 10m⁴ 10.4m⁵ 8.9s 10f* 8.1g* 8g* 9d] lengthy, rather angular
gelding: has a powerful, roundish action: fair performer: off course over 2 months
and really found his form, winning handicaps (2 apprentice events) at Pontefract,
Haydock and Newmarket in August: well backed but edgy and raced too freely in
Cambridgeshire at Newmarket 5 weeks later: needs strong pace at 1m, and stays
1½m: acts on firm and soft going: ran poorly when blinkered earlier in career:
sometimes sweats: idles, and is held up: sold 15,500 gns Newmarket Autumn Sales.
Mrs J. R. Ramsden

VAGUE NANCY (IRE)   4 b.f. Mazaad 106 – Noble Nancy (Royal And Regal   –
(USA)) [1991 5g a5g 10g 1992 a7g 10g] close-coupled, workmanlike filly: no worthwhile form, including in sellers. *C. J. Hill*

VAIGLY SUNTHYME   2 ch.g. (Feb 11) Vaigly Great 127 – Red Roses (FR) (Roi   **55**
Dagobert 128) [1992 8.5m 8d 8v⁴] 1,100Y: rather leggy gelding: half-brother to 3
winners abroad: dam won at up to 6f in France: progressive form in maidens: stays
1m: acts on heavy ground. *J. M. Carr*

VAILMONT (USA)   3 ch.f. Diesis 133 – Annie Edge 118 (Nebbiolo 125) [1991   **88**
6m² 5m* 5.3g³ 1992 6g* 5g* 5m 5.1m³] tall filly: fairly useful performer at her best:
beat small fields in 2 minor events at Kempton in May, idling in front on second
occasion: ran badly at Newcastle (reportedly in season, hung left throughout) and
Chepstow (pulled too hard for claimer) afterwards: will prove best at sprint
distances: headstrong: best held up. *I. A. Balding*

VAIN PRINCE   5 b.h. Sandhurst Prince 128 – Vain Deb 66 (Gay Fandango (USA)   **53** p
132) [1991 12s 12.3s 16.5m³ 16.5m 13d 14.1f² 15.9m 1992 16f³ 16.2d* 14.1d* 16.1g*]
rangy horse: modest form: completed hat-trick in 19 days in handicaps at Beverley
(amateurs), Nottingham and Newcastle in August: stays 2m: acts on any going: ran
creditably in blinkers earlier in career: winner of 3 novice chases in the autumn:
probably capable of better. *N. Tinkler*

VALATCH   4 ch.g. Valiyar 129 – Love Match (USA) (Affiliate (USA)) [1991 10f   –
12f⁴ 12m* 16.2g 1992 10.3g a12g] big, strong, lengthy gelding: rated 60 at 3 yrs: no
form in the spring at 4 yrs, trained reappearance (visored) by D. Smith: stays 1½m:
acts on firm ground. *J. L. Harris*

VALERE KNIGHT (IRE)   2 b.c. (Apr 28) Heraldiste (USA) 121 – Kix 71 (King   **46**
Emperor (USA)) [1992 5g⁴ 6g⁵ 6s 6.1d] IR 4,800F, IR 4,800Y: rather leggy colt:
half-brother to several winners, including fair 7f handicapper Glen Na Smole (by
Ballymore): dam in frame in early-season maidens at 2 yrs: plating-class maiden:
best effort on debut: sold 400 gns Doncaster September Sales. *C. G. Cox*

VALIANT COMMANDER   2 b.g. (May 11) War Hero 116 – Polola 42 (Aragon   **57** p
118) [1992 10g⁴] workmanlike gelding: second foal: half-brother to 3-y-o Sting In
The Tail (by Scorpio): dam ran 3 times at 2 yrs, third once at 5f: 50/1, burly and
green, 7 lengths fourth of 11 to Manaarah in maiden at Nottingham in October, held
up and late progress: mulish stalls: will improve. *P. R. Hedger*

VALIANT WARRIOR   4 br.g. Valiyar 129 – Jouvencelle 68 (Rusticaro (FR)   –
124) [1991 8g 8f⁴ 10s⁶ 10m³ 10f⁵ 9m⁵ 11.9g² 11.9m⁵ 12.1d* 12d⁴ 1992 16d 12.3g
12.3d 14d] workmanlike gelding: rated 77 at 3 yrs for H. Candy: no form on flat in
1992, trained by D. Nicholson first outing: stays 1½m: best efforts on an easy
surface: often bandaged: untrustworthy winning novice hurdler. *M. D. Hammond*

VALIANT WORDS   5 br.g. Valiyar 129 – Wild Words 76 (Galivanter 131) [1991   –
10d* 10m* 10.2d² 10g 11.5m² 11.4m³ 12g 1992 10m 8.5g 8.1m⁵ 10m 8.5d a10g] leggy
gelding: rated 72 at 4 yrs: no worthwhile form (including in blinkers once) in 1992:
stays 1½m: acts on firm and dead going. *R. Akehurst*

VALLANCE   4 b.c. Top Ville 129 – Kindjal 84 (Kris 135) [1991 10d² 10.5g⁴ 1992   **88**
12g 12.3v 10d 10m* 10m* 10f* 10d² 10.1m² 10.4s³] robust colt: much improved
handicapper: found his form in the summer, winning at Lingfield, Ripon and, despite
carrying head high and swishing tail under pressure, at Newmarket: will prove at
least as effective at 1½m as 1¼m: acts on good to firm and dead ground, fair effort
on very soft. *P. W. Harris*

VALLEY OF FIRE   3 b.f. Dancing Brave (USA) 140 – Glowing Embers 107   **89**
(Nebbiolo 125) [1991 NR 1992 8d* 10.1d³ 10m⁴ 10s* 10s 11s] useful-looking, rather
unfurnished filly: third foal: dam Irish 7f and 1¼m winner, is half-sister to Kalaglow:
fairly useful performer at best: won maiden at Warwick in April and handicap at

Sandown in August: weakened quickly 1½f out in quite valuable handicaps last 2 starts: stayed 1¼m: acted on good to firm and soft ground: visits Persian Heights. *J. R. Fanshawe*

VALLEY OF TIME (FR)   4 br.f. In Fijar (USA) 121 – Vallee Sarthoise (FR) (Val de Loir 133) [1991 7f 7g 8.2m 7g 8.3d³ 11g 8g³ 8.3d⁴ 9.2d 9m⁴ 9.2s⁶ 1992 8.3v 8.1m³ 7.1f* 8.3m⁴ 7g⁴ 7.1d 7.1g] sturdy filly: poor handicapper: trained reappearance by P. Monteith: made all in Edinburgh apprentice handicap in June: below form last 2 starts, off course 6 weeks before each of them: effective from 7f to 9f: best form on a sound surface: headstrong when tried blinkered once: tongue tied down final start: has been mulish at stalls: has won for 7-lb claimer: has joined D. Nolan. *T. Craig*   **44**

VALSEUR (USA)   3 ch.c. Lyphard (USA) 132 – Vachti (FR) 114 (Crystal Palace (FR) 132) [1991 8.1s* 1992 12m⁴ 11.6g] small, lengthy colt: fair handicapper: ran well when fourth at Newbury, poorly when well-backed favourite at Windsor later in the summer: should stay further: sold to join L. Lungo 2,000 gns Newmarket Autumn Sales. *Mrs J. Cecil*   **70**

VALUED FRIEND (USA)   4 b.g. Ziggy's Boy (USA) – Tuvalu (USA) (Our Native (USA)) [1991 10m 12f⁴ 10m 15.4m a12g⁶ 1992 a12g 12g] close-coupled, angular gelding: seems of little account: sold 500 gns Ascot November Sales. *J. J. Bridger*   **–**

VANART   3 b.g. Precocious 126 – Red Spider 78 (Red God 128§) [1991 NR 1992 8f³ 7f⁶ 8.5s³ 7m³ 8v⁶ a8g] 6,400F, 6,100Y: tall gelding: half-brother to several middle-distance winners, including 1¼m winner Volcanoes Spark (by Touching Wood) and November Handicap winner Abu Kadra (by Blakeney), both temperamental: dam 1m winner: disappointing maiden: may well be ungenuine: retained 3,000 gns Doncaster November Sales. *W. W. Haigh*   **70 d**

VANBOROUGH LAD   3 b.g. Precocious 126 – Lustrous 73 (Golden Act (USA)) [1991 5v* 5d³ 6g 6m 6.1g* 5m⁴ 8g 8g² 7d 1992 8d³ 10d 7.6s² 7g 7m⁶ 8s⁵ 7.6m⁶ 8g 8d² 7.6s² 8s⁴ 7.1s⁵] lengthy gelding: has a round action: fair but none too consistent handicapper: suited by 1m: best efforts with give in the ground, acts on heavy: visored once at 2 yrs. *M. J. Haynes*   **69**

VANDA'S GIRL   4 b.f. Noalto 120 – Concorde Lady 66 (Hotfoot 126) [1991 10d 1992 a12g] sparely-made filly: seems of little account these days. *A. Bailey*   **–**

VANDERVALLY   3 ch.g. Van Der Linden (FR) – Sannavally (Sagaro 133) [1991 NR 1992 7f 7g 9g⁴] 900 2-y-o: small gelding: third foal: half-brother to useful 5-y-o 6f to 8.5f winner Croft Valley (by Crofthall): dam ran once: sire (by Bold Lad) 6f to 15f winner in Italy: no worthwhile form, including in seller: sold 580 gns Doncaster November Sales. *R. M. Whitaker*   **–**

VANISKI   5 b.g. Niniski (USA) 125 – Voltigeuse (USA) (Filiberto (USA) 123) [1991 10f 16m 16m* 16m⁵ 18.1m 17.2g⁶ 1992 a13g⁴] leggy gelding: plating-class handi-capper: never-nearer fourth in claimer on equitrack in February: better suited by 2m than shorter: acts on good to firm ground: visored last 3 starts. *Mrs Barbara Waring*   **–**

VANROY   8 b.g. Formidable (USA) 125 – Princess Tavi (Sea Hawk II 131) [1991 a8g² a7g* a7g a8g⁴ a8g⁶ 8d 8g 9d⁴ 8m a10g a11g⁵ a8g* a8g 1992 10m³ 10g² 7g 8.5g* 10m⁵ 8.3g⁴ 8.3d² 10m* 10m⁴ 10.1d 10.1d 9d] sturdy gelding: carries plenty of condition: fair handicapper: won at Epsom and Windsor (claimer, by 5 lengths) in midsummer: probably needs further than 7f and stays 1¼m: best on a sound surface or all-weather tracks: is held up: best visored. *J. R. Jenkins*   **67**

VANUATU (IRE)   3 b.f. Orchestra 118 – Owey (Sovereign Gleam 117) [1991 NR 1992 8g 10g⁴ 10.1d⁵ 10.2s⁵] leggy filly: sister to 1¼m to 15f winner/smart jumper Pat's Jester and Irish 1986 2-y-o 5f winner Lovely Band, and half-sister to Irish 2-y-o winners by Red Alert and Ahonoora: dam unraced half-sister to smart Irish sprinter Quisling: showed signs of ability though well beaten all starts: worth a try over 1½m. *T. Thomson Jones*   **–**

VARDY (IRE)   2 ch.g. (Feb 9) King Persian 107 – Jolie Brise (Tumble Wind (USA)) [1992 5d 5m 6d⁴ 7f] 1,750Y: short-backed, good-topped gelding: half-brother to quite modest 5f winner First Fastnet (by Ahonoora) and a winner in Denmark: dam unraced daughter of half-sister to Swing Easy: poor form in varied events, including a seller: off course nearly 3 months and backward, stiff task in Redcar nursery final start: stays 6f: best efforts on dead ground: blinkered third start. *P. C. Haslam*   **36**

VASILIEV   4 b.g. Sadler's Wells (USA) 132 – Poquito Queen (CAN) 113 (Explodent (USA)) [1991 10m⁶ 12g* 13.3g 12d² 11.4m 11.7g⁴ 13.3g² 1992 12g 13.8g² 10m 12f² 12m 14d⁶ 11.8d 12d⁴ 12.4v] big gelding: inconsistent handicapper: capable   **78 d**

of fair form, but reluctant to race on occasions and best left alone: will stay 1¾m: acts on dead ground: probably best in blinkers/visor: temperamental. *J. P. Leigh*

VA UTU   4 b.g. Balliol 125 – Flame 49 (Firestreak 125) [1991 10.1s 8m 9m³ 8f4 8g*   **53** 7.5m 10g 8m 10m 10.5g 8m⁶ 1992 a11g a10g a10g³ a10g* a10g³ a10g⁶] angular gelding: hobdayed as a juvenile: modest performer: trained reappearance by R. Woodhouse: won apprentice handicap at Lingfield late in year: stays 1¼m: acts on firm going and equitrack: tried visored once. *M. R. Channon*

VAYAVAIG   2 b.f. (Jan 20) Damister (USA) 123 – Dervaig 90 (Derring-Do 131)   **65** p [1992 6d³ 6d* 6v] 36,000Y: leggy, quite attractive filly: closely related to useful 7f and 1m winner Hello Vaigly (by Hello Gorgeous) and half-sister to several winners, notably smart sprinter Vaigly Great (by Great Nephew): dam 2-y-o 5f winner: well-backed favourite after promising debut, won 19-runner maiden at Haydock in fine style: very stiff task, never got into Racecall Gold Trophy at Redcar later in October: will stay 1m: should do better. *J. R. Fanshawe*

VELASCO (IRE)   2 b.g. (Feb 28) Nordico (USA) – Donnarella (Dom Racine (FR)   **43** 121) [1992 6.1m⁶ a5g 6g 5d] IR 23,000Y: close-coupled, good-topped gelding: second living foal: brother to 1990 Irish 2-y-o 7f winner Donnarico: dam Irish maiden: plating-class maiden: tended to wander and looked a tricky ride at Lingfield final outing: will be better suited by 7f: twice slowly away. *Sir Mark Prescott*

VELLANDRUCHA   3 b.f. Cragador 110 – Shadha 57 (Shirley Heights 130) [1991   **42** 5m⁵ 5m 1992 8.9g4 8m 10s 6.1s⁵ 6.1g 6.9v] leggy, shallow-girthed filly: inconsistent maiden: should stay at least 7f: acts on soft ground. *J. A. Bennett*

VELOCE (IRE)   4 b.g. Kafu 120 – Joanns Goddess (Godswalk (USA) 130) [1991   **64** 6m 7.5m* 8m 7.1g 7.6g⁶ 7.5f 6.1d 1992 8d4 8s 8g³ 8m² 8f 7.5g⁵ 7.1m³ 7.1f³ 7.6g 7d² 6d³ 7s⁵ 6s4 6d⁶ 7.6v 6.1s a7g² a8g4 a8g] lengthy, robust gelding: modest handicapper: joined present trainer (with M. O'Neill previously) after ninth start and generally ran creditably: effective from a testing 6f to 1m: acts on firm and soft ground: below form when blinkered/visored: suitable mount for apprentice. *A. Bailey*

VELVETEEN BOY   4 b.g. Enchantment 115 – Penny Bazaar 67 (Native Bazaar   **–** 122) [1991 NR 1992 8.5g 8g⁶] heavy-topped gelding: fifth foal: half-brother to poor 1¼m winner Bee-Kay-Ess (by Porto Bello): dam 7f winner: behind in maiden at Beverley (started slowly) and in useful company at Pontefract in April: has joined T. Donnelly. *B. W. Lunness*

VENDREDI TREIZE   9 b. or br.g. Lucky Wednesday 124 – Angel Row 96   **26** (Prince Regent (FR) 129) [1991 NR 1992 5.1g 6.1m⁵ 7g 6.1g 5.1m] tall gelding: bad mover: poor handicapper: stays 7f: acts on firm and dead going: blinkered earlier in career: often bandaged. *S. R. Bowring*

VENTIQUATTROFOGLI (IRE)   2 b.c. (Apr 5) Persian Bold 123 – India   **101** Atlanta (Ahonoora 122) [1992 6m² 5.7f* 5.9f* 7f* 7.5g* 8d* 8v] 14,500Y: compact colt: second foal: dam never ran: progressed really well between June and September, winning maiden at Bath, minor event at Carlisle, nursery (impressively) at Redcar and listed races at Florence and Rome: well beaten in Gran Criterium at Milan 4 weeks later: stays 1m: acts on firm and dead ground, well beaten on heavy. *J. L. Dunlop*

VENTURE CAPITALIST   3 ch.g. Never So Bold 135 – Brave Advance (USA)   **101** 98 (Bold Laddie (USA)) [1991 6d³ 6d² 1992 6m³ 6s² 6g* 6m⁵ 6m² 6g⁶ 6g4 6f* 5m³ 6g* 5.6m² 6d 6m] lengthy, deep-girthed gelding: moderate mover: progressed into a useful handicapper: won at Salisbury in May (maiden) and July (claimer) and at Newcastle in August: easily best of last 3 starts when neck second to Lochsong in Portland Handicap at Doncaster: stays 6f: best efforts on a sound surface: blinkered last 6 starts. *R. Hannon*

VENTURE FOURTH   3 b.c. Hotfoot 126 – Four Lawns 77 (Forlorn River 124)   **47** [1991 5m 5m 5m⁵ 7m 8m 7.6d 1992 10.5d 7m³ 7g⁵ 7g4 8m 7s] leggy colt: plating-class maiden: well beaten last 2 starts: should stay 1m: acts on good to firm ground. *E. J. Alston*

VENTURE PRINTS   2 b.c. (Mar 14) Presidium 124 – Bar Gold 80 (Lucky Brief   **44** 128) [1992 6f 6g⁶ 5m 6g 8g] 3,300Y, 7,800 2-y-o: leggy colt: half-brother to several winners here and abroad, including fair 1985 2-y-o Lily Fogg (by Swing Easy) and stayer Gold Rifle (by Scottish Rifle): dam won twice at around 1¼m: poor maiden: well beaten last 3 starts, in selling event final one: should stay 1m. *R. Champion*

VENTURINA (IRE)   3 b.f. Taufan (USA) 119 – Love Resolved 55 (Dan Cupid   **88** 132) [1991 6m⁵ 6m* 7.5f* 7g² 8m 1992 8d³ 11.5d³] sturdy filly: fairly useful performer: third in £9,900 event at Kempton (edgy, made most) and listed race at Lingfield in the spring: probably stays 1½m: acts on firm and dead going. *B. W. Hills*

VENUS OBSERVED   4 ch.f. Sharpo 132 – Fair And Wise 75 (High Line 125)   **94** d
[1991 8g 7m⁴ 7m⁵ 10m 8m* 7.9g² 1992 8g* 8.1m 8g 7.9m 7.3g 7m] leggy, angular filly: fairly useful on her day: won Jubilee Handicap at Kempton in May: no form after: best at 1m: acts on good to firm ground: ridden by 7-lb claimer A. Armes: sold 14,000 gns Newmarket December Sales. *H. Candy*

VERDANT BOY   9 br.g. Green Dancer (USA) 132 – Favorite Prospect (USA)   **49** (Mr Prospector (USA)) [1991 a7g² a7g² a7g a7g³ 7g* 6m² 6m 6g⁵ 8.5m 8d² 1992 a7g⁶ 8.1m⁵ a7g 6f⁵ 6m⁵ 7g⁶ 7.5m³ 7.1d⁶ 8.3s² 8s 8g⁶ 6s³ 7.1g 6v] quite attractive gelding: carries condition: moderate walker: modest handicapper: has won one of last 39 starts: effective from 6f to around 1m: acts on any going: suitable mount for apprentice. *M. P. Naughton*

VERDE ALITALIA (IRE)   3 ch.c. Fayruz 116 – Soul of Discretion (Tumble   **59** + Wind (USA)) [1991 6g 5m³ 5m* 1992 5g 5g⁶] lengthy, good-quartered colt: moderate mover: rated 77 at 2 yrs: shaped encouragingly on reappearance and not given hard race from modest draw (looked really well, never dangerous) later in the spring: looked capable of better and remains in training. *J. L. Dunlop*

VERMONT MAGIC   4 b.g. Elegant Air 119 – Jove's Voodoo (USA) 74 (Northern   – Jove (CAN)) [1991 11.7m⁵ 11.9m⁴ 12f 11.7f⁴ 10.4m* 1992 9.7v a10g] lengthy gelding: bought out of Lord Huntingdon's stable 15,000 gns after winning York selling handicap at 3 yrs, when rated 79: tailed off in modest company year later: seems suited by 1¼m: acts on firm going: has worn crossed noseband. *R. J. Hodges*

VERONIA   3 b.f. Bustino 136 – Neenah 107 (Bold Lad (IRE) 133) [1991 7.1m⁶   – 1992 10g 10s⁴ 10.3f 8d 8d a8g] leggy, workmanlike filly: well beaten all starts but has shown signs of ability: likely to prove suited by middle distances: sold 8,600 gns Newmarket December Sales. *J. H. M. Gosden*

VERRO (USA)   5 ch.h. Irish River (FR) 131 – Royal Rafale (USA) (Reneged)   **43** [1991 a6g⁵ a7g a8g⁴ a6g* a6g⁴ a7g⁴ 6d³ 6m 7m 6.1d a12g a8g⁶ 1992 a7g a6g⁴   a34 a7g⁴ a10g a7g 5.1d³ 5s* 5d a7g⁴ 6d a8g 7s 6.1s 6v⁴ a7g] robust, good-quartered horse: carries condition: inconsistent in handicaps after winning at Hamilton in May: effective from testing 5f to 7f: acts on heavy ground and fibresand: usually blinkered nowadays: sometimes carries head awkwardly and looks difficult ride. *J. A. Bennett*

VERSAILLESPRINCESS   4 b.f. Legend of France (USA) 124 – Naamullah   – (Reform 132) [1991 NR 1992 a10g] second foal: dam unraced: 33/1, showed little in maiden claimer at Lingfield in December. *K. O. Cunningham-Brown*

VERT AMANDE (FR)   4 ch.c. Kenmare (FR) 125 – Lady Berry (FR) 121   **126** (Violon d'Ingres (FR)) [1991 10d² 10.5g* 10g⁵ 12.5m³ 15d⁴ 1992 10s 12g* 12g² 12.5g* 12.5s⁴ 12s³ 12f]

The Fabre stable once again dominated French racing—the trainer headed the list for the sixth consecutive year—but the Lellouche yard also

Prix Maurice de Nieuil, Maisons-Laffitte—Vert Amande beats Mashaallah (rails) a neck, with Songlines (noseband) third and Merzouk fourth

had another good season. Lellouche, who finished second in the trainers' table, suffered misfortune when stable star Pistolet Bleu, one of the major contenders for the Prix de l'Arc, was injured before his final warm-up race. But the stable still took a share of the prize money when the 75/1-chance Vert Amande came from well back to reach third, beaten a neck and two lengths by Subotica and User Friendly. Vert Amande had made steady progress since joining Lellouche after being sold out of J. Beguigne's stable for 620,000 francs (about £62,500) at the end of his three-year-old career, but nothing he had achieved suggested he'd be good enough to get so close in an Arc. Vert Amande's only victory in five starts as a three-year-old had come in a maiden race at Maisons-Laffitte and he'd managed only fourth to the useful Stoute-trained filly Sought Out in the Prix de Lutece at Longchamp on Arc weekend on his final start. He gained the first of two pattern race victories as a four-year-old in the four-runner Prix d'Hedouville at Longchamp in April, after which he ran Dear Doctor to three quarters of a length in the Prix Jean de Chaudenay at Saint-Cloud in May. Vert Amande confirmed his advancement with a narrow victory—starting favourite—in the eight-runner Prix Maurice de Nieuil at Maisons-Laffitte in July. He came from last to first in the straight to beat the British-trained Mashaallah, who was giving 7 lb, by a neck with the subsequent Prix Niel winner Songlines a length away third. If Vert Amande's improved form in the Arc suggested he was one of the best middle-distance horses in Europe, he showed nothing to substantiate it in his runs either side of the Arc, finishing fourth behind the Prix du Jockey-Club fifth Modhish in the Grand Prix de Deauville in August and thirteenth of fourteen in the Japan Cup in November.

		Kalamoun	Zeddaan
	Kenmare (FR)	(gr 1975)	Khairunissa
	(gr 1975)	Belle of Ireland	Milesian
Vert Amande (FR)		(ch 1964)	Belle of The Ball
(ch.c. 1988)		Violon d'Ingres	Tourment
	Lady Berry (FR)	(b 1959)	Flute Enchantee
	(ch 1970)	Moss Rose	Mossborough
		(ch 1963)	Damasi

Vert Amande is by the good-class French miler Kenmare, who is now based in Australia but will stand a season at Coolmore in 1993 (IR 12,500 guineas, no foal no fee), out of that fine staying filly the Prix Royal-Oak winner Lady Berry, a very genuine and consistent racemare who met defeat only in the Prix de Diane and the Prix de l'Arc. Lady Berry has bred several other winners including Le Nain Jaune (by Pharly), a winner of the Grand Prix de Paris and sire of Magic Night, and Woolskin (by Wollow), a Grand Prix de Paris runner-up, both of them in the days when the Grand Prix was run over fifteen furlongs. Vert Amande, who has a good turn of foot, stays a mile and a half well and should prove at least as effective at a mile and three quarters given the chance. He has shown his best form with some give in the ground. *E. Lellouche, France*

VERVEINE (USA) 3 br.f. Lear Fan (USA) 130 – Venise (USA) (Nureyev (USA) 131) [1991 7g* 7m* 8d³ 1992 8g³ 10g³ 10.5g³ 10m⁵ 12m⁴ 12s] small, attractive French filly: smart and consistent performer: close up in frame in Prix de la Grotte and Prix Saint-Alary (to Rosefinch) at Longchamp, Prix de Diane Hermes (length third behind Jolypha) at Chantilly and Prix Vermeille at Longchamp (around ½-length fourth to Jolypha): also ran creditably when 7 lengths ninth of 18 in Prix de l'Arc de Triomphe at Longchamp: stays 1½m: acts on good to firm ground and soft. *E. Lellouche, France* **117**

VERY DICEY 4 b.g. Tremblant 112 – Party Game 70 (Red Alert 127) [1991 6m 5m⁴ 6g 5g² 5.3f² 5g⁶ 5.7m⁴ 5s⁵ 8.3g 5.3f* 5f* 5d 5d 5g³ 1992 a5g⁴ a6g² a5g³ a6g* 6g⁵ 5g² 5.1g 5g a5g² 5m⁵ 5.1d 5.2s a5g⁶ a6g⁴ a5g³ a5g⁴ a6g⁶] strong, workmanlike gelding: fairly useful performer: claimed out of S. Dow's stable £6,595 after winning Lingfield claimer in March: effective at 5f and easy 6f: best efforts on a sound surface or on all-weather tracks: has won for 7-lb claimer: has had tongue tied down: has hung: speedy: suited by forcing tactics. *W. R. Muir* **82**

VERY EVIDENT (IRE) 3 b.g. Glenstal (USA) 118 – Royal Daughter (High Top 131) [1991 7g⁶ 1992 8.2d³ 10g 12g⁴ 10.1f] lengthy, sturdy gelding: failed to progress after third in Nottingham minor event, and not seen out after June: should stay 1¼m: sold to join R. O'Leary 9,200 gns Newmarket Autumn Sales. *B. W. Hills* **62 d**

VERY GOOD   3 b.f. Noalto 120 – Sew Nice 71 (Tower Walk 130) [1991 6g 5m 1992   –
6m 5g 5m 5m 8.2s] lengthy, good-topped filly: of little account. *N. Tinkler*

VIA BORGHESE (USA)   3 b.f. Seattle Dancer (USA) 119 – Angela Serra **105** p
(Arctic Tern (USA) 126) [1991 6.3m* 7d³ 1992 10m⁴ 8g* 8g* 8g*] useful Irish filly:
successful in 1992 in listed races at the Curragh and Leopardstown and Group 3
contest (by head from Gdansk's Honour) at the Curragh: never-dangerous fourth to
Market Booster in Pretty Polly Stakes at the Curragh: probably stays 1¼m. *M. V.
O'Brien, Ireland*

VIAGGIO   4 b.c. High Line 125 – Al Washl (USA) 79 (The Minstrel (CAN) 135)   –
[1991 10v 10s 12f³ 12m⁴ 16g⁴ 12s 1992 12g⁵ 12s 11.4g⁶ 12s] leggy, workmanlike colt:
fourth foal: half-brother to fairly useful sprinter Hufoof (by Known Fact) and a
winner in Germany by Chief Singer: dam placed over 5f and 6f at 3 yrs: ex-Irish
maiden (in frame in handicaps at 3 yrs for N. Meade): poor handicapper here: stays
1½m: acts on firm ground, not on soft: blinkered second start: won novice hurdle in
December. *J. Akehurst*

VIARDOT (IRE)   3 b.c. Sadler's Wells (USA) 132 – Vive La Reine (Vienna 127)   **92**
[1991 8d³ 1992 10.1s* 12g² 10.5d* 10m 10d] rangy colt: has a quick, round action:
easy winner in small-field maiden at Newcastle and minor event at Haydock in
spring: creditable seventh of 9 in listed race at Goodwood but well beaten in £50,800
handicap at Sandown after: probably stays 1½m: has form on good to firm ground,
but may prove ideally suited by a soft surface: soon off bridle, and worth a try in
blinkers/visor: has joined M. Pipe. *M. R. Stoute*

VICEROY   5 b.g. Indian King (USA) 128 – Bold Polly 67 (Bold Lad (IRE) 133) **109**
[1991 6m 5f² 5m 5m⁴ 5g³ 5.2f² 5.1m⁴ 5.6m⁶ 5.2f* 5g² 1992 5m³ 5m⁶ 5g* 5.1m
5g* 5m* 6m 5d⁴ 5m 5g] strong, well-made gelding: much improved in handicaps in
1992: successful in quite valuable events at Epsom and Newcastle (2, including
Gosforth Park Cup): ran creditably eighth and final starts, moderately in listed race
in between: effective at 5f and 6f: acts on firm and dead ground: used to be blinkered,
but visored nowadays: sometimes slowly away/wears crossed noseband and tongue
strap: good mount for claimer: trained first 9 starts by W. Pearce/B. Beasley. *Mrs L.
Piggott*

*Carmelites Kildare 7th Centenary Desmond Stakes, the Curragh—
Via Borghese wins narrowly from Gdansk's Honour (not in picture);
Sure Sharp (right) is third*

VICEROY GEM (IRE)   4 ch.g. Sallust 134 – Gang Plank 84 (Tower Walk 130)   –
[1991 10g 12f⁶ 10.2g 6.1d 8g⁴ 8f⁶ 7g³ 7m 1992 9.7v 10m] leggy, workmanlike gelding:
has a round action: poor maiden nowadays: stays 1m: best efforts on good ground. *R.
J. Holder*

VICKY'S MARK   3 b.f. Petong 126 – London Fling (Jaazeiro (USA) 127) [1991 NR   –
1992 8f] sturdy, plain filly: first foal: dam unraced: last of 9 in claimer at Newmarket
in June. *J. M. P. Eustace*

VICTOIRE BLEUE   5 b.m. Legend of France (USA) 124 – Vosges 117 (Youth **106**
(USA) 135) [1991 10.5g 12g 10.5d³ 12g* 16g² 15.5m* 20d* 1992 16.2d 15.5g⁵ 14g*]
small, rather sparely-made French mare: rated 114p at 4 yrs when successful in
excellent style on final start in Prix du Cadran: below that form in 1992, disappointing favourite (heavily bandaged and unimpressive in appearance) in Sagaro Stakes
at Ascot on first run and only neck winner from Great Marquess of minor event at
Vichy in July: stayed 2½m: acted on good to firm ground and dead (never raced on
anything more extreme): had good turn of foot: has been retired. *A. Fabre, France*

VICTORIA HALL   2 b.f. (May 8) Hallgate 127 – Thorganby Victory 82 (Burglar   **56**
128) [1992 5g⁵ 5d³ 6s³ 6.1s² 6m³] 2,200Y: good-bodied filly: eighth foal: half-sister
to 7f and 1m winer Absolute Steal (by Absalom) and 6f and 7f winner Taskforce
Victory (by Record Token): dam 2-y-o 5f winner: off course 3½ months before
running very well on last 2 starts in nursery at Chepstow and maiden at Pontefract:
stays 6f: probably acts on any going. *W. G. M. Turner*

VICTORIAN STAR   2 br.f. (Apr 7) King Among Kings 60 – Santo Star 55   –
(Monsanto (FR) 121) [1992 6s 5.3f⁶ 6f 5h 5.3f a6g] close-coupled filly: third foal: dam
half-sister to Ebor winner Another Sam: well beaten, including in sellers. *P. Butler*

VICTORIA ROAD (IRE)   4 b.g. Runnett 125 – That's Swiss (Thatching 131)   –
[1991 6d⁵ 7.5g³ 7m² 7d² 7m* 7f³ 8.5f³ 7.6g³ 7.6m 1992 6v 5.9d 8f 7g 6s] lengthy,
workmanlike gelding: has a round action: rated 80 at 3 yrs: on the downgrade.
M. H. Easterby

VICTOR ROMEO   3 b.c. Nomination 125 – Be My Sweet 78 (Galivanter 131)   **46** §
[1991 5m⁶ 5m 5m⁴ 6g⁴ 6.1m* 7m² 8.2m³ 7m a8g 1992 a10g⁵ 9.2d 12.2g⁴ 10d⁶
7.5m⁵ 9.2d 8d 10s] good-topped colt: good walker: plater: stays 1m: acts on good to
firm ground: effective blinkered or not: sold out of W. Pearce's stable 1,500 gns
Doncaster June Sales and off course 4 months after sixth start: seems irresolute.
R. C. Spicer

VICTORY GATE (USA)   7 b.g. Lydian (FR) 120 – Pago Miss (USA) (Pago   –
Pago) [1991 NR 1992 11.9m 9.7v] lengthy gelding: fair hurdler/chaser: only poor on
flat nowadays. *A. Moore*

VIENNA BOUND   2 b.c. (Apr 22) Dowsing (USA) 124 – Crimson Ring (Persian   – p
Bold 123) [1992 6m] 5,400Y: workmanlike colt: half-brother to 8.2f winner Fistful of
Bucks (by Lochnager): dam lightly raced: burly and never a factor in 29-runner
seller at Newmarket in October: should do better. *C. F. Wall*

VIEW FROM ABOVE   6 b.m. Dara Monarch 128 – Organdy 84 (Blakeney 126)   ?
[1991 12g² 11.7g* 11.7g* 12g 1992 11.8g* 12d 12g] strong mare: rated 91 at 3 yrs:
successful several times in Jersey in 1992, including over 1¾m, and at Le Pin-Au-
Haras in October: never dangerous in Doncaster handicaps last 2 runs: effective
from 1½m to 1¾m: acts on firm ground: sometimes wears tongue strap. *Paul Green,
Jersey*

VIKING VENTURE   7 ch.g. Viking (USA) – Mattira (FR) (Rheffic (FR) 129)   –
[1991 NR 1992 11.6g 11.6g] small, lengthy, workmanlike gelding: on the downgrade.
D. A. Wilson

VILLA CAPRI   3 b.f. Cragador 110 – La Troienne (Henbit (USA) 130) [1991 6d   –
1992 7g 8s] workmanlike filly: poor maiden: looks one to treat with caution. *C. E.
Brittain*

VILLAGE GREEN (FR)   2 gr.c. (Apr 13) Village Star (FR) 131 – Betera (FR)   **74** ?
(Green Dancer (USA) 132) [1992 7d⁵ 8g⁶ 8m⁴ a8g] 85,000 francs (approx £8,500) Y:
rather leggy, quite attractive colt: half-brother to 2 winners in France: dam French
4-y-o 11.5f winner: sire French middle-distance colt: kept useful company at Ascot
first 2 starts, better effort when sixth in strongly-run listed event: well-backed
favourite, well below form in maidens at Pontefract and Lingfield (beat only one)
afterwards: will stay 1¼m: best form on easy ground: tends to carry head high:
difficult to assess. *C. E. Brittain*

VILLAGE PET   4 b.c. Tina's Pet 121 – Village Lass (No Mercy 126) [1991 a5g a6g   – §
a5g⁶ 5g³ 5m 5d 5g 5.1g a6g a5g a5g 1992 5m 5.1m] leggy, plain colt: has a round

Prix des Tourelles, Longchamp—Villandry asserts from Stani River

action: inconsistent sprint handicapper: acts on firm ground: ran poorly when blinkered once: sold out of R. Bennett's stable 675 gns Ascot March Sales before first run. *P. J. Hobbs*

VILLANDRY (USA)   4 ch.f. Lyphard's Wish (FR) 124 – Valhalla 83 (New **113** Chapter 106) [1991 10d* 10.5s⁴ 10.5g⁶ 10.5g* 12d⁴ 12.5d⁵ 1992 10g⁴ 12.5g⁵ 12s* 12.5s 12g*] very useful French filly: won listed race at Longchamp in September: below form in Prix de Royallieu there before landing Grade 2 Long Island Handicap at Belmont for best effort in 1992: effective at 1¼m to 1½m: yet to race on top-of-the-ground. *A. Fabre, France*

VILLAVINA   2 b.f. (Feb 8) Top Ville 129 – Karavina (Karabas 132) [1992 5f⁵ 7g⁵ **59** 8g⁵ 8.2d 7g a7g⁶] 23,000F: smallish filly: moderate walker: half-sister to useful 1986 2-y-o 6f winner Kalorama (by Bold Lad) and 2 winners abroad: dam Irish 6f and 7f winner: consistent until running moderately (in an eyeshield) on equitrack: will stay beyond 1m. *S. Dow*

VINSTAN   6 gr.g. Rabdan 129 – Pretty Fast 52 (Firestreak 125) [1991 a12g 1992   – a14g 14.6d a12s 12.3m 14.1d] big, lengthy gelding: on the downgrade. *C. A. Smith*

VINTAGE   7 b.g. Noalcoholic (FR) 128 – Good To Follow 82 (Wollow 132) [1991 **84** 12m* 11.7m² 12g⁴ 11.6m² 12m⁵ 11.5f* 1992 12g 11.5m⁶ a10g⁴ a10g⁴ a13g²] strong, lengthy gelding: has round action: fairly useful handicapper: off course a year before reappearance: best efforts in 1992 at Lingfield final 2 starts: better at 1½m/13f than shorter: acts on firm and dead going and on equitrack: wears tongue strap: sometimes sweats: usually held up. *Major W. R. Hern*

VINTAGE CROP   5 ch.g. Rousillon (USA) 133 – Overplay 107 (Bustino **119** p 136) [1991 16g* 1992 14s* 9g³ 14s* 14s⁵ 18m*]

One-time Melbourne Cup entry Vintage Crop won the Tote Cesarewitch like a good horse, and, although he looked thrown in at the weights beforehand, he probably is one. The 5/1 favourite following a sustained ante-post gamble, he drew right away over the last two furlongs and had eight lengths to spare over next-home Specificity. The previous month, on his last start, Vintage Crop had shown much improved form when a staying-on fifth of nine behind Mashaallah, Snurge, Drum Taps and Rock Hopper in the Irish St Leger, finishing within six lengths of Mashaallah. It was a performance which would have earned him around a stone more than he actually received in the Cesarewitch had the handicapper been in a position to take account of it. But the weights were already published. All that the official had had to go on for Vintage Crop when he framed his handicap was a total of four races on the flat

Tote Cesarewitch, Newmarket—
Vintage Crop lands a gamble in style from Specificity (right) and Farat

in Ireland, in particular three handicaps in the current season. The horse had been running well and had easily landed the odds over a distance of ground at Gowran Park in May and Tralee in August. On the strength of these performances Vintage Crop was put in 13 lb behind the top weight Further Flight, a non-acceptor who will be hard pushed to beat him at levels in future. Plans to run in the Melbourne Cup were abandoned well before the Cesarewitch, reportedly because of varied obstacles, bureaucratic, veterinary and financial, which cropped up as the trip was being organized. Immediately after the Cesarewitch it was announced that Vintage Crop, a big, lengthy, long-striding galloper, would be returned to hurdling in the winter—he won two out of two races over timber in December, 1991—and would be aimed at the Champion Hurdle. There are surely more flat races to be won with him though, valuable races at that, with more improvement to come.

	Rousillon (USA) (b 1981)	Riverman (b 1969)	Never Bend
			River Lady
		Belle Dorine (b or br 1977)	Marshua's Dancer
Vintage Crop (ch.g. 1987)			Palsy Walsy
	Overplay (b 1978)	Bustino (b 1971)	Busted
			Ship Yard
		Melodramatic (b 1970)	Tudor Melody
			Irish Flight

The Cesarewitch revealed two things about Vintage Crop that had had to be taken on trust by his backers—that he acts as well on good to firm ground as on soft and is as effective at two and a quarter miles as at a mile and three quarters. The way he finished the course at Newmarket, he will have no difficulty staying two and a half miles, which is surprising for a horse by Rousillon. The dam Overplay was a useful middle-distance filly; she finished third in the Ribblesdale and ran well in the Yorkshire Oaks on another visit to Britain, but was probably too highly tried in the Irish St Leger on her only attempt at further. Matings with Known Fact, Cure The Blues and Flash of Steel have produced minor winners in Ireland and on the Continent. The next dam Melodramatic, a miler, was out of a half-sister to the top-class middle-distance colt Carnoustie and the very useful stayer Philemon, the last-named third in the Irish St Leger in 1963 and winner of the Brown Jack Stakes a couple of seasons later. *D. K. Weld, Ireland*

VIRGINIA COTTAGE 3 b.f. Lomond (USA) 128 – Bermuda Classic 98 (Double **39** Form 130) [1991 6.1f 7m 1992 8d 8.1d⁶ 5s⁴ 6g⁵ 5h 5m 6g⁵ 6f 6m 7.1s 6.1g] leggy filly: poor mover: headstrong maiden: bred to stay 1m: acts on soft ground: stiff tasks when blinkered. *B. A. McMahon*

VIRILIS 2 b.c. (Feb 19) Niniski (USA) 125 – Valiant Cry (Town Crier 119) [1992 **–** 6m⁶] 98,000Y: angular colt: has scope: half-brother to fairly useful Irish sprinter Mitsubishi Vision (by Cure The Blues) and a minor winner over middle distances in France: dam French 9f winner: 33/1 and in need of race, tailed-off last of 6 in Middle Park Stakes at Newmarket in October. *C. E. Brittain*

VIRKON VENTURE (IRE) 4 b.g. Auction Ring (USA) 123 – Madame Fair **–** (Monseigneur (USA) 127) [1991 10g 8.5f⁵ 8g 9d* 10d* 10d³ 9g⁵ 1992 10d 8.9m 9d 10m 10.5s⁶ 11.8s] leggy, angular gelding: rated 83 in 1992: well below that form in handicaps in 1992: should prove at least as effective at 1½m as shorter: best efforts with give in the ground: sometimes bandaged. *M. H. Tompkins*

VIS-A-VIS 3 gr.g. Efisio 120 – River Vixen (Sagaro 133) [1991 5m 5m 6g 7s 6m **–** 1992 10d 6d] tall, workmanlike gelding: seems of little account. *D. Burchell*

VISIMOTION (USA) 2 ch.c. (Feb 5) Imp Society (USA) – Ditdad (USA) (Tudor **65** Grey 119) [1992 5g⁴ 5.1m³] $20,000Y: lengthy colt: half-brother to a minor winner in North America: dam won at up to 7f: modest maiden: not seen out after May: will be suited by further. *M. J. Heaton-Ellis*

VISION OF WONDER 8 b.g. Tyrnavos 129 – Valeur (Val de Loir 133) [1991 **27** 12s⁶ 14.6m 1992 11.5f 14.1g⁵ 18g 18.2m⁴ 18.2g] angular gelding: good mover: inconsistent staying handicapper: acts on any going. *J. S. King*

VISTEC EXPRESS (IRE) 2 b.c. (Mar 22) Salse (USA) 128 – Kriswick 72 (Kris **60** p 135) [1992 8d] 12,000F, 31,000Y: leggy colt: first live foal: dam, successful at 15f at 4 yrs in France, is half-sister to Queen's Vase winner Santella Man: very easy to back, shaped encouragingly when 11 lengths ninth of 18 to Dyab in maiden at Leicester in October, good headway over 2f out, having been slowly away and not knocked about once held: reared and fell over in paddock beforehand: sure to improve. *H. R. A. Cecil*

VISTO SI STAMPI (IRE) 2 b.c. (Mar 10) Ahonoora 122 – Jardiniere (Nijinsky **91** p (CAN) 138) [1992 7g⁴ 7g* 8.1s*] 38,000Y: strong, good-topped colt: third foal: dam, showed a little ability in Ireland, is sister to Kings Lake, closely related to Salmon Leap and half-sister to Cloonlara (dam of Glenstal): most progressive colt: quickened in good style when winning maiden at Ayr (by 4 lengths) in August and minor event at Haydock (looked extremely well, beat Shrewd Idea by short head) following month: will stay at least 1¼m: can make his mark in stronger company at 3 yrs. *J. L. Dunlop*

VITAL VOLTAGE (IRE) 3 ch.g. Soughaan (USA) 111 – Damariscotta (Aho- **–** noora 122) [1991 5m 6m 7.5f³ 7m³ 7m 1992 10m 8g 8f 8h 9.9d⁴ 7d 7g⁶ 7.5d] small, leggy gelding: poor plater: should stay 1¼m: acts on firm ground: below form blinkered/visored. *M. W. Ellerby*

VITE VITE 6 ch.g. Kind of Hush 118 – Swiftacre (Bay Express 132) [1991 a11g⁵ **–** a10g a8g⁵ a7g³ a8g² a8g⁶ 10s 7.5g 8m 7.6g a7g⁶ 8f 8.2d 1992 8s] strong, workman-like gelding: poor handicapper: stays 1¼m: acts on firm ground. *R. C. Spicer*

VIVA DARLING 3 b.g. King Luthier 113 – Be My Darling 82 (Windjammer **67** (USA)) [1991 5g⁴ 5m³ 7m 1992 10.5s² 10g⁵ 8d⁴ 10.1m³ 10m² 12h³ 12.3d* 10.3m] quite attractive gelding: consistent handicapper in first half of 1992, not seen out after July: won apprentice event at Wolverhampton: stays 12.3f: acts on any going. *B. A. McMahon*

VIVE LE ROI (IRE) 3 b. or br.g. Mister Majestic 122 – Vivungi (USA) (Exbury **–** 138) [1991 NR 1992 6d³] IR 7,000F, 25,000Y: lengthy gelding: closely related to 2 winners by Tumble Wind, including fairly useful 1983 2-y-o 5f winner El Gazebo, later successful at up to 1m in USA, and half-brother to several other winners: dam placed at around 7f in France and Ireland: 12½ lengths third of 4 in maiden at Newcastle in March: dead. *Mrs J. R. Ramsden*

VIVITZ (IRE) 3 b.c. Alzao (USA) 117 – Stapelea (FR) (Faraway Son (USA) 130) **56** [1991 6d 7.1s⁵ 7s 7m⁵ 8g 1992 8d 10d 10g² 10f⁶ 10m] leggy colt: modest maiden: pulled up lame final start: stayed 1¼m: acted on good to firm and soft ground: dead. *G. B. Balding*

VIV'S PET 2 b.f. (Feb 18) Petong 126 – Doppio 62 (Dublin Taxi) [1992 6g⁶ 5d⁶ 6d **41** 6s 6g] 8,600Y: neat filly: third foal: sister to 3-y-o 6f winner Wandering Stranger and

1990 2-y-o 5f winner Garth: dam 2-y-o 5f winner: went the wrong way, blinkered last 2 starts: sold 1,000 gns Ascot November Sales. *A. Hide*

VLADIVOSTOK 2 gr.c. (Feb 24) Siberian Express (USA) 125 – Tsungani 64 **66** (Cure The Blues (USA)) [1992 6f² 6.1d 7g] 11,000Y: leggy colt: has scope: first foal: dam 2-y-o 6f winner, is half-sister to useful 1983 2-y-o 6f winner Keep Tapping: off course 3 months after promising second in Newbury maiden in May: ran moderately after: sold 9,600 gns Newmarket Autumn Sales. *B. W. Hills*

VOLUNTEER POINT (IRE) 2 b.c. (Jan 18) Mister Majestic 122 – Lola Sharp **33** (Sharpen Up 127) [1992 5m 6g⁶ 5f 7m] 3,000F, 17,500Y: compact, good-topped colt: sixth foal: half-brother to 3 winners, including 6f (at 2 yrs) and 1¼m winner Dawson City (by Glint of Gold): dam won in Italy: poor form. *Mrs S. A. Bramall*

VRATISLAV (USA) 3 ch.c. Nijinsky (CAN) 138 – Mizima (USA) (Damascus **96** p (USA)) [1991 NR 1992 10g* 12m²] angular, quite good-topped colt: first living foal: dam, daughter of Oaks winner Monade, won 6f maiden in USA: won maiden at Windsor by 10 lengths: 1½ lengths second of 6 to Colorific in minor event at Newmarket later in July: seemed sure to improve again and win races at 1½m + . *J. H. M. Gosden*

VUCHTERBACHER 6 b.g. Longleat (USA) 109 – Queensbury Star 76 **–** (Wishing Star 117) [1991 7.5f 8f⁵ a7g* a7g* 7m² 6m 7f a7g* 7m* 7m a7g a7g³ a7g* a60 d 1992 a7g⁴ a7g⁵ a7g² a8g a8g⁵ a7g⁵ 7f 10g a7g³ a7g⁶ a8g⁴ a7g⁴] leggy, close-coupled gelding: has a round action: modest handicapper: somewhat disappointing after third outing: best at 7f: acts on good to firm ground and all-weather surfaces: tailed off when visored: sometimes bandaged: excellent mount for an apprentice. *P. F. Tulk*

W

WAAREE (USA) 2 ro.c. (Mar 28) Risen Star (USA) – Flight Dancer (USA) 109 **50** (Misty Flight) [1992 7f 8.1d] $300,000Y: close-coupled, quite attractive colt: moderate walker: half-brother to several winners, notably Minstrella (by The Minstrel) and high-class Misty Gallore (by Halo), winner of 11 races and best from 6f to 9f: dam won 4 times over 5f and 6f at 2 yrs, and stayed 1¼m: sire (by Secretariat) won Preakness and Belmont Stakes: plating-class form in moderately-run minor event on debut: well beaten on dead ground. *A. A. Scott*

WAAZA (USA) 3 b.g. Danzig Connection (USA) – Nishig (USA) (Naskra (USA)) **70** d [1991 NR 1992 8f⁴ 9m⁴ 10m 10.5g 11g 11d² 11.7d⁴ 10d⁶] $45,000Y: lengthy gelding: first foal: dam, unplaced from 5 starts in North America, is half-sister to 4-time stakes winner Dairy Bar: fair form first 2 starts: well below form most starts afterwards (including in blinkers twice) though not entirely discredited when second in claimer at Wolverhampton: probably stays 11f: usually slowly away: trained until after penultimate start by A. Scott: has been gelded: one to treat with a deal of caution. *Miss L. C. Siddall*

WADERS DREAM (IRE) 3 b.g. Doulab (USA) 115 – Sea Mistress (Habitat **76** 134) [1991 6m 5m 6f* 5m 1992 6g⁶ 7f² 7g a6g³ 6m⁶] leggy gelding: good walker: fair handicapper: may prove ideally suited by 7f: acts on firm ground: blinkered (ran creditably) penultimate start: has run well when sweating, and for apprentice. *J. E. Banks*

WAFI (USA) 3 b.c. Lyphard (USA) 132 – Dictina (FR) (Dictus (FR) 126) [1991 NR **68** 1992 8g 7g³ 8m³ 8d 8g³ 6s 7g 7d⁶ 6m²] $100,000Y: smallish colt: moderate mover: third foal: half-brother to a winner in Norway by Sharpen Up and to 4-y-o 9f winner Legal View (by Riverman): dam winner of 4 races, including 9f Grade 3 event, from family of Caro: fair maiden at best: below form last 4 starts, not completely discredited in blinkers last time: probably stays 1m: sold to Mrs M. Reveley 5,200 gns Newmarket Autumn Sales. *B. Hanbury*

WAHEM (IRE) 2 b.c. (May 19) Lomond (USA) 128 – Pro Patria 86 (Petingo 135) **70** [1992 5g 5g⁴ 5s² 6g 8.5d³ 8f* 8d] 17,000Y: angular, unfurnished colt: good mover: half-brother to top-class middle-distance filly Unite (by Kris) and 7.2f seller winner Palletine (by African Sky): dam, sister to smart miler Patris, won over 5f and 6f at 2 yrs from 4 starts: fair performer: trained first 3 starts by N. Callaghan, off course nearly 4 months afterwards: made all in small group on far side when winning 21-runner nursery at Doncaster in September: well out of depth in Racing Post Trophy following month: better at 1m than shorter. *C. E. Brittain*

WAINWRIGHT (USA) 3 ch.c. Bering 136 – Crystal Bright 75 (Bold Lad (IRE) –
133) [1991 7m² 1992 8g⁵] quite attractive colt: looked promising on debut, but
soundly beaten in maiden at Newmarket in August, 1992: bred to stay 1¼m. *J. H. M.
Gosden*

WAJEEB (USA) 3 b.c. Majestic Light (USA) – Reham 67 (Mill Reef (USA) 141) 70 p
[1991 NR 1992 11.8s³] rangy, good sort: fifth foal: half-brother to modest 1987 2-y-o
Fleur de Foret (by Green Forest), later ungenuine, and to a stakes-placed winner in
North America by Coastal: dam, placed from 1¼m to 1½m, is half-sister to both
Smoggy, smart winner at up to 9f in France and USA, and Ribblesdale winner Dish
Dash: 7/1 and carrying condition, 6½ lengths third of 10 to Sayh in minor event at
Leicester in June, held up then chasing leader under hands and heels final 2f:
showed knee action to post: seemed sure to improve. *B. Hanbury*

WAKIL (IRE) 3 br.c. Tate Gallery (USA) 117 – Arena 86 (Sallust 134) [1991 6g 7d 56
1992 8d 9g 10f 10d⁴ 8f³ 8.3g² 9.7m*] good-bodied colt: moderate mover: modest
handicapper: sold out of J. Benstead's stable 8,200 gns Newmarket July Sales after
fourth start: best efforts last 2 starts, always front rank when winning at Folkestone
in August: should prove better at around 1¼m than shorter: acts on good to firm
ground. *L. G. Cottrell*

WAKT 2 b.f. (Feb 22) Akarad (FR) 130 – Nasara (FR) (Home Guard (USA) 129) 39 p
[1992 8d] first foal: dam, lightly-raced French 11f winner, is half-sister to Natroun
(by Akarad), family also of Yashgan, Vayraan and Valiyar: 16/1, around 16 lengths
eighth of 20 to Lille Hammer in maiden at Yarmouth in October: likely to improve.
D. Morley

WALID'S PRINCESS (IRE) 2 b.f. (Mar 31) Waajib 121 – Glomach (USA) 73 52
(Majestic Light (USA)) [1992 5g³ 5g 6.1g 6m⁴ 7g 6.1m* 7g⁵ 6d⁴ a6g] 1,800F, IR
2,100Y: sturdy filly: moderate walker: sixth living foal: half-sister to 3-y-o Ferrycrosthemersey (by Red Sunset): dam 7f winner, is out of half-sister to top-class
American horses Fort Marcy and Key To The Mint: modest performer: landed
gamble in seller (retained 3,400 gns) at Nottingham in August, despite wandering: *J.
Wharton*

WALIMU (IRE) 3 b.f. Top Ville 129 – Summer Impressions (USA) 70 (Lyphard 82
(USA) 132) [1991 NR 1992 8g³ 8g* 8.1d³ 9d⁵ 10g* 10m⁵ 12m* 12g] lengthy, angular
filly: carries condition: shows knee action: third live foal: half-sister to 9f winner
Princess Zepoli (by Persepolis): dam minor winner at 1m at 4 yrs in France, is
daughter of Roussalka: generally progressive performer: won maiden at Wolverhampton in July and handicaps at Sandown and Newmarket (quickening clear over 2f
out, held on by a head) in the autumn: below form final start: suited by middle
distances: acted on good to firm and dead ground: visits Mtoto. *C. F. Wall*

WALI (USA) 2 b.c. (Feb 10) Lomond (USA) 128 – Magic Slipper 97 (Habitat 134) 63 p
[1992 6g⁴ 6s] sturdy, medium-sized colt: third foal: half-brother to 3-y-o 6.9f winner
Ahbab (by Persian Bold): dam 1¼m and 11.5f winner, is half-sister to Light Cavalry
and Fairy Footsteps: similar form in newcomers event at Ascot (raced keenly) and
maiden at Newbury (headed well over 1f out) in October: will stay at least 7f: may
well improve. *P. T. Walwyn*

WALKING ON WATER 3 ch.g. Celestial Storm (USA) 132 – Maiden Pool 85 72
(Sharpen Up 127) [1991 6m⁴ 6d 6m* 6g² 6s³ 6g 6g 1992 7m 7g 9m 10f³ 11.6g 12d⁴
11.9f 12d] quite good-topped gelding: has a free, rather round action: inconsistent
handicapper: stays 1¼m: acts on any going: probably best blinkered/visored:
sometimes sweats: tends to carry head high, and not an easy ride. *R. F. Johnson
Houghton*

WALKING POSSESSION 3 b.c. Faustus (USA) 118 – Pepeke 78 (Mummy's 75
Pet 125) [1991 a5g² 7m 5m⁴ 6g 5m* 5d* 5d³ 6s² 1992 6g 5.1g⁴ 5m² 5g 6m⁵ 6m 5m*
5f* 6m 5d 5d³] lengthy colt: moderate mover: fair form on his day: got up close
home in claimers at Beverley and Pontefract in the summer: effective at 5f and 6f:
acts on any going: has form without blinkers, but wore them when successful: sold
5,400 gns Newmarket September Sales. *R. Boss*

WALKING SAINT 5 b.m. Godswalk (USA) 130 – Saintly Tune (Welsh Saint
126) [1991 9g 8g 8.3m³ 8f 9d⁵ 10m³ 7.9m⁶ 10.3g 1992 10.8d 8g 16f² 11.8d⁶ a12g
17.2h⁴ 10.2g 14.6g] close-coupled mare: rated 57 at 4 yrs: little form in 1992. *Graeme
Roe*

WALKING THE PLANK 3 b.g. Daring March 116 – Pirate Maid (Auction Ring –
(USA) 123) [1991 5.7f⁴ 8g* 8d² 8g⁶ 1992 8d] tall, rather unfurnished gelding: fair

907

performer as a juvenile (rated 78) and shaped as if retaining ability in strongly-run handicap at Kempton in April: stays 1m: acts on dead ground. *P. T. Walwyn*

WALK IN THE PARK 3 ch.f. Valiyar 129 – Tripolitaine (FR) (Nonoalco (USA) 131) [1991 5.3f4 5g3 6m5 5.2g* 6m* 6g2 7g3 6d* 5.7f2 6g4 5g4 6m 1992 7m4 6d 5g5 6m2 5m2 7g3 6g 5.1m2 6g2 5.2d2 5d* 5m4 5d 5d* 6d6 5.6m4 5.2g4] small, strong filly: fairly useful and consistent sprinter: won 2 claimers at Sandown in the summer: particularly good efforts in Portland Handicap at Doncaster and £7,000 event at Newbury last 2 starts: won on firm and dead ground: normally ridden by 5-lb claimer A. Tucker: tough and genuine. *R. Simpson* **91**

WALKONTHEMOON 3 ch.f. Coquelin (USA) 121 – Lunar Eclipse 95 (Hot Spark 126) [1991 5g4 a7g6 1992 a8g5 a7g3 a7g* 7.5g 8f3 6.9g 7m 8f4 7g 8d 8d] leggy, close-coupled filly: inconsistent plater: made all in maiden at Lingfield in February: stays 1m: acts on firm ground (seemingly not on a soft surface) and equitrack: below form when blinkered/visored. *M. McCormack* **47**

WALK THAT WALK 3 b.f. Hadeer 118 – Che Gambe (USA) (Lyphard (USA) 132) [1991 5m4 5m* 7.6d 7d 1992 8d] leggy, workmanlike filly: off course 6 months after winning maiden in spring at 2 yrs for C. Brittain: very stiff tasks, below that form in handicap company since, in April on only outing in 1992: should stay 1m: sold 800 gns Newmarket September Sales. *N. C. Wright* **–**

WALK THE BEAT 2 b.c. (May 9) Interrex (CAN) – Plaits 93 (Thatching 131) [1992 5s6 5d*] 3,200Y: fourth foal: half-brother to middle-distance plater Headbee (by Head For Heights): dam unreliable maiden, stayed 7f: won maiden auction at Edinburgh in November, doing particularly well as reared stalls, swerved left and lost several lengths: will improve again. *R. Simpson* **67 p**

WALNUT BURL (IRE) 2 b.c. (Apr 26) Taufan (USA) 119 – Hay Knot (Main Reef 126) [1992 5m4 6m 6d3 6m5 6s4 6s] 8,200 2-y-o: rather leggy, quite attractive colt: moderate walker: third foal: dam, never ran, from family of Wassl: modest form in varied events: will stay 7f: acts on good to firm and soft ground. *L. J. Holt* **57**

WALSHAM WITCH 2 b.f. (Apr 12) Music Maestro 119 – Makinlau 88 (Lauso) [1992 6g4 6m* 7m6 6f* 6d4 6m 6m6] 1,100Y: workmanlike filly: moderate mover: closely related to a winner abroad by Song: dam won from 1m to 1½m: modest performer: won maiden auction at Yarmouth and nursery (making most and battling on gamely) at Pontefract in the summer: ran moderately last 2 starts: should stay 7f: acts on firm and dead ground. *M. H. Tompkins* **61**

WALSTEAD (IRE) 3 b.c. Fairy King (USA) – Tecmessa (Home Guard (USA) 129) [1991 5m* 6.3s 6g 1992 5g 6d 6m6 5m5 a6g6 6d4 7g 7g 6m 5.2s6 6.1s 6.9v] strong colt: inconsistent performer: trained until after third start by W. Jarvis: should stay beyond 6f: has form on good to firm ground and dead. *D. A. Wilson* **56**

WALTERS WONDER 2 b.c. (Mar 5) Welsh Captain 113 – Romana 72 (Roman Warrior 132) [1992 5g 6f] sturdy colt: first foal: dam stayed very well: well beaten in minor event at Windsor (backward) and seller at Warwick (bolted at start) in May. *J. R. Jenkins* **–**

WANDA 5 b.m. Taufan (USA) 119 – Pitaka (Pitskelly 122) [1991 5g3 5f6 6g* 6g4 5d* 5g3 6.1m 6m 5.1m 5g 5.1s5 5.1d4 5d 1992 5s*dis 5d] close-coupled, angular mare: moderate mover: fair handicapper: comfortably made all at Lingfield in April, but disqualified after failing a dope test: effective at 5f and 6f: acted on any going, but best efforts with give in the ground: not blinkered since 3 yrs: reportedly covered by Salse. *K. R. Burke* **73**

WANDERING STRANGER 3 gr.f. Petong 126 – Doppio 62 (Dublin Taxi) [1991 5m2 5m2 5g3 1992 6m3 5g3 6m* 6g] deep-girthed, workmanlike filly: fair performer: won maiden at Windsor in July, edging left: tailed-off last of 19 in Newmarket handicap month later: stays 6f: acts on good to firm going, yet to race on a soft surface. *P. J. Makin* **68**

WAND (IRE) 3 b.f. Reference Point 139 – Fairy Dancer (USA) (Nijinsky (CAN) 138) [1991 7g 1992 12g3 12.2g2 11.9m4 14s*] sturdy, attractive filly: moderate mover: won maiden at Haydock in September, leading over 3f out and battling on well: will stay 2m: acts on good to firm and soft ground: consistent. *H. R. A. Cecil* **69**

WANZA 2 b.g. (Apr 7) Petoski 135 – Lovers Light (Grundy 137) [1992 6f4 6g 8m4 7g 7d] 7,000F, 6,200Y: sturdy, lengthy, quite attractive colt: fifth foal: half-brother to 1½m winner Eliki (by Nishapour): dam out of half-sister to Main Reef: modest maiden: will stay middle distances: best form on top-of-the-ground. *J. Hanson* **53**

WAR BEAT 4 b.g. Wolver Heights 99 – Branitska (Mummy's Pet 125) [1991 14.1g a12g* 14.1f6 11.9g3 12.1s a12g 1992 14.1m4 15.8g5 14.6d6] sturdy gelding: has a quick **–**

action: modest handicapper, rated 58 at 3 yrs: below form in 1992 in midsummer: should stay 2m: acts on firm ground, not dead: has taken good hold: joined B. Baugh and won novice hurdle in August. *P. J. Bevan*

WARKWORTH (USA) 2 ch.c. (Apr 9) Tejano (USA) – Plum Quick (USA) **65** (Terresto) [1992 5g 5d² 6f 7g⁵ 7m 7g⁴ 6m³] $23,000Y: compact colt: fourth reported foal: half-brother to a minor winner by Magesterial: dam won at up to 7f: sire (by Caro) high-class winner from 6f to 1m at 2 yrs: fair form in varied events, including a nursery and a seller: stays 7f: best form in blinkers or visor: tends to sweat and get on edge: sold 7,200 gns Newmarket Autumn Sales. *J. W. Watts*

WARM SPELL 2 b.g. (Mar 11) Northern State (USA) 91 – Warm Wind 84 **66** (Tumble Wind (USA)) [1992 5m 6g* 7m 7f 5g⁴ 7g² 8d*] 7,400Y: good-quartered gelding: fourth foal: dam, 7f to 1¼m winner, is half-sister to Yorkshire Oaks winners Sally Brown and Untold: fair performer: led line in seller (sold out of Lord Huntingdon's stable 4,500 gns) at Leicester in July and nursery (having been set plenty to do) at Goodwood in October: will stay at least 1¼m: acts well on a soft surface, and is probably unsuited by firm ground. *R. Simpson*

WAR REQUIEM (IRE) 2 b.c. (Mar 11) Don't Forget Me 127 – Ladiz (Persian **50** Bold 123) [1992 5g⁶ 5g 5.3f² 7.3g 6.1s⁵ 7d 7.3g 7g⁵ 8d 7.3s⁶ a7g a7g] good-quartered colt: carries condition: second foal: dam poor daughter of half-sister to smart Jeroboam and Mirabeau: inconsistent maiden: should stay 1m: probably acts on any going. *G. B. Balding*

WARRIOR PRINCE 4 b.g. Prince Sabo 123 – Choral Park (Music Boy 124) **– §** [1991 5g² 5m 5f 6m 7d 6g 5d⁶ 7m a8g 1992 a7g] sturdy, lengthy gelding: poor walker: no worthwhile form for long time and is untrustworthy: sold 1,500 gns Ascot February Sales. *R. M. Whitaker*

WARSPITE 2 b.c. (Mar 14) Slip Anchor 136 – Valkyrie 87 (Bold Lad (IRE) 133) **59 p** [1992 7m 8.2s⁶] sturdy colt: fourth foal: half-brother to 1m winner Clipping and 1989 2-y-o 6f winner Flamberge (both by Kris) and 1987 2-y-o 6f to 1¼m winner Valentine (by Cure The Blues): dam half-sister to smart middle-distance performer Sabre Dance, ran only at 2 yrs, winning at 5f: modest form in maidens at Newmarket (scratched to post) and Nottingham in October: will do better over middle distances. *P. T. Walwyn*

WASEELA (IRE) 3 b.f. Ahonoora 122 – Wassl's Sister (Troy 137) [1991 6f 7m² **74** 1992 8g⁴ 8f⁴ 10.1m 8f² 6.9h* 8.5s⁴ 8g* 8m* 9f 8g⁶ 8.1g] rangy filly: fair handicapper: won at Carlisle (maiden), Yarmouth and Newcastle (made all) in midsummer: well below best afterwards: stayed 8.5f: not discredited on soft ground, but best efforts on a sound surface: visits Soviet Star. *A. A. Scott*

WASHINGTON RED 3 ch.g. Tickled Pink 114 – Apple Queen (Behistoun 131) **–** [1991 6.1m 1992 8g a5g 14.6s⁴] smallish, sturdy gelding: seems of little account: blinkered on fibresand: sold to join R. Lee 1,250 gns Ascot June Sales. *M. F. Barraclough*

WASSL THIS THEN (IRE) 3 b.f. Wassl 125 – Dancing Decoy 78 (Troy 137) **74** [1991 6.1m 7g⁶ 6d⁵ 1992 8f³ 8g² 10m² 10.2f³ 11.6d* 11.6m² 10g] smallish-looking filly: consistent handicapper: dead-heated at Windsor in July: not seen out again after finishing last at Newmarket following month: will stay 1½m: acts on firm and dead ground: game. *D. W. P. Arbuthnot*

WATCH ME GO (IRE) 3 b.g. On Your Mark 125 – Nighty Night (Sassafras **58** (FR) 135) [1991 5g 6m⁵ 7g 7.5f⁶ 7g⁵ 7.5f* 8m⁶ 8m 7m 7m 1992 9.9g⁵ 8.5m 7m⁵ 8m⁴ 8m* 8m 8g 12.2g 8g 9d³ 7d 8.2s] quite attractive gelding: inconsistent handicapper: won 4-runner race at Redcar in August: stays 1m: acts on firm ground: visored twice, running creditably first occasion: headstrong on occasions. *Bob Jones*

WATCH TOWER BAY (IRE) 4 ch.g. Kings Lake (USA) 133 – Noon Bells **–** (Ballymore 123) [1991 12g 18.1m 1992 a12g⁵] tall gelding: poor form at 2 yrs: none afterwards: dead. *R. Boss*

WATER DIVINER 2 b.g. (Mar 30) Dowsing (USA) 124 – Prudence 68 (Grundy **52** 137) [1992 5.3m⁵ 5m 5d 6m 7m 7d* 7g⁶ 7m a7g] 15,000Y, 15,500F, 15,000Y: leggy, light-framed gelding: has a roundish action: fourth foal: half-brother to 1991 2-y-o 8.1f winner Cautionary Tale (by Sharrood), and winners in Holland and Germany: dam, seemed to stay middle distances, is half-sister to Ribblesdale winner Strigida: inconsistent performer: won seller (no bid) at Wolverhampton in July: will stay 1m: acts on good to soft ground: wears blinkers: sold 1,050 gns Ascot September Sales. *R. F. Johnson Houghton*

WATERFOWL CREEK (IRE) 3 b. or br.f. Be My Guest (USA) 126 – On **88** Show 92 (Welsh Pageant 132) [1991 NR 1992 8v* 8d⁴ 8m² 7.1s⁵ 8m* 7s³ 7g⁴ 7g²] leggy, quite attractive filly: sister to very useful 1m winner Guest Artiste, closely related to very useful miler Inchmurrin (by Lomond) and half-sister to 7f winner Sohrab (by Shernazar) and very useful 2-y-o 6f winner Welney (by Habitat): dam 1¼m winner: fairly useful performer: won maiden at Warwick in March and minor event at Leicester in September: effective at 7f and 1m: acted on good to firm and heavy ground: to stud. *G. Wragg*

WATERLORD (IRE)   2 b.c. (Jan 23) Bob Back (USA) 124 – Ringtail 102   **61** (Auction Ring (USA) 123) [1992 5d 6f² 6g⁴ 7d 5.7g² 6m 5.1m² 6g 5g 6.1v4] IR 4,000Y: small, sturdy colt: third foal: half-brother to fairly useful 1990 2-y-o 6f winner Mohawk Chief (by Ahonoora): dam 2-y-o 5f winner: fair maiden: good second in 5.1f nursery at Chester, staying on well having been outpaced: probably acts on any going: stay 7f (steadied stalls and not knocked about when tried): joined M. Heaton-Ellis and retained 12,000 gns Ascot December Sales. *C. G. Cox*

WATERLOW PARK   10 ch.g. Wollow 132 – Caraquenga (USA) 92 (Cyane) [1991   – NR 1992 12g] big gelding: good mover: rated 76 at 8 yrs: shaped as if retaining ability when behind at Kempton in May, 1992: effective at 1m in strongly-run race and stays well: suited by a sound surface: has broken blood vessels: excellent mount for inexperienced rider: genuine. *I. A. Balding*

WATERMILL GIRL   4 b.f. Blakeney 126 – Absurd 60 (Absalom 128) [1991 8g   – 10g 7f 1992 a7g a8g a12g 8g⁶ 7g 10m⁶ 8.3g 12.1s] smallish filly: inconsistent maiden handicapper: stays 1¼m: acts on good to firm ground: tried visored: sold 600 gns Newmarket Autumn Sales. *D. T. Thom*

WATER SKIER   2 b.c. (Mar 21) Nishapour (FR) 125 – Wave Dancer 76 (Dance In   **54** p Time (CAN)) [1992 7m] rangy colt: third foal: half-brother to 3-y-o Surf Boat (by Master Willie) and French 9f winner Toby Henry (by Jalmood): dam 11.7f winner, is sister to very useful middle-distance horse Sailor's Dance and half-sister to Gold Cup winner Longboat: 50/1 and in need of race, better than fifteenth-of-17 position suggests in Newmarket maiden won by Placerville in October, travelling smoothly 5f then stumbling and losing action: will improve. *B. W. Hills*

WATHIK (USA)   2 ch.c. (Jan 31) Ogygian (USA) – Copper Creek 78 (Habitat 134)   **89** [1992 6g² 7m* 7d4 6g*] $280,000Y: strong, lengthy colt: has plenty of scope: has a quick action: second foal: half-brother to 3-y-o 5f winner My Sovereign (by Sovereign Dancer): dam 6f winner from good family: sire (by Damascus) high class, best at up to 1m: fairly useful performer: won moderately-run maiden at Newmarket in July and minor event at Doncaster in October: should stay 1m: acts on good to firm and dead ground. *H. Thomson Jones*

WAVEBAND   3 br.f. Thatching 131 – Waveguide 76 (Double Form 130) [1991 5d*   – 6m4 1992 6d⁶ 6g 8g 6d] neat filly: moderate mover: rated 62 at 2 yrs: stiff tasks, no worthwhile form (including in blinkers) in 1992: should stay 6f: possibly unsuited by good to firm ground: sold 1,100 gns Newmarket Autumn Sales. *B. W. Hills*

WAVE HILL   3 b.c. Sizzling Melody 117 – Trikymia 68 (Final Straw 127) [1991   **85** 5g² 6f² 5.8d* 7d² 6m² 6m3 6.1m⁵ 6m* 1992 6s⁶ 6m 8.5d² 8f* 8m² 8g² 8f 7.9m 8d⁶ 9d] close-coupled colt: fairly useful performer in first half of season, winning claimer (claimed out of H. Cecil's stable £16,950) at Newmarket in June: below form after finishing second in valuable handicaps following month: will prove best at up to 1m: acts on firm and dead ground: tongue tied down final start. *R. Hannon*

WAVE MASTER   5 b.g. Chief Singer 131 – Sea Fret 96 (Habat 127) [1991 7.1m⁶   **40** 9.7g³ 10.3g 1992 a8g 10f³ 11.6g⁴ a10g 16d] sturdy, close-coupled gelding: has a roundish action: inconsistent plater: tailed off last 2 starts: stays 11.6f: acts on firm going: below form when blinkered once earlier in career. *R. J. Hodges*

WAVERLEY STAR   7 br.g. Pitskelly 122 – Quelle Blague (Red God 128§) [1991   **57** a5g⁴ 5d⁴ 6d 5f⁴ 5g 5f⁵ 5m3 6m 5d⁶ 5.9m⁴ a5g³ 5s⁵ 5d³ 5.2g 6g⁵ 5m 6m3 5f 5m 5m 6m⁵ 5m3 5m⁵ 6m⁴ 1992 a5g⁴ 6f³ a6g³ 5.3d* 5.1d⁴ a6g] big, workmanlike gelding: poor mover: formerly inconsistent handicapper, much more consistent in 1992: neck winner at Brighton in September: unlucky at Chepstow next time: best at sprint distances: acts on firm and dead ground, and on fibresand: often blinkered (has been tried in visor), not last 3 starts: has edged left: trained first 3 starts by S. Norton. *K. O. Cunningham-Brown*

WAVE TO ME   3 ch.g. Risk Me (FR) 127 – Songs Jest (Song 132) [1991 NR 1992   – a7g a8g] big, plain, angular gelding: moderate mover: half-brother to several winning sprinters, including smart Reesh (by Lochnager) and useful Tadwin (by Never So Bold): dam unraced close relation to Jester: looked of little account: dead. *N. Tinkler*

WAYWARD SON 3 gr.g. Risk Me (FR) 127 – Mummy's Chick 77 (Mummy's Pet –
125) [1991 6d 5.7f 1992 5m 7d 8f 6.1g 8g 8f⁵ a10g² 11.5m⁴ 11.9g a13g] sparely-made, a42
plain gelding: has a round action: inconsistent plater, trained until after penultimate
start by G. Lewis: stays 1¼m: possibly temperamental. *J. J. Bridger*

WEALTHYWOO 2 ch.f. (Mar 9) Rich Charlie 117 – Woomargama 69 (Creetown **44**
123) [1992 5.1s³ 6m 6m⁶ 6d³ 6g⁵ 5g* 5m⁵ 5g 5d a6g⁴ a7g] good-topped filly: has
a round action: fourth foal: dam poor maiden: poor performer: won 4-runner nursery
at Folkestone in July: acts on good to firm ground, but probably
ideally suited by an easy surface: effective with or without blinkers: trained first 10
starts by J. S. Moore. *H. J. Collingridge*

WEAPON EXHIBITION 5 ch.m. Exhibitioner 111 – Weapon (Prince Ippi **42**
(GER)) [1991 7.8g 9.5m⁶ 8g 7.8g 9d 9g² 1992 a8g 10d a10g⁴ 10m] leggy, workmanlike ex-Irish mare: third foal: dam placed twice at 2 yrs in Ireland: trained by V.
Kennedy at 4 yrs: form here only when fourth in Lingfield selling handicap: stays
1¼m: no improvement in blinkers/visor. *G. A. Ham*

WE ARE DOOMED 2 ch.c. (Apr 8) Primo Dominie 121 – Divetta 72 (Ribero **42**
126) [1992 6.1d⁴ 7g 6m 7.1s 8.2d 7d] workmanlike colt: half-brother to 1990 2-y-o 7f
winner Copper Burn (by Electric) and a winner abroad by Henbit: dam won at 6f and
1m: poor plater: visored, well beaten at Redcar final start: stays 8.2f: acts on dead
ground. *J. R. Fanshawe*

WEAVER BIRD 2 b.f. (Apr 22) Master Willie 129 – Sweet Snow (USA) (Lyphard **66** p
(USA) 132) [1992 6s³ 6.1d*] 1,000Y: leggy, unfurnished filly: has a round action:
third living foal: sister to 3-y-o Miss Cresta: dam 10.5f winner in France, is out of
Kentucky Oaks winner Sun And Snow: favourite, won 22-runner maiden auction at
Nottingham in August, leading 2f out on stand side and running on well: can improve
again over further. *H. Candy*

WEAVER GEORGE (IRE) 2 b.g. (Apr 6) Flash of Steel 120 – Nephrite 106 **45**
(Godswalk (USA) 130) [1992 6d 6f⁴ 6.9h² 7.5s² 7f 8g 7.5m] IR 7,200Y: leggy gelding:
shows knee action: fourth foal: half-brother to 6f winner Emerald Ring (by Auction
Ring): dam, 6f winner, is daughter of half-sister to top sprinter Double Form:
modest plater: stays 7.5f: acts on any going: has joined N. Chamberlain. *M. H.
Easterby*

WEDDING OF THE SEA (USA) 3 ch.f. Blushing Groom (FR) 131 – Sweet **109**
Mover (USA) 95 (Nijinsky (CAN) 138) [1991 5m² 6d* 5.5g² 6g² 1992 7d² 5d³ 6d*
6s³] very useful French filly: won Group 3 Prix de Ris-Orangis at Evry in July by 1½
lengths from Central City: 2¾ lengths third behind Elbio and Twafeaj in Group 2
race at Baden-Baden 2 months later: stayed 7f but best form at 6f: acted on soft
going: visits Machiavellian. *A. Fabre, France*

WEDDING VOW (USA) 4 b.f. Nijinsky (CAN) 138 – Wedding Picture (USA) –
(Blushing Groom (FR) 131) [1991 NR 1992 12g⁵] strong, good-topped filly: second
foal: dam 6f stakes winner at 3 and 4 yrs: 8/1, bandaged behind, burly and green,
nearly 25 lengths fifth of 6 in maiden at Beverley in April, never getting into race
after slow start: moved poorly to post. *J. H. M. Gosden*

WEDNESDAYS AUCTION (IRE) 4 b.c. Mazaad 106 – Happy Always 48 –
(Lucky Wednesday 124) [1991 10g 9m* 1992 10g 10m 12.3d] workmanlike colt: rated
52 + at 3 yrs: no form in August, 1992, looking none too keen once: should stay
1¼m: acts on good to firm ground: sold to join R. Rowe 2,100 gns Newmarket
Autumn Sales. *B. Hanbury*

WEEHEBY (USA) 3 ch.c. Woodman (USA) 126 – Fearless Dame (USA) (Fear- **65**
less Knight) [1991 8m 1992 10g 9.7m⁵ 8.9g² 10f 8.2g* 8m 9.9m³ 10g 10g³ 9g 9.7g
10s²] strong colt: impresses in appearance: good walker: inconsistent performer:
won 3-runner apprentice maiden at Nottingham in July, carrying head high: easily
best subsequent efforts when placed in ladies handicaps and celebrity event: stays
1¼m: acts on good to firm and soft ground: blinkered (below form, hung under
pressure) once: has had tongue tied down. *A. A. Scott*

WEEKDAY CROSS (IRE) 4 b.g. Taufan (USA) 119 – Isoldes Tower (Balliol –
125) [1991 a10g² 12.2d³ 10g 9.2d³ 8m 1992 10.8v 10d 10.8f] good-topped gelding:
rated 56 at 3 yrs: no form in the spring at 4 yrs: stays 1½m: acts on dead ground:
blinkered (ran poorly) once. *J. R. Jenkins*

WEEKEND GIRL 3 b.f. Vorvados 118 – Mrs Scattercash (Northfields (USA)) –
[1991 6f 6f 7m 10.5d 6.1m 1992 a6g 8s 6s 5.1d a7g 8.1m⁴ 10d 6.1g 6g] leggy filly: of
little account. *W. M. Brisbourne*

WELCOMING ARMS 5 b.m. Free State 125 – The Guzzler 69 (Behistoun 131) –
[1991 12.3s 13.8g 16.5m a14g* a12g a14g 12m⁴ 16.1m³ 16.9m* 16m⁵ 18.1m⁶ a14g

Ladbroke Chester Cup (Handicap)—
Welshman gallops on gamely to hold Bardolph and Line Drummer

1992 17.1m] angular, workmanlike mare: rated 50 at 4 yrs: burly, signs of retaining ability at Pontefract in May: needs further than 1½m: acts on good to firm going and fibresand: won when blinkered once: sold only 580 gns Doncaster September Sales. *P. Calver*

WELL AHEAD   3 b.f. Last Tycoon 131 – Sistabelle (Bellypha 130) [1991 NR 1992 **60** 8g 11g² 11.1f² 12.2g⁶ 11.9d² 14.1g] lengthy, unfurnished filly: second foal: dam unraced sister to Bella Colora and half-sister to Colorspin: modest maiden: clipped leader's heels and fell over 3f out at Carlisle in September final start: worth another try over 1¾m: easily best effort on firm ground: tends to sweat. *M. Johnston*

WELL BEYOND (IRE)   3 ch.f. Don't Forget Me 127 – Mariakova (USA) 84 **101** (The Minstrel (CAN) 135) [1991 5g* 6m⁵ 6m 1992 7.1s* 8m⁵ 8g* 8g] strong, lengthy filly: shows knee action: useful performer: won minor event at Chepstow in August and, putting up best effort, 7-runner listed race (set slow pace, battled on well to hold Jdaayel by a head) at Ascot in October: below form in listed event final start: stays 1m: acts on good to firm and soft ground: to stud. *B. W. Hills*

WELL BOUGHT (IRE)   3 b.f. Auction Ring (USA) 123 – Knighton House 113 **–** (Pall Mall 132) [1991 NR 1992 a8g² a8g a7g⁵] half-sister to several winners, including very useful middle-distance winner Open Day (by Northfields) and smart 1977 French 2-y-o 6f and 1m winner River Knight (by Riverman): dam, sister to Reform, was very useful at up to 1¼m: no worthwhile form early in the year. *C. V. Lines*

WELL DIRECTED (IRE)   3 b.c. Sadler's Wells (USA) 132 – So Directed 98 **–** (Homing 130) [1991 NR 1992 10.5d 12s 10s] 76,000Y: smallish colt: second foal: half-brother to modest 1¼m winner Harbour Knight (by Caerleon): dam Irish 2-y-o 5f winner: always behind in maidens: blinkered final start, looking irresolute: sold 1,700 gns Newmarket Autumn Sales. *J. L. Dunlop*

WELLINGTON ROCK (USA)   3 ch.c. Lyphard's Wish (FR) 124 – Cuz's Star **81** (USA) (Galaxy Libra 104) [1991 7g⁴ 7d 1992 8m³ 8.3f* 8h* 8g⁵] tall, useful-looking colt: fluent mover: fairly useful form: landed odds in maiden at Hamilton and median auction match at Carlisle in June: fair fifth in £9,600 handicap at Newmarket following month: should stay 1¼m: possibly unsuited by dead ground: wears crossed noseband. *J. A. R. Toller*

WELL SADDLED (IRE)   3 b.c. Sadler's Wells (USA) 132 – Ukraine Girl 121 **94 ?** (Targowice (USA) 130) [1991 7g* 1992 8m⁵ 12g 10m 12.1d] well-made colt: capable of fairly useful form: improved form when never-dangerous twelfth of 18 in the Derby at Epsom: off course nearly 4 months, and ran as if something amiss both starts afterwards: sold 16,000 gns Newmarket Autumn Sales. *D. R. C. Elsworth*

WELL SUITED   2 b.g. (May 7) Elegant Air 119 – Gay Appeal 76 (Star Appeal 133) **57** [1992 6m⁵] 21,000Y: leggy gelding: third foal: dam 1½m winner: 5/1, over 10 lengths fifth of 10 to Firm Pledge in maiden at Goodwood in May: bred to stay middle distances: looked sure to improve. *R. Hannon*

WELLSY LAD (USA)   5 ch.g. El Baba (USA) – Iwishiknew (USA) (Damascus **53** (USA)) [1991 a7g⁵ a8g⁶ a6g⁶ a7g 6d 7.5f a6g* 6g³ 6f a7g a6g* a6g⁵ 6m a7g 6g 6d 6s² **a60** a6g³ a7g a6g* a6g* a6g⁶ 1992 a7g² a6g a5g a6g a7g⁴ a6g⁴ 6v³ 6.1d a7g a7g² a7g⁴ a7g³ a6g⁵ a7g⁵ a7g a7g 6.1s 6v² 6.9v⁵ a6g² a6g a6g] leggy, angular gelding:

moderate walker: modest handicapper, best on all-weather: effective at 6f and 7f: best turf form with give in the ground. *D. W. Chapman*

WELL TRIED (IRE) 2 b.f. (Feb 19) Thatching 131 – Good Effort (Try My Best **43** (USA) 130) [1992 5.1m⁶ 5g 6m a5g⁶] first foal: dam Irish 2-y-o 6f winner: poor maiden: stays 6f. *R. Hollinshead*

WELSH HERITAGE (IRE) 2 b.f. (Mar 16) Slip Anchor 136 – Mohibbah (USA) **48** p 86 (Conquistador Cielo (USA)) [1992 7g⁶] 27,000Y: first foal: dam 2-y-o 5f winner: 16/1 around 10 lengths sixth of 16 to Sueboog in minor event at Newbury in September: will improve. *Lord Huntingdon*

WELSHMAN 6 ch.g. Final Straw 127 – Joie de Galles 72 (Welsh Pageant 132) **68** [1991 14m³ 18.4d⁵ 17.6m⁵ 18f³ 14d* 14g² 16.2g⁵ 14g⁵ 15.9m³ 14m 14g⁵ 14.6g² 1992 12g² 16d⁴ 18.5g* 15.9m⁵ 14g 16.2s 16.2g 18m] close-coupled, workmanlike gelding: fair handicapper: in very good heart in the spring, winning Ladbroke Chester Cup by 3 lengths from Bardolph: subsequently off course 3½ months and well beaten last 4 starts: effective at 1½m and stays very well: acts on good to firm going, but best efforts with give in the ground: suited by racing up with pace. *M. Blanshard*

WELSH MILL (IRE) 3 b.c. Caerleon (USA) 132 – Gay Milly (FR) 74 (Mill Reef **92** (USA) 141) [1991 7.9m⁴ 1992 10m* 12d² 12d² 13.3g² 13.3s³] close-coupled, attractive colt: fairly useful and consistent performer: won minor event at Windsor in June: ran well all outings afterwards, second to Castoret in Autumn Cup at Newbury penultimate start: will stay 1¾m: acts on good to firm and soft ground. *Lord Huntingdon*

WELSH PET 2 b.f. (Mar 27) Petong 126 – Glyn Rhosyn (Welsh Saint 126) [1992 **48** 6m³ 6s 6.1g a6g] small filly: has a quick action: fifth foal: half-sister to 1988 2-y-o 6f winner Ipo (by Mummy's Game): dam poor maiden: well beaten except on debut: blinkered last time: sold 1,700 gns Newmarket Autumn Sales. *P. J. Makin*

WELSH SECRET 4 b.f. Welsh Captain 113 – Bridge of Gold 68 (Balidar 133) **–** [1991 6d⁴ 5m* 5g* 6f* 5g* 6m⁵ 6g 6g 6g⁴ 6d 6m 1992 6v] strong, workmanlike filly: poor mover: rated 85 at 3 yrs: backward and poorly drawn, last of 17 at Pontefract in April, 1992: should prove ideally suited to 5f: acts on firm going, twice shaped well on dead. *Mrs J. R. Ramsden*

WEMYSS BRIGHT 2 b.f. (Apr 6) Dancing Brave (USA) 140 – Bahamian 115 (Mill **?** Reef (USA) 141) [1992 9s*] first foal: dam, 1½m winner stayed 15f, is half-sister to smart miler Captivator out of disqualified Irish Oaks winner Sorbus: won 7-runner newcomers race at Maisons-Laffitte in November by 5 lengths: a promising staying filly. *A. Fabre, France*

WENTBRIDGE LAD (IRE) 2 b.c. (Apr 5) Coquelin (USA) 121 – Cathryn's **49** Song (Prince Tenderfoot (USA) 126) [1992 5m⁶ 6g 6g⁶ 7m⁵ 7.5s* 7d⁴] IR 3,000F, IR 2,000Y, resold 4,100Y: lengthy, rather leggy colt: fourth foal: half-brother to 4-y-o 6f to 1m winner Stairway To Heaven (by Godswalk) and fair 5-y-o 1¼m handicapper Katy's Lad (by Camden Town): dam never ran: lowered in class, won seller (no bid) at Beverley in July, running on strongly having been tailed off entering straight: will be better suited by 1¼m: acts on good to firm and soft ground: possibly best in blinkers: not an easy ride. *B. A. McMahon*

WE'RE ALL GAME 3 b.f. Mummy's Game 120 – Swynford's Pride 95 (Rapid **64** River 127) [1991 5m 5m⁶ 6g⁵ 6.1m⁶ 5d³ 1992 5s³ 5g⁵ 5g² 5g 5g⁶ 5d* 5d 5s] tall, leggy filly: fair sprinter: improved form to win handicap at Ayr in September, running on strongly having been outpaced early on: failed to reproduce that form: best with some give in the ground: sweating and on toes final start. *B. C. Morgan*

WESAAM (USA) 3 b.c. Riverman (USA) 131 – Share The Fantasy (USA) **95** (Exclusive Native (USA)) [1991 6g² 6m² 8m* 8g² 1992 8d⁶ 10.3m⁶ 8.1m 8g⁵ 8.5d* 8m² 8d³ 8m 10m] strong, close-coupled colt: moderate mover: useful handicapper: made all in 3-runner race at Beverley in July: below form last 2 starts: stays 8.5f: acts on good to firm and dead ground: blinkered twice, running creditably second occasion: finds little off bridle: has joined T. Skiffington in USA. *Major W. R. Hern*

WESSEX MILORD 7 ch.g. Stanford 121§ – Miss Osprey 93 (Sea Hawk II 131) **–** [1991 NR 1992 16d 6f⁶ 6.1m 7.1f³ 8m⁵ 7m 7.1s 9d a8g⁵] strong, lengthy gelding: of little account. *J. A. Bennett*

WESSHAUN 2 b.f. (May 18) Shaunicken – Wessex Flyer (Pony Express 85) **41** [1992 7d a5g⁶ a5g⁶] leggy, plain filly: second reported foal: dam had extremely bad reputation in points: poor maiden. *W. G. M. Turner*

WEST AUCKLAND 3 br.g. Silly Prices 110 – Elitist 72 (Keren 100) [1991 NR 1992 10d 13.8g] big gelding: third foal: brother to 2 poor animals: dam promised to stay 1¼m: burly, tailed off in maiden and claimer in September. *N. Chamberlain* –

WEST END GIRL 2 b.f. (Mar 5) Absalom 128 – City Ditty (Camden Town 125) [1992 7m⁵ 7g 7.5m 10.5d] 3,000Y: big, strong filly: has a round action: first reported foal: dam no sign of ability over hurdles or in points: modest plater: best effort when keeping-on fifth at Newmarket: will stay at least 1m. *R. J. R. Williams* 44

WESTERING 2 b.f. (Feb 12) Auction Ring (USA) 123 – Westerlake (Blakeney 126) [1992 6g⁶] strong filly: third foal: half-sister to 3-y-o 1m and 8.2f winner Legend Dulac (by Legend of France) and 1¼m winner Western Loch (by Reesh): dam twice-raced, from family of Lyric Fantasy: 33/1 and carrying condition, slow-starting 10 lengths sixth of 10 to Lake Pleasant in maiden at Newmarket in July, held up taking keen hold then keeping on well, not knocked about: showed a moderate action: looked certain to improve. *W. Jarvis* –

WESTERN APPROACH (USA) 3 b.f. Gone West (USA) – Devon Diva (USA) (The Minstrel (CAN) 135) [1991 6m² 1992 5m* 6f* 5m 5m* 5m] workmanlike filly: smart performer on her day: easily made all in maiden at Doncaster and minor event at Newmarket in June and (putting up easily best effort when beating Bunty Boo by 3½ lengths under 9-7) £11,200 handicap at York in August: disappointing in Group 3 event and listed race otherwise: best at 5f: yet to race with give in the ground: has joined R. Frankel in USA. *J. H. M. Gosden* 115

WESTERN CAPE (USA) 2 b.c. (Feb 15) Gone West (USA) – Blue Bell Pearl (FR) (Pharly (FR) 130) [1992 7g⁴] $150,000Y: smallish, sturdy colt: fourth foal: half-brother to winners (at 3 yrs) in France by Shirley Heights and Glint of Gold: dam, best at 1m, won Group 3 Prix de Sandringham: sire very smart at up to 9f: 4¾ lengths fourth of 16 to Emperor Jones in maiden at Newmarket in August, waited with in touch taking good hold, outpaced over 2f out then keeping on steadily: looked sure to do better and win races. *R. Charlton* 75 p

WESTERN DANCER 11 b.g. Free State 125 – Polyandrist 92 (Polic 126) [1991 12v⁴ 16g⁵ 16.1g⁶ 1992 14.9d² 17.2s⁶ 14s] lengthy gelding: usually looks well: good mover: rated 98 in his heyday: just a poor handicapper nowadays: ideally suited by good test of stamina: acts on any going: well served by strong gallop. *C. A. Horgan* 49

WESTERN DYNASTY 6 ch.g. Hotfoot 126 – Northern Dynasty 65 (Breeders Dream 116) [1991 12s 12m⁶ 11d⁶ 11.1g³ 10m⁵ 11.5s² 10.1g⁵ 11.8m⁴ 12d a12g⁵ a14g⁵ 1992 12d* 10d 11.9d⁵ 12g 12m² 11.8g² 12m³ 11.9m 12g⁴ 11.4g³ 12d⁴ 12g 11.8s] big, lengthy gelding: carries condition: moderate mover: fair handicapper: won at Kempton in April: modest efforts last 2 starts, visored on final one: ideally suited by 1½m: probably acts on any going: has run well for apprentice. *M. J. Ryan* 71

WESTERN VALLEY 2 ch.f. (Mar 21) Valiyar 129 – Another Western 58 (Good Times (ITY)) [1992 7g 6d⁵ a6g⁴ a6g] lengthy filly: easy mover: second foal: dam, out of a 1¼m winner, ran 5 times over sprint distances: poor maiden: should stay 7f + . *K. O. Cunningham-Brown* 51

WESTFIELD MOVES (IRE) 4 b.c. Montelimar (USA) 122 – Rathcoffey Daisy (Pampapaul 12 I) [1991 10g⁴ 10d⁶ 12d⁶ 10.2f⁴ 9g² 8.9m 9f³ 10.3m⁵ 8.9m⁶ 8.1d⁵ 8g9.7s³ 1992 a11g³ a12g* a12g* a12g⁴ 10.3g 14.1d⁴ 14.6g 10g*] leggy, lengthy colt: modest handicapper: won at Southwell in February and, after 10-week break, 19-runner event at Pontefract (sweating) in July: effective from 1¼m to 1¾m: acts on any 62

Falmouth Stakes (Handicap), York — top-weight Western Approach makes all in fine style

going: effective visored or not, didn't wear one in 1992: has won for apprentice: rather lazy, but game. *H. J. Collingridge*

WESTHOLME (USA) 4 ch.g. Lyphard's Wish (FR) 124 – Shroud (USA)   **76**
(Vaguely Noble 140) [1991 10g* 12.3d² 10.6g 11.9m³ 11.9m⁵ 12g² 13.9g 10.3m⁵ 11.9d 10.3d 1992 11.9d 10f³ 12.4f 10.4d⁴ 12m 12.3m² 12.3g⁵ 10.5d⁴ 10.4s⁴ 10.3s* 12g⁴] lengthy gelding: fair handicapper in second half of season: won at Chester in October: creditable fourth in November Handicap at Doncaster: stays 1½m: acts on any going: is held up. *M. H. Easterby*

WESTMEAD NICK 2 b.c. (Mar 3) Dreams To Reality (USA) 113 – Starchy   **–**
(Crisp And Even 116) [1992 5g 5.1m⁴ a6g⁵ 6.1m] 2,000Y: angular colt: half-brother to middle-distance staying plater Vestige (by Remainder Man): dam well beaten both starts: bad plater: will stay 1m +. *J. Berry*

WESTRAY (FR) 2 b.c. (Mar 31) Caerwent 123 – Mindena (FR) (Bellman (FR)   **–**
123) [1992 7g] workmanlike colt: second reported foal: dam French provincial 10.5f winner: 50/1 and very green, slowly away and never dangerous in minor event at Kempton in August: reared over in paddock, and became coltish: sold 500 gns Ascot December Sales. *Dr J. D. Scargill*

WEST STOW 3 b.c. Rainbow Quest (USA) 134 – Favoletta 115 (Baldric II 131)   **69**
[1991 NR 1992 9.9g² 10.1s² 11.7s 12.2g* 12.3f⁵ 12.1m³ 14.6g⁶ 12.1g⁵ 12g] small, attractive colt: has a quick action: half-brother to numerous winners, including Favoridge (by Riva Ridge), very smart at up to 1m, and Amaranda (by Bold Lad), smart 5f performer: dam won Irish 1000 Guineas and is half-sister to Furioso, the dam of Teenoso: inconsistent performer: made all in maiden at Catterick in June: ran creditably in apprentice handicap at Hamilton penultimate start: stays 12.2f: acts on good to firm and soft ground. *M. R. Stoute*

WEST WITH THE WIND 5 b. or br.g. Glint of Gold 128 – Mighty Fly 117   **49**
(Comedy Star (USA) 121) [1991 10.2s 12.1g* 11.9d 1992 12g 16.1s 12.3g⁵ 12.3d] workmanlike gelding: modest form on his day: first outing for nearly 6 months, easily best run in handicaps in 1992 when fifth at Ripon: should stay beyond 1½m: acts on good to firm ground, has won on soft over hurdles: has joined M. Dods. *G. M. Moore*

WHARF (USA) 2 ch.c. (Feb 4) Storm Bird (CAN) 134 – Dockage (USA) **107** p
(Riverman (USA) 131) [1992 6f* 6g*]
    The July Stakes winner Wharf was the forgotten member of Khalid Abdulla's quartet of pattern-race-winning two-year-old colts. Just as he looked set to consolidate his reputation in the top summer events, a training set-back cut short his first season after two races, leaving us still in the dark as to how good he might be. Wharf is coming back in training as a three-year-old, and if all goes well with him he should prove worthy of a higher rating than his form so far merits. Wharf's racecourse experience as a two-year-old was limited to appearances in quick succession on his local July course at Newmarket. Reputed to be one of Cecil's best youngsters before he made his first appearance in public in the Champagne Pommery Maiden Stakes over six furlongs in June, Wharf substantiated the racecourse rumours with a sparkling performance, comfortably landing the odds by three lengths from Right

July Stakes, Newmarket—Wharf sticks on determinedly to hold Canaska Star

Win with a largely backward-looking bunch twelve lengths and more behind. Twelve days later, Wharf lined up as 6/4-on favourite against the Coventry Stakes third Pips Pride, the progressive Fortune Cay, the Chesham Stakes fourth Aljazzaf, the Ripon winner Majestic Hawk and the well-regarded maiden Canaska Star in a typically-small turnout for the Group 3 July Stakes. Wharf had to fight hard to maintain his unbeaten record. Looking really well again, he broke much more sharply than he had first time up, and raced in third place as Fortune Cay and Pips Pride matched strides two lengths clear. Wharf had made up the ground with two furlongs to run, where Majestic Hawk also came through to make a line of four, but no sooner had he shaken off that trio than Canaska Star, benefiting from a more patient ride than he was given in the Coventry, came with a storming run on the outside. Despite drifting off a true line, Wharf gamely kept his head in front, and, in a rousing finish, won by a neck, Pip's Pride beating Majestic Hawk for third over three lengths behind. Wharf's subsequent training problems—he suffered from sore shins and was turned out after the July Stakes—ensured that he ended the season still very much a 'dark horse', an odd state of affairs for a colt who'd won one of the first two-year-old pattern races of the season.

In common with Zafonic, Wharf was bred at the Kentucky arm of Juddmonte Farms. He's a son of the top-class two-year-old and good-class stallion Storm Bird, sire of such as Indian Skimmer and Magical Wonder in Europe and Summer Squall and Storm Cat in America, out of the useful Riverman mare Dockage, a winner over a mile and nine furlongs in France. Dockage, whose only previous foal Docklands (by Theatrical) ran once for Gosden in 1992, showing little, is one of three winners from Golden Alibi in a chequered career at stud that saw her either barren or not covered in five of the six seasons after she foaled the minor American winner Desert Peace in 1985. Golden Alibi was the second highest-priced yearling filly sold at public auction in 1979, fetching 1,100,000 dollars, and was sold again three years later as an unraced four-year-old, carrying the modest stayer Ightham, for $750,000. The main reason that Golden Alibi attracted so much attention at the sales is that she is a close relative of the brilliant racemare and high-class broodmare Dahlia. Dahlia won fifteen races in all in a long career at the highest level on both sides of the Atlantic. She won seven Group 1 races in Europe, including the Benson and Hedges Gold Cup and the King George VI and Queen Elizabeth II Diamond Stakes on two separate occasions, before carrying on in the same vein in North America where her four Grade 1 victories included the Washington D.C. International. Dahlia has produced three notable winners at stud, namely the middle-distance performers Dahar and Wajd and the French mile-and-a-quarter and fifteen-furlong winner Rivlia, later a high-class performer in the States.

		Northern Dancer	Nearctic
	Storm Bird (CAN)	(b 1961)	Natalma
	(b 1978)	South Ocean	New Providence
Wharf (USA)		(b 1967)	Shining Sun
(ch.c. Feb 4, 1990)		Riverman	Never Bend
	Dockage (USA)	(b 1969)	River Lady
	(b 1984)	Golden Alibi	Empery
		(ch 1978)	Charming Alibi

We don't expect to see Wharf campaigned much at six furlongs as a three-year-old; even in the July Stakes the manner of his performance indicated that he really needed further and he can be expected to stay a mile and a quarter. A lengthy, useful-looking colt, a grand walker, too, Wharf has raced only on good or good to firm ground. *H. R. A. Cecil*

WHAT A CARD 4 b.f. Myjinski (USA) – Ventrex 95 (Henry The Seventh 125) [1991 8f 12m 12g⁶ 11m⁶a 12g³ 13d⁶ 12fa 11g⁵ 1992 a14g⁴] sparely-made filly: probably of little account these days. *R. Johnson* –

WHAT BLISS 2 ch.f. (Feb 9) Kabour 80 – Wedded Bliss 76 (Relko 136) [1992 5g 5d] close-coupled filly: moderate walker: fifth foal: dam won from 1½m to 2m at 5 and 6 yrs: soundly beaten in seller at Doncaster and minor event at Catterick (blinkered) in the spring. *D. W. Chapman* –

WHATCOMESNATURALLY (USA) 3 ch.f. Arctic Tern (USA) 126 – Reina –
Real (ARG) (Escudo Real) [1991 8.9d 8s 1992 10.2m 11.7m³ a14g 14.1m⁵ 16.1s] leggy
filly: modest mover: little worthwhile form: sold out of J. Hills's stable 2,600 gns
Newmarket July Sales after second 3-y-o start: stays 11.7f: acts on good to firm
ground: has joined M. Hammond. *M. C. Chapman*

WHATEVER'S RIGHT (IRE) 3 b.g. Doulab (USA) 115 – Souveniers (Relko 62
136) [1991 NR 1992 8d² 10s] IR 5,400F, 3,000Y, 1,000 2-y-o: workmanlike gelding:
third foal: half-brother to Irish 6f winner Just A Memory (by Kafu): dam, placed over
1m at 2 yrs in Ireland, is daughter of Princess Royal winner Aloft: 50/1, backward
and ridden by 7-lb claimer, easily better effort in maidens at Leicester in October
when 5 lengths second of 16 in apprentice event, having been outpaced early on. *M.
D. I. Usher*

WHAT KATY DID (USA) 3 b.f. Nureyev (USA) 131 – Katies 125 (Nonoalco 87 p
(USA) 131) [1991 NR 1992 7.9g* 9g*] $450,000Y: lengthy, sparely-made filly: third
foal: half-sister to very useful sprinter Katies First (by Kris) and U.S. winner Jet
Route (by Alydar): dam won Coronation Stakes and Irish 1000 Guineas: bandaged
behind, led about 1f out to win maiden at York and handicap at Newbury (just held
on) in September: will stay 1¼m: looked sure to improve again: joined J. Pease in
France. *J. H. M. Gosden*

WHEELER'S WONDER (IRE) 3 br.f. Sure Blade (USA) 130 – Querida 41
(Habitat 134) [1991 8.2m 6m⁶ 7.1d a8g a7g 1992 10g 8m⁵ 11.5g⁴ 11.9f 11.8g] leggy,
rather angular filly: poor maiden: stays 1m: acts on good to firm ground, ran
moderately on all-weather surfaces: visored (well beaten) final start: sold to join B.
Llewellyn 800 gns Newmarket Autumn Sales. *N. C. Wright*

WHEELS OF WEETMAN 5 b.g. Stanford 121§ – Miss Legend (USA) (Bold –
Legend) [1991 6m 6g 5m 6g 7g 5.1g 1992 8.9g 12m 10.5g 10.5g] heavy-topped
gelding: no worthwhile form. *Miss S. J. Wilton*

WHERE'S RUTH (IRE) 3 b.f. Bluebird (USA) 125 – Mannevillette (USA) –
(Foolish Pleasure (USA)) [1991 5m 5d³ 6d⁶ a7g* 7g³ 7m 1992 a7g a8g 8.2g] lengthy
filly: rated 58 at 2 yrs: no worthwhile form in handicaps in 1992, racing too freely in
blinkers second start: should stay beyond 7f. *M. W. Easterby*

WHERE'S THE DANCE 2 b.f. (Mar 27) Alzao (USA) 117 – Pu Yi (Habitat 134) 61
[1992 6f² 7.1d² 7.1g⁴ 6.5m 5.2g 7m] strong, good-bodied filly: carries plenty of
condition: first foal: dam once-raced sister to Habibti: modest maiden: stays 7.1f:
acts on firm and dead ground. *C. E. Brittain*

WHIMSICAL NOTION 2 br.f. (Apr 30) Macmillion 110 – My Charade 79 –
(Cawston's Clown 113) [1992 6d 8.2s] leggy, sparely-made filly: third foal (all by
Macmillion): sister to winning stayer Smilingatstrangers: dam, 1¾m winner, is
half-sister to very useful 6f to 7f performer Step Ahead: in rear in maidens at
Goodwood and Nottingham (ran wide bend, tailed off) in the autumn. *Mrs Barbara
Waring*

WHIPPET 8 b.h. Sparkler 130 – St Louis Sue (FR) 79 (Nonoalco (USA) 131) [1991 58 d
5g⁶ 6g 6m⁴ 6m 6g 6s 7d 6d a6g a8g 1992 5.1d⁴ 5.1d 7g⁴ 7f⁶ 7g 10g 6.1s] lengthy,
good-quartered horse: bad mover: one-time useful performer for C. Austin (sold
2,800 gns Ascot February Sales): very much on the downgrade: best form at sprint
distances: acts on any going: has worn visor/blinkers. *J. A. Bennett*

WHIRL 3 ro.f. Bellypha 130 – Spin Turn (Homing 130) [1991 NR 1992 8g² 8m⁵ 79
10.1g³ 10.5g* 11.9d³ 10s⁴ 11.9s⁴] leggy, angular filly: third foal: half-sister to a
winner in Italy by Niniski: dam unraced daughter of Oaks third The Dancer: fair
handicapper: won maiden at Haydock in August: stays 1½m: acts on good ground:
consistent. *J. R. Fanshawe*

WHIRLYGIG 3 b.f. Gorytus (USA) 132 – Avant-Garde (Pas de Seul 133) [1991 –
5d⁴ 5f³ 6g 5.1g⁶ 7f a8g 1992 a7g³ a8g⁶ 8g 6.9g 9.9m 12.2d] smallish filly: of little
account these days. *J. S. Wainwright*

WHISKEY BLUES 7 b.g. Cure The Blues (USA) – Ozone (Auction Ring (USA) –
123) [1991 NR 1992 10s a12g] tall gelding: half-brother to 8-y-o Cronk's Quality (by
Main Reef): dam Irish 7f and 9f winner: blinkered when placed at up to 9f in Ireland
as 3-y-o for D. Weld: no form in 2 claimers here. *B. Richmond*

WHISPERDALES 2 gr.g. (Jun 4) Chilibang 120 – Gangawayhame 91 56 §
(Lochnager 132) [1992 5m* 5m³ 5g 5g 5g⁶ 5g] 1,000Y: small, sparely-made gelding:
sixth foal: half-brother to 5.8f winner Awa'Wi'Ye and 1989 2-y-o 5f sellers winner
Guthrie Court (both by Daring March): dam 2-y-o 6f winner stayed 7f: won median
auction at Beverley in May: in-and-out form after and looked ungenuine,

Sunset Boulevard Solario Stakes, Sandown—White Crown continues to progress

particularly when blinkered and sweating profusely once: one to treat with caution. *M. W. Ellerby*

WHISPER'S SHADOW   3 b.f. Northern Baby (CAN) 127 – Sir Ivor's Sorrow   **68** (USA) (Sir Ivor 135) [1991 8.2m 7m 8s³ 1992 11.5g⁴ 10.8m⁵ a12g² 14.1g⁵ 10f] tall, rather angular filly: modest handicapper: stays 1½m: acts on good to firm and soft ground and on fibresand: below form when visored final start. *M. H. Tompkins*

WHITECHAPEL (USA)   4 b.g. Arctic Tern (USA) 126 – Christchurch (FR) 88   **87** (So Blessed 130) [1991 11g 10g² a12g* 14m 13.3g³ 1992 12g* 12d* 12g* a14g⁵ 13.9m⁴ 12s³ 16.2g⁵ 12g] big, lengthy gelding: consistent and much improved handicapper in 1992: successful at Doncaster, Ascot (apprentices) and Salisbury: in frame in Tote Ebor at York and Krug Trophy at Ascot: effective from 1½m to 2m: acts on fibresand and good to firm and soft ground: held up. *Lord Huntingdon*

WHITE CREEK (IRE)   2 gr.g. (Apr 6) Don't Forget Me 127 – Zanskar (Gods-   **40** walk (USA) 130) [1992 6m 6f] angular, workmanlike gelding: sixth foal: half-brother to winning 6-y-o sprinter Iron King (by Tender King) and an ungenuine animal by Rusticaro: dam Irish 2-y-o 5f winner: well beaten in maidens at York and Hamilton: not seen out after June. *J. Berry*

WHITE CROWN (USA)   2 ch.c. (Jan 22) Secreto (USA) 128 – Won't She Tell **104** (USA) (Banner Sport (USA)) [1992 5g⁴ 6f* 6m³ 7g² 7d* 7.1d*] $65,000Y: strong,   **p** lengthy colt: first reported foal: dam, multiple winner in North America, stayed at least 9f: most progressive colt: successful in maiden at Redcar in May, Mtoto Donnington Castle Stakes (by 4 lengths from Geisway, making all) at Newbury in July and Solario Stakes (led over 2f out, held King Paris by 1½ lengths) at Sandown in August: should stay 1¼m: has won on firm ground but best efforts on dead: strong-galloping sort: an admirable colt, with the scope to improve further at 3 yrs. *B. Hanbury*

WHITEHALL (IRE)   3 ch.g. Don't Forget Me 127 – Starlust 79 (Sallust 134)   **66** [1991 NR 1992 11d 7m⁴ a7g⁵ 7.1f⁵ a7g² a7g* 7m⁶ a7g³ a7g⁶] 31,000F, IR 44,000Y: sturdy, short-legged gelding: poor mover: half-brother to 3 winners, including useful 6f and 1m winner Bronzewing (by Beldale Flutter) and 1¼m winner Travel Storm (by Lord Gayle): dam 2-y-o 5f winner, is half-sister to Welsh Pearl, very useful at up to 1m: none too consistent performer: won maiden at Southwell in July: stays 7f: acts on good to firm ground and all-weather surfaces: flashes tail: sold 3,800 gns Newmarket Autumn Sales. *C. R. Nelson*

WHITE MUZZLE   2 b.c. (Mar 21) Dancing Brave (USA) 140 – Fair of The Furze   **84** 112 (Ela-Mana-Mou 132) [1992 8g³ 7m³] 40,000Y: lengthy, good-bodied colt: third   **p** foal: half-brother to useful 1¼m performer Elfaslah (by Green Desert): dam Irish 1m and 1¼m winner stayed 1½m: shaped with plenty of promise when beaten around 2 lengths by Pembroke in Newbury minor event and Barathea in Newmarket

918

maiden in autumn: will be well suited by middle distances: has plenty of scope, and will win a race or two. *P. W. Chapple-Hyam*

WHITE RIVER 6 ch.h. Pharly (FR) 130 – Regain 86 (Relko 136) [1991 14d² 14m⁵ **43** 14.8m³ 14g 13.8m 1992 14.1d 17.2s⁵a14g⁴ 14.1g² 14.1m² 14.6m² 14.6d⁵ 14.6g² 13.1f⁶ 14.1d] smallish, lengthy horse: poor mover: largely consistent handicapper: stays 15.3f: acts on firm and dead ground: sometimes bandaged off-hind: best visored. *D. Haydn Jones*

WHITE SHADOW (IRE) 2 b.f. (Feb 7) Last Tycoon 131 – Welsh Daylight **87** p (Welsh Pageant 132) [1992 5f⁴ 6m² 6g* 6g² 6s*] leggy, rather unfurnished filly: has scope: half-sister to 3-y-o Brecon Beacons (by Shirley Heights) and 3 winners abroad, including very useful French middle-distance performer Ordinance (by Henbit): dam won twice over 1¼m in Ireland: most progressive filly: won maiden at Kempton in July and listed race (led close home under strong ride to beat Yakin by a neck) at Ayr in September: will be well suited by 1m: acts on good to firm and soft ground: sure to improve further. *R. Charlton*

WHITE WEDDING 3 ch.f. Dominion 123 – Sledge 80 (Young Generation 129) **64** d [1991 5g³ 7g⁶ 6f 1992 11.7d² 11.9f³ 12.2d³ 12m² 11.7m² 14.6g⁶ 12v] small, good-quartered filly: modest maiden at best: stays 1½m: best with give in the ground: sometimes bandaged: sold 2,300 gns Newmarket Autumn Sales. *P. F. I. Cole*

WHITE WILLOW 3 br.g. Touching Wood (USA) 127 – Dimant Blanche (USA) **75** 77 (Gummo (USA) 117) [1991 NR 1992 10.1s² 12.1g² 12.1d* 11.9s 12m 12d] sturdy gelding: third foal: half-brother to a winner in Germany by Mummy's Pet: dam 5f winner: won 3-runner maiden at Hamilton in May: off course 5 months and never dangerous in handicaps after, not disgraced final outing: stays 1½m: acts on soft ground: trained first 2 starts by B. Hanbury. *Mrs M. Reveley*

WHITLEY GORSE 2 b.c. (Mar 15) Glint of Gold 128 – Martin-Lavell News 90 **53** (Song 132) [1992 5s* 5m² 7f⁵ 7g⁶ 5m] 4,400Y: compact colt: fourth foal: closely related to 3-y-o Fragrant Hackette (by Simply Great) and half-brother to 5f winner Musical Flash (by Music Boy): dam won twice over 5f from 4 starts at 2 yrs: showed little after winning maiden at Newcastle and second of 3 to Star Family Friend in minor event at Pontefract in spring: should stay beyond 5f: sold 1,300 gns Doncaster October Sales. *J. Etherington*

WHITRIGG LAD 3 b. or br.c. Skyliner 117 – Whitmarsh 56 (Hessonite 88) [1991 **–** NR 1992 7.5m 7m⁴ 7.5m 8h 10m] leggy colt: fifth reported foal: half-brother to plating-class 1¼m winner Leacroft (by Domitor), also successful over jumps: dam in frame over 7f and 1m from only 3 starts: little worthwhile form, including in seller. *W. W. Haigh*

WHITTINGHAM (IRE) 3 b.c. Fayruz 116 – Bohemian Rhapsody 86 (On Your **102** Mark 125) [1991 5g* 5f* 5d* 5g* 6g³ 5g² 6g⁴ 6g² 5v* 5d⁵ 1992 5v² 5d* 5g² 5g⁴ 5m] strong, compact colt: useful Italian sprinter: won minor event in April then good efforts in frame in Premio Certosa and listed race, all at Milan: visored and looking

Shadwell Stud Firth of Clyde Stakes, Ayr—
White Shadow (right) gets up to beat Yakin (centre) and Star Family Friend

really well, last of 11 in King George Stakes at Goodwood final outing: stays 6f: acts on any going. *O. Pessi, Italy*

WHITWELL HILL 3 gr.f. Damister (USA) 123 – Nullah 71 (Riverman (USA) 131) [1991 NR 1992 12m⁴ a12s 12m] 1,600Y: smallish, angular filly: fourth foal: half-sister to 11f to 1½m winner Chiefs Babu (by Chief Singer): dam third over 1¼m on only start: no promise, including in seller. *Mrs V. A. Aconley* –

WHITWORTH GREY 4 gr.g. Marching On 101 – Grey Morley 78 (Pongee 106) [1991 11m 9g 7f 6.9f 1992 12.1g] leggy, angular gelding: moderate mover: poor maiden: should stay 1m: acts on firm and dead ground: below form blinkered. *M. Dods* –

WHO'S TEF (IRE) 4 b.g. Muscatite 122 – Eternal Optimist (Relko 136) [1991 7g⁵ 6f 7.5f² 8.5m 8g 7f⁶ 8.5f* 8f⁴ 7.5f* 7.5f⁴ 10f* 8f⁴ 8.5f⁴ 8.9m 8m 1992 9.9g 9.9m⁴ 8f⁴ 9.9g⁴ 10f² 8f 9.9d³ 10m⁵ 8f² 7.5m⁴ 9f⁶ 8g 8.5m] rather leggy, close-coupled gelding: moderate mover: modest handicapper: stays 1¼m: acts on firm and dead ground: below form when visored/blinkered: usually claimer ridden nowadays. *M. H. Easterby* **61**

WHO'S THAT LADY 3 b.f. Nordance (USA) – Piccadilly Etta 76 (Floribunda 136) [1991 5d⁶ 5f³ 1992 7d 5v³ 7s* 6.9d⁵ 7g a7g a7g a7g⁶] small, leggy filly: below form after winning handicap at Newcastle in April: off course 6 months after fourth start: best effort at 7f on soft ground. *M. H. Easterby* **60**

WHO'S THE BEST (IRE) 2 b.c. (Jan 30) Wassl 125 – Rip Roaring (Royal And Regal (USA)) [1992 6g 7g⁵ 7g⁶ 6m 7d 6d] IR 5,800Y: close-coupled colt: good mover: fourth foal: brother to a winner in Italy: dam, unraced, from family of Ardross: modest maiden: will be better suited by 1m: below form blinkered final outing. *A. P. Jarvis* **58**

WHO'S TOM (IRE) 2 b.c. (Mar 12) Tate Gallery (USA) 117 – Clover Princess 110 (Right Tack 131) [1992 5g⁵ 6m 5d 6m 6g] IR 14,500F, 12,000Y: smallish, work-manlike colt: half-brother to several winners abroad: dam Irish 7f/1m performer: poor form, including in sellers: stays 6f: bandaged. *W. J. Musson* **48**

WHYALLA RAIN 2 br.f. (Apr 14) Chief Singer 131 – Nullah 71 (Riverman (USA) 131) [1992 6d 7g a8g] leggy filly: fifth foal: sister to fair middle-distance colt Chiefs Babu: dam third over 1¼m on only start: well beaten in late-season maidens. *R. Hollinshead* –

WHY SO HASTY 11 b.g. Proverb 127 – Well Caught (Golden Vision 105) [1991 NR 1992 10d] moderate chaser nowadays: tailed off in celebrity event at Wetherby. *M. C. Chapman* –

WICKINS 2 b.c. (Apr 8) Petong 126 – Bo' Babbity 75 (Strong Gale 116) [1992 5.2d 5m 5.1m 6g 6d 7.1s⁶ 5.3d⁴ a6g² 6d] 6,200Y: tall colt: moderate mover: second foal: dam 2-y-o 5f winner, is half-sister to high-class sprinter Anita's Prince: modest maiden: best efforts at 6f: acts on dead ground: best form blinkered. *G. Lewis* **52**

WICK POUND 6 b.g. Niniski (USA) 125 – Hors Serie (USA) 103 (Vaguely Noble 140) [1991 a10g 14.8m* 14.8d³ 17.2f 18.8f⁴ 14.9m² 13.1f 11.9f 1992 14m* 14m³] small, lightly-made gelding: poor mover: very easy winner of handicap at Sandown in June and ran well there (out of handicap and got poor run) following month: won over fences in October: stays 1¾m: acts on good to firm and dead going: blinkered nowadays. *J. A. B. Old* **56**

WIDE SUPPORT 7 b.g. Be My Guest (USA) 126 – Riva Ring (USA) (Riva Ridge (USA)) [1991 10v 12d³ 10m⁴ 12g⁵ 14g 1992 16d 12.1d 12.1s 9.7v] big, good-topped ex-Irish handicapper, rated 76 as 6-y-o when with D. Weld: soundly beaten in 1992, pulled up final run: stays 1½m: acts on good to firm and dead ground: best form blinkered. *A. Moore* –

WIDYAN (USA) 4 b.c. Fappiano (USA) – Hotel Street (USA) 93 (Alleged (USA) 138) [1991 11g* 12.3d⁴ 12g 10g⁴ 10.5f 1992 10m 11.9f 8.1s] rangy, good sort: has a fluent, round action: rated 105 as 3-y-o: little sparkle in 1992, not seen out after July: better at 1½m than 1¼m: acts on any going: below form when blinkered: sold 16,000 gns Newmarket September Sales. *P. F. I. Cole* –

WIEDNIU (USA) 3 b.f. Danzig Connection (USA) – Nicole Mon Amour (USA) (Bold Bidder) [1991 6g³ 1992 7.3d² 8d⁴ 8f⁴ 8g³ 8g²] strong, lengthy filly: useful performer: ran well in 1992 in Fred Darling Stakes at Newbury (length second to Musicale), Group 2 event at Dusseldorf, Coronation Stakes at Royal Ascot and Falmouth Stakes at Newmarket (third to Gussy Marlowe): long way below form (chipped knee bone) in Warwick maiden final start: stays 1m: acts on firm and dead going. *Lord Huntingdon* **106**

WILCO 3 ch.g. Bay Express 132 – Solo Singer 66 (Song 132) [1991 5g 5s⁴ 5g⁴ 5m³ 5g 5f⁴ 5d a5g⁴ a6g² 1992 6g 5m 5.7f⁴ 5g 5g] strong, workmanlike gelding: moderate mover: rated 65 at 2 yrs: seems on the downgrade: stays 6f: acts on firm ground and equitrack: sold 1,250 gns Ascot September Sales. *Andrew Turnell* **51**

WILD AND LOOSE 4 b.g. Precocious 126 – Regain 86 (Relko 136) [1991 7g⁴ 8g* 10g⁴ 8m³ 10m 8m³ 10d⁶ 8d* 8g⁶ 1992 7g 8f 8s 7g] big, lengthy, good-topped gelding: moderate mover: rated 90 at 3 yrs: never dangerous but not knocked about in handicaps in 1992 and shaped as if retains his ability: off course over 4 months after second run: best at 1m to 1¼m: acts on good to firm and dead ground: held up. *D. R. C. Elsworth* **– p**

WILD APPLAUSE (IRE) 3 b.f. Sadler's Wells (USA) 132 – Noble Mark 120 (On Your Mark 125) [1991 NR 1992 10g 10g⁶ 10m⁵ 10s³ 10s 12.2d*] rather leggy filly: closely related to several winners, including good miler The Noble Player (by The Minstrel) and useful 1987 2-y-o 5f and 7f over Border Guard (by Nureyev), and half-sister to several winners, including over middle distances: dam very smart sprinter: modest performer: won maiden at Catterick in October: stays 1½m: best efforts on a soft surface: usually bandaged behind. *J. H. M. Gosden* **71**

WILDE RUFO 3 ro.c. Sharrood (USA) 124 – Wanton 106 (Kris 135) [1991 5g³ 6m* 6g 6m³ 5.2g 7m³ 7m³ 8s 1992 7g²ᵈⁱˢ 8g 8m³ 6f 7f⁵ 6m 6g² 6g 6d⁵ 7f 7d⁴] small, sturdy colt: carries condition: useful but inconsistent performer: best 3-y-o efforts when second to Pursuit of Love in Free Handicap at Newmarket (weighed in 6 lb too light) and third to Prince Ferdinand in listed race at Haydock: stays 1m: acts on any going: sold 31,000 gns Newmarket Autumn Sales. *P. A. Kelleway* **99**

WILD EXPRESSION 2 ch.c. (Apr 7) Then Again 126 – Pleasure Island 57 (Dalsaan 125) [1992 7.5d 7.5d 8g 7g] 6,400F, 8,200Y: big, good-topped, workmanlike colt: third foal: half-brother to 3-y-o Elysian Sprite (by Petorius), sprint winner in Austria in 1992: dam 7.5f winner: always behind in auction events. *C. Tinkler* **42**

WILD FIRE 3 ch.c. Kalaglow 132 – Bundu (FR) 88 (Habitat 134) [1991 7g⁶ 7f² 8f* 1992 9.9g⁵ 10g⁴ 10.1m* 12f² 10.4d 10m² 10g³ 10.1m* 10m] leggy, lengthy colt: doesn't take the eye in appearance: good mover: fairly useful handicapper: won at Yarmouth in June and (£7,700 contest) September: good second in valuable events at Royal Ascot (to Source of Light) and Goodwood (to Party Cited): effective at 1¼m and 1½m: needs top-of-the-ground: sold 42,000 gns Newmarket Autumn Sales. *G. Wragg* **94**

WILD HONOUR (IRE) 3 b.g. Fayruz 116 – Hurricane Hazel (Lorenzaccio 130) [1991 5f² 5.1m⁶ 5d² 5.7m⁵ 6m* 5m² 6m² 5m² 5g* 5m* 6d³ 5.7f* 6g³ 5m* 5g 5m 1992 a7g 5g 5g² 5g⁵ 5m 5f⁴ 5d] compact gelding: poor mover: fair handicapper: effective at 5f and 6f: best on a sound surface: ran creditably when visored: sometimes gave trouble at stalls: sold 6,400 gns Newmarket Autumn Sales, reportedly to race in Scandinavia. *W. R. Muir* **83**

WILD PERSIAN (IRE) 3 b.f. Persian Bold 123 – Recapture 58 (Sassafras (FR) 135) [1991 6g a6g⁶ 1992 6.9g 11.5m 7m] leggy filly: seems of little account. *Pat Mitchell* **–**

WILD POPPY 3 br.f. Norwick (USA) 120 – Brandon Creek 79 (Be My Guest (USA) 126) [1991 NR 1992 8.3g⁶ 8g 8g 10d] 3,000Y: small, sturdy filly: sister to 6f and 1m winner Ciboure and half-sister to 3 winners, including 1m and 1¼m winner Patience Creek (by Mummy's Game): dam suited by 1½m: no sign of ability. *E. A. Wheeler* **–**

WILD PRINCESS (USA) 2 b.f. (Feb 10) Wild Again (USA) – Bonnie Blade (USA) (Blade (USA)) [1992 7s² 7d*] $80,000Y: leggy, close-coupled, quite attractive filly: has a quick action: tenth foal: all 8 others to have raced have won, including restricted stakes winner (Grade 1-placed) Bullet Blade (by Amber Pass): dam minor winner at 2 yrs: sire easily best at 4 yrs when Breeders' Cup Classic winner: length winner from Imaginary of 16-runner maiden at Leicester in October, kicking on 2f out but having little left at line: should improve further. *L. M. Cumani* **74 p**

WILD PROSPECT 4 b.c. Homing 130 – Cappuccilli 111 (Lorenzaccio 130) [1991 a8g 7d 8g 7.5g² 7g² 7f² 8m 7f 7f* 7f* 7f* 7.5f* 7.6m 7.5f⁵ 7m 8m 7d 1992 8g 7d 7g² 7f⁵ 7m⁴ 7m⁴ 7g⁴ 7m⁴ 8.2d 7d 8g] smallish, good-quartered colt: bad mover: modest handicapper: well below form last 3 starts, visored final one: best form at around 7f on a sound surface: has gone well on a turning track: front runner. *C. Tinkler* **67**

WILD SABLE (IRE) 4 ch.f. Kris 135 – Fur Hat (Habitat 134) [1991 10d* 10.8d² 1992 10d] tall, leggy filly: rated 88 at 3 yrs: not seen in 1992 after running in Rosebery Handicap at Kempton in April: stays 10.8f: acts on dead ground: sold 49,000 gns Newmarket December Sales. *M. R. Stoute* **–**

WILD STRAWBERRY 3 ro.f. Ballacashtal (CAN) – Pts Fairway (Runnymede **68** d
123) [1991 5g⁶ 6d⁵ 6m⁵ 6m* 6m 1992 8g⁶ 7f 8m⁴ 10m⁵ 8m 11.8g 11g 8.9d 8d] tall,
workmanlike filly: modest handicapper: below form in second half of 1992, tried
visored: best form at 1m: acts on good to firm ground: trained until after penultimate
start by J. Eustace. *D. A. Wilson*

WILEYS FOLLY 6 ch.m. Krayyan 117 – Friend's Folly (Sweet Revenge 129) **38**
[1991 a7g a5g⁵ a5g⁶ a8g⁵ 7g 6f⁶ 8f⁶ 7f 6m 6f a7g⁵ 8m² 8f* 10f a10g a8g² a10g⁴ 1992
a10g a10g a8g⁴ a10g⁴ 10d 7g] angular mare: poor mover: poor handicapper: best at
1m to 1¼m: acts on firm ground and equitrack: best without blinkers or visor. *S.
Dow*

WILKINS 3 b.g. Master Willie 129 – Segos 81 (Runnymede 123) [1991 7.1d 1992 **74**
10v 10g 12.3d³ 14.6g* 14s* 16.2s²] strong gelding: progressed well in 1992: clear-
cut winner of handicaps at Wolverhampton and Salisbury in summer: will stay
beyond 2m: acts on soft ground: usually races prominently. *J. R. Fanshawe*

WILLESDON (USA) 8 ch.h. Master Willie 129 – Dona Maya (USA) (Reviewer –
(USA)) [1991 7v 10.2f 8.9m² 10s 12.1g 1992 10m 8g] angular horse: hobdayed:
successful over hurdles in August but no show on flat in summer: stays 11f: probably
unsuited by soft going, acts on any other: ran well when blinkered. *A. Barrow*

WILL HE OR WONT HE (IRE) 4 b.c. The Noble Player (USA) 126 – Dusty – §
Highway (High Top 131) [1991 a8g* a8g* a7g³ 10m 11.6m a8g a8g a10g⁴ a10g 1992
a10g⁶ a10g] sturdy, quite attractive colt: has a round action: on the downgrade, and
refused to race final start: best left alone. *B. J. McMath*

WILLIE SPARKLE 6 b.g. Roi Guillaume (FR) 119 – Adamay (Florescence 120) –
[1991 NR 1992 13.1s] half-brother to 1981 2-y-o 6f and 7f winner Martialis (by
Martinmas): dam won maiden hurdle: modest hurdler (stays 2¼m): bandaged,
showed signs of ability in amateurs race at Ayr in September on debut on flat. *Mrs S.
C. Bradburne*

WILL-O-BAY 4 b.f. Bay Express 132 – Will Be Wanton 64 (Palm Track 122) –
[1991 NR 1992 a5g a7g 6.9h⁶] workmanlike filly: second foal: dam maiden plater on
flat seemed to stay 1¼m, won a selling hurdle: thrice raced, and no worthwhile
form. *R. Hollinshead*

WILL OF STEEL 3 ch.g. Master Willie 129 – Collapse 107 (Busted 134) [1991 **81**
NR 1992 6.1d² 7g² 8f³ 7d 6s* 6d² 7.1s⁴ 7g] 8,400F, 9,000Y: workmanlike gelding:
poor mover: closely related to 1m winner Collide and winning Irish stayer Carricero
(both by High Line) and half-brother to several winners, including fair 6f winner
Lapse (by Bold Lad): dam won from 5f to 1m: fair handicapper: won at Salisbury in
September for 7-lb claimer: very good second of 23 to Densben in £13,100 handicap
at York but below form after: should prove as effective at 1m: acts on soft ground:
sold out of H. Candy's stable 17,000 gns Newmarket Autumn Sales after penultimate start. *Mrs J. R. Ramsden*

WILLOW BLUE 5 gr.g. Full of Hope 125 – Paddock Princess 80 (Dragonara –
Palace (USA) 115) [1991 10m³ 10m⁵ 8g⁴ 9.5m⁵ 12g 10.8m⁶ 8.1d 10.1s 1992 11.9d]
leggy, close-coupled gelding: ex-Irish handicapper: thrice raced on flat here and no
worthwhile form: stays 1½m: acts on firm ground: ran well when blinkered once. *T.
P. McGovern*

WILLSHE GAN 2 b.f. (May 1) Precocious 126 – Quisissanno 76 (Be My Guest **83**
(USA) 126) [1992 5f² 5f* 5f³ 6m² 7d4 6m⁴ 6g³ 5g⁴ 5d³ 5s³ 6v] 4,800Y: good-topped
filly: has scope: carries condition: usually looks well: fifth foal: sister to 3-y-o Euro
Festival, successful at 6f (at 2 yrs) and 7f, and half-sister to 3 winners here and
abroad, including Irish 1½m and 1¾m winner Montezuma (by Commanche Run):
dam 1½m winner: fair performer: won maiden auction at Redcar in May: ran very
well in £7,600 event at York and listed race at Ayr eighth and ninth starts but below
form after, visored first occasion: stays 6f: acts on firm and dead ground. *Denys
Smith*

WILL'S LEGACY 2 ch.c. (Feb 9) Northern Tempest (USA) 120 – Crosby **39**
Triangle 72 (Windjammer (USA)) [1992 5g⁶ 5m⁶] workmanlike colt: third foal: dam
sprinter: poor form in minor event at Windsor and maiden at Lingfield: not seen out
after June. *W. Carter*

WILL SOON 3 ch.c. Nicholas Bill 125 – Henceforth 58 (Full of Hope 125) [1991 **69**
7m 7g⁵ 1992 7s⁶ 8.2g² 8f⁴ 10.5g⁴ 9g 9g³ 7.6s 10s⁶] leggy, close-coupled colt: modest
maiden: acts on soft going. *H. Candy*

WINDPOWER (IRE) 3 ch.g. Sharpo 132 – Night of Wind 101 (Tumble Wind **82**
(USA)) [1991 5m* 6g² 6f⁵ 6g 8m 1992 6d4 6g* 6m 6m³ 6f 6f⁶ 6.1d² 6.1m 6g 8s 6d
6.1s] strong gelding: poor mover: inconsistent handicapper: won at Pontefract in

April: stays 6f: acts on firm and dead ground: below form when visored once: sold 12,000 gns Newmarket Autumn Sales. *J. Berry*

WINDRUSH BOY 2 br.c. (Apr 19) Dowsing (USA) 124 – Bridge Street Lady 93 **68** (Decoy Boy 129) [1992 5.1m^2 5g^2 5f 5m^5] lengthy, leggy colt: second foal: dam sprinter: consistent in maidens until running moderately at Chester final start: speedy: acts on firm ground: drifted markedly left once. *M. McCormack*

WINDSOR HIGHNESS 5 ch.m. Glenstal (USA) 118 – Mrs Simpson (USA) – (Windsor Ruler (USA)) [1991 a7g* a7g^2 a7g 8f 10.1s^2 11.5g^6 10m^4 a12g^5 11.7m^4 10f 7m 1992 a7g a10g^6 a13g a10g^6 10d] lengthy, rather sparely-made ex-Irish mare: no worthwhile form on flat early in 1992: best form at 1¼m: has gone well on soft ground: below form in blinkers: often slowly away and soon behind: won selling hurdle (sold to join K. Wingrove's stable 5,800 gns) in September. *M. P. Muggeridge*

WINDSOR PARK (USA) 6 br.g. Bold Forbes (USA) – Round Tower 93 (High – Top 131) [1991 a12g^6 a10g^4 a10g^4 a8g^6 a10g^2 a12g^4 a13g^2 12s^6 12m 10.8m^5 11.8g a12g^3 a13g^3 a14g^3 1992 a12g 12g 14.1d] leggy, quite attractive gelding: good walker: poor handicapper: stays 1¾m: acts on good to firm going: ran poorly in visor. *K. S. Bridgwater*

WINGED BAYARD 3 b.c. Arctic Tern (USA) 126 – Fabulous Rina (FR) **66** (Fabulous Dancer (USA) 124) [1991 NR 1992 12g^3 11.9m^5] tall, leggy colt: second foal: dam French 1¼m and 10.5f winner: staying-on third in maiden at Salisbury: not seen again after running moderately at Haydock in May and sold 1,000 gns Newmarket Autumn Sales. *R. F. Johnson Houghton*

WINGED WHISPER (USA) 3 ch.g. Air Forbes Won (USA) – Soft Reply **62 d** (USA) (Personality (USA)) [1991 5d 5g 5g^5 6m^4 7.5f* 7m^4 7.5f^4 8m 1992 8.9s^3 10f^3 11.6m 8.2d^3 8g^2 8.9g^4 8m 8.2d 7g^6 8d 10.1d^6] sturdy gelding: carries condition: well below form after fifth outing: stays 1¼m: acts on any going: has looked irresolute: claimed out of C. Thornton's stable £7,011 second start. *C. A. Smith*

WINGFIELD (USA) 4 b.c. Devil's Bag (USA) – Tennis Partner (USA) **79 d** (Northern Dancer (CAN)) [1991 7g^6 9m^2 7g^4 10m^2 10d* 10.2s^4 8d* 9d 1992 a10g^6 8d 9d^3 8m 9s 9d 7.5g] compact, quite attractive colt: dam reported foal: dam unraced sister to Ajdal, from family also of Arazi: fair handicapper at 3 yrs for J. Oxx: disappointing at 4 yrs, trained first 4 starts by D. Elsworth: stays 1¼m: acts on good to firm ground and dead: blinkered final start. *J. Oxx, Ireland*

WING PARK 8 ch.h. Golden Dipper 119 – Puente Primera 90 (Primera 131) [1991 – NR 1992 7f] strong, lengthy horse: rated 97 as 6-y-o (effective at 5f to 7f and acted on any going): tailed off in handicap in June, only subsequent run. *G. A. Pritchard-Gordon*

WINGS COVE 2 b.c. (Feb 28) Elegant Air 119 – Bel Esprit (Sagaro 133) [1992 7g **51** 8s] 18,000Y: good-bodied colt: sixth foal: half-brother to several winners here and abroad, including Fille d'Esprit (by Cragador), at 6f and 7.3f, and 3-y-o miler Tynron Doon (by Cragador): dam no form: soundly beaten in maidens at Newmarket and Warwick in autumn: sold 5,800 gns Newmarket Autumn Sales. *M. R. Stoute*

WINGS OF FREEDOM (IRE) 4 b.g. Fairy King (USA) – Wingau (FR) 70 – (Hard To Beat 132) [1991 8g 8d 11.7d 10g 10s 12.4f^4 11.6m^3 12s 12d^5 11.8m 14.1m^3 16.1g^2 15.8g^4 13.8m^4 1992 18g 14.9d^5] rangy gelding: poor mover: modest handicapper at best: not seen out on flat in 1992 after May: stays 2m: probably acts on any going: below form blinkered: won over hurdles in September. *J. R. Jenkins*

WINNIE RECKLESS 3 ch.f. Local Suitor (USA) 128 – Bereeka (Main Reef – 126) [1991 NR 1992 8g 8m^4] sturdy, quite attractive filly: first foal: dam unraced half-sister to top-class 6f to 10.5f winner Wollow: tailed off in maidens at Warwick and Yarmouth: not seen out after July. *C. E. Brittain*

WINOSKI 4 b.g. Petoski 135 – Persevering 95 (Blakeney 126) [1991 a8g a10g^4 – a10g* 12v^2 a10g* 12.3d^4 10.5m^3 1992 a12g^4 a13g 17.1d] strong, compact gelding: rated 74 at 3 yrs: on the downgrade. *D. L. Williams*

WINTERING (IRE) 2 ch.c. (Feb 25) Sharpo 132 – Winter Lady (Bonne Noel **72 p** 115) [1992 5s*] 5,800F, 46,000Y: half-brother to winners in Italy and France: dam unraced sister to Noelino and Little Bonny: won maiden at Folkestone in October by 1½ lengths from Glen Miller, running on well: will stay 6f: will improve. *Sir Mark Prescott*

WINTER LIGHTNING 3 b.f. Dominion 123 – Shaft of Sunlight 58 (Sparkler **54** 130) [1991 6g a8g^5 a8g 1992 13.1m 14g^6 18.2m* a12g^6] sturdy, angular filly: won handicap at Chepstow in June: subsequently sold out of P. Walwyn's stable 6,400 gns Newmarket July Sales and well beaten in Southwell claimer: stays well: acts on good to firm ground. *D. J. Wintle*

WIORNO   4 b.c. Wassl 125 – Just You Wait (Nonoalco (USA) 131) [1991 8s* 10g² **123** 10d* 10g⁶ 9.7d* 1992 10s 10m² 10.5d* 10s⁵ 9.7s² 12d³] tall colt: good-class French performer: beat Snurge by ½ length in Grade 1 Rothmans International at Woodbine on final start in October but demoted to third for hampering third close home: also winner of Group 3 race at Longchamp (by ½ length from Runyon) and length second to both Opera House in Brigadier Gerard Stakes at Sandown and to Sillery, running on, in Ciga Prix Dollar at Longchamp: stays 1½m well: acts on good to firm and soft going: sweating when below form fourth start. *A. Fabre, France*

WIRED FOR SOUND   2 b.c. (May 21) Sharpo 132 – Swift Return 79 (Double   – Form 130) [1992 6s 7.1s] 2,300F, 5,200Y: fifth foal: half-brother to fair sprinter Abom Swift (by Absalom) and a winner in Italy: dam 2-y-o 6f winner, is half-sister to smart Skyliner: well beaten in October maidens at Lingfield and Chepstow. *M. R. Channon*

WISE FRIEND (USA)   4 b.g. Sagace (FR) 135 – Swalthee (FR) (Sword Dancer   – (USA)) [1991 a10g a12g 1992 a13g a12g a16g 11.9m 17.2s] leggy gelding: no worthwhile form. *C. P. Wildman*

WISE PORTIA   3 b.f. Quadratic (USA) – Pervenche (Latest Model 115) [1991   – 5.7f⁵ 1992 7g 10m 8.3g⁵ 9.7g⁶ 10.8s] small, sparely-made filly: plater: should stay beyond 1m: sold 600 gns Newmarket Autumn Sales. *H. Candy*

WISHAM (USA)   2 ch.c. (Apr 11) Be My Guest (USA) 126 – Massorah (FR) 108 **71** p .(Habitat 134) [1992 6g⁵ 7g³] tall, good-topped colt: has plenty of scope: fifth foal: closely related to 3-y-o 6f winner Massiba and 2 winners in France, including (at 7.5f and 1m) Monaiya (all by Shareef Dancer): dam French sprinter: retained by trainer 32,000 gns Newmarket July Sales: burly still, much better effort in October when 4 lengths third of 14, niggled along at halfway and staying on strongly close home, to Pamzig in maiden at Doncaster: will be well suited by 1m: will improve again. *B. Hanbury*

WISHES   2 b.f. (Apr 26) Caerleon (USA) 132 – Talon d'Aiguille (USA) (Big Spruce   – p (USA)) [1992 7g] first foal: dam, French 1¼m winner, is half-sister to Korveya (dam of Hector Protector and Shanghai) and Proskona out of 1000 Guineas runner-up Konafa: 25/1, never dangerous in maiden at Newmarket in October: should do better. *J. R. Fanshawe*

WISHING CAP (USA)   2 b.c. (Feb 9) Lyphard's Wish (FR) 124 – Phils Fancy **56** 102 (Irish Love 117) [1992 5.9f⁶ 6f³ 6g* a7g² 7f* 7g⁵ 7g³ 7m] $26,000Y: well-made colt: half-brother to 1990 Irish 2-y-o 5f winner Downeaster Alexa (by Red Ryder) and a winner in Germany: dam useful sprinter at 2 yrs in Ireland: successful in Catterick claimer in July and nursery at Thirsk in August: last of 8 in nursery final run: will be better suited by 1m: acts on firm ground, ran respectably on fibresand: below form with tongue strap (very edgy) once: sold 8,500 gns Newmarket Autumn Sales. *Sir Mark Prescott*

WISHING WELL   3 ch.f. Sharpo 132 – Acclimatise 116 (Shirley Heights 130)   – [1991 5d³ 1992 7d⁵] angular, leggy filly: reportedly chipped knee bone after debut: ran as if something amiss in 7-runner minor event at Leicester in June, first run for nearly a year: sold 26,000 gns Newmarket December Sales. *Mrs J. Cecil*

La Coupe, Longchamp—Wiorno and Runyon are six lengths clear

WITCHES COVEN   3 gr.f. Sharrood (USA) 124 – Tricky 66 (Song 132) [1991 7g⁴ **52**
7.5f² 1992 a8g³ 10g 8.9g⁴ a12g² a12g³ a14g* 14.1g⁴ᵈⁱˢ 16.9d⁵] leggy, rather unfurnished filly: modest handicapper: won at Southwell in August: stays 1¾m: acts on all-weather surfaces, below form on dead ground: suitable mount for inexperienced rider: sold to join Mrs A. Knight 4,000 gns Newmarket Autumn Sales. *M. Bell*

WITCHWAY NORTH   2 b.f. (May 9) Northern State (USA) 91 – Petulengra 98 **–**
(Mummy's Pet 125) [1992 a7g] 1,000Y: eighth foal: half-sister to 1m seller winner Northern Warrior (by Petong): dam 5f and 6f winner at 2 yrs: soon struggling in claimer at Southwell in November. *M. J. Camacho*

WITH GUSTO   5 b.g. Taufan (USA) 119 – Finesse 87 (Miralgo 130) [1991 12s 12g³ **39**
a13g⁶ 1992 a10g* a10g⁴ 9d 10g] good-topped gelding: poor handicapper: won a50 apprentice maiden at Lingfield in March: stays 13f: acts on good to firm and dead ground and equitrack: sometimes bandaged: not seen out after May. *K. O. Cunningham-Brown*

WITH LOVE   3 ch.f. Be My Guest (USA) 126 – Royal Caprice (USA) (Swaps) **–**
[1991 NR 1992 10.5d⁵] IR 50,000Y: leggy, sparely-made filly: half-sister to several winners, including smart 1986 2-y-o 6f and 7f winner Genghiz (by Sir Ivor), later successful at 1¼m: dam won at up to 1m: well beaten in maiden at Haydock in September on belated debut. *L. M. Cumani*

WITHOUT A FLAG (USA)   2 ch.g. (Feb 13) Stately Don (USA) 122 – **52**
Northerly Cheer (USA) (Northjet 136) [1992 5d⁵ 6g⁴ 6g⁶ 6g 6m⁶ a7g³] $25,000F, $35,000Y: smallish, sturdy gelding: first foal: dam unraced: modest maiden: will be better suited by 1m: acts on equitrack. *C. A. Cyzer*

WITNESS BOX (USA)   5 b.h. Lyphard (USA) 132 – Excellent Alibi (USA) **112**
(Exceller (USA) 129) [1991 9g³ 11.8g⁴ 12g 11.5d³ 14g* 16.2g* 13.9g* 13.3m 1992 14g 16g* 14g² 16.1f* 16m² 18f² 20s⁴ 15.5s⁵]

The whip and the guidelines for its use are seldom out of the racing news nowadays. Inconsistencies in stewards' decisions make for bewilderment sometimes. Take Steve Cauthen's suspension following so-called 'improper' use of the whip at the prestigious Goodwood meeting. The former champion, a universally respected jockey, is not a vigorous user of the whip and had never previously been called to account for contravening the guidelines. The four-day suspension imposed by the Goodwood stewards after Cauthen had

Newcastle Brown Ale Northumberland Plate (Handicap), Newcastle—
the very genuine Witness Box gains a deserved big-race success,
narrowly holding off Cabochon (almost hidden), with Satin Lover (white bridle)
and Hawait Al Barr close up

Sheikh Mohammed's "Witness Box"

struck Witness Box more than the 'recommended' ten times in a rousing finish with Further Flight to the Goodwood Cup was therefore a surprise. Cauthen also fell foul of the stewards for using the whip down the shoulder on Witness Box, something which also incurred their displeasure when he rode Daru to victory in the last race of the afternoon. The action of the Goodwood stewards in both cases—Cauthen was sent on to Portman Square after the second—was over-doing it to say the least. The Jockey Club's whip guidelines were originally introduced because of concern in some quarters about the effect of the use of the whip on racing's public image. In fact, the publicity surrounding some of the most famous cases has served only to leave the way racing has sought to deal with a relatively insignificant problem open to ridicule. The subsequent decision of the Jockey Club's Disciplinary Committee to add a six-day suspension for Cauthen's riding of Daru struck a jarring note. Eddery and Roberts, locked in a tight battle for the championship, both gave up an afternoon's rides to support Cauthen at the Disciplinary Committee hearing at which the trainer of Witness Box and Daru also backed the jockey. Given the mild nature of the offence it had been widely expected that Cauthen, who decided not to appeal against the suspension imposed for his riding of Witness Box, would receive a sympathetic hearing. Alas, the treatment of Cauthen served only to fan the flames of discontent that many jockeys and trainers feel about the way the present rules are interpreted. The guidelines recommend only that stewards 'should consider enquiring into any case where a rider has used his whip more than ten times' but in the case of Witness Box the Goodwood stewards seemed to interpret this particular guideline as a rule. Cauthen used his whip correctly on Witness Box, keeping perfectly in rhythm with his mount who responded with great determination only to be caught virtually on the line. Knowing when and how frequently to use the whip is a matter for judgement—split-second judgement in a tight finish—and it's always wisest to give a top jockey the benefit of any doubt. Commonsense dictates that horses can be abused more by being hit three or four times when they have nothing more to give, than by being struck a dozen or more times when running on strongly; a jockey of Cauthen's calibre can be relied on not to hit a horse any more than necessary. The guidelines also draw the attention of stewards to the hitting of horses down the shoulder, which is forbidden except 'in very exceptional cases'; Cauthen did little more than give Daru a couple of flicks down the shoulder close home to keep him straight, a corrective measure.

Witness Box (USA) (b.h. 1987)	Lyphard (USA) (b 1969)	Northern Dancer (b 1961)	Nearctic / Natalma
		Goofed (ch 1960)	Court Martial / Barra II
	Excellent Alibi (USA) (b 1981)	Exceller (b 1973)	Vaguely Noble / Too Bald
		Charming Alibi (ch 1963)	Honeys Alibi / Adorada II

Further Flight and Witness Box, two of the gamest horses in training, staged a repeat finish six weeks later in the Doncaster Cup over two furlongs further. Witness Box again went down by a short head, Cauthen dictating the pace from the start and keeping Witness Box going strongly under firm riding only to be pipped on the post. The Goodwood Cup and Doncaster Cup were the first pattern races Witness Box had contested (he came fourth in the Prix du Cadran and fifth in the Prix Royal-Oak in two later pattern events). A progressive stayer as a four-year-old, Witness Box spent the first part of the latest season in handicap company, winning at Newmarket on One Thousand Guineas day and taking the very competitive Newcastle Brown Ale Northumberland Plate in June. Ridden by Duffield, he got home in a driving finish with Cabochon and Satin Lover at Newcastle, taking some time to wear down the leaders and then just holding the late challenge of the runner-up. The rangy, attractive Witness Box, who usually takes the eye in the paddock, is the first reported foal of the French mile-and-a-quarter to mile-and-a-half winner Excellent Alibi, a daughter of Exceller closely related to the remarkable Dahlia. Dahlia was by Exceller's sire Vaguely Noble out of Excellent Alibi's dam Charming Alibi. This American family is renowned for producing racehorses who stand up well to a long and hard career on the racecourse—Charming Alibi herself won sixteen of her seventy-one races—and Witness Box, who stays in training, is following in the tradition for toughness and reliability. He'll presumably be trained for the Gold Cup as a six-year-old. He stays two and a half miles and, although his round action might mislead some into thinking he's a soft-ground performer, he acts on any going. He's a credit to all associated with him. *J. H. M. Gosden*

WIXON (FR) 2 b.f. (May 11) Fioravanti (USA) 115 – Forli's Fair (CAN) (Thatch **114** (USA) 136) [1992 6g* 6s⁴ 5d² 6.5s² 5s* 7s²] second foal: half-sister to French 3-y-o

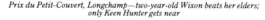

Prix du Petit-Couvert, Longchamp—two-year-old Wixon beats her elders; only Keen Hunter gets near

1¼m winner Cariellor's Miss (by Cariellor): dam lightly-raced half-sister to Fair Salinia: successful in listed newcomers race at Deauville in August and Prix du Petit-Couvert (by ¾ length from Keen Hunter, pair 6 lengths clear) at Longchamp in October: creditable second to Kadounor in Criterium de Maisons-Laffitte in November: stays 7f, but best form at 5f: has raced only on an easy surface. *F. Boutin, France*

WOLFHOUND (USA)   3 ch.c. Nureyev (USA) 131 – Lassie Dear (USA)   **120** (Buckpasser) [1991 6m* 6m* 1992 7g3 5f4 6g6 6d3 5.2g* 6d* 7d*]
There was plenty of evidence in 1992 that Sheikh Mohammed made the right decision in encouraging John Gosden back from the United States. In his fourth season at Newmarket, the trainer sent out easily his best total of winners, 111, and recouped about £1,175,000 in win and place prize money in Great Britain. A huge string such as his—160-strong according to the 1992 *Horses In Training*—backed by the sport's top owners should, of course, contain more than a smattering of pattern-class talent. Gosden's yard did not disappoint in this respect. His older horses included Mashaallah, Keen Hunter, Red Bishop, Witness Box and Knifebox, while Sonus, Wolfhound, Muhtarram, Pollen Count, Western Approach, Toussaud and Landowner figured among the three-year-olds. Marillette, Taos and Beggarman Thief won good two-year-old races and if the likes of Tinners Way, Pembroke, Azilian, Catrail, Storm Canyon and Emperor Jones all fail to figure in pattern company in 1993 it will be a surprise. There are horses of all disciplines in that list and more than one in five runners from Stanley House were winners, a strike-rate bettered only by Cecil and Charlton in the top forty trainers. Patience, allied with the ability to send a horse out fit after a long lay-off, has played an integral part in the success of many of Gosden's older horses, but he is not averse to a more attacking policy as he showed with the two-year-old Marillette.

The career of Wolfhound has been one testament to Gosden's judgement. On several occasions in the latest season one could be excused for thinking that Wolfhound was being kept in too high company and at the wrong trip, but the trainer's opinion of this colt was vindicated in fine style in the autumn. As a two-year-old, Wolfhound won his only two starts, both at six furlongs, in a maiden at Redcar and a minor event at Doncaster, having been outpaced and niggled along in the early stages at Doncaster. Clearly bound for much better things, he made his reappearance in the European Free Handicap at Newmarket in April and passed the post fourth of nine, basically never able to challenge but putting up a good effort judged on his previous form. Many expected his next appearance to be at a mile. Instead, Wolfhound was pitched in at the deep end against most of the best sprinters in the five-furlong King's Stand Stakes at Royal Ascot. This looked to be flying very high but Wolfhound was beaten only about three quarters of a length behind the winner Sheikh Albadou, finishing best of all. Although the proximity of 100/1-shot El Yasaf one place behind Wolfhound raised eyebrows, it was hard to dispute the trainer's assessment of Wolfhound's class now. It was a promising effort, particularly so for his prospects at six furlongs, but we had to wait a while before that promise was realised. In the July Cup at Newmarket three weeks later Wolfhound was very disappointing, beaten about nine lengths behind

Diadem Stakes, Ascot—Wolfhound beats Lochsong and Montendre in good style

Prix de la Foret, Longchamp—Wolfhound continues to progress;
he makes all and holds off Silicon Bavaria by a neck

the principals, and although a second try at six furlongs in the Haydock Park
Sprint Cup two months after that resulted in a rather better display, Wolfhound was still some way off recapturing his Royal Ascot form and Sheikh
Albadou beat him eight and a half lengths; chasing the leaders until outpaced
under two out, Wolfhound stayed on again to take third near the line.

The promise of Royal Ascot was beginning to fade in the memory but
Wolfhound was to end the season a Group 1 winner himself. First, though,
came a near-£7,000 event over five furlongs at Newbury in which there was
only one possible danger, the King George Stakes third Artistic Reef, whom
Wolfhound saw off by two lengths, followed by the Group 3 Diadem Stakes at
Ascot. Second favourite at 4/1, Wolfhound looked in magnificent shape before
the Diadem, a strong good-topped individual continuing to impress with his
physical progress. In the race, his chief opponents all quickly showed their
hands—the Prix de Meautry first and second Twafeaj and Thourios, the Duke
of York and Cork and Orrery winner Shalford and the rapidly improving handicapper Lochsong were four in line up front by halfway. Wolfhound, however,
was stalking them on the outside and Cauthen didn't have to ask him for his
effort until the furlong marker. Lochsong had gone on but Wolfhound looked
to have her measure and, though he didn't go right away, he soon had a length-
and-a-half advantage and was never in danger of relinquishing it. This was the
Wolfhound we'd been promised on the same course over three months
earlier. The crowning of his season was the Prix de la Foret at Longchamp.
Each of Wolfhound's seven opponents there had won at least one pattern race
and they included the classic-placed three-year-olds Hydro Calido, Kenbu,
Lion Cavern and Pursuit of Love, but it was Wolfhound, under a masterly ride
from Pat Eddery, who ran out the winner. Having set a steady pace,
Wolfhound had a clear advantage and was still travelling well within himself
just over a furlong and a half out, then Eddery set him alight with only the
five-year-old outsider Silicon Bavaria and Kenbu able to produce anything like
the same response. At the post Wolfhound was a neck up on Silicon Bavaria
with Kenbu, who hadn't had the best of runs, also closing another length and a
half back in third.

Wolfhound is from a superb family which also features in the essay on
Shuailaan, as Shuailaan is out of one of Wolfhound's half-sisters. All of Lassie
Dear's nine foals prior to Wolfhound were winners, including the very useful
1988 middle-distance colt Al Mufti (by Roberto) who has since won graded
races in South Africa, and another of her daughters Weekend Surprise (by
Secretariat) is the dam of Summer Squall and A P Indy. Lassie Dear, a Grade 3
winner over an extended mile at two years, is a half-sister to the high-class
French middle-distance colt Gay Mecene and their dam Gay Missile is a
half-sister to Raja Baba. Lassie Dear's first foal and Wolfhound's close
relative Presto Lad (by Nijinsky) won only a maiden race from nineteen starts

Sheikh Mohammed's "Wolfhound"

		Northern Dancer (b 1961)	Nearctic
			Natalma
	Nureyev (USA) (b 1977)	Special (b 1969)	Forli
Wolfhound (USA) (ch.c. 1989)			Thong
		Buckpasser (b 1963)	Tom Fool
	Lassie Dear (USA) (b 1974)		Busanda
		Gay Missile (b 1967)	Sir Gaylord
			Missy Baba

but was still sent to stud. On pedigree, no wonder. Wolfhound's sire Nureyev was reportedly standing at a fee of 150,000 dollars in 1992, 100,000 dollars down on that of two years before. Other good winners for him in Europe in the latest season were Red Slippers, Oumaldaaya, Kitwood, Hydro Calido, Trishyde and Rudimentary. Gosden must be hoping that Wolfhound, like Rudimentary, will be an improved horse again as a four-year-old. The two are very different sorts in other respects but in this the story could well turn out the same. Wolfhound's efforts at the back-end of 1992 are certainly no discouragement. An easy mover, Wolfhound put up his best efforts in the Diadem and Foret over a stiff six furlongs and seven. Both were on dead ground, but the importance of the ground for him is probably not so great. *J. H. M. Gosden*

WOLF POWER (IRE) 2 b.c. (Apr 9) Taufan (USA) 119 – Heather Lark (Red **64** Alert 127) [1992 6g 6m³ 5f² 6m² 6s⁵ 6m] IR 12,500F, IR 26,000Y: lengthy, unfurnished colt: fifth foal: brother to useful 1988 Irish 2-y-o sprinter Heather Seeker: dam Irish 2-y-o 5f winner: easily best effort in Pontefract maiden fourth start: should be better suited by 1m: possibly unsuited by soft ground. *T. Thomson Jones*

WONDERFUL YEARS (USA) 2 ch.c. (Feb 9) Key To The Mint (USA) – **44** p
Velvet Storm (USA) (Wajima (USA)) [1992 8.1d⁵ 8d 8.1d⁵] $55,000F: leggy colt:
moderate mover: half-brother to 3 minor winners in USA: dam ran once: sire top
class at up to 1½m: poor form in autumn maidens, though gives impression capable
of better: will be well suited by middle distances. *Mrs J. R. Ramsden*

WOODCHAT (USA) 2 b.c. (Mar 2) Woodman (USA) 126 – Theriot's Treasure **97**
(USA) (Mac Diarmida (USA)) [1992 7d⁷ 7g* 8d³] $220,000Y: strong, rangy colt: has
a powerful, round action: third foal: dam won at up to 1¼m: progressive colt:
successful in Salisbury maiden and Deploy Acomb Stakes (by a head from Salatin) at
York in August: odds on, over a length third of 6 to Blush Rambler in listed race at
Goodwood: will be better suited by 1¼m. *P. F. I. Cole*

WOODCOCK WENDY 3 br.f. Myjinski (USA) – Deandar (Communication 119) – §
[1991 NR 1992 10g⁵ 10.2d 9.7g] long-backed, unfurnished filly: second foal: half-
sister to middle-distance performer Woodcock Wonder (by Royal Vulcan): dam of no
account over jumps: no sign of ability and has looked most reluctant. *M. J. Bolton*

WOODENVILLE (USA) 2 ch.c. (Apr 7) Woodman (USA) 126 – Classy Compo- **86** p
sition (USA) (Monteverdi 129) [1992 6d³ 6g* 7d² 7m⁶] $145,000Y: close-coupled,
robust colt: good mover: first foal: dam, minor winner at 2 yrs in North America, is
half-sister to dam of Robellino: ¾-length winner of maiden at Newmarket in June,
making all: progressed after, sixth of 10 to Maroof in Lanson Champagne Vintage
Stakes at Goodwood following month: will be better suited by 1m. *L. M. Cumani*

WOODHAUNTER (USA) 2 ch.c. (Feb 28) Woodman (USA) 126 – Naughti- **86** p
ness (USA) (Cox's Ridge (USA)) [1992 7f² 7g² 7d* 7g³] $205,000F: tall, rangy colt:
has a round action: first foal: dam unraced: progressive colt: 4-length winner of
maiden at Ayr in July, making all: kept on well when 1½ lengths last of 3 to Antester
in minor event there following month: will be better suited by 1¼m: likeable sort
with plenty of scope who'll keep improving. *J. H. M. Gosden*

WOODLAND RIDE 3 b.f. Northern Tempest (USA) 120 – On A Bit 66 –
(Mummy's Pet 125) [1991 7g 7m 6g 1992 9.9f] workmanlike filly: has a round action:
no sign of ability: sold 820 gns Doncaster October Sales. *J. G. FitzGerald*

WOODLANDS CROWN 9 ch.g. Milford 119 – Town Girl 99 (Town Crier 119) –
[1991 a12g 8f 9d 8.1g⁴ 8.2g 8f 12f² 13.1f 1992 12d 12.3s] leggy, quite good-topped
gelding: bad handicapper: stays 1½m: acts on firm ground. *D. C. Tucker*

WOODLANDS ELECTRIC 2 b.g. (Apr 10) Rich Charlie 117 – Hallowed –
(Wolver Hollow 126) [1992 5s⁶ 6v a7g] neat gelding: first reported foal: dam,
maiden, stayed 1½m, later won over jumps: well beaten in late-season maidens. *P.
A. Pritchard*

WOODLANDS GREY 6 gr.g. Nishapour (FR) 125 – Topling 85 (High Top 131) –
[1991 8.2m 8m a8g 1992 8.9g 8f] close-coupled, workmanlike gelding: no worthwhile
form: blinkered once. *P. A. Pritchard*

WOODLANDS LEGEND 3 b.c. Sayf El Arab (USA) 127 – Vernair (USA) 73 –
(Super Concorde 128) [1991 8.1g 1992 8g 10s 10f] good-topped, plain colt: no
worthwhile form. *D. C. Tucker*

WOODSIDE HEATH 5 ch.g. King Persian 107 – Saga's Humour (Bustino 136) –
[1991 NR 1992 10d 8.9d] neat gelding: has a round action: on the downgrade. *J. S.
Moore*

WOODURATHER 6 br.g. Touching Wood (USA) 127 – Rather Warm 103 **70**
(Tribal Chief 125) [1991 10.2s 10.2g³ 12.5g⁴ 10.3d 10.1s* 10.8d² 12.3g²] small,
light-framed gelding: moderate walker: fair handicapper: not seen out after April:
stays 12.5f: goes particularly well on soft surface: keen sort: pulled hard in blinkers
once. *M. C. Pipe*

WOODWARDIA (USA) 2 ch.f. (Feb 13) El Gran Senor (USA) 136 – Chain Fern **76** p
(USA) (Blushing Groom (FR) 131) [1992 6d² 7g³] unfurnished filly: first foal: dam
unraced sister to Al Bahathri: shaped well in large-field maidens at Kempton (raced
keenly when second to Mithl Al Hawa) and Newmarket (well-backed favourite, kept
on well 2 lengths behind Fayfa) in autumn: will stay 1m: will improve again. *B. W.
Hills*

WOOLAW GIRL 4 br.f. Sayf El Arab (USA) 127 – Pacific Princess 82 (Dom –
Racine (FR) 121) [1991 NR 1992 a6g] first foal: dam 6f (at 2 yrs) and 1m winner: tailed
off in Southwell claimer in December on belated debut. *A. W. Potts*

WOOTTON RIVERS (USA) 2 ch.c. (Mar 1) Woodman (USA) 126 – Mount **106**
Holyoke 93 (Golden Fleece (USA) 133) [1992 7g⁴ 7d* 7f³ 8s* 6m⁵ 8d³ 9v* 10s*]
medium-sized, useful-looking colt: shows knee action: second foal: dam, 1m winner,

is daughter of smart sprinter Amaranda, herself daughter of Favoletta: progressive colt: successful in second half of 1992 in maiden at Goodwood, minor event at Ayr and at Rome in listed race (trained until after then by P. Chapple-Hyam) and Group 2 event (beat Mr Richard by 3½ lengths) in November: also ran well when fifth of 6 in Middle Park Stakes at Newmarket and third of 7 in Juddmonte EBF Beresford Stakes at the Curragh: will stay 1½m: acts on good to firm ground, and clearly goes extremely well on a soft surface. *G. Pucciatti, Italy*

WORDSMITH (IRE) 2 b.g. (May 6) Cyrano de Bergerac 120 – Cordon 89 **63** (Morston (FR) 125) [1992 7d 7g⁵ 7s 10g] 10,500F, 9,400Y: compact, good-quartered gelding: tenth foal: half-brother to several winners here and abroad, including fair 1¼m winner Fayette (by Dom Racine) and 3-y-o 8.5f winner Haroldon (by Heraldiste): dam won over 7f and 1½m: failed to progress after strong-finishing fifth in Leicester maiden in September: should be suited by middle distances: sold to join Mrs J. Ramsden's stable 8,200 gns Newmarket Autumn Sales and gelded. *G. Harwood*

WORKINGFORPEANUTS (IRE) 2 ch.f. (Apr 6) Entitled 126 – Tracy's **53** Sundown (Red Sunset 120) [1992 6f⁴ 6f³ 7m² 7d 7g² 7f 7d⁴ 7d 8g 6g] IR 750F, IR 1,600Y, 4,000 2-y-o: close-coupled filly: second foal: dam Irish 11f winner: fair plater: will be very well suited by 1¼m+: acts on firm and dead ground: usually starts slowly and gets behind (best runs given strong handling). *C. A. Smith*

WORKING TITLE (IRE) 2 b.c. (Feb 4) Prince Rupert (FR) 121 – Occupation **51** (Homing 130) [1992 8v 7g⁶ a8g] IR 13,000F, 14,500Y: sturdy colt: half-brother to 1½m winner There You Are (by Kings Lake) and a winner in USA: dam, placed over 6f at 2 yrs in Ireland, is half-sister to Irish St Leger winner Mountain Lodge: shaped encouragingly when sixth of 18 in maiden at Doncaster but ran poorly at Southwell later in November: should be suited by middle distances. *J. W. Hills*

WORLD EXPRESS (IRE) 2 b.c. (Feb 9) Jareer (USA) 115 – Eight Mile Rock **75** 76 (Dominion 123) [1992 5g 5.1d⁶ 6f 5.7g 8.1s* 9g⁵] 4,800Y: rather leggy colt: first foal: dam 7f winner: vastly improved when visored first time in Chepstow maiden in August, winning by 2½ lengths: not entirely discredited when visored again in Sandown nursery following month: will be suited by middle distances: easily best form on soft ground. *B. R. Millman*

WORTHY MEMORIES 3 b.f. Don't Forget Me 127 – Intrinsic (Troy 137) [1991 **–** NR 1992 8g] 2,600F: tall, unfurnished filly: second foal: dam, out of a half-sister to Prix du Jockey-Club second Patch, showed signs of ability but looked none too tractable: moved poorly to post when well beaten in maiden at Warwick in August on belated debut. *C. F. Wall*

WOTAMONA 4 b.f. Another Realm 118 – Meadow Wood (Meadow Court 129) **–** [1991 10g 12.2m⁵ 15.3m a12g² a12g 14.1m 14.1f³ 14.1m 10.8g 1992 12.5s⁶ 12.1s 12.1v a16g⁶ a14g] leggy, sparely-made filly: none too consistent maiden: stays 1¾m. *B. Palling*

WRETS 3 b.g. Kalaglow 132 – Hayley Warren (Habitat 134) [1991 8s 1992 8g² **76** 10m⁴ 8.9d⁵ 9m* 10g² 10s] angular, lengthy gelding: good mover: fair handicapper: won maiden at Newcastle in July: stays 1¼m: acts on good to firm and dead ground, unsuited by very soft: sold to join Mrs. P. Joynes' stable 6,400 gns Newmarket Autumn Sales. *M. R. Stoute*

WRIGHTMILL (IRE) 2 b.g. (Feb 25) Taufan (USA) 119 – Anita's Princess **51** (Miami Springs 121) [1992 5g⁶ 6f 8g 7.5m 6.1g 6d] 5,000Y: leggy, close-coupled gelding: has a round action: third foal: brother to plating-class 4-y-o So Apt: dam unraced half-sister to Anita's Prince: modest maiden: best form at 6f in visor. *C. Tinkler*

WRITTEN AGREEMENT 4 ch.g. Stanford 121§ – Covenant 75 (Good Bond **–** 122) [1991 NR 1992 8g] fifth foal: half-brother to modest 1¼m winner Royal Treaty (by Tower Walk): dam 7f winner at 2 yrs, stayed 1½m: tailed off in Lingfield seller in August. *R. E. Peacock*

WRYCREST 3 b.f. Sharpo 132 – Wryneck 89 (Niniski (USA) 125) [1991 6.1f 6f 6g **–** 1992 8.9s 8.1d] leggy filly: has quick, moderate action: rated 49 at 2 yrs: no form in 1992: sold 780 gns Newmarket September Sales. *R. Charlton*

WSOM (IRE) 4 b.g. Tate Gallery (USA) 117 – April Bride (USA) (Run The **–** Gantlet (USA)) [1991 6m 7m* 7.2m² 7m 7.6d⁴ 8m 7m a7g 1992 8d 9f 12f⁶ 7g] lengthy gelding: rated 62 at 3 yrs: below form in 1992: should stay beyond 1½m: acts on good to firm ground and dead: below form when visored once. *J. M. Carr*

WUFUD (USA) 2 b. or br.c. (Mar 11) Woodman (USA) 126 – Olden Damoiselle **78** (USA) (Olden Times) [1992 6d 6f² 7f* 7m² 7g 7d⁶] $240,000Y: well-made colt: good mover: half-brother to 2 minor winners in North America: dam minor sprint winner in USA: won maiden at Brighton in July: stayed on unable to challenge when good second of 4 in minor event at Newcastle and seventh of 14 in £12,100 nursery at York after: will be well suited by 1¼m: acts on firm ground, seems unsuited by dead. *J. L. Dunlop*

WYLAM 5 b.g. What A Guest 119 – Wish You Wow (Wolver Hollow 126) [1991 a7g a14g 1992 14.1d] lengthy, rather sparely-made gelding: poor maiden on flat: won over fences in October: subsequently joined C. Williams. *G. H. Eden* —

WYNDOM EARLE (IRE) 2 b.c. (Mar 15) Good Times (ITY) – Georgian Melody (Hello Gorgeous (USA) 128) [1992 8d] 1,700Y: first foal: dam little sign of ability: tailed off in maiden auction at Redcar in October. *R. Earnshaw* —

WYNONA (IRE) 2 b.f. (Feb 19) Cyrano de Bergerac 120 – Highdrive (Ballymore 123) [1992 7g⁴ 7m² 8.1d⁴ 7m* 7m] leggy, angular filly: moderate mover: third foal: dam well beaten: progressed well, successful at Newmarket in seller (retained 8,500 gns) in July and nursery (came from well off pace) in September, until last of 7 in Rockfel Stakes there, flashing tail under pressure: stays 1m: acts on good to firm and dead ground. *G. C. Bravery* **89**

Y

YAAFOOR (USA) 3 b.g. Northern Baby (CAN) 127 – Second Glance (USA) (Big Burn (USA)) [1991 7g⁵ 7d⁵ 1992 10.8g 12.5g 10f] leggy gelding: no worthwhile form in 1992: should stay at least 1m: has worn tongue strap: sold to join P. Hedger 4,600 gns Newmarket July Sales. *A. A. Scott* —

YAAKUM 3 b.g. Glint of Gold 128 – Nawadder 73 (Kris 135) [1991 7d 8m 8.3g⁴ 10m 1992 12.3s 6.9d² 7.5m] robust, angular gelding: plating-class maiden: blinkered, not entirely discredited in seller (claimed to join J. Banks £5,800) final start, in May: stays 1¼m: acts on good to firm and soft ground: has been gelded. *B. Hanbury* —

YAHMI (IRE) 2 b.c. (Jan 24) Law Society (USA) 130 – Hogan's Sister (USA) (Speak John) [1992 7g 8f 8d⁵] 27,000F, IR 84,000Y: useful-looking colt: has scope: brother to Irish middle-distance winner Lynch Law and half-brother to several winners, notably top-class 6f/7f performer Salieri (by Accipiter): dam unraced half-sister to Father Hogan: fair maiden: best effort when close fifth at Redcar, front rank throughout and keeping on well: will be well suited by 1¼m +. *Major W. R. Hern* **74**

YAJEED (USA) 2 ch.c. (Mar 26) Seattle Dancer (USA) 119 – Dona Maya (USA) (Reviewer (USA)) [1992 7m⁵ 7m* 7s 8.2g⁴] 750,000 francs (approx £75,300) Y: lengthy, angular colt: has scope: good mover: half-brother to 4 winners here and abroad, including useful 1982 2-y-o 7f and 1m winner Ashmolean (by Vaguely Noble) and smart 1986 French 2-y-o 1m winner Willesdon (by Master Willie), later 11f winner: dam, minor stakes winner, won at up to 9f: fair performer: won maiden at Newmarket in August, having come off bridle at halfway: better suited by 1m than 7f: acts on good to firm ground, well beaten in valuable race in France on soft: may do better. *A. A. Scott* **72**

YAKIN (USA) 2 b.f. (Mar 18) Nureyev (USA) 131 – Looks Sensational (USA) (Majestic Light (USA)) [1992 5.1m² 5g* 6s² 5g] 300,000Y: workmanlike filly: second foal: dam twice-raced half-sister to high-class colt Awe Inspiring (stayed 1¼m) from family of Zilzal (by Nureyev) and Polish Precedent: fairly useful performer: heavily-backed favourite, won maiden at Wolverhampton in September, leading 2f out and soon clear: excellent second in listed race at Ayr 11 days later, making most: last of 13 in Cornwallis Stakes at Ascot in October: much better suited by 6f than 5f, and should stay 1m: best effort on soft ground. *H. Thomson Jones* **86**

YAMANOUCHI 8 b.g. Hard Fought 125 – Noreena (Nonoalco (USA) 131) [1991 8.5f⁴ 8h⁵ 8m³ 9m 10.9g* 9m 10.2m⁵ 8m 1992 10s] short-backed ex-Irish gelding: rated 50 at 7 yrs: tailed off in selling handicap in September, 1992: better at around 11f than shorter: acts on good to firm ground: modest winning hurdler in 1991/2. *D. Moffatt* —

YANKEE FLYER 5 b.m. Henbit (USA) 130 – Yankee Special 60 (Bold Lad (IRE) 133) [1991 7g² 7.6m³ 8g⁴ 8.9m² 1992 8g⁶ 10g] sparely-made mare: poor mover: poor maiden on flat and not one to trust: stays 1m: acts on good to firm ground: poor winning hurdler in 1991/2. *Miss S. J. Wilton* — §

YARDLEY COURT 2 b.c. (Feb 12) Today And Tomorrow 78 – Zarnina 56 (The –
Brianstan 128) [1992 6f] leggy, quite attractive colt: fifth foal: dam 2-y-o 5f seller
winner: 66/1 and freely to post, tailed off in 10-runner maiden at Ripon in June, tiring
over 2f from home: wasn't seen out again. *B. Beasley*

YATOO (IRE) 3 ch.g. Ballad Rock 122 – Phar Lapa 59 (Grundy 137) [1991 5g 6d –
6.1m³ 7m⁴ 7.6m 1992 6.9v 7s 7m 6g] lengthy gelding: rated 68 at 2 yrs: no form in
1992: should stay middle distances: has joined B. Llewellyn. *R. Hannon*

YAWL 2 b.f. (Apr 22) Rainbow Quest (USA) 134 – Bireme 127 (Grundy 137) **112** p
[1992 7d³ 7d* 7m*]
    Given their respective opportunities, it was always much more likely
that a Derby winner would sire a Derby winner than an Oaks winner would
produce an Oaks winner. The latter feat has been achieved on just nine
occasions, the last time in 1912 by Mirska, a daughter of the 1899 winner
Musa. The 1980 winner Bireme, however, has prospects of becoming the
ninth mare (the 1863 winner Queen Bertha foaled both the 1875 winner
Spinaway and the 1879 winner Wheel of Fortune) to achieve the distinction, as
her daughter Yawl, a winner of two of her three races as a two-year-old,
including the Group 3 Rockfel Stakes at Newmarket, looks set for a good
season in 1993. It's far too early to say whether Yawl is up to classic standard,
but her first-season performances were most encouraging in that respect, and
as she comes from a family that's notable for producing late-developing,
middle-distance stayers, there's every reason to imagine that she'll do better
as a three-year-old.
    Yawl's first appearance on the racecourse, when she finished five and a
half lengths third of seven to Kusamba, beaten also by her lesser-fancied
stable-companion Black Dragon, in a seven-furlong minor event at York in
September, was a promising one; but her second effort, in the six-runner Oh
So Sharp Stakes over the same distance at Newmarket the following month,
was that of a very useful filly. Starting at 5/1 in a field which also contained the
previous winners Gustavia, Nuryandra and Self Assured, who last time out
had been runner-up to Marillette in the May Hill Stakes at Doncaster, Yawl
was sent on after a furlong and a half and proceeded to make the rest of the
running, forging clear in excellent style from the Bushes to win by six lengths
from the newcomer Rumpus with Self Assured another four lengths back in
third. There's little doubt that with both Self Assured, who looked past her
best for the season, and Gustavia, who didn't seem at ease on the dead ground,
well below form, Yawl is flattered by a literal interpretation of the result; but,
back over the same course and distance in the Rockfel Stakes two weeks
later, Yawl confirmed what a useful young stayer she is. Opposed by six,
including Queen's View and Felawnah, first and second respectively in the

*Rockfel Stakes, Newmarket — Yawl stays on strongly to beat Queen's View
and puts herself bang in the Oaks picture*

Blue Seal Stakes at Ascot, the Queen Mary and Cherry Hinton-placed Mystic Goddess and the dual six-furlong winner Katiba, Yawl won gamely, quickening a modest gallop after half a furlong and staying on strongly when challenged by Queen's View on the rise to the line to earn the verdict by three quarters of a length. From a handicapping point of view, it wasn't by any stretch of the imagination a top-class performance—after all, Mystic Goddess, exposed as just a fairly useful filly, was only two lengths away in third—but under conditions which were much quicker than she'd encountered previously, and which could reasonably have been anticipated to have favoured some of her opponents, it was a thoroughly encouraging one. Make no mistake, Yawl will be even more effective over middle distances in the coming season.

Yawl (b.f. Apr 22, 1990)	Rainbow Quest (USA) (b 1981)	Blushing Groom (ch 1974)	Red God
			Runaway Bride
		I Will Follow (b 1975)	Herbager
			Where You Lead
	Bireme (ch 1977)	Grundy (ch 1972)	Great Nephew
			Word From Lundy
		Ripeck (br 1959)	Ribot
			Kyak

With an Arc winner for her sire as well as an Oaks winner for her dam Yawl is bred to win just about anything. Doubtless the same has been said or written somewhere about some of Bireme's six previous foals; their combined total of two wins on the flat proves, if nothing else, that there's no guarantee of success where the breeding of racehorses is concerned. Bireme's two other winners are the three-year-old mile-and-a-half winner Quadrireme (by Rousillon) and Yawl's full brother Trireme, who split a pastern after a promising success over seven furlongs as a two-year-old; visits to Kris, Bustino, Posse and Final Straw produced only two minor winners over hurdles. As we've said, Bireme is from a well-known family, a large proportion of whose members have been late developers. Her dam Ripeck is a daughter of Kyak, who together with her half-sisters Ark Royal and Cutter was one of three Park Hill winners bred by Dick Hollingsworth's famous broodmare Felucca. Ripeck, a winner over a mile and a quarter as a three-year-old, though equally effective at a mile and a half, has bred a line of winners too long to mention individually, most of whom showed at least useful form once their two-year-old days were behind; but they include the good middle-distance stayer Buoy, the out-and-out stayer Balinger and the smart sprinter Fluke. Bireme, incidentally, was one of the better Oaks winners of the last twenty years, but she was injured after Epsom and never ran again. In all, Bireme ran just four times; she also won the Musidora Stakes at York and over seven furlongs as a two-year-old. Yawl, a tall, unfurnished filly, acts on good to firm and good to soft ground. The 20/1 on offer for the Oaks at the time of writing could well turn out to be good value. *B. W. Hills*

YAZALY (USA) 3 ch.c. Blushing Groom (FR) 131 – Capricorn Belle 115 **71 §** (Nonoalco (USA) 131) [1991 6s² 6d² 1992 6d 8s 8m² 7m³ 7g] strong, lengthy colt: capable of fair form: easily best effort in 1992 when second in handicap at Pontefract but looked a decidedly hard ride: moved poorly to post next start and soundly beaten final one, in July: stays 1m: acts on good to firm and soft ground: visored last 3 starts: not one to trust. *A. A. Scott*

YELLOW RATTLE 2 ch.f. (Feb 7) Local Suitor (USA) 128 – Pine (Supreme **–** Sovereign 119) [1992 7d] rangy filly: has scope: fifth foal: sister to 3-y-o Affa and half-sister to 1¼m winner Firgrove (by Relkino): dam twice: weak 16/1-chance and very green, slowly away and always behind in 14-runner maiden at Salisbury in July: moved moderately down. *Major W. R. Hern*

YELTSIN 2 ch.c. (Mar 31) Soviet Star (USA) 128 – Mill On The Floss 117 (Mill **85 p** Reef (USA) 141) [1992 7m⁶ 8s*] compact colt: fluent mover: third foal: half-brother to useful 3-y-o 10.3f winner Hatta's Mill (by Green Desert) and 10.2f and 1½m winner Top Mill (by High Top): dam 7f (at 2 yrs) and 1½m winner from very good family: well-backed 7/2-shot, and looking very well, won 12-runner maiden at Newcastle by a neck from Bin Ajwaad, pair clear, held up travelling smoothly then running on well from 2f out: will stay beyond 1m: wears a dropped noseband: will improve again. *H. R. A. Cecil*

YENOORA (IRE) 3 b.g. Ahonoora 122 – Beijing (USA) 89 (Northjet 136) [1991 **78**
8.2f 8s 10m 1992 14.6g3 14.9f* 12d3 13.1m* a16g* a16g* 16d2 16m] big, lengthy
gelding: has a round action: fair handicapper: won at Warwick (2-runner race) in
May, then at Bath and twice at Lingfield in the summer: off course 7 weeks,
sweating and probably in need of race when well beaten final start: suited by test of
stamina: acts on firm and dead going, goes well on equitrack: has worn dropped
noseband: has worn bandages: has been gelded. *P. F. I. Cole*

YEOMAN BID 5 b.g. Longleat (USA) 109 – Bounding (Forlorn River 124) [1991 –
a7g5 a10g 7g 8.3g 10f5 10g a7g5 a8g 1992 8m 8.5d] big, angular gelding: has a
roundish action: probably no longer of much account. *J. Dooler*

YEOMAN BOUND 4 b.g. Norwick (USA) 120 – Bounding (Forlorn River 124) –
[1991 10.1g 8d 1992 a10g 12g 8.3g 6m 12f 10s 9d] workmanlike gelding: seems of little
account. *K. T. Ivory*

YEOMAN FORCE 6 b.g. Crofter (USA) 124 – High Voltage 82 (Electrify) [1991 –
7m a6g 1992 a6g4] tall, angular gelding: has a long stride: moderate handicapper at
best nowadays: fourth at Lingfield in February, for 7-lb claimer: suited by 6f:
probably acts on any going: has worn blinkers, often visored. *J. M. Bradley*

YES 4 b.f. Blakeney 126 – Arrapata (Thatching 131) [1991 6g 7g 5g5 6g 6d4 5g3 5m **57**
a5g 6s 6f3 5.2f2 6g* 6m 7s 1992 5.9d4 5g3 5m 6g* 5m 5m3 7.1f4 5s2 6g3 6g 5.2g2 5d3
5g 6d 5m 5.1s] compact filly: moderate mover: modest handicapper: won at
Yarmouth (apprentices) in June: well below form last 4 starts: best at stiff 5f/6f: acts
on firm and soft ground: tried visored: often claimer ridden: sometimes slowly away.
D. T. Thom

YET TO DANCE 2 b.f. (Apr 9) Mashhor Dancer (USA) – Fayette 80 (Dom –
Racine (FR) 121) [1992 5.7f4] fifth foal: dam 1¼m winner: 10/1, soundly-beaten
fourth of 5 in median auction at Bath in June. *R. J. Holder*

YEVEED (IRE) 2 b.f. (Feb 3) Wassl 125 – Teresa Deevey 50 (Runnett 125) **58**
[1992 5g5 5f5 6.1g2 7f a7g3 a7g5 7.1s* 8s] leggy, angular filly: moderate mover: first
foal: dam twice-raced 6f winner: moderate performer: much improved effort to win
selling nursery at Sandown (no bid) in August, pushed along in last 3f and staying on
well: ran moderately in similar event at Pontefract 6 weeks later: should be suited
by 1m: best form on soft ground: flashed tail and carried head awkwardly once. *M. H.
Easterby*

YFOOL 2 b.f. (Mar 22) Persian Bold 123 – Raiwand 106 (Tap On Wood 130) [1992 **63**
5g 6g3 7d3 7m] smallish, leggy, close-coupled filly: has a quick action: first foal: dam
1m to 1¼m winner probably stayed 1½m: progressive form in maidens first 3 starts:
creditable thirteenth of 21 in nursery at Newmarket in September: will be better
suited by 1m. *J. R. Fanshawe*

YILDIZ 3 b.f. Be My Guest (USA) 126 – Yldizlar 77 (Star Appeal 133) [1991 7m3 **100** ?
1992 10m2 10.3g2 10m2 10g3 10.3g* 14.6m 10d5 12.2d*] rangy, good-topped filly:
good walker: moderate mover: useful at her best (beaten short head by Feminine
Wiles in listed race at Newbury third start) but well below that form last 5 starts:
odds on and nowhere near best to land maiden at Chester in August and apprentice
race at Catterick in October: should prove best at up to 1½m: acts on good to firm
ground, has won on dead. *B. W. Hills*

YIMKIN BOOKRA 4 b.g. Nomination 125 – Top Stream 87 (Highland Melody –
112) [1991 8d 8m4 8g 10g6 10.2g3 12f5 10.2g 10.5g 1992 10d 14.6g6] sturdy, lengthy
gelding: rated 73 at 3 yrs: signs of retaining some ability on second start in April:
unlikely to stay beyond 1½m: acts on good to firm ground. *W. R. Muir*

YONGE TENDER 5 b.m. Tender King 123 – St Clair Star (Sallust 134) [1991 a6g **56** d
6d 7m* 7d3 7m5 7m2 7.6d 7g* 6m4 6.1m* 7f2 7m* 6f 1992 a7g a7g 7g5 8.5g2 7.5m4 **a–**
8m2 6g6 7f 7.6m6 7g 6g6 7m 7g 8m3 7s 7d5] small, close-coupled mare: carries
condition: moderate mover: consistent handicapper when with J. Wharton (claimed
out of his stable £6,153 sixth start): largely disappointing afterwards: effective at
6f to 8.5f: acts on firm and dead going, possibly unsuited by very soft: usually
blinkered. *C. N. Williams*

YORK HILL 2 ch.c. (Feb 28) Stanford 121§ – New Way 103 (Klairon 131) [1992 **78**
6m3 8s 8g] 8,200Y: medium-sized, good-topped colt: half-brother to several
winners, including smart miler Star Way (by Star Appeal): dam won over 5f and 6f at
2 yrs: carrying condition, similar level of form in maiden at York (soon chased
along), Royal Lodge Stakes at Ascot (never a factor) and minor event at Newmarket:
stays 1m: acts on good to firm and soft ground. *P. A. Kelleway*

YORKSHIRE FISHER (IRE) 4 b.g. Anita's Prince 126 – Sericana Run (Run –
The Gantlet (USA)) [1991 NR 1992 13.8d 14.1g⁶ 10f] second reported foal: dam
unraced: no sign of ability in 3 starts. *Miss Gay Kelleway*

YORKSHIRE HOLLY 9 br.g. Bivouac 114 – Holly Doon (Doon 124) [1991 18s² 50
16.1m 15.8g 1992 17.1d⁴ 16d 17.1m⁴ 13.8m⁶ 16.2m³] smallish, workmanlike gelding:
moderate mover: modest staying handicapper: joined R. Wood. *M. Avison*

YORKSHIRE ROCK 2 b.c. (May 13) Ballad Rock 122 – Bombshell 76 (Le 46
Levanstell 122) [1992 6f 7.5d³] 9,400Y: well-made colt: dishes off-fore: brother to
3-y-o Bold Surprise and half-brother to several winners, including 1988 2-y-o 1m
winner Future Glory (by Ile de Bourbon) and 1¾m winner Orlandoland (by Reliance
II): dam 8.5f winner: similar form in Redcar maiden and Beverley minor event (last
of 3) in early-summer: will stay middle distances. *M. H. Easterby*

YOUNG ABSALOM 2 gr.g. (Feb 19) Absalom 128 – Archaic 65 (Relic) [1992 5g –
5g 6f a6g 8.1s] 10,000Y: smallish, compact gelding: brother to 1989 2-y-o 5f winner
Seven Sons and half-brother to several winners, including very smart 1978 2-y-o 5f
performer Schweppeshire Lad (by Decoy Boy), later good sprinter in New Zealand:
dam maiden: well beaten, including in a seller: sold 700 gns Ascot September Sales.
L. G. Cottrell

YOUNG BUSTER (IRE) 4 b.c. Teenoso (USA) 135 – Bustara 92 (Busted 120
134) [1991 10d² 12m* 11.5g² 11.1m* 12g³ 10m⁶ 1992 12d 10m³ 10m² 10s 10.3m*
10.5d⁶ 10d]

The campaign for Sunday racing was highlighted when the Jockey Club
staged an experimental first Sunday meeting in Britain at Doncaster on July
26th. Whether the publicity surrounding the day, in itself, brought regular
Sunday racing any nearer must be doubted. The concept of Sunday trading of
any sort still incurs enormous hostility from church bodies, some trade unions
and a small section of the general public, and the powerful 'Keep Sunday
Special' lobby received a boost with a long-awaited European Court judgement late in the year that restrictions on Sunday shop-opening contained in
the Shops Act of 1950 are lawful. Sunday trading reforms, including legalising

*Mail On Sunday Trophy Stakes, Doncaster —
Young Buster is given a cheeky ride by Michael Hills*

Mollers Racing's "Young Buster"

the opening of shops on Sunday, now depend on Parliament which would also
have to make changes to the Betting, Gaming and Lotteries Act before
on-course and off-course betting could take place on Sunday racing as it does
on other days of the week. There was no on-course betting at Doncaster and
the nation's betting shops remained closed. In truth, the meeting was more a
summer fete which included horsey attractions than a typical day at the races;
the event attracted a crowd of 23,000 with the entrance fee (£5) ostensibly
paid for a 'musical entertainment' in order to circumvent the Sunday Observ-
ance Act of 1784. In logic, of course, the law should be reformed to allow
proper race meetings—with betting—to take place on Sunday as on any other
day. But previous attempts in Parliament to bring about reforms in the Sunday
trading laws—of which another is planned towards the end of 1993—have
proved disastrous, making the British a laughing-stock to foreigners. The
unfair moralistic restraints imposed by the present laws are unpopular with
the vast majority of the population. You'd think, therefore, that it would be a
simple matter to repeal or change them in a democracy. How wrong you'd be!
Governments of all colours have so far been reluctant to introduce even a
measure of reform to the outmoded Sunday trading laws. Racing, and betting
on horse racing, did, however, take a small step forward with the announce-
ment that betting shops are to be allowed to open in the evenings between
April 1st and August 31st each year, starting in 1993. It is the first change in

938

regulations governing opening hours since off-course cash betting was legalised in 1960, and comes after years of lobbying.

The administration of the day at Doncaster wasn't without its snags for the organisers, but a shambles over the deadline for the declaration of runners should have been avoided. After one or two trainers apparently failed to realise that the deadline was forty-eight hours, instead of the usual twenty-four, the Stewards of the Jockey Club amazingly suspended the *Rules of Racing* and extended the deadline by almost five hours as efforts were made to contact all trainers who had originally entered horses but had not declared them. Young Buster was one of only three who came in — his trainer saying it had always been the intention to run — and his presence boosted the field for the most valuable race on the programme, the Mail On Sunday Trophy Stakes, to six. Young Buster had shown progressive form in the second half of his three-year-old career and looked sure to win more good races at four. However, he arrived at Doncaster without a victory in four starts, all of them in pattern company, and with something of a question mark over his enthusiasm. He'd put up his best performance, blinkered for the first time, when passing the post third (promoted to second) in the Prince of Wales's Stakes at Royal Ascot, but had then folded quickly, again blinkered, in the Coral-Eclipse. The Derby fifth Twist And Turn, who had finished well ahead of Young Buster at Sandown, started favourite for the Mail On Sunday Trophy — his closing odds from the Tote-Coral pool, based on bets struck the day before or by telephone clients, were 5/2-on. Young Buster's performance couldn't be faulted this time: waited with, and still with plenty to do three furlongs out, he came with a smooth run to lead inside the final furlong and was barely off the bridle to beat the front-running Twist And Turn by a length. Young Buster was unplaced in two pattern races on good to soft after Doncaster and his overall record suggests he needs a sound surface. He's effective at a mile and a quarter to a mile and a half and is a tricky ride, needing to be brought with a late run. He didn't wear blinkers at Doncaster or in his two subsequent races.

		Youth	Ack Ack
	Teenoso (USA)	(b 1973)	Gazala II
	(b or br 1980)	Furioso	Ballymoss
Young Buster (IRE)		(b 1971)	Violetta III
(b.c. 1988)	Bustara	Busted	Crepello
	(b 1983)	(b 1963)	Sans Le Sou
		Romara	Bold Lad
		(ch 1976)	Peaceful

The rather angular, quite attractive Young Buster, who has a quick action, remains in training. Details of his pedigree can be briefly updated from those that appeared in *Racehorses of 1991*. Young Buster is the first foal of Bustara, a six-furlong two-year-old winner who later showed she stayed a mile and a quarter; Sheikh Mohammed owns her second and third foals, the modest maiden El Taranda (by Ela-Mana-Mou) and the unraced two-year-old Rising Wolf (by Shirley Heights) who were both in training at Abington Place stables in the latest season. Young Buster's grandam Romara took her stud record to eight winners from eight foals to race when her three-year-old Romansh (by Shernazar) won a maiden race at Catterick in March. *G. Wragg*

YOUNG DUKE (IRE) 4 gr.c. Double Schwartz 128 – Princess Pamela 70 (Dragonara Palace (USA) 115) [1991 6m² 6f² 7m* 8m³ 7m³ 8f² 7.1m5 1992 7d] leggy colt: rated 75 at 3 yrs: well beaten only run in 1992, in August: stays 1m: acts on firm ground: effective blinkered, visored or not: sometimes carries head awkwardly and wanders under pressure. *M. McCormack* —

YOUNG ERN 2 b.c. (Apr 28) Efisio 120 – Stardyn (Star Appeal 133) [1992 6m 5m² 6h* 7d⁴ 6f 6d* 6v³] good-topped colt: has a round action: second reported foal: half-brother to 4-y-o 1m winner Crown Reserve (by Another Realm): dam maiden suited by 1½m: useful performer: easily won maiden at Folkestone in June and minor event at Leicester in October: excellent third of 24 to Pips Pride in Racecall Gold Trophy at Redcar: will stay 1m: acts on any going. *S. Dow* 99

YOUNG FREEMAN (USA) 3 b.c. Nijinsky (CAN) 138 – Committed (USA) 128 (Hagley (USA)) [1991 8d² 1992 10m* 10m⁴ 12g 11.6g³ 10g5 10m] big, rangy, good sort: impresses in appearance: has a markedly round action: most impressive 98 winner of Brighton maiden and good fourth to Jeune in Goodwood listed race in May: failed to progress, running as if something amiss in the Derby and last in Newmarket handicap final run: may prove ideally suited by 1¼m: acts on good to firm and dead going. *G. Harwood*

YOUNG GENINSKY 2 b.f. (Feb 11) Myjinski (USA) – Costock Bunny (Young Generation 129) [1992 5g 8g a6g 7d 5d a7g] lengthy filly: has a round action: second live foal: dam of little account: no sign of ability: tried blinkered. *R. J. Weaver* –

YOUNG GEORGE 5 b.g. Camden Town 125 – Young Grace (Young Emperor 133) [1991 8d 10f² 11f⁵ 12m³ 10g 10d² 9.9f² 10f* 10f⁵ 10.1m⁵ 9.9f4 10.9m² 10.5d 1992 11m* 9.9m 12.1m* 11.9f 11d⁶ 12.1m⁵ 12.3m³ 12.3g 10.1m⁶ 12m 14.1d 13.8d] good-topped, close-coupled gelding: carries condition: successful in handicaps at Redcar and Edinburgh in spring: below best in second half of 1992: seems best at up to 1½m: acts on firm ground, possibly unsuited by very soft: sometimes wanders in front. *M. Dods* 60

YOUNG INDIA 5 br.m. Indian King (USA) 128 – Marfisa (Green God 128) [1991 8m 1992 9.2d 7.1m] big, workmanlike mare: inconsistent handicapper: probably stays 1m and acts on any going: below form blinkered once. *D. Burchell* –

YOUNG JASON 9 ch.g. Star Appeal 133 – Smarten Up 119 (Sharpen Up 127) [1991 8d 7.6d 8m 8m⁵ 8g⁶ 8f 8m 7.5f* 8f 9m 8m 1992 8d⁵ 8m³ 8m⁶ 10g⁶ 9d* 8m⁶ 9f³ 8g 8g 8.5m 9g⁵ 9d⁶ 10.3s] small, good-bodied gelding: moderate mover: modest handicapper: won at Redcar in July: best at 1m/9f: acts on any going: below form when blinkered once: tends to carry head high, and not easiest of rides but has won for claimer: tough. *F. H. Lee* 53

YOUNG MAX 3 b.c. Nomination 125 – Hollow Heart 89 (Wolver Hollow 126) [1991 5m 6m 1992 7g⁶ 7s⁴] deep-girthed colt: fair maiden, best effort on reappearance: not seen out after April: stays 7f. *D. R. C. Elsworth* 69

YOUNG MUSICIAN (IRE) 3 b.g. Cyrano de Bergerac 120 – Gentalyn (Henbit (USA) 130) [1991 6m 6.1m³ 1992 8f 7.5m 6m] big, plain gelding: poor maiden: well below form blinkered final start, in July: should stay 1m. *J. G. FitzGerald* –

YOUNG POKEY 7 b.g. Uncle Pokey 116 – Young Romance (King's Troop 118) [1991 NR 1992 13.1s] good-topped gelding: brother to fair miler Romantic Uncle (later winner over hurdles) and half-brother to several minor winners: dam pulled up on only outing is out of a winning sprinter: leading novice chaser in 1991/2, successful in Arkle Chase: not knocked about in mid-division of amateurs race at Ayr in September on debut on flat. *O. Sherwood* –

YOUNG SAM 3 b.g. Seymour Hicks (FR) 125 – Aphrodisiac 69 (He Loves Me 120) [1991 NR 1992 11m⁶] first foal: dam 7.2f (at 2 yrs) and 5f winner: always behind in seller at Wolverhampton in August. *P. D. Evans* –

YOUNG SENOR (USA) 3 b.c. El Gran Senor (USA) 136 – Liturgism (USA) (Native Charger) [1991 5g² 6g* 6m 7m² 7d³ 7m* 7m 1992 9g² 10.4m⁴] sturdy, good-bodied colt: very useful performer: ran very well when beaten head by Twist And Turn in listed race at Newmarket in April: not discredited in Dante Stakes (7 lengths behind Alnasr Alwasheek) at York month after, stumbling markedly leaving stalls: stays 1¼m: has form on dead ground, but seems better suited by a sound surface: tends to be mulish at stalls, and not seen again after refusing to enter them for the Derby. *G. Wragg* 113

YOUNG SHADOWFAX 5 gr.h. Absalom 128 – Miss Twiggy 80 (Tycoon II) [1991 a6g⁴ a6g³ a8g a6g⁵ 9g 6m⁶ 6g 7d 7m 6f⁴ 6g⁴ 5m⁶ 5g⁵ 5m² a5g 5m 1992 5.1g⁴ 6m⁴ 6m⁴ a6g⁴ 7m⁴ 7m 6g] sturdy, good-quartered horse: modest handicapper: effective at up to 7f: best turf efforts on a sound surface, also acts on equitrack: effective with or without visor: often bandaged near-hind: sometimes has tongue tied down: sold 600 gns Newmarket Autumn Sales. *C. N. Allen* 55

YOUNG SPARKIE 2 ch.c. (Mar 4) Superlative 118 – Aspark (Sparkler 130) [1992 6m a6g a8g] angular colt: third foal: half-brother to fair sprinter Arturian (by Vaigly Great): dam little form: poor maiden. *R. F. Johnson Houghton* 38

YOUNG TESS 2 b.f. (Apr 8) Teenoso (USA) 135 – Bundu (FR) 88 (Habitat 134) [1992 8m⁵ 7s 7d⁴] 3,000Y: smallish filly: fifth foal: sister to 1¼m winner Bushy Tailed and half-sister to 3-y-o Wild Fire (by Kalaglow), successful at 1m (at 2 yrs) and 10.1f, and 6-y-o 1m to 10.1f winner Mbulwa (by Be My Guest): dam 10.6f winner: only modest form but ran far better than position indicates all starts, going on really well without being at all hard ridden each time: will be suited by middle distances: most definitely capable of better, and is one to look out for. *Miss S. E. Hall* 55 p

YOUNG VALENTINE 3 ch.g. Bairn (USA) 126 – Spinner 59 (Blue Cashmere **64**
129) [1991 5m* 5f4 6g5 1992 6m 6.1m6 8.5d4 7g² 7g 7m6 7d 7d] angular, quite
attractive gelding: inconsistent handicapper: stays 8.5f: acts on good to firm and
dead ground. *R. M. Whitaker*

YOURS BY RIGHT 2 ch.f. (May 3) Entitled 126 – Super Style (Artaius (USA) **79** p
129) [1992 6m* 6g* 6d*] close-coupled filly: third known foal: half-sister to French
11f to 15f winner New Style (by Saint Cyrien): dam French 11f winner: most
progressive filly: successful in maiden claimer at Brighton in July and nurseries at
Windsor in August and Ascot (always prominent when gamely beating Top Pet by
short head) in September: refused to enter stalls on first appearance: will stay 1m:
sure to improve again. *W. G. M. Turner*

YOURS OR MINE (IRE) 4 b.f. Exhibitioner 111 – Mahele (USA) (Hawaii) **54**
[1991 6m5 6m* 1992 7m 7.9m4 7f 8f² 7.1d 7.6d6] leggy, quite attractive filly: has
half-sister to 2 minor sprint winners by Wolverlife, including Wolver Gold, later
winner over hurdles: dam showed poor form: not seen out until 1992, but had good
season in handicaps: successful at Thirsk, Ripon and Leicester: best form at 6f and
7f: acts on good to firm and soft ground: has seemed headstrong. *D. W. Chapman*

YOUSEFIA (USA) 3 b.f. Danzig (USA) – Foreign Courier (USA) (Sir Ivor 135) **84**
[1991 6m5 6m* 1992 7m 7.9m4 7f 8f² 7.1d 7.6d6] leggy, quite attractive filly: has
smooth action: fair handicapper: ran poorly last 2 starts, and not seen out after July:
best effort at 1m: acts on firm ground, seems unsuited by dead: visored penultimate
run. *M. R. Stoute*

YOXALL LODGE 2 b.c. (Feb 12) Aragon 118 – Opal Fancy 83 (Kibenka 119) **66**
[1992 7s 6.9v² 7g] 3,000Y: big, lengthy colt: half-brother to fair miler Cuvee Charlie
(by Treboro): dam placed over 1m: best effort in autumn maidens when beaten a
neck by easy winner Semillon at Folkestone: still needed race when around 10
lengths ninth of 18, eased considerably, at Doncaster after: should stay 1m. *H. J.
Collingridge*

YUNUS EMRE (IRE) 2 ch.c. (May 4) Lomond (USA) 128 – Thrifty Trio (USA) –
116 (Groton) [1992 7s6 6v] 3,400F: workmanlike colt: poor walker: has a round
action: brother to a winner in USA and half-brother to 3 winners, including sprinters
Luck Penny (by Bustino) and Saturnian (by Sallust): dam smart sprinter: well
beaten in maidens at Warwick and Folkestone in October. *M. Bell*

Z

ZAAHI (USA) 3 b. or br.c. Slew O' Gold (USA) – Alghuzaylah 90 (Habitat **121**
134) [1991 7.1m* 7m5 1992 8g² 8g4 8.5g* 8m² 10g² 10s³ 10m5]
Zaahi fell short of the standard required to win a Group 1 race, but only
just. The margin between victory and defeat in the St James's Palace Stakes at
Royal Ascot was a short head. Looking in fine shape beforehand, Zaahi was
quickly sent to the front under a skilful from Richard Hills and had the field
stretched entering the straight where the market leaders Arazi and Rodrigo
de Triano were fifth and sixth. It gradually became clear that that pair were

*Diomed Stakes, Epsom—only win of the year for the very smart Zaahi;
Misterioso (second left) chases him home*

Hamdan Al-Maktoum's "Zaahi"

unable to find the turn of speed expected of them and that Zaahi was not stopping up front, but 25/1-shot Brief Truce summoned up a finishing effort that denied Zaahi on the post. Zaahi started at 8/1 at Royal Ascot in a field of eight. He represented the Poule d'Essai des Poulains classic form having gone on from a head second to Jeune in the Thirsk Classic Trial to be fourth of nine at Longchamp a month later, putting up an excellent effort to be beaten just over one and three quarter lengths, always near the front, behind Shanghai. Zaahi had already had one chance to confirm the form before Royal Ascot. The Group 3 Diomed Stakes at Epsom was the race in question and Zaahi started favourite, though not a clear one, surprisingly. The five-year-old mare Susurration shared the honour, fresh from a narrow triumph in a listed race. Also in the line up were the impressive three-year-old handicapper Mizaaya, the surprise 1991 Diomed winner Sylva Honda and the four-year-olds Flashfoot and Mohican Girl. For Zaahi, this was a gilt-edged opportunity and he took it in good style, going on two furlongs out and clear soon afterwards, the second home (at a distance of two and a half lengths) being the 20/1-shot Misterioso.

Zaahi's season after Royal Ascot comprised three runs at a mile and a quarter, our conclusion afterwards being that he stays the trip when conditions aren't testing. When the ground was soft in the Prix Guillaume d'Ornano at Deauville, Zaahi was some way below his best in third after he had looked the chief threat to Great Palm, weakening in a manner that suggested it was a combination of the ground and trip which found him out and not just the ground. His three-quarters-of-a-length second to Kooyonga in a Group 1 event at Munich thirteen days earlier and four-and-three-quarter-lengths fifth of ten to Rodrigo de Triano in the Champion Stakes at Newmarket two months later were much more his true form, particularly the latter. The pace in the

Champion Stakes, though, was not a strong one; Zaahi had set it and he appeared to falter close home, all of which confirmed this as the limit of his stamina. A mile may even prove ideal when Zaahi returns to action in 1993.

Zaahi (USA) (b. or br.c. 1989)	Slew O' Gold (USA) (b 1980)	Seattle Slew (b or br 1974)	Bold Reasoning
			My Charmer
		Alluvial (ch 1969)	Buckpasser
			Bayou
	Alghuzaylah (ch 1981)	Habitat (b 1966)	Sir Gaylord
			Little Hut
		Asian Princess (ch 1969)	Native Prince
			Valadier

A strong, good-bodied colt who impresses in appearance, Zaahi will certainly be an imposing four-year-old. He is a son of the seven-time Grade 1 winner Slew O'Gold, born in the year that Slew O'Gold's first crop were three-year-olds and included four Group or Grade 1 winners, among them the Coronation Stakes winner Golden Opinion. Zaahi's dam Alghuzaylah had two previous foals, a colt by Damascus successful in the United States and the useful 1990 sprinter Kadim (by Diesis) who has since gained further victories in Australia. Alghuzaylah's 1990 foal is the Topsider filly Wanisa and she produced a filly by Shadeed in 1991. Alghuzaylah won a five-furlong race at Beverley as a two-year-old and showed fairly useful form in being placed twice, at seven furlongs and a mile, as a three-year-old. She was acquired for 330,000 Irish guineas as a yearling, her attraction on pedigree lying chiefly as a half-sister to Pitasia, the 1978 Prix Robert Papin and Criterium des Pouliches winner who was also placed in three other Group 1 races, the Prix Morny, Prix Saint-Alary and Prix Vermeille. The second dam Asian Princess was virtually useless on the racecourse, the third Valadier a two-year-old one-mile winner. The latter is half-sister to the Yorkshire Oaks and Musidora winner Palatch, herself the dam of that high-class middle-distance colt Patch. *H. Thomson Jones*

ZAFARRANCHO (IRE) 3 ch.g. Bluebird (USA) 125 – Claretta (USA) 82   – p
(Roberto (USA) 131) [1991 NR 1992 12.3s⁴ 10.5d 14.1g] 44,000F: rangy gelding: moderate mover: half-brother to 5-y-o 1¼m winner Saville Way (by Gorytus), very smart 6-y-o middle-distance stayer Sapience (by Niniski) and 3 winners abroad: dam 2-y-o 7f winner: bandaged, well beaten in maidens in the autumn, though showed signs of ability first 2 starts: may do better. *J. G. FitzGerald*

ZAFONIC (USA) 2 b.c. (Apr 1) Gone West (USA) – Zaizafon (USA) 119 **126** p
(The Minstrel (CAN) 135) [1992 6.5s* 6s* 7m* 7m*]
While the result of the Dewhurst Stakes might have had considerably more influence upon the top spot in the Free Handicap than it has the outcome of the Two Thousand Guineas in the last twenty-five years—twelve of its winners have headed the Free Handicap in that period, only Nijinsky, Wollow and El Gran Senor have gone on to success at Newmarket—we'll take some convincing that the 1993 Guineas winner isn't going to be the same horse that ran away with the Dewhurst in October. Zafonic, unbeaten in all his four races, looked in a different league to his rivals in the Dewhurst, just as he had when bolting up in another Group 1 event, the Prix de la Salamandre, at Longchamp on his previous appearance. There hasn't been a more impressive Dewhurst winner since El Gran Senor in 1983, and while Zafonic might not have achieved so much as his illustrious predecessor did when beating Rainbow Quest, Siberian Express and Superlative in 1983, he won with such authority that, at 5/4 at the time of writing, he's the shortest-priced winter favourite for the Guineas since Tudor Minstrel in 1947. El Gran Senor, of course, went on to show himself a brilliant three-year-old, winning the most hotly-contested Guineas for many years—the next three home were Chief Singer, Lear Fan and Rainbow Quest—before compensating for his narrow defeat in the Derby by accounting for Rainbow Quest again in the Irish Derby. Zafonic is unlikely to be raced over middle distances—he looks purely and simply a miler—but, like El Gran Senor before him, has a chance in the Guineas second to none, and unless something untoward happens before the first Saturday in May we shouldn't care to look elsewhere for the Two Thousand Guineas winner.

*Prix Morny Agence Francaise, Deauville—still getting the hang of things;
Zafonic beats Secrage by three quarters of a length*

If Zafonic's was a name which meant little to racegoers outside France before he ran in the Prix de la Salamandre at Longchamp in September, the widespread coverage given to his exhilarating victory there left few unaware of his existence afterwards. He wasn't exactly an unexposed horse going into the race, having won both the six-and-a-half-furlong Prix de Toncarville and the six-furlong Prix Morny Agence Francaise at Deauville the previous month, but he'd not caught the imagination in either, particularly not in the Morny where he'd had to work hard to overcome the Prix de Cabourg winner Secrage and the Princess Margaret winner Marina Park by three quarters of a length and half a length. Three weeks later in the Salamandre, though, in conditions which were very different from the soft, sticky ground that had prevailed at Deauville, Zafonic looked a colt right out of the top drawer. The devastating turn of foot with which he rapidly swept aside such useful opposition as the Gimcrack winner Splendent, the Prix Robert Papin winner Didyme, the July and Richmond Stakes runner-up Canaska Star and the Cabourg second Kingmambo, was unfortunately denied to television viewers on account of some rather indifferent camera work, but from the stands there was no mistaking its immediate impact. From a position four or five lengths down entering the short home straight, the early leaders having gone only a steady gallop, Zafonic surged past his five opponents to gain an advantage of three lengths with more than a furlong still to run and then stayed on strongly to win in terrific style. One small criticism of Zafonic's performance might be that he hadn't increased his advantage over the runner-up Kingmambo by the line—Splendent took third spot, incidentally, Canaska Star fourth—but the first-class acceleration he showed, frequently the hallmark of a top-quality horse, couldn't be faulted. It came as no surprise to find that the 8/1 at which he was offered for the Guineas immediately after the race had been cut to 4/1 by the end of the following day.

It's easy to get carried away by one performance but in the Dewhurst at Newmarket five weeks later, with the ground still riding on top, Zafonic re-emphasized his classic prospects with a display which, if anything, was even more impressive than his victory in the Salamandre. The ten-runner field that lined up against him undoubtedly had more strength in depth to it than the one he'd left for dead at Longchamp, but neither the Coventry and Laurent-Perrier Champagne winner Petardia, the highly promising twice-successful Inchinor, the unbeaten National Stakes winner Fatherland, bidding

Prix de la Salamandre, Longchamp—
Kingmambo and Splendent have no answer to Zafonic's breathtaking acceleration

to give Vincent O'Brien an eighth winner of the race he dominated in the 'seventies and 'eighties, the Royal Lodge third Lost Soldier, the Mill Reef fifth Carbon Steel, the highly-impressive Newbury winner Sueboog, supplemented into the race at a cost of £12,500, nor the highly-regarded Firm Pledge, was able to prevent his running away with the Dewhurst by the widest margin for ten years. Zafonic outshone his rivals from the moment he walked into the paddock. A big, strong, imposing colt, a real powerhouse on looks, Zafonic constantly took the eye (his two attendants ensured he stayed more relaxed than he had been at Longchamp) and was no less impressive in the canter to the start, showing a powerful yet wonderfully athletic action. Once the race was under way the 11/10-on Zafonic gave his supporters little cause for worry. Soon cantering along at the rear of the field as Sueboog and the 50/1-shot Zind quickened what had been a modest early pace—the eleven runners were covered by barely five lengths at halfway—Zafonic, travelling ominously well, moved upsides Sueboog with two and a half furlongs to run as

Dewhurst Stakes, Newmarket—Zafonic wins by four lengths
and becomes the shortest-priced winter favourite for the Guineas since Tudor Minstrel

the filly, in company with those behind her, came under severe pressure. As soon as Eddery, riding his fifth Dewhurst winner, let out an inch of rein Zafonic quickened into an unassailable lead; allowed to drift to his right as Firm Pledge and Inchinor joined Sueboog in a keenly-contested battle for second place, which Inchinor won in a three-way photo, he passed the post four lengths clear, hand ridden. In routing his field Zafonic fully justified all the acclaim he'd received at Longchamp. His performance was as striking as we've seen from a two-year-old in Europe in recent years, and points to his being well up to Guineas-winning standard.

		Mr Prospector	Raise A Native
Zafonic (USA) (b.c. Apr 1, 1990)	Gone West (USA) (b 1984)	(b 1970)	Gold Digger
		Secrettame	Secretariat
		(ch 1978)	Tamerett
	Zaizafon (USA) (ch 1982)	The Minstrel	Northern Dancer
		(ch 1974)	Fleur
		Mofida	Right Tack
		(ch 1974)	Wold Lass

    Zafonic was bred by Juddmonte Farms Incorporated, the breeding operation in Kentucky where two of Khalid Abdulla's other 1992 Group 1 winners, All At Sea and Jolypha, were also raised. He's a son of the second-crop Mr Prospector stallion Gone West, who is a full brother to the 1991 Middle Park runner-up Lion Cavern and from the same family as the Two Thousand Guineas winner Known Fact and the high-class six-furlong to nine-and-a-half-furlong winner Tentam. Gone West was a very smart racehorse who gained his most notable success in the Grade 1 Dwyer Stakes over nine furlongs, at which distance he also ran second to Gulch in the Grade 1 Wood

Mr K. Abdulla's "Zafonic"

Memorial Invitational Stakes, but he was widely considered to be more suited to shorter distances—*Principal American Racehorses of 1987* called him a 'natural miler', whose runaway victory in the Dwyer was the result of a 'powerful rail-favouring bias at Belmont Park'—and at a mile he won the Grade 2 Gotham Stakes and the Grade 2 Withers Stakes. Zafonic's breeding on his dam's side isn't particularly impressive; apart from the Coral-Eclipse and Phoenix Champion Stakes winner Elmaamul, whose grandam is also Mofida, there isn't another top-class animal in his immediate pedigree. However, Zafonic's dam Zaizafon was a very useful animal in her racing days; she won the seven-furlong Seaton Delaval Stakes and another race besides as a two-year-old but was a much better filly in her second season when she ran two particularly good races at a mile—probably her ideal distance—to be fourth to Al Bahathri in the Child Stakes and third to Shadeed in the Queen Elizabeth II Stakes. Zaizafon ended her racing career with John Gosden in the States, and has remained there since; her first two foals, Roneo (by Secretariat) and Botanic (by Mr Prospector) both showed fair form in France without winning, and since Zafonic, her third foal, she's had a colt by Private Account and a filly by Elmaamul's sire Diesis. Zaizafon is the best foal produced by the very tough and smart racemare Mofida. A daughter of the largely undistinguished stallion Right Tack, Mofida won seven races at up to an extended seven furlongs, missing the frame on only four occasions from twenty-seven starts in her first two seasons and keeping her form well enough to run second in the Duke of York Stakes and fifth in the July Cup in another hard campaign as a four-year-old. Besides being the grandam of Elmaamul, Mofida has thrown several winners herself, including the latest Middle Park third Factual and his three-year-old brother Modernise, a very useful miler; she's done at least as well in that respect as her own dam Wold Lass, a plating-class half-sister to the speedy two-year-olds Chebs Lad and Reet Lass. *A. Fabre, France*

ZAFRA   4 b.f. Dunbeath (USA) 127 – White's Ferry (Northfields (USA)) [1991 16.1g   –
17.2g 1992 8f 8.3m] neat filly: has a round action: seems of little account. *G. F. H. Charles-Jones*

ZAIRE   3 b.g. Riverman (USA) 131 – Pelf (USA) 79 (Al Nasr (FR) 126) [1991 NR   –
1992 8f5 10.3m3 8f 9.7m6 10s 9.7s4] first foal: dam 7f winner in Italy, is half-sister to very useful Kanz, smart Diomedia and Crown Treasure, dam of Glint of Gold and Diamond Shoal: little worthwhile form: sold out of J. W. Watts's stable 5,200 gns Newmarket July Sales after second start: tried visored and blinkered: resold 2,200 gns Newmarket Autumn Sales. *A. N. Lee*

ZALON (IRE)   3 gr.c. Flash of Steel 120 – Negligence 66 (Roan Rocket 128) [1991   **99**
7m2 1992 7g4 8g* 8.9g5 10f* 10s 10.1m5 12m] tall, lengthy colt: useful performer: heavily-backed favourite, won maiden at Newmarket in April and £7,200 handicap (made most) at Sandown in June: apparently acted as pacemaker in listed race final start: should stay beyond 1¼m: acts on firm going, never travelling well on soft: joined G. Jones in USA. *J. H. M. Gosden*

ZAMAAN YA ZAMAAN (IRE)   3 b.g. Persian Bold 123 – Unbidden Melody   **72**
(USA) (Chieftain II) [1991 8m 1992 10m3 12m2 12.3f4 14.1d4] leggy gelding: has a quick action: fair maiden: well below form last 2 starts: stays 1½m: acts on good to firm ground: sold 6,400 gns Newmarket July Sales. *M. A. Jarvis*

ZAMIRAH (IRE)   3 b.f. Trojan Fen 118 – Sweet Pleasure 88 (Sweet Revenge   **77**
129) [1991 7m* 7g3 8.1m3 1992 8d4 8m 7.9m 10s3 12m3 11.8s5] workmanlike filly: fair handicapper: good third at Ayr (£10,400 event) and (stayed on strongly from rear) Newmarket in the autumn: stays 1½m: acts on good to firm and soft going: sold 15,500 gns Newmarket December Sales. *G. Wragg*

ZANY ZANNA (IRE)   2 b.f. (Feb 24) Petorius 117 – Zany (Junius (USA) 124)   **83**
[1992 5g6 5g6 6f5 5h* 5g* 5m* 5m4 6.5m 5.2g2 5m3 5d2 5g] IR 4,600Y: workmanlike filly: first foal: dam Irish 9.5f and 1¼m winner at 4 yrs: generally progressive form: won sellers at Folkestone (no bid) and Lingfield (retained 4,600 gns) and nurseries for 5-lb claimer at Goodwood and Redcar, all in the summer: may be worth another try at 6f: yet to race on very soft going, acts on any other: genuine: sold 15,000 gns Newmarket December Sales. *G. A. Pritchard-Gordon*

ZANZE (USA)   2 b.f. (Feb 14) Dixieland Band (USA) – Charming Tiara (USA)   **55** p
(Alydar (USA)) [1992 7g] $320,000Y: first foal: dam unraced half-sister to Seattle

Slew, Lomond and Seattle Dancer: 10/1, around 9 lengths fifteenth of 24 in Newmarket maiden in October won by Fayfa, prominent until eased when beaten: sure to do better. *J. H. M. Gosden*

ZARANI SIDI ANNA (USA)   2 b.f. (May 6) Danzig (USA) – Emmaline (USA)   **77 p** (Affirmed (USA)) [1992 6s*] $450,000Y: close-coupled filly: fourth foal: half-sister to fairly useful 1¼m and 1½m winner My Ballerina (by Sir Ivor): dam winner at up to 9f in USA, is closely related to smart middle-distance horse Hatim and half-sister to Super Asset and Bates Motel: 13/2, and better for race, won 16-runner maiden at Newbury in October by ¾ length from The Little Ferret, chasing leaders, niggled along 2f out and staying on well: will improve, particularly over further. *M. R. Stoute*

ZAWAAHY (USA)   3 b.f. El Gran Senor (USA) 136 – Exotic Treat (USA)   **89** (Vaguely Noble 140) [1991 NR 1992 8s² 9m³ 8f* 8m⁴ 10g² 11.4d² 10.5s³ 12s] 420,000Y: angular, lightly-made filly: progressed into a fairly useful performer: won maiden at Salisbury in June: best effort when third in £11,400 handicap at Haydock: close up long way in £60,500 handicap at Ascot later in September: probably suited by about 1¼m: acts on any going. *A. A. Scott*

ZEALOUS KITTEN (USA)   4 ch.f. The Minstrel (CAN) 135 – Zealous Cat   **58** (USA) (Cougar (CHI)) [1991 12d² 12g⁴ 12m⁶ 10.1d⁴ 11.7m 8.9m 12m⁶ 10g⁵ 11.8g 12f a16g 1992 12.5g⁵ 14.6g* 17.2s* 16m] leggy, close-coupled filly: moderate mover: modest handicapper: ridden by claimer, won at Wolverhampton (by 5 lengths) and Bath (gamely) before soon struggling on good to firm ground at Goodwood later in spring: stays 17f: best efforts with give in the ground, and acts on soft: visored (below form) twice at 3 yrs. *R. J. Price*

ZEBOIM   6 ch.g. Stanford 121§ – Solarina (Solinus 130) [1991 6f² 6g* 6m* 5f 6m*   **75** 7f³ 6m⁴ 6m* 1992 6g³ 6m 6m³ 6g⁶ 6g* 7s³ 7g³] big, lengthy, workmanlike gelding: consistent handicapper: won at Folkestone in September and good efforts in big fields at Newbury and Newmarket afterwards: best at 6f/7f: acts on any going: effective with or without blinkers or visor: has won when sweating and for apprentice: is held up. *W. R. Muir*

ZENITH   2 b.f. (Feb 19) Shirley Heights 130 – Soprano 112 (Kris 135) [1992 6m³   **77** 7m² 7s² 8.5m*] lengthy, quite attractive filly: fourth foal: half-sister to 3-y-o 1½m winner Trumpet (by Dominion): dam 7.6f and 1m winner, is out of close relation to smart Rhyme Royal: fairly useful performer: well-backed odds-on chance, comfortable winner of maiden at Beverley in September, leading over 1f out and running on well under hands and heels: will stay at least 1¼m: may do better. *I. A. Balding*

ZEPPEKI (IRE)   4 b.g. Taufan (USA) 119 – Avital (Pitskelly 122) [1991 6g³ a7g⁵   **–** 7m³ 8f* 8m* 1992 8d] lengthy, good-quartered gelding: rated 70 at 3 yrs: behind only run in 1992, in April: should stay beyond 1m: probably acts on any going: below form in blinkers. *M. D. Hammond*

ZHAAB   2 b.f. (Feb 5) Shareef Dancer (USA) 135 – Pumpona (USA) (Sharpen Up   **38** 127) [1992 6d 6d 6v a8g] 620 2-y-o: stocky filly: first foal: dam, unraced, from fast family: poor maiden: stays 1m. *M. Madgwick*

ZIETEN (USA)   2 b.c. (Mar 23) Danzig (USA) – Blue Note (FR) 122 **118 p** (Habitat 134) [1992 5.5g* 6m* 5d* 6m*]

For the second time in three seasons, leading French trainer Andre Fabre sent out the winner of the Newgate Stud Middle Park Stakes at Newmarket in October, the progressive colt Zieten swooping late to keep his unbeaten record. By our reckoning, Zieten has better form to his credit than Fabre's 1990 winner Lycius at the same stage of his career, and better, too, than Lion Cavern whom Fabre saddled to finish an unfortunate second to Rodrigo de Triano in the race in 1991. The fact that Lycius and Lion Cavern went on to be placed in the Two Thousand Guineas and the Poule d'Essai des Poulains respectively might lead one to view Zieten's classic prospects in an extremely rosy light, but he's far from certain to stay a mile, and while there was talk after the Middle Park of his returning to Newmarket for the Two Thousand Guineas in May perhaps the most significant clue to his future vocation lay in his engagement in the five-furlong Prix de l'Abbaye.

Zieten went to post at Newmarket having won all his three races in France. His first two victories, in the five-and-a-half-furlong Prix Saint-Crespin, which he won by three lengths, and the six-furlong Prix La Fleche, a listed event in which he beat Creaking Board by half a length, were gained at

Newgate Stud Middle Park Stakes, Newmarket—
Zieten remains unbeaten, quickening past Pips Pride (rails) close home

Evry in early-summer, but he was then laid low by a bout of coughing and didn't make his third appearance until September when, in the five-furlong Prix d'Arenberg at Longchamp, he accounted for the subsequent Prix du Petit Couvert winner Wixon by three quarters of a length, quickening well, according to his regular rider Cauthen, until tiring as lack of condition told in the softish ground. From a choice of engagements—the five-year-old Keen Hunter eventually represented his owner Sheikh Mohammed in the Abbaye —Zieten was routed to Newmarket where he started a 5/2-shot to give the Sheikh his first Group 1 winner of the season in Britain. It also turned out to be one of the last big winners for the Sheikh's successful partnership with Steve Cauthen who was unable to agree terms for a retainer to ride for Sheikh Mohammed in 1993. Zieten's trainer Fabre, incidentally, has singlehandedly revived the French challenge that used to be such a dominant feature of the Middle Park in its heyday. The reasons behind the French shunning the race for so long can only be guessed at, but it's still surprising that French trainers, who are provided with so few opportunities within the pattern system to run their two-year-old sprinters at home, should fail to take advantage of the more plentiful, and often better endowed, options available abroad. While there were seventeen pattern races open to two-year-olds over five or six furlongs in Britain in 1992, there were only eight in France. The shortcomings in the structure of the French two-year-old pattern worked to the benefit of the Middle Park for the third year running as Zieten's participation gave the contest a much-needed boost. Apart from Silver Wizard, a very useful colt who'd beaten the subsequent Mill Reef winner Forest Wind comfortably in the BonusPrint Sirenia Stakes at Kempton and who started a heavily-backed odds-on favourite, only four other runners were declared: the tough and genuine 'Heinz 57' Phoenix Stakes winner Pips Pride, fourth to Forest Wind in the Mill Reef last time out; the well-regarded Doncaster minor event winner Factual; the seven-furlong and one-mile soft-ground winner Wootton Rivers; and the Clive Brittain-trained newcomer Virilis. Zieten won comfortably enough in the end, but only after he'd been made to fight hard. Held up in fifth place, just in front of the hard-pulling Silver Wizard, who was already giving his supporters an anxious time, Zieten was asked to take closer order as Pips Pride quickened the tempo and poached a clear advantage passing halfway. As Pips Pride kept up the gallop, Zieten couldn't make any impression initially, but upon meeting the rising ground and being shown the whip he began to pull back the leader and in the last sixty yards had too much strength for Pips Pride and won by half a length, Factual keeping on willingly to finish two and a half lengths back in third just ahead of the disappointing Silver Wizard. With Pips Pride and, more particularly, Factual running well above

949

Sheikh Mohammed's "Zieten"

their earlier form and Wootton Rivers not beaten far in fifth place, the Middle Park form looked a bit suspect at first, but the subsequent performances of Pips Pride, and, to a lesser extent, Wootton Rivers, illustrated that, if anything, it was better than it had seemed on first inspection.

Zieten, a small, angular colt who possesses a powerful round action and acts on good to firm and dead ground, is a product of a mating between the 1991 champion sire Danzig and the good French mare Blue Note. Danzig has been a regular in the top fifteen of the General Sire List in North America since his first crop were three-year-olds in 1985 and at the time of writing was well on the way to becoming the first stallion since Mr Prospector to top the General Sire List in successive seasons. Danzig's success in 1991 meant that he became only the third horse in the twentieth century to be crowned champion sire to have not won a stakes race himself: knee trouble restricted his appearances on the racecourse to just three, all of which he won by at least five lengths, and eventually forced his retirement with his three-year-old season only halfway through. Many of Danzig's runners in the States stay quite well, but he's regarded first and foremost as an influence for speed in Europe and there's not much doubt in our minds that Zieten will prove best at up to a mile, perhaps even be ideally suited by sprint distances. Zieten's dam Blue Note, a daughter of Habitat, was never raced beyond a mile in any of her thirteen starts in England and France and showed her best form at seven furlongs or less. She was very useful at two, when she won three races in minor and listed company and finished a good third in the five-furlong Prix du Petit Couvert, but was even better in her second season when she won the seven-furlong Prix de la Porte Maillot and defeated Cadeaux Genereux in the six-and-a-half-furlong Prix Maurice de Gheest, ending the year as the highest-rated home-trained filly in the five-to-seven-furlong category of the French Classifications. Blue Note is a half-sister to several winners in France, including the five-furlong to one-mile winner Balakhana, subsequently the dam of the useful 1987 French two-year-old sprinter Balawaki. Her dam Balsamique won several races on the Flat at up to eleven and a half furlongs and ended her career over jumps; her grandam Bruyere neither ran nor bred anything of note.

	Danzig (USA) (b 1977)	Northern Dancer (b 1961)	Nearctic
Zieten (USA) (b.c. Mar 23, 1990)			Natalma
		Pas de Nom (b or br 1968)	Admiral's Voyage
			Petitioner
	Blue Note (FR) (b 1985)	Habitat (b 1966)	Sir Gaylord
			Little Hut
		Balsamique (b 1973)	Tourangeau
			Bruyere

With his stable-companion Zafonic holding a first-rate chance in the Two Thousand Guineas, there's no guarantee that Zieten will even be sent to Newmarket; if he's to run in any of the classics it looks most likely to be the Poule d'Essai des Poulains in which the competition is unlikely to be so strong. If Zieten doesn't stay a mile there will be plenty of opportunities either here or in France for him to make a name for himself over shorter distances, especially as few of the better older sprinters are remaining in training and those that aren't of vintage quality. Whatever his ideal distance turns out to be, Zieten will probably make further improvement as a three-year-old. *A. Fabre, France*

ZIGGY'S PEARL (USA) 4 b.f. Ziggy's Boy – Kobette (Cyane) [1991 NR 1992 9.2m] second foal: dam won twice at up to 1m in minor company in USA as 3-y-o: successful once in sprint claimer from 8 starts on flat in USA as 2-y-o: tailed-off last over hurdles here before soundly beaten in Hamilton claimer later in May. *W. G. M. Turner*   –

ZILFI (USA) 2 b.c. (May 8) Lyphard (USA) 132 – Over Your Shoulder (USA) 77 (Graustark) [1992 a6g* 8.1s] lengthy colt: well-related to Harbour Club (by Danzig), winner in North America from 6f to 8.5f, and half-brother to a winner in USA by Mr Prospector: dam, sister to very smart American 6f to 1¼m winner Proctor, was middle-distance stayer: ½-length winner of maiden at Southwell in June: well-beaten last of 11 in minor event at Sandown over 2 months after but hampered over 2f out and not discredited: will stay 1¼m: should improve. *P. F. I. Cole*   **60 p**

ZIMZALABIM 2 b.c. (Mar 17) Damister (USA) 123 – Galaxie Dust (USA) 86 (Blushing Groom (FR) 131) [1992 5g4 6m* 6.1g2 7m 7.3s] 2,200Y: tall, good-bodied colt: has scope: third living foal: brother to 3-y-o 1¼m winner Galactic Miss: dam 2-y-o 6f winner: appeared to run excellent race (only previous success in Chester maiden auction in May) when facing very stiff task on first run for 2 months in Dewhurst Stakes at Newmarket, coming off bridle early and staying on into ninth of 11, around 12 lengths down on Zafonic: never a threat and beaten around 14 lengths in Vodafone Horris Hill Stakes at Newbury 6 days after: will stay 1m: sold 36,000 gns Newmarket Autumn Sales. *B. W. Hills*   **98 ?**

ZINAAD 3 b.c. Shirley Heights 130 – Time Charter 131 (Saritamer (USA) 130) [1991 8m* 1992 12m* 12s3] finely-made, quite attractive colt: fluent mover: 14/1 on first run for over 12 months having chipped knee bone in the spring, beat Sonus 1½ lengths in 8-runner listed race at Newmarket in October, held up, hampered 2f out then renewing challenge to win going away: favourite, creditable 3 lengths third of 8 to Up Anchor in St Simon Stakes at Newbury 23 days later, keeping on steadily from rear: will stay beyond 1½m: probably capable of better. *M. R. Stoute*   **114 p**

ZINBAQ 6 ch.h. Ahonoora 122 – Zaiyundeen (FR) (Exbury 138) [1991 a7g4 6v* 6d* 6g 7m3 7m4 6m 6g5 6m4 6v4 6m5 7g5 7g3 7.1g 7m 7g 7g 1992 a7g3 6v4 a7g 6.1d5 7g 7.1f* 8.1g 7f4 7m3 7g2 7d6 7.1s4 6s5 7s 7g] quite attractive horse: moderate mover: consistent handicapper: successful at Chepstow in June: best at 6f/7f: acts on any going, including equitrack: suitable mount for inexperienced rider: tough. *C. J. Benstead*   **42**

ZIND (IRE) 2 b.c. (Apr 3) Law Society (USA) 130 – Rose Red (USA) 92 (Northern Dancer (CAN)) [1992 8f4 8m2 7m 8d3] 78,000Y: attractive, good-topped colt: good   **108**

walker: half-brother to a winner in USA by Seattle Slew and to the dam of very useful Irish sprinter Archway and Derby winner Dr Devious: dam, Irish 2-y-o 6f winner unraced at 3 yrs, is half-sister to high-class 1m to 1½m winner Critique: very useful maiden: ran excellent races last 2 starts when around 7 lengths seventh of 11 to Zafonic in Dewhurst Stakes at Newmarket and 10 lengths third of 10 to Armiger in Racing Post Trophy at Doncaster: will be suited by middle distances: has plenty of scope, and sure to win a race. *P. W. Chapple-Hyam*

ZINGER 4 b.g. Lucky Wednesday 124 – Starkist 81 (So Blessed 130) [1991 7d* 7m 6d⁶ 6s⁴ 7g⁵ a8g 7m 8m 1992 6.9h⁵ 9f⁵ 12g 9.9m] leggy, quite good-topped gelding: poor mover: poor and inconsistent handicapper: stays 9f: probably acts any any going: often blinkered/visored. *T. Fairhurst* —

ZINJAAL (IRE) 2 b.c. (Feb 12) Jareer (USA) 115 – Penny Suprise (Tumble Wind (USA)) [1992 5s⁶ 5s 5m⁴ 7f⁶] IR 3,100F, IR 8,500Y: compact colt: second foal: half-brother to Irish 3-y-o 6f winner Recollection (by Seclude): dam unraced: poor maiden: tailed off in seller final start: sold 1,200 gns Newmarket July Sales. *B. Hanbury* **35**

ZOMAN (USA) 5 ch.h. Affirmed (USA) – A Little Affection (USA) (King Emperor (USA)) [1991 8g² 10g* 9m³ 10g² 10d* 10d5 9.7d⁴ 10v³ 1992 8.1g² 10g² 9.2d* 10s⁶ 10.4g⁶ 10d* a10f] **122**

Last, but by no means least. Five-year-old Zoman's continued good form makes him fully deserving of another *Racehorses* essay. The Prix d'Ispahan at Longchamp in May saw him gain a well-deserved first Group 1 victory, and he also won the extremely valuable Budweiser International at Laurel in October. Zoman is a tough and genuine racehorse who nearly always gives his best, but he's a few pounds below top class. His splendid record—he'd won four other pattern races earlier in his career and finished second in a classic (the Poule d'Essai des Poulains)—reflects greatly on the skill and enterprise of his trainer. Opportunities in Britain for a horse like Zoman are limited but there is no shortage of suitable races abroad. Five of Zoman's seven wins so far have been gained overseas, the only race he has won in Britain since his two-year-old days being the fairly weakly-contested Scottish Classic at Ayr as a four-year-old. Zoman showed himself clearly as good as ever when runner-up in the Forte Mile at Sandown and the Tattersalls Rogers Gold Cup at the Curragh (a race he'd won as a four-year-old) on his first two outings. Even so, it looked as if he would have to surpass himself to win the Prix d'Ispahan, in which he had finished an excellent third the previous year to Sanglamore and Priolo when the race had been run at Chantilly. Fortunately for Zoman, four of those who might have figured prominently—Selkirk, Tel Quel, Magic Night and Caerlina, all Group 1 winners—ran some way below their best. Zoman is usually prominent from the start in his races, and often makes the running. He can be a tough nut to crack once in front and kept on gamely in heavy rain at Longchamp to hold off the strong-finishing Arcangues by a neck after quickening clear early in the straight; Exit To Nowhere was one and a half lengths further away in third. Zoman's efforts in Group 1 company in Britain on his next two starts—in the Coral-Eclipse and the Juddmonte International—were slightly disappointing but he wasn't finished yet.

Prix d'Ispahan, Longchamp—
Zoman holds Arcangues in the driving rain for a first Group 1 success

Budweiser International, Laurel—Zoman finds extra to hold off Sillery

Zoman bounced back in the Budweiser International at Laurel in October, becoming the first British-trained winner of this famous Grade 1 race since Karabas, in the days when it was run as the Washington D.C. International. The Washington International, founded by the zealous John D. Schapiro, was first staged in 1952 and pioneered regular competition on turf between North American horses and horses from other continents. British-trained Wilwyn won the first running, his success surprising many sceptics in Europe who believed good horses couldn't retain their form after being flown across the Atlantic. French trainers, in particular, supported the Washington International with fervour. In thirty-six runnings before the race changed to the Budweiser International in 1988, French representatives won fourteen, only three fewer than the number of winners that represented the United States; there were two winners for Britain, and one each for Ireland (Sir Ivor), Australia and Venezuela. The race is well endowed—Zoman earned £266,273 —but its prestige has fallen off. The Washington International usually attracted a field representative of the world's finest middle-distance horses on turf and its winners regularly won end-of-season recognition as champions. However, since the distance of the race was reduced from a mile and a half to a mile and a quarter in 1986 in an attempt to bolster its flagging appeal, Sunshine Forever in 1988 is the only winner to receive an Eclipse award. Those awards, instituted in 1971, had been given to Washington International winners Run The Gantlet, Dahlia (though not in the year she won the International), Youth, Johnny D., Mac Diarmida, Bowl Game, April Run, All Along and Vanlandingham. The North American fixture list had to be revised to accommodate the Breeders' Cup, and the International was moved from its traditional November date in 1984; its timing now puts it much closer to top races in Europe, particularly to the Prix de l'Arc upon which it used to rely to produce runners. The field wasn't outstanding in 1992. Zoman survived an injury scare—he was found to have knocked a hind leg in his box overnight —and went on to put up a performance at least as good as any he'd achieved previously. Sent into the lead at around halfway, Zoman stuck to his task in typical style to hold off Sillery by a head. Sillery the third and fourth, Contested Bid and Leariva (winner of the race the previous year), were all French-trained. Zoman was sent back to the States the following month for the Breeders' Cup Classic but, starting at 75/1, he managed only twelfth to A P Indy, pushed along some way from home.

Zoman (USA) (ch.h. 1987)	Affirmed (USA) (ch 1975)	Exclusive Native (ch 1965)	Raise A Native
			Exclusive
		Won't Tell You (b 1962)	Crafty Admiral
			Scarlet Ribbon
	A Little Affection (USA) (ch 1977)	King Emperor (b 1966)	Bold Ruler
			Irish Jay
		Chicken Little (b 1966)	Olympia
			Dashing By

In appearance, Zoman is tall and lengthy, though rather sparely made. An extensive review of his pedigree antecedents isn't necessary here, as he'll be in training again in the next season. Zoman and leading American turf mare

Flawlessly were the most successful representatives in 1992 of their sire Affirmed, whose record at stud suffers by comparison to his deeds as a racehorse. He won twenty-two of his twenty-nine starts, including the triple crown, and was twice voted Horse of the Year. Zoman's dam the smart American sprinter A Little Affection was also fully tested on the racecourse, winning seven of her twenty-eight races over four seasons. Easily the pick of A Little Affection's other foals is Zoman's close relative Love And Affection (by Exclusive Era, like Affirmed a son of Exclusive Native). Love And Affection was runner-up in a Grade 1 race, the Spinaway Stakes, as a two-year-old and went on to show smart form at around a mile as a three-year-old. Zoman is effective at a mile to a mile and a quarter, and has shown his form on ground ranging from good to firm to heavy. He occasionally gives trouble being put into the stalls but is thoroughly reliable once racing. *P. F. I. Cole*

ZONK   2 ch.c. (Feb 28) Nishapour (FR) 125 – Liberty Tree 96 (Dominion 123)   **51** [1992 8d 8d] 7,400Y: sturdy colt: fourth foal: half-brother to fair sprinter Tango Time (by Music Boy) and 1m winner Take A Liberty (by Aragon): dam 6f to 1m winner: green and burly, in midfield in maidens at Redcar in October. *J. Pearce*

ZOOM LENS (IRE)   3 ch.f. Caerleon (USA) 132 – Photo 83 (Blakeney 126) [1991   **65** 7m³ 7g⁵ 1992 10g⁴ 12.2d⁴ 16s a14g⁶] small filly: modest maiden: should have proved suited by further than 1½m: acted on good to firm and dead ground: stud. *J. L. Dunlop*

ZUHAL   4 b.f. Busted 134 – Divine Thought 102 (Javelot 124) [1991 9.9f³ 7.1g⁵   **60** 10m⁶ 12.1s 1992 14d³ 13.3g⁶] lengthy, angular filly: maiden handicapper: not seen out again after running moderately in June: will stay 2m: acts on good to firm and dead ground, seemingly not soft: sold 4,400 gns Newmarket December Sales. *H. Thomson Jones*

ZUNO WARRIOR   2 b.c. (Mar 28) Dominion 123 – Hanglands (Bustino 136)   **96** [1992 5s⁴ 5g* 5d³ 6.1d* 6g² 7f²] 15,500Y: sturdy, good-quartered colt: good mover: third foal: brother to a poor maiden: dam lightly raced: progressive colt: successful in Warwick maiden in April and minor event at Chester in July: second in nurseries after at Ascot and Brighton: will be better suited by 1m: strong-galloping sort. *G. Lewis*

EVERY TWO MONTHS
COMPLETE INFORMATION
ON FRENCH GROUP RACES,
SALES AND MAJOR EVENTS,
PEDIGREES OF ALL GROUP
WINNERS, UP-TO-DATE
STATISTICS.

SUBSCRIPTION FORM :
1 YEAR SUBSCRIPTION
FOR 6 ISSUES INCLUDING
ETALONS 1993 :

☐ E.C., CH, A : 580 FF
☐ OTHER EUROPE : 650 FF
☐ USA, CANADA, MIDDLE-
EAST : 750 FF
☐ SOUTH AMERICA, AFRICA,
JAPAN, ASIA : 850 F
☐ AUSTRALIA,
NEW ZEALAND : 900 FF

M. _____

ADDRESS _____

_____

COUNTRY _____

☐ BY CHEQUE, MADE OUT TO:
ETALONS
☐ BY VISA CARD
CARD NUMBER :

⌷⌷⌷⌷⌷⌷⌷⌷⌷⌷⌷⌷⌷⌷⌷⌷

VALID DATE :　　　⌷⌷⌷⌷
SIGNATURE

COURSES & ELEVAGE

THE FRENCH PERSPECTIVE ON HORSE RACING AND BREEDING.
SINCE 1954

Published by ETALONS: 6, rond-point des Champs-Elysées 75008 Paris - France
Tel: (33) 1 43 59 94 14 - Fax: (33) 1 43 59 94 41

ST JOVITE

TIMEFORM
HORSE OF
THE YEAR

TIMEFORM CHAMPIONS OF 1992

HORSE OF THE YEAR
BEST MIDDLE-DISTANCE HORSE
(RATED AT 135)

ST JOVITE (USA)

3 b.c. Pleasant Colony – Northern Sunset (Northfields)
Owner Mrs V. Kraft Payson   Trainer J. Bolger

BEST TWO-YEAR-OLD COLT (RATED AT 131p)

ARMIGER

2 ch.c. Rainbow Quest – Armeria (Northern Dancer)
Owner Mr K. Abdulla   Trainer H. Cecil

BEST TWO-YEAR-OLD FILLY (RATED AT 116p)

SAYYEDATI

2 b.f. Shadeed – Dubian (High Line)
Owner Mr M. Obaida   Trainer C. Brittain

BEST THREE-YEAR-OLD FILLY (RATED AT 128)

USER FRIENDLY

3 b.f. Slip Anchor – Rostova (Blakeney)
Owner Mr W. J. Gredley   Trainer C. Brittain

BEST SPRINTER (RATED AT 128)

SHEIKH ALBADOU

4 b.c. Green Desert – Sanctuary (Welsh Pageant)
Owner Mr H. Salem   Trainer A. Scott

BEST MILERS (RATED AT 129)

LAHIB (USA)

4 b.c. Riverman – Lady Cutlass (Cutlass)
Owner Hamdan Al-Maktoum   Trainer J. Dunlop

SELKIRK (USA)

4 ch.c. Sharpen Up – Annie Edge (Nebbiolo)
Owner Mr G. Strawbridge   Trainer I. Balding

BEST STAYING PERFORMANCE (RATED AT 123)

MASHAALLAH (USA)

4 b.c. Nijinsky – Homespun (Round Table)
Owner Sheikh Ahmed Al-Maktoum   Trainer J. Gosden

THE TIMEFORM 'TOP HUNDRED'

Here are listed the 'Top 100' two-year-olds, three-year-olds and older horses in the annual.

Two-Year-Olds

131p	Armiger
126p	Zafonic
125p	Tenby
119p	Blush Rambler
119	Basim
118p	Zieten
117p	Kadounor
116p	Sayyedati
115p	Inchinor
115	Firm Pledge
115	Lyric Fantasy
115	Pips Pride
114	Wixon
113p	Fatherland
113p	Ivanka
113p	Seaton Delaval
113	Marchand de Sable
113	Pelder
112p	Beggarman Thief
112p	Gold Splash
112p	Yawl
112	Arinthod
112	Chancetobewild
112	Infrasonic
112	Silver Wizard
111p	Corrazona
111p	Dernier Empereur
111p	Forest Wind
111p	Kindergarten
111p	Mil Foil
111p	Richard of York
111p	Shemaka
111	Dancienne
111	Didyme
111	Ranger
111	Revelation
110	Borodislew
110	Devil's Rock
110	Kingmambo
110	Love of Silver
110	Sharp Prod
109p	Elizabeth Bay
109p	Sueboog
108p	Ardkinglass
108p	Bin Ajwaad
108p	Factual
108	Cox Orange
108	Glorieux Dancer
108	Petardia
108	Rouquette
108	Splendent
108	Zind
107p	Barathea
107p	Scribe
107p	Wharf
107	Frenchpark
107	Marillette
107	Maroof
107	Master Peace

107	Nominator
107	Son Pardo
106p	Up And At 'Em
106	Berdansk
106	Desert Secret
106	Firm Friend
106	Lorelie
106	Poker Chip
106	Rain Brother
106	Right Win
106	Wootton Rivers
105p	Blues Traveller
105p	Madeleine's Dream
105	Canaska Star
105	Geisway
105	Green's Bid
105	Marina Park
104P	Criquette
104p	White Crown
104	Fastness
104	Honor And Pride
104	Secrage
103p	Saint Express
103p	Satank
103	Fyfield Flyer
103	Urgent Request
102p	Lindon Lime
102	Fitzcarraldo
102	Sissingaya
101p	Sumoto
101	Ajfan
101	Ventiquattrofogli
100P	Taos
100p	Khoraz
100p	Thawakib
100	Ansellman
100	Darbonne
100	King Paris
100	Lost Soldier
100	Niche
100	Sabre Rattler
100	Shahik

Three-Year-Olds

135	St Jovite
130	Rodrigo de Triano
128	User Friendly
127	Dr Devious
126	Brief Truce
124	All At Sea
124	Arazi
124	Marling
124	Pursuit of Love
123	Jolypha
123	Silver Wisp
122	Alhijaz
122	My Memoirs
122	Shuailaan
121	Jeune

121	Petit Loup
121	Songlines
121	Zaahi
120p	Inner City
120	Apple Tree
120	Contested Bid
120	Daros
120	Ezzoud
120	Hatoof
120	Homme de Loi
120	Polytain
120	Seattle Rhyme
120	Sonus
120	Wolfhound
119p	Masad
119	Bonny Scot
119	Cardoun
119	Kitwood
119	Platini
119	Shanghai
119	Silvernesian
119	Steinbeck
118p	Cunning
118	Assessor
118	Culture Vulture
118	Lucky Lindy
118	Rainbow Corner
117p	Garden of Heaven
117	Alnasr Alwasheek
117	Free Flyer
117	Hydro Calido
117	Lion Cavern
117	Marble Maiden
117	Marignan
117	Market Booster
117	Modhish
117	Muhtarram
117	Rosefinch
117	Sheba Dancer
117	Sporades
117	Thourios
117	Urban Sea
117	Verveine
116p	Andros Bay
116	Beyton
116	Prince Ferdinand
116	Showbrook
116	Take Risks
116	Trishyde
116	Twist And Turn
116§	Adieu Au Roi
115	Aljadeer
115	Calling Collect
115	Dadarissime
115	Dilum
115	Good To Dance
115	Guislaine
115	Johann Quatz
115	Kenbu
115	La Favorita
115	Modernise

115	Pollen Count	119p	Vintage Crop
115	Western Approach	119	Blyton Lad
114p	Zinaad	119	Keen Hunter
114	Absurde	119	Perpendicular
114	Bold N'Flashy	119	Ruby Tiger
114	Freddie Lloyd	119	Sought Out
114	Great Palm	119	Star of Cozzene
114	In A Tiff	118p	Serrant
114	Perfect Circle	118	Knifebox
114	River Nymph	118	Monde Bleu
114	Up Anchor	118	Red Bishop
113p	Hazaam	118	Rudimentary
113	Arrikala	117	Corrupt
113	Bezelle	117	Diamonds Galore
113	Djais	117	Erdelistan
113	Euphonic	117	Suave Dancer
113	King's Loch	117	Toulon
113	Sharpitor	116	Acteur Francais
113	Spartan Shareef	116	Dream Talk
113	Torrey Canyon	116	Fortune's Wheel
113	Young Senor	116	Further Flight
112	Alflora	116	Goofalik
112	Captain Horatius	116	Man From Eldorado
112	Dajraan	115	Dariyoun
112	Ivyanna	115	George Augustus
112	Linnga	115	Half A Tick
112	Mack The Knife	115	Luchiroverte
112	Mojave	115	Silicon Bavaria
112	Palomelle	114	Flowing
112	Spring	114	Jahafil
112	Stubass	114	Northern Crystal
		114	Snaadee
		114§	Arcadian Heights
Older Horses		113	Approach The Bench
		113	Caerlina
133	Pistolet Bleu	113	Dampierre
131	Subotica	113	Karinga Bay
129	Lahib	113	Robin des Pins
129	Selkirk	113	Runyon
128	Sheikh Albadou	113	Star of Gdansk
127	Dear Doctor	113	Villandry
127	Second Set	113?	Gussy Marlowe
126	Saddlers' Hall	112p	Mellottie
126	Vert Amande	112	Cherry Grove Lad
125	Kooyonga	112	Fabulous Hostess
125	Mr Brooks	112	Ile de Chypre
125	Opera House	112	Lara's Idea
124	Rock Hopper	112	Leariva
124	Sapience	112	Mohican Girl
124§	Shalford	112	Montendre
123	Mashaallah	112	Witness Box
123	Sikeston	111p	Lochsong
123	Tel Quel	111	Always Friendly
123	Wiorno	111	Commendable
122	Environment Friend	111	Desert Sun
122	Exit To Nowhere	111	Norwich
122	Magic Night	111	Secret Haunt
122	Sillery	111	Turgeon
122	Snurge	110	Amigo Menor
122	Zoman	110	Arranvanna
121	Arcangues	110	Cardmania
121	Drum Taps	110	Notley
121	Elbio	110	Rambo's Hall
121	Lomitas	110	Shambo
120	Misil	110	Spaniards Close
120	Saganeca	110	Spinning
120	Terimon	110	Steerforth
120	Young Buster	110	Street Rebel

TIMEFORM COMPUTER TIMEFIGURES

Timefigures measure the performance of horses not on their form one against another but in terms of time, in seconds (per five furlongs) faster or slower than a certain fixed standard. The following tables show the best timefigure recorded by the leading horses—judged on time—in each category in 1992. Next to the timefigure is the equivalent timerating in pounds, directly comparable with the Timeform Ratings in this annual volume.

TWO-YEAR-OLDS

1	ARMIGER	−1.00	125
2	LYRIC FANTASY	−0.62	116
3	BARATHEA	−0.56	114
4	PETARDIA	−0.55	114
5	IVANKA	−0.54	114
6	ZAFONIC	−0.53	113
7	MAROOF	−0.50	113
8	HUMAM	−0.42	111
9	UP AND AT 'EM	−0.40	110
10	AJFAN	−0.36	109
11	RIGHT WIN	−0.36	109
12	ZEITEN	−0.31	108
13	SPLENDENT	−0.29	107
14	TENBY	−0.28	107
15	TAOS	−0.27	107
16	BEGGARMAN THIEF	−0.27	107
17	SO FACTUAL	−0.26	107
18	NEEDLE GUN	−0.26	107
19	STORM CANYON	−0.25	106
20	WHARF	−0.24	106
21	FITZCARRALDO	−0.23	106
22	SILVER WIZARD	−0.22	106
23	CANASKA STAR	−0.21	105
24	ARDKINGLASS	−0.21	105
25	GREEN'S BID	−0.19	105
26	PIPS PRIDE	−0.18	105
27	INCHINOR	−0.17	104
28	SHEBL	−0.16	104
29	YAWL	−0.14	104
30	SAYYEDATI	−0.13	103

THREE-YEAR-OLD SPRINTERS

1	WESTERN APPROACH	−0.72	118
2	FREDDIE LLOYD	−0.53	113
3	PURSUIT OF LOVE	−0.28	107
4	PRINCE FERDINAND	−0.25	106
5	WOLFHOUND	−0.22	106
6	ORTHORHOMBUS	−0.20	105
7	KAYVEE	−0.17	104
8	PARIS HOUSE	−0.13	103
9	KING'S SYGNET	−0.11	103
10	SPLICE	−0.08	102

THREE-YEAR-OLD MILERS

1	DR DEVIOUS	−1.07	127
2	ALNASR ALWASHEEK	−1.02	126
3	BRIEF TRUCE	−0.96	124
4	MARLING	−0.79	120
5	YOUNG SENOR	−0.78	120
6	IRISH MEMORY	−0.62	116
7	ZAAHI	−0.61	115
8	TWIST AND TURN	−0.59	115
9	EZZOUD	−0.54	114
10	ALHIJAZ	−0.53	113

THREE-YEAR-OLD MIDDLE DISTANCE

1	RODRIGO DE TRIANO	−1.21	130
2	ALL AT SEA	−1.01	125
3	DR DEVIOUS	−0.90	123
4	SEATTLE RHYME	−0.90	123
5	INNER CITY	−0.83	121
6	POLLEN COUNT	−0.78	120
7	ALJADEER	−0.77	119
8	USER FRIENDLY	−0.77	119
9	MASAD	−0.67	117
10	ALNASR ALWASHEEK	−0.62	116

THREE-YEAR-OLD STAYERS

1	RAIN RIDER	−0.35	109
2	BRIER CREEK	−0.22	106
3	ALLEGAN	−0.18	105
4	LANDOWNER	−0.12	103
5	THREE WELLS	0.02	100
6	AL KARNAK	0.02	100
7	DARU	0.12	97
8	NOT IN DOUBT	0.14	97
9	USER FRIENDLY	0.15	96
10	BELGRAN	0.18	96

OLDER HORSE
SPRINTERS

1	SHALFORD	−0.95	124
2	MR BROOKS	−0.90	123
3	SHEIKH ALBADOU	−0.79	120
4	DIAMONDS GALORE	−0.66	117
5	VICEROY	−0.65	116
6	ELBIO	−0.62	116
7	BLYTON LAD	−0.38	110
8	MEDAILLE D'OR	−0.37	109
9	TBAB	−0.35	109
10	SIZZLING SAGA	−0.33	108

OLDER HORSE
MILERS

1	LAHIB	−1.17	129
2	RUDIMENTARY	−1.04	126
3	SELKIRK	−0.98	125
4	SECOND SET	−0.90	123
5	SIKESTON	−0.81	120
6	SHEIKH ALBADOU	−0.70	118
7	EXIT TO NOWHERE	−0.57	114
8	SURE SHARP	−0.50	113
9	STAR OF COZZENE	−0.50	113
10	ILE DE CHYPRE	−0.50	113

OLDER HORSE
MIDDLE DISTANCE

1	OPERA HOUSE	−0.78	120
2	KOOYONGA	−0.78	120
3	SADDLERS' HALL	−0.68	117
4	SAPIENCE	−0.66	117
5	SPINNING	−0.62	116
6	DEAR DOCTOR	−0.61	115
7	ROCK HOPPER	−0.59	115
8	ZOMAN	−0.59	115
9	SUBOTICA	−0.56	114
10	TERIMON	−0.54	114

OLDER HORSE
STAYERS

1	DRUM TAPS	−0.38	110
2	ARCADIAN HEIGHTS	−0.37	109
3	STEERFORTH	−0.37	109
4	VINTAGE CROP	−0.36	109
5	TURGEON	−0.17	104
6	ENDOLI	−0.13	103
7	WITNESS BOX	−0.08	102
8	HAWAIT AL BARR	−0.06	102
9	GONDOLIER	−0.05	101
10	CASTLE COURAGEOUS	0.03	99

1992 STATISTICS (TURF SEASON)

The following tables show the leading owners, trainers, breeders, jockeys, horses and sires of winners during the 1992 turf season, under Jockey Club Rules. The tables are reproduced by permission of *The Sporting Life*.

OWNERS

		Horses	Races Won	Stakes £
1.	Sheikh Mohammed	230	185	1,194,368
2.	Hamdan Al-Maktoum	174	103	694,894
3.	R. E. Sangster	76	47	677,228
4.	K. Abdulla	90	76	620,351
5.	Maktoum Al-Maktoum	79	34	435,151
6.	W. J. Gredley	15	9	415,621
7.	Sidney H. Craig	1	1	355,000
8.	Lord Weinstock	20	21	295,231
9.	Lord Carnarvon	12	14	265,167
10.	Mrs Virginia Kraft Payson	1	1	261,216
11.	Fahd Salman	69	51	259,207
12.	Sheikh Ahmed Al-Maktoum	65	34	213,184

TRAINERS

		Horses	Races Won	Stakes £
1.	R. Hannon	198	147	1,154,201
2.	P. W. Chapple-Hyam	66	41	989,499
3.	C. E. Brittain	126	63	972,327
4.	M. R. Stoute	131	74	863,611
5.	H. R. A. Cecil	112	109	735,358
6.	J. H. M. Gosden	133	111	727,778
7.	J. L. Dunlop	116	75	524,173
8.	I. A. Balding	69	36	499,096
9.	G. Wragg	45	42	494,689
10.	P. F. I. Cole	119	84	429,687
11.	Lord Huntingdon	70	53	380,015
12.	L. M. Cumani	85	54	357,579

BREEDERS

		Individ'l Winners	Races Won	Stakes £
1.	Swettenham Stud	33	49	759,532
2.	Juddmonte Farms	49	68	568,675
3.	Stetchworth Park Stud Ltd	9	15	429,787
4.	Lyonstown Stud	3	3	359,791
5.	Ballymacoll Stud Farm Ltd	16	26	317,196
6.	Sheikh Mohammed	31	53	292,168
7.	Hamdan Al-Maktoum	2	4	269,218
8.	Mrs Virginia Kraft Payson	1	1	261,216

JOCKEYS

		1st	2nd	3rd	Unpl	Total Mts	Per Cent
1.	M. Roberts	206	146	113	603	1068	19.3
2.	Pat Eddery	178	118	76	359	731	24.4
3.	W. Carson	125	120	107	504	856	14.6

		1st	2nd	3rd	Unpl	Total Mts	Per Cent
4.	T. Quinn	108	121	81	468	778	13.9
5.	G. Duffield	108	70	59	466	703	15.4
6.	S. Cauthen	107	85	72	293	557	19.2
7.	L. Dettori	101	82	76	420	679	14.9
8.	R. Cochrane	100	96	104	479	779	12.8
9.	W. Ryan	96	103	91	401	691	13.9
10.	J. Reid	95	78	89	442	704	13.5
11.	K. Darley	91	85	61	325	562	16.2
12.	W. R. Swinburn	82	86	76	279	523	15.7

HORSES

		Races Won	Stakes £
1.	Rodrigo de Triano 3 ch.c.		
	El Gran Senor – Hot Princess	3	494,764
2.	User Friendly 3 b.f.		
	Slip Anchor – Rostova	5	402,905
3.	Dr Devious 3 ch.c.		
	Ahonoora – Rose of Jericho	1	355,000
4.	Lahib 4 b.c.		
	Riverman – Lady Cutlass	2	263,311
5.	St Jovite 3 b.c.		
	Pleasant Colony – Northern Sunset	1	261,216
6.	Lyric Fantasy 2 b.f.		
	Tate Gallery – Flying Melody	5	185,605
7.	Marling 3 b.f.		
	Lomond – Marwell	2	184,586
8.	Saddlers' Hall 4 b.c.		
	Sadler's Wells – Sunny Valley	4	179,323

SIRES OF WINNERS

		Horses	Races Won	Stakes £
1.	El Gran Senor (1981) by Northern Dancer	11	19	564,008
2.	Sadler's Wells (1981) by Northern Dancer	30	49	563,048
3.	Slip Anchor (1982) by Shirley Heights	16	29	529,304
4.	Ahonoora (1975) by Lorenzaccio	20	28	519,763
5.	Riverman (1969) by Never Bend	10	15	353,532
6.	Green Desert (1983) by Danzig	28	42	350,501
7.	Persian Bold (1975) by Bold Lad	17	28	283,332
8.	Rainbow Quest (1981) by Blushing Groom	24	35	267,338

FIRST SEASON SIRES OF WINNERS

		Horses	Races Won	Stakes £
1.	Chilibang (1984) by Formidable	6	9	25,431
2.	Persian Heights (1985) by Persian Bold	5	7	25,183
3.	Jareer (1983) by Northern Dancer	6	9	20,096
4.	Salt Dome (1983) by Blushing Groom	4	5	16,495
5.	Mtoto (1983) by Busted	4	4	16,290
6.	Soviet Star (1984) by Nureyev	4	5	15,097
7.	Interrex (1984) by Vice Regent	5	6	14,890
8.	Entitled (1984) by Mill Reef	1	3	14,196

THE FREE HANDICAP

TWO-YEAR-OLDS

The following are the weights allotted in the European Free Handicap published on 14th January. The race is to be run over seven furlongs at Newmarket on 14th April, 1993.

	st	lb		st	lb		st	lb
Zafonic	9	7	Love of Silver	8	7	Power of Polly	8	3
Armiger	9	6	Pips Pride	8	7	Ribbonwood	8	3
Lyric Fantasy	9	4	Secrage	8	7	Wootton Rivers	8	3
Tenby	9	4	White Crown	8	7	Bright Generation	8	2
Basim	9	0	Beggarman Thief	8	6	Colyan	8	2
Blush Rambler	9	0	Berdansk	8	6	Emperor Jones	8	2
Son Pardo	8	13	Borodislew	8	6	Factual	8	2
Ardkinglass	8	12	Dancienne	8	6	Katiba	8	2
Creaking Board	8	12	Dancing Bloom	8	6	Lost Soldier	8	2
Firm Pledge	8	12	Dernier Empereur	8	6	Majestic Hawk	8	2
Inchinor	8	12	Didyme	8	6	Pembroke	8	2
Wharf	8	12	Geisway	8	6	Poker Chip	8	2
Canaska Star	8	11	Ivanka	8	6	Redenham	8	2
Sayyedati	8	11	Marina Park	8	6	Revelation	8	2
Fatherland	8	10	Millyant	8	6	Sabre Rattler	8	2
Forest Wind	8	10	Ranger	8	6	Shebl	8	2
Kadounor	8	10	Shemaka	8	6	Ansellman	8	1
Kingmambo	8	10	Sueboog	8	6	Bob's Return	8	1
Seaton Delaval	8	10	Taos	8	6	Criquette	8	1
Wixon	8	10	Thawakib	8	6	Declassified	8	1
Yawl	8	10	Up And At 'Em	8	6	Fortune Cay	8	1
Zieten	8	10	Zind	8	6	Needle Gun	8	1
Barathea	8	9	Darbonne	8	5	Planetary Aspect	8	1
Gold Splash	8	9	Marillette	8	5	Saint Express	8	1
Maroof	8	9	Nominator	8	5	Satank	8	1
Mil Foil	8	9	Perfect Halo	8	5	Sea Gazer	8	1
Pelder	8	9	Right Win	8	5	Storm Canyon	8	1
Petardia	8	9	Sumoto	8	5	Urgent Request	8	1
Sharp Prod	8	9	Woodchat	8	5	Antester	8	0
Splendent	8	9	Ajfan	8	4	Carbon Steel	8	0
Earl of Barking	8	8	Bashayer	8	4	Dahyah	8	0
Elizabeth Bay	8	8	Blues Traveller	8	4	Felawnah	8	0
Green's Bid	8	8	Chaddleworth	8	4	Felucca	8	0
Kindergarten	8	8	Fyfield Flyer	8	4	Finmental	8	0
Marchand de Sable	8	8	Gabr	8	4	First Veil	8	0
Queen's View	8	8	King Paris	8	4	Fitzcarraldo	8	0
Richard of York	8	8	Mystic Goddess	8	4	Iviza	8	0
Silver Wizard	8	8	Niche	8	4	Kamaatera	8	0
So Factual	8	8	Placerville	8	4	Kharaj	8	0
Arinthod	8	7	Salatin	8	4	Little Too Much	8	0
Chancetobewild	8	7	Toocando	8	4	Lord President	8	0
Corrazona	8	7	Bin Ajwaad	8	3	Mukhamedov	8	0
Desert Secret	8	7	Catrail	8	3	Port Lucaya	8	0
Devil's Rock	8	7	Lindon Lime	8	3	Roger The Butler	8	0
Glorieux Dancer	8	7	Newton's Law	8	3	Tioman Island	8	0
Humam	8	7	Palacegate			Wathik	8	0
Infrasonic	8	7	Episode	8	3			

BRITISH CLASSIFICATIONS

The following were published on 14th January, 1993 and contain horses trained in Great Britain which ran during 1992, and were assessed at a rating of 100 or above by the Official Handicappers. Horses racing over different distances and being top rated, are credited with those performances by inclusion in the appropriate division.

THREE-YEAR-OLDS

5 furlongs plus
121 Pursuit of Love
116 Freddie Lloyd
113 Paris House
110 Swing Low
110 Twafeaj
110 Western
    Approach
109 Central City
109 Hamas
106 Fylde Flyer
106 Rose Indien
105 Artistic Reef
104 Garah
104 Harvest Girl
102 Heather Bank
100 Colway Bold
100 Spanish Storm

7 furlongs plus
126 Marling
122 Alhijaz
121 Zaahi
119 Inner City
119 Thourios
118 Ezzoud
118 Lucky Lindy
118 Rainbow Corner
117 Culture Vulture
117 Prince Ferdinand
117 Wolfhound
116 Dilum
116 Modernise
115 Perfect Circle
114 Calling Collect

114 Hazaam
113 Fair Cop
112 Toussaud
111 Casteddu
111 Mojave
111 Young Senor
110 Rokeby
110 Spartan Shareef
110 Torrey Canyon
109 Feminine Wiles
109 Night
    Manoeuvres
108 Storm Dove
108 Tik Fa
107 Musicale
106 A-To-Z
106 Reported
105 Cloud of Dust
105 Katakana
105 Wiedniu
103 Distinct
    Thatcher
103 John Rose
103 Midnight Air
103 River Falls
103 Speaker's House
102 Amwag
102 Badie
102 Misterioso
102 Soiree
102 Wilde Rufo
100 King Olaf

9½ furlongs plus
127 Rodrigo
    de Triano

121 Shuailaan
119 Seattle Rhyme
118 Alnasr
    Alwasheek
118 Free Flyer
118 Masad
118 Twist And Turn
114 Great Palm
113 Pollen Count
113 Sharpitor
112 Aljadeer
112 Party Cited
111 Oumaldaaya
108 Red Slippers
107 Fast Manouvre
107 King's Loch
106 Peto
103 Highland Dress
102 Arbusha
101 Bobzao
100 Citiqueen
100 Mystery Play

11 furlongs plus
125 Dr Devious
124 User Friendly
122 My Memoirs
121 Silver Wisp
119 Bonny Scot
118 Cunning
117 Garden of
    Heaven
117 Silvernesian
116 Jeune
116 Muhtarram
115 Daros

114 Beyton
112 Captain Horatius
111 Alflora
111 Armarama
110 Bineyah
110 Guilty Secret
109 Binkhaldoun
109 Niodini
107 Mack The Knife
107 Zinaad
106 Colorific
106 Only Royale
106 Spring
106 Up Anchor
105 Saratoga Source
103 Alphard
103 Blushing Storm
101 Anne Bonny
101 Kasmayo
100 Daru
100 Pearl Angel
100 Tapis Rouge

14 furlongs plus
122 User Friendly
119 Sonus
115 Assessor
110 Landowner
110 Rain Rider
108 Jape
107 Anna of Saxony
106 Allegan
103 Shirley Valentine
101 Brier Creek

FOUR-YEAR-OLDS AND UPWARDS

5 furlongs plus
127 Sheikh Albadou
122 Shalford
121 Mr Brooks
117 Elbio
117 Keen Hunter
116 Blyton Lad
114 Snaadee
112 Montendre
111 Lochsong
110 Notley
109 Amigo Menor
107 Spaniards Close
107 Viceroy
106 Case Law
105 Medaille d'Or
104 Night Jar
101 Chicarica
100 Sizzling Saga

7 furlongs plus
128 Selkirk
126 Lahib
126 Second Set
122 Sikeston
118 Rudimentary
112 Mellottie
111 Flying Brave

111 Sure Sharp
110 Desert Sun
110 Gussy Marlowe
109 Bog Trotter
109 Norwich
109 Susurration
108 Enharmonic
108 Melpomene
106 Crystal Path
106 Lech
106 Mystiko
106 Norton
     Challenger
105 Rambo's Hall
103 Lovealoch
102 Ajaad
102 Pfalz
101 Consigliere
101 Military Fashion
101 Two Left Feet
100 Badawi
100 Sylva Honda

9 ½ furlongs plus
121 Environment
     Friend
120 Ruby Tiger
119 Zoman

118 Knifebox
118 Perpendicular
117 Young Buster
114 Corrupt
111 Half A Tick
110 Karinga Bay
108 Ile de Chypre
108 Mohican Girl
106 Flashfoot
105 Fair Average
105 Jura
103 Revif
101 Lupescu
101 St Ninian
100 Linpac West
100 Mesleh

11 furlongs plus
124 Saddlers' Hall
123 Opera House
122 Rock Hopper
122 Sapience
121 Terimon
120 Mashaallah
117 Always Friendly
115 Red Bishop
114 Spinning
113 Jahafil

112 Luchiroverte
110 Secret Haunt
108 Adam Smith
107 Surrealist
104 Matador
103 Marcus Thorpe
102 Parting Moment
100 Fragrant Hill

14 furlongs plus
119 Rock Hopper
118 Snurge
117 Drum Taps
115 Further Flight
113 Arcadian Heights
112 Witness Box
109 Endoli
106 Shambo
106 Tyrone Bridge
105 Michelozzo
104 Al Mutahm
104 Per Quod
103 Supreme Choice
101 Duke of Paducah
101 Steerforth
100 Hieroglyphic
100 Romany Rye

INTERNATIONAL CLASSIFICATIONS

The following were published on 14th January, 1993 and contain horses which, during 1992, ran in France, Germany, Great Britain, Ireland or Italy, and were jointly assessed at a rating of 110 or above by the Official Handicappers. Horses racing over different distances and being top rated, are credited with those performances by inclusion in the appropriate division.

TWO-YEAR-OLDS

125 Zafonic	114 Wixon	112 Richard of York	111 Borodislew
124 Armiger	114 Yawl	112 Silver Wizard	110 Creaking Board
122 Lyric Fantasy	114 Zieten	112 So Factual	110 Dancienne
122 Tenby	113 Barathea	111 Arinthod	110 Dancing Bloom
118 Basim	113 Gold Splash	111 Chancetobewild	110 Dernier
118 Blush Rambler	113 Maroof	111 Corrazona	Empereur
117 Son Pardo	113 Mil Foil	111 Desert Secret	110 Didyme
116 Ardkinglass	113 Pelder	111 Devil's Rock	110 Geisway
116 Firm Pledge	113 Petardia	111 Glorieux Dancer	110 Ivanka
116 Inchinor	113 Sharp Prod	111 Humam	110 Marina Park
116 Wharf	113 Splendent	111 Infrasonic	110 Millyant
115 Canaska Star	112 Earl of Barking	111 Love of Silver	110 Ranger
115 Sayyedati	112 Elizabeth Bay	111 Pip's Pride	110 Shemaka
114 Fatherland	112 Green's Bid	111 Secrage	110 Sueboog
114 Forest Wind	112 Kindergarten	111 White Crown	110 Taos
114 Kadounor	112 Marchand	110 Beggarman	110 Thawakib
114 Kingmambo	de Sable	Thief	110 Up And At 'Em
114 Seaton Delaval	112 Queen's View	110 Berdansk	110 Zind

THREE-YEAR-OLDS

5 furlongs plus	117 Lion Cavern	9½ furlongs plus	11 furlongs plus
121 Pursuit of Love	117 Prince Ferdinand	127 Rodrigo	135 St Jovite
116 Freddie Lloyd	117 Steinbeck	de Triano	125 Dr Devious
114 Bold N'Flashy	117 Wolfhound	121 Shuailaan	124 User Friendly
114 Showbrook	116 Dilum	120 Jolypha	122 My Memoirs
113 Paris House	116 Kenbu	119 Homme de Loi	121 Silver Wisp
112 Bezelle	116 Marble Maiden	119 Seattle Rhyme	120 Platini
110 Park Dream	116 Modernise	118 Alnasr	119 Bonny Scot
110 Swing Low	115 Judge Decision	Alwasheek	119 Polytain
110 Twafeaj	115 Perfect Circle	118 Free Flyer	118 Apple Tree
110 Wedding of	115 River Majesty	118 Masad	118 Cunning
The Sea	114 Calling Collect	118 Twist And Turn	117 Garden of
110 Western	114 Hazaam	117 Sheba Dancer	Heaven
Approach	114 Hydro Calido	117 Verveine	117 Market Booster
	114 Sporades	115 Adieu Au Roi	117 Silvernesian
7 furlongs plus	113 Fair Cop	115 Johann Quatz	117 Songlines
126 Marling	113 Highest Ody	114 Great Palm	117 Urban Sea
123 Brief Truce	113 Take Risks	114 Guislaine	116 Jeune
122 Alhijaz	112 Absurde	114 Rosefinch	116 Marignan
122 Arazi	112 La Favorita	113 Pollen Count	116 Muhtarram
121 All At Sea	112 Toussaud	113 Sharpitor	116 Petit Loup
121 Zaahi	111 Casteddu	112 Aljadeer	116 Trishyde
119 Cardoun	111 Euphonic	112 Fast Cure	115 Contested Bid
119 Hatoof	111 Mojave	112 Guado	115 Daros
119 Inner City	111 Stubass	d'Annibale	115 Modhish
119 Shanghai	111 Young Senor	112 Party Cited	114 Arrikala
119 Thourios	110 Luazur	111 Arastou	114 Beyton
118 Ezzoud	110 Rokeby	111 Khanata	114 Pik Konig
118 Kitwood	110 Spartan Shareef	111 Oumaldaaya	113 In A Tiff
118 Lucky Lindy	110 Tertian	111 River Nymph	113 Revasser
118 Rainbow Corner	110 Torrey Canyon	110 Break Bread	113 Trampoli
117 Culture Vulture	110 Wedding Ring		112 Captain Horatius

112 Carlton
112 Merzouk
112 Natiello
112 Rougeur
111 Alflora
111 Armarama

111 Good To Dance
110 Andros Bay
110 Bineyah
110 Colon
110 Grand Plaisir
110 Guilty Secret

110 Ivyanna
110 Linnga
110 Non Partisan

14 furlongs plus
122 User Friendly

119 Sonus
115 Assessor
110 Dadarissime
110 Landowner
110 Rain Rider

FOUR-YEAR-OLDS AND UPWARDS

5 furlongs plus
127 Sheikh Albadou
122 Shalford
121 Mr Brooks
117 Diamonds Galore
117 Elbio
117 Keen Hunter
116 Blyton Lad
116 Monde Bleu
114 Cardmania
114 Dream Talk
114 Snaadee
112 Flowing
112 Montendre
111 Lochsong
110 Arranvanna
110 Ganges
110 Notley
110 Reference Light
110 Street Rebel

7 furlongs plus
128 Selkirk
126 Lahib
126 Second Set
122 Misil
122 Sikeston
121 Exit To Nowhere
118 Rudimentary
118 Star of Cozzene

116 Luthier
   Enchenteur
113 Caerlina
113 Irish Stew
113 Silicon Bavaria
112 Mellottie
111 Flying Brave
111 Rezon
111 Robin des Pins
111 Sure Sharp
110 Acteur Francais
110 Approach
   The Bench
110 As Que To
110 Desert Sun
110 Gussy Marlowe
110 Metal Storm

9½ furlongs plus
125 Dear Doctor
122 Kooyonga
121 Environment
   Friend
120 Ruby Tiger
119 Sillery
119 Zoman
118 Arcangues
118 Knifebox
118 Perpendicular
117 Young Buster

116 Suave Dancer
115 Fortune's Wheel
115 George Augustus
114 Corrupt
114 Glity
112 Funny Baby
112 Goofalik
112 Leariva
111 Half A Tick
110 Karinga Bay
110 Passing Sale
110 Past Master
110 Star of Gdansk

11 furlongs plus
129 Pistolet Bleu
128 Subotica
124 Saddlers' Hall
124 Vert Amande
123 Opera House
122 Lomitas
122 Rock Hopper
122 Sapience
121 Terimon
120 Mashaallah
119 Saganeca
119 Tel Quel
118 Art Bleu
118 Magic Night
118 Toulon

117 Always Friendly
117 Wiorno
116 Serrant
115 Hondo Mondo
115 Red Bishop
114 Spinning
113 Jahafil
112 Deja
112 Erdelistan
112 Fabulous Hostess
112 Lara's Idea
111 Luchiroverte
110 Myrakalu
110 Runyon
110 Secret Haunt

14 furlongs plus
119 Rock Hopper
118 Snurge
118 Sought Out
117 Drum Taps
115 Dariyoun
115 Further Flight
113 Arcadian Heights
112 Turgeon
112 Vintage Crop
112 Witness Box
110 Commendable

IRISH CLASSIFICATIONS

For horses rated 100 or more (95 or more for two-year-olds), which were trained in Ireland in 1992. Horses trained outside Ireland are included if they won, or achieved their rating, in Ireland.

TWO-YEAR-OLDS

118 Basim	107 Scribe	101 Wangola	97 Pinch The Devil
115 Sayyedati	106 Asema	100 Massyar	97 Reliable
114 Fatherland	106 Bright	100 Preponderance	96 Mr Martini
113 Maroof	Generation	100 Shandon Lake	96 Nicea
112 Earl of Barking	106 Tahdeed	99 Moumayaz	96 Nordic Fox
111 Pips Pride	104 Tropical	98 Bint Albadou	96 Staviski
110 Up And At 'Em	103 Alouette	98 Biyik	95 Alaija
109 Shahik	103 Ancestral	98 Miami Sands	95 Captain Le Saux
108 Frenchpark	Dancer	97 Colour Party	95 Eurostorm
107 Ivory Frontier	103 Chanzi	97 Foresee	95 Idris
107 Khoraz	103 Rondelli	97 Just Speculation	95 L'Ecrivain
107 Newton's Law	102 Little Munchkin	97 Master Tribe	95 Timourid

THREE-YEAR-OLDS

5 furlongs plus	108 Irish Memory	9½ furlongs plus	11 furlongs plus
116 Freddie Lloyd	106 A-To-Z	127 Rodrigo	135 St Jovite
112 Bezelle	106 Reported	de Triano	124 User Friendly
110 Park Dream	106 Thyer	125 Dr Devious	117 Market Booster
109 Bradawn	105 Cloud of Dust	111 Alflora	114 Arrikala
Breever	105 Equal Eloquence	111 Khanata	113 In A Tiff
108 Poolesta	105 Tarwiya	110 Bineyah	110 Andros Bay
106 Maledetto	104 Nordic Brief	109 Firing Line	110 Ivyanna
	103 Miznah	107 Mining Tycoon	108 Ebaziya
7 furlongs plus	102 Soiree	107 Ormsby	101 Dabtiya
126 Marling	101 Nordic Pageant	107 Vasarelli	100 Yukon Gold
123 Brief Truce	101 Treasure Hope	106 Misako-Togo	
118 Ezzoud	100 Americarr	102 Tijara	14 furlongs plus
109 Portico	100 Caurselle	100 Riszard	101 Sinntara
109 Via Borghese	100 Dashing Colours		
108 Gdansk's			
Honour			

FOUR-YEAR-OLDS AND UPWARDS

5 furlongs plus	109 Norwich	119 Zoman	100 Gaelic Myth
121 Mr Brooks	109 Rami	115 George Augustus	
112 Flowing	107 Committed	110 Star of Gdansk	14 furlongs plus
110 Street Rebel	Dancer	105 Dowland	119 Mashaallah
104 Title Roll	104 Ballykett Prince	104 Lifewatch Vision	118 Snurge
102 Malvernico	104 Pre-Eminent	102 Thornberry	117 Drum Taps
101 Chicarica	103 Milieu		112 Vintage Crop
	101 Salmon Eile	11 furlongs plus	105 Persian Halo
7 furlongs plus	101 Two Left Feet	123 Opera House	101 Coolcullen
122 Sikeston	100 Winning Heart	120 Mashaallah	101 Sleet Skier
111 Sure Sharp		113 Jahafil	100 Lord Noble
110 Approach	9½ furlongs plus	110 Runyon	100 Onesixnine
The Bench	122 Kooyonga	107 Cherry Grove	
		Lad	

YOUR KEY
to Europe's Premier
Bloodstock Nursery

SATURDAY MORNING'S ODDS-ON FAVOURITE
Ireland's International Racing
and Bloodstock Weekly

THE IRISH FIELD

11-15 D'Olier Street, Dublin 2
Telephone: Dublin 6792022   FAX: 6793029

SELECTED BIG RACES 1992

Prize money for racing abroad has been converted to £ Sterling at the exchange rate current at the time of the race. The figures are correct to the nearest £.

1   CRAVEN STAKES (Gr 3)   1m
    (3yo c + g)
£18,801   Newmarket   16 April
    Alnasr Alwasheek 8-9
      SCauthen 1
    Dr Devious (Ire) 9-0
      CAsmussen 1½.2
    Irish Memory 8-9
      CRoche 2½.3
    Muhtarram (USA) 8-9
      WCarson 2.4
    Badie (USA) 8-9 JReid ¾.5
    Bold Pursuit (Ire) 8-9
      LPiggott 8.6
    Torrey Canyon (USA) 8-9
      PatEddery 5.7
    Forest Tiger (USA) 8-9
      LDettori 10.8

11/4 Forest Tiger, 7/2 Dr Devious, 5/1 ALNASR ALWASHEEK, Muhtarram, 6/1 Bold Pursuit, 15/2 Torrey Canyon, 16/1 Irish Memory, 33/1 Badie
  Sheikh Ahmed Al-Maktoum (M. R. Stoute) 8ran 1m37.39 (Good)

2   GENERAL ACCIDENT   1m
    1000 GUINEAS STAKES
    (Gr 1) (3yo f)
£111,387   Newmarket   30 April
    Hatoof (USA) 9-0
      WRSwinburn 1
    Marling (Ire) 9-0
      SCauthen hd.2
    Kenbu (Fr) 9-0 FHead ¾.3
    Perfect Circle 9-0
      RCochrane ½.4
    Culture Vulture (USA) 9-0
      TQuinn 8.5
    A-To-Z (Ire) 9-0 MHills ¾.6
    Pearl Angel 9-0 LPiggott ½.7
    Soiree (Ire) 9-0
      DHolland sh.8
    Musicale (USA) 9-0
      MRoberts 1.9
    Harvest Girl (Ire) 9-0
      AMunro nk.10
    Skimble (USA) 9-0
      PatEddery 2.11
    Mahasin (USA) 9-0
      WCarson 5.12
    Central City 9-0
      BRaymond 1½.13
    Nimble Deer 9-0
      GDuffield 8.14

7/2 Musicale, 5/1 HATOOF, Marling, 13/2 Soiree, 10/1 A-To-Z, 11/1 Kenbu, 12/1 Perfect Circle, 14/1 Culture Vulture, 16/1 Mahasin, 25/1 Skimble, 33/1 Central

City, 40/1 Harvest Girl, 100/1 Pearl Angel, 150/1 Nimble Deer
  Maktoum Al-Maktoum (Mrs C. Head) 14ran 1m39.45 (Good)

3   GENERAL ACCIDENT   1m
    2000 GUINEAS STAKES
    (Gr 1) (3yo c + f)
£113,736   Newmarket   2 May
    Rodrigo de Triano (USA) 9-0
      LPiggott 1
    Lucky Lindy (Ire) 9-0
      MJKinane 1½.2
    Pursuit of Love 9-0
      MRoberts ½.3
    Silver Wisp (USA) 9-0
      PaulEddery hd.4
1   Muhtarram (USA) 9-0
      WCarson ½.5
    Tertian (USA) 9-0
      PatEddery 1½.6
    Thourios 9-0 RCochrane ¾.7
    Swing Low 9-0
      WRSwinburn 2.8
1*   Alnasr Alwasheek 9-0
      SCauthen 2½.9
1   Badie (USA) 9-0
      LDettori nk.10
    Steinbeck (USA) 9-0
      TJarnet hd.11
    Cardoun (Fr) 9-0 DBoeuf 1.12
    Wilde Rufo 9-0 TQuinn ... 1½.13
    River Falls 9-0
      BRaymond 3.14
    Dilum (USA) 9-0
      AMunro 5.15
    Artic Tracker (USA) 9-0
      JReid 1½.16

5/2 Alnasr Alwasheek, 9/2 Pursuit of Love, 6/1 RODRIGO DE TRIANO, 8/1 Cardoun, 12/1 Tertian, 14/1 Dilum, 16/1 Steinbeck, 20/1 River Falls, Swing Low, 25/1 Muhtarram, Silver Wisp, 50/1 Lucky Lindy, Thourios, 66/1 Artic Tracker, Badie, 100/1 Wilde Rufo
  R. E. Sangster (P. W. Chapple-Hyam) 16ran 1m38.37 (Good)

4   PRIX GANAY (Gr 1) 1¼m 110y
    (4yo + c + f)
£50,556   Longchamp   3 May
    Subotica (Fr) 4-9-2 TJarnet .. 1
    Pistolet Bleu (Ire) 4-9-2
      DBoeuf nk.2
    Suave Dancer (USA) 4-9-2
      CAsmussen 3.3
    Fortune's Wheel (Ire) 4-9-2
      MBoutin ½.4
    Art Bleu 5-9-2 CAubert 2.5

Passing Sale (Fr) 5-9-2
    ALequeux 2½.6
    Glity (USA) 4-9-2 ELegrix .. nk.7
2/5 Suave Dancer, 7/2 Art Bleu and
Pistolet Bleu, 57/10 Fortune's Wheel,
74/10 SUBOTICA, 24/1 Passing Sale,
29/1 Glity
    O. Lecerf (A. Fabre) 7ran 2m09.30
(Good)

5   DUBAI POULE D'ESSAI   1m
    DES POULAINS (Gr 1)
    (3yo c)
£101,317   Longchamp   10 May
    Shanghai (USA) 9-2
      FHead 1
    Rainbow Corner 9-2
      PatEddery sn.2
    Lion Cavern (USA) 9-2
      SCauthen ¾.3
    Zaahi (USA) 9-2 RHills 1.4
    Judge Decision (Fr) 9-2
      WRSwinburn sh.5
    Take Risks (Fr) 9-2
      TJarnet 1.6
    Highest Ody (Fr) 9-2
      ELegrix sh.7
    Bakari (Ire) 9-2 DBoeuf 6.8
    Lucet (USA) 9-2 CAubert 3.9
Evens Rainbow Corner, 4/1 Highest
Ody, Lion Cavern, 7/1 Bakari, Lucet,
117/10 SHANGHAI, 17/1 Judge Decision,
Zaahi, 18/1 Take Risks
    S. Niarchos (F. Boutin) 9ran 1m38.20
(Good)

6   DUKE OF YORK STAKES   6f
    (Gr 3) (3yo +)
£23,220   York   14 May
    Shalford (Ire) 4-9-4
      MRoberts 1
    Mr Brooks 5-9-6
      LPiggott 3½.2
    Amigo Menor 6-9-4
      CRutter 1½.3
    Colway Bold 3-8-3
      WCarson 1½.4
    Stack Rock 5-8-11 KFallon ... 1.5
    Montendre 5-9-0 JReid 1.6
    Fylde Flyer 3-8-3 JCarroll 5.7
    Norwich 5-9-4 SCauthen nk.8
    Line Engaged (USA) 4-9-0
      RCochrane 7.9
7/2 Norwich, 4/1 Mr Brooks, 9/2 Fylde
Flyer, 6/1 SHALFORD, 8/1 Montendre,
17/2 Stack Rock, 10/1 Amigo Menor, 14/1
Colway Bold, 25/1 Line Engaged
    D. F. Cock (R. Hannon) 9ran 1m08.82
(Good to Firm)

7   JUDDMONTE   1m
    LOCKINGE STAKES
    (Gr 2) (3yo +)
£41,538   Newbury   15 May
    Selkirk (USA) 4-9-5
      RCochrane 1

    Lahib (USA) 4-9-0
      TQuinn 2½.2
    Rudimentary (USA) 4-9-3
      SCauthen 2.3
    Flying Brave 4-9-3 JReid 5.4
    Mystiko (USA) 4-9-5
      MRoberts 1.5
    Fair Average 4-9-0
      WNewnes 1.6
    Leariva (USA) 5-9-2
      DBoeuf 2½.7
    Desert Sun 4-9-0
      PatEddery 1½.8
    Mukaddamah (USA) 4-9-3
      WCarson 3½.9
    Ajaad (USA) 4-9-0
      WRSwinburn 15.10
9/4 Rudimentary, 5/2 SELKIRK, 9/2
Desert Sun, 5/1 Mystiko, 12/1 Ajaad,
Mukaddamah, 16/1 Lahib, Leariva, 33/1
Fair Average, Flying Brave
    George Strawbridge (I. A. Balding)
10ran 1m36.99 (Good to Firm)

8   AIRLIE/COOLMORE   1m
    IRISH 2000 GUINEAS
    (Gr 1) (3yo c)
£111,927   Curragh   16 May
3*   **Rodrigo de Triano (USA)** 9-0
      LPiggott 1
    Ezzoud (Ire) 9-0
      WRSwinburn 1.2
    Brief Truce (USA) 9-0
      MJKinane 1½.3
3²   Lucky Lindy (Ire) 9-0
      JReid ½.4
1³   Irish Memory 9-0 CRoche 5.5
    Portico (USA) 9-0
      SCauthen 3.6
8/11 RODRIGO DE TRIANO, 5/1
Ezzoud, 13/2 Lucky Lindy, 8/1 Portico,
11/1 Brief Truce, 20/1 Irish Memory
    R. E. Sangster (P. W. Chapple-Hyam)
6ran 1m41.70 (Good)

9   DUBAI POULE D'ESSAI   1m
    DES POULICHES (Gr 1)
    (3yo f)
£101,317   Longchamp   17 May
2   **Culture Vulture (USA)** 9-2
      TQuinn 1
    Hydro Calido (USA) 9-2
      FHead ½.2
    Guislaine (Fr) 9-2
      CAsmussen ¾.3
    Absurde (Fr) 9-2
      ESaint-Martin nk.4
    Euphonic (USA) 9-2
      PatEddery nk.5
2*   Hatoof (USA) 9-2
      WRSwinburn 1½.6
2³   Kenbu (Fr) 9-2
      ALequeux ½.7
    Symphorine (USA) 9-2
      TJarnet 2½.8

Plume Magique 9-2
  BRaymond 2½.9

18/10 Hatoof and Plume Magique, 5/2
Hydro Calido, 73/10 Guislaine, 73/10
Euphonic, 79/10 Symphorine, 94/10
Absurde, 12/1 Kenbu, 131/10 CULTURE
VULTURE
  C. Wright (P. Cole) 9ran 1m37.00
(Good to Firm)

10	GOFFS IRISH 1000	1m
	GUINEAS (Gr 1) (3yo f)	
£111,009	Curragh	23 May

2²	**Marling (Ire)** 9-0	
	WRSwinburn	1
	Market Booster (USA) 9-0	
	MJKinane	1.2
	Tarwiya (Ire) 9-0	
	TJarnet	1.3
2	A-To-Z (Ire) 9-0 MHills	¾.4
	Cattermole (USA) 9-0	
	CAsmussen	hd.5
	Khanata (USA) 9-0	
	JPMurtagh	sh.6
	Caurselle (Ire) 9-0	
	KJManning	1½.7
	Gdansk's Honour (USA) 9-0	
	CRoche	3.8
	Bezelle 9-0 PShanahan	1½.9

4/5 MARLING, 7/2 Bezelle, 10/1
Khanata, 11/1 A-To-Z, 20/1 Cattermole,
Gdansk's Honour, Market Booster,
Tarwiya, 100/1 Caurselle
  E. J. Loder (G. Wragg) 9ran 1m41.50
(Good)

11	PRIX SAINT-ALARY	1¼m
	(Gr 1) (3yo f)	
£58,539	Longchamp	24 May

	Rosefinch (USA) 9-2	
	SCauthen	1
	Jolypha (USA) 9-2	
	PatEddery	sh.2
	Verveine (USA) 9-2	
	DBoeuf	hd.3
	Trishyde (USA) 9-2	
	FHead	½.4
	Trampoli (USA) 9-2	
	SGuillot	1½.5
	Good To Dance (Ire) 9-2	
	TJarnet	hd.6
	Sheba Dancer (Fr) 9-2	
	ALequeux	4.7
	Winnetka (USA) 9-2	
	CAsmussen	sn.8
	Shannkara (Ire) 9-2	
	WMongil	5.9
	Irish Source 9-2	
	ESaint-Martin	2½.10
	Badiane (USA) 9-2	
	YTalamo	11

29/10 Badiane and Verveine, 33/10
Jolypha, Trishyde, 53/10 Good To Dance
and Trampoli, 13/2 Sheba Dancer, 68/10
Shannkara, 182/10 ROSEFINCH, 25/1
Irish Source, 27/1 Winnetka

Sheikh Mohammed (A. Fabre) 11ran
2m05.00 (Good)

12	PRIX JEAN PRAT (Gr 1) 1m 1f55y	
	(3yo c + f)	
£50,658	Longchamp	31 May

	Kitwood (USA) 9-2	
	SCauthen	1
8	**Lucky Lindy (Ire)** 9-2	
	PatEddery	sn.2
5*	**Shanghai (USA)** 9-2	
	FHead	nk.3
	Calling Collect (USA) 9-2	
	DBoeuf	2.4
	Heligoland (Ire) 9-2	
	SGuillot	6.5

11/10 Shanghai, 5/2 Heligoland and
KITWOOD, 26/10 Calling Collect, 32/10
Lucky Lindy
  Sheikh Mohammed (A. Fabre) 5ran
1m58.00 (Good to Soft)

13	PRIX D'ISPAHAN (Gr 1) 1m 1f55y	
	(4yo + c + f)	
£50,658	Longchamp	31 May

	Zoman (USA) 5-9-2 AMunro .	1
	Arcangues (USA) 4-9-2	
	TJarnet	nk.2
	Exit To Nowhere (USA) 4-9-2	
	FHead	1½.3
	Funny Baby (Fr) 4-9-2	
	ALequeux	2½.4
	Tel Quel (Fr) 4-9-2	
	SCauthen	hd.5
7*	Selkirk (USA) 4-9-2	
	RCochrane	1½.6
	Magic Night (Fr) 4-8-13	
	ABadel	2.7
7	Leariva (USA) 5-8-13	
	CAsmussen	6.8
	Caerlina (Ire) 4-8-13	
	ELegrix	2.9
	Metal Storm (Fr) 4-9-2	
	PatEddery	6.10
	L'Amour Fou (Ire) 4-8-13	
	KVaillant	20.11

6/4 Selkirk, 43/10 Exit To Nowhere,
58/10 Caerlina, 63/10 L'Amour Fou and
Magic Night, 69/10 Tel Quel, 123/10
ZOMAN, 126/10 Arcangues, 16/1
Leariva, 26/1 Metal Storm, 33/1 Funny
Baby
  F. Salman (P.F.I. Cole) 11ran 1m54.60
(Good to Soft)

14	EVER READY DERBY	1½m 10y
	(Gr 1) (3yo c + f)	
£355,000	Epsom	3 June

1²	**Dr Devious (Ire)** 9-0 JReid	1
	St Jovite (USA) 9-0	
	CRoche	2.2
3	Silver Wisp (USA) 9-0	
	PaulEddery	sh.3
3	Muhtarram (USA) 9-0	
	WCarson	3½.4

Twist And Turn 9-0
MJKinane 2½.5
Alflora (Ire) 9-0
TQuinn 2½.6
3   Alnasr Alwasheek 9-0
SCauthen hd.7
Great Palm (USA) 9-0
AMunro 1.8
8*   Rodrigo de Triano (USA) 9-0
LPiggott 2.9
3   Thourios 9-0
MRoberts 2½.10
5²   Rainbow Corner 9-0
PatEddery nk.11
Well Saddled (Ire) 9-0
JWilliams 2.12
Assessor (Ire) 9-0
WRSwinburn 6.13
Paradise Navy 9-0
GDuffield 10.14
Lobilio (USA) 9-0 RHills 2.15
Pollen Count (USA) 9-0
LDettori 1½.16
Ninja Dancer (USA) 9-0
MHills ¾.17
Young Freeman (USA) 9-0
BRaymond 20.18

13/2 Rodrigo de Triano, 8/1 DR
DEVIOUS, 9/1 Alnasr Alwasheek,
Assessor, Muhtarram, Rainbow Corner,
10/1 Great Palm, 11/1 Silver Wisp, 12/1
Twist And Turn, 14/1 Pollen Count, St
Jovite, 50/1 Thourios, 66/1 Young
Freeman, 100/1 Ninja Dancer, 150/1 Well
Saddled, 200/1 Alflora, 250/1 Lobilio,
Paradise Navy
    Sidney H. Craig (P. W. Chapple-
Hyam) 18ran 2m36.19 (Good)

15   HANSON   1½m10y
       CORONATION CUP
       (Gr 1) (4yo +)
£90,282   Epsom   4 June
       Saddlers' Hall (Ire) 4-9-0
WRSwinburn 1
       Rock Hopper 5-9-0
PatEddery ¾.2
       Terimon 6-9-0
MRoberts ¾.3
4*   Subotica (Fr) 4-9-0
TJarnet nk.4
Always Friendly 4-8-11
AMunro sh.5
Saganeca (USA) 4-8-11
WMongil 2½.6
Snurge 5-9-0 TQuinn ¾.7
Sapience 6-9-0 RCochrane 2.8
Mellaby (USA) 4-9-0
BRaymond dist.9

5/4 SADDLERS' HALL, 11/4 Subotica,
7/1 Rock Hopper, 8/1 Snurge, 12/1
Terimon, 16/1 Sapience, 25/1 Saganeca,
40/1 Always Friendly, 150/1 Mellaby
    Lord Weinstock (M. R. Stoute) 9ran
2m35.73 (Good)

16   GOLD SEAL OAKS   1½m10y
       (Gr 1) (3yo f)
£147,500   Epsom   6 June
       User Friendly 9-0
GDuffield 1
       All At Sea (USA) 9-0
PatEddery 3½.2
2   Pearl Angel 9-0
LPiggott 20.3
Saratoga Source (USA) 9-0
RCochrane 2½.4
Shining Bright 9-0
TJarnet 1½.5
Fawaayid (USA) 9-0
CRoche 8.6
2   Perfect Circle 9-0
WRSwinburn 25.7

11/10 All At Sea, 9/2 Perfect Circle, 5/1
USER FRIENDLY, 7/1 Fawaayid, 20/1
Shining Bright, 33/1 Pearl Angel,
Saratoga Source
    W. J. Gredley (C. E. Brittain) 7ran
2m39.77 (Good to Soft)

17   PRIX DU JOCKEY-CLUB   1½m
       LANCIA (Gr 1) (3yo c + f)
£255,102   Chantilly   7 June
       Polytain (Fr) 9-2 LDettori 1
       Marignan (USA) 9-2
DBoeuf 1½.2
       Contested Bid (USA) 9-2
PatEddery ¾.3
Johann Quatz (Fr) 9-2
FHead ¾.4
Modhish (Ire) 9-2
MJKinane 2.5
Binkhaldoun (USA) 9-2
RHills ns.6
Apple Tree (Fr) 9-2
TJarnet 2½.7
Adieu Au Roi (Ire) 9-2
MBoutin nk.8
Dajraan (Ire) 9-2
SCauthen sh.9
Paix Blanche (Fr) 8-13
ALequeux nk.10
Silver Kite (USA) 9-2
SGuillot 2.11
Jape (USA) 9-2 AMunro ½.12
Glanville (USA) 9-2
WMongil ½.13
Jamshid (Jpn) 9-2
MdeSmyter 3.14
Break Bread (USA) 9-2
CAsmussen nk.15
Prince Polino (USA) 9-2
ELegrix 2½.16
Grand Plaisir (Ire) 9-2
GGuignard dist.17

38/10 Apple Tree and Marignan and Paix
Blanche, 39/10 Johann Quatz, 68/10
Dajraan and Modhish, 97/10 Grand
Plaisir, 10/1 Break Bread, 13/1 Jape,
136/10 Contested Bid, 166/10 Adieu Au
Roi, 28/1 Prince Polino, 32/1 Glanville,
365/10 POLYTAIN, 41/1 Binkhaldoun,
50/1 Silver Kite, 55/1 Jamshid

974

Mme B. Houillion (A. Spanu) 17ran
2m30.30 (Good)

18 PRIX DE DIANE 1¼m110y
HERMES (Gr 1) (3yo f)
£142,857 Chantilly 14 June
11² **Jolypha (USA)** 9-2
PatEddery 1
11 **Sheba Dancer (Fr)** 9-2
ELegrix 1.2
11³ **Verveine (USA)** 9-2
DBoeuf sh.3
9³ Guislaine (Fr) 9-2
CAsmussen 1½.4
11* Rosefinch (USA) 9-2
SCauthen sn.5
Urban Sea (USA) 9-2
MBoutin ½.6
11 Trishyde (USA) 9-2
FHead 3.7
11 Good To Dance (Ire) 9-2
TJarnet ½.8
Oumaldaaya (USA) 9-2
WCarson ns.9
Decided Air (Ire) 9-2
WRSwinburn 10.10
African Peace (USA) 9-2
SGuillot 11
Garendare 9-2 WMongil 12
23/10 Trishyde, 36/10 JOLYPHA, 41/10
Guislaine, 48/10 African Peace and
Decided Air and Rosefinch, 52/10
Garendare and Verveine, 95/10
Oumaldaaya, 167/10 Good To Dance,
24/1 Urban Sea, 29/1 Sheba Dancer
K. Abdulla (A. Fabre) 12ran 2m09.50
(Good)

19 QUEEN ANNE STAKES 1m
(Gr 2) (3yo +)
£54,972 Ascot 16 June
7² **Lahib (USA)** 4-9-2 WCarson .. 1
Second Set (Ire) 4-9-8
LDettori hd.2
Sikeston (USA) 6-9-8
MRoberts ½.3
13³ Exit To Nowhere (USA) 4-9-2
FHead sh.4
Approach The Bench (Ire) 4-9-2
JReid 3.5
7³ Rudimentary (USA) 4-9-5
PatEddery 1½.6
Goofalik (USA) 5-9-5
SCauthen 2½.7
Star of Gdansk (USA) 4-9-2
CRoche sh.8
Lovealoch (Ire) 4-8-13
MHills 10.9
10/3 LAHIB, 4/1 Second Set, 5/1 Exit To
Nowhere, 11/2 Rudimentary, 15/2
Goofalik, 11/1 Star of Gdansk, 20/1
Approach The Bench, Sikeston, 25/1
Lovealoch
Hamdan Al-Maktoum (J. L. Dunlop)
9ran 1m38.64 (Good to Firm)

20 PRINCE OF WALES'S 1¼m
STAKES (Gr 2) (3yo +)
£58,536 Ascot 16 June
Order as they passed the post
(Kooyonga was subsequently disqual-
ified and placed third)
Kooyonga (Ire) 4-9-4
WJO'Connor 1
Perpendicular 4-9-3
WRyan 1½.2
Young Buster (Ire) 4-9-3
WRSwinburn hd.3
15³ Terimon 6-9-7 MRoberts .. 1½.4
12² Lucky Lindy (Ire) 3-8-5
MJKinane 1½.5
Opera House 4-9-5
SCauthen 1½.6
7 Desert Sun 4-9-3
PatEddery nk.7
14 Thourios 3-8-5 AClark 2.8
Gussy Marlowe 4-9-0
LDettori 2½.9
Karinga Bay 5-9-3
BRouse hd.10
13 Tel Quel (Fr) 4-9-7
WCarson sh.11
5/2 Opera House, 6/1 Lucky Lindy,
Terimon, 7/1 Tel Quel, 9/1 Kooyonga,
Young Buster, 10/1 Desert Sun, 20/1
PERPENDICULAR, 25/1 Gussy
Marlowe, Thourios, 40/1 Karinga Bay
Lord Howard de Walden (H. R. A.
Cecil) 11ran 2m04.13 (Good to Firm)

21 ST JAMES'S PALACE 1m
STAKES (Gr 1) (3yo c + f)
£118,188 Ascot 16 June
8³ **Brief Truce (USA)** 9-0
MJKinane 1
5 **Zaahi (USA)** 9-0 RHills sh.2
8² **Ezzoud (Ire)** 9-0
PatEddery 1½.3
14 Rodrigo de Triano (USA) 9-0
LPiggott sh.4
Arazi (USA) 9-0
SCauthen ¾.5
Casteddu 9-0 AMunro 3.6
3 River Falls 9-0
BRaymond 4.7
Beldi (USA) 9-0
MRoberts 8.8
10/11 Arazi, 4/1 Rodrigo de Triano, 6/1
Ezzoud, 8/1 Zaahi, 20/1 Casteddu, 25/1
BRIEF TRUCE, 40/1 River Falls, 100/1
Beldi
Moyglare Stud Farms Ltd (D. K.
Weld) 8ran 1m39.32 (Good to Firm)

22 QUEEN MARY STAKES 5f
(Gr 3) (2yo f)
£23,976 Ascot 17 June
Lyric Fantasy (Ire) 8-8
MRoberts 1
Mystic Goddess (USA) 8-8
PatEddery 5.2

975

Toocando (Ire) 8-8
RCochrane 1½.3
Marina Park 8-8
DeanMcKeown 2½.4
Lucky Parkes 8-8
JCarroll ½.5
Holly Golightly 8-8
JReid sh.6
Star Family Friend (Ire) 8-8
PRobinson sh.7
Toledo Queen (Ire) 8-8
PaulEddery 1½.8
Moodiesburn (Ire) 8-8
AMackay 1.9
Carranita (Ire) 8-8
JWilliams 2.10
Hamsah (Ire) 8-8
SCauthen 3½.11
Belle Soiree 8-8 TQuinn 8.12
Amirati (USA) 8-8
WRSwinburn 3.13

11/8 LYRIC FANTASY, 7/1 Hamsah, 15/2 Mystic Goddess, 8/1 Amirati, 10/1 Toocando, 12/1 Lucky Parkes, 14/1 Star Family Friend, 20/1 Holly Golightly, 20/1 Toledo Queen, 33/1 Carranita, Marina Park, 100/1 Belle Soiree, Moodiesburn
Lord Carnarvon (R. Hannon) 13ran 59.72secs (Firm)

23   CORONATION STAKES   1m
(Gr 1) (3yo f)
£107,886   Ascot   17 June
10*   **Marling (Ire)** 9-0
WRSwinburn 1
9*   **Culture Vulture (USA)** 9-0
TQuinn ¾.2
Katakana (USA) 9-0
SCauthen 6.3
Wiedniu (USA) 9-0
MRoberts sh.4
9   Absurde (Fr) 9-0 FHead sh.5
2   Mahasin (USA) 9-0
WCarson 12.6
2   Soiree (Ire) 9-0
DHolland 10.7

8/11 MARLING, 9/2 Culture Vulture, 9/1 Absurde, Mahasin, 14/1 Wiedniu, 16/1 Katakana, 33/1 Soiree
E. J. Loder (G. Wragg) 7ran 1m39.01 (Firm)

24   GOLD CUP (Gr 1) (4yo +)   2½m
£108,549   Ascot   18 June
Drum Taps (USA) 6-9-2
LDettori 1
Arcadian Heights 4-9-0
WRSwinburn 2.2
Turgeon (USA) 6-9-2
SCauthen 3.3
Endoli (USA) 5-9-2
MRoberts 1.4
Mardonius 6-9-2 PatEddery .. 8.5
Tyrone Bridge 6-9-2
PShanahan 2½.6

7/4 DRUM TAPS, 4/1 Endoli, 5/1 Turgeon, 11/2 Arcadian Heights, 9/1 Mardonius, 10/1 Tyrone Bridge
Yoshio Asakawa (Lord Huntingdon) 6ran 4m 18.29 (Firm)

25   KING'S STAND STAKES   5f
(Gr 2) (3yo +)
£59,368   Ascot   19 June
Sheikh Albadou 4-9-3
WRSwinburn 1
6²   **Mr Brooks** 5-9-3 LPiggott . ½.2
Elbio 5-9-3 LDettori nk.3
Wolfhound (USA) 3-8-10
SCauthen hd.4
El Yasaf (Ire) 4-9-3
JWilliams ½.5
Flowing (USA) 4-9-0
MJKinane hd.6
Monde Bleu 4-9-3
PatEddery sh.7
Paris House 3-8-10 JCarroll .. 5.8
Blyton Lad 6-9-3 SWebster ... 5.9
Another Episode (Ire) 3-8-10
GCarter 12.10

7/2 Monde Bleu, SHEIKH ALBADOU, 9/2 Elbio, 6/1 Paris House, 15/2 Mr Brooks, 11/1 Wolfhound, 12/1 Flowing, 16/1 Blyton Lad, 50/1 Another Episode, 100/1 El Yasaf
Hilal Salem (A. A. Scott) 10ran 1m00.50 (Firm)

26   GRAN PREMIO DI   1½m
MILANO (Gr 1) (3yo +)
£153,585   Milan   21 June
Mashaallah (USA) 4-9-6
SCauthen 1
15   **Saganeca (USA)** 4-9-3
TJarnet ¾.2
Lara's Idea (Ire) 4-9-3
VMezzatesta 1½.3
15   Always Friendly 4-9-3
AMunro nk.4
15   Snurge 5-9-6 TQuinn nk.5
Erdelistan (Fr) 5-9-6
JHeloury 4.6
Marcus Thorpe (USA) 4-9-6
PRobinson hd.7
Deja 4-9-6 FHead ... 1½.8
4   Passing Sale (Fr) 5-9-6
ALequeux nk.9
Jack Lang 4-9-6 EBotti 12.10

32/10 Snurge, 33/10 Always Friendly, 39/10 MASHAALLAH, 47/10 Deja, 64/10 Passing Sale, 67/10 Jack Lang and Lara's Idea, 75/10 Saganeca, 10/1 Saganeca, 60/1 Marcus Thorpe
Ahmed Al-Maktoum (J. H. M. Gosden) 10ran 2m31.50 (Good to Soft)

27   BUDWEISER IRISH   1½m
DERBY (Gr 1) (3yo c + f)
£328,991   Curragh   28 June
14²   **St Jovite (USA)** 9-0
CRoche 1

976

14* **Dr Devious (Ire)** 9-0
JReid 12.2
17³ **Contested Bid (USA)** 9-0
PatEddery 1.3
Dive For Cover (USA) 9-0
DHolland 3.4
21³ Ezzoud (Ire) 9-0
WRSwinburn ¾.5
17² Marignan (USA) 9-0
DBoeuf nk.6
Ormsby (Ire) 9-0
MJKinane 5.7
Boloardo 9-0 MRoberts 10.8
Landowner (Ire) 9-0
RCochrane sh.9
Mining Tycoon (Ire) 9-0
KJManning 4½.10
Appealing Bubbles (Ire) 9-0
CEverard 6.11
4/5 Dr Devious, 7/2 ST JOVITE, 7/1
Landowner, 10/1 Ezzoud, 11/1 Contested
Bid, Marignan, 20/1 Ormsby, 66/1
Boloardo, Dive For Cover, 100/1 Mining
Tycoon, 200/1 Appealing Bubbles
Mrs Virginia Kraft Payson (J. S.
Bolger) 11ran 2m26.66 (Good to Firm)

28   IDEE HANSA-PREIS   1m3f
(Gr 2) (3yo +)
£48,110   Hamburg   28 June
Lomitas 4-9-8 ABoschert 1
Captain Horatius (Ire) 3-8-2
WRyan 4.2
Capwell 3-7-12 ABest 3.3
Silvestro 7-9-4 WBuick sh.4
Leone (Ger) 4-9-6
KWoodburn 4.5
Pigeon Voyageur (Ire) 4-9-6
LMader 1¾.6
Gestut Fahrhof (A. Wohler) 6ran
2m18.80 (Good to Firm)

29   GRAND PRIX DE PARIS   1¼m
LOUIS VUITTON (Gr 1)
(3yo c + f)
£152,749   Longchamp   28 June
Homme de Loi (Ire) 9-2
TJarnet 1
12* **Kitwood (USA)** 9-2
SCauthen ¾.2
18   Guislaine (Fr) 8-13
CAsmussen ½.3
17   Adieu Au Roi (Ire) 9-2
MBoutin 1.4
18³ Verveine (USA) 8-13
WMongil sn.5
Olanthe (USA) 9-2
SGuillot ½.6
14   Pollen Count (USA) 9-2
WCarson ½.7
17   Johann Quatz (Fr) 9-2
FHead sh.8
Vasarelli (Ire) 9-2
AMunro 1½.9
Alhijaz 9-2 LPiggott ½.10

2/1 Johann Quatz, 24/10 Kitwood and
Olanthe and Pollen Count, 37/10
HOMME DE LOI, 64/10 Verveine, 68/10
Guislaine, 102/10 Alhijaz, 18/1 Adieu Au
Roi, 29/1 Vasarelli
P. de Moussac (A. Fabre) 10ran
2m03.90 (Good to Firm)

30   CORAL-ECLIPSE   1¼m7y
STAKES (Gr 1) (3yo +)
£152,356   Sandown   4 July
20³ **Kooyonga (Ire)** 4-9-4
WJO'Connor 1
20   **Opera House** 4-9-7
SCauthen 1½.2
15   **Sapience** 6-9-7
RCochrane 1½.3
Free Flyer (Ire) 3-8-10
RHills ½.4
14   Twist And Turn 3-8-10
MJKinane nk.5
13* Zoman (USA) 5-9-7
AMunro hd.6
15² Rock Hopper 5-9-7
WRSwinburn 1½.7
13² Arcangues (USA) 4-9-7
TJarnet nk.8
20   Terimon 6-9-7 MRoberts 5.9
20² Young Buster (Ire) 4-9-7
MHills 12.10
15   Mellaby (USA) 4-9-7
BRaymond 15.11
Hailsham (Can) 4-9-7
WCarson 15.12
7/2 KOOYONGA, 5/1 Arcangues, 11/2
Zoman, 8/1 Opera House, Rock Hopper,
Twist And Turn, 9/1 Terimon, 14/1
Sapience, Young Buster, 33/1 Free
Flyer, 66/1 Hailsham, 200/1 Mellaby
Mitsuo Haga (M. Kauntze) 12ran
2m10.83 (Soft)

31   GRAND PRIX DE   1½m
SAINT-CLOUD (Gr 1)
(3yo + c + f)
£153,374   Saint-Cloud   5 July
4² **Pistolet Bleu (Ire)** 4-9-8
DBoeuf 1
13   Magic Night (Fr) 4-9-5
ABadel 5.2
15   Subotica (Fr) 4-9-8
TJarnet 2½.3
26² Saganeca (USA) 4-9-5
GMosse 3.4
Danae de Brule (Fr) 5-9-5
RLaplanche 10.5
4   Art Bleu 5-9-8 CAubert 2.6
L'Oiseau Bleu Roi (USA) 5-9-8
PBruneau 8.7
Evens Subotica, 14/10 Art Bleu and
L'Oiseau Bleu Roi and PISTOLET
BLEU, 32/10 Magic Night, 92/10
Saganeca, 21/1 Danae de Brule
D. Wildenstein (E. Lellouche) 7ran
2m30.30 (Good to Soft)

32   JULY CUP (Gr 1) (3yo +)   6f
£92,620   Newmarket   9 July

25²   **Mr Brooks** 5-9-6 LPiggott **1**
3³   **Pursuit of Love** 3-8-13
    PatEddery hd.**2**
25*   **Sheikh Albadou** 4-9-6
    WRSwinburn nk.**3**
25³   Elbio 5-9-6 LDettori 1½.**4**
25   Paris House 3-8-13 JCarroll .. 6.**5**
25   Wolfhound (USA) 3-8-13
    SCauthen 1½.**6**
6*   Shalford (Ire) 4-9-6
    MRoberts 3.**7**
    Tbab (Ire) 4-9-6
    BRaymond dh.**7**

15/8 Sheikh Albadou, 9/4 Shalford, 5/1 Wolfhound, 13/2 Pursuit of Love, 9/1 Elbio, 16/1 MR BROOKS, 33/1 Paris House, 50/1 Tbab
P. Green (R. Hannon) 8ran 1m11.80 (Good)

33   KILDANGAN STUD   1½m
    IRISH OAKS (Gr 1) (3yo f)
£112,037   Curragh   11 July

16*   **User Friendly** 9-0
    GDuffield **1**
10²   **Market Booster (USA)** 9-0
    MJKinane nk.**2**
    Arrikala (Ire) 9-0
    KJManning ½.**3**
    Bineyah (Ire) 9-0
    WRSwinburn 2½.**4**
10   Khanata (USA) 9-0
    JPMurtagh 10.**5**
    Armarama 9-0
    PRobinson 4½.**6**
    Ebony And Ivory (Ire) 9-0
    RJGriffiths 1½.**7**
17   Paix Blanche (Fr) 9-0
    DBoeuf 7.**8**
    Ivyanna (Ire) 9-0 CRoche 5.**9**

8/11 USER FRIENDLY, 9/2 Market Booster, 11/2 Ivyanna, 10/1 Khanata, 14/1 Armarama, 25/1 Arrikala, Bineyah, Paix Blanche, 100/1 Ebony And Ivory
W. J. Gredley (C. E. Brittain) 9ran 2m33.70 (Good)

34   PRIX MAURICE DE   1½m110y
    NIEUIL (Gr 2) (3yo +)
£41,623   Maisons-Laffitte   24 July

    Vert Amande (Fr) 4-9-2
    DBoeuf **1**
26*   **Mashaallah (USA)** 4-9-9
    JReid nk.**2**
    Songlines (Fr) 3-8-5
    OBenoist 1.**3**
    Merzouk (USA) 3-8-5
    ESaint-Martin ½.**4**
    Villandry (USA) 4-8-13
    TJarnet 2.**5**
    Embarcadero (Ger) 4-9-2
    MRimmer 1.**6**
    Lights Out (Fr) 6-9-2
    GMosse sh.**7**

    Gloria Mundi (Fr) 5-8-13
    BMarcus hd.**8**

24/10   VERT   AMANDE,   28/10 Songlines, 38/10 Merzouk, 42/10 Mashaallah, 59/10 Villandry, 10/1 Lights Out, 20/1 Embarcadero, 36/1 Gloria Mundi
E. Sarasola (E. Lellouche) 8ran 2m36.80 (Good)

35   KING GEORGE VI AND   1½m
    QUEEN ELIZABETH
    DIAMOND STAKES
    (Gr 1) (3yo +)
£261,216   Ascot   25 July

27*   **St Jovite (USA)** 3-8-9
    SCraine **1**
15*   **Saddlers' Hall (Ire)** 4-9-7
    WCarson 6.**2**
30²   **Opera House** 4-9-7
    SCauthen ½.**3**
30³   Sapience 6-9-7 RCochrane .. ½.**4**
30   Rock Hopper 5-9-7
    WRSwinburn hd.**5**
30   Terimon 6-9-7 MRoberts 8.**6**
14³   Silver Wisp (USA) 3-8-9
    PaulEddery ¾.**7**
    Jeune 3-8-9 MHills ¾.**8**

4/5 ST JOVITE, 7/2 Saddlers' Hall, 8/1 Silver Wisp, 10/1 Opera House, 16/1 Sapience, 22/1 Rock Hopper, 33/1 Terimon
Mrs Virginia Kraft Payson (J. S. Bolger) 8ran 2m30.85 (Good)

36   SUSSEX STAKES (Gr 1)   1m
    (3yo +)
£76,700   Goodwood   29 July

23*   **Marling (Ire)** 3-8-10
    PatEddery **1**
13   **Selkirk (USA)** 4-9-7
    RCochrane hd.**2**
19²   **Second Set (Ire)** 4-9-7
    LDettori ¾.**3**
32³   Sheikh Albadou 4-9-7
    WRSwinburn 2.**4**
19³   Sikeston (USA) 6-9-7
    MRoberts sh.**5**
    Star of Cozzene (USA) 4-9-7
    CAsmussen 2.**6**
19   Rudimentary (USA) 4-9-7
    SCauthen ½.**7**
20   Thourios 3-8-13 WCarson 5.**8**

11/10 MARLING, 7/2 Second Set, Selkirk, 11/1 Sheikh Albadou, 16/1 Sikeston, 20/1 Rudimentary, Thourios, 33/1 Star of Cozzene
E. J. Loder (G. Wragg) 8ran 1m36.68 (Good to Firm)

37   GOODWOOD CUP (Gr 3)   2m
    (3yo +)
£29,952   Goodwood   30 July

    Further Flight 6-9-5 MHills . **1**
    Witness Box (USA) 5-9-0
    SCauthen sh.**2**

27   **Landowner (Ire)** 3-8-3
      WCarson 1½.3
24²   Arcadian Heights 4-9-3
      WRSwinburn 3½.4
    Luchiroverte (Ire) 4-9-0
      MRoberts 2½.5
    Elsurimo (Ger) 5-9-7
      MRimmer 2.6
    Duke of Paducah (USA) 5-9-0
      JReid nk.7
24   Tyrone Bridge 6-9-3
      LPiggott hd.8
    Le Corsaire (USA) 4-9-0
      LDettori 1½.9
    Tetradonna (Ire) 4-8-11
      PaulEddery 1.10
    Parting Moment (USA) 5-9-5
      RCochrane 8.11

9/2 Arcadian Heights, Luchiroverte, 5/1
Landowner, Witness Box, 7/1
FURTHER FLIGHT, 10/1 Tyrone
Bridge, 12/1 Le Corsaire, 16/1 Duke of
Paducah, 25/1 Tetradonna, 33/1 Parting
Moment
  S. Wingfield Digby (B. W. Hills) 11ran
3m24.04 (Good to Firm)

38   PRIX MAURICE DE   6f110y
    GHEEST (Gr 2) (3yo +)
£26,015   Deauville   2 August
32²   **Pursuit of Love** 3-8-9
      MJKinane 1
3   **Cardoun (Fr)** 3-8-9
      DBoeuf 1½.2
    Twafeaj (USA) 3-8-6
      WRSwinburn ½.3
    Ganges (USA) 4-8-13
      FHead ¾.4
    Crack Regiment (USA) 4-8-13
      ASCruz 1½.5
32   Elbio 5-8-13 RCochrane ½.6
5³   Lion Cavern 3-8-9
      SCauthen 1½.7
3   Tertian (USA) 3-8-9
      PatEddery nk.8
    Reference Light (USA) 5-8-13
      MPlanard 6.9
    Worldwide (Ire) 3-8-9
      ELegrix ½.10
    Bradawn Breever (Ire) 3-8-9
      RJGriffiths 6.11

19/10 PURSUIT OF LOVE, 23/10 Lion
Cavern, 52/10 Cardoun, 72/10 Elbio,
98/10 Tertian, 118/10 Ganges, 13/1
Reference Light, 29/1 Twafeaj, 32/1
Crack Regiment, 35/1 Worldwide, 45/1
Bradawn Breever
  Lord Howard de Walden (H. R. A.
Cecil) 11ran 1m16.30 (Good)

39   GROSSER MERCEDES 1¼m
    BENZ PREIS BAYERISCHES
    ZUCHTRENNEN (Gr 1) (3yo +)
£98,592   Munich   2 August
30*   **Kooyonga (Ire)** 4-9-2
      WJO'Connor 1
21²   **Zaahi (USA)** 3-8-7 RHills .. ¾.2

20*   **Perpendicular** 4-9-6
      WRyan 1¼.3
    Dear Doctor (Fr) 5-9-6
      CAsmussen sh.4
4   Fortune's Wheel (Ire) 4-9-6
      MBoutin 2½.5
    Hondo Mondo (Ire) 4-9-6
      AHelfenbein 3.6
    Maitre (Ire) 4-9-6
      WBuick 4½.7
Mitsuo Haga (M. Kauntze) 7ran
2m05.80 (Good)

40   PRIX DE POMONE   1m5f110y
    (Gr 2) (3yo + f)
£26,096   Deauville   9 August
31²   **Magic Night (Fr)** 4-9-2
      ABadel 1
    Sought Out (Ire) 4-9-2
      CAsmussen 1.2
26   **Always Friendly** 4-9-2
      AMunro sn.3
    Linnga (Ire) 3-8-7
      GGuignard 1½.4
11   Trampoli (USA) 3-8-7
      TJarnet 2½.5
11   Winnetka (USA) 3-8-7
      FHead 8.6
    Magnificent Star (USA) 4-9-2
      ASCruz 10.7
    Miss Plum 3-8-7 PatEddery .. 5.8
13   L'Amour Fou (Ire) 4-9-2
      PBruneau dist.9

6/10 L'Amour Fou and MAGIC NIGHT,
9/2 Trampoli, 46/10 Linnga, 117/10
Sought Out, 13/1 Magnificent Star,
164/10 Miss Plum, 18/1 Always Friendly,
28/1 Winnetka
  H. Yokoyama (P. Demercastel) 9ran
3m07.10 (Soft)

41   GROSSER PREIS VON 6f110y
    BERLIN (Gr 3) (3yo +)
£70,671   Baden-Baden 9 August
32*   **Mr Brooks** 5-9-6 LPiggott 1
25   **Monde Bleu** 4-9-6
      SGuillot ½.2
    Dream Talk 5-9-6 GMosse . 1.3
    Silicon Bavaria (Fr) 5-9-2
      MBoutin 3½.4
    Be Happy (Ger) 3-8-7
      LPyritz 1½.5
    Roman Prose 7-9-6 CBlack .. ns.6
    My Corncrake (Ire) 6-9-6
      FDiaz 2½.7
    Dawson Place (USA) 4-9-6
      WBuick 8
    Windreiter 3-8-10 WNewnes ... 9
    Astica 3-8-6 GHuber 10
    Cardmania (USA) 6-9-6
      ALequeux 11
    Sambit 3-8-10 ABoschert 12

P. Green (R. Hannon) 12ran 1m14.60
(Good)

42 PRIX DU HARAS DE 1m
FRESNAY-LE-BUFFARD
JACQUES LE MAROIS
(Gr 1) (3yo + c + f)
£105,042 Deauville 16 August

19	**Exit To Nowhere (USA)** 4-9-4	
	CAsmussen 1	
19*	**Lahib (USA)** 4-9-4	
	WCarson 1.2	
38²	**Cardoun (Fr)** 3-8-11	
	DBoeuf hd.3	
36	Star of Cozzene (USA) 4-9-4	
	GMosse nk.4	
9	Hatoof (USA) 3-8-8	
	WRSwinburn 2.5	
38	Lion Cavern (USA) 3-8-11	
	TJarnet 1½.6	
	El Prado (Ire) 3-8-11	
	CRoche 1½.7	
	Misil (USA) 5-9-4	
	LDettori 1½.8	
5	Take Risks (Fr) 3-8-11	
	MBoutin nk.9	
9²	Hydro Calido (USA) 3-8-8	
	FHead 1½.10	
3	Dilum (USA) 3-8-11	
	AMunro 4.11	
36	Sikeston (USA) 6-9-4	
	MRoberts 2.12	
29²	Kitwood (USA) 3-8-11	
	PatEddery 1.13	
	Hazm (USA) 3-8-11 RHills .. 1.14	

23/10 EXIT TO NOWHERE and Hydro
Calido, 47/10 Kitwood and Lion Cavern,
51/10 Dilum, 7/1 Misil, 91/10 Cardoun,
10/1 Sikeston, 126/10 Hazm and Lahib,
16/1 Hatoof, Take Risks, 26/1 El Prado,
36/1 Star of Cozzene
  S. S. Niarchos (F. Boutin) 14ran
1m40.82 (Soft)

43 JUDDMONTE 1¼m85y
INTERNATIONAL
STAKES (Gr 1) (3yo +)
£164,852 York 18 August

21	**Rodrigo de Triano (USA)** 3-8-12	
	LPiggott 1	
16²	**All At Sea (USA)** 3-8-9	
	PatEddery 1.2	
	Seattle Rhyme (USA) 3-8-12	
	CAsmussen 3.3	
27²	Dr Devious (Ire) 3-8-12	
	JReid sh.4	
	Masad (Ire) 3-8-12 LDettori .. 3.5	
30	Zoman (USA) 5-9-6	
	AMunro 2½.6	
14	Alnasr Alwasheek 3-8-12	
	SCauthen 1½.7	
	Ruby Tiger 5-9-3 TQuinn 8.8	
20	Gussy Marlowe 4-9-3	
	WCarson 5.9	
35	Terimon 6-9-6 MRoberts .. hd.10	
	Bobzao (Ire) 3-8-12	
	JCarroll 3.11	
39*	Kooyonga (Ire) 4-9-3	
	WJO'Connor dist.12	

2/1 Kooyonga, 5/1 All At Sea, 7/1 Alnasr
Alwasheek, 8/1 Dr Devious, RODRIGO
DE TRIANO, 9/1 Ruby Tiger, 16/1
Masad, Seattle Rhyme, 20/1 Zoman, 25/1
Terimon, 100/1 Gussy Marlowe, 200/1
Bobzao
  R. E. Sangster (P. W. Chapple-Hyam)
12ran 2m07.19 (Good)

44 ASTON UPTHORPE 1m3f195y
YORKSHIRE OAKS (Gr 1)
(3yo + f + m)
£77,728 York 19 August

33*	**User Friendly** 3-8-11	
	GDuffield 1	
33	**Bineyah (Ire)** 3-8-11	
	PatEddery 2½.2	
	Guilty Secret (Ire) 3-8-11	
	PaulEddery sh.3	
	Niodini (USA) 3-8-11	
	SCauthen nk.4	
16³	Pearl Angel 3-8-11	
	LPiggott 10.5	
26³	Lara's Idea 4-9-7 JReid ¾.6	
	Midnight Air (USA) 3-8-11	
	RCochrane sh.7	
40	Magnificent Star (USA) 4-9-7	
	LDettori 2.8	

8/11 USER FRIENDLY, 8/1 Bineyah,
Magnificent Star, Midnight Air, Niodini,
12/1 Lara's Idea, 33/1 Guilty Secret,
Pearl Angel
  W. J. Gredley (C. E. Brittain) 8ran
2m29.41 (Good to Firm)

45 KEENELAND 5f
NUNTHORPE STAKES
(Gr 1) (2yo +)
£93,528 York 20 August

22*	**Lyric Fantasy (Ire)** 2-7-8	
	MRoberts 1	
41*	**Mr Brooks** 5-9-6 LPiggott . ½.2	
	Diamonds Galore (Can)	
	7-9-6 AGryder 1½.3	
38	Elbio 5-9-6 WRSwinburn nk.4	
	Freddie Lloyd (USA) 3-9-3	
	PatEddery nk.5	
32	Paris House 3-9-3	
	SCauthen 2½.6	
	Farfelu 5-9-6 TQuinn 1½.7	
2	Harvest Girl (Ire) 3-9-0	
	WCarson hd.8	
	Medaille d'Or 4-9-6	
	LDettori 1.9	
25	El Yasaf (Ire) 4-9-6	
	JWilliams 3½.10	
25	Blyton Lad 6-9-6	
	SWebster 2½.11	

8/11 LYRIC FANTASY, 9/2 Mr Brooks,
8/1 Freddie Lloyd, 10/1 Elbio, 11/1 Paris
House, 25/1 Blyton Lad, 33/1 Diamonds
Galore, 50/1 Medaille d'Or, 66/1 El Yasaf,
Farfelu, Harvest Girl
  Lord Carnarvon (R. Hannon) 11ran
57.39secs (Good to Firm)

46 PRIX MORNY AGENCE   6f
    FRANCAISE (Gr 1) (2yo c + f)
£104,932   Deauville   23 August
    Zafonic (USA) 8-11
    PatEddery 1
    Secrage (USA) 8-8
    BJovine ¾.2
22 **Marina Park** 8-8
    DeanMcKeown ½.3
    Wixon (Fr) 8-8
    ESaint-Martin 1½.4
    Didyme (USA) 8-11
    GMosse nk.5
    Kingmambo (USA) 8-11
    FHead 1.6
    Namaqualand (USA) 8-11
    SCauthen nk.7
    Future Storm (USA) 8-11
    VMezzatesta 1½.8
    Port Lucaya 8-11 JReid nk.9
    Creaking Board 8-8
    ELegrix 3.10
6/5 Didyme, 27/10 ZAFONIC, 56/10
Creaking Board and Future Storm, 7/1
Kingmambo, 112/10 Secrage, 12/1
Namaqualand, 163/10 Marina Park, 22/1
Wixon, 56/1 Port Lucaya
    K. Abdulla (A. Fabre) 10ran 1m14.80
(Soft)

47 PRIX KERGORLAY   1m7f
    (Gr 2) (3yo +)
£26,233   Deauville   23 August
40² **Sought Out (Ire)** 4-9-1
    CAsmussen 1
24* **Drum Taps (USA)** 6-9-11
    LDettori 5.2
    Michelozzo (USA) 6-9-4
    JReid 4.3
    In Quarto 3-8-7 DBoeuf 1½.4
    Shambo 5-9-9 MRoberts 5.5
24³ Turgeon (USA) 6-9-11
    SCauthen 5.6
    Hateel 6-9-4 WCarson 6.7
    Supreme Choice (USA) 4-9-4
    PatEddery 8.8
    Triple Tiara (USA) 3-9-4
    TJarnet 8.9
11/10 Drum Taps, 29/10 SOUGHT OUT,
4/1 Triple Tiara and Turgeon, 66/10 In
Quarto, 105/10 Shambo, 13/1 Supreme
Choice, 33/1 Hateel, 40/1 Michelozzo
    Lord Weinstock (J. E. Hammond) 9ran
3m25.40 (Soft)

48 BEEFEATER GIN   1m
    CELEBRATION MILE
    (Gr 2) (3yo +)
£50,035   Goodwood   29 August
36² **Selkirk (USA)** 4-9-3
    RCochrane 1
3   **Steinbeck (USA)** 3-8-8
    SCauthen 2½.2
36   Rudimentary (USA) 4-9-3
    LPiggott hd.3
29   Alhijaz 3-9-0 WCarson nk.4

Flashfoot 4-9-0
    PaulEddery 10.5
7   Mystiko (USA) 4-9-0 JReid . hd.6
    Sylva Honda 4-9-0
    GCarter 3½.7
1/2 SELKIRK, 5/1 Steinbeck, 7/1
Rudimentary, 10/1 Mystiko, 20/1 Alhijaz,
50/1 Flashfoot, 100/1 Sylva Honda
    George Strawbridge (I. A. Balding)
7ran 1m41.72 (Good to Soft)

49 JACOBS GOLDENE   6f
    PEITSCHE (Gr 2) (3yo +)
£34,172   Baden-Baden   2 September
45   **Elbio** 5-9-3 JReid 1
38³ **Twafeaj (USA)** 3-8-7
    BRaymond 1.2
    Wedding of The Sea (USA)
    3-8-7 TJarnet 1¾.3
41   Silicon Bavaria (Fr) 5-8-13
    MBoutin nk.4
41³ Dream Talk 5-9-3 GMosse 3.5
    Rocky Waters (USA) 3-8-11
    BRouse 3½.6
    Litron (Ger) 3-8-11 DIlic ¾.7
    Montepulciano (USA) 3-8-11
    AHelfenbein 8
    Hatta Fort 5-9-3 ABest 9
3 1/10 Wedding of The Sea, 32/10 Litron,
38/10 Dream Talk, ELBIO, 61/10
Twafeaj, 87/10 Silicon Bavaria, 13/1
Montepulciano, 20/1 Rocky Waters, 37/1
Hatta Fort
    B. Brackpool (P. J. Makin) 9ran
1m12.99 (Soft)

50 HAYDOCK PARK   6f
    SPRINT CUP (Gr 1) (2yo +)
£75,150   Haydock   5 September
36   **Sheikh Albadou** 4-9-9
    BRaymond 1
45² **Mr Brooks** 5-9-9
    LPiggott 2½.2
32   **Wolfhound (USA)** 3-9-6
    SCauthen 6.3
3   Shalford (Ire) 4-9-9 JReid 4.4
    Wilde Rufo 3-9-6 KDarley . 2½.5
    Sizzling Saga (Ire) 4-9-9
    JCarroll 2½.6
32   Tbab (Ire) 4-9-9 MBirch 5.7
    Bletchley Park (Ire) 3-9-6
    RHills 10.8
9/4 Mr Brooks, SHEIKH ALBADOU,
5/2 Shalford, 7/1 Wolfhound, 33/1 Tbab,
66/1 Bletchley Park, Sizzling Saga, 100/1
Wilde Rufo
    Hilal Salem (A. A. Scott) 8ran 1m14.17
(Good to Soft)

51 BONUSPRINT   1m3f30y
    SEPTEMBER STAKES
    (Gr 3) (3yo +)
£21,573   Kempton   5 September
35   **Jeune** 3-8-6 RCochrane 1
    Red Bishop (USA) 4-9-0
    WCarson 3½.2

43³ **Seattle Rhyme (USA)** 3-8-6
CAsmussen nk.**3**
Corrupt (USA) 4-9-5
LDettori 1½.**4**
Ile de Chypre 7-9-7 AClark . 10.5

8/11 Seattle Rhyme, 11/2 Corrupt, Red
Bishop, 6/1 JEUNE, 16/1 Ile de Chypre
Sir Robin McAlpine (G. Wragg) 5ran
2m22.61(Good)

52　BEVERLY D　　　1m1f110y
STAKES (GRADE 1)
(3yo + f + m)
£167,213　Arlington　5 September
Kostroma 6-8-11
KDesormeaux **1**
43　**Ruby Tiger** 5-8-11
TQuinn 1¼.**2**
Dance Smartly (Can) 4-8-11
PDay nk.**3**
Marble Maiden 3-8-5
TJarnet 2.4
Polemic (USA) 4-8-11
MSmith hd.5
Super Staff (USA) 4-8-11
CMcCarron 1½.6
Julie La Rousse (Ire) 4-8-11
CAntley hd.7
Elegance (USA) 5-8-11
GGomez ns.8
Crystal Path (Fr) 4-8-11
EFires 2½.9
13　Caerlina (Ire) 4-8-11
ELegrix ½.10
Olden Rijn (USA) 4-8-11
JVelasquez 1.11
Alcando 6-8-11 SSellers .. 4½.12
Radiant Ring (Can) 4-8-11
JLauzon 1¼.13

8/5 Dance Smartly and Radiant Ring, 5/2
KOSTROMA, 58/10 Ruby Tiger, 82/10
Polemic and Super Staff, 11/1 Alcando,
14/1 Marble Maiden, 16/1 Julie La
Rousse, 29/1 Caerlina, 54/1 Olden Rijn,
59/1 Elegance, 60/1 Crystal Path
W. De Burgh/R. Sangster/Preston-
wood Farms (G. Jones) 13ran 1m54.00
(Firm)

53　GROSSER PREIS VON　　1½m
BADEN (Gr 1) (3yo +)
£102,678　Baden-Baden　6 September
34²　**Mashaallah (USA)** 4-9-6
JReid **1**
Platini (Ger) 3-8-9
MRimmer 1¼.**2**
35　**Sapience** 6-9-6 WCarson . 1½.**3**
39　Hondo Mondo (Ire) 4-9-6
ABest ¾.4
Pik Konig (Ger) 3-8-9
ABoschert .... pu

6/5 Platini, 22/10 Sapience, 36/10 Pik
Konig, 6/1 Mashaallah, 63/10 Hondo
Mondo
Sheikh Ahmed Al-Maktoum (J. H. M.
Gosden) 5ran 2m37.83 (Soft)

54　EMIRATES PRIX DU　　1m
MOULIN DE
LONGCHAMP (Gr 1)
(3yo + c + f)
£90,215　Longchamp　6 September
43²　**All At Sea (USA)** 3-8-8
PatEddery **1**
21*　**Brief Truce (USA)** 3-8-11
MJKinane nk.**2**
42　**Hatoof (USA)** 3-8-8
GMosse 2½.**3**
42　Misil (USA) 4-9-2
RCochrane 2.4
42　Kitwood (USA) 3-8-11
TJarnet 1.5
42³　Cardoun (Fr) 3-8-11
DBoeuf ¾.6
42　Take Risks (Fr) 3-8-11
MBoutin ½.7
12³　Shanghai (USA) 3-8-11
ALequeux 2.8
Sharp Review (Ire) 4-9-2
PShanahan 1.9
42　El Prado (Ire) 3-8-11
LPiggott 4.10

21/10 Brief Truce and Sharp Review,
29/10 ALL AT SEA, 6/1 Kitwood, 62/10
Hatoof, 7/1 Cardoun, 78/10 Shanghai,
105/10 Misil, 20/1 El Prado, 25/1 Take
Risks
K. Abdulla (H. R. A. Cecil) 10ran
1m40.70 (Soft)

55　ARLINGTON　　1¼m (Turf)
MILLION (GRADE 1) (3yo +)
£334,427　Arlington　6 September
39　**Dear Doctor (Fr)** 5-9-0
CAsmussen **1**
Sky Classic (Can) 5-9-0
PDay hd.**2**
Golden Pheasant (USA) 6-9-0
GStevens nk.**3**
42*　Exit To Nowhere (USA) 4-9-0
FHead 2¼.4
El Trenzador (Arg) 4-9-0
EDelahoussaye 1¼.5
Quest For Fame 5-9-0
CMcCarron 1½.6
Chenin Blanc (USA) 6-9-0
MSmith ½.7
36³　Second Set (Ire) 4-9-0
LDettori ¾.8
42　Star of Cozzene (USA) 4-9-0
CAntley 1½.9
Marquetry (USA) 5-9-0
DFlores ½.10
River Verdon 5-9-0
BMarcus 3.11
John Rose 3-8-8
GayKelleway 13.12

6/5 Sky Classic, 37/10 Marquetry AND
Quest For Fame, 67/1 Golden
Pheasant, 91/10 River Verdon, 108/10
Exit To Nowhere, 139/10 DEAR
DOCTOR, 169/10 Second Set, 226/10
Chenin Blanc, 261/10 El Trenzador,

345/10 Star of Cozzene, 744/10 John Rose
Henri Chalhoub (J. E. Hammond) 12ran 1m59.80 (Firm)

56   KIVETON PARK   7f
STAKES (Gr 3) (3yo +)
£23,733   Doncaster   10 September
38*   **Pursuit of Love** 3-9-3
      RCochrane **1**
      Prince Ferdinand 3-9-0
      JReid 2.**2**
      Storm Dove (USA) 3-8-7
      PatEddery nk.**3**
42   Dilum (USA) 3-9-0
      AMunro sh.**4**
6   Norwich 5-9-4 SCauthen ... 3½.**5**
21   River Falls 3-8-10
      BRaymond 2½.**6**
      Bog Trotter (USA) 4-9-4
      LPiggott sh.**7**
50   Wilde Rufo 3-8-10 JCarroll 2.**8**
      Reported (Ire) 3-8-10
      PaulEddery 1½.**9**
48   Sylva Honda 4-9-4
      GDuffield ½.**10**
9/4 Storm Dove, 7/2 Dilum, 4/1 PURSUIT OF LOVE, 5/1 Prince Ferdinand, 12/1 Bog Trotter, 14/1 Norwich, 16/1 Reported, 25/1 River Falls, 50/1 Sylva Honda, 100/1 Wilde Rufo
Lord Howard de Walden (H. R. A. Cecil) 10ran 1m23.95 (Firm)

57   COALITE ST LEGER   1¾m 132y
STAKES (Gr 1) (3yo c + f)
£161,368   Doncaster   12 September
44*   **User Friendly** 8-11
      GDuffield **1**
      Sonus (Ire) 9-0
      SCauthen 3½.**2**
      Bonny Scot (Ire) 9-0
      LDettori nk.**3**
      Shuailaan (USA) 9-0
      MRoberts ¾.**4**
      Mack The Knife 9-0
      LPiggott 6.**5**
14   Assessor (Ire) 9-0 JReid 5.**6**
      Rain Rider 9-0 WCarson ¾.**7**
7/4 USER FRIENDLY, 5/2 Bonny Scot, 5/1 Rain Rider, 15/2 Sonus, 14/1 Assessor, Mack The Knife, 18/1 Shuailaan
W. J. Gredley (C. E. Brittain) 7ran 3m05.48 (Good to Firm)

58   KERRY GROUP IRISH   1¼m
CHAMPION STAKES
(Gr 1) (3yo + c + f)
£82,190   Leopardstown   13 September
43   **Dr Devious (Ire)** 3-8-11
      JReid **1**
35*   **St Jovite (USA)** 3-8-11
      CRoche sh.**2**

14   **Alflora (Ire)** 3-8-11
      MRoberts 9.**3**
43   Kooyonga (Ire) 4-9-3
      WJO'Connor 6.**4**
      Malvernico (Ire) 4-9-6
      KJManning 2.**5**
14   Great Palm (USA) 3-8-11
      TQuinn 15.**6**
      Dowland (USA) 4-9-6
      PVGilson 8.**7**
      Magic Carr (USA) 3-8-11
      CEverard dist.**8**
4/7 St Jovite, 7/2 DR DEVIOUS, 4/1 Kooyonga, 11/1 Great Palm, 50/1 Alflora, 100/1 Malvernico, 200/1 Dowland, Magic Carr
Sidney H. Craig (P. W. Chapple-Hyam) 8ran 2m 10.00 (Good to Soft)

59   PRIX NIEL ESCADA   1½m
(Gr 2) (3yo c + f)
£42,017   Longchamp   13 September
34³   **Songlines (Fr)** 9-2
      OBenoist **1**
      Petit Loup (USA) 9-2
      CAsmussen ns.**2**
17   **Apple Tree (Fr)** 9-2
      TJarnet ½.**3**
27³   Contested Bid (USA) 9-2
      PatEddery 1.**4**
27   Marignan (USA) 9-2
      DBoeuf 2.**5**
17   Glanville (USA) 9-2
      ELegrix hd.**6**
29   Johann Quatz (Fr) 9-2
      FHead hd.**7**
17*   Polytain (Fr) 9-2 LDettori 2.**8**
6/4 Polytain, 31/10 Marignan, 37/10 Contested Bid, 62/10 Petit Loup, 74/10 Apple Tree, 118/10 SONGLINES, 15/1 Johann Quatz, 41/1 Glanville
Sir R. McAlpine (E. Bartholomew) 8ran 2m32.80 (Good to Firm)

60   PRIX VERMEILLE   1½m
ESCADA (Gr 1) (3yo f)
£105,042   Longchamp   13 September
18*   **Jolypha (USA)** 9-2
      PatEddery **1**
      Cunning 9-2 LDettori hd.**2**
18   **Urban Sea (USA)** 9-2
      MBoutin ½.**3**
29   Verveine (USA) 9-2
      DBoeuf ns.**4**
33²   Market Booster (USA) 9-2
      MJKinane hd.**5**
18   Trishyde (USA) 9-2
      FHead sn.**6**
      Palomelle (Fr) 9-2
      TJarnet 2½.**7**
      River Nymph (USA) 9-2
      ELegrix 1½.**8**
40   Linnga (Ire) 9-2
      GGuignard 1.**9**
      Ionian Sea 9-2 CBlack 1½.**10**

8/5 JOLYPHA, 26/10 Market Booster, 11/2 Cunning, 10/1 Verveine, 103/10 Trishyde, 12/1 Linnga, 17/1 Palomelle, River Nymph, Urban Sea, 31/1 Ionian Sea
K. Abdulla (A. Fabre) 10ran 2m32.80 (Good to Firm)

61	PRIX DE LA SALAMANDRE (Gr 1) (2yo c + f)	7f
£52,521	Longchamp	13 September
46*	**Zafonic (USA)** 8-11 PatEddery	1
46	**Kingmambo (USA)** 8-11 FHead	3.2
	Splendent (USA) 8-11 AMunro	½.3
	Canaska Star 8-11 SCauthen	1½.4
46	Didyme (USA) 8-11 ELegrix	sh.5
	Tenga (USA) 8-8 ESaint-Martin	3.6

1/2 ZAFONIC, 38/10 Splendent, 43/10 Didyme, 98/10 Kingmambo, 112/10 Canaska Star, 116/10 Tenga
K. Abdulla (A. Fabre) 6ran 1m23.30 (Good to Firm)

62	PRIX FOY ESCADA (Gr 3) (4yo +)	1½m
£21,008	Longchamp	13 September
40*	**Magic Night (Fr)** 4-8-13 ABadel	1
31³	**Subotica (Fr)** 4-9-2 TJarnet	¾.2
20	**Tel Quel (Fr)** 4-9-2 SCauthen	sh.3
31	Saganeca (USA) 4-8-13 CAsmussen	4.4

7/10 MAGIC NIGHT, 14/10 Subotica, 46/10 Tel Quel, 9/1 Saganeca
H. Yokoyama (P. Demercastel) 4ran 2m40.50 (Good to Firm)

63	ROKEBY FARMS MILL REEF STAKES (Gr 2) (2yo)	6f8y
£30,716	Newbury	19 September
	Forest Wind (USA) 8-11 LDettori	1
46³	**Marina Park** 8-6 DeanMcKeown	½.2
	Sharp Prod (USA) 9-1 AMunro	2.3
	Pips Pride 9-1 BRaymond	1.4
	Carbon Steel (Ire) 8-11 PRobinson	1.5
	Aradanza 8-11 JWilliams	3½.6
	Green's Bid 8-11 MRoberts	2.7

5/4 Marina Park, 7/2 Green's Bid, 11/2 FOREST WIND, 6/1 Sharp Prod, 8/1 Pips Pride, 12/1 Carbon Steel, 50/1 Aradanza

Ecurie Fustok (M. Moubarak) 7ran 1m14.80 (Good)

64	JEFFERSON SMURFIT MEMORIAL IRISH ST LEGER (Gr 1) (3yo +)	1¾m
£80,571	Curragh	19 September
53*	**Mashaallah (USA)** 4-9-8 SCauthen	1
26	**Snurge** 5-9-8 TQuinn	nk.2
47²	**Drum Taps (USA)** 6-9-8 JReid	¾.3
35	Rock Hopper 5-9-8 PatEddery	2½.4
	Vintage Crop 5-9-8 MJKinane	2.5
33³	Arrikala (Ire) 3-8-9 CRoche	4½.6
	Dabtiya (Ire) 3-8-9 RHughes	1½.7
	Tropicarr (USA) 3-8-12 KJManning	dist.8
	Jahafil 4-9-8 WCarson	15.9

11/4 MASHAALLAH, 9/2 Drum Taps, 5/1 Snurge, 6/1 Rock Hopper, 7/1 Arrikala, Jahafil, 20/1 Dabtiya, Vintage Crop, 100/1 Tropicarr
Sheikh Ahmed Al-Maktoum (J. H. M. Gosden) 9ran 3m02.01 (Soft)

65	GRAN PREMIO D'ITALIA (Gr 1) (3yo)	1½m
£103,059	Milan	20 September
43	**Masad (Ire)** 9-2 LDettori	1
17	**Modhish (Ire)** 9-2 PatEddery	¾.2
	In A Tiff (Ire) 9-2 MJKinane	1.3
	Silvernesian (USA) 9-2 WCarson	3.4
27	Mining Tycoon (Ire) 9-2 CRoche	5.5
	Big Tobin (Ity) 9-2 AParravani	5.6
29	Vasarelli (Ire) 9-2 LPiggott	7.7

Evens Modhish, 26/10 MASAD, 3/1 In A Tiff, 13/1 Mining Tycoon, 15/1 Vasarelli, 18/1 Silvernesian, 25/1 Big Tobin
Scuderia Gabriella (L. M. Cumani) 7ran 2m30.00 (Good to Soft)

66	HOOVER CUMBERLAND LODGE STAKES (Gr 3) (3yo +)	1½m
£26,640	Ascot	24 September
35³	**Opera House** 4-9-5 SCauthen	1
51²	**Red Bishop (USA)** 4-9-0 PatEddery	1½.2
	Garden of Heaven (USA) 3-8-6 MRoberts	¾.3
57³	Bonny Scot (Ire) 3-8-11 LDettori	1½.4
53³	Sapience 6-9-5 WCarson	7.5

9/4 OPERA HOUSE, 5/2 Red Bishop, 3/1 Bonny Scot, 4/1 Sapience, 25/1 Garden of Heaven

Sheikh Mohammed (M. R. Stoute)
5ran 2m40.47 (Soft)

67	QUEEN ELIZABETH II STAKES (Gr 1) (3yo +)	1m
£208,339	Ascot	26 September
42²	**Lahib (USA)** 4-9-4 WCarson .. 1	
54²	**Brief Truce (USA)** 3-9-0	
	MJKinane 2.2	
48*	**Selkirk (USA)** 4-9-4	
	JReid 1½.3	
54*	All At Sea (USA) 3-8-11	
	PatEddery 2½.4	
55	Second Set (Ire) 4-9-4	
	LDettori 3½.5	
48	Mystiko (USA) 4-9-4	
	MRoberts 8.6	
36*	Marling (Ire) 3-8-11	
	WRSwinburn hd.7	
54	Sharp Review (Ire) 4-9-4	
	PShanahan 2.8	
	Hamas (Ire) 3-9-0 RHills ... 1½.9	

5/4 Selkirk, 4/1 All At Sea, 9/2 Marling, 7/1 Brief Truce, 8/1 LAHIB, 14/1 Second Set, 50/1 Mystiko, 200/1 Hamas, Sharp Review

Hamdan Al-Maktoum (J. L. Dunlop)
9ran 1m44.50 (Soft)

68	FILLIES' MILE (Gr 1) (2yo f)	1m
£93,015	Ascot	26 September
	Ivanka (Ire) 8-10	
	MRoberts 1	
	Ajfan (USA) 8-10	
	RHills 1½.2	
	Iviza (Ire) 8-10	
	SCauthen 3.3	
	Bright Generation (Ire) 8-10	
	AMunro ½.4	
	Abury (Ire) 8-10 JReid 1.5	
	Magique Rond Point (USA) 8-10	
	PatEddery ¾.6	
22²	Mystic Goddess (USA) 8-10	
	WCarson 7.7	
	Comme d'Habitude (USA) 8-10	
	TQuinn 25.8	

11/4 Iviza, 7/2 Bright Generation, Magique Rond Point, 11/2 Mystic Goddess, 6/1 IVANKA, 14/1 Comme d'Habitude, 16/1 Ajfan, 33/1 Abury

Ali Saeed (C. E. Brittain) 8ran
1m46.65 (Soft)

69	TATTERSALLS CHEVELEY PARK STAKES (Gr 1) (2yo f)	6f
£74,998	Newmarket	30 September
	Sayyedati 8-11	
	WRSwinburn 1	
45*	**Lyric Fantasy (Ire)** 8-11	
	MRoberts 2.2	

Poker Chip 8-11
MHills 1½.3
Anonymous 8-11 LDettori 6.4

1/2 Lyric Fantasy, 5/2 SAYYEDATI, 9/1 Poker Chip, 50/1 Anonymous

Mohamed Obaida (C. E. Brittain) 4ran
1m11.82 (Good to Firm)

70	NEWGATE STUD MIDDLE PARK STAKES (Gr 1) (2yo c)	6f
£58,035	Newmarket	1 October
	Zieten (USA) 9-0	
	SCauthen 1	
63	Pips Pride 9-0 LDettori 1.2	
	Factual (USA) 9-0	
	PatEddery 2½.3	
	Silver Wizard (USA) 9-0	
	WCarson ¾.4	
	Wootton Rivers (USA) 9-0	
	DHolland 3.5	
	Virilis 9-0 MRoberts 30.6	

8/13 Silver Wizard, 5/2 ZIETEN, 12/1 Pips Pride, 14/1 Factual, 20/1 Wootton Rivers, 33/1 Virilis

Sheikh Mohammed (A. Fabre) 6ran
1m11.28 (Good to Firm)

71	CIGA PRIX DU CADRAN (Gr 1) (4yo +)	2½m
£58,892	Longchamp	3 October
47*	**Sought Out (Ire)** 4-8-13	
	CAsmussen 1	
64³	**Drum Taps (USA)** 6-9-2	
	AMunro 4.2	
	Dariyoun (USA) 4-9-2	
	FHead 1½.3	
37²	Witness Box (USA) 5-9-2	
	SCauthen 2½.4	
	Great Marquess 5-9-2	
	MJKinane 5.5	
	Le Montagnard (Fr) 4-9-2	
	CJPhelippeau hd.6	
	Proud Panther (Fr) 6-9-2	
	ABadel dist.7	

11/10 SOUGHT OUT, 17/10 Drum Taps, 7/2 Great Marquess and Witness Box, 92/10 Le Montagnard, 16/1 Dariyoun, Proud Panther

Lord Weinstock (J. E. Hammond) 7ran
4m41.10 (Soft)

72	CIGA GRAND CRITERIUM (Gr 1) (2yo c + f)	1m
£141,343	Longchamp	3 October
	Tenby 8-11 PatEddery 1	
	Blush Rambler (USA) 8-11	
	SCauthen 2½.2	
	Basim (USA) 8-11	
	CRoche sh.3	
	Seaton Delaval (USA) 8-11	
	TJarnet 2½.4	
61²	Kingmambo (USA) 8-11	
	FHead 1½.5	
	Lindon Lime (USA) 8-11	
	TQuinn 3.6	

61   Canaska Star 8-11
      MJKinane 1.7
61[3] Splendent (USA) 8-11
      AMunro 8.8
    Kadounor (Fr) 8-11
      GGuignard ns.9
    Master Peace (Fr) 8-11
      ELegrix 1½.10
    Fastness (Ire) 8-11
      CAsmussen 1½.11

17/10 TENBY, 7/2 Fastness, 39/10 Blush Rambler and Seaton Delaval, 49/10 Kadounor, 68/10 Basim, 10/1 Kingmambo, 14/1 Master Peace, 15/1 Lindon Lime and Splendent, 42/1 Canaska Star
  K. Abdulla (H. R. A. Cecil) 11ran
1m46.90 (Soft)

73   CIGA PRIX DOLLAR 1m 1f 165y
    (Gr 2) (3yo +)
£34,819   Longchamp   3 October
    Sillery (USA) 4-9-0 FHead 1
    Wiorno 4-9-0 TJarnet 1.2
51   Corrupt (USA) 4-9-0
      CAsmussen 1½.3
    Half A Tick (USA) 4-9-0
      TQuinn 5.4
    Spartan Shareef (Ire) 3-8-10
      AMunro nk.5
    Knifebox (USA) 4-9-0
      MJKinane 10.6
43   Alnasr Alwasheek 3-9-0
      PatEddery 1½.7
29   Pollen Count (USA) 3-9-0
      SCauthen 1½.8

2/1 SILLERY, 24/10 Knifebox and Pollen Count, 36/10 Alnasr Alwasheek, 4/1 Corrupt, 79/10 Wiorno, 114/10 Half A Tick, 26/1 Spartan Shareef
  Mme A. Head (Mme C. Head) 8ran
2m 11.60 (Soft)

74   CIGA PRIX DU   1m
    ROND-POINT (Gr 2) (3yo +)
£47,114   Longchamp   4 October
21   Arazi (USA) 3-8-11
      SCauthen 1
12   Calling Collect (USA) 3-8-11
      LDettori 4.2
48   Alhijaz 3-9-4 JReid hd.3
20   Lucky Lindy (Ire) 3-8-11
      MJKinane 1½.4
    Acteur Francais (USA) 4-8-13
      DBoeuf 1.5
    Dampierre (USA) 4-8-13
      TJarnet 1½.6
    Tik Fa (USA) 3-8-11
      WRSwinburn ½.7
17   Silver Kite (USA) 3-8-11
      GMosse nk.8
    Primer Amor (Spa) 5-8-13
      WCarson 5.9
    Code Breaker (Fr) 3-8-11
      ELegrix sn.10
    Mojave 3-8-11
      PatEddery 2½.11

6/5 ARAZI, 32/10 Dampierre, 57/10 Calling Collect, 15/2 Mojave, 14/1 Lucky Lindy, Tik Fa, 17/1 Acteur Francais, 25/1 Alhijaz, 26/1 Silver Kite, 31/1 Primer Amor, 34/1 Code Breaker
  Sheikh Mohammed (F. Boutin) 11ran
1m44.00 (Soft)

75   PRIX MARCEL   1m
    BOUSSAC (Gr 1) (2yo f)
£94,229   Longchamp   4 October
    Gold Splash (USA) 8-11
      GMosse 1
    Kindergarten 8-11
      SCauthen sn.2
    Love of Silver (USA) 8-11
      MRoberts ¾.3
    Rouquette 8-11 ABadel 1.4
    Marillette (USA) 8-11
      PatEddery hd.5
    Lorelie (Fr) 8-11
      FHead 2½.6
46[2] Secrage (USA) 8-11
      BJovine hd.7
    Sissingaya (USA) 8-11
      DBoeuf ½.8
    Marviah (USA) 8-11
      CAsmussen 1.9
    Nemea (USA) 8-11
      LDettori ½.10
    Cox Orange (USA) 8-11
      TJarnet dist.11

1/2 Cox Orange and Kindergarten and Marillette, 39/10 Secrage, 68/10 Love of Silver, 114/10 GOLD SPLASH, 17/1 Lorelie, Rouquette, 25/1 Marviah, 35/1 Sissingaya, 70/1 Nemea
  J. Wertheimer (Mme C. Head) 11ran
1m44.90 (Soft)

76   CIGA PRIX DE   5f
    L'ABBAYE (Gr 1) (2yo + c + f)
£82,449   Longchamp   4 October
50[2] Mr Brooks 5-9-11 LPiggott ... 1
    Keen Hunter (USA) 5-9-11
      SCauthen 2.2
49* Elbio 5-9-11 JReid nk.3
10   Bezelle 3-9-8 PShanahan 1.4
25   Flowing (USA) 4-9-8
      MJKinane sn.5
    Bold n'Flashy (Can) 3-9-11
      RDosRamos nk.6
49[2] Twafeaj (USA) 3-9-8
      WRSwinburn 2.7
49   Dream Talk 5-9-11
      GMosse 1½.8
    Peperonata (Ire) 2-8-5
      JLowe 3.9

9/10 MR BROOKS, 27/10 Keen Hunter, 57/10 Elbio, 67/10 Flowing, 13/1 Bold n'Flashy, 17/1 Dream Talk, 27/1 Twafeaj, 39/1 Bezelle, 64/1 Peperonata
  P. Green (R. Hannon) 9ran 1m02.30 (Soft)

77 CIGA PRIX DE L'ARC DE 1½m
  TRIOMPHE (Gr 1) (3yo + c + f)
£588,929 Longchamp 4 October
62² **Subotica (Fr)** 4-9-4 TJarnet .. 1
57* **User Friendly** 3-8-8
  GDuffield nk.2
34* **Vert Amande (Fr)** 4-9-4
  ELegrix 2.3
58² St Jovite (USA) 3-8-11
  CRoche 1½.4
62 Saganeca (USA) 4-9-1
  WMongil sh.5
58* Dr Devious (Ire) 3-8-11
  JReid ¾.6
30 Arcangues (USA) 4-9-4
  GMosse 2.7
60* Jolypha (USA) 3-8-8
  PatEddery nk.8
60 Verveine (USA) 3-8-8
  DBoeuf ns.9
55* Dear Doctor (Fr) 5-9-4
  CAsmussen ¾.10
64* Mashaallah (USA) 4-9-4
  SCauthen ½.11
59² Petit Loup (USA) 3-8-11
  WRSwinburn nk.12
62* Magic Night (Fr) 4-9-1
  ABadel nk.13
66 Sapience 6-9-4 TQuinn ... 1½.14
35² Saddlers' Hall (Ire) 4-9-4
  WCarson 1½.15
60 Market Booster (USA) 3-8-8
  MJKinane 1½.16
51³ Seattle Rhyme (USA) 3-8-11
  MRoberts ½.17
59 Polytain (Fr) 3-8-11
  LDettori 18

33/10 User Friendly, 9/2 Magic Night, 54/10 Jolypha, 13/2 St Jovite, 7/1 Dr Devious, 88/10 SUBOTICA, 12/1 Arcangues and Verveine, 16/1 Dear Doctor, 21/1 Saddlers' Hall, 26/1 Mashaallah, 31/1 Petit Loup, 32/1 Market Booster, 37/1 Polytain, 55/1 Seattle Rhyme, 75/1 Vert Amande, 104/1 Saganeca, 132/1 Sapience
O. Lecerf (A. Fabre) 18ran 2m39.00 (Soft)

78 CIGA PRIX DE 1m 1f55y
  L'OPERA (Gr 2) (3yo + f + m)
£47,114 Longchamp 4 October
54³ **Hatoof (USA)** 3-8-13
  WRSwinburn 1
  La Favorita (Fr) 3-8-9
  GMosse ½.2
52² **Ruby Tiger** 5-9-1 TQuinn 1.3
  Sporades (USA) 3-8-9
  TJarnet ns.4
13 Leariva (USA) 5-8-13
  CAsmussen sh.5
60 Palomelle (Fr) 3-8-9
  LDettori 2.6
  Wedding Ring (Ire) 3-8-9
  MBoutin nk.7
60 Trishyde (USA) 3-8-11
  FHead 1.8

  Melpomene (USA) 4-8-13
  MRoberts ¾.9
18 Rosefinch (USA) 3-8-13
  SCauthen 1.10
18 Garendare 3-8-9 DBoeuf 11
  Formidable Flight 3-8-9
  ELegrix 12

18/10 HATOOF, 2/1 Leariva, 38/10 Ruby Tiger, 5/1 Sporades, 63/10 Rosefinch, 15/2 Trishyde, 12/1 Melpomene, 29/1 Formidable Flight, 34/1 Wedding Ring, 36/1 Palomelle, 56/1 Garendare, 57/1 La Favorita
Maktoum Al-Maktoum (Mme C. Head) 12ran 2m02.40 (Soft)

79 PRIX DE LA FORET 7f
  (Gr 1) (2yo + c + f)
£60,827 Longchamp 11 October
50³ **Wolfhound (USA)** 3-9-10
  PatEddery 1
49 **Silicon Bavaria (Fr)** 5-9-9
  MBoutin nk.2
9 **Kenbu (Fr)** 3-9-7
  CAsmussen 1½.3
42 Lion Cavern (USA) 3-9-10
  SCauthen 4.4
41² Monde Bleu 4-9-12
  TJarnet ¾.5
56* Pursuit of Love 3-9-10
  RCochrane nk.6
42 Hydro Calido (USA) 3-9-7
  FHead ½.7
21 Casteddu 3-9-10 AMunro 5.8

6/4 Pursuit of Love, 24/10 Hydro Calido, 36/10 Lion Cavern and WOLFHOUND, 53/10 Monde Bleu, 11/2 Kenbu, 25/1 Silicon Bavaria, 38/1 Casteddu
Sheikh Mohammed (J. H. M. Gosden) 8ran 1m24.80 (Good to Soft)

80 PREMIO VITTORIO DI 1m
  CAPUA (Gr 1) (3yo +)
£66,011 Milan 11 October
74³ **Alhijaz** 3-8-9 WCarson 1
48³ **Rudimentary (USA)** 4-8-11
  JReid 3½.2
54 **Misil** 4-8-11
  LDettori 2½.3
  Golden Mintage (USA) 4-8-11
  AParravani 12.4
54 Shanghai (USA) 3-8-9
  ESaint-Martin 2.5
  Candy Glen 5-8-11
  VMezzatesta 15.6

Prince A. A. Faisal (J. L. Dunlop) 6ran 1m46.10 (Soft)

81 CHALLENGE STAKES 7f
  (Gr 2) (3yo +)
£35,028 Newmarket 15 October
67³ **Selkirk (USA)** 4-9-3
  RCochrane 1
36 **Thourios** 3-8-11
  WCarson 2½.2

67 **Second Set (Ire)** 4-9-3
LDettori 1½.**3**
56² Prince Ferdinand 3-8-11
JReid 2.**4**
16 Perfect Circle 3-8-8
WRSwinburn 1.**5**
56 Norwich 5-9-0 SCauthen ½.**6**
56 Dilum (USA) 3-8-11
AMunro 2.**7**
67 Mystiko (USA) 4-9-3
MRoberts 4.**8**

5/6 SELKIRK, 7/2 Second Set, 8/1
Prince Ferdinand, 9/1 Mystiko, 16/1
Perfect Circle, 16/1 Dilum, 33/1
Norwich, Thourios
    George Strawbridge (I. A. Balding)
8ran 1m22.27 (Good to Firm)

82 DEWHURST STAKES   7f
    (Gr 1) (2yo c + f)
£95,051   Newmarket   16 October
61* **Zafonic (USA)** 9-0
PatEddery **1**
Inchinor 9-0 TQuinn 4.**2**
Firm Pledge (USA) 9-0
AMunro sh.**3**
Sueboog (Ire) 8-9
WRSwinburn hd.**4**
Fatherland (Ire) 9-0
LPiggott ½.**5**
Petardia 9-0 MHills 2½.**6**
Zind (Ire) 9-0 MRoberts hd.**7**
Blues Traveller (Ire) 9-0
DHolland 1.**8**
Zimzalabim 9-0 WCarson 3.**9**
Lost Soldier (USA) 9-0
LDettori nk.**10**
63 Carbon Steel (Ire) 9-0
SCauthen 5.**11**

10/11 ZAFONIC, 5/1 Inchinor, 13/2
Inchinor, 8/1 Petardia, 12/1 Firm Pledge,
14/1 Sueboog, 33/1 Lost Soldier, 50/1
Zind, 66/1 Blues Traveller, Carbon
Steel, 100/1 Zimzalabim
    K. Abdulla (A. Fabre) 11ran 1m23.61
(Good to Firm)

83 DUBAI CHAMPION   1¼m
    STAKES (Gr 1) (3yo +)
£216,176   Newmarket   17 October
43* **Rodrigo de Triano (USA)** 3-8-12
LPiggott **1**
67* **Lahib (USA)** 4-9-3
WCarson nk.**2**
Environment Friend 4-9-3
GDuffield 3.**3**
57 Shuailaan (USA) 3-8-12
MRoberts sh.**4**
39² Zaahi (USA) 3-8-12 RHills . 1½.**5**
65* Masad (Ire) 3-8-12
LDettori sh.**6**
48² Steinbeck (USA) 3-8-12
SCauthen hd.**7**
77 Seattle Rhyme (USA) 3-8-12
JWilliams 1½.**8**
73³ Corrupt (USA) 4-9-3 JReid .. ¾.**9**

73 Pollen Count (USA) 3-8-12
RCochrane 15.**10**

11/8 RODRIGO DE TRIANO, 2/1 Lahib,
11/1 Masad, 12/1 Steinbeck, 14/1
Shuailaan, 16/1 Zaahi, 20/1 Environment
Friend, Seattle Rhyme, 40/1 Pollen
Count, 66/1 Corrupt
    R. E. Sangster (P. W. Chapple-Hyam)
10ran 2m02.46 (Good to Firm)

84 BUDWEISER   1¼m
    INTERNATIONAL
    (GRADE 1) (3yo +)
£266,273   Laurel   17 October
43 **Zoman (USA)** 5-9-0 AMunro . **1**
73* **Sillery (USA)** 4-9-0
FHead hd.**2**
59 **Contested Bid (USA)** 3-8-10
PatEddery 1¾.**3**
78 Leariva (USA) 5-8-11
DBoeuf 2¼.**4**
Stark South (USA) 4-9-0
LPincayjnr 1.**5**
Senor Tomas (USA) 3-8-10
AGryder 4.**6**
Thakib (USA) 5-9-0
RMigliore 1¾.**7**
30 Young Buster (Ire) 4-9-0
MHills nk.**8**

7/5 Sillery, 32/10 Contested Bid, 48/10
Senor Thomas, 15/2 ZOMAN, 77/10
Stark South, 13/1 Leariva, 17/1 Thakib,
28/1 Young Buster
    Fahd Salman (P. F. I. Cole) 8ran
2m01.40 (Good to Soft)

85 GRAN PREMIO DEL   1½m
    JOCKEY CLUB E COPPA
    D'ORO (Gr 1) (3yo +)
£209,744   Milan   18 October
65 **Silvernesian (USA)** 3-8-12
LPiggott **1**
66² **Red Bishop (USA)** 4-9-3
WCarson 1½.**2**
Erdelistan (Fr) 5-9-3
SSoto 2½.**3**
Patrik of Ireland (Ire) 4-9-3
MPlanard 7.**4**
Green Senor (USA) 4-9-3
MTellini 1¾.**5**
44 Lara's Idea 4-9-0 DZarroli ... hd.**6**
77 Saganeca (USA) 4-9-0
LDettori 5½.**7**

Gerecon Italia (J. L. Dunlop) 7ran
2m39.90 (Soft)

86 E. P. TAYLOR   1¼m
    STAKES (GRADE 2)
    (3yo + f + m)
£100,457   Woodbine   18 October
78* **Hatoof (USA)** 3-8-6
WRSwinburn **1**
60³ **Urban Sea (USA)** 3-8-6
MBoutin 1¼.**2**
Hero's Love (USA) 4-8-11
DSeymour 1¼.**3**

988

78[3]	Ruby Tiger 5-8-11 TQuinn .. hd.4
	Party Cited (USA) 3-8-6
	ASolis 2½.5
	Prominent Feather (USA) 3-8-6
	JLauzon 1½.6
52	Radiant Ring 4-8-11
	DPenna 2½.7
	Bally Vaughn 3-8-6
	RDosRamos 3.8
	Dance For Donna 3-8-6
	RSabourin ns.9
	Plenty of Grace (USA) 5-8-11
	HMcCauley 2½.10
	Red Journey (USA) 4-8-11
	RGriffith 7.11
	Country Stage (USA) 4-8-11
	RLandry 3.12

2/1 HATOOF, 63/20 Urban Sea, 41/10
Ruby Tiger, 89/10 Radiant Ring, 109/10
Plenty of Grace, 14/1 Hero's Love and
Prominent Feather, 19/1 Red Journey,
23/1 Bally Vaughn, 25/1 Party Cited, 40/1
Dance For Donna, 68/1 Country Stage
   Maktoum Al Maktoum (Mme C.
Head) 12ran 2m07.40 (Good to Soft)

87	ROTHMANS 1½m
	INTERNATIONAL (GRADE 1)
	(3yo +)
£302,857   Woodbine   10 October

Order as they passed the post (Wiorno
was subsequently disqualified and
placed third)

73[2]	Wiorno 4-9-0 TJarnet 1
64[2]	Snurge 5-9-0 TQuinn ½.2
	Ghazi (USA) 3-8-7
	RDavis 1¼.3
	Wolf (Chi) 5-9-0
	EDelahoussaye 1½.4
77	Saddlers' Hall (Ire) 4-9-0
	WRSwinburn nk.5
	Beyton (USA) 3-8-7 ASolis . hd.6
	Cozzene's Prince (Can) 5-9-0
	EMaple hd.7
	Tot of Rum (Can) 6-9-0
	DDavid 1½.8
	Seattle Bound (Can) 4-9-0
	DSeymour 2.9
	Aptakisic (Ire) 4-9-0
	JVelasquez nk.10
77	Mashaallah (USA) 4-9-0
	SCauthen ½.11
	Spinning 5-9-0
	RCochrane 1¼.12
	Beau Fasa (USA) 6-9-0
	RLandry 13
	Rainbows For Life (Can) 4-9-0
	DPenna 14

23/10 Mashaallah, 5/1 SNURGE, 6/1
Saddlers' Hall, Wolf, 9/1 Cozzene's
Prince, 11/1 Rainbows For Life and Tot of
Rum, 12/1 Wiorno, 16/1 Spinning, 29/1
Beyton, 38/1 Ghazi, 47/1 Seattle Bound,
64/1 Aptakisic, 68/1 Beau Fasa
   M. Arbib (P. F. I. Cole) 14ran 2m39.00
(Good to Soft)

| 88 | VODAFONE HORRIS   7f64y |
| | HILL STAKES (Gr 3) (2yo c + g) |
£25,580   Newbury   22 October
	Beggarman Thief (USA) 8-12
	RCochrane 1
	Bin Ajwaad (Ire) 8-12
	SCauthen 2.2
46	Port Lucaya 8-12 JReid 3.3
	Nominator 9-1 WCarson hd.4
	Kusamba (USA) 8-12
	MHills 3.5
	Urgent Request (Ire) 8-12
	PatEddery 2.6
	Desert Shot 8-12
	WRSwinburn ¾.7
82	Zimzalabim 8-12
	JWilliams 2½.8
63[3]	Sharp Prod (USA) 9-3
	LPiggott 1½.9
	New Capricorn (USA) 8-12
	BRaymond 5.10
	Press Gallery 8-12
	PaulEddery 1½.11

3/1 Urgent Request, 5/1 BEGGARMAN
THIEF, Desert Shot, 7/1 Bin Ajwaad, 8/1
Sharp Prod, 10/1 Nominator, 11/1
Kusamba, 14/1 Zimzalabim, 25/1 Port
Lucaya, Press Gallery, 33/1 New
Capricorn
   Landon Knight (J. H. M. Gosden)
11ran 1m35.24 (Soft)

| 89 | RACING POST TROPHY   1m |
| | (Gr 1) (2yo c + f) |
£104,396   Doncaster   24 October
	Armiger 9-0 PatEddery 1
68*	Ivanka (Ire) 8-9
	SCauthen 6.2
82	Zind (Ire) 9-0 GDuffield 4.3
	Desert Secret (Ire) 9-0
	WRSwinburn 1.4
	Noyan 9-0 MHills 5.5
	Newton's Law (Ire) 9-0
	LPiggott ½.6
	Redenham (USA) 9-0
	JReid sh.7
	Mukhamedov 9-0
	CAsmussen ½.8
75	Marillette (USA) 8-9
	WCarson 5.9
	Wahem (Ire) 9-0
	KDarley 15.10

5/4 ARMIGER, 9/2 Ivanka, 5/1 Desert
Secret, Marillette, 12/1 Redenham, 14/1
Newton's Law, 25/1 Zind, 33/1
Mukhamedov, 66/1 Noyan, 100/1 Wahem
   K. Abdulla (H. R. A. Cecil) 10ran
1m39.70 (Good to Soft)

| 90 | PRIX DU PETIT   5f |
| | COUVERT (Gr 3) (2yo +) |
£24,242   Longchamp   25 October
46	Wixon (Fr) 2-8-6 FHead 1
76[2]	Keen Hunter (USA) 5-9-11
	SCauthen ¾.2

Dauberval (USA) 3-9-11
  TJarnet 6.3
La Pitie (USA) 3-9-8
  ODoleuze sn.4
Mot de France (Fr) 4-9-11
  ABadel ns.5
Celtic River (Ire) 3-9-8
  ESaint-Martin 5.6
Avrilana (Fr) 4-9-8
  GGuignard 5.7
Rayon Bleu (Fr) 5-9-11
  PatEddery 1.8
Parios (Fr) 4-10-0
  FJohansson 2½.9

1/2 Keen Hunter and Dauberval, 39/10 WIXON, 44/10 Parios, 98/10 Mot de France, 21/1 La Pitie, 23/1 Rayon Bleu, 29/1 Celtic River, 33/1 Avrilana
  Allen E. Paulson (F. Boutin) 9ran 1m00.90 (Soft)

91	PRIX ROYAL-OAK	1m7f110y

(Gr 1) (3yo +)
£48,486   Longchamp   25 October

57	**Assessor (Ire)** 3-8-11	
	TQuinn 1	
40³	**Always Friendly** 4-9-0	
	AMunro 2½.2	
71*	**Sought Out (Ire)** 4-9-0	
	CAsmussen 6.3	
	Sheikh Dancer 5-9-3	
	DBoeuf 8.4	
71	Witness Box (USA) 5-9-3	
	SCauthen 5.5	
	Allegan (USA) 3-8-11	
	PatEddery 8.6	
71³	Dariyoun (USA) 4-9-3	
	FHead 5.7	
33	Ivyanna (Ire) 3-8-8	
	KJManning 20.8	
17	Jamshid (Jpn) 3-8-11	
	TJarnet ns.9	
	Balnibarbi 3-8-11 WRyan 8.10	
	Justice (Fr) 4-9-3 SGuillot 11	
	Dadarissime (Fr) 3-8-11	
	ESaint-Martin .... pu	

4/5 Sought Out, 19/4 Allegan and Balnibarbi, 13/2 Dadarissime, 15/2 Jamshid, 9/1 Witness Box, 15/1 Always Friendly, 20/1 Dariyoun, 37/1 Ivyanna, 39/1 Sheikh Dancer, 427/10 ASSESSOR, 52/1 Justice
  B. E. Nielsen (R. Hannon) 12ran 3m35.80 (Soft)

92	BREEDERS' CUP	6f (Dirt)

SPRINT (Grade 1) (3yo +)
£325,000 Gulfstream Park 31 October

	Thirty Slews 5-9-0	
	EDelahoussaye 1	
	Meafara (USA) 3-8-8	
	JVelasquez nk.2	
	Rubiano (USA) 5-9-0	
	JulieKrone 3.3	
50*	Sheikh Albadou 4-9-0	
	WRSwinburn ns.4	

76³	Elbio 5-9-0 PatEddery 1.5	
	King Corrie (Can) 4-9-0	
	DPenna ½.6	
	Arrowtown (USA) 4-9-0	
	LPincayjnr ½.7	
	Senor Speedy (USA) 5-9-0	
	JChavez 1.8	
	Superstrike 3-8-11	
	DSorenson 1.9	
	Furiously (USA) 3-8-11	
	JBailey 1.10	
	Gray Slewpy (USA) 4-9-0	
	KDesormeaux ½.11	
41	Cardmania (USA) 6-9-0	
	CMcCarron nk.12	
	Salt Lake (USA) 3-8-11	
	MSmith 2.13	
76*	Mr Brooks 5-9-0 LPiggott .... f	

21/10 Rubiano, 3/1 Sheikh Albadou, 7/1 Salt Lake, 11/10 Mr Brooks, 13/1 Gray Slewpy, 138/10 Meafara, 17/1 Senor Speedy, 18/1 Superstike, 187/10 THIRTY SLEWS, 22/1 Furiously, 25/1 King Corrie, 32/1 Arrowtown and Cardmania and Elbio
  M. Degroot, Dutch Masters II and M. Pegram (R. Baffert) 14ran 1m08.20 (Fast)

93	BREEDERS' CUP	1m 1f (Dirt)

DISTAFF (Grade 1)
(3yo + f + m)
£325,000 Gulfstream Park 31 October

	Paseana (Arg) 5-8-11	
	CMcCarron 1	
	Versailles Treaty (USA)	
	4-8-11 MSmith 4.2	
	Magical Maiden (USA) 3-8-7	
	GStevens ½.3	
	Queen of Triumph (USA) 3-8-7	
	JChavez 1½.4	
67	Marling (Ire) 3-8-7	
	WRSwinburn nk.5	
	Lite Light (USA) 4-8-11	
	EDelahoussaye ½.6	
	Meadow Star (USA) 4-8-11	
	PDay 1.7	
	Exchange (USA) 4-8-11	
	LPincayjnr 1½.8	
	Fowda (USA) 4-8-11	
	PValenzuela nk.9	
23²	Culture Vulture (USA) 3-8-7	
	TQuinn ½.10	
	Shared Interest (USA) 4-8-11	
	JulieKrone 1½.11	
	Saratoga Dew (USA) 3-8-7	
	HMcCauley 2.12	
	Diamond Duo (USA) 3-8-7	
	TTurner 12.13	
	Harbour Club (USA) 5-8-11	
	JBailey 1¼.14	

2/1 Saratoga Dew, 27/10 Exchange and PASEANA, 37/10 Versailles Treaty, 83/10 Fowda, 17/2 Marling, 15/1 Lite Light, 31/1 Magical Maiden, 36/1 Harbour Club, 37/1 Meadow Star, 44/1 Shared Interest, 48/1 Culture Vulture,

50/1 Diamond Duo and Queen of Triumph
Sidney H. Craig (R. McAnally) 14ran 1m48.00 (Fast)

94   BREEDERS' CUP   1m
    MILE (GRADE 1) (3yo +)
£325,000 Gulfstream Park 31 October

	Lure (USA) 3-8-10 MSmith ...	1
	Paradise Creek (USA) 3-8-10	
	PDay	3.2
67[2]	**Brief Truce (USA)** 3-8-10	
	MJKinane	nk.3
	Val Des Bois (Fr) 6-9-0	
	EDelahoussaye	1½.4
81*	Selkirk (USA) 4-9-0	
	RCochrane	½.5
	Luthier Enchanteur (USA) 5-9-0	
	KDesormeaux	1.6
	Forty Niner Days (USA) 5-9-0	
	CNakatani	1½.7
55	Exit To Nowhere (USA) 4-9-0	
	FHead	ns.8
	Fourstars Allstar (USA) 4-9-0	
	JBailey	hd.9
	Lotus Pool (USA) 5-9-0	
	CWoodsJnr	ns.10
74*	Arazi (USA) 3-8-10	
	PValenzuela	1.11
54	Cardoun (Fr) 3-8-10	
	CAntley	4.12
	Thunder Regent (Can) 5-9-0	
	CLopez	nk.13
	Bistro Garden (USA) 4-9-0	
	CMcCarron	4.14

6/4 Arazi, 38/10 Selkirk, 54/10 LURE, 82/10 Brief Truce, 98/10 Lotus Pool, 13/1 Exit To Nowhere, 14/1 Luthier Enchanteur and Val de Bois, 21/1 Forty Niner Days, 30/1 Cardoun and Paradise Creek, 42/1 Bistro Garden, 66/1 Fourstars Allstar, 75/1 Thunder Regent
Claiborne Farm (C. McGaughey III) 14ran 1m32.80 (Firm)

95   BREEDERS' CUP   1½m
    TURF (GRADE 1) (3yo +)
£650,000 Gulfstream Park 31 October

	Fraise (USA) 4-9-0	
	PValenzuela	1
55[2]	**Sky Classic (Can)** 5-9-0	
	PDay	ns.2
55	**Quest For Fame** 5-9-0	
	PatEddery	2.3
77	Dr Devious (Ire) 3-8-9 JReid .	1.4
77*	Subotica (Fr) 4-9-0	
	TJarnet	½.5
78	Trishyde (USA) 3-8-6	
	FHead	2.6
	Navarone (USA) 4-9-0	
	CMcCarron	½.7
	Daros 3-8-9	
	EDelahoussaye	4½.8
83	Corrupt (USA) 4-9-0	
	MRoberts	12½.9
	Solar Splendor (USA) 5-9-0	
	HMcCauley	3½.10

9/10 Sky Classic, 33/10 Navarone, 15/2 Subotica, 91/10 Dr Devious, 10/1 Solar Splendor, 14/1 FRAISE, 17/1 Quest For Fame, 42/1 Daros, 79/1 Trishyde, 118/1 Corrupt
Mrs A. E. Paulson (W. Mott) 10ran 2m24.00 (Firm)

96   BREEDERS' CUP   1¼m (Dirt)
    CLASSIC (GRADE 1) (3yo +)
£975,000 Gulfstream Park 31 October

	A P Indy (USA) 3-8-9	
	EDelahoussaye	1
	Pleasant Tap (USA) 5-9-0	
	GStevens	2.2
77	**Jolypha (USA)** 3-8-6	
	PatEddery	½.3
	Reign Road (USA) 4-9-0	
	KDesormeaux	1½.4
	Sultry Song (USA) 4-9-0	
	JBailey	nk.5
	Defensive Play (USA) 5-9-0	
	PDay	hd.6
	Thunder Rumble (USA) 3-8-9	
	HMcCauley	1½.7
	Strike The Gold (USA) 4-9-0	
	CPerret	5½.8
	Twilight Agenda (USA) 6-9-0	
	CMcCarron	nk.9
	Jolie's Halo (USA) 5-9-0	
	EPrado	3.10
55	Marquetry (USA) 5-9-0	
	DFlores	1½.11
84*	Zoman (USA) 5-9-0	
	AMunro	3.12
	Technology (USA) 3-8-9	
	LPincayJnr	2½.13
83*	Rodrigo de Triano (USA) 3-8-9	
	WRSwinburn	12.14

21/10 A P INDY, 5/2 Pleasant Tap, 59/10 Sultry Song, 62/10 Rodrigo de Triano, 77/10 Strike The Gold, 15/1 Twilight Agenda, 16/1 Defensive Play and Jolypha and Marquetry, 37/1 Technology, 38/1 Reign Road, 41/1 Thunder Rumble, 70/1 Jolie's Halo, 75/1 Zoman
T. Tsurumaki, W. S. Farish, W. S. Kilroy and H. Good (N. Drysdale) 14ran 2m00.20 (Firm)

97   CRITERIUM DE   7f
    MAISONS-LAFFITTE
    (Gr 2) (2yo c + f)
£43,050 Maisons-Laffitte 6 November

72	**Kadounor (Fr)** 8-11	
	ODeleuze	1
90*	**Wixon (Fr)** 8-8 FHead	1½.2
	Chancetobewild (USA)	
	8-11 CAsmussen	½.3
	Firm Friend (Ire) 8-8	
	DBoeuf	1½.4
	Auvergne (Can) 8-11	
	TJarnet	2½.5

6/4 Wixon, 22/10 Chancetobewild, 28/10 KADOUNOR, 39/10 Auvergne, 15/2 Firm Friend

Mme H. Rabatel (J. Laumain) 5ran
1m35.40 (Soft)

98   CRITERIUM DE   1¼m
SAINT-CLOUD (Gr 1) (2yo c + f)
£61,500   Saint-Cloud   8 November
   Marchand de Sable (USA)
    8-11 DBoeuf 1
   Infrasonic 8-11
    PatEddery nk.2
   Arinthod (Fr) 8-11
    FHead hd.3
   Ranger (Fr) 8-11
    CAsmussen 1.4
   Frenchpark 8-11
    PShanahan 2.5
   Samakatan (Ire) 8-11
    GDubroeucq 4.6
   Dardjini (USA) 8-11
    WMongil 2.7
   Lencloitre (Fr) 8-8
    OPeslier 1½.8

13/10 Dardjini and Samakatan, 2/1
Infrasonic, 3/1 MARCHAND DE
SABLE, 11/1 Frenchpark, Ranger, 19/1
Arinthod, 26/1 Lencloitre
  L. de Angeli (E. Lellouche) 8ran
2m 19.10 (Soft)

99   PREMIO ROMA (Gr 1)   1¼m
(3yo + c + f)
£110,245   Rome   15 November
80³ **Misil (USA)** 4-8-13 LDettori .. 1
80* **Alhijaz** 3-8-12 WCarson ... 5½.2
   Guado d'Annibale (Ire) 3-8-12
    JacquelineFreda ½.3
65   Vasarelli (Ire) 3-8-12
    VMezzatesta 5.4
85   Green Senor (USA) 4-8-13
    MTellini 2.5
85³ Erdelistan (Fr) 5-8-13
    EBotti ½.6
85² Red Bishop (USA) 4-8-13
    PatEddery 2.7
65³ In A Tiff (Ire) 3-8-12
    PShanahan 3½.8
   Astro di Luce (USA) 3-8-12
    DZarroli .... 1¾.9.
   Bateau Rouge (Ire) 5-8-13
    FJovine 6.10

Laghi SRL (V. Caruso) 10ran 2m07.40
(Heavy)

100   JAPAN CUP (Gr 1)   1½m
(3yo +)
£920,813   Tokyo   29 November
   Tokai Teio (Jpn) 4-8-13
    YOkabe 1
   Naturalism (NZ) 4-8-13
    LDittman nk.2
77   **Dear Doctor (Fr)** 5-8-13
    CAsmussen ½.3
   Legacy World (Jpn) 3-8-9
    HKoyauchi 3½.4
   Hishi Masaru (Jpn) 3-8-9
    YTake ¾.5

77² User Friendly 3-8-5
    GDuffield ¾.6
   Let's Elope (NZ) 5-8-9
    DBeadman 4.7
   Let's Go Tarquin (Jpn) 5-8-13
    SOsaki 1¾.8
   Ikuno Dictus (Jpn) 5-8-9
    YMuramoto nk.9
95   Dr Devious (Ire) 3-8-9
    CMcCarron ns.10
95³ Quest For Fame 5-8-13
    PatEddery nk.11
   Yamanin Global (Jpn) 5-8-13
    HKawachi ns.12
77³ Vert Amande (Fr) 4-8-13
    DBoeuf 1½.13
   Hashiru Shogun (Jpn) 4-8-13
    KSuzuki 3.14

22/10 User Friendly, 57/10 Naturalism,
7/1 Let's Elope, 8/1 Dear Doctor, 9/1
TOKAI TEIO, 94/10 Quest For Fame,
109/10 Dr Devious, 134/10 Hishi Masaru,
168/10 Vert Amande, 169/10 Legacy
World, 277/10 Let's Go Tarquin, 278/10
Yamanin Global, 449/10 Hashiru
Shogun, 64/1 Ikuno Dictus
  M. Uchimura (S. Matsumoto) 14ran
2m24.60 (Firm)

INDEX TO SELECTED BIG RACES

Absurde 9, 23
Abury 68
Acteur Francais 74
Adieu Au Roi 17, 29
African Peace 18
Ajaad 7
Ajfan 68²
Alcando 52
Alflora 14, 58³
Alhijaz 29, 48, 74³, 80*, 99²
All At Sea . 16², 43², 54*, 67
Allegan 91
Alnasr Alwasheek
          1*, 3, 14, 43, 73
Always Fr'dly 15, 26, 40³, 91²
Amigo Menor 6³
Amirati 22
Anonymous 69
Another Episode 25
A P Indy 96*
Appealing Bubbles 27
Apple Tree 1
Approach The Bench 19
Aptakisic 87
Aradanza 63
Arazi 21, 74*, 94
Arcadian Heights 24², 27
Arcangues 13², 30, 77
Arinthod 98³
Armarama 33
Armiger 89*
Arrikala 33³, 64
Arrowtown 92
Art Bleu 4, 31
Artic Tracker 3
Assessor 14, 57, 91*
Astica 41
Astro di Luce 99
A-To-Z 2, 10
Auvergne 97
Avrilana 90

Badiane 11
Badie 1,3
Bakari 5
Bally Vaughn 86
Balnibarbi 91
Basim 72³
Bateau Rouge 99
Beau Fasa 87
Beggarman Thief 88*
Be Happy 41
Beldi 21
Belle Soiree 22
Beyton 87
Bezelle 10, 76
Big Tobin 65
Bin Ajwaad 88²
Bineyah 33, 44²
Binkhaldoun 17
Bistro Garden 94
Bletchley Park 50
Blues Traveller 82
Blush Rambler 72²
Blyton Lad 25, 45
Bobzao 43

Bog Trotter 56
Bold n'Flashy 76
Bold Pursuit 1
Boloardo 27
Bonny Scot 57³, 66
Bradawn Breever 38
Break Bread 17
Brief Truce
         8³, 21*, 54², 67², 94³
Bright Generation 68

Caerlina 13, 52
Calling Collect 12, 74²
Canaska Star 61, 72
Candy Glen 80
Captain Horatius 28²
Capwell 28³
Carbon Steel 63, 82
Cardmania 41, 92
Cardoun .. 3, 38², 42³, 54, 94
Carranita 22
Casteddu 21, 79
Cattermole 10
Caurselle 10
Celtic River 90
Central City 2
Chancetobewild 97³
Chenin Blanc 55
Code Breaker 74
Colway Bold 6
Comme d'Habitude 68
Contested B. 17³, 27³, 59, 84³
Corrupt 51, 73³, 83, 95
Country Style 86
Cox Orange 75
Cozzene's Prince 87
Crack Regiment 38
Creaking Board 46
Crystal Path 52
Culture Vulture 2, 9*, 23², 93
Cunning 60²

Dabtiya 64
Dadarissime 91
Dajraan 17
Dampierre 74
Danae de Brule 31
Dance For Donna 86
Dance Smartly 52³
Dardjini 98
Dariyoun 71³, 91
Daros 95
Dauberval 90³
Dawson Place 41
Dear Doctor 39, 55*, 77, 100³
Decided Air 18
Defensive Play 96
Deja 26
Desert Secret 89
Desert Shot 88
Desert Sun 7, 20
Diamond Duo 93
Diamonds Galore 45³
Didyme 46, 61
Dilum 3, 42, 56, 81
Dive For Cover 27

Dowland 58
Dr Devious 1², 14*, 27²,
          43, 58*, 77, 95, 100
Dream Talk 41³, 49, 76
Drum Taps 24*, 47², 64³, 71²
Duke of Paducah 37

Ebony And Ivory 33
Elbio 25³, 32, 38, 45,
                 49*, 76³, 92
Elegance 52
El Prado 42, 54
Elsurimo 37
El Trenzador 55
El Yasaf 25, 45
Embarcadero 34
Endoli 24
Environment Friend 83³
Erdelistan 26, 85³, 99
Euphonic 9
Exchange 93
Exit To Nowhere
          13³, 19, 42*, 55, 94
Ezzoud 8², 21³, 27

Factual 70³
Fair Average 7
Farfelu 45
Fastness 72
Fatherland 82
Fawaayid 16
Firm Friend 97
Firm Pledge 82³
Flashfoot 48
Flowing 25, 76
Flying Brave 7
Forest Tiger 1
Forest Wind 63*
Formidable Flight 78
Fortune's Wheel 4, 39
Forty Niner Days 94
Fourstars Allstar 94
Fowda 93
Fraise 95*
Freddie Lloyd .... ⸍⁻¹
Free Flyer 30
Frenchpark 98
Funny Baby 13
Furiously 92
Further Flight 37*
Future Storm 46
Fylde Flyer 6

Ganges 38
Garden of Heaven 66³
Garendare 18, 78
Gdansk's Honour 10
Ghazi 87²
Glanville 17, 59
Glity 4
Gloria Mundi 34
Golden Mintage 80
Golden Pheasant 55³
Gold Splash 75*
Good To Dance 11, 18
Goofalik 19

Grand Plaisir 17
Gray Slewpy 92
Great Marquess 71
Great Palm 14, 58
Green's Bid 63
Green Senor 85, 99
Guado d'Annibale 99³
Guilty Secret 44³
Guislaine 9³, 18, 29³
Gussy Marlowe 20, 43

Hailsham 30
Half A Tick 73
Hamas 67
Hamsah 22
Harbour Club 93
Harvest Girl 2, 45
Hashiru Shogun 100
Hateel 47
Hatoof2*, 9, 42, 54³, 78*, 86*
Hatta Fort 49
Hazm 42
Heligoland 12
Hero's Love 86³
Highest Ody 5
Hishi Masaru 100
Holly Golightly 22
Homme de Loi 29*
Hondo Mondo 39, 53
Hydro Calido 9², 42, 79

Ikuno Dictus 100
Ile de Chypre 51
In A Tiff 65³, 99
Inchinor 82²
Infrasonic 98²
In Quarto 47
Ionian Sea 60
Irish Memory 1³, 8
Irish Source 11
Ivanka 68*, 89²
Ivisa 68³
Ivyanna 33, 91

Jack Lang 26
Jahafil 64
Jamshid 17, 91
Jape 17
Jeune 35, 51*
Johann Quatz 17, 29, 59
John Rose 55
Jolie's Halo 96
Jolypha 11², 18*, 60*, 77, 96³
Judge Decision 5
Julie La Rousse 52
Justice 91

Kadounor 72, 97*
Karinga Bay 20
Katakana 23³
Keen Hunter 76², 90²
Kenbu 2³, 9, 79³
Khanata 10, 33
Kindergarten 75²
King Corrie 92
Kingmambo 46, 61², 72
Kitwood 12*, 29², 42, 54
Knifebox 73

Kooyonga 20³, 30*, 39*, 43, 58
Kostroma 52*
Kusamba 88

La Favorita 78²
Lahib . 7², 19*, 42², 67*, 83²
L'Amour Fou 13, 40
Landowner 27, 37³
La Pitie 90
Lara's Idea 26³, 44, 85
Leariva 7, 13, 78, 84
Le Corsaire 37
Legacy World 100
Le Montagnard 71
Lencloitre 98
Leone 28
Let's Elope 100
Let's Go Tarquin 100
Lights Out 34
Lindon Lime 72
Line Engaged 6
Linnga 40, 60
Lion Cavern ... 5³, 38, 42, 79
Lite Light 93
Litron 49
Lobilio 14
L'Oiseau Bleu Roi 31
Lomitas 28*
Lorelie 75
Lost Soldier 82
Lotus Pool 94
Lovealoch 19
Love of Silver 75³
Lucet 5
Luchiroverte 37
Lucky Lindy3², 8, 12², 20, 74
Lucky Parkes 22
Lure 94*
Luthier Enchanteur 94
Lyric Fantasy . 22*, 45*, 69²

Mack The Knife 57
Magical Maiden 93³
Magic Carr 58
Magic Night
        13, 31², 40*, 62*, 77
Magique Rond Point 68
Magnificent Star 40, 44
Mahasin 2, 23
Maitre 39
Malvernico 58
Marble Maiden 52
Marchand de Sable 98*
Marcus Thorpe 26
Mardonius 24
Marignan 17², 27, 59
Marillette 75, 89
Marina Park 22, 46³, 63²
Marling
        2², 10*, 23*, 36*, 67, 93
Market Booster
            10², 33², 60, 77
Marquetry 55, 96
Marviah 75
Masad 43, 65*, 83
Mashaallah
    26*, 34², 53*, 64*, 77, 87
Master Peace 72

Meadow Star 93
Meafara 92²
Medaille d'Or 45
Mellaby 15, 30
Melpomene 78
Merzouk 34
Metal Storm 13
Michelozzo 47³
Midnight Air 44
Mining Tycoon 27, 65
Misil 42, 54, 80³, 99*
Miss Plum 40
Modhish 17, 65²
Mojave 74
Monde Bleu 25, 41², 79
Montendre 6
Montepulciano 49
Moodiesburn 22
Mot de France 90
Mr Brooks 6², 25², 32*,
        41*, 45², 50², 76*, 92
Muhtarram 1, 3, 14
Mukaddamah 7
Mukhamedov 89
Musicale 2
My Corncrake 41
Mystic Goddess 22², 68
Mystiko 7, 48, 67, 81

Namaqualand 46
Naturalism 100²
Navarone 95
Nemea 75
New Capricorn 88
Newton's Law 89
Nimble Deer 2
Ninja Dancer 14
Niodini 44
Nominator 88
Norwich 6, 56, 81
Noyan 89
Olanthe 29
Olden Rijn 52
Opera House20, 30², 35³, 66*
Ormsby 27
Oumaldaaya 18

Paix Blanche 17, 33
Palomelle 60, 78
Paradise Creek 94²
Paradise Navy 14
Parios 90
Paris House 25, 32, 45
Parting Moment 37
Party Cited 86
Paseana 93*
Passing Sale 4, 26
Patrik of Ireland 85
Pearl Angel 2, 16³, 44
Peperonata 76
Perfect Circle ... 2, 16, 81
Perpendicular 20*, 39³
Petardia 82
Petit Loup 59², 77
Pigeon Voyageur 28
Pik Konig 53
Pips Pride 63, 70²
Pistolet Bleu 4², 31*

Platini 53²
Pleasant Tap 96²
Plenty of Grace 86
Plume Magique 9
Poker Chip 69³
Polemic 52
Pollen Count ... 14, 29, 73, 83
Polytain 17*, 59, 77
Portico 8
Port Lucaya 46, 88³
Press Gallery 88
Primer Amor 74
Prince Ferdinand 56², 81
Prince Polino 17
Prominent Feather 86
Proud Panther 71
Pursuit of Love
      3³, 32², 38*, 56*, 79

Queen of Triumph 93
Quest For Fame 55, 95³, 100

Radiant Ring 52, 86
Rainbow Corner 5², 14
Rainbow For Life 87
Rain Rider 57
Ranger 98
Rayon Bleu 90
Red Bishop . 51², 66², 85², 99
Redenham 89
Red Journey 86
Reference Light 38
Reign Road 96
Reported 56
River Falls 3, 21, 56
River Nymph 60
River Verdon 55
Rock Hopper .. 15², 30, 35, 64
Rocky Waters 49
Rodrigo de Triano
      3*, 8*, 14, 21, 43*, 83*, 96
Roman Prose 41
Rosefinch 11*, 18, 78
Rouquette 75
Rubiano 92³
Ruby Tiger ... 43, 52², 78³, 86
Rudimentary
      7³, 19, 36, 48³, 80²

Saddlers' Hall 15*, 35², 77, 87
Saganeca
      15, 26², 31, 62, 77, 85
Salt Lake 92
Samakatan 98
Sambit 41
Sapience
      15, 30³, 35, 53³, 66, 77
Saratoga Dew 93
Saratoga Source 16
Sayyedati 69*
Seaton Delaval 72
Seattle Bound 87
Seattle Rhyme
      43³, 51³, 77, 83
Second Set
      19², 36³, 55, 67, 81³
Secrage 46², 75

Selkirk
      7*, 13, 36², 48*, 67³, 81*, 94
Senor Speedy 92
Senor Tomas 84
Shalford 6*, 32, 50
Shambo 47
Shanghai 5*, 12³, 54, 80
Shannkara 11
Shared Interest 93
Sharp Prod 63³, 88
Sharp Review 54, 67
Sheba Dancer 11, 18²
Sheikh Albadou
      25*, 32³, 36, 50*, 92
Sheikh Dancer 91
Shining Bright 16
Shuailaan 57, 83
Sikeston 19³, 36, 42
Silicon Bavaria ... 41, 49, 79²
Sillery 73*, 84²
Silver Kite 17, 74
Silvernesian 65, 85*
Silver Wisp 3, 14³, 35
Silver Wizard 70
Silvestro 28
Sissingura 75
Sizzling Saga 50
Skimble 2
Sky Classic 55², 95²
Snurge 15, 26, 64², 87*
Soiree 2, 23
Solar Splendour 95
Songlines 34³, 59*
Sonus 57²
Sought Out 40², 47*, 71*, 91³
Spartan Shareef 73
Spinning 87
Splendent 61³, 72
Sporades 78
Stack Rock 6
Star Family Friend 22
Stark South 84
Star of Cozzene 36, 42, 55
Star of Gdansk 19
Steinbeck 3, 48², 83
St Jovite 14², 27*, 35*, 58², 77
Storm Dove 56³
Strike The Gold 96
Suave Dancer 4³
Subotica
      ... 4*, 15, 31³, 62², 77*, 95
Sueboog 82
Sultry Song 96
Super Staff 52
Superstrike 92
Supreme Choice 47
Swing Low 3
Sylva Honda 48, 56
Symphorine 9

Take Risks 5, 42, 54
Tarwiya 10³
Tbab 32, 50
Technology 96
Tel Quel 13, 20, 62³
Tenby 72*
Tenga 61
Terimon ... 15³, 20, 30, 35, 43

Tertian 3, 38
Tetradonna 37
Thakib 84
Thirty Slews 92*
Thourios 3, 14, 20, 36, 81²
Thunder Regent 94
Thunder Rumble 96
Tik Fa 74
Tokai Teio 100*
Toledo Queen 22
Toocando 22³
Torrey Canyon 1
Tot of Rum 87
Trampoli 11, 40
Triple Tiara 47
Trishyde 11, 18, 60, 78, 95
Tropicarr 64
Turgeon 24³, 47
Twafeaj 38³, 49², 76
Twilight Agenda 96
Twist And Turn 14, 30
Tyrone Bridge 24, 37

Urban Sea ... 18, 60³, 86²
Urgent Request 88
User Friendly
      16*, 33*, 44*, 57*, 77², 100

Val Des Bois 94
Vasarelli 29, 65, 99
Versailles Treaty 93²
Vert Amande 34*, 77³, 100
Verveine . 11³, 18³, 29, 60, 77
Villandry 34
Vintage Crop 64
Virilis 70

Wahem 89
Wedding of The Sea 49³
Wedding Ring 78
Well Saddled 14
Wiedniu 23
Wilde Rufo 3, 50, 56
Windreiter 41
Winnetka 11, 40
Wiorno 73², 87³
Witness Box 37², 71, 91
Wixon 46, 90*, 97²
Wolf 87
Wolfhound 25, 32, 50³, 79*
Wootton Rivers 70
Worldwide 38

Yamanin Global 100
Young Buster 20², 30, 84
Young Freeman 14

Zaahi 5, 21², 39², 83
Zafonic 46*, 61*, 82*
Zeiten 70*
Zimzalabim 82, 88
Zind 82, 89³
Zoman ... 13*, 30, 43, 84*, 96

TRAINERS

The figures in brackets are the number of winners each trainer has had on the flat (turf and all-weather) in Britain over the past five years from 1988 to 1992 inclusive. Quarters and telephone numbers are given.

Aconley, Mrs V. A. (—:—:0:1:0)
Westow (065381) 594 and (0653) 695042 (home)
Akehurst, J. (—:—:4:13:6)
Lambourn (0488) 72688
Akehurst, R. P. J. (25:33:34:42:30)
Epsom (0372) 748800 and fax (0372) 739410
Allan, A. R. (1:1:1:1:2)
Cornhill-on-Tweed (089082) 581
Allen, C. N. (7:8:19:16:7)
Newmarket (0638) 667870 and mobilephone (0831) 349629
Alston, E. J. (10:1:6:12:15)
Preston (0772) 612120
Arbuthnot, D. W. P. (3:10:20:12:12)
Newbury (0635) 578427
Armstrong, R. W. (36:21:26:10:15)
Newmarket (0638) 663333 or 663334
Austin, Mrs S. M. (—:—:0:0:0)
Malton (065385) 200
Avison, M. (1:0:4:0:0)
Nawton (0439) 71672

Bailey, A. (21:12:10:11:16)
Tarporley (0829) 760762
Bailey, K. C. (0:1:0:2:0)
Lambourn (0488) 71483
Baker, R. J. (—:—:—:—:2)
Tiverton (0398) 5317
Balding, G. B. (7:15:18:18:15)
Whitcombe (0305) 260724
Balding, I. A. (43:41:48:53:36)
Kingsclere (0635) 298210
Balding, J. (2:5:7:4:0)
Doncaster (0302) 710096 and (0777) 818407 (stable)
Banks, J. E. (—:—:—:3:4)
Newmarket (0638) 667997 (office) and 661472 (home)
Barker, Mrs P. A. (—:—:0:1:0)
Wetherby (0937) 582151
Barker, W. L. (—:—:—:0:1)
Scorton (0325) 378266 and mobilephone (0836) 260149
Barons, D. H. (0:0:0:0:0)
Kingsbridge (0548) 550326 and 550411
Barr, R. E. (—:—:—:0:0)
Stokesley (0642) 710687
Barraclough, M. F. (—:—:—:0:2)
Claverdon (092684) 3332
Barratt, L. J. (4:0:0:1:0)
Oswestry (069188) 209
Barron, T. D. (18:24:58:39:41)
Thirsk (0845) 587435
Barrow, A. K. (—:0:0:0:0)
Bridgwater (0278) 732522
Barwell, C. R. (—:—:0:0:0)
Tiverton (03985) 537 and 224

Bastiman, R. (3:7:12:14:10)
Wetherby (0937) 583050
Beaumont, P. (0:0:0:0:0)
Brandsby (03475) 208
Beever, C. R. (—:0:1:1:1)
Grantham (0476) 870177
Bell, M. L. W. (—:18:21:43:39)
Newmarket (0638) 666567
Bennett, J. A. (0:0:0:2:1)
Sparsholt (023559) 635
Bennett, R. A. (0:1:4:1:1)
Maidenhead (0628) 30290
Benstead, C. J. (14:9:6:5:9)
Epsom (037 22) 73152
Bentley, W. (0:1:1:0:0)
Middleham (0969) 22289
Berry, J. (70:92:127:143:107)
Lancaster (0524) 791179
Bethell, J. D. W. (4:11:10:11:5)
Middleham (0969) 22962 and 23321
Bevan, P. J. (0:0:0:1:2)
Kingstone (0889) 500647 (yard) or 500670 (home)
Bishop, K. S. (0:0:0:0:0)
Bridgwater (0278) 671437
Blanshard, M. T. W. (3:8:5:6:8)
Lambourn (0488) 71091
Blum, G. (3:1:2:6:4)
Newmarket (0638) 713916
Bolton, M. J. (0:0:2:1:5)
East Grinstead (0980) 621059
Booth, C. B. B. (7:4:4:5:3)
Flaxton (065 381) 586
Bosley, J. R. (0:0:0:0:0)
Bampton (0993) 850212
Boss, R. (23:23:36:18:9)
Newmarket (0638) 661335
Bostock, J. R. (—:—:1:3:0)
Swaffham (0366) 47870
Bottomley, J. F. (—:4:5:4:3)
Malton (0653) 694597 (stable)
Bower, Miss L. J. (0:0:0:0:0)
Alresford (0962) 771552
Bowring, S. R. (7:2:4:2:9)
Mansfield (0623) 822451
Bradburne, Mrs S. (—:—:—:—:0)
Cupar (033781) 325
Bradley, J. M. (2:1:4:2:3)
Chepstow (0291) 622486
Bradstock, M. F. (0:0:0:0:0)
East Garston (048839) 8801
Bramall, Mrs S. A. (—:—:—:0:0)
Hutton Sessay (0845) 401333
Bravery, G. C. (—:—:—:0:5)
Newmarket (0638) 668985
Brazington, R. G. (0:0:0:0:1)
Redmarley, Glos. (0452) 840384
Brennan, O. (2:0:2:0:0)
Newark (063 686) 332

Bridger, J. J. (0:0:2:0:2)
Chichester (0428) 722528
Bridgwater, K. S. (1:0:0:2:2)
Solihull (056478) 2895
Brisbourne, W. M. (—:—:—:0:2)
Shrewsbury (074381) 536 and 360
Brittain, C. E. (40:36:42:53:63)
Newmarket (0638) 663739 and 664347
Brittain, M. A. (44:26:27:21:7)
Warthill (0759) 71472
Broad, C. D. (—:—:—:1:1)
Westbury-upon-Severn, Glos. (0452)
760835 (office) and 830015 (home)
Brooks, C. P. E. (0:1:0:1:0)
Lambourn (0488) 72077 (office) and
72909 (home)
Brotherton, R. (—:—:—:—:0)
Evesham (0386) 710772
Burchell, W. D. (0:1:7:4:1)
Ebbw Vale (0495) 302551
Burgoyne, P. V. J. P. (0:0:0:0:0)
Upper Lambourn (023 559) 688
Burke, K. R. (—:—:—:0:2:0)
Broadway (0386) 858153 (office) and
858489 (home)
Butler, P. (0:0:0:0:3)
Lewes (0273) 890124
Bycroft, N. (10:2:2:6:4)
Brandsby (034 75) 641

Caldwell, T. H. (—:0:0:0:1)
Warrington (0565) 777275
Callaghan, N. A. (27:32:31:30:21)
Newmarket (0638) 664040
Calver, P. (7:7:18:8:6)
Ripon (0765) 600313
Camacho, M. J. C. (8:12:20:15:20)
Malton (0653) 694901
Cambidge, B. R. (2:1:2:4:0)
Shifnal (095 276) 249
Campbell, I. (4:3:7:1:5)
Newmarket (0638) 660829
Candy, H. D. N. B. (20:16:23:16:21)
Wantage (0367) 820276
Carr, J. M. (—:—:—:—:2)
Malton (0653) 694671
Carter, W. Y. (2:23:20:15:19)
Leatherhead (0372) 377209
Casey, W. T. (3:1:4:5:5)
Lambourn (0488) 73004
Cecil, H. R. A. (112:117:111:119:109)
Newmarket (0638) 662192 or 662387
(home)
Cecil, Mrs J. (—:—:—:19:30)
Newmarket (0638) 560634 (office) and
662420 (home) and fax (0638) 560636
Chamberlain, A. J. (—:—:0:0:0)
Swindon (0285) 861347
Chamberlain, N. (0:0:0:0:1)
West Auckland (0388) 832 465 and
834636 (office)
Champion, R. (0:1:0:0:0)
Newmarket (0638) 666546
Channon, M. R. (—:—:16:22:27)
Lambourn (0264) 810225 (home) and
(0488) 71149 (stable)
Chapman, D. W. (36:29:22:24:15)
Stillington (0347) 21683

Chapman, M. C. (0:0:1:7:1)
Market Rasen (0673) 843663
Chapple-Hyam, P. W. (—:—:—:27:41)
Manton (0672) 514901
Charles, M. J. (0:0:1:0:0)
Warwick (0926) 493878
Charles-Jones, G. F. H. (—:—:—:—:1)
Wantage (0235) 767713
Charlton, J. I. A. (0:0:0:0:0)
Stocksfield (0661) 843 247
Charlton, R. J. (—:—:37:26:43)
Beckhampton (06723) 533 (office) and
330 (home)
Cheesbrough, P. (—:—:—:—:0)
Bishop Auckland (0388) 720213 and
720432 (hostel)
Christian, S. P. L. (1:0:0:0:0)
Kinnersley (0905) 371233
Clay, W. (0:0:0:0:0)
Fulford (0782) 392 131
Codd, L. J. (—:3:0:3:1)
Nantwich (0270) 610172
Cole, P. F. I. (43:51:53:73:86)
Whatcombe (04882) 433 or 434
Collingridge, H. J. (7:12:7:9:10)
Newmarket (0638) 665454
Cosgrove, D. J. S. (—:—:—:—:3)
Newmarket (0638) 661961 and mobile
(0831) 508753
Cottrell, L. G. (19:12:4:10:8)
Cullompton (088 46) 320
Craig, T. (1:4:1:1:1)
Dunbar (0368) 62583
Cumani, L. M. (73:88:109:72:54)
Newmarket (0638) 665432
Cundell, P. D. (5:1:0:1:1)
Newbury (0635) 578267
Cunningham-Brown, K. O.
(0:7:4:2:18)
Stockbridge (0264) 781611
Curley, B. J. (1:0:3:3:0)
Newmarket (0638) 508251
Curtis, R. (3:3:4:3:3)
Epsom (0372) 277645
Cuthbert, T. A. K. (—:—:—:—:0)
Carlisle (0228) 560822 and 561317
(stables)
Cyzer, C. A. (—:14:9:20:27)
Horsham (0403) 730255

Dalton, P. T. (—:—:—:—:0)
Burton-on-Trent (0283) 701318
Davison, A. R. (2:0:0:0:1)
Caterham (0883) 344523
Dawe, Mrs J. C. (0:1:0:0:3)
Bridgwater (027874) 588
Denson, A. W. (0:1:0:0:2)
Epsom (03727) 29398
Dickin, R. (0:0:1:5:3)
Dymock (0531) 890644
Dixon, M. (—:—:—:0:5)
Epsom (0372) 279308
Dods, M. J. K. (—:—:—:3:7)
Darlington (0325) 374270
Donnelly, T. W. (—:—:—:0:0)
Hartshorne (0283) 226046 and 216965
(office)

997

Dooler, J. (—:0:0:0:1)
Goole (0405) 861903
Douglass, G. W. (—:—:—:—:0)
Snailwell (0638) 720500
Dow, S. L. (6:7:5:17:17)
Epsom (0372) 721490 (home)
Dunlop, J. L. (66:66:78:58:75)
Arundel (0903) 882194 (office) or
882106 (home)

Earnshaw, R. (0:3:4:2:0)
Harrogate (0423) 567790
Easterby, M. H. (64:57:61:58:38)
Malton (065 386) 566
Easterby, M. W. (25:19:25:14:12)
Sheriff Hutton (03477) 368
Eckley, M. W. (4:1:1:2:1)
Ludlow (058472) 372
Eden, G. H. (—:—:2:4:5)
Newmarket (0638) 667938
Edwards, J. A. C. (6:1:0:0:1)
Ross-on-Wye (098987) 259 and 639
(home)
Ellerby, M. W. (0:1:0:0:2)
Pickering (0751) 74092
Ellison, B. (—:—:0:3:4)
Burythorpe (0653) 600158
Elsey, C. C. (—:3:8:7:9)
Lambourn (0488) 71242
Elsey, C. W. C. (10:10:9:4:9)
Malton (0653) 693149
Elsworth, D. R. C. (28:35:44:40:32)
Fordingbridge (07253) 220 (home) or
528 (office)
Enright, G. P. (0:1:0:0:0)
Haywards Heath (0273) 479183
Etherington, J. (11:18:17:9:15)
Malton (0653) 692842
Eustace, J. M. P. (—:0:6:10:7)
Newmarket (0638) 664277
Evans, P. D. (—:0:0:3:6)
Welshpool (0938) 570288 and (0831)
815603 (mobile)
Eyre, J. L. (—:—:—:—:1)
Mirfield (0924) 492058

Fairhurst, T. (10:11:12:15:9)
Middleham (0969) 23362
Fanshawe, J. R. (—:0:18:22:28)
Newmarket (0638) 660153 and 664525
Feilden, P. J. (1:7:6:5:5)
Newmarket (0638) 577637
Felgate, P. S. (17:12:10:6:10)
Melton Mowbray (0664) 812019
Fetherston-Godley, M. J. (10:2:7:13:7)
East Ilsley (063 528) 250
Ffitch-Heyes, J. R. (0:0:1:2:3)
Lewes (0273) 480804
Fisher, R. F. (2:1:0:0:0)
Ulverston (0229) 55664 and 55819
(office)
FitzGerald, J. G. (20:22:21:12:9)
Malton (0653) 692718
Fleming, G. (—:—:—:—:0)
Louth (0507) 363525
Forsey, B. (1:0:0:1:0)
Crowcombe (098 48) 270

Forster, T. A. (0:0:0:0:0)
Letcombe Bassett (023 57) 3092
Franks, D. R. (—:—:—:0:0)
Esh 091-373 5460 (office) and 091-
3840989 and 091-373 0459
Frost, R. G. (0:0:0:0:0)
Buckfastleigh (03644) 2267

Gandolfo, D. R. (0:0:0:0:0)
Wantage (023 57) 3242
Gaselee, N. A. D. C. (3:2:0:0:0)
Lambourn (0488) 71503
Gifford, J. T. (0:0:3:0:0)
Findon (0903) 872226
Glover, J. A. (12:3:5:4:25)
Worksop (0909) 475962 or 475425
(stable)
Gosden, J. H. M. (—:28:87:86:113)
Newmarket (0638) 669944
Graham, N. A. (11:—:6:7:6)
Newmarket (0638) 665202 (office) and
667851 (home)
Gubby, B. (1:0:7:0:2)
Bagshot (0276) 63282 and 71030
(evenings)
Guest, R. (—:7:7:5:15)
Newmarket (0638) 661508

Haggas, W. J. (14:16:21:27:13)
Newmarket (0638) 667013
Haigh, W. W. (3:3:5:6:9)
Malton (0653) 694428
Haine, Mrs D. E. S. (0:1:0:0:0)
Newmarket (0638) 561001
Haldane, J. S. (1:0:0:1:0)
Kelso (0573) 224956
Hall, Miss S. E. (7:6:12:6:9)
Middleham (0969) 40223
Hallett, T. B. (0:0:0:0:0)
Saltash (0752) 846829
Ham, G. A. (—:—:0:1:1)
Axbridge (0934) 750331
Hammond, M. D. (—:—:5:1:9)
Middleham (0969) 40228
Hanbury, B. (40:42:36:36:39)
Newmarket (0638) 663193 (stable) and
(0440) 820396 (home) or fax (0638)
667209
Hannon, R. M. (43:55:73:126:154)
Marlborough (0264) 850254
Hanson, J. (1:2:—:—:1)
Wetherby (0937) 582841 and 586776
(yard)
Harris, J. L. (0:0:6:8:9)
Melton Mowbray (0949) 60671
Harris, P. W. (0:2:8:3:13)
Berkhamsted (0442) 842 480
Harrison, R. A. (—:—:7:4:3)
Middleham (0969) 23788
Harwood, G. (73:109:69:55:29)
Pulborough (0798) 873011 or 873012
Haslam, P. C. (22:—:—:14:29)
Middleham (0969) 24351
Haynes, M. J. (11:6:9:9:4)
Epsom (073 73) 51140
Hayward, P. A. (0:1:1:0:0)
Netheravon (0980) 70585

998

Heaton-Ellis, M. J. B. (—:—:—:0:8)
Wroughton (0793) 815009
Hedger, P. R. (—:—:—:—:0)
Arundel (0243) 543863
Henderson, N. J. (0:0:0:0:0)
Lambourn (0488) 72259
Hern, W. R. (30:45:30:23:17)
Lambourn (0488) 73300 (office) and
(063528) 251 (home) and fax (0488)
71728
Herries, Lady (6:9:4:14:6)
Arundel (090674) 421
Hide, A. G. (8:11:10:15:5)
Newmarket (0638) 662063
Hill, C. J. (5:3:11:16:19)
Barnstaple (0271) 42048
Hillen, S. M. A. (—:—:—:—:1)
Eldersfield (0452) 840386
Hills, B. W. (93:73:113:99:63)
Lambourn (0488) 71548 and fax (0488)
72823
Hills, J. W. (14:16:28:20:25)
Lambourn (0488) 73144 and fax (0488)
73099
Hoad, R. P. C. (1:0:2:0:0)
Lewes (0273) 477124
Hobbs, P. J. (0:0:0:0:2)
Watchet (0984) 40366
Hodges, R. J. (8:12:25:27:21)
Somerton (045822) 3922
Holden, W. (4:3:1:3:2)
Newmarket (0638) 577384
Hollinshead, R. (33:30:41:31:60)
Upper Longdon (0543) 490298 and
490490
Holt, L. J. (6:13:6:4:12)
Tunworth (0256) 463376
Horgan, C. A. (6:9:3:4:5)
Billingbear (0344) 425382
Houghton, R. F. J. (36:24:25:13:10)
Blewbury (0235) 850480
Howling, P. (9:5:6:6:3)
Brook (042868) 4065
Huntingdon, Lord (31:26:20:36:60)
West Ilsley (0635) 28747 (office) or
28725 (home)

Incisa, D. E. (2:0:2:4:1)
Leyburn (0969) 40653
Ingram, R. (—:—:—:2:1)
Fiskerton (0636) 815742
Ivory, K. T. (7:7:7:5:9)
Radlett (0923) 855337

Jackson, C. F. C. (2:0:0:0:0)
Malvern (0886) 880463
James, A. P. (0:0:0:0:0)
Evesbatch (0885) 410240
James, C. J. (6:1:1:3:4)
Newbury (048839) 280
James, M. B. C. (2:0:0:0:0)
Whitchurch (0948) 4067
Jarvis, A. P. (—:—:—:1:2)
Abingdon (0235) 851341
Jarvis, M. A. (31:28:28:24:28)
Newmarket (0638) 661702 and 662519

Jarvis, W. (26:32:31:29:22)
Newmarket (0638) 669873 (office) or
662677 (home)
Jefferson, J. M. (4:1:0:0:0)
Malton (0653) 697225
Jenkins, J. R. (15:10:13:12:12)
Royston (0763) 241141 (office) and
246611 (home)
Jermy, D. C. (0:0:0:1:0)
Warminster (0985) 213155
Johnson, J. H. (0:0:1:0:1)
Bishop Auckland (0388) 762113 and
730872
Johnston, M. S. (5:15:28:31:53)
Middleham (0969) 22237
Jones, A. P. (—:—:—:0:0)
Lambourn (0488) 72263
Jones, A. W. (0:1:1:0:1)
Oswestry (0691) 659720
Jones, D. H. (6:3:7:2:5)
Pontypridd (0443) 202515
Jones, G. H. (0:0:0:0:0)
Tenbury Wells (056887) 676 and 305
(stable)
Jones, H. Thomson (41:37:34:37:27)
Newmarket (0638) 664884
Jones, P. J. (0:0:0:0:0)
Marlborough (067286) 427
Jones, R. W. (—:—:—:4:11)
Wickhambrook (0440) 820342
Jones, T. M. (4:0:2:0:0)
Guildford (048641) 2604
Jones, T. Thomson (—:7:8:7:5)
Lambourn (0488) 71596 and 72933
Jordan, F. T. J. (1:3:1:0:0)
Leominster (056882) 281
Jordan, Mrs J. (—:—:—:3:1)
Lambourn (0488) 73446
Juckes, R. T. (0:0:0:0:0)
Abberley, Worcs. (0299) 896471

Kelleway, Miss G. M. (—:—:—:—:0)
Newmarket (0638) 669511 and mobile
(0860) 860198
Kelleway, P. A. (16:13:8:13:16)
Newmarket (0638) 661461
Kelly, G. P. (0:0:0:0:0)
Sheriff Hutton (03477) 518 and 770
Kemp, W. T. (0:0:0:0:0)
Duns (03615) 242
Kersey, T. (0:1:0:2:0)
West Melton (0709) 873166
Kettlewell, S. E. (0:0:1:2:5)
Middleham (0969) 40295
King, Mrs A. L. M. (0:0:1:3:2)
Stratford-on-Avon (0789) 205087
King, J. S. (0:4:2:0:5)
Swindon (0793) 731481
Knight, Mrs A. J. (0:0:0:4:12)
Cullompton (0823) 680959
Knight, Miss H. C. (—:—:—:0:1:1)
Wantage (0235) 833535

Laing, D. R. (19:—:—:4:8)
Lambourn (0488) 72381
Lamb, R. R. (—:—:—:—:0)
Seahouses (0665) 720260

999

Leach, M. R. (1:0:0:0:0)
Newark (0636) 626518
Leach, P. S. (—:0:1:0:0)
Taunton (0823) 433249
Leadbetter, S. J. (0:0:0:0:0)
Ladykirk (0289) 382519
Lee, A. N. (2:8:7:4:2)
Newmarket (0638) 662734 (home)
Lee, F. H. (8:27:25:30:27)
Wilmslow (0625) 529672 and 533250
(stud)
Lee, R. A. (0:0:0:2:3)
Presteigne (0544) 267672 and
mobilephone (0836) 537145
Leigh, J. P. (3:1:4:5:1)
Willoughton, Lincs. (0427) 668210
Lewis, G. (32:23:26:41:54)
Epsom (037 22) 77662 or 77366
Loder, D. R. (—:—:—:—:2)
Newmarket (0638) 662233
Long, J. E. (0:0:0:0:0)
Plumpton (0273) 890244
Lungo, L. (—:—:0:1:0)
Carrutherstown (0387) 84691

Macauley, Mrs N. J. (6:14:24:21:12)
Sproxton (0476) 860578 and 860090
(office)
Mackie, W. J. W. (9:6:8:3:4)
Derby (0283) 585604
Madgwick, M. J. (2:3:5:0:0)
Denmead (0705) 258313
Makin, P. J. (24:29:27:23:12)
Ogbourne Maisey (0672) 512973
Manning, R. J. (—:—:0:0:0)
Winterbourne, Avon (0454) 773274
Marks, D. (1:2:1:0:8)
Lambourn (0488) 71767
Marvin, R. F. (—:—:0:0:0)
Newark (0623) 822714
McCain, D. (0:0:0:0:0)
Cholmondeley (0829) 720352
McConnochie, J. C. (—:0:0:0:0)
Stratford-on-Avon (0789) 450607
McCormack, M. (4:12:5:16:16)
Wantage (023 559) 433
McCourt, M. (1:3:2:1:3)
Letcombe Regis (023 57) 4456
McEntee, P. M. (—:—:—:—:1)
Bracknell (0344) 891211
McGovern, T. P. (—:—:0:2:0)
Haywards Heath (0444) 881594
McKie, Mrs V. J. (—:—:—:0:0)
Buckingham (0296) 730707
McMahon, B. A. (20:21:22:14:31)
Tamworth (0827) 62901
McMath, B. J. (—:—:0:0:1)
Newmarket (0638) 665868
Meehan, B. J. (—:—:—:—:0)
Lambourn
Mellor, S. T. E. (2:2:0:0:0)
Wanborough (0793) 790230
Millman, B. R. (—:—:12:9:7)
Cullompton (0884) 6620 and carphone
(0860) 661854
Mitchell, N. R. (0:0:0:0:0)
Piddletrenthide (0300) 4739

Mitchell, P. (12:15:13:8:5)
Epsom (037 22) 73729
Mitchell, P. (Pat) K. (2:6:11:5:10)
Newmarket (0638) 660013
Moffatt, D. (0:2:1:7:5)
Cartmel (05395) 36689
Monteith, P. (3:1:2:2:0)
Rosewell (031-440) 2309
Moore, A. (0:4:3:1:6)
Woodingdean (0273) 681679
Moore, G. M. (12:18:10:8:10)
Middleham (0969) 23823
Moore, J. S. (—:—:0:1:2)
Thruxton (0264) 88538 (office) and
(0380) 728526 (home) and
mobilephone (0831) 256532
Morgan, B. C. (6:3:2:0:3)
Barton-under-Needwood (028 375)
304
Morgan, K. A. (0:0:0:0:0)
Waltham-on-the-Wolds (066478) 711
Morley, M. F. D. (30:26:25:20:19)
Newmarket (0638) 667175
Morris, D. (—:—:2:6:8)
Newmarket (0638) 667959
Muggeridge, M. P. (—:—:1:3:2)
Fyfield (0264) 850872
Muir, W. R. (—:—:—:13:9)
Chaddleworth (04882) 463
Murphy, F. (—:—:—:—:0)
Woodbridge (072876) 243 or 554
Murphy, P. G. (—:—:—:—:3)
Portbury (0275) 372192 and fax 374185
Murray, B. W. (—:—:0:1:0)
Malton (0653) 692879
Murray-Smith, D. J. G. (9:8:9:7:2)
Upper Lambourn (0488) 71041
Musson, W. J. (10:6:4:9:6)
Newmarket (0638) 663371

Nash, C. T. (—:—:—:0:0)
Wantage (0367) 820510
Naughton, M. P. (8:19:12:21:32)
Richmond, N. Yorks (0748) 822803
and mobilephone (0831) 414217
Naughton, T. J. (—:—:—:6:8)
Epsom (0372) 745112
Nelson, C. R. (22:19:30:11:7)
Lambourn (0488) 71391
Nicholls, P. F. (—:—:—:—:0)
Ditcheat (074986) 656 and mobile
(0860) 225692
Nicholson, D. (0:0:0:0:1)
Temple Guiting (038673) 209/219 or
fax 218
Norton, J. (2:0:0:0:0)
Barnsley (0226) 387633
Norton, S. G. (33:11:20:19:27)
Barnsley (0924) 830450 and 830406
(office)

O'Donoghue, J. (0:0:0:1:0)
Reigate (073 72) 45241
O'Gorman, W. A. (24:10:51:29:27)
Newmarket (0638) 663330
Old, J. A. B. (1:0:1:1:3)
Barbury Castle (0793) 845200 or
845900

1000

O'Leary, R. M. (1:2:0:1:0)
Malton (065386) 684 and 404
O'Mahony, F. J. (—:—:0:0:3)
Dormansland (0342) 833278
O'Neill, J. J. (1:0:8:2:1)
Penrith (07684) 84555
O'Neill, M. J. (—:9:12:13:2)
Lydiate 051-5319616 (office), 6887
(home) and 5269115 (evening)
O'Neill, O. (1:0:2:1:0)
Cheltenham (024 267) 3275
O'Shea, J. G. M. (0:0:0:0:0)
Wythall (0564) 794631
O'Sullivan, R. J. (0:7:6:11:9)
Bognor (02432) 67563
Owen, E. H. (0:1:0:0:0)
Denbigh (0824) 790264 and 790356

Palling, B. (1:4:4:1:8)
Cowbridge (0446) 772089
Parker, C. (0:0:0:0:1)
Lockerbie (05765) 232
Parkes, J. E. (1:6:2:4:4)
Malton (0653) 697570
Parrott, Mrs H. K. (—:—:0:0:1)
Deerhurst (0684) 292214
Payne, J. W. (9:5:4:12:9)
Newmarket (0638) 668675
Payne, S. G. (—:0:0:0:0)
Carlisle (06973) 20010
Peacock, R. E. (2:3:1:3:2)
Tetbury (0666) 577238
Pearce, J. N. (3:5:13:11:21)
Newmarket (0638) 664669
Perratt, Miss L. A. (—:—:—:6:10)
Ayr (0292) 266232
Perrin, Mrs J. S. (—:—:—:—:0)
Royston (0763) 848113
Pickering, J. A. (—:—:—:—:1)
Wigston (0455) 220535
Piggott, Mrs S. E. (17:34:13:15:10)
Newmarket (0638) 662584
Pipe, M. C. (5:2:10:17:15)
Wellington (Somerset) (0884) 840715
Pitman, Mrs J. S. (2:2:1:0:0)
Lambourn (0488) 71714
Popham, C. R. (0:0:0:0:0)
Bishop's Lydeard (0823) 432769
Potts, A. W. (0:0:0:0:1)
Barton-on-Humber (065 261) 750
Preece, W. G. (2:0:0:0:0)
Telford (095 286) 249
Prescott, Sir Mark (34:40:48:48:50)
Newmarket (0638) 662117
Price, R. J. (—:—:—:—:2)
Leominster (0568) 615638 and 612333
Pritchard, P. A. (0:0:0:0:0)
Shipston-on-Stour (0295) 680689
Pritchard-Gordon, G. A.
(20:16:18:14:17)
Newmarket (0638) 662824

Ramsden, Mrs L. E. (14:32:26:38:23)
Sandhutton (0845) 587226
Reid, A. S. (—:—:—:0:1)
Thurleigh 071-7231824
Retter, Mrs J. G. (—:—:—:—:0)
Whitestone (0392) 81410

Reveley, Mrs M. (12:15:15:34:68)
Saltburn (0287) 650456 and 652000
(hostel)
Richards, G. W. (1:0:2:0:0)
Greystoke (07684) 83392
Richmond, B. A. (0:0:0:0:0)
Wellingore (0522) 810578
Ringer, D. J. (0:0:0:0:0)
Newmarket (0638) 662653 and 666021
(home)
Roe, C. G. A. M. (0:0:0:0:0)
Chalford (0453) 885487
Rothwell, B. S. (—:—:—:—:0:3)
Catwick (0964) 542583
Rowe, R. (—:—:—:—:1)
Storrington (0903) 742871
Ryan, M. J. (22:13:32:23:22)
Newmarket (0638) 664172

Sanders, Miss B. V. J. (14:7:4:7:4)
Epsom (03722) 78453
Sasse, D. J. G. (—:—:—:—:0)
Newmarket (0638) 507032
Scargill, Dr J. D. (9:8:18:7:9)
Newmarket (0638) 663254
Scott, A. A. (—:24:29:23:38)
Newmarket (0638) 661998
Scudamore, M. J. (0:0:0:0:0)
Hoarwithy (0432) 840253
Sharpe, Mrs N. S. A. (0:0:0:0:0)
Clifford (0497) 3465
Shaw, D. (—:—:—:0:2)
Ashington (0903) 893031
Sherwood, O. M. C. (2:0:0:0:0)
Upper Lambourn (0488) 71411
Sherwood, S. E. H. (—:—:0:0:0)
East Ilsley (063528) 678
Siddall, Miss L. C. (9:8:4:2:4)
York (090 484) 291
Simpson, R. (8:7:6:5:11)
Swindon
Smart, B. (0:0:0:0:2)
Lambourn (0488) 71632
Smith, A. (3:1:1:1:3)
Beverley (0482) 882520
Smith, C. (—:—:—:—:0)
Wellingore (0526) 833245
Smith, C. A. (—:—:—:2:0)
Malvern (06845) 5900
Smith, D. (14:15:8:9:15)
Bishop Auckland (0388) 603317 and
606180
Smith, J. P. (0:1:0:0:2)
Rugeley (054 36) 6587
Smith, N. A. (—:—:0:0:0)
Evesham (0386) 793263
Smith, Mrs S. J. (—:—:—:0:0)
Bingley (0274) 564930
Spearing, J. L. (3:8:13:12:14)
Alcester (0789) 772639
Spicer, R. C. (—:—:—:—:5)
Spalding (077587) 444
Stevens, B. (0:2:0:0:0)
Winchester (0962) 883030
Stewart, A. C. (40:30:41:29:22)
Newmarket (0638) 667323
Storey, W. L. (0:0:0:2:2)
Consett (0207) 55259

1001

Stoute, M. R. (99:116:78:83:74)
Newmarket (0638) 663801
Stringer, A. P. (—:2:5:4:6)
Carlton Husthwaite (0845) 401329
Sutcliffe, J. R. E. (12:18:17:3:14)
Epsom (037 22) 72825
Swinbank, Mrs A. (—:—:—:—:0)
Darlington (0325) 377318

Tate, F. M. (0:0:0:0:0)
Kidderminster (0562) 777243
Tate, T. P. (—:—:—:—:0)
Tadcaster (0937) 836036
Thom, D. T. (10:6:11:3:7)
Newmarket (0638) 577288
Thompson, R. (0:4:1:0:0)
Grantham (0780) 410812
Thompson, Ronald (7:5:7:4:3)
Doncaster (0302) 842 857, 845904 and
840174
Thompson, V. (0:0:0:0:0)
Alnwick (0665) 576272
Thorner, G. E. (0:0:—:0:0)
Letcombe Regis (02357) 3003
Thornton, C. W. (15:12:12:9:2)
Middleham (0969) 23350
Tinkler, C. H. (24:35:29:15:5)
Malton (0653) 695981
Tinkler, N. D. (24:24:17:13:9)
Malton (065385) 245 and 5 12
Toller, J. A. R. (6:7:7:4:9)
Newmarket (0638) 668503
Tompkins, M. H. (16:44:46:42:42)
Newmarket (0638) 661434
Trietline, C. C. (0:0:0:0:0)
Welford-on-Avon (0789) 750 294
Tucker, D. C. (0:0:0:0:0)
Frome (0373) 62383
Tucker, D. R. (0:0:0:0:1)
Cullompton (0823) 680159
Tulk, P. F. (—:—:—:6:0)
Newmarket (0638) 663209
Turnell, A. (2:4:2:4:0)
East Hendred (0235 833) 297
Turner, W. G. (0:0:0:0:0)
Tavistock (0822) 810237
Turner, W. (Bill) G. M. (3:6:2:2:11)
Corton Denham (096322) 523
Twiston-Davies, N. A. (—:0:0:0:0)
Cheltenham (045 1) 850278

Upson, J. R. (—:—:—:0:0) Towcester
(0327) 860043
Usher, M. D. I. (8:14:12:4:3)
East Garston (0488) 398953/4 (office)
and 7 1307 (home)

Voorspuy, R. (2:0:1:5:2)
Polegate (032 12) 7133

Wainwright, J. S. (2:4:3:5:1)
Malton (065385) 537
Wall, C. F. (13:9:15:7:7)
Newmarket (0638) 661999 (office) and
668896 (home)
Walwyn, P. T. (30:36:48:24:22)
Lambourn (0488) 71347

Waring, Mrs B. H. (2:1:5:6:3)
Malmesbury (0225) 742044
Watson, F. (0:1:0:0:0)
Sedgefield (0740) 20582
Watts, J. W. (23:25:27:14:17)
Richmond (0748) 850444
Weaver, R. J. (—:0:0:0:0)
Leicester (0533) 414112
Webber, J. H. (0:0:0:0:0)
Banbury (0295) 750226 and 750466
(stable) and mobilephone (0836)
580129
Weedon, C. V. (—:—:0:1:0)
Chiddingfold (0428) 683344
Weymes, E. (10:6:5:2:12)
Leyburn (0969) 40229
Wharton, J. (9:13:15:11:18)
Melton Mowbray (0664) 78334
(stable) and 65225 (home)
Wheeler, E. A. (4:2:7:8:6)
Lambourn (0488) 7 1650 and carphone
(0836) 201356
Whitaker, R. M. (49:29:36:24:23)
Wetherby (0532) 892265 and (0937)
582122 (office)
White, J. R. (0:5:2:5:9)
Wendover (0296) 623387
White, K. B. (1:0:1:3:0)
Craven Arms (058 476) 200
Whitfield, Miss A. J. (—:0:4:3:7)
Lambourn (0488) 72342
Wigham, P. (0:0:1:1:4)
Malton (094 42) 332
Wightman, W. G. R. (3:8:3:5:14)
Upham (0489) 892565
Wildman, C. P. (1:3:3:3:3)
Salisbury (0980) 52226
Wilkinson, B. E. (0:0:0:0:0)
Middleham (0969) 23385
Wilkinson, M. J. (0:0:0:0:0)
Chipping Warden (029586) 713
Williams, C. N. (1:2:4:2:3)
Newmarket (0638) 665116
Williams, D. L. (0:0:0:0:0)
Lambourn (0488) 2636 and 38530 and
(0836) 547894
Williams, M. (—:—:—:—:0)
Wellington (0823) 665156
Williams, R. J. R. (18:17:15:20:14)
Newmarket (0638) 663 218
Williams, W. R. (0:—:0:0:0)
Idestone (0392) 81558
Willis, H. (—:—:—:—:0)
Twyford (Hants) (0962) 712159
Wilson, A. J. (0:0:0:0:0)
Cheltenham (0242) 244713
Wilson, D. A. (7:15:19:11:10)
Headley (03722) 78327 (office) and
73839 (home)
Wilson, Capt. J. H. (11:8:7:12:5)
Preston (0772) 812780
Wilton, Miss S. J. (0:0:0:1:0)
Stoke-on-Trent (0782) 550861
Wingrove, K. G. (—:0:0:0:0)
Norwich (0263) 735299 and 733685
Wintle, D. J. (0:0:0:1:0)
Westbury-on-Severn (0452) 760459
and 760825

1002

Woodhouse, R. D. E. (0:0:0:2:0)
York (065 38 1) 637
Woodman, S. (0:0:0:0:0)
Chichester (0243) 527 136
Woods, S. P. C. (—:—:—:—:10)
Newmarket (0638) 711067
Wragg, G. (31:25:32:5 1:45)
Newmarket (0638) 662328
Wright, N. C. (—:—:—:—:2)
Dullingham Lay (0638) 508144

Yardley, F. J. (1:1:1:0:0)
Ombersley (0905) 620477
Yardley, G. H. (—:—:—:—:0)
Malvern (0905) 830245

The following relinquished their
licence during the season

Beasley, B. J. (—:—:—:—:13)
Blockley, P. A. (3:2:3:1:0)
Cox, C. G. (—:—:—:—:3)
Fox, J. C. (1:3:2:0:0)
Garraton, D. T. (—:—:0:0:0)
Harris, S. T. (0:0:2:0:0)
Holder, R. J. (8:17:16:18:11)
Holmes, C. J. (0:0:0:0:0)
Jones, Mrs G. E. (0:0:0:0:0:0)
Liddle, P. (—:0:0:0:0)
Lunness, B. W. (—:—:—:0:0)
Miller, N. (—:—:—:—:0)
Moubarak, M. Y. (1:1:15:18:18)
Oldroyd, G. R. (2:0:1:5:0)
Oliver, Mrs S. (0:1:0:0:0)
Pearce, W. J. the late (18:24:2 1:29:14)
Roberts, J. D. (0:1:0:3:0)
Robinson, M. H. B. (0:0:0:0:0)
Stephenson, W. A. the late (0:0:0:0:0:1)

JOCKEYS

The figures in brackets show the number of winners each jockey has
ridden on the flat (turf and all-weather) in Britain during the past five years,
from 1988 to 1992 inclusive. Also included are telephone numbers and riding
weights.

Adams, N. M. (17:23:36:15:20) 7   7
(0488) 72004 and carphone (0836)
787881 and (agent) (0903) 873780
Armytage, Miss G.
(—:—:—:—:0) 7   10
c/o (063528) 203 and 273

Bacon, A. E. (8:8:0:0:0) 8   0
071-25 16666 (office) and (0708)
229168 (home) (agent)
Bardwell, G. S. (39:10:26:17:34) . 7   7
(0638) 561452 (home) and (agent)
668484 or (0860) 864864 and fax
(0638) 660946
Baxter, G. E. (19:21:30:24:18) 8   2
(0903) 873780 (agent)
Berry, R. J. (—:0:—:—:0) 8   4
c/o (03722) 77662
Biggs, D. D. (8:11:12:34:60) 7   10
(0638) 561287 and (agent) (0638)
743938 and (0860) 766903
Birch, M. (95:91:61:55:40) 8   3
(0653) 628578 and 628683 and
carphone (0860) 245768
Brown, J. H. (3:3:0:0:0) 8   1
(0653) 6977 68
Burke, P. A. (23:14:12:8:4) 7   9
(075 1) 77 142 and fax 77 124

Carlisle, N. A. (9:17:20:27:2 1) 7   8
(0638) 663863 and (agent) (0638)
66643 1 and 667336

Carroll, J. (49:62:50:87:68) 8   2
(0253) 8 12299 and carphone (083 1)
801770
Carson, W. F. H.
(130:138:187:155:125) 7   10
(0638) 660947, (0285) 65 89 19 and
(agent) 08 1-748-9746 or (0836) 3 15000
Carter, G. A. (42:49:89:75:73) 7   12
(0638) 665950 (home) and (agent)
668484 or (0860) 864864 and fax
(0638) 660946
Cauthen, S. M.
(104:164:142:107:107) 8   8
(02357) 2450 and (0860) 407 107
(agent's mobile) and
fax (02357) 72 14 1
Charnock, L. (18:15:18:17:19) 7   7
(0653) 695004
Clark, A. S. (20:38:23:20:16) 8   2
(07982) 3028 and (agent) (0222)
615594
Cochrane, R.
(120:120:109:102:100) 8   6
(0638) 743045 and mobilephone
(0860) 343400
Connorton, N. B.
(34:2 1:26:26:29) 8   1
(0748) 824059 (home) and (0850)
707330 and (agent) (075 1) 77 142 and
fax 77 124
Crealock, G. A. (—:—:—:6:3) 8   0
(0638) 663739 or 668164

Crossley, B. G. (9:16:20:11:6) 7 10
(0638) 751367 (home) and
mobilephone (0836) 366739
Culhane, P. A. (38:24:20:29:16) ... 8 2
(0937) 836171 and mobilephone (0831)
201425
Curant, J. A. (2:2:1:0:0) 7 12
(01876) 0250 and (0638) 780027

D'Arcy, P. W. (7:5:6:3:5) 8 2
(0638) 750005
Darley, K. P. (38:70:83:66:91) 8 0
(0347) 22588 and mobilephone (0860)
926556
Dawson, S. (14:16:12:11:11) 7 9
(0672) 40031 (home) and (0903)
873780 (agent)
Day, N. P. (26:22:39:28:31) 8 3
agent (0638) 730012 and (0831) 336611
Dettori, L. (22:75:141:94:101) 8 4
(0638) 666431 and 667336 (agent)
Dicks, A. C. (1:0:0:1:0) 8 4
(0272) 519184 and (027581) 2192
Duffield, G. P.
(77:87:84:88:108) 8 0
(0638) 668484 or (0860) 864864 or fax
(0638) 660946 (agent) and 507544
(home)
Dwyer, C. A. (3:3:1:2:2) 8 8
(0638) 668869

Eddery, P. J. J.
(183:171:209:165:178) 8 5
(0844) 290282 and 201427
Elliott, R. P. (10:19:22:14:10) 8 0
(0969) 22884

Fallon, K. F. (31:28:39:29:45) 8 1
(0751) 77142 and fax 77124 (agent) and
(0653) 693087 (home)
Fanning, J. K. (0:0:17:45:45) 7 7
(09442) 419 or 8879
Fortune, J. J. (8:29:46:32:26) 8 0
(0347) 22410 and mobile (0836)
326084
Fox, R. D. S. (16:11:6:13:2) 7 7
(0353) 723236 and (0733) 263816
(agent)

Gibson, D. (16:30:30:22:23) 7 9
(0235) 835184 and mobilephone (0831)
103354
Greaves, Miss A. A.
(—:3:49:34:23) 8 1
(0609) 776489 (home) and (0347)
810825 (agent)

Hillis, R. P. (10:7:11:4:0) 8 4
(0831) 236748 and (agent) (0733)
263816
Hills, M. P. (76:77:61:65:91) 8 2
(0284) 850805 and mobilephone
(0860) 235151 (agent)
Hills, R. J. (52:63:56:67:52) 8 0
(0284) 850805 and mobilephone
(0860) 235151 (agent)
Hind, G. E. P. (2:23:28:26:16) 8 0
(0638) 741060 and mobile (0836)
789919 and fax (0638) 743846 (agent)

Holland, D. P. (—:—:30:79:68) 8 0
(0488) 71548 and (agent) (0403)
259345 or mobile (0850) 300449
Hood, W. (1:4:7:5:1) 8 5
(0638) 778366
Houston, Miss J. (0:3:4:1:3) 7 7
(0638) 669839
Howe, N. J. (5:4:8:7:3) 8 2
(02357) 68227 (home) and (agent)
(0733) 263816

Johnson, E. (10:4:4:1:2) 7 8
(0638) 720960 and mobile (0831)
345360

Keightley, S. L. (3:6:0:2:0) 9 0
Kelleway, Miss G. M.
(—:—:—:—:2) 8 3
(0638) 669511
King, G. N. (0:0:0:—:0) 7 10
(0638) 661998

Lang, T. L. (0:1:0:2:0) 8 4
(0296) 625310
Lappin, R. T. (6:4:22:8:6) 8 0
(0625) 533250 (stable) or mobile
(0831) 620475
Lowe, J. J. (41:36:45:54:33) 7 8
(0904) 708871 (home) and
mobilephone (0860) 244284 or (agent)
(0609) 748241 and mobilephone (0836)
229366 and fax (0609) 748749
Lucas, T. G. (—:—:—:1:10) 8 6
(03477) 697

Mackay, A. (36:10:14:18:8) 7 8
(0638) 665512 and mobile (0831)
844206 and (agent) (0831) 865974
McGlone, A. D. (16:15:25:24:17) . 7 12
(0264) 790421 and carphone (0836)
242788 and (agent) (0423) 871624 or
mobilephone (0860) 401683
McKeown, D. R.
(59:86:87:72:59) 8 2
(0977) 681247 and mobilephone (0860)
685439 and (agent) (0306) 888318 and
mobile (0860) 243068
McKinley, E. M. (—:—:—:—:0) .. 8 10
McLaughlin, J. F. S.
(—:—:—:1:0) 8 7
(0638) 668115
Mellor, Miss. A. D. (11:7:3:2:0) ... 7 7
(0793) 790230 and carphone (0836)
278602
Mercer, A. (2:5:3:1:0) 8 0
c/o (0748) 850444
Morris, A. (1:3:1:—:0) 8 2
(0403) 891339
Morris, Mrs C. L. (0:—:1:0:0) 8 0
(0273) 681679
Morris, S. D. (7:2:1:0:3) 8 0
(0653) 692098
Munro, A. K. (33:38:95:110:84) ... 7 12
(0954) 781783 (home) and
mobilephone (0831) 364757 and
(agent) (0536) 412144 and (0831)
630363

1004

Murray, J. G. (4:3:0:3:0) 8 3
c/o (0403) 730255 and (09442) 419 and
8879 (agent)

Newnes, W. A. P.
(44:40:53:30:27) 8 3
(023559) 272 and mobilephone (0831)
171809 and Fax (023559) 611 and
(agent) 071-2402963 and (0850)
369112
Nicholls, D. (32:28:26:30:17) 8 6
(0347) 23094, (0845) 401470 and
(agent) (0751) 77142 and fax (77124)
Nutter, C. (1:2:5:2:3) 7 13
(0638) 668153

Oldroyd, G. R. (—:—:—:—:2) 8 7
c/o (065381) 586

Perks, S. J. (18:34:29:23:2) 8 0
(0543) 490298
Perrett, M. E. (—:—:—:—:1) 8 13
079-887 4894 (home), agent (0367)
820214 and (0793) 522359
Piggott, L. K. (—:—:3:48:35) 8 6
(0638) 662584 and mobilephone
(0836) 222269
Price, R. W. (2:10:6:6:16) 7 11
(0831) 865974 (agent)
Procter, B. T. (2:4:1:2:0) 8 2
(063528) 596
Proud, A. (12:7:4:7:2) 7 10
(0949) 43350 (home) and 50099
(office) and mobilephone (0860)
913063

Quinn, J. A. (23:19:31:32:48) 7 7
(0638) 730445 mobilephone (0831)
321813 and (agent) (0751) 77142 and
fax 77124
Quinn, T. R. (46:63:90:99:117) 8 2
(0635) 200530 and fax (0635) 202051
and (agent) (0788) 832958 and mobile
(0831) 821100

Radmore, W. (—:—:—:—:0) 7 7
(0635) 578879
Raymond, B. H.
(77:66:75:74:53) 8 5
(0638) 730387 (home) and (agent)
666431 and 667336
Raymont, S. J. (1:1:5:7:1) 7 13
(06723) 533 and (0249) 817007
Reid, J. A. (79:84:67:80:96) 8 6
(0367) 820214 and fax 820533 (agent)
or (0367) 820711 and (0836) 243285
Roberts, M. L.
(121:107:128:118:206) 8 0
(0638) 661026 (home) and (agent)
(0860) 702322 (mobile) or (0932)
347382 or fax 343378
Robinson, P. P. (10:—:—:—:52) .. 8 0
(0638) 668484 and (0860) 864864 and
fax (0638) 660946 (agent) or (0638)
561716 (home)
Rogers, T. (—:—:0:5:3) 8 7
(0635) 864853 and mobile (0831)
856969 or (agent) (0831) 865974

Rouse, B. A. (51:56:36:13:26) 8 3
(0293) 871547
Rutter, C. L. P. (15:14:28:24:17) . 7 11
023 559 614 and (0836) 760769
(mobile)
Ryan, W. (58:49:59:72:105) 8 2
(0638) 741060 and (0836) 789919 and
fax (0638) 743846 (agent)

Sedgwick, P. (—:0:3:2:0) 8 2
c/o (0759) 71472
Shoults, A. F. (4:4:7:2:2) 7 12
(0638) 731238 and (agent) (0709)
866276 or (0831) 300935
Skingle, A. T. (—:—:—:0:0) 7 13
c/o (0638) 668675
Smith, V. (3:0:1:3:4) 8 6
(0638) 668972 and (agent) 668974 or
(0831) 865974
Sprake, T. J. (4:8:12:—:22) 7 11
(0793) 870606 (agent)
Street, R. (6:3:0:2:0) 7 7
(0488) 71412 and 71548 and (agent)
(0273) 23889 or (0850) 725039
Swinburn, W. R. J.
(88:93:112:68:82) 8 6
(0440) 820277 (home) and (0638)
660811 and 660258 (agent)

Tebbutt, M. J. (2:8:23:15:19) 8 4
(0638) 668484 and mobilephone
(0860) 864864 and fax (0638) 660946
Tinkler, Mrs K. A.
(16:12:13:8:0) 7 7
(065385) 245 and 512

Vincent, Miss L. J.
(—:—:—:1:0) 8 5
(0793) 782286 and mobilephone
(0836) 647725

Webster, S. G. (19:23:19:12:10) .. 8 1
(0904) 608458
Wernham, R. A. (12:6:7:0:0) 8 4
(0235) 833754
Whitworth, S. J.
(31:24:34:26:20) 8 0
(0672) 40961 (home) and (0831)
674707
Wigham, M. (23:33:27:9:8) 8 4
(0638) 560507 and carphone (0831)
456426
Williams, J. A. N.
(25:35:62:64:50) 8 3
(0454) 218622 and carphone (0836)
520252
Williams, T. L. (28:38:27:19:13) .. 7 9
(0488) 72734 (home) and carphone
(0860) 589885 and (agent) (0423)
871624 and (0860) 401683
Wood, M. (1:2:1:4:0) 8 0
(065385) 412
Wood, S. (17:12:15:23:19) 7 7
(0347) 224410 and mobilephone (0836)
326084 (agent)
Woods, E. W. J. (—:—:—:—:10) .. 8 2
(0638) 663025

1005

The following relinquished their
licence during the season

Eddery, J. D. (—:4:1:2:0)
Eddery, P. A. (52:44:50:72:73)
Wharton, W. J. (0:1:0:0:0)

APPRENTICES

The following list shows the employer and riding weight of every apprentice who holds a current licence to ride on the flat, and the number of winners he or she has ridden, wins in apprentice races being recorded separately.

Apprentices may claim 7 lb until they have won 20 races, 5 lb until they have won 50 races and 3 lb until they have won 95 races (any win in any kind of race in any country included). The allowance each apprentice is entitled to claim is shown in brackets. The claim may be exercised in all handicaps and selling races, and in all other races with guaranteed prize money of not more than £8,000.

Adams, R. N. (7) .... 7　8
(M. Bell)
Adamson, C. N. (7) .... 7　0
(P. Calver)
Addington, C. (7) .... 7　10
(J. Jenkins)
Ahern, Miss K. E. (7) .... 7　7
(J. Dunlop)
Aldwincle, W. J. (7) .... 7　7
(Mrs S. Piggott)
Allinson, P. A. (7) .... 8　2
(Mrs J. Jordan)
Andrew, G. (7) .... 8　3
(P. Chapple-Hyam)
Armes, Miss A. C. (7) 8 + 8 ap ...... 7　0
(H. Candy)
Arrowsmith, F. P. (7) 6 + 9 ap ..... 8　5
(I. Balding)
Ashley, T. L. (7) 2 .... 7　10
(R. Akehurst)
Avery, C. M. (7) 4 + 5 ap .... 7　7
(L. Holt) (0256) 463376 or 471680

Baird, M. J. (7) 2 .... 7　0
(M. Johnston)
Balding, Miss Claire
(7) 2 + 3 ap .... 7　0
(J. Balding) (0302) 710096 and (0777)
818407 (agent)
Bastiman, H. J. (7) 10 + 2 ap .... 8　2
(R. Bastiman)
Bates, A. (7) 5 .... 9　0
(P. Kelleway) (0638) 560464 and
mobilephone (0831) 390708
Beaver, T. H. (7) .... 7　10
(M. Ryan)
Benney, Miss S. J. (7) .... 7　7
(C. Cyzer)
Bentley, E. (7) 2 + 4 ap .... 7　12
(D. Morley)

Berry, R. K. (7) 1 ap .... 7　9
(D. Elsworth)
Biggs, Miss D. D. M. (7) 2 + 1 ap .. 8　0
(P. Howling)
Bott, R. P. (7) .... 7　0
(W. Holden)
Bowe, P. D. P. (7) 2 + 2 ap .... 7　10
(W. Musson)
Bowen, Miss A. J. (7) .... 8　5
(G. Lewis)
Bradley, Michael (7) .... 7　12
(J. Bradley)
Bramhill, J. A. (7) 1 .... 7　5
(B. McMahon)
Bray, V. (7) 1 + 3 ap .... 7　10
(B. Hanbury)
Bream, Miss R. (7) .... 7　4
(R. Simpson)
Bressington, M. P. (7) 1 ap .... 7　11
(K. Cunningham-Brown)
Brett, Miss. B. N. (7) .... 7　7
(Mrs S. Piggott)
Bridger, Miss R. J. (7) .... 8　8
(J. Bridger)

Cairns, A. (7) 2 .... 7　12
(M. Bell)
Carson, D. A. (7) 2 + 1 ap .... 7　7
(R. Hollinshead)
(0543) 490298
Carter, L. A. (7) 2 + 1 ap .... 8　0
(R. Akehurst)
Copp, S. L. (7) .... 7　6
(Mrs G. Reveley)
Cotgrave, Miss P. (7) .... 7　4
(Miss B. Sanders)
Coulter, Miss R. E. (7) 1 ap .... 7　2
(M. Heaton-Ellis)
Cripps, D. (7) .... 7　10
(P. Mitchell)

1006

Daly, A. T. (7) 7 0
  (J. Berry) (0524) 791179
Davies, S. G. (5) 19 + 13 ap 7 12
  (H. Cecil) (0638) 561952 and (agent)
  (0245) 362394
Davison, Miss C. A. (7) 7 7
  (Mrs A. Swinbank)
Denaro, Mark (7) 2 ap 7 12
  (R. Hannon)
Dennis, J. P. (7) 1 ap 7 4
  (R. Hollinshead) (0543) 490298
Dobbin, A. G. (5) 2 + 3 ap 9 0
  (J. O'Neill)
Doyle, B. (5) 35 + 4 ap 7 5
  (C. Brittain)
Drake, S. T. (7) 7 10
  (H. Candy)
Drowne, S. J. (7) 8 + 5 ap 7 10
  (R. Holder)
Dunnachie, D. D. (7) 2 + 3 ap 8 0
  (J. Gosden)
Dwyer, M. J. (7) 6 8
  (I. Balding)

Eblet, G. G. (7) 7 0
  (J. Wharton)
Edmunds, J. P. (7) 7 12
  (J. Balding)
Eiffert, S. (7) 2 .... 8 4
  (R. Guest)

Fifield, D. G. A. (7) 7 8
  (C. Horgan)
Forletta, Miss E. (7) 8 4
  (A. Stewart)
Forster, G. (7) 11 + 4 ap 7 12
  (C. Allen) (0949) 51179 and (0860)
  707563 (agent)
Frost, W. D. (7) 1ap 8 4
  (M. O'Neill)
Fullelove, Miss R. E. (7) 7 7
  (R. Holder)

Gallimore, Miss A. (7) 7 0
  (A. Bailey)
Garth, A. R. (5) 17 + 6 ap 7 4
  (R. Hollinshead) (0543) 490298
Gent, Miss R. J. (7) 7 0
  (R. Charlton)
Gibbons, Miss A. L. (7) 7 2
  (J. Wilson)
Gibbs, D. (7) 1 + 2 ap 7 7
  (R. Hannon)
Godsafe, M. S. B. (7) 3 ap 8 2
  (Miss G. Kelleway) (0327) 349700
Grantham, I. (7) 7 0
  (A. Harrison)
Griffiths, D. C. (7) 7 9
  (I. Balding)
Gwilliams, N. L. (5) 23 + 1 ap 7 8
  (W. Carter) (0372) 377209 and 377240
  and (agent) (0793) 870606

Hall, N. V. (7) 1 + 1 ap 7 10
  (G. Wragg) 071-25 16666 and (0708)
  229168 (home)
Halliday, V. (7) 7 .... 7 11
  (T. Barron)

Harris, J. C. (7) 7 12
  (L. Cumani)
Harris, M.P. (7) 3 + 1 ap 7 12
  (S. Bowring)
Harrison, D. P. (3) 60 + 10 ap 7 4
  (Lord Huntingdon)
Harwood, Miss G. M. (7) 1 .... 8 3
  (G. Harwood)
Havlin, R. (7) 4 + 3ap 7 7
  (Miss L. Perratt) (09442) 419 or 8879
Hawksley, C. L. (7) 11 + 2 ap 7 2
  (H. Collingridge) (0831) 865974
  (agent)
Hawksley, W. A. (7) 7 7
  (H. Collingridge)
Haworth, S. M. (7) 2 + 5 ap 8 1
  (J. Berry)
Hayman, Miss D. M. (7) 1 + 2 ap .. 7 4
  (M. Moubarak)
Henry, M. P. (7) 7 0
  (J. W. HIlls)
Hollick, W. J. (7) 7 9
  (A. Bailey)
Houghton, P. (7) 2 .... 8 10
  (G. Harwood)
Humphries, M. B. (7) 6 + 4 ap 7 6
  (R. Hollinshead) (0543) 490298
Hunt, Michael (7) 2 ap 7 7
  (J. FitzGerald)
  (0904) 647213 (agent)
Hunt, M. R. (7) 2 ap 7 10
  (R. Hannon)
Hunter, J. J. (7) 5 + 5 ap 7 9
  (D. Elsworth)
Husband, E. L. (7) 1 + 8 ap 8 2
  (R. Hollinshead) (0543) 490298

Jacobs, Miss L. A. (7) 7 10
  (H. Thomson Jones)
Johnson, P. A. (7) 1 + 3 ap 8 7
  (M. W. Easterby)
Jones, J. (7) 7 12
  (M. Stoute)
Jones, Miss W. J. (7) 7 3
  (R. Hannon)

Kennedy, N. A. (5) 37 + 3 ap 7 6
  (F. Lee) (0751) 77142 and fax 77124
  (agent)
Knott, S. T. (7) 7 12
  (E. Alston)

Lane, B. B. (7) 6 + 7 ap 8 0
  (J. W. Payne) (0638) 663254
Law, Miss A. E. (7) 7 0
  (J. Wilson)
Liggins, A. (7) 7 2
  (S. Woods)
Llewellyn, C. (7) 7 8
  (R. Hollinshead) (0543) 490298
Long, Miss L. G. (7) 8 7
  (J. Long)
Lynagh, Miss T. D. (7) 7 10
  (P. Haslam)

Maloney, S. J. (3) 54 + 4 ap 7 6
  (M. H. Easterby) (agent) (0751) 77142
  and fax 77124

Martinez, A. L. (7) 1 + 1 ap 7 10
(S. Dow)
Mason, Miss K. L. (7) 7 7
(P. Howling)
McCabe, D. R. (7) 1 + 1 ap 7 9
(W. Musson)
McCabe, P. A. (7) 2 + 4 ap 7 4
(M. Ryan)
McCarthy, S. B. (7) 2 ap 7 0
(B. Hills)
McCormick, P. (7) 8 0
(P. Cole)
McDonnell, Miss K. S.
(7) 6 + 5 ap 7 0
(W. Muir)
McLaughlin, T. G. (7) 9 + 3 ap 7 11
(P. Cole) (0793) 870606 (agent)
McLaughlin, Mrs W. H. (7) 8 0
(A. Bailey)
Meredith, D. (5) 3 + 2 ap 9 0
(R. Dickin)
Middleton, D. J. (7) 7 13
(P. Makin)
Millard, Miss S. C. (7) 7 0
(D. Wilson)
Milligan, G. E. H. (7) 1 + 1 ap 7 0
(Mrs S. Piggott)
Milligan, Miss H. (7) 7 4
(A. Scott)
Mitchell, G. C. (7) 1 + 5 ap 7 9
(I. Campbell)
Moffatt, D. (7) 13 + 5 ap 7 0
(Mrs G. Reveley) (0287) 650456
Moorhouse, Miss P. J. T. (7) 7 12
(S. Norton)
Mulvey, S. (7) 3 + 4 ap 7 10
(M. Tompkins) (0245) 362394 (agent)

Newton, L. (5) 16 + 4 ap 7 9
(Mrs J. Cecil)
Norton, F. (3) 72 + 11 ap 7 7
(G. Wragg) (0751) 77142 and fax 77124
(agent)

O'Dwyer, J. J. (7) 3 .... 7 12
(M. Bell)
O'Gorman, Miss E. S.
(3) 57 + 2 ap 8 1
(W. O'Gorman)
O'Gorman, S. M. (3) 63 + 5 ap 7 8
(I. Balding)
O'Leary, T. (7) 8 2
(M. Bell)
O'Neill, D. W. (7) 7 7
(R. Hannon)

Painter, R. B. (7) 1 ap 8 4
(M. Channon)
Parkin, G. (7) 1 + 5 ap 7 12
(R. Whitaker) (0937) 582122
Pattinson, K. (7) 1 ap 8 2
(M. Stoute)
Payne, M. (7) 8 2
(G. Lewis)
Pears, O. J. (5) 20 + 5 ap 7 12
(S. Norton) (0924) 830450 and (0977)
620264 (evenings) (agent)

Perham, R. (3) 62 + 6 ap 8 2
(R. Hannon) (0733) 263816 (agent) or
(0264) 850254 and 850523 or mobile
(0836) 521636
Plowright, Miss M. (7) 7 9
(Mrs A. Knight)
Porritt, S. (7) 7 12
(J. Berry)
Procter, A. R. (7) 8 + 6 ap 8 12
(D. Elsworth) (07253) 504/520 and
mobile (0860) 718654
Prys-Jones, Miss B. L. (7) 7 8
(J. Berry)
Purseglove, Miss T. N. (7) 2 + 1
ap 8 1
(G. Balding)

Radford-Howes, Miss S. (7) 1 + 1
ap 7 0
(W. Haggas)
Roberts, P. B. (7) 1 ap 7 2
(J. Berry)
Rothwell, G. (7) 7 0
(M. Channon)
Russell, B. J. (7) 4 + 8 ap 7 8
(G. Lewis)
Rutter, K. (5) 20 + 7 ap 7 13
(M. Jarvis) (0638) 668459 and (0903)
873780 (agent)

Salt, D. (7) 7 2
(Lord Huntingdon)
Sanders, S. (7) 7 + 8 ap 7 7
(B. McMahon)
Savage, F. M. (7) 6 6
(R. Hollinshead)
Scally, C. (7) 1 + 1 ap 8 0
(K. Ivory)
Scotland, J. R. (7) 7 7
(Miss L. Perratt)
Sked, K. P. (7) 7 0
(C. Thornton)
Smith, J. D. (7) 6 + 5 ap 7 0
(P. Cole)
Smith, Miss M. J. (7) 1 + 1 ap 7 5
(N. Macauley)

Tate, J. D. (7) 8 + 2 ap 7 11
(A. Scott) (0347) 22410 and (0836)
326084 (agent)
Taylor, A. F. (7) 7 12
(R. Hollinshead)
Teague, C. (7) 1 .... 6 7
(Denys Smith)
Thomas, W. (7) 7 7
(N. Callaghan)
Thompson, T. P. (7) 9 0
(R. Hodges)
Toole, D. J. (7) 1 ap 7 0
(M. Haynes)
Tucker, A. P. (3) 41 + 16 ap 7 10
(R. Simpson) (0831) 865974 (agent)
Turner, P. J. (7) 12 + 6 ap 7 7
(M. Bell)
Turner, R. D. (7) 7 10
(Pat Mitchell)
Turner, S. (7) 9 1
(R. Whitaker)

Varley, N. G. (7) 5 + 3 ap 7 5
  (J. Fanshawe)

Wands, Miss I. J. C. (7) 7 7
  (G. Balding)
Waterfield, R. J. (7) 1 ap 7 7
  (R. Holder)
Weaver, J. C. (3) 46 + 17 ap 7 12
  (L. Cumani) (0423) 87 1624 and (0860)
  40 1683 (mobile) (agent)
Webb, C. (7) 7 11
  (P. Makin)
Whelan, A. W. E. (7) 7 2
  (R. Hannon)
Wilkinson, J. (7) 6 10
  (Lord Huntingdon)
Williams, J. A. (7) 7 7
  (R. Bastiman)
Williams, S. D. (5) 21 + 6 ap 8 6
  (J. Glover) (0709) 866276 and (0831)
  300935 (agent)
Wilson, T. G. A. (7) 4 + 3 ap 7 3
  (C. Wall) (0638) 66 1999 or 66 1467
Wright, D. T. (7) 6 + 2 ap 7 0
  (A. Bailey) (0831) 865974 (agent)
Wynne, S. (5) 2 + 1 ap 8 11
  (R. Hollinshead) (0543) 490298

The following relinquished their
licence during the season

Denaro, M. J. (7) 10 + 3 ap
Giles, S. M. (7) 4 + 9 ap
Hodgson, C. A. (5) 32 + 10 ap
Howarth, Miss N. (7) 3 ap
Husband, G. I. (3) 42 + 10 ap
Jermy, M. (7) 1 + 2 ap
Lakeman, A. (7) 2 ap
Lanigan, S. (7) 1 ap
Mahoney, L. D. (7) 1 + 1 ap
Marshall, J. (7) 4 + 8 ap
Munday, C. J. A. (7) 6 + 5 ap
Simpson, M. (7) 1 + 1 ap
Thomas, B. (7) 3 + 3 ap
Thompson, D. R. (7) 1
Tierney, D. P. (7) 1 ap
Williams, David (7) 1
Williams, Miss. H. M. (7) 1 ap

1993 FLAT RACING FIXTURES

(a) Denotes All-Weather meeting
* Denotes evening meeting

March

1 Mon.	Southwell (a)
4 Thu.	Lingfield (a)
5 Fri.	Southwell (a)
6 Sat.	Lingfield (a)
8 Mon.	Southwell (a)
16 Tue.	Lingfield (a)
18 Thu.	Southwell (a)
24 Wed.	Southwell (a)
25 Thu.	Doncaster
26 Fri.	Doncaster
27 Sat.	Doncaster, Lingfield (a), Warwick
29 Mon.	Folkestone, Hamilton
30 Tue.	Leicester, Newcastle
31 Wed.	Catterick

April

1 Thu.	Brighton, Southwell
2 Fri.	Beverley, Kempton
3 Sat.	Beverley, Lingfield (a)
5 Mon.	Southwell
6 Tue.	Folkestone, Pontefract
7 Wed.	Ripon
8 Thu.	Brighton, Hamilton, Leicester
10 Sat.	Haydock, Kempton
12 Mon.	Kempton, Newcastle, Nottingham, Warwick
13 Tue.	Newcastle, Newmarket, Warwick
14 Wed.	Newmarket, Pontefract
15 Thu.	Newmarket, Ripon
16 Fri.	Newbury, Thirsk
17 Sat.	Newbury, Thirsk
19 Mon.	Brighton, Edinburgh, Nottingham
20 Tue.	Folkestone
21 Wed.	Catterick
22 Thu.	Beverley
23 Fri.	Carlisle, Sandown
24 Sat.	Leicester, Ripon, Sandown (mixed)
26 Mon.	Pontefract, Southwell, Windsor*
27 Tue.	Bath, Nottingham
28 Wed.	Ascot
29 Thu.	Hamilton, Newmarket, Salisbury
30 Fri.	Hamilton, Newmarket

May

1 Sat.	Haydock, Newmarket, Thirsk
3 Mon.	Doncaster, Kempton, Newcastle, Warwick
4 Tue.	Chester
5 Wed.	Chester, Edinburgh, Salisbury
6 Thu.	Brighton, Carlisle, Chester
7 Fri.	Beverley, Carlisle, Lingfield
8 Sat.	Beverley, Lingfield
10 Mon.	Redcar, Southwell, Windsor*

11 Tue.	York
12 Wed.	Kempton*, York
13 Thu.	Brighton, York
14 Fri.	Newbury, Thirsk
15 Sat.	Hamilton*, Lingfield*, Newbury, Southwell, Thirsk
17 Mon.	Bath, Edinburgh
18 Tue.	Beverley, Goodwood
19 Wed.	Goodwood, Nottingham
20 Thu.	Goodwood, Newcastle
21 Fri.	Catterick, Hamilton, Newmarket
22 Sat.	Ayr, Carlisle*, Catterick, Lingfield, Newmarket
24 Mon.	Ayr, Leicester
25 Tue.	Folkestone, Newbury*, Southwell
26 Wed.	Brighton, Hamilton, Ripon*
27 Thu.	Brighton, Carlisle
28 Fri.	Haydock, Pontefract*, Salisbury
29 Sat.	Doncaster, Haydock, Kempton, Lingfield*, Southwell*, Warwick*
31 Mon.	Chepstow, Doncaster, Leicester, Redcar, Sandown

June

1 Tue.	Leicester, Redcar, Sandown*
2 Wed.	Beverley*, Epsom, Sandown
3 Thu.	Beverley, Epsom
4 Fri.	Catterick, Epsom, Haydock*, Goodwood*, Southwell
5 Sat.	Edinburgh, Epsom, Haydock, Leicester*, Wolverhampton*
7 Mon.	Nottingham, Pontefract
8 Tue.	Pontefract, Salisbury
9 Wed.	Beverley, Hamilton*, Kempton*, Yarmouth
10 Thu.	Chepstow*, Hamilton, Newbury
11 Fri.	Doncaster*, Goodwood*, Sandown, Southwell, York
12 Sat.	Bath, Lingfield*, Nottingham*, Sandown, Wolverhampton*, York
14 Mon.	Brighton, Edinburgh, Windsor*
15 Tue.	Royal Ascot, Thirsk
16 Wed.	Nottingham, Ripon, Royal Ascot
17 Thu.	Ripon, Royal Ascot
18 Fri.	Ayr, Goodwood*, Newmarket*, Redcar, Royal Ascot
19 Sat.	Ascot, Ayr, Lingfield*, Redcar, Southwell*, Warwick
21 Mon.	Edinburgh, Pontefract, Windsor*
22 Tue.	Brighton, Newbury*, Yarmouth
23 Wed.	Carlisle, Chester*, Kempton*, Salisbury
24 Thu.	Carlisle, Salisbury, Wolverhampton
25 Fri.	Bath*, Doncaster, Goodwood*, Lingfield, Newcastle*, Newmarket

26 Sat.	Chepstow, Doncaster*, Lingfield*, Newcastle, Newmarket, Warwick*
28 Mon.	Hamilton*, Nottingham, Windsor*, Wolverhampton
29 Tue.	Chepstow, Folkestone
30 Wed.	Catterick, Epsom*, Warwick, Yarmouth

July

1 Thu.	Brighton, Catterick, Haydock*, Yarmouth
2 Fri.	Beverley*, Haydock, Sandown, Southwell
3 Sat.	Bath, Beverley, Haydock, Nottingham*, Sandown
5 Mon.	Edinburgh, Leicester, Ripon*, Windsor*
6 Tue.	Newmarket, Pontefract
7 Wed.	Bath, Kempton*, Newmarket, Redcar*
8 Thu.	Chepstow*, Newmarket, Nottingham, Redcar
9 Fri.	Chester*, Lingfield, Warwick, York
10 Sat.	Chester, Lingfield, Salisbury, Southwell*, York
12 Mon.	Beverley*, Edinburgh, Windsor*, Wolverhampton
13 Tue.	Beverley, Folkestone, Leicester*
14 Wed.	Catterick, Sandown*, Southwell, Yarmouth*
15 Thu.	Catterick, Chepstow*, Hamilton, Sandown
16 Fri.	Hamilton*, Newbury, Newmarket*, Southwell, Thirsk
17 Sat.	Ayr, Lingfield*, Newbury, Newmarket, Ripon, Wolverhampton*
19 Mon.	Ayr, Bath, Windsor*
20 Tue.	Edinburgh, Folkestone
21 Wed.	Doncaster, Redcar*, Sandown*, Yarmouth
22 Thu.	Brighton, Doncaster*, Hamilton, Yarmouth
23 Fri.	Ascot, Ayr*, Carlisle, Pontefract*, Yarmouth
24 Sat.	Ascot, Ayr, Newcastle, Southwell*, Warwick*, Wolverhampton*
26 Mon.	Lingfield, Newcastle, Windsor*, Wolverhampton*
27 Tue.	Beverley, Goodwood, Leicester*
28 Wed.	Catterick, Epsom*, Goodwood, Southwell
29 Thu.	Goodwood, Hamilton, Salisbury*, Yarmouth
30 Fri.	Edinburgh*, Goodwood, Newmarket*, Thirsk
31 Sat.	Goodwood, Newmarket, Thirsk, Windsor*

August

| 2 Mon. | Nottingham*, Ripon |
| 3 Tue. | Brighton, Nottingham*, Redcar |

4 Wed.	Brighton, Kempton*, Pontefract
5 Thu.	Bath, Brighton, Pontefract
6 Fri.	Haydock*, Newmarket*, Redcar, Wolverhampton
7 Sat.	Ayr, Haydock, Lingfield*, Newmarket, Redcar, Southwell
9 Mon.	Leicester*, Thirsk*, Windsor
10 Tue.	Bath, Catterick*, Yarmouth
11 Wed.	Beverley, Salisbury, Sandown*
12 Thu.	Beverley, Salisbury
13 Fri.	Haydock*, Folkestone, Newbury, Southwell
14 Sat.	Lingfield*, Newbury, Ripon
16 Mon.	Hamilton, Windsor
17 Tue.	Folkestone, York
18 Wed.	Carlisle, Kempton*, Yarmouth, York
19 Thu.	Ayr, Salisbury*, Yarmouth, York
20 Fri.	Chester, Sandown
21 Sat.	Chester, Ripon, Sandown
23 Mon.	Nottingham
24 Tue.	Brighton, Pontefract
25 Wed.	Brighton, Redcar
26 Thu.	Edinburgh, Lingfield
27 Fri.	Goodwood, Newmarket, Thirsk
28 Sat.	Goodwood, Newcastle, Newmarket, Windsor*
30 Mon.	Chepstow, Epsom, Newcastle, Ripon, Warwick, Wolverhampton
31 Tue.	Epsom, Ripon

September

1 Wed.	York
2 Thu.	Salisbury, Wolverhampton, York
3 Fri.	Haydock, Kempton
4 Sat.	Haydock, Kempton, Thirsk
6 Mon.	Hamilton, Wolverhampton
7 Tue.	Leicester, Lingfield
8 Wed.	Doncaster
9 Thu.	Doncaster, Folkestone
10 Fri.	Doncaster, Goodwood
11 Sat.	Chepstow, Doncaster, Goodwood
13 Mon.	Bath, Leicester
14 Tue.	Sandown, Yarmouth
15 Wed.	Beverley, Sandown, Yarmouth
16 Thu.	Ayr, Beverley, Lingfield, Yarmouth
17 Fri.	Ayr, Newbury, Southwell
18 Sat.	Ayr, Catterick, Newbury
20 Mon.	Edinburgh, Folkestone, Nottingham, Pontefract
21 Tue.	Kempton, Nottingham
22 Wed.	Brighton
23 Thu.	Ascot
24 Fri.	Ascot, Haydock, Redcar
25 Sat.	Ascot, Haydock, Redcar
27 Mon.	Bath, Hamilton, Wolverhampton
28 Tue.	Brighton, Newcastle
29 Wed.	Newmarket, Salisbury
30 Thu.	Lingfield, Newmarket

October

| 1 Fri. | Goodwood, Newmarket |

2 Sat.	Goodwood, Newmarket
4 Mon.	Pontefract, Warwick
5 Tue.	Folkestone, Redcar, Warwick
6 Wed.	Haydock, York
7 Thu.	Haydock, York
8 Fri.	Ascot
9 Sat.	Ascot, York
11 Mon.	Leicester
12 Tue.	Chepstow, Leicester
13 Wed.	Redcar
14 Thu.	Newmarket
15 Fri.	Catterick, Newmarket
16 Sat.	Catterick, Newmarket
18 Mon.	Folkestone, Nottingham
19 Tue.	Chepstow, Chester
20 Wed.	Chester
21 Thu.	Newbury, Pontefract
22 Fri.	Doncaster
23 Sat.	Doncaster, Newbury
25 Mon.	Leicester, Lingfield
26 Tue.	Leicester, Redcar
27 Wed	Yarmouth
28 Thu.	Nottingham
29 Fri.	Newmarket
30 Sat.	Newmarket

November

1 Mon.	Newcastle, Wolverhampton (a)
2 Tue.	Redcar
4 Thu.	Edinburgh, Lingfield (a)
5 Fri.	Doncaster
6 Sat.	Doncaster
8 Mon.	Folkestone, Wolverhampton (a)
10 Wed.	Lingfield (a)
13 Sat.	Lingfield (a)
16 Tue.	Southwell (a)
22 Mon.	Wolverhampton (a)
23 Tue.	Southwell (a)
27 Sat.	Lingfield (a)
29 Mon.	Lingfield (a)

December

1 Wed.	Southwell (a)
2 Thu.	Lingfield (a)
8 Wed.	Lingfield (a)
14 Tue.	Southwell (a)
15 Wed.	Lingfield (a)
16 Thu.	Southwell (a)
18 Sat.	Lingfield (a)
21 Tue.	Lingfield (a)
27 Mon.	Wolverhampton (a)
28 Tue.	Wolverhampton (a)
31 Fri.	Lingfield (a)

Join us at the races in 1993 . . .

'Timeform Day' at Bath
Monday May 17th

'Timeform Day' at Pontefract
Tuesday August 24th

Timeform customers are being invited to join us
at Bath on May 17th or at Pontefract on August 24th
and meet members of the Timeform team.
In conjunction with both racecourses
we're offering an exclusive package
including reduced-price admission
and complimentary
Timeform Race Card.

Further details from:
Timeform   Halifax   West Yorkshire

CHARACTERISTICS OF RACECOURSES

ASCOT—The Ascot round course is a right-handed, triangular circuit of 1m 6f and 34 yds, with a run-in of 2½f. There is a straight mile course, over which the Royal Hunt Cup is run, and the Old mile course which joins the round course in Swinley Bottom. All races shorter than a mile are decided on the straight course. From the 1½-mile starting gate the round course runs downhill to the bend in Swinley Bottom, where it is level, then rises steadily to the turn into the straight, from where it is uphill until less than a furlong from the winning post, the last hundred yards being more or less level. The straight mile is slightly downhill from the start and then rises to the 5f gate, after which there is a slight fall before the junction with the round course. Despite the downhill run into Swinley Bottom and the relatively short run-in from the final turn, the Ascot course is galloping in character; the turns are easy, there are no minor surface undulations to throw a long-striding horse off balance, and all races are very much against the collar over the last half-mile. The course is, in fact, quite a testing one, and very much so in soft going, when there is a heavy premium on stamina. In such circumstances races over 2 miles to 2¾ miles are very severe tests.
DRAW: The draw seems of little consequence nowadays.

AYR—The Ayr round course is a left-handed, oval track, about twelve furlongs in extent, with a run-in of half a mile. Eleven-furlong races start on a chute, which joins the round course after about a furlong. There is a straight six-furlong course of considerable width. The course is relatively flat, but there are gentle undulations throughout, perhaps more marked in the straight. It has a good surface and well-graded turns, and is a fine and very fair track, on the whole galloping in character.
DRAW: On the straight course a low draw is an advantage in big fields, particularly when the ground is soft.

BATH—The Bath round course is a left-handed, oval track, just over a mile and a half in extent, with a run-in of nearly half a mile. There is an extension for races over five furlongs and five furlongs and 161 yards. The run-in bends to the left, and is on the rise all the way. The mile and the mile-and-a-quarter courses have been designed to give over a quarter of a mile straight at the start, and the track generally is galloping rather than sharp.
DRAW: The draw seems of little consequence nowadays.

BEVERLEY—The Beverley round course is a right-handed, oval track, just over a mile and three furlongs in extent, with a run-in of two and a half furlongs. The five-furlong track bends right at halfway. The general galloping nature of the track is modified by the downhill turn into the straight and the relatively short run-in. The five-furlong course is on the rise throughout, and so is rather testing even in normal conditions; in soft going it takes some getting, particularly for two-year-olds early in the season.
DRAW: High numbers have an advantage over the five-furlong course.

BRIGHTON—The Brighton course takes the shape of an extended 'U' and is 1½ miles in length. The first three furlongs are uphill, following which there is a slight descent followed by a slight rise to about four furlongs from home; the track then runs more sharply downhill until a quarter of a mile out, from where it rises to the last hundred yards, the finish being level. The run-in is about 3½ furlongs, and there is no straight course. This is essentially a sharp track. While the turns are easy enough, the pronounced gradients make Brighton an unsuitable course for big, long-striding horses, resolute gallopers or round-actioned horses. Handy, medium-sized, fluent movers, and quick-actioned horses are much more at home on the course. There are no opportunities for long-distance plodders at Brighton.
DRAW: In sprint races a low number is advantageous, and speed out of the gate even more so.

CARLISLE—Carlisle is a right-handed, pear-shaped course, just over a mile and a half in extent, with a run-in of a little more than three furlongs. The six-furlong course, of which the five-furlong course is a part, the mile course, and the mile-and-a-half course start on three separate off-shoot extensions. For the first three furlongs or so the course runs downhill, then rises for a short distance,

FIXTURES
1993

AYR

SCOTLAND'S PREMIER COURSE

JANUARY	Saturday 2nd	N.H.
	Thursday 21st	N.H.
	Saturday 30th	N.H.
FEBRUARY	Friday 12th	N.H.
	Saturday 13th	N.H.
MARCH	Friday 12th	N.H.
	Saturday 13th	N.H.
APRIL	Friday 16th	N.H.
	Saturday 17th	N.H.
MAY	Saturday 22nd	FLAT
	Monday 24th	FLAT
JUNE	Friday 18th	FLAT
	Saturday 19th	FLAT
JULY	Saturday 17th	FLAT
	Monday 19th	FLAT
	Friday 23rd (EVE)	FLAT
	Saturday 24th	FLAT
AUGUST	Saturday 7th	FLAT
	Thursday 19th	FLAT
SEPTEMBER	Thursday 16th	FLAT
	Friday 17th	FLAT
	Saturday 18th	FLAT
OCTOBER	Saturday 9th	N.H.
NOVEMBER	Friday 12th	N.H.
	Saturday 13th	N.H.
DECEMBER	Tuesday 28th	N.H.

How to get there

Glasgow Airport *1 Hour by Car*
Prestwick Airport *10 Minutes by Car*
Racecourse Landing Ground *Helicopters Only*
Train Service *Every 30 Minutes from Glasgow*

**All Enquiries to The Racecourse Office
2 Whitletts Road, Ayr.
Telephone Ayr (0292) 264179**

levelling out just beyond the mile post. From there until the turn into the straight the course is flat, apart from minor undulations. The six-furlong course, which bears right soon after the start, and again at the turn into the straight, is level for two furlongs, then rises fairly steeply until the distance, from which point it is practically level. The track is galloping in character, and the six-furlong course is a stiff test of stamina for a two-year-old.

DRAW: High numbers have an advantage which is more marked in the shorter races.

CATTERICK—The Catterick round course is a left-handed, oval track, measuring just under nine furlongs, with a run-in of three furlongs. The five-furlong course bears left before and at the junction with the round course. From the seven-furlong starting gate the round course is downhill almost all the way, and there is a sharp turn on the falling gradient into the straight. The five-furlong course is downhill throughout, quite steeply to start with, and less so thereafter. Catterick is an exceedingly sharp track with pronounced undulations of surface, and it is therefore an impossible course for a big, long-striding animal. Experience of the track counts for a great deal, and jockeyship is of the utmost importance.

DRAW: A low number gives a slight advantage over five furlongs, but in races over six furlongs and seven furlongs a slow beginner on the inside is almost certain to be cut off.

CHEPSTOW—The Chepstow round course is a left-handed, oval track, about two miles in extent, with a run-in of five furlongs. There is a straight mile course, over which all races up to a mile are run. The round course has well-marked undulations, and the straight course is generally downhill and level alternately as far as the run-in, thereafter rising sharply for over two furlongs, and then gradually levelling out to the winning post. Notwithstanding the long run-in and general rise over the last five furlongs, this is not an ideal galloping track because of the changing gradients.

DRAW: Of little consequence nowadays.

CHESTER—Chester is a left-handed, circular course, only a few yards over a mile round, the smallest circuit of any flat-race course in Great Britain. It is quite flat and on the turn almost throughout, and although the run-in is nearly straight, it is less than two furlongs in length. Apart from extreme distance events, such as the Chester Cup and other 2¼m races, the course is against the long-striding, resolute galloper and greatly favours the handy, medium-sized, sharp-actioned horse.

DRAW: Given a good start, the draw is of little consequence. A slow start is virtually impossible to overcome in sprint races.

DONCASTER—Doncaster is a left-handed, pear-shaped course, over 15 furlongs round and quite flat, except for a slight hill about 1¼ miles from the finish. There is a perfectly straight mile, and a round mile starting on an off-shoot of the round course. The run-in from the turn is about 4½ furlongs. This is one of the fairest courses in the country, but its flat surface and great width, its sweeping turn into the straight, and long run-in, make it galloping in character, and ideal for the big, long-striding stayer.

DRAW: The draw seems of little consequence nowadays.

EDINBURGH—The Edinburgh round course is a right-handed oval track, nearly a mile and a quarter in extent, with a run-in of half a mile. There is a straight five-furlong course. The track is flat, with slight undulations and a gentle rise from the distance to the winning post. The turns at the top end of the course and into the straight are very sharp, and handiness and adaptability to negotiate the bends are of the utmost importance. The big, long-striding, cumbersome horse is at a distinct disadvantage on the round track, especially in races at up to a mile and three furlongs, but to a lesser extent in races over longer distances.

DRAW: Over five furlongs low numbers have a considerable advantage when the stalls are on the stand side and high numbers have a slight advantage when the stalls are on the far side. High numbers have an advantage in seven-furlong and mile races.

EPSOM—Epsom is a left-handed, U-shaped course, 1½ miles in extent. The Derby course is decidedly uphill for the first half-mile, level for nearly two furlongs and then quite sharply downhill round the bend to Tattenham Corner and all the way up the straight until approaching the final furlong, from where there is a fairish rise to the winning post. The run-in is less than four furlongs. The 7f and 6f courses start on tangential extensions. The 5f course is quite straight and sharply downhill to the junction with the round course. Races over 1½ miles can be testing if the pace over the first uphill four furlongs is strong, as it frequently is in the Derby. Otherwise the track is not really testing in itself, and races up to 8½ furlongs are very sharp indeed, the sprint courses being the fastest in the world. Owing to its bends and pronounced downhill gradients, Epsom favours the handy, fluent-actioned, medium-sized horse: big horses sometimes handle the course well enough, but cumbersome horses, long-striding gallopers, or those with pronounced 'knee-action' are not suited by it and are frequently quite unable to act upon it, especially when the going is firm or hard. Any hesitation at the start or slowness into stride results in considerable loss of ground over the first furlong in sprint races. For this reason Epsom is no course for a green and inexperienced two-year-old, slow to realise what is required.

DRAW: Nowadays a high draw is a considerable advantage over five furlongs and a slight advantage over six. A low number is an advantage over distances of seven furlongs to a mile and a quarter. A quick start is desirable at up to seven furlongs at least.

FOLKESTONE—The Folkestone round course is a right-handed, pear-shaped track, about ten and a half furlongs in extent, with a run-in of two and a half furlongs. There is a straight six-furlong course. The course is undulating, with the last part slightly on the rise, but notwithstanding its width, the easy turns, and the uphill finish, it is by no means a galloping track.

DRAW: No advantage.

GOODWOOD—The Goodwood track consists of a nearly straight six-furlong course, with a triangular right-handed loop circuit. Races over two and a half miles start near the winning post: the horses run the reverse way of the straight, branch left at the first or lower bend, go right-handed round the loop and return to the straight course via the top bend. Races over two miles, one and three quarter miles and one and a half miles are also run on this course. Over distances between seven furlongs and a mile and a quarter all running is done in the direction of the finish, with all but the mile and a quarter races using the lower bend. Although there is a five-furlong run-in from the top bend, the turns and, more specially, the pronounced downhill gradients from the turn, make Goodwood essentially a sharp track, favouring the active, handy, fluent-mover rather than the big, long-striding horse. This is of lesser importance in long-distance races, where the emphasis is on sound stamina, and of great importance in the shorter-distance races, particularly in sprints and especially when the going is on top. The five-furlong course is one of the fastest in the country.

DRAW: A low number is regarded as advantageous in sprint races when the ground is soft. Alacrity out of the gate is certainly of importance in five-furlong races.

HAMILTON—The Hamilton track is a perfectly straight six-furlong course, with a pear-shaped, right-handed loop, the whole being a mile and five furlongs in extent from a start in front of the stands, round the loop and back to the winning post. The run-in is five furlongs. The turns are very easy, and the course is undulating for the most part, but just over three furlongs from the winning post there are steep gradients into and out of a pronounced hollow, followed by a severe hill to the finish.

DRAW: Middle to high numbers have an advantage in races over the straight course.

HAYDOCK PARK—Haydock Park is a left-handed, oval-shaped course, about thirteen furlongs round, with a run-in of 4½ furlongs, and a straight 6-furlong course. The alternative 6-furlong course and all races of 1½ miles start on tangential extensions to the round course. Haydock is rather galloping in character.

DRAW: When conditions are testing there is a considerable advantage in racing close to the stand rail in the straight. Whatever the conditions, in races over 7 furlongs and a mile a good start and a handy position on the home turn are important.

KEMPTON—Kempton is a right-handed, triangular course, just over 13 furlongs round. The ten-furlong Jubilee Course starts on an extension to the round course. Sprint races are run over a separate diagonal course. The Kempton track is perfectly flat with normal characteristics, being neither a sharp track nor a galloping one.

DRAW: On the sprint course a draw near the rails is advantageous when the ground is soft; when the stalls are placed on the far side a high draw is an enormous advantage nowadays whatever the going.

LEICESTER—The Leicester round course is a right-handed, oval track, about a mile and three quarters in extent, with a run-in of four and a half furlongs. The straight mile course, on which all races of up to a mile are run, is mainly downhill to halfway, then rises gradually for over two furlongs, finishing on the level. The track is galloping. For two-year-olds early in the season it poses quite a test of stamina.

DRAW: Low numbers have an advantage in races at up to a mile and the advantage seems to be more marked when the going is on the soft side.

LINGFIELD (Turf)—The Lingfield Park round course is a left-handed loop, which intersects the straight of seven furlongs and 140 yards nearly half a mile out. For nearly half its length the round course is quite flat, then rises with easy gradients to the summit of a slight hill, after which there is a downhill turn to the straight. The straight course has a considerable downhill gradient to halfway, and is slightly downhill for the rest of the way. The straight course is very easy, and the track as a whole is sharp, putting a premium on speed and adaptability, and making relatively small demands upon stamina, though this does not, of course, apply to races over two miles. The mile and a half course, over which the Derby Trial is run, bears quite close resemblance to the Epsom Derby course.

DRAW: On the straight course a position close to either rail is advantageous.

LINGFIELD (All-Weather)—The all-weather track is laid out inside the turf track, following much the same line in the straight and the back straight then turning sharply for home at the top corner, so that it is only a mile and a quarter in extent, a chute in the straight providing a thirteen-furlong start. There is no straight sprint course, the fields at five furlongs and six furlongs having two bends to negotiate. The surface is Equitrack, whereas Southwell's is Fibresand.

DRAW: A low number seems an advantage in sprints, but the ability to lie handy is probably even more important.

NEWBURY—The Newbury round course is a left-handed, oval track, about a mile and seven furlongs in extent, with a run-in of nearly five furlongs. There is a straight mile course, which is slightly undulating throughout. Races on the round mile and over the extended seven furlongs start on an extension from the round course. Notwithstanding the undulations this is a good galloping track.

DRAW: A high number used to be a fairly considerable advantage over the straight course, but since the narrowing of the track the advantage seems to have disappeared.

NEWCASTLE—Newcastle is a left-handed, oval-shaped course of a mile and six furlongs in circumference. There is also a straight course, over which all races of seven furlongs or less are run. The course is decidedly galloping in character, and a steady climb from the turn into the straight makes Newcastle a testing track, particularly for two-year-olds early in the season. Ability to see the journey out thoroughly is most important.

DRAW: On the straight course, the softer the ground the bigger the advantage the lower numbers enjoy. On a sound surface, horses racing up the middle seem to be at a disadvantage with those racing towards either rail.

NEWMARKET ROWLEY MILE COURSE—The Cesarewitch course is two and a quarter miles in extent, with a right-handed bend after a mile, the last mile and a quarter being the straight Across the Flat. From the Cesarewitch start the course runs generally downhill to a sharp rise just before the turn. There are undulations throughout the first mile of the straight, then the course runs downhill for a furlong to the Dip, and uphill for the last furlong to the winning post. This is an exceedingly wide, galloping track, without minor irregularities of surface, so it is ideal for the big, long-striding horse, except for the descent into the Dip, which is more than counterbalanced by the final hill.

DRAW: Little advantage normally.

NEWMARKET SUMMER (JULY) COURSE—The Newmarket Summer Course is two miles and a furlong in extent, with a right-handed bend at halfway, the first mile being part of the Cesarewitch course, and the last the straight Bunbury

Mile. The course runs generally downhill to a sharp rise just before the turn. There are undulations for the first three quarters of a mile of the straight, then the course runs downhill for a furlong to a dip and uphill for the last furlong to the winning post. This is an exceedingly wide, galloping track, ideal for the big, long-striding horse, except for the descent into the dip, which is more than counterbalanced by the final hill.
DRAW: The draw confers little advantage.

NOTTINGHAM—The Nottingham round course is a left-handed, oval track, about a mile and a half in extent, with a run-in of four and a half furlongs. There is a straight 6f course, but no longer a straight mile. The course is flat and the turns are easy.
DRAW: In sprints when the stalls are placed on the stand side high numbers have a clear advantage, increasing as the ground softens. With the stalls on the far side low numbers are preferred.

PONTEFRACT—Pontefract is a left-handed, oval track, about two miles in extent. There is no straight course, and the run-in is only just over two furlongs. There are considerable gradients and a testing hill over the last three furlongs. The undulations, the sharp bend into the straight, and the short run-in disqualify it from being described as a galloping track, but there is a premium on stamina.
DRAW: A low number is advantageous particularly over five furlongs but it becomes a decided disadvantage if a horse fails to jump off well.

REDCAR—Redcar is a narrow, left-handed, oval track, about a mile and three quarters in extent, with a run-in of five furlongs, which is part of the straight mile course. The course is perfectly flat with normal characteristics, and provides an excellent gallop.
DRAW: Middle to high numbers usually have some advantage on the straight course.

RIPON—The Ripon course is a right-handed, oval circuit of 13 furlongs, with a run-in of 5f, and a straight 6f course. Owing to the rather cramped bends and the surface undulations in the straight, the Ripon track is rather sharp in character.
DRAW: On the straight course the draw is of no importance but in races on the mile course, horses drawn in the high numbers seem to have an advantage.

SALISBURY—The Salisbury track is a right-handed loop course, with a run-in of seven furlongs, which, however, is not straight, for the mile course, of which it is a part, has a right-handed elbow after three furlongs. For races over a mile and three quarters horses start opposite the Club Enclosure, and running away from the stands, bear to the left, and go round the loop. The course, which is uphill throughout the last half-mile, is galloping and rather testing.
DRAW: Low numbers are favoured in sprints when the going is soft.

SANDOWN—Sandown is a right-handed, oval-shaped course of 13 furlongs, with a straight run-in of 4f. There is a separate straight course which runs across the main circuit over which all 5f races are decided. From the 1¼m starting gate, the Eclipse Stakes course, the track is level to the turn into the straight, from where it is uphill until less than a furlong from the winning post, the last hundred yards being more or less level. The 5f track is perfectly straight and rises steadily throughout. Apart from the minor gradients between the main winning post and the 1¼m starting gate, there are no undulations to throw a long-striding horse off balance, and all races over the round course are very much against the collar from the turn into the straight. The course is, in fact, a testing one, and over all distances the ability to see the trip out well is of the utmost importance.
DRAW: On the five-furlong course high numbers have a considerable advantage in big fields when the ground is soft, and high numbers are favoured when the stalls are placed on the far side whatever the ground. Low numbers are favoured when the stalls are on the stand side.

SOUTHWELL—The left-handed course is laid out in a tight, level, mile-and-a-quarter oval, a spur to the three-furlong run-in providing a straight five furlongs. There are two types of surface, the all-weather track on the outside of the turf track. Nearly all races here are truly run. The all-weather surface is Fibresand, whereas Lingfield's is Equitrack.
DRAW: No advantage on the straight five furlongs. Over six and seven furlongs on the round course a low draw is probably advantageous, a quick beginning definitely so.

THIRSK—The Thirsk round course is a left-handed, oval track, just over a mile and a quarter in extent, with a run-in of half a mile. There is a straight six-furlong course, which is slightly undulating throughout. The round course itself is almost perfectly flat, but though the turns are relatively easy and the ground well levelled all round, the track is on the sharp side and by no means ideal for a horse that requires time to settle down, and time and space to get down to work in the straight.
DRAW: On the straight course a position close to either rail is advantageous.

WARWICK—Warwick is a broad, left-handed, oval track, just over a mile and three quarters in extent, with a run-in of about three and a half furlongs. There is no straight course, the five-furlong course having a left-hand elbow at the junction with the round course. Mile races start on an extension from the round course, the first four and a half furlongs being perfectly straight. This is a sharp track, with the emphasis on speed and adaptability rather than stamina. The laboured galloper is at a disadvantage, especially in races at up to a mile.
DRAW: A high number is advantageous in races up to a mile when the ground is soft, but a quick beginning is also important.

WINDSOR—Windsor racecourse, laid out in the form of a figure eight, is 12½ furlongs in extent. In races of around 1½ miles both left-handed and right-handed turns are met. The last five furlongs of the course are straight, except for a slight bend to the right three furlongs from the finish. The six-furlong start is now on an extension of the straight. Although perfectly flat throughout, the bends make this track rather sharp in character. However, as there is a nearly straight 5f run-in the relative sharpness of the track is of no consequence in the longer races. Big, long-striding horses which normally require a more galloping course are at little or no disadvantage over these trips.
DRAW: No material advantage.

WOLVERHAMPTON—The Wolverhampton round course is a left-handed, pear-shaped or triangular track, just over a mile and a half in extent, with a run-in of five furlongs. There is a straight course of five furlongs. The course is level throughout, with normal characteristics.
DRAW: The draw confers no advantage.

YARMOUTH—The Yarmouth round course is a narrow, left-handed, oval track, about thirteen furlongs in extent, with a run-in of five furlongs. There is a straight mile course. Apart from a slight fall just before the run-in, the track is perfectly flat, with normal characteristics.
DRAW: Middle to high numbers have an advantage on the straight course.

YORK—York is a left-handed, U-shaped course, 2 miles in extent, and quite flat throughout. There is also a perfectly flat straight course, over which all 5f and 6f races are run. 7f races start on a spur which joins the round course after about two furlongs. The run-in from the turn is nearly 5 furlongs. This is one of the best courses in the country, of great width throughout and with a sweeping turn into the long straight. The entire absence of surface undulations makes it ideal for a long-striding, resolute galloper, but it is really a splendid track, bestowing no great favours on any type of horse.
DRAW: The draw seemed of little consequence in 1992.

York
1993 Fixtures

Great Races Great Racing

MAY
TUESDAY 11th●WEDNESDAY 12th●THURSDAY 13th

JUNE
FRIDAY 11th●SATURDAY 12th

JULY
FRIDAY 9th●SATURDAY 10th

AUGUST
TUESDAY 17th●WEDNESDAY 18th●THURSDAY 19th

SEPTEMBER
WEDNESDAY 1st●THURSDAY 2nd

OCTOBER
WEDNESDAY 6th●THURSDAY 7th●SATURDAY 9th

Fifteen Days Racing

See it Live . . .

York Races

York Race Committee, The Racecourse, York YO2 1EX

Telephone: (0904) 620911   Fax: (0904) 611071

ERRATA & ADDENDA

'RACEHORSES OF 1991'

Ballerina Bay	second foal: dam maiden, suited by 1½m +
Berseto (USA)	won at Doncaster, not Newmarket
Culture Vulture (USA)	dam is by Gallant Romeo or Far North
Drummer Hicks	dam won at 1½m and 2m
Drum Taps (USA)	P243 Irish *Guinness* Oaks
Environment Friend	P265 Meadow *Meats* Irish Champion Stakes
Failand	delete 'to join R. Brotherton's stable'
Firefighter	dam ran *6* times
Innerglow	won at Wolverhampton, not Bath
Libk	York event was worth £13,940
Magnificent Star (USA)	penultimate line 'race over *one mile*'
Metternich	half-brother to several winners here and abroad, including Irish Oaks winner Princess Pati (by Top Ville) and high-class middle-distance performer Seymour Hicks (by Ballymore): dam won Irish 1000 Guineas and Yorkshire Oaks. Dam rated 122
Misaka Togo	Misak*o* Togo
Monarda	also won at Lingfield
Mystic Panther	dam ran at 2 yrs
Owler	sold 11,500 gns Newmarket December Sales
Qualitair Rhythm (Ire)	delete 'to join J. Bottomley's stable'
Rainbow Corner	P683 Bold Fantasy is daughter of Ribot's Fantasy
Second Set (Ire)	P760 reports of breaking blood vessels were incorrect
Shirl	second foal: dam sister to French 6.5f to 1m winner Boreale
Spring Saint	wasn't dead
Very Dicey	trainer R. Smyth
Walk That Walk	dam won over 6f at 3 yrs in USA
Big race results	Race 43 Shamshir S.P. 7/2, Race 62 Subotica S.P. 5/2

Index to photographs — copyright as follows

Maledetto (Jacqueline O'Brien), Mamma's Too (Timeform), Marju (Rex Coleman), Mukaddamah (W. W. Rouch & Co), Mystery Play (Rex Coleman), Mystiko (John Crofts), Nibbs Point (John Crofts)

'RACEHORSES OF 1992'

Culture Vulture (USA) and Ibraz (USA)

dam is by Gallant Romeo or Far North

STALLION
SECTION

Standing at Britton House Stud

FORZANDO

bay 1981 by FORMIDABLE - PRINCELY MAID by King's Troop

Multiple Group Winner
Won 12 races including
Metropolitan H'cap Gr.1
Won 5 consecutive races as a 2-year-old

Sire of 3 crops
2-y-old Stakes Winners from each including
UP AND AT'EM (Cornwallis S. **Gr.3**, Round Tower S. **LR** at 2 in 1992)

Fee: £2,000 October 1st NFNF

Standing at Thornton Stud

KRIS

chesnut 1976 by SHARPEN UP - DOUBLY SURE by Reliance

CHAMPION EUROPEAN MILER
in 1979 and 1980
CHAMPION SIRE of Group 1 winners:

**OH SO SHARP, COMMON GROUNDS, UNITE, FITNAH, FLASH OF
STEEL, SUDDEN LOVE, RAFHA, SHAVIAN, SHAMSHIR**
LEADING SIRE of BLACK TYPE PERFORMERS to Runners

Fee:£20,000 October 1st NFNF (Limited to 51 mares)

John Day, Thornton Stud, Thornton-le-Street, Thirsk, Yorkshire.
Telephone: (0845) 522522.

Enquiries to:
LONDON THOROUGHBRED SERVICES LTD.,
44 St Leonard's Terrace, London SW3 4QH.
Telephone: 071 - 351 - 2181. Fax: 071 - 352 - 8958.

Standing at Woodland Stud

PHARLY

chestnut 1974 by Lyphard - Comely by Boran

Winner of 3 Group 1 races at 2 and 3 years

Highly Successful Sire
with Lifetime Earnings of £4.9 Million

including

35 Group / Stakes Winners
His First 10 crops have produced
53% Winners to Foals

Fee: £3,000 October 1st NFNF (Limited to 48 mares)

Woodland Stud, Snailwell Road, Newmarket, Suffolk.
Telephone: Newmarket (0638) 663081.

Enquiries to:
LONDON THOROUGHBRED SERVICES LTD.,
44 St Leonard's Terrace, London SW3 4QH.
Telephone: 071 - 351 - 2181. Fax: 071 - 352 - 8958.

Standing at Plantation Stud

PURSUIT OF LOVE

bay 1989 by GROOM DANCER - DANCE QUEST by Green Dancer

Winner of 4 races £162,190, 6½ - 7F, 2 - 3 years

Prix Maurice de Gheest **Gr.2**
Kiveton Park Stakes **Gr.3**
European Free Handicap **LR**
2nd July Cup **Gr.1** (beaten a head)
3rd General Accident 2000 Guineas **Gr.1**

Fee: £5,000 October 1st NFNF (Limited to 48 mares)

Leslie Harrison, Plantation Stud, Exning, Newmarket, Suffolk CB8 7LJ
Telephone: (0638) 577341. Fax: (0638) 578474.
Enquiries to:
LONDON THOROUGHBRED SERVICES LTD.,
44 St Leonard's Terrace, London SW3 4QH.
Telephone: 071 - 351 - 2181. Fax: 071 - 352 - 8958.

Standing at Littleton Stud

ROBELLINO

bay 1979 by Roberto - Isobelline by Pronto
Dual Group Winner, broke course record at Ascot at 2

Champion First Season Sire
in England 1985 (when standing in USA)

A Leading 2yo Sire in Europe in 1992
of 14 individual 2yo winners

Lifetime Earnings of over £2,250,000

Fee: £4,000 October 1st NFNF (refundable if no live foal)

Standing at Lanwades Stud

SELKIRK

chesnut 1988 by SHARPEN UP - ANNIE EDGE by Nebbiolo

Champion European 3-y-old Miler
Winner of 6 races £477,379, 7 - 8F, 2 - 4 years
Queen Elizabeth II Stakes Gr.1
Juddmonte Lockinge Stakes Gr.2
Beefeater Gin Celebration Mile Stakes Gr.2
Challenge Stakes Gr.2
2nd Sussex Stakes Gr.1 (beaten head by Marling)

Fee: £8,000 October 1st NFNF (Limited to 48 mares)

Kirsten Rausing, Lanwades Stud, Moulton, Newmarket, Suffolk CB8 8QS
Telephone: (0638) 750222. Fax: (0638) 751186.
Enquiries to:
LONDON THOROUGHBRED SERVICES LTD.,
44 St Leonard's Terrace, London SW3 4QH.
Telephone: 071 - 351 - 2181. Fax: 071 - 352 - 8958.

Standing at Woodland Stud

SHARPO

chesnut 1977 by SHARPEN UP - MOIETY BIRD by Falcon

One of EUROPE's LEADING SIRES
of 2-year-olds in 1991 and 1992

Sire in 1992 of
42 individual Winners of 85 races
and £585,000

Fee: £4,000 October 1st NFNF (Limited to 50 mares)

Woodland Stud, Snailwell Road, Newmarket, Suffolk.
Telephone: Newmarket (0638) 663081.
Enquiries to:
LONDON THOROUGHBRED SERVICES LTD.,
44 St Leonard's Terrace, London SW3 4QH.
Telephone: 071 - 351 - 2181. Fax: 071 - 352 - 8958.

Standing at Plantation Stud

SLIP ANCHOR

bay 1982 by SHIRLEY HEIGHTS - SAYONARA by Birkhahn

Champion European 3-year-old in 1985

Leading British Based Sire in 1992
Sire of:
**USER FRIENDLY, IONIAN SEA, KASMAYO,
FIRING LINE, LUCHIROVERTE, UP ANCHOR.**

Fee: £12,500 October 1st NFNF (Limited to 50 mares)

Leslie Harrison, Plantation Stud, Exning, Newmarket, Suffolk CB8 7LJ.
Telephone: (0638) 577341. Fax: (0638) 578474.
Enquiries to:
**LONDON THOROUGHBRED SERVICES LTD.,
44 St Leonard's Terrace, London SW3 4QH.
Telephone: 071 - 351 - 2181. Fax: 071 - 352 - 8958.**

LAW SOCIETY - (Alleged - Bold Bikini)

MASTERCLASS - (The Minstrel - Monroe)

NIGHT SHIFT - (Northern Dancer - Ciboulette) New for '93

PERSIAN HEIGHTS - (Persian Bold - Ready and Willing)

ROYAL ACADEMY - (Nijinsky - Crimson Saint)

SADLER'S WELLS - (Northern Dancer - Fairy Bridge)

SCENIC - (Sadler's Wells - Idyllic)

SHALFORD - (Thatching - Enigma) New for '93

THATCHING - (Thatch - Abella)

TIROL - (Thatching - Alpine Niece)

WAAJIB - (Try My Best - Coryana)

U.S.A. STALLIONS

EL GRAN SENOR - (Northern Dancer - Sex Appeal)

GEIGER COUNTER - (Mr. Prospector - Thong)

LOMOND - (Northern Dancer - My Charmer)

SEATTLE DANCER - (Nijinsky - My Charmer)

STORM BIRD - (Northern Dancer - South Ocean)

WOODMAN - (Mr. Prospector - Playmate)

EUROPE'S FINEST SOURCE OF PROVEN STALLIONS

Paul Shanahan: 353-52-31298/31645 (home) Tom Gaffney: 353-52-31966.
David Magnier /Joe Hernon/Albert Sherwood: 353-25-31966/31689. David Magnier 353-25-31465 (home)
Joe Hernon: 353-22-26275 (home) Albert Sherwood 353-25-31230 (home)

STALLIONS FOR 1993

AL HAREB - (El Gran Senor - Icing)

ALZAO - (Lyphard - Lady Rebecca)

ARCHWAY - (Thatching - Rose of Jericho)

BE MY GUEST - (Northern Dancer - What a Treat)

BLUEBIRD - (Storm Bird - Ivory Dawn)

CAERLEON - (Nijinsky - Foreseer)

CLASSIC MUSIC - (Northern Dancer - Fairy Bridge)

DANEHILL - (Danzig - Razyana)

DISTINCTLY NORTH - (Minshaanshu Amad - Distinctiveness)

DON'T FORGET ME - (Ahonoora - African Doll)

FAIRY KING - (Northern Dancer - Fairy Bridge)

HIGH ESTATE - (Shirley Heights - Regal Beauty)

KENMARE - (Kalamoun - Belle of Ireland) New for '93

LAST TYCOON - (Try My Best - Mill Princess)

COOLMORE

CONTACT: **COOLMORE STUD**, FETHARD, CO. TIPPERARY, IRELAND.
TEL: 353-52-31298. TELEX: 80695. FAX: 353-52-31382.
BOB LANIGAN: 353-52-31298. **CHRISTY GRASSICK:** 353-52-31313.

DARLEY STUD MANAGEMENT
STALLIONS FOR 1993

Standing at Dalham Hall Stud, Newmarket

ARAZI 1989 by

Blushing Groom - Danseur Fabuleux
Champion 2yo in Europe and North America.
Won 9 Group/Listed races £674,474 at 2 and 3

MACHIAVELLIAN 1987 by

Mr Prospector - Coup de Folie
Unbeaten Champion European 2yo 1989.
1st Yearlings 1993.

OLD VIC 1986

by Sadler's Wells - Cockade. Champion European
3yo 1989, won French and Irish Derbies **G.1.**
1st Yearlings 1993.

POLISH PRECEDENT 1986 by

Danzig - Past Example
Won 7 in 1989 including 2 Group 1 races.
1st 2-year-olds 1993.

SHAREEF DANCER 1980 by

Northern Dancer - Sweet Alliance
A Leading European Sire.

SOVIET STAR 1984 by

Nureyev - Veruschka
Champion European Sprinter 1988. Won 5 Gr.1
races.
Sire of 5 2-year-old winners 1992.

Standing at Aston Upthorpe Stud, Oxfordshire

MTOTO 1983 by Busted - Amazer

Champion European 4yo in 1987. Won King George VI & Queen Elizabeth Diamond S.
G.1, Coral-Eclipse S. **G.1** (x2), Prince of Wales's S. **G.2** (x2).
Sire of 5 2-y-old winners 1992.

Standing at Ragusa Stud, Co. Kildare.

IN THE WINGS 1986 by

Sadler's Wells - High Hawk
Group 1 winner in USA, England and France of
Breeders' Cup Turf **G.1**, Hanson Coronation
Cup **G.1**, Grand Prix de Saint-Cloud **G.1**.
1st Yearlings 1993.

LYCIUS 1988 by

Mr Prospector - Lypatia
Record breaking Group 1 winner at 2 and placed
in 5 G.1 races at 3, defeated the winners of 16
G.1 races.
Retired to stud in 1992.

Enquiries to: Mrs Blackwell,
Darley Stud Management Company Ltd.,
Dalham Hall Stud, Duchess Drive, Newmarket,
Suffolk. CB8 9HD.
Telephone: Newmarket (0638) 730070.
Fax: (0638) 730167.

Champions

from the 'Racehorses' series

Horse of the Year

1969	Levmoss	**133**
1970	Nijinsky	**138**
1971	Brigadier Gerard	**141**
	Mill Reef	**141**
1972	Brigadier Gerard	**144**
1973	Apalachee	**137**
	Rheingold	**137**
1974	Allez France	**136**
1975	Grundy	**137**
1976	Youth	**135**
1977	Alleged	**137**
1978	Alleged	**138**
1979	Troy	**137**
1980	Moorestyle	**137**
1981	Shergar	**140**
1982	Ardross	**134**
1983	Habibti	**136**
1984	Provideo	**112**
1985	Pebbles	**135**
1986	Dancing Brave	**140**
1987	Reference Point	**139**
1988	Warning	**136**
1989	Zilzal	**137**
1990	Dayjur	**137**
1991	Generous	**139**
1992	St Jovite	**135**

Best Two-Year-Old Colt

1969	Nijinsky	131	1982	Diesis	133
1970	My Swallow	134	1983	El Gran Senor	131
1971	Deep Diver	134	1984	Kala Dancer	129
1972	The Go-Between	129	1985	Huntingdale	132
1973	Apalachee	137	1986	Reference Point	132
1974	Grundy	134	1987	Warning	127p
1975	Manado	130	1988	Prince of Dance	128
1976	Blushing Groom	131		Scenic	128
1977	Try My Best	130p	1989	Be My Chief	123p
1978	Tromos	134	1990	Hector Protector	122p
1979	Monteverdi	129	1991	Arazi	135
1980	Storm Bird	134	1992	Armiger	131p
1981	Wind & Wuthering	132			

Best Two-Year-Old Filly

1969	Mange Tout	125	1982	Ma Biche	123
1970	Cawston's Pride	131	1983	Treizieme	121
1971	Rose Dubarry	127	1984	Triptych	125
1972	Jacinth	133	1985	Femme Elite	124
1973	Melchbourne	125	1986	Forest Flower	127
1974	Cry of Truth	129	1987	Ravinella	121p
1975	Theia	128	1988	Tessla	116p
1976	Cloonlara	130		Pass The Peace	116p
1977	Cherry Hinton	125	1989	Negligent	118p
1978	Sigy	132	1990	Shadayid	117p
1979	Aryenne	120	1991	Midnight Air	111p
1980	Marwell	124	1992	Sayyedati	116p
1981	Circus Ring	122			

Best Sprinter

1969	Song	132	1981	Marwell	133
1970	Amber Rama	133	1982	Sharpo	130
1971	Joshua	129	1983	Habibti	136
1972	Deep Diver	134	1984	Chief Singer	131
1973	Sandford Lad	133	1985	Never So Bold	135
1974	Saritamer	130	1986	Last Tycoon	131
1975	Flirting Around	134	1987	Ajdal	130
1976	Lochnager	132	1988	Soviet Star	128
1977	Gentilhombre	131	1989	Cadeaux Genereux	131
1978	Solinus	130	1990	Dayjur	137
1979	Thatching	131	1991	Polish Patriot	128
1980	Moorestyle	137	1992	Sheikh Albadou	128

Best Miler

1969	Habitat	134	1982	Green Forest	134
1970	Welsh Pageant	130	1983	Luth Enchantee	130
1971	Brigadier Gerard	141	1984	El Gran Senor	136
1972	Brigadier Gerard	144	1985	Shadeed	135
1973	Thatch	136	1986	Dancing Brave	140
1974	Nonoalco	131	1987	Miesque	131
1975	Bolkonski	134	1988	Warning	136
1976	Wollow	132	1989	Zilzal	137
1977	Blushing Groom	131	1990	Markofdistinction	130
1978	Homing	130		Royal Academy	130
1979	Kris	135	1991	Selkirk	129
1980	Known Fact	135	1992	Lahib	129
1981	Northjet	136		Selkirk	129

Best Middle-Distance Horse

1969	Park Top	131	1982	Assert	134
1970	Nijinsky	138	1983	Shareef Dancer	135
1971	Mill Reef	141	1984	Teenoso	135
1972	Mill Reef	141		Sagace	135
1973	Rheingold	137	1985	Slip Anchor	136
1974	Allez France	136	1986	Dancing Brave	140
1975	Grundy	137	1987	Reference Point	139
1976	Youth	135	1988	Mtoto	134
1977	Alleged	137		Tony Bin	134
1978	Alleged	138	1989	Old Vic	136
1979	Troy	137	1990	Saumarez	132
1980	Argument	133	1991	Generous	139
1981	Shergar	140	1992	St Jovite	135

Best Stayer

1969	Levmoss	133	1980	Le Moss	135
1970	High Line	125	1981	Ardross	131
1971	Rock Roi	127	1982	Ardross	134
1972	Rock Roi	127	1983	Little Wolf	127
1973	Parnell	130	1984	Commanche Run	129
1974	Ragstone	128	1985	Oh So Sharp	131
1975	Bruni	132	1986	Moon Madness	128
1976	Sagaro	129	1987	Reference Point	139
1977	Dunfermline	133	1988	Minster Son	130
	Sagaro	133	1989	Michelozzo	127p
1978	Buckskin	133	1990	Snurge	130
1979	Buckskin	131	1991	Toulon	125
	Le Moss	131	1992	Mashaallah	123